ENVIRONMENTAL LAW HANDBOOK

Volume 2

ENVIRONMENTAL LAW HANDBOOK

Volume 2

General Editor

Andrew Waite
Solicitor

Bloomsbury Professional

Bloomsbury Professional Ltd, Maxwelton House, 41–43 Boltro Road, Haywards Heath, West Sussex, RH16 1BJ

Bloomsbury Professional is an imprint of Bloomsbury Publishing plc

A CIP Catalogue record for this book is available from the British Library.

ISBN 978 1 78043 006 5

Typeset by Phoenix Photosetting, Chatham, Kent
Printed and bound by CPI Group (UK) Ltd, Croydon, CR0 4YY

CONTENTS

Part 2B Statutory Instruments

Part 2B

Statutory Instruments

ENVIRONMENTAL DAMAGE (PREVENTION AND REMEDIATION) (WALES) REGULATIONS 2009

SI 2009/995

PART 1
INTRODUCTORY PROVISIONS

1 Title, commencement and application

(1) The title of these Regulations is the Environmental Damage (Prevention and Remediation) (Wales) Regulations 2009. They come into force on 6 May 2009.

(2) These Regulations apply in relation to Wales and the areas specified in regulation 6.

2 Interpretation

(1) In these Regulations—

"activity" ("gweithgaredd") means any economic activity, whether public or private and whether or not carried out for profit;

"groundwater" ("dŵ r daear") means all water that is below the surface of the ground in the saturation zone and in direct contact with the ground or subsoil;

"local authority" ("awdurdod lleol") means a county council or a county borough council;

"natural habitat" ("cynefin naturiol") means—

(a) the habitats of species mentioned in Article 4(2) of, or Annex I to, Council Directive 79/409/EEC on the conservation of wild birds or listed in Annex II to Council Directive 92/43/EEC on the conservation of natural habitats and of wild fauna and flora;

(b) the natural habitats listed in Annex I to Council Directive 92/43/EEC; and

(c) the breeding sites or resting places of the species listed in Annex IV to Council Directive 92/43/EEC;

"natural resource" ("adnoddyn naturiol") means—

(a) protected species;

(b) natural habitats;

(c) species or habitats on a site of special scientific interest for which the site has been notified under section 28 of the Wildlife and Countryside Act 1981;

(d) water; and

(e) land;

"operator" ("gweithredwr") means a person who operates or controls an activity, the holder of a permit or authorisation relating to that activity or the person registering or notifying such an activity;

"protected species" ("rhywogaethau a warchodir") means the species mentioned in Article 4(2) of Council Directive 79/409/EEC or listed in Annex I to that Directive or Annexes II and IV to Council Directive 92/43/EEC;

"services" ("gwasanaethau") means the functions performed by a natural resource for the benefit of another natural resource or the public;

"Wales" ("Cymru") has the meaning given under section 158 of the Government of Wales Act 2006.

(2) Unless otherwise defined in these Regulations, expressions used in Directive 2004/35/EC of the European Parliament and of the Council on environmental liability with regard to the prevention and remedying of environmental damage have the same meaning in these Regulations.

(3) In relation to the deliberate release and placing on the market of genetically modified organisms, "operator" ("gweithredwr") and "responsible operator" ("gweithredwr cyfrifol") includes—

(a) the holder of a relevant consent issued under Directive 2001/18/EC of the European Parliament and of the Council on the deliberate release into the environment of genetically modified organisms;

(b) the holder of a relevant consent for the deliberate release of genetically modified organisms granted by the Welsh Ministers under section 111(1) of the Environmental Protection Act 1990; or

(c) the holder of a relevant authorisation issued under Regulation (EC) No 1829/2003 of the European Parliament and of the Council on genetically modified food and feed.

3 References to [EU][1] instruments

Reference in these Regulations to [EU][1] instruments are references to those instruments as amended from time to time.

Amendment

1 Substituted by the Treaty of Lisbon (Changes in Terminology) Order 2011, SI 2011/1043, art 10(1)(d).

4 Meaning of "environmental damage"

(1) These Regulations apply in relation to the prevention and remediation of environmental damage; and "environmental damage" ("difrod amgylcheddol") is damage to—

(a) protected species or natural habitats, or a site of special scientific interest,

(b) surface water or groundwater, or

(c) land,

as specified in this regulation.

(2) Environmental damage to protected species or natural habitats or a site of special scientific interest means damage of a kind specified in Schedule 1.

(3) Environmental damage to surface water means damage to a surface water body classified as such pursuant to Directive 2000/60/EC of the European Parliament and of the Council establishing a framework for Community action in the field of water policy such that—

(a) a biological quality element listed in Annex V to that Directive,

(b) the level of a chemical listed in the legislation in Annex IX or a chemical listed in Annex X to that Directive, or

(c) a physicochemical quality element listed in Annex V to that Directive,

changes sufficiently to lower the status of the water body in accordance with Directive 2000/60/EC of the European Parliament and of the Council (whether or not the water body is in fact reclassified as being of lower status).

(4) Environmental damage to groundwater means any damage to a body of groundwater such that its conductivity, level or concentration of pollutants changes sufficiently to lower its status pursuant to Directive 2000/60/EC of the European Parliament and of the Council (and for pollutants Directive 2006/118/EC of the European Parliament and of the Council on the protection of groundwater against pollution and deterioration) (whether or not the body of groundwater is in fact reclassified as being of lower status).

(5) Environmental damage to land means contamination of land by substances, preparations, organisms or micro-organisms that results in a significant risk of adverse effects on human health.

5 Environmental damage to which these Regulations apply

(1) These Regulations apply in relation to environmental damage if it is caused by an activity in Schedule 2.

(2) In the case of environmental damage to protected species or natural habitats or a site of special scientific interest the Regulations also apply in relation to environmental damage caused by any other activity if the operator—
(a) intended to cause environmental damage; or
(b) was negligent as to whether environmental damage would be caused.

6 Areas of application

(1) The damage must be in an area specified in the following table—

Type of damage	*Area in which these Regulations apply*
Damage to water	Wales and all water up to one nautical mile seaward from the baseline in Wales
Damage in a site of special scientific interest	Wales
Damage to protected species or natural habitats	Wales
Damage to land	Wales

(2) In this regulation, "the baseline" means the baselines from which the breadth of the territorial sea is measured for the purposes of the Territorial Sea Act 1987.

7 Other legislation

(1) These Regulations are without prejudice to any other enactment concerning damage to the environment.

(2) They are without prejudice to the right of an operator to limit liability in accordance with the Convention on Limitation of Liability for Maritime Claims 1976.

8 Exemptions

(1) These Regulations do not apply in relation to—
(a) damage that took place before the coming into force of these Regulations;
(b) damage that takes place after that date, or is threatened after that date, but is caused by an incident, event or emission that took place before that date; or
(c) damage caused by an incident, event or emission that takes place after that date if it derives from an activity that took place and finished before that date.

(2) They do not apply in relation to environmental damage caused by—
(a) an act of terrorism;
(b) an exceptional natural phenomenon, provided the operator of the activity concerned took all reasonable precautions to protect against damage being caused by such an event;
(c) activities the sole purpose of which is to protect from natural disasters;
(d) an incident in respect of which liability or compensation falls within the scope of—

(i) the International Convention of 27 November 1992 on Civil Liability for Oil Pollution Damage;
(ii) the International Convention of 27 November 1992 on the Establishment of an International Fund for Compensation for Oil Pollution Damage; or
(iii) the International Convention on Civil Liability for Bunker Oil Pollution Damage 2001;

(e) activities the main purpose of which is to serve national defence or international security;
(f) radioactivity from an activity covered by the Treaty establishing the European Atomic Energy Community or caused by an incident or activity in respect of which liability or compensation falls within the scope of the Paris Convention of 29 July 1960 on Third Party Liability in the Field of Nuclear Energy and the Brussels Supplementary Convention of 31 January 1963; or
(g) damage caused in the course of commercial sea fishing if all legislation relating to that fishing was complied with.

(3) They only apply to environmental damage caused by pollution of a diffuse character if it is possible to establish a causal link between the damage and specific activities.

9 Exemption from damage to water

(1) Damage to water does not include—
(a) damage caused by new modifications to the physical characteristics of a surface water body,
(b) an alteration to the level of a body of groundwater pursuant to Directive 2000/60/EC of the European Parliament and of the Council, or
(c) deterioration from high status to good status of a body of surface water resulting from new sustainable human development activities pursuant to that Directive,
if all the conditions in paragraph (2) are fulfilled.

(2) The conditions are—
(a) all practicable steps are taken to mitigate the adverse impact on the status of the body of water;
(b) the reasons for those modifications or alterations are specifically set out and explained in the river basin management plan required under Article 13 of Directive 2000/60/EC of the European Parliament and of the Council and the objectives are reviewed every six years;
(c) the reasons for those modifications or alterations are of overriding public interest, or the result of the damage is outweighed by the benefits of the new modifications or alterations to human health, to the maintenance of human safety or to sustainable development; and
(d) the beneficial objectives served by those modifications or alterations of the water body cannot for reasons of technical feasibility or disproportionate cost be achieved by other means.

10 [Enforcing authorities under the Environmental Permitting (England and Wales) Regulations 2010][1]

(1) These Regulations are enforced in accordance with this regulation if the damage is caused by [an activity][1] that requires a permit or registration under the Environmental Permitting (England and Wales) Regulations [2010][1].

(2) If the Environment Agency is responsible for granting the permit, they are enforced by the Environment Agency in all cases.

(3) If the local authority is responsible for granting the permit—
(a) Part 2 is enforced by the local authority;
(b) Part 3 is enforced by—
(i) the local authority if the damage is to land;
(ii) the Environment Agency if the damage is to water;
(iii) Countryside Council for Wales if the damage is to natural habitats or protected species or a site of special scientific interest.

Amendment

1 Substituted by the Environmental Permitting (England and Wales) (Amendment) Regulations 2012, SI 2012/630, reg 19(1), (2)(b).

11 Enforcing authorities in other cases

(1) If the damage is caused by an activity that does not require a permit or registration under the Environmental Permitting (England and Wales) Regulations [2010][1] these Regulations are enforced in accordance with the following table.

Type of environmental damage	*Area of damage*	*Enforcing Authority*
Damage to water—		Environment Agency
Damage to protected species or natural habitats or a site of special scientific interest—	land	Countryside Council for Wales
	water but not in the sea[(1)]	Environment Agency
	the sea	— if the damage is due to an activity authorised by the Environment Agency, the Environment Agency; — otherwise the Welsh Ministers
Damage to land—		Local authority

(1) "Sea" includes—
(a) any area submerged at mean high water spring tide; and
(b) each of the following, so far as the tide flows at mean high water spring tide—
(i) every estuary or arm of the sea; and
(ii) the waters of any channel, creek, bay or river.

(2) The Welsh Ministers may give directions to an enforcing authority of a general or specific character with respect to the carrying out of its functions under these Regulations.

(3) An enforcing authority must comply with a direction given to it under these Regulations.

Amendment

1 Substituted by the Environmental Permitting (England and Wales) (Amendment) Regulations 2012, SI 2012/630, reg 19(1), (3).

12 Enforcement

(1) If there is more than one type of damage, so that there is more than one enforcing authority, these Regulations are enforced by any or all of the specified enforcing authorities.

(2) An enforcing authority may enter into an arrangement with any other enforcing authority to act on its behalf.

PART 2
PREVENTING ENVIRONMENTAL DAMAGE

13 Preventing environmental damage

(1) An operator of an activity that causes an imminent threat of environmental damage, or an imminent threat of damage in relation to which there are reasonable grounds to believe willbecome environmental damage, must immediately—
(a) take all practicable steps to prevent the damage; and
(b) (unless the threat has been eliminated) notify all relevant details to the enforcing authority appearing to be the appropriate one.

(2) The enforcing authority may serve a notice on that operator that—
(a) describes the threat;
(b) specifies the measures required to prevent the damage; and
(c) requires the operator to take those measures, or measures at least equivalent to them, within the period specified in the notice.

(3) Failure to comply with paragraph (1) or a notice served under paragraph (2) is an offence.

14 Preventing further environmental damage

(1) An operator of an activity that has caused environmental damage, or has caused damage where there are reasonable grounds to believe that the damage is or will become environmental damage, must immediately—
(a) take all practicable steps to prevent further damage; and
(b) notify all relevant details to the enforcing authority appearing to be the appropriate one.

(2) The enforcing authority may serve a notice on that operator that—
(a) describes the damage;
(b) requires the operator to provide additional information on any damage that has occurred;
(c) specifies the measures required to prevent further damage; and
(d) requires the operator to take those measures, or measures at least equivalent to them, within the period specified in the notice.

(3) Failure to comply with paragraph (1) or a notice served under paragraph (2) is an offence.

15 Action by the enforcing authority

Any duty in this Part on the operator of an activity may be carried out by the enforcing authority instead of the operator—
(a) in an emergency;
(b) if the operator cannot be ascertained; or
(c) if the operator fails to comply with a notice.

16 Following instructions from a public authority

When an operator acts in accordance with the instructions of a public authority, and as a result causes or threatens to cause environmental damage, and accordingly action is taken under regulations 13, 14 or 15 then, unless the instructions related to an emission or incident caused by the operator's own activities, the operator may recover the costs of actions under those regulations from that public authority.

PART 3
REMEDIATION

17 Assessment of damage

Where damage has been caused, and there are reasonable grounds for believing that it is, or may be, environmental damage, the enforcing authority must establish whether or not it is environmental damage.

18 Determining liability to remediate

(1) If the enforcing authority decides that the damage is environmental damage it must notify the operator or operators of any activity or activities that caused the damage (referred to in these Regulations as "the responsible operator" ("y gweithredwr cyfrifol")) that—

(a) the damage is environmental damage;
(b) the responsible operator's activity was a cause of the environmental damage;
(c) the responsible operator must submit proposals, within a time specified by the enforcing authority, for measures that will achieve the remediation of the environmental damage in accordance with Schedule 4; and
(d) the responsible operator has a right to appeal.

(2) The enforcing authority may withdraw or vary the notification if it is satisfied that the notification should not have been served or that an appeal against the notification is likely to succeed.

19 Appeals against liability to remediate

(1) A person served with notification under regulation 18 may notify the Welsh Ministers that that person intends to appeal against that notification.

(2) Notice of appeal must be served on the Welsh Ministers within 28 days of service of the notification under regulation 18 unless the time limit is extended by the Welsh Ministers.

(3) The grounds of appeal are—

(a) the operator's activity was not a cause of the environmental damage;
(b) the enforcing authority has acted unreasonably in deciding that the damage is environmental damage;
(c) the environmental damage resulted from compliance with an instruction from a public authority (except an instruction relating to an emission or incident caused by the operator's own activities);
(d) the responsible operator was not at fault or negligent and the environmental damage was caused by an emission or event expressly authorised by, and fully in accordance with the conditions of a permit listed in Schedule 3;
(e) the responsible operator was not at fault or negligent and the environmental damage was caused by an emission or activity or any manner of using a product in the course of an activity that the operator demonstrates was not considered likely to cause environmental damage according to the state of scientific and technical knowledge at the time when the emission was released or the activity took place;
(f) the environmental damage was the result of an act of a third party and occurred despite the fact that the responsible operator took all appropriate safety measures.

(4) Paragraph 3(e) does not apply in relation to the deliberate release of genetically modified organisms.

(5) Schedule 5 contains procedures for the appeal.

(6) The person deciding the appeal may confirm or quash the notice.

20 Remediation notices

(1) Once it receives the proposals from the responsible operator (or, if a proposal is not received within the specified time limit, at any time after the time limit has expired), the enforcing authority must, so far as is practicable, consult—
(a) anyone who has notified an enforcing authority under regulation 29, and
(b) any person on whose land the remedial measures will be carried out,
and may consult any other person appearing to be necessary.

(2) Following consultation the enforcing authority must serve a remediation notice on the responsible operator that specifies—
(a) the damage;
(b) the measures necessary for remediation of the damage, together with the reasons;
(c) the period within which those measures must be taken;
(d) any additional monitoring or investigative measures that the responsible operator must carry out during remediation; and
(e) the right of appeal against the remediation notice.

(3) The enforcing authority may withdraw or vary the remediation notice if it is satisfied that the remediation notice should not have been served or that an appeal against the remediation notice is likely to succeed.

(4) Failure to comply with a remediation notice is an offence.

21 Appeal against the remediation notice

(1) The responsible operator may notify the Welsh Ministers that that person intends to appeal against the remediation notice on the grounds that its contents are unreasonable.

(2) An appeal may only be brought against those parts of the remediation notice that are different from proposals made by the responsible operator.

(3) Notice of appeal must be served on the Welsh Ministers within 28 days of service of the remediation notice unless the time limit is extended by the Welsh Ministers.

(4) Schedule 5 contains procedures for the appeal.

(5) The Welsh Ministers or the appointed person may confirm, vary or quash the notice, and must give written notification of the final decision and the reasons for it, and may, if appropriate, add further compensatory remediation requirements necessitated by the lapse of time since the remediation notice was served.

(6) A remediation notice need not be complied with pending determination of an appeal unless the person hearing the appeal directs otherwise.

22 Further provisions on remediation notices

An enforcing authority may serve further remediation notices at any time while remediation is being carried out or, if remediation has not been achieved, at the end of the remediation period, requiring further or different remediation.

23 Action by the enforcing authority

Once it has established that in its opinion damage is environmental damage, the enforcing authority may carry out any reasonable works—

(a) at any time if a responsible operator cannot be identified;
(b) if a responsible operator fails to comply with a remediation notice, whether or not an appeal is pending; or
(c) if the responsible operator is not required to remediate under these Regulations.

PART 4
ADMINISTRATION AND ENFORCEMENT

24 Costs when the enforcing authority acts instead of the operator

(1) An operator liable to carry out works under Part 2 is liable for any reasonable costs incurred by the enforcing authority in taking any reasonable action under regulation 15.

(2) The responsible operator is liable for the reasonable costs of the enforcing authority for any action taken under regulation 23 unless the responsible operator was not liable for the action taken.

25 Costs concerned with administration

(1) An operator liable to carry out works under Part 2 is liable for the reasonable costs incurred by the enforcing authority in preparing any notice under Part 2, or in ensuring compliance with that Part.

(2) The responsible operator is responsible for the costs incurred by the enforcing authority under Part 3 of—
(a) assessing whether the damage is environmental damage;
(b) establishing who is the responsible operator;
(c) establishing what remediation is appropriate;
(d) carrying out necessary consultation; and
(e) monitoring the remediation, both during and after the work.

(3) Costs means costs that are justified by the need to ensure the proper and effective enforcement of these Regulations.

26 Proceedings for costs by an enforcing authority

No proceedings for the recovery of costs may be commenced by the enforcing authority under these Regulations after a period of 5 years has elapsed since—
(a) the completion of the measures to which the proceedings relate, or
(b) the identification of the operator liable to carry out the measures,
whichever is the later.

27 Costs recoverable from owner to be a charge on premises

(1) Where any costs are recoverable under these Regulations by an enforcing authority from a person who is the owner of premises and the enforcing authority serves a notice on that person under this regulation—
(a) the costs carry interest, at such reasonable rate as the authority may determine, from the date of service of the notice until the whole amount is paid; and
(b) subject to the following, the costs and accrued interest are a charge on the premises.

(2) A notice served under this regulation must—
(a) specify the amount of the costs that the enforcing authority claims is recoverable;
(b) state the effect of paragraph (1) and the rate of interest determined by the enforcing authority under that paragraph; and
(c) state the effect of paragraphs (4) to (6).

(3) On the date on which an enforcing authority serves a notice on a person under this regulation the authority must also serve a copy of the notice on every other person who, to the knowledge of the authority, has an interest in the premises capable of being affected by the charge.

(4) Subject to any order under paragraph (7)(b) or (c) below, the amount of any costs specified in a notice under this regulation and the accrued interest is a charge on the premises—
(a) as from the end of the period of 21 days beginning with the date of service of the notice, or
(b) where an appeal is brought under paragraph (6), as from the final determination of the appeal,
until the costs and interest are recovered.

(5) For the purposes of paragraph (4), the withdrawal of an appeal has the same effect as a final determination of the appeal.

(6) A person served with a notice or copy of a notice under this regulation may appeal against the notice to the county court within the period of 21 days beginning with the date of service.

(7) On such an appeal the court may—
(a) confirm the notice without modification;
(b) order that the notice is to have effect with the substitution of a different amount for the amount originally specified in it; or
(c) order that the notice is to be of no effect.

(8) An enforcing authority has, for the purpose of enforcing a charge under this regulation, all the same powers and remedies under the Law of Property Act 1925, and otherwise, as if it were a mortgagee by deed having powers of sale and lease, of accepting surrenders of leases and of appointing a receiver.

(9) In this regulation, "owner" ("perchennog"), in relation to any premises, means a person (other than a mortgagee not in possession) who, whether in that person's own right or as trustee for any other person, is entitled to receive the rack rent of the premises or, where the premises are not let at a rack rent, would be so entitled if they were so let.

28 Recovery of costs from other persons

An operator who incurs liability to the enforcing authority under these Regulations (whether in carrying out work or in payment to the enforcing authority) may recover all or some of those costs from any other person who also caused the damage.

29 Requests for action by interested parties

(1) Any person—
(a) who is affected or likely to be affected by environmental damage, or
(b) who otherwise has a sufficient interest,
may notify the appropriate enforcing authority of any environmental damage which is being, or has been caused or of which there is an imminent threat.

(2) A notification must be accompanied by—
(a) a statement explaining the way the notifier will be affected by the damage, or the reason that the notifier has a sufficient interest; and
(b) sufficient information to enable the enforcing authority to identify the location and nature of the incident.

(3) The enforcing authority must consider the notification and inform the notifier as to the action, if any, that it intends to take.

(4) Before taking any decision the enforcing authority must, if practicable—
(a) notify the operator concerned of the notification and the accompanying information; and
(b) invite that operator to submit comments on them.

(5) Paragraphs (3) and (4) do not apply if—
(a) the notifier is not likely to be affected or does not have a sufficient interest;
(b) in the opinion of the enforcing authority the information provided does not disclose any environmental damage or threat of environmental damage; or
(c) as a result of the urgency of the situation, it is not practicable for the enforcing authority to comply with those paragraphs.

30 Grant of and compensation for rights of entry etc.

(1) Any person whose consent is required before any works required by these Regulations may be carried out must grant, or join in granting, such rights in relation to any land or water as will enable the operator, or a person acting on behalf of the operator, to carry out that work.

(2) A person who grants, or joins in granting, any rights as required by paragraph (1) is entitled to compensation from the operator determined in accordance with Schedule 6.

31 Powers of authorised persons

(1) Enforcing authorities may authorise persons for the purposes of enforcing these Regulations.

(2) The powers in section 108 of the Environment Act 1995 apply in relation to these Regulations, and the powers of persons authorised by the Environment Agency in that section are exercisable by persons authorised by any enforcing authority.

(3) Those powers are extended to all areas to which these Regulations apply.

(4) In addition, a person authorised by the Welsh Ministers enforcing these Regulations in relation to the sea may at any time board and inspect a ship or marine installation.

(5) For the purposes of exercising the powers in this regulation, the authorised person may require a ship or marine installation—
(a) to stop; or
(b) to do anything else that will facilitate the boarding of that or any other ship or marine installation.

(6) An authorised person who has boarded a ship or marine installation may, for the purposes of disembarking from the ship or installation, require that or any other ship or marine installation—
(a) to stop; or
(b) to do anything else that will enable the authorised person, and any person accompanying that person, to disembark.

(7) An authorised person may require any person on board a vessel or marine installation to afford such facilities and assistance with respect to matters under that person's control as the authorised person considers would facilitate the exercise of any power conferred by this regulation.

(8) It is an offence to fail to comply with instructions given under this regulation, or knowingly to provide false or misleading information.

32 Provision of information to the enforcing authority

An enforcing authority may require an operator to provide such information as it may reasonably require to enable the enforcing authority to carry out its functions under these Regulations, and failure to provide such information is an offence.

33 Enforcement

No enforcement action may be taken under these Regulations 30 years or more after the emission, event or incident concerned.

34 Penalties

(1) A person guilty of an offence under these Regulations is liable—

(a) on summary conviction, to a fine not exceeding the statutory maximum or to imprisonment for a term not exceeding three months or both; or

(b) on conviction on indictment, to a fine or to imprisonment for a term not exceeding two years or both.

(2) Where a body corporate is guilty of an offence under these Regulations, and that offence is proved to have been committed with the consent or connivance of, or to have been attributable to any neglect on the part of—

(a) any director, manager, secretary or other similar person of the body corporate, or

(b) any person who was purporting to act in any such capacity,

that person is guilty of the offence as well as the body corporate.

(3) For the purposes of paragraph (2), "director" ("cyfarwyddwr"), in relation to a body corporate whose affairs are managed by its members, means a member of the body corporate.

SCHEDULE 1
DAMAGE TO PROTECTED SPECIES, NATURAL HABITATS AND SITES OF SPECIAL SCIENTIFIC INTEREST

Regulation 4

1 Damage to protected species and natural habitats

(1) In the case of protected species or natural habitat (other than damage on a site of special scientific interest to which paragraph 4 applies) the damage must be such that it has a significant adverse effect on reaching or maintaining the favourable conservation status of the protected species or natural habitat taking into account—

(a) the conservation status at the time of the damage;

(b) the services provided by the amenities they produce;

(c) their capacity for natural regeneration;

(d) the number of individuals, their density or the area covered;

(e) the role of the particular individuals or of the damaged area in relation to the species or to the habitat conservation and the rarity of the species or habitat assessed at the relevant level whether local, regional or Community-wide;

(f) the capacity of the species for propagation, its viability or the capacity of the habitat for natural regeneration; and

(g) the capacity of the species or habitat to recover within a short time of the damage being caused to a condition that leads to its state at the time of the damage or better without any intervention other than increased protection measures.

2 Conservation status of natural habitats

(1) A natural habitat's conservation status is the sum of the influences acting on that habitat and its typical species that may affect its long term natural distribution, structure and functions as well as the long term survival of its typical species.

(2) Its conservation status is favourable if—
(a) the natural range and areas covered within that natural range are stable or increasing;
(b) the specific structure and functions which are necessary for the long term maintenance of the natural habitat exist and are likely to continue to exist for the foreseeable future; and
(c) the conservation status of its typical species is favourable.

3 Conservation status of species

(1) A species' conservation status is the sum of the influences acting on the species concerned that may affect the long term distribution and abundance of its populations.

(2) The conservation status is favourable if—
(a) the population dynamics data on the species concerned indicate that it is maintaining itself on a long term basis as a viable component of its natural habitat;
(b) the natural range of the species is neither being reduced nor is likely to be reduced for the foreseeable future; and
(c) there is, and will probably continue to be, a sufficiently large habitat to maintain its populations on a long term basis.

4 Sites of special scientific interest

(1) In the case of a site of special scientific interest, the damage must be to—
(a) the species or habitats notified under section 28 of the Wildlife and Countryside Act 1981; or
(b) protected species or natural habitats.

(2) The damage must have an adverse effect on the integrity of the site (that is, the coherence of its ecological structure and function, across its whole area, that enables it to sustain the habitat, complex of habitats or the levels of populations of the species affected).

5 Express authorisation

Damage to protected species and natural habitats, and damage on a site of special scientific interest, does not include damage caused by an act expressly authorised by the relevant authorities in accordance with the Conservation (Natural Habitats, etc.) Regulations 1994 or Part II of the Wildlife and Countryside Act 1981.

SCHEDULE 2
ACTIVITIES CAUSING DAMAGE

Regulation 5

1 Operations to which this Schedule applies

This Schedule lists the activities for which there is liability under regulation 5(1).

2 Operation of permitted installations

The operation of installations subject to permit in pursuance of Directive 2008/1/EC of the European Parliament and of the Council concerning integrated pollution prevention and control (all activities listed in Annex I to that Directive with the exception of installations or parts of installations used for research, development and testing of new products and processes).

3 Waste management operations

(1) Waste management operations, including the collection, transport, recovery and disposal of waste and hazardous waste, including the supervision of such operations and after—care of disposal sites, subject to permit or registration in pursuance of [Directive 2008/98/EC of the European Parliament and of the Council on waste][1].

(2) The operation of landfill sites under Council Directive 1999/31/EC on the landfill of waste and the operation of incineration plants under Directive 2000/76/EC of the European Parliament and of the Council on the incineration of waste.

(3) This does not include the spreading of sewage sludge from urban waste water treatment plants, treated to an approved standard, for agricultural purposes.

Amendment

1 Substituted by the Waste (Miscellaneous Provisions) (Wales) Regulations 2011, SI 2011/971, reg 6.

4 Mining waste

The management of extractive waste under Directive 2006/21/EC of the European Parliament and of the Council on the management of waste from extractive industries.

5 Discharges requiring authorisation

(1) All discharges into the inland surface water that require prior authorisation in pursuance of Directive 2006/11/EC of the European Parliament and of the Council on pollution caused by certain dangerous substances discharged into the aquatic environment of the Community.

(2) All discharges of substances into groundwater that require prior authorisation in pursuance of Council Directive 80/68/EEC on the protection of groundwater against pollution caused by certain dangerous substances.

(3) All discharges or injections of pollutants into surface water or groundwater that require a permit, authorisation or registration under Directive 2000/60/EC of the European Parliament and of the Council of establishing a framework for Community action in the field of water policy.

6 Water abstraction and impoundment

Water abstraction and impoundment of water subject to prior authorisation in pursuance of Directive 2000/60/EC of the European Parliament and of the Council establishing a framework for Community action in the field of water policy.

7 Dangerous substances, plant protection products and biocidal products

Manufacture, use, storage, processing, filling, release into the environment and onsite transport of—

(a) dangerous substances as defined in Article 2(2) of Council Directive 67/548/EEC on the approximation of the laws, regulations and administrative provisions of the Member States relating to the classification, packaging and labelling of dangerous substances;

(b) dangerous preparations as defined in Article 2(2) of Directive 1999/45/EC of the European Parliament and of the Council concerning the approximation of the laws, regulations and administrative provisions of the Member States relating to the classification, packaging and labelling of dangerous preparations;

(c) plant protection products [which has the same meaning as in Article 2(1) of Regulation (EC) No 1107/2009 of the European Parliament and of the Council concerning the placing of plant protection products on the market and repealing Council Directives 79/117/EEC and 91/414/EEC][1]; and

(d) biocidal products as defined in Article 2(1)(a) of Directive 98/8/EC of the European Parliament and of the Council concerning the placing of biocidal products on the market.

Amendment

1 Substituted by the Plant Protection Products Regulations 2011, SI 2011/2131, reg 31(1), Sch 4.

8 Transport

Transport by road, rail, inland waterways, sea or air of dangerous goods or polluting goods as defined in—

(a) Annex A to Council Directive 94/55/EC on the approximation of the laws of the Member States with regard to the transport of dangerous goods by road;

(b) the Annex to Council Directive 96/49/EC on the approximation of the laws of the Member States with regard to the transport of dangerous goods by rail; and

(c) Council Directive 93/75/EEC concerning minimum requirements for vessels bound for or leaving Community ports and carrying dangerous or polluting goods.

9 Genetically modified organisms

(1) Any contained use, including transport, involving genetically modified organisms (including genetically modified micro-organisms as defined by Council Directive 90/219/EEC on the contained use of genetically modified micro-organisms).

(2) Any deliberate release into the environment, transport and placing on the market of genetically modified organisms as defined by Directive 2001/18/EC of the European Parliament and of the Council on the deliberate release into the environment of genetically modified organisms.

10 Transboundary shipment of waste

Transboundary shipment of waste within, into or out of the Community, requiring an authorisation or prohibited under Regulation (EC) No 1013/2006 of the European Parliament and of the Council on shipments of waste.

SCHEDULE 3
PERMITS, ETC.

Regulation 19

1

The following are permits for the purposes of regulation 19(3) in so far as they relate to an activity in Schedule 2—

(a) a permit granted under the Environmental Permitting (England and Wales) Regulations [2010][1] or a registration under those Regulations;

[(b) a marine licence granted under Part 4 of the Marine and Coastal Access Act 2009;][2]

(c) ...[3] an ordinary or emergency drought order or a drought permit under the Water Resources Act 1991;

(d) ...[3]

(e) a water abstraction or impoundment licence under the Water Resources Act 1991;

(f) [an authorisation of, or permission for, a plant protection product granted, or deemed to be granted, in accordance with Regulation (EC) No 1107/2009 of the European Parliament and of the Council concerning the placing of plant protection products on the market and repealing Council Directives 79/117/EEC and 91/414/EEC.][4]

Amendments

1 Substituted by the Environmental Permitting (England and Wales) (Amendment) Regulations 2012, SI 2012/630, reg 19(1), (4)(b)(i).

2 Substituted by the Marine and Coastal Access Act 2009 (Commencement No.5, Consequential and Transitional Provisions) Order 2011, SI 2011/556, art 5, Schedule, para 10(1), (2)(a).

3 Repealed by the Environmental Permitting (England and Wales) (Amendment) Regulations 2012, SI 2012/630, reg 19(1), (4)(b)(ii), (iii).

4 Substituted by the Plant Protection Products Regulations 2011, SI 2011/2131, reg 31(1), Sch 4.

SCHEDULE 4
REMEDIATION

Regulation 18

PART 1
REMEDIATION OF DAMAGE TO NATURAL RESOURCES OTHER THAN LAND

1 Application of Part 1

This Part relates to remediation of damage to natural resources other than land.

2 Risk to human health

Remediation must remove any significant risk to human health.

3 Objective

The objective of remediation is to achieve the same level of natural resource or services as would have existed if the damage had not occurred.

4 Primary and complementary remediation

(1) The remediation must consist of such primary remediation or complementary remediation or both as will achieve the objective.

(2) Primary remediation is any remedial measure which returns the damaged natural resources or impaired services to, or towards, the state that would have existed if the damage had not occurred (natural recovery is a permitted form of primary remediation in appropriate cases).

(3) Complementary remediation is any remedial measure taken in relation to natural resources or services to compensate for the fact that primary remediation does not result in fully restoring the damaged natural resources or impaired services to the state that would have existed if the damage had not occurred.

5 Compensatory remediation

(1) In addition compensatory remediation must be provided to compensate for interim losses of natural resources or services that occur from the date of damage until remediation has achieved its objective; and in this paragraph "interim losses" ("colledion interim") means losses which result from the fact that the damaged natural resources or services are not able to perform their ecological functions or provide services to other natural resources or to the public until the primary or complementary remediation has been carried out.

(2) Compensatory remediation does not include financial compensation.

6 Choice of remediation

(1) The remediation options must be evaluated using best available methods, and based on—

(a) the effect of each option on public health and safety;

(b) the cost of implementing the option;

(c) the likelihood of success of each option;

(d) the extent to which each option will prevent future damage, and avoid collateral damage as a result of implementing the option;

(e) the extent to which each option benefits each component of the natural resource or service;

(f) the extent to which each option takes account of relevant social, economic and cultural concerns and other relevant factors specific to the locality;

(g) the length of time it will take for the restoration of the environmental damage to be effective;

(h) the extent to which each option achieves the restoration of the site of the environmental damage; and

(i) the geographical linkage to the damaged site.

7 Identification of complementary and compensatory remediation

(1) If possible, complementary and compensatory remedial measures must provide natural resources or services of the same type, quality and quantity as those damaged.

(2) Where this is not possible, similar but different natural resources or services must be provided (for example, by offsetting a reduction in the quality of natural resources or services by increasing their quantity).

(3) Where this is not possible, different natural resources or services may be provided, and the remedial measures must have the same monetary valuation as the lost natural resources or services.

(4) If valuation of the lost natural resources or services is practicable, but valuation of the remedial measures cannot be made within a reasonable time or at a reasonable cost, then remedial measures may be provided whose cost (instead of monetary valuation) is equivalent to the value of the lost natural resources or services.

(5) In the case of complementary remediation at a new site, where possible and appropriate this site should be geographically linked to the damaged site.

8 Options

(1) When evaluating the different identified remedial options, primary remedial measures that do not fully restore the damaged water or protected species or natural habitat to its state at the time of the incident or that restore it more slowly may be decided on (for example, when the equivalent natural resources or services could be provided elsewhere at a lower cost).

(2) This decision can be taken only if the natural resources or services foregone as a result of the decision are compensated for by increasing complementary or compensatory actions to provide a similar level of natural resources or services.

(3) The enforcing authority may at any time decide that no further remedial measures need be taken if—

(a) the remedial measures already taken have removed any significant risk of adversely affecting human health, water or protected species and natural habitats; and

(b) the cost of the remedial measures needed for restoration to its state before the incident would be disproportionate to the environmental benefits to be obtained.

PART 2
REMEDIATION OF DAMAGE TO LAND

9 Remediation of damage to land

(1) This Part applies in relation to damage to land.

(2) The remediation must ensure, as a minimum, that the relevant contaminants are removed, controlled, contained or diminished so that the land, taking account of its lawful current use or any planning permission in existence at the time of the damage, no longer poses any significant risk of adverse effects on human health.

(3) The presence of such risks must be assessed through risk-assessment procedures taking into account the characteristic and function of the soil, the type and concentration of the harmful substances, preparations, organisms or micro-organisms, their risk and the possibility of their dispersion.

(4) Natural recovery is a permitted form of remediation in appropriate cases.

SCHEDULE 5
APPEALS

Regulations 19 and 21

PART 1
APPEALS WHEN THE WELSH MINISTERS ARE NOT THE ENFORCING AUTHORITY

1

This Part applies when the Welsh Ministers are not the enforcing authority.

2

Notification of appeal must contain—
(a) a copy of the notification or remediation notice appealed against; and
(b) the grounds of appeal.

3

When notification is received, the Welsh Ministers must send a copy of the notification of appeal to the enforcing authority, and the enforcing authority must immediately send a copy to any person who appears to it to have a particular interest in the subject matter of the appeal, and notify the Welsh Ministers whom it has notified.

4

The Welsh Ministers must notify the appellant of the time limit within which the appellant must provide in writing—
(a) a statement of case; and
(b) all relevant correspondence.

5

When these are received, the Welsh Ministers must send all the documents to the enforcing authority, giving the enforcing authority a time limit within which it must provide a written response.

6

At the same time the Welsh Ministers must notify any person notified under paragraph 3 of the time limit under paragraph 5 and invite them to make representations before that date.

7

The Welsh Ministers must then decide whether further evidence is needed, and give directions accordingly.

8

The Welsh Ministers must then refer the appeal to a person appointed by the Welsh Ministers to deal with the appeal, and specify to the appointed person whether or not the appeal must be dealt with by written procedure or whether a hearing must be held.

9

Following the conclusion of the appeal by the appointed person, the appointed person must decide the matter or, if so directed by the Welsh Ministers at any stage before the decision is made, make a recommendation to the Welsh Ministers, who must decide the appeal.

10

The person deciding the appeal may make such order as to the costs of the parties (including parties who make representation) as is fit.

PART 2
APPEALS WHEN THE WELSH MINISTERS ARE THE ENFORCING AUTHORITY

11

If the Welsh Ministers are the enforcing authority, the procedures in Part 1 apply except that—
(a) the Welsh Ministers must appoint a person as soon as notification of appeal is received;
(b) the appointed person must carry out the functions of the Welsh Ministers specified in that Part; and
(c) the appointed person must in all cases decide the appeal.

SCHEDULE 6
COMPENSATION

Regulation 30

1 Compensation for grant of rights

This Schedule prescribes—
(a) the period within which a person who grants, or joins in granting, any rights pursuant to regulation 30 may apply for compensation for the grant of those rights;
(b) the manner in which, and the person to whom, such an application may be made; and
(c) the manner of determining such compensation, for determining the amount of such compensation and for making supplemental provision relating to such compensation.

2 Interpretation

In this Schedule—

"the grantor" ("y grantwr") means the person who grants, or joins in granting, any right; and

"relevant interest" ("buddiant perthnasol") means an interest in land out of which a right has been granted or which is bound by a right granted.

3 Period for making an application

An application for compensation must be made before the expiry of a period of 12 months beginning with—
(a) the date of the grant of the rights in respect of which compensation is claimed, or
(b) where there is an appeal against the notice in relation to which those rights were granted, the date on which the appeal is determined or withdrawn,

whichever is the later date.

4 Manner of making an application

(1) An application for compensation must be made in writing and delivered at or sent by pre-paid post to the last known address for correspondence of the person to whom the right was granted.

(2) The application must contain—
(a) a copy of the grant of rights in respect of which the grantor is applying for compensation and of any plans attached to such grant;
(b) a description of the exact nature of any interest in land in respect of which compensation is applied for; and

(c) a statement of the amount of compensation applied for, distinguishing the amounts applied for under each of sub-paragraphs (a) to (e) of paragraph 5 and showing how the amount applied for under each sub-paragraph has been calculated.

5 Loss and damage for which compensation payable

Compensation is payable for loss and damage of the following descriptions—

(a) any depreciation in the value of any relevant interest to which the grantor is entitled which results from the grant of the right;

(b) loss or damage, in relation to any relevant interest to which the grantor is entitled, which—

 (i) is attributable to the grant of the right or the exercise of it;

 (ii) does not consist of depreciation in the value of that interest; and

 (iii) is loss or damage for which the grantor would have been entitled to compensation by way of compensation for disturbance, if that interest had been acquired compulsorily under the Acquisition of Land Act 1981, in pursuance of a notice to treat served on the date on which the grant of the right was made;

(c) damage to any interest in land to which the grantor is entitled which is not a relevant interest and which results from the grant of the right or from the exercise of it;

(d) any loss or damage sustained by the grantor, other than in relation to any interest in land to which the grantor is entitled, which is attributable to the grant of the right or the exercise of it; and

(e) the amount of any valuation and legal costs reasonably incurred by the grantor in granting the right and in the preparation of the application for and the negotiation of the amount of compensation.

6 Basis on which compensation assessed

(1) The rules set out in section 5 of the Land Compensation Act 1961 (rules for assessing compensation) have effect, so far as applicable and subject to any necessary modifications, for the purpose of assessing any compensation as they have effect for the purpose of assessing compensation for the compulsory acquisition of an interest in land.

(2) Where the relevant interest in respect of which any compensation is to be assessed is subject to a mortgage—

(a) the compensation must be assessed as if the interest were not subject to the mortgage;

(b) no compensation is payable in respect of the interest of the mortgagee (as distinct from the interest which is subject to the mortgage); and

(c) any compensation payable in respect of the interest that is subject to the mortgage must be paid to the mortgagee or, if there is more than one mortgagee, to the first mortgagee and must, in either case, be applied as if it were proceeds of sale.

7 Determination of disputes

(1) Any question of disputed compensation must be referred to and determined by the Lands Tribunal.

(2) In relation to the determination of any such question of compensation the provisions of sections 2 and 4 of the Land Compensation Act 1961 (procedure on references to the Lands Tribunal and costs) shall apply as if—

(a) the reference in section 2 of the Land Compensation Act 1961 to section 1 of that Act were a reference to sub-paragraph (1) of this paragraph; and

(b) references in section 4 of that Act to the acquiring authority were references to the person to whom the rights were granted.

LANDFILL TAX (PRESCRIBED LANDFILL SITE ACTIVITIES) ORDER 2009

SI 2009/1929

1 Citation and commencement

This Order may be cited as The Landfill Tax (Prescribed Landfill Site Activities) Order 2009 and comes into force on 1st September 2009.

2 Interpretation

In this Order—

"cell bund" means a structure within a disposal area which separates units of waste;

"disposal area" means any area of a landfill site where any landfill disposal takes place;

"hard standing" means a base within a landfill site on which any landfill site activity such as sorting, treatment, processing, storage or recycling is carried out;

"haul road" means any road within a landfill site which gives access to a disposal area;

"screening bund" means any structure on a landfill site (whether below or above ground) put in place to protect or conceal any landfill site activity or to reduce nuisance from noise.

3 Prescribed landfill site activities

(1) The following landfill site activities are prescribed for the purposes of section 65A of the Finance Act 1996 (activities to be treated as disposals):

(a) the use of material to cover the disposal area during a short term cessation in landfill disposal activity;
(b) the use of material to create or maintain a temporary haul road;
(c) the use of material to create or maintain temporary hard standing;
(d) the use of material to create or maintain a cell bund;
(e) the use of material to create or maintain a temporary screening bund except where the material so used is naturally occurring material extracted from the landfill site in which the temporary screening bund is located;
(f) the temporary storage of ashes (including pulverised fuel ash and furnace bottom ash);
(g) the use of material placed against the drainage layer or liner of the disposal area to prevent damage to that layer or liner;
(h) any other landfill site activity if in relation to that activity—
    (i) paragraph 1B of Part 1 of Schedule 5 to the Finance Act 1996 requires a person to notify or give information, or under regulation 16A of the Landfill Tax Regulations 1996 a person is required to designate a part of a landfill site as an "information area", give information or maintain a record in respect of the area; and
    (ii) that requirement is not complied with.

(2) Paragraph (1) does not apply to any landfill site activity if, or to the extent that, it involves material that is or has been otherwise chargeable to landfill tax or exempted from landfill tax.

CONSERVATION OF HABITATS AND SPECIES REGULATIONS 2010

SI 2010/490

PART 1
INTRODUCTORY AND GENERAL PROVISIONS

1 Citation and commencement

(1) These Regulations may be cited as the Conservation of Habitats and Species Regulations 2010.

(2) Except as provided by paragraphs (3) and (4), these Regulations come into force on 1st April 2010.

(3) In regulation 6 (relevant authorities in relation to marine areas and European marine sites), paragraph (i) (inshore fisheries and conservation authority) comes into force immediately after section 153 of the Marine Act (management of inshore fisheries) comes into force.

(4) The following provisions come into force immediately after section 134 of the Marine Act (orders for protection of marine conservation zones in Wales) comes into force (so far as not already brought into force)—

(a) paragraph (2) of regulation 38 (European marine sites: byelaws and orders), and paragraphs (3), (4) and (5) of that regulation in so far as they relate to paragraph (2); and

(b) paragraph (3) of regulation 133 (revocations), in so far as that paragraph relates to the revocation, as regards Wales, of—

(i) the entry "sections 36 and 37 of the Wildlife and Countryside Act 1981 (marine nature reserves)," in paragraph (3) of regulation 3 (implementation of Directive) of the 1994 Regulations, and

(ii) regulation 36 (byelaws for protection of European marine site) of the 1994 Regulations.

2 Extent

(1) Except as provided in this regulation, these Regulations extend to England and Wales only.

(2) The following provisions also extend to Scotland—

(a) regulation 3(8) (interpretation in relation to adjacent sea);

[(b) regulations 9 (duties relating to compliance with the Directives) and 9A (duties in relation to wild bird habitat), in so far as those regulations apply in relation to the exercise of a function which relates to a reserved matter (within the meaning of Schedule 5 to the Scotland Act 1998 (reserved matters));][1]

(c) regulation 39(4) (statement under Planning Act 2008);

[(ca) Chapter 1 of Part 6 (assessment of plans and projects: general provisions), in so far as that Chapter applies in relation to plans and projects—

(i) which do not relate to a matter specified in Chapters 2 to 9 of that Part, and

(ii) which relate to a reserved matter (within the meaning of Schedule 5 to the Scotland Act 1998);][2]

(d) in regulation 68 (grant of planning permission)—

(i) paragraph (1)(e)(ii) and (iii) (deemed grant of planning permission under section 57(2) of the Town and Country Planning (Scotland) Act 1997 and section 5(1) of the Pipe-lines Act 1962), and

(ii) paragraph (2) in so far as that paragraph relates to paragraph (1)(e)(ii) and (iii) of that regulation;

(e) in regulation 69 (planning permission: duty to review), in paragraph (3)—

(i) sub-paragraph (b) (direction under section 5(1) of the Pipe-lines Act 1962), and

(ii) sub-paragraph (d) in so far as that sub-paragraph relates to a direction under section 57(2) of the Town and Country Planning (Scotland) Act 1997;

(f) regulations 81, 82 and 83(2) (development consent under Planning Act 2008);

(g) Chapter 4 of Part 6 (electricity);

(h) Chapter 5 of Part 6 (pipe-lines);

[(ha) regulation 100 (marine works) in so far as it applies to the granting of a licence under Part 2 of the Food and Environment Protection Act 1985;][3]

(i) regulation 106 (national policy statements under Planning Act 2008), and regulations 102, 103 and 105 in so far as they apply in relation to a national policy statement by virtue of regulation 106; …[4]

[(ia) regulation 107A, in so far as it applies in relation to the exercise of any power by the Secretary of State, and regulations 102, 103 and 105 in so far as they apply to marine policy statements by virtue of regulation 107A;][3]

(j) in Schedule 6 (amendments of legislation)—

(i) sub-paragraph (3) of paragraph 5 (amendment of section 123 of the Marine Act),

(ii) sub-paragraph (5) of that paragraph (amendment of section 237 of that Act), and

(iii) paragraph 7 (amendment of the 2007 Regulations),

and regulation 132 in so far as it relates to those provisions.

(3) The following provisions also extend to Scotland in so far as they have effect in relation to the provisions specified in paragraph (2)—

(a) regulations [1 (citation and commencement) and 2 (extent),][3] 3 (interpretation), 5 (nature conservation bodies), 7 (competent authorities) and 8 (European sites and European marine sites);

(b) Chapter 1 of Part 6 (general provisions in relation to Part 6 (assessment of plans and projects)); and

(c) regulations 128 (advisory role of the Joint Nature Conservation Committee), 129(3) (advisory role of Scottish Natural Heritage) and 131 (notices).

[(4) The following provisions also extend to Northern Ireland—

(a) regulations 9 and 9A, in so far as those regulations apply in relation to the exercise of a function which relates to an excepted matter (within the meaning given by section 4(1) of the Northern Ireland Act 1998);

(b) Chapter 1 of Part 6, in so far as that Chapter applies in relation to plans and projects—

(i) which do not relate to a matter specified in Chapters 2 to 9 of that Part, and

(ii) which relate to an excepted matter (within the meaning given by section 4(1) of the Northern Ireland Act 1998);

(c) regulation 100, in so far as it applies in relation to a marine licence under Part 4 of the Marine Act in respect of anything done in the course of carrying on an activity which relates to a matter which is an excepted matter by virtue of paragraph 4 of Schedule 2 to the Northern Ireland Act 1998 (defence of the realm etc.);

(d) regulation 107A, in so far as it applies in relation to the exercise of any power by the Secretary of State, and regulations 102, 103 and 105 in so far as they apply to marine policy statements by virtue of regulation 107A; and

(e) in Schedule 6—

(i) sub-paragraphs (3) and (5) of paragraph 5, and sub-paragraph (1) of paragraph 5 in so far as it relates to those sub-paragraphs, and

(ii) paragraph 7,

and regulation 132 in so far as it relates to those provisions.][1]

[(4A) This regulation and regulations 1, 3, 5, 7, 8, 128 and 131 also extend to Northern Ireland in so far as they have effect in relation to the provisions specified in paragraph (4).

(4B) Chapter 1 of Part 6 also extends to Northern Ireland in so far as it has effect in relation to the provision specified in paragraph (4)(c).][2]

(5) …[5]

(6) The revocation of an enactment by any provision of regulation 133 (revocations) or Schedule 7 (revocations) has the same extent as the enactment revoked, except that the following provisions do not extend to Scotland—

(a) paragraph (3) of that regulation, and paragraph (1) of that regulation so far as it relates to paragraph (3); and

(b) paragraph (4)(b) of that regulation and Part 2 of that Schedule.

Amendments

1 Substituted by the Conservation of Habitats and Species (Amendment) Regulations 2012, SI 2012/1927, regs 2, 3(1), (2)(a), (3).

2 Inserted by the Conservation of Habitats and Species (Amendment) Regulations 2012, SI 2012/1927, regs 2, 3(1), (2)(b), (3).

3 Inserted by the Conservation of Habitats and Species (Amendment) Regulations 2011, SI 2011/625, regs 2, 3(a)(i), (iii), (b).

4 Repealed by the Conservation of Habitats and Species (Amendment) Regulations 2011, SI 2011/625, regs 2, 3(a)(ii).

5 Repealed by the Conservation of Habitats and Species (Amendment) Regulations 2012, SI 2012/1927, regs 2, 3(1), (4).

3 Interpretation

(1) In these Regulations—

"the 1949 Act" means the National Parks and Access to the Countryside Act 1949;

"the 1994 Regulations" means the Conservation (Natural Habitats, &c.) Regulations 1994;

"the 2007 Regulations" means the Offshore Marine Conservation (Natural Habitats, &c.) Regulations 2007;

["the appropriate authority" means the Secretary of State in relation to England and the Welsh Ministers in relation to Wales (but see modifications of the meaning of that term in regulations 9(4) and 9A(12)(a), and modifications of references to that term in regulations 67(1)(b), (3)(c), (5) and (8)(b), 94(6), 106(3)(b) and 107A(3)(c)), and any person exercising any function of the Secretary of State or the Welsh Ministers;][1]

"competent authority" is to be construed in accordance with regulation 7 (competent authorities);

"conservation" has the meaning given by Article 1(a) of the Habitats Directive;

"conservation status" and "favourable conservation status" have the meanings given by paragraphs (e) (in relation to habitats) and (i) (in relation to species) of Article 1 of the Habitats Directive;

"destroy", in relation to an egg, includes doing anything to the egg which is calculated to prevent it from hatching, and "destruction" is to be construed accordingly;

"the devolved administrations" means the Welsh Ministers, the Department of the Environment in Northern Ireland and the Scottish Ministers;

["the Directives" means the Habitats Directive and the new Wild Birds Directive;][2]

"enactment" includes a local enactment and an enactment contained in subordinate legislation, and "subordinate legislation" has the same meaning as in the Interpretation Act 1978 (see section 21 of that Act);

"English inshore region" means the area of sea within the seaward limits of the territorial sea adjacent to England;

"European marine site" has the meaning given by paragraph (4) of regulation 8 (European sites and European marine sites);

"European offshore marine site" means a European offshore marine site within the meaning of regulation 15 of the 2007 Regulations (meaning of European offshore marine site);

"European site" has the meaning given by regulation 8 (European sites and European marine sites);

"functions" includes powers and duties;

"the Habitats Directive" means Council Directive 92/43/EEC on the conservation of natural habitats and of wild fauna and flora;

"land" includes land covered by water;

"local planning authority" means, except as otherwise provided, any authority having any function as a local planning authority or mineral planning authority under the TCPA 1990;

"management agreement" means an agreement made, or having effect as if made, under regulation 16 (management agreements);

"the Marine Act" means the Marine and Coastal Access Act 2009;

"marine area" means (subject to [regulations 9(5) and 9A(12)(b)][1]) the English inshore region and the Welsh inshore region;

"Natura 2000" means the European network of special areas of conservation, and special protection areas under the old Wild Birds Directive or the new Wild Birds Directive, provided for by Article 3(1) of the Habitats Directive;

"natural habitats" has the meaning given by Article 1(b) of the Habitats Directive;

"nature conservation body" and "appropriate nature conservation body" have the meaning given by regulation 5 (nature conservation bodies);

"the new Wild Birds Directive" means Directive 2009/147/EC of the European Parliament and of the Council on the conservation of wild birds;

["Northern Ireland inshore region" means the area of sea within the seaward limits of the territorial sea adjacent to Northern Ireland;][2]

"officer"—

(a) in relation to a body corporate, means a director, member of the committee of management, chief executive, manager, secretary or other similar officer of the body, and

(b) in relation to an unincorporated body, means any member of its governing body or a chief executive, manager or other similar officer of the body;

"the old Wild Birds Directive" means Council Directive 79/409/EEC on the conservation of wild birds;

"priority natural habitat types" has the meaning given by Article 1(d) of the Habitats Directive;

"priority species" has the meaning given by Article 1(h) of the Habitats Directive;

"the register" means the register of European sites provided for by regulation 13 (register of European sites);

"relevant authorities", in relation to marine areas and European marine sites, is to be construed in accordance with regulation 6 (relevant authorities in relation to marine areas and European marine sites);

"relevant licensing body" has the meaning given by regulation 56 (relevant licensing body);

"research" includes inquiries and investigations;

"restricted English inshore region" means so much of the English inshore region as lies to seaward of mean low water mark;

"sample" means a sample of blood, tissue or other biological material;

"Scottish inshore region" means the area of sea within the seaward limits of the territorial sea adjacent to Scotland;

"sea" includes—

(a) any area submerged at mean high water spring tide, and

(b) the waters of every estuary, river or channel, so far as the tide flows at mean high water spring tide,

and any reference to an area of sea includes the bed and subsoil of the sea within that area;

"ship" means any vessel (including hovercraft, submersible craft and other floating craft) other than one which permanently rests on, or is permanently attached to, the seabed;

"site" has the meaning given by Article 1(j) of the Habitats Directive;

"site of Community importance" has the meaning given by Article 1(k) of the Habitats Directive;

"special area of conservation" has the meaning given by Article 1(l) of the Habitats Directive;

"specimen"—

(a) for the purposes of Part 7 (enforcement), means any animal or plant, or any part of, or anything derived from, an animal or plant, and

(b) for all other purposes has the meaning given by Article 1(m) of the Habitats Directive;

"statutory undertaker" means a person who is, or is deemed to be, a statutory undertaker for the purposes of any provision of Part 11 of the TCPA 1990 (statutory undertakers);

"the TCPA 1990" means the Town and Country Planning Act 1990;

"the WCA 1981" means the Wildlife and Countryside Act 1981; …[3]

"Welsh inshore region" means the area of sea within the seaward limits of the territorial sea adjacent to [Wales;][1]

["wild bird" means a bird which is—

(a) a member of a species referred to in Article 1 of the new Wild Birds Directive, and

(b) wild.][2]

(2) The area of sea referred to in sub-paragraph (a) of the definition of "sea" in paragraph (1) includes waters in any area—

(a) which is closed, whether permanently or intermittently, by a lock or other artificial means against the regular action of the tide, but

(b) into and from which seawater is caused or permitted to flow, whether continuously or from time to time.

(3) Terms not defined in paragraph (1) which are used in these Regulations and also in the Habitats Directive have the meaning they bear in that Directive.

(4) In these Regulations, any reference to an Annex to the Habitats Directive is a reference to that Annex to that Directive as amended from time to time.

(5) Subject to regulation 83(1)(which relates to the construction of provisions of Chapter 2 of Part 6 as one with the TCPA 1990), these Regulations apply to the Isles of Scilly as if the Isles were a county and the Council of the Isles were a county council.

(6) Except as provided by paragraph (7), for the purposes of these Regulations—
(a) any reference to England includes the English inshore region;
(b) any reference to Wales includes the Welsh inshore region;
(c) any reference to Scotland includes the Scottish inshore region; …[3]
(d) any reference to Great Britain includes the English inshore region, the Welsh inshore region and the [Scottish inshore region;][1]
[(e) any reference to Northern Ireland includes the Northern Ireland inshore region; and
(f) any reference to the United Kingdom includes its internal waters and the English inshore region, the Welsh inshore region, the Scottish inshore region and the Northern Ireland inshore region.][2]

(7) Paragraph (6) does not apply for the purposes of—
(a) in paragraph (1), the definitions of "English inshore region", ["Welsh inshore region", "Scottish inshore region" and "Northern Ireland inshore region"][1]; …[3]
[(b) paragraph (8); or
(c) regulation 4(2)(a)(ii).][2]

(8) For the purposes of these Regulations—
[(a) the territorial sea adjacent to England is so much of the territorial sea adjacent to the United Kingdom as is not the territorial sea adjacent to Wales, the territorial sea adjacent to Scotland or the territorial sea adjacent to Northern Ireland;][1]
(b) ["the territorial sea adjacent to Wales"][1] is to be construed in accordance with article 6 of and Schedule 3 to the National Assembly for Wales (Transfer of Functions) Order 1999 (the sea adjacent to Wales); …[3]
(c) ["the territorial sea adjacent to Scotland"][1] is to be construed in accordance with article 3 of and Schedule 1 to the Scottish Adjacent Waters Boundaries [Order 1999; and][1]
[(d) "the territorial sea adjacent to Northern Ireland" is to be construed in accordance with article 2 of the Adjacent Waters Boundaries (Northern Ireland) Order 2002.][2]

(9) Nothing in these Regulations is to be construed as excluding the application of the provisions of Part 1 of the WCA 1981 (wildlife) in relation to animals or plants also protected under Part 3, 4 or 5 of these Regulations.

Amendments

1 Substituted by the Conservation of Habitats and Species (Amendment) Regulations 2012, SI 2012/1927, regs 2, 4(1), (2)(a), (c), (f), (3)(b), (4)(a), (c), (5)(a), (b)(i), (c).

2 Inserted by the Conservation of Habitats and Species (Amendment) Regulations 2012, SI 2012/1927, regs 2, 4(1), (2)(b), (d), (g), (3)(c), (5)(d).

3 Repealed by the Conservation of Habitats and Species (Amendment) Regulations 2012, SI 2012/1927, regs 2, 4(1), (2)(e), (3)(a), (4)(b), (5)(b)(ii).

4 Plans or projects relating to offshore marine area or offshore marine installations

(1) Nothing in these Regulations requires an appropriate assessment of any plan or project so far as that plan or project is to be carried out on, in or in relation to any part of the sea in the offshore marine area, or on or in relation to an offshore marine installation.

(2) In paragraph (1)—
(a) "offshore marine area" means—

(i) any part of the seabed and subsoil situated in any area designated under subsection (7) of section 1 of the Continental Shelf Act 1964 (exploration and exploitation of continental shelf), and
(ii) any part of the waters within British fishery limits (except the internal waters of, and the territorial sea adjacent to, the United Kingdom, the Channel Islands and the Isle of Man); and

(b) "offshore marine installation" means any artificial island, installation or structure (other than a ship) which is situated—
(i) in any part of the waters in any area designated under section 1(7) of the Continental Shelf Act 1964, or
(ii) in any part of the waters in any area designated under subsection (4) of section 84 of the Energy Act 2004 (exploitation of areas outside the territorial sea for energy production).

5 Nature conservation bodies

(1) Except as provided by [paragraphs (2) to (4)][1], in these Regulations—
(a) "nature conservation body" means Natural England or the Countryside Council for Wales; and
(b) "the appropriate nature conservation body" means—
(i) Natural England, in relation to England, or
(ii) the Countryside Council for Wales, in relation to Wales.

[(2) In regulations 48 (surveillance of conservation status of habitats and species) and 50 (monitoring of incidental capture and killing), "nature conservation body" means Natural England, the Countryside Council for Wales or the Joint Nature Conservation Committee.

(3) In a provision of Part 6 (assessment of plans and projects) which extends to England and Wales only, "the appropriate nature conservation body" means—
(a) Natural England, in relation to England, or
(b) the Countryside Council for Wales, in relation to Wales,
except in relation to an effect on a European offshore marine site, in which case it means the Joint Nature Conservation Committee.][1]

[(4) In a provision of Part 6 which extends to Scotland or Northern Ireland, "the appropriate nature conservation body" means—
(a) Natural England, in relation to England,
(b) the Countryside Council for Wales, in relation to Wales,
(c) Scottish Natural Heritage, in relation to Scotland, or
(d) the Department of the Environment in Northern Ireland, in relation to Northern Ireland,
except in relation to an effect on a European offshore marine site, in which case it means the Joint Nature Conservation Committee.][2]

Amendments

1 Substituted by the Conservation of Habitats and Species (Amendment) Regulations 2012, SI 2012/1927, regs 2, 5.
2 Inserted by the Conservation of Habitats and Species (Amendment) Regulations 2012, SI 2012/1927, regs 2, 5(b).

6 Relevant authorities in relation to marine areas and European marine sites

For the purposes of these Regulations the relevant authorities, in relation to a marine area or European marine site, are such of the following as have functions in relation to land or waters within or adjacent to that area or site—
(a) a nature conservation body;

(b) a county council, county borough council, district council or London borough council;
(c) the Environment Agency;
(d) the Marine Management Organisation;
(e) a water undertaker or sewerage undertaker, or an internal drainage board;
(f) a navigation authority within the meaning of the Water Resources Act 1991;
(g) a harbour authority within the meaning of the Harbours Act 1964;
(h) a lighthouse authority;
[(i) an inshore fisheries and conservation authority established under Part 6 of the Marine Act (management of inshore fisheries); and][1]
(j) …[2]
(k) a National Park authority.

Amendments

1 Substituted by the Marine and Coastal Access Act 2009 (Transitional and Savings Provisions) Order 2011, SI 2011/603, art 9(a), Sch 2, Pt 1, para 12(a).

2 Repealed by the Marine and Coastal Access Act 2009 (Transitional and Savings Provisions) Order 2011, SI 2011/603, art 9(a), Sch 2, Pt 1, para 12(b).

7 Competent authorities

(1) For the purposes of these Regulations, "competent authority" includes—
(a) any Minister of the Crown (as defined in the Ministers of the Crown Act 1975), government department, statutory undertaker, public body of any description or person holding a public office;
(b) the Welsh Ministers; and
(c) any person exercising any function of a person mentioned in sub-paragraph (a) or (b).

(2) In the following provisions (and as provided in regulation 67(3)(a)), "competent authority" includes the Scottish Ministers—
(a) paragraph (2) of regulation 68 (grant of planning permission), in so far as that paragraph relates to a deemed grant of planning permission under—
  (i) section 57(2) of the Town and Country Planning (Scotland) Act 1997, as mentioned in regulation 68(1)(e)(ii), or
  (ii) section 5(1) of the Pipe-lines Act 1962, as mentioned in regulation 68(1)(e)(iii);
(b) Chapter 4 of Part 6 (electricity); and
(c) Chapter 5 of Part 6 (pipe-lines).

(3) In paragraph (1)—
(a) "public body" includes [the Broads Authority and][1] any local authority, joint board, joint committee or National Park authority; and
(b) "public office" means—
  (i) an office under the Crown,
  (ii) an office created or continued in existence by a public general Act or by legislation passed by the National Assembly for Wales, or
  (iii) an office the remuneration in respect of which is paid out of money provided by Parliament or the National Assembly for Wales.

(4) In paragraph (3)(a)—
"local authority" means—
(a) in relation to England, a county council, a district council, a parish council, a London borough council, the Common Council of the City of London, the sub-treasurer of the Inner Temple or the under treasurer of the Middle Temple, and

(b) in relation to Wales, a county council, a county borough council or a community council;

"joint board" means a joint planning board within the meaning of section 2 of the TCPA 1990 (joint planning boards); and

"joint committee" means a joint committee appointed under subsection (1)(b) of section 102 of the Local Government Act 1972 (appointment of committees).

Amendment

1 Inserted by the Conservation of Habitats and Species (Amendment) Regulations 2012, SI 2012/1927, regs 2, 6.

8 European sites and European marine sites

(1) Subject to paragraph (2), in these Regulations a "European site" means—

(a) a special area of conservation;

(b) a site of Community importance which has been placed on the list referred to in the third sub-paragraph of Article 4(2) of the Habitats Directive;

(c) a site hosting a priority natural habitat type or priority species protected in accordance with Article 5(4) of the Habitats Directive (a site in respect of which consultation has been initiated under Article 5(1) of that Directive, during the consultation period or pending a decision of the Council under Article 5(3));

(d) an area classified pursuant to Article 4(1) or (2) of the old Wild Birds Directive or the new Wild Birds Directive; or

(e) a site which has been proposed to the European Commission under regulation 10 (selection of sites eligible for identification as of Community importance), until such time as—

(i) the site is placed on the list of sites of Community importance referred to in the third sub-paragraph of Article 4(2) of the Habitats Directive, or

(ii) agreement is reached or a decision is taken pursuant to Article 4(2) of that Directive not to place the site on that list.

(2) In these Regulations, a reference to a European site—

(a) in Part 6 (assessment of plans and projects), is a reference to a European site in [the United Kingdom][1]; and

(b) in any other provision of these Regulations, except where otherwise indicated, is a reference to a European site in England or Wales.

(3) In any enactment other than these Regulations, a reference to a European site within the meaning of these Regulations is a reference to a European site as defined in paragraph (1).

(4) In these Regulations a "European marine site" means a European site so far as consisting of marine areas.

Amendment

1 Substituted by the Conservation of Habitats and Species (Amendment) Regulations 2012, SI 2012/1927, regs 2, 7.

[9 Duties relating to compliance with the Directives

(1) The appropriate authority, the nature conservation bodies and, in relation to the marine area, a competent authority must exercise their functions which are relevant to nature conservation, including marine conservation, so as to secure compliance with the requirements of the Directives.

(2) Paragraph (1) applies, in particular, to functions under the following enactments—

the Dockyard Ports Regulation Act 1865,

subsection (2) of section 2 of the Military Lands Act 1900 (provision as to byelaws relating to the sea, tidal water or shore),
Part 3 of the 1949 Act (nature conservation),
the Harbours Act 1964,
section 15 of the Countryside Act 1968 (areas of special scientific interest),
Part 2 of the Control of Pollution Act 1974 (pollution of water),
Part 1 (wildlife) and sections 28 to 28S and 31 to 35A of the WCA 1981 (which relate to sites of special scientific interest),
sections 131, 132 and 134 of the Environmental Protection Act 1990 (which relate to nature conservation functions of the Countryside Council for Wales),
the Water Resources Act 1991,
the Land Drainage Act 1991,
the Sea Fisheries Acts within the meaning of section 1 of the Sea Fisheries (Wildlife Conservation) Act 1992 (conservation in the exercise of sea fisheries functions),
the Natural Environment and Rural Communities Act 2006,
the Planning Act 2008,
the Marine Act, in particular any functions under Parts 3, 4, 5 and 6 of that Act (marine planning, marine licensing, nature conservation and management of inshore fisheries, respectively), and
these Regulations.

(3) Without prejudice to the preceding provisions, a competent authority, in exercising any of their functions, must have regard to the requirements of the Directives so far as they may be affected by the exercise of those functions.

(4) The reference in paragraph (1) to the appropriate authority—
(a) to the extent that that paragraph applies in relation to Scotland, includes the Secretary of State exercising functions in relation to Scotland; and
(b) to the extent that that paragraph applies in relation to Northern Ireland, includes the Secretary of State exercising functions in relation to Northern Ireland.

(5) In paragraph (1), "marine area" includes—
(a) the Northern Ireland inshore region; and
(b) the Scottish inshore region.][1]

Amendment

1 Substituted by the Conservation of Habitats and Species (Amendment) Regulations 2012, SI 2012/1927, regs 2, 8.

[9A Duties in relation to wild bird habitat

(1) Without prejudice to regulation 9(1), the appropriate authority, the nature conservation bodies and, in relation to the marine area, a competent authority must take such steps in the exercise of their functions as they consider appropriate to secure the objective in paragraph (3), so far as lies within their powers.

(2) Except in relation to the marine area, the Environment Agency, the Forestry Commissioners, local authorities, the Broads Authority and National Park authorities must take such steps in the exercise of their functions as they consider appropriate to contribute to the achievement of the objective in paragraph (3).

(3) The objective is the preservation, maintenance and re-establishment of a sufficient diversity and area of habitat for wild birds in the United Kingdom, including by means of the upkeep, management and creation of such habitat, as appropriate, having regard to the requirements of Article 2 of the new Wild Birds Directive.

(4) Paragraph (1) applies, in particular, to—
(a) functions under the following enactments—
sections 17, 18, 20 and 21(6) of the 1949 Act (which relate to nature reserves),
section 7 (management agreements) of the Natural Environment and Rural Communities Act 2006,
Parts 3, 4, 5 and 6 (marine planning, marine licensing, nature conservation and management of inshore fisheries, respectively) of the Marine Act, and
these Regulations; and
(b) any function exercisable in relation to town and country planning.

(5) Paragraph (2) applies, in particular, to—
(a) functions under the following enactments—
sections 21 and 90 of the 1949 Act (which relate to nature reserves and local authority byelaws, respectively),
sections 3 (management of forestry land) and 10 (application for felling licence and decision of Commissioners thereon) of the Forestry Act 1967,
sections 3 and 6 of the Norfolk and Suffolk Broads Act 1988 (the Broads Plan and byelaws, respectively);
section 66 of the Environment Act 1995 (National Park Management Plans);
sections 38 and 39 of the Flood and Water Management Act 2010 (which relate to incidental flooding or coastal erosion), and
these Regulations; and
(b) any function exercisable in relation to town and country planning.

(6) In subsection (3)(a) of section 123 of the Marine Act (creation of network of conservation sites), as it applies in relation to the marine area, the reference to "the conservation or improvement of the marine environment" includes the objective in paragraph (3), and accordingly the duty in section 124 of the Marine Act (report) applies in relation to that objective.

(7) In considering which measures may be appropriate for the purpose of securing or contributing to the objective in paragraph (3), appropriate account must be taken of economic and recreational requirements.

(8) So far as lies within their powers, a competent authority in exercising any function in or in relation to the United Kingdom must use all reasonable endeavours to avoid any pollution or deterioration of habitats of wild birds (except habitats beyond the outer limits of the area to which the new Wild Birds Directive applies).

(9) The appropriate authority must take any steps they consider necessary to facilitate or co-ordinate arrangements to secure the taking of steps under paragraphs (1) and (2) by the bodies mentioned in those paragraphs.

(10) After consultation with the appropriate nature conservation body, the appropriate authority must give guidance to the Environment Agency, the Forestry Commissioners, local authorities, the Broads Authority, National Park authorities and any other competent authority they consider appropriate—
(a) to facilitate the determination by those bodies of the extent to which the diversity and area of habitat for wild birds is sufficient; and
(b) on the steps that it may be appropriate to take under paragraph (1) or (2).

(11) In exercising a function to which paragraph (1) or (2) applies, a body to which guidance has been given under paragraph (10) must have regard to that guidance.

(12) In this regulation—

(a) references in paragraphs (1), (9) and (10) to the appropriate authority—
 (i) to the extent that this regulation applies in relation to Scotland, include the Secretary of State exercising functions in relation to Scotland, and
 (ii) to the extent that this regulation applies in relation to Northern Ireland, include the Secretary of State exercising functions in relation to Northern Ireland;
(b) in paragraphs (1) and (2), "marine area" includes—
 (i) the Northern Ireland inshore region, and
 (ii) the Scottish inshore region; and
(c) "local authority" has the same meaning as in regulation 7.][1]

Amendment

1 Inserted by the Conservation of Habitats and Species (Amendment) Regulations 2012, SI 2012/1927, regs 2, 8.

[9B Review by appropriate nature conservation body

(1) The appropriate nature conservation body must, from time to time—
(a) review the extent to which the objective in regulation 9A(3) has been met, other than in relation to the marine area;
(b) set out the conclusions of the review in a report, including any recommendations for further action; and
(c) send the report to the appropriate authority.

(2) In carrying out the review, the nature conservation bodies must, so far as is reasonable, take account of any measures taken which contribute to the achievement of that objective, whether or not taken pursuant to a requirement imposed by any enactment.

(3) The nature conservation bodies may act together to fulfil the duty under paragraph (1).][1]

Amendment

1 Inserted by the Conservation of Habitats and Species (Amendment) Regulations 2012, SI 2012/1927, regs 2, 8.

PART 2
CONSERVATION OF NATURAL HABITATS AND HABITATS OF SPECIES

European sites

10 Selection of sites eligible for identification as of Community importance

(1) On the basis of the criteria set out in Annex III (Stage 1) to the Habitats Directive, and relevant scientific information, the appropriate authority must propose a list of sites in England or Wales which are eligible for identification as of Community importance, indicating with respect to each site—
(a) which natural habitat types in Annex I to the Habitats Directive the site hosts; and
(b) which species in Annex II to the Habitats Directive that are native to Great Britain the site hosts.

(2) For animal species ranging over wide areas these sites must correspond to the places within the natural range of such species which present the physical or biological factors essential to their life and reproduction.

(3) For aquatic species which range over wide areas, such sites are to be proposed only where there is a clearly identifiable area representing the physical and biological factors essential to their life and reproduction.

(4) The appropriate authority may propose modification of the list in the light of the results of the surveillance referred to in Article 11 of the Habitats Directive.

(5) The list, and any new site included in that list, must be transmitted to the European Commission together with information on each site including—
(a) a map of the site,
(b) its name, location and extent, and
(c) the data resulting from application of the criteria specified in Annex III (Stage 1) to the Habitats Directive,
provided in a format established by the European Commission.

11 Designation of special areas of conservation

(1) Once a site of Community importance in England or Wales has been adopted in accordance with the procedure laid down in Article 4(2) of the Habitats Directive, the appropriate authority must designate that site as a special area of conservation as soon as possible and no later than six years from the date of adoption of that site.

(2) The appropriate authority must establish priorities for the designation of sites in the light of—
(a) the importance of the sites for the maintenance or restoration at a favourable conservation status of—
   (i) a natural habitat type specified in Annex I to the Habitats Directive, or
   (ii) a species specified in Annex II to the Habitats Directive,
   and for the coherence of Natura 2000; and
(b) the threats of degradation or destruction to which the sites are exposed.

12 Consultation as to inclusion of site omitted from the list

If consultation is initiated by the European Commission in accordance with Article 5(1) of the Habitats Directive with respect to a site in England or Wales hosting a priority natural habitat type or priority species, and—
(a) the appropriate authority and the European Commission agree, within the period of six months mentioned in Article 5(2) of the Habitats Directive, that the site should be selected as a site of Community importance, or
(b) the European Council, acting on a proposal from the European Commission in pursuance of Article 5(2) of the Habitats Directive, decides that the site should be so selected in accordance with Article 5(3) of that Directive,
for the purposes of these Regulations the site is to be treated as having been placed on the list referred to in the third sub-paragraph of Article 4(2) of the Habitats Directive as from the date of the agreement referred to in paragraph (a) or the decision referred to in paragraph (b).

[12A Classification of sites as special protection areas

(1) The appropriate authority must classify as special protection areas such sites in England and Wales as the authority considers necessary to ensure that the objective in paragraph (2) is met.

(2) The objective referred to in paragraph (1) is that those sites across the United Kingdom's territory which are most suitable in number and size for—
(a) the conservation of the species listed in Annex 1 to the new Wild Birds Directive which naturally occur in that territory, and
(b) the conservation of regularly occurring migratory species of birds not listed in Annex 1 which naturally occur in that territory,
are classified as special protection areas.

(3) The appropriate authority must make a decision as to the sites to be classified for the purpose mentioned in paragraph (1) only on the basis of relevant scientific information and—

(a) in the case of a site to be classified for the purpose mentioned in paragraph (2)(a), on the basis of the criteria set out in Article 4(1) of the new Wild Birds Directive; and

(b) in the case of a site to be classified for the purpose mentioned in paragraph (2)(b), on the basis of the criteria set out in Article 4(2) of the new Wild Birds Directive.

(4) Where a site is classified under paragraph (1), the appropriate authority must provide information on that site to the Commission including—

(a) a map or chart of the site;

(b) its name, location and extent; and

(c) the data resulting from application of the criteria set out in Article 4(1) or Article 4(2) of the new Wild Birds Directive.

(5) The information specified in paragraph (4) must be provided in such format as is established by the Commission.

[(6) In this regulation "the United Kingdom's territory" means the United Kingdom and the offshore marine area (as defined in regulation 4(2)(a)).][1]][2]

Amendments

1 Substituted by the Conservation of Habitats and Species (Amendment) Regulations 2012, SI 2012/1927, regs 2, 9.

2 Inserted by the Conservation of Habitats and Species (Amendment) Regulations 2011, SI 2011/625, regs 2, 4.

[12B Notification of a proposal to classify a special protection area

(1) If the appropriate authority proposes to classify a site as a special protection area under regulation 12A, the authority must give to the appropriate nature conservation body—

(a) notice of that proposal; and

(b) an accompanying statement of the reasons for that proposal.

(2) Where the appropriate nature conservation body is given notice of a proposal under paragraph (1), the body must give notice of that proposal and provide a copy of the appropriate authority's statement of reasons for that proposal to—

(a) any of the following who in its opinion ought to be notified—

  (i) competent authorities which exercise functions in relation to the site;

  (ii) competent authorities which exercise functions in relation to an area adjacent to the site; and

  (iii) every owner and occupier of the site;

(b) such other persons as in its opinion ought to be notified; and

(c) such other persons as the appropriate authority directs.

(3) A notice under paragraph (2) must specify the date (being not less than 12 weeks from the date of the giving of the notice) by which representations with respect to the proposal may be made to the appropriate nature conservation body.

(4) The appropriate nature conservation body must provide to the appropriate authority a report describing the representations duly made, if any, that it received about the proposal, or, where no such representations have been received, stating that fact.

(5) The appropriate authority must consider the report provided under paragraph (4).

(6) The appropriate authority may issue guidance to the appropriate nature conservation body for the purposes of its functions under this regulation, and the appropriate nature

conservation body must have regard to that guidance in discharging any of those functions.

(7) The appropriate authority may vary or revoke a direction under paragraph (2)(c).][1]

Amendment

1 Inserted by the Conservation of Habitats and Species (Amendment) Regulations 2011, SI 2011/625, regs 2, 4.

Register of European sites

13 Register of European sites

(1) A register of European sites, in an appropriate format, must be compiled and maintained by—
(a) the Secretary of State, in relation to European sites in England; and
(b) the Welsh Ministers, in relation to European sites in Wales.

(2) The registers must include—
(a) special areas of conservation, as soon as they are designated by the appropriate authority;
(b) sites of Community importance as soon as they are placed on the list referred to in the third sub-paragraph of Article 4(2) of the Habitats Directive, until they are designated as special areas of conservation;
(c) any site hosting a priority natural habitat type or priority species in respect of which consultation is initiated under Article 5(1) of the Habitats Directive, during the consultation period or pending a Council decision under Article 5(3);
(d) areas classified pursuant to Article 4(1) or (2) of the old Wild Birds Directive or the new Wild Birds Directive, as soon as they are classified by the appropriate authority; and
(e) any site which has been proposed to the European Commission under regulation 10 (selection of sites eligible for identification as of Community importance), until such time as paragraph (i) or (ii) of regulation 8(1)(e) applies.

(3) The appropriate authority, in relation to the register for which that authority is responsible—
(a) may amend any entry;
(b) must remove any entry relating to a site which is no longer a European site; and
(c) must keep a copy available for public inspection at all reasonable hours and free of charge.

(4) An entry in the register in respect of a European site other than a European marine site is a local land charge.

14 Notification of changes to the register

(1) As soon as possible after including a European site in the register or amending an entry in the register, the appropriate authority must notify the appropriate nature conservation body and send to that body a copy of the new or amended entry.

(2) As soon as possible after removing an entry from the register, the appropriate authority must notify the appropriate nature conservation body.

(3) The nature conservation bodies must keep a copy of the register entries relating to European sites in their area available for public inspection at all reasonable hours and free of charge.

15 Notice to landowners and other bodies

(1) As soon as practicable after a nature conservation body receive notification under regulation 14 in relation to a European site, they must give notice to—
(a) every owner or occupier of land within that site;
(b) every local planning authority in whose area that site, or any part of it, is situated;
(c) the Marine Management Organisation, if that site is a European marine site; and
(d) such other persons as the appropriate authority may direct.

(2) Where, under paragraph (1), a nature conservation body give notice to a person ("P") that a site has been included in the register, or that a register entry relating to a site has been amended, the nature conservation body must provide P with a copy of the register entry.

(3) In paragraph (2) the register entry a copy of which must be provided to P—
(a) in the case of notice given under paragraph (1)(a), is the register entry (or that part of an entry) which relates to the land owned or occupied by P; and
(b) in the case of notice given under paragraph (1)(b), is the register entry (or that part of an entry) which relates to the land within P's area.

(4) The appropriate authority may give directions as to the form and content of notices under this regulation.

Management agreements

16 Management agreements

(1) The appropriate nature conservation body may, for the purposes specified in paragraph (2), make an agreement (a "management agreement") with a person who has an interest in—
(a) land which forms part of a European site, or
(b) land adjacent to such a site,
about the management or use of the land.

(2) A management agreement may be made for the purposes of the management, conservation, restoration or protection of the site, or any part of it.

(3) A management agreement may, in particular—
(a) impose on the person who has an interest in the land obligations in respect of the use of the land;
(b) impose on the person who has an interest in the land restrictions on the exercise of rights over the land;
(c) provide for the carrying out of such work as may be expedient for the purposes of the agreement by any person or persons;
(d) provide for any matter for which a management scheme relating to a site of special scientific interest provides (or could provide);
(e) provide for the making of payments by either party to the other party or to any other person;
(f) contain incidental and consequential provision.

(4) A management agreement is, unless the agreement otherwise provides—
(a) binding on persons deriving title under or from the person with whom the appropriate nature conservation body make the agreement; and
(b) enforceable by the appropriate nature conservation body against those persons.

(5) Paragraphs 1 to 3 of Schedule 2 to the Forestry Act 1967 (which makes provision for certain persons to enter into forestry dedication covenants) apply to management agreements as they apply to forestry dedication covenants.

(6) In this regulation—
(a) "interest in land" has the same meaning as in the 1949 Act; and
(b) "management scheme" and "site of special scientific interest" have the same meaning as in Part 2 (nature conservation, countryside and national parks) of the WCA 1981.

17 Existing agreements

(1) For the purposes of these Regulations, any agreement made before 1st April 2010 in relation to land in England or Wales which on or after that date becomes land within a European site, or adjacent to such a site, being an agreement made under—
(a) section 16 of the 1949 Act (agreements for management of nature reserves),
(b) section 15 of the Countryside Act 1968 (areas of special scientific interest), or
(c) section 7 of the Natural Environment and Rural Communities Act 2006 (management agreements),
has effect upon the designation of the site as if it were a management agreement entered into by Natural England or the Countryside Council for Wales (as the case may be) under regulation 16.

(2) Any other thing done or deemed to have been done under—
(a) any provision of Part 3 (nature conservation) of the 1949 Act, or under Part 6 (general, financial and supplementary) of that Act so far as it applies for the purposes of Part 3, or
(b) section 15 of the Countryside Act 1968,
in respect of any land prior to that land becoming land within a European site, or adjacent to such a site, continues to have effect as if done under the corresponding provision of these Regulations.

(3) Any reference in a relevant enactment to a nature reserve within the meaning of section 15 (meaning of "nature reserve") of the 1949 Act is to be construed as including a reference to a European site, and in this paragraph "a relevant enactment" means an enactment not contained in, or in an instrument made under, the 1949 Act or the WCA 1981.

18 Certain payments under management agreements

(1) This regulation applies where the appropriate nature conservation body offer to enter into a management agreement providing for the making of payments by them to—
(a) a person who has given notice under [section 28E(1)(a) of the WCA 1981 (duties in relation to sites of special scientific interest)][1] or paragraph (5)(a)(ii) or (b) of regulation 26 (restriction on carrying out operations specified in order); or
(b) a person whose application for a farm capital grant within the meaning of regulation 24 has been refused in consequence of an objection by that body.

(2) Subject to paragraph (3), such payments must be of such amounts as may be determined by the appropriate nature conservation body in accordance with guidance given by the appropriate authority.

(3) If the person with whom the agreement is to be made so requires within one month of receiving the offer, the determination of those amounts must be referred to an arbitrator to be appointed, in default of agreement, by the appropriate authority.

(4) Where the amounts determined by the arbitrator exceed those determined by the appropriate nature conservation body, that body must—
(a) amend the offer so as to give effect to the arbitrator's determination; or

(b) except in the case of an offer made to a person whose application for a farm capital grant has been refused in consequence of an objection by the appropriate nature conservation body, withdraw the offer.

Amendment

1 Substituted by the Conservation of Habitats and Species (Amendment) Regulations 2012, SI 2012/1927, regs 2, 10.

Control of potentially damaging operations

19 Notification of potentially damaging operations

(1) This regulation and [regulation 21][1] apply where a notification is in force under section 28 of the WCA 1981 (sites of special scientific interest) in relation to land which is or forms part of a European site.

(2) The appropriate nature conservation body may, for the purpose of securing compliance with the requirements of the [Directives][1], at any time [vary][1] the notification with respect to—

(a) the flora, fauna or geological or physiographical features by reason of which the land is of special interest; or

(b) any operations appearing to the appropriate nature conservation body to be likely to damage that flora or fauna or those features.

(3) …[2]

(4) …[2]

Amendments

1 Substituted by the Conservation of Habitats and Species (Amendment) Regulations 2012, SI 2012/1927, regs 2, 11(a), (b).

2 Repealed by the Conservation of Habitats and Species (Amendment) Regulations 2012, SI 2012/1927, regs 2, 11(c).

[*Regulation 20 was repealed by the Conservation of Habitats and Species (Amendment) Regulations 2012, SI 2012/1927, regs 2, 12.*]

21 Assessment of implications for European sites

(1) Where it appears to the appropriate nature conservation body that [a notice of a proposal under section 28E(1)(a) of the WCA 1981][1] relates to an operation which is or forms part of a plan or project which—

(a) is likely to have a significant effect on a European site (either alone or in combination with other plans or projects), and

(b) is not directly connected with or necessary to the management of that site,

they must make an appropriate assessment of the implications for that site in view of that site's conservation objectives.

(2) In the light of the conclusions of the assessment, they may give consent for the operation only after having ascertained that the plan or project will not adversely affect the integrity of the site.

(3) This regulation does not apply in relation to a site which is a European site by reason of regulation 8(1)(c) (site protected in accordance with Article 5(4) of the Habitats Directive).

Amendment

1 Substituted by the Conservation of Habitats and Species (Amendment) Regulations 2012, SI 2012/1927, regs 2, 13.

[*Regulation 22 was repealed by the Conservation of Habitats and Species (Amendment) Regulations 2012, SI 2012/1927, regs 2, 14.*]

[23 Sites of special scientific interest which become European sites: duty to review

(1) This regulation applies where a consent for an operation has been given under section 28E(3)(a) of the WCA 1981 (or having effect as if given under that section in relation to land included in a site of special scientific interest which, after the date of that consent, becomes land within a European site.

(2) The appropriate nature conservation body must, as soon as reasonably practicable, review the consent and affirm, modify or withdraw it.

(3) Regulation 21 applies for the purposes of paragraph (2), with the following modifications—
(a) as if the reference in regulation 21(1) to a notice of a proposal under section 28E(1)(a) of the WCA 1981 were a reference to a consent under section 28E(3)(a) of that Act; and
(b) as if the reference to giving consent in regulation 21(2) were a reference to affirming that the consent should remain in force.][1]

Amendment
1 Substituted by the Conservation of Habitats and Species (Amendment) Regulations 2012, SI 2012/1927, regs 2, 15.

24 Farm capital grants

(1) Where an application for a farm capital grant is made as respects expenditure incurred or to be incurred for the purpose of activities on land within a European site, the appropriate authority—
(a) must, so far as may be consistent with the purposes of the grant provisions, exercise their functions so as to further the conservation of the flora, fauna, or geological or physiographical features by reason of which the land is a European site; and
(b) where the appropriate nature conservation body have objected to the making of the grant on the ground that the activities in question have destroyed or damaged or will destroy or damage that flora or fauna or those features, must not make the grant except after considering the objection.

(2) Where in consequence of an objection by the appropriate nature conservation body, an application for a grant as respects expenditure to be incurred is refused on the ground that the activities in question will have such an effect as is mentioned in paragraph (1)(b), the appropriate nature conservation body must, within three months of their receiving notice of the appropriate authority's decision, offer to enter into a management agreement—
(a) imposing restrictions as respects those activities, and
(b) providing for the making by them of payments to the applicant,
in the terms of a draft submitted to the applicant.

(3) In this regulation—
(a) "farm capital grant" means—
    (i) a grant under a scheme made under section 29 of the Agriculture Act 1970 (farm capital grants), or
    (ii) a grant under regulations made under section 2(2) of the European Communities Act 1972 to a person carrying on an agricultural business within the meaning of those regulations in respect of expenditure incurred or to be incurred for the purposes of or in connection with that business, being

expenditure of a capital nature or incurred in connection with expenditure of a capital nature; and

(b) "grant provisions" means—

(i) in the case of a grant of a kind described in sub-paragraph (a)(i), the scheme under which the grant is made and section 29 of the Agriculture Act 1970, and

(ii) in the case of a grant of a kind described in sub-paragraph (a)(ii), the regulations under which the grant is made and the EU instrument in pursuance of which the regulations were made.

Special nature conservation orders

25 Power to make special nature conservation order

(1) The appropriate authority may, after consultation with the appropriate nature conservation body, make in respect of any land within a European site an order (a "special nature conservation order") specifying operations (whether on land specified in that order or elsewhere and whether or not within the European site) which appear to the appropriate authority to be of a kind which, if carried out in certain circumstances or in a particular manner, would be likely to destroy or damage the flora, fauna, or geological or physiographical features by reason of which the land is a European site.

(2) A special nature conservation order may be amended or revoked by a further order.

(3) Schedule 1 has effect with respect to the making, confirmation and coming into operation of special nature conservation orders and amending or revoking orders.

(4) A special nature conservation order specifying operations on land is a local land charge.

(5) If an order under paragraph (1) specifies any operation of a kind not carried out, or proposed to be carried out, on land within a European site, the order must specify the operation by reference to the place where it is being, or is proposed to be, carried out.

26 Restriction on carrying out operations specified in order

(1) In respect of any land within a European site in respect of which a special nature conservation order is made, the appropriate authority may serve a notice (a "stop notice") on any person carrying out, or proposing to carry out, any operation of a kind specified in that order which appears to the appropriate authority to be likely to destroy or damage the flora, fauna, or geological or physiographical features by reason of which the land is a European site.

(2) The stop notice must specify—

(a) details of the operation;

(b) details of the European site to which the notice relates; and

(c) the date on which the notice takes effect.

(3) Where the identity of a person carrying out, or proposing to carry out, the operation is not reasonably ascertainable, the appropriate authority may, instead of serving a stop notice, publish a notice in at least one local newspaper circulating in the area in which the land to which the notice relates is situated, and affix a copy or copies of the notice to some conspicuous object or objects on the land to which the notice relates.

(4) A person on whom a stop notice is served must not carry out on any land within a European site in respect of which a special nature conservation order is in force, or in the place by reference to which the operation is specified, any operation specified in the

order, unless the notice condition specified in paragraph (5) and the consent condition specified in paragraph (6) are fulfilled.

(5) The notice condition is—
(a) where the operation is carried out on land, that—
  (i) the operation is carried out, or caused or permitted to be carried out, by the owner or occupier of the land, and
  (ii) after service of the stop notice, one of them has given the appropriate nature conservation body written notice of a proposal to carry out the operation, specifying its nature and where it is proposed to carry it out; and
(b) in any other case, that after service of the stop notice, the person proposing to carry out the operation has given the appropriate nature conservation body written notice of a proposal to carry out the operation, specifying its nature and where it is proposed to carry it out.

(6) The consent condition is—
(a) that the operation is carried out with the written consent of the appropriate nature conservation body; or
(b) that the operation is carried out in accordance with the terms of a management agreement.

(7) A consent under paragraph (6)(a) may be given—
(a) subject to conditions, and
(b) for a limited period,
specified in the consent.

(8) A person who, without reasonable excuse, contravenes paragraph (4) commits an offence and is liable—
(a) on summary conviction, to a fine not exceeding the statutory maximum;
(b) on conviction on indictment, to a fine.

(9) For the purposes of paragraph (8) it is a reasonable excuse for a person to carry out an operation if—
(a) the operation was an emergency operation particulars of which (including details of the emergency) were notified to the appropriate nature conservation body as soon as practicable after the commencement of the operation; or
(b) the operation was authorised by a planning permission granted on an application under Part 3 (control over development) of the TCPA 1990.

(10) For the purposes of this regulation and regulations 27 and 28—
(a) a "stop notice" means a notice served under paragraph (1);
(b) references to the service of a stop notice are taken to mean (in an appropriate case) the publication and affixing of a notice under paragraph (3); and
(c) where a notice is published and affixed under paragraph (3), any person carrying out an operation specified in the notice is taken to be a person on whom a stop notice is served.

27 Assessment of implications for European sites after service of stop notice

(1) Where it appears to the appropriate nature conservation body that an application for consent under regulation 26(6)(a) relates to an operation which is or forms part of a plan or project which—
(a) is likely to have a significant effect on a European site (either alone or in combination with other plans or projects), and
(b) is not directly connected with or necessary to the management of that site,

they must make an appropriate assessment of the implications for that site in view of that site's conservation objectives.

(2) In the light of the conclusions of the assessment, they may give consent for the operation only after having ascertained that the plan or project will not adversely affect the integrity of the site.

(3) Where the appropriate nature conservation body refuse consent they must give reasons for their decision.

(4) A person on whom a stop notice is served may—
(a) within two months of receiving notice of the refusal of consent, or
(b) if no notice of a decision is received by that person within three months of an application for consent being made,
by notice in writing to the appropriate nature conservation body require them to refer the matter as soon as possible to the appropriate authority.

(5) If, following a referral under paragraph (4), the appropriate authority are satisfied that, there being no alternative solutions, the plan or project must be carried out for imperative reasons of overriding public interest (which, subject to paragraph (6), may be of a social or economic nature), the appropriate authority may direct the appropriate nature conservation body to give consent to the operation.

(6) Where the site concerned hosts a priority natural habitat type or a priority species, the reasons referred to in paragraph (5) must be either—
(a) reasons relating to human health, public safety or beneficial consequences of primary importance to the environment; or
(b) any other reasons which the appropriate authority, having due regard to the opinion of the European Commission, consider to be imperative reasons of overriding public interest.

(7) Where the appropriate authority direct the appropriate nature conservation body to give consent under paragraph (5), the appropriate authority must secure that such compensatory measures are taken as are necessary to ensure that the overall coherence of Natura 2000 is protected.

(8) This regulation does not apply in relation to a site which is a European site by reason of regulation 8(1)(c) (site protected in accordance with Article 5(4) of the Habitats Directive).

28 Compensation for effect of stop notice

(1) Where the appropriate authority have served a stop notice on any person, the appropriate nature conservation body must pay compensation to any person who—
(a) at the time at which the notice is served has an interest in affected relevant land; and
(b) on a claim duly made to the appropriate nature conservation body, shows that the value of that interest is less than it would have been if the notice had not been served.

(2) No claim for compensation may be made in respect of an order unless the appropriate authority have given notice of the decision in respect of that order under paragraph 6(1) or (2) of Schedule 1 (special nature conservation orders: procedure).

(3) The amount of the compensation payable is the difference between the value of the interest and what that value would have been had a stop notice not been served.

(4) For this purpose—
(a) an interest in land is to be valued at the time when the stop notice is served; and
(b) where a person, by reason of having more than one interest in affected relevant land, makes more than one claim in respect of the same restriction having effect by virtue of a stop notice being served, the various interests in respect of which that person claims compensation are to be valued together.

(5) Section 10 of the Land Compensation Act 1973 (mortgages, trusts of land and settlements) applies in relation to compensation under this regulation as it applies in relation to compensation under Part 1 of that Act.

(6) For the purposes of assessing compensation under this regulation, the rules set out in section 5 of the Land Compensation Act 1961 (rules for assessing compensation on a compulsory acquisition) have effect, so far as applicable and subject to any necessary modifications, as they have effect for the purpose of assessing compensation for the compulsory acquisition of an interest in land.

(7) Interest is payable in relation to compensation, at the rate for the time being prescribed under section 32 of the Land Compensation Act 1961 (rate of interest after entry on land), from the date of the claim until payment.

(8) In the case of any dispute as to compensation—
(a) the Upper Tribunal has the function of determining the dispute; and
(b) section 4 of the Land Compensation Act 1961 (costs) applies in relation to the determination, subject to any necessary modifications.

(9) In this regulation—
(a) "affected relevant land" means land which forms part of an agricultural unit which comprises land to which the stop notice relates; and
(b) "agricultural unit" means land which is occupied by a person as a unit for agricultural purposes, including any dwelling or other building occupied by that person for the purpose of farming the land.

29 Restoration orders

(1) Where a person ("P") is convicted of an offence under regulation 26 (restriction on carrying out operations specified in order), the court may, in addition to dealing with P in any other way, make an order (a "restoration order") requiring P to carry out, within such period as may be specified in the order, such operations for the purpose of restoring the land to its former condition as may be so specified.

(2) A restoration order made on conviction on indictment is to be treated for the purposes of section 30 of the Criminal Appeal Act 1968 (restitution of property) as an order for the restitution of property.

(3) In the case of a restoration order made by a magistrates' court, the period specified in the order does not begin to run—
(a) in any case until the end of the period for the time being prescribed by law for the giving of notice of appeal against a decision of a magistrates' court; and
(b) where notice of appeal is given within the period so prescribed, until determination of the appeal.

(4) At any time before a restoration order has been fully complied with, the court may, on the application of the person subject to the order, discharge or vary the order if it appears to the court that a change in circumstances has made compliance with the order impracticable or unnecessary.

(5) A person who fails without reasonable excuse to comply with a restoration order commits an offence and is liable on summary conviction to a fine not exceeding level 5 on the standard scale.

(6) A person who continues to fail to comply with a restoration order, following conviction under paragraph (5), may be proceeded against for a further offence from time to time until the order is complied with.

(7) If, within the period specified in a restoration order, any operations specified in the order have not been carried out, the appropriate nature conservation body may enter the land and carry out those operations and recover from the person subject to the order any expenses reasonably incurred by them in doing so.

Byelaws

30 Power to make byelaws

(1) The appropriate nature conservation body may make byelaws for the protection of a European site under section 20 of the 1949 Act (byelaws for protection of nature reserves).

(2) Such byelaws may, in particular, make the kinds of provision mentioned in this regulation, subject to regulation 31(1).

(3) Byelaws may—
(a) provide for prohibiting or restricting the entry into, or movement within, the site of persons, vehicles, boats or animals;
(b) prohibit or restrict the killing, taking, molesting or disturbance of living creatures of any description in the site, the taking, destruction or disturbance of eggs of any such creature, the taking of, or interference with, vegetation of any description in the site, or the doing of anything in the site which will interfere with the soil or damage any object in the site;
(c) contain provisions prohibiting the depositing of rubbish and the leaving of litter in the site; and
(d) prohibit or restrict, or provide for prohibiting or restricting, the lighting of fires in the site or the doing of anything likely to cause a fire in the site.

(4) Byelaws may prohibit or restrict any activity referred to in paragraph (3) within such area surrounding or adjoining the site as appears to the appropriate nature conservation body necessary for the protection of the site.

(5) Byelaws may provide for the issue, on such terms and subject to such conditions as may be specified in the byelaws, of permits authorising—
(a) entry into the site or any such surrounding or adjoining area as is mentioned in paragraph (4), or
(b) the doing of anything within the site, or any such surrounding or adjoining area,
where such entry, or doing that thing, would otherwise be unlawful under the byelaws.

(6) Byelaws may be made so as to relate either to the whole or to any part of the European site, or of any such surrounding or adjoining area as is mentioned in paragraph (4), and may make different provision for different parts of the site.

(7) This regulation does not apply in relation to a European marine site (but see regulation 38 (European marine sites: byelaws and orders)).

31 Byelaws: supplementary provisions

(1) Relevant byelaws must not interfere with—

(a) the exercise by any person of a right vested in that person as owner, lessee or occupier of land in the European site, or in any such surrounding or adjoining area as is mentioned in regulation 30(4);
(b) the exercise of any public right of way;
(c) the exercise of any functions of statutory undertakers;
(d) the exercise of any functions of an internal drainage board or the Commissioners appointed under the Tweed Fisheries Act 1969; or
(e) the provision of an electronic communications code network or the exercise of any right conferred by or in accordance with the electronic communications code on the provider of any such network.

(2) Sections 236 to 238 of the Local Government Act 1972 (procedure, etc., for byelaws; offences against byelaws; evidence of byelaws) apply to all relevant byelaws as if the appropriate nature conservation body were a local authority within the meaning of that Act.

(3) In relation to relevant byelaws, the confirming authority for the purposes of section 236 of the Local Government Act 1972 is the appropriate authority.

(4) The appropriate nature conservation body may take such steps as may be necessary for the purpose of enforcing byelaws made by them.

(5) In this regulation and in regulations 32 and 33, "relevant byelaws" means byelaws under section 20 of the 1949 Act as it applies by virtue of regulation 30.

32 Compensation for effect of byelaws

(1) Where the exercise of any right vested in a person ("P"), whether by reason of P's being entitled to any interest in land or by virtue of a licence or agreement, is prevented or hindered by the coming into operation of relevant byelaws, P is entitled to receive compensation from the appropriate nature conservation body.

(2) Any dispute arising on a claim for any such compensation is to be determined by the Upper Tribunal.

(3) For the purposes of any such reference to the Upper Tribunal, section 4 of the Land Compensation Act 1961 (costs) has effect with the substitution for references to the acquiring authority of references to the authority from whom the compensation in question is claimed.

(4) Rules (2) to (4) of the Rules set out in section 5 of that Act (rules for assessing compensation on a compulsory acquisition) apply to the calculation of any such compensation, in so far as it is calculated by reference to the depreciation of the value of an interest in land.

(5) In the case of an interest in land subject to a mortgage—
(a) any such compensation in respect of the depreciation of that interest is to be calculated as if the interest were not subject to the mortgage;
(b) a claim or application for the payment of any such compensation may be made by any person who when the byelaws giving rise to the compensation were made was the mortgagee of the interest, or by any person claiming under such a person, but without prejudice to the making of a claim or application by any other person;
(c) subject to sub-paragraph (d), a mortgagee is not entitled to any such compensation in respect of that mortgagee's interest as such; and
(d) any compensation payable in respect of the interest subject to the mortgage must be paid to the mortgagee or, where there is more than one mortgagee, to the first mortgagee, and must in either case be applied by the mortgagee as if it were proceeds of sale.

33 Continuation in force of existing byelaws

Any byelaws in force under section 20 of the 1949 Act in relation to land which on or after 1st April 2010 becomes land within a European site, or adjacent to such a site—
(a) have effect as if they are relevant byelaws; and
(b) are to be construed as if originally made as such byelaws.

Powers of compulsory acquisition

34 Powers of compulsory acquisition

(1) Where the appropriate nature conservation body are satisfied—
(a) that they are unable, as respects any interest in land within a European site, to conclude a management agreement on terms appearing to them to be reasonable, or
(b) where they have entered into a management agreement as respects such an interest, that a breach of the agreement has occurred which prevents or impairs the satisfactory management of the European site,
they may acquire that interest compulsorily.

(2) Such a breach as is mentioned in paragraph (1)(b) is not to be treated as having occurred by virtue of any act or omission capable of remedy unless there has been default in remedying it within a reasonable time after notice given by the appropriate nature conservation body requiring that act or omission to be remedied.

(3) Any dispute arising as to whether there has been such a breach of a management agreement is to be determined by an arbitrator appointed by the Lord Chancellor.

(4) The power of compulsory acquisition conferred by paragraph (1) on the appropriate nature conservation body may be exercised in any particular case only after authorisation by the appropriate authority.

(5) In relation to any acquisition of land under this regulation, the Acquisition of Land Act 1981 applies; and in relation to any such acquisition of any interest in land, the Compulsory Purchase Act 1965 applies.

(6) In this regulation—
(a) "land" includes any interest in land; and
(b) an "interest", in relation to land, includes any estate in land and any right over land, whether the right is exercisable by virtue of the ownership of an interest in land or by virtue of a licence or agreement, and in particular includes sporting rights.

European marine sites

35 Marking of site and advice by nature conservation bodies

(1) The appropriate nature conservation body may [deposit or remove][1] markers indicating the existence and extent of a European marine site.

[(2) This power is exercisable subject to the obtaining of any necessary marine licence under Part 4 of the Marine Act or any approval required to be obtained from the appropriate authority under article 26(2) of the Marine Licensing (Exempted Activities) Order 2011 or article 25(2) of the Marine Licensing (Exempted Activities) (Wales) Order 2011.][1]

(3) As soon as possible after a site becomes a European marine site, the appropriate nature conservation body must advise other relevant authorities as to—
(a) the conservation objectives for that site; and

(b) any operations which may cause deterioration of natural habitats or the habitats of species, or disturbance of species, for which the site has been designated.

Amendment

1 Substituted by the Conservation of Habitats and Species (Amendment) Regulations 2011, SI 2011/625, regs 2, 5.

36 Management scheme for European marine site

(1) The relevant authorities, or any of them, may establish for a European marine site a management scheme under which their functions (including any power to make byelaws) are to be exercised so as to secure in relation to that site compliance with the requirements of the [Directives][1].

(2) Only one management scheme may be made for each European marine site.

(3) A management scheme may be amended from time to time.

(4) As soon as a management scheme has been established, or is amended, a copy of it must be sent by the relevant authority or authorities concerned to the appropriate nature conservation body.

Amendment

1 Substituted by the Conservation of Habitats and Species (Amendment) Regulations 2012, SI 2012/1927, regs 2, 16.

37 Direction to establish or amend management scheme

(1) The appropriate authority may give directions to the relevant authorities, or any of them, as to the establishment of a management scheme for a European marine site.

(2) Directions may, in particular—

(a) require conservation measures specified in the direction to be included in the scheme;

(b) appoint one of the relevant authorities to co-ordinate the establishment of the scheme;

(c) set time limits within which any steps are to be taken;

(d) provide that the approval of the appropriate authority is required before the scheme is established; and

(e) require any relevant authority to supply to the appropriate authority such information concerning the establishment of the scheme as may be specified in the direction.

(3) The appropriate authority may give directions to the relevant authorities, or any of them, as to the amendment of a management scheme for a European marine site, either generally or in any particular respect.

(4) Any direction under this regulation must be in writing and may be varied or revoked by a further direction.

38 European marine sites: byelaws and orders

(1) The Marine Management Organisation may make byelaws for the protection of a European marine site in England under section 129 of the Marine Act (byelaws for protection of marine conservation zones in England).

(2) The Welsh Ministers may make orders for the protection of a European marine site in Wales under section 134 of that Act (orders for protection of marine conservation zones in Wales).

(3) The provisions of Chapter 1 (marine conservation zones) of Part 5 of that Act relating to byelaws under section 129 or orders under section 134 apply, with the modifications described in paragraph (4), in relation to byelaws made by virtue of paragraph (1) or (as the case may be) orders made by virtue of paragraph (2).

(4) The modifications are—
(a) any reference to an MCZ is to be read as a reference to a European marine site;
(b) in sections 129(1) and 134(1), the reference to furthering the conservation objectives stated for an MCZ is to be read as a reference to protecting a European marine site;
(c) the reference in section 129(3)(c) to hindering the conservation objectives stated for an MCZ is to be read as a reference to damaging a European marine site.

(5) …[1]

Amendment

1 Repealed by the Conservation of Habitats and Species (Amendment) Regulations 2012, SI 2012/1927, regs 2, 17.

Nature conservation policy in planning contexts

39 Nature conservation policy in planning contexts

(1) For the purposes of—
(a) subsection (3) of section 17 (local development documents) of the Planning and Compulsory Purchase Act 2004,
(b) subsection (2)(b) of section 62 (local development plan) of that Act, and
(c) subsection (2)(b) of section 70 (regional strategy) of the Local Democracy, Economic Development and Construction Act 2009,
policies relating to the development and use of land are to be taken to include policies encouraging the management of features of the landscape which are of major importance for wild fauna and flora.

(2) For the purposes of—
(a) subsection (3A) of section 12 (preparation of unitary development plan) of the TCPA 1990;
(b) subsection (3) of section 31 (structure plans: continuity, form and content) of that Act; and
(c) subsection (3) of section 36 (local plans) of that Act,
policies in respect of the conservation of the natural beauty and amenity of the land are to be taken to include policies encouraging the management of features of the landscape which are of major importance for wild fauna and flora.

(3) The features of the landscape referred to in paragraphs (1) and (2) are those which, by virtue of their linear and continuous structure (such as rivers with their banks or the traditional systems of marking field boundaries) or their function as "stepping stones" (such as ponds or small woods), are essential for the migration, dispersal and genetic exchange of wild species.

(4) Where the Secretary of State considers it necessary, the Secretary of State must include in a national policy statement under Part 2 (national policy statements) of the Planning Act 2008 policy that encourages the management of such features of the landscape (as mentioned in paragraph (3)) which are of major importance for wild fauna and flora.

PART 3
PROTECTION OF SPECIES

Protection of animals

40 European protected species of animals

(1) Schedule 2 (European protected species of animals) lists those species of animals listed in Annex IV(a) to the Habitats Directive which have a natural range which includes any area in Great Britain.

(2) References in this Part to a "European protected species" of animal are to any of those species.

41 Protection of certain wild animals: offences

(1) A person who—
(a) deliberately captures, injures or kills any wild animal of a European protected species,
(b) deliberately disturbs wild animals of any such species,
(c) deliberately takes or destroys the eggs of such an animal, or
(d) damages or destroys a breeding site or resting place of such an animal,
is guilty of an offence.

(2) For the purposes of paragraph (1)(b), disturbance of animals includes in particular any disturbance which is likely—
(a) to impair their ability—
  (i) to survive, to breed or reproduce, or to rear or nurture their young, or
  (ii) in the case of animals of a hibernating or migratory species, to hibernate or migrate; or
(b) to affect significantly the local distribution or abundance of the species to which they belong.

(3) It is an offence for any person—
(a) to be in possession of, or to control,
(b) to transport,
(c) to sell or exchange, or
(d) to offer for sale or exchange,
anything to which this paragraph applies.

(4) Paragraph (3) applies to—
(a) any live or dead animal or part of an animal—
  (i) which has been taken from the wild, and
  (ii) which is of a species or subspecies listed in Annex IV(a) to the Habitats Directive; and
(b) anything derived from such an animal or any part of such an animal.

(5) Paragraphs (1) and (3) apply regardless of the stage of the life of the animal in question.

(6) Unless the contrary is shown, in any proceedings for an offence under paragraph (1) the animal in question is presumed to have been a wild animal.

(7) In any proceedings for an offence under paragraph (3), where it is alleged that an animal or a part of an animal was taken from the wild, it is presumed, unless the contrary is shown, that that animal or part of an animal was taken from the wild.

(8) A person guilty of an offence under this regulation is liable on summary conviction to imprisonment for a term not exceeding six months or to a fine not exceeding level 5 on the standard scale, or to both.

(9) Guidance as to the application of the offences in paragraph (1)(b) or (d) in relation to particular species of animals or particular activities may be published by—
(a) the appropriate authority; or
(b) the appropriate nature conservation body, with the approval of the appropriate authority.

(10) In proceedings for an offence under paragraph (1)(b) or (d), a court must take into account any relevant guidance published under paragraph (9).

(11) In deciding upon the sentence for a person convicted of an offence under paragraph (1)(d), the court must in particular have regard to whether that person could reasonably have avoided the damage to or destruction of the breeding site or resting place concerned.

42 Protection of certain wild animals: defences

(1) A person ("P") is not guilty of the offence under regulation 41(1)(a) of deliberately capturing a wild animal of a European protected species, or an offence under regulation 41(3)(a) or (b), if P shows that the act in question—
(a) was in relation to an animal that had been disabled otherwise than by P's unlawful act; and
(b) was done solely for one or both of the purposes of—
  (i) tending it and releasing it when no longer disabled, or
  (ii) releasing it after it had been tended.

(2) A person ("P") is not guilty of an offence under regulation 41(1)(a) or 41(3)(a) or (b) if P shows that the act in question—
(a) was in relation to an animal that had been seriously disabled otherwise than by P's unlawful act and that there was no reasonable chance of its recovering; and
(b) was done solely for one or both of the purposes of—
  (i) ending the animal's life, or
  (ii) disposing of it (otherwise than by sale or exchange) as soon as practicable after it was dead.

(3) A person is not guilty of the offence under regulation 41(1)(a) of deliberately injuring a wild animal of a European protected species if that person shows that this was done solely—
(a) for the purpose of taking a sample by virtue of any of the sampling provisions; or
(b) for the purpose of taking a sample to be used in evidence in any criminal proceedings in respect of an offence specified in paragraph (11) (wherever the offence was committed).

(4) A person is not guilty of an offence under regulation 41(3)(a) or (b) if that person shows that the act in question was done solely for one or more of the purposes of—
(a) investigating whether an offence specified in paragraph (11) is being or has been committed (wherever the offence was committed);
(b) bringing, conducting, or giving evidence in, any criminal proceedings in respect of any such offence; or
(c) giving effect to an order under any of the forfeiture provisions.

(5) Subject to paragraph (6), a person who shows that the animal or part of the animal in question, or the animal or part of the animal from which the thing in question is derived, was lawfully taken from the wild is not guilty of an offence under regulation 41(3).

(6) The defence in paragraph (5) does not apply—

(a) in respect of the offences in regulation 41(3)(a) and (b) if—

(i) the animal or part in question is an animal, or part of an animal, of a European protected species or of the species Lacerta vivipara pannonica (viviparous lizard) or Lycaena dispar (the large copper butterfly), or the thing in question is derived from such an animal, and

(ii) the animal, part or thing in question was in the defendant's possession or control, or transported by the defendant, for the purpose of sale or exchange; or

(b) in respect of the offences in regulation 41(3)(c) and (d), if the animal or part in question is an animal, or part of an animal, of any of the species referred to in sub-paragraph (a)(i), or the thing in question is derived from such an animal.

(7) For the purposes of paragraph (5) an animal, or part of an animal, is treated as having been lawfully taken from the wild if—

(a) it was taken from the wild in the European territory of a member State, being territory to which the TFEU applies, without contravention of the law of that member State and before the implementation date; or

(b) it was taken from the wild elsewhere.

(8) A person is not guilty of an offence under regulation 41(3) if that person shows that the animal or part of the animal, or the animal from which the thing in question is derived—

(a) is of a species listed in the second column of Schedule 3 (excluded populations of certain species) and was from a population occurring in a country or area which is specified in respect of that species in the third column of that Schedule;

(b) is of the species Capra aegagrus (wild goat) and was not from a naturally occurring population;

(c) is of the subspecies Ovis gmelini musimon (European mouflon) and was not from a naturally occurring population in Corsica or Sardinia; or

(d) is of the species Coregonus oxyrhynchus (houting) and either was from Finland or was not from an anadromous population.

(9) The defences in paragraphs (1) to (4) do not apply where it is shown by the prosecution that the defendant's action did not satisfy the conditions in paragraph (10).

(10) Those conditions are that—

(a) there was no satisfactory alternative; and

(b) the action was not detrimental to the maintenance of the population of the species concerned at a favourable conservation status in their natural range.

(11) For the purposes of paragraphs (3)(b) and (4)(a) and (b), the specified offences are—

(a) an offence under section 9 (protection of certain wild animals), 11 (prohibition of certain methods of killing or taking wild animals) or 17 (false statements made for obtaining registration or licence etc.) of the WCA 1981, or an offence under section 18 of that Act (attempts to commit offences etc.) which relates to an offence under section 9 or 11;

(b) an offence under the following provisions of these Regulations—

(i) regulation 41 (protection of certain wild animals: offences),

(ii) regulation 43 (prohibition of certain methods of capturing or killing wild animals),

(iii) regulation 57 (false statements made for obtaining licence), where that offence relates to the obtaining of a licence under regulation 53 (licences for certain activities relating to animals or plants), or

(iv) regulation 116 (attempts and possession of means of committing offence), where that offence relates to an offence under regulation 41 or 43;

(c) an offence under the 1997 Regulations or an offence of attempting to commit such an offence; or

(d) an offence under regulation 39 (protection of wild animals listed in Annex IV(a) to the Habitats Directive), 41 (prohibition of certain methods of capturing or killing wild animals) or 51 (false statements made for obtaining licence) of the 2007 Regulations, an offence of attempting to commit an offence under regulation 39 or 41 of those Regulations, or an offence under regulation 64 of those Regulations (possession of means of committing offence) which relates to an offence under regulation 39 or 41 of those Regulations.

(12) For the purposes of any proceedings for an offence under regulation 41(3), the common names given in parentheses in paragraphs (6) and (8) are to be disregarded.

43 Prohibition of certain methods of capturing or killing wild animals

(1) This regulation applies in relation to the capturing or killing of a wild animal—

(a) of any of the species listed in Schedule 4 (which lists those species listed in Annex V(a) to the Habitats Directive, and to which Article 15 of that Directive applies, which have a natural range which includes any area of Great Britain); or

(b) of a European protected species, where the capturing or killing of such animals is permitted in accordance with these Regulations.

(2) It is an offence to use for the purpose of capturing or killing any such wild animal—

(a) any of the means listed in paragraph (3) or (4);

(b) any form of capturing or killing from the modes of transport listed in paragraph (5); or

(c) any other means of capturing or killing which is indiscriminate and capable of causing the local disappearance of, or serious disturbance to, a population of any species of animal listed in Schedule 4 or any European protected species of animal.

(3) The prohibited means of capturing or killing mammals are—

(a) the use of blind or mutilated animals as live decoys;

(b) tape recorders;

(c) electrical and electronic devices capable of killing or stunning;

(d) artificial light sources;

(e) mirrors and other dazzling devices;

(f) devices for illuminating targets;

(g) sighting devices for night shooting comprising an electronic image magnifier or image converter;

(h) explosives;

(i) nets which are non-selective according to their principle or their conditions of use;

(j) traps which are non-selective according to their principle or their conditions of use;

(k) crossbows;

(l) poisons and poisoned or anaesthetic bait;

(m) gassing or smoking out;

(n) semi-automatic or automatic weapons with a magazine capable of holding more than two rounds of ammunition.

(4) The prohibited means of capturing or killing fish are—

(a) poison;

(b) explosives.

(5) The prohibited modes of transport are—

(a) aircraft;
(b) moving motor vehicles.

(6) A person guilty of an offence under this regulation is liable on summary conviction to imprisonment for a term not exceeding six months or to a fine not exceeding level 5 on the standard scale, or to both.

Protection of plants

44 European protected species of plants

(1) Schedule 5 (European protected species of plants) lists those species of plants listed in Annex IV(b) to the Habitats Directive which have a natural range which includes any area in Great Britain.

(2) References in this Part to a "European protected species" of plant are to any of those species.

45 Protection of certain wild plants: offences

(1) It is an offence deliberately to pick, collect, cut, uproot or destroy a wild plant of a European protected species.

(2) It is an offence for any person—
(a) to be in possession of, or to control,
(b) to transport,
(c) to sell or exchange, or
(d) to offer for sale or exchange,
anything to which this paragraph applies.

(3) Paragraph (2) applies to—
(a) any live or dead plant or part of a plant—
 (i) which has been taken in the wild, and
 (ii) which is of a species or subspecies listed in Annex II(b) (other than any bryophyte) or Annex IV(b) to the Habitats Directive; and
(b) anything derived from such a plant or any part of such a plant.

(4) Paragraphs (1) and (2) apply regardless of the stage of the biological cycle of the plant in question.

(5) Unless the contrary is shown, in any proceedings for an offence under paragraph (1) the plant in question is presumed to have been a wild plant.

(6) In any proceedings for an offence under paragraph (2), where it is alleged that a plant or a part of a plant was taken in the wild, it is presumed, unless the contrary is shown, that that plant or part of a plant was taken in the wild.

(7) A person guilty of an offence under this regulation is liable on summary conviction to imprisonment for a term not exceeding six months or to a fine not exceeding level 5 on the standard scale, or to both.

46 Protection of certain wild plants: defences

(1) A person is not guilty of the offence under regulation 45(1) of picking or cutting a wild plant of a European protected species if this was done solely—
(a) for the purpose of taking a sample by virtue of any of the sampling provisions; or

(b) for the purpose of taking a sample to be used in evidence in any criminal proceedings in respect of an offence specified in paragraph (6) (wherever the offence was committed).

(2) A person is not guilty of an offence under regulation 45(2)(a) or (b) if that person shows that the act in question was done solely for one or more of the purposes of—

(a) investigating whether an offence specified in paragraph (6) is being or has been committed (wherever the offence was committed);

(b) bringing, conducting, or giving evidence in, any criminal proceedings in respect of any such offence; or

(c) giving effect to an order under any of the forfeiture provisions.

(3) Subject to paragraph (4), a person who shows that the plant or part of the plant in question, or the plant or part of the plant from which the thing in question is derived, was lawfully taken in the wild, is not guilty of an offence under regulation 45(2).

(4) The defence in paragraph (3) does not apply—

(a) in respect of the offences in regulation 45(2)(a) and (b) if—

   (i) the plant or part in question is a plant, or part of a plant, of a European protected species, or the thing in question is derived from such a plant, and

   (ii) the plant, part or thing in question was in the defendant's possession or control, or transported by the defendant, for the purpose of sale or exchange; or

(b) in respect of the offences in regulation 45(2)(c) and (d), if the plant or part in question is a plant, or part of a plant, of a European protected species, or the thing in question is derived from such a plant.

(5) For the purposes of paragraph (3) a plant, or part of a plant, is treated as having been lawfully taken in the wild if—

(a) it was taken in the wild in the European territory of a member State, being territory to which the TFEU applies, without contravention of the law of that member State and before the implementation date; or

(b) it was taken in the wild elsewhere.

(6) For the purposes of paragraphs (1)(b) and (2)(a) and (b), the specified offences are—

(a) an offence under section 13 (protection of wild plants) or 17 (false statements made for obtaining registration or licence etc.) of the WCA 1981, or an offence under section 18 of that Act (attempts to commit offences etc.) which relates to an offence under section 13;

(b) an offence under the following provisions of these Regulations—

   (i) regulation 45 (protection of certain wild plants: offences),

   (ii) regulation 57 (false statements made for obtaining licence), where that offence relates to the obtaining of a licence under regulation 53 (licences for certain activities relating to animals or plants), or

   (iii) regulation 116 (attempts and possession of means of committing offence), where that offence relates to an offence under regulation 45;

(c) an offence under the 1997 Regulations or an offence of attempting to commit such an offence; or

(d) an offence under regulation 43 (offences relating to wild plants listed in Annex IV(b) to the Habitats Directive) or 51 (false statements made for obtaining licence) of the 2007 Regulations, an offence of attempting to commit an offence under regulation 43 of those Regulations, or an offence under regulation 64 of those Regulations (possession of means of committing offence) which relates to an offence under regulation 43 of those Regulations.

Interpretation of Part 3

47 Interpretation of Part 3

In this Part—

(a) "the 1997 Regulations" means the Control of Trade in Endangered Species (Enforcement) Regulations 1997;

(b) "the forfeiture provisions" means—
  (i) subsection (6) of section 21 (penalties, forfeitures etc.) of the WCA 1981,
  (ii) regulation 122 (forfeiture) of these Regulations, or
  (iii) regulation 11 (forfeiture) of the 1997 Regulations;

(c) "the implementation date" means—
  (i) where the relevant State became a member State before 10th June 1994, 10th June 1994, and
  (ii) in any other case, the date on which the relevant State became a member State;

(d) "relevant State" means the State in whose territory—
  (i) the animal, or part of it, was taken from the wild, or
  (ii) the plant, or part of it, was taken in the wild,

  as the case may be;

(e) "the sampling provisions" means—
  (i) section 18C (Group 1 offences and licences: examining specimens and taking samples), 18E (Group 2 offences: examining specimens and taking samples) or 19XA (constables' powers in connection with samples) of the WCA 1981,
  (ii) regulation 113 (powers in relation to samples: constables) or 114 (powers in relation to specimens and samples: wildlife inspectors) of these Regulations,
  (iii) paragraph (3) or (5) of regulation 9 (powers of entry) of the 1997 Regulations, or
  (iv) paragraph (2) of regulation 56 (powers relating to specimens) of the 2007 Regulations; and

(f) "the TFEU" means the Treaty on the Functioning of the European Union.

PART 4
ADDITIONAL PROTECTION OF HABITATS AND WILD ANIMALS AND PLANTS

Surveillance and monitoring

48 Surveillance of conservation status of habitats and species

(1) The appropriate authority must make arrangements in accordance with paragraphs (4) to (6) for the surveillance of the conservation status of natural habitat types of Community interest and species of Community interest, and in particular priority natural habitat types and priority species.

(2) In respect of the arrangements made by the Secretary of State under paragraph (1), the Secretary of State must, from time to time—

(a) consult the devolved administrations;

(b) provide the devolved administrations with such information as the Secretary of State considers appropriate that has been derived from the surveillance which has been arranged; and

(c) review those arrangements and, if appropriate, revise them.

(3) In respect of the arrangements made by the Welsh Ministers under paragraph (1), the Welsh Ministers must, from time to time—
(a) consult the Secretary of State and the other devolved administrations;
(b) provide the Secretary of State and the other devolved administrations with such information as the Welsh Ministers consider appropriate that has been derived from the surveillance which has been arranged; and
(c) review those arrangements and, if appropriate, revise them.

(4) The appropriate nature conservation body must—
(a) assess how and to what extent surveillance of the conservation status of each relevant habitat and species is to be carried out, having regard to—
(i) whether a habitat or species is a priority natural habitat type or priority species, and
(ii) the conservation status of the habitat or species; and
(b) advise the appropriate authority as to the need for such surveillance.

(5) The appropriate authority must ensure that the necessary surveillance is carried out on an ongoing basis.

(6) Surveillance for the purposes of this regulation may be carried out by—
(a) a nature conservation body;
(b) any other person acting pursuant to, and in accordance with, an agreement with the appropriate authority or a nature conservation body.

(7) In paragraph (4), a "relevant" habitat or species means a habitat or species of a type referred to in paragraph (1).

(8) In this regulation—
(a) "natural habitat types of Community interest" has the meaning given by Article 1(c) of the Habitats Directive; and
(b) "species of Community interest" has the meaning given by Article 1(g) of the Habitats Directive.

49 Protection of certain animals and plants from exploitation

(1) The appropriate authority must, as required in the light of information derived from surveillance arranged under regulation 48 or otherwise arranged for the purpose of Article 11 of the Habitats Directive, ensure that measures are taken for the purpose specified in paragraph (2).

(2) The purpose is to ensure that—
(a) the taking in the wild of specimens of a species listed in Annex V to the Habitats Directive, and
(b) the exploitation of such specimens,
are compatible with the maintenance of that species at a favourable conservation status.

(3) Where measures are required under paragraph (1), the appropriate authority must make arrangements for surveillance for the purpose of establishing whether the taking in the wild of specimens of the species concerned, and the exploitation of specimens of that species, are compatible with the maintenance of that species at a favourable conservation status.

50 Monitoring of incidental capture and killing

(1) The appropriate authority must make arrangements in accordance with paragraphs (4) to (6) to establish a system to monitor the incidental capture or killing of animals of the species listed in Annex IV(a) to the Habitats Directive.

(2) In respect of the arrangements made by the Secretary of State under paragraph (1), the Secretary of State must, from time to time—
(a) consult the devolved administrations;
(b) provide the devolved administrations with such information as the Secretary of State considers appropriate that has been derived from the monitoring which has been arranged; and
(c) review those arrangements and, if appropriate, revise them.

(3) In respect of the arrangements made by the Welsh Ministers under paragraph (1), the Welsh Ministers must, from time to time—
(a) consult the Secretary of State and the other devolved administrations;
(b) provide the Secretary of State and the other devolved administrations with such information as the Welsh Ministers consider appropriate that has been derived from the monitoring which has been arranged; and
(c) review those arrangements and, if appropriate, revise them.

(4) The appropriate nature conservation body must, in relation to the species of animals listed in Annex IV(a) to the Habitats Directive which are found in England or Wales—
(a) identify the risks of incidental capture and killing to which those species are subject, and the activities which give rise to such risks;
(b) maintain a record of instances of incidental capture or killing of animals of those species of which the nature conservation body are aware as a result of the surveillance carried out under regulation 48 (surveillance of conservation status of habitats and species), the monitoring carried out under this regulation or otherwise;
(c) assess to what extent monitoring of incidental capture and killing is needed, having regard to—
  (i) the risks identified under sub-paragraph (a),
  (ii) the instances of incidental capture or killing recorded under sub-paragraph (b),
  (iii) whether the species is a priority species, and
  (iv) the conservation status of the species; and
(d) advise the appropriate authority as to the need for such monitoring.

(5) The appropriate authority must ensure that the necessary monitoring of incidental capture and killing is carried out.

(6) Monitoring for the purposes of this regulation may be carried out by—
(a) a nature conservation body;
(b) any other competent authority;
(c) any other person acting pursuant to, and in accordance with—
  (i) an agreement with the appropriate authority or a nature conservation body, or
  (ii) a condition of a licence or other authorisation granted by a competent authority.

51 Protection from incidental capture and killing

(1) The appropriate authority, as required in the light of information derived from monitoring arranged under regulation 50 or otherwise arranged for the purpose of Article 12(4) of the Habitats Directive, must make arrangements for further research for, or ensure that conservation measures are taken for, the purpose specified in paragraph (2).

(2) The purpose is to ensure that any incidental capture or killing of animals of a species listed in Annex IV(a) to the Habitats Directive does not have a significant negative impact on that species.

Introduction of new species

52 Introduction of new species from ships

(1) It is an offence for any person on board a ship in any relevant part of the marine area deliberately to introduce into that area, other than in accordance with paragraph (3), any live animal or plant of a kind having a natural range which does not include any area in Great Britain.

(2) For the purposes of paragraph (1), "relevant part" means any part where the introduction would give rise to a risk of prejudice to natural habitats within their natural range or a risk of prejudice to wild native flora or fauna (whether in the place of introduction or elsewhere).

(3) An introduction is in accordance with this paragraph if—
(a) it resulted from a discharge of water carried as ballast and the discharge was necessary for the purpose of protecting the safety of any person or ship; and
(b) all reasonably practicable steps were taken—
 (i) to avoid its occurring in an area where it would give rise to a risk of prejudice to natural habitats within their natural range or a risk of prejudice to wild native flora or fauna (whether in the place of introduction or elsewhere), and
 (ii) to minimise any risk of such prejudice.

(4) In any proceedings for an offence under this regulation, it is for the defendant to show that the introduction in question was in accordance with paragraph (3).

(5) The appropriate authority may issue guidance about steps which may be taken to avoid committing an offence under this regulation.

(6) In any proceedings for an offence under this regulation—
(a) where the offence is alleged to have been committed in England, a court must have regard to any guidance issued by the Secretary of State under paragraph (5); and
(b) where the offence is alleged to have been committed in Wales, a court must have regard to any guidance issued by the Welsh Ministers under paragraph (5).

(7) A person guilty of an offence under this regulation is liable—
(a) on summary conviction, to a fine not exceeding the statutory maximum; or
(b) on conviction on indictment, to a fine.

(8) Section 14 of the WCA 1981 (introduction of new species etc.) does not apply in relation to any act which is an offence under this regulation.

PART 5
LICENCES

Grant of licences

53 Licences for certain activities relating to animals or plants

(1) Subject to the provisions of this regulation, the relevant licensing body may grant a licence for the purposes specified in paragraph (2).

(2) The purposes are—
(a) scientific or educational purposes;

(b) ringing or marking, or examining any ring or mark on, wild animals;
(c) conserving wild animals or wild plants or introducing them to particular areas;
(d) protecting any zoological or botanical collection;
(e) preserving public health or public safety or other imperative reasons of overriding public interest including those of a social or economic nature and beneficial consequences of primary importance for the environment;
(f) preventing the spread of disease; or
(g) preventing serious damage to livestock, foodstuffs for livestock, crops, vegetables, fruit, growing timber or any other form of property or to fisheries.

(3) Regulations 41 (protection of certain wild animals: offences), 43 (prohibition of certain methods of capturing or killing wild animals) and 45 (protection of certain wild plants: offences) do not apply to anything done under and in accordance with the terms of a licence granted under paragraph (1).

(4) Subject to the provisions of this regulation, the relevant licensing body may grant a licence to permit the taking or the possession or control of certain specimens of any of the species or subspecies listed in Annex II(b) (other than any bryophyte) or Annex IV to the Habitats Directive notwithstanding that the licence is for a purpose not specified in paragraph (2).

(5) Regulations 41, 43 and 45 do not apply to anything done under and in accordance with the terms of a licence granted under paragraph (4).

(6) A licence under paragraph (4) may be granted only to such persons as are named in the licence.

(7) The relevant licensing body may grant a licence under paragraph (4) only if they are satisfied that the grant of the licence would be consistent with the restrictions in Article 16(1)(e) of the Habitats Directive (namely "under strictly supervised conditions, on a selective basis and to a limited extent" and "in limited numbers").

(8) A licence under paragraph (4) must specify—
(a) the species or subspecies of animal or plant to which the licence relates;
(b) the maximum number of specimens which may be taken or be in the possession or control of the person authorised by the licence, or which particular specimens may be taken or be in the possession or control of that person; and
(c) the conditions subject to which the action authorised by the licence may be taken and in particular—
 (i) the methods, means or arrangements by which specimens may be taken or be in the possession or control of the person authorised by the licence,
 (ii) when or over what period the action authorised by the licence may be taken, and
 (iii) where the licence authorises any person to take specimens, the area from which they may be taken.

(9) The relevant licensing body must not grant a licence under this regulation unless they are satisfied—
(a) that there is no satisfactory alternative; and
(b) that the action authorised will not be detrimental to the maintenance of the population of the species concerned at a favourable conservation status in their natural range.

(10) A licence under this regulation which authorises any person to kill wild animals must specify the area within which and the methods by which the wild animals may be killed and must not be granted for a period of more than two years.

(11) Where the appropriate authority exercise any functions under this regulation (see regulation 56(3)), the appropriate authority must from time to time consult the appropriate nature conservation body as to the exercise of those functions, and must not grant a licence of any description unless the appropriate nature conservation body have advised as to the circumstances in which, in their opinion, licences of that description should be granted.

(12) Where the Marine Management Organisation exercises any functions under this regulation (see regulation 56(2)(a)(i)), it must from time to time consult Natural England as to the exercise of those functions, and must not grant a licence of any description unless Natural England have advised as to the circumstances in which, in their opinion, licences of that description should be granted.

(13) It is a defence in proceedings for an offence under section 8(b) of the Protection of Animals Act 1911 (which restricts the placing on land of poison and poisonous substances) to show that—
(a) the act alleged to constitute the offence was done under and in accordance with the terms of a licence granted under this regulation; and
(b) any conditions specified in the licence were complied with.

(14) In paragraph (2) "livestock" includes any animal which is kept—
(a) for the provision of food, skins or fur;
(b) for the purpose of its use in the carrying on of any agricultural activity; or
(c) for the provision or improvement of shooting or fishing.

54 Licences for the introduction of new species

(1) Subject to paragraph (3), the relevant licensing body may grant a licence in relation to the introduction of new species from ships.

(2) Regulation 52 (introduction of new species from ships) does not apply to anything done under and in accordance with the terms of a licence granted under paragraph (1).

(3) The relevant licensing body must not grant a licence under this regulation unless they are satisfied that the action authorised by the licence will not prejudice natural habitats within their natural range or wild native flora and fauna.

55 Licences: general provisions

(1) This regulation applies in relation to a licence under regulation 53 or 54.

(2) A licence—
(a) may be, to any degree, general or specific;
(b) (subject to regulation 53(6)) may be granted either to persons of a class or to a particular person; and
(c) may be subject to compliance with any specified conditions.

(3) For the purposes of a licence the definition of a class of persons may be framed by reference to any circumstances whatever including, in particular, their being authorised by any other person.

(4) A licence may be modified or revoked at any time by the authority which granted it, but is otherwise valid for the period stated in the licence.

(5) The relevant licensing body may charge for a licence such reasonable sum (if any) as they may determine.

Relevant licensing body

56 Relevant licensing body

(1) For the purposes of regulations 53, 54 and 55, "relevant licensing body" has the meaning given in this regulation.

(2) In the case of a licence granted under regulation 53(1) for a purpose specified in any of sub-paragraphs (a) to (d) of paragraph (2) of that regulation, "relevant licensing body" means—
(a) in relation to England—
 (i) so far as the licence relates to the restricted English inshore region, the Marine Management Organisation, and
 (ii) otherwise, Natural England; or
(b) in relation to Wales, the Countryside Council for Wales.

(3) In the case of a licence granted—
(a) under regulation 53(1) for a purpose specified in any of sub-paragraphs (e) to (g) of paragraph (2) of that regulation,
(b) under regulation 53(4), or
(c) under regulation 54,
"relevant licensing body" means the appropriate authority.

Offences

57 False statements made for obtaining licence

(1) A person ("P") commits an offence if, for the purposes of obtaining, whether for P or another, the grant of a licence under regulation 53 or 54, P—
(a) makes a statement or representation, or supplies a document or information, which P knows to be false in a material particular; or
(b) recklessly makes a statement or representation, or supplies a document or information, which is false in a material particular.

(2) A person guilty of an offence under this regulation is liable on summary conviction to imprisonment for a term not exceeding six months or to a fine not exceeding level 5 on the standard scale, or to both.

58 Offence of breaching licence condition

[(1) It is an offence for a person to contravene or fail to comply with a licence condition.][1]

(2) Paragraph (1) applies to a licence under regulation 53 granted on or after 21st August 2007.

(3) A person ("P") is not guilty of an offence under paragraph (1) if P shows that—
(a) P took all reasonable precautions and exercised all due diligence to avoid commission of the offence; or
(b) the commission of the offence was otherwise due to matters beyond P's control.

(4) A person guilty of an offence under paragraph (1) is liable on summary conviction to imprisonment for a term not exceeding six months or to a fine not exceeding level 5 on the standard scale, or to both.

Amendment

1 Substituted by the Conservation of Habitats and Species (Amendment) Regulations 2012, SI 2012/1927, regs 2, 18.

PART 6
ASSESSMENT OF THE PLANS AND PROJECTS

Chapter 1
General provisions

Introductory provisions

59 Interpretation of Part 6

In this Part—

(a) "the assessment provisions" means regulations 61 (assessment of implications for European sites and European offshore marine sites) and 62 (considerations of overriding public interest); ...[1]

(b) "the review provisions" means regulations 63 (review of existing decisions and consents) and 64 (consideration on review);

[(c) any reference to—

(i) the giving or granting of any consent, permission or other authorisation (except in the heading to any regulation or in any reference to any such heading), or

(ii) directing that planning permission is deemed to be granted,

is to be taken, in relation to any authorisation which is capable of being varied or modified, to include a reference to the variation or modification of such a consent, permission or authorisation; and

(d) the reference in regulation 61(1) to deciding to undertake a plan or project is to be taken to include a reference to deciding to vary any plan or project undertaken or to be undertaken by the competent authority.][2]

Amendments

1 Repealed by the Conservation of Habitats and Species (Amendment) Regulations 2011, SI 2011/625, regs 2, 6(a).

2 Inserted by the Conservation of Habitats and Species (Amendment) Regulations 2011, SI 2011/625, regs 2, 6(b).

60 Application of provisions of Chapter 1

[(1) The requirements of the assessment provisions and the review provisions apply—

(a) subject to and in accordance with the provisions of Chapters 2 to 7, in relation to the matters specified in those provisions; and

(b) subject to regulation 61(7)(c), in relation to all other plans and projects not relating to matters specified in Chapters 2 to 9.][1]

(2) Supplementary provision is made by regulations 65 to 67.

Amendment

1 Substituted by the Conservation of Habitats and Species (Amendment) Regulations 2012, SI 2012/1927, regs 2, 19.

General provisions for protection of European sites and European offshore marine sites

61 Assessment of implications for European sites and European offshore marine sites

(1) A competent authority, before deciding to undertake, or give any consent, permission or other authorisation for, a plan or project which—

(a) is likely to have a significant effect on a European site or a European offshore marine site (either alone or in combination with other plans or projects), and
(b) is not directly connected with or necessary to the management of that site,
must make an appropriate assessment of the implications for that site in view of that site's conservation objectives.

(2) A person applying for any such consent, permission or other authorisation must provide such information as the competent authority may reasonably require for the purposes of the assessment or to enable them to determine whether an appropriate assessment is required.

(3) The competent authority must for the purposes of the assessment consult the appropriate nature conservation body and have regard to any representations made by that body within such reasonable time as the authority specify.

(4) They must also, if they consider it appropriate, take the opinion of the general public, and if they do so, they must take such steps for that purpose as they consider appropriate.

(5) In the light of the conclusions of the assessment, and subject to regulation 62 (considerations of overriding public interest), the competent authority may agree to the plan or project only after having ascertained that it will not adversely affect the integrity of the European site or the European offshore marine site (as the case may be).

(6) In considering whether a plan or project will adversely affect the integrity of the site, the authority must have regard to the manner in which it is proposed to be carried out or to any conditions or restrictions subject to which they propose that the consent, permission or other authorisation should be given.

[(7) This regulation does not apply in relation to—
(a) a site which is a European site by reason of regulation 8(1)(c);
(b) a site which is a European offshore marine site by reason of regulation 15(c) of the 2007 Regulations; or
(c) a plan or project to which any of the following apply—
  (i) the Offshore Petroleum Activities (Conservation of Habitats) Regulations 2001 (in so far as this regulation is not disapplied by regulation 4 (plans or projects relating to offshore marine area or offshore marine installations) in relation to plans or projects to which those Regulations apply),
  (ii) the Environmental Impact Assessment (Agriculture) (England) (No 2) Regulations 2006,
  (iii) the Environmental Impact Assessment (Agriculture) (Wales) Regulations 2007, or
  (iv) the Merchant Shipping (Ship-to-Ship Transfers) Regulations 2010.][1]

(8) Where a plan or project requires an appropriate assessment both under this regulation and under the 2007 Regulations, the assessment required by this regulation need not identify those effects of the plan or project that are specifically attributable to that part of it that is to be carried out in [the United Kingdom][1], provided that an assessment made for the purpose of this regulation and the 2007 Regulations assesses the effects of the plan or project as a whole.

Amendment
1 Substituted by the Conservation of Habitats and Species (Amendment) Regulations 2012, SI 2012/1927, regs 2, 20.

62 Considerations of overriding public interest

(1) If the competent authority are satisfied that, there being no alternative solutions, the plan or project must be carried out for imperative reasons of overriding public interest

(which, subject to paragraph (2), may be of a social or economic nature), they may agree to the plan or project notwithstanding a negative assessment of the implications for the European site or the European offshore marine site (as the case may be).

(2) Where the site concerned hosts a priority natural habitat type or a priority species, the reasons referred to in paragraph (1) must be either—
(a) reasons relating to human health, public safety or beneficial consequences of primary importance to the environment; or
(b) any other reasons which the competent authority, having due regard to the opinion of the European Commission, consider to be imperative reasons of overriding public interest.

(3) Where a competent authority other than the Secretary of State or the Welsh Ministers desire to obtain the opinion of the European Commission as to whether reasons are to be considered imperative reasons of overriding public interest, they may submit a written request to the appropriate authority—
(a) identifying the matter on which an opinion is sought; and
(b) accompanied by any documents or information which may be required.

(4) The appropriate authority—
(a) may seek the opinion of the European Commission concerning the plan or project; and
(b) where such an opinion is received, must send it to the competent authority.

(5) Where a competent authority other than the Secretary of State or the Welsh Ministers propose to agree to a plan or project under this regulation notwithstanding a negative assessment of the implications for the site concerned—
(a) they must notify the appropriate authority; and
(b) they must not agree to the plan or project before the end of the period of 21 days beginning with the day notified by the appropriate authority as that on which their notification was received, unless the appropriate authority notify them that they may do so.

(6) Without prejudice to any other power, the appropriate authority may give directions to the competent authority in any such case prohibiting them from agreeing to the plan or project, either indefinitely or during such period as may be specified in the direction.

63 Review of existing decisions and consents

(1) Where before the date on which a site becomes a European site or a European offshore marine site a competent authority have decided to undertake, or have given any consent, permission or other authorisation for, a plan or project to which regulation 61(1) would apply if it were to be reconsidered as of that date, the authority must, as soon as reasonably practicable—
(a) review their decision or, as the case may be, the consent, permission or other authorisation; and
(b) affirm, modify or revoke it.

(2) They must for that purpose make an appropriate assessment of the implications for the site in view of that site's conservation objectives; and the provisions of regulation 61(2) to (4) apply, with the appropriate modifications, in relation to such a review.

(3) Subject to the provisions of Chapters 2 to 7, any review required by this regulation must be carried out under existing statutory procedures where such procedures exist, and if none exists, the appropriate authority may give directions as to the procedure to be followed.

(4) Nothing in this regulation affects anything done in pursuance of the decision, or the consent, permission or other authorisation, before the date mentioned in paragraph (1).

64 Consideration on review

(1) The following provisions apply where a decision, or a consent, permission or other authorisation, falls to be reviewed under regulation 63.

(2) Subject as follows, the provisions of regulations 61(5) and (6) and 62 apply, with the appropriate modifications, in relation to the decision on the review.

(3) The decision, or the consent, permission or other authorisation, may be affirmed if it appears to the competent authority reviewing it that other action taken or to be taken by them, or by another authority, will secure that the plan or project does not adversely affect the integrity of the site.

(4) Where that object may be attained in a number of ways, the competent authority or authorities concerned must seek to secure that the action taken is the least onerous to those affected.

(5) The appropriate authority may issue guidance to competent authorities for the purposes of paragraph (3) as to the manner of determining which of different ways should be adopted for securing that the plan or project does not have any such effect, and in particular—

(a) the order of application of different controls; and

(b) the extent to which account should be taken of the possible exercise of other powers.

(6) The competent authorities concerned must have regard to any such guidance.

(7) Any modification or revocation of a decision, or a consent, permission or other authorisation, must be carried out under existing statutory procedures where such procedures exist, and if none exists, the appropriate authority may give directions as to the procedure to be followed.

65 Co-ordination where more than one competent authority involved

(1) This regulation applies where a plan or project—

(a) is undertaken by more than one competent authority;

(b) requires the consent, permission or other authorisation of more than one competent authority; or

(c) is undertaken by one or more competent authorities and requires the consent, permission or other authorisation of one or more other competent authorities.

(2) Nothing in regulation 61(1) or 63(2) requires a competent authority to assess any implications of a plan or project which would be more appropriately assessed under that provision by another competent authority.

(3) The appropriate authority may issue guidance to competent authorities for the purposes of regulations 61 to 64 as to the circumstances in which a competent authority may or should adopt the reasoning or conclusions of another competent authority as to whether a plan or project—

(a) is likely to have a significant effect on a European site or a European offshore marine site; or

(b) will adversely affect the integrity of a European site or a European offshore marine site.

(4) The competent authorities concerned must have regard to any such guidance.

(5) In determining whether a plan or project should be agreed to under regulation 62 (considerations of overriding public interest), a competent authority other than the Secretary of State or the Welsh Ministers must seek and have regard to the views of the other competent authority or authorities involved.

66 Compensatory measures

Where in accordance with regulation 62 (considerations of overriding public interest)—
(a) a plan or project is agreed to, notwithstanding a negative assessment of the implications for a European site or a European offshore marine site, or
(b) a decision, or a consent, permission or other authorisation, is affirmed on review, notwithstanding such an assessment,
the appropriate authority must secure that any necessary compensatory measures are taken to ensure that the overall coherence of Natura 2000 is protected.

67 Modifications of regulations 61 to 66 in certain cases

(1) Where any provision of regulations 61 to 66 (a "general provision") applies in relation to a provision specified in paragraph (2), that general provision applies with the following modifications—
(a) any reference to the Welsh Ministers is omitted; and
(b) for any reference to the appropriate authority, substitute a reference to the Secretary of State.

(2) The provisions specified for the purposes of paragraph (1) are—
(a) paragraphs (1)(e)(i) and (2) of regulation 68 (grant of planning permission) in so far as those provisions relate to a direction given by the Secretary of State under section 90 of the TCPA 1990 (development with government authorisation) that planning permission is deemed to be granted; and
(b) regulations 81 and 82 (development consent under Planning Act 2008).

(3) Where a general provision applies in relation to a provision specified in paragraph (4), that general provision applies with the following modifications—
(a) any reference to a competent authority is taken to include the Scottish Ministers;
(b) for any reference to the Welsh Ministers, substitute a reference to the Scottish Ministers; and
(c) for any reference to the appropriate authority—
  (i) in a case where the competent authority for the purposes of a provision specified in paragraph (4) are the Scottish Ministers, substitute a reference to the Scottish Ministers, and
  (ii) in any other case, substitute a reference to the Secretary of State.

(4) The provisions specified for the purposes of paragraph (3) are—
(a) in regulation 68—
  (i) paragraph (1)(e)(ii) and (iii) (deemed grant of planning permission under section 57(2) of the Town and Country Planning (Scotland) Act 1997 and section 5(1) of the Pipe-lines Act 1962), and
  (ii) paragraph (2) in so far as that paragraph relates to paragraph (1)(e)(ii) and (iii) of that regulation;
(b) Chapter 4 (electricity); and
(c) Chapter 5 (pipe-lines).

(5) Where a general provision applies in relation to regulation 100 (marine works), and confers a function on the appropriate authority, that provision applies with the following modifications—

(a) in a case to which paragraph (6) applies, for any reference to the appropriate authority, substitute a reference to the Welsh Ministers; and
(b) in any other case, for any reference to the appropriate authority, substitute a reference to the Secretary of State.

(6) This paragraph applies where the function in question is exercisable in relation to—
(a) any application to the Welsh Ministers for an authorisation in respect of marine works;
(b) any application to any other authority for—
  (i) an authorisation in respect of marine works, the refusal of which gives rise to a right of appeal to the Welsh Ministers,
  (ii) an authorisation in respect of marine works in relation to which the Welsh Ministers exercise any power of direction or call-in,
  [(iii) an authorisation of harbour works which are, or are to be, carried out in relation to a fishery harbour in Wales under legislation of a kind mentioned in regulation 100(6)(c);][1]
(c) the grant of any application of a kind mentioned in sub-paragraph (a) or (b)[; or][1]
[(d) harbour works which—
  (i) are, or are to be, carried out in relation to a fishery harbour in Wales, and
  (ii) are authorised by, and are, or are to be, carried out in accordance with, any legislation of a kind mentioned in regulation 100(6)(c).][2]

(7) In paragraph (6)—
(a) "authorisation" means any licence, consent or other approval; and
(b) ["marine works" and "harbour works" have][3] the same meaning as in regulation 100.

[(8) Where a general provision applies in relation to a plan or project which does not relate to a matter specified in Chapters 2 to 9, to the extent that that general provision applies in relation to Scotland or Northern Ireland, that provision applies with the following modifications—
(a) any reference to the Welsh Ministers is omitted; and
(b) for any reference to the appropriate authority, substitute a reference to the Secretary of State.][4]

Amendments

1 Substituted by the Conservation of Habitats and Species (Amendment) Regulations 2011, SI 2011/625, regs 2, 7(a), (b).
2 Inserted by the Conservation of Habitats and Species (Amendment) Regulations 2011, SI 2011/625, regs 2, 7(c).
3 Substituted by the Conservation of Habitats and Species (Amendment) Regulations 2012, SI 2012/1927, regs 2, 21(a).
4 Inserted by the Conservation of Habitats and Species (Amendment) Regulations 2012, SI 2012/1927, regs 2, 21(b).

Chapter 2
Planning

Planning permission

68 Grant of planning permission

(1) The assessment provisions apply in relation to—
(a) granting planning permission on an application under Part 3 of the TCPA 1990 (control over development);

(b) granting planning permission on an application under section 293A of that Act (urgent Crown development);
(c) granting planning permission, or upholding a decision of the local planning authority to grant planning permission (whether or not subject to the same conditions and limitations as those imposed by the local planning authority), on determining an appeal under section 78 of that Act (right to appeal against planning decisions) in respect of such an application;
(d) granting planning permission under—
    (i) section 141(2)(a) of that Act (action in relation to purchase notice), or
    (ii) section 177(1)(a) of that Act (grant or modification of planning permission on appeals against enforcement notices);
(e) directing under the following provisions that planning permission is deemed to be granted—
    (i) subsection (1), (2) or (2A) of section 90 of that Act (development with government authorisation),
    (ii) section 57(2) of the Town and Country Planning (Scotland) Act 1997 (deemed grant of planning permission in relation to development for which a consent has been granted under section 36 or 37 of the Electricity Act 1989), or
    (iii) section 5(1) of the Pipe-lines Act 1962 (provisions with respect to planning permission concerning pipe-lines);
(f) making—
    (i) an order under section 102 of the TCPA 1990 (orders requiring discontinuance of use or alteration or removal of buildings or works), including an order made under that section by virtue of section 104 of that Act (powers in relation to section 102 orders) which grants planning permission, or confirming any such order under section 103 of that Act (confirmation of section 102 orders), or
    (ii) an order under paragraph 1 of Schedule 9 to that Act (order requiring discontinuance of mineral working), including an order made under that paragraph by virtue of paragraph 11 of that Schedule to that Act (powers in relation to orders under Schedule 9) which grants planning permission; or
(g) directing under the following provisions that if an application is made for planning permission it must be granted—
    (i) section 141(3) of that Act (action in relation to purchase notice), or
    (ii) section 35(5) of the Planning (Listed Buildings and Conservation Areas) Act 1990 (action in relation to listed building purchase notice).

(2) Where the assessment provisions apply, the competent authority may, if they consider that any adverse effects of the plan or project on the integrity of a European site or a European offshore marine site would be avoided if the planning permission were subject to conditions or limitations, grant planning permission or, as the case may be, take action which results in planning permission being granted or deemed to be granted subject to those conditions or limitations.

(3) Where the assessment provisions apply, outline planning permission must not be granted unless the competent authority are satisfied (whether by reason of the conditions and limitations to which the outline planning permission is to be made subject, or otherwise) that no development likely adversely to affect the integrity of a European site or a European offshore marine site could be carried out under the permission, whether before or after obtaining approval of any reserved matters.

(4) In paragraph (3), "outline planning permission" and "reserved matters" have the same meanings as in section 92 of the TCPA 1990 (outline planning permission).

69 Planning permission: duty to review

(1) Subject to the following provisions of this regulation, the review provisions apply to any planning permission or deemed planning permission, unless—

(a) the development to which it related has been completed;

(b) it was granted subject to a condition as to the time within which the development to which it related was to be begun and that time has expired without the development having been begun; or

(c) it was granted for a limited period and that period has expired.

(2) The review provisions do not apply to planning permission granted or deemed to have been granted—

(a) by a development order (but see regulations 73 to 78);

(b) by virtue of the adoption of a simplified planning zone scheme or of alterations to such a scheme (but see regulation 79); or

(c) by virtue of the taking effect of an order designating an enterprise zone under paragraph 5 of Schedule 32 to the Local Government, Planning and Land Act 1980 (enterprise zones), or by virtue of the approval of a modified enterprise zone scheme (but see regulation 80).

(3) Planning permission deemed to be granted by virtue of—

(a) a direction under section 90(1) of the TCPA 1990 in respect of development for which an authorisation has been granted under section 1 of the Pipe-lines Act 1962 (pipe-line construction authorisations),

(b) a direction under section 5(1) of the Pipe-lines Act 1962,

(c) a direction under section 90(1) of the TCPA 1990 in respect of development for which a consent has been granted under section 36 or 37 of the Electricity Act 1989 (consents required in relation to generating stations and overhead lines),

(d) a direction under section 90(2) of the TCPA 1990 or section 57(2) of the Town and Country Planning (Scotland) Act 1997 (which relate to development for which a consent has been granted under section 36 or 37 of the Electricity Act 1989), or

(e) a direction under section 90(2A) of the TCPA 1990 (which relates to development in pursuance of an order under section 1 or 3 of the Transport and Works Act 1992 (orders as to railways, tramways or inland waterways)),

must be reviewed in accordance with Chapter 4 (electricity), Chapter 5 (pipe-lines) or Chapter 6 (transport and works) (as the case may be) in conjunction with the review of the underlying authorisation, consent or order.

(4) In the case of planning permission deemed to have been granted in any other case by a direction under section 90(1) of the TCPA 1990, the local planning authority must—

(a) identify any such permission which they consider falls to be reviewed under the review provisions, and

(b) refer the matter to the government department or person which made the direction,

and the department or person must, if in agreement that the planning permission does fall to be so reviewed, review the direction in accordance with the review provisions.

(5) Except as otherwise expressly provided, the review provisions do not apply to planning permission granted or deemed to be granted by a public general Act of Parliament.

(6) Subject to paragraphs (3) and (4), where planning permission granted by the appropriate authority falls to be reviewed under the review provisions—

(a) it must be reviewed by the local planning authority; and

(b) the power conferred by section 97 of the TCPA 1990 (power to revoke or modify planning permission) is exercisable by that local planning authority as in relation to planning permission granted on an application under Part 3 of that Act (control over development).

(7) In a non-metropolitan county in England the function of reviewing any such planning permission is to be exercised by the district planning authority unless it relates to a county matter (within the meaning of paragraph 1 of Schedule 1 to the TCPA 1990), in which case it is exercisable by the county planning authority.

70 Planning permission: consideration on review

(1) In reviewing any planning permission or deemed planning permission under the review provisions, the competent authority must—
(a) consider whether any adverse effects could be overcome by planning obligations under section 106 of the TCPA 1990 (planning obligations) being entered into; and
(b) if they consider that those effects could be so overcome, invite those concerned to enter into such obligations.

(2) So far as the adverse effects are not thus overcome, the authority must make such order as may be required under—
(a) section 97 of that Act (power to revoke or modify planning permission); or
(b) section 102 of or paragraph 1 of Schedule 9 to that Act (orders requiring discontinuance of use etc.).

(3) Where the authority ascertain that the carrying out or, as the case may be, the continuation of the development would adversely affect the integrity of a European site or a European offshore marine site, they nevertheless need not proceed under the review provisions if and so long as they consider that there is no likelihood of the development being carried out or continued.

71 Planning permission: effect of orders made on review

(1) An order under section 97 of the TCPA 1990 made pursuant to regulation 69 (duty to review) takes effect upon the service of the notices required by section 98(2) of that Act (procedure for section 97 orders) or, where there is more than one such notice and those notices are served at different times, upon the service of the last such notice to be served.

(2) Where the appropriate authority determine not to confirm such an order—
(a) the order ceases to have effect as from the time of that determination;
(b) the permission revoked or modified by the order thereafter has effect as if the order had never been made;
(c) any period specified in the permission for the taking of any action, being a period which had not expired prior to the date upon which the order took effect under paragraph (1), is extended by a period equal to that during which the order had effect; and
(d) there is substituted for any date specified in the permission as being a date by which any action should be taken ("the specified date"), not being a date falling prior to the date upon which the order took effect under paragraph (1), such later date as postpones the specified date by a period equal to that during which the order had effect.

(3) An order under section 102 of or paragraph 1 of Schedule 9 to the TCPA 1990 made pursuant to regulation 69, in so far as it requires the discontinuance of a use of land or imposes conditions upon the continuance of a use of land, takes effect upon the service of the notices required by section 103(3) (confirmation of section 102 orders) or, where there is more than one such notice and those notices are served at different times, upon the service of the last such notice to be served.

(4) Where the appropriate authority determine not to confirm any such order, the order ceases to have effect as from the time of that determination and the use which by the order was discontinued or upon which conditions were imposed—

(a) may thereafter be continued as if the order had never been made; and
(b) is to be treated for the purposes of the TCPA 1990 as if it had continued without interruption or modification throughout the period during which the order had effect.

(5) An order under section 97 of that Act made in pursuance of regulation 69 does not affect so much of the development authorised by the permission as was carried out prior to the order taking effect.

(6) An order under section 102 of or paragraph 1 of Schedule 9 to that Act made in pursuance of regulation 69 does not affect anything done prior to the site becoming a European site or European offshore marine site.

72 Planning permission: supplementary provisions as to compensation

(1) Where the appropriate authority determine not to confirm an order under section 97 of the TCPA 1990 which has taken effect under regulation 71(1), any claim for compensation under section 107 of that Act (compensation where planning permission revoked or modified) is limited to any loss or damage directly attributable to the permission being suspended or temporarily modified for the duration of the period between the order so taking effect and the appropriate authority's determination not to confirm the order.

(2) Where the appropriate authority determine not to confirm an order under section 102 of the TCPA 1990 (orders requiring discontinuance of use or alteration or removal of buildings or works) which has taken effect under regulation 71(3), any claim for compensation under section 115 of that Act (compensation in respect of orders under section 102) is limited to any loss or damage directly attributable to any right to continue a use of the land being, by virtue of the order, suspended or subject to conditions for the duration of the period between the order so taking effect and the appropriate authority's determination not to confirm the order.

(3) Paragraph (4) applies where—
(a) compensation is payable in respect of—
  (i) an order under section 97 of the TCPA 1990, or
  (ii) any order mentioned in section 115(1) of that Act or to which that section applies by virtue of section 115(5); and
(b) the order has been made pursuant to regulation 63 (review of existing decisions and consents).

(4) Where this paragraph applies, the authority liable to pay the compensation must refer the question as to the amount of the compensation to the Upper Tribunal for its determination, unless and to the extent that in any particular case the appropriate authority have indicated in writing that such a reference and determination may be dispensed with.

General development orders

73 General development orders

(1) It is a condition of any planning permission granted by a general development order, whether made before or after 1st April 2010, that development which—
(a) is likely to have a significant effect on a European site or a European offshore marine site (either alone or in combination with other plans or projects), and
(b) is not directly connected with or necessary to the management of the site,
must not be begun until the developer has received written notification of the approval of the local planning authority under regulation 75 (approval of local planning authority).

(2) It is a condition of any planning permission granted by a general development order made before 1st April 2010 that development which—

(a) is likely to have a significant effect on a European site (either alone or in combination with other plans or projects),

(b) is not directly connected with or necessary to the management of the site, and

(c) was begun but not completed before that date,

must not be continued until the developer has received written notification of the approval of the local planning authority under regulation 75.

(3) Nothing in this regulation affects anything done pursuant to any such planning permission before 1st April 2010.

74 General development orders: opinion of appropriate nature conservation body

(1) Where it is intended to carry out development in reliance on the permission granted by a general development order, application may be made in writing to the appropriate nature conservation body for their opinion as to whether the development is likely to have a relevant effect.

(2) The application must give details of the development which is intended to be carried out.

(3) On receiving such an application, the appropriate nature conservation body must consider whether the development is likely to have such an effect.

(4) Where they consider that they have sufficient information to conclude that the development will, or will not, have such an effect, they must notify the applicant and the local planning authority in writing of their opinion.

(5) If the appropriate nature conservation body consider that they have insufficient information to reach either of those conclusions, they must notify the applicant in writing indicating in what respects they consider the information insufficient, and the applicant may supply further information with a view to enabling them to reach a decision on the application.

(6) The opinion of the appropriate nature conservation body, notified in accordance with paragraph (4), that the development is not likely to have a relevant effect is conclusive of that question for the purpose of reliance on the planning permission granted by a general development order.

(7) In this regulation and in regulation 75 "a relevant effect" means such an effect as is mentioned in regulation 73(1)(a) or (2)(a).

75 General development orders: approval of local planning authority

(1) An application to the local planning authority for approval, as mentioned in regulation 73 (general development orders), must—

(a) give details of the development which is intended to be carried out; and

(b) be accompanied by—

  (i) a copy of any relevant notification by the appropriate nature conservation body under regulation 74 (opinion of appropriate nature conservation body), and

  (ii) any fee required to be paid.

(2) For the purposes of their consideration of the application the local planning authority must assume that the development is likely to have a relevant effect.

(3) The authority must send a copy of the application to the appropriate nature conservation body and must take account of any representations made by them.

(4) If in their representations the appropriate nature conservation body state their opinion that the development is not likely to have a relevant effect, the local planning authority must send a copy of the representations to the applicant.

(5) The sending of the copy of the representations to the applicant under paragraph (4) has the same effect as a notification by the appropriate nature conservation body of their opinion under regulation 74(4).

(6) In any other case in which the application has been sent to the appropriate nature conservation body, the local planning authority must, taking account of any representations made by the appropriate nature conservation body, make an appropriate assessment of the implications of the development for the European site or European offshore marine site in view of that site's conservation objectives.

(7) In the light of the conclusions of the assessment the local planning authority may approve the development only after having ascertained that it will not adversely affect the integrity of the site.

76 General development orders: supplementary

(1) The local planning authority for the purposes of regulations 73 to 75 are the authority to which an application for approval under regulation 75 (approval of local planning authority) would fall to be made if it were an application for planning permission.

(2) The fee payable in connection with an application for such approval is £30.

(3) Approval required by regulation 73 (general development orders) is to be treated—
(a) for the purposes of the provisions of the TCPA 1990 relating to appeals, as approval required by a condition imposed on a grant of planning permission; and
(b) for the purposes of the provisions of any general development order relating to the time within which notice of a decision should be given, as approval required by a condition attached to a grant of planning permission.

Special development orders

77 Special development orders

(1) A special development order may not grant planning permission for development which—
(a) is likely to have a significant effect on a European site (either alone or in combination with other plans or projects); and
(b) is not directly connected with or necessary to the management of the site.

(2) A special development order made before 1st April 2010 is not to be taken to grant planning permission for development of a kind mentioned in paragraph (1), whether or not the development authorised by the permission has been begun.

(3) Nothing in this regulation affects anything done pursuant to a special development order before 1st April 2010.

(4) A special development order may not grant planning permission for development which is likely to have a significant effect on a European offshore marine site (either alone or in combination with other plans or projects).

Local development orders

78 Local development orders

A local development order may not grant planning permission for development which—
(a) is likely to have a significant effect on a European site or a European offshore marine site (either alone or in combination with other plans or projects); and
(b) is not directly connected with or necessary to the management of the site.

Neighbourhood development orders

[78A Neighbourhood development orders

A neighbourhood development order may not grant planning permission for development which—
(a) is likely to have a significant effect on a European site or a European offshore marine site (either alone or in combination with other plans or projects); and
(b) is not directly connected with or necessary to the management of the site.][1]

Amendment

1 Inserted by the Neighbourhood Planning (General) Regulations 2012, SI 2012/637, reg 2, Sch 2, paras 2, 3.

Simplified planning zones and enterprise zones

79 Simplified planning zones

(1) Where a simplified planning zone scheme is adopted or approved, that scheme is not to be taken to grant planning permission for development which—
(a) is likely to have a significant effect on a European site (either alone or in combination with other plans or projects); and
(b) is not directly connected with or necessary to the management of the site.

(2) A simplified planning zone scheme in force before 1st April 2010 is not to be taken to grant planning permission for development of a kind mentioned in paragraph (1), whether or not the development authorised by the permission has been begun.

(3) Where a simplified planning zone scheme is adopted or approved, that scheme is not to be taken to grant planning permission for development which is likely to have a significant effect on a European offshore marine site (either alone or in combination with other plans or projects).

(4) A simplified planning zone scheme adopted or approved on or after 21st August 2007 and before 1st April 2010 is not to be taken to grant planning permission for development of a kind mentioned in paragraph (3).

80 Enterprise zones

(1) Where an order designating an enterprise zone is made, or where a modified enterprise zone scheme is approved, that order or scheme is not to be taken to grant planning permission for development which—
(a) is likely to have a significant effect on a European site (either alone or in combination with other plans or projects); and
(b) is not directly connected with or necessary to the management of the site.

(2) Where such an order was made or such a scheme was approved before 1st April 2010, that order or scheme is not to be taken to grant planning permission for development of

a kind mentioned in paragraph (1), whether or not the development authorised by the permission has been begun.

(3) Where an order designating an enterprise zone is made, or where a modified enterprise zone scheme is approved, that order or scheme is not to be taken to grant planning permission for development which is likely to have a significant effect on a European offshore marine site (either alone or in combination with other plans or projects).

(4) Where such an order was made or such a scheme was approved on or after 21st August 2007 and before 1st April 2010, that order or scheme is not to be taken to grant planning permission for development of a kind mentioned in paragraph (3).

Development consent under Planning Act 2008

81 Grant of development consent

(1) The assessment provisions apply in relation to the making of an order granting development consent under the Planning Act 2008.

(2) Where those provisions apply, the competent authority may, if they consider that any adverse effects of the plan or project on the integrity of a European site or a European offshore marine site would be avoided if the order granting development consent included requirements under section 120 of the Planning Act 2008 (what may be included in order granting development consent), make an order subject to those requirements.

82 Development consent: review

(1) The review provisions apply to any order granting development consent under the Planning Act 2008 unless—

(a) the development to which it related has been completed before the site becomes a European site or a European offshore marine site;

(b) it included a requirement as to the time within which the development to which it related was to be begun and that time has expired without the development having been begun; or

(c) the development consent was granted for a limited period and that period has expired.

(2) …[1]

(3) …[1]

(4) In any such review of an order granting development consent, the competent authority must—

(a) consider whether any adverse effects could be overcome by imposing requirements under paragraph 5(4)(c), (d) or (e) of Schedule 6 to the Planning Act 2008 (changes to, and revocation of, orders granting development consent); and

(b) if they consider that those effects could be so overcome, impose those requirements by making such an order under paragraph 3(1) of Schedule 6 to that Act as may be required.

(5) …[1]

(6) …[1]

Amendment

1 Repealed by the Localism Act 2011(Infrastructure Planning) (Consequential Amendments) Regulations 2012, SI 2012/635, reg 9(1), (2).

Interpretation of Chapter 2

83 Interpretation of Chapter 2

(1) This Chapter, except regulations 81 and 82, is to be construed as one with the TCPA 1990.

[(2) In regulations 81 and 82, the terms "development" and "development consent" have the meanings given by the Planning Act 2008.][1]

Amendment

1 Substituted by the Localism Act 2011(Infrastructure Planning) (Consequential Amendments) Regulations 2012, SI 2012/635, reg 9(1), (3).

Chapter 3
Highways and roads

84 Construction or improvement of highways or roads

(1) The assessment provisions apply in relation to any plan or project—

(a) by the appropriate authority to construct a new highway or to improve, within the meaning of the Highways Act 1980, an existing highway; or

(b) by a local highway authority to carry out within the boundaries of a road any works required for the improvement of the road.

(2) The review provisions apply to any such plan or project as is mentioned in paragraph (1) unless—

(a) the works have been completed before the site became a European site or a European offshore marine site; or

(b) the works were completed before 30th October 1994.

85 Cycle tracks and other ancillary works

Subsection (10) of section 3 of the Cycle Tracks Act 1984 (conversion of footpaths into cycle tracks) is not to be taken to deem planning permission to be granted for development which—

(a) is likely to have a significant effect on a European site (either alone or in combination with other plans or projects), and

(b) is not directly connected with or necessary to the management of the site,

whether or not the development authorised by the permission has been begun.

Chapter 4
Electricity

86 Consents under Electricity Act 1989: application of assessment and review provisions

(1) The assessment provisions apply in relation to the granting of—

(a) consent under section 36 of the Electricity Act 1989 (consent required for construction etc. of generating stations) to construct, extend or operate a generating station in Great Britain; or

(b) consent under section 37 of that Act (consent required for overhead lines) to install an electric line above ground.

(2) Where in such a case the competent authority consider that any adverse effects of the plan or project on the integrity of a European site or a European offshore marine site

would be avoided if the consent were subject to conditions, the competent authority may grant consent subject to those conditions.

(3) The review provisions apply to a consent mentioned in paragraph (1) unless—
(a) the works to which the consent relates—
  (i) have been completed before the site became a European site or a European offshore marine site (as the case may be), or
  (ii) were completed before 30th October 1994; or
(b) the consent was granted—
  (i) subject to a condition as to the time within which the works to which it relates were to be begun and that time has expired without those works having been begun, or
  (ii) for a limited period and that period has expired.

(4) Where the consent is for, or includes, the operation of a generating station, the works are to be treated as completed when, in reliance on the consent, the generating station is first operated.

(5) Where on the review of such a consent the competent authority consider that any adverse effects on the integrity of a European site or a European offshore marine site of the carrying out or, as the case may be, the continuation of the plan or project would be avoided by a variation of the consent, the authority may vary the consent accordingly.

(6) In conjunction with the review of any such consent the competent authority must review any direction deeming planning permission to be granted for the plan or project and may vary or revoke it.

87 Consents under Electricity Act 1989: procedure on review

(1) Where the competent authority decide in pursuance of regulation 86(3), (5) or (6) to revoke or vary a consent under the Electricity Act 1989 or a direction deeming planning permission to be granted, the authority must serve notice on—
(a) the person to whom the consent was granted or, as the case may be, in whose favour the direction was made,
(b) in the case of a consent under section 36 of the Electricity Act 1989, any other person proposing to operate the generating station in question, and
(c) any other person who in the authority's opinion will be affected by the revocation or variation,

informing them of the decision and specifying a period of not less than 28 days within which any person on whom the notice is served may make representations to the authority.

(2) The competent authority must also serve notice on—
(a) the relevant planning authority within the meaning of paragraph 2(6) of Schedule 8 to the Electricity Act 1989 (consents under sections 36 and 37 of that Act), and
(b) the appropriate nature conservation body,

informing them of the decision and inviting their representations within the specified period.

(3) The competent authority must consider whether to proceed with the revocation or variation, and must have regard to any representations made in accordance with paragraph (1) or (2).

(4) If within the specified period a person on whom notice was served under paragraph (1), or the relevant planning authority, so requires, the competent authority must before deciding whether to proceed with the revocation or variation give—
(a) to that person or the relevant planning authority (as the case may be), and

(b) to any other person on whom notice under paragraph (1) or (2) was required to be served,

an opportunity of appearing before, and being heard by, a person appointed by the competent authority for the purpose.

88 Consents under Electricity Act 1989: effect of review

(1) The revocation or variation pursuant to regulation 86(3), (5) or (6) of a consent under the Electricity Act 1989 or a direction deeming planning permission to be granted takes effect upon the service of the notices required by regulation 87(1) or, where there is more than one such notice and those notices are served at different times, upon the service of the last such notice to be served.

(2) Where the competent authority decide not to proceed with the revocation or variation, the consent or direction has effect again as from the time of that decision, and thereafter has effect as if—

(a) any period specified in the consent or direction for the taking of any action, being a period which had not expired prior to the date mentioned in paragraph (1), were extended by a period equal to that during which the revocation or variation had effect; and

(b) there were substituted for any date specified in the consent or direction as being a date by which any action should be taken ("the specified date"), not being a date falling prior to the date mentioned in paragraph (1), such later date as postpones the specified date by a period equal to that during which the revocation or variation had effect.

(3) The revocation or variation of a consent or direction as mentioned in paragraph (1) does not affect anything done under the consent or direction prior to the revocation or variation taking effect.

89 Consents under Electricity Act 1989: compensation

(1) Where a direction deeming planning permission to be granted is revoked or varied pursuant to regulation 86(6), that permission is to be treated—

(a) for the purposes of Part 4 of the TCPA 1990 (compensation for effects of certain orders, notices etc.) as having been revoked or modified by order under section 97 of that Act (power to revoke or modify planning permission); or

(b) for the purposes of Part 4 of the Town and Country Planning (Scotland) Act 1997 (compensation for effects of certain orders, notices etc.) as having been revoked or modified by order under section 65 of that Act (power to revoke or modify planning permission).

(2) Where a consent under the Electricity Act 1989 is revoked or varied pursuant to regulation 86(3) or (5), Part 4 of the TCPA 1990 or Part 4 of the Town and Country Planning (Scotland) Act 1997 (as the case may be) applies as if—

(a) the consent had been planning permission granted on an application under that Act and had been revoked or modified by order under section 97 of the TCPA 1990 or section 65 of the Town and Country Planning (Scotland) Act 1997; and

(b) that Part provided that the competent authority was the person liable to pay any compensation provided for by that Part.

(3) Paragraph (2) does not confer any right to compensation for any expenditure, loss or damage for which compensation is payable by virtue of paragraph (1).

(4) Where the competent authority decide not to proceed with the revocation or variation of a consent under the Electricity Act 1989 or a direction deeming planning permission to

be granted, any claim for compensation by virtue of this regulation is limited to any loss or damage directly attributable to the consent or direction ceasing to have effect or being varied for the duration of the period between the revocation or variation taking effect under regulation 88(1) and the competent authority's decision not to proceed with it.

(5) Where compensation is payable by virtue of this regulation, the question as to the amount of the compensation must be referred to and determined by the Upper Tribunal, or the Lands Tribunal for Scotland, unless and to the extent that in any particular case the competent authority have indicated in writing that such a reference and determination may be dispensed with.

Chapter 5
Pipe-lines

90 Authorisations under Pipe-lines Act 1962: application of assessment and review provisions

(1) The assessment provisions apply in relation to the granting of a pipe-line construction authorisation under the Pipe-lines Act 1962.

(2) Where in such a case the competent authority consider that any adverse effects of the plan or project on the integrity of a European site or a European offshore marine site would be avoided by granting an authorisation for the execution of works for the placing of the proposed pipe-line along a modified route, the competent authority may, subject to the provisions of Schedule 1 to the Pipe-lines Act 1962 (which relates to applications for pipe-line construction authorisations), grant such an authorisation.

(3) The review provisions apply to an authorisation mentioned in paragraph (1) unless—

(a) the works to which the authorisation relates—

  (i) have been completed before the site became a European site or a European offshore marine site (as the case may be), or

  (ii) were completed before 30th October 1994; or

(b) the authorisation was granted—

  (i) subject to a condition as to the time within which the works to which it relates were to be begun and that time has expired without those works having been begun, or

  (ii) for a limited period and that period has expired.

(4) Where on the review of such an authorisation the competent authority consider that any adverse effects on the integrity of a European site or a European offshore marine site of the carrying out or, as the case may be, the continuation of the plan or project would be avoided by a variation of the authorisation, the authority may vary it accordingly.

(5) In conjunction with the review of any such authorisation the competent authority must review any direction deeming planning permission to be granted for the plan or project and may vary or revoke it.

91 Authorisations under Pipe-lines Act 1962: procedure on review

(1) Where the competent authority decide in pursuance of regulation 90(3), (4) or (5) to revoke or vary an authorisation under the Pipe-lines Act 1962 or a direction deeming planning permission to be granted, the authority must serve notice on—

(a) the person to whom the authorisation was granted or, as the case may be, in whose favour the direction was made, and

(b) any other person who in the authority's opinion will be affected by the revocation or variation, informing them of the decision and specifying a period of not less than 28 days within which any person on whom the notice is served may make representations to the authority.

(2) The competent authority must also serve notice on—
(a) the local planning authority, and
(b) the appropriate nature conservation body,
informing them of the decision and inviting their representations within the specified period.

(3) The competent authority must consider whether to proceed with the revocation or variation, and must have regard to any representations made in accordance with paragraph (1) or (2).

(4) If within the specified period a person on whom notice was served under paragraph (1), or the local planning authority, so requires, the competent authority must before deciding whether to proceed with the revocation or variation give—
(a) to that person or the local planning authority (as the case may be), and
(b) to any other person on whom notice under paragraph (1) or (2) was required to be served,
an opportunity of appearing before, and being heard by, a person appointed by the competent authority for the purpose.

92 Authorisations under Pipe-lines Act 1962: effect of review

(1) The revocation or variation pursuant to regulation 90(3), (4) or (5) of an authorisation under the Pipe-lines Act 1962 or a direction deeming planning permission to be granted takes effect upon the service of the notices required by regulation 91(1) or, where there is more than one such notice and those notices are served at different times, upon the service of the last such notice to be served.

(2) Where the competent authority decide not to proceed with the revocation or variation, the authorisation or direction has effect again as from the time of that decision, and thereafter has effect as if—
(a) any period specified in the authorisation or direction for the taking of any action, being a period which had not expired prior to the date mentioned in paragraph (1), were extended by a period equal to that during which the revocation or variation had effect; and
(b) there were substituted for any date specified in the authorisation or direction as being a date by which any action should be taken ("the specified date"), not being a date falling prior to the date mentioned in paragraph (1), such later date as postpones the specified date by a period equal to that during which the revocation or variation had effect.

(3) The revocation or variation of an authorisation or direction as mentioned in paragraph (1) does not affect anything done under the authorisation or direction prior to the revocation or variation taking effect.

93 Authorisations under Pipe-lines Act 1962: compensation

(1) Where a direction deeming planning permission to be granted is revoked or varied pursuant to regulation 90(5), that permission is to be treated—
(a) for the purposes of Part 4 of the TCPA 1990 (compensation for effects of certain orders, notices etc.) as having been revoked or modified by order under section 97 of that Act (power to revoke or modify planning permission); or
(b) for the purposes of Part 4 of the Town and Country Planning (Scotland) Act 1997 (compensation for effects of certain orders, notices etc.) as having been revoked

or modified by order under section 65 of that Act (power to revoke or modify planning permission).

(2) Where an authorisation under the Pipe-lines Act 1962 is revoked or varied pursuant to regulation 90(3) or (4), Part 4 of the TCPA 1990 or Part 4 of the Town and Country Planning (Scotland) Act 1997 (as the case may be) applies as if—

(a) the authorisation had been planning permission granted on an application under that Act and had been revoked or modified by order under section 97 of the TCPA 1990 or section 65 of the Town and Country Planning (Scotland) Act 1997; and

(b) that Part provided that the competent authority was the person liable to pay any compensation provided for by that Part.

(3) Paragraph (2) does not confer any right to compensation for any expenditure, loss or damage for which compensation is payable by virtue of paragraph (1).

(4) Where the competent authority decide not to proceed with the revocation or variation of an authorisation under the Pipe-lines Act 1962 or a direction deeming planning permission to be granted, any claim for compensation by virtue of this regulation is limited to any loss or damage directly attributable to the authorisation or direction ceasing to have effect or being varied for the duration of the period between the revocation or variation taking effect under regulation 92(1) and the competent authority's decision not to proceed with it.

(5) Where compensation is payable by virtue of this regulation, the question as to the amount of the compensation must be referred to and determined by the Upper Tribunal, or the Lands Tribunal for Scotland, unless and to the extent that in any particular case the competent authority have indicated in writing that such a reference and determination may be dispensed with.

Chapter 6
Transport and works

94 Orders under Transport and Works Act 1992: application of assessment and review provisions

(1) The assessment provisions apply in relation to the making of an order under section 1 (orders as to railways, tramways etc.) or 3 (orders as to inland waterways etc.) of the Transport and Works Act 1992.

(2) Where in such a case the appropriate authority consider that any adverse effects of the plan or project on the integrity of a European site or a European offshore marine site would be avoided by making modifications to the proposals, the appropriate authority may make an order subject to those modifications.

(3) The review provisions apply to an order mentioned in paragraph (1) unless the works to which the order relates have been completed before the site became a European site or a European offshore marine site.

(4) Where on the review of such an order the appropriate authority consider that any adverse effects on the integrity of a European site or a European offshore marine site of the carrying out or, as the case may be, the continuation of the plan or project would be avoided by a variation of the order, the appropriate authority may vary it accordingly.

(5) In conjunction with the review of any such order the appropriate authority must review any direction deeming planning permission to be granted for the plan or project and may vary or revoke it.

(6) In relation to an order mentioned in paragraph (1) which has effect or would have effect in both England and Wales, for any reference in this Chapter to the appropriate authority substitute a reference to the Secretary of State.

95 Orders under Transport and Works Act 1992: procedure on review

(1) Where the appropriate authority decide in pursuance of regulation 94(3), (4) or (5) to revoke or vary an order under the Transport and Works Act 1992 or a direction deeming planning permission to be granted, the authority must serve notice on—

(a) the person (if any) on whose application the order was made or, as the case may be, in whose favour the direction was made, and

(b) any other person who in the authority's opinion will be affected by the revocation or variation,

informing them of the decision and specifying a period of not less than 28 days within which any person on whom the notice is served may make representations to the appropriate authority.

(2) The appropriate authority must also serve notice on—

(a) the local planning authority, and

(b) the appropriate nature conservation body,

informing them of the decision and inviting their representations within the specified period.

(3) The appropriate authority must consider whether to proceed with the revocation or variation, and must have regard to any representations made in accordance with paragraph (1) or (2).

(4) If within the specified period a person on whom notice was served under paragraph (1), or the local planning authority, so requires, the appropriate authority must before deciding whether to proceed with the revocation or variation of the order or direction give—

(a) to that person or the local planning authority (as the case may be), and

(b) to any other person on whom notice under paragraph (1) or (2) was required to be served,

an opportunity of appearing before, and being heard by, a person appointed by the appropriate authority for the purpose.

96 Orders under Transport and Works Act 1992: effect of review

(1) The revocation or variation pursuant to regulation 94(3), (4) or (5) of an order under the Transport and Works Act 1992 or a direction deeming planning permission to be granted takes effect upon the service of the notices required by regulation 95(1) or, where there is more than one such notice and those notices are served at different times, upon the service of the last such notice to be served.

(2) Where the appropriate authority decide not to proceed with the revocation or variation, the order or direction has effect again as from the time of that decision, and thereafter has effect as if—

(a) any period specified in the order or direction for the taking of any action, being a period which had not expired prior to the date mentioned in paragraph (1), were extended by a period equal to that during which the revocation or variation had effect; and

(b) there were substituted for any date specified in the order or direction as being a date by which any action should be taken ("the specified date"), not being a date falling prior to the date mentioned in paragraph (1), such later date as postpones the specified date by a period equal to that during which the revocation or variation had effect.

(3) The revocation or variation of an order or direction as mentioned in paragraph (1) does not affect anything done under the order or direction prior to the revocation or variation taking effect.

97 Orders under Transport and Works Act 1992: compensation

(1) Where a direction deeming planning permission to be granted is revoked or varied pursuant to regulation 94(5), that permission is to be treated for the purposes of Part 4 of the TCPA 1990 (compensation for effects of certain orders, notices etc.) as having been revoked or modified by order under section 97 of that Act (power to revoke or modify planning permission).

(2) Where an order under the Transport and Works Act 1992 is revoked or varied pursuant to regulation 94(3) or (4), Part 4 of the TCPA 1990 applies as if—

(a) the order had been planning permission granted on an application under that Act and had been revoked or modified by order under section 97 of that Act; and

(b) that Part provided that the appropriate authority was the person liable to pay any compensation provided for by that Part.

(3) Paragraph (2) does not confer any right to compensation for any expenditure, loss or damage for which compensation is payable by virtue of paragraph (1).

(4) Where the appropriate authority decide not to proceed with the revocation or variation of an order under the Transport and Works Act 1992 or a direction deeming planning permission to be granted, any claim for compensation by virtue of this regulation is limited to any loss or damage directly attributable to the order or direction ceasing to have effect or being varied for the duration of the period between the revocation or variation taking effect under regulation 96(1) and the appropriate authority's decision not to proceed with it.

(5) Where compensation is payable by virtue of this regulation, the question as to the amount of the compensation must be referred to and determined by the Upper Tribunal unless and to the extent that in any particular case the appropriate authority have indicated in writing that such a reference and determination may be dispensed with.

Chapter 7
Environmental controls

98 Environmental permits

(1) The assessment provisions apply in relation to the granting of an environmental permit under the Environmental Permitting (England and Wales) Regulations [2010][1].

(2) Where in such a case the competent authority consider that any adverse effects of the plan or project on the integrity of a European site or a European offshore marine site would be avoided if the permit were subject to conditions, they may grant a permit, or cause a permit to be granted, subject to those conditions.

(3) The review provisions apply to a permit described in paragraph (1).

(4) Where on the review of such a permit the competent authority consider that any adverse effects on the integrity of a European site or a European offshore marine site of the carrying out or, as the case may be, the continuation of activities authorised by it would be avoided by a variation of the permit, they may vary it, or cause it to be varied, accordingly.

(5) Where any question arises as to agreeing to a plan or project, or affirming a permit on review, under regulation 62 (considerations of overriding public interest), the competent authority must refer the matter to the appropriate authority which must determine the matter in accordance with that regulation and give directions to the competent authority accordingly.

Amendment

1 Substituted by Environmental Permitting (England and Wales) (Amendment) Regulations 2012/630 reg 22.

99 Abstraction and works authorised under water legislation

(1) The assessment provisions apply in relation to the granting of an authorisation by virtue of—

(a) the granting of a licence under Chapter 2 of Part 2 of the WRA (abstraction and impounding);

(b) the making of an order under section 27A of the WRA (variation of small quantity threshold);

(c) the making of regulations under section 33A of the WRA (power to provide for further exemptions), where those regulations relate to—

 (i) a prescribed geographical area,

 (ii) a prescribed source of supply (in the case of an exemption from the restriction on abstraction or the other restrictions imposed by section 24 of the WRA (restrictions on abstraction)), or

 (iii) prescribed inland waters (in the case of an exemption from the restriction on impounding works);

(d) any consent given under paragraph (2);

(e) the making of an order under section 73 of the WRA (power to make ordinary and emergency drought orders) which has the effect of authorising—

 (i) an abstraction or additional abstraction, or

 (ii) a discharge or additional discharge;

(f) the granting of a permit under section 79A of that Act (drought permits);

(g) any consent given under section 166 of the WIA (consents for certain discharges under section 165) or section 164 of the WRA (consents for certain discharges under section 163); or

(h) the making of an order under section 167 of the WIA (compulsory works orders) or section 168 of the WRA (compulsory works orders).

(2) An exemption conferred by regulations under section 33A of the WRA, other than regulations referred to in paragraph (1)(c), does not apply in relation to any particular abstraction or impounding works unless the Environment Agency has given consent in writing to the abstraction or impounding works being carried out.

(3) Where, in relation to any plan or project authorised by any means referred to in sub-paragraphs (a) to (h) of paragraph (1), the competent authority consider that any adverse effects of the plan or project on the integrity of a European site or a European offshore marine site would be avoided if the authorisation were subject to conditions, they may grant the authorisation, or cause it to be granted, subject to those conditions.

(4) Where, by virtue of paragraph (1)(g), the assessment provisions apply in relation to the granting of an authorisation by virtue of a consent under section 166 of the WIA or section 164 of the WRA, the section in question has effect as if in each case—

(a) in subsection (3), the words "and, subject to that subsection, where an application for any consent is required to be determined within the period specified in paragraph (a) above and is not so determined, the consent applied for shall be deemed to have been given unconditionally." were omitted; and

(b) in paragraph (a) of that subsection, for the words "the period of seven days" there were substituted the words "the period of fourteen days".

(5) The review provisions apply to any authorisation mentioned in paragraph (1)(a), (b), (c), (d) or (h).

(6) Where on the review of any such authorisation the competent authority consider that any adverse effects on the integrity of a European site or a European offshore marine site of the carrying out or, as the case may be, the continuation of the activities authorised by it would be avoided by a variation of the authorisation, they may vary it, or cause it to be varied, accordingly.

(7) In this regulation—
(a) "the WIA" means the Water Industry Act 1991; and
(b) "the WRA" means the Water Resources Act 1991.

100 Marine works

(1) The assessment provisions apply in relation to the granting of a licence, consent or other approval for marine works.

(2) Where the assessment provisions apply, the competent authority may, if they consider that any adverse effects of the plan or project on the integrity of a European site or a European offshore marine site would be avoided if the licence, consent or other approval were subject to conditions or requirements, grant the licence, consent or other approval subject to those conditions or requirements.

(3) The review provisions apply to any licence, consent or other approval for marine works.

(4) Where on the review of any such licence, consent or other approval the competent authority consider that any adverse effects on the integrity of a European site or a European offshore marine site of the carrying out or, as the case may be, the continuation of activities authorised by it would be avoided by a variation of the licence, consent or other approval, they may vary it accordingly.

[(5) In this regulation, "marine works" means—
(a) any activity or proposed activity requiring —
  (i) a marine licence under Part 4 of the Marine Act;
  (ii) a licence under Part 2 of the Food and Environment Protection Act 1985 (deposits in the sea);
  (iii) an authorisation under the Aquatic Animal Health (England and Wales) Regulations 2009; or
  (iv) an approval or consent for harbour works under legislation falling within paragraph (6); or
(b) harbour works authorised by, and carried out in accordance with, any legislation falling within paragraph (6).

(6) The legislation referred to in paragraph (5)(a)(iv) and (b) is—
(a) a local Act;
(b) such an Act read together with a notice given and published under section 9 of the Harbours Transfer Act 1862 (power to Admiralty to retain authority over ports, etc. where dockyards, etc. are situate); or
(c) an order made under section 14 (powers, on application of harbour authorities, or others, to make orders for securing harbour efficiency etc.) or 16 (powers, on application of intending undertakers, or others, to make orders conferring powers for improvement, construction, etc., of harbours) of the Harbours Act 1964.][1]

[(7) In paragraph (5)(a)(iv) and (b), "harbour works" means—
(a) works involved in the construction of a harbour;
(b) works involving the making of modifications to an existing harbour;
(c) any dredging operation undertaken by or on behalf of a harbour authority within the meaning of the Harbours Act 1964; and
(d) works involving the deposit of spoil from any such dredging operation.][2]

Amendments

1 Substituted by the Conservation of Habitats and Species (Amendment) Regulations 2011, SI 2011/625, regs 2, 8.

2 Inserted by the Conservation of Habitats and Species (Amendment) Regulations 2011, SI 2011/625, regs 2, 8.

101 Derogations in relation to nitrate pollution prevention legislation

(1) The assessment provisions apply in relation to the granting of a derogation—
(a) under Part 3A of the Nitrate Pollution Prevention Regulations 2008; or
(b) under Part 3A of the Nitrate Pollution Prevention (Wales) Regulations 2008.

(2) Where the assessment provisions apply, the competent authority may, if they consider any adverse effects of the plan or project on the integrity of a European site or a European offshore marine site would be avoided if the derogation were subject to conditions, grant the derogation, subject to those conditions.

Chapter 8
Land use plans

Land use plans

102 Assessment of implications for European sites and European offshore marine sites

(1) Where a land use plan—
(a) is likely to have a significant effect on a European site or a European offshore marine site (either alone or in combination with other plans or projects), and
(b) is not directly connected with or necessary to the management of the site,
the plan-making authority for that plan must, before the plan is given effect, make an appropriate assessment of the implications for the site in view of that site's conservation objectives.

(2) The plan-making authority must for the purposes of the assessment consult the appropriate nature conservation body and have regard to any representations made by that body within such reasonable time as the authority specify.

(3) They must also, if they consider it appropriate, take the opinion of the general public, and if they do so, they must take such steps for that purpose as they consider appropriate.

(4) In the light of the conclusions of the assessment, and subject to regulation 103 (considerations of overriding public interest), the plan-making authority or, in the case of a regional strategy, the Secretary of State must give effect to the land use plan only after having ascertained that it will not adversely affect the integrity of the European site or the European offshore marine site (as the case may be).

(5) A plan-making authority must provide such information as the appropriate authority may reasonably require for the purposes of the discharge of the obligations of the appropriate authority under this Chapter.

(6) This regulation does not apply in relation to a site which is—

(a) a European site by reason of regulation 8(1)(c), or
(b) a European offshore marine site by reason of regulation 15(c) of the 2007 Regulations

(site protected in accordance with Article 5(4) of the Habitats Directive).

[102A Assessment of implications for European site: neighbourhood development plans

(1) A qualifying body which submits a proposal for a neighbourhood development plan must provide such information as the competent authority may reasonably require for the purposes of the assessment under regulation 102 or to enable them to determine whether that assessment is required.

(2) In this regulation, "qualifying body" means a parish council, or an organisation or body designated as a neighbourhood forum, authorised for the purposes of a neighbourhood development plan to act in relation to a neighbourhood area as a result of section 61F of the TCPA 1990, as applied by section 38C of the 2004 Planning Act.

(3) Where the competent authority decide to revoke or modify a neighbourhood development plan after it has been made, they must for that purpose make an appropriate assessment of the implications for any European site likely to be significantly affected in view of that site's conservation objectives; and regulation 102 and this regulation apply with the appropriate modifications in relation to such a revocation or modification.][1]

Amendment

1 Inserted by the Neighbourhood Planning (General) Regulations 2012, SI 2012/637, reg 2, Sch 2, paras 2, 4.

103 Considerations of overriding public interest

(1) If the plan-making authority are satisfied that, there being no alternative solutions, the land use plan must be given effect for imperative reasons of overriding public interest (which, subject to paragraph (3), may be of a social or economic nature), they may give effect to the land use plan notwithstanding a negative assessment of the implications for the European site or the European offshore marine site (as the case may be).

(2) In relation to a regional strategy, paragraph (1) applies to the Secretary of State as it applies to a plan-making authority in the case of any other land use.

(3) Where the site concerned hosts a priority natural habitat type or a priority species, the reasons referred to in paragraph (1) must be either—

(a) reasons relating to human health, public safety or beneficial consequences of primary importance to the environment; or
(b) any other reasons which the plan-making authority, having due regard to the opinion of the European Commission, consider to be imperative reasons of overriding public interest.

(4) Where a plan-making authority other than the Secretary of State or the Welsh Ministers desire to obtain the opinion of the European Commission as to whether reasons are to be considered imperative reasons of overriding public interest, they may submit a written request to the appropriate authority—

(a) identifying the matter on which an opinion is sought; and
(b) accompanied by any documents or information which may be required.

(5) The appropriate authority—

(a) may seek the opinion of the European Commission concerning the plan; and
(b) where such an opinion is received, must send it to the plan-making authority.

(6) Where a plan-making authority other than the Secretary of State or the Welsh Ministers propose to give effect to a land use plan under this regulation notwithstanding a negative assessment of the implications for the site concerned—
(a) they must notify the appropriate authority; and
(b) they must not give effect to the land use plan before the end of the period of 21 days beginning with the day notified by the appropriate authority as that on which their notification was received, unless the appropriate authority notify them that they may do so.

(7) Without prejudice to any other power, the appropriate authority may give directions to the plan-making authority in any such case prohibiting them from giving effect to the land use plan, either indefinitely or during such period as may be specified in the direction.

104 Co-ordination for land use plan prepared by more than one authority

(1) The following provisions apply where two or more local planning authorities prepare a joint local development document under section 28 (joint local development documents) or a joint local development plan under section 72 (joint local development plans) of the 2004 Planning Act.

(2) Nothing in paragraph (1) of regulation 102 (assessment of implications for European sites and European offshore marine sites) requires a local planning authority to assess any implications of a joint local development document or plan which would be more appropriately assessed under that provision by another local planning authority.

(3) The appropriate authority may issue guidance to local planning authorities for the purposes of regulation 102(1) as to the circumstances in which a local planning authority may or should adopt the reasoning or conclusions of another local planning authority as to whether a joint local planning document or plan—
(a) is likely to have a significant effect on a European site or a European offshore marine site; or
(b) will adversely affect the integrity of a European site or a European offshore marine site.

(4) The local planning authorities concerned must have regard to any such guidance.

(5) In determining whether a joint local development document or plan should be adopted under regulation 103 (considerations of overriding public interest), a local planning authority must seek and have regard to the views of the other local planning authorities concerned.

105 Compensatory measures

Where in accordance with regulation 103 (considerations of overriding public interest) a land use plan is given effect notwithstanding a negative assessment of the implications for a European site or a European offshore marine site, the appropriate authority must secure that any necessary compensatory measures are taken to ensure that the overall coherence of Natura 2000 is protected.

Planning Act 2008

106 National policy statements

(1) This Chapter applies—
(a) in relation to a national policy statement under Part 2 (national policy statements) of the Planning Act 2008 as it applies in relation to a land use plan, and

(b) in relation to the Secretary of State when exercising powers under Part 2 of that Act as it applies in relation to a plan-making authority,

with the modifications specified in paragraphs (2) and (3).

(2) Any reference in this Chapter to giving effect to a land use plan, in relation to a national policy statement, is to be taken to be a reference to the designation of a statement as a national policy statement or an amendment of a national policy statement under Part 2 of the Planning Act 2008.

(3) Where this Chapter applies by virtue of paragraph (1)—

(a) regulations 102(5), 103(4) to (7) and 104 do not apply; and

(b) in regulation 105, for the reference to the appropriate authority substitute a reference to the Secretary of State.

Interpretation of Chapter 8

107 Interpretation of Chapter 8

(1) In this Chapter—

"the 1999 Act" means the Greater London Authority Act 1999;

"the 2004 Planning Act" means the Planning and Compulsory Purchase Act 2004;

"the 2005 Order" means the Planning and Compulsory Purchase Act 2004 (Commencement No. 3 and Consequential and Transitional Provisions) (Wales) Order 2005;

"the 2009 Act" means the Local Democracy, Economic Development and Construction Act 2009;

"land use plan" means—

(a) the regional strategy under Part 5 (regional strategy) of the 2009 Act;

(b) the spatial development strategy under section 334 (the spatial development strategy) of the 1999 Act;

(c) a local development document as provided for in Part 2 (local development) of the 2004 Planning Act other than a statement of community involvement under section 18 (statement of community involvement) of that Act;

(d) a local development plan as provided for in Part 6 (Wales) of the 2004 Planning Act;

(e) the Wales Spatial Plan under section 60 (Wales Spatial Plan) of the 2004 Planning Act;

(f) an alteration or replacement of a structure plan, unitary development plan, local plan, minerals local plan, or waste local plan under Part 2 (development plans) of the TCPA 1990 to the extent permitted by Schedule 8 (transitional provisions) to the 2004 Planning Act; …[1]

(g) a unitary development plan as provided for in Part 2 of the TCPA 1990 to the extent permitted by article 4 (transitional provisions) of the 2005 Order; [or

(h) a neighbourhood development plan as defined in section 38A (neighbourhood development plans) of the 2004 Planning Act;][2]

"plan-making authority" means—

(a) responsible regional authorities as defined in section 72 (responsible regional authorities) of the 2009 Act;

(b) the Mayor of London when exercising powers under subsection (1) or (2) of section 341 (alteration or replacement) of the 1999 Act;

(c) an authority which, by virtue of Part 1 (planning authorities) of the TCPA 1990 or an order under subsection (2) of section 29 (joint committees) of the 2004 Planning Act, is a local planning authority;

(d) the Secretary of State when exercising powers under—
(i) section 21 (intervention by Secretary of State) or section 27 (Secretary of State's default power) of the 2004 Planning Act, or
(ii) section 19 (approval of a unitary development plan), subsection (4) of section 35A (calling in of proposal for approval by the Secretary of State) or section 45 (approval of proposals by the Secretary of State) of the TCPA 1990 to the extent permitted by Schedule 8 to the 2004 Planning Act; ...[1]
(e) the Welsh Ministers when exercising powers under—
(i) section 60(3), section 65 (intervention by Assembly) or subsection (4) of section 71 (Assembly's default power) of the 2004 Planning Act, or
(ii) section 19 of the TCPA 1990 to the extent permitted by article 4 of the 2005 Order; [or][3]
[(f) the local planning authority when exercising powers under Schedule 4B to the TCPA 1990 (as applied by section 38A(3) of the 2004 Planning Act); and][2]

"regional strategy" has the same meaning as in section 70 (regional strategy) of the 2009 Act.

(2) References in this Chapter to giving effect to a land use plan are to—
(a) the publication, under subsection (5) of section 78 (approval of revision by Secretary of State) of the 2009 Act, of a revision of a regional strategy;
(b) the approval, under section 21(9) or 27(4) of the 2004 Planning Act, of a local development document;
(c) the adoption, under section 23 (adoption of local development documents) of the 2004 Planning Act, of a local development document other than a statement of community involvement under section 18 of that Act;
(d) the publication, under section 341 of the 1999 Act, of alterations of the spatial development strategy or a new spatial development strategy to replace it;
(e) the publication, under section 60 of the 2004 Planning Act, of a revision of the Wales Spatial Plan;
(f) the adoption, under section 67 (adoption of local development plan) of the 2004 Planning Act, of a local development plan;
(g) the approval, under section 65(9) or 71(4) of the 2004 Planning Act, of a local development plan;
(h) the adoption, under section 35(1) (adoption of proposals), or approval under section 35A(4) of the TCPA 1990, of an alteration or replacement of a structure plan to the extent permitted by paragraph 2(2) of Schedule 8 to the 2004 Planning Act;
(i) the adoption, under section 15 (adoption of unitary development plans by local planning authority) and that provision as applied by subsection (2) of section 21 (alteration or replacement of unitary development plans) of the TCPA 1990, of an alteration or replacement of a unitary development plan to the extent permitted by paragraph 4 of Schedule 8 to the 2004 Planning Act;
(j) the approval, under section 19 and that provision as applied by section 21(2) of the TCPA 1990, of an alteration or replacement of a unitary development plan to the extent permitted by paragraph 4 of Schedule 8 to the 2004 Planning Act;
(k) the adoption, under section 43 (adoption of proposals) or approval under section 45 of the TCPA 1990, of an alteration or replacement of a local plan, minerals local plan or waste local plan to the extent permitted by paragraph 9, 10 or 14 of Schedule 8 to the 2004 Planning Act;

(l) the adoption, under section 15 of the TCPA 1990, of a unitary development plan to the extent permitted by article 4 of the 2005 Order; …[1]

(m) the approval, under section 19 of the TCPA 1990, of a unitary development plan to the extent permitted by article 4 of the 2005 Order; [or

(n) the holding of a referendum in accordance with paragraph 12(4) of Schedule 4B to the TCPA 1990 (as applied by section 38A(3) of the 2004 Planning Act).][2]

Amendments

1 Repealed by the Neighbourhood Planning (General) Regulations 2012, SI 2012/637, reg 2, Sch 2, paras 2, 5.

2 Inserted by the Neighbourhood Planning (General) Regulations 2012, SI 2012/637, reg 2, Sch 2, paras 2, 5.

3 Substituted by the Neighbourhood Planning (General) Regulations 2012, SI 2012/637, reg 2, Sch 2, paras 2, 5(a)(ii).

[Chapter 9
Marine policy statement and marine plans][1]

[107A Marine policy statement

(1) Chapter 8 applies—

(a) in relation to a marine policy statement under Chapter 1 of Part 3 (marine planning) of the Marine Act as it applies in relation to a land use plan, and

(b) in relation to a policy authority when exercising powers under Part 3 of that Act as it applies in relation to a plan-making authority,

with the modifications specified in paragraphs (2) and (3).

(2) Any reference in Chapter 8 to giving effect to a land use plan, in relation to a marine policy statement, is to be taken to be a reference to the adoption and publication of a marine policy statement in accordance with Schedule 5 to the Marine Act or any amendment of a marine policy statement under section 47 of that Act.

(3) Where Chapter 8 applies by virtue of paragraph (1)—

(a) in regulation 102(2), after "the appropriate nature conservation body" insert "and the Joint Nature Conservation Committee";

(b) regulations 102(5), 103(4) to (7) and 104 do not apply; and

(c) in regulation 105, for the reference to the appropriate authority substitute a reference to the policy authority.

(4) In this regulation "policy authority" means the Secretary of State or the Welsh Ministers.][1]

Amendment

1 Inserted by the Conservation of Habitats and Species (Amendment) Regulations 2011, SI 2011/625, regs 2, 9.

[107B Marine plan

(1) Chapter 8 applies—

(a) in relation to a marine plan as it applies in relation to a land use plan, and

(b) in relation to a marine plan authority when exercising powers under Part 3 of the Marine Act as it applies in relation to a plan-making authority,

with the modifications specified in paragraphs (2) and (3).

(2) Any reference in Chapter 8 to giving effect to a land use plan, in relation to a marine plan, is to be taken to be a reference to the adoption and publication of a marine plan in accordance with Schedule 6 to the Marine Act or any amendment of a marine plan under section 52 of that Act.

(3) Where Chapter 8 applies by virtue of paragraph (1), regulations 102(5), 103(4) to (7) and 104 do not apply.

(4) In this regulation—
(a) "marine plan" means a marine plan under Chapter 2 of Part 3 of the Marine Act; and
(b) "marine plan authority" has the meaning given by Part 3 of the Marine Act.][1]

Amendment

1 Inserted by the Conservation of Habitats and Species (Amendment) Regulations 2011, SI 2011/625, regs 2, 9.

PART 7
ENFORCEMENT

Wildlife inspectors

108 Wildlife inspectors

(1) In this Part, "wildlife inspector" means a person authorised in writing under this regulation by the appropriate authority.

(2) An authorisation under paragraph (1) is subject to any conditions or limitations specified in it.

Powers of entry

109 Powers of entry: constables

(1) If a constable suspects with reasonable cause that any person is committing or has committed an offence specified in paragraph (4), the constable may, for the purposes of exercising the powers conferred by regulation 112 (constables' powers of search, etc.) or arresting a person in accordance with section 24 of the Police and Criminal Evidence Act 1984 (arrest without warrant: constables) for such an offence, enter any premises other than a dwelling.

(2) A constable may—
(a) be accompanied by any other person that the constable considers necessary; and
(b) bring any equipment or materials that the constable considers necessary.

(3) If a justice of the peace, on sworn information in writing, is satisfied that there are reasonable grounds for suspecting that an offence specified in paragraph (4) has been committed and that evidence of the offence may be found on any premises, the justice may by signed warrant authorise a constable to enter and search those premises for the purpose of obtaining that evidence.

(4) The offences specified for the purposes of this regulation are—
(a) a species offence;
(b) an offence under regulation 52 (introduction of new species from ships);
(c) an offence under regulation 57 (false statements made for obtaining licence); and
(d) an offence under regulation 116(1) or (2) (attempts and possession of means of committing offence).

110 Powers of entry: wildlife inspectors

(1) A wildlife inspector may, at all reasonable hours, enter and inspect any premises other than a dwelling—

(a) for the purpose of ascertaining whether a species offence is being or has been committed; or
(b) for the purpose of verifying any statement or representation made, or document or information supplied, by an occupier of the premises in connection with an application for, or the holding of, a licence granted under regulation 53 (licences for certain activities relating to animals or plants).

(2) The power in paragraph (1) to enter and inspect premises includes power to board and inspect a ship within the marine area, subject to paragraphs (3) to (6).

(3) Paragraph (4) applies in relation to—
(a) a third country ship;
(b) a warship which is being used by the government of a State other than the United Kingdom (whether or not it is a third country ship); and
(c) any other ship which is being used by the government of a State other than the United Kingdom for any non-commercial purpose.

(4) A wildlife inspector must not, in the exercise of the power in paragraph (1), board or inspect a ship to which this paragraph applies unless—
(a) in the case of a third country ship (other than a ship which is being used as mentioned in paragraph (3)(b) or (c)), the United Kingdom is entitled under international law to exercise that power without the consent of the flag state; or
(b) the Commissioners have given authority to exercise that power.

(5) The Commissioners must not give their authority under paragraph (4)(b) unless the flag state has consented to the United Kingdom exercising that power (whether generally or in relation to the ship in question).

(6) In giving their authority under paragraph (4)(b), the Commissioners must impose such conditions or limitations on the exercise of the power as may be necessary to give effect to any conditions or limitations imposed by the flag state.

(7) A wildlife inspector must, if requested to do so, produce a duly authenticated authorisation document before entering any premises.

(8) A wildlife inspector may be accompanied by a veterinary surgeon if the wildlife inspector has reasonable grounds for believing that such a person will be needed for the exercise of powers under regulation 114 (powers in relation to specimens and samples: wildlife inspectors).

(9) In this regulation—

"the Commissioners" means the Commissioners for Her Majesty's Revenue and Customs;

"flag state", in relation to a ship, means the State whose flag that ship is flying or is entitled to fly; and

"third country ship" means a ship which—
(a) is flying the flag of, or is registered in, any State or territory (other than Gibraltar) which is not a member State; and
(b) is not registered in a member State.

111 Powers of entry: other authorised persons

(1) A person authorised in writing by the appropriate nature conservation body may, at all reasonable hours, enter any land except a dwelling—
(a) to ascertain whether a special nature conservation order should be made under regulation 25 (power to make special nature conservation order), whether a stop notice should be served under paragraph (1) of regulation 26 (restriction on

carrying out operations specified in order) or whether an offence under regulation 26(8) is being, or has been, committed on that land;
(b) to ascertain the amount of any compensation payable under regulation 28 (compensation for effect of stop notice) in respect of an interest in that land; or
(c) to affix a notice in accordance with regulation 26(3) or paragraph 2(5) of Schedule 1 (procedure in connection with special conservation orders).

(2) An officer of the Valuation Office or a person authorised in writing by the appropriate nature conservation body may enter any land for the purpose of surveying it, or of estimating its value, in connection with any claim for compensation under regulation 32 (compensation for effect of byelaws) in respect of that or any other land.

(3) A person authorised in writing by the authority having power to acquire land or an interest in land may enter that land for the purpose of surveying it in connection with the acquisition of that land or of any interest in that land, whether by agreement or compulsorily, in the exercise of any power conferred by these Regulations.

(4) A person authorised under this regulation must, if requested to do so, produce a duly authenticated authorisation document before entering any land.

(5) A person authorised under paragraph (1) may not demand admission as of right to any land which is occupied unless either—
(a) 24 hours' notice of the intended entry has been given to the occupier; or
(b) the purpose of the entry is to ascertain whether an offence under regulation 26(8) is being, or has been, committed on that land.

(6) A person authorised under paragraph (2) or (3) may not demand admission as of right to any land which is occupied unless at least 14 days' notice in writing of the intended entry has been given to the occupier.

Powers of search, etc.

112 Constables' powers of search, etc.

(1) If a constable suspects with reasonable cause that any person is committing or has committed an offence specified in paragraph (2), the constable may without warrant—
(a) stop and search that person if the constable suspects with reasonable cause that evidence of the commission of the offence is to be found on that person;
(b) search or examine anything which that person may be using or which is in that person's possession if the constable suspects with reasonable cause that evidence of the commission of the offence is to be found on that thing; or
(c) seize and detain, for the purposes of proceedings in relation to an offence specified in paragraph (2), anything which may be evidence of the commission of the offence or may be liable to be forfeited under regulation 122 (forfeiture).

(2) The offences specified for the purposes of this regulation are—
(a) a species offence;
(b) an offence under regulation 52 (introduction of new species from ships);
(c) an offence under regulation 57 (false statements made for obtaining licence); and
(d) an offence under regulation 116(1) or (2) (attempts and possession of means of committing offence).

Powers in relation to specimens and samples

113 Powers in relation to samples: constables

(1) If a constable suspects with reasonable cause that a specimen found in the exercise of powers conferred by this Part is one in respect of which an offence specified in paragraph

(5) is being or has been committed, the constable may require a sample to be taken from the specimen.

(2) If a constable suspects with reasonable cause that an offence specified in paragraph (5) is being or has been committed in respect of any specimen ("the relevant specimen"), the constable may require any person to make available for the taking of a sample any other specimen in that person's possession or control which—

(a) is alleged to be, or

(b) the constable suspects with reasonable cause to be,

a specimen a sample from which will tend to establish the identity or ancestry of the relevant specimen.

(3) Where a sample from a live animal or plant is to be taken, any person who has possession or control of the animal or plant must give the person taking the sample such assistance as that person may reasonably require for that purpose.

(4) This regulation is subject to regulation 115 (restrictions on taking samples from live specimens).

(5) The offences specified for the purposes of this regulation are—

(a) a species offence;

(b) an offence under regulation 57 (false statements made for obtaining licence), where that offence relates to the obtaining of a licence under regulation 53 (licences for certain activities relating to animals or plants); and

(c) an offence under regulation 116(1) or (2) (attempts and possession of means of committing offence).

114 Powers in relation to specimens and samples: wildlife inspectors

(1) The powers conferred by this regulation are exercisable where a wildlife inspector has entered premises for a purpose mentioned in paragraph (1)(a) or (b) of regulation 110 (powers of entry: wildlife inspectors).

(2) The wildlife inspector, or accompanying veterinary surgeon, may—

(a) for any such purpose, examine any specimen; and

(b) subject to paragraph (3) and regulation 115 (restrictions on taking samples from live specimens), take a sample from it.

(3) No sample may be taken under paragraph (2) from a live animal or plant except for the purpose of establishing its ancestry or identity.

(4) The wildlife inspector may require an occupier of the premises to give such assistance as is reasonable in the circumstances for the purpose of—

(a) making an examination under paragraph (2)(a); or

(b) taking a sample under paragraph (2)(b).

(5) The wildlife inspector may take and remove from the premises a specimen which is not a live animal or plant, if there are reasonable grounds for believing that it is evidence of a species offence.

115 Restrictions on taking samples from live specimens

(1) No sample may be taken by virtue of regulation 113 or 114 from a live animal except by a veterinary surgeon.

(2) No sample may be taken by virtue of those regulations from a live animal or plant unless the person taking it is satisfied on reasonable grounds that taking it will not cause lasting harm to the specimen.

Offences

116 Attempts and possession of means of committing offence

(1) A person who attempts to commit an offence specified in paragraph (3) is guilty of an offence and punishable in the same manner as for that offence.

(2) A person who, for the purposes of committing an offence specified in paragraph (3), is in possession of anything capable of being used for committing such an offence, is guilty of an offence and punishable in the same manner as for that offence.

(3) The offences specified for the purposes of this regulation are—
(a) a species offence; and
(b) an offence under regulation 57 (false statements made for obtaining licence), where that offence relates to the obtaining of a licence under regulation 53 (licences for certain activities relating to animals or plants).

117 Obstruction of persons exercising powers of entry under regulation 111

A person who intentionally obstructs a person exercising powers under regulation 111 (powers of entry: other authorised persons) commits an offence and is liable on summary conviction to a fine not exceeding level 3 on the standard scale.

118 Obstruction in connection with constables' powers to take samples

(1) A person who, without reasonable excuse, fails—
(a) to make available any specimen in accordance with a requirement under paragraph (2) of regulation 113 (powers in relation to samples: constables), or
(b) to give any assistance reasonably required under paragraph (3) of that regulation,
commits an offence.

(2) A person guilty of an offence under paragraph (1) is liable on summary conviction to a fine not exceeding level 5 on the standard scale.

119 Offences in connection with wildlife inspectors' enforcement powers

(1) A person who—
(a) intentionally obstructs a wildlife inspector acting in the exercise of powers conferred by regulation 110 (powers of entry: wildlife inspectors) or paragraph (2) or (5) of regulation 114 (powers in relation to specimens and samples: wildlife inspectors), or
(b) fails without reasonable excuse to give any assistance reasonably required under regulation 114(4),
commits an offence.

(2) A person who, with intent to deceive, falsely pretends to be a wildlife inspector, commits an offence.

(3) A person guilty of an offence under paragraph (1) is liable on summary conviction to a fine not exceeding level 5 on the standard scale.

(4) A person guilty of an offence under paragraph (2) is liable—
(a) on summary conviction, to imprisonment for a term not exceeding six months or a fine not exceeding the statutory maximum, or to both; or
(b) on conviction on indictment, to imprisonment not exceeding two years or to a fine, or to both.

Codes of practice

120 Codes of practice

(1) The appropriate authority may—
(a) issue a code of practice in connection with any of the provisions of regulations 108 (wildlife inspectors), 110 (powers of entry: wildlife inspectors), 114 (powers in relation to specimens and samples: wildlife inspectors), 115 (restrictions on taking samples from live specimens), 118 (obstruction in connection with constables' powers to take samples) and 119 (offences in connection with wildlife inspectors' enforcement powers); and
(b) revise or replace such a code.

(2) In discharging any function under the regulations specified in paragraph (1)(a)—
(a) a wildlife inspector authorised by the Secretary of State must have regard to any relevant provision of a code issued by the Secretary of State;
(b) a wildlife inspector authorised by the Welsh Ministers must have regard to any relevant provision of a code issued by them.

(3) But a wildlife inspector's failure to have regard to any provision of a code does not make that inspector liable to criminal or civil proceedings.

(4) A code—
(a) is admissible in evidence in any proceedings; and
(b) must be taken into account by any court in any case in which it appears to the court to be relevant.

Miscellaneous

121 Advice and assistance from nature conservation bodies

(1) The appropriate nature conservation body may advise or assist any constable or wildlife inspector in, or in connection with, enforcement action in relation to an offence specified in paragraph (2).

(2) The offences specified for the purposes of this regulation are—
(a) a species offence;
(b) an offence under regulation 57 (false statements made for obtaining licence), where that offence relates to the obtaining of a licence under regulation 53 (licences for certain activities relating to animals or plants); and
(c) an offence under regulation 116(1) or (2) (attempts and possession of means of committing offence).

122 Forfeiture

(1) The court by which a person is convicted of an offence specified in paragraph (3)—
(a) must order the forfeiture of any animal, plant or other thing in respect of which the offence was committed; and
(b) may order the forfeiture of any vehicle, animal, weapon or other thing which was used to commit the offence.

(2) In paragraph (1)(b) "vehicle" includes any aircraft, hovercraft or boat.

(3) The offences specified for the purposes of this regulation are—
(a) a species offence;
(b) an offence under regulation 57 (false statements made for obtaining licence), where that offence relates to the obtaining of a licence under regulation 53 (licences for certain activities relating to animals or plants); and

(c) an offence under regulation 116(1) or (2) (attempts and possession of means of committing offence).

123 Proceedings for offences: venue and time limits

(1) For the purposes of conferring jurisdiction, an offence specified in paragraph (5) is deemed to have been committed in any place where the offender is found or to which the offender is first brought after the commission of the offence.

(2) Summary proceedings for such an offence may be commenced within the period of six months from the date on which the prosecutor first knows of evidence sufficient, in the prosecutor's opinion, to justify proceedings.

(3) But no such proceedings may be commenced more than two years after the commission of the offence.

(4) For the purposes of paragraph (2)—
(a) a certificate signed by or on behalf of the prosecutor and stating the date on which the prosecutor first knew of evidence sufficient to justify the proceedings is conclusive evidence of that fact; and
(b) a certificate stating that matter and purporting to be so signed is deemed to be so signed unless the contrary is proved.

(5) The offences specified for the purposes of this regulation are—
(a) a species offence;
(b) an offence under regulation 52 (introduction of new species from ships);
(c) an offence under regulation 57 (false statements made for obtaining licence); and
(d) an offence under regulation 116(1) or (2) (attempts and possession of means of committing offence).

124 Offences by bodies corporate etc.

(1) If an offence under these Regulations committed by a body corporate (other than a limited liability partnership or a Scottish partnership) is proved—
(a) to have been committed with the consent or connivance of an officer, or
(b) to be attributable to any neglect on the part of an officer,
the officer, as well as the body corporate, is guilty of the offence and liable to be proceeded against and punished accordingly.

(2) If the affairs of a body corporate are managed by its members, paragraph (1) applies in relation to the acts and defaults of a member in connection with the member's functions of management as it applies to an officer of a body corporate.

(3) If an offence under these Regulations committed by a partnership (including a limited liability partnership and a Scottish partnership) is proved—
(a) to have been committed with the consent or connivance of a partner, or
(b) to be attributable to any neglect on the part of a partner,
the partner, as well as the partnership, is guilty of the offence and liable to be proceeded against and punished accordingly.

(4) If an offence under these Regulations committed by an unincorporated body (other than an unincorporated partnership) is proved—
(a) to have been committed with the consent or connivance of an officer of the body, or
(b) to be attributable to any neglect on the part of such an officer,
the officer, as well as the body, is guilty of the offence and liable to be proceeded against and punished accordingly.

(5) In this regulation—
(a) "officer" includes a person purporting to act as an officer; and
(b) "partner" includes a person purporting to act as a partner.

125 Application of criminal offences to the Crown

(1) No contravention by the Crown of any provision of these Regulations makes the Crown criminally liable, but the High Court may, on the application of any person appearing to the Court to have an interest, declare unlawful an act or omission of the Crown which constitutes such a contravention.

(2) Notwithstanding paragraph (1), these Regulations apply to persons in the public service of the Crown as they apply to any other person.

Interpretation of Part 7

126 Interpretation of Part 7

In this Part—
(a) a "species offence" means an offence under—
  (i) regulation 41 (protection of certain wild animals: offences),
  (ii) regulation 43 (prohibition of certain methods of capturing or killing wild animals),
  (iii) regulation 45 (protection of certain wild plants: offences), or
  (iv) regulation 58 (offence of breaching licence condition); and
(b) "premises" includes land (including buildings), movable structures, vehicles, vessels, aircraft and other means of transport.

PART 8
FINAL PROVISIONS

127 Powers of drainage authorities

(1) Where the appropriate nature conservation body or any other person enter into an agreement with a drainage authority for the doing by that authority of any work on land in a European site, no limitation imposed by law on the capacity of the drainage authority by virtue of its constitution operates so as to prevent the authority carrying out the agreement.

(2) In paragraph (1) "drainage authority" means the Environment Agency or an internal drainage board.

128 Advisory role of the Joint Nature Conservation Committee

(1) The Joint Nature Conservation Committee may provide advice or make representations to any competent authority in relation to—
(a) any question as to whether that authority is obliged to carry out an appropriate assessment in relation to a European offshore marine site under these Regulations;
(b) any appropriate assessment on which that authority is obliged to consult the Committee under these Regulations;
(c) any application made pursuant to regulation 75 (general development orders: approval of local planning authority) and sent to the Committee by that authority pursuant to regulation 75(3);
(d) any decision of the Secretary of State in respect of which notice has been served on the Committee under paragraph (2)(b) of regulation 87 (consents under Electricity

Act 1989: procedure on review) or 91 (authorisations under Pipe-lines Act 1962: procedure on review); and

(e) any decision of the appropriate authority in respect of which notice has been served on the Committee under paragraph (2)(b) of regulation 95 (orders under Transport and Works Act 1992: procedure on review).

(2) The Joint Nature Conservation Committee may undertake, commission or support (whether by financial means or otherwise) such research and scientific work as they consider is required for the purposes of providing advice or making representations under this regulation.

129 Advisory role of Natural England, the Countryside Council for Wales and Scottish Natural Heritage

(1) Natural England may—

(a) provide advice and assistance, or make representations, to any competent authority on any matter which relates to England and is connected with the discharge of the competent authority's functions under these Regulations; and

(b) undertake, commission or support (whether by financial means or otherwise) such research and scientific work as they consider is required for the purposes of providing advice or assistance or making representations under sub-paragraph (a).

(2) The Countryside Council for Wales may—

(a) provide advice and assistance, or make representations, to any competent authority on any matter which relates to Wales and is connected with the discharge of the competent authority's functions under these Regulations; and

(b) undertake, commission or support (whether by financial means or otherwise) such research and scientific work as they consider is required for the purposes of providing advice or assistance or making representations under sub-paragraph (a).

(3) Scottish Natural Heritage may—

(a) provide advice and assistance, or make representations, to any competent authority on any matter which relates to Scotland and is connected with the discharge of the competent authority's functions under these Regulations; and

(b) undertake, commission or support (whether by financial means or otherwise) such research and scientific work as they consider is required for the purposes of providing advice or assistance or making representations under sub-paragraph (a).

[129A Research

(1) The appropriate authority must take such steps to encourage research and scientific work as they consider necessary—

(a) having regard to the objectives in Article 2, and the obligation in Article 11, of the Habitats Directive; and

(b) for the purpose of the protection or management, and in relation to the use, of any population of wild birds.

(2) The appropriate authority must supply such information as they consider appropriate to the European Commission and, in the case of information supplied for the purposes of the Habitats Directive, to member States, to further the proper co-ordination of research carried out by member States or by the European Commission for the purposes of the Directives.

(3) In deciding what steps to take under paragraph (1), the appropriate authority must have particular regard to the need for research and scientific work—

(a) on the subjects listed in Annex V to the new Wild Birds Directive; or

(b) which may be required to implement Articles 4 and 10 of the Habitats Directive.][1]

Amendment

1 Inserted by the Conservation of Habitats and Species (Amendment) Regulations 2012, SI 2012/1927, regs 2, 22.

130 Local inquiries

(1) The appropriate authority may cause a local inquiry to be held for the purposes of the exercise of any of their functions under these Regulations.

(2) The provisions of section 250(2) to (5) of the Local Government Act 1972 (which relate to evidence and costs in inquiries) apply in relation to an inquiry held under this regulation.

131 Notices

(1) Any notice required or authorised to be served under these Regulations to any person may be given by—

(a) delivering it to the person;
(b) leaving it at the person's proper address; or
(c) sending it by post to the person at that address.

(2) Any such notice may—

(a) in the case of a body corporate, be served on an officer of the body;
(b) in the case of a limited liability partnership, Scottish partnership or unincorporated partnership, be served on a partner or a person having the control or management of the partnership business; and
(c) in the case of an unincorporated body other than an unincorporated partnership, be served on an officer of that body.

(3) For the purposes of this regulation and section 7 of the Interpretation Act 1978 (service of documents by post) in its application to this regulation, the proper address of any person on whom a notice is to be served is—

(a) in the case of a body corporate, the address of the registered or principal office of the body;
(b) in the case of a limited liability partnership or a Scottish partnership, the address of the registered or principal office of the partnership;
(c) in the case of an unincorporated partnership or any other unincorporated body, the address of the principal office of the partnership or body;
(d) in the case of a person on whom the notice is served in reliance on paragraph (2), the proper address of the body corporate, partnership or other unincorporated body in question; and
(e) in any other case, the last known address of the person in question.

(4) If a person on whom a notice is to be served under these Regulations has specified an address for service of such a notice, that address is also to be treated, for the purposes of this regulation and section 7 of the Interpretation Act 1978 in its application to this regulation, as that person's proper address.

(5) If the name or address of any occupier of premises on whom a notice is to be served under these Regulations cannot, after reasonable inquiry, be ascertained, the notice may be served by leaving it conspicuously affixed to a building or object on the premises.

(6) This regulation is subject to any provision of these Regulations, or to any direction given under these Regulations, which relates to the service of any notice under these Regulations.

(7) This regulation does not apply to the service of any notice required or authorised to be served under the Acquisition of Land Act 1981, as applied by these Regulations (see regulation 34 (powers of compulsory acquisition)).

(8) In this regulation—

(a) "body corporate" does not include a limited liability partnership or a Scottish partnership; and

(b) references to serving include references to similar expressions (such as giving or sending).

[*Regulations 132 and 133 are not reproduced.*]

134 Transitional provisions

(1) Any licence granted by Natural England under any of sub-paragraphs (a) to (d) of regulation 44(2) of the 1994 Regulations (grant of licences for certain purposes) before 1st April 2010, to the extent that it relates to the restricted English inshore region, is to have effect from that date as a licence granted by the Marine Management Organisation under regulation 53(1) of these Regulations (licences for certain activities relating to animals or plants) for a purpose specified in the corresponding sub-paragraph of paragraph (2) of that regulation.

(2) Any application to Natural England for a licence under any of sub-paragraphs (a) to (d) of regulation 44(2) of the 1994 Regulations, to the extent that it relates to the restricted English inshore region, and which was made, but not determined or withdrawn, before 1st April 2010, is to be treated as an application made to the Marine Management Organisation on or after 1st April 2010 under regulation 53(1) of these Regulations for a purpose specified in the corresponding sub-paragraph of paragraph (2) of that regulation.

(3) Any licence granted before 1st April 2010—

(a) under regulation 37D of the 1994 Regulations (licensing the introduction of new species),

(b) under any of sub-paragraphs (a) to (d) of regulation 44(2) of the 1994 Regulations—

  (i) by Natural England, to the extent that the licence relates to an area other than the restricted English inshore region, or

  (ii) by the Countryside Council for Wales,

(c) under any of sub-paragraphs (e) to (g) of regulation 44(2) of the 1994 Regulations, or

(d) under regulation 44(2A) of those Regulations,

is to have effect from that date as a licence granted under regulation 53(1) (for a purpose specified in the corresponding sub-paragraph of paragraph (2) of that regulation), regulation 53(4) or 54 of these Regulations (whichever is the corresponding provision).

(4) Any application—

(a) for a licence under regulation 37D of the 1994 Regulations,

(b) for a licence under any of sub-paragraphs (a) to (d) of regulation 44(2) of the 1994 Regulations—

  (i) made to Natural England, to the extent that the licence relates to an area other than the restricted English inshore region, or

  (ii) made to the Countryside Council for Wales,

(c) for a licence under any of sub-paragraphs (e) to (g) of regulation 44(2) of the 1994 Regulations, or

(d) for a licence under regulation 44(2A) of those Regulations,

which was made, but not determined or withdrawn, before 1st April 2010 is to be treated as an application made on or after 1st April 2010 under regulation 53(1) (for a purpose specified in the corresponding sub-paragraph of paragraph (2) of that regulation), regulation 53(4) or 54 of these Regulations (whichever is the corresponding provision).

(5) Any agreement previously entered into by Natural England or the Countryside Council for Wales under regulation 16 of the 1994 Regulations (management agreements), or having effect as if it had been entered into by either of those bodies under that provision, and which is in force immediately before 1st April 2010, has effect as if it were a management agreement entered into by Natural England or the Countryside Council for Wales (as the case may be) under regulation 16 (management agreements) of these Regulations.

(6) Nothing in this regulation prejudices the application of section 16 (general savings) or 17 (repeal and re-enactment) of the Interpretation Act 1978 to any case not provided for in this regulation.

[135 Review

(1) In relation to England, the Secretary of State must from time to time—
(a) carry out a review of these Regulations;
(b) set out the conclusions of the review in a report; and
(c) publish the report.

(2) In carrying out the review the Secretary of State must, so far as is reasonable, have regard to how the Directives are implemented in other member States.

(3) The report must in particular—
(a) set out the objectives intended to be achieved by the regulatory system established by these Regulations;
(b) assess the extent to which those objectives are achieved; and
(c) assess whether those objectives remain appropriate and, if so, the extent to which they could be achieved with a system that imposes less regulation.

(4) The first report under this regulation must be published before the end of the period of five years beginning with 16th August 2012.

(5) Reports under this regulation are afterwards to be published at intervals not exceeding five years.][1]

Amendment

1 Inserted by the Conservation of Habitats and Species (Amendment) Regulations 2012, SI 2012/1927, regs 2, 23.

SCHEDULE 1
SPECIAL NATURE CONSERVATION ORDERS: PROCEDURE

Regulation 25(3)

Coming into operation

1

(1) An original order or a restrictive amending order takes effect on its being made.

(2) The appropriate authority must consider every such order, and the order ceases to have effect nine months after it is made unless—
(a) that authority have previously given notice under paragraph 6 that the order has been considered and that it is not proposed to amend or revoke it; or
(b) the order has been revoked.

(3) Subject to paragraphs 3(2) and 4(4), a revoking order, or an amending order which is not restrictive, does not take effect until confirmed by the appropriate authority.

(4) An amending or revoking order requiring confirmation is to be treated as being revoked if the appropriate authority give notice under paragraph 6 that it is not to be confirmed.

Publicity for orders

2

(1) The appropriate authority must, where an order has been made, give notice setting out the order (or describing its general effect) and stating that it has taken effect or, as the case may be, that it has been made and requires confirmation.

(2) The notice must—
(a) name a place in the area in which the land to which the order relates is situated where a copy of the order may be inspected free of charge at all reasonable hours; and
(b) specify the time (not being less than 28 days from the date of the first publication of the notice) within which, and the manner in which, representations or objections with respect to the order may be made.

(3) The notice must be given—
(a) by publication in the London Gazette and also at least one local newspaper circulating in the area in which the land to which the order relates is situated;
(b) by serving an equivalent notice—
(i) on every owner and occupier of that land (subject to sub-paragraph (4)); and
(ii) on the local planning authority within whose area the land is situated.

(4) The appropriate authority may, in any particular case, direct that it is not necessary to comply with sub-paragraph (3)(b)(i).

(5) Where the appropriate authority give a direction under paragraph (4) in the case of an order specifying any operation carried out, or proposed to be carried out, on any land—
(a) in addition to publication the notice must be addressed to "The owners and any occupiers" of the land (describing it), describing details of the operation and the details of the European site to which the order relates; and
(b) a copy or copies of the notice must be affixed to some conspicuous object or objects on the land.

Unopposed orders

3

(1) Where an order has taken effect immediately and no representations or objections are duly made in respect of it, or any so made are withdrawn, the appropriate authority must, as soon as practicable after considering the order, decide either to take no action on it or to make an order amending or revoking it.

(2) Where an amending or revoking order is made under sub-paragraph (1)—
(a) it takes effect immediately;
(b) it does not require confirmation; and
(c) it is not necessary to consider any representation or objection made in respect of it.

(3) Where an order requiring confirmation (in accordance with paragraph 1(3)) is made and no representations or objections are duly made in respect of it, or any so made are withdrawn, the appropriate authority may confirm the order (with or without modifications).

Opposed orders

4

(1) If any representation or objection duly made with respect to an order is not withdrawn, the appropriate authority must, as soon as practicable (in the case of an order having immediate effect) or (in the case of an order requiring confirmation) before confirming the order—

(a) cause a local inquiry to be held; or
(b) afford any person by whom a representation or objection has been duly made and not withdrawn an opportunity of being heard by a person appointed by the appropriate authority for the purpose.

(2) On considering any representations or objections duly made and the report of any person appointed to hold the inquiry or to hear representations or objections, the appropriate authority—
(a) if the order has already taken effect, must decide either to take no action on the order or to make an order amending or revoking it as appropriate in the light of the report, representations or objections; and
(b) if the order requires confirmation, may confirm it (with or without modifications).

(3) The provisions of section 250(2) to (5) of the Local Government Act 1972 (which relate to evidence and costs in inquiries) apply in relation to an inquiry held under this paragraph.

(4) Where an amending or revoking order is made under sub-paragraph (2)(a)—
(a) it takes effect immediately;
(b) it does not require confirmation; and
(c) it is not necessary to consider any representation or objection made in respect of it.

Restriction on power to amend orders or confirm them with modifications

5

The appropriate authority may not, by virtue of paragraph 3(1) or 4(2), amend an order which has taken effect, or confirm any other order with modifications, so as to extend the area to which the order applies.

Notice of final decision on order

6

(1) The appropriate authority must, as soon as practicable after making an order under paragraph 3(1) or 4(2)(a), give notice—
(a) setting out the order (or describing its effect) and stating that it has taken effect; and
(b) naming a place in the area in which the land to which the order relates is situated where a copy of the order may be inspected free of charge at all reasonable hours.

(2) The appropriate authority must give notice of any of the following decisions as soon as practicable after making the decision—
(a) a decision under paragraph 3(1) or 4(2)(a) to take no action on an order which has already taken effect;
(b) a decision to confirm or not to confirm an order requiring confirmation under this Schedule.

(3) A notice under this paragraph of a decision to confirm an order must—
(a) set out the order as confirmed (or describe its general effect) and state the day on which the order took effect; and
(b) name a place in the area in which the land to which the order relates is situated where a copy of the order as confirmed may be inspected free of charge at all reasonable hours.

(4) Any notice under this paragraph must be given by publishing it in accordance with paragraph 2(3)(a) and serving a copy of it on any person on whom a notice was required to be served under paragraph 2(3)(b).

Proceedings for questioning validity of orders

7

(1) This paragraph applies to any order which has taken effect and as to which the appropriate authority have given notice under paragraph 6 of a decision to take no action or to amend the order in accordance with paragraph 4 ("the relevant notice").

(2) If any person is aggrieved by an order to which this paragraph applies and desires to question its validity on the ground that it is not within the powers of regulation 25 (power to make special nature conservation order), or that any of the requirements of this Schedule have not been complied with in relation to it, that person may within six weeks from the date of the relevant notice make an application to the High Court.

(3) On any such application the High Court may, if satisfied that the order is not within those powers or that the interests of the applicant have been substantially prejudiced by a failure to comply with any of those requirements, quash the order, or any provision of the order, either generally or in so far as it affects the interests of the applicant.

(4) Except as provided by this paragraph, the validity of an order may not be questioned in any legal proceedings whatsoever.

Interpretation

8

In this Schedule—

"amending order" and "revoking order" mean an order which amends or, as the case may be, revokes a previous order;

"order" means an order under regulation 25 (special nature conservation order);

"original order" means an order other than an amending or revoking order; and

"restrictive", in relation to an amending order, means extending the area to which a previous order applies.

SCHEDULE 2
EUROPEAN PROTECTED SPECIES OF ANIMALS

Regulation 40(1)

Common name	*Scientific name*
Bats, Horseshoe (all species)	Rhinolophidae
Bats, Typical (all species)	Vespertilionidae
Butterfly, Large Blue	Maculinea arion
Cat, Wild	Felis silvestris
Dolphins, porpoises and whales (all species)	Cetacea
Dormouse	Muscardinus avellanarius
Frog, Pool	Rana lessonae
Lizard, Sand	Lacerta agilis
Moth, Fisher's Estuarine	Gortyna borelii lunata
Newt, Great Crested (or Warty)	Triturus cristatus
Otter, Common	Lutra lutra
Snail, Lesser Whirlpool Ram's-horn	Anisus vorticulus
Snake, Smooth	Coronella austriaca

Common name	*Scientific name*
Sturgeon	Acipenser sturio
Toad, Natterjack	Bufo calamita
Turtles, Marine	Caretta caretta
	Chelonia mydas
	Lepidochelys kempii
	Eretmochelys imbricata
	Dermochelys coriacea

NOTE. The common name or names given in the first column of this Schedule are included by way of guidance only; in the event of any dispute or proceedings, the common name or names must not be taken into account.

SCHEDULE 3
EXCLUDED POPULATIONS OF CERTAIN SPECIES

Regulation 42(8)(a)

(1) Common name	*(2) Scientific name*	*(3) Excluded countries and areas*
Beaver, Eurasian	Castor fiber	Estonia, Finland, Latvia, Lithuania, Poland and Sweden
Hamster, Common (or Black bellied)	Cricetus cricetus	Hungary
Wolf, Grey	Canis lupus	Bulgaria, Estonia, Greece north of the 39th parallel, Latvia, Lithuania, Poland, Slovakia, Spain north of the River Duero, and the reindeer management area in Finland as defined in paragraph 2 of Finnish Act No. 848/90 of 14th September 1990 on reindeer management
Lynx, Eurasian	Lynx lynx	Estonia
Viper, Seoane's	Vipera seoanni	Spain

NOTE: The common name or names given in the first column to this Schedule are included by way of guidance only; in the event of any dispute or proceedings, the common name or names must not be taken into account.

SCHEDULE 4
ANIMALS WHICH MAY NOT BE CAPTURED OR KILLED IN CERTAIN WAYS

Regulation 43(1)(a)

Common name	*Scientific name*
Barbel	Barbus barbus
Grayling	Thymallus thymallus
Hare, Mountain	Lepus timidus
Lamprey, River	Lampetra fluviatilis
Marten, Pine	Martes martes

Common name	*Scientific name*
Polecat	Mustela putorius (otherwise known as Putorius putorius)
Salmon, Atlantic	Salmo salar (only in fresh water)
Seal, Bearded	Erignathus barbatus
Seal, Common	Phoca vitulina
Seal, Grey	Halichoerus grypus
Seal, Harp	Phoca groenlandica (otherwise known as Pagophilus groenlandicus)
Seal, Hooded	Cystophora cristata
Seal, Ringed	Phoca hispida (otherwise known as Pusa hispida)
Shad, Allis	Alosa alosa
Shad, Twaite	Alosa fallax
Vendace	Coregonus albula
Whitefish	Coregonus lavaretus

NOTE. The common name or names given in the first column of this Schedule are included by way of guidance only; in the event of any dispute or proceedings, the common name or names must not be taken into account.

SCHEDULE 5
EUROPEAN PROTECTED SPECIES OF PLANTS

Regulation 44(1)

Common name	*Scientific name*
Dock, Shore	Rumex rupestris
Fern, Killarney	Trichomanes speciosum
Gentian, Early	Gentianella anglica
Lady's-slipper	Cypripedium calceolus
Marshwort, Creeping	Apium repens
Naiad, Slender	Najas flexilis
Orchid, Fen	Liparis loeselii
Plantain, Floating-leaved water	Luronium natans
Saxifrage, Yellow Marsh	Saxifraga hirculus

NOTE. The common name or names given in the first column of this Schedule are included by way of guidance only; in the event of any dispute or proceedings, the common name or names must not be taken into account.

[*Schedules 6 and 7 are not reproduced.*]

WATER RESOURCES (CONTROL OF POLLUTION) (SILAGE, SLURRY AND AGRICULTURAL FUEL) (ENGLAND) REGULATIONS 2010

SI 2010/639

1 Citation, commencement and application

These Regulations—

(a) may be cited as the Water Resources (Control of Pollution) (Silage, Slurry and Agricultural Fuel Oil) (England) Regulations 2010;

(b) apply to England only; and

(c) come into force on 6th April 2010.

2 Interpretation

(1) In these Regulations—

"construct" includes install;

"fuel oil" means oil intended for use as a fuel for the production of heat or power but does not include oil intended for use exclusively as a fuel for heating a farmhouse or other residential premises on a farm and stored separately from other oil;

"livestock" means—

(a) animals kept for the production of food or wool, or

(b) birds kept for the production of food;

"reception pit" means a pit used for the collection of slurry before it is transferred into a slurry storage tank or for the collection of slurry discharged from such a tank;

"silage" includes a crop being made into silage;

"silage effluent" means effluent from silage …[1];

"silo" means a structure used for making or storing silage;

"slurry" means liquid or semi-liquid matter composed of—

(a) excreta produced by livestock while in a yard or building (including that held in wood chip corrals); or

(b) a mixture wholly or mainly consisting of livestock excreta, livestock bedding, rainwater and washings from a building or yard used by livestock,

of a consistency that allows it to be pumped or discharged by gravity at any stage in the handling process;

"slurry storage tank" includes a lagoon, a pit (other than a reception pit) or tower used for the storage of slurry.

(2) A reference in these Regulations to a slurry storage system includes a slurry storage tank and—

(a) any reception pit and any effluent tank used in connection with the tank; and

(b) any channels and pipes used in connection with the tank, any reception pit or any effluent tank.

(3) A requirement in these Regulations for a silo or slurry storage tank to conform to a British Standard (in whole or in part) is satisfied if the silo or tank conforms to a standard or specification that provides an equivalent level of protection and performance and is recognised for use in a member State, Iceland, Liechtenstein, Norway or Turkey.

Amendment

1 Repealed by the Water Resources (Control of Pollution) (Silage, Slurry and Agricultural Fuel Oil) (England) (Amendment) Regulations 2010, SI 2010/1091, regs 2, 3.

3 Making or storage of silage

(1) Subject to paragraph (3), a person who has custody or control of silage that is being made or stored must ensure that—

(a) the silage is kept in a silo that satisfies the requirements of Schedule 1; or

(b) ...[1] the silage is compressed into bales that—

(i) are wrapped and sealed into impermeable membranes, or enclosed in impermeable bags; and

(ii) are stored at least 10 metres from any inland freshwaters or coastal waters that effluent escaping from the bales could enter; or

(c) if the silage is a crop being made into field silage (that is, silage made on open land by a method different from the baling method referred to in paragraph (b)) or silage that is being stored on open land—

(i) the Agency is given notice of the place where the silage is to be made or stored at least 14 days before the place is first used for that purpose; and

(ii) the place is at least 10 metres from any inland freshwaters or coastal waters, and at least 50 metres from the nearest relevant abstraction point of any protected water supply source that silage effluent could enter if it escaped.

(2) For paragraph (1)(c)(ii), a water supply source is a protected water supply source if—

(a) any relevant water abstraction from the source is licensed under Part II of the Water Resources Act 1991; or

(b) the person making or storing the silage was aware of the source's location—

(i) before the making of the silage began; or

(ii) if the silage was made elsewhere, before it was stored on the land in question.

(3) Paragraph (1) does not apply to silage while it is stored temporarily in a container, trailer or vehicle in connection with its transport about the farm or elsewhere.

[(4) A person who has custody or control of a silage bale must not open or remove the wrapping of the bale within 10 metres of any inland freshwaters or coastal waters which silage effluent could enter as a result.][2]

(5) In this regulation—

(a) "relevant water abstraction" means the abstraction of water for use for—

(i) human consumption, or

(ii) domestic purposes (within the meaning given by section 218 of the Water Industry Act 1991) other than human consumption, or

(iii) manufacturing food or drink for human consumption; and

(b) "water supply source" means inland freshwaters or ground waters from which a relevant abstraction is made or licensed to be made.

Amendments

1 Repealed by the Water Resources (Control of Pollution) (Silage, Slurry and Agricultural Fuel Oil) (England) (Amendment) Regulations 2010, SI 2010/1091, regs 2, 4(a).

2 Substituted by the Water Resources (Control of Pollution) (Silage, Slurry and Agricultural Fuel Oil) (England) (Amendment) Regulations 2010, SI 2010/1091, regs 2, 4(b).

4 Storage of slurry

(1) Subject to paragraph (2), a person having custody or control of slurry must store it only in a slurry storage system that satisfies the requirements of Schedule 2.

(2) Paragraph (1) does not apply to slurry while it is stored temporarily in a tanker that is used for transporting slurry on roads or about a farm.

5 Storage of fuel oil on farms

(1) Subject to paragraph (2), a person who has custody or control of fuel oil on a farm must ensure that it is stored—
(a) in a fuel storage tank within a storage area or facility that satisfies the requirements of Schedule 3;
(b) in drums within such a storage area; or
(c) in an underground fuel storage tank.

(2) Paragraph (1) does not apply—
(a) to the temporary storage of fuel oil in a tanker used for transporting fuel oil on roads or about a farm; or
(b) where the total quantity of fuel oil stored on the farm does not exceed 1,500 litres.

6 Exemptions

(1) Subject to paragraph (2), these Regulations do not apply to a silo, slurry storage system or fuel storage tank—
(a) which, before 1st March 1991, was being used for the purpose of making silage, storing slurry or, as the case may be, storing fuel oil;
(b) where it was not used before 1st March 1991 for that purpose, it was constructed before that date for such use; or
(c) in relation to which—
(i) a contract for its construction, substantial enlargement or substantial reconstruction was entered into before 1st March 1991, or
(ii) such work was commenced before that date, and
and in either case the work was completed before 1st September 1991.

(2) These Regulations apply to a silo, slurry storage system or fuel storage tank meeting the requirements of paragraph (1) if any requirement of a notice under regulation 7 is not complied with within the period stated in the notice.

(3) Any reference in paragraph (2) to the period stated in a notice is to that period as extended if it has been extended under regulation 7(5)(b) or by virtue of regulation 8(6) and any reference in those paragraphs to a requirement of a notice is to that requirement as modified if it has been modified under regulation 7(5).

7 Notice requiring works etc.

(1) The Agency may serve, on a person who has custody or control of silage, slurry or fuel oil or is responsible for the silo, slurry storage system or fuel oil storage tank, in circumstances in which these Regulations apply, a notice ("regulation 7 notice") requiring the person to carry out works, or take precautions or other steps, specified in the notice.

(2) The works, precautions or other steps must be, in the opinion of the Agency, appropriate, having regard to the requirements of these Regulations, for reducing to a minimum any significant risk of pollution of controlled waters.

(3) The notice must—
(a) specify or describe the works, precautions or other steps that the person is required to carry out or take;
(b) state the period within which any such requirement is to be complied with; and
(c) inform the person of the effect of regulation 8.

(4) The period for compliance stated in the notice is—
(a) 28 days; or
(b) such longer period as is reasonable in the circumstances.

[(4A) A person on whom a regulation 7 notice has been served must comply with the requirements of that notice.][1]

(5) The Agency may at any time (including a time after the period for compliance has ended)—
(a) withdraw the notice;
(b) extend the period for compliance with any requirement of the notice; or
(c) with the consent of the person on whom the notice is served, modify the requirements of the notice.

(6) The Agency must withdraw the notice, extend the period for compliance, or modify the requirements of the notice if so directed by the Secretary of State under regulation 8(5).

Amendment
1 Inserted by the Water Resources (Control of Pollution) (Silage, Slurry and Agricultural Fuel Oil) (England) (Amendment) Regulations 2010, SI 2010/1091, regs 2, 5.

8 Appeals against regulation 7 notices

(1) A person served with a regulation 7 notice may, within the period of 28 days beginning on the day after the date on which the notice is served (or such longer period as the Secretary of State allows), appeal to the Secretary of State against the notice.

(2) An appeal under this regulation must be made by the appellant serving notice on the Secretary of State.

(3) The notice must contain or be accompanied by a statement of the grounds of appeal.

(4) Before determining an appeal under this regulation, the Secretary of State must, if requested to do so by the appellant or the Agency, afford them an opportunity of appearing before and being heard by a person appointed by the Secretary of State for the purpose.

(5) On determining an appeal under this regulation, the Secretary of State may direct the Agency to—
(a) withdraw the regulation 7 notice;
(b) modify any of its requirements;
(c) extend the period for compliance with any requirement; or
(d) dismiss the appeal.

(6) The period for compliance with a regulation 7 notice against which an appeal has been made is, subject to any direction under paragraph (5), extended so that it expires on the date on which the Secretary of State finally determines the appeal or, if the appeal is withdrawn, the date on which it is withdrawn.

9 Notice of construction etc

A person who proposes to have custody or control of silage, slurry or fuel oil that is to be kept or stored on a farm in a silo, slurry storage system or fuel storage area constructed, substantially enlarged or substantially reconstructed on or after the date these Regulations come into force must give the Agency notice specifying the type of structure to be used and its location at least 14 days before the structure is to be used for such keeping or storage.

10 Offences and penalties

(1) A person who contravenes regulation 3(1) or (4), 4(1), 5(1) or [7(4A)][1] of these Regulations is guilty of an offence and liable—
(a) on summary conviction, to a fine not exceeding the statutory maximum;
(b) on conviction on indictment, to a fine.

(2) A person who contravenes regulation 9 is guilty of an offence and liable on summary conviction to a fine not exceeding level 2 on the standard scale.

Amendment

1 Substituted by the Water Resources (Control of Pollution) (Silage, Slurry and Agricultural Fuel Oil) (England) (Amendment) Regulations 2010, SI 2010/1091, regs 2, 6.

[*Regulation 11 is not reproduced.*]

SCHEDULE 1
REQUIREMENTS FOR SILOS

Regulation 3(1)(a)

1

The requirement to be satisfied in relation to a silo is that it complies with the following provisions of this Schedule.

2

The base of the silo must—
(a) extend beyond any walls of the silo;
(b) be provided at its perimeter with channels designed and constructed so as to collect any silage effluent that escapes from the silo; and
(c) have adequate provision for the drainage of that effluent from those channels to an effluent tank through a channel or pipe.

3

The capacity of the effluent tank must not be less than—
(a) in the case of a silo with a capacity of less than 1,500 cubic metres, 20 litres for each cubic metre of silo capacity; and
(b) in the case of a silo with a capacity of 1,500 cubic metres or more, 30 cubic metres plus 6.7 litres for each cubic metre of silo capacity in excess of 1,500 cubic metres.

4

(1) The base of the silo must be—
(a) designed in accordance with the code of practice for design of concrete structures for retaining aqueous liquids published by the British Standards Institution and numbered BS 8007: 1987; or
(b) constructed using appropriate hot-rolled asphalt in accordance with the code of practice for selection and use of construction materials published by the British Standards Institution and numbered BS 5502:Part 21: 1990.

(2) The base of the silo, the base and walls of its effluent tank and channels and walls of any pipes must be impermeable.

5

The base and walls of the silo, its effluent tank and channels and the walls of any pipes must, so far as reasonably practicable, be resistant to attack by silage effluent.

6

No part of the silo, its effluent tank or channels or any pipes may be situated within 10 metres of any inland freshwaters or coastal waters into which silage effluent could enter if it were to escape.

7

If the silo has retaining walls—

(a) the retaining walls must be capable of withstanding minimum wall loadings calculated on the assumptions and in the manner indicated by paragraphs 15.6 of the code of practice on buildings and structures for agriculture published by the British Standards Institution and numbered BS 5502: Part 22: 2003;

(b) the silo must at no time be loaded to a depth exceeding the maximum depth consistent with the design assumption made in respect of the loadings of the retaining walls; and

(c) notices must be displayed on the retaining walls in accordance with paragraph 18 of that code of practice.

8

Subject to paragraph 9, the silo, its effluent tank and channels and any pipes must be designed and constructed so that with proper maintenance they are likely to continue to satisfy the requirements of paragraphs 2 to 5 and, if applicable, paragraph 7(a) for at least 20 years.

9

If any part of an effluent tank is below ground level, the tank must be designed and constructed so that it is likely to continue to satisfy the requirements of paragraphs 4 and 5 for at least 20 years without maintenance.

SCHEDULE 2
REQUIREMENTS FOR SLURRY STORAGE SYSTEMS

Regulation 4

1

The requirements to be satisfied in relation to a slurry storage system are as follows.

2

The base of the slurry storage tank, the base and walls of any effluent tank, channels and reception pit, and the walls of any pipes, must be impermeable.

3

The base and walls of the slurry storage tank, any effluent tank, channels and reception pit, and the walls of any pipes, must be protected against corrosion in accordance with paragraph 7 of the code of practice on buildings and structures for agriculture published by the British Standards Institution and numbered BS 5502: Part 50: 1993.

4

The base and walls of the slurry storage tank and of any reception pit must be capable of withstanding characteristic loads calculated on the assumptions and in the manner indicated by paragraph 5 of the code of practice on buildings and structures for agriculture published by the British Standards Institution and numbered BS 5502: Part 50: 1993.

5

(1) Any facilities used for the temporary storage of slurry before it is transferred to a slurry storage tank must have adequate capacity to store—
(a) the maximum quantity of slurry that (disregarding any slurry which will be transferred directly into a slurry storage tank) is likely to be produced on the premises in any two day period; or
(b) a lesser capacity that the Agency agrees in writing is adequate to avoid any significant risk of pollution of controlled waters.

(2) Where slurry flows into a channel before discharging into a reception pit and the flow of slurry out of the channel is controlled by means of a sluice, the capacity of the reception pit must be adequate to hold the maximum quantity of slurry that can be released by opening the sluice.

6

(1) Subject to sub-paragraph (2), the slurry storage tank must have adequate storage capacity for the likely quantities of slurry produced from time to time on the premises in question, taking into account—
(a) the proposed method of utilising the slurry, and the likely rates and times of utilisation; and
(b) the matters mentioned in sub-paragraph (3).

(2) If it is proposed to utilise the slurry on the premises by spreading it on the land, the tank need not have a greater storage capacity than is adequate, taking into account the matters mentioned in sub-paragraph (3), to hold the maximum quantity of slurry likely to be produced in any four month period.

(3) The matters to be taken into account for sub-paragraphs (1) and (2) are—
(a) the storage capacity of any other slurry storage tank on the premises;
(b) the likely quantities of rainfall (including snow, hail or sleet) that may fall or drain into the slurry storage tank during the likely maximum storage period; and
(c) the need to provide at least 750 millimetres of freeboard in the case of a tank with walls made of earth and 300 millimetres of freeboard in all other cases.

7

No part of the slurry storage tank or any effluent tank, channels or reception pit may be situated within 10 metres of any inland freshwaters or coastal waters into which slurry could enter if it were to escape unless precautions are taken that the Agency agrees in writing are adequate to avoid any significant risk of pollution of controlled waters.

8

The slurry storage tank and any effluent tank, channels, pipes and reception pit must be designed and constructed so that with proper maintenance they are likely to continue to satisfy the requirements of paragraphs 2 to 4 for at least 20 years.

9

If the walls of the slurry storage tank are not impermeable, the base of the tank must—
(a) extend beyond the walls;
(b) be provided with channels designed and constructed so as to collect any slurry that escapes from the tank;
(c) have adequate provision for the drainage of the slurry from those channels to an effluent tank through a channel or pipe.

10

(1) Subject to sub-paragraph (3), if the slurry storage tank or any effluent tank or reception pit is fitted with a drainage pipe there must be two valves in series on the pipe with each valve separated from the other by a minimum distance of 1 metre.

(2) Each valve must be capable of shutting off the flow of slurry through the pipe and must be kept shut and locked in that position when not in use.

(3) Sub-paragraph (1) does not apply in relation to a slurry storage tank that drains through the pipe into another slurry storage tank if the other tank is of equal or greater capacity or if the tops of the tanks are at the same level.

11

In the case of a slurry storage tank with walls made of earth the tank must not be filled to a level that allows less than 750 millimetres of freeboard.

SCHEDULE 3
REQUIREMENTS FOR FUEL OIL STORAGE AREAS

Regulation 5(1)

1

The requirements to be satisfied in relation to a fuel oil storage area are as follows.

2

The storage area must be surrounded by a bund capable of retaining within the area—

(a) if there is only one fuel storage tank within the area and fuel oil is not otherwise stored there, a volume of fuel oil not less than 110 per cent of the capacity of the tank;

(b) if there is more than one fuel storage tank within the area and fuel oil is not otherwise stored there, a volume of fuel oil not less than the greater of—
  - (i) 110 per cent of the capacity of the largest tank within the area; or
  - (ii) 25 per cent of the total volume of such oil which could be stored in the tanks within the area;

(c) if there is no fuel storage tank within the area, a volume of fuel oil not less than 25 per cent of the total of such oil at any time stored within the area;

(d) in any other case, a volume of fuel oil not less than the greater of—
  - (i) 110 per cent of the capacity of the fuel storage tank or, as the case may be, of the largest tank within the area;
  - (ii) if there is more than one fuel storage tank within the area, 25 per cent of the total volume of such oil that could be stored in the tanks within the area; or
  - (iii) 25 per cent of the total volume of such oil at any time stored within the area.

3

The bund and the base of the area must be—

(a) impermeable to water and oil; and

(b) designed and constructed so that they are of sufficient strength and structural integrity so that with proper maintenance they are likely to remain so for at least 20 years.

4

Every part of any fuel storage tank must be within the bund.

5

Any tap or valve permanently fixed to the fuel storage tank through which fuel oil can be discharged to the open must—

(a) also be within the bund;
(b) be so arranged as to discharge vertically downwards; and
(c) be shut and locked in that position when not in use.

6

If fuel from the tank is delivered through a flexible pipe that is permanently attached to the tank, the pipe must be—
(a) fitted with a tap or valve at its end that closes automatically when not in use; and
(b) locked in a way that ensures that it is kept within the bund when not in use.

7

No part of the fuel storage area or the bund enclosing it may be situated within 10 metres of any inland freshwaters or coastal waters that fuel oil could enter if it were to escape.

ENVIRONMENTAL PERMITTING (ENGLAND AND WALES) REGULATIONS 2010

SI 2010/675

PART 1
GENERAL

1 Citation, commencement, extent and application

(1) These Regulations—

(a) may be cited as the Environmental Permitting (England and Wales) Regulations 2010;

(b) come into force on 6th April 2010, immediately after the coming into force of the Environmental Permitting (England and Wales) (Amendment) (No 2) Regulations 2009; and

(c) extend to England and Wales only.

(2) These Regulations apply to the sea adjacent to England and Wales out as far as the seaward boundary of the territorial sea; and for that purpose—

(a) the sea adjacent to England is so much of the sea adjacent to Great Britain as is not the sea adjacent to Wales or the sea adjacent to Scotland;

(b) the sea adjacent to Wales has the same meaning as it has by virtue of section 158(3) or (4) of the Government of Wales Act 2006; and

(c) the sea adjacent to Scotland has the same meaning as the internal waters and territorial sea of the United Kingdom adjacent to Scotland has by virtue of section 126(2) of the Scotland Act 1998.

2 Interpretation: general

(1) In these Regulations—

"the 1980 Act" means the Highways Act 1980;

"the 1990 Act" means the Environmental Protection Act 1990;

"the 1991 Act" means the Water Resources Act 1991;

"the 1993 Act" means the Radioactive Substances Act 1993;

"the 1995 Act" means the Environment Act 1995;

"the 2007 Regulations" means the Environmental Permitting (England and Wales) Regulations 2007;

"the 2009 Regulations" means the Groundwater (England and Wales) Regulations 2009;

"the Agency" means the Environment Agency;

"agricultural waste" means waste from premises used for agriculture within the meaning of the Agriculture Act 1947;

...[1]

"appropriate authority" means—

(a) in relation to England, the Secretary of State, and

(b) in relation to Wales, the Welsh Ministers;

"Category A mining waste facility" means a mining waste facility that is classified as Category A under Article 9 of the Mining Waste Directive;

"class", in relation to a regulated facility, is to be construed in accordance with regulation 8;

"coastal waters" has the meaning given in section 104 of the 1991 Act;

"confidential information" means information that is commercially or industrially confidential in relation to any person;

"date of registration" has the meaning given in paragraph 1 of Schedule 2;

"directly associated activity"—

(a) in relation to a SED activity, has the meaning given in paragraph 2 of Schedule 14,

(b) in relation to any other activity falling within Part 2 of Schedule 1, has the meaning given in paragraph 1 of Part 1 of that Schedule;

"disposal"—

(a) except in relation to a radioactive substances activity, has the meaning given in paragraph 2 of Schedule 9,

(b) in relation to a radioactive substances activity, has the meaning given in paragraph 1 of Part 2 of Schedule 23;

"effluent" has the same meaning as in the 1991 Act;

"emission" means—

(a) in relation to a Part A installation, the direct or indirect release of substances, vibrations, heat or noise from individual or diffuse sources in the installation into the air, water or land,

(b) in relation to a Part B installation, the direct release of substances or heat from individual or diffuse sources in the installation into the air,

(c) in relation to Part A mobile plant, the direct or indirect release of substances, vibrations, heat or noise from the mobile plant into the air, water or land,

(d) in relation to Part B mobile plant, the direct release of substances or heat from the mobile plant into the air,

(e) in relation to a waste operation, the direct or indirect release of substances, vibrations, heat or noise from individual or diffuse sources related to the operation into the air, water or land,

(f) in relation to a mining waste operation, the direct or indirect release of substances, vibrations, heat or noise from individual or diffuse sources related to the operation into the air, water or land, and

(g) in relation to a radioactive substances activity, the direct or indirect release of radioactive material or radioactive waste;

"enforcement notice" means a notice served under regulation 36;

"environmental permit" has the meaning given in regulation 13(1);

"environmental permit condition" means a condition of an environmental permit;

"establishment" has the same meaning as in the Waste Framework Directive;

"excluded waste operation" means any part of a waste operation not carried on at an installation or by means of Part A mobile plant or Part B mobile plant that—

(a) is the subject of a licence under Part 2 of the Food and Environment Protection Act 1985 or does not require such a licence by virtue of an order under section 7 of that Act, or

(b) relates to waste described in [regulation 3(2) of the Controlled Waste (England and Wales) Regulations 2012][2];

"exempt facility" has the meaning given in regulation 5;

"exempt groundwater activity" has the meaning given in regulation 5;

"exempt waste operation" has the meaning given in regulation 5;

"exempt water discharge activity" has the meaning given in regulation 5;

"exemption registration authority" has the meaning given in paragraph 2 of Schedule 2;

"existing mining waste facility" means a mining waste facility in operation on 1st May 2008;

"extractive waste" means waste within the meaning of Article 2(1) of the Mining Waste Directive, except where it is excluded from the scope of that Directive by Article 2(2)(a) and (b);

"groundwater" means all water which is below the surface of the ground in the saturation zone and in direct contact with the ground or subsoil;

"groundwater activity" has the meaning given in paragraph 3 of Schedule 22;

"hazardous substance" has the meaning given in paragraph 4 of Schedule 22;

"hazardous waste", except in Section 5.1 of Part 2 of Schedule 1—

(a) in relation to England, has the meaning given in regulation 6 of the Hazardous Waste (England and Wales) Regulations 2005,

(b) in relation to Wales, has the meaning given in regulation 6 of the Hazardous Waste (Wales) Regulations 2005;

"highway drain" means a drain which a highway authority or other person is entitled to keep open by virtue of section 100 of the 1980 Act;

"household waste" has the meaning given in section 75(5) of the 1990 Act;

"inland freshwaters" has the meaning given in section 104 of the 1991 Act;

"installation" has the meaning given in paragraph 1 of Part 1 of Schedule 1;

"lake or pond" and "waters of any lake or pond" have the same meaning as in section 104 of the 1991 Act;

"landfill" has the meaning given in paragraph 2(1)(d) of Schedule 10;

"landfill closure notice" means a closure notice served under paragraph 10 of Schedule 10;

"local authority" has the meaning given in regulation 6;

"mining waste facility" has the meaning given in paragraph 2(1) of Schedule 20;

"mining waste facility closure notice" means a closure notice served under paragraph 10 of Schedule 20;

"mining waste operation" has the meaning given in paragraph 2(1) of Schedule 20;

"mobile plant" means any of the following—

(a) Part A mobile plant,

(b) Part B mobile plant,

(c) waste mobile plant;

"mobile radioactive apparatus" has the meaning given in paragraph 1 of Part 2 of Schedule 23;

"net rated thermal input" has the meaning given in paragraph 1 of Part 1 of Schedule 1;

"non-hazardous waste", except in Section 5.1 of Part 2 of Schedule 1, means waste which is not hazardous waste;

"nuclear site", in relation to a radioactive substances activity, has the meaning given in paragraph 1 of Part 2 of Schedule 23;

"operate a regulated facility" and "operator" have the meaning given in regulation 7;

"Part A activity" and "Part B activity" have the meaning given in paragraph 1 of Part 1 of Schedule 1;

"Part A installation", "Part A(1) installation, "Part A(2) installation" and "Part B installation" have the meaning given in paragraph 1 of Part 1 of Schedule 1;

"Part A mobile plant", "Part A(1) mobile plant", "Part A(2) mobile plant" and "Part B mobile plant" have the meaning given in paragraph 1 of Part 1 of Schedule 1;

"pollutant" means any substance liable to cause pollution;

"pollution", in relation to a water discharge activity or groundwater activity, means the direct or indirect introduction, as a result of human activity, of substances or heat into the air, water or land which may—

(a) be harmful to human health or the quality of aquatic ecosystems or terrestrial ecosystems directly depending on aquatic ecosystems,

(b) result in damage to material property, or
(c) impair or interfere with amenities or other legitimate uses of the environment;

"pollution", other than in relation to a water discharge activity or groundwater activity, means any emission as a result of human activity which may—
(a) be harmful to human health or the quality of the environment,
(b) cause offence to a human sense,
(c) result in damage to material property, or
(d) impair or interfere with amenities or other legitimate uses of the environment;

"prescribed statutory provision" means—
(a) Part 2 of the Food and Environment Protection Act 1985,
(b) section 163 of the 1991 Act,
(c) section 165 of the Water Industry Act 1991, or
(d) any local statutory provision (within the meaning given in section 221 of the 1991 Act) or statutory order which expressly confers power to discharge effluent into water;

"prohibition notice" means a notice served under paragraph 9 of Schedule 22;

"proposed transferee" means the person to whom an operator [or a regulator][3] proposes to transfer an environmental permit in whole or in part;

"public participation provisions" means regulations 26, 29 and 59, and paragraphs 6 and 8 of Part 1 of Schedule 5;

"public register" has the meaning given in regulation 46(1);

"radioactive material" has the meaning given in [paragraph 3][4] of Part 2 of Schedule 23;

"radioactive substances activity" has the meaning given in [paragraph 11][4] of Part 2 of Schedule 23;

["radioactive substances exemption" means an exemption under Part 7 of Schedule 23 from the requirement for an environmental permit in respect of a radioactive substances activity;][5]

"radioactive waste" has the meaning given in [paragraph 3][4] of Part 2 of Schedule 23;

"recovery" has the meaning given in paragraph 2 of Schedule 9;

"register" and "registered", in relation to an exempt facility, have the meaning given in paragraph 1 of Schedule 2;

"regulated facility" has the meaning given in regulation 8;

["Regulation (EC) No 1069/2009" means Regulation (EC) No. 1069/2009 of the European Parliament and of the Council laying down health rules as regards animal by-products and derived products not intended for human consumption and repealing Regulation (EC) No. 1774/2002 (Animal by-products Regulation);][6]

"regulator" means the authority on whom functions are conferred by regulation 32, or by a direction under regulation 33;

"regulator-initiated variation" means the variation of an environmental permit on the initiative of the regulator under regulation 20(1);

"relevant function" has the meaning given in regulation 9;

"relevant territorial waters" has the meaning given in section 104(1) of the 1991 Act;

"revocation notice" means a notice served under regulation 22(3);

"rule-making authority" means—
(a) in relation to a regulated facility for which a local authority is the regulator, the appropriate authority, and
(b) in relation to any other regulated facility, the Agency;

"SED activity" means an activity falling within Section 7 of Part 2 of Schedule 1;
"SED installation" has the meaning given in Schedule 14;
"sewage effluent" has the meaning given in section 221 of the 1991 Act;
"sewer" has the same meaning as in the 1991 Act;
"standard facility" means a regulated facility described in standard rules published under regulation 26(5);
"stand-alone groundwater activity" means a groundwater activity that is not carried on as part of the operation of a regulated facility of another class;
"stand-alone water discharge activity" means a water discharge activity that is not carried on as part of the operation of a regulated facility of another class;
"statutory order" means any order, byelaw, scheme or award made under any enactment, including an order or scheme confirmed by Parliament or brought into operation in accordance with special parliamentary procedure;
"suspension notice" means a notice served under regulation 37;
"trade effluent" has the meaning given in section 221 of the 1991 Act;
"undertaking", except in relation to a radioactive substances activity, has the same meaning as in the Waste Framework Directive;
"vessel", except in Schedule 1, Part 2, Chapter 2, Section 2.2 and in Schedule 23, Part 2, paragraph 7, has the same meaning as in the 1991 Act;
["waste", except where otherwise defined, and subject to [paragraph (5) where it applies][4], means anything that—
(a) is waste within the meaning of Article 3(1) of the Waste Framework Directive; and
(b) is not excluded from the scope of that Directive by Article 2(1), (2) or (3);][7]
"waste battery or accumulator" has the meaning given in Article 3(7) of the Batteries Directive, but does not include any waste which is excluded from the scope of that Directive by Article 2(2);
"waste mobile plant" means plant that is—
(a) designed to move or be moved whether on roads or other land,
(b) used to carry on a waste operation, and
(c) not an installation, Part A mobile plant or Part B mobile plant;
"waste oil" means mineral-based lubricating or industrial oil which has become unfit for the use for which it was originally intended and, in particular, used combustion engine oil, gearbox oil, mineral lubricating oil, oil for turbines and hydraulic oil;
"waste operation" means recovery or disposal of waste;
"water discharge activity" has the meaning given in paragraph 3 of Schedule 21;
"WEEE" has the meaning given in Article 3(b) of the WEEE Directive; and
"working day" means a day other than—
(a) a Saturday or a Sunday,
(b) Good Friday or Christmas Day, or
(c) a day which is a bank holiday under the Banking and Financial Dealings Act 1971.

(2) For the purpose of calculating a period of time from one event to another event, that period—
(a) starts on the day on which the first event occurs; and
(b) ends on the day on which the second event occurs.

(3) In these Regulations, a power to give a direction includes a power to vary or revoke it.

[[(4) Paragraph (5) applies where a person ("A")—

(a) carries on a radioactive substances activity described in paragraph 11(2)(b) or (c) or (4) of Part 2 of Schedule 23 in respect of radioactive waste;
(b) is exempt under regulation 12(3) from the requirement for an environmental permit in respect of that activity and that waste ("the relevant exemption"); and
(c) the waste ("the applicable radioactive waste") is—
(i) NORM waste (as that term is defined in Part 7 of Schedule 23); or
(ii) the waste described in the first, second or sixth row of column 1 of table 6 in Part 7 of Schedule 23.][4]][8]

[(5) Where this paragraph applies, for so long as the relevant exemption applies to A, the applicable radioactive waste must be treated for the purposes of these Regulations as if it were waste other than radioactive waste.][5]

Amendments

1 Repealed by the Animal By-Products (Enforcement) (England) Regulations 2011, SI 2011/881, reg 27, Sch 2, para 18(1), (2)(a).
2 Substituted by the Controlled Waste (England and Wales) Regulations 2012, SI 2012/811, reg 6, Sch 2, para 5.
3 Inserted by the Environmental Permitting (England and Wales) (Amendment) Regulations 2012, SI 2012/630, reg 3.
4 Substituted by the Environmental Permitting (England and Wales) (Amendment) Regulations 2011, SI 2011/2043, regs 3, 4(1)-(3), (5)-(7).
5 Inserted by the Environmental Permitting (England and Wales) (Amendment) Regulations 2011, SI 2011/2043, regs 3, 4(1), (4), (8).
6 Inserted by the Animal By-Products (Enforcement) (England) Regulations 2011, SI 2011/881, reg 27, Sch 2, para 18(1), (2)(b).
7 Substituted by the Waste (England and Wales) Regulations 2011, SI 2011/988, reg 48(2), Sch 3, paras 1, 2(a).
8 Inserted by the Waste (England and Wales) Regulations 2011, SI 2011/988, reg 48(2), Sch 3, paras 1, 2(b).

3 Interpretation: Directives

In these Regulations—

"the Batteries Directive" means Directive 2006/66/EC of the European Parliament and of the Council on batteries and accumulators and waste batteries and accumulators and repealing Directive 91/157/EEC;

"the End-of-Life Vehicles Directive" means Directive 2000/53/EC of the European Parliament and of the Council on end-of-life vehicles;

"the IPPC Directive" means Directive 2008/1/EC of the European Parliament and of the Council concerning integrated pollution prevention and control;

"the Landfill Directive" means Council Directive 1999/31/EC on the landfill of waste, as read with Council Decision 2003/33/EC establishing criteria and procedures for the acceptance of waste at landfills pursuant to Article 16 of, and Annex II to, Directive 1999/31/EC;

"the Mining Waste Directive" means Directive 2006/21/EC of the European Parliament and of the Council on the management of waste from extractive industries and amending Directive 2004/35/EC;

["the Waste Framework Directive" means Directive 2008/98/EC of the European Parliament and of the Council on waste;][1]

"the Waste Incineration Directive" means Directive 2000/76/EC of the European Parliament and of the Council on the incineration of waste;

"the Water Framework Directive" means Directive 2000/60/EC of the European Parliament and of the Council establishing a framework for Community action in the field of water policy; and

"the WEEE Directive" means Directive 2002/96/EC of the European Parliament and of the Council on waste electrical and electronic equipment.

Amendment

1 Substituted by the Waste (England and Wales) Regulations 2011, SI 2011/988, reg 48(2), Sch 3, paras 1, 3.

4 Exempt facilities

Schedule 2 (exempt facilities: general) has effect.

5 Interpretation: exempt facilities

(1) In these Regulations—

"exempt facility" means—

(a) an exempt waste operation,

(b) an exempt water discharge activity, or

(c) an exempt groundwater activity;

["exempt groundwater activity" means—

(a) a stand-alone groundwater activity that meets the requirements of paragraph 5 of Schedule 2; or

(b) a groundwater activity that—

(i) is a groundwater tracer test as defined in paragraph 1 of Part 3 of Schedule 3;

(ii) is also a radioactive substances activity by virtue of the using of radioactive material as a part of that test; and

(iii) meets the requirements of paragraph 5 of Schedule 2;][1]

"exempt waste operation" means a waste operation—

(a) that—

(i) is not carried on at an installation, or

(ii) is an activity that falls within Section 5.3 or Section 5.4 of Part 2 of Schedule 1 and is carried on at an installation, and

(b) that meets the requirements of paragraph 3(1) of Schedule 2; and

"exempt water discharge activity" means a stand-alone water discharge activity that meets the requirements of paragraph 4 of Schedule 2.

(2) In these Regulations, in relation to an exempt waste operation, a reference to any of paragraphs U1 to U16, T1 to T33, D1 to D8 or S1 to S3 has the meaning given in paragraph 1(8) of Chapter 1 of Part 1 of Schedule 3.

Amendment

1 Substituted by the Environmental Permitting (England and Wales) (Amendment) Regulations 2011, SI 2011/2043, regs 3, 5.

6 Interpretation: local authority

(1) In these Regulations, "local authority" means—

(a) in England outside Greater London—

(i) a district council,

(ii) where there is a county council but no district council, the county council, or

(iii) the Council of the Isles of Scilly;

(b) in Greater London—

(i) the council of a London borough,

(ii) the Common Council of the City of London,

(iii) the Sub-Treasurer of the Inner Temple, or

(iv) the Under-Treasurer of the Middle Temple;

(c) in Wales—

(i) a county council, or

(ii) a county borough council.

(2) Where a port health authority has been constituted for a port health district by an order under section 2 of the Public Health (Control of Disease) Act 1984 that authority is the local authority for the area covered by that district in relation to a Part B installation.

7 Interpretation: operate a regulated facility and operator

In these Regulations—

"operate a regulated facility" means—

(a) operate an installation or mobile plant, or

(b) carry on a waste operation, mining waste operation, radioactive substances activity, water discharge activity or groundwater activity; and

"operator", in relation to a regulated facility, means—

(a) the person who has control over the operation of the regulated facility,

(b) if the regulated facility has not yet been put into operation, the person who will have control over the regulated facility when it is put into operation, or

(c) if a regulated facility authorised by an environmental permit ceases to be in operation, the person who holds the environmental permit.

8 Interpretation: regulated facility and class of regulated facility

(1) In these Regulations, "regulated facility" means any of the following—

(a) an installation,

(b) mobile plant,

(c) a waste operation,

(d) a mining waste operation,

(e) a radioactive substances activity,

(f) a water discharge activity,

(g) a groundwater activity.

(2) But the following are not regulated facilities—

(a) an exempt facility,

(b) an excluded waste operation,

(c) the disposal or recovery of household waste from a domestic property within the curtilage of that property by a person other than an establishment or undertaking.

(3) In these Regulations, a reference to a class of regulated facility is a reference to a class in paragraph (1).

(4) A regulated facility of any of the following classes may be carried on as part of the operation of a regulated facility of another class—

(a) waste operation;

(b) mining waste operation;

(c) water discharge activity;

(d) groundwater activity.

9 Interpretation: relevant function

In these Regulations, "relevant function" means any of the following functions—

(a) determining an application—

(i) for the grant of an environmental permit under regulation 13(1),

(ii) for the variation of an environmental permit under regulation 20(1),

(iii) for the transfer of an environmental permit in whole or in part under regulation 21(1),

(iv) for the surrender of an environmental permit in whole or in part under regulation 25(2),

(b) varying an environmental permit—
 (i) on the initiative of the regulator under regulation 20(1),
 (ii) in relation to a transfer in whole or in part under regulation 21(1) or (3),
 (iii) in relation to a partial revocation under regulation 22(1),
 (iv) in relation to a partial surrender under regulation 24(2) or 25(2),
(c) revoking an environmental permit in whole or in part under regulation 22(1),
(d) exercising the power to serve a notice under Schedule 21 or 22 requiring a person to hold an environmental permit,
(e) exercising the following powers or duty—
 (i) any power in relation to standard rules in Chapter 4 of Part 2,
 (ii) the duty to vary an environmental permit after revocation of standard rules in regulation 30(3),
(f) exercising any of the following powers relating to enforcement—
 (i) the power to serve an enforcement notice,
 (ii) the power to serve a suspension notice,
 (iii) the power to serve a prohibition notice,
 (iv) the power to serve a landfill closure notice,
 (v) the power to serve a mining waste facility closure notice.

10 Giving notices, notifications and directions, and the submission of forms

(1) In this regulation, "instrument" means a notice, notification, certificate, direction or form under these Regulations.

(2) An instrument must be in writing.

(3) An instrument may be served on or given to a person by—
(a) personal delivery;
(b) leaving it at the person's proper address; or
(c) sending it by post or electronic means to the person's proper address.

(4) In the case of a body corporate, an instrument may be served on or given to the secretary or clerk.

(5) In the case of a partnership, an instrument may be served on or given to a partner or a person having control or management of the partnership business.

(6) For the purposes of this regulation, "proper address" means—
(a) in the case of a body corporate or their secretary or clerk—
 (i) the registered or principal office of that body, or
 (ii) the email address of the secretary or clerk,
(b) in the case of a partnership or a partner or person having control or management of the partnership business—
 (i) the principal office of the partnership, or
 (ii) the email address of a partner or a person having that control or management,
(c) in any other case, a person's last known address, which includes an email address.

(7) For the purposes of paragraph (6), the principal office of a company registered outside the United Kingdom or of a partnership established outside the United Kingdom is their principal office in the United Kingdom.

(8) A form provided by the regulator which specifies an electronic address for submission may be submitted electronically to that address.

(9) A form provided by the regulator for completion and submission through a website may be submitted through that site.

PART 2
ENVIRONMENTAL PERMITS

Chapter 1
Application to the Crown and requirement for an environmental permit

11 Application to the Crown

Schedule 4 (application of these Regulations to the Crown) has effect.

12 Requirement for environmental permit

(1) A person must not, except under and to the extent authorised by an environmental permit—
(a) operate a regulated facility; or
(b) cause or knowingly permit a water discharge activity or groundwater activity.

(2) Paragraph (1)(b) does not apply if the water discharge activity or groundwater activity is an exempt facility.

[(3) In respect of a radioactive substances activity, paragraph (1) does not apply to a person to whom a radioactive substances exemption applies for that activity.][1]

[(4) Paragraph (5) applies to a person ("A") who—
(a) receives radioactive waste from another person ("B") for the purposes of A disposing of that waste; and
(b) subsequently disposes of that waste.

(5) Where this paragraph applies, A does not require an environmental permit—
(a) for the receipt of waste from B, where B holds an environmental permit which allows B to dispose of the waste to A; or
(b) for the subsequent disposal of that waste by A, where the waste is disposed of in accordance with the permit held by B.][2]

Amendments
1 Substituted by the Environmental Permitting (England and Wales) (Amendment) Regulations 2011, SI 2011/2043, regs 3, 6.
2 Inserted by the Environmental Permitting (England and Wales) (Amendment) Regulations 2011, SI 2011/2043, regs 3, 6.

Chapter 2
Grant of an environmental permit

13 Grant of an environmental permit

(1) On the application of an operator, the regulator may grant the operator a permit (an "environmental permit") authorising—
(a) the operation of a regulated facility; and
(b) that operator as the person authorised to operate that regulated facility.

(2) Regulation 17 applies in relation to the grant of a single permit authorising the operation of more than one regulated facility by the same operator.

(3) Part 1 of Schedule 5 applies in relation to an application for the grant of an environmental permit.

14 Content and form of an environmental permit

(1) An environmental permit must specify—

(a) the regulated facility whose operation it authorises; and
(b) the operator of that regulated facility.

(2) An environmental permit that authorises the operation of a regulated facility ("regulated facility A") need not specify any regulated facility of another class that is carried on as part of the operation of regulated facility A.

(3) An environmental permit may be in electronic form.

(4) An environmental permit must include a map, plan or other description of the site showing the geographical extent of the site of the regulated facility.

(5) But if there is more than one regulated facility on the site, the map, plan or other description need show only the combined extent of all the facilities.

(6) Paragraphs (4) and (5) do not apply to an environmental permit authorising—
(a) the operation of mobile plant; or
(b) the carrying on of a radioactive substances activity described in [paragraph 11(5)][1] of Part 2 of Schedule 23.

Amendment

1 Substituted by the Environmental Permitting (England and Wales) (Amendment) Regulations 2011, SI 2011/2043, regs 3, 7.

15 Conditions in relation to certain land

(1) Conditions in an environmental permit may require the operator to carry out works or do other things in relation to land which the operator is not entitled to do without obtaining the consent of another person.

(2) If an environmental permit contains such a condition, the person whose consent is required must grant the operator such rights as are necessary to enable the operator to comply with the condition.

(3) Part 2 of Schedule 5 applies where such rights are granted.

16 Mobile plant operating on the site of another regulated facility: conflict of permit conditions

If—
(a) an environmental permit ("permit A") authorises the operation of mobile plant on the site of another regulated facility the operation of which is authorised under a separate environmental permit ("permit B"); and
(b) there is an inconsistency between the requirements imposed by permit A and those imposed by permit B,

the requirements imposed by permit B prevail.

17 Single site permits etc.

(1) Except as otherwise provided by this regulation, a regulator may not authorise the operation of more than one regulated facility under a single environmental permit.

(2) The regulator may authorise, under a single environmental permit, the operation by the same operator—
(a) of more than one mobile plant;
(b) of more than one standard facility (other than a standard facility to which the IPPC Directive applies); …[1]
(c) subject to paragraph (3) and (4), of more than one regulated facility on the same site[; or

(d) of more than one radioactive substances activity described in paragraph 11(6) of Part 2 of Schedule 23, where all such activities are in respect of the use or potential use of the same premises for underground disposal (within the meaning of paragraph 11(7) of that Schedule).][2]

(3) If one of the regulated facilities mentioned in paragraph (2)(c) is a radioactive substances activity described in [paragraph 11(5)][3] of Part 2 of Schedule 23, the permit may authorise the operation of that regulated facility on more than one site.

(4) If a groundwater activity is carried on as part of a radioactive substances activity—
(a) the regulator must authorise the carrying on of the groundwater activity under the same environmental permit that authorises the carrying on of the radioactive substances activity; and
(b) a separate permit must not be granted in relation to the groundwater activity.

Amendments

1 Repealed by the Environmental Permitting (England and Wales) (Amendment) Regulations 2012, SI 2012/630, reg 4(a).
2 Inserted by the Environmental Permitting (England and Wales) (Amendment) Regulations 2012, SI 2012/630, reg 4(b).
3 Substituted by the Environmental Permitting (England and Wales) (Amendment) Regulations 2011, SI 2011/2043, regs 3, 8.

18 Consolidation of an environmental permit

(1) Paragraph (2) applies if the same operator is authorised by more than one environmental permit to operate—
(a) more than one mobile plant;
(b) more than one standard facility, not being a standard facility to which the IPPC Directive applies; or
(c) more than one regulated facility on the same site.

(2) The regulator may replace the environmental permits ("old permits") with a consolidated environmental permit—
(a) applying to the same regulated facilities; and
(b) subject to the same conditions that applied to the old permits, but varied as the regulator thinks fit.

(3) The regulator may replace a consolidated environmental permit ("old permit") with 2 or more environmental permits ("new permits").

(4) Each of the new permits is subject to whichever conditions of the old permit are relevant, varied as the regulator thinks fit.

(5) The regulator may replace a single environmental permit ("old permit") which has been varied with a consolidated environmental permit subject to the same conditions that applied to the old permit.

(6) A variation made by a regulator under this regulation—
(a) is taken to be a regulator-initiated variation under regulation 20(1); and
(b) may only be made in accordance with regulation 20.

(7) Paragraphs 17, 18 and 19 of Part 1 of Schedule 5 apply in relation to the decision to make a regulator-initiated variation and the notification of such a decision.

19 Subsistence of an environmental permit

Once granted an environmental permit continues in force until—
(a) it is revoked in whole in accordance with regulation 22;

[(b) it is surrendered in whole in accordance with—
  (i) regulation 24, or
  (ii) regulation 25 and Part 1 of Schedule 5;
(c) it is replaced with a consolidated permit in accordance with any of the following—
  (i) regulation 18(2),
  (ii) regulation 22(5),
  (iii) paragraph 19(2) of Part 1 of Schedule 5; or
(d) it ceases to have effect in accordance with regulation 67A(3), (4) or (5).][1]

Amendment

1 Substituted by the Environmental Permitting (England and Wales) (Amendment) Regulations 2012, SI 2012/630, reg 5.

Chapter 3
Variation, transfer, revocation and surrender of an environmental permit

20 Variation of an environmental permit

(1) The regulator may vary an environmental permit on the application of the operator or on its own initiative.

(2) A variation under this regulation must not reduce the extent of the site of a regulated facility.

(3) Paragraph (2) does not apply if the variation relates to any part of an environmental permit (or if applicable, the whole permit) that authorises the operation of a regulated facility of the following description—
(a) a Part B installation, except to the extent that it relates to a waste operation;
(b) a stand-alone water discharge activity or stand-alone groundwater activity.

(4) With respect to any part of an environmental permit (or if applicable, the whole permit) that authorises the carrying on of a stand-alone water discharge activity, a regulator must not, without the agreement of the operator, on its own initiative—
(a) within 4 years after the grant of the permit, vary any condition of the permit that relates to the water discharge activity; or
(b) within 4 years after the variation of a condition of the permit that relates to the water discharge activity, further vary that condition.

(5) Paragraph (4) does not apply if—
(a) the regulated facility is a standard facility; or
(b) the regulator, on its own initiative, varies an environmental permit, or any condition of a permit, in order to comply with—
  (i) an obligation of the United Kingdom under the [EU Treaties][1]; or
  (ii) a direction given by the appropriate authority under regulation 61.

(6) Part 1 of Schedule 5 applies in relation to an application for the variation of an environmental permit or a proposal to vary an environmental permit on the initiative of the regulator under paragraph (1).

Amendment

1 Substituted by the Environmental Permitting (England and Wales) (Amendment) Regulations 2012, SI 2012/630, reg 6.

21 Transfer of an environmental permit

[(1) The regulator may transfer to a proposed transferee an environmental permit or any part of an environmental permit—

(a) if the operator is one individual (A) and the regulator is satisfied that A cannot be found, on the application of the proposed transferee only,
(b) if the operator is two or more individuals (A and B) and the regulator is satisfied that A cannot be found, on the joint application of B and the proposed transferee, or
(c) otherwise, on the joint application of the operator and the proposed transferee.][1]

(2) Part 1 of Schedule 5 applies in relation to an application for the transfer of an environmental permit in whole or in part.

(3) Paragraph (1) does not apply to an environmental permit (or any part of a permit) that authorises the carrying on of a stand-alone water discharge activity or stand-alone groundwater activity.

[(4) The regulator may transfer to a proposed transferee an environmental permit to which paragraph (1) does not apply, or any part of that permit—
(a) if the operator is one individual (A) and the regulator is satisfied that A cannot be found, on the notification of the proposed transferee only;
(b) unless sub-paragraph (c) applies, if the operator is two or more individuals (A and B) and the regulator is satisfied that A cannot be found, on the joint notification of B and the proposed transferee;
(c) if the operator is two or more individuals (A and B) and the proposed transferee is two or more individuals (B and C), where B is both an operator and a proposed transferee—
 (i) on the joint notification of A and C, or
 (ii) if the regulator is satisfied that A cannot be found, on the notification of C only; or
(d) otherwise, on the joint notification of the operator and the proposed transferee.][1]

(5) A notification must—
(a) be made on the form provided by the regulator;
(b) include such information as is specified on the form; and
(c) specify a date on which the transfer is to take place, which must be not less than 20 working days after the date on which the notification is given.

(6) A transfer following a notification takes effect on the date specified in the notification.

(7) If—
(a) an enforcement notice is in force in respect of an environmental permit; and
(b) the permit is transferred to another person, either in whole or in part,
the duty to comply with the enforcement notice is also transferred to the other person to the extent that it relates to the permit or part transferred.

[(8) Unless a proposed transferee makes a joint application or gives a joint notification, the regulator may not transfer to the proposed transferee an environmental permit or any part of an environmental permit in respect of a regulated facility that ceased to be in operation more than 6 months before the proposed date of transfer.][2]

Amendments

1 Substituted by the Environmental Permitting (England and Wales) (Amendment) Regulations 2012, SI 2012/630, reg 7(a), (b).

2 Inserted by the Environmental Permitting (England and Wales) (Amendment) Regulations 2012, SI 2012/630, reg 7(c).

22 Revocation of an environmental permit: general

(1) The regulator may revoke an environmental permit in whole or in part.

(2) If the regulator revokes a permit in part, it may vary the permit conditions to the extent that it considers necessary to take account of the revocation.

(3) Where the regulator decides to revoke an environmental permit it must serve a notice on the operator specifying—

(a) the reasons for the revocation;

(b) in the case of a partial revocation—

  (i) the extent to which the environmental permit is being revoked, and

  (ii) any variation to the conditions of the environmental permit; and

(c) the date on which the revocation will take place, which must not be less than 20 working days after the date on which the notice is served.

(4) Unless the regulator withdraws a revocation notice, an environmental permit ceases to have effect on the date specified in the notice—

(a) in the case of a revocation in whole, entirely; or

(b) in the case of a partial revocation, to the extent of the part revoked.

(5) In the case of a partial revocation, the regulator may replace the environmental permit with a consolidated environmental permit reflecting the variation.

(6) Any variation made by a regulator under this regulation—

(a) is taken to be a regulator-initiated variation under regulation 20(1); and

(b) may only be made in accordance with regulation 20.

(7) Paragraphs 17, 18 and 19 of Part 1 of Schedule 5 apply in relation to the decision to make a regulator-initiated variation and the notification of such a decision.

(8) If a waste operation, stand-alone water discharge activity or stand-alone groundwater activity is registered as an exempt facility, that part of an environmental permit (or if applicable, the whole permit) that relates to the waste operation, water discharge activity or groundwater activity is revoked on the date of registration.

23 Revocation of an environmental permit: steps to be taken after the revocation takes effect

(1) This regulation applies where the regulator has decided to revoke an environmental permit, or part of a permit, and the regulator considers that, after the revocation takes effect, it is appropriate for the operator to take steps—

(a) to avoid a pollution risk resulting from the operation of the regulated facility; or

(b) to return the site of the regulated facility to a satisfactory state, having regard to the state of the site before the facility was put into operation.

(2) But this regulation does not apply if the revocation relates to any part of an environmental permit (or if applicable, the whole permit) that authorises the operation of a regulated facility of the following description—

(a) a Part B installation, except to the extent that it relates to a waste operation;

(b) mobile plant;

(c) a stand-alone water discharge activity or stand-alone groundwater activity.

(3) If the operator is already required to take the steps mentioned in paragraph (1) under the environmental permit, the revocation notice must specify the regulator's view under paragraph (1) and state that paragraph (4) applies.

(4) The environmental permit continues to have effect to the extent that it requires the steps to be taken until the regulator issues a certificate stating that it is satisfied that all the steps have been taken.

(5) If the operator is not already required to take the steps mentioned in s paragraph (1) under the environmental permit, the revocation notice must specify the regulator's view under paragraph (1) and the steps to be taken.

(6) If paragraph (5) applies, unless the regulator issues a certificate stating that it is satisfied that all the steps have been taken, the steps must be treated as if they were conditions of an environmental permit for the purposes of—
(a) regulation 20;
(b) regulation 36; and
(c) the offence in regulation 38(2).

24 Notification of the surrender of an environmental permit

(1) This regulation applies to any part of an environmental permit (or if applicable, the whole permit) that authorises the operation of a regulated facility of the following description or class—
(a) a Part B installation, except to the extent that it relates to a waste operation;
(b) mobile plant;
(c) a stand-alone water discharge activity or stand-alone groundwater activity.

(2) By notification to the regulator, the operator may surrender that part of an environmental permit (or if applicable, the whole permit) to which this regulation applies.

(3) A notification must—
(a) be made on the form provided by the regulator;
(b) include such information as is specified in the form; and
(c) specify the date on which the surrender is to take place, which must not be less than 20 working days after the date on which the notification is given.

(4) Subject to paragraph (7), the environmental permit ceases to have effect on the date specified in the notification to the extent specified there.

(5) Paragraphs (6) and (7) apply to a partial surrender if the regulator considers it necessary to vary the environmental permit conditions to take account of that surrender.

(6) The regulator must serve a notice on the operator specifying—
(a) the regulator's view under paragraph (5);
(b) the variation; and
(c) the date the variation takes effect.

(7) If the date specified in the notice under paragraph (6)(c) is later than the date specified in the notification under paragraph (3)(c), the variation and partial surrender both take effect on the later date.

25 Application for the surrender of an environmental permit

(1) This regulation applies to an environmental permit, or any part of a permit, to which regulation 24 does not apply.

(2) By application to the regulator, an operator may surrender an environmental permit, or that part of a permit, to which this regulation applies.

(3) Part 1 of Schedule 5 applies in relation to an application for the surrender of an environmental permit in whole or in part.

Chapter 4
Standard rules

26 Preparation and revision of standard rules

(1) A rule-making authority may prepare standard rules for such regulated facilities as are described in those rules.

(2) In preparing or revising standard rules the authority must consult—

(a) such persons as it considers are representative of the interests of communities likely to be affected by, or persons operating, the regulated facilities described in the rules; and

(b) such other persons as it considers are likely to be affected by or have an interest in the rules.

(3) But the duty in paragraph (2) does not apply in relation to revisions which comprise only minor administrative changes.

(4) The authority must keep under review all standard rules published by it under this regulation and revise those rules when it considers necessary.

(5) The authority must publish on its website all standard rules prepared or revised by it under this regulation.

(6) The duty in paragraph (2) may be satisfied by a consultation carried out partially or wholly before the coming into force of these Regulations.

27 Standard rules as conditions of an environmental permit

(1) This regulation applies where a rule-making authority has published standard rules under regulation 26(5).

(2) At the request of the operator of a standard facility the regulator may include in the environmental permit authorising the operation of the facility a term providing that the relevant rules are conditions of the permit.

(3) If the regulator includes such a term, the relevant rules are conditions of the permit for the purposes of these Regulations, but there is no right of appeal under regulation 31 in relation to such a condition or the relevant rules.

(4) In this regulation, "relevant rules" means the standard rules which apply to the standard facility.

28 Notification of revisions of standard rules

(1) This regulation applies where the rule-making authority proposes to revise standard rules under regulation 26(4).

(2) Before the rule-making authority complies with regulation 26(5), the regulator must notify any operator who holds a relevant environmental permit—

(a) of the proposed revisions;

(b) of the date when the revised rules will be published, which must not be less than 3 months after the date the notification is served; and

(c) that on this date the revised rules will become conditions of the environmental permit.

(3) But the authority may publish the revised rules before 3 months after the date the notification is served if the revisions comprise only minor administrative changes.

(4) The revised rules take effect when published under regulation 26(5).

(5) In this regulation, "relevant environmental permit" means an environmental permit which will be affected by the proposed revisions.

29 Revocation of standard rules

The rule-making authority may revoke standard rules, but before doing so must consult the persons referred to in regulation 26(2).

30 Variation of an environmental permit: revocation of standard rules

(1) This regulation applies to an environmental permit which includes a standard rules term if the standard rules applying by virtue of that term have been revoked by the regulator.

(2) The revoked rules continue to have effect until the regulator varies the permit under paragraph (3).

(3) As soon as reasonably practicable after the revocation of the rules, the regulator must vary the permit so as to—
(a) remove the standard rules term; and
(b) include such alternative conditions as it considers appropriate.

(4) In this regulation, "standard rules term" means a term of the type mentioned in regulation 27(2).

Chapter 5
Appeals in relation to environmental permits

31 Appeals to an appropriate authority

(1) In this regulation, "application" has the meaning given in paragraph 1 of Part 1 of Schedule 5.

(2) Subject to paragraphs (4) and (5), the following persons may appeal to the appropriate authority—
(a) a person whose application is refused;
(b) a person who is aggrieved by a decision to impose an environmental permit condition following that person's application;
(c) a person who is aggrieved by a decision to impose a condition on an environmental permit held by that person—
 (i) as a result of a regulator-initiated variation, or
 (ii) to take account of the partial transfer, partial revocation or partial surrender of that environmental permit;
(d) a person who is aggrieved by the deemed withdrawal under paragraph 4(2) of Part 1 of Schedule 5 of that person's duly-made application;
(e) a person who is aggrieved by a decision relating to an environmental permit held by that person not to authorise the closure procedure mentioned in—
 (i) Article 13 of the Landfill Directive after a request referred to in Article 13(a)(ii) of that Directive, or
 (ii) Article 12 of the Mining Waste Directive after a request referred to in Article 12(2)(b) of that Directive;
(f) a person on whom an enforcement notice, a revocation notice, suspension notice, prohibition notice, landfill closure notice or mining waste facility closure notice is served.

(3) In paragraph (2), "person" includes a person to whom an environmental permit is transferred after—
(a) an application or a decision mentioned in that paragraph is made, or
(b) a notice mentioned in that paragraph is served.

(4) Paragraph (2) does not apply where—
(a) the relevant decision or notice implements a direction of the appropriate authority given under—
 (i) regulation 61(1),

(ii) regulation 62(1) or (6), or
(iii) paragraph (7) of this regulation; or

(b) an application for the grant or variation of an environmental permit in relation to a Category A mining waste facility that is an existing mining waste facility is refused pursuant to paragraph 14(2) of Schedule 20.

(5) Paragraph (2)(f) does not apply to the extent that a revocation notice or suspension notice is served because of a failure to pay a charge prescribed in a scheme made under regulation 65(1) in respect of the subsistence of an environmental permit.

(6) On the determination of an appeal in respect of a notice, the appropriate authority—
(a) may quash or affirm the notice; and
(b) if it affirms the notice, may affirm it, with or without modifications.

(7) When determining an appeal in respect of a decision, the appropriate authority has the same powers as the regulator had when making the decision.

(8) On the determination of an appeal in respect of a decision, unless the appropriate authority affirms the decision the authority must direct the regulator to give effect to its determination when sending a copy of it to the regulator under paragraph 6(2)(a) of Schedule 6.

(9) Except as otherwise provided by this regulation—
(a) an appeal does not have the effect of suspending a decision or notice; but
(b) if an appeal is brought against a revocation notice, the notice does not take effect until the final determination or the withdrawal of the appeal.

(10) Subject to paragraph (13), paragraph (9)(b) does not apply if the revocation notice—
(a) relates to any part of an environmental permit (or if applicable, the whole permit) that authorises the carrying on of a stand-alone water discharge activity; and
(b) states that, in the opinion of the regulator, the revocation is necessary for the purpose of preventing or, where that is not practicable, minimising, pollution.

(11) If an appeal is brought under paragraph (2)(c)(i) in respect of a decision to impose a condition on an environmental permit in relation to a stand-alone water discharge activity, the imposition of the environmental permit condition does not take effect, subject to paragraphs (12) and (13), until the final determination or the withdrawal of the appeal.

(12) Paragraph (11) does not apply if the notice effecting the decision includes a statement that, in the opinion of the regulator, the imposition of the condition is necessary for the purpose of preventing or, where that is not practicable, minimising, pollution.

(13) If the appropriate authority, on the application of the appellant, determines that the regulator acted unreasonably in excluding the application of paragraph (9)(b) or (11), then—
(a) if the appeal is still pending at the end of the day on which the determination is made, paragraph (9)(b) or (11) applies to the decision or notice from the end of that day;
(b) the appellant is entitled to recover compensation from the regulator in respect of any loss suffered in consequence of that exclusion; and
(c) any dispute as to a person's entitlement to such compensation or as to the amount of it is to be determined by a single arbitrator appointed—
(i) by agreement between the parties to the dispute; or
(ii) in the absence of agreement, by the appropriate authority.

(14) Schedule 6 (appeals to the appropriate authority) has effect in relation to the making and determination of appeals under this regulation.

PART 3
DISCHARGE OF FUNCTIONS IN RELATION TO A REGULATED FACILITY

32 Discharge of functions

(1) Subject to regulation 33, functions in relation to a regulated facility, other than a regulated facility mentioned in paragraph (2), are exercisable by the Agency.

(2) Functions in relation to a regulated facility of the following description or class are exercisable by the local authority in whose area the regulated facility is or will be operated—
(a) a Part A(2) installation or Part A(2) mobile plant;
(b) a Part B installation or Part B mobile plant, but not in respect of any of the following regulated facilities carried on at the installation or by means of mobile plant—
  (i) a waste operation (unless it is a Part B activity),
  (ii) a mining waste operation,
  (iii) a water discharge activity,
  (iv) a groundwater activity.

(3) If the principal place of business of the operator of Part A(2) mobile plant or Part B mobile plant is in England and Wales, functions in relation to that regulated facility are exercisable by the local authority in whose area the place of business is.

(4) If the principal place of business of the operator of Part A(2) mobile plant or Part B mobile plant is not in England and Wales, functions in relation to that regulated facility are exercisable by—
(a) the local authority which granted the environmental permit authorising the operation of the regulated facility; or
(b) if no permit has been granted, the local authority in whose area the regulated facility is first operated, or is intended to be first operated.

(5) In this regulation, "functions" includes relevant functions.

33 Direction to a regulator: discharge of functions by a different regulator

(1) An appropriate authority may direct—
(a) the Agency to exercise such local authority functions as are, and for such period as is, specified in the direction; or
(b) a local authority to exercise such Agency functions as are, and for such period as is, specified in the direction.

(2) A direction under this regulation may include such saving and transitional provisions as the appropriate authority considers necessary or expedient.

(3) A direction under this regulation may be made in respect of a description or class of regulated facility or a specific regulated facility.

(4) A direction under paragraph (1)(b) may only be made in respect of—
(a) an installation, but not in respect of a mining waste operation carried on at an installation; or
(b) mobile plant.

(5) When giving a direction under this regulation the appropriate authority must notify the persons in paragraph (6) of the direction and publish the direction on its website.

(6) The persons are—
(a) the Agency; and

(b) any local authority or other person whom the appropriate authority considers is affected by the direction.

(7) An appropriate authority must not comply with a duty under paragraph (5) in a case where the authority considers that to do so would be contrary to the interests of national security.

(8) In this regulation (ignoring any direction under this regulation)—
"Agency functions" means functions which are exercisable by the Agency by virtue of regulation 32 or paragraph 2 of Schedule 2; and
"local authority functions" means functions which are exercisable by a local authority by virtue of regulation 32 or paragraph 2 of Schedule 2.

34 Review of environmental permits and inspection of regulated facilities

(1) The regulator must periodically review environmental permits.

(2) The regulator must make appropriate periodic inspections of regulated facilities.

35 Specific provisions applying to environmental permits

(1) Schedules 7 to 23 have effect.

(2) To the extent that the operation of a regulated facility of a description or class mentioned in any of the following Schedules requires an environmental permit, the requirements of that Schedule apply in relation to that regulated facility—
(a) Schedule 7 (Part A installations and Part A mobile plant);
(b) Schedule 8 (Part B installations and Part B mobile plant);
(c) Schedule 9 (waste operations);
(d) Schedule 10 (landfill);
(e) Schedule 11 (waste motor vehicles);
(f) Schedule 12 (waste electrical and electronic equipment);
(g) Schedule 13 (waste incineration);
(h) Schedule 14 (SED installations);
(i) Schedule 15 (large combustion plants);
(j) Schedule 16 (asbestos);
(k) Schedule 17 (titanium dioxide);
(l) Schedule 18 (petrol vapour recovery);
(m) Schedule 19 (waste batteries and accumulators);
(n) Schedule 20 (mining waste operations);
(o) Schedule 21 (water discharge activities);
(p) Schedule 22 (groundwater activities);
(q) Schedule 23 (radioactive substances activities).

PART 4
ENFORCEMENT AND OFFENCES

36 Enforcement notices

(1) If the regulator considers that an operator has contravened, is contravening, or is likely to contravene an environmental permit condition, the regulator may serve a notice (an "enforcement notice") on the operator under this regulation.

(2) An enforcement notice must—
(a) state the regulator's view under paragraph (1);
(b) specify the matters constituting the contravention or making a contravention likely;

(c) specify the steps that must be taken to remedy the contravention or to ensure that the likely contravention does not occur; and
(d) specify the period within which those steps must be taken.

(3) Steps that may be specified in an enforcement notice include steps—
(a) to make the operation of a regulated facility comply with the environmental permit conditions; and
(b) to remedy the effects of pollution caused by the contravention.

(4) The regulator may withdraw an enforcement notice at any time by further notice served on the operator.

37 Suspension notices

(1) The regulator may suspend an environmental permit by serving a notice (a "suspension notice") on the operator under this regulation.

(2) If the regulator considers that the operation of a regulated facility under an environmental permit involves a risk of serious pollution, it may serve a suspension notice on the operator.

(3) Paragraph (2) applies whether or not the manner of operating the regulated facility which involves the risk is subject to or contravenes an environmental permit condition.

(4) A suspension notice served for the purpose of paragraph (2) must—
(a) specify—
(i) the risk of serious pollution mentioned in that paragraph,
(ii) the steps that must be taken to remove that risk, and
(iii) the period within which the steps must be taken;
(b) state that the environmental permit ceases to have effect to the extent specified in the notice until the notice is withdrawn; and
(c) if the environmental permit continues to authorise the operation of a regulated facility, state any steps (in addition to those already required to be taken by the environmental permit conditions) that are to be taken when operating that regulated facility.

(5) The regulator may suspend an environmental permit under regulation 65(5) by serving a suspension notice on the operator.

(6) A suspension notice served for the purpose of paragraph (5) must—
(a) specify the reason for the suspension;
(b) state the sum payable by the operator and the period within which it is to be paid; and
(c) state that the environmental permit ceases to have effect to the extent specified in the notice until the notice is withdrawn.

(7) If a suspension notice is served, the environmental permit ceases to have effect to the extent stated in the notice.

(8) The regulator—
(a) may withdraw a suspension notice at any time by further notice served on the operator; and
(b) must withdraw a notice when satisfied that the steps specified in it have been taken.

38 Offences

(1) It is an offence for a person to—
(a) contravene regulation 12(1); or
(b) knowingly cause or knowingly permit the contravention of regulation 12(1)(a).

(2) It is an offence for a person to fail to comply with or to contravene an environmental permit condition.

(3) It is an offence for a person to fail to comply with the requirements of an enforcement notice or of a prohibition notice, suspension notice, landfill closure notice or mining waste facility closure notice.

(4) It is an offence for a person—
(a) to fail to comply with a notice under regulation 60(1) requiring the provision of information, without reasonable excuse;
(b) to make a statement which the person knows to be false or misleading in a material particular, or recklessly to make a statement which is false or misleading in a material particular, where the statement is made—
 (i) in purported compliance with a requirement to provide information imposed by or under a provision of these Regulations,
 (ii) for the purpose of obtaining the grant of an environmental permit to any person, or the variation, transfer in whole or in part, or surrender in whole or in part of an environmental permit, or
 (iii) for the purpose of obtaining, renewing or amending the registration of an exempt facility;
(c) intentionally to make a false entry in a record required to be kept under an environmental permit condition;
(d) with intent to deceive—
 (i) to forge or use a document issued or authorised to be issued or required for any purpose under an environmental permit condition, or
 (ii) to make or have in the person's possession a document so closely resembling such a document as to be likely to deceive.

(5) It is an offence for an establishment or undertaking to—
(a) fail to comply with paragraph 14(3) or (4) of Schedule 2; or
(b) intentionally make a false entry in a record required to be kept under that paragraph.

(6) If an offence committed by a person under this regulation is due to the act or default of some other person, that other person is also guilty of the offence and liable to be proceeded against and punished accordingly, whether or not proceedings for the offence are taken against the firstmentioned person.

39 Penalties

(1) A person guilty of an offence under regulation 38(1), (2) or (3) is liable—
(a) on summary conviction to a fine not exceeding £50,000 or imprisonment for a term not exceeding 12 months, or to both; or
(b) on conviction on indictment to a fine or imprisonment for a term not exceeding 5 years, or to both.

(2) In relation to an offence committed before the commencement of section 154(1) of the Criminal Justice Act 2003, paragraph (1)(a) has effect as if for "12 months" there were substituted "6 months".

(3) A person guilty of an offence under regulation 38(4) is liable—
(a) on summary conviction to a fine not exceeding the statutory maximum; or
(b) on conviction on indictment to a fine or imprisonment for a term not exceeding 2 years, or to both.

(4) An establishment or undertaking guilty of an offence under regulation 38(5) is liable on summary conviction to a fine not exceeding level 2 on the standard scale.

40 Defences

(1) It is a defence for a person charged with an offence under regulation 38(1), (2) or (3) to prove that the acts alleged to constitute the contravention were done in an emergency in order to avoid danger to human health in a case where—
(a) the person took all such steps as were reasonably practicable in the circumstances for minimising pollution; and
(b) particulars of the acts were furnished to the regulator as soon as reasonably practicable after they were done.

(2) A person who knowingly permits a water discharge activity or groundwater activity where the discharge is water from an abandoned mine or an abandoned part of a mine is not guilty of an offence under regulation 38(1) unless—
(a) the person is the owner or former operator of the mine or that part of it; and
(b) the mine or the part of the mine was abandoned after 31st December 1999.

(3) In paragraph (2), "abandoned", in relation to a mine, and "mine" have the meaning given in section 91A of the 1991 Act.

41 Offences by bodies corporate

(1) If an offence committed under these Regulations by a body corporate is proved—
(a) to have been committed with the consent or connivance of an officer; or
(b) to be attributable to any neglect on the part of an officer,
the officer as well as the body corporate is guilty of the offence and liable to be proceeded against and punished accordingly.

(2) If the affairs of a body corporate are managed by its members, paragraph (1) applies in relation to the acts and defaults of a member in connection with the member's functions of management as if the member were a director of the body.

(3) In this regulation, "officer", in relation to a body corporate, means a director, member of the committee of management, chief executive, manager, secretary or other similar officer of the body, or a person purporting to act in any such capacity.

42 Enforcement by the High Court

If the regulator considers that proceedings against a person for an offence under regulation 38(3) would afford an ineffectual remedy against the person, the regulator may take proceedings in the High Court for the purpose of securing compliance with the enforcement notice, suspension notice, prohibition notice, landfill closure notice or mining waste facility closure notice.

43 Admissibility of evidence

Where, pursuant to an environmental permit granted by a local authority, an entry is required to be made in any record as to the observance of a condition of the environmental permit and the entry has not been made, that fact is admissible as evidence that the condition has not been observed.

44 Power of court to order cause of offence to be remedied

(1) This regulation applies where a person is convicted of an offence under regulation 38(1), (2) or (3) in respect of a matter which appears to the court to be a matter which it is in the person's power to remedy.

(2) In addition to or instead of a punishment imposed under regulation 39 the court may order the person to take such steps for remedying the matter within such period as may be specified in the order.

(3) The period may be extended, or further extended, by order of the court on an application made before the end of the period or the extended period, as the case may be.

(4) If a person is ordered to remedy a matter, that person is not liable under regulation 38 in respect of that matter during the period or the extended period.

PART 5
PUBLIC REGISTERS

45 Interpretation of this Part

In this Part—

"final confidentiality decision" means—

(a) a determination under regulation 50,
(b) a determination under section 22(2) or 66(2) of the 1990 Act,
(c) a determination under regulation 31(2) of the 2000 Regulations, or
(d) the determination or withdrawal of an appeal in relation to a determination referred to in paragraphs (a) to (c);

"the information subject" means the person to whom information relates; and

"objection notice" means a notice given under regulation 48(1)(b).

46 Duty of the regulator to maintain a public register

(1) Subject to regulations 47 and 48, the regulator must maintain a register (a "public register") containing the information in paragraph 1 of Schedule 24 (public registers).

(2) Nothing in paragraph (1) requires a public register to contain information relating to criminal proceedings, or anything which is the subject matter of criminal proceedings, before those proceedings are finally disposed of.

(3) In paragraph (2), "criminal proceedings" includes prospective criminal proceedings.

(4) A local authority must also include on its public register any information which is included on the Agency's public register in respect of a regulated facility (other than mobile plant or a stand-alone water discharge activity or stand-alone groundwater activity)—

(a) for which the Agency is the regulator; and
(b) which is in the area of the authority.

(5) But—

(a) paragraph (4) does not apply to a port health authority; and
(b) every local authority whose area adjoins that of a port health authority must comply with paragraph (4) as if the port health authority had not been constituted.

(6) The Agency must provide the local authority with the information necessary to comply with paragraph (4).

(7) The regulator must enter information on its public register as soon as reasonably practicable after it comes within the regulator's possession.

(8) Where information of any description is excluded from any public register under regulation 48, a statement must be entered on the register indicating the existence of information of that description.

(9) The regulator must—

(a) make its public register available for public inspection at all reasonable times, free of charge; and

(b) enable members of the public to obtain copies of entries on its public register on payment of a reasonable charge.

(10) A public register may be kept in any form.

47 Exclusion from public registers of information affecting national security

(1) The appropriate authority may direct the regulator that in the interests of national security specified information or information of a specified description must be excluded from a public register.

(2) The regulator must notify the appropriate authority of any information (other than information relating to a radioactive substances activity) that it excludes from a public register pursuant to such a direction.

(3) The appropriate authority may direct the regulator that in the interests of national security information of a specified description—

(a) must be referred to the authority for its determination as to whether or not the information may be included on a public register; and

(b) must not be included on a public register unless the appropriate authority determines that it may be included.

(4) A person may give a notice to the appropriate authority stating that, in the person's opinion, the inclusion of information on a public register would be contrary to the interests of national security.

(5) A notice under paragraph (4) must specify the information and indicate its apparent nature.

(6) A person giving a notice under paragraph (4) must at the same time notify the regulator.

(7) The regulator must not include information notified under paragraph (4) on a public register unless the appropriate authority determines that it may be included.

48 Exclusion from public registers of confidential information

(1) The regulator must exclude information from a public register, unless a condition in paragraph (2) is met, if it—

(a) considers that the information may be confidential information; or

(b) receives notice from the information subject which—

   (i) states that the information subject considers the information is confidential information, and

   (ii) gives reasons for that view.

(2) The conditions are that—

(a) in relation to paragraph (1)(a), the regulator has given a notice under regulation 49(1) and the information subject has given notice of consent under regulation 49(2)(a);

(b) in relation to paragraph (1)(a) or (b)—

   (i) a final confidentiality decision that the information should be included on the register has been made, or

   (ii) the appropriate authority has given a direction under regulation 56(1) which requires the information to be included on the register.

49 Procedure if the regulator considers that information may be confidential

(1) If the regulator considers that information may be confidential information but has not received an objection notice, it must give notice of that view to the information subject.

(2) The information subject may within 15 working days after the date of the notice given by the regulator under paragraph (1)—
(a) give notice to the regulator consenting to the regulator including the information on the register; or
(b) give an objection notice to the regulator.

50 Duty to determine confidentiality

The regulator must determine whether information must be included on the public register, or excluded from the public register because it is confidential information, if—
(a) having given notice under regulation 49(1), it does not receive notice of consent in accordance with regulation 49(2)(a); or
(b) it receives an objection notice.

51 Determination of confidentiality

(1) When making a determination under regulation 50, the regulator must comply with this regulation.

(2) In making the determination, the regulator must—
(a) take any reasons given in an objection notice into account;
(b) apply a presumption in favour of including the information on the public register; and
(c) determine to exclude the information from the public register if it considers that—
  (i) the information is commercial or industrial information,
  (ii) its confidentiality is provided by law to protect a legitimate economic interest, and
  (iii) in all the circumstances, the public interest in maintaining the confidentiality of the information outweighs the public interest in including it on the register.

(3) But, to the extent that information relates to emissions, the regulator must determine to include it on the public register.

(4) Nothing in this regulation authorises the exclusion from the public register of information contained in or otherwise held with other information excluded from the register unless the information is not reasonably capable of being separated for the purposes of inclusion on the register.

52 Procedure following a determination

(1) The regulator must give notice of its determination, the reasons for it and the details of the appeals procedure to the information subject within—
(a) a period of 20 working days beginning with the date its duty under regulation 50 arises; or
(b) such longer period as it agrees with the information subject.

(2) If the regulator fails to give notice under paragraph (1) within the period required by that paragraph, the information subject may give notice to the regulator of that failure, and on such notice—
(a) the regulator is deemed to have determined that the information must be included on the register; and
(b) the deemed determination is subject to the right of appeal in regulation 53(1).

(3) If the regulator determines that the information must be included on the public register, it must not include the information before the expiry of the period of 15 working days after—

(a) it has given notice of the determination; or

(b) a notice under paragraph (2) resulting in a deemed determination is given,

but must include it after the expiry of that period if notice of appeal has not been given.

53 Appeals in relation to confidentiality

(1) The information subject may give notice of appeal to the appropriate authority against a determination made under regulation 50 within 15 working days after the regulator has given notice of it.

(2) A notice of appeal must—

(a) be in writing;

(b) include a statement of the grounds of appeal;

(c) state whether the information subject wishes the appeal to be in the form of a hearing or to be disposed of through written representations; and

(d) be copied to the regulator.

(3) If the information subject gives notice of appeal, the regulator must not include the information on the public register before the appeal is decided.

(4) The appropriate authority—

(a) may give the information subject and the regulator an opportunity of appearing before and being heard by a person appointed by it; and

(b) must do so in a case where the notice of appeal states that the information subject wishes the appeal to be in the form of a hearing.

(5) A hearing under paragraph (4) of this regulation is subject to paragraphs 5(2) to 5(6) and 6 of Schedule 6 (except paragraph 5(3)(c)) as if it were a hearing under paragraph 5(1) of that Schedule, save that "the appellant" is to be read as "the information subject".

54 Consequences of an appeal

(1) If the appropriate authority allows the appeal, the regulator must exclude the information from the public register.

(2) If the appropriate authority rejects the appeal or the appeal is withdrawn, the regulator must include the information on the public register.

55 Reconsideration of confidentiality

(1) The regulator must cease to treat information as confidential information at the expiry of—

(a) a period of 4 years after the final confidentiality decision; or

(b) such shorter period as is specified in that decision.

(2) But if the person to whom the information relates gives notice to the regulator before the expiry of that period that the person considers that the information remains confidential information—

(a) regulation 48 applies in respect of the information and the regulator must treat the notice as an objection notice; and

(b) regulations 50 to 54 apply notwithstanding any previous compliance with those regulations in relation to the information.

56 Directions of the appropriate authority in relation to confidentiality

(1) The appropriate authority may direct the regulator that specified information, or information of a specified description, must be included on the public register even though it is confidential information.

(2) The appropriate authority must not give a direction under paragraph (1) unless it considers that the public interest in including such information on the register outweighs the public interest in maintaining its confidentiality.

PART 6
POWERS AND FUNCTIONS OF THE REGULATOR AND THE APPROPRIATE AUTHORITY

57 Power of the regulator to prevent or remedy pollution

(1) If the regulator considers that the operation of a regulated facility under an environmental permit involves a risk of serious pollution, it may arrange for steps to be taken to remove that risk.

(2) The regulator may arrange for steps to be taken to remedy the effects of pollution if—
(a) the commission of an offence under regulation 38(1), (2) or (3) causes pollution; or
(b) the regulator suspects that an offence under that regulation is being or has been committed and that pollution is being or has been caused as a result.

(3) If the regulator intends to arrange for steps to be taken under paragraph (2), it must notify the operator of the steps not less than 5 working days before they are taken.

(4) If the regulator arranges for steps to be taken under this regulation, it may recover the cost of taking those steps from the operator.

(5) But costs are not recoverable under paragraph (4)—
(a) if the steps referred to in paragraph (1) are taken and the operator shows that there was no risk of serious pollution; or
(b) to the extent that the operator shows that the costs were unnecessarily incurred by the regulator.

58 Environment Agency: notices in relation to emissions to water

(1) This regulation applies to Part A installations and Part A mobile plant for which a local authority is the regulator.

(2) At any time the Agency may give notice to the local authority specifying the emission limit values or the conditions it considers appropriate for preventing or reducing emissions into water from the installation or mobile plant.

(3) If such a notice is issued, the local authority must exercise its functions under these Regulations to ensure the environmental permit for the installation or mobile plant includes—
(a) the emission limit values or conditions specified in the notice; or
(b) such stricter limit values or more onerous conditions as the authority thinks fit.

(4) In this regulation, "emission limit value" means the mass, expressed in terms of specific parameters, concentration or level of an emission, which must not be exceeded during a period of time.

59 Environment Agency: public participation statement

(1) The Agency must prepare and publish a statement of its policies for complying with its public participation duties.

(2) In preparing or revising the statement the Agency must consult such persons as it considers are affected by, are likely to be affected by, or have an interest in, the statement.

(3) The Agency must—
(a) keep the statement under review;
(b) revise the statement when it considers necessary; and
(c) publish any revised statement.

(4) The Agency must comply with any published statement when exercising its functions under the public participation provisions.

(5) The duty in paragraph (2) may be satisfied by a consultation carried out partially or wholly before the coming into force of these Regulations.

(6) In this regulation, "public participation duties" means the duties in the following provisions—
(a) regulation 26;
(b) regulation 29;
(c) paragraphs 6 and 8(2) of Part 1 of Schedule 5.

60 Power to require the provision of information

(1) For the purposes of discharging its functions under these Regulations, an appropriate authority, regulator or exemption registration authority, by notice served on any person, may require that person to provide such information in such form and within such period as is specified in the notice.

(2) A notice under paragraph (1) may require a person to provide any information on emissions where that requirement is reasonable, including the provision of information—
(a) not in the person's possession; and
(b) which would not usually come into the person's possession.

(3) For the purposes of this regulation the discharge by the appropriate authority of—
(a) an obligation of the United Kingdom under the [EU Treaties][1]; or
(b) an international obligation of the United Kingdom,
must be treated as a function of the authority under these Regulations.

(4) For the purposes of this regulation the compilation of an inventory of emissions (whether or not from a regulated facility) must be treated as a function of the regulator under these Regulations.

Amendment

1 Substituted by the Environmental Permitting (England and Wales) (Amendment) Regulations 2012, SI 2012/630, reg 8.

61 Directions to regulators and exemption registration authorities: general

(1) An appropriate authority may give directions to a regulator or exemption registration authority of a general or specific character with respect to the carrying out of its functions under these Regulations.

(2) Without prejudice to the generality of the power in paragraph (1), a direction may direct the regulator or exemption registration authority to exercise or not to exercise—
(a) specified powers;

(b) its powers in specified circumstances; or
(c) its powers in a specified manner.

(3) Except in an emergency, an appropriate authority may give a direction to the Agency under paragraph (1) only after consultation with the Agency.

(4) The regulator or exemption registration authority must comply with a direction given to it under these Regulations.

62 Reference of applications to an appropriate authority

(1) An appropriate authority may give directions to a regulator requiring that a particular application or class of application be referred to it for determination.

(2) The regulator must—
(a) inform the applicant of the fact that the application is being referred to the appropriate authority; and
(b) forward to the appropriate authority any representations made in respect of the application.

(3) When an application is referred to an appropriate authority, the appropriate authority—
(a) may afford the applicant and the regulator an opportunity of appearing before and being heard by a person appointed by the appropriate authority, and
(b) must do so in any case where a request is duly made by the applicant or the regulator to be so heard.

(4) A request under paragraph (3)(b) must be made in writing within 15 working days after the day on which the applicant is informed that the application is being referred to the appropriate authority.

(5) A hearing under paragraph (3) is subject to paragraphs 5(2) to (6) and 6 of Schedule 6 (except paragraph 5(3)(c)) as if it were a hearing under paragraph 5(1) of that Schedule with the following modifications—
(a) "the appellant" is to be read as "the applicant";
(b) "the appeal" is to be read as "the application".

(6) On determining an application referred to it under this regulation the appropriate authority must give to the regulator a direction as to whether the regulator is to grant the application and, if so, the conditions that are to be attached to the environmental permit.

(7) In this regulation, "application" means an application—
(a) for the grant of an environmental permit, or
(b) for the variation of an environmental permit.

63 Directions to the Agency: installations outside the United Kingdom

(1) This regulation applies where an appropriate authority receives information pursuant to Article 18(1) of the IPPC Directive in relation to the operation of an installation outside the United Kingdom which is likely to have a significant negative effect on the environment of England or Wales.

(2) For the purpose of complying with Article 18(2) of the IPPC Directive, the appropriate authority must direct the Agency to take such steps as it considers appropriate to—
(a) bring the information to the attention of persons likely to be affected by the operation of the installation; and
(b) provide them with an opportunity to comment on the information.

64 Guidance to regulators and exemption registration authorities

(1) An appropriate authority may issue guidance to a regulator or exemption registration authority with respect to the exercise of its functions under these Regulations.

(2) In the exercise of those functions the regulator or exemption registration authority must have regard to the guidance.

65 Fees and charges in relation to the exercise of regulator's functions by local authorities

(1) An appropriate authority may make, and from time to time revise, a scheme prescribing—
(a) fees payable to a regulator in respect of applications—
 (i) for the grant of an environmental permit,
 (ii) for the variation of an environmental permit,
 (iii) for the transfer of an environmental permit in whole or in part,
 (iv) for the surrender of an environmental permit in whole or in part;
(b) fees payable to a regulator in respect of a regulator-initiated variation; and
(c) charges payable to a regulator in respect of the subsistence of an environmental permit.

(2) A scheme may in particular—
(a) prescribe specific fees and charges or the methods by which they are to be calculated;
(b) make different provision for different cases, including different provision in relation to different persons, circumstances or localities;
(c) subject to the requirements of these Regulations, provide for the time when, and the manner in which, payments required by the scheme are to be made; and
(d) make such incidental, supplementary and transitional provision as appears necessary or expedient to the appropriate authority.

(3) In making or revising a scheme, so far as practicable the appropriate authority must ensure that the fees and charges payable are sufficient to cover expenditure by a regulator—
(a) in exercising its functions under these Regulations;
(b) in making payment to any person who prepares guidance in relation to an installation or mobile plant that is—
 (i) mentioned in regulation 32(2), or
 (ii) specified in a direction under regulation 33;
(c) in making payment to the Agency in relation to the exercise of the Agency's functions under regulation 58.

(4) A scheme must provide for the payment of sums by the regulator to the Agency where those sums are related to expenditure by the Agency under regulation 58 or in preparing guidance referred to in paragraph (3)(b).

(5) If a regulator considers that an operator has failed to pay a charge specified in a scheme in respect of the subsistence of the operator's permit, the regulator may revoke or suspend the permit.

(6) A revocation or suspension must be by way of notice served under regulation 22(3) or regulation 37.

(7) In this regulation, "regulator" means a local authority on which functions are conferred by regulation 32 or by a direction under regulation 33.

66 Plans relating to emissions

(1) Subject to paragraph (3), an appropriate authority may make plans for—

(a) the setting of limits on the total amount, or the total amount in any period, of emissions from all or any description of source; or

(b) the allocation of quotas relating to such emissions.

(2) If the appropriate authority allocates a quota in a plan made under paragraph (1) it may also make a scheme for the trading or other transfer of that quota.

(3) This regulation does not apply to an emission plan.

(4) In this regulation—

"emission" means the direct or indirect release of any substance from individual or diffuse sources into the air, water or land; and

"emission plan" has the meaning given in the Large Combustion Plants (National Emission Reduction Plan) Regulations 2007.

PART 7
MISCELLANEOUS PROVISIONS

Chapter 1
Interpretation

67 Interpretation of this Part

In this Part—

"2007 transitional application" means a transitional application within the meaning of Part 7 of the 2007 Regulations;

["article" and "substance" have the meaning given to them in Schedule 23 to these Regulations;][1]

"authorisation" means an authorisation under section 13 or 14 of the 1993 Act;

"closure and after-care obligations" means any environmental permit condition—

(a) which implements Article 13 of the Landfill Directive, or

(b) which is otherwise related to closure and after-care of a landfill site or to ensuring that it does not cause pollution;

"determination date"—

(a) for an application mentioned in regulation 70 of the 2007 Regulations (other than an application to which regulation 71 of those Regulations applied), has the meaning given in paragraph (2) of that regulation,

(b) for an application to which regulation 71 of those Regulations applied, has the meaning given in paragraph (4) of that regulation;

"discharge consent" means a consent under Chapter 2 of Part 3 of the 1991 Act;

"disposal licence" means a disposal licence issued under section 5 of the Control of Pollution Act 1974;

"existing" means in force at the relevant time;

"existing environmental permit" means an environmental permit under the 2007 Regulations in force at the relevant time;

"existing notice" means, for the purposes of Chapter 3, a notice in force at the relevant time served or given by the Agency under a former enactment in relation to—

(a) an authorisation, registration, discharge consent or groundwater permit, or

(b) the requirement for a discharge consent or groundwater permit;

"existing permit" means an existing authorisation, registration, discharge consent or groundwater permit;

"former enactment" means the 1991 Act, the 1993 Act or the 2009 Regulations;

"former PPC or waste legislation" means any provision of the following enactments repealed or revoked by the 2007 Regulations—

(a) the 1990 Act,

(b) the Waste Management Licensing Regulations 1994,

(c) the PPC Regulations,

(d) the Landfill (England and Wales) Regulations 2002;

"groundwater permit" means a permit under regulation 13 of the 2009 Regulations;

"licence" means a disposal licence or a waste management licence;

"outstanding appeal" means an appeal made, but not determined, by the relevant time;

"PPC permit" means a permit granted under regulation 10 of the PPC Regulations;

"the PPC Regulations" means the Pollution Prevention and Control (England and Wales) Regulations 2000;

. . .[2]

"registration" means a registration under section 7 or 10 of the 1993 Act;

"related activity" means any of the following activities relating to the operation of a landfill—

(a) storage or treatment of leachate;

(b) utilization or flaring of landfill gas;

"relevant time" means immediately before the coming into force of these Regulations;

"transfer notice" means any of the following notices given before the coming into force of these Regulations in respect of a transfer which, at the relevant time, had not taken effect—

(a) a joint notice given under paragraph 11(6)(a) of Schedule 10 to the 1991 Act for the purpose of the transfer of a discharge consent,

(b) a notice mentioned in paragraph (a) given for the purpose of the transfer of a groundwater permit;

"transitional application" means any of the following applications not determined by the relevant time—

(a) an application for an authorisation or registration,

(b) an application for the variation of an authorisation or registration,

(c) an application under section 16A of the 1993 Act for the transfer of an authorisation,

(d) an application under section 12 of the 1993 Act to cancel a registration,

(e) an application under section 17 of the 1993 Act to revoke an authorisation,

(f) an application for a discharge consent,

(g) an application for the variation of a discharge consent,

(h) an application for a groundwater permit; and

"waste management licence" means a licence granted under section 35 of the 1990 Act.

Amendments

1 Inserted by the Environmental Permitting (England and Wales) (Amendment) Regulations 2011, SI 2011/2043, regs 3, 9(1), (2).

2 Repealed by the Environmental Permitting (England and Wales) (Amendment) Regulations 2011, SI 2011/2043, regs 3, 9(1), (3).

[Chapter 1A
Further provision – death of sole operator][1]

[67A Death of sole operator

(1) This regulation applies if—
(a) an environmental permit authorising the operation of a regulated facility is held by one individual ("A"); and
(b) A dies.

(2) On the death of A, the environmental permit—
(a) forms part of A's personal estate;
(b) vests in A's personal representatives;
(c) continues to have effect subject to the conditions that applied at the time of A's death; and
(d) must be read as if it contained the following condition—

"As soon as is practicable after the death of the operator, the personal representatives of the operator must notify the regulator that the environmental permit has vested in them.".

(3) The environmental permit ceases to have effect 6 months after the day on which A dies, unless, by that time—
(a) the permit has been transferred under regulation 21; or
(b) the regulator has received from A's personal representatives a duly-made application under regulation 21(1) for the transfer of the permit, and the application has not been withdrawn or finally determined.

(4) If paragraph (3)(b) applies, the environmental permit continues in effect until the application—
(a) is withdrawn; or
(b) on determination, is refused.][1]

Amendments
1 Inserted by the Environmental Permitting (England and Wales) (Amendment) Regulations 2012, SI 2012/630, reg 9.

Chapter 2
Further provision - waste and extractive waste

68 Further provision in relation to waste and extractive waste

(1) Schedule 25 (waste and extractive waste) has effect.

(2) Section 33(1)(a) of the 1990 Act (prohibition on unauthorised deposit of waste)—
(a) does not apply to an operation which—
  (i) falls within a description in Part 3 of Schedule 25, and
  (ii) meets the conditions specified in that Part for an operation of that description; and
(b) does not apply to extractive waste at any time before the requirement for an environmental permit under regulation 12 applies in respect of the deposit of that waste.

Chapter 3
Transitional provisions - former enactments

69 Existing permits

On the coming into force of these Regulations an existing permit—

(a) becomes an environmental permit authorising the operation of a regulated facility under these Regulations; and
(b) has effect subject to any conditions that applied to it at the relevant time.

70 Site plans not required for existing permits

Regulation 14(4) does not apply in relation to a regulated facility—
(a) authorised by an environmental permit by virtue of regulation 69(a); or
(b) authorised by an environmental permit granted on the determination of—
  (i) a transitional application, or
  (ii) an outstanding appeal.

71 Review of existing groundwater permits

(1) Any environmental permit that, at the relevant time, was a permit within the meaning of the 2009 Regulations and was granted before the coming into force of those Regulations must be reviewed before 22nd December 2012.

(2) The regulator must on review assess compliance with the conditions of the permit.

(3) If the operator fails to comply with any condition of the permit, the regulator must take appropriate steps to ensure compliance.

[*Regulation 72 was repealed by the Environmental Permitting (England and Wales) (Amendment) Regulations 2011, SI 2011/2043, regs 3, 10.*]

[72A Previously excluded radioactive material and radioactive waste

(1) Paragraph (3) applies to a person ("A") who was carrying on an activity ("the continuing activity") described in paragraph (2) immediately before 1st October 2011 and who continues to carry on the activity on or after that date.

(2) The continuing activity referred to in paragraph (1) means an activity carried on by A—
(a) in respect of a substance or article which—
  (i) immediately before 1st October 2011 was not defined as radioactive material or radioactive waste; but
  (ii) on that date became defined as radioactive material or radioactive waste by virtue of the amendments made to those definitions on that date ("the relevant amendments");

  and
(b) which on that date became a radioactive substances activity described in paragraph 11(2), (4) or (5) of Part 2 of Schedule 23 by virtue of the relevant amendments.

(3) Where this paragraph applies, A is exempt from the requirement to hold an environmental permit in respect of the continuing activity until the end time set out in regulation 72C.][1]

Amendment

1 Inserted by the Environmental Permitting (England and Wales) (Amendment) Regulations 2011, SI 2011/2043, regs 3, 11.

[72B Previously exempt radioactive substances activities

(1) Paragraph (3) applies to a person ("A") who was carrying on an activity ("the continuing activity") described in paragraph (2) immediately before 1st October 2011 and who continues to carry on the activity on or after that date.

(2) The continuing activity referred to in paragraph (1) means an activity—

(a) described in paragraph 11(2), (4) or (5) of Part 2 of Schedule 23; and
(b) in respect of which, immediately before 1st October 2011, A was exempted under regulation 72 (as in force at that time) from the requirement to hold an environmental permit ("the existing exemption").

(3) Where this paragraph applies, the existing exemption continues to apply to A until the time set out in paragraph (4), subject to any conditions which applied to that exemption.

(4) The time referred to in paragraph (3) is—
(a) if A does not become exempt in respect of the continuing activity under a radioactive substances exemption before 1st April 2012, the end time set out in regulation 72C; or
(b) if A does become so exempt, the time at which the exemption begins to apply.][1]

Amendment

1 Inserted by the Environmental Permitting (England and Wales) (Amendment) Regulations 2011, SI 2011/2043, regs 3, 11.

[72C End time: regulations 72A and 72B

(1) For the purposes of regulations 72A and 72B, the end time is—
(a) where, before 1st April 2012, A makes a permit application—
   (i) if that application is granted, the time of grant;
   (ii) if that application is refused and—
      (aa) A appeals against the refusal under regulation 31, the time at which the appeal is determined or withdrawn;
      (bb) A does not appeal against the refusal, the end of the day which is the final appeal date;

   or
(b) where no such application is made, the earliest of—
   (i) 1st April 2012;
   (ii) the time at which A ceases to carry on the continuing activity; or
   (iii) for the purposes of regulation 72A only, the time a radioactive substances exemption first applies to A in respect of the continuing activity.

(2) In paragraph (1)—

"final appeal date" means the last day on which an appeal against a refusal to grant an environmental permit could have been brought under regulation 31, but not including any extension of the time limit for making an appeal allowed by the appropriate authority under paragraph 3(2) of Schedule 6; and

"permit application" means—
   (a) an application for an environmental permit under regulation 13 in respect of (as applicable) the continuing activity under regulation 72A or 72B; or
   (b) an application under regulation 20 for a variation of an existing environmental permit, in respect of the inclusion in the permit of that continuing activity.][1]

Amendment

1 Inserted by the Environmental Permitting (England and Wales) (Amendment) Regulations 2011, SI 2011/2043, regs 3, 11.

[72D Existing radioactive substances permits

(1) Paragraph (4) applies to a person ("A") who was carrying on an activity described in paragraph (2) ("the continuing excluded activity") or paragraph (3) ("the continuing exempt activity") immediately before 1st October 2011 and who—

(a) continues to carry on that activity after that date; and
(b) holds an environmental permit in respect of the activity ("permit A").

(2) The continuing excluded activity referred to in paragraph (1) means an activity which—
(a) was a radioactive substances activity immediately before 1st October 2011; but
(b) ceases to be such an activity on that date because it was carried on in respect of a substance or article which ceased to be defined as radioactive material or radioactive waste on that date by virtue of the amendments made to the definitions in these Regulations of radioactive material and radioactive waste on that date.

(3) The continuing exempt activity referred to in paragraph (1) means an activity—
(a) described in paragraph 11(2), 11(4) or 11(5) of Part 2 of Schedule 23 to these Regulations; and
(b) in respect of which A—
    (i) immediately before 1st October 2011, was not exempt under regulation 72 (as it was in force at that time); but
    (ii) is exempt under a radioactive substances exemption.

(4) Where this paragraph applies, subject to paragraph (5), A may surrender any part of permit A that applies to the continuing excluded activity or the continuing exempt activity by notification to the regulator.

(5) A notification under paragraph (4) must be made to the regulator on or before 31st March 2012.

(6) Regulation 24(3) to (7) applies as if the notification were made under that regulation.][1]

Amendment

1 Inserted by the Environmental Permitting (England and Wales) (Amendment) Regulations 2011, SI 2011/2043, regs 3, 11.

73 Exempt water discharge activities

(1) In this regulation, "small sewage effluent water discharge activity" means the discharge from a sewage treatment plant of 5 cubic metres per day or less of sewage effluent into inland freshwaters, coastal waters or relevant territorial waters.

(2) On the coming into force of these Regulations, a small sewage effluent water discharge activity authorised by an existing permit is taken to be an exempt facility.

74 Exempt groundwater activities

(1) In this regulation, "small sewage effluent groundwater activity" means the discharge from a septic tank or sewage treatment plant of 2 cubic metres per day or less of sewage effluent that results in the input of pollutants to groundwater.

(2) On the coming into force of these Regulations, a small sewage effluent groundwater activity authorised by an existing permit is taken to be an exempt facility.

(3) From the coming into force of these Regulations until 1st January 2012, a person carrying on a groundwater activity taken to be an exempt facility under paragraph (2) does not require an environmental permit unless a notice is served on that person under paragraph 10 of Schedule 22 and has taken effect.

(4) From the coming into force of these Regulations until 1st January 2012, a small sewage effluent groundwater activity that, at the relevant time, was not authorised by an existing permit does not need to be authorised by an environmental permit or registered as an exempt facility unless—

(a) a notice was served under the 2009 Regulations prohibiting the carrying on of the activity and that notice continues in effect under these Regulations; or
(b) a notice under paragraph 10 of Schedule 22 is served on the person carrying on the activity and the notice has taken effect.

(5) A small sewage effluent groundwater activity that is begun after the coming into force of these Regulations does not need to be authorised by an environmental permit or registered as an exempt facility until 1st January 2012 unless a notice under paragraph 10 of Schedule 22 is served on the person carrying on the activity and the notice has taken effect.

(6) On and after 1st January 2012, a person must not carry on a small sewage effluent groundwater activity unless it is—
(a) authorised by an environmental permit; or
(b) registered as an exempt facility.

75 Transitional applications

(1) On the coming into force of these Regulations, a transitional application is taken to be an application for the grant, variation, transfer or surrender of an environmental permit.

(2) The application is taken to be made on the date the transitional application was made.

(3) Anything done under a former enactment in relation to a transitional application before the coming into force of these Regulations is taken to be done under these Regulations.

(4) The public participation provisions apply to a transitional application under a former enactment unless—
(a) the transitional application relates to a radioactive substances activity; or
(b) under the former enactment there was no requirement for public participation in the application process.

76 Transfer notices under former enactments

(1) On the coming into force of these Regulations, a transfer notice is taken to be a joint notification under regulation 21(4).

(2) The joint notification is taken to be made on the date the transfer notice was made.

(3) Anything done under a former enactment in relation to a transfer notice before the coming into force of these Regulations is taken to be done under these Regulations.

77 Existing notices under former enactments

On the coming into force of these Regulations—
(a) an existing notice given under section 86(1)(b) of the 1991 Act in relation to a discharge from a highway drain or a discharge into the waters of any lake or pond which are not inland freshwaters becomes an environmental permit and has effect subject to any conditions that applied to it at the relevant time;
(b) any requirements imposed under an existing notice served under section 20 of the 1993 Act in relation to an existing authorisation or registration which becomes an environmental permit by virtue of regulation 69(a) are taken to be conditions of the environmental permit;
(c) an existing notice served under section 90B of the 1991 Act or section 21 of the 1993 Act is taken to be an enforcement notice served under these Regulations;
(d) an existing notice served under section 22 of the 1993 Act is taken to be a suspension notice served under these Regulations;

(e) an existing notice served under regulation 18 of the 2009 Regulations prohibiting a course of action is taken to be a prohibition notice served under these Regulations; and

(f) each of the following existing notices is taken to be a revocation notice served under these Regulations—

  (i) an existing notice served under paragraph 7(2)(a) of Schedule 10 to the 1991 Act (discharge consents),

  (ii) an existing notice served under regulation 16(5) of the 2009 Regulations (groundwater permits),

  (iii) an existing notice given under section 12(2)(a) of the 1993 Act (registrations) in relation to the cancellation of a registration,

  (iv) an existing notice given under section 17(3)(a) of the 1993 Act (authorisations) in relation to the revocation of an authorisation.

78 Outstanding appeals against existing notices

(1) Any outstanding appeal made under a former enactment against an existing notice is taken to be made under these Regulations.

(2) A notice of appeal under Schedule 6 is taken to be given on the date the outstanding appeal was made under the former enactment.

(3) Anything done under the former enactment in relation to the outstanding appeal is taken to be done under these Regulations.

(4) The time limits in Schedule 6 for doing anything in relation to an appeal apply in relation to the outstanding appeal unless, in any case, a longer time limit applied under the former enactment, in which case that time limit applies.

79 Appeals under these Regulations against existing notices

(1) An appeal may be made under these Regulations against an existing notice if, by the relevant time, the time for making an appeal under the former enactment had not expired.

(2) If an appeal is made under these Regulations against an existing notice, the applicable time limit for giving notice of appeal runs from the date the existing notice was served under the former enactment.

(3) In this regulation, the applicable time limit is—

(a) the time limit in paragraph 3 of Schedule 6; or

(b) if a longer time limit applied under the former enactment, that time limit.

80 Decisions under former enactments

A decision by a regulator or appropriate authority under a former enactment is taken to be made under these Regulations.

81 Outstanding appeals against decisions under former enactments

(1) Any outstanding appeal made under a former enactment against a decision under that enactment is taken to be made under these Regulations.

(2) A notice of appeal under Schedule 6 is taken to be given on the date the outstanding appeal was made under the former enactment.

(3) Anything done under the former enactment in relation to the outstanding appeal is taken to be done under these Regulations.

(4) The time limits in Schedule 6 for doing anything in relation to an appeal apply in relation to the outstanding appeal unless, in any case, a longer time limit applied under the former enactment, in which case that time limit applies.

82 Appeals under these Regulations against decisions under former enactments

(1) An appeal may be made under these Regulations against a decision under a former enactment if, by the relevant time, the time for making an appeal under the former enactment had not expired.

(2) If an appeal is made under these Regulations against a decision made under a former enactment, the applicable time limit for giving notice of appeal runs from the date the decision under the former enactment was made.

(3) In this regulation, the applicable time limit is—
(a) the time limit in paragraph 3 of Schedule 6; or
(b) if a longer time limit applied under the former enactment, that time limit.

83 Existing directions under former enactments

On the coming into force of these Regulations—
(a) an existing direction given to the Agency by the Secretary of State under section 23(1) of the 1993 Act is taken to be given under regulation 61; and
(b) an existing direction given to the Agency by the Secretary of State under section 24(1) of the 1993 Act is taken to be given under regulation 62.

84 Public registers under former enactments

(1) On the coming into force of these Regulations, the following information is taken to be information contained on a public register under these Regulations—
(a) any information that, at the relevant time—
  (i) was kept under section 39 of the 1993 Act, and
  (ii) was publicly available;
(b) any information in relation to discharge consents or groundwater permits that, at the relevant time, was kept under section 190 of the 1991 Act.

(2) The following decisions are taken to be final confidentiality decisions for the purposes of Part 5—
(a) a decision by the Agency under section 191B of the 1991 Act that information is commercially confidential in relation to any person;
(b) a decision by the Agency under section 39(1) of the 1993 Act not to disclose information relating to any relevant process or trade secret.

(3) For the purposes of regulation 55, a final confidentiality decision by virtue of paragraph (2) is taken to be made on the coming into force of these Regulations.

(4) The following directions are taken to be given under regulation 47(1)—
(a) a direction given under section 191A of the 1991 Act;
(b) a direction given under section 25 of the 1993 Act.

(5) A notification by the Agency under section 191A(3) of the 1991 Act is taken to be a notification under regulation 47(2).

85 Recovery of expenses for disposal of radioactive waste

(1) If, before the coming into force of these Regulations, the regulator disposed of radioactive waste in the exercise of its powers under section 30 of the 1993 Act but did

not recover all expenses reasonably incurred by it under that section, the regulator may recover expenses under paragraph 4(2) of Part 3 of Schedule 23 to these Regulations.

(2) If, before the coming into force of these Regulations, the regulator disposed of radioactive waste in the exercise of its powers under section 30A of the 1993 Act but did not recover all expenses reasonably incurred by it under that section, the regulator may recover expenses under paragraph 8(2) of Part 4 of Schedule 23 to these Regulations.

Chapter 4
Transitional provisions - the 2007 Regulations and former PPC or waste legislation

86 Existing environmental permits

On the coming into force of these Regulations, an existing environmental permit—
(a) becomes an environmental permit authorising the operation of a regulated facility under these Regulations; and
(b) has effect subject to any conditions that applied to it at the relevant time.

87 Applications under the 2007 Regulations

(1) If an application for the grant, variation, transfer or surrender of an environmental permit under the 2007 Regulations was not determined by the relevant time, the application is taken to be made under these Regulations.

(2) The application is taken to be made on the date the application was made under the 2007 Regulations.

(3) Anything done under the 2007 Regulations in relation to the application before the coming into force of these Regulations is taken to be done under these Regulations.

88 Applications for grant of PPC permit or waste management licence

(1) If the determination date for an application mentioned in regulation 70(1)(a) or (b) of the 2007 Regulations was not reached by the relevant time, the application is taken to be an application for the grant of an environmental permit.

(2) The application is taken to be made on the date the application was made under former PPC or waste legislation.

(3) Anything done under former PPC or waste legislation in relation to the application before the coming into force of these Regulations is taken to be done under these Regulations.

89 2007 transitional applications for grant of PPC permit, other than in relation to landfill

(1) This regulation applies where, by the relevant time—
(a) an existing licence, other than a licence the whole or part of which authorises the operation of a landfill and the carrying on of any related activity, was the subject of an application to which regulation 71 of the 2007 Regulations applied; and
(b) the determination date had not been reached.

(2) On the coming into force of these Regulations—
(a) the application is taken to be an application for the grant of an environmental permit; and

(b) pending determination of the application, the licence has effect—
  (i) as if it were an environmental permit, and
  (ii) subject to any conditions that applied to it at the relevant time.

(3) If on the determination of the application an environmental permit is granted, the licence—
(a) becomes an environmental permit; and
(b) has effect subject to any conditions imposed on it under these Regulations.

(4) If the application is withdrawn, or on the determination of the application an environmental permit is not granted, the licence no longer has effect.

90 2007 transitional applications for grant of PPC permit in relation to landfill

(1) This regulation applies where, by the relevant time—
(a) an existing licence the whole or part of which authorises the operation of a landfill and the carrying on of any related activity was the subject of an application to which regulation 71 of the 2007 Regulations applied; and
(b) the determination date had not been reached.

(2) On the coming into force of these Regulations—
(a) the application is taken to be an application for the grant of an environmental permit; and
(b) pending determination of the application, the licence (or that part of the licence relating to the landfill and any related activity) has effect—
  (i) as if it were an environmental permit, and
  (ii) subject to any conditions that applied to it at the relevant time.

(3) If on the determination of the application an environmental permit is granted, the licence—
(a) becomes an environmental permit authorising the operation of the landfill and the carrying on of any related activity; and
(b) has effect subject to any conditions imposed on it under these Regulations.

(4) If the application is withdrawn, or on the determination of the application an environmental permit is not granted, the licence (or that part of the licence relating to the landfill and any related activity)—
(a) becomes an environmental permit authorising the carrying on of any related activity; and
(b) has effect subject to closure and after-care obligations.

91 2007 transitional applications for grant of PPC permit in relation to landfill: applications determined under the 2007 Regulations

(1) This regulation applies where—
(a) an existing licence (or any part of an existing licence) authorising the operation of a landfill and the carrying on of any related activity was the subject of an application to which regulation 71 of the 2007 Regulations applied;
(b) the application was determined under those Regulations; and
(c) on the determination date, the licence did not become an environmental permit under those Regulations.

(2) On the coming into force of these Regulations, the licence (or that part of the licence relating to the landfill and any related activity)—
(a) becomes an environmental permit authorising the carrying on of any related activity; and
(b) has effect subject to closure and after-care obligations.

92 2007 transitional applications not relating to grant of PPC permit

(1) If a PPC permit or waste management licence was the subject of a 2007 transitional application for variation, transfer or surrender and by the relevant time the determination date had not been reached—

(a) on the coming into force of these Regulations, the permit or licence—
  (i) becomes an environmental permit, and
  (ii) has effect subject to any conditions that applied to it at the relevant time; and

(b) the application is taken to be an application for the variation, transfer or surrender of an environmental permit under these Regulations.

(2) If a waste management licence was the subject of a 2007 transitional application for modification and by the relevant time the determination date had not been reached—

(a) on the coming into force of these Regulations, the licence—
  (i) becomes an environmental permit, and
  (ii) has effect subject to any conditions that applied to it at the relevant time; and

(b) the application is taken to be an application for the variation of an environmental permit under these Regulations.

(3) The application is taken to be made on the date the 2007 transitional application was made.

(4) Anything done before the coming into force of these Regulations under the 2007 Regulations or former PPC or waste legislation in relation to a 2007 transitional application is taken to be done under these Regulations.

93 Notifications of surrender

On the coming into force of these Regulations, a notification that was given under regulation 24(2) of the 2007 Regulations that had not taken effect by the relevant time is taken to be a notification under regulation 24(2).

94 Existing notices under the 2007 Regulations or former PPC or waste legislation

On the coming into force of these Regulations—

(a) the following are taken to be enforcement notices—
  (i) an existing enforcement notice served under the 2007 Regulations,
  (ii) an existing notice served under regulation 24 of the PPC Regulations,
  (iii) an existing notice served under section 42(5) of the 1990 Act;

(b) the following are taken to be suspension notices—
  (i) an existing suspension notice served under the 2007 Regulations,
  (ii) an existing notice served under regulation 25 of the PPC Regulations,
  (iii) an existing notice served under section 38(6) of the 1990 Act;

(c) the following are taken to be revocation notices—
  (i) an existing revocation notice served under the 2007 Regulations,
  (ii) an existing notice served under regulation 21 of the PPC Regulations,
  (iii) an existing notice served under section 38(3) or (4) of the 1990 Act;

(d) an existing closure notice served under regulation 16 of the Landfill (England and Wales) Regulations 2002 is taken to be a landfill closure notice.

95 Outstanding appeals against existing notices

(1) Any outstanding appeal made under the 2007 Regulations or former PPC or waste legislation against an existing notice mentioned in regulation 94 is taken to be made under these Regulations.

(2) A notice of appeal under Schedule 6 is taken to be given on the date the outstanding appeal was made under the 2007 Regulations or former PPC or waste legislation.

(3) Anything done under the 2007 Regulations or former PPC or waste legislation in relation to the outstanding appeal is taken to be done under these Regulations.

(4) The time limits in Schedule 6 for doing anything in relation to an appeal apply in relation to the outstanding appeal unless, in any case, a longer time limit applied under the 2007 Regulations or former PPC or waste legislation, in which case that time limit applies.

96 Appeals under these Regulations against existing notices

(1) An appeal may be made under these Regulations against an existing notice mentioned in regulation 94 if, by the relevant time, the time for making an appeal under the 2007 Regulations or former PPC or waste legislation had not expired.

(2) If an appeal is made under these Regulations against an existing notice, the applicable time limit for giving notice of appeal runs from the date the existing notice was served under the 2007 Regulations or former PPC or waste legislation.

(3) In this regulation, the applicable time limit is—
(a) the time limit in paragraph 3 of Schedule 6; or
(b) if a longer time limit applied under the 2007 Regulations or former PPC or waste legislation, that time limit.

97 Decisions under the 2007 Regulations or former PPC or waste legislation

The following decisions are taken to be made under these Regulations—
(a) a decision by a regulator or appropriate authority under the 2007 Regulations;
(b) a decision by a regulator or appropriate authority under former PPC or waste legislation.

98 Outstanding appeals against decisions under the 2007 Regulations or former PPC or waste legislation

(1) Any outstanding appeal made under the 2007 Regulations or former PPC or waste legislation against a decision mentioned in regulation 97 is taken to be made under these Regulations.

(2) A notice of appeal under Schedule 6 is taken to be given on the date the outstanding appeal was made under the 2007 Regulations or former PPC or waste legislation.

(3) Anything done under the 2007 Regulations or former PPC or waste legislation in relation to the outstanding appeal is taken to be done under these Regulations.

(4) The time limits in Schedule 6 for doing anything in relation to an appeal apply in relation to the outstanding appeal unless, in any case, a longer time limit applied under the 2007 Regulations or former PPC or waste legislation, in which case that time limit applies.

99 Appeals under these Regulations against decisions under the 2007 Regulations or former PPC or waste legislation

(1) An appeal may be made under these Regulations against a decision mentioned in regulation 97 if, by the relevant time, the time for making an appeal under the 2007 Regulations or former PPC or waste legislation had not expired.

(2) If an appeal is made under these Regulations against a decision mentioned in regulation 97, the applicable time limit for giving notice of appeal runs from the date the decision was made under the 2007 Regulations or former PPC or waste legislation.

(3) In this regulation, the applicable time limit is—
(a) the time limit in paragraph 3 of Schedule 6; or
(b) if a longer time limit applied under the 2007 Regulations or former PPC or waste legislation, that time limit.

100 Other existing notices and instruments

(1) On the coming into force of these Regulations—
(a) an existing notice served under regulation 26(3) of the PPC Regulations is taken to be served under regulation 57(3);
(b) an existing notice served under regulation 28(1) of the PPC Regulations is taken to be a notice served under regulation 60(1); and
(c) any existing instrument served or given under the 2007 Regulations and not otherwise provided for in this Chapter is taken to be served or given under these Regulations.

(2) An existing notice or existing instrument remains in force—
(a) for the period (if any) specified in it; or
(b) until it is withdrawn, revoked or expires under these Regulations.

(3) In this regulation, "instrument" has the meaning given in regulation 10 of the 2007 Regulations.

101 Existing directions under the 2007 Regulations

(1) On the coming into force of these Regulations, any existing direction given to a regulator by the appropriate authority under any of the following provisions of the 2007 Regulations is taken to be given under the equivalent provision in these Regulations—
(a) regulation 31(7);
(b) regulation 33(1);
(c) regulation 47(1) or (3);
(d) regulation 56(1);
(e) regulation 61;
(f) regulation 62(1) or (6);
(g) regulation 63(2).

(2) Any information excluded from a public register pursuant to an existing direction given under regulation 47(1) of the 2007 Regulations is taken to be notified under regulation 47(2) of these Regulations.

102 Public registers

(1) Any information that, at the relevant time, was contained in a public register maintained by a regulator under the 2007 Regulations, or was deemed to be information kept on that register, is taken to be information contained in the public register maintained by the regulator under these Regulations.

(2) Any information that, at the relevant time, was within a regulator's possession for the purposes of regulation 46 of the 2007 Regulations but was not entered on a public register under those Regulations is taken to be in the regulator's possession for the purposes of these Regulations and must be entered on the register as soon as reasonably practicable.

103 Existing exempt waste operations

(1) This regulation applies to any establishment or undertaking which was carrying on an exempt waste operation under the 2007 Regulations as in force on 5th April 2010.

(2) The establishment or undertaking is taken to carry on an exempt waste operation under these Regulations until—

(a) the date mentioned in paragraph (3); or

(b) if before that date the waste operation ceases to be an exempt waste operation within the meaning of the 2007 Regulations as in force on 5th April 2010, the date on which it ceases to be such.

(3) The date mentioned in this paragraph is—

(a) if an application for the grant or variation of an environmental permit is made in relation to the waste operation on or before the date shown in the table set out below for the operation ("the indicated date")—

(i) if the application is granted, the date of the grant,

(ii) if the application is refused, and the applicant appeals against the refusal, the date the appeal is determined or withdrawn, or

(iii) if the application is refused, and the applicant does not appeal against the refusal, the day after the last day on which an appeal could have been brought under these Regulations;

(b) if the establishment or undertaking seeks to be registered in relation to the waste operation on or before the indicated date, the date of registration; or

(c) otherwise, the indicated date.

Waste operation	*Date*
A waste operation described in paragraph 9, 10, 12 or 19 of Part 1 of previous Schedule 3 that does not involve the disposal or recovery of agricultural waste on agricultural land	1st October 2011
A waste operation described in paragraph 13 or 21 of Part 1 of previous Schedule 3 that does not involve the disposal or recovery of agricultural waste on agricultural land	6th April 2012
A waste operation described in paragraph 7 of Part 1 of previous Schedule 3 that does not involve the disposal or recovery of agricultural waste on agricultural land	1st October 2012
A waste operation described in paragraph 4 to 6, 11, 14, 15, 17, 18, 20, 22, 23, 25, 29 to 32, 38, 40 to 42 or 46 of Part 1 of previous Schedule 3 that does not involve the disposal or recovery of waste on agricultural land	1st October 2012
A waste operation described in paragraph 2, 3, 8, 24 or 43 to 45 of Part 1 of previous Schedule 3	1st October 2013
A waste operation described in paragraph 7, 9, 10, 12, 13, 16, 19, 21, 28, 36, 37 or 47 of Part 1 of previous Schedule 3 that involves the disposal or recovery of agricultural waste on agricultural land	1st October 2013
Any other waste operation described in Part 1 of previous Schedule 3 that involves the disposal or recovery of waste on agricultural land	1st October 2013

(4) In this regulation—

"agricultural land" means land used for agriculture within the meaning of section 109(3) of the Agriculture Act 1947;

"previous Schedule 3" means Schedule 3 to the 2007 Regulations as in force on 5th April 2010;

"registered" has the meaning given in paragraph 1 of Schedule 2; and
"relevant particulars" has the meaning given in paragraph 6(3) of Schedule 2.

104 Existing Part A(1) installations

On the coming into force of these Regulations, an installation that, at the relevant time, carried on a Part A(1) activity under the 2007 Regulations by virtue of paragraph 2(4) of Part 1 of Schedule 1 to those Regulations is taken to be a Part A(1) installation for the purpose of these Regulations.

105 Existing mining waste operations

(1) Regulation 12(1) does not apply to an existing mining waste operation involving an existing mining waste facility until the date mentioned in paragraph (2).

(2) The date is—
(a) if an application for the grant or variation of an environmental permit is made on or before 1st May 2011—
   (i) if the application is granted, the date of the grant,
   (ii) if the application is refused, and the applicant appeals against the refusal, the date the appeal is determined or withdrawn,
   (iii) if the application is refused, and the applicant does not appeal against the refusal, the day after the last day on which an appeal could have been brought under these Regulations, or
   (iv) if the application is for the grant or variation of an environmental permit in relation to a Category A mining waste facility that is an existing mining waste facility and the application is refused pursuant to paragraph 14(2) of Schedule 20, the date of the refusal; or
(b) if no such application is made, 1st May 2011.

(3) Where an existing mining waste operation is not covered by paragraph (1), regulation 12(1) does not apply to that operation until the date mentioned in paragraph (4).

(4) The date is—
(a) if an application for the grant or variation of an environmental permit is made on or before 30th December 2010—
   (i) if the application is granted, the date of the grant,
   (ii) if the application is refused, and the applicant appeals against the refusal, the date the appeal is determined or withdrawn, or
   (iii) if the application is refused, and the applicant does not appeal against the refusal, the day after the last day on which an appeal could have been brought under these Regulations; or
(b) if no such application is made, 30th December 2010.

(5) In this regulation, "existing mining waste operation" means a mining waste operation subsisting on 1st May 2008.

Chapter 5
Savings and consequential provisions

106 Savings

(1) Despite the revocation of the 2007 Regulations, and the revocation of regulation 12(10) of the PPC Regulations by the 2007 Regulations, any condition implied in a permit by that regulation that continued in effect under the 2007 Regulations and had effect at the relevant time continues to have effect under these Regulations.

(2) Despite the revocation of regulation 44 of the End-of-Life Vehicles Regulations 2003 by the 2007 Regulations, any modification to a waste management licence that continued in effect under the 2007 Regulations and had effect at the relevant time continues to have effect under these Regulations.

(3) Despite the amendments made by regulation 6 of the Environmental Permitting (England and Wales) (Amendment) (No 2) Regulations 2009 (which amend regulation 38 of the 2007 Regulations), regulation 38(2) of the 2007 Regulations, as in force at the relevant time, continues in force for the purposes of regulation 103 of these Regulations.

(4) Despite the amendments made by regulation 13(2) of the Environmental Permitting (England and Wales) (Amendment) (No 2) Regulations 2009 (which amend section 41 of the 1995 Act by omitting subsection (2A) and by omitting the definition of "relevant environmental licence" in subsection (10)), those subsections, as in force at the relevant time, continue in force for the purposes of regulation 103 of these Regulations.

(5) Despite the substitution made by regulation 13(3) of the Environmental Permitting (England and Wales) (Amendment) (No 2) Regulations 2009 (which substitutes paragraph (j) in the definition of "environmental licence" in section 56(1) of the 1995 Act), the definition of "environmental licence" in that paragraph, as in force at the relevant time, continues in force for the purposes of regulation 103 of these Regulations.

[*Regulation 107 is not reproduced.*]

108 Revocations

(1) The instruments in Schedule 27 (revocations) are revoked to the extent specified.

(2) Despite the revocation of regulations 10 and 11 of the Environmental Permitting (England and Wales) (Amendment) (No 2) Regulations 2009, and of Schedules 2 and 3 to the 2007 Regulations, those Schedules (as in force at the relevant time) continue in force for the purpose of regulation 103 of these Regulations.

(3) Despite the revocation of regulation 68A of the 2007 Regulations, a condition implied in a permit by that regulation that had effect at the relevant time continues to have effect under these Regulations.

(4) Despite the revocation of regulation 69(5) and (6) of the 2007 Regulations, a condition implied in a permit by regulation 69(6) of those Regulations that had effect at the relevant time continues to have effect under these Regulations.

[*Regulation 109 is not reproduced.*]

[Chapter 6
Review][1]

[110 Review

(1) The Secretary of State, in relation to England, must from time to time—

(a) carry out a review of these Regulations;

(b) set out the conclusions of the review in a report; and

(c) publish the report.

(2) The report must in particular—

(a) set out the objectives intended to be achieved by the regulatory system established by these Regulations;

(b) assess the extent to which the objectives have been achieved; and

(c) assess whether the objectives remain appropriate and, if so, the extent to which they could be achieved with a system that imposes less regulation.

(3) The first report under this regulation must be published before the end of the period of 5 years beginning with 6th April 2012.

(4) Reports under this regulation are afterwards to be published at intervals not exceeding 5 years.]1

Amendment

1 Inserted by the Environmental Permitting (England and Wales) (Amendment) Regulations 2012, SI 2012/630, reg 11.

SCHEDULE 1
ACTIVITIES, INSTALLATIONS AND MOBILE PLANT

Regulation 2(1)

PART 1
INTERPRETATION AND APPLICATION: GENERAL

1 Interpretation

In this Schedule—

"activity" means, subject to this Part, an activity listed in Part 2 of this Schedule;

"background quantity" means, in relation to the release of a substance resulting from an activity, such quantity of that substance as is present in—

(a) water supplied to the site where the activity is carried on,

(b) water abstracted for use in the activity, and

(c) precipitation onto the site on which the activity is carried on;

"controlled waters" has the meaning given in section 104 of the 1991 Act;

"directly associated activity", in relation to an activity other than a SED activity, means an operation which—

(a) has a technical connection with the activity,

(b) is carried on on the same site as the activity, and

(c) could have an effect on pollution;

"installation" means (except where used in the definition of "excluded plant" in Section 5.1 of Part 2 of this Schedule)—

(a) a stationary technical unit where one or more activities are carried on, and

(b) any other location on the same site where any other directly associated activities are carried on,

and references to an installation include references to part of an installation;

"net rated thermal input" means the rate at which fuel can be burned at the maximum continuous rating of the appliance multiplied by the net calorific value of the fuel and expressed as megawatts thermal;

"Part A activity" means a Part A(1) activity or a Part A(2) activity;

"Part A(1) activity" means an activity falling within Part A(1) of any Section in Part 2 of this Schedule;

"Part A(2) activity" means an activity falling within Part A(2) of any Section in Part 2 of this Schedule;

"Part A installation" means a Part A(1) installation or a Part A(2) installation;

"Part A(1) installation" means an installation where there is carried on—

(a) a Part A(1) activity,

(b) a Part A(1) activity and either a Part A(2) activity or a Part B activity, or

(c) a Part A(1) activity, a Part A(2) activity and a Part B activity;

"Part A(2) installation" means an installation, not being a Part A(1) installation, where there is carried on—

(a) a Part A(2) activity, or
(b) a Part A(2) activity and a Part B activity;

"Part A mobile plant" means Part A(1) mobile plant or Part A(2) mobile plant;

"Part A(1) mobile plant" means plant, other than an installation, that is used to carry on—

(a) a Part A(1) activity,
(b) a Part A(1) activity and either a Part A(2) activity or a Part B activity, or
(c) a Part A(1) activity, a Part A(2) activity and a Part B activity;

"Part A(2) mobile plant" means plant, other than an installation, that is used to carry on—

(a) a Part A(2) activity, or
(b) a Part A(2) activity and a Part B activity;

"Part B activity" means an activity falling within Part B of any Section in Part 2 of this Schedule;

"Part B installation" means, subject to Sections 2.2, 5.1 and 6.4 of Part 2 of this Schedule, an installation, not being a Part A installation, where a Part B activity is carried on; and

"Part B mobile plant" means plant, not being Part A mobile plant, that is designed to move or be moved whether on roads or other land and that is used to carry on a Part B activity.

2 Activities falling within more than one Part description

(1) Where, in Part 2 of this Schedule, an activity falls within a description in Part A(1) and a description in Part A(2) that activity must be regarded as falling only within that description which fits it most aptly.

(2) Where, in Part 2 of this Schedule, an activity falls within a description in Part A(1) and a description in Part B (other than a description in Section 7) that activity must be regarded as falling only within the description in Part A(1).

(3) Where, in Part 2 of this Schedule, an activity falls within a description in Part A(2) and a description in Part B (other than a description in Section 7) that activity must be regarded as falling only within the description in Part A(2).

3 Application of activities falling within Sections 1.1 to 6.9 of Part 2

An activity is not to be taken to be an activity falling within Sections 1.1 to 6.9 of Part 2 of this Schedule if it is—

(a) carried on in a working museum to demonstrate an industrial activity of historic interest;
(b) carried on for educational purposes in a school as defined in section 4(1) of the Education Act 1996;
(c) carried on at an installation or by means of Part A mobile plant or Part B mobile plant solely used for research, development and testing of new products and processes;
(d) the running on or within an aircraft, hovercraft, mechanically propelled road vehicle, railway locomotive or ship or other vessel of an engine which propels or provides electricity for it;
(e) the running of an engine in order to test it before it is installed or in the course of its development; or
(f) carried on as a domestic activity in connection with a private dwelling.

4 Capacity: Part A(1) and A(2) descriptions

(1) This paragraph applies for the purpose of determining whether an activity carried on in a stationary technical unit falls within a description in Part A(1) or Part A(2) of Part 2 of this Schedule which refers to capacity, other than design holding capacity.

(2) Where a person carries out several activities falling within the same description in Part A(1) or Part A(2) in different parts of the same stationary technical unit or in different stationary technical units on the same site, the capacities of each part or unit, as the case may be, must be added together and the total capacity must be attributed to each part or unit for the purpose of determining whether the activity carried on in each part or unit falls within a description in Part A(1) or Part A(2).

(3) For the purpose of sub-paragraph (2), no account must be taken of capacity when determining whether activities fall within the same description.

(4) Where an activity falls within a description in Part A(1) or Part A(2) by virtue of this paragraph it is not to be taken to be an activity falling within a description in Part B (other than a description in Section 7).

5 Operation below thresholds: effect on the installation

Where an operator is authorised by an environmental permit to operate an installation at which Part A(1) activities, Part A(2) activities or Part B activities which are described in Part 2 of this Schedule by reference to a threshold (whether in terms of capacity or otherwise) are carried on, the installation does not cease to be a Part A(1) installation, a Part A(2) installation or a Part B installation, as the case may be, by virtue of the installation being operated below the relevant threshold unless the permit ceases to have effect in accordance with these Regulations.

6 Application of Part B activities: releases into the air

(1) Subject to sub-paragraph (2), an activity is not to be taken to be a Part B activity within Part 2 of this Schedule if it cannot result in the release into the air of a substance listed in sub-paragraph (3) or there is no likelihood that it will result in the release into the air of any such substance except in a quantity which is so trivial that it is incapable of causing pollution or its capacity to cause pollution is insignificant.

(2) Sub-paragraph (1) does not apply to—
(a) a SED activity; or
(b) an activity which may give rise to an offensive smell noticeable outside the site where the activity is carried on.

(3) References to, or to the release into the air of, a substance listed in this paragraph are to any of the following substances—
(a) oxides of sulphur and other sulphur compounds;
(b) oxides of nitrogen and other nitrogen compounds;
(c) oxides of carbon;
(d) organic compounds and partial oxidation products;
(e) metals, metalloids and their compounds;
(f) asbestos (suspended particulate matter and fibres), glass fibres and mineral fibres;
(g) halogens and their compounds;
(h) phosphorus and its compounds;
(i) particulate matter.

7 References to releases into water

References in Part 2 of this Schedule to a substance, or to the release into water of a substance, listed in this paragraph or to its release in a quantity which, in any 12-month period, is greater than the background quantity by an amount specified in this paragraph are references to the following substances and amounts—

Substance	*Amount greater than the background quantity (in grammes) in any 12-month period*
Mercury and its compounds	200 (expressed as metal)
Cadmium and its compounds	1,000 (expressed as metal)
All isomers of hexachlorocyclohexane	20
All isomers of DDT	5
Pentachlorophenol and its compounds	350 (expressed as PCP)
Hexachlorobenzene	5
Hexachlorobutadiene	20
Aldrin	2
Dieldrin	2
Endrin	1
Polychlorinated Biphenyls	1
Dichlorvos	0.2
1, 2—Dichloroethane	2,000
All isomers of trichlorobenzene	75
Atrazine	350*
Simazine	350*
Tributyltin compounds	4 (expressed as TBT)
Triphenyltin compounds	4 (expressed as TPT)
Trifluralin	20
Fenitrothion	2
Azinphos-methyl	2
Malathion	2
Endosulfan	0.5

* Where both Atrazine and Simazine are released, the figure for both substances in aggregate is 350 grammes.

8 References to certain substances

(1) References in Part 2 of this Schedule to a substance listed in this paragraph are to any of the following substances—

(a) alkali metals and their oxides and alkaline earth metals and their oxides;
(b) organic solvents;
(c) azides;
(d) halogens and their covalent compounds;
(e) metal carbonyls;
(f) organo-metallic compounds;
(g) oxidising agents;
(h) polychlorinated dibenzofuran and any congener thereof;
(i) polychlorinated dibenzo-p-dioxin and any congener thereof;
(j) polyhalogenated biphenyls, terphenyls and naphthalenes;
(k) phosphorus;
(l) pesticides.

(2) In this paragraph, "pesticide" means any chemical substance or preparation prepared or used for destroying any pest, including those used for—

(a) protecting plants or wood or other plant products from harmful organisms;
(b) regulating the growth of plants;
(c) giving protection against harmful creatures or rendering such creatures harmless;

(d) controlling organisms with harmful or unwanted effects on water systems, buildings or other structures, or on manufactured products; or
(e) protecting animals against ectoparasites.

PART 2
ACTIVITIES

Chapter 1
Energy activities

Section 1.1
Combustion activities

Interpretation of Section 1.1

[1

In this Section—

"anaerobic digestion" means the mesophilic and thermophilic biological decomposition and stabilisation of biodegradable materials which—

(a) is carried on under controlled anaerobic conditions,
(b) produces a methane-rich gas mixture, and
(c) results in stable sanitised material that can be applied to land for the benefit of agriculture or to improve the soil structure or nutrients in land; and

"recovered oil" means waste oil which has been processed but which has not ceased to be waste.][1]

Amendment

1 Inserted by the Environmental Permitting (England and Wales) (Amendment) Regulations 2012, SI 2012/630, reg 12(1), (2)(a).

Part A(1)

(a) Burning any fuel in an appliance with a rated thermal input of 50 or more megawatts.
(b) Unless carried on as part of a Part A(2) or Part B activity, burning any—
(i) waste oil;
(ii) recovered oil; or
(iii) fuel manufactured from, or comprising, any other waste,
in an appliance with a rated thermal input of 3 or more megawatts, but less than 50 megawatts.

Interpretation and application of Part A(1)

1

For the purpose of Part A(1)(a) of this Section, where 2 or more appliances with an aggregate rated thermal input of 50 megawatts or more are operated on the same site by the same operator those appliances must be treated as a single appliance with a rated thermal input of 50 megawatts or more.

2

Nothing in this Part of this Section applies to burning fuels in an appliance installed on an offshore platform situated on, above or below those parts of the sea adjacent to England and Wales from the low water mark to the seaward baseline of the United Kingdom territorial sea.

3

In paragraph 2, "offshore platform" means any fixed or floating structure which—

(a) is used for the purposes of or in connection with the production of petroleum; and

(b) in the case of a floating structure, is maintained on a station during the course of production,

but does not include any structure where the principal purpose of the use of the structure is the establishment of the existence of petroleum or the appraisal of its characteristics, quality or quantity or the extent of any reservoir in which it occurs.

4

In paragraph 3, "petroleum" includes any mineral oil or relative hydrocarbon and natural gas existing in its natural condition in strata but does not include coal or bituminous shales or other stratified deposits from which oil can be extracted by destructive distillation.

[5

In Part A(1)(b)(iii) of this Section, "fuel" excludes—

(a) gas produced by biological degradation of waste in a landfill that is not listed in Part 2 of this Schedule,

(b) gas produced as a result of the anaerobic digestion of biodegradable waste, and

(c) fuel which has ceased to be waste.][1]

[6

Nothing in this Part of this Section applies to burning fuels in an appliance installed on a storage or unloading platform as defined in regulation 2 of the Offshore Combustion Installations (Prevention and Control of Pollution) Regulations 2001.][2]

Amendments

1 Substituted by the Environmental Permitting (England and Wales) (Amendment) Regulations 2012, SI 2012/630, reg 12(1), (2)(b).

2 Inserted by the Environmental Permitting (England and Wales) (Amendment) Regulations 2012, SI 2012/630, reg 12(1), (2)(c).

Part B

Unless falling within Part A(1)(a) of this Section—

(a) Burning any fuel (other than a fuel mentioned in Part A(1)(b)) in—

  (i) a boiler;

  (ii) a furnace;

  (iii) a gas turbine; or

  (iv) a compression ignition engine,

  with a net rated thermal input of 20 or more megawatts, but a rated thermal input of less than 50 megawatts.

(b) Burning any—

  (i) waste oil;

  (ii) recovered oil;

  (iii) solid fuel which has been manufactured from waste by an activity involving the application of heat,

  in an appliance with a rated thermal input of less than 3 megawatts.

(c) Burning fuel manufactured from or including waste (other than a fuel mentioned in paragraph (b)) in an appliance with a net rated thermal input of 0.4 or more megawatts, but a rated thermal input of less than 3 megawatts.

(d) Burning fuel manufactured from or including waste (other than a fuel mentioned in paragraph (b)) in 2 or more appliances which have a combined net rated thermal input of 0.4 or more megawatts, but a rated thermal input of less than 3 megawatts.

Interpretation and application of Part B

1

Part B does not apply to any activity falling within Part A(1) or Part A(2) of Section 5.1.

[2

In Part B(b)(iii), (c) or (d) of this Section—
"fuel" excludes—

(a) gas produced by biological degradation of waste, and
(b) fuel which has ceased to be waste.][1]

Amendment

1 Substituted by the Environmental Permitting (England and Wales) (Amendment) Regulations 2012, SI 2012/630, reg 12(1), (2)(d).

Section 1.2
Gasification, Liquefaction and Refining Activities

Part A(1)

(a) Refining gas where this is likely to involve the use of 1,000 or more tonnes of gas in any 12-month period.
(b) Reforming natural gas.
(c) Operating coke ovens.
(d) Coal or lignite gasification.
[(e) Producing gas from oil or other carbonaceous material or from mixtures of oil and other carbonaceous material, unless the production is carried on as part of an activity which is a combustion activity (whether or not that combustion activity is described in Section 1.1), or the gas is produced as a result of—
  (i) the anaerobic digestion of biodegradable material, none of which is waste, or
  (ii) the anaerobic digestion of biodegradable waste in an installation with a waste treatment capacity not exceeding 100 tonnes per day.][1]
(f) Purifying or refining any product of any of the activities falling within paragraphs (a) to (e) or converting it into a different product.
(g) Refining mineral oils.
(h) The loading, unloading, handling or storage of, or the physical, chemical or thermal treatment of—
  (i) crude oil;
  (ii) stabilised crude petroleum;
  (iii) crude shale oil;
  (iv) where related to another activity described in this paragraph, any associated gas or condensate; or
  (v) emulsified hydrocarbons intended for use as a fuel.
(i) The further refining, conversion or use (otherwise than as a fuel or solvent) of the product of any activity falling within paragraph (g) or (h) in the manufacture of a chemical.
(j) Activities involving the pyrolysis, carbonisation, distillation, liquefaction, gasification, partial oxidation or other heat treatment of—
  (i) coal (other than the drying of coal);
  (ii) lignite;
  (iii) oil;
  (iv) other carbonaceous material; or
  (v) mixtures of any of these,
  otherwise than with a view to making charcoal.

(k) Odorising natural gas or liquefied petroleum gas where that activity is related to a Part A activity.

Amendment

1 Substituted by the Environmental Permitting (England and Wales) (Amendment) Regulations 2012, SI 2012/630, reg 12(1), (3)(a).

Interpretation and application of Part A(1)

1

Part A(1)(j) does not include—

(a) the use of any substance as a fuel;

(b) the incineration of any substance as a waste;

[(c) any activity for the treatment of sewage or sewage sludge;

(d) the anaerobic digestion of biodegradable material, none of which is waste; or

(e) the anaerobic digestion of biodegradable waste in an installation with a waste treatment capacity not exceeding 100 tonnes per day.][1]

2

In Part A(1)(j), the heat treatment of oil, other than distillation, does not include the heat treatment of waste oil or waste emulsions containing oil in order to recover the oil from aqueous emulsions.

[3

In Part A(1)—

"anaerobic digestion" means the mesophilic and thermophilic biological decomposition and stabilisation of biodegradable materials which—

(a) is carried on under controlled anaerobic conditions,

(b) produces a methane-rich gas mixture, and

(c) results in stable sanitised material that can be applied to land for the benefit of agriculture or to improve the soil structure or nutrients in land; and

"carbonaceous material" includes such materials as charcoal, coke, peat, rubber and wood, but does not include wood which has not been chemically treated or sewage.][1]

Amendment

1 Substituted by the Environmental Permitting (England and Wales) (Amendment) Regulations 2012, SI 2012/630, reg 12(1), (3)(b), (c).

Part A(2)

(a) Refining gas where this activity does not fall within Part A(1)(a) of this Section.

Part B

(a) Blending odorant for use with natural gas or liquefied petroleum gas.

(b) The storage of petrol in stationary storage tanks at a terminal, or the loading or unloading at a terminal of petrol into or from road tankers, rail tankers or inland waterway vessels.

(c) The unloading of petrol into stationary storage tanks at a service station, if the total quantity of petrol unloaded into such tanks at the service station in any 12-month period is likely to be $500m^3$ or more.

[(d) Motor vehicle refuelling activities at an existing service station after the prescribed date, if the throughput of petrol at that service station in any 12 month period is in excess of $3000\ m^3$.

(e) Motor vehicle refuelling activities at a new service station, if the throughput of petrol at that service station in any 12 month period is, or is intended to be in excess of 500 m^3.][1]

[(f) Motor vehicle refuelling activities at a new service station if the throughput of petrol at that service station in any 12 month period is, or is likely to be in excess of 100 m^3 and it is situated under permanent living quarters or working areas.

(g) Any service station which undergoes a major refurbishment must be treated as a new service station.][2]

Amendments

1 Substituted by the Environmental Permitting (England and Wales) (Amendment) (No. 2) Regulations 2011, SI 2011/2933, reg 2(1), (2)(a).

2 Inserted by the Environmental Permitting (England and Wales) (Amendment) (No. 2) Regulations 2011, SI 2011/2933, reg 2(1), (2)(b).

Interpretation of Part B

1

In Part B—

"existing service station" means a service station—

(a) which was put into operation; or

(b) for which planning permission under the Town and Country Planning Act 1990 was granted,

before 31st December 2009;

"inland waterway vessel" means a vessel, other than a sea-going vessel, having a total dead weight of 15 or more tonnes;

["new service station" means, in relation to service stations to which paragraph (e) of Part B applies, those which are put into operation on or after 1st January 2010, and in relation to service stations to which paragraph (f) of Part B applies, those which are put into operation on or after 1st January 2012;][1]

"petrol" means any petroleum derivative (other than liquefied petroleum gas), with or without additives, having a Reid vapour pressure of 27.6 or more kilopascals, which is intended for use as a fuel for motor vehicles;

["prescribed date" means 31st December 2011 if the throughput is in excess of 3500 m^3 and 31st December 2018 if the throughput is in excess of 3000 m^3;][1]

"service station" means any premises where petrol is dispensed to motor vehicle fuel tanks from stationary storage tanks[but does not include any service station exclusively used in association with the construction and delivery of new motor vehicles][2];

"terminal" means any premises which are used for the storage and loading of petrol into road tankers, rail tankers or inland waterway vessels.

[2

Any other expressions used in Part B which, in relation to paragraphs (b) and (c), are also used in Directive 94/63/EC on the control of volatile organic compound (VOC) emissions resulting from the storage of petrol and its distribution from terminals to service stations, or in relation to paragraphs (d) to (g), are also used in Directive 2009/126/EC on Stage II petrol vapour recovery during refuelling of motor vehicles at service stations have the same meaning as in those Directives.][1]

Amendments

1 Substituted by the Environmental Permitting (England and Wales) (Amendment) (No. 2) Regulations 2011, SI 2011/2933, reg 2(1), (3)(a), (b), (d).

2 Inserted by the Environmental Permitting (England and Wales) (Amendment) (No. 2) Regulations 2011, SI 2011/2933, reg 2(1), (3)(c).

Chapter 2
Production and Processing of Metals

Section 2.1
Ferrous Metals

Interpretation of Section 2.1

1

In this Section, "ferrous alloy" means an alloy of which iron is the largest constituent, or equal to the largest constituent, by weight, whether or not that alloy also has a non-ferrous metal content greater than any percentage specified in Section 2.2.

Part A(1)

(a) Roasting or sintering metal ore, including sulphide ore, or any mixture of iron ore with or without other materials.
(b) Producing, melting or refining iron or steel or any ferrous alloy, including continuous casting, except where the only furnaces used are—
  (i) electric arc furnaces with a designed holding capacity of less than 7 tonnes, or
  (ii) cupola, crucible, reverbatory, rotary, induction, vacuum, electro-slag or resistance furnaces.
(c) Processing ferrous metals and their alloys by using hot-rolling mills with a production capacity of more than 20 tonnes of crude steel per hour.
(d) Loading, unloading or otherwise handling or storing more than 500,000 tonnes in total in any 12-month period of iron ore, except in the course of mining operations, or burnt pyrites.

Part A(2)

(a) Unless falling within Part A(1)(b) of this Section, producing pig iron or steel, including continuous casting, in a plant with a production capacity of more than 2.5 tonnes per hour.
(b) Operating hammers in a forge, the energy of which is more than 50 kilojoules per hammer, where the calorific power used is more than 20 megawatts.
(c) Applying protective fused metal coatings with an input of more than 2 tonnes of crude steel per hour.
(d) Casting ferrous metal at a foundry with a production capacity of more than 20 tonnes per day.

Part B

(a) Unless falling within Part A(1)(b) of this Section, producing pig iron or steel, including continuous casting, in a plant with a production capacity of 2.5 or less tonnes per hour.
(b) Unless falling within Part A(2)(a) or (d) of this Section, producing, melting or refining iron or steel or any ferrous alloy (other than producing pig iron or steel, including continuous casting) using—
  (i) one or more electric arc furnaces, none of which has a designed holding capacity of 7 or more tonnes; or
  (ii) a cupola, crucible, reverberatory, rotary, induction, electro-slag or resistance furnace.
(c) Desulphurising iron, steel or any ferrous alloy.
(d) Heating iron, steel or any ferrous alloy (whether in a furnace or other appliance) to remove grease, oil or any other non-metallic contaminant (including such operations as the removal by heat of plastic or rubber covering from scrap cable) unless—

(i) it is carried on in one or more furnaces or other appliances the primary combustion chambers of which have in aggregate a rated thermal input of less than 0.2 megawatts;

(ii) it does not involve the removal by heat of plastic or rubber covering from scrap cable or of any asbestos contaminant; and

(iii) it is not related to any other activity falling within this Part of this Section.

(e) Unless falling within Part A(1) or Part A(2) of this Section, casting iron, steel or any ferrous alloy from deliveries of 50 or more tonnes of molten metal.

Section 2.2
Non-Ferrous Metals

Interpretation and application of Section 2.2

1

In this Section "non-ferrous metal alloy" means an alloy which is not a ferrous alloy, as defined in Section 2.1.

2

Part A(1)(c) to (h) and Part B do not apply to hand soldering, flow soldering or wave soldering.

Part A(1)

(a) Unless falling within Part A(2) of this Section, producing non-ferrous metals from ore, concentrates or secondary raw materials by metallurgical, chemical or electrolytic activities.

(b) Melting, including making alloys, of non-ferrous metals, including recovered products (such as refining or foundry casting) where—

(i) the plant has a melting capacity of more than 4 tonnes per day for lead or cadmium or 20 tonnes per day for all other metals; and

(ii) any furnace (other than a vacuum furnace), bath or other holding vessel used in the plant for the melting has a design holding capacity of 5 or more tonnes.

(c) Except where the activity is related to an activity described in Part A(2)(a), or Part B(a), (d) or (e) of this Section, refining any non-ferrous metal or alloy, other than the electrolytic refining of copper.

(d) Producing, melting or recovering by chemical means or by the use of heat, lead or any lead alloy, if—

(i) the activity may result in the release into the air of lead; and

(ii) in the case of lead alloy, the percentage by weight of lead in the alloy in molten form is more than 23 per cent if the alloy contains copper and 2 per cent in other cases.

(e) Recovering any gallium, indium, palladium, tellurium or thallium if the activity may result in their release into the air.

(f) Producing, melting or recovering (whether by chemical means or by electrolysis or by the use of heat) cadmium or mercury or any alloy containing more than 0.05 per cent by weight of either of those metals or both in aggregate.

(g) Mining zinc- or tin-bearing ores where the activity may result in the release into water of cadmium or any compound of cadmium in a concentration which is greater than the background concentration.

(h) Manufacturing or repairing involving the use of beryllium or selenium or an alloy containing one or both of those metals, if the activity may result in the release into the air of any substance in paragraph 6(3) of Part 1 of this Schedule; but an activity does not fall within this paragraph by reason of it involving an alloy that contains beryllium if that alloy in molten form contains less than 0.1 per cent by weight of beryllium and the activity falls within Part B(a) or (d) of this Section.

(i) Pelletising, calcining, roasting or sintering any non-ferrous metal ore or any mixture of such ore and other materials.

Interpretation of Part A(1)

1

In Part A(1)(g), "background concentration" means any concentration of cadmium or any compound of cadmium which would be present in the release irrespective of any effect the activity may have had on the composition of the release and includes such concentration of those substances as is present in—

(a) water supplied to the site where the activity is carried on;
(b) water abstracted for use in the activity; and
(c) precipitation onto the site on which the activity is carried on.

Part A(2)

[(a) Melting, including making alloys, of non-ferrous metals, including recovered products (such as refining or foundry casting) where the plant has a melting capacity of more than 4 tonnes per day for lead or cadmium or 20 tonnes per day for all other metals, and
  (i) no furnace (other than a vacuum furnace), bath or other holding vessel used in the plant for the melting has a design holding capacity of 5 or more tonnes; or
  (ii) the plant uses a vacuum furnace of any design holding capacity.][1]

Amendment

1 Substituted by the Environmental Permitting (England and Wales) (Amendment) (No. 2) Regulations 2010, SI 2010/2172, reg 2(1), (2).

Part B

(a) Melting, including making alloys, of non-ferrous metals (other than tin or any alloy which in molten form contains 50 per cent or more by weight of tin), including recovered products (such as refining or foundry casting) in plant with a melting capacity of 4 tonnes or less per day for lead or cadmium or 20 tonnes or less per day for all other metals.
(b) The heating in a furnace or any other appliance of any non-ferrous metal or non-ferrous metal alloy for the purpose of removing grease, oil or any other non-metallic contaminant, including such operations as the removal by heat of plastic or rubber covering from scrap cable, if not related to another activity described in this Part of this Section; but an activity does not fall within this paragraph if—
  (i) it involves the use of one or more furnaces or other appliances the primary combustion chambers of which have in aggregate a net rated thermal input of less than 0.2 megawatts; and
  (ii) it does not involve the removal by heat of plastic or rubber covering from scrap cable or of any asbestos contaminant.
(c) Melting zinc or a zinc alloy in conjunction with a galvanising activity at a rate of 20 or less tonnes per day.
(d) Melting zinc, aluminium or magnesium or an alloy of one or more of these metals in conjunction with a die-casting activity at a rate of 20 or less tonnes per day.
(e) Unless falling within Part A(1) or Part A(2) of this Section, the separation of copper, aluminium, magnesium or zinc from mixed scrap by differential melting.

Interpretation and application of Part B

1

When determining the extent of an installation carrying on an activity within Part B(e), any location where the associated storage or handling of scrap which is to be heated as part of that activity is carried on, other than a location where scrap is loaded into a furnace, is to be ignored.

Section 2.3
Surface Treating Metals and Plastic Materials

Part A(1)

(a) Unless falling within Part A(2) of this Section, surface treating metals and plastic materials using an electrolytic or chemical process where the aggregated volume of the treatment vats is more than $30m^3$.

Part A(2)

(a) Surface treating metals and plastic materials using an electrolytic or chemical process where the aggregated volume of the treatment vats is more than $30m^3$ and where the activity is carried on at the same installation as one or more activities falling within—
  (i) Part A(2) or Part B of Section 2.1;
  (ii) Part A(2) or Part B of Section 2.2; or
  (iii) Part A(2) or Part B of Section 6.4.

Part B

(a) Any process for the surface treatment of metal which is likely to result in the release into air of any acid-forming oxide of nitrogen and which does not fall within Part A(1) or Part A(2) of this Section.

Chapter 3
Mineral Industries

Section 3.1
Production of Cement and Lime

Part A(1)

(a) Producing cement clinker or producing and grinding cement clinker.
(b) Producing lime—
  (i) in kilns or other furnaces with a production capacity of more than 50 tonnes per day; or
  (ii) if the activity is likely to involve the heating in any 12-month period of 5,000 or more tonnes of calcium carbonate or calcium magnesium carbonate or both in aggregate.

Part A(2)

(a) Unless falling with Part A(1) of this Section, grinding cement clinker.
(b) Unless falling within Part A(1) of Section 2.1 or 2.2, grinding metallurgical slag in plant with a grinding capacity of more than 250,000 tonnes in any 12-month period.

Part B

(a) Storing, loading or unloading cement or cement clinker in bulk prior to further transportation in bulk.
(b) Blending cement in bulk or using cement in bulk other than at a construction site, including the bagging of cement and cement mixtures, the batching of ready-mixed concrete and the manufacture of concrete blocks and other cement products.
(c) Slaking lime for the purpose of making calcium hydroxide or calcium magnesium hydroxide.
(d) Producing lime where the activity is not likely to involve the heating in any 12-month period of 5,000 or more tonnes of calcium carbonate or calcium magnesium carbonate or both in aggregate.

Section 3.2
Activities Involving Asbestos

Interpretation of Section 3.2

1

In this Section "asbestos" means any of the following fibrous silicates: actinolite, amosite, anthophyllite, chrysotile, crocidolite and tremolite.

Part A(1)

(a) Producing asbestos or manufacturing products based on or containing asbestos.
(b) Stripping asbestos from railway vehicles except—
 (i) in the course of the repair or maintenance of the vehicle;
 (ii) in the course of recovery operations following an accident; or
 (iii) where the asbestos is permanently bonded in cement or in any other material (including plastic, rubber or resin).
(c) Destroying a railway vehicle by burning if asbestos has been incorporated in, or sprayed on to, its structure.

Part B

(a) Unless related to an activity falling within Part A(1) of this Section, the industrial finishing of—
 (i) asbestos cement;
 (ii) asbestos cement products;
 (iii) asbestos fillers;
 (iv) asbestos filters;
 (v) asbestos floor coverings;
 (vi) asbestos friction products;
 (vii) asbestos insulating board;
 (viii) asbestos jointing, packaging or reinforcement material;
 (ix) asbestos packing;
 (x) asbestos paper or card; or
 (xi) asbestos textiles.

Section 3.3
Manufacturing Glass and Glass Fibre

Part A(1)

(a) Manufacturing glass fibre.
(b) Manufacturing glass frit or enamel frit and its use in any activity where that activity is related to its manufacture and the aggregate quantity of such substances manufactured in any 12-month period is likely to be 100 or more tonnes.

Part A(2)

(a) Manufacturing glass, unless falling within Part A(1) of this Section, where the melting capacity of the plant is more than 20 tonnes per day.

Part B

Unless falling within Part A(1) or Part A(2) of this Section—
(a) Manufacturing glass at any location with the capacity to make 5,000 or more tonnes of glass in any 12-month period, and any activity involving the use of glass which is carried on at any such location in conjunction with its manufacture.

(b) Manufacturing glass where the use of lead or any lead compound is involved.
(c) Manufacturing any glass product where lead or any lead compound has been used in the manufacture of the glass except—
  (i) making products from lead glass blanks; or
  (ii) melting, or mixing with another substance, glass manufactured elsewhere to produce articles such as ornaments or road paint.
(d) Polishing or etching glass or glass products in the course of any manufacturing activity if—
  (i) hydrofluoric acid is used; or
  (ii) hydrogen fluoride may be released into the air.
(e) Manufacturing glass frit or enamel frit and its use in any activity where that activity is related to its manufacture.

Section 3.4
Production of Other Mineral Fibres

Part A(1)

(a) Unless falling within Part A(1) or Part A(2) of Section 3.3, melting mineral substances in plant with a melting capacity of more than 20 tonnes per day.
(b) Unless falling within Part A(1) of Section 3.3, producing any fibre from any mineral.

Section 3.5
Other Mineral Activities

Part A(2)

(a) Manufacturing cellulose fibre reinforced calcium silicate board using unbleached pulp.

Part B

(a) Unless falling within Part A(1) or Part A(2) of any Section, the crushing, grinding or other size reduction, other than the cutting of stone, or the grading, screening or heating of any designated mineral or mineral product except where the operation of the activity is unlikely to result in the release into the air of particulate matter.
(b) Any of the following activities unless carried on at an exempt location—
  (i) crushing, grinding or otherwise breaking up coal, coke or any other coal product;
  (ii) screening, grading or mixing coal, coke or any other coal product;
  (iii) loading or unloading petroleum coke, coal, coke or any other coal product except unloading on retail sale.
(c) The crushing, grinding or other size reduction, with machinery designed for that purpose, of bricks, tiles or concrete.
(d) Screening the product of any activity described in paragraph (c).
(e) Coating road stone with tar or bitumen.
(f) Loading, unloading or storing pulverised fuel ash in bulk prior to further transportation in bulk.
(g) The fusion of calcined bauxite for the production of artificial corundum.

Interpretation and application of Part B

1

In Part B—
"coal" includes lignite;
"designated mineral or mineral product" means—

(a) clay, sand or any other naturally occurring mineral other than coal;
(b) metallurgical slag;
(c) boiler or furnace ash produced from the burning of coal, coke or any other coal product;
(d) gypsum which is a by-product of any activity;

"exempt location" means—

(a) any premises used for the sale of petroleum coke, coal, coke or any coal product where the throughput of such substances at those premises in any 12-month period is in aggregate likely to be less than 10,000 tonnes; or
(b) any premises to which petroleum coke, coal, coke or any coal product is supplied only for use there;

"retail sale" means sale to the final customer.

2

Part B does not apply to any activity carried on underground.

Section 3.6
Ceramic Production

Part A(1)

(a) Manufacturing ceramic products (including roofing tiles, bricks, refractory bricks, tiles, stoneware or porcelain) by firing in kilns, where—
(i) the kiln production capacity is more than 75 tonnes per day; or
(ii) the kiln capacity is more than $4m^3$ and the setting density is more than 300 kg/m^3,

and a reducing atmosphere is used other than for the purposes of colouration.

Part A(2)

(a) Unless falling within Part A(1) of this Section, manufacturing ceramic products (including roofing tiles, bricks, refractory bricks, tiles, stoneware or porcelain) by firing in kilns, where—
(i) the kiln production capacity is more than 75 tonnes per day; or
(ii) the kiln capacity is more than $4m^3$ and the setting density is more than 300 kg/m^3.

Part B

(a) Unless falling within Part A(1) or A(2) of this Section, firing heavy clay goods or refractory materials (other than heavy clay goods) in a kiln.
(b) Vapour glazing earthenware or clay with salts.

Interpretation of Part B

1

In Part B—

"clay" includes a blend of clay with ash, sand or other materials;

"refractory material" means material (such as fireclay, silica, magnesite, chrome-magnesite, sillimanite, sintered alumina, beryllia and boron nitride) which is able to withstand high temperatures and to function as a furnace lining or in other similar high temperature applications.

Chapter 4
The Chemical Industry

Interpretation of Chapter 4

1

In Part A(1) of the Sections of this Chapter, "producing" means producing in a chemical plant by chemical processing for commercial purposes substances or groups of substances listed in the relevant Sections.

Section 4.1
Organic Chemicals

Interpretation of Section 4.1

1

In this Section, "pre-formulated resin or pre-formulated gel coat" means any resin or gel coat which has been formulated before being introduced into polymerisation or co-polymerisation activity, whether or not the resin or gel coat contains a colour pigment, activator or catalyst.

Part A(1)

(a) Producing organic chemicals such as—
  (i) hydrocarbons (linear or cyclic, saturated or unsaturated, aliphatic or aromatic);
  (ii) organic compounds containing oxygen (for example alcohols, aldehydes, ketones, carboxylic acids, esters, ethers, peroxides, phenols, epoxy resins);
  (iii) organic compounds containing sulphur (for example sulphides, mercaptans, sulphonic acids, sulphonates, sulphates and sulphones and sulphur heterocyclics);
  (iv) organic compounds containing nitrogen (for example amines, amides, nitrous-, nitroor azo-compounds, nitrates, nitriles, nitrogen heterocyclics, cyanates, isocyanates, diisocyanates and di-isocyanate prepolymers);
  (v) organic compounds containing phosphorus (for example substituted phosphines and phosphate esters);
  (vi) organic compounds containing halogens (for example halocarbons, halogenated aromatic compounds and acid halides);
  (vii) organometallic compounds (for example lead alkyls, Grignard reagents and lithium alkyls);
  (viii) plastic materials (for example polymers, synthetic fibres and cellulose-based fibres);
  (ix) synthetic rubbers;
  (x) dyes and pigments;
  (xi) surface-active agents.

(b) Producing any other organic compounds not described in paragraph (a).

(c) Polymerising or co-polymerising any unsaturated hydrocarbon or vinyl chloride (other than a pre-formulated resin or pre-formulated gel coat which contains any unsaturated hydrocarbon) which is likely to involve, in any 12-month period, the polymerisation or co-polymerisation of 50 or more tonnes of any of those materials, or any combination of those materials in aggregate.

(d) Any activity involving the use in any 12-month period of 1 or more tonnes of toluene diisocyanate or other di-isocyanate of comparable volatility or, where partly polymerised, the use of partly polymerised di-isocyanates or prepolymers containing 1 or more tonnes of those monomers, if the activity may result in a release into the air which contains such a di-isocyanate monomer.

(e) The flame bonding of polyurethane foams or polyurethane elastomers.

(f) Recovering—
  (i) carbon disulphide;
  (ii) pyridine or any substituted pyridine.
(g) Recovering or purifying acrylic acid, substituted acrylic acid or any ester of acrylic acid or of substituted acrylic acid.

Part B

(a) Unless falling within Part A(1) of this Section, any activity where the carrying on of the activity by the person concerned at the location in question is likely to involve the use in any 12-month period of 5 tonnes or more of any di-isocyanate or of any partly polymerised di-isocyanate or, in aggregate, of both.
(b) Cutting polyurethane foams or polyurethane elastomers with heated wires.
(c) Any activity for the polymerisation or co-polymerisation of any pre-formulated resin or pre-formulated gel coat which contains any unsaturated hydrocarbon, where the activity is likely to involve, in any 12-month period, the polymerisation or co-polymerisation of 100 or more tonnes of unsaturated hydrocarbon.
(d) Unless falling within Part A(1) of this Section, any activity involving the use of toluene di-isocyanate or partly polymerised di-isocyanate if—
  (i) less than 1 tonne of toluene di-isocyanate monomer is likely to be used in any 12-month period; and
  (ii) the activity may result in a release into the air which contains toluene di-isocyanate.

Section 4.2
Inorganic Chemicals

Part A(1)

(a) Producing inorganic chemicals such as—
  (i) gases (for example ammonia, hydrogen chloride, hydrogen fluoride, hydrogen cyanide, hydrogen sulphide, oxides of carbon, sulphur compounds, oxides of nitrogen, hydrogen, oxides of sulphur, phosgene);
  (ii) acids (for example chromic acid, hydrofluoric acid, hydrochloric acid, hydrobromic acid, hydroiodic acid, phosphoric acid, nitric acid, sulphuric acid, oleum and chlorosulphonic acid);
  (iii) bases (for example ammonium hydroxide, potassium hydroxide, sodium hydroxide);
  (iv) salts (for example ammonium chloride, potassium chlorate, potassium carbonate, sodium carbonate, perborate, silver nitrate, cupric acetate, ammonium phosphomolybdate);
  (v) non-metals, metal oxides, metal carbonyls or other inorganic compounds (for example calcium carbide, silicon, silicon carbide, titanium dioxide);
  (vi) halogens or interhalogen compounds comprising 2 or more of halogens, or any compound comprising one or more of those halogens and oxygen.
(b) Unless falling within any other Section, any manufacturing activity which is likely to result in the release into the air of any hydrogen halide (other than the manufacture of glass or the coating, plating or surface treatment of metal) or which is likely to result in the release into the air or water of any halogen or any of the compounds mentioned in paragraph (a)(vi) (other than the treatment of water).
(c) Unless falling within any other Section, any manufacturing activity involving the use of hydrogen cyanide or hydrogen sulphide.
(d) Unless falling within any other Section, any manufacturing activity (other than the application of a glaze or vitreous enamel) involving the use of, or the use or recovery of, any compound of any of the following elements—
  (i) antimony;
  (ii) arsenic;

(iii) beryllium;
(iv) gallium;
(v) indium;
(vi) lead;
(vii) palladium;
(viii) platinum;
(ix) selenium;
(x) tellurium;
(xi) thallium,

where the activity may result in the release into the air of any of those elements or compounds or the release into water of any substance listed in paragraph 7 of Part 1 of this Schedule.

(e) Recovering any compound of cadmium or mercury.

(f) Unless falling within any other Section, any manufacturing activity involving the use of mercury or cadmium or any compound of either element or which may result in the release into air of either of those elements or their compounds.

(g) Unless carried on as part of any other activity within this Schedule—
(i) recovering, concentrating or distilling sulphuric acid or oleum;
(ii) recovering nitric acid;
(iii) purifying phosphoric acid.

(h) Unless falling within any other Section, any activity (other than the combustion or incineration of carbonaceous material as defined in the Interpretation of Part A(1) of Section 1.2) which is likely to result in the release into the air of any acid-forming oxide of nitrogen.

(i) Unless carried on as part of any other activity within this Schedule, recovering ammonia.

(j) Extracting any magnesium compound from sea water.

Section 4.3
Chemical Fertiliser Production

Part A(1)

(a) Producing (including any blending which is related to their production) phosphorus-, nitrogen-or potassium-based fertilisers (simple or compound fertilisers).

(b) Converting chemical fertilisers into granules.

Section 4.4
Plant Health Products and Biocides

Part A(1)

(a) Producing plant health products or biocides.

(b) Formulating such products if this may result in the release into water of any substance listed in paragraph 7 of Part 1 of this Schedule in a quantity which, in any 12-month period, is greater than the background quantity by more than the amount specified in that paragraph for that substance.

Section 4.5
Pharmaceutical Production

Part A(1)

(a) Producing pharmaceutical products using a chemical or biological process.

(b) Formulating such products if this may result in the release into water of any substance listed in paragraph 7 of Part 1 of this Schedule in a quantity which, in any 12-month period, is greater than the background quantity by more than the amount specified in that paragraph for that substance.

Section 4.6
Explosives Production

Part A(1)

(a) Producing explosives.

Section 4.7
Manufacturing Activities Involving Carbon Disulphide or Ammonia

Part A(1)

(a) Unless falling within Part A(2) of Section 6.7, any manufacturing activity which may result in the release of carbon disulphide into the air.
(b) Any activity for the manufacture of a chemical which may result in the release of ammonia into the air other than an activity in which ammonia is only used as a refrigerant.

Section 4.8
The Storage of Chemicals in Bulk

Part B

(a) The storage in tanks, other than in tanks for the time being forming part of a powered vehicle, of any of the substances listed below except where the total storage capacity of the tanks installed at the location in question in which the relevant substance may be stored is less than the figure specified below in relation to that substance—
   (i) one or more acrylates, 20 tonnes (in aggregate);
   (ii) acrylonitrile, 20 tonnes;
   (iii) anhydrous ammonia, 100 tonnes;
   (iv) anhydrous hydrogen fluoride, 1 tonne;
   (v) toluene di-isocyanate, 20 tonnes;
   (vi) vinyl chloride monomer, 20 tonnes;
   (vii) ethylene, 8,000 tonnes.

Chapter 5
Waste Management

Section 5.1
Incineration and Co-incineration of Waste

Interpretation of Section 5.1

1

In this Section—
"co-incineration" means the use of wastes as a regular or additional fuel in a co-incineration plant or the thermal treatment of waste for the purpose of disposal in a co-incineration plant;
"co-incineration plant" means any stationary or mobile plant whose main purpose is the generation of energy or production of material products, and—
   (a) which uses wastes as a regular or additional fuel; or
   (b) in which waste is thermally treated for the purpose of disposal.
   If co-incineration takes place in such a way that the main purpose of the plant is not the generation of energy or production of material products but rather the thermal treatment of waste, the plant must be regarded as an incineration plant.

This definition covers the site and the entire plant including all co-incineration lines, waste reception, storage, on site pre-treatment facilities, waste-, fuel- and air-supply systems, boiler, facilities for the treatment of exhaust gases, on-site facilities for treatment or storage of residues and waste water, stack devices and systems for controlling incineration operations, recording and monitoring incineration conditions, but does not cover co-incineration in an excluded plant;

"excluded plant" means—

(a) a plant treating only the following wastes—

(i) vegetable waste from agriculture and forestry,

(ii) vegetable waste from the food processing industry, if the heat generated is recovered,

(iii) fibrous vegetable waste from virgin pulp production and from production of paper from pulp, if it is co-incinerated at the place of production and the heat generated is recovered,

(iv) wood waste with the exception of wood waste which may contain halogenated organic compounds or heavy metals as a result of treatment with wood-preservatives or coating, and which includes in particular such wood waste originating from construction and demolition waste,

(v) cork waste,

(vi) radioactive waste,

[(vii) animal carcasses as regulated by Regulation (EC) No 1069/2009;][1]

(viii) waste resulting from the exploration for, and the exploitation of, oil or gas resources from off-shore installations and incinerated on board the installation; or

(b) an experimental plant used for research, development and testing in order to improve the incineration process and which treats less than 50 tonnes of waste per year;

"hazardous waste", in relation to any solid or liquid waste, has the meaning given in regulation 6 of (in relation to England) the Hazardous Waste (England and Wales) Regulations 2005 or (in relation to Wales) regulation 6 of the Hazardous Waste (Wales) Regulations 2005, but does not include—

(a) combustible liquid wastes including waste oils, provided that they meet the following criteria—

(i) the mass content of polychlorinated aromatic hydrocarbons, for example polychlorinated biphenyls or pentachlorinated phenol amounts to concentrations not higher than those set out in the relevant [EU][2] legislation,

(ii) these wastes are not rendered hazardous by virtue of containing other constituents listed in Schedule 2 to (in relation to England) the Hazardous Waste (England and Wales) Regulations 2005, or (in relation to Wales) Schedule 2 to the Hazardous Waste (Wales) Regulations 2005 in quantities or in concentrations which are inconsistent with the achievement of the objectives set out in [Article 13][3] of the Waste Framework Directive, and

(iii) the net calorific value amounts to at least 30 MJ per kilogramme;

(b) any combustible liquid wastes which cannot cause, in the flue gas directly resulting from their combustion, emissions other than those from gasoil as defined in Article 1(1) of Council Directive 93/12/EEC relating to the sulphur content of certain liquid fuels or a higher concentration of emissions than those resulting from the combustion of gasoil as so defined;

"incineration plant" means any stationary or mobile technical unit and equipment dedicated to the thermal treatment of wastes with or without recovery of the combustion heat generated, including—

(a) the incineration by oxidation of waste; and
(b) other thermal treatment processes such as pyrolysis, gasification or plasma processes in so far as the substances resulting from the treatment are subsequently incinerated.

This definition covers the site and the entire incineration plant including all incineration lines, waste reception, storage, on site pre-treatment facilities, waste-fuel and air-supply systems, boiler, facilities for the treatment of exhaust gases, on-site facilities for treatment or storage of residues and waste water, stack, devices and systems for controlling incineration operations, recording and monitoring incineration conditions, but does not cover incineration in an excluded plant;

"non-hazardous waste" means waste which is not hazardous waste;

"relevant Community legislation" has the same meaning as in Article 3(2)(a)(i) of the Waste Incineration Directive;

"waste" means any solid or liquid waste as defined in [Article 3(1)][3] of the Waste Framework Directive.

Amendments

1 Substituted by the Animal By-Products (Enforcement) (England) Regulations 2011, SI 2011/881, reg 27, Sch 2, para 18(1), (3).
2 Substituted by the Treaty of Lisbon (Changes in Terminology) Order 2011, SI 2011/1043, art 6(2)(b).
3 Substituted by the Waste (England and Wales) Regulations 2011, SI 2011/988, reg 48(2), Sch 3, paras 1, 5(a).

Part A(1)

(a) The incineration of hazardous waste in an incineration plant.
(b) Unless carried on as part of any other Part A(1) activity, the incineration of hazardous waste in a co-incineration plant.
(c) The incineration of non-hazardous waste in an incineration plant with a capacity of 1 tonne or more per hour.
(d) Unless carried on as part of any other activity in Part A(1), the incineration of hazardous waste in a plant which is not an incineration plant or a co-incineration plant.
(e) Unless carried on as part of any other activity in Part A(1), the incineration of nonhazardous waste in a plant which is not an incineration plant or a co-incineration plant but which has a capacity of 1 tonne or more per hour.
(f) The incineration, other than incidentally in the course of burning landfill gas or solid or liquid waste, of any gaseous compound containing halogens in a plant which is not an incineration plant or a co-incineration plant.

Part A(2)

(a) The incineration of non-hazardous waste in an incineration plant with a capacity of less than 1 tonne per hour.
(b) Unless carried on as part of any other Part A activity, the incineration of non-hazardous waste in a co-incineration plant.
(c) The incineration of animal carcasses in a plant, which is not an incineration plant or a coincineration plant, with a capacity of more than 10 tonnes per day but less than 1 tonne per hour.

Part B

(a) The incineration of non-hazardous waste in a plant which is—
    (i) not an incineration plant or a co-incineration plant, and
    (ii) on premises where there is plant, other than incineration plant or co-incineration plant, which has an aggregate capacity of 50 kilogrammes or more per hour but less than 1 tonne per hour.
(b) The cremation of human remains.

Application of Part B

1

When determining the extent of an installation carrying on an activity within Part B, any location of the following description is to be ignored: any location where the associated storage or handling of wastes and residues which are to be incinerated as part of that activity is carried on, other than a location where the associated storage or handling of animal remains intended for burning in an incinerator used wholly or mainly for the incineration of such remains or residues from the burning of such remains in such an incinerator is carried on.

Section 5.2
Disposal of Waste by Landfill

Part A(1)

(a) The disposal of waste in a landfill—
 (i) receiving more than 10 tonnes of waste in any day, or
 (ii) with a total capacity of more than 25,000 tonnes,
 but excluding disposals in a landfill taking only inert waste.

Section 5.3
Disposal of Waste other than by Incineration or Landfill

Part A(1)

(a) The disposal of hazardous waste (other than by incineration or landfill) in a facility with a capacity of more than 10 tonnes per day.
(b) The disposal of waste oils (other than by incineration or landfill) in a facility with a capacity of more than 10 tonnes per day.
(c) Disposal of non-hazardous waste in a facility with a capacity of more than 50 tonnes per day by—
 (i) biological treatment, not being treatment specified in any paragraph other than paragraph D8 of [Annex I][1] to the Waste Framework Directive, which results in final compounds or mixtures which are discarded by means of any of the operations numbered D1 to D12 in that Annex (D8), or
 (ii) physico-chemical treatment, not being treatment specified in any paragraph other than paragraph D9 in [Annex I][1] to the Waste Framework Directive, which results in final compounds or mixtures which are discarded by means of any of the operations numbered D1 to D12 in that Annex (for example, evaporation, drying, calcination, etc) (D9).

Amendment
1 Substituted by the Waste (England and Wales) Regulations 2011, SI 2011/988, reg 48(2), Sch 3, paras 1, 5(b).

Interpretation and application of Part A(1)

1

In Part A(1)(b)"disposal" means the processing or destruction of waste oil as well as its storage and tipping above ground.

2

Part A(1) does not apply to the treatment, by means of mobile plant, of—
(a) waste soil; or

(b) contaminated material, substances or products, for the purpose of remedial action with respect to land or controlled waters.

3

The reference to a D paragraph number in brackets at the end of Part A(1)(c)(i) and (ii) is a reference to the number of the corresponding paragraph in [Annex I][1] to the Waste Framework Directive (disposal operations).

Amendment

1 Substituted by the Waste (England and Wales) Regulations 2011, SI 2011/988, reg 48(2), Sch 3, paras 1, 5(b).

Section 5.4
Recovery of Waste

Part A(1)

(a) Recovering by distillation of any oil or organic solvent.
(b) Cleaning or regenerating carbon, charcoal or ion exchange resins by removing matter which is, or includes, any substance listed in paragraphs 6 to 8 of Part 1 of this Schedule.
(c) Unless carried on as part of any other Part A activity, recovering hazardous waste in a plant with a capacity of more than 10 tonnes per day by means of the following operations—
  (i) the use principally as a fuel or other means to generate energy (R1),
  (ii) solvent reclamation/regeneration (R2),
  (iii) recycling/reclamation of inorganic materials other than metals and metal compounds (R5),
  (iv) regeneration of acids or bases (R6),
  (v) recovering components used for pollution abatement (R7),
  (vi) recovery of components from catalysts (R8),
  (vii) oil re-refining or other reuses of oil (R9).

Interpretation and application of Part A(1)

1

Part A(1)(a) and (b) do not apply to any of the following activities, except where the activity involves distilling more than 100 tonnes per day—
(a) distilling oil for the production or cleaning of vacuum pump oil;
(b) an activity which is ancillary to and related to another activity, whether described in this Schedule or not, which involves the production or use of the substance which is recovered, cleaned or regenerated.

2

Part A(1) does not apply to the treatment, by means of mobile plant, of—
(a) waste soil; or
(b) contaminated material, substances or products, for the purpose of remedial action with respect to land or controlled waters.

3

The reference to an R paragraph number in brackets at the end of Part A(1)(c)(i) to (vii) is a reference to the number of the corresponding paragraph in [Annex II][1] to the Waste Framework Directive (recovery operations).

Amendment

1 Substituted by the Waste (England and Wales) Regulations 2011, SI 2011/988, reg 48(2), Sch 3, paras 1, 5(c).

Section 5.5
The Production of Fuel from Waste

Part A(1)

(a) Making solid fuel (other than charcoal) from waste by any process involving the use of heat.

Chapter 6
Other Activities

Section 6.1
Paper, Pulp and Board Manufacturing Activities

Part A(1)

(a) Producing, in industrial plant, pulp from timber or other fibrous materials.
(b) Producing, in industrial plant, paper and board where the plant has a production capacity of more than 20 tonnes per day.
(c) Any activity associated with making paper pulp or paper, including activities connected with the recycling of paper such as de-inking, if the activity may result in the release into water of any substance in paragraph 7 of Part 1 of this Schedule in a quantity which, in any 12-month period, is greater than the background quantity by more than the amount specified in that paragraph in relation to that substance.

Interpretation of Part A(1)

1

In Part A(1)(c), "paper pulp" includes pulp made from wood, grass, straw or similar materials and references to the making of paper are to the making of any product using paper pulp.

Part A(2)

(a) Manufacturing wood particleboard, oriented strand board, wood fibreboard, plywood, cement-bonded particleboard or any other composite wood-based board.

Section 6.2
Carbon Activities

Part A(1)

(a) Producing carbon or hard-burnt coal or electro-graphite by means of incineration or graphitisation.

Section 6.3
Tar and Bitumen Activities

Part A(1)

(a) The following activities—
   (i) distilling tar or bitumen in connection with any process of manufacture, or
   (ii) heating tar for the manufacture of electrodes or carbon-based refractory materials,

   where the activity is likely to involve the use in any 12-month period of 5 or more tonnes of tar or of bitumen or both in aggregate.

Part B

(a) Any activity not falling within Part A(1) of this Section or of Section 6.2 involving—
  (i) heating, but not distilling, tar or bitumen in connection with any manufacturing activity, or
  (ii) oxidising bitumen by blowing air through it, at plant where no other activities described in any Section in this Schedule are carried on,

where the carrying on of the activity is likely to involve the use in any 12-month period of 5 or more tonnes of tar or bitumen or both in aggregate.

Interpretation of Part B

1

In Part B, "tar" and "bitumen" include pitch.

Section 6.4
Coating Activities, Printing and Textile Treatments

Part A(1)

(a) Applying or removing a coating material containing any tributyltin compound or triphenyltin compound, if carried on at a shipyard or boatyard where vessels of a length of 25 metres or more can be built, maintained or repaired.
(b) Pre-treating (by operations such as washing, bleaching or mercerization) or dyeing fibres or textiles in plant with a treatment capacity of more than 10 tonnes per day.
(c) Treating textiles if the activity may result in the release into water of any substance in paragraph 7 of Part 1 of this Schedule in a quantity which, in any 12-month period, is greater than the background quantity by more than the amount specified in that paragraph in relation to that substance.

Part A(2)

(a) Unless falling within Part A(1) of this Section, surface treating substances, objects or products using organic solvents, in particular for dressing, printing, coating, degreasing, waterproofing, sizing, painting, cleaning or impregnating, in plant with a consumption capacity of more than 150 kg per hour or more than 200 tonnes per year.

Part B

(a) Unless falling within Part A(1) or Part A(2) of this Section or Part A(2)(c) of Section 2.1, any process (other than for the re-painting or re-spraying of or of parts of aircraft or road or railway vehicles) for applying to a substrate, or drying or curing after such application, printing ink or paint or any other coating material as, or in the course of, a manufacturing activity, where the process may result in the release into the air of particulate matter or of any volatile organic compound and is likely to involve the use in any 12-month period of—
  (i) 20 or more tonnes of printing ink, paint or other coating material which is applied in solid form,
  (ii) 20 or more tonnes of any metal coating which is sprayed on in molten form,
  (iii) 25 or more tonnes of organic solvents in respect of any cold set web offset printing activity or any sheet fed offset litho printing activity, or
  (iv) 5 or more tonnes of organic solvents in respect of any activity not mentioned in sub-paragraph (iii).
(b) Unless falling within Part A(2) of this Section, re-painting or re-spraying road vehicles or parts of them if the activity may result in the release into the air of particulate matter

or of any volatile organic compound and the carrying on of the activity is likely to involve the use of 1 or more tonne of organic solvents in any 12-month period.

(c) Re-painting or re-spraying aircraft or railway vehicles or parts of them if the activity may result in the release into the air of particulate matter or of any volatile organic compound and the carrying on of the activity is likely to involve the use in any 12-month period of—
   (i) 20 or more tonnes of any paint or other coating material which is applied in solid form,
   (ii) 20 or more tonnes of any metal coatings which are sprayed on in molten form, or
   (iii) 5 or more tonnes of organic solvents.

Interpretation and application of Part B

1

In Part B—

"aircraft" includes gliders and missiles;

"coating material" means paint, printing ink, varnish, lacquer, dye, any metal oxide coating, any adhesive coating, any elastomer coating, any metal or plastic coating and any other coating material.

2

The amount of organic solvents used in an activity must be calculated as—

(a) the total input of organic solvents into the process, including both solvents contained in coating materials and solvents used for cleaning or other purposes; less

(b) any organic solvents that are removed from the process for re-use or for recovery for reuse.

3

When determining the extent of an installation carrying on an activity within Part B any location where the associated cleaning of used storage drums prior to painting or their incidental handling in connection with such cleaning is carried on is to be ignored, unless that location forms part of a SED installation.

Section 6.5
The Manufacture of Dyestuffs, Printing Ink and Coating Materials

Part B

(a) Unless falling within Part A(1) or Part A(2) of any other Section—
   (i) manufacturing or formulating printing ink or any other coating material containing, or involving the use of, an organic solvent, where the carrying on of the activity is likely to involve the use of 100 or more tonnes of organic solvents in any 12-month period,
   (ii) manufacturing any powder for use as a coating material [where the process uses lead chromate or triglycidyl isocyanurate and][1] where there is the capacity to produce 200 tonnes or more of such powder in any 12-month period.

Amendment

1 Inserted by the Environmental Permitting (England and Wales) (Amendment) (No. 2) Regulations 2010, SI 2010/2172, reg 2(1), (3).

Interpretation of Part B

1

In Part B, "coating material" has the same meaning as in Section 6.4.

2

The amount of organic solvents used in an activity must be calculated as—

(a) the total input of organic solvents into the process, including both solvents contained in coating materials and solvents for cleaning or other purposes; less

(b) any organic solvents, not contained in coating materials, that are removed from the process for re-use or for recovery for re-use.

Section 6.6
Timber Activities

Part A(1)

(a) Curing, or chemically treating, as part of a manufacturing process, timber or products wholly or mainly made of wood if any substance in paragraph 7 of Part 1 of this Schedule is used.

Part B

(a) Unless falling within Part A(2) of Section 6.1, manufacturing products wholly or mainly of wood at any works if the activity involves a relevant activity and the throughput of the works in any 12-month period is likely to be more than—
  (i) 10,000 cubic metres in the case of works at which wood is only sawed, or wood is sawed and subjected to excluded activities, or
  (ii) 1,000 cubic metres in any other case.

Interpretation of Part B

1

In Part B—

"excluded activity" means any relevant activity (other than sawing) which, ignoring any sawing carried on at the works, would be unlikely to result in the release into the air of any substance in paragraph 6(3) of Part 1 of this Schedule in a quantity capable of causing significant harm;

"relevant activity" means the sawing, drilling, sanding, shaping, turning, planing, curing or chemical treatment of wood;

"throughput" means the amount of wood which is subjected to a relevant activity, but where wood is subject to 2 or more relevant activities at the same works, the second and any subsequent activity is to be ignored;

"wood" includes any product consisting wholly or mainly of wood; and

"works" includes a sawmill or any other premises where relevant activities are carried on.

Section 6.7
Activities Involving Rubber

Part A(2)

(a) Manufacturing new tyres (but not remoulds or retreads) if this involves the use in any 12-month period of 50,000 or more tonnes of one or more of the following—
  (i) natural rubber,
  (ii) synthetic organic elastomers,
  (iii) other substances mixed with them.

Part B

(a) Unless falling within Part A(1) or Part A(2) of any Section, the mixing, milling or blending of—

(i) natural rubber, or
(ii) synthetic organic elastomers,
if carbon black is used.

(b) Any activity which converts the product of an activity falling within paragraph (a) into a finished product if related to an activity falling within that paragraph.

Section 6.8
The Treatment of Animal and Vegetable Matter and Food Industries

Interpretation of Section 6.8

1

In this Section—
"animal" includes a bird or a fish;
"excluded activity" means—
(a) any activity carried on on a farm or agricultural holding other than—
(i) the manufacture of goods for sale,
(ii) the production of compost for growing mushrooms,
(b) the manufacture or preparation of food or drink for human consumption but excluding—
(i) the extraction, distillation or purification of animal or vegetable oil or fat otherwise than as an activity incidental to the cooking of food for human consumption,
(ii) any activity involving the use of green offal or the boiling of blood except the cooking of food (other than tripe) for human consumption,
(iii) the cooking of tripe for human consumption elsewhere than on premises on which it is to be consumed,
(c) the fleshing, cleaning and drying of pelts of fur-bearing mammals,
(d) any activity carried on in connection with the operation of a collection centre for animal by-products,
(e) any activity for the manufacture of soap not falling within Part A(1) of Section 4.1,
(f) the storage of vegetable matter not falling within any other Section,
(g) …[1]
(h) the manufacture of starch,
(i) …[1]
(j) the salting of hides or skins, unless related to any other activity listed in this Schedule,
(k) any activity for composting animal or vegetable matter or a combination of both, except where that activity is carried on for the purposes of cultivating mushrooms,
(l) any activity for cleaning, and any related activity for drying or dressing, seeds, bulbs, corms or tubers (and "related activity" means an activity being carried on by the same person at the same site),
(m) the drying of grain or pulses,
(n) any activity for the production of cotton yarn from raw cotton or for the conversion of cotton yarn into cloth,
[(o) the drying of green crops;][2]
"food" includes—
(a) drink,
(b) articles and substances of no nutritional value which are used for human consumption, and
(c) articles and substances used as ingredients in the preparation of food;
["green crops" means alfalfa (Lucerne), clover, grass, perennial ryegrass, tall fescue and other similar crops;][2]

"green offal" means the stomach and intestines of any animal, other than poultry or fish, and their contents.

Amendments

1 Repealed by the Animal By-Products (Enforcement) (England) Regulations 2011, SI 2011/881, reg 27, Sch 2, para 18(1), (4).

2 Inserted by the Environmental Permitting (England and Wales) (Amendment) (No. 2) Regulations 2010, SI 2010/2172, reg 2(1), (4).

Part A(1)

(a) Tanning hides and skins at a plant with a treatment capacity of more than 12 tonnes of finished products per day.

(b) Slaughtering animals at a plant with a carcass production capacity of more than 50 tonnes per day.

(c) Disposing of or recycling animal carcasses or animal waste, other than by rendering or by incineration falling within Section 5.1, at a plant with a treatment capacity exceeding 10 tonnes per day of animal carcasses or animal waste or both in aggregate.

(d) Treating and processing materials intended for the production of food products from—
  (i) animal raw materials (other than milk) at a plant with a finished product production capacity of more than 75 tonnes per day; or
  (ii) vegetable raw materials at a plant with a finished product production capacity of more than 300 tonnes per day (average value on a quarterly basis).

(e) Treating and processing milk, the quantity of milk received being more than 200 tonnes per day (average value on an annual basis).

(f) Processing, storing or drying by the application of heat the whole or part of any dead animal or any vegetable matter (other than the treatment of effluent so as to permit its discharge into controlled waters or into a sewer unless the treatment involves the drying of any material with a view to its use as animal feedstuff) if the processing, storing or drying—
  (i) does not fall within any other Section, or Part A(2) of this Section, and is not an excluded activity; and
  (ii) may result in the release into water of any substance in paragraph 7 of Part 1 of this Schedule in a quantity which, in any 12-month period, is greater than the background quantity by more than the amount specified in relation to the substance in that paragraph.

Part A(2)

(a) Disposing of or recycling animal carcasses or animal waste by rendering at plant with a treatment capacity exceeding 10 tonnes per day of animal carcasses or animal waste or both in aggregate.

Part B

(a) Processing, storing or drying by the application of heat the whole or part of any dead animal or any vegetable matter (other than the treatment of effluent so as to permit its discharge into controlled waters or into a sewer unless the treatment involves the drying of any material with a view to its use as animal feedstuff) if the processing, storing or drying—
  (i) does not fall within another Section, or Part A(1) or Part A(2) of this Section;
  (ii) is not an excluded activity; and
  (iii) may result in the release into the air of—
    (aa) any substance in paragraph 6(3) of Part 1 of this Schedule, or
    (bb) any offensive smell noticeable outside the premises on which the activity is carried on.

(b) Breeding maggots in any case where 5 or more kg of animal matter, vegetable matter or both in aggregate, are introduced into the process in any week.

Section 6.9
Intensive Farming

Part A(1)

(a) Rearing poultry or pigs intensively in an installation with more than—
  (i) 40,000 places for poultry;
  (ii) 2,000 places for production pigs (over 30 kg); or
  (iii) 750 places for sows.

[Section 6.10
Carbon capture and storage

This version in force from: August 12, 2011 to present

Part A(1)]

(a) Capture of carbon dioxide streams from an installation for the purposes of geological storage pursuant to Directive 2009/31/EC of the European Parliament and of the Council on the geological storage of carbon dioxide.][1]

Amendment

1 Inserted by the Environmental Permitting (England and Wales) (Amendment) Regulations 2011, SI 2011/2043, regs 3, 12.

Section 7
SED Activities

Part B

(a) The activities listed in the table below if they are operated above the solvent consumption threshold for the activity.

Activity	*Solvent consumption threshold in tonnes/ year*
Heatset web offset printing	15
Publication rotogravure	25
Other rotogravure, flexography, rotary screen printing, laminating or varnishing units	15
Rotary screen printing on textile or cardboard	30
Surface cleaning using substances or preparations which because of their content of volatile organic compounds classified as carcinogens, mutagens or toxic to reproduction under Directive 67/548/EEC on the approximation of laws, regulations and administrative provisions relating to the classification, packaging and labelling of dangerous substances are assigned or need to carry one or more of the risk phrases R45, R46, R49, R60 or R61, or halogenated VOCs which are assigned or need to carry the risk phrase R40	1
Other surface cleaning	2
Vehicle coating and vehicle refinishing	0.5
Coil coating	25
Other coating activities, including metal, plastic, textile (except rotary screen printing on textile), fabric, film and paper coating	5
Winding wire coating	5
Coating activity applied to wooden surfaces	15

Activity	*Solvent consumption threshold in tonnes/ year*
Dry cleaning	0
Wood impregnation	25
Coating activity applied to leather	10
Footwear manufacture	5
Wood and plastic lamination	5
Adhesive coating	5
Manufacture of coating preparations, varnishes, inks and adhesives	100
Rubber conversion	15
Vegetable oil and animal fat extraction and vegetable oil refining activities	10
Manufacturing of pharmaceutical products	50

Interpretation and application of Part B

1

For the purposes of Part B—

"adhesive" means any preparation, including all the organic solvents or preparations containing organic solvents necessary for its proper application, which is used to adhere separate parts of a product;

"adhesive coating" means any activity in which an adhesive is applied to a surface, excluding the application of adhesive and laminating associated with printing activities;

"coating" means any preparation, including all the organic solvents or preparations containing organic solvents necessary for its proper application, which is used to provide a decorative, protective or other functional effect on a surface;

"coating activity" means any activity in which a single or a multiple application of a continuous film of a coating is applied (including a step in which the same article is printed using any technique) but does not include the coating of substrate with metals by electrophoretic or chemical spraying techniques;

"coil coating" means any activity where coiled steel, stainless steel, coated steel copper alloys or aluminium strip is coated with either a film forming or laminate coating in a continuous process;

"consumption" means the total input of organic solvents into an installation per calendar year, or any other 12-month period, less any volatile organic compounds that are recovered for reuse;

"dry cleaning" means any industrial or commercial activity using volatile organic compounds to clean garments, furnishing and similar consumer goods excluding the manual removal of stains and spots in the textile and clothing industry;

"flexography" means a printing activity using an image carrier of rubber or elastic photopolymers on which the printing areas are above the non-printing areas, and liquid inks which dry through evaporation;

"footwear manufacture" means any activity of producing complete footwear or parts of footwear;

"heat web offset printing" means a web-fed printing activity using an image carrier in which the printing and non-printing area are in the same plane, where—

(a) the non-printing area is treated to attract water and reject ink,

(b) the printing area is treated to receive and transmit ink to the surface to be printed, and

(c) evaporation takes place in the oven where hot air is used to heat the printed material;

"ink" means a preparation, including all the organic solvents or preparations containing organic solvents necessary for its proper application which is used in a printing activity to impress text or images on to a surface;

"laminating associated to a printing activity" means the adhering together of 2 or more flexible materials to produce laminates;

"manufacturing of coating preparations, varnishes, inks and adhesives" means the manufacture of coating preparations, varnishes, inks and adhesives as final products and where carried on at the same site, the manufacture of intermediates by the mixing of pigments, resins and adhesive materials with organic solvent or other carrier, including—

(a) dispersion and pre-dispersion activities,
(b) viscosity and tint adjustments, and
(c) operations for filling the final product into its container;

"manufacturing of pharmaceutical products" means an activity that involves the—

(a) chemical synthesis,
(b) fermentation,
(c) extraction, or
(d) formulation and finishing,

of pharmaceutical products and, where carried on at the same site, the manufacture of intermediate products;

["the Motor Vehicle Directive" means Directive 2007/46/EC of the European Parliament and of the Council establishing a framework for the approval of motor vehicles and their trailers, and of systems, components and separate technical units intended for such vehicles;][1]

"organic compound" means any compound containing at least the element carbon and one or more of hydrogen, halogens, oxygen, sulphur, phosphorus, silicon or nitrogen, with the exception of carbon oxides and inorganic carbonates and bicarbonates;

"organic solvents" means any volatile organic compound which is used alone or in combination with other agents, and without undergoing a chemical change to dissolve raw materials, products or waste materials, as a—

(a) cleaning agent to dissolve contaminants,
(b) dissolver,
(c) dispersion medium,
(d) viscosity adjuster,
(e) surface tension adjuster,
(f) plasticiser, or
(g) preservative;

"other coating activities" means a coating activity applied to—

(a) trailers, defined in categories O1, O2, O3, and O4 in the Motor Vehicle Directive,
(b) metallic and plastic surfaces including surfaces of airplanes, ships, trains, or
(c) textile, fabric, film and paper surfaces;

"printing activity" means any activity (not being a step in a coating activity) for reproducing text and/or images in which, with the use of an image carrier, ink is transferred onto any type of surface, including the use of associated varnishing, coating and laminating techniques;

"publication rotogravure" means a rotogravure printing activity used for printing paper for magazines, brochures, catalogues or similar products, using toluene-based inks;

"reuse" means the use of organic solvents recovered from an installation for any technical or commercial purpose and including use as a fuel but excluding the final disposal of such recovered organic solvent as waste;

"rotary screen printing" means a web-fed printing activity in which liquid ink which dries only through evaporation is passed onto the surface to be printed by forcing it through a porous image carrier, in which the printing area is open and the non-printing area is sealed off;

"rotogravure" means a printing activity, using a cylindrical image carrier in which the printing area is below the non-printing area and liquid inks which dry through evaporation, and in which the recesses are filled with ink and the surplus is cleaned off the non-printing area before the surface to be printed contacts the cylinder and lifts the ink from the recesses;

"rubber conversion" means—

(a) any activity of mixing, milling, blending, calendering, extrusion or vulcanisation of natural or synthetic rubber, or

(b) any ancillary operations for converting natural or synthetic rubber into a finished product;

"surface cleaning" means any activity, except dry cleaning, using organic solvents to remove contamination from the surface of material including degreasing but excluding the cleaning of equipment; and a cleaning activity consisting of more than one step before or after any other activity is to be considered as one surface cleaning activity;

"varnish" means a transparent coating;

"varnishing" means an activity by which varnish or an adhesive coating for the purpose of sealing the packaging material is applied to a flexible material;

"vegetable oil and animal fat extraction and vegetable oil refining activities" means any activity to extract vegetable oil from seeds and other vegetable matter, the processing of dry residues to produce animal feed, the purification of fats and vegetable oils derived from seeds, vegetable matter or animal matter;

"vehicle coating" means a coating activity applied to the following vehicles—

(a) new cars, defined as vehicles of category M1 in the Motor Vehicle Directive, and of category N1 in so far as they are coated at the same installation as M1 vehicles,

(b) truck cabins, defined as the housing for the driver, and all integrated housing for the technical equipment, of vehicles of category N2 or N3 in the Motor Vehicle Directive,

(c) vans and trucks, defined as vehicles of category N1, N2 or N3 in the Motor Vehicle Directive, but not including truck cabins, or

(d) buses, defined as vehicles in category M2 or M3 in the Motor Vehicle Directive;

"vehicle refinishing" means any industrial or commercial coating activity and associated degreasing activities performing—

(a) the original coating of road vehicles as defined in the Motor Vehicle Directive or part of them with refinishing-type materials, where this is carried on away from the original manufacturing line, or

(b) the coating of trailers (including semi-trailers) (category O in the Motor Vehicle Directive);

"volatile organic compound" or "VOC" means—

(a) any organic compound having a vapour pressure of 0.01 or more kPa at 293.15K or having a corresponding volatility under the particular conditions of use, or

(b) the fraction of creosote which exceeds a vapour pressure of 0.01 kPA at 293.15K;

"web-fed" means that the material to be printed is fed to the machine from a reel as distinct from separate sheets;

"winding wire coating" means any coating activity of metallic conductors used for winding the coils in transformers and motors, etc;

"wood and plastic lamination" means any activity to adhere together wood or plastic to produce laminated products;

"wood impregnation" means any activity giving a loading of preservative in timber.

2

An activity is deemed to be operated above the solvent consumption threshold specified for that activity under Part B if the activity is likely to be operated above that threshold in any 12-month period.

3

An activity listed in Part B includes the cleaning of equipment but, except for a surface cleaning activity, not the cleaning of products.

Amendment

1 Substituted by the Environmental Permitting (England and Wales) (Amendment) Regulations 2012, SI 2012/630, reg 12(1), (4).

SCHEDULE 2
EXEMPT FACILITIES: GENERAL

Regulation 4

1 Interpretation: general

(1) In this Schedule—

"applicable fee" means—

(a) a fee imposed by the Agency under paragraph 11 until such date as it is superseded by a charging scheme referred to in that paragraph, or

(b) on and after that date, the fee prescribed under such a scheme;

"date of registration" means the date on which the relevant particulars first appear on the register;

"occupier" means a person who is or has been the occupier of the land on which an exempt water discharge activity or exempt groundwater activity is carried on;

"operator" means the person carrying on a water discharge activity or groundwater activity;

"register" means the register which the exemption registration authority is required to establish and maintain under paragraph 7(1);

"registered" means—

(a) in relation to a waste operation, that the relevant particulars appear on the register during a valid registration period,

(b) in relation to a water discharge activity or groundwater activity, that the relevant particulars appear on the register,

and "registration" is to be construed accordingly;

"relevant particulars" has the meaning given in paragraph 6(3);

"valid registration period", for an exempt waste operation, means the period of validity of a registration referred to in paragraph 12(1), as read with paragraph 12(2); and

"WEEE operation" means a waste operation falling within a description in paragraph T11.

2 Interpretation: exemption registration authority

(1) Subject to sub-paragraphs (2) and (3), the exemption registration authority in relation to a waste operation falling within a description in Part 1 of Schedule 3 is the Agency.

(2) The exemption registration authority in relation to a waste operation falling within a description in paragraph T3 or T7 is—

(a) for a waste operation carried on by waste mobile plant by an establishment or undertaking whose principal place of business is in England and Wales, the local authority in whose area it has its principal place of business;

(b) for a waste operation carried on by waste mobile plant by an establishment or undertaking whose principal place of business is not in England and Wales, the local authority in whose area the operation is first carried on;
(c) for a waste operation not carried on by waste mobile plant, the local authority in whose area the operation is carried on.

(3) …[1]

(4) The exemption registration authority in relation to a water discharge activity falling within a description in Part 2 of Schedule 3 is the Agency.

(5) The exemption registration authority in relation to a groundwater activity falling within a description in Part 3 of Schedule 3 is the Agency.

Amendment
1 Repealed by the Waste (England and Wales) Regulations 2011, SI 2011/988, reg 48(2), Sch 3, paras 1, 6(a).

3 Exempt waste operations

(1) For the purpose of the definition of "exempt waste operation", the requirements are—
(a) that a waste operation—
  (i) falls within a description in Part 1 of Schedule 3, and
  (ii) satisfies the general and specific conditions specified in Part 1 of that Schedule in relation to the description;
(b) subject to sub-paragraph (2) and paragraph 9(10) of this Schedule—
  (i) that the waste operation is registered, and
  (ii) an establishment or undertaking is registered in relation to it; and
(c) that the type and quantity of waste submitted to the waste operation, and the method of disposal or recovery, are consistent with the need to attain the objectives mentioned in [Article 13][1] of the Waste Framework Directive.

(2) The registration requirements in sub-paragraph (1)(b) do not apply in respect of a waste operation carried on by a person who is not an establishment or undertaking.

Amendment
1 Substituted by the Waste (England and Wales) Regulations 2011, SI 2011/988, reg 48(2), Sch 3, paras 1, 6(b).

4 Exempt water discharge activities

For the purpose of the definition of "exempt water discharge activity", the requirements are—
(a) that a water discharge activity—
  (i) falls within a description in Part 2 of Schedule 3, and
  (ii) satisfies, in relation to an activity of that description, the relevant conditions specified in Part 2 of that Schedule;
(b) that the water discharge activity is registered and, subject to paragraph 9(10) of this Schedule, for a water discharge activity that falls within a description in—
  (i) paragraph 1 of Part 2 of Schedule 3, the operator is registered in relation to the activity, or
  (ii) paragraph 2 of Part 2 of that Schedule, the occupier is registered in relation to the activity; and
(c) that the water discharge activity does not cause pollution of inland freshwaters, coastal waters or relevant territorial waters.

5 Exempt groundwater activities

For the purpose of the definition of "exempt groundwater activity", the requirements are—
(a) that a groundwater activity—
  (i) falls within a description in Part 3 of Schedule 3;

(ii) satisfies, in relation to an activity of that description, the relevant conditions specified in Part 3 of that Schedule;

(b) that the groundwater activity is registered and, subject to paragraph 9(10) of this Schedule, for a groundwater activity that falls within a description in—

(i) paragraph 2 of Part 3 of Schedule 3, the operator is registered in relation to the activity, or

(ii) paragraph 3 of Part 3 of that Schedule, the occupier is registered in relation to the activity; and

(c) that the groundwater activity does not cause pollution of groundwater.

6 Procedure for registering an exempt facility

(1) An establishment or undertaking seeking to be registered in relation to a waste operation described in Part 1 of Schedule 3, or seeking to renew such a registration, must notify the exemption registration authority of—

(a) the relevant particulars; and

(b) the information specified in sub-paragraph (4).

(2) An occupier or operator seeking to be registered in relation to a water discharge activity described in Part 2 of Schedule 3 or a groundwater activity described in Part 3 of that Schedule must notify the exemption registration authority of the relevant particulars.

(3) The relevant particulars are—

(a) the name and address of—

(i) for a waste operation, the establishment or undertaking, or

(ii) for a water discharge activity or groundwater activity, the occupier or operator;

(b) a description of the waste operation, water discharge activity or groundwater activity;

(c) the place where the waste operation, water discharge activity or groundwater activity is carried on, including—

(i) the post code (if applicable), or

(ii) the Ordnance Survey National Grid reference point; and

(d) if the waste operation is a WEEE operation, the type and quantity of waste subject to the operation.

(4) The information in this sub-paragraph is the name and contact details of an individual officer or employee designated by the establishment or undertaking to be the primary contact for the purposes of registration.

(5) Notification under sub-paragraph (1) or (2) must be in the form specified by the exemption registration authority.

(6) If a notification under sub-paragraph (1) relates to a waste operation that is a WEEE operation, the notification must be accompanied by the applicable fee.

7 Register of exempt facilities

(1) Every exemption registration authority must establish and maintain a register of exempt facilities in relation to which it is the exemption registration authority.

(2) Subject to sub-paragraphs (3), (4) and (5), the exemption registration authority must ensure the register contains the relevant particulars—

(a) for an exempt waste operation, within 5 working days after the date that it receives—

(i) notification of the relevant particulars and the information specified in paragraph 6(4), and

(ii) for a WEEE operation, payment of the applicable fee in accordance with paragraph 6(6); and

(b) for an exempt water discharge activity or exempt groundwater activity, within 15 working days after the date that it receives notification of the relevant particulars.

(3) The exemption registration authority must ensure the register is updated to reflect any changes notified under paragraph 13(1) of this Schedule or under Part 2 or 3 of Schedule 3—

(a) for exempt waste operations, within 5 working days after the date that it receives the notification, or

(b) for exempt water discharge activities and exempt groundwater activities, within 15 working days after that date.

(4) The exemption registration authority must not enter the relevant particulars on the register in relation to a WEEE operation until it has carried out an inspection in relation to the operation that complies with the second and third paragraphs of Article 6(2) of the WEEE Directive.

(5) Every exemption registration authority must—

(a) ensure that its register is open to inspection by the public free of charge at all reasonable hours; and

(b) provide reasonable facilities to the public for obtaining a copy of an entry on payment of a reasonable charge.

(6) A register may be kept in any form.

8 Duty to remove entries from the register

(1) The duty to maintain a register in paragraph 7(1) includes a duty to remove an entry from the register if—

(a) the exemption registration authority becomes aware that the exempt facility is no longer in operation at the place stated in the relevant particulars;

(b) the facility ceases to be an exempt facility; or

(c) in the case of a WEEE operation, the exemption registration authority—

 (i) has carried out an inspection in accordance with paragraph 15(2), and

 (ii) is not satisfied as to the particulars to be verified pursuant to the third paragraph of Article 6(2) of the WEEE Directive.

(2) If the exemption registration authority removes an entry from the register under sub-paragraph (1), it must notify without delay the occupier, operator or other person registered in relation to the exempt facility.

(3) Sub-paragraph (2) does not apply if the exemption registration authority was notified by the person registered in relation to the facility that the facility is no longer in operation at the place stated in the relevant particulars.

9 Exclusion from the register of information affecting national security

(1) The appropriate authority may direct the exemption registration authority that, in the interests of national security, specified information or information of a specified description must be excluded from the register.

(2) The exemption registration authority must notify the appropriate authority of any information it excludes from the register pursuant to such a direction.

(3) The appropriate authority may direct the exemption registration authority that, in the interests of national security, before information of a specified description is included on the register, the information must be referred to the appropriate authority for determination as to whether or not it should be excluded from the register.

(4) A determination by the appropriate authority under sub-paragraph (3) to exclude information from the register must be given effect by a direction under sub-paragraph (1).

(5) A person may give a notice to the appropriate authority stating that, in the person's opinion, the inclusion of information on the register would be contrary to the interests of national security.

(6) A notice under sub-paragraph (5) must specify the information and indicate its apparent nature.

(7) A person giving a notice under sub-paragraph (5) must at the same time notify the exemption registration authority.

(8) The exemption registration authority must not include information notified under sub-paragraph (5) on the register unless the appropriate authority determines that it may be included.

(9) A determination by the appropriate authority to exclude information notified under sub-paragraph (5) from the register must be given effect by a direction under sub-paragraph (1).

(10) In relation to an exempt facility that is the subject of a direction or notice given under this paragraph, the requirement in paragraph 3(1)(b), 4(b) or 5(b)—
(a) does not apply where a direction or notice requires the exclusion of all relevant particulars from the register; and
(b) is satisfied where—
(i) a direction under sub-paragraph (1) requires the exclusion of some, but not all, relevant particulars from the register,
(ii) a direction under sub-paragraph (3) requires the exclusion of relevant particulars from the register, or
(iii) a notice under sub-paragraph (5) which is pending a determination under sub-paragraph (8) requires the exclusion of relevant particulars from the register,
and where any relevant particulars which are not subject to a direction or notice are included on the register.

10 Restrictions on registering exempt waste operations carried on at the same place

(1) An establishment or undertaking may not be registered more than once during a valid registration period in relation to any one waste operation described in Part 1 of Schedule 3 that is carried on or is to be carried on at the same place.

(2) If an establishment or undertaking is registered more than once in contravention of sub-paragraph (1), the second and any subsequent registration is invalid.

(3) Subject to sub-paragraph (7), not more than one establishment or undertaking may be registered at the same time in relation to the same waste operation described in Part 1 of Schedule 3 if the operation is carried on or is to be carried on at the same place.

(4) If more than one establishment or undertaking is registered in contravention of sub-paragraph (3), only the registration specified in sub-paragraph (5) is valid.

(5) The registration in this sub-paragraph is the registration of the establishment or undertaking in respect of which the relevant particulars first appeared on the register in the relevant period.

(6) In this paragraph, "relevant period" means the period during which the relevant particulars appear on the register.

(7) Sub-paragraph (3) does not apply in relation to a waste operation falling within a description in paragraph D2.

11 Fee for registration relating to WEEE operations

(1) Notwithstanding the power to make a charging scheme under section 41 of the 1995 Act, the Agency may impose a fee in accordance with sub-paragraph (2) until—
(a) the fee is superseded by such a charging scheme; or
(b) 1st April 2013,
whichever is the earlier.

(2) The fee referred to in sub-paragraph (1) is £840 in respect of the registration of an establishment or undertaking in relation to a WEEE operation.

12 Validity of registration of waste operations

(1) A first registration or a registration in relation to a WEEE operation is valid for 3 years.

(2) Any other registration in relation to a waste operation is valid until the end of validity of the first registration.

(3) For the purposes of sub-paragraphs (1) and (2), the period of validity of a registration commences on the date of registration or on the most recent renewal date, as the case may be.

(4) An establishment or undertaking may renew a registration at any time in the month prior to the registration becoming invalid (and the registration procedure specified in paragraph 6 applies in relation to any such renewal).

(5) Where an establishment or undertaking has renewed a registration, the renewal takes effect on the day after the day on which the previous registration becomes invalid.

(6) In this paragraph—

"first registration" means—

(a) the first appearance on the register of relevant particulars for an establishment or undertaking in relation to a waste operation other than a WEEE operation, or

(b) in the case of a renewal, the first such appearance following the end of validity of the registration, other than the end of validity of the registration of a WEEE operation;

"renewal date" means the date that the renewal of a registration takes effect.

13 Changes to relevant particulars relating to waste operations

(1) An establishment or undertaking registered in relation to a waste operation must notify the exemption registration authority without delay of any changes to—

(a) any of the relevant particulars; and

(b) any of the information specified in paragraph 6(4).

(2) If an establishment or undertaking does not comply with sub-paragraph (1)(a), the exemption registration authority may remove from the register the entry made in respect of the establishment or undertaking.

(3) Notification under sub-paragraph (1) must be in the form specified by the exemption registration authority.

(4) The exemption registration authority must notify the establishment or undertaking in question without delay if it removes an entry from the register pursuant to sub-paragraph (2).

14 Record keeping for exempt waste operations

(1) This paragraph applies to every exempt waste operation where the waste operation—

(a) is a WEEE operation; or

(b) falls within a description in—

(i) subject to sub-paragraph (2), paragraph U10 or U11,

(ii) paragraph T9,

(iii) paragraph T3 or T7 where the operation is carried on by waste mobile plant.

(2) But it does not apply in relation to an exempt waste operation where—

(a) the waste operation falls within a description in paragraph U10 or U11; and

(b) the establishment or undertaking is required to keep records in relation to the operation and the waste that is subject to that operation under the Nitrate Pollution Prevention Regulations 2008 or the Nitrate Pollution Prevention (Wales) Regulations 2008.

(3) An establishment or undertaking which carries on an exempt waste operation to which this paragraph applies must—

(a) keep [chronological][1] records of the quantity, nature, origin and, where relevant, the destination and treatment method of all waste disposed of or recovered in the course of that operation; and

(b) where the waste operation falls within a description in paragraph T3 or T7 and is carried on by waste mobile plant, keep records of the places where the operation is carried on.

(4) An establishment or undertaking which carries on an exempt waste operation to which this paragraph applies must—

[(a) retain any records that it is required to keep under sub-paragraph (3) for a period of—

(i) 3 years, if the operation involves the treatment of hazardous waste;

(ii) otherwise 2 years;][2]

(b) during that period make those records available to the exemption registration authority on request.

Amendments

1 Inserted by the Waste (England and Wales) Regulations 2011, SI 2011/988, reg 48(2), Sch 3, paras 1, 6(c)(i).

2 Substituted by the Waste (England and Wales) Regulations 2011, SI 2011/988, reg 48(2), Sch 3, paras 1, 6(c)(ii).

15 Periodic inspections of establishments and undertakings

(1) Every exemption registration authority must carry out appropriate periodic inspections of establishments and undertakings carrying on exempt waste operations in respect of which it is the exemption registration authority.

(2) If an exempt waste operation involves a WEEE operation, the exemption registration authority must discharge the duty in sub-paragraph (1) by carrying out an inspection that complies with the third and fourth paragraphs of Article 6(2) of the WEEE Directive.

SCHEDULE 3
EXEMPT FACILITIES: DESCRIPTIONS AND CONDITIONS

Schedule 2, paragraph 3(1)(a)

PART 1
EXEMPT WASTE OPERATIONS: DESCRIPTIONS AND CONDITIONS (SPECIFIC AND GENERAL)

Chapter 1
Interpretation of Part 1

1 Interpretation

(1) In this Part—

"agricultural land" has the meaning given in section 109(1) of the Agriculture Act 1947 and, for the purposes of the descriptions in paragraphs U10 and U11, this includes land used for the production of timber or other non-food crops;

"anaerobic digestion" means the mesophilic and thermophilic biological decomposition and stabilisation of biodegradable waste which—

(a) is carried on under controlled anaerobic conditions, and

(b) results in stable sanitised material that can be applied to land for the benefit of agriculture or to improve the soil structure or nutrients in land;

"associated storage" means storage of waste that—

(a) is associated with the use, treatment or disposal of waste, and

(b) takes place at the place where the use, treatment or disposal is carried on;

"bank" means a bank, wall or embankment adjoining or confining, or constructed for the purposes of or in connection with, any channel and includes all land between the bank and low-watermark;

"construction" means the carrying on of building or engineering work which includes the repair, alteration, maintenance or improvement of an existing work and preparatory or landscaping works;

"impermeable surface" means a surface or pavement constructed and maintained to a standard sufficient to prevent the transmission of liquids beyond the surface;

"inland waters" has the meaning given in section 221(1) of the 1991 Act;

"place of production" means, in relation to any waste, the place where the waste was originally produced;

"Plant Health notice" means a notice served under—

(a) article 12 of the Plant Health (Phytophthora ramorum) (England) Order 2004,

(b) article 13 of the Plant Health (Phytophthora ramorum) (Wales) Order 2006,

(c) article 31 of the Plant Health (Forestry) Order 2005,

(d) article 32 of the Plant Health (England) Order 2005,

(e) article 32 of the Plant Health (Wales) Order 2006;

"relevant waste", where it appears in any paragraph in this Part, means waste that—

(a) falls within a code specified in the first column of the table in the paragraph, and

(b) is of a type specified in the second column of the table;

"scrap metal" has the meaning given in section 9(2) of the Scrap Metal Dealers Act 1964;

"sealed drainage" means a drainage system with an impermeable surface which ensures that—

(a) no liquid will run off the surface otherwise than via the system, and

(b) except where they may be lawfully discharged, all liquids entering the system are collected in a sealed sump;

"secondary containment" means a bund or any other system for preventing waste which has leaked from the primary container from escaping from the place where it is stored or treated.

(2) In this Part, a 6 digit code used to refer to a waste is a reference to the waste specified by the 6 digit code—

(a) in England, in the List of Wastes (England) Regulations 2005;

(b) in Wales, in the List of Wastes (Wales) Regulations 2005,

except insofar as the waste specified in this Part in relation to such a code does not include some of the types of waste specified by that code in those Regulations.

(3) Where a bund is used as secondary containment—

(a) the bund must have an impermeable lining and—

(i) have a capacity of not less than 110% of the original container's storage capacity, or

(ii) if there is more than one container within the containment system, have a capacity of not less than 110% of the largest container's storage capacity or 25% of their aggregate storage capacity, whichever is the greater, and

(b) reasonable precautions must be taken to ensure that the capacities specified in paragraph (a) are maintained at all times.

(4) When interpreting this Part, a container, lagoon or other place is secure in relation to waste kept in it if—

(a) all reasonable precautions are taken to ensure that the waste cannot escape from it; and

(b) members of the public are unable to gain access to the waste.

(5) Where a quantity limit is specified in relation to more than one operation (storage, use or treatment) in any one specific or additional condition, that quantity limit applies to all of those operations on an aggregate basis.

(6) Where a waste operation is carried on by waste mobile plant, the quantity limits specified in any specific or additional specific condition in any Chapter of this Part apply in relation to each place where the operation is carried on.

(7) The quantity limits specified in any specific condition in paragraphs U1, U2, U10, U11, U12 and U15 that relate to the use or storage of waste over a specified period apply for that period regardless of whether more than one establishment or undertaking carries on the operation at the same place over that period.

(8) In this Part—
(a) a reference to any of paragraphs U1 to U16 is a reference to a paragraph numbered 1 to 16 in Section 2 of Chapter 2 (use of waste);
(b) a reference to any of paragraphs T1 to T33 is a reference to a paragraph numbered 1 to 33 in Section 2 of Chapter 3 (treatment of waste);
(c) a reference to any of paragraphs D1 to D8 is a reference to a paragraph numbered 1 to 8 in Section 2 of Chapter 4 (disposal of waste);
(d) a reference to any of paragraphs S1 to S3 is a reference to a paragraph numbered 1 to 3 in Section 2 of Chapter 5 (storage of waste).

Chapter 2
Use of waste

Section 1
Introductory

1

The descriptions in this Chapter—
(a) are set out in the first sub-paragraph of paragraphs U1 to U16; and
(b) include associated storage.

2

The specific conditions for each description in this Chapter are set out in the third sub-paragraph of paragraphs U1 to U16.

3

The general conditions for all descriptions in this Chapter are as follows—
(a) the operation is for the purposes of recovering or reusing the waste, unless otherwise stated in the specific conditions;
(b) the waste used is suitable for the purposes of the operation;
(c) no more waste is used than is necessary to carry on the operation.

Section 2
Descriptions and specific conditions

1 Use of waste in construction (U1)

(1) The use of relevant waste in construction.

(2) The tables specifying relevant waste for the purposes of this paragraph are set out below.

Table 1

Codes	*Waste types*	*Quantity limit*	*Additional specific conditions*
010102	Waste from mineral non-metalliferous excavation	5,000 tonnes	
010408	Waste gravel and crushed rock other than those mentioned in 010407		
010409	Waste sand and clays		
020202	Shellfish shells from which the soft tissue or flesh has been removed only		
101208	Waste ceramics, bricks, tiles and construction products (after thermal processing)		
101314	Waste concrete and concrete sludge		
170101	Concrete		
170102	Bricks		
170103	Tiles and ceramics		
170107	Mixtures of concrete, bricks, tiles and ceramics other than those mentioned in 170106		
170506	Dredging spoil other than those mentioned in 170505		A
170508	Track ballast other than those mentioned in 170507		
191205	Glass		
191209	Minerals (for example sand, stones)		
191212	Aggregates only		

Table 2

Codes	*Waste types*	*Quantity limit*	*Additional specific conditions*
020399, 020401	Soil from cleaning and washing fruit and vegetables only	1,000 tonnes	
170302	Bituminous mixtures other than those mentioned in 170301	1,000 tonnes	B
170504	Soil and stones other than those mentioned in 170503	1,000 tonnes	
170506	Dredging spoil other than those mentioned in 170505	1,000 tonnes	
191302	Solid wastes from soil remediation other than those mentioned in 191301	1,000 tonnes	
200202	Soil and stones	1,000 tonnes	
020103	Plant tissue waste	1,000 tonnes	B
030101, 030301	Untreated waste bark, cork and wood only	1,000 tonnes	B
030105	Untreated wood including sawdust, shavings and cuttings from untreated wood only	1,000 tonnes	B
170201	Untreated wood only	1,000 tonnes	B
191207	Untreated wood other than those mentioned in 191206 only	1,000 tonnes	B
200138	Untreated wood other than those mentioned in 200137 only	1,000 tonnes	B][1]

Table 3

Codes	*Waste types*	*Quantity limit*	*Additional specific conditions*
170302	Bituminous mixtures other than those mentioned in 170301	50,000 tonnes	C
170504	Road sub base only		C

(3) For the purposes of this paragraph, the specific conditions are that—

(a) where the relevant waste falls within the first column of a table in sub-paragraph (2), the total quantity of waste used or stored over any 3-year period does not exceed the limit indicated in the third column of that table;

(b) where one or more waste type falling within the first column of any one table in sub-paragraph (2) is used or stored, the total quantity for all the waste types used or stored does not exceed the limit indicated in the third column of that table over any 3-year period;

(c) no waste is stored for longer than 12 months prior to use; and

(d) the operation complies with such of the following additional conditions as are specified in the fourth column of the table and for these purposes—

A the waste is used only for drainage work carried on for the purposes of the Land Drainage Act 1991, the 1991 Act or the 1995 Act,

B the waste is used only for the construction of tracks, paths, bridleways or car parks and must be processed into chipped form prior to use,

C the waste is used only for the construction of roads.

Amendments

1 Substituted by the Environmental Permitting (England and Wales) (Amendment) Regulations 2012, SI 2012/630, reg 13(1), (2)(a).

2 Use of baled end-of-life tyres in construction (U2)

(1) The use of relevant waste in construction.

(2) The table specifying relevant waste for the purposes of this paragraph is set out below.

Codes	*Waste types*
160103	Baled end-of-life tyres only

(3) For the purposes of this paragraph, the specific conditions are that—

(a) the total quantity of waste used or stored during the construction does not exceed 50 tonnes of baled tyres;

(b) the waste is not used more than once;

(c) the bales comply with standard PAS108; and

(d) no waste is stored for longer than 3 months prior to use.

3 Use of waste in the construction of entertainment or educational installations etc (U3)

(1) The use of relevant waste in the construction of installations, exhibits, sets or demonstrations for entertainment or educational purposes.

(2) The table specifying relevant waste for the purposes of this paragraph is set out below.

Codes	*Waste types*
170102	Bricks
170103	Tiles and ceramics
170201, 200138	Wood
170203, 200139	Plastic

Codes	*Waste types*
170401 to 170407, 170411, 200140	Metals including their alloys
200101	Paper and cardboard
200111	Textiles

(3) For the purposes of this paragraph, the specific condition is that the total quantity of waste used or stored prior to use does not exceed 20 tonnes at any one time.

4 Burning of waste as a fuel in a small appliance (U4)

(1) The burning of relevant waste as a fuel in an appliance if the requirements in sub-paragraph (4) are met.

(2) The table specifying relevant waste for the purposes of this paragraph is set out below.

Codes	*Waste types*
020103, 200201	Plant tissue waste only
020107, 170201	Untreated wood only
020304	Vegetable waste unsuitable for consumption or processing
030101	Waste bark and cork
030105	Untreated sawdust and wood shavings other than those mentioned in 030104 only
030301	Waste bark and wood
030310	Fibre rejects (fibrous vegetable waste from virgin pulp preparation or paper pulp production) only
150103	Untreated wooden packaging only

(3) For the purposes of this paragraph, the specific conditions are that—
(a) the total quantity of waste burned over any period of 1 hour is less than 50kg;
(b) the total quantity of waste stored at any one time does not exceed 10 tonnes; and
(c) the waste is stored in a secure place.

(4) The requirements in this sub-paragraph are that—
(a) the appliance has a net rated thermal input of less than 0.4 megawatts; and
(b) where it is used together with other appliances (whether or not it is operated simultaneously with such other appliances), the aggregate net rated thermal input of all the appliances is less than 0.4 megawatts.

5 Use of waste derived biodiesel as fuel (U5)

(1) The use of biodiesel derived from relevant waste as a fuel in a portable generator if the requirements in sub-paragraph (4) are met or in a motor vehicle and the storage of such biodiesel—
(a) in or on a motor vehicle or in such a portable generator; or
(b) at a place that is owned or occupied by the owner or user of the biodiesel.

(2) The table specifying relevant waste for the purposes of this paragraph is set out below.

Codes	*Waste types*
190210	Waste derived biodiesel only

(3) For the purposes of this paragraph, the specific conditions are that—
(a) the total quantity of biodiesel stored in or on a motor vehicle or in a portable generator at any one time does not exceed 1,000 litres;
(b) the total quantity of biodiesel stored at a place owned or occupied by the owner or user of the biodiesel at any one time does not exceed 5,000 litres; and
(c) the biodiesel is stored with secondary containment.

(4) The requirements in this sub-paragraph are that—
(a) the portable generator has a net rated thermal input of less than 0.4 megawatts; and
(b) where it is used together with other portable generators (whether or not it is operated simultaneously with such other generators) the aggregate net rated thermal input of all the generators is less than 0.4 megawatts.

6 Use of sludge for the purposes of re-seeding a waste water treatment plant (U6)

(1) The use of relevant waste at a waste water treatment plant for the purposes of re-seeding the plant.

(2) The table specifying relevant waste for the purposes of this paragraph is set out below.

Codes	*Waste types*
190805	Sludges from treatment of urban waste water
190812	Sludges from biological treatment of industrial waste water other than those mentioned in 190811

(3) For the purposes of this paragraph, the specific conditions are that—
(a) the total quantity of waste used or stored at the plant at any one time does not exceed 1,000 cubic metres; and
(b) the waste was not produced at the plant.

7 Use of effluent to clean a highway gravel bed (U7)

(1) The use of relevant waste from a water treatment works or a waste water treatment plant to clean a highway gravel bed.

(2) The table specifying relevant waste for the purposes of this paragraph is set out below.

Codes	*Waste types*
190899	Effluent only

(3) For the purposes of this paragraph, the specific conditions are that—
(a) the total quantity of waste used over any 24-hour period does not exceed 10 cubic metres;
(b) the highway gravel bed has sealed drainage to ensure that the condition in paragraph (c) can be met;
(c) all waste used in and produced by the cleaning operation is collected; and
(d) the waste meets any relevant conditions specified in the environmental permit authorising the operation of the water treatment works or waste water treatment plant.

8 Use of waste for a specified purpose (U8)

(1) The use of relevant waste for a specified purpose.

(2) For the purposes of this paragraph—
(a) the table specifying relevant waste and the limits referred to in sub-paragraph (3)(a) and (b) is set out below;
(b) "specified purpose" is a purpose specified in the third column of the table.

[Codes	*Waste types*	*Specified purpose*	*Quantity limit (at any one time)*
030105, 191207	Untreated wood (including shavings, woodchip and sawdust) and oversized compost only	Use in horse menages	1,000 tonnes

[Codes	*Waste types*	*Specified purpose*	*Quantity limit (at any one time)*
191204	Shredded or granulated rubber and end-of-life tyres only	Use in horse menages	1,000 tonnes
191201	Shredded paper and cardboard	Use as animal bedding	100 tonnes
030305, 030310, 030311	Paper fibre, de-inked paper pulp and de-inked paper sludge from paper manufacturing only	Use as animal bedding	100 tonnes
030105, 191207	Untreated wood (including shavings, woodchip and sawdust) and oversized compost only	Use as animal bedding	100 tonnes
160103	End-of-life tyres	Use as a weight on cover sheeting on agricultural premises or use as crash barriers	40 tonnes
150102	Geotextile bags (flexible intermediate bulk containers) only	Use as reinforcement in construction	100 bags
020202	Shellfish shells from which the soft tissue or flesh has been removed only	Use for ornamental purposes	50 tonnes
191205	Crushed glass only	Use for ornamental purposes	50 tonnes
200127*, 200128, 080111*, 080112	Paints (excluding specialist and industrial paints, wood preservatives, aerosol and spray paints, inks, adhesives and resins)	Use as paint	1,000 litres
190599	Compost produced for the purposes of growing mushrooms only	Use in growing mushrooms	1,000 tonnes
170102, 170904	Stones and bricks capable of being used in their existing state only	Use in construction of buildings, fencing, barriers, containment or similar above ground construction	100 tonnes
170201, 191207, 200138	Non-hazardous wood including telegraph poles and railway sleepers and lock gates and associated balance beams	Use in construction of buildings, fencing, barriers, containment or similar above ground construction	100 tonnes
110105*, 110107*	Ferric chloride and aluminium hydroxide only	Use in treating municipal waste water effluent	50 cubic metres
110105*, 110107*	Ferric chloride and aluminium hydroxide only	Use in potable water treatment processes	50 cubic metres
190902, 190903, 190906	Sludges/solutions from the treatment of water only	Use in treating municipal waste water effluent	50 cubic metres
100201, 100202, 170504, 191209	Blast furnace slag and stones only	Use as filter media at waste water treatment works	50,000 tonnes

[Codes	*Waste types*	*Specified purpose*	*Quantity limit (at any one time)*
170204*, 191206*, 200137*	Hazardous wooden telegraph poles and railway sleepers and lock gates and associated balance beams only	Use in construction of buildings, fencing, barriers, containment or similar above ground construction	100 tonnes]

(3) For the purposes of this paragraph, the specific conditions are that—

(a) the total amount of waste used or stored at any one time does not exceed the quantity limit specified in the fourth column;

(b) in relation to any relevant waste to which code 160103 applies (end-of-life tyres), within the quantity limit specified for that waste type, not more than 10 tonnes is stored together;

(c) the waste is not treated or required to be treated prior to use; and

[(d) in relation to any relevant waste to which code 110105* (ferric chloride), 110107* (aluminium hydroxide), 190902, 190903, 190906 (sludges/solutions from the treatment of water) applies, the waste is stored—

(i) with secondary containment, and

(ii) in a location with sealed drainage; and

(e) in relation to any relevant waste to which code 110105* (ferric chloride), 110107* (aluminium hydroxide) applies, within the quantity limit specified for that waste type, not more than 10 tonnes of waste may be used per day.]

Amendment

1 Substituted by the Environmental Permitting (England and Wales) (Amendment) Regulations 2012, SI 2012/630, reg 13(1), (2)(b), (c).

9 Use of waste to manufacture finished goods (U9)

(1) The use of relevant waste to manufacture finished goods.

(2) The table specifying relevant waste for the purposes of this paragraph and the quantity limits referred to in sub-paragraph (3)(a) is set out below.

Codes	*Waste types*	*Quantity limit (at any one time)*	*Additional specific conditions*
100101, 100102	Ash only	500 tonnes	A
101208	Ceramics	100 tonnes	A
101112, 150107, 191205, 200102	Glass	5,000 tonnes	A
100105	Gypsum only	500 tonnes	A
200199	Lion faeces only	5 tonnes	B
120101, 120103, 150104, 160117, 160118, 191001, 191002, 191202, 191203, 200140	Metals	500 tonnes	A
150101, 191201, 200101	Paper and cardboard	15,000 tonnes	C, D
070213, 120105, 150102, 191204, 200139	Plastics	500 tonnes	E
191204	Rubber only	30 tonnes	E, F
. . .[1]			

Codes	*Waste types*	*Quantity limit (at any one time)*	*Additional specific conditions*
040221, 040222, 150109, 191208, 200110, 200111	Textiles	1,000 tonnes	B
030105, 030301, 150103, 191207, 200138	Wood, bark, cork, sawdust, shavings, cuttings, particle board	100 tonnes	B

(3) For the purposes of this paragraph, the specific conditions are that—

(a) the total quantity of waste used or stored at any one time does not exceed the quantity limit specified in the third column of the table in sub-paragraph (2);

(b) the waste is stored in a secure location at the place where the manufacturing is carried on;

(c) the operation does not involve any activity falling within a description in Part A(1) or Part A(2) of Part 2 of Schedule 1; and

(d) the operation complies with such of the following additional specific conditions as are specified in the fourth column of the table—

A the waste is stored at a location with sealed drainage,

B the waste is stored indoors or in a secure container,

C the waste is stored in a baled form, in a container or indoors,

D within the quantity limit specified in the third column of the table and notwithstanding additional specific condition C, up to 1,000 tonnes may be stored outdoors so long as it is stored in an enclosure designed and maintained to prevent the escape of litter,

E the waste is not subject to heat treatment,

F the total quantity of waste stored together does not exceed 10 tonnes.

(4) For the purposes of this paragraph, "finished goods" means goods that are ready for use by an end consumer without any further processing.

Amendment

1 Repealed by the Waste (England and Wales) Regulations 2011, SI 2011/988, reg 48(2), Sch 3, paras 1, 7(a).

10 Spreading waste on agricultural land to confer benefit (U10)

(1) The spreading of relevant waste on agricultural land to confer benefit to the land for the purposes of providing, maintaining or improving the soil's ability to provide a growing medium by adding nutrients, lime or biomass.

(2) The table specifying relevant waste for the purposes of this paragraph and the quantity and storage limits referred to in sub-paragraph (3) is set out below.

Codes	*Waste types*	*Quantity limit*	*Storage limit (at any one time)*	*Period*	*Additional specific conditions*
010102, 010408, 170504	Chalk only	50 tonnes per hectare	200 tonnes	12 months	A
[020101	Sludges from washing and cleaning fruit and vegetables on farm only	50 tonnes per hectare	200 tonnes	12 months	A, F
020199, 020399	Untreated wash waters from cleaning fruit and vegetables on farm only	100 tonnes per hectare	200 tonnes	12 months	A, F

Codes	*Waste types*	*Quantity limit*	*Storage limit (at any one time)*	*Period*	*Additional specific conditions*
020305	Effluent from the on-site treatment of wash waters from cleaning fruit and vegetables on farm only	100 tonnes per hectare	200 tonnes	12 months	A, F][1]
...[2]	...[2]	...[2]	...[2]	...[2]	...[2]
020401, 020399	Soil from cleaning and washing fruit and vegetables only	50 tonnes per hectare	200 tonnes	12 months	A
020199	Milk from agricultural premises only	50 cubic metres of diluted milk per hectare	200 tonnes	24 hours	A, B, E
100101	Ash from wood chip boilers produced pursuant to an operation described in paragraph U4 only	1 tonne per hectare	10 tonnes	12 months	A
170506	Dredging spoil (other than those mentioned in 170505) generated from the creation or maintenance of habitats, ditches or ponds within parks, gardens, fields and forests only	150 tonnes per hectare	1,250 tonnes	12 months	C
020199	Spent compost from the growing of mushrooms [only][2]	50 tonnes per hectare	500 tonnes	12 months	A
190599	Compost produced pursuant to a treatment described in paragraph T23 or T26 only	50 tonnes per hectare	500 tonnes	12 months	A
190604	Digestate produced pursuant to a treatment described in paragraph T24 or T25 only	50 tonnes per hectare	200 tonnes	12 months	A
190812	Waste consisting of biobed or biofilter material produced pursuant to a treatment described in paragraph T32 only	50 tonnes per hectare	200 tonnes	12 months	A, D

(3) For the purposes of this paragraph, the specific conditions are that—

(a) the total quantity of waste spread does not exceed the limit specified in the third column of the table in sub-paragraph (2) over the period specified in the fifth column;

(b) the total quantity of waste stored at any one time does not exceed the limit specified in the fourth column of the table;
(c) subject to additional specific conditions D and E in sub-paragraph (f), where they apply, no waste is stored for longer than 12 months prior to spreading;
(d) the waste is stored in a secure location prior to spreading;
(e) at the time the spreading begins—
 (i) the land has not been frozen for 12 hours or more in the preceding 24 hours,
 (ii) the land is not waterlogged, frozen or snow-covered; and
(f) the operation complies with such of the following additional specific conditions as are specified in the sixth column of the table—
 A the location of any waste which is stored or land which is spread is at least 10 metres from a watercourse and 50 metres from a spring, well or borehole,
 B prior to spreading, the waste is diluted with not less than an equal quantity of water or slurry and the land is spread not more than once in any 4-week period,
 C the waste is spread adjacent to the place from which it was dredged,
 D the waste is stored for at least 12 months prior to spreading,
 E the waste is not stored for longer than 24 hours prior to spreading,
 [F the waste is spread at the place where it is produced.][1]

Amendments

1 Inserted by the Environmental Permitting (England and Wales) (Amendment) Regulations 2012, SI 2012/630, reg 13(1), (2)(d)(i), (e).

2 Repealed by the Waste (England and Wales) Regulations 2011, SI 2011/988, reg 48(2), Sch 3, paras 1, 7(b).

11 Spreading waste on non-agricultural land to confer benefit (U11)

(1) The spreading of relevant waste on land that is not agricultural land for the purposes of providing, maintaining or improving the soil's ability to provide a growing medium by adding nutrients, lime or biomass.

(2) The table specifying relevant waste for the purposes of this paragraph and the quantity and storage limits referred to in sub-paragraph (3) is set out below.

Codes	*Waste types*	*Quantity limit (over 12 months)*	*Storage limit (at any one time)*	*Additional specific conditions*
010102, 010408, 170504	Chalk only	50 tonnes per hectare	200 tonnes	A
…[1]	…[1]	…[1]	…[1]	…[1]
020202	Shellfish shells from which the soft tissue or flesh has been removed only	50 tonnes per hectare	200 tonnes	A
020399, 020401	Soil from cleaning and washing fruit and vegetables only	50 tonnes per hectare	200 tonnes	A
100101	Ash from wood chip boilers produced pursuant to an operation described in paragraph U4 only	1 tonne per hectare	10 tonnes	A
170506	Dredging spoil (other than those mentioned in 170505) generated from the creation or maintenance of habitats, ditches or ponds within parks, gardens, fields and forests only	150 tonnes per hectare	1,250 tonnes	B

Codes	*Waste types*	*Quantity limit (over 12 months)*	*Storage limit (at any one time)*	*Additional specific conditions*
020199	Spent compost from the growing of mushrooms only	50 tonnes per hectare	500 tonnes	A
190599	Compost produced pursuant to a treatment described in paragraph T23 or T26 only	50 tonnes per hectare	500 tonnes	A
190604	Digestate produced pursuant to a treatment described in paragraph T24 or T25 only	50 tonnes per hectare	200 tonnes	A
190812	Waste consisting of biobed or biofilter material produced pursuant to a treatment described in paragraph T32 only	50 tonnes per hectare	200 tonnes	A, C
200108	Coffee grounds only	50 tonnes per hectare	200 tonnes	A

(3) For the purposes of this paragraph, the specific conditions are that—

(a) the total quantity of waste spread does not exceed the limit specified in the third column of the table in sub-paragraph (2) over any 12-month period;

(b) the total quantity of waste stored at any one time does not exceed the limit specified in the fourth column of the table;

(c) subject to additional specific condition C in sub-paragraph (f), where it applies, no waste is stored for longer than 12 months prior to spreading;

(d) the waste is stored in a secure location prior to spreading;

(e) at the time the spreading begins—

(i) the land has not been frozen for 12 hours or more in the preceding 24 hours,

(ii) the land is not waterlogged, frozen or snow-covered; and

(f) the operation complies with such of the following additional specific conditions as are specified in the fifth column of the table—

A the location of any waste which is stored or land which is spread is at least 10 metres from a watercourse and 50 metres from a spring, well or borehole,

B the waste is spread adjacent to the place from which it was dredged,

C the waste is stored for at least 12 months prior to spreading.

Amendment

1 Repealed by the Waste (England and Wales) Regulations 2011, SI 2011/988, reg 48(2), Sch 3, paras 1, 7(b).

12 Use of mulch (U12)

(1) The use of relevant waste as a mulch.

(2) The table specifying relevant waste for the purposes of this paragraph is set out below.

Codes	*Waste types*
020103, 191207, 200201	Untreated wood and plant matter

(3) For the purposes of this paragraph, the specific conditions are that—

(a) the total quantity of waste used or stored over any period of 1 month does not exceed 100 tonnes; and

(b) the waste is stored in a secure location prior to use.

13 Spreading of plant matter to confer benefit (U13)

(1) The spreading of relevant waste at the place of production to confer benefit.

(2) The table specifying relevant waste for the purposes of this paragraph is set out below.

Codes	*Waste types*
020103, 020107, 020304, 200201	Plant tissue only

(3) For the purposes of this paragraph, the specific conditions are that—

(a) the total quantity of waste spread over any 12-month period does not exceed 50 tonnes per hectare;

(b) at the time the spreading begins—

(i) the land has not been frozen for 12 hours or more in the preceding 24 hours,

(ii) the land is not waterlogged, frozen or snow-covered; and

(c) except for waste which is spread on the banks of the waters from which it was produced, no waste is spread within 50 metres of any watercourse, spring, well or borehole.

14 Incorporation of ash into soil (U14)

(1) The incorporation of ash which is relevant waste into soil resulting from a qualifying operation.

(2) The table specifying relevant waste for the purposes of this paragraph is set out below.

Codes	*Waste types*
020103, 020107, 200201	Ash from burning of plant tissue only

(3) For the purposes of this paragraph, the specific conditions are that—

(a) the total quantity of waste incorporated into soil does not exceed 10 tonnes per hectare; and

(b) ashes of burnt cereal, straw or cereal stubble are not allowed, without reasonable excuse, proof of which lies on the establishment or undertaking carrying on the operation, to remain on the soil for longer than 24 hours after the commencement of the burning but must be incorporated into the soil—

(i) within that period, or

(ii) in a case where, having regard to wind conditions to do so would be likely to cause nuisance, as soon as conditions allow.

(4) For the purposes of this paragraph, a "qualifying operation" is one that—

(a) involves the burning of cereal straw or cereal stubble;

(b) falls within a description in paragraph D7; and

(c) complies with the specific conditions specified in that paragraph and the general conditions specified in Chapter 3.

15 Pig and poultry ash (U15)

(1) The spreading of relevant waste on agricultural land at the place of production.

(2) The table specifying relevant waste for the purposes of this paragraph is set out below.

Codes	*Waste types*
190112	Ash from the incineration of pig and poultry carcasses only

(3) For the purposes of this paragraph, the specific conditions are that—

(a) the total quantity of waste spread over any 12-month period does not exceed 150kg per hectare;

(b) the waste is mixed with an equal volume or more of manure or slurry prior to spreading;

(c) the waste is stored in a secure place prior to spreading;

(d) the location of the waste which is stored or land which is spread is at least—

(i) 10 metres from a watercourse,

(ii) 50 metres from a spring, well or borehole; and

(e) at the time of the spreading—
   (i) the land has not been frozen for 12 hours or more in the preceding 24 hours,
   (ii) the land is not waterlogged, frozen or snow-covered.

16 Use of depolluted end-of-life vehicles for vehicle parts (U16)

(1) The use of relevant waste for vehicle parts.

(2) The table specifying relevant waste for the purposes of this paragraph is set out below.

Codes	*Waste types*
160106	End-of-life vehicles, containing neither liquids nor other hazardous components
160122	Non-hazardous components from end-of-life vehicles only

(3) For the purposes of this paragraph, the specific conditions are that—
(a) no more than two depolluted end-of-life vehicles are stored at any one time;
(b) in relation to relevant waste to which code 160122 applies (non-hazardous components from end-of-life vehicles), the total quantity of waste stored at any one time does not exceed 5 cubic metres;
(c) the waste is stored in a secure place;
(d) the waste is stored on an impermeable surface; and
(e) the operation is for the purposes of re-using the waste.

[(4) In this paragraph—
"depolluted" means that the vehicle has been subjected to all of the operations described in paragraph 3 of Annex 1 to the End-of-Life Vehicles Directive;
"end-of-life vehicle" has the meaning given in paragraph 2(2)(b) of Schedule 11.][1]

Amendment

1 Substituted by the Environmental Permitting (England and Wales) (Amendment) Regulations 2012, SI 2012/630, reg 13(1), (2)(f).

Chapter 3
Treatment of waste

Section 1
Introductory

1

The descriptions in this Chapter—
(a) are set out in the first sub-paragraph of paragraphs T1 to T33; and
(b) include associated storage.

2

The specific conditions for each description in this Chapter are set out in the third sub-paragraph of paragraphs T1 to T33.

3

The general condition for the descriptions in this Chapter is that the operation is for the purposes of recovering the waste, unless otherwise stated in the specific conditions.

Section 2
Descriptions and specific conditions

1 Cleaning, washing, spraying or coating relevant waste (T1)

(1) The treatment of relevant waste by cleaning, washing, spraying or coating it, subject to sub-paragraph (4).

(2) The table specifying relevant waste for the purposes of this paragraph is set out below.

Codes	*Waste types*
150105	Composite packaging
160120, 150107, 170202, 191205, 200102	Glass
150101	Paper and cardboard packaging
020104, 070213, 150102, 160119, 170203, 200139	Plastic
150109	Textile packaging

(3) For the purposes of this paragraph, the specific conditions are that—
(a) the total quantity of waste treated over any 7-day period does not exceed 300 tonnes;
(b) subject to paragraph (e), the total quantity of waste stored at any one time does not exceed 300 tonnes;
(c) the waste is stored and treated in a location with sealed drainage;
(d) no waste is stored for longer than 3 months prior to treatment;
(e) where the waste consists of containers that have been used to contain a dangerous substance, the total quantity of waste stored does not exceed 1 tonne over any 7-day period; and
(f) the waste is not contaminated by more than 1% of its original volume prior to treatment.

(4) The description in sub-paragraph (1) does not include cleaning, washing, spraying or coating of any relevant waste if this falls within Part B of section 6.4 of Part 2 of Schedule 1.

(5) In this paragraph, "dangerous substance" has the meaning given in regulation 2(1) of the Chemicals (Hazard Information and Packaging for Supply) Regulations 2009.

(6) References in this paragraph to quantity limits by weight include the weight of any contamination.

2 Recovery of textiles (T2)

(1) The treatment of relevant waste by laundering or otherwise cleaning it.

(2) The table specifying relevant waste for the purposes of this paragraph is set out below.

Codes	*Waste types*
191208	Textiles
200110	Clothes
200111	Textiles

(3) For the purposes of this paragraph, the specific conditions are that—
(a) the total quantity of waste treated or stored at any one time does not exceed 20,000 tonnes; and
(b) the waste is treated and stored at a location with sealed drainage.

3 Treatment of waste metals and metal alloys by heating for the purposes of removing grease etc (T3)

(1) The treatment of relevant waste for the purposes of removing grease, oil or any other non-metallic contaminant by heating it in an appliance where the requirements of sub-paragraph (4) are met using a process that is not an excluded process.

(2) The table specifying relevant waste for the purposes of this paragraph is set out below.

Codes	*Waste types*
160117	Ferrous metal
160118	Non ferrous metal
191001	Iron and steel waste
191002	Non ferrous waste
191202	Ferrous metal
191203	Non ferrous metal
200140	Metals

(3) For the purposes of this paragraph, the specific conditions are that—
(a) the total quantity of waste stored or treated at any one time does not exceed 10 tonnes; and
(b) the waste is stored in a secure location with sealed drainage.

(4) The requirements in this sub-paragraph are that—
(a) the appliance has a net rated thermal input of less than 0.2 megawatts; and
(b) where it is used together with other appliances (whether or not it is operated simultaneously with such other appliances), the aggregate net rated thermal input of all the appliances is less than 0.2 megawatts.

(5) The processes that are excluded processes for the purposes of sub-paragraph (1) are—
(a) the removal by heat of plastic or rubber covering from scrap cable or any asbestos contaminant;
(b) a process that is an activity listed in Section 2.1 (other than paragraph (d) of Part B) of Part 2 of Schedule 1 involving the heating of iron, steel or ferrous alloy; and
(c) a process that is an activity described in Part A(1) or A(2) of Section 2.2 of Part 2 of Schedule 1 involving the heating of any non-ferrous metal or non-ferrous metal alloy.

4 Preparatory treatments (baling, sorting, shredding etc) (T4)

(1) The treatment of relevant waste by baling, sorting, shredding, pulverising, densifying, crushing or compacting it.

(2) The table specifying relevant waste for the purposes of this paragraph and the quantity limits referred to in sub-paragraph (3) is set out below.

Codes	*Waste types*	*Treatment limit (over 7 days)*	*Storage limit (at any one time)*
150104, 200140	Cans and foils only	100 tonnes where treatment is carried on outdoors 500 tonnes where treatment is carried on indoors	500 tonnes
070213, 150102, 150105	Food and drink cartons only	100 tonnes where treatment is carried on outdoors 3,000 tonnes where treatment is carried on indoors	500 tonnes
150107, 160120, 170202, 191205, 200102	Glass	5,000 tonnes	5,000 tonnes

Codes	*Waste types*	*Treatment limit (over 7 days)*	*Storage limit (at any one time)*
030308, 030307, 150101, 191201, 200101	Paper and cardboard (excluding food and drink cartons)	500 tonnes where treatment is carried on outdoors 3,000 tonnes where treatment is carried on indoors	15,000 tonnes
020104, 070213, 120105, 150102, 160119, 170203, 191204, 200139	Plastic	100 tonnes where treatment is carried on outdoors 3000 tonnes where treatment is carried on indoors	500 tonnes
040222, 150109, 191208, 200110, 200111	Textiles and clothes	1,000 tonnes where treatment is carried on outdoors 3,000 tonnes where treatment is carried on indoors	1,000 tonnes

(3) For the purposes of this paragraph, the specific conditions are that—

(a) subject to paragraph (d), the total quantity of waste treated over any 7-day period does not exceed the limit specified in the third column of the table in sub-paragraph (2);

(b) the total quantity of waste stored at any one time does not exceed the limit specified in the fourth column of the table;

(c) no waste is stored for longer than 12 months;

(d) where the treatment involves pulverising waste—

  (i) the total quantity of waste treated over any 7-day period does not exceed 5 tonnes,

  (ii) the treatment is carried on indoors;

(e) where the treatment involves densifying waste, the treatment does not involve the application of heat;

(f) the treatment and storage are carried on in a secure place;

(g) the waste arrives at the place where the operation is carried on unmixed with any other type of waste;

(h) the waste is treated and stored in an unmixed state; and

(i) in relation to relevant waste to which codes 030308, 030307, 150101, 191201, 200101 apply (paper and cardboard)—

  (i) the waste is stored in a baled form, in a container or indoors,

  (ii) within the storage limit specified in the fourth column of the table, up to 1,000 tonnes may be stored outdoors so long as it is stored in an enclosure designed and maintained to prevent the escape of litter.

5 Screening and blending of waste (T5)

(1) The treatment of relevant waste by screening and blending it for the purposes of producing an aggregate or soil and associated prior treatment.

(2) The table specifying relevant waste for the purposes of this paragraph is set out below.

Codes	*Waste types*
010408	Waste gravel and crushed rocks other than those mentioned in 010407
010409	Waste sand and clays
020202	Shellfish shells from which the soft tissue or flesh has been removed only
030101	[Untreated waste bark and cork only][1]

Codes	*Waste types*
030301	[Untreated waste][1] bark and wood
100101	Bottom ash, slag and boiler dust (excluding boiler dust mentioned in 100104)
100115	Bottom ash, slag and boiler dust from co-incineration other than those mentioned in 100114
170101	Concrete
170102	Bricks
170103	Tiles and ceramics
170107	Mixtures of concrete, bricks, tiles and ceramics other than those mentioned in 170106
170201	[Untreated wood only][1]
170302	Bituminous mixtures other than those mentioned in 170301
170504	Soil and stones other than those mentioned in 170503
170506	Dredging spoil other than those mentioned in 170505
170508	Track ballast other than those mentioned in 170507
190599	Compost produced pursuant to a treatment described in paragraphs T23 or T26 only
191205	Glass
191209	Aggregates only
191212	Gypsum recovered from construction materials only
191302	Solid wastes from soil remediation other than those mentioned in 191301
191304	Sludges from soil remediation other than those mentioned in 191303
200202	Soil and stones

(3) For the purposes of this paragraph, the specific conditions are that—

(a) in relation to any relevant waste to which code 170302 applies (bituminous mixtures other than those mentioned in 170301) where the treatment is for the purposes of manufacturing roadstone, the total quantity of waste treated or stored over any 3-year period does not exceed 50,000 tonnes;

(b) in relation to relevant waste not covered by paragraph (a), the total quantity of waste treated or stored over any 3-year period does not exceed 5,000 tonnes;

(c) no waste is stored for longer than 12 months; and

(d) the treatment is carried on at the place—

 (i) of production, or

 (ii) where the treated waste is to be used.

(4) In this paragraph, "associated prior treatment" means crushing relevant waste for the purposes of screening or blending it but does not include crushing of any relevant waste which falls within Part B of Section 3.5 of Part 2 of Schedule 1 or within paragraph T7.

Amendment

1 Substituted by the Environmental Permitting (England and Wales) (Amendment) Regulations 2012, SI 2012/630, reg 13(1), (3)(a).

6 Treatment of waste wood and waste plant matter by chipping, shredding, cutting or pulverising (T6)

(1) The treatment of relevant waste by chipping, shredding, cutting or pulverising it.

(2) The table specifying relevant waste for the purposes of this paragraph is set out below.

Codes	*Waste types*
020103, 200201	Plant tissue waste
030101,030301, 170201	Wood
150103	[Wooden][1] packaging only

(3) For the purposes of this paragraph, the specific conditions are that—

(a) the total quantity of waste treated or stored over any 7-day period does not exceed 500 tonnes; and

(b) no waste is stored for longer than 3 months after treatment.

Amendment

1 Substituted by the Environmental Permitting (England and Wales) (Amendment) Regulations 2012, SI 2012/630, reg 13(1), (3)(b).

7 Treatment of waste bricks, tiles and concrete by crushing, grinding or reducing in size (T7)

(1) The treatment of relevant waste by crushing, grinding or reducing it in size but not including any treatment activity covered by paragraph (c) in Part B of Section 3.5 of Part 2 of Schedule 1.

(2) The table specifying relevant waste for the purposes of this paragraph is set out below.

Codes	*Waste types*
170101	Concrete
170102	Bricks
170103	Tiles and ceramics
170107	Mixtures of concrete, bricks, tiles and ceramics (other than those mentioned in 170106*)

(3) For the purposes of this paragraph, the specific conditions are that—

(a) the total quantity of waste treated over any period of 1 hour does not exceed 20 tonnes;

(b) the total quantity of waste stored at any one time does not exceed 200 tonnes;

(c) the waste is stored in a secure place prior to treatment;

(d) the treatment is carried on—

- (i) at the place of production, or
- (ii) at the place where the treated waste is to be used; and

(e) the operation does not result in the release into the air of a substance listed in paragraph 6(3) of Part 1 of Schedule 1 except in a quantity which is so trivial that it is incapable of causing pollution or its capacity to cause pollution is insignificant.

8 Mechanical treatment of end-of-life tyres (T8)

(1) The treatment of end-of-life tyres, including such tyres in a shredded or granulated form, that are relevant waste by a relevant treatment operation and associated prior treatment.

(2) The table specifying relevant waste and relevant treatment operations for the purposes of this paragraph is set out below.

Codes	*Waste types*	*Relevant treatment operation*
160103	End-of-life tyres	Granulating, baling, peeling, shaving, shredding and re-treading of tyres
191204	Shredded or granulated end-of-life tyres only	Granulating

(3) For the purposes of this paragraph, the specific conditions are that—

(a) the total quantity of waste stored or treated over any 7-day period does not exceed—

- (i) 60 tonnes of truck tyres, or
- (ii) 40 tonnes of any other tyres;

(b) within the limits in paragraph (a), the total quantity stored together does not exceed 10 tonnes;

(c) in relation to any relevant treatment operation that is granulating, the treatment is carried on indoors; and

(d) in relation to any relevant treatment operation that is re-treading, the treatment is for the purposes of re-using the waste.

(4) In this paragraph, "associated prior treatment" means cleaning tyres and separating rims from them prior to treatment.

9 Recovery of scrap metal (T9)

(1) The recovery of scrap metal consisting of relevant waste by—
(a) sorting, grading, shearing by manual feed, baling or crushing it; or
(b) cutting it with hand-held equipment.

(2) The table specifying relevant waste for the purposes of this paragraph is set out below.

Codes	*Waste types*
020110	Waste metal
150104	Metallic packaging
160117, 191202	Ferrous metal
160118, 191203	Non ferrous metal
170401	Copper, bronze, brass
170402	Aluminium
170403	Lead
170404	Zinc
170405	Iron and steel
170406	Tin
170407	Mixed metals
170411	Cables other than those mentioned in 170410
200140	Metals

(3) For the purposes of this paragraph, the specific conditions are that—
(a) the total quantity of waste treated or stored at any one time does not exceed 1,000 tonnes;
(b) within the limit in paragraph (a), the total quantity of any cables stored or treated does not exceed 50 tonnes;
(c) no waste is stored for longer than 24 months;
(d) the recovery is carried on at a location with sealed drainage; and
(e) the height of any pile or stack of waste does not exceed 5 metres.

10 Sorting mixed waste (T10)

(1) The sorting of one type of relevant waste from one or more other types of relevant waste.

(2) The table specifying relevant waste for the purposes of this paragraph is set out below.

Codes	*Waste types*
150101, 200101	Paper and cardboard
150102, 200139	Plastics
150104, 200140	Metals
150105	Composite packaging
150106	Mixed packaging
150107, 200102	Glass
150109, 200110, 200111	Textiles and clothing only

(3) For the purposes of this paragraph, the specific conditions are that—

(c) the operation complies with such of the following additional specific conditions as is specified in the fifth column of the table—
   A the operation is for the purposes of reusing the waste,
   B no waste is stored for longer than 12 months,
   C treatment and storage are carried on indoors.

13 Treatment of waste food (T13)

(1) The treatment of waste food that is relevant waste by decanting or unwrapping it, bulking it up and sorting it.

(2) The table specifying relevant waste for the purposes of this paragraph is set out below.

Codes	*Waste types*
...[1]	
020304, 020501, 020601, 020704	Materials unsuitable for consumption or processing ...[1]
200199	Non liquid foods unsuitable for consumption or processing ...[1]

(3) For the purposes of this paragraph, the specific conditions are that—
(a) the total quantity of waste treated or stored at any one time does not exceed 30 tonnes;
(b) the treatment and storage are carried on—
   (i) indoors,
   (ii) in a secure place;
(c) no waste is stored for longer than 7 days;
(d) in relation to relevant waste specified in the first row of the table in sub-paragraph (2) (milk only), the operation is carried on in a dairy which has sealed drainage; and
(e) any resultant waste packaging is bulked up for the purposes of recovery.

Amendment

1 Repealed by the Waste (England and Wales) Regulations 2011, SI 2011/988, reg 48(2), Sch 3, paras 1, 8(a).

14 Crushing and emptying waste vehicle oil filters (T14)

(1) The treatment of waste vehicle oil filters consisting of relevant waste by crushing and emptying them.

(2) The table specifying relevant waste for the purposes of this paragraph is set out below.

Codes	*Waste types*
160107*	Oil filters

(3) For the purposes of this paragraph, the specific conditions are that—
(a) the total quantity of waste stored after treatment does not exceed 1 tonne of crushed and emptied oil filters at any one time;
(b) the treatment is carried on at the place of production;
(c) the equipment used to treat the waste is—
   (i) designed for the purposes of crushing oil filters,
   (ii) designed and maintained to ensure that oil does not escape during treatment; and
(d) the treatment takes place as soon as practicable after the oil filter is removed from a vehicle.

15 Treatment of waste aerosol cans (T15)

(1) The treatment of empty used waste aerosol cans consisting of relevant waste by puncturing and crushing them.

(2) The table specifying relevant waste for the purposes of this paragraph is set out below.

Codes	Waste types
160504*	Aerosol cans containing residues of or contaminated by dangerous substances only
160505	Aerosol cans only

(3) For the purposes of this paragraph, the specific conditions are that—

(a) the total quantity of waste treated or stored in any 12-month period does not exceed 3,000 cans;

(b) the waste is stored in a secure location in vented containers prior to treatment;

(c) the treatment and storage are carried on—

  (i) at the place of production,

  (ii) in a well-ventilated area; and

(d) the equipment used to treat the waste is designed for that purpose.

16 [Treatment of waste toner cartridges and waste ink cartridges by sorting, dismantling, cleaning or refilling (T16)][1]

(1) The treatment of waste toner cartridges [and waste ink cartridges][2] consisting of relevant waste by sorting, dismantling, cleaning or refilling them.

(2) The table specifying relevant waste for the purposes of this paragraph is set out below.

Codes	Waste types
[080313	Waste ink other than that mentioned in 080312*][2]
080318	Waste printing toner other than those mentioned in 080317
150102	Plastic packaging
160216	Cartridges taken from discarded equipment other than those mentioned in 160215 only
200139	Plastics

(3) For the purposes of this paragraph, the specific conditions are that—

(a) the total quantity of waste treated or stored at any one time does not exceed [150 tonnes][1]; and

(b) the treatment is carried on—

  (i) indoors,

  (ii) at a location with sealed drainage.

Amendments

1 Substituted by the Environmental Permitting (England and Wales) (Amendment) Regulations 2012, SI 2012/630, reg 13(1), (3)(d)(iii).

2 Inserted by the Environmental Permitting (England and Wales) (Amendment) Regulations 2012, SI 2012/630, reg 13(1), (3)(d)(i), (ii).

17 Crushing waste fluorescent tubes (T17)

(1) The crushing of relevant waste for the purposes of volume reduction prior to collection.

(2) The table specifying relevant waste for the purposes of this paragraph is set out below.

Codes	Waste types
200121*	Fluorescent tubes only

(3) For the purposes of this paragraph, the specific conditions are that—

(a) the total quantity of waste crushed over any period of 24 hours does not exceed 3 tonnes;

(b) the crushing is carried on at the place of production;

(c) the equipment used for crushing is designed for the purposes of crushing and volume reduction;

(d) the mercury concentration in any resultant emissions does not exceed 25 microgrammes per cubic metre; and
(e) any glass or mercury released after crushing is stored in a secure container under weatherproof covering.

18 Dewatering using flocculants (T18)

(1) The treatment of relevant waste by dewatering using flocculants.

(2) The table specifying relevant waste for the purposes of this paragraph is set out below.

Codes	*Waste types*
010409	Clay effluent resulting from the manufacture of ceramics only
080120	Water based paint wash waters only

(3) For the purposes of this paragraph, the specific conditions are that—
(a) the total quantity of waste stored or treated at any one time does not exceed 30,000 litres; and
(b) the waste is stored in a container with secondary containment.

19 [Physical and chemical treatment of waste edible oil and fat to produce biodiesel (T19)][1]

(1) The physical [and chemical][2] treatment of relevant waste for the purposes of producing biodiesel.

(2) The table specifying relevant waste for the purposes of this paragraph is set out below.

Codes	*Waste types*
200125	Edible oil and fat

(3) For the purposes of this paragraph, the specific conditions are that—
[(a) the total quantity of waste physically treated or stored at any one time does not exceed 5,000 litres;
(aa) the total quantity of waste chemically treated at any one time does not exceed 250 litres;][1]
(b) the waste is treated and stored in a container with secondary containment;
(c) no waste is stored for longer than 3 months; and
(d) the operation is for the purposes of reusing the waste.

Amendments

1 Substituted by the Environmental Permitting (England and Wales) (Amendment) Regulations 2012, SI 2012/630, reg 13(1), (3)(e)(ii).

2 Inserted by the Environmental Permitting (England and Wales) (Amendment) Regulations 2012, SI 2012/630, reg 13(1), (3)(e)(i).

20 Treatment of waste at a water treatment works (T20)

(1) The treatment of relevant waste at a water treatment works.

(2) The table specifying relevant waste for the purposes of this paragraph is set out below.

Codes	*Waste types*
190902	Sludges from water clarification
190903	Sludges from decarbonation
190906	Solutions and sludges from regeneration of ion exchangers
190999	Waste water and bore hole flushings only

(3) For the purposes of this paragraph, the specific conditions are that—

(a) the total quantity of waste treated at the works over any period of 12 months does not exceed 10,000 cubic metres; and

(b) the waste is treated and stored in a secure location with sealed drainage.

21 Recovery of waste at a waste water treatment works (T21)

(1) The recovery of relevant waste at a waste water treatment works.

(2) The table specifying relevant waste for the purposes of this paragraph is set out below.

Codes	*Waste types*
190801	Screenings
190802	Sewage grit (waste from desanding) only
190805	Sludges from treatment of urban waste water
190899	Centrate liquor only
190902	Sludges from water clarification
190903	Sludges from decarbonation
190906	Solutions and sludges from regeneration of ion exchangers
200304	Septic tank sludge

(3) For the purposes of this paragraph, the specific conditions are that—

(a) the total quantity of waste brought to the works over any period of 12 months does not exceed 100,000 cubic metres; and

(b) the waste is treated and stored in a secure location with sealed drainage.

[Schedule 3, Pt 1, Ch 3, Section 2, para 22 was repealed by the Waste (England and Wales) Regulations 2011, SI 2011/988, reg 48(2), Sch 3, paras 1, 8(b).]

23 Aerobic composting and associated prior treatment (T23)

(1) The treatment of relevant waste by aerobic composting and associated prior treatment.

(2) The tables specifying relevant waste for the purposes of this paragraph are set out below.

Table 1

Codes	*Waste types*
170506	Plant tissue waste from inland waters only
020103, 200201	Plant tissue waste
020106	Horse manure and farmyard manure only
020107	Biodegradable waste from forestry only
[020199	Fully biodegradable animal bedding][1]
200101	Paper and cardboard
200201	Biodegradable waste plant matter only

Table 2

Codes	*Waste types*
020202	Animal tissue waste
020501, 020601	Materials unsuitable for consumption or processing
200108	Biodegradable kitchen and canteen waste
200302	Biodegradable waste from markets only

(3) For the purposes of this paragraph, the specific conditions are—

(a) the total quantity of waste treated or stored at any one time does not exceed 80 tonnes where—

(i) the operation is carried on at the place of production, and
(ii) the treated waste is being or is to be used at that place;
(b) the total quantity of waste treated or stored at any one time does not exceed 60 tonnes where—
(i) the waste is produced at a place other than where the operation is carried on, or
(ii) the treated waste is not to be used at the place where the operation is carried on;
(c) within the quantity limits in paragraphs (a) and (b), the waste does not consist at any one time of more than the following quantities—
(i) 10 tonnes of paper or cardboard,
(ii) 20 tonnes of manure,
(iii) 10 tonnes of any relevant waste listed in Table 2;
(d) in relation to relevant waste listed in Table 1, no waste is stored for longer than 1 month prior to treatment;
(e) in relation to relevant waste listed in Table 2, no waste is stored for longer than 7 days prior to treatment;
(f) no waste is stored for a period of longer than 12 months after treatment; and
(g) the treatment results in a stable sanitised material that can be applied to land for the benefit of agriculture or to improve the soil structure or nutrients in land.

(4) In this paragraph—
"aerobic composting" means the autothermic and thermophilic biological decomposition and stabilisation of biodegradable waste under controlled conditions that are aerobic;
"associated prior treatment" means screening, chipping, shredding, cutting, pulverising or sorting waste for the purposes of aerobic composting.

Amendment

1 Inserted by the Environmental Permitting (England and Wales) (Amendment) Regulations 2012, SI 2012/630, reg 13(1), (3)(f).

24 Anaerobic digestion at premises used for agriculture and burning of resultant biogas (T24)

(1) The treatment by anaerobic digestion of relevant waste at premises used for agriculture and associated prior treatment and the burning of any resultant biogas.

(2) The table specifying relevant waste for the purposes of this paragraph is set out below.

Codes	*Waste types*
020103, 020107, 170506, 200201	Plant tissue waste
020106	Horse and farmyard manure, slurry only
[020199	Fully biodegradable animal bedding][1]

(3) For the purposes of this paragraph, the specific conditions are that—
(a) the total quantity of waste treated or stored at any one time does not exceed 1,250 cubic metres;
(b) the minimum retention time for the waste in the digester is 28 days; and
(c) any gas resulting from the operation is collected and then burnt in an appliance—
(i) where the requirements of sub-paragraph (5) are met, and
(ii) the appliance is for the purposes of producing energy.

(4) In this paragraph, "associated prior treatment" means screening, chipping, shredding, cutting, pulverising or sorting waste for the purposes of anaerobic digestion.

(5) The requirements in this sub-paragraph are that—
(a) the appliance has a net rated thermal input of less than 0.4 megawatts; and
(b) where it is used together with other appliances (whether or not it is operated simultaneously with such other appliances), the aggregate net rated thermal input of all the appliances is less than 0.4 megawatts.

Amendment

1 Inserted by the Environmental Permitting (England and Wales) (Amendment) Regulations 2012, SI 2012/630, reg 13(1), (3)(g).

25 Anaerobic digestion at premises not used for agriculture and burning of resultant biogas (T25)

(1) The treatment by anaerobic digestion of relevant waste at premises not used for agriculture and associated prior treatment and the burning of any resultant biogas.

(2) The table specifying relevant waste for the purposes of this paragraph is set out below.

Codes	*Waste types*
020103, 020107, 170506, 200201	Plant tissue waste
020106	Horse and farmyard manure only
[020199	Fully biodegradable animal bedding][1]
200101	Paper and cardboard
200108	Biodegradable kitchen and canteen waste
020202	Animal tissue waste
020501, 020601	Materials unsuitable for consumption or processing
200302	Biodegradable waste from markets only

(3) For the purposes of this paragraph, the specific conditions are that—

(a) the total quantity of waste treated or stored at any one time does not exceed 50 cubic metres;

(b) the minimum retention time for the waste in the digester is 28 days; and

(c) any gas resulting from the operation is collected and then burnt in an appliance—

(i) where the requirements of sub-paragraph (5) are met, and

(ii) the appliance is for the purposes of producing energy.

(4) In this paragraph, "associated prior treatment" means screening, chipping, shredding, cutting, pulverising or sorting waste for the purposes of anaerobic digestion.

(5) The requirements in this sub-paragraph are that—

(a) the appliance has a net rated thermal input of less than 0.4 megawatts; and

(b) where it is used together with other appliances (whether or not it is operated simultaneously with such other appliances), the aggregate net rated thermal input of all the appliances is less than 0.4 megawatts.

Amendment

1 Inserted by the Environmental Permitting (England and Wales) (Amendment) Regulations 2012, SI 2012/630, reg 13(1), (3)(g).

26 Treatment of kitchen waste in a wormery (T26)

(1) The treatment in a wormery of relevant waste originating from a kitchen.

(2) The table specifying relevant waste for the purposes of this paragraph is set out below.

Codes	*Waste types*
200101	Paper and cardboard
200108	Biodegradable kitchen and canteen waste

(3) For the purposes of this paragraph, the specific conditions are that—

(a) the total quantity of waste treated over any 12-month period does not exceed 6 tonnes; and

(b) the treatment results in a stable sanitised vermicompost that can be applied to land for the benefit of agriculture or to improve the soil structure or nutrients in land.

27 [Treatment of sheep dip using organophosphate-degrading enzyme (T27)]1

(1) The treatment of used organophosphate sheep dip consisting of relevant waste for the purposes of its disposal.

(2) The table specifying relevant waste for the purposes of this paragraph is set out below.

Codes	*Waste types*
020109	Organophosphate sheep dip only

(3) For the purposes of this paragraph, the specific conditions are that—
(a) total quantity of waste treated or stored over any 24-hour period does not exceed 8,000 litres;
(b) the waste is treated using organophosphate-degrading enzyme in accordance with the enzyme manufacturer's instructions;
(c) the treatment and storage are carried on at the place of production; and
[(d) the treatment is carried on in a secure container located within a drain pen or in a secure sheep dip bath.][1]

[(4) In this paragraph, "drain pen" means an impermeable area draining back to the sheep dip bath where newly-dipped sheep are held while they continue to drip.][2]

Amendments

1 Substituted by the Environmental Permitting (England and Wales) (Amendment) Regulations 2012, SI 2012/630, reg 13(1), (3)(h)(i).

2 Inserted by the Environmental Permitting (England and Wales) (Amendment) Regulations 2012, SI 2012/630, reg 13(1), (3)(h)(ii).

28 Sorting and de-naturing of controlled drugs for disposal (T28)

(1) The treatment of controlled drugs consisting of relevant waste by sorting and denaturing them prior to their disposal.

(2) The table specifying relevant waste for the purposes of this paragraph is set out below.

Codes	*Waste types*
180109	Medicines from natal care, diagnosis, treatment or prevention of disease in humans
180208	Medicines from research, diagnosis, treatment or prevention of disease involving animals
200132	Medicines separately collected as municipal waste

(3) For the purposes of this paragraph, the specific conditions are that—
(a) the total quantity of waste treated or stored at any one time does not exceed 1 cubic metre;
(b) the treatment and storage are carried on at the place of production; and
(c) no waste is stored for longer than 6 months.

(4) In this paragraph, "controlled drug" means a controlled drug specified in Schedules 1 to 5 to the Misuse of Drugs Regulations 2001.

29 Treatment of non-hazardous pesticide washings by carbon filtration for disposal (T29)

(1) The treatment of non-hazardous pesticide washings that are relevant waste by carbon filtration for the purposes of disposal.

(2) The table specifying relevant waste for the purposes of this paragraph is set out below.

Codes	*Waste types*
020109, 160509	Non-hazardous pesticide washings only

(3) For the purposes of this paragraph, the specific conditions are that—
(a) the total quantity of waste treated or stored over any 24-hour period does not exceed 8,000 litres;
(b) the treatment and storage are carried on at the place of production; and
(c) the treatment is carried on in a location with sealed drainage.

30 Recovery of silver (T30)

(1) The recovery of silver from relevant waste produced in connection with printing or photographic processes.

(2) The table specifying relevant waste for the purposes of this paragraph is set out below.

Codes	*Waste types*
[090106*	Wastes containing silver from on-site treatment of photographic wastes][1]
090107	Photographic film or paper containing silver or silver compounds

(3) For the purposes of this paragraph, the specific conditions are that—
(a) the total quantity of waste stored or treated at any one time does not exceed 1,000 litres; and
(b) the treatment and storage are carried on in a location with sealed drainage.

Amendment
1 Inserted by the Environmental Permitting (England and Wales) (Amendment) Regulations 2012, SI 2012/630, reg 13(1), (3)(i).

31 Recovery of monopropylene glycol from aircraft antifreeze fluids (T31)

(1) The recovery of monopropylene glycol by filtering and distilling relevant waste collected following de-icing of aircraft.

(2) The table specifying relevant waste for the purposes of this paragraph is set out below.

Codes	*Waste types*
160115	Antifreeze fluids other than those mentioned in 160114

(3) For the purposes of this paragraph, the specific conditions are that—
(a) the total quantity of waste treated or stored over any 7-day period does not exceed 250 cubic metres;
(b) the waste is treated in a location with sealed drainage;
(c) the operation is carried on at the place where the waste is produced; and
(d) the waste is stored with secondary containment.

32 Treatment of waste in a biobed or biofilter (T32)

(1) The treatment of relevant waste in a lined biobed or above ground biofilter.

(2) The table specifying relevant waste for the purposes of this paragraph is set out below.

Codes	*Waste types*
020109, 160509	Non-hazardous pesticide washings only

(3) For the purposes of this paragraph, the specific conditions are that—
(a) the total quantity of waste treated or stored over any 12-month period does not exceed 15,000 litres;
(b) the biobed or biofilter is located at a secure place that is—
(i) at least 10 metres from a watercourse,
(ii) at least 50 metres from a spring or well or from any borehole not used to supply water for domestic or food production purposes,
(iii) at least 250 metres from any borehole used to supply water for domestic or food production purposes,

(iv) not within a zone defined by a 50-day travel time for groundwater to reach a groundwater abstraction that is used to supply water for domestic or food production purposes;

(c) the biobed or biofilter—

(i) is designed and maintained for the treatment operation,

(ii) has an impermeable lining; and

(d) the treatment is carried on at the place of production.

33 Recovery of central heating oil by filtration (T33)

(1) The recovery of central heating oil by filtering relevant waste.

(2) The table specifying relevant waste for the purposes of this paragraph is set out below.

Codes	*Waste types*
130701*	Central heating oil only

(3) For the purposes of this paragraph, the specific conditions are that—

(a) the total quantity of waste treated over any 7-day period does not exceed 400 litres;

(b) the waste is stored with secondary containment;

(c) the treatment is carried on at a location with sealed drainage; and

(d) the operation is for the purposes of reusing the waste.

Chapter 4
Disposal of waste

Section 1
Introductory

1

The descriptions in this Chapter—

(a) are set out in the first sub-paragraph of paragraphs D1 to D8; and

(b) include associated storage.

2

The specific conditions for each description in this Chapter are set out in the third sub-paragraph of paragraphs D1 to D8.

3

The general condition for all descriptions in this Chapter is that the operation is carried on at the place of production.

Section 2
Descriptions and specific conditions

1 Deposit of waste from dredging of inland waters (D1)

(1) The deposit of relevant waste arising from the dredging of inland waters and associated screening and dewatering.

(2) The table specifying relevant waste for the purposes of this paragraph is set out below.

Codes	*Waste types*
170506	Dredging spoil other than those mentioned in 170505

(3) For the purposes of this paragraph, the specific conditions are that—

(a) the total quantity of waste deposited or treated over any 12-month period does not exceed 50 cubic metres for each metre of land on which the waste is deposited; and
(b) the waste is deposited at the closest possible point to where the waste was produced on—
 (i) the bank of the inland waters from which the waste was produced, or
 (ii) such width of land adjoining the inland waters so as to enable the waste to be removed and deposited by mechanical means in one operation.

2 Deposit of waste from a railway sanitary convenience (D2)

(1) The deposit of relevant waste on to a railway track.

(2) The table specifying relevant waste for the purposes of this paragraph is set out below.

Codes	*Waste types*
200399	Wastes from railway sanitary conveniences only

(3) For the purposes of this paragraph, the specific condition is that the total quantity of waste deposited per discharge does not exceed 25 litres.

(4) In this paragraph, "railway sanitary convenience" means a sanitary convenience or sink forming part of a vehicle used for the carriage of passengers on a railway.

3 Deposit of waste from a portable sanitary convenience (D3)

(1) The deposit of relevant waste by burying it.

(2) The table specifying relevant waste for the purposes of this paragraph is set out below.

Codes	*Waste types*
200399	Waste from portable sanitary conveniences only

(3) For the purposes of this paragraph, the specific conditions are that—
(a) the total quantity of waste deposited over any 12-month period does not exceed 1 cubic metre; and
(b) no waste is deposited within—
 (i) 10 metres of any watercourse,
 (ii) 50 metres of any spring, well or borehole.

4 Deposit of agricultural waste consisting of plant tissue under a Plant Health notice (D4)

(1) The deposit of agricultural waste that is relevant waste.

(2) The table specifying relevant waste for the purposes of this paragraph is set out below.

Codes	*Waste types*
020103	Plant tissue waste

(3) For the purposes of this paragraph, the specific conditions are that—
(a) the deposit is required under a Plant Health notice;
(b) where waste is deposited into a pile, the pile—
 (i) does not exceed 250 tonnes, and
 (ii) is not immediately adjacent to another pile of the same type of waste;
(c) at the time the deposit is made—
 (i) the land has not been frozen for 12 hours or more in the preceding 24 hours,
 (ii) the land is not waterlogged, frozen or snow-covered; and
(d) no waste is deposited within—
 (i) 10 metres of any watercourse,
 (ii) 50 metres of any spring, well or borehole.

5 Depositing samples of waste for the purposes of testing or analysing them (D5)

(1) The deposit and subsequent storage of relevant samples of waste at any place where the samples are being or are to be tested or analysed.

(2) For the purposes of sub-paragraph (1), "relevant samples of waste" means samples of waste that are taken—

(a) in the exercise of any power under—
 (i) the 1993 Act,
 (ii) the Control of Pollution Act 1974,
 (iii) section 5 of the Control of Pollution (Amendment) Act 1989,
 (iv) the 1990 Act,
 (v) the 1991 Act,
 (vi) the Water Industry Act 1991,
 (vii) the Waste Electrical and Electronic Equipment Regulations 2006,
 (viii) the Producer Responsibility Obligations (Packaging Waste) Regulations 2007,
 (ix) regulation 88 of the Waste Batteries and Accumulators Regulations 2009;
(b) by or on behalf of the holder of an environmental permit;
(c) by or on behalf of a person carrying on in relation to the waste—
 (i) an operation described in this Part, or
 (ii) an excluded waste operation;
(d) by or on behalf of the owner or occupier of the land from which the samples are taken;
(e) by or on behalf of any person to whom section 34(1) or (1A) of the 1990 Act applies in connection with that person's duties under that section;
(f) by or on behalf of any person to whom the Transfrontier Shipment of Waste Regulations 2007 apply in connection with that person's powers under those Regulations; or
(g) for the purposes of research.

(3) For the purposes of this paragraph, the specific conditions are that—
(a) the total quantity of waste deposited or stored at any one time does not exceed 10 tonnes; and
(b) the waste is not stored for longer than 12 months or such other period as may be ordered in court proceedings.

6 Disposal by incineration (D6)

(1) The disposal by incineration of the waste described in sub-paragraph (2) in an incinerator where the requirements in sub-paragraph (4) are met.

(2) The waste described in this paragraph is the waste mentioned in Article 2(2)(a)(i) to (viii) of the Waste Incineration Directive, but excluding the waste mentioned in sub-paragraph (vi) (radioactive waste) of that Article.

(3) For the purposes of this paragraph, the specific conditions are that—
(a) the total quantity of waste stored prior to incineration does not exceed 5 tonnes at any one time; and
(b) the operation is carried on by the person who produced the waste.

(4) The requirements in this sub-paragraph are—
(a) the incinerator has a capacity of less than 50kg per hour and a net rated thermal input of less than 0.4 megawatts; and
(b) where it is used together with other incinerators (whether or not it is operated simultaneously with such other incinerators), the aggregate net rated thermal input of all the incinerators is less than 0.4 megawatts.

7 Burning waste in the open (D7)

(1) The burning of relevant waste on open land.

(2) The table specifying relevant waste for the purposes of this paragraph is set out below.

Codes	*Waste types*
020103, 020107, 200201	Plant tissue
030105	Sawdust, shavings and cuttings from untreated wood only
030301	Waste bark and wood

(3) For the purposes of this paragraph, the specific conditions are that—
(a) the total quantity of waste burned over any period of 24 hours does not exceed 10 tonnes;
(b) the total quantity of waste stored at any one time does not exceed 20 tonnes; and
(c) no waste is stored for longer than 6 months.

8 Burning waste at a port under a Plant Health notice (D8)

(1) The burning of relevant waste at a port.

(2) The table specifying relevant waste for the purposes of this paragraph is set out below.

Codes	*Waste types*
020103, 020107, 020304, 200201	Plant tissue only
150103, 200138	Wood used to wedge or support parts of cargo, including packing material, spacers and pallets only

(3) For the purposes of this paragraph, the specific conditions are that—
(a) the total quantity of waste burned or stored over any period of 24 hours does not exceed 10 tonnes;
(b) the burning and storage of waste takes place in a secure place at the port where the waste was unloaded; and
(c) the burning is required under a Plant Health notice.

(4) In this paragraph, "port" means a port appointed by order made under section 19 of the Customs and Excise Management Act 1979.

Chapter 5
Storage of waste

Section 1
Introductory

1

The descriptions in this Chapter are set out in the first sub-paragraph of paragraphs S1 to S3.

2

The specific conditions for each of the descriptions in this Chapter are set out in the third sub-paragraph of paragraphs S1 to S3.

3

The general conditions for all descriptions in this Chapter are that the storage is carried on—
(a) at a place other than the place of production, and
(b) pending the recovery of the waste.

Section 2
Descriptions and specific conditions

1 Storage of waste in secure containers (S1)

(1) The storage of relevant waste at a place in a secure container or containers for the purposes of its recovery elsewhere.

(2) The table specifying relevant waste for the purposes of this paragraph and the storage limits referred to in sub-paragraph (3) is set out below.

Codes	*Waste types*	*Storage limit (at any one time)*
130109* to 130113* 130204* to 130208* 130401* to 130403* 130701*	Waste oils	[3 cubic metres][1]
150101, 200101	Cartons	400 cubic metres
150102, 200139	Plastics and plastic packaging	400 cubic metres
150104, 200140	Cans and foil only	400 cubic metres
150101, 200101	Paper and cardboard	400 cubic metres
150107, 200102	Glass	400 cubic metres
150109, 200110, 200111	Textiles and clothes	400 cubic metres
150202*	Absorbents, filter materials (including oil filters not otherwise specified) wiping cloths, protective clothing contaminated by dangerous substances	3 cubic metres
150203	Absorbents, filter materials, wiping cloths and protective clothing other than those mentioned in 150202	3 cubic metres
160107*	Oil filters	3 cubic metres

(3) For the purposes of this paragraph, the specific conditions are that—
(a) the total quantity of waste stored at any one time does not exceed the limit specified in the third column in the table in sub-paragraph (2);
(b) the total quantity of storage containers at the storage place at any one time does not exceed 20;
(c) no waste is stored for longer than 12 months;
[(d) the person storing the waste is the owner of the container or containers or has the consent of the owner;
(e) in respect of any waste oils and waste to which code 160107* (oil filters) applies, the waste is stored with secondary containment; and
(f) each waste type is stored separately.][2]

Amendments
1 Substituted by Environmental Permitting (England and Wales) (Amendment) Regulations 2010/676 reg 2.
2 Substituted by the Environmental Permitting (England and Wales) (Amendment) Regulations 2012, SI 2012/630, reg 13(1), (4).

2 Storage of waste in a secure place (S2)

(1) The storage of relevant waste in a secure place for the purposes of its recovery elsewhere.

(2) The table specifying relevant waste for the purposes of this paragraph and the quantity limits referred to in sub-paragraph (3) is set out below.

Codes	*Waste types*	*Storage limit (at any one time)*	*Period*	*Additional specific conditions*
161002	Aqueous paint related waste only	1,000 litres	6 months	A, C
160601*, 160602*, 160603*, 160604, 160605, 200133*, 200134	Batteries	10 tonnes	6 months	A, B
150104, 200140	Cans and foil only	500 tonnes	12 months	
140601*	CFCs, HCFCs and HFCs	18 tonnes	6 months	A, C
170101, 170102, 170103,170107, 170202, 170203, 170401 to 170407, 170504, 170604, 170802	Construction and demolition waste capable of being used in its existing state (non hazardous) only	100 tonnes	12 months	
200125	Edible oil and fat only	5,000 tonnes	12 months	A, C
100207*	Electric arc furnace dust only	2,500 tonnes	3 months	D, E, F
020104	Farm plastics (non packaging) only	500 tonnes	12 months	D
070213, 150101, 150102, 150105, 200139	Food and drink cartons only	500 tonnes	12 months	
101112, 150107, 160120, 170202, 191205, 200102	Glass	5,000 tonnes	12 months	B
020102	Mammalian protein only	60,000 tonnes	12 months	D
020202	Mammalian tallow only	45,000 tonnes	12 months	D
200307	Mattresses only	5 tonnes	3 months	D
010408, 191209	Marble chips only	5,000 tonnes	12 months	
020304	Olive pulp/pellet only	5,000 tonnes	3 months	B, C, E
200127*, 200128, 080111*, 080112	Paints (excluding specialist and industrial paints, wood preservatives, aerosol and spray paints, inks, adhesives and resins) pending reuse as paints only	10,000 litres	6 months	A, C
150101, 191201, 200101, 030308, 030307	Paper and cardboard (excluding food and drink cartons) only	15,000 tonnes	12 months	J, K
090107, 090108	Photographic films and papers	50 tonnes	12 months	J
070213, 120105, 150102, 160119, 191204, 200139	Plastic	500 tonnes	12 months	
100101	Poultry litter ash only	3,000 tonnes	12 months	D, E
080318, 150102, 160216, 200139	Printer cartridges only	5,000 units	6 months	D

Codes	*Waste types*	*Storage limit (at any one time)*	*Period*	*Additional specific conditions*
170301*, 170302, 170504	Road planings, waste road chippings, road sub-base only	500 tonnes	12 months	
020110, 160117, 160118, 191203, 170401, 170402, 170403, 170404, 170405, 170406, 170407, 191202, 170411	Scrap metal	15,000 tonnes	6 months	B, E
090110, 090111*, 090112	Single use cameras	400 cubic metres	6 months	
020401, 020399	Soils from cleaning fruit and vegetables only	100 tonnes	6 months	
100316, 100405*, 100504, 100511, 100604, 100811, 100899	Solder metal, skimmings, ashes and residues	100 tonnes	3 months	G
140602*, 140603*, 200113*	Solvents and solvent mixtures	5 cubic metres	6 months	A, C
100101, 100102, 100105, 100115	Synthetic gypsum and pulverised fuel ash only	2,500 tonnes	3 months	D, E, F
040222, 150109, 191208, 200110, 200111	Textiles and clothes	1,000 tonnes	12 months	
160103, 191204	Tyres, tyre chip and crumb	40 tonnes	3 months	H
110113*, 120301*, 160708*	Waste cleaning solution containing 2% sodium metasilicate and 1–2% waste oil only	3 tonnes	3 months	A, C
160211*,160213*, 160214, 160216, 200121*, 200123*, 200135*, 200136	WEEE	400 cubic metres	6 months	I
030301, 150102, 150103, 200138	Wine bottle corks only	500 tonnes	12 months	
030105, 170201, 170204*,191206*, 191207, 200137*, 200138	Wood including telegraph poles and railway sleepers (hazardous and non hazardous)	100 tonnes	12 months	

(3) For the purposes of this paragraph, the specific conditions are that—

(a) the total quantity of waste stored at any one time does not exceed the limit specified in the third column of the table in sub-paragraph (2);

(b) no waste is stored for longer than the period specified in the fourth column of the table;

(c) each type of waste is stored separately; and

(d) the operation complies with such of the following additional conditions as are specified in the fifth column of the table—

A the waste is stored in a container,

B the storage place has sealed drainage,

C the waste is stored with secondary containment,

D the waste is stored indoors,
E the waste is stored at a dock prior to being exported or after being imported,
F the waste must arrive at the storage place in bags and must be stored there in bags or in drums,
G the waste is stored in bags or in drums,
H the total quantity of waste stored together does not exceed 10 tonnes,
I the requirements in paragraph 1 of Annex III to the WEEE Directive must be complied with,
J the waste is stored in a baled form, in a container or indoors,
K within the quantity limit specified in the third column of the table and notwithstanding additional specific condition J, up to 1,000 tonnes may be stored outdoors so long as it is stored in an enclosure designed and maintained to prevent the escape of litter.

3 Storage of sludge (S3)

(1) The storage of relevant waste.

(2) The table specifying relevant waste for the purposes of this paragraph is set out below.

Codes	*Waste types*
190805	Residual sludge from sewage plants treating domestic or urban waste waters and from other sewage plants treating waste waters of a composition similar to domestic and urban waste waters only
200304	Residual sludge from septic tanks and other similar installations for the treatment of sewage only

(3) For the purposes of this paragraph, the specific conditions are that—
(a) the total quantity of waste stored at any one time does not exceed 1,250 tonnes;
(b) no waste is stored for longer than 12 months;
(c) the waste is stored in a secure location at the place where it is to be used;
(d) the waste is stored at least—
(i) 10 metres from any watercourse,
(ii) 50 metres from any spring or well, or from any borehole not used to supply water for domestic or food production purposes,
(iii) 250 metres from any borehole used to supply water for domestic or food production purposes;
(e) no waste is stored—
(i) within a zone defined by a 50-day travel time for groundwater to reach a groundwater abstraction that is used to supply water for domestic or food production purposes,
(ii) within 0.3 metres of the top of an open storage container or within 0.75 metres of the top of an earthbank tank or lagoon; and
(f) after storage, the waste is to be used in accordance with the Sludge (Use in Agriculture) Regulations 1989.

PART 2
EXEMPT WATER DISCHARGE ACTIVITIES: DESCRIPTIONS AND CONDITIONS

1 Vegetation management activities

(1) For the purpose of paragraph 4(a)(i) of Schedule 2, the description is cutting or uprooting a substantial amount of vegetation in any inland freshwaters or so near to any such waters that it falls into them and failure to take reasonable steps to remove the vegetation from these waters.

(2) For the purpose of paragraph 4(a)(ii) of that Schedule, the conditions in relation to a water discharge activity described in sub-paragraph (1) are—

(a) that vegetation removed from the waters must be deposited in accordance with guidance issued by the appropriate authority; and

(b) that where it is necessary to allow vegetation to pass downstream—

  (i) prior notice of the dates of the water discharge activity is given, in accordance with guidance issued by the appropriate authority, to persons likely to be affected by such an activity, and

  (ii) the activity is not carried on if there is insufficient flow to convey the vegetation.

2 Small discharges of sewage effluent

(1) For the purpose of paragraph 4(a)(i) of Schedule 2, the description is the discharge from a sewage treatment plant of 5 cubic metres per day or less of sewage effluent into inland freshwaters, coastal waters or relevant territorial waters.

(2) For the purpose of paragraph 4(a)(ii) of that Schedule, the conditions in relation to a water discharge activity described in sub-paragraph (1) are—

(a) that all works and equipment used for the treatment of sewage effluent and its discharge comply with the requirements specified in guidance issued by the appropriate authority in relation to—

  (i) design and manufacturing standards,

  (ii) construction, installation and operation specifications, and

  (iii) siting and installation;

(b) that the discharge cannot reasonably, at the time it is first made, be made to the foul sewer;

(c) that the discharge does not contain trade effluent;

(d) that all works and equipment used for the treatment of sewage effluent and its discharge are maintained in accordance with the manufacturer's specification;

(e) that records of maintenance work are kept by the person who is the occupier of the land on which the discharge is made ("the occupier") for at least 5 years after the work is carried out;

(f) that the occupier must notify the exemption registration authority if an exempt water discharge activity ceases to be in operation;

(g) that the occupier must ensure that all works and equipment used for the treatment of sewage effluent and its discharge are appropriately decommissioned when the exempt facility ceases to be in operation so that there is no risk of pollutants entering inland freshwaters or coastal waters;

(h) that, before an occupier ceases to be in occupation of land on which an exempt water discharge activity is carried on, the occupier must give to the person who will next be in occupation of the land a written notice—

  (i) stating that an exempt water discharge activity is being carried on on the land;

  (ii) containing a description of the exempt facility;

  (iii) stating the conditions that must be satisfied in relation to the exempt facility; and

  (iv) accompanied by any records of maintenance mentioned in paragraph (e).

Part 3
Exempt groundwater activities: descriptions and conditions

1 Interpretation of Part 3

In this Part—

"groundwater tracer test" means a study of—

  (a) the behaviour or movement of water, or

  (b) a contaminant below ground,

  which involves the addition to groundwater of a distinguishable material which has nearly identical properties to the contaminant or water being studied;

"small quantity of substance" is to be construed in accordance with the final paragraph of Article 11(3)(j) of the Water Framework Directive;

"specified groundwater remediation scheme" means a remediation scheme which involves the addition of a substance or preparation to groundwater which enhances the rate of remediation of groundwater contaminants;

"water features" includes boreholes, wells, adits, springs, seepage and wetland areas, ponds, lakes and watercourses; and

"water features survey" means a survey of all water features within 1 kilometre of the proposed activity that may be affected by it.

2 Discharge of small quantities of substances for scientific purposes

(1) For the purpose of paragraph 5(a)(i) of Schedule 2, the description is the discharge of small quantities of substances for scientific purposes as part of—

(a) a specified groundwater remediation scheme; or

(b) a groundwater tracer test.

(2) For the purpose of paragraph 5(a)(ii) of that Schedule, the conditions in relation to a groundwater activity of that description are—

(a) that a water features survey has demonstrated that the discharge will not cause pollution;

(b) that the prior consent of every person having a right to abstract water in the vicinity of the discharge has been obtained;

(c) that the exemption registration authority is notified before the commencement of the discharge;

(d) that in the case of discharges as part of a specified groundwater remediation scheme, monitoring of the discharge, to determine whether pollution has been caused, is undertaken.

3 Small discharges of sewage effluent

(1) For the purpose of paragraph 5(a)(i) of Schedule 2, the description is a discharge from a septic tank or sewage treatment plant of 2 cubic metres per day or less of sewage effluent that results in the input of pollutants to groundwater.

(2) For the purpose of paragraph 5(a)(ii) of that Schedule, the conditions in relation to a groundwater activity of that description are—

(a) that all works and equipment used for the treatment of sewage effluent and its discharge comply with the requirements specified in guidance issued by the appropriate authority in relation to—

 (i) design and manufacturing standards,

 (ii) construction, installation and operation specifications, and

 (iii) siting and installation of infiltration systems;

(b) that the discharge cannot reasonably, at the time it is first made, be made to the foul sewer;

(c) that the discharge does not contain trade effluent;

(d) that the discharge does not result in an input of pollutants to groundwater—

 (i) within 50 metres of a point at which water is abstracted from underground strata, or

 (ii) within a zone defined by a 50-day travel time for groundwater to reach a groundwater abstraction point that is used to supply water for domestic or food production purposes;

(e) that all works and equipment used for the treatment of sewage effluent and its discharge are maintained in accordance with the manufacturer's specification;

(f) that records of maintenance work are kept by the person who is the occupier of the land on which the discharge is made ("the occupier") for at least 5 years after the work is carried out;

(g) that the occupier must notify the exemption registration authority if an exempt groundwater activity ceases to be in operation;

(h) that the occupier must ensure that all works and equipment for the treatment of sewage effluent and its discharge are appropriately decommissioned when the exempt facility ceases to be in operation so that there is no risk of pollutants entering groundwater;

(i) that before an occupier ceases to be in occupation of land on which an exempt groundwater activity is carried on, the occupier must give to the person who will next be in occupation of the land a written notice—

  (i) stating that an exempt groundwater activity is being carried on on the land;

  (ii) containing a description of the exempt facility;

  (iii) stating the conditions that must be satisfied in relation to the exempt facility; and

  (iv) accompanied by any records of maintenance mentioned in paragraph (f).

SCHEDULE 4
APPLICATION TO THE CROWN

Regulation 11

1 Crown application

Subject to paragraphs 2 to 5, these Regulations bind the Crown.

2 Contravention of these Regulations by the Crown

(1) If the Crown contravenes a provision of these Regulations—

(a) it is not criminally liable under regulation 38; and

(b) no proceedings may be taken against it under regulation 42.

(2) But—

(a) on the application of a regulator, the High Court may declare a contravention of these Regulations by the Crown to be unlawful; and

(b) these Regulations apply to persons in the public service of the Crown as they apply to other persons.

3 Entry to Crown premises

(1) If the appropriate authority considers that in the interests of national security particular powers of entry must not be used in relation to particular Crown premises it may certify that those powers must not be used in relation to those premises.

(2) In this paragraph—

"Crown premises" means premises held or used by or on behalf of the Crown; and

"power of entry" means a power of entry exercisable under section 108 of the 1995 Act, in relation to a function under these Regulations.

4 Service on certain Crown operators

(1) This paragraph applies in relation to a regulated facility controlled or operated by a person acting on behalf of—

(a) the Royal Household;

(b) the Duchy of Lancaster; or

(c) the Duke of Cornwall or other possessor of the Duchy of Cornwall.

(2) When serving or giving notices or notifications, or instituting proceedings, the following person must be treated as the operator—

(a) in relation to sub-paragraph (1)(a), the Keeper of the Privy Purse;

(b) in relation to sub-paragraph (1)(b), the person appointed by the Chancellor of the Duchy of Lancaster;

(c) in relation to sub-paragraph (1)(c), the person appointed by the Duke of Cornwall or other possessor of the Duchy of Cornwall.

5 Application of this Schedule to certain radioactive substances activities

(1) These Regulations do not bind the Crown in relation to a radioactive substances activity carried on at premises—

(a) occupied on behalf of the Crown for naval, military or air force purposes or for the purposes of the department of the Secretary of State having responsibility for defence; or

(b) occupied by or for the purposes of visiting forces.

(2) In this paragraph, "visiting force" has the meaning given in section 12(1) of the Visiting Forces Act 1952.

SCHEDULE 5
ENVIRONMENTAL PERMITS

Regulations 13(3) and 15(3)

PART 1
GRANT, VARIATION, TRANSFER AND SURRENDER OF ENVIRONMENTAL PERMITS

1 Interpretation

…[1] In this Part—

"applicant" means—

(a) in the case of an application for the transfer of an environmental permit in whole or in part, the operator and the proposed transferee,

(b) in every other case, the operator;

"application" means an application—

[(a) in the case of an application for the transfer of an environmental permit in whole or in part—

(i) the operator and the proposed transferee, or

(ii) the proposed transferee,][2]

(b) by an operator for the variation of an environmental permit under regulation 20(1),

(c) for the transfer, in whole or in part, of an environmental permit under regulation 21(1), or

(d) for the surrender, in whole or in part, of an environmental permit under regulation 25(2); and

"public consultee" means a person whom the regulator considers is affected by, is likely to be affected by, or has an interest in, an application.

Amendments

1 Repealed by the Environmental Permitting (England and Wales) (Amendment) Regulations 2012, SI 2012/630, reg 14(a).

2 Substituted by the Environmental Permitting (England and Wales) (Amendment) Regulations 2012, SI 2012/630, reg 14(b).

2 Making an application

(1) An application must—

(a) be made by the applicant on the form provided by the regulator; and

[(b) include—

(i) such information as is specified on the form, and

(ii) any additional information required by the regulator.][1]

(2) Every application must be accompanied by any fee prescribed in a charging scheme made by the regulator under section 41 of the 1995 Act or by the appropriate authority under regulation 65.

Amendment

1 Substituted by the Environmental Permitting (England and Wales) (Amendment) Regulations 2012, SI 2012/630, reg 14(d).

3 Withdrawing an application

(1) A duly-made application may be withdrawn by the applicant before it is determined.

(2) If an application is withdrawn the applicant is not entitled to the return of any fee which accompanied it.

4 Further information in respect of a duly-made application

(1) If the regulator considers that it requires further information to determine a duly-made application, it may serve a notice on the applicant specifying the further information and the period within which it must be provided.

(2) If the applicant fails to provide the further information in accordance with the notice, the regulator may serve a further notice on the applicant stating that the application is deemed to be withdrawn, upon which the application is deemed to be withdrawn.

(3) If an application is deemed to be withdrawn, the applicant is not entitled to the return of any fee which accompanied it.

5 Public participation: scope

(1) Paragraph 6 applies to every application for the grant of an environmental permit except an application in relation to—

(a) mobile plant;

(b) a radioactive substances activity described in [paragraph 11(5)][1] of Part 2 of Schedule 23;

(c) a standard facility, unless the facility is a Part A installation; or

(d) a mining waste operation not involving a mining waste facility to which Article 7 of the Mining Waste Directive applies.

(2) Paragraph 6 applies to every application for the variation of an environmental permit if—

(a) it would entail a substantial change; or

(b) the regulator determines that the paragraph should apply.

(3) Paragraph 8 applies to every regulator-initiated variation if—

(a) it would entail a substantial change; or

(b) the regulator determines that the paragraph should apply.

(4) But paragraphs 6 and 8 do not apply to the extent that the application or regulator-initiated variation relates to—

(a) the burning of waste oil in an appliance with a rated thermal input of less than 0.4 megawatts;

(b) dry cleaning;

(c) the unloading of petrol into stationary storage tanks at a service station if it is an activity within paragraph (c) of Part B of Section 1.2 of Part 2 of Schedule 1; or

(d) any motor vehicle refuelling activity within paragraph (d) or (e) of Part B of Section 1.2 of Part 2 of Schedule 1.

(5) In this paragraph—

"change in operation" means a change in the nature or functioning, or an extension, of an installation, which may have consequences for the environment;

"co-incineration plant" has the meaning given in Section 5.1 of Part 2 of Schedule 1;

"dry cleaning" has the meaning given in Part B of Section 7 of Part 2 of Schedule 1;
"incineration plant" has the meaning given in Section 5.1 of Part 2 of Schedule 1; and
"substantial change" means a change in operation of an installation which in the regulator's opinion may have significant negative effects on human beings or the environment and includes—

(a) in relation to a Part A installation, a change in operation which in itself meets the thresholds, if any, set out in Part 2 of Schedule 1, and
(b) in relation to an incineration plant or co-incineration plant for non-hazardous waste, a change in operation which would involve the incineration or co-incineration of hazardous waste.

(6) When assessing whether a change in operation of a Part B installation has significant effects on the environment, the regulator must consider only its emissions to air.

Amendment

1 Substituted by the Environmental Permitting (England and Wales) (Amendment) Regulations 2011, SI 2011/2043, regs 3, 13.

6 Public participation in relation to certain applications

(1) Subject to sub-paragraphs (2) and (3), if this paragraph applies the regulator must, within the consultation communication period—

(a) take the steps it considers appropriate to inform the public consultees of the application and the place and times its public register can be inspected free of charge;
(b) invite the public consultees to make representations on the application; and
(c) specify to the public consultees the address to which and the period within which representations are to be made.

(2) The regulator must not inform the public consultees of information which is to be excluded from a public register in the interests of national security unless the appropriate authority directs that it must do so.

(3) The regulator must not inform the public consultees of information which is to be excluded from a public register because it is confidential information, unless the public consultee is—

(a) a public authority and the information is necessary for the exercise of its functions; or
(b) a sewerage undertaker and the information relates to the release of any substance into a sewer vested in that undertaker.

7 Calculation of the consultation communication period

(1) In paragraph 6, "the consultation communication period" means a period of 30 working days starting on the day the regulator receives a duly-made application.

(2) But if—

(a) a determination in relation to national security or confidentiality is to be made under regulation 47 or 50; or
(b) the regulator gives notice under regulation 49(1) that it considers information in an application may be confidential information,

"the consultation communication period" means a period of 30 working days starting on the determination date or on the day the applicant gives notice of consent under regulation 49(2), as the case may be.

(3) In sub-paragraph (2), "determination date" means—

(a) the date of a determination under regulation 47(3) or (7);
(b) if the regulator determines under regulation 50 that the information must be excluded from the public register, the date of the determination; or
(c) if the regulator determines otherwise under that regulation—
    (i) if an appeal is brought, the date of determination or withdrawal of that appeal, or
    (ii) if no appeal is brought, the date on which the period for bringing an appeal expires.

8 Public participation in relation to regulator-initiated variations

(1) If this paragraph applies, the regulator must notify the operator—
(a) that the public participation procedures in sub-paragraph (2) apply;
(b) of the variation it proposes to the environmental permit; and
(c) of any fee prescribed in respect of this paragraph in a charging scheme made by the regulator under section 41 of the 1995 Act or by the appropriate authority under regulation 65.

(2) The regulator must—
(a) take the steps it considers appropriate to inform the public consultees of the proposed variation;
(b) invite the operator and the public consultees to make representations on the proposed variation; and
(c) specify to the operator and the public consultees the address to which and the period within which representations are to be made.

9 Consultation: conditions mentioned in regulation 15(1)

(1) This paragraph applies if the regulator proposes to include a condition mentioned in regulation 15(1) in an environmental permit.

(2) If this paragraph applies, the regulator must serve a notice which complies with sub-paragraph (3) on every person appearing to it to fall within sub-paragraph (4).

(3) The notice must specify—
(a) the proposed condition;
(b) the works or other things which the condition would require; and
(c) the address to which and the period within which representations on the proposed condition are to be made (which period must not expire less than 20 working days after the day the notice is served).

(4) A person falls within this sub-paragraph if—
(a) the person is the owner, lessee or occupier of land; and
(b) regulation 15(2) would require the person to grant the rights mentioned there if the proposed condition were included in the environmental permit.

(5) In sub-paragraph (4)(a), "owner" means the person who—
(a) is receiving the rack-rent of the land, whether on the person's own account or as agent or trustee for another person; or
(b) would receive the rack-rent if the land were let at a rack-rent,
but does not include a mortgagee not in possession.

10 Consultation with other member States

(1) This paragraph applies if—
(a) an appropriate authority is aware that the grant of a relevant application or regulatorinitiated variation is likely to have significant negative effects on the environment of another member State; or
(b) another member State requests information about a relevant application or about a proposal for a regulator-initiated variation.

(2) As soon as is reasonably practicable the appropriate authority must—
(a) send the particulars of the relevant application or regulator-initiated variation to that member State to serve as the basis for bilateral consultations of the type referred to in the relevant Article;
(b) inform that member State of the relevant information; and
(c) notify the operator and the regulator that it has complied with paragraphs (b) and (c).

(3) If a regulator receives notification under sub-paragraph (2)(c), it must not determine the application or make the regulator-initiated variation until the appropriate authority has—
(a) notified it that the bilateral consultations have been completed; and
(b) sent it any representations made by the member State.

(4) In this paragraph—

"member State" includes Iceland, Liechtenstein and Norway but only to the extent that there is a relevant application or regulator-initiated variation which relates to the carrying on at an installation of an activity listed in the IPPC Directive;

"relevant application" means an application for the grant or variation of an environmental permit in relation to an installation described in sub-paragraph (5) or a Category A mining waste facility;

"relevant Article" means—
(a) in the case of an application in relation to an installation described in sub-paragraph (5), Article 18 of the IPPC Directive,
(b) in the case of an application in relation to a Category A mining waste facility, Article 16 of the Mining Waste Directive; and

"relevant information" means—
(a) where the relevant application or regulator-initiated variation relates to an installation described in sub-paragraph (5), a matter in paragraph 1 of Annex V to the IPPC Directive,
(b) where it relates to a Category A mining waste facility, the information required under Article 16 of the Mining Waste Directive.

(5) The description in this sub-paragraph is an installation where an activity listed in Annex 1 to the IPPC Directive is carried on.

11 Duty to consider representations

Before it determines an application or makes a regulator-initiated variation, the regulator must consider any representation—
(a) made pursuant to paragraph 6(1)(b), 8(2)(b) or 9(3)(c); or
(b) sent to it under paragraph 10(3)(b).

12 Duty to determine an application

(1) The regulator must grant or refuse a duly-made application.

(2) Except in the case of an application for the surrender of an environmental permit in whole, the regulator may grant an application subject to such conditions as it sees fit.

(3) But—
(a) variations of an environmental permit in relation to the grant of an application for variation, transfer in whole or in part, or partial surrender must be in consequence of the variation, transfer or partial surrender, as the case may be; and
(b) if granting an application for partial transfer, the regulator must grant a new environmental permit to the transferee subject to the same conditions as the original permit, varied in consequence of the partial transfer.

13 Identity and competence of the operator

(1) Subject to sub-paragraph (3), the regulator must refuse an application for the grant of an environmental permit or for the transfer in whole or in part of an environmental permit if it considers that, if the permit is granted or transferred, the requirements in sub-paragraph (2) will not be satisfied.

(2) The requirements are that the applicant for the grant of an environmental permit, or the proposed transferee, on the transfer of an environmental permit (in whole or in part), must—

(a) be the operator of the regulated facility; and
(b) operate the regulated facility in accordance with the environmental permit.

(3) The requirement in sub-paragraph (2)(b) does not apply to an applicant for the grant of an environmental permit authorising the carrying on of only a stand-alone water discharge activity or stand-alone groundwater activity.

14 Surrender applications

(1) The regulator must accept an application for the surrender of an environmental permit in whole or in part under regulation 25(2) if it is satisfied that the necessary measures have been taken—
(a) to avoid a pollution risk resulting from the operation of the regulated facility; and
(b) to return the site of the regulated facility to a satisfactory state, having regard to the state of the site before the facility was put into operation.

(2) Sub-paragraph (1) does not apply to an application for the surrender of any part of an environmental permit (or if applicable, the whole permit) that authorises the carrying on of a radioactive substances activity at a nuclear site.

15 Time limits for determination

(1) If—
(a) the regulator has not determined an application within the relevant period; and
(b) the applicant serves a notice on the regulator which refers to this paragraph,
the application is deemed to have been refused on the day on which the notice is served.

(2) Sub-paragraph (1) does not apply—
(a) to an application for the grant of an environmental permit that, if granted, would authorise the carrying on of a radioactive substances activity at a nuclear site; or
(b) to an application for the transfer of an environmental permit where the permit authorises the carrying on of a radioactive substances activity at a nuclear site.

(3) In sub-paragraph (1) "the relevant period" means a period, calculated in accordance with paragraph 16, of—
(a) in the case of an application for the transfer of an environmental permit in whole or in part, 2 months;
(b) in a case where paragraph 6 applies, 4 months; or
(c) in any other case, 3 months,
or in any case, a longer period than the period in paragraph (a), (b) or (c), if it is agreed by the regulator and the applicant.

16 Calculation of the relevant period

(1) This paragraph provides for the calculation of a period referred to in paragraph 15(3).

(2) The period starts—
(a) in the case of an application for the grant or variation of an environmental permit in relation to a Category A mining waste facility—
  (i) on the day the regulator is notified by the relevant emergency planner of the matters referred to in paragraph 14(1) of Schedule 20, and for these purposes "relevant emergency planner" has the meaning given in paragraph 2 of that Schedule, or
  (ii) if paragraph 10 of this Schedule applies, on the day mentioned in sub-paragraph (i) of this paragraph or, if the day on which the appropriate authority complies with paragraph 10(3) of this Schedule is later, on that day;
(b) if paragraph 10 of this Schedule applies and the application is not one covered by paragraph (a), on the day the appropriate authority complies with paragraph 10(3) of this Schedule;

(c) in all other cases, on the day the regulator receives a duly-made application.

(3) In calculating the period the following periods must be ignored—

(a) a period beginning with the service of a notice requiring further information under paragraph 4(1) to the receipt by the regulator of that information;

(b) a period for representations mentioned in paragraph 9(3)(c) to the extent that it does not overlap with a period for representations mentioned in paragraph 6(1)(c);

(c) a period during which national security or confidentiality is being considered in relation to the application, that is to say—

(i) any period during which a determination under regulation 47(3), 47(7) or 50 is being considered (including any appeal), or

(ii) a period of 15 working days after the service of a notice under regulation 49(1);

(d) if the regulator informs the public in relation to a draft decision in accordance with paragraph 1(d) of Annex V to the IPPC Directive, a period of 20 working days.

17 Notification of a determination or decision

(1) As soon as is reasonably practicable after it determines an application or decides to make a regulator-initiated variation, the regulator must comply with sub-paragraph (2).

(2) The regulator must—

(a) notify the applicant or, for a regulator-initiated variation, the operator of—

(i) its determination or decision,

(ii) the rights of appeal the applicant or operator has under regulation 31, and

(iii) the requirements relating to the exercise of those rights in paragraphs 2 and 3 of Schedule 6; and

(b) if paragraph 10 applies, notify the appropriate authority of the determination or decision.

(3) In this paragraph, "determination" and "decision" include the reasons for the determination or decision.

18 Date of effect of certain determinations and decisions

(1) This paragraph applies to—

(a) a determination by which the regulator grants an application which—

(i) varies an environmental permit in consequence of an application for variation, transfer in whole or in part, or partial surrender, or

(ii) grants a new environmental permit in consequence of an application for partial transfer; and

(b) a decision to make a regulator-initiated variation.

(2) The determination or decision must specify any variation and the date it is to take effect.

(3) If the regulator grants an application for the transfer of an environmental permit in whole or in part, the determination must specify the date agreed between the regulator and the applicant that the transfer is to take effect.

19 Form of certain determinations and decisions: consolidation of permits

(1) This paragraph applies to every determination and decision to which paragraph 18 applies.

(2) A determination or decision may comprise—

(a) a consolidated permit reflecting the variations; and

(b) a notice specifying the variations included in that consolidated permit.

(3) Only the variations specified are subject to the right of appeal in regulation 31(2)(b) or (c).

PART 2
COMPENSATION IN RELATION TO CONDITIONS AFFECTING CERTAIN INTERESTS IN LAND

1 Interpretation

In this Part—

"grantor" means a person who grants the operator rights pursuant to regulation 15(2);

"relevant interest" means an interest in land out of which rights have been granted pursuant to regulation 15(2); and

"rights" means the rights granted by the grantor.

2 Entitlement to compensation

A grantor is entitled to be paid compensation under this Part by the operator.

3 Loss and damage for which compensation is payable

(1) Subject to paragraph 6(3) and (5)(b), compensation is payable for loss and damage of the following descriptions—

(a) depreciation in the value of any relevant interest to which the grantor is entitled which results from the grant of the rights;

(b) depreciation in the value of any other interest in land to which the grantor is entitled which results from the exercise of the rights;

(c) loss or damage, in relation to any relevant interest to which the grantor is entitled, which—

(i) is attributable to the grant of the rights or the exercise of them,

(ii) does not consist of depreciation in the value of that interest, and

(iii) is loss or damage for which the grantor would have been entitled to compensation by way of compensation for disturbance if the circumstances specified in sub-paragraph (2) applied;

(d) damage to, or injurious affection of, any interest in land to which the grantor is entitled which—

(i) is not a relevant interest, and

(ii) results from the grant of the rights or the exercise of them;

(e) loss in respect of work carried out by or on behalf of the grantor which is rendered abortive by the grant of the rights or the exercise of them.

(2) For the purpose of sub-paragraph (1)(c)(iii), the circumstances are that the relevant interest was acquired compulsorily—

(a) under the Acquisition of Land Act 1981; and

(b) in pursuance of a notice to treat served on the date on which the rights were granted.

4 Date when entitlement to compensation arises

(1) An entitlement to compensation under this Part arises on the date of the grant of the rights.

(2) But if an appeal against the conditions of the environmental permit which rendered the grant of rights necessary is refused, the entitlement to compensation arises on the date the appeal is determined.

5 Application for compensation

(1) An application for compensation under this Part must be made by the grantor—

(a) within 12 months after the date on which the entitlement to compensation arises; or

(b) within 6 months after the date on which the rights are first exercised.

(2) An application must be—

(a) made in writing;

(b) made to the operator to whom the rights were granted; and
(c) delivered at or sent by pre-paid post to the last known address for correspondence of that operator.

(3) The application must contain, or be accompanied by—
(a) a copy of the grant of rights in respect of which the grantor's entitlement arises and any plans attached to that grant;
(b) a description of the exact nature of any interest in land in respect of which compensation is applied for;
(c) a statement of the amount of compensation applied for—
 (i) distinguishing the amounts applied for under each of paragraphs 3(a) to (e), and
 (ii) showing how the amount applied for under each paragraph has been calculated; and
(d) if the date on which the entitlement to compensation arises is ascertained in accordance with paragraph 4(2), a copy of the notice of the final determination of the appeal.

6 Assessment of the amount to be paid by way of compensation

(1) The amount to be paid by way of compensation under this Part must be assessed in accordance with this paragraph.

(2) The rules set out in section 5 of the Land Compensation Act 1961 have effect for the purposes of this paragraph as they have effect for the purpose of assessing compensation for the compulsory acquisition of an interest in land, so far as applicable and subject to any necessary modifications.

(3) No account is to be taken of any enhancement of the value of an interest in land by reason of any building erected, work done, or improvement or alteration made on land in which the grantor is, or was at the time the building or other work was carried out, directly or indirectly concerned, if the work carried out—
(a) was not reasonably necessary; and
(b) was undertaken with a view to obtaining compensation or increased compensation.

(4) In calculating the amount of a loss under paragraph 3(e), expenditure incurred in the preparation of plans or on other similar preparatory matters is to be taken into account.

(5) Where the interest in respect of which compensation is to be assessed is subject to a mortgage—
(a) the compensation must be assessed as if the interest were not subject to the mortgage; and
(b) no compensation is payable in respect of the interest of the mortgagee (as distinct from the interest which is subject to the mortgage).

(6) Compensation must include an amount equal to the grantor's reasonable valuation and legal expenses.

7 Payment of compensation

(1) Compensation in respect of an interest which is subject to a mortgage must be paid—
(a) to the mortgagee; or
(b) if there is more than one mortgagee, to the first mortgagee,
and must, in either case, be applied by the mortgagee as if it were proceeds of sale.

(2) Amounts of compensation determined under this Part are payable—
(a) where the operator and either the grantor or mortgagee agree that a single payment is to be made on a specified date, on that date;
(b) where the operator and either the grantor or mortgagee agree that payment is to be made in instalments at different dates, on the date agreed as regards each instalment;
(c) in any other case, subject to any direction of the Upper Tribunal or the court, as soon as reasonably practicable after the amount of the compensation has been determined.

(3) Any question of the application of paragraph 6(3) or dispute as to the amount of compensation must be referred to and determined by the Upper Tribunal.

(4) In relation to the determination of such a question, section 4 of the Land Compensation Act 1961 applies as if the reference in section 2(1) of that Act to section 1 of that Act were a reference to sub-paragraph (3) of this paragraph.

8 Interest payable on compensation

(1) Compensation payable under this Part carries interest at the rate for the time being prescribed under section 32 of the Land Compensation Act 1961 from the date specified in sub-paragraph (2) to payment.

(2) The date is—
(a) in the case of compensation payable under paragraph 3(a) or (b), the date of depreciation;
(b) in the case of compensation payable under paragraph 3(c), (d) or (e), the date on which the loss is sustained, the damage is done, or the injurious affection occurs, as the case may be;
(c) in the case of compensation payable under paragraph 6(6), the date on which the expenses become payable.

(3) If it appears to a person ("A") that A may become liable to pay to another person ("B") compensation under this Schedule or interest under this paragraph, on the written request of B, A may make one or more payments on account of such compensation or interest.

(4) A may recover the payment or excess if, after A makes a payment under sub-paragraph (3)—
(a) it is agreed or determined that A is not liable to pay compensation or interest; or
(b) by reason of any agreement or determination, the payment is shown to be excessive.

SCHEDULE 6
APPEALS TO THE APPROPRIATE AUTHORITY

Regulation 31(14)

1 Interpretation

In this Schedule—
"appeal" means an appeal to the appropriate authority;
"appointed person" means the person appointed under paragraph 5; and
"determination" includes the reasons for the determination.

2 Making an appeal

(1) A person making an appeal must—
(a) send the appropriate authority written notice of the appeal and the documents specified in sub-paragraph (2); and
(b) at the same time send the regulator copies of the notice and documents.

(2) The documents are—
(a) a statement of the grounds of appeal;
(b) a copy of any relevant application;
(c) a copy of any relevant environmental permit;
(d) a copy of any relevant correspondence between the appellant and the regulator;
(e) a copy of any decision or notice which is the subject matter of the appeal; and
(f) a statement indicating whether the appellant wishes the appeal to be in the form of a hearing or to be dealt with by way of written representations.

(3) An appellant may withdraw an appeal by notifying the appropriate authority in writing and must send a copy of that notification to the regulator.

3 Time limit for making an appeal

(1) A notice of appeal must be given—
(a) in relation to an appeal against a revocation notice, before the revocation notice takes effect;
(b) in relation to the withdrawal of a duly-made application under paragraph 4(2) of Part 1 of Schedule 5, not later than 15 working days after the date of the further notice served under that paragraph;
(c) in relation to an enforcement notice, a regulator-initiated variation, suspension notice, mining waste facility closure notice or landfill closure notice, not later than 2 months after the date of the variation or notice;
(d) in relation to a prohibition notice, not later than 21 days after the date of the notice; or
(e) in any other case, not later than 6 months after the date of the decision or deemed decision.

(2) The appropriate authority may in a particular case allow notice of appeal to be given after the periods mentioned in sub-paragraph (1)(b) to (e) have expired.

4 Notice to affected and interested persons

(1) The regulator must, within 10 working days after receipt of a copy of a notice of appeal, give notice of it to any person whom the regulator considers is affected by, is likely to be affected by, or has an interest in, the subject matter of the appeal.

(2) A notice must include—
(a) a description of the subject matter of the appeal; and
(b) a statement that representations in writing may be made to the appropriate authority within a period of 15 working days after the date of the notice.

(3) The regulator must notify the appropriate authority of the persons to whom, and the date on which, such a notice was sent, within 10 working days after sending it.

(4) The regulator must give notice of the withdrawal of an appeal to every person given such a notice.

5 Hearing before an appointed person

(1) Before determining an appeal the appropriate authority may give the appellant and the regulator an opportunity of appearing before and being heard by a person appointed by the appropriate authority, and must do so in a case where a request is duly made by the appellant or the regulator to be so heard.

(2) If the appointed person so decides, a hearing may be held wholly or to any extent in private.

(3) The persons entitled to be heard at a hearing are—
(a) the appellant;
(b) the regulator; and
(c) a person who has made representations to the regulator in respect of the subject matter of the appeal within the period mentioned in paragraph 4(2)(b).

(4) The appointed person may permit other persons to be heard and such permission must not be unreasonably withheld.

(5) After the hearing, the appointed person must make a report in writing to the appropriate authority which must include the appointed person's—
(a) conclusions; and
(b) recommendations or reasons for not making recommendations.

(6) Subsections (2) to (5) of section 250 of the Local Government Act 1972 apply to hearings held under this paragraph by an appointed person as they apply to inquiries caused to be held under that section by a Minister with the following modifications—
(a) the substitution in subsection (2) for the reference to the person appointed to hold the inquiry with a reference to the appointed person;
(b) the substitution in subsection (4) for the references to the Minister causing the inquiry to be held with references to the appropriate authority;
(c) the substitution of the reference in that subsection to a local authority with a reference to the regulator;
(d) the substitution in subsection (5) for the reference to the Minister causing the inquiry to be held with a reference to the appropriate authority.

6 Notice of determination of an appeal

(1) The appropriate authority must give notice to the appellant of its determination and provide the appellant with a copy of the report mentioned in paragraph 5(5).

(2) At the same time the appropriate authority must send—
(a) a copy of the documents mentioned in sub-paragraph (1) to the regulator; and
(b) a copy of its determination to any person who made representations in respect of the subject matter of the appeal to the authority, or at any hearing.

7 Procedure following the quashing of a determination of an appropriate authority

(1) If a determination is quashed in proceedings before a court, the appropriate authority—
(a) must send to the persons notified of its determination under paragraph 6 a statement of the matters in relation to which further representations are invited;
(b) must give those persons the opportunity of making written representations in respect of those matters within 20 working days after the date of the statement; and
(c) may cause a hearing to be held or reopened.

(2) If a hearing is held or reopened under sub-paragraph (1)(c), paragraphs 5(2) to 5(6) apply as they apply to a hearing held under paragraph 5(1).

(3) Paragraph 6 applies to the re-determination of an appeal as it applies to the determination of that appeal.

SCHEDULE 7
PART A INSTALLATIONS AND PART A MOBILE PLANT

Regulation 35(2)(a)

1 Application

This Schedule applies in relation to every Part A installation or Part A mobile plant.

2 Interpretation

When interpreting the IPPC Directive for the purposes of this Schedule—
(a) except where otherwise defined in this paragraph, an expression that is defined in Part 1 of these Regulations has the meaning given in that Part;
(b) "installation" means "Part A installation or Part A mobile plant";
(c) "permit" means "environmental permit";
(d) the competent authority is the regulator; and
(e) "substance" is to be read as including, after the words "its compounds" in Article 2(1) of the IPPC Directive, the words "and any biological entity or micro-organism".

3 Exercise of regulator's functions: general

The regulator must exercise its functions under these Regulations for the purpose of achieving a high level of protection of the environment taken as a whole by, in particular, preventing or, where that is not practicable, reducing emissions into the air, water and land.

4 Applications for the grant of an environmental permit

(1) The regulator must ensure that every application for the grant of an environmental permit includes the information specified in Article 6(1) of the IPPC Directive.

(2) But when interpreting Article 6(1), the regulator must ignore the fourth indent in the case of Part A mobile plant.

5 Exercise of relevant functions

(1) The regulator must exercise its relevant functions so as to ensure compliance with the following provisions of the IPPC Directive—

(a) Article 3, ignoring the words "provide that the competent authorities" contained in the first sentence of Article 3(1);
(b) Article 9(1) to (6);
(c) Article 10;
(d) Article 12;
(e) Article 14 point (b);
(f) Article 19(2).

(2) But when interpreting the IPPC Directive for the purposes of this paragraph, the regulator must—

(a) ignore the second and fourth paragraphs of Article 9(3);
(b) in the case of Part A mobile plant, in Article 9(4), ignore the words "its geographical location and the local environmental conditions";
(c) ignore the second paragraph of Article 9(5);
(d) ignore the second paragraph of Article 9(6); and
(e) in the case of Part A mobile plant, ignore Article 12.

6 Public participation

The regulator must exercise its functions under the public participation provisions in relation to Part A installations so as to meet the requirements of Article 15(1) of the IPPC Directive.

7 Review of environmental permits

The regulator must review an environmental permit if any of the circumstances in Article 13(2) of the IPPC Directive apply in relation to the Part A installation or Part A mobile plant whose operation it authorises.

8 Developments in best available techniques

(1) The regulator must ensure that it is informed of developments in best available techniques.

(2) In this paragraph, "best available techniques" has the meaning given in Article 2(12) of the IPPC Directive.

SCHEDULE 8
PART B INSTALLATIONS AND PART B MOBILE PLANT

Regulation 35(2)(b)

1 Application

This Schedule applies in relation to every Part B installation and Part B mobile plant.

2 Interpretation

When interpreting the IPPC Directive for the purposes of this Schedule—
(a) except where otherwise defined in this paragraph, an expression that is defined in Part 1 of these Regulations has the meaning given in that Part;
(b) "installation" means "Part B installation" or "Part B mobile plant";
(c) "permit" means "environmental permit";
(d) a reference to "emission limit values" is to be read as a reference to those values which are relevant to air pollution;
(e) the competent authority is the regulator; and
(f) "substance" is to be read as including, after the words "its compounds" in Article 2(1) of that Directive, the words "and any biological entity or micro-organism".

3 Exercise of regulator's functions: general

The regulator must exercise its functions under these Regulations for the purpose of preventing or, where that is not practicable, reducing emissions into the air.

4 Applications for the grant of an environmental permit

(1) The regulator must ensure that every application for the grant of an environmental permit includes the information specified in Article 6(1) of the IPPC Directive.

(2) But, when interpreting Article 6(1), the regulator must—
(a) ignore points (b), (d) and (g);
(b) ignore points (c) and (e) to the extent that the application relates to the carrying on of dry cleaning at a Part B installation;
(c) in point (e), the reference to "each medium" is to be read as a reference to "air";
(d) ignore point (f) to the extent that the application relates to the burning of waste oil in an appliance with a net rated thermal input of less than 0.4 megawatts at a Part B installation;
(e) in point (h), read the reference to "Article 3" as a reference to "Article 3(1)(a) and (1)(b)".

(3) In this paragraph, "dry cleaning" has the meaning given in Part B of Section 7 of Part 2 of Schedule 1.

5 Exercise of relevant functions

(1) The regulator must exercise its relevant functions so as to ensure compliance with the following provisions of the IPPC Directive—
(a) Article 3(1)(a) and (b);
(b) Article 9(1) to (4);
(c) Article 10;
(d) Article 12;
(e) Article 19(2).

(2) But when interpreting the IPPC Directive for the purposes of this paragraph, the regulator must—
(a) in Article 3(1), ignore the words "provide that the competent authorities";
(b) in Article 9(1) read—
  (i) the reference to "Article 3" as a reference to "Article 3(1)(a) and (b)", and
  (ii) the words from "in order" to the end of the Article as "for the purpose of preventing or, where that is not practicable, reducing emissions into the air";
(c) in Article 9(3), ignore the words "and their potential to transfer pollution from one medium to another (water, air and land)";
(d) in Article 9(4)—
  (i) in the case of Part B mobile plant, ignore the words "its geographical location and the local environmental conditions", and

(ii) ignore the last sentence;
(e) in the case of Part B mobile plant, ignore Article 12;
(f) in Annex III, ignore the section headed "WATER".

6 Review of environmental permits

The regulator must review an environmental permit if any of the circumstances in Article 13(2) of the IPPC Directive apply in relation to the Part B installation or Part B mobile plant whose operation it authorises.

7 Developments in best available techniques

(1) The regulator must ensure that it is informed of developments in best available techniques.

(2) In this paragraph, "best available techniques" has the meaning given in Article 2(12) of the IPPC Directive, save that the reference to "Annex IV" in that Article is to be read as a reference to "paragraphs 4 to 8 of Annex IV".

SCHEDULE 9
WASTE OPERATIONS

Regulation 35(2)(c)

1 Application

This Schedule applies in relation to every waste operation.

2 Interpretation

In this Schedule—
"disposal" has the same meaning as in the Waste Framework Directive and related terms are to be construed accordingly; and
"recovery" has the same meaning as in the Waste Framework Directive and related terms are to be construed accordingly.

3 Grant of an environmental permit for a relevant waste operation: requirement for prior planning permission

(1) Following an application under regulation 13(1), the regulator must not grant an environmental permit that relates to a relevant waste operation if—
(a) use of the site for carrying on the relevant waste operation requires planning permission or development consent under the Planning Act 2008; and
(b) no such permission or consent is in force.

(2) In this paragraph—
"planning permission" means planning permission under the Town and Country Planning Act 1990 and includes—
(a) a certificate under section 191 of that Act, and
(b) an established use certificate under section 192 of that Act, as originally enacted, which continues to have effect for the purposes of subsection (4) of that section; and
"relevant waste operation" means—
(a) a waste operation that is not carried on at an installation or by means of Part A mobile plant or Part B mobile plant, or
(b) a specified waste management activity.

(3) In sub-paragraph (2)(b), "specified waste management activity" means one of the following activities—
(a) the disposal of waste in a landfill falling within Section 5.2 of Part 2 of Schedule 1;

(b) the disposal of waste falling within Section 5.3 of Part 2 of Schedule 1;
(c) the recovery of waste falling within Part A(1)(c)(i), (ii), (v) or (vii) of Section 5.4 of Part 2 of Schedule 1.

(4) But "specified waste management activity" does not include any activity specified in sub-paragraph (3)(b) or (c) if that activity—
(a) is carried on at the same installation as a Part A(1) activity not specified in sub-paragraph (3); and
(b) is not the activity which constitutes the primary purpose for operating the installation.

[4 Exercise of relevant functions

(1) The regulator must exercise its relevant functions—
(a) for the purposes of ensuring that—
 (i) the waste hierarchy referred to in Article 4 of the Waste Framework Directive is applied to the generation of waste by a waste operation;
 (ii) waste generated by a waste operation is treated in accordance with Article 4 of the Waste Framework Directive;
(b) for the purposes of implementing Article 13 of the Waste Framework Directive, but not in respect of nuisances and hazards arising from traffic beyond the site of a waste operation;
(c) so as to ensure that the requirements in the second paragraph of Article 23(1) of the Waste Framework Directive are met;
(d) so as to ensure compliance with the following Articles of the Waste Framework Directive—
 (i) Article 18(2)(b) and (c);
 (ii) Article 23(3);
 (iii) Article 23(4);
 (iv) Article 35(1).

(2) But the following duties take effect in relation to an environmental permit which is in force on the date of coming into force of the Waste (England and Wales) Regulations 2011 on the first review of the permit by the regulator (under regulation 34(1)) after that date—
(a) the duty in paragraphs (1)(a), (1)(d)(i) and (1)(d)(iii);
(b) the duty in paragraph (1)(c), to the extent that it is imposed in relation to Article 23(1)(e) and (f).][1]

Amendment

1 Substituted by the Waste (England and Wales) Regulations 2011, SI 2011/988, reg 48(2), Sch 3, paras 1, 9(a).

[Schedule 9, para 4 was repealed by the Waste (England and Wales) Regulations 2011, SI 2011/988, reg 48(2), Sch 3, paras 1, 9(b).]

SCHEDULE 10
LANDFILL

Regulation 35(2)(d)

1 Application

This Schedule applies in relation to every landfill except a landfill which finally ceased to accept waste for disposal before 16th July 2001.

2 Interpretation: general

(1) In this Schedule—
(a) unless otherwise provided, an expression that is defined in the Landfill Directive has the meaning given in that Directive;

(b) "the Decision" means Council Decision 2003/33/EC;
(c) "the Decision Annex" means the Annex to the Decision; and
(d) "landfill" has the meaning given in Article 2(g) of the Landfill Directive, but does not include any operation excluded from the scope of that Directive by Article 3(2).

(2) When interpreting the Landfill Directive and the Decision for the purposes of this Schedule—
(a) an expression that is defined in Part 1 of these Regulations has the meaning given in that Part;
(b) "landfill permit" means environmental permit;
(c) "nature protection zone" means any—
  (i) site of special scientific interest within the meaning given in section 52 of the Wildlife and Countryside Act 1981, or
  (ii) European site within the meaning given in [regulation 8(1) of the Conservation of Habitats and Species Regulations 2010][1];
(d) "PAHs (polycyclic aromatic hydrocarbons)" means [Naphthalene][1], Acenaphthylene, Acenaphthene, Anthracene, Benzo(a)anthracene, Benzo(b)fluoranthene, Benzo(k) fluoranthene, Benzo(g,h,i)perylene, Benzo(a)pyrene, Chrysene, Coronene, Dibenzo(a,h) anthracene, Fluorene, Fluoranthene, Indeno(1,2,3-c,d)pyrene, Phenanthrene and Pyrene;
(e) "permit" means environmental permit;
(f) "SIC code" means the UK Standard Industrial Classification of Economic Activities 2007 (SIC 2007) published by the Office for National Statistics on 14th December 2007 and implemented on 1st January 2008; and
(g) the competent authority is the regulator.

Amendment

1 Substituted by the Environmental Permitting (England and Wales) (Amendment) Regulations 2012, SI 2012/630, reg 15.

3 Applications for the grant of an environmental permit

The regulator must require that every application for the grant of an environmental permit includes the information specified in Article 7 of the Landfill Directive.

4 Inspection prior to operation

The regulator must inspect every landfill site so as to comply with the requirements in Article 8(c) of the Landfill Directive.

5 Exercise of relevant functions

(1) The regulator must exercise its relevant functions so as to ensure compliance with the following provisions of the Landfill Directive—
(a) Article 4;
(b) Article 5(3) and (4);
(c) Article 6;
[(d) Article 8, but not in respect of nuisances and hazards arising from traffic beyond the site of a landfill;][1]
(e) Article 9;
(f) Article 10;
(g) Article 11(1);
(h) Article 12;
(i) Article 13;
(j) Article 14.

(2) The regulator must exercise those relevant functions having regard to Article 1 of the Landfill Directive.

(3) The regulator must exercise those relevant functions so as to ensure compliance with the requirements imposed on the Member State by the following provisions of the Decision—
(a) Article 2;
(b) Article 3;
(c) Article 4.

Amendment

1 Substituted by the Waste (England and Wales) Regulations 2011, SI 2011/988, reg 48(2), Sch 3, paras 1, 10.

6 Interpretation of the Landfill Directive for the exercise of relevant functions

When interpreting the Landfill Directive for the purposes of paragraph 5(1)—
(a) in Article 6(a), the words "This provision may not apply to" is to be read as "This provision does not apply to";
(b) in Article 8(a)(iv), ignore the last sentence;
(c) the last sentence of paragraph 2 of Annex I is to be read as "The above provisions do not apply to inert landfills."; and
(d) in paragraph 3(3) of Annex I, ignore the sentence immediately following the table headed "Leachate collection and bottom sealing".

7 Interpretation of the Decision Annex for the exercise of relevant functions: general

When interpreting the Decision Annex for the purposes of paragraph 5(3)—
(a) in points 1.1.1 and 1.2, the periods referred to as to be defined or determined by the Member State are in each case 2 years;
(b) point 1.1.2(b) is to be read as requiring the SIC code of the process producing the waste to be part of the information referred to;
(c) in point 1.1.2(g), ignore the words "in case of mirror entries";
(d) ignore the third sentence of section 2;
(e) in points 2.1.2.1, 2.2.2, 2.3.1 and 2.4.1 the table columns headed "L/S = 10 l/kg" must be used to determine limit values;
(f) in the table in point 2.1.2.2, the limit value for PAHs (polycyclic aromatic hydrocarbons) is set at 100 mg/kg;
(g) in point 2.2.3, the first reference to "gypsum-based materials" is to be read as "gypsumbased and other high sulphate-bearing materials";
(h) in point 2.3.3, the first reference to "suitable asbestos waste" is to be read as "suitable materials"; and
(i) in the table in point 2.4.1, the limit values are subject to the qualification that the regulator may include conditions in an environmental permit authorising limit values for specific parameters (other than Dissolved Organic Carbon) up to 3 times higher than those listed for specified wastes accepted at a landfill, taking into account the characteristics of the landfill and its surroundings and provided a risk assessment demonstrates that emissions (including leachate) from the landfill will present no additional risk to the environment.

8 Interpretation of the Decision Annex for the exercise of relevant functions: additional acceptance criteria relating to physical stability and bearing capacity of granular waste

When interpreting the Decision Annex for the purposes of paragraph 5(3)—
(a) in point 2.3.2, the criteria to ensure that granular waste will have sufficient physical stability and bearing capacity are that it has either—
  (i) if it is cohesive waste, a mean in situ shear strength of at least 50kPa, or
  (ii) if it is non-cohesive waste, an in situ bearing ratio of at least 5%;
(b) point 2.4.2 is to be read as if, in addition to the criteria listed, it requires the satisfaction of the criteria in paragraph (a)(i) and (a)(ii).

9 Interpretation of the Decision Annex for the exercise of relevant functions: additional acceptance criteria in relating to monolithic waste

When interpreting the Decision Annex for the purposes of paragraph 5(3)—

(a) point 2.3.1 is to be read as if, in addition to the criteria listed, it requires the satisfaction of the following criteria in relation to stable, non-reactive monolithic hazardous waste and non-hazardous waste which is to be landfilled in the same cell with such waste—

(i) it meets either—

(aa) the limit values for leaching set out in the table in point 2.3.1, or

(bb) the limit values for leaching set out in the following table—

Component	*Symbol*	*mg/m²*
Arsenic	As	1.3
Barium	Ba	45
Cadmium	Cd	0.2
Total Chromium	Cr_{total}	5
Copper	Cu	45
Mercury	Hg	0.1
Molybdenum	Mo	7
Nickel	Ni	6
Lead	Pb	6
Antimony	Sb	0.3
Selenium	Se	0.4
Zinc	Zn	30
Chloride	Cl-	10,000
Fluoride	F-	60
Sulphate	$SO_4$2-	10,000
Dissolved Organic Carbon	DOC	Must be evaluated

(ii) it meets the additional criteria set out in the following table—

Parameter	*Value*
pH of the eluate from the monolith or crushed monolith	Must be evaluated
Electrical conductivity (μ S.cm-1m-2) of the eluate from the monolith or crushed monolith	Must be evaluated
Acid Neutralisation Capacity (ANC) of the crushed monolith	Must be evaluated

(iii) it has a mean unconfined compressive strength of at least 1Mpa after 28 days curing;

(iv) it has either—

(aa) dimensions of greater than 40cm along each side, or

(bb) a depth and fracture spacing when hardened of greater than 40cm; and

(v) where the waste was subjected to treatment to render it monolithic, prior to such treatment it met the following limit values—

(aa) loss on ignition of 10%, or

(bb) total organic carbon of 6%;

(b) point 2.4.1 in the Decision Annex is to be read as if, in addition to the criteria listed, it requires the satisfaction of the following criteria in relation to monolithic waste to be accepted at a landfill for hazardous waste—

(i) it complies with paragraphs (a)(ii) to (a)(v), and

(ii) it meets either—

(aa) the limit values for leaching set out in the table in point 2.4.1, or

(bb) the limit values for leaching set out in the following table—

Component	*Symbol*	*mg/m*$^{2(1)}$
Arsenic	As	20
Barium	Ba	150
Cadmium	Cd	1
Total Chromium	Crtotal	25
Copper	Cu	60
Mercury	Hg	0.4
Molybdenum	Mo	20
Nickel	Ni	15
Lead	Pb	20
Antimony	Sb	2.5
Selenium	Se	5
Zinc	Zn	100
Chloride	Cl-	20,000
Fluoride	F-	200
Sulphate	SO42-	20,000
Dissolved Organic Carbon	DOC	Must be evaluated

(1) The regulator may include conditions in an environmental permit authorising limit values for specific parameters (other than Dissolved Organic Carbon) up to 3 times higher for specified wastes accepted in a landfill, taking into account the characteristics of the landfill and its surroundings and provided a risk assessment demonstrates that emissions (including leachate) from the landfill will present no additional risk to the environment.

10 Closure of a landfill

(1) The regulator must set out any reasoned decision under Article 13(a)(iii) of the Landfill Directive in a closure notice served on the operator.

(2) A closure notice must, in addition to stating the regulator's reasons for requiring initiation of the closure procedure, specify—

(a) the steps the operator is required to take to initiate the procedure; and

(b) the period within which they must be taken.

(3) The regulator may withdraw a closure notice at any time by further notice served on the operator.

(4) Closure of a landfill does not relieve the operator of liability under the conditions of the environmental permit.

11 Surrender applications

When determining an application for the surrender, in whole or in part, of an environmental permit, the regulator must exercise its functions so as to ensure the operator complies with the requirements in Article 13(d) of the Landfill Directive.

SCHEDULE 11
WASTE MOTOR VEHICLES

Regulation 35(2)(e)

1 Application

This Schedule applies in relation to waste motor vehicles.

2 Interpretation

(1) In this Schedule—

"waste" means waste within the meaning of Article 1(1)(a) of the Waste Framework Directive; and

"waste motor vehicle" means a motor vehicle that is waste.

(2) When interpreting the End-of-Life Vehicles Directive for the purposes of this Schedule—

(a) except where otherwise defined in this paragraph, an expression that is defined in Part 1 of these Regulations has the meaning given in that Part;

(b) "end-of-life vehicle" means waste motor vehicle;

(c) "vehicle" means any motor vehicle;

(d) "waste" means waste within the meaning of [Article 3(1)][1] of the Waste Framework Directive.

Amendment

1 Substituted by the Waste (England and Wales) Regulations 2011, SI 2011/988, reg 48(2), 11.

3 Exercise of relevant functions

(1) The regulator must exercise its relevant functions so as to ensure compliance with Article 6(1) and (3) of the End-of-Life Vehicles Directive.

(2) When interpreting the End-of-Life Vehicles Directive for the purposes of this paragraph, "establishment or undertaking" is to be read as "operator".

SCHEDULE 12
WASTE ELECTRICAL AND ELECTRONIC EQUIPMENT

Regulation 35(2)(f)

1 Application

This Schedule applies in relation to waste electrical and electronic equipment which is within the scope of the WEEE Directive by virtue of Article 2 of that Directive.

2 Interpretation

(1) In this Schedule, "waste electrical and electronic equipment" has the meaning given in Article 3(b) of the WEEE Directive.

(2) When interpreting the WEEE Directive for the purposes of this Schedule—

(a) an expression that is defined in Part 1 of these Regulations has the meaning given in that Part;

(b) "permit" means environmental permit; and

(c) "waste" means waste within the meaning of [Article 3(1)][1] of the Waste Framework Directive.

Amendment

1 Substituted by the Waste (England and Wales) Regulations 2011, SI 2011/988, reg 48(2), 12.

3 Exercise of relevant functions

(1) The regulator must exercise its relevant functions so as to ensure compliance with Article 6(1) first paragraph and Article 6(3) and (4) of the WEEE Directive.

(2) But when interpreting the WEEE Directive for the purposes of this paragraph, ignore the following words in Article 6(4)—

(a) "or the registration referred to in paragraph 2"; and

(b) "and for the achievement of the recovery targets set out in Article 7".

SCHEDULE 13
WASTE INCINERATION

Regulation 35(2)(g)

1 Application

This Schedule applies in relation to every waste incineration installation.

2 Interpretation

(1) In this Schedule, "waste incineration installation" means that part of an installation or Part A mobile plant in which any of the following activities is carried on—

(a) the incineration of waste falling within the following provisions of Section 5.1 of Part 2 of Schedule 1—
  (i) paragraphs (a) to (c) of Part A(1), or
  (ii) paragraph (a) or (b) of Part A(2); or

(b) any other activity falling within Part 2 of Schedule 1 which is carried on in a coincineration plant (as that term is defined in Section 5.1 of Part 2 of Schedule 1).

(2) When interpreting the Waste Incineration Directive for the purposes of this Schedule—

(a) an expression that is defined in Section 5.1 of Part 2 of Schedule 1 has the meaning given in that Section;

(b) except where also defined in Section 5.1 of Part 2 of Schedule 1, an expression that is defined in Part 1 of these Regulations has the meaning given in that Part;

(c) "permit" means environmental permit; and

(d) the competent authority is the regulator.

3 Applications for the grant of an environmental permit

The regulator must require that every application for the grant of an environmental permit includes the information specified in Article 4(2) of the Waste Incineration Directive.

4 Exercise of relevant functions

(1) The regulator must exercise its relevant functions so as to ensure compliance with the following provisions of the Waste Incineration Directive—

(a) Article 4(3) to (5);

(b) Article 5;

(c) Article 6, except the last indent of 6(4);

(d) Article 7(1) to (4);

(e) Article 8(1) to (7);

(f) Article 9;

(g) Article 10;

(h) Article 11, except for 11(1) and (13);

(i) Article 12(2), to the extent that it relates to the provision of annual reports by the operator;

(j) Article 13.

(2) But when interpreting the Waste Incineration Directive for the purposes of this paragraph—

(a) in Article 6(4), ignore the words "Member States may lay down rules governing these authorisations" in both places they occur;

(b) in Article 11(1), ignore the words "either" and "or by general binding rules";

(c) Article 11(2)(c) is to be read as if the words "and dioxin-like polychlorinated biphenyls and poly-cyclic aromatic hydrocarbons" appeared after the word "furans"; and

(d) Annex V is to be read as if every reference to an exemption which "may" be authorised by the competent authority was a reference to an exemption which "must" be authorised by the competent authority.

SCHEDULE 14
SED INSTALLATIONS

Regulation 35(2)(h)

1 Application

This Schedule applies in relation to every SED installation.

2 Interpretation

(1) In this Schedule—

"directly associated activity", in relation to a SED activity, means an operation which—

(a) has a technical connection with the SED activity,

(b) is carried on on the same site as the SED activity, and

(c) could have an effect on a discharge of volatile organic compounds into the environment;

"SED installation" means—

(a) a stationary technical unit where one or more SED activities are carried on, and

(b) any other location on the same site where any other directly associated activities are carried on; and

"the Solvent Emissions Directive" means Council Directive 1999/13/EC on the limitation of emissions of volatile organic compounds due to the use of organic solvents in certain activities and installations.

(2) When interpreting the Solvent Emissions Directive for the purposes of this Schedule—

(a) an expression that is defined in Section 7 of Part 2 of Schedule 1 has the meaning given in that Section;

(b) except where also defined in that Section or in this paragraph, an expression that is defined in Part 1 of these Regulations has the meaning given in that Part;

(c) "authorisation" means environmental permit;

(d) "emission" has the meaning given in the Solvent Emissions Directive;

(e) "installation" means SED installation;

(f) the competent authority is the regulator.

3 Exercise of relevant functions

(1) The regulator must exercise its relevant functions so as to ensure compliance with the following provisions of the Solvent Emissions Directive—

(a) Article 4(4);

(b) Article 5, except for the last sentence of 5(3), and 5(13);

(c) Article 7(2);

(d) Article 8(1) to (4);

(e) Article 9;

(f) Article 10.

(2) When interpreting the Solvent Emissions Directive for the purposes of this paragraph—

(a) in Article 5(1), ignore the words "either" and "or by general binding rules";

(b) in Article 7(2), ignore the words "and during the formulation of general binding rules"; and

(c) in point 1 of Annex IIB, ignore the last sentence.

SCHEDULE 15
LARGE COMBUSTION PLANTS

Regulation 35(2)(i)

1 Application

This Schedule applies in relation to every combustion plant to which the Large Combustion Plants Directive applies by virtue of Article 1 of that Directive.

2 Interpretation

(1) In this Schedule—

"combustion plant" has the meaning given in Article 2(7) of the Large Combustion Plants Directive;

"existing plant" has the meaning given in Article 2(10) of the Large Combustion Plants Directive; and

"the Large Combustion Plants Directive" means Directive 2001/80/EC of the European Parliament and of the Council on the limitation of emissions of certain pollutants into the air from large combustion plants.

(2) When interpreting the Large Combustion Plants Directive for the purposes of this Schedule—

(a) except where also defined in this paragraph, an expression that is defined in Part 1 of these Regulations has the meaning given in that Part;

(b) the competent authority is—

  (i) for the purposes of exercising a judgment of whether there is an overriding need to maintain energy supplies under Article 7(1) or (3) of the Large Combustion Plants Directive, the appropriate authority,

  (ii) otherwise, the regulator;

(c) the national emission reduction plan referred to in Article 4(6) of the Large Combustion Plants Directive is the emission plan, as amended from time to time, published under regulation 4(1) of the Large Combustion Plants (National Emission Reduction Plan) Regulations 2007;

(d) "emission" has the meaning given in the Large Combustion Plants Directive;

(e) "licence" means environmental permit;

(f) "permit" means environmental permit; and

(g) in Article 4(4), ignore the words "and from their inclusion in the national emission reduction plan".

3 Exercise of relevant functions

(1) The regulator must exercise its relevant functions so as to ensure compliance with the following provisions of the Large Combustion Plants Directive—

(a) Article 4(1), (2) and (4);

(b) Article 5(1);

(c) Article 6;

(d) Article 7, except the last sentence of 7(2) and the last sentence of 7(3);

(e) Article 8;

(f) Article 9;

(g) Article 10;

(h) Article 12;

(i) Article 13;

(j) Article 14(1), (2) and (4).

(2) The regulator must—

(a) exercise its relevant functions in relation to a regulated facility which—

  (i) is an existing plant, and

  (ii) elects to comply with the emission limit values established under Article 4(1) of the Large Combustion Plants Directive, so as to ensure compliance with Article 4(3)(a) of that Directive; and

(b) exercise its relevant functions in relation to a regulated facility which is included in the national emission reduction plan referred to in Article 4(6) of the Large Combustion Plants Directive so as to ensure compliance with Article 4(3)(b) of that Directive, to the extent that such compliance is not ensured by the Large Combustion Plants (National Emission Reduction Plan) Regulations 2007.

(3) The regulator must—

(a) immediately inform the appropriate authority of any suspension under Article 7(2) or derogation under Article 7(3) of the Large Combustion Plants Directive;

(b) immediately inform the appropriate authority if it considers that the appropriate authority must make a judgment of whether there is an overriding need to maintain energy supplies under Article 7(1) or (3) of the Large Combustion Plants Directive; and

(c) exercise its relevant functions in relation to such a judgment in accordance with the decision of that authority.

SCHEDULE 16
ASBESTOS

Regulation 35(2)(j)

1 Application

This Schedule applies in relation to every regulated facility.

2 Interpretation

(1) In this Schedule, "the Asbestos Directive" means Council Directive 87/217/EEC on the prevention and reduction of environmental pollution by asbestos.

(2) When interpreting the Asbestos Directive for the purposes of this Schedule—

(a) except where otherwise defined in this paragraph, an expression that is defined in Part 1 of these Regulations has the meaning given in that Part;

(b) the competent authority is the regulator;

(c) "waste" has the meaning given in the Asbestos Directive.

3 Exercise of relevant functions

(1) The regulator must exercise its relevant functions so as to ensure compliance with the following provisions of the Asbestos Directive—

(a) Article 3;

(b) Article 4(1);

(c) Article 5;

(d) Article 6(1) and (2);

(e) Article 8.

(2) When interpreting the Asbestos Directive for the purposes of this paragraph, in Article 6(1), "regular intervals" means, for the purposes of a regulated facility to which Article 4 applies, intervals of not more than 6 months.

SCHEDULE 17
TITANIUM DIOXIDE

Regulation 35(2)(k)

1 Application

This Schedule applies in relation to every regulated facility where the chlorine process or the sulphate process is carried on.

2 Interpretation

(1) In this Schedule—

"the Titanium Dioxide Directive" means Council Directive 92/112/EEC on procedures for harmonizing the programmes for the reduction and eventual elimination of pollution caused by waste from the titanium dioxide industry; and

"chlorine process" and "sulphate process" have the same meaning as in Article 2 of the Titanium Dioxide Directive.

(2) When interpreting the Titanium Dioxide Directive for the purposes of this Schedule, an expression that is defined in Part 1 of these Regulations has the meaning given in that Part.

3 Exercise of relevant functions

The regulator must exercise its relevant functions so as to ensure compliance with the following provisions of the Titanium Dioxide Directive—

(a) Article 4;
(b) Article 6;
(c) Article 9;
(d) Article 10;
(e) Article 11.

[SCHEDULE 18
PETROL VAPOUR RECOVERY

Regulation 35(2)(l)

PART 1
PVR I][1]

[1 Application

This Part applies in relation to every Part B activity falling within paragraphs (b) and (c) of Part B of Section 1.2 of Part 2 of Schedule 1.][1]

Amendment

1 Substituted by the Environmental Permitting (England and Wales) (Amendment) (No. 2) Regulations 2011, SI 2011/2933, reg 2(1), (4).

[2 Interpretation

In this Part, "PVR I" means European Parliament and Council Directive 94/63/EC on the control of volatile organic compound (VOC) emissions resulting from the storage of petrol and its distribution from terminals to service stations.][1]

Amendment

1 Substituted by the Environmental Permitting (England and Wales) (Amendment) (No. 2) Regulations 2011, SI 2011/2933, reg 2(1), (4).

[3 Exercise of relevant functions

(1) The regulator must exercise its relevant functions so as to ensure compliance with the following provisions of PVR I—

(a) Article 3(1), first paragraph;
(b) Article 4(1), first and last paragraphs, and 4(3);
(c) Article 6(1), first paragraph.

(2) When interpreting PVR I for the purposes of this paragraph—

(a) in point 1 of Annex I, "special landscape areas which have been designated by national authority" includes the Broads, the New Forest and any National Park or Area of Outstanding Natural Beauty; and
(b) ignore points 2.3, 3.2, and 3.5 of Annex IV.][1]

Amendment

1 Substituted by the Environmental Permitting (England and Wales) (Amendment) (No. 2) Regulations 2011, SI 2011/2933, reg 2(1), (4).

[PART 2
PVR II][1]

[1 Application

This Part applies in relation to every Part B activity falling within paragraphs (d) to (g) of Part B of Section 1.2 of Part 2 of Schedule 1.][1]

Amendment

1 Substituted by the Environmental Permitting (England and Wales) (Amendment) (No. 2) Regulations 2011, SI 2011/2933, reg 2(1), (4).

[2 Interpretation

In this Part, "PVR II" means Directive 2009/126/EC of the European Parliament and of the Council on Stage II petrol vapour recovery during refuelling of motor vehicles at service stations.][1]

Amendment

1 Substituted by the Environmental Permitting (England and Wales) (Amendment) (No. 2) Regulations 2011, SI 2011/2933, reg 2(1), (4).

[3 Exercise of relevant functions

(1) The regulator must exercise its relevant functions so as to ensure compliance with the following provisions of PVR II—
(a) Article 3;
(b) Article 4;
(c) Article 5.

(2) But when interpreting PVR II for the purposes of this paragraph—
(a) in Articles 3, 4 and 5, ignore the words "member states shall ensure that" where they occur;
(b) in Article 4, ignore the words "with effect from the date on which Stage II petrol vapour recovery systems become mandatory pursuant to Article 3".][1]

Amendment

1 Substituted by the Environmental Permitting (England and Wales) (Amendment) (No. 2) Regulations 2011, SI 2011/2933, reg 2(1), (4).

SCHEDULE 19
WASTE BATTERIES AND ACCUMULATORS

Regulation 35(2)(m)

1 Application

This Schedule applies in relation to waste batteries and accumulators.

2 Exercise of relevant functions

The regulator must exercise its relevant functions so as to ensure compliance with Article 12(2) of the Batteries Directive.

SCHEDULE 20
MINING WASTE OPERATIONS

Regulation 35(2)(n)

1 Application

This Schedule applies in relation to every mining waste operation.

2 Interpretation

(1) In this Schedule—

"mining waste facility" means a "waste facility" as defined in Article 3(15) of the Mining Waste Directive but excludes those facilities mentioned in Article 24(2) or in the first paragraph of Article 24(4) of that Directive;

"mining waste operation" means the management of extractive waste, whether or not involving a mining waste facility, but does not include the activities in Article 2(2)(c) of the Mining Waste Directive;

"relevant emergency planner" means, in relation to an application for a mining waste facility that is located in—

(a) London, the London Fire and Emergency Planning Authority,

(b) an area where there is a fire and civil defence authority, that authority,

(c) the Isles of Scilly, the Council of the Isles of Scilly,

(d) an area in the rest of England, the county council for that area or where there is no county council for that area, the district council for that area,

(e) an area in Wales, the county council or county borough council for that area; and

"waste management plan" means a plan of the type described in Article 5(1) of the Mining Waste Directive which has the objectives in Article 5(2) and contains the elements and information set out in Article 5(3) of that Directive.

(2) When interpreting the Mining Waste Directive for the purposes of this Schedule—

(a) except where otherwise defined in this paragraph, an expression that is defined in Part 1 of these Regulations has the meaning given in that Part;

(b) "permit" means an environmental permit; and

(c) the competent authority is the regulator.

3 Applications for grant or variation of an environmental permit

(1) The regulator must require that every application for the grant or variation of an environmental permit in relation to a mining waste operation involving a mining waste facility to which Article 7 of the Mining Waste Directive applies includes—

(a) the information specified in Article 7(2) of that Directive; and

(b) where Article 6 of the Directive applies, the information mentioned in the second sentence of the third paragraph of Article 6(3).

(2) Where the regulator receives an application for the grant or variation of an environmental permit and that application includes the information required under sub-paragraph (1)(b), the regulator must immediately forward the information to the relevant emergency planner.

(3) The regulator must require that every application for the grant or variation of an environmental permit in relation to any other mining waste operation includes a waste management plan.

(4) For the purposes of this paragraph, the regulator may accept a waste management plan produced pursuant to other legislation which complies with Article 5(1) to (4) of the Mining Waste Directive if it has been reviewed and amended in accordance with Article 5(4) of that Directive.

4 Review of environmental permits

The regulator must periodically review an environmental permit relating to a mining waste facility if Article 7 of the Mining Waste Directive applies in respect of that facility and any of the circumstances in Article 7(4) of the Directive apply in relation to it.

5 Classification of mining waste facilities

The regulator must exercise its functions so as to ensure compliance with Article 9 of the Mining Waste Directive in respect of any mining waste facility to which Article 7 of that Directive does not apply.

6 Inspections

The regulator must inspect every mining waste facility to which Article 7 of the Mining Waste Directive applies so as to comply with the requirements of Article 17(1) of that Directive.

7 Exercise of relevant functions

The regulator must exercise its relevant functions so as to ensure compliance with the following requirements of the Mining Waste Directive—

(a) Article 2(4);
(b) Article 4;
(c) Article 5(4) and (6);
(d) Article 6(2), the first and second paragraphs of Article 6(3), the first paragraph of Article 6(4) to the extent that it relates to plans prepared under the first paragraph of Article 6(3) and the second paragraph of Article 6(4) to the extent that it relates to the regulator's functions;
(e) Article 7(1) and (3)(a);
(f) Article 10;
(g) Article 11;
(h) Article 12;
(i) Article 13;
(j) Article 14 (1) to (3);
(k) Article 17(2);
(l) Article 24(1).

8 Public participation

The regulator must exercise its functions under the public participation provisions in relation to mining waste facilities to which Article 7 of the Mining Waste Directive applies so as to meet the requirements of Article 8 of that Directive.

9 Derogation from requirements

(1) The regulator must exercise its functions to ensure that the requirements mentioned in the first paragraph of Article 2(3) of the Mining Waste Directive do not apply to the substances mentioned in that paragraph where they result from an operation mentioned in that paragraph, to the extent allowed by that paragraph.

(2) The regulator must waive the requirements of the Mining Waste Directive in relation to the deposit of the substances mentioned in the second paragraph of Article 2(3) of that Directive if the regulator is satisfied that the requirements of Article 4 of that Directive are met.

(3) The regulator must waive the requirements mentioned in the third paragraph of Article 2(3) of the Mining Waste Directive in relation to the waste mentioned in that paragraph to the extent allowed by that paragraph.

10 Closure of a mining waste facility

(1) The regulator must set out any reasoned decision under Article 12(2)(c) of the Mining Waste Directive in a closure notice served on the operator.

(2) A closure notice must, in addition to stating the regulator's reasons for requiring initiation of the closure procedure, specify—
(a) the steps the operator is required to take to initiate the procedure; and
(b) the period within which they must be taken.

(3) The regulator may withdraw a closure notice at any time by further notice served on the operator.

(4) Closure of a mining waste facility does not relieve the operator of liability under the environmental permit conditions that relate to the facility.

(5) The regulator must exercise its functions so as to ensure compliance with Article 14(4) of the Mining Waste Directive.

11 Inventory of closed mining waste facilities

The regulator must maintain and make available to the public an inventory of closed mining waste facilities so as to ensure compliance with Article 20 of the Mining Waste Directive.

12 Developments in best available techniques

(1) The regulator must ensure that it is informed of developments in best available techniques.

(2) In this paragraph, "best available techniques" has the meaning given in Article 2(12) of the IPPC Directive.

13 Planning permission requirements and conditions

(1) Following an application under regulation 13(1), the regulator must not grant an environmental permit in relation to a mining waste facility to which Article 7 of the Mining Waste Directive applies if use of the site as a mining waste facility requires planning permission and no such permission is in force.

(2) Where—
(a) a mining waste operation is the subject of an environmental permit;
(b) that operation has been granted planning permission subject to conditions ("planning conditions"); and
(c) there is an inconsistency between the environmental permit conditions and the planning conditions,

the environmental permit conditions prevail.

(3) In this paragraph, "planning permission" means planning permission under the Town and Country Planning Act 1990 and includes—
(a) a certificate under section 191 of that Act; and
(b) an established use certificate under section 192 of that Act, as originally enacted, which continues to have effect for the purposes of subsection (4) of that section.

14 Applications for grant or variation of an environmental permit for a Category A mining waste facility

(1) The regulator must not grant an application for the grant or variation of an environmental permit relating to a Category A mining waste facility until it has been notified by the relevant emergency planner that it has the information necessary to enable it to draw up an external emergency plan.

(2) The regulator must refuse an application relating to a Category A mining waste facility that is an existing mining waste facility upon receipt of a notice by the relevant emergency

planner stating that the operator has not provided the information necessary to enable the relevant emergency planner to draw up an external emergency plan.

(3) In this paragraph, "external emergency plan" means a plan as required under the third paragraph of Article 6(3) of the Mining Waste Directive that has the objectives specified in the first paragraph of Article 6(4) of that Directive.

SCHEDULE 21
WATER DISCHARGE ACTIVITIES

Regulation 35(2)(o)

1 Application

This Schedule applies in relation to every water discharge activity.

2 Interpretation

In this Schedule—

"discharging sewer" means the sewer or works from which sewage effluent is discharged;

"discharging undertaker" means the sewerage undertaker in which a discharging sewer is vested;

"main connection" has the same meaning as in section 110A of the Water Industry Act 1991;

"pipe" has the same meaning as in the 1991 Act;

"sending undertaker" means a sewerage undertaker which discharges sewage effluent into the discharging sewer or other sewer or works vested in the discharging undertaker; and

"waste" in the term "waste matter" includes—

(a) anything that is waste for the purposes of the Waste Framework Directive and is not excluded from the scope of that Directive by Article 2(1)[, (2) or (3)][1] of that Directive,

(b) anything that is waste for the purposes of the Mining Waste Directive and is not excluded from the scope of that Directive by Article 2(2) of that Directive.

Amendment

1 Inserted by the Waste (England and Wales) Regulations 2011, SI 2011/988, reg 48(2), Sch 3, paras 1, 13.

3 Meaning of "water discharge activity"

(1) A "water discharge activity" means any of the following—

(a) the discharge or entry to inland freshwaters, coastal waters or relevant territorial waters of any—

(i) poisonous, noxious or polluting matter,

(ii) waste matter, or

(iii) trade effluent or sewage effluent;

(b) the discharge from land through a pipe into the sea outside the seaward limits of relevant territorial waters of any trade effluent or sewage effluent;

(c) the removal from any part of the bottom, channel or bed of any inland freshwaters of a deposit accumulated by reason of any dam, weir or sluice holding back the waters, by causing it to be carried away in suspension in the waters, unless the activity is carried on in the exercise of a power conferred by or under any enactment relating to land drainage, flood prevention or navigation;

(d) the cutting or uprooting of a substantial amount of vegetation in any inland freshwaters or so near to any such waters that it falls into them and failure to take reasonable steps to remove the vegetation from these waters;

(e) an activity in respect of which a notice under paragraph 4 or 5 has been served and has taken effect.

(2) A discharge or an activity that might lead to a discharge is not a "water discharge activity"—
(a) if the discharge is made, or authorised to be made, by or under any prescribed statutory provision; or
(b) if the discharge is of trade effluent or sewage effluent from a vessel.

(3) In determining whether a discharge or an activity is a water discharge activity, no account must be taken of any radioactivity possessed by any substance or article or by any part of any premises.

4 Highway drains — notice requiring environmental permit

(1) This paragraph applies where—
(a) a person is operating a highway drain; and
(b) that activity might lead to a discharge mentioned in paragraph 3(1)(a) or (b).

(2) The regulator may serve a notice on the person operating the highway drain requiring the person, from the date the notice takes effect, to hold an environmental permit authorising the carrying on of that activity.

(3) A notice under this paragraph takes effect on the date specified in it, which must be at least 6 months after it is served.

5 Discharge of trade effluent or sewage effluent into lake or pond — notice requiring environmental permit

(1) The regulator may serve a notice on a person who discharges trade effluent or sewage effluent into the waters of any lake or pond which are not inland freshwaters requiring the person, from the date the notice takes effect, to hold an environmental permit authorising the carrying on of that activity.

(2) A notice under this paragraph takes effect on the date specified in it, which must be at least 3 months after it is served.

6 Liability resulting from discharge of sewage effluent from public sewer

(1) This paragraph applies for the purpose of determining liability for a water discharge activity that consists of a discharge of sewage effluent from a discharging sewer vested in a discharging undertaker.

(2) A discharging undertaker causes a discharge of sewage effluent if—
(a) matter included in the discharge is received by the discharging undertaker into the discharging sewer or into any other sewer or works vested in it;
(b) the discharging undertaker was bound (either unconditionally or subject to conditions which were observed) to receive the matter into the discharging sewer or other sewer or works; and
(c) sub-paragraph (3) does not apply.

(3) This sub-paragraph applies if, before the discharging undertaker discharges the sewage effluent from the discharging sewer, the sending undertaker, under an agreement with the discharging undertaker under section 110A of the Water Industry Act 1991, discharges the sewage effluent through a main connection into—
(a) the discharging sewer; or
(b) any other sewer or works vested in the discharging undertaker.

(4) If sub-paragraph (3) applies, the sending undertaker causes the discharge if—
(a) matter included in the discharge is received by the sending undertaker into a sewer or works vested in it; and

(b) it was bound (either conditionally or subject to conditions which were observed) to receive that matter into that sewer or works.

(5) A sewerage undertaker is not guilty of an offence under regulation 38(1) in relation to a water discharge activity that consists of a discharge of sewage effluent from a sewer or works vested in it if—

(a) the contravention is attributable to a discharge which another person caused or knowingly permitted to be made into the sewer or works;

(b) the undertaker either was not bound to receive the discharge into the sewer or works or was bound to receive it there subject to conditions which were not observed; and

(c) the undertaker could not reasonably have been expected to prevent the discharge into the sewer or works.

(6) A person is not guilty of an offence under regulation 38(1) in relation to a discharge which the person caused or knowingly permitted to be made into a sewer or works vested in a sewerage undertaker if that undertaker was bound to receive the discharge, either unconditionally or subject to conditions which were observed.

SCHEDULE 22
GROUNDWATER ACTIVITIES

Regulation 35(2)(p)

1 Application

This Schedule applies in relation to every groundwater activity.

2 Interpretation

In this Schedule—

"body of groundwater" has the same meaning as in the Water Framework Directive;

"direct input" in relation to groundwater means the introduction of a pollutant to groundwater without percolation through soil or subsoil;

"Groundwater Daughter Directive" means Directive 2006/118/EC of the European Parliament and of the Council on the protection of groundwater against pollution and deterioration;

"Groundwater Directive" means Council Directive 80/68/EEC on the protection of groundwater against pollution caused by certain dangerous substances;

"indirect input" in relation to groundwater means the introduction of a pollutant to groundwater after percolation through soil or subsoil; and

"surface waters" has the same meaning as in the Water Framework Directive.

3 Meaning of "groundwater activity"

(1) Subject to sub-paragraphs (2) and (3), "groundwater activity" means any of the following—

(a) the discharge of a pollutant that results in the direct input of that pollutant to groundwater;

(b) the discharge of a pollutant in circumstances that might lead to an indirect input of that pollutant to groundwater;

(c) any other discharge that might lead to the direct or indirect input of a pollutant to groundwater;

(d) an activity in respect of which a notice under paragraph 10 has been served and has taken effect;

(e) an activity that might lead to a discharge mentioned in paragraph (a), (b) or (c), where that activity is carried on as part of the operation of a regulated facility of another class.

(2) A discharge or an activity that might lead to a discharge is not a "groundwater activity" if the discharge is—

(a) made, or authorised to be made, by or under any prescribed statutory provision; or

(b) of trade effluent or sewage effluent from a vessel.

(3) The regulator may determine that a discharge, or an activity that might lead to a discharge, is not a groundwater activity if the input of the pollutant—

(a) is the consequence of an accident or exceptional circumstances of natural cause that could not reasonably have been foreseen, avoided or mitigated;
(b) is or would be of a quantity and concentration so small as to obviate any present or future danger of deterioration in the quality of the receiving groundwater; or
(c) is or would be incapable, for technical reasons, of being prevented or limited without using—
   (i) measures that would increase risks to human health or to the quality of the environment as a whole, or
   (ii) disproportionately costly measures to remove quantities of pollutants from, or otherwise control their percolation in, contaminated ground or subsoil.

(4) The regulator must keep a record of all determinations under sub-paragraph (3).

4 Meaning of "hazardous substance"

(1) A hazardous substance is any substance or group of substances that are toxic, persistent and liable to bio-accumulate.

(2) This includes in particular the following when they are toxic, persistent and liable to bioaccumulate—

(a) organohalogen compounds and substances which may form such compounds in the aquatic environment,
(b) organophosphorous compounds,
(c) organotin compounds,
(d) substances and preparations, or the breakdown products of such, which have been proved to possess carcinogenic or mutagenic properties or properties which may affect steroidogenic, thyroid, reproduction or other endocrine-related functions in or via the aquatic environment,
(e) persistent hydrocarbons and persistent and bioaccumulable organic toxic substances,
(f) cyanides,
(g) metals (in particular, cadmium and mercury) and their compounds,
(h) arsenic and its compounds,
(i) biocides and plant protection products.

(3) The regulator must publish a list of substances that it considers to be hazardous substances.

5 Meaning of "non-hazardous pollutant"

A non-hazardous pollutant is any pollutant other than a hazardous substance.

6 Exercise of relevant functions

For the purposes of implementing the Groundwater Directive, the Water Framework Directive and the Groundwater Daughter Directive, the regulator must, in exercising its relevant functions, take all necessary measures—

(a) to prevent the input of any hazardous substance to groundwater; and
(b) to limit the input of non-hazardous pollutants to groundwater so as to ensure that such inputs do not cause pollution of groundwater.

7 Applications for grant of environmental permit

(1) This paragraph applies to an application for the grant of an environmental permit relating to—

(a) a discharge mentioned in paragraph 3(1)(a), (b) or (c); or
(b) an activity that might lead to such a discharge.

(2) When the regulator receives an application, it must ensure that all necessary investigations have been carried out to ensure that it grants any permit in accordance with paragraph 6.

(3) If it grants the permit, it must include conditions requiring all necessary technical precautions to be observed to ensure the objectives of paragraph 6 are achieved.

(4) A permit may not be granted—
(a) without examination of—
  (i) the hydrogeological conditions of the area concerned,
  (ii) the possible purifying powers of the soil and subsoil, and
  (iii) the risk of pollution and alteration of the quality of the groundwater from the discharge, and
(b) without establishing whether the input of pollutants to groundwater is a satisfactory solution from the point of view of the environment.

(5) A permit may only be granted if the regulator has checked that the groundwater (and, in particular, its quality) will undergo the requisite surveillance.

8 Groundwater activities for which a permit may be granted

Despite paragraph 6, provided it does not compromise the achievement of any of the environmental objectives relating to groundwater in Article 4 of the Water Framework Directive, the regulator may grant an environmental permit for—
(a) the injection of water containing substances resulting from the operations for exploration and extraction of hydrocarbons or mining activities, and injection of water for technical reasons, into geological formations from which hydrocarbons or other substances have been extracted or into geological formations which for natural reasons are permanently unsuitable for other purposes, provided that the injection does not contain substances other than those resulting from the above operations,
(b) the reinjection of pumped groundwater from mines and quarries or associated with the construction or maintenance of civil engineering works,
(c) the injection of natural gas or liquefied petroleum gas for storage purposes into geological formations which for natural reasons are permanently unsuitable for other purposes,
[(ca) the injection of carbon dioxide streams for storage purposes into geological formations which for natural reasons are permanently unsuitable for other purposes, provided that such injection is made in accordance with Directive 2009/31/EC of the European Parliament and of the Council on the geological storage of carbon dioxide, or excluded from the scope of that Directive pursuant to Article 2(2) of that Directive,][1]
(d) the injection of natural gas or liquefied petroleum gas for storage purposes into other geological formations where there is an overriding need for security of gas supply, and where the injection is such as to prevent any present or future danger of deterioration in the quality of any receiving groundwater,
(e) construction, civil engineering and building works and similar activities on or in the ground which come into contact with groundwater,
(f) discharges of small quantities of substances for scientific purposes for characterisation, protection or remediation of bodies of water limited to the amount strictly necessary for the purposes concerned,
(g) interventions in surface waters for the purposes, amongst others, of mitigating the effects of floods and droughts, and for the management of waters and waterways,
(h) the artificial recharge or augmentation of a body of groundwater for the purposes of groundwater management,
(i) reinjection into the same aquifer of water used for geothermal purposes.

Amendment

1 Inserted by the Environmental Permitting (England and Wales) (Amendment) Regulations 2011, SI 2011/2043, regs 3, 14.

9 Prohibition notice

(1) This paragraph applies where—
(a) any person is carrying on, or proposing to carry on, any activity on or in the ground; and
(b) that activity might lead to a discharge mentioned in paragraph 3(1)(a), (b) or (c).

(2) The regulator may serve a notice on the person prohibiting the carrying on of the activity.

(3) The regulator may withdraw a prohibition notice at any time by further notice served on the person.

10 Notice requiring environmental permit

(1) This paragraph applies where—
(a) any person is carrying on, or proposing to carry on, any activity on or in the ground; and
(b) that activity might lead to a discharge mentioned in paragraph 3(1)(a), (b) or (c).

(2) The regulator may serve a notice on the person requiring the person, from the date the notice takes effect, to hold an environmental permit authorising the carrying on of the activity.

(3) A notice under paragraph (1) takes effect on the date specified in it, but—
(a) a notice served for the purpose of paragraph 11 must not take effect until at least 6 months after it is served; and
(b) a notice served for the purpose of paragraph 12, or for any other purpose, must not take effect until at least 3 months after it is served.

11 Notice in relation to a highway drain

A highway authority or other person entitled to keep open a highway drain by virtue of section 100 of the 1980 Act who operates a highway drain other than under and in accordance with an environmental permit is not guilty of an offence under regulation 38(1) unless—
(a) the regulator has served a notice on that person under paragraph 10 of this Schedule; and
(b) the notice has taken effect.

12 Notice in relation to a domestic septic tank or sewage treatment plant

Before 1st January 2012, a person who, other than under and in accordance with an environmental permit, uses a septic tank or sewage treatment plant with a discharge of 2 cubic metres per day or less of sewage effluent that results in the input of pollutants to groundwater is not guilty of an offence under regulation 38(1) unless—
(a) the regulator has served a notice on that person under paragraph 10 of this Schedule; and
(b) the notice has taken effect.

13 Guidance

(1) The appropriate authority may issue guidance to persons causing or liable to cause inputs of pollutants to groundwater with respect to the steps they must take to prevent or limit those pollutants from entering groundwater.

(2) The regulator must take into account whether or not such guidance is or is likely to be complied with before taking any enforcement action under these Regulations.

(3) Guidance must be publicised as the appropriate authority sees fit.

14 Liability resulting from discharge of sewage effluent from public sewer

(1) This paragraph applies for the purpose of determining liability for a groundwater activity that consists of a discharge of sewage effluent from a discharging sewer vested in a discharging undertaker.

(2) A discharging undertaker causes a discharge of sewage effluent if—
(a) matter included in the discharge is received by the discharging undertaker into the discharging sewer or into any other sewer or works vested in it;
(b) the discharging undertaker was bound (either unconditionally or subject to conditions which were observed) to receive the matter into the discharging sewer or other sewer or works; and
(c) sub-paragraph (3) does not apply.

(3) This sub-paragraph applies if, before the discharging undertaker discharges the sewage effluent from the discharging sewer, the sending undertaker, under an agreement with the discharging undertaker under section 110A of the Water Industry Act 1991, discharges the sewage effluent through a main connection into—
(a) the discharging sewer; or
(b) any other sewer or works vested in the discharging undertaker.

(4) If sub-paragraph (3) applies, the sending undertaker causes the discharge if—
(a) matter included in the discharge was received by the sending undertaker into a sewer or works vested in it; and
(b) it was bound (either conditionally or subject to conditions which were observed) to receive that matter into that sewer or works.

(5) A sewerage undertaker is not guilty of an offence under regulation 38(1) in relation to a groundwater activity that consists of a discharge of sewage effluent from a sewer or works vested in it if—
(a) the contravention is attributable to a discharge which another person caused or knowingly permitted to be made into the sewer or works;
(b) the undertaker either was not bound to receive the discharge into the sewer or works or was bound to receive it there subject to conditions which were not observed; and
(c) the undertaker could not reasonably have been expected to prevent the discharge into the sewer or works.

(6) A person is not guilty of an offence under regulation 38(1) in relation to a discharge which the person caused or knowingly permitted to be made into a sewer or works vested in a sewerage undertaker if that undertaker was bound to receive the discharge, either unconditionally or subject to conditions which were observed.

[SCHEDULE 23
RADIOACTIVE SUBSTANCES ACTIVITIES

Regulation 35(2)(q)

PART 1
APPLICATION][1]

[1 Application

This Schedule applies in relation to every radioactive substances activity.][1]

Amendment

1 Substituted by the Environmental Permitting (England and Wales) (Amendment) Regulations 2011, SI 2011/2043, regs 3, 15, Sch 1.

[PART 2
INTERPRETATION][1]

[1 Interpretation

(1) In this Schedule—

"article" includes a part of an article;

"the Basic Safety Standards Directive" means Council Directive 96/29/EURATOM laying down basic safety standards for the protection of the health of workers and the general public against the dangers arising from ionising radiation;

"Bq" means becquerels;

"contamination"occurs where a substance or article is so affected by—

(a) absorption, admixture or adhesion of radioactive material or radioactive waste; or

(b) the emission of neutrons or ionising radiation,

as to become radioactive or to possess increased radioactivity;

"disposal" in relation to waste includes its removal, deposit, destruction, discharge (whether into water or into the air or into a sewer or drain or otherwise) or burial (whether underground or otherwise) and "dispose of" is to be construed accordingly;

"m", where it appears after a radionuclide, means a radionuclide in a metastable state of radioactive decay in which gamma photons are emitted;

"mobile radioactive apparatus" means any apparatus, equipment, appliance or other thing which is radioactive material and—

(a) is constructed or adapted for being transported from place to place; or

(b) is portable and designed or intended to be used for releasing radioactive material into the environment or introducing it into organisms;

"nuclear site" means—

(a) any site in respect of which a nuclear site licence is for the time being in force; or

(b) any site in respect of which, after the revocation or surrender of a nuclear site licence, the period of responsibility of the licensee has not yet come to an end,

and "licensee", when used in relation to a nuclear site, and "period of responsibility" have the same meaning as in the Nuclear Installations Act 1965;

"premises" includes any land, whether covered by buildings or not, including any place underground and any land covered by water;

"relevant liquid" means a liquid which—

(a) is non-aqueous; or

(b) is classified (or would be so classified in the absence of its radioactivity) under Council Regulation No. 1272/2008 as having any of the following hazard classes and hazard categories (as defined in that Regulation)—

(i) acute toxicity: categories 1, 2 or 3;

(ii) skin corrosion/irritation: category 1 corrosive, sub-categories: 1A, 1B or 1C; or

(iii) hazardous to the aquatic environment: acute category 1 or chronic categories 1 or 2;

"substance" means any natural or artificial substance, whether in solid or liquid form or in the form of a gas or vapour;

"Table 1", "Table 2", "Table 3" mean the tables with those numbers in Part 3 of this Schedule;

"undertaking" includes any trade, business or profession and—

(a) in relation to a public or local authority, includes any of the powers or duties of that authority, and

(b) in relation to any other body of persons (whether corporate or unincorporate), includes any of the activities of that body; and

"waste" should be construed in accordance with paragraph 3(2).

(2) In this Schedule, where any reference is made to a substance or article possessing a concentration or quantity of radioactivity which exceeds the value specified in a column in either of Tables 1 and 2, or either of Tables 5 and 7 in Part 7 of this Schedule, that value is exceeded if—

(a) where only one radionuclide which is listed or described in the relevant table is present in the substance or article, the concentration or quantity of that radionuclide exceeds the concentration or quantity specified in the appropriate entry of that column in that table; or

(b) where more than one radionuclide which is listed or described in the relevant table is present, the sum of the quotient values of all such radionuclides in the substance or article, as determined by the summation rule following the table (as it applies to that column), is greater than one,

and any reference to a concentration or quantity of radioactivity not exceeding such a value shall be construed accordingly.][1]

Amendment

1 Substituted by the Environmental Permitting (England and Wales) (Amendment) Regulations 2011, SI 2011/2043, regs 3, 15, Sch 1.

[2 Interpretation: NORM industrial activity

(1) Subject to sub-paragraph (2), in this Schedule—

"type 1 NORM industrial activity" means—

(a) the production and use of thorium, or thorium compounds, and the production of products where thorium is deliberately added; or

(b) the production and use of uranium or uranium compounds, and the production of products where uranium is deliberately added; and

"type 2 NORM industrial activity" means—

(a) the [extraction and production][1] and use of rare earth elements and rare earth element alloys;

(b) the mining and processing of ores other than uranium ore;

(c) the production of oil and gas;

(d) the removal and management of radioactive scales and precipitates from equipment associated with industrial activities;

(e) any industrial activity utilising phosphate ore;

(f) the manufacture of titanium dioxide pigments;

(g) the extraction and refining of zircon and manufacture of zirconium compounds;

(h) the production of tin, copper, aluminium, zinc, lead and iron and steel;

(i) any activity related to coal mine de-watering plants;

(j) china clay extraction;

(k) water treatment associated with provision of drinking water; or

(l) the remediation of contamination from any type 1 NORM industrial activity or any of the activities listed above.

(2) An activity which involves the processing of radionuclides of natural terrestrial or cosmic origin for their radioactive, fissile or fertile properties is not a type 1 NORM industrial activity or a type 2 NORM industrial activity.][2]

Amendments

1 Substituted by the Environmental Permitting (England and Wales) (Amendment) Regulations 2012, SI 2012/630, reg 16(1), (2).

2 Substituted by the Environmental Permitting (England and Wales) (Amendment) Regulations 2011, SI 2011/2043, regs 3, 15, Sch 1.

[3 Interpretation: "radioactive material", "radioactive waste" and "waste"

(1) In this Schedule, except as provided by paragraph 7, 8, 9 or 10—

"radioactive material" means a substance or article which is not waste, and which satisfies the requirements of paragraph 4, 5 or 6 as they apply to such a substance or article;

"radioactive waste" means a substance or article which is waste, and which satisfies the requirements of paragraph 4, 5 or 6.

(2) In this Schedule—

(a) "waste" includes—

(i) any substance which constitutes scrap material or an effluent or other unwanted surplus substance arising from the application of any process, and

(ii) any substance or article which requires to be disposed of as being broken, worn out, contaminated or otherwise spoilt;

and

(b) any substance or article which, in the course of carrying on any undertaking, is discharged, discarded or otherwise dealt with as if it were waste is presumed to be waste unless the contrary is proved.][1]

Amendment

1 Substituted by the Environmental Permitting (England and Wales) (Amendment) Regulations 2011, SI 2011/2043, regs 3, 15, Sch 1.

[4 NORM industrial activities

(1) Sub-paragraph (2) applies to a substance or article which—

(a) arises from or is used in a type 1 NORM industrial activity;

(b) is waste which arises from a type 2 NORM industrial activity; or

(c) is contaminated by a substance or article described in paragraph (a) or (b), including where such contamination occurs indirectly through another contaminated substance or article.

(2) A substance or article to which this sub-paragraph applies is radioactive material or radioactive waste where it has a concentration of radioactivity which exceeds the following values in Table 1—

(a) for a substance or article which is a solid or a substance which is a relevant liquid, the value specified in column 2;

(b) for a substance which is any other liquid, the value specified in column 3; or

(c) for a substance which is a gas, the value specified in column 4.][1]

Amendment

1 Substituted by the Environmental Permitting (England and Wales) (Amendment) Regulations 2011, SI 2011/2043, regs 3, 15, Sch 1.

[5 Processed radionuclides of natural terrestrial or cosmic origin

A substance or article is radioactive material or radioactive waste where—

(a) the substance or article contains one or more of the radionuclides of natural terrestrial or cosmic origin which are listed in column 1 of Table 2;

(b) the substance or article—

(i) is processed or is intended to be processed for the radioactive, fissile or fertile properties of those radionuclides; or

(ii) is contaminated by a substance or article to which sub-paragraph (i) applies, including where such contamination occurs indirectly through another contaminated substance or article;

and

(c) the substance or article is—

(i) a solid or a relevant liquid and it has a concentration of radioactivity which exceeds the value specified in column 2 of Table 2; or

(ii) any other liquid or a gas.][1]

Amendment

1 Substituted by the Environmental Permitting (England and Wales) (Amendment) Regulations 2011, SI 2011/2043, regs 3, 15, Sch 1.

[6 Radionuclides not of natural terrestrial or cosmic origin

A substance or article which contains one or more radionuclides that are not of natural terrestrial or cosmic origin is radioactive material or radioactive waste where—

(a) the substance or article is a solid or a relevant liquid and it has a concentration of radioactivity which exceeds the value specified in column 2 of Table 2; or
(b) the substance is any other liquid or a gas.][1]

Amendment

1 Substituted by the Environmental Permitting (England and Wales) (Amendment) Regulations 2011, SI 2011/2043, regs 3, 15, Sch 1.

[7 Radionuclides with a short half-life

A substance or article is not radioactive material or radioactive waste where none of the radionuclides which it contains or which it consists of has a half-life exceeding 100 seconds.][1]

Amendment

1 Substituted by the Environmental Permitting (England and Wales) (Amendment) Regulations 2011, SI 2011/2043, regs 3, 15, Sch 1.

[8 Radionuclides not of natural terrestrial or cosmic origin in background radioactivity

(1) A substance or article is not radioactive material or radioactive waste where—
(a) the substance or article is contaminated as a result of a climatic process, or a combination of such processes, by radionuclides which—
(i) are not of natural terrestrial or cosmic origin; and
(ii) are not present in the substance or article at a concentration that exceeds that found normally in such a substance or article in the United Kingdom;
and
(b) in the absence of such contamination, the substance or article would not otherwise be radioactive material or radioactive waste under this Schedule.

(2) In this paragraph, a "climatic process" includes wind, precipitation and the general circulation of the atmosphere and oceans.][1]

Amendment

1 Substituted by the Environmental Permitting (England and Wales) (Amendment) Regulations 2011, SI 2011/2043, regs 3, 15, Sch 1.

[9 Contaminated substances or articles

(1) Subject to sub-paragraph (2), a substance or article is not radioactive material where—
(a) the substance or article is contaminated, but has not been so contaminated with the intention of utilising its radioactive, fissile or fertile properties; and
(b) in the absence of such contamination, the substance or article would not otherwise be radioactive material under this Schedule.

(2) Sub-paragraph (1) only applies while the substance or article is kept on the premises on which the contamination occurred.][1]

Amendment

1 Substituted by the Environmental Permitting (England and Wales) (Amendment) Regulations 2011, SI 2011/2043, regs 3, 15, Sch 1.

[10 Substances or articles after disposal

(1) A substance or article is not radioactive material or radioactive waste during the excluded period where—
(a) the substance or article has been disposed of lawfully, and at the time of the disposal no further act of disposal is intended in respect of it; or
(b) the substance or article—
(i) is contaminated by a substance or article to which paragraph (a) applies, including where such contamination occurs indirectly through another contaminated substance or article;

(ii) in the absence of such contamination, would not otherwise be radioactive material or radioactive waste under this Schedule; and

(iii) is not contaminated with the intention of using its radioactive, fissile or fertile properties.

(2) In sub-paragraph (1), "the excluded period" means the period—

(a) beginning at the relevant start time; and

(b) ending at the time that there is an increase in the radiation exposure of the public or of any plant or animal which is caused by the substance or article being subject to a process after the relevant start time.

(3) Sub-paragraph (4) applies to a substance or article which—

(a) is disposed of by burial (whether underground or otherwise) on premises in respect of which an environmental permit in respect of the radioactive substances activity in paragraph 11(2)(b) is held at the time of disposal;

(b) is disposed of in accordance with that permit; and

(c) is solid at the time of the disposal.

(4) Where this sub-paragraph applies, the relevant start time is—

(a) where the environmental permit in sub-paragraph (3)(a) is surrendered, the time at which the surrender takes effect; or

(b) where that permit is revoked and—

(i) regulation 23 applies to that permit, the time at which the regulator issues the certificate described in paragraph (4) or (6) of that regulation; or

(ii) regulation 23 does not apply to that permit, the time at which the revocation takes effect.

(5) Sub-paragraph (6) applies to a substance or article ("A") described in sub-paragraph (1)(b), where the substance or article ("B") which contaminates it (directly or indirectly) is described in sub-paragraph (3).

(6) Where this sub-paragraph applies, the relevant start time for A is the later of—

(a) the time at which A becomes contaminated; and

(b) the relevant start time for B.

(7) In respect of a substance or article ("C") to which sub-paragraphs (4) and (6) do not apply, the relevant start time is—

(a) where sub-paragraph (1)(a) applies to C, the time at which C is disposed of; or

(b) where sub-paragraph (1)(b) applies to C, the time at which C becomes contaminated.][1]

Amendment

1 Substituted by the Environmental Permitting (England and Wales) (Amendment) Regulations 2011, SI 2011/2043, regs 3, 15, Sch 1.

[11 Interpretation: radioactive substances activity

(1) Subject to paragraphs 12 and 13, "radioactive substances activity" means an activity described in sub-paragraph (2), (4), (5) or (6).

(2) A radioactive substances activity is carried on where a person uses premises for the purposes of an undertaking and that person—

(a) except where sub-paragraph (5) applies, keeps or uses radioactive material on those premises;

(b) disposes of radioactive waste on or from those premises; or

(c) accumulates radioactive waste on those premises,

knowing or having reasonable grounds for believing the material or waste to be radioactive material or radioactive waste.

(3) For the purposes of sub-paragraph (2)(c), where—

(a) radioactive material is produced, kept or used on any premises;

(b) any substance arising from the production, keeping or use of that material is accumulated in a part of the premises appropriated for the purpose; and

(c) that substance is retained there for a period of not less than 3 months,

that substance, unless the contrary is proved, is presumed to be radioactive waste.

(4) A radioactive substances activity is carried on where, in the course of a person carrying on an undertaking, that person—

(a) receives radioactive waste for the purposes of disposing of that waste; and

(b) knows or has reasonable grounds for believing the waste to be radioactive waste.

(5) A radioactive substances activity is carried on where a person keeps or uses mobile radioactive apparatus for—

(a) testing, measuring or otherwise investigating any of the characteristics of substances or articles; or

(b) releasing quantities of radioactive material into the environment or introducing such material into organisms.

(6) A radioactive substances activity is carried on where a person carries out intrusive investigation work or other excavation, construction or building work—

(a) to determine the suitability of any premises; or

(b) to enable the use of any premises,

as a place that may be used wholly or substantially for underground disposal.

(7) In sub-paragraph (6)—

"intrusive investigation work" means the drilling of boreholes into, or excavation of, sub-soil or rock to determine geological or hydrogeological conditions; and

"underground disposal" means—

(a) the disposal of solid radioactive waste in an engineered facility, or in part of an engineered facility, which is beneath the surface of the ground, and

(b) where the natural environment which surrounds the facility acts, in combination with any engineered measures, to inhibit the transit of radionuclides from the facility to the surface,

and does not include the disposal of radioactive waste in a facility which is beneath the surface of the ground only by virtue of the placing of rocks or soil above it.][1]

Amendment

1 Substituted by the Environmental Permitting (England and Wales) (Amendment) Regulations 2011, SI 2011/2043, regs 3, 15, Sch 1.

[12 Nuclear sites

(1) Paragraph 11(2)(a) does not apply to the activity carried on by a licensee of a nuclear site on any premises situated on that site at any time—

(a) while a nuclear site licence is in force in respect of that site; and

(b) after the revocation or surrender of such a licence but before the period of responsibility of the licensee has come to an end.

(2) In respect of any premises which—

(a) are situated on a nuclear site; but

(b) have ceased to be used for the purposes of an undertaking carried on by the licensee,

paragraph 11(2)(b) applies to those premises as if the premises were used for the purposes of an undertaking carried on by the licensee.

(3) Paragraph 11(2)(c) does not apply to the accumulation of radioactive waste on any premises situated on a nuclear site.][1]

Amendment

1 Substituted by the Environmental Permitting (England and Wales) (Amendment) Regulations 2011, SI 2011/2043, regs 3, 15, Sch 1.

[13 Vehicles, vessels and aircraft

In determining whether any radioactive material is kept or used on any premises, no account must be taken of any radioactive material kept or used in or on any railway vehicle, road vehicle, vessel or aircraft if—

(a) the vehicle, vessel or aircraft is on the premises in the course of a journey; or

(b) in the case of a vessel which is on those premises otherwise than in the normal course of a journey, the material is used in propelling the vessel or is kept in or on the vessel for use in propelling it.][1]

Amendment

1 Substituted by the Environmental Permitting (England and Wales) (Amendment) Regulations 2011, SI 2011/2043, regs 3, 15, Sch 1.

[PART 3
TABLES OF RADIONUCLIDES AND SUMMATION RULES

Table 1][1]

[1

The Table 1 referred to in paragraph 4 (NORM industrial activities) of Part 2 is—

Table 1
Concentration of radionuclides: NORM industrial activities

Radionuclide	*Solid or relevant liquid concentration in becquerels per gram (Bq/g)*	*Any other liquid concentration in becquerels per litre (Bq/l)*	*Gaseous concentration in becquerels per cubic metre (Bq/m^3)*
U-238sec	0.5	0.1	0.001
U-238+	5	10	0.01
U-234	5	10	0.01
Th-230	10	10	0.001
Ra-226+	0.5	1	0.01
Pb-210+	5	0.1	0.01
Po-210	5	0.1	0.01
U-235sec	1	0.1	0.0001
U-235+	5	10	0.01
Pa-231	5	1	0.001
Ac-227+	1	0.1	0.001
Th-232sec	0.5	0.1	0.001
Th-232	5	10	0.001
Ra-228+	1	0.1	0.01
Th-228+	0.5	1	0.001

2

The Table 1 summation rule in respect of column 2, 3 or 4 means the sum of the quotients A/B where—

(a) "A" means the concentration of each radionuclide listed in column 1 of Table 1 that is present in the substance or article; and

(b) "B" means the concentration of that radionuclide specified in column 2, 3 or 4 (as appropriate) of Table 1.][1]

Amendment

1 Substituted by the Environmental Permitting (England and Wales) (Amendment) Regulations 2011, SI 2011/2043, regs 3, 15, Sch 1.

[Table 2][1]

[3

The Table 2 referred to in paragraphs 5 (processed radionuclides of natural terrestrial or cosmic origin) and 6 (radionuclides not of natural terrestrial or cosmic origin) of Part 2 is—

Table 2
Concentration of radionuclides

Radionuclide	*Concentration in becquerels per gram (Bq/g)*
H-3	102
Be-7	10
C-14	10
F-18	1
Na-22	0.1
Na-24	0.1
Si-31	102
P-32	102
P-33	102
S-35	102
Cl-36	1
Cl-38	1
K-42	10
K-43	1
Ca-45	102
Ca-47	1
Sc-46	0.1
Sc-47	10
Sc-48	0.1
V-48	0.1
Cr-51	10
Mn-51	1
Mn-52	0.1
Mn-52m	1
Mn-53	103
Mn-54	0.1
Mn-56	1
Fe-52+	1
Fe-55	102
Fe-59	0.1
Co-55	1
Co-56	0.1
Co-57	1
Co-58	0.1
Co-58m	102
Co-60	0.1

Radionuclide	*Concentration in becquerels per gram (Bq/g)*
Co-60m	103
Co-61	102
Co-62m	1
Ni-59	102
Ni-63	102
Ni-65	1
Cu-64	10
Zn-65	1
Zn-69	102
Zn-69m+	1
Ga-72	1
Ge-71	104
As-73	102
As-74	1
As-76	1
As-77	102
Se-75	1
Br-82	0.1
Rb-86	10
Sr-85	1
Sr-85m	10
Sr-87m	10
Sr-89	10
Sr-90+	1
Sr-91+	1
Sr-92	1
Y-90	102
Y-91	10
Y-91m	1
Y-92	10
Y-93	10
Zr-93	10
Zr-95+	0.1
Zr-97+	1
Nb-93m	102
Nb-94	0.1
Nb-95	1
Nb-97+	1
Nb-98	1
Mo-90	1
Mo-93	10
Mo-99+	1
Mo-101+	1
Tc-96	0.1
Tc-96m	10
Tc-97	10

Radionuclide	*Concentration in becquerels per gram (Bq/g)*
Tc-97m	10
Tc-99	1
Tc-99m	102
Ru-97	1
Ru-103+	1
Ru-105+	1
Ru-106+	1
Rh-103m	104
Rh-105	10
Pd-103+	103
Pd-109+	102
Ag-105	1
Ag-108m+	0.1
Ag-110m+	0.1
Ag-111	10
Cd-109+	10
Cd-115+	1
Cd-115m+	10
In-111	1
In-113m	10
In-114m+	1
In-115m	10
Sn-113+	1
Sn-125	1
Sb-122	1
Sb-124	0.1
Sb-125+	1
Te-123m	1
Te-125m	102
Te-127	102
Te-127m+	10
Te-129	10
Te-129m+	10
Te-131	10
Te-131m+	1
Te-132+	0.1
Te-133+	1
Te-133m+	1
Te-134	1
I-123	10
I-125	1
I-126	1
I-129	0.1
I-130	1
I-131+	1
I-132	1

Radionuclide	*Concentration in becquerels per gram (Bq/g)*
I-133	1
I-134	1
I-135	1
Cs-129	1
Cs-131	103
Cs-132	1
Cs-134	0.1
Cs-134m	103
Cs-135	10
Cs-136	0.1
Cs-137+	1
Cs-138	1
Ba-131	1
Ba-140	0.1
La-140	0.1
Ce-139	1
Ce-141	10
Ce-143	1
Ce-144+	10
Pr-142	10
Pr-143	102
Nd-147	10
Nd-149	10
Pm-147	102
Pm-149	102
Sm-151	102
Sm-153	10
Eu-152	0.1
Eu-152m	10
Eu-154	0.1
Eu-155	10
Gd-153	10
Gd-159	10
Tb-160	0.1
Dy-165	102
Dy-166	10
Ho-166	10
Er-169	102
Er-171	10
Tm-170	10
Tm-171	102
Yb-175	10
Lu-177	10
Hf-181	1
Ta-182	0.1
W-181	10

Radionuclide	*Concentration in becquerels per gram (Bq/g)*
W-185	102
W-187	1
Re-186	102
Re-188	10
Os-185	1
Os-191	10
Os-191m	103
Os-193	10
Ir-190	0.1
Ir-192	0.1
Ir-194	10
Pt-191	1
Pt-193m	102
Pt-197	102
Pt-197m	102
Au-198	1
Au-199	10
Hg-197	10
Hg-197m	10
Hg-203	1
Tl-200	1
Tl-201	10
Tl-202	1
Tl-204	10
Pb-203	1
Pb-210+	0.01
Pb-212+	1
Bi-206	0.1
Bi-207	0.1
Bi-210	10
Bi-212+	1
Po-203	1
Po-205	1
Po-207	1
Po-210	0.01
At-211	102
Ra-223+	1
Ra-224+	1
Ra-225	1
Ra-226+	0.01
Ra-227	10
Ra-228+	0.01
Ac-227+	0.01
Ac-228	1
Th-226+	102
Th-227	1

Radionuclide	*Concentration in becquerels per gram (Bq/g)*
Th-228+	0.1
Th-229+	0.1
Th-230	0.1
Th-231	102
Th-232	0.01
Th-232+	0.01
Th-232sec	0.01
Th-234+	10
Pa-230	1
Pa-231	0.01
Pa-233	1
U-230+	1
U-231	10
U-232+	0.1
U-233	1
U-234	1
U-235+	1
U-235sec	0.01
U-236	1
U-237	10
U-238+	1
U-238sec	0.01
U-239	102
U-240+	10
Np-237+	0.1
Np-239	10
Np-240	1
Pu-234	102
Pu-235	102
Pu-236	0.1
Pu-237	10
Pu-238	0.1
Pu-239	0.1
Pu-240	0.1
Pu-241	1
Pu-242	0.1
Pu-243	102
Pu-244+	0.1
Am-241	0.1
Am-242	102
Am-242m+	0.1
Am-243+	0.1
Cm-242	1
Cm-24	30.1
Cm-244	0.1
Cm-245	0.1

Radionuclide	*Concentration in becquerels per gram (Bq/g)*
Cm-246	0.1
Cm-247+	0.1
Cm-248	0.1
Bk-249	10
Cf-246	10
Cf-248	1
Cf-249	0.1
Cf-250	0.1
Cf-251	0.1
Cf-252	0.1
Cf-253	1
Cf-253+	1
Cf-254	0.1
Es-253	1
Es-254+	0.1
Es-254m+	1
Fm-254	102
Fm-255	10
Any other solid or [relevant liquid][2] radionuclide that is not of natural terrestrial or cosmic origin	0.01 or that concentration which gives rise to a dose to a member of the public of 10 microsieverts per year calculated by reference to guidance by Euratom in RP 122 part 1.

4

The Table 2 column 2 summation rule means the sum of the quotients A/B where—

(a) "A" means the concentration of each radionuclide listed in column 1 of Table 2 that is present in the substance or article, and

(b) "B" means the concentration of that radionuclide specified in column 2 of Table 2.][1]

Amendments

1 Substituted by the Environmental Permitting (England and Wales) (Amendment) Regulations 2011, SI 2011/2043, regs 3, 15, Sch 1.

2 Substituted by the Environmental Permitting (England and Wales) (Amendment) Regulations 2012, SI 2012/630, reg 16(1), (3).

[References in Table 1 and Table 2 to + and sec][1]

[5

Where any radionuclide carries the suffix "+" or "sec" in Table 1 or Table 2—

(a) that radionuclide represents the parent radionuclide in secular equilibrium with the corresponding daughter radionuclides which are identified in column 2 of Table 3 in respect of that parent radionuclide; and

(b) a concentration value given in a table in this Part in respect of such a parent radionuclide is the value for the parent radionuclide alone, but already takes into account the daughter radionuclides present.][1]

Amendment

1 Substituted by the Environmental Permitting (England and Wales) (Amendment) Regulations 2011, SI 2011/2043, regs 3, 15, Sch 1.

[Table 3][1]

[6

The Table 3 referred to in paragraph 5 is—

Table 3
Radionuclides in secular equilibrium

Parent radionuclide	*Daughter radionuclides*
Fe-52+	Mn-52m
Zn-69m+	Zn-69
Sr-90+	Y-90
Sr-91+	Y-91m
Zr-95+	Nb-95m
Zr-97+	Nb-97m, Nb-97
Nb-97+	Nb-97m
Mo-99+	Tc-99m
Mo-101+	Tc-101
Ru-103+	Rh-103m
Ru-105+	Rh-105m
Ru-106+	Rh-106
Pd-103+	Rh-103m
Pd-109+	Ag-109m
Ag-108m+	Ag-108
Ag-110m+	Ag-110
Cd-109+	Ag-109m
Cd-115+	In-115m
Cd-115m+	In-115m
In-114m+	In-114
Sn-113+	In-113m
Sb-125+	Te-125m
Te-127m+	Te-127
Te-129m+	Te-129
Te-131m+	Te-131
Te-132+	I-132
Te-133+	I-133, Xe-133m, Xe-133
Te-133m+	Te-133, I-133, Xe-133m, Xe-133
I-131+	Xe-131m
Cs-137+	Ba-137m
Ce-144+	Pr-144, Pr-144m
Pb-210+	Bi-210, Po-210
Pb-212+	Bi-212, Tl-208
Bi-212+	Tl-208
Ra-223+	Rn-219, Po-215, Pb-211, Bi-211, Tl-207
Ra-224+	Rn-220, Po-216, Pb-212, Bi-212, Tl-208
Ra-226+	Rn-222, Po-218, Pb-214, Bi-214, Po-214
Ra-228+	Ac-228
Ac-227+	Th-227, Fr-223, Ra-223, Rn-219, Po-215, Pb-211, Bi-211, Tl-207, Po-211

Parent radionuclide	*Daughter radionuclides*
Th-226+	Ra-222, Rn-218, Po-214
Th-228+	Ra-224, Rn-220, Po-216, Pb-212, Bi-212, Tl-208
Th-229+	Ra-225, Ac-225, Fr-221, At-217, Bi-213, Tl-209, Pb-209
Th-232+	Ra-228, Ac-228, Th-228, Ra-224, Rn-220, Po-216, Pb-212, Bi-212, Tl-208
Th-232sec	Ra-228, Ac-228, Th-228, Ra-224, Rn-220, Po-216, Pb-212, Bi-212, Po-212, Tl-208
Th-234+	Pa-234m, Pa-234
U-230+	Th-226, Ra-222, Rn-218, Po-214
U-232+	Th-228, Ra-224, Rn-220, Po-216, Pb-212, Bi-212, Tl-208
U-235+	Th-231
U-235sec	Th-231, Pa-231, Ac-227, Th-227, Fr-223, Ra-223, Rn-219, Po-215, Pb-211, Bi-211, Tl-207, Po-211
U-238+	Th-234, Pa-234m, Pa-234
U-238sec	Th-234, Pa-234m, Pa-234, U-234, Th-230, Ra-226, Rn-222, Po-218, Pb-214, Bi-214, Po-214, Pb-210, Bi-210, Po-210
U-240+	Np-240m, Np-240
Np-237+	Pa-233
Pu-244+	U-240, Np-240m, Np-240
Am-242m+	Np-238
Am-243+	Np-239
Cm-247+	Pu-243
Cf-253+	Cm-249
Es-254+	Bk-250
Es-254m+	Fm-254][1]

Amendment

1 Substituted by the Environmental Permitting (England and Wales) (Amendment) Regulations 2011, SI 2011/2043, regs 3, 15, Sch 1.

[PART 4
THE BASIC SAFETY STANDARDS DIRECTIVE

Section 1
Exposures and doses][1]

[1 Optimisation and dose limits

In respect of a radioactive substances activity that relates to radioactive waste, the regulator must exercise its relevant functions to ensure that—

(a) all exposures to ionising radiation of any member of the public and of the population as a whole resulting from the disposal of radioactive waste are kept as low as reasonably achievable, taking into account economic and social factors; and

(b) the sum of the doses resulting from the exposure of any member of the public to ionising radiation does not exceed the dose limits set out in Article 13 of the Basic Safety Standards Directive subject to the exclusions set out in Article 6(4) of that Directive.][1]

Amendment

1 Substituted by the Environmental Permitting (England and Wales) (Amendment) Regulations 2011, SI 2011/2043, regs 3, 15, Sch 1.

[2 Specific dose limits and calculation

(1) In exercising those relevant functions in relation to the planning stage of radiation protection, the regulator must have regard to the following maximum doses to individuals which may result from a defined source—

(a) 0.3 millisieverts per year from any source from which radioactive discharges are first made on or after 13th May 2000; or

(b) 0.5 millisieverts per year from the discharges from any single site.

(2) In exercising those relevant functions, the regulator must observe the requirements of the following provisions of the Basic Safety Standards Directive—

(a) in estimating effective dose and equivalent dose, Articles 15 and 16;

(b) in estimating population doses, Article 45; and

(c) in relation to the responsibilities of undertakings, Article 47.][1]

Amendment

1 Substituted by the Environmental Permitting (England and Wales) (Amendment) Regulations 2011, SI 2011/2043, regs 3, 15, Sch 1.

[Section 2
Interventions][1]

[3 Radioactive waste: power of the Secretary of State to provide facilities for disposal or accumulation

(1) If it appears to the Secretary of State that adequate facilities are not available for the safe disposal or accumulation of radioactive waste, the Secretary of State may—

(a) provide such facilities; or

(b) make arrangements for their provision by such persons as the Secretary of State may think fit.

(2) Before exercising the power under sub-paragraph (1), the Secretary of State must consult with—

(a) any local authority in whose area the facilities would be situated; and

(b) such other public or local authorities (if any) as appear to the Secretary of State to be proper to be consulted.

(3) Reasonable charges for the use of any facilities provided under sub-paragraph (1) may be made by—

(a) the Secretary of State; or

(b) the person providing such facilities, unless the arrangements made by the Secretary of State with that person provide to the contrary.][1]

Amendment

1 Substituted by the Environmental Permitting (England and Wales) (Amendment) Regulations 2011, SI 2011/2043, regs 3, 15, Sch 1.

[4 Radioactive waste: power of disposal by the regulator

(1) Sub-paragraph (2) applies if there is radioactive waste on any premises and the regulator is satisfied that the waste ought to be disposed of but that it is unlikely that the waste will be lawfully disposed of—

(a) because the premises are unoccupied;

(b) because the occupier is absent or insolvent; or

(c) for any other reason.

(2) The regulator may dispose of the waste and recover any expenses it reasonably incurs in that disposal from—

(a) the occupier of the premises; or

(b) if the premises are unoccupied, the owner of the premises.

(3) In sub-paragraph (2)—

(a) "owner" has the same meaning as in section 343 of the Public Health Act 1936; and

(b) the provisions of section 294 of that Act (which limits the liability of owners who are only agents or trustees) apply but as if reference in that section to a council recovering expenses under that Act were to the regulator recovering expenses under sub-paragraph (2).][1]

Amendment

1 Substituted by the Environmental Permitting (England and Wales) (Amendment) Regulations 2011, SI 2011/2043, regs 3, 15, Sch 1.

[PART 5
THE HASS DIRECTIVE

Section 1
Security of sources][1]

[1 Interpretation

In this Part—

"the HASS Directive" means Council Directive 2003/122/EURATOM on the control of high-activity sealed radioactive sources and orphan sources;

"high-activity or similar source" means—

(a) a high-activity source; or

(b) such other sealed source which, in the opinion of the regulator, is of a similar level of potential hazard to a high-activity source;

"high-activity source" has the same meaning as in the HASS Directive but excluding any such source once its activity level has fallen below the exemption levels specified in column 2 of Table A to Annex I to the Basic Safety Standards Directive;

"orphan source" has the same meaning as in the HASS Directive; and

"sealed source" has the same meaning as in the HASS Directive.][1]

Amendment

1 Substituted by the Environmental Permitting (England and Wales) (Amendment) Regulations 2011, SI 2011/2043, regs 3, 15, Sch 1.

[2 Site security: inspection

(1) In exercising relevant functions in relation to a radioactive substances activity, the regulator must comply with sub-paragraph (3) where a high-activity or similar source is, or will be, kept, used, disposed of or accumulated on any premises.

(2) Sub-paragraph (1) does not apply where the premises are, or are part of, a nuclear site.

(3) In considering if the measures taken, or to be taken, by the operator ensure the adequate security of any premises, the regulator must where appropriate inspect those premises.

(4) Where the regulator inspects any premises under sub-paragraph (3), it may be accompanied by such other persons as are appropriate to assist it in assessing the measures.

(5) An operator must permit the regulator (and any person accompanying it) reasonable access to any premises the regulator wishes to inspect under sub-paragraph (3).

(6) If the operator fails to comply with sub-paragraph (5), the regulator may refuse the application or revoke the permit insofar as it relates to the sources referred to in subparagraph (1).][1]

Amendment

1 Substituted by the Environmental Permitting (England and Wales) (Amendment) Regulations 2011, SI 2011/2043, regs 3, 15, Sch 1.

[3 Site security: security measures and advice

(1) In exercising relevant functions in relation to a radioactive substances activity, the regulator must comply with sub-paragraph (2) where a high-activity or similar source is, or will be, kept, used, disposed of or accumulated on any premises.

(2) The regulator—
(a) must satisfy itself that there are in place measures concerning site security, including the security measures in sub-paragraph (3), as are appropriate to the source and premises in question;
(b) where it considers it appropriate to do so, must consult the police, security services or other appropriate persons on site security;
(c) must have regard to any advice given by them, if it is issued within such time as the regulator believes is reasonable before it exercises a relevant function; and
(d) must impose appropriate environmental permit conditions concerning site security.

(3) The security measures referred to in sub-paragraph (2)(a) are—
(a) measures to ensure the physical security of the premises, including the installation of alarm and detection systems, and the retaining of documentary evidence of those measures;
(b) measures, which are evidenced in writing—
(i) to prevent unauthorised access to, or loss or theft of, a high-activity or similar source;
(ii) to detect such matters; and
(iii) to review and enhance the physical security of the premises in response to any increased risk of unauthorised access, loss or theft;
(c) written procedures to ensure that before a person is authorised to have access to a high-activity or similar source—
(i) that person has passed checks to verify their identity, and
(ii) satisfactory written references have been obtained which confirm, as far as reasonably practicable, that there is no information to indicate that the person presents any security risk to the sources; and
(d) measures to keep secure, and prevent unauthorised access to, information relating to—
(i) a high-activity or similar source, and
(ii) the measures referred to in paragraphs (a), (b) and (c).][1]

Amendment

1 Substituted by the Environmental Permitting (England and Wales) (Amendment) Regulations 2011, SI 2011/2043, regs 3, 15, Sch 1.

[Section 2
Advice and assistance in relation to orphan sources][1]

[4 Advice and assistance in respect of orphan sources

(1) The relevant person must ensure that specialised technical advice and assistance is promptly made available to persons who—
(a) are not normally involved in operations subject to radiation protection requirements, and
(b) suspect the presence of an orphan source.

(2) The relevant person must ensure that the primary aim of such advice and assistance is—
(a) the safety of the source; and
(b) protecting the public and workers from radiation.

(3) The relevant person means—
(a) in relation to the protection of workers, the Secretary of State;
(b) in relation to the protection of the public (other than workers)—

(i) in England, the Secretary of State,
(ii) in Wales, the Welsh Ministers.][1]

Amendment

1 Substituted by the Environmental Permitting (England and Wales) (Amendment) Regulations 2011, SI 2011/2043, regs 3, 15, Sch 1.

[Section 3
Exercise of relevant functions and matters in relation to orphan sources][1]

[5 General

(1) In exercising relevant functions in relation to a radioactive substances activity, the regulator must comply with the following provisions of the HASS Directive—
(a) Article 3(2) and (3);
(b) Article 4;
(c) Article 5(1) and (2);
(d) Article 6;
(e) subject to sub-paragraph (2), Article 7(1) and (2).

(2) In relation to a high-activity source placed on the market before 31st December 2005, sub-paragraph (1)(e) has effect as if it referred to the provisions contained in Article 16(1)(b) of the HASS Directive.][1]

Amendment

1 Substituted by the Environmental Permitting (England and Wales) (Amendment) Regulations 2011, SI 2011/2043, regs 3, 15, Sch 1.

[6 Records and inspections

In relation to a high-activity source, the regulator must—
(a) keep records of those matters—
(i) required by Article 5(3) and (4) of the HASS Directive; and
(ii) notified to it under Article 6 of that Directive;
and
(b) establish or maintain a system of inspections to enforce the following provisions of the HASS Directive—
(i) Articles 3 to 6;
(ii) as appropriate, Article 7(1) and (2) or Article 16(1)(b).][1]

Amendment

1 Substituted by the Environmental Permitting (England and Wales) (Amendment) Regulations 2011, SI 2011/2043, regs 3, 15, Sch 1.

[7 Training and information

(1) In relation to a high-activity source, the appropriate training and adequate information required by the Ionising Radiations Regulations 1999 must include—
(a) specific requirements for the safe management of such a source;
(b) particular emphasis on the necessary safety requirements in relation to such a source; and
(c) specific information on possible consequences of the loss of adequate control of such a source.

(2) The training and information on the matters in sub-paragraph (1) must be repeated at regular intervals and documented, with a view to preparing the employees and other persons referred to in those Regulations for such matters.][1]

Amendment

1 Substituted by the Environmental Permitting (England and Wales) (Amendment) Regulations 2011, SI 2011/2043, regs 3, 15, Sch 1.

[8 Orphan sources

(1) The regulator must—
(a) be prepared, or have made provision (including the assignment of responsibilities), to recover any orphan source; and
(b) have drawn up appropriate response plans and measures.

(2) The regulator may recover any expenses reasonably incurred by it in the recovery and disposal of an orphan source from—
(a) the person carrying on the radioactive substances activity involving that source; or
(b) the occupier or owner of the premises where the source is located.

(3) In relation to sub-paragraph (2)—
(a) "owner" has the same meaning as in section 343 of the Public Health Act 1936; and
(b) the provisions of section 294 of that Act (which limits the liability of owners who are only agents or trustees) apply but as if reference in that section to a council recovering expenses under that Act were to the regulator recovering expenses under sub-paragraph (2).][1]

Amendment

1 Substituted by the Environmental Permitting (England and Wales) (Amendment) Regulations 2011, SI 2011/2043, regs 3, 15, Sch 1.

[PART 6
CONDITIONS IN ENVIRONMENTAL PERMITS][1]

[1 Posting on premises of environmental permits

(1) Subject to sub-paragraph (3), the regulator must impose environmental permit display conditions on an environmental permit granted under these Regulations if the permit—
(a) relates to a radioactive substances activity described in paragraph 11(2) of Part 2 of this Schedule; and
(b) does not relate to a sealed source.

(2) Where an existing radioactive substances permit—
(a) becomes an environmental permit by virtue of regulation 69(a); and
(b) does not relate to a sealed source,
the environmental permit has effect subject to environmental permit display conditions in addition to any conditions that apply to it by virtue of regulation 69(b).

(3) The regulator, if required to do so on the grounds of national security by any direction issued to it under these Regulations or under any other enactment—
(a) must vary or revoke environmental permit display conditions or any similar environmental permit conditions that applied to an existing radioactive substances permit at the relevant time; or
(b) must not impose such conditions.

(4) In this paragraph—

"environmental permit display conditions" means a requirement that the operator—
(a) keep copies of the permit posted on the premises, and
(b) post the permit in such characters and positions as to be conveniently read by persons who have duties on the premises which are or could be affected by the matters set out in the permit; and

"existing radioactive substances permit" means—
(a) an authorisation under section 13 or 14 of the 1993 Act, or
(b) a registration under section 7 of the 1993 Act.][1]

Amendment

1 Substituted by the Environmental Permitting (England and Wales) (Amendment) Regulations 2011, SI 2011/2043, regs 3, 15, Sch 1.

[PART 7
RADIOACTIVE SUBSTANCES ACTIVITY EXEMPTIONS

Section 1
General][1]

[1 Interpretation

In this Part—

"Ba-137m eluting source" means a source which consists of Cs-137 in a sealed container which is designed and constructed to allow the elution of Ba-137m, and which is radioactive material or radioactive waste solely because of that Cs-137;

"Class A gaseous tritium light device" means a gaseous tritium light device where the activity of the device does not exceed 2×10^{10} Bq of tritium;

"Class B gaseous tritium light device" means a gaseous tritium light device which is installed or intended to be installed on premises and where the activity—

(a) in each sealed container in the device does not exceed 8×10^{10} Bq of tritium; and

(b) of the device does not exceed 1×10^{12} Bq of tritium;

"Class C gaseous tritium light device" means a gaseous tritium light device installed or intended to be installed—

(a) in a vessel or aircraft; or

(b) in a vehicle or other equipment used or intended to be used by the armed forces of the Crown;

"disposal permit" means—

(a) an environmental permit to carry on the radioactive substances activity described in paragraph 11(2)(b) of Part 2 of this Schedule; or

(b) an authorisation under the 1993 Act to dispose of radioactive waste held in respect of premises situated in Northern Ireland or Scotland;

"electrodeposited source" means an article where radionuclides are electrodeposited onto a metal substrate and which is radioactive material or radioactive waste solely because it contains Ni-63 or Fe-55;

"gaseous tritium light device" means a sealed source in a device which is an illuminant, instrument, sign or indicator which—

(a) incorporates tritium in one or more sealed containers constructed to prevent dispersion of that tritium in normal use; and

(b) is radioactive material solely because it contains that tritium;

"luminised article" means an article which is made wholly or partly from a luminescent substance in the form of a film or a paint and which—

(a) is radioactive material or radioactive waste solely because it contains Pm-147 or H-3; and

(b) is not a sealed source;

"management", in respect of waste, means—

(a) the preparation by checking, cleaning or repairing that waste for its re-use without further processing;

(b) the recovery of that waste;

(c) the disposal of that waste; or

(d) the application of any treatment process to that waste which is preparatory to the recovery or disposal of it,

and cognate expressions shall be construed accordingly;

"relevant river" means a river or a part of a river which—

(a) is not a part of the sea; and

(b) at the place and time of any disposal into it of aqueous radioactive waste from a sewage disposal works or directly from premises, has a flow-rate which is not less than $1 m^3 s\text{-}1$;

"relevant sewer" means—

(a) a public sewer; or
(b) a disposal main which leads to a sewage disposal works that—
(i) has the capacity to handle a minimum of $100m^3$ of effluent per day; and
(ii) discharges treated effluent only to the sea or to a relevant river,

and "public sewer", "disposal main", "sewage disposal works" and "effluent" have the same meaning as in the Water Industry Act 1991;

"relevant standard conditions" has the meaning given in paragraph 10;

"sea" includes any area submerged at mean high water springs and also includes, so far as the tide flows at mean high water springs, an estuary or arm of the sea and the waters of any channel, creek, bay or river;

"sealed source" means a radioactive source containing radioactive material where the structure is designed to prevent, under normal use, any dispersion of radioactive substances, excluding such a source where it is an electrodeposited source or a tritium foil source;

"stored in transit" means the storage in the course of transit of radioactive material or radioactive waste but does not include any storage of such material or waste where it is removed from its container;

"Table 4", "Table 5", "Table 6", "Table 7" or "Table 8" means the table with that number in this Part;

"a tritium foil source" means an article which—
(a) has a mechanically tough surface into which tritium is incorporated; and
(b) is radioactive material or radioactive waste solely because of that tritium;

"uranium or thorium compound" means a substance or article which is radioactive material or radioactive waste solely because it is or contains metallic uranium or thorium or prepared compounds of uranium or thorium, and in respect of which metal or compound the proportion of—
(a) U-235 in the uranium it contains is no more than 0.72% by mass; and
(b) any isotope of thorium it contains is present in the isotopic proportions found in nature;

"waste permitted person" means, in relation to the radioactive waste where the term appears, a person who holds—
(a) an environmental permit to carry on the radioactive substances activity described in paragraph 11(2)(b) or (c) of Part 2 of this Schedule; or
(b) in respect of premises in Scotland or Northern Ireland, an authorisation under section 13 or 14 of the 1993 Act;

"week" means any period of seven consecutive days; and

"year" means a calendar year.][1]

Amendment

1 Substituted by the Environmental Permitting (England and Wales) (Amendment) Regulations 2011, SI 2011/2043, regs 3, 15, Sch 1.

[2 Interpretation: NORM

(1) In this Part, "NORM waste" means a substance or article which is solid radioactive waste under—
(a) paragraph 4 of Part 2 of this Schedule; or
(b) except where sub-paragraph (2) applies, paragraph 5 of that Part where the waste arises from the remediation of land.

(2) Land is not contaminated under sub-paragraph (1)(b) where the land is on a site in respect of which a nuclear site licence is or has been in force and the contamination occurred—
(a) when that licence was in force; or
(b) before that licence was granted, when the site was used for the purpose of installing or operating an installation described in subsection (1) of section 1 of the Nuclear

Installations Act 1965 (restriction of certain nuclear installations to licensed sites) or in regulations made under that subsection.

(3) In these Regulations, "NORM waste concentration" means, in respect of radionuclides contained in NORM waste, the sum of the concentrations of the single radionuclide with the highest concentration in each of the natural decay chains beginning with—

(a) U-238;

(b) U-235; and

(c) Th-232.][1]

Amendment

1 Substituted by the Environmental Permitting (England and Wales) (Amendment) Regulations 2011, SI 2011/2043, regs 3, 15, Sch 1.

[Section 2

Exemption for keeping and using radioactive material and accumulating radioactive waste][1]

[3 Exemption for keeping and using radioactive material

(1) A person ("A") is exempt from the requirement for an environmental permit to carry on the radioactive substances activity described in paragraph 11(2)(a) of Part 2 of this Schedule in respect of—

(a) subject to sub-paragraph (2), the radioactive material described in paragraph 5, where A complies with the relevant standard conditions and—

  (i) in respect of radioactive material described in paragraph 5(1)(a), the condition in paragraph 6(1); and

  (ii) in respect of radioactive material described in paragraph 5(1)(b), the condition in paragraph 6(2);

or

(b) radioactive material stored in transit.

(2) A is not exempt from the requirement for an environmental permit under subparagraph (1) (a) in respect of a high activity source where A takes possession of it.][1]

Amendment

1 Substituted by the Environmental Permitting (England and Wales) (Amendment) Regulations 2011, SI 2011/2043, regs 3, 15, Sch 1.

[4 Exemption for accumulating radioactive waste

(1) This paragraph applies to the following radioactive substances activities—

(a) the activity described in paragraph 11(2)(c) of Part 2 of this Schedule ("Activity A"); and

(b) the activity described in paragraph 11(4) of Part 2 of this Schedule ("Activity B").

(2) In this paragraph, "paragraph 5 waste" means radioactive waste described in paragraph 5.

(3) A person ("A") is exempt from the requirement for an environmental permit to carry on Activity A or B, in respect of radioactive waste which is stored in transit.

(4) Subject to sub-paragraph (5), a person ("B") is exempt from the requirement for an environmental permit to carry on Activity A or B in respect of paragraph 5 waste where—

(a) B receives that waste for accumulation on premises (with a view to its subsequent management by B on those premises);

(b) in respect of those premises B manages substantial quantities of waste which is not radioactive waste; and

(c) the management of the radioactive waste will be completed by B as soon as is reasonably practicable, with the radioactive waste dispersed in non-radioactive waste.

(5) B is not exempt under sub-paragraph (4) from the requirement for an environmental permit to carry on Activity B where the waste received by B is or contains a high-activity source.

(6) A person ("C") is exempt from the requirement for an environmental permit to carry on Activity A in respect of paragraph 5 waste, where C complies with the relevant standard conditions and—

(a) in respect of radioactive waste described in paragraph 5(1)(a), the condition in paragraph 6(1); and

(b) in respect of radioactive waste described in paragraph 5(1)(b), the condition in paragraph 6(2).

(7) A person ("D") is exempt from the requirement for an environmental permit to carry on Activity A in respect of radioactive waste which is a sealed source, an electrodeposited source or a tritium foil source which—

(a) contains a quantity of radionuclides which exceeds the value specified in column 2 of Table 4 in respect of the relevant type of source;

(b) immediately before it became radioactive waste, was radioactive material in the form of a sealed source, an electrodeposited source or a tritium foil source (as appropriate); and

(c) has not been received by D for the purpose of D disposing of it,

where D complies with the relevant standard conditions.][1]

Amendment

1 Substituted by the Environmental Permitting (England and Wales) (Amendment) Regulations 2011, SI 2011/2043, regs 3, 15, Sch 1.

[5 Radioactive substances exempted under paragraphs 3 and 4

(1) Subject to sub-paragraph (2), paragraphs 3(1)(a) and 4(4) and (6) apply to—

(a) a substance or article described in an entry in column 1 of Table 4 which contains a quantity of radionuclides that does not exceed the value specified in column 2 of Table 4 in respect of that substance or article; or

(b) any substance or article which is not described in an entry in column 1 of Table 4.

(2) Sub-paragraph (1) does not apply to NORM waste with a NORM waste concentration which is less than or equal to 10 Bq/g.][1]

Amendment

1 Substituted by the Environmental Permitting (England and Wales) (Amendment) Regulations 2011, SI 2011/2043, regs 3, 15, Sch 1.

[6 Conditions in respect of the total quantity or concentration of radioactive substances on any premises

(1) The condition referred to in paragraphs 3(1)(a)(i) and 4(6)(a) is that, in respect of the total amount of a substance or article described in paragraph 5(1)(a) (including any mobile radioactive apparatus) on the premises, the quantity of radionuclides must not exceed the value specified for that substance or article in column 3 of Table 4.

(2) The condition referred to in paragraphs 3(1)(a)(ii) and 4(6)(b) in respect of a substance or article described in paragraph 5(1)(b) is that—

(a) in respect of the total amount of such substances and articles on the premises, the quantity of radioactivity does not exceed the value specified in column 2 of Table 5; or

(b) no such substance or article on the premises contains a concentration of radioactivity that exceeds the value specified in column 3 of Table 5.][1]

Amendment

1 Substituted by the Environmental Permitting (England and Wales) (Amendment) Regulations 2011, SI 2011/2043, regs 3, 15, Sch 1.

[7 Exemption for accumulating NORM waste

(1) This paragraph applies—

(a) to the following radioactive substances activities—

(i) the activity described in paragraph 11(2)(c) of Part 2 of this Schedule ("Activity A");

(ii) the activity described in paragraph 11(4) of Part 2 of this Schedule ("Activity B");

and

(b) where Activity A or B is carried on in respect of NORM waste with a NORM waste concentration that does not exceed 10 Bq/g ("Qualifying NORM Waste").

(2) Subject to sub-paragraph (5) where it applies, a person ("A") is exempt from the requirement for an environmental permit to carry on Activity A or Activity B in respect of Qualifying NORM Waste, where another person ("B") transfers that waste to A—

(a) in accordance with—

(i) a disposal permit held by B; or

(ii) an exemption from holding such a permit that applied to B in respect of the transfer to A;

and

(b) for the purpose of its accumulation by A with a view to its subsequent management by A on the premises on which it is received by A.

(3) Subject to sub-paragraph (5) where it applies, a person ("C") is exempt from the requirement for an environmental permit to carry on Activity A in respect of Qualifying NORM Waste where C complies with the relevant standard conditions.

(4) Sub-paragraph (5) applies to a person ("D") who holds an environmental permit to carry on Activity A on premises ("the relevant premises") in respect of NORM waste with a NORM waste concentration which is more than 10 Bq/g.

(5) The exemptions in sub-paragraphs (2) and (3) do not apply to D in respect of Qualifying NORM waste—

(a) with a NORM waste concentration which exceeds 5 Bq/g; and

(b) which is accumulated on the relevant premises.][1]

Amendment

1 Substituted by the Environmental Permitting (England and Wales) (Amendment) Regulations 2011, SI 2011/2043, regs 3, 15, Sch 1.

[Section 3
Exemption for keeping or using mobile radioactive apparatus][1]

[8 Exemption for keeping or using mobile radioactive apparatus

(1) A person ("A") is exempt from the requirement for an environmental permit to carry on the radioactive substances activity described in paragraph 11(5) of Part 2 of this Schedule in respect of—

(a) a mobile radioactive apparatus described in an entry in column 1 of Table 4 where—

(i) that apparatus contains a quantity of radionuclides that does not exceed the value specified in column 2 of Table 4 in respect of an apparatus of that description; and

(ii) A complies with the conditions in sub-paragraph (2);

or

(b) mobile radioactive apparatus stored in transit.

(2) The conditions in this sub-paragraph are that A must—

(a) ensure that in relation to the total amount of all such mobile radioactive apparatus that A holds, the quantity of radionuclides does not exceed the value specified, in respect of an apparatus of that description, in column 3 of Table 4; and

(b) comply with the relevant standard conditions.][1]

Amendment

1 Substituted by the Environmental Permitting (England and Wales) (Amendment) Regulations 2011, SI 2011/2043, regs 3, 15, Sch 1.

[Section 4
Relevant standard conditions][1]

[9 Interpretation of this section

In this section, "radioactive substances" means radioactive material, mobile radioactive apparatus and radioactive waste, and "exempt radioactive substances" means radioactive substances in respect of which an exemption in section 2 or 3 of this Part applies.][1]

Amendment

1 Substituted by the Environmental Permitting (England and Wales) (Amendment) Regulations 2011, SI 2011/2043, regs 3, 15, Sch 1.

[10 Relevant standard conditions

(1) Reference to the relevant standard conditions in sections 1 to 3 of this Part, means in respect of the exemption provided for in—

(a) paragraph 3(1)(a), the conditions in paragraphs 11 and 12;
(b) paragraph 4(6), 4(7) or 7(3), the conditions in paragraphs 11, 12 and 14;
(c) paragraph 8(1)(a), the conditions in paragraphs 11 …[1] and 13.

(2) A condition in paragraph 11, 12 or 13 does not apply in respect of an exemption in section 2 or 3 of this Part unless that condition is a relevant condition in respect of that exemption.][2]

Amendments

1 Repealed by the Environmental Permitting (England and Wales) (Amendment) Regulations 2012, SI 2012/630, reg 16(1), (4)(a).
2 Substituted by the Environmental Permitting (England and Wales) (Amendment) Regulations 2011, SI 2011/2043, regs 3, 15, Sch 1.

[11 General conditions

A person ("A") to whom the conditions in this paragraph apply must—

(a) keep an adequate record of any exempt radioactive substances which A holds, and—
  (i) in respect of exempt radioactive substances which are mobile radioactive apparatus, the locations at which they are kept or used;
  (ii) in respect of other exempt radioactive substances, the location within the premises where A holds them;
(b) ensure that where reasonably practicable exempt radioactive substances or the containers of such radioactive substances, are marked or labelled as radioactive;
(c) in respect of exempt radioactive substances which are sealed sources, electrodeposited sources or tritium foil sources, not modify or mutilate those sources or cause a loss of containment such that radioactive material or radioactive waste may be released outside the source;
(d) allow the regulator access to such records or such premises as the regulator may request in order to determine that all of the conditions in respect of the relevant exemption are complied with;
(e) hold the exempt radioactive substances safely and securely to prevent, so far as reasonably practicable—
  (i) accidental removal, loss or theft from the premises where they are held; or
  (ii) loss of containment;
  and
(f) in respect of exempt radioactive substances in a container—
  (i) not modify or mutilate that container; and
  (ii) prevent any uncontrolled or unintended release of radioactive material or radioactive waste from the container.][1]

Amendment

1 Substituted by the Environmental Permitting (England and Wales) (Amendment) Regulations 2011, SI 2011/2043, regs 3, 15, Sch 1.

[12 Loss or theft conditions

(1) Subject to sub-paragraph (2), in the event of an incident of loss or theft (or suspected loss or theft) of exempt radioactive substances (except mobile radioactive apparatus) from the premises where they are held, a person to whom the condition in this paragraph applies must—

(a) notify the incident to the regulator as soon as reasonably practicable; and

(b) include in that notification the details of any other incidents of loss or theft (or suspected loss or theft) of any radioactive substances from those premises over the 12 months preceding the incident being notified.

(2) In respect of an incident described in sub-paragraph (1), a notification to the regulator is not required where in respect of the aggregated total amount of exempt radioactive substances (excluding mobile radioactive apparatus) lost or stolen (or suspected to have been lost or stolen) from the premises in the incident and in all other such incidents in the 12 months preceding it, the total quantity of radioactivity does not exceed the value that is ten times the value in column 2 of Table 5.][1]

Amendment

1 Substituted by the Environmental Permitting (England and Wales) (Amendment) Regulations 2011, SI 2011/2043, regs 3, 15, Sch 1.

[13 Loss or theft conditions: mobile radioactive apparatus

(1) Subject to sub-paragraph (2), in the event of an incident of loss or theft (or suspected loss or theft) of mobile radioactive apparatus from a person ("A") to whom the condition in this paragraph applies, A must—

(a) notify the incident to the regulator as soon as reasonably practicable; and

(b) include in that notification the details of any other incidents of loss or theft (or suspected loss or theft) of any mobile radioactive apparatus from A over the 12 months preceding the incident being notified.

(2) In respect of an incident described in sub-paragraph (1), a notification to the regulator is not required where in respect of the aggregated total amount of mobile radioactive apparatus lost or stolen (or suspected to have been lost or stolen) from A in the incident and in all other such incidents in the 12 months preceding it, the total quantity of radioactivity does not exceed the value that is ten times the value in column 2 of Table 5.][1]

Amendment

1 Substituted by the Environmental Permitting (England and Wales) (Amendment) Regulations 2011, SI 2011/2043, regs 3, 15, Sch 1.

[14 Condition to dispose of accumulated waste

A person to whom the condition in this paragraph applies must dispose of the radioactive waste which is the subject of the exemption to which this condition applies—

(a) as soon as reasonably practicable after it has become waste; and

(b) in the case of such waste where it is a sealed source, a tritium foil source or an electrodeposited source, in any event within 26 weeks after it has become waste unless the regulator advises in writing that a longer period of accumulation is allowed.][1]

Amendment

1 Substituted by the Environmental Permitting (England and Wales) (Amendment) Regulations 2011, SI 2011/2043, regs 3, 15, Sch 1.

[Section 5
Exemption for disposing of solid radioactive waste][1]

[15 Exemption for receiving and disposing of solid radioactive waste

(1) This paragraph applies to the following radioactive substances activities—
(a) the activity described in paragraph 11(2)(b) of Part 2 of this Schedule ("Activity A");
(b) the activity described in paragraph 11(4) of Part 2 of this Schedule ("Activity B").

(2) A person ("A") is exempt from the requirement for an environmental permit to carry on Activity A or Activity B in respect of solid radioactive waste described in paragraph 16(1)(a) where—
(a) A receives the waste on premises for the purpose of it being managed by A on those premises;
(b) in respect of those premises A manages substantial quantities of waste which is not radioactive waste; and
(c) the radioactive waste will be disposed of by A as soon as is reasonably practicable with the radioactive waste dispersed in non-radioactive waste.

(3) A person ("B") is exempt from the requirement for an environmental permit to carry on Activity A in respect of solid radioactive waste described in paragraph 16(1) where—
(a) in respect of a sealed source, an electrodeposited source or a tritium foil source, B complies with the conditions in paragraph 17(2); and
(b) in respect of any other waste described in paragraph 16(1)(a), B complies with the conditions in paragraph 17(1) and (2).][1]

Amendment
1 Substituted by the Environmental Permitting (England and Wales) (Amendment) Regulations 2011, SI 2011/2043, regs 3, 15, Sch 1.

[16 Solid radioactive waste

(1) Solid radioactive waste referred to in paragraph 15 means—
(a) subject to sub-paragraph (2), solid radioactive waste described in an entry in column 1 of Table 6 which does not contain a concentration of radionuclides that exceeds the value specified in column 2 of that table in respect of that kind of waste; or
(b) a sealed source, an electrodeposited source or a tritium foil source which is not described in paragraph (a).

(2) Sub-paragraph (1)(a) does not apply to waste—
(a) where, prior to the disposal of that waste, a person has diluted it with the intention of ensuring that sub-paragraph (1)(a) is met; or
(b) which is NORM waste with a NORM waste concentration which is less than or equal to 10 Bq/g.][1]

Amendment
1 Substituted by the Environmental Permitting (England and Wales) (Amendment) Regulations 2011, SI 2011/2043, regs 3, 15, Sch 1.

[17 Conditions in respect of solid radioactive waste

(1) The condition referred to in paragraph 15(3)(b) is that B must ensure that, in respect of the total amount of a waste to which this condition applies that is disposed of on or from the premises, the quantity of radioactivity which that waste contains must not exceed the value specified in column 3 of Table 6 in respect of that waste during the period stated in that column.

(2) The conditions referred to in paragraph 15(3)(a) and (b) are that B must—
(a) keep an adequate record of the solid radioactive waste which B disposes of on or from any premises under that paragraph;

(b) dispose of the waste by any of the routes described in sub-paragraph (3);
(c) where the disposal route in sub-paragraph (3)(a) is used, ensure that where reasonably practicable any marking or labelling of the waste or its container is removed before the person disposes of that waste;
(d) where the waste is or was a high-activity source, notify the details of the disposal to the regulator within 14 days of the disposal (including the information required by Annex II of the HASS Directive), in such form as may be required by the regulator; and
(e) allow the regulator access to such records or such premises as the regulator may request in order to determine that all of the conditions that apply in respect of the relevant exemption in paragraph 15(3) are complied with.

(3) The routes referred to in sub-paragraph (2)(b) are that the waste is transferred to—
(a) subject to sub-paragraph (4), a person who manages substantial quantities of nonradioactive waste and where the radioactive waste will be so managed with the radioactive waste dispersed in non-radioactive waste;
(b) a waste permitted person; or
(c) where the waste is a sealed source, an electrodeposited source or a tritium foil source, to a licensee of a nuclear site or to a person who is situated in another country and who is lawfully entitled to receive such waste.

(4) The route in sub-paragraph (3)(a) does not apply in respect of waste—
(a) described in paragraph 16(1)(b); or
(b) which is described in paragraph 16(1)(a) and which is a sealed source, an electrodeposited source or a tritium foil source, where in respect of the total amount of such a source which is disposed of on or from the premises under paragraph 15(3), the quantity of radioactivity which that waste contains exceeds the value specified in column 3 of Table 6 in respect of that source during the period stated in that column.][1]

Amendment

1 Substituted by the Environmental Permitting (England and Wales) (Amendment) Regulations 2011, SI 2011/2043, regs 3, 15, Sch 1.

[Section 6
Exemption for disposing of NORM waste][1]

[18 Exemption for receiving and disposing of NORM waste

(1) This paragraph applies—
(a) to the following radioactive substances activities—
 (i) the activity described in paragraph 11(2)(b) of Part 2 of this Schedule ("Activity A");
 (ii) the activity described in paragraph 11(4) of Part 2 of this Schedule ("Activity B");

 and
(b) where Activity A or B is carried on in respect of NORM waste—
 (i) with a NORM waste concentration that does not exceed 5 Bq/g ("type 1 NORM Waste"); or
 (ii) with a NORM waste concentration that exceeds 5 Bq/g but does not exceed 10 Bq/g ("type 2 NORM waste").

(2) Subject to sub-paragraph (6), a person ("A") is exempt from the requirement for an environmental permit to carry on Activity A or Activity B in respect of type 1 NORM waste or type 2 NORM waste where another person ("B") transfers that waste to A—
(a) in accordance with—
 (i) a disposal permit held by B; or
 (ii) an exemption from holding such a permit that applied to B in respect of the transfer to A;

 and

(b) for the purpose of its disposal by A on the premises on which A receives it.

(3) Where a person ("C") disposes of—
(a) type 1 NORM waste on or from premises, sub-paragraph (4) applies to C; or
(b) type 2 NORM waste on or from premises, sub-paragraph (5) applies to C.

(4) C is exempt from the requirement for an environmental permit to carry on Activity A in respect of type 1 NORM waste where in relation to the total amount of such waste disposed of on or from the premises by C per year—
(a) the quantity of radionuclides does not exceed 5×10^{10} Bq, and C complies with the conditions in paragraph 19(1); or
(b) subject to sub-paragraph (6), the quantity of radionuclides exceeds 5×10^{10} Bq, and C complies with—
   (i) the conditions in paragraph 19(1); and
   (ii) where C intends to dispose of the waste by one of the methods in paragraph 19(2)(a), the conditions in paragraph 19(3).

(5) Subject to sub-paragraph (6), C is exempt from the requirement for an environmental permit to carry on Activity A in respect of type 2 NORM waste where C complies with the conditions in paragraph 19(1) and (3).

(6) Sub-paragraph (7) applies to a person ("E") where E holds an environmental permit to carry on Activity A for the disposal on or from premises ("the relevant premises") of NORM waste with a NORM waste concentration which exceeds 10 Bq/g.

(7) The following exemptions do not apply to E—
(a) the exemptions in sub-paragraph (2) in respect of type 2 NORM waste;
(b) the exemption in sub-paragraph (4)(b); and
(c) the exemption in sub-paragraph (5).][1]

Amendment

1 Substituted by the Environmental Permitting (England and Wales) (Amendment) Regulations 2011, SI 2011/2043, regs 3, 15, Sch 1.

[19 Conditions in respect of NORM waste

(1) The conditions referred to in the exemptions in paragraph 18(4)(a) and (b)(i) and (5) are that C must—
(a) keep an adequate record of the NORM waste which C disposes of under those exemptions;
(b) dispose of the waste by any of the methods described in sub-paragraph (2);
(c) where the disposal method in sub-paragraph (2)(a) or (b) is used, ensure that where reasonably practicable any marking or labelling of the waste or its container is removed before C disposes of that waste; and
(d) allow the regulator access to such records or such premises as the regulator may request in order to determine that all of the conditions that apply to C in respect of the relevant exemption in that paragraph are complied with.

(2) The methods referred to in sub-paragraph (1)(b) are that the waste is disposed of—
(a) subject to sub-paragraph (3) where it applies, by burial in landfill or by the transfer of the waste to a person for the purpose of—
   (i) the burial in landfill of the waste; or
   (ii) the application of a treatment process to the waste which is preparatory to the burial in landfill of that waste;
(b) by incineration (or transfer to a person for such incineration or treatment which is preparatory to the incineration of the waste), but not in respect of—
   (i) type 1 NORM waste, where in respect of the total amount of that waste that is incinerated (or transferred to a person for preparation or incineration) per year the quantity of radionuclides in the total amount of that waste exceeds 1×10^8 Bq; or

(ii) type 2 NORM waste;

or

(c) by transfer to a waste permitted person.

(3) The conditions referred to in paragraph 18(4)(b)(ii) and (5) are that C must—

(a) make a written radiological assessment of the reasonably foreseeable pathways for the exposure of the public and workers to radiation in respect of—

(i) the application of any treatment process to the waste which is preparatory to its burial in landfill, at the place of that treatment; and

(ii) the burial in landfill of that waste, at the place of disposal;

(b) be satisfied that the assessment demonstrates that radiation doses are not expected to exceed—

(i) 1 millisievert per year to any worker at the place of treatment or disposal; and

(ii) 300 microsievert per year to any member of the public;

(c) provide that assessment to the regulator at least 28 days before the first disposal is made; and

(d) not dispose of that waste (or continue to do so) if the regulator objects in writing to that assessment.][1]

Amendment

1 Substituted by the Environmental Permitting (England and Wales) (Amendment) Regulations 2011, SI 2011/2043, regs 3, 15, Sch 1.

[Section 7
Exemption for disposing of aqueous radioactive waste][1]

[20 Exemption for disposing of aqueous radioactive waste in Table 6

(1) Subject to sub-paragraph (2), a person ("A") is exempt from the requirement for an environmental permit to carry on the radioactive substances activity described in paragraph 11(2)(b) of Part 2 of this Schedule in respect of aqueous radioactive waste described in an entry in column 1 of Table 6, where A complies with the conditions in sub-paragraph (3).

(2) A is not exempt under sub-paragraph (1) where the person who generated that waste did not minimise the quantity of radionuclides generated as waste to the extent reasonably practicable.

(3) The conditions referred to in sub-paragraph (1) are that, in respect of the waste described in that sub-paragraph, A must—

(a) ensure that in respect of the total amount of that waste that is disposed of on or from the premises in a year, the quantity of radioactivity which that waste contains does not exceed the value specified in column 3 of Table 6 in respect of that waste;

(b) dispose of that waste to a relevant sewer or to a waste permitted person;

(c) keep an adequate record of that waste which A disposes of on or from the premises; and

(d) allow the regulator access to such records or such premises as the regulator may request in order to determine that the preceding conditions in this sub-paragraph are complied with.][1]

Amendment

1 Substituted by the Environmental Permitting (England and Wales) (Amendment) Regulations 2011, SI 2011/2043, regs 3, 15, Sch 1.

[21 Exemption for disposing of other aqueous radioactive waste

(1) Subject to sub-paragraph (2), a person ("A") is exempt from the requirement for an environmental permit to carry on the radioactive substances activity described in paragraph 11(2)(b) of Part 2 of this Schedule in respect of aqueous radioactive waste described in sub-paragraph (3) where A disposes of that waste in accordance with the conditions in paragraph 22(1).

(2) A is not exempt under sub-paragraph (1) in respect of premises, where A holds an environmental permit to carry on the radioactive substances activity described in paragraph 11(2)(b) of Part 2 of this Schedule for the disposal of aqueous radioactive waste on or from those premises.

(3) Subject to sub-paragraph (4), the waste referred to in sub-paragraph (1) is aqueous radioactive waste—
(a) which is not described in an entry in column 1 of Table 6; and
(b) with a total concentration of radioactivity which does not exceed 100 Bq/ml.

(4) Sub-paragraph (3) does not apply to aqueous radioactive waste—
(a) which a person has diluted with the intention that—
  (i) the waste has a concentration of radioactivity which is below the value in subparagraph (3)(b); or
  (ii) the condition in paragraph 22(3)(a) or (4)(b) is complied with in respect of that waste;

  or
(b) where the person who generated that waste did not minimise the quantity of radionuclides generated as waste to the extent reasonably practicable.][1]

Amendment

1 Substituted by the Environmental Permitting (England and Wales) (Amendment) Regulations 2011, SI 2011/2043, regs 3, 15, Sch 1.

[22 Conditions in respect of aqueous radioactive waste in paragraph 21

(1) The conditions referred to in paragraph 21(1) are that A must—
(a) subject to sub-paragraph (2), dispose of the waste to which that paragraph applies—
  (i) directly into a relevant river or the sea;
  (ii) to a relevant sewer; or
  (iii) to a waste permitted person.
(b) keep an adequate record of the waste which A disposes of from the premises under that paragraph;
(c) in respect of the disposal of aqueous non-table 6 waste, comply with sub-paragraph (3) or (4) as appropriate; and
(d) allow the regulator access to such records or such premises as the regulator may request in order to determine that all of the preceding conditions are complied with.

(2) In respect of aqueous non-Table 6 waste disposed of from the premises, A must not use both of the disposal routes described in sub-paragraph (1)(a)(i) and (ii) in a year and where—
(a) A uses the route in sub-paragraph (1)(a)(i), the conditions in sub-paragraph (3) apply to A; or
(b) A uses the route in sub-paragraph (1)(a)(ii), or A does not use the route in either sub-paragraph (1)(a)(i) or (ii), the conditions in sub-paragraph (4) apply to A.

(3) Where this sub-paragraph applies and A disposes of the aqueous non-table 6 waste directly into a relevant river or the sea, A must—
(a) in respect of any aqueous non-Table 6 waste which A disposes of, ensure that the concentration of radioactivity does not exceed the value specified in column 2 of Table 7; and
(b) in respect of the total amount of aqueous non-Table 6 waste which A disposes of from the premises in a year, ensure that the quantity of radioactivity does not exceed the value specified in column 4 of Table 7.

(4) Where this sub-paragraph applies and A disposes of the aqueous non-table 6 waste to a relevant sewer (or only to a waste permitted person), A must ensure that, in respect of the total amount of aqueous non-Table 6 waste which is disposed of from those premises in a year, the total quantity of radioactivity does not exceed—

(a) where any of that waste has a concentration of radioactivity which exceeds the value specified in column 2 of Table 7, the value in sub-paragraph (5); or

(b) where none of that waste has a concentration of radioactivity which exceeds the value specified in column 2 of Table 7, the value in sub-paragraph (5) or (6).

(5) The value referred to in sub-paragraph (4)(a) and (b) is—

(a) 1×10^8 Bq for the sum of the following radionuclides: H-3, C-11, C-14, F-18, P-32, P-33, S-35, Ca-45, Cr-51, Fe-55, Ga-67, Sr-89, Y-90, Tc-99m, In-111, I-123, I-125, I-131, Sm-153, Tl-201; and

(b) 1×10^6 Bq for the sum of all other radionuclides.

(6) The value referred to in sub-paragraph (4)(b) is the value specified in column 3 of Table 7.

(7) In this paragraph, "aqueous non-Table 6 waste" means aqueous radioactive waste which is not described in an entry in column 1 of Table 6.][1]

Amendment

1 Substituted by the Environmental Permitting (England and Wales) (Amendment) Regulations 2011, SI 2011/2043, regs 3, 15, Sch 1.

[Section 8
Exemption for disposal of gaseous radioactive waste][1]

[23 Exemption for disposal of gaseous radioactive waste

(1) Subject to sub-paragraph (2), a person ("A") is exempt from the requirement for an environmental permit to carry on the radioactive substances activity described in paragraph 11(2)(b) of Part 2 of this Schedule in respect of gaseous radioactive waste where—

(a) the only radionuclide contained in that waste is Kr-85 and A—

  (i) ensures that in respect of the total amount of such waste which is disposed of from the premises in a year, the total quantity of radioactivity does not exceed 1011 Bq; and

  (ii) complies with the conditions in paragraph 24(1);

  or

(b) subject to sub-paragraph (3), that waste—

  (i) is released from within a container at the time that the container is opened; and

  (ii) is emitted by solid or liquid radioactive material within the container,

and A complies with the conditions in paragraph 24(1).

(2) Sub-paragraph (1) does not apply to waste where the person who generated that waste did not minimise the quantity of radionuclides generated as waste to the extent reasonably practicable.

(3) Sub-paragraph (1)(b) does not apply in respect of any gas which arises as a result of a process applied by a person to the contained radioactive material.][1]

Amendment

1 Substituted by the Environmental Permitting (England and Wales) (Amendment) Regulations 2011, SI 2011/2043, regs 3, 15, Sch 1.

[24 Conditions in respect of gaseous radioactive waste

(1) The conditions referred to in paragraph 23(1) are that A must—

(a) to the extent that is reasonably practicable—

  (i) in respect of relevant gaseous waste which arises in a building, cause the waste to be disposed of by an extraction system which removes the waste from the area where it arose and which vents the waste into the atmosphere; and

  (ii) prevent the entry or, where sub-paragraph (i) applies, the re-entry, of relevant gaseous waste into a building;

  and

(b) allow the regulator access to such records or such premises as the regulator may request in order to determine that all of the conditions that apply to A in respect of the relevant exemption in that paragraph are complied with.

(2) In this paragraph "relevant gaseous waste" means waste which is described in paragraph 23(1) and disposed of under the exemption in that paragraph.][1]

Amendment

1 Substituted by the Environmental Permitting (England and Wales) (Amendment) Regulations 2011, SI 2011/2043, regs 3, 15, Sch 1.

[Section 9
Tables and summation rules in this Part

Table 4][1]

[25

The Table 4 referred to in sections 2 and 3 of this Part—

Table 4
Radioactive material and accumulated radioactive waste: values of maximum quantities

Substance or article	*Maximum quantity of radionuclides for each substance or article*	*Maximum quantity of radionuclides:* *(a) on any premises in items which satisfy the limit in column 2; or* *(b) in mobile radioactive apparatus held by a person*
A sealed source of a type not described in any other row of this table.	4×10^6 Bq	2×10^8 Bq
A Class A gaseous tritium light device.	2×10^{10} Bq	5×10^{12} Bq
A Class B gaseous tritium light device.	1×10^{12} Bq	3×10^{13} Bq
A Class C gaseous tritium light device.	1×10^{12} Bq	No limit.
Any sealed source which is solely radioactive material or radioactive waste because it contains tritium.	2×10^{10} Bq	5×10^{12} Bq
A tritium foil source.	2×10^{10} Bq	5×10^{12} Bq
A smoke detector affixed to premises.	4×10^6 Bq	No limit.
An electrodeposited source.	6×10^8 Bq Ni-63 or 2×10^8 Bq Fe-55	6×10^{11} Bq
A luminised article.	8×10^7 Bq Pm-147 or 4×10^9 Bq H-3	4×10^{10} Bq Pm-147 or 2×10^{11} Bq H-3
A Ba-137m eluting source.	4×10^4 Bq Cs-137+	4×10^5 Bq Cs-137+

Substance or article	*Maximum quantity of radionuclides for each substance or article*	*Maximum quantity of radionuclides:* *(a) on any premises in items which satisfy the limit in column 2; or* *(b) in mobile radioactive apparatus held by a person*
A substance or article which is or contains magnesium alloy or thoriated tungsten in which the thorium concentration does not exceed 4% by mass.	No limit.	No limit.
A uranium or thorium compound.	Up to a total of 5 kg of uranium and thorium.	Up to a total of 5 kg of uranium and thorium.
A substance or article (other than a sealed source) which is [, used for, or arises from] 2 medical or veterinary diagnosis or treatment or clinical or veterinary trials.	1×10^9 Bq Tc-99m and in respect of the total for all other radionuclides– (i) 1×10^8 Bq if the substance or article is radioactive material; or (ii) 2×10^8 Bq if the substance or article is radioactive waste.	1×10^9 Bq Tc-99m and 2×10^8 Bq of all other radionuclides, (no more than 1×10^8 Bq of which is contained in radioactive material).][1]

1. Substituted by the Environmental Permitting (England and Wales) (Amendment) Regulations 2011, SI 2011/2043, regs 3, Sch.1 para.1.
2. Words inserted by the Environmental Permitting (England and Wales) (Amendment) Regulations 2012, SI 2012/630, reg 16(1), (4)(b).

Amendment

1 Substituted by the Environmental Permitting (England and Wales) (Amendment) Regulations 2011, SI 2011/2043, regs 3, 15, Sch 1.

[Table 5][1]

[26

The Table 5 referred to in sections 2 and 4 of this Part is—

Table 5
Radionuclides: values of quantities and concentrations

Radionuclides	*Maximum quantity of radioactivity (Bq) on any premises*	*Maximum concentration (Bq/g)*
H-3	10^9	10^6
Be-7	10^7	10^3
C-14	10^7	10^4
O-15	10^9	10^2
F-18	10^6	10
Na-22	10	10
Na-24	10	10
Si-31	10^6	10^3

Radionuclides	*Maximum quantity of radioactivity (Bq) on any premises*	*Maximum concentration (Bq/g)*
P-32	10^5	10^3
P-33	10^8	10^5
S-35	10^8	10^5
Cl-36	10^6	10^4
Cl-38	10^5	10
Ar-37	10^8	10^6
Ar-41	10^9	10^2
K-42	10^6	10^2
K-43	10^6	10
Ca-45	10^7	10^4
Ca-47	10^6	10
Sc-46	10^6	10
Sc-47	10^6	10^2
Sc-48	10^5	10
V-48	10^5	10
Cr-51	10^7	10^3
Mn-51	10^5	10
Mn-52	10^5	10
Mn-52m	10^5	10
Mn-53	10^9	10^4
Mn-54	10^6	10
Mn-56	10^5	10
Fe-52	10^6	10
Fe-55	10^6	10^4
Fe-59	10^6	10
Co-55	10^6	10
Co-56	10^5	10
Co-57	10^6	10^2
Co-58	10^6	10
Co-58m	10^7	10^4
Co-60	10^5	10
Co-60m	10^6	10^3
Co-61	10^6	10^2
Co-62m	10^5	10
Ni-59	10^8	10^4
Ni-63	10^8	10^5
Ni-65	10^6	10
Cu-64	10^6	10^2
Zn-65	10^6	10
Zn-69	10^6	10^4
Zn-69m	10^6	10^2
Ga-72	10^5	10
Ge-71	10^8	10^4
As-73	10^7	10^3
As-74	10^6	10

Radionuclides	*Maximum quantity of radioactivity (Bq) on any premises*	*Maximum concentration (Bq/g)*
As-76	10^5	10^2
As-77	10^6	10^3
Se-75	10^6	10^2
Br-82	10^6	10
Kr-74	10^9	10^2
Kr-76	10^9	10^2
Kr-77	10^9	10^2
Kr-79	10^5	10^3
Kr-81	10^7	10^4
Kr-83m	10^{12}	10^5
Kr-85	10^4	10^5
Kr-85m	10^{10}	10^3
Kr-87	10^9	10^2
Kr-88	10^9	10^2
Rb-86	10^5	10^2
Sr-85	10^6	10^2
Sr-85m	10^7	10^2
Sr-87m	10^6	10^2
Sr-89	10^6	10^3
Sr-90+	10^4	10^2
Sr-91	10^5	10
Sr-92	10^6	10
Y-90	10^5	10^3
Y-91	10^6	10^3
Y-91m	10^6	10^2
Y-92	10^5	10^2
Y-93	10^5	10^2
Zr-93+	10^7	10^3
Zr-95	10^6	10
Zr-97+	10^5	10
Nb-93m	10^7	10^4
Nb-94	10^6	10
Nb-95	10^6	10
Nb-97	10^6	10
Nb-98	10^5	10
Mo-90	10^6	10
Mo-93	10^8	10^3
Mo-99	10^6	10^2
Mo-101	10^6	10
Tc-96	10^6	10
Tc-96m	10^7	10^3
Tc-97	10^8	10^3
Tc-97m	10^7	10^3
Tc-99	10^7	10^4
Tc-99m	10^7	10^2

Radionuclides	*Maximum quantity of radioactivity (Bq) on any premises*	*Maximum concentration (Bq/g)*
Ru-97	10^7	10^2
Ru-103	10^6	10^2
Ru-105	10^6	10
Ru-106+	10^5	10^2
Rh-103m	10^8	10^4
Rh-105	10^7	10^2
Pd-103	10^8	10^3
Pd-109	10^6	10^3
Ag-105	10^6	10^2
Ag-108m+	10^6	10
Ag-110m	10^6	10
Ag-111	10^6	10^3
Cd-109	10^6	10^4
Cd-115	10^6	10^2
Cd-115m	10^6	10^3
In-111	10^6	10^2
In-113m	10^6	10^2
In-114m	10^6	10^2
In-115m	10^6	10^2
Sn-113	10^7	10^3
Sn-125	10^5	10^2
Sb-122	10^4	10^2
Sb-124	10^6	10
Sb-125	10^6	10^2
Te-123m	10^7	10^2
Te-125m	10^7	10^3
Te-127	10^6	10^3
Te-127m	10^7	10^3
Te-129	10^6	10^2
Te-129m	10^6	10^3
Te-131	10^5	10^2
Te-131m	10^6	10
Te-132	10^7	10^2
Te-133	10^5	10
Te-133m	10^5	10
Te-134	10^6	10
I-123	10^7	10^2
I-125	10^6	10^3
I-126	10^6	10^2
I-129	10^5	10^2
I-130	10^6	10
I-131	10^6	10^2
I-132	10^5	10
I-133	10^6	10
I-134	10^5	10

Radionuclides	Maximum quantity of radioactivity (Bq) on any premises	Maximum concentration (Bq/g)
I-135	10^6	10
Xe-131m	10^4	10^4
Xe-133	10^4	10^3
Xe-135	10^{10}	10^3
Cs-129	10^5	10^2
Cs-131	10^6	10^3
Cs-132	10^5	10
Cs-134m	10^5	10^3
Cs-134	10^4	10
Cs-135	10^7	10^4
Cs-136	10^5	10
Cs-137+	10^4	10
Cs-138	10^4	10
Ba-131	10^6	10^2
Ba-140+	10^5	10
La-140	10^5	10
Ce-139	10^6	10^2
Ce-141	10^7	10^2
Ce-143	10^6	10^2
Ce-144+	10^5	10^2
Pr-142	10^5	10^2
Pr-143	10^6	10^4
Nd-147	10^6	10^2
Nd-149	10^6	10^2
Pm-147	10^7	10^4
Pm-149	10^6	10^3
Sm-151	10^8	10^4
Sm-153	10^6	10^2
Eu-152	10^6	10
Eu-152m	10^6	10^2
Eu-154	10^6	10
Eu-155	10^7	10^2
Gd-153	10^7	10^2
Gd-159	10^6	10^3
Tb-160	10^6	10
Dy-165	10^6	10^3
Dy-166	10^6	10^3
Ho-166	10^5	10^3
Er-169	10^7	10^4
Er-171	10^6	10^2
Tm-170	10^6	10^3
Tm-171	10^8	10^4
Yb-175	10^7	10^3
Lu-177	10^7	10^3
Hf-181	10^6	10

Radionuclides	*Maximum quantity of radioactivity (Bq) on any premises*	*Maximum concentration (Bq/g)*
Ta-182	10^4	10
W-181	10^7	10^3
W-185	10^7	10^4
W-187	10^6	10^2
Re-186	10^6	10^3
Re-188	10^5	10^2
Os-185	10^6	10
Os-191	10^7	10^2
Os-191m	10^7	10^3
Os-193	10^6	10^2
Ir-190	10^6	10
Ir-192	10^4	10
Ir-194	10^5	10^2
Pt-191	10^6	10^2
Pt-193m	10^7	10^3
Pt-197	10^6	10^3
Pt-197m	10^6	10^2
Au-198	10^6	10^2
Au-199	10^6	10^2
Hg-197	10^7	10^2
Hg-197m	10^6	10^2
Hg-203	10^5	10^2
Tl-200	10^6	10
Tl-201	10^6	10^2
Tl-202	10^6	10^2
Tl-204	10^4	10^4
Pb-203	10^6	10^2
Pb-210+	10^4	10
Pb-212+	10^5	10
Bi-206	10^5	10
Bi-207	10^6	10
Bi-210	10^6	10^3
Bi-212+	10^5	10
Po-203	10^6	10
Po-205	10^6	10
Po-207	10^6	10
Po-210	10^4	10
At-211	10^7	10^3
Rn-220+	10^7	10^4
Rn-222+	10^8	10
Ra-223+	10^5	10^2
Ra-224+	10^5	10
Ra-225	10^5	10^2
Ra-226+	10^4	10
Ra-227	10^6	10^2

Radionuclides	*Maximum quantity of radioactivity (Bq) on any premises*	*Maximum concentration (Bq/g)*
Ra-228+	10^5	10
Ac-228	10^6	10
Th-226+	10^7	10^3
Th-227	10^4	10
Th-228+	10^4	1
Th-229+	10^3	1
Th-230	10^4	1
Th-231	10^7	10^3
Th-232 sec	10^3	1
Th-234+	10^5	10^3
Pa-230	10^6	10
Pa-231	10^3	1
Pa-233	10^7	10^2
U-230+	10^5	10
U-231	10^7	10^2
U-232+	10^3	1
U-233	10^4	10
U-234	10^4	10
U-235+	10^4	10
U-236	10^4	10
U-237	10^6	10^2
U-238+	10^4	10
U-238 sec	10^3	1
U-239	10^6	10^2
U-240	10^7	10^3
U-240+	10^6	10
Np-237+	10^3	1
Np-239	10^7	10^2
Np-240	10^6	10
Pu-234	10^7	10^2
Pu-235	10^7	10^2
Pu-236	10^4	10
Pu-237	10^7	10^3
Pu-238	10^4	1
Pu-239	10^4	1
Pu-240	10^3	1
Pu-241	10^5	10^2
Pu-242	10^4	1
Pu-243	10^7	10^3
Pu-244	10^4	1
Am-241	10^4	1
Am-242	10^6	10^3
Am-242m+	10^4	1
Am-243+	10^3	1
Cm-242	10^5	10^2

Radionuclides	*Maximum quantity of radioactivity (Bq) on any premises*	*Maximum concentration (Bq/g)*
Cm-243	10^4	1
Cm-244	10^4	10
Cm-245	10^3	1
Cm-246	10^3	1
Cm-247	10^4	1
Cm-248	10^3	1
Bk-249	10^6	10^3
Cf-246	10^6	10^3
Cf-248	10^4	10
Cf-249	10^3	1
Cf-250	10^4	10
Cf-251	10^3	1
Cf-252	10^4	10
Cf-253	10^5	10^2
Cf-254	10^3	1
Es-253	10^5	10^2
Es-254	10^4	10
Es-254m	10^6	10^2
Fm-254	10^7	10^4
Fm-255	10^6	10^3
Any other radionuclide that is: (a) not of natural terrestrial or cosmic origin; or (b) listed in Table 2 in this Schedule.	10^3, or the quantity given in respect of that radionuclide in the Health Protection Agency's publication 'Exempt Concentrations and Quantities for Radionuclides not Included in the European Basic Safety Standards Directive'.	1, or the concentration given in respect of that radionuclide in the publication referenced in column 2.

27

The summation rule in respect of column 2 of Table 5 is the sum of the quotients A/B where—

(a) "A" means the quantity of each radionuclide listed in column 1 of Table 5 that is present in the material and waste; and

(b) "B" means the quantity of that radionuclide specified in column 2 of Table 5.

28

The summation rule in respect of column 2 of Table 5 is the sum of the quotients C/D where—

(a) "C" means the concentration of each radionuclide listed in column 1 of Table 5 that is present in the material and waste; and

(b) "D" means the concentration of that radionuclide specified in column 3 of Table 5.][1]

Amendment

1 Substituted by the Environmental Permitting (England and Wales) (Amendment) Regulations 2011, SI 2011/2043, regs 3, 15, Sch 1.

[Table 6][1]

[29

The Table 6 referred to in sections 5 and 7 of this Part is—

Table 6
Radioactive waste: values of quantities and concentrations

Radioactive waste	*Maximum concentration of radionuclides*	*Maximum quantity of radioactivity to be disposed of in the period stated*
Solid radioactive waste, with no single item > 4×10^4 Bq.	4×10^5 Bq for the sum of all radionuclides per 0.1m^3.	2×10^8 Bq/year.
Solid radioactive waste containing tritium and C-14 only, with no single item > 4×10^5 Bq.	4×10^6 Bq of tritium and C-14 per 0.1m^3.	2×10^9 Bq/year.
Individual sealed sources.	2×10^5 Bq for the sum of all radionuclides per 0.1m^3.	1×10^7 Bq/year.
Individual sealed sources which are solely radioactive waste because they contain tritium.	2×10^{10} Bq of tritium per 0.1m^3.	1×10^{13} Bq/year.
Luminised articles with no single item containing > 8×10^7 Bq of Pm-147 or > 4×10^9 of tritium.	8×10^7 Bq per 0.1m^3 of Pm-147 or 4×10^9 Bq per 0.1m^3 for tritium.	2×10^9 Bq/year of Pm-147 or 1×10^{11} Bq/year of tritium.
Solid radioactive waste which consists of magnesium alloy, thoriated tungsten or dross from hardener alloy in which the thorium concentration does not exceed 4% by mass.	No limit.	No limit.
Solid uranium or thorium compound.	No limit.	0.5 kg of uranium or thorium per week.
Aqueous liquid uranium or thorium compound.	No limit.	0.5 kg of uranium or thorium per year.
Aqueous liquid human excreta.	No limit.	1×10^{10} Bq/year of Tc-99m and 5×10^9 Bq/year for the sum of all other radionuclides.][1]

Amendment

1 Substituted by the Environmental Permitting (England and Wales) (Amendment) Regulations 2011, SI 2011/2043, regs 3, 15, Sch 1.

[Table 7][1]

[30

The Table 7 referred to in section 7 of this Part is—

Table 7
Aqueous radioactive waste values

Radionuclide	*Concentration in Bq/litre*	*Maximum annual quantity of radionuclides to a relevant sewer (Bq/year)*	*Maximum annual quantity of radionuclides directly into a relevant river or the sea (Bq/year)*
H-3	103	10^{10}	10^{10}
Be-7	1	10^{7}	10^{7}
C-14	0.1	10^{6}	10^{6}
F-18	0.1	10^{6}	10^{6}
Na-22	1	10^{6}	10^{7}
Na-24	1	10^{7}	10^{7}
Si-31	10	10^{8}	10^{8}
P-32	0.001	10^{4}	10^{4}
P-33	0.001	10^{4}	10^{4}
S-35	10	3×10^{7}	10^{8}
Cl-36	10	10^{7}	10^{8}
Cl-38	0.1	10^{6}	10^{6}
K-42	0.01	10^{4}	10^{4}
K-43	0.01	10^{4}	10^{4}
Ca-45	1	10^{7}	10^{7}
Ca-47	0.1	10^{6}	10^{6}
Sc-46	0.001	10^{4}	10^{4}
Sc-47	0.01	10^{4}	10^{4}
Sc-48	0.001	10^{4}	10^{4}
V-48	1	10^{7}	10^{7}
Cr-51	10	10^{8}	10^{8}
Mn-51	0.001	10^{4}	10^{4}
Mn-52	0.001	10^{4}	10^{4}
Mn-52m	0.001	10^{4}	10^{4}
Mn-53	1	10^{7}	10^{7}
Mn-54	0.01	10^{4}	10^{4}
Mn-56	0.001	10^{4}	10^{4}
Fe-52	0.01	10^{4}	10^{4}
Fe-55	1	10^{7}	10^{7}
Fe-59	0.01	10^{4}	10^{4}
Co-55	0.001	10^{4}	10^{4}
Co-56	0.001	10^{4}	10^{4}
Co-57	0.1	10^{6}	10^{6}
Co-58	0.1	10^{6}	10^{6}
Co-58m	1	10^{7}	10^{7}
Co-60	0.01	10^{4}	10^{4}
Co-60m	1	10^{7}	10^{7}
Co-61	0.1	10^{6}	10^{6}
Co-62m	0.001	10^{4}	10^{4}
Ni-59	1	10^{7}	10^{7}
Ni-63	102	10^{9}	10^{9}
Ni-65	0.01	10^{4}	10^{4}
Cu-64	0.1	10^{6}	10^{6}

Radionuclide	*Concentration in Bq/litre*	*Maximum annual quantity of radionuclides to a relevant sewer (Bq/year)*	*Maximum annual quantity of radionuclides directly into a relevant river or the sea (Bq/year)*
Zn-65	0.1	3×10^4	10^6
Zn-69	10	10^8	10^8
Zn-69m	0.1	10^6	10^6
Ga-67	0.1	10^6	10^6
Ga-72	0.001	10^4	10^4
Ge-71	1	10^7	10^7
As-73	10	10^8	10^8
As-74	1	10^7	10^7
As-76	1	10^7	10^7
As-77	1	10^7	10^7
Se-75	0.1	3×10^4	10^6
Br-82	0.1	10^6	10^6
Rb-86	0.1	10^6	10^6
Sr-85	0.1	10^6	10^6
Sr-85m	0.1	10^6	10^6
Sr-87m	0.1	10^6	10^6
Sr-89	1	10^7	10^7
Sr-90+	0.1	3×10^4	10^6
Sr-91	0.01	10^4	10^4
Sr-92	0.01	10^4	10^4
Y-90	1	10^7	10^7
Y-91	1	10^7	10^7
Y-91m	0.01	10^4	10^4
Y-92	0.1	10^6	10^6
Y-93	0.1	10^6	10^6
Zr-93	10	10^8	10^8
Zr-95+	0.001	10^4	10^4
Zr-97	0.01	10^4	10^4
Nb-93m	10	10^8	10^8
Nb-94	0.1	10^6	10^6
Nb-95	1	10^7	10^7
Nb-97	1	10^7	10^7
Nb-98	0.1	10^6	10^6
Mo-90	0.1	10^6	10^6
Mo-93	1	10^7	10^7
Mo-99	0.1	10^6	10^6
Mo-101	0.01	10^4	10^4
Tc-96	1	10^7	10^7
Tc-96m	102	10^9	10^9
Tc-97	102	10^9	10^9
Tc-97m	10	10^8	10^8
Tc-99	10	10^7	10^8
Tc-99m	10	3×10^7	10^8

Radionuclide	*Concentration in Bq/litre*	*Maximum annual quantity of radionuclides to a relevant sewer (Bq/year)*	*Maximum annual quantity of radionuclides directly into a relevant river or the sea (Bq/year)*
Ru-97	0.01	10^4	10^4
Ru-103	0.01	10^4	10^4
Ru-105	0.01	10^4	10^4
Ru-106+	0.1	10^6	10^6
Rh-103m	10	10^8	10^8
Rh-105	1	10^7	10^7
Pd-103	0.1	10^6	10^6
Pd-109	0.1	10^6	10^6
Ag-105	1	10^7	10^7
Ag-108m	0.1	10^6	10^6
Ag-110m	0.1	10^6	10^6
Ag-111	10	10^8	10^8
Cd-109	1	10^7	10^7
Cd-115	0.1	10^6	10^6
Cd-115m	1	10^7	10^7
In-111	0.01	10^4	10^4
In-113m	0.01	10^4	10^4
In-114m	0.01	10^4	10^4
In-115m	0.01	10^4	10^4
Sn-113	0.1	10^6	10^6
Sn-125	0.01	10^4	10^4
Sb-122	0.1	10^6	10^6
Sb-124	0.1	10^6	10^6
Sb-125	1	10^7	10^7
Te-123m	1	10^7	10^7
Te-125m	1	10^7	10^7
Te-127	10	10^8	10^8
Te-127m	1	10^7	10^7
Te-129	10	10^8	10^8
Te-129m	1	10^7	10^7
Te-131	1	10^7	10^7
Te-131m	1	10^7	10^7
Te-132	0.1	10^6	10^6
Te-133	1	10^7	10^7
Te-133m	1	10^7	10^7
Te-134	1	10^7	10^7
I-123	1	10^7	10^7
I-125	1	10^7	10^7
I-126	0.1	10^6	10^6
I-129	0.1	10^6	10^6
I-130	0.1	10^6	10^6
I-131	0.1	10^6	10^6
I-132	0.1	10^6	10^6

Radionuclide	*Concentration in Bq/litre*	*Maximum annual quantity of radionuclides to a relevant sewer (Bq/year)*	*Maximum annual quantity of radionuclides directly into a relevant river or the sea (Bq/year)*
I-133	0.1	10^6	10^6
I-134	0.1	10^6	10^6
I-135	0.1	10^6	10^6
Cs-129	0.01	10^4	10^4
Cs-131	0.1	10^6	10^6
Cs-132	0.01	10^4	10^4
Cs-134	0.01	10^4	10^4
Cs-134m	0.1	10^6	10^6
Cs-135	0.1	10^6	10^6
Cs-136	0.001	10^4	10^4
Cs-137+	0.01	10^4	10^4
Cs-138	0.001	10^4	10^4
Ba-131	0.1	10^6	10^6
Ba-140	0.1	10^6	10^6
La-140	0.001	10^4	10^4
Ce-139	0.1	10^6	10^6
Ce-141	0.1	10^6	10^6
Ce-143	0.01	10^4	10^4
Ce-144	0.1	10^6	10^6
Pr-142	0.1	10^6	10^6
Pr-143	10	10^8	10^8
Nd-147	0.01	10^4	10^4
Nd-149	0.01	10^4	10^4
Pm-147	10	10^8	10^8
Pm-149	1	10^7	10^7
Sm-151	102	10^9	10^9
Sm-153	0.1	10^6	10^6
Eu-152	0.01	10^4	10^4
Eu-152m	0.01	10^4	10^4
Eu-154	0.01	10^4	10^4
Eu-155	0.1	10^6	10^6
Gd-153	0.1	10^6	10^6
Gd-159	0.1	10^6	10^6
Tb-160	0.01	10^4	10^4
Dy-165	0.1	10^6	10^6
Dy-166	0.1	10^6	10^6
Ho-166	0.1	10^6	10^6
Er-169	10	10^8	10^8
Er-171	0.01	10^4	10^4
Tm-170	1	10^7	10^7
Tm-171	10	10^8	10^8
Yb-175	0.1	10^6	10^6
Lu-177	0.1	10^6	10^6

Radionuclide	*Concentration in Bq/litre*	*Maximum annual quantity of radionuclides to a relevant sewer (Bq/year)*	*Maximum annual quantity of radionuclides directly into a relevant river or the sea (Bq/year)*
Hf-181	0.01	10^4	10^4
Ta-182	0.001	10^4	10^4
W-181	0.1	10^6	10^6
W-185	1	10^7	10^7
W-187	0.01	10^4	10^4
Re-186	1	10^7	10^7
Re-188	1	10^7	10^7
Os-185	0.01	10^4	10^4
Os-191	0.1	10^6	10^6
Os-191m	1	10^7	10^7
Os-193	0.1	10^6	10^6
Ir-190	0.001	10^4	10^4
Ir-192	0.01	10^4	10^4
Ir-194	0.1	10^6	10^6
Pt-191	0.01	10^4	10^4
Pt-193m	1	10^7	10^7
Pt-197	0.1	10^6	10^6
Pt-197m	0.1	10^6	10^6
Au-198	1	10^7	10^7
Au-199	1	10^7	10^7
Hg-197	1	10^7	10^7
Hg-197m	0.1	10^6	10^6
Hg-203	0.1	10^6	10^6
Tl-200	0.01	10^4	10^4
Tl-201	0.1	10^6	10^6
Tl-202	0.01	10^4	10^4
Tl-204	0.1	10^6	10^6
Pb-203	0.01	10^4	10^4
Pb-210	0.001	10^4	10^4
Pb-212	0.1	10^6	10^6
Bi-206	0.01	10^4	10^4
Bi-207	0.1	10^6	10^6
Bi-210	10	10^8	10^8
Bi-212	1	10^7	10^7
Po-203	0.001	10^4	10^4
Po-205	0.001	10^4	10^4
Po-207	0.001	10^4	10^4
Po-210	0.001	10^4	10^4
At-211	1	10^7	10^7
Ra-223	0.01	10^4	10^4
Ra-224+	0.01	10^4	10^4
Ra-225	0.01	10^4	10^4
Ra-226+	0.01	10^4	10^4

Radionuclide	*Concentration in Bq/litre*	*Maximum annual quantity of radionuclides to a relevant sewer (Bq/year)*	*Maximum annual quantity of radionuclides directly into a relevant river or the sea (Bq/year)*
Ra-227	1	10^7	10^7
Ra-228	0.01	10^4	10^4
Ac-227	0.1	10^6	10^6
Ac-228	0.001	10^4	10^4
Th-226	0.1	10^6	10^6
Th-227	0.01	10^4	10^4
Th-228	1	10^7	10^7
Th-229	0.01	10^4	10^4
Th-230	1	10^7	10^7
Th-231	0.1	10^6	10^6
Th-232	1	10^6	10^7
Th-234	0.1	10^6	10^6
Pa-230	0.01	10^4	10^4
Pa-231	0.01	10^4	10^4
Pa-233	0.1	10^6	10^6
U-230	0.1	10^6	10^6
U-231	10	10^8	10^8
U-232	0.1	10^6	10^6
U-233	0.1	10^6	10^6
U-234	0.1	10^6	10^6
U-235+	0.1	10^6	10^6
U-236	0.1	10^6	10^6
U-237	10	10^8	10^8
U-238+	0.1	10^6	10^6
U-239	10	10^8	10^8
U-240	10	10^8	10^8
Np-237	0.1	10^6	10^6
Np-239	1	10^7	10^7
Np-240	0.1	10^6	10^6
Pu-234	0.01	10^4	10^4
Pu-235	0.01	10^4	10^4
Pu-236	1	10^7	10^7
Pu-237	0.1	10^6	10^6
Pu-238	0.1	10^6	10^6
Pu-239	0.1	10^6	10^6
Pu-240	0.1	10^6	10^6
Pu-241	10	10^8	10^8
Pu-242	0.1	10^6	10^6
Pu-243	0.1	10^6	10^6
Pu-244	0.1	10^6	10^6
Am-241	0.1	10^6	10^6
Am-242	0.1	10^6	10^6
Am-242m	0.1	10^6	10^6

Radionuclide	*Concentration in Bq/litre*	*Maximum annual quantity of radionuclides to a relevant sewer (Bq/year)*	*Maximum annual quantity of radionuclides directly into a relevant river or the sea (Bq/ year)*
Am-243	0.1	10^6	10^6
Cm-242	1	10^7	10^7
Cm-243	0.1	10^6	10^6
Cm-244	0.1	10^6	10^6
Cm-245	0.01	10^4	10^4
Cm-246	0.1	10^6	10^6
Cm-247	0.01	10^4	10^4
Cm-248	0.1	10^6	10^6
Bk-249	102	10^9	10^9
Cf-246	1	10^7	10^7
Cf-248	1	10^7	10^7
Cf-249	0.01	10^4	10^4
Cf-250	0.1	10^6	10^6
Cf-251	0.01	10^4	10^4
Cf-252	0.1	10^6	10^6
Cf-253	10	10^8	10^8
Cf-254	0.0001	10^3	10^3
Es-253	1	10^7	10^7
Es-254	0.1	10^6	10^6
Es-254m	0.01	10^4	10^4
Fm-254	1	10^7	10^7
Fm-255	0.1	10^6	10^6
	0.0001	10^3	10^3
Any other radionuclide that is not of natural terrestrial or cosmic origin	or that concentration which gives rise to a dose to a member of the public of 10 microsieverts per year calculated in accordance with the methodology used to calculate other concentrations in this table.	or that quantity which corresponds to $3000m^3$ of aqueous radioactive waste up to the appropriate concentration as calculated in accordance with column 2.	or that quantity which corresponds to $10000m^3$ of aqueous radioactive waste up to the appropriate concentration as calculated in accordance with column 2.

31

The summation rule in respect of column 2 of Table 7 is the sum of the quotients A/B where—

(a) "A" means the concentration in Bq/ litre of each radionuclide listed in column 1 of Table 7 that is present in aqueous waste which is not described in a row in column 1 of Table 6; and

(b) "B" means the concentration of that radionuclide specified in column 2 of Table 7.

32

The summation rule in respect of column 3 of Table 7 is the sum of the quotients C/D where—

(a) "C" means the quantity in Bq of each radionuclide listed in column 1 of Table 7 that is present in the aqueous waste which is not described in a row in column 1 of Table 6 which is disposed of in the year; and

(b) "D" means the quantity of that radionuclide specified in column 3 of Table 7.

33

The summation rule in respect of column 4 of Table 7 is the sum of the quotients C/E where—

(a) "C" means the quantity in Bq of each radionuclide listed in column 1 of Table 7 that is present in the aqueous waste which is not described in a row in column 1 of Table 6 which is disposed of in the year; and

(b) "E" means the quantity of that radionuclide specified in column 4 of Table 7.

Amendment

1 Substituted by the Environmental Permitting (England and Wales) (Amendment) Regulations 2011, SI 2011/2043, regs 3, 15, Sch 1.

[34 Interpretation of this section

In this section, where any radionuclide carries the suffix "+" or "sec"—

(a) that radionuclide represents the parent radionuclide in secular equilibrium with the corresponding daughter radionuclides which are identified in column 2 of Table 8 adjacent to that parent radionuclide; and

(b) a concentration or activity value given in respect of such a parent radionuclide is the value for the parent radionuclide alone, but already takes into account the daughter radionuclides in column 2 that are present.][1]

Amendment

1 Substituted by the Environmental Permitting (England and Wales) (Amendment) Regulations 2011, SI 2011/2043, regs 3, 15, Sch 1.

[Table 8][1]

[35

The Table 8 referred to in paragraph 34 is—

Table 8
Radionuclides in secular equilibrium

Parent radionuclide	*Daughter radionuclides*
Sr-90+	Y-90
Zr-93+	Nb-93m
Zr-95+	Nb-95
Zr-97+	Nb-97
Ru-106+	Rh-106
Ag-108m+	Ag-108
Cs-137+	Ba-137m
Ba-140+	La-140
Ce-144+	Pr-144
Pb-210+	Bi-210, Po-210
Pb-212+	Bi-212, Tl-208, Po-212
Bi-212+	Tl-208, Po-212

Parent radionuclide	*Daughter radionuclides*
Rn-220+	Po-216
Rn-222+	Po-218, Pb-214, Bi-214, Po-214
Ra-223+	Rn-219, Po-215, Pb-211, Bi-211, Tl-207
Ra-224+	Where Ra-224+ is referred to in Table 5: Rn-220, Po-216, Pb-212, Bi-212, Tl-208, Po-212
	Where Ra-224+ is referred to in Table 7: Pb-212
Ra-226+	Where Ra-226+ is referred to in Table 5: Rn-222, Po-218, Pb-214, Bi-214, Pb-210, Bi-210, Po-210, Po-214
	Where Ra-226+ is referred to in Table 7: Rn-222, Po-218, Pb-214, Bi-214, Po-214
Ra-228+	Ac-228
Th-226+	Ra-222, Rn-218, Po-214
Th-228+	Ra-224, Rn-220, Po-216, Pb-212, Bi-212, Po-212, Tl-208
Th-229+	Ra-225, Ac-225, Fr-221, At-217, Bi-213, Po-213, Pb-209
Th-232 sec	Ra-228, Ac-228, Th-228, Ra-224, Rn-220, Po-216, Pb-212, Bi-212, Po-212, Tl-208
Th-234+	Pa-234m
U-230+	Th-226, Ra-222, Rn-218, Po-214
U-232+	Th-228, Ra-224, Rn-220, Po-216, Pb-212, Bi-212, Tl-208, Po-212
U-235+	Th-231
U-238+	Th-234, Pa-234m, Pa-234
U-238 sec	Th-234, Pa-234m, U-234, Th-230, Ra-226, Rn-222, Po-218, Pb-214, Bi-214, Pb-210, Bi-210, Po-210, Po-214
U-240+	Np-240
Np-237+	Pa-233
Am-242m+	Am-242
Am-243+	Np-239][1]

Amendment

1 Substituted by the Environmental Permitting (England and Wales) (Amendment) Regulations 2011, SI 2011/2043, regs 3, 15, Sch 1.

[PART 8
RADIOACTIVITY TO BE DISREGARDED

Section 1
Provisions

Interpretation][1]

[1

(1) For the purposes of the matters referred to in sub-paragraph (2), no account is to be taken of any radioactivity possessed by a substance or article or by a part of any premises.

(2) The matters are—

(a) the operation of a provision to which this Part applies;

(b) the exercise of a power conferred by, or for the enforcement of, a provision to which this Part applies; and

(c) the performance of a duty imposed by, or for the enforcement of, a provision to which this Part applies.

2

(1) This Part applies to a provision—
(a) specified in paragraph 3;
(b) contained in an instrument made under a provision so specified;
(c) which has effect by virtue of a provision so specified; or
(d) which extends or applies a provision so specified.

(2) This Part also applies to a provision of a local enactment (whenever passed or made and however expressed) in so far as it—
(a) prohibits or restricts—
(i) the disposal or accumulation of waste;
(ii) the disposal or accumulation of a substance which is or causes a nuisance; or
(iii) a disposal or accumulation which causes pollution; or
(b) confers a power, or imposes a duty, on a public authority or an officer of a public authority to take action to prevent, restrict or abate a disposal or accumulation of a description given in paragraph (a).

(3) In sub-paragraph (2)—
(a) a reference to "disposal" in relation to a provision to which this Part applies, means—
(i) the discharge or deposit of a substance; or
(ii) the allowing of a substance to escape or to enter a stream or other place,
as may be mentioned in that provision; and
(b) "local enactment" means—
(i) a local or private Act;
(ii) an order confirmed by Parliament or brought into operation in accordance with special parliamentary procedure; or
(iii) an order confirmed by the National Assembly for Wales or brought into operation in accordance with special procedure in the Assembly.][1]

Amendment

1 Substituted by the Environmental Permitting (England and Wales) (Amendment) Regulations 2011, SI 2011/2043, regs 3, 15, Sch 1.

[Provisions of enactments][1]

[3

(1) The provisions referred to in paragraph 2(1) are those listed in table 9 below.

(2) References to provisions of the Water Resources Act 1991 have effect subject to the power conferred by section 98 of that Act.

Table 9
Statutory provisions in respect of which radioactivity is to be disregarded

Act	*Provisions*
Public Health Act 1936 (c. 49)	Sections 48, 79, 81, 82, 141, 259 and 261.
Water Act 1945 (c. 42)	Section 18 so far as it continues to have effect by virtue of Schedule 2 to the Water Consolidation (Consequential Provisions) Act 1991 or by virtue of provisions of the Control of Pollution Act 1974 not having been brought into force.
Salmon and Freshwater Fisheries Act 1975 (c. 51)	Section 4.
Building Act 1984 (c. 55)	Section 59.

Act	*Provisions*
The Planning (Hazardous Substances) Act 1990 (c. 10)	The whole Act.
Environmental Protection Act 1990 (c. 43)	Part III (subject to regulation 47(3) of the Waste (England and Wales) Regulations 2011).
Water Industry Act 1991 (c. 56)	Sections 72, 111, and 113(6); In Part IV, Chapter III; In Schedule 8, paragraphs 2 to 4 so far as they re-enact provisions of sections 43 and 44 of the Control of Pollution Act 1974.
Water Resources Act 1991 (c. 57)	Sections 82, 84, 92, 93, 161–161D, 190, 202, and 203; In Schedule 25, paragraph 6.
Clean Air Act 1993 (c. 11)	Section 16.
Marine and Coastal Access Act 2009 (c. 23)	Section 155.][1]

Amendment

1 Substituted by the Environmental Permitting (England and Wales) (Amendment) Regulations 2011, SI 2011/2043, regs 3, 15, Sch 1.

SCHEDULE 24
PUBLIC REGISTERS

Regulation 46(1)

1 Matters to be included in a public register

(1) A public register must contain a copy of—

(a) every application for—
   (i) the grant of an environmental permit,
   (ii) the variation of an environmental permit,
   (iii) the transfer of an environmental permit in whole or in part, or
   (iv) the surrender of an environmental permit in whole or in part;

(b) every notice requesting further information under paragraph 4(1) of Part 1 of Schedule 5;

(c) all representations made in respect of an application for the grant or variation of an environmental permit;

(d) every environmental permit, variation, transfer in whole or in part, or surrender in whole or in part granted or made by the regulator;

(e) every determination or decision notified under paragraph 17(2)(a) of Part 1 of Schedule 5;

(f) every prohibition notice, enforcement notice, revocation notice, suspension notice, landfill closure notice, mining waste facility closure notice or notice withdrawing such a notice served by the regulator;

(g) in relation to an appeal to an appropriate authority, every—
   (i) notice of appeal,
   (ii) document relating to the appeal,
   (iii) representation made in respect of the appeal, and
   (iv) determination of the authority, including any report accompanying that determination;

(h) all information obtained by the regulator—
   (i) as a result of its own monitoring,
   (ii) as a result of monitoring required under an environmental permit condition, or
   (iii) under regulation 60 in relation to monitoring;

(i) all other information given to the regulator in compliance with—
   (i) an environmental permit condition,
   (ii) an enforcement notice,
   (iii) a suspension notice,
   (iv) a landfill closure notice,
   (v) a mining waste facility closure notice, or
   (vi) regulation 60;
(j) every report published by the regulator relating to an assessment of the environmental consequences of the operation of an installation;
(k) every direction given to the regulator or the exemption registration authority by an appropriate authority under these Regulations, other than a direction given under regulation 47 or paragraph 9 of Schedule 2.

(2) A public register must also contain—
(a) details of any conviction or formal caution for an offence under regulation 38 in respect of an environmental permit granted by the regulator or a failure to apply to the regulator for the grant of an environmental permit;
(b) an inventory of closed mining waste facilities as required under Article 20 of the Mining Waste Directive;
(c) a list identifying all waste incineration installations—
   (i) which have a capacity of less than 2 tonnes per hour, and
   (ii) whose operation is authorised by an environmental permit containing conditions which give effect to the Waste Incineration Directive; and
(d) details of—
   (i) all fees and charges paid to a regulator within the meaning of regulation 65 pursuant to a scheme under that regulation, and
   (ii) the total expenditure of that regulator in exercising its functions under these Regulations.

(3) The regulator may omit any representation referred to in sub-paragraph (1) from its public register at the request of the person making the representation, but the regulator must then include in the public register a statement that a representation was made and was the subject of such a request.

(4) The regulator may omit from its public register any representation which substantially duplicates a representation already included in the public register, but the regulator must then include on the register a statement of the number of representations that have been omitted on this basis.

(5) If the regulator omits from its public register information referred to in sub-paragraph (1)(h) on the grounds that it is commercially or industrially confidential, the regulator must include in the public register a statement indicating whether or not there has been compliance with any environmental permit condition related to that information and requiring compliance with emission limit values.

(6) In this paragraph, "waste incineration installation" has the meaning given in Schedule 13.

2 Information no longer relevant for public participation

A regulator is not required to keep in its public register information which is no longer relevant for the purposes of public participation required under these Regulations.

3 Formal cautions

A regulator must remove details of any formal caution from its public register 5 years after the caution was given.

SCHEDULE 25
WASTE AND EXTRACTIVE WASTE

Regulation 68

PART 1
INTERPRETATION

1 Interpretation: general

(1) In this Schedule—

. . .[1]

["collection" has the same meaning as in Article 3(10) of the Waste Framework Directive;][2]

"collection point" means a place which is used for the collection of waste by an establishment or undertaking where the establishment or undertaking does not—

(a) receive payment for collecting the waste, or

(b) collect waste as its main business activity;

. . .[1]

"place of production" means, in relation to any waste, the place where the waste was originally produced;

. . .[1]

(2) For the purposes of this Schedule, a container, lagoon or other place is secure in relation to waste kept in it if—

(a) all reasonable precautions are taken to ensure that the waste cannot escape from it; and

(b) members of the public are unable to gain access to the waste.

Amendments

1 Repealed by the Waste (England and Wales) Regulations 2011, SI 2011/988, reg 48(2), Sch 3, paras 1, 14(a).

2 Substituted by the Waste (England and Wales) Regulations 2011, SI 2011/988, reg 48(2), Sch 3, paras 1, 14(b).

[Schedule 25, para 2 was repealed by the Waste (England and Wales) Regulations 2011, SI 2011/988, reg 48(2), Sch 3, paras 1, 14(c).]

[Schedule 25, Pt 2 was repealed by the Waste (England and Wales) Regulations 2011, SI 2011/988, reg 48(2), Sch 3, paras 1, 14(c).]

PART 3
OPERATIONS TO WHICH SECTION 33(1)(A) OF THE 1990 ACT DOES NOT APPLY: DESCRIPTIONS AND CONDITIONS

1 General

(1) The descriptions in this Part are set out in the first sub-paragraph of each paragraph.

(2) The conditions for an operation of each description are set out in the second sub-paragraph of each paragraph.

2 Temporary storage at the place of production

(1) The temporary storage of any waste at the place of production, pending its collection.

(2) For the purposes of this paragraph, the conditions are—

(a) no waste is stored for longer than 12 months; and

(b) the waste is stored in a secure place.

3 Temporary storage of waste at a place controlled by the producer

(1) The temporary storage of any waste, pending its collection, at a place controlled by the producer of the waste.

(2) For the purposes of this paragraph, the conditions are—
(a) the producer has control over the waste and the storage place;
(b) the waste does not contain or consist of—
  (i) unbonded asbestos, or
  (ii) any substance with a flash point of less than 21 degrees Celsius;
(c) the operation is not carried on in the course of providing a waste management service to another person;
(d) the waste is stored in a secure place;
(e) where more than one type of waste is stored, the types are not mixed;
(f) no waste is stored for longer than 3 months;
(g) in relation to non-liquid waste, the total quantity stored at any one time does not exceed 50 cubic metres; and
(h) in relation to liquid waste—
  (i) the total quantity stored at any one time does not exceed 1,000 litres,
  (ii) the waste is stored in a container with secondary containment.

4 Temporary storage at a collection point

(1) The temporary storage of waste at a collection point for the purposes of recovering or disposing of the waste elsewhere.

(2) For the purposes of this paragraph, the conditions are that—
(a) the waste does not contain or consist of—
  (i) asbestos,
  (ii) any substance with a flash point of less than 21 degrees Celsius;
(b) the waste is stored in a secure container;
(c) where more than one type of waste is stored, the types are not mixed;
(d) in relation to WEEE, the total quantity of waste stored at any one time does not exceed 30 cubic metres;
(e) in relation to non-hazardous waste that—
  (i) is not WEEE, and
  (ii) is to be recovered elsewhere,
  the total quantity of waste stored any one time does not exceed 50 cubic metres; and
(f) in relation to waste not covered by paragraph (d) or (e), the total quantity of waste stored at any one time does not exceed 5 cubic metres.

[*Schedules 26 to 28 is not reproduced.*]

CRC ENERGY EFFICIENCY SCHEME ORDER 2010

SI 2010/768

PART 1
INTRODUCTION

Chapter 1
General

1 Citation and commencement

This Order may be cited as the CRC Energy Efficiency Scheme Order 2010 and comes into force on the fifth day after it is made.

2 The trading scheme: phases and application

[(1) This Order establishes a trading scheme in relation to scheme activities for a trading period of seven phases which comprise—

(a) a first phase of four years commencing on 1st April 2010;

(b) five subsequent phases of six years commencing as shown in the following table—

Second to seventh phases: commencement dates

	Commencement date of phase
Second phase	1st April 2013
Third phase	1st April 2018
Fourth phase	1st April 2023
Fifth phase	1st April 2028
Sixth phase	1st April 2033

(c) a seventh phase of five years commencing on 1st April 2038.][1]

(2) This Order does not apply to an organisation which enjoys an exemption or relief from taxes under Schedule 1 to the International Organisations Act 1968.

Amendment

1 Substituted by the CRC Energy Efficiency Scheme (Amendment) Order 2011, SI 2011/234, art 2.

3 Interpretation

In this Order—

"the 2000 Act" means the Freedom of Information Act 2000;

"account holder" means the public body, undertaking or other person in whose name an account in the Registry is held;

"achievement table" has the meaning given by article 75(3);

"the Act" means the Climate Change Act 2008;

"the administrator" has the meaning given by article 9;

"allowance" means a tradeable allowance issued under regulations made by the Treasury under section 21 of the Finance Act 2008;

"annual report" means the report described in article 49;

["annual reporting year" means each year of a phase;][1]

"applicant" means—

(a) a public body or group of public bodies; or

(b) an undertaking or group of undertakings,

required to submit an application for registration as a participant under Part 2 or Schedule 6;

"authorised supplier" means—

(a) in respect of electricity, a person who is licensed to supply electricity (or is exempt from requiring a licence to do so) as defined by—
  (i) section 64(1) of the Electricity Act 1989; or
  (ii) Article 8(1)(c) of the Electricity (Northern Ireland) Order 1992;

(b) in respect of gas, a person who is licensed to supply gas (or is exempt from requiring a licence to do so) as defined by—
  (i) section 48(1) of the Gas Act 1986; or
  (ii) Article 6(1)(c) of the Gas (Northern Ireland) Order 1996;

"blocking" has the meaning given by article 105(3);

"cancellation account" means the account provided by the administrator into which allowances must be surrendered by a participant in compliance with article 53;

"CCA" means a climate change agreement within the meaning given in paragraph 46 of Schedule 6 to the Finance Act 2000;

"CCA emissions" has the meanings given by paragraph 12(3) of Schedule 5;

"CCA facility" means a facility which is subject to a CCA target;

"CCA target" means a target in respect of energy use or carbon emissions under a CCA;

"CCA target period" means a period referred to as a target period in a CCA or in any rules applicable to a CCA in which a CCA target is to be achieved;

"charitable purpose" has the meaning given by—

(a) section 2 of the Charities Act 2006 in relation to England and Wales;
(b) section 7(2) of the Charities and Trustee Investment (Scotland) Act 2005 in relation to Scotland;
(c) section 2 of the Charities Act (Northern Ireland) 2008 in relation to Northern Ireland;

"charge" and "charging" have the meanings given in Part 11;

"Chief inspector" means the Chief inspector constituted under regulation 8(3) of the Pollution Prevention and Control Regulations (Northern Ireland) 2003;

"civil penalty" means a penalty which may be imposed under Part 14;

"Community tradeable emissions allowances" has the meaning given by Article 3a of the EU ETS Directive;

"compliance account" means the account of a participant from which allowances must be surrendered to the cancellation account in compliance with article 53;

"core emissions" has the meaning given by article 42(3);

"core supply" means a supply of electricity or gas described in Schedule 2;

"CRC" means carbon reduction commitment;

"CRC emissions" has the meaning given by article 50(1);

"CRC supplies" has the meaning given by article 50(2);

"day" means a working day unless provided to the contrary;

"daily meter" applies in relation to a supply of gas and has the meaning given by paragraph 7 of Schedule 2;

"domestic accommodation" has the meaning given by paragraph 16(3) of Schedule 1;

"dynamic supply" means a supply of electricity described in paragraph 5 of Schedule 2;

"early action" has the meaning given by paragraph 5(2) of Schedule 8;

"electricity generating credit" has the meaning given by article 31(2) but where it applies other than in Part 3, reference to "applicant" in that expression is to be read as a reference to "participant";

"enforcement notice" has the meaning given by article 91;

"EU ETS Directive" means Directive 2003/87/EC of the European Parliament and of the Council establishing a scheme for greenhouse gas emission allowance trading within the Community and amending Council Directive 96/61/EC, as amended from time to time;

"EU ETS emissions" has the meanings given by paragraph 12(2) of Schedule 5;

"EU ETS installation" means—

(a) an activity or installation within scope of the EU ETS Directive; and

(b) any additional activity not included within Annex I of that Directive but approved in the United Kingdom under Article 24,

but not an installation approved as excluded in the United Kingdom under Article 27;

"exemption CCA target period" has the meaning given by article 29;

"footprint emissions" has the meaning given by article 41;

"footprint report" has the meaning given by article 39(1)(a);

["footprint supplies" has the meaning given by article 41(5);][2]

"footprint year" means the first year of each phase;

"franchise" and the related expressions, "franchise agreement", "franchise premises", "franchisee" and "franchisor" have the meanings given in section 3 of Schedule 1;

"fuel" has the meaning given by paragraph 3(3) of Schedule 1;

"general CCA exemption" has the meaning given by article 33;

"generated and supplied electricity" has the meaning given by article 31(1)(d);

"government decision" has the meaning given by paragraph 14 of Schedule 3;

"group" has the meaning given by—

(a) paragraph 6 of Schedule 3, in respect of public bodies;

(b) paragraph 1 of Schedule 4, in respect of undertakings;

"group CCA exemption" has the meaning given by article 34;

"group undertaking" has the meaning given by paragraph 1 of Schedule 4;

"highest parent undertaking" has the meaning given by paragraph 1 of Schedule 4;

"hourly meter" applies in relation to a supply of gas and has the meaning given by paragraph 8(1) of Schedule 2;

"independent college group" has the meaning given by article 21(1)(b)(ii);

"kWh" means kilowatt hour or hours;

"local authority decision" has the meaning given by paragraph 16 of Schedule 3;

"member CCA exemption" has the meaning given by article 32;

"MWh" means megawatt hour or hours;

"non-settled half hourly meter" applies in relation to a supply of electricity and has the meaning given by paragraph 3(1) of Schedule 2;

"participant" means the following registered by the administrator as a participant—

(a) a public body or group of public bodies; or

(b) an undertaking or group of undertakings,

which carries out a scheme activity; and where a participant is a group, subject to Schedule 6, the participant constitutes the members from time to time of that group;

"performance table" has the meaning given by article 77(1);

"phase" means one of the seven phases of the scheme described in article 2(1);

"post-qualification period" has the meaning given by article 27;

"premises" means any—

(a) land, vehicle or vessel; or

(b) plant which is designed to move or be moved whether on roads or otherwise;

"principal place of activity" means the principal place in the United Kingdom—

(a) where the applicant or participant carries on the scheme activity applicable to it; or
(b) if an applicant or participant carries on more than one scheme activity, where it carries on the main scheme activity;

"publication" has the meaning given by article 105(3);
"public function" means any activity carried out by a public body;
"public body" has the meaning given in section 1 of Schedule 3;
"qualification day" means the last day of a qualification year;
"qualification criteria" means that—
(a) an applicant is supplied with electricity by a settled half hourly meter;
(b) qualifying electricity is supplied to it for the purposes of a scheme activity; and
(c) the amount of that qualifying electricity satisfies the qualifying amount;

"qualification year" means—
(a) in respect of the first phase, the 2008 calendar year;
(b) in respect of the second and subsequent phases, the year immediately before the beginning of the phase;

"qualifying amount" means 6000 MWh or more;
"qualifying electricity" means electricity supplied to a public body or undertaking in accordance with sections 1 to 5 of Schedule 1—
(a) measured by a meter described in paragraph 1 of Schedule 2 except a non-domestic meter; or
(b) which is a dynamic supply;

"the Registry" has the meaning given by article 68;
"relative change" has the meaning given by paragraph 2 of Schedule 8;
"renewables generation" has the meaning given by paragraph 28 of Schedule 1;
"residual measurement list" has the meaning given by article 44(4);
"residual supplies" has the meaning given by article 44(5);
"ROC" means a renewables obligation certificate issued further to an order made under—
(a) sections 32 to 32M of the Electricity Act 1989; or
(b) Articles 52 to 55F of the Energy (Northern Ireland) Order 2003;

"scheme" means the trading scheme established by this Order;
"scheme activity" means to carry on a business or a public function or an activity which has a charitable purpose;
"settled half hourly meter" applies in relation to a supply of electricity and has the meaning given by paragraph 2(1) of Schedule 2;
"significant group undertaking" has the meaning given by paragraphs 2 and 4 of Schedule 4;
"tCO_2" means tonne or tonnes of carbon dioxide;
"third party" means a person, other than a participant, for whom the administrator has opened an account in the Registry;
"total emissions" has the meaning given by article 30;
"transport consumption" has the meaning given by paragraph 19 of Schedule 1;
"turnover" means—
(a) where a participant is an undertaking or group of undertakings, its turnover as defined in section 474(1) of the Companies Act 2006 as if that section—
(i) applied to undertakings as defined in this Order; but
(ii) did not apply to turnover arising outside the United Kingdom;

or
(b) where a participant is a public body or group of public bodies, the revenue expenditure of the participant;

"undertaking" has the meaning given in paragraph 1 of Schedule 4;
"unit of turnover" means turnover expressed in pounds sterling rounded up to the nearest pound;
"vessel" means, except under paragraph 22 of Schedule 1, any boat or ship;
"working day" means 9 am to 5 pm on Mondays to Fridays excluding—
- (a) bank holidays within the meaning of section 1 of the Banking and Financial Dealings Act 1971, including those bank holidays in part only of the United Kingdom;
- (b) Good Friday; and
- (c) when it falls on a day that would otherwise be a working day, Christmas Day;

"year" means (except for the qualification year in respect of the first phase) 1st April to the following 31st March, inclusive of those dates.

Amendments

1 Substituted by the CRC Energy Efficiency Scheme (Amendment) Order 2011, SI 2011/234, art 3(1), (2).
2 Inserted by the CRC Energy Efficiency Scheme (Amendment) Order 2011, SI 2011/234, art 3(1), (3).

4 Supplies and emissions

As provided under this Order, Schedule 1 (supplies and emissions) has effect concerning—
- (a) whether a supply is made of electricity, gas or fuel;
- (b) the amount of such a supply; and
- (c) the emissions from such a supply.

5 Registration and requirements of participants and others

(1) Part 2 provides for registration as a participant for a phase of the scheme.

(2) Part 3 provides for exemptions from certain requirements of this Order.

(3) Subject to any exemption, in respect of a phase a participant must comply with—
- (a) Part 4 to provide a footprint report and to compile a residual measurement list;
- (b) Part 5 to provide annual reports on CRC supplies;
- (c) Part 6 to surrender allowances equal to the participant's CRC emissions;
- (d) Part 7 to keep and audit records relating to the requirements of Parts 2 to 6.

(4) The following have effect in respect of Parts 2 to 7—
- (a) Schedule 2 (core supplies);
- (b) Schedule 3 (public bodies);
- (c) Schedule 4 (undertakings and significant group undertakings);
- (d) Schedule 5 (information);
- (e) Schedule 6 (changes to participants).

(5) Part 8 provides for persons to provide information and assistance to participants and the administrator.

6 Powers and duties of the administrator

The administrator has the powers and duties set out under the following Parts of this Order—
- (a) Part 9 to administer the scheme;
- (b) Part 10 to compile and publish achievement and performance tables;
- (c) Part 11 to impose charges;
- (d) Part 12 to monitor compliance;
- (e) Part 13 to enforce failures to comply with this Order.

7 Penalties, offences and appeals

(1) A participant which fails to comply with this Order may be liable under—
(a) Part 14 to a civil penalty;
(b) Part 15 to a criminal penalty.

(2) Part 16 provides for appeals.

8 Groups: liability to comply with this Order

(1) Paragraph (2) applies where an applicant or a participant is—
(a) a group of undertakings; or
(b) an independent college group.

(2) Each member of a group described in paragraph (1)—
(a) is jointly and severally liable to comply with requirements placed on the group under Parts 2 to 14;
(b) may be liable to a criminal penalty under Part 15.

(3) For a group of public bodies (except an independent college group)—
(a) the body listed in article 73(4) which is a member of that group is liable to comply with Part 2 and not any other member of the group;
(b) the body in whose name the compliance account is set up is liable to comply with requirements placed on the group under Parts 4 to 14 and not any other member of the group;
(c) subject to article 110, any member of that group may be liable to a criminal penalty under Part 15.

Chapter 2
The administrator and co-operation

9 The administrator

(1) Reference to "the administrator" in the provisions which appear in—
(a) column 1 of the following table, means the Environment Agency;
(b) column 2 of the following table, subject to paragraphs (2) and (3), means—
(i) the Environment Agency, in respect of England and Wales;
(ii) the Scottish Environment Protection Agency, in respect of Scotland;
(iii) the Chief inspector, in respect of Northern Ireland.

[Table of provisions

Column 1	*Column 2*
Part 2 except articles 18(1) and 28	Articles 18(1), 28, 39(3), 47(3), 57(4), 64 and 74
Parts 4 to 6 except articles 39(3) and 47(3)	Parts 11 to 16
Articles 59(2), 68 to 73	
Part 10][1]	

(2) Where the administrator is a participant, reference to "the administrator" in Parts 12 to 14 means, where the participant is—
(a) the Environment Agency, the Secretary of State;
(b) the Scottish Environment Protection Agency, the Scottish Ministers;
(c) the Chief inspector, the Department of the Environment.

(3) The administrator may exercise the powers in Parts 12 to 14 anywhere in the United Kingdom.

Amendment

1 Substituted by the CRC Energy Efficiency Scheme (Amendment) Order 2011, SI 2011/234, art 4.

10 Co-operation and provision of information

(1) The bodies constituting the administrator must—

(a) co-operate with each other; and

(b) provide each other with such of the information provided to or obtained by them under any of Parts 2 to 6, 8 to 10, 12 or 13 of this Order as they may require to enable them to carry out their duties as an administrator under this Order.

(2) The administrator must provide to a national authority such of the information described in paragraph (1)(b) as that authority may lawfully require in relation to compliance with and enforcement of this Order.

PART 2
REGISTRATION AS A PARTICIPANT

Chapter 1
General

11 Applications, information and charges

(1) A requirement to apply for registration as a participant means that an application for registration must—

(a) be made to the administrator and, unless otherwise agreed by the administrator, be made using the Registry; and

(b) include—

  (i) the information in section 1 of Schedule 5; and

  (ii) the charge for registration as a participant under article 81.

(2) When requested by the administrator, the applicant must provide such suitable and up to date evidence of identity as the administrator may require in respect of—

(a) the intended account holder of the compliance account; and

(b) the individuals who will access the compliance account.

(3) The administrator may require other information from applicants or any particular applicant in order to effect a registration.

(4) The requirements to apply for registration as a participant under this Part apply in respect of each phase.

12 Time for applications

An application for registration as a participant under this Part must be made in respect of—

(a) the first phase, on or before 30th September 2010;

(b) the second and subsequent phases, within 6 months of the beginning of the phase.

13 Registration and certificates

(1) Where the administrator is satisfied that an application has been duly made, it must—

(a) register the applicant as a participant;

(b) issue a certificate of registration to the participant, the certificate to be in such form as the administrator thinks fit.

(2) An applicant registered under paragraph (1) is a participant for the relevant phase, unless the administrator cancels that registration.

(3) The administrator must maintain an up to date list of participants.

Chapter 2
Public bodies

14 Government departments and the devolved administrations

(1) The following public bodies must apply for registration as a participant—
(a) a government department;
(b) the Scottish Ministers;
(c) the Welsh Assembly Government;
(d) a Northern Ireland Department;
(e) a public body in respect of which a local authority decision is made.

(2) Where a public body listed in paragraph (1) is a member of a group, paragraph (1) applies to that group.

(3) Paragraph (1) is not satisfied in respect of a body described in sub-paragraphs (a) to (d) where part only of that body is registered as a participant.

15 Other public bodies

(1) Paragraph (2) applies to a public body except a public body to which article 14 or chapter 3 applies.

(2) Except where a government decision provides to the contrary, for the purposes of articles 16 and 17, whether—
(a) a group exists or not; and
(b) whether a public body is or is not a member of a group,
are matters determined on the qualification day of the qualification year, whatever applied earlier in that year.

16 Public bodies: applications by groups

(1) Paragraph (2) applies to a group of public bodies except a group to which article 14(2) or chapter 3 applies.

(2) Where this paragraph applies, the group must apply for registration as a participant where during the qualification year for the phase or any part of that year, it meets the qualification criteria.

17 Public bodies: applications other than by groups

(1) Paragraph (2) applies to a public body which is not a member of a group and is not a body to which article 14(1) or chapter 3 applies.

(2) Where this paragraph applies, the public body must apply for registration as a participant in respect of a phase where during the qualification year for that phase or any part of that year, it meets the qualification criteria.

18 Determinations by the administrator

(1) Subject to [paragraph (2)][1], the administrator may determine whether or not a public body is a member of a group.

(2) Paragraph (1) does not apply to a public body or group to which any of the following apply—
(a) chapter 3;
(b) paragraph 7, 8 or 9 of section 2 of Schedule 3;
(c) a government decision or local authority decision.

Amendment
1 Substituted by the CRC Energy Efficiency Scheme (Amendment) Order 2011, SI 2011/234, art 5.

Chapter 3
Universities and colleges: England

19 Universities and colleges: England

(1) This chapter applies to governing bodies of a college of a university and a university—
(a) described in Part IV of Schedule 1 to the 2000 Act; and
(b) where the university is wholly or mainly situated in England.

(2) For the purposes of this chapter, whether a college is a college of a university is determined on the qualification day of the qualification year, whatever applied earlier in that year.

20 Qualifying electricity

(1) The governing bodies of colleges of a university and the university ("the university and colleges") are a group for the purposes of paragraph (2) whether or not those bodies have a legal identity separate from each other.

(2) Articles 21 and 22 apply where the university and colleges meet the qualification criteria.

(3) Where the university and colleges do not meet the qualification criteria, none of them are required to apply for registration as a participant in respect of a phase.

21 Universities and colleges: groups

(1) Where this article applies—
(a) the governing body of a college of the university which has a legal identity separate from the governing body of the university is "an independent college";
(b) for the purposes of article 22—
 (i) the university and colleges are a group but that group does not include an independent college unless the university and colleges and the independent college otherwise agree;
 (ii) an independent college which is not part of the group under [paragraph (1)(b)(i)][1] may agree with another such independent college to form a group ("an independent college group").

(2) Any agreement under [paragraph (1)(b)][1] must be made before the group makes an application for registration.

Amendment
1 Substituted by the CRC Energy Efficiency Scheme (Amendment) Order 2011, SI 2011/234, art 6.

22 Applications

(1) Where this article applies, the following which exist must apply for registration as separate participants in respect of a phase—
(a) the university and colleges;

(b) an independent college group;
(c) an independent college which is not a member of (a) or (b).

(2) The administrator must be notified with the application—
(a) by the university and colleges—
  (i) whether or not an independent college is a member of the group; and
  (ii) if not, the identity of the college;
(b) by an independent college or an independent college group, the identity of the university.

Chapter 4
Undertakings

23 Groups of undertakings

(1) This article applies to undertakings.

(2) For the purposes of articles 24 to 26—
(a) whether a group exists or not; and
(b) whether an undertaking is or is not a member of a group,
are matters determined on the qualification day of the qualification year, whatever applied earlier in that year.

(3) Subject to article 27, any change in the members of a group after the qualification day is to be ignored for the purposes of this Part.

24 Undertakings: applications by groups

(1) This article applies to a group of undertakings but is subject to article 27.

(2) The group must apply for registration as a participant in respect of a phase where during the qualification year for the phase or any part of that year, it meets the qualification criteria.

25 Undertakings: applications by significant group undertakings

(1) Paragraph (2) applies where a group ("A") includes a significant group undertaking ("B") and A—
(a) satisfies article 24(2) and would do so if it did not include B;
(b) is not subject to article 27; and
(c) complies with article 11 at least 3 months before the time required under article 12.

(2) Where this paragraph applies, A may in the application under article 11 request the administrator to register A and B as separate participants.

(3) Where such a request is made—
(a) the administrator must notify A and B as soon as possible whether or not it agrees to it; and
(b) if it does, B may make an application in accordance with article 11 if it does so by the time required under article 12.

(4) Where—
(a) the request is not agreed; or
(b) it is but B does not make an application or not in the time required,
the application by A under article 11 includes B as a member of A.

26 Undertakings: applications other than by groups

Subject to article 27, an undertaking must apply for registration as a participant in respect of a phase where—
(a) it is not a member of a group; and
(b) during the qualification year for that phase or any part of that year, it meets the qualification criteria.

27 Changes to undertakings and groups

(1) Paragraph (2) applies where—
(a) a requirement to register applies to a group or undertaking under article 24 or 26; and
(b) a change described in section 1 of Part 3 of Schedule 6 applies to that group or undertaking after the qualification day but before the group or undertaking makes an application for registration within the time provided under article 12 ("the post-qualification period").

(2) Where this paragraph applies—
(a) a group or undertaking to which article 24 or 26 would otherwise apply must instead register as a participant as provided by section 1 of Part 3 of Schedule 6; and
(b) other undertakings affected by such change must comply with that section.

28 Determinations by the administrator

The administrator may determine whether or not—
(a) an undertaking is a member of a group;
(b) article 27(2) applies to a group or an undertaking.

PART 3
EXEMPTIONS

29 CCA emissions and target periods

(1) In this Part—
(a) an applicant or, where an applicant is a group, a member of that applicant has CCA emissions where it operates a CCA facility;
(b) subject to article 36, "exemption CCA target period" means the CCA target period which ends in the qualification year for the phase.

(2) Where, in respect of the first phase, the exemption CCA target period ends at the end of 31st December 2008, that target period is deemed to end within the qualification year.

(3) [Articles 32 to 38 do][1] not apply to a public body to which article 14 applies.

Amendment

1 Substituted by the CRC Energy Efficiency Scheme (Amendment) Order 2011, SI 2011/234, art 7.

30 Total emissions

(1) "Total emissions" means—
(a) the sum of—
  (i) EU ETS emissions and CCA emissions as defined by one of the ways given in paragraph 12 of Schedule 5 as chosen by the applicant; and
  (ii) emissions calculated in accordance with paragraph 29 of Schedule 1 in respect of the amount of electricity, gas and fuel supplied to the applicant

calculated in accordance with sections 1 to 5 of Schedule 1 but excluding any supplies in respect of which emissions are included under paragraph (i);

and

(b) deducting any electricity generating credit of the applicant.

(2) In this Part, total emissions are calculated in respect of the exemption CCA target period.

31 Electricity generating credit

(1) In article 30, "electricity generating credit" applies where—

(a) an applicant generates electricity;

(b) the applicant is not issued with a ROC and is not in receipt of a financial incentive made by virtue of section 41 of the Energy Act 2008 in respect of that generation;

(c) the generation does not occur at a place described in paragraph (3); and

(d) the electricity generated is supplied to a public body or undertaking and that supply is a supply of electricity under paragraph 1 or 6 of Schedule 1, such electricity being "the generated and supplied electricity".

(2) Electricity generating credit is the amount of emissions calculated in accordance with paragraph 29 of Schedule 1 in respect of the generated and supplied electricity.

(3) The places referred to in paragraph (1) are—

(a) an EU ETS installation where electricity is generated;

(b) a nuclear power station;

(c) a hydro-generating station which was ineligible for a ROC.

(4) In paragraph (3), "hydro-generating station" has the meaning given by article 2(1) of the Renewables Obligation Order 2009 and as if that article applied to Scotland and Northern Ireland.

32 Member CCA exemptions

(1) Paragraph (2) applies where an applicant—

(a) consists of a group; and

(b) during the exemption CCA target period, a member of the group has CCA emissions which are more than 25% of the total emissions of that member.

(2) Where this paragraph applies and where the applicant complies with article 35 or 36, as a participant it has a member CCA exemption in respect of such a member.

33 General CCA exemptions

(1) Paragraph (2) applies where an applicant—

(a) does not consist of a group; and

(b) during the CCA target period, has CCA emissions which are more than 25% of its total emissions.

(2) Where this paragraph applies and where the applicant complies with article 35 or 36, as a participant it has a general CCA exemption.

34 Group CCA exemptions

(1) Paragraph (3) applies where—

(a) an applicant consists of a group; and

(b) X minus Y is less than 1000 MWh.

(2) In paragraph (1)—

"X" means the amount of qualifying electricity supplied to the applicant;

"Y" means—

(a) where a member of the group satisfies article 32(1)(b), the amount of X which is supplied to each member of the group which satisfies that article; or

(b) where no member of the group satisfies article 32(1)(b), zero.

(3) Where this paragraph applies and where the applicant complies with article 35 or 36, as a participant it has a group CCA exemption.

35 Requirements for exemptions to apply: general

Where an applicant intends that an exemption applies to it, the applicant must provide the following information with the application for registration under article 11—

(a) which exemption applies; and

(b) the information required under paragraph 7 of Schedule 5, as applicable to the exemption.

36 Requirements for exemption to apply: exception

(1) Paragraph (2) applies where—

(a) a participant does not comply with article 35; and

(b) an exemption applies to the participant under articles 32 to 34 if the exemption CCA target period means the CCA target period which ends in the footprint year.

(2) Where this paragraph applies and a participant intends that an exemption applies to it, the participant must provide the information in article 35(a) and (b) when it complies with article 39.

37 Effect of exemptions and records

(1) Subject to article 38—

(a) except where sub-paragraph (b) applies, as a participant, an applicant is exempt from Parts 4 to 7 of this Order for the phase where a general CCA exemption or a group CCA exemption applies to it;

(b) where a participant complies with article 36, the participant is exempt from Parts 5 to 7 of this Order for that phase where a general CCA exemption or a group CCA exemption applies to it.

(2) In respect of each year of the phase where the participant is exempt under paragraph (1), it must keep records of the information in paragraph 7 of Schedule 5.

38 Loss of exemptions and further exemptions

(1) Where—

(a) a participant has a member CCA exemption; and

(b) the member to which the exemption applies ceases to be a member of the participant,

the member CCA exemption does not apply for the subsequent years of the phase after the year in which sub-paragraph (b) applies.

(2) Where in a year of a phase, the member of a participant to which a member CCA exemption applies does not have energy use or carbon emissions subject to a CCA target, the member CCA exemption does not apply—

(a) in the next year of the phase; and

(b) any subsequent year where the member does not have energy use or carbon emissions subject to a CCA target.

(3) Where in a year of a phase, a participant which has a general CCA exemption does not have energy use or carbon emissions subject to a CCA target, the general CCA exemption does not apply—
(a) in the next year of the phase; and
(b) any subsequent year where the participant does not have energy use or carbon emissions subject to a CCA target.

(4) Where in a year of a phase, a participant has a group CCA exemption and—
(a) paragraph (1) or (2) applies;
(b) the calculation in article 34(1) is made excluding the members to which a member CCA exemption is not to apply by reason of those paragraphs; and
(c) by that calculation, a group CCA exemption would not apply,
the group CCA exemption does not apply in the next year of the phase and any subsequent year where by such a calculation, a group CCA exemption would not apply.

(5) Where an exemption does not apply as provided under this article, the participant must notify the administrator of that fact when it provides, as applicable, the footprint report or the annual report.

(6) Where article 46 or 51 applies, further exemptions apply under section 2 of Part 3 of Schedule 6.

PART 4
FOOTPRINT REPORTS AND RESIDUAL MEASUREMENT LISTS

39 Provision of footprint reports

(1) Subject to articles 37 and 40, a participant must—
(a) provide to the administrator the information in section 2 of Schedule 5 ("a footprint report"); and
(b) unless otherwise agreed by the administrator, provide the footprint report using the Registry.

(2) A participant must comply with paragraph (1) by no later than the last working day of July after the end of the footprint year.

(3) Where by 40 days after the due date, a participant has failed to provide a footprint report, the administrator may determine the footprint report.

40 Member CCA exemptions

Where a participant has a member CCA exemption—
(a) the provision of information on supplies and emissions in the footprint report; and
(b) reference to supplies or emissions of the participant under the following articles in this Part,
excludes any supplies or emissions of a member of the group to which a member CCA exemption applies.

41 Footprint emissions

(1) "Footprint emissions" means the emissions listed in paragraph (2) during the footprint year but deducting any electricity generating credit of the participant during that year.

(2) The emissions referred to in paragraph (1) are—
(a) EU ETS emissions;
(b) CCA emissions;
(c) emissions calculated in accordance with paragraph 29 of Schedule 1 from footprint supplies.

(3) The lowest value of footprint emissions is zero.

(4) In paragraph (2), EU ETS emissions and CCA emissions are such emissions as defined by one of the ways given in paragraph 12 of Schedule 5 as chosen by the participant.

(5) In paragraph (2)(c), "footprint supplies" means—
(a) the amount of electricity, gas and fuel supplied to the participant calculated in accordance with sections 1 to 6 of Schedule 1; but
(b) excluding—
(i) supplies of gas and fuel made to an EU ETS installation; [and][1]
(ii) supplies of electricity, gas and fuel made to a CCA facility to which a member CCA exemption does not apply.

Amendment

1 Substituted by the CRC Energy Efficiency Scheme (Amendment) Order 2011, SI 2011/234, art 8.

42 Requirement for residual measurement lists

(1) Subject to article 37, a participant must compile a residual measurement list where the percentage which its emissions described in paragraph (2) bear to footprint emissions is less than the residual percentage.

(2) The emissions referred to in paragraph (1) are—
(a) core emissions;
(b) EU ETS emissions; and
(c) CCA emissions.

(3) In paragraph (2), "core emissions" means—
(a) emissions calculated in accordance with paragraph 29 of Schedule 1 in respect of core supplies less the deductions from those supplies under sections 4 and 5 of Schedule 1; but
(b) excluding—
(i) core supplies of gas made to an EU ETS installation; or
(ii) core supplies of electricity and gas made to a CCA facility to which a member CCA exemption does not apply.

43 Residual percentage

(1) Subject to paragraph (3), "the residual percentage" referred to in article 42(1) is 90%.

(2) Paragraph (3) applies—
(a) to the second and subsequent phases; and
(b) where a participant compiled a residual measurement list for the immediately previous phase.

(3) Where this paragraph applies, "the residual percentage" referred to in paragraph (1) is the higher of—
(a) 90%; or
(b) where it applies, the percentage which the sum of emissions described in paragraph (4) bears to footprint emissions.

(4) The emissions referred to in paragraph (3) are—
(a) the emissions from residual supplies in the residual measurement list in the penultimate year of the previous phase; and
(b) the emissions described in article 42(2) in the footprint year.

44 Content of residual measurement lists

(1) Paragraph (2) applies where a participant is required to compile a residual measurement list under article 42.

(2) Where this paragraph applies, a participant must compile a list of residual supplies such that the percentage which—
(a) the emissions from those supplies; and
(b) the emissions described in article 42(2),
bear to footprint emissions is at least equal to the residual percentage referred to in article 43.

(3) A participant may—
(a) include in its list of residual supplies more residual supplies than required under paragraph (2);
(b) compile a list of residual supplies although it is not required to do so under article 42.

(4) The list of residual supplies compiled under—
(a) paragraph (2) including any additional residual supplies under paragraph (3)(a); or
(b) paragraph (3)(b),
is the participant's residual measurement list.

(5) "Residual supplies" means supplies which the participant expects to be made to it during the annual reporting years of a phase which if made in the footprint year would be the participant's footprint supplies other than core supplies.

45 Compilation of residual measurement lists

The residual measurement list must be compiled by the last working day of July after the end of the footprint year.

46 Changes affecting participants

Subject to article 37, where changes affecting a participant take place in a footprint year as described in Part 1 or 2 or section 2 of Part 3 of Schedule 6—
(a) the participant; and
(b) in respect of section 2 of Part 3 of Schedule 6, undertakings which are not participants,
must comply with such of those provisions as are applicable to them.

PART 5
ANNUAL REPORTS

47 Provision of annual reports

(1) Subject to articles 37 and 48, a participant must provide to the administrator a report which complies with article 49 on its CRC supplies during an annual reporting year ("an annual report").

(2) A participant must provide the annual report—
(a) unless otherwise agreed by the administrator, using the Registry; and
(b) by no later than the last working day of July after the end of the annual reporting year.

(3) Where by 40 days after the due date a participant has failed to provide the annual report, the administrator may determine the report.

PART 5
ANNUAL REPORTS

48 Member CCA exemptions

Where a participant has a member CCA exemption, core supplies and residual supplies under article 50 excludes any supplies or emissions of a member of the group to which a member CCA exemption applies.

49 Annual report

(1) A participant must provide in the annual report—

(a) the amount of the supplies under article 50(3);

(b) whether or not the following apply to the participant—
   (i) an estimation adjustment; or
   (ii) renewables generation,

   and, if so, the amount of each supply to which the adjustment applies and the amount of the renewables generation;

(c) whether or not electricity generating credit applies to the participant and, if so, the amount of the generated and supplied electricity; and

(d) where the participant wishes to be included in the early action or relative change tables, the information required to determine early action or relative change in relation to the participant.

(2) Where the administrator receives the annual report in accordance with article 47, it must calculate the participant's CRC emissions.

50 CRC emissions

(1) "CRC emissions" means the emissions calculated in accordance with paragraph 29 of Schedule 1 from CRC supplies.

(2) "CRC supplies" means—

(a) the supplies listed in paragraph (3) during an annual reporting year; and

(b) in respect of those supplies during that year—
   (i) applying the additions under section 6 of Schedule 1; and
   (ii) deducting any electricity generating credit.

(3) The supplies referred to in paragraph (2)(a) are—

(a) the participant's core supplies less the deductions from those supplies under sections 4 and 5 of Schedule 1 but excluding—
   (i) core supplies of gas made to an EU ETS installation; and
   (ii) core supplies of electricity and gas made to a CCA facility to which a member CCA exemption does not apply;

(b) residual supplies included in the participant's residual measurement list, where such a list is required under article 42.

51 Changes affecting participants

Subject to article 37, where changes affecting a participant take place in an annual reporting year as described in Part 1 or 2 or section 2 of Part 3 of Schedule 6—

(a) the participant; and

(b) in respect of section 2 of Part 3 of Schedule 6, undertakings which are not participants,

must comply with such of those provisions as are applicable to them.

PART 6
ALLOWANCES AND CRC EMISSIONS

52 Validity of allowances

(1) Subject to paragraph (2), an allowance is valid for the purposes of compliance with article 53—
(a) for the year in respect of which it was issued; and
(b) for any subsequent year,
but an allowance issued in the first phase is not valid in respect of CRC emissions made in a subsequent phase.

(2) Where—
(a) a participant is required to acquire and surrender additional allowances under article 97(4)(b) or 100(2)(a) in respect of an annual reporting year; and
(b) the participant holds an allowance which is valid for the following year ("year 2"),
the participant may surrender the allowance which is valid for year 2 in order to comply with those articles.

(3) An allowance is not valid for any purpose other than a purpose for which it is valid under paragraphs (1) and (2).

53 Allowances and CRC emissions

(1) Subject to paragraph (2) and article 37, for—
(a) the second and [subsequent][1] years of the first phase; and
(b) the [second][1] and subsequent years of a subsequent phase,
the participant must …[2] surrender a quantity of allowances from its compliance account to the cancellation account which is at least equal to the participant's CRC emissions for that year.

(2) Paragraph (1) does not apply in respect of a year where the participant's CRC emissions for that year are less than one tCO_2.

(3) A surrender of allowances must be made by the participant—
(a) by the last working day of July after the end of the applicable year; and
(b) using the Registry.

Amendments
1 Substituted by the CRC Energy Efficiency Scheme (Amendment) Order 2011, SI 2011/234, art 9(1)-(3).
2 Repealed by the CRC Energy Efficiency Scheme (Amendment) Order 2011, SI 2011/234, art 9(1), (4).

54 Cancellation of allowances and surplus surrendered allowances

(1) The administrator must in respect of a participant cancel such quantity of allowances in the cancellation account which is equal to the participant's CRC emissions for the relevant year of the phase—
(a) except where sub-paragraph (b) or (c) applies, as stated in the annual report;
(b) further to a determination under article 47(3); or
(c) as provided under article 97(4)(a), 97(5), 100(2)(a), 100(3) or 101(2)(a).

(2) Where a participant surrenders to the cancellation account more allowances ("surplus allowances") than required under paragraph (1), the surplus allowances—
(a) must remain in the cancellation account;
(b) subject to article 52,—
 (i) are surrendered in respect of the subsequent year ("year 2") in which the participant is required to comply with article 53; and
 (ii) must be cancelled before any other allowances which are surrendered.

(3) Where the surplus allowances exceed the quantity required to be surrendered in year 2, subject to article 52, paragraph (2)(b) applies to the years after year 2 until no surplus allowances remain.

55 Allowances and trading

(1) Subject to paragraphs (2) and (3), the administrator must maintain a record in respect of an allowance which shows—
(a) the year in which it was issued;
(b) the allocation in which it was issued;
(c) the date of issue;
(d) to whom it was issued;
(e) the account in which it is held from time to time;
(f) transfers of it;
(g) when it is cancelled.

(2) Trading in allowances is permitted by participants and third parties to enable participants to comply with article 53(1).

(3) This article does not apply to Community tradeable emissions allowances.

56 Community tradeable emissions allowances

(1) Subject to paragraph (2), the Environment Agency has the power to acquire Community tradeable emissions allowances as may be required to comply with requirements imposed on it under regulations made under section 21 of the Finance Act 2008.

(2) No acquisition must be made under paragraph (1) by taking part in an allocation conducted pursuant to section 16 of the Finance Act 2007.

PART 7
RECORDS

57 General

(1) Subject to article 37, a participant must maintain the records provided by this Part.

(2) Except where paragraph (3) applies, those records must be kept for at least seven years after the end of the phase to which they relate.

(3) The records in relation to the following must be kept for so long as the participant is part of the scheme—
(a) the participant's position in the performance table drawn up for the first year of the scheme in which the participant takes part;
(b) the participant's first footprint report and first annual report.

(4) Records must be—
(a) adequate to show to the satisfaction of the administrator that the participant has complied with its obligations under this Order;
(b) up to date and, so far as possible, kept together; and
(c) available for inspection by the administrator at any time.

58 Records: general

A participant must maintain records in respect of the information—
(a) in paragraph 7 and section 2 of Schedule 5, as applicable to the participant;
(b) used to compile its footprint report and annual report;
(c) relevant to any of the changes described in Schedule 6.

59 Records: residual measurements lists and public disclosure

(1) Where a participant is required to compile a residual measurement list under article 42, that list must be kept with the records described in article 58.

(2) Where a participant has informed the administrator that—
(a) it discloses publicly each year—
(i) its emissions reduction targets; and
(ii) its performance against them;
(b) a person with management control has responsibility in respect of those matters; or
(c) it operates an employee engagement programme to reduce its emissions,
the participant must maintain records of the disclosure, the person or the programme, as applicable.

(3) In paragraph (2)(c), "employee engagement programme" means a programme organised or supported by the participant which enables employees of that participant to make regular contributions to the ways in which the participant may reduce the emissions made or caused by the participant.

60 Audit of records

(1) A participant must carry out regular audits of the records required to be maintained under this Part and do so to ensure its compliance with those requirements.

(2) The satisfactory completion of such an audit must be evidenced in writing ("an audit certificate").

(3) The audit certificate may be in such form as the participant sees fit but must be—
(a) signed by a person who exercises management control in respect of the activities of the participant; and
(b) kept with its records.

PART 8
INFORMATION AND ASSISTANCE REQUIREMENTS

61 Supplies of electricity, gas and fuel under Part 8

In this Part except articles 62 and 63, information which may be requested or required in respect of a supply of electricity, gas or fuel includes information relating to all sections of Schedule 1.

[*Regulation 62 was repealed by the CRC Energy Efficiency Scheme (Amendment) Order 2011, SI 2011/234, art 10.*]

63 Information on electricity and gas supplied from authorised suppliers holding a licence

(1) A participant may request in writing the following information from those authorised suppliers of electricity or gas which hold a licence to make such a supply—
(a) the amount of electricity or gas supplied to the participant in the year in which the request is made; and
(b) how much, if any, of that supply has been estimated by the supplier and the period to which such an estimate relates.

(2) Where such an authorised supplier receives such a request, the supplier must reply in writing within 6 weeks of the end of the year of the phase to which the information relates.

64 Information from electricity suppliers

(1) The administrator may by notice require an electricity supplier to provide it with information as if—
(a) it was a notice provided for in paragraph 2 of Schedule 4 to the Act; but
(b) in respect of such a notice—
 (i) section 50(2) of the Act did not apply; and
 (ii) the modifications in paragraph (2) apply.

(2) The modifications referred to in paragraph (1) are that—
(a) the purpose for which the power may be exercised is to identify public bodies or undertakings which should or should not be participants in the scheme;
(b) reference to the environmental authority in paragraph 2 of Schedule 4 to the Act is a reference to the administrator;
(c) in paragraph 4(2) of Schedule 4 to the Act, the date referred to must not be earlier than two months after the date of the notice; and
(d) paragraphs 4(3) and 5 of that Schedule do not apply.

65 Assistance by occupiers

(1) Where paragraph 14 of Schedule 1 applies, A may request B (where A and B are as described in that paragraph) to provide A with such reasonable assistance as A may require to comply with Part 2 or to comply with A's obligations as a participant.

(2) B must comply with the request within a reasonable time.

66 Information and assistance by franchisees

(1) Where [paragraph 9 of Schedule 1][1] applies, the franchisor may request the franchisee to provide it with such reasonable information and assistance as it may require to comply with Part 2 or to comply with the franchisor's obligations as a participant.

(2) The franchisee must comply with the request within a reasonable time.

Amendment

1 Substituted by the CRC Energy Efficiency Scheme (Amendment) Order 2011, SI 2011/234, art 11.

67 Information and assistance: public bodies

(1) This article applies where an applicant or a participant is a group of public bodies.

(2) In paragraph (3), "A" means the public body under article 73(4) or (5) in whose name the compliance account in the Registry is, or is to be, set up.

(3) A may request any other member ("B") of the group to provide A with such reasonable information and assistance as A may require to comply with Part 2 or to comply with its obligations as a participant.

(4) B must comply with the request within a reasonable time.

PART 9
ADMINISTRATION OF THE SCHEME

68 The Registry

(1) The administrator must establish and operate an electronic system ("the Registry") and Schedule 7 has effect.

(2) Communications between—
(a) the administrator;
(b) a participant; and
(c) a third party account holder,
must, so far as possible, take place using the Registry.

(3) The administrator—
(a) must take reasonable steps to ensure the Registry is available to those entitled to use it during each working day; and
(b) may make it available at such other times as the administrator believes reasonable.

(4) The administrator may establish administrative rules in relation to the operation of the Registry.

69 Security of the Registry

The administrator—
(a) must take reasonable steps to ensure that the operation of the Registry is secure from misuse, including use by those not entitled to use it;
(b) may suspend the operation of the Registry or any account where it believes security of the Registry may be at risk by not doing so;
(c) must ensure that information which relates to an account holder or a participant (other than information to which article 78 or 80 applies) is not accessible by another account holder or participant whilst using the Registry.

70 Security and identities

(1) A participant must not allow an individual to operate its compliance account on its behalf unless the administrator has notified it that it is satisfied as to the identity of that individual.

(2) The administrator must take reasonable steps to check the identity of—
(a) any such individual; and
(b) the intended account holder of the compliance account.

(3) The administrator may determine—
(a) to prevent or suspend any individual from operating a compliance account where it has reason to believe that evidence of the individual's identity may be incorrect or incomplete;
(b) to refuse to open a compliance account where the administrator has not been able to satisfy itself of the identity of—
(i) an individual whom the participant intends will operate that account on its behalf; or
(ii) the intended account holder of that account,
and the administrator has given the participant a reasonable opportunity to provide suitable and up to date evidence of such identity.

71 Preventing or suspending use of the Registry

(1) The administrator may suspend or restrict a participant's use of the Registry if that participant or any individual acting on its behalf—
(a) is in breach of this Order or any administrative rules concerning the operation of the Registry; or
(b) in the belief of the administrator, is using or intends to use the Registry for or in connection with a criminal offence.

(2) The administrator must give notice to the participant of such suspension or restriction except in relation to the registration of an applicant or where paragraph (1)(b) applies.

72 Cancellation of registrations of participants

(1) Subject to paragraphs (2) and (3), the administrator must cancel the registration of a participant where the administrator is satisfied that a participant no longer carries on a scheme activity.

(2) The administrator must give a participant notice that it intends to cancel its registration and unless the participant agrees otherwise, the registration must not be cancelled earlier than 3 months after the date of the notice.

(3) Cancellation of the registration of a participant must be made by removing the participant from the list of participants held by the administrator and notice that the cancellation has been made must be given in writing to the former participant as soon as possible.

(4) Where the registration of a participant is cancelled, the compliance account must be closed and any allowances held in the account immediately prior to its closure must be cancelled by the administrator.

(5) The administrator is not required to cancel a registration until such time as the administrator is satisfied that the participant has complied with any outstanding requirement under this Order applicable to that participant.

(6) Where cancellation of a registration is required under section 2 of Part 3 of Schedule 6, the administrator must comply with paragraphs (3) and (4).

73 Account holders

(1) The account holder in respect of the compliance account for a group of undertakings is, as the applicant or participant chooses—
(a) the highest parent undertaking of the group; or
(b) a member of the group,
with its principal place of activity in the United Kingdom.

(2) Where no undertaking exists as provided under paragraph (1), the highest parent undertaking of the group must appoint a representative with a principal place of activity in the United Kingdom as the account holder.

(3) Where a participant is a group of undertakings and it intends to change the account holder—
(a) the participant must notify the administrator of the intended new account holder;
(b) that account holder must be an undertaking which complies with paragraph (1) or, as appropriate, paragraph (2); and
(c) the administrator must approve the change.

(4) Where a group of public bodies includes the following—
(a) a government department;
(b) the Scottish Ministers;
(c) the Welsh Assembly Government;
(d) a Northern Ireland Department;
(e) a local authority;
(f) a university,
subject to paragraph (5), the account holder in respect of the compliance account is that body.

(5) Where—
(a) a body listed in paragraph (4) is part of more than one group; or
(b) a public body other than one listed in paragraph (4) is a participant,
the account holder in respect of the compliance account is such body as the administrator agrees.

74 Determinations

(1) This article applies in respect of a determination by the administrator under—
(a) article 18(1), [28][1], 39(3), 47(3), 70(3) or 86(5); or
(b) paragraph 8 of Part 3 of Schedule 6.

(2) A determination must be made in writing by the administrator and, within 10 days of making the determination, notified to such persons as the administrator decides may be affected by it.

Amendment

1 Substituted by the CRC Energy Efficiency Scheme (Amendment) Order 2011, SI 2011/234, art 12.

PART 10
ACHIEVEMENT AND PERFORMANCE TABLES, PUBLICATION AND VERIFICATION

75 Achievement tables

(1) The administrator must in accordance with this article compile the following tables—
(a) early action for each of the annual reporting years of the first phase; and
(b) absolute change and relative change for the annual reporting years in paragraph (2),

and Schedule 8 has effect to calculate early action, absolute change and relative change.

(2) The annual reporting years referred to in paragraph (1)(b) [are the second and subsequent annual reporting years of each phase][1].

(3) The tables compiled under paragraph (1) are achievement tables.

(4) An achievement table must rank participants such that—
(a) where a participant ("A") has achieved x%; and
(b) another participant ("B") has achieved less than x%,

B ranks lower than A.

(5) Participants which achieve the same percentage have equal ranking.

(6) A participant's ranking in an achievement table must be given a score, with the lowest ranking having a score of one.

Amendment

1 Substituted by the CRC Energy Efficiency Scheme (Amendment) Order 2011, SI 2011/234, art 13.

76 No information on relative change and early action

Where the administrator has not been provided by a participant with the information required to calculate for an annual reporting year early action or relative change, the participant does not appear in the relevant table for that year.

77 Performance tables

(1) Subject to paragraph (2), the administrator must in accordance with this article compile a table ("a performance table") in respect of—
(a) each of the annual reporting years of the first phase; and
(b) the second and subsequent annual reporting years of subsequent phases.

(2) For the first annual reporting year of the first phase, the early action table is also the performance table.

(3) Except for the first annual reporting year of the first phase, the administrator must—
(a) for the annual reporting year—
(i) calculate a participant's scores in each applicable achievement table for that year; or
(ii) where a participant is not listed in the early action or relative change table for that year, apply to it a score of zero in respect of the table where it does not appear;
(b) apply to those scores the applicable weighting percentage; and
(c) add those scores as weighted to determine the total weighted score for a participant.

(4) A performance table must rank participants such that—
(a) where a participant ("A") has achieved a total weighted score of x; and
(b) another participant ("B") has achieved a total weighted score less than x,
B ranks lower than A.

(5) Participants which achieve the same total weighted score have equal ranking.

(6) In paragraph (3), "the weighting percentage" means the percentage stated in the following table—

Weighting percentages

	Second year: first phase	*Third year: first phase*	*[Fourth year: first phase and each year of the second to seventh phases]*[1]
Early action table	40%	20%	—
Absolute change table	45%	60%	75%
Relative change table	15%	20%	25%

Amendment
1 Substituted by the CRC Energy Efficiency Scheme (Amendment) Order 2011, SI 2011/234, art 14.

78 Publication

(1) The administrator must publish the matters set out in paragraph (3) for each annual reporting year to the extent that it holds information on those matters.

(2) Publication must be made as soon as possible after the last working day of July subsequent to the end of the annual reporting year.

(3) The matters referred to in paragraph (1) are—
(a) the performance table;
(b) in respect of each participant—
(i) its name or its trading or other name by which it is commonly known;
(ii) its CRC emissions and CRC emissions per unit of turnover;
(iii) absolute change;
(iv) relative change;
(v) if applicable, early action;
(c) where a participant is a group of undertakings, the significant group undertakings (if any) which are members of that participant;
(d) where a significant group undertaking is a participant separate from the group in which it would otherwise be a participant, that fact;
(e) the achievement tables;
(f) where applicable, that a participant has informed the administrator that—
(i) it discloses publicly each year—
(aa) its emissions reduction targets; and

(bb) its performance against them;

(ii) a person with management control has responsibility in respect of those matters; or

(iii) it operates an employee engagement programme to reduce its emissions.

(4) The administrator may publish—

(a) the information provided in the annual report;

(b) tables concerning the performance of participants in the scheme, other than the achievement and performance tables.

(5) Where a participant is required to provide for the same year—

(a) an annual report in respect of the last year of one phase ("the first report"); and

[(b) an annual report in respect of the first year of the subsequent phase,][1]

the administrator must publish the matters in paragraph (3) using the information in the first report only, so far as those matters are included in that report.

Amendment

1 Substituted by the CRC Energy Efficiency Scheme (Amendment) Order 2011, SI 2011/234, art 15.

79 Verification

(1) A participant may request the administrator to carry out a verification of the participant's position in the performance table published under article 78.

(2) Such a request must be made in writing within 40 days of publication.

(3) Where such a request is made—

(a) the verification must be carried out by an independent person;

(b) the participant and the administrator must each pay half that person's reasonable costs incurred in carrying out the verification; and

(c) the administrator must—

(i) seek the verification within 20 days of receiving the request; and

(ii) comply with the result of the verification.

(4) The independent person is such person as the administrator and participant agree or, in default of agreement within a reasonable time, as appointed by the administrator.

(5) In this article, "verification" means to check that the administrator has correctly calculated any of—

(a) the participant's CRC emissions under article 49(2) and any adjustments to those emissions under paragraph 4 of Schedule 8;

(b) the scores which are used to rank the participant in the performance table under article 77(3);

(c) absolute change and relative change under paragraphs 1 and 2 of Schedule 8;

(d) early action under paragraph 5 of Schedule 8,

as the participant believes may have been incorrectly calculated.

80 Further publication

(1) Paragraph (2) applies where—

(a) an appeal is made against—

(i) a determination under article 47(3); or

(ii) the penalty imposed under article 97(4)(a)(ii);

(b) a request for verification is made under article 79.

(2) Where this paragraph applies—

(a) the administrator may publish a list of those participants which have in respect of the annual reporting year made any such appeal or request;

(b) subject to paragraph (3), where any such appeal or request results in a participant's position in the performance table being changed, the administrator must as soon as possible publish an amended table.

(3) Publication under paragraph (2)(b) must not take place until the completion of all such appeals or requests made by all participants.

(4) The administrator may publish an amended performance table at any time where it discovers any error or omission in the table.

PART 11
CHARGING

81 Charges

(1) The administrator may charge an applicant or participant for the chargeable activities in article 82.

(2) Payment of a charge is not received by the administrator until the administrator has cleared funds for the full amount due and a charge if unpaid may be recovered by the administrator as a civil debt.

(3) A charge must be calculated by reference to the costs of administering the scheme.

(4) The administrator may apply different charges for—
(a) the same chargeable activity;
(b) different classes of applicant or participant in respect of the same chargeable activity.

82 Chargeable activities

(1) In article 81, "chargeable activity" means any of the following—
(a) registration of a participant;
(b) maintaining a participant for each year of a phase where it is a participant;
(c) establishing an account, other than a compliance account;
(d) maintaining such account for each year of a phase where it is required;
(e) making a determination under article 39(3) or 47(3).

(2) The administrator—
(a) must require the charge for registration as a participant to be paid before it makes the registration;
(b) in respect of any other charge, may require it to be paid before it carries out the relevant chargeable activity;
(c) is not required to reimburse a charge paid where—
  (i) the chargeable activity is not completed; or
  (ii) an applicant or participant liable to pay it does not remain within the scheme for all the period in respect of which the charge is payable or has been calculated.

83 Amount of charges

(1) The amount of a charge payable under article 81(1) is that set out in—
(a) version 1 of the document named "CRC Energy Efficiency Scheme Charges" made available by the administrator on or before this Order is made; or
(b) any replacement or revision of that document ("revised charging document").

(2) Article 81(3) must be complied with in respect of the amount of a charge under paragraph (1).

84 Revised charges

(1) The administrator may draw up a revised charging document.

(2) Subject to paragraph (3), the administrator must not apply a revised charging document unless—

(a) in such manner as it considers appropriate for bringing a proposed document to the attention of those likely to be affected by it, the administrator—
  (i) sets out its proposals; and
  (ii) specifies the period within which representations or objections must be made to it;

  and

(b) it receives approval to the revised charging document from the Secretary of State.

(3) The Secretary of State must consider any representations or objections made by any person to the proposed revised charging document before the Secretary of State decides whether or not to approve it.

(4) The administrator must not take the steps required under paragraph (2)(a) unless it first consults the following on its proposals—

(a) the Secretary of State;
(b) the Scottish Ministers;
(c) the Welsh Ministers; and
(d) the Northern Ireland departments.

(5) A revised charging document must be published and made available before it is to take effect.

85 Collection and remittance of charges

(1) An administrator (other than the Environment Agency) must pay to the Agency any charge received by it.

(2) The Environment Agency—

(a) may collect a charge on behalf of another administrator;
(b) must remit charges received to the Secretary of State or, where the Secretary of State directs, as directed to—
  (i) the Scottish Ministers;
  (ii) the Welsh Ministers; or
  (iii) the Department of the Environment.

PART 12
MONITORING COMPLIANCE

86 Compliance notices

(1) The administrator may request a person to provide it with such information as it believes it requires in relation to monitoring compliance with Parts 2 to 11 of this Order.

(2) The administrator must request the information referred to in paragraph (1) by a written notice ("a compliance notice") served on the person to whom it is addressed.

(3) A compliance notice may be in such form as the administrator sees fit but must state the date by which compliance with the notice is required.

(4) A compliance notice may be varied or revoked in writing by the administrator at any time.

(5) Where a person—
(a) fails to comply with a compliance notice; or
(b) in the opinion of the administrator, supplies incomplete or inaccurate information,
the administrator may instead determine the information requested.

87 Inspections

(1) Subject to the following paragraphs, the administrator may inspect any premises and any thing in or on those premises in order to monitor compliance with Parts 2 to 11 of this Order.

(2) Reasonable prior notice must be given before exercising the power of inspection.

(3) A person in control of the premises to which the administrator requires access must allow the administrator to have access to those premises.

(4) A person acting on behalf of the administrator may, when inspecting premises,—
(a) require the production of any record;
(b) take measurements, photographs, recordings or copies of any thing;
(c) require any person at the premises to provide facilities and assistance to the extent that is within that person's control.

(5) An administrator may delegate another body which is an administrator to exercise the power of inspection on its behalf.

(6) The power of inspection does not apply to—
(a) a prohibited place for the purposes of the Official Secrets Act 1911; or
(b) any other premises to which the Crown restricts access on the grounds of national security,
except to the extent agreed by the person in control of such place or premises.

PART 13
ENFORCEMENT

88 Powers of the administrator in respect of enforcement

The powers of enforcement in this Part may be exercised where the administrator reasonably believes that there has been a failure (except in respect of this article) to comply with a provision of this Order.

89 Authorised persons

(1) The administrator may—
(a) exercise the powers of entry and inspection in Schedule 9 and authorise in writing such persons ("authorised persons") who appear suitable to act on its behalf to do so;
(b) make such authorisation subject to any limitations or conditions as the administrator sees fit.

(2) Paragraph (3) applies in respect of—
(a) any of the bodies which comprise the administrator; and
(b) a person authorised by such a body to exercise any of the functions of that body otherwise than under this Order.

(3) Where this paragraph applies, a person referred to in paragraph (2)(b) is an authorised person for the purposes of paragraph (1)(a) in respect of that body unless the administrator provides otherwise.

90 Notices to provide information: compliance with articles 58 and 59

The administrator may, by a written notice served on a participant, require that participant—

(a) to furnish information in relation to a failure or suspected failure to comply with article 58 or 59; and

(b) to do so in the form specified in the notice and within such period following service of the notice or at such time as is specified in the notice.

91 Enforcement notices

(1) The administrator may serve an enforcement notice on any person who fails to comply with a provision of this Order.

(2) An enforcement notice must be in writing and specify—

(a) the provision of this Order in respect of which there has been a failure;

(b) the matters constituting the failure;

(c) the steps that must be taken to remedy the failure; and

(d) the period within which those steps must be taken.

(3) An enforcement notice may be withdrawn at any time.

(4) If a person fails to comply with an enforcement notice, the administrator—

(a) may do what that person was required to do; and

(b) may recover from an applicant or participant served with a notice the costs of doing so.

PART 14
CIVIL PENALTIES

92 Civil penalties

(1) The administrator—

(a) may impose a civil penalty as set out in this Part; and

(b) where it does so, it must give written notice of such penalty to the persons affected.

(2) In respect of a financial penalty, a notice of such penalty must state—

(a) the amount due;

(b) where the amount due includes a daily penalty, what that daily penalty is; and

(c) to whom the penalty must be paid.

(3) The administrator must remit a financial penalty received to the Secretary of State.

93 Recovery of civil penalties

(1) Except for a financial penalty, a civil penalty has effect once the notice of that penalty is given unless that notice provides otherwise.

(2) A financial penalty—

(a) is due 60 days after notice of that penalty is given; and

(b) if unpaid, is recoverable as a civil debt by the administrator.

94 Waiver and modification of civil penalties

(1) Paragraph (2) applies in respect of a person ("A") on whom a civil penalty may be or has been imposed and where the administrator is satisfied that A has provided evidence to the administrator within a reasonable time that—

(a) A took all reasonable steps—
  (i) to comply with the relevant provision of this Order; or
  (ii) to rectify any failure in compliance as soon as it came to A's notice;
  and
(b) in all the other circumstances it is reasonable to exercise the powers in paragraph (2) in relation to A.

(2) Where this paragraph applies, the administrator may—
(a) waive a penalty;
(b) allow additional time to pay;
(c) impose a lower financial penalty or substitute a lower financial penalty where one has already been imposed; or
(d) modify the application of a publication or blocking penalty.

95 Failures in respect of registration

(1) The penalties in paragraph (2) apply where a public body or undertaking—
(a) fails to apply for registration as a participant contrary to—
  (i) article 11; or
  (ii) Schedule 6, where an application for registration is required under that Schedule;
  or
(b) applies late for registration as a participant contrary to—
  (i) article 12; or
  (ii) paragraph 2(1) of Part 1, paragraph 2(1) of Part 2 or paragraph 1 or 7 of Part 3 of Schedule 6, where an application for registration is required under those Parts of that Schedule.

(2) The penalties are—
(a) the financial penalties of—
  (i) £5000; and
  (ii) £500 for each day until the application for registration is made, subject to a maximum of 80 days;
  and
(b) publication.

[(3) The penalties in paragraph (4) apply where—
(a) a public body or undertaking fails to report details of each settled half hourly meter under paragraph 6 of Schedule 5 where an application for registration is required under Part 2 of Schedule 6; or
(b) an undertaking fails to provide the information required under paragraph 3(2)(d) of Part 3 of Schedule 6.][1]

(4) The penalties are—
(a) the financial penalty of £500 for each meter not reported; and
(b) publication.

Amendment

1 Substituted by the CRC Energy Efficiency Scheme (Amendment) Order 2011, SI 2011/234, art 16.

96 Failures in respect of footprint reports

(1) The penalties in paragraph (2) apply where a participant—
(a) fails to provide a footprint report contrary to article 39(1); or
(b) provides late a footprint report contrary to article 39(2).

(2) The penalties are—
(a) a financial penalty of £5000 and publication; and
(b) where the report is provided—
(i) no more than 40 days after the due date, a financial penalty of £500 for each day the report is provided after the due date; or
(ii) more than 40 days after the due date or not at all, a financial penalty of £40,000.

97 Failures in respect of annual reports

(1) The penalties in the following paragraphs apply where a participant—
(a) fails to provide an annual report contrary to article 47(1); or
(b) provides late an annual report contrary to article 47(2)(b).

(2) The penalties are—
(a) a financial penalty of £5000 and publication; and
(b) where the report is provided—
(i) no more than 40 days after the due date, a financial penalty of £500 for each day the report is provided after the due date; or
(ii) more than 40 days after the due date or not at all, a financial penalty of £40,000..

(3) Paragraphs (4) and (5) apply where the annual report is provided more than 40 days after the due date or not at all.

(4) Where this paragraph applies, the following additional penalties apply to the participant—
(a) the CRC emissions of the participant for the year to which the annual report relates are—
(i) double the CRC emissions reported in the annual report of the previous year; or
(ii) where no such report exists, double the CRC emissions which the administrator calculates the participant made in the year for which the annual report is not provided;
(b) the participant must immediately acquire allowances and surrender them in accordance with Part 6 equal to the CRC emissions which apply under sub-paragraph (a) (or such additional allowances having regard to any allowances surrendered on time for the annual reporting year);
(c) a financial penalty of £40 per tCO_2 of so much of the CRC emissions which apply under sub-paragraph (a) but—
(i) deducting the emissions represented by those allowances (if any) which are surrendered by the participant on time for the year to which the annual report relates; and
(ii) before the doubling is applied;
(d) for the annual reporting year, the participant achieves the lowest ranking in the achievement and performance tables; and
(e) blocking.

(5) Where this paragraph applies and a participant—
(a) fails to comply with paragraph (4)(b) by the 31st March after the annual report was due; and
(b) continues in the scheme,
the allowances required to be surrendered under paragraph (4)(b) are added to the quantity of allowances required to be surrendered in the next year that compliance with Part 6 is required.

98 Failures to provide information or notifications

(1) The penalties in paragraph (2) apply where a participant—

(a) fails to provide the information in section 1 of Schedule 5 where required under Part 2 or Schedule 6;

(b) in purported compliance with the requirements in sub-paragraph (a), provides inaccurate information;

(c) fails to provide a notification to the administrator as required under—

(i) article 38(5); or

(ii) Part 1, 2 or 3 of Schedule 6.

(2) The penalties are—

(a) the financial penalty of £5000 and publication; and

(b) where the participant provides inaccurate information and—

(i) achieves a higher position in the performance table than it would have done had it provided the information accurately; and

(ii) in consequence the participant received a grant under section 53(1)(b) of the Act from the Secretary of State which is greater than it would otherwise have done,

a penalty of double the amount of the grant which the participant should not have received.

99 Inaccurate footprint reports and annual reports

(1) The penalties in paragraph (3) apply where a participant provides an inaccurate—

(a) footprint report contrary to article 39; or

(b) annual report contrary to article 47.

(2) In paragraph (1), "inaccurate" means where any of the supplies or emissions reported differ by more than 5% from the supplies or emissions which should have been reported, ignoring any estimation adjustment under paragraph 26 or 27 of section 6 of Schedule 1.

(3) The penalties are—

(a) a financial penalty of £40 per tCO_2 of so much of those supplies or emissions which were inaccurately reported; and

(b) publication.

(4) Where the provision of an inaccurate footprint report causes a participant to provide an inaccurate annual report, a penalty must be imposed only in respect of the former.

100 Failures to surrender allowances contrary to Part 6

(1) The penalties in paragraphs (2) and (3) apply where—

(a) a participant fails to surrender sufficient allowances contrary to Part 6; and

(b) that failure is apparent to the administrator at the time compliance is required,

but do not apply where a penalty is imposed under article 97(4) or (5).

(2) The penalties are—

(a) the participant must—

(i) immediately acquire such additional allowances as are equal to the amount which should have been surrendered ("the shortfall allowances"); and

(ii) surrender the shortfall allowances in accordance with Part 6;

(b) a financial penalty of £40 per tCO_2 of so much of the emissions represented by the shortfall allowances;

(c) publication; and

(d) blocking.

(3) Where a participant—
(a) fails to comply with paragraph (2)(a) by the 31st March after the surrender should have been made; and
(b) continues in the scheme,
the shortfall allowances are added to the quantity of allowances required to be surrendered in the next year that compliance with Part 6 is required.

101 Later discovered failures to surrender allowances contrary to Part 6

(1) The penalties in paragraph (2) apply where—
(a) by reference to its annual report, a participant complied with Part 6;
(b) the administrator finds, within five years of the date on which compliance with Part 6 is required in respect of that report, that the participant reported fewer CRC supplies in that report than it should have done; and
(c) in consequence, the participant surrendered fewer allowances than it should have done to comply with Part 6 ("the shortfall allowances").

(2) The penalties are—
(a) where the participant is a participant at the time paragraph (1)(b) applies—
  (i) the shortfall allowances are added to the quantity of allowances required to be surrendered in the next annual reporting year that the shortfall is found; and
  (ii) publication;
  or
(b) where the participant is not a participant at the time paragraph (1)(b) applies, a financial penalty which represents the value of the shortfall allowances.

(3) The value under paragraph (2)(b) means the value of allowances in the auction or sale of allowances by the Environment Agency immediately before the shortfall was found.

102 Failures to maintain records

(1) The penalties in paragraph (2) apply where—
(a) the administrator has given notice under article 90 in respect of a failure to comply with article 58; and
(b) the participant has failed to comply by the time stated in that notice.

(2) The penalties are—
(a) a financial penalty at the rate of £40 per tCO_2 of so much of the CRC emissions of the participant in the annual reporting year immediately preceding the year in which the non-compliance is discovered; and
(b) publication.

(3) Where a participant fails to keep records as provided by article 59, the penalties are a financial penalty of £5000 and publication.

[*Regulation 103 was repealed by the CRC Energy Efficiency Scheme (Amendment) Order 2011, SI 2011/234, art 17.*]

104 Failures to provide information under article 64

(1) The penalties in paragraph (2) apply where—
(a) the administrator has served a notice as provided under article 64 on an electricity supplier or distributor; and
(b) at least one previous such notice has not been complied with by that supplier.

(2) The penalties are—
(a) a financial penalty of £500,000 or, if lower, 0.5% of the supplier's turnover; and
(b) publication.

105 Blocking and publication

(1) The administrator may impose the penalty of blocking until—
(a) the failure is remedied; and
(b) any financial penalty imposed in respect of the same failure is paid.

(2) Publication—
(a) must not take place until the time to appeal against the penalty under Part 16 has expired and—
 (i) no appeal against the penalty has been made; or
 (ii) where an appeal against the penalty has been made and the participant is unsuccessful in that appeal, until after the disposal of that appeal;
(b) lasts for one year but the administrator may impose the penalty for a longer period, if it believes the seriousness of the failure justifies such longer period.

(3) In this Part—
"blocking" means to prevent or restrict the operation of an account of a participant;
"publication" means to publish on a part of the Registry which is accessible to the public—
 (a) the name of the participant; and
 (b) details of the failure in respect of which a civil penalty has been imposed.

PART 15
CRIMINAL OFFENCES AND PENALTIES

106 Offences

(1) It is an offence for a person—
(a) intentionally to obstruct an authorised person in the exercise of the powers or duties of the authorised person under Schedule 9; or
(b) to make a statement—
 (i) which that person knows to be false or misleading in a material particular; or
 (ii) recklessly and which is false or misleading in a material particular,
 where the statement is made in purported compliance with a provision of this Order.

(2) It is an offence for a person—
(a) to fail to comply with an enforcement notice;
(b) where an authorised person exercises the powers or duties under Schedule 9—
 (i) to fail or refuse to provide facilities or assistance or to permit any inspection, when reasonably required by an authorised person; or
 (ii) to prevent any other person from appearing before an authorised person or answering any question to which an authorised person may require an answer.

(3) It is a defence for a person charged with an offence under paragraph (2) to prove that such person had a reasonable excuse for the matters charged.

(4) It is an offence for a person to pretend to be an authorised person.

(5) It is an offence for a person in control of any premises to refuse to allow the administrator access to those premises contrary to article 87(3) where such access is reasonably required.

107 Penalties

(1) A person guilty of an offence under article 106(1)(b) or (2)(a) is liable—

(a) in England and Wales or Northern Ireland—
  (i) on summary conviction to a fine not exceeding £50,000 or to a term of imprisonment not exceeding 3 months, or both;
  (ii) on conviction on indictment, to a fine or to a term of imprisonment not exceeding 2 years, or both;

and

(b) in Scotland—
  (i) on summary conviction to a fine not exceeding £50,000 or to a term of imprisonment not exceeding 12 months, or both;
  (ii) on conviction on indictment, to a fine or to a term of imprisonment not exceeding 2 years, or both.

(2) A person guilty of an offence under article 106(1)(a), (2)(b), (4) or (5) is liable—

(a) in England and Wales or Northern Ireland—
  (i) on summary conviction to a fine not exceeding the statutory maximum or to a term of imprisonment not exceeding 3 months, or both;
  (ii) on conviction on indictment, to a fine or to a term of imprisonment not exceeding 2 years, or both;

and

(b) in Scotland—
  (i) on summary conviction to a fine not exceeding the statutory maximum or to a term of imprisonment not exceeding 12 months, or both;
  (ii) on conviction on indictment, to a fine or to a term of imprisonment not exceeding 2 years, or both.

108 Bodies corporate

(1) Where an offence under this Part is committed by a body corporate and—

(a) it is committed with the consent or connivance of an officer; or

(b) it is attributable to any neglect on the officer's part,

the officer as well as the body corporate is guilty of the offence and is liable to be proceeded against and punished accordingly.

(2) "Officer", in relation to a body corporate, means a director, manager, secretary or other similar officer of the body, or a person purporting to act in any such capacity.

(3) If the affairs of a body corporate are managed by its members, paragraph (1) applies in relation to the acts or defaults of a member in connection with that member's functions of management as if the member were a director of the body corporate.

109 Scottish partnerships

(1) Where an offence under this Part is committed by a Scottish partnership and—

(a) it is committed with the consent or connivance of a partner; or

(b) it is attributable to any neglect on the partner's part,

the partner as well as the partnership is guilty of the offence and is liable to be proceeded against and punished accordingly.

(2) In paragraph (1) "partner" includes a person purporting to act as a partner.

110 The Crown

(1) This Order applies to the Crown but no contravention of it by the Crown makes the Crown criminally liable.

(2) Notwithstanding paragraph (1), this Order applies to persons in the public service of the Crown as it applies to other persons.

PART 16
APPEALS, SERVICE OF NOTICES AND NATIONAL SECURITY

111 Appeals

In accordance with Schedule 10—

(a) a public body or undertaking notified of a determination referred to in article 74(1) may appeal against that determination;

(b) a person served with an enforcement notice may appeal against that notice;

(c) a public body or undertaking given notice that they are liable to a civil penalty may appeal against the imposition of that penalty.

112 Service of documents and periods to comply

Schedule 11 (service of documents and periods to comply) has effect.

113 National security

No provision of this Order requires the Crown to provide information to the administrator or to any other person where to do so would, in the opinion of the person who holds or controls the information, be contrary to the interests of national security.

SCHEDULE 1
SUPPLIES AND EMISSIONS

Article 4

SECTION 1
ELECTRICITY, GAS AND FUELS: GENERAL

1 Electricity

(1) Subject to section 3, a public body or undertaking ("A") is supplied with electricity by a person ("B") where—

(a) A agrees with B that B will supply electricity to A and that A will pay B for that supply;

(b) A receives a supply further to that agreement; and

(c) that supply is measured by a metering device or is a dynamic supply.

(2) A supply of electricity is made at the time it is received.

(3) In sub-paragraph (1)(c) "metering device" is a device where the electricity supplied is charged for as measured by the device.

2 Gas

(1) Subject to section 3, a public body or undertaking ("A") is supplied with gas by a person ("B") where—

(a) A agrees with B that B will supply gas to A and that A will pay B for that supply;

(b) A receives a supply further to that agreement; and

(c) that supply is measured by a metering device.

(2) A supply of gas is made at the time it is received.

(3) In sub-paragraph (1)(c), a "metering device" is a device where the gas supplied is charged for as measured by the device.

3 Fuels

(1) Subject to sub-paragraph (2) and section 3, a public body or undertaking ("A") is supplied with fuel by a person ("B") where—
(a) A agrees with B that B will supply fuel to A and that A will pay B for that supply; and
(b) A receives a supply further to that agreement.

(2) No supply of fuel is made under sub-paragraph (1) where that fuel is supplied under paragraph 2.

(3) A supply is made to A—
(a) at the time the supply is delivered to A; or
(b) if later, at the time that B provides written confirmation to A of the delivery.

(4) In this paragraph—
"fuel" means any of the fuels listed in column 1 of the table in paragraph 4 ("fuels table");
"waste"(including in "waste oil" and "waste solvents" in that table)—
(a) has the meaning given in section 75(2) of the Environmental Protection Act 1990; but
(b) excludes—
(i) any other fuel (except waste oil or waste solvents);
(ii) biomass; or
(iii) gas derived from a landfill site or produced from the treatment of sewage.

(5) In sub-paragraph (4), "biomass" has the same meaning it has under article 4 of the Renewables Obligation Order 2009 and as if that article applied in Scotland and Northern Ireland.

4 Fuels table

The fuels table referred to in paragraph 3—

Fuels table

Fuel	*Measurement unit*
Aviation spirit	tonnes
Aviation turbine fuel	tonnes
Basic Oxygen Steel (BOS) gas	kWh
Blast furnace gas	kWh
Burning oil/kerosene/paraffin	litres
Cement industry coal	tonnes
Coke oven gas	kWh
Commercial and public sector coal	tonnes
Coking coal	tonnes
Colliery methane	kWh
Diesel	litres
Fuel oil	tonnes
Gas oil	litres
Industrial coal	tonnes
Lignite	tonnes
Liquid petroleum gas (LPG)	litres
Peat	tonnes

Fuel	*Measurement unit*
Naphtha	tonnes
Natural gas	kWh
Other petroleum gas	kWh
Petrol	litres
Petroleum coke	tonnes
Scrap tyres	tonnes
Solid smokeless fuel	tonnes
Sour gas	kWh
Waste (other than waste oil or waste solvents)	tonnes
Waste oil	tonnes
Waste solvents	tonnes

5 Measurement units

(1) Where in this Order information must be provided concerning a supply of electricity, gas or fuel, the amount of that supply must be expressed in the applicable measurement unit.

(2) The following measurement units apply—
(a) electricity and gas, kWh;
(b) fuels, as stated in column 2 of the fuels table.

SECTION 2
ELECTRICITY AND GAS: SELF-SUPPLY

6 Self-supply of electricity by generators, transmitters, distributors and authorised suppliers

(1) Where a public body or undertaking—
(a) is described in sub-paragraph (3); and
(b) supplies electricity to itself,
subject to sub-paragraph (2), it is supplied with that electricity.

(2) Sub-paragraph (1) does not apply to the extent that the electricity is used directly for the generation, transmission or distribution of electricity.

(3) The public bodies or undertakings referred to in sub-paragraph (1) are—
(a) an authorised supplier of electricity;
(b) in Great Britain, a public body or undertaking which—
 (i) holds a generation, transmission or distribution licence within the meaning of section 6 of the Electricity Act 1989; or
 (ii) generates, transmits or distributes electricity and which is exempt under that Act from the requirement to hold a licence to do so;
(c) in Northern Ireland, a public body or undertaking which—
 (i) holds a generation or a distribution and transmission licence made under Article 10 of the Electricity (Northern Ireland) Order 1992; or
 (ii) generates, distributes or transmits electricity and which is exempt under that Order from the requirement to hold a licence to do so.

7 Self-supply by authorised gas suppliers

Where an authorised supplier of gas supplies gas to itself, it is supplied with that gas except to the extent which it uses that gas directly for the transport, supply or shipping of gas.

SECTION 3
FRANCHISE AGREEMENTS

8 Supplies under franchise agreements

(1) This section applies to supplies of electricity, gas or fuel in relation to franchise agreements and varies the provisions under section 1 concerning to whom a supply is made.

(2) The variation applies only where provided under this Order.

9 Franchise agreements

(1) A "franchise agreement" exists where one undertaking ("the franchisee") and another undertaking ("the franchisor") agree that—

(a) the franchisee carries on a business activity which is the sale or distribution of goods or the provision of services ("the franchise business");

(b) the franchise business is carried on under a name which the franchisor provides to the franchisee;

(c) the premises where the franchise business is carried on are used exclusively for that business by the franchisee; and

(d) those premises have an internal or external appearance agreed by the franchisor and that appearance is similar to that of other premises in respect of which the franchisor has entered into a franchise agreement.

(2) Where a franchise agreement exists, "franchise premises" means—

(a) the premises described in sub-paragraph (1); and

(b) other premises used by the franchisee in relation to carrying on the franchise business.

10 Franchise agreements not existing

A franchise agreement does not exist where—

(a) the franchisee and the franchisor are group undertakings in relation to each other; or

(b) in relation to franchise premises, the franchisee occupies those premises with the permission of the franchisor.

11 Supplies to franchisees regarded as supplies to franchisors

(1) Sub-paragraphs (2) and (3) apply where—

(a) there is a franchise agreement; and

(b) the franchisee is supplied with electricity, gas or fuel under section 1 of this Schedule in relation to the franchise premises ("a franchise supply").

(2) For the purposes of Part 2 of this Order, where—

(a) the franchise agreement exists on the qualification day; and

(b) during the qualification year there is a franchise supply of electricity which is qualifying electricity,

that franchise supply of electricity is a supply to the franchisor and not the franchisee.

(3) For the purposes of Parts 4 and 5 of this Order, where—

(a) the franchisor is a participant or is a member of a group which is a participant; and

(b) the franchise agreement exists during a year of a phase,

the franchise supply during that year is a supply to the franchisor and not the franchisee.

SECTION 4
DEDUCTIONS FROM SUPPLIES

12 Deductions from supplies

(1) This section provides for deductions in calculating the amount of a supply of electricity, gas or fuel under section 1, 2 or 3 of this Schedule.

(2) The deductions apply only where provided under this Order.

13 Unconsumed supply

(1) Sub-paragraph (3) applies where A does not consume for its own use some or all of the supply to it of electricity, gas or fuel.

(2) The amount not consumed by A is "unconsumed supply".

(3) Subject to paragraph 14, A is not supplied with the unconsumed supply.

14 Occupation of premises

(1) [Subject to sub-paragraph (3), this sub-paragraph applies][1] where—
(a) A has an unconsumed supply; and
(b) that unconsumed supply is consumed by a person ("B") in respect of premises which B occupies with the permission of A.

(2) Paragraph 13(3) does not apply to an unconsumed supply to which sub-paragraph (1) applies.

[(3) Sub-paragraph (1) does not apply where B is a Northern Ireland Department which occupies premises with the permission of A, and A is another Northern Ireland Department.][2]

Amendments
1 Substituted by the CRC Energy Efficiency Scheme (Amendment) Order 2011, SI 2011/234, art 18(1), (2).
2 Inserted by the CRC Energy Efficiency Scheme (Amendment) Order 2011, SI 2011/234, art 18(1), (3).

15 Consumption outside the United Kingdom

A is not supplied with electricity, gas or fuel to the extent that supply is consumed by A outside the United Kingdom.

16 Domestic accommodation

(1) Subject to sub-paragraph (2), A is not supplied with electricity, gas or fuel—
(a) to the extent that supply is consumed by A for the purposes of domestic accommodation; and
(b) where the conditions in sub-paragraph (4) are satisfied concerning that accommodation.

(2) A is supplied with electricity, gas or fuel in respect of common areas described in sub-paragraph (5)(b) where a decision has been made under sub-paragraph (6) that those common areas are not part of the domestic accommodation.

(3) "Domestic accommodation" means premises or that part of premises intended to be used as a person's permanent home.

(4) The conditions referred to in sub-paragraph (1)—
(a) the accommodation is not provided in relation to a person's education, employment or service; and
(b) no services are provided for the care of a person in residence in that accommodation by the person to whom the supply of electricity, gas or fuel is made.

(5) Where common areas of premises are used in relation to domestic accommodation and the premises are used—
(a) solely for domestic accommodation; or
(b) partly for domestic accommodation,
the common areas are part of that accommodation.

(6) A may decide that the common areas where sub-paragraph (5)(b) applies are not part of the domestic accommodation.

(7) A decision made under sub-paragraph (6)—

(a) may be made in respect of—

 (i) the supply in the qualification year of a phase and where so made, applies to the phase;

 (ii) a phase where it was not made in respect of the qualification year, where such a decision is made on or before the participant submits its footprint report;

(b) must not be altered during the phase.

17 Caravan sites: accommodation

(1) A is not supplied with electricity, gas or fuel to the extent that supply is consumed by A directly for the purposes of accommodation at a caravan site.

(2) "Caravan site" means—

(a) in England and Wales and Scotland, a caravan site within the meaning of section 1(4) of the Caravan Sites and Control of Development Act 1960 which is in accordance with Part 1 of that Act—

 (i) licensed;

 (ii) exempt from requiring a licence; or

 (iii) provided by a local authority as defined by that Part;

(b) in England and Wales, land licensed under section 269 of the Public Health Act 1936 for use as a site for a moveable dwelling within the meaning of that section;

(c) in Northern Ireland, a caravan site within the meaning of section 1(4) of the Caravans Act (Northern Ireland) 1963 which is—

 (i) licensed in accordance with section 1(1) of that Act;

 (ii) exempt from requiring a licence under section 2 of that Act;

 (iii) provided by a district council as defined by section 21 of that Act; or

 (iv) provided by the Northern Ireland Housing Executive pursuant to Article 28A of the Housing (Northern Ireland) Order 1981.

18 Emergency and temporary accommodation

(1) Where A is a housing body, A is not supplied with electricity, gas or fuel to the extent the supply is consumed by A for the purposes of emergency or temporary accommodation.

(2) In sub-paragraph (1)—

(a) "emergency or temporary accommodation" means accommodation provided in discharge of a duty on the housing body under—

 (i) in England and Wales, Part VII of the Housing Act 1996;

 (ii) in Scotland, Part II of the Housing (Scotland) Act 1987;

 (iii) in Northern Ireland, Part II of the Housing (Northern Ireland) Order 1988;

(b) "housing body" means—

 (i) in England and Wales, a local housing authority within the meaning of Part VII of the Housing Act 1996;

 (ii) in Scotland, a local authority within the meaning of Part II of the Housing (Scotland) Act 1987;

 (iii) in Northern Ireland, the Northern Ireland Housing Executive.

19 Transport consumption

(1) Subject to sub-paragraph (2), A is not supplied with electricity, gas or fuel to the extent that supply is consumed by A for the purposes of transport ("transport consumption").

(2) A is supplied with an un-metered electricity or gas transport supply where a decision has been made that such a supply is not consumed for the purposes of transport under paragraph 20 or 21.

20 Un-metered transport supply: electricity

(1) Sub-paragraph (2) applies where—
(a) A has consumed a supply of electricity for the purposes of transport; and
(b) part of that supply so consumed was not measured by a meter of any sort ("un-metered electricity transport supply").

(2) Where this sub-paragraph applies, A may decide that un-metered electricity transport supply is not consumed for the purposes of transport.

(3) A decision made under sub-paragraph (2)—
(a) may be made in respect of—
 (i) qualifying electricity in the qualification year of a phase and where so made, applies also to supplies of electricity during the phase;
 (ii) a phase where it was not made in respect of the qualification year, where such a decision is made on or before the participant submits its footprint report;
(b) must not be altered during the phase.

21 Un-metered transport supply: gas

(1) Sub-paragraph (2) applies where—
(a) A has consumed gas for the purposes of transport; and
(b) part of that supply so consumed was not measured by a meter of any sort ("un-metered gas transport supply").

(2) Where this sub-paragraph applies, A may decide that un-metered gas transport supply during a phase is not consumed for the purposes of transport.

(3) A decision made under sub-paragraph (2)—
(a) may be made in respect of a phase where such a decision is made on or before the participant submits its footprint report;
(b) must not be altered during the phase.

22 Purposes of transport

(1) In paragraph 19, electricity, gas or fuel is consumed for the purposes of transport where it is used—
(a) by a road going vehicle, a vessel, an aircraft or a train; or
(b) in relation to railways, for network services except where electricity, gas or fuel is used to provide power, heat or light to a building.

(2) The following definitions have effect for the purposes of sub-paragraph (1)—
"aircraft" means a self-propelled machine that can move through the air other than against the earth's surface;
"network services" has the same meaning it has in section 82 of the Railways Act 1993 but as if section 82(3)(h) of that Act did not apply;
"road going vehicle" means any vehicle—
 (a) in respect of which a vehicle licence is required under the Vehicle Excise and Registration Act 1994;
 (b) which is an exempt vehicle under that Act; or
 (c) which is required to display a certificate of Crown exemption under regulation 31 of the Road Vehicles (Registration and Licensing) Regulations 2002;
"train" has the same meaning it has in section 83 of the Railways Act 1993;
"vessel" means any boat or ship which is self-propelled and operates in or under water.

SECTION 5
DEDUCTIONS FROM SUPPLIES DURING THE FIRST PHASE IN NORTHERN IRELAND

23 Application of section 5

(1) This section provides for deductions in calculating the amount of a supply of electricity, gas or fuel under section 1, 2 or 3 of this Schedule in Northern Ireland.

(2) The deductions apply only for the first phase and where provided under this Order.

24 Public lighting supplies

(1) A is not supplied with electricity, gas or fuel to the extent that supply is consumed by A for the purposes of public lighting.

(2) In sub-paragraph (1) "public lighting" means lighting to illuminate—
(a) a public accessway, being a street, footpath, footway, cycle track or pedestrian subway open to public access;
(b) a traffic sign or bollard provided in connection with a public accessway; or
(c) a car park,
but only where such lighting is provided by or on behalf of the Department for Regional Development.

SECTION 6
ADDITIONS TO SUPPLIES: ESTIMATION ADJUSTMENTS

25 Additions to supplies

(1) This section provides for additions in calculating the amount of a supply of electricity, gas or fuel under section 1, 2 or 3 of this Schedule.

(2) The additions apply only where provided under this Order.

26 Estimation adjustment: electricity and gas

(1) Sub-paragraph (2) applies—
(a) to a supply to A of electricity or gas measured by a specific metering device ("device 1") during a year;
(b) for at least half of the year in which the supply is made, the amount of that supply is estimated by the supplier; and
(c) A cannot provide evidence to the satisfaction of the administrator that A has measured such estimated supply by a meter reading from device 1.

(2) Where this sub-paragraph applies, the "estimation adjustment" is 10% of the amount of the supply during the year which is measured by device 1.

27 Estimation adjustment: fuels

(1) Sub-paragraph (2) applies where—
(a) A is supplied with fuel during a year;
(b) for at least half of the year in which the supply is made, the amount of that supply consumed by A is estimated by A; and
(c) A cannot provide evidence to the satisfaction of the administrator of that amount.

(2) Where this sub-paragraph applies, the "estimation adjustment" is 10% of that amount which has been estimated.

SECTION 7
RENEWABLES GENERATION AND AMOUNT OF EMISSIONS FROM SUPPLIES

28 Renewables generation: electricity

(1) Sub-paragraph (2) applies where—
(a) A generates electricity;
(b) in respect of that generation,—
 (i) A is issued with a ROC; or
 (ii) A is in receipt of a financial incentive made by virtue of section 41 of the Energy Act 2008; and
(c) A supplies some or all of that generated electricity to itself under paragraph 6 of this Schedule at the premises where it is generated.

(2) Where this sub-paragraph applies, "renewables generation" is the amount of the electricity generated which A supplies to itself.

29 Amount of emissions

(1) The emissions in tCO_2 from an amount of electricity, gas or fuel supplied is found by applying to that amount the relevant conversion factor.

(2) Where in respect of fuel, the amount supplied is a blend of fuels, the requirement in sub-paragraph (1) applies in proportion to the fuels supplied.

30 Conversion factors

In paragraph 29, "relevant conversion factor" means a factor listed—
(a) in version 1 of the document named "CRC Energy Efficiency Scheme Order: Table of Conversion Factors" published by the Secretary of State and made available on the website address at, www.decc.gov.uk, on or before the date this Order is made; or
(b) in any replacement or revision of the document described in sub-paragraph (a) which is published and made available in the same way as that document ("a revised document").

31 Revisions to conversion factors

(1) Only the Secretary of State may draw up a revised document.

(2) The Secretary of State must—
(a) consult publicly on a draft of a revised document; and
(b) carry out that consultation for a minimum of 12 weeks.

(3) The Secretary of State must consult—
(a) the Scottish Ministers;
(b) the Welsh Ministers; and
(c) the Northern Ireland departments,
before complying with sub-paragraph (2).

(4) A revised document must be published and made available at least 90 days before the end of the year of the phase in which the factors are to have effect.

SCHEDULE 2
CORE SUPPLIES

Article 5

SECTION 1
CORE ELECTRICITY SUPPLIES

1 Core electricity supplies

A core supply of electricity means a supply to which sections 1 to 3 of Schedule 1 apply where the supply is—

(a) measured by the following type of meter—
   (i) a settled half hourly meter;
   (ii) a non-settled half hourly meter, where paragraph 3 is satisfied; or
   (iii) a non-domestic meter;
   or
(b) a dynamic supply.

2 Settled half hourly meters

(1) In paragraph 1, "a settled half hourly meter" is a meter which—
(a) is able to measure electricity supplied at least every half hour; and
(b) enables the supplier to comply with provisions of its licence to determine charges between that supplier and another licence holder in respect of the transmission and trading of wholesale electricity.

(2) In sub-paragraph (1), "licence" means—
(a) in Great Britain, a licence within the meaning of section 6(1) of the Electricity Act 1989;
(b) in Northern Ireland, a licence within the meaning of Article 10(1) or (2) of the Electricity (Northern Ireland) Order 1992.

3 Non-settled half hourly meters

(1) In paragraph 1, "a non-settled half hourly meter" is a meter which—
(a) is able to measure electricity supplied at least every half hour; and
(b) subject to sub-paragraph (3), in respect of a phase has been read remotely.

(2) In sub-paragraph (1)(b), "read remotely" means where the meter is read remotely by the public body or undertaking to which the supply is made (or by a person acting on its behalf) at any time during—
(a) the qualification year for the phase; or
(b) a year of that phase.

(3) Sub-paragraph (1)(b) is satisfied in and from the year in which the remote reading first takes place.

4 Non-domestic meters

In paragraph 1, "a non-domestic meter" means a meter which—
(a) is designed to measure supplies to non-domestic premises;
(b) measures such supplies; and
(c) is capable of measuring maximum electricity demand.

5 Dynamic supply

In paragraph 1, a "dynamic supply" means a supply where—
(a) a device, which is not a metering device, records daily when electricity is supplied or not to one item of a set of equipment on premises; and
(b) that record is used to determine the half hourly supply of electricity to the whole set of equipment.

SECTION 2
CORE GAS SUPPLIES

6 Core gas supplies

(1) A core supply of gas means a supply to which sections 1 to 3 of Schedule 1 apply measured by a meter which is—
(a) a daily meter;

(b) an hourly meter; or
(c) a large gas point meter.

(2) A meter under sub-paragraph (1) includes any ancillary device used in connection with that meter which allows the amount of the supply measured by that meter to be read.

7 Daily meters

In paragraph 6, "a daily meter" is a meter which—
(a) is able to measure gas supplied at least daily; and
(b) is read in Great Britain by an authorised supplier or an authorised transporter under section 48(1) of the Gas Act 1986 or in Northern Ireland by a licence holder under Article 3(1) of the Gas (Northern Ireland) Order 1996.

8 Hourly meters

(1) In paragraph 6, "an hourly meter" is a meter which—
(a) is able to measure gas at least hourly; and
(b) subject to sub-paragraph (3), in respect of a phase has been read remotely.

(2) In sub-paragraph (1), "read remotely" has the same meaning it has in paragraph 3(2).

(3) Sub-paragraph (1)(b) is satisfied in respect of the year in which the remote reading first takes place and each subsequent year of the phase.

9 Large gas point meters

In paragraph 6, "a large gas point meter" means a meter which during a footprint year of a phase measured greater than 73,200 kWh of gas supplied.

SCHEDULE 3
PUBLIC BODIES

Article 5

SECTION 1
INTERPRETATION

1 Public bodies

In this Order, "public body" means a public body described in this section.

2 Public authorities and the National Assembly for Wales Commission

(1) A public authority is a public body.

(2) In sub-paragraph (1), a "public authority" means—
(a) a public authority within the meaning of section 3(1)(a) of the Freedom of Information Act 2000 ("the 2000 Act"); and
(b) a Scottish public authority within the meaning of section 3(1)(a) of the Freedom of Information (Scotland) Act 2002("the 2002 Act"),
but not any such authority listed in sub-paragraph (4) or paragraph 4.

(3) Where a public authority is included within the 2000 Act or the 2002 Act subject to a limitation, that limitation does not apply in respect of this Order.

(4) The public authorities referred to in sub-paragraph (2) are—
(a) the House of Commons;
(b) the House of Lords;
(c) the force or any unit described in sub-paragraph (a) or (b) of paragraph 6 (the armed forces of the Crown) of Schedule 1 to the 2000 Act;

(d) a person described in paragraph 64 (persons nominating special constables) of Schedule 1 to the 2000 Act;
(e) the National Assembly for Wales.

(5) The National Assembly for Wales Commission is a public body.

3 Public bodies: bodies corporate

(1) A body corporate is a public body where it is a body in which a public body under paragraph 2 is a majority member.

(2) A public body is a majority member of a body ("body A") under sub-paragraph (1) where—
(a) the member;
(b) a person acting on behalf of the member; or
(c) a body corporate in which the member or person acting on its behalf is a majority member,
(any of whom is "person B") satisfies the provisions in sub-paragraph (3).

(3) The provisions referred to in sub-paragraph (2) are—
(a) person B holds a majority of the voting rights in body A;
(b) person B is a member of body A and has the right to appoint or remove a majority of its board of directors; or
(c) person B is a member of body A and controls alone, pursuant to an agreement with other members, a majority of the voting rights in body A.

4 Public bodies: proprietors of Academies and colleges

(1) The proprietor of—
(a) an Academy within the meaning of section 482 of the Education Act 1996;
(b) a city technology college or city college for the technology of the arts within the meaning of section 482 of that Act as originally enacted,
is a public body.

(2) Where—
(a) a proprietor described in sub-paragraph (1) is the proprietor of more than one Academy or college; and
(b) those Academies or colleges are situated in more than one local authority area,
the proprietor is a separate public body in respect of those Academies or colleges in different local authority areas.

(3) Where a proprietor would be required to register as a participant under Part 2—
(a) if it were not a public body under sub-paragraph (1); and
(b) excluding the scheme activities in respect of which it is such a public body,
the proprietor is, as applicable, a separate public body or undertaking in respect of its other scheme activities.

5 Public bodies: one public body part of another

(1) Except where paragraph 4(2) or (3) applies, where a public body ("A") is part of another public body ("B")—
(a) A is not a public body; and
(b) B including A is a public body.

(2) A government department is not part of another government department.

SECTION 2
PUBLIC BODIES: GROUPS

6 Groups and members

In relation to public bodies—

"group" means those public bodies which are members of a group—
- (a) as provided by paragraphs 7 to 9;
- (b) further to—
  - (i) a government decision under paragraph 14;
  - (ii) a local authority decision under paragraph 16;

  or
- (c) as provided under article 20 for the purposes of that article or under article 21;

"member" means a public body which is part of a group together with one or more other public bodies.

7 Bodies corporate

Subject to a government decision under paragraph 14, where a body corporate is a public body and where the majority member is—
- (a) a government department, that body is a member of a group with that department;
- (b) the Scottish Ministers, that body is a member of a group with the Ministers;
- (c) the Welsh Ministers, the First Minister for Wales or the Counsel General, that body is a member of a group with the Welsh Assembly Government;
- (d) a relevant Northern Ireland department, that body is a member of a group with the relevant department.

8 Educational bodies: England and Wales

(1) In England and Wales—
- (a) where a public body is the governing body of a maintained school or a maintained nursery school, that public body is member of a group with the local authority which maintains the school;
- (b) a public body described in paragraph 4(1) is a member of a group with the local authority which exercises educational functions in the area in which the Academy or college is situated.

(2) In this paragraph, the following have the same meanings given to them in the 2000 Act—

"local authority";

"maintained nursery school";

"maintained school".

9 Grant-aided schools: Northern Ireland

(1) This paragraph applies in Northern Ireland and to a public body which is a grant-aided school within the meaning of Article 2(2) of the of the Education and Libraries (Northern Ireland) Order 1986 ("a grant-aided school").

(2) Subject to sub-paragraph (3), a grant-aided school is a member of a group with the Education and Library Board which funds that school.

(3) Where the Education and Skills Authority has been established, subject to sub-paragraph (4), a grant-aided school is a member of a group with that Authority.

(4) Sub-paragraph (3) does not apply in respect of a phase where that phase has commenced before the Authority is established.

SECTION 3
PUBLIC BODIES: GOVERNMENT AND LOCAL AUTHORITY DECISIONS

10 Government and local authority decisions

(1) Except in relation to the Treasury, the Secretary of State may make a government decision in relation to a government department.

(2) The Treasury may make a government decision in relation to the Treasury.

(3) Where—
(a) the Secretary of State or the Treasury intend to make a government decision described in paragraph 14(2)(a) in relation to a public authority described in Part VI of Schedule 1 to the 2000 Act; and
(b) that authority exercises functions partly other than in England,
the Secretary of State or the Treasury must consult, as applicable, the Scottish Ministers, the Welsh Ministers or the relevant Northern Ireland department before making the decision.

(4) The Secretary of State or the Treasury must not make a government decision in relation to a public body which exercises functions wholly in Scotland, Wales or Northern Ireland.

(5) A local authority decision may be made by—
(a) the Secretary of State in relation to a local government public body or a local government group in England;
(b) the Welsh Ministers in relation to a local government public body or a local government group in Wales.

(6) A government decision—
(a) must not be made such that a public body, on its own or part of a group,—
  (i) which is a participant, is no longer a participant;
  (ii) which is required to be a participant, is no longer required to be a participant;
(b) may be made for the better administration of the scheme.

11 The Scottish Ministers

(1) The Scottish Ministers may make a government decision as if reference in paragraph 14(2) to "a government department" were a reference to the Scottish Ministers.

(2) The Scottish Ministers may make a government decision described in paragraph 14(2)(a) only in respect of the public bodies described in the following paragraphs of this Schedule—
(a) paragraph 2(2)(b);
(b) paragraph 3 where the majority member is a body described in paragraph 2(2)(b).

12 The Welsh Assembly Government and Welsh Ministers

(1) The Welsh Ministers may make a government decision as if reference in paragraph 14(2) to "a government department" were a reference to the Welsh Assembly Government.

(2) The Welsh Ministers must not make a government decision under paragraph 14(2)(a) unless the public body exercises functions in or as regards Wales and—
[(a)][1] those functions are exercised in relation to matters within the legislative competence of the National Assembly for Wales; or
[(b)][1] functions are exercisable in relation to that body by the Welsh Ministers, the First Minister for Wales or the Counsel General.

Amendment
1 Substituted by the CRC Energy Efficiency Scheme (Amendment) Order 2011, SI 2011/234, art 19.

13 Northern Ireland departments

(1) The relevant Northern Ireland department may make a government decision as if reference in paragraph 14(2) to "a government department" were a reference to a relevant department.

(2) The relevant Northern Ireland department must not make a government decision under paragraph 14(2)(a) unless the Northern Ireland Assembly has legislative competence in respect of the functions of the public body.

14 Government decisions

(1) "A government decision" means any decision described in sub-paragraph (2) in relation to—

(a) qualification for a phase; or
(b) participation during a phase or any part of a phase.

(2) The decisions referred to in sub-paragraph (1) are—
(a) that a public body (which is not a government department) is or is not a member of a group together with the department;
(b) that any part of a government department as described in the decision must register as a participant separately from the remainder of the department;
(c) subject to paragraph 15(2), that a government department is a member of a group with another government department;
(d) under paragraph 13 only and where the Education and Skills Authority referred to in paragraph 9(3) has been established, that—
  (i) paragraph 9(2) does not apply to a grant-aided school referred to in that sub-paragraph; and
  (ii) such a school is a member of a group with the Authority.

15 Government decisions: supplies and departments

(1) A government decision under paragraph 14(2)(b) must state—
(a) which supplies of electricity, gas or fuel are supplied to which part of the department for the phase;
(b) where a public body is a member of a group with the department, with which part of the department it is a group member.

(2) A government decision under paragraph 14(2)(c) must only be made in respect of a department which, had it been subject to article 17 on qualification for the phase, would not have been required to register as a participant.

16 Local authority decisions

(1) In paragraph 10(5), a "local authority decision" means a decision described in sub-paragraph (2) in relation to qualification for a phase in respect of—
(a) a public body ("a local government public body") which is—
  (i) in England, a public authority described in paragraphs 7(a) and 8 to 11 of Part II (local government) of Schedule 1 to the 2000 Act; or
  (ii) in Wales, a public authority described in paragraph 7(b) of that Part;

  or
(b) where the local government public body is a member of a group under section 2 of this Schedule ("the local government group"), such a group.

(2) A decision referred to in sub-paragraph (1) means that a local government public body or group is a public body to which article 14(1)(e) applies.

(3) Where such a decision is made, the decision may also provide—
(a) that the body or group is a member of a group with another public body required to register as a participant;
(b) where applicable, that the decision only applies to the local government public body and not any other member of the local government group.

(4) Where a decision is made under sub-paragraph (3)(b)—
(a) the local government group ceases to exist; and
(b) other members of the group are separate public bodies.

17 Notification of government and local authority decisions

(1) The administrator must be notified in writing with the application for registration as a participant in respect of—
(a) a government decision in relation to qualification for a phase;
(b) a local authority decision.

(2) A government decision in relation to participation during a phase or any part of a phase must be notified in writing as soon as possible to the administrator.

(3) A notification required under sub-paragraph (1) or (2) must—
(a) state the period for which the decision has effect, which may commence before the date of the notification but must not commence in a phase which has completed; and
(b) identify the public bodies affected.

(4) A government decision or local authority decision may be varied or revoked in writing.

SCHEDULE 4
UNDERTAKINGS AND SIGNIFICANT GROUP UNDERTAKINGS

Article 5

Undertakings and significant group undertakings

1 Undertakings

In this Order, subject to paragraph 4—
(a) in relation to an undertaking, "group" means those undertakings which are group undertakings in respect of each other;
(b) "group undertaking" has the meaning given by section 1161(5) of the Companies Act 2006 but where "undertaking" has the meaning given in this Order;
(c) "highest parent undertaking" is the undertaking in the group which is not a subsidiary of any other undertaking in the group;
(d) "member" in relation to group undertakings means an undertaking which is part of a group;
(e) "parent undertaking", "subsidiary undertaking" and related expressions have the same meanings as in Part 38 of the Companies Act 2006 but where "undertaking" has the meaning given in this Order;
(f) "undertaking" means—
(i) an undertaking as defined in section 1161(1) of the Companies Act 2006; and
(ii) as if that definition included an unincorporated association which carries on a charitable activity,
but an undertaking does not include a public body.

2 Significant group undertakings

(1) An undertaking is a "significant group undertaking" of a group when so provided under this paragraph—
(a) for the purposes of Part 2; and
(b) during a phase.

(2) Sub-paragraph (3) applies—
(a) to a group of undertakings ("G");
(b) to an undertaking ("U") which is a group undertaking of G; and
(c) where U is a subsidiary of another undertaking of G.

(3) Subject to sub-paragraph (4), for the purposes of Part 2 where—
(a) U; and
(b) any subsidiary undertakings of U,
would, if U was not a member of G, have been required to register as a participant under Part 2, U is a significant group undertaking as a member of G, together with U's subsidiary undertakings, if any.

(4) Where—
(a) U would be a significant undertaking as a member of G under sub-paragraph (3); but
(b) G is subject to article 27(2),
the provisions of section 1 of Part 3 of Schedule 6 vary sub-paragraph (3).

(5) Subject to paragraph 3, where U is a significant group undertaking as a member of—
(a) G for the purposes of Part 2 under sub-paragraph (3); or
(b) another group, where sub-paragraph (4) applies,
U is a significant group undertaking as a member of G or that other group for that phase, together with U's subsidiary undertakings from time to time, if any.

3 Significant group undertakings: movement between groups during a phase

(1) Subject to paragraph 4, where—
(a) U was a significant group undertaking as a member of a group under paragraph 2; and
(b) during a phase U becomes a member of another group of undertakings ("G2"),
U is a significant group undertaking as a member of G2 for the remainder of that phase, together with U's subsidiary undertakings from time to time, if any.

(2) Paragraphs 10 and 12 of section 2 of Part 3 of Schedule 6 make provision in relation to the change described in sub-paragraph (1).

4 Significant group undertakings as participants

Where during a phase a significant group undertaking—
(a) is a member of a group; but
(b) is a participant separate from the group,
for such time as it is a participant separate from the group, it must be treated as if it was not a member of the group for the phase.

SCHEDULE 5
INFORMATION

Article 5

SECTION 1
INFORMATION ON REGISTRATION

General

1

Information in this section is required under Part 2 and Schedule 6.

Contact information

2

Subject to paragraph 4, as applicable to the applicant—
(a) name, postal address, email address and telephone number;
(b) the principal place of activity;
(c) any company registration number and registered office;
(d) any trading or other name by which the applicant is commonly known.

3

Where the applicant is a group of undertakings—
(a) the information in paragraph 2 in respect of—
  (i) each significant group undertaking; and
  (ii) the highest parent undertaking;
  and
(b) where an undertaking other than the highest parent undertaking is to be the account holder of the compliance account, the information in paragraph 2 in respect of that undertaking.

4

Where the applicant is a group of public bodies, the information in paragraph 2 is required only in respect of the following in that group—
(a) a government department;
(b) the Scottish Ministers;
(c) the Welsh Assembly Government;
(d) a Northern Ireland Department;
(e) a local authority;
(f) a university;
(g) for a group which does not include a public body described in sub-paragraphs (a) to (f), the body in the group intended to be the account holder in respect of the compliance account.

5

The name, postal address, email address and telephone number of at least three individuals who will act as contacts for the applicant, one of whom must exercise management control in respect of the public body or undertaking which is to be the account holder of the compliance account.

Total supplies of qualifying electricity

6

(1) A list of all settled half hourly meters which measured the supply of qualifying electricity to the applicant in the qualification year.

(2) The total amount of qualifying electricity in the qualification year.

(3) The amount of electricity under sub-paragraph (2) may be estimated.

Exemptions

7

Where the participant intends to claim—
(a) a member CCA exemption, in respect of the member its total emissions and its CCA emissions;
(b) a general CCA exemption, the participant's total emissions and CCA emissions;
(c) a group CCA exemption, "X" and "Y" referred to in article 34(2).

SECTION 2
INFORMATION IN FOOTPRINT YEARS

General

8

Information in this section is required from a participant under Part 4.

Supplies

9

(1) The amount of electricity, gas and fuel supplied to the participant in the footprint year calculated in accordance with sections 1 to 5 of Schedule 1 but excluding any such supplies to—

(a) an EU ETS installation; or
(b) a CCA facility to which a member CCA exemption does not apply.

(2) Core supplies calculated in accordance with sections 1 to 5 of Schedule 1 but excluding such supplies made to—
(a) an EU ETS installation; or
(b) a CCA facility to which a member CCA exemption does not apply.

(3) The amount of any supply of energy during the footprint year except electricity, gas or fuel, identifying the energy source.

Residual measurement list and residual supplies

10

Whether or not the participant has compiled a residual measurement list and, if it has, the residual supplies in that list.

Electricity generating credit and renewables generation

11

The amount, if any, of electricity generating credit and renewables generation.

EU ETS and CCA emissions

12

(1) The emissions from the participant's—
(a) EU ETS installations ("EU ETS emissions");
(b) CCA facilities ("CCA emissions") excluding a facility to which a member CCA exemption applies.

(2) "EU ETS emissions" means—
(a) the emissions required to be reported by the participant to comply with the EU ETS Directive in the calendar year commencing on the 1st January immediately before the start of the footprint year; or
(b) the emissions in respect of the amount of electricity, gas and fuel supplied at the EU ETS installations and where—
  (i) those supplies are calculated in accordance with sections 1 to 5 of Schedule 1; and
  (ii) the emissions from those supplies are calculated in accordance with paragraph 29 of Schedule 1.

(3) "CCA emissions" means—
[(za) where an exemption is claimed under article 35, the emissions required to be reported by the participant under the CCA for the CCA facilities, where those facilities are subject to a CCA target period ending in the qualification year;][1]
(a) [where an exemption is claimed under article 36,][1] the emissions required to be reported by the participant under the CCA for the CCA facilities, where those facilities are subject to a CCA target period ending in the footprint year; or
(b) the emissions in respect of the amount of electricity, gas and fuel supplied at the CCA facilities and where—
  (i) those supplies are calculated in accordance with sections 1 to 5 of Schedule 1; and
  (ii) the emissions from those supplies are calculated in accordance with paragraph 29 of Schedule 1.

Amendment
1 Inserted by the CRC Energy Efficiency Scheme (Amendment) Order 2011, SI 2011/234, art 20.

Decisions in respect of domestic accommodation and un-metered transport supplies

13

Whether or not it has made a decision—

(a) under paragraph 16 of Schedule 1 that common areas are not part of domestic accommodation;

(b) under paragraph 20 of Schedule 1 that un-metered electricity transport supply is not consumed for the purposes of transport;

(c) under paragraph 21 of Schedule 1 that un-metered gas transport supply is not consumed for the purposes of transport.

SCHEDULE 6
CHANGES TO PARTICIPANTS

Article 5

PART 1
PUBLIC BODIES: GOVERNMENT

Section 1

Government departments, Northern Ireland departments, the Scottish Ministers and the Welsh Assembly Government

1 Application of Part 1

(1) Where the changes described in sections 2 to 5 of this Part occur in a year of a phase ("year 1") in relation to a participant which is or includes—

(a) a government department or part of it;

(b) a relevant Northern Ireland department or part of it,

such a participant must comply with the requirements in those sections.

(2) Under sub-paragraph (1)(b), in relation to a relevant Northern Ireland department, reference in paragraphs 7 and 11 to the Secretary of State includes reference to the relevant department.

(3) Where the changes described in sections 3 to 5 occur in year 1 in relation to a participant which is or includes the Scottish Ministers or part of that body, such a participant must comply with the requirements in those sections.

(4) Under sub-paragraph (3), in relation to the Scottish Ministers, reference to—

(a) the Secretary of State in paragraph 11 includes the Scottish Ministers;

(b) a department in paragraph 12 includes those Ministers or part of that body.

(5) Where the changes described in section 4 or 5 occur in year 1 in relation to a participant which is or includes the Welsh Assembly Government or part of that body, such a participant must comply with the requirements in those sections.

(6) Under sub-paragraph (5), in relation to the Welsh Assembly Government, reference to a department in paragraph 12 includes the Welsh Assembly Government or part of that body.

2 Notifications and applications: time to comply and the administrator

(1) A notification or application for registration required under this Part must be made using the Registry and within 3 months of the change occurring.

(2) Subject to receipt of such notification or application for registration, the administrator must amend the information it holds in respect of the relevant participants.

Section 2
Creation of new departments

3 Creation of a new department

This section applies where—
(a) from part of a participant ("A") and part of another participant ("B"), a department ("C") is created in year 1; and
(b) A and B continue as participants.

4 Creation of a new department: year 1

In year 1—
(a) C must—
  (i) apply for registration as a participant in accordance with article 11; and
  (ii) comply with Part 5 as if C existed for the whole of year 1;
(b) A and B must comply with this Order as if C had not been created.

5 Creation of a new department: year 2

In the year after year 1 ("year 2")—
(a) C must comply with Parts 4 and 5 of this Order; and
(b) A and B must comply with this Order as if C had not been created.

6 Creation of a new department: after year 2

(1) In the years after year 2—
(a) C must comply with this Order as applicable to the years after year 2; and
(b) A and B must comply with this Order as applicable to the years after year 2 but where A and B do not include C.

(2) In the year after year 2, where A or B have a residual measurement list, that list must be amended to exclude any residual supplies of C.

7 Deemed supplies of the new department

(1) For the purposes of this section, the Secretary of State may declare in writing that a supply of electricity, gas or fuel—
(a) to A or B is deemed to be a supply to C;
(b) to C is deemed to be a supply to A or B.

(2) A declaration made under sub-paragraph (1) must be provided by the Secretary of State to the administrator as soon as possible.

Section 3
Transfers of parts of government departments, Northern Ireland departments or the Scottish Ministers

8 Transfer of part of a department to another department

This section applies where from a participant ("D"), a part ("E") transfers to another participant ("F") in year 1 ("the transfer").

9 Transfers: year 1

In year 1, D and F must—
(a) notify the administrator of—
  (i) the transfer; and
  (ii) as soon as possible, the percentage of the emissions of D which are attributable to E;
(b) comply with this Order as if the transfer had not occurred.

10 Transfers: year 2

(1) In the year after year 1 ("year 2"), where D has a residual measurement list, it must amend that list to exclude any residual supplies of E.

(2) In year 2 where—
(a) D and F have residual measurement lists; and
(b) residual supplies of E were included in D's list,
F must amend its list to include the residual supplies of E which were in D's list.

(3) In year 2 where—
(a) D has a residual measurement list and residual supplies of E were included in D's list; and
(b) F does not have a residual measurement list,
F must compile a residual measurement list to include the residual supplies of E which were in D's list.

11 Deemed supplies

(1) For the purposes of this section, the Secretary of State may declare in writing that a supply of electricity, gas or fuel—
(a) to D which is attributable to E is deemed to be a supply to F;
(b) to F which is attributable to E is deemed to be a supply to D.

(2) A declaration made under sub-paragraph (1) must be provided by the Secretary of State to the administrator as soon as possible.

Section 4
Mergers in respect of government departments, Northern Ireland departments, the Scottish Ministers or the Welsh Assembly Government

12 Mergers of departments

(1) Sub-paragraphs (2) to (5) apply where a participant ("G") merges with another participant ("H") in year 1 ("the merger") to form a new department ("J").

(2) J must notify the administrator of the merger.

(3) Where G or H had a residual measurement list before the merger, J must compile such a list from the residual supplies of G or H or, as appropriate, both.

(4) J must—
(a) apply for registration as a participant in accordance with article 11; and
(b) comply with this Order as if J existed for the whole of year 1.

(5) Subject to the registration of J, the administrator must cancel the registration of G and H for the remainder of the phase.

Section 5
Government decisions and separate participation

13 Government decisions

This section applies where a government decision is made in respect of a participant ("K") that a part of K is a separate participant ("L").

14 Separate participants: year 1

In year 1,—
(a) L must—
 (i) apply for registration as a participant in accordance with article 11; and

(ii) comply with Parts 4, 5 and 7 as if L existed for the whole of year 1;
(b) K must comply with this Order as if the government decision had not been made.

PART 2
OTHER PUBLIC BODIES

1 Application of Part 2

This Part applies where the change described occurs in a year of a phase ("year 1") and to a participant which is or includes a public body other than a public body to which Part 1 applies.

2 Notifications and applications: time to comply and the administrator

(1) The notification and application for registration required under this Part must be made using the Registry and within 3 months of the change occurring.

(2) Subject to receipt of such notification or application for registration, the administrator must amend the information it holds in respect of the relevant participants.

3 Mergers of public bodies

(1) Sub-paragraphs (2) to (5) apply where a participant ("A") merges with another participant ("B") in year 1 ("the merger") to form a new public body ("C").

(2) C must notify the administrator of the merger.

(3) Where A or B had a residual measurement list before the merger, C must compile such a list from the residual supplies of A or B or, as appropriate, both.

(4) C must—
(a) apply for registration as a participant in accordance with article 11; and
(b) comply with this Order as if C existed for the whole of year 1.

(5) Subject to the registration of C, the administrator must cancel the registration of A and B for the remainder of the phase.

PART 3
UNDERTAKINGS

Section 1
Post-qualification period

1 Time for applications

Where an application for registration is required under this section, that application must be made by the time provided under article 12.

2 Significant group undertakings leaving a group but not joining another group

(1) Sub-paragraph (2) applies to a group ("A") where the following change occurs in the post-qualification period—
(a) a significant group undertaking ("B") leaves A; and
(b) B does not become a member of another group.

(2) In respect of the change—
(a) B must—
(i) apply to be registered as a participant in accordance with article 11; and
(ii) when doing so notify the administrator that it was a member of A and when it ceased to be so;

(b) A must—
 (i) apply to be registered as a participant in accordance with article 11;
 (ii) when doing so notify the administrator that B was a member of A and when it ceased to be so; and
 (iii) in respect of the information required under paragraph 6 of Schedule 5, include the information which applied to B in the qualification year.

3 Joining of undertakings with a group which is not required to register as a participant

(1) Sub-paragraph (2) applies to a group or undertaking ("C") where the following change occurs in the post-qualification period—
(a) C becomes a significant group undertaking as a member of another group ("D"); and
(b) D is not required to register under article 24.

(2) In respect of the change—
(a) D must—
 (i) apply for registration as a participant in accordance with article 11; and
 (ii) when doing so notify the administrator that C is a member of D and when that occurred;
(b) C must not apply for registration as a participant;
(c) D is only a participant in respect of C; and
(d) D must with the application for registration provide in respect of the qualification year the information in sub-paragraph (3).

(3) The information referred to in sub-paragraph (2)—
(a) a list of the settled half hourly meters which measured the supply of electricity to D and the identification numbers of those meters; and
(b) in respect of the supply of electricity to D measured by settled half hourly meters and non-settled half hourly meters—
 (i) whether or not the supply equalled or exceeded 3000 MWh and, if it did, the amount of the supply; and
 (ii) if the supply equalled or exceeded 6000 MWh—
  (aa) why D was not required to register as a participant; and
  (bb) which deductions from a supply in section 4 and, if applicable, section 5 of Schedule 1 are applicable to the supply.

4 Joining of undertakings with a group which is required to register as a participant

(1) Sub-paragraphs (2) to (4) apply to a group or undertaking ("E") where the following change occurs in the post-qualification period—
(a) E becomes a significant group undertaking as a member of another group ("F"); and
(b) F is required to register under article 24 but has not applied for registration.

(2) In respect of the change F must—
(a) apply for registration as a participant in accordance with article 11;
(b) when doing so notify the administrator that E is a member of F and when that occurred;
(c) in that notification F must inform the administrator whether or not F requests that E may apply for registration as a separate participant; and
(d) in respect of the information required under paragraph 6 of Schedule 5, include the information which applied to E in the qualification year.

(3) Where a request is made under sub-paragraph (2)(c), that must be treated as a request under article 25(2) and paragraphs (3) and (4) of that article apply.

(4) Except where sub-paragraph (3) applies, E must not apply for registration as a participant.

5 Significant group undertakings transferring between groups

(1) Sub-paragraphs (2) to (4) apply to a significant group undertaking ("G") of a group ("H") where—

(a) G becomes a significant group undertaking as a member of another group ("J") in the post-qualification period; and
(b) H and J are groups to which article 27(2) applies.

(2) In respect of the change H and J must—
(a) apply for registration as participants in accordance with article 11;
(b) when doing so notify the administrator of the change and when it occurred; and
(c) in the notification by J, it must inform the administrator whether or not J requests that G may apply for registration as a separate participant.

(3) Where a request is made under sub-paragraph (2)(c), that must be treated as a request under article 25(2) and [paragraphs (3) and (4)][1] of that article apply.

(4) In respect of the information required under paragraph 6 of Schedule 5—
(a) H must include the information which applied to G in the qualification year;
(b) J must not include that information.

Amendment

1 Substituted by the CRC Energy Efficiency Scheme (Amendment) Order 2011, SI 2011/234, art 21.

Section 2
Footprint years and annual reporting years

6 Application and general changes during footprint years and annual reporting years

(1) This section does not apply to a participant where—
(a) any of the changes occurs to that participant in the post-qualification period which falls within a footprint year; and
(b) the participant has complied with section 1 of this Part in respect of those changes.

(2) Where in respect of the year in which a change occurs, a participant has a general or a group CCA exemption, a requirement imposed on a participant under this section does not apply to such a participant.

(3) Subject to sub-paragraph (4), where a participant is a group—
(a) the members of the group are those members from time to time during the year;
(b) a footprint report and CRC supplies must be determined in relation to the supplies of electricity, gas or fuel to members of the group only for such time as they are members during the year.

(4) Except in respect of paragraph 7(1) or (3), a change as described in this section where it does not occur on the first day of the year of a phase, is deemed to take place on that day.

7 Notifications and applications: time to comply and the administrator

(1) A notification or application for registration required under this section must be made using the Registry and within 3 months of the change occurring.

(2) Subject to receipt of such notification or application for registration, the administrator must amend the information it holds in respect of the relevant participants.

(3) Where under this section a participant must compile or amend a residual measurement list, that compilation or amendment must be made within 3 months of the change occurring.

8 Determinations

The administrator may make a determination—
(a) whether any change as described in this section has occurred;
(b) whether a notification or application for registration is required as provided under this section.

9 Significant group undertakings becoming participants

(1) Sub-paragraphs (2) and (3) apply where the following change occurs—
(a) a participant ("A") consists of a group;
(b) a significant group undertaking ("B") leaves that group; and
(c) B does not become a member of another group.

(2) Subject to sub-paragraph (4), in respect of the change—
(a) B must apply for registration as a participant in accordance with article 11;
(b) A and B must notify the administrator of the change and when it occurred;
(c) where the change occurs in a footprint year, B must comply with Part 4 of this Order as if B was a participant for the whole of the year in which the change occurs.

(3) Subject to sub-paragraph (4), where the change occurs in an annual reporting year—
(a) B must provide an annual report in respect of the annual reporting year as if B was a participant for the whole of that year; and
(b) where A has a residual measurement list ("list A") which includes the residual supplies of B—
(i) list A must be amended to exclude the residual supplies of B;
(ii) B must compile a residual measurement list from B's residual supplies in list A.

(4) Where A has a member CCA exemption in respect of B—
(a) sub-paragraph (2)(a) applies but otherwise sub-paragraphs (2) and (3) do not apply to B;
(b) where B is—
(i) a group of undertakings, B has a group CCA exemption;
(ii) not such a group, B has a general CCA exemption;
and
(c) subject to article 38, B is exempt from Parts 4 to 7 of this Order for the phase where the applicable exemption applies to B.

10 Joining of a participant or significant group undertaking with a non-participant

(1) Sub-paragraphs (2) and (3) apply where the following change occurs—
(a) a participant or significant group undertaking ("C") of a participant becomes a member of a group ("D"); and
(b) D is not a participant.

(2) Subject to sub-paragraph (6), in respect of the change—
(a) D must apply for registration as a participant in accordance with article 11;
(b) where C is a participant, C must notify the administrator of the change and when it occurred;
(c) where C is a significant group undertaking as a member of a participant, that participant must notify the administrator of the change and when it occurred;
(d) where the change occurs in a footprint year, D must comply with Part 4 of this Order but only in respect of those supplies of electricity, gas or fuel which relate to C and as if C was part of D for the whole of the year in which the change occurs;
(e) C is a significant group undertaking as a member of D for the phase and as if C was a member of D for the whole of the year in which the change occurs;
(f) subject to the registration of D, and where C is a participant, the administrator must cancel the registration of C for the remainder of the phase.

(3) Subject to sub-paragraph (6), where the change occurs in an annual reporting year—
(a) D must provide an annual report in respect of the year but only in respect of those emissions which relate to C and as if C was a member of D for the whole of the year;
(b) where C is a participant and C had a residual measurement list before the change occurred, D must compile such a list from the residual supplies of C.

(4) Subject to sub-paragraph (6), sub-paragraph (5) applies where—
(a) the change occurs in an annual reporting year; and
(b) C is a significant group undertaking of a participant and that participant has a residual measurement list ("list A") which includes residual supplies of C.

(5) Where this sub-paragraph applies—
(a) list A must be amended to exclude the residual supplies of C;
(b) D must compile a residual measurement list from the residual supplies of C in list A.

(6) Where C is a significant group undertaking of a participant and that participant has a member CCA exemption in respect of C—
(a) sub-paragraph (2) applies except paragraphs (b) and (d);
(b) sub-paragraphs (3) to (5) do not apply to D;
(c) where D is—
  (i) a group of undertakings, D has a group CCA exemption;
  (ii) not such a group, D has a general CCA exemption;
  and
(d) subject to article 38, D is exempt from Parts 4 to 7 of this Order for the phase where the applicable exemption applies to D.

11 Joining of a participant as a member of another participant

(1) Sub-paragraphs (2) to (4) apply where the following change occurs—
(a) a participant ("E") becomes a member of a group ("F"); and
(b) F is a participant.

(2) In respect of the change—
(a) E and F must notify the administrator of the change and when it occurred; and
(b) in the notification by F, F must inform the administrator whether or not F requests that E continues as a separate participant.

(3) Where—
(a) F requests that E continues as a separate participant; and
(b) the administrator agrees and so notifies E and F,
E and F continue as separate participants.

(4) Where E and F do not continue as separate participants—
(a) E is a significant group undertaking as a member of F for the phase and as if E was a member of F for the whole of the year in which the change occurs;
(b) subject to the administrator being satisfied that E and F are complying with this Order, the administrator must cancel the registration of E for the remainder of the phase.

(5) Subject to sub-paragraph (7), sub-paragraph (6) applies where the change occurs in an annual reporting year and E and F do not continue as separate participants.

(6) Where this sub-paragraph applies and—
(a) where—
  (i) F did not have a residual measurement list; and
  (ii) E did have a residual measurement list,
  E's residual measurement list becomes F's list;
(b) where E and F each had a residual measurement list before the change occurred, F must amend its list to include the residual supplies from E's list.

(7) Where E and F do not continue as separate participants and E had a general or group CCA exemption—
(a) F has a member CCA exemption in respect of E; and
(b) sub-paragraph (6) does not apply.

12 Significant group undertakings transferring to another participant

(1) Sub-paragraphs (2) to (5) apply where the following change occurs—
(a) a participant ("G") consists of a group;
(b) a significant group undertaking ("H") which was a member of G becomes a significant group undertaking as a member of another participant ("J").

(2) In respect of the change—
(a) G and J must notify the administrator of the change and when it occurred;
(b) in the notification of J, J must inform the administrator whether or not J requests that H may apply for registration as a separate participant; and
(c) if such a request is made, H may make an application to be a participant and if it does, must do so in accordance with article 11.

(3) Where H is registered as a participant separate from J, H must comply with Part 4 as if H had been a participant for the whole of the year in which the change occurs.

(4) Where H is not registered as a separate participant, H is treated as if it was a significant group undertaking as a member of J for the whole of the year in which the change occurs.

(5) Where the change occurs in an annual reporting year and—
(a) G has a residual measurement list, G must amend its residual measurement list to exclude any residual supplies of H;
(b) subject to sub-paragraph (6), where H is not registered as a separate participant and—
(i) where—
(aa) J does not have a residual measurement list; and
(bb) G has a residual measurement list including residual supplies of H, J must compile a residual measurement list from those residual supplies of H;
(ii) where J has a residual measurement list, J must amend its list to include the residual supplies of H.

(6) Sub-paragraph (5)(b) does not apply where—
(a) H is not registered as a separate participant; and
(b) G has a group CCA exemption or had a member CCA exemption in respect of H.

(7) Where G has a group CCA exemption or had a member CCA exemption in respect of H, J has a member CCA exemption in respect of H.

SCHEDULE 7
THE REGISTRY

Article 68

1 Setting up accounts

(1) The administrator must ensure the Registry allows the following accounts to be held—
(a) a compliance account for a participant; and
(b) as agreed by it—
(i) additional accounts for a participant; and
(ii) accounts for third parties.

(2) The administrator may—
(a) limit the number of accounts in respect of a participant or third party; and
(b) set up other accounts.

(3) The administrator must set up one compliance account for a participant where—
(a) it has registered an applicant as a participant; and
(b) it has completed to its satisfaction the identity checks required under article 70(2).

(4) The public body or undertaking in whose name an account is held is the account holder.

2 Account holders and information

The administrator must ensure that the Registry provides the following information—

(a) to an account holder—

(i) the number of allowances it holds; and

(ii) a summary of any transfer, surrender or cancellation of allowances relating to that account holder made during the previous five years;

(b) to a participant, its CRC emissions—

(i) where provided, from CRC supplies in its most recent annual report;

(ii) from CRC supplies determined under article 47(3); or

(iii) applied under article 97(4)(a);

(c) to a participant—

(i) the number of allowances in its compliance account which are available to comply with Part 6; and

(ii) matters notified to the participant by the administrator.

3 Recording of transfers between accounts

The administrator must ensure that the Registry records the transfer of allowances between accounts made by account holders and to make that record—

(a) for a transfer made on a working day, if possible that working day or otherwise the following working day;

(b) for a transfer made on a non-working day, if possible the following working day or otherwise the next following working day.

4 Updating of accounts

The administrator must ensure that the cancellation and surrender of allowances is recorded in the relevant accounts and that record is made as soon as practicable.

5 Non-compliance accounts and third party accounts

(1) A participant may request the administrator to provide accounts for it in the Registry in addition to a compliance account, on terms agreed by the administrator.

(2) A person who is not a participant ("a third party") may request the administrator to provide accounts for it in the Registry on terms agreed by the administrator.

(3) Such terms must require that the participant or third party complies with any administrative rules drawn up by the administrator under article 68(4).

SCHEDULE 8
ACHIEVEMENT AND PERFORMANCE TABLES

Article 75

1 Absolute change in CRC emissions

The percentage change in the CRC emissions of a participant for an annual reporting year ("year A") compared to—

(a) where it exists, the historic average of CRC emissions of that participant; or

(b) otherwise, the relevant CRC emissions of that participant for the annual reporting year ("year B") before year A,

is the "absolute change" in CRC emissions for year A.

2 Relative change in CRC emissions

(1) The percentage change in the CRC emissions of a participant per unit of turnover for year A compared to—

(a) where it exists, the historic average of CRC emissions of that participant per unit of turnover; or

(b) otherwise, the relevant CRC emissions of that participant per unit of turnover in year B,

is the "relative change" in CRC emissions for year A.

(2) In sub-paragraph (1), "year A" and "year B" have the meaning given in paragraph 1.

3 Historic average of CRC emissions and reported or determined CRC emissions

(1) In paragraphs 1 and 2, an "historic average of CRC emissions" applies where during the previous five years before year A—

(a) there are at least two annual reports where the participant reported CRC supplies ("the historic sequence"); and

(b) those reports have not been found to be inaccurate by the administrator.

(2) The "historic average of CRC emissions" means the average of the CRC emissions in the historic sequence.

(3) In paragraphs 1, 2 and 4, "relevant CRC emissions" means the CRC emissions calculated from the CRC supplies in the annual report, as determined by the administrator under article 47(3) or applied under article 97(4)(a).

(4) In this paragraph—

(a) "year A" has the meaning given in paragraph 1; and

(b) an historic sequence exists even where one or more of the years in that sequence are in different phases.

4 Adjustments to CRC emissions

(1) Where any of the following applies to a participant in an annual reporting year—

(a) a change in its eligibility criteria for a CCA; or

(b) a change in the application of EU ETS to it,

the participant must notify the change to the administrator within three months of that change.

(2) Sub-paragraph (3) applies where a notification is made under—

(a) sub-paragraph (1); or

(b) Parts 1 or 2 or section 2 of Part 3 of Schedule 6.

(3) Where this sub-paragraph applies, the administrator must calculate, in respect of the participants which may be affected by the change, the appropriate adjustments to—

(a) where it exists, the historic average of CRC emissions; or

(b) otherwise, the relevant CRC emissions in the relevant annual reporting years.

(4) The adjustments made under sub-paragraph (3) must be applied by the administrator when it calculates absolute change and relative change.

(5) The administrator may make adjustments equivalent to those in sub-paragraph (4) where a participant enters into a new CCA or an existing CCA is modified such that a CCA applies to emissions which would be CRC emissions of the participant.

5 Early action

(1) Sub-paragraphs (2) to (6) apply only to the first phase.

(2) "Early action" is the average of these percentages—

(a) the percentage which the amount during the first year of the phase of—

  (i) electricity and gas supplied measured by automatic meters; and

  (ii) electricity supplied which is a dynamic supply,

  bears to the amount of all electricity and gas supplied during that year, excluding the supply of electricity measured by a settled half hourly meter required to be installed and the supply of gas measured by a daily meter required to be installed;

(b) the percentage which certified CRC emissions during a year of the phase bears to all CRC emissions in that year.

(3) Where under sub-paragraph (2)(a)—
(a) all of the electricity is measured by a settled half hourly meter required to be installed; and
(b) all of the gas supplied is measured by a daily meter required to be installed,
the percentage under sub-paragraph (2)(a) is 50%.

(4) In sub-paragraph (2)(a) "automatic meter" means—
(a) in respect of electricity—
  (i) a settled half hourly meter not required to be installed; or
  (ii) a non-settled half hourly meter;
(b) in respect of gas—
  (i) a daily meter not required to be installed; or
  (ii) an hourly meter.

(5) In sub-paragraph (2)(b), "certified CRC emissions" means—
(a) CRC emissions or emissions calculated in an equivalent way to the calculation of CRC emissions; and
(b) where a certification in respect of such emissions is valid on the last day of the relevant year of the phase.

(6) In sub-paragraph (5), "certification" means certification under—
(a) the Carbon Trust Standard Rules version 1.0 dated June 2008; or
(b) such other rules concerning the certification of emissions which the administrator and the participant agree.

SCHEDULE 9
POWERS OF ENTRY AND INSPECTION

Article 89

SECTION 1

Powers of entry and inspection

1

The powers of the administrator and an authorised person acting on its behalf are—
(a) to enter at any reasonable time any premises which that person has reason to believe it is necessary to enter;
(b) on entering any premises by virtue of sub-paragraph (a), to—
  (i) be accompanied by any other person duly authorised by the administrator and, if the authorised person has reasonable cause to apprehend any serious obstruction in the execution of the authorised person's duty, a constable;
  (ii) take any equipment or materials required for any purpose for which the power of entry is being exercised;
(c) to make such examination and investigation as may in any circumstances be necessary;
(d) as regards any premises which the authorised person has power to enter, to direct that those premises or any part of them, or anything in them, shall be left undisturbed (whether generally or in particular respects) for so long as is reasonably necessary for the purpose of any examination or investigation under sub-paragraph (c);
(e) to take such measurements and photographs and make such recordings as the authorised person considers necessary for the purpose of any examination or investigation under sub-paragraph (c);
(f) to take samples, or cause samples to be taken, of any thing found in or on any premises which the authorised person has power to enter, and of the air, water or land in, on, or in the vicinity of, the premises;
(g) in the case of any thing found in or on any premises which the authorised person has power to enter and which appears to that person to be in contravention of a provision of

this Order, to cause it to be dismantled or subjected to any process or test (but not so as to destroy or damage it, unless that is necessary);

(h) in the case of any thing mentioned in sub-paragraph (g), to take possession of it and detain it for so long as is necessary for all or any of the following purposes—
  (i) to examine it, or cause it to be examined, and to do, or cause to be done, to it anything which the authorised person has power to do under that sub-paragraph;
  (ii) to ensure that it is not tampered with before examination of it is completed; and
  (iii) to ensure that it is available for use in any proceedings for an offence under this Order;

(i) to require any person whom the authorised person has reasonable cause to believe to be able to give any information relevant to any examination or investigation under sub-paragraph (c) to answer (in the absence of persons other than a person nominated by that person to be present and any persons whom the authorised person may allow to be present) such questions as the authorised person thinks fit to ask and to sign a declaration of the truth of that person's answers;

(j) to require the production of, or where the information is recorded in computerised form, the furnishing of extracts from, any records which it is necessary for the authorised person to see for the purposes of an examination or investigation under sub-paragraph (c) and to inspect, and take copies of, or of any entry in, the records; and

(k) to require any person to afford the authorised person such facilities and assistance with respect to any matters or things within the other person's control or in relation to which that person has responsibilities as are necessary to enable the authorised person to exercise any of the powers conferred on the authorised person by this section.

2

In any case where it is proposed to enter any premises used for residential purposes, or to take heavy equipment on to any premises which are to be entered, any entry by virtue of paragraph 1 must only be effected—

(a) after the expiration of at least seven days' notice of the proposed entry given to a person who appears to the authorised person in question to be in occupation of the premises in question; and

(b) either—
  (i) with the consent of the person who is in occupation of those premises; or
  (ii) under the authority of a warrant by virtue of section 2 of this Schedule.

3

Where an authorised person proposes to enter any premises and—

(a) entry has been refused and the authorised person apprehends on reasonable grounds that the use of force may be necessary to effect entry; or

(b) the authorised person apprehends on reasonable grounds that entry is likely to be refused and that the use of force may be necessary to effect entry,

any entry on to those premises by virtue of paragraph 1 must only be effected under the authority of a warrant by virtue of section 2 of this Schedule.

4

In relation to any premises belonging to or used for the purposes of the United Kingdom Atomic Energy Authority, the powers under paragraph 1 have effect subject to section 6(3) of the Atomic Energy Authority Act 1954 (which restricts entry to such premises where they have been declared to be prohibited places for the purposes of the Official Secrets Act 1911).

5

Where an authorised person proposes to exercise the power conferred by paragraph 1(g), that person must, if so requested by a person who at the time is present on and has responsibilities in relation to the premises, cause anything which is to be done by virtue of that power to be done in the presence of that other person.

6

Before exercising the power conferred by paragraph 1(g), an authorised person must consult—
(a) such persons having duties on the premises where the thing is to be dismantled or subject to the process or test; and
(b) such other persons,
as appear to the authorised person to be appropriate for the purpose of ascertaining what dangers, if any, there may be in doing anything which it is proposed to do or cause to be done under the power.

7

No answer given by a person in pursuance of a requirement imposed under paragraph 1(i) is admissible in evidence in England and Wales or Northern Ireland against that person in any proceedings, or in Scotland against that person in any criminal proceedings.

8

Nothing in paragraph 1 compels the production by any person of a document of which—
(a) in England and Wales or Northern Ireland, that person would on grounds of legal professional privilege be entitled to withhold production on an order for discovery in an action in the County Court or High Court; or
(b) in Scotland, that person would on grounds of confidentiality of communications be entitled to withhold production on an order for the production of documents in an action in the Court of Session.

Section 2
Warrants, evidence and compensation

Entry and inspection under warrant

9

Subject to paragraph 11, if it is shown to the satisfaction, in England and Wales of a justice of the peace, in Scotland of the sheriff or a justice of the peace, or in Northern Ireland of a lay magistrate, on sworn information in writing—
(a) that there are relevant grounds for the exercise in relation to any premises of the powers under paragraph 1 ("the power"); and
(b) that one or more of the conditions specified in paragraph 10 is fulfilled in relation to those premises,
the justice, sheriff or lay magistrate may by warrant authorise the administrator to designate a person who is authorised to exercise the power in relation to those premises, in accordance with the warrant.

10

The conditions mentioned in paragraph 9 are—
(a) that the exercise of the power in relation to the premises has been refused;
(b) that such a refusal is reasonably apprehended;
(c) that the premises are unoccupied;
(d) that the occupier is temporarily absent from the premises and the case is one of urgency; or
(e) that an application for admission to the premises would defeat the object of the proposed entry.

11

In a case where paragraph 2 applies, a justice of the peace, sheriff or lay magistrate must not issue a warrant under paragraph 9 by virtue only of being satisfied that the exercise of the power in relation to any premises has been refused, or that a refusal is reasonably apprehended, unless the justice of the peace, sheriff or lay magistrate is also satisfied that the notice required by paragraph 2 has been given and that the period of that notice has expired.

12

Every warrant under paragraph 9 continues in force until the purposes for which the warrant was issued have been fulfilled.

13

An authorised person must produce evidence of that person's authorisation or designation and other authority before exercising the power.

14

A person who, in exercise of the power, enters on any premises which are unoccupied or whose occupier is temporarily absent must leave the premises as effectively secured against trespassers as that person found them.

Compensation in respect of entry and inspection

15

Where any person exercises any power conferred by paragraph 1(a) or (b), it is the duty of the administrator under whose authorisation that person acts to make full compensation to any person who has sustained loss or damage by reason of—

(a) the exercise of a power under paragraph 1 by the authorised person; or

(b) the performance of, or failure of the authorised person to perform, the duty imposed under paragraph 14.

16

Compensation is not payable by virtue of paragraph 15 in respect of any loss or damage if—

(a) it is attributable to the default of the person who sustained it; or

(b) it is loss or damage in respect of which compensation is payable by virtue of any other enactment.

17

Any dispute as to a person's entitlement to compensation under paragraph 15, or as to the amount of any such compensation—

(a) in England and Wales, must be referred to the arbitration of a single arbitrator appointed by agreement between the administrator and the person who claims to have sustained the loss or damage or, in default of agreement, appointed by the Secretary of State;

(b) in Scotland, must be referred to the arbitration of an arbiter, appointed by agreement between the administrator and the person who claims to have sustained the loss or damage or, in default of agreement, appointed by the Scottish Ministers; or

(c) in Northern Ireland, must be referred to and determined by the Lands Tribunal for Northern Ireland.

18

An authorised person is not to be liable in any civil proceedings for anything done in the purported exercise of the powers under paragraph 1 if the court is satisfied that the act was done in good faith and that there were reasonable grounds for doing it.

SCHEDULE 10
APPEALS

Article 111

1

Except where paragraph 4, 5 or 6 applies, the appeal body means the body provided under paragraph 2 in respect of an appeal referred to in article 111.

2

Under paragraph 1, where the determination, notice or penalty is made or given by—
(a) the Environment Agency and the determination, notice or penalty relates—
  (i) only to Wales, the appeal body is the Welsh Ministers;
  (ii) other than only to Wales, the appeal body is the Secretary of State;
(b) the Scottish Environment Protection Agency, the appeal body is the Scottish Ministers;
(c) the Chief inspector, the appeal body is the relevant Northern Ireland department.

3

Paragraph 4 applies where an appeal is made by an applicant or participant which is or includes—
(a) a government department;
(b) the Scottish Ministers;
(c) the Welsh Assembly Government.

4

Where this paragraph applies, the appeal body is an independent person which the following appoints in writing—
(a) the Secretary of State, in respect of an appeal by a government department;
(b) the Scottish Ministers, in respect of an appeal by those Ministers;
(c) the Welsh Ministers, in respect of an appeal by the Welsh Assembly Government.

5

Where an appeal is made by an applicant or participant which is or includes a Northern Ireland department, the appeal body is an independent person which the Department of the Environment appoints in writing.

6

Where a determination, notice or penalty is made or given by—
(a) the Secretary of State;
(b) the Scottish Ministers; or
(c) the Department of the Environment,
the appeal body is an independent person which that body appoints in writing.

7

An appellant must give written notice of the appeal together with a statement of the grounds of appeal to the appeal body and the appeal body must as soon as is reasonably practicable send to the administrator a copy of that notice together with the statement of the grounds of appeal.

8

An appeal must be received by the appeal body no later than 40 days after the date of—
(a) the determination referred to in article 74(1);
(b) service of an enforcement notice;
(c) imposition of the civil penalty.

9

The appeal body may decide an appeal received late.

10

An appellant may withdraw an appeal by notifying the appeal body, and as soon as is reasonably practicable the appeal body must notify the administrator.

11

The bringing of an appeal—
(a) except where the appeal body has given the appellant notice under paragraph 15, suspends an enforcement notice, financial penalty or publication taking effect;
(b) does not suspend a determination referred to in article 74(1) or a civil penalty not described in sub-paragraph (a) taking effect.

12

The appeal body may—
(a) in respect of a determination, enforcement notice or civil penalty—
 (i) cancel or affirm it; and
 (ii) if it affirms it, may do so either in its original form or with such modifications as the appeal body sees fit;
(b) instruct the administrator to do or not to do any thing which is within the power of the administrator.

13

The appeal body may publicise the appeal where it considers it appropriate to do so.

14

The appeal body may—
(a) adopt such procedures as it sees fit to determine an appeal, taking into account any requests of the parties to the appeal;
(b) appoint a person to hear an appeal on behalf of that body;
(c) request a person to make a recommendation in relation to any subject matter of the appeal.

15

On request by the administrator, the appeal body may award the administrator its reasonable costs of an appeal where the appeal body has given the appellant written notice that in its opinion—
(a) the appeal is frivolous or vexatious or otherwise has no reasonable prospects of success; or
(b) the appeal is conducted in an unreasonable or vexatious manner.

16

The costs under paragraph 15—
(a) are those agreed by the parties to the appeal or in default of agreement, as found by the appeal body;
(b) if unpaid, are recoverable as a civil debt by the administrator.

17

In this Schedule, "independent person" means a person who has no individual interest in the matter subject to the appeal and is independent of the parties to the appeal.

SCHEDULE 11
SERVICE OF DOCUMENTS

Article 112

1

The provisions of this Schedule apply to the service of a document except where a contrary provision applies under Schedule 9.

2

A document must be in writing.

3

Subject to paragraph 5, a document may be served on or given to a person (which includes a member of an unincorporated association) by—
(a) delivering it to that person in person;
(b) leaving it at that person's proper address; or
(c) sending it by post or electronic means to that person's proper address.

4

For the purposes of paragraph 3, a document is served on or given to a person under paragraph 3 in the case of—
(a) a body corporate, where it is served on or given to the director, secretary or clerk of that body;
(b) a partnership, where it is served on or given to a partner or a person having control or management of the partnership business;
(c) an unincorporated association, where it is served on or given to a person having management responsibilities in respect of the association.

5

A document may be served on an applicant or participant by sending it to the email address provided under paragraph 2, 3(a)(ii), 3(b) or 4 of section 1 of Schedule 5, as applicable to the applicant or participant.

6

Except where paragraph 5 applies, if a person to be served with or given a document has specified an address in the United Kingdom (other than that person's proper address) at which that person or someone on that person's behalf will accept documents of that description, that address must instead be treated as that person's proper address.

7

In paragraphs 3 and 6, "proper address" means in the case of—
(a) a body corporate or their director, secretary or clerk—
  (i) the registered or principal office of that body; or
  (ii) the email address of the director, secretary or clerk;
(b) a partnership or a partner or person having control or management of the partnership business—
  (i) the principal office of the partnership; or
  (ii) the email address of a partner or a person having that control or management;
(c) any other person, that person's last known address, which includes an email address.

8

For the purposes of paragraph 7, the principal office of a company registered outside the United Kingdom or of a partnership established outside the United Kingdom is its principal office in the United Kingdom.

9

Where—

(a) a participant is a group; and

(b) the administrator gives any communication to the public body or undertaking in whose name the compliance account is set up under article 73,

that communication is made to each member of the group.

ENVIRONMENTAL CIVIL SANCTIONS (ENGLAND) ORDER 2010

SI 2010/1157

PART 1
INTRODUCTION

1 Citation, application and commencement

This Order may be cited as the Environmental Civil Sanctions (England) Order 2010; it applies in England and comes into force on 6th April 2010.

2 Regulators

These are the regulators for the purposes of this Order in relation to the offences under the provisions specified in Schedule 5 which are enforced by them—

(a) the Environment Agency, and

(b) Natural England.

PART 2
CIVIL SANCTIONS, NOTICES AND UNDERTAKINGS

3 Civil sanctions, notices and undertakings

(1) Schedule 1 makes provision for fixed monetary penalties.

(2) Schedule 2 makes provision for variable monetary penalties, compliance notices, restoration notices and third party undertakings.

(3) Schedule 3 makes provision for stop notices.

(4) Schedule 4 makes provision for enforcement undertakings.

(5) Those terms have the meanings specified in those Schedules.

4 Scope

Schedule 5 sets out the provisions creating the offences to which this Order relates.

5 Combination of penalties

(1) A regulator may not serve a notice of intent relating to a fixed monetary penalty if a variable monetary penalty has been imposed or a compliance notice, restoration notice or stop notice has been served on that person relating to the same act or omission.

(2) A regulator may not serve a notice of intent relating to a variable monetary penalty, compliance notice or restoration notice, or serve a stop notice, on any person if, in relation to the same act or omission—

(a) a fixed monetary penalty has been imposed on that person, or

(b) that person has discharged liability for a fixed monetary penalty following service of a notice of intent to impose that penalty.

PART 3
NON-COMPLIANCE AND ENFORCEMENT

6 Recovery of payments

The regulator may recover any fixed monetary penalty, variable monetary penalty or non-compliance penalty on the order of a court, as if payable under a court order.

7 Non-compliance penalties

(1) If a person fails to comply with a compliance notice, a restoration notice or a third party undertaking, the regulator may serve a notice on that person imposing a monetary penalty ("a non-compliance penalty") in respect of the same offence irrespective of whether a variable monetary penalty was also imposed in respect of that offence.

(2) The amount of the penalty must be determined by the regulator, and must be a percentage of the costs of fulfilling the remaining requirements of the notice or third party undertaking.

(3) The percentage must be determined by the regulator having regard to all the circumstances of the case and may, if appropriate, be 100%.

(4) The notice must include information as to—
(a) the grounds for imposing the non-compliance penalty;
(b) the amount to be paid;
(c) how payment must be made;
(d) the period in which payment must be made, which must not be less than 28 days;
(e) the right of appeal;
(f) the consequences of failure to make payment in the specified period;
(g) any circumstances in which the regulator may reduce the amount of the penalty.

(5) If the requirements of the compliance notice or restoration notice are complied with or a third party undertaking is fulfilled before the time set for payment of the non-compliance penalty, the penalty is not payable.

(6) The person on whom the notice imposing the non-compliance penalty is served may appeal against it.

(7) The grounds of appeal are—
(a) that the decision to serve the notice was based on an error of fact;
(b) that the decision was wrong in law;
(c) that the decision was unfair or unreasonable for any reason
(d) that the amount of the penalty was unreasonable;
(e) any other reason.

8 Enforcement cost recovery notices

(1) A regulator may serve a notice ("an enforcement cost recovery notice") on a person on whom a variable monetary penalty notice, compliance notice, restoration notice or stop notice has been served requiring that person to pay the costs incurred by the regulator in relation to the imposition of that notice up to the time of its imposition.

(2) Costs include in particular—
(a) investigation costs;
(b) administration costs;
(c) costs of obtaining expert advice (including legal advice).

(3) The enforcement cost recovery notice must specify—
(a) how payment must be made;
(b) the amount required to be paid and the period in which payment must be made, which must not be less than 28 days;
(c) the grounds for imposing the notice;
(d) the right of appeal; and
(e) the consequences of failure to comply with the notice in the specified period.

(4) The person on whom the notice is served may require the regulator to provide a detailed breakdown of the amount.

(5) The person required to pay costs is not liable to pay any costs shown by that person to have been unnecessarily incurred.

(6) The person required to pay costs may appeal—
(a) against the decision of the regulator to impose the requirement to pay costs;
(b) against the decision of the regulator as to the amount of those costs; or
(c) for any other reason.

PART 4
ADMINISTRATION

9 Withdrawing or amending a notice

A regulator may at any time in writing—
(a) withdraw a fixed monetary penalty notice;
(b) withdraw a variable monetary penalty notice, a non-compliance penalty notice or an enforcement cost recovery notice or reduce the amount specified in the notice;
(c) withdraw a compliance notice, restoration notice or stop notice or amend the steps so as to reduce the amount of work necessary to comply with the notice.

10 Appeals

(1) An appeal under this Order is to the First-tier Tribunal.

(2) In any appeal (except in relation to a stop notice) where the commission of an offence is an issue requiring determination, the regulator must prove that offence according to the same burden and standard of proof as in a criminal prosecution.

(3) In any other case the tribunal must determine the standard of proof.

(4) All notices (other than stop notices) are suspended pending appeal.

(5) The Tribunal may suspend or vary a stop notice.

(6) The Tribunal may, in relation to the imposition of a requirement or service of a notice—
(a) withdraw the requirement or notice;
(b) confirm the requirement or notice;
(c) vary the requirement or notice;
(d) take such steps as the regulator could take in relation to the act or omission giving rise to the requirement or notice;
(e) remit the decision whether to confirm the requirement or notice, or any matter relating to that decision, to the regulator.

11 Guidance as to use of civil sanctions

(1) Where power is conferred on a regulator in this Order to impose a civil sanction in relation to an offence—

(a) the regulator must publish guidance about its use of the sanction;
(b) in the case of guidance relating to a fixed monetary penalty, variable monetary penalty, compliance notice, restoration notice or stop notice, the guidance must contain the relevant information;
(c) the regulator must revise the guidance where appropriate;
(d) the regulator must have regard to the guidance or revised guidance in exercising its functions.

(2) In the case of guidance relating to a fixed monetary penalty, the relevant information referred to in paragraph (1)(b) is information as to—
(a) the circumstances in which the penalty is likely to be imposed;
(b) the circumstances in which it may not be imposed;
(c) the amount of the penalty;
(d) how liability for the penalty may be discharged and the effect of discharge; and
(e) rights to make representations and objections and rights of appeal.

(3) In the case of guidance relating to a variable monetary penalty, a compliance notice or a restoration notice, the relevant information referred to in paragraph (1)(b) is information as to—
(a) the circumstances in which the requirement is likely to be imposed;
(b) the circumstances in which it may not be imposed;
(c) in the case of a variable monetary penalty, the matters likely to be taken into account by the regulator in determining the amount of the penalty (including voluntary reporting by any person of their own non-compliance); and
(d) rights to make representations and objections and rights of appeal.

(4) In the case of guidance relating to a stop notice, the relevant information referred to in paragraph (1)(b) is information as to—
(a) the circumstances in which the regulator is likely to serve the notice;
(b) the circumstances in which it may not be imposed; and
(c) rights of appeal.

12 Additional guidance

The regulator must issue guidance relating to the use of non-compliance penalties and enforcement cost recovery notices specifying—
(a) the circumstances in which they are likely to be imposed;
(b) the circumstances in which they may not be imposed;
(c) matters to be taken into account in establishing the amount involved;
(d) rights of appeal.

13 Consultation on guidance

The regulator must consult such persons as it considers appropriate before publishing any guidance or revised guidance under this Order.

14 Publication of enforcement action

(1) Where a power is conferred on a regulator to impose a civil sanction under this Order in relation to an offence, the regulator must from time to time publish—
(a) the cases in which the civil sanction has been imposed,
(b) where the civil sanction is a fixed monetary penalty, the cases in which liability to the penalty has been discharged by payment of the penalty following the notice of intent and without further action being taken;
(c) where the civil sanction is a variable monetary penalty, restoration notice or compliance notice, the cases in which a third party undertaking has been accepted;
(d) cases in which an enforcement undertaking has been entered into.

(2) In paragraph (1)(a) the reference to cases in which the civil sanction has been imposed does not include cases where the sanction has been imposed but overturned on appeal.

(3) This article does not apply in cases where the regulator considers that publication would be inappropriate.

15 Power of entry

(1) Any person authorised in writing to do so by Natural England may, on producing the authorisation if required, enter any premises (other than premises used exclusively as domestic premises) at any reasonable time to ascertain whether a compliance notice, restoration notice or stop notice has been complied with or an undertaking accepted under this Order has been fulfilled.

(2) For the avoidance of doubt this power does not include a power to seize any property.

SCHEDULE 1
FIXED MONETARY PENALTIES

Article 3

1 Power to impose a fixed monetary penalty

(1) A regulator may by notice impose a fixed monetary penalty on a person in relation to an offence under a provision specified in Schedule 5 if the table in that Schedule indicates that such penalty is possible for that offence.

(2) Before doing so the regulator must be satisfied beyond reasonable doubt that the person has committed the offence.

(3) "Fixed monetary penalty" means a requirement to pay to a regulator a penalty of £100 for an individual or £300 for a body corporate.

2 Notice of intent

(1) Where a regulator proposes to impose a fixed monetary penalty on a person, the regulator must serve on that person a notice of what is proposed (a "notice of intent").

(2) The notice of intent must include—
(a) the grounds for the proposal to impose the fixed monetary penalty;
(b) the amount of the penalty;
(c) a statement that liability for the penalty can be discharged by paying 50% of the penalty within 28 days beginning with the day on which the notice was received;
(d) information as to—
  (i) the effect of that discharge payment;
  (ii) the right to make representations and objections within 28 days beginning with the day on which the notice of intent was received.
  (iii) the circumstances in which the regulator may not impose the requirement (including any defences relating to the offence in relation to which the notice is served).

3 Discharge of liability

The penalty is discharged if a person who receives a notice of intent pays 50% of the amount of the penalty within 28 days beginning with the day on which the notice was received.

4 Making representations and objections

A person on whom a notice of intent is served may within 28 days beginning with the day on which the notice was received make written representations and objections to the regulator in relation to the proposed imposition of the fixed monetary penalty.

5 Service of final notice

(1) If the person who has received a notice of intent does not discharge liability within 28 days the regulator may serve a final notice imposing a fixed monetary penalty.

(2) The regulator may not serve a final notice on a person where the regulator is satisfied that the person would not, by reason of any defence, be liable to be convicted of the offence to which the notice relates.

(3) A regulator who serves a final notice relating to a fixed monetary penalty may not serve any other notice under this Order in relation to the offence.

6 Contents of final notice

A final notice must include information as to—
(a) the amount of the penalty;
(b) the grounds for imposing the penalty;
(c) how payment may be made;
(d) the period of 56 days within which payment must be made;
(e) details of the early payment discounts and late payment penalties;
(f) rights of appeal; and
(g) the consequences of non-payment.

7 Discount for early payment

If a person who was served with a notice of intent made representations or objections concerning that notice within the time limit, that person may discharge the final notice by paying 50% of the penalty within 28 days beginning with the day on which the final notice was received.

8 Grounds of appeal

(1) The person receiving the final notice may appeal against it.

(2) The grounds for appeal are—
(a) that the decision was based on an error of fact;
(b) that the decision was wrong in law;
(c) that the decision was unreasonable;
(d) any other reason.

9 Non-payment after 56 days

(1) The penalty must be paid within 56 days of receipt of the final notice.

(2) If the penalty is not paid within 56 days the amount payable is increased by 50%.

(3) In the case of an appeal it is payable within 28 days of the determination of the appeal (if the appeal is unsuccessful), and if it is not paid within 28 days the amount of the penalty is increased by 50%.

10 Criminal proceedings

(1) If a notice of intent for a fixed monetary penalty is served on any person—
(a) no criminal proceedings for the offence may be instituted against that person in respect of the act or omission to which the notice relates before 28 days from the date the notice of intent is received, and
(b) if that person so discharges liability, that person may not at any time be convicted of the offence in relation to that act or omission.

(2) If a fixed monetary penalty is imposed on any person, that person may not at any time be convicted of the offence in respect of the act or omission giving rise to the penalty.

SCHEDULE 2
VARIABLE MONETARY PENALTIES, COMPLIANCE NOTICES, RESTORATION NOTICES AND THIRD PARTY UNDERTAKINGS

Article 3

1 Imposition of a variable monetary penalty, compliance notice or restoration notice

(1) A regulator may by notice impose—

(a) a requirement to pay a monetary penalty to a regulator of such amount as the regulator may determine ("a variable monetary penalty"),

(b) a requirement to take such steps as a regulator may specify, within such period as it may specify, to secure that the offence does not continue or recur ("a compliance notice"), or

(c) a requirement to take such steps as a regulator may specify, within such period as it may specify, to secure that the position is, so far as possible, restored to what it would have been if the offence had not been committed ("a restoration notice"),

in relation to an offence under a provision specified in Schedule 5 if the table in that Schedule indicates that such penalty or notice is possible for that offence.

(2) Before doing so the regulator must be satisfied beyond reasonable doubt that the person has committed the offence.

(3) A requirement under this paragraph may not be imposed on a person on more than one occasion in relation to the same act or omission.

(4) Where a variable monetary penalty is imposed in relation to an offence that is—

(a) triable summarily only, and

(b) punishable on summary conviction by a fine (whether or not it is also punishable by a term of imprisonment),

the amount of the variable monetary penalty may not exceed the maximum amount of that fine.

(5) In any event the amount of a variable monetary penalty must not exceed £250,000.

(6) Before serving a notice relating to a variable monetary penalty the regulator may require the person to provide such information as is reasonable to establish the amount of any financial benefit arising as a result of the offence.

2 Notice of intent

(1) Where a regulator proposes to serve a notice under this Schedule on a person, the regulator must serve on that person a notice of what is proposed (a "notice of intent").

(2) In the case of a proposed restoration notice or compliance notice the notice of intent must include—

(a) the grounds for the proposed notice;

(b) the requirement of the notice;

(c) information as to—

(i) the right to make representations and objections within 28 days beginning with the day on which the notice of intent was received;

(ii) the circumstances in which the regulator may not impose the notice (including any defences relating to the offence in relation to which the notice is served).

(3) In the case of a proposed variable monetary penalty the notice of intent must include—

(a) the grounds for imposing the variable monetary penalty;

(b) the amount of the penalty;

(c) information as to—

(i) the right to make representations and objections within 28 days beginning with the day on which the notice of intent was received;

(ii) the circumstances in which the regulator may not impose the penalty (including any defences relating to the offence in relation to which the notice is served).

3 Making representations and objections

A person on whom a notice of intent is served may within 28 days beginning with the day on which the notice was received make written representations and objections to the regulator in relation to the proposed imposition of a variable monetary penalty, restoration notice or compliance notice.

4 Third party undertakings

(1) A person on whom a notice of intent is served may offer an undertaking as to action to be taken by that person (including the payment of a sum of money) to benefit any third party affected by the offence ("a third party undertaking").

(2) The regulator may accept or reject such a third party undertaking.

5 Final notice

(1) After the end of the period for making representations and objections, the regulator must decide whether to—

(a) impose the requirements in the notice of intent, with or without modifications, or

(b) impose any other requirement that the regulator has power to impose under this Schedule.

(2) Where the regulator decides to impose a requirement, the notice imposing it (the "final notice") must comply with paragraph 6 or 7.

(3) The regulator may not impose a final notice on a person where the regulator is satisfied that the person would not, by reason of any defence, be liable to be convicted of the offence to which the notice relates.

(4) The regulator must take into account any third party undertaking that it accepts in deciding—

(a) whether or not to serve a final notice; and

(b) the amount of any variable monetary penalty it imposes.

6 Contents of final notice — variable monetary penalty

A final notice for a variable monetary penalty must include information as to—

(a) the grounds for imposing the penalty;

(b) the amount to be paid;

(c) how payment may be made;

(d) the period within which payment must be made which must be not less than 28 days;

(e) rights of appeal; and

(f) the consequences of failing to comply with the notice.

7 Contents of final notice — compliance notice or restoration notice

A final notice relating to a compliance notice or restoration notice must include information as to—

(a) the grounds for imposing the notice;

(b) what compliance or restoration is required and the period within which it must be completed;

(c) the rights of appeal; and

(d) the consequences of failing to comply with the notice.

8 Appeals against a final notice

(1) The person receiving the final notice may appeal against it.

(2) The grounds for appeal are—

(a) that the decision was based on an error of fact;

(b) that the decision was wrong in law;
(c) in the case of a variable monetary penalty, that the amount of the penalty is unreasonable;
(d) in the case of a non-monetary requirement, that the nature of the requirement is unreasonable;
(e) that the decision was unreasonable for any other reason;
(f) any other reason.

9 Criminal proceedings

(1) If—
(a) a variable monetary penalty, compliance notice or restoration notice is imposed on any person, or
(b) a third party undertaking is accepted from any person,
that person may not at any time be convicted of the offence in respect of the act or omission giving rise to the variable monetary penalty, compliance notice, restoration notice or third party undertaking except in a case referred to in sub-paragraph (2).

(2) The case referred to in sub-paragraph (1) is a case where—
(a) a restoration notice or compliance notice is imposed on a person or a third party undertaking is accepted from a person,
(b) no variable monetary penalty is imposed on that person, and
(c) that person fails to comply with the restoration notice, compliance notice or third party undertaking.

(3) Criminal proceedings for offences triable summarily to which a notice or undertaking in sub-paragraph (2) relates may be instituted at any time up to six months from the date when the regulator notifies the person that such person has failed to comply with that notice or undertaking.

SCHEDULE 3
STOP NOTICES

Article 3

1 Stop notices

(1) The regulator may serve a stop notice on any person in accordance with this Schedule in relation to an offence under a provision specified in Schedule 5 if the table in that Schedule indicates that such notice is possible for that offence.

(2) A "stop notice" is a notice prohibiting a person from carrying on an activity specified in the notice until the person has taken the steps specified in the notice.

(3) A stop notice may only be served in a case falling within sub-paragraph (4) or (5).

(4) A case falling within this sub-paragraph is a case where—
(a) the person is carrying on the activity,
(b) the regulator reasonably believes that the activity as carried on by that person is causing, or presents a significant risk of causing, serious harm to any of the matters referred to in sub-paragraph (6), and
(c) the regulator reasonably believes that the activity as carried on by that person involves or is likely to involve the commission of an offence under a provision specified in Schedule 5 by that person.

(5) A case falling within this sub-paragraph is a case where the regulator reasonably believes that—
(a) the person is likely to carry on the activity,
(b) the activity as likely to be carried on by that person will cause, or will present a significant risk of causing, serious harm to any of the matters referred to in sub-paragraph (6), and

(c) the activity as likely to be carried on by that person will involve or will be likely to involve the commission of an offence under a provision specified in Schedule 5 by that person.

(6) The matters referred to in sub-paragraphs (4)(b) and (5)(b) are—
(a) human health,
(b) the environment (including the health of animals and plants).

(7) The steps referred to in sub-paragraph (2) must be steps to remove or reduce the harm or risk of harm referred to in sub-paragraph (4)(b) or (5)(b).

2 Contents of a stop notice

A stop notice must include information as to—
(a) the grounds for serving the stop notice;
(b) the steps the person must take to comply with the stop notice;
(c) rights of appeal; and
(d) the consequences of non-compliance.

3 Appeals

(1) The person on whom a stop notice is served may appeal against the decision to serve it.

(2) The grounds for appeal are—
(a) that the decision was based on an error of fact;
(b) that the decision was wrong in law;
(c) that the decision was unreasonable;
(d) that any step specified in the notice is unreasonable;
(e) that the person has not committed the offence and would not have committed it had the stop notice not been served;
(f) that the person would not, by reason of any defence, have been liable to be convicted of the offence had the stop notice not been served;
(g) any other reason.

4 Completion certificates

(1) Where, after service of a stop notice, the regulator is satisfied that the person has taken the steps specified in the notice, the regulator must issue a certificate to that effect (a "completion certificate").

(2) The stop notice ceases to have effect on the issue of a completion certificate.

(3) The person on whom the stop notice is served may at any time apply for a completion certificate.

(4) The regulator must make a decision as to whether to issue a completion certificate within 14 days of such an application.

(5) The person on whom the stop notice was served may appeal against a decision not to issue a completion certificate on the grounds that—
(a) the decision was based on an error of fact;
(b) the decision was wrong in law;
(c) the decision was unfair or unreasonable;
(d) the decision was wrong for any other reason.

5 Compensation

(1) A regulator must compensate a person for loss suffered as the result of the service of the stop notice or the refusal of a completion certificate if that person has suffered loss as a result of the notice or refusal and—
(a) a stop notice is subsequently withdrawn or amended by the regulator because the decision to serve it was unreasonable or any step specified in the notice was unreasonable;

(b) the operator successfully appeals against the stop notice and the First-tier Tribunal finds that the service of the notice was unreasonable; or
(c) the operator successfully appeals against the refusal of a completion certificate and the Tribunal finds that the refusal was unreasonable.

(2) A person may appeal against a decision not to award compensation or the amount of compensation—
(a) on the grounds that the regulator's decision was unreasonable;
(b) on the grounds that the amount offered was based on incorrect facts;
(c) for any other reason.

6 Offences

(1) Where a person on whom a notice is served does not comply with it within the time limit specified in the notice, the person is guilty of an offence and liable—
(a) on summary conviction, to a fine not exceeding £20,000, or imprisonment for a term not exceeding twelve months, or both, or
(b) on conviction on indictment, to imprisonment for a term not exceeding two years, or a fine, or both.

(2) In the application of this paragraph in relation to an offence committed before the commencement of section 154(1) of the Criminal Justice Act 2003 the reference in sub-paragraph (1)(a) to twelve months is to be read as a reference to six months.

SCHEDULE 4
ENFORCEMENT UNDERTAKINGS

Article 3

1 Enforcement undertakings

(1) A regulator may accept an enforcement undertaking from a person in a case where the regulator has reasonable grounds to suspect that the person has committed an offence under a provision specified in Schedule 5 and the table in that Schedule indicates that an enforcement undertaking may be accepted in relation to that offence.

(2) For the purposes of this Schedule, an "enforcement undertaking" is a written undertaking to take such action as may be specified in the undertaking within such period as may be so specified.

2 Contents of an enforcement undertaking

(1) An enforcement undertaking must specify—
(a) action to secure that the offence does not continue or recur,
(b) action to secure that the position is, so far as possible, restored to what it would have been if the offence had not been committed,
(c) action (including the payment of a sum of money) to benefit any person affected by the offence, or
(d) where restoration of the harm arising from the offence is not possible, action that will secure equivalent benefit or improvement to the environment.

(2) It must specify the period within which the action must be completed.

(3) It must include—
(a) a statement that the undertaking is made in accordance with this Schedule;
(b) the terms of the undertaking;
(c) how and when a person is considered to have discharged the undertaking.

(4) The enforcement undertaking may be varied, or the period within which the action must be completed may be extended, if both parties agree in writing.

3 Acceptance of an enforcement undertaking

If a regulator has accepted an enforcement undertaking then, unless the person from whom the undertaking is accepted has failed to comply with the undertaking or any part of it—

(a) that person may not at any time be convicted of the offence in respect of the act or omission to which the undertaking relates,

(b) the regulator may not impose on that person any fixed monetary penalty, variable monetary penalty, compliance notice or restoration notice in respect of that act or omission.

4 General provisions on enforcement undertakings

(1) A regulator must establish and publish the procedure for entering into an enforcement undertaking.

(2) The regulator must consult such persons as it considers appropriate before doing so.

(3) When it accepts an undertaking the regulator may publish it in whatever manner it sees fit.

5 Discharge of an enforcement undertaking

(1) A regulator who is satisfied that an enforcement undertaking has been complied with must issue a certificate to that effect.

(2) A regulator may require the person who has given the undertaking to provide sufficient information to determine that the undertaking has been complied with.

(3) The person who gave the undertaking may at any time apply for such a certificate.

(4) The regulator must make a decision as to whether to issue such a certificate, and give written notice of the decision to the applicant, within 14 days of such an application.

(5) The person to whom the notice is given may appeal against a decision not to issue a certificate on the grounds that the decision—

(a) was based on an error of fact;

(b) was wrong in law;

(c) was unfair or unreasonable

(d) was wrong for any other reason.

6 Inaccurate, incomplete or misleading information

(1) A person who has given inaccurate, misleading or incomplete information in relation to an enforcement undertaking is regarded as not having complied with it.

(2) A regulator may by notice in writing revoke a certificate issued under paragraph 5 if it was issued on the basis of inaccurate, incomplete or misleading information.

7 Non-compliance with an enforcement undertaking

(1) If an enforcement undertaking is not complied with the regulator may either—

(a) serve a variable monetary penalty notice, compliance notice or restoration notice, or

(b) bring criminal proceedings.

(2) If a person has complied partly but not fully with an undertaking, that part-compliance must be taken into account in the imposition of any criminal or other sanction on the person.

(3) Criminal proceedings for offences triable summarily to which an enforcement undertaking relates may be instituted at any time up to six months from the date when the regulator notifies the person that such person has failed to comply with that undertaking.

SCHEDULE 5
OFFENCES

Article 4

In the following table—
"FMP" is a fixed monetary penalty;
"VMP" is a variable monetary penalty;
"CN" is a compliance notice;
"RN" is a restoration notice;
"SN" is a stop notice;
"EU" is an enforcement undertaking.

Provision creating an offence		*FMP*	*VMP*	*CN*	*RN*	*SN*	*EU*
Destructive Imported Animals Act 1932							
	section 6(1)(c), limited to acting in contravention of or failure to comply with the terms of a licence	No	Yes	Yes	Yes	Yes	Yes
	section 6(1)(e)	No	Yes	No	No	No	No
Pests Act 1954							
	section 4(2)	No	Yes	No	No	No	No
Weeds Act 1959							
	section 2(1)	No	Yes	No	No	No	No
	section 4(2)	No	Yes	No	No	No	No
Salmon and Freshwater Fisheries Act 1975							
	section 2(1)	No	Yes	No	No	No	No
	section 2(2)	No	Yes	No	No	No	No
	section 2(4)	No	Yes	No	Yes	Yes	Yes
	section 4(1)	No	Yes	No	Yes	Yes	Yes
	section 5(4)	No	Yes	No	Yes	Yes	Yes
	section 9(2)	No	Yes	No	Yes	No	Yes
	section 12(1)	No	Yes	No	Yes	Yes	Yes
	section 12(3)	No	Yes	No	Yes	Yes	Yes
	section 13(2)	No	Yes	No	Yes	Yes	Yes
	section 14(8)	No	Yes	No	Yes	Yes	Yes
	section 15(2)	No	Yes	No	Yes	Yes	Yes
	section 18(1)	No	Yes	No	No	No	No
	section 27	No	Yes	No	No	No	No
	section 31(2)	No	Yes	No	No	No	No
Wildlife and Countryside Act 1981							
	section 1(1)	No	Yes	Yes	Yes	Yes	No
	section 1(2)	No	Yes	Yes	Yes	Yes	No
	section 1(5)	No	Yes	Yes	Yes	Yes	No
	section 5(1)	No	Yes	No	Yes	Yes	No
	section 6(1)	No	Yes	Yes	Yes	Yes	No
	section 6(2)	No	Yes	Yes	Yes	Yes	No
	section 6(3)	No	Yes	Yes	Yes	Yes	No
	section 7(1)	No	Yes	Yes	Yes	Yes	No
	section 7(3)	No	Yes	Yes	Yes	Yes	No
	section 7(4)	No	Yes	Yes	Yes	Yes	No

Provision creating an offence		*FMP*	*VMP*	*CN*	*RN*	*SN*	*EU*
	section 8(1)	No	Yes	Yes	Yes	Yes	No
	section 8(3)	No	Yes	Yes	Yes	Yes	No
	section 9(1)	No	Yes	Yes	Yes	Yes	No
	section 9(2)	No	Yes	Yes	Yes	Yes	No
	section 9(4)	No	Yes	Yes	Yes	Yes	No
	section 9(4A)	No	Yes	Yes	Yes	Yes	No
	section 9(5)	No	Yes	Yes	Yes	Yes	No
	section 11(1)	No	Yes	No	Yes	Yes	No
	section 11(2)	No	Yes	Yes	Yes	Yes	No
	section 11(3)	No	Yes	Yes	Yes	Yes	No
	section 13(1)	No	Yes	Yes	Yes	Yes	No
	section 13(2)	No	Yes	Yes	Yes	Yes	No
	section 14(1)	No	Yes	Yes	Yes	Yes	No
	section 14(2)	No	Yes	Yes	Yes	Yes	No
	section 17	No	Yes	No	No	No	No
	section 19XB(1)	No	Yes	No	No	No	No
	section 19XB(2)	No	Yes	No	No	No	No
	section 19XB(3)	No	Yes	No	No	No	No
	section 19XB(4)	No	Yes	No	No	No	No
	section 28P(1)	Yes	Yes	Yes	Yes	Yes	Yes
	section 28P(2)	Yes	Yes	Yes	Yes	Yes	Yes
	section 28P(3)	Yes	Yes	Yes	Yes	Yes	Yes
	section 28P(5A)	Yes	Yes	Yes	Yes	Yes	Yes
	section 28P(6)	No	Yes	Yes	Yes	Yes	Yes
	section 28P(6A)	No	Yes	Yes	Yes	Yes	Yes
	section 28P(8)	No	Yes	No	No	No	No
	section 28S(3)	No	Yes	No	No	No	No
	section 51(4)	No	Yes	No	No	No	No
Salmon Act 1986							
	section 32	No	Yes	No	No	No	No
Environmental Protection Act 1990							
	section 33(6)	No	No	No	No	Yes	No
	section 71(3)	No	Yes	No	No	No	No
Water Resources Act 1991							
	section 24(4)(a)	Yes	Yes	Yes	Yes	Yes	Yes
	section 24(4)(b)	Yes	Yes	Yes	Yes	Yes	Yes
	section 25(2)(a)	Yes	Yes	Yes	Yes	Yes	Yes
	section 25(2)(b)	Yes	Yes	Yes	Yes	Yes	Yes
	section 25C	No	Yes	No	No	No	No
	section 80(1)	Yes	Yes	Yes	Yes	Yes	Yes
	section 80(2)	Yes	Yes	Yes	Yes	Yes	Yes
	section 161D(1)	No	Yes	No	No	No	No
	section 199(4)	No	Yes	No	No	No	No
	section 201(3)	No	Yes	No	No	No	No
	section 202(4)	No	Yes	No	No	No	No

Provision creating an offence	*FMP*	*VMP*	*CN*	*RN*	*SN*	*EU*
section 206(1)	No	Yes	No	No	No	No
section 206(3)	No	Yes	No	No	No	No
section 206(3A)	No	Yes	No	No	No	No
section 206(4)	No	Yes	No	No	No	No
Schedule 20, paragraph 7	No	Yes	No	No	No	No
Water Industry Act 1991						
section 120(9)	Yes	Yes	Yes	Yes	No	Yes
section 130(7)	Yes	Yes	Yes	Yes	No	Yes
section 133(5)	No	Yes	No	Yes	No	No
section 135A(2)(a)	No	Yes	No	No	No	No
Deer Act 1991						
section 8(5)	Yes	Yes	No	No	Yes	Yes
Land Drainage Act 1991						
section 53(2)	No	Yes	No	No	No	No
section 64(6)	No	Yes	No	No	No	No
section 69(4)	No	Yes	No	No	No	No
Protection of Badgers Act 1992						
section 3	Yes	Yes	Yes	Yes	Yes	Yes
section 10(8)	Yes	Yes	Yes	Yes	Yes	Yes
Environment Act 1995						
section 110(1)	No	Yes	No	No	No	No
section 110(2)(a)	No	Yes	No	No	No	No
section 110(2)(b)	No	Yes	No	No	No	No
section 110(2)(c)	No	Yes	No	No	No	No
section 110(3)	No	Yes	No	No	No	No
Water Act 2003						
Section 4(4)	No	Yes	No	No	No	No

ANIMAL BY-PRODUCTS (ENFORCEMENT) (ENGLAND) REGULATIONS 2011

SI 2011/881

PART 1
INTRODUCTION

Citation, commencement and application

1

These Regulations—
(a) may be cited as the Animal By-Products (Enforcement) (England) Regulations 2011;
(b) come into force on 23rd March 2011; and
(c) apply in England.

Interpretation

2

(1) In these Regulations—

"EU Control Regulation" means Regulation (EC) No. 1069/2009 of the European Parliament and of the Council laying down health rules as regards animal by-products and derived products not intended for human consumption and repealing Regulation (EC) No. 1774/2002 (Animal by-products Regulation);

"EU Implementing Regulation" means Commission Regulation (EU) No. 142/2011 implementing Regulation (EC) No. 1069/2009 of the European Parliament and of the Council laying down health rules as regards animal by-products and derived products not intended for human consumption and implementing Council Directive 97/78/EC as regards certain samples and items exempt from veterinary checks at the border under that Directive as amended from time to time;

"animal by-product requirement" has the meaning given in regulation 17(2);

"authorised person" means a person authorised under regulation 22;

"competent authority" has the meaning given in regulation 3;

"enforcement authority" means a body exercising functions under regulation 21(1) or (2);

"premises" includes—
(a) any land, building, shed or pen;
(b) any receptacle or container;
(c) any ship; or
(d) a vehicle of any description;

"ship" includes a hovercraft, submersible craft or any other floating craft but not a vessel which—
(a) permanently rests on or is permanently attached to the seabed; or
(b) is an installation within section 16 of the Energy Act 2008.

(2) Expressions used in these Regulations that are also used in the EU Control Regulation or the EU Implementing Regulation have the same meaning in these Regulations as they have in the EU Control Regulation or in the EU Implementing Regulation.

PART 2
THE COMPETENT AUTHORITY AND MISCELLANEOUS PROVISIONS

The competent authority

3

The competent authority for the purposes of the EU Control Regulation and the EU Implementing Regulation is the Secretary of State.

Access

4

In relation to a prohibition on feeding in Article 11(1)(a), (b) or (d) (restrictions on use) of the EU Control Regulation, the requirements of [regulation 5][1] apply.

Amendment

1 Substituted by the Animal By-Products (Enforcement) and Transmissible Spongiform Encephalopathies (England) (Amendment) Regulations 2011, SI 2011/2681, reg 2(a).

5

(1) Animal by-products, including catering waste, must not be brought on to any premises if farmed animals would have access to such animal by-products.

(2) Paragraph (1) does not apply to derived products, except for—
(a) products derived from catering waste; or
(b) meat and bone meal derived from Category 2 material and processed animal proteins intended to be used as or in organic fertilisers and soil improvers that do not comply with the requirements of Article 32(1)(d) (placing on the market and use) of the EU Control Regulation.

6

A carcase or part of a carcase of any farmed animal that has not been slaughtered for human consumption must be held, pending consignment or disposal, in such manner as to ensure that any animal or bird will not have access to it.

Use of organic fertilisers and soil improvers

7

(1) Where organic fertilisers or soil improvers are applied to land, no person may allow pigs to have access to that land or to be fed cut herbage from such land for a period of 60 days beginning with the application of the organic fertiliser or soil improver.

(2) Paragraph (1) does not apply to the following organic fertilisers or soil improvers—
(a) manure;
(b) milk;
(c) milk-based products;
(d) milk-derived products;
(e) colostrum;
(f) colostrum products; or
(g) digestive tract content.

Collection centres

8

A processing plant for Category 2 material which is approved for the purpose of being a collection centre for Category 2 material is authorised as a collection centre.

Remote areas

9

The following areas are remote areas for the purposes of Article 19(1)(b) of the EU Control Regulation (collection, transport and disposal)—
(a) Lundy Island;
(b) the Isles of Scilly;
(c) …[1]

Amendment

1 Repealed by the Animal By-Products (Enforcement) and Transmissible Spongiform Encephalopathies (England) (Amendment) Regulations 2011, SI 2011/2681, reg 2(b).

Placing on the market

10

The placing on the market of untreated wool and untreated hair from farms or from establishments or plants is authorised except where they present a risk of any disease communicable through those products to humans or animals.

PART 3
REGISTRATION AND APPROVAL

Procedure for registration of plants and establishments

11

A notification must be made in writing to the competent authority, where it is made—
(a) with a view to registration in accordance with Article 23(1) (registration of operators, establishments or plants) of the EU Control Regulation; or
(b) to inform the authority of changes in accordance with Article 23(2) of that Regulation.

Notifications of competent authority in respect of registration

12

The competent authority must give notice in writing to—
(a) the operator who has notified in accordance with regulation 11, of—
 (i) the registration of such an operator; or
 (ii) the decision not to register;
(b) a registered operator, of—
 (i) a prohibition made under Article 46(2) (prohibition on operations) of the EU Control Regulation;

(ii) a requirement to comply with Article 23(1)(b) or (2) of the EU Control Regulation (information on activities and up-to-date information);
(iii) the amendment of the registration or the ending of the registration where an operator has notified the competent authority of the closure of an establishment in accordance with Article 23(2) (up to date information) of the EU Control Regulation.

Procedure for approval

13

Operators to whom Article 24(1) (approval of establishments or plants) of the EU Control Regulation applies, must apply in writing to the competent authority to be approved, including approval after the grant of temporary approval where Article 33 of the EU Implementing Regulation (re-approval of plants and establishments after the grant of temporary approval) applies.

Notification in respect of decisions on approval

14

The competent authority must give notice in writing to—
(a) the applicant for approval, of the—
(i) grant of approval in accordance with Articles 24 (approval) and 44 (procedure for approval) of the EU Control Regulation;
(ii) grant of conditional approval in accordance with Articles 24 and 44 of the EU Control Regulation, or the extension of such approval in accordance with that Article; or
(iii) refusal to grant approval in respect of an initial application or extension;
(b) where conditional approval has been granted in accordance with Articles 24 and 44 of the EU Control Regulation, the operator of the plant or establishment subject to such approval, of the—
(i) grant of full approval;
(ii) extension of such approval;
(iii) imposition of conditions in accordance with Article 46(1)(c) (suspensions, withdrawals and prohibitions on operators) of the EU Control Regulation;
(iv) suspension of such approval in accordance with Article 46(1)(a) of the EU Control Regulation;
(v) withdrawal of such approval in accordance with Article 46(1)(b) of the EU Control Regulation;
(vi) making of a prohibition in accordance with Article 46(2) of the EU Control Regulation; or
(vii) refusal to extend or grant full approval; or
(c) the operator of an approved plant or establishment, of the—
(i) imposition of conditions in accordance with Article 46(1)(c) of the EU Control Regulation (suspension, withdrawal);
(ii) suspension of such approval in accordance with Article 46(1)(a) of the EU Control Regulation;
(iii) making of a prohibition in accordance with Article 46(2) of the EU Control Regulation; or
(iv) withdrawal of such approval in accordance Article 46(1)(b) of the EU Control Regulation.

Reasons for decisions

15

(1) Where a decision is made by the competent authority and notified in accordance with regulation 12 or regulation 14, the competent authority must give reasons in writing for that decision.

(2) Paragraph (1) does not apply to decisions notified under—
(a) regulation 12(a)(i);
(b) regulation 14(a)(i); or
(c) regulation 14(b)(i) or (ii).

Appeals procedure

16

(1) Where the competent authority has made a notification to which regulation 15(1) applies, a person may appeal against it by making written representations, within 21 days of the notification of that decision, to a person appointed for the purpose by the Secretary of State.

(2) The competent authority may also make written representations to the appointed person concerning the decision.

(3) The appointed person must then report in writing to the Secretary of State.

(4) The Secretary of State must give to the applicant written notification of the final determination of the Secretary of State and the reasons for it.

PART 4
OFFENCES AND PENALTIES

Offences in respect of the EU Control Regulation and the EU Implementing Regulation

17

(1) A person who fails to comply with an animal by-product requirement commits an offence.

(2) "Animal by-product requirement" means any requirement in Column 2 of Schedule 1 to these Regulations as read with the provisions in Column 3 to that Schedule.

Offence of obstruction

18

It is an offence—
(a) intentionally to obstruct an authorised person;
(b) without reasonable cause, to fail to give to an authorised person any information or assistance or to provide any facilities that such person may reasonably require;
(c) knowingly or recklessly to give false or misleading information to an authorised person; or
(d) to fail to produce a record or document when required to do so by an authorised person.

Corporate, partnership and unincorporated association offences

19

(1) Where—

(a) an offence under these Regulations has been committed by a body corporate or a partnership or Scottish partnership or other unincorporated association; and

(b) it is proved that the offence was committed with the consent or connivance of, or was attributable to any neglect on the part of, a relevant individual (including an individual purporting to act in the capacity of a relevant individual),

the relevant individual as well as the body corporate, partnership, Scottish partnership or unincorporated association, is guilty of the offence and is liable to be proceeded against and punished accordingly.

(2) In paragraph (1), "relevant individual" means—

(a) in relation to a body corporate—

  (i) a director, manager, secretary or other similar officer of the body;

  (ii) where the affairs of the body are managed by its members, a member;

(b) in relation to a partnership or Scottish partnership, a partner;

(c) in relation to an unincorporated association other than a Scottish partnership, a person who is concerned in the management or control of the association.

(3) Proceedings for an offence under these Regulations alleged to have been committed by a partnership or an unincorporated association may be brought against the partnership or association in the name of the partnership or association.

(4) For the purpose of proceedings in paragraph (3)—

(a) rules of court relating to the service of documents have effect as if the partnership or unincorporated association were a body corporate; and

(b) the following provisions apply as they apply in relation to a body corporate—

  (i) section 33 of the Criminal Justice Act 1925; and

  (ii) Schedule 3 to the Magistrates' Courts Act 1980.

(5) A fine imposed on a partnership or unincorporated association on its conviction of an offence under these Regulations is to be paid out of the funds of the partnership or association

Penalties

20

A person guilty of an offence under these Regulations is liable—

(a) on summary conviction, to a fine not exceeding the statutory maximum or to imprisonment not exceeding three months or both; or

(b) on conviction on indictment, to a fine or to imprisonment for a term not exceeding two years, or both.

PART 5
ENFORCEMENT

Enforcement authority

21

(1) These Regulations are enforced by—

(a) the local authority;

(b) the port health authority in relation to—
  (i) the London port health district (within the meaning given by section 7(1) of the Public Health (Control of Disease) Act 1984), or
  (ii) a port health district constituted by order under section 2(3) of that Act; or
(c) the Secretary of State in relation to a food hygiene establishment.

(2) Paragraph (1)(a) and (b) does not apply where the Secretary of State directs that the enforcement duty is to be exercised in relation to cases of a particular description or any particular case by the Secretary of State.

(3) In paragraph (1)(a) "local authority" means—
(a) where there is a unitary authority, within the meaning of the Local Government Changes for England Regulations 1994, that authority;
(b) where there is not a unitary authority—
  (i) in a metropolitan district, the council of that district;
  (ii) in a non-metropolitan county, the council of that county or the council of a district within the county area;
  (iii) in each London borough, the council of that borough;
(c) in the City of London, the Common Council; or
(d) the Council of the Isles of Scilly.

(4) In paragraph (1)(b) "port health authority" means—
(i) in relation to the London port health district, the Common Council of the City of London; or
(ii) in relation to any other port health district, the port health authority for that district.

(5) In paragraph (1)(c), "food hygiene establishment" means an establishment referred to in regulation 5(2) of the Food Hygiene (England) Regulations 2006 in respect of which the Food Standards Agency has enforcement functions under those Regulations.

Authorised person

22

An enforcement authority may authorise in writing such persons as the authority considers appropriate to act for the purpose of enforcing these Regulations.

Powers of entry and additional powers

23

(1) An authorised person may, on production of that person's authority if so required—
(a) enter and inspect premises (except a dwelling-house) at all reasonable hours;
(b) take such other persons and any equipment or materials as necessary;
(c) make such examination or investigation as necessary;
(d) direct that the premises, or part of them, are left undisturbed (whether generally or in particular respects) for so long as is reasonably necessary for the purpose of any examination or investigation under sub-paragraph (c);
(e) take such measurements and photographs and make such recordings as are considered necessary for the purpose of any examination or investigation under sub-paragraph (c);
(f) in the case of any article or substance found in or on the premises—
  (i) take samples;
  (ii) test or subject it to any process, where it appears that it has caused or is likely to cause harm to human health or to the health of animals or plants;

(iii) take possession of it and retain it for so long as is necessary—
(aa) to examine it and to exercise the power within paragraph (ii);
(bb) to ensure that it is not tampered with before examination of it is completed; and
(cc) to ensure that it is available for use as evidence in any proceedings for an offence under these Regulations;

(g) require the production of, or where the information is recorded in computerised form the furnishing of extracts from, any records which it is necessary to see for the purposes of any examination or investigation under sub-paragraph (c) and to inspect and take copies of, or of any entry in, the records;

(h) require any person to afford such facilities and assistance with respect to any matters or things within that person's control or in relation to which that person has responsibilities as are necessary to enable the authorised person to exercise any of the powers conferred by this regulation; or

(i) mark any animal or animal by-product as the authorised person considers necessary.

(2) Where an authorised person proposes to exercise the power in paragraph (1)(f)(ii), the authorised person must—

(a) if so requested by a person who at the time is present and has responsibilities in relation to those premises, cause anything which is to be done by virtue of that power to be done in that person's presence;

(b) consult such persons as appear to the authorised person appropriate for the purpose of ascertaining what dangers, if any, there may be in doing anything which is proposed under that power.

(3) Where an authorised person in respect of the power in paragraph (1)(f)(iii)—

(a) proposes to exercise that power, the authorised person must, if it is practicable to do so, take a sample of it and give to a responsible person at the premises a portion of the sample marked in a manner sufficient to identify it; or

(b) exercises that power, the authorised person must leave a notice giving particulars of the article or substance sufficient to identify it and stating that possession has been taken, such notice to be left either—
(i) with a responsible person; or
(ii) if that is impracticable, fixed in a conspicuous place at those premises.

(4) Nothing in this regulation compels the production by any person of a document which that person would be entitled to withhold production of on the grounds of legal professional privilege on an order for discovery in an action in the High Court.

Warrant

24

(1) If, in relation to the power to enter premises under regulation 23, a justice of the peace, on written information on oath—

(a) is satisfied that there are reasonable grounds to believe that any information or material relevant to the examination or investigation under regulation 23(1)(c) is on any such premises; and

(b) is satisfied that—
(i) entry to such premises has been, or is likely to be, refused, and that notice of intention to apply for a warrant has been given to the occupier; or
(ii) an application for entry, or the giving of such a notice would defeat the object of the entry, or that the case is one of urgency, or that such premises are unoccupied or the occupier is temporarily absent,

the justice may by warrant, which continues in force for a period of one month, authorise an authorised person to enter the premises, if necessary by force.

(2) If, in relation to a dwelling-house, a justice of the peace on written information on oath—

(a) is satisfied that there are reasonable grounds to believe that information or material relevant to an examination or investigation for the purpose of enforcing the EU Control Regulation, the EU Implementing Regulation and these Regulations is on such premises; and

(b) is satisfied that—

  (i) entry to such premises has been, or is likely to be, refused, and that notice of intention to apply for a warrant has been given to the occupier; or

  (ii) an application for entry, or the giving of such a notice would defeat the object of the entry, or that the case is one of urgency, or that such premises are unoccupied or the occupier is temporarily absent,

the justice may by warrant, which continues in force for a period of one month, authorise an authorised person to enter such premises, if necessary by force, and inspect them.

(3) Where an authorised person has been authorised under paragraph (2) to enter by warrant, the authorised person has the powers in regulation 23(1)(b) to (i).

Notices served by an authorised person

25

(1) An authorised person may serve a notice in accordance with paragraph (2) where that person—

(a) considers that there is a contravention of, or failure to comply with an animal by-product requirement; or

(b) reasonably suspects that as a result of such contravention or failure to comply, premises constitute a risk to human or animal health.

(2) Notices may be served on the occupier of any premises, or the person in charge of the premises—

(a) requiring the disposal and, where applicable, storage pending such disposal of—

  (i) animal by-products and derived products;

  (ii) material in premises to which paragraph (1)(b) applies;

(b) requiring the cleansing and disinfection of premises to which paragraph (1)(b) applies and, where applicable, specifying the method for such cleansing and disinfection;

(c) prohibiting animal by-products and derived products being—

  (i) moved in or brought on to premises;

  (ii) moved in or brought on to premises unless in accordance with conditions specified in the notice, including a condition as to the satisfactory completion of the cleansing and disinfection in accordance with a notice as provided in sub-paragraph (b).

(3) A notice served under paragraph (2) must be complied with at the expense of the person on whom the notice is served and, if it is not complied with, an authorised person may arrange for it to be complied with at the expense of that person.

(4) Paragraph (1) does not apply where Article 46(1) (suspensions, withdrawals and prohibitions on operations) of the EU Control Regulation applies.

Power to disclose information for enforcement purposes

26

(1) This regulation applies to information received by an enforcement authority or an authorised person in the course of enforcing these Regulations.

(2) That person may disclose the information to any comparable enforcement authority or authorised person (appointed elsewhere within the United Kingdom to enforce the EU Control Regulation and the EU Implementing Regulation) for the purposes of their enforcement role.

(3) For the purposes of this regulation, "an enforcement authority" includes the Food Standards Agency.

[*Regulation 27 is not reproduced.*]

PART 7
REVOCATIONS AND TRANSITIONAL PROVISION

[*Regulation 28 is not reproduced.*]

Transitional provision

29

(1) The collection, transport and disposal of Category 3 material in Article 10(f) of the EU Control Regulation (Category 3 material) is authorised for the period ending on 31 December 2012, where the requirements of paragraph (2) are satisfied.

(2) The requirements are—
(a) the material satisfies Article 36(3) of, and paragraphs (a) to (c) of Chapter 4 of Annex 6 to, the EU Implementing Regulation; and
(b) the means of disposal for such material, in addition to the means in Article 14 of the EU Control Regulation (disposal and use of Category 3 material), are disposal—
  (i) in an authorised landfill without prior processing; or
  (ii) where Article 21 of the EU Control Regulation is satisfied, to a biogas or composting plant for transformation in accordance with an authorisation under paragraph 2 of Section 2 of Chapter 3 of Annex 5 to the EU Implementing Regulation.

[Review of these Regulations][1]

[30

(1) The Secretary of State must from time to time—
(a) carry out a review of these Regulations;
(b) set out the conclusions of the review in a report; and
(c) publish the report.

(2) In carrying out the review the Secretary of State must, so far as is reasonable, have regard to how the EU Control Regulation and the EU Implementing Regulation are implemented in other member States.

(3) The report must in particular—
(a) set out the objectives intended to be achieved by these Regulations;
(b) assess the extent to which those objectives are achieved; and
(c) assess whether those objectives remain appropriate and, if so, the extent to which they could be achieved in a less burdensome way.

(4) The first report under this regulation must be published before the end of the period of five years beginning with 30th November 2011.

(5) Reports under this regulation are afterwards to be published at intervals not exceeding five years.][1]

Amendment

1 Inserted by the Animal By-Products (Enforcement) and Transmissible Spongiform Encephalopathies (England) (Amendment) Regulations 2011, SI 2011/2681, reg 2(c).

SCHEDULE 1
ANIMAL BY-PRODUCT REQUIREMENTS

Regulation 17

Column 1 *Subject matter of requirement*	*Column 2* *Provisions containing the basic requirement*	*Column 3* *Provisions to be read with the provision(s) mentioned in Column 2*
1. General Obligation	Article 4(1) or (2) of the EU Control Regulation	Article 3 of the EU Implementing Regulation
2. General animal health restrictions	Article 6(1) of the EU Control Regulation	Article 4 of the EU Implementing Regulation
3. Restrictions on use for feeding purposes	Article 11 of the EU Control Regulation	Regulations 4 to 7 of these Regulations and Article 5 of the EU Implementing Regulation
[3A. Restrictions on access to carcases	Articles 12, 13 and 21(1) of the EU Control Regulation	Regulation 6 of these Regulations][1]
4. Disposal and use of Category 1 material	Article 12 of the EU Control Regulation, subject to Article 16 (b) to (e) of that Regulation and Article 7 of the EU Implementing Regulation	Articles 6(3) to (5), 8(1), 9(b) and (c), 11(2), 12(2) and 15 of the EU Implementing Regulation
5. Disposal and use of Category 2 material	Article 13 of the EU Control Regulation, subject to Articles 15(2)(b) and 16(b) to (f) and (h) of that Regulation	Regulation 8 of these Regulations and Articles 6(3) to (5), 8(1), 9(b) and (c), 10(1), 11(2), 12(2), 13(1) and 15 of the EU Implementing Regulation
6. Disposal and use of Category 3 material	Article 14 of the EU Control Regulation, subject to Article 16 (b) to (h) of that Regulation and Article 7 of the EU Implementing Regulation	Regulation 29 of these Regulations and Articles 6(3) to (5), 8(1), 9(b) and (c), 10(1), 11(2), 12(2), 13(2), 15 and 36(3) of the EU Implementing Regulation
7. Collection and identification as regards category and transport	Article 21(1) to (4) of the EU Control Regulation	Article 17 of the EU Implementing Regulation
8. Traceability	Article 22(1) and (2) of the EU Control Regulation	Article 17 of the EU Implementing Regulation
9. Registration of operators, establishments and plants	Articles 23(1) and (2) and 55 of the EU Control Regulation	Regulation 11 of these Regulations and Articles 20(1) and (2) and 32(7) of the EU Implementing Regulation

Column 1 *Subject matter of requirement*	*Column 2* *Provisions containing the basic requirement*	*Column 3* *Provisions to be read with the provision(s) mentioned in Column 2*
10. Approval of establishments and plants	Articles 24, 44(3) and 55 of the EU Control Regulation	Regulation 13 of these Regulations and Articles 19, 32(7) and 33 of the EU Implementing Regulation
11. General hygiene conditions	Article 25 of the EU Control Regulation	Articles 9(a), 19 and 20 of the EU Implementing Regulation
12. Handling of animal by-products within food businesses	Article 26 of the EU Control Regulation	
13. Own checks	Article 28 of the EU Control Regulation	
14. Hazard analysis and critical control points	Article 29(1) to (3) of the EU Control Regulation	
15. Placing on the market animal by-products and derived products for feeding to farmed animals excluding fur animals	Article 31(1) of the EU Control Regulation	Articles 21 and 24(2) of the EU Implementing Regulation
16. Placing on the market and use of organic fertilisers and soil improvers	Article 32(1) and (2) of the EU Control Regulation	Regulation 7(1) of these Regulations and Articles 22(1) to (3) and 36(1) of the EU Implementing Regulation
17. Collection and movement for manufacture of derived products	Article 34 of the EU Control Regulation except in so far as it relates to imports	Article 33 of the EU Control Regulation and Article 23 of the EU Implementing Regulation
18. Prohibition on use for manufacture for products not within Article 33 or 36 of the EU Control Regulation	Article 24(1) of the EU Implementing Regulation	Articles 33 and 36 of the EU Control Regulation
19. Placing on the market of pet food	Article 35 of the EU Control Regulation	Articles 3 and 24(3) of the EU Implementing Regulation
20. Placing on the market of other derived products	Article 36 of the EU Control Regulation	Regulation 10 of these Regulations and Articles 3 and 24(1), (2) and (4) of the EU Implementing Regulation
21. Safe sourcing	Article 37(2) of the EU Control Regulation	
22. Export	Article 43 of the EU Control Regulation	
23. Controls for dispatch	Article 48 of the EU Control Regulation	Articles 11(3), 12(3) and 31 of the EU Implementing Regulation

[*Schedule 2 is not reproduced.*]

WASTE (ENGLAND AND WALES) REGULATIONS 2011

SI 2011/988

PART 1
GENERAL

1 Citation, commencement and extent

(1) These Regulations may be cited as the Waste (England and Wales) Regulations 2011.

(2) Subject to paragraph (3), they come into force on the day after the day on which they are made.

(3) Regulation 12 comes into force at the end of the period of 6 months beginning with the day on which these Regulations are made.

(4) These Regulations extend to England and Wales.

2 Application

Subject to regulation 47(2), these Regulations do not apply in relation to waste which is excluded from the scope of the Waste Framework Directive by Article 2(1), (2) or (3) of that Directive.

3 Interpretation

(1) In these Regulations—

"appropriate authority" means—

(a) in relation to England, the Secretary of State;

(b) in relation to Wales, the Welsh Ministers;

"controlled waste" has the meaning given in section 75(4) of the Environmental Protection Act 1990;

"hazardous waste"—

(a) in relation to England has the meaning given in regulation 6 of the Hazardous Waste (England and Wales) Regulations 2005;

(b) in relation to Wales has the meaning given in regulation 6 of the Hazardous Waste (Wales) Regulations 2005;

"national waste management plan" means a waste management plan prepared by an appropriate authority;

"waste collection authority" means an authority which is a waste collection authority for the purposes of Part 2 of the Environmental Protection Act 1990;

"the Waste Framework Directive" means Directive 2008/98/EC of the European Parliament and of the Council on waste;

"waste management plan" has the meaning given in regulation 7(1);

"waste prevention programme" has the meaning given in regulation 4(1) and (2).

(2) Terms which are used but not defined in these Regulations and are used in the Waste Framework Directive have the same meaning as in that Directive.

PART 2
WASTE PREVENTION PROGRAMMES

4 Establishment of waste prevention programmes

(1) The appropriate authority must, not later than 12th December 2013—

(a) evaluate the usefulness of the waste prevention measures set out as examples in Annex IV of the Waste Framework Directive and any other such measures the authority thinks fit; and
(b) establish one or more programmes of waste prevention measures (each a "waste prevention programme").

(2) A programme established before the coming into force of these Regulations may be a waste prevention programme.

(3) In this regulation, "waste prevention measures" means measures taken before a substance, material or product has become waste that reduce—
(a) the quantity of waste, including through the re-use of products or the extension of the life span of products;
(b) the adverse impacts of generated waste on the environment and human health; or
(c) the content of harmful substances in materials and products.

5 Purposes etc. of waste prevention programmes

The appropriate authority must ensure that a waste prevention programme—
(a) is compatible with the objectives in paragraphs 1 and 2 of Schedule 1;
(b) has as its purpose a contribution towards breaking the link between economic growth and the environmental impacts associated with the generation of waste;
(c) is expressed in writing and—
 (i) sets out the objectives of the programme and a description of existing waste prevention measures; and
 (ii) if it is integrated into a waste management plan or other programme, clearly identifies the programme's waste prevention measures.

6 Monitoring and evaluation of waste prevention programmes

(1) An appropriate authority—
(a) must establish qualitative or quantitative benchmarks; and
(b) may establish qualitative or quantitative targets and indicators,
against which to assess the value of waste prevention programmes.

(2) An appropriate authority must publish the benchmarks and any targets or indicators it establishes.

PART 3
WASTE MANAGEMENT PLANS

7 Requirement for waste management plans

(1) The appropriate authority must ensure that there are one or more plans containing policies in relation to waste management in England or Wales, as the case may be (each a "waste management plan").

(2) A waste management plan may form part of a document and, where this is the case, any requirement of law in relation to the plan applies only to that part.

(3) In this Part—
(a) "England" includes the sea adjacent to England out as far as the seaward boundary of the territorial sea;
(b) "Wales" includes the sea adjacent to Wales out as far as the seaward boundary of the territorial sea;

(c) the sea adjacent to England is so much of the sea adjacent to Great Britain as is not the sea adjacent to Wales or the sea adjacent to Scotland;
(d) the sea adjacent to Wales has the same meaning as it has by virtue of section 158(3) or (4) of the Government of Wales Act 2006; and
(e) the sea adjacent to Scotland has the same meaning as the internal waters and territorial sea of the United Kingdom adjacent to Scotland by virtue of section 126(2) of the Scotland Act 1998.

8 Content of waste management plans

(1) The appropriate authority must ensure that the waste management plans (taken together) cover the whole of England or Wales, as the case may be.

(2) The appropriate authority must ensure that the waste management plans (taken together)—
(a) include a statement of the authority's policies for attaining the objectives specified in Part 1 of Schedule 1; and
(b) include the matters set out in Part 2 of Schedule 1.

(3) The appropriate authority must consider, in particular, whether the matters set out in Part 3 of Schedule 1 should be included in the waste management plans.

(4) An appropriate authority must ensure that the waste management plans conform to the strategy for the reduction of biodegradable waste going to landfill—
(a) in relation to England, required by section 17(1) of the Waste and Emissions Trading Act 2003;
(b) in relation to Wales, required by section 19(1) of that Act.

(5) A statement of policy made before the coming into force of these Regulations may be, or form part of, a waste management plan.

PART 4
WASTE PREVENTION PROGRAMMES AND WASTE MANAGEMENT PLANS: GENERAL PROVISION

9 Directions to the Environment Agency

(1) The appropriate authority may give directions to the Environment Agency requiring it—
(a) to advise the authority on the measures or policies which are to be included in a waste prevention programme or waste management plan;
(b) to carry out a survey or investigation into any other matter in connection with the preparation of such a programme or plan or any modification of it, and report its findings to the authority.

(2) A direction given under paragraph (1)(b)—
(a) must specify or describe the matters which are to be the subject of the survey or investigation;
(b) may specify bodies or persons to be consulted before carrying out the survey or investigation; and
(c) may make provision in relation to the manner in which—
  (i) the survey or investigation is to be carried out; or
  (ii) the findings are to be reported and made available.

(3) The Environment Agency must comply with a direction given under paragraph (1).

(4) Where a direction is given under paragraph (1)(b), the Environment Agency must also consult any body or person that it considers appropriate but is not specified in the direction.

(5) The Environment Agency must make its findings available to the bodies and persons it consults.

10 Review and modification of programmes and plans

(1) The appropriate authority—
(a) must review each waste prevention programme and national waste management plan at least every sixth year;
(b) may from time to time modify a programme or plan.

(2) The appropriate authority must ensure that the Environment Agency and the bodies or persons mentioned in paragraph (3) are consulted during the preparation of—
(a) proposals for a waste prevention programme or national waste management plan; or
(b) proposals to modify such a programme or plan.

(3) They are such bodies or persons appearing to be representative of—
(a) the interests of local government; and
(b) the interests of industry,
as the authority considers appropriate.

(4) This regulation does not apply to a national waste management plan containing only provision relating to paragraph 8, 9, 10 or 11 of Schedule 1.

(5) Steps taken before the coming into force of these Regulations in relation to a waste prevention programme or national waste management plan may be steps for the purposes of this regulation.

11 Public participation in programmes and plans

(1) Part 4 of Schedule 1 (public participation in the preparation or modification of a waste prevention programme or national waste management plan) has effect, but does not apply to a programme or plan—
(a) designed for the sole purpose of serving national defence or taken in case of civil emergencies;
(b) for which a public participation procedure is carried out under—
(i) Part 3 of the Environmental Assessment of Plans and Programmes Regulations 2004, or
(ii) Part 3 of the Environmental Assessment of Plans and Programmes (Wales) Regulations 2004; or
(c) containing only provision relating to paragraph 8, 9, 10 or 11 of Schedule 1.

(2) The appropriate authority must ensure that waste prevention programmes and national waste management plans are available on a publicly available website.

(3) Steps taken before the coming into force of these Regulations in relation to a waste prevention programme or national waste management plan may be steps for the purposes of Part 4 of Schedule 1.

PART 5
DUTIES IN RELATION TO WASTE MANAGEMENT AND IMPROVED USE OF WASTE AS A RESOURCE

12 Duty in relation to the waste hierarchy

(1) An establishment or undertaking which imports, produces, collects, transports, recovers or disposes of waste, or which as a dealer or broker has control of waste must,

on the transfer of waste, take all such measures available to it as are reasonable in the circumstances to apply the following waste hierarchy as a priority order—
(a) prevention;
(b) preparing for re-use;
(c) recycling;
(d) other recovery (for example energy recovery);
(e) disposal.

(2) But an establishment or undertaking may depart from the priority order in paragraph (1) so as to achieve the best overall environmental outcome where this is justified by life-cycle thinking on the overall impacts of the generation and management of the waste.

(3) When considering the overall impacts mentioned in paragraph (2), the following considerations must be taken into account—
(a) the general environmental protection principles of precaution and sustainability;
(b) technical feasibility and economic viability;
(c) protection of resources;
(d) the overall environmental, human health, economic and social impacts.

[13 Duties in relation to collection of waste

(1) This regulation applies from 1st January 2015.

(2) Subject to paragraph (4), an establishment or undertaking which collects waste paper, metal, plastic or glass must do so by way of separate collection.

(3) Subject to paragraph (4), every waste collection authority must, when making arrangements for the collection of waste paper, metal, plastic or glass, ensure that those arrangements are by way of separate collection.

(4) The duties in this regulation apply where separate collection—
(a) is necessary to ensure that waste undergoes recovery operations in accordance with Articles 4 and 13 of the Waste Framework Directive and to facilitate or improve recovery; and
(b) is technically, environmentally and economically practicable.][1]

Amendment
1 Substituted by the Waste (England and Wales) (Amendment) Regulations 2012, SI 2012/1889, reg 2(1), (2).

14 Duty in relation to collected waste

(1) An establishment or undertaking which collects, transports or receives waste paper, metal, plastic or glass must, from 1st January 2015, take all such measures available to it in that capacity as are reasonable in the circumstances to ensure that where that waste has been separately collected it is not mixed with other waste or other material with different properties.

[(2) This duty applies where keeping waste separate is necessary to ensure that waste undergoes recovery operations in accordance with Articles 4 and 13 of the Waste Framework Directive and to facilitate or improve recovery.][1]

Amendment
1 Substituted by the Waste (England and Wales) (Amendment) Regulations 2012, SI 2012/1889, reg 2(1), (3).

15 Guidance

(1) The appropriate authority may give guidance on the discharge of the duties in regulations 12 to 14.

(2) An establishment or undertaking discharging any of the duties in regulations 12 to 14 must, in doing so, have regard to any such guidance.

PART 6
DUTIES OF PLANNING AUTHORITIES

16 General interpretation

(1) In this Part—

"the 1990 Act" means the Town and Country Planning Act 1990;
"the 2004 Act" means the Planning and Compulsory Purchase Act 2004;
"the 2008 Act" means the Planning Act 2008;
"local planning authority" has the same meaning as in 1990 Act;
"mineral planning authority" has the same meaning as in section 1 of the 1990 Act;
"planning permission" has the meaning given in section 336 of the 1990 Act.

(2) In this Part, "the planning Acts" means—
(a) the 1990 Act;
(b) the Planning (Listed Buildings and Conservation Areas) Act 1990;
(c) the Planning (Hazardous Substances) Act 1990;
(d) the Planning (Consequential Provisions) Act 1990;
(e) the 2004 Act; and
(f) the 2008 Act.

(3) In this Part, "planning authority" means—
(a) a local planning authority;
(b) a joint committee constituted under section 29 of the 2004 Act;
(c) a person appointed under paragraph 1 of Schedule 6 to the 1990 Act;
(d) a government department in respect of its functions under the planning Acts; or
(e) an appropriate authority in respect of its functions under the planning Acts.

17 Meaning of planning functions

(1) In this Part, "planning functions" means any of the following functions, other than a function which must be discharged by statutory instrument—
(a) determining—
(i) an application for planning permission under section 70 of the 1990 Act, or
(ii) an appeal made under section 78 of the 1990 Act in relation to the determination of such an application;
(b) deciding whether to take action under section 141(2) or (3) or 177(1)(a) or (b) of the 1990 Act, or under section 35(5) of the Planning (Listed Buildings and Conservation Areas) Act 1990;
(c) deciding whether to direct under section 90(1), (2) or (2A) of the 1990 Act that planning permission must be deemed to be granted;
(d) deciding whether—
(i) in making or confirming a discontinuance order, to include in the order any grant of planning permission, or
(ii) to confirm (with or without modifications) a discontinuance order insofar as it grants planning permission;
(e) making a local development order under section 61A of the 1990 Act;
(f) discharging functions under Part 2 of the 1990 Act;
(g) discharging functions in relation to England under—
(i) Part 2 of and Schedule 8 to the 2004 Act, or
(ii) Part 5 of the Local Democracy, Economic Development and Construction Act 2009;
(h) discharging functions in relation to Wales under Part 6 of and Schedule 8 to the 2004 Act;

(i) deciding whether to—
   (i) make a development consent order under section 104 or 105 of the 2008 Act, or
   (ii) make changes to, or revoke, such an order under section 153 of that Act, other than in accordance with paragraph 2 of Schedule 6 to that Act.

(2) In paragraph (1)(d), "discontinuance order" means an order under—
(a) section 102 of the 1990 Act (including an order made under that section by virtue of section 104 of that Act); or
(b) paragraph 1 of Schedule 9 to the 1990 Act (including an order made under that paragraph by virtue of paragraph 11 of that Schedule).

18 Exercise of planning functions

A planning authority must have regard to the following provisions of the Waste Framework Directive when exercising its planning functions to the extent that those functions relate to waste management—
(a) Article 13;
(b) the first paragraph of Article 16(1), ignoring the words "in cooperation with other Member States where this is necessary or advisable" and "taking into account best available techniques";
(c) Article 16(2) and (3).

19 Inspections

(1) This regulation applies where a planning authority has planning functions in relation to establishments or undertakings carrying on disposal or recovery of waste.

(2) The planning authority must ensure that appropriate periodic inspections of those establishments or undertakings are made.

20 Further duties in relation to planning permission

(1) A planning authority must not grant planning permission or development consent for a landfill unless it has taken into consideration the requirements of—
(a) paragraph 1.1 of Annex I to Council Directive 1999/31/EC on the landfill of waste;
(b) paragraph 5 of that Annex, but only in respect of nuisances and hazards arising from traffic beyond the site of the landfill.

(2) A mineral planning authority must not grant planning permission for a mining waste facility to which Article 7 of Directive 2006/21/EC of the European Parliament and of the Council on the management of waste from extractive industries applies unless it is satisfied that—
(a) the operator of that facility will meet the requirements of Article 11(2)(a) of that Directive; and
(b) the management of waste at that facility will not conflict directly or otherwise interfere with the implementation of the plans referred to in Article 7(3)(b) of that Directive.

(3) In this regulation—
"landfill" has the meaning given in Article 2(g) of Directive 1999/31/EC, but does not include any operation excluded from the scope of that Directive by Article 3(2);
"mining waste facility" means a "waste facility" as defined in Article 3(15) of Directive 2006/21/EC, but does not include those facilities mentioned in Article 24(2) or in the first paragraph of Article 24(4).

PART 7
DEPOSITS IN THE SEA

21 Interpretation

In this Part, "offshore licensing functions" means—
(a) functions under Part 2 of the Food and Environment Protection Act 1985;
(b) functions under Part 4 of the Marine and Coastal Access Act 2009,
other than functions which must be exercised by statutory instrument.

22 Exercise of offshore licensing functions

An appropriate authority must exercise its offshore licensing functions—
(a) so far as material, for the purposes of implementing the waste management plans;
(b) for the purposes of ensuring that—
  (i) the waste hierarchy referred to in Article 4 of the Waste Framework Directive is applied to the generation of waste; and
  (ii) waste generated by the disposal or recovery of waste is treated in accordance with Article 4 of the Waste Framework Directive;
(c) for the purposes of implementing Article 13 of the Waste Framework Directive;
(d) so as to ensure that the requirements in the second paragraph of Article 23(1) of the Waste Framework Directive are met; and
(e) so as to ensure compliance with the following Articles of the Waste Framework Directive—
  (i) Article 18(2)(b) and (c),
  (ii) Article 23(3) and (4),
  (iii) Article 35(1).

23 Inspections

(1) This regulation applies where an appropriate authority has offshore licensing functions in relation to establishments or undertakings carrying on disposal or recovery of waste.

(2) The appropriate authority must ensure that appropriate periodic inspections of those establishments or undertakings are made.

PART 8
REGISTRATION OF CARRIERS, BROKERS AND DEALERS

24 Interpretation

(1) The regulations in this Part, to the extent that they relate to carriers of controlled waste, have effect as if they were made in exercise of the powers in sections 1(3), 2 and 4(6) of the Control of Pollution (Amendment) Act 1989.

(2) Sections 3 and 4 of the Control of Pollution (Amendment) Act 1989 have effect as if—
(a) references to carriers of controlled waste in those sections included references to brokers of and to dealers in controlled waste;
(b) references to the transport of controlled waste included references to acting as a broker of or dealer in controlled waste; and
(c) regulations 26 and 28 to 34, to the extent that they relate to brokers and dealers, were made in exercise of the powers in sections 2 and 4(6) of that Act.

(3) Section 3(5) and (6) of the Control of Pollution (Amendment) Act 1989 (in its application to carriers, brokers and dealers) has effect as if—

(a) references to provision made by virtue of subsection (1) or (2) include a reference to regulations 29(5) and 32(1); and

(b) references to a prescribed offence include an offence specified in regulation 29(5)(b).

(4) Section 7(1) of the Control of Pollution (Amendment) Act 1989 has effect as if the words "the provisions of this Act" included a reference to regulation 25.

(5) In this Part—

"the relevant time" means immediately before the coming into force of these Regulations;

"specified person" means—

(a) a charity or voluntary organisation;

(b) a waste collection authority;

(c) an authority which is a waste disposal authority for the purposes of Part 2 of the Environmental Protection Act 1990;

(d) an authority which is a waste regulation authority for the purposes of Part 2 of the Environmental Protection Act 1990;

(e) a carrier which only transports waste produced by the carrier itself, except where it is construction or demolition waste (and "construction" includes improvement, repair and alteration);

(f) a carrier which only transports, a broker which only arranges for the recovery or disposal of, or a dealer which only deals in—

(i) animal by-products;

(ii) waste from a mine or quarry; or

(iii) waste from premises used for agriculture.

25 Registration of brokers and dealers in controlled waste

No person may act as a broker of or dealer in controlled waste unless registered with the Environment Agency.

26 Exemptions in relation to carriers

(1) The following are not required to be a registered carrier of controlled waste for the purposes of section 1 of the Control of Pollution (Amendment) Act 1989—

(a) a carrier who is a specified person and who does not normally and regularly transport controlled waste;

(b) the operator of a vessel, aircraft, hovercraft, floating container or vehicle, in relation to its use, after it has been loaded with waste in circumstances in which a marine licence is required or would be required but for a marine exemption order for transporting the waste in order to carry out a specified marine operation.

(2) In paragraph (1)(b)—

"marine licence" means—

(a) a licence under Part 2 of the Food and Environment Protection Act 1985; or

(b) a marine licence under Part 4 of the Marine and Coastal Access Act 2009;

"marine exemption order" means an order under—

(a) section 7 of the Food and Environment Protection Act 1985 (exemptions from licensing); or

(b) section 74 of the Marine and Coastal Access Act 2009 (which provides for exemptions from marine licensing);

"specified marine operation" means an operation mentioned in—

(a) section 5 or 6 of the Food and Environment Protection Act 1985 (deposits in the sea or incineration); or

(b) an item numbered 1 to 6 or 11 to 13 in section 66(1) of the Marine and Coastal Access Act 2009 (which specifies licensable marine activities).

27 Transitional exemptions

(1) Until the end of 2013, a transitionally exempt carrier is not required to be registered as a carrier of controlled waste for the purposes of section 1 of the Control of Pollution (Amendment) Act 1989.

(2) Until the end of 2013, a transitionally exempt broker is not required to be registered as a broker of controlled waste for the purposes of regulation 25.

(3) In this regulation—

"transitionally exempt carrier" means a carrier who—

(a) at the relevant time was not required to be registered as a carrier of controlled waste for the purposes of—

(i) section 1 of the Control of Pollution (Amendment) Act 1989, and

(ii) paragraph 12(1) of Schedule 4 to the Waste Management Licensing Regulations 1994; or

(b) had they been a carrier of controlled waste at the relevant time, would not have been required to be registered for those purposes;

"transitionally exempt broker" means a broker who—

(a) at the relevant time was not required to be registered as a broker of controlled waste for the purposes of—

(i) regulation 20(1) of the Waste Management Licensing Regulations 1994, and

(ii) paragraph 12(2) of Schedule 4 to those Regulations, or

(b) had they been a broker of controlled waste at the relevant time, would not have been required to be registered for those purposes.

28 The register

(1) The Environment Agency must establish and maintain a register of carriers, brokers and dealers.

(2) A register of carriers or brokers held at the relevant time for the purposes of the Control of Pollution (Amendment) Act 1989 or the Waste Management Licensing Regulations 1994 is a register for the purposes of these Regulations.

29 Procedure for registration

(1) This regulation applies to—

(a) registration of a carrier for the purposes of the Control of Pollution (Amendment) Act 1989; and

(b) registration of a broker or dealer for the purposes of regulation 25.

(2) Registration must be made using the form provided by the Environment Agency.

(3) All the information required by the form must be provided, together with any fee prescribed in a charging scheme made by the Environment Agency under section 41 of the Environment Act 1995.

(4) The Agency may require additional information to be provided.

(5) Registration may be refused if, in the opinion of the Agency—

(a) it is undesirable for the applicant to be authorised to transport controlled waste or to act as a broker or dealer of controlled waste (as the case may be); and

(b) the applicant or another relevant person has been convicted of an offence under—

- (i) regulation 42,
- (ii) section 1, 5 or 7(3) of the Control of Pollution (Amendment) Act 1989,
- (iii) section 33 or 34 of the Environmental Protection Act 1990,
- (iv) section 110(2) of the Environment Act 1995,
- (v) the Hazardous Waste (England and Wales) Regulations 2005,
- (vi) the Hazardous Waste (Wales) Regulations 2005,
- (vii) the Transfrontier Shipment of Waste Regulations 2007,
- (viii) regulation 38 of the Environmental Permitting (England and Wales) Regulations 2007, or
- (ix) regulation 38 of the Environmental Permitting (England and Wales) Regulations 2010.

(6) On registration the Agency must provide a certificate of registration to the applicant.

(7) If registration is refused the Agency must notify the applicant and give written reasons for the refusal.

30 Updating the register

(1) A registered carrier, broker or dealer must within 28 days inform the Environment Agency of any change of circumstance affecting information in the entry relating to that carrier, broker or dealer.

(2) If the Agency becomes aware that the information held on the register is incorrect in respect of any carrier, broker or dealer, it may remove that person from the register where it is reasonable to do so.

(3) Where the Agency has the person's address, it must notify them of the removal and request the correct information.

(4) The Agency must restore the person to the register if the correct information comes to its notice.

31 Duration of a registration

(1) Unless revoked, registration of a specified person is indefinite.

(2) For other persons registration is for three years unless revoked.

(3) But registration is not valid during any period of removal from the register under regulation 30(2).

32 Revocation of registration

(1) A registration may be revoked if—

(a) the registered person or another relevant person has been convicted of an offence specified in regulation 29(5)(b); and

(b) in the opinion of the Agency, it is undesirable for the registered carrier, broker or dealer to continue to be authorised to act as a carrier or broker of, or a dealer in, controlled waste (as the case may be).

(2) If a registration is revoked the Agency must notify the registered person and give written reasons for the revocation.

(3) A revocation comes into force—
(a) where no appeal is made, 28 days after the date the notification is received; or
(b) where an appeal is made, when it is withdrawn or refused.

33 Appeals

An appeal under section 4 of the Control of Pollution (Amendment) Act 1989 must be received by the Secretary of State or the Welsh Ministers (as the case may be) within 28 days of the refusal or revocation that is the subject of the appeal.

34 Inspections

(1) The Environment Agency must ensure that appropriate periodic inspections of registered carriers, brokers and dealers are made.

(2) If the inspection relates to collection or transport of controlled waste, the Environment Agency must ensure that it covers the origin, nature, quantity and destination of that waste.

(3) In paragraph (2), "collection or transport" includes an operation where waste is transported following transfer between different carriers.

PART 9
TRANSFER OF WASTE

35 The transfer note

(1) This regulation takes effect as if it were made in exercise of the power in section 34(5) of the Environmental Protection Act 1990.

(2) When controlled waste is transferred in accordance with section 34(1)(c) of that Act the written description of the waste ("the transfer note") must—
(a) identify the waste to which it relates by reference to the appropriate codes in the List of Wastes (England) Regulations 2005 or, as the case may be, the List of Wastes (Wales) Regulations 2005, give a description of the waste and state—
(i) its quantity and whether it is loose or in a container,
(ii) if in a container, the kind of container,
(iii) the time and place of transfer, and
(iv) the SIC code of the transferor;
(b) give the name and address of the transferor and the transferee and be signed by them;
(c) state whether each of the transferor and transferee are—
(i) the producer of the waste,
(ii) the importer of the waste,
(iii) the transporter of the waste,
(iv) a local authority,
(v) a holder of an environmental permit under the Environmental Permitting (England and Wales) Regulations 2010, in which case the note must include the permit number (if any),
(vi) a person carrying on an operation to which section 33(1)(a) of the Environmental Protection Act 1990 does not apply by virtue of regulation 68(2) of the Environmental Permitting (England and Wales) Regulations 2010,
(vii) a person registered as a carrier of controlled waste under the Control of Pollution (Amendment) Act 1989, in which case the note must include the registration number (if any),

(viii) a person registered as a broker of or dealer in controlled waste, in which case the note must include the registration number (if any);

(d) confirm that the transferor has discharged the duty in regulation 12.

(3) Until the end of the period of 6 months beginning with the day on which these Regulations are made, a transfer note may omit the information required by paragraph (2)(a)(iv) and (d).

(4) The transfer note may be in electronic form if the person producing it can do so in a visible and legible documentary form.

(5) Where the transfer note is in electronic form, the signature required by paragraph (2)(b) must be an electronic signature (and "electronic signature" means data in electronic form which are attached to or logically associated with the transfer note and which serve as a method of authentication).

(6) The transferor and the transferee must keep a transfer note, or a copy of it, for at least 2 years and produce it to an officer of the Environment Agency or of a waste collection authority on demand within 7 days.

(7) This regulation does not apply where the waste transferred is hazardous waste and the consignment note and, where appropriate, schedule required by the Hazardous Waste (England and Wales) Regulations 2005 or the Hazardous Waste (Wales) Regulations 2005 are completed and dealt with in accordance with those Regulations.

(8) In this regulation "SIC code" means a code included in the UK Standard Industrial Classification of Industrial Activities 2007 (SIC 2007) published by the Office for National Statistics on 14th December 2007.

PART 10
ENFORCEMENT

36 Interpretation

In this Part—

"the 1989 Act" means the Control of Pollution (Amendment) Act 1989;
"compliance notice" has the meaning given in regulation 38(1);
"regulation authority" has the meaning given in section 9 of the 1989 Act;
"restoration notice" has the meaning given in regulation 40(1);
"specified person" has the meaning given in regulation 24(5);
"stop notice" has the meaning given in regulation 39(1).

37 Enforcement authority

The Environment Agency enforces Part 5 and regulation 25.

38 Compliance notices

(1) A "compliance notice" is a notice requiring a person to take specified steps within a specified period to secure that a contravention does not continue or recur.

(2) If the Environment Agency considers that a person has contravened or is contravening regulation 12(1), [13(2)][1], 14(1) or 25 it may serve a compliance notice on that person.

(3) If a regulation authority considers that a person has contravened or is contravening section 1 of the 1989 Act it may serve a compliance notice on that person.

(4) A compliance notice must—
(a) state the authority's reason for serving it;
(b) specify the matters constituting the contravention;
(c) specify the steps which must be taken to secure that the contravention does not continue or recur;
(d) specify the period within which those steps must be taken;
(e) give information as to the rights of appeal (including the period within which an appeal must be brought).

Amendment
1 Substituted by the Waste (England and Wales) (Amendment) Regulations 2012, SI 2012/1889, reg 2(1), (4).

39 Stop notices

(1) A "stop notice" is a notice prohibiting a person from carrying on an activity specified in the notice until the person has taken the steps specified in the notice.

(2) If the Environment Agency considers that a person is carrying on an activity in contravention of regulation 12(1), [13(2)][1], 14(1) or 25 it may serve a stop notice on that person.

(3) If a regulation authority considers that a person is carrying on an activity in contravention of section 1 of the 1989 Act it may serve a stop notice on that person.

(4) A stop notice must—
(a) state the authority's reason for serving it;
(b) specify the matters constituting the contravention;
(c) specify the steps which must be taken to remedy the contravention;
(d) give information as to the rights of appeal (including the period within which an appeal must be brought).

Amendment
1 Substituted by the Waste (England and Wales) (Amendment) Regulations 2012, SI 2012/1889, reg 2(1), (4).

40 Restoration notices

(1) A "restoration notice" is a notice requiring a person to take specified steps within a specified period to secure that the position is, so far as possible, restored to what it would have been if a contravention had not occurred.

(2) If the Environment Agency considers that a person has contravened regulation 14(1) it may serve a restoration notice on that person.

(3) A restoration notice must—
(a) state the Environment Agency's reason for serving it;
(b) specify the matters constituting the contravention;
(c) specify the steps which must be taken to secure restoration, so far as possible;
(d) specify the period within which those steps must be taken;
(e) give information as to the rights of appeal (including the period within which an appeal must be brought).

41 Appeals

(1) A person on whom a compliance notice, stop notice or restoration notice is served may appeal against the decision to serve it.

(2) The grounds for appeal are—
(a) that the decision was wrong in fact;
(b) that the decision was wrong in law;

(c) that the decision was unreasonable;
(d) that any step specified in the notice is unreasonable;
(e) any other reason.

(3) The right of appeal is to the First-tier tribunal.

(4) The tribunal must determine the standard of proof.

(5) A notice, and any requirement in a notice, is not suspended pending an appeal unless the tribunal directs otherwise.

(6) The tribunal may—
(a) withdraw the requirement or notice;
(b) confirm the requirement or notice;
(c) vary the requirement or notice;
(d) take such steps as the authority serving the notice could take in relation to the act or omission giving rise to the requirement or notice;
(e) remit the decision whether to confirm the requirement or notice, or any matter relating to that decision, to the authority.

42 Offence and penalties

(1) A person is guilty of an offence who—
(a) if they are not a specified person, fails to comply with regulation 25; or
(b) fails to comply with a compliance notice, stop notice or restoration notice.

(2) A person guilty of an offence under—
(a) paragraph (1)(a); or
(b) paragraph (1)(b) in relation to contravention of regulation 25,
is liable on summary conviction to a fine not exceeding level 5 on the standard scale.

(3) A person guilty of an offence under paragraph (1)(b) in relation to contravention of regulation 12(1), [13(2)][1] or 14(1) is liable—
(a) on summary conviction, to a fine not exceeding the statutory maximum;
(b) on conviction on indictment, to a fine.

Amendment

1 Substituted by the Waste (England and Wales) (Amendment) Regulations 2012, SI 2012/1889, reg 2(1), (4).

43 Proceedings against partnerships and unincorporated associations

(1) Proceedings for an offence under regulation 42(1) alleged to have been committed by a partnership or unincorporated association may be brought against the partnership or association in the name of the partnership or association.

(2) For the purposes of such proceedings the following apply as if the partnership or unincorporated association were a body corporate—
(a) rules of court relating to the service of documents; and
(b) section 33 of the Criminal Justice Act 1925 and Schedule 3 to the Magistrates' Courts Act 1980.

(3) A fine imposed on a partnership or unincorporated association is to be paid out of the funds of the partnership or association.

44 Offences by bodies corporate, partnerships and unincorporated associations

(1) Where a body corporate is guilty of an offence under regulation 42(1), and that offence is proved to have been committed with the consent or connivance of, or to have been attributable to any neglect on the part of—

(a) any director, manager, secretary or other similar officer of the body corporate; or
(b) any person who was purporting to act in any such capacity,
that person, as well as the body corporate, is guilty of the offence.

(2) In paragraph (1) "director", in relation to a body corporate whose affairs are managed by its members, means a member of the body corporate.

(3) Where a partnership is guilty of an offence under regulation 42(1), and that offence is proved to have been committed with the consent or connivance of, or to have been attributable to any neglect on the part of a partner, the partner, as well as the partnership, is guilty of the offence.

(4) In paragraph (3) "partner" includes a person purporting to act as a partner.

(5) Where an unincorporated association is guilty of an offence under regulation 42(1), and that offence is proved to have been committed with the consent or connivance of, or to have been attributable to any neglect on the part of an officer of the association, that officer, as well as the association, is guilty of the offence.

(6) In paragraph (5) "officer", in relation to an unincorporated association, means—
(a) an officer of the association or a member of its governing body; or
(b) a person purporting to act in such a capacity.

45 Proceedings for contravention of section 1 of the Control of Pollution (Amendment) Act 1989

A regulation authority must not institute proceedings against a specified person for contravention of section 1 of the 1989 Act unless—
(a) the authority has served a compliance notice or stop notice on the person in respect of the contravention; and
(b) the person has failed to comply with the notice.

PART 11
FINAL PROVISIONS

46 Registration: reduction of administrative burden

(1) This regulation applies to the Environment Agency in relation to registration of—
(a) carriers and brokers of, and dealers in, controlled waste (see Part 8); and
(b) establishments and undertakings carrying on exempt waste operations under Schedule 2 to the Environmental Permitting (England and Wales) Regulations 2010.

(2) The Environment Agency must, where possible, use existing records held by it to obtain information for the registration process in order to reduce the administrative burden.

47 Radioactive waste

[(1) This regulation applies to radioactive waste—
(a) which is a specified waste; and
(b) in respect of which a person—
  (i) is carrying on a radioactive substances activity described in paragraph 11(2)(b) or (c) or (4) of Part 2 of Schedule 23 to the Environmental Permitting (England and Wales) Regulations 2010; and
  (ii) is exempt from the requirement for an environmental permit under regulation 12(2A) of those Regulations for that activity.][1]

(2) Radioactive waste to which this regulation applies must be treated as waste for the purposes of these Regulations.

(3) Sections 33 to 34C of the Environmental Protection Act 1990 apply to radioactive waste to which this regulation applies.

(4) In this regulation—

"environmental permit" has the meaning given in regulation 13(1) of the Environmental Permitting (England and Wales) Regulations 2010;

["radioactive substances exemption" means an exemption under Part 7 of Schedule 23 to the Environmental Permitting (England and Wales) Regulations 2010 from the requirement for an environmental permit under regulation 12 of those regulations in respect of a radioactive substances activity;][2]

"radioactive waste" and "radioactive substances activity" have the meanings given in [paragraphs 3 and 11][1] of Part 2 of Schedule 23 to the Environmental Permitting (England and Wales) Regulations 2010;

...[3]

["specified waste" means—

(a) NORM waste (as that term is defined in Part 7 of Schedule 23 to the Environmental Permitting (England and Wales) Regulations 2010; or

(b) the waste described in the first, second or sixth row of column 1 of table 6 in Part 7 of Schedule 23 to the Environmental Permitting (England and Wales) Regulations 2010.][2]

Amendments

1 Substituted by the Environmental Permitting (England and Wales) (Amendment) Regulations 2011, SI 2011/2043, reg 16, Sch 2, Pt 2, para 6(1), (2), (3)(a).

2 Inserted by the Environmental Permitting (England and Wales) (Amendment) Regulations 2011, SI 2011/2043, reg 16, Sch 2, Pt 2, para 6(1), (3)(c).

3 Repealed by the Environmental Permitting (England and Wales) (Amendment) Regulations 2011, SI 2011/2043, reg 16, Sch 2, Pt 2, para 6(1), (3)(b).

[*Regulation 48 is not reproduced.*]

[49 Review

(1) The Secretary of State must from time to time—

(a) carry out a review of these Regulations in relation to England;

(b) set out the conclusions of the review in a report; and

(c) publish the report.

(2) In carrying out the review the Secretary of State must, so far as is reasonable, have regard to how the Waste Framework Directive (which is implemented in part by means of these Regulations) is implemented in other member States.

(3) The report must in particular—

(a) set out the objectives intended to be achieved by the regulatory system established by these Regulations;

(b) assess the extent to which those objectives are achieved; and

(c) assess whether those objectives remain appropriate and, if so, the extent to which they could be achieved with a system that imposes less regulation.

(4) The first report under this regulation must be published before the end of the period of 5 years beginning with 1st October 2012.

(5) Reports under this regulation are afterwards to be published at intervals not exceeding 5 years.][1]

Amendment

1 Inserted by the Waste (England and Wales) (Amendment) Regulations 2012, SI 2012/1889, reg 2(1), (5).

SCHEDULE 1
WASTE PREVENTION PROGRAMMES AND WASTE MANAGEMENT PLANS

Regulations 5, 8 and 11

PART 1
OBJECTIVES

1 Overall objective

To protect the environment and human health by preventing or reducing the adverse impacts of the generation and management of waste and by reducing overall impacts of resource use and improving the efficiency of such use.

2 Application of the waste hierarchy

(1) To apply the following waste hierarchy as a priority order in waste prevention and management policy—
(a) prevention;
(b) preparing for re-use;
(c) recycling;
(d) other recovery (for example energy recovery);
(e) disposal.

(2) When applying the waste hierarchy in sub-paragraph (1), the appropriate authority must ensure that it—
(a) encourages the options that deliver the best overall environmental outcome, which may require specific waste streams to depart from the hierarchy where this is justified by life-cycle thinking on the overall impacts of the generation and management of such waste;
(b) takes into account—
(i) the general environmental protection principles of precaution and sustainability,
(ii) technical feasibility and economic viability,
(iii) protection of resources, and
(iv) the overall environmental, human health, economic and social impacts.

3 Protection of human health and the environment

To ensure that waste management is carried out without endangering human health, without harming the environment and, in particular—
(a) without risk to water, air, soil, plants or animals;
(b) without causing a nuisance through noise or odours; and
(c) without adversely affecting the countryside or places of special interest.

4 Principles of self-sufficiency and proximity

(1) To establish an integrated and adequate network of waste disposal installations and of installations for the recovery of mixed municipal waste collected from private households, including, where such collection also covers such waste from other producers, taking into account best available techniques.

(2) The network must be designed to enable the European Union as a whole to become self-sufficient in waste disposal and in the recovery of mixed municipal waste collected from private households, and to enable the United Kingdom to move towards that aim taking into account geographical circumstances or the need for specialised installations for certain types of waste.

(3) The network must enable waste to be disposed of and mixed municipal waste collected from private households to be recovered in one of the nearest appropriate installations, by means of the most appropriate technologies, in order to ensure a high level of protection for the environment and human health.

(4) This paragraph does not require that the full range of final recovery facilities be located in England or in Wales or in England and Wales together.

PART 2
MATTERS WHICH MUST BE INCLUDED IN WASTE MANAGEMENT PLANS

5 Analysis of the current waste management situation etc.

An analysis of the current waste management situation in England or Wales, as the case may be, the measures to be taken to improve environmentally sound preparing for re-use, recycling, recovery and disposal of waste and an evaluation of how the plan will support the implementation of the objectives and provisions of the Waste Framework Directive.

6 General policies in relation to waste

As appropriate and taking into account the geographical level and geographical area to which the plan relates, provisions relating to—

(a) the type, quantity and source of waste generated within the territory, the waste likely to be shipped from or to the United Kingdom, and an evaluation of the development of waste streams in the future;

(b) existing waste collection schemes and major disposal and recovery installations, including any special arrangements for waste oils, hazardous waste or waste streams addressed by specific European Union legislation;

(c) an assessment of the need for new collection schemes, the closure of existing waste installations, additional waste installation infrastructure (in accordance with the objective in paragraph 4), and, if necessary the related investments;

(d) sufficient information on the location criteria for site identification and on the capacity of future disposal or major recovery installations, if necessary;

(e) general waste management policies, including planned waste management technologies and methods, or policies for waste posing specific management problems.

7 Policies in relation to packaging waste

In pursuance of the objectives and measures in Directive 94/62/EC of the European Parliament and of the Council on packaging and packaging waste, a chapter on the management of packaging and packaging waste, including measures taken pursuant to Articles 4 and 5 of that Directive.

8 Policies in relation to separate collection of waste

Measures to promote high quality recycling including the setting up of separate collections of waste where technically, environmentally and economically practicable and appropriate to meet the necessary quality standards for the relevant recycling sectors.

9 Policies in relation to bio-waste

As appropriate, measures to encourage the separate collection of bio-waste with a view to the composting and digestion of bio-waste.

10 Policies in relation to re-use

As appropriate, measures to be taken to promote the re-use of products and preparing for re-use activities, in particular—

(a) measures to encourage the establishment and support of re-use and repair networks;
(b) the use of economic instruments;
(c) the use of procurement criteria;
(d) the setting of quantitative objectives.

11 Preparing for re-use, recovery and recycling targets

(1) Measures to be taken to ensure that, by 2020, at least 50% by weight of waste from households is prepared for re-use or recycled.

(2) Measures to be taken to ensure that, by 2020, at least 70% by weight of the waste mentioned in paragraph (3) is subjected to material recovery.

(3) That waste is construction and demolition waste excluding—

(a) hazardous waste;
(b) naturally occurring material falling within code 17 05 04 in Schedule 1 to—
    (i) the List of Wastes (England) Regulations 2005, or
    (ii) the List of Wastes (Wales) Regulations 2005.

PART 3
MATTERS WHICH MAY BE INCLUDED IN WASTE MANAGEMENT PLANS

12 Matters which may be included in a waste management plan

Taking into account the geographical level and geographical area to which the plan relates—

(a) organisational aspects related to waste management including a description of the allocation of responsibilities between public and private actors carrying out waste management;
(b) an evaluation of the usefulness and suitability of the use of economic and other instruments in tackling various waste problems, taking into account the need to maintain the smooth functioning of the internal market;
(c) the use of awareness campaigns and information provision directed at the general public or at a specific set of consumers;
(d) historical contaminated waste disposal sites and measures for their rehabilitation.

PART 4
PUBLIC PARTICIPATION IN THE PREPARATION OR MODIFICATION OF A WASTE PREVENTION PROGRAMME OR NATIONAL WASTE MANAGEMENT PLAN

13 Interpretation

In this Part—

"consultation bodies" means—

(a) in relation to a waste prevention programme or national waste management plan relating to England—
    (i) Natural England, and
    (ii) the Historic Buildings and Monuments Commission for England (English Heritage);
(b) in relation to a waste prevention programme or national waste management plan relating to Wales, the Countryside Council for Wales;

"public consultees" means the persons to whose attention proposals for a programme or plan are brought by the appropriate authority pursuant to paragraph 14(1)(b).

14 Public participation procedures

(1) As soon as reasonably practicable after preparing proposals for a waste prevention programme or national waste management plan or for the modification of such a programme or plan, the appropriate authority must—
(a) send a copy of the proposals to the consultation bodies;
(b) take such steps as it considers appropriate to bring the proposals to the attention of the persons who in the authority's opinion—
  (i) are, or are likely to be, affected by the programme or plan, or
  (ii) have an interest in the programme or plan;
(c) inform the public consultees of the address (which may include a website)—
  (i) at which a copy of the proposals may be viewed, and
  (ii) from which a copy of the proposals may be obtained;
(d) invite the consultation bodies and public consultees to express their opinion on the proposals, specifying the address to which, and the period within which, opinions must be sent.

(2) The period referred to in paragraph (1)(d) must be of such length as will ensure that the consultation bodies and the public consultees are given an effective opportunity to express their opinion on the proposals.

(3) The appropriate authority must keep a copy of the proposals at its principal office for inspection by the public at all reasonable times free of charge.

(4) Nothing in paragraph (1)(c) requires the appropriate authority to provide copies free of charge, but where a charge is made it must be reasonable.

15 Procedures following public participation

(1) Before decisions on a waste prevention programme or national waste management plan are made, the appropriate authority must take account of any opinion expressed by a consultation body or public consultee.

(2) As soon as reasonably practicable after making decisions on a waste prevention programme or national waste management plan, the appropriate authority must—
(a) inform the consultation bodies and the public consultees of the matters in paragraph (3);
(b) take such steps as it considers appropriate to bring those matters to the attention of the public; and
(c) if it has adopted the programme or plan, make a copy available at its principal office for inspection by the public at all reasonable times free of charge.

(3) The matters are—
(a) the decisions made by the appropriate authority on the programme or plan;
(b) the reasons and considerations on which those decisions are based; and
(c) information about the public participation procedure.

(4) Nothing in paragraph (2)(c) requires the appropriate authority to provide copies free of charge, but where a charge is made it must be reasonable.

[*Schedule 2 to 5 are not reproduced.*]

ENVIRONMENTAL PROTECTION (CONTROLS ON OZONE-DEPLETING SUBSTANCES) REGULATIONS 2011

SI 2011/1543

PART 1
INTRODUCTION

1 Title, commencement and extent

(1) These Regulations may be cited as the Environmental Protection (Controls on Ozone-Depleting Substances) Regulations 2011.

(2) They come into force on 20th July 2011.

(3) They only extend to Northern Ireland in so far as they relate to import and export under the EU Regulation.

2 Interpretation

In these Regulations—

"authorised person" means a person authorised under regulation 8(1);

"controlled substances" means the substances in Annex I of the EU Regulation as amended from time to time;

"enforcement notice" has the meaning given by regulation 9(1);

"enforcing authority" means a body enforcing the EU Regulation under regulation 7;

"export" and "import" have the meaning given in Article 3 of the EU Regulation;

"the EU Regulation" means Regulation (EC) No 1005/2009 of the European Parliament and of the Council on substances that deplete the ozone layer;

"offshore installation" has the meaning given by Schedule 1.

3 The competent authority

The Secretary of State is the competent authority for the purposes of the EU Regulation.

PART 2
OFFENCES, PENALTIES AND ENFORCEMENT

4 Offences

(1) Any person who breaches a provision of the EU Regulation set out in Schedule 2 is guilty of an offence.

(2) Failure to comply with any of the following is an offence—

(a) an enforcement notice;

(b) a notice under regulation 11.

(3) It is an offence—

(a) intentionally to obstruct any person acting in the execution or enforcement of the EU Regulation;

(b) without reasonable cause, to fail to give to any such person any assistance or information which that person may reasonably require for those purposes;

(c) to furnish to any such person any information knowing it to be false or misleading; or

(d) to fail to produce a document or record to any such person when required to do so.

5 Penalties

A person guilty of an offence under these Regulations is liable—

(a) on summary conviction, to a fine not exceeding the statutory maximum; or

(b) on conviction on indictment, to a fine.

6 Offences by bodies corporate

(1) If an offence under these Regulations committed by a body corporate is proved—

(a) to have been committed with the consent or connivance of an officer; or

(b) to be attributable to any neglect on the part of an officer,

the officer, as well as the body corporate, is guilty of the offence and liable to be proceeded against and punished accordingly.

(2) In paragraph (1) "officer", in relation to a body corporate, means—

(a) a director, manager, secretary or other similar officer of the body; or

(b) a person purporting to act in any such capacity.

(3) If the affairs of a body corporate are managed by its members, paragraph (1) applies in relation to the acts and defaults of a member in connection with the member's functions of management as it applies to an officer of a body corporate.

(4) If an offence under these Regulations committed by a partnership in Scotland is proved—

(a) to have been committed with the consent or connivance of a partner; or

(b) to be attributable to any neglect on the part of a partner,

the partner, as well as the partnership, is guilty of the offence and liable to be proceeded against and punished accordingly.

(5) In paragraph (4) "partner" includes a person purporting to act as a partner.

7 Enforcement

(1) The Agency and the local authority enforce the EU Regulation.

(2) In relation to—

(a) cases of a particular description; or

(b) a particular case,

the Secretary of State, as regards England, the Welsh Ministers as regards Wales, the Scottish Ministers as regards Scotland, or the Department of the Environment as regards Northern Ireland, may direct that the EU Regulation be enforced by them instead.

(3) The Secretary of State enforces the EU Regulation in relation to offshore installations.

(4) Nothing in these Regulations authorises an enforcing authority to bring proceedings in Scotland for an offence.

(5) In this regulation—

"the Agency" means—

(a) as regards England and Wales, the Environment Agency, and

(b) as regards Scotland, the Scottish Environment Protection Agency;

"local authority" means—

(a) in England, where there is, within the meaning of the Local Government Changes for England Regulations 1994, a unitary authority, that authority;

(b) otherwise in England—
  (i) a district council,
  (ii) a London borough council,
  (iii) the Common Council of the City of London, or
  (iv) the Council of the Isles of Scilly;
(c) in relation to Wales—
  (i) a county council, or
  (ii) a county borough council;
(d) in relation to Scotland, a council constituted under section 2 of the Local Government etc. (Scotland) Act 1994;
(e) in relation to Northern Ireland, a district council.

8 Authorisation by the enforcing authority

(1) An enforcing authority may authorise persons in writing for the purposes of enforcing the EU Regulation.

(2) The following are authorised for the purposes of paragraph (1)—
(a) in England, Scotland and Wales a person authorised under section 108 of the Environment Act 1995;
(b) in Northern Ireland a person authorised under Article 72 of the Waste and Contaminated Land (Northern Ireland) Order 1997.

(3) The powers in section 108 of the Environment Act 1995 (powers of enforcing authorities and persons authorised by them) are extended to the offshore area for the purposes of enforcing the EU Regulation.

9 Enforcement notices

(1) An enforcement notice is a notice requiring a person to take specified steps to remedy or avert a contravention.

(2) An authorised person who is of the opinion that a person has contravened, is contravening or is likely to contravene a provision of the EU Regulation may serve an enforcement notice on that person.

(3) An enforcement notice must—
(a) state that the authorised person is of that opinion;
(b) specify the matters constituting the contravention or the matters making it likely that the contravention will arise, as the case may be;
(c) specify the steps that must be taken to remedy or avert the contravention;
(d) specify the period within which those steps must be taken;
(e) state—
  (i) that the person on whom the notice is served has the right of appeal to a magistrates' court or the sheriff; and
  (ii) the period within which the appeal may be brought.

(4) An authorised person may at any time withdraw an enforcement notice.

(5) A person on whom an enforcement notice is served must comply with it at their own expense.

(6) If an enforcement notice is not complied with, the enforcing authority may arrange for it to be complied with at the expense of the person on whom it was served.

10 Appeals against enforcement notices

(1) A person who is aggrieved by an enforcement notice may appeal against it.

(2) The right of appeal is to a magistrates' court or, in Scotland, to the sheriff.

(3) The procedure on an appeal to a magistrates' court is by way of complaint, and the Magistrates' Courts Act 1980 applies to the proceedings.

(4) An appeal to the sheriff is by summary application.

(5) An appeal may be brought not later than 28 days after the date on which the enforcement notice is served.

(6) An enforcement notice is not suspended pending an appeal unless the court or sheriff orders otherwise.

(7) On an appeal the court or sheriff may either cancel the notice or confirm it, with or without modification.

11 Powers of the Secretary of State

The Secretary of State may by notice require a person in possession of a controlled substance, or a product or equipment containing or relying on a controlled substance, that has been produced, placed on the market or imported or is intended to be or is being exported, in contravention of the EU Regulation, to dispose of it or otherwise render it harmless in accordance with the notice.

12 Power to seize and detain

(1) A customs official may seize and detain any controlled substance or product or equipment containing or relying on a controlled substance which the official believes is being—
(a) imported in contravention of Article 15 of the EU Regulation; or
(b) exported in contravention of Article 17 of the EU Regulation.

(2) Anything seized and detained under paragraph (1) may be detained for no longer than 5 working days and must be dealt with during the period of its detention in such manner as the Secretary of State may direct under section 5 of the 2009 Act.

(3) In this regulation—
"the 2009 Act" means the Borders, Citizenship and Immigration Act 2009;
"customs official" means a general customs official designated under section 3(1) of the 2009 Act, or a customs revenue official designated under section 11(1) of that Act;
"working day" means any day other than a Saturday, a Sunday, Christmas Day, Good Friday or a day which is a bank holiday under the Banking and Financial Dealings Act 1971 in any part of the United Kingdom.

PART 3
REVIEW, REVOCATIONS AND AMENDMENTS

13 Review

(1) Before the end of each review period, the Secretary of State must—
(a) carry out a review of these Regulations;
(b) set out the conclusions of the review in a report; and
(c) publish the report.

(2) The report must in particular—
(a) set out the objectives intended to be achieved by these Regulations;
(b) assess the extent to which the objectives have been achieved;

(c) assess whether the objectives remain appropriate and, if so, the extent to which they could be achieved in a less burdensome way.

(3) The first review period is the period of five years beginning with the day on which these Regulations come into force.

(4) Each subsequent review period is a period of five years beginning with the date on which the report of the preceding review was published.

[*Regulations 14 and 15 are not reproduced.*]

SCHEDULE 1
MEANING OF "OFFSHORE INSTALLATION"

Regulation 2

1

(1) "Offshore installation" means an installation or structure, other than a ship, used for carrying on an activity in sub-paragraph (2) which is situated in the waters of, or on or under the seabed in, the marine area; and "marine area" means—

(a) the tidal waters and parts of the sea in or adjacent to the United Kingdom up to the seaward limits of the territorial sea; and

(b) the area designated by an Order in Council under section 1(7) of the Continental Shelf Act 1964.

(2) The activities are—

(a) the exploitation, or the exploration with a view to exploitation, of mineral resources in or under the shore or bed of waters in the marine area;

(b) the exploration of a place in, under or over such waters with a view to the storage of gas;

(c) the conversion of a place under the shore or bed of such waters for the purpose of storing gas;

(d) the storage of gas in, under or over such waters or the recovery of gas so stored;

(e) the unloading of gas at a place in, under or over such waters;

(f) the conveyance of things by means of a pipe, or system of pipes, constructed or placed on, in or under the shore or bed of such waters;

(g) the provision of accommodation for persons who work on or from an installation which is or has been maintained, or is intended to be established, for the carrying on of an activity in this sub-paragraph.

(3) In sub-paragraph (2)—

(a) references (in whatever form) to storing gas include storing gas with a view to its permanent disposal;

(b) "gas" means—

  (i) gas within the meaning of the Energy Act 2008; or

  (ii) carbon dioxide.

SCHEDULE 2
OFFENCES FOR BREACH OF THE EU REGULATION

Regulation 4(1)

Provision of the EU Regulation	*Subject matter*
Article 4	Production of controlled substances
Article 5(1)	Placing on the market and use of controlled substances
Article 5(2)	Placing on the market of controlled substances in non-refillable containers

Provision of the EU Regulation	*Subject matter*
Article 6(1)	Placing on the market of products and equipment containing or relying on controlled substances
Article 6(2)	Prohibition and decommissioning of fire protection systems and fire extinguishers containing halons
Article 13(3)	Decommissioning of fire protection systems and fire extinguishers containing halons
Article 15(1)	Imports of controlled substances and products and equipment containing or relying on controlled substances
Article 17(1)	Exports of controlled substances or products and equipment containing or relying on controlled substances
Article 20	Trade with a State not party to the Montreal Protocol on substances that deplete the ozone layer or a territory not covered by that Protocol
Article 22(1), (2) and (4)	Recovery and destruction, recycling and reclamation of controlled substances
Article 23(1)	Precautionary measures to prevent and minimise leakages and emissions of controlled substances
Article 23(2)	Requirements for specified stationary equipment or systems
Article 23(3)	Record keeping by undertakings
Article 23(5)	Precautionary measures to prevent and minimise leakages and emissions of controlled substances used as feedstock or process agents
Article 23(6)	Precautionary measures to prevent and minimise leakages and emissions of controlled substances inadvertently produced in the manufacture of other chemicals
Article 24(1)	Production, import, placing on the market, use or export of new substances

WATER INDUSTRY (SCHEMES FOR ADOPTION OF PRIVATE SEWERS) REGULATIONS 2011

SI 2011/1566

1 Citation, commencement and expiry

(1) These Regulations may be cited as the Water Industry (Schemes for Adoption of Private Sewers) Regulations 2011 and come into force on 1st July 2011.

(2) They cease to have effect at the end of 30th June 2018.

2 Interpretation

In these Regulations—

"the Act" means the Water Industry Act 1991;

"adoptable", in relation to a private sewer or private lateral drain, means a sewer or lateral drain in relation to which a sewerage undertaker must perform the relevant duty;

"declaration" means a declaration of vesting under subsection (1) of section 102 of the Act (adoption of sewers and disposal works);

"exempt", in relation to a private sewer or private lateral drain, means a sewer or lateral drain which is exempt under regulation 5;

"main scheme" means a scheme under regulation 3;

"private lateral drain" means the whole or part of a lateral drain which is not vested in a sewerage undertaker in its capacity as such;

"private sewer" means the whole or part of a foul, combined or surface water private sewer, but does not include a highway drain or sewer;

"pumping station" means that part of a sewer or lateral drain which is a pumping station used or intended to be used in connection with that sewer or lateral drain, and includes the rising main (the pressurised pipe that connects the pumping station with the rest of the sewer or lateral drain);

"the relevant date" means the date of commencement (in full) of section 42(1) of the Flood and Water Management Act 2010;

"the relevant duty" means the duty under section 105A(4) of the Act (duty on sewerage undertakers to exercise their powers under section 102 of the Act with a view to making a declaration pursuant to a scheme);

"scheme" means a scheme described in section 105A of the Act (schemes for the adoption of sewers, lateral drains and sewage disposal works);

"the supplementary adoption date" means the date which is the day after the end of the period of 6 months beginning with the relevant date; and

"supplementary scheme" means a scheme under regulation 4.

3 Main schemes

(1) The Secretary of State must make a scheme (a "main scheme") for the adoption of private sewers and private lateral drains by every sewerage undertaker whose area is wholly or mainly in England.

(2) The Welsh Ministers must make a scheme (a "main scheme") for the adoption of private sewers and private lateral drains by every sewerage undertaker whose area is wholly or mainly in Wales.

(3) The making of a main scheme is the circumstance giving rise to the relevant duty pursuant to that scheme.

(4) Paragraphs (5) to (7) specify criteria relevant to the performance of that duty.

(5) Each sewerage undertaker must perform the relevant duty pursuant to a main scheme in relation to any private sewer—
(a) which is situated within the area of that undertaker; and
(b) which, immediately before 1st July 2011, communicates with a public sewer.

(6) Each sewerage undertaker must perform the relevant duty pursuant to a main scheme in relation to any private lateral drain which, immediately before 1st July 2011, communicates with a public sewer which is vested in that undertaker.

(7) The relevant duty pursuant to a main scheme is not owed in relation to any private sewer or private lateral drain—
(a) which is exempt; or
(b) which is, immediately before 1st July 2011, the subject of a declaration.

(8) Each main scheme must provide that any declaration which is made pursuant to that scheme in relation to a private sewer or private lateral drain—
(a) must specify 1st October 2011 as the date of vesting of that sewer or lateral drain (except any part of that sewer or lateral drain which is a pumping station), and
(b) must specify a date no later than 1st October 2016 as the date of vesting of any pumping station which forms part of that sewer or lateral drain,

except where it is not possible, in respect of a particular sewer or lateral drain, to make a declaration specifying such a date because a proposal to make a declaration in respect of that sewer or lateral drain is subject to an outstanding appeal under section 105B of the Act (adoption schemes: appeals).

(9) Any number of declarations may be made pursuant to a main scheme.

4 Supplementary schemes

(1) On or as soon as reasonably practicable after the relevant date, the Secretary of State must make a scheme (a "supplementary scheme") for the adoption of private sewers and private lateral drains by every sewerage undertaker whose area is wholly or mainly in England.

(2) On or as soon as reasonably practicable after the relevant date, the Welsh Ministers must make a scheme (a "supplementary scheme") for the adoption of private sewers and private lateral drains by every sewerage undertaker whose area is wholly or mainly in Wales.

(3) The making of a supplementary scheme is the circumstance giving rise to the relevant duty pursuant to that scheme.

(4) Paragraphs (5) to (7) specify criteria relevant to the performance of that duty.

(5) Each sewerage undertaker must perform the relevant duty pursuant to a supplementary scheme in relation to any private sewer—
(a) which is situated within the area of that undertaker;
(b) which, immediately before the relevant date, communicates with a public sewer; and
(c) in relation to which the relevant duty is not owed pursuant to a main scheme.

(6) Each sewerage undertaker must perform the relevant duty pursuant to a supplementary scheme in relation to any private lateral drain—
(a) which, immediately before the relevant date, communicates with a public sewer which is vested in that undertaker; and
(b) in relation to which the relevant duty is not owed pursuant to a main scheme.

(7) The relevant duty pursuant to a supplementary scheme is not owed in relation to any private sewer or private lateral drain—
(a) which is exempt; or
(b) which is, immediately before the relevant date, the subject of a declaration.

(8) Each supplementary scheme must provide that any declaration which is made pursuant to that scheme in relation to a private sewer or private lateral drain—
(a) must specify the supplementary adoption date as the date of vesting of that sewer or lateral drain (except any part of that sewer or lateral drain which is a pumping station), and
(b) must specify a date no later than 1st October 2016 as the date of vesting of any pumping station which forms part of that sewer or lateral drain,
except where it is not possible, in respect of a particular sewer or lateral drain, to make a declaration specifying such a date because a proposal to make a declaration in respect of that sewer or lateral drain is subject to an outstanding appeal under section 105B of the Act.

(9) Any number of declarations may be made pursuant to a supplementary scheme.

5 Exempt private sewers and exempt private lateral drains

(1) A private sewer or private lateral drain is exempt for the purposes of a main scheme or a supplementary scheme if that sewer or lateral drain is owned by a railway undertaker.

(2) A private sewer or private lateral drain is exempt for the purposes of a main scheme if—
(a) that sewer or lateral drain is situated on or under Crown land; and
(b) the sewerage undertaker within whose area that sewer or lateral drain is situated has received notice in writing before 1st July 2011 from the appropriate authority in relation to that land that that sewer or lateral drain should be exempt.

(3) A private sewer or private lateral drain is exempt for the purposes of a supplementary scheme if—
(a) that sewer or lateral drain is situated on or under Crown land; and
(b) the sewerage undertaker within whose area that sewer or lateral drain is situated has received notice in writing before the relevant date from the appropriate authority in relation to that land that that sewer or lateral drain should be exempt.

(4) In this regulation "Crown land" means land an interest in which—
(a) belongs to Her Majesty in right of the Crown; or
(b) belongs to a government department or is held in trust for Her Majesty for the purposes of a government department.

(5) In this regulation "the appropriate authority" means—
(a) in the case of land which belongs to Her Majesty in right of the Crown, the Crown Estate Commissioners or other government department having management of the land in question;
(b) in the case of land which belongs to a government department or is held in trust for Her Majesty for the purposes of a government department, that department.

6 Publication of proposal to make a declaration

In exercising its powers under subsection (4) of section 102 of the Act (as modified by section 105A(6)(a) of the Act) pursuant to the relevant duty, a sewerage undertaker must publish notice of its proposal to make a declaration—
(a) in the London Gazette; and
(b) in as many local or regional newspapers circulating in that undertaker's area as may be required to cover the whole of that area.

7 Existing proposals to make declarations, and existing declarations

(1) Paragraph (2) applies where—

(a) a private sewer or private lateral drain which would be adoptable pursuant to a main scheme is, immediately before 1st July 2011, the subject of a proposal (under section 102(4) of the Act) to make a declaration; or

(b) a private sewer or private lateral drain which would be adoptable pursuant to a supplementary scheme is, immediately before the relevant date, the subject of such a proposal.

(2) Where this paragraph applies—

(a) that proposal, in so far as it relates to that sewer or lateral drain, is treated as having been withdrawn; and

(b) any appeal under subsection (1)(a) of section 105 of the Act (appeals with respect to adoption) in relation to that sewer or lateral drain which is outstanding immediately before—

(i) 1st July 2011, in relation to a sewer or lateral drain to which this paragraph applies by virtue of paragraph (1)(a), or

(ii) the relevant date, in relation to a sewer or lateral drain to which this paragraph applies by virtue of paragraph (1)(b),

is to be discontinued.

(3) Where—

(a) (if it were not for regulation 3(7)(b)) a private sewer or private lateral drain would be adoptable pursuant to a main scheme, and

(b) that sewer or lateral drain is, immediately before 1st July 2011, the subject of a declaration which specifies 2nd October 2011 or a later date as the date of vesting of that sewer or lateral drain,

the date of vesting of that sewer or lateral drain pursuant to that declaration is treated as being 1st October 2011.

(4) Where—

(a) (if it were not for regulation 4(7)(b)) a private sewer or private lateral drain would be adoptable pursuant to a supplementary scheme, and

(b) that sewer or lateral drain is, immediately before the relevant date, the subject of a declaration which specifies a date later than the supplementary adoption date as the date of vesting of that sewer or lateral drain,

the date of vesting of that sewer or lateral drain pursuant to that declaration is treated as being the supplementary adoption date.

8 Outstanding appeals under section 105(1)(b) of the Act

Where an appeal under section 105(1)(b) of the Act—

(a) is outstanding, immediately before 1st July 2011, in relation to a private sewer or private lateral drain which would be adoptable pursuant to a main scheme, or

(b) is outstanding, immediately before the relevant date, in relation to a private sewer or private lateral drain which would be adoptable pursuant to a supplementary scheme,

that appeal is to be discontinued.

9 Existing applications for agreements, and existing agreements, under section 104 of the Act

(1) Paragraph (2) applies where—

(a) a private sewer or private lateral drain which would be adoptable pursuant to a main scheme is, immediately before 1st July 2011, the subject of an application, under subsection (2) of section 104 of the Act (agreements to adopt sewer, drain or sewage disposal works at future date), for an agreement; or

(b) a private sewer or private lateral drain which would be adoptable pursuant to a supplementary scheme is, immediately before the relevant date, the subject of such an application.

(2) Where this paragraph applies—

(a) that application, in so far as it relates to that sewer or lateral drain, is treated as having been withdrawn; and

(b) any appeal under section 105(2) of the Act in relation to that sewer or lateral drain which is outstanding immediately before—

(i) 1st July 2011, in relation to a sewer or lateral drain to which this paragraph applies by virtue of paragraph (1)(a), or

(ii) the relevant date, in relation to a sewer or lateral drain to which this paragraph applies by virtue of paragraph (1)(b),

is to be discontinued.

(3) Paragraph (4) applies where—

(a) a private sewer or private lateral drain which would be adoptable pursuant to a main scheme is, immediately before 1st July 2011, the subject of an agreement; or

(b) a private sewer or private lateral drain which would be adoptable pursuant to a supplementary scheme is, immediately before the relevant date, the subject of an agreement.

(4) Where this paragraph applies—

(a) that sewer or lateral drain vests in the relevant sewerage undertaker on the earlier of—

(i) the date specified as the date of vesting of that sewer or lateral drain in a declaration made pursuant to a main scheme or a supplementary scheme (as the case may be), or

(ii) the date of vesting under the agreement in question;

(b) that agreement, in so far as it relates to that sewer or lateral drain, is treated as terminating on the vesting date; and

(c) the relevant sewerage undertaker may continue to benefit from any term of that agreement relating to the provision by any other party to the agreement of security for the discharge of obligations in connection with that sewer or lateral drain, in recompense for expenditure incurred prior to the vesting date by that undertaker in relation to—

(i) any works carried out on that sewer or lateral drain by that undertaker prior to the vesting date, or

(ii) any contract entered into by that undertaker with another party for the carrying out of such works.

(5) In this regulation—

(a) "agreement" means an agreement under section 104 of the Act;

(b) "the relevant sewerage undertaker" means the sewerage undertaker which is a party to the agreement in question; and

(c) "the vesting date", in relation to a sewer or lateral drain, means the date on which that sewer or lateral drain vests in the relevant sewerage undertaker, as determined by paragraph (4)(a).

CONTROLLED WASTE (ENGLAND AND WALES) REGULATIONS 2012

SI 2012/811

1 Citation, extent and commencement

(1) These Regulations may be cited as the Controlled Waste (England and Wales) Regulations 2012.

(2) They extend to England and Wales.

(3) They come into force on 6th April 2012.

2 Interpretation

In these Regulations—

"the Act" means the Environmental Protection Act 1990;

"Directive waste" means anything that—

(a) is waste within the meaning of Article 3(1) of Directive 2008/98/EC of the European Parliament and of the Council on waste and repealing certain Directives; and

(b) is not excluded from the scope of that Directive by Article 2(1), (2) or (3);

"septic tank sludge" and "sludge" have the meaning given in regulation 2(1) of the Sludge (Use in Agriculture) Regulations 1989.

3 Waste which is not to be treated as household waste, industrial waste or commercial waste

(1) Waste which is not Directive waste is not to be treated as household waste, industrial waste or commercial waste for the purposes of Part 2 of the Act.

(2) The following waste (where it is Directive waste) is not to be treated as household waste, industrial waste or commercial waste for the purposes of Part 2 of the Act—

(a) sewage, sludge or septic tank sludge which is treated, kept or disposed of (otherwise than by means of mobile plant) within the curtilage of a sewage treatment works as an integral part of the operation of those works;

(b) sludge which is supplied or used in accordance with the Sludge (Use in Agriculture) Regulations 1989;

(c) septic tank sludge which is used on agricultural land within the meaning of those Regulations.

(3) Animal by-products (where they are Directive waste) which are collected and transported in accordance with Article 21(1) to (3) of the Animal By-Products Regulation are not to be treated as household waste, industrial waste or commercial waste for the purposes of section 34 of the Act.

(4) In this regulation—

(a) "animal by-products" has the meaning given in Article 3(1) of the Animal By-Products Regulation;

(b) "the Animal By-Products Regulation" means Regulation (EC) No 1069/2009 of the European Parliament and of the Council laying down health rules as regards animal by-products and derived products not intended for human consumption and repealing Regulation (EC) No 1774/2002 (Animal by-products Regulation).

4 Household, industrial and commercial waste

Subject to regulation 3 [and regulation 4A][1], Schedule 1 (household, industrial and commercial waste) has effect.

Amendment

1 Inserted by the Controlled Waste (England and Wales) (Amendment) Regulations 2012, SI 2012/2320, reg 2(1), (2).

[4A Restriction on charging for disposal of waste

(1) This regulation applies in England only.

(2) Nothing in regulation 4 has the effect of making a person liable to pay a charge under section 45(4) of the Act for the disposal of waste if the first and second conditions are satisfied.

(3) The first condition is that no charge would have been payable under section 45(4) of the Act for the disposal of that waste had it been collected under section 45(1) of the Act before 6th April 2012.

(4) The second condition is that the waste is from a hereditament as regards which the person is subject to a non-domestic rate under section 43(1) of the Local Government Finance Act 1988, for which the chargeable amount payable is calculated in accordance with section 43(4A)(a) of that Act.][1]

Amendment

1 Inserted by the Controlled Waste (England and Wales) (Amendment) Regulations 2012, SI 2012/2320, reg 2(1), (3).

5 Litter and refuse

Part 2 of the Act has effect as if references to controlled waste collected under section 45 include references to litter and refuse collected under sections 89(1)(a) and (c), 92(9) and 92C(3) of the Act.

[*Regulations 6 and 7 are not reproduced.*]

SCHEDULE 1
HOUSEHOLD, INDUSTRIAL AND COMMERCIAL WASTE

Regulation 4

1 Interpretation

In this Schedule—

"camp site" means land on which tents are pitched for the purpose of human habitation and land the use of which is incidental to that purpose;

"charity shop" means a hereditament used wholly or mainly for the sale of goods donated to a charity where the proceeds of sale (after deduction of expenses) are applied for the purposes of a charity;

"clinical waste" means waste from a healthcare activity (including veterinary healthcare) that—

(a) contains viable micro-organisms or their toxins which are known or reliably believed to cause disease in humans or other living organisms,

(b) contains or is contaminated with a medicine that contains a biologically active pharmaceutical agent, or

(c) is a sharp, or a body fluid or other biological material (including human and animal tissue) containing or contaminated with a dangerous substance within the meaning of Council Directive 67/548/EEC on the approximation of laws, regulations and administrative provisions relating to the classification, packaging and labelling of dangerous substances,

and waste of a similar nature from a non-healthcare activity;

"composite hereditament" has the same meaning as in section 64(9) of the Local Government Finance Act 1988;

"construction" includes improvement, repair or alteration;

"factory" has the meaning given in section 175 of the Factories Act 1961;

"general medical practitioner" means a person registered in the General Practitioner Register kept by the General Medical Council under section 34C of the Medical Act 1983;

"gypsies and travellers"—

(a) in relation to England, has the same meaning as in regulation 2 of the Housing (Assessment of Accommodation Needs) (Meaning of Gypsies and Travellers) (England) Regulations 2006;

(b) in relation to Wales, has the same meaning as in regulation 2 of the Housing (Assessment of Accommodation Needs) (Meaning of Gypsies and Travellers) (Wales) Regulations 2007;

"hazardous waste"—

(a) in relation to England, has the meaning given in regulation 6 of the Hazardous Waste (England and Wales) Regulations 2005;

(b) in relation to Wales, has the meaning given in regulation 6 of the Hazardous Waste (Wales) Regulations 2005;

"not for profit body" means a body which, by virtue of its constitution or any enactment—

(a) is required (after payment of outgoings) to apply the whole of its income, and any capital which it expends, for charitable or public purposes; and

(b) is prohibited from directly or indirectly distributing among its members any part of its assets (otherwise than for charitable or public purposes);

"offensive waste" means waste that—

(a) is not clinical waste,

(b) contains body fluids, secretions or excretions, and

(c) falls within code 18 01 04, 18 02 03 or 20 01 99 in Schedule 1 to—

(i) the List of Wastes (England) Regulations 2005, in relation to England, or

(ii) the List of Wastes (Wales) Regulations 2005, in relation to Wales;

"place of worship" means a hereditament exempt from local non-domestic rating by virtue of paragraph 11 of Schedule 5 to the Local Government Finance Act 1988;

"scientific research association" has the meaning given in section 469 of the Corporation Tax Act 2010;

"scrap metal" has the meaning given in section 9(2) of the Scrap Metal Dealers Act 1964;

"vessel" includes a hovercraft within the meaning of section 4(1) of the Hovercraft Act 1968;

"waste oil" means any mineral or synthetic lubrication or industrial oil which is unfit for its original purpose.

2 Sources of household, industrial and commercial waste

(1) This paragraph describes waste which is to be treated as household waste, industrial waste or commercial waste because of the place where it is produced.

(2) The second column of the table describes the places at which waste is produced.

(3) The waste must be treated for the purposes of Part 2 of the Act as the type of waste mentioned in the third column, subject to any exception in the fourth column.

(4) But in a case where paragraph 3 or 4(3) requires waste to be treated inconsistently with sub-paragraph (3), the requirements of those paragraphs take precedence.

Classification by place of production

No.	*Description*	*Classification*	*Exceptions*
1	Private storage premises used wholly or mainly for the storage of articles of domestic use	Household waste	
2	Land belonging to or used wholly or mainly in connection with domestic property or a caravan where waste from that property or caravan is to be treated as household waste	Household waste	
3	A private garage	Household waste	Where the garage has a floor area exceeding $25m^2$ or is not used wholly or mainly for the accommodation of a private motor vehicle, the waste is to be treated as commercial waste
4	A vehicle or vessel used wholly for the purposes of living accommodation	Household waste	Where the vehicle or vessel is used in the course of a business for the provision of self-catering accommodation, the waste is to be treated as commercial waste
5	A place of worship	Household waste	
6	A residential hostel which provides accommodation only to persons with no other permanent address or who are unable to live at their permanent address	Household waste	
7	A penal institution	Household waste	
8	A charity shop selling donated goods originating from domestic property	Household waste	
9	A caravan or mobile home site for gypsies and travellers	Household waste	
10	Premises used wholly or mainly for public meetings	Household waste	
11	Domestic property used in the course of a business for the provision of self-catering accommodation	Commercial waste	
12	A caravan— (a) used in the course of a business for the provision of self-catering accommodation, or (b) which is not allowed to be used for human habitation throughout the year by virtue of a licence or planning permission	Commercial waste	

No.	*Description*	*Classification*	*Exceptions*
13	Premises occupied by a charity and wholly or mainly used for charitable purposes	Commercial waste	Where the waste is from a place of worship or from premises used wholly or mainly for public meetings, it is to be treated as household waste
14	A camp site or a tent pitched on land other than a camp site	Commercial waste	Where the waste is from domestic premises at a camp site, it is to be treated as household waste
15	A royal palace	Commercial waste	
16	Premises occupied by a club, society or any association of persons in which activities are conducted for the benefit of the members	Commercial waste	
17	Premises occupied by— (a) a court; (b) a government department; (c) a local authority; (d) a person appointed by or under any enactment to discharge public functions; (e) a body incorporated by Royal Charter	Commercial waste	Waste classified as household waste or industrial waste because it is from a place— (a) otherwise described in this table (except for entry 27); or (b) described in section 75(5) or (6) of the Act (household waste or industrial waste)
18	A hotel	Commercial waste	
19	Any part of a composite hereditament used for the purposes of a trade or business	Commercial waste	
20	A market or fair	Commercial waste	
21	The practice of a general medical practitioner	Commercial waste	
22	A workshop or similar premises which is not a factory only because— (a) those working there are not employees; or (b) the work carried on there is not carried on by way of trade or for purposes of gain	Industrial waste	Where the principal activities at the premises are computer operations or the copying of documents by photographic or lithographic means the waste is to be treated as commercial waste
23	Waste from a laboratory	Industrial waste	
24	Waste from a scientific research association	Industrial waste	
25	Waste from premises used for the breeding, boarding or stabling of animals	Industrial waste	
26	Waste imported into England or Wales	Industrial waste	

No.	*Description*	*Classification*	*Exceptions*
27	Directive waste from a place (including any vehicle, vessel or aircraft) not otherwise described in this table or in section 75(5) or (7) of the Act (household waste and commercial waste)	Industrial waste	

3 Nature of waste and activities producing waste

(1) This paragraph describes waste which is to be treated as household waste, commercial waste or industrial waste because of its nature or the activity which produces it notwithstanding the place where it is produced.

(2) The second column of the table describes the nature of the waste or the activity which produces it.

(3) The waste must be treated for the purposes of Part 2 of the Act as the type of waste mentioned in the third column, subject to any exception in the fourth column.

(4) But in a case where paragraph 4(3) requires waste to be treated inconsistently with sub-paragraph (3), the requirements of that paragraph take precedence.

Classification by nature of waste or activity producing waste

No.	*Description*	*Classification*	*Exceptions*
1	Waste arising from the discharge of duties under section 89(1)(a), (c) or (f) of the Act (duties to collect litter and refuse)	Household waste	
2	Waste arising from the discharge by a local authority of its duty under section 89(2) of the Act (duty to ensure highways and roads are kept clean)	Household waste	
3	Waste arising from the discharge of duties under sections 89(1)(d), 92(9), 92C(3) and 93 of the Act (duties and powers in relation to the collection of litter and refuse)	Commercial waste	
4	Waste collected under section 22(3) of the Control of Pollution Act 1974 (street cleaning)	Commercial waste	
5	Waste arising from the discharge of duties under section 89(1) (b) and (e) of the Act (duties to collect litter and refuse)	Industrial waste	
6	Waste arising from the discharge by the Secretary of State or the Welsh Ministers of the duty under section 89(2) of the Act (duty to ensure highways and roads are kept clean)	Industrial waste	

No.	*Description*	*Classification*	*Exceptions*
7	Hazardous waste arising from the following activities carried on at premises used for the purposes of a trade or business— (a) mixing or selling paints; (b) sign writing; (c) laundering or dry cleaning; (d) developing photographic film or making photographic prints; (e) selling petrol, diesel fuel, paraffin, kerosene, heating oil or similar substances; (f) selling pesticides, herbicides or fungicides	Industrial waste	
8	Waste oil, waste solvent or scrap metal	Industrial waste	Where the waste is produced at the following places it is to be treated as household waste— (a) a residential home; (b) domestic property, a caravan or land belonging to or used in connection with such a place; (c) a private garage which has a floor area of $25m^2$ or less or is used wholly or mainly for the accommodation of a private motor vehicle; (d) private storage premises used wholly or mainly for the storage of articles of domestic use; (e) a vehicle or vessel used wholly for the purposes of living accommodation, except where it is used in the course of a business for the provision of self-catering accommodation
9	Waste from construction or demolition works, including preparatory works	Industrial waste	The waste is to be treated as household waste for the purposes of section 34(2) and (2A) of the Act only (disapplication of section 34(1) and duty on the occupier of domestic property to transfer household waste only to an authorised person or for authorised transport purposes)
10	Septic tank sludge	Industrial waste	The waste is to be treated as household waste for the purposes of section 34(2) and (2A) of the Act only

No.	*Description*	*Classification*	*Exceptions*
11	Sewage	Industrial waste	
12	Clinical waste and offensive waste	Industrial waste	Clinical waste and offensive waste produced at domestic property, a residential home, a caravan or a vehicle or vessel used wholly for the purposes of living accommodation is to be treated as household waste, except that where such a vehicle or vessel is used in the course of a business for the provision of self-catering accommodation, such waste is to be treated as commercial waste Clinical waste and offensive waste collected under section 22(3) of the Control of Pollution Act 1974 or section 89, 92(9), 92C(3) or 93 of the Act is to be treated as household waste or commercial waste in accordance with entries 1 to 6

4 Household waste for which collection and disposal charges may be made

(1) The second column of the table in this paragraph describes waste which is household waste (by virtue of section 75(5) of the Act) or waste which is to be treated as household waste (by virtue of paragraph 2 or 3).

(2) The third column indicates which household waste is prescribed for the purposes of section 45(3) of the Act (cases in respect of which a charge for collection may be made).

(3) Subject to [sub-paragraph][1] (8), the fourth column indicates which waste must be treated as commercial waste for the purposes of the following provisions of the Act—

(a) section 45(4) to the extent that it concerns liability to pay a reasonable charge for disposal of commercial waste and the recovery of such a charge; and

(b) section 52(9) (which entitles waste disposal authorities to reimbursement by waste collection authorities in relation to costs incurred in arranging the disposal of commercial and industrial waste).

(4) [Sub-paragraph (8) applies][1] in England only.

(5) …[2]

(6) …[2]

(7) …[2]

(8) In relation to entry 15 of the table (waste from premises forming part of a university, school or other educational establishment), nothing in [sub-paragraph (3)][1] has the effect of making a person liable to pay a charge under section 45(4) of the Act for the disposal of waste from premises forming part of—

(a) a school maintained by a local authority (within the meaning of section 142(1) of the School Standards and Framework Act 1998),

(b) an institution within the further education sector (within the meaning of section 91 of the Further and Higher Education Act 1992), or

(c) an Academy (within the meaning of section 1(10) of the Academies Act 2010),

if, immediately before the coming into force of these Regulations, the collection of waste from those premises was being undertaken pursuant to arrangements made under section 45(1) of the Act.

Collection and disposal charges

No.	*Description of household waste*	*Collection charge*	*Disposal charge*
1	Any article of waste which exceeds 25kg in weight	Yes	No, subject to entries 11 to 17
2	Any article of waste which does not fit or cannot be fitted into— (a) a receptacle for household waste provided in accordance with section 46 of the Act; or (b) where no such receptacle is provided, a cylindrical container 750mm in diameter and 1m in length	Yes	No, subject to entries 11 to 17
3	Garden waste	Yes	No, subject to entries 11 to 17
4	Dead domestic pets	Yes	No, subject to entries 11 to 17
5	Waste oil or grease	Yes	No, subject to entries 11 to 17
6	Asbestos	Yes	No, subject to entries 11 to 17
7	Waste which may not be put into a receptacle provided under section 46 of the Act because of a notice served under that section	Yes	No, subject to entries 11 to 17
8	Waste from premises used wholly or mainly for public meetings	Yes	No
9	Clinical waste and offensive waste produced at a domestic property, a caravan or a vehicle or vessel used wholly for the purposes of living accommodation	Yes	No
10	Waste from a residential hostel which provides accommodation only to persons with no other permanent address or who are unable to live at their permanent address	Yes	No
11	Waste from a charity shop selling donated goods originating from domestic property	Yes	Yes, but only to the extent that the waste originated from non-domestic property

No.	*Description of household waste*	*Collection charge*	*Disposal charge*
12	Waste from premises occupied by— (a) a community interest company (being a company which is registered as such with the registrar of companies), or (b) a charity or other not for profit body, which collects goods for re-use or waste to prepare for re-use from domestic property	Yes	Yes, but only to the extent that the waste originated from non-domestic property
13	Litter and refuse collected under section 89(1)(f) of the Act	Yes	Yes
14	Waste from a residential home or land belonging to or wholly or mainly used in connection with a residential home	Yes	Yes
15	Waste from premises forming part of a university, school or other educational establishment	Yes	In Wales: yes In England: yes, subject to paragraph 4(8)
16	Waste from premises forming part of a hospital or nursing home except for waste from a residential hostel forming such part which provides accommodation only to persons with no other permanent address	Yes	Yes
17	Waste from a penal institution	Yes	Yes

Amendments

1 Substituted by the Controlled Waste (England and Wales) (Amendment) Regulations 2012, SI 2012/2320, reg 2(1), (4)(a), (b), (d).

2 Repealed by the Controlled Waste (England and Wales) (Amendment) Regulations 2012, SI 2012/2320, reg 2(1), (4)(c).

[*Schedule 2 is not reproduced.*]

GREENHOUSE GAS EMISSIONS TRADING SCHEME REGULATIONS 2012

SI 2012/3038

PART 1
GENERAL

1 Citation and commencement

These Regulations may be cited as the Greenhouse Gas Emissions Trading Scheme Regulations 2012 and come into force on 1st January 2013.

2 Duty to review these Regulations

(1) The Secretary of State must from time to time—
(a) carry out a review of these Regulations;
(b) set out the conclusions of the review in a report; and
(c) publish the report.

(2) In carrying out the review the Secretary of State must, so far as is reasonable, have regard to how the Directive, and measures adopted under it by the European Commission, are implemented in other member States.

(3) The report must in particular—
(a) set out the objectives intended to be achieved by the regulatory system established by these Regulations;
(b) assess the extent to which those objectives are achieved; and
(c) assess whether those objectives remain appropriate and, if so, the extent to which they could be achieved with a system that imposes less regulation.

(4) The first report under this regulation must be published before the end of the period of five years beginning with the day on which these Regulations come into force.

(5) Reports under this regulation are afterwards to be published at intervals not exceeding five years.

3 Interpretation

(1) In these Regulations—
"the 2005 Regulations" means the Greenhouse Gas Emissions Trading Scheme Regulations 2005;
"the 2010 Regulations" means the Aviation Greenhouse Gas Emissions Trading Scheme Regulations 2010;
"allocation", in relation to an allowance, means allocation free of charge in accordance with Chapter 1 or 2 of the Directive;
"allowance"—
(a) in this regulation, has the meaning given in Article 3(a) of the Directive, but
(b) otherwise (and subject to regulations 54(7) and 82(1)) means an allowance other than an aviation allowance;
"annual reportable emissions" means the reportable emissions arising in any scheme year;
"authority" means—
(a) in relation to an installation which is (or will be) situated in England or an offshore installation, the Secretary of State;

(b) in relation to an installation, other than an offshore installation, which is (or will be) situated in—
(i) Scotland, the Scottish Ministers;
(ii) Wales, the Welsh Ministers;
(iii) Northern Ireland, the Department of the Environment;
(c) in relation to a UK administered operator, the authority defined in regulation 20;
(d) in relation to a banned non-UK operator, the Secretary of State;

"aviation activity" means an aviation activity listed in Annex 1 to the Directive;

"aviation allowance" means any allowance allocated in accordance with Article 3e or 3f of the Directive or auctioned in accordance with Article 3d of the Directive;

"aviation emissions" means emissions, arising from an aviation activity, of gases specified in respect of that activity by Annex 1 to the Directive;

"aviation emissions plan" means an emissions plan as defined by regulation 20;

"banned non-UK operator" means a person on whom an operating ban has been imposed under Article 16(10) of the Directive and who is not a UK administered operator;

"bioliquids" has the meaning given in Article 2(h) of the Renewable Energy Directive;

"cease operation", in relation to an installation, has the meaning given in paragraph (3);

"chief inspector" means the chief inspector constituted under regulation 8(3) of the Northern Ireland Regulations;

"current operator" has the meaning given by regulation 12(1);

"the Directive" means Directive 2003/87/EC of the European Parliament and of the Council establishing a scheme for greenhouse gas emissions allowance trading within the Community and amending Council Directive 96/61/EC, as amended from time to time and as adapted by Annex 20 to the EEA agreement;

"duly made", in relation to an application, means made in accordance with the requirements of these Regulations;

"emissions" has the meaning given in Article 3(b) of the Directive;

"excluded installation" means an installation the exclusion of which is deemed to be approved by the European Commission under the first sub-paragraph of Article 27(2) of the Directive, unless a notice has been given to the operator under paragraph 8(1) or (4) or paragraph 9(1) of Schedule 5 (in which case the installation ceases to be an excluded installation as from the date specified in the notice);

"excluded installation emissions permit" means a permit—
(a) granted following an application under regulation 10(2), or
(b) which results from a variation under paragraph 2 of Schedule 5;

"fee", in relation to any matter, means the fee or charge prescribed in respect of that matter by a scheme, or regulations, made under—
(a) regulation 18;
(b) section 41A of the Environment Act 1995;
(c) regulation 4 of the Greenhouse Gas Emissions Trading Scheme Charging Scheme Regulations (Northern Ireland) 2010; or
(d) Article 127 of the Planning (Northern Ireland) Order 1991;

"the Free Allocation Decision" means Commission Decision 2011/278/EU of 27 April 2011 determining transitional Union-wide rules for harmonised free allocation of emission allowances pursuant to Article 10a of Directive 2003/87/EC;

"greenhouse gas emissions permit" means a permit granted following an application under—
(a) regulation 10(1); or
(b) regulation 8 of the 2005 Regulations;

"installation" has the meaning given in Article 3(e) of the Directive (and references to an "installation" include a reference to a part of an installation);

"KP registry administrator" has the meaning given by regulation 81(1);

"monitoring and reporting conditions" has the meaning given by paragraph 3(8) of Schedule 5;
"monitoring and reporting requirements" has the meaning given by paragraph 2(3) of Schedule 4;
"the Monitoring and Reporting Regulation" means Commission Regulation (EU) No 601/2012 of 21 June 2012 on the monitoring and reporting of greenhouse gas emissions pursuant to Directive 2003/87/EC of the European Parliament and of the Council, as amended from time to time;
"new operator" has the meaning given by regulation 12(1);
"Northern Ireland Regulations" means the Pollution Prevention and Control Regulations (Northern Ireland) 2003;
"notice of surrender" has the meaning given in regulation 13(7);
"offshore installation" means—
(a) an offshore petroleum installation; or
(b) an offshore storage or unloading installation;
"offshore petroleum installation" means an installation which—
(a) is used for purposes connected with the exploration for, or exploitation of, petroleum (within the meaning of section 1 of the Petroleum Act 1998); and
(b) is, or will be, situated in the area (together with places above and below it) comprising—
(i) those parts of the sea adjacent to England and Wales from the low water mark to the landward baseline of the United Kingdom territorial sea;
(ii) the United Kingdom territorial sea apart from those areas comprised in any controlled waters within the meaning of section 30A(1) of the Control of Pollution Act 1974; and
(iii) those areas of sea in any area for the time being designated under section 1(7) of the Continental Shelf Act 1964;
"the Offshore Regulations" means the Offshore Combustion Installations (Prevention and Control of Pollution) Regulations 2001;
"offshore storage or unloading installation" means an installation which—
(a) is used for purposes connected with an activity within section 2(3) or section 17(2) of the Energy Act 2008; and
(b) is, or will be, situated in the area (together with places above and below it) comprising—
(i) those parts of the sea adjacent to England from the low water mark to the landward baseline of the United Kingdom territorial sea;
(ii) the United Kingdom territorial sea, other than the territorial sea adjacent to Scotland or Wales; and
(iii) those areas of sea in a Gas Importation and Storage Zone (within the meaning of section 1(5) of that Act);
"operator", in relation to an installation, has the meaning given in paragraph (2) (and "operate" has the corresponding meaning);
"partial transfer" has the meaning given by regulation 12(2);
"permit" (except in paragraph 1(2)(b) of Schedule 4 and paragraph 7(12) of Schedule 6) means—
(a) a greenhouse gas emissions permit; or
(b) an excluded installation emissions permit;
"the Planning Appeals Commission" means the Planning Appeals Commission established under article 110 of the Planning (Northern Ireland) Order 1991;
"prescribed" (in relation to a fee) means specified in, or determined under, the scheme or regulations in question;

"the Registries Regulation 2010" means Commission Regulation (EU) No 920/2010 of 7 October 2010 for a standardised and secured system of registries pursuant to Directive 2003/87/EC of the European Parliament and of the Council and Decision No 280/2004/EC of the European Parliament and of the Council;

"the Registries Regulation 2011" means Commission Regulation (EU) No 1193/2011 of 18 November 2011 establishing a Union Registry for the trading period commencing on 1 January 2013, and subsequent trading periods, of the Union emissions trading scheme pursuant to Directive 2003/87/EC of the European Parliament and of the Council and Decision No 280/2004/EC of the European Parliament and of the Council and amending Commission Regulations (EC) No 2216/2004 and (EU) No 920/2010, as amended from time to time;

"registry administrator" has the meaning given by regulation 8(1);

"registry account" means an operator holding account or an aircraft operator holding account in the Union Registry (and "open", "blocked" or "excluded" status, in relation to such an account, have the meanings given by Article 9 of the Registries Regulation 2011);

"regulated activity" means an activity (other than an aviation activity) that—

(a) is listed in Annex 1 to the Directive, and

(b) results in specified emissions;

"regulator" means, in relation to—

(a) an installation (other than an offshore installation) which is, or will be, situated in—

  (i) England and Wales, the Environment Agency;

  (ii) Scotland, SEPA;

  (iii) Northern Ireland, the chief inspector;

(b) an offshore installation, the Secretary of State;

(c) a UK administered operator, the regulator specified in regulations 27 to 29;

(d) a banned non-UK operator, the Environment Agency;

"the Renewable Energy Directive" means Directive 2009/28/EC of the European Parliament and of the Council on the promotion of the use of energy from renewable sources and amending and subsequently repealing Directives 2001/77/EC and 2003/30/EC, as amended from time to time;

"reportable emissions" means—

(a) in relation to an installation, the total specified emissions (expressed in tonnes of carbon dioxide equivalent) which arise from the regulated activities carried out at that installation; or

(b) in relation to a UK aircraft operator, the total aviation emissions of that aircraft operator (expressed in tonnes of carbon dioxide equivalent);

"revocation notice" has the meaning given by regulation 14(1);

"scheme year" means the year beginning with 1st January 2013 or any subsequent calendar year;

"SEPA" means the Scottish Environment Protection Agency;

"specified emissions", in relation to an activity listed in Annex 1 to the Directive, means emissions of gases specified in Annex 1 in respect of that activity;

"sub-installation" has the meaning given by Article 3(b), (c), (d) and (h) and Article 6 of the Free Allocation Decision;

"surrender requirements" has the meaning given by paragraph 2(4) of Schedule 4;

"tonne of carbon dioxide equivalent" has the meaning given in Article 3(j) of the Directive;

"trading period" means one of the following eight-year periods—

(a) 2013 to 2020; and

(b) subsequent consecutive periods of eight calendar years;

"UK administered operator" has the meaning given in regulation 20;

"UK aircraft operator" has the meaning given by regulation 26;

"the Union Registry" means the registry established by Article 4 of the Registries Regulation 2011;

"the UK Registry" means the registry operated by the Environment Agency for the purposes specified in Article 3(1) of the Registries Regulation 2010 immediately before the coming into force of these Regulations;

"variation", in relation to a permit or a plan, means the amendment of its provisions (and "vary" has the corresponding meaning);

"the Verification Regulation" means Commission Regulation (EU) No 600/2012 of 21 June 2012 on the verification of greenhouse gas emission reports and tonne-kilometre reports and the accreditation of verifiers pursuant to Directive 2003/87/EC of the European Parliament and of the Council, as amended from time to time;

"working day" means any day other than—

(a) a Saturday, Sunday, Good Friday, or Christmas Day; or

(b) a day which is a bank holiday under the Banking and Financial Dealings Act 1971;

"written procedures" means the written procedures required by Article 11(1) of the Monitoring and Reporting Regulation.

(2) The "operator" of an installation is the person who has control over its operation; but where—

(a) an installation has not been put into operation, the operator is the person who will have control over the operation of the installation when it is put into operation;

(b) an installation has ceased operation, the operator is the person who holds the permit relating to the installation; and

(c) the holder of a permit has ceased to have control of the installation to which it relates, the operator is that permit holder.

(3) An installation ceases operation where—

(a) the conditions in paragraph 7(1)(b) or (c) of Schedule 6 apply in relation to that installation; or

(b) the installation is a relevant installation, and has permanently ceased the carrying out of regulated activities for the purposes of paragraph 7 of that Schedule.

(4) For the purposes of paragraph (3), a relevant installation is any installation other than—

(a) an excluded installation; or

(b) an installation that, by virtue of Article 10a(3) of the Directive, is not eligible for an allocation.

(5) References in these Regulations to anything taking effect (or ceasing to have effect) on a particular date are to be read as references to it taking effect (or ceasing to have effect) as from the beginning of that date.

4 Application to the Crown etc.

Schedule 1 (application to the Crown etc.) has effect.

5 Notices etc.

Schedule 2 (notices etc.) has effect.

6 Applications etc.

Schedule 3 (applications etc.) has effect.

7 Functions of the regulator: Northern Ireland

(1) Regulation 8(4) of the Northern Ireland Regulations (delegation of functions) has effect as if the reference to the chief inspector's functions included a reference to the chief inspector's functions under these Regulations.

(2) Regulation 37(1) of the Northern Ireland Regulations (power of the Department to give directions) has effect as if the reference to functions under those Regulations included a reference to functions under these Regulations.

(3) Any direction of the Department of the Environment that is given by virtue of paragraph (2) must be published in such manner as the Department of the Environment considers appropriate.

8 Commission Regulations: designations

(1) The Environment Agency is the national administrator designated by the United Kingdom for the purposes of the Registries Regulation 2011, and in these Regulations is referred to in that capacity as the "registry administrator".

(2) Subject to paragraph (3), the regulator is the competent authority designated by the United Kingdom for the purposes of the Registries Regulation 2010.

(3) The Secretary of State is the competent authority so designated for the purposes of—
(a) Article 26(2);
(b) Article 27(6),
(c) Article 28(1); and
(d) Article 64a(1).

(4) Subject to paragraph (5), the regulator is the competent authority designated by the United Kingdom for the purposes of the Registries Regulation 2011 (other than Articles 23(3) and 31(6)).

(5) The Secretary of State is the competent authority so designated for the purposes of—
(a) Article 17;
(b) Article 29(2);
(c) Article 30(1);
(d) Article 31(7); and
(e) Article 71(1).

(6) Subject to paragraph (7), the regulator is the competent authority designated by the United Kingdom for the purposes of the Monitoring and Reporting Regulation.

(7) The Secretary of State is the competent authority so designated for the purposes of Article 68(3).

(8) Subject to paragraph (9), the regulator is the competent authority designated by the United Kingdom for the purposes of the Verification Regulation.

(9) The Secretary of State is the competent authority so designated for the purposes of Article 64(3), and is designated as the focal point authorised by the United Kingdom for the purposes of Article 69(2).

PART 2
STATIONARY INSTALLATIONS

Chapter 1
Permits

9 Requirement for permit to carry out regulated activities

No person may carry out a regulated activity at an installation except to the extent authorised by a permit held by the operator of the installation.

10 Applications for and grant of permits

(1) The operator of an installation (other than an excluded installation) may apply to the regulator for a greenhouse gas emissions permit to carry out a regulated activity at the installation.

(2) The operator of an excluded installation may apply to the regulator for an excluded installation emissions permit to carry out a regulated activity at the installation.

(3) However, an application may not be made—

(a) under paragraph (1) or (2) where a permit has already been granted in respect of the installation and continues to have effect; or

(b) under paragraph (2) where an excluded installation emissions permit has been granted in respect of the installation and has been surrendered or revoked.

(4) Following an application under paragraph (1) or (2), the permit must be granted if the regulator is satisfied that—

(a) the application is duly made, and

(b) at the time that the permit is granted (or, if later, has effect) the applicant will be capable of monitoring and reporting emissions from the installation in accordance with—

(i) the monitoring and reporting requirements of the greenhouse gas emissions permit, or

(ii) the monitoring and reporting conditions of the excluded installations permit,

but must otherwise be refused.

(5) A permit may be granted under this regulation in respect of more than one installation on the same site, provided that they are operated by the same operator.

(6) Paragraph 1 of Schedule 4 makes further provision about applications for permits.

(7) Paragraph 2 of Schedule 4 makes provision about the contents of greenhouse gas emissions permits, and paragraph 3 of Schedule 5 makes provision about the contents of excluded installation emissions permits.

11 Review, variation and consolidation of permits

(1) The regulator must review a permit before the end of the period of five years beginning with the date on which the permit was granted, and afterwards at intervals not exceeding five years.

(2) The regulator may, by giving notice to the operator, vary a permit at any time and may in particular make any variation of the permit that the regulator considers necessary in consequence of—

(a) a review under paragraph (1);

(b) any report made by the operator under Article 69 of the Monitoring and Reporting Regulation; or

(c) any notification as mentioned in paragraph 2(7)(b) of Schedule 4 (notification of planned changes in operation etc).

(3) The regulator may by giving notice to the operator vary a permit where the operator—

(a) applies to the regulator for such a variation pursuant to a provision of the permit; or

(b) has failed to comply with a requirement of the permit to apply for such a variation.

(4) The regulator may by giving notice to the operator vary a permit in order to comply with regulator's duty under—

(a) regulation 88(6); or

(b) any of the following provisions of Schedule 5—

(i) paragraph 2(1);
(ii) paragraph 3(3);
(iii) paragraph 6(5) or (6);
(iv) paragraph 7(4)(b), (6)(b) or (7)(b);
(v) paragraph 8(6).

(5) A notice given under paragraph (2), (3)(b) or (4) may specify a period within which a fee for the variation of the permit must be paid.

(6) The regulator may by giving notice to the operator replace a permit with a consolidated permit applying to the same regulated activities, and containing the same or equivalent provisions, in the following circumstances—
(a) where the permit has been varied;
(b) where there is more than one permit applying to installations on the same site operated by the same operator.

12 Transfer of permits

(1) Subject to paragraph (6), the holder of a permit ("the current operator") and another person may jointly apply to the regulator for the permit to be transferred to that other person ("the new operator").

(2) An application may also be made under paragraph (1) for the partial transfer of a permit; and for that purpose a "partial transfer" is a transfer in respect of—
(a) some only of the installations to which the permit relates; or
(b) some only of the parts of an installation to which the permit relates.

(3) Paragraph 3 of Schedule 4 makes further provision about the transfer, or partial transfer, of a permit.

(4) Subject to paragraph 3(2)(b) of Schedule 4, an application under paragraph (1) must be granted if the regulator is satisfied that—
(a) the application is duly made, and
(b) the new operator will (from the relevant date) be the operator of the installation and will be capable of monitoring and reporting emissions from the installation in accordance with—
(i) the monitoring and reporting requirements of the greenhouse gas emissions permit, or
(ii) the monitoring and reporting conditions of the excluded installations emissions permit,

but must otherwise be refused.

(5) For the purposes of paragraph (4), the relevant date is the date mentioned in paragraph 3(6), (8) or (10) of Schedule 4 as the case may be.

(6) An application for the transfer (or partial transfer) of a permit may not be made in respect of any installation (or part of an installation) that has ceased operation.

13 Surrender of permits

(1) Subject to paragraph (4), if an installation has ceased operation the operator must apply to the regulator to surrender the permit authorising regulated activities at the installation.

(2) Such an application must be made within the period specified by paragraph (3), or such longer period as may be agreed with the regulator.

(a) determining whether the requirements, restrictions or prohibitions imposed under or by virtue of these Regulations are being, or have been, complied with;
(b) discharging one or more of the functions conferred or imposed upon the Secretary of State under or by virtue of these Regulations; or
(c) determining whether and, if so, how such a function should be discharged.

(2) The powers exercisable under paragraph (1) are the powers in sub-paragraphs (a) to (k) of regulation 13(2) of the Offshore Regulations (but subject to paragraphs (3) to (4) of that regulation).

(3) Regulation 18(1)(h) of the Offshore Regulations applies to a failure to comply with an obligation imposed pursuant to a power exercisable under paragraph (1) as it applies to a failure to comply with an obligation imposed pursuant to regulation 13(2) of the Offshore Regulations.

18 Charging schemes

(1) The Secretary of State may make, and from time to time revise, a scheme prescribing charges in relation to offshore installations in respect of the matters to which paragraph (2) applies.

(2) This paragraph applies to—
(a) the performance by the Secretary of State of functions conferred under or by virtue of these Regulations, as regulator in relation to offshore installations; and
(b) the subsistence of an account required to be held in a trading scheme registry by the operator of an offshore installation.

(3) In this regulation, "trading scheme registry" has the meaning given by section 41A(7) of the Environment Act 1995.

(4) The charges prescribed by a scheme under paragraph (1) must be paid to the Secretary of State.

19 Charging schemes: supplementary

(1) On making, or revising, a scheme the Secretary of State must lay before each House of Parliament a copy of (as the case may be)—
(a) the scheme; or
(b) the revisions made to the scheme (or the scheme as so revised).

(2) A scheme may, in particular—
(a) make different provision for different cases, including different provision in relation to different persons in different circumstances or localities;
(b) allow for reduced charges payable in respect of permits granted to the same operator;
(c) provide for the times at which and the manner in which the payments required by the scheme are to be made (subject to any requirements in these Regulations as to times at which payment is required); and
(d) make such incidental, supplementary and transitional provisions as appear to the Secretary of State to be appropriate.

(3) The Secretary of State must take such steps as the Secretary of State considers appropriate for bringing the provisions of a scheme which is for the time being in force to the attention of persons likely to be affected by it.

(4) In this regulation, "scheme" means a scheme made under regulation 18(1).

PART 3
AVIATION

Chapter 1
General

20 Interpretation

In this Part (and in Schedules 7 to 10)—

"the 2009 Regulations" means the Aviation Greenhouse Gas Emissions Trading Scheme Regulations 2009;

"area", in relation to a regulator, means—
- (a) in respect of the Environment Agency, England and Wales;
- (b) in respect of SEPA, Scotland;
- (c) in respect of the chief inspector, Northern Ireland;

"authority", in relation to a UK administered operator ("P") means—
- (a) the Welsh Ministers, where—
  - (i) P's regulator is the Environment Agency; and
  - (ii) P's registered office is in Wales;
- (b) the Scottish Ministers, where P's regulator is SEPA;
- (c) the Department of the Environment in Northern Ireland, where P's regulator is the chief inspector;
- (d) otherwise, the Secretary of State;

"benchmarking plan" has the meaning given by paragraph 2 of Schedule 7;

"benchmarking year", in relation to a trading period, means the calendar year ending 24 months before the beginning of the period;

"Commission list" means the list of operators set out in Commission Regulation (EC) No 748/2009 on the list of aircraft operators which performed an aviation activity listed in Annex I to Directive 2003/87/EC on or after 1 January 2006 specifying the administering Member State for each aircraft operator, as amended from time to time;

"emissions plan" means a plan issued under—
- (a) regulation 34(1)(a);
- (b) regulation 19(1)(a) of the 2010 Regulations; or
- (c) regulation 15(1)(a) of the 2009 Regulations;

"member State" includes an EEA state;

"registered office" (except in Schedule 9) means the registered office in the United Kingdom that a company is required to have under section 86 of the Companies Act 2006;

"tonne-kilometre" and "tonne-kilometre data" have the same meaning as in the Monitoring and Reporting Regulation;

"UK administered operator" means (subject to regulations 22 to 25) a person who is—
- (a) identified in the Commission list, and
- (b) specified in that list as an aircraft operator to be administered by the United Kingdom;

"unlisted operator" means a person who is—
- (a) not identified in the Commission list, and
- (b) the user or owner of an aircraft used to perform an aviation activity.

21 Civil Aviation Authority

(1) The Civil Aviation Authority must provide such assistance and advice as the regulator may require in connection with any of the regulator's functions under this Part (including Schedules 7 to 10) or under regulation 44.

(2) The Civil Aviation Authority is entitled to recover from the regulator a sum equal to any expense reasonably incurred by it in providing the regulator with assistance or advice under paragraph (1).

22 UK administered operators: power to designate

(1) This paragraph applies where the Secretary of State is satisfied that, under Article 18a(1) of the Directive, the United Kingdom is to be regarded as the administering member State in respect of an unlisted operator ("P").

(2) Where paragraph (1) applies the Secretary of State must—
(a) designate P as an operator to whom these Regulations apply; and
(b) give notice to P of that designation.

(3) From the date of service of the notice under paragraph (2), P is to be treated as a UK administered operator for the purposes of these Regulations.

(4) Before making a designation under paragraph (2), the Secretary of State must consult—
(a) P;
(b) the relevant regulator;
(c) the relevant authority; and
(d) such other persons as the Secretary of State considers appropriate.

(5) For the purposes of paragraph (4)—
(a) the relevant regulator is the person who will be the regulator of P if the designation is made; and
(b) the relevant authority is a person (other than the Secretary of State) who will then be the authority in relation to P.

(6) A designation under paragraph (2)—
(a) must (subject to paragraph (7)) be revoked by the Secretary of State if paragraph (1) no longer applies in relation to P, and
(b) ceases to have effect once P is identified in the Commission list,
but this is without prejudice to any specification of P in that list as an aircraft operator to be administered by the United Kingdom.

(7) A designation may not be revoked solely because P has ceased to perform an aviation activity.

(8) Paragraphs (2)(b), (3) and (4) apply to the revocation of a designation as they apply to the designation itself, except that the reference in paragraph (3) to being treated as a UK administered operator is to be read (subject to the proviso in paragraph (6)) as a reference to no longer being so treated.

Chapter 2
UK administered operators, UK aircraft operators and regulators

23 Application to be designated as a UK administered operator

(1) An unlisted operator ("Q") may apply to the Secretary of State to be designated as a UK administered operator.

(2) Where such an application is made the Secretary of State must, after consulting the relevant persons—
(a) designate Q in accordance with regulation 22(1) and (2); or
(b) refuse the application.

(3) For the purposes of paragraph (2) the relevant persons are—
(a) the person who will be the regulator of Q if the designation is made;
(b) a person (other than the Secretary of State) who will then be the authority in relation to Q; and
(c) such other persons as the Secretary of State considers appropriate.

(4) An application under this regulation must be accompanied by evidence that the United Kingdom is to be regarded as the administering member State in respect of Q.

24 Transfers of operators between member States

(1) This regulation applies where a person (a "transferred operator")—
(a) was a non-UK operator at the beginning of a scheme year but, in the course of that year, ceased to be a non-UK operator and became a UK administered operator, or
(b) was a UK administered operator at the beginning of a scheme year but, in the course of that year, ceased to be a UK administered operator and became a non-UK operator.

(2) For those purposes, "non-UK operator" means a person who is—
(a) identified in the Commission list, and
(b) specified in that list as an aircraft operator to be administered by a member State other than the United Kingdom ("the other State").

(3) Subject to paragraphs (4) and (5), a regulator ("R") in performing any of R's functions under these Regulations may (if it appears to R appropriate to do so) treat the transferred operator—
(a) as a person who, for the whole of that scheme year, is not a UK administered operator, or
(b) as a person who is a UK administered operator for the whole of that scheme year.

(4) R may not so treat a transferred operator unless R has—
(a) consulted the other State and the transferred operator, and
(b) given both of them notice of that decision.

(5) R may not treat the transferred operator as a UK administered operator under paragraph (3)(b) for the purposes of imposing a civil penalty in respect of any failure to comply with these Regulations that occurred—
(a) while the transferred operator was still a non-UK operator, or
(b) after the transferred operator became a non-UK operator.

25 Gibraltar operators

(1) This paragraph applies where—
(a) a person ("P") is specified in the Commission list as an aircraft operator to be administered by the United Kingdom;
(b) the Commission list identifies P's State as "Gibraltar (UK)"; and
(c) the Secretary of State is satisfied that P is regulated for the purposes of the Directive under legislation implementing the Directive that is applicable in Gibraltar.

(2) Where paragraph (1) applies, the Secretary of State—
(a) may designate P as a Gibraltar operator, and
(b) must in that case give notice to P of the designation.

(3) From the date of service of the notice under paragraph (2), P is to be treated for the purposes of these Regulations as a person who is not a UK administered operator.

(4) Where regulation (1)(b) or (c) no longer applies in relation to P, the Secretary of State may revoke P's designation; and in that case—

(a) the Secretary of State must give notice to P of the revocation, and
(b) from the date following the date of service of that notice (and for as long as paragraph (1)(a) continues to apply in relation to P) P is to be treated as a UK administered operator for the purposes of these Regulations.

(5) Before making a designation under paragraph (2), the Secretary of State must consult—
(a) P;
(b) the regulator of P;
(c) a person (other than the Secretary of State) who is the authority in relation to P; and
(d) the Government of Gibraltar.

(6) Before revoking a designation under paragraph (4), the Secretary of State must consult—
(a) P;
(b) the person who will be the regulator of P if the revocation is made;
(c) a person (other than the Secretary of State) who will then be the authority in relation to P; and
(d) the Government of Gibraltar.

26 UK aircraft operators

(1) A person ("P") is a UK aircraft operator in relation to a scheme year where, in respect of that year, P—
(a) is a UK administered operator; and
(b) performs an aviation activity (or is deemed to perform an aviation activity in accordance with paragraph (5)).

(2) Where the regulator cannot identify the person that performed an aviation activity the regulator may, where the owner of the aircraft at the time it was used to perform the activity ("the owner") is a UK administered operator or an unlisted operator, serve a notice on the owner.

(3) A notice under paragraph (2) must—
(a) where this information is available to the regulator, specify the dates, times and locations of the activity;
(b) be accompanied by such evidence relevant to the activity as the regulator considers appropriate; and
(c) require the owner to inform the regulator of the identity of the person who performed the activity, by the deadline specified in the notice.

(4) The regulator may extend the deadline specified in a notice under paragraph (2).

(5) Where the owner does not comply with a notice under paragraph (2) by the deadline as so specified or extended, the owner is on the expiry of that deadline deemed to be the person that performed the aviation activity.

27 Regulators: general

Subject to regulations 28 and 29, the regulator of a UK administered operator ("P") is—
(a) the Environment Agency, where—
 (i) P has its registered office in England or Wales; or
 (ii) P does not have a registered office;
(b) SEPA, where P has its registered office in Scotland;
(c) the chief inspector, where P has its registered office in Northern Ireland.

28 Regulators: assessment of emissions

(1) Where—

(a) a UK aircraft operator ("A") does not have a registered office, and
(b) the regulator ("B") is in possession of the necessary data,
B must by 1st September in the final year of each trading period make an assessment in accordance with paragraph (2).

(2) The assessment must—
(a) determine whether the highest percentage of A's aviation emissions is attributable to the area of a different regulator ("C"); and
(b) in doing so take into account data from the two scheme years preceding the year in which the assessment is made (if received by B before the date that it is made).

(3) Where that assessment shows that the highest percentage of emissions is attributable to the area of C, B must give notice to A and C by 21st December in the final year of the trading period.

(4) Where—
(a) B has given notice under paragraph (3), and
(b) the regulator for the trading period following that notice is not determined under regulation 29,
C is the regulator of A from the beginning of that trading period.

29 Regulators: change in registered office

(1) This paragraph applies where a UK administered operator ("A") with a registered office in the area of one regulator changes, in the course of a trading period, the address of its registered office to the area of a different regulator ("R").

(2) Where paragraph (1) applies, R is the regulator of A from the beginning of the next trading period.

(3) Where—
(a) a UK administered operator ("B") which did not have a registered office at the beginning of a trading period acquires a registered office in the course of that period, and
(b) that registered office is in the area of a regulator ("S") who is not the regulator of B in that trading period,
S is the regulator of B from the beginning of the next trading period.

Chapter 3
Allocation of aviation allowances

30 Allocation of aviation allowances

The following Schedules have effect—
(a) Schedule 7 (allocation of aviation allowances);
(b) Schedule 8 (allocation of aviation allowances from the special reserve).

Chapter 4
Monitoring and reporting aviation emissions

31 Interpretation

In this Chapter, any reference to a numbered Article is to that Article of the Monitoring and Reporting Regulation.

32 Application for an emissions plan by a UK administered operator

(1) Subject to paragraphs (3), (4) and (6), a UK administered operator ("A") must apply to the regulator for a monitoring plan in accordance with Article 51(1).

(2) That application must contain a plan to monitor A's aviation emissions (together with supporting documents) submitted under Article 12(1).

(3) If A has previously been issued with an emissions plan—
(a) an application under paragraph (1) may not be made without the agreement of the regulator; and
(b) any plan issued under regulation 34(1)(a) replaces the plan that has previously been issued.

(4) Where an application is made by virtue of the second or third sub-paragraphs of Article 51(1), the application must include a satisfactory explanation of why it could not have been made earlier.

(5) Without prejudice to paragraph (1), a UK administered operator who has not previously been issued with an emissions plan may make an application in accordance with paragraph (2) at any time.

(6) If A is a transferred operator within regulation 24(1)(a), and has previously applied to another member State for a monitoring plan in accordance with Article 51(1)—
(a) this regulation applies to A as it applies to a UK administered operator who is not a transferred operator; but
(b) the application to the regulator may be made within the period of 8 weeks beginning with the date on which A became a UK administered operator.

33 Requirement to notify the regulator if an emissions plan is not applied for

(1) Without prejudice to regulation 32(1), a person ("B") who becomes a UK administered operator after 31st December 2012 must by the relevant date—
(a) apply to the regulator in accordance with regulation 32, or
(b) notify the regulator in accordance with paragraph (2).

(2) The notification must state that B does not expect to commence an aviation activity within the four-month period beginning with the relevant date.

(3) For the purposes of this regulation, "the relevant date" is the last day of the period of 12 weeks beginning with the date on which B became a UK administered operator.

34 Issue of an emissions plan

(1) Where a UK administered operator ("A") has made an application under regulation 32 the regulator must, by the notice of determination of the application—
(a) issue to A a plan setting out how A's aviation emissions must be monitored; or
(b) where paragraph (2) applies, refuse the application.

(2) This paragraph applies where—
(a) the regulator is not satisfied that the plan proposed in the application complies with the Monitoring and Reporting Regulation; and
(b) A has not agreed to amendments of the plan that so satisfy the regulator.

(3) A plan issued under paragraph (1)(a) must contain—
(a) the provisions of the plan as proposed in the application, or with amendments as mentioned in paragraph (2)(b); and
(b) any conditions included pursuant to regulation 36(1).

(4) Where the application is refused—

(a) the regulator must state in the notice under paragraph (1)(b) what changes must be made to the application if a plan is to be issued; and

(b) A must (or, in the case of an application under regulation 32(5), may) resubmit the amended application within the period of 31 days beginning with the date of service of that notice.

(5) This regulation applies to the resubmission of an application as it applies to the original application, but for that purpose the references to the period of two months in paragraph 2(1)(a) and (2)(b) of Schedule 3 are to be read as a reference to a period of 24 days.

35 Monitoring and reporting emissions

(1) Once a UK administered operator ("A") has been issued with an emissions plan, A must monitor aviation emissions for each scheme year in which A is a UK aircraft operator.

(2) Monitoring under paragraph (1) must be carried out in accordance with—

(a) the Monitoring and Reporting Regulation; and

(b) A's emissions plan (including the written procedures supplementing that plan).

(3) A must prepare a verified report of aviation emissions, for the whole of each such scheme year, in accordance with the Monitoring and Reporting Regulation and the Verification Regulation.

(4) The report prepared under paragraph (3) must be submitted to the regulator by 31st March in the year following that scheme year.

36 Emissions plan conditions

(1) Each regulator ("R") must ensure that the emissions plan of a UK administered operator ("A") for which R is the regulator includes any conditions that R from time to time considers necessary to give proper effect to—

(a) the Monitoring and Reporting Regulation; and

(b) the Verification Regulation.

(2) A must comply with any condition included in A's emissions plan.

37 Variation of an emissions plan

(1) The regulator may, by giving notice to a UK administered operator ("A"), make any variation of A's emissions plan that the regulator considers necessary in consequence of a report made by A under Article 69.

(2) The regulator may, by giving notice to A, vary A's emissions plan where—

(a) A applies to the regulator for an amendment to the emissions plan, pursuant to a condition of the plan; or

(b) A has failed to comply with a requirement in the emissions plan to apply for such an amendment.

(3) The regulator may, by giving notice to a UK administered operator, vary an emissions plan in order to comply with the regulator's duty under regulation 36(1) or 89(4).

(4) A notice given under paragraph (1), (2)(b) or (3) may specify a period within which a fee for the variation of the emissions plan must be paid.

38 Variation of a benchmarking plan

The regulator may, by giving notice to a UK administered operator ("B"), vary B's benchmarking plan where B applies to the regulator under paragraph 4(1) of Schedule 7 or paragraph 4(1) of Schedule 8.

Chapter 5
Sanctions (other than civil penalties)

39 Detention and sale of aircraft

(1) Where a person ("P") is—

(a) a UK administered operator who has not paid a civil penalty within the period of 6 months beginning with the date by which it is due, or

(b) the subject of an operating ban imposed under Article 16(10) of the Directive,

the regulator may detain a relevant aircraft.

(2) For the purposes of paragraph (1)—

(a) a "civil penalty" is any penalty imposed—

 (i) under Part 7; or

 (ii) under the 2010 Regulations in respect of a failure to comply with those Regulations on or after 1st January 2012; and

(b) a "relevant aircraft" is any aircraft of which the regulator has reason to believe that P is the operator.

(3) Schedule 9 makes further provision about the detention of aircraft under this regulation, and about the sale of aircraft following such detention.

(4) For the purposes of paragraph (2), and of Schedules 9 and 10, the operator of an aircraft is the person using the aircraft to perform an aviation activity (and "operate" has the corresponding meaning).

40 Aircraft operating bans

Schedule 10 has effect in relation to—

(a) requests to the European Commission made by the Secretary of State under Article 16(5) of the Directive for the imposition of an operating ban on a UK administered operator; and

(b) the enforcement of any operating ban imposed under Article 16(10) of the Directive.

PART 4
SURRENDER OF ALLOWANCES

41 Surrender of allowances: operators of installations

For each scheme year, the operator of an installation must surrender allowances in accordance with the surrender requirements of the permit for the installation.

42 Surrender of allowances: UK aircraft operators

(1) For each scheme year a UK aircraft operator ("P") must, by the following 30th April, surrender a number of allowances or aviation allowances equal to P's annual reportable emissions in that scheme year.

(2) For the purposes of the requirement in paragraph (1) the amount of the annual reportable emissions in a recovery year is deemed to be increased by an amount equal to

the amount of annual reportable emissions, arising in the non-compliance year, in respect of which P failed to comply with that requirement.

(3) For the purposes of paragraph (2)—

(a) a "non-compliance year" is any scheme year for which P fails to comply with the requirement in paragraph (1); and

(b) the "recovery year" is—

(i) the scheme year following the non-compliance year; or

(ii) where the non-compliance results from an error in the verified emissions report submitted by P, the scheme year in which the error is discovered.

PART 5
ENFORCEMENT ETC.

43 Enforcement notices

(1) Where the regulator considers that a person ("P") has contravened, is contravening, or is likely to contravene a relevant provision, the regulator may serve a notice ("enforcement notice") on P.

(2) For the purpose of paragraph (1), a "relevant provision" is any provision of—

(a) these Regulations;

(b) the Monitoring and Reporting Regulation;

(c) a permit; or

(d) an aviation emissions plan.

(3) An enforcement notice must—

(a) state the regulator's view under paragraph (1);

(b) specify the matters constituting the contravention or making a contravention likely;

(c) specify the steps that must be taken to remedy the contravention or to ensure that the likely contravention does not occur; and

(d) specify the period within which those steps must be taken.

(4) P must comply with the requirements of the notice within the period so specified.

(5) The regulator may withdraw an enforcement notice at any time by further notice served on P.

44 Power to determine reportable emissions

(1) A power of the regulator to make a conservative estimate of emissions in accordance with Article 70 of the Monitoring and Reporting Regulation (a "determination of emissions") may also be exercised where—

(a) an operator fails to comply with the requirement to submit—

(i) a surrender report in accordance with paragraph 4(1)(a) and (b) of Schedule 4; or

(ii) a revocation report in accordance with paragraph 5(1)(a) and (b) of Schedule 4;

(b) an operator has failed to satisfy the regulator as required pursuant to paragraph 2(3)(c) of Schedule 4 or paragraph 3(8)(c) of Schedule 5;

(c) a request has been made under regulation 54(5)(b); or

(d) the regulator considers that such a determination is necessary for the purpose of imposing, or considering whether to impose, a penalty under Part 7.

(2) In the case referred to in paragraph (1)(b), in making the determination the regulator may substitute an emissions factor of greater than zero for the factor reported in respect of the bioliquids concerned.

(3) The regulator may make a determination of emissions where—
(a) the operator has failed to submit a report as required pursuant to paragraph 3(8)(b) of Schedule 5; or
(b) the regulator has reason to believe that the report submitted is incorrect.

(4) A determination of emissions—
(a) must be notified to the operator or UK aircraft operator concerned; and
(b) is to be treated as determining all of the reportable emissions from the installation (or of the UK aircraft operator) for the period to which the determination relates.

(5) A notice under paragraph (4)—
(a) except where it relates to an excluded installation, must be served on the registry administrator (and is in that case to be regarded as an instruction to the registry administrator for the purposes of Article 32(6) of the Registries Regulation 2011); and
(b) must, where required by Article 70(2) of the Monitoring and Reporting Regulation, specify the corrections that are required to the verified report mentioned in regulation 35(3) or in paragraph 2(3)(b) of Schedule 4.

(6) A regulator who makes a determination of emissions under the Monitoring and Reporting Regulation, or by virtue of this regulation, may recover the cost of doing so from the operator or UK aircraft operator concerned.

PART 6
INFORMATION

45 Provision of information

(1) An authority or the Secretary of State may, by notice served on a regulator ("R"), require R to furnish such information about the discharge of R's functions as the authority or the Secretary of State may require.

(2) For the purposes mentioned in paragraph (4), an authority, the Secretary of State, the registry administrator, the KP registry administrator or a regulator (a "relevant body") may, by notice served on any person, require that person ("P") to furnish such information as is specified in the notice, in such form and within such period following service of the notice or at such time as is so specified.

(3) The information which P may be required to furnish by a notice under paragraph (2) includes information, which, although it is not in P's possession or would not otherwise come into P's possession, is information which it is reasonable to require P to compile for the purpose of complying with the notice.

(4) The purposes referred to in paragraph (2) are—
(a) the discharge of the relevant body's functions; and
(b) applying, seeking to apply, or assessing whether to seek to apply emission allowance trading to activities or greenhouse gases which are not listed in Annex 1 to the Directive, in accordance with Article 24 of the Directive.

(5) Where the Secretary of State is entitled to serve a notice on a person under paragraph (2)—
(a) in relation to England and Wales, the regulator, and
(b) in relation to Scotland and Northern Ireland, the regulator or the Environment Agency,
may serve that notice for the purpose of assisting the Secretary of State.

(6) In this regulation, "functions" means functions under or by virtue of—
(a) these Regulations;
(b) the Monitoring and Reporting Regulation;
(c) the Verification Regulation;
(d) the Registries Regulation 2010; or
(e) the Registries Regulation 2011.

46 Disclosure of information

(1) Subject to paragraph (2) a relevant body (within the meaning of regulation 45(2)) must not disclose or publish any information provided to the relevant body under these Regulations except where—
(a) disclosure or publication is—
  (i) required in these Regulations or otherwise by law;
  (ii) necessary for the performance of the relevant body's functions (as defined by regulation 45(6)); or
  (iii) made with the consent of the person by or on behalf of whom the information was provided; or
(b) disclosure is between one relevant body and another.

(2) The Secretary of State may use any information held or obtained for the purposes of these Regulations, and may share such information with other government bodies, for the purpose of preparing and publishing national energy and emissions statistics, including the preparation and publication of a national inventory.

(3) For the purpose of paragraph (2), "national inventory" means the estimation, under Article 4(1)(a) of the United Nations Framework Convention on Climate Change 1, of anthropogenic emissions of greenhouse gases by sources and removals of all greenhouse gases by sinks not controlled by the Montreal Protocol.

47 National security

(1) No information may be published—
(a) by the Secretary of State under regulation 16(6), paragraph 8 of Schedule 7 or paragraph 8 of Schedule 8, or
(b) by the regulator under regulation 71,
if, in the opinion of the Secretary of State, the publication of that information would be contrary to the interests of national security.

(2) For the purposes of paragraph (1)(b), the Secretary of State may give to the regulator directions specifying information which may not be published under regulation 71.

(3) The regulator must notify the Secretary of State of any information which is excluded from publication in accordance with directions under paragraph (2).

PART 7
CIVIL PENALTIES

48 Interpretation

In this Part—
"carbon price", in relation to a tonne of carbon dioxide equivalent, is the price referred to in regulation 49;
"penalty notice" means a notice served under regulation 50(1);
"additional penalty notice" means a notice served under regulation 50(3).

49 Carbon Price

(1) In respect of the scheme year beginning with 1st January 2013, the carbon price is £6.70.

(2) For each subsequent scheme year, the Secretary of State must determine a price as the carbon price for that year, based on the sterling equivalent of the average end of day settlement price (in Euro per tonne of carbon dioxide equivalent) of the December futures contracts for that scheme year.

(3) For that purpose—
"average end of day settlement price" means the average over the 12 months ending with the relevant date;
"futures contract" means the futures contract as traded on the single largest carbon market exchange (as determined by volume of sales in the 12 months ending with the relevant date);
"sterling equivalent" means the sterling equivalent converted by reference to the Bank of England annual average spot exchange rate for the 12 months ending with the relevant date;
"the relevant date", in relation to the year for which the carbon price is set, is 11th November in the preceding year.

(4) The Secretary of State must publish a determination made under paragraph (2) one month before the beginning the scheme year in question.

50 Penalty notices

(1) Where the regulator is satisfied that a person ("P") is liable to a civil penalty under this Part the regulator must (subject to regulation 51) serve a notice on P.

(2) The penalty notice must specify—
(a) the regulation under which that liability arises;
(b) the amount of the civil penalty due;
(c) where appropriate, how that amount is calculated;
(d) whether or not P may be liable to a civil penalty in accordance with regulation 53(2)(b), 56(2)(b), 60(2)(b), 62(2)(b), 63(2)(b), 64(2)(b), 67(2)(b), 68(2)(b), or 69(2)(b) (an "additional daily penalty"); and
(e) if P will not be liable to an additional daily penalty, the date by which the penalty for which P is liable must be paid.

(3) Subject to regulation 51 and to paragraph (4), where the regulator is satisfied that P is liable to an additional daily penalty the regulator must, when the amount of that additional daily penalty can be determined, serve a notice on P specifying—
(a) the total amount of the civil penalties due; and
(b) the date by which that amount must be paid.

(4) In the case of an additional daily penalty under regulation 67(2)(b), a notice under paragraph (3) stating the amount of additional daily penalty that has accrued by the date of the notice may be served at such intervals as the regulator thinks fit.

(5) A civil penalty imposed by a penalty notice or an additional penalty notice must be paid to the regulator by the date specified in the notice.

(6) Any such civil penalty is recoverable by the regulator—
(a) as a civil debt; and
(b) where applicable, in accordance with regulation 39 and Schedule 9.

(7) the regulator must, as soon as is reasonably practicable—

(a) give notice to the authority of the service of any penalty notice or additional penalty notice; and
(b) pass to the authority any civil penalty that has been paid to the regulator.

51 Discretion in imposing civil penalties

(1) Where the regulator considers it appropriate to do so, the regulator may (subject to paragraph (2))—
(a) refrain from imposing a civil penalty;
(b) reduce the amount of a penalty (including the amount of an additional daily penalty);
(c) extend the time for payment specified in the penalty notice or additional penalty notice;
(d) withdraw a penalty notice or an additional penalty notice;
(e) modify the notice by substituting a lower penalty.

(2) The powers under paragraph (1) do not apply in relation to any penalty arising under regulation 54(1).

52 Carrying out a regulated activity contrary to regulation 9

(1) Where in any scheme year a regulated activity is carried out that is not authorised by a permit, contrary to regulation 9, the operator of the installation ("P") is at the end of that year liable to the civil penalty in paragraph (2).

(2) For each such year, the civil penalty is
$A + (B \times C)$,
where—
A is the estimated amount of the costs avoided by P in that year as a result of carrying out a regulated activity without such authorisation;
B is the estimated amount of reportable emissions from the installation in the period during which a regulated activity was carried out without such authorisation;
C is the carbon price for that year.

(3) In exercising powers under regulation 51 in relation to the penalty in paragraph (2), the regulator must ensure that the penalty imposed exceeds the amount of any economic benefit that P has obtained as a result of carrying out a regulated activity that is not authorised by a permit.

(4) The authority must exercise powers under section 40 of the Environment Act 1995 or regulation 37 of the Northern Ireland Regulations to give the regulator directions as to—
(a) the estimation by the regulator of A and B in paragraph (2); and
(b) the exercise of the regulator's powers in accordance with paragraph (3).

53 Failure to comply with a condition of a permit

(1) An operator is liable to the civil penalties in paragraph (3) where the operator fails to comply (or comply on time) with a condition of a permit included pursuant to—
(a) paragraph 2(1)(e)(ii) or (iv) of Schedule 4 (but excluding the condition mentioned in paragraph (4) below);
(b) paragraph 3(1)(g), (h) or (i) of Schedule 5; or
(c) regulation 10 of the 2005 Regulations, other than regulation 10(3) and (4) (or such a condition as modified by virtue of regulation 88(6) or (7) of these Regulations).

(2) However, an operator is not liable to those civil penalties where the failure to comply gives rise to a penalty under regulation 57.

(3) The civil penalties are—
(a) £3,750; and
(b) £375 for each day that the operator fails to comply with the condition following service of a penalty notice, up to a maximum of £33,750.

(4) An operator is liable to a civil penalty of £5,000 where the operator fails to comply with a condition of a permit included pursuant to paragraph 2(7)(a) of Schedule 4.

54 Failure to surrender allowances

(1) A person ("P") is liable to the civil penalty in paragraph (2) where P fails to surrender sufficient allowances, contrary to regulation 41 or regulation 42.

(2) The civil penalty ("excess emissions penalty") is the sterling equivalent of 100 Euros for each allowance that P failed so to surrender.

(3) But paragraph (1) is subject to paragraphs (4) to (6).

(4) Where paragraph (5) applies, P is not liable to the excess emissions penalty for a failure to surrender allowances in respect of those reportable emissions in a scheme year that—
(a) were not reported in the verified emissions report submitted for that year, but
(b) have been determined by the regulator following a request under paragraph (5)(b).

(5) This paragraph applies where P, before the regulator serves on P a penalty notice imposing an excess emissions penalty in respect of emissions in that scheme year (or a notice of the regulator's intention to do so)—
(a) notifies the regulator that there are annual reportable emissions not included in the report that has been submitted for that year,
(b) requests the regulator to make a determination of the annual reportable emissions for that year, and
(c) has surrendered allowances equal to the reportable emissions as so determined.

(6) Where paragraph (5) applies, P is liable to the civil penalty of the sterling equivalent of 20 Euros for each allowance that P failed to surrender in respect of the unreported emissions by the relevant date.

(7) In this regulation—
(a) "allowance", where P is a UK aircraft operator, includes an aviation allowance;
(b) "relevant date" means 30th April in the year following the scheme year mentioned in paragraph (4);
(c) "unreported emissions" means the emissions mentioned in paragraph (4);
(d) "sterling equivalent" means, subject to paragraph (8), the sterling equivalent converted by reference to the applicable rate of conversion; and
(e) for that purpose the applicable rate is the first rate of conversion to be published in September of the year preceding the scheme year in which P is liable to the penalty in the C series of the Official Journal of the European Union, adjusted in accordance with paragraph (8).

(8) If the last Harmonised Index of Consumer Prices for the member States of the European Union ("HICP") published by Eurostat before the end of April in the year in which P failed to surrender the allowances shows an average percentage price increase as compared with the last HICP published before the end of April 2012, the sterling equivalent is increased by the same percentage.

55 Exceeding an emissions target for an excluded installation

(1) An operator of an excluded installation is liable to the civil penalty in paragraph (2) where in any scheme year the operator fails to comply with paragraph 5 of Schedule 5.

(2) The civil penalty is

$(A - B) \times C$

, where—

A is the amount of annual reportable emissions arising in the scheme year;

B is the emissions target for that year;

C is the carbon price for that year.

56 Failure to pay a penalty for exceeding an emissions target for an excluded installation

(1) An operator of an excluded installation is liable to the civil penalties in paragraph (2) where the operator fails to pay a penalty imposed under regulation 55 by the date specified in the penalty notice.

(2) The civil penalties are—

(a) 10% of the penalty imposed under regulation 55; and

(b) £150 for each day that the operator fails to pay that penalty following service of a penalty notice in respect of the penalty under sub-paragraph (a), up to a maximum of £13,500.

57 Under-reporting of emissions from an excluded installation

(1) An operator of an excluded installation is liable to the civil penalty in paragraph (2) where there are reportable emissions in a scheme year ("the unreported emissions") that—

(a) were not reported in the report submitted for that year under paragraph 3(8)(b) of Schedule 5; but

(b) have been determined by the regulator under regulation 44(3).

(2) The civil penalty is

$A + (B \times C)$

where—

A is £3,750;

B is the amount of the unreported emissions;

C is the carbon price for that year.

58 Failure to notify when an excluded installation ceases to meet the criteria for being excluded

(1) An operator of an excluded installation ("P") is liable to the civil penalties in paragraphs (2) and (3) where P fails to comply (or comply on time) with a notification requirement under—

(a) a condition of a permit included pursuant to paragraph 3(4) or (5) of Schedule 5; or

(b) paragraph 4(1) or (2) of Schedule 5.

(2) For the first scheme year in which P fails to comply with the requirement to notify by 31st March in that year, the civil penalty is £2,500.

(3) For the first and each subsequent scheme year in which P has still failed to comply with the notification requirement by 31st October in that year, P is at the end of the following scheme year ("S") liable to the civil penalty in paragraph (4).

(4) The civil penalty is

$2 \times (A + B)$

, where—

A is £2,500;

B is the avoided compliance costs.

(5) In paragraph (4) "avoided compliance costs" means

$((W - X) \times Y) - Z$

, where—

W is the amount of annual reportable emissions arising in S;

X is the number of allowances for S to which P would have been entitled in accordance with Article 10a of the Directive, if the installation had not been an excluded installation and had been carrying out regulated activities;

Y is the carbon price for S;

Z is any penalty due under regulation 55 in respect of S.

59 Failure to surrender a permit

Where an operator fails to make an application to surrender a permit, contrary to regulation 13(1) and (2), the operator is liable to a civil penalty of £5,000.

60 Failure to submit or resubmit an application for an emissions plan

(1) A UK administered operator ("A") is liable to the civil penalties in paragraph (2) where A fails to—

(a) submit (or to submit on time) an application for an emissions plan, contrary to regulation 32(1);

(b) provide a satisfactory explanation, contrary to regulation 32(4); or

(c) resubmit (or to resubmit on time) an application for an emissions plan, where required to do so by regulation 34(4).

(2) The civil penalties are—

(a) £1,500; and

(b) £150 for each day that the application or resubmission of an application is not provided, following the service of a penalty notice, up to a maximum of £13,500.

61 Failure to notify the regulator if an emissions plan is not applied for

(1) A UK administered operator ("A") is liable to the civil penalty in paragraph (2) where A fails to comply with the requirements of regulation 33(1).

(2) The civil penalty is £5,000.

62 Failure to comply with a condition of an emissions plan

(1) A UK administered operator ("A") is liable to the civil penalties in paragraph (2) where A fails to comply (or to comply on time) with a condition in an emissions plan, contrary to regulation 36(2).

(2) The civil penalties are—

(a) £1,500; and

(b) £150 for each day that A fails to comply with the condition following the service of a penalty notice, up to a maximum of £13,500.

63 Failure to monitor aviation emissions

(1) A UK administered operator ("A") is liable to the civil penalties in paragraph (2) where A fails to monitor aviation emissions, contrary to regulation 35(1).

(2) The civil penalties are—

(a) £1,500; and

(b) £150 for each day that A fails to monitor aviation emissions following the service of a penalty notice, up to a maximum of £13,500.

64 Failure to report aviation emissions

(1) A UK administered operator ("A") is liable to the civil penalties in paragraph (2) where A fails to report (or to report on time) aviation emissions, contrary to regulation 35(4).

(2) The civil penalties are—
(a) £3,750; and
(b) £375 for each day that the report is not submitted, following the service of a penalty notice, up to a maximum of £33,750.

65 Failure to provide assistance and advice

Where an aerodrome operator fails to provide reasonable assistance and advice, contrary to paragraph 7(1) of Schedule 9, the aerodrome operator is liable to a civil penalty of £50,000.

66 Failure to comply with a direction relating to an operating ban

Where a person fails to comply with a direction, contrary to paragraph 2(4)(a) of Schedule 10, that person is liable to a civil penalty of £50,000.

67 Failure to return allowances

(1) An operator or a UK administered operator ("P") is liable to the civil penalties in paragraph (2) where P—
(a) receives allowances or aviation allowances to which P is not entitled; and
(b) fails to return (or return on time) such allowances or aviation allowances, contrary to—
 (i) paragraph 11(4) of Schedule 6; or
 (ii) paragraph 10(4) of Schedule 7.

(2) The civil penalties are—
(a) £20,000; and
(b) £1,000 for each day that P fails to return the allowances following the service of a penalty notice.

68 Failure to comply with an enforcement notice

(1) A person ("P") is liable to the civil penalties in paragraph (2) where P fails to comply (or to comply on time) with the requirements of an enforcement notice, contrary to regulation 43(4).

(2) The civil penalties are—
(a) £20,000; and
(b) £1,000 for each day that P fails to comply with the requirements of the enforcement notice, following service of a penalty notice, up to a maximum of £30,000.

69 Failure to comply with an information notice

(1) A person ("P") is liable to the civil penalties in paragraph (2) where P fails to comply (or to comply on time) with the requirements of notice served under regulation 45(2) (an "information notice").

(2) The civil penalties are—
(a) £1,500; and
(b) £150 for each day that P fails to comply with the requirements of the information notice, following service of a penalty notice, up to a maximum of £13,500.

70 Providing false or misleading information

(1) A person ("P") is liable to the civil penalty in paragraph (2) where P provides false or misleading information, or makes a statement which is false or misleading in a material particular, where the statement is made or the information is provided—
(a) in any application made under these Regulations, or in response to a notice served under paragraph 1(12) of Schedule 3;
(b) in a notice under regulation 33(1)(b);
(c) in an aviation emissions report prepared under regulation 35(3);
(d) in response to a notice served under regulation 45(2);
(e) pursuant to a requirement mentioned in regulation 80(2) or (4);
(f) in purported compliance with the conditions of a permit or an aviation emissions plan; or
(g) pursuant to paragraph 6(2), 7(9), 8(4)(a), 8(5) or 11 of Schedule 6.

(2) The civil penalty is £1,000.

71 Publication of names of persons subject to penalties under regulation 54(1)

(1) As soon as possible after—
(a) the expiry of the period for appealing the imposition of a penalty by the regulator under regulation 54(1), or
(b) if such an appeal is made, the determination or withdrawal of the appeal,
the regulator must (subject to paragraph (2)) publish the name of the person on whom that penalty was imposed.

(2) The name must not be published if, following such an appeal, the person is found not to be liable to any of the penalty imposed under regulation 54(1).

(3) Paragraph (1) is subject to regulation 47 (national security).

PART 8
APPEALS

Chapter 1
General

72 Interpretation

In this Part—
(a) "appeal body" has the meaning given by regulation 75;
(b) "decision" means—
  (i) a notice or deemed refusal under these Regulations; or
  (ii) an action or decision of the registry administrator or the KP registry administrator;
(c) "notice" includes—
  (i) in the case of a notice determining an application for a permit or the transfer of the permit, the provisions of any permit attached to the notice; and
  (ii) in the case of a notice determining an application for an aviation emissions plan, the conditions included in the plan issued by the notice.

73 Rights of appeal

(1) Subject to paragraph (3), the following persons may appeal to the appeal body—
(a) a person who is aggrieved by a decision determining any application made by them under these Regulations;

(b) a person who is aggrieved by a notice served on them under any provision mentioned in paragraph (2).

(2) Those provisions are—
(a) regulation 11(2), (3)(b) or (4);
(b) regulation 14(1);
(c) regulation 26(2);
(d) regulation 37(1), (2)(b) or (3);
(e) regulation 43(1);
(f) regulation 44(4);
(g) regulation 45(2);
(h) regulation 50(1) or (3);
(i) paragraph 8(1) or (4) of Schedule 5;
(j) paragraph 6(7)(a) of Schedule 6, in relation to a decision to make a request under paragraph 6(5)(a) or (b) of that Schedule;
(k) paragraph 7(11)(a) of Schedule 6, in relation to a decision to make a request under paragraph 7(9)(a) of that Schedule;
(l) paragraph 7(11)(b) of Schedule 6;
(m) paragraph 8(11)(a) of Schedule 6, in relation to a decision to make a request under paragraph 8(9)(a) or (b) of that Schedule;
(n) paragraph 11(2) of Schedule 6;
(o) paragraph 10(2) of Schedule 7.

(3) An appeal under paragraph (1) may not be made to the extent that the decision implements—
(a) a direction given by the authority under section 40 of the Environment Act 1995 or regulation 37 of the Northern Ireland Regulations, or
(b) a direction given by an appeal body under these Regulations.

74 Rights of appeal: registries

(1) A person who is aggrieved by a decision of the registry administrator referred to in a provision of the Registries Regulation 2011 mentioned in paragraph (2) may exercise the right to object given by that provision by appealing to the appeal body.

(2) Those provisions are—
(a) Article 20(3);
(b) Article 22(6);
(c) Article 23(3);
(d) Article 30(5);
(e) Article 31(6).

(3) A person who is aggrieved by a decision of the KP registry administrator referred to in a provision of the Registries Regulation 2010 mentioned in paragraph (4) may exercise the right to object given by that provision by appealing to the appeal body.

(4) Those provisions are—
(a) Article 18(3);
(b) Article 20(4)
(c) Article 21(1);
(d) Article 27(5);
(e) Article 28(5).

(5) On receiving notice under regulation 80(10), the account holder may appeal to the appeal body against the decision to set a registry account to blocked status.

75 Appeal body

(1) In the case of an appeal against a decision of SEPA, the appeal body is the Scottish Ministers.

(2) In the case of an appeal against a decision of the chief inspector, the appeal body is the Planning Appeals Commission.

(3) In the case of an appeal against any other decision the appeal body is the First-tier Tribunal.

76 Effect of an appeal

(1) Subject to paragraphs (2) to (4), the bringing of an appeal under regulation 73 suspends the effect of the decision pending the final determination or withdrawal of the appeal.

(2) The bringing of an appeal does not suspend the effect of—
(a) a decision refusing an application;
(b) a deemed refusal;
(c) a notice under—
    (i) regulation 11(2), (3)(b) or (4);
    (ii) regulation 37(1), (2)(b) or (3);
    (iii) regulation 43(1);
    (iv) paragraph 8(1) or (4) of Schedule 5; or
    (v) paragraphs 6(7)(a), 7(11)(a) or (b), or 8(11)(a) of Schedule 6.

(3) Where (following an application for a permit or for the transfer of a permit) a permit has been granted or varied, the bringing of an appeal against the provisions of the permit or the terms of the variation does not suspend the effect of those provisions or terms.

(4) Where an aviation emissions plan has been issued following an application under regulation 32, the bringing of an appeal against the conditions included in the plan does not suspend the effect of those conditions.

(5) The bringing of an appeal against a determination of emissions under regulation 44(4) suspends the effect of the decision only for the purpose of assessing whether there has been compliance with regulation 41 or 42.

(6) The bringing of an appeal under regulation 74 does not suspend the effect of the decision pending the final determination or withdrawal of the appeal.

77 Determination of an appeal

(1) In determining an appeal under regulation 73(1) the appeal body may, subject to paragraph (3)—
(a) affirm the decision;
(b) quash the decision or vary any of its terms;
(c) substitute a deemed refusal with a decision of the appeal body; or
(d) give directions to the regulator as to the exercise of the regulator's functions under these Regulations.

(2) In determining an appeal under regulation 74 the appeal body may give directions to—
(a) the registry administrator as to the exercise of its functions under the Registries Regulation 2011, or
(b) the KP administrator as to the exercise of its functions under the Registries Regulation 2010.

(3) The appeal body may not make a determination that would result in a decision which could not otherwise have been made under these Regulations or under the Registries Regulation 2010 or 2011.

Chapter 2
Appeals: Scotland and Northern Ireland

78 Procedure for appeals

(1) Schedule 11, Part 1, has effect in relation to the making and determination of an appeal to the Scottish Ministers.

(2) The Scottish Ministers may—
(a) appoint any person to exercise on their behalf, with or without payment, the function of determining an appeal under this Part or any matter or question involved in such an appeal; or
(b) refer any matter or question involved in such an appeal to such person as they may appoint for the purpose, with or without payment.

(3) Schedule 11, Part 2, has effect in relation to appointments under paragraph (2)(a).

(4) Schedule 12 has effect in relation to the making and determination of an appeal to the Planning Appeals Commission.

PART 9
THE UNION REGISTRY AND THE UK REGISTRY

79 Interpretation

(1) In this regulation and regulation 80, a reference to a numbered Article is to that Article of the Registries Regulation 2011.

(2) In regulation 80—
"the allocation table" means the national allocation table notified to the European Commission by the United Kingdom under Article 49;
"the aviation allocation table" means the national aviation allocation table notified by the United Kingdom to the European Commission under Article 53(1).

80 The Union Registry

(1) The registry administrator may require users of the Union Registry to comply with reasonable terms and conditions in relation to that registry.

(2) It is the duty of the account holder to comply with the requirement to enter emissions data in accordance with Article 32(2); furthermore, an amount of zero must be entered by the account holder if the latter is—
(a) an operator who carried out no regulated activity in the year to which the data would relate; or
(b) a UK administered operator who carried out no aviation activity in that year.

(3) The verifier is responsible under Articles 32(4) and (5) for—
(a) approving the annual verified emissions; and
(b) marking the emissions as verified.

(4) The operator or the UK administered operator is responsible for complying with the requirement under Article 14(1) or 15(1) to provide information to the registry administrator and request the opening of a registry account.

(5) In complying with the requirement mentioned in paragraph (4), the operator or the UK administered operator must provide such evidence of identity and address as may be required by the registry administrator.

(6) Where—
(a) an operator fails to comply with regulation 41, or
(b) a UK aircraft operator fails to comply with regulation 42,
the registry administrator must set the relevant registry account to blocked status until the compliance status figure for the installation or UK aircraft operator, calculated in accordance with Article 34, is greater than or equal to zero.

(7) This paragraph applies where—
(a) an operator is required to submit a report to the regulator by the terms of a notice of surrender or a revocation notice; and
(b) the operator—
(i) fails to submit the report to the regulator within the time specified in the report;
(ii) submits an incomplete report to the regulator within the time so specified; or
(iii) submits within the time so specified a report to the regulator that cannot be verified in whole or in part in accordance with the monitoring and reporting requirements for the installation.

(8) Where paragraph (7) applies, the registry administrator must set the relevant operator holding account to blocked status until—
(a) the report has been prepared and verified in accordance with the requirements of paragraph 4(1)(b) or 5(1)(b) of Schedule 4 and has been submitted to the regulator; or
(b) the regulator has notified, in accordance with regulation 44(4)(a), a determination of the reportable emissions referred to in paragraph 4(1)(a) or 5(1)(a) of that Schedule.

(9) Where an operator is in breach of the requirement to comply with a notice given under paragraph 11(2) of Schedule 6 or paragraph 10(2) of Schedule 7, the registry administrator must set the operator holding account to blocked status until that notice has been complied with.

(10) Where the registry administrator sets a registry account to blocked status pursuant to paragraph (6), (8) or (9) it must notify the account holder specifying the reason why, and the period during which, the relevant registry account will be blocked.

(11) The regulator must, as soon as is reasonably practicable, notify the registry administrator where a change to the allocation table or aviation allocation table becomes necessary—
(a) by virtue of Article 50(1) or 54(1), or
(b) for any other reason (and in particular in consequence of paragraph 5 or 10 of Schedule 6).

(12) The registry administrator must, as soon as is reasonably practicable, notify the European Commission in accordance with Article 50(2) or 54(2) of any changes to the allocation table or aviation allocation table (other than those falling within paragraph (11)(a)).

(13) This paragraph applies where—
(a) a notice of surrender or a revocation notice has been given and has taken effect; and
(b) the operator is unable to comply with the requirement to surrender allowances imposed by that notice by the date specified in the notice, due to the suspension of access to the relevant registry account by the registry administrator pursuant to Article 31.

(14) Where paragraph (13) applies, the registry administrator must, if so requested by the operator, surrender the number of allowances specified in the notice of surrender or the revocation notice.

(15) The registry administrator or the KP registry administrator may refuse to—
(a) open any account in the Union Registry or the UK Registry, or
(b) approve an authorised representative or an additional authorised representative in relation to such an account,
where it is satisfied that the proposed account holder, authorised representative or additional authorised representative is not a fit and proper person to hold such an account or, as the case may be, act as such a representative.

(16) The registry administrator may extend the suspension of the running of delays under Article 36(3) to all days in a scheme year that are not working days, provided that the decision to do so is published by the registry administrator by 1st December in the previous scheme year.

81 The UK Registry

(1) The Environment Agency must continue to operate the UK Registry for the purposes of meeting the obligations of the United Kingdom referred to in Article 3(1) of the Registries Regulation 2010 (obligations as a Party to the Kyoto Protocol 1 and under Article 6 of Decision No 280/2004/EC), and in that capacity is referred to in these Regulations as the "KP registry administrator".

(2) The Environment Agency may require users of the UK Registry to comply with reasonable terms and conditions in relation to that registry.

PART 10
SUPPLEMENTARY

82 Recovery of fees

(1) In this regulation "allowances" includes aviation allowances.

(2) Any fee payable by virtue of these Regulations may be recovered by the regulator—
(a) as a civil debt; or
(b) by the seizure and sale of a number of allowances held by the operator or UK administered operator liable to the fee ("the debtor") in accordance with paragraph (3).

(3) Where the regulator proposes to recover an unpaid fee by the seizure and sale of allowances held by the debtor, the regulator must—
(a) notify the registry administrator and the debtor;
(b) instruct the registry administrator to transfer a number of allowances sufficient to cover the unpaid fee, and any expenses incurred in recovering it from the debtor, to the regulator's person holding account in the Union Registry;
(c) sell the allowances transferred under sub-paragraph (b) for the best price that can reasonably be obtained, though a failure to do so does not make a sale under this paragraph void or voidable; and
(d) apply the proceeds of sale in the following order—
 (i) in payment of the unpaid fee in respect of which the allowances were seized and sold;
 (ii) in payment of any expenses incurred by the regulator in seizing and selling the allowances,
and pay any residue from the proceeds of sale to the debtor.

83 Consequences of non-payment

The regulator is not required to perform a function for which a fee is payable in relation to a person who has not paid a fee which that person is liable to pay.

84 Guidance

(1) The authority may issue guidance to the regulator with respect to the carrying out of any of the regulator's functions under these Regulations, the Monitoring and Reporting Regulation or the Verification Regulation.

(2) The Secretary of State may issue guidance to the registry administrator or the KP registry administrator with respect to the carrying out of any of its functions under these Regulations, the Registries Regulation 2011 or the Registries Regulation 2010.

(3) The regulator, the registry administrator or the KP registry administrator must have regard to any guidance issued under paragraph (1) or (2).

PART 11
REVOCATIONS, SAVINGS AND TRANSITIONAL PROVISIONS.

[*Regulation 85 is not reproduced.*]

86 Savings and transitional provisions: the 2005 Regulations

(1) Notwithstanding the revocations made by regulation 85, the following provisions of the 2005 Regulations ("the relevant provisions") continue to have effect to the extent specified below.

(2) Part 1 and Schedule 1 have effect for the purpose of the relevant provisions.

(3) Regulations 16 and 17 have effect for the purposes of making an application for the surrender of a permit, or the service of a notice of revocation in respect of a failure to make such an application, where the circumstances giving rise to the requirement to make the application occurred before 1st January 2013.

(4) Regulation 18(3) to (5) has effect in relation to the charging schemes referred to in that regulation.

(5) Regulation 22 (other than paragraph (2)) has effect for the purpose of allowing an operator to make an application for an allocation from the new entrant reserve (as defined by regulation 2 of the 2005 Regulations).

(6) But for the purpose of paragraph (5) above, the reference in regulation 22(22) to regulation 15(1) of the 2005 Regulations is to be read as a reference to regulation 12(1) of these Regulations (and the reference to the proposed transferee is accordingly to be read as a reference to the new operator).

(7) Subject to paragraph (8) below, regulation 26 has effect for all purposes relating to the registry referred to in Article 3(2) of the Registries Regulation 2010.

(8) In regulation 26—
(a) paragraphs (2) to (5) do not have effect; and
(b) paragraph (8) has effect as if the references to Articles 18, 20(4) and 27(5) were omitted.

(9) The following provisions have effect in so far as they relate to any activities carried out, or emissions arising, prior to 1st January 2013—
(a) regulation 27A;
(b) Part 4.

(10) Subject to paragraph (11) below, Part 5 and Schedules 2 to 4 have effect in relation to any appeal brought against a decision or notice specified in regulation 32(1) to (5) of the 2005 Regulations.

(11) Regulation 32(4) has effect as if the reference to the appropriate authority were a reference to the First-tier tribunal (and the reference to the appropriate authority in regulation 32(7) is to be construed accordingly).

(12) Regulation 35 has effect in so far as it relates to functions carried out before 1st January 2013 or under the relevant provisions.

(13) Regulation 36 has effect in so far as it relates to a civil penalty in respect of emissions arising before 1st January 2013.

(14) Regulation 37 has effect.

(15) Paragraph (1)(c) to (f) of regulation 38 has effect in so far as it relates to the relevant provisions, but where the conduct giving rise to the offence occurs after 31st December 2012 the following civil penalties apply instead of the offences under that paragraph—
(a) the penalty in regulation 59 above applies instead of the offence of failing to making an application to surrender a permit;
(b) the penalties in regulation 53 above apply instead of the offence of failing to comply with a notice under regulation 22(13)(a) (and for that purpose the condition of the notice is deemed to be a condition falling within paragraph (1)(c) of regulation 53);
(c) the penalties in regulation 68 above apply instead of the offence of failing to comply with an enforcement notice; and
(d) the penalty in regulation 70 above applies instead of an offence under paragraph (1)(f) of regulation 38.

(16) Subject to paragraph (17) below, regulation 38(2) and (3) has effect.

(17) No prosecution may be brought in respect of an offence under regulation 38(1)(a) if—
(a) the conduct that gave rise to the offence continues after 31st December 2012; and
(b) the person who has committed the offence will be liable to a civil penalty under regulation 52 above.

(18) Regulations 39 to 41 have effect in relation to a failure to surrender allowances in respect of emissions arising before 1st January 2013, and regulation 40 has effect in relation to an understatement of such emissions.

(19) Parts 8 to 10 have effect in so far as they relate to functions carried out, or powers exercised, under the relevant provisions or as national administrator under the Registries Regulation 2010.

87 Savings and transitional provisions: the 2010 Regulations

(1) Notwithstanding the revocations made by regulation 85, the following provisions of the 2010 Regulations ("the relevant provisions") continue to have effect to the extent specified below.

(2) Part 1 has effect for the purpose of the relevant provisions.

(3) The time period in regulation 18(1) has effect in relation to a person who became an aircraft operator under the 2010 Regulations before 1st January 2013, but the application for an emissions plan must otherwise be made under regulation 32 of these Regulations.

(4) Regulations 21 and 22 have effect in relation to aviation emissions arising before 1st January 2013.

(5) Regulations 26 and 27 have effect in relation to aviation emissions arising before 1st January 2013.

(6) Regulation 28 has effect in relation to the charging schemes referred to in that regulation.

(7) Regulation 29 has effect in relation to the functions referred to in that regulation.

(8) The following have effect in relation to civil penalties arising under the 2010 Regulations—
(a) Part 8;
(b) regulation 49.

(9) Part 11 and Schedules 3 to 5 have effect in relation to any appeal brought against any decision made or notice served under the 2010 Regulations.

(10) The following have effect in relation to decisions or functions of the regulator under the 2010 Regulations—
(a) Part 12;
(b) regulations 58 and 59.

(11) Regulations 55 to 57, and Schedule 6, have effect in relation to information provided, reports submitted, or notices served under the 2010 Regulations.

(12) Paragraph (3), and (5) to (8), of regulation 60 have effect.

88 Transitional provisions: permits

(1) An application under regulation 8 of the 2005 Regulations for a greenhouse gas emissions permit that is made to the regulator before 1st January 2013, and not determined before that date, may be treated by the regulator as an application made under—
(a) regulation 10(1) above; or
(b) if the installation to which the application relates is an excluded installation, regulation 10(2) above.

(2) An application under regulation 14 of the 2005 Regulations for the variation of a permit that is made to the regulator before 1st January 2013, and not determined before that date, may be treated by the regulator as an application made under regulation 11(3)(a) above.

(3) An application under regulation 15 of the 2005 Regulations for the transfer of a permit (other than for a partial transfer) that is made to the regulator before 1st January 2013, and not determined before that date, may be treated by the regulator as an application made under regulation 12(1) above.

(4) An application under regulation 15 of the 2005 Regulations for the partial transfer of a permit that is made to the regulator before 1st January 2013 and not determined before that date may be treated by the regulator as an application made under regulation 12(1) above, provided that the application has been amended to the satisfaction of the regulator (and is otherwise deemed to have been withdrawn).

(5) Subject to paragraphs (6) and (7), a permit granted under regulation 9 of the 2005 Regulations that is in force immediately before 1st January 2013 ("the permit") continues to have effect until it is revoked or surrendered under these Regulations.

(6) The regulator must vary the permit as necessary to bring it into a form in which it could have been granted under regulation 10 above.

(7) Until such variations are made, the permit has effect in relation to emissions in the year beginning with 1st January 2013, or in any subsequent scheme year, as if—

(a) any reference in the permit to Commission Decision 2007/589/EC of 18 July 2007 were a reference to the Monitoring and Reporting Regulation, and any reference to Section 5.2, 5.3 or Section 9 of Annex 1 to that Decision were a reference to the corresponding provision of that Regulation;

(b) any reference in the permit to Annex 5 to the Directive were a reference to the Verification Regulation;

(c) any reference in the permit to the Emission Trading Registry for the UK were a reference to the Union Registry; and

(d) any requirement of the permit to submit a report to the regulator by 30th June each year, setting out proposed improvements in monitoring at the installation, applied only in relation to the report required to be submitted by 30th June 2013.

(8) Notwithstanding the variations made pursuant to paragraph (6), the permit as it had effect immediately before 1st January 2013 continues to have such effect in relation to any emissions arising before that date and any obligations relating to them.

89 Transitional provisions: aviation emissions plans

(1) An application for an emissions plan under regulation 18 of the 2010 Regulations that has not been determined under those Regulations may be treated by the regulator as an application made under regulation 32 above.

(2) An application for the variation of an emissions plan, pursuant to a condition of the plan, that is made to the regulator before 1st January 2013 may be treated by the regulator as an application made under regulation 37(2)(a) above.

(3) Subject to paragraph (4) and (5), an aviation emissions plan that is in force immediately before 1st January 2013 ("the plan") continues to have effect.

(4) The regulator must vary the plan as necessary to bring it into a form in which it could have been issued under regulation 34 above.

(5) Until such variations are made, the plan has effect in relation to emissions in the year beginning with 1st January 2013, or in any subsequent scheme year, as if—

(a) any reference in the plan to Commission Decision 2007/589/EC of 18 July 2007 were a reference to the Monitoring and Reporting Regulation, and any reference to Section 9 of Annex 1 and Sections 2, 3 and 4 of Annex 14 to that Decision were a reference to the corresponding provision of that Regulation; and

(b) any requirement of the plan to submit a report to the regulator by 30th June each year, setting out proposed improvements in monitoring of aviation activities, applied only in relation to the report required to be submitted by 30th June 2013.

SCHEDULE 1
APPLICATION TO THE CROWN ETC.

Regulation 4

1 Crown application

Subject to paragraphs 2 and 3, these Regulations bind the Crown.

2 Entry to Crown premises

(1) If the Secretary of State considers that in the interests of national security particular powers of entry must not be used in relation to particular Crown premises, the Secretary of State may certify that those powers must not be used in relation to those premises.

(2) In this paragraph—

"Crown premises" means premises held or used by or on behalf of the Crown;

"power of entry" means a power of entry exercisable under section 108 of the Environment Act 1995 or regulation 27 of the Northern Ireland Regulations, in relation to a function under these Regulations.

3 Service on certain Crown operators

(1) This paragraph applies in relation to an installation operated by a person acting on behalf of—

(a) the Royal Household;

(b) the Duchy of Lancaster; or

(c) the Duke of Cornwall or other possessor of the Duchy of Cornwall.

(2) In relation to the serving or giving of notices or other documents under these Regulations, the following person must be treated as the operator—

(a) in relation to sub-paragraph (1)(a), the Keeper of the Privy Purse;

(b) in relation to sub-paragraph (1)(b), the person appointed by the Chancellor of the Duchy of Lancaster;

(c) in relation to sub-paragraph (1)(c), the person appointed by the Duke of Cornwall or other possessor of the Duchy of Cornwall.

SCHEDULE 2
NOTICES ETC.

Regulation 5

1

In this Schedule, "instrument" means any notice or direction served or given under these Regulations (but does not include a notice or direction required to be given to the regulator or registry administrator).

2

An instrument must be in writing.

3

An instrument may be served on or given to a person ("P") by—

(a) delivering it to P in person;

(b) sending it to a postal or email address n provided by P for the purpose of service of instruments;

(c) leaving it at P's proper address; or

(d) sending it by post or electronic means to P's proper address.

4

In the case of a body corporate, an instrument may be served on or given to the secretary or clerk of that body.

5

In the case of a partnership, an instrument may be served on or given to a partner or a person having control or management of the partnership business.

6

If a person ("Q") to be served with or given an instrument has specified an address in the United Kingdom (other than Q's proper address) at which Q or someone on Q's behalf will accept instruments of that description, that address must instead be treated as Q's proper address.

7

For the purposes of this Schedule, "proper address" means (subject to paragraph 6)—
(a) in the case of a body corporate or its secretary or clerk—
(i) the registered or principal office of that body, or
(ii) the email address of the secretary or clerk;
(b) in the case of a partnership or a partner or person having control or management of the partnership business—
(i) the principal office of the partnership, or
(ii) the email address (or, in the case of a partnership established outside the United Kingdom, the last known address) of a partner or a person having that control or management;
(c) in any other case, a person's last known address (which for the purpose of this paragraph and paragraph (b) includes an email address).

8

For the purposes of paragraph 7, where a body corporate registered outside the United Kingdom or a partnership established outside the United Kingdom has an office in the United Kingdom, the principal office of that body corporate or partnership is its principal office in the United Kingdom.

9

(1) Where for the purposes of paragraph 7 the person giving or serving an instrument is not able to ascertain a proper address in relation to a UK administered operator, a relevant address may instead be treated as the proper address.

(2) For that purpose, "relevant address" means an address derived from information supplied to the regulator by Eurocontrol (or any other organisation) at the request of the European Commission.

10

The provisions of this Schedule do not apply where a contrary provision applies under paragraph 8 of Schedule 9.

SCHEDULE 3
APPLICATIONS ETC.

Regulation 6

1 Applications etc.: general

(1) This paragraph applies—
(a) to any application, notice or report submitted to the regulator under any provision of—
(i) these Regulations,
(ii) a permit, or
(iii) an aviation emissions plan; and
(b) notwithstanding any further provision made under or by virtue of these Regulations in respect of such application, notice or report.

(2) Sub-paragraph (10) also applies to applications—
(a) to the registry administrator to open an account in the Union Registry, and
(b) to the KP registry administrator to open an account in the UK Registry,
and for that purpose the provision of updated information in relation to such an account is to be treated as an application.

(3) For the purposes of this paragraph, an application includes any proposed plan required to be submitted as part of the application.

(4) An application, report or notice—
(a) must be in writing; and
(b) unless agreed otherwise in writing with the regulator, must be submitted on a form made available by the regulator for that purpose.

(5) Such a form must specify, as the case may be—
(a) the information required by the regulator to determine the application; or
(b) the matters required to be included in the report.

(6) Unless agreed otherwise in writing with the regulator, the form must be sent to the regulator electronically.

(7) A form provided by the regulator which specifies an electronic address for submission must, if submitted electronically, be sent to that address.

(8) A form provided by the regulator for submission through a website must, unless the regulator agrees otherwise in writing, be submitted through that site and in accordance with the instructions given there for completion and submission.

(9) Unless the information has been provided in a previous application made to the regulator, an application must contain the name, postal address (including postcode) and telephone number of the applicant, together with—
(a) an email address for service, or
(b) a postal address for service (including postcode) in the United Kingdom,
and in the case of an application under regulation 12 (transfer of permits) those requirements apply to each of the joint applicants.

(10) An application must be accompanied by the fee prescribed, but—
(a) where the application is sent electronically, the fee may be sent to the regulator separately from the application (and in that case the application is deemed not to have been received by the regulator until the fee has also been received); and
(b) where the application relates to an offshore installation, the fee need not be paid until the end of the period of 28 days beginning with the date on which the regulator serves a notice on the operator requesting payment of the fee.

(11) An application may be withdrawn at any time before it is determined.

(12) The regulator may, by notice to the applicant, require the applicant to provide such further information specified in the notice, within the period so specified, as the regulator may require for the purpose of determining the application.

(13) The application is deemed to have been withdrawn where—
(a) the applicant has failed to provide that information by the end of that period (or by such later date as may be agreed with the regulator); and
(b) the regulator gives notice to the applicant that the application is treated as having been withdrawn.

2 Determination of applications

(1) Subject to sub-paragraph (2), where an application to the regulator under these Regulations is duly made it must be determined by the regulator within—
(a) the period of two months beginning with the date on which the application was received, or
(b) such longer period as may be agreed in writing with the applicant.

(2) For the purposes of sub-paragraph (1)—
(a) an application is determined when notice of the determination is given to the applicant by the regulator; and
(b) in calculating the period of two months, no account is to be taken of any period beginning with the date on which a notice under paragraph 1(12) is served on the applicant and ending with the date on which the applicant provides the information specified in the notice.

(3) If the regulator fails to determine the application within the period allowed by sub-paragraphs (1) and (2)—

(a) the applicant may give to the regulator notice that the applicant treats the application as having been refused, and

(b) the application is then deemed to have been refused at the end of that period.

(4) Where the application is an application for a permit or the transfer of a permit, any permit that is granted as a result of the application must be attached to the notice given under sub-paragraph (2)(a).

SCHEDULE 4
PERMITS

Regulations 10, 12, 13 and 14

1 Applications for permits

(1) An application for a permit must contain—

(a) as well as the address for service required under Schedule 3, any address to which correspondence relating to the application should be sent; and (if the applicant is a body corporate)—

  (i) its registered number and the postal address of its registered or principal office, and

  (ii) if that body corporate is a subsidiary of a holding company within the meaning of section 1159 of the Companies Act 2006, the name of the holding company (other than a holding company which is itself a subsidiary) and the postal address of its registered or principal office;

(b) in relation to the site of the installation—

  (i) the postal address and national grid reference of the site (or equivalent information identifying the installation and its location);

  (ii) a description of the site and the location of the installation on it; and

  (iii) the name of any local authority in whose area the site is situated;

(c) a description of the installation, including a description of—

  (i) the regulated activities to be carried out at the installation and the specified emissions from those activities; and

  (ii) any directly associated activities (within Article 3(e) of the Directive) that are also to be carried out;

(d) a description of the raw and auxiliary materials used in carrying out regulated activities in the installation, the use of which is likely to lead to specified emissions;

(e) a description of the sources of specified emissions from the regulated activities carried out in the installation;

(f) a monitoring plan submitted under Article 12 of the Monitoring and Reporting Regulation, together with—

  (i) the supporting documents under Article 12(1) of that Regulation;

  (ii) the summary of a procedure ensuring fulfilment of the requirements referred to in Article 12(3)(a) and (b) of that Regulation; and

  (iii) the uncertainty assessment carried out under Article 28(1)(a) of that Regulation;

(g) a description, including the reference number, of any environmental licence issued in relation to the installation;

(h) any additional information which the applicant wishes the regulator to take into account in considering the application; and

(i) a non-technical summary of the information referred to in paragraphs (c) to (h).

(2) For the purposes of sub-paragraph (1)(g), "environmental licence" means—

(a) an authorisation under Part 1 of the Environmental Protection Act 1990 or the Industrial Pollution Control (Northern Ireland) Order 1997; or

(b) a permit under—

(i) the Environmental Permitting (England and Wales) Regulations 2010;
(ii) the Pollution Prevention and Control (Scotland) Regulations 2000;
(iii) the Offshore Regulations; or
(iv) the Northern Ireland Regulations.

(3) Where an application is for a permit in respect of more than one installation, the application must contain the information required by sub-paragraph (1) in respect of each installation.

2 Content of a greenhouse gas emissions permit

(1) A greenhouse gas emissions permit granted under regulation 10 must contain—
(a) the name and postal address in the United Kingdom (including postcode) of the operator;
(b) the postal address and national grid reference of the installation (or equivalent information identifying the installation and its location);
(c) a description of the installation, including—
(i) the regulated activities to be carried out at the installation and the specified emissions from those activities; and
(ii) any directly associated activities (within Article 3(e) of the Directive) that are also to be carried out;
(d) a description of the site and the location of the installation on that site; and
(e) as defined below—
(i) the monitoring plan;
(ii) the monitoring and reporting requirements;
(iii) the surrender requirements; and
(iv) the supplementary requirements.

(2) The monitoring plan is the plan approved in accordance with Articles 11 to 13 of the Monitoring and Reporting Regulation.

(3) The monitoring and reporting requirements are—
(a) a requirement to monitor the annual reportable emissions of the installation in accordance with—
(i) the Monitoring and Reporting Regulation; and
(ii) the monitoring plan (including the written procedures supplementing that plan);
(b) a requirement to prepare, for each scheme year, a verified report of those emissions in accordance with the Monitoring and Reporting Regulation and the Verification Regulation, and to submit that report to the regulator by 31st March in the following year;
(c) a requirement to satisfy the regulator, if an emission factor of zero has been reported in respect of the use of bioliquids, that the sustainability criteria set out in Article 17(2) to (5) of the Renewable Energy Directive have been fulfilled in accordance with Article 18(1) of that Directive; and
(d) any further conditions that the regulator considers necessary to give proper effect to the Monitoring and Reporting Regulation or the Verification Regulation.

(4) The surrender requirements are conditions obliging the operator to surrender, by the 30th April following a scheme year, a number of allowances equal to the annual reportable emissions of the installation in that scheme year.

(5) For the purposes of the surrender requirements the amount of the annual reportable emissions of the installation in a recovery year is deemed to be increased by an amount equal to the amount of annual reportable emissions, arising in the non-compliance year, in respect of which the operator failed to comply with the surrender requirements.

(6) For the purposes of sub-paragraph (5)—
(a) a "non-compliance year" is a scheme year in respect of which an operator fails to comply with the surrender requirements; and
(b) the "recovery year" is—

(i) the scheme year following the non-compliance year; or
(ii) where the non-compliance results from an error in the verified emissions report submitted by the operator, the scheme year in which the error is discovered.

(7) The supplementary requirements are—
(a) notification requirements corresponding to the requirements in paragraphs 6(2) and 8(4)(a) and (5) of Schedule 6 (except in the case of the installations mentioned in paragraph 1(3)(b) of that Schedule);
(b) any other conditions that the regulator considers necessary to ensure that the operator notifies the regulator of any planned or effective changes to the capacity, activity level or operation of the installation, by 31st December in the year in which the change was planned or has occurred; and
(c) any other conditions that the regulator considers appropriate to include in the permit.

3 Transfer of permits

(1) An application under regulation 12 must—
(a) contain the information mentioned in sub-paragraph (3); and
(b) identify the installations, or parts of an installation, to which the application relates ("the transferred units") and the regulated activities authorised to be carried out at them ("the transferred activities").

(2) In the case of a partial transfer—
(a) the application must also state—
(i) the amount of allowances that are to be transferred to the transferred units; and
(ii) the initial installed capacity of all sub-installations to which the permit relates, identifying those that correspond to the transferred units; and
(b) the application may not be granted unless the regulator is satisfied that—
(i) the amount mentioned in paragraph (a)(i) reflects the historical activity levels of the transferred units, calculated in accordance with Article 9 of the Free Allocation Decision; and
(ii) the capacities mentioned in paragraph (a)(ii) have been calculated in accordance with Article 7(3) of the Free Allocation Decision.

(3) The information referred to in sub-paragraph (1)(a) is—
(a) in relation to each applicant, as well as the address for service required under Schedule 3 any address to which correspondence relating to the application should be sent;
(b) in relation to the new operator, the information mentioned in paragraph 1(1)(a)(i) and (ii); and
(c) a monitoring plan and other information mentioned in paragraph 1(1)(f) submitted by the new operator, or a specification by that operator of the parts of the existing monitoring plan that it is proposed should be varied and any necessary corresponding updating of that information.

(4) Where the application relates to a partial transfer, a transfer of the permit is effected by the regulator giving notice—
(a) granting a permit to the new operator ("the new permit") which—
(i) authorises the carrying out of the transferred activities;
(ii) identifies the transferred units at which they may be carried out; and
(iii) includes such other provisions as the regulator (subject to sub-paragraph (5)) considers appropriate; and
(b) making such corresponding variations to the provisions of the permit held by the current operator ("the original permit") as the regulator (subject to sub-paragraph (5)) considers appropriate.

(5) In exercising the powers given by sub-paragraph (4)(a)(iii) and (b), the regulator must ensure that the conditions of the new permit, or the original permit as varied, are (so far as relevant) the same as the conditions that were included in the original permit, subject to such modifications as in the opinion of the regulator are necessary to take account of the transfer.

(6) For the purposes of sub-paragraph (4) the new permit, and the variations of the original permit, have effect from a date agreed with the applicants and specified in the new permit and in the original permit as so varied.

(7) Where the application does not relate to a partial transfer, the transfer of the permit is effected by the regulator giving notice varying the permit so that it includes—
(a) the name and other particulars of the new operator;
(b) the date referred to in sub-paragraph (8); and
(c) such variations to the monitoring plan as the regulator considers appropriate.

(8) From a date agreed with the applicants, the new operator is to be treated as the holder of the permit as varied under sub-paragraph (7).

(9) If the new operator already holds a permit (an "existing permit") for an installation that is on the same site as the transferred unit the regulator may effect a transfer within sub-paragraph (7) by—
(a) giving notice of such variations to the existing permit as in the opinion of the regulator are necessary to take account of the transfer; and
(b) cancelling the permit held by the current operator.

(10) For the purposes of sub-paragraph (9)—
(a) the variations of the existing permit have effect from a date agreed with the applicants and specified in the existing permit as so varied; and
(b) the cancelled permit ceases to have effect on that date.

(11) A regulator who effects the transfer of a permit in accordance with this paragraph must notify the registry administrator of the transfer.

(12) Upon receipt of a notice under sub-paragraph (11) the registry administrator must carry out any necessary changes to the national allocation table pursuant to Article 50(1)(d) or (e) of the Registries Regulation 2011.

4 Surrender of permits

(1) The notice of surrender must require the operator, in relation to the scheme year in which it takes effect ("the relevant year"), to—
(a) submit to the regulator by a date specified in the notice a report ("the surrender report") specifying the reportable emissions from the beginning of the relevant year until the date on which the notice takes effect;
(b) ensure that the surrender report is prepared and verified in accordance with the monitoring and reporting requirements of the greenhouse gas emissions permit to which the application to surrender relates ("the permit"); and
(c) by a date specified in the notice, surrender allowances equal to—
 (i) the reportable emissions specified in the surrender report;
 (ii) where an operator has failed to comply with the surrender requirements of the permit imposed in respect of the last scheme year for which the date for surrendering allowances in accordance with those requirements has passed, the annual reportable emissions in respect of which the operator failed so to comply;
 (iii) where the notice of surrender is served in a scheme year in which an error in the report submitted by an operator under the monitoring and reporting requirements in relation to any earlier scheme year has been discovered, the annual reportable emissions in respect of which, as a result of that error, the operator failed to comply with the surrender requirements of the permit in respect of the scheme year to which the error relates; and
 (iv) where an operator has failed to comply with regulation 13(2), the total number of allowances which by the date on which the notice of surrender is served have been issued in respect of the installation which would not have been issued if the operator had so complied.

(2) From the date on which the notice of surrender takes effect—

(a) the permit ceases to have effect to authorise the carrying out of a regulated activity or to require the monitoring of emissions; but

(b) any conditions of the permit continue to have effect so far as they are not superseded by the requirements of that notice in accordance with sub-paragraphs (5) to (7) until the regulator certifies—

(i) that those requirements and any surrender requirements of the permit have been complied with, or

(ii) that there is no reasonable prospect of further allowances being surrendered by the operator in respect of the installation to which the notice relates.

(3) From the scheme year following the relevant year, for the purposes of assessing compliance with any surrender requirements of the permit the amount of reportable emissions of the installation (before any increase in accordance with paragraph 2(5)) is deemed to be zero.

(4) Where the regulator certifies in accordance with sub-paragraph (2)(b)(ii) that there is no reasonable prospect of further allowances being surrendered by the operator, the regulator must notify the registry administrator.

(5) The requirements specified in a notice of surrender pursuant to sub-paragraph (1)(a) and (b) are to be treated as if they were monitoring and reporting requirements of the permit.

(6) Subject to paragraph (7), the requirements specified in a notice of surrender pursuant to sub-paragraph (1)(c) are to be treated as if—

(a) they were surrender requirements of the permit, and

(b) the number of allowances required to be surrendered by the notice of surrender were the annual reportable emissions of the installation in respect of the scheme year to which the notice relates.

(7) Where the surrender report understates any reportable emissions, the requirement to surrender allowances equal to the amount of the understatement is not superseded by the requirements specified in the notice of surrender.

(8) Where the operator fails to comply with the requirements of a notice of surrender included pursuant to sub-paragraph (1), the regulator must notify the registry administrator.

5 Revocation of permits

(1) The revocation notice must require the operator, in relation to the scheme year in which it takes effect ("the relevant year"), to—

(a) submit to the regulator by a date specified in the notice a report ("the revocation report") specifying the reportable emissions from the beginning of the relevant year until the date on which the notice takes effect;

(b) ensure that the revocation report is prepared and verified in accordance with the monitoring and reporting requirements of the greenhouse gas emissions permit to which the revocation notice relates ("the permit"); and

(c) by a date specified in the notice, surrender allowances equal to—

(i) the reportable emissions specified in the revocation report;

(ii) where an operator has failed to comply with the surrender requirements of the permit imposed in respect of the last scheme year for which the date for surrendering allowances in accordance with those requirements has passed, the annual reportable emissions in respect of which the operator failed so to comply;

(iii) where the revocation notice is served in a scheme year in which an error in the report submitted by an operator under the monitoring and reporting requirements in relation to any earlier scheme year has been discovered, the annual reportable emissions in respect of which, as a result of that error, the operator failed to comply with the surrender requirements of the permit in respect of the scheme year to which the error relates; and

(iv) where the notice has been served under regulation 14(1)(b), the total number of allowances which by the date on which the revocation notice is served have been issued in respect of the installation which would not have been issued if the operator had so complied.

(2) A revocation notice must specify a period within which the fee for the revocation of the permit must be paid.

(3) From the date on which the revocation notice takes effect—

(a) the permit ceases to have effect to authorise the carrying out of a regulated activity or to require the monitoring of emissions; but

(b) any conditions of the permit continue to have effect so far as they are not superseded by the requirements of that notice in accordance with sub-paragraphs (6) to (8) until the regulator certifies—

(i) that those requirements and any surrender requirements of the permit imposed have been complied with, or

(ii) that there is no reasonable prospect of further allowances being surrendered by the operator in respect of the installation to which the notice relates.

(4) From the scheme year following the relevant year, for the purposes of assessing compliance with the surrender requirements of the permit the amount of reportable emissions of the installation (before any increase in accordance with paragraph 2(5)) is deemed to be zero.

(5) Where the regulator certifies in accordance with sub-paragraph (3)(b)(ii) that there is no reasonable prospect of further allowances being surrendered by the operator, the regulator must notify the registry administrator.

(6) The requirements specified in a revocation notice pursuant to sub-paragraph (1)(a) and (b) are to be treated as if they were monitoring and reporting requirements of the permit.

(7) Subject to paragraph (8), the requirements specified in a revocation notice pursuant to sub-paragraph (1)(c) are to be treated as if—

(a) they were surrender requirements of the permit, and

(b) the number of allowances required to be surrendered by the revocation notice were the annual reportable emissions of the installation in respect of the scheme year to which the notice relates.

(8) Where the revocation report understates any reportable emissions, the requirement to surrender allowances equal to the amount of the understatement is not superseded by the requirements specified in the revocation notice.

(9) Where the operator fails to comply with the requirements of a revocation notice included pursuant to sub-paragraph (1), the regulator must notify the registry administrator.

(10) A regulator who has served a revocation notice may, at any time before the date on which it takes effect, withdraw the notice.

SCHEDULE 5
EXCLUDED INSTALLATIONS

Regulations 10(7) and 15

1 Interpretation

(1) In this paragraph, "hospital" means—

(a) any institution for the reception and treatment of persons suffering from illness;

(b) any maternity home;

(c) any institution for the reception and treatment of persons during convalescence or persons requiring medical rehabilitation;

(d) any clinics, dispensaries or out-patient departments maintained in connection with an establishment mentioned in paragraphs (a) to (c);
(e) any research or teaching facility that is associated with an establishment mentioned in paragraphs (a) to (c) which has as its primary purpose medical research or medical teaching;
(f) any other facility which has as its primary purpose the provision of such services as are necessary to maintain the proper functioning of any establishment mentioned in paragraphs (a) to (d), including in particular—
  (i) blood transfusion services,
  (ii) catering services,
  (iii) laundry services, or
  (iv) medical sanitisation services.

(2) For the purposes of sub-paragraph (1), "illness" includes any disorder or disability of the mind and any injury or disability requiring medical or dental treatment or nursing.

(3) For the purposes of this Schedule, an installation primarily provides services to a hospital in a scheme year—
(a) where no more than 15% of heat produced by the installation is exported to an establishment other than a hospital in that year; or
(b) if the installation is not owned by a hospital, not less than 85% of heat produced by the installation is supplied to one or more hospitals in that year.

(4) In this Schedule—
"emissions report" has the meaning given by paragraph 3(8)(b)(i);
"emissions target", in relation to a scheme year, means an amount of reportable emissions specified in an excluded installation emissions permit as the target for the excluded installation in that year;
"maximum amount" means annual reportable emissions of 24,999 tonnes of carbon dioxide equivalent in any scheme year.

2 Conversion of a greenhouse gas emissions permit

(1) Where a greenhouse gas emissions permit has been granted in respect of an installation that is an excluded installation, the regulator must vary the greenhouse gas emissions permit (with effect from a date to be included in the permit) so that the provisions of the permit are replaced by provisions that satisfy the requirements of paragraph 3.

(2) When a permit is varied under sub-paragraph (1)—
(a) the regulator may make only such variations as appear to the regulator to be necessary in consequence of the installation being an excluded installation; but
(b) that is without prejudice to the duty to vary the permit in accordance with regulation 88(6).

(3) A variation of a permit under this paragraph does not affect any obligations of the operator under the permit in respect of emissions arising prior to 1st January 2013.

3 Content of an excluded installation emissions permit

(1) An excluded installation emissions permit must contain—
(a) the name and postal address in the United Kingdom (including postcode) of the operator and any other address for correspondence specified by the operator;
(b) the postal address and national grid reference of the installation (or for offshore installations equivalent information identifying the installation and its location);
(c) a description of the installation, including—
  (i) the regulated activities to be carried out at the installation and the specified emissions from those activities; and
  (ii) the directly associated activities (within Article 3(e) of the Directive) that are also to be carried out;

(d) a description of the site and the location of the installation on that site;
(e) an emissions target for each scheme year prior to 2021;
(f) a monitoring plan (as defined in sub-paragraph (7));
(g) the monitoring and reporting conditions (as defined in sub-paragraph (8));
(h) the record keeping requirements (as defined in sub-paragraph (9)); and
(i) any other conditions that the regulator considers appropriate to include in the permit.

(2) The authority must exercise powers under section 40 of the Environment Act 1995, or regulation 37 of the Northern Ireland Regulations, to give the regulator directions as to the calculation of the emissions targets included under sub-paragraph (1)(e).

(3) If the regulator has been directed to do so under an enactment mention in sub-paragraph (2) before 30th September in any scheme year, the regulator must vary the permit by substituting new emissions targets for the existing targets for each subsequent scheme year in order to take into account (to the extent and in the manner specified in the direction)—
(a) any amendments to the Directive;
(b) any amendments to the list adopted by the European Commission under Article 10a(13) of the Directive;
(c) any amendments to Decision No. 406/2009/EC of the European Parliament and the Council of 23 April 2009 on the effort of Member States to reduce their greenhouse gas emissions to meet the Community's greenhouse gas emission reduction commitments up to 2020;
(d) any measures relating to carbon budgets under the Climate Change Act 2008; or
(e) any other matters mentioned in the direction.

(4) An excluded installation emissions permit that is granted in respect of an installation which does not primarily provide services to a hospital must contain a condition requiring the operator to give notice to the regulator by the relevant date if the annual reportable emissions from the installation in any scheme year exceed the maximum amount.

(5) An excluded installation emissions permit granted in respect of an installation which primarily provides services to a hospital must contain a condition requiring the operator to give notice to the regulator by the relevant date if the installation ceases to do so in any scheme year.

(6) For the purposes of sub-paragraphs (4) and (5), the relevant date is 31st March in the year following the scheme year in question.

(7) The monitoring plan is the plan approved in accordance with Articles 11 to 13 of the Monitoring and Reporting Regulation.

(8) The monitoring and reporting conditions are—
(a) a requirement to monitor the annual reportable emissions of the installation in accordance with—
  (i) the relevant provisions of the Monitoring and Reporting Regulation; and
  (ii) the monitoring plan (including the written procedures supplementing that plan);
(b) a requirement to submit to the regulator, for each scheme year, by 31st March in the following year a report of the annual reportable emissions from the installation in accordance with the relevant provisions of the Monitoring and Reporting Regulation ("the emissions report") that is either—
  (i) verified in accordance with the Verification Regulation, or
  (ii) accompanied by a notice declaring that—
    (aa) in preparing the emissions report the operator has complied with the relevant provisions of the Monitoring and Reporting Regulation;
    (bb) the operator has complied with the monitoring plan for the installation; and
    (cc) the report is free from material misstatements;
(c) a requirement to satisfy the regulator, if an emission factor of zero has been reported in respect of the use of bioliquids, that the sustainability criteria set out in Article 17(2) to

(5) of the Renewable Energy Directive have been fulfilled in accordance with Article 18(1) of that Directive; and

(d) any further conditions that the regulator considers necessary to ensure that the operator complies with the relevant provisions of the Monitoring and Reporting Regulation.

(9) The record keeping requirements are any conditions requiring the operator of an installation referred to in sub-paragraph (5) who has not given notice in accordance with that provision to—

(a) maintain records demonstrating that it continues to primarily provide services to a hospital; and

(b) comply with requests from the regulator to inspect those records for the purpose of verifying the accuracy of the records and of the emissions report.

(10) In this paragraph, "relevant provisions" means the provisions specified in the permit as relevant for the purposes of monitoring and reporting emissions from excluded installations.

(11) The authority must exercise powers under section 40 of the Environment Act 1995, or regulation 37 of the Northern Ireland Regulations, to give the regulator directions as to the provisions that are to be specified in accordance with sub-paragraph (10).

4 Activities during 2012: duty to notify regulator

(1) An operator of an excluded installation which primarily provided services to a hospital before 2013, but ceased to do so during 2012, must give notice to the regulator of that cessation no later than 31stMarch 2013.

(2) The operator of a relevant installation must give notice to the regulator no later than 31st March 2013 where the annual reportable emissions from the installation during 2012 exceeded the maximum amount.

(3) For the purposes of sub-paragraph (2) an installation is a "relevant installation" if—

(a) it is an excluded installation that does not primarily provides services to a hospital; and

(b) the operator of the installation was, prior to 2013, not under any obligation to report its annual reportable emissions to the regulator.

5 Emissions target: duty not to exceed

An operator must ensure that annual reportable emissions from an excluded installation in a scheme year do not exceed the emissions target for that year.

6 Emissions target: increase in the capacity of an excluded installation

(1) Where a capacity increase has occurred at an excluded installation after 30th June 2011, the operator may apply to the regulator for an increase in the emissions targets for the installation.

(2) An application under sub-paragraph (1) must be made—

(a) by 31st December in the year during which the capacity increase occurred or within 3 months of the date of the capacity increase, whichever is later; or

(b) where the capacity increase occurred before 1st January 2013, by 30th June 2013.

(3) The application must contain evidence demonstrating the following—

(a) the date on which the capacity increase was put into operation;

(b) that the increase is not temporary;

(c) that the increase is in operation and is required for the purpose of carrying out the operator's primary business activities;

(d) in the case of a capacity increase at a heat sub-installation where measurable heat is produced otherwise than within the installation's boundaries, that the increase is solely associated with measurable heat produced at the installation; and

(e) any further matters that the regulator is required to take into account by a direction referred to in sub-paragraph (8).

(4) Where the regulator receives an application under sub-paragraph (1), and is satisfied with information provided by the operator under sub-paragraph (3), the regulator may calculate new emissions targets for that and subsequent scheme years.

(5) Where the regulator calculates new emissions targets pursuant to sub-paragraph (4), the regulator must vary the permit by substituting the new emissions targets for the existing targets.

(6) Where after having varied the permit under sub-paragraph (5) the regulator is subsequently satisfied that the evidence provided by the operator under sub-paragraph (3) is incorrect or incomplete, the regulator may recalculate those new emissions targets and vary the permit accordingly by making a new substitution of emissions targets.

(7) However, except where the excluded installation primarily provides services to a hospital, the increase in an emissions target under sub-paragraph (4) or (6) may not result in an emissions target which exceeds the maximum amount.

(8) The authority must exercise powers under section 40 of the Environment Act 1995, or regulation 37 of the Northern Ireland Regulations, to give the regulator directions as to—
(a) the further matters required to be taken into account when considering an application under sub-paragraph (1); and
(b) the calculation or recalculation of emissions targets under sub-paragraphs (4) or (6).

(9) In this paragraph—
(a) "capacity increase" means an increase in a sub-installation's installed capacity whereby one or more identifiable physical changes relating to its technical configuration and functioning other than a replacement of an existing production line takes place;
(b) "installed capacity" means—
 (i) the sub-installation's installed capacity on 30 June 2011; or
 (ii) in the case of an installation which has had a capacity increase since 30th June 2011, the installed capacity of the sub-installation following the last capacity increase;
(c) "measurable heat" has the same meaning as in Article 3(e) of the Free Allocation Decision;
(d) "sub-installation" has the meaning given in Article 3(b), (c), (d) and (h) and Article 6 of the Free Allocation Decision.

7 Banking an overachieved emissions target

(1) Subject to sub-paragraph (2), in this paragraph "bankable amount" in relation to a scheme year means the difference between—
(a) the emissions target for that year; and
(b) the amount of reportable emissions stated in the emissions report for that year.

(2) Where the carrying out of regulated activities at an excluded installation has been suspended for a period, in circumstances where the installation would be deemed to have permanently ceased the carrying out of regulated activities were it an installation to which Schedule 6 applied, the bankable amount is zero in relation to any scheme year in which that period (or any part of that period) falls.

(3) For the purposes of deciding whether the circumstances mentioned in sub-paragraph (2) apply, the operator may make an application under paragraph 7(2) of Schedule 6.

(4) Subject to sub-paragraph (5), where for any scheme year ("S") the bankable amount is greater than zero the regulator—
(a) may increase the emissions target for the installation for the following scheme year by the bankable amount; and
(b) must in that case vary the permit by substituting that increased emissions target for the existing target.

(5) Except where the excluded installation primarily provides services to a hospital, if increasing the emissions target under sub-paragraph (4) would result in an emissions target which exceeds the maximum amount, the increased emissions target must instead be equal to the maximum amount.

(6) Where the amount of reportable emissions stated in the emissions report for S is amended following a determination of emissions under regulation 44(3), the regulator must—
(a) calculate the bankable amount using the data as so determined; and
(b) where an increased emissions target has been substituted under sub-paragraph (4)(b), make a further variation of the permit to substitute a revised emissions target.

(7) Where an increased emissions target for a scheme year has been substituted following an application under paragraph 6(1), but the application was determined in the following year, the regulator must—
(a) calculate any bankable amount for the scheme year using that increased target; and
(b) vary the permit to substitute a revised emissions target for the following year, based on the amount so calculated.

8 Termination of an excluded installation emissions permit

(1) Where the regulator is satisfied that—
(a) the annual reportable emissions from an excluded installation which does not primarily provide services to a hospital have exceeded the maximum amount, or
(b) an excluded installation has ceased to primarily provide services to a hospital,
the regulator must, as soon as is reasonably practicable, give a notice to the operator.

(2) A notice under sub-paragraph (1) must state that, from the beginning of the scheme year following the year in which the notice is given—
(a) the installation will not be treated as an excluded installation; and
(b) the operator will be required to comply with the conditions of a greenhouse gas emissions permit in respect of the installation.

(3) This sub-paragraph applies where the regulator is satisfied that the operator of an excluded installation has—
(a) committed a sufficiently serious breach of the conditions of the excluded installation emissions permit, or
(b) failed to pay to the regulator the penalty imposed under regulation 56 within one month after the date specified in the penalty notice.

(4) Where sub-paragraph (3) applies the regulator may revoke the permit under regulation 14 or give a notice to the operator in accordance with sub-paragraph (5).

(5) The notice must state that, from the beginning of the scheme year following the year in which notice is given—
(a) the installation will not be treated as an excluded installation; and
(b) the operator will be required to comply with the conditions of a greenhouse gas emissions permit in respect of the installation.

(6) Where notice is given under sub-paragraph (1) or (4), the regulator must vary the excluded installation emissions permit, with effect from the 1st January in the scheme year following the year in which the notice was given ("the date of conversion"), so that the provisions of the permit that satisfy the requirements of paragraph 3 are replaced by provisions satisfying the requirements of paragraph 2 of Schedule 4.

(7) In varying a permit under sub-paragraph (6), the regulator may make only such variations as appear to the regulator to be necessary in consequence of the installation ceasing to be treated as an excluded installation.

(8) A variation of a permit under sub-paragraph (6) does not affect any obligations of the operator under the permit in respect of emissions arising from activities prior to the date of conversion.

(9) Where—
(a) notice is given under sub-paragraph (1) or (4), and
(b) the operator holds a registry account with excluded status in respect of the installation,
the regulator must give notice to the registry administrator, in accordance with the Registries Regulation 2011, to change the status of the account to open from the year beginning with the date of conversion.

(10) Where sub-paragraph (3) applies and the permit is revoked, the regulator must give notice to the registry administrator in accordance with the Registries Regulation 2011 to close the account.

9 End of excluded installation status

(1) By 1st July 2020 the regulator must give a notice to each operator of an excluded installation stating that, from 1st January 2021—
(a) the installation will not be treated as an excluded installation; and
(b) the operator will be required to comply with the conditions of a greenhouse gas emissions permit in respect of the installation.

(2) Sub-paragraphs (6) to (9) of paragraph 8 apply in respect of a notice given under sub-paragraph (1) of this paragraph as they apply to in respect of a notice give under paragraph 8(1).

SCHEDULE 6
ALLOCATION AND ADJUSTMENT OF ALLOWANCES

Regulation 16(3)

1 Interpretation

(1) In this Schedule—
(a) "the allocation table" has the meaning given by regulation 79(2);
(b) "new entrant reserve" means the reserve of allowances provided for under Article 10a(7) of the Directive;
(c) "preliminary total annual amount of allowances" is that amount as calculated in accordance with Article 19(3) of the Free Allocation Decision;
(d) "verified" means verified as satisfactory in accordance with Article 8 of the Free Allocation Decision (except that the reference to Decision 2007/589/EC in Article 8(3) is to be read as a reference to the Verification Regulation);
(e) "year" means a scheme year in the trading period 2013 to 2020.

(2) In this Schedule, the following expressions have the meanings given to them in Article 3 of the Free Allocation Decision—
"added capacity" (see Article 3(l));
"incumbent installation" (see Article 3(a));
"reduced capacity" (see Article 3(m));
"significant capacity extension" (see Article 3(i));
"significant capacity reduction" (see Article 3(j));
"start of changed operation" (see Article 3(o));
"start of normal operation" (see Article 3(n)).

(3) This Schedule does not apply to—
(a) an excluded installation (see regulation 15(3)(b)); or
(b) an installation that, by virtue of Article 10a(3) of the Directive, is not eligible for an allocation.

2 Application for an allocation from the new entrant reserve: new entrants

(1) Subject to sub-paragraph (2), where—

(a) the permit for an installation was granted on or after 30th June 2011, or
(b) the permit was granted before 30th June 2011, but the start of normal operation was on or after that date,

the operator of the installation may apply to the regulator for an allocation of allowances in respect of that installation from the new entrant reserve.

(2) Such an application may not be made where—
(a) the start of normal operation was before 30th June 2011; or
(b) the installation has already been included in the list referred to regulation 16(2).

(3) Any application under sub-paragraph (1) must be made—
(a) before the end of the period of twelve months beginning with the start of normal operation of the installation, or
(b) if that period expired before 1st February 2013, by that date.

(4) The application must contain—
(a) all relevant information regarding each parameter listed in Annex 5 to the Free Allocation Decision for each separate sub-installation;
(b) the initial installed capacity for each sub-installation calculated by the operator in accordance with Article 17(4) of the Free Allocation Decision; and
(c) subject to paragraph (5), a statement that the data referred to in paragraphs (a) and (b) have been verified.

(5) If the date for the submission of the application in accordance with sub-paragraph (3) falls before 30th May 2013, the statement may be submitted separately from the application and by the latter date.

(6) If the regulator approves the calculations of initial installed capacity the regulator must calculate—
(a) the activity levels of the installation in accordance with Article 18(1) and (2) of the Free Allocation Decision;
(b) the preliminary annual number of allowances to be allocated as from the start of normal operation of the installation for each sub-installation in accordance with Article 19(1) to (3) of the Free Allocation Decision; and
(c) the preliminary total annual amount of allowances to be allocated to the installation.

(7) The result of any calculation under sub-paragraph (6) must be included in the notice of the determination of an application under sub-paragraph (1).

3 Application for an allocation from the new entrant reserve: significant capacity extensions

(1) Where an installation had a significant capacity extension—
(a) after 30th June 2011, or
(b) on or before that date, but where the added capacity was capable of determination only after 30th September 2011,

the operator of the installation may (subject to sub-paragraph (2)) apply to the regulator for an allocation of allowances from the new entrant reserve.

(2) Any application under sub-paragraph (1) must be made—
(a) before the end of the period of twelve months beginning with—
  (i) the start of changed operation of the installation, or
  (ii) in the case mentioned in paragraph (1)(b), the date of determination of added capacity; or
(b) if that period expired before 1st February 2013, by that date.

(3) The application must contain—
(a) all relevant information regarding each parameter listed in Annex 5 to the Free Allocation Decision for each separate sub-installation;

(b) the installed capacity, and a calculation of the added capacity, for each such sub-installation;
(c) any other evidence necessary to demonstrate that the criteria for a significant capacity extension have been met; and
(d) subject to sub-paragraph (4), a statement that the data referred to in paragraphs (a) to (c) have been verified.

(4) If the date for the submission of the application in accordance with sub-paragraph (2) falls before 30th May 2013, the statement may be submitted separately from the application and by the latter date.

(5) If the regulator approves the calculation of added capacity the regulator must calculate—
(a) the activity levels (for the added capacity only) of the sub-installations to which the significant capacity extension applies in accordance with Article 18(1) and (2) of the Free Allocation Decision;
(b) the preliminary number of allowances to be allocated for each sub-installation insofar as the extension is concerned in accordance with Articles 19(1) to (3) and 20 of the Free Allocation Decision; and
(c) the preliminary total annual amount of allowances to be allocated to the installation insofar as the extension is concerned.

(6) The result of any calculation under sub-paragraph (5) must be included in the notice of the determination of an application under sub-paragraph (1).

4 Notification of preliminary annual number of allowances: new entrants and significant capacity extensions

(1) The regulator must, within 28 days after the date of the notice referred to in paragraph 2(6) or 3(5) notify the preliminary total annual amount calculated under paragraph 2(5)(c) or 3(4)(c) to—
(a) the authority;
(b) the Secretary of State (where the Secretary of State is not the authority); and
(c) the European Commission, pursuant to Article 19(4) of the Free Allocation Decision.

(2) Where the European Commission notifies the regulator that the preliminary total annual amount is rejected the regulator must, as soon as is reasonably practicable, notify the operator giving the reasons for rejection provided by the European Commission.

5 Calculation of final total annual amount of allowances allocated free of charge: new entrants and significant capacity extensions

(1) Where the European Commission approves the preliminary total annual amount notified under paragraph 4(1), the regulator must calculate the final total annual amount of allowances allocated to the installation concerned.

(2) The regulator must, as soon as is reasonably practicable, notify the final total annual amount to—
(a) the operator;
(b) the authority;
(c) the registry administrator; and
(d) the Secretary of State (where the Secretary of State is not the authority).

(3) For the purpose of this paragraph, the final total annual amount is the preliminary total annual amount, adjusted annually by the linear reduction factor referred to in Article 10a(7) of the Directive (using the preliminary total annual amount for 2013 as a reference).

6 Adjustment of allocation: significant capacity reductions

(1) This sub-paragraph applies where a sub-installation has had a significant capacity reduction—

(a) after 30th June 2011, or
(b) on or before that date, but the extent of the reduction could not be determined before 30th September 2011.

(2) Where sub-paragraph (1) applies the operator of the installation must, by the relevant date, submit to the regulator a notice containing—
(a) a statement of the reduced capacity, and of the installed capacity of the sub-installation after taking into account the capacity reduction; and
(b) a statement that the data submitted under paragraph (a) have been verified.

(3) For that purpose—
(a) the relevant date is the later of—
 (i) the last day of the period of 7 months following the date of the change of capacity;
 (ii) 31st December in the year in which that change occurred; or
 (iii) 1st February 2013; but
(b) where the relevant date falls before 30th May 2013, the statement referred to in sub-paragraph (2)(b) need only be submitted by the latter date.

(4) Once the operator has submitted the information required by sub-paragraph (2) the regulator must—
(a) in accordance with Article 18 of the Free Allocation Decision, calculate the activity levels for the reduced capacity of the sub-installation to which the significant capacity reduction relates in accordance with Article 18(3) of the Free Allocation Decision;
(b) in accordance with Article 21(2) of the Free Allocation Decision, reduce the preliminary annual number of allowances allocated to each sub-installation by the preliminary annual number of allowances allocated to the sub-installation concerned calculated in accordance with Article 19(1) of the Free Allocation Decision insofar as the significant capacity reduction is concerned; and
(c) in accordance with Article 21(2) of the Free Allocation Decision, revise the preliminary total annual amount for the installation concerned in accordance with the methodology applied to determine the preliminary total annual amount prior to the significant capacity reduction.

(5) The regulator must request the registry administrator to withhold the allocation of allowances to the operator of an installation for as long as any of the following circumstances obtains—
(a) the regulator is investigating whether or not there has been a significant capacity reduction in relation to the installation;
(b) the information required under sub-paragraph (2)—
 (i) has not been submitted in accordance with that sub-paragraph; or
 (ii) has been submitted but is insufficient;
(c) the operator has submitted a notice under sub-paragraph (2)(a), but has not yet submitted the statement under sub-paragraph (2)(b);
(d) the regulator is carrying out functions under sub-paragraph (4);
(e) a notification has been given to the European Commission pursuant to paragraph 9(3)(d) and the notified amount of allowances has not yet been approved by the European Commission; or
(f) a notification has been made to the registry administrator under regulation 80(11) but the necessary changes to the national allocation table have not yet been made.

(6) The registry administrator must comply with a request made under sub-paragraph (5).

(7) Where the regulator makes a request under sub-paragraph (5) the regulator—
(a) must notify the operator of the decision to do so as soon as is reasonably practicable; and
(b) may, if the regulator considers it appropriate to do so, subsequently notify the operator that—
 (i) the allocation of allowances will be permanently reduced; or
 (ii) the allowances (or a proportion of them) will be issued.

(8) Where the European Commission approves the preliminary total annual amount of allowances notified under paragraph 9(1), the regulator must treat the installed capacity of the sub-installation after having had a significant capacity reduction as the sub-installation's initial installed capacity when assessing any subsequent significant capacity change.

7 Adjustment of allocation to an installation: permanent cessations of regulated activities

(1) For the purposes of this paragraph, an installation permanently ceases the carrying out of regulated activities where any of the following conditions are met—

(a) the permit or a licence for the installation has been surrendered or revoked, or otherwise ceased to have effect;

(b) the operation of regulated activities at the installation is technically impossible;

(c) the installation was, but is no longer, carrying out regulated activities and it is technically impossible for it to resume doing so;

(d) subject to sub-paragraphs (2) and (3), the operator—

(i) has suspended the carrying out of regulated activities at the installation, and

(ii) the carrying out of regulated activities has not recommenced within the period of 6 months following the date of the suspension.

(2) The operator may apply to the regulator for the period of 6 months mentioned in sub-paragraph (1)(d) to be extended to a period not exceeding 18 months, on the ground that the carrying out of regulated activities at the installation cannot be recommenced within that period of 6 months due to exceptional and unforeseeable circumstances that could not have been avoided even if all due care had been exercised, and were beyond the control of the operator.

(3) Sub-paragraph (1)(d) does not apply to an installation if it is kept in reserve or on standby, or is operated on a seasonal basis, provided that—

(a) the operator holds a permit and a licence for the installation;

(b) it is technically possible to commence the carrying out of regulated activities without making physical changes to the installation; and

(c) regular maintenance of the installation is carried out.

(4) Subject to sub-paragraph (5), no allocation of allowances to an installation may be made for any year following the year in which the installation has permanently ceased the carrying out of regulated activities.

(5) Notwithstanding the provisions of paragraph 2(2)(b), where regulated activities at the installation recommence after the expiry of the period of 6 months following the date of suspension or any longer period allowed pursuant to sub-paragraph (2) ("the relevant period"), the operator may apply for an allocation of allowances under paragraph 2.

(6) This sub-paragraph applies where the operator—

(a) has suspended the carrying out of regulated activities at the installation; and

(b) intends to recommence regulated activities before the expiry of relevant period.

(7) Where sub-paragraph (6) applies, the operator may within a period of one month beginning with the date of suspension apply to the regulator for the suspension to be treated as temporary; and if the application is granted—

(a) allowances may be issued to the installation notwithstanding that the relevant period has not expired; but

(b) such an issue of allowances is without prejudice to sub-paragraph (4) and paragraph 11(1).

(8) An application under sub-paragraph (7) must provide evidence that the carrying out of regulated activities will recommence within the relevant period.

(9) The regulator must request the registry administrator to withhold the allocation of allowances to the operator of an installation for as long as any of the following circumstances obtains—

(a) the regulator is investigating whether or not the installation has permanently ceased the carrying out of regulated activities;
(b) an application under sub-paragraph (7) has been made but the application—
  (i) has not yet been determined, or
  (ii) has been refused and the relevant period has not yet expired;
(c) an application under regulation 12(1) has been made but has not yet been determined;
(d) a notice of surrender or revocation notice has been given but has not yet taken effect;
(e) an appeal against such a notice has been made but has not been determined or withdrawn;
(f) a notification has been made to the registry administrator under regulation 80(11) but the necessary changes to the allocation table have not yet been made.

(10) The registry administrator must comply with a request made under sub-paragraph (9).

(11) Where the regulator makes a request under sub-paragraph (9) the regulator—
(a) must notify the operator of the decision to do so as soon as is reasonably practicable; and
(b) may, if the regulator considers it appropriate to do so, subsequently notify the operator that—
  (i) the allocation of allowances will be permanently reduced; or
  (ii) the allowances (or a proportion of them) will be issued.

(12) In this paragraph—
(a) a "licence" for an installation is a permit in force issued in relation to that installation in accordance with—
  (i) Directive 2008/1/EC of the European Parliament and of the Council concerning integrated pollution prevention and control, as amended for time to time; or
  (ii) Directive 2010/75/EU of the European Parliament and of the Council on industrial emissions (integrated pollution prevention and control), as amended for time to time;
(b) "relevant period" has the meaning given in sub-paragraph (5).

8 Adjustment of allocation to an installation: partial cessation of regulated activities

(1) For the purposes of this paragraph, an installation partially ceases regulated activities where sub-paragraph (2) applies in relation to that installation.

(2) This sub-paragraph applies where one sub-installation of the installation which contributes to—
(a) at least 30% of the final annual amount of allowances allocated to the installation, or
(b) the allocation of more than 50,000 allowances,
reduces its activity level in a given year by at least 50% compared to the activity level originally used for calculating the sub-installation's allocation ("initial activity level").

(3) However, following a partial transfer, sub-paragraph (2) applies as follows—
(a) the amount of allowances transferred to the transferred units, in accordance with paragraph 3(2) of Schedule 4, is to be treated as the final annual amount of allowances allocated to the installation for the purposes of this paragraph; and
(b) the activity level calculated in accordance with paragraph 3(2)(b)(i) of Schedule 4 is to be treated as the initial activity level for the purposes of this paragraph.

(4) Where an installation partially ceases regulated activities—
(a) the operator must notify the regulator that such a reduction in activity level has occurred, stating the amount of that reduction and the sub-installation to which it applies—
  (i) by 31st December in the year in which the reduction occurred, or
  (ii) within one month after the date on which it occurred, if later; and
(b) the regulator must—
  (i) adjust the allocation of allowances in accordance with sub-paragraph (6),
  (ii) revise the preliminary annual number of allowances allocated to each sub-installation; and

(iii) revise the preliminary total annual amount of allowances to be allocated, commencing with the year following the year in which the reduction in activity level occurred.

(5) Where a sub-installation of an installation that contributes as described in sub-paragraph (2)(a) or (b) reduced its activity level in 2012 by at least 50% compared to the initial activity level—

(a) the operator must by 1st February 2013 notify the regulator that such a reduction in activity level has occurred, stating the amount of that reduction and the sub-installation to which it applies; and

(b) the regulator must take the action described in sub-paragraph (4)(b).

(6) Where the activity level of a sub-installation is reduced—

(a) by 50% or more but less than 75% compared to the initial activity level, the operator is entitled to receive a quantity of allowances representing half of the final annual amount of allocated allowances in respect of that sub-installation, commencing with the year following the year during which the reduction took place;

(b) by 75% or more but less than 90% compared to the initial activity level, the operator is entitled to receive a quantity of allowances representing 25% of the final annual amount of allocated allowances in respect of that sub-installation, commencing with the year following the year during which the reduction took place;

(c) by 90% or more, the operator is entitled to no allowances in respect of that sub-installation, commencing with the year following the year during which the reduction took place.

(7) Where, following such reduction, the activity level of a sub-installation subsequently reaches more than—

(a) 50% compared to the initial activity level, the operator is entitled to receive a quantity of allowances equal to the full quantity of the final annual amount of allowances allocated in respect of that sub-installation, commencing with the year following the year during which the activity level exceeded 50%;

(b) 25% compared to the initial activity level, the operator is entitled to receive a quantity of allowances equal to half of the final annual amount of allowances allocated in respect of that sub-installation, commencing with the year following the year during which the activity level exceeded 25%.

(8) Where sub-paragraph (7) applies—

(a) the operator must take the action described in sub-paragraph (4)(a) in relation to the subsequent change; and

(b) the regulator must—

(i) adjust the allocation of allowances in accordance with sub-paragraph (7);

(ii) revise the preliminary annual number of allowances allocated to each sub-installation; and

(iii) revise the preliminary total annual amount of allowances to be allocated, commencing with the year following the year in which the subsequent change occurred.

(9) The regulator must request the registry administrator to withhold the allocation of allowances to the operator of an installation for as long as any of the following circumstances obtains—

(a) the regulator is investigating whether or not the installation has partially ceased regulated activities;

(b) the information required under sub-paragraph (4)—

(i) has not been submitted in accordance with that sub-paragraph; or

(ii) has been submitted but is insufficient;

(c) the regulator is carrying out functions under sub-paragraph (4)(b);

(d) a notification has been given to the European Commission pursuant to paragraph 9(3)(d) and the notified amount of allowances has not yet been approved by it;

(e) a notification has been made to the registry administrator under regulation 80(11) but the necessary changes to the allocation table have not yet been made.

(10) The registry administrator must comply with a request made under sub-paragraph (9).

(11) Where the regulator has made a request under sub-paragraph (9) the regulator—
(a) must notify the operator of the decision to do so as soon as is reasonably practicable; and
(b) may, if the regulator considers it appropriate to do so, subsequently notify the operator that—
 (i) the allocation of allowances will be permanently reduced; or
 (ii) the allowances (or a proportion of them) will be issued.

(12) In this paragraph "activity level" means (subject to sub-paragraph (3)(b)) the activity level used for calculating the sub-installation's allocation in accordance with Article 9 of the Free Allocation Decision (or, where applicable, Article 18).

9 Notification of preliminary annual number of allowances: significant capacity reductions and partial cessation of regulated activities

(1) The regulator must, within 28 days after the date of making a calculation under—
(a) paragraph 6(4)(c) (significant capacity reductions); or
(b) paragraph 8(4)(b) or (8)(b) (partial cessation of regulated activities),
notify the revised preliminary total annual amount of allowances to the persons mentioned in sub-paragraph (3).

(2) A notice given to the operator under paragraph (1) may specify a period within which a fee for making the calculation must be paid.

(3) Those persons are—
(a) the operator;
(b) the authority;
(c) the Secretary of State (where the Secretary of State is not the authority); and
(d) the European Commission, pursuant to Article 24(2) of the Free Allocation Decision.

(4) Where the European Commission notifies the regulator that the revised preliminary total annual amount of allowances is rejected the regulator must, as soon as is reasonably practicable, notify the operator giving the reasons for rejection provided by the European Commission.

10 Calculation of final total annual amount of allowances: significant capacity reductions and partial cessation of regulated activities

(1) Where the European Commission approves the revised preliminary total annual amount of allowances notified under paragraph 9(1), the regulator must calculate the revised final total annual amount of allowances allocated to the installation concerned.

(2) For the purposes of sub-paragraph (1) the final total annual amount is—
(a) the revised preliminary total annual amount notified under paragraph 9(1), but
(b) in the case of a significant capacity reduction, that amount as adjusted by multiplying that number of allowances by the cross-sectoral correction factor under Article 10(9) of the Free Allocation Decision.

(3) The regulator must, as soon as is reasonably practicable, notify the final total annual amount to—
(a) the operator;
(b) the registry administrator;
(c) the authority; and
(d) the Secretary of State (where the Secretary of State is not the authority).

11 Recovery of allowances

(1) This sub-paragraph applies where an operator ("P") has been issued allowances to which P is not entitled as a result, in particular, of—
(a) a failure to notify the regulator of any change to an installation's capacity, activity level or operation;
(b) the installation's allocation not being adjusted in sufficient time to prevent such an over-allocation of allowances;
(c) the installation having permanently ceased the carrying out of regulated activities despite allowances having been issued under paragraph 7(7); or
(d) an error of the regulator or registry administrator.

(2) Where sub-paragraph (1) applies, the regulator must give a notice to P instructing P to return a sum of allowances equal to those to which P is not entitled.

(3) The notice under sub-paragraph (1) must specify—
(a) the number of allowances to which the operator is not entitled;
(b) the reasons why the operator is not entitled to those allowances;
(c) the process by which those allowances must be returned; and
(d) the date by which those allowances must be returned.

(4) An operator must comply with a notice given under sub-paragraph (2).

SCHEDULE 7
ALLOCATION OF AVIATION ALLOWANCES

Regulation 30(a)

1 Purpose of this Schedule

(1) This Schedule sets out the requirements that must be satisfied by a UK administered operator ("P") who wishes to apply for an allocation of aviation allowances issued under Article 3e of the Directive in any trading period other than 2013 to 2020.

(2) Paragraph 10 provides for the recovery of aviation allowances to which a UK administered operator is not entitled, and applies to aviation allowances issued following an application made under Schedule 8 as well as one made under this Schedule.

2 Application for a benchmarking plan

(1) P must apply to the regulator for a plan in accordance with Article 51(2) of the Monitoring and Reporting Regulation (a "benchmarking plan").

(2) That application must contain a plan to monitor tonne-kilometre data from P's aviation activity (together with supporting documents) submitted under Article 12(1) of the Monitoring and Reporting Regulation.

3 Issue of a benchmarking plan

(1) Where P has made an application under paragraph 2 the regulator must, by notice given to P—
(a) issue a benchmarking plan to P; or
(b) where sub-paragraph (2) applies, refuse the application.

(2) This sub-paragraph applies where—
(a) the regulator is not satisfied that the plan proposed in the application complies with the Monitoring and Reporting Regulation; and
(b) P has not agreed to amendments of the plan that so satisfy the regulator.

(3) Where the regulator by notice refuses to issue a benchmarking plan under sub-paragraph (1)(b), the notice must state what changes must be made to the proposed plan for the purposes of any fresh application under paragraph 2.

4 Amendment of a benchmarking plan

(1) P must apply to the regulator to vary P's benchmarking plan where any significant modifications of that plan are necessary by virtue of Articles 14 and 15 of the Monitoring and Reporting Regulation.

(2) Where the regulator varies the plan following an application under paragraph (1), any reference in this paragraph or in paragraph 5 to a benchmarking plan is a reference to the plan as so varied.

5 Monitoring tonne-kilometre data

P must monitor tonne-kilometre data from P's aviation activity carried out in the benchmarking year in accordance with—
(a) the benchmarking plan issued under paragraph 3 (including the written procedures supplementing that plan); and
(b) the Monitoring and Reporting Regulation.

6 Reporting tonne-kilometre data

P must—
(a) prepare a verified report of tonne-kilometre data monitored in accordance with paragraph 5;
(b) ensure that the report complies with the Monitoring and Reporting Regulation and the Verification Regulation; and
(c) make an application for an allocation by submitting the report to the regulator by 31st March in the year after the benchmarking year.

7 Submission of the report to the Secretary of State and the European Commission

(1) Where P has made an application under paragraph 6(c) the regulator must—
(a) grant the application and submit the report to the Secretary of State; or
(b) subject to sub-paragraph (2), refuse the application where the regulator is not satisfied that P has complied with the requirements of this Schedule.

(2) The regulator may grant the application under sub-paragraph (1)(a) where P has otherwise complied with the requirements of this Schedule but failed to comply with the deadline in Article 51(2) of the Monitoring and Reporting Regulation or in paragraph 6(c).

(3) Where the regulator refuses the application under sub-paragraph (1)(b), the notice of determination must state the regulator's reasons for doing so.

(4) The Secretary of State must, by 30th June in the year after the benchmarking year, submit to the European Commission any report submitted under sub-paragraph (1)(a).

8 Publication of aviation allowances

(1) Within the period of 3 months beginning with the date on which the Commission adopts a decision under Article 3e(3) of the Directive in respect of a trading period, the Secretary of State must (in accordance with Article 3e(4)) calculate and publish—
(a) the total allocation of aviation allowances for the period to each UK administered operator whose report was submitted under paragraph 7(4); and
(b) the allocation of aviation allowances to each such UK administered operator for each year of the period.

(2) Sub-paragraph (1) is subject to regulation 47 (national security).

9 Force majeure

(1) Paragraphs 4 to 8 are subject to the provisions of Article 68 of the Monitoring and Reporting Regulation (which apply where a person cannot monitor and report tonne-kilometre data because of serious and unforeseeable circumstances outside that person's control).

(2) The Secretary of State must notify to the registry administrator any revised allocation of aviation allowances published by the Secretary of State under Article 68(3) of that Regulation.

10 Recovery of allowances

(1) This sub-paragraph applies where a UK administered operator ("Q")—
(a) has a duty to return excess aviation allowances under Article 68(3) of the Monitoring and Reporting Regulation; or
(b) has otherwise been issued aviation allowances to which Q is no longer entitled as a result, in particular, of—
(i) Q having ceased to perform an aviation activity; or
(ii) an error of the regulator or registry administrator.

(2) Where sub-paragraph (1) applies, the regulator must give notice to Q instructing Q to return a sum of aviation allowances equal to those to which Q is not entitled.

(3) The notice under sub-paragraph (2) must specify—
(a) the number of aviation allowances to which Q is not entitled;
(b) the reason why Q is not entitled to them;
(c) the process by which they must be returned; and
(d) the date by which they must be returned.

(4) Q must comply with a notice given under sub-paragraph (2).

SCHEDULE 8
ALLOCATION OF AVIATION ALLOWANCES FROM THE SPECIAL RESERVE

Regulation 30(b)

1 Purpose of this Schedule

(1) This Schedule sets out the requirements that must be satisfied by an eligible person ("R") who wishes to apply for an allocation of allowances issued from the special reserve under Article 3f of the Directive in any trading period.

(2) For that purpose, and subject to sub-paragraphs (3) and (4), an eligible person in a trading period is—
(a) a person who becomes a UK aircraft operator after the benchmarking year for that trading period; or
(b) a UK aircraft operator whose tonne-kilometre data in the second calendar year in the trading period exceeds by more than 93.9% its tonne-kilometre data in the benchmarking year for that trading period.

(3) A person is not an eligible person by virtue of sub-paragraph (2)(a) if that person has previously received an allocation of aviation allowances for that trading period.

(4) A person within sub-paragraph (2)(a), or a UK aircraft operator within sub-paragraph (2)(b), who would otherwise qualify as an eligible person by virtue of performing an aviation activity does not so qualify where that aviation activity is in whole or part a continuation of an activity previously performed by another person who is or has been a person falling within the definition of "aircraft operator" in Article 3(o) of the Directive.

2 Application for a benchmarking plan

(1) R must apply to the regulator for a benchmarking plan in accordance with Article 51(2) of the Monitoring and Reporting Regulation.

(2) That application must contain a plan to monitor tonne-kilometre data from R's aviation activity (together with supporting documents) submitted under Article 12(1) of the Monitoring and Reporting Regulation.

3 Issue of a benchmarking plan

(1) Where R has made an application under paragraph 2 the regulator must, by notice given to R—
(a) issue a benchmarking plan to R; or
(b) where sub-paragraph (2) applies, refuse to issue such a plan.

(2) This sub-paragraph applies where—
(a) the regulator is not satisfied that the plan proposed in the application complies with the Monitoring and Reporting Regulation; and
(b) P has not agreed to amendments of the plan that satisfy the regulator.

(3) Where the regulator by notice refuses to issue a benchmarking plan under sub-paragraph (1)(b), the notice must state what changes must be made to the proposed plan for the purposes of any fresh application under paragraph 2.

4 Amendment of a benchmarking plan

(1) R must apply to the regulator to the vary the benchmarking plan where any significant modifications of that plan are necessary by virtue of Articles 14 and 15 of the Monitoring and Reporting Regulation.

(2) Where the regulator varies the plan following an application under sub-paragraph (1), any reference in this paragraph or in paragraph 5 to a benchmarking plan is a reference to the plan as so varied.

5 Monitoring tonne-kilometre data

R must monitor tonne-kilometre data from R's aviation activity carried out in the benchmarking year in accordance with—
(a) the benchmarking plan issued under paragraph 3 (including the written procedures supplementing that plan); and
(b) the Monitoring and Reporting Regulation.

6 Application for an allocation of allowances

(1) R must apply to the regulator by 30th June in the third year of a trading period.

(2) That application must—
(a) contain evidence that R is an eligible person under paragraph 1(2);
(b) include a verified report of R's tonne-kilometre data monitored in accordance with paragraph 5;
(c) ensure that the report complies with the Monitoring and Reporting Regulation and the Verification Regulation; and
(d) where R is eligible by virtue of paragraph 1(2)(b), include evidence of—
(i) the percentage increase in R's tonne-kilometres from the benchmarking year to the second calendar year in the trading period;
(ii) the increase in R's tonne-kilometres from the benchmarking year to the second calendar year in the trading period; and
(iii) the amount in tonne-kilometres by which R exceeds the percentage in paragraph 1(2)(b) in the second calendar year in the trading period.

7 Submission of an application to the Secretary of State and to the European Commission

(1) Where R has made an application under paragraph 6 the regulator must—
(a) grant the application and forward it to the Secretary of State; or
(b) subject to sub-paragraph (2), refuse the application where the regulator is not satisfied that R has complied with the requirements of this Schedule.

(2) The regulator may grant the application under sub-paragraph (1)(a) where R has otherwise complied with the requirements of this Schedule but failed to comply with the deadline in Article 51(2) of the Monitoring and Reporting Regulation or in paragraph 6(1).

(3) Where the regulator refuses the application under sub-paragraph (1)(b), the notice of determination must state the regulator's reasons for doing so.

(4) The Secretary of State must submit an application received under sub-paragraph (1)(a) to the European Commission within 6 months of the deadline in paragraph 6(1).

8 Publication of aviation allowances from the special reserve

(1) Within the period of 3 months beginning with the date on which the Commission adopts a decision under Article 3f(5) of the Directive in respect of a trading period, the Secretary of State must (in accordance with Article 3f(7)) calculate and publish—

(a) the total allocation of aviation allowances for the period from the special reserve to each UK administered operator whose application was submitted under paragraph 7(4); and

(b) the allocation of aviation allowances to each such UK administered operator for each remaining year of the period.

(2) Sub-paragraph (1) is subject to regulation 47 (national security).

SCHEDULE 9
DETENTION AND SALE OF AIRCRAFT

Regulation 39(3)

1 Interpretation

In this Schedule—

"aerodrome" has the meaning given to it in section 105(1) of the Civil Aviation Act 1982;

"aerodrome operator" means the person for the time being having the management or control of an aerodrome;

"aircraft documents" has the meaning given by section 88(10) of the Civil Aviation Act 1982;

"airport charges" means charges payable to the owner or manager of an aerodrome for the use of, or for services provided at, an aerodrome (but does not include charges payable by virtue of section 73 of the Transport Act 2000);

"civil penalty" means any civil penalty which is due under regulation 50, under regulation 21 of the 2009 Regulations or regulation 30 of the 2010 Regulations (even where the failure giving rise to that civil penalty arose before 1st January 2012);

"the court" means—

(a) in relation to England, Wales and Northern Ireland, the High Court; and

(b) in relation to Scotland, the Court of Session;

"defaulting operator" means a person who falls under regulation 39(1)(a) or (b);

"operating ban" means an operating ban imposed under Article 16(10) of the Directive;

"regulator expenses" means any expenses incurred by the regulator in detaining, keeping or selling an aircraft, including—

(a) any sums recovered from the regulator under paragraph 7(2) or regulation 21(2), or any sums under paragraph 2(4)(b) of Schedule 10 that have not been recovered under paragraph 2(5) of that Schedule;

(b) any expenses in connection with the application to the court under paragraph 4; and

(c) any regulator expenses that are deemed to be added by virtue of paragraph 3(2).

2 Sale following detention of aircraft

Where an aircraft has been detained—

(a) under regulation 39(1)(a) and the defaulting operator has not paid the civil penalty and regulator expenses within the period of—

(i) 56 days beginning with the date on which the detention began; or
(ii) 21 days beginning with the date of service of a notice under paragraph 8(2), if later; or

(b) under regulation 39(1)(b) and—
(i) the operating ban has not been lifted within the period of 56 days beginning with the date on which the detention began; and
(ii) the defaulting operator has not paid the regulator expenses,

the regulator may, subject to the following provisions of this Schedule, sell that aircraft.

3 Release of aircraft

(1) The regulator must not detain, or continue to detain, or sell an aircraft if—

(a) following detention, the regulator no longer has reason to believe the defaulting operator is the operator of the aircraft;
(b) in relation to a detention under regulation 39(1)(a), the defaulting operator—
(i) has exercised a right of appeal in respect of the civil penalty for which the aircraft has been detained;
(ii) gives to the regulator, pending the determination or withdrawal of the appeal, sufficient security for the payment of that civil penalty and any other civil penalty that the defaulting operator has not paid; and
(iii) pays to the regulator the regulator expenses;
(c) the defaulting operator or any other person claiming an interest in the aircraft demonstrates to the satisfaction of the regulator that the defaulting operator is no longer entitled to possession of the detained aircraft, or no longer entitled to possession of a part of it, in particular by virtue of the termination of any lease of the aircraft or of any part;
(d) in relation to a detention under regulation 39(1)(a), the defaulting operator pays to the regulator—
(i) the civil penalty for which the aircraft has been detained;
(ii) any other civil penalty that the defaulting operator has not paid; and
(iii) the regulator expenses;
(e) in relation to a detention under regulation 39(1)(b)—
(i) the operating ban imposed on the defaulting operator is lifted; and
(ii) the defaulting operator pays to the regulator any regulator expenses; or
(f) in relation to a detention under regulation 39(1)(b)—
(i) the regulator is satisfied that the aircraft will not be flown from the aerodrome in contravention of the operating ban; and
(ii) the defaulting operator pays to the regulator any regulator expenses.

(2) Where an aircraft has been detained, but subsequently released under sub-paragraph (1)(c), any unpaid regulator expenses incurred in relation to that detention are deemed to be added to any regulator expenses that may subsequently be incurred in relation to an aircraft of which the defaulting operator is the operator.

4 Court procedures

(1) The regulator must not sell an aircraft under paragraph 2 without the leave of the court.

(2) The court must not give leave under sub-paragraph (1) in relation to a detention under regulation 39(1)(a) except where it is satisfied that—

(a) a civil penalty is due to the regulator;
(b) the UK administered operator has not paid the civil penalty to the regulator; and
(c) the regulator is entitled to apply to the court for leave to sell the aircraft.

(3) The court must not give leave under sub-paragraph (1) in relation to a detention under regulation 39(1)(b) except where it is satisfied that—

(a) an operating ban has been imposed on the person who is the operator of the aircraft;

(b) the operating ban has not been lifted before the expiry of the period mentioned in paragraph 2(b); and
(c) the regulator is entitled to apply to the court for leave to sell the aircraft.

(4) Before applying to the court for leave under sub-paragraph (1) the regulator must, in accordance with the procedure set out in paragraph 8—
(a) take steps for bringing the proposed application to the notice of any person who may have an interest in the aircraft; and
(b) afford those persons an opportunity of becoming a party to the proceedings.

(5) Where leave is given under sub-paragraph (1) the regulator must sell the aircraft for the best price that can be reasonably obtained.

(6) Failure to comply with sub-paragraph (4) or (5) does not make a sale void or voidable.

5 Proceeds of sale

(1) The proceeds of any sale under this Schedule must be applied by the regulator in the following order—
(a) in payment of any customs duty which is due in consequence of the aircraft having been brought into the United Kingdom;
(b) in payment of any regulator expenses that remain unpaid;
(c) in payment of any charges in respect of any aircraft operated by the defaulting operator which the court has found to be due by virtue of section 73(1) of the Transport Act 2000;
(d) in payment of any airport charges incurred in respect of the aircraft which are due from the defaulting operator to the person entitled to levy charges in respect of the aerodrome at which the aircraft was detained under regulation 39(1);
(e) in relation to a detention under regulation 39(1)(a), in payment of the civil penalty in respect of which the aircraft was detained and sold;
(f) in payment of any other civil penalty that the defaulting operator has not paid.

(2) The regulator must, after making the payments under sub-paragraph (1), pay any residue from the proceeds of sale to the person or persons whose interests have been divested by reason of the sale.

6 Equipment and documents

(1) The power to detain and sell an aircraft under regulation 39 and this Schedule includes the power to detain and sell equipment and stores carried in the aircraft provided it is the property of the defaulting operator; and for that purpose references to the aircraft include references to any such equipment and stores.

(2) The power of detention under regulation 39 extends to any aircraft documents carried in the aircraft, and any such documents may, if the aircraft is sold under these Regulations, be transferred by the regulator to the purchaser.

7 Assistance of aerodrome operator

(1) An aerodrome operator must provide such reasonable assistance and advice as the regulator may require in connection with any of the regulator's functions under this Schedule.

(2) An aerodrome operator is entitled to recover from the regulator a sum equal to any expense reasonably incurred in providing the regulator with assistance or advice under sub-paragraph (1).

8 Procedure for applying for leave to sell an aircraft

(1) The following procedure applies where the regulator proposes to apply to the court for leave to sell an aircraft under paragraph 4.

(2) At least 21 days before applying to the court the regulator must, unless it is impracticable to so do, serve a notice in accordance with sub-paragraph (5) on—
(a) the person in whose name the aircraft is registered;
(b) any person who appears to the regulator to be the owner of the aircraft;
(c) any person who appears to the regulator to be a charterer of the aircraft whether or not by demise;
(d) any person who appears to the regulator to have the management of the aircraft for the time being;
(e) any person who appears to the regulator to be the operator of the aircraft;
(f) any person who is registered as a mortgagee of the aircraft under an Order in Council made under section 86 of the Civil Aviation Act 1982 or who appears to the regulator to be a mortgagee of the aircraft under the law of any country other than the United Kingdom;
(g) any other person who appears to the regulator to have a proprietary interest in the aircraft or any part of it.

(3) Where a person who has been served with a notice in accordance with sub-paragraph (2) informs the regulator within the period of 14 days beginning with the day following service of the notice of the person's desire to become a party to the proceedings, the regulator must make that person a party to the application.

(4) At the same time as serving any notice under sub-paragraph (2), the regulator must publish a copy of that notice—
(a) in the London Gazette and—
(i) if the aircraft is detained in Scotland, the Edinburgh Gazette, or
(ii) if it is detained in Northern Ireland, the Belfast Gazette; and
(b) in one or more local newspapers circulating in the locality in which the aircraft is detained.

(5) A notice under sub-paragraph (2) must—
(a) state the nationality and registration marks of the aircraft;
(b) state the type of aircraft;
(c) state, as the case may be, the matters mentioned in sub-paragraph (6) or (7);
(d) invite the person to whom the notice is given to inform the regulator within 14 days after the date of service of the notice if the person wishes to become a party to the proceedings on the application.

(6) The matters mentioned in this sub-paragraph are that—
(a) by reason of default in the payment of a civil penalty, the regulator, on a date specified in the notice, detained the aircraft under these Regulations; and
(b) unless payment of the sum so due is made within a period of—
(i) 56 days beginning with the date when the detention began, or
(ii) 21 days after the date of service of the notice, if later,
the regulator may (subject to the provisions of this Schedule) apply to the court for leave to sell the aircraft.

(7) The matters mentioned in this sub-paragraph are that—
(a) by reason of an operating ban having been imposed on the operator of the aircraft under Article 16(10) of the Directive the regulator, on a date specified in the notice, detained the aircraft under these Regulations; and
(b) unless the operating ban has been lifted within the period of 56 days beginning with the date on which the detention began and the operator of the aircraft has paid the regulator expenses by a date specified in the notice, the regulator may (subject to the provisions of this Schedule) apply to the court for leave to sell the aircraft.

(8) A notice under sub-paragraph (2) must be served by the regulator—
(a) delivering it to the person to whom it is to be sent;
(b) leaving it at that person's usual or last known place of business or abode;

(c) sending it, addressed to that person at that person's usual or last known place of business or abode, by a registered post service or by a postal service which provided for the delivery of the notice by post to be recorded; or
(d) if the person to whom it is to be sent is an incorporated company or body, delivering it to the secretary, clerk or other appropriate officer of the company or body at its registered or principal office or sending it, addressed to the secretary, clerk or other officer of the company or body at that office, by a registered post service or by a postal service which provides for the delivery of the notice by post to be recorded.

(9) In sub-paragraph (8), "registered post service" and "postal service" have the meaning given in section 125(1) of the Postal Services Act 2000; and any notice which is sent by a postal service in accordance with that sub-paragraph to a place outside the United Kingdom must be sent by air mail or by some other equally expeditious means.

SCHEDULE 10
AIRCRAFT OPERATING BANS

Regulation 40

1 Application for an operating ban

(1) Where the Secretary of State intends to make a request to the European Commission under Article 16(5) of the Directive to impose an operating ban on a UK administered operator ("A"), the Secretary of State must first—
(a) receive consent from—
 (i) the Scottish Ministers, where SEPA is the regulator;
 (ii) the Welsh Ministers, where A's registered office is in Wales;
 (iii) the Department of the Environment in Northern Ireland, where the chief inspector is the regulator; and
(b) give notice to the regulator.

(2) A notice under sub-paragraph (1)(b) may require relevant information to be provided to the Secretary of State by a deadline specified in the notice, and may require in particular—
(a) evidence that A has not complied with obligations under these Regulations; and
(b) details of any enforcement action against A that has been taken by the regulator.

(3) Following the giving of notice under sub-paragraph (1)(b) and, where applicable, the provision of information under sub-paragraph (2), the Secretary of State must give notice to A.

(4) A notice under sub-paragraph (3) must—
(a) include a copy of any information provided under sub-paragraph (2);
(b) include a copy of the request that the Secretary of State intends to send to the European Commission;
(c) give A an opportunity to make representations before the Secretary of State makes the request; and
(d) set out the deadline by which those representations must be made.

2 Enforcement of an operating ban

(1) Where the European Commission has adopted a decision to impose an operating ban on a person ("P") under Article 16(10) of the Directive, the regulator must take all reasonable steps to ensure that P does not operate a flight that departs from or arrives in the United Kingdom.

(2) The steps a regulator may take under sub-paragraph (1) include—
(a) subject to sub-paragraph (3), issuing to aerodrome operators (or to any other person) any direction that the regulator deems necessary to enforce the ban;
(b) detaining and selling any aircraft of which P is the operator, in accordance with regulation 39(1)(b) and Schedule 9.

(3) Before issuing a direction under sub-paragraph (2)(a) the regulator must receive approval from the authority and (where different) the relevant authority.

(4) A person to whom a direction is issued under sub-paragraph (2)(a)—
(a) must comply with that direction, but
(b) is entitled to recover from the regulator a sum equal to any expense reasonably incurred by that person in complying with the direction.

(5) The regulator is entitled to recover as a civil debt from the operator concerned all sums incurred under sub-paragraph (4).

(6) In sub-paragraph (3) "relevant authority" means, where the principal place of business of the person to be directed is—
(a) in Wales, the Welsh Ministers;
(b) in Scotland, the Scottish Ministers;
(c) in Northern Ireland, the Department of the Environment in Northern Ireland;
(d) not in Wales, Scotland or Northern Ireland, the Secretary of State.

SCHEDULE 11
APPEALS TO THE SCOTTISH MINISTERS

Regulation 78(1) and (3)

PART 1

1

(1) Any person who wishes to appeal to the Scottish Ministers ("the appeal body") under regulation 73(1) against a decision of SEPA must—
(a) give to the appeal body written notice of the appeal together with the documents specified in sub-paragraph (2); and
(b) at the same time, send to the regulator a copy of that notice together with copies of the documents specified in sub-paragraph (2)(a) and (e).

(2) The documents mentioned in sub-paragraph (1) are—
(a) a statement of the grounds of appeal;
(b) a copy of any relevant application;
(c) a copy of any relevant monitoring plan, aviation emissions plan, or benchmarking plan (as defined by regulation 20);
(d) a copy of any relevant correspondence between the appellant and the regulator;
(e) a copy of any notice (or particulars of any deemed refusal) which is the subject matter of the appeal; and
(f) a statement indicating whether the appellant wishes the appeal to be in the form of a hearing or to be disposed of on the basis of written representations.

(3) An appellant may withdraw an appeal by notifying the appeal body in writing and must send a copy of that notification to the regulator.

2

(1) Subject to sub-paragraph (2), notice of appeal in accordance with paragraph 1 is to be given before the expiry of the period of 24 days beginning with the date that the decision takes effect.

(2) The appeal body may in a particular case allow notice of appeal to be given after the expiry of the period in sub-paragraph (1) where they are satisfied that there was good reason for the applicant's failure to bring the appeal in time.

3

(1) The regulator must, within 16 days of receipt of the copy of the notice of appeal sent in accordance with paragraph 1, give notice of it to any person who appears to the regulator to have a particular interest in the subject matter of the appeal.

(2) A notice under sub-paragraph (1) must—
(a) state that notice of appeal has been given;
(b) state the name of the appellant;
(c) describe the decision or notice to which the appeal relates;
(d) state that if a hearing is to be held wholly or partly in public, an interested party will be notified of the date of the hearing; and
(e) state that an affected party may request to be heard at a hearing.

(3) An interested party may request the regulator to provide a copy of the documents set out in paragraph 1(2) for the purposes of the appeal only and where such a request is made the regulator must provide the documents as soon as is reasonably practicable.

(4) An interested party—
(a) may make representations with respect to the appeal to the appeal body in writing within 16 days beginning with the date of the notice under sub-paragraph (1);
(b) must, when making those representations, state whether or not their civil rights will be determined in the appeal, and, if so, which civil rights will be determined.

(5) The appeal body must provide a copy of any representations made under sub-paragraph (4) to the appellant and the regulator.

(6) The regulator must, within 8 days of sending a notice under sub-paragraph (1), notify the appeal body of the persons to whom and the date on which the notice was sent.

(7) The appeal body must, as soon as possible after receiving representations under sub-paragraph (4), determine whether an interested party is an affected party.

(8) In the event of an appeal being withdrawn, the regulator must give notice of the withdrawal to all interested parties.

4

(1) Before determining an appeal, the appeal body may afford the appellant, the regulator and any affected party an opportunity of appearing before and being heard by a person appointed by the appeal body (the "person holding the hearing") and it must do so in any case where a request is made by the appellant, the regulator or any affected party.

(2) A hearing held under sub-paragraph (1) may, if the person holding the hearing so decides, be held wholly or partly in private.

(3) Where the appeal body causes a hearing to be held under sub-paragraph (1) it must give the appellant, the regulator and any affected party at least 24 days notice (or such shorter period of notice as they may agree) of the date, time and place fixed for the holding of the hearing.

(4) In the case of a hearing which is to be held wholly or partly in public, the appeal body must, at least 24 days before the date fixed for the holding of the hearing—
(a) publish a copy of the notice referred to in sub-paragraph (3) in a newspaper circulating in the locality in which the installation is operated, or (as the case may be) in an appropriate international aviation publication; and
(b) serve a copy of that notice on every interested party who has made representations in writing to the appeal body.

(5) The appeal body may vary the date fixed for the holding of any hearing and sub-paragraphs (3) and (4) apply to the variation of a date as they applied to the date originally fixed.

(6) The appeal body may vary the time or place for the holding of a hearing and must give such notice of any such variation as appears to the appeal body to be reasonable.

(7) The persons entitled to be heard at a hearing are the appellant, the regulator and any affected party.

(8) Nothing in sub-paragraph (7) prevents the person holding the hearing from permitting any other persons to be heard at the hearing and such permission must not be unreasonably withheld.

(9) After the conclusion of a hearing, the person holding the hearing must make a report in writing to the appeal body which must include that person's conclusions and recommendations, or decision not to make any recommendation and in all cases the reasons supporting the report.

(10) Paragraph 13(5) applies to hearings held under this paragraph as if references to the appointed person in that paragraph were references to the person holding the hearing under this paragraph.

5

(1) Where an appeal under regulation 73(1) is to be disposed of on the basis of written representations, the regulator must submit any written representations to the appeal body not later than 24 days after receiving a copy of the documents mentioned in paragraph 1(2)(a) and (e).

(2) The appellant must make any further representations by way of reply to any representations from the regulator not later than 16 days after the date of submission of those representations by the regulator.

(3) Any representations made by the appellant or the regulator must bear the date on which they are submitted to the appeal body.

(4) When the regulator or the appellant submits any representations to the appeal body they must at the same time send a copy of them to the other party.

(5) The appeal body must send to the appellant and the regulator a copy of any representations made to the appeal body by any interested party and must allow the appellant and the regulator a period of not fewer than 16 days in which to make representations on them.

(6) The appeal body may in a particular case—
(a) set earlier or later time limits than those mentioned in this Part;
(b) require or permit exchanges of representations between the parties in addition to those mentioned in sub-paragraphs (1) and (2).

6

(1) The appeal body must give notice to the appellant of the determination of the appeal and must provide the appellant with a copy of any report mentioned in paragraph 4(9).

(2) The appeal body must at the same time send—
(a) a copy of the documents mentioned in sub-paragraph (1) to the regulator; and
(b) a copy of the determination of the appeal to any interested party who made representations to the appeal body and, if a hearing was held, to any other person who made representations at the hearing.

7

Where an appeal is made against the refusal of an application for an allocation under Schedule 7 or Schedule 8, the appeal body must, where practicable, determine the appeal before the deadline in paragraph 7(4) of Schedule 7 or Schedule 8, as appropriate.

8

Where the appeal body's determination of an appeal is quashed in proceedings before any court, the appeal body—

(a) must send to the persons notified of the determination under paragraph 6 a statement of the matters with respect to which further representations are invited for the purposes of the further consideration of the appeal;
(b) must afford to those persons the opportunity of making, within 31 days of the date of the statement, written representations in respect of those matters; and
(c) may, as the appeal body thinks fit, cause a hearing to be held or reopened and, if it does so, paragraphs 4(2) to (10) apply to the hearing or the reopened hearing as they apply to a hearing held under paragraph 4(1),

and paragraph 6 applies to the re-determination of the appeal as it applies to the determination of an appeal.

9

In this Part—
(a) "affected party" means an interested party—
  (i) who has stated in representations under paragraph 3(4) that their civil rights will be determined in an appeal; and
  (ii) whose civil rights the appeal body is satisfied will be so determined;
(b) "interested party" means a person notified under paragraph 3(1).

PART 2

10

In this Part—
"appointed person" means a person appointed under regulation 78(2)(a);
"appointment", in the case of any appointed person, means appointment under regulation 78(2)(a).

11

An appointment must be in writing and—
(a) may relate to any particular appeal, matters or questions specified in the appointment or to appeals, matters or questions of a description so specified;
(b) may provide for any function to which it relates to be exercisable by the appointed person either unconditionally or subject to the fulfilment of such conditions as may be specified in the appointment; and
(c) may, by notice in writing to the appointed person, be revoked at any time by the appeal body in respect of any appeal, matter or question which has not been determined by the appointed person before that time.

12

Subject to the provisions of this Part, an appointed person, in relation to any appeal, matter or question to which the appointed person's appointment relates, has the same powers and duties as the appeal body, other than any function of appointing a person for the purpose—
(a) of enabling persons to appear before and be heard by the person so appointed; or
(b) of referring any question or matter to that person.

13

(1) If the appellant, the regulator or any person whose civil rights are to be determined in the appeal expresses a wish to appear before and be heard by the appointed person, the appointed person must give them an opportunity of appearing and being heard.

(2) Whether or not a person under sub-paragraph (1) has asked for an opportunity to appear and be heard, the appointed person—

(a) may hold a local inquiry or other hearing in connection with the appeal, matter or question; and
(b) must if the appeal body so directs, hold a local inquiry in connection with an appeal, matter or question.

(3) Where an appointed person holds a local inquiry or other hearing by virtue of this Part, an assessor may be appointed by the appeal body to sit with the appointed person at the inquiry or hearing and advise the appeal body on any matters arising, notwithstanding that the appointed person is to determine the appeal, matter or question.

(4) Subject to sub-paragraphs (5) and (6), the costs of a local inquiry held under this Part must be defrayed by the appeal body.

(5) Subsections (3) to (8) of section 210 of the Local Government (Scotland) Act 1973 (which relates to the costs of and holding of local inquiries) apply to hearings held under this Part by an appointed person as they apply to inquiries held under that section, but with the following modifications, that is to say—
(a) with the substitution in subsection (3) (notice of inquiry) for the reference to the person appointed to hold the inquiry of a reference to the appointed person;
(b) with the substitution in subsection (4) (evidence) for the reference to the person appointed to hold the inquiry and, in paragraph (b), the reference to the person holding the inquiry of references to the appointed person;
(c) with the substitution in subsection (6) (expenses of witnesses etc) for the references to the Minister causing the inquiry to be held of a reference to the appointed person or the Scottish Ministers;
(d) with the substitution in subsection (7) (expenses)—
  (i) for the first reference to the Minister of a reference to the Scottish Ministers; and
  (ii) for the second reference to the Minister of a reference to the appointed person or the Scottish Ministers;
(e) with the substitution in subsection (7A) (recovery of entire administrative expense)—
  (i) for the first reference to the Minister of a reference to the appointed person or the Scottish Ministers;
  (ii) in paragraph (a), for the reference to the Minister of a reference to the Scottish Ministers; and
  (iii) in paragraph (b), for the reference to the Minister holding the inquiry of a reference to the Scottish Ministers;
(f) with the substitution in subsection (7B) (power to prescribe daily amount)—
  (i) for the first reference to the Minister of a reference to the Scottish Ministers;
  (ii) in paragraphs (a) and (c), for the references to the person appointed to hold the inquiry of references to the appointed person; and
  (iii) in paragraph (d), for the reference to the Minister of a reference to the appointed person or the Scottish Ministers; and
(g) with the substitution in subsection (8) (certification of expenses)—
  (i) for the words "the Minister has", of the words "the Scottish Ministers have";
  (ii) for the reference to him and the reference to the Crown of references to the appointed person or the Scottish Ministers.

14

(1) Where—
(a) under paragraph 11(c) the appointment of the appointed person is revoked in respect of any appeal, matter or question, and
(b) the appeal body does not itself propose to determine that appeal, matter or question,
the appeal body must appoint another person under regulation 78(2)(a) to determine the appeal, matter or question.

(2) Where such a new appointment is made, the consideration of the appeal, matter or question, or any hearing in connection with it, must be begun afresh.

15

(1) Anything done or omitted to be done by an appointed person in, or in connection with, the exercise of any function to which the appointment relates is for all purposes to be treated as done or omitted to be done by the appeal body in its capacity as such.

(2) Sub-paragraph (1) does not apply—

(a) for the purposes of so much of any contract made between the appeal body and the appointed person as relates to the exercise of the function; or

(b) for the purposes of any criminal proceedings brought in respect of anything done or omitted to be done by an appointed person in, or in connection with, the exercise or purported exercise of any function to which the appointment relates.

SCHEDULE 12
APPEALS (NORTHERN IRELAND)

Regulation 78(4)

1

(1) A person who wishes to appeal to the Planning Appeals Commission ("the appeals commission") under regulation 73(1) against a decision of the chief inspector must give to the appeals commission written notice of the appeal together with a statement of the grounds of appeal.

(2) The appeals commission must as soon as is reasonably practicable send to the regulator a copy of that notice and that statement.

(3) An appellant may withdraw an appeal by notifying the appeals commission; and the appeals commission must as soon as is reasonably practicable notify the regulator of that withdrawal.

2

Notice of appeal in accordance with paragraph 1 is to be given before the expiry of the period of 47 days beginning with the date on which the decision takes effect.

3

(1) The appeals commission must determine the appeal and paragraphs (1), (3), (4) and (5) of Article 111 of the Planning (Northern Ireland) Order 1991 apply in relation to the determination of the appeal as they apply in relation to the determination of an appeal under that Order.

(2) The appeals commission must determine the process for determining appeals taking into account any requests of either party to the appeal.

4

An appeal under this Schedule must be accompanied by a fee; and Article 127(2)(b) of the Planning (Northern Ireland) Order 1991 has effect as if the reference to an appeal under that Order included a reference to an appeal under these Regulations.

ENERGY PERFORMANCE OF BUILDINGS (ENGLAND AND WALES) REGULATIONS 2012

SI 2012/3118

PART 1
INTRODUCTORY

1 Citation, application, extent and commencement

(1) These Regulations may be cited as the Energy Performance of Buildings (England and Wales) Regulations 2012.

(2) Subject to regulation 5 and any other exemptions in these Regulations, and notwithstanding section 4 of the Building Act 1984, these Regulations apply to all buildings including buildings which are exempt from building regulations by virtue of that section.

(3) These Regulations extend to England and Wales.

(4) These Regulations shall come into force on 9th January 2013.

2 Interpretation

(1) In these Regulations—

"accreditation scheme" means a scheme approved by the Secretary of State in accordance with—
- (a) regulation 22; or
- (b) regulation 30 of the Building Regulations 2010;

"air-conditioning system" means a combination of all the components required to provide a form of air treatment in which the temperature is controlled or can be lowered, and includes systems which combine such air treatment with the control of ventilation, humidity and air cleanliness;

"asset rating" means a numerical indicator of the amount of energy estimated to meet the different needs associated with a standardised use of a building, calculated according to the methodology approved by the Secretary of State pursuant to regulation 24 of the Building Regulations 2010;

"authorised recipient" means—
- (a) either House of Parliament (or a member or officer thereof);
- (b) a government department;
- (c) a person or body (other than a government department or the Welsh Ministers) to which section 6 of the National Audit Act 1983 applies;
- (d) the Welsh Ministers;
- (e) the National Assembly for Wales;
- (f) the Scottish Parliament, the Scottish Executive, an office-holder in the Scottish Administration or a Scottish Public Authority;
- (g) the Northern Ireland Assembly or a Northern Ireland Department;
- (h) a county council, district council or parish council in England;
- (i) a London borough council;
- (j) the Common Council of the City of London;
- (k) the Greater London Authority;
- (l) a local authority within the meaning of section 61 of the Local Government in Scotland Act 2003;

(m) a local authority within the meaning of section 175 of the Local Government (Wales) Measure 2011;
(n) a council of a district or borough within the meaning of the Local Government Act (Northern Ireland) 1972;
(o) a university, including a university college (or any institution in the nature of a college in a university) or a school or hall of a university;
(p) a provider of higher education as defined in section 579(1) of the Education Act 1996 ("the 1996 Act") (other than one mentioned in paragraph (o) above);
(q) a provider of further education as defined in section 2(3) to (5) of the 1996 Act;
(r) a charity whose purposes include—
(i) the conduct of research into the earth's climate or environment or research into the construction, design or use of buildings, or
(ii) the promotion of energy efficiency in buildings;
(s) a registered provider of social housing;
(t) a person who operates an accreditation scheme approved by the Secretary of State under regulation 22;
(u) a green deal relevant person;
(v) the holder of a licence under section 6(1)(c) or (d) of the Electricity Act 1989 (distribution and supply licences) which has been modified by the Secretary of State under section 41(1) of the Energy Act 2008 (power to amend licence conditions etc: feed-in tariffs); and
(w) a person (other than a natural person) who is certificated under the scheme known as the "Microgeneration Certification Scheme";

"building" means a roofed construction having walls, for which energy is used to condition the indoor climate;
"building envelope" means the integrated elements of a building which separate its interior from the outdoor environment;
"building unit" means a section, floor or apartment within a building which is designed or altered to be used separately;
"bulk access data" means any data entered onto a register as required by regulation 27(2);
"display energy certificate" means a certificate which complies with regulation 15;
"dwelling" means a building or part of a building occupied or intended to be occupied as a separate dwelling;
"energy assessor" means an individual who is a member of an accreditation scheme;
"energy from renewable sources" means energy from renewable non-fossil sources, namely wind, solar, aerothermal, geothermal, hydrothermal and ocean energy, hydropower, biomass, landfill gas, sewage treatment plant gas and biogases;
"energy performance certificate" means a certificate which—
(a) in the case of a certificate entered on the register before 9th January 2013 complied with the requirements of regulation 11(1) of the Energy Performance of Buildings (Certificates and Inspections) (England and Wales) Regulations 2007;
(b) in the case of a certificate entered on the register on or after 9th January 2013 complies with the requirements of regulation 9(1) of these Regulations; or
(c) complies with the requirements of regulation 29 of the Building Regulations 2010;

"general access data" means information that is required by these Regulations to be included in an energy performance certificate, a display energy certificate, an inspection report, or a recommendation report;
"green deal plan" means an energy plan which is a green deal plan in accordance with section 1(3) of the Energy Act 2011;

"green deal relevant person" means a person who, after the coming into force of framework regulations made under section 3(1) of the Energy Act 2011—
(a) is authorised by the Secretary of State to act as a green deal provider pursuant to those regulations,
(b) is a body specified or authorised for the purposes of subsection (1)(a) of that section, or
(c) operates a scheme for the purpose of assessing whether persons are qualified to act as advisors in relation to green deal plans;

"inspection report" means a report issued by an energy assessor in accordance with regulation 19(1);

"keeper of the register" means the Secretary of State, or the person keeping a register on the Secretary of State's behalf;

"nominated date", in relation to a display energy certificate, means a date no later than three months after the end of the period over which the operational rating is calculated, which is nominated by the energy assessor who issued the certificate;

"operational rating" means a numeric indicator of the amount of energy consumed during the occupation of the building over a period of 12 months ending no earlier than three months before the nominated date, calculated according to the methodology approved by the Secretary of State for the purposes of regulation 24 of the Building Regulations 2010;

"penalty charge notice" means a notice given pursuant to regulation 36;

"personal data" has the meaning given in section 1(1) of the Data Protection Act 1998;

"register" means a register required to be maintained under regulation 27;

"relevant person" (other than in the phrase "green deal relevant person") means—
(a) in relation to a building which is to be sold, the seller;
(b) in relation to a building which is to be rented out, the prospective landlord;
(c) in relation to an air-conditioning system, the person who has control of the operation of the system; and
(d) in relation to a building which is constructed, the person who carries out the construction;

"report reference number" means the unique number assigned by the keeper of the register to each energy performance certificate or display energy certificate;

"total useful floor area" means the gross floor area as measured in accordance with the guidance issued from time to time by the Royal Institution of Chartered Surveyors or by any body replacing that Institution.

3 Meaning of "prospective buyer or tenant"

A person becomes a prospective buyer or tenant in relation to a building when he or she—
(a) requests any information about the building from the relevant person or the relevant person's agent for the purpose of deciding whether to buy or rent the building;
(b) makes a request to view the building for the purpose of deciding whether to buy or rent the building; or
(c) makes an offer, whether oral or written, to buy or rent the building.

4 Recommendation reports

(1) In these Regulations, a "recommendation report" means recommendations made by an energy assessor for the cost-effective improvement of the energy performance of a building or building unit.

(2) A recommendation report made on or after 9th January 2013 must include—
(a) recommended cost-effective measures that could be carried out in connection with a major renovation of the building envelope or technical building systems;

(b) recommended cost-effective measures for individual building elements that could be carried out without the necessity for a major renovation of the building envelope or technical building systems;

(c) an indication as to how the owner or tenant can obtain more detailed information about improving the energy efficiency of the building, including more detailed information about the cost-effectiveness of the recommendations; and

(d) information on the steps to be taken to implement the recommendations.

(3) Any cost-effective measure which the energy assessor recommends must be technically feasible for the building to which the recommendation report relates.

(4) A recommendation report made on or after 9th January 2013 ceases to be valid at the end of the following periods—

(a) for a report which is included in an energy performance certificate, ten years from the date of that certificate;

(b) for a report which is required to be held in respect of the building under regulation 14(3)(a)—

  (i) where the nominated date applying to the report is before 9th January 2013, seven years, or

  (ii) where the nominated date applying to the report is on or after 9th January 2013, ten years.

(5) In this regulation—

(a) "building envelope" has the meaning given in regulation 29A(4) of the Building Regulations 2010.

(b) "major renovation" means the renovation of a building where more than 25% of the surface area of the building envelope undergoes renovation; and

(c) "technical building systems" means technical equipment for the heating, cooling, ventilation, hot water, lighting (or for any combination thereof) of a building or building unit.

PART 2
DUTIES RELATING TO ENERGY PERFORMANCE CERTIFICATES

5 Application of Part 2

(1) This Part does not apply to—

(a) buildings officially protected as part of a designated environment or because of their special architectural or historical merit, in so far as compliance with certain minimum energy performance requirements would unacceptably alter their character or appearance;

(b) buildings used as places of worship and for religious activities;

(c) temporary buildings with a time of use of two years or less;

(d) industrial sites, workshops and non-residential agricultural buildings with low energy demand;

(e) non-residential agricultural buildings which are in use by a sector covered by a national sectoral agreement on energy performance;

(f) residential buildings which are used or intended to be used—

  (i) for less than four months of the year, or

  (ii) for a limited annual time of use and with an expected energy consumption of less than 25% of what would be the result of all-year use; and

(g) stand-alone buildings with a total useful floor area of less than $50m^2$.

(2) Nothing in this Part requires an energy performance certificate to be given or made available to a prospective buyer or tenant at any time before the construction of the building has been completed.

6 Energy performance certificates on sale and rent

(1) Subject to regulation 8, this regulation applies where a building is to be sold or rented out.

(2) The relevant person shall make available free of charge a valid energy performance certificate to any prospective buyer or tenant—

(a) at the earliest opportunity; and

(b) in any event no later than whichever is the earlier of—

(i) in the case of a person who requests information about the building, the time at which the relevant person first makes available any information in writing about the building to the person; or

(ii) in the case of a person who makes a request to view the building, the time at which the person views the building.

(3) Paragraph (2) does not apply if the relevant person believes on reasonable grounds that the prospective buyer or tenant—

(a) is unlikely to have sufficient means to buy or rent the building;

(b) is not genuinely interested in buying or renting a building of a general description which applies to the building; or

(c) is not a person to whom the relevant person is likely to be prepared to sell or rent out the building.

(4) Nothing in paragraph (3) authorises the doing of anything which constitutes an unlawful act of discrimination.

(5) The relevant person must ensure that a valid energy performance certificate has been given free of charge to the person who ultimately becomes the buyer or tenant.

7 Energy performance certificates on marketing

(1) Subject to regulation 8, this regulation applies where—

(a) a building is to be sold or rented out; and

(b) no valid energy performance certificate is available for that building.

(2) Before the building is put on the market, the relevant person must secure that an energy performance certificate is commissioned for the building.

(3) Before marketing the building, a person acting on behalf of the relevant person must be satisfied that an energy performance certificate has been commissioned for the building.

(4) The relevant person and a person acting on behalf of the relevant person must use all reasonable efforts to secure that a valid energy performance certificate is obtained for the building before the end of a period of 7 days starting with the day on which the building was first put on the market.

(5) Where any person subject to the duty in paragraph (4) is unable, despite using all reasonable efforts, to secure that a valid energy performance certificate is obtained for the building before the end of the 7 day period specified in that paragraph, the person shall secure that the certificate is obtained before the end of the period of 21 days immediately following the 7 day period.

(6) In this regulation—

(a) "the market" means the property market in England and Wales;

(b) a building is put on the market when the fact that it is or may become available for sale or rent is, with the intention of marketing the building, first made public in England and Wales by or on behalf of the relevant person;

(c) a fact is made public when it is advertised or otherwise communicated (in whatever form and by whatever means) to the public or to a section of the public;
(d) an energy performance certificate is commissioned when a request is made—
 (i) which is properly addressed to an energy assessor who is accredited to produce energy performance certificates for the category of building in question, and
 (ii) which is in such form, contains all such information and is accompanied by such payment or undertaking to make such payment as is usually necessary to obtain a certificate.

8 Buildings to be demolished

(1) Regulations 6 and 7 do not apply in relation to a dwelling which is to be sold or rented out where the relevant person can demonstrate that—
(a) the dwelling is suitable for demolition;
(b) the resulting site is suitable for redevelopment;
(c) all the relevant planning permissions, listed building consents and conservation area consents exist in relation to the demolition; and
(d) in relation to the redevelopment—
 (i) either outline planning permission or planning permission exists, or both; and
 (ii) where relevant, listed building consent exists.

(2) Regulation 6 does not apply in relation to any prospective buyer or tenant of a building other than a dwelling which is to be sold or rented out where—
(a) the relevant person can demonstrate that—
 (i) the building is to be sold or rented out with vacant possession;
 (ii) the building is suitable for demolition; and
 (iii) the resulting site is suitable for redevelopment; and
(b) the relevant person believes on reasonable grounds that the prospective buyer or tenant intends to demolish the building.

(3) Regulation 7 does not apply in relation to a building other than a dwelling which is to be sold or rented out where the relevant person can demonstrate that—
(a) the building is to be sold or rented out with vacant possession;
(b) the building is suitable for demolition;
(c) the resulting site is suitable for redevelopment;
(d) all the relevant planning permissions, listed building consents and conservation area consents exist in relation to the demolition; and
(e) in relation to the development—
 (i) either outline planning permission or planning permission exists, or both; and
 (ii) where relevant, listed building consent exists.

9 Energy performance certificates

(1) An energy performance certificate entered on the register on or after 9th January 2013 must—
(a) express the asset rating of the building in a way approved by the Secretary of State under regulation 24 of the Building Regulations 2010;
(b) include a reference value such as a current legal standard or benchmark;
(c) be issued by an energy assessor who is accredited to produce energy performance certificates for the category of building to which the certificate relates;
(d) include a recommendation report unless there is no reasonable potential for energy performance improvements compared to the energy performance requirements in force;

(e) include the following information—
   (i) the reference number under which the set of data from which the certificate may be produced has been entered onto the register in accordance with regulation 27;
   (ii) the address of the building;
   (iii) an estimate of the total useful floor area of the building; and
   (iv) the date on which it was issued; and
(f) be valid in accordance with paragraph (2).

(2) An energy performance certificate is only valid for the purposes of this Part if—
(a) it was entered on the register no more than 10 years before the date on which it is made available; and
(b) no other energy performance certificate for the building has since been entered on the register.

(3) An energy performance certificate must not contain any information or data (except for the address of the building) from which a living individual (other than the energy assessor or his employer) can be identified.

(4) Certification for building units on or after 9th January 2013 may be based—
(a) for a non-residential building, on a common certification of the whole building for blocks with a common heating system; or
(b) on the assessment of another representative apartment or unit in the same block..

(5) Certification on or after 9th January 2013 for a building which consists of a single dwelling may be based on the assessment of another representative building of similar design and size with a similar actual energy performance quality if such correspondence is guaranteed by the energy assessor issuing the energy performance certificate.

10 Display of energy performance certificates

(1) This regulation applies to a building, other than a dwelling, which satisfies all the following requirements—
(a) it has a total useful floor area of more than $500m^2$;
(b) it is frequently visited by the public; and
(c) an energy performance certificate has been made available in accordance with—
   (i) regulation 6, or
   (ii) regulation 29(2) of the Building Regulations 2010.

(2) In a building to which this regulation applies, the energy performance certificate must be valid, and must be displayed in a prominent place clearly visible to members of the public who visit the building.

11 Statement of energy performance indicator

(1) This regulation applies to—
(a) a building having a valid energy performance certificate
(b) a building unit in such a building, and
(c) a building unit having a valid energy performance certificate.

(2) Where a building or building unit to which this regulation applies is offered for sale or rent on or after 9th January 2013, the asset rating of the building expressed in the energy performance certificate must be stated in any advertisement of the sale or rental in commercial media.

12 Production of copies of energy performance certificates

Where this Part requires a relevant person to give or make available a valid energy performance certificate to any person, it is sufficient for the relevant person to give or make available a copy of a valid certificate.

13 Electronic production of energy performance certificates

Where regulation 6(2) or 6(5) requires a valid energy performance certificate to be given or made available to any person, the certificate may be given or made available electronically if the intended recipient consents to receiving the certificate electronically.

PART 3
DISPLAY ENERGY CERTIFICATES

14 Duties relating to display energy certificates and recommendation reports

(1) This regulation applies on and after the specified date to buildings occupied by public authorities and frequently visited by the public.

(2) In this regulation the specified date is—
(a) for buildings with a total useful floor area of over $500m^2$, 9th January 2013; and
(b) for buildings with a total useful floor area of between $250m^2$ and less than $500m^2$, 9th July 2015.

(3) Every occupier of a building to which this regulation applies must—
(a) have in its possession or control at all times a valid recommendation report relating to the building unless there is no reasonable potential for energy performance improvements compared to the energy performance requirements in force; and
(b) display at all times a valid display energy certificate in a prominent place clearly visible to members of the public who visit the building.

(4) A display energy certificate for a building to which this regulation applies is valid for the following period—
(a) 12 months beginning with the nominated date where the total useful floor area of the building is over $1,000m^2$; or
(b) 10 years beginning with the nominated date in the case of any other building.

15 Display energy certificates

A display energy certificate must—
(a) subject to regulation 16, express the operational rating of the building in a way approved by the Secretary of State under regulation 24 of the Building Regulations 2010;
(b) show the operational ratings for the building which were expressed in any certificates displayed by the occupier during the two years before the nominated date;
(c) include a reference value such as a current legal standard or benchmark;
(d) be issued by an energy assessor who is accredited to produce display energy certificates for that category of building;
(e) include the following information—
(i) the reference number under which the set of data from which the certificate may be produced has been entered onto the register in accordance with regulation 27;
(ii) the address of the building;

(iii) the total useful floor area of the building;
(iv) the name of the energy assessor who issued it;
(v) the name and address of the energy assessor's employer, or, if he is self-employed, the name under which he trades and his address;
(vi) the date on which it was issued;
(vii) the nominated date; and
(viii) the name of the approved accreditation scheme of which the energy assessor is a member.

16 Change of occupier

Regulation 15(a) does not apply in relation to a display energy certificate which is displayed by an occupier of a building at any time before that occupier has been in occupation of the building for 15 months.

PART 4
INSPECTION OF AIR-CONDITIONING SYSTEMS

17 Application and interpretation of Part 4

(1) This Part applies to air-conditioning systems with an effective rated output of more than 12kW.

(2) Where the relevant person has the power to control the temperature of more than one individual air-conditioning unit in a building, each unit shall be considered to be a component of a single air-conditioning system for the purposes of paragraph (1).

(3) In this Part, "effective rated output" means the maximum calorific output specified and guaranteed by the manufacturer of the system as being deliverable during continuous operation while complying with the useful efficiency indicated by the manufacturer.

18 Inspections of air-conditioning systems

(1) It is the duty of the relevant person in relation to an air-conditioning system to which this Part applies to ensure that the system is inspected by an energy assessor at regular intervals not exceeding five years.

(2) The first inspection of the system must take place before the relevant date.

(3) In this regulation, "the relevant date"—
(a) where the system is first put into service on or after 1st January 2008, means the last day of the period of five years beginning with the date on which the system is first put into service; and
(b) where paragraph (a) does not apply—
(i) in the case of a system with an effective rated output of more than 250kW, means 4th January 2009; or
(ii) in the case of a system with an effective rated output of more than 12kW, means 4th January 2011.

19 Reports

(1) Where an energy assessor undertakes an inspection of the system he must make a written report of the inspection and give it to the relevant person as soon as practicable after completing the inspection.

(2) The inspection report must include an assessment of the air-conditioning efficiency and the sizing of the system compared to the cooling requirements of the building, and

contain appropriate advice on possible improvements to the system, replacement of the system and alternative solutions.

(3) The inspection report must be in a form including the following information—

(a) the reference number under which the set of data from which the report may be produced has been entered onto the register in accordance with regulation 27;

(b) the address of the building in which the system is located;

(c) the name of the energy assessor;

(d) the name and address of the energy assessor's employer, or, if such a person is self-employed, the name under which that person trades and their address;

(e) the date on which the inspection occurred; and

(f) the name of the approved accreditation scheme of which the energy assessor is a member.

20 Keeping of records etc

(1) The relevant person must keep the most recent inspection report made by an energy assessor pursuant to regulation19.

(2) Where the relevant person changes, the previous relevant person must give to the new relevant person any inspection report kept by him under this regulation.

21 Changes of relevant person

Where—

(a) the relevant person changes; and

(b) the new relevant person is not given any inspection report,

the new relevant person must ensure that the system is inspected within three months of the day on which he becomes the relevantperson.

PART 5
ENERGY ASSESSORS

22 Accreditation schemes

(1) An energy assessor must be a member of an accreditation scheme approved by the Secretary of State.

(2) The terms of approval of any accreditation scheme may be limited in relation to—

(a) the categories of building for which members may produce certificates; and

(b) the types of air-conditioning systems members may inspect.

(3) Before approving an accreditation scheme the Secretary of State must be satisfied that the scheme contains adequate provision—

(a) for ensuring that members of the scheme carry out consistent and accurate energy assessments in an independent manner;

(b) for ensuring that members of the scheme are fit and proper persons who are qualified (by their education, training and experience) to carry out energy assessments;

(c) for requiring members of the scheme to prepare energy performance certificates, display energy certificates, recommendation reports and inspection reports using a standard form for each type of document;

(d) for ensuring that a code is produced and published as regards the conduct required of its members;

(e) for indemnity arrangements in relation to relevant person and prospective or actual buyers or tenants;

(f) for facilitating the resolution of complaints against members of the scheme;
(g) for requiring the sets of data from which may be produced energy performance certificates, display energy certificates, recommendation reports and inspection reports prepared by members of the scheme to be entered onto the relevant register maintained by the Secretary of State pursuant to regulation 27; and
(h) for the keeping of a register of the members of the scheme.

23 Related party disclosures

An energy assessor must include in an energy performance certificate or inspection report a declaration of any personal or business relationship (other than in relation to producing the certificate or inspection report) that he has with—
(a) the person who commissioned the certificate or inspection report;
(b) any person on whose behalf the certificate or inspection report was commissioned; and
(c) any person who he believes—
  (i) has or may have a personal or business relationship with a person referred to in paragraph (a) or (b); or
  (ii) has or may have an interest in the building.

24 Duty of care

(1) Energy assessors must carry out energy assessments with reasonable care and skill.

(2) The duty imposed by paragraph (1) shall be enforceable by the following persons—
(a) the relevant person;
(b) in the case of an energy performance certificate, any prospective or actual buyer or tenant during the period of validity of the certificate; and
(c) in the case of a display energy certificate, the occupier of the building.

(3) Any cause of action arising in relation to the duty imposed by paragraph (1) is deemed not to be an action founded on tort for the purposes of the Limitation Act 1980.

25 Right to copy documents

Any person may, for the purpose of complying with any duty imposed by these Regulations, copy or issue a copy of any document produced by an energy assessor.

26 Meaning of energy assessment

In this Part, a reference to "energy assessment" includes a reference to—
(a) the preparation and issuing of energy performance certificates;
(b) the preparation and issuing of display energy certificates;
(c) the preparation and issuing of recommendation reports;
(d) the preparation and issuing of inspection reports;
(e) the carrying out of any inspections undertaken for the purposes of preparing any of the documents referred to in paragraphs (a) to (d).

PART 6
REGISTRATION AND DISCLOSURE OF DATE RELATING TO CERTIFICATES AND REPORTS

27 Registration of certificates etc

(1) The Secretary of State shall maintain one or more registers of data from which the following documents may be produced—

(a) energy performance certificates;
(b) display energy certificates; and
(c) inspection reports.

(2) An energy assessor who issues a document referred to in paragraph (1)(a) or (b) must ensure that the data which, in accordance with the methodology of calculation of the energy performance of buildings approved by the Secretary of State under regulation 24 of the Building Regulations 2010, was used to calculate any asset rating or operational rating, and to produce the document, is entered onto the relevant register before the assessor gives the document to the person who requested that it be issued.

(3) An energy assessor who issues an inspection report must ensure that the data required by regulation 19(3) to be included in the report is entered onto the relevant register before the assessor gives the document to the relevant person.

(4) Each set of data entered onto the register from which a particular document may be produced—
(a) shall be registered under a unique reference number; and
(b) shall not be altered once registered.

(5) Any data entered on the register must be kept on the register for a period of at least 20 years beginning on the date on which it is entered onto the register.

28 Fees for entering data onto register

The keeper of the register may charge the following fees for entering data onto the register on or after 9th January 2013—
(a) for entering data from which an energy performance certificate which relates to a dwelling may be produced, a fee of £1.15;
(b) for entering data from which—
  (i) an energy performance certificate which relates to a building other than a dwelling,
  (ii) a display energy certificate, or
  (iii) an inspection report,
  may be produced, a fee of £5.36.

29 Disclosure of data: general

(1) A person keeping a register on the Secretary of State's behalf must not disclose data that has been entered onto a register to any other person unless the disclosure is in accordance with regulation 30, 31 or 32.

(2) It is an offence for a person to disclose, or permit the disclosure of, data otherwise than in accordance with paragraph (1).

(3) A person guilty of an offence under paragraph (2) is liable on summary conviction to a fine not exceeding level 5 on the standard scale.

30 Disclosure of general access data

(1) The keeper of the register may disclose general access data to any person if the conditions in paragraph (2) are met.

(2) The conditions are that—
(a) a request for disclosure of the data to the person has been made by means of a website operated by the keeper;
(b) the request includes at least one of the following—
  (i) the full postcode of that building;

(ii) the name of the road or street on which, and the name of the city, town, village or parish in which that building is located; or

(iii) the report reference number of the valid energy performance certificate that relates to the building.

(c) where the request is for data other than data required to be included in a display energy certificate, there is no opt-out in effect in respect of the data; and

(d) the particular building to which the data relates is not an excluded building.

(3) In this regulation—

(a) an opt-out is in effect in respect of data where—

(i) the owner or occupier of the building to which the data relates has notified the keeper that the data is not to be disclosed,

(ii) the notice was given in writing, or by electronic communication sent to an address or location specified by the keeper for the purpose of the receipt of such notices, and

(iii) the notice has not been withdrawn by the owner or occupier (by the means referred to in this sub-paragraph); and

(b) "excluded building" means a building owned, occupied or used from time to time by or for the purposes of—

(i) the Security Service, the Secret Intelligence Service or the Government Communications Headquarters;

(ii) any of the armed forces;

(iii) the Royal Family;

(iv) a prison;

(v) a contracted out prison within the meaning of the Criminal Justice Act 1991; or

(vi) a young offender institution.

31 Disclosure of bulk access data

(1) The keeper of the register may disclose—

(a) bulk access data which relates solely to a display energy certificate to any person if the condition in paragraph (2)(c) is met;

(b) other bulk access data to an authorised recipient if all of the conditions in paragraph (2) are met.

(2) The conditions are that—

(a) the authorised recipient has made a request for one or more specific descriptions of data to the keeper;

(b) the request was made in writing, or by electronic communication sent to an address or location specified by the keeper for the purpose of the receipt of such requests;

(c) the authorised recipient (other than one falling within paragraph (a), (b), (d), (e), (f) or (g) of the definition of that term in regulation 2 has paid a fee to the keeper, in the amount determined in accordance with regulation 33;

(d) the data is disclosed in summary form and does not include any information revealing the location of an excluded building (or any information from which the location of such a building can be deduced), or revealing the address or postcode of an identifiable person where an opt-out has effect under regulation 30;

(e) the disclosure is made subject to the condition that the data is to be used by the recipient solely for one or more of the purposes described in Part 1 of Schedule 1; and

(f) the disclosure is made subject to the conditions set out in Part 2 of that Schedule.

(3) The keeper of the register may refuse to disclose information under paragraph (1)(b) where the person who requests the disclosure has previously failed to comply with a condition of the kind referred to in paragraph (2)(e) or (f).

(4) In this regulation, "excluded building" has the same meaning as in regulation 30.

32 Disclosure by keeper of register

(1) The keeper of the register may disclose general access data or bulk access data—
(a) to an enforcement authority for the purposes of their duty under regulation 34(2);
(b) to a local authority for the purposes of their duty under section 91 of the Building Act 1984;
(c) to an approved inspector for the purposes of the inspector's functions under Part 2 of the Building Act 1984; or
(d) for the purpose of—
  (i) the prevention or detection of crime;
  (ii) the apprehension or prosecution of alleged offenders;
  (iii) any proceedings in a court or tribunal; or
  (iv) complying with an order or a court or tribunal.

(2) A person keeping a register on the Secretary of State's behalf may disclose general access data or bulk access data to the Secretary of State for the purpose of enabling the Secretary of State to carry out any function under or in connection with these Regulations, or for statistical or research purposes.

33 Fee for disclosure of bulk access data

(1) The amount of the fee referred to in regulation 31(2)(c) is the sum of—
(a) the number of small data packs requested multiplied by one penny (1p);
(b) the number of medium data packs requested multiplied by five pence (5p); and
(c) the number of large data packs requested multiplied by ten pence (10p).

(2) In this regulation, "small data pack", "medium data pack" and "large data pack"have the meanings given in Schedule 2.

PART 7
ENFORCEMENT

34 Enforcement authorities

(1) Every local weights and measures authority is an enforcement authority for the purpose of this Part.

(2) It is the duty of each enforcement authority to enforce in their area the duties under regulations 6(2), 6(5), 7(2), 7(3), 7(4), 7(5), 14(3), 18(1), 20, 21 and 35(5), and the EPC construction duty.

(3) In this regulation, "the EPC construction duty" means the duty specified in paragraph (4) applying to a building specified in paragraph (5).

(4) The duty is the requirement in accordance with the provisions of regulation 29 of the Building Regulations 2010 that a relevant person must, no later than five days after construction work has been completed on a building, give to the owner of the building an energy performance certificate for the building.

(5) The buildings to which the duty in paragraph (4) applies are those specified in regulation 34(1)(a) and (b) of the Building Regulations 2010.

35 Power to require production of documents

(1) An authorised officer of an enforcement authority may require a person who appears to him to be or to have been subject to any of the duties under regulation 6, 14(3), 18(1) or 20, or the EPC construction duty, to produce for inspection a copy of—
(a) a valid energy performance certificate;
(b) a recommendation report; or
(c) an inspection report.

(2) An authorised officer of an enforcement authority may require a person who appears to him to have been subject to the duty under regulation 7(3) to produce for inspection a copy of any request made in accordance with regulation 7(6)(d).

(3) The powers conferred by paragraphs (1) and (2) include power to take copies of any document produced for inspection.

(4) A requirement under this regulation may not be imposed more than six months after the last day on which the person concerned was subject to such a duty in relation to the building.

(5) It is the duty of a person subject to such a requirement to comply with it within the period of seven days beginning with the day after that on which it is imposed.

(6) A person is not required to comply with such a requirement if he has a reasonable excuse for not complying with the requirement.

(7) In this regulation, "the EPC construction duty" means the duty specified in paragraph (8) applying to a building specified in paragraph (9).

(8) The duty is the requirement in accordance with the provisions of regulation 29 of the Building Regulations 2010 that a relevant person must, no later than five days after construction work has been completed on a building, give to the owner of the building an energy performance certificate for the building.

(9) The buildings to which the duty in paragraph (4) applies are those specified in regulation 34(1)(a) and (b) of the Building Regulations 2010.

36 Penalty charge notices

(1) An authorised officer of an enforcement authority may, if he believes that a person has committed a breach of any duty under regulation 6(2), 6(5), 7(2), 7(3), 7(4), 7(5), 14(3), 18(1), 20, 21, or 35(5), or the EPC construction duty, give a penalty charge notice to that person.

(2) A penalty charge notice may not be given after the end of the period of six months beginning with the day (or in the case of a continuing breach the last day) on which the breach of duty was committed.

(3) A penalty charge notice must—
(a) state the officer's belief that the person has committed a breach of duty;
(b) give such particulars of the circumstances as may be necessary to give reasonable notice of the breach of duty;
(c) require that person, within a period specified in the notice—
  (i) to pay a penalty charge specified in the notice; or
  (ii) to give notice to the enforcement authority that he wishes the authority to review the notice;
(d) state the effect of regulation 41;
(e) specify the person to whom and the address at which the penalty charge may be paid and the method or methods by which payment may be made; and

(f) specify the person to whom and the address at which a notice requesting a review may be sent (and to which any representations relating to the review may be addressed).

(4) The period specified under paragraph (3)(c) must not be less than 28 days beginning with the day after that on which the penalty charge notice was given.

(5) The enforcement authority may extend the period for complying in any particular case if they consider it appropriate to do so.

(6) The enforcement authority may, if they consider that the penalty charge notice ought not to have been given, give the recipient a notice withdrawing the penalty charge notice.

(7) The enforcement authority must withdraw a penalty charge notice where the recipient can demonstrate that—

(a) he took all reasonable steps and exercised all due diligence to avoid breaching the duty; or

(b) regulation 37 (defence) applies.

(8) In this regulation, "the EPC construction duty" means the duty specified in paragraph (9) applying to a building specified in paragraph (10).

(9) The duty is the requirement in accordance with the provisions of regulation 29 of the Building Regulations 2010 that a relevant person must, no later than five days after construction work has been completed on a building, give to the owner of the building an energy performance certificate for the building.

(10) The buildings to which the duty in paragraph (4) applies are those specified in regulation 34(1)(a) and (b) of the Building Regulations 2010.

37 Defence when energy performance certificate unobtainable

(1) A relevant person shall not be liable to a penalty charge notice for a breach of the duty imposed by regulation 6 where he can demonstrate that—

(a) he is not a person to whom the duty under regulation 7(2) previously applied and he made a request for an energy performance certificate as soon as possible after he became subject to the duty, and, despite all reasonable efforts and enquiries by the relevant person, he did not have in his possession or control a valid energy performance certificate at the relevant time; or

(b) in the case of a failure to make available an energy performance certificate to a prospective tenant—

(i) the prospective tenant was seeking to rent the building due to an emergency which required the tenant's urgent relocation;

(ii) at the relevant time the relevant person did not have in his possession or control a valid energy performance certificate;

(iii) there was insufficient time in which the relevant person could reasonably have been expected to obtain a certificate before renting out the building to the prospective tenant; and

(iv) the relevant person has given a valid energy performance certificate to the tenant as soon as reasonably practicable after renting out the building.

(2) A relevant person shall not be liable to a penalty charge notice for a breach of the duty imposed by regulation 6 where he can demonstrate that—

(a) he is a person to whom the duty under regulation 7(2) applies;

(b) he complied with that duty; and

(c) despite all reasonable efforts and enquiries by the relevant person he did not have in his possession or control a valid energy performance certificate at the relevant time.

(3) In paragraph (1)(a) the reference to a request is to a request properly addressed to a person who usually provides or is likely to provide an energy performance certificate for the category of building in question and which includes such payment or an undertaking to make such payment as is usually necessary to obtain an energy performance certificate.

(4) In this regulation, "relevant time" means the point in time by which the relevant person is required to have made an energy performance certificate available to a prospective buyer or tenant by virtue of regulation 6(2).

38 Penalty amount

(1) The penalty charge specified in the notice shall be—

(a) in relation to a breach of a duty under regulation 6(2), 6(5), 7(2), 7(3), (4), or 7(5), or of the EPC construction duty—

- (i) where the building is a dwelling, £200;
- (ii) where the building is not a dwelling, calculated in accordance with the formula in paragraph (2);

(b) in relation to a breach of a duty under regulation 14(3)(a), £1000;

(c) in relation to a breach of a duty under regulation 14(3)(b), £500;

(d) in relation to a breach of a duty under regulation 18(1), 20(1), 20(2) or 21, £300; and

(e) in relation to a breach of a duty under regulation 35(5), £200.

(2) Subject to the minimum and maximum penalty charges prescribed by paragraph (3), the penalty charge for the purposes of paragraph (1)(a)(ii) shall be—

(a) where the building constitutes a hereditament, 12.5% of the rateable value of the hereditament;

(b) where no other building (other than a building which is exempt from Part 2 by virtue of—

- (i) regulation 5(1)(a), (b), (d) or (e), or
- (ii) for a building which is not a dwelling, regulation 5(1)(c) or (g)),

forms a part of the same hereditament, 12.5% of the rateable value of the hereditament of which the building forms a part;

(c) where the building comprises more than one hereditament, 12.5% of the sum of the rateable values of each hereditament that comprise the building; and

(d) where—

- (i) one or more buildings (other than a building which is exempt from Part 2 by virtue of—
  - (aa) regulation 5(1)(a), (b),, (d) or (e), or
  - (bb) for a building which is not a dwelling, regulation 5(1)(c) or (g)) form part of the same hereditament; or
- (ii) the building is not, or does not form part of, a hereditament which appears on a local non-domestic rating list at the relevant time,

£750.

(3) The minimum and maximum penalty charges for the purposes of paragraph (2) are £500 and £5000 respectively.

(4) In this regulation—

(a) "the EPC construction duty" means the duty specified in sub-paragraph (b) applying to a building specified in sub-paragraph (c);

(b) the duty is the requirement in accordance with the provisions of regulation 29 of the Building Regulations 2010 that a relevant person must, no later than five days after construction work has been completed on a building, give to the owner of the building an energy performance certificate for the building; and

(c) the buildings to which the duty in paragraph (4) applies are those specified in regulation 34(1)(a) and (b) of the Building Regulations 2010.

(5) In this regulation the following definitions also apply—

"hereditament" means a hereditament which, pursuant to section 42 of the Local Government Finance Act 1988, is shown on a local non-domestic rating list in force at the relevant time;

"local non-domestic rating list" means a local non-domestic rating list maintained in accordance with section 41 of the Local Government Finance Act 1988;

"rateable value" means the rateable value shown for a hereditament on a local non-domestic rating list at the relevant time; and

"relevant time" means the time at which the penalty charge notice is given.

39 Reviews

(1) If, within the period specified under regulation 36(3)(c) (or that period as extended under regulation 36(5)), the recipient of the penalty charge notice gives notice to the enforcement authority requesting a review, the authority shall—

(a) consider any representations made by the recipient and all other circumstances of the case;

(b) decide whether to confirm or withdraw the notice; and

(c) give notice of their decision to the recipient.

(2) A notice confirming the penalty charge notice must also state the effect of regulations 40 and 41.

(3) If the authority are not satisfied that—

(a) the recipient committed the breach of duty specified in the notice;

(b) the notice was given within the time allowed by regulation 36(2) and complies with the other requirements imposed by these Regulations; and

(c) in the circumstances of the case it was appropriate for a penalty charge notice to be given to the recipient,

they shall withdraw the penalty charge notice.

40 Appeal to the county court

(1) If, after a review, the penalty charge notice is confirmed by the enforcement authority, the recipient may, within the period of 28 days beginning with the day after that on which the notice under regulation 39(1)(c) is given, appeal to the county court against the penalty charge notice.

(2) The county court may extend the period for appealing against the notice.

(3) Such an appeal must be on one (or more) of the following grounds—

(a) that the recipient did not commit the breach of duty specified in the penalty charge notice;

(b) that the notice was not given within the time allowed by regulation 36(2) or does not comply with any other requirement imposed by these Regulations; or

(c) that in the circumstances of the case it was inappropriate for the notice to be given to the recipient.

(4) An appeal against a penalty charge notice shall be by way of a rehearing; and the court shall either uphold the notice or quash it.

(5) If the penalty charge notice is withdrawn or quashed, the authority shall repay any amount previously paid as a penalty charge in pursuance of the notice.

41 Recovery of penalty charges

(1) The amount of the penalty charge is recoverable from the recipient of the penalty charge notice as a debt owed to the authority unless—
(a) the notice has been withdrawn or quashed; or
(b) the charge has been paid.

(2) Proceedings for the recovery of the penalty charge may not be commenced before the end of the period mentioned in regulation 39(1).

(3) If within that period the recipient of the penalty charge notice gives notice to the authority that he wishes the authority to review the penalty charge notice, such proceedings may not be commenced—
(a) before the end of the period mentioned in regulation 40(1); and
(b) where the recipient appeals against the penalty charge notice, before the end of the period of 28 days beginning with the day on which the appeal is withdrawn or determined.

(4) In proceedings for the recovery of the penalty charge, a certificate which—
(a) purports to be signed by or on behalf of the person having responsibility for the financial affairs of the enforcement authority; and
(b) states that payment of the penalty charge was or was not received by a date specified in the certificate,

is evidence of the facts stated.

42 Service of documents

(1) A penalty charge notice and any other notice mentioned in this Part may be given by post.

(2) Any such notice may be given—
(a) in the case of a body corporate, to the secretary or clerk of that body; and
(b) in the case of a partnership, to any partner or to a person having control or management of the partnership business.

43 Offences relating to enforcement officers

(1) A person who obstructs an officer of an enforcement authority acting in pursuance of regulation 35 is guilty of an offence.

(2) A person who, not being an authorised officer of an enforcement authority, purports to act as such in pursuance of this Part is guilty of an offence.

(3) A person guilty of an offence under this regulation is liable on summary conviction to a fine not exceeding level 5 on the standard scale.

PART 8
MISCELLANEOUS

44 Application to the Crown

(1) Subject to paragraph (2), these Regulations, other than regulation 45(2)(a), bind the Crown.

(2) No act or omission by or on behalf of the Crown shall constitute an offence or make the Crown liable to a penalty charge notice under these Regulations, but the High Court may, on the application of an enforcement authority, declare unlawful any act or omission of the Crown which constitutes a contravention of these Regulations.

45 Duty to cooperate

(1) This regulation applies where these Regulations impose a duty on a person to—

(a) make available, give or display an energy performance certificate or a display energy certificate in relation to a building; or

(b) ensure an air-conditioning system is inspected.

(2) It shall be the duty of every person with an interest in, or in occupation of, the building to—

(a) allow such access to any energy assessor appointed by the person referred to in paragraph (1) ("the responsible person") as is reasonably necessary to inspect the building for the purposes of—

(i) preparing an energy performance certificate;

(ii) preparing a display energy certificate;

(iii) preparing a recommendation report; or

(iv) inspecting an air-conditioning system; and

(b) cooperate with the responsible person so far as is reasonably necessary to enable him to comply with the duty referred to in paragraph (1).

[*Section 46 is not reproduced.*]

47 Review

(1) Before the end of each review period, the Secretary of State must—

(a) carry out a review of these Regulations;

(b) set out the conclusions of the review in a report; and

(c) publish the report.

(2) In carrying out the review the Secretary of State must, so far as is reasonable, have regard to how Directive 2010/31/EU of the European Parliament and of the Council on the energy performance of buildings of 19th May 2010 (recast) is implemented in other member States.

(3) The report must in particular—

(a) set out the objectives intended to be achieved by these Regulations;

(b) assess the extent to which those objectives are achieved; and

(c) assess whether those objectives remain appropriate and, if so, the extent to which they could be achieved with a system that imposes less regulation.

(4) "Review period" means—

(a) the period of five years beginning with the day on which these Regulations come into force; and

(b) subject to paragraph (5), each successive period of five years.

(5) If a report under this regulation is published before the last day of the review period to which it relates, the following review period is to begin with the day on which that report is published.

SCHEDULE 1

Regulation 31

PART 1

The purposes are—

1

Promoting energy efficiency improvements (as defined in section 2 of the Energy Act 2011) ("energy efficiency improvements") in relation to buildings.

2

Conducting research into, or developing or analysing policy (or policy proposals) in relation to, the energy efficiency of buildings.

3

Conducting research into the effectiveness or impact of energy efficiency improvements.

4

Identifying geographic areas where the energy efficiency of buildings is low relative to other areas, or conducting research into the extent, causes or consequences of such lower levels of efficiency.

5

Promoting and marketing energy efficiency improvements that may be made pursuant to a green deal plan.

6

Identifying and analysing the impact of carbon emissions on the environment resulting from buildings with low levels of energy efficiency.

7

Determining whether energy efficiency improvements that may be made pursuant to a green deal plan have or have not been made in respect of a particular building or buildings.

PART 2

The conditions are—

1

The authorised recipient is, until the data is deleted from the authorised recipient's records and systems (so that the personal data is no longer accessible by any means by the authorised recipient), a data controller within the meaning of section 1(1) of the Data Protection Act 1998 in relation to the information disclosed.

2

The authorised recipient must not—

(a) disclose any personal data contained in or derived from data disclosed to it under regulation 31 to any other person without the consent of the person who is the subject of the data;

(b) use such personal data in order to contact an individual for the purpose of marketing or promoting products or services which do not relate to energy efficiency.

3

The authorised recipient must not make contact with any person ("the subject") whose identity or contact details (or both) have become known to the authorised recipient from data disclosed to the authorised recipient under regulation 31 unless—

(a) the authorised recipient advises the subject, at the time contact is first made, that—

  (i) their identity or contact details (or both) have been obtained from the keeper of the register under that regulation, and

  (ii) the subject is entitled to refuse to receive any further communications from the authorised recipient; and

(b) the first contact with the subject is made by means of written communication (including electronic communication) only.

4

The authorised recipient must not make further contact with a person if the person has informed the authorised recipient that they do not wish to receive any further communications from the authorised recipient.

5

In paragraphs 6 and 7, "the subject" means a person whose identity or contact details (or both) have become known to the authorised recipient from data disclosed to it under regulation 31.

6

If the authorised recipient has on three separate occasions made contact with the subject and received no response from the subject within fourteen days of the third contact, the authorised recipient—

(a) must not attempt to contact the subject again; and

(b) must, as soon as reasonably practicable (and in any event within fourteen days of the receipt of a request made by or on behalf of the subject to do so), delete any personal data contained in or derived from data disclosed to the authorised recipient under regulation 31 from its records and systems (so that the personal data is no longer accessible by any means to the authorised recipient).

7

The authorised recipient must, as soon as reasonably practicable (and in any event within fourteen days of the receipt of a request made by or on behalf of the subject), delete any personal data contained in or derived from data disclosed to the authorised recipient under regulation 31 from its records and systems (so that the personal data is no longer accessible by any means by the authorised recipient) if the subject requests the authorised recipient to do so.

8

The authorised recipient must ensure that its officers and employees comply with the conditions in paragraphs 1 to 7 of this Part.

SCHEDULE 2
MEANINGS OF SMALL, MEDIUM AND LARGE DATA PACKS

Regulation 33

PART 1
ENERGY PERFORMANCE CERTIFICATES

1

In this Part, "residential property" means premises in England and Wales consisting of a single dwelling, including ancillary land.

2

For data from which an energy performance certificate for a residential property may be produced—

(a) a small data pack means a set of data containing the following information concerning the property: the address (including the postcode), the energy rating, the potential energy rating, the energy efficiency, the potential energy efficiency, the property type, the inspection date, the region, local authority area, constituency and county where it is located and the date the data was entered onto the register;

(b) a medium data pack means a set of data containing the data described in paragraph 2(a), together with the following additional information concerning the property: the transaction type, the current environment impact, the potential environment impact, the current energy consumption, the potential energy consumption, the current Co2 emissions, the current Co2 emissions per floor area, the potential Co2 emissions, the current lighting cost, the potential lighting cost, the current heating cost, the potential heating cost, the current hot water cost, the potential hot water cost, the total floor area, the energy tariff, whether the property is connected to the gas network, the floor level, whether the property is on the top floor (for flats), if the property is a flat not on the top floor the story count for the property, the overall dimensions and size of the building, the type of heating controls, the proportion of windows which are multi-glazed, the types of glazing and the area glazed, the number of extensions to the property, the number of habitable rooms, the number of heated rooms, the proportion of low energy light and the number of open fireplaces; and

(c) a large data pack means a set of data containing the data described in paragraphs 2(a) and (b), together with any additional data entered onto the register pursuant to regulation 27 from which an energy performance certificate (or any information contained within such a certificate) may be produced in relation to the property.

3

For data from which an energy performance certificate for a property other than a residential property may be produced—

(a) a small data pack means a set of data containing the following information concerning the property: the address (including the postcode), the energy rating, the property type, the inspection date, the region, local authority area, constituency and county where it is located and the date the data was entered onto the register;

(b) a medium data pack means a set of data containing the data described in paragraph 3(a), together with the following additional information concerning the property: the transaction type, the benchmark against other new build or existing properties as appropriate, whether the property is a level 3, 4 or 5 building, the main heating fuel, the other fuel description, whether the property is air-conditioned, whether the property has specialised energy requirements, the energy from renewable sources (if any) used by the property and the floor area; and

(c) a large data pack means a set of data containing the data described in paragraphs 3(a) and (b), together with any additional data entered onto the register pursuant to regulation 27 from which an energy performance certificate (or any information contained within such a certificate) may be produced in relation to the property.

PART 2
DISPLAY ENERGY CERTIFICATES

4

For data from which a display energy certificate may be produced—

(a) a small data pack means a set of data containing the following information concerning the property in question: the address (including the postcode), the energy rating, the proportion of Co2 emissions attributable to electricity used in the property, the proportion of Co2 emissions from energy used to heat the property, the proportion of Co2 emissions from energy from renewable sources (if any) used in the property, the property type, the inspection date, the region, local authority area, constituency and county where it is located and the date the data was entered onto the register;

(b) a medium data pack means a set of data containing the data described in paragraph 4(a), together with the following additional information concerning the property: the benchmark against other new build or existing properties as appropriate, whether the property is a level 3, 4 or 5 building, the main heating fuel, the other fuel description, whether the building is air-conditioned, whether the building has specialised energy requirements, the energy from renewable sources (if any) used in the property, the floor area and the building level; and

(c) a large data pack means a set of data containing the data described in paragraphs 4(a) and (b) together with any additional data entered onto the register pursuant to regulation 27 from which a display energy certificate (or any information contained within such a certificate) may be produced in relation to the property in question.

PART 3
AIR-CONDITIONING INSPECTION REPORTS

5

For data from which an inspection report may be produced—

(a) a small data pack means a set of data containing the following information concerning the property in question: the address (including the postcode), the property type, the inspection date, the region, local authority area, constituency and county where it is located and the date the data was entered onto the register;

(b) a medium data pack means a set of data containing the data described in paragraph 5(a), together with the following additional information: the name of the equipment owner, their telephone number, the name of their organisation, the equipment owner's address, (including the town, city or parish and postcode), the person responsible for the operation of the air-conditioning equipment, the operator's employer, the operator's address (including the town, city or parish and postcode) and the name of the building; and

(c) a large data pack means a set of data containing the data described in paragraphs 5(a) and (b), together with any additional data entered onto the register pursuant to regulation 27 from which the inspection report (or any information contained within the report) may be produced.

SCHEDULE 3
REVOCATION OF REGULATIONS

Regulation 46

Regulations revoked	*References*	*Extent of revocation*
The Energy Performance of Buildings (Certificates and Inspections) (England and Wales) Regulations 2007	SI 2007/991	The whole Regulations.
The Energy Performance of Buildings (Certificates and Inspections) (England and Wales) (Amendment) Regulations 2007	SI 2007/1669	The whole Regulations.
The Energy Performance of Buildings (Certificates and Inspections) (England and Wales) (Amendment No. 2) Regulations 2007	SI 2007/3302	The whole Regulations.
The Energy Performance of Buildings (Certificates and Inspections) (England and Wales) (Amendment) Regulations 2008	SI 2008/647	The whole Regulations.

Regulations revoked	*References*	*Extent of revocation*
The Energy Performance of Buildings (Certificates and Inspections) (England and Wales) (Amendment No. 2) Regulations 2008	SI 2008/2363	The whole Regulations.
The Energy Performance of Buildings (Certificates and Inspections) (England and Wales) (Amendment) Regulations 2009	SI 2009/1900	The whole Regulations.
The Energy Performance of Buildings (Certificates and Inspections) (England and Wales) (Amendment) Regulations 2010	SI 2010/1456	The whole Regulations.
The Building Regulations 2010	SI 2010/2214	Regulation 54(1) and Schedule 5, insofar as they relate to the Energy Performance of Buildings (Certificates and Inspections) (England and Wales) Regulations 2007, and regulation 54(2) insofar as it relates to paragraph 2 of Schedule 6 to the Building Regulations 2010.
The Building (Amendment) Regulations 2011	SI 2011/1515	Regulation 2.
The Energy Performance of Buildings (Certificates and Inspections) (England and Wales) (Amendment) Regulations 2011	SI 2011/2452	The whole regulations.
The Energy Performance of Buildings (Certificates and Inspections) (England and Wales) (Amendment) Regulations 2012	SI 2012/809	The whole regulations.

ENVIRONMENTAL PERMITTING (ENGLAND AND WALES) (AMENDMENT) REGULATIONS 2013

[This is draft legislation.]

PART 1
GENERAL

1 Citation

These Regulations may be cited as the Environmental Permitting (England and Wales) (Amendment) Regulations 2013.

2 Commencement

(1) Save as provided in paragraphs (2), (3) and (4), these Regulations come into force on the seventh day after the day on which they are made.

(2) Regulation 58(2) comes into force on 7th January 2014.

(3) Regulation 58(3) comes into force on 1st January 2016.

(4) Regulation 4(6), (8), (12) and (15) and regulation 5 come into force in relation to existing installations on 7th January 2014.

(5) In these Regulations—

(a) "existing installation" means an installation where a Part A activity is carried on—

(i) which is in operation on or before 7th January 2013, or

(ii) in respect of which a duly made application for an environmental permit is submitted before 7th January 2013 and which commences operation on or before 7th January 2014,

provided that an environmental permit has been granted in respect of such operation;

(b) "environmental permit" and "installation" have the same definition as in the principal Regulations;

(c) "Part A activity" has the same definition as in the principal Regulations and does not include operating small waste incineration plants.

3 Interpretation

In these Regulations, "the principal Regulations" means the Environmental Permitting (England and Wales) Regulations 2010.

PART 2
AMENDMENTS OF THE PRINCIPAL REGULATIONS

4 Regulation 2 (interpretation: general)

(1) Regulation 2(1) of the principal Regulations is amended in accordance with paragraphs (2) to (14).

(2) Omit the definition of "directly associated activity".

(3) In the definition of "emission"—

(a) for paragraph (c) substitute—

"(c) in relation to a solvent emission activity, the direct or indirect release of substances from individual or diffuse sources in the regulated facility into the air;";

(b) omit "and" immediately preceding paragraph (g) and at the end insert—
",

(h) in relation to a small waste incineration plant, the direct or indirect release of substances from individual or diffuse sources in the regulated facility to air or water;".

(4) In the definition of "excluded waste operation" omit "Part A mobile plant or".

(5) After the definition of "exemption registration authority", insert—
""existing installation" means an installation carrying on a Part A activity—

(a) which is in operation on or before 7th January 2013, or

(b) in respect of which a duly made application for an environmental permit is submitted before 7th January 2013 and which commences operation on or before 7th January 2014,

provided that an environmental permit has been granted in respect of such operation;.".

(6) In the definition of "hazardous waste" for "except in Section 5.1 of Part 2 of Schedule 1" substitute "subject to paragraph (6)".

(7) In the definition of "mobile plant" omit paragraph (a).

(8) In the definition of "non-hazardous waste" for "except in Section 5.1 of Part 2 of Schedule 1" substitute "subject to paragraph (6)".

(9) For the definition of "Part A mobile plant", "Part A(1) mobile plant", "Part A(2) mobile plant" and "Part B mobile plant" substitute—
""Part B mobile plant" has the meaning given in paragraph 1 of Part 1 of Schedule 1;".

(10) Omit the definitions of "SED activity" and "SED installation".

(11) After the definition of "sewer" insert—
""small waste incineration plant" means a waste incineration plant or waste co-incineration plant with a capacity less than or equal to 10 tonnes per day for hazardous waste or 3 tonnes per hour for non-hazardous waste;

"solvent emission activity" means an activity to which Chapter V of the Industrial Emissions Directive applies;".

(12) For the definition of "waste" substitute—
""waste", subject to paragraph (5) where it applies, and except where otherwise defined—

(a) in relation to Chapter 5 of Part 2 of Schedule 1, Schedule 13 or 13A, Schedule 14, Schedule 15 or 15A, or Schedule 17 or 17A, means anything that—
   (i) is waste within the meaning of Article 3(1) of the Waste Framework Directive; and
   (ii) is not excluded from the scope of that Directive by Article 2(1)(d) of that Directive;

(b) in any other case means anything that—
   (i) is waste within the meaning of Article 3(1) of the Waste Framework Directive; and
   (ii) is not excluded from the scope of that Directive by Article 2(1), (2) or (3) of that Directive;".

(13) After the definition of "waste battery or accumulator" insert—
""waste co-incineration plant" means a stationary or mobile technical unit whose main purpose is the generation of energy or production of material products and which uses waste as a regular or additional fuel or in which waste is thermally treated for the purpose of disposal through the incineration by oxidation of waste as well as

other thermal treatment processes, such as pyrolysis, gasification or plasma process, if the substances resulting from the treatment are subsequently incinerated;

"waste incineration plant" means a stationary or mobile technical unit and equipment dedicated to the thermal treatment of waste, with or without recovery of the combustion heat generated, through the incineration by oxidation of waste as well as other thermal treatment processes, such as pyrolysis, gasification or plasma process, if the substances resulting from the treatment are subsequently incinerated;".

(14) In the definition of "waste mobile plant", in paragraph (c) omit ", Part A mobile plant".

(15) After paragraph (5) of regulation 2 insert—

"(6) In relation to an activity that falls within Chapter 5 of Part 2 of Schedule 1 or Schedule 13 or 13A, hazardous waste means waste which displays any of the characteristics listed in Annex IIIto the Waste Framework Directive.".

5 Regulation 3 (interpretation: Directives)

In regulation 3 of the principal Regulations—

(a) for the definition of "the IPPC Directive" substitute—

""the Industrial Emissions Directive" means Directive 2010/75/EU of the European Parliament and of the Council on industrial emissions (integrated pollution prevention and control) (Recast);";

(b) omit the definition of "the Waste Incineration Directive".

6 Regulation 5 (interpretation: exempt facilities)

In regulation 5(1) of the principal Regulations, in the definition of "exempt waste operation", for paragraph (a) substitute—

"(a) that is not carried on at an installation, and".

7 Regulation 6 (interpretation: local authority)

In regulation 6(2) of the principal Regulations, after "Part B installation" insert ", a small waste incineration plant or a solvent emission activity".

8 Regulation 7 (interpretation: operate a regulated facility and operator)

In regulation 7 of the principal Regulations, in the definition of "operate a regulated facility", for "or groundwater activity" substitute ", groundwater activity, small waste incineration plant operation or solvent emission activity".

9 Regulation 8 (interpretation: regulated facility and class of regulated facility)

(1) At the end of regulation 8(1) of the principal Regulations, insert—

",

(h) a small waste incineration plant;

(i) a solvent emission activity".

(2) At the end of regulation 8(4) of the principal Regulations, insert—

";

(e) small waste incineration plant;

(f) solvent emission activity".

10 Regulation 12 (requirement for an environmental permit)

In regulation 12 of the principal Regulations, after paragraph (5) insert—

"(6) Paragraph (1)(a) does not apply until 7th July 2015 in relation to the Part A activities to which paragraph (7) applies, provided that—
(a) the installation at which the activity is carried on is in operation before 7th January 2013, and
(b) the activity is not a Part A activity before that date.

(7) The Part A activities to which this paragraph applies are those falling within—
(a) paragraph (d) of Section 1.2 (in relation to the gasification or liquefaction of fuels other than coal);
(b) Chapter 4 (in relation to the biological processing of chemicals);
(c) Section 5.3 (in relation to the recovery of hazardous waste in an installation with a capacity over 10 tonnes per day by biological or physico-chemical treatment, blending, mixing or repackaging, or surface impoundment);
(d) paragraph (a) of Section 5.4 (in relation to the disposal of non-hazardous waste by biological or physico-chemical treatment, pre-treatment for incineration or co-incineration, treatment of slags and ashes or treatment in shredders of metal waste);
(e) paragraph (b) of Section 5.4 (in relation to the recovery or a mix of recovery and disposal of non-hazardous waste by biological treatment, pre-treatment for incineration or co-incineration, treatment of slags and ashes or treatment in shredders of metal waste);
(f) Section 5.6 (temporary or underground storage of hazardous waste);
(g) Section 5.7 (independently operated treatment of waste water);
(h) Section 6.6 (preservation of wood and wood based products with chemicals);
(i) paragraph (d) of Section 6.8 (treatment and processing of animal and vegetable raw materials for food and feed).".

11 Regulation 17 (single site permits)

In regulation 17(2)(b) of the principal Regulations, omit "(other than a standard facility to which the IPPC Directive applies)".

12 Regulation 18 (consolidation of an environmental permit)

In regulation 18(1)(b) of the principal Regulations, omit ", not being a standard facility to which the IPPC Directive applies".

13 Regulation 32 (discharge of functions)

(1) In regulation 32(2) of the principal Regulations—
(a) in sub-paragraph (a) omit "or Part A(2) mobile plant";
(b) at the end insert—
";
(c) a small waste incineration plant;
(d) a solvent emission activity".

(2) In regulation 32(3) and (4) omit "Part A(2) mobile plant or".

14 Regulation 35 (specific provisions applying to environmental permits)

In regulation 35(2) of the principal Regulations—
(a) in sub-paragraph (a) for "and Part A mobile plant" substitute "and Schedule 7A (Part A installations: Industrial Emissions Directive)";
(b) in sub-paragraph (b) after "mobile plant" insert "etc.";

(c) in sub-paragraph (g) after "(waste incineration)" insert "and Schedule 13A (waste incineration: industrial emissions directive)";
(d) in sub-paragraph (h) for "SED installations" substitute "solvent emission activities";
(e) in sub-paragraph (i), after "(large combustion plants)" insert "and Schedule 15A (large combustion plants: industrial emissions directive)";
(f) in sub-paragraph (k), after "(titanium dioxide)" insert "and Schedule 17A (titanium dioxide: industrial emissions directive)".

15 Regulation 36 (enforcement notices)

In regulation 36 of the principal Regulations—
(a) in paragraph (1) omit "(an "enforcement notice")" and "under this regulation";
(b) in paragraph (2) for "An enforcement notice" substitute "The notice";
(c) in paragraph (3) for "an enforcement notice" substitute "the notice";
(d) for paragraph (4) substitute—

"(4) In the case of a regulated facility to which Schedule 7A, 13A or 14 applies, if the regulator considers that an incident or accident significantly affecting the environment has occurred as the result of the operation of that regulated facility, the regulator may serve a notice on the operator of that facility.

(5) A notice served under paragraph (4) must—
(a) specify the measures necessary to limit the environmental consequences of the incident or accident, and
(b) specify the measures necessary to prevent further incidents or accidents.

(6) The regulator may withdraw the notice at any time by further notice served on the operator.".

16 Regulation 40 (defences)

In regulation 40 of the principal Regulations, after paragraph (3) insert—

"(4) Subject to paragraph (5), it is a defence for a person charged with an offence under regulation 38(1) in relation to an activity listed in regulation 12(7), to prove that a duly-made application for a permit was submitted to the regulator by—
(a) 30th September 2014 where the activity is listed in sub-paragraph (a), (b) or (e) of regulation 12(7);
(b) 31st December 2014 where the activity is listed in sub-paragraph (c),(d) or (h) of regulation 12(7);
(c) 31st March 2015 where the activity is listed in sub-paragraph (f), (g) or (i) of regulation 12(7).

(5) Where a permit has been refused, paragraph (4) does not apply—
(a) if the applicant appeals against the refusal, after the date the appeal is determined or withdrawn, or
(b) if the applicant does not appeal, after the day after the last day on which an appeal could have been brought under these Regulations.".

17 Regulation 58 (Environment Agency: notices in relation to emissions to water)

In regulation 58(1) of the principal Regulations, omit "and Part A mobile plant".

18 Regulation 63 (directions to the Agency: installations outside the United Kingdom)

(1) In regulation 63(1) of the principal Regulations for "Article 18(1) of the IPPC Directive" substitute "Article 26(1) of the Industrial Emissions Directive".

(2) In regulation 63(2) of the principal Regulations, for "Article 18(2) of the IPPC Directive" substitute "Article 26(2) of the Industrial Emissions Directive".

19 Part 1 of Schedule 1 (activities, installations and mobile plant—interpretation and application: general)

(1) Part 1 of Schedule 1 to the principal Regulations is amended as follows.

(2) In paragraph 1 (interpretation)—
(a) in the definition of "directly associated activity", omit ", in relation to an activity other than a SED activity,";
(b) in the definition of "installation", omit "(except where used in the definition of "excluded plant" in Section 5.1 of Part 2 of this Schedule)";
(c) for the definition of "Part A(1) installation" substitute—
""Part A(1) installation" means an installation where a Part A(1) activity is carried on either alone or in combination with any or all of the following—
(a) an A(2) activity;
(b) a Part B activity;
(c) the operation of a small waste incineration plant;
(d) a solvent emission activity;";
(d) for the definition of "Part A(2) installation" substitute—
""Part A(2) installation" means an installation where a Part A(2) activity is carried on either alone or in combination with any or all of the following—
(a) a Part B activity;
(b) the operation of a small waste incineration plant;
(c) a solvent emission activity;";
(e) omit the definitions of "Part A mobile plant", "Part A(1) mobile plant" and "Part A(2) mobile plant";
(f) in the definition of "Part B installation", after "is carried on" insert—
"either alone or in combination with either or both of the following—
(a) the operation of a small waste incineration plant;
(b) a solvent emission activity";
(g) in the definition of "Part B mobile plant" omit ", not being Part A mobile plant,".

(3) In paragraph 2(2) and (3) (activities falling within more than one Part description) omit "(other than a description in Section 7)".

(4) In paragraph 3 (application of activities falling within Sections 1.1 to 6.9 of Part 2)—
(a) in the heading and first line of the paragraph, omit "Sections 1.1 to 6.9 of";
(b) for sub-paragraph (c) substitute—
"(c) carried on at an installation, other than a waste incineration plant or a waste co-incineration plant, or by means of Part B mobile plant, where the installation or plant is used solely for research, development and testing of new products or processes;";
(c) omit "or" immediately preceding sub-paragraph (f) and at the end insert—
"; or
(g) carried on at a waste incineration plant or a waste co-incineration plant used for research, development and testing in order to improve the incineration process and which treats less than 50 tonnes of waste per year".

(5) For paragraph 4 substitute—

"4 Application of thresholds in Part 2

For the purposes of assessing whether an activity is above any of the thresholds given in Part 2 of this Schedule, where several activities falling under the same description of activity containing a threshold are operated in the same installation, the capacities of those activities must be added together.".

(6) In paragraph 6 (application of Part B activities: releases into the air) omit sub-paragraph (2)(a).

20 Part 2 of Schedule 1 (activities)

Part 2 of Schedule 1 to the principal Regulations is amended in accordance with regulations 21 to 45.

21 Combustion activities

In Section 1.1 (combustion activities)—
(a) in Part A(1) omit paragraph (b);
(b) in interpretation and application of Part A(1), omit paragraph 5;
(c) in paragraph (a) of Part B, omit "(other than a fuel mentioned in Part A(1)(b))".

22 Gasification, liquefaction and refining activities

(1) In Section 1.2 (gasification, liquefaction and refining activities), in Part A(1)—
(a) omit paragraph (b);
(b) for paragraph (d) substitute—
"(d) Gasification or liquefaction of coal or other fuels in installations with a total rated thermal input of 20 megawatts or more.";
(c) omit paragraphs (e) and (f);
(d) in paragraph (h), omit sub-paragraphs (iii) to (v);
(e) omit paragraph (i);
(f) omit paragraph (k);
(g) in interpretation and application—
(i) in paragraph 1(b), after "incineration" insert "in a waste incineration plant or waste co-incineration plant";
(ii) in paragraph 1(d) for "none of which is waste; or" substitute "whether or not containing or comprising waste.";
(iii) omit paragraph 1(e).

(2) In Section 1.2, in Part B—
(a) in paragraph (d), after "any 12 month period is" insert "or is likely to be";
(b) in paragraph (f), for "is likely to be" substitute "is intended to be";
(c) in interpretation of Part B—
(i) in the definition of "existing service station" for "31st December 2009" substitute "1st January 2010";
(ii) in the definition of "new service station", after "1st January 2012" insert "but does not include an existing service station".

23 Non-ferrous metals

In Section 2.2 (non-ferrous metals)—
(a) in interpretation and application, in paragraph 2 for "Part A(1)(c) to (h) substitute "Part A(1) (a), (b) and (f).";
(b) in Part A(1)—
(i) in paragraph (b), for "(such as refining or foundry casting)" substitute "and the operation of non-ferrous metal foundries";
(ii) omit paragraphs (c) to (e);
(iii) omit paragraphs (g) to (i);

(c) omit the paragraph headed Interpretation of Part A(1);
(d) in Part A(2), in paragraph (a), for "(such as refining or foundry casting)" substitute "and operating of non-ferrous metal foundries".

24 Production of cement and lime

In Section 3.1 (production of cement and lime)—
(a) in Part A(1)—
  (i) in paragraph (a) for "or producing and grinding cement clinker" substitute "in rotary kilns with a production capacity exceeding 500 tonnes per day or in other kilns with a production capacity exceeding 50 tonnes per day";
  (ii) for paragraph (b) substitute—
"(b) Producing lime or magnesium oxide in kilns with a production capacity of more than 50 tonnes per day.".
(b) in Part A(2)—
  (i) for paragraph (a) substitute—
"(a) Grinding cement clinker";
  (ii) omit paragraph (b);
(c) in Part B, for paragraph (d) substitute—
"(d) Producing lime or magnesium oxide where the activity does not involve the heating of more than 50 tonnes per day of calcium carbonate or calcium magnesium carbonate or both in aggregate.".

25 Activities involving asbestos

In Section 3.2 (activities involving asbestos), in Part A(1), omit paragraph (c).

26 Manufacturing glass and glass fibre

In Section 3.3 (manufacturing glass and glass fibre), in Part A(1)—
(a) in paragraph (a), after "glass fibre" insert "in plant with a melting capacity exceeding 20 tonnes per day";
(b) omit paragraph (b).

27 Production of other mineral fibres

In Section 3.4 (production of other mineral fibres), in Part A(1)—
(a) for paragraph (a) substitute—
"(a) Melting mineral substances including the production of mineral fibres in plants with a melting capacity exceeding 20 tonnes per day.";
(b) omit paragraph (b).

28 The chemical industry

In Chapter 4 (the chemical industry), in paragraph 1 (interpretation of Chapter 4), for "producing in a chemical plant by chemical processing for commercial purposes substances or groups of substances" substitute "producing on an industrial scale by chemical or biological processing of substances or groups of substances".

29 Organic chemicals

In Section 4.1 (organic chemicals)—
(a) in Part A(1) omit paragraphs (b) to (g);
(b) for paragraph (b) of Part B, substitute—
"(b) The flame bonding or cutting with heated wires of polyurethane foams or polyurethane elastomers.".

30 Inorganic chemicals

In Section 4.2 (inorganic chemicals), in Part A(1) omit paragraphs (c), (g), (i) and (j).

31 Chemical fertiliser production

In Section 4.3 (chemical fertiliser production), in Part A(1) omit paragraph (b).

32 Plant health products and biocides

In Section 4.4 (plant health products and biocides), in Part A(1) omit paragraph (b).

33 Pharmaceutical production

In Section 4.5 (pharmaceutical production), in Part A(1)—
(a) in paragraph (a), omit "using a chemical or biological process";
(b) omit paragraph (b).

34 Manufacturing activities involving carbon disulphide or ammonia

In Section 4.7 (manufacturing activities involving carbon disulphide or ammonia), in Part A(1) omit paragraph (a).

35 Incineration and co-incineration of waste

In Section 5.1 (incineration and co-incineration of waste)—
(a) omit the paragraph headed "Interpretation of Section 5.1";
(b) for Part A(1) substitute—

"Part A(1)
(a) The incineration of hazardous waste in a waste incineration plant or waste co-incineration plant with a capacity exceeding 10 tonnes per day.
(b) The incineration of non-hazardous waste in a waste incineration plant or waste co-incineration plant with a capacity exceeding 3 tonnes per hour.
(c) The incineration, other than incidentally in the course of burning landfill gas or solid or liquid waste, of any gaseous compound containing halogens.";
(c) omit Part A(2);
(d) in Part B, for paragraph (a) substitute—
"(a) The incineration in a small waste incineration plant with an aggregate capacity of 50 kilogrammes or more per hour of the following waste—
(i) vegetable waste from agriculture and forestry;
(ii) vegetable waste from the food processing industry, if the heat generated is recovered;
(iii) fibrous vegetable waste from virgin pulp production and from production of paper from pulp, if it is co-incinerated at the place of production and the heat generated is recovered;
(iv) cork waste;
(v) wood waste with the exception of wood waste which may contain halogenated organic compounds or heavy metals as a result of treatment with wood preservatives or coatings;
(vi) animal carcasses.".

36 New section 5.3 (disposal or recovery of hazardous waste)

For Section 5.3 (disposal of waste other than by incineration or landfill), substitute—

"Section 5.3
Disposal or recovery of hazardous waste

Part A(1)

(a) Disposal or recovery of hazardous waste with a capacity exceeding 10 tonnes per day involving one or more of the following activities—
   (i) biological treatment;
   (ii) physico-chemical treatment;
   (iii) blending or mixing prior to submission to any of the other activities listed in this Section or in Section 5.1;
   (iv) repackaging prior to submission to any of the other activities listed in this Section or in Section 5.1;
   (v) solvent reclamation or regeneration;
   (vi) recycling or reclamation of inorganic materials other than metals or metal compounds;
   (vii) regeneration of acids or bases;
   (viii) recovery of components used for pollution abatement;
   (ix) recovery of components from catalysts;
   (x) oil re-refining or other reuses of oil;
   (xi) surface impoundment.".

37 New section 5.4 (disposal, recovery or a mix of disposal and recovery of non-hazardous waste)

For Section 5.4 (recovery of waste), substitute—

"Section 5.4
Disposal, recovery or a mix of disposal and recovery of non-hazardous waste

Part A(1)

(a) Disposal of non-hazardous waste with a capacity exceeding 50 tonnes per day (or 100 tonnes per day if the only waste treatment activity is anaerobic digestion) involving one or more of the following activities, and excluding activities covered by Council Directive 91/271/EEC concerning urban waste-water treatment—
   (i) biological treatment;
   (ii) physico-chemical treatment;
   (iii) pre-treatment waste for incineration or co-incineration;
   (iv) treatment of slags and ashes;
   (v) treatment in shredders of metal waste, including waste electrical and electronic equipment and end-of-life vehicles and their components.

(b) Recovery or a mix of recovery and disposal of non-hazardous waste with a capacity exceeding 75 tonnes per day (or 100 tonnes per day if the only waste treatment activity is anaerobic digestion) involving one or more of the following activities, and excluding activities covered by Council Directive 91/271/EEC—
   (i) biological treatment;
   (ii) pre-treatment of waste for incineration or co-incineration;
   (iii) treatment of slags and ashes;
   (iv) treatment in shredders of metal waste, including waste electrical and electronic equipment and end-of-life vehicles and their components.".

38 New section 5.6 (temporary or underground storage of hazardous waste)

After Section 5.5 (the production of fuel from waste), insert—

"Section 5.6
Temporary or underground storage of hazardous waste

Part A(1)

(a) Temporary storage of hazardous waste with a total capacity exceeding 50 tonnes pending any of the activities listed in Sections 5.1, 5.2, 5.3 and paragraph (b) of this Section, except—
   (i) temporary storage, pending collection, on the site where the waste is generated, or
   (ii) activities falling within Section 5.2.

(b) Underground storage of hazardous waste with a total capacity exceeding 50 tonnes.".

39 New section 5.7 (treatment of waste water)

After Section 5.6 (temporary or underground storage of hazardous waste), insert—

"Section 5.7
Treatment of waste water

Part A(1)

(a) Independently operated treatment of waste water not covered by Directive 91/271/EEC and discharged by an installation carrying out any other Part A(1) or A(2) activity.".

40 Paper, pulp and board manufacturing activities

In Section 6.1 (paper, pulp and board manufacturing activities)—

(a) in Part A(1)—
   (i) omit paragraph (c);
   (ii) omit the paragraph headed Interpretation of Part A(1);

(b) in Part A(2), for paragraph (a) substitute—

"(a) Producing, in an industrial plant, one or more of the following wood-based panels with a production capacity exceeding 600m3 per day: oriented strand board, particleboard or fibreboard.".

41 Coating activities, printing and textile treatments

In Section 6.4 (coating activities, printing and textile treatments)—

(a) in Part A(1), omit paragraphs (a) and (c);

(b) in Interpretation and application of Part B, in paragraph 3, for "a SED installation" substitute "a regulated facility at which a solvent emission activity is carried out".

42 Timber activities

In Section 6.6 (timber activities), for Part A(1) substitute—

"Part A(2)

(a) Preservation of wood and wood products with chemicals with a production capacity exceeding 75 m3 per day other than exclusively treating against sapstain.".

43 Treatment of animal and vegetable matter and food industries

In Section 6.8 (treatment of animal and vegetable matter and food industries), in Part A(1)—

(a) for paragraph (d) substitute—

"(d) Treatment and processing, other than exclusively packaging, of the following raw materials, whether previously processed or unprocessed, intended for the production of food or feed (where the weight of the finished product excludes packaging)—

(i) only animal raw materials (other than milk only) with a finished product production capacity greater than 75 tonnes per day;

(ii) only vegetable raw materials with a finished product production capacity greater than 300 tonnes per day or 600 tonnes per day where the installation operates for a period of no more than 90 consecutive days in any year;

(iii) animal and vegetable raw materials (other than milk only), both in combined and separate products, with a finished product production capacity in tonnes per day greater than—

(aa) 75 if A is equal to 10 or more, or

(bb) 300 – (22.5 × A) in any other case,

where 'A' is the portion of animal material in percent of weight of the finished product production capacity;";

(b) omit paragraph (f).

44 SED activities

Omit Section 7 (SED activities).

45 Schedule 3 (exempt facilities: descriptions and conditions)

In Schedule 3 to the principal Regulations—

(a) in paragraph 3 of Section 1 of Chapter 2 of Part 1 (general conditions), after sub-paragraph (c), insert—

";

(d) the operation is not an activity that falls within Chapter 5 of Part 2 of Schedule 1 (waste management)";

(b) in paragraph 6 of Section 2 of Chapter 4 of Part 1 (disposal by incineration)—

(i) in sub-paragraph (1) for "an incinerator" substitute "a small waste incineration plant";

(ii) for sub-paragraph (2) substitute—

"(2) The waste described in this paragraph is the waste mentioned in Article 42(2)(a)(i) and (iii) of the Industrial Emissions Directive.";

(iii) in sub-paragraph (4)(a) for "incinerator" substitute "small waste incineration plant";

(iv) in sub-paragraph (4)(b) for "incinerators" wherever it occurs, substitute "small waste incineration plants".

46 Schedule 5 (environmental permits)

(1) Part 1 of Schedule 5 to the principal Regulations is amended as follows.

(2) In paragraph 5(1)(c) omit ", unless the facility is a Part A installation".

(3) In paragraph 5(4)(d)for "paragraph (d) or (e)" substitute "paragraphs (d) to (g)".

(4) In paragraph 5(5)—

(a) for the definition of "dry cleaning" substitute—

""dry cleaning" means an industrial or commercial activity using volatile organic compounds to clean garments, furnishing and similar consumer goods excluding the manual removal of stains and spots in the textile or clothing industry;";

(b) omit the definitions of "co-incineration plant" and "incineration plant";

(c) in the definition of "substantial change", in paragraph (b) for "an incineration plant or co-incineration plant" substitute "a waste incineration plant or waste co-incineration plant".

(5) In paragraph 10 (consultation with other member States)—
(a) in sub-paragraph (4)—
(i) in the definition of "member State", for "the IPPC Directive" substitute "Annex I to the Industrial Emissions Directive";
(ii) in the definition of "relevant Article", for "Article 18 of the IPPC Directive" substitute "Article 26 of the Industrial Emissions Directive";
(iii) in the definition of "relevant information", for "Annex V to the IPPC Directive" substitute "Annex IV to the Industrial Emissions Directive";
(b) in sub-paragraph (5) for "IPPC Directive" substitute "Industrial Emissions Directive".

(6) In paragraph 16(3)(d) for "IPPC Directive" substitute "Industrial Emissions Directive".

(7) After paragraph 19 insert—

"20 Incidents and accidents: deemed condition of a permit

Every environmental permit in relation to a regulated facility to which Schedule 7A, 13A or 14 applies is deemed to contain the following conditions, unless such conditions are included in the permit—
(a) in the event that the operation of a regulated facility gives rise to an incident or accident which significantly affects the environment, the operator of that regulated facility must immediately—
(i) inform the regulator,
(ii) take the measures necessary to limit the environmental consequences of such an incident or accident, and
(iii) take the measures necessary to prevent further possible incidents or accidents;
(b) in the event of a breach of any condition of a permit, the operator of a regulated facility must immediately—
(i) inform the regulator, and
(ii) take the measures necessary to ensure that compliance is restored within the shortest possible time;
(c) in the event of a breach of any condition of a permit which poses an immediate danger to human health or threatens to cause an immediate significant adverse effect on the environment, the operator of a regulated facility must immediately suspend the operation of the regulated facility or the relevant part of it until compliance with the condition of the permit has been restored.".

47 Amendment to Schedule 7 (Part A installations)

(1) In Schedule 7 to the principal Regulations—
(a) in the heading omit "and Part A mobile plant";
(b) for paragraph 1 substitute—

"1

(1) This Schedule applies until 7th January 2014 in relation to every existing installation.

(2) This Schedule ceases to apply on 7th January 2014.";
(c) in paragraph 2(b) omit "or Part A mobile plant";
(d) omit paragraph 4 (b);
(e) omit paragraph 5(2)(b) and (e);
(f) in paragraph 7 omit "or Part A mobile plant".

(2) After Schedule 7 to the principal Regulations, insert—

"SCHEDULE 7A
PART A INSTALLATIONS: INDUSTRIAL EMISSIONS DIRECTIVE

Regulation 35(2)(a)

1 Application

This Schedule applies—
(a) in relation to every new installation;
(b) from 7th January 2014 in relation to every existing installation.

2 Interpretation

(1) In this Schedule, "new installation" means a Part A installation which is not an existing installation.

(2) When interpreting the Industrial Emissions Directive for the purposes of this Schedule—
(a) except where defined in this paragraph, an expression that is defined in Part 1 of these Regulations has the meaning given in that Part;
(b) "installation" means Part A installation;
(c) "permit" means environmental permit;
(d) the competent authority is the regulator;
(e) "substance" is to be read as including, after the words "its compounds" in Article 3(1) of the Industrial Emissions Directive, the words "and any biological entity or micro-organism";
(f) "general binding rule" means a standard rule published under regulation 26.

3 Exercise of regulator's functions: general

The regulator must exercise its functions under these Regulations for the purpose of achieving a high level of protection of the environment taken as a whole by, in particular, preventing or, where that is not practicable, reducing emissions into the air, water and land.

4 Applications for the grant of an environmental permit

The regulator must ensure that every application for the grant of an environmental permit includes the information specified in Article 12 of the Industrial Emissions Directive.

5 Exercise of relevant functions

The regulator must exercise its relevant functions so as to ensure compliance with the following provisions of the Industrial Emissions Directive—
(a) Article 5(1) and (3);
(b) Article 7;
(c) Article 8(2);
(d) Article 9;
(e) Article 11;
(f) Article 13(7);
(g) Article 14;
(h) Article 15 (excluding the penultimate sub-paragraph of Article 15(4));
(i) Article 16;
(j) Article 17;
(k) Article 18;
(l) Article 20(1) and (2);
(m) Article 22 (excluding the last sub-paragraph of Article 22(2));
(n) Article 26(4).

6 Developments in best available techniques

(1) The regulator must ensure that it is informed of developments in best available techniques and of the publication of any new or updated BAT conclusions and where appropriate must

exercise its functions so as to encourage the application of emerging techniques, in particular those identified in BAT reference documents.

(2) In this paragraph—

(a) "BAT conclusions" has the meaning given in Article 3(12) of the Industrial Emissions Directive;

(b) "BAT reference document" has the meaning given in Article 3(11) of the Industrial Emissions Directive;

(c) "best available techniques" has the meaning given in Article 3(10) of the Industrial Emissions Directive;

(d) "emerging technique" has the meaning given in Article 3(14) of the Industrial Emissions Directive.

7 Review of environmental permits

The regulator must review an environmental permit in accordance with Article 21 of the Industrial Emissions Directive if any of the circumstances in that Article applies in relation to the Part A installation whose operation the permit authorises.

8 Public participation

The regulator must exercise its functions so as to meet the requirements of Article 24 of the Industrial Emissions Directive.

9 Inspections

When inspecting a regulated facility in accordance with regulation 34(2) the regulator must comply with Article 23 of the Industrial Emissions Directive.".

48 Schedule 8 (part B installations and part B mobile plant)

For Schedule 8 to the principal Regulations substitute—

"SCHEDULE 8
PART B INSTALLATIONS AND PART B MOBILE PLANT ETC.

Regulation 35(2)(b)

1 Application

(1) In England and Wales, this Schedule applies in relation to every Part B installation.

(2) In Wales only this Schedule also applies in relation to every small waste incineration plant (in addition to the provisions in Schedule 13 or 13A) and in relation to every solvent emission activity (in addition to the provisions in Schedule 14).

2 Interpretation

For the purposes of this Schedule—

(a) "best available techniques" means the most effective and advanced stage in the development of activities and their methods of operation which indicates the practical suitability of particular techniques for providing in principle the basis for emission limit values relevant to air pollution designed to prevent and, where that is not practicable, generally to reduce emissions and the impact on the environment as a whole; where—

(i) "techniques" includes both the technology used and the way in which the installation is designed, built, maintained, operated and decommissioned;

(ii) "available techniques" means those techniques developed on a scale which allows implementation in the relevant industrial sector, under economically and technically viable conditions, taking into consideration the costs and advantages, and which are reasonably accessible to the operator;

(iii) "best" means most effective in achieving a high general level of protection of the environment as a whole;

(b) "installation" means a Part B installation, Part B mobile plant, small waste incineration plant or solvent emission activity.

3 Exercise of regulator's functions: general

The regulator must exercise its functions under these Regulations for the purpose of preventing or, where that is not practicable, reducing emissions into the air.

4 Applications for the grant of an environmental permit

(1) The regulator must ensure that every application for the grant of an environmental permit includes the following information—

(a) the installation and its activities;

(b) the sources of emissions to air from the installation;

(c) the nature and quantities of foreseeable emissions into the air from the installation as well as identification of significant effects of those emissions on the environment;

(d) the proposed technology or other techniques for preventing, or where that is not possible, reducing emissions to air from the installation;

(e) further measures planned to ensure that the installation is operated in such a way that—

(i) all appropriate preventive measures are taken against pollution, in particular through the application of best available techniques; and

(ii) no significant pollution is caused;

(f) measures planned to monitor emissions into the air;

(g) the main alternatives, if any, to the techniques or measures required in paragraphs (d) to (f);

(h) a non-technical summary of the details referred to in paragraphs (a) to (g).

(2) Paragraph (1)(d) does not apply to the extent that the application relates to the burning of waste oil in an appliance with a net rated thermal input of less than 0.4 megawatts at a Part B installation.

(3) In the case of a new installation or a substantial change where Article 4 of Directive 85/337/EEC applies, any relevant information obtained or conclusion arrived at pursuant to Articles 5, 6 or 7 of that Directive shall be taken into consideration by the regulator for the purposes of granting the environmental permit.

5 Exercise of relevant functions

(1) The regulator must, for the purpose of preventing or, where that is not practicable, reducing emissions into the air, exercise its relevant functions in relation to the installations to which this Schedule applies—

(a) so as to ensure that they are operated in such a way that—

(i) appropriate preventive measures are taken against air pollution, in particular through the application of best available techniques;

(ii) no significant air pollution is caused;

(b) where an environmental quality standard requires stricter conditions than those achievable by the use of best available techniques, additional measures are required by the permit, without prejudice to other measures which might be taken to comply with environmental quality standards;

(c) permits include emission limit values, which may if appropriate be supplemented or replaced by equivalent parameters or technical measures, for polluting substances likely to be emitted into the air from the installation concerned in significant quantities;

(d) where emissions of a greenhouse gas from an installation are specified in Annex 1 to Directive 2003/87/EC of the European Parliament and of the Council establishing a scheme for greenhouse gas emission allowance trading within the European Union in relation to an activity carried out in that installation, the permit does not include an emission limit value for direct emissions of that gas unless it is necessary to ensure that no significant local pollution is caused.

(2) The regulator must ensure that emission limit values or equivalent parameters or technical measures are based on best available techniques without prescribing the use of any technique or specific technology, but taking into account the technical characteristics of the installation, including (except in the case of mobile plant) its geographical location and the local environmental conditions.

(3) In this paragraph "substance" means any chemical element and its compounds and any biological entity or micro-organism, with the exception of the following substances—

(a) radioactive substances as defined in Article 1 of Council Directive 96/29/Euratom laying down basic safety standards for the protection of the health of workers and the general public against the dangers arising from ionising radiation;

(b) genetically modified micro-organisms as defined in Article 2(b) of Directive 2009/41/EC of the European Parliament and of the Council on the contained use of genetically modified micro-organisms;

(c) genetically modified organisms as defined in point 2 of Article 2 of Directive 2001/18/EC of the European Parliament and of the Council on the deliberate release into the environment of genetically modified organisms.

6 Change in operation

(1) Operators holding environmental permits for installations to which this Schedule applies must notify the regulator of any substantial change in the operation of that installation.

(2) Where there is a substantial change in the operation of an installation, the regulator must ensure that the environmental permit is reviewed and, if necessary, updated.

7 Review of permits

The regulator must review an environmental permit where—

(a) the air pollution caused by the installation is of such significance that the existing emission limit values of the permit need to be revised or new values need to be included in the permit;

(b) substantial changes in best available techniques make it possible to reduce emissions significantly without imposing excessive costs;

(c) the operational safety of the process or activity requires other techniques to be used; or

(d) new legislation necessitates a review.

8 Developments in best available techniques

The regulator must ensure that it is informed of developments in best available techniques.".

49 Schedule 9 (waste operations)

(1) Schedule 9 to the principal Regulations is amended as follows.

(2) In paragraph 3(2), in the definition of "relevant waste operation" in paragraph (a) omit "Part A mobile plant or".

(3) For sub-paragraph 3(3)(b) and (c) substitute—

"(b) the disposal of hazardous waste (other than by incineration or landfill) in a facility with a capacity of more than 10 tonnes per day;

(c) the recovery of hazardous waste falling within sub-paragraph (i) to (v), (viii) or (x) of paragraph (a) of Part A(1) of Section 5.3 of Part 2 of Schedule 1;

(d) the disposal of non-hazardous waste falling within paragraph (a) of Part A(1) of Section 5.4 of Part 2 of Schedule 1;

(e) the recovery or a mix of recovery and disposal of non-hazardous waste falling within paragraph (b) of Part A(1) of Section 5.4 of Part 2 of Schedule 1;

(f) temporary or underground storage of hazardous waste falling within Part A(1) of Section 5.6 of Part 2 of Schedule 1.".

(4) In paragraph 3(4), after paragraph (a) omit "and" and at the end insert—
", or
(c) is an exempt waste operation".

50 Schedule 13 (waste incineration)

(1) In Schedule 13 to the principal Regulations—
(a) for paragraph 1 substitute—

"1

(1) This Schedule applies until 7th January 2014 in relation to every existing installation that is a waste incineration plant or waste co-incineration plant except those treating only the waste mentioned in Article 42(2)(a)(i) and (iii) of the Industrial Emissions Directive.

(2) This Schedule ceases to apply on 7th January 2014.";
(b) omit paragraph 2(1) and (2)(a) and (b).

(2) After Schedule 13 to the principal Regulations, insert—

"SCHEDULE 13A
WASTE INCINERATION: INDUSTRIAL EMISSIONS DIRECTIVE

Regulation 35(2)(g)

1 Application

(1) This Schedule applies in relation to—
(a) every small waste incineration plant, and
(b) every new waste incineration plant or new waste co-incineration plant,
to which Chapter IV of the Industrial Emissions Directive applies, except those which are operated as a domestic activity in connection with a private dwelling.

(2) It applies from 7th January 2014 in relation to every existing installation that is a waste incineration plant or waste co-incineration plant and to which Chapter IV of the Industrial Emissions Directive applies, except those which are operated as a domestic activity in connection with a private dwelling.

2 Interpretation

(1) In this Schedule "new waste incineration plant" or "new waste co-incineration plant" means a waste incineration plant or co-incineration plant which is not an existing installation.

(2) When interpreting Chapter IV of the Industrial Emissions Directive for the purposes of this Schedule—
(a) an expression that is defined in Part 1 of these Regulations has the meaning given in that Part;
(b) the competent authority is the regulator;
(c) "permit" means environmental permit;
(d) "general binding rule" means a standard rule published under regulation 26.

3 Applications for the grant of an environmental permit

The regulator must ensure that every application for the grant of an environmental permit includes the information specified in Article 44 of the Industrial Emissions Directive.

4 Exercise of relevant functions

(1) The regulator must exercise its relevant functions so as to ensure compliance with the following provisions of the Industrial Emissions Directive—

(a) Article 5(1) and (3);
(b) Article 7;
(c) Article 8(2);
(d) Article 9;
(e) Article 42(1)
(f) Article 43;
(g) Article 45(1), (2) and (4);
(h) Article 46;
(i) Article 47;
(j) Article 48(1) to (4);
(k) Article 49;
(l) Article 50;
(m) Article 51(1) to (3);
(n) Article 52;
(o) Article 53;
(p) Article 54;
(q) Article 55;
(r) Article 82(5) and (6).

(2) But when interpreting the Industrial Emissions Directive for the purposes of this Schedule—
(a) in Article 51(1) ignore the words "Member states may lay down rules governing these authorisations";
(b) paragraph 2.1(c) of Part 6 of Annex VI is to be read as if the words "and dioxin-like polychlorinated biphenyls and polycyclic aromatic hydrocarbons" appeared after the word "furans", but only in the case of particular plants where the regulator can demonstrate that emissions of those additional substances are, or are likely to be, significant.".

51 Schedule 14 (solvent emission activities)

For Schedule 14 to the principal Regulations substitute—

"SCHEDULE 14
SOLVENT EMISSION ACTIVITIES

Regulation 35(2)(h)

1 Application

This Schedule applies in relation to every solvent emission activity.

2 Interpretation

When interpreting Chapter V of the Industrial Emissions Directive for the purposes of this Schedule—
(a) except where defined in this paragraph, an expression that is defined in Part 1 of these Regulations has the meaning given in that Part;
(b) the competent authority is the regulator;
(c) "installation" means a stationary technical unit within which a solvent emission activity is carried out, and any other directly associated activities on the same site which have a technical connection with the solvent emission activity and which could have an effect on emission of volatile organic compounds;
(d) "permit" means environmental permit;
(e) "general binding rule" means a standard rule published under regulation 26.

3 Exercise of relevant functions

The regulator must exercise its relevant functions so as to ensure compliance with the following provisions of the Industrial Emissions Directive—

(a) Article 5(1) and (3);
(b) Article 7;
(c) Article 8(2);
(d) Article 9;
(e) Article 57;
(f) Article 58;
(g) Article 59 (except article 59(4));
(h) Article 60;
(i) Article 61;
(j) Article 62;
(k) Article 63;
(l) Article 65;
(m) Article 82(7), (8) and (9).".

52 Schedule 15 (large combustion plants)

(1) In Schedule 15 to the principal Regulations, for paragraph 1 substitute—

"1

(1) This Schedule applies until 1st January 2016 in relation to every existing installation that is a combustion plant to which the Large Combustion Plants Directive applies by virtue of Article 1 of that Directive.

(2) This Schedule ceases to apply on 1st January 2016.".

(2) After Schedule 15 to the principal Regulations, insert—

"SCHEDULE 15A
LARGE COMBUSTION PLANTS: INDUSTRIAL EMISSIONS DIRECTIVE

Regulation 35(2)(i)

1 Application

This Schedule applies—
(a) in relation to every new large combustion plant;
(b) from 1st January 2016 in relation to every existing installation that is a large combustion plant.

2 Interpretation

(1) In this Schedule—
"combustion plant" has the meaning given in Article 3(25) of the Industrial Emissions Directive;
"large combustion plant" means a combustion plant with a total rated thermal input of 50 megawatts or more to which chapter III of the Industrial Emissions Directive applies;
"new large combustion plant" means a large combustion plant which is not an existing installation.

(2) When interpreting the Industrial Emissions Directive for the purposes of this Schedule—
(a) except where defined in this paragraph, an expression that is defined in Part 1 of these Regulations has the meaning given in that Part;
(b) the competent authority is—
  (i) for the purposes of exercising a judgement as to whether there is an overriding need to maintain energy supplies under Articles 30(6) and 37 the Industrial Emissions Directive, the appropriate authority;
  (ii) otherwise, the regulator;
(c) "permit" means environmental permit.

3 Exercise of relevant functions

The regulator must exercise its relevant functions so as to ensure compliance with the following provisions of the Industrial Emissions Directive—

(a) Article 29;

(b) Article 30(1) to (8), except the second sub-paragraph of 30(5) and the last sub-paragraph of 30(6);

(c) Article 31(1) and (2);

(d) Article 32(2) and (3);

(e) Article 33 except 33(2);

(f) Article 34(1) and (2);

(g) Article 35(1);

(h) Article 37;

(i) Article 38;

(j) Article 39;

(k) Article 40.

4 Interruption in supply of fuel

The regulator must—

(a) immediately inform the appropriate authority of any derogation under Article 30(5) of the Industrial Emissions Directive;

(b) immediately inform the appropriate authority if it considers that a derogation in accordance with Articles 30(6) or 37(2) of the Industrial Emissions Directive is or might be appropriate.".

53 Schedule 17 (titanium dioxide)

(1) In Schedule 17 to the principal Regulations, for paragraph 1 substitute—

"1

(1) This Schedule applies until 7th January 2014 in relation to every existing installation where the chlorine process or the sulphate process in carried on.

(2) This Schedule ceases to apply on 7th January 2014.".

(2) After Schedule 17 to the principal Regulations, insert—

"SCHEDULE 17A
TITANIUM DIOXIDE: INDUSTRIAL EMISSIONS DIRECTIVE

Regulation 35(2)(k)

1 Application

This Schedule applies—

(a) in relation to every new installation in which titanium dioxide is produced; and

(b) from 7th January 2014 in relation to every existing installation in which titanium dioxide is produced.

2 Interpretation

(1) In this Schedule "new installation" means a Part A installation which is not an existing installation.

(2) When interpreting Chapter VI of the Industrial Emissions Directive for the purposes of this Schedule—

(a) an expression that is defined in Part 1 of these Regulations has the meaning given in that Part;

(b) the competent authority is the regulator;
(c) "permit" means environmental permit.

3 Exercise of relevant functions

The regulator must exercise its relevant functions so as to ensure compliance with the following provisions of the Industrial Emissions Directive—
(a) Article 67;
(b) Article 68;
(c) Article 69;
(d) Article 70.".

54 Schedule 20 (mining waste operations)

In paragraph 12(2) of Schedule 20 to the principal Regulations, for "Article 2(12) of the IPPC Directive" substitute "Article 3(10) of the Industrial Emissions Directive".

PART 3
TRANSITIONAL PROVISIONS AND REVOCATIONS

55 Activities no longer requiring permits

(1) Where the activity to which an environmental permit relates falls only within a description in Part 2 of Schedule 1 to the principal Regulations which by virtue of the coming into force of these Regulations is no longer included in that Schedule, that permit ceases to have effect.

(2) Where an environmental permit contains any condition which relates solely to a description of an activity which was included in Part 2 of Schedule 1 to the principal Regulations but which by virtue of the coming into force of these Regulations is no longer included in that Schedule, that condition ceases to have effect.

56 Former Part A activities

(1) This regulation applies where an environmental permit is for an activity—
(a) which, immediately before the coming into force of these Regulations, was a Part A activity, and
(b) which, on the coming into force of these Regulations, becomes a Part B activity or any other regulated facility.

(2) Where this regulation applies—
(a) the permit is deemed to be granted under the principal Regulations as amended by these Regulations; and
(b) any conditions of that permit which are applicable only to Part A installations cease to have effect.

(3) In this regulation, "Part B activity" and "regulated facility" have the same definition as in the principal Regulations as amended by these Regulations.

57 Consequential amendment

(1) The Volatile Organic Compounds in Paints, Varnishes and Vehicle Refinishing Products Regulations 2012 are amended as follows.

(2) In regulation 3(3) for "an SED (Solvent Emission Directive) activity" substitute "a solvent emission activity".

(3) In regulation 3(4)—
(a) for "SED (Solvent Emission Directive) Activity" substitute "solvent emission activity";
(b) for sub-paragraph (a) substitute—
"(a) Schedule 14 to the Environmental Permitting (England and Wales) Regulations 2010.".

58 Revocations

(1) The following Regulations are revoked—

(a) the Clean Air Enactments (Repeals and Modifications) Regulations 1974;

(b) the Control of Industrial Air Pollution (Transfer of Powers of Enforcement) Regulations 1987;

(c) the Control of Asbestos in the Air Regulations 1990.

(2) Schedules 7, 13 and 17 to the principal Regulations are revoked.

(3) Schedule 15 to the principal Regulations is revoked.

Part 3
Statutory Guidance

WASTE MANAGEMENT: THE DUTY OF CARE: A CODE OF PRACTICE ENVIRONMENTAL PROTECTION ACT 1990 SECTION 34

(Revised 1996)

Introduction

i This code of practice consists of the guidance in Sections 1-7 together with their related Annexes. It is issued by the Secretary of State for the Environment, the Secretary of State for Scotland and the Secretary of State for Wales in accordance with section 34(7) and (8) of the Environmental Protection Act 1990 ("the 1990 Act"). This code supersedes that issued in December 1991 which is hereby revoked. This introduction is not part of the code of practice.

ii Section 34 of the 1990 Act imposes a duty of care on persons concerned with **controlled waste**. The duty applies to any person who produces, imports, carries, keeps, treats or disposes of controlled waste, or as a broker has control of such waste. Breach of the duty of care is an offence, with a penalty of an unlimited fine if convicted on indictment.

iii Waste poses a threat to the environment and to human health if it is not managed properly and recovered or disposed of safely. The duty of care is designed to be an essentially self regulating system which is based on good business practice. It places a duty on anyone who in any way has a responsibility for controlled waste to ensure that it is managed properly and recovered or disposed of safely. The purpose of this code is to provide practical guidance for waste holders and brokers subject to the duty of care. It has been revised to take account of changes in waste management law since the code was first issued in December 1991. These changes include the application of the duty of care to the scrap metal industry from 1 October 1995.

iv The code recommends a series of steps which should normally be enough to meet the duty. The code cannot cover every contingency. The legal obligation is to comply with the duty of care itself rather than with the code. **Annex A** gives a detailed explanation of the law.

v The Code makes reference to the Environment Agency and to the Scottish Environment Protection Agency. In England and Wales, local authorities' waste regulation functions are transferred to the Environment Agency by section 2 of the Environment Act 1995 with effect from 1 April 1996. Until that date, waste regulation is a function of the local authorities designated in section 30(1) of the Environmental Protection Act 1990.

vi In Scotland, local authorities' waste regulation functions are transferred to the Scottish Environment Protection Agency by section 21 of the Environment Act 1995 with effect from 1 April 1996.

vii The code is divided into:-

— Sections 1-7: Step by step guidance on following the duty;

— A summary check list; and

Annexes

A: the law on the duty of care;

B: responsibilities under the duty;

C: Regulations on keeping records;

D: an outline of some other legal requirements; and

E: a glossary of terms used in the code.

viii Guidance on the definition of waste, which does not form part of the code of practice, is contained in the Appendix.

Is it "waste"?

ix The duty of care applies to waste which is controlled waste (see paragraphs 1.1-1.2 below). The first question, therefore, is whether any particular substance is "waste". Since 1 May 1994 the common European definition of waste in the Framework Directive[1] on waste has been in force. The legal definition of waste is:-

> "any substance or object...which the producer[2] or the person in possession of it discards or intends or is required to discard."

x Whether or not a substance is waste must be determined on the facts of the case; and interpretation of the law is a matter for the Courts. The Departments[3] have provided guidance on the interpretation of the definition of waste in DOE Circular 11/94[4]. In the Departments' view the purpose of the Framework Directive is to treat as waste, and accordingly to supervise the collection, transport, storage, recovery and disposal of, those substances or objects which fall out of the commercial cycle or out of the chain of utility. The Departments have suggested, therefore, that to determine whether a substance or object has been discarded the following question may be asked:-

> Has the substance or object been discarded so that it is no longer part of the normal commercial cycle or chain of utility?

xi An answer of "no" to this question should provide a reasonable indication that the substance or object concerned is not waste. As indicated, however, the purpose of the Framework Directive is to supervise the collection, transport, storage, recovery and disposal of waste; and these are activities which themselves may be of a commercial nature. A distinction must be drawn, therefore, between the normal commercial cycle and the commercial cycle which exists for the purpose of collecting, transporting, storing, recovering and disposing of waste. It is also essential to bear in mind that a substance or object does not cease to be waste as soon as it is transferred for collection, transport, storage, recovery or disposal. A substance or object which is waste at the point of its original production should be regarded as waste until it is recovered or disposed of.

The Appendix provides a summary of the main questions which need to be addressed in reaching a view on whether a particular substance or object is waste; and when it may cease to be waste.

Notes

1 Council Directive 75/442/EEC as amended by Directives 91/156/EEC and 91/692/EEC.

2 "Producer" means anyone whose activities produce waste or who carries out preprocessing, mixing or other operations resulting in a change in its nature or composition.

3 The Department of the Environment, the Welsh Office and The Scottish Office Agriculture, Environment and Fisheries Department.

4 Welsh Office Circular 26/94 and The Scottish Office Environment Department Circular 10/94.

STEP BY STEP GUIDANCE

Section 1
Identify and describe the controlled waste

1.1

The duty of care applies to anyone who is the holder[1] of controlled waste[2]. The only exception to this is for the occupiers of domestic property for the household waste which comes from their home. Anyone subject to the duty of care who has some "controlled waste" must identify and describe the kind of waste it is.

Notes

1 "Holder" means a person who imports, produces, carries, keeps, treats, or disposes of controlled waste or, as a broker, has control of it.

2 Only waste which is "Directive waste" is treated as controlled waste – see the glossary of terms at **Annex E**.

Is it "controlled waste"?

1.2

"Controlled waste" means waste from households[1], commerce or industry. At present, the main kinds of waste that are not "controlled waste" are waste from agricultural premises, waste from mines and quarries, explosives and most radioactive waste. However, the Departments intend to issue a consultation paper containing proposals for the extension of the definition of controlled waste to include certain categories of agricultural waste and of mines and quarries waste. Unless the context indicates otherwise, subsequent references in the code to "waste" should be read as references to "controlled waste".

Note

1 Householders are exempt from the duty of care for their own household waste (**Annex A** paragraph A.9).

What are the problems of the waste?

1.3

Waste cannot be simply divided between the safe and the hazardous. There are safe ways of dealing with any waste. Equally, any waste can be hazardous to human health or the environment if it is wrongly managed. Deciding whether any waste poses a problem requires consideration not only of its composition but of what will happen to it. For most waste it is not necessary to know more than what it is in very general terms. But subsequent holders must be provided with a description of the waste that is full enough to enable them to manage the waste properly. Even everyday items may cause problems in handling or treatment.

1.4

In looking for waste problems it may help to ask such questions as:-

(a) does the waste need a special container to prevent its escape or to protect it from the elements;

(b) what type of container suits it and what material can the container be made of;

(c) can it safely be mixed with any other waste or are there wastes with which it should not be mixed;

(d) can it safely be crushed and transferred from one vehicle to another;

(e) can it safely be incinerated or are there special requirements for its incineration, such as minimum temperature and combustion time;

(f) can it be disposed of safely in a landfill site with other waste; and

(g) is it likely to change its physical state during storage or transport?

1.5

Anything unusual in waste can pose a problem. So can anything which is out of proportion. Ordinary household waste, and waste from shops or offices, often contains small amounts of potentially hazardous substances. This may not matter if they are mixed in a large quantity of other waste. What should be identified as potential problems in a consignment of waste, are significant quantities of an unexpected substance, or unusual amounts of an expected substance.

1.6

Note that certain particularly dangerous or difficult wastes are subject to strict legal controls quite apart from and additional to the requirements of the duty of care. These wastes are known as "special wastes" (see **Annex D** paragraphs D.16-D.18).

What goes in a description?

1.7

A transfer note must be completed, signed and kept by the parties involved if waste is transferred. This is a requirement of the Environmental Protection (Duty of Care) Regulations 1991 ("the 1991 Regulations"). Any breach of the 1991 Regulations is an offence (see **Annex C** on keeping records). Amongst other things, the transfer note must state:-

(a) the quantity of waste transferred – most waste management companies, in particular landfill operators, receive quantities of waste by weight. Wherever possible, therefore, a transfer note should record the weight of waste transferred;
(b) how it is packed – whether loose or in a container; and
(c) if in a container, the kind of container.

1.8

There must also be a description of the waste. This may be provided separately or combined as a single document with the transfer note. At the time of the publication of this code, a national waste classification scheme is the subject of consultation. One of the aims of the scheme is to provide a comprehensive list of waste types which may be generally accepted as the reference point for describing waste. The description of waste should, therefore, wherever possible refer to the appropriate entry in the national waste classification scheme when, subject to consultation, it is introduced. It is good practice to label drums or similar closed containers with a description of the waste. Under the 1991 Regulations the parties must keep the transfer note and the description for two years. The description should always mention any **special problems**, requirements or knowledge. In addition it should include some combination of:-

(a) the type of premises or business from which the waste comes;
(b) the name of the substance or substances;
(c) the process that produced the waste; and
(d) a chemical and physical analysis.

1.9

The description must provide enough information to enable subsequent holders to avoid mismanaging the waste. When writing a description it is open to the holder to ask the manager who will handle the waste what he needs to know. For most wastes, those that need only a simple description, either 1.8(a) or (b) above will do. However, in some cases it may not be enough simply to describe the waste as "household", "commercial" or "industrial" waste without providing a clearer idea of what the substance is or providing details about the premises from which it originated. Each element of the description is dealt with in paragraphs 1.11-1.17 below.

Special problems

1.10

The description should always contain any information which might affect the handling of the waste. This should include:-

(a) special problems identified under paragraphs 1.3 to 1.6 above;

(b) any information, advice or instructions about the handling, recovery or disposal of the waste given to the holder by the Environment Agency or by the Scottish Environment Protection Agency[1] or the suppliers of material or equipment;

(c) details of problems previously encountered with the waste;

(d) changes to the description since a previous load.

Note

1 In the case of processes regulated under Integrated Pollution Control in England and Wales, the Environment Agency may give advice to the producer of waste that is relevant to its subsequent management prior to its final disposal or treatment. In Scotland the Integrated Pollution control authority is the Scottish Environment Protection Agency. This advice should also be included in the description.

A) Source of the waste: type of premises or business

1.11

It may sometimes be enough to describe the source of the waste by referring either to the use of the premises where the waste is produced or to the occupation of the waste producer.

1.12

Such a "source of waste" description is recommended as the commonsense simple description where businesses produce a mixture of wastes none of which has special handling or disposal requirements; or where there are no special handling or disposal requirements which cannot be identified from such a simple description. Such a description must make it clear what type of wastes are produced and the contents of the wastes; and their proportions must be only such as might be expected.

B) Name of the substance

1.13

The waste may be described by saying what it is made of. This may be in physical and chemical terms or by the common name of the waste where this is equally helpful. Such a description by name is recommended for waste composed of a single simple material or a simple mixture.

C) Process producing the waste

1.14

The waste may be described by saying how it was produced. Such a description would include details of materials used or processed, the equipment used and the treatment and changes that produced the waste. If necessary this would include information obtained from the supplier of the materials and equipment.

1.15

This should form part of the description for most industrial wastes and some commercial wastes.

D) Chemical and physical analysis

1.16

A description based on the process producing the waste (C) will not go far enough where the holder does not know enough about the source of the waste. It will often not be adequate where:-

(a) wastes, especially industrial wastes, from different activities or processes are mixed; or

(b) the activity or process alters the properties or composition of the materials put in.

1.17

For such wastes an analysis will usually be needed. In cases of doubt, the holder may find it helpful to consult the intended waste manager as to whether he needs an analysis to manage the waste properly. Where it is necessary the holder should detail the physical and chemical composition of the waste itself including, where different substances are mixed, their dilutions or proportions. The holder might either provide this information himself or obtain a physical or chemical analysis from a laboratory or from a waste management contractor.

Section 2
Keep the waste safely

The problem

2.1

All waste holders must act to keep waste safe against:-

(a) corrosion or wear of waste containers;

(b) accidental spilling or leaking or inadvertent leaching from waste unprotected from rainfall;

(c) accident or weather breaking contained waste open and allowing it to escape;

(d) waste blowing away or falling while stored or transported;

(e) scavenging of waste by vandals, thieves, children, trespassers or animals.

2.2

Holders should protect waste against these risks while it is in their possession. They should also protect it for its future handling requirements. Waste should reach not only its next holder but a licensed facility or other appropriate destination without escape. Where waste is to be mixed immediately, for example in a transfer station, a civic amenity site or a municipal collection vehicle, it only needs to be packed well enough to reach that immediate destination.

Preventing its escape after that stage is up to the next holder. However, there are wastes that may need to reach a disposal or treatment site in their original containers. For example, drummed waste. In such cases, holders will need to know through how many subsequent hands; under what conditions; for how long; and to what ultimate treatment their waste will go in order to satisfy themselves that it is packed securely enough to reach its final destination intact. If an intermediate holder alters waste in any way, by mixing, treating or repacking it, then he will be responsible for observing all this guidance on keeping waste safe.

Storing waste securely

2.3

Security precautions at sites where waste is stored should prevent theft, vandalism or scavenging of waste. Holders should take particular care to secure waste material attractive to scavengers, for example, building and demolition materials and scrap metal. Special care should also be taken to secure waste which has a serious risk attached to it, for example certain types of clinical waste. Waste holders should undertake regular reviews of the waste in their possession to ensure that it has not been disturbed or tampered with.

2.4

Segregation of different categories of waste where they are produced may be necessary to prevent the mixing of incompatible wastes. For example, avoiding reactions in mixtures. Segregation may assist the disposal of waste to specialist outlets. Where segregation is practised on sites, the waste holder should ensure that his employees and anyone else handling waste there are aware of the locations and uses of each segregated waste container.

Containers

2.5

Waste handed over to another person should be in some sort of container, which might include a skip. The only reasonable exception would be loose material loaded into a vehicle and then covered sufficiently to prevent escape before being moved. Waste containers should suit the material put in them.

2.6

It is good practice to label drums or similar closed containers with a note of the contents when stored or handed over. This could be a copy of the waste description. To avoid confusion, old labels should be removed from drums which are reused.

Waste left for collection

2.7

Waste left for collection outside premises should be in containers that are strong and secure enough to resist not only wind and rain but also animal disturbance, especially for food waste. All containers left outside for collection will therefore need to be secured or sealed. For example, drums with lids, bags tied up, skips covered. To minimise the risks, waste should not be left outside for collection longer than is necessary. Waste should only be put out for collection on or near the advertised collection times.

Section 3
Transfer to the right person

3.1

Waste may be handed on only to authorised persons or to persons for authorised transport purposes. This **Section** of the code advises on who these persons are; and what checks to carry out *before* making an arrangement or contract for transferring waste.

3.2

Section 34(3) of the 1990 Act sets out those who are authorised persons. The list of authorised persons is:-

(a) any authority which is a waste collection authority for the purposes of Part II of the 1990 Act;

(b) any person who is the holder of a waste management licence under section 35 of the 1990 Act;

(c) any person who does not need a waste management licence because the activity he carries out is exempt from licensing by virtue of regulation 16 or 17 of and Schedule 3 to the Waste Management Licensing Regulations 1994[1] ("the 1994 Regulations");

(d) any person who is registered as a carrier of controlled waste under section 2 of the Control of Pollution (Amendment) Act 1989 ("the 1989 Act");

(e) any person exempt from registration as a carrier of controlled waste under regulation 2 of the Controlled Waste (Registration of Carriers and Seizure of Vehicles) Regulations 1991[2]; and

(f) In Scotland, a waste disposal authority acting in accordance with a resolution made under section 54 of the Environmental Protection Act 1990 (see paragraphs 3.20-3.21).

3.3

The list of authorised transport purposes is set out in section 34(4) of the 1990 Act which is reproduced at the end of **Annex A**.

3.4

It should be noted that it is an offence under Regulation 20 of the 1994 Regulations (subject to various provisions) for anyone to arrange on behalf of another person for the disposal or recovery of controlled waste if he is not a registered broker. Anyone subject to the duty of care must ensure that insofar as they use a broker when transferring waste, they use a registered broker (that is any person registered as a waste broker in accordance with regulation 20 of the 1994 Regulations) or one exempt from the registration requirements (in accordance with regulation 20 of the 1994 Regulations) (see Annex paragraphs D.11-D.15).

Notes

1 As amended by the Waste Management Licensing (Amendment etc.) Regulations 1995.

2 SI 1991/1624 as amended by the Controlled Waste Regulations 1992 (SI 1992/588) and the Waste Management Licensing Regulations 1994 (SI 1994/1056).

Public waste collection

3.5

Local authorities collect waste from households and from some commercial premises. They do this either with their own labour or using private contractors who will be registered carriers (**Annex D** paragraphs D.7-D.10). Private persons are exempt from the duty in connection with their own household waste produced on their premises (**Annex A** paragraph A.9). If there is any doubt about whether or not a particular waste can go in the normal collection, the producer should ask the local authority (the borough or district council or in Scotland on 1 April 1996, the council, or in Wales on 1 April 1996, the county or county borough council).

Using a waste carrier

3.6

A waste holder or broker may transfer waste to someone who transports it – a waste carrier – who may or may not also be a waste manager (**Annex D** paragraphs D.7-D.10). Subject to certain exemptions, anyone carrying waste in the course of their business, or in any other way for profit, must be registered with the Environment Agency or with the Scottish Environment Protection Agency. The Agencies' register of carriers is open to public inspection. For the purpose of the duty of care, holders may use these registers as a reference list of carriers who are authorised to transport waste. However, inclusion on the Agencies' register is not a recommendation or guarantee of a carrier's suitability to accept any particular type of waste. The holder or broker should remain alert to any sign that the waste may not be legally dealt with by a carrier.

3.7

Anyone intending to transfer waste to a carrier will need to check that the carrier is registered or is exempt from registration. A registered carrier's authority for transporting waste is either his certificate of registration or a copy of his certificate of registration if *it was provided by the Agencies (or before 1 April 1996 by the relevant waste regulation authority).* The certificate or copy certificate will show the date on which the carrier's registration expires. All copy certificates must be numbered and marked to show that they are copies and have been provided by the Agencies (or before 1 April 1996 by the relevant waste regulation authority). Photocopies are not valid and **do not** provide evidence of the carrier's registration.

3.8

In all cases other than those involving repeated transfers of waste, the holder should ask to see, and should check the details of, the carrier's certificate or copy certificate of registration. In addition, before using any carrier for the first time, the holder should check with the Environment Agency or the Scottish Environment Protection Agency that the carrier's registration is still valid, even if his certificate appears to be current. The holder should provide the appropriate Agency with the carrier's name and registration number as shown on the certificate.

3.9

In practice, the only exempt carriers who might take waste from a holder are:-

(a) charities and voluntary organisations;

(b) waste collection authorities (local authorities) collecting any waste themselves (though an authority's contractors are not exempt); waste disposal authorities and the Agencies;

(c) wholly owned subsidiaries of British Rail when carrying waste by rail[1];

(d) ship operators where waste is to be disposed of under licence at sea;

(e) persons who are authorised under the Animal By-Products Order 1992 to hold or deal with animal waste or the holder of a knackers yard licence[2].

3.10

It should be noted that animal waste which is collected and transported in accordance with Schedule 2 to the Animal By- Products Order 1992 is not controlled waste for the purposes of the duty of care (see **Annex A** paragraph A.10).

3.11

Charities and voluntary organisations, waste collection, disposal authorities and the Agencies and British Rail subsidiaries need to be registered as exempt carriers in the Agencies' register of professional collectors and transporters of waste[3].

3.12

In all cases other than those involving repeated transfers of waste, the holder should ask the carrier to confirm the type of exemption under which he transports waste. In addition, before using for the first time a carrier who claims to be exempt, the holder should ask the carrier to provide evidence that the exemption which he claims is valid.

Notes

1 Regulation 23(2) of the 1994 Regulations amends the controlled Waste (Registration of Carriers and Seizure of Vehicles) Regulations 1991 to provide an exemption from carrier registration for any wholly owned subsidiary of the British Railways Board which has applied for registration as a carrier of controlled waste. The exemption applies only where the subsidiary of the British Railways Board is registered under the provisions of para 12 of Sch 4 to the 1994 Regulations, and for the period whilst its application for registration under the Controlled Waste Regulations 1991 is pending.

2 That is, a knackers yard licence which in England and Wales has the same meaning as in s 34 of the Slaughterhouses Act 1974 and in Scotland means a licence under s 6 of the Slaughter of Animals (Scotland) Act 1980.

3 See paragraphs 1.70-1.84 of DOE Circular 11/94 (Welsh Office Circular 26/94 and The Scottish Office Environment Department Circular 10/94).

Sending waste for disposal, treatment or recovery

3.13

A "waste manager" is anyone:-

(a) who stores waste or who processes it in some intermediate way short of final disposal[1];

(b) who carries out a waste recovery operation[2]; or

(c) who carries out a waste disposal operation[3].

3.14

All of these activities are subject to the waste management licensing requirements of Part II of the 1990 Act. Where a licence is necessary it is issued by the Agencies (and before 1 April 1996 by the relevant waste regulation authority). The licence will usually set out the types and quantities of waste that the operator may deal with and the way in which the waste is managed. It may also cover such matters as operating hours and pollution control on site.

3.15

Before choosing a waste manager as the next person to take waste, a holder will need to:-

(a) check that the manager has a licence; and

(b) establish that the licence permits the manager to take the type and quantity of waste involved.

3.16

A waste holder should check this not merely by asking the waste manager but by examining his licence. The holder in turn should show the manager the description of the waste involved. If the holder doubts whether the licence covers his particular waste he can ask the waste manager or, if he is still not satisfied, the Agency which issued the licence.

3.17

Some forms of waste disposal, treatment or recovery do not require a licence because the activity concerned has been exempted from licensing[4]. If a selected waste manager is not licensed because what he is doing is exempt then he should say so and state which type of exemption he comes under. It is not taking enough care for a holder to consign waste to a contractor who states that he is exempt but does not give the grounds. The holder delivering waste to an exempt waste manager should check that the waste is within the scope of the exemption. The exemptions are limited to specific circumstances and types of waste. If in doubt about the exemption of a particular activity the holder may seek advice from the Agencies. (For more information on licensing and exemptions see **Annex D** paragraphs D.2-D.4).

3.18

A holder of waste should make these same checks on licences and exemptions wherever he delivers waste even if he is not the producer. A carrier should always check that the next holder he delivers to is an authorised person and that the description of the waste he carries is within the licence or exemption of any waste manager to whom he delivers, unless he is only providing the transport to a contract directly between the producer and the waste manager. In that case the producer should make all the checks on the waste manager.

Notes

1 These activities may involve the deposit of waste under s 33(1)(a) of the 1990 Act or they may be a recovery or disposal operation.
2 Waste recovery operations are listed in Pt IV of Sch 4 to the 1994 Regulations.
3 Waste disposal operations are listed in Pt III of Sch 4 to the 1994 Regulations.
4 By virtue of regs 16 and 17 of and Sch 3 to the 1994 Regulations as amended by the Waste Management Licensing (Amendment Etc.) Regulations 1995.

Responsibility of brokers

3.19

A broker, by arranging for the transfer of waste, shares responsibility for its proper transfer with the two holders directly involved. He should follow the relevant part of the guidance in paragraphs 3.6-3.18 above when undertaking checks in connection with arrangements he intends to make, or has made, for waste.

Waste disposal authorities in Scotland, England and Wales

3.20

In Scotland, local authorities may operate their own disposal sites for publicly collected waste. In some cases, such sites may also take waste directly from commerce or industry. Sites of this kind are not licensed but are operated subject to the terms and conditions of resolutions passed by the authorities which are broadly similar to those in waste management licences. In relation to these sites, it is necessary to:-

(a) check that they are operated by the local waste disposal authority; and
(b) establish that the resolution permits the authority to take the type and quantity of waste involved.

3.21

The Environment Act 1995 transfers waste regulation functions to the Scottish Environment Protection Agency on 1 April 1996. A period of six months will be allowed from this date for an authority operating a site under a resolution to apply for a waste management licence under Part II of the 1990 Act. Thereafter, the resolution will continue to operate only for so long as it takes to deal with the licence application including the time taken to settle any appeal.

3.22

In England and Wales, waste disposal authorities will not normally be responsible for the operation of waste facilities. The Environment Act 1995 nevertheless provides that, from the transfer on 1 April 1996 of waste regulation functions to the Environment Agency, any waste facilities still operated by waste disposal authorities are to be subject to the waste management licensing system under Part II of the 1990 Act.

Checks on repetitive transfers

3.23

Full checks on carriers and waste managers do not need to be repeated if transfers of waste are repetitive – the same type of waste from the same origin to the same destination. The obvious example is waste collection from commercial premises. However, it would be advisable to make occasional checks to ensure that the contents or composition of the waste which is being transferred under cover of a season ticket remains consistent with the waste description.

3.24

For a series of identical loads making up one transaction there is no need to see every time a load of waste is transferred the licence of a waste manager or, in Scotland, the local authority's resolution (see paragraphs 3.20-3.21 above); or the registration certificate of a waste carrier. However, licences, resolutions, registration or evidence of exemption should be examined afresh in the following cases:-

(a) whenever a new transaction is involved, that is if the description or destination of the waste has changed;
(b) where several different carriers or disposers are collecting waste at one place and there might be a danger of an unauthorised carrier collecting a load. For example, a construction or demolition site from which several hauliers are taking waste away;
(c) as a minimum precaution, the licence, resolution, registration or evidence of exemption should be seen and checked at least once a year even if nothing has changed in a series of transfers;
(d) where there has been a change in the licence or resolution conditions of the destination; or
(e) where there has been a change in the waste carrier transporting the waste.

Section 4
Receiving waste

4.1

The previous three **Sections** of this code look at transfers from the point of view of the person transferring the waste to someone else. This **Section** offers guidance to persons receiving waste, whether at its ultimate destination or as an intermediate holder.

Checking on the source of waste

4.2

Checking is not only in one direction. No-one should accept waste from a source that seems to be in breach of the duty of care. Waste may only come *either* from the person who first produces *or* imports it or from someone who has received it. The person who receives it must be one of the persons entitled to receive waste – that is an authorised person or a person for authorised transport purposes (**Section 3**). On the handover of waste, the previous holder and the recipient will complete a transfer note in which the previous holder will declare which category of person entitled to hold waste he is. The recipient should ensure that this is properly completed before accepting waste. Checking back in this way need not be as thorough as checking forward.

4.3

Recipients should not normally need to see any waste management licence of the previous holder; and there is no explicit requirement for a person receiving waste from a waste carrier to check on whether or not the carrier is registered. In the Departments' view, it is not an offence under section 34(1) of the 1990 Act for a recipient to accept waste from an unregistered carrier. However, an offence might have been committed earlier in the chain. For example, a waste producer who transfers waste to someone who is not authorised to accept it. This may be a carrier who was required to be registered but was not. The carrier himself would also be in breach of the carrier registration legislation if he was required to be registered but was not. Paragraphs 5.10-5.12 below provide guidance on reporting to the Agencies.

4.4

However, the first time a carrier delivers waste, the recipient should satisfy himself that he dealing with someone who is properly registered to transport the waste. In this case, it would be reasonable to ask to see either the carrier's registration certificate or official copy certificate, or to request confirmation of the type of exemption under which the carrier is transporting the waste.

4.5

Before receiving any waste, a holder should establish that it is contained in a manner suitable for its subsequent handling and final disposal or recovery. Where the recipient provides containers he should advise what waste may be placed in them.

4.6

The recipient should also look at the description and seek more information from the previous holder if this is necessary to manage the waste.

Co-operation with the previous holder

4.7

Anyone receiving waste should co-operate with the previous holder in any steps they are taking to comply with the duty. That means in particular supplying correct and adequate information that the previous holder may *need.*

4.8

The previous holder needs to know enough about the later handling of his waste – how it is likely to be carried, stored and treated – to pack and describe it properly. The recipient should give such information.

4.9

Under the 1991 Regulations (**Annex C**) anyone receiving waste must receive a description and complete a transfer note. The recipient must declare on the transfer note which category of authorised person he is, with details. Before making any arrangement to receive waste, a waste manager should show to the previous holder his waste management licence or a statement of the type of exemption from licensing under which he is operating; and a carrier should show his certificate of registration, an official copy of his certificate of registration or evidence of the type of exemption from registration under which he transports waste. It would be sensible for every waste management site office to hold a copy of the waste management licence or a statement of the type of exemption; and for every vehicle used by a carrier to carry an official copy of the carrier's certificate of registration or evidence of the type of exemption under which he transports waste. Where an establishment or undertaking is carrying out an exempt activity, the statement of the type of exemption may take the form of a copy of its entry in the Agencies' register of exempt activities[1].

4.10

A broker, by arranging for the transfer of waste, shares responsibility for its proper transfer with the two holders directly involved. To enable the broker and the other parties to the transfer to discharge their duty of care, information may need to be exchanged between the broker and the previous holder or recipient of the waste, in line with the guidance in this **Section**.

Notes

1 Regulation 18(8) of the 1994 Regulations requires the Agencies to provide reasonable facilities for obtaining, on payment of reasonable charges, copies of entries in their register of exempt activities.

Section 5
Checking up

5.1

The previous **Sections** describe normal procedures for transferring waste from the producer to its final destination. Most of the checking that is reasonable is already built into these procedures and the transfer note system (**Annex C**). This **Section** gives guidance on what further checks are advisable and the action to take when checks show that something is wrong.

Checks after transfer

5.2

Most waste transfers require no further action from the person transferring waste after the waste has been transferred. A producer is under no specific duty to audit his waste's final destination. However, undertaking such an audit and subsequent periodic site visits would be a prudent means of protecting his position by being able to demonstrate the steps he had taken to prevent illegal treatment of his waste.

5.3

One exception is where a holder makes arrangements with more than one party. For example, a producer arranges two contracts, one for disposal and another for transport to the disposal site. In that case the producer should establish that he not only handed the waste to the carrier but that it reached the disposer. Similar considerations apply to a broker who may make arrangements on behalf of a waste producer with several parties (carrier, disposer etc).

Checks after receipt

5.4

Any waste holder, but especially a waste manager receiving waste, has a strong practical interest in the description being correct and containing adequate information. A waste management licence will control the quantities and types of waste that may be accepted and how they may be managed. It is within his capacity as a waste manager to ensure that descriptions of waste received are indeed correct. Anyone receiving waste should make at least a quick visual check that it appears to match the description. For a waste manager it would be good practice to go beyond this by fully checking the composition of samples of waste received.

Causes for concern

5.5

Every waste holder should be alert for any evidence that suggests that the duty of care is not being observed or that illegal waste handling is taking place. Obvious causes for concern that any holder should notice when he accepts or transfers waste include:-

(a) waste that is wrongly or inadequately described being delivered to a waste management site;
(b) waste being delivered or taken away without proper packing so that it is likely to escape;
(c) failure of the person delivering or taking waste to complete a transfer note properly, or an apparent falsehood on the transfer note;
(d) an unsupported claim of exemption from licensing or registration as a carrier; and
(e) failure of waste consigned via a carrier to arrive at a destination with whom the transferring holder has an arrangement; or
(f) damage to, or interference with containers.

5.6

Other causes of concern may come to light. Waste holders do not have to check up after waste is handed on, but they may become aware of where it is going, and should act on such information if it suggests illegal or careless waste management. Similarly, a broker who suspects mismanagement of waste for which he has made arrangements should take appropriate action. For instance, he may need to make further checks to establish the facts, or use different waste carriers and managers unless and until problems are remedied. Paragraphs 5.10-5.12 give guidance on informing the Environment Agency or the Scottish Environment Protection Agency.

Action to take with other holders

5.7

A holder who only suspects that his waste is not being dealt with properly should first of all check his facts, in the first place with the next (or sometimes the previous) holder. This may involve asking that further details should be added to a waste description, for more information about the exact status of the holder for the purposes of waste management licensing or carrier registration, why they may be entitled to an exemption, or simply where waste went to or came from.

5.8

If a holder is not satisfied with the information or is certain that waste he handles is being wrongly managed by another person then his first action should normally be to refuse to transfer or accept further consignments of the waste in question to or from that person, unless and until the problem is remedied. Such a step may not be practicable in all cases. For example, to avoid breach of a contract to deliver or accept waste or because there is no other outlet immediately available for the waste. Steps should be taken to minimise such inflexibility. One possible measure would be for new waste contracts to provide for termination if a breach of the duty occurs and a notice to rectify is not complied with.

5.9

If an arrangement that has proved wrong in some respect has to continue temporarily then the holder should take stringent precautions. For example, where waste has been misdescribed he should analyse further consignments; where waste has been collected or delivered without being properly packed he should inspect each further load; and where it has not reached its legitimate destination he should check that each subsequent load arrives at the appointed place. He should also, if appropriate, bring the situation to the attention of the Agencies, which may be able to offer guidance.

Reporting to the Environment Agency or to the Scottish Environment Protection Agency

5.10

The Environment Agency and the Scottish Environment Protection Agency are responsible for the licensing of waste management facilities; the registration of establishments or undertakings carrying out activities exempt from licensing; the registration of waste carriers; and the registration of waste brokers.

5.11

The Agencies do not have a specific duty to enforce the duty of care. However, they have a major interest in breaches of the duty which might contribute to illegal waste management. They are also equipped with the powers and expertise to prevent or pursue offences and to advise on the legal and environmentally sound management of waste. Fly tipping (ie disposing of waste without a waste management licence or an exemption from licensing) is one such offence. Fly tipping is a serious offence, and the Courts may impose fines and/or imprison those responsible. The Government is keen to ensure that fly-tipping does not increase following the introduction of the landfill tax in October 1996. The Departments therefore expect the Agencies to give a high priority to the prevention of fly-tipping and to draw the financial gains made by perpetrators to the attention of the Courts.

5.12

Any person who imports, produces, carries, keeps, treats or disposes of waste or who has control of it as a broker is required to take all reasonable measures to prevent the unlawful deposit, recovery or disposal of the waste by themselves or another person. Holders should tell the Agencies where they know or suspect that:-

(a) there is a breach of the duty of care; or
(b) waste is carried by an unregistered carrier not entitled to exemption; or
(c) waste is stored, disposed of, treated or recovered:-
  (i) without a licence or in a way not permitted by the licence;
  (ii) contrary to the terms or conditions of a licence exemption; or
  (iii) in Scotland, contrary to the terms and conditions of an authority's resolution.

Section 6
Expert help and guidance

6.1

A waste holder may not always have the knowledge or expertise to discharge his duty of care. He should then seek expert help and guidance. The holder is still the person responsible for discharging his own duty of care, a responsibility that cannot be transferred to an expert adviser.

Help with analysing, describing and handling waste

6.2

Waste consultants and waste managers offer services to examine waste problems, identify wastes and recommend storage and handling methods. A waste holder may also use an analytical laboratory to establish the nature of unknown waste that he needs to describe. A consultant or laboratory acting in this way can only advise, and cannot take over the duty of care from the holder. However reliable the expert, the holder himself needs to ask the right questions. Where he is faced with an unknown substance or a known waste but no disposal outlet, he needs to establish not only what it is but what special needs it has for storage, transport or treatment, and what the possible outlets for it may be, whether disposal or reclamation.

Help with choosing a destination

6.3

A consultant may put a waste holder in touch with a legitimate outlet for his waste. Alternatively, waste managers or carriers themselves may offer expert advice on a destination for a waste. A large waste management organisation with a variety of disposal or recovery methods under its control may be able to provide all the waste management services a holder needs. Otherwise it may be necessary to ask several firms for advice on whether or not they would accept a waste. If a consultant arranges a waste transfer to such an extent that he controls what happens to the waste, he is a broker, and shares responsibility with the two holders directly involved for the proper transfer of the waste (**Section 3** paragraph 3.19 and **Annex B** paragraph B.12).

6.4

If the next holder is himself a source of advice he may sometimes undertake the analysis and write the waste description on behalf of the previous holder. What he may not do is to undertake the checks or complete a transfer note for which the previous holder is responsible.

Help from relevant authorities

6.5

A *waste collection authority* will be able to tell a waste holder whether a particular waste may or will be collected by the authority as part of its normal public waste collection.

6.6

The *Environment Agency and the Scottish Environment Protection Agency* have expertise in the management of all types of controlled waste. Although the Agencies will help as far as possible, they are not in a position to offer advice to every waste holder on how he should deal with his waste. Information that is held by the Agencies and is available for any enquirer to examine on request is:-

(a) the register which the Agencies[1] are required to maintain under section 64 of the 1990 Act as amended by the 1995 Act. The information on the register includes details of current or recently current waste management licences;[2]

(b) the register which the Agencies are required to maintain under regulation 18 of the 1994 Regulations of establishments or undertakings carrying on exempt activities involving the recovery or disposal of waste;

(c) the register of waste carriers which the Agencies are required to maintain under regulation 3 of the Controlled Waste (Registration of Carriers and Seizure of Vehicles) Regulations 1991;

(d) the register of waste brokers which the Agencies are required to maintain under regulation 20 of and Schedule 5 to the 1994 Regulations; and

(e) the register of professional collectors, transporters, dealers and brokers of waste which the Agencies are required to maintain under paragraph 12 of Part I of Schedule 4 to the 1994 Regulations.

Notes

1 And waste collection authorities in England and, from 1 April 1996, waste collection authorities in Wales

2 Regulation 10 of the 1994 Regulations sets out the information which the register must contain.

Waste Management Papers

6.7

Detailed advice on good practice is given in the series of Waste Management Papers issued by the Departments and published by HMSO. These cover subjects including the handling, disposal, treatment and recovery of particular wastes and waste management licensing.

Section 7
The duty of care and scrap metal

7.1

Scrap metal became a controlled waste for the purposes of the duty of care from 1 October 1995[1]. The duty of care and the guidance in the previous **Sections** of this code therefore apply to holders of scrap metal as they do to holders of other types of controlled waste. The purpose of this **Section** is to supplement that guidance and, in so doing, to take account of the distinctive features of scrap metal and the circumstances in which it is recovered.

7.2

Metal recycling sites (MRSs) are classified as recovery operations for the purposes of waste management licensing. In this context, the Secretary of State has advised in DOE Circular 6/95[2] that waste regulation authorities (which from 1 April 1996 should be taken to mean the Environment Agency or the Scottish Environment Protection Agency):-

"(a) should have regard to the fact that scrap metal recovery and waste motor vehicle dismantling are a source of benefit to the environment and sustainable development;

(b) should strike an appropriate balance between advice and encouragement and regulation and legal enforcement; and

(c) should distinguish between and act proportionately in relation to 'technical' breaches of the Regulations[3], the 1994 Regulations[4] or Part II of the 1990 Act where there is no threat of pollution to the environment or harm to human health; and breaches which do give rise to such a threat. In the former case waste regulation authorities' main aim should be to ensure that the person responsible is made aware of his legal responsibilities and that steps are taken by the authority or the person concerned to prevent the commission of any further 'technical' offences."

7.3

The Secretary of State has also recognised the distinctive nature of MRSs in the guidance on the licensing of these facilities which he has issued in Waste Management Paper No.4A (see paragraph 6.7 above). For example, the operator of a MRS is likely to have a sound knowledge of the materials he receives; and unlike many other types of controlled waste, a significant proportion of the scrap metal which he receives will have a positive value both to the person transferring it and the person to whom it is transferred. A consequence of this is that the operator of a MRS is likely to have a direct interest in taking measures "to prevent the escape of waste from his control"[5]. Many MRSs operate under the terms of exemptions from waste management licensing. The terms of these exemptions require that the activity concerned is carried on at a "**secure place** designed or adapted for the recovery of scrap metal or the dismantling of waste motor vehicles…."[6]

Notes

1 Regulations 3(2) and 7(2) of the Controlled Waste Regulation 1992 (SI 1992/588) as amended by reg 2(1) of the Waste Management Licensing (Amendment etc.) Regulations 1995 (SI 1995/288).
2 Welsh Office Circular 25/95 and The Scottish Office Environment Department Circular 8/95.
3 The Waste Management Licensing (Amendment etc.) Regulations 1995.
4 The Waste Management Licensing Regulations 1994.
5 Section 34(1)(b) of the 1990 Act.
6 Paragraph 45(1) and (2) of Sch 3 to the Waste Management Licensing Regulations 1994 (inserted by reg 3(16) of the Waste Management (Amendment etc) Regulations 1995).

The transfer note system

7.4

As explained in paragraphs 1.7-1.9 above, if waste is transferred from one person to another a transfer note must be completed, signed and kept by the parties to the transfer. The format of the transfer note is not prescriptive. However, the transfer note must include the information shown on the suggested standard form for voluntary use at **Annex C**.

7.5

Operators of MRSs are well placed to meet the requirements of the 1991 Regulations because of the records which they are required to keep under the Scrap Metal Dealers Act 1964 ("the 1964 Act")[1]. In this respect, section 2 of the 1964 Act requires every scrap

metal dealer to keep, at each place occupied by him as a scrap metal store, a book[2] and to enter in the book specified particulars with respect to:-
(a) all scrap metal received at that place, and
(b) all scrap metal either processed at, or despatched from, that place.

7.6

Section 2(2) and (3) of the 1964 Act specifies the particulars to be entered in the book as follows:-

In the case of scrap metal received at the place occupied by the dealer
"(a) the description and weight of the scrap metal;
(b) the date and time of the receipt of the scrap metal;
(c) if the scrap metal is received from another person, the full name and address of that person;
(d) the price, if any, payable in respect of the receipt of the scrap metal, if that price has been ascertained at the time when the entry in the book relating to that scrap metal is to be made;
(e) where the last preceding paragraph does not apply, the value of the scrap metal at the time when the entry is to be made as estimated by the dealer;
(f) in the case of scrap metal delivered at the place in question by means of a mechanically propelled vehicle bearing a registration mark (whether the vehicle belongs to the dealer or not), the registration mark borne by the vehicle."

In the case of scrap metal either processed at, or despatched from, the place occupied by the dealer
"(a) the description and weight of the scrap metal;
(b) the date of processing or, as the case may be, despatch of the scrap metal, and, if processed, the process applied;
(c) in the case of scrap metal despatched on sale or exchange, the full name and address of the person to whom the scrap metal is sold or with whom it is exchanged, and the consideration for which it is sold or exchanged;
(d) in the case of scrap metal processed or despatched otherwise than on sale or exchange, the value of the scrap metal immediately before its processing or dispatch as estimated by the dealer."

7.7

As indicated at paragraph 7.4 above, the form of the transfer note required for the purposes of the duty of care is not prescribed in the 1991 Regulations. The purpose of this was to allow each sector of industry to use or adapt its existing systems. This approach enables the scrap metal industry to use the records which dealers are required to keep under the 1964 Act[3] as a basis to fulfil the requirements of the 1991 Regulations.

7.8

The only other information required by the 1991 Regulations is:-
(a) how the material is contained on its transfer (ie whether it is loose or in a container and the kind of any container eg in sacks a skip or drums);
(b) whether the person transferring the waste is the producer or importer of that material;
(c) to which category of authorised persons[4] the person transferring the waste and the person receiving the waste belongs; and
(d) the place of transfer[5].

7.9

Annex C paragraph C.8 provides guidance on the completion of transfer notes.

Notes

1 The equivalent provision in Scotland is s 30 of the Civic Government (Scotland) Act 1982 (the 1982 Act).

2 Section 30(3)(b) of the 1982 Act provides that in Scotland records may alternatively be kept by "the use of a device for storing and processing information."

3 In Scotland the Civic Government (Scotland) Act 1982.

4 If the transfer is to a person for authorised transport purposes, it is necessary to specify which of those purposes.

5 Regulation 2(2)(a)(iii) of the 1991 Regulations. In the case of scrap metal despatched from the place occupied by the dealer, the transfer note should also record the time of transfer.

Keeping a record of transactions

7.10

Section 2(5) of the 1964 Act[1] requires scrap metal dealers to retain the book containing records of dealings for two years beginning from the day on which the last entry was made in the book. This is similar to the requirement under the 1991 Regulations. The 1991 Regulations do not specify which of the two parties must complete the transfer note. It may be completed by either party. However, both parties are required to ensure that it is completed and must sign it and keep a copy.

7.11

Scrap metal dealers may wish, therefore, to assist those who transfer scrap metal to them by providing prepared documentation including the required information which the transferor may then complete and sign. If prepared documentation is provided the transferor should ensure that he is advised by the dealer that the details are correct.

Note

1 In Scotland s 30(4) of the 1982 Act.

Records kept by itinerant traders

7.12

Among other matters, section 3 of the 1964 Act makes provision for dealers who carry on their business as part of the business of an itinerant collector. This sets out the particular record keeping requirements for itinerant collectors, although it remains the case that transaction receipts should be kept for two years. From 1 October 1995 itinerant collectors are subject to the duty of care in the same way as anyone else who deals in scrap metal. Itinerant collectors must therefore ensure that a transfer note is completed and that they retain a copy when they collect or hand on scrap metal. An important exception to this relates to householders' own waste collected from their home (see paragraph 7.15 below).

7.13

In Scotland, the equivalent term for an itinerant collector is an itinerant metal dealer. Provisions covering itinerant metal dealers are contained in sections 32 and 33 of the Civic Government (Scotland) Act 1982 (the 1982 Act). Section 33(3) of the 1982 Act provides that ".. an itinerant metal dealer shall keep a record in respect of each sale to him of metal…" section 33(4) goes on to say "any such records shall be kept by the dealer for a period of 6 months from the date of the sale to which it relates". Therefore, if itinerant metal dealers in Scotland wish to use these record for the purpose of the duty of care provisions they must keep them for two years.

Records kept by motor vehicle dismantlers

7.14

Any motor vehicle dismantler who falls outside the provisions of the 1964 Act because the materials in which he deals are not scrap metal, should follow the guidance on transfer notes provided in paragraphs 1.7-1.9 above and in **Annex C** of this Code of Practice[1].

Note

1 Section 9(1) of the Scrap Metal Dealers Act 1964 defines a scrap metal dealer as follows:-"For the purposes of this Act a person carries on business as a scrap metal dealer if he carries on a business which consists wholly or partly of buying and selling scrap metal, whether the scrap metal sold is in the form in which it was bought or otherwise, other than a business in the course of which scrap metal is not bought except as materials for the manufacture of other articles and is not sold except as a by-product of such manufacture or as surplus materials bought but not required for such manufacture; and 'scrap metal dealer' (where that expression is used in this Act otherwise than in a reference to carrying on business as a scrap metal dealer) means a person who (in accordance with the preceding provisions of this subsection) carries on business as a scrap metal dealer."

Householders

7.15

Householders are **exempt** from the duty of care for their own household waste (**Annex A** paragraph A.9). This means that a transfer note does not need to be completed when a householder brings his own household waste to a MRS; or when a householder's own scrap metal is collected from his home.

Season tickets

7.16

For regular customers and suppliers there is provision to agree a "season ticket". In other words, one transfer note which will cover multiple transfers over a given period of time. The use of a season ticket is, however, only permissible where the parties involved in the series of transfers do not change and where the description of the waste transferred remains the same (see **Annex C** paragraph C.4).

Transferring and receiving waste

7.17

The guidance provided in **Section 3** (Transfer to the right person) and **Section 4** (Receiving waste) applies to anyone subject to the duty of care, including operators of MRSs. As those **Sections** explain, controlled waste may be transferred only to authorised persons or to persons for authorised transport purposes. A full list of authorised persons is at **Section 3**, paragraph 3.2.

7.18

It is recognised that the scrap metal industry receives its material from diverse sources and that it could take considerable time to verify carriers' or suppliers' credentials at a site which undertakes a great number of transactions each day. The code is not intended to place dealers in the position where they have to seek excessive verification from their suppliers to an extent that in time, discourages them from transferring scrap metal for recovery.

7.19

As **Section 4** explains, checking back when waste is received need not be as thorough as checking forward. There is no explicit requirement for a person receiving waste from a waste carrier to check on whether or not the carrier is registered. In the Departments' view, it is not an offence under section 34(1) of the 1990 Act for a scrap metal dealer[1] to accept waste from an unregistered carrier. However, an offence might have been committed earlier in the chain. For example, a waste producer who transfers waste to someone who is not authorised to accept it. This may be a carrier who was required to be registered but was not. The carrier himself would also be in breach of the carrier registration legislation if he was required to be registered but was not.

7.20

However, the first time a carrier delivers waste, the recipient should satisfy himself that he is dealing with someone who is properly registered to transport the waste. In this case it would be reasonable to ask to see either the carrier's registration certificate or official copy certificate, or to request confirmation of the type of exemption under which the carrier is transporting the waste.

Note

1 Or any other person subject to the duty of care.

Role of the Environment Agency and the Scottish Environment Protection Agency

7.21

Section 5 (paragraphs 5.10-5.11) explains that, whilst the Agencies do not have a specific duty to enforce the duty of care. they have a major interest in breaches of the duty which might contribute to illegal waste management. The Agencies can, as can anyone else, bring a prosecution if they have evidence that the duty of care has been breached. In their dealings with the scrap metal industry, the Agencies have been asked to have regard to the considerations referred to in paragraph 7.2 above.

Summary checklist

This section draws together in one place a simple checklist of the main steps that are normally necessary to meet the duty of care. As with the code itself, *this does not mean that completing the steps listed here is all that needs to be done under the duty of care.* The checklist cross-refers to key sections of the code, to the introduction to the code and to the Appendix for fuller guidance.

It should be noted that the introduction to the code and the Appendix do not form part of the code of practice itself.

		Refer to paragraphs
(a)	Is what you have waste? If yes,	Introduction and the Appendix
(b)	is it controlled waste? If yes,	1.2
(c)	while you have it, protect and store it properly,	2.1-2.4
(d)	write a proper description of the waste, covering:-	1.7-1.9
	— any problems it poses;	1.3-1.6 & 1.10

		Refer to paragraphs
	and, *as necessary to others who might deal with it later*, one or more of:-	
	— the type of premises the waste comes from;	1.11-1.12
	— what the waste is called;	1.13
	— the process that produced the waste; and	1.14-1.15
	— a full analysis;	1.16-1.17
(e)	select someone else to take the waste. They must be an authorised person or authorised for transport purposes. As such they should be one or more of the following and must prove that they are:-	
	— a registered waste carrier;	3.6-3.8
	— exempt from waste carrier registration;	3.9-3.12
	— a waste manager licensed to accept the waste;	3.13-3.16
	— exempt from waste management licensing;	3.17-3.18
	— a waste collection authority;	3.5
	— In Scotland, a waste disposal authority operating under the terms of a resolution;	3.20-3.21
	— authorised transport purposes;	3.3
(f)	anyone arranging on behalf of another person for the disposal or recovery of controlled waste must be:-	
	— a registered waste broker or	3.4, 3.19, 4.10
	— an exempt waste broker	3.4
(g)	pack the waste safely when transferring it and keep it in your possession until it is to be transferred;	2.5-2.7
(h)	check the next person's credentials when transferring waste to them;	3.7-3.12, 3.15-3.19
(I)	complete and sign a transfer note;	**Annex C**, C.3-C.4
(j)	hand over the description and complete a transfer note when transferring the waste;	1.7-1.9, **Annex C**, C.3-C.4
(k)	keep a copy of the transfer note signed by the person the waste was given to, and a copy of the description, for two years;	**Annex C**, C.5
(l)	when receiving waste, check that the person who hands it over is one of those listed in (e), or the producer of the waste, obtain a description from them, complete a transfer note and keep the documents for two years.	4.2-4.10, 5.4
(m)	whether transferring or receiving waste, be alert for any evidence or suspicion that the waste you handle is being dealt with illegally at any stage, in case of doubt question the person involved and if not satisfied, alert the Environment Agency or the Scottish Environment Protection Agency.	5.5-5.11
(n)	supplementary guidance for holders of scrap metal	Section 7

ANNEX A
THE LAW ON THE DUTY OF CARE

What the duty requires

A.1

The duty of care is set out in section 34 of the 1990 Act (a copy is printed at the end of this **Annex**). Those subject to the duty must try to achieve the following four things:-

(a) to prevent any other person committing the offences of depositing, disposing of or recovering controlled waste without a waste management licence[1]; contrary to the conditions of a licence[2]; or in a manner likely to cause environmental pollution or harm to health[3] (It should also be noted that, where a person purports to be carrying on an activity which is exempt from licensing but he fails to comply with the terms and conditions of the exemption, he may be prosecuted under section 33(1) of the 1990 Act for carrying out a licensable activity without a licence.);

(b) to prevent the escape of waste, that is, to contain it;

(c) to ensure that, if the waste is transferred, it goes only to an "authorised person" or to a person for "authorised transport purposes". **A list of authorised persons is provided at paragraph 3.2.** The list of authorised transport purposes is set out in section 34(4) of the 1990 Act which is printed at the end of this **Annex**;

(d) when waste is transferred, to make sure that there is also transferred a written description of the waste, a description good enough to enable each person receiving it to avoid committing any of the offences under (a) above; and to comply with the duty at (b) above to prevent the escape of waste.

A.2

Those subject to the duty must also comply with the 1991 Regulations which require them to keep records and make them available to the Agencies. The 1991 Regulations are additional to the code of practice and are summarised at **Annex C**.

A.3

Failing to observe the duty of care or the 1991 Regulations is a criminal offence.

Notes

1 Section 33(1)(a) and (b) of the 1990 Act as modified by para 9 of Sch 4 to the 1994 Regulations.
2 Section 33(6) of the 1990 Act.
3 Section 33(1)(c) of the 1990 Act.

Amendments to section 34

A.4

Since section 34 of the 1990 Act was originally brought into force there have been two amendments to it:-

(a) section 33 of the Deregulation and Contracting Out Act 1994 clarifies the transfer note requirements relating to multiple transfers of waste (the "season ticket" arrangements – see also **Annex C** paragraph C.4 and **Section 7** paragraph 7.16). This amendment was made because section 34 of the 1990 Act might have been construed as requiring a separate description to be supplied with each load of waste. Section 33 (4A) of the 1994 Act therefore provides that:-

> "(a) a transfer of waste in stages shall be treated as taking place when the first stage of the transfer takes place; and
>
> (b) a series of transfers between the same parties of waste of the same description shall be treated as a single transfer taking place when the first of the transfers in the series takes place".

(b) Paragraph 65 of Schedule 22 of The Environment Act 1995 amends section 34 of the 1990 Act to allow the Secretary of State to make regulations to specify persons as authorised persons under the duty of care as follows:

"(3A) The Secretary of State may by regulations amend subsection (3) above so as to add, whether generally or in such circumstances as may be prescribed in the regulations, any person specified in the regulations, or any description of person so specified, to the persons who are authorised persons for the purposes of subsection (1) (c) above."

Who is under the duty?

A.5

The duty and therefore this code apply to any person who:-
(a) imports, produces or carries controlled waste;
(b) keeps, treats or disposes of controlled waste (a"waste manager"); or
(c) as a broker has control of controlled waste.

A.6

In this code and its **Annexes** all the persons referred to in paragraph A.5 above are referred to as "holders" of waste. Brokers are included in this term for convenience. However, the description in paragraph A.7 below should be borne in mind by users of the code.

A.7

Section 34 of the 1990 Act does not define "broker". However regulation 20 of the 1994 Regulations describes a broker as a person who arranges "for the disposal or recovery of controlled waste on behalf of another person". A broker does not handle waste himself or have it in his own physical possession but he controls what happens to it.

A.8

Employers are responsible for the acts and omissions of their employees. They therefore should provide adequate equipment, training and supervision to ensure that their employees observe the duty of care.

Exemption for householders

A.9

The only exception to the duty is for occupiers of domestic property for "household waste" (see entry for "controlled waste" in the Glossary of terms) from the property. Note that this does *not* exempt:-
(a) a householder disposing of waste that is not from his property (for example, waste from his workplace; or waste from his neighbour's property); or
(b) someone who is not the occupier of the property (for example, a builder carrying out works to a house he does not occupy is subject to the duty for the waste he produces).

Exemption for animal by-products

A.10

Animal waste which is collected and transported in accordance with Schedule 2 to the Animal By-Products Order 1992 is not subject to the duty of care. The 1994 regulations amend the Controlled Waste Regulations 1992 so that this type of waste is not treated as controlled waste for the purposes of the duty of care[1]. Schedule 2 of the Animal By-Products Order contains a system of control on the transfer of waste which achieves broadly the same objective as the duty of care.

Note

1 Regulation 24(7) of the Waste Management Licensing Regulations 1994 amends reg 7 of the Controlled Waste Regulations 1992 (SI 1992/588).

What each waste holder has to do

A.11

A waste holder is not responsible for ensuring that all the aims of the duty of care (listed in paragraph A.1) are fulfilled. A holder is only expected to take measures that are:-
(a) reasonable in the circumstances, *and*
(b) applicable to him in his capacity.

A.12

The *circumstances* that affect what is reasonable include:-
(a) what the waste is;
(b) the dangers it presents in handling and treatment;
(c) how it is dealt with; and
(d) what the holder might reasonably be expected to know or foresee.

A.13

The *capacity* of the holder is who he is, how much control he has over what happens to the waste and in particular what his connection with the waste is. Different measures will be reasonable depending on whether his connection with the waste is as an importer, producer, carrier, keeper, treater, disposer, dealer or broker.

A.14

Waste holders can be responsible only for waste which is at some time under their control. It is not a breach of the duty to fail to take steps to prevent someone else from mishandling any other waste. However, a holder's responsibility for waste which he at any stage controls extends to what happens to it at other times, insofar as he knows or might reasonably foresee. Further guidance on the reasonable limits of responsibilities is in **Annex B**.

Offences and penalties

A.15

Breach of the duty of care is a criminal offence. It is an offence irrespective of whether or not there has been any other breach of the law or any consequent environmental pollution or harm to human health. The offence is punishable by a fine of up to £5,000 on summary conviction or an unlimited fine on conviction on indictment.

The Code of Practice

A.16

This code of practice has statutory standing. The Secretary of State is obliged by section 34 of the 1990 Act to issue practical guidance on how to discharge the duty. This code constitutes that guidance. The code is admissible in evidence in court. Section 34(10) of the 1990 Act provides that if a provision of the code appears to the court to be relevant to any question arising in the proceedings, it must be taken into account in determining that question. The code may therefore be used by a Court in deciding whether or not an accused has complied with his duty of care.

Environmental Protection Act 1990

34 Duty of care etc. as respects waste

(1) Subject to subsection (2) below, it shall be the duty of any person who imports, produces, carries, keeps treats or disposes of controlled waste or, as a broker, has control of such waste, to take all such measures applicable to him in that capacity as are reasonable in the circumstances -

(a) to prevent any contravention by any other person of section 33 above;
(b) to prevent the escape of waste from his control or that of any other person; and
(c) on the transfer of the waste to secure -
 (i) that the transfer is only to an authorised person or to a person for authorised transport purposes; and
 (ii) that there is transferred such a written description of the waste as will enable other persons to avoid a contravention of that section and to comply with the duty under this subsection as respects the escape of waste.

(2) The duty imposed by subsection (1) above does not apply to an occupier of domestic property as respects the household waste produced on the property.

(3) The following are authorised persons for the purpose of subsection (1)(c) above -

(a) any authority which is a waste collection authority for the purposes of this Part;
(b) any person who is the holder of a waste management licence under section 35 below or of a disposal licence under section 5 of the Control of Pollution Act 1974;
(c) any person to whom section 33(1) above does not apply by virtue of regulations under subsection (3) of that section;
(d) any person registered as a carrier of controlled waste under section 2 of the Control of Pollution (Amendment) Act 1989;
(e) any person who is not required to be so registered by virtue of regulations under section 1(3) of that Act; and
(f) a waste disposal authority in Scotland.

(3A) The Secretary of State may by regulations amend subsection (3) above so as to add, whether generally or in such circumstances as may be prescribed in the regulations, any person specified in the regulations, or any description of person so specified, to the persons who are authorised persons for the purposes of subsection (1) (c) above.

(4) The following are authorised transport purposes for the purposes of subsection (1)(c) above -

(a) the transport of controlled waste within the same premises between different places in those premises;
(b) the transport to a place in Great Britain of controlled waste which has been brought from a country or territory outside Great Britain not having been landed in Great Britain until it arrives at that place; and
(c) the transport by air or sea of controlled waste from a place in Great Britain to a place outside Great Britain; and "transport"has the same meaning in this subsection as in the Control of Pollution (Amendment) Act 1989.

(4A) For the purposes of subsection (1)(c)(ii) above -

(a) a transfer of waste in stages shall be treated as taking place when the first stage of the transfer takes place, and
(b) a series of transfers between the same parties of waste of the same description shall be treated as a single transfer taking place when the first of the transfers in the series takes place.

(5) The Secretary of State may, by regulations, make provision imposing requirements on any person who is subject to the duty imposed by subsection (1) above as respects the making and retention of documents and the furnishing of documents or copies of documents.

(6) Any person who fails to comply with the duty imposed by subsection (1) above or with any requirement imposed under subsection (5) above shall be liable -

(a) on summary conviction, to a fine not exceeding the statutory maximum; and

(b) on conviction on indictment, to a fine.

(7) The Secretary of State shall, after consultation with such persons or bodies as appear to him representative of the interests concerned, prepare and issue a code of practice for the purpose of providing to persons practical guidance on how to discharge the duty imposed on them by subsection (1) above.

(8) The Secretary of State may from time to time revise a code of practice issued under subsection (7) above by revoking, amending or adding to the provisions of the code.

(9) The code of practice prepared in pursuance of subsection (7) above shall be laid before both Houses of Parliament.

(10) A code of practice issued under subsection (7) above shall be admissible in evidence and if any provision of such a code appears to the court to be relevant to any question arising in the proceedings it shall be taken into account in determining that question.

(11) Different codes of practice may be prepared and issued under subsection (7) above for different areas.

ANNEX B
RESPONSIBILITIES UNDER THE DUTY OF CARE

B.1

The main **Sections** of the code address all waste holders who are subject to the duty of care. In law all the responsibilities for waste under the duty are spread among all those who hold that waste at any stage. But responsibilities are not spread evenly. Some holders will have greater or less responsibility for some aspects of the duty, according to their connection with the waste (see **Annex A** paragraphs A.11-A.14). This **Annex** offers guidance for each category of waste holder on their particular responsibilities. This **Annex** is neither comprehensive nor self-contained guidance for particular categories of waste holder. It only draws out questions of the allocation of responsibility. All waste holders should follow the guidance in the main sections of the code of practice.

Waste producers

B.2

The duty of care applies to a person who "produces" waste. Section 34 of the 1990 Act does not define this term. However, in relation to the definition of waste, regulation 1(3) of the 1994 Regulations provides that "'producer' means anyone whose activities produce [Directive] waste or who carries out preprocessing, mixing or other operations resulting in a change in its nature or composition". This definition is also reflected in paragraph 88 of Schedule 22 of the Environment Act 1995.

B.3

Waste producers are solely responsible for the care of their waste while they hold it. Waste producers are normally best placed to know what their waste is and to choose the disposal, treatment or recovery method, if necessary with expert help and advice. They bear the main responsibility for ensuring that the description of the waste which leaves them is accurate and contains all the information necessary for safe handling, disposal, treatment or recovery. If they also select a final disposal, treatment or recovery destination then they share with the waste manager of that destination responsibility for ensuring that the waste falls within the terms of any licence or exemption relevant to that final destination.

B.4

Producers bear the main responsibility for packing waste to prevent its escape in transit. Waste leaving producers should be packed in a way that subsequent holders can rely on.

B.5

Using a registered or exempt carrier does not necessarily let a producer out of all responsibility for checking the later stages of the disposal of his waste. The producer and the disposer may sometimes make all the arrangements for the disposal or recovery of waste, and then contract with a carrier simply to convey the waste from one to the other. Such a case is very little different in practice from that where there is no intermediate carrier involved. If a producer arranges disposal or recovery then he should exercise the same care in selecting the disposer or recoverer as if he were delivering the waste himself.

B.6

It is not possible to draw a line at the gate of producers' premises and say that their responsibility for waste ends there. A producer is responsible according to what he knows or should have foreseen. So if he hands waste to a carrier not only should it be properly packed when transferred, but the producer should take account of anything he sees or learns about the way in which the carrier is subsequently handling it. The producer would not be expected to follow the carrier but he should be able to see whether the waste is loaded securely for transport when it leaves, and he may come to learn or suspect that it is not ending up at a legitimate destination. A producer may notice a carrier's lorries returning empty for further loads in a shorter time than they could possibly have taken to reach and return from the nearest lawful disposal site; or a producer may notice his carrier apparently engaged in the unlawful dumping of someone else's waste. These would be grounds for suspecting illegal disposal of his own waste. The same reasoning applies when a producer makes arrangements with a waste manager for the disposal, treatment or recovery of waste. The producer shares the blame for illegal treatment of his waste if he ignores evidence of mistreatment. A producer should act on knowledge to stop the illegal handling of waste (see paragraphs 5.5-5.12).

Waste importers

B.7

Revised legislative requirements mean that waste importers and exporters face stringent controls and in some cases, prohibitions on transfrontier shipments of waste. Consent to movements of waste must be obtained from the competent authorities involved and full details about each shipment must be given on a consignment note (**Annex D** vi. D.21 -D.22).

Waste carriers

B.8

A waste carrier is responsible for the adequacy of packaging while waste is under his control. He should not rely totally on how it is packed or handed over by the previous holder. He should at least look at how it is contained to ensure that it is not obviously about to escape. His own handling in transferring and transporting waste should take account of how it is packed, or if necessary he may need to repack it or have it repacked to withstand handling.

B.9

A waste carrier would not normally be expected to take particular measures to provide a new description of the waste he carried unless he altered it in some way. The description would normally be provided by the waste producer, unless the producer is a householder not subject to the duty, in which case the person first taking waste from the householder would have to ensure that a description was furnished to the next holder. When accepting any waste a carrier should make at least a quick visual inspection to see that it appears to match the description, but he need not analyse the waste unless there is reason to suspect an anomaly or the waste is to be treated in some way not foreseen by the producer.

B.10

If a carrier or any other intermediate holder does alter waste in any way, by mixing, treating or repacking it, he will need to consider whether a new description is necessary. The description received may continue to serve for waste that is merely compacted or mixed with similar waste, but if it has deteriorated or decomposed or if it has been altered in any way that matters for handling and disposal then a new description should be written.

B.11

Where there is a contract between the producer and the waste manager and a carrier is contracted solely to provide transport, he may rely on the producer checking the scope of the licence or exemption of the waste manager to whom the waste is delivered. In other cases the carrier should check this himself.

Waste brokers

B.12

A waste broker arranging the transfer of waste between a producer and a waste manager, to such an extent that he controls what happens to the waste, is taking responsibility for the legality of the arrangement. He should ensure that he is as well informed about the nature of the waste as if he were discharging the responsibilities of both producer and waste manager. He is as responsible as either for ensuring that a correct and adequate description is transferred, that the waste is within the scope of any waste licence or exemption, that it is carried only by a registered or exempt carrier and that documentation is properly completed. As he does not directly handle the waste, he cannot be held responsible for its packaging. However, he may be in a position to advise producers on appropriate methods of packaging or containment if he has greater knowledge of how the waste will be handled once it is removed from the producers premises. He should also undertake the same level of checks after transfer, and the same action on any cause for suspicion, as a waste holder.

Waste managers

B.13

Waste managers, like waste carriers, should normally be able to rely on the description of waste supplied to them. However in disposing, treating or recovering waste they are in a stronger position to notice discrepancies between the description and the waste and therefore bear a greater responsibility for checking descriptions of waste they receive. Sample checks on the composition of waste received would be good practice.

B.14

Waste managers are also in a good position to notice that waste has not been properly dealt with or falsely documented before it reaches them. For example, a waste manager may receive waste which is documented as coming directly from one producer but which shows signs of having been mixed or treated at some intermediate stage. A manager is to some extent responsible for following up evidence of previous misconduct just as he is for subsequent mismanagement of waste, that is to the extent that he knew or should have foreseen it and to the extent that he can control what happens.

ANNEX C
REGULATIONS ON KEEPING RECORDS

C.1

The 1991 Regulations[1] are made under section 34(5) of the 1990 Act and require all those subject to the duty to make records of waste they receive and consign, to keep the records and to make them available to the Environment Agency or to the Scottish Environment Protection Agency.

C.2

The 1991 Regulations require each party to any transfer to keep a copy of the description which is transferred. An individual holder might transfer onward the description of the waste that he received unchanged in which case it would be advisable for the sake of clarity to endorse the description for onward transfer to the effect that the waste was sent onwards as received. If a different description of waste is transferred onwards, whether or not this reflects any change in the nature or composition of the waste, then copies of both descriptions must be made. The holder making the copy need not be the author of the description, which will often be written only by the producer or broker and reused unchanged by each subsequent holder.

C.3

The Regulations also require the parties to complete, sign and keep a transfer note. The transfer note contains information about the waste and about the parties to the transfer.

Notes

1 The Environmental Protection (Duty of Care) Regulations 1991 (SI 1991/2839).

Season ticket provisions

C.4

While all transfers of waste must be documented, the 1991 Regulations do not require each individual transfer to be separately documented. Where a series of transfers of waste of the same description is being made between the same parties, provision is made for the parties to agree a "season ticket" – ie one transfer note covering a series of transfers (see paragraph A.4 above). A season ticket might be used, for example, for the weekly or daily collections of waste from shops or commercial premises, or the removal of a large heap of waste by multiple lorry trips. In the Departments' view, however, a season ticket should not extend for a period of more than 12 months from the date on which the first of the transfers subject to the arrangements takes place.

Duty of care: Controlled waste transfer note

C.5

The 1991 Regulations require these records (both the descriptions and the transfer notes) to be kept for at least two years. Holders (which includes where relevant, brokers) must provide copies of these records if requested by the Agencies.

C.6

One purpose of documentation is to create an information source of use to other holders. It is open to holders (including where relevant, brokers) to ask each other for details from records, especially to check what happened to waste after it was consigned. A holder or broker might draw conclusions and alert the Agencies to any suspected breach of the duty if such a request were refused.

Format of the record

C.7

There is no compulsory form for keeping these records. It is recognised that a number of holders already keep records of waste in a manner that meets the requirements of the 1991 Regulations with little or no further adaptation. For example, scrap metal dealers may adapt the system of books they are obliged to keep under the Scrap Metal Dealers Act 1964 or in Scotland the Civic Government (Scotland) Act 1982 (see **Section 7** paragraphs 7.5-7.13). The consignment note for special waste can be properly completed so as to fulfil the duty of care requirements (**Annex D** paragraphs D.16- D.18). Similarly, the consignment note system for transfrontier shipments of waste which involves the use of movement and tracking forms should, if properly completed satisfy the duty of care arrangements (**Annex D** paragraphs D.21-D.22).

C.8

A suggested standard form for voluntary use is included in this **Annex**. It should be noted that the boxes on the model form are consistent with the requirements of section 34(1) of the 1990 Act and with the requirements of the 1991 Regulations. This means that where existing documentation systems are adapted to meet the transfer note requirements of the duty of care, all of this information should be included.

C.9

Breach of any provision of the 1991 Regulations is an offence.

Duty of Care: Controlled Waste Transfer Note

Section A - Description of Waste

1. Please describe the waste being transferred:

2. How is the waste contained?

Loose ☐ *Sacks* ☐ *Skip* ☐ *Drum* ☐ *Other* ☐ → *please describe:*

3. What is the quantity of waste (number of sacks, weight etc):

Section B - Current holder of the waste (Transferor)

1. Full Name (BLOCK CAPITALS):

2. Name and address of Company:

3. Which of the following are you? (Please ✓ one or more boxes)

producer of the waste ☐ *holder of waste disposal or waste management licence* ☐ → *Licence number: Issued by:*

importer of the waste ☐ *exempt from requirement to have a waste disposal or waste management licence* ☐ → *Give reason:*

waste collection authority ☐ *registered waste carrier* ☐ → *Registration number: Issued by:*

waste disposal authority (Scotland only) ☐ *exempt from requirement to register* ☐ → *Give reason:*

Section C - Person collecting the waste (Transferee)

1. Full Name (BLOCK CAPITALS):

2. Name and address of Company:

3. Which of the following are you? (Please ✓ one or more boxes)

authorised for transport purposes ☐ → *Specify which of those purposes:*

waste collection authority ☐ *holder of waste disposal or waste management licence* ☐ → *Licence number: Issued by:*

waste disposal authority (Scotland only) ☐ *exempt from requirement to have a waste management licence* ☐ → *Give reason:*

registered waste carrier ☐ → *Registration number: Issued by:*

exempt from requirement to register ☐ → *Give reason:*

Section D

1. Address of place of transfer/collection point:

2. Date of transfer:

3. Time(s) of transfer (for multiple consignments, give 'between' dates):

4. Name and address of broker who arranged this waste transfer (if applicable):

	Transferor	**Transferee**
5.	Signed:	Signed:
	Full name: (BLOCK CAPITALS)	Full Name: (BLOCK CAPITALS)
	Representing:	Representing:

FED 0443 (02/96 DDP)

ANNEX D
OTHER LEGAL CONTROLS

D.1

This code offers guidance on the discharge of a waste holder's duty of care under section 34 of the 1990 Act. Holders are also subject to other statutory requirements, some of the most important of which are set out here.

I WASTE MANAGEMENT LICENSING

D.2

In *England*, *Wales* and *Scotland* a new system of waste management licensing under Part II of the 1990 Act came into force on 1 May 1994 and replaced the system of licensing set up under the Control of Pollution Act 1974. (The new system applied to the recovery of scrap metal and waste motor vehicle dismantling from 1 April 1995). The new system is the main means by which the Government's obligations under the amended EC Framework Directive on waste are fulfilled.

D.3

Under the 1990 Act *waste management licences* are required to authorise the:-

(a) deposit of controlled waste in or on land;

(b) the disposal or recovery of controlled waste (ie a disposal operation or a recovery operation);

(c) the use of certain mobile plant to dispose of or recover controlled waste.

D.4

Exemptions from the requirement to have a waste management licence for any of the activities listed above are to be found in regulations 16 and 17 of and Schedule 3 to the 1994 Regulations[1].

Notes

1 As amended by the Waste Management Licensing (Amendment Etc.) Regulations 1995 (SI 1995/288) and by the Waste Management Licensing (Amendment No 2) Regulations 1995 (SI 1995/1950).

New controls

D.5

The Environment Act 1995 transfers waste regulation functions in *England and Wales* from waste regulation authorities to the Environment Agency, and in *Scotland* to the Scottish Environment Protection Agency on 1 April 1996.

D.6

Paragraph 65 of Schedule 22 of the Environment Act 1995 also provides that additions may be made to the list of "authorised persons" (listed in **Section 3** paragraph 3.2), for the purpose of the duty of care.

II THE REGISTRATION OF WASTE CARRIERS

D.7

Subject to certain provisions, section 1(1) of the Control of Pollution (Amendment) Act 1989 ("the 1989 Act") makes it an offence to transport controlled waste without being registered as a waste carrier. The requirement to register applies to any person who transports controlled waste which that person has not produced themselves, to or from any place in Great Britain in the course of any business of his or otherwise with a view to profit. For this purpose, "transport" includes the transport of waste by road, rail, air, sea or inland waterway. It should be noted that construction (which includes improvement, repair or alteration) and demolition contractors would have to be registered as carriers if they wished to transport such waste, even if they had produced it themselves, and the transport of such waste when not registered would constitute a breach of the duty of care. The Controlled Waste (Registration of Carriers and Seizure of Vehicles) Regulations 1991[1] require the Agencies to establish and maintain a register of waste carriers; and set out the basis on which the registration system operates. Guidance on registration is provided in DOE Circular 11/91[2].

D.8

Paragraph 12 of Schedule 4 to the 1994 Regulations requires any waste carrier exempted from the waste carrier registration requirements (ie charities, voluntary organisations, waste collection/ British Rail subsidiaries and the Agencies) to register as an exempt carrier with the Environment Agency or with the Scottish Environment Protection Agency.

D.9

Anyone subject to the duty of care must ensure that, if waste is transferred, it is transferred only to an authorised person or to a person for authorised transport purposes. Among those who are "authorised persons" are:-

(a) any person registered with the Agencies as a carrier of controlled waste; and
(b) any person who is exempt from registration by virtue of regulations made under section 1(3) of the 1989 Act. The exemptions at present in force are set out in regulation 2 of the Controlled Waste (Registration of Carriers and Seizure of Vehicles) Regulations 1991.

D.10

It is not an offence under section 1(1) the 1989 Act to transport controlled waste without being registered in the circumstances set out in (a)-(c) below. The following are also "authorised transport purposes" for the duty of care:

(a) the transport of controlled waste between different places within the same premises;
(b) the transport to a place in Great Britain of controlled waste which has been brought from a country or territory outside Great Britain and is not landed in Great Britain until it arrives at that place. This means that the requirement to register as a carrier applies only from the point at which imported waste is landed in Great Britain; and
(c) the transport by air or sea of controlled waste being exported from Great Britain.

Notes

1 SI 1991/1624 as amended by SI 1992/588 and SI 1994/1056.
2 Welsh Office Circular 34/91 and The Scottish Office Environment Department Circular 18/91.

III THE REGISTRATION OF WASTE BROKERS

D.11

Subject to various provisions, regulation 20 of the 1994 Regulations makes it an offence for anyone to arrange on behalf of another person for the disposal or recovery of controlled waste if he is not registered as a broker. Anyone subject to the duty of care must ensure that, insofar as they use a broker when transferring waste, they use a registered broker or one exempt from the registration requirements.

D.12

The Transfrontier Shipment of Waste Regulations 1994 (S.I. 1994 No.1137) require waste brokers making international arrangements for the disposal or recovery of controlled waste within Great Britain or abroad to be registered.

D.13

Registered waste carriers transporting waste to or from any place in Great Britain as part of the arrangement do not need to be registered as a broker.

D.14

Paragraph 12 of Schedule 4 to the 1994 Regulations requires any undertaking which acts as a waste broker or dealer, is exempted under regulation 20 (ie a charity, voluntary organisation, waste collection/disposal/regulation authority) and possesses no other relevant permit for carrying on this activity, to register with the Agencies.

D.15

Anyone subject to the duty of care must ensure that, if waste is transferred, it is transferred only to an authorised person or to a person for authorised transport purposes. Authorised persons are discussed and listed in **Section 3** paragraph 3.2 and at **Annex A**.

IV SPECIAL WASTE

D.16

Certain particularly difficult or dangerous wastes ("special wastes") are subject to additional requirements in The Control of Pollution (Special Waste) Regulations 1980 (S.I. 1980 No.1709) made under the Control of Pollution Act 1974. The 1980 Regulations will be replaced by new Special Waste Regulations made under section 62 of the 1990 Act. The new Regulations are planned to come into force in 1996.

D.17

Special waste is subject to the duty of care, including the guidance in the code of practice and the requirements of the 1991 Regulations, in the same way as other controlled waste. Compliance with the duty of care does not in any way discharge the need also to comply with the Special Waste Regulations.

D.18

The consignment note for special waste can be properly completed so as to fulfil the duty of care requirements; a separate transfer note is not then required.

V ROAD TRANSPORT OF DANGEROUS SUBSTANCES

D.19

Waste holders have obligations in respect of the regulations and associated codes of practice concerned with the transport of dangerous substances. For national transport the primary regulations are:-

(a) The Road Traffic (Carriage of Dangerous Substances in Road Tankers and Tank Containers) Regulations 1992 (S.I. 1992 No.743 as amended by S.I. 1992 No.1213, S.I. 1993 No.1746 and S.I. 1994 No.669;

(b) The Carriage of Dangerous Goods by Road and Rail (Classification, Packaging and Labelling) Regulations 1994 (S.I. 1994 No.669);

(c) The Road Traffic (Carriage of Dangerous Substances in Packages etc.) Regulations 1992 (S.I. 1992 No.742 as amended by S.I. 1992 No.1213, S.I. 1993 No.1746 and S.I. 1994 No.669);

(d) The Road Traffic (Training of Drivers of Vehicles Carrying Dangerous Goods) Regulations 1992 (S.I. 1992 No.744 as amended by S.I. 1992 No.1213, S.I. 1993 No.1122, S.I. 1993 No.1746, S.I. 1994 No.397 and S.I. 1994 No.669);

(e) The Dangerous Substances in Harbour Areas Regulations 1987 (S.I. 1987 No.37).

D.20

The regulations listed above are supplemented by the Approved Carriage List – Information approved for the classification, packaging and labelling of dangerous goods for carriage by road and rail (ISBN 0 7176 0745 3, available from Health and Safety Executive (HSE) Books.) The regulations are also supplemented by the Approved Methods for the Classification and Packaging of Dangerous Goods for Carriage by Road and Rail (ISBN 0 7176 0744 5, available from HSE Books).

VI INTERNATIONAL WASTE TRANSFERS

D.21

Waste importers or exporters must act according to the requirements of the EC Waste Shipments Regulation (259/93/EEC) and the associated Transfrontier Shipment of Waste Regulations 1994 (S.I. 1994 No 1137).

D.22

The EC Regulation requires pre-notification of and consent to movements of waste, with the details of each shipment set out on a consignment note. (Non-hazardous waste moving for recovery does not need to be pre-notified). The consignment note adopted by the EC is the OECD notification and movement/tracking form. It is generally agreed in the UK that copies of both documents should accompany each shipment. These two documents together should satisfy the duty of care requirements. Forms are issued by UK/EC competent authorities of dispatch or destination, except for imports of waste for recovery into the EC from an OECD country where they are issued by the competent authority of dispatch in that country.

VII HEALTH AND SAFETY

D.23

Waste holders have a duty to ensure, so far as is reasonably practicable, the health and safety of their employees and other persons who may be affected by their actions in connection with the use, handling, storage or transport of waste, by virtue of sections 2 and 3 of the Health and Safety at Work etc Act 1974.

D.24

Holders also have specific duties under health and safety regulations, including the Control of Substances Hazardous to Health Regulations 1994 (S.I. 1994 No.3246), and in particular the requirement to carry out an assessment of the risks of their activities as required by the Management of Health and Safety at Work Regulations 1992 (S.I. 1992 No 2051).

ANNEX E
GLOSSARY OF TERMS USED IN THIS CODE OF PRACTICE

The 1995 Act: The Environment Act 1995.

The 1990 Act: the Environmental Protection Act 1990.

The 1989 Act: the Control of Pollution (Amendment) Act 1989.

The 1982 Act: The Civic Government (Scotland) Act 1982.

The 1964 Act: The Scrap Metal Dealers Act 1964.

The Agencies: The Environment Agency and the Scottish Environment Protection Agency. These are the waste regulation authorities in Great Britain from 1 April 1996.

Broker: a person who arranges for the disposal or recovery of controlled waste on behalf of another. Such arrangements will include those for the transfer of waste. He does not handle waste himself or have it in his own physical possession, but he controls what happens to it. However, for convenience, brokers are included within the term "waste holder" as it is used in the code of practice.

A registered broker is registered with a waste regulation authority in accordance with regulation 20 of the Waste Management Licensing Regulations 1994.

An exempt broker is a waste broker who by virtue of regulation 20(2), (3) or (4) of the Waste Management Licensing Regulations 1994 is not required to be registered under regulation 20.

Carrier: a person who transports controlled waste, within Great Britain, including journeys into and out of Great Britain.

A registered carrier is registered with a waste regulation authority under the 1989 Act.

An exempt carrier is a waste carrier who is not required to register under the 1989 Act because:-

(a) he is exempt from registration by virtue of regulation 2 of the Controlled Waste (Registration of Carriers and Seizure of Vehicles) Regulations 1991; or

(b) he is transporting waste in the circumstances set out in section 1(2) of the 1989 Act. These circumstances are also "authorised transport purposes" as defined in section 34(4) of the 1990 Act.

Controlled waste: as defined in section 30 of the Control of Pollution Act 1974, section 75 of the 1990 Act and the Controlled Waste Regulations 1992 (as amended). That is, household, commercial and industrial waste. Paragraphs 9(2) and 10(3) to Schedule 4 of the Waste Management Licensing Regulations 1994 provides that any reference to "waste" in Part I of the 1974 Act or Part II of the 1990 Act includes a reference to Directive Waste.

Dealer: a dealer in controlled waste acquires waste and sells it on. He may be a holder of the waste, or he may (as a broker does) make arrangements for its transfer without holding it.

A registered dealer is registered with a waste regulation authority in accordance with regulation 20 of the Waste Management Licensing Regulations 1994.

A registered dealer in scrap metal: A scrap metal dealer registered with the local authority in accordance with the Scrap Metal Dealers Act 1964. For the purposes of that Act a scrap metal dealer is defined as a person who "carries on a business which consists wholly or partly of buying and selling scrap metal …."

Directive waste: as defined in regulation 1(3) of the Waste Management Licensing Regulations 1994. Directive waste is subject to control as household, industrial or commercial waste (ie as "controlled waste").

Disposal operation: "disposal" as defined in Regulation 1(3) of the Waste Management Licensing Regulations 1994. A list of disposal operations is set out at Part III of Schedule 4 to those Regulations.

The Framework Directive on waste: Council Directive 75/442/EEC as amended by Directives 91/156/EEC and 91/692/EEC. The Framework Directive provides a common European definition of waste; it requires the control through licensing of waste recovery and disposal operations; and defines the circumstances under which exemptions from licensing may be made.

Holder: means a person who imports, produces, carries, keeps, treats, or disposes of controlled waste or, as a broker, has control of it.

Licensed waste manager is one in possession of a licence under section 35 of the 1990 Act or, for a transitional period, under section 5 of the Control of Pollution Act 1974.

An exempt waste manager is one exempted from licensing by regulations under section 33(3) of the 1990 Act.

Metal recycling site (MRS): a site for the recovery scrap metal or waste motor vehicle dismantling. The site may either be subject to waste management licensing or operated under the terms and conditions of an exemption from licensing.

Producer: means anyone whose activities produce [Directive] waste or who carries out preprocessing, mixing or other operations resulting in a change in its nature or composition (regulation 1(3) of the Waste Management Licensing Regulations 1994 (S.I. 1994 No.1056)).

Recovery operation: "recovery" as defined in regulation 1(3) of the Waste Management Licensing Regulations 1994. A list of recovery operations is set out in Part 1V of Schedule 4 to the Waste Management Licensing Regulations 1994.

The 1991 Regulations: The Environmental Protection (Duty of Care) Regulations 1991 (S.I. 1991 No 2839).

The 1994 Regulations: The Waste Management Licensing Regulations 1994 (S.I. 1994 No 1056).

The 1995 Regulations: The Waste Management Licensing (Amendment etc) Regulations 1995 (S.I. 1995 No 288).

Transferee: The person to whom waste is transferred.

Transferor: The person transferring the waste to another person.

Waste collection authority: local authority responsible for collecting waste; as defined in section 30(3) of the 1990 Act.

Waste disposal authority: as defined in section 30(2) of the 1990 Act. That is a local authority responsible for arranging the disposal of publicly collected waste. In Scotland, a waste disposal authority may itself act as a waste manager.

Waste regulation authority: as defined in section 30(1) of the 1990 Act. The authority formerly charged with the issue of waste management licences under section 35 of the 1990 Act. Section 30(1) of the 1990 Act originally designated waste regulation as a local authority function. The 1995 Act transfers on 1 April 1996, responsibility for waste regulation to two new Agencies – the Environment Agency in England and Wales and the Scottish Environment Protection Agency in Scotland. Section 30(1) of the 1990 Act is amended accordingly.

APPENDIX
THE DEFINITION OF WASTE

The following is re-produced from DOE Circular 11/94[1]. The highlighted paragraph references are references to paragraphs of DOE Circular 11/94. This Appendix is not part of the code of practice.

"SUMMARY

What Is Waste?

2.53

The following paragraphs are intended to provide a helpful summary of the Departments' guidance on the definition of waste; and to draw attention to some of the main questions which should be addressed in reaching a view on whether a particular substance or object is waste. However, the Departments caution against reaching a view on whether any particular substance or object is waste until all of the relevant issues have been considered. The main questions are:-

(a) does the substance or object fall into one of the categories set out in Part II of Schedule 4 to the Regulations; **and**

(b) if so, has it been discarded by its holder, does he have any intention of discarding it or is he required to discard it (**paragraphs 2.18 and 2.19**)?

When Is A Substance Or Object Discarded?

2.54

Waste appears to be perceived in the Directive as posing a threat to human health or the environment which is different from the threat posed by substances or objects which are not waste. This threat arises from the particular propensity of waste to be disposed of or recovered in ways which are potentially harmful to human health or the environment and from the fact that the producers of the substances or objects concerned may no longer have the self interest necessary to ensure the provision of appropriate safeguards. The purpose of the Directive, therefore, is to treat as waste those substances or objects which fall out of the normal commercial cycle or out of the chain of utility (**paragraph 2.14**). To determine whether a substance or object has been discarded the following question should be asked:-

— has the substance or object been discarded so that it is no longer part of the normal commercial cycle or chain of utility?

2.55

An answer of "no" to this question should provide a reasonable indication that the substance or object concerned is not waste (**paragraphs 2.20 and 2.21**). A substance or object should **not** be regarded as waste:-

(a) solely on the grounds that it falls into one of the categories listed in Part II of Schedule 4 to the Regulations (**paragraph 2.19**);

(b) solely on the grounds that it has been consigned to a recovery operation listed in Part IV of Schedule 4 to the Regulations (**paragraphs 2.25 and 2.26**);

(c) if it is sold or given away and can be used in its present form (albeit after repair) or in the same way as any other raw material without being subjected to a specialised recovery operation (**paragraphs 2.28(a), 2.30-2.31, 2.32, 2.33(a), 2.33(b)(I), 2.35 and 2.36**);

(d) if its producer puts it to beneficial use (**paragraph 2.40**); or

(e) solely on the grounds that its producer would be unlikely to seek a substitute for it if it ceased to become available to him as, say, a by-product (**paragraph 2.42**).

2.56

A substance or object **should be** regarded as waste if it falls into one of the categories listed in Part II of Schedule 4 to the Regulations and:-

(a) it is consigned to a disposal operation listed in Part III of Schedule 4 to the Regulations (**paragraph 2.33**);

(b) it can be used only after it has been consigned to a *specialised recovery operation* (**paragraphs 2.28(b), 2.30-2.31 and 2.33(c)**);

(c) the holder pays someone to provide him with a service, and that service is the collection [and taking away] of a substance or object which the holder does not want and wishes to get rid of (**paragraph 2.33(d)**);

(d) the purpose of any [beneficial] use is wholly or mainly to relieve the holder of the burden of disposing of it and the user would be unlikely to seek a substitute for it if it ceased to become available to him as, say, a by-product (**paragraphs 2.37, 2.38, 2.41 and 2.42**);

(e) it is discarded or otherwise dealt with as if it were waste (**paragraphs 2.33(b)(ii) and 2.52**); or

(f) it is abandoned or dumped (**paragraph 2.24**).

Can Waste Cease To Be Waste?

2.57

A substance or object which is waste **does not** cease to be waste as soon as it is transferred for collection, transport, storage, *specialised recovery* or disposal; or as soon as it reaches a *specialised recovery establishment or undertaking*. A substance or object which is waste, and is not fit for use in its present form or in the same way as any other raw material, may cease to be waste when it has been recovered within the meaning of the Directive (**paragraphs 2.46-2.49**).

2.58

The recovery of waste occurs when its processing produces a material of sufficient beneficial use to eliminate or sufficiently diminish the threat posed by the original production of the waste. This will generally take place when the recovered material can be used as a raw material in the same way as raw materials of non-waste origin by a natural or legal person other than a *specialised recovery establishment or undertaking* (**paragraphs 2.47-2.49**).

2.59

In a few cases, a change of intention by the person to whom waste has been transferred may be sufficient to result in the substance or object concerned ceasing to be waste. This is likely to occur only where it transpires that the substance or object which has been transferred as waste is in fact fit for use in its present form (albeit after repair) or in the same way as any other raw material without being subjected to a *specialised recovery operation* (**paragraph 2.50**)."

Notes

1 Welsh Office Circular 26/94 and The Scottish Office Environment Department Circular 10/94.

ENVIRONMENTAL PROTECTION ACT 1990: PART 2A CONTAMINATED LAND STATUTORY GUIDANCE

April 2012

INTRODUCTION

1

This statutory guidance ("this Guidance") is issued by the Secretary of State for Environment, Food and Rural Affairs in accordance with section 78YA of the Environmental Protection Act 1990 ("the 1990 Act"). Section 57 of the Environment Act 1995 created Part 2A of the Environmental Protection Act 1990 ("Part 2A") which establishes a legal framework for dealing with contaminated land in England. This Guidance applies only in England.

2

This Guidance is intended to explain how local authorities should implement the regime, including how they should go about deciding whether land is contaminated land in the legal sense of the term. It also elaborates on the remediation provisions of Part 2A, such as the goals of remediation, and how regulators should ensure that remediation requirements are reasonable. This Guidance also explains specific aspects of the Part 2A liability arrangements, and the process by which the enforcing authority may recover the costs of remediation from liable parties in certain circumstances.

3

This Guidance is legally binding on enforcing authorities, and relevant sections of Part 2A which form the basis of this Guidance are mentioned in specific Sections of this Guidance below. This Guidance has been subject to Parliamentary scrutiny under the negative resolution parliamentary procedure, in accordance with section 78YA of the 1990 Act. The Environment Agency and other relevant bodies in the land contamination sector have been consulted in relation to this Guidance, as required by section 78YA(1) of the 1990 Act, and a full public consultation was held between December 2010 and March 2011. This Guidance should be read in accordance with Part 2A.

4

This Guidance replaces the previous statutory guidance which was published as Annex 3 of Defra Circular 01/2006, and was issued in accordance with section 78YA of the 1990 Act. The previous statutory guidance, as it relates to non-radioactive contaminated land, and the Circular of which it was a part are obsolete from the date on which this Guidance is issued.

Radioactive contamination of land

5

This Guidance does not apply to radioactive contamination of land. Radioactive contaminated land is covered by separate statutory guidance. In the event that land is affected by both radioactive and non-radioactive contaminants both sets of statutory guidance will apply, and the enforcing authority should decide what is a reasonable course of action having due regard for the relevant primary legislation and advice from the Environment Agency.

Terminology

6

Most of the specific terms used in this Guidance are defined within the text. Some general aspects of terminology are:

— "contaminated land" is used to mean land which meets the Part 2A definition of contaminated land. Other terms, such as "land affected by contamination" or "land contamination", are used to describe the much broader categories of land where contaminants are present but usually not at a sufficient level of risk to be contaminated land.

— "Part 2A" means Part 2A of the Environmental Protection Act 1990 (as amended).

— The terms "contaminant", "pollutant" and "substance" as used in this Guidance have the same meaning – i.e. they all mean a substance relevant to the Part 2A regime which is in, on or under the land and which has the potential to cause significant harm to a relevant receptor, or to cause significant pollution of controlled waters. This Guidance mainly uses the term "contaminant" and associated terms such as "contaminant linkage". However it recognises that some non-statutory technical guidance relevant to land contamination uses alternative terms such as "pollutant", "substance" and associated terms in effect to mean the same thing.

— "unacceptable risk" means a risk of such a nature that it would give grounds for land to be considered contaminated land under Part 2A.

SECTION 1: OBJECTIVES OF THE PART 2A REGIME

1.1

This Guidance should be read and applied with Part 2A and the following points in mind.

1.2

England has a considerable legacy of historical land contamination involving a very wide range of substances. On all land there are background levels of substances, including substances that are naturally present as a result of our varied and complex geology and substances resulting from diffuse human pollution. On some land there are greater concentrations of contaminants, often associated with industrial use and waste disposal. In a minority of cases there may be sufficient risk to health or the environment for such land to be considered contaminated land.

1.3

Part 2A provides a means of dealing with unacceptable risks posed by land contamination to human health and the environment, and enforcing authorities should seek to find and deal with such land. Under Part 2A the starting point should be that land is not contaminated land unless there is reason to consider otherwise. Only land where unacceptable risks are clearly identified, after a risk assessment has been undertaken in accordance with this Guidance, should be considered as meeting the Part 2A definition of contaminated land.

1.4

The overarching objectives of the Government's policy on contaminated land and the Part 2A regime are:

(a) To identify and remove unacceptable risks to human health and the environment.
(b) To seek to ensure that contaminated land is made suitable for its current use.
(c) To ensure that the burdens faced by individuals, companies and society as a whole are proportionate, manageable and compatible with the principles of sustainable development.

1.5

Enforcing authorities should seek to use Part 2A only where no appropriate alternative solution exists. The Part 2A regime is one of several ways in which land contamination can be addressed. For example, land contamination can be addressed when land is developed (or redeveloped) under the planning system, during the building control process, or where action is taken independently by landowners. Other legislative regimes may also provide a means of dealing with land contamination issues, such as building regulations; the regimes for waste, water, and environmental permitting; and the Environmental Damage (Prevention and Remediation) Regulations 2009.

1.6

Under Part 2A , the enforcing authority may need to decide whether and how to act in situations where such decisions are not straightforward, and where there may be unavoidable uncertainty underlying some of the facts of each case. In so doing, the authority should use its judgement to strike a reasonable balance between: (a) dealing with risks raised by contaminants in land and the benefits of remediating land to remove or reduce those risks; and (b) the potential impacts of regulatory intervention including financial costs to whoever will pay for remediation (including the taxpayer where relevant), health and environmental impacts of taking action, property blight, and burdens on affected people. The authority should take a precautionary approach to the risks raised by contamination, whilst avoiding a disproportionate approach given the circumstances of each case. The aim should be to consider the various benefits and costs of taking action, with a view to ensuring that the regime produces net benefits, taking account of local circumstances.

SECTION 2: LOCAL AUTHORITY INSPECTION DUTIES

2.1

Part 2A requires that local authorities cause their areas to be inspected with a view to identifying contaminated land, and to do this in accordance with this Guidance. Relevant sections of the Act include:

a) Section 78B(1): Every local authority shall cause its area to be inspected from time to time for the purpose – (a) of identifying contaminated land; and (b) of enabling the authority to decide whether any such land is land which is required to be designated as a special site.
b) Section 78B(2): In performing [these] functions… a local authority shall act in accordance with any guidance issued for the purpose by the Secretary of State.

2.2

This Guidance recognises that there are two broad types of "inspection" likely to be carried out by local authorities: (a) strategic inspection, for example collecting information to make a broad assessment of land within an authority's area and then identifying priority land for more detailed consideration; and (b) carrying out the detailed inspection of particular land to obtain information on ground conditions and carrying out the risk assessments which support decisions under the Part 2A regime relevant to that land. This Guidance refers to the former as "strategic inspection" and the latter as "detailed inspection".

Strategic inspection

2.3

The local authority should take a strategic approach to carrying out its inspection duty under section 78B(1). This approach should be rational, ordered and efficient, and it should reflect local circumstances. Strategic approaches may vary between local authorities.

2.4

The local authority should set out its approach as a written strategy, which it should formally adopt and publish to a timescale to be set by the authority. Strategies produced in accordance with previous versions of this Guidance should be updated or replaced to reflect this Guidance. The authority may choose to have a separate strategy document and/or to include its strategy as part of a wider document.

2.5

The local authority should keep its written strategy under periodic review to ensure it remains up to date. It is for the authority to decide when its strategy should be reviewed, although as good practice it should aim to review its strategy at least every five years.

2.6

The local authority should include in its strategy:

(a) Its aims, objectives and priorities, taking into account the characteristics of its area.

(b) A description of relevant aspects of its area.

(c) Its approach to strategic inspection of its area or parts of it.

(d) Its approach to the prioritisation of detailed inspection and remediation activity.

(e) How its approach under Part 2A fits with its broader approach to dealing with land contamination. For example, its broader approach may include using the planning system to ensure land is made suitable for use when it is redeveloped; and/or encouraging polluters/owners of land affected by contamination to deal with problems without the need for Part 2A to be used directly; and/or encouraging problematic land to be dealt with as part of wider regeneration work.

(f) Broadly, how the authority will seek to minimise unnecessary burdens on the taxpayer, businesses and individuals; for example by encouraging voluntary action to deal with land contamination issues as far as it considers reasonable and practicable.

Prioritisation of detailed inspection activity

2.7

When the local authority is carrying out detailed inspection of land in accordance with Part 2A, it should seek to give priority to particular areas of land that it considers most likely to pose the greatest risk to human health or the environment.

2.8

In some cases the process of strategic inspection, including prioritisation of detailed inspection activities, may give rise to property blight issues. The local authority should seek to minimise or reduce such potential blight as far as it considers reasonable. The authority should also be open to moves by the land owner (or some other interested party) to help resolve the status of the land themselves. For example, the authority may decide that the land is, or is not, contaminated land on the basis of information provided by the land owner or other interested party, provided the authority is satisfied with the robustness of the information.

Detailed inspection of particular areas of land

2.9

If the local authority identifies land where it considers there is a reasonable possibility that a significant contaminant linkage (as defined in paragraphs 3.8 and 3.9) exists, it should inspect the land to obtain sufficient information to decide whether it is contaminated land, having regard to section 3 of this Guidance. The timing of such inspection should be subject to the authority's approach to prioritisation of detailed inspection.

2.10

The authority should consult the landowner before inspecting the land unless there is a particular reason why this is not possible, for example because it has not been possible to identify or locate the landowner. Where the owner refuses access, or the landowner cannot be found, the authority should consider using statutory powers of entry.

2.11

If the local authority intends to carry out an inspection using statutory powers of entry under section 108 of the Environment Act 1995 it should first be satisfied that there is a reasonable possibility that a significant contaminant linkage may exist on the land. The authority should not use statutory powers of entry to undertake intrusive investigations, including the taking of sub-surface samples, if:

(a) it has already been provided with appropriate, detailed information on the condition of the land (e.g. by the Environment Agency or some other person such as the owner of the land) which provides sufficient information for the authority to decide whether or not the land is contaminated land; or

(b) a relevant person (e.g. the owner of the land, or a person who may be liable for the contamination) offers to provide such information within a reasonable and specified time, and then provides such information within that time.

2.12

The local authority should carry out any intrusive investigation in accordance with appropriate good practice technical procedures for such investigations.

2.13

If at any stage the local authority considers, on the basis of information obtained from inspection activities, that there is no longer a reasonable possibility that a significant contaminant linkage exists on the land, the authority should not carry out any further inspection in relation to that linkage.

2.14

If the local authority identifies land which it considers (if the land were to be determined as contaminated land) would be likely to meet one or more of the descriptions of a special site set out in the Contaminated Land (England) Regulations 2006, it should consult the Environment Agency and, subject to the Agency's advice and agreement, arrange for the Agency to carry out any intrusive inspection of the land on behalf of the authority. If the Agency is to carry out such an inspection, the authority should where necessary authorise a person nominated by the Agency to exercise the powers of entry conferred by section 108 of the Environment Act 1995.

2.15

Where the Environment Agency carries out an inspection on behalf of a local authority, the authority's regulatory functions under section 78B and 78C of the 1990 Act (including the inspection duty and the decision as to whether land is contaminated land) and the need to comply with the related provisions of this Guidance remain the sole responsibility of the authority. The Agency should advise the authority of its findings in order to enable the authority to carry out these functions. The Agency should carry out any intrusive investigations in accordance with appropriate good practice technical procedures for such investigations.

SECTION 3: RISK ASSESSMENT

3.1

Part 2A takes a risk-based approach to defining contaminated land. For the purposes of this Guidance, "risk" means the combination of: (a) the likelihood that harm, or pollution of water, will occur as a result of contaminants in, on or under the land; and (b) the scale and seriousness of such harm or pollution if it did occur.

3.2

All soils contain substances that could be harmful to human or environmental receptors, although in the very large majority of cases the level of risk is likely to be very low. In conducting risk assessment under the Part 2A regime, the local authority should aim to focus on land which might pose an unacceptable risk.

3.3

Local authorities should have regard to good practice guidance on risk assessment and they should ensure they undertake risk assessment in a way which delivers the results needed to make robust decisions in line with Part 2A and this Guidance.

3.4

Risk assessments should be based on information which is: (a) scientifically-based; (b) authoritative; (c) relevant to the assessment of risks arising from the presence of contaminants in soil; and (d) appropriate to inform regulatory decisions in accordance with Part 2A and this Guidance.

Current use

3.5

Under Part 2A, risks should be considered only in relation to the current use of the land. For the purposes of this Guidance, the "current use" means:

(a) The use which is being made of the land currently.

(b) Reasonably likely future uses of the land that would not require a new or amended grant of planning permission.
(c) Any temporary use to which the land is put, or is likely to be put, from time to time within the bounds of current planning permission.
(d) Likely informal use of the land, for example children playing on the land, whether authorised by the owners or occupiers, or not.
(e) In the case of agricultural land, the current agricultural use should not be taken to extend beyond the growing or rearing of the crops or animals which are habitually grown or reared on the land.

3.6

In assessing risks the local authority should disregard any receptors which are not likely to be present given the current use of the land or other land which might be affected. In considering the timescale over which a risk should be assessed the authority should take into account any evidence that the current use of the land will cease in the relevant foreseeable future (e.g. within the period of exposure assumed for relevant receptors in a contaminant linkage).

3.7

When considering risks in relation to any future use or development which falls within the description of a "current use", the local authority should assume that the future use or development would be carried out in accordance with any existing planning permission. In particular, the authority should assume:
(a) That any remediation which is the subject of a condition attached to that planning permission, or is the subject of any planning obligation, will be carried out in accordance with that permission or obligation.
(b) Where a planning permission has been given subject to conditions which require steps to be taken to prevent problems which might be caused by contamination, and those steps are to be approved by the local planning authority, that the local planning authority will ensure that those steps include adequate remediation.

Contaminant linkages

3.8

Under Part 2A, for a relevant risk to exist there needs to be one or more contaminant-pathway-receptor linkagse – "contaminant linkage" – by which a relevant receptor might be affected by the contaminants in question. In other words, for a risk to exist there must be contaminants present in, on or under the land in a form and quantity that poses a hazard, and one or more pathways by which they might significantly harm people, the environment, or property; or significantly pollute controlled waters. For the purposes of this Guidance:
(a) A "contaminant" is a substance which is in, on or under the land and which has the potential to cause significant harm to a relevant receptor, or to cause significant pollution of controlled waters.
(b) A "receptor" is something that could be adversely affected by a contaminant, for example a person, an organism, an ecosystem, property, or controlled waters. The various types of receptors that are relevant under the Part 2A regime are explained in later sections.
(c) A "pathway" is a route by which a receptor is or might be affected by a contaminant.

3.9

The term "contaminant linkage" means the relationship between a contaminant, a pathway and a receptor. All three elements of a contaminant linkage must exist in relation to particular land before the land can be considered potentially to be contaminated land under Part2A, including evidence of the actual presence of contaminants. The term "significant contaminant linkage", as used in this Guidance, means a contaminant linkage which gives rise to a level of risk sufficient to justify a piece of land being determined as contaminated land. The term "significant contaminant" means the contaminant which forms part of a significant contaminant linkage.

3.10

In some cases the local authority may encounter land where risks are presented by groups of substances which are likely to behave in the same manner, or a substantially very similar manner, in relation to the risks they may present (e.g. as may be the case with organic substances found in oils). For the purposes of identifying and assessing contaminant linkages and taking regulatory decisions in relation to such linkages, the local authority may treat such groups of contaminants as being in effect a single contaminant and multiple contaminant linkages as being in effect a single contaminant linkage. The authority should only do this if there is a scientifically robust reason for doing so, and it should state clearly why this approach has been taken in relevant documentation (including the risk summary discussed later in this Section) if the land is later determined as contaminated land.

3.11

In considering contaminant linkages, the local authority should consider whether:

(a) The existence of several different potential pathways linking one or more potential contaminants to a particular receptor, or to a particular class of receptors, may result in a significant contaminant linkage.

(b) There is more than one significant contaminant linkage on any land. If there are, the authority should consider whether or not each should be dealt with separately, since different people may be responsible for the remediation of individual contaminant linkages.

The process of risk assessment

3.12

The process of risk assessment involves understanding the risks presented by land, and the associated uncertainties. In practice, this understanding is usually developed and communicated in the form of a "conceptual model". The understanding of the risks is developed through a staged approach to risk assessment, often involving a preliminary risk assessment informed by desk-based study; a site visit and walkover; a generic quantitative risk assessment; and various stages of more detailed quantitative risk assessment. The process should normally continue until it is possible for the local authority to decide: (a) that there is insufficient evidence that the land might be contaminated land to justify further inspection and assessment; and/or (b) whether or not the land is contaminated land.

3.13

For land to proceed to the next stage of risk assessment there should be evidence that an unacceptable risk could reasonably exist. If the authority considers there is little reason to consider that the land might pose an unacceptable risk, inspection activities should stop at that point. In such cases the authority should have regard to paragraphs 5.2–5.4 of this Guidance.

3.14

It may become apparent during the course of detailed inspection of land that the assumptions that led to the prioritisation of the land prove to be incorrect, and that the risks posed by the land are lower than expected. In such cases the authority should consider whether (and if so how) to proceed with its inspection, having regard to the need to prioritise inspection activities in accordance with Section 2. There may be good reason to continue until a decision can be taken on whether or not the land is contaminated land. However, as soon as it becomes clear to the authority that the land is unlikely to be contaminated land, it should bring its inspection and risk assessment to an end, and redirect its efforts to the inspection of other land in line with its approach to prioritisation.

3.15

As a general rule, inspections should be conducted as quickly, and with as little disruption, as reasonably possible whilst ensuring that a sufficiently robust assessment is carried out. The local authority should seek to avoid or minimise the impacts of long inspections on affected persons, in particular significant disruption and stress to directly affected members of the public in the case of inspections involving residential land.

3.16

The local authority should seek to ensure that its risk assessment is relevant to the land in question, and that it is based on risks that are reasonably likely to exist. In the course of risk assessment the authority may consider possible exposure scenarios or situations which are very unlikely to occur. However, regulatory decisions should be based on what is reasonably likely, not what is hypothetically possible.

3.17

In undertaking risk assessments, local authorities should ensure that the time and resource put into assessment is sufficient to provide a robust basis for regulatory decisions. In some cases, there may be a need for detailed and lengthy assessments, particularly in complex cases where regulatory decisions are not straightforward. However, in other cases a less detailed and shorter assessment may be appropriate. For example, if it becomes evident early in risk assessment that there is clearly a high or low risk (to the extent that the decision on whether or not land is contaminated land is straightforward) the authority should normally take the decision on the basis of this evidence alone.

Using external expertise during risk assessment

3.18

Developing an understanding of risks in complex cases may raise issues which are beyond the expertise of any one person, and may require the involvement of others to conduct a robust risk assessment. There may be little need to consult others in cases where risks are clearly high or low or where the authority has sufficient internal expertise, but in more complex cases the authority may consider it necessary to bring in external expertise.

3.19

The question of who to consult depends largely on the circumstances of the land, and the expertise and gaps in expertise of the person doing the assessment. When choosing specialist consultants, local authorities should strive as far as possible to ensure that they are appropriately qualified and competent to undertake the work. Authorities, or consultants working on their behalf, may also consider seeking advice from other relevant experienced practitioners.

3.20

External experts may advise the local authority on regulatory decisions under the Part 2A regime, but the decisions themselves remain the sole responsibility of the local authority.

"Normal" presence of contaminants

3.21

The Part 2A regime was introduced to help identify and deal with land which poses unacceptable levels of risk. It is not intended to apply to land with levels of contaminants in soil that are commonplace and widespread throughout England or parts of it, and for which in the very large majority of cases there is no reason to consider that there is an unacceptable risk.

3.22

Normal levels of contaminants in soil should not be considered to cause land to qualify as contaminated land, unless there is a particular reason to consider otherwise. Therefore, if it is established that land is at or close to normal levels of particular contaminants, it should usually not be considered further in relation to the Part 2A regime and the local authority should have regard to paragraphs 5.2 to 5.4 of this Guidance.

3.23

For the purpose of this Guidance, "normal" levels of contaminants in soil may result from:

(a) The natural presence of contaminants (e.g. caused by soil formation processes and underlying geology) at levels that might reasonably be considered typical in a given area and have not been shown to pose an unacceptable risk to health or the environment.

(b) The presence of contaminants caused by low level diffuse pollution, and common human activity other than specific industrial processes. For example, this would include diffuse pollution caused by historic use of leaded petrol and the presence of benzo(a)pyrene from vehicle exhausts, and the spreading of domestic ash in gardens at levels that might reasonably be considered typical.

3.24

In deciding whether land has normal levels of contaminants, the local authority should consider whether contamination is within the bounds of what might be considered typical or widespread: (a) locally, if there is sufficient information to make a reasonable consideration of what is normal within a local area; and/or (b) regionally or nationally in broadly similar circumstances, having due regard to similarity in terms of land use and other relevant factors such as soil type, hydrogeology, and the form of the contaminants.

3.25

The local authority should decide that normal levels of contaminants exist in relation to land where: (a) those levels are not significantly different to those likely to be typical or widespread within the authority's area, or in other similar areas; and/or (b) those levels are common or usual in similar land use situations across England or parts of it; and (c) there is no specific reason to consider that those levels of contaminants are likely to pose an unacceptable risk.

3.26

It is possible that specific pieces of land at or slightly above normal levels of contamination with regard to specific substances may pose sufficient risk to be contaminated land, and that remediation of such land may bring significant net benefits. However, such cases are likely to be very unusual and the authority should take particular care to explain why the decision has been taken, and to ensure that it is supported by robust scientifically-based evidence.

Use of generic assessment criteria and other technical tools

3.27

It is common practice in contaminated land risk assessment to use "generic assessment criteria" (GACs) as screening tools in generic quantitative human health risk assessment to help assessors decide when land can be excluded from the need for further inspection and assessment, or when further work may be warranted.

3.28

Local authorities may use GACs and other technical tools to inform certain decisions under the Part 2A regime, provided: (i) they understand how they were derived and how they can be used appropriately; (ii) they have been produced in an objective, scientifically robust and expert manner by reputable organisations; and (iii) they are only used in a manner that is in accordance with Part 2A and this Guidance.

3.29

GACs[1] relating to human health risk assessment represent cautious estimates of levels of contaminants in soil at which there is considered to be no risk to health or, at most, a minimal risk to health. With regard to such GACs:

(a) They may be used to indicate when land is very unlikely to pose a significant possibility of significant harm to human health. This is on the basis that they are designed to estimate levels of contamination at which risks are likely to be negligible or minimal and far from posing a significant possibility of significant harm to human health.

(b) They should not be used as direct indicators of whether a significant possibility of significant harm to human health may exist. Also, the local authority should not view the degree by which GACs are exceeded (in itself) as being particularly relevant to this consideration, given that the degree of risk posed by land would normally depend on many factors other than simply the amount of contaminants in soil[2].

(c) They should not be seen as screening levels which describe the boundary between Categories 3 and 4 in terms of Section 4 (i.e. the two Categories in which land would not be contaminated land on grounds of risks to human health). In the very large majority of cases, these SGVs/GACs describe levels of contamination from which risks should be considered to be comfortably within Category 4[3].

(d) They should not be viewed as indicators of levels of contamination above which detailed risk assessment would automatically be required under Part 2A.

(e) They should not be used as generic remediation targets under the Part 2A regime. Nor should they be used in this way under the planning system, for example in relation to ensuring that land affected by contamination does not meet the Part 2A definition of contaminated land after it has been developed.

3.30

New technical tools and advice may be developed and used in accordance with paragraph 3.28 above to help regulators and others apply and conform to this Guidance. This may be undertaken by government bodies, regulators or other organisations in the land contamination sector. Tools might be developed to help assessors apply the Category 1-4 approach (as described in Section 4 of this Guidance) in relation to specific substances or situations. For example, this might include the development of generic screening levels to help assessors decide when land might be assumed to be in Category 4; or tools to help describe how estimates of risk and/or bodily uptake of a contaminant might indicate that land should be placed within certain Categories.

Notes

1 Paragraph 3.27 refers specifically to the Soil Guideline Values produced by the Environment Agency, and other published GACs produced on similar basis by LQM/Chartered Institute of Environmental Health and the Environmental Industries Commission using the Agency's Contaminated Land Exposure Assessment methodology as existed when this Guidance came into force.

2 The level of risk raised by land contamination will depend on more than simply the amount of contaminants in the soil. For example, it will also depend on what form the contaminants take, where they are in the soil, the efficiency of the pathway by which receptors may be exposed, the sensitivity of receptors, the likely degree and duration of exposure, the dose-response relationship, etc. These factors will vary from case to case, sometimes very substantially.

3 The question of how comfortably land at the SGV/GAC levels would fall into Category 4 depends on the specific GAC in question and the site circumstances, given that different GACs have different levels of precaution built into them and that risks will depend on many factors other than merely the amount of contaminants in soil. In some cases it may be that GAC levels can be exceeded by a substantial degree (sometimes by orders of magnitude) and the land might still fall within Category 4, but in other cases there may be a considerably smaller margin and in some cases it may be that GAC levels are exceeded by only a few times and land would fall outside of Category 4.

Recognising and dealing with uncertainty

3.31

All risk assessments of potentially contaminated land will involve uncertainty, for example due to scientific uncertainty over the effects of substances, and the assumptions that lie behind predicting what might happen in the future. When building an understanding of the risks relating to land, the local authority should recognise that uncertainty exists. The authority should seek to minimise uncertainty as far as it considers to be relevant, reasonable and practical; and it should recognise remaining uncertainty, which is likely to exist in almost all cases. It should be aware of the assumptions and estimates that underlie the risk assessment, and the effect of these on its conclusions.

3.32

The uncertainty underlying risk assessments means there is unlikely to be any single "correct" conclusion on precisely what is the level of risk posed by land, and it is possible that different suitably qualified people could come to different conclusions when presented with the same information. It is for the local authority to use its judgement to form a reasonable view of what it considers the risks to be on the basis of a robust assessment of available evidence in line with this Guidance.

Risk summaries

3.33

Once the local authority has completed its detailed inspection and assessment of particular land it should be satisfied it has sufficient understanding of the risks to take relevant regulatory decisions.

3.34

The local authority should produce a risk summary for any land where, on the basis of its risk assessment, the authority considers it is likely that the land in question may be determined as contaminated land. The risk summary should explain the authority's understanding of the risks and other factors the authority considers to be relevant. The authority should seek to ensure that the risk summary is understandable to the layperson, including the owners of the land and members of the public who may be affected by the decision. The authority should not proceed to formal determination of land as contaminated land unless a risk summary has been prepared.

3.35

Risk summaries should as a minimum include:

(a) A summary of the authority's understanding of the risks, including a description of: the contaminants involved; the identified contaminant linkage(s), or a summary of such linkages; the potential impact(s); the estimated possibility that the impact(s) may occur; and the timescale over which the risk may become manifest.

(b) A description of the authority's understanding of the uncertainties behind its assessment.

(c) A description of the risks in context, for example by setting the risk in local or national context, or describing the risk from land contamination relative to other risks that receptors might be expected to be exposed to in any case. This need not involve a detailed comparison of relative risks, but the authority should aim to explain the risks in a way which is understandable and relevant to the layperson.

(d) A description of the authority's initial views on possible remediation. This need not be a detailed appraisal, but it should include a description of broadly what remediation might entail; how long it might take; likely effects of remediation works on local people and businesses; how much difference it might be expected to make to the risks posed by the land; and the authority's initial assessment of whether remediation would be likely to produce a net benefit, having regard to the broad objectives of the regime set out in Section 1. In the case of land which (if it were determined as contaminated land) would be likely to be a special site, the authority should seek the views of the Environment Agency, and take any views provided into account in producing this description.

3.36

Local authorities are not required to produce risk summaries:

(a) For land which will not be determined as contaminated land (e.g. land that would be in Categories 3 and 4 in terms of Section 4 of this Guidance). In such cases the authority should have regard to paragraphs 5.2–5.4 of this Guidance.

(b) For land which has been prioritised for detailed inspection (in accordance with Section 2 of this Guidance) but which has not yet been subject to risk assessment in accordance with Section 3 above.

(c) For land determined as contaminated land before this Guidance came into force.

SECTION 4: DEFINITION OF CONTAMINATED LAND

4.1

Part 2A of the 1990 Act defines "contaminated land", and provides for the Secretary of State to issue guidance (i.e. this Guidance) on how local authorities should determine which land is contaminated land and which is not.

4.2

Relevant sections of the Act include:

— Section 78A(2): "contaminated land" is any land which appears to the local authority in whose area it is situated to be in such a condition, by reason of substances in, on or under the land that – (a) significant harm is being caused or there is a significant possibility of such harm being caused; or (b) significant pollution of controlled waters is being caused, or there is a significant possibility of such pollution being caused;

— Section 78A(4): "Harm" means harm to the health of living organisms or other interference with the ecological systems of which they form part and, in the case of man, includes harm to his property.

— Section 78A(5): The questions – (a) what harm or pollution of controlled waters is to be regarded as "significant", and (b) whether the possibility of significant harm or of significant pollution of controlled waters being caused is "significant", shall be determined in accordance with guidance issued for the purpose by the Secretary of State in accordance with section 78YA below.

— Section 78A(6): Without prejudice to the guidance that may be issued under sub-section (5) above, guidance under paragraph (a) of that sub-section may make provision for different degrees of importance to be assigned to, or for the disregard of (a) different descriptions of living organisms or ecological systems or of poisonous, noxious or polluting matter or solid waste matter; (b) different descriptions of places or controlled waters, or different degrees of pollution; or (c) different descriptions of harm to health or property, or other interference; and guidance under paragraph (b) of that subsection may make provision for different degrees of possibility to be regarded as "significant" (or as not being "significant") in relation to different descriptions of significant harm or of significant pollution.

Section 4.1: Significant harm to human health

4.3

The paragraphs below set out categories of harm that should be considered to be significant harm to human health. In all cases the harm should be directly attributable to the effects of contaminants in, on or under the land on the body(ies) of the person(s) concerned.

4.4

Conditions for determining that land is contaminated land on the basis that significant harm is being caused would exist where: (a) the local authority has carried out an appropriate, scientific and technical assessment of all the relevant and available evidence; and (b) on the basis of that assessment, the authority is satisfied on the balance of probabilities that significant harm is being caused (i.e. that it is more likely than not that such harm is being caused) by a significant contaminant(s).

4.5

The following health effects should always be considered to constitute significant harm to human health: death; life threatening diseases (e.g. cancers); other diseases likely to have serious impacts on health; serious injury[1]; birth defects; and impairment of reproductive functions.

4.6

Other health effects may be considered by the local authority to constitute significant harm. For example, a wide range of conditions may or may not constitute significant harm (alone or in combination) including: physical injury; gastrointestinal disturbances; respiratory tract effects; cardio-vascular effects; central nervous system effects; skin ailments; effects on organs such as the liver or kidneys; or a wide range of other health impacts. In deciding whether or not a particular form of harm is significant harm, the local authority should consider the seriousness of the harm in question: including the impact on the health, and quality of life, of any person suffering the harm; and the scale of the harm. The authority should only conclude that harm is significant if it considers that treating the land as contaminated land would be in accordance with the broad objectives of the regime as described in Section 1.

4.7

If the local authority decides that harm is occurring but it is not significant harm, it should consider whether such harm might be relevant to consideration of whether or not the land poses a significant possibility of significant harm (see sub-section 4.2 below). For example, this might be the case if there is evidence that the harm may be a precursor to, or indicative or symptomatic of, a more serious form of harm, or that repeated episodes of minor harm (e.g. repeated skin ailments) might lead to more serious harm in the longer term.

4.8

In cases where the local authority considers that: (i) significant harm may be being caused, or is likely to have been caused in the past; and (ii) there is a significant possibility that it may happen again, the authority may choose to consider whether to determine the land on grounds of significant possibility of significant harm (as an alternative to consideration that significant harm is being caused).

Notes

1 Physical injury in relation to significant harm would include injury caused by chemical and biochemical properties of substances, such as injury resulting from explosive or asphyxiating properties of gases. It would not extend to injury caused by only physical properties of substances, such as injury caused by falling onto sharp or hard objects made of relevant substances.

Section 4.2: Significant possibility of significant harm to human health

4.9

In deciding whether or not a significant possibility of significant harm to human health exists, the local authority should first understand the possibility of significant harm from the relevant contaminant linkage(s) and the levels of uncertainty attached to that understanding, before it goes on to decide whether or not the possibility of significant harm is significant.

Possibility of significant harm to human health

4.10

In assessing the possibility of significant harm to human health from the land and associated issues, the local authority should act in accordance with the advice on risk assessment in Section 3 and the guidance in this section.

4.11

The term "possibility of significant harm" as it applies to human health, for the purposes of this guidance, means the risk posed by one or more relevant contaminant linkage(s) relating to the land. It comprises:

(a) The estimated likelihood that significant harm might occur to an identified receptor, taking account of the current use of the land in question.

(b) The estimated impact if the significant harm did occur i.e. the nature of the harm, the seriousness of the harm to any person who might suffer it, and (where relevant) the extent of the harm in terms of how many people might suffer it.

4.12

In estimating the likelihood that a specific form of significant harm might occur the local authority should, among other things, consider:

(a) The estimated probability that the significant harm might occur: (i) if the land continues to be used as it is currently being used; and (ii) where relevant, if the land were to be used in a different way (or ways) in the future having regard to the guidance on "current use" in Section 3.

(b) The strength of evidence underlying the risk estimate. It should also consider the key assumptions on which the estimate of likelihood is based, and the level of uncertainty underlying the estimate.

4.13

In some cases the local authority's assessment of possibility of significant harm may be based, solely or partially, on a possible risk that may exist if circumstances were to change in the future within the bounds of the current use of the land. For example, an assessment may be based on a possible risk if a more sensitive receptor were to move onto the land at some point in the future. In such cases the authority should ensure that the possibility of the future circumstance occurring is taken into account in estimating the overall possibility of significant harm.

4.14

The local authority should estimate the timescale over which the significant harm might become manifest, to the extent that this is possible and practicable (and recognising that often it may only be possible and practicable to give a broad indication of the estimated timescale).

4.15

Having completed its estimation of the possibility of significant harm, the local authority should produce a risk summary in accordance with Section 3.

Deciding whether a possibility of significant harm is significant (human health)

4.16

The decision on whether the possibility of significant harm being caused is significant is a regulatory decision to be taken by the relevant local authority. In deciding whether the possibility of significant harm being caused is significant, the authority is deciding whether the possibility of significant harm posed by contamination in, on or under the land is sufficiently high that regulatory action should be taken to reduce it, with all that would entail. In taking such decisions, the local authority should take account of the broad aims of the regime set out in Section 1 of this Guidance.

4.17

In deciding whether or not land is contaminated land on grounds of significant possibility of significant harm to human health, the local authority should use the categorisations described in paragraphs 4.19–4.30 below. Categories 1 and 2 would encompass land which is capable of being determined as contaminated land on grounds of significant possibility of significant harm to human health. Categories 3 and 4 would encompass land which is not capable of being determined on such grounds.

4.18

In considering whether a significant possibility of significant harm exists, the local authority should consider the number of people who might be exposed to the risk in question and/or the number of people it estimates would be likely to suffer harm. In some cases, the authority may decide that this is not a particularly relevant consideration: it is quite possible that land could be determined as contaminated land on the basis of a significant possibility of significant harm to an individual or a small number of people. However in other cases the authority may consider that the number of people affected is an important consideration, for example if the number of people at risk substantially alters the authority's view of the likelihood of significant harm or the scale and seriousness of such harm if it did occur.

Category 1: Human Health

4.19

The local authority should assume that a significant possibility of significant harm exists in any case where it considers there is an unacceptably high probability, supported by robust science-based evidence, that significant harm would occur if no action is taken to stop it. For the purposes of this Guidance, these are referred to as "Category 1: Human Health" cases. Land should be deemed to be a Category 1: Human Health case where:

(a) the authority is aware that similar land or situations are known, or are strongly suspected on the basis of robust evidence, to have caused such harm before in the United Kingdom or elsewhere; or

(b) the authority is aware that similar degrees of exposure (via any medium) to the contaminant(s) in question are known, or strongly suspected on the basis of robust evidence, to have caused such harm before in the United Kingdom or elsewhere;

(c) the authority considers that significant harm may already have been caused by contaminants in, on or under the land, and that there is an unacceptable risk that it might continue or occur again if no action is taken. Among other things, the authority may decide to determine the land on these grounds if it considers that it is likely that significant harm is being caused, but it considers either: (i) that there is insufficient evidence to be sure of meeting the "balance of probability" test for demonstrating that significant harm is being caused; or (ii) that the time needed to demonstrate such a level of probability would cause unreasonable delay, cost, or disruption and stress to affected people particularly in cases involving residential properties.

Category 4: Human Health

4.20

The local authority should not assume that land poses a significant possibility of significant harm if it considers that there is no risk or that the level of risk posed is low. For the purposes of this Guidance, such land is referred to as a "Category 4: Human Health" case. The authority may decide that the land is a Category 4: Human Health case as soon as it considers it has evidence to this effect, and this may happen at any stage during risk assessment including the early stages.

4.21

The local authority should consider that the following types of land should be placed into Category 4: Human Health:

(a) Land where no relevant contaminant linkage has been established.

(b) Land where there are only normal levels of contaminants in soil, as explained in Section 3 of this Guidance.

(c) Land that has been excluded from the need for further inspection and assessment because contaminant levels do not exceed relevant generic assessment criteria in accordance with Section 3 of this Guidance, or relevant technical tools or advice that may be developed in accordance with paragraph 3.30 of this Guidance.

(d) Land where estimated levels of exposure to contaminants in soil are likely to form only a small proportion of what a receptor might be exposed to anyway through other sources of environmental exposure (e.g. in relation to average estimated national levels of exposure to substances commonly found in the environment, to which receptors are likely to be exposed in the normal course of their lives).

4.22

The local authority may consider that land other than the types described in paragraph 4.21 should be placed into Category 4: Human Health if following a detailed quantitative risk assessment it is satisfied that the level of risk posed is sufficiently low.

4.23

Local authorities may decide that particular land apparently matching the descriptions of paragraph 4.21 (b) or (d) immediately above poses sufficient risk to human health to fall into Categories other than Category 4. However, such cases are likely to be very unusual and the authority should take particular care to explain why the decision has been taken, and to ensure that it is supported by robust evidence.

Categories 2 and 3: Human Health

4.24

For land that cannot be placed into Categories 1 or 4, the local authority should decide whether the land should be placed into either: (a) Category 2: Human Health, in which case the land would be capable of being determined as contaminated land on grounds of significant possibility of significant harm to human health; or (b) Category 3: Human Health, in which case the land would not be capable of being determined on such grounds.

4.25

The local authority should consider this decision in the context of the broad objectives of the regime and of the Government's policy as set out in Section 1. It should also be mindful of the fact that the decision is a positive legal test, meaning that the starting assumption should be that land does not pose a significant possibility of significant harm unless there is reason to consider otherwise. The authority should then, in accordance with paragraphs 4.26 to 4.29 below, decide which of the following two categories the land falls into:

(a) Category 2: Human Health. Land should be placed into Category 2 if the authority concludes, on the basis that there is a strong case for considering that the risks from the land are of sufficient concern, that the land poses a significant possibility of significant harm, with all that this might involve and having regard to Section 1. Category 2 may include land where there is little or no direct evidence that similar land, situations or levels of exposure have caused harm before, but nonetheless the authority considers on the basis of the available evidence, including expert opinion, that there is a strong case for taking action under Part 2A on a precautionary basis.

(b) Category 3: Human Health. Land should be placed into Category 3 if the authority concludes that the strong case described in 4.25(a) does not exist, and therefore the legal test for significant possibility of significant harm is not met. Category 3 may include land where the risks are not low, but nonetheless the authority considers that regulatory intervention under Part 2A is not warranted. This recognises that placing land in Category 3 would not stop others, such as the owner or occupier of the land, from taking action to reduce risks outside of the Part 2A regime if they choose. The authority should consider making available the results of its inspection and risk assessment to the owners/occupiers of Category 3 land.

4.26

In making its decision on whether land falls into Category 2 or Category 3, the local authority should first consider its assessment of the possibility of significant harm to human health, including the estimated likelihood of such harm, the estimated impact if it did occur, the timescale over which it might occur, and the levels of certainty attached to these estimates. If the authority considers, on the basis of this consideration alone, that the strong case described in paragraph 4.25(a) does or does not exist, the authority should make its decision on whether the land falls into Category 2 or Category 3 on this basis regardless of the other factors discussed in paragraph 4.27.

4.27

If the authority considers that it cannot make a decision in line with paragraph 4.26, it should consider other factors which it considers are relevant to achieving the objectives set out in Section 1. This should include consideration of:

(a) The likely direct and indirect health benefits and impacts of regulatory intervention. This would include benefits of reducing or removing the risk posed by contamination. It would also include any risks from contaminants being mobilised during remediation (which would in any case have to be considered under other relevant legislation); and any indirect impacts such as stress-related health effects that may be experienced by affected people, particularly local residents. If it is not clear to the authority that the health benefits of remediation would outweigh the health impacts, the authority should presume the land falls into Category 3 unless there is strong reason to consider otherwise.

(b) The authority's initial estimate of what remediation would involve; how long it would take; what benefit it would be likely to bring; whether the benefits would outweigh the financial and economic costs; and any impacts on local society or the environment from taking action that the authority considers to be relevant.

4.28

In making its consideration in regard to paragraph 4.27(a) and (b), the local authority is not required to make a detailed assessment. For example, the consideration should not necessarily involve quantification of the impacts, particularly if the authority considers it is not possible or reasonable to do so, and the authority is not expected to produce a detailed cost-benefit or sustainability analysis. Rather it is expected to make a broad consideration of factors it considers relevant to achieving the aims of Section 1.

4.29

If, having taken the above factors into account, the local authority still cannot decide whether or not a significant possibility of significant harm exists, it should conclude that the legal test has not been met and the land should be placed in Category 3.

Section 4.3: Significant harm and significant possibility of such harm (non-human receptors)

4.30

In considering non-human receptors, the local authority should only regard receptors described in Tables 1 and 2 as being relevant for the purposes of Part 2A (e.g. harm to an ecological system outside the description in Table 1 should not be considered to be significant harm). Similarly, in considering whether significant harm is being caused or there is a significant possibility of such harm, the authority should only regard the forms of harm described in Tables 1 and 2 as being relevant.

4.31

Tables 1 and 2 below give guidance on how the local authority should go about deciding whether or not: (i) significant harm is being caused; or (ii) there is a significant possibility of such harm to non-human receptors. In making such decisions the authority should have close regard to Section 1 and should only consider determining land as contaminated land if it is satisfied it would be in accordance with the broad aims set out in Section 1.

4.32

In Tables 1 and 2, references to "relevant information" mean information which is: (a) scientifically-based; (b) authoritative; (c) relevant to the assessment of risks arising from the presence of contaminants in soil; and (d) appropriate to inform the determination of whether any land is contaminated land.

4.33

In considering "ecological system effects" described in Table 1, the local authority should consult Natural England and have regard to its comments before deciding whether or not to make a determination.

Table 1: Ecological system effects

Relevant types of receptor	*Significant harm*	*Significant possibility of significant harm*
Any ecological system, or living organism forming part of such a system, within a location which is: — a site of special scientific interest (under section 28 of the Wildlife and Countryside Act 1981) — a national nature reserve (under s.35 of the 1981 Act) — a marine nature reserve (under s.36 of the 1981 Act) — an area of special protection for birds (under s.3 of the 1981 Act) — a "European site" within the meaning of regulation 8 of the Conservation of Habitats and Species Regulations 2010 — any habitat or site afforded policy protection under paragraph 6 of Planning Policy Statement (PPS 9) on nature conservation (i.e. candidate Special Areas of Conservation, potential Special Protection Areas and listed Ramsar sites); or — any nature reserve established under section 21 of the National Parks and Access to the Countryside Act 1949.	The following types of harm should be considered to be significant harm: — harm which results in an irreversible adverse change, or in some other substantial adverse change, in the functioning of the ecological system within any substantial part of that location; or — harm which significantly affects any species of special interest within that location and which endangers the long-term maintenance of the population of that species at that location. In the case of European sites, harm should also be considered to be significant harm if it endangers the favourable conservation status of natural habitats at such locations or species typically found there. In deciding what constitutes such harm, the local authority should have regard to the advice of Natural England and to the requirements of the Conservation of Habitats and Species Regulations 2010.	Conditions would exist for considering that a significant possibility of significant harm exists to a relevant ecological receptor where the local authority considers that: — significant harm of that description is more likely than not to result from the contaminant linkage in question; or — there is a reasonable possibility of significant harm of that description being caused, and if that harm were to occur, it would result in such a degree of damage to features of special interest at the location in question that they would be beyond any practicable possibility of restoration. Any assessment made for these purposes should take into account relevant information for that type of contaminant linkage, particularly in relation to the ecotoxicological effects of the contaminant.

Table 2: Property effects

Relevant types of receptor	*Significant harm*	*Significant possibility of significant harm*
Property in the form of: — crops, including timber; — produce grown domestically, or on allotments, for consumption; — livestock; — other owned or domesticated animals; — wild animals which are the subject of shooting or fishing rights.	For crops, a substantial diminution in yield or other substantial loss in their value resulting from death, disease or other physical damage. For domestic pets, death, serious disease or serious physical damage. For other property in this category, a substantial loss in its value resulting from death, disease or other serious physical damage. The local authority should regard a substantial loss in value as occurring only when a substantial proportion of the animals or crops are dead or otherwise no longer fit for their intended purpose. Food should be regarded as being no longer fit for purpose when it fails to comply with the provisions of the Food Safety Act 1990. Where a diminution in yield or loss in value is caused by a contaminant linkage, a 20% diminution or loss should be regarded as a benchmark for what constitutes a substantial diminution or loss. In this Chapter, this description of significant harm is referred to as an "animal or crop effect".	Conditions would exist for considering that a significant possibility of significant harm exists to the relevant types of receptor where the local authority considers that significant harm is more likely than not to result from the contaminant linkage in question, taking into account relevant information for that type of contaminant linkage, particularly in relation to the ecotoxicological effects of the contaminant.
Property in the form of buildings. For this purpose, "building" means any structure or erection, and any part of a building including any part below ground level, but does not include plant or machinery comprised in a building, or buried services such as sewers, water pipes or electricity cables.	Structural failure, substantial damage or substantial interference with any right of occupation. The local authority should regard substantial damage or substantial interference as occurring when any part of the building ceases to be capable of being used for the purpose for which it is or was intended.	Conditions would exist for considering that a significant possibility of significant harm exists to the relevant types of receptor where the local authority considers that significant harm is more likely than not to result from the contaminant linkage in question during the expected economic life of the building (or in the case of a scheduled

Relevant types of receptor	*Significant harm*	*Significant possibility of significant harm*
	In the case of a scheduled Ancient Monument, substantial damage should also be regarded as occurring when the damage significantly impairs the historic, architectural, traditional, artistic or archaeological interest by reason of which the monument was scheduled. In this Chapter, this description of significant harm is referred to as a "building effect".	Ancient Monument the foreseeable future), taking into account relevant information for that type of contaminant linkage.

Section 4.4: Significant pollution of controlled waters and significant possibility of such pollution

4.34

This sub-section gives Guidance on how the local authority should go about deciding whether significant pollution of controlled waters is being caused, or whether there is a significant possibility of such pollution being caused. This sub-section deals with controlled waters as a receptor in contaminant linkages, and not as a pathway.

4.35

In establishing whether significant pollution of controlled waters is being caused, or whether there is a significant possibility of such pollution being caused, the local authority should have regard for any technical guidance issued by the Environment Agency to support this Guidance. If the authority considers it likely that land might be contaminated land on such grounds, it should consult the Agency and have strong regard to the Agency's advice.

Pollution of controlled waters

4.36

Under section 78A(9) of Part 2A the term "pollution of controlled waters" means the entry into controlled waters of any poisonous, noxious or polluting matter or any solid waste matter. The term "controlled waters" in relation to England has the same meaning as in Part 3 of the Water Resources Act 1991, except that "ground waters" does not include waters contained in underground strata but above the saturation zone.

4.37

Given that the Part 2A regime seeks to identify and deal with significant pollution (rather than lesser levels of pollution), the local authority should seek to focus on pollution which: (i) may be harmful to human health or the quality of aquatic ecosystems or terrestrial ecosystems directly depending on aquatic ecosystems; (ii) which may result in damage to material property; or (iii) which may impair or interfere with amenities and other legitimate uses of the environment.

Significant pollution of controlled waters

4.38

The following types of pollution should be considered to constitute significant pollution of controlled waters:

(a) Pollution equivalent to "environmental damage" to surface water or groundwater as defined by The Environmental Damage (Prevention and Remediation) Regulations 2009, but which cannot be dealt with under those Regulations.

(b) Inputs resulting in deterioration of the quality of water abstracted, or intended to be used in the future, for human consumption such that additional treatment would be required to enable that use.

(c) A breach of a statutory surface water Environment Quality Standard, either directly or via a groundwater pathway.

(d) Input of a substance into groundwater resulting in a significant and sustained upward trend in concentration of contaminants (as defined in Article 2(3) of the Groundwater Daughter Directive (2006/118/EC)[1]).

4.39

In some circumstances, the local authority may consider that the following types of pollution may constitute significant pollution: (a) significant concentrations[2] of hazardous substances or non-hazardous pollutants in groundwater; or (b) significant concentrations of priority hazardous substances, priority substances or other specific polluting substances in surface water; at an appropriate, risk-based compliance point[3]. The local authority should only conclude that pollution is significant if it considers that treating the land as contaminated land would be in accordance with the broad objectives of the regime as described in Section 1. This would normally mean that the authority should conclude that less serious forms of pollution are not significant. In such cases the authority should consult the Environment Agency.

4.40

The following types of circumstance should not be considered to be contaminated land on water pollution grounds:

(a) The fact that substances are merely entering water and none of the conditions for considering that significant pollution is being caused set out in paragraphs 4.38 and 4.39 above are being met.

(b) The fact that land is causing a discharge that is not discernible at a location immediately downstream or down-gradient of the land (when compared to upstream or up-gradient concentrations).

(c) Substances entering water in compliance with a discharge authorised under the Environmental Permitting Regulations.

Notes

1 Relating to paragraph 4.41(d), Article 2(3) says, "significant and sustained upward trend means any statistically and environmentally significant increase of concentration of a pollutant, group of pollutants, or indicator of pollution in groundwater for which trend reversal is identified as being necessary in accordance with Article 5."

2 Significant concentrations must be determined on a site and substance specific basis.

3 Appropriate compliance points must be determined on a site and substance specific basis.

Significant pollution of controlled waters is being caused

4.41

In deciding whether significant pollution of controlled waters is being caused, the local authority should consider that this test is only met where it is satisfied that the substances in question are continuing to enter controlled waters; or that they have already entered the waters and are likely to do so again in such a manner that past and likely future entry in effect constitutes ongoing pollution. For these purposes, the local authority should:

(a) Regard substances as having entered controlled waters where they are dissolved or suspended in those waters, or (if they are immiscible with water) they have direct contact with those waters on or beneath the surface of the water.
(b) Take the term "continuing to enter" to mean any measurable entry of the substance(s) into controlled waters additional to any which has already occurred.
(c) Take the term "likely to do so again" to mean more likely than not to occur again.

4.42

Land should not be determined as contaminated land on grounds that significant pollution of controlled waters is being caused where: (a) the relevant substance(s) are already present in controlled waters; (b) entry into controlled waters of the substance(s) from land has ceased; and (c) it is not likely that further entry will take place.

Significant possibility of significant pollution of controlled waters

4.43

In deciding whether or not a significant possibility of significant pollution of controlled waters exists, the local authority should first understand the possibility of significant pollution of controlled waters posed by the land, and the levels of certainty/uncertainty attached to that understanding, before it goes on to decide whether or not that possibility is significant. The term "possibility of significant pollution of controlled waters" means the estimated likelihood that significant pollution of controlled waters might occur. In assessing the possibility of significant pollution of controlled waters from land, the local authority should act in accordance with the advice on risk assessment in Section 3 and the guidance in this sub-section.

4.44

In deciding whether the possibility of significant pollution of controlled waters is significant the local authority should bear in mind that Part 2A makes the decision a positive legal test. In other words, for particular land to meet the test the authority needs reasonably to believe that there is a significant possibility of such pollution, rather than to demonstrate that there is not.

4.45

Before making its decision on whether a given possibility of significant pollution of controlled waters is significant, the local authority should consider:

(a) The estimated likelihood that the potential significant pollution of controlled waters would become manifest; the strength of evidence underlying the estimate; and the level of uncertainty underlying the estimate.

(b) The estimated impact of the potential significant pollution if it did occur. This should include consideration of whether the pollution would be likely to cause a breach of European water legislation, or make a major contribution to such a breach.
(c) The estimated timescale over which the significant pollution might become manifest.
(d) The authority's initial estimate of whether remediation is feasible, and if so what it would involve and the extent to which it might provide a solution to the problem; how long it would take; what benefit it would be likely to bring; and whether the benefits would outweigh the costs and any impacts on local society or the environment from taking action.

4.46

The local authority should consider these factors in the context of the broad objectives of the regime as set out in Section 1. It should also consider how the factors interrelate (e.g. likelihood relative to impact). The authority should then decide which of the following categories the land falls into. Categories 1 and 2 would comprise cases where the authority considers that a significant possibility of significant pollution of controlled waters exists. Categories 3 and 4 would comprise cases where the authority considers that a significant possibility of such pollution does not exist.
(a) **Category 1 (Water):** This covers land where the authority considers that there is a strong and compelling case for considering that a significant possibility of significant pollution of controlled waters exists. In particular this would include cases where there is robust science-based evidence for considering that it is likely that high impact pollution (such as the pollution described in paragraph 4.38) would occur if nothing were done to stop it.
(b) **Category 2 (Water):** This covers land where: (i) the authority considers that the strength of evidence to put the land into Category 1 does not exist; but (ii) nonetheless, on the basis of the available scientific evidence and expert opinion, the authority considers that the risks posed by the land are of sufficient concern that the land should be considered to pose a significant possibility of significant pollution of controlled waters on a precautionary basis, with all that this might involve (e.g. likely remediation requirements, and the benefits, costs and other impacts of regulatory intervention). Among other things, this category might include land where there is a relatively low likelihood that the most serious types of significant pollution might occur.
(c) **Category 3 (Water):** This covers land where the authority concludes that the risks are such that (whilst the authority and others might prefer they did not exist) the tests set out in Categories 1 and 2 above are not met, and therefore regulatory intervention under Part 2A is not warranted. This category should include land where the authority considers that it is very unlikely that serious pollution would occur; or where there is a low likelihood that less serious types of significant pollution might occur.
(d) **Category 4 (Water):** This covers land where the authority concludes that there is no risk, or that the level of risk posed is low. In particular, the authority should consider that this is the case where: (a) no contaminant linkage has been established in which controlled waters are the receptor in the linkage; or (b) the possibility only relates to types of pollution described in paragraph 4.40 above (i.e. types of pollution that should not be considered to be significant pollution); or (c) the possibility of water pollution similar to that which might be caused by "background" contamination as explained in Section 3.

SECTION 5: DETERMINATION OF CONTAMINATED LAND

5.1

Section 78A(2) of the 1990 Act says that in determining whether any land appears to be contaminated land, a local authority shall, "...act in accordance with guidance issued by the Secretary of State...with respect to the manner in which that determination is to be made." This section provides such Guidance.

Deciding that land is not contaminated land

5.2

In implementing the Part 2A regime, the local authority is likely to inspect land that it then considers is not contaminated land. For example, this will be the case where the authority has ceased its inspection and assessment of land on grounds that there is little or no evidence to suggest that it is contaminated land. In such cases, the authority should issue a written statement to that effect (rather than coming to no formal conclusion) to minimise unwarranted blight. The statement should make clear that on the basis of its assessment, the authority has concluded that the land does not meet the definition of contaminated land under Part 2A. The authority may choose to qualify its statement (e.g. given that its Part 2A risk assessment may only be relevant to the current use of the land).

5.3

Paragraph 5.2 recognises that the nature of soil contamination means it is never possible to know the exact contamination status of any land with absolute certainty, and that scientific understanding of risks may evolve over time. However, such a lack of certainty should not stop the authority from deciding that land is not contaminated land. The starting assumption of Part 2A is that land is not contaminated land unless there is reason to consider otherwise.

5.4

The local authority should keep a record of its reasons for deciding that land is not contaminated land. The authority should inform the owners of the land of its conclusion and give them a copy of the written statement referred to in paragraph 5.2. The authority should also consider informing other interested parties (for example occupiers of the land and owners and occupiers of neighbouring land) and whether to publish the statement. The statement should be issued within a timescale that the authority considers to be a reasonable, having regard to the need to minimise unwarranted burdens to persons likely to be directly affected, in particular the landowner, and occupiers or users of the land where relevant.

Determining that land is contaminated land

5.5

The local authority has the sole responsibility for determining whether any land appears to be contaminated land. It cannot delegate this responsibility (except in accordance with section 101 of the Local Government Act 1972). However, in making such decisions the authority may rely on information or advice provided by another body such as the Environment Agency, or a suitably qualified experienced practitioner appointed for that purpose.

5.6

There are four possible grounds for the determination of land as contaminated land (with regard to non-radioactive contamination):

(a) Significant harm is being caused to a human, or relevant non-human, receptor.
(b) There is a significant possibility of significant harm being caused to a human, or relevant non-human, receptor.
(c) Significant pollution of controlled waters is being caused.
(d) There is a significant possibility of significant pollution of controlled waters being caused.

5.7

Before making any determination, the local authority should have identified one or more significant contaminant linkage(s), and carried out a robust, appropriate, scientific and technical assessment of all the relevant and available evidence. If the authority considers that conditions for considering land to be contaminated land do not exist it should not decide that the land is contaminated land.

5.8

In the case of any land which, following determination as contaminated land, would be likely to meet one or more of the descriptions of a "Special Site" set out in the Contaminated Land Regulations 2006, the local authority should consult the Environment Agency before deciding whether or not to determine the land, providing the Agency with a draft record of the determination that the authority is required to prepare in accordance with paragraphs 5.17–5.19 below. The authority should take the Agency's views into full consideration and it should strive to ensure it has the Agency's agreement to its decision (although the decision is for the authority to make subject to the provisions of Part 2A).

Physical extent of land to be determined

5.9

It is for the local authority to decide the physical extent of land that should be determined. The authority should strive to ensure that there are grounds to consider that all the land in question can reasonably be considered to be contaminated land. In practice, often it is likely that contamination will not be uniformly spread across land, and it may not be clear precisely where the boundaries of the contamination lie. In such cases the authority should use its judgement on the extent of land it might reasonably consider to be contaminated land.

5.10

The local authority should review its decision on the physical extent of the land to be determined (or that has been determined) if at a later date it becomes aware of relevant further information. For example this may be the case if, during remediation, it becomes clear that the extent of contamination is significantly greater or less than was thought when the determination was made.

Sub-division of land for the purposes of determination

5.11

The local authority may sub-divide the relevant land for the purposes of determination by issuing separate determinations for smaller areas of land which form part of a larger area of contaminated land. In deciding whether (and if so how) to do this, the authority should take into account: (i) the nature of the contamination; (ii) the degree of risk posed, and whether this varies across the land; (iii) the nature of the remediation which might be required; (iv) the ownership of the land; and (v) the likely identity of those who may bear responsibility for the remediation.

Making determinations in urgent cases

5.12

If the local authority considers there is an urgent need to determine particular land, it should make the determination in a timescale it considers appropriate to the urgency of the situation.

Informing interested parties

5.13

Before making a determination, the local authority should inform the owners and occupiers of the land and any other person who appears to the authority to be liable to pay for remediation of its intention to determine the land (to the extent that the authority is aware of these parties at the time) unless the authority considers there is an overriding reason for not doing so. The authority should also consider:

(a) Whether to give such persons time to make representations (for example to seek clarification of the grounds for determination, or to propose a solution that might avoid the need for formal determination) taking into account: the broad aims of regime; the urgency of the situation; any need to avoid unwarranted delay; and any other factor the authority considers to be appropriate.

(b) Whether to inform other interested parties as it considers necessary, for example owners and occupiers of neighbouring land.

5.14

If the local authority determines land as contaminated land, it shall give notice of that fact to (a) the Environment Agency; (b) the owner of the land; (c) any person who appears to the authority to be in occupation of the whole or any part of the land; and (d) each person who appears to the authority to be an appropriate person; in accordance with section 78B(3) of Part 2A. In respect of point (d) this Guidance recognises that in some cases the authority may not have identified the appropriate person(s) at the time the determination is made, in which case the requirement to give notice to such persons would not apply.

Postponing determination

5.15

The local authority may postpone determination of contaminated land if the land owner or some other person undertakes to deal with the problem without determination, and the authority is satisfied that the remediation will happen to an appropriate standard and timescale. If the authority chooses to do this, any agreement it enters into should not affect its ability to determine the land in future (e.g. if the person fails to carry out the remediation as agreed).

5.16

The local authority may postpone determination of contaminated land if a significant contaminant linkage would only exist if the circumstances of the land were to change in the future within the bounds of the current use of the land as described in paragraph 3.5 of this Guidance (e.g. if a more sensitive receptor were to move onto the land or a temporarily interrupted pathway were to be reactivated). If the authority chooses to do this, it should keep the status of the land under review and take reasonable measures to ensure that the postponement does not create conditions under which significant risks could go unaddressed in future. Alternatively the authority may decide to determine the land but postpone remediation.

Record of the determination of contaminated land

5.17

The local authority should prepare a written record of any determination that land is contaminated land. The record should clearly and accurately identify the location, boundaries and area of the land in question, making appropriate reference to Ordnance Survey grid references and/or Global Positioning co-ordinates. The record should be made publicly available by means to be decided by the authority.

5.18

The record should explain why the determination has been made, including:

(a) The risk summary required by Section 3 of this Guidance, and where not already covered in the risk summary: (i) a relevant conceptual model comprising text, plans, cross sections, photographs and tables as necessary in the interests of making the description understandable to the layperson; and (ii) a summary of the relevant assessment of this evidence.

(b) A summary of why the authority considers that the requirements of relevant sections of this Guidance have been satisfied

5.19

The local authority should seek to ensure (as far as reasonable) that all aspects of the record of determination are understandable to non-specialists, including affected members of the public.

Reconsideration, revocation and variation of determinations

5.20

The local authority should reconsider any determination that land is contaminated land if it becomes aware of further information which it considers significantly alters the basis for its original decision. In such cases the authority should decide whether to retain, vary or revoke the determination.

5.21

The local authority should reconsider any determination of contaminated land if remediation action has been taken which, in the view of the authority, stops the land being contaminated land. In such cases the authority should issue a statement to this effect, having regard to paragraphs 5.2 to 5.4 above.

5.22

If the local authority varies or revokes a determination, or issues a statement in accordance with paragraph 5.21, it should record its reasons for doing so alongside the initial record of determination in a way that ensures the changed status of the land is made clear. If the reconsideration results in relevant documentation, such as a revised determination notice or a statement in accordance with paragraph 5.21, copies of this documentation should also be recorded. The authority should ensure that interested parties are informed of the decisions and the reasons for it, including the owner of the land; any person who appears to the authority to be in occupation of the whole or any part of the land; any person who was previously identified by the authority to be an appropriate person; and the Environment Agency.

SECTION 6: REMEDIATION OF CONTAMINATED LAND

6.1

Once land has been determined as contaminated land, the enforcing authority must consider how it should be remediated and, where appropriate, it must issue a remediation notice to require such remediation. The enforcing authority for the purposes of remediation may be the local authority which determined the land, or the Environment Agency, which takes on responsibility once land has been determined if the land is deemed to be a "special site". The rules on what land is to be regarded as special sites, and various rules on the issuing of remediation notices, are set out in the Contaminated Land (England) Regulations 2006.

6.2

Relevant provisions of Part 2A include:

- Section 78A(7): Defines "remediation" as: "(a) the doing of anything for the purpose of assessing the condition of – (i) the contaminated land in question; or (ii) any controlled waters affected by that land; or (iii) any land adjoining or adjacent to that land; (b) the doing of any works, the carrying out of any operations or the taking of any steps in relation to any such land for the purpose – (i) of preventing or minimising, or remedying or mitigating the effects of, any significant harm (or significant pollution of controlled waters), by reason of which the contaminated land is such land; or (ii) of restoring the land or waters to their former state; or (c) the making of subsequent inspections from time to time for the purpose of keeping under review the condition of the land or waters."
- Section 78E(1): "In any case where [the local authority has identified contaminated land]…the enforcing authority shall… serve on each person who is an appropriate person a…"remediation notice"…specifying what that person is to do by way of remediation and the periods within which he is required to do each of the things so specified."
- Section 78E(4): "The only things by way of remediation which the enforcing authority may do, or require to be done, under or by virtue of [Part 2A] are things which it considers reasonable, having regard to – (a) the cost which is likely to be involved; and (b) the seriousness of the harm, or pollution of controlled waters, in question."
- Section 78E(5): "In determining for any purpose of this Part – (a) what is to be done (whether by an appropriate person, the enforcing authority, or any other person) by way of remediation in any particular case, (b) the standard to which any land is, or waters are, to be remediated pursuant to [a remediation] notice, or (c) what is, or is not, to be regarded as reasonable for the purposes of subsection (4) above, the enforcing authority shall have regard to any guidance issued for the purpose by the Secretary of State."

6.3

The enforcing authority should have regard to this Guidance when it is: (a) deciding what remediation action it should specify in a remediation notice as being required to be carried out; (b) satisfying itself that appropriate remediation is being, or will be, carried out without the service of a notice; or (c) deciding what remediation action it should carry out itself.

6.4

The guidance in this Section does not attempt to set out detailed technical procedures or working methods. In considering such matters, the enforcing authority may consult relevant technical documents (e.g. produced by the Environment Agency or other professional and technical organisations). It may also act on the advice of a suitably qualified experienced practitioner.

Section 6(a): Remediation techniques

6.5

The broad aim of remediation should be: (a) to remove identified significant contaminant linkages, or permanently to disrupt them to ensure they are no longer significant and that risks are reduced to below an unacceptable level; and/or (b) to take reasonable measures to remedy harm or pollution that has been caused by a significant contaminant linkage.

6.6

Remediation may involve a range of treatment, assessment and monitoring actions, sometimes with different remediation actions being used in combination or sequentially to secure the overall remediation of the land.

6.7

In cases where the aim of remediation is to remove or permanently disrupt significant contaminant linkages, remediation treatment should involve demonstrable disruption or removal of the significant contaminant linkage(s) that led to land being determined as contaminated land, in order to reduce or remove unacceptable risks to receptors. This might involve one or more of the following:

(a) Reducing or treating the contaminant part of the linkage (e.g. by physically removing contaminants or contaminated soil or water, or by treating the soil or water to reduce levels of contaminants, or by altering the chemical or physical form of the contaminants).

(b) Breaking, removing or disrupting the pathway parts of the linkage (e.g. a pathway could be disrupted by removing or reducing the chance that receptors might be exposed to contaminants, for example by installing gas membranes in a property, or by sealing land with a material such as clay or concrete).

(c) Protecting or removing the receptor. For example, by changing the land use or restricting access to land it may be possible to reduce risks to below an unacceptable level.

6.8

Assessment or monitoring actions may also be required as part of remediation. For example, assessment actions may be needed to characterise the nature of significant contaminant linkage(s) to help the authority decide what remediation should involve. Assessment may also be needed whilst other remediation actions are being carried out, or after other actions have been carried out (e.g. to assess the effectiveness of the other measures, or to inform the need for possible further remediation actions). Monitoring actions may be needed after remediation has taken place (e.g. to check whether remedial action has been successful, or whether there is a need for further assessment or action).

6.9

Assessment and monitoring action should not be required for any purpose other than the remediation of the land in relation to the reason why it was determined as contaminated land.

Phased remediation

6.10

Remediation may require a phased approach, with different remediation actions being carried out in sequence or in parallel.

6.11

In some cases, it may not be possible or reasonable for a single remediation notice to specify all the remediation actions which might eventually be needed. In such cases, the enforcing authority should specify in the notice the remediation action(s) which it considers to be appropriate at the time, and further remediation notices may need to be issued later regarding further phases of action.

6.12

If a phased approach is taken to remediation, before serving any further remediation notice, the enforcing authority should be satisfied that previous action has not already achieved the remediation of the land (i.e. to a standard to which remediation can reasonably be required, having regard to the advice below), and that further action is still necessary to achieve the remediation of the land in question.

Remediation of multiple significant contaminant linkages

6.13

Where more than one significant contaminant linkage has been identified on the land, the enforcing authority should consider whether reasonable actions for addressing each linkage individually would result in the optimum approach for achieving the overall remediation of the land. If a more integrated approach would be more practicable and more cost effective whilst still delivering the same (or a better) overall standard of remediation the enforcing authority should generally favour this approach. However, in cases where more than one party has been found responsible for linkages, the enforcing authority should not impose an approach which is more costly for any responsible party than addressing the linkages separately.

Section 6(b): Securing remediation without a remediation notice

6.14

Before serving a remediation notice, the enforcing authority should consider section 78H(5)(a)–(d) of Part 2A. The authority should not serve a remediation notice if it is satisfied that appropriate measures are being taken by way of remediation without the serving of a remediation notice. The authority should assume that appropriate measures are being taken if: (a) it is satisfied that steps are being taken that are likely to achieve a standard of remediation equal to, or better than, what the authority would otherwise have specified in a remediation notice; and (b) the authority is satisfied that the timescale in which remediation is planned to take place is appropriate.

6.15

The enforcing authority should actively consider the merits and likelihood of achieving remediation without recourse to a remediation notice before issuing a remediation notice.

Section 6(c): Standard of remediation

6.16

Part 2A states that the enforcing authority may only require (or undertake itself in cases where direct enforcing authority intervention is deemed necessary) actions in a remediation notice which are reasonable with regard to the cost and the seriousness of the pollution or harm. This requirement is in addition to the broader responsibility on the enforcing authority, as a public regulator, to act in a reasonable manner.

6.17

In cases where the aim of remediation is to remove or permanently to disrupt significant contaminant linkages, the enforcing authority should aim to ensure that remediation achieves a standard sufficient to ensure the land no longer poses sufficient risk to qualify as contaminated land. In using powers under Part 2A, the authority should not require a higher standard of remediation. The appropriate person or some other person might choose to carry out remediation to a higher standard (e.g. to increase the value or utility of the land, or to prepare it for redevelopment) but it should not be required by the authority.

6.18

Where the authority considers that it is not practicable or reasonable to remediate land to a degree where it stops being contaminated land, the authority should consider whether it would be reasonable to require remediation to a lesser standard. The broad aim should be to manage or remediate the land in such a way that risks are minimised as far as is reasonably practicable.

6.19

In cases where the purpose of remediation is to remedy harm or pollution that has already been caused, the enforcing authority should decide what is a suitable standard of remediation having regard to the guidance on reasonableness below. In some cases it may be reasonable to require land or waters to be restored to their former state. In other cases it may not be practicable and/or reasonable to do this. In such cases the authority should consider whether it would be reasonable to require remediation to a lesser standard.

Section 6(d): Reasonableness of remediation

6.20

The enforcing authority may only require remediation action in a remediation notice if it is satisfied that those actions are reasonable. In deciding what is reasonable, the authority must consider various factors, having particular regard to: (a) the practicability, effectiveness and durability of remediation; (b) the health and environmental impacts of the chosen remedial options; (c) the financial cost which is likely to be involved; and (d) the benefits of remediation with regard to the seriousness of the harm or pollution of controlled waters in question.

6.21

The paragraphs below explain how the enforcing authority should consider these factors in reaching a judgement on what is reasonable. The enforcing authority should regard a remediation action as being reasonable if it is satisfied that the benefits of remediation are likely to outweigh the costs of remediation.

6.22

In some cases, it might be that there is more than one potential approach to remediation that would be reasonable. In such cases the authority should choose what it considers to be the "best practicable technique" having regard to the factors above. Unless there are strong grounds to consider otherwise, the best practicable technique in such circumstances is likely to be the technique that achieves the required standard of remediation to the appropriate timescale, whilst imposing the least cost on the persons who will pay for the remediation.

Practicability, effectiveness and durability of remediation

6.23

The enforcing authority should ensure that any requirement it makes in regard to remediation is practicable and effective – i.e. it should be possible, within reasonable limits, for the person to undertake the required actions, and the actions should be effective in addressing the problem at hand. This applies both to the remediation scheme as a whole and the individual remediation actions of which it is comprised.

6.24

In assessing the practicability of any remediation, the authority should consider, in particular: (i) technical constraints, such as whether the technical capacity and resources needed to undertake the work exist, and could reasonably be made available; (ii) site constraints, such as access to the relevant land or waters, the presence of buildings or other structures in, on or under the land; (iii) time constraints, such as whether it would be possible to carry out the remediation within the required time period; and (iv) regulatory constraints, such as whether the remediation can be carried out within relevant statutory or similar controls.

6.25

The enforcing authority should consider the durability of remediation. In some cases it will be reasonable to require (or otherwise ensure) a permanent solution to the problem. In other cases this may not be possible or reasonable, in which case the authority should consider how to ensure a reasonable standard of durability. The aim should be to ensure (as far as practical and reasonable) that the scheme as a whole would continue to be effective during the time over which the significant contaminant linkage would continue to exist or recur.

6.26

In considering durability, the enforcing authority should consider whether it is likely that some other future action (such as redevelopment) will resolve or control the problem. If the authority feels that such action is likely to occur within a reasonable timescale, the authority may consider whether it would be appropriate to require remediation of limited durability, pending a more durable solution later.

6.27

Where a remediation scheme cannot reasonably and practicably continue to be effective during the whole of the expected duration of the problem, the enforcing authority should require the remediation to be effective for as long as can reasonably and practicably be achieved. In such circumstances, additional monitoring actions may be required.

6.28

Where a remediation method requires on-going management and maintenance in order to continue to be effective (for example, the maintenance of gas venting or alarm systems), these on-going requirements should be specified in any remediation notice (or similar remediation agreement if remediation is being taken forward without such a notice) as well as any monitoring actions necessary to keep the effectiveness of the remediation under review.

Financial cost of remediation

6.29

In considering the costs likely to be involved in carrying out any remediation action, the enforcing authority should take into account the direct financial costs likely to be caused by remediation. This would include:

(a) The cost of preparing for remediation to take place (e.g. feasibility studies, design of remedial actions, management costs, and the cost of relevant assessment actions).

(b) The cost of undertaking the remediation actions and making good afterwards, including any tax payable.

(c) The cost of managing the land after the main remediation action has taken place (e.g. on-going requirements to manage or maintain the remediation action, and the cost of any monitoring or assessment action).

(d) Relevant disruption costs (e.g. depreciation in the value of land or other interests, or other loss or damage, which is likely to result from the carrying out of the remediation action in question).

(e) The above costs relative to any estimated increase in the financial value and utility of the land as a result of remediation, and whether such increase in value and utility would accrue to the person(s) bearing the cost of remediation.

6.30

The identity or financial standing of any person who may be required to pay for a remediation action are not relevant to the consideration of whether the costs of a remediation action are reasonable (although they may be relevant in deciding whether the cost of remediation can be imposed on such persons).

Benefits of remediation

6.31

In considering the benefits of remediation, the enforcing authority should consider: (a) the seriousness of any harm or pollution of controlled waters and the various factors that led the land to be determined (e.g. the scale of harm or pollution that might already be occurring; or the likelihood of potential future harm or pollution and the likely impact if it were to occur); (b) the context in which the effects are occurring or might occur; and (c) any estimated increase in the financial value and utility of the land as a result of remediation, and who would benefit from such an increase. In considering such benefits it is for the authority to decide whether or not to describe such benefits (whether direct or indirect) in terms of monetary value or whether to make a qualitative consideration.

6.32

Where the significant harm is an "ecological system effect" (as defined in Table 1 in Section 4) the enforcing authority should take into account any advice received from Natural England. Where the enforcing authority is the local authority, it should take into account any advice received from the Environment Agency when it is considering the significance of any pollution of controlled waters and the benefits of any remediation.

Health and environmental impacts of remediation

6.33

In considering the costs of remediation and the seriousness of harm or pollution, the enforcing authority should also consider other costs and impacts that may, directly or indirectly, result from remediation. This should include consideration of: (a) potential health impacts of remediation; and (b) environmental impacts of remediation. In considering such impacts it is for the authority to decide whether or not to describe such costs in terms of monetary value or whether to make a qualitative consideration.

6.34

The enforcing authority's consideration of potential health impacts of remediation should include: (a) direct health effects (e.g. resulting from contaminants being mobilised during remediation, and worker safety); and (b) indirect health effects such as stress-related effects that may be experienced by affected people, particularly local residents. In making this consideration the authority should also be mindful of the health benefits of remediation and the potential health impacts of not remediating the land.

6.35

With regard to environmental impacts of remediation, the enforcing authority should consider whether remediation can be carried out without disproportionate damage to the environment, and in particular: (a) without significant risk to water, air, soil and plants and animals; (b) without causing a nuisance through noise or odours; (c) without adversely affecting the countryside or places of special interest; and (d) without adversely affecting a building of special architectural or historic interest.

6.36

The enforcing authority should strive to minimise impacts of remediation on health and the environment (and comply with any relevant regimes that might require this, for example the health and safety, planning and environmental permitting regimes). If the authority considers that health or environmental impacts of a particular remediation approach are likely to outweigh the likely benefits of dealing with the risk posed by the contamination, it should consider whether an alternative approach to remediation is preferable, even if it may deliver a lower standard of remediation than other techniques.

Section 6(e): Revision of remediation notices

6.37

The enforcing authority should consider revising a remediation notice if it considers it is reasonable to do so. In particular this would apply to cases where new information comes to light which calls into question the reasonableness of an existing remediation notice. For example, this might be the case where information that comes to light during remediation shows that some remediation actions are no longer necessary, or that additional or alternative actions are necessary.

6.38

If the enforcing authority has issued a remediation notice but the person concerned later proposes an alternative remediation scheme, the authority should consider whether to amend or revoke the remediation notice. It is for the authority to decide the degree of consideration it gives to such a proposal. If the authority decides to do this, it should be satisfied that the standard of remediation and the timescale in which it would take place are in line with the guidance in this chapter.

Section 6(f): Verification

6.39

Any remedial treatment action should include appropriate verification measures. In arranging for such measures, the enforcing authority should ensure that the person responsible for verification is a suitably qualified experienced practitioner.

SECTION 7: LIABILITY

7.1

The main provisions for the establishment of liability are set out in Part 2A, and the enforcing authority (and anyone else interested in liability) should refer directly to Part 2A. This Section (as with all of this Guidance) should be read in conjunction with the 1990 Act.

7.2

The statutory guidance in this Section relates in particular to circumstances where two or more persons are liable to bear the responsibility for any particular thing by way of remediation. It deals with the questions of who should be excluded from liability, and how the cost of each remediation action should be apportioned between those who remain liable after any such exclusion. It is issued under section 78F(6) and (7) of the 1990 Act, which provides that:

— Section 78F(6): Where two or more persons would, apart from this sub-section, be appropriate persons in relation to any particular thing which is to be done by way of remediation, the enforcing authority shall determine in accordance with guidance issued for the purpose by the Secretary of State whether any, and if so which, of them is to be treated as not being an appropriate person in relation to that thing.

— Section 78F(7): Where two or more persons are appropriate persons in relation to any particular thing which is to be done by way of remediation, they shall be liable to bear the cost of doing that thing in proportions determined by the enforcing authority in accordance with guidance issued for the purpose by the Secretary of State.

7.3

In summary, this Section sets out a process involving:

(a) **Initial identification of liable persons:** The authority makes an initial identification of persons who may be responsible for paying for remediation actions. In doing this, each significant contaminant linkage is treated separately (unless it is reasonable to treat more than one linkage together because the same parties are liable). The authority first looks for persons who caused or knowingly permitted each linkage in terms of section 78F(2) of Part 2A (who this Guidance refers to as "Class A" persons). If no Class A persons can be found, the authority usually seeks to identify the owners or occupiers of the land in terms of section 78F(4) of Part 2A (who this Guidance refers to as "Class B" persons), although this step does not apply to linkages that relate solely to the pollution of controlled waters. The persons responsible for each linkage make up a "liability group" for that linkage. Liability groups may consist of one or more persons, and this Guidance sometimes uses the terms "Class A liability group" or a "Class B liability group" to reflect the nature of persons in the group.

(b) **Orphan linkages:** If no Class A or Class B persons can be found liable for a linkage, that linkage becomes known as an "orphan linkage" for which there are separate procedures set out at the end of this Section.

(c) **Remediation actions:** The authority decides what remediation actions relate to which linkages. This Guidance uses the term "remediation action" to mean any individual thing which is being, or is to be, done by way of remediation. A "remediation package" is all the remediation actions which relate to a particular linkage. A "remediation scheme" is the complete set of remediation actions (relating to one or more linkages) to be carried out with respect to the relevant land or waters.

(d) **Attribution of liability to liability groups:** The authority attributes responsibility between liability groups. This Guidance uses the term "attribution" to mean the process of apportionment between liability groups.

(e) **Exclusions:** The authority considers (with regard to any liability group with two or more members) whether members of the group should be excluded, in accordance with the rules for exclusion set out in Section 7(c) with regard to Class A persons, and Section 7(e) with regard to Class B persons. This Guidance uses the term "exclusion" to mean any decision by the enforcing authority that a person is to be treated as not being an appropriate person in accordance with section 78F(6) of Part 2A.

(f) **Apportioning liability between members of liability groups:** The authority decides how apportion liability between the members of each liability group who remain after any exclusions have been made. This Guidance uses the term "apportionment" to mean a decision by the authority dividing the costs of carrying out any remediation action between two or more appropriate persons in accordance with section 78F(7) of Part 2A.

Section 7(a): Procedure for determining liabilities

7.4

For some land, the process of determining liabilities will consist simply of identifying either a single person (either an individual or a corporation such as a limited company) who has caused or knowingly permitted the presence of a single significant contaminant, or the owner of the land. The history of other land may be more complex. A succession of different occupiers or of different industries, or a variety of substances may all have contributed to the problems which have made the land "contaminated land" as defined for the purposes of Part 2A. Numerous separate remediation actions may be required, which may not correlate neatly with those who are to bear responsibility for the costs. The degree of responsibility for the state of the land may vary widely. Determining liability for the costs of each remediation action can be correspondingly complex.

Step 1: Identifying potential appropriate persons and liability groups

7.5

As part of the process of determining that the land is "contaminated land" (see Chapters A and B), the enforcing authority will have identified at least one significant contaminant linkage (contaminant, pathway and receptor), resulting from the presence of at least one contaminant.

7.6

Where there is a single significant contaminant linkage:

(a) The enforcing authority should identify all persons who would be appropriate persons to pay for any remediation action relevant to the contaminant which forms part of the significant contaminant linkage. These persons constitute the "liability group" for that significant contaminant linkage.

(b) To achieve this, the enforcing authority should make reasonable enquiries to find all those who have caused or knowingly permitted the contaminant in question to be in, on or under the land. Any such persons constitute a "Class A liability group" for the significant contaminant linkage.

(c) If no such Class A persons can be found for any significant contaminant, the enforcing authority should consider whether the significant contaminant linkage of which it forms part relates solely to the significant pollution of controlled waters (rather than to any significant harm to human or relevant environmental receptors). If this is the case, there will be no liability group for that significant contaminant linkage, and it should be treated as an "orphan linkage" (see paragraphs 7.92–7.98 below).

(d) In any other case where no Class A persons can be found for a significant contaminant, the enforcing authority should identify all of the current owners or occupiers of the contaminated land in question. These persons then constitute a "Class B liability group" for the significant contaminant linkage.

(e) If the enforcing authority cannot find any Class A persons or any Class B persons in respect of a significant contaminant linkage, there will be no liability group for that linkage and it should be treated as an "orphan linkage" (see paragraphs 7.92–7.98 below).

7.7

Where there are two or more significant contaminant linkages, the enforcing authority should consider each significant contaminant linkage in turn, carrying out the steps set out in paragraph 7.6 above, to identify the liability group (if one exists) for each of the linkages.

7.8

Having identified one or more liability groups, the enforcing authority should consider whether any of the members of those groups are exempted from liability under the provisions in Part 2A. This could apply where:

(a) A person who would otherwise be a Class A person is exempted from liability arising with respect to water pollution from an abandoned mine (see section 78J(3) of Part 2A).
(b) A Class B person is exempted from liability arising from the escape of a contaminant from one piece of land to other land (see section 78K of Part 2A).
(c) A person is exempted from liability by virtue of his being a person "acting in a relevant capacity" (such as acting as an insolvency practitioner) as defined in section 78X(4) of Part 2A.

7.9

If all of the members of any liability group benefit from one or more of these exemptions, the enforcing authority should treat the significant contaminant linkage in question as an orphan linkage (see paragraphs 7.92–7.98 below).

7.10

Persons may be members of more than one liability group (e.g. if they caused or knowingly permitted the presence of more than one significant contaminant).

7.11

Where the membership of all of the liability groups is the same, there may be opportunities for the enforcing authority to abbreviate the remaining stages of this procedure. However, the tests for exclusion and apportionment may produce different results for different significant contaminant linkages, and so the enforcing authority should exercise caution before trying to simplify the procedure in any case.

Step 2: Characterising remediation actions

7.12

Each remediation action will be carried out to achieve a particular purpose with respect to one or more defined significant contaminant linkages. Where there is a single significant contaminant linkage on the land in question, all the remediation actions will be referable to that linkage, and there is no need to consider how the different actions relate to different linkages. This step and Step 3 of the procedure therefore do not need to be carried out in where there is only a single significant contaminant linkage. However, where there are two or more significant contaminant linkages on the land in question, the enforcing authority should establish whether each remediation action is: (a) referable solely to the significant contaminant in a single significant contaminant linkage (a "single-linkage action"); or (b) referable to the significant contaminant in more than one significant contaminant linkage (a "shared action").

7.13

Where a remediation action is a shared action, there are two possible relationships between it and the significant contaminant linkages to which it is referable. The enforcing authority should establish whether the shared action is:
(a) a "common action" – i.e. an action which addresses together all of the significant contaminant linkages to which it is referable, and which would have been part of the remediation package for each of those linkages if each of them had been addressed separately.

(b) a "collective action" – i.e. an action which addresses together all of the significant contaminant linkages to which it is referable, but which would not have been part of the remediation package for every one of those linkages if each of them had been addressed separately, because: (i) the action would not have been appropriate in that form for one or more of the linkages (since some different solution would have been more appropriate); (ii) the action would not have been needed to the same extent for one or more of the linkages (since a less far-reaching version of that type of action would have sufficed); or (iii) the action represents a more economic way of addressing the linkages together which would not be possible if they were addressed separately.

7.14

A collective action replaces actions that would have been appropriate for the individual significant contaminant linkages if they had been addressed separately, as it achieves the purposes which those other actions would have achieved.

Step 3: Attributing responsibility between liability groups

7.15

This stage of the procedure does not apply in simpler cases. Where there is only a single significant contaminant linkage, the liability group for that linkage bears the full cost of carrying out any remediation action. Where the linkage is an orphan linkage, the enforcing authority has the power to carry out the remediation action itself, at its own cost.

7.16

Similarly, for any single-linkage action, the liability group (i.e. the group that remains after the exclusions in paragraph 7.8 have been applied) for the significant contaminant linkage in question bears the full cost of carrying out that action.

7.17

However, the enforcing authority should apply the guidance in Section 7(g) below with respect to each shared action, in order to attribute to each of the different liability groups their share of responsibility for that action.

7.18

After the guidance in Section 7(g) has been applied to all shared actions, it may be the case that a Class B liability group which has been identified does not have to bear the costs for any remediation actions. Where this is the case, the enforcing authority does not need to apply any of the rest of the guidance in this Chapter to that liability group.

Step 4: Excluding members of a liability group

7.19

The enforcing authority should now consider, for each liability group which has two or more members, whether any of those members should be excluded from liability: (a) for each Class A liability group with two or more members, the enforcing authority should apply the guidance on exclusion in Section 7(c); and (b) for each Class B liability group with two or more members, the enforcing authority should apply the guidance on exclusion in Section 7(e).

Step 5: Apportioning liability between members of a liability group

7.20

The enforcing authority should now determine how any costs attributed to each liability group should be apportioned between the members of that group who remain after any exclusions have been made.

7.21

For any liability group (after the exclusions in paragraph 7.8 have been applied) which has only a single remaining member, that person bears all of the costs falling to that liability group (i.e. both the cost of any single-linkage action referable to the significant contaminant linkage in question; and the share of the cost of any shared action attributed to the group as a result of the attribution process set out in Section 7(g)).

7.22

For any liability group which has two or more remaining members, the enforcing authority should apply the relevant guidance on apportionment between those members. Each of the remaining members of the group will then bear the proportion determined under that guidance of the total costs falling to the group, that is both the cost of any single-linkage action referable to the significant contaminant linkage in question, and the share of the cost of any shared action attributed to the group as a result of the attribution process set out in Part 9. The relevant apportionment guidance is: (a) for any Class A liability group, the guidance set out in Section 7(d); and (b) for any Class B liability group, the guidance set out in Section 7(f).

Section 7(b): General considerations relating to exclusion, apportionment and attribution procedures

7.23

This sub-section sets out general guidance about the application of the exclusion, apportionment and attribution procedures set out in the rest of this Chapter. It is issued under both section 78F(6) and section 78F(7).

7.24

The enforcing authority should ensure that any person who might benefit from an exclusion, apportionment or attribution is aware of the guidance in this Chapter, so that they may make appropriate representations to the enforcing authority.

7.25

The enforcing authority should apply the tests for exclusion (in Section 7(c) and (e)) with respect to the members of each liability group. If a person, who would otherwise be an appropriate person to bear responsibility for a particular remediation action, has been excluded from the liability groups for all of the significant contaminant linkages to which that action is referable, he should be treated as not being an appropriate person in relation to that remediation action.

Financial circumstances

7.26

The financial circumstances of those concerned should have no bearing on the application of the procedures for exclusion, apportionment and attribution in this Chapter, except where the circumstances in paragraph 7.74 below apply (the financial circumstances of those concerned are taken into account in the separate consideration under section 78P(2) on hardship and cost recovery). In particular, it should be irrelevant in the context of decisions on exclusion and apportionment: (a) whether those concerned would benefit from any limitation on the recovery of costs under the provisions on hardship and cost recovery in section 78P(2); or (b) whether those concerned would benefit from any insurance or other means of transferring their responsibilities to another person.

Information and decisions

7.27

The enforcing authority should make reasonable endeavours to consult those who may be affected by any exclusion, apportionment or attribution. In all cases, however, it should seek to obtain only such information as it is reasonable to seek, having regard to: (a) how the information might be obtained; (b) the cost of obtaining the information for all parties involved; and (c) the potential significance of the information for any decision.

7.28

The statutory guidance in this Section should be applied in the light of the circumstances as they appear to the enforcing authority on the basis of the evidence available to it at that time. Where the enforcing authority is presented with conflicting evidence, it should make decisions with regard to the balance of probabilities. The enforcing authority should take into account the information that it has acquired in the light of the guidance in the previous paragraph, but the burden of providing the authority with any further information needed to establish an exclusion or to influence an apportionment or attribution should rest on any person seeking such a benefit. The enforcing authority should consider any relevant information which has been provided by those potentially liable under these provisions. Where any such person provides such information, any other person who may be affected by an exclusion, apportionment or attribution based on that information should be given a reasonable opportunity to comment on that information before the determination is made.

Agreements on liabilities

7.29

In any case where:

(a) two or more persons are appropriate persons and thus responsible for all or part of the costs of a remediation action;

(b) they agree, or have agreed, the basis on which they wish to divide that responsibility; and

(c) a copy of the agreement is provided to the enforcing authority and none of the parties to the agreement informs the authority that it challenges the application of the agreement;

the enforcing authority should generally make such determinations on exclusion, apportionment and attribution as are needed to give effect to this agreement, and should not apply the remainder of this guidance for exclusion, apportionment or attribution between the parties to the agreement. However, the enforcing authority should apply the guidance to determine any exclusions, apportionments or attributions between any or all of those parties and any other appropriate persons who are not parties to the agreement.

7.30

However, where giving effect to such an agreement would increase the share of the costs theoretically to be borne by a person who would benefit from a limitation on recovery of remediation costs under the provision on hardship in section 78P(2)(a) or under the guidance on cost recovery issued under section 78P(2)(b), the enforcing authority should disregard the agreement.

Section 7(c): Exclusion of members of a Class A liability group

7.31

This sub-section of the Guidance sets out the tests for determining whether to exclude from liability a person who would otherwise be a Class A person. The tests are intended to establish whether, in relation to other members of the liability group, it is fair that relevant persons should bear any part of that responsibility.

7.32

The exclusion tests below are subject to the following overriding guidance:

(a) the exclusions that the enforcing authority should make are solely in respect of the significant contaminant linkage giving rise to the liability of the liability group in question; an exclusion in respect of one significant contaminant linkage has no necessary implication in respect to any other such linkage, and a person who has been excluded with respect to one linkage may still be liable to meet all or part of the cost of carrying out a remediation action by reason of his membership of another liability group;

(b) the tests should be applied in the sequence in which they are set out; and

(c) if the result of applying a test would be to exclude all of the members of the liability group who remain after any exclusions resulting from previous tests, that further test should not be applied, and consequently the related exclusions should not be made.

7.33

The effect of any exclusion made under Test 1, or Tests 4 to 6 below should be to remove completely any liability that would otherwise have fallen on the person benefiting from the exclusion. Where the enforcing authority makes any exclusion under one of these tests, it should therefore apply any subsequent exclusion tests, and make any apportionment within the liability group, in the same way as it would have done if the excluded person had never been a member of the liability group.

7.34

The effect of any exclusion made under Test 2 (Payments made for remediation) or Test 3 (Sold with information), on the other hand, is intended to be that the person who received the payment or bought the land, as the case may be, (the "payee or buyer") should bear the liability of the person excluded (the "payer or seller") in addition to any liability which the person is to bear in respect of their own actions or omissions. To achieve this, the enforcing authority should:

(a) complete the application of the other exclusion tests and then apportion liability between the members of the liability group, as if the payer or seller were not excluded as a result of Test 2 or Test 3; and
(b) then apportion any liability of the payer or seller, calculated on this hypothetical basis, to the payee or buyer, in addition to the liability (if any) that the payee or buyer has in respect of his own actions or omissions; this should be done even if the payee or buyer would otherwise have been excluded from the liability group by one of the other exclusion tests.

Related companies

7.35

Before applying any of the exclusion tests, the enforcing authority should establish whether two or more of the members of the liability group are "related companies".

7.36

Where the question to be considered in any exclusion test concerns the relationship between, or the relative positions of, two or more related companies, the enforcing authority should not apply the test so as to exclude any of the related companies. For example, in Test 3 (Sold with information), if the "seller" and the "buyer" are related companies, the "seller" would not be excluded by virtue of that Test.

7.37

For these purposes, "related companies" are those which are, or were at the "relevant date", members of a group of companies consisting of a "holding company" and its "subsidiaries". The "relevant date" is that on which the enforcing authority first served on anyone a notice under section 78B(3) identifying the land as contaminated land, and the terms "holding company" and "subsidiaries" have the same meaning as in Section 1159 of the Companies Act 2006.

Exclusion tests for Class A persons

Test 1: Excluded activities

7.38

The purpose of Test 1 is to exclude persons who have been identified as members of a Class A liability group solely on grounds of having carried out certain activities. The activities are ones which, in the Government's view, carry such limited responsibility (if any) that exclusion would be justified even where the activity is held to amount to "causing or knowingly permitting" under Part 2A. This is not intended to imply that the carrying out of such activities necessarily amounts to "causing or knowingly permitting".

7.39

In applying Test 1, the enforcing authority should exclude any appropriate person who is a member of a liability group solely by reason of one or more of the activities listed in (a) to (k) below.
(a) Providing (or withholding) financial assistance to another person (whether or not that other person is a member of the liability group), in the form of any one or more of the following: (i) making a grant; (ii) making a loan or providing any other form of credit, including instalment credit, leasing arrangements and mortgages;

(iii) guaranteeing the performance of a person's obligations; (iv) indemnifying a person in respect of any loss, liability or damage; (v) investing in the undertaking of a body corporate by acquiring share capital or loan capital of that body without thereby acquiring such control as a "holding company" has over a "subsidiary" as defined in section 736 of the Companies Act 1985; or (vi) providing a person with any other financial benefit (including the remission in whole or in part of any financial liability or obligation).

(b) Underwriting an insurance policy under which another person was insured in respect of any occurrence, condition or omission by reason of which that other person has been held to have caused or knowingly permitted the significant contaminant to be in, on or under the land in question. For the purposes of this sub-paragraph: (i) underwriting an insurance policy is to be taken to include imposing any conditions on the person insured, for example relating to the manner in which he carries out the insured activity; and (ii) it is irrelevant whether or not the insured person can now be found.

(c) As a provider of financial assistance or as an underwriter, carrying out any action for the purpose of deciding whether or not to provide such financial assistance or underwrite such an insurance policy as is mentioned above. This sub-paragraph does not apply to the carrying out of any intrusive investigation in respect of the land in question for the purpose of making that decision where: (i) the carrying out of that investigation is itself a cause of the existence, nature or continuance of the significant contaminant linkage in question; and (ii) the person who applied for the financial assistance or insurance is not a member of the liability group.

(d) Consigning, as waste, to another person the substance which is now a significant contaminant, under a contract under which that other person knowingly took over responsibility for its proper disposal or other management on land not under the control of the person seeking to be excluded from liability. For the purpose of this sub-paragraph, it is irrelevant whether or not the person to whom the waste was consigned can now be found.

(e) Creating at any time a tenancy over the land in question in favour of another person who has subsequently caused or knowingly permitted the presence of the significant contaminant linkage in question (whether or not the tenant can now be found).

(f) As owner of the land in question, licensing at any time its occupation by another person who has subsequently caused or knowingly permitted the presence of the significant contaminant in question (whether or not the licensee can now be found). This test does not apply in a case where the person granting the licence operated the land as a site for the disposal or storage of waste at the time of the grant of the licence.

(g) Issuing any statutory permission, licence or consent required for any action or omission by reason of which some other person appears to the enforcing authority to have caused or knowingly permitted the presence of the significant contaminant in question (whether or not that other person can now be found). This test does not apply in the case of statutory undertakers granting permission for their contractors to carry out works.

(h) Taking, or not taking, any statutory enforcement action: (i) with respect to the land, or (ii) against some other person who appears to the enforcing authority to have caused or knowingly permitted the presence of the significant contaminant in question, whether or not that other person can now be found.

(i) Providing legal, financial, engineering, scientific or technical advice to (or design, contract management or works management services for) another person (the "client"), whether or not that other person can now be found: (i) in relation to an action or omission (or a series of actions and/or omissions) by reason of which the client has been held to have caused or knowingly permitted the presence of the significant contaminant; (ii) for the purpose of assessing the condition of the land, for example whether it might be contaminated; or (iii) for the purpose of establishing what might be done to the land by way of remediation.

(j) As a person providing advice or services as described in sub-paragraph (i) above carrying out any intrusive investigation in respect of the land in question, except where: (i) the investigation is itself a cause of the existence, nature or continuance of the significant contaminant linkage in question; and (ii) the client is not a member of the liability group.

(k) Performing any contract by providing a service (whether the contract is a contract of service (employment), or a contract for services) or by supplying goods, where the contract is made with another person who is also a member of the liability group in question. For the purposes of this sub-paragraph the person providing the service or supplying the goods is referred to as the "contractor" and the other party as the "employer". This sub-paragraph applies to subcontracts where either the ultimate employer or an intermediate contractor is a member of the liability group. This sub-paragraph does not apply where: (i) the activity under the contract is of a kind referred to in a previous sub-paragraph of this paragraph; (ii) the action or omission by the contractor by virtue of which he has been identified as an appropriate person was not in accordance with the terms of the contract; or (iii) where:
- the employer is a body corporate;
- the contractor was a director, manager, secretary or other similar officer of the body corporate, or a person purporting to act in any such capacity, at the time when the contract was performed; and
- the action or omissions by virtue of which the employer has been identified as an appropriate person were carried out or made with the consent or connivance of the contractor, or were attributable to any neglect on his part.

Test 2: Payments for remediation

7.40

The purpose of this test is to exclude from liability those who have already, in effect, met their responsibilities by making certain kinds of payment to some other member of the liability group, which would have been sufficient to pay for adequate remediation.

7.41

In applying this test, the enforcing authority should consider whether all the following circumstances exist: (a) one of the members of the liability group has made a payment to another member of that liability group for the purpose of carrying out particular remediation on the land in question; only payments of the kinds set out in paragraph 7.42 immediately below are to be taken into account; (b) that payment would have been sufficient at the date when it was made to pay for the remediation in question; (c) if the remediation for which the payment was intended had been carried out effectively, the land in question would not now be in such a condition that it has been identified as contaminated land by reason of the significant contaminant linkage in question; and (d) the remediation in question was not carried out or was not carried out effectively.

7.42

Payments of the following kinds alone should be taken into account: (a) a payment made voluntarily, or to meet a contractual obligation, in response to a claim for the cost of the particular remediation; (b) a payment made in the course of a civil legal action, or arbitration, mediation or dispute resolution procedure, covering the cost of the particular remediation, whether paid as part of an out-of-court settlement, or paid under the terms of a court order; or (c) a payment as part of a contract (including a group of interlinked contracts) for the transfer of ownership of the land in question which is either specifically provided for in the contract to meet the cost of carrying out the particular remediation or which consists of a reduction in the contract price explicitly stated in the contract to be for that purpose.

7.43

For the purposes of this test, payments include consideration of any form.

7.44

However, no payment should be taken into account where the person making the payment retained any control after the date of the payment over the condition of the land in question (that is, over whether or not the substances by reason of which the land is regarded as contaminated land were permitted to be in, on or under the land). For this purpose, neither of the following should be regarded as retaining control over the condition of the land: (a) holding contractual rights to ensure the proper carrying out of the remediation for which the payment was made; nor (b) holding an interest or right of any of the following kinds: (i) easements for the benefit of other land, where the contaminated land in question is the servient tenement, and statutory rights of an equivalent nature; (ii) rights of statutory undertakers to carry out works or install equipment; (iii) reversions upon expiry or termination of a long lease; or (iv) the benefit of restrictive covenants or equivalent statutory agreements.

7.45

If all of the circumstances set out in paragraph 7.41 above apply, the enforcing authority should exclude the person who made the payment in respect of the remediation action in question. (See paragraph 7.34 above for guidance on how this exclusion should be made.)

Test 3: Sold with information

7.46

The purpose of this test is to exclude from liability those who, although they have caused or knowingly permitted the presence of a significant contaminant in, on or under some land, have disposed of that land in circumstances where it is reasonable that another member of the liability group, who has acquired the land from them, should bear the liability for remediation of the land.

7.47

In applying this test, the enforcing authority should consider whether all the following circumstances exist:

(a) one of the members of the liability group (the "seller") has sold the land in question to a person who is also a member of the liability group (the "buyer");

(b) the sale took place at arms' length (that is, on terms which could be expected in a sale on the open market between a willing seller and a willing buyer);

(c) before the sale became binding, the buyer had information that would reasonably allow that particular person to be aware of the presence on the land of the contaminant identified in the significant contaminant linkage in question, and the broad measure of that presence; and the seller did nothing material to misrepresent the implications of that presence; and

(d) after the date of the sale, the seller did not retain any interest in the land in question or any rights to occupy or use that land.

7.48

In determining whether these circumstances exist:

(a) a sale of land should be regarded as being either the transfer of the freehold or the grant or assignment of a long lease; for this purpose, a "long lease" means a lease (or sub-lease) granted for a period of more than 21 years under which the lessee satisfies the definition of "owner" set out in section 78A(9);

(b) the question of whether persons are members of a liability group should be decided on the circumstances as they exist at the time of the determination (and not as they might have been at the time of the sale of the land);

(c) where there is a group of transactions or a wider agreement (such as the sale of a company or business) including a sale of land, that sale of land should be taken to have been at arms' length where the person seeking to be excluded can show that the net effect of the group of transactions or the agreement as a whole was a sale at arms' length;

(d) in transactions since the beginning of 1990 where the buyer is a large commercial organisation or public body, permission from the seller for the buyer to carry out his own investigations of the condition of the land should normally be taken as sufficient indication that the buyer had the information referred to in paragraph 7.47(c) above; and

(e) for the purposes of paragraph 7.47(d) above, the following rights should be disregarded in deciding whether the seller has retained an interest in the contaminated land in question or rights to occupy or use it: (i) easements for the benefit of other land, where the contaminated land in question is the servient tenement, and statutory rights of an equivalent nature, (ii) rights of statutory undertakers to carry out works or install equipment, (iii) reversions upon expiry or termination of a long lease, and (iv) the benefit of restrictive covenants or equivalent statutory agreements.

7.49

If all of the circumstances in paragraph 7.47 above apply, the enforcing authority should exclude the seller. (See paragraph 7.34 above for guidance on how this exclusion should be made.)

7.50

This test does not imply that the receipt by the buyer of the information referred to in paragraph 7.47(c) above necessarily means that the buyer has "caused or knowingly permitted" the presence of the significant contaminant in, on or under the land.

Test 4: Changes to substances

7.51

The purpose of this test is to exclude from liability those who are members of a liability group solely because they caused or knowingly permitted the presence in, on or under the land of a substance which has only led to the creation of a significant contaminant linkage because of its interaction with another substance which was later introduced to the land by another person.

7.52

In applying this test, the enforcing authority should consider whether all the following circumstances exist:

(a) The substance forming part of the significant contaminant linkage in question is present, or has become a significant contaminant, only as the result of a chemical reaction, biological process, radioactive decay or other change (the "intervening change") involving: (i) both a substance (the "earlier substance") which would not have formed part of the significant contaminant linkage if the intervening change had not occurred; and (ii) one or more other substances (the "later substances").

(b) The intervening change would not have occurred in the absence of the later substances;

(c) A person (the "first person") is a member of the liability group because he/she caused or knowingly permitted the presence in, on or under the land of the earlier substance, but he/she did not cause or knowingly permit the presence of any of the later substances.

(d) One or more other persons are members of the liability group because they caused or knowingly permitted the later substances to be in, on or under the land.

(e) Before the date when the later substances started to be introduced in, on or under the land, the first person: (i) could not reasonably have foreseen that the later substances would be introduced onto the land; (ii) could not reasonably have foreseen that, if they were, the intervening change would be likely to happen; or (iii) took what, at that date, were reasonable precautions to prevent the introduction of the later substances or the occurrence of the intervening change, even though those precautions have, in the event, proved to be inadequate.

(f) After that date, the first person did not: (i) cause or knowingly permit any more of the earlier substance to be in, on or under the land in question; (ii) do anything which has contributed to the conditions that brought about the intervening change; or (iii) fail to do something which he could reasonably have been expected to do to prevent the intervening change happening.

7.53

If all of the circumstances in paragraph 7.52 above apply, the enforcing authority should exclude the first person (or persons, if more than one member of the liability group meets this description).

Test 5: Escaped substances

7.54

The purpose of this test is to exclude from liability those who would otherwise be liable for the remediation of contaminated land which has become contaminated as a result of the escape of substances from other land, where it can be shown that another member of the liability group was actually responsible for that escape.

7.55

In applying this test, the enforcing authority should consider whether all the following circumstances exist:

(a) a significant contaminant is present in, on or under the contaminated land in question wholly or partly as a result of its escape from other land;

(b) a member of the liability group for the significant contaminant linkage of which that contaminant forms part: (i) caused or knowingly permitted the contaminant to be present in, on or under that other land (that is, the person is a member of that liability group by reason of section 78K(1)), and (ii) is a member of that liability group solely for that reason; and

(c) one or more other members of that liability group caused or knowingly permitted the significant contaminant to escape from that other land and its escape would not have happened but for their actions or omissions.

7.56

If all of the circumstances in paragraph 7.55 above apply, the enforcing authority should exclude any person meeting the description in paragraph 7.55(b) above.

Test 6: Introduction of pathways or receptors

7.57

The purpose of this test is to exclude from liability those who would otherwise be liable solely because of the subsequent introduction by others of the relevant pathways or receptors (as defined in Section 3) in the significant contaminant linkage.

7.58

In applying this test, the enforcing authority should consider whether all the following circumstances exist:

(a) One or more members of the liability group have carried out a relevant action, and/or made a relevant omission ("the later actions"), either: (i) as part of the series of actions and/or omissions which amount to their having caused or knowingly permitted the presence of the contaminant in a significant contaminant linkage; or (ii) in addition to that series of actions and/or omissions.

(b) The effect of the later actions has been to introduce the pathway or the receptor which form part of the significant contaminant linkage in question.

(c) If those later actions had not been carried out or made, the significant contaminant linkage would either not have existed, or would not have been a significant contaminant linkage, because of the absence of a pathway or of a receptor.

(d) A person is a member of the liability group in question solely by reason of having carried out other actions or making other omissions ("the earlier actions") which were completed before any of the later actions were carried out or made.

7.59

For the purpose of this test:

(a) A "relevant action" means: (i) the carrying out at any time of building, engineering, mining or other operations in, on, over or under the land in question; and/or (ii) the making of any material change in the use of the land in question for which a specific application for planning permission was required to be made (as opposed to permission being granted, or deemed to be granted, by general legislation or by virtue of a development order, the adoption of a simplified planning zone or the designation of an enterprise zone) at the time when the change in use was made.

(b) A "relevant omission" means: (i) in the course of a relevant action, failing to take a step which would have ensured that a significant contaminant linkage was not brought into existence as a result of that action, and/or (ii) unreasonably failing to maintain or operate a system installed for the purpose of reducing or managing the risk associated with the presence on the land in question of the significant contaminant in the significant contaminant linkage in question.

7.60

This test applies only with respect to developments on, or changes in the use of, the contaminated land itself. It does not apply where the relevant acts or omissions take place on other land, even if they have the effect of introducing pathways or receptors.

7.61

If all of the circumstances in paragraph 7.58 above apply, the enforcing authority should exclude any person meeting the description at paragraph 7.58(d) above.

Section 7(d): Apportionment between members of a single Class A liability group

7.62

The statutory guidance in this Part is issued under section 78F(7) and sets out the principles on which liability should be apportioned within each Class A liability group as it stands after any members have been excluded from liability with respect to the relevant significant contaminant linkage as a result of the application of the exclusion tests in Section 7(c).

7.63

The history and circumstances of different areas of contaminated land, and the nature of the responsibility of each of the members of any Class A liability group for a significant contaminant linkage, are likely to vary greatly. It is therefore not possible to prescribe detailed rules for the apportionment of liability between those members which would be fair and appropriate in all cases.

General principles

7.64

In apportioning costs between the members of a Class A liability group who remain after any exclusions have been made, the enforcing authority should follow the general principle that liability should be apportioned to reflect the relative responsibility of each of those members for creating or continuing the risk now being caused by the significant contaminant linkage in question. In applying this principle, the enforcing authority should follow, where appropriate, the specific approaches set out in paragraphs 7.66-7.75 below.

7.65

If appropriate information is not available to enable the enforcing authority to make such an assessment of relative responsibility (and, following the guidance at paragraph 7.27 above, such information cannot reasonably be obtained) the authority should apportion liability in equal shares among the remaining members of the liability group for any significant contaminant linkage, subject to the specific guidance in paragraph 7.74 below.

Specific approaches

Partial applicability of an exclusion test

7.66

If, for any member of the liability group, the circumstances set out in any of the exclusion tests in Section 7(c) above apply to some extent, but not sufficiently to mean that an exclusion should be made, the enforcing authority should assess that person's degree of responsibility as being reduced to the extent which is appropriate in the light of all the circumstances and the purpose of the test in question. For example, in considering Test 2, a payment may have been made which was sufficient to pay for only half of the necessary remediation at that time – the authority could therefore reduce the payer's responsibility by half.

Entry of a substance vs. its continued presence

7.67

In assessing the relative responsibility of a person who has caused or knowingly permitted the entry of a significant contaminant into, onto or under land (the "first person") and another person who has knowingly permitted the continued presence of that same contaminant in, on or under that land (the "second person"), the enforcing authority should consider the extent to which the second person had the means and a reasonable opportunity to deal with the presence of the contaminant in question or to reduce the seriousness of the implications of that presence. The authority should then assess the relative responsibilities on the following basis: (a) if the second person had the necessary means and opportunity, they should bear the same responsibility as the first person; (b) if the second person did not have the means and opportunity, their responsibility relative to that of the first person should be substantially reduced; and (c) if the second person had some, but insufficient, means or opportunity, their responsibility relative to that of the first person should be reduced to an appropriate extent.

Persons who have caused or knowingly permitted the entry of a significant contaminant

7.68

Where the enforcing authority is determining the relative responsibilities of members of the liability group who have caused or knowingly permitted the entry of the significant contaminant into, onto or under the land, it should follow the approach set out in paragraphs 7.69 to 7.72 below.

7.69

If the nature of the remediation action points clearly to different members of the liability group being responsible for particular circumstances at which the action is aimed, the enforcing authority should apportion responsibility in accordance with that indication. In particular, where different persons were in control of different areas of the land in question, and there is no interrelationship between those areas, the enforcing authority should regard the persons in control of the different areas as being separately responsible for the events which make necessary the remediation actions or parts of actions referable to those areas of land.

7.70

If the circumstances in paragraph 7.69 above do not apply, but the quantity of the significant contaminant present is a major influence on the cost of remediation, the enforcing authority should regard the relative amounts of that contaminant which are referable to the different persons as an appropriate basis for apportioning responsibility.

7.71

If it is deciding the relative quantities of contaminant which are referable to different persons, the enforcing authority should consider first whether there is direct evidence of the relative quantities referable to each person. If there is such evidence, it should be used. In the absence of direct evidence, the enforcing authority should see whether an appropriate surrogate measure is available. Such surrogate measures can include: (a) the relative periods during which the different persons carried out broadly equivalent operations on the land; (b) the relative scale of such operations carried out on the land by the different persons (a measure of such scale may be the quantities of a product that were produced); (c) the relative areas of land on which different persons carried out their operations; and (d) combinations of the foregoing measures.

7.72

In cases where the circumstances in neither paragraph 7.69 nor 7.70 above apply, the enforcing authority should consider the nature of the activities carried out by the appropriate persons concerned from which the significant contaminant arose. Where these activities were broadly equivalent, the enforcing authority should apportion responsibility in proportion to the periods of time over which the different persons were in control of those activities. It would be appropriate to adjust this apportionment to reflect circumstances where the persons concerned carried out activities which were not broadly equivalent, for example where they were on a different scale.

Persons who have knowingly permitted the continued presence of a contaminant

7.73

Where the enforcing authority is determining the relative responsibilities of members of the liability group who have knowingly permitted the continued presence, over a period of time, of a significant contaminant in, on or under land, it should apportion that responsibility in proportion to: (a) the length of time during which each person controlled the land; (b) the area of land which each person controlled; (c) the extent to which each person had the means and a reasonable opportunity to deal with the presence of the contaminant in question or to reduce the seriousness of the implications of that presence; or (d) a combination of the foregoing factors.

Companies and officers

7.74

If, following the application of the exclusion tests (and in particular the specific guidance at paragraph 7.39(k)(iii)) both a company and one or more of its relevant officers remain as members of the liability group, the enforcing authority should apportion liability on the following bases:

(a) the enforcing authority should treat the company and its relevant officers as a single unit for the purposes of: (i) applying the general principle in paragraph 7.64 above (i.e. it should consider the responsibilities of the company and its relevant officers as a whole, in comparison with the responsibilities of other members of the liability group), and (ii) making any apportionment required by paragraph 7.65 above; and

(b) having determined the share of liability falling to the company and its relevant officers together, the enforcing authority should apportion responsibility between the company and its relevant officers on a basis which takes into account the degree of personal responsibility of those officers, and the relative levels of resources which may be available to them and to the company to meet the liability.

7.75

For the purposes of paragraph 7.74 immediately above, the "relevant officers" of a company are any director, manager, secretary or other similar officer of the company, or any other person purporting to act in any such capacity.

Section 7(e): Exclusion of members of a Class B liability group

7.76

The guidance in this sub-section is issued under section 78F(6) and sets out the test which should be applied in determining whether to exclude from liability a person who would otherwise be a Class B person (that is, a person liable to meet remediation costs solely by reason of ownership or occupation of the land in question). The purpose of the test is to exclude from liability those who do not have an interest in the capital value of the land in question.

7.77

The test applies where two or more persons have been identified as Class B persons for a significant contaminant linkage.

7.78

In such circumstances, the enforcing authority should exclude any Class B person who either:

(a) occupies the land under a licence, or other agreement, of a kind which has no marketable value or which he is not legally able to assign or transfer to another person (for these purposes the actual marketable value, or the fact that a particular licence or agreement may not actually attract a buyer in the market, are irrelevant); or

(b) is liable to pay a rent which is equivalent to the rack rent for such of the land in question as he occupies and holds no beneficial interest in that land other than any tenancy to which such rent relates; where the rent is subject to periodic review, the rent should be considered to be equivalent to the rack rent if, at the latest review, it was set at the full market rent at that date.

7.79

However, the test should not be applied, and consequently no exclusion should be made, if it would result in the exclusion of all of the members of the liability group.

Section 7(f): Apportionment between the members of a dingle Class B liability group

7.80

The statutory guidance in this Part is issued under section 78F(7) and sets out the principles on which liability should be apportioned within each Class B liability group as it stands after any members have been excluded from liability with respect to the relevant significant contaminant linkage as a result of the application of the exclusion test in Section 7(e) above.

7.81

Where the whole or part of a remediation action for which a Class B liability group is responsible clearly relates to a particular area within the land to which the significant contaminant linkage as a whole relates, liability for the whole, or the relevant part, of that action should be apportioned amongst those members of the liability group who own or occupy that particular area of land.

7.82

Where those circumstances do not apply, the enforcing authority should apportion liability for the remediation actions necessary for the significant contaminant linkage in question amongst all of the members of the liability group.

7.83

Where the enforcing authority is apportioning liability amongst some or all of the members of a Class B liability group, it should do so in proportion to the capital values of the interests in the land in question, which include those of any buildings or structures on the land:

(a) where different members of the liability group own or occupy different areas of land, each such member should bear responsibility in the proportion that the capital value of their area of land bears to the aggregate of the capital values of all the areas of land; and

(b) where different members of the liability group have an interest in the same area of land, each such member should bear responsibility in the proportion which the capital value of their interest bears to the aggregate of the capital values of all those interests; and

(c) where both the ownership or occupation of different areas of land and the holding of different interests come into the question, the overall liability should first be apportioned between the different areas of land and then between the interests within each of those areas of land, in each case in accordance with the last two sub-paragraphs.

7.84

The capital value used for these purposes should be that estimated by the enforcing authority, on the basis of the available information, disregarding the existence of any contamination. The value should be estimated in relation to the date immediately before the enforcing authority first served a notice under section 78B(3) in relation to that land. Where the land in question is reasonably uniform in nature and amenity and is divided among a number of owner-occupiers, it can be an acceptable approximation of this basis of apportionment to make the apportionment on the basis of the area occupied by each.

7.85

Where part of the land in question is land for which no owner or occupier can be found, the enforcing authority should deduct the share of costs attributable to that land on the basis of the respective capital values of that land and the other land in question before making a determination of liability.

7.86

If appropriate information is not available to enable the enforcing authority to make an assessment of relative capital values (and, following the guidance at paragraph 7.27 above, such information cannot reasonably be obtained), the enforcing authority should apportion liability in equal shares among all the members of the liability group.

Section 7(g): Attribution of responsibility between liability groups

7.87

The statutory guidance in this sub-section is issued under section 78F(7) and applies where one remediation action is referable to two or more significant contaminant linkages (i.e. it is a "shared action"). This can occur either where both linkages require the same action (that is, it is a "common action") or where a particular action is part of the best combined remediation scheme for two or more linkages (that is, it is a "collective action"). This Part provides statutory guidance on the attribution of responsibility for the costs of any shared action between the liability groups for the linkages to which it is referable.

Attributing responsibility for the cost of shared actions between liability groups

7.88

The enforcing authority should attribute responsibility for the costs of any common action among the liability groups for the significant contaminant linkages to which it is referable on the following basis:

(a) If there is a single Class A liability group, then the full cost of carrying out the common action should be attributed to that group, and no cost should be attributed to any Class B liability group.

(b) If there are two or more Class A liability groups, then an equal share of the cost of carrying out the common action should be attributed to each of those groups, and no cost should be attributed to any Class B liability group.

(c) If there is no Class A liability group and there are two or more Class B liability groups, then the enforcing authority should treat those liability groups as if they formed a single liability group, attributing the cost of carrying out the common action to that combined group, and applying the guidance on exclusion and apportionment set out in sub-sections 7(e) and 7(f) above as between all of the members of that combined group.

7.89

The enforcing authority should attribute responsibility for the cost of any collective action among the liability groups for the significant contaminant linkages to which it is referable on the same basis as for the costs of a common action, except that where the costs fall to be divided among several Class A liability groups, instead of being divided equally, they should be attributed on the following basis:

(a) Having estimated the costs of the collective action, the enforcing authority should also estimate the hypothetical cost for each of the liability groups of carrying out the actions which are subsumed by the collective action and which would be necessary if the significant contaminant linkage for which that liability group is responsible were to be addressed separately; these estimates are the "hypothetical estimates" of each of the liability groups.

(b) The enforcing authority should then attribute responsibility for the cost of the collective action between the liability groups in the proportions which the hypothetical estimates of each liability group bear to the aggregate of the hypothetical estimates of all the groups.

Confirming the attribution of responsibility

7.90

If any appropriate person demonstrates, before the service of a remediation notice, to the satisfaction of the enforcing authority that the result of an attribution made on the basis set out in paragraphs 7.88 and 7.89 above would have the effect of the liability group of which they are a member having to bear a liability which is so disproportionate (taking into account the overall relative responsibilities of the persons or groups concerned for the condition of the land) as to make the attribution of responsibility between all the liability groups concerned unjust when considered as a whole, the enforcing authority should reconsider the attribution. In doing so, the enforcing authority should consult the other appropriate persons concerned.

7.91

If the enforcing authority then agrees that the original attribution would be unjust it should adjust the attribution between the liability groups so that it is just and fair in the light of all the circumstances. An adjustment under this paragraph should be necessary only in very exceptional cases.

Orphan linkages

7.92

As explained above (e.g. in paragraphs 7.6 and 7.9), an "orphan linkage" may arise where: (a) the significant contaminant linkage relates solely to the significant pollution of controlled waters (and not to significant harm) and no Class A person can be found; (b) no Class A or Class B persons can be found; or (c) those who would otherwise be liable are exempted by one of the relevant statutory provisions (i.e. sections 78J(3), 78K or 78X(3)).

7.93

In any case where only one significant contaminant linkage has been identified, and that is an orphan linkage, the enforcing authority should itself bear the cost of any remediation which is carried out.

7.94

In more complicated cases, there may be two or more significant contaminant linkages, of which some are orphan linkages. Where this applies, the enforcing authority will need to consider each remediation action separately.

7.95

For any remediation action which is referable to an orphan linkage, and is not referable to any other linkage for which there is a liability group, the enforcing authority should itself bear the cost of carrying out that action.

7.96

For any shared action which is referable to an orphan linkage and also to a single significant contaminant linkage for which there is a Class A liability group, the enforcing authority should attribute all of the cost of carrying out that action to that Class A liability group.

7.97

For any shared action which is referable to an orphan linkage and also to two or more significant contaminant linkages for which there are Class A liability groups, the enforcing authority should attribute the costs of carrying out that action between those liability groups in the same way as it would do if the orphan linkage did not exist.

7.98

For any shared action which is referable to an orphan linkage and also to a significant contaminant linkage for which there is a Class B liability group (and not to any significant contaminant linkage for which there is a Class A liability group) the enforcing authority should adopt the following approach:

(a) where the remediation action is a common action the enforcing authority should attribute all of the cost of carrying out that action to the Class B liability group; and

(b) where the remediation action is a collective action, the enforcing authority should estimate the hypothetical cost of the action which would be needed to remediate separately the effects of the linkage for which that group is liable. The enforcing authority should then attribute the costs of carrying out the collective action between itself and the Class B liability group so that the expected liability of that group does not exceed that hypothetical cost.

SECTION 8: RECOVERY OF THE COSTS OF REMEDIATION

8.1

The statutory guidance in this Section is issued under section 78P(2) of the 1990 Act. It provides guidance on the extent to which the enforcing authority should seek to recover the costs of remediation which it has carried out and which it is entitled to recover.

8.2

The main relevant sections of the 1990 Act are:

— Section 78P(1): "Where, by virtue of section 78N(3)(a), (c), (e) or (f)... the enforcing authority does any particular thing by way of remediation, it shall be entitled, subject to sections 78J(7) and 78K(6)..., to recover the reasonable cost incurred in doing it from the appropriate person or, if there are two or more appropriate persons in relation to the thing in question, from those persons in proportions determined pursuant to section 78F(7)..."

— Section 78P(2): "In deciding whether to recover the cost, and, if so, how much of the cost, which it is entitled to recover under subsection (1) above, the enforcing authority shall have regard – (a) to any hardship which the recovery may cause to the person from whom the cost is recoverable; and (b) to any guidance issued by the Secretary of State for the purposes of this subsection."

8.3

This Section also explains when the enforcing authority is prevented from serving a remediation notice under section 78H(5), under which the authority may not serve a remediation notice if the authority has the power to carry out remediation itself, by virtue of section 78N. Under that latter section, the authority asks the hypothetical question of whether it would seek to recover all of the reasonable costs it would incur if it carried out the remediation itself. The authority then has the power to carry out that remediation itself if it concludes that, having regard to hardship and the guidance in this Chapter, it would either not seek to recover its costs, or seek to recover only a part of its costs. The relevant sections of the 1990 Act are:

— Section 78H(5): "The enforcing authority shall not serve a remediation notice on a person if and so long as... (d) the authority is satisfied that the powers conferred on it by section 78 below to do what is appropriate by way of remediation are exercisable..."

— Section 78N(3) provides that the enforcing authority has the power to carry out remediation: "(e) where the enforcing authority considers that, were it to do some particular thing by way of remediation, it would decide, by virtue of subsection (2) of section 78P... or any guidance issued under that subsection, – (i) not to seek to recover under subsection (1) of that section any of the reasonable cost incurred by it in doing that thing; or (ii) to seek so to recover only a portion of that cost;..."

Section 8(a): Cost recovery decisions

8.4

This Section sets out considerations to which the enforcing authority should have regard when making any cost recovery decision. In view of the wide variation in situations which are likely to arise (e.g. due to variations in the history and ownership of land, and liability for its remediation) the guidance in this section sets out principles and approaches, rather than detailed rules. The enforcing authority should have regard to the circumstances of each individual case.

8.5

In making any cost recovery decision, the enforcing authority should have regard to the following general principles:

(a) The authority should aim for an overall result which is as fair and equitable as possible to all who may have to meet the costs of remediation, including national and local taxpayers.

(b) The "polluter pays" principle should be applied with a view that, where possible, the costs of remediating pollution should be borne by the polluter. The authority should therefore consider the degree and nature of responsibility of the relevant appropriate person(s) for the creation, or continued existence, of the circumstances which lead to the land in question being identified as contaminated land.

8.6

In general the enforcing authority should seek to recover all of its reasonable costs. However, the authority should waive or reduce the recovery of costs to the extent that it considers this appropriate and reasonable, either: (i) to avoid any undue hardship which the recovery may cause to the appropriate person; or (ii) to reflect one or more of the specific considerations set out in the statutory guidance in sub-sections 8(b), 8(c) and 8(d) below. In making such decisions, the authority should bear in mind that recovery is not necessarily an "all or nothing" matter (i.e. where reasonable, appropriate persons can be made to pay part of the authority's costs even if they cannot reasonably be made to pay all of the costs).

8.7

In deciding how much of its costs it should recover, the enforcing authority should consider whether it could recover more of the costs by deferring recovery and securing them by a charge on the land in question under section 78P. Such deferral may lead to payment from the appropriate person either in instalments (see section 78P(12)) or when the land is next sold.

Information for making decisions

8.8

In general, the enforcing authority should expect anyone who is seeking a waiver or reduction in the recovery of remediation costs to present any information needed to support such a request.

8.9

In making any cost recovery decision, the enforcing authority should consider any relevant information provided by the appropriate person(s). The authority should also seek to obtain such information as is reasonable, having regard to: (i) accessibility of the information; (ii) the cost, for any of the parties involved, of obtaining the information; and (iii) the likely significance of the information for any decision.

8.10

The enforcing authority should, in all cases, inform the appropriate person of any cost recovery decisions taken, explaining the reasons for those decisions.

Cost recovery policies

8.11

The enforcing authority may choose to adopt and make available a policy statement about the general approach it intends to take in making cost recovery decisions.

Section 8(b): Considerations Applying both to Class A & Class B Persons

8.12

Paragraphs 8.13–8.22 below set out considerations to which the enforcing authority should have regard when making any cost recovery decisions, irrespective of whether the appropriate person is a Class A person or a Class B person. They apply in addition to the general issue of the "hardship" which the cost recovery may cause to the appropriate person.

Commercial Enterprises

8.13

Subject to the specific circumstances set out below, the enforcing authority should adopt the same approach to all types of commercial or industrial enterprises which are identified as appropriate persons. This applies whether the appropriate person is a public corporation, a limited company (whether public or private), a partnership (whether limited or not) or an individual operating as a sole trader.

Threat of business closure or insolvency

8.14

In cases where a small or medium-sized enterprise is the appropriate person, or is run by the appropriate person, the enforcing authority should consider: (i) whether recovery of the full cost attributable to that person would mean that the enterprise is likely to become insolvent and thus cease to exist; and (ii) if so, the cost to the local economy of such a closure.

8.15

Where the cost of that closure to the local economy appears to be greater than the costs of remediation which the enforcing authority would have to bear itself, the authority should consider waiving or reducing its costs recovery to the extent needed to avoid making the enterprise insolvent.

8.16

However, the enforcing authority should not waive or reduce its costs recovery where: (a) it is satisfied that an enterprise has deliberately arranged matters so as to avoid responsibility for the costs of remediation; (b) it appears that the enterprise would be likely to become insolvent whether or not recovery of the full cost takes place; or (c) it appears that the enterprise could be kept in, or returned to, business even it does become insolvent under its current ownership.

8.17

For these purposes, a "small or medium-sized enterprise" should be taken to mean an independent enterprise which matches the definition of a "micro, small and medium-sized enterprise" as established by the European Commission Recommendation of 6 May 2003, and any updates of that definition as may happen in future. (Under the 2003 definition this would cover any such enterprise with fewer than 250 employees, and either an annual turnover less than or equal to €50 million, or an annual balance sheet total less than or equal to €43 million).

8.18

Local authorities may wish to take account in cost recovery decisions of any relevant policy on assisting enterprise or promoting economic development. In cases where the Environment Agency is the enforcing authority, it should seek to be consistent with the policy of the local authority in whose area the contaminated land is situated (if such a policy exists). The Agency should consult the local authority and take its views into consideration in making its own cost recovery decisions.

Trusts

8.19

Where the appropriate persons include persons acting as trustees, the enforcing authority should assume that such trustees will exercise all the powers which they have, or may reasonably obtain, to make funds available from the trust, or from borrowing that can be made on behalf of the trust, for the purpose of paying for remediation. The authority should, nevertheless, consider waiving or reducing its costs recovery to the extent that the costs of remediation to be recovered from the trustees would otherwise exceed the amount that can be made available from the trust to cover those costs.

8.20

However, the enforcing authority should not waive or reduce its costs recovery: (a) where it is satisfied that the trust was formed for the purpose of avoiding paying the costs of remediation; or (b) to the extent that trustees have personally benefited, or will personally benefit, from the trust.

Charities

8.21

Since charities are intended to operate for the benefit of the community, the enforcing authority should consider the extent to which any recovery of costs from a charity would detrimentally impact that charity's activities. Where this is the case, the authority should consider waiving or reducing its costs recovery to the extent needed to avoid such a consequence. This approach applies equally to charitable trusts and to charitable companies.

Social housing landlords

8.22

The enforcing authority should consider waiving or reducing its costs recovery if: (a) the appropriate person is a body eligible for registration as a social housing landlord under section 2 of the Housing Act 1996 (for example, a housing association); (b) its liability relates to land used for social housing; and (c) full recovery would lead to significant financial difficulties for the appropriate person, such that the provision or upkeep of the social housing would be jeopardised significantly. The extent of the waiver or reduction should be sufficient to avoid any such financial difficulties.

Section 8(c): Specific considerations applying to Class A persons

8.23

This sub-section sets out specific considerations to which the enforcing authority should have regard in cost recovery decisions where the appropriate person is a Class A person.

8.24

In applying the approach in this sub-section, the enforcing authority should consider whether or not the Class A person is likely to have profited financially from the activity which led to the land being determined to be contaminated land (e.g. as might be the case if the contamination resulted from a business activity). If the person did profit, the authority should generally be less willing to waive or reduce costs recovery than if no such profits were made.

Where other potentially appropriate persons have not been found

8.25

In some cases where a Class A person has been found, it may be possible to identify another person who caused or knowingly permitted the presence of the significant contaminant in question, but who cannot now be found for the purposes of treating that person as an appropriate person (as might be the case if a company has been dissolved). In such cases, the enforcing authority should consider waiving or reducing its costs recovery from a Class A person if that person demonstrates that:

(a) another identified person, who cannot now be found, also caused or knowingly permitted the significant contaminant to be in, on or under the land; and
(b) if that other person could be found, the Class A person seeking the waiver or reduction of the authority's costs recovery would either: (i) be excluded from liability by virtue of one or more of the exclusion tests set out in the Section 7 of this Guidance; or (ii) the proportion of the cost of remediation which the appropriate person has to bear would have been significantly less, by virtue of the guidance on apportionment set out in Section 7.

8.26

Where an appropriate person is making a case for the enforcing authority's costs recovery to be waived or reduced by virtue of paragraph 8.25 above, that person should provide evidence to the authority that a particular person, who cannot now be found, caused or knowingly permitted the significant contaminant to be in, on or under the land. The authority should not regard it as sufficient for the appropriate person concerned merely to state that such a person must have existed.

Section 8(d): Specific considerations applying to Class B persons

8.27

This sub-section sets out specific considerations relating to cost recovery decisions where the appropriate person is a Class B person.

Costs in Relation to Land Values

8.28

In some cases, the costs of remediation may exceed the likely value of the land in its current use (as defined in Section 3 of this Guidance) after the required remediation has been carried out. In such cases, the enforcing authority should consider waiving or reducing its costs recovery from a Class B person if that person demonstrates that the costs of remediation are likely to exceed the value of the land. In this context, the "value" should be taken to be the value that the remediated land would have on the open market, at the time the cost recovery decision is made, disregarding any possible blight arising from the contamination.

8.29

In general, the extent of the waiver or reduction in costs recovery should be sufficient to ensure that the costs of remediation borne by the Class B person do not exceed the value of the land. However, the enforcing authority should seek to recover more of its costs to the extent that the remediation would result in an increase in the value of any other land from which the Class B person would benefit.

Precautions taken before acquiring a freehold or a leasehold interest

8.30

In some cases, the Class B person may have been unaware that the land in question may be contaminated land when they acquired it. Alternatively, the person may have taken a risk that the land was not contaminated, or they may have taken some precautions to reduce the risk of acquiring land which is contaminated.

8.31

The enforcing authority should consider reducing its costs recovery where a Class B person who is the owner of the land demonstrates that:

(a) the person took such steps (prior to acquiring the freehold or accepting the grant of assignment of a leasehold) as would have been reasonable at that time to establish the presence of any contaminants;

(b) when the person acquired the land (or accepted the grant of assignment of the leasehold) they were nonetheless unaware of the presence of the significant contaminant now identified, and could not reasonably have been expected to have been aware of its presence; and

(c) the authority considers it would be reasonable, taking into account the interests of national and local taxpayers, that the person should not bear the whole cost of remediation.

8.32

The enforcing authority should bear in mind that the safeguards which might reasonably be expected to be taken will be different in different types of transaction (for example, acquisition of recreational land as compared with commercial land transactions) and as between buyers of different types (for example, private individuals as compared with major commercial undertakings).

Owner-occupiers of dwellings

8.33

Where a Class B person owns and occupies a dwelling on the contaminated land in question, the enforcing authority should consider waiving or reducing its costs recovery if the person satisfies the authority that, at the time the person purchased the dwelling, the person did not know, and could not reasonably have been expected to have known, that the land was adversely affected by presence of the contaminant(s) in question. Any such waiver or reduction should be to the extent needed to ensure that the Class B person in question bears no more of the cost of remediation than it appears reasonable to impose, having regard to the person's income, capital and outgoings. Where the person has inherited the dwelling or received it as a gift, the authority should consider the situation at the time when the person received the property.

8.34

Where the contaminated land in question extends beyond the dwelling and its curtilage, and is owned or occupied by the same appropriate person, the approach in paragraph 8.33 above should be applied only to the dwelling and its curtilage.

MANAGEMENT STATEMENT ISSUED TO THE ENVIRONMENT AGENCY BY THE SECRETARY OF STATE FOR ENVIRONMENT, FOOD AND RURAL AFFAIRS AND THE WELSH ASSEMBLY GOVERNMENT

July 2002

1 INTRODUCTION

Purpose of Management Statement

1.1

The purpose of this Management Statement is to set out: the relationships between the Secretary of St ate for Environment, Food and Rural Affairs (the Secretary of State), the Welsh Assembly Government (the Assembly Government) exercising powers delegated by the National Assembly of Wales (the National Assembly) and the Environment Agency (the Agency); the framework within which the Agency will operate; and other guidance relevant to the exercise of its functions. The Management Statement has been drawn up in consultation with the Environment Agency. The Financial Memorandum issued by the Department for Environment, Food and Rural Affairs (DEFRA), in conjunction with the Assembly Government sets out the conditions under which funds are paid to the Agency, the limits of delegations, and how the Agency will be held to account for these funds.

Publication

1.2

Copies of this Management Statement will be placed in the libraries of both Houses of Parliament and the National Assembly.

Review and amendment

1.3

The Management Statement will usually be amended in the context of a Financial Management and Policy Review of the Agency (see paragraph 4.13 below). The Secretary of State, the Assembly Government or the Agency may however propose amendments at any time. The Secretary of State, in agreement with the Assembly Government will decide what changes, if any, are to be made. Legislative changes take precedence over the terms of the Management Statement.

2 ROLE AND STATUS OF THE AGENCY

Status of the Agency

2.1

The Agency is a Non-Departmental Public Body (NDPB), responsible to the Secretary of State. It is also an Assembly Sponsored Public Body, responsible to the National Assembly. It was established as a public body corporate, and took over its functions from the National Rivers Authority, Her Majesty's Inspectorate of Pollution and waste regulation authorities on 1 April 1996, in accordance with the provisions of the Environment Act 1995 (the 1995 Act) and related legislation. The 1995 Act has since been amended by the Government of Wales Act 1998.

Functions and duties

2.2

The Agency's principal functions and duties may be categorised as follows:

— **Flood Defence:** To supervise all matters relating to flood defence, to undertake certain measures approved by Regional Flood Defence Committees including surveying flood defences and flood risk areas. Also to educate and inform about flood risk and advise local government about development in flood plains and provide warning and response to flooding incidents.

— **Water Resources:** To conserve, distribute, augment and secure the proper use of water resources and regulate licensed water abstractions. Also to publish information about the demand for water and available resources.

— **Water Quality:** To preserve and improve the quality of rivers, estuaries, coastal waters and groundwaters, through pollution control powers and the regulation of discharge consents, and to monitor sewage treatment works and trade discharges. Also to monitor the quality of freshwater, groundwater and tidal waters (up to three miles from the coast).

— **Waste Management:** To regulate the treating, keeping, movement and disposal of controlled waste by operators, carriers and brokers and at waste management sites, and to provide technical guidance on waste management and survey waste disposal needs and priorities.

— **Process Industry Regulation:** To provide an integrated approach to regulating the environmental impacts of major industry, to regulate industrial processes with the greatest pollution potential and to be responsible for implementing Integrated Pollution Prevention and Control (IPPC).

— **Fisheries:** To maintain and improve salmon, trout, freshwater and eel fisheries, to regulate these and to inform DEFRA and the Assembly Government of outbreaks of notifiable fish disease.

— **Radioactive Substances:** To regulate the disposal of radioactive waste and the keeping and use of radioactive substances at non-nuclear sites. Also to carry out monitoring of radioactivity levels in the environment.

— **Land Contamination:** To regulate the remediation of contaminated land designated as special sites and to report on the state of contaminated land.

— **Navigation:** To maintain and improve navigation on the navigable waters (mostly rivers) for which it has responsibility and licence boats using these waters.

— **Recreation:** To promote recreational use of and access along water.

— **Conservation:** To conserve and enhance the water environment, including areas of natural beauty or environmental sensitivity and to encourage biodiversity.

2.3

The Agency also has statutory responsibilities in relation to the collection and dissemination of environmental information, assessing the environmental impacts of pollution, and promoting an understanding of methods for environmental protection and management, including:

— Assembling and disseminating environmental data, from its own monitoring and other sources. This enables it to form an overview of and to communicate the general state of the environment.

— Following developments in technology for preventing or reducing pollution.
— Assessing the environmental impacts of pollution or options for avoiding, limiting, or cleaning up pollution, when Central Government and/or the Assembly Government request it to do so.
— Carrying out or promoting research in relation to its activities.

The Agency's principal aim

2.4

Section 4 of the 1995 Act defines the principal aim of the Agency: in discharging its functions the Agency is required so to protect or enhance the environment, taken as a whole, as to make the contribution that the Secretary of State and the National Assembly consider appropriate towards achieving sustainable development. Guidance on the nature of the Agency's contribution to sustainable development is set out in statutory guidance to the Agency issued by the Secretary of State and the National Assembly.

The wider policy framework

2.5

The Agency is expected to play a central part in delivering the environmental priorities of Central Government and the Assembly Government, through its various functions and its roles as:
— an environmental regulator;
— an environmental operator;
— a monitor of the state of the environment;
— an advisor on the development of environmental policy; and
— a promoter of scientific research in support of these roles.

2.6

The Agency's functions and roles underpin Central Government.s and the National Assembly's objectives for the Agency. These are set out in Guidance issued under section 4 of the 1995 Act. The Guidance identifies the key environmental priorities which the Agency is expected to deliver, or help to deliver, over the five years or so from when the guidance is issued, and which will form the context for decisions on Agency resources.

Partnership

2.7

The Agency is expected to work closely with Central Government departments in England, in particular DEFRA; with the Assembly Government in Wales; and with other statutory agencies. It is expected that Central Government and the Agency will share the same desired outcomes in relation to England and that the Assembly Government and the Agency should share the same desired outcomes in relation to Wales. The Agency has a contribution to make to the development of policy, although this is ultimately a matter for Central Government in England and the National Assembly acting through the Assembly Government in Wales. The Agency will support, as appropriate, DEFRA and the Assembly Government, by means of technical and scientific advice as required.

2.8

In pursuit of its objectives the Agency will need to work closely with a wide range of partners in the public, private and voluntary sectors. An inclusive approach will be important in ensuring that the Agency is responsive to the views and policies of those with whom it deals, that it can receive and give advice, and that relative responsibilities are well understood and properly co-ordinated. In some cases a memorandum of understanding with another body may be useful.

2.9

The Agency has wide-ranging functions, and many people have a direct or indirect interest in its work, at the local, regional and national levels. The Agency should operate in an open and transparent way and should develop its approach to consultation and to customer liaison in accordance with its published Customer Charter standards of service. It should have in mind its main business needs and its organisational priorities, in order to achieve effective liaison and value for money.

2.10

The Agency will need special links with:

— **Regulated organisations**, most of which are charge-payers. They must have the information and advice they need on the development, operation and financing of the Agency's regulatory regimes, and on its approach to enforcement and how to comply with requirements. The Agency should ensure that its staff are aware of the published Code of Practice on the exercise of its regulatory responsibilities, and implement its principles in their work. It should monitor compliance with the Code, and have arrangements for reviewing complaints of non-compliance.

— **Other enforcement agencies:** The Agency should work closely with other enforcement agencies (including local authorities, the Health and Safety Executive, the Maritime and Coastguard Agency, English Nature, the Food Standards Agency, the Countryside Council for Wales, the Welsh Development Agency, the Scottish Environment Protection Agency, and the Northern Ireland Environment and Heritage Service) to minimise and, if possible, to eliminate duplication and conflict in applying legislation, guidance and standards. Where there are overlapping responsibilities, the Agency should consult other agencies on proposed actions or statements, other than in exceptional circumstances such as an emergency.

— **Other bodies with responsibilities for protection of public health**, including the Department of Health, the Health Department of the Assembly Government, the National Health Service, the Drinking Water Inspectorate, and local authority Environmental Health Departments.

— **Bodies dealing with accidents and emergencies:** The Agency should liaise and establish effective working relationships with other bodies dealing with accidents and emergencies, including those responsible for emergency planning in central and local government, the Assembly Government, the Department of Transport, Local Government and the Regions and the emergency services.

— **Its Regional Flood Defence Committees:** The Agency's regional flood defence committees are responsible for carrying out all of the Agency's flood defence functions, other than the issuing of levies, making drainage charges or borrowing money.

— **Its Regional Advisory Committees:** The Agency's regional advisory committees are an important source of local input and of external expertise and challenge.

— **Regional bodies:** The Agency should work closely with English regional bodies, including the regional development agencies and regional chambers, and other organisations with a strategic role at the regional level. The Agency works with regional bodies to produce regional sustainable development frameworks, and contributes to regional planning guidance and regional development agencies. regional strategies.

— **Local authorities** are key partners in areas such as flood defence, planning and development control, control of air pollution, and waste issues. The Agency is a statutory consultee in relation to planning and development control issues. The Agency should work in partnership with local authorities as they develop their community strategies (local sustainable development strategies).

3 THE STRUCTURAL FRAMEWORK

Accountability

3.1

The Agency is accountable for its activities in England to the Secretary of State. The Secretary of State is in turn accountable to Parliament for these activities, for the Agency's charging regimes in England and Wales, and for its expenditure in England, whether from monies voted by Parliament or from charges or levies.

3.2

The Agency is accountable to the National Assembly for its activities and expenditure in Wales. The Secretary of State.s functions for approval of charging schemes are exercisable only after consultation with the Assembly Government.

Role of Secretary of State

3.3

The role of the Secretary of State is:

— to set the policy framework for the Agency in England;

— to agree in conjunction with the Assembly Government a corporate strategy for the Agency every five years which will set the strategic context for the corporate planning process;

— through the corporate planning process, to agree the Agency's overall priorities and objectives for England each year;

— to allocate resources to the Agency for its activities in England and to approve changes to levels of charges for environmental regulation;

— with Treasury Ministers, to approve the Agency's charging schemes or amendments to such schemes;

— to monitor the performance of the Agency in England in relation to agreed objectives and targets;

— to appoint in consultation with the Assembly Government the Chairman and members of the Agency (other than the Chief Executive, who acts as an ex officio member of the Board) and to set the terms and conditions of such appointments;

— to appoint the Chairs of the Agency's Regional Environmental Protection Advisory Committees, Regional Flood Defence Committees and Regional Fisheries, Ecology, Recreation and Conservation Committees in England;

— to confirm the appointment of the Chief Executive as Accounting Officer;

— to issue any general guidance or specific directions; and

— to lay copies of the Agency's annual report and accounts before Parliament each year.

3.4

The Permanent Secretary of DEFRA is principal Accounting Officer and adviser to the Secretary of State on questions of expenditure allocation and finance. The Permanent

Secretary is accountable for the payment of grant-in-aid to the Agency and for ensuring that the Agency has adequate systems in place to secure the propriety and regularity of expenditure, including expenditure funded from charges and levies, as well as prudent and economical administration. He is also responsible for ensuring that the financial and management controls in the Department are appropriate.

Role of the Assembly Government

3.5

The role of the Assembly Government is:
- to set the policy framework for the Agency's activities in Wales;
- through the corporate planning process, to agree the Agency's overall priorities and objectives for its activities in Wales;
- to allocate resources to the Agency for its activities in Wales and to consider the effects on Wales of the Secretary of State.s proposals to approve changes to levels of charges for environmental regulation;
- to monitor the performance of the Agency in Wales in relation to agreed objectives and targets;
- to appoint the Chairs of the Agency's Environmental Protection Advisory Committee, the Regional Flood Defence Committees and the Fisheries, Ecology, Recreation and Conservation Committees in Wales;
- to issue any general guidance or specific directions; and
- to lay the Agency's accounts, together with the financial statements regarding their functions in Wales, before the National Assembly.

Role of the Principal Accounting Officer to the National Assembly for Wales

3.6

The Permanent Secretary to the National Assembly is the Principal Accounting Officer of the National Assembly on terms specified by HM Treasury. The Principal Accounting Officer of the National Assembly is accountable to the National Assembly and to Parliament for the issue of grant-in-aid to the Agency in respect of its activities in Wales, and is responsible for ensuring that it is within the ambit and the amount of the National Assembly's Budget, and that the National Assembly's authority has been sought and given.

3.7

The Principal Accounting Officer of the National Assembly for Wales is also responsible for ensuring that the financial and other management controls applied by the National Assembly for Wales, are appropriate and sufficient to safeguard public funds and that those being applied by the Agency conform with the requirements both of propriety and good financial management; that there is an adequate statement of the financial relationship between the National Assembly for Wales and the Agency in respect of its activities in Wales and that this statement is reviewed regularly; that the conditions attached to grant in aid conform with the terms of the Budgets; and that arrangements are in place to monitor compliance with those conditions.

Dealings with Parliament and the National Assembly

3.8

Members of Parliament and National Assembly Members may approach, or may be approached by, the Chairman or Chief Executive of the Agency, or members of its staff.

At all times it is important for the Agency to be objective and even-handed in its dealings with Parliament and the Assembly, to consult DEFRA and the Assembly Government where appropriate and to keep them informed of action taken.

3.9

Whenever it is appropriate to do so, Ministers will refer enquiries and representations from Members of Parliament, National Assembly Members and others about the discharge of the Agency's responsibilities to its Chairman or Chief Executive. They must keep Ministers and their Departments or the Assembly Government, and where appropriate Parliament and the National Assembly, informed of action taken in such cases.

Appointment of the Chairman and members

3.9

In accordance with the provisions of section 1 of the 1995 Act, the Secretary of State is responsible for appointing a Chairman, Deputy Chairman and members of the Agency (collectively known as the Board). The Board consists of no less than eight and no more than 15 members. The Assembly Government is responsible for appointing one Board Member. The Chairman, Deputy Chairman and members are salaried and may receive reasonable expenses, including travelling and subsistence costs. Salaries, allowances, pensions, gratuities, compensation and expenses are approved by the Secretary of State with the consent of the Treasury and the agreement of the Assembly Government.

3.10

Appointments to the Board are made in accordance with guidelines issued by the independent Commissioner for Public Appointments. Appointments are for a fixed term – normally three years on initial appointment – and serving members may be reappointed to serve a second term. Only in exceptional circumstances would a reappointment for a third term be agreed; a Board member would need to apply for a third term in competition with others.

Role of Chairman

3.11

The Chairman is responsible to the Secretary of State for the overall direction and management of the Agency within the policy framework set by the Secretary of State for the Agency's activities in England. The Chairman is responsible to the National Assembly for the overall direction and management of the Agency in Wales. The Chairman will represent the Agency, and will be the primary contact with Ministers, raising issues with them as appropriate.

3.12

The Chairman is responsible for ensuring that the Board works effectively, and for ensuring that Board members are aware of the terms of their appointment, their duties and responsibilities. He is required to monitor the performance of other Board members, to provide an assessment of the performance of individual board members, and to advise the Secretary of State and the Assembly Government when they are being considered for reappointment or for appointment to another public body. When appointments are being made, the Chairman advises the Secretary of State or the Assembly Government about the needs of the Agency, with a view to ensuring a proper balance of professional and financial expertise.

Role of the Board

3.13

In legal terms it is the Board members, including the Chairman and Deputy Chairman, who form the Agency. They are collectively responsible for:

— the overall strategic direction of the Agency;
— shaping its policies and promoting them to external audiences;
— ensuring that the policies and activities of the Agency are consistent with provisions of legislation; with the statutory guidance issued to the Agency and any other guidance or direction given by the Secretary of State or the National Assembly; with the policy framework set by Secretary of State and the Assembly Government; and with policies of Central Government and the Assembly Government generally; and ensuring delivery of the Agency's objectives;
— the quality of the management of the Agency (generally delegated to the Chief Executive and Directors);
— ensuring that the requirements of propriety, regularity and value for money are met in the Agency's use of resources;
— approving the Agency's Corporate Plan as agreed by the Secretary of State and the Assembly Government; and
— approving the Agency's Annual Report and Accounts for presentation to the Secretary of State and the National Assembly ahead of laying before Parliament.

3.14

A key role of the Board is to monitor the performance of the Agency, in particular in relation to the delivery of its statutory objectives. This is at the heart of their accountability to the Secretary of State and the National Assembly.

3.15

Board members may delegate to an Audit Committee, as a sub-committee of the Board their collective responsibility for monitoring that the Agency complies with any statutory or administrative requirements for the use of public funds, and for maintaining high standards of corporate governance. The role of the Audit Committee will be determined by the Board, which will receive regular reports on the work of that committee.

3.16

The Agency is required to adopt, keep under review and observe a Code of Practice for members based on the Cabinet Office Guidance on Codes of Best Practice for Board Members of Public Bodies.

3.17

In addition to their collective responsibilities, Board members have an individual responsibility to:

— contribute to decision-making;
— regularly attend board meetings;
— keep up-to-date on relevant issues;
— comply with the Board.s Code of Practice and with rules relating to the use of public funds;

— accept corporate decisions once made; and
— act at all times in good faith and in the best interests of the Board.

3.18

Board members and staff are expected to conduct their dealings with the public in an open and responsible way, ensuring compliance with the principles of Service First and the Code of Practice on Access to Government Information.

Role of Chief Executive

3.19

The Chief Executive is designated as the Agency's Accounting Officer by DEFRA.s Accounting Officer and as such is responsible to Parliament and the Accounting Officer of DEFRA and to the Principal Accounting Officer of the National Assembly – in respect of its activities in Wales – for the Agency's resources. The essence of the role of the Agency's Accounting Officer is a personal responsibility for the propriety and regularity of the public finances for which the Chief Executive is answerable; for the keeping of proper accounts and for signing the accounts; for prudent and economical administration; for the avoidance of waste and extravagance; and for the efficient and effective use of all resources. The Accounting Officer has a responsibility to see that appropriate advice is tendered to Board members on all these matters.

3.20

With the Secretary of State.s agreement, the Chief Executive acts as an ex officio member of the Board.

3.21

The Chief Executive is responsible for delivering the Agency's business planning process, including:
— the development of the Agency's five-year Corporate Strategy describing how the Agency intends to deliver, and monitor the delivery of, Central Government and the National Assembly's objectives for the Agency in England and Wales over the medium term;
— the development of a Corporate Plan for England and Wales; and
— the overall organisation, management, and staffing of the Agency.

3.22

The Chief Executive is responsible for advising the Board on the discharge of its responsibilities under the relevant Acts, this Management Statement, the Financial Memorandum and other guidance. The Chief Executive should ensure that:
— adequate internal management and financial controls are in place and reviewed regularly;
— the Agency takes no action which would infringe the requirements of propriety or regularity, or which does not represent prudent or economical administration or efficiency or effectiveness;
— appropriate personnel management policies are developed and observed; and that the Agency achieves high standards of personnel management;
— a comprehensive system of internal delegated authority is in place;
— procedures on financial and other matters, including security, and staff conduct and discipline, are in place; and
— there are effective procedures for handling complaints.

3.23

The appointment of the Chief Executive is by recruitment through open competition. It is made by the Agency and is subject to approval by the Secretary of State following consultation with the Assembly Government. The Board should set performance objectives for the Chief Executive which reflect both the Accounting Officer responsibilities and the Chief Executive.s role in delivering the policy framework set by the Secretary of State and the Assembly Government.

Maladministration

3.24

The Parliamentary Commissioner for Administration may investigate all functions of the Agency other than land drainage and flood defence. These are subject to the jurisdiction of the Local Government Ombudsman, as they are funded to a large extent by levies on local authorities. The Welsh Administration Ombudsman can investigate all functions of the Environment Agency in Wales except action in respect of its land drainage and flood defence functions which are within the jurisdiction of the Local Government Ombudsman, as in England.

4 ORGANISATION AND OPERATION

4.1

The Agency's headquarters are in Bristol. Some headquarters functions – including Parliamentary and media relations work – are also located in London. It has seven regional offices in England and the main office of Environment Agency Wales is in Cardiff.

4.2

Central Government Ministers wish to give the Agency a measure of freedom to determine and adjust regional and local boundaries in England in the light of operational needs. However, Ministers should be consulted on proposals that would significantly change the existing regional boundaries of the Agency.

4.3

The Assembly Government wishes to see the retention of an office of the Agency that has operational responsibility for the whole or for the large majority of Wales and to retain a public face responsibility that coincides with the boundary of Wales. The Assembly Government should be consulted on any proposals which would significantly change the operation, public face or area boundaries in Wales.

Staffing and conditions of service

4.4

The Agency is, in general, responsible for the appointment and management of its staff. However, DEFRA and Treasury approval is required for its pay and grading system and any major structural change to it. The Assembly Government should be consulted as appropriate. Annual pay remits require the approval of DEFRA and the Treasury, as do changes in terms and conditions which have major financial implications.

4.5

The Agency will ensure appropriate non-pay related terms and conditions of employment are in place.

4.6

The Agency is an equal opportunities employer and is required to ensure that all its employment practices and policies comply with equal opportunity legislation and good practice guidelines. The Board is required to adopt, observe and keep under review a Code of Conduct for staff, based on the Cabinet Office Model Code for Staff of Executive Non- Departmental Public Bodies.

Strategic and business planning

4.7

The Agency is required to produce and agree with its sponsors a Corporate Strategy describing how it intends to deliver the objectives set out in the statutory guidance given in respect of England by the Secretary of State and in respect of Wales by the National Assembly under section 4 of the 1995 Act. This forms the context for the Agency's business planning process, including corporate planning and business management. It will also be a defining document for Central Government and National Assembly decisions on resources, in setting charging levels, and in corporate planning rounds. The strategy should be reviewed periodically and should include a description of priorities, objectives and targets over a five-year period.

Corporate planning

4.8

The Agency will each year, in consultation with DEFRA and the Assembly Government, prepare and submit for agreement a Corporate Plan in accordance with guidance issued by DEFRA and the Assembly Government, including the Financial Memorandum. The Plan must provide information on objectives, performance indicators, performance targets, efficiency targets, timing and costs, and must be published. It must take account of planned resource allocations to the Agency and charging decisions, and provide any further information about resource requirements and assumptions requested by DEFRA or the Assembly Government. The Agency will also submit annually to the Assembly Government a Corporate Plan covering the Agency's activities in Wales in more detail. The detailed Corporate Planning timetable is set out in the Financial Memorandum.

The monitoring and review framework

4.9

To complement the Annual Report, the Agency should provide DEFRA with a high level in-year performance management report which will enable DEFRA to monitor the Agency's performance against its objectives, its in-year performance against the Corporate Plan, and its compliance with all relevant delegations and directions. In Wales the Agency should submit quarterly performance reports to the Assembly Government. This will allow monitoring of performance against the targets and objectives set in respect of their activities in Wales by the Assembly Government in the annual Remit letter.

Annual Report and Accounts

4.10

Sections 45 and 46 of the 1995 Act require the Agency to submit audited accounts to the Secretary of State and the National Assembly in accordance with an Accounts Direction and other guidance that the Secretary of State and the Treasury issue from time to time. Section 52 requires the Agency to prepare an annual report to the Secretary of State and the National Assembly.

4.11

The Annual Report and Accounts should describe the Agency's activities; state the extent to which objectives and agreed financial and other performance targets have been met; list the names of the current members of the Agency and senior staff; and provide details of remuneration of members and senior staff in accordance with Treasury guidance. The Annual Report should state how to obtain a copy of the Members Registers of Interests.

4.12

The Secretary of State, having seen and endorsed the report and accounts, is required to submit the Agency's statement of accounts to the Comptroller and Auditor General, who examines, certifies and reports on them. The Secretary of State also arranges to have them laid before both Houses of Parliament. The Auditor General for Wales may inspect the Agency's accounts and all related papers in respect of the Agency's activities in Wales. The Assembly Government will arrange for copies of the report and accounts to be placed in the library of the National Assembly. At the same time as the Agency submits to Parliament its accounts it should also arrange to submit to the Assembly Government a financial statement in respect of its activities in Wales. The form and content of the statement will be agreed between the Agency and the Assembly Government

4.13

Accounts laid before Parliament are subject to scrutiny by the Committee on Public Accounts (PAC) – a committee of the House of Commons which has responsibility to oversee the propriety and value for money of public expenditure. This is one of the central planks of an NDPB.s accountability to Parliament. The Audit Committee of the National Assembly may examine any report laid before the National Assembly by the Auditor General for Wales in respect of the Agency's functions in Wales.

Audit

4.14

It is Government policy that the accounts of all Non-Departmental Public Bodies will be audited by the National Audit Office (NAO), or by auditors appointed by the NAO, and it is intended that this will apply to the Agency from 2002/03. The Chief Executive is responsible for the arrangements for internal audit, which should operate to the standards specified in the Treasury's Government Internal Audit Manual. The operation of audit is detailed in the Agency's Financial Memorandum.

Financial Management and Policy reviews

4.15

The Agency will be reviewed critically at least every five years (or as Cabinet Office guidance directs) to examine:

- the continuing need for the functions carried out by the Agency and the extent to which these could be more effectively undertaken in other ways;
- the efficiency and effectiveness with which the Agency carries out its activities and uses its resources; and
- the effectiveness of the Agency's working relationship with Central Government, the Assembly Government and other statutory agencies.

Part 4
EU Materials

TREATY ON THE FUNCTIONING OF THE EUROPEAN UNION

[Articles 1 to 25 are not reproduced.]

PART THREE
UNION POLICIES AND INTERNAL ACTIONS

[Articles 26 to 190 are not reproduced.]

Title XX
Environment

Article 191

1. Union policy on the environment shall contribute to pursuit of the following objectives:
— preserving, protecting and improving the quality of the environment,
— protecting human health,
— prudent and rational utilisation of natural resources,
— promoting measures at international level to deal with regional or worldwide environmental problems, and in particular combating climate change.

2. Union policy on the environment shall aim at a high level of protection taking into account the diversity of situations in the various regions of the Union. It shall be based on the precautionary principle and on the principles that preventive action should be taken, that environmental damage should as a priority be rectified at source and that the polluter should pay.

In this context, harmonisation measures answering environmental protection requirements shall include, where appropriate, a safeguard clause allowing Member States to take provisional measures, for non-economic environmental reasons, subject to a procedure of inspection by the Union.

3. In preparing its policy on the environment, the Union shall take account of:
— available scientific and technical data,
— environmental conditions in the various regions of the Union,
— the potential benefits and costs of action or lack of action,
— the economic and social development of the Union as a whole and the balanced development of its regions.

4. Within their respective spheres of competence, the Union and the Member States shall cooperate with third countries and with the competent international organisations. The arrangements for Union cooperation may be the subject of agreements between the Union and the third parties concerned.

The previous subparagraph shall be without prejudice to Member States' competence to negotiate in international bodies and to conclude international agreements.

Article 192

1. The European Parliament and the Council, acting in accordance with the ordinary legislative procedure and after consulting the Economic and Social Committee and the Committee of the Regions, shall decide what action is to be taken by the Union in order to achieve the objectives referred to in Article 191.

2. By way of derogation from the decision-making procedure provided for in paragraph 1 and without prejudice to Article 114, the Council acting unanimously in accordance with a special legislative procedure and after consulting the European Parliament, the Economic and Social Committee and the Committee of the Regions, shall adopt:

(a) provisions primarily of a fiscal nature;
(b) measures affecting:
- town and country planning,
- quantitative management of water resources or affecting, directly or indirectly, the availability of those resources,
- land use, with the exception of waste management;

(c) measures significantly affecting a Member State's choice between different energy sources and the general structure of its energy supply.

The Council, acting unanimously on a proposal from the Commission and after consulting the European Parliament, the Economic and Social Committee and the Committee of the Regions, may make the ordinary legislative procedure applicable to the matters referred to in the first subparagraph.

3. General action programmes setting out priority objectives to be attained shall be adopted by the European Parliament and the Council, acting in accordance with the ordinary legislative procedure and after consulting the Economic and Social Committee and the Committee of the Regions.

The measures necessary for the implementation of these programmes shall be adopted under the terms of paragraph 1 or 2, as the case may be.

4. Without prejudice to certain measures adopted by the Union, the Member States shall finance and implement the environment policy.

5. Without prejudice to the principle that the polluter should pay, if a measure based on the provisions of paragraph 1 involves costs deemed disproportionate for the public authorities of a Member State, such measure shall lay down appropriate provisions in the form of:
- temporary derogations, and/or
- financial support from the Cohesion Fund set up pursuant to Article 177.

Article 193

The protective measures adopted pursuant to Article 192 shall not prevent any Member State from maintaining or introducing more stringent protective measures. Such measures must be compatible with the Treaties. They shall be notified to the Commission.

[Articles 194 to 358 are not reproduced.]

COUNCIL DIRECTIVE 91/271/EEC

of 21 May 1991

CONCERNING URBAN WASTE WATER TREATMENT

THE COUNCIL OF THE EUROPEAN COMMUNITIES,

Having regard to the Treaty establishing the European Economic Community, and in particular 130s thereof,

Having regard to the proposal from the Commission,

Having regard to the opinion of the European Parliament,

Having regard to the opinion of the Economic and Social Committee,

Whereas the Council Resolution of 28 June 1988 on the protection of the North Sea and of other waters in the Community invited the Commission to submit proposals for measures required at Community level for the treatment of urban waste water;

Whereas pollution due to insufficient treatment of waste water in one Member State often influences other Member States' waters; whereas in accordance with Article 130r, action at Community level is necessary;

Whereas to prevent the environment from being adversely affected by the disposal of insufficiently-treated urban waste water, there is a general need for secondary treatment of urban waste water;

Whereas it is necessary in sensitive areas to require more stringent treatment; whereas in some less sensitive areas a primary treatment could be considered appropriate;

Whereas industrial waste water entering collecting systems as well as the discharge of waste water and disposal of sludge from urban waste water treatment plants should be subject to general rules or regulations and/or specific authorizations;

Whereas discharges from certain industrial sectors of biodegradable industrial waste water not entering urban waste water treatment plants before discharge to receiving waters should be subject to appropriate requirements;

Whereas the recycling of sludge arising from waste water treatment should be encouraged; whereas the disposal of sludge to surface waters should be phased out;

Whereas it is necessary to monitor treatment plants, receiving waters and the disposal of sludge to ensure that the environment is protected from the adverse effects of the discharge of waste waters;

Whereas it is important to ensure that information on the disposal of waste water and sludge is made available to the public in the form of periodic reports;

Whereas Member States should establish and present to the Commission national programmes for the implementation of this Directive;

Whereas a Committee should be established to assist the Commission on matters relating to the implementation of this Directive and to its adaptation to technical progress,

HAS ADOPTED THIS DIRECTIVE:

Article 1

This Directive concerns the collection, treatment and discharge of urban waste water and the treatment and discharge of waste water from certain industrial sectors.

The objective of the Directive is to protect the environment from the adverse effects of the abovementioned waste water discharges.

Article 2

For the purpose of this Directive:

1. "urban waste water" means domestic waste water or the mixture of domestic waste water with industrial waste water and/or run-off rain water;

2. "domestic waste water" means waste water from residential settlements and services which originates predominantly from the human metabolism and from household activities;

3. "industrial waste water" means any waste water which is discharged from premises used for carrying on any trade or industry, other than domestic waste water and run-off rain water;

4. "agglomeration" means an area where the population and/or economic activities are sufficiently concentrated for urban waste water to be collected and conducted to an urban waste water treatment plant or to a final discharge point;

5. "collecting system" means a system of conduits which collects and conducts urban waste water;

6. "1 p.e. (population equivalent)" means the organic biodegradable load having a five-day biochemical oxygen demand (BOD5) of 60 g of oxygen per day;

7. "primary treatment" means treatment of urban waste water by a physical and/or chemical process involving settlement of suspended solids, or other processes in which the BOD5 of the incoming waste water is reduced by at least 20 % before discharge and the total suspended solids of the incoming waste water are reduced by at least 50 %;

8. "secondary treatment" means treatment of urban waste water by a process generally involving biological treatment with a secondary settlement or other process in which the requirements established in Table 1 of Annex I are respected;

9. "appropriate treatment" means treatment of urban waste water by any process and/or disposal system which after discharge allows the receiving waters to meet the relevant quality objectives and the relevant provisions of this and other Community Directives;

10. "Sludge" means residual sludge, whether treated or untreated, from urban waste water treatment plants;

11. "eutrophication" means the enrichment of water by nutrients, especially compounds of nitrogen and/or phosphorus, causing an accelerated growth of algae and higher forms of plant life to produce an undesirable disturbance to the balance of organisms present in the water and to the quality of the water concerned;

12. "estuary" means the transitional area at the mouth of a river between fresh-water and coastal waters. Member States shall establish the outer (seaward) limits of estuaries for the purposes of this Directive as part of the programme for implementation in accordance with the provisions of Article 17 (1) and (2);

13. "coastal waters" means the waters outside the low-water line or the outer limit of an estuary.

Article 3

1. Member States shall ensure that all agglomerations are provided with collecting systems for urban waste water,

— at the latest by 31 December 2000 for those with a population equivalent (p.e.) of more than 15000, and

— at the latest by 31 December 2005 for those with a p.e. of between 2000 and 15000.

For urban waste water discharging into receiving waters which are considered "sensitive areas" as defined under Article 5, Member States shall ensure that collection systems are provided at the latest by 31 December 1998 for agglomerations of more than 10000 p.e.

Where the establishment of a collecting system is not justified either because it would produce no environmental benefit or because it would involve excessive cost, individual systems or other appropriate systems which achieve the same level of environmental protection shall be used.

2. Collecting systems described in paragraph 1 shall satisfy the requirements of Annex I (A). These requirements may be amended in accordance with the procedure laid down in Article 18.

Article 4

1. Member States shall ensure that urban waste water entering collecting systems shall before discharge be subject to secondary treatment or an equivalent treatment as follows:
— at the latest by 31 December 2000 for all discharges from agglomerations of more than 15000 p.e.,
— at the latest by 31 December 2005 for all discharges from agglomerations ofbetween 10000 and 15000 p.e.,
— at the latest by 31 December 2005 for discharges to fresh-water and estuaries from agglomerations of between 2000 and 10000 p.e.

2. Urban waste water discharges to waters situated in high mountain regions (over 1500 m above sea level) where it is difficult to apply an effective biological treatment due to low temperatures may be subjected to treatment less stringent than that prescribed in paragraph 1, provided that detailed studies indicate that such discharges do not adversely affect the environment.

3. Discharges from urban waste water treatment plants described in paragraphs 1 and 2 shall satisfy the relevant requirements of Annex I.B. These requirements may be amended in accordance with the procedure laid down in Article 18.

4. The load expressed in p.e. shall be calculated on the basis of the maximum average weekly load entering the treatment plant during the year, excluding unusual situations such as those due to heavy rain.

Article 5

1. For the purposes of paragraph 2, Member States shall by 31 December 1993 identify sensitive areas according to the criteria laid down in Annex II.

2. Member States shall ensure that urban waste water entering collecting systems shall before discharge into sensitive areas be subject to more stringent treatment than that described in Article 4, by 31 December 1998 at the latest for all discharges from agglomerations of more than 10000p.e.

3. Discharges from urban waste water treatment plants described in paragraph 2 shall satisfy the relevant requirements of Annex I B. These requirements may be amended in accordance with the procedure laid down in Article 18.

4. Alternatively, requirements for individual plants set out in paragraphs 2 and 3 above need not apply in sensitive areas where it can be shown that the minimum percentage of reduction of the overall load entering all urban waste water treatment plants in that area is at least 75 % for total phosphorus and at least 75 % for total nitrogen.

5. Discharges from urban waste water treatment plants which are situated in the relevant catchment areas of sensitive areas and which contribute to the pollution of these areas shall be subject to paragraphs 2, 3 and 4.

In cases where the above catchment areas are situated wholly or partly in another Member State Article 9 shall apply.

6. Member States shall ensure that the identification of sensitive areas is reviewed at intervals of no more than four years.

7. Member States shall ensure that areas identified as sensitive following review under paragraph 6 shall within seven years meet the above requirements.

8. A Member State does not have to identify sensitive areas for the purpose of this Directive if it implements the treatment established under paragraphs 2, 3 and 4 over all its territory.

Article 6

1. For the purposes of paragraph 2, Member States may by 31 December 1993 identify less sensitive areas according to the criteria laid down in Annex II.

2. Urban waste water discharges from agglomerations of between 10000 and 150000 p.e. to coastal waters and those from agglomaterions of between 2000 and 10000 p.e. to estuaries situated in areas described in paragraph 1 may be subjected to treatment less stringent than that prescribed in Article 4 providing that:

— such discharges receive at least primary treatment as defined in Article 2 (7) in conformity with the control procedures laid down in Annex I D,

— comprehensive studies indicate that such discharges will not adversely affect the environment.

Member States shall provide the Commission with all relevant information concerning the abovementioned studies.

3. If the Commission considers that the conditions set out in paragraph 2 are not met, it shall submit to the Council an appropriate proposal.

4. Member States shall ensure that the identification of less sensitive areas is reviewed at intervals of not more than four years.

5. Member States shall ensure that areas no longer identified as less sensitive shall within seven years meet the requirements of Articles 4 and 5 as appropriate.

Article 7

Member States shall ensure that, by 31 December 2005, urban waste water entering collecting systems shall before discharge be subject to appropriate treatment as defined in Article 2 (9) in the following cases:

— for discharges to fresh-water and estuaries from agglomerations of less than 2000 p.e.,

— for discharges to coastal waters from agglomerations of less than 10000 p.e.

Article 8

1. Member States may, in exceptional cases due to technical problems and for geographically defined population groups, submit a special request to the Commission for a longer period for complying with Article 4.

2. This request, for which grounds msut be duly put forward, shall set out the technical difficulties experienced and must propose an action programme with an appropriate timetable to be undertaken to implement the objective of this Directive. This timetable shall be included in the programme for implementation referred to in Article 17.

3. Only technical reasons can be accepted and the longer period referred to in paragraph 1 may not extend beyond 31 December 2005.

4. The Commission shall examine this request and take appropriate measures in accordance with the procedure laid down in Article 18.

5. In exceptional circumstances, when it can be demonstrated that more advanced treatment will not produce any environmental benefits, discharges into less sensitive areas of waste waters from agglomerations of more than 150000 p.e. may be subject to the treatment provided for in Article 6 for waste water from agglomerations of between 10000 and 150000 p.e.

In such circumstances, Member States shall submit beforehand the relevant documentation to the Commission. The Commission will examine the case and take appropriate measures in accordance with the procedure laid down in Article 18.

Article 9

Where waters within the area of jurisdiction of a Member State are adversely affected by discharges of urban waste water from another Member State, the Member State whose waters are affected may notify the other Member State and the Commission of the relevant facts.

The Member States concerned shall organize, where appropriate with the Commission, the concertation necessary to identify the discharges in question and the measures to be taken at source to protect the waters that are affected in order to ensure conformity with the provisions of this Directive.

Article 10

Member States shall ensure that the urban waste water treatment plants built to comply with the requirements of Articles 4, 5, 6 and 7 are designed, constructed, operated and maintained to ensure sufficient performance under all normal local climatic conditions. When designing the plants, seasonal variations of the load shall be taken into account.

Article 11

1. Member States shall ensure that, before 31 December 1993, the discharge of industrial waste water into collecting systems and urban waste water treatment plants is subject to prior regulations and/or specific authorizations by the competent authority or appropriate body.

2. Regulations and/or specific authorization shall satisfy the requirements of Annex I C. These requirements may be amended in accordance with the procedure laid down in Article 18.

3. Regulations and specific authorization shall be reviewed and if necessary adapted at regular intervals.

Article 12

1. Treated waste water shall be reused whenever appropriate. Disposal routes shall minimize the adverse effects on the environment.

2. Competent authorities or appropriate bodies shall ensure that the disposal of waste water from urban waste water treatment plants is subject to prior regulations and/or specific authorization.

3. Prior regulations and/or specific authorization of discharges from urban waste water treatment plants made pursuant to paragraph 2 within agglomerations of 2000 to 10000 p.e. in the case of discharges to fresh waters and estuaries, and of 10000p.e. or more in respect of all discharges, shall contain conditions to satisfy the relevant requirements of Annex I B. These requirements may be amended in accordance with the procedure laid down in Article 18.

4. Regulations and/or authorization shall be reviewed and if necessary adapted at regular intervals.

Article 13

1. Member States shall ensure that by 31 December 2000 biodegradable industrial waste water from plants belonging to the industrial sectors listed in Annex III which does not enter

urban waste water treatment plants before discharge to receiving waters shall before discharge respect conditions established in prior regulations and/or specific authorization by the competent authority or appropriate body, in respect of all discharges from plants representing 4000 p.e. or more.

2. By 31 December 1993 the competent authority or appropriate body in each Member State shall set requirements appropriate to the nature of the industry concerned for the discharge of such waste water.

3. The Commission shall carry out a comparison of the Member States' requirements by 31 December 1994. It shall publish the results in a report and if necessary make an appropriate proposal.

Article 14

1. Sludge arising from waste water treatment shall be re-used whenever appropriate. Disposal routes shall minimize the adverse effects on the environment.

2. Competent authorities or appropriate bodies shall ensure that before 31 December 1998 the disposal of sludge from urban waste water treatment plants is subject to general rules or registration or authorization.

3. Member States shall ensure that by 31 December 1998 the disposal of sludge to surface waters by dumping from ships, by discharge from pipelines or by other means is phased out.

4. Until the elimination of the forms of disposal mentioned in paragraph 3, Member States shall ensure that the total amount of toxic, persistent or bioaccumulable materials in sludge disposed of to surface waters is licensed for disposal and progressively reduced.

Article 15

1. Competent authorities or appropriate bodies shall monitor:

— discharges from urba waste water treatment plants to verify compliance with the requirements of Annex I.B in accordance with the control procedures laid down in Annex I.D,

— amounts and composition of sludges disposed of to surface waters.

2. Competent authorities or appropriate bodies shall monitor waters subject to discharges from urban waste water treatment plants and direct discharges as described in Article 13 in cases where it can be expected that the receiving environment will be significantly affected.

3. In the case of a discharge subject to the provisions of Article 6 and in the case of disposal of sludge to surface waters, Member States shall monitor and carry out any other relevant studies to verify that the discharge or disposal does not adversely affect the environment.

4. Information collected by competent authorities or appropriate bodies in complying with paragraphs 1, 2 and 3 shall be retained in the Member State and made available to the Commission within six months of receipt of a request.

5. Guidelines on the monitoring referred to in paragraphs 1, 2 and 3 may be formulated in accordance with the procedure laid down in Article 18.

Article 16

Without prejudice to the implementation of the provisions of Council Directive 90/313/EEC of 7 June 1990 on the freedom of access to information on the environment [5], Member States shall ensure that every two years the relevant authorities or bodies publish situation reports on the disposal of urban waste water and sludge in their areas. These reports shall be transmitted to the Commission by the Member States as soon as they are published.

Article 17

1. Member States shall by 31 December 1993 establish a programme for the implementation of this Directive.

2. Member States shall by 30 June 1994 provide the Commission with information on the programme.

3. Member States shall, if necessary, provide the Commission by 30 June every two years with an update of the information described in paragraph 2.

4. The methods and formats to be adopted for reporting on the national programmes shall be determined in accordance with the procedure laid down in Article 18. Any amendments to these methods and formats shall be adopted in accordance with the same procedure.

5. The Commission shall every two years review and assess the information received pursuant to paragraphs 2 and 3 above and publish a report thereon.

Article 18

1. The Commission shall be assisted by a Committee composed of the representatives of the Member States and chaired by the representative of the Commission.

2. The representative of the Commission shall submit to the committee a draft of the measures to be taken. The committee shall deliver its opinion on the draft within a time limit which the chairman may lay down according to the urgency of the matter. The opinion shall be delivered by the majority laid down in Article 148 (2) of the Treaty in the case of decisions which the Council is required to adopt on a proposal from the Commission. The votes of the representatives of the Member States within the committee shall be weighted in the manner set out in that Article. The chairman shall not vote.

3.

(a) The Commission shall adopt the measures envisaged if they are in accordance with the opinion of the committee.

(b) If the measures envisaged are not in accordance with the opinion of the committee, or if no opinion is delivered, the Commission shall, without delay, submit to the Council a proposal relating to the measures to be taken. The Council shall act by a qualified majority.

If, on the expiry of a period of three months from the date of referral to the Council, the Council has not acted, the proposed measures shall be adopted by the Commission, save where the Council has decided against the said measures by a simple majority.

Article 19

1. Member States shall bring into force the laws, regulations and administrative provisions necessary to comply with this Directive no later than 30 June 1993. They shall forthwith inform the Commission thereof.

2. When Member States adopt the measures referred to in paragraph 1, they shall contain a reference to this Directive or shall be accompanied by such a reference on the occasion of their official publication. The methods of making such a reference shall be laid down by the Member States.

3. Member States shall communicate to the Commission the texts of the main provisions of national law which they adopt in the field governed by this Directive.

Article 20

This Directive is addressed to the Member States.

ANNEX I
REQUIREMENTS FOR URBAN WASTE WATER

A. COLLECTING SYSTEMS

Collecting systems shall take into account waste water treatment requirements.

The design, construction and maintenance of collecting systems shall be undertaken in accordance with the best technical knowledge not entailing excessive costs, notably regarding:
— volume and characteristics of urban waste water,
— prevention of leaks,
— limitation of pollution of receiving waters due to storm water overflows.

B. DISCHARGE FROM URBAN WASTE WATER TREATMENT PLANTS TO RECEIVING WATERS

1. Waste water treatment plants shall be designed or modified so that representative samples of the incoming waste water and of treated effluent can be obtained before discharge to receiving waters.

2. Discharges from urban waste water treatment plants subject to treatment in accordance with Articles 4 and 5 shall meet the requirements shown in Table 1.

3. Discharges from urban waste water treatment plants to those sensitive areas which are subject to eutrophication as identified in Annex IIA (a) shall in addition meet the requirements shown in Table 2 of this Annex.

4. More stringent requirements than those shown in Table 1 and/or Table 2 shall be applied where required to ensure that the receiving waters satisfy any other relevant Directives.

5. The points of discharge of urban waste water shall be chosen, as far as possible, so as to minimize the effects on receiving waters.

C. INDUSTRIAL WASTE WATER

Industrial waste water entering collecting systems and urban waste water treatment plants shall be subject to such pre-treatment as is required in order to:
— protect the health of staff working in collecting systems and treatment plants,
— ensure that collecting systems, waste water treatment plants and associated equipment are not damaged,
— ensure that the operation of the waste water treatment plant and the treatment of sludge are not impeded,
— ensure that discharges from the treatment plants do not adversely affect the environment, or prevent receiving water from complying with other Community Directives,
— ensure that sludge can be disposed of safety in an environmentally acceptable manner.

D. REFERENCE METHODS FOR MONITORING AND EVALUATION OF RESULTS

1. Member States shall ensure that a monitoring method is applied which corresponds at least with the level of requirements described below.

Alternative methods to those mentioned in paragraphs 2; 3 and 4 may be used provided that it can be demonstrated that equivalent results are obtained.

Member States shall provide the Commission with all relevant information concerning the applied method. If the Commission considers that the conditions set out in paragraphs 2, 3 and 4 are not met, it will submit an appropriate proposal to the Council.

2. Flow-proportional or time-based 24-hour samples shall be collected at the same well-defined point in the outlet and if necessary in the inlet of the treatment plant in order to monitor compliance with the requirements for discharged waste water laid down in this Directive.

Good international laboratory practices aiming at minimizing the degradation of samples between collection and analysis shall be applied.

3. The minimum annual number of samples shall be etermined according to the size of the treatment plant and be collected at regular intervals during the year

—	2 000 to 9 999 p.e.	12 samples during the first year four samples in subsequent years, if it can be shown that the water during the first year complies with the provisions of the Directive; if one sample of the four fails, 12 samples must be taken in the year that follows
—	10 000 to 49 999 p.e.	12 samples
—	50 000 p.e. or over	24 samples

4. The treated waste water shall be assumed to conform to the relevant parameters if, for each relevant parameter considered individually, samples of the water show that it complies with the relevant para metric value in the following way:

(a) for the parameters specified in Table 1 and Article 2 (7), a maximum number of samples which are allowed to fail the requirements, expressed in concentrations and/or percentage reductions in Table 1 and Article 2 (7), is specified in Table 3 ;

(b) for the parameters of Table 1 expressed in concentrations, the failing samples taken under normal operating conditions must not deviate from the parametric values by more than 100 %. For the parametric values in concentration relating to total suspended solids deviations of up to 150 % may be accepted ;

(c) for those parameters specified in Table 2 the annual mean of the samples for each parameter shall conform to the relevant parametric values.

5. Extreme values for the water quality in question shall not be taken into consideration when they are the result of unusual situations such as those due to heavy rain.

Table 1
Requirements for discharges from urban waste water treatment plants subject to Articles 4 and 5 of the Directive. The values for concentration or for the percentage of reduction shall apply.

Parameters	*Concentration*	*Minimum percentage of reduction*[(1)]	*Reference method of measurement*
Biochemical oxygen demand (BODS at 20°C) without nitrification[(2)]	25 mg/l O_2	70–90 40 under Article 4(2)	Homogenised, unfiltered, undecanted sample. Determination of dissolved oxygen before and after five-day incubation at 20°C ± 1°C, in complete darkness. Addition of a nitrification inhibitor.
Chemical oxygen demand (COD)	125 mg/l O_2	75	Homogenised, unfiltered, undecanted sample. Potassium dichromate.

Parameters	*Concentration*	*Minimum percentage of reduction*[(1)]	*Reference method of measurement*
Total suspended solids	35 mg/l[(3)] 35 under Article 4(2) (more than 10 000 p.e.) 60 under Article 4(2) (2 000–10 000 p.e.)	90[(3)] 90 under Article 4(2) (more than 10 000 p.e.) 70 under Article 4(2) (2 000–10 000 p.e.)	— Filtering of a representative sample through a 0,45 μm filter membrane. Drying at 105°C and weighing. — Centrifuging of a representative sample (for at least five mins with mean acceleration of 2 800 to 3 200 g), drying at 105°C and weighing.

(1) Reduction in relation to the load of the influent.
(2) The parameter can be replaced by another parameter: total organic carbon (TOC) or total oxygen demand (TOD) if a relationship can be established between BODS and the substitute parameter.
(3) This requirement is optional.

Analyses concerning discharges from lagooning shall be carried out on filtered samples; however, the concentration of total suspended solids in unfiltered water samples shall not exceed 150 mg/l.

Table 2
Requirements for discharges from urban waste water treatment plants to sensitive areas which are subject to eutrophication as identified in Annex IIA (a). One or both parameters may be applied depending on the local situation. The values for concentration or for the percentage of reduction shall apply.

Parameters	*Concentration*	*Minimum percentage of reduction*[(1)]	*Reference method of measurement*
Total phosphorus	2 mg/l P (10 000 – 100 000 p.e.) 1 mg/l P (more than 100 000 p.e.)	80	Molecular absorption spectrophotometry
Total nitrogen[(2)]	15 mg/l P (10 000 – 100 000 p.e.) 10 mg/l P (more than 100 000 p.e.)[(3)]	70–80	Molecular absorption spectrophotometry

(1) Reduction in relation to the load of the influent.
(2) Total nitrogen means: the sum of total Kjeldahl-nitrogen (organic N + NH_3), nitrate (NO3)-nitrogen and nitrite (NO_2)-nitrogen.
(3) Alternatively, the daily average must not exceed 20 mg/l N. This requirement refers to a water treatment plant. As a substitute for the condition concerning the temperature, it is possible to apply a limited time of operation, which takes into account the regional climatic conditions. This alternative applies if it can be shown that paragraph 1 of Annex 1.0 is fulfilled.

Table 3

Series of samples taken in any one year	*Maximum permitted number of samples which fail to conform*
4–7	1
8–16	2
17–28	3
29–40	4
41–53	5
54–67	6
68–81	7
82–95	8
96–110	9
111–125	10
126–140	11
141–155	12
156–171	13
172–187	14
188–203	15
204–219	16
220–235	17
236–251	18
252–268	19
269–284	20
285–300	21
301–317	22
318–334	23
335–350	24
351–365	25

ANNEX II
CRITERIA FOR IDENTIFICATION OF SENSITIVE AND LESS SENSITIVE AREAS

A. SENSITIVE AREAS

A water body must be identified as a sensitive area if it falls into one of the following groups:

(a) natural freshwater lakes, other freshwater bodies, estuaries and coastal waters which are found to be eutrophic or which in the near future may become eutrophic if protective action is not taken.

The following elements might be taken into account when considering which nutrient should be reduced by further treatment:

(i) lakes and streams reaching lakes/reservoirs/closed bays which are found to have a poor water exchange, whereby accumulation may take place. In these areas, the removal of phosphorus should be included unless it can be demonstrated that the removal will have no effect on the level of eutrophication. Where discharges from large agglomerations are made, the removal of nitrogen may also be considered ;

(ii) estuaries, bays and other coastal waters which are found to have a poor water exchange, or which receive large quantities of nutrients. Discharges from small agglomerations are usually of minor importance in those areas, but for large agglomerations, the removal of phosphorus and/or nitrogen should be included unless it can be demonstrated that the removal will have no effect on the level of eutrophication ;

(b) surface freshwaters intended for the abstraction of drinking water which could contain more than the concentration of nitrate laid down under the relevant provisions of Council Directive 75/440/EEC of 16 June 1975 concerning the quality required of surface water intended for the abstraction of drinking water in the Member States if action is not taken;

(c) areas where further treatment than that prescribed in Article 4 of this Directive is necessary to fulfil Council Directives.

B. LESS SENSITIVE AREAS

A marine water body or area can be identified as a less sensitive area if the discharge of waste water does not adversely affect the environment as a result of morphology, hydrology or specific hydraulic condi tions which exist in that area.

When identifying less sensitive areas, Member States shall take into account the risk that the discharged load may be transferred to adjacent areas where it can cause detrimental environmental effects. Member States shall recognize the presence of sensitive areas outside their national jurisdiction.

The following elements shall be taken into consideration when identifying less sensitive areas:

open bays, estuaries and other coastal waters with a good water exchange and not subject to eutrophica tion or oxygen depletion or which are considered uhlikely to become eutrophic or to develop oxygen depletion due to the discharge of urban waste water.

ANNEX III
INDUSTRIAL SECTORS

1. Milk-processing
2. Manufacture of fruit and vegetable products
3. Manufacture and bottling of soft drinks
4. Potato-processing
5. Meat industry
6. Breweries
7. Production of alcohol and alcoholic beverages
8. Manufacture of animal feed from plant products
9. Manufacture of gelatine and of glue from hides, skin and bones
10. Malt-houses
11. Fish-processing industry

COUNCIL DIRECTIVE 91/676/EEC

of 12 December 1991

CONCERNING THE PROTECTION OF WATERS AGAINST POLLUTION CAUSED BY NITRATES FROM AGRICULTURAL SOURCES

THE COUNCIL OF THE EUROPEAN COMMUNITIES,

Having regard to the Treaty establishing the European Economic Community, and in particular Article 130s thereof,

Having regard to the proposal from the Commission,

Having regard to the opinion of the European Parliament,

Having regard to the opinion of the Economic and Social Committee,

Whereas the nitrate content of water in some areas of Member States is increasing and is already high as compared with standards laid down in Council Directive 75/440/EEC of 16 June 1975 concerning the quality required of surface water intended for the abstraction of drinking water in the Member States, as amended by Directive 79/869/EEC, and Council Directive 80/778/EEC of 15 July 1980 relating to the quality of water intended for human consumption, as amended by the 1985 Act of Accession;

Whereas the fourth programme of action of the European Economic Communities on the environment indicated that the Commission intended to make a proposal for a Directive on the control and reduction of water pollution resulting from the spreading or discharge of livestock effluents and the excessive use of fertilizers;

Whereas the reform of the common agricultural policy set out in the Commission's green paper "Perspectives for the common agricultural policy" indicated that, while the use of nitrogen-containing fertilizers and manures is necessary for Community agriculture, excessive use of fertilizers constitutes an environmental risk, that common action is needed to control the problem arising from intensive livestock production and that agricultural policy must take greater account of environmental policy;

Whereas the Council resolution of 28 June 1988 of the protection of the North Sea and of other waters in the Community invites the Commission to submit proposals for measures at Community level;

Whereas the main cause of pollution from diffuse sources affecting the Community's waters in nitrates from agricultural sources;

Whereas it is therefore necessary, in order to protect human health and living resources and aquatic ecosystems and to safeguard other legitimate uses of water, to reduce water pollution caused or induced by nitrates from agricultural sources and to prevent further such pollution; whereas for this purpose it is important to take measures concerning the storage and the application on land of all nitrogen compounds and concerning certain land management practices;

Whereas since pollution of water due to nitrates on one Member State can influence waters in other Member States, action at Community level in accordance with Article 130r is therefore necessary;

Whereas, by encouraging good agricultural practices, Member States can provide all waters with a general level of protection against pollution in the future;

Whereas certain zones, draining into waters vulnerable to pollution from nitrogen compounds, require special protection;

Whereas it is necessary for Member States to identify vulnerable zones and to establish and implement action programmes in order to reduce water pollution from nitrogen compounds in vulnerable zones;

Whereas such action programmes should include measures to limit the land-application of all nitrogen-containing fertilizers and in particular to set specific limits for the application of livestock manure;

Whereas it is necessary to monitor waters and to apply reference methods of measurement for nitrogen compounds to ensure that measures are effective;

Whereas it is recognized that the hydrogeology in certain Member States is such that it may be many years before protection measures lead to improvements in water quality;

Whereas a Committee should be established to assist the Commission on matters relating to the implementation of this Directive and to its adaptation to scientific and technical progress;

Whereas Member States should establish and present to the Commission reports on the implementation of this Directive;

Whereas the Commission should report regularly on the implementation of this Directive by the Member States,

HAS ADOPTED THIS DIRECTIVE:

Article 1

This Directive has the objective of:

— reducing water pollution caused or induced by nitrates from agricultural sources and - preventing further such pollution.

Article 2

For the purpose of this Directive:

(a) "groundwater": means all water which is below the surface of the ground in the saturation zone and in direct contact with the ground or subsoil;

(b) "freshwater": means naturally occurring water having a low concentration of salts, which is often acceptable as suitable for abstraction and treatment to produce drinking water;

(c) "nitrogen compound": means any nitrogen-containing substance except for gaseous molecular nitrogen;

(d) "livestock": means all animals kept for use or profit;

(e) "fertilizer": means any substance containing a nitrogen compound or nitrogen compounds utilized on land to enhance growth of vegetation; it may include livestock manure, the residues from fish farms and sewage sludge;

(f) "chemical fertilizer": means any fertilizer which is manufactured by an industrial process;

(g) "livestock manure": means waste products excreted by livestock or a mixture of litter and waste products excreted by livestock, even in processed form;

(h) "land application": means the addition of materials to land whether by spreading on the surface of the land, injection into the land, placing below the surface of the land or mixing with the surface layers of the land;

(i) "eutrophication": means the enrichment of water by nitrogen compounds, causing an accelerated growth of algae and higher forms of plant life to produce an undesirable disturbance to the balance of organisms present in the water and to the quality of the water concerned;

(j) "pollution": means the discharge, directly or indirectly, of nitrogen compounds from agricultural sources into the aquatic environment, the results of which are such as to cause hazards to human health, harm to living resources and to aquatic ecosystems, damage to amenities or interference with other legitimate uses of water;

(k) "vulnerable zone": means an area of land designated according to Article 3 (2).

Article 3

1. Waters affected by pollution and waters which could be affected by pollution if action pursuant Article 5 is not taken shall be identified by the Member States in accordance with the criteria set out in Annex I.

2. Member States shall, within a two-year period following the notification of this Directive, designate as vulnerable zones all known areas of land in their territories which drain into the waters identified according to paragraph 1 and which contribute to pollution. They shall notify the Commission of this initial designation within six months.

3. When any waters identified by a Member State in accordance with paragraph 1 are affected by pollution from waters from another Member State draining directly or indirectly in to them, the Member States whose waters are affected may notify the other Member States and the Commission of the relevant facts.

The Member States concerned shall organize, where appropriate with the Commission, the concertation necessary to identify the sources in question and the measures to be taken to protect the waters that are affected in order to ensure conformity with this Directive.

4. Member States shall review if necessary revise or add to the designation of vulnerable zones as appropriate, and at last every four years, to take into account changes and factors unforeseen at the time of the previous designation. They shall notify the Commission of any revision or addition to the designations within six months.

5. Member States shall be exempt from the obligation to identify specific vulnerable zones, if they establish and apply action programmes referred to in Article 5 in accordance with this Directive throughout their national territory.

Article 4

1. With the aim of providing for all waters a general level of protection against pollution, Member States shall, within a two-year period following the notification of this Directive:

(a) establish a code or codes of good agricultural practice, to be implemented by farmers on a voluntary basis, which should contain provisions covering at least the items mentioned in Annex II A;

(b) set up where necessary a programme, including the provision of training and information for farmers, promoting the application of the code(s) of good agricultural practice.

2. Member States shall submit to the Commission details of their codes of good agricultural practice and the Commission shall include information on these codes in the report referred to in Article 11. In the light of the information received, the Commission may, if it considers it necessary, make appropriate proposals to the Council.

Article 5

1. Within a two-year period following the initial designation referred to in Article 3 (2) or within one year of each additional designation referred to in Article 3 (4), Member States shall, for the purpose of realizing the objectives specified in Article 1, establish action programmes in respect of designated vulnerable zones.

2. An action programme may relate to all vulnerable zones in the territory of a Member State or, where the Member State considers it appropriate, different programmes may be established for different vulnerable zones or parts of zones.

3. Action programmes shall take into account:

(a) available scientific and technical data, mainly with reference to respective nitrogen contributions originating from agricultural and other sources;
(b) environmental conditions in the relevant regions of the Member State concerned.

4. Action programmes shall be implemented within four years of their establishment and shall consist of the following mandatory measures:
(a) the measures in Annex III;
(b) those measures which Member States have prescribed in the code(s) of good agricultural practice established in accordance with Article 4, except those which have been superseded by the measures in Annex III.

5. Member States shall moreover take, in the framework of the action programmes, such additional measures or reinforced actions as they consider necessary if, at the outset or in the light of experience gained in implementing the action programmes, it becomes apparent that the measures referred to in paragraph 4 will not be sufficient for achieving the objectives specified in Article 1. In selecting these measures or actions, Member States shall take into account their effectiveness and their cost relative to other possible preventive measures.

6. Member States shall draw up and implement suitable monitoring programmes to assess the effectiveness of action programmes established pursuant to this Article.

Member States which apply Article 5 throughout their national territory shall monitor the nitrate content of waters (surface waters and groundwater) at selected measuring points which make it possible to establish the extent of nitrate pollution in the waters from agricultural sources.

7. Member States shall review and if necessary revise their action programmes, including any additional measures taken pursuant to paragraph 5, at least every four years. They shall inform the Commission of any changes to the action programmes.

Article 6

1. For the purpose of designating and revising the designation of vulnerable zones, Member States shall:
(a) within two years of notification of the Directive, monitor the nitrate concentration in freshwaters over a period of one year:
   (i) at surface water sampling stations, laid down in Article 5 (4) of Directive 75/440/EEC and/or at other sampling stations which are representative of surface waters of Member States, at least monthly and more frequently during flood periods;
   (ii) at sampling stations which are representative of the groundwater aquifers of Member States, at regular intervals and taking into account the provisions of Directive 80/778/EEC;
(b) repeat the monitoring programme outlined in (a) at least every four years, except for those sampling stations where the nitrate concentration in all previous samples has been below 25 mg/l and no new factor likely to increase the nitrage content has appeared, in which case the monitoring programme need be repeated only every eight years;
(c) review the eutrophic state of their fresh surface waters, estuarial and coastal waters every four years.

2. The reference methods of measurement set out in Annex IV shall be used.

[Article 7][1]

[The Commission may draw up guidelines for the monitoring referred to in Articles 5 and 6 in accordance with the regulatory procedure referred to in Article 9(2).][1]

Amendment

1 Substituted by Regulation 1137/2008 of the European Parliament and of the Council of 22 October 2008 adapting a number of instruments subject to the procedure laid down in Article 251 of the Treaty to Council Decision 1999/468/EC, with regard to the regulatory procedure with scrutiny, Article 1, Annex, Pt 4.3, para 1.

[Article 8][1]

[The Commission may adapt the Annexes to this Directive to scientific and technical progress.

Those measures, designed to amend non-essential elements of this Directive, shall be adopted in accordance with the regulatory procedure with scrutiny referred to in Article 9(3).][1]

Amendment

1 Substituted by Regulation 1137/2008 of the European Parliament and of the Council of 22 October 2008 adapting a number of instruments subject to the procedure laid down in Article 251 of the Treaty to Council Decision 1999/468/EC, with regard to the regulatory procedure with scrutiny, Article 1, Annex, Pt 4.3, para 1.

[Article 9][1]

[1. The Commission shall be assisted by a committee.

2. Where reference is made to this Article, Articles 5 and 7 of Decision 1999/468/EC shall apply, having regard to the provisions of Article 8 thereof.

The period laid down in Article 5(6) Decision 1999/468/EC shall be set at three months.

[3. Where reference is made to this paragraph, Article 5a(1) to (4) and Article 7 of Decision 1999/468/EC shall apply, having regard to the provisions of Article 8 thereof.][2]][1]

Amendments

1 Substituted by Regulation 1882/2003 of the European Parliament and of the Council of 29 September 2003 adapting to Council Decision 1999/468/EC the provisions relating to committees which assist the Commission in the exercise of its implementing powers laid down in instruments subject to the procedure referred to in Article 251 of the EC Treaty, Article 3, Annex III, para 25.

2 Substituted by Regulation 1137/2008 of the European Parliament and of the Council of 22 October 2008 adapting a number of instruments subject to the procedure laid down in Article 251 of the Treaty to Council Decision 1999/468/EC, with regard to the regulatory procedure with scrutiny, Article 1, Annex, Pt 4.3, para 1.

Article 10

1. Member States shall, in respect of the four-year period following the notification of this Directive and in respect of each subsequent four-year period, submit a report to the Commission containing the information outlined in Annex V.

2. A report pursuant to this Article shall be submitted to the Commission within six months of the end of the period to which it relates.

Article 11

On the basis of the information received pursuant to Article 10, the Commission shall publish summary reports within six months of receiving the reports from Member States and shall communicate them to the European Parliament and to the Council. In the light of the implementation of the Directive, and in particular the provisions of Annex III, the Commission shall submit to the Council by 1 January 1998 a report accompanied where appropriate by proposals for revision of this Directive.

Article 12

1. The Member States shall bring into force the laws, regulations and administrative provisions necessary to comply with this Directive within two years of its notification. They shall forthwith inform the Commission thereof.

2. When Member States adopt these measures, they shall contain a reference to this Directive or shall be accompanied by such reference on the occasion of their official publication. The methods of making such a reference shall be laid down by the Member States.

3. Member States shall communicate to the Commission the texts of the provisions of national law which they adopt in the field governed by this Directive.

Article 13

This Directive is addressed to the Member States.

ANNEX I
CRITERIA FOR IDENTIFYING WATERS REFERRED TO IN ARTICLE 3 (1)

A. Waters referred to in Article 3 (1) shall be identified making use, inter alia, of the following criteria:

1. whether surface freshwaters, in particular those used or intended for the abstraction of drinking water, contain or could contain, if action pursuant to Article 5 is not taken, more than the concentration of nitrates laid down in accordance with Directive 75/440/ EEC;
2. whether groundwaters contain more than 50 mg/l nitrates or could contain more than 50 mg/l nitrates if action pursuant to Article 5 is not taken;
3. whether natural freshwater lakes, other freshwater bodies, estuaries, coastal waters and marine waters are found to be eutrophic or in the near future may become euthropic if action pursuant to Article 5 is not taken.

B. In applying these criteria, Member States shall also take account of:

1. the pyhsical and environmental characteristics of the waters and land;
2. the current understanding of the behaviour of nitrogen compounds in the environment (water and soil);
3. the current understanding of the impact of the action taken pursuant to Article 5.

ANNEX II
CODE(S) OF GOOD AGRICULTURAL PRACTICE

A. A code or codes of good agricultural practice with the objective of reducing pollution by nitrates and taking account of conditions in the different regions of the Community should certain provisions covering the following items, in so far as they are relevant:

1. periods when the land application of fertilizer is inappropriate;
2. the land application of fertilizer to steeply sloping ground;
3. the land application of fertilizer to water-saturated, flooded, frozen or snow-covered ground;
4. the conditions for land application of fertilizer near water courses;
5. the capacity and construction of storage vessels for livestock manures, including measures to prevent water pollution by run-off and seepage into the groundwater and surface water of liquids containing livestock manures and effluents from stored plant materials such as silage;
6. procedures for the land application, including rate and uniformity of spreading, of both chemical fertilizer and livestock manure, that will maintain nutrient losses to water at an acceptable level.

B. Member States may also include in their code(s) of good agricultural practices the following items:

7. land use management, including the use of crop rotation systems and the proportion of the land area devoted to permanent crops relative to annual tillage crops;
8. the maintenance of a minimum quantity of vegetation cover during (rainy) periods that will take up the nitrogen from the soil that could otherwise cause nitrate pollution of water;
9. the establishment of fertilizer plans on a farm-by-farm basis and the keeping of records on fertilizer use;
10. the prevention of water pollution from run-off and the downward water movement beyond the reach of crop roots in irrigation systems.

ANNEX III
MEASURES TO BE INCLUDED IN ACTION PROGRAMMES AS REFERRED TO IN ARTICLE 5 (4) (A)

1. The measures shall include rules relating to:

1. periods when the land application of certain types of fertilizer is prohibited;
2. the capacity of storage vessels for livestock manure; this capacity must exceed that required for storage throughout the longest period during which land application in the vulnerable zone is prohibited, except where it can be demonstrated to the competent authority that any quantity of manure in excess of the actual storage capacity will be disposed of in a manner which will not cause harm to the environment;
3. limitation of the land application of fertilizers, consistent with good agricultural practice and taking into account the characteristics of the vulnerable zone concerned, in particular:
   (a) soil conditions, soil type and slope;
   (b) climatic conditions, rainfall and irrigation;
   (c) land use and agricultural practices, including crop rotation systems;

   and to be based on a balance between:
   (i) the foreseeable nitrogen requirements of the crops, and
   (ii) the nitrogen supply to the crops from the soil and from fertilization corresponding to:
   — the amount of nitrogen present in the soil at the moment when the crop starts to use it to a significant degree (outstanding amounts at the end of winter),
   — the supply of nitrogen through the net mineralization of the reserves of organic nitrogen in the soil,
   — additions of nitrogen compounds from livestock manure,
   — additions of nitrogen compounds from chemical and other fertilizers.

2. These measures will ensure that, for each farm or livestock unit, the amount of livestock manure applied to the land each year, including by the animals themselves, shall not exceed a specified amount per hectare.

The specified amount per hectare be the amount of manure containing 170 kg N. However:

(a) for the first four year action programme Member States may allow an amount of manure containing up to 210 kg N;

(b) during and after the first four-year action programme, Member States may fix different amounts from those referred to above. These amounts must be fixed so as not to prejudice the achievement of the objectives specified in Article 1 and must be justified on the basis of objectives criteria, for example:
   — long growing seasons,
   — crops with high nitrogen uptake,
   — high net precipitation in the vulnerable zone,
   — soils with exceptionally high denitrification capacity.

   [If a Member State allows a different amount under point (b) of the second subparagraph, it shall inform the Commission, which shall examine the justification in accordance with the regulatory procedure referred to in Article 9(2).][1]

3. Member States may calculate the amounts referred to in paragraph 2 on the basis of animal numbers.

4. Member States shall inform the Commission of the manner in which they are applying the provisions of paragraph 2. In the light of the information received, the Commission may, if it considers necessary, make appropriate proposals to the Council in accordance with Article 11.

Amendment

1 Substituted by Regulation 1137/2008 of the European Parliament and of the Council of 22 October 2008 adapting a number of instruments subject to the procedure laid down in Article 251 of the Treaty to Council Decision 1999/468/EC, with regard to the regulatory procedure with scrutiny, Article 1, Annex, Pt 4.3, para 1.

ANNEX IV
REFERENCE METHODS OF MEASUREMENT

Chemical fertilizer

Nitrogen compounds shall be measured using the method described in Commission Directive 77/535/EEC of 22 June 1977 on the approximation of the laws of the Member States relating to methods of sampling and analysis for fertilizers (as amended by Directive 89/519/EEC).

Freshwaters, coastal waters and marine waters

Nitrate concentration shall be measured in accordance with Article 4a of Council Decision 77/795/EEC of 12 December 1977 establishing a common procedure for the exchange of information on the quality of surface fresh water in the Community (as amended by Decision 86/574/EEC).

ANNEX V
INFORMATION TO BE CONTAINED IN REPORTS TO ARTICLE 10

1. A statement of the preventive action taken pursuant to Article 4.

2. A map showing the following:
(a) waters identified in accordance with Article 3 (1) and Annex I indicating for each water which of the criteria in Annex I was used for the purpose of identification;
(b) the location of the designed vulnerable zones, distinguishing between existing zones and zones designated since the previous report.

3. A summary of the monitoring results obtained pursuant to Article 6, including a statement of the considerations which led to the designation of each vulnerable zone and to any revision of or addition to designations of vulnerable zones.

4. A summary of the action programmes drawn up pursuant to Article 5 and, in particular:
(a) the measures required by Article 5 (4) (a) and (b);
(b) the information required by Annex III (4);
(c) any additional measures or reinforced actions taken pursuant to Article 5 (5);
(d) a summary of the results of the monitoring programmes implemented pursuant to Article 5 (6);
(e) the assumptions made by the Member States about the likely timescale within which the waters identified in accordance with Article 3 (1) are expected to respond to the measure in the action programme, along with an indication of the level of uncertainty incorporated in these assumptions.

COUNCIL DIRECTIVE 92/43/EEC

of 21 May 1992

ON THE CONSERVATION OF NATURAL HABITATS AND OF WILD FAUNA AND FLORA

THE COUNCIL OF THE EUROPEAN COMMUNITIES,

Having regard to the Treaty establishing the European Economic Community, and in particular Article 130s thereof,

Having regard to the proposal from the Commission,

Having regard to the opinion of the European Parliament,

Having regard to the opinion of the Economic and Social Committee,

Whereas the preservation, protection and improvement of the quality of the environment, including the conservation of natural habitats and of wild fauna and flora, are an essential objective of general interest pursued by the Community, as stated in Article 130r of the Treaty;

Whereas the European Community policy and action programme on the environment (1987 to 1992) makes provision for measures regarding the conservation of nature and natural resources;

Whereas, the main aim of this Directive being to promote the maintenance of biodiversity, taking account of economic, social, cultural and regional requirements, this Directive makes a contribution to the general objective of sustainable development; whereas the maintenance of such biodiversity may in certain cases require the maintenance, or indeed the encouragement, of human activities;

Whereas, in the European territory of the Member States, natural habitats are continuing to deteriorate and an increasing number of wild species are seriously threatened; whereas given that the threatened habitats and species form part of the Community's natural heritage and the threats to them are often of a transboundary nature, it is necessary to take measures at Community level in order to conserve them;

Whereas, in view of the threats to certain types of natural habitat and certain species, it is necessary to define them as having priority in order to favour the early implementation of measures to conserve them;

Whereas, in order to ensure the restoration or maintenance of natural habitats and species of Community interest at a favourable conservation status, it is necessary to designate special areas of conservation in order to create a coherent European ecological network according to a specified timetable;

Whereas all the areas designated, including those classified now or in the future as special protection areas pursuant to Council Directive 79/409/EEC of 2 April 1979 on the conservation of wild birds, will have to be incorporated into the coherent European ecological network;

Whereas it is appropriate, in each area designated, to implement the necessary measures having regard to the conservation objectives pursued;

Whereas sites eligible for designation as special areas of conservation are proposed by the Member States but whereas a procedure must nevertheless be laid down to allow the designation in exceptional cases of a site which has not been proposed by a Member State but which the Community considers essential for either the maintenance or the survival of a priority natural habitat type or a priority species;

Whereas an appropriate assessment must be made of any plan or programme likely to have a significant effect on the conservation objectives of a site which has been designated or is designated in future;

Whereas it is recognized that the adoption of measures intended to promote the conservation of priority natural habitats and priority species of Community interest is a common responsibility of all Member States; whereas this may, however, impose an excessive financial burden on certain Member States given, on the one hand, the uneven distribution of such habitats and species throughout the Community and, on the other hand, the fact that the "polluter pays" principle can have only limited application in the special case of nature conservation;

Whereas it is therefore agreed that, in this exceptional case, a contribution by means of Community co-financing should be provided for within the limits of the resources made available under the Community's decisions;

Whereas land-use planning and development policies should encourage the management of features of the landscape which are of major importance for wild fauna and flora;

Whereas a system should be set up for surveillance of the conservation status of the natural habitats and species covered by this Directive;

Whereas a general system of protection is required for certain species of flora and fauna to complement Directive 79/409/EEC; whereas provision should be made for management measures for certain species, if their conservation status so warrants, including the prohibition of certain means of capture or killing, whilst providing for the possibility of derogations on certain conditions;

Whereas, with the aim of ensuring that the implementation of this Directive is monitored, the Commission will periodically prepare a composite report based, inter alia, on the information sent to it by the Member States regarding the application of national provisions adopted under this Directive;

Whereas the improvement of scientific and technical knowledge is essential for the implementation of this Directive; whereas it is consequently appropriate to encourage the necessary research and scientific work;

Whereas technical and scientific progress mean that it must be possible to adapt the Annexes; whereas a procedure should be established whereby the Council can amend the Annexes;

Whereas a regulatory committee should be set up to assist the Commission in the implementation of this Directive and in particular when decisions on Community co-financing are taken;

Whereas provision should be made for supplementary measures governing the reintroduction of certain native species of fauna and flora and the possible introduction of non-native species;

Whereas education and general information relating to the objectives of this Directive are essential for ensuring its effective implementation,

HAS ADOPTED THIS DIRECTIVE:

Definitions

Article 1

For the purpose of this Directive:

(a) *conservation* means a series of measures required to maintain or restore the natural habitats and the populations of species of wild fauna and flora at a favourable status as defined in (e) and (i);

(b) *natural habitats* means terrestrial or aquatic areas distinguished by geographic, abiotic and biotic features, whether entirely natural or semi-natural;

(c) *natural habitat types of Community interest* means those which, within the territory referred to in Article 2:

(i) are in danger of disappearance in their natural range;

or

(ii) have a small natural range following their regression or by reason of their intrinsically restricted area;

or

[(iii) present outstanding examples of typical characteristics of one or more of the five following biogeographical regions: Alpine, Atlantic, Continental, Macaronesian and Mediterranean.][1]

Such habitat types are listed or may be listed in Annex I;

(d) *priority natural habitat types* means natural habitat types in danger of disappearence, which are present on the territory referred to in Article 2 and for the conservation of which the Community has particular responsibility in view of the proportion of their natural range which falls within the territory referred to in Article 2; these priority natural habitat types are indicated by an asterisk (*) in Annex I;

(e) *conservation status of a natural habitat* means the sum of the influences acting on a natural habitat and its typical species that may affect its long-term natural distribution, structure and functions as well as the long-term survival of its typical species within the territory referred to in Article 2.

The conservation status of a natural habitat will be taken as "favourable" when:

— its natural range and areas it covers within that range are stable or increasing, and

— the specific structure and functions which are necessary for its long-term maintenance exist and are likely to continue to exist for the foreseeable future, and

— the conservation status of its typical species is favourable as defined in (i);

(f) *habitat of a species* means an environment defined by specific abiotic and biotic factors, in which the species lives at any stage of its biological cycle;

(g) *species of Community interest* means species which, within the territory referred to in Article 2, are:

(i) endangered, except those species whose natural range is marginal in that territory and which are not endangered or vulnerable in the western palearctic region; or

(ii) vulnerable, i.e. believed likely to move into the endangered category in the near future if the causal factors continue operating; or

(iii) rare, i.e. with small populations that are not at present endangered or vulnerable, but are at risk. The species are located within restricted geographical areas or are thinly scattered over a more extensive range; or

(iv) endemic and requiring particular attention by reason of the specific nature of their habitat and/or the potential impact of their exploitation on their habitat and/or the potential impact of their exploitation on their conservation status.

Such species are listed or may be listed in Annex II and/or Annex IV or V;

(h) *priority species* means species referred to in (g) (i) for the conservation of which the Community has particular responsibility in view of the proportion of their natural range which falls within the territory referred to in Article 2; these priority species are indicated by an asterisk (*) in Annex II;

(i) *conservation status of a species* means the sum of the influences acting on the species concerned that may affect the long-term distribution and abundance of its populations within the territory referred to in Article 2;

The conservation status will be taken as "favourable" when:

— population dynamics data on the species concerned indicate that it is maintaining itself on a long-term basis as a viable component of its natural habitats, and

— the natural range of the species is neither being reduced nor is likely to be reduced for the foreseeable future, and

— there is, and will probably continue to be, a sufficiently large habitat to maintain its populations on a long-term basis;

(j) *site* means a geographically defined area whose extent is clearly delineated;

(k) *site of Community importance* means a site which, in the biogeographical region or regions to which it belongs, contributes significantly to the maintenance or restoration at a favourable conservation status of a natural habitat type in Annex I or of a species in Annex II and may also contribute significantly to the coherence of Natura 2000 referred to in Article 3, and/or contributes significantly to the maintenance of biological diversity within the biogeographic region or regions concerned.

For animal species ranging over wide areas, sites of Community importance shall correspond to the places within the natural range of such species which present the physical or biological factors essential to their life and reproduction;

(l) *special area of conservation* means a site of Community importance designated by the Member States through a statutory, administrative and/or contractual act where the necessary conservation measures are applied for the maintenance or restoration, at a favourable conservation status, of the natural habitats and/or the populations of the species for which the site is designated;

(m) *specimen* means any animal or plant, whether alive or dead, of the species listed in Annex IV and Annex V, any part or derivative thereof, as well as any other goods which appear, from an accompanying document, the packaging or a mark or label, or from any other circumstances, to be parts or derivatives of animals or plants of those species;

(n) *the committee* means the committee set up pursuant to Article 20.

Amendment

1 Substituted by Council Directive 2006/105/EC of 20 November 2006 adapting Directives 79/409/EEC, 92/43/EEC, 97/68/EC, 2001/80/EC and 2001/81/EC in the field of environment, by reason of the accession of Bulgaria and Romania, Article 1, Annex, Pt A, para 2(a).

Article 2

1. The aim of this Directive shall be to contribute towards ensuring bio-diversity through the conservation of natural habitats and of wild fauna and flora in the European territory of the Member States to which the Treaty applies.

2. Measures taken pursuant to this Directive shall be designed to maintain or restore, at favourable conservation status, natural habitats and species of wild fauna and flora of Community interest.

3. Measures taken pursuant to this Directive shall take account of economic, social and cultural requirements and regional and local characteristics.

Conservation of natural habitats and habitats of species

Article 3

1. A coherent European ecological network of special areas of conservation shall be set up under the title Natura 2000. This network, composed of sites hosting the natural habitat types listed in Annex I and habitats of the species listed in Annex II, shall enable the natural habitat types and the species' habitats concerned to be maintained or, where appropriate, restored at a favourable conservation status in their natural range.

The Natura 2000 network shall include the special protection areas classified by the Member States pursuant to Directive 79/409/EEC.

2. Each Member State shall contribute to the creation of Natura 2000 in proportion to the representation within its territory of the natural habitat types and the habitats of species referred to in paragraph 1. To that effect each Member State shall designate, in accordance with Article 4, sites as special areas of conservation taking account of the objectives set out in paragraph 1.

3. Where they consider it necessary, Member States shall endeavour to improve the ecological coherence of Natura 2000 by maintaining, and where appropriate developing, features of the landscape which are of major importance for wild fauna and flora, as referred to in Article 10.

Article 4

1. On the basis of the criteria set out in Annex III (Stage 1) and relevant scientific information, each Member State shall propose a list of sites indicating which natural habitat types in Annex I and which species in Annex II that are native to its territory the sites host. For animal species ranging over wide areas these sites shall correspond to the places within the natural range of such species which present the physical or biological factors essential to their life and reproduction. For aquatic species which range over wide areas, such sites will be proposed only where there is a clearly identifiable area representing the physical and biological factors essential to their life and reproduction. Where appropriate, Member States shall propose adaptation of the list in the light of the results of the surveillance referred to in Article 11.

The list shall be transmitted to the Commission, within three years of the notification of this Directive, together with information on each site. That information shall include a map of the site, its name, location, extent and the data resulting from application of the criteria specified in Annex III (Stage 1) provided in a format established by the Commission in accordance with the procedure laid down in Article 21.

2. On the basis of the criteria set out in Annex III (Stage 2) and in the framework both of each of the [nine][1] biogeographical regions referred to in Article 1 (c) (iii) and of the whole of the territory referred to in Article 2 (1), the Commission shall establish, in agreement with each Member State, a draft list of sites of Community importance drawn from the Member States' lists identifying those which host one or more priority natural habitat types or priority species.

Member States whose sites hosting one or more priority natural habitat types and priority species represent more than 5 % of their national territory may, in agreement with the Commission, request that the criteria listed in Annex III (Stage 2) be applied more flexibly in selecting all the sites of Community importance in their territory.

The list of sites selected as sites of Community importance, identifying those which host one or more priority natural habitat types or priority species, shall be adopted by the Commission in accordance with the procedure laid down in Article 21.

3. The list referred to in paragraph 2 shall be established within six years of the notification of this Directive.

4. Once a site of Community importance has been adopted in accordance with the procedure laid down in paragraph 2, the Member State concerned shall designate that site as a special area of conservation as soon as possible and within six years at most, establishing priorities in the light of the importance of the sites for the maintenance or restoration, at a favourable conservation status, of a natural habitat type in Annex I or a species in Annex II and for the coherence of Natura 2000, and in the light of the threats of degradation or destruction to which those sites are exposed.

5. As soon as a site is placed on the list referred to in the third subparagraph of paragraph 2 it shall be subject to Article 6 (2), (3) and (4).

Amendment

1 Substituted by Council Directive 2006/105/EC of 20 November 2006 adapting Directives 79/409/EEC, 92/43/EEC, 97/68/EC, 2001/80/EC and 2001/81/EC in the field of environment, by reason of the accession of Bulgaria and Romania, Article 1, Annex, Pt A, para 2(b).

Article 5

1. In exceptional cases where the Commission finds that a national list as referred to in Article 4 (1) fails to mention a site hosting a priority natural habitat type or priority species which, on the basis of relevant and reliable scientific information, it considers to be essential for the maintenance of that priority natural habitat type or for the survival of that priority species, a bilateral consultation procedure shall be initiated between that Member State and the Commission for the purpose of comparing the scientific data used by each.

2. If, on expiry of a consultation period not exceeding six months, the dispute remains unresolved, the Commission shall forward to the Council a proposal relating to the selection of the site as a site of Community importance.

3. The Council, acting unanimously, shall take a decision within three months of the date of referral.

4. During the consultation period and pending a Council decision, the site concerned shall be subject to Article 6 (2).

Article 6

1. For special areas of conservation, Member States shall establish the necessary conservation measures involving, if need be, appropriate management plans specifically designed for the sites or integrated into other development plans, and appropriate statutory, administrative or contractual measures which correspond to the ecological requirements of the natural habitat types in Annex I and the species in Annex II present on the sites.

2. Member States shall take appropriate steps to avoid, in the special areas of conservation, the deterioration of natural habitats and the habitats of species as well as disturbance of the species for which the areas have been designated, in so far as such disturbance could be significant in relation to the objectives of this Directive.

3. Any plan or project not directly connected with or necessary to the management of the site but likely to have a significant effect thereon, either individually or in combination with other plans or projects, shall be subject to appropriate assessment of its implications for the site in view of the site's conservation objectives. In the light of the conclusions of the assessment of the implications for the site and subject to the provisions of paragraph 4, the competent national authorities shall agree to the plan or project only after having ascertained that it will not adversely affect the integrity of the site concerned and, if appropriate, after having obtained the opinion of the general public.

4. If, in spite of a negative assessment of the implications for the site and in the absence of alternative solutions, a plan or project must nevertheless be carried out for imperative reasons of overriding public interest, including those of a social or economic nature, the Member State shall take all compensatory measures necessary to ensure that the overall coherence of Natura 2000 is protected. It shall inform the Commission of the compensatory measures adopted.

Where the site concerned hosts a priority natural habitat type and/or a priority species, the only considerations which may be raised are those relating to human health or public safety, to beneficial consequences of primary importance for the environment or, further to an opinion from the Commission, to other imperative reasons of overriding public interest.

Article 7

Obligations arising under Article 6 (2), (3) and (4) of this Directive shall replace any obligations arising under the first sentence of Article 4 (4) of Directive 79/409/EEC in respect of areas classified pursuant to Article 4 (1) or similarly recognized under Article 4 (2) thereof, as from the date of implementation of this Directive or the date of classification or recognition by a Member State under Directive 79/409/EEC, where the latter date is later.

Article 8

1. In parallel with their proposals for sites eligible for designation as special areas of conservation, hosting priority natural habitat types and/or priority species, the Member States shall send, as appropriate, to the Commission their estimates relating to the Community co-financing which they consider necessary to allow them to meet their obligations pursuant to Article 6 (1).

2. In agreement with each of the Member States concerned, the Commission shall identify, for sites of Community importance for which co-financing is sought, those measures essential for the maintenance or re-establishment at a favourable conservation status of the priority natural habitat types and priority species on the sites concerned, as well as the total costs arising from those measures.

3. The Commission, in agreement with the Member States concerned, shall assess the financing, including co-financing, required for the operation of the measures referred to in paragraph 2, taking into account, amongst other things, the concentration on the Member State's territory of priority natural habitat types and/or priority species and the relative burdens which the required measures entail.

4. According to the assessment referred to in paragraphs 2 and 3, the Commission shall adopt, having regard to the available sources of funding under the relevant Community instruments and according to the procedure set out in Article 21, a prioritized action framework of measures involving co-financing to be taken when the site has been designated under Article 4 (4).

5. The measures which have not been retained in the action framework for lack of sufficient resources, as well as those included in the abovementioned action framework which have not received the necessary co-financing or have only been partially co-financed, shall be reconsidered in accordance with the procedure set out in Article 21, in the context of the two-yearly review of the action framework and may, in the maintime, be postponed by the Member States pending such review. This review shall take into account, as appropriate, the new situation of the site concerned.

6. In areas where the measures dependent on co-financing are postponed, Member States shall refrain from any new measures likely to result in deterioration of those areas.

Article 9

The Commission, acting in accordance with the procedure laid down in Article 21, shall periodically review the contribution of Natura 2000 towards achievement of the objectives set out in Article 2 and 3. In this context, a special area of conservation may be considered for declassification where this is warranted by natural developments noted as a result of the surveillance provided for in Article 11.

Article 10

Member States shall endeavour, where they consider it necessary, in their land-use planning and development policies and, in particular, with a view to improving the ecological coherence of the Natura 2000 network, to encourage the management of features of the landscape which are of major importance for wild fauna and flora.

Such features are those which, by virtue of their linear and continuous structure (such as rivers with their banks or the traditional systems for marking field boundaries) or their function as stepping stones (such as ponds or small woods), are essential for the migration, dispersal and genetic exchange of wild species.

Article 11

Member States shall undertake surveillance of the conservation status of the natural habitats and species referred to in Article 2 with particular regard to priority natural habitat types and priority species.

Protection of species

Article 12

1. Member States shall take the requisite measures to establish a system of strict protection for the animal species listed in Annex IV (a) in their natural range, prohibiting:

(a) all forms of deliberate capture or killing of specimens of these species in the wild;
(b) deliberate disturbance of these species, particularly during the period of breeding, rearing, hibernation and migration;
(c) deliberate destruction or taking of eggs from the wild;
(d) deterioration or destruction of breeding sites or resting places.

2. For these species, Member States shall prohibit the keeping, transport and sale or exchange, and offering for sale or exchange, of specimens taken from the wild, except for those taken legally before this Directive is implemented.

3. The prohibition referred to in paragraph 1 (a) and (b) and paragraph 2 shall apply to all stages of life of the animals to which this Article applies.

4. Member States shall establish a system to monitor the incidential capture and killing of the animal species listed in Annex IV (a). In the light of the information gathered, Member States shall take further research or conservation measures as required to ensure that incidental capture and killing does not have a significant negative impact on the species concerned.

Article 13

1. Member States shall take the requisite measures to establish a system of strict protection for the plant species listed in Annex IV (b), prohibiting:
(a) the deliberate picking, collecting, cutting, uprooting or destruction of such plants in their natural range in the wild;
(b) the keeping, transport and sale or exchange and offering for sale or exchange of specimens of such species taken in the wild, except for those taken legally before this Directive is implemented.

2. The prohibitions referred to in paragraph 1 (a) and (b) shall apply to all stages of the biological cycle of the plants to which this Article applies.

Article 14

1. If, in the light of the surveillance provided for in Article 11, Member States deem it necessary, they shall take measures to ensure that the taking in the wild of specimens of species of wild fauna and flora listed in Annex V as well as their exploitation is compatible with their being maintained at a favourable conservation status.

2. Where such measures are deemed necessary, they shall include continuation of the surveillance provided for in Article 11. Such measures may also include in particular:
— regulations regarding access to certain property,
— temporary or local prohibition of the taking of specimens in the wild and exploitation of certain populations,
— regulation of the periods and/or methods of taking specimens,
— application, when specimens are taken, of hunting and fishing rules which take account of the conservation of such populations,
— establishment of a system of licences for taking specimens or of quotas,
— regulation of the purchase, sale, offering for sale, keeping for sale or transport for sale of specimens,
— breeding in captivity of animal species as well as artificial propagation of plant species, under strictly controlled conditions, with a view to reducing the taking of specimens of the wild,
— assessment of the effect of the measures adopted.

Article 15

In respect of the capture or killing of species of wild fauna listed in Annex V (a) and in cases where, in accordance with Article 16, derogations are applied to the taking, capture or killing of species listed in Annex IV (a), Member States shall prohibit the use of all indiscriminate means capable of causing local disappearance of, or serious disturbance to, populations of such species, and in particular:

(a) use of the means of capture and killing listed in Annex VI (a);

(b) any form of capture and killing from the modes of transport referred to in Annex VI (b).

Article 16

1. Provided that there is no satisfactory alternative and the derogation is not detrimental to the maintenance of the populations of the species concerned at a favourable conservation status in their natural range, Member States may derogate from the provisions of Articles 12, 13, 14 and 15 (a) and (b):

(a) in the interest of protecting wild fauna and flora and conserving natural habitats;

(b) to prevent serious damage, in particular to crops, livestock, forests, fisheries and water and other types of property;

(c) in the interests of public health and public safety, or for other imperative reasons of overriding public interest, including those of a social or economic nature and beneficial consequences of primary importance for the environment;

(d) for the purpose of research and education, of repopulating and re-introducing these species and for the breedings operations necessary for these purposes, including the artificial propagation of plants;

(e) to allow, under strictly supervised conditions, on a selective basis and to a limited extent, the taking or keeping of certain specimens of the species listed in Annex IV in limited numbers specified by the competent national authorities.

2. Member States shall forward to the Commission every two years a report in accordance with the format established by the Committee on the derogations applied under paragraph 1. The Commission shall give its opinion on these derogations within a maximum time limit of 12 months following receipt of the report and shall give an account to the Committee.

3. The reports shall specify:

(a) the species which are subject to the derogations and the reason for the derogation, including the nature of the risk, with, if appropriate, a reference to alternatives rejected and scientific data used;

(b) the means, devices or methods authorized for the capture or killing of animal species and the reasons for their use;

(c) the circumstances of when and where such derogations are granted;

(d) the authority empowered to declare and check that the required conditions obtain and to decide what means, devices or methods may be used, within what limits and by what agencies, and which persons are to carry out the task;

(e) the supervisory measures used and the results obtained.

Information

Article 17

1. Every six years from the date of expiry of the period laid down in Article 23, Member States shall draw up a report on the implementation of the measures taken under this Directive. This report shall include in particular information concerning the conservation measures referred to in Article 6 (1) as well as evaluation of the impact of those measures on the conservation status of the natural habitat types of Annex I and the species in Annex II and the main results of the surveillance referred to in Article 11. The report, in accordance with the format established by the committee, shall be forwarded to the Commission and made accessible to the public.

2. The Commission shall prepare a composite report based on the reports referred to in paragraph 1. This report shall include an appropriate evaluation of the progress achieved and, in particular, of the contribution of Natura 2000 to the achievement of the objectives set out in Article 3. A draft of the part of the report covering the information supplied by a Member State shall be forwarded to the Member State in question for verification. After submission to

the committee, the final version of the report shall be published by the Commission, not later than two years after receipt of the reports referred to in paragraph 1, and shall be forwarded to the Member States, the European Parliament, the Council and the Economic and Social Committee.

3. Member States may mark areas designated under this Directive by means of Community notices designed for that purpose by the committee.

Research

Article 18

1. Member States and the Commission shall encourage the necessary research and scientific work having regard to the objectives set out in Article 2 and the obligation referred to in Article 11. They shall exchange information for the purposes of proper coordination of research carried out at Member State and at Community level.

2. Particular attention shall be paid to scientific work necessary for the implementation of Articles 4 and 10, and transboundary cooperative research between Member States shall be encouraged.

Procedure for amending the Annexes

Article 19

Such amendments as are necessary for adapting Annexes I, II, III, V and VI to technical and scientific progress shall be adopted by the Council acting by qualified majority on a proposal from the Commission.

Such amendments as are necessary for adapting Annex IV to technical and scientific progress shall be adopted by the Council acting unanimously on a proposal from the Commission.

Committee

[Article 20][1]

[The Commission shall be assisted by a committee.][1]

Amendment

1 Substituted by Regulation 1882/2003 of the European Parliament and of the Council of 29 September 2003 adapting to Council Decision 1999/468/EC the provisions relating to committees which assist the Commission in the exercise of its implementing powers laid down in instruments subject to the procedure referred to in Article 251 of the EC Treaty, Article 3, Annex III, para 30.

[Article 21][1]

[1. Where reference is made to this Article, Artiles 5 and 7 of Decision 1999/468/EC shall apply, having regard to the provisions of Article 8 thereof.

The period laid down in article 5(6) of Decision 1999/468/EC shall be set at three months.

2. The Commission shall adopt its rules of procedure.][1]

Amendment

1 Substituted by Regulation 1882/2003 of the European Parliament and of the Council of 29 September 2003 adapting to Council Decision 1999/468/EC the provisions relating to committees which assist the Commission in the exercise of its implementing powers laid down in instruments subject to the procedure referred to in Article 251 of the EC Treaty, Article 3, Annex III, para 30.

Supplementary provisions

Article 22

In implementing the provisions of this Directive, Member States shall:

(a) study the desirability of re-introducing species in Annex IV that are native to their territory where this might contribute to their conservation, provided that an investigation, also taking into account experience in other Member States or elsewhere, has established that such re-introduction contributes effectively to re-establishing these species at a favourable conservation status and that it takes place only after proper consultation of the public concerned;

(b) ensure that the deliberate introduction into the wild of any species which is not native to their territory is regulated so as not to prejudice natural habitats within their natural range or the wild native fauna and flora and, if they consider it necessary, prohibit such introduction. The results of the assessment undertaken shall be forwarded to the committee for information;

(c) promote education and general information on the need to protect species of wild fauna and flora and to conserve their habitats and natural habitats.

Final provisions

Article 23

1. Member States shall bring into force the laws, regulations and administrative provisions necessary to comply with this Directive within two years of its notification. They shall forthwith inform the Commission thereof.

2. When Member States adopt such measures, they shall contain a reference to this Directive or be accompanied by such reference on the occasion of their official publication. The methods of making such a reference shall be laid down by the Member States.

3. Member States shall communicate to the Commission the main provisions of national law which they adopt in the field covered by this Directive.

Article 24

This Directive is addressed to the Member States.

[ANNEX I NATURAL HABITAT TYPES OF COMMUNITY INTEREST WHOSE CONSERVATION REQUIRES THE DESIGNATION OF SPECIAL AREAS OF CONSERVATION

Interpretation][1]

[Guidance on the interpretation of habitat types is given in the "Interpretation Manual of European Union Habitats" as approved by the committee set up under Article 20 ("Habitats Committee") and published by the European Commission.

The code corresponds to the NATURA 2000 code.

The sign "*" indicates priority habitat types.][1]

Amendment

1 Substituted by Council Directive 2006/105/EC of 20 November 2006 adapting Directives 79/409/EEC, 92/43/EEC, 97/68/EC, 2001/80/EC and 2001/81/EC in the field of environment, by reason of the accession of Bulgaria and Romania, Article 1, Annex, Pt A, para 2(a).

[1. COASTAL AND HALOPHYTIC HABITATS][1]

[11 Open sea and tidal areas

1110 Sandbanks which are slightly covered by sea water all the time

1120 * *Posidonia* beds (*Posidonion oceanicae*)

1130 Estuaries

1140 Mudflats and sandflats not covered by seawater at low tide
1150 * Coastal lagoons
1160 Large shallow inlets and bays
1170 Reefs
1180 Submarine structures made by leaking gases

12 Sea cliffs and shingle or stony beaches
1210 Annual vegetation of drift lines
1220 Perennial vegetation of stony banks
1230 Vegetated sea cliffs of the Atlantic and Baltic coasts
1240 Vegetated sea cliffs of the Mediterranean coasts with endemic *Limonium* spp.
1250 Vegetated sea cliffs with endemic flora of the Macaronesian coasts

13 Atlantic and continental salt marshes and salt meadows
1310 *Salicornia* and other annuals colonizing mud and sand
1320 *Spartina* swards (*Spartinion maritimae*)
1330 Atlantic salt meadows (*Glauco-Puccinellietalia maritimae*)
1340 * Inland salt meadows

14 Mediterranean and thermo-Atlantic salt marshes and salt meadows
1410 Mediterranean salt meadows (*Juncetalia maritimi*)
1420 Mediterranean and thermo-Atlantic halophilous scrubs (*Sarcocornetea fruticosi*)
1430 Halo-nitrophilous scrubs (*Pegano-Salsoletea*)

15 Salt and gypsum inland steppes
1510 * Mediterranean salt steppes (*Limonietalia*)
1520 * Iberian gypsum vegetation (*Gypsophiletalia*)
1530 * Pannonic salt steppes and salt marshes

16 Boreal Baltic archipelago, coastal and landupheaval areas
1610 Baltic esker islands with sandy, rocky and shingle beach vegetation and sublittoral vegetation
1620 Boreal Baltic islets and small islands
1630 * Boreal Baltic coastal meadows
1640 Boreal Baltic sandy beaches with perennial vegetation
1650 Boreal Baltic narrow inlets][1]

Amendment

1 Substituted by Council Directive 2006/105/EC of 20 November 2006 adapting Directives 79/409/EEC, 92/43/EEC, 97/68/EC, 2001/80/EC and 2001/81/EC in the field of environment, by reason of the accession of Bulgaria and Romania, Article 1, Annex, Pt A, para 2(a).

[2. COASTAL SAND DUNES AND INLAND DUNES][1]

[21 Sea dunes of the Atlantic, North Sea and Baltic coasts
2110 Embryonic shifting dunes
2120 Shifting dunes along the shoreline with *Ammophila arenaria* ("white dunes")
2130 * Fixed coastal dunes with herbaceous vegetation ("grey dunes")
2140 * Decalcified fixed dunes with *Empetrum nigrum*
2150 * Atlantic decalcified fixed dunes (*Calluno-Ulicetea*)
2160 Dunes with *Hippophaë rhamnoides*
2170 Dunes with *Salix repens* ssp. *argentea* (*Salicion arenariae*)
2180 Wooded dunes of the Atlantic, Continental and Boreal region
2190 Humid dune slacks
21A0 Machairs (* in Ireland)

22 Sea dunes of the Mediterranean coast
2210 *Crucianellion maritimae* fixed beach dunes
2220 Dunes with *Euphorbia terracina*

2230 *Malcolmietalia* dune grasslands
2240 *Brachypodietalia* dune grasslands with annuals
2250 * Coastal dunes with *Juniperus* spp.
2260 *Cisto-Lavenduletalia* dune sclerophyllous scrubs
2270 * Wooded dunes with *Pinus pinea* and/or *Pinus pinaster*

23 Inland dunes, old and decalcified
2310 Dry sand heaths with *Calluna* and *Genista*
2320 Dry sand heaths with *Calluna* and *Empetrum nigrum*
2330 Inland dunes with open *Corynephorus* and Agrostis grasslands
2340 * Pannonic inland dunes][1]

Amendment

1 Substituted by Council Directive 2006/105/EC of 20 November 2006 adapting Directives 79/409/EEC, 92/43/EEC, 97/68/EC, 2001/80/EC and 2001/81/EC in the field of environment, by reason of the accession of Bulgaria and Romania, Article 1, Annex, Pt A, para 2(a).

[3. FRESHWATER HABITATS][1]

[31 Standing water
3110 Oligotrophic waters containing very few minerals of sandy plains (*Littorelletalia uniflorae*)
3120 Oligotrophic waters containing very few minerals generally on sandy soils of the West Mediterranean, with *Isoetes* spp.
3130 Oligotrophic to mesotrophic standing waters with vegetation of the *Littorelletea uniflorae* and/or of the *Isoëto-Nanojuncetea*
3140 Hard oligo-mesotrophic waters with benthic vegetation of *Chara* spp.
3150 Natural eutrophic lakes with *Magnopotamion* or *Hydrocharition* — type vegetation
3160 Natural dystrophic lakes and ponds
3170 * Mediterranean temporary ponds
3180 * Turloughs
3190 Lakes of gypsum karst
31A0 * Transylvanian hot-spring lotus beds

32 Running water - sections of water courses with natural or semi-natural dynamics (minor, average and major beds) where the water quality shows no significant deterioration
3210 Fennoscandian natural rivers
3220 Alpine rivers and the herbaceous vegetation along their banks
3230 Alpine rivers and their ligneous vegetation with *Myricaria germanica*
3240 Alpine rivers and their ligneous vegetation with *Salix elaeagnos*
3250 Constantly flowing Mediterranean rivers with *Glaucium flavum*
3260 Water courses of plain to montane levels with the *Ranunculion fluitantis* and *Callitricho-Batrachion* vegetation
3270 Rivers with muddy banks with *Chenopodion rubri* p.p. and *Bidention* p.p. vegetation
3280 Constantly flowing Mediterranean rivers with *Paspalo-Agrostidion* species and hanging curtains of *Salix* and *Populus alba*
3290 Intermittently flowing Mediterranean rivers of the *Paspalo-Agrostidion*][1]

Amendment

1 Substituted by Council Directive 2006/105/EC of 20 November 2006 adapting Directives 79/409/EEC, 92/43/EEC, 97/68/EC, 2001/80/EC and 2001/81/EC in the field of environment, by reason of the accession of Bulgaria and Romania, Article 1, Annex, Pt A, para 2(a).

[4. TEMPERATE HEATH AND SCRUB][1]

[4010 Northern Atlantic wet heaths with *Erica tetralix*
4020 * Temperate Atlantic wet heaths with *Erica ciliaris* and *Erica tetralix*
4030 European dry heaths
4040 * Dry Atlantic coastal heaths with *Erica vagans*

4050 * Endemic macaronesian heaths
4060 Alpine and Boreal heaths
4070 * Bushes with *Pinus mugo* and *Rhododendron hirsutum* (*Mugo-Rhododendretum hirsuti*)
4080 Sub-Arctic *Salix* spp. Scrub
4090 Endemic oro-Mediterranean heaths with gorse
40A0 * Subcontinental peri-Pannonic scrub
40B0 Rhodope *Potentilla fruticosa* thickets
40C0 * Ponto-Sarmatic deciduous thickets][1]

Amendment

1 Substituted by Council Directive 2006/105/EC of 20 November 2006 adapting Directives 79/409/EEC, 92/43/EEC, 97/68/EC, 2001/80/EC and 2001/81/EC in the field of environment, by reason of the accession of Bulgaria and Romania, Article 1, Annex, Pt A, para 2(a).

[5. SCLEROPHYLL OUS SCRUB (MATORRAL)][1]

[51 Sub-Mediterranean and temperate scrub
5110 Stable xerothermophilous formations with Buxus sempervirens on rock slopes (*Berberidion* p.p.)
5120 Mountain *Cytisus purgans* formations
5130 *Juniperus communis* formations on heaths or calcareous grasslands
5140 * *Cistus palhinhae* formations on maritime wet heaths

52 Mediterranean arborescent matorral
5210 Arborescent matorral with *Juniperus* spp.
5220 * Arborescent matorral with *Zyziphus*
5230 * Arborescent matorral with *Laurus nobilis*

53 Thermo-Mediterranean and pre-steppe brush
5310 *Laurus nobilis* thickets
5320 Low formations of Euphorbia close to cliffs
5330 Thermo-Mediterranean and pre-desert scrub

54 Phrygana
5410 West Mediterranean clifftop phryganas (*Astragalo-Plantaginetum subulatae*)
5420 Sarcopoterium spinosum phryganas
5430 Endemic phryganas of the *Euphorbio-Verbascion*][1]

Amendment

1 Substituted by Council Directive 2006/105/EC of 20 November 2006 adapting Directives 79/409/EEC, 92/43/EEC, 97/68/EC, 2001/80/EC and 2001/81/EC in the field of environment, by reason of the accession of Bulgaria and Romania, Article 1, Annex, Pt A, para 2(a).

[6. NATURAL AND SEMI-NATURAL GRASSLAND FORMATIONS][1]

[61 Natural grasslands
6110 Rupicolous calcareous or basophilic grasslands of the *Alysso-Sedion albi*
6120 * Xeric sand calcareous grasslands
6130 Calaminarian grasslands of the *Violetalia calaminariae*
6140 Siliceous Pyrenean *Festuca eskia* grasslands
6150 Siliceous alpine and boreal grasslands
6160 Oro-Iberian *Festuca indigesta* grasslands
6170 Alpine and subalpine calcareous grasslands
6180 Macaronesian mesophile grasslands
6190 Rupicolous pannonic grasslands (*Stipo-Festucetalia pallentis*)

62 Semi-natural dry grasslands and scrubland facies
6210 Semi-natural dry grasslands and scrubland facies on calcareous substrates (*Festuco-Brometalia*) (* important orchid sites)

6220 * Pseudo-steppe with grasses and annuals of the *Thero-Brachypodietea*
6230 * Species-rich *Nardus* grasslands, on silicious substrates in mountain areas (and submountain areas in Continental Europe)
6240 * Sub-Pannonic steppic grasslands
6250 * Pannonic loess steppic grasslands
6260 * Pannonic sand steppes
6270 * Fennoscandian lowland species-rich dry to mesic grasslands
6280 * Nordic alvar and precambrian calcareous flatrocks
62A0 Eastern sub-Mediterranean dry grasslands (*Scorzoneratalia villosae*)
62B0 * Serpentinophilous grassland of Cyprus
62C0 Ponto-Sarmatic steppes
62D0 Oro-Moesian acidophilous grasslands

63 Sclerophillous grazed forests (dehesas)
6310 Dehesas with evergreen *Quercus* spp.

64 Semi-natural tall-herb humid meadows
6410 *Molinia* meadows on calcareous, peaty or clayey-silt-laden soils (*Molinion caeruleae*)
6420 Mediterranean tall humid grasslands of the *Molinio-Holoschoenion*
6430 Hydrophilous tall herb fringe communities of plains and of the montane to alpine levels
6440 Alluvial meadows of river valleys of the *Cnidion dubii*
6450 Northern boreal alluvial meadows
6460 Peat grasslands of Troodos

65 Mesophile grasslands
6510 Lowland hay meadows (*Alopecurus pratensis*, *Sanguisorba officinalis*)
6520 Mountain hay meadows
6530 * Fennoscandian wooded meadows][1]

Amendment

1 Substituted by Council Directive 2006/105/EC of 20 November 2006 adapting Directives 79/409/EEC, 92/43/EEC, 97/68/EC, 2001/80/EC and 2001/81/EC in the field of environment, by reason of the accession of Bulgaria and Romania, Article 1, Annex, Pt A, para 2(a).

[7. RAISED BOGS AND MIRES AND FENS][1]

[71 Sphagnum acid bogs
7110 * Active raised bogs
7120 Degraded raised bogs still capable of natural regeneration
7130 Blanket bogs (* if active bog)
7140 Transition mires and quaking bogs
7150 Depressions on peat substrates of the *Rhynchosporion*
7160 Fennoscandian mineral-rich springs and springfens

72 Calcareous fens
7210 * Calcareous fens with *Cladium mariscus* and species of the *Caricion davallianae*
7220 * Petrifying springs with tufa formation (*Cratoneurion*)
7230 Alkaline fens
7240 * Alpine pioneer formations of the *Caricion bicoloris-atrofuscae*

73 Boreal mires
7310 * Aapa mires
7320 * Palsa mires][1]

Amendment

1 Substituted by Council Directive 2006/105/EC of 20 November 2006 adapting Directives 79/409/EEC, 92/43/EEC, 97/68/EC, 2001/80/EC and 2001/81/EC in the field of environment, by reason of the accession of Bulgaria and Romania, Article 1, Annex, Pt A, para 2(a).

[8. ROCKY HABITATS AND CAVES][1]

[81 Scree

8110 Siliceous scree of the montane to snow levels (*Androsacetalia alpinae* and *Galeopsietalia ladani*)

8120 Calcareous and calcshist screes of the montane to alpine levels (*Thlaspietea rotundifolii*)

8130 Western Mediterranean and thermophilous scree

8140 Eastern Mediterranean screes

8150 Medio-European upland siliceous screes

8160 * Medio-European calcareous scree of hill and montane levels

82 Rocky slopes with chasmophytic vegetation

8210 Calcareous rocky slopes with chasmophytic vegetation

8220 Siliceous rocky slopes with chasmophytic vegetation

8230 Siliceous rock with pioneer vegetation of the *Sedo-Scleranthion* or of the *Sedo albi-Veronicion dillenii*

8240 * Limestone pavements

83 Other rocky habitats

8310 Caves not open to the public

8320 Fields of lava and natural excavations

8330 Submerged or partially submerged sea caves

8340 Permanent glaciers][1]

Amendment

1 Substituted by Council Directive 2006/105/EC of 20 November 2006 adapting Directives 79/409/EEC, 92/43/EEC, 97/68/EC, 2001/80/EC and 2001/81/EC in the field of environment, by reason of the accession of Bulgaria and Romania, Article 1, Annex, Pt A, para 2(a).

[9. FORESTS][1]

[(Sub)natural woodland vegetation comprising native species forming forests of tall trees, with typical undergrowth, and meeting the following criteria: rare or residual, and/or hosting species of Community interest.

90 Forests of Boreal Europe

9010 * Western Taïga

9020 * Fennoscandian hemiboreal natural old broad-leaved deciduous forests (*Quercus, Tilia, Acer, Fraxinus* or *Ulmus*) rich in epiphytes

9030 * Natural forests of primary succession stages of landupheaval coast

9040 Nordic subalpine/subarctic forests with *Betula pubescens* ssp. *czerepanovii*

9050 Fennoscandian herb-rich forests with *Picea abies*

9060 Coniferous forests on, or connected to, glaciofluvial eskers

9070 Fennoscandian wooded pastures

9080 * Fennoscandian deciduous swamp woods

91 Forests of temperate Europe

9110 *Luzulo-Fagetum* beech forests

9120 Atlantic acidophilous beech forests with *Ilex* and sometimes also *Taxus* in the shrublayer (*Quercion robori-petraeae* or *Ilici-Fagenion*)

9130 *Asperulo-Fagetum* beech forests

9140 Medio-European subalpine beech woods with *Acer* and *Rumex arifolius*

9150 Medio-European limestone beech forests of the *Cephalanthero-Fagion*

9160 Sub-Atlantic and medio-European oak or oak-hornbeam forests of the *Carpinion betuli*

9170 *Galio-Carpinetum* oak-hornbeam forests

9180 * *Tilio-Acerion* forests of slopes, screes and ravines

9190 Old acidophilous oak woods with *Quercus robur* on sandy plains

91A0 Old sessile oak woods with *Ilex* and *Blechnum* in the British Isles

91B0 Thermophilous *Fraxinus angustifolia* woods

91C0 * Caledonian forest
91D0 * Bog woodland
91E0 * Alluvial forests with *Alnus glutinosa* and *Fraxinus excelsior* (*Alno-Padion*, *Alnion incanae*, *Salicion albae*)
91F0 Riparian mixed forests of *Quercus robur*, *Ulmus laevis* and *Ulmus minor*, *Fraxinus excelsior* or *Fraxinus angustifolia*, along the great rivers (*Ulmenion minoris*)
91G0 * Pannonic woods with *Quercus petraea* and *Carpinus betulus*
91H0 * Pannonian woods with *Quercus pubescens*
91I0 * Euro-Siberian steppic woods with *Quercus* spp.
91J0 * *Taxus baccata* woods of the British Isles
91K0 Illyrian *Fagus sylvatica* forests (*Aremonio-Fagion*)
91L0 Illyrian oak-hornbeam forests (*Erythronio-Carpinion*)
91M0 Pannonian-Balkanic turkey oak –sessile oak forests
91N0 * Pannonic inland sand dune thicket (*Junipero-Populetum albae*)
91P0 Holy Cross fir forest (*Abietetum polonicum*)
91Q0 Western Carpathian calcicolous *Pinus sylvestris* forests
91R0 Dinaric dolomite Scots pine forests (*Genisto januensis-Pinetum*)
91S0 * Western Pontic beech forests
91T0 Central European lichen Scots pine forests
91U0 Sarmatic steppe pine forest
91V0 Dacian Beech forests (*Symphyto-Fagion*)
91W0 Moesian beech forests
91X0 * Dobrogean beech forests
91Y0 Dacian oak & hornbeam forests
91Z0 Moesian silver lime woods
91AA * Eastern white oak woods
91BA Moesian silver fir forests
91CA Rhodopide and Balkan Range Scots pine forests

92 Mediterranean deciduous forests
9210 * Apeninne beech forests with *Taxus* and *Ilex*
9220 * Apennine beech forests with *Abies alba* and beech forests with *Abies nebrodensis*
9230 Galicio-Portuguese oak woods with *Quercus robur* and *Quercus pyrenaica*
9240 *Quercus faginea* and *Quercus canariensis* Iberian woods
9250 *Quercus trojana* woods
9260 *Castanea sativa* woods
9270 Hellenic beech forests with *Abies borisii-regis*
9280 *Quercus frainetto* woods
9290 *Cupressus* forests (*Acero-Cupression*)
92A0 *Salix alba* and *Populus alba* galleries
92B0 Riparian formations on intermittent Mediterranean water courses with *Rhododendron ponticum*, *Salix* and others
92C0 *Platanus orientalis* and *Liquidambar orientalis* woods (*Platanion orientalis*)
92D0 Southern riparian galleries and thickets (*Nerio-Tamaricetea* and *Securinegion tinctoriae*)

93 Mediterranean sclerophyllous forests
9310 Aegean *Quercus brachyphylla* woods
9320 *Olea* and *Ceratonia* forests
9330 *Quercus suber* forests
9340 *Quercus ilex* and *Quercus rotundifolia* forests
9350 *Quercus macrolepis* forests
9360 * Macaronesian laurel forests (*Laurus*, *Ocotea*)
9370 * Palm groves of *Phoenix*
9380 Forests of *Ilex aquifolium*
9390 * Scrub and low forest vegetation with *Quercus alnifolia*
93A0 Woodlands with *Quercus infectoria* (*Anagyro foetidae-Quercetum infectoriae*)

94 Temperate mountainous coniferous forests
9410 Acidophilous *Picea* forests of the montane to alpine levels (*Vaccinio-Piceetea*)
9420 Alpine *Larix decidua* and/or *Pinus cembra* forests
9430 Subalpine and montane *Pinus uncinata* forests (* if on gypsum or limestone)

95 Mediterranean and Macaronesian mountainous coniferous forests
9510 * Southern Apennine *Abies alba* forests
9520 *Abies pinsapo* forests
9530 * (Sub-) Mediterranean pine forests with endemic black pines
9540 Mediterranean pine forests with endemic Mesogean pines
9550 Canarian endemic pine forests
9560 * Endemic forests with *Juniperus* spp.
9570 * *Tetraclinis articulata* forests
9580 * Mediterranean *Taxus baccata* woods
9590 * *Cedrus brevifolia* forests (*Cedrosetum brevifoliae*)
95A0 High oro-Mediterranean pine forests][1]

Amendment

1 Substituted by Council Directive 2006/105/EC of 20 November 2006 adapting Directives 79/409/EEC, 92/43/EEC, 97/68/EC, 2001/80/EC and 2001/81/EC in the field of environment, by reason of the accession of Bulgaria and Romania, Article 1, Annex, Pt A, para 2(a).

[ANNEX II
ANIMAL AND PLANT SPECIES OF COMMUNITY INTEREST WHOSE CONSERVATION REQUIRES THE DESIGNATION OF SPECIAL AREAS OF CONSERVATION

Interpretation][1]

[(a) Annex II follows on from Annex I for the establishment of a consistent network of special areas of conservation.

(b) The species listed in this Annex are indicated:
— by the name of the species or subspecies, or
— by all the species belonging to a higher taxon or to a designated part of that taxon.

The abbreviation "spp." after the name of a family or genus designates all the species belonging to that family or genus.

(c) Symbols

An asterisk (*) before the name of a species indicates that it is a priority species.

Most species listed in this Annex are also listed in Annex IV. Where a species appears in this Annex but does not appear in either Annex IV or Annex V, the species name is followed by the symbol (o); where a species which appears in this Annex also appears in Annex V but does not appear in Annex IV, its name is followed by the symbol (V).][1]

Amendment

1 Substituted by Council Directive 2006/105/EC of 20 November 2006 adapting Directives 79/409/EEC, 92/43/EEC, 97/68/EC, 2001/80/EC and 2001/81/EC in the field of environment, by reason of the accession of Bulgaria and Romania, Article 1, Annex, Pt A, para 2(a).

[(A) ANIMALS

Vertebrates][1]

Mammals

INSECTIVORA
Talpidae
Galemys pyrenaicus

CHIROPTERA
Rhinolophidae
Rhinolophus blasii
Rhinolophus euryale
Rhinolophus ferrumequinum
Rhinolophus hipposideros
Rhinolophus mehelyi
Vespertilionidae
Barbastella barbastellus
Miniopterus schreibersii
Myotis bechsteinii
Myotis blythii
Myotis capaccinii
Myotis dasycneme
Myotis emarginatus
Myotis myotis
Pteropodidae
Rousettus aegyptiacus

RODENTIA
Gliridae
Myomimus roachi
Sciuridae
* *Marmota marmota latirostris*
* *Pteromys volans* (*Sciuropterus russicus*)
Spermophilus citellus (*Citellus citellus*)
* *Spermophilus suslicus* (*Citellus suslicus*)
Castoridae
Castor fiber (except the Estonian, Latvian, Lithuanian, Finnish and Swedish populations)
Cricetidae
Mesocricetus newtoni
Microtidae
Microtus cabrerae
**Microtus oeconomus arenicola*
* *Microtus oeconomus mehelyi*
Microtus tatricus
Zapodidae
Sicista subtilis

CARNIVORA
Canidae
* *Alopex lagopus*
**Canis lupus* (except the Estonian population; Greek populations: only those south of the 39th parallel; Spanish populations: only those south of the Duero; Latvian, Lithuanian and Finnish populations)
Ursidae
**Ursus arctos* (except the Estonian, Finnish and Swedish populations)
Mustelidae
* *Gulo gulo*
Lutra lutra
Mustela eversmanii
* *Mustela lutreola*
Vormela peregusna
Felidae
Lynx lynx (except the Estonian, Latvian and Finnish populations)
* *Lynx pardinus*

Phocidae

Halichoerus grypus (V)
* *Monachus monachus*
Phoca hispida bottnica (V)
* *Phoca hispida saimensis*
Phoca vitulina (V)

ARTIODACTYLA
Cervidae

* *Cervus elaphus corsicanus*
Rangifer tarandus fennicus (o)

Bovidae

* *Bison bonasus*
Capra aegagrus (natural populations)
* *Capra pyrenaica pyrenaica*
Ovis gmelini musimon (*Ovis ammon musimon*) (natural populations — Corsica and Sardinia)
Ovis orientalis ophion (*Ovis gmelini ophion*)
* *Rupicapra pyrenaica ornata* (*Rupicapra rupicapra ornata*)
Rupicapra rupicapra balcanica
* *Rupicapra rupicapra tatrica*

CETACEA

Phocoena phocoena
Tursiops truncatus][1]

Amendment

1 Substituted by Council Directive 2006/105/EC of 20 November 2006 adapting Directives 79/409/EEC, 92/43/EEC, 97/68/EC, 2001/80/EC and 2001/81/EC in the field of environment, by reason of the accession of Bulgaria and Romania, Article 1, Annex, Pt A, para 2(a).

[Reptiles

CHELONIA (TESTUDINES)
Testudinidae

Testudo graeca
Testudo hermanni
Testudo marginata

Cheloniidae

* *Caretta caretta*
* *Chelonia mydas*

Emydidae

Emys orbicularis
Mauremys caspica
Mauremys leprosa

SAURIA
Lacertidae

Lacerta bonnali (*Lacerta monticola*)
Lacerta monticola
Lacerta schreiberi
Gallotia galloti insulanagae
**Gallotia simonyi*
Podarcis lilfordi
Podarcis pityusensis

Scincidae

Chalcides simonyi (*Chalcides occidentalis*)

Gekkonidae

Phyllodactylus europaeus

OPHIDIA (SERPENTES)
Colubridae
 * *Coluber cypriensis*
 Elaphe quatuorlineata
 Elaphe situla
 * *Natrix natrix cypriaca*
Viperidae
 * *Macrovipera schweizeri* (*Vipera lebetina schweizeri*)
 Vipera ursinii (except *Vipera ursinii rakosiensis*)
 * *Vipera ursinii rakosiensis*][1]

Amendment

1 Substituted by Council Directive 2006/105/EC of 20 November 2006 adapting Directives 79/409/EEC, 92/43/EEC, 97/68/EC, 2001/80/EC and 2001/81/EC in the field of environment, by reason of the accession of Bulgaria and Romania, Article 1, Annex, Pt A, para 2(a).

[Amphibians

CAUDATA
Salamandridae
 Chioglossa lusitanica
 Mertensiella luschani (Salamandra luschani)
 * *Salamandra aurorae (Salamandra atra aurorae)*
 Salamandrina terdigitata
 Triturus carnifex (Triturus cristatus carnifex)
 Triturus cristatus (Triturus cristatus cristatus)
 Triturus dobrogicus (Triturus cristatus dobrogicus)
 Triturus karelinii (Triturus cristatus karelinii)
 Triturus montandoni
 Triturus vulgaris ampelensis
Proteidae
 Proteus anguinus
Plethodontidae
 Hydromantes (Speleomantes) ambrosii
 Hydromantes (Speleomantes) flavus
 Hydromantes (Speleomantes) genei
 Hydromantes (Speleomantes) imperialis
 Hydromantes (Speleomantes) strinatii
 Hydromantes (Speleomantes) supramontis

ANURA
Discoglossidae
 * *Alytes muletensis*
 Bombina bombina
 Bombina variegata
 Discoglossus galganoi (including Discoglossus jeanneae)
 Discoglossus montalentii
 Discoglossus sardus
Ranidae
 Rana latastei
Pelobatidae
 **Pelobates fuscus insubricus]*[1]

Amendment

1 Substituted by Council Directive 2006/105/EC of 20 November 2006 adapting Directives 79/409/EEC, 92/43/EEC, 97/68/EC, 2001/80/EC and 2001/81/EC in the field of environment, by reason of the accession of Bulgaria and Romania, Article 1, Annex, Pt A, para 2(a).

[Fish

PETROMYZONIFORMES
Petromyzonidae
Eudontomyzon spp. (o)
Lampetra fluviatilis (V) (except the Finnish and Swedish populations)
Lampetra planeri (o) (except the Estonian, Finnish and Swedish populations)
Lethenteron zanandreai (V)
Petromyzon marinus (o) (except the Swedish populations)

ACIPENSERIFORMES
Acipenseridae
**Acipenser naccarii*
**Acipenser sturio*

CLUPEIFORMES
Clupeidae
Alosa spp. (V)

SALMONIFORMES
Salmonidae
Hucho hucho (natural populations) (V)
Salmo macrostigma (o)
Salmo marmoratus (o)
Salmo salar (only in fresh water) (V) (except the Finnish populations)
Coregonidae
* *Coregonus oxyrhynchus* (anadromous populations in certain sectors of the North Sea)
Umbridae
Umbra krameri (o)

CYPRINIFORMES
Cyprinidae
Alburnus albidus (o) (*Alburnus vulturius*)
Anaecypris hispanica
Aspius aspius (V) (except the Finnish populations)
Barbus comiza (V)
Barbus meridionalis (V)
Barbus plebejus (V)
Chalcalburnus chalcoides (o)
Chondrostoma genei (o)
Chondrostoma lusitanicum (o)
Chondrostoma polylepis (o) (including *C. willkommi*)
Chondrostoma soetta (o)
Chondrostoma toxostoma (o)
Gobio albipinnatus (o)
Gobio kessleri (o)
Gobio uranoscopus (o)
Iberocypris palaciosi (o)
* *Ladigesocypris ghigii* (o)
Leuciscus lucumonis (o)
Leuciscus souffia (o)
Pelecus cultratus (V)
Phoxinellus spp. (o)
* *Phoxinus percnurus*
Rhodeus sericeus amarus (o)
Rutilus pigus (V)
Rutilus rubilio (o)
Rutilus arcasii (o)

Rutilus macrolepidotus (o)
Rutilus lemmingii (o)
Rutilus frisii meidingeri (V)
Rutilus alburnoides (o)
Scardinius graecus (o)

Cobitidae
Cobitis elongata (o)
Cobitis taenia (o) (except the Finnish populations)
Cobitis trichonica (o)
Misgurnus fossilis (o)
Sabanejewia aurata (o)
Sabanejewia larvata (o) (*Cobitis larvata* and *Cobitis conspersa*)

SILURIFORMES
Siluridae
Silurus aristotelis (V)

ATHERINIFORMES
Cyprinodontidae
Aphanius iberus (o)
Aphanius fasciatus (o)
* *Valencia hispanica*
* *Valencia letourneuxi (Valencia hispanica)*

PERCIFORMES
Percidae
Gymnocephalus baloni
Gymnocephalus schraetzer (V)
* *Romanichthys valsanicola*
Zingel spp. ((o) except *Zingel asper* and *Zingel zingel* (V))

Gobiidae
Knipowitschia (Padogobius) panizzae (o)
Padogobius nigricans (o)
Pomatoschistus canestrini (o)

SCORPAENIFORMES
Cottidae
Cottus gobio (o) (except the Finnish populations)
Cottus petiti (o)][1]

Amendment

1 Substituted by Council Directive 2006/105/EC of 20 November 2006 adapting Directives 79/409/EEC, 92/43/EEC, 97/68/EC, 2001/80/EC and 2001/81/EC in the field of environment, by reason of the accession of Bulgaria and Romania, Article 1, Annex, Pt A, para 2(a).

[Invertebrates][1]

[Arthropods

CRUSTACEA
Decapoda
Austropotamobius pallipes (V)
Austropotamobius torrentium (V)

Isopoda
* *Armadillidium ghardalamensis*

INSECTA
Coleoptera
Agathidium pulchellum (o)
Bolbelasmus unicornis

Boros schneideri (o)
Buprestis splendens
Carabus hampei
Carabus hungaricus
* *Carabus menetriesi pacholei*
* *Carabus olympiae*
Carabus variolosus
Carabus zawadszkii
Cerambyx cerdo
Corticaria planula (o)
Cucujus cinnaberinus
Dorcadion fulvum cervae
Duvalius gebhardti
Duvalius hungaricus
Dytiscus latissimus
Graphoderus bilineatus
Leptodirus hochenwarti
Limoniscus violaceus (o)
Lucanus cervus (o)
Macroplea pubipennis (o)
Mesosa myops (o)
Morimus funereus (o)
* *Osmoderma eremita*
Oxyporus mannerheimii (o)
Pilemia tigrina
* *Phryganophilus ruficollis*
Probaticus subrugosus
Propomacrus cypriacus
* *Pseudogaurotina excellens*
Pseudoseriscius cameroni
Pytho kolwensis
Rhysodes sulcatus (o)
* *Rosalia alpina*
Stephanopachys linearis (o)
Stephanopachys substriatus (o)
Xyletinus tremulicola (o)

Hemiptera

Aradus angularis (o)

Lepidoptera

Agriades glandon aquilo (o)
Arytrura musculus
**Callimorpha (Euplagia, Panaxia) quadripunctaria* (o)
Catopta thrips
Chondrosoma fiduciarium
Clossiana improba (o)
Coenonympha oedippus
Colias myrmidone
Cucullia mixta
Dioszeghyana schmidtii
Erannis ankeraria
Erebia calcaria
Erebia christi
Erebia medusa polaris (o)
Eriogaster catax
Euphydryas (Eurodryas, Hypodryas) aurinia (o)

Glyphipterix loricatella
Gortyna borelii lunata
Graellsia isabellae (V)
Hesperia comma catena (o)
Hypodryas maturna
Leptidea morsei
Lignyoptera fumidaria
Lycaena dispar
Lycaena helle
Maculinea nausithous
Maculinea teleius
Melanargia arge
* *Nymphalis vaualbum*
Papilio hospiton
Phyllometra culminaria
Plebicula golgus
Polymixis rufocincta isolata
Polyommatus eroides
Pseudophilotes bavius
Xestia borealis (o)
Xestia brunneopicta (o)
* *Xylomoia strix*

Mantodea
Apteromantis aptera

Odonata
Coenagrion hylas (o)
Coenagrion mercuriale (o)
Coenagrion ornatum (o)
Cordulegaster heros
Cordulegaster trinacriae
Gomphus graslinii
Leucorrhinia pectoralis
Lindenia tetraphylla
Macromia splendens
Ophiogomphus cecilia
Oxygastra curtisii

Orthoptera
Baetica ustulata
Brachytrupes megacephalus
Isophya costata
Isophya harzi
Isophya stysi
Myrmecophilus baronii
Odontopodisma rubripes
Paracaloptenus caloptenoides
Pholidoptera transsylvanica
Stenobothrus (Stenobothrodes) eurasius

ARACHNIDA
Pseudoscorpiones
Anthrenochernes stellae (o)][1]

Amendment

1 Substituted by Council Directive 2006/105/EC of 20 November 2006 adapting Directives 79/409/EEC, 92/43/EEC, 97/68/EC, 2001/80/EC and 2001/81/EC in the field of environment, by reason of the accession of Bulgaria and Romania, Article 1, Annex, Pt A, para 2(a).

[Molluscs

GASTROPODA

Anisus vorticulus
Caseolus calculus
Caseolus commixta
Caseolus sphaerula
Chilostoma banaticum
Discula leacockiana
Discula tabellata
Discus guerinianus
Elona quimperiana
Geomalacus maculosus
Geomitra moniziana
Gibbula nivosa
* *Helicopsis striata austriaca* (o)
Hygromia kovacsi
Idiomela (Helix) subplicata
Lampedusa imitatrix
* *Lampedusa melitensis*
Leiostyla abbreviata
Leiostyla cassida
Leiostyla corneocostata
Leiostyla gibba
Leiostyla lamellosa
* *Paladilhia hungarica*
Sadleriana pannonica
Theodoxus transversalis
Vertigo angustior (o)
Vertigo genesii (o)
Vertigo geyeri (o)
Vertigo moulinsiana (o)

BIVALVIA

Unionoida

Margaritifera durrovensis (Margaritifera margaritifera) (V)
Margaritifera margaritifera (V)
Unio crassus

Dreissenidae

Congeria kusceri][1]

Amendment

1 Substituted by Council Directive 2006/105/EC of 20 November 2006 adapting Directives 79/409/EEC, 92/43/EEC, 97/68/EC, 2001/80/EC and 2001/81/EC in the field of environment, by reason of the accession of Bulgaria and Romania, Article 1, Annex, Pt A, para 2(a).

[(B) PLANTS][1]

[Pteridophyta

ASPLENIACEAE

Asplenium jahandiezii (Litard.) Rouy
Asplenium adulterinum Milde

BLECHNACEAE

Woodwardia radicans (L.) Sm.

DICKSONIACEAE

Culcita macrocarpa C. Presl

DRYOPTERIDACEAE

Diplazium sibiricum (Turcz. ex Kunze) Kurata
* *Dryopteris corleyi* Fraser-Jenk.
Dryopteris fragans (L.) Schott

HYMENOPHYLLACEAE

Trichomanes speciosum Willd.

ISOETACEAE

Isoetes boryana Durieu
Isoetes malinverniana Ces. & De Not.

MARSILEACEAE

Marsilea batardae Launert
Marsilea quadrifolia L.
Marsilea strigosa Willd.

OPHIOGLOSSACEAE

Botrychium simplex Hitchc.
Ophioglossum polyphyllum A. Braun][1]

Amendment

1 Substituted by Council Directive 2006/105/EC of 20 November 2006 adapting Directives 79/409/EEC, 92/43/EEC, 97/68/EC, 2001/80/EC and 2001/81/EC in the field of environment, by reason of the accession of Bulgaria and Romania, Article 1, Annex, Pt A, para 2(a).

[Gymnospermae

PINACEAE

* *Abies nebrodensis* (Lojac.) Mattei][1]

Amendment

1 Substituted by Council Directive 2006/105/EC of 20 November 2006 adapting Directives 79/409/EEC, 92/43/EEC, 97/68/EC, 2001/80/EC and 2001/81/EC in the field of environment, by reason of the accession of Bulgaria and Romania, Article 1, Annex, Pt A, para 2(a).

[Angiospermae

ALISMATACEAE

* *Alisma wahlenbergii* (Holmberg) Juz.
Caldesia parnassifolia (L.) Parl.
Luronium natans (L.) Raf.

AMARYLLIDACEAE

Leucojum nicaeense Ard.
Narcissus asturiensis (Jordan) Pugsley
Narcissus calcicola Mendonça
Narcissus cyclamineus DC.
Narcissus fernandesii G. Pedro
Narcissus humilis (Cav.) Traub
* *Narcissus nevadensis* Pugsley
Narcissus pseudonarcissus L.subsp. *nobilis* (Haw.) A. Fernandes
Narcissus scaberulus Henriq.
Narcissus triandrus L. subsp. *capax* (Salisb.) D. A. Webb.
Narcissus viridiflorus Schousboe

ASCLEPIADACEAE

Vincetoxicum pannonicum (Borhidi) Holub

BORAGINACEAE

* *Anchusa crispa* Viv.
Echium russicum J.F.Gemlin

* *Lithodora nitida* (H. Ern) R. Fernandes
Myosotis lusitanica Schuster
Myosotis rehsteineri Wartm.
Myosotis retusifolia R. Afonso
Omphalodes kuzinskyanae Willk.
* *Omphalodes littoralis* Lehm.
* *Onosma tornensis* Javorka
Solenanthus albanicus (Degen & al.) Degen & Baldacci
* *Symphytum cycladense* Pawl.

CAMPANULACEAE
Adenophora lilifolia (L.) Ledeb.
Asyneuma giganteum (Boiss.) Bornm.
* *Campanula bohemica* Hruby
* *Campanula gelida* Kovanda
Campanula romanica Săvul.
* *Campanula sabatia* De Not.
* *Campanula serrata* (Kit.) Hendrych
Campanula zoysii Wulfen
Jasione crispa (Pourret) Samp. subsp. *serpentinica* Pinto da Silva
Jasione lusitanica A. DC.

CARYOPHYLLACEAE
Arenaria ciliata L. subsp. *pseudofrigida* Ostenf. & O.C. Dahl
Arenaria humifusa Wahlenberg
* *Arenaria nevadensis* Boiss. & Reuter
Arenaria provincialis Chater & Halliday
* *Cerastium alsinifolium* Tausch *Cerastium dinaricum* G. Beck & Szysz.
Dianthus arenarius L. subsp. *arenarius*
* *Dianthus arenarius* subsp. *bohemicus* (Novak) O.Schwarz
Dianthus cintranus Boiss. & Reuter subsp. *cintranus* Boiss. & Reuter
* *Dianthus diutinus* Kit.
* *Dianthus lumnitzeri* Wiesb.
Dianthus marizii (Samp.) Samp.
* *Dianthus moravicus* Kovanda
* *Dianthus nitidus* Waldst. et Kit.
Dianthus plumarius subsp. *regis-stephani* (Rapcs.) Baksay
Dianthus rupicola Biv.
* *Gypsophila papillosa* P. Porta
Herniaria algarvica Chaudhri
* *Herniaria latifolia* Lapeyr. subsp. *litardierei* Gamis
Herniaria lusitanica (Chaudhri) subsp. *berlengiana* Chaudhri
Herniaria maritima Link
* *Minuartia smejkalii* Dvorakova
Moehringia jankae Griseb. ex Janka
Moehringia lateriflora (L.) Fenzl.
Moehringia tommasinii Marches.
Moehringia villosa (Wulfen) Fenzl
Petrocoptis grandiflora Rothm.
Petrocoptis montsicciana O. Bolos & Rivas Mart.
Petrocoptis pseudoviscosa Fernández Casas
Silene furcata Rafin. subsp. *angustiflora* (Rupr.) Walters
* *Silene hicesiae* Brullo & Signorello
Silene hifacensis Rouy ex Willk.
* *Silene holzmanii* Heldr. ex Boiss.
Silene longicilia (Brot.) Otth.

Silene mariana Pau
* *Silene orphanidis* Boiss.
* *Silene rothmaleri* Pinto da Silva
* *Silene velutina* Pourret ex Loisel.

CHENOPODIACEAE
* *Bassia (Kochia) saxicola* (Guss.) A. J. Scott
* *Cremnophyton lanfrancoi* Brullo et Pavone
* *Salicornia veneta* Pignatti & Lausi

CISTACEAE
Cistus palhinhae Ingram
Halimium verticillatum (Brot.) Sennen
Helianthemum alypoides Losa & Rivas Goday
Helianthemum caput-felis Boiss.
* *Tuberaria major* (Willk.) Pinto da Silva & Rozeira

COMPOSITAE
* *Anthemis glaberrima* (Rech. f.) Greuter
Artemisia campestris L. subsp. *bottnica* A.N. Lundström ex Kindb.
* *Artemisia granatensis* Boiss.
* *Artemisia laciniata* Willd.
Artemisia oelandica (Besser) Komaror
* *Artemisia pancicii* (Janka) Ronn.
* *Aster pyrenaeus* Desf. ex DC
* *Aster sorrentinii* (Tod) Lojac.
Carlina onopordifolia Besser
* *Carduus myriacanthus* Salzm. ex DC.
* *Centaurea alba* L. subsp. *heldreichii* (Halacsy) Dostal
* *Centaurea alba* L. subsp. *princeps* (Boiss. & Heldr.) Gugler
* *Centaurea akamantis* T. Georgiadis & G. Chatzikyriakou
* *Centaurea attica* Nyman subsp. *megarensis* (Halacsy & Hayek) Dostal
* *Centaurea balearica* J. D. Rodriguez
* *Centaurea borjae* Valdes-Berm. & Rivas Goday
* *Centaurea citricolor* Font Quer
Centaurea corymbosa Pourret
Centaurea gadorensis G. Blanca
* *Centaurea horrida* Badaro
Centaurea immanuelis-loewii Degen
Centaurea jankae Brandza
* *Centaurea kalambakensis* Freyn & Sint.
Centaurea kartschiana Scop.
* *Centaurea lactiflora* Halacsy
Centaurea micrantha Hoffmanns. & Link subsp. *herminii* (Rouy) Dostál
* *Centaurea niederi* Heldr.
* *Centaurea peucedanifolia* Boiss. & Orph.
* *Centaurea pinnata* Pau
Centaurea pontica Prodan & E. I. Nyárády
Centaurea pulvinata (G. Blanca) G. Blanca
Centaurea rothmalerana (Arènes) Dostál
Centaurea vicentina Mariz
Cirsium brachycephalum Juratzka
* *Crepis crocifolia* Boiss. & Heldr.
Crepis granatensis (Willk.) B. Blanca & M. Cueto
Crepis pusilla (Sommier) Merxmüller
Crepis tectorum L. subsp. *nigrescens*
Erigeron frigidus Boiss. ex DC.

* *Helichrysum melitense* (Pignatti) Brullo et al
Hymenostemma pseudanthemis (Kunze) Willd.
Hyoseris frutescens Brullo et Pavone
* *Jurinea cyanoides* (L.) Reichenb.
* *Jurinea fontqueri* Cuatrec.
* *Lamyropsis microcephala* (Moris) Dittrich & Greuter
Leontodon microcephalus (Boiss. ex DC.) Boiss.
Leontodon boryi Boiss.
* *Leontodon siculus* (Guss.) Finch & Sell
Leuzea longifolia Hoffmanns. & Link
Ligularia sibirica (L.) Cass.
* *Palaeocyanus crassifolius* (Bertoloni) Dostal
Santolina impressa Hoffmanns. & Link
Santolina semidentata Hoffmanns. & Link
Saussurea alpina subsp. *esthonica* (Baer ex Rupr) Kupffer
* *Senecio elodes* Boiss. ex DC.
Senecio jacobea L. subsp. *gotlandicus* (Neuman) Sterner
Senecio nevadensis Boiss. & Reuter
* *Serratula lycopifolia* (Vill.) A.Kern
Tephroseris longifolia (Jacq.) Griseb et Schenk subsp. *moravica*

CONVOLVULACEAE
* *Convolvulus argyrothamnus* Greuter
* *Convolvulus fernandesii* Pinto da Silva & Teles

CRUCIFERAE
Alyssum pyrenaicum Lapeyr.
* *Arabis kennedyae* Meikle
Arabis sadina (Samp.) P. Cout.
Arabis scopoliana Boiss
* *Biscutella neustriaca* Bonnet
Biscutella vincentina (Samp.) Rothm.
Boleum asperum (Pers.) Desvaux
Brassica glabrescens Poldini
Brassica hilarionis Post
Brassica insularis Moris
* *Brassica macrocarpa* Guss.
Braya linearis Rouy
* *Cochlearia polonica* E. Fröhlich
* *Cochlearia tatrae* Borbas
* *Coincya rupestris* Rouy
* *Coronopus navasii* Pau
Crambe tataria Sebeok
Diplotaxis ibicensis (Pau) Gómez-Campo
* *Diplotaxis siettiana* Maire
Diplotaxis vicentina (P. Cout.) Rothm.
Draba cacuminum Elis Ekman
Draba cinerea Adams
Draba dorneri Heuffel.
Erucastrum palustre (Pirona) Vis.
* *Erysimum pieninicum* (Zapal.) Pawl.
* *Iberis arbuscula* Runemark
Iberis procumbens Lange subsp. *microcarpa* Franco & Pinto da Silva
* *Jonopsidium acaule* (Desf.) Reichenb.
Jonopsidium savianum (Caruel) Ball ex Arcang.

Rhynchosinapis erucastrum (L.) Dandy ex Clapham subsp. *cintrana* (Coutinho) Franco & P. Silva (*Coincya cintrana* (P. Cout.) Pinto da Silva)
Sisymbrium cavanillesianum Valdés & Castroviejo
Sisymbrium supinum L.
Thlaspi jankae A.Kern.

CYPERACEAE
Carex holostoma Drejer
* *Carex panormitana* Guss.
Eleocharis carniolica Koch

DIOSCOREACEAE
* *Borderea chouardii* (Gaussen) Heslot

DROSERACEAE
Aldrovanda vesiculosa L.

ELATINACEAE
Elatine gussonei (Sommier) Brullo et al

ERICACEAE
Rhododendron luteum Sweet

EUPHORBIACEAE
* *Euphorbia margalidiana* Kuhbier & Lewejohann
Euphorbia transtagana Boiss.

GENTIANACEAE
* *Centaurium rigualii* Esteve
* *Centaurium somedanum* Lainz
Gentiana ligustica R. de Vilm. & Chopinet
Gentianella anglica (Pugsley) E. F. Warburg
* *Gentianella bohemica* Skalicky

GERANIACEAE
* *Erodium astragaloides* Boiss. & Reuter
Erodium paularense Fernández-González & Izco
* *Erodium rupicola* Boiss.

GLOBULARIACEAE
* *Globularia stygia* Orph. ex Boiss.

GRAMINEAE
Arctagrostis latifolia (R. Br.) Griseb.
Arctophila fulva (Trin.) N. J. Anderson
Avenula hackelii (Henriq.) Holub
Bromus grossus Desf. ex DC.
Calamagrostis chalybaea (Laest.) Fries
Cinna latifolia (Trev.) Griseb.
Coleanthus subtilis (Tratt.) Seidl
Festuca brigantina (Markgr.-Dannenb.) Markgr.-Dannenb.
Festuca duriotagana Franco & R. Afonso
Festuca elegans Boiss.
Festuca henriquesii Hack.
Festuca summilusitana Franco & R. Afonso
Gaudinia hispanica Stace & Tutin
Holcus setiglumis Boiss. & Reuter subsp. *duriensis* Pinto da Silva
Micropyropsis tuberosa Romero — Zarco & Cabezudo
Poa granitica Br.-Bl. subsp. *disparilis* (E. I. Nyárády) E. I. Nyárády
* *Poa riphaea* (Ascher et Graebner) Fritsch

Pseudarrhenatherum pallens (Link) J. Holub
Puccinellia phryganodes (Trin.) Scribner + Merr.
Puccinellia pungens (Pau) Paunero
* *Stipa austroitalica* Martinovsky
* *Stipa bavarica* Martinovsky & H. Scholz
Stipa danubialis Dihoru & Roman
* *Stipa styriaca* Martinovsky
* *Stipa veneta* Moraldo
* *Stipa zalesskii* Wilensky
Trisetum subalpestre (Hartman) Neuman

GROSSULARIACEAE
* *Ribes sardoum* Martelli

HIPPURIDACEAE
Hippuris tetraphylla L. Fil.

HYPERICACEAE
* *Hypericum aciferum* (Greuter) N. K. B. Robson

IRIDACEAE
Crocus cyprius Boiss. et Kotschy
Crocus hartmannianus Holmboe
Gladiolus palustris Gaud.
Iris aphylla L. subsp. *hungarica* Hegi
Iris humilis Georgi subsp. *arenaria* (Waldst. et Kit.) A. et D.Löve

JUNCACEAE
Juncus valvatus Link
Luzula arctica Blytt

LABIATAE
Dracocephalum austriacum L.
* *Micromeria taygetea* P. H. Davis
Nepeta dirphya (Boiss.) Heldr. ex Halacsy
* *Nepeta sphaciotica* P. H. Davis
Origanum dictamnus L.
Phlomis brevibracteata Turril
Phlomis cypria Post
Salvia veneris Hedge
Sideritis cypria Post
Sideritis incana subsp. *glauca* (Cav.) Malagarriga
Sideritis javalambrensis Pau
Sideritis serrata Cav. ex Lag.
Teucrium lepicephalum Pau
Teucrium turredanum Losa & Rivas Goday
* *Thymus camphoratus* Hoffmanns. & Link
Thymus carnosus Boiss.
* *Thymus lotocephalus* G. López & R. Morales (*Thymus cephalotos* L.)

LEGUMINOSAE
Anthyllis hystrix Cardona, Contandr. & E. Sierra
* *Astragalus algarbiensis* Coss. ex Bunge
* *Astragalus aquilanus* Anzalone
Astragalus centralpinus Braun-Blanquet
* *Astragalus macrocarpus* DC. subsp. lefkarensis
* *Astragalus maritimus* Moris
Astragalus peterfii Jáv.
Astragalus tremolsianus Pau

* *Astragalus verrucosus* Moris
* *Cytisus aeolicus* Guss. ex Lindl.
Genista dorycnifolia Font Quer
Genista holopetala (Fleischm. ex Koch) Baldacci
Melilotus segetalis (Brot.) Ser. subsp. *fallax* Franco
* *Ononis hackelii* Lange
Trifolium saxatile All.
* *Vicia bifoliolata* J.D. Rodríguez

LENTIBULARIACEAE
* *Pinguicula crystallina* Sm.
Pinguicula nevadensis (Lindb.) Casper

LILIACEAE
Allium grosii Font Quer
* *Androcymbium rechingeri* Greuter
* *Asphodelus bento-rainhae* P. Silva
* *Chionodoxa lochiae* Meikle in Kew Bull.
Colchicum arenarium Waldst. et Kit.
Hyacinthoides vicentina (Hoffmans. & Link) Rothm.
* *Muscari gussonei* (Parl.) Tod.
Scilla litardierei Breist.
* *Scilla morrisii* Meikle
Tulipa cypria Stapf
Tulipa hungarica Borbas

LINACEAE
* *Linum dolomiticum* Borbas
* *Linum muelleri* Moris (*Linum maritimum muelleri*)

LYTHRACEAE
* *Lythrum flexuosum* Lag.

MALVACEAE
Kosteletzkya pentacarpos (L.) Ledeb.

NAJADACEAE
Najas flexilis (Willd.) Rostk. & W. L. Schmidt
Najas tenuissima (A. Braun) Magnus

OLEACEAE
Syringa josikaea Jacq. Fil. ex Reichenb.

ORCHIDACEAE
Anacamptis urvilleana Sommier et Caruana Gatto
Calypso bulbosa L.
* *Cephalanthera cucullata* Boiss. & Heldr.
Cypripedium calceolus L.
Dactylorhiza kalopissii E.Nelson
Gymnigritella runei Teppner & Klein
Himantoglossum adriaticum Baumann
Himantoglossum caprinum (Bieb.) V.Koch
Liparis loeselii (L.) Rich.
* *Ophrys kotschyi* H.Fleischm. et Soo
* *Ophrys lunulata* Parl.
Ophrys melitensis (Salkowski) J et P Devillers-Terschuren
Platanthera obtusata (Pursh) subsp. *oligantha* (Turez.) Hulten

OROBANCHACEAE
Orobanche densiflora Salzm. ex Reut.

PAEONIACEAE

Paeonia cambessedesii (Willk.) Willk.
Paeonia clusii F. C. Stern subsp. *rhodia* (Stearn) Tzanoudakis
Paeonia officinalis L. subsp. *banatica* (Rachel) Soo
Paeonia parnassica Tzanoudakis

PALMAE

Phoenix theophrasti Greuter

PAPAVERACEAE

Corydalis gotlandica Lidén
Papaver laestadianum (Nordh.) Nordh.
Papaver radicatum Rottb. subsp. *hyperboreum* Nordh.

PLANTAGINACEAE

Plantago algarbiensis Sampaio (*Plantago bracteosa* (Willk.) G. Sampaio)
Plantago almogravensis Franco

PLUMBAGINACEAE

Armeria berlengensis Daveau
* *Armeria helodes* Martini & Pold
Armeria neglecta Girard
Armeria pseudarmeria (Murray) Mansfeld
* *Armeria rouyana* Daveau
Armeria soleirolii (Duby) Godron
Armeria velutina Welw. ex Boiss. & Reuter
Limonium dodartii (Girard) O. Kuntze subsp. *lusitanicum* (Daveau) Franco
* *Limonium insulare* (Beg. & Landi) Arrig. & Diana
Limonium lanceolatum (Hoffmans. & Link) Franco
Limonium multiflorum Erben
* *Limonium pseudolaetum* Arrig. & Diana
* *Limonium strictissimum* (Salzmann) Arrig.

POLYGONACEAE

Persicaria foliosa (H. Lindb.) Kitag.
Polygonum praelongum Coode & Cullen
Rumex rupestris Le Gall

PRIMULACEAE

Androsace mathildae Levier
Androsace pyrenaica Lam.
* *Cyclamen fatrense* Halda et Sojak
* *Primula apennina* Widmer
Primula carniolica Jacq.
Primula nutans Georgi
Primula palinuri Petagna
Primula scandinavica Bruun
Soldanella villosa Darracq.

RANUNCULACEAE

* *Aconitum corsicum* Gayer (*Aconitum napellus* subsp. *corsicum*)
Aconitum firmum (Reichenb.) Neilr subsp. *moravicum* Skalicky
Adonis distorta Ten.
Aquilegia bertolonii Schott
Aquilegia kitaibelii Schott
* *Aquilegia pyrenaica* D.C. subsp. *cazorlensis* (Heywood) Galiano
* *Consolida samia* P.H. Davis
* *Delphinium caseyi* B.L.Burtt
Pulsatilla grandis Wenderoth *Pulsatilla patens* (L.) Miller

* *Pulsatilla pratensis* (L.) Miller subsp. *hungarica* Soo
* *Pulsatilla slavica* G.Reuss.
* *Pulsatilla subslavica* Futak ex Goliasova
Pulsatilla vulgaris Hill. subsp. *gotlandica* (Johanss.) Zaemelis & Paegle
Ranunculus kykkoensis Meikle
Ranunculus lapponicus L.
* *Ranunculus weyleri* Mares

RESEDACEAE
* *Reseda decursiva* Forssk.

ROSACEAE
Agrimonia pilosa Ledebour
Potentilla delphinensis Gren. & Godron
Potentilla emilii-popii Nyárády
* *Pyrus magyarica* Terpo
Sorbus teodorii Liljefors

RUBIACEAE
Galium cracoviense Ehrend.
* *Galium litorale* Guss.
Galium moldavicum (Dobrescu) Franco
* *Galium sudeticum* Tausch
* *Galium viridiflorum* Boiss. & Reuter

SALICACEAE
Salix salvifolia Brot. subsp. *australis* Franco

SANTALACEAE
Thesium ebracteatum Hayne

SAXIFRAGACEAE
Saxifraga berica (Beguinot) D.A. Webb
Saxifraga florulenta Moretti
Saxifraga hirculus L.
Saxifraga osloënsis Knaben
Saxifraga tombeanensis Boiss. ex Engl.

SCROPHULARIACEAE
Antirrhinum charidemi Lange
Chaenorrhinum serpyllifolium (Lange) Lange subsp. *lusitanicum* R. Fernandes
* *Euphrasia genargentea* (Feoli) Diana
Euphrasia marchesettii Wettst. ex Marches.
Linaria algarviana Chav.
Linaria coutinhoi Valdés
Linaria loeselii Schweigger
* *Linaria ficalhoana* Rouy
Linaria flava (Poiret) Desf.
* *Linaria hellenica* Turrill
Linaria pseudolaxiflora Lojacono
* *Linaria ricardoi* Cout.
Linaria tonzigii Lona
* *Linaria tursica* B. Valdés & Cabezudo
Odontites granatensis Boiss.
* *Pedicularis sudetica* Willd.
Rhinanthus oesilensis (Ronniger & Saarsoo) Vassilcz
Tozzia carpathica Wol.
Verbascum litigiosum Samp.
Veronica micrantha Hoffmanns. & Link
* *Veronica oetaea* L.-A. Gustavsson

SOLANACEAE
* *Atropa baetica* Willk.

THYMELAEACEAE
* *Daphne arbuscula* Celak
Daphne petraea Leybold
* *Daphne rodriguezii* Texidor

ULMACEAE
Zelkova abelicea (Lam.) Boiss.

UMBELLIFERAE
* *Angelica heterocarpa* Lloyd
Angelica palustris (Besser) Hoffm.
* *Apium bermejoi* Llorens
Apium repens (Jacq.) Lag.
Athamanta cortiana Ferrarini
* *Bupleurum capillare* Boiss. & Heldr.
* *Bupleurum kakiskalae* Greuter
Eryngium alpinum L.
* *Eryngium viviparum* Gay
* *Ferula sadleriana* Lebed.
Hladnikia pastinacifolia Reichenb.
* *Laserpitium longiradium* Boiss.
* *Naufraga balearica* Constans & Cannon
* *Oenanthe conioides* Lange
Petagnia saniculifolia Guss.
Rouya polygama (Desf.) Coincy
* *Seseli intricatum* Boiss.
Seseli leucospermum Waldst. et Kit
Thorella verticillatinundata (Thore) Briq.

VALERIANACEAE
Centranthus trinervis (Viv.) Beguinot

VIOLACEAE
Viola delphinantha Boiss.
* *Viola hispida* Lam.
Viola jaubertiana Mares & Vigineix
Viola rupestris F.W. Schmidt subsp. *relicta* Jalas][1]

Amendment

1 Substituted by Council Directive 2006/105/EC of 20 November 2006 adapting Directives 79/409/EEC, 92/43/EEC, 97/68/EC, 2001/80/EC and 2001/81/EC in the field of environment, by reason of the accession of Bulgaria and Romania, Article 1, Annex, Pt A, para 2(a).

[Lower plants]

[BRYOPHYTA
Bruchia vogesiaca Schwaegr. (o)
Bryhnia novae-angliae (Sull & Lesq.) Grout (o)
* *Bryoerythrophyllum campylocarpum* (C. Müll.) Crum. (*Bryoerythrophyllum machadoanum* (Sergio) M. O. Hill) (o)
Buxbaumia viridis (Moug.) Moug. & Nestl. (o)
Cephalozia macounii (Aust.) Aust. (o)
Cynodontium suecicum (H. Arn. & C. Jens.) I. Hag. (o)
Dichelyma capillaceum (Dicks.) Myr. (o)
Dicranum viride (Sull. & Lesq.) Lindb. (o)
Distichophyllum carinatum Dix. & Nich. (o)

Drepanocladus (Hamatocaulis) vernicosus (Mitt.) Warnst. (o)
Encalypta mutica (I. Hagen) (o)
Hamatocaulis lapponicus (Norrl.) Hedenäs (o)
Herzogiella turfacea (Lindb.) I. Wats. (o)
Hygrohypnum montanum (Lindb.) Broth. (o)
Jungermannia handelii (Schiffn.) Amak. (o)
Mannia triandra (Scop.) Grolle (o)
* *Marsupella profunda* Lindb. (o)
Meesia longiseta Hedw. (o)
Nothothylas orbicularis (Schwein.) Sull. (o)
Ochyraea tatrensis Vana (o)
Orthothecium lapponicum (Schimp.) C. Hartm. (o)
Orthotrichum rogeri Brid. (o)
Petalophyllum ralfsii (Wils.) Nees & Gott. (o)
Plagiomnium drummondii (Bruch & Schimp.) T. Kop. (o)
Riccia breidleri Jur. (o)
Riella helicophylla (Bory & Mont.) Mont. (o)
Scapania massolongi (K. Müll.) K. Müll. (o)
Sphagnum pylaisii Brid. (o)
Tayloria rudolphiana (Garov) B. & S. (o)
Tortella rigens (N. Alberts) (o)][1]

Amendment

1 Substituted by Council Directive 2006/105/EC of 20 November 2006 adapting Directives 79/409/EEC, 92/43/EEC, 97/68/EC, 2001/80/EC and 2001/81/EC in the field of environment, by reason of the accession of Bulgaria and Romania, Article 1, Annex, Pt A, para 2(a).

[Species for Macaronesia][1]

[Pteridophyta

HYMENOPHYLLACEAE
Hymenophyllum maderensis Gibby & Lovis

DRYOPTERIDACEAE
* *Polystichum drepanum* (Sw.) C. Presl.

ISOETACEAE
Isoetes azorica Durieu & Paiva ex Milde

MARSILEACEAE
* *Marsilea azorica* Launert & Paiva][1]

Amendment

1 Substituted by Council Directive 2006/105/EC of 20 November 2006 adapting Directives 79/409/EEC, 92/43/EEC, 97/68/EC, 2001/80/EC and 2001/81/EC in the field of environment, by reason of the accession of Bulgaria and Romania, Article 1, Annex, Pt A, para 2(a).

[Angiospermae

ASCLEPIADACEAE
Caralluma burchardii N. E. Brown
* *Ceropegia chrysantha* Svent.

BORAGINACEAE
Echium candicans L. fil.
* *Echium gentianoides* Webb & Coincy
Myosotis azorica H. C. Watson
Myosotis maritima Hochst. in Seub.

CAMPANULACEAE

* *Azorina vidalii* (H. C. Watson) Feer
Musschia aurea (L. f.) DC.
* *Musschia wollastonii* Lowe

CAPRIFOLIACEAE

* *Sambucus palmensis* Link

CARYOPHYLLACEAE

Spergularia azorica (Kindb.) Lebel

CELASTRACEAE

Maytenus umbellata (R. Br.) Mabb.

CHENOPODIACEAE

Beta patula Ait.

CISTACEAE

Cistus chinamadensis Banares & Romero
* *Helianthemum bystropogophyllum* Svent.

COMPOSITAE

Andryala crithmifolia Ait.
* *Argyranthemum lidii* Humphries
Argyranthemum thalassophylum (Svent.) Hump.
Argyranthemum winterii (Svent.) Humphries
* *Atractylis arbuscula* Svent. & Michaelis
Atractylis preauxiana Schultz.
Calendula maderensis DC.
Cheirolophus duranii (Burchard) Holub
Cheirolophus ghomerytus (Svent.) Holub
Cheirolophus junonianus (Svent.) Holub
Cheirolophus massonianus (Lowe) Hansen & Sund.
Cirsium latifolium Lowe
Helichrysum gossypinum Webb
Helichrysum monogynum Burtt & Sund.
Hypochoeris oligocephala (Svent. & Bramw.) Lack
* *Lactuca watsoniana* Trel.
* *Onorpordum nogalesii* Svent.
* *Onopordum carduelinum* Bolle
* *Pericallis hadrosoma* (Svent.) B. Nord.
Phagnalon benettii Lowe
Stemmacantha cynaroides (Chr. Son. in Buch) Ditt
Sventenia bupleuroides Font Quer
* *Tanacetum ptarmiciflorum* Webb & Berth

CONVOLVULACEAE

* *Convolvulus caput-medusae* Lowe
* *Convolvulus lopez-socasii* Svent.
* *Convolvulus massonii* A. Dietr.

CRASSULACEAE

Aeonium gomeraense Praeger
Aeonium saundersii Bolle
Aichryson dumosum (Lowe) Praeg.
Monanthes wildpretii Banares & Scholz
Sedum brissemoretii Raymond-Hamet

CRUCIFERAE

* *Crambe arborea* Webb ex Christ

Crambe laevigata DC. ex Christ
* *Crambe sventenii* R. Petters ex Bramwell & Sund.
* *Parolinia schizogynoides* Svent.
Sinapidendron rupestre (Ait.) Lowe

CYPERACEAE
Carex malato-belizii Raymond

DIPSACACEAE
Scabiosa nitens Roemer & J. A. Schultes

ERICACEAE
Erica scoparia L. subsp. *azorica* (Hochst.) D. A. Webb

EUPHORBIACEAE
* *Euphorbia handiensis* Burchard
Euphorbia lambii Svent.
Euphorbia stygiana H. C. Watson

GERANIACEAE
* *Geranium maderense* P. F. Yeo

GRAMINEAE
Deschampsia maderensis (Haeck. & Born.) Buschm.
Phalaris maderensis (Menezes) Menezes

GLOBULARIACEAE
* *Globularia ascanii* D. Bramwell & Kunkel
* *Globularia sarcophylla* Svent.

LABIATAE
* *Sideritis cystosiphon* Svent.
* *Sideritis discolor* (Webb ex de Noe) Bolle
Sideritis infernalis Bolle
Sideritis marmorea Bolle
Teucrium abutiloides L'Hér
Teucrium betonicum L'Hér

LEGUMINOSAE
* *Anagyris latifolia* Brouss. ex Willd.
Anthyllis lemanniana Lowe
* *Dorycnium spectabile* Webb & Berthel
* *Lotus azoricus* P. W. Ball
Lotus callis-viridis D. Bramwell & D. H. Davis
* *Lotus kunkelii* (E. Chueca) D. Bramwell & al.
* *Teline rosmarinifolia* Webb & Berthel.
* *Teline salsoloides* Arco & Acebes.
Vicia dennesiana H. C. Watson

LILIACEAE
* *Androcymbium psammophilum* Svent.
Scilla maderensis Menezes
Semele maderensis Costa

LORANTHACEAE
Arceuthobium azoricum Wiens & Hawksw

MYRICACEAE
* *Myrica rivas-martinezii* Santos.

OLEACEAE
Jasminum azoricum L.
Picconia azorica (Tutin) Knobl.

ORCHIDACEAE

Goodyera macrophylla Lowe

PITTOSPORACEAE

* *Pittosporum coriaceum* Dryand. ex Ait.

PLANTAGINACEAE

Plantago malato-belizii Lawalree

PLUMBAGINACEAE

* *Limonium arborescens* (Brouss.) Kuntze
Limonium dendroides Svent.
* *Limonium spectabile* (Svent.) Kunkel & Sunding
* *Limonium sventenii* Santos & Fernández Galván

POLYGONACEAE

Rumex azoricus Rech. fil.

RHAMNACEAE

Frangula azorica Tutin

ROSACEAE

* *Bencomia brachystachya* Svent.
Bencomia sphaerocarpa Svent.
* *Chamaemeles coriacea* Lindl.
Dendriopoterium pulidoi Svent.
Marcetella maderensis (Born.) Svent.
Prunus lusitanica L.subsp. *azorica* (Mouillef.) Franco
Sorbus maderensis (Lowe) Dode

SANTALACEAE

Kunkeliella subsucculenta Kammer

SCROPHULARIACEAE

* *Euphrasia azorica* H.C. Watson
Euphrasia grandiflora Hochst. in Seub.
* *Isoplexis chalcantha* Svent. & O'Shanahan
Isoplexis isabelliana (Webb & Berthel.) Masferrer
Odontites holliana (Lowe) Benth.
Sibthorpia peregrina L.

SOLANACEAE

* *Solanum lidii* Sunding

UMBELLIFERAE

Ammi trifoliatum (H. C. Watson) Trelease
Bupleurum handiense (Bolle) Kunkel
Chaerophyllum azoricum Trelease
Ferula latipinna Santos
Melanoselinum decipiens (Schrader & Wendl.) Hoffm.
Monizia edulis Lowe
Oenanthe divaricata (R. Br.) Mabb.
Sanicula azorica Guthnick ex Seub.

VIOLACEAE

Viola paradoxa Lowe][1]

Amendment

1 Substituted by Council Directive 2006/105/EC of 20 November 2006 adapting Directives 79/409/EEC, 92/43/EEC, 97/68/EC, 2001/80/EC and 2001/81/EC in the field of environment, by reason of the accession of Bulgaria and Romania, Article 1, Annex, Pt A, para 2(a).

[Lower plants][1]

[BRYOPHYTA

* *Echinodium spinosum* (Mitt.) Jur. (o)

* *Thamnobryum fernandesii* Sergio (o)][1]

Amendment

1 Substituted by Council Directive 2006/105/EC of 20 November 2006 adapting Directives 79/409/EEC, 92/43/EEC, 97/68/EC, 2001/80/EC and 2001/81/EC in the field of environment, by reason of the accession of Bulgaria and Romania, Article 1, Annex, Pt A, para 2(a).

ANNEX III
CRITERIA FOR SELECTING SITES ELIGIBLE FOR IDENTIFICATION AS SITES OF COMMUNITY IMPORTANCE AND DESIGNATION AS SPECIAL AREAS OF CONSERVATION

STAGE 1: ASSESSMENT AT NATIONAL LEVEL OF THE RELATIVE IMPORTANCE OF SITES FOR EACH NATURAL HABITAT TYPE IN ANNEX I AND EACH SPECIES IN ANNEX II (INCLUDING PRIORITY NATURAL HABITAT TYPES AND PRIORITY SPECIES)

A. *Site assessment criteria for a given natural habitat type in Annex I*

(a) Degree of representativity of the natural habitat type on the site.

(b) Area of the site covered by the natural habitat type in relation to the total area covered by that natural habitat type within national territory.

(c) Degree of conservation of the structure and functions of the natural habitat type concerned and restoration possibilities.

(d) Global assessment of the value of the site for conservation of the natural habitat type concerned.

B. *Site assessment criteria for a given species in Annex II*

(a) Size and density of the population of the species present on the site in relation to the populations present within national territory.

(b) Degree of conservation of the features of the habitat which are important for the species concerned and restoration possibilities.

(c) Degree of isolation of the population present on the site in relation to the natural range of the species.

(d) Global assessment of the value of the site for conservation of the species concerned.

C. On the basis of these criteria, Member States will classify the sites which they propose on the national list as sites eligible for identification as sites of Community importance according to their relative value for the conservation of each natural habitat type in Annex I or each species in Annex II.

D. That list will show the sites containing the priority natural habitat types and priority species selected by the Member States on the basis of the criteria in A and B above.

STAGE 2: ASSESSMENT OF THE COMMUNITY IMPORTANCE OF THE SITES INCLUDED ON THE NATIONAL LISTS

1. All the sites identified by the Member States in Stage 1 which contain priority natural habitat types and/or species will be considered as sites of Community importance.

2. The assessment of the Community importance of other sites on Member States' lists, i.e. their contribution to maintaining or re-establishing, at a favourable conservation status, a natural habitat in Annex I or a species in Annex II and/or to the coherence of Natura 2000 will take account of the following criteria:

(a) relative value of the site at national level;

(b) geographical situation of the site in relation to migration routes of species in Annex II and whether it belongs to a continuous ecosystem situated on both sides of one or more internal Community frontiers;

(c) total area of the site;

(d) number of natural habitat types in Annex I and species in Annex II present on the site;

(e) global ecological value of the site for the biogeographical regions concerned and/or for the whole of the territory referred to in Article 2, as regards both the characteristic or unique aspect of its features and the way they are combined.

[ANNEX IV
ANIMAL AND PLANT SPECIES OF COMMUNITY INTEREST IN NEED OF STRICT PROTECTION][1]

[The species listed in this Annex are indicated:

— by the name of species or subspecies, or

— by the body of species belonging to a higher taxon or to a designated part of that taxon.

The abbreviation "spp." after the name of a family or genus designates all the species belonging to that family or genus.][1]

Amendment

1 Substituted by Council Directive 2006/105/EC of 20 November 2006 adapting Directives 79/409/EEC, 92/43/EEC, 97/68/EC, 2001/80/EC and 2001/81/EC in the field of environment, by reason of the accession of Bulgaria and Romania, Article 1, Annex, Pt A, para 2(a).

[(A) ANIMALS

Vertebrates][1]

[Mammals

INSECTIVORA

Erinaceidae

Erinaceus algirus

Soricidae

Crocidura canariensis

Crocidura sicula

Talpidae

Galemys pyrenaicus

MICROCHIROPTERA

All species

MEGACHIROPTERA

Pteropodidae

Rousettus aegyptiacus

RODENTIA

Gliridae

All species except *Glis glis* and *Eliomys quercinus*

Sciuridae

Marmota marmota latirostris

Pteromys volans (*Sciuropterus russicus*)

Spermophilus citellus (*Citellus citellus*)

Spermophilus suslicus (*Citellus suslicus*)

Sciurus anomalus

Castoridae

Castor fiber (except the Estonian, Latvian, Lithuanian, Polish, Finnish and Swedish populations)

Cricetidae

Cricetus cricetus (except the Hungarian populations)

Mesocricetus newtoni

Microtidae

Microtus cabrerae

Microtus oeconomus arenicola

Microtus oeconomus mehelyi

Microtus tatricus

Zapodidae

Sicista betulina

Sicista subtilis

Hystricidae

Hystrix cristata

CARNIVORA

Canidae

Alopex lagopus

Canis lupus (except the Greek populations north of the 39th parallel; Estonian populations, Spanish populations north of the Duero; Bulgarian, Latvian, Lithuanian, Polish, Slovak populations and Finnish populations within the reindeer management area as defined in paragraph 2 of the Finnish Act No 848/90 of 14 September 1990 on reindeer management)

Ursidae

Ursus arctos

Mustelidae

Lutra lutra

Mustela eversmanii

Mustela lutreola

Vormela peregusna

Felidae

Felis silvestris

Lynx lynx (except the Estonian population)

Lynx pardinus

Phocidae

Monachus monachus

Phoca hispida saimensis

ARTIODACTYLA

Cervidae

Cervus elaphus corsicanus

Bovidae

Bison bonasus

Capra aegagrus (natural populations)

Capra pyrenaica pyrenaica

Ovis gmelini musimon (*Ovis ammon musimon*) (natural populations — Corsica and Sardinia)

Ovis orientalis ophion (*Ovis gmelini ophion*)

Rupicapra pyrenaica ornata (*Rupicapra rupicapra ornata*)

Rupicapra rupicapra balcanica

Rupicapra rupicapra tatrica

CETACEA

All species][1]

Amendment

1 Substituted by Council Directive 2006/105/EC of 20 November 2006 adapting Directives 79/409/EEC, 92/43/EEC, 97/68/EC, 2001/80/EC and 2001/81/EC in the field of environment, by reason of the accession of Bulgaria and Romania, Article 1, Annex, Pt A, para 2(a).

[Reptiles

TESTUDINATA

Testudinidae

Testudo graeca

Testudo hermanni

Testudo marginata

Cheloniidae

Caretta caretta

Chelonia mydas

Lepidochelys kempii

Eretmochelys imbricata

Dermochelyidae

Dermochelys coriacea

Emydidae

Emys orbicularis

Mauremys caspica

Mauremys leprosa

SAURIA

Lacertidae

Algyroides fitzingeri

Algyroides marchi

Algyroides moreoticus

Algyroides nigropunctatus

Gallotia atlantica

Gallotia galloti

Gallotia galloti insulanagae

Gallotia simonyi

Gallotia stehlini

Lacerta agilis

Lacerta bedriagae

Lacerta bonnali (*Lacerta monticola*)

Lacerta monticola

Lacerta danfordi

Lacerta dugesi

Lacerta graeca

Lacerta horvathi

Lacerta schreiberi

Lacerta trilineata

Lacerta viridis

Lacerta vivipara pannonica

Ophisops elegans

Podarcis erhardii

Podarcis filfolensis

Podarcis hispanica atrata

Podarcis lilfordi

Podarcis melisellensis

Podarcis milensis

Podarcis muralis

Podarcis peloponnesiaca

Podarcis pityusensis

Podarcis sicula

Podarcis taurica

Podarcis tiliguerta

Podarcis wagleriana

Scincidae
Ablepharus kitaibelii
Chalcides bedriagai
Chalcides ocellatus
Chalcides sexlineatus
Chalcides simonyi (*Chalcides occidentalis*)
Chalcides viridianus
Ophiomorus punctatissimus
Gekkonidae
Cyrtopodion kotschyi
Phyllodactylus europaeus
Tarentola angustimentalis
Tarentola boettgeri
Tarentola delalandii
Tarentola gomerensis
Agamidae
Stellio stellio
Chamaeleontidae
Chamaeleo chamaeleon
Anguidae
Ophisaurus apodus

OPHIDIA
Colubridae
Coluber caspius
Coluber cypriensis
Coluber hippocrepis
Coluber jugularis
Coluber laurenti
Coluber najadum
Coluber nummifer
Coluber viridiflavus
Coronella austriaca
Eirenis modesta
Elaphe longissima
Elaphe quatuorlineata
Elaphe situla
Natrix natrix cetti
Natrix natrix corsa
Natrix natrix cypriaca
Natrix tessellata
Telescopus falax
Viperidae
Vipera ammodytes
Macrovipera schweizeri (*Vipera lebetina schweizeri*)
Vipera seoanni (except Spanish populations)
Vipera ursinii
Vipera xanthina
Boidae
Eryx jaculus][1]

Amendment

1 Substituted by Council Directive 2006/105/EC of 20 November 2006 adapting Directives 79/409/EEC, 92/43/EEC, 97/68/EC, 2001/80/EC and 2001/81/EC in the field of environment, by reason of the accession of Bulgaria and Romania, Article 1, Annex, Pt A, para 2(a).

[Amphibians

CAUDATA

Salamandridae

Chioglossa lusitanica
Euproctus asper
Euproctus montanus
Euproctus platycephalus
Mertensiella luschani (*Salamandra luschani*)
Salamandra atra
Salamandra aurorae
Salamandra lanzai
Salamandrina terdigitata
Triturus carnifex (Triturus cristatus carnifex)
Triturus cristatus (Triturus cristatus cristatus)
Triturus italicus
Triturus karelinii (Triturus cristatus karelinii)
Triturus marmoratus
Triturus montandoni
Triturus vulgaris ampelensis

Proteidae

Proteus anguinus

Plethodontidae

Hydromantes (Speleomantes) ambrosii
Hydromantes (Speleomantes) flavus
Hydromantes (Speleomantes) genei
Hydromantes (Speleomantes) imperialis
Hydromantes (Speleomantes) strinatii (Hydromantes (Speleomantes) italicus)
Hydromantes (Speleomantes) supramontis

ANURA

Discoglossidae

Alytes cisternasii
Alytes muletensis
Alytes obstetricans
Bombina bombina
Bombina variegata
Discoglossus galganoi (including *Discoglossus jeanneae*)
Discoglossus montalentii
Discoglossus pictus
Discoglossus sardus

Ranidae

Rana arvalis
Rana dalmatina
Rana graeca
Rana iberica
Rana italica
Rana latastei
Rana lessonae

Pelobatidae

Pelobates cultripes
Pelobates fuscus
Pelobates syriacus

Bufonidae

Bufo calamita
Bufo viridis

Hylidae

Hyla arborea
Hyla meridionalis
Hyla sarda][1]

Amendment

1 Substituted by Council Directive 2006/105/EC of 20 November 2006 adapting Directives 79/409/EEC, 92/43/EEC, 97/68/EC, 2001/80/EC and 2001/81/EC in the field of environment, by reason of the accession of Bulgaria and Romania, Article 1, Annex, Pt A, para 2(a).

[Fish

ACIPENSERIFORMES
Acipenseridae

Acipenser naccarii
Acipenser sturio

SALMONIFORMES
Coregonidae

Coregonus oxyrhynchus (anadromous populations in certain sectors of the North Sea, except the Finnish populations)

CYPRINIFORMES
Cyprinidae

Anaecypris hispanica
Phoxinus percnurus

ATHERINIFORMES
Cyprinodontidae

Valencia hispanica

PERCIFORMES
Percidae

Gymnocephalus baloni
Romanichthys valsanicola
Zingel asper][1]

Amendment

1 Substituted by Council Directive 2006/105/EC of 20 November 2006 adapting Directives 79/409/EEC, 92/43/EEC, 97/68/EC, 2001/80/EC and 2001/81/EC in the field of environment, by reason of the accession of Bulgaria and Romania, Article 1, Annex, Pt A, para 2(a).

[Invertebrates][1]

[Arthropods

CRUSTACEA
Isopoda

Armadillidium ghardalamensis

INSECTA
Coleoptera

Bolbelasmus unicornis
Buprestis splendens
Carabus hampei
Carabus hungaricus
Carabus olympiae
Carabus variolosus
Carabus zawadszkii
Cerambyx cerdo
Cucujus cinnaberinus

Dorcadion fulvum cervae
Duvalius gebhardti
Duvalius hungaricus
Dytiscus latissimus
Graphoderus bilineatus
Leptodirus hochenwarti
Pilemia tigrina
Osmoderma eremita
Phryganophilus ruficollis
Probaticus subrugosus
Propomacrus cypriacus
Pseudogaurotina excellens
Pseudoseriscius cameroni
Pytho kolwensis
Rosalia alpina

Lepidoptera

Apatura metis
Arytrura musculus
Catopta thrips
Chondrosoma fiduciarium
Coenonympha hero
Coenonympha oedippus
Colias myrmidone
Cucullia mixta
Dioszeghyana schmidtii
Erannis ankeraria
Erebia calcaria
Erebia christi
Erebia sudetica
Eriogaster catax
Fabriciana elisa
Glyphipterix loricatella
Gortyna borelii lunata
Hypodryas maturna
Hyles hippophaes
Leptidea morsei
Lignyoptera fumidaria
Lopinga achine
Lycaena dispar
Lycaena helle
Maculinea arion
Maculinea nausithous
Maculinea teleius
Melanargia arge
Nymphalis vaualbum
Papilio alexanor
Papilio hospiton
Parnassius apollo
Parnassius mnemosyne
Phyllometra culminaria
Plebicula golgus
Polymixis rufocincta isolata
Polyommatus eroides
Proserpinus proserpina
Pseudophilotes bavius

Xylomoia strix
Zerynthia polyxena

Mantodea

Apteromantis aptera

Odonata

Aeshna viridis
Cordulegaster heros
Cordulegaster trinacriae
Gomphus graslinii
Leucorrhinia albifrons
Leucorrhinia caudalis
Leucorrhinia pectoralis
Lindenia tetraphylla
Macromia splendens
Ophiogomphus cecilia
Oxygastra curtisii
Stylurus flavipes
Sympecma braueri

Orthoptera

Baetica ustulata
Brachytrupes megacephalus
Isophya costata
Isophya harzi
Isophya stysi
Myrmecophilus baronii
Odontopodisma rubripes
Paracaloptenus caloptenoides
Pholidoptera transsylvanica
Saga pedo
Stenobothrus (Stenobothrodes) eurasius

ARACHNIDA

Araneae

Macrothele calpeiana][1]

Amendment

1 Substituted by Council Directive 2006/105/EC of 20 November 2006 adapting Directives 79/409/EEC, 92/43/EEC, 97/68/EC, 2001/80/EC and 2001/81/EC in the field of environment, by reason of the accession of Bulgaria and Romania, Article 1, Annex, Pt A, para 2(a).

[Molluscs

GASTROPODA

Anisus vorticulus
Caseolus calculus
Caseolus commixta
Caseolus sphaerula
Chilostoma banaticum
Discula leacockiana
Discula tabellata
Discula testudinalis
Discula turricula
Discus defloratus
Discus guerinianus
Elona quimperiana
Geomalacus maculosus
Geomitra moniziana

Gibbula nivosa
Hygromia kovacsi
Idiomela (Helix) subplicata
Lampedusa imitatrix
Lampedusa melitensis
Leiostyla abbreviata
Leiostyla cassida
Leiostyla corneocostata
Leiostyla gibba
Leiostyla lamellosa
Paladilhia hungarica
Patella ferruginea
Sadleriana pannonica
Theodoxus prevostianus
Theodoxus transversalis

BIVALVIA
Anisomyaria
Lithophaga lithophaga
Pinna nobilis
Unionoida
Margaritifera auricularia
Unio crassus
Dreissenidae
Congeria kusceri

ECHINODERMATA
Echinoidea
Centrostephanus longispinus][1]

Amendment

1 Substituted by Council Directive 2006/105/EC of 20 November 2006 adapting Directives 79/409/EEC, 92/43/EEC, 97/68/EC, 2001/80/EC and 2001/81/EC in the field of environment, by reason of the accession of Bulgaria and Romania, Article 1, Annex, Pt A, para 2(a).

[(B) PLANTS][1]

Annex IV (b) contains all the plant species listed in Annex II (b) plus those mentioned below][1]

Amendment

1 Substituted by Council Directive 2006/105/EC of 20 November 2006 adapting Directives 79/409/EEC, 92/43/EEC, 97/68/EC, 2001/80/EC and 2001/81/EC in the field of environment, by reason of the accession of Bulgaria and Romania, Article 1, Annex, Pt A, para 2(a).

[Pteridophyta

ASPLENIACEAE
Asplenium hemionitis L.][1]

Amendment

1 Substituted by Council Directive 2006/105/EC of 20 November 2006 adapting Directives 79/409/EEC, 92/43/EEC, 97/68/EC, 2001/80/EC and 2001/81/EC in the field of environment, by reason of the accession of Bulgaria and Romania, Article 1, Annex, Pt A, para 2(a).

[Angiospermae

AGAVACEAE
Dracaena draco (L.) L.

AMARYLLIDACEAE
Narcissus longispathus Pugsley
Narcissus triandrus L.

BERBERIDACEAE
Berberis maderensis Lowe

CAMPANULACEAE
Campanula morettiana Reichenb.
Physoplexis comosa (L.) Schur.

CARYOPHYLLACEAE
Moehringia fontqueri Pau

COMPOSITAE
Argyranthemum pinnatifidum (L.f.) Lowe subsp. *succulentum* (Lowe) C. J. Humphries
Helichrysum sibthorpii Rouy
Picris willkommii (Schultz Bip.) Nyman
Santolina elegans Boiss. ex DC.
Senecio caespitosus Brot.
Senecio lagascanus DC. subsp. *lusitanicus* (P. Cout.) Pinto da Silva
Wagenitzia lancifolia (Sieber ex Sprengel) Dostal

CRUCIFERAE
Murbeckiella sousae Rothm.

EUPHORBIACEAE
Euphorbia nevadensis Boiss. & Reuter

GESNERIACEAE
Jankaea heldreichii (Boiss.) Boiss.
Ramonda serbica Pancic

IRIDACEAE
Crocus etruscus Parl.
Iris boissieri Henriq.
Iris marisca Ricci & Colasante

LABIATAE
Rosmarinus tomentosus Huber-Morath & Maire
Teucrium charidemi Sandwith
Thymus capitellatus Hoffmanns. & Link
Thymus villosus L. subsp. villosus L.

LILIACEAE
Androcymbium europaeum (Lange) K. Richter
Bellevalia hackelli Freyn
Colchicum corsicum Baker
Colchicum cousturieri Greuter
Fritillaria conica Rix
Fritillaria drenovskii Degen & Stoy.
Fritillaria gussichiae (Degen & Doerfler) Rix
Fritillaria obliqua Ker-Gawl.
Fritillaria rhodocanakis Orph. ex Baker
Ornithogalum reverchonii Degen & Herv.-Bass.
Scilla beirana Samp.
Scilla odorata Link

ORCHIDACEAE
Ophrys argolica Fleischm.
Orchis scopulorum Simsmerh.
Spiranthes aestivalis (Poiret) L. C. M. Richard

PRIMULACEAE

Androsace cylindrica DC.
Primula glaucescens Moretti
Primula spectabilis Tratt.

RANUNCULACEAE

Aquilegia alpina L.

SAPOTACEAE

Sideroxylon marmulano Banks ex Lowe

SAXIFRAGACEAE

Saxifraga cintrana Kuzinsky ex Willk.
Saxifraga portosanctana Boiss.
Saxifraga presolanensis Engl.
Saxifraga valdensis DC.
Saxifraga vayredana Luizet

SCROPHULARIACEAE

Antirrhinum lopesianum Rothm.
Lindernia procumbens (Krocker) Philcox

SOLANACEAE

Mandragora officinarum L.

THYMELAEACEAE

Thymelaea broterana P. Cout.

UMBELLIFERAE

Bunium brevifolium Lowe

VIOLACEAE

Viola athois W. Becker
Viola cazorlensis Gandoger][1]

Amendment

1 Substituted by Council Directive 2006/105/EC of 20 November 2006 adapting Directives 79/409/EEC, 92/43/EEC, 97/68/EC, 2001/80/EC and 2001/81/EC in the field of environment, by reason of the accession of Bulgaria and Romania, Article 1, Annex, Pt A, para 2(a).

[ANNEX V
ANIMAL AND PLANT SPECIES OF COMMUNITY INTEREST WHOSE TAKING IN THE WILD AND EXPLOITATION MAY BE SUBJECT TO MANAGEMENT MEASURES][1]

[The species listed in this Annex are indicated:

— by the name of the species or subspecies, or
— by the body of species belonging to a higher taxon or to a designated part of that taxon.

The abbreviation "spp." after the name of a family or genus designates all the species belonging to that family or genus.][1]

Amendment

1 Substituted by Council Directive 2006/105/EC of 20 November 2006 adapting Directives 79/409/EEC, 92/43/EEC, 97/68/EC, 2001/80/EC and 2001/81/EC in the field of environment, by reason of the accession of Bulgaria and Romania, Article 1, Annex, Pt A, para 2(a).

[(A) ANIMALS

***Vertebrates]*[1]**

[Mammals

RODENTIA
Castoridae
Castor fiber (Finnish, Swedish, Latvian, Lithuanian, Estonian and Polish populations)
Cricetidae
Cricetus cricetus (Hungarian populations)

CARNIVORA
Canidae
Canis aureus
Canis lupus (Spanish populations north of the Duero, Greek populations north of the 39th parallel Finnish populations within the reindeer management area as defined in paragraph 2 of the Finnish Act No 848/90 of 14 September 1990 on reindeer management, Bulgarian, Latvian, Lithuanian, Estonian, Polish and Slovak populations)
Mustelidae
Martes martes
Mustela putorius
Felidae
Lynx lynx (Estonian population)
Phocidae
All species not mentioned in Annex IV
Viverridae
Genetta genetta
Herpestes ichneumon

DUPLICIDENTATA
Leporidae
Lepus timidus

ARTIODACTYLA
Bovidae
Capra ibex
Capra pyrenaica (except *Capra pyrenaica pyrenaica*)
Rupicapra rupicapra (except *Rupicapra rupicapra balcanica*, *Rupicapra rupicapra ornata* and *Rupicapra rupicapra tatrica*)][1]

Amendment
1 Substituted by Council Directive 2006/105/EC of 20 November 2006 adapting Directives 79/409/EEC, 92/43/EEC, 97/68/EC, 2001/80/EC and 2001/81/EC in the field of environment, by reason of the accession of Bulgaria and Romania, Article 1, Annex, Pt A, para 2(a).

[Amphibians

ANURA
Ranidae
Rana esculenta
Rana perezi
Rana ridibunda
Rana temporaria][1]

Amendment
1 Substituted by Council Directive 2006/105/EC of 20 November 2006 adapting Directives 79/409/EEC, 92/43/EEC, 97/68/EC, 2001/80/EC and 2001/81/EC in the field of environment, by reason of the accession of Bulgaria and Romania, Article 1, Annex, Pt A, para 2(a).

[Fish

PETROMYZONIFORMES
Petromyzonidae
Lampetra fluviatilis
Lethenteron zanandrai

ACIPENSERIFORMES
Acipenseridae
All species not mentioned in Annex IV

CLUPEIFORMES
Clupeidae
Alosa spp.

SALMONIFORMES
Salmonidae
Thymallus thymallus
Coregonus spp. (except *Coregonus oxyrhynchus* - anadromous populations in certain sectors of the North Sea)
Hucho hucho
Salmo salar (only in fresh water)

CYPRINIFORMES
Cyprinidae
Aspius aspius
Barbus spp.
Pelecus cultratus
Rutilus friesii meidingeri
Rutilus pigus

SILURIFORMES
Siluridae
Silurus aristotelis

PERCIFORMES
Percidae
Gymnocephalus schraetzer
Zingel zingel][1]

Amendment

1 Substituted by Council Directive 2006/105/EC of 20 November 2006 adapting Directives 79/409/EEC, 92/43/EEC, 97/68/EC, 2001/80/EC and 2001/81/EC in the field of environment, by reason of the accession of Bulgaria and Romania, Article 1, Annex, Pt A, para 2(a).

[Invertebrates][1]

[Coelenterata

CNIDARIA
Corallium rubrum][1]

Amendment

1 Substituted by Council Directive 2006/105/EC of 20 November 2006 adapting Directives 79/409/EEC, 92/43/EEC, 97/68/EC, 2001/80/EC and 2001/81/EC in the field of environment, by reason of the accession of Bulgaria and Romania, Article 1, Annex, Pt A, para 2(a).

[Mollusca

GASTROPODA - STYLOMMATOPHORA
Helix pomatia

BIVALVIA - UNIONOIDA
Margaritiferidae
Margaritifera margaritifera
Unionidae
Microcondylaea compressa
Unio elongatulus][1]

Amendment
1 Substituted by Council Directive 2006/105/EC of 20 November 2006 adapting Directives 79/409/EEC, 92/43/EEC, 97/68/EC, 2001/80/EC and 2001/81/EC in the field of environment, by reason of the accession of Bulgaria and Romania, Article 1, Annex, Pt A, para 2(a).

[Annelida

HIRUDINOIDEA - ARHYNCHOBDELLAE
Hirudinidae
Hirudo medicinalis][1]

Amendment
1 Substituted by Council Directive 2006/105/EC of 20 November 2006 adapting Directives 79/409/EEC, 92/43/EEC, 97/68/EC, 2001/80/EC and 2001/81/EC in the field of environment, by reason of the accession of Bulgaria and Romania, Article 1, Annex, Pt A, para 2(a).

[Arthropoda

CRUSTACEA - DECAPODA
Astacidae
Astacus astacus
Austropotamobius pallipes
Austropotamobius torrentium
Scyllaridae
Scyllarides latus

INSECTA - LEPIDOPTERA
Saturniidae
Graellsia isabellae][1]

Amendment
1 Substituted by Council Directive 2006/105/EC of 20 November 2006 adapting Directives 79/409/EEC, 92/43/EEC, 97/68/EC, 2001/80/EC and 2001/81/EC in the field of environment, by reason of the accession of Bulgaria and Romania, Article 1, Annex, Pt A, para 2(a).

[(B) PLANTS][1]

[Algae

RHODOPHYTA

CORALLINACEAE
Lithothamnium coralloides Crouan frat.
Phymatholithon calcareum (Poll.) Adey & McKibbin][1]

Amendment
1 Substituted by Council Directive 2006/105/EC of 20 November 2006 adapting Directives 79/409/EEC, 92/43/EEC, 97/68/EC, 2001/80/EC and 2001/81/EC in the field of environment, by reason of the accession of Bulgaria and Romania, Article 1, Annex, Pt A, para 2(a).

[Lichenes

CLADONIACEAE
Cladonia L. subgenus *Cladina* (Nyl.) Vain.][1]

Amendment

1 Substituted by Council Directive 2006/105/EC of 20 November 2006 adapting Directives 79/409/EEC, 92/43/EEC, 97/68/EC, 2001/80/EC and 2001/81/EC in the field of environment, by reason of the accession of Bulgaria and Romania, Article 1, Annex, Pt A, para 2(a).

[Brypohyta

MUSCI

LEUCOBRYACEAE

Leucobryum glaucum (Hedw.) Ångstr.

SPHAGNACEAE

Sphagnum L. spp. (except *Sphagnum pylaisii* Brid.)][1]

Amendment

1 Substituted by Council Directive 2006/105/EC of 20 November 2006 adapting Directives 79/409/EEC, 92/43/EEC, 97/68/EC, 2001/80/EC and 2001/81/EC in the field of environment, by reason of the accession of Bulgaria and Romania, Article 1, Annex, Pt A, para 2(a).

[Pteridophyta

Lycopodium spp.][1]

Amendment

1 Substituted by Council Directive 2006/105/EC of 20 November 2006 adapting Directives 79/409/EEC, 92/43/EEC, 97/68/EC, 2001/80/EC and 2001/81/EC in the field of environment, by reason of the accession of Bulgaria and Romania, Article 1, Annex, Pt A, para 2(a).

[Angiospermae

AMARYLLIDACEAE

Galanthus nivalis L.
Narcissus bulbocodium L.
Narcissus juncifolius Lagasca

COMPOSITAE

Arnica montana L.
Artemisia eriantha Tem
Artemisia genipi Weber
Doronicum plantagineum L. subsp. *tournefortii* (Rouy) P. Cout.
Leuzea rhaponticoides Graells

CRUCIFERAE

Alyssum pintadasilvae Dudley.
Malcolmia lacera (L.) DC. subsp. *graccilima* (Samp.) Franco
Murbeckiella pinnatifida (Lam.) Rothm. subsp. *herminii* (Rivas-Martinez) Greuter & Burdet

GENTIANACEAE

Gentiana lutea L.

IRIDACEAE

Iris lusitanica Ker-Gawler

LABIATAE

Teucrium salviastrum Schreber subsp. *salviastrum* Schreber

LEGUMINOSAE

Anthyllis lusitanica Cullen & Pinto da Silva
Dorycnium pentaphyllum Scop. subsp. *transmontana* Franco
Ulex densus Welw. ex Webb.

LILIACEAE

Lilium rubrum Lmk
Ruscus aculeatus L.

PLUMBAGINACEAE

Armeria sampaio (Bernis) Nieto Feliner

ROSACEAE

Rubus genevieri Boreau subsp. *herminii* (Samp.) P. Cout.

SCROPHULARIACEAE

Anarrhinum longipedicelatum R. Fernandes
Euphrasia mendonçae Samp.
Scrophularia grandiflora DC.subsp. *grandiflora* DC.
Scrophularia berminii Hoffmanns & Link
Scrophularia sublyrata Brot.][1]

Amendment

1 Substituted by Council Directive 2006/105/EC of 20 November 2006 adapting Directives 79/409/EEC, 92/43/EEC, 97/68/EC, 2001/80/EC and 2001/81/EC in the field of environment, by reason of the accession of Bulgaria and Romania, Article 1, Annex, Pt A, para 2(a).

ANNEX VI
PROHIBITED METHODS AND MEANS OF CAPTURE AND KILLING AND MODES OF TRANSPORT

(a) Non-selective means

MAMMALS

— Blind or mutilated animals used as live decoys
— Tape recorders
— Electrical and electronic devices capable of killing or stunning
— Artificial light sources
— Mirrors and other dazzling devices
— Devices for illuminating targets
— Sighting devices for night shooting comprising an electronic image magnifier or image converter
— Explosives
— Nets which are non-selective according to their principle or their conditions of use
— Traps which are non-selective according to their principle or their conditions of use
— Crossbows
— Poisons and poisoned or anaesthetic bait
— Gassing or smoking out
— Semi-automatic or automatic weapons with a magazine capable of holding more than two rounds of ammunition

FISH

— Poison
— Explosives

(b) Modes of transport

— Aircraft
— Moving motor vehicles

EUROPEAN PARLIAMENT AND COUNCIL DIRECTIVE 94/62/EC

of 20 December 1994

ON PACKAGING AND PACKAGING WASTE

THE EUROPEAN PARLIAMENT AND THE COUNCIL OF THE EUROPEAN UNION,

Having regard to the Treaty establishing the European Community, and in particular Article 100a thereof,

Having regard to the proposal from the Commission,

Having regard to the opinion of the Economic and Social Committee,

Acting in accordance with the procedure laid down in Article 189b of the Treaty,

Whereas the differing national measures concerning the management of packaging and packaging waste should be harmonized in order, on the one hand, to prevent any impact thereof on the environment or to reduce such impact, thus providing a high level of environmental protection, and, on the other hand, to ensure the functioning of the internal market and to avoid obstacles to trade and distortion and restriction of competition within the Community;

Whereas the best means of preventing the creation of packaging waste is to reduce the overall volume of packaging;

Whereas it is important, in relation of the objectives of this Directive, to respect the general principle that measures taken in one Member State to protect the environment should not adversely affect the ability of other Member States to achieve the objectives of the Directive;

Whereas the reduction of waste is essential for the sustainable growth specifically called for by the Treaty on European Union;

Whereas this Directive should cover all types of packaging placed on the market and all packaging waste; whereas; therefore, Council Directive 85/339/EEC of 27 June 1985 on containers of liquids for human consumption should be repealed;

Whereas packaging has a vital social and economic function and therefore measures provided for in this Directive should apply without prejudice to other relevant legislative requirements affecting quality and transport of packaging or packaged goods;

Whereas, in line with the Community strategy for waste management set out in Council resolution of 7 May 1990 on waste policy and Council Directive 75/442/EEC of 15 July 1975 on waste (6), the management of packaging and packaging waste should include as a first priority, prevention of packaging waste and, as additional fundamental principles, reuse of packaging, recycling and other forms of recovering packaging waste and, hence, reduction of the final disposal of such waste;

Whereas, until scientific and technological progress is made with regard to recovery processes, reuse and recycling should be considered preferable in terms of environmental impact; whereas this requires the setting up in the Member States of systems guaranteeing the return of used packaging and/or packaging waste; whereas life-cycle assessments should be completed as soon as possible to justify a clear hierarchy between reusable, recyclable and recoverable packaging;

Whereas prevention of packaging waste shall be carried out through appropriate measures, including initiatives taken within the Member States in accordance with the objectives of this Directive;

Whereas Member States may encourage, in accordance with the Treaty, reuse systems of packaging which can be reused in an environmentally sound manner, in order to take advantage of the contribution of such systems to environmental protection;

Whereas from an environmental point of view recycling should be regarded as an important part of recovery with a particular view to reducing the consumption of energy and of primary raw materials and the final disposal of waste;

Whereas energy recovery is one effective means of packaging waste recovery;

Whereas targets set in Member States for the recovery and recycling of packaging waste should be confined within certain ranges so as to take account of the different situations in Member States and to avoid creating barriers to trade and distortion of competition;

Whereas, in order to achieve results in the medium term and to give economic operators, consumers and public authorities the necessary perspective for the longer term, a medium-term deadline should be set for attaining the aforementioned targets and a long-term deadline set for targets to be determined at a later stage with a view to substantially increasing those targets;

Whereas the European Parliament and the Council should, on the basis of reports by the Commission, examine the practical experience gained in Member States in working towards the aforementioned targets and the findings of scientific research and evaluation techniques such as eco-balances;

Whereas Member States which have, or will set, programmes going beyond such target ranges should be permitted to pursue those targets in the interest of a high level of environmental protection on condition shat such measures avoid disturbances on the internal market and do not prevent other Member States from complying with this Directive; whereas the Commission should confirm such measures after appropriate verification;

Whereas, on the other hand, certain Member States may be allowed to adopt lower targets because of the specific circumstances in those Member States, on condition that they achieve a minimum target for recovery within the standard deadline, and the standard targets by a later deadline;

Whereas the management of packaging and packaging waste requires the Member States to set up return, collection and recovery systems; whereas such systems should be open to the participation of all interested parties and be designed to avoid discrimination against imported products and barriers to trade or distortions of competition and to guarantee the maximum possible return of packaging and packaging waste, in accordance with the Treaty;

Whereas the issue of Community marking of packaging requires further study, but should be decided by the Community in the near future;

Whereas, in order to minimize the impact of packaging and packaging waste on the environment and to avoid barriers to trade and distortion of competition, it is also necessary to define the essential requirements governing the composition and the reusable and recoverable (including recyclable) nature of packaging;

Whereas the presence of noxious metals and other substances in packaging should be limited in view of their environmental impact (in particular in the light of their likely presence in emissions or ash when packaging is incinerated, or in leachate when packaging is landfilled); whereas it is essential, as a first step towards reducing the toxicity of packaging waste, to prevent the addition of noxious heavy metals to packaging and ensure that such substances are not released into the environment, with appropriate exemptions which should be determined by the Commission in specific cases under a Committee procedure;

Whereas, if a high level of recycling is to be attained and health and safety problems are to be avoided by those employed to collect and process packaging waste, it is essential for such waste to be sorted at source;

Whereas the requirements for the manufacturing of packaging should not apply to packaging used for a given product before the date of entry into force of this Directive; whereas a transition period for the marketing of packaging is also required;

Whereas the timing of the provision on the placing on the market of packaging which meets all essential requirements should take account of the fact that European standards are being prepared by the competent standardization body; whereas, however, the provisions on means of proof of conformity of national standards should apply without delay;

Whereas the preparation of European standards for essential requirements and other related issues should be promoted;

Whereas the measures provided for in this Directive imply the development of recovery and recycling capacities and market outlets for recycled packaging materials;

Whereas the inclusion of recycled material in packaging should not contradict relevant provisions on hygiene, health and consumer safety;

Whereas Community-wide data on packaging and packaging waste are needed in order to monitor the implementation of the objectives of this Directive;

Whereas it is essential that all those involved in the production, use, import and distribution of packaging and packaged products become more aware of the extent to which packaging becomes waste, and that in accordance with the polluter-pays principle they accept responsibility for such waste; whereas the development and implementation of the measures provided for in this Directive should involve and require the close cooperation of all the partners, where appropriate, within a spirit of shared responsibility;

Whereas consumers play a key role in the management of packaging and packaging waste and thus have to be adequately informed in order to adapt their behaviour and attitudes;

Whereas the inclusion of a specific chapter on the management of packaging and packaging waste in the waste management plans required pursuant to Directive 75/442/EEC will contribute to the effective implementation of this Directive;

Whereas, in order to facilitate the achievement of the objectives of this Directive, it may be appropriate for the Community and the Member States to use economic instruments in accordance with the provisions of the Treaty, so as to avoid new forms of protectionism;

Whereas Member States should, without prejudice to Council Directive 83/189/EEC of 28 March 1983 laying down a procedure for the provision of information in the field of technical standards and regulations, notify the Commission of drafts of any measures they intend to adopt before adopting them, so that it can be established whether or not they comply with the Directive;

Whereas the adaptation to scientific and technical progress of the packaging identification system and the formats relating to a database system should be ensured by the Commission under a committee procedure;

Whereas it is necessary to provide for specific measures to be taken to deal with any difficulties encountered in the implementation of this Directive in accordance, where appropriate, with the same committee procedure,

HAVE ADOPTED THIS DIRECTIVE:

Article 1

Objectives

1. This Directive aims to harmonize national measures concerning the management of packaging and packaging waste in order, on the one hand, to prevent any impact thereof on

the environment of all Member States as well as of third countries or to reduce such impact, thus providing a high level of environmental protection, and, on the other hand, to ensure the functioning of the internal market and to avoid obstacles to trade and distortion and restriction of competition within the Community.

2. To this end this Directive lays down measures aimed, as a first priority, at preventing the production of packaging waste and, as additional fundamental principles, at reusing packaging, at recycling and other forms of recovering packaging waste and, hence, at reducing the final disposal of such waste.

Article 2

Scope

1. This Directive covers all packaging placed on the market in the Community and all packaging waste, whether it is used or released at industrial, commercial, office, shop, service, household or any other level, regardless of the material used.

2. This Directive shall apply without prejudice to existing quality requirements for packaging such as those regarding safety, the protection of health and the hygiene of the packed products or to existing transport requirements or to the provisions of Council Directive 91/689/EEC of 12 December 1991 on hazardous waste.

Article 3

Definitions

For the purposes of this Directive:

1. "packaging" shall mean all products made of any materials of any nature to be used for the containment, protection, handling, delivery and presentation of goods, from raw materials to processed goods, from the producer to the user or the consumer. "Non-returnable" items used for the same purposes shall also be considered to constitute packaging.

   "Packaging" consists only of:

   (a) sales packaging or primary packaging, i. e. packaging conceived so as to constitute a sales unit to the final user or consumer at the point of purchase;

   (b) grouped packaging or secondary packaging, i. e. packaging conceived so as to constitute at the point of purchase a grouping of a certain number of sales units whether the latter is sold as such to the final user or consumer or whether it serves only as a means to replenish the shelves at the point of sale; it can be removed from the product without affecting its characteristics;

   (c) transport packaging or tertiary packaging, i. e. packaging conceived so as to facilitate handling and transport of a number of sales units or grouped packagings in order to prevent physical handling and transport damage. Transport packaging does not include road, rail, ship and air containers;

   [The definition of "packaging" shall be further based on the criteria set out below. The items listed in Annex I are illustrative examples of the application of these criteria.

   (i) Items shall be considered to be packaging if they fulfil the abovementioned definition without prejudice to other functions which the packaging might also perform, unless the item is an integral part of a product and it is necessary to contain, support or preserve that product throughout its lifetime and all elements are intended to be used, consumed or disposed of together.

   (ii) Items designed and intended to be filled at the point of sale and "disposable" items sold, filled or designed and intended to be filled at the point of sale shall be considered to be packaging provided they fulfil a packaging function.

   (iii) Packaging components and ancillary elements integrated into packaging shall be considered to be part of the packaging into which they are integrated.

Ancillary elements hung directly on, or attached to, a product and which perform a packaging function shall be considered to be packaging unless they are an integral part of this product and all elements are intended to be consumed or disposed of together.

[The Commission shall, as appropriate, examine and, where necessary, review the illustrative examples for the definition of packaging given in Annex I. As a priority, the following items shall be addressed: CD and video cases, flower pots, tubes and cylinders around which flexible material is wound, release paper of self-adhesive labels and wrapping paper. Those measures, designed to amend non-essential elements of this Directive, shall be adopted in accordance with the regulatory procedure with scrutiny referred to in Article 21(3).][1][2]

2. "packaging waste" shall mean any packaging or packaging material covered by the definition of waste in Directive 75/442/EEC, excluding production residues;
3. "packaging waste management" shall mean the management of waste as defined in Directive 75/442/EEC;
4. "prevention" shall mean the reduction of the quantity and of the harmfulness for the environment of:
   - materials and substances contained in packaging and packaging waste,
   - packaging and packaging waste at production process level and at the marketing, distribution, utilization and elimination stages,

   in particular by developing "clean" products and technology;
5. "reuse" shall mean any operation by which packaging, which has been conceived and designed to accomplish within its life cycle a minimum number of trips or rotations, is refilled or used for the same purpose for which it was conceived, with or without the support of auxiliary products present on the market enabling the packaging to be refilled; such reused packaging will become packaging waste when no longer subject to reuse;
6. "recovery" shall mean any of the applicable operations provided for in Annex II.B to Directive 75/442/EEC;
7. "recycling" shall mean the reprocessing in a production process of the waste materials for the original purpose or for other purposes including organic recycling but excluding energy recovery;
8. "energy recovery" shall mean the use of combustible packaging waste as a means to generate energy through direct incineration with or without other waste but with recovery of the heat;
9. "organic recycling" shall mean the aerobic (composting) or anaerobic (biomethanization) treatment, under controlled conditions and using micro-organisms, of the biodegradable parts of packaging waste, which produces stabilized organic residues or methane. Landfill shall not be considered a form of organic recycling;
10. "disposal" shall mean any of the applicable operations provided for in Annex II.A to Directive 75/442/EEC;
11. "economic operators" in relation to packaging shall mean suppliers of packaging materials, packaging producers and converters, fillers and users, importers, traders and distributors, authorities and statutory organizations;
12. "voluntary agreement" shall mean the formal agreement concluded between the competent public authorities of the Member State and the economic sectors concerned, which has to be open to all partners who wish to meet the conditions of the agreement with a view to working towards the objectives of this Directive.

Amendments

1 Substituted by Regulation (EC) No 219/2009 of the European Parliament and of the Council of 11 March 2009 adapting a number of instruments subject to the procedure referred to in Article 251 of the Treaty to Council Decision 1999/468/EC with regard to the regulatory procedure with scrutiny, Article 1, Annex, Pt 3.3, para 1.

2 Inserted by Directive 2004/12/EC of the European Parliament and of the Council of 11 February 2004 amending Directive 94/62/EC on packaging and packaging waste, Article 1.1.

[Article 4

Prevention][1]

[1. Member States shall ensure that, in addition to the measures to prevent the formation of packaging waste taken in accordance with Article 9, other preventive measures are implemented.

Such other measures may consist of national programmes, projects to introduce producer responsibility to minimise the environmental impact of packaging or similar actions adopted, if appropriate in consultation with economic operators, and designed to bring together and take advantage of the many initiatives taken within Member States as regards prevention. They shall comply with the objectives of this Directive as defined in Article 1(1).

2. The Commission shall help to promote prevention by encouraging the development of suitable European standards, in accordance with Article 10. The standards shall aim to minimise the environmental impact of packaging in accordance with Articles 9 and 10.

3. The Commission shall, as appropriate, present proposals for measures to strengthen and complement the enforcement of the essential requirements and to ensure that new packaging is put on the market only if the producer has taken all necessary measures to minimise its environmental impact without compromising the essential functions of the packaging.][1]

Amendment

1 Substituted by Directive 2004/12/EC of the European Parliament and of the Council of 11 February 2004 amending Directive 94/62/EC on packaging and packaging waste, Article 1.2.

Article 5

Member States may encourage reuse systems of packaging, which can be reused in an environmentally sound manner, in conformity with the Treaty.

[Article 6

Recovery and recycling][1]

[1. In order to comply with the objectives of this Directive, Member States shall take the necessary measures to attain the following targets covering the whole of their territory:

(a) no later than 30 June 2001 between 50 % as a minimum and 65 % as a maximum by weight of packaging waste will be recovered or incinerated at waste incineration plants with energy recovery;
(b) no later than 31 December 2008 60 % as a minimum by weight of packaging waste will be recovered or incinerated at waste incineration plants with energy recovery;
(c) no later than 30 June 2001 between 25 % as a minimum and 45 % as a maximum by weight of the totality of packaging materials contained in packaging waste will be recycled with a minimum of 15 % by weight for each packaging material;
(d) no later than 31 December 2008 between 55 % as a minimum and 80 % as a maximum by weight of packaging waste will be recycled;
(e) no later than 31 December 2008 the following minimum recycling targets for materials contained in packaging waste will be attained:
    (i) 60 % by weight for glass;
    (ii) 60 % by weight for paper and board;
    (iii) 50 % by weight for metals;
    (iv) 22,5 % by weight for plastics, counting exclusively material that is recycled back into plastics;
    (v) 15 % by weight for wood.

2. Packaging waste exported out of the Community in accordance with Council Regulations (EEC) No 259/93, (EC) No 1420/1999 and Commission Regulation (EC) No 1547/1999, shall only count for the achievement of the obligations and targets of paragraph 1 if there is sound

evidence that the recovery and/or recycling operation took place under conditions that are broadly equivalent to those prescribed by the Community legislation on the matter.

3. Member States shall, where appropriate, encourage energy recovery, where it is preferable to material-recycling for environmental and cost-benefit reasons. This could be done by considering a sufficient margin between national recycling and recovery targets.

4. Member States shall, where appropriate, encourage the use of materials obtained from recycled packaging waste for the manufacturing of packaging and other products by:
(a) improving market conditions for such materials;
(b) reviewing existing regulations preventing the use of those materials.

5. Not later than 31 December 2007, the European Parliament and the Council shall, acting by qualified majority and on a proposal from the Commission, fix targets for the third five-year phase 2009 until 2014, based on the practical experience gained in the Member States in pursuit of the targets laid down in paragraph 1 and the findings of scientific research and evaluation techniques such as life-cycle assessments and cost-benefit analysis.

This process shall be repeated every five years.

6. The measures and targets referred to in paragraph 1 shall be published by the Member States and shall be the subject of an information campaign for the general public and economic operators.

7. Greece, Ireland and Portugal may, because of their specific situations, namely respectively the large number of small islands, the presence of rural and mountain areas and the current low level of packaging consumption, decide to:
(a) attain, no later than 30 June 2001, lower targets than those fixed in paragraphs 1(a) and (c), but shall at least attain 25 % for recovery or incineration at waste incineration plants with energy recovery;
(b) postpone at the same time the attainment of the targets in paragraphs 1(a) and (c) to a later deadline which shall not, however, be later than 31 December 2005;
(c) postpone the attainment of the targets referred to in paragraphs 1(b), (d) and (e) until a date of their own choice which shall not be later than 31 December 2011.

8. The Commission shall, as soon as possible and no later than 30 June 2005, present a report to the European Parliament and the Council on the progress of the implementation of this Directive and its impact on the environment, as well as on the functioning of the internal market. The report shall take into account individual circumstances in each Member State. It shall cover the following:
(a) an evaluation of the effectiveness, implementation and enforcement of the essential requirements;
(b) additional prevention measures to reduce the environmental impact of packaging as far as possible without compromising its essential functions;
(c) the possible development of a packaging environment indicator to render packaging waste prevention simpler and more effective;
(d) packaging waste prevention plans;
(e) encouragement of reuse and, in particular, comparison of the costs and benefits of reuse and those of recycling;
(f) producer responsibility including its financial aspects;
(g) efforts to reduce further and, if appropriate, ultimately phase out heavy metals and other hazardous substances in packaging by 2010.

This report shall, as appropriate, be accompanied by proposals for revision of the related provisions of this Directive, unless such proposals have, by that time, been presented.

9. The report shall address the issues in paragraph 8 as well as other relevant issues in the framework of the different elements of the Sixth Environmental Action Programme, in particular the thematic strategy on recycling and the thematic strategy on the sustainable use of resources.

The Commission and the Member States shall, as appropriate, encourage studies and pilot projects concerning points 8(b), (c), (d), (e) and (f) and other prevention instruments.

10. Member States which have, or will, set programmes going beyond the maximum targets of paragraph 1 and which provide to this effect appropriate capacities for recycling and recovery shall be permitted to pursue those targets in the interest of a high level of environmental protection, on condition that these measures avoid distortions of the internal market and do not hinder compliance by other Member States with this Directive. Member States shall inform the Commission of such measures. The Commission shall confirm these measures, after having verified, in cooperation with the Member States, that they are consistent with the abovementioned considerations and do not constitute an arbitrary means of discrimination or a disguised restriction on trade between Member States.

[11. Member States having acceded to the European Union by virtue of the Accession Treaty of 16 April 2003 may postpone the attainment of the targets referred to in paragraph 1(b), (d) and (e) until a date of their own choosing which shall not be later than 31 December 2012 for the Czech Republic, Estonia, Cyprus, Lithuania, Hungary, Slovenia and Slovakia; 31 December 2013 for Malta; 31 December 2014 for Poland; and 31 December 2015 for Latvia.][2]][1]

Amendments

1 Substituted by Directive 2004/12/EC of the European Parliament and of the Council of 11 February 2004 amending Directive 94/62/EC on packaging and packaging waste, Article 1.3.

2 Inserted by Directive 2005/20/EC of the European Parliament and of the Council of 9 March 2005 amending Directive 94/62/EC on packaging and packaging waste, Article 1.

Article 7

Return, collection and recovery systems 1. Member States shall take the necessary measures to ensure that systems are set up to provide for:

(a) the return and/or collection of used packaging and/or packaging waste from the consumer, other final user, or from the waste stream in order to channel it to the most appropriate waste management alternatives;

(b) the reuse or recovery including recycling of the packaging and/or packaging waste collected,

in order to meet the objectives laid down in this Directive.

These systems shall be open to the participation of the economic operators of the sectors concerned and to the participation of the competent public authorities. They shall also apply to imported products under non-discriminatory conditions, including the detailed arrangements and any tariffs imposed for access to the systems, and shall be designed so as to avoid barriers to trade or distortions of competition in conformity with the Treaty.

2. The measures referred to in paragraph 1 shall form part of a policy covering all packaging and packaging waste and shall take into account, in particular, requirements regarding the protection of environmental and consumer health, safety and hygiene; the protection of the quality,the authenticity and the technical characteristics of the packed goods and materials used; and the protection of industrial and commercial property rights.

Article 8

Marking and identification system

1. The Council shall, in accordance with the conditions laid down in the Treaty, decide no later than two years after the entry into force of this Directive on the marking of packaging.

[2. To facilitate collection, reuse and recovery including recycling, packaging shall indicate for the purposes of its identification and classification by the industry concerned the nature of the packaging material(s) used on the basis of Commission Decision 97/129/EC.][1]

3. Packaging shall bear the appropriate marking either on the packaging itself or on the label. It shall be clearly visible and easily legible. The marking shall be appropriately durable and lasting, including when the packaging is opened.

Amendment

1 Substituted by Directive 2004/12/EC of the European Parliament and of the Council of 11 February 2004 amending Directive 94/62/EC on packaging and packaging waste, Article 1.4.

Article 9

Essential requirements

1. Member States shall ensure that three years from the date of the entry into force of this Directive, packaging may be placed on the market only if it complies with all essential requirements defined by this Directive including Annex II.

2. Member States shall, from the date set out in Article 22 (1), presume compliance with all essential requirements set out in this Directive including Annex II in the case of packaging which complies:

(a) with the relevant harmonized standards, the reference numbers of which have been published in the Official Journal of the European Communities. Member States shall publish the reference numbers of national standards transposing these harmonized standards;

(b) with the relevant national standards referred to in paragraph 3 in so far as, in the areas covered by such standards, no harmonized standards exist.

3. Member States shall communicate to the Commission the text of their national standards, as referred to in paragraph 2 (b), which they deem to comply with the requirements referred to in this Article. The Commission shall forward such texts forthwith to the other Member States.

Member States shall publish the references of these standards. The Commission shall ensure that they are published in the Official Journal of the European Communities.

4. Where a Member State or the Commission considers that the standards referred to in paragraph 2 do not entirely meet the essential requirements referred to in paragraph 1, the Commission or the Member State concerned shall bring the matter before the Committee set up by Directive 83/189/EEC giving the reasons therefor. This Committee shall deliver an opinion without delay.

In the light of the Committee's opinion, the Commission shall inform Member States whether or not it is necessary to withdraw those standards from the publications referred to in paragraphs 2 and 3.

Article 10

Standardization

The Commission shall promote, as appropriate, the preparation of European standards relating to the essential requirements referred to in Annex II.

The Commission shall promote, in particular, the preparation of European standards relating to:

— criteria and methodologies for life-cycle analysis of packaging,
— the methods for measuring and verifying the presence of heavy metals and other dangerous substances in the packaging and their release into the environment from packaging and packaging waste,
— criteria for a minimum content of recycled material in packaging for appropriate types of packaging,
— criteria for recycling methods,
— criteria for composting methods and produced compost,
— criteria for the marking of packaging.

Article 11

Concentration levels of heavy metals present in packaging

1. Member States shall ensure that the sum of concentration levels of lead, cadmium, mercury and hexavalent chromium present in packaging or packaging components shall not exceed the following:
— 600 ppm by weight two years after the date referred to in Article 22 (i);
— 250 ppm by weight three years after the date referred to in Article 22 (i);
— 100 ppm by weight five years after the date referred to in Article 22 (i).

2. The concentration levels referred to in paragraph 1 shall not apply to packaging entirely made of lead crystal glass as defined in Directive 69/493/EEC.

[3. The Commission shall determine the conditions under which the concentration levels referred to in paragraph 1 will not apply to recycled materials and to product loops which are in a closed and controlled chain, as well as the types of packaging which are exempted from the requirement referred to in the third indent of paragraph 1.

Those measures, designed to amend non-essential elements of this Directive by supplementing it, shall be adopted in accordance with the regulatory procedure with scrutiny referred to in Article 21(3).][1]

Amendment
1 Substituted by Regulation (EC) No 219/2009 of the European Parliament and of the Council of 11 March 2009 adapting a number of instruments subject to the procedure referred to in Article 251 of the Treaty to Council Decision 1999/468/EC with regard to the regulatory procedure with scrutiny, Article 1, Annex, Pt 3.3, para 2.

Article 12

Information systems

1. Member States shall take the necessary measures to ensure that databases on packaging and packaging waste are established, where not already in place, on a harmonized basis in order to contribute to enabling Member States and the Commission to monitor the implementation of the objectives set out in this Directive.

2. To this effect, the databases shall provide in particular information on the magnitude, characteristics and evolution of the packaging and packaging waste flows (including information on the toxicity or danger of packaging materials and components used for their manufacture) at the level of individual Member States.

[3. In order to harmonise the characteristics and presentation of the data prod uced and to make the data of the Member States compatible, Member States shall provide the Commission with their available data in formats which shall be adopted on the basis of Annex I II, in accordance with the regulatory procedure referred to in Article 21(2).][1]

4. Member States shall take into account the particular problems of small and medium-sized enterprises in providing detailed data.

5. The data obtained shall be made available with the national reports referred to in Article 17 and shall be updated in subsequent reports.

6. Member States shall require all economic operators involved to provide competent authorities with reliable data on their sector as required in this Article.

Amendment
1 Substituted by Regulation (EC) No 219/2009 of the European Parliament and of the Council of 11 March 2009 adapting a number of instruments subject to the procedure referred to in Article 251 of the Treaty to Council Decision 1999/468/EC with regard to the regulatory procedure with scrutiny, Article 1, Annex, Pt 3.3, para 3.

Article 13

Information for users of packaging

Member States shall take measures, within two years of the date referred to in Article 22 (1), to ensure that users of packaging, including in particular consumers, obtain the necessary information about:

— the return, collection and recovery systems available to them,
— their role in contributing to reuse, recovery and recycling of packaging and packaging waste,
— the meaning of markings on packaging existing on the market,
— the appropriate elements of the management plans for packaging and packaging waste as referred to in Article 14.

[Member States shall also promote consumer information and awareness campaigns.][1]

Amendment

1 Substituted by Directive 2004/12/EC of the European Parliament and of the Council of 11 February 2004 amending Directive 94/62/EC on packaging and packaging waste, Article 1.5.

Article 14

Management Plans

In pursuance of the objectives and measures referred to in this Directive, Member States shall include in the waste management plans required pursuant to Article 17 of Directive 75/442/EEC, a specific chapter on the management of packaging and packaging waste, including measures taken pursuant to Articles 4 and 5.

Article 15

Economic instruments

Acting on the basis of the relevant provisions of the Treaty, the Council adopts economic instruments to promote the implementation of the objectives set by this Directive. In the absence of such measures, the Member States may, in accordance with the principles governing Community environmental policy, inter alia, the polluter-pays principle, and the obligations arising out of the Treaty, adopt measures to implement those objectives.

Article 16

Notification

1. Without prejudice to Directive 83/189/EEC, before adopting such measures, Member States shall notify the drafts of measures which they intend to adopt within the framework of this Directive to the Commission, excluding measures of a fiscal nature, but including technical specifications linked to fiscal measures which encourage compliance with such technical specifications, in order to permit the latter to examine them in the light of existing provisions following in each case the procedure under the above Directive.

2. If the proposed measure is also a technical matter within the meaning of Directive 83/189/EEC, the Member State concerned may indicate, when following the notification procedures referred to in this Directive, that the notification is equally valid for Directive 83/189/EEC.

Article 17

Obligation to report

Member States shall report to the Commission on the application of this Directive in accordance with Article 5 of Council Directive 91/692/EEC of 23 December 1991 standardizing and rationalizing reports on the implementation of certain Directives relating to the environment. The first report shall cover the period 1995 to 1997.

Article 18

Freedom to place on the market

Member States shall not impede the placing on the market of their territory of packaging which satisfies the provisions of this Directive.

[Article 19

Adaptation to scientific and technical progress][1]

[1. The amendments necessary for adapting to scientific and technical progress the identification system (as referred to in Article 8(2) and Article 10, second paragraph, last indent) and the formats relating to the database system (as referred to in Article 12(3) and Annex III) shall be adopted in accordance with the regulatory procedure referred to in Article 21(2).

2. The Commission shall adopt the amendments necessary for adapting to scientific and technical progress the illustrative examples on the definition of packaging (as referred to in Annex I). Those measures, designed to amend non-essential elements of this Directive, shall be adopted in accordance with the regulatory procedure with scrutiny referred to in Article 21(3).][1]

Amendment

1 Substituted by Regulation (EC) No 219/2009 of the European Parliament and of the Council of 11 March 2009 adapting a number of instruments subject to the procedure referred to in Article 251 of the Treaty to Council Decision 1999/468/EC with regard to the regulatory procedure with scrutiny, Article 1, Annex, Pt 3.3, para 4.

Article 20

Specific measures

[1. The Commission shall determine the technical measures necessary to deal with any difficulties encountered in applying the provisions of this Directive, in particular, to inert packaging materials placed on the market in very small quantities (i.e. approximately 0,1 % by weight) in the Community, primary packaging for medical devices and pharmaceutical products, small packaging and luxury packaging. Those measures, designed to amend non-essential elements of this Directive by supplementing it, shall be adopted in accordance with the regulatory procedure with scrutiny referred to in Article 21(3).][1]

2. The Commission shall also present a report to the European Parliament and the Council on any other measure to be taken, if appropriate accompanied by a proposal.

Amendment

1 Substituted by Regulation (EC) No 219/2009 of the European Parliament and of the Council of 11 March 2009 adapting a number of instruments subject to the procedure referred to in Article 251 of the Treaty to Council Decision 1999/468/EC with regard to the regulatory procedure with scrutiny, Article 1, Annex, Pt 3.3, para 5.

[Article 21

Committee procedure][1]

[1. The Commission shall be assisted by a committee.

2. Where reference is made to this paragraph, Articles 5 and 7 of Decision 1999/468/EC shall apply, having regard to the provisions of Article 8 thereof.

The period laid down in Article 5(6) of Decision 1999/468/EC shall be set at three months.

[3. Where reference is made to this paragraph, Article 5a(1) to (4) and Article 7 of Decision 1999/468/EC shall apply, having regard to the provisions of Article 8 thereof.][2]][1]

Amendment

1 Substituted by Directive 2004/12/EC of the European Parliament and of the Council of 11 February 2004 amending Directive 94/62/EC on packaging and packaging waste, Article 1.8.

2 Substituted by Regulation (EC) No 219/2009 of the European Parliament and of the Council of 11 March 2009 adapting a number of instruments subject to the procedure referred to in Article 251 of the Treaty to Council Decision 1999/468/EC with regard to the regulatory procedure with scrutiny, Article 1, Annex, Pt 3.3, para 6.

Article 22

Implementation in national law

1. Member States shall bring into force the laws, regulations and administrative provisions necessary to comply with this Directive before 30 June 1996. They shall immediately inform the Commission thereof.

2. When Member States adopt these measures, they shall contain a reference to this Directive or shall be accompanied by such reference on the occasion of their official publication. the methods for making such reference shall be laid down by the Member States.

3. In addition, Member States shall communicate to the Commission all existing laws, regulations and administrative provisions adopted within the scope of this Directive.

[3a. Provided that the objectives set out in Article 6 are achieved, Member States may transpose the provisions of Article 7 by means of agreements between the competent authorities and the economic sectors concerned.

Such agreements shall meet the following requirements:
(a) agreements shall be enforceable;
(b) agreements shall specify objectives with the corresponding deadlines;
(c) agreements shall be published in the national official journal or an official document equally accessible to the public, and transmitted to the Commission;
(d) the results achieved shall be monitored regularly, reported to the competent authorities and the Commission and made available to the public under the conditions set out in the agreement;
(e) the competent authorities shall ensure that the progress achieved under the agreement is examined;
(f) in the event of non-compliance with the agreement, Member States shall implement the relevant provisions of this Directive by legislative, regulatory or administrative measures.][1]

4. The requirements for the manufacturing of packaging shall in no case apply to packaging used for a given product before the date of entry into force of this Directive.

5. Member States shall, for a period not exceeding five years from the date of the entry into force of the present Directive, allow the placing on the market of packaging manufactured before this date and which is in conformity with their existing national law.

Amendment

1 Inserted by Directive 2004/12/EC of the European Parliament and of the Council of 11 February 2004 amending Directive 94/62/EC on packaging and packaging waste, Article 1.9.

Article 23

Directive 85/339/EEC is hereby repealed with effect from the date referred to in Article 22 (1).

Article 24

This Directive shall enter into force on the day of its publication in the Official Journal of the European Communities.

Article 25

This Directive is addressed to the Member States.

[ANNEX I ILLUSTRATIVE EXAMPLES FOR CRITERIA REFERRED TO IN ARTICLE 3(1)][1]

[Illustrative examples for criterion (i)

Packaging

Sweet boxes

Film overwrap around a CD case

Non-packaging

Flower pots intended to stay with the plant throughout its life

Tool boxes

Tea bags

Wax layers around cheese

Sausage skins][1]

Amendment

1 Substituted by Directive 2004/12/EC of the European Parliament and of the Council of 11 February 2004 amending Directive 94/62/EC on packaging and packaging waste, Article 1.10.

[Illustrative examples for criterion (ii)

Packaging, if designed and intended to be filled at the point of sale

Paper or plastic carrier bags

Disposable plates and cups

Cling film

Sandwich bags

Aluminium foil

Non-packaging

Stirrer

Disposable cutlery][1]

Amendment

1 Substituted by Directive 2004/12/EC of the European Parliament and of the Council of 11 February 2004 amending Directive 94/62/EC on packaging and packaging waste, Article 1.10.

[Illustrative examples for criterion (iii)

Packaging

Labels hung directly on or attached to a product

Part of packaging

Mascara brush which forms part of the container closure

Sticky labels attached to another packaging item

Staples

Plastic sleeves

Device for measuring dosage which forms part of the container closure for detergents.][1]

Amendment

1 Substituted by Directive 2004/12/EC of the European Parliament and of the Council of 11 February 2004 amending Directive 94/62/EC on packaging and packaging waste, Article 1.10.

ANNEX II
ESSENTIAL REQUIREMENTS ON THE COMPOSITION AND THE REUSABLE AND RECOVERABLE, INCLUDING RECYCLABLE, NATURE OF PACKAGING

1. Requirements specific to the manufacturing and composition of packaging

— Packaging shall be so manufactured that the packaging volume and weight be limited to the minimum adequate amount to maintain the necessary level of safety, hygiene and acceptance for the packed product and for the consumer.

— Packaging shall be designed, produced and commercialized in such a way as to permit its reuse or recovery, including recycling, and to minimize its impact on the environment when packaging waste or residues from packaging waste management operations are disposed of.

— Packaging shall be so manufactured that the presence of noxious and other hazardous substances and materials as constituents of the packaging material or of any of the packaging components is minimized with regard to their presence in emissions, ash or leachate when packaging or residues from management operations or packaging waste are incinerated or landfilled.

2. Requirements specific to the reusable nature of packaging

The following requirements must be simultaneously satisfied:

— the physical properties and characteristics of the packaging shall enable a number of trips or rotations in normally predictable conditions of use,

— possiblity of processing the used packaging in order to meet health and safety requirements for the workforce,

— fulfil the requirements specific to recoverable packaging when the packaging is no longer reused and thus becomes waste.

3. Requirements specific to the recoverable nature of packaging

(a) Packaging recoverable in the form of material recycling Packaging must be manufactured in such a way as to enable the recycling of a certain percentage by weight of the materials used into the manufacture of marketable products, in compliance with current standards in the Community. The establishment of this percentage may vary, depending on the type of material of which the packaging is composed.

(b) Packaging recoverable in the form of energy recovery Packaging waste processed for the purpose of energy recovery shall have a minimum inferior calorific value to allow optimization of energy recovery.

(c) Packaging recoverable in the form of composting Packaging waste processed for the purpose of composting shall be of such a biodegradable nature that it should not hinder the separate collection and the composting process or activity into which it is introduced.

(d) Biodegradable packaging Biodegradable packaging waste shall be of such a nature that it is capable of undergoing physical, chemical, thermal or biological decomposition such that most of the finished compost ultimately decomposes into carbon dioxide, biomass and water.

ANNEX III
DATA TO BE INCLUDED BY MEMBER STATES IN THEIR DATABASES ON PACKAGING AND PACKAGING WASTE IN ACCORDANCE WITH TABLES 1 TO 4)

1. For primary, secondary and tertiary packaging:

(a) quantities, for each broad category of material, of packaging consumed within the country (produced + imported − exported) (Table 1);

(b) quantities reused (Table 2).

2. For household and non-household packaging waste:

(a) quantities for each broad category of material, recovered and disposed of within the country (produced + imported − exported) (Table 3);

(b) quantities recycled and quantities recovered for each broad category of material (Table 4).

Table 1
Quantity of packaging (primary, secondary and tertiary) consumed within the national territory

	Tonnage produced	*– Tonnage exported*	*+ Tonnage imported*	*= Total*
Glass				
Plastic				
Paper/cardboard (including composite)				
Metal				
Wood				
Other				
Total				

Table 2
Quantity of packaging (primary, secondary and tertiary) reused within the national territory

	Tonnage of packaging consumed	*Packaging reused*	
		Tonnage	*Percentage*
Glass			
Plastic			
Paper/cardboard (including composite)			
Metal			
Wood			
Other			
Total			

Table 3
Quantity of packaging waste recovered and disposed of within the national territory

	Tonnage of waste produced	*– Tonnage of waste exported*	*+ Tonnage of waste imported*	*= Total*
Household waste				
Glass packaging				
Plastic packaging				
Paper/cardboard packaging				
Cardboard composite packaging				
Metal packaging				
Wood packaging				
Total Household packaging waste				
Non-household waste				
Glass packaging				
Plastic packaging				
Paper/cardboard packaging				
Cardboard composite packaging				
Metal packaging				
Wood packaging				
Total non-household packaging waste				

Table 4
Quantity of packaging waste recycled or recovered within the national territory

	Total tonnage recovered and disposed of	*Quantity recycled*		*Quanatity recovered*	
		Tonnage	*Percentage*	*Tonnage*	*Percentage*
Household waste					
Glass packaging					
Plastic packaging					
Paper/cardboard packaging					
Cardboard composite packaging					
Metal packaging					
Wood packaging					
Total household packaging waste					
Non-household waste					
Glass packaging					
Plastic packaging					

	Total tonnage recovered and disposed of	*Quantity recycled*		*Quanatity recovered*	
		Tonnage	*Percentage*	*Tonnage*	*Percentage*
Paper/cardboard packaging					
Cardboard composite packaging					
Metal packaging					
Wood packaging					
Total non-household packaging waste					

COUNCIL DIRECTIVE 96/29/EURATOM

of 13 May 1996

LAYING DOWN BASIC SAFETY STANDARDS FOR THE PROTECTION OF THE HEALTH OF WORKERS AND THE GENERAL PUBLIC AGAINST THE DANGERS ARISING FROM IONIZING RADIATION

THE COUNCIL OF THE EUROPEAN UNION,

Having regard to the Treaty establishing the European Atomic Energy Community, and in particular Articles 31 and 32 thereof,

Having regard to the proposal from the Commission, drawn up after obtaining the opinion of a group of persons appointed by the Scientific and Technical Committee from among scientific experts in the Member States,

Having regard to the opinion of the European Parliament,

Having regard to the opinion of the Economic and Social Committee

Whereas Article 2b of the Treaty provides for the establishment of uniform basic safety standards to protect the health of workers and of the general public;

Whereas Article 30 of the Treaty defines the »basic standards« for the protection of the health of workers and the general public against the dangers arising from ionizing radiation as:
(a) maximum permissible doses compatible with adequate safety;
(b) maximum permissible levels of exposure and contamination;
(c) the fundamental principles governing the health surveillance of workers;

Whereas Article 33 of the Treaty requires each Member State to lay down the appropriate provisions, whether by legislation, regulation or administrative action, to ensure compliance with the basic standards which have been established and shall take the necessary measures with regard to teaching, education and vocational training;

Whereas in order to perform its task the Community laid down basic standards for the first time in 1959 pursuant to Article 218 of the Treaty by means of Directives of 2 February 1959 laying down the basic standards for the protection of the health of workers and the general public against the dangers arising from ionizing radiations; whereas the Directives were revised in 1962 by Directive of 5 March 1962, in 1966 by Directive 66/45/Euratom, in 1976 by Directive 76/579Euratom, in 1979 by Directive 79/343/Euratom, in 1980 by Directive 80/836/Euratom and in 1984 by Directive 84/467/Euratom;

Whereas the basic standards directives have been supplemented by Council Directive 84/466/ Euratom of 3 September 1984 laying down basic measures for the radiation protection of persons undergoing medical examination or treatment; Council Decision 87/600/Euratom of 14 December 1987 on Community arrangements for the early exchange of information in the event of a radiological emergency; Council Regulation (Euratom) No 3954/87 of 22 December 1987 laying down maximum permitted levels of radioactive contamination of foodstuffs and of feedingstuffs following a nuclear accident or any other case of radiological emergency; Council Directive 89/618Euratom of 27 November 1989 on informing the general public about health protection measures to be applied and steps to be taken in the event of a radiological emergency; Council Directive 90/641/Euratom of 4 December 1990 on the operational protection of outside workers exposed to the risk of ionizing radiation during their activities in controlled areas; Council Directive 92/3/Euratom of 3 February 1992 on the supervision and control of shipments of radioactive waste between Member States and into and out of the Community; and Council Regulation (Euratom) No 1493/93 of 8 June 1993 on shipments of radioactive substances between Member States;

Whereas the development of scientific knowledge concerning radiation protection, as expressed in particular in Recommendation No 60 of the International Commission on Radiological Protection, makes it convenient to revise the basic standards and to lay them down in a new legal instrument;

Whereas the basic standards are of special significance as to ionizing radiation risks with regard to other Directives concerned with other types of risks and it is important to make progress in applying them in a uniform manner within the Community;

Whereas it is desirable to take into account in the scope of the basic standards the practices or work activities which may result in a significant increase in exposure for workers and members of the public, which cannot be disregarded from the radiation protection point of view, due to ionizing radiation from artificial radiation sources or natural radiation sources, as well as appropriate protection in cases of intervention;

Whereas the Member States, in order to ensure compliance with the basic standards, are required to submit certain practices involving a hazard from ionizing radiation to a system of reporting and prior authorization or to prohibit certain practices;

Whereas a system of radiation protection for practices should continue to be based on the principles of justification of exposure, optimization of protection and dose limitation; whereas, limitations of doses must be fixed taking into account the particular situation of the different groups of persons exposed such as workers, apprentices, students and members of the public;

Whereas the operational protection of exposed workers, apprentices and students requires the implementation of measures at the workplace; whereas these measures must include prior evaluation of the hazard involved, classification of workplaces and workers, monitoring of areas and working conditions and medical surveillance;

Whereas the Member States should be required to identify work activities involving significantly increased levels of exposure for workers or members of the public to natural radiation sources which cannot be disregarded from a radiation protection point of view; whereas the Member States should take appropriate protective measures in respect of the work activities declared to be of concern;

Whereas the operational protection of the population in normal circumstances requires the establishment by Member States of a system of inspection to keep under review the radiation protection of the population and to check compliance with the basic standards;

Whereas the Member States should be prepared for the likelihood of potential radiological emergencies on their territory and should cooperate with other Member States and with third countries in order to facilitate the preparedness and management of those situations;

Whereas the basic standards directives as last revised by Directive 84/467/Euratom should be repealed with effect from the date that this Directive becomes applicable,

HAS ADOPTED THIS DIRECTIVE:

Title I
Definitions

Article 1

For the purpose of this Directive, the following terms have the meaning hereby assigned to them.

Absorbed dose (D): the energy absorbed per unit mass

Where
$D = d\bar{\varepsilon}/ dm$

— $d\bar{\varepsilon}/$ is the mean energy imparted by ionizing radiation to the matter in a volume element,
— dm is the mass of the matter in this volume element.

In this Directive absorbed dose denotes the dose averaged over a tissue or an organ. The unit for absorbed dose is the gray.

Accelerator: apparatus or installation, in which particles are accelerated, emitting ionizing radiation with an energy higher than 1 mega-electron volt (MeV).

Accidental exposure: an exposure of individuals as a result of an accident. It does not include emergency exposure.

Activation: process through which a stable nuclide is transformed into a radionuclide by irradiating with particles or high-energy gamma rays the material in which it is contained.

Activity (A): the activity, A, of an amount of a radionuclide in a particular energy state at a given time is the quotient of dN by dt, where dN is the expectation value of the number of spontaneous nuclear transitions from that energy state in the time interval dt:

$A = dN / dt$

The unit of activity is the becquerel.

Apprentice: a person receiving training or instruction within an undertaking with a view to exercising a specific skill.

Approved dosimetric service: a body responsible for the calibration, reading or interpretation of individual monitoring devices, or for the measurement of radioactivity in the human body or in biological samples, or for assessment of doses, whose capacity to act in this respect is recognized by the competent authorities.

Approved medical practioner: a medical practitioner responsible for the medical surveillance of category A workers, as defined in Article 21, whose capacity to act in that respect is recognized by the competent authorities.

Approved occupational health services: a body or bodies to which may be assigned responsibility for the radiation protection of exposed workers and/or medical surveillance of category A workers. Its capacity to act in that respect is recognized by the competent authorities.

Artificial sources: radiation sources other than natural radiation sources.

Authorization: a permission granted in a document by the competent authority, on application, or granted by national legislation, to carry out a practice or any other action within the scope of this Directive.

Becquerel (Bq): the special name of the unit of activity. One becquerel is equivalent to one transition per second:

$1\ Bq = 1\ s^{-1}$

Clearance levels: values, established by national competent authorities, and expressed in terms of activity concentrations and/or total activity, at or below which radioactive substances or materials containing radioactive substances arising from any practice subject to the requirement of reporting or authorization may be released from the requirements of this Directive.

Committed effective dose: ($E(\tau)$): the sum of the committed organ or tissue equivalent doses ($H_T(\tau)$) resulting from an intake, each multiplied by the appropriate tissue weighting factor w_T. It is defined by:

$$E(t) = \sum_T w_T H_T(t)$$

In specifying E(τ), τ is given in the number of years over which the integration is made. The unit for committed effective dose is the sievert.

Committed equivalent dose ($H_T(\tau)$): the integral over time (t) of the equivalent dose rate in tissue or organ T that will be received by an individual as a result of an intake. It is given by:

$$H_T(t) = \int_{t_0}^{t_0+t} H_T(t)td$$

for an intake at time t_0 where

— $H_T(t)$ is the relevant equivalent dose rate in organ or tissue T at time t,
— τ is the time over which the integration is performed.

In specifying $H_T(\tau)$, τ is given in years. When τ is not given, a period of 50 years is assumed for adults and up to age 70 for children. The unit for committed equivalent dose is the sievert.

Competent authorities: any authority designated by a Member State.

Controlled area: an area subject to special rules for the purpose of protection against ionizing radiation or of preventing the spread of radioactive contamination and to which access is controlled.

Disposal: the emplacement of waste in a repository, or a given location, without the intention of retrieval. Disposal also covers the approved direct discharge of wastes into the environment, with subsequent dispersion.

Dose constraint: a restriction on the prospective doses to individuals which may result from a defined source, for use at the planning stage in radiation protection whenever optimization is involved.

Dose limits: maximum references laid down in Title IV for the doses resulting from the exposure of workers, apprentices and students and members of the public to ionizing radiation covered by this Directive that apply to the sum of the relevant doses from external exposures in the specified period and the 50-year committed doses (up to age 70 for children) from intakes in the same period.

Effective dose (E): the sum of the weighted equivalent doses in all the tissues and organs of the body specified in Annex II from internal and external irradiation. It is defined by the expression:

$$E = \sum_T w_T H_T = \sum_T w_T \sum_R w_R D_{T,R}$$

where

— $D_{T,R}$ is the absorbed dose averaged over tissue or organ T, due to radiation R,
— W_R is the radiation weighting factor and
— W_T is the tissue weighting factor for tissue or organ T.

The appropriate W_T and W_R values are specified in Annex II. The unit for effective dose is the sievert.

Emergency exposure: an exposure of individuals implementing the necessary rapid action to bring help to endangered individuals, prevent exposure of a large number of people or save a valuable installation or goods, whereby one of the individual dose limits equal to that laid down for exposed workers could be exceeded. Emergency exposure shall apply only to volunteers.

Equivalent dose (H_T): the absorbed dose, in tissue or organ T weighted for the type and quality of radiation R. It is given by:

$H_{T,R} = w_R D_{T,R}$

where

— DT,R is the absorbed dose averaged over tissue or organ T, due to radiation R,

— wR is the radiation weighting factor.

When the radiation field is composed of types and energies with different values of w_R, the total equivalent dose, H_T, is given by:

$$H_T = \sum_R w_R D_{T,R}$$

The appropriate wR values are specified in Annex II. The unit for equivalent dose is the sievert.

Exposed workers: persons, either self-employed or working for an employer, subject to an exposure incurred at work from practices covered by this Directive and liable to result in doses exceeding one or other of the dose levels equal to the dose limits for members of the public.

Exposure: the process of being exposed to ionizing radiation.

Gray (Gy): the special name of the unit of absorbed dose. One gray is equal to one joule per kilogram:

$1 \text{ Gy} = 1 \text{ J kg}^{-1}$

Health detriment: an estimate of the risk of reduction in length and quality of life occurring in a population following exposure to ionizing radiations. This includes loss arising from somatic effects, cancer and severe genetic disorder.

Intake: the activities of radionuclides entering the body from the external environment.

Intervention: a human activity that prevents or decreases the exposure of individuals to radiation from sources which are not part of a practice or which are out of control, by acting on sources, transmission pathways and individuals themselves.

Intervention level: a value of avertable equivalent dose, avertable effective dose or a derived value, at which intervention measures should be considered. The avertable dose or derived value is solely that associated with the exposure pathway to which the intervention measure is to be applied.

Ionizing radiation: the transfer of energy in the form of particles or electromagnetic waves of a wavelength of 100 nanometer or less or a frequency of 3×10^{15} Hertz or more capable of producing ions directly or indirectly.

Members of the public: individuals in the population, excluding exposed workers, apprentices and students during their working hours and individuals during the exposures referred to in Article 6(4)(a), (b) and (c).

Natural radiation sources: sources of ionizing radiation from natural terrestrial or cosmic origin.

Potential exposure: exposure, that is not expected to be delivered with certainty, with a probability of occurrence that can be estimated in advance.

Practice: a human activity that can increase the exposure of individuals to radiation from an artificial source, or from a natural radiation source where natural radionuclides are processed for their radioactive, fissile or fertile properties, except in the case of an emergency exposure.

Qualified experts: Persons having the knowledge and training needed to carry out physical, technical or radiochemical tests enabling doses to be assessed, and to give advice in order to ensure effective protection of individuals and the correct operation of protective equipment, whose capacity to act as a qualified expert is recognized by the competent authorities. A qualified expert may be assigned the technical responsibility for the tasks of radiation protection of workers and members of the public.

Radioactive contamination: the contamination of any material, surface or environment or of an individual by radioactive substances. In the specific case of the human body, this radioactive contamination includes both external skin contamination and internal contamination, irrespective of route of intake.

Radioactive substance: any substance that contains one or more radionuclides the activity or concentration of which cannot be disregarded as far as radiation protection is concerned.

Radiological emergency: a situation that requires urgent action in order to protect workers, members of the public or the population either partially or as a whole.

Reference group of the population: a group comprising individuals whose exposure to a source is reasonably uniform and representative of that of the individuals in the population who are the more highly exposed to that source.

Reporting: requirement of submitting a document to the competent authority to notify the intention to carry out a practice or any other action within the scope of this Directive.

Sealed source: a source whose structure is such as to prevent, under normal conditions of use, any dispersion of the radioactive substances into the environment.

Sievert: the special name of the unit of equivalent or effective dose. One sievert is equivalent to one joule per kilogram:

$1\ Sv = 1\ J\ kg^{-1}$

Source: an apparatus, a radioactive substance or an installation capable of emitting ionizing radiation or radioactive substances.

Supervised area: an area subject to appropriate supervision for the purpose of protection against ionizing radiation.

Undertaking: any natural or legal person who carries out the practices or work activities referred to in Article 2 of this Directive and who has the legal responsibility under national law for such practices or work activities.

Title II
Scope

Article 2

1. This Directive shall apply to all practices which involve a risk from ionizing radiation emanating from an artificial source or from a natural radiation source in cases where natural radionuclides are or have been processed in view of their radioactive, fissile or fertile properties, namely:

(a) the production, processing, handling, use, holding, storage, transport, import to and export from the Community and disposal of radioactive substances;

(b) the operation of any electrical equipment emitting ionizing radiation and containing components operating at a potential difference of more than 5 kV;

(c) any other practice specified by the Member State.

2. In accordance with Title VII it shall also apply to work activities which are not covered by paragraph 1 but which involve the presence of natural radiation sources and lead to a significant increase in the exposure of workers or members of the public which cannot be disregarded from the radiation protection point of view.

3. In accordance with Title IX it shall also apply to any intervention in cases of radiological emergencies or in cases of lasting exposure resulting from the after-effects of a radiological emergency or a past or old practice or work activity.

4. This Directive shall not apply to exposure to radon in dwellings or to the natural level of radiation, i.e. to radionuclides contained in the human body, to cosmic radiation prevailing at ground level or to aboveground exposure to radionuclides present in the undisturbed earth's crust.

Title III
Reporting and authorization of practices

Article 3

Reporting

1. Each Member State shall require the carrying out of the practices referred to in Article 2 (1) to be reported, except as provided for in this Article.

2. No reporting need be required for practices involving the following:

(a) radioactive substances where the quantities involved do not exceed in total the exemption values set out in column 2 of Table A to Annex I or, in exceptional circumstances in an individual Member State, different values authorized by the competent authorities that nevertheless satisfy the basic general criteria set out in Annex I; or

(b) radioactive substances where the concentrations of activity per unit mass do not exceed the exemption values set out in column 3 of Table A to Annex I or, in exceptional circumstances in an individual Member State, different values authorized by the competent authorities that nevertheless satisfy the basic general criteria set out in Annex I; or

(c) apparatus containing radioactive substances exceeding the quantities or concentration values specified in subparagraphs (a) or (b), provided that:
  (i) it is of a type approved by the competent authorities of the Member State; and
  (ii) it is constructed in the form of a sealed source; and
  (iii) it does not cause, in normal operating conditions, a dose rate exceeding 1 $\mu Sv\ h^{-1}$ at a distance of 0,1 m from any accessible surface of the apparatus; and
  (iv) conditions for disposal have been specified by the competent authorities; or

(d) the operation of any electrical apparatus to which this Directive applies, other than that referred to in subparagraph (e) provided that:
  (i) it is of a type approved by the competent authorities of the Member State; and
  (ii) it does not cause, in normal operating conditions, a dose rate exceeding 1 $\mu Sv\ h^{-1}$ at a distance of 0,1 m from any accessible surface of the apparatus; or

(e) the operation of any cathode ray tube intended for the display of visual images, or other electrical apparatus operating at a potential difference not exceeding 30 kV, provided that this operation does not cause, in normal operating conditions, a dose rate exceeding 1 $\mu Sv\ h^{-1}$ at a distance of 0,1 m from any accessible surface of the apparatus; or

(f) material contaminated with radioactive substances resulting from authorized releases which competent authorities have declared not to be subject to further controls.

Article 4

Authorization

1. Except as provided for in this Article, each Member State shall require prior authorization for the following practices:

(a) operation and decommissioning of any facility of the nuclear fuel cycle and exploitation and closure of uranium mining;

(b) the deliberate addition of radioactive substances in the production and manufacture of medicinal products and the import or export of such goods;

(c) the deliberate addition of radioactive substances in the production and manufacture of consumer goods and the import or export of such goods;

(d) the deliberate administration of radioactive substances to persons and, in so far as radiation protection of human beings is concerned, animals for the purpose of medical or veterinary diagnosis, treatment or research;

(e) the use of X-ray sets or radioactive sources for industrial radiography or processing of products or research or the exposure of persons for medical treatment and the use of accelerators except electron microscopes;

2. Prior authorization may be required for practices other than those listed in paragraph 1.

3. Member States may specify that a practice shall not require authorization where:
(a) in the case of the practices described in paragraph 1 (a), (c) and (e), the practice is exempt from reporting; or
(b) in cases where a limited risk of exposure of human beings does not necessitate the examination of individual cases the practice is undertaken in accordance with conditions laid down in national legislation.

Article 5

Authorization and clearance for disposal, recycling or reuse

1. The disposal, recycling or reuse of radioactive substances or materials containing radioactive substances arising from any practice subject to the requirement of reporting or authorization is subject to prior authorization.

2. However, the disposal, recycling or reuse of such substances or materials may be released from the requirements of this Directive provided they comply with clearance levels established by national competent authorities. These clearance levels shall follow the basic criteria used in Annex I and shall take into account any other technical guidance provided by the Community.

Title IV
Justification, optimization and dose limitation for practices

Chapter I
General Principles

Article 6

1. Member States shall ensure that all new classes or types of practice resulting in exposure to ionizing radiation are justified in advance of being first adopted or first approved by their economic, social or other benefits in relation to the health detriment they may cause.

2. Existing classes or types of practice may be reviewed as to justification whenever new and important evidence about their efficacy or consequences is acquired.

3. In addition each Member State shall ensure that:
(a) in the context of optimization all exposures shall be kept as low as reasonably achievable, economic and social factors being taken into account;
(b) without prejudice to Article 12, the sum of the doses from all relevant practices shall not exceed the dose limits laid down in this Title for exposed workers, apprentices and students and members of the public.

4. The principle set out in paragraph 3 (a) shall apply to all exposures to ionizing radiation resulting from the practices referred to in Article 2 (1). The principle set out in paragraph 3 (b) shall not apply to any of the following exposures:
(a) exposure of individuals as part of their own medical diagnosis or treatment;
(b) exposure of individuals knowingly and willingly helping (other than as part of their occupation) in the support and comfort of patients undergoing medical diagnosis or treatment;
(c) exposure of volunteers participating in medical and biomedical research programmes.

5. Member States shall permit neither the deliberate addition of radioactive substances in the production of foodstuffs, toys, personal ornaments and cosmetics nor the import or export of such goods.

Article 7

Dose constraints

1. Dose constraints should be used, where appropriate, within the context of optimization of radiological protection.

2. Guidance established by each Member State on the appropriate procedures to be applied to individuals exposed in accordance with Article 6 (4) (b) and (c) may include dose constraints.

Chapter II
Limitation of doses

Article 8

Age limit for exposed workers

Subject to Article 11 (2), persons under 18 years of age may not be assigned to any work which would result in their being exposed workers.

Article 9

Dose limits for exposed workers

1. The limit on effective dose for exposed workers shall be 100 millisieverts ("mSv") in a consecutive five-year period, subject to a maximum effective dose of 50 mSv in any single year. Member States may decide an annual amount.

2. Without prejudice to paragraph 1:
(a) the limit on equivalent dose for the lens of the eye shall be 150 mSv in a year;
(b) the limit on equivalent dose for the skin shall be 500 mSv in a year. This limit shall apply to the dose averaged over any area of 1 cm^2, regardless of the area exposed;
(c) the limit on equivalent dose for the hands, forearms, feet and ankles shall be 500 mSv in a year.

Article 10

Special protection during pregnancy and breastfeeding

1. As soon as a pregnant woman informs the undertaking, in accordance with national legislation and/or national practice, of her condition, the protection of the child to be born shall be comparable with that provided for members of the public. The conditions for the pregnant woman in the context of her employment shall therefore be such that the equivalent dose to the child to be born will be as low as reasonably achievable and that it will be unlikely that this dose will exceed 1 mSv during at least the remainder of the pregnancy.

2. As soon as a nursing woman informs the undertaking of her condition she shall not be employed in work involving a significant risk of bodily radioactive contamination.

Article 11

Dose limits for apprentices and students

1. The dose limits for apprentices aged 18 years or over and students aged 18 years or over who, in the course of their studies, are obliged to use sources shall be the same as the dose limits for exposed workers laid down in Article 9.

2. The limit for effective dose for apprentices aged between 16 and 18 years and for students aged between 16 and 18 years who, in the course of their studies, are obliged to use sources shall be 6 mSv per year.

Without prejudice to this dose limit:

(a) the limit on equivalent dose for the lens of the eye shall be 50 mSv in a year;

(b) the limit on equivalent dose for the skin shall be 150 mSv in a year. This limit shall apply to the dose averaged over any area of 1 cm^2, regardless of the area exposed;

(c) the limit on equivalent dose for the hands, forearms, feet and ankles shall be 150 mSv in a year.

3. The dose limits for apprentices and students who are not subject to the provisions of paragraphs 1 and 2 shall be the same as the dose limits for members of the public specified in Article 13.

Article 12

Specially authorized exposures

1. In exceptional circumstances, excluding radiological emergencies and evaluated case by case, the competent authorities may, where some specific operation so requires, authorize individual occupational exposures of some identified workers exceeding the dose limits set out in Article 9, provided that such exposures are limited in time, confined to certain working areas and within maximum exposure levels defined for the particular case by the competent authorities. The following conditions shall be taken into account:

(a) only category A workers as defined in Article 21 may be subject to specially authorized exposures;

(b) apprentices, students, pregnant women and breastfeeding women who are likely to be bodily contaminated shall be excluded from such exposures;

(c) the undertaking shall carefully justify these exposures in advance and thoroughly discuss them with the voluntary workers, their representatives, the approved medical practitioner, the approved occupational health services or the qualified expert;

(d) information about the risks involved and the precautions to be taken during the operation shall be provided to the relevant workers in advance;

(e) all doses relating to such exposures shall be separately recorded in the medical record referred to in Article 34 and the individual record referred to in Article 28.

2. The exceeding of dose limits as a result of specially authorized exposures shall not necessarily constitute a reason by the employer for excluding from his usual occupation or relocating the worker, without the agreement of the worker.

Article 13

Dose limits for members of the public

1. Without prejudice to Article 14, the dose limits for members of the public shall be as laid down in paragraphs 2 and 3.

2. The limit for effective dose shall be 1 mSv in a year. However, in special circumstances, a higher effective dose may be authorized in a single year, provided that the average over five consecutive years does not exceed 1 mSv per year.

3. Without prejudice to paragraph 2:

(a) the limit on equivalent dose for the lens of the eye shall be 15 mSv in a year;

(b) the limit on equivalent dose for the skin shall be 50 mSv in a year averaged over any 1 cm^2 area of skin, regardless of the area exposed.

Article 14

Exposure of the population as a whole

Each Member State shall take reasonable steps to ensure that the contribution to the exposure of the population as a whole from practices is kept as low as reasonably achievable, economic and social factors being taken into account.

The total of all such contributions shall be regularly assessed.

Title V
Estimation of effective dose

Article 15

For the estimation of effective and equivalent doses the values and relationships referred to in this Title shall be used. The competent authorities may authorize the use of equivalent methods.

Article 16

Without prejudice to the provisions of Article 15:

(a) For external radiation, the values and relationships given in Annex II shall be used to estimate the relevant effective and equivalent doses;

(b) For internal exposure from a radionuclide or from a mixture of radionuclides, the values and relationships given in Annexes II and III may be used to estimate the effective doses.

Title VI
Fundamental principles governing operational protection of exposed workers, apprentices and students for practices

Article 17

Operational protection of exposed workers shall be based in particular on the following principles:

(a) prior evaluation to identify the nature and magnitude of the radiological risk to exposed workers and implementation of the optimization of radiation protection in all working conditions;

(b) classification of workplaces into different areas, where appropriate, by reference to an assessment of the expected annual doses and the probability and magnitude of potential exposures;

(c) classification of workers into different categories;

(d) implementation of control measures and monitoring relating to the different areas and working conditions, including, where necessary, individual monitoring;

(e) medical surveillance.

Chapter I
Measures for the restriction of exposure

Section 1
Classification and delineation of areas

Article 18

Arrangements in workplaces

1. For the purposes of radiation protection, arrangements shall be made as regards all workplaces where there is a possibility of exposure to ionizing radiation in excess of 1 mSv per year or an equivalent dose of one-tenth of the dose limits for the lens of the eyes, skin and extremities laid down in Article 9 (2). Such arrangements must be appropriate to the nature of the installations and sources and to the magnitude and nature of the risks. The scope of the precautions and monitoring, as well as their type and quality, must be appropriate to the risks associated with the work involving exposure to ionizing radiation.

2. A distinction shall be made between controlled areas and supervised areas.

3. The competent authorities shall establish guidance on the classification of controlled and supervised areas which is relevant to the particular circumstances.

4. The undertaking shall keep under review the working conditions in controlled and supervised areas.

Article 19

Requirements for controlled areas

1. The minimum requirements for a controlled area are as follows:

(a) the controlled area shall be delineated and access to it shall be restricted to individuals who have received appropriate instructions and shall be controlled in accordance with written procedures provided by the undertaking. Wherever there is a significant risk of the spread of radioactive contamination, specific arrangements shall be made, including access and exit of individuals and goods;

(b) taking into account the nature and extent of radiological risks in the controlled area, radiological surveillance of the working environment shall be organized in accordance with the provisions of Article 24;

(c) signs indicating type of area, nature of the sources and their inherent risks shall be displayed;

(d) working instructions appropriate to the radiological risk associated with the sources and the operations involved shall be laid down.

2. The implementation of these duties will be carried out under the responsibility of the undertaking following consultations with the approved occupational health services or the qualified experts.

Article 20

Requirements for supervised areas

1. The requirements for a supervised area are as follows:

(a) as a minimum, taking into account the nature and extent of radiological risks in the supervised area, radiological surveillance of the working environment shall be organized in accordance with the provisions of Article 24;

(b) if appropriate, signs indicating type of area, nature of the sources and their inherent risks shall be displayed;

(c) if appropriate, working instructions appropriate to the radiological risk associated with the sources and the operations involved shall be laid down.

2. The implementation of these duties will be carried out under the responsibility of the undertaking following consultations with the qualified experts or the approved occupational health services.

Section 2
Classification of exposed workers, apprentices and students

Article 21

Categorization of exposed workers

For the purposes of monitoring and surveillance, a distinction shall be made between two categories of exposed workers:

(a) *category A:* those exposed workers who are liable to receive an effective dose greater than 6 mSv per year or an equivalent dose greater than 3/10 of the dose limits for the lens of the eye, skin and extremities laid down in Article 9 (2);

(b) *category B:* those exposed workers who are not classified as exposed category A workers.

Article 22

Information and training

1. Member States shall require the undertaking to inform exposed workers, apprentices and students who, in the course of their studies, are obliged to use sources on:

(a) the health risks involved in their work:
- — the general radiation protection procedures and precautions to be taken and, in particular, those involved with operational and working conditions in respect of both the practice in general and each type of work station or job to which they may be assigned,
- — the importance of complying with the technical, medical and administrative requirements;

(b) in the case of women, the need for early declaration of pregnancy in view of the risks of exposure for the child to be born and the risk of contaminating the nursing infant in case of bodily radioactive contamination.

2. Member States shall require the undertaking to arrange for relevant training in the field of radiation protection to be given to exposed workers, apprentices and students.

Section 3
Assessment and implementation of arrangements for the radiological protection of exposed workers

Article 23

1. The undertaking shall be responsible for assessing and implementing arrangements for the radiological protection of exposed workers.

2. Member States shall require the undertaking to consult the qualified experts or the approved occupational health services on the examination and testing of protective devices and measuring instruments comprising in particular:

(a) prior critical examination of plans for installations from the point of view of radiation protection;

(b) the acceptance into service of new or modified sources from the point of view of radiation protection;

(c) regular checking of the effectiveness of protective devices and techniques;

(d) regular calibration of measuring instruments and regular checking that they are serviceable and correctly used.

Chapter II
Assessment of exposure

Section 1
Monitoring of the workplace

Article 24

1. The radiological surveillance of the working environment referred to in Articles 19 (1) (b) and 20 (1) (a) shall comprise, where appropriate:

(a) the measurement of external dose rates, indicating the nature and quality of the radiation in question;

(b) the measurement of air activity concentration and surface density of contaminating radioactive substances, indicating their nature and their physical and chemical states.

2. The results of these measurements shall be recorded and shall be used, if necessary, for estimating individual doses, as provided for in Article 25.

Section 2
Individual monitoring

Article 25

Monitoring - General

1. Individual monitoring shall be systematic for exposed category A workers. This monitoring shall be based on individual measurements which are established by an approved dosimetric service. In cases where category A workers are liable to receive significant internal contamination an adequate system for monitoring should be set up; the competent authorities may provide general guidance for identifying such workers.

2. Monitoring for category B workers shall be at least sufficient to demonstrate that such workers are correctly classified in category B. Member States may require individual monitoring and if necessary individual measurements, established by an approved dosimetric service, for category B workers.

3. In cases where individual measurements are impossible or inadequate, the individual monitoring shall be based on an estimate arrived at either from individual measurements made on other exposed workers or from the results of the surveillance of the workplace provided for in Article 24.

Section 3
Monitoring in the case of accidental or emergency exposure

Article 26

In the case of accidental exposure the relevant doses and their distribution in the body shall be assessed.

Article 27

In the case of emergency exposure, individual monitoring or assessment of the individual doses shall be carried out as appropriate to the circumstances.

Section 4
Recording and reporting of results

Article 28

1. A record containing the results of the individual monitoring, shall be made for each exposed category A worker.

2. For the purposes of paragraph 1 the following shall be retained during the working life involving exposure to ionizing radiation of exposed workers, and afterwards until the individual has or would have attained the age of 75 years, but in any case not less than 30 years from the termination of the work involving exposure:

(a) a record of the exposures measured or estimated, as the case may be, of individual doses pursuant to Articles 12, 25, 26 and 27;

(b) in the case of exposures referred to in Articles 26 and 27, the reports relating to the circumstances and the action taken;

(c) the results of workplace monitoring used to assess individual doses where necessary.

3. Exposure referred to in Articles 12, 26 and 27 shall be recorded separately in the dose record referred to in paragraph 1.

Article 29

1. The results of the individual monitoring required by Articles 25, 26 and 27 shall be:

(a) made available to the competent authorities, and to the undertaking;
(b) made available to the worker concerned in accordance with Article 38 (2);
(c) submitted to the approved medical practitioner or approved occupational health services in order to interpret their implications for human health, as provided for in Article 31.

2. Member States shall determine the arrangements under which the results of individual monitoring are conveyed.

3. In the case of an accidental or emergency exposure, the results of individual monitoring shall be submitted without delay.

Chapter III
Medical surveillance of exposed workers

Article 30

The medical surveillance of exposed workers shall be based on the principles that govern occupational medicine generally.

Section 1
Medical surveillance of category A workers

Article 31

Medical surveillance

1. Notwithstanding the overall responsibility of the undertaking, the medical surveillance of category A workers shall be the responsibility of approved medical practitioners or approved occupational health services.

This medical surveillance must allow for ascertaining the state of health of workers under surveillance as regards their fitness for the tasks assigned to them. To this end the approved medical practitioner or approved occupational health services must have access to any relevant information they require including the environmental conditions existing in the working premises.

2. Medical surveillance shall include:
(a) a medical examination prior to employment or classification as category A worker. The purpose of this thorough examination shall be to determine the worker's fitness for a post as category A worker for which he is being considered;
(b) periodic reviews of health. The state of health of each category A worker shall be reviewed at least once a year, in order to determine whether they remain fit to perform their duties. The nature of these reviews, which can be performed as many times as the approved medical practitioner considers necessary, shall depend on the type of work and on the individual worker's state of health.

3. The approved medical practitioner or approved occupational health services may indicate the need for medical surveillance to continue after cessation of work for as long as they consider it necessary to safeguard the health of the person concerned.

Article 32

Medical classification

The following medical classification shall be adopted with respect to fitness for work as a category A worker:
(a) fit;
(b) fit, subject to certain conditions;
(c) unfit.

Article 33

No worker may be employed or classified for any period in a specific post as a category A worker if the medical findings deem him unfit for that specific post.

Article 34

Medical records

1. A medical record shall be opened for each category A worker and kept up to date so long as he remains a worker of that category. Thereafter it shall be retained until the individual has or would have attained the age of 75 years, but in any case not less than 30 years from the termination of the work involving exposure to ionizing radiation.

2. The medical record shall include information regarding the nature of the employment, the results of the medical examinations prior to employment or classification as category A worker, the periodic reviews of health and the record of doses required by Article 28.

Section 2
Special surveillance of exposed workers

Article 35

1. Special medical surveillance shall be provided in each case where one of the dose limits laid down in Article 9 has been exceeded.

2. Subsequent conditions of exposure shall be subject to the agreement of the approved medical practitioner or approved occupational health services.

Article 36

In addition to the medical surveillance of exposed workers provided for in Articles 30 and 31, provision shall be made for any further action in relation to the health protection of the exposed individual considered necessary by the approved medical practitioner or approved occupational health services such as further examinations, decontamination measures or urgent remedial treatment.

Section 3
Appeals

Article 37

Each Member State shall lay down the procedure for appeal against the findings and decisions made in pursuance of Articles 32, 33 and 35.

Chapter IV
Tasks of Member States in respect of protection of exposed workers

Article 38

1. Each Member State shall establish a system or systems of inspection to enforce the provisions introduced in compliance with this Directive and to initiate surveillance and intervention measures wherever necessary.

2. Each Member State shall require that workers have access at their request to the results of their individual monitoring, including the results of measurements which may have been used in estimating them, or of the assessments of their doses made as a result of workplace measurements.

3. Each Member State shall make the necessary arrangements to recognize, as appropriate, the capacity of:
— the approved medical practitioners,
— the approved occupational health services,
— the approved dosimetric services,
— the qualified experts.

To this end, each Member State shall ensure that the training of such specialists is arranged.

4. Each Member State shall require that the means necessary for proper radiation protection are placed at the disposal of the units responsible. A specialized radiation protection unit, distinct from production and operation units in the case of an internal unit, authorized to perform radiation protection tasks and provide specific advice shall be required for the installations which the competent authorities consider necessary. This unit may be shared by several installations.

5. Each Member State shall facilitate the exchange amongst competent authorities, or approved medical practitioners, or approved occupational health services, or qualified experts, or approved dosimetric services within the European Community of all relevant information on the doses previously received by a worker in order to perform the medical examination prior to employment or classification as a category A worker pursuant to Article 31 and to control the further exposure of workers.

Chapter V
Operational protection of apprentices and students

Article 39

1. The exposure conditions and operational protection of apprentices and students aged 18 years or over referred to in Article 11 (1) shall be equivalent to that of exposed workers of category A or B as appropriate.

2. The exposure conditions and operational protection of apprentices and students aged between 16 and 18 years referred to in Article 11 (2) shall be equivalent to that of exposed workers of category B.

Title VII
Significant increase in exposure due to natural radiation sources

Article 40

Application

1. This Title shall apply to work activities not covered by Article 2 (1) within which the presence of natural radiation sources leads to a significant increase in the exposure of workers or of members of the public which cannot be disregarded from the radiation protection point of view.

2. Each Member State shall ensure the identification, by means of surveys or by any other appropriate means, of work activities which may be of concern. These include, in particular:
(a) work activities where workers and, where appropriate, members of the public are exposed to thoron or radon daughters or gamma radiation or any other exposure in workplaces such as spas, caves, mines, underground workplaces and aboveground workplaces in identified areas;
(b) work activities involving operations with, and storage of, materials, not usually regarded as radioactive but which contain naturally occurring radionuclides, causing a significant increase in the exposure of workers and, where appropriate, members of the public;

(c) work activities which lead to the production of residues not usually regarded as radioactive but which contain naturally occurring radionuclides, causing a significant increase in the exposure of members of the public and, where appropriate, workers;
(d) aircraft operation.

3. Articles 41 and 42 shall apply to the extent that the Member States have declared that exposure to natural radiation sources due to work activities identified in accordance with paragraph 2 of this Article needed attention and had to be subject to control.

Article 41

Protection against exposure from terrestrial natural radiation sources

For each work activity declared by them to be of concern, the Member States shall require the setting-up of appropriate means for monitoring exposure and as necessary:
(a) the implementation of corrective measures to reduce exposure pursuant to all or part of Title IX;
(b) the application of radiation protection measures pursuant to all or part of Titles III, IV, V, VI and VIII.

Article 42

Protection of air crew

Each Member State shall make arrangements for undertakings operating aircraft to take account of exposure to cosmic radiation of air crew who are liable to be subject to exposure to more than 1 mSv per year. The undertakings shall take appropriate measures, in particular:
— to assess the exposure of the crew concerned,
— to take into account the assessed exposure when organizing working schedules with a view to reducing the doses of highly exposed aircrew,
— to inform the workers concerned of the health risks their work involves,
— to apply Article 10 to female air crew.

Title VIII
Implementation of radition protection for the population in normal circumstances

Article 43

Basic principles

Each Member State shall create the conditions necessary to ensure the best possible protection of the population based on the principles set out in Article 6 and to apply the fundamental principles governing operational protection of the population.

Article 44

Conditions for authorization of practices involving a risk from ionizing radiation for the population

Operational protection of the population in normal circumstances from practices subject to prior authorization means all arrangements and surveys for detecting and eliminating the factors which, in the course of any operation involving exposure to ionizing radiation, are liable to create a risk of exposure for the population which cannot be disregarded from the radiation protection point of view. Such protection shall include the following tasks:
(a) examination and approval of plans for installations involving an exposure risk, and of the proposed siting of such installations within the territory concerned, from the point of view of radiation protection;

(b) acceptance into service of such new installations subject to adequate protection being provided against any exposure or radioactive contamination liable to extend beyond the perimeter, taking into account, if relevant, demographic, meteorological, geological, hydrological and ecological conditions;
(c) examination and approval of plans for the discharge of radioactive effluents.

These tasks shall be carried out in accordance with rules laid down by the competent authorities on the basis of the extent of the exposure risk involved.

Article 45

Estimates of population doses

The competent authorities shall:
(a) ensure that dose estimates from practices referred to in Article 44 are made as realistic as possible for the population as a whole and for reference groups of the population in all places where such groups may occur;
(b) decide on the frequency of assessments and take all necessary steps to identify the reference groups of the population, taking into account the effective pathways of transmission of the radioactive substances;
(c) ensure, taking into account the radiological risks, that the estimates of the population doses include:
 — assessment of the doses due to external radiation, indicating, where appropriate, the quality of the radiation in question,
 — assessment of the intake of radionuclides, indicating the nature of the radionuclides and, where necessary, their physical and chemical states, and determination of the activity and concentrations of these radionuclides,
 — assessment of the doses that the reference groups of the population are liable to receive and specification of the characteristics of these groups.
(d) require records to be kept relating to measurements of external exposure, estimates of intakes of radionuclides and radioactive contamination as well as the results of the assessment of the doses received by reference groups and by the population.

Article 46

Inspection

As regards health protection of the population each Member State shall establish a system of inspection to enforce the provisions introduced in compliance with this Directive and to initiate surveillance in the area of radiation protection.

Article 47

Responsibilities of undertakings

1. Each Member State shall require the undertaking responsible for practices as referred to in Article 2 to conduct them in accordance with the principles of health protection of the population in the area of radiation protection and in particular to carry out the following tasks within its installations:
(a) achieving and maintaining an optimal level of protection of the environment and the population;
(b) checking the effectiveness of technical devices for protecting the environment and the population;
(c) acceptance into service, from the point of view of surveillance of radiation protection, of equipment and procedures for measuring and assessing, as appropriate, exposure and radioactive contamination of the environment and the population;

(d) regular calibration of measuring instruments and regular checking that they are serviceable and correctly used.

2. Qualified experts and, as appropriate, the specialized radiation protection unit referred to in Article 38 (4) shall be concerned in the discharge of these duties.

Title IX
Intervention

Article 48

Application

1. This Title shall apply to intervention in cases of radiological emergencies or in cases of lasting exposure resulting from the after-effects of a radiological emergency or a past or old practice or work activity.

2. The implementation and extent of any intervention shall be considered in compliance with the following principles:
— intervention shall be undertaken only if the reduction in detriment due to radiation is sufficient to justify the harm and costs, including social costs, of the intervention,
— the form, scale and duration of the intervention shall be optimized so that the benefit of the reduction in health detriment less the detriment associated with the intervention, will be maximized,
— dose limits, as laid down in Articles 9 and 13, shall not apply to intervention; however, the intervention levels established in application of Article 50 (2) constitute indications as to the situations in which intervention is appropriate; furthermore, in cases of long term exposure covered by Article 53, the dose limits set out in Article 9 should normally be appropriate for workers involved in interventions.

Section 1
Intervention in cases of radiological emergency

Article 49

Potential exposures

The Member States shall, where appropriate, require:
— that the possibility of radiological emergencies resulting from practices subject to the system of reporting or authorization laid down in Title III be considered,
— that the spatial and temporal distribution of the radioactive substances dispersed in the event of a possible radiological emergency be assessed,
— that the corresponding potential exposures be assessed.

Article 50

Intervention preparation

1. Each Member State shall ensure that account is taken of the fact that radiological emergencies may occur in connection with practices on or outside its territory and affect it.

2. Each Member State shall ensure that appropriate intervention plans, taking account of the general principles of radiation protection for intervention referred to in Article 48 (2) and of the appropriate intervention levels established by the competent authorities, are drawn up at national or local level, including within installations, in order to deal with various types of radiological emergency and that such plans are tested to an appropriate extent at regular intervals.

3. Each Member State shall ensure, where appropriate, that provision is made for the creation and appropriate training of special teams for technical, medical and health intervention.

4. Each Member State shall seek to cooperate with other Member States or non-Member States in relation to possible radiological emergencies at installations on its own territory which may affect other Member States or non-Member States, in order to facilitate the organization of radiological protection in these States.

Article 51

Implementation of intervention

1. Each Member State shall make provision for the immediate notification to its competent authorities by the undertaking responsible for the practices involved of any radiological emergency occurring in its territory and shall require all appropriate action to reduce the consequences.

2. Each Member State shall ensure that in the event of a radiological emergency on its own territory, the undertaking responsible for the practices involved makes an initial provisional assessment of the circumstances and consequences of the emergency and assists with intervention.

3. Each Member State shall ensure that provision is made, if the situation so requires, for intervention related to:
— the source, to reduce or stop the direct radiation and emission of radionuclides,
— the environment, to reduce the transfer of radioactive substances to individuals,
— individuals, to reduce exposure and organize the treatment of victims.

4. In the event of a radiological emergency on or outside its territory, each Member State shall require:
(a) the organization of appropriate intervention, taking account of the real characteristics of the emergency;
(b) the assessment and recording of the consequences of the radiological emergency and of the effectiveness of the intervention.

5. Each Member State shall, in the event of a radiological emergency occurring at an installation on its territory or being likely to have radiological consequences on its territory, establish relations to obtain cooperation with any other Member State or non-Member State which may be involved.

Article 52

Emergency occupational exposure

1. Each Member State shall make provision for situations where workers or intervention personnel involved in different kinds of intervention are liable to be subjected to emergency exposure resulting in doses in excess of the dose limits for exposed workers. To this end, each Member State shall establish exposure levels taking into account the technical obligations and health risks. These levels shall be operational guides. An exposure above these special levels may be admitted exceptionally to save human lives and only for volunteers who are informed about the risks involved in their intervention.

2. Each Member State shall require radiological monitoring and medical surveillance of the special emergency intervention teams.

Section II
Intervention in cases of lasting exposure

Article 53

Where the Member States have identified a situation leading to lasting exposure resulting from the after-effects of a radiological emergency or a past practice, they shall, if necessary and to the extent of the exposure risk involved, ensure that:

(a) the area concerned is demarcated;
(b) arrangements for the monitoring of exposure are made;
(c) any appropriate intervention is implemented, taking account of the real characteristics of the situation;
(d) access to or use of land or buildings situated in the demarcated area is regulated.

TITLE X
FINAL PROVISIONS

Article 54

1. This Directive establishes the basic safety standards for the protection of the health of workers and the general public against the dangers arising from ionizing radiation with the aim of their uniform implementation by Member States. If a Member State is to adopt dose limits which are stricter than those laid down in this Directive, it shall inform the Commission and the Member States.

Article 55

Implementation

1. Member States shall bring into force the laws, regulations and administrative provisions necessary to comply with this Directive before 13 May 2000. They shall forthwith inform the Commission thereof.

When Member States adopt these provisions, they shall contain a reference to this Directive or shall be accompanied by such reference on the occasion of their official publication. The methods of making such reference shall be laid down by Member States.

2. Member States shall communicate to the Commission the text of the main laws, regulations or administrative provisions which they adopt in the field governed by this Directive.

Article 56

Repeals

The Directives of 2 February 1959, the Directive of 5 March 1962, Directives 66/45/Euratom, 76/579/Euratom, 79/343/Euratom, 80/836/Euratom and 84/467/Euratom shall be repealed with effect from 13 May 2000.

Article 57

This Directive is addressed to the Member States.

ANNEX I
CRITERIA TO BE CONSIDERED FOR THE APPLICATION OF ARTICLE 3

1. A practice may be exempted from the requirement to report without further consideration, in compliance with Article 3 (2) (a) or (b) respectively, if either the quantity or the activity concentration, as appropriate, of the relevant radionuclides does not exceed the values in column 2 or 3 of Table A.

2. The basic criteria for the calculation of the values in Table A, for the application of exemptions for practices, are as follows:
(a) the radiological risks to individuals caused by the exempted practice are sufficiently low as to be of no regulatory concern; and
(b) the collective radiological impact of the exempted practice is sufficiently low as to be of no regulatory concern under the prevailing circumstances; and
(c) the exempted practice is inherently without radiological significance, with no appreciable likelihood of scenarios that could lead to a failure to meet the criteria in (a) and (b).

3. Exceptionally, as provided in Article 3, individual Member States may decide that a practice may be exempted where appropriate without further consideration, in accordance with the basic criteria, even if the relevant radionuclides deviate from the values in Table A, provided that the following criteria are met in all feasible circumstances:

(a) the effective dose expected to be incurred by any member of the public due to the exempted practice is of the order of 10 μSv or less in a year;
and

(b) either the collective effective dose committed during one year of performance of the practice is no more than about 1 man × Sv or an assessment of the optimization of protection shows that exemption is the optimum option.

4. For radionuclides not listed in Table A, the competent authority shall assign appropriate values for the quantities and concentrations of activity per unit mass where the need arises. Values thus assigned shall be complementary to those in Table A.

5. The values laid down in Table A apply to the total inventory of radioactive substances held by a person or undertaking as part of a specific practice at any point in time.

6. Nuclides carrying the suffix "+" or "sec" in Table A represent parent nuclides in equilibrium with their correspondent daughter nuclides as listed in Table B. In this case the values given in Table A refer to the parent nuclide alone, but already take account of the daughter nuclide(s) present.

7. In all other cases of mixtures of more than one nuclide, the requirement for reporting may be waived if the sum of the ratios for each nuclide of the total amount present divided by the value listed in Table A is less than or equal to 1. This summation rule also applies to activity concentrations where the various nuclides concerned are contained in the same matrix.

Table A

Nuclide	*Quantity (Bq)*	*Concentration (kBq/kg)*
H-3	10^9	10^6
Be-7	10^7	10^3
C-14	10^7	10^4
O-15	10^9	10^2
F-18	10^6	10
Na-22	10^6	10
Na-24	10^5	10
Si-31	10^6	10^3
P-32	10^5	10^3
P-33	10^8	10^5
S-35	10^8	10^5
Cl-36	10^6	10^4
Cl-38	10^5	10
Ar-37	10^8	10^6
Ar-41	10^9	10^2
K-40	10^6	10^2
K-42	10^6	10^2
K-43	10^6	10
Ca-45	10^7	10^4
Ca-47	10^6	10
Sc-46	10^6	10
Sc-47	10^6	10^2
Sc-48	10^5	10

Nuclide	*Quantity (Bq)*	*Concentration (kBq/kg)*
V-48	10^5	10
Cr-51	10^7	10^3
Mn-51	10^5	10
Mn-52	10^5	10
Mn-52m	10^5	10
Mn-53	10^9	10^4
Mn-54	10^6	10
Mn-56	10^5	10
Fe-52	10^6	10
Fe-55	10^6	10^4
Fe-59	10^6	10
Co-55	10^6	10
Co-56	10^5	10
Co-57	10^6	10^2
Co-58	10^6	10
Co-58m	10^7	10^4
Co-60	10^5	10
Co-60m	10^6	10^3
Co-61	10^6	10^2
Co-62m	10^5	10
Ni-59	10^8	10^4
Ni-63	10^8	10^5
Ni-65	10^6	10
Cu-64	10^6	10^2
Zn-65	10^6	10
Zn-69	10^6	10^4
Zn-69m	10^6	10^2
Ga-72	10^5	10
Ge-71	10^8	10^4
As-73	10^7	10^3
As-74	10^6	10
As-76	10^5	10^2
As-77	10^6	10^3
Se-75	10^6	10^2
Br-82	10^6	10
Kr-74	10^9	10^2
Kr-76	10^9	10^2
Kr-77	10^9	10^2
Kr-79	10^5	10^3
Kr-81	10^7	10^4
Kr-83m	10^{12}	10^5
Kr-85	10^4	10^5
Kr-85m	10^{10}	10^3
Kr-87	10^9	10^2
Kr-88	10^9	10^2
Rb-86	10^5	10^2

Nuclide	*Quantity (Bq)*	*Concentration (kBq/kg)*
Sr-85	10^6	10^2
Sr-85m	10^7	10^2
Sr-87m	10^6	10^2
Sr-89	10^6	10^3
Sr-90 +	10^4	10^2
Sr-91	10^5	10
Sr-92	10^6	10
Y-90	10^5	10^3
Y-91	10^6	10^3
Y-91m	10^6	10^2
Y-92	10^5	10^2
Y-93	10^5	10^2
Zr-93 +	10^7	10^3
Zr-95	10^6	10
Zr-97 +	10^5	10
Nb-93m	10^7	10^4
Nb-94	10^6	10
Nb-95	10^6	10
Nb-97	10^6	10
Nb-98	10^5	10
Mo-90	10^6	10
Mo-93	10^8	10^3
Mo-99	10^6	10^2
Mo-101	10^6	10
Tc-96	10^6	10
Tc-96m	10^7	10^3
Tc-97	10^8	10^3
Tc-97m	10^7	10^3
Tc-99	10^7	10^4
Tc-99m	10^7	10^2
Ru-97	10^7	10^2
Ru-103	10^6	10^2
Ru-105	10^6	10
Ru-106 +	10^5	10^2
Rh-103m	10^8	10^4
Rh-105	10^7	10^2
Pd-103	10^8	10^3
Pd-109	10^6	10^3
Ag-105	10^6	10^2
Ag-108m +	10^6	10
Ag-110m	10^6	10
Ag-111	10^6	10^3
Cd-109	10^6	10^4
Cd-115	10^6	10^2
Cd-115m	10^6	10^3
In-111	10^6	10^2

Nuclide	*Quantity (Bq)*	*Concentration (kBq/kg)*
In-113m	10^6	10^2
In-114m	10^6	10^2
In-115m	10^6	10^2
Sn-113	10^7	10^3
Sn-125	10^5	10^2
Sb-122	10^4	10^2
Sb-124	10^6	10
Sb-125	10^6	10^2
Te-123m	10^7	10^2
Te-125m	10^7	10^3
Te-127	10^6	10^3
Te-127m	10^7	10^3
Te-129	10^6	10^2
Te-129m	10^6	10^3
Te-131	10^5	10^2
Te-131m	10^6	10
Te-132	10^7	10^2
Te-133	10^5	10
Te-133m	10^5	10
Te-134	10^6	10
I-123	10^7	10^2
I-125	10^6	10^3
I-126	10^6	10^2
I-129	10^5	10^2
I-130	10^6	10
I-131	10^6	10^2
I-132	10^5	10
I-133	10^6	10
I-134	10^5	10
I-135	10^6	10
Xe-131m	10^4	10^4
Xe-133	10^4	10^3
Xe-135	1010	10^3
Cs-129	10^5	10^2
Cs-131	10^6	10^3
Cs-132	10^5	10
Cs-134m	10^5	10^3
Cs-134	10^4	10
Cs-135	10^7	10^4
Cs-136	10^5	10
Cs-137 +	10^4	10
Cs-138	10^4	10
Ba-131	10^6	10^2
Ba-140 +	10^5	10
La-140	10^5	10
Ce-139	10^6	10^2

Nuclide	*Quantity (Bq)*	*Concentration (kBq/kg)*
Ce-141	10^7	10^2
Ce-143	10^6	10^2
Ce-144 +	10^5	10^2
Pr-142	10^5	10^2
Pr-143	10^6	10^4
Nd-147	10^6	10^2
Nd-149	10^6	10^2
Pm-147	10^7	10^4
Pm-149	10^6	10^3
Sm-151	10^8	10^4
Sm-153	10^6	10^2
Eu-152	10^6	10
Eu-152m	10^6	10^2
Eu-154	10^6	10
Eu-155	10^7	10^2
Gd-153	10^7	10^2
Gd-159	10^6	10^3
Tb-160	10^6	10
Dy-165	10^6	10^3
Dy-166	10^6	10^3
Ho-166	10^5	10^3
Er-169	10^7	10^4
Er-171	10^6	10^2
Tm-170	10^6	10^3
Tm-171	10^8	10^4
Yb-175	10^7	10^3
Lu-177	10^7	10^3
Hf-181	10^6	10
Ta-182	10^4	10
W-181	10^7	10^3
W-185	10^7	10^4
W-187	10^6	10^2
Re-186	10^6	10^3
Re-188	10^5	10^2
Os-185	10^6	10
Os-191	10^7	10^2
Os-191m	10^7	10^3
Os-193	10^6	10^2
Ir-190	10^6	10
Ir-192	10^4	10
Ir-194	10^5	10^2
Pt-191	10^6	10^2
Pt-193m	10^7	10^3
Pt-197	10^6	10^3
Pt-197m	10^6	10^2
Au-198	10^6	10^2

Nuclide	*Quantity (Bq)*	*Concentration (kBq/kg)*
Au-199	10^6	10^2
Hg-197	10^7	10^2
Hg-197m	10^6	10^2
Hg-203	10^5	10^2
Tl-200	10^6	10
Tl-201	10^6	10^2
Tl-202	10^6	10^2
Tl-204	10^4	10^4
Pb-203	10^6	10^2
Pb-210 +	10^4	10
Pb-212 +	10^5	10
Bi-206	10^5	10
Bi-207	10^6	10
Bi-210	10^6	10^3
Bi-212 +	10^5	10
Po-203	10^6	10
Po-205	10^6	10
Po-207	10^6	10
Po-210	10^4	10
At-211	10^7	10^3
Rn-220 +	10^7	10^4
Rn-222 +	10^8	10
Ra-223 +	10^5	10^2
Ra-224 +	10^5	10
Ra-225	10^5	10^2
Ra-226 +	10^4	10
Ra-227	10^6	10^2
Ra-228 +	10^5	10
Ac-228	10^6	10
Th-226 +	10^7	10^3
Th-227	10^4	10
Th-228 +	10^4	1
Th-229 +	10^3	1
Th-230	10^4	1
Th-231	10^7	10^3
Th-232sec	10^3	1
Th-234 +	10^5	10^3
Pa-230	10^6	10
Pa-231	10^3	1
Pa-233	10^7	10^2
U-230 +	10^5	10
U-231	10^7	10^2
U-232 +	10^3	1
U-233	10^4	10
U-234	10^4	10
U-235 +	10^4	10

Nuclide	*Quantity (Bq)*	*Concentration (kBq/kg)*
U-236	10^4	10
U-237	10^6	10^2
U-238 +	10^4	10
U-238sec	10^3	1
U-239	10^6	10^2
U-240	10^7	10^3
U-240 +	10^6	10
Np-237 +	10^3	1
Np-239	10^7	10^2
Np-240	10^6	10
Pu-234	10^7	10^2
Pu-235	10^7	10^2
Pu-236	10^4	10
Pu-237	10^7	10^3
Pu-238	10^4	1
Pu-239	10^4	1
Pu-240	10^3	1
Pu-241	10^5	10^2
Pu-242	10^4	1
Pu-243	10^7	10^3
Pu-244	10^4	1
Am-241	10^4	1
Am-242	10^6	10^3
Am-242m +	10^4	1
Am-243 +	10^3	1
Cm-242	10^5	10^2
Cm-243	10^4	1
Cm-244	10^4	10
Cm-245	10^3	1
Cm-246	10^3	1
Cm-247	10^4	1
Cm-248	10^3	1
Bk-249	10^6	10^3
Cf-246	10^6	10^3
Cf-248	10^4	10
Cf-249	10^3	1
Cf-250	10^4	10
Cf-251	10^3	1
Cf-252	10^4	10
Cf-253	10^5	10^2
Cf-254	10^3	1
Es-253	10^5	10^2
Es-254	10^4	10
Es-254m	10^6	10^2
Fm-254	10^7	10^4
Fm-255	10^6	10^3

TableB
List of nuclides in secular equilibrium as referred to in point 6 of this Annex

Parent nuclide	*Daughter nuclides*
Sr-80 +	Rb-80
Sr-90 +	Y-90
Zr-93 +	Nb-93m
Zr-97 +	Nb-97
Ru-106 +	Rh-106
Ag-108m +	Ag-108
Cs-137 +	Ba-137
Ba-140 +	La-140
Ce-134 +	La-134
Ce-144 +	Pr-144
Pb-210 +	Bi-210, Po-210
Pb-212 +	Bi-212, Tl-208, Po-212
Bi-212 +	Tl-208, Po-212
Rn-220 +	Po-216
Rn-222 +	Po-218, Pb-214, Bi-214, Po-214
Ra-223 +	Rn-219, Po-215, Pb-211, Bi-211, Tl-207
Ra-224 +	Rn-220, Po-216, Pb-212, Bi-212, Tl-208, Po-212
Ra-226 +	Rn-222, Po-218, Pb-214, Bi-214, Pb-210, Bi-210, Po-210, Po-214
Ra-228 +	Ac-228
Th-226 +	Ra-222, Rn-218, Po-214
Th-228 +	Ra-224, Rn-220, Po-216, Pb-212, Bi-212, Tl-208, Po-212
Th-229 +	Ra-225, Ac-225, Fr-221, At-217, Bi-213, Po-213, Pb-209
Th-232sec	Ra-228, Ac-228, Th-228, Ra-224, Rn-220, Po-216, Pb-212, Bi-212, Tl-208, Po-212
Th-234 +	Pa-234m
U-230 +	Th-226, Ra-222, Rn-218, Po-214
U-232 +	Th-228, Ra-224, Rn-220, Po-216, Pb-212, Bi-212, Tl-208, Po-212
U-235 +	Th-231
U-238 +	Th-234, Pa-234m
U-238sec	Th-234, Pa-234m, U-234, Th-230, Ra-226, Rn-222, Po-218, Pb-214, Bi-214, Pb-210, Bi-210, Po-210, Po-214
U-240 +	Np-240
Np-237 +	Pa-233
Am-242m +	Am-242
Am-243 +	Np-239

ANNEX II

A. DEFINITIONS OF TERMS USED IN THIS ANNEX

*Ambient dose equivalent H** (d): the dose equivalent at a point in a radiation field that would be produced by the corresponding expanded and aligned field in the ICRU sphere at a depth, d, on the radius opposing the direction of the aligned field. The special name for the unit of ambient dose equivalent is sievert (Sv).

Directional dose equivalent H' (d, Ω): the dose equivalent at a point in a radiation field that would be produced by the corresponding expanded field, in the ICRU sphere at a depth, d, on a radius in a specified direction, Ω. The special name for the unit of directional dose equivalent is sievert (Sv).

Expanded and aligned field: a radiation field in which the fluence and its directional and energy distribution are the same as in the expanded field, but the fluence is unidirectional.

Expanded field: a field derived from the actual field, where the fluence and its directional and energy distributions have the same values throughout the volume of interest as in the actual field at the point of reference.

Fluence, ϕ: the quotient of dN by da, where dN is the number of particles which enter a sphere of cross-sectional area da:

$\phi = dN / da$

Mean quality factor $\bar{Q}$: average value of the quality factor at a point in tissue where the absorbed dose is delivered by particles with different L values. It is calculated according to the expression:

$$\bar{Q} = 1/\bar{D} \int_0^\infty Q(L)D(L)dt$$

where D(L)dL is the absorbed dose at 10 mm between linear energy transfer L and L + dL; and Q(L) is the corresponding quality factor at the point of interest. The Q-L relationships are given in C.

Personal dose equivalent, Hp (d): the dose equivalent in soft tissues, at an appropriate depth, d, below a specified point in the body. The special name for the unit of personal dose equivalent is sievert (Sv).

Quality factor (Q): a function of linear energy transfer (L) used to weight absorbed doses at a point in such a way as to take into account the quality of a radiation.

Radiation weighting factor (w_R): a dimensionless factor used to weight the tissue or organ absorbed dose. The appropriate (w_R) values are given in B.

Tissue or organ absorbed dose (DT): the quotient of the total energy imparted in a tissue or organ and the mass of that tissue or organ.

Tissue weighting factor (w_T): a dimensionless factor used to weight the equivalent dose in a tissue or organ (T). The appropriate (w_T) values are specified in D.

Unrestricted linear energy transfer (L ∞;): a quantity defined as:

$L_\infty = dE / dl$

where dE is the mean energy lost by a particle of energy E in traversing a distance dl in water. In this Directive L ∞; is denoted by L.

ICRU sphere: a body introduced by the International Commission on Radiation Units (ICRU) to approximate the human body as regards energy absorption from ionizing radiation; it consists of a 30 cm diameter tissue equivalent sphere with a density of 1 g cm-3 and a mass composition of 76,2 % oxygen, 11,1 % carbon, 10,1 % hydrogen and 2,6 % nitrogen.

B. VALUES OF RADIATION WEIGHTING FACTOR, W_R

Values of radiation weighting factor, w_R, depend on the type and quality of the external radiation field or on the type and quality of the radiation emitted by an internally deposited radionuclide.

When the radiation field is composed of types and energies with different values of w_R, the absorbed dose must be subdivided into blocks, each with its own value of w_R and added to give the total equivalent dose. Alternatively, it may be expressed as a continuous distribution in energy where each element of absorbed dose from the energy element between E and E + dE is multiplied by the value of w_R from the relevant entry in the Table below.

Type and energy range	*Radiation weighting factor, w_R*
Photons, all energies	1
Electrons and muons, all energies	1
Neutrons, energy < 10 keV	5
10 keV to 100 keV	10
> 100 keV to 2 MeV	20
> 2 MeV to 20 MeV	10
> 20 MeV	5
Protons, other than recil protons, energy > 2 MeV	5
Alpha particles, fission fragments, heavy nuclei	20

In calculations involving neutrons, difficulties may arise in applying step function values. In these cases it may be preferable to use the continuous function described by the following mathematical relationship:

$W_R = 5 + 17e^{(\ln(2E))2/6}$

where E is the neutron energy in MeV.

A direct comparison of the two approaches is given, in Figure 1.

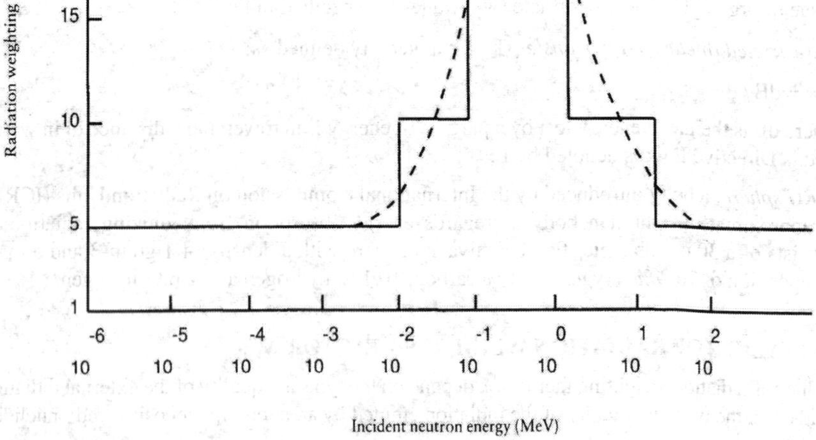

Figure 1
Radiation weighting factors for neutrons. The smooth curve is to be treated as an approximation

For radiation types and energy which are not included in the table, an approximation of wR may be obtained by calculating the mean quality factor $\bar{Q}$ at a depth of 10 mm in a ICRU sphere.

C. RELATIONSHIP BETWEEN THE QUALITY FACTOR, Q(L), AND UNRESTRICTED LINEAR ENERGY TRANSFER, L

Unrestricted linear energy transfer, L in water (keV μm^{-1})	*Q(L)*
< 10	1
10–100	0,32L-2,2
> 100	300/ $\sqrt{L}$

D. VALUES OF TISSUE WEIGHTING FACTOR, WT (*)

Values of tissue weighting factor, wT, are shown below:

Tissue or organ	*Tissue weighting factors, w_T*
Gonads	0,2
Bone marrow (red)	0,12
Colon	0,12
Lung	0,12
Stomach	0,12
Bladder	0,05
Breast	0,05
Liver	0,05
Oesophagus	0,05
Thyroid	0,05
Skin	0,01
Bone surface	0,01
Remainder	0,05 (**) (***)

(*) The values have been developed from a reference population of equal numbers of both sexes and a wide range of ages. In the definition of effective does they apply to workers, to the whole population and to either sex.

(**) For the purposes of calculation, the remainder is composed of the following additional tissues and organs: adrenals, brain, upper large intestine, small intestine, kidney, muscle, pancreas, spleen, thymus and uterus. The list includes organs which are known to be susceptible to can cer induction. If other tissues and organs subsequently become identified as having a significant risk of induced cancer they will then be included either with a specific wT or in this additional list constituting the remainder. The latter may also include other tissues or organs selectively irradiated.

(***) In those exceptional cases in which a single one of the remainder tissues or organs receives and equivalent dose in excess of the highest dose in any one of the 12 organs for which a weighting factor is specified, a weighting factor of 0,025 should be applied to that tissue or organ and a weighting factor of 0,025 to the average dose in the rest of the remainder as defined above.

E. OPERATIONAL QUANTITIES FOR EXTERNAL RADIATION

Operational quantities for external radiation are used for individual monitoring for radiation protection purposes:

1. Individual monitoring:
personal dose equivalent Hp(d),
d: depth in mm in the body.

2. Area monitoring:
ambient dose equivalent H* (d),
directional dose equivalent H' (d, Ω),
d: depth in mm under the surface of the sphere given in A,
Ω: angle of incidence.

3. For strongly penetrating radiation a depth of 10 mm, for weakly penetrating radiation a depth of 0,07 mm for the skin and 3 mm for the eye is recommended.

ANNEX III

A. Throughout the Directive, unless otherwise specified, requirements on doses apply to the sum of the relevant doses from external exposure in a specified period and the relevant 50-year committed doses (up to age 70 for children) from intakes in the same period. The specified period is that given in Articles 9 and 13 in relation to the dose limits.

In general the effective dose E incurred by an individual in the group of age g will be determined according to the following formula:

$$E = E_{external} + \sum_j h(g)_{j,ing} J_{j,ing} + \sum_j h(g)_{j,inh} J_{j,inh}$$

Where $E_{external}$ is the relevant effective dose from external exposure; $h(g)_{j,ing}$ and $h(g)_{j,inh}$ are the committed effective dose per unit-intake for ingested or inhaled radionuclide j (Sv/Bq) by an individual in the group of age g; $J_{j,ing}$ and $J_{j,inh}$ respectively are the relevant intake via ingestion or inhalation of the radionuclide j (Bq).

B. Except for radon progeny and thoron progeny, values of the committed effective dose for unit intake for ingestion and inhalation are given for members of the public and for apprentices and students aged between 16 and 18 years in Tables (A) and (B) to this Annex.

Except for radon progeny and thoron progeny, values of the committed effective dose for unit intake for ingestion and inhalation are given for exposed workers and for apprentices and students aged 18 years or more in Table (C) to this Annex.

For exposure of members of the public, Table (A) for ingestion includes values corresponding to different gut transfer factors f_1 for infants and for older persons. Also for exposure of members of the public, Table (B) for inhalation includes values for different lung retention types with appropriate f_1 values for the component of the intake cleared to the gastrointestinal tract. If information is available on these parameters, the appropriate value shall be used; if not, the most restrictive value shall be used. For occupational exposure, Table (C) includes values for ingestion corresponding to different gut transfer factors f_1 and values for inhalation for different lung retention types with appropriate f_1 values for the component of the intake cleared to the gastrointestinal tract.

Table (D) presents gut transfer factors f_1 by element and compounds for workers and where appropriate members of the public for intake by ingestion. Table (E) presents lung absorption types and gut transfer factors f_1, also by element and compounds and also for exposed workers and for apprentices and students aged 18 years or more, for intake by inhalation.

For members of the public the lung absorption types and gut transfer factors f_1, shall take into account the chemical form of the element on the basis of available international guidance. In general, if no information is available on these parameters, the most conservative value should be used.

C. For radon progeny and thoron progeny the following conventional conversion factors apply, effective dose per unit potential alpha-energy exposure (Sv per $J.h.m^{-3}$):
Radon at home:1,1
Radon at work: 1,4
Thoron at work: 0,5

Potential alpha energy (of radon progeny and thoron progeny): The total alpha energy ultimately emitted during the decay of radon progeny and thoron progeny through the decay chain, up to but not including 210Pb for progeny of 222Rn and up to stable 208Pb for progeny of 220Rn. The unit is J (Joule). For the exposure to a given concentration for a given time the unit is $J.h.m^{-3}$.

D. Tables:
(A) Ingestion dose coefficients for members of the public.
(B) Inhalation dose coefficients for members of the public.
(C) Inhalation and ingestion dose coefficients for workers.
(D) Values for f_1 for the calculation of ingestion dose coefficients.
(E) Lung absorption types and f_1 values for chemical forms of the elements for the calculation of inhalation dose coefficients.

Table (A)

Committed effective dose per unit intake via ingestion (Sv Bq^{-1}) for members of the public

Nuclide	*Physical half-life*	*Age ≤ 1 a*		*Age*	*1—2 a*	*2—7 a*	*7—12 a*	*12—17 a*	*4 17 a*
		f_1 for ≤ 1 a	*h(g)*	*f_1 for g > 1 a*	*h(g)*	*h(g)*	*h(g)*	*h(g)*	*h(g)*
Hydrogen									
Tritiated water	12,3 a	1,000	$6,4\ 10^{-11}$	1,000	$4,8\ 10^{-11}$	$3,1\ 10^{-11}$	$2,3\ 10^{-11}$	$1,8\ 10^{-11}$	$1,8\ 10^{-11}$
OBT	12,3 a	1,000	$1,2\ 10^{-10}$	1,000	$1,2\ 10^{-10}$	$7,3\ 10^{-11}$	$5,7\ 10^{-11}$	$4,2\ 10^{-11}$	$4,2\ 10^{-11}$
Beryllium									
Be-7	53,3 d	0,020	$1,8\ 10^{-10}$	0,005	$1,3\ 10^{-10}$	$7,7\ 10^{-11}$	$5,3\ 10^{-11}$	$3,5\ 10^{-11}$	$2,8\ 10^{-11}$
Be-10	$1,60\ 10^{6}$ a	0,020	$1,4\ 10^{-8}$	0,005	$8,0\ 10^{-9}$	$4,1\ 10^{-9}$	$2,4\ 10^{-9}$	$1,4\ 10^{-9}$	$1,1\ 10^{-9}$
Carbon									
C-11	0,340 h	1,000	$2,6\ 10^{-10}$	1,000	$1,5\ 10^{-10}$	$7,3\ 10^{-11}$	$4,3\ 10^{-11}$	$3,0\ 10^{-11}$	$2,4\ 10^{-11}$
C-14	$5,73\ 10^{3}$ a	1,000	$1,4\ 10^{-9}$	1,000	$1,6\ 10^{-9}$	$9,9\ 10^{-10}$	$8,0\ 10^{-10}$	$5,7\ 10^{-10}$	$5,8\ 10^{-10}$
Fluorine									
F-18	1,83 h	1,000	$5,2\ 10^{-10}$	1,000	$3,0\ 10^{-10}$	$1,5\ 10^{-10}$	$9,1\ 10^{-11}$	$6,2\ 10^{-11}$	$4,9\ 10^{-11}$
Sodium									
Na-22	2,60 a	1,000	$2,1\ 10^{-8}$	1,000	$1,5\ 10^{-8}$	$8,4\ 10^{-9}$	$5,5\ 10^{-9}$	$3,7\ 10^{-9}$	$3,2\ 10^{-9}$
Na-24	15,0 h	1,000	$3,5\ 10^{-9}$	1,000	$2,3\ 10^{-9}$	$1,2\ 10^{-9}$	$7,7\ 10^{-10}$	$5,2\ 10^{-10}$	$4,3\ 10^{-10}$
Magnesium									
Mg-28	20,9 h	1,000	$1,2\ 10^{-8}$	0,500	$1,4\ 10^{-8}$	$7,4\ 10^{-9}$	$4,5\ 10^{-9}$	$2,7\ 10^{-9}$	$2,2\ 10^{-9}$
Aluminium									
Al-26	$7,16\ 10^{5}$ a	0,020	$3,4\ 10^{-8}$	0,010	$2,1\ 10^{-8}$	$1,1\ 10^{-8}$	$7,1\ 10^{-9}$	$4,3\ 10^{-9}$	$3,5\ 10^{-9}$
Silicon									
Si-31	2,62 h	0,020	$1,9\ 10^{-9}$	0,010	$1,0\ 10^{-9}$	$5,1\ 10^{-10}$	$3,0\ 10^{-10}$	$1,8\ 10^{-10}$	$1,6\ 10^{-10}$
Si-32	$4,50\ 10^{2}$ a	0,020	$7,3\ 10^{-9}$	0,010	$4,1\ 10^{-9}$	$2,0\ 10^{-9}$	$1,2\ 10^{-9}$	$7,0\ 10^{-10}$	$5,6\ 10^{-10}$
Phosphorus									
P-32	14,3 d	1,000	$3,1\ 10^{-8}$	0,800	$1,9\ 10^{-8}$	$9,4\ 10^{-9}$	$5,3\ 10^{-9}$	$3,1\ 10^{-9}$	$2,4\ 10^{-9}$

Nuclide	Physical half-life	Age ≤ 1 a		Age	1—2 a	2—7 a	7—12 a	12—17 a	4 17 a
		f_1 for ≤ 1 a	h(g)	f_1 for g > 1 a	h(g)	h(g)	h(g)	h(g)	h(g)
P-33	25,4 d	1,000	$2,7\ 10^{-9}$	0,800	$1,8\ 10^{-9}$	$9,1\ 10^{-10}$	$5,3\ 10^{-10}$	$3,1\ 10^{-10}$	$2,4\ 10^{-10}$
Sulphur									
S-35 (inorganic)	87,4 d	1,000	$1,3\ 10^{-9}$	1,000	$8,7\ 10^{-10}$	$4,4\ 10^{-10}$	$2,7\ 10^{-10}$	$1,6\ 10^{-10}$	$1,3\ 10^{-10}$
S-35 (organic)	87,4 d	1,000	$7,7\ 10^{-9}$	1,000	$5,4\ 10^{-9}$	$2,7\ 10^{-9}$	$1,6\ 10^{-9}$	$9,5\ 10^{-10}$	$7,7\ 10^{-10}$
Chlorine									
Cl-36	$3,01\ 10^{5}$ a	1,000	$9,8\ 10^{-9}$	1,000	$6,3\ 10^{-9}$	$3,2\ 10^{-9}$	$1,9\ 10^{-9}$	$1,2\ 10^{-9}$	$9,3\ 10^{-10}$
Cl-38	0,620 h	1,000	$1,4\ 10^{-9}$	1,000	$7,7\ 10^{-10}$	$3,8\ 10^{-10}$	$2,2\ 10^{-10}$	$1,5\ 10^{-10}$	$1,2\ 10^{-10}$
Cl-39	0,927 h	1,000	$9,7\ 10^{-10}$	1,000	$5,5\ 10^{-10}$	$2,7\ 10^{-10}$	$1,6\ 10^{-10}$	$1,1\ 10^{-10}$	$8,5\ 10^{-11}$
Potassium									
K-40	$1,28\ 10^{9}$ a	1,000	$6,2\ 10^{-8}$	1,000	$4,2\ 10^{-8}$	$2,1\ 10^{-8}$	$1,3\ 10^{-8}$	$7,6\ 10^{-9}$	$6,2\ 10^{-9}$
K-42	12,4 h	1,000	$5,1\ 10^{-9}$	1,000	$3,0\ 10^{-9}$	$1,5\ 10^{-9}$	$8,6\ 10^{-10}$	$5,4\ 10^{-10}$	$4,3\ 10^{-10}$
K-43	22,6 h	1,000	$2,3\ 10^{-9}$	1,000	$1,4\ 10^{-9}$	$7,6\ 10^{-10}$	$4,7\ 10^{-10}$	$3,0\ 10^{-10}$	$2,5\ 10^{-10}$
K-44	0,369 h	1,000	$1,0\ 10^{-9}$	1,000	$5,5\ 10^{-10}$	$2,7\ 10^{-10}$	$1,6\ 10^{-10}$	$1,1\ 10^{-10}$	$8,4\ 10^{-11}$
K-45	0,333 h	1,000	$6,2\ 10^{-10}$	1,000	$3,5\ 10^{-10}$	$1,7\ 10^{-10}$	$9,9\ 10^{-11}$	$6,8\ 10^{-11}$	$5,4\ 10^{-11}$
Calcium[(a)]									
Ca-41	$1,40\ 10^{5}$ a	0,600	$1,2\ 10^{-9}$	0,300	$5,2\ 10^{-10}$	$3,9\ 10^{-10}$	$4,8\ 10^{-10}$	$5,0\ 10^{-10}$	$1,9\ 10^{-10}$
Ca-45	163 d	0,600	$1,1\ 10^{-8}$	0,300	$4,9\ 10^{-9}$	$2,6\ 10^{-9}$	$1,8\ 10^{-9}$	$1,3\ 10^{-9}$	$7,1\ 10^{-10}$
Ca-47	4,53 d	0,600	$1,3\ 10^{-8}$	0,300	$9,3\ 10^{-9}$	$4,9\ 10^{-9}$	$3,0\ 10^{-9}$	$1,8\ 10^{-9}$	$1,6\ 10^{-9}$
Scandium									
Sc-43	3,89 h	0,001	$1,8\ 10^{-9}$	$1,0\ 10^{-4}$	$1,2\ 10^{-9}$	$6,1\ 10^{-10}$	$3,7\ 10^{-10}$	$2,3\ 10^{-10}$	$1,9\ 10^{-10}$
Sc-44	3,93 h	0,001	$3,5\ 10^{-9}$	$1,0\ 10^{-4}$	$2,2\ 10^{-9}$	$1,2\ 10^{-9}$	$7,1\ 10^{-10}$	$4,4\ 10^{-10}$	$3,5\ 10^{-10}$
Sc-44m	2,44 d	0,001	$2,4\ 10^{-8}$	$1,0\ 10^{-4}$	$1,6\ 10^{-8}$	$8,3\ 10^{-9}$	$5,1\ 10^{-9}$	$3,1\ 10^{-9}$	$2,4\ 10^{-9}$
Sc-46	83,8 d	0,001	$1,1\ 10^{-8}$	$1,0\ 10^{-4}$	$7,9\ 10^{-9}$	$4,4\ 10^{-9}$	$2,9\ 10^{-9}$	$1,8\ 10^{-9}$	$1,5\ 10^{-9}$
Sc-47	3,35 d	0,001	$6,1\ 10^{-9}$	$1,0\ 10^{-4}$	$3,9\ 10^{-9}$	$2,0\ 10^{-9}$	$1,2\ 10^{-9}$	$6,8\ 10^{-10}$	$5,4\ 10^{-10}$
Sc-48	1,82 d	0,001	$1,3\ 10^{-8}$	$1,0\ 10^{-4}$	$9,3\ 10^{-9}$	$5,1\ 10^{-9}$	$3,3\ 10^{-9}$	$2,1\ 10^{-9}$	$1,7\ 10^{-9}$

Nuclide	Physical half-life	*Age ≤ 1 a*		*Age*	*1—2 a*	*2—7 a*	*7—12 a*	*12—17 a*	*4 17 a*
		f_1 *for ≤ 1 a*	*h(g)*	f_1 *for g > 1 a*	*h(g)*	*h(g)*	*h(g)*	*h(g)*	*h(g)*
Sc-49	0,956 h	0,001	$1,0\ 10^{-9}$	$1,0\ 10^{-4}$	$5,7\ 10^{-10}$	$2,8\ 10^{-10}$	$1,6\ 10^{-10}$	$1,0\ 10^{-10}$	$8,2\ 10^{-11}$
Titanium									
Ti-44	47,3 a	0,020	$5,5\ 10^{-8}$	0,010	$3,1\ 10^{-8}$	$1,7\ 10^{-8}$	$1,1\ 10^{-8}$	$6,9\ 10^{-9}$	$5,8\ 10^{-9}$
Ti-45	3,08 h	0,020	$1,6\ 10^{-9}$	0,010	$9,8\ 10^{-10}$	$5,0\ 10^{-10}$	$3,1\ 10^{-10}$	$1,9\ 10^{-10}$	$1,5\ 10^{-10}$
Vanadium									
V-47	0,543 h	0,020	$7,3\ 10^{-10}$	0,010	$4,1\ 10^{-10}$	$2,0\ 10^{-10}$	$1,2\ 10^{-10}$	$8,0\ 10^{-11}$	$6,3\ 10^{-11}$
V-48	16,2 d	0,020	$1,5\ 10^{-8}$	0,010	$1,1\ 10^{-8}$	$5,9\ 10^{-9}$	$3,9\ 10^{-9}$	$2,5\ 10^{-9}$	$2,0\ 10^{-9}$
V-49	330 d	0,020	$2,2\ 10^{-10}$	0,010	$1,4\ 10^{-10}$	$6,9\ 10^{-11}$	$4,0\ 10^{-11}$	$2,3\ 10^{-11}$	$1,8\ 10^{-11}$
Chromium									
Cr-48	23,0 h	0,200	$1,4\ 10^{-9}$	0,100	$9,9\ 10^{-10}$	$5,7\ 10^{-10}$	$3,8\ 10^{-10}$	$2,5\ 10^{-10}$	$2,0\ 10^{-10}$
		0,020	$1,4\ 10^{-9}$	0,010	$9,9\ 10^{-10}$	$5,7\ 10^{-10}$	$3,8\ 10^{-10}$	$2,5\ 10^{-10}$	$2,0\ 10^{-10}$
Cr-49	0,702 h	0,200	$6,8\ 10^{-10}$	0,100	$3,9\ 10^{-10}$	$2,0\ 10^{-10}$	$1,1\ 10^{-10}$	$7,7\ 10^{-11}$	$6,1\ 10^{-11}$
		0,020	$6,8\ 10^{-10}$	0,010	$3,9\ 10^{-10}$	$2,0\ 10^{-10}$	$1,1\ 10^{-10}$	$7,7\ 10^{-11}$	$6,1\ 10^{-11}$
Cr-51	27,7 d	0,200	$3,5\ 10^{-10}$	0,100	$2,3\ 10^{-10}$	$1,2\ 10^{-10}$	$7,8\ 10^{-11}$	$4,8\ 10^{-11}$	$3,8\ 10^{-11}$
		0,020	$3,3\ 10^{-10}$	0,010	$2,2\ 10^{-10}$	$1,2\ 10^{-10}$	$7,5\ 10^{-11}$	$4,6\ 10^{-11}$	$3,7\ 10^{-11}$
Manganese									
Mn-51	0,770 h	0,200	$1,1\ 10^{-9}$	0,100	$6,1\ 10^{-10}$	$3,0\ 10^{-10}$	$1,8\ 10^{-10}$	$1,2\ 10^{-10}$	$9,3\ 10^{-11}$
Mn-52	5,59 d	0,200	$1,2\ 10^{-8}$	0,100	$8,8\ 10^{-9}$	$5,1\ 10^{-9}$	$3,4\ 10^{-9}$	$2,2\ 10^{-9}$	$1,8\ 10^{-9}$
Mn-52m	0,352 h	0,200	$7,8\ 10^{-10}$	0,100	$4,4\ 10^{-10}$	$2,2\ 10^{-10}$	$1,3\ 10^{-10}$	$8,8\ 10^{-11}$	$6,9\ 10^{-11}$
Mn-53	$3,70\ 10^{6}$ a	0,200	$4,1\ 10^{-10}$	0,100	$2,2\ 10^{-10}$	$1,1\ 10^{-10}$	$6,5\ 10^{-11}$	$3,7\ 10^{-11}$	$3,0\ 10^{-11}$
Mn-54	312 d	0,200	$5,4\ 10^{-9}$	0,100	$3,1\ 10^{-9}$	$1,9\ 10^{-9}$	$1,3\ 10^{-9}$	$8,7\ 10^{-10}$	$7,1\ 10^{-10}$
Mn-56	2,58 h	0,200	$2,7\ 10^{-9}$	0,100	$1,7\ 10^{-9}$	$8,5\ 10^{-10}$	$5,1\ 10^{-10}$	$3,2\ 10^{-10}$	$2,5\ 10^{-10}$
Iron[(b)]									
Fe-52	8,28 h	0,600	$1,3\ 10^{-8}$	0,100	$9,1\ 10^{-9}$	$4,6\ 10^{-9}$	$2,8\ 10^{-9}$	$1,7\ 10^{-9}$	$1,4\ 10^{-9}$
Fe-55	2,70 a	0,600	$7,6\ 10^{-9}$	0,100	$2,4\ 10^{-9}$	$1,7\ 10^{-9}$	$1,1\ 10^{-9}$	$7,7\ 10^{-10}$	$3,3\ 10^{-10}$

Nuclide	*Physical half-life*	*Age ≤ 1 a*		*Age*	*1—2 a*	*2—7 a*	*7—12 a*	*12—17 a*	*4 17 a*
		f_1 *for ≤ 1 a*	*h(g)*	f_1 *for g > 1 a*	*h(g)*	*h(g)*	*h(g)*	*h(g)*	*h(g)*
Fe-59	44,5 d	0,600	3,9 10^{-8}	0,100	1,3 10^{-8}	7,5 10^{-9}	4,7 10^{-9}	3,1 10^{-9}	1,8 10^{-9}
Fe-60	1,00 10^{5} a	0,600	7,9 10^{-7}	0,100	2,7 10^{-7}	2,7 10^{-7}	2,5 10^{-7}	2,3 10^{-7}	1,1 10^{-7}
Cobalt[(c)]									
Co-55	17,5 h	0,600	6,0 10^{-9}	0,100	5,5 10^{-9}	2,9 10^{-9}	1,8 10^{-9}	1,1 10^{-9}	1,0 10^{-9}
Co-56	78,7 d	0,600	2,5 10^{-8}	0,100	1,5 10^{-8}	8,8 10^{-9}	5,8 10^{-9}	3,8 10^{-9}	2,5 10^{-9}
Co-57	271 d	0,600	2,9 10^{-9}	0,100	1,6 10^{-9}	8,9 10^{-10}	5,8 10^{-10}	3,7 10^{-10}	2,1 10^{-10}
Co-58	70,8 d	0,600	7,3 10^{-9}	0,100	4,4 10^{-9}	2,6 10^{-9}	1,7 10^{-9}	1,1 10^{-9}	7,4 10^{-10}
Co-58m	9,15 h	0,600	2,0 10^{-10}	0,100	1,5 10^{-10}	7,8 10^{-11}	4,7 10^{-11}	2,8 10^{-11}	2,4 10^{-11}
Co-60	5,27 a	0,600	5,4 10^{-8}	0,100	2,7 10^{-8}	1,7 10^{-8}	1,1 10^{-8}	7,9 10^{-9}	3,4 10^{-9}
Co-60m	0,174 h	0,600	2,2 10^{-11}	0,100	1,2 10^{-11}	5,7 10^{-12}	3,2 10^{-12}	2,2 10^{-12}	1,7 10^{-12}
Co-61	1,65 h	0,600	8,2 10^{-10}	0,100	5,1 10^{-10}	2,5 10^{-10}	1,4 10^{-10}	9,2 10^{-11}	7,4 10^{-11}
Co-62m	0,232 h	0,600	5,3 10^{-10}	0,100	3,0 10^{-10}	1,5 10^{-10}	8,7 10^{-11}	6,0 10^{-11}	4,7 10^{-11}
Nickel									
Ni-56	6,10 d	0,100	5,3 10^{-9}	0,050	4,0 10^{-9}	2,3 10^{-9}	1,6 10^{-9}	1,1 10^{-9}	8,6 10^{-10}
Ni-57	1,50 d	0,100	6,8 10^{-9}	0,050	4,9 10^{-9}	2,7 10^{-9}	1,7 10^{-9}	1,1 10^{-9}	8,7 10^{-10}
Ni-59	7,50 10^{4} a	0,100	6,4 10^{-10}	0,050	3,4 10^{-10}	1,9 10^{-10}	1,1 10^{-10}	7,3 10^{-11}	6,3 10^{-11}
Ni-63	96,0 a	0,100	1,6 10^{-9}	0,050	8,4 10^{-10}	4,6 10^{-10}	2,8 10^{-10}	1,8 10^{-10}	1,5 10^{-10}
Ni-65	2,52 h	0,100	2,1 10^{-9}	0,050	1,3 10^{-9}	6,3 10^{-10}	3,8 10^{-10}	2,3 10^{-10}	1,8 10^{-10}
Ni-66	2,27 d	0,100	3,3 10^{-8}	0,050	2,2 10^{-8}	1,1 10^{-8}	6,6 10^{-9}	3,7 10^{-9}	3,0 10^{-9}
Copper									
Cu-60	0,387 h	1,000	7,0 10^{-10}	0,500	4,2 10^{-10}	2,2 10^{-10}	1,3 10^{-10}	8,9 10^{-11}	7,0 10^{-11}
Cu-61	3,41 h	1,000	7,1 10^{-10}	0,500	7,5 10^{-10}	3,9 10^{-10}	2,3 10^{-10}	1,5 10^{-10}	1,2 10^{-10}
Cu-64	12,7 h	1,000	5,2 10^{-10}	0,500	8,3 10^{-10}	4,2 10^{-10}	2,5 10^{-10}	1,5 10^{-10}	1,2 10^{-10}
Cu-67	2,58 d	1,000	2,1 10^{-9}	0,500	2,4 10^{-9}	1,2 10^{-9}	7,2 10^{-10}	4,2 10^{-10}	3,4 10^{-10}

Nuclide	Physical half-life	Age ≤ 1 a		Age	1—2 a	2—7 a	7—12 a	12—17 a	4 17 a
		f_1 for ≤ 1 a	h(g)	f_1 for g > 1 a	h(g)	h(g)	h(g)	h(g)	h(g)
Zinc									
Zn-62	9,26 h	1,000	4,2 10^{-9}	0,500	6,5 10^{-9}	3,3 10^{-9}	2,0 10^{-9}	1,2 10^{-9}	9,4 10^{-10}
Zn-63	0,635 h	1,000	8,7 10^{-10}	0,500	5,2 10^{-10}	2,6 10^{-10}	1,5 10^{-10}	1,0 10^{-10}	7,9 10^{-11}
Zn-65	244 d	1,000	3,6 10^{-8}	0,500	1,6 10^{-8}	9,7 10^{-9}	6,4 10^{-9}	4,5 10^{-9}	3,9 10^{-9}
Zn-69	0,950 h	1,000	3,5 10^{-10}	0,500	2,2 10^{-10}	1,1 10^{-10}	6,0 10^{-11}	3,9 10^{-11}	3,1 10^{-11}
Zn-69m	13,8 h	1,000	1,3 10^{-9}	0,500	2,3 10^{-9}	1,2 10^{-9}	7,0 10^{-10}	4,1 10^{-10}	3,3 10^{-10}
Zn-71m	3,92 h	1,000	1,4 10^{-9}	0,500	1,5 10^{-9}	7,8 10^{-10}	4,8 10^{-10}	3,0 10^{-10}	2,4 10^{-10}
Zn-72	1,94 d	1,000	8,7 10^{-9}	0,500	8,6 10^{-9}	4,5 10^{-9}	2,8 10^{-9}	1,7 10^{-9}	1,4 10^{-9}
Gallium									
Ga-65	0,253 h	0,010	4,3 10^{-10}	0,001	2,4 10^{-10}	1,2 10^{-10}	6,9 10^{-11}	4,7 10^{-11}	3,7 10^{-11}
Ga-66	9,40 h	0,010	1,2 10^{-8}	0,001	7,9 10^{-9}	4,0 10^{-9}	2,5 10^{-9}	1,5 10^{-9}	1,2 10^{-9}
Ga-67	3,26 d	0,010	1,8 10^{-9}	0,001	1,2 10^{-9}	6,4 10^{-10}	4,0 10^{-10}	2,4 10^{-10}	1,9 10^{-10}
Ga-68	1,13 h	0,010	1,2 10^{-9}	0,001	6,7 10^{-10}	3,4 10^{-10}	2,0 10^{-10}	1,3 10^{-10}	1,0 10^{-10}
Ga-70	0,353 h	0,010	3,9 10^{-10}	0,001	2,2 10^{-10}	1,0 10^{-10}	5,9 10^{-11}	4,0 10^{-11}	3,1 10^{-11}
Ga-72	14,1 h	0,010	1,0 10^{-8}	0,001	6,8 10^{-9}	3,6 10^{-9}	2,2 10^{-9}	1,4 10^{-9}	1,1 10^{-9}
Ga-73	4,91 h	0,010	3,0 10^{-9}	0,001	1,9 10^{-9}	9,3 10^{-10}	5,5 10^{-10}	3,3 10^{-10}	2,6 10^{-10}
Germanium									
Ge-66	2,27 h	1,000	8,3 10^{-10}	1,000	5,3 10^{-10}	2,9 10^{-10}	1,9 10^{-10}	1,3 10^{-10}	1,0 10^{-10}
Ge-67	0,312 h	1,000	7,7 10^{-10}	1,000	4,2 10^{-10}	2,1 10^{-10}	1,2 10^{-10}	8,2 10^{-11}	6,5 10^{-11}
Ge-68	288 d	1,000	1,2 10^{-8}	1,100	8,0 10^{-9}	4,2 10^{-9}	2,6 10^{-9}	1,6 10^{-9}	1,3 10^{-9}
Ge-69	1,63 d	1,000	2,0 10^{-9}	1,000	1,3 10^{-9}	7,1 10^{-10}	4,6 10^{-10}	3,0 10^{-10}	2,4 10^{-10}
Ge-71	11,8 d	1,000	1,2 10^{-10}	1,000	7,8 10^{-11}	4,0 10^{-11}	2,4 10^{-11}	1,5 10^{-11}	1,2 10^{-11}
Ge-75	1,38 h	1,000	5,5 10^{-10}	1,000	3,1 10^{-10}	1,5 10^{-10}	8,7 10^{-11}	5,9 10^{-11}	4,6 10^{-11}
Ge-77	11,3 h	1,000	3,0 10^{-9}	1,000	1,8 10^{-9}	9,9 10^{-10}	6,2 10^{-10}	4,1 10^{-10}	3,3 10^{-10}
Ge-78	1,45 h	1,000	1,2 10^{-9}	1,000	7,0 10^{-10}	3,6 10^{-10}	2,2 10^{-10}	1,5 10^{-10}	1,2 10^{-10}

Nuclide	*Physical half-life*	*Age ≤ 1 a*		*Age*	*1—2 a*	*2—7 a*	*7—12 a*	*12—17 a*	*4 17 a*
		f_1 *for ≤ 1 a*	*h(g)*	f_1 *for g > 1 a*	*h(g)*	*h(g)*	*h(g)*	*h(g)*	*h(g)*
Arsenic									
As-69	0,253 h	1,000	$6,6\ 10^{-10}$	0,500	$3,7\ 10^{-10}$	$1,8\ 10^{-10}$	$1,1\ 10^{-10}$	$7,2\ 10^{-11}$	$5,7\ 10^{-11}$
As-70	0,876 h	1,000	$1,2\ 10^{-9}$	0,500	$7,8\ 10^{-10}$	$4,1\ 10^{-10}$	$2,5\ 10^{-10}$	$1,7\ 10^{-10}$	$1,3\ 10^{-10}$
As-71	2,70 d	1,000	$2,8\ 10^{-9}$	0,500	$2,8\ 10^{-9}$	$1,5\ 10^{-9}$	$9,3\ 10^{-10}$	$5,7\ 10^{-10}$	$4,6\ 10^{-10}$
As-72	1,08 d	1,000	$1,1\ 10^{-8}$	0,500	$1,2\ 10^{-8}$	$6,3\ 10^{-9}$	$3,8\ 10^{-9}$	$2,3\ 10^{-9}$	$1,8\ 10^{-9}$
As-73	80,3 d	1,000	$2,6\ 10^{-9}$	0,500	$1,9\ 10^{-9}$	$9,3\ 10^{-10}$	$5,6\ 10^{-10}$	$3,2\ 10^{-10}$	$2,6\ 10^{-10}$
As-74	17,8 d	1,000	$1,0\ 10^{-8}$	0,500	$8,2\ 10^{-9}$	$4,3\ 10^{-9}$	$2,6\ 10^{-9}$	$1,6\ 10^{-9}$	$1,3\ 10^{-9}$
As-76	1,10 d	1,000	$1,0\ 10^{-8}$	0,500	$1,1\ 10^{-8}$	$5,8\ 10^{-9}$	$3,4\ 10^{-9}$	$2,0\ 10^{-9}$	$1,6\ 10^{-9}$
As-77	1,62 d	1,000	$2,7\ 10^{-9}$	0,500	$2,9\ 10^{-9}$	$1,5\ 10^{-9}$	$8,7\ 10^{-10}$	$5,0\ 10^{-10}$	$4,0\ 10^{-10}$
As-78	1,51 h	1,000	$2,0\ 10^{-9}$	0,500	$1,4\ 10^{-9}$	$7,0\ 10^{-10}$	$4,1\ 10^{-10}$	$2,7\ 10^{-10}$	$2,1\ 10^{-10}$
Selenium									
Se-70	0,683 h	1,000	$1,0\ 10^{-9}$	0,800	$7,1\ 10^{-10}$	$3,6\ 10^{-10}$	$2,2\ 10^{-10}$	$1,5\ 10^{-10}$	$1,2\ 10^{-10}$
Se-73	7,15 h	1,000	$1,6\ 10^{-9}$	0,800	$1,4\ 10^{-9}$	$7,4\ 10^{-10}$	$4,8\ 10^{-10}$	$2,5\ 10^{-10}$	$2,1\ 10^{-10}$
Se-73m	0,650 h	1,000	$2,6\ 10^{-10}$	0,800	$1,8\ 10^{-10}$	$9,5\ 10^{-11}$	$5,9\ 10^{-11}$	$3,5\ 10^{-11}$	$2,8\ 10^{-11}$
Se-75	120 d	1,000	$2,0\ 10^{-8}$	0,800	$1,3\ 10^{-8}$	$8,3\ 10^{-9}$	$6,0\ 10^{-9}$	$3,1\ 10^{-9}$	$2,6\ 10^{-9}$
Se-79	$6,50\ 10^{4}$ a	1,000	$4,1\ 10^{-8}$	0,800	$2,8\ 10^{-8}$	$1,9\ 10^{-8}$	$1,4\ 10^{-8}$	$4,1\ 10^{-9}$	$2,9\ 10^{-9}$
Se-81	0,308 h	1,000	$3,4\ 10^{-10}$	0,800	$1,9\ 10^{-10}$	$9,0\ 10^{-11}$	$5,1\ 10^{-11}$	$3,4\ 10^{-11}$	$2,7\ 10^{-11}$
Se-81m	0,954 h	1,000	$6,0\ 10^{-10}$	0,800	$3,7\ 10^{-10}$	$1,8\ 10^{-10}$	$1,1\ 10^{-10}$	$6,7\ 10^{-11}$	$5,3\ 10^{-11}$
Se-83	0,375 h	1,000	$4,6\ 10^{-10}$	0,800	$2,9\ 10^{-10}$	$1,5\ 10^{-10}$	$8,7\ 10^{-11}$	$5,9\ 10^{-11}$	$4,7\ 10^{-11}$
Bromine									
Br-74	0,422 h	1,000	$9,0\ 10^{-10}$	1,000	$5,2\ 10^{-10}$	$2,6\ 10^{-10}$	$1,5\ 10^{-10}$	$1,1\ 10^{-10}$	$8,4\ 10^{-11}$
Br-74m	0,691 h	1,000	$1,5\ 10^{-9}$	1,000	$8,5\ 10^{-10}$	$4,3\ 10^{-10}$	$2,5\ 10^{-10}$	$1,7\ 10^{-10}$	$1,4\ 10^{-10}$
Br-75	1,63 h	1,000	$8,5\ 10^{-10}$	1,000	$4,9\ 10^{-10}$	$2,5\ 10^{-10}$	$1,5\ 10^{-10}$	$9,9\ 10^{-11}$	$7,9\ 10^{-11}$
Br-76	16,2 h	1,000	$4,2\ 10^{-9}$	1,000	$2,7\ 10^{-9}$	$1,4\ 10^{-9}$	$8,7\ 10^{-10}$	$5,6\ 10^{-10}$	$4,6\ 10^{-10}$
Br-77	2,33 d	1,000	$6,3\ 10^{-10}$	1,000	$4,4\ 10^{-10}$	$2,5\ 10^{-10}$	$1,7\ 10^{-10}$	$1,1\ 10^{-10}$	$9,6\ 10^{-11}$

Nuclide	Physical half-life	Age ≤ 1 a		Age	1—2 a	2—7 a	7—12 a	12—17 a	4 17 a
		f_1 for ≤ 1 a	h(g)	f_1 for g > 1 a	h(g)	h(g)	h(g)	h(g)	h(g)
Br-80	0,290 h	1,000	$3,9\ 10^{-10}$	1,000	$2,1\ 10^{-10}$	$1,0\ 10^{-10}$	$5,8\ 10^{-11}$	$3,9\ 10^{-11}$	$3,1\ 10^{-11}$
Br-80m	4,42 h	1,000	$1,4\ 10^{-9}$	1,000	$8,0\ 10^{-10}$	$3,9\ 10^{-10}$	$2,3\ 10^{-10}$	$1,4\ 10^{-10}$	$1,1\ 10^{-10}$
Br-82	1,47 d	1,000	$3,7\ 10^{-9}$	1,000	$2,6\ 10^{-9}$	$1,5\ 10^{-9}$	$9,5\ 10^{-10}$	$6,4\ 10^{-10}$	$5,4\ 10^{-10}$
Br-83	2,39 h	1,000	$5,3\ 10^{-10}$	1,000	$3,0\ 10^{-10}$	$1,4\ 10^{-10}$	$8,3\ 10^{-11}$	$5,5\ 10^{-11}$	$4,3\ 10^{-11}$
Br-84	0,530 h	1,000	$1,0\ 10^{-9}$	1,000	$5,8\ 10^{-10}$	$2,8\ 10^{-10}$	$1,6\ 10^{-10}$	$1,1\ 10^{-10}$	$8,8\ 10^{-11}$
Rubidium									
Rb-79	0,382 h	1,000	$5,7\ 10^{-10}$	1,000	$3,2\ 10^{-10}$	$1,6\ 10^{-10}$	$9,2\ 10^{-11}$	$6,3\ 10^{-11}$	$5,0\ 10^{-11}$
Rb-81	4,58 h	1,000	$5,4\ 10^{-10}$	1,000	$3,2\ 10^{-10}$	$1,6\ 10^{-10}$	$1,0\ 10^{-10}$	$6,7\ 10^{-11}$	$5,4\ 10^{-11}$
Rb-81m	0,533 h	1,000	$1,1\ 10^{-10}$	1,000	$6,2\ 10^{-11}$	$3,1\ 10^{-11}$	$1,8\ 10^{-11}$	$1,2\ 10^{-11}$	$9,7\ 10^{-12}$
Rb-82m	6,20 h	1,000	$8,7\ 10^{-10}$	1,000	$5,9\ 10^{-10}$	$3,4\ 10^{-10}$	$2,2\ 10^{-10}$	$1,5\ 10^{-10}$	$1,3\ 10^{-10}$
Rb-83	86,2 d	1,000	$1,1\ 10^{-8}$	1,000	$8,4\ 10^{-9}$	$4,9\ 10^{-9}$	$3,2\ 10^{-9}$	$2,2\ 10^{-9}$	$1,9\ 10^{-9}$
Rb-84	32,8 d	1,000	$2,0\ 10^{-8}$	1,000	$1,4\ 10^{-8}$	$7,9\ 10^{-9}$	$5,0\ 10^{-9}$	$3,3\ 10^{-9}$	$2,8\ 10^{-9}$
Rb-86	18,7 d	1,000	$3,1\ 10^{-8}$	1,000	$2,0\ 10^{-8}$	$9,9\ 10^{-9}$	$5,9\ 10^{-9}$	$3,5\ 10^{-9}$	$2,8\ 10^{-9}$
Rb-87	$4,70\ 10^{10}$ a	1,000	$1,5\ 10^{-8}$	1,000	$1,0\ 10^{-8}$	$5,2\ 10^{-9}$	$3,1\ 10^{-9}$	$1,8\ 10^{-9}$	$1,5\ 10^{-9}$
Rb-88	0,297 h	1,000	$1,1\ 10^{-9}$	1,000	$6,2\ 10^{-10}$	$3,0\ 10^{-10}$	$1,7\ 10^{-10}$	$1,2\ 10^{-10}$	$9,0\ 10^{-11}$
Rb-89	0,253 h	1,000	$5,4\ 10^{-10}$	1,000	$3,0\ 10^{-10}$	$1,5\ 10^{-10}$	$8,6\ 10^{-11}$	$5,9\ 10^{-11}$	$4,7\ 10^{-11}$
Strontium[(d)]									
Sr-80	1,67 h	0,600	$3,7\ 10^{-9}$	0,300	$2,3\ 10^{-9}$	$1,1\ 10^{-9}$	$6,5\ 10^{-10}$	$4,2\ 10^{-10}$	$3,4\ 10^{-10}$
Sr-81	0,425 h	0,600	$8,4\ 10^{-10}$	0,300	$4,9\ 10^{-10}$	$2,4\ 10^{-10}$	$1,4\ 10^{-10}$	$9,6\ 10^{-11}$	$7,7\ 10^{-11}$
Sr-82	25,0 d	0,600	$7,2\ 10^{-8}$	0,300	$4,1\ 10^{-8}$	$2,1\ 10^{-8}$	$1,3\ 10^{-8}$	$8,7\ 10^{-9}$	$6,1\ 10^{-9}$
Sr-83	1,35 d	0,600	$3,4\ 10^{-9}$	0,300	$2,7\ 10^{-9}$	$1,4\ 10^{-9}$	$9,1\ 10^{-10}$	$5,7\ 10^{-10}$	$4,9\ 10^{-10}$
Sr-85	64,8 d	0,600	$7,7\ 10^{-9}$	0,300	$3,1\ 10^{-9}$	$1,7\ 10^{-9}$	$1,5\ 10^{-9}$	$1,3\ 10^{-9}$	$5,6\ 10^{-10}$
Sr-85m	1,16 h	0,600	$4,5\ 10^{-11}$	0,300	$3,0\ 10^{-11}$	$1,7\ 10^{-11}$	$1,1\ 10^{-11}$	$7,8\ 10^{-12}$	$6,1\ 10^{-12}$
Sr-87m	2,80 h	0,600	$2,4\ 10^{-10}$	0,300	$1,7\ 10^{-10}$	$9,0\ 10^{-11}$	$5,6\ 10^{-11}$	$3,6\ 10^{-11}$	$3,0\ 10^{-11}$
Sr-89	50,5 d	0,600	$3,6\ 10^{-8}$	0,300	$1,8\ 10^{-8}$	$8,9\ 10^{-9}$	$5,8\ 10^{-9}$	$4,0\ 10^{-9}$	$2,6\ 10^{-9}$

Nuclide	Physical half-life	Age ≤ 1 a		Age	1—2 a	2—7 a	7—12 a	12—17 a	4 17 a
		f_1 for ≤ 1 a	h(g)	f_1 for g > 1 a	h(g)	h(g)	h(g)	h(g)	h(g)
Sr-90	29,1 a	0,600	2,3 10^{-7}	0,300	7,3 10^{-8}	4,7 10^{-8}	6,0 10^{-8}	8,0 10^{-8}	2,8 10^{-8}
Sr-91	9,50 h	0,600	5,2 10^{-9}	0,300	4,0 10^{-9}	2,1 10^{-9}	1,2 10^{-9}	7,4 10^{-10}	6,5 10^{-10}
Sr-92	2,71 h	0,600	3,4 10^{-9}	0,300	2,7 10^{-9}	1,4 10^{-9}	8,2 10^{-10}	4,8 10^{-10}	4,3 10^{-10}
Yttrium									
Y-86	14,7 h	0,001	7,6 10^{-9}	1,0 10^{-4}	5,2 10^{-9}	2,9 10^{-9}	1,9 10^{-9}	1,2 10^{-9}	9,6 10^{-10}
Y-86m	0,800 h	0,001	4,5 10^{-10}	1,0 10^{-4}	3,1 10^{-10}	1,7 10^{-10}	1,1 10^{-10}	7,1 10^{-11}	5,6 10^{-11}
Y-87	3,35 d	0,001	4,6 10^{-9}	1,0 10^{-4}	3,2 10^{-9}	1,8 10^{-9}	1,1 10^{-9}	7,0 10^{-10}	5,5 10^{-10}
Y-88	107 d	0,001	8,1 10^{-9}	1,0 10^{-4}	6,0 10^{-9}	3,5 10^{-9}	2,4 10^{-9}	1,6 10^{-9}	1,3 10^{-9}
Y-90	2,67 d	0,001	3,1 10^{-8}	1,0 10^{-4}	2,0 10^{-8}	1,0 10^{-8}	5,9 10^{-9}	3,3 10^{-9}	2,7 10^{-9}
Y-90m	3,19 h	0,001	1,8 10^{-9}	1,0 10^{-4}	1,2 10^{-9}	6,1 10^{-10}	3,7 10^{-10}	2,2 10^{-10}	1,7 10^{-10}
Y-91	58,5 d	0,001	2,8 10^{-8}	1,0 10^{-4}	1,8 10^{-8}	8,8 10^{-9}	5,2 10^{-9}	2,9 10^{-9}	2,4 10^{-9}
Y-91m	0,828 h	0,001	9,2 10^{-11}	1,0 10^{-4}	6,0 10^{-11}	3,3 10^{-11}	2,1 10^{-11}	1,4 10^{-11}	1,1 10^{-11}
Y-92	3,54 h	0,001	5,9 10^{-9}	1,0 10^{-4}	3,6 10^{-9}	1,8 10^{-9}	1,0 10^{-9}	6,2 10^{-10}	4,9 10^{-10}
Y-93	10,1 h	0,001	1,4 10^{-8}	1,0 10^{-4}	8,5 10^{-9}	4,3 10^{-9}	2,5 10^{-9}	1,4 10^{-9}	1,2 10^{-9}
Y-94	0,318 h	0,001	9,9 10^{-10}	1,0 10^{-4}	5,5 10^{-10}	2,7 10^{-10}	1,5 10^{-10}	1,0 10^{-10}	8,1 10^{-11}
Y-95	0,178 h	0,001	5,7 10^{-10}	1,0 10^{-4}	3,1 10^{-10}	1,5 10^{-10}	8,7 10^{-11}	5,9 10^{-11}	4,6 10^{-11}
Zirconium									
Zr-86	16,5 h	0,020	6,9 10^{-9}	0,010	4,8 10^{-9}	2,7 10^{-9}	1,7 10^{-9}	1,1 10^{-9}	8,6 10^{-10}
Zr-88	83,4 d	0,020	2,8 10^{-9}	0,010	2,0 10^{-9}	1,2 10^{-9}	8,0 10^{-10}	5,4 10^{-10}	4,5 10^{-10}
Zr-89	3,27 d	0,020	6,5 10^{-9}	0,010	4,5 10^{-9}	2,5 10^{-9}	1,6 10^{-9}	9,9 10^{-10}	7,9 10^{-10}
Zr-93	1,53 106 a	0,020	1,2 10^{-9}	0,010	7,6 10^{-10}	5,1 10^{-10}	5,8 10^{-10}	8,6 10^{-10}	1,1 10^{-9}
Zr-95	64,0 d	0,020	8,5 10^{-9}	0,010	5,6 10^{-9}	3,0 10^{-9}	1,9 10^{-9}	1,2 10^{-9}	9,5 10^{-10}
Zr-97	16,9 h	0,020	2,2 10^{-8}	0,010	1,4 10^{-8}	7,3 10^{-9}	4,4 10^{-9}	2,6 10^{-9}	2,1 10^{-9}
Niobium									
Nb-88	0,238 h	0,020	6,7 10^{-10}	0,010	3,8 10^{-10}	1,9 10^{-10}	1,1 10^{-10}	7,9 10^{-11}	6,3 10^{-11}

Nuclide	Physical half-life	Age ≤ 1 a		Age	1—2 a	2—7 a	7—12 a	12—17 a	4 17 a
		f_1 for ≤ 1 a	h(g)	f_1 for g > 1 a	h(g)	h(g)	h(g)	h(g)	h(g)
Nb-89	2,03 h	0,020	$3,0\ 10^{-9}$	0,010	$2,0\ 10^{-9}$	$1,0\ 10^{-9}$	$6,0\ 10^{-10}$	$3,4\ 10^{-10}$	$2,7\ 10^{-10}$
Nb-89	1,10 h	0,020	$1,5\ 10^{-9}$	0,010	$8,7\ 10^{-10}$	$4,4\ 10^{-10}$	$2,7\ 10^{-10}$	$1,8\ 10^{-10}$	$1,4\ 10^{-10}$
Nb-90	14,6 h	0,020	$1,1\ 10^{-8}$	0,010	$7,2\ 10^{-9}$	$3,9\ 10^{-9}$	$2,5\ 10^{-9}$	$1,6\ 10^{-9}$	$1,2\ 10^{-9}$
Nb-93m	13,6 a	0,020	$1,5\ 10^{-9}$	0,010	$9,1\ 10^{-10}$	$4,6\ 10^{-10}$	$2,7\ 10^{-10}$	$1,5\ 10^{-10}$	$1,2\ 10^{-10}$
Nb-94	$2,03\ 10^{4}$ a	0,020	$1,5\ 10^{-8}$	0,010	$9,7\ 10^{-9}$	$5,3\ 10^{-9}$	$3,4\ 10^{-9}$	$2,1\ 10^{-9}$	$1,7\ 10^{-9}$
Nb-95	35,1 d	0,020	$4,6\ 10^{-9}$	0,010	$3,2\ 10^{-9}$	$1,8\ 10^{-9}$	$1,1\ 10^{-9}$	$7,4\ 10^{-10}$	$5,8\ 10^{-10}$
Nb-95m	3,61 d	0,020	$6,4\ 10^{-9}$	0,010	$4,1\ 10^{-9}$	$2,1\ 10^{-9}$	$1,2\ 10^{-9}$	$7,1\ 10^{-10}$	$5,6\ 10^{-10}$
Nb-96	23,3 h	0,020	$9,2\ 10^{-9}$	0,010	$6,3\ 10^{-9}$	$3,4\ 10^{-9}$	$2,2\ 10^{-9}$	$1,4\ 10^{-9}$	$1,1\ 10^{-9}$
Nb-97	1,20 h	0,020	$7,7\ 10^{-10}$	0,010	$4,5\ 10^{-10}$	$2,3\ 10^{-10}$	$1,3\ 10^{-10}$	$8,7\ 10^{-11}$	$6,8\ 10^{-11}$
Nb-98	0,858 h	0,020	$1,2\ 10^{-9}$	0,010	$7,1\ 10^{-10}$	$3,6\ 10^{-10}$	$2,2\ 10^{-10}$	$1,4\ 10^{-10}$	$1,1\ 10^{-10}$
Molybdenum									
Mo-90	5,67 h	1,000	$1,7\ 10^{-9}$	1,000	$1,2\ 10^{-9}$	$6,3\ 10^{-10}$	$4,0\ 10^{-10}$	$2,7\ 10^{-10}$	$2,2\ 10^{-10}$
Mo-93	$3,50\ 10^{3}$ a	1,000	$7,9\ 10^{-9}$	1,000	$6,9\ 10^{-9}$	$5,0\ 10^{-9}$	$4,0\ 10^{-9}$	$3,4\ 10^{-9}$	$3,1\ 10^{-9}$
Mo-93m	6,85 h	1,000	$8,0\ 10^{-10}$	1,000	$5,4\ 10^{-10}$	$3,1\ 10^{-10}$	$2,0\ 10^{-10}$	$1,4\ 10^{-10}$	$1,1\ 10^{-10}$
Mo-99	2,75 d	1,000	$5,5\ 10^{-9}$	1,000	$3,5\ 10^{-9}$	$1,8\ 10^{-9}$	$1,1\ 10^{-9}$	$7,6\ 10^{-10}$	$6,0\ 10^{-10}$
Mo-101	0,244 h	1,000	$4,8\ 10^{-10}$	1,000	$2,7\ 10^{-10}$	$1,3\ 10^{-10}$	$7,6\ 10^{-11}$	$5,2\ 10^{-11}$	$4,1\ 10^{-11}$
Technetium									
Tc-93	2,75 h	1,000	$2,7\ 10^{-10}$	0,500	$2,5\ 10^{-10}$	$1,5\ 10^{-10}$	$9,8\ 10^{-11}$	$6,8\ 10^{-11}$	$5,5\ 10^{-11}$
Tc-93m	0,725 h	1,000	$2,0\ 10^{-10}$	0,500	$1,3\ 10^{-10}$	$7,3\ 10^{-11}$	$4,6\ 10^{-11}$	$3,2\ 10^{-11}$	$2,5\ 10^{-11}$
Tc-94	4,88 h	1,000	$1,2\ 10^{-9}$	0,500	$1,0\ 10^{-9}$	$5,8\ 10^{-10}$	$3,7\ 10^{-10}$	$2,5\ 10^{-10}$	$2,0\ 10^{-10}$
Tc-94m	0,867 h	1,000	$1,3\ 10^{-9}$	0,500	$6,5\ 10^{-10}$	$3,3\ 10^{-10}$	$1,9\ 10^{-10}$	$1,3\ 10^{-10}$	$1,0\ 10^{-10}$
Tc-95	20,0 h	1,000	$9,9\ 10^{-10}$	0,500	$8,7\ 10^{-10}$	$5,0\ 10^{-10}$	$3,3\ 10^{-10}$	$2,3\ 10^{-10}$	$1,8\ 10^{-10}$
Tc-95m	61,0 d	1,000	$4,7\ 10^{-9}$	0,500	$2,8\ 10^{-9}$	$1,6\ 10^{-9}$	$1,0\ 10^{-9}$	$7,0\ 10^{-10}$	$5,6\ 10^{-10}$
Tc-96	4,28 d	1,000	$6,7\ 10^{-9}$	0,500	$5,1\ 10^{-9}$	$3,0\ 10^{-9}$	$2,0\ 10^{-9}$	$1,4\ 10^{-9}$	$1,1\ 10^{-9}$
Tc-96m	0,858 h	1,000	$1,0\ 10^{-10}$	0,500	$6,5\ 10^{-11}$	$3,6\ 10^{-11}$	$2,3\ 10^{-11}$	$1,6\ 10^{-11}$	$1,2\ 10^{-11}$

Nuclide	*Physical half-life*	*Age ≤ 1 a*		*Age*	*1—2 a*	*2—7 a*	*7—12 a*	*12—17 a*	*4 17 a*
		f_1 *for ≤ 1 a*	*h(g)*	f_1 *for g > 1 a*	*h(g)*	*h(g)*	*h(g)*	*h(g)*	*h(g)*
Tc-97	2,60 10^{6} a	1,000	9,9 10^{-10}	0,500	4,9 10^{-10}	2,4 10^{-10}	1,4 10^{-10}	8,8 10^{-11}	6,8 10^{-11}
Tc-97m	87,0 d	1,000	8,7 10^{-9}	0,500	4,1 10^{-9}	2,0 10^{-9}	1,1 10^{-9}	7,0 10^{-10}	5,5 10^{-10}
Tc-98	4,20 10^{6} a	1,000	2,3 10^{-8}	0,500	1,2 10^{-8}	6,1 10^{-9}	3,7 10^{-9}	2,5 10^{-9}	2,0 10^{-9}
Tc-99	2,13 10^{5} a	1,000	1,0 10^{-8}	0,500	4,8 10^{-9}	2,3 10^{-9}	1,3 10^{-9}	8,2 10^{-10}	6,4 10^{-10}
Tc-99m	6,02 h	1,000	2,0 10^{-10}	0,500	1,3 10^{-10}	7,2 10^{-11}	4,3 10^{-11}	2,8 10^{-11}	2,2 10^{-11}
Tc-101	0,237 h	1,000	2,4 10^{-10}	0,500	1,3 10^{-10}	6,1 10^{-11}	3,5 10^{-11}	2,4 10^{-11}	1,9 10^{-11}
Tc-104	0,303 h	1,000	1,0 10^{-9}	0,500	5,3 10^{-10}	2,6 10^{-10}	1,5 10^{-10}	1,0 10^{-10}	8,0 10^{-11}
Ruthenium									
Ru-94	0,863 h	0,100	9,3 10^{-10}	0,050	5,9 10^{-10}	3,1 10^{-10}	1,9 10^{-10}	1,2 10^{-10}	9,4 10^{-11}
Ru-97	2,90 d	0,100	1,2 10^{-9}	0,050	8,5 10^{-10}	4,7 10^{-10}	3,0 10^{-10}	1,9 10^{-10}	1,5 10^{-10}
Ru-103	39,3 d	0,100	7,1 10^{-9}	0,050	4,6 10^{-9}	2,4 10^{-9}	1,5 10^{-9}	9,2 10^{-10}	7,3 10^{-10}
Ru-105	4,44 h	0,100	2,7 10^{-9}	0,050	1,8 10^{-9}	9,1 10^{-10}	5,5 10^{-10}	3,3 10^{-10}	2,6 10^{-10}
Ru-106	1,01 a	0,100	8,4 10^{-8}	0,050	4,9 10^{-8}	2,5 10^{-8}	1,5 10^{-8}	8,6 10^{-9}	7,0 10^{-9}
Rhodium									
Rh-99	16,0 d	0,100	4,2 10^{-9}	0,050	2,9 10^{-9}	1,6 10^{-9}	1,0 10^{-9}	6,5 10^{-10}	5,1 10^{-10}
Rh-99m	4,70 h	0,100	4,9 10^{-10}	0,050	3,5 10^{-10}	2,0 10^{-10}	1,3 10^{-10}	8,3 10^{-11}	6,6 10^{-11}
Rh-100	20,8 h	0,100	4,9 10^{-9}	0,050	3,6 10^{-9}	2,0 10^{-9}	1,4 10^{-9}	8,8 10^{-10}	7,1 10^{-10}
Rh-101	3,20 a	0,100	4,9 10^{-9}	0,050	2,8 10^{-9}	1,6 10^{-9}	1,0 10^{-9}	6,7 10^{-10}	5,5 10^{-10}
Rh-101m	4,34 d	0,100	1,7 10^{-9}	0,050	1,2 10^{-9}	6,8 10^{-10}	4,4 10^{-10}	2,8 10^{-10}	2,2 10^{-10}
Rh-102	2,90 a	0,100	1,9 10^{-8}	0,050	1,0 10^{-8}	6,4 10^{-9}	4,3 10^{-9}	3,0 10^{-9}	2,6 10^{-9}
Rh-102m	207 d	0,100	1,2 10^{-8}	0,050	7,4 10^{-9}	3,9 10^{-9}	2,4 10^{-9}	1,4 10^{-9}	1,2 10^{-9}
Rh-103m	0,935 h	0,100	4,7 10^{-11}	0,050	2,7 10^{-11}	1,3 10^{-11}	7,4 10^{-12}	4,8 10^{-12}	3,8 10^{-12}
Rh-105	1,47 d	0,100	4,0 10^{-9}	0,050	2,7 10^{-9}	1,3 10^{-9}	8,0 10^{-10}	4,6 10^{-10}	3,7 10^{-10}
Rh-106m	2,20 h	0,100	1,4 10^{-9}	0,050	9,7 10^{-10}	5,3 10^{-10}	3,3 10^{-10}	2,0 10^{-10}	1,6 10^{-10}
Rh-107	0,362 h	0,100	2,9 10^{-10}	0,050	1,6 10^{-10}	7,9 10^{-11}	4,5 10^{-11}	3,1 10^{-11}	2,4 10^{-11}

Nuclide	Physical half-life	Age ≤ 1 a		Age	1—2 a	2—7 a	7—12 a	12—17 a	4 17 a
		f_1 for ≤ 1 a	h(g)	f_1 for g > 1 a	h(g)	h(g)	h(g)	h(g)	h(g)
Palladium									
Pd-100	3,63 d	0,050	7,4 10^{-9}	0,005	5,2 10^{-9}	2,9 10^{-9}	1,9 10^{-9}	1,2 10^{-9}	9,4 10^{-10}
Pd-101	8,27 h	0,050	8,2 10^{-10}	0,005	5,7 10^{-10}	3,1 10^{-10}	1,9 10^{-10}	1,2 10^{-10}	9,4 10^{-11}
Pd-103	17,0 d	0,050	2,2 10^{-9}	0,005	1,4 10^{-9}	7,2 10^{-10}	4,3 10^{-10}	2,4 10^{-10}	1,9 10^{-10}
Pd-107	6,50 10^{6} a	0,050	4,4 10^{-10}	0,005	2,8 10^{-10}	1,4 10^{-10}	8,1 10^{-11}	4,6 10^{-11}	3,7 10^{-11}
Pd-109	13,4 h	0,050	6,3 10^{-9}	0,005	4,1 10^{-9}	2,0 10^{-9}	1,2 10^{-9}	6,8 10^{-10}	5,5 10^{-10}
Silver									
Ag-102	0,215 h	0,100	4,2 10^{-10}	0,050	2,4 10^{-10}	1,2 10^{-10}	7,3 10^{-11}	5,0 10^{-11}	4,0 10^{-11}
Ag-103	1,09 h	0,100	4,5 10^{-10}	0,050	2,7 10^{-10}	1,4 10^{-10}	8,3 10^{-11}	5,5 10^{-11}	4,3 10^{-11}
Ag-104	1,15 h	0,100	4,3 10^{-10}	0,050	2,9 10^{-10}	1,7 10^{-10}	1,1 10^{-10}	7,5 10^{-11}	6,0 10^{-11}
Ag-104m	0,558 h	0,100	5,6 10^{-10}	0,050	3,3 10^{-10}	1,7 10^{-10}	1,0 10^{-10}	6,8 10^{-11}	5,4 10^{-11}
Ag-105	41,0 d	0,100	3,9 10^{-9}	0,050	2,5 10^{-9}	1,4 10^{-9}	9,1 10^{-10}	5,9 10^{-10}	4,7 10^{-10}
Ag-106	0,399 h	0,100	3,7 10^{-10}	0,050	2,1 10^{-10}	1,0 10^{-10}	6,0 10^{-11}	4,1 10^{-11}	3,2 10^{-11}
Ag-106m	8,41 d	0,100	9,7 10^{-9}	0,050	6,9 10^{-9}	4,1 10^{-9}	2,8 10^{-9}	1,8 10^{-9}	1,5 10^{-9}
Ag-108m	1,27 10^{2} a	0,100	2,1 10^{-8}	0,050	1,1 10^{-8}	6,5 10^{-9}	4,3 10^{-9}	2,8 10^{-9}	2,3 10^{-9}
Ag-110m	250 d	0,100	2,4 10^{-8}	0,050	1,4 10^{-8}	7,8 10^{-9}	5,2 10^{-9}	3,4 10^{-9}	2,8 10^{-9}
Ag-111	7,45 d	0,100	1,4 10^{-8}	0,050	9,3 10^{-9}	4,6 10^{-9}	2,7 10^{-9}	1,6 10^{-9}	1,3 10^{-9}
Ag-112	3,12 h	0,100	4,9 10^{-9}	0,050	3,0 10^{-9}	1,5 10^{-9}	8,9 10^{-10}	5,4 10^{-10}	4,3 10^{-10}
Ag-115	0,333 h	0,100	7,2 10^{-10}	0,050	4,1 10^{-10}	2,0 10^{-10}	1,2 10^{-10}	7,7 10^{-11}	6,0 10^{-11}
Cadmium									
Cd-104	0,961 h	0,100	4,2 10^{-10}	0,050	2,9 10^{-10}	1,7 10^{-10}	1,1 10^{-10}	7,2 10^{-11}	5,4 10^{-11}
Cd-107	6,49 h	0,100	7,1 10^{-10}	0,050	4,6 10^{-10}	2,3 10^{-10}	1,3 10^{-10}	7,8 10^{-11}	6,2 10^{-11}
Cd-109	1,27 a	0,100	2,1 10^{-8}	0,050	9,5 10^{-9}	5,5 10^{-9}	3,5 10^{-9}	2,4 10^{-9}	2,0 10^{-9}
Cd-113	9,30 10^{15} a	0,100	1,0 10^{-7}	0,050	4,8 10^{-8}	3,7 10^{-8}	3,0 10^{-8}	2,6 10^{-8}	2,5 10^{-8}
Cd-113m	13,6 a	0,100	1,2 10^{-7}	0,050	5,6 10^{-8}	3,9 10^{-8}	2,9 10^{-8}	2,4 10^{-8}	2,3 10^{-8}

Nuclide	Physical half-life	Age ≤ 1 a		Age	1—2 a	2—7 a	7—12 a	12—17 a	4 17 a
		f_1 for ≤ 1 a	h(g)	f_1 for g > 1 a	h(g)	h(g)	h(g)	h(g)	h(g)
Cd-115	2,23 d	0,100	$1,4\ 10^{-8}$	0,050	$9,7\ 10^{-9}$	$4,9\ 10^{-9}$	$2,9\ 10^{-9}$	$1,7\ 10^{-9}$	$1,4\ 10^{-9}$
Cd-115m	44,6 d	0,100	$4,1\ 10^{-8}$	0,050	$1,9\ 10^{-8}$	$9,7\ 10^{-9}$	$6,9\ 10^{-9}$	$4,1\ 10^{-9}$	$3,3\ 10^{-9}$
Cd-117	2,49 h	0,100	$2,9\ 10^{-9}$	0,050	$1,9\ 10^{-9}$	$9,5\ 10^{-10}$	$5,7\ 10^{-10}$	$3,5\ 10^{-10}$	$2,8\ 10^{-10}$
Cd-117m	3,36 h	0,100	$2,6\ 10^{-9}$	0,050	$1,7\ 10^{-9}$	$9,0\ 10^{-10}$	$5,6\ 10^{-10}$	$3,5\ 10^{-10}$	$2,8\ 10^{-10}$
Indium									
In-109	4,20 h	0,040	$5,2\ 10^{-10}$	0,020	$3,6\ 10^{-10}$	$2,0\ 10^{-10}$	$1,3\ 10^{-10}$	$8,2\ 10^{-11}$	$6,6\ 10^{-11}$
In-110	4,90 h	0,040	$1,5\ 10^{-9}$	0,020	$1,1\ 10^{-9}$	$6,5\ 10^{-10}$	$4,4\ 10^{-10}$	$3,0\ 10^{-10}$	$2,4\ 10^{-10}$
In-110	1,15 h	0,040	$1,1\ 10^{-9}$	0,020	$6,4\ 10^{-10}$	$3,2\ 10^{-10}$	$1,9\ 10^{-10}$	$1,3\ 10^{-10}$	$1,0\ 10^{-10}$
In-111	2,83 d	0,040	$2,4\ 10^{-9}$	0,020	$1,7\ 10^{-9}$	$9,1\ 10^{-10}$	$5,9\ 10^{-10}$	$3,7\ 10^{-10}$	$2,9\ 10^{-10}$
In-112	0,240 h	0,040	$1,2\ 10^{-10}$	0,020	$6,7\ 10^{-11}$	$3,3\ 10^{-11}$	$1,9\ 10^{-11}$	$1,3\ 10^{-11}$	$1,0\ 10^{-11}$
In-113m	1,66 h	0,040	$3,0\ 10^{-10}$	0,020	$1,8\ 10^{-10}$	$9,3\ 10^{-11}$	$6,2\ 10^{-11}$	$3,6\ 10^{-11}$	$2,8\ 10^{-11}$
In-114m	49,5 d	0,040	$5,6\ 10^{-8}$	0,020	$3,1\ 10^{-8}$	$1,5\ 10^{-8}$	$9,0\ 10^{-9}$	$5,2\ 10^{-9}$	$4,1\ 10^{-9}$
In-115	$5,10\ 10^{15}$ a	0,040	$1,3\ 10^{-7}$	0,020	$6,4\ 10^{-8}$	$4,8\ 10^{-8}$	$4,3\ 10^{-8}$	$3,6\ 10^{-8}$	$3,2\ 10^{-8}$
In-115m	4,49 h	0,040	$9,6\ 10^{-10}$	0,020	$6,0\ 10^{-10}$	$3,0\ 10^{-10}$	$1,8\ 10^{-10}$	$1,1\ 10^{-10}$	$8,6\ 10^{-11}$
In-116m	0,902 h	0,040	$5,8\ 10^{-10}$	0,020	$3,6\ 10^{-10}$	$1,9\ 10^{-10}$	$1,2\ 10^{-10}$	$8,0\ 10^{-11}$	$6,4\ 10^{-11}$
In-117	0,730 h	0,040	$3,3\ 10^{-10}$	0,020	$1,9\ 10^{-10}$	$9,7\ 10^{-11}$	$5,8\ 10^{-11}$	$3,9\ 10^{-11}$	$3,1\ 10^{-11}$
In-117m	1,94 h	0,040	$1,4\ 10^{-9}$	0,020	$8,6\ 10^{-10}$	$4,3\ 10^{-10}$	$2,5\ 10^{-10}$	$1,6\ 10^{-10}$	$1,2\ 10^{-10}$
In-119m	0,300 h	0,040	$5,9\ 10^{-10}$	0,020	$3,2\ 10^{-10}$	$1,6\ 10^{-10}$	$8,8\ 10^{-11}$	$6,0\ 10^{-11}$	$4,7\ 10^{-11}$
Tin									
Sn-110	4,00 h	0,040	$3,5\ 10^{-9}$	0,020	$2,3\ 10^{-9}$	$1,2\ 10^{-9}$	$7,4\ 10^{-10}$	$4,4\ 10^{-10}$	$3,5\ 10^{-10}$
Sn-111	0,588 h	0,040	$2,5\ 10^{-10}$	0,020	$1,5\ 10^{-10}$	$7,4\ 10^{-11}$	$4,4\ 10^{-11}$	$3,0\ 10^{-11}$	$2,3\ 10^{-11}$
Sn-113	115 d	0,040	$7,8\ 10^{-9}$	0,020	$5,0\ 10^{-9}$	$2,6\ 10^{-9}$	$1,6\ 10^{-9}$	$9,2\ 10^{-10}$	$7,3\ 10^{-10}$
Sn-117m	13,6 d	0,040	$7,7\ 10^{-9}$	0,020	$5,0\ 10^{-9}$	$2,5\ 10^{-9}$	$1,5\ 10^{-9}$	$8,8\ 10^{-10}$	$7,1\ 10^{-10}$
Sn-119m	293 d	0,040	$4,1\ 10^{-9}$	0,020	$2,5\ 10^{-9}$	$1,3\ 10^{-9}$	$7,5\ 10^{-10}$	$4,3\ 10^{-10}$	$3,4\ 10^{-10}$
Sn-121	1,13 d	0,040	$2,6\ 10^{-9}$	0,020	$1,7\ 10^{-9}$	$8,4\ 10^{-10}$	$5,0\ 10^{-10}$	$2,8\ 10^{-10}$	$2,3\ 10^{-10}$

Nuclide	*Physical half-life*	*Age ≤ 1 a*		*Age*	*1—2 a*	*2—7 a*	*7—12 a*	*12—17 a*	*4 17 a*
		f_1 for ≤ 1 a	*h(g)*	*f_1 for g > 1 a*	*h(g)*	*h(g)*	*h(g)*	*h(g)*	*h(g)*
Sn-121m	55,0 a	0,040	4,6 10^{-9}	0,020	2,7 10^{-9}	1,4 10^{-9}	8,2 10^{-10}	4,7 10^{-10}	3,8 10^{-10}
Sn-123	129 d	0,040	2,5 10^{-8}	0,020	1,6 10^{-8}	7,8 10^{-9}	4,6 10^{-9}	2,6 10^{-9}	2,1 10^{-9}
Sn-123m	0,668 h	0,040	4,7 10^{-10}	0,020	2,6 10^{-10}	1,3 10^{-10}	7,3 10^{-11}	4,9 10^{-11}	3,8 10^{-11}
Sn-125	9,64 d	0,040	3,5 10^{-8}	0,020	2,2 10^{-8}	1,1 10^{-8}	6,7 10^{-9}	3,8 10^{-9}	3,1 10^{-9}
Sn-126	1,00 10^{5} a	0,040	5,0 10^{-8}	0,020	3,0 10^{-8}	1,6 10^{-8}	9,8 10^{-9}	5,9 10^{-9}	4,7 10^{-9}
Sn-127	2,10 h	0,040	2,0 10^{-9}	0,020	1,3 10^{-9}	6,6 10^{-10}	4,0 10^{-10}	2,5 10^{-10}	2,0 10^{-10}
Sn-128	0,985 h	0,040	1,6 10^{-9}	0,020	9,7 10^{-10}	4,9 10^{-10}	3,0 10^{-10}	1,9 10^{-10}	1,5 10^{-10}
Antimony									
Sb-115	0,530 h	0,200	2,5 10^{-10}	0,100	1,5 10^{-10}	7,5 10^{-11}	4,5 10^{-11}	3,1 10^{-11}	2,4 10^{-11}
Sb-116	0,263 h	0,200	2,7 10^{-10}	0,100	1,6 10^{-10}	8,0 10^{-11}	4,8 10^{-11}	3,3 10^{-11}	2,6 10^{-11}
Sb-116m	1,00 h	0,200	5,0 10^{-10}	0,100	3,3 10^{-10}	1,9 10^{-10}	1,2 10^{-10}	8,3 10^{-11}	6,7 10^{-11}
Sb-117	2,80 h	0,200	1,6 10^{-10}	0,100	1,0 10^{-10}	5,6 10^{-11}	3,5 10^{-11}	2,2 10^{-11}	1,8 10^{-11}
Sb-118m	5,00 h	0,200	1,3 10^{-9}	0,100	1,0 10^{-9}	5,8 10^{-10}	3,9 10^{-10}	2,6 10^{-10}	2,1 10^{-10}
Sb-119	1,59 d	0,200	8,4 10^{-10}	0,100	5,8 10^{-10}	3,0 10^{-10}	1,8 10^{-10}	1,0 10^{-10}	8,0 10^{-11}
Sb-120	5,76 d	0,200	8,1 10^{-9}	0,100	6,0 10^{-9}	3,5 10^{-9}	2,3 10^{-9}	1,6 10^{-9}	1,2 10^{-9}
Sb-120	0,265 h	0,200	1,7 10^{-10}	0,100	9,4 10^{-11}	4,6 10^{-11}	2,7 10^{-11}	1,8 10^{-11}	1,4 10^{-11}
Sb-122	2,70 d	0,200	1,8 10^{-8}	0,100	1,2 10^{-8}	6,1 10^{-9}	3,7 10^{-9}	2,1 10^{-9}	1,7 10^{-9}
Sb-124	60,2 d	0,200	2,5 10^{-8}	0,100	1,6 10^{-8}	8,4 10^{-9}	5,2 10^{-9}	3,2 10^{-9}	2,5 10^{-9}
Sb-124m	0,337 h	0,200	8,5 10^{-11}	0,100	4,9 10^{-11}	2,5 10^{-11}	1,5 10^{-11}	1,0 10^{-11}	8,0 10^{-12}
Sb-125	2,77 a	0,200	1,1 10^{-8}	0,100	6,1 10^{-9}	3,4 10^{-9}	2,1 10^{-9}	1,4 10^{-9}	1,1 10^{-9}
Sb-126	12,4 d	0,200	2,0 10^{-8}	0,100	1,4 10^{-8}	7,6 10^{-9}	4,9 10^{-9}	3,1 10^{-9}	2,4 10^{-9}
Sb-126m	0,317 h	0,200	3,9 10^{-10}	0,100	2,2 10^{-10}	1,1 10^{-10}	6,6 10^{-11}	4,5 10^{-11}	3,6 10^{-11}
Sb-127	3,85 d	0,200	1,7 10^{-8}	0,100	1,2 10^{-8}	5,9 10^{-9}	3,6 10^{-9}	2,1 10^{-9}	1,7 10^{-9}
Sb-128	9,01 h	0,200	6,3 10^{-9}	0,100	4,5 10^{-9}	2,4 10^{-9}	1,5 10^{-9}	9,5 10^{-10}	7,6 10^{-10}
Sb-128	0,173 h	0,200	3,7 10^{-10}	0,100	2,1 10^{-10}	1,0 10^{-10}	6,0 10^{-11}	4,1 10^{-11}	3,3 10^{-11}

Nuclide	*Physical half-life*	*Age ≤ 1 a*		*Age*	*1—2 a*	*2—7 a*	*7—12 a*	*12—17 a*	*4 17 a*
		f_1 *for ≤ 1 a*	*h(g)*	f_1 *for g > 1 a*	*h(g)*	*h(g)*	*h(g)*	*h(g)*	*h(g)*
Sb-129	4,32 h	0,200	4,3 10^{-9}	0,100	2,8 10^{-9}	1,5 10^{-9}	8,8 10^{-10}	5,3 10^{-10}	4,2 10^{-10}
Sb-130	0,667 h	0,200	9,1 10^{-10}	0,100	5,4 10^{-10}	2,8 10^{-10}	1,7 10^{-10}	1,2 10^{-10}	9,1 10^{-11}
Sb-131	0,383 h	0,200	1,1 10^{-9}	0,100	7,3 10^{-10}	3,9 10^{-10}	2,1 10^{-10}	1,4 10^{-10}	1,0 10^{-10}
Tellurium									
Te-116	2,49 h	0,600	1,4 10^{-9}	0,300	1,0 10^{-9}	5,5 10^{-10}	3,4 10^{-10}	2,1 10^{-10}	1,7 10^{-10}
Te-121	17,0 d	0,600	3,1 10^{-9}	0,300	2,0 10^{-9}	1,2 10^{-9}	8,0 10^{-10}	5,4 10^{-10}	4,3 10^{-10}
Te-121m	154 d	0,600	2,7 10^{-8}	0,300	1,2 10^{-8}	6,9 10^{-9}	4,2 10^{-9}	2,8 10^{-9}	2,3 10^{-9}
Te-123	1,00 10^{13} a	0,600	2,0 10^{-8}	0,300	9,3 10^{-9}	6,9 10^{-9}	5,4 10^{-9}	4,7 10^{-9}	4,4 10^{-9}
Te-123m	120 d	0,600	1,9 10^{-8}	0,300	8,8 10^{-9}	4,9 10^{-9}	2,8 10^{-9}	1,7 10^{-9}	1,4 10^{-9}
Te-125m	58,0 d	0,600	1,3 10^{-8}	0,300	6,3 10^{-9}	3,3 10^{-9}	1,9 10^{-9}	1,1 10^{-9}	8,7 10^{-10}
Te-127	9,35 h	0,600	1,5 10^{-9}	0,300	1,2 10^{-9}	6,2 10^{-10}	3,6 10^{-10}	2,1 10^{-10}	1,7 10^{-10}
Te-127m	109 d	0,600	4,1 10^{-8}	0,300	1,8 10^{-8}	9,5 10^{-9}	5,2 10^{-9}	3,0 10^{-9}	2,3 10^{-9}
Te-129	1,16 h	0,600	7,5 10^{-10}	0,300	4,4 10^{-10}	2,1 10^{-10}	1,2 10^{-10}	8,0 10^{-11}	6,3 10^{-11}
Te-129m	33,6 d	0,600	4,4 10^{-8}	0,300	2,4 10^{-8}	1,2 10^{-8}	6,6 10^{-9}	3,9 10^{-9}	3,0 10^{-9}
Te-131	0,417 h	0,600	9,0 10^{-10}	0,300	6,6 10^{-10}	3,5 10^{-10}	1,9 10^{-10}	1,2 10^{-10}	8,7 10^{-11}
Te-131m	1,25 d	0,600	2,0 10^{-8}	0,300	1,4 10^{-8}	7,8 10^{-9}	4,3 10^{-9}	2,7 10^{-9}	1,9 10^{-9}
Te-132	3,26 d	0,600	4,8 10^{-8}	0,300	3,0 10^{-8}	1,6 10^{-8}	8,3 10^{-9}	5,3 10^{-9}	3,8 10^{-9}
Te-133	0,207 h	0,600	8,4 10^{-10}	0,300	6,3 10^{-10}	3,3 10^{-10}	1,6 10^{-10}	1,1 10^{-10}	7,2 10^{-11}
Te-133m	0,923 h	0,600	3,1 10^{-9}	0,300	2,4 10^{-9}	1,3 10^{-9}	6,3 10^{-10}	4,1 10^{-10}	2,8 10^{-10}
Te-134	0,696 h	0,600	1,1 10^{-9}	0,300	7,5 10^{-10}	3,9 10^{-10}	2,2 10^{-10}	1,4 10^{-10}	1,1 10^{-10}
Iodine									
I-120	1,35 h	1,000	3,9 10^{-9}	1,000	2,8 10^{-9}	1,4 10^{-9}	7,2 10^{-10}	4,8 10^{-10}	3,4 10^{-10}
I-120m	0,883 h	1,000	2,3 10^{-9}	1,000	1,5 10^{-9}	7,8 10^{-10}	4,2 10^{-10}	2,9 10^{-10}	2,1 10^{-10}
I-121	2,12 h	1,000	6,2 10^{-10}	1,000	5,3 10^{-10}	3,1 10^{-10}	1,7 10^{-10}	1,2 10^{-10}	8,2 10^{-11}
I-123	13,2 h	1,000	2,2 10^{-9}	1,000	1,9 10^{-9}	1,1 10^{-9}	4,9 10^{-10}	3,3 10^{-10}	2,1 10^{-10}

Nuclide	Physical half-life	Age ≤ 1 a		Age	1—2 a	2—7 a	7—12 a	12—17 a	4 17 a
		f_1 for ≤ 1 a	h(g)	f_1 for g > 1 a	h(g)	h(g)	h(g)	h(g)	h(g)
I-124	4,18 d	1,000	1,2 10^{-7}	1,000	1,1 10^{-7}	6,3 10^{-8}	3,1 10^{-8}	2,0 10^{-8}	1,3 10^{-8}
I-125	60,1 d	1,000	5,2 10^{-8}	1,000	5,7 10^{-8}	4,1 10^{-8}	3,1 10^{-8}	2,2 10^{-8}	1,5 10^{-8}
I-126	13,0 d	1,000	2,1 10^{-7}	1,000	2,1 10^{-7}	1,3 10^{-7}	6,8 10^{-8}	4,5 10^{-8}	2,9 10^{-8}
I-128	0,416 h	1,000	5,7 10^{-10}	1,000	3,3 10^{-10}	1,6 10^{-10}	8,9 10^{-11}	6,0 10^{-11}	4,6 10^{-11}
I-129	1,57 10^{7} a	1,000	1,8 10^{-7}	1,000	2,2 10^{-7}	1,7 10^{-7}	1,9 10^{-7}	1,4 10^{-7}	1,1 10^{-7}
I-130	12,4 h	1,000	2,1 10^{-8}	1,000	1,8 10^{-8}	9,8 10^{-9}	4,6 10^{-9}	3,0 10^{-9}	2,0 10^{-9}
I-131	8,04 d	1,000	1,8 10^{-7}	1,000	1,8 10^{-7}	1,0 10^{-7}	5,2 10^{-8}	3,4 10^{-8}	2,2 10^{-8}
I-132	2,30 h	1,000	3,0 10^{-9}	1,000	2,4 10^{-9}	1,3 10^{-9}	6,2 10^{-10}	4,1 10^{-10}	2,9 10^{-10}
I-132m	1,39 h	1,000	2,4 10^{-9}	1,000	2,0 10^{-9}	1,1 10^{-9}	5,0 10^{-10}	3,3 10^{-10}	2,2 10^{-10}
I-133	20,8 h	1,000	4,9 10^{-8}	1,000	4,4 10^{-8}	2,3 10^{-8}	1,0 10^{-8}	6,8 10^{-9}	4,3 10^{-9}
I-134	0,876 h	1,000	1,1 10^{-9}	1,000	7,5 10^{-10}	3,9 10^{-10}	2,1 10^{-10}	1,4 10^{-10}	1,1 10^{-10}
I-135	6,61 h	1,000	1,0 10^{-8}	1,000	8,9 10^{-9}	4,7 10^{-9}	2,2 10^{-9}	1,4 10^{-9}	9,3 10^{-10}
Caesium									
Cs-125	0,750 h	1,000	3,9 10^{-10}	1,000	2,2 10^{-10}	1,1 10^{-10}	6,5 10^{-11}	4,4 10^{-11}	3,5 10^{-11}
Cs-127	6,25 h	1,000	1,8 10^{-10}	1,000	1,2 10^{-10}	6,6 10^{-11}	4,2 10^{-11}	2,9 10^{-11}	2,4 10^{-11}
Cs-129	1,34 d	1,000	4,4 10^{-10}	1,000	3,0 10^{-10}	1,7 10^{-10}	1,1 10^{-10}	7,2 10^{-11}	6,0 10^{-11}
Cs-130	0,498 h	1,000	3,3 10^{-10}	1,000	1,8 10^{-10}	9,0 10^{-11}	5,2 10^{-11}	3,6 10^{-11}	2,8 10^{-11}
Cs-131	9,69 d	1,000	4,6 10^{-10}	1,000	2,9 10^{-10}	1,6 10^{-10}	1,0 10^{-10}	6,9 10^{-11}	5,8 10^{-11}
Cs-132	6,48 d	1,000	2,7 10^{-9}	1,000	1,8 10^{-9}	1,1 10^{-9}	7,7 10^{-10}	5,7 10^{-10}	5,0 10^{-10}
Cs-134	2,06 a	1,000	2,6 10^{-8}	1,000	1,6 10^{-8}	1,3 10^{-8}	1,4 10^{-8}	1,9 10^{-8}	1,9 10^{-8}
Cs-134m	2,90 h	1,000	2,1 10^{-10}	1,000	1,2 10^{-10}	5,9 10^{-11}	3,5 10^{-11}	2,5 10^{-11}	2,0 10^{-11}
Cs-135	2,30 10^{6} a	1,000	4,1 10^{-9}	1,000	2,3 10^{-9}	1,7 10^{-9}	1,7 10^{-9}	2,0 10^{-9}	2,0 10^{-9}
Cs-135m	0,883 h	1,000	1,3 10^{-10}	1,000	8,6 10^{-11}	4,9 10^{-11}	3,2 10^{-11}	2,3 10^{-11}	1,9 10^{-11}
Cs-136	13,1 d	1,000	1,5 10^{-8}	1,000	9,5 10^{-9}	6,1 10^{-9}	4,4 10^{-9}	3,4 10^{-9}	3,0 10^{-9}
Cs-137	30,0 a	1,000	2,1 10^{-8}	1,000	1,2 10^{-8}	9,6 10^{-9}	1,0 10^{-8}	1,3 10^{-8}	1,3 10^{-8}

Nuclide	*Physical half-life*	*Age ≤ 1 a*		*Age*	*1—2 a*	*2—7 a*	*7—12 a*	*12—17 a*	*4 17 a*
		f_1 for ≤ 1 a	*h(g)*	*f_1 for g > 1 a*	*h(g)*	*h(g)*	*h(g)*	*h(g)*	*h(g)*
Cs-138	0,536 h	1,000	1,1 10^{-9}	1,000	5,9 10^{-10}	2,9 10^{-10}	1,7 10^{-10}	1,2 10^{-10}	9,2 10^{-11}
Barium[e]									
Ba-126	1,61 h	0,600	2,7 10^{-9}	0,200	1,7 10^{-9}	8,5 10^{-10}	5,0 10^{-10}	3,1 10^{-10}	2,6 10^{-10}
Ba-128	2,43 d	0,600	2,0 10^{-8}	0,200	1,7 10^{-8}	9,0 10^{-9}	5,2 10^{-9}	3,0 10^{-9}	2,7 10^{-9}
Ba-131	11,8 d	0,600	4,2 10^{-9}	0,200	2,6 10^{-9}	1,4 10^{-9}	9,4 10^{-10}	6,2 10^{-10}	4,5 10^{-10}
Ba-131m	0,243 h	0,600	5,8 10^{-11}	0,200	3,2 10^{-11}	1,6 10^{-11}	9,3 10^{-12}	6,3 10^{-12}	4,9 10^{-12}
Ba-133	10,7 a	0,600	2,2 10^{-8}	0,200	6,2 10^{-9}	3,9 10^{-9}	4,6 10^{-9}	7,3 10^{-9}	1,5 10^{-9}
Ba-133m	1,62 d	0,600	4,2 10^{-9}	0,200	3,6 10^{-9}	1,8 10^{-9}	1,1 10^{-9}	5,9 10^{-10}	5,4 10^{-10}
Ba-135m	1,20 d	0,600	3,3 10^{-9}	0,200	2,9 10^{-9}	1,5 10^{-9}	8,5 10^{-10}	4,7 10^{-10}	4,3 10^{-10}
Ba-139	1,38 h	0,600	1,4 10^{-9}	0,200	8,4 10^{-10}	4,1 10^{-10}	2,4 10^{-10}	1,5 10^{-10}	1,2 10^{-10}
Ba-140	12,7 d	0,600	3,2 10^{-8}	0,200	1,8 10^{-8}	9,2 10^{-9}	5,8 10^{-9}	3,7 10^{-9}	2,6 10^{-9}
Ba-141	0,305 h	0,600	7,6 10^{-10}	0,200	4,7 10^{-10}	2,3 10^{-10}	1,3 10^{-10}	8,6 10^{-11}	7,0 10^{-11}
Ba-142	0,177 h	0,600	3,6 10^{-10}	0,200	2,2 10^{-10}	1,1 10^{-10}	6,6 10^{-11}	4,3 10^{-11}	3,5 10^{-11}
Lanthanum									
La-131	0,983 h	0,005	3,5 10^{-10}	5,0 10^{-4}	2,1 10^{-10}	1,1 10^{-10}	6,6 10^{-11}	4,4 10^{-11}	3,5 10^{-11}
La-132	4,80 h	0,005	3,8 10^{-9}	5,0 10^{-4}	2,4 10^{-9}	1,3 10^{-9}	7,8 10^{-10}	4,8 10^{-10}	3,9 10^{-10}
La-135	19,5 h	0,005	2,8 10^{-10}	5,0 10^{-4}	1,9 10^{-10}	1,0 10^{-10}	6,4 10^{-11}	3,9 10^{-11}	3,0 10^{-11}
La-137	6,00 10^{-4} a	0,005	1,1 10^{-9}	5,0 10^{-4}	4,5 10^{-10}	2,5 10^{-10}	1,6 10^{-10}	1,0 10^{-10}	8,1 10^{-11}
La-138	1,35 10^{11} a	0,005	1,3 10^{-8}	5,0 10^{-4}	4,6 10^{-9}	2,7 10^{-9}	1,9 10^{-9}	1,3 10^{-9}	1,1 10^{-9}
La-140	1,68 d	0,005	2,0 10^{-8}	5,0 10^{-4}	1,3 10^{-8}	6,8 10^{-9}	4,2 10^{-9}	2,5 10^{-9}	2,0 10^{-9}
La-141	3,93 h	0,005	4,3 10^{-9}	5,0 10^{-4}	2,6 10^{-9}	1,3 10^{-9}	7,6 10^{-10}	4,5 10^{-10}	3,6 10^{-10}
La-142	1,54 h	0,005	1,9 10^{-9}	5,0 10^{-4}	1,1 10^{-9}	5,8 10^{-10}	3,5 10^{-10}	2,3 10^{-10}	1,8 10^{-10}
La-143	0,237 h	0,005	6,9 10^{-10}	5,0 10^{-4}	3,9 10^{-10}	1,9 10^{-10}	1,1 10^{-10}	7,1 10^{-11}	5,6 10^{-11}
Cerium									
Ce-134	3,00 d	0,005	2,8 10^{-8}	5,0 10^{-4}	1,8 10^{-8}	9,1 10^{-9}	5,5 10^{-9}	3,2 10^{-9}	2,5 10^{-9}

Nuclide	Physical half-life	Age ≤ 1 a		Age	1—2 a	2—7 a	7—12 a	12—17 a	4 17 a
		f_1 for ≤ 1 a	h(g)	f_1 for g > 1 a	h(g)	h(g)	h(g)	h(g)	h(g)
Ce-135	17,6 h	0,005	7,0 10^{-9}	5,0 10^{-4}	4,7 10^{-9}	2,6 10^{-9}	1,6 10^{-9}	1,0 10^{-9}	7,9 10^{-10}
Ce-137	9,00 h	0,005	2,6 10^{-10}	5,0 10^{-4}	1,7 10^{-10}	8,8 10^{-11}	5,4 10^{-11}	3,2 10^{-11}	2,5 10^{-11}
Ce-137m	1,43 d	0,005	6,1 10^{-9}	5,0 10^{-4}	3,9 10^{-9}	2,0 10^{-9}	1,2 10^{-9}	6,8 10^{-10}	5,4 10^{-10}
Ce-139	138 d	0,005	2,6 10^{-9}	5,0 10^{-4}	1,6 10^{-9}	8,6 10^{-10}	5,4 10^{-10}	3,3 10^{-10}	2,6 10^{-10}
Ce-141	32,5 d	0,005	8,1 10^{-9}	5,0 10^{-4}	5,1 10^{-9}	2,6 10^{-9}	1,5 10^{-9}	8,8 10^{-10}	7,1 10^{-10}
Ce-143	1,38 d	0,005	1,2 10^{-8}	5,0 10^{-4}	8,0 10^{-9}	4,1 10^{-9}	2,4 10^{-9}	1,4 10^{-9}	1,1 10^{-9}
Ce-144	284 d	0,005	6,6 10^{-8}	5,0 10^{-4}	3,9 10^{-8}	1,9 10^{-8}	1,1 10^{-8}	6,5 10^{-9}	5,2 10^{-9}
Praseodymium									
Pr-136	0,218 h	0,005	3,7 10^{-10}	5,0 10^{-4}	2,1 10^{-10}	1,0 10^{-10}	6,1 10^{-11}	4,2 10^{-11}	3,3 10^{-11}
Pr-137	1,28 h	0,005	4,1 10^{-10}	5,0 10^{-4}	2,5 10^{-10}	1,3 10^{-10}	7,7 10^{-11}	5,0 10^{-11}	4,0 10^{-11}
Pr-138m	2,10 h	0,005	1,0 10^{-9}	5,0 10^{-4}	7,4 10^{-10}	4,1 10^{-10}	2,6 10^{-10}	1,6 10^{-10}	1,3 10^{-10}
Pr-139	4,51 h	0,005	3,2 10^{-10}	5,0 10^{-4}	2,0 10^{-10}	1,1 10^{-10}	6,5 10^{-11}	4,0 10^{-11}	3,1 10^{-11}
Pr-142	19,1 h	0,005	1,5 10^{-8}	5,0 10^{-4}	9,8 10^{-9}	4,9 10^{-9}	2,9 10^{-9}	1,6 10^{-9}	1,3 10^{-9}
Pr-142m	0,243 h	0,005	2,0 10^{-10}	5,0 10^{-4}	1,2 10^{-10}	6,2 10^{-11}	3,7 10^{-11}	2,1 10^{-11}	1,7 10^{-11}
Pr-143	13,6 d	0,005	1,4 10^{-8}	5,0 10^{-4}	8,7 10^{-9}	4,3 10^{-9}	2,6 10^{-9}	1,5 10^{-9}	1,2 10^{-9}
Pr-144	0,288 h	0,005	6,4 10^{-10}	5,0 10^{-4}	3,5 10^{-10}	1,7 10^{-10}	9,5 10^{-11}	6,5 10^{-11}	5,0 10^{-11}
Pr-145	5,98 h	0,005	4,7 10^{-9}	5,0 10^{-4}	2,9 10^{-9}	1,4 10^{-9}	8,5 10^{-10}	4,9 10^{-10}	3,9 10^{-10}
Pr-147	0,227 h	0,005	3,9 10^{-10}	5,0 10^{-4}	2,2 10^{-10}	1,1 10^{-10}	6,1 10^{-11}	4,2 10^{-11}	3,3 10^{-11}
Neodymium									
Nd-136	0,844 h	0,005	1,0 10^{-9}	5,0 10^{-4}	6,1 10^{-10}	3,1 10^{-10}	1,9 10^{-10}	1,2 10^{-10}	9,9 10^{-11}
Nd-138	5,04 h	0,005	7,2 10^{-9}	5,0 10^{-4}	4,5 10^{-9}	2,3 10^{-9}	1,3 10^{-9}	8,0 10^{-10}	6,4 10^{-10}
Nd-139	0,495 h	0,005	2,1 10^{-10}	5,0 10^{-4}	1,2 10^{-10}	6,3 10^{-11}	3,7 10^{-11}	2,5 10^{-11}	2,0 10^{-11}
Nd-139m	5,50 h	0,005	2,1 10^{-9}	5,0 10^{-4}	1,4 10^{-9}	7,8 10^{-10}	5,0 10^{-10}	3,1 10^{-10}	2,5 10^{-10}
Nd-141	2,49 h	0,005	7,8 10^{-11}	5,0 10^{-4}	5,0 10^{-11}	2,7 10^{-11}	1,6 10^{-11}	1,0 10^{-11}	8,3 10^{-12}
Nd-147	11,0 d	0,005	1,2 10^{-8}	5,0 10^{-4}	7,8 10^{-9}	3,9 10^{-9}	2,3 10^{-9}	1,3 10^{-9}	1,1 10^{-9}

Nuclide	Physical half-life	Age ≤ 1 a		Age	1—2 a	2—7 a	7—12 a	12—17 a	4 17 a
		f_1 for ≤ 1 a	h(g)	f_1 for g > 1 a	h(g)	h(g)	h(g)	h(g)	h(g)
Nd-149	1,73 h	0,005	1,4 10^{-9}	5,0 10^{-4}	8,7 10^{-10}	4,3 10^{-10}	2,6 10^{-10}	1,6 10^{-10}	1,2 10^{-10}
Nd-151	0,207 h	0,005	3,4 10^{-10}	5,0 10^{-4}	2,0 10^{-10}	9,7 10^{-11}	5,7 10^{-11}	3,8 10^{-11}	3,0 10^{-11}
Promethium									
Pm-141	0,348 h	0,005	4,2 10^{-10}	5,0 10^{-4}	2,4 10^{-10}	1,2 10^{-10}	6,8 10^{-11}	4,6 10^{-11}	3,6 10^{-11}
Pm-143	265 d	0,005	1,9 10^{-9}	5,0 10^{-4}	1,2 10^{-9}	6,7 10^{-10}	4,4 10^{-10}	2,9 10^{-10}	2,3 10^{-10}
Pm-144	363 d	0,005	7,6 10^{-9}	5,0 10^{-4}	4,7 10^{-9}	2,7 10^{-9}	1,8 10^{-9}	1,2 10^{-9}	9,7 10^{-10}
Pm-145	17,7 a	0,005	1,5 10^{-9}	5,0 10^{-4}	6,8 10^{-10}	3,7 10^{-10}	2,3 10^{-10}	1,4 10^{-10}	1,1 10^{-10}
Pm-146	5,53 a	0,005	1,0 10^{-8}	5,0 10^{-4}	5,1 10^{-9}	2,8 10^{-9}	1,8 10^{-9}	1,1 10^{-9}	9,0 10^{-10}
Pm-147	2,62 a	0,005	3,6 10^{-9}	5,0 10^{-4}	1,9 10^{-9}	9,6 10^{-10}	5,7 10^{-10}	3,2 10^{-10}	2,6 10^{-10}
Pm-148	5,37 d	0,005	3,0 10^{-4}	5,0 10^{-4}	1,9 10^{-8}	9,7 10^{-9}	5,8 10^{-9}	3,3 10^{-9}	2,7 10^{-9}
Pm-148m	41,3 d	0,005	1,5 10^{-8}	5,0 10^{-4}	1,0 10^{-8}	5,5 10^{-9}	3,5 10^{-9}	2,2 10^{-9}	1,7 10^{-9}
Pm-149	2,21 d	0,005	1,2 10^{-8}	5,0 10^{-4}	7,4 10^{-9}	3,7 10^{-9}	2,2 10^{-9}	1,2 10^{-9}	9,9 10^{-10}
Pm-150	2,68 h	0,005	2,8 10^{-9}	5,0 10^{-4}	1,7 10^{-9}	8,7 10^{-10}	5,2 10^{-10}	3,2 10^{-10}	2,6 10^{-10}
Pm-151	1,18 d	0,005	8,0 10^{-9}	5,0 10^{-4}	5,1 10^{-9}	2,6 10^{-9}	1,6 10^{-9}	9,1 10^{-10}	7,3 10^{-10}
Samarium									
Sm-141	0,170 h	0,005	4,5 10^{-10}	5,0 10^{-4}	2,5 10^{-10}	1,3 10^{-10}	7,3 10^{-11}	5,0 10^{-11}	3,9 10^{-11}
Sm-141m	0,377 h	0,005	7,0 10^{-10}	5,0 10^{-4}	4,0 10^{-10}	2,0 10^{-10}	1,2 10^{-10}	8,2 10^{-11}	6,5 10^{-11}
Sm-142	1,21 h	0,005	2,2 10^{-9}	5,0 10^{-4}	1,3 10^{-9}	6,2 10^{-10}	3,6 10^{-10}	2,4 10^{-10}	1,9 10^{-10}
Sm-145	340 d	0,005	2,4 10^{-9}	5,0 10^{-4}	1,4 10^{-9}	7,3 10^{-10}	4,5 10^{-10}	2,7 10^{-10}	2,1 10^{-10}
Sm-146	1,03 10^{8} a	0,005	1,5 10^{-6}	5,0 10^{-4}	1,5 10^{-7}	1,0 10^{-7}	7,0 10^{-8}	5,8 10^{-8}	5,4 10^{-8}
Sm-147	1,06 10^{11} a	0,005	1,4 10^{-6}	5,0 10^{-4}	1,4 10^{-7}	9,2 10^{-8}	6,4 10^{-8}	5,2 10^{-8}	4,9 10^{-8}
Sm-151	90,0 a	0,005	1,5 10^{-9}	5,0 10^{-4}	6,4 10^{-10}	3,3 10^{-10}	2,0 10^{-10}	1,2 10^{-10}	9,8 10^{-11}
Sm-153	1,95 d	0,005	8,4 10^{-9}	5,0 10^{-4}	5,4 10^{-9}	2,7 10^{-9}	1,6 10^{-9}	9,2 10^{-10}	7,4 10^{-10}
Sm-155	0,368 h	0,005	3,6 10^{-10}	5,0 10^{-4}	2,0 10^{-10}	9,7 10^{-11}	5,5 10^{-11}	3,7 10^{-11}	2,9 10^{-11}
Sm-156	9,40 h	0,005	2,8 10^{-9}	5,0 10^{-4}	1,8 10^{-9}	9,0 10^{-10}	5,4 10^{-10}	3,1 10^{-10}	2,5 10^{-10}

Nuclide	Physical half-life	Age ≤ 1 a		Age	1—2 a	2—7 a	7—12 a	12—17 a	4 17 a
		f_1 for ≤ 1 a	h(g)	f_1 for g > 1 a	h(g)	h(g)	h(g)	h(g)	h(g)
Europium									
Eu-145	5,94 d	0,005	5,1 10^{-9}	5,0 10^{-4}	3,7 10^{-9}	2,1 10^{-9}	1,4 10^{-9}	9,4 10^{-10}	7,5 10^{-10}
Eu-146	4,61 d	0,005	8,5 10^{-9}	5,0 10^{-4}	6,2 10^{-9}	3,6 10^{-9}	2,4 10^{-9}	1,6 10^{-9}	1,3 10^{-9}
Eu-147	24,0 d	0,005	3,7 10^{-9}	5,0 10^{-4}	2,5 10^{-9}	1,4 10^{-9}	8,9 10^{-10}	5,6 10^{-10}	4,4 10^{-10}
Eu-148	54,5 d	0,005	8,5 10^{-9}	5,0 10^{-4}	6,0 10^{-9}	3,5 10^{-9}	2,4 10^{-9}	1,6 10^{-9}	1,3 10^{-9}
Eu-149	93,1 d	0,005	9,7 10^{-10}	5,0 10^{-4}	6,3 10^{-10}	3,4 10^{-10}	2,1 10^{-10}	1,3 10^{-10}	1,0 10^{-10}
Eu-150	34,2 a	0,005	1,3 10^{-8}	5,0 10^{-4}	5,7 10^{-9}	3,4 10^{-9}	2,3 10^{-9}	1,5 10^{-9}	1,3 10^{-9}
Eu-150	12,6 h	0,005	4,4 10^{-9}	5,0 10^{-4}	2,8 10^{-9}	1,4 10^{-9}	8,2 10^{-10}	4,7 10^{-10}	3,8 10^{-10}
Eu-152	13,3 a	0,005	1,6 10^{-8}	5,0 10^{-4}	7,4 10^{-9}	4,1 10^{-9}	2,6 10^{-9}	1,7 10^{-9}	1,4 10^{-9}
Eu-152m	9,32 h	0,005	5,7 10^{-9}	5,0 10^{-4}	3,6 10^{-9}	1,8 10^{-9}	1,1 10^{-9}	6,2 10^{-10}	5,0 10^{-10}
Eu-154	8,80 a	0,005	2,5 10^{-8}	5,0 10^{-4}	1,2 10^{-8}	6,5 10^{-9}	4,1 10^{-9}	2,5 10^{-9}	2,0 10^{-9}
Eu-155	4,96 a	0,005	4,3 10^{-9}	5,0 10^{-4}	2,2 10^{-9}	1,1 10^{-9}	6,8 10^{-10}	4,0 10^{-10}	3,2 10^{-10}
Eu-156	15,2 d	0,005	2,2 10^{-8}	5,0 10^{-4}	1,5 10^{-8}	7,5 10^{-9}	4,6 10^{-9}	2,7 10^{-9}	2,2 10^{-9}
Eu-157	15,1 h	0,005	6,7 10^{-9}	5,0 10^{-4}	4,3 10^{-9}	2,2 10^{-9}	1,3 10^{-9}	7,5 10^{-10}	6,0 10^{-10}
Eu-158	0,765 h	0,005	1,1 10^{-9}	5,0 10^{-4}	6,2 10^{-10}	3,1 10^{-10}	1,8 10^{-10}	1,2 10^{-10}	9,4 10^{-11}
Gadolinium									
Gd-145	0,382 h	0,005	4,5 10^{-10}	5,0 10^{-4}	2,6 10^{-10}	1,3 10^{-10}	8,1 10^{-11}	5,6 10^{-11}	4,4 10^{-11}
Gd-146	48,3 d	0,005	9,4 10^{-9}	5,0 10^{-4}	6,0 10^{-9}	3,2 10^{-9}	2,0 10^{-9}	1,2 10^{-9}	9,6 10^{-10}
Gd-147	1,59 d	0,005	4,5 10^{-9}	5,0 10^{-4}	3,2 10^{-9}	1,8 10^{-9}	1,2 10^{-9}	7,7 10^{-10}	6,1 10^{-10}
Gd-148	93,0 a	0,005	1,7 10^{-6}	5,0 10^{-4}	1,6 10^{-7}	1,1 10^{-7}	7,3 10^{-8}	5,9 10^{-8}	6,6 10^{-8}
Gd-149	9,40 d	0,005	4,0 10^{-9}	5,0 10^{-4}	2,7 10^{-9}	1,5 10^{-9}	9,3 10^{-10}	5,7 10^{-10}	4,5 10^{-10}
Gd-151	120 d	0,005	2,1 10^{-9}	5,0 10^{-4}	1,3 10^{-9}	6,8 10^{-10}	4,2 10^{-10}	2,4 10^{-10}	2,0 10^{-10}
Gd-152	1,08 10^{14} a	0,005	1,2 10^{-6}	5,0 10^{-4}	1,2 10^{-7}	7,7 10^{-8}	5,3 10^{-8}	4,3 10^{-8}	4,1 10^{-8}
Gd-153	242 d	0,005	2,9 10^{-9}	5,0 10^{-4}	1,8 10^{-9}	9,4 10^{-10}	5,8 10^{-10}	3,4 10^{-10}	2,7 10^{-10}
Gd-159	18,6 h	0,005	5,7 10^{-9}	5,0 10^{-4}	3,6 10^{-9}	1,8 10^{-9}	1,1 10^{-9}	6,2 10^{-10}	4,9 10^{-10}

Nuclide	Physical half-life	Age ≤ 1 a		Age	1—2 a	2—7 a	7—12 a	12—17 a	4 17 a
		f_1 for ≤ 1 a	h(g)	f_1 for g > 1 a	h(g)	h(g)	h(g)	h(g)	h(g)
Terbium									
Tb-147	1,65 h	0,005	$1,5\ 10^{-9}$	$5,0\ 10^{-4}$	$1,0\ 10^{-9}$	$5,4\ 10^{-10}$	$3,3\ 10^{-10}$	$2,0\ 10^{-10}$	$1,6\ 10^{-10}$
Tb-149	4,15 h	0,005	$2,4\ 10^{-9}$	$5,0\ 10^{-4}$	$1,5\ 10^{-9}$	$8,0\ 10^{-10}$	$5,0\ 10^{-10}$	$3,1\ 10^{-10}$	$2,5\ 10^{-10}$
Tb-150	3,27 h	0,005	$2,5\ 10^{-9}$	$5,0\ 10^{-4}$	$1,6\ 10^{-9}$	$8,3\ 10^{-10}$	$5,1\ 10^{-10}$	$3,2\ 10^{-10}$	$2,5\ 10^{-10}$
Tb-151	17,6 h	0,005	$2,7\ 10^{-9}$	$5,0\ 10^{-4}$	$1,9\ 10^{-9}$	$1,0\ 10^{-9}$	$6,7\ 10^{-10}$	$4,2\ 10^{-10}$	$3,4\ 10^{-10}$
Tb-153	2,34 d	0,005	$2,3\ 10^{-9}$	$5,0\ 10^{-4}$	$1,5\ 10^{-9}$	$8,2\ 10^{-10}$	$5,1\ 10^{-10}$	$3,1\ 10^{-10}$	$2,5\ 10^{-10}$
Tb-154	21,4 h	0,005	$4,7\ 10^{-9}$	$5,0\ 10^{-4}$	$3,4\ 10^{-9}$	$1,9\ 10^{-9}$	$1,3\ 10^{-9}$	$8,1\ 10^{-10}$	$6,5\ 10^{-10}$
Tb-155	5,32 d	0,005	$1,9\ 10^{-9}$	$5,0\ 10^{-4}$	$1,3\ 10^{-9}$	$6,8\ 10^{-10}$	$4,3\ 10^{-10}$	$2,6\ 10^{-10}$	$2,1\ 10^{-10}$
Tb-156	5,34 d	0,005	$9,0\ 10^{-9}$	$5,0\ 10^{-4}$	$6,3\ 10^{-9}$	$3,5\ 10^{-9}$	$2,3\ 10^{-9}$	$1,5\ 10^{-9}$	$1,2\ 10^{-9}$
Tb-156m	1,02 d	0,005	$1,5\ 10^{-9}$	$5,0\ 10^{-4}$	$1,0\ 10^{-9}$	$5,6\ 10^{-10}$	$3,5\ 10^{-10}$	$2,2\ 10^{-10}$	$1,7\ 10^{-10}$
Tb-156m	5,00 h	0,005	$8,0\ 10^{-10}$	$5,0\ 10^{-4}$	$5,2\ 10^{-10}$	$2,7\ 10^{-10}$	$1,7\ 10^{-10}$	$1,0\ 10^{-10}$	$8,1\ 10^{-11}$
Tb-157	$1,50\ 10^2$ a	0,005	$4,9\ 10^{-10}$	$5,0\ 10^{-4}$	$2,2\ 10^{-10}$	$1,1\ 10^{-10}$	$6,8\ 10^{-11}$	$4,1\ 10^{-11}$	$3,4\ 10^{-11}$
Tb-158	$1,50\ 10^2$ a	0,005	$1,3\ 10^{-8}$	$5,0\ 10^{-4}$	$5,9\ 10^{-9}$	$3,3\ 10^{-9}$	$2,1\ 10^{-9}$	$1,4\ 10^{-9}$	$1,1\ 10^{-9}$
Tb-160	72,3 d	0,005	$1,6\ 10^{-8}$	$5,0\ 10^{-4}$	$1,0\ 10^{-8}$	$5,4\ 10^{-9}$	$3,3\ 10^{-9}$	$2,0\ 10^{-9}$	$1,6\ 10^{-9}$
Tb-161	6,91 d	0,005	$8,3\ 10^{-9}$	$5,0\ 10^{-4}$	$5,3\ 10^{-9}$	$2,7\ 10^{-9}$	$1,6\ 10^{-9}$	$9,0\ 10^{-10}$	$7,2\ 10^{-10}$
Dysprosium									
Dy-155	10,0 h	0,005	$9,7\ 10^{-10}$	$5,0\ 10^{-4}$	$6,8\ 10^{-10}$	$3,8\ 10^{-10}$	$2,5\ 10^{-11}$	$1,6\ 10^{-10}$	$1,3\ 10^{-10}$
Dy-157	8,10 h	0,005	$4,4\ 10^{-10}$	$5,0\ 10^{-4}$	$3,1\ 10^{-10}$	$1,8\ 10^{-10}$	$1,2\ 10^{-10}$	$7,7\ 10^{-11}$	$6,1\ 10^{-11}$
Dy-159	144 d	0,005	$1,0\ 10^{-9}$	$5,0\ 10^{-4}$	$6,4\ 10^{-10}$	$3,4\ 10^{-10}$	$2,1\ 10^{-10}$	$1,3\ 10^{-10}$	$1,0\ 10^{-10}$
Dy-165	2,33 h	0,005	$1,3\ 10^{-9}$	$5,0\ 10^{-4}$	$7,9\ 10^{-10}$	$3,9\ 10^{-10}$	$2,3\ 10^{-10}$	$1,4\ 10^{-10}$	$1,1\ 10^{-10}$
Dy-166	3,40 d	0,005	$1,9\ 10^{-8}$	$5,0\ 10^{-4}$	$1,2\ 10^{-8}$	$6,0\ 10^{-9}$	$3,6\ 10^{-9}$	$2,0\ 10^{-9}$	$1,6\ 10^{-9}$
Holmium									
Ho-155	0,800 h	0,005	$3,8\ 10^{-10}$	$5,0\ 10^{-4}$	$2,3\ 10^{-10}$	$1,2\ 10^{-10}$	$7,1\ 10^{-11}$	$4,7\ 10^{-11}$	$3,7\ 10^{-11}$
Ho-157	0,210 h	0,005	$5,8\ 10^{-11}$	$5,0\ 10^{-4}$	$3,6\ 10^{-11}$	$1,9\ 10^{-11}$	$1,2\ 10^{-11}$	$8,1\ 10^{-12}$	$6,5\ 10^{-12}$
Ho-159	0,550 h	0,005	$7,1\ 10^{-11}$	$5,0\ 10^{-4}$	$4,3\ 10^{-11}$	$2,3\ 10^{-11}$	$1,4\ 10^{-11}$	$9,9\ 10^{-12}$	$7,9\ 10^{-12}$

Nuclide	*Physical half-life*	*Age ≤ 1 a*		*Age*	*1—2 a*	*2—7 a*	*7—12 a*	*12—17 a*	*4 17 a*
		f_1 *for ≤ 1 a*	*h(g)*	f_1 *for g > 1 a*	*h(g)*	*h(g)*	*h(g)*	*h(g)*	*h(g)*
Ho-161	2,50 h	0,005	1,4 10^{-10}	5,0 10^{-4}	8,1 10^{-11}	4,2 10^{-11}	2,5 10^{-11}	1,6 10^{-11}	1,3 10^{-11}
Ho-162	0,250 h	0,005	3,5 10^{-11}	5,0 10^{-4}	2,0 10^{-11}	1,0 10^{-11}	6,0 10^{-12}	4,2 10^{-12}	3,3 10^{-12}
Ho-162m	1,13 h	0,005	2,4 10^{-10}	5,0 10^{-4}	1,5 10^{-10}	7,9 10^{-11}	4,9 10^{-11}	3,3 10^{-11}	2,6 10^{-11}
Ho-164	0,483 h	0,005	1,2 10^{-10}	5,0 10^{-4}	6,5 10^{-11}	3,2 10^{-11}	1,8 10^{-11}	1,2 10^{-11}	9,5 10^{-12}
Ho-164m	0,625 h	0,005	2,0 10^{-10}	5,0 10^{-4}	1,1 10^{-10}	5,5 10^{-11}	3,2 10^{-11}	2,1 10^{-11}	1,6 10^{-11}
Ho-166	1,12 d	0,005	1,6 10^{-8}	5,0 10^{-4}	1,0 10^{-8}	5,2 10^{-9}	3,1 10^{-9}	1,7 10^{-9}	1,4 10^{-9}
Ho-166m	1,20 10^{3} a	0,005	2,6 10^{-8}	5,0 10^{-4}	9,3 10^{-9}	5,3 10^{-9}	3,5 10^{-9}	2,4 10^{-9}	2,0 10^{-9}
Ho-167	3,10 h	0,005	8,8 10^{-10}	5,0 10^{-4}	5,5 10^{-10}	2,8 10^{-10}	1,7 10^{-10}	1,0 10^{-10}	8,3 10^{-11}
Erbium									
Er-161	3,24 h	0,005	6,5 10^{-10}	5,0 10^{-4}	4,4 10^{-10}	2,4 10^{-10}	1,6 10^{-10}	1,0 10^{-10}	8,0 10^{-11}
Er-165	10,4 h	0,005	1,7 10^{-10}	5,0 10^{-4}	1,1 10^{-10}	6,2 10^{-11}	3,9 10^{-11}	2,4 10^{-11}	1,9 10^{-11}
Er-169	9,30 d	0,005	4,4 10^{-9}	5,0 10^{-4}	2,8 10^{-9}	1,4 10^{-9}	8,2 10^{-10}	4,7 10^{-10}	3,7 10^{-10}
Er-171	7,52 h	0,005	4,0 10^{-9}	5,0 10^{-4}	2,5 10^{-9}	1,3 10^{-9}	7,6 10^{-10}	4,5 10^{-10}	3,6 10^{-10}
Er-172	2,05 d	0,005	1,0 10^{-8}	5,0 10^{-4}	6,8 10^{-9}	3,5 10^{-9}	2,1 10^{-9}	1,3 10^{-9}	1,0 10^{-9}
Thulium									
Tm-162	0,362 h	0,005	2,9 10^{-10}	5,0 10^{-4}	1,7 10^{-10}	8,7 10^{-11}	5,2 10^{-11}	3,6 10^{-11}	2,9 10^{-11}
Tm-166	7,70 h	0,005	2,1 10^{-9}	5,0 10^{-4}	1,5 10^{-9}	8,3 10^{-10}	5,5 10^{-10}	3,5 10^{-10}	2,8 10^{-10}
Tm-167	9,24 d	0,005	6,0 10^{-9}	5,0 10^{-4}	3,9 10^{-9}	2,0 10^{-9}	1,2 10^{-9}	7,0 10^{-10}	5,6 10^{-10}
Tm-170	129 d	0,005	1,6 10^{-8}	5,0 10^{-4}	9,8 10^{-9}	4,9 10^{-9}	2,9 10^{-9}	1,6 10^{-9}	1,3 10^{-9}
Tm-171	1,92 a	0,005	1,5 10^{-9}	5,0 10^{-4}	7,8 10^{-10}	3,9 10^{-10}	2,3 10^{-10}	1,3 10^{-10}	1,1 10^{-10}
Tm-172	2,65 d	0,005	1,9 10^{-8}	5,0 10^{-4}	1,2 10^{-8}	6,1 10^{-9}	3,7 10^{-9}	2,1 10^{-9}	1,7 10^{-9}
Tm-173	8,24 h	0,005	3,3 10^{-9}	5,0 10^{-4}	2,1 10^{-9}	1,1 10^{-9}	6,5 10^{-10}	3,8 10^{-10}	3,1 10^{-10}
Tm-175	0,253 h	0,005	3,1 10^{-10}	5,0 10^{-4}	1,7 10^{-10}	8,6 10^{-11}	5,0 10^{-11}	3,4 10^{-11}	2,7 10^{-11}
Ytterbium									
Yb-162	0,315 h	0,005	2,2 10^{-10}	5,0 10^{-4}	1,3 10^{-10}	6,9 10^{-11}	4,2 10^{-11}	2,9 10^{-11}	2,3 10^{-11}

Nuclide	Physical half-life	Age ≤ 1 a		Age	1—2 a	2—7 a	7—12 a	12—17 a	4 17 a
		f_1 for ≤ 1 a	h(g)	f_1 for g > 1 a	h(g)	h(g)	h(g)	h(g)	h(g)
Yb-166	2,36 d	0,005	7,7 10^{-9}	5,0 10^{-4}	5,4 10^{-9}	2,9 10^{-9}	1,9 10^{-9}	1,2 10^{-9}	9,5 10^{-10}
Yb-167	0,292 h	0,005	7,0 10^{-11}	5,0 10^{-4}	4,1 10^{-11}	2,1 10^{-11}	1,2 10^{-11}	8,4 10^{-12}	6,7 10^{-12}
Yb-169	32,0 d	0,005	7,1 10^{-9}	5,0 10^{-4}	4,6 10^{-9}	2,4 10^{-9}	1,5 10^{-9}	8,8 10^{-10}	7,1 10^{-10}
Yb-175	4,19 d	0,005	5,0 10^{-9}	5,0 10^{-4}	3,2 10^{-9}	1,6 10^{-9}	9,5 10^{-10}	5,4 10^{-10}	4,4 10^{-10}
Yb-177	1,90 h	0,005	1,0 10^{-9}	5,0 10^{-4}	6,8 10^{-10}	3,4 10^{-10}	2,0 10^{-10}	1,1 10^{-10}	8,8 10^{-11}
Yb-178	1,23 h	0,005	1,4 10^{-9}	5,0 10^{-4}	8,4 10^{-10}	4,2 10^{-10}	2,4 10^{-10}	1,5 10^{-10}	1,2 10^{-10}
Lutetium									
Lu-169	1,42 d	0,005	3,5 10^{-9}	5,0 10^{-4}	2,4 10^{-9}	1,4 10^{-9}	8,9 10^{-10}	5,7 10^{-10}	4,6 10^{-10}
Lu-170	2,00 d	0,005	7,4 10^{-9}	5,0 10^{-4}	5,2 10^{-9}	2,9 10^{-9}	1,9 10^{-9}	1,2 10^{-9}	9,9 10^{-10}
Lu-171	8,22 d	0,005	5,9 10^{-9}	5,0 10^{-4}	4,0 10^{-9}	2,2 10^{-9}	1,4 10^{-9}	8,5 10^{-10}	6,7 10^{-10}
Lu-172	6,70 d	0,005	1,0 10^{-8}	5,0 10^{-4}	7,0 10^{-9}	3,9 10^{-9}	2,5 10^{-9}	1,6 10^{-9}	1,3 10^{-9}
Lu-173	1,37 a	0,005	2,7 10^{-9}	5,0 10^{-4}	1,6 10^{-9}	8,6 10^{-10}	5,3 10^{-10}	3,2 10^{-10}	2,6 10^{-10}
Lu-174	3,31 a	0,005	3,2 10^{-9}	5,0 10^{-4}	1,7 10^{-9}	9,1 10^{-10}	5,6 10^{-10}	3,3 10^{-10}	2,7 10^{-10}
Lu-174m	142 d	0,005	6,2 10^{-9}	5,0 10^{-4}	3,8 10^{-9}	1,9 10^{-9}	1,1 10^{-9}	6,6 10^{-10}	5,3 10^{-10}
Lu-176	3,60 10^{10} a	0,005	2,4 10^{-8}	5,0 10^{-4}	1,1 10^{-8}	5,7 10^{-9}	3,5 10^{-9}	2,2 10^{-9}	1,8 10^{-9}
Lu-176m	3,68 h	0,005	2,0 10^{-9}	5,0 10^{-4}	1,2 10^{-9}	6,0 10^{-10}	3,5 10^{-10}	2,1 10^{-10}	1,7 10^{-10}
Lu-177	6,71 d	0,005	6,1 10^{-9}	5,0 10^{-4}	3,9 10^{-9}	2,0 10^{-9}	1,2 10^{-9}	6,6 10^{-10}	5,3 10^{-10}
Lu-177m	161 d	0,005	1,7 10^{-8}	5,0 10^{-4}	1,1 10^{-8}	5,8 10^{-9}	3,6 10^{-9}	2,1 10^{-9}	1,7 10^{-9}
Lu-178	0,473 h	0,005	5,9 10^{-10}	5,0 10^{-4}	3,3 10^{-10}	1,6 10^{-10}	9,0 10^{-11}	6,1 10^{-11}	4,7 10^{-11}
Lu-178m	0,378 h	0,005	4,3 10^{-10}	5,0 10^{-4}	2,4 10^{-10}	1,2 10^{-10}	7,1 10^{-11}	4,9 10^{-11}	3,8 10^{-11}
Lu-179	4,59 h	0,005	2,4 10^{-9}	5,0 10^{-4}	1,5 10^{-9}	7,5 10^{-10}	4,4 10^{-10}	2,6 10^{-10}	2,1 10^{-10}
Hafnium									
Hf-170	16,0 h	0,020	3,9 10^{-9}	0,002	2,7 10^{-9}	1,5 10^{-9}	9,5 10^{-10}	6,0 10^{-10}	4,8 10^{-10}
Hf-172	1,87 a	0,020	1,9 10^{-8}	0,002	6,1 10^{-9}	3,3 10^{-9}	2,0 10^{-9}	1,3 10^{-9}	1,0 10^{-9}
Hf-173	24,0 h	0,020	1,9 10^{-9}	0,002	1,3 10^{-9}	7,2 10^{-10}	4,6 10^{-10}	2,8 10^{-10}	2,3 10^{-10}

Nuclide	Physical half-life	Age ≤ 1 a		Age	1—2 a	2—7 a	7—12 a	12—17 a	4 17 a
		f_1 for ≤ 1 a	h(g)	f_1 for g > 1 a	h(g)	h(g)	h(g)	h(g)	h(g)
Hf-175	70,0 d	0,020	$3,8\ 10^{-9}$	0,002	$2,4\ 10^{-9}$	$1,3\ 10^{-9}$	$8,4\ 10^{-10}$	$5,2\ 10^{-10}$	$4,1\ 10^{-10}$
Hf-177m	0,856 h	0,020	$7,8\ 10^{-10}$	0,002	$4,7\ 10^{-10}$	$2,5\ 10^{-10}$	$1,5\ 10^{-10}$	$1,0\ 10^{-10}$	$8,1\ 10^{-11}$
Hf-178m	31,0 a	0,020	$7,0\ 10^{-8}$	0,002	$1,9\ 10^{-8}$	$1,1\ 10^{-8}$	$7,8\ 10^{-9}$	$5,5\ 10^{-9}$	$4,7\ 10^{-9}$
Hf-179m	25,1 d	0,020	$1,2\ 10^{-8}$	0,002	$7,8\ 10^{-9}$	$4,1\ 10^{-9}$	$2,6\ 10^{-9}$	$1,6\ 10^{-9}$	$1,2\ 10^{-9}$
Hf-180m	5,50 h	0,020	$1,4\ 10^{-9}$	0,002	$9,7\ 10^{-10}$	$5,3\ 10^{-10}$	$3,3\ 10^{-10}$	$2,1\ 10^{-10}$	$1,7\ 10^{-10}$
Hf-181	42,4 d	0,020	$1,2\ 10^{-8}$	0,002	$7,4\ 10^{-9}$	$3,8\ 10^{-9}$	$2,3\ 10^{-9}$	$1,4\ 10^{-9}$	$1,1\ 10^{-9}$
Hf-182	$9,00\ 10^{6}$ a	0,020	$5,6\ 10^{-8}$	0,002	$7,9\ 10^{-9}$	$5,4\ 10^{-9}$	$4,0\ 10^{-9}$	$3,3\ 10^{-9}$	$3,0\ 10^{-9}$
Hf-182m	1,02 h	0,020	$4,1\ 10^{-10}$	0,002	$2,5\ 10^{-10}$	$1,3\ 10^{-10}$	$7,8\ 10^{-11}$	$5,2\ 10^{-11}$	$4,2\ 10^{-11}$
Hf-183	1,07 h	0,020	$8,1\ 10^{-10}$	0,002	$4,8\ 10^{-10}$	$2,4\ 10^{-10}$	$1,4\ 10^{-10}$	$9,3\ 10^{-11}$	$7,3\ 10^{-11}$
Hf-184	4,12 h	0,020	$5,5\ 10^{-9}$	0,002	$3,6\ 10^{-9}$	$1,8\ 10^{-9}$	$1,1\ 10^{-9}$	$6,6\ 10^{-10}$	$5,2\ 10^{-10}$
Tantalum									
Ta-172	0,613 h	0,010	$5,5\ 10^{-10}$	0,001	$3,2\ 10^{-10}$	$1,6\ 10^{-10}$	$9,8\ 10^{-11}$	$6,6\ 10^{-11}$	$5,3\ 10^{-11}$
Ta-173	3,65 h	0,010	$2,0\ 10^{-9}$	0,001	$1,3\ 10^{-9}$	$6,5\ 10^{-10}$	$3,9\ 10^{-10}$	$2,4\ 10^{-10}$	$1,9\ 10^{-10}$
Ta-174	1,20 h	0,010	$6,2\ 10^{-10}$	0,001	$3,7\ 10^{-10}$	$1,9\ 10^{-10}$	$1,1\ 10^{-10}$	$7,2\ 10^{-11}$	$5,7\ 10^{-11}$
Ta-175	10,5 h	0,010	$1,6\ 10^{-9}$	0,001	$1,1\ 10^{-9}$	$6,2\ 10^{-10}$	$4,0\ 10^{-10}$	$2,6\ 10^{-10}$	$2,1\ 10^{-10}$
Ta-176	8,08 h	0,010	$2,4\ 10^{-9}$	0,001	$1,7\ 10^{-9}$	$9,2\ 10^{-10}$	$6,1\ 10^{-10}$	$3,9\ 10^{-10}$	$3,1\ 10^{-10}$
Ta-177	2,36 d	0,010	$1,0\ 10^{-9}$	0,001	$6,9\ 10^{-10}$	$3,6\ 10^{-10}$	$2,2\ 10^{-10}$	$1,3\ 10^{-10}$	$1,1\ 10^{-10}$
Ta-178	2,20 h	0,010	$6,3\ 10^{-10}$	0,001	$4,5\ 10^{-10}$	$2,4\ 10^{-10}$	$1,5\ 10^{-10}$	$9,1\ 10^{-11}$	$7,2\ 10^{-11}$
Ta-179	1,82 a	0,010	$6,2\ 10^{-10}$	0,001	$4,1\ 10^{-10}$	$2,2\ 10^{-10}$	$1,3\ 10^{-10}$	$8,1\ 10^{-11}$	$6,5\ 10^{-11}$
Ta-180	$1,00\ 10^{13}$ a	0,010	$8,1\ 10^{-9}$	0,001	$5,3\ 10^{-9}$	$2,8\ 10^{-9}$	$1,7\ 10^{-9}$	$1,1\ 10^{-9}$	$8,4\ 10^{-10}$
Ta-180m	8,10 h	0,010	$5,8\ 10^{-10}$	0,001	$3,7\ 10^{-10}$	$1,9\ 10^{-10}$	$1,1\ 10^{-10}$	$6,7\ 10^{-11}$	$5,4\ 10^{-11}$
Ta-182	115 d	0,010	$1,4\ 10^{-8}$	0,001	$9,4\ 10^{-9}$	$5,0\ 10^{-9}$	$3,1\ 10^{-9}$	$1,9\ 10^{-9}$	$1,5\ 10^{-9}$
Ta-182m	0,264 h	0,010	$1,4\ 10^{-10}$	0,001	$7,5\ 10^{-11}$	$3,7\ 10^{-11}$	$2,1\ 10^{-11}$	$1,5\ 10^{-11}$	$1,2\ 10^{-11}$
Ta-183	5,10 d	0,010	$1,4\ 10^{-8}$	0,001	$9,3\ 10^{-9}$	$4,7\ 10^{-9}$	$2,8\ 10^{-9}$	$1,6\ 10^{-9}$	$1,3\ 10^{-9}$
Ta-184	8,70 h	0,010	$6,7\ 10^{-9}$	0,001	$4,4\ 10^{-9}$	$2,3\ 10^{-9}$	$1,4\ 10^{-9}$	$8,5\ 10^{-10}$	$6,8\ 10^{-10}$

Nuclide	*Physical half-life*	*Age ≤ 1 a*		*Age*	*1—2 a*	*2—7 a*	*7—12 a*	*12—17 a*	*4 17 a*
		f_1 for ≤ 1 a	*h(g)*	*f_1 for g > 1 a*	*h(g)*	*h(g)*	*h(g)*	*h(g)*	*h(g)*
Ta-185	0,816 h	0,010	8,3 10^{-10}	0,001	4,6 10^{-10}	2,3 10^{-10}	1,3 10^{-10}	8,6 10^{-11}	6,8 10^{-11}
Ta-186	0,175 h	0,010	3,8 10^{-10}	0,001	2,1 10^{-10}	1,1 10^{-10}	6,1 10^{-11}	4,2 10^{-11}	3,3 10^{-11}
Tungsten									
W-176	2,30 h	0,600	6,8 10^{-10}	0,300	5,5 10^{-10}	3,0 10^{-10}	2,0 10^{-10}	1,3 10^{-10}	1,0 10^{-10}
W-177	2,25 h	0,600	4,4 10^{-10}	0,300	3,2 10^{-10}	1,7 10^{-10}	1,1 10^{-10}	7,2 10^{-11}	5,8 10^{-11}
W-178	21,7 d	0,600	1,8 10^{-9}	0,300	1,4 10^{-9}	7,3 10^{-10}	4,5 10^{-10}	2,7 10^{-10}	2,2 10^{-10}
W-179	0,625 h	0,600	3,4 10^{-11}	0,300	2,0 10^{-11}	1,0 10^{-11}	6,2 10^{-12}	4,2 10^{-12}	3,3 10^{-12}
W-181	121 d	0,600	6,3 10^{-10}	0,300	4,7 10^{-10}	2,5 10^{-10}	1,6 10^{-10}	9,5 10^{-11}	7,6 10^{-11}
W-185	75,1 d	0,600	4,4 10^{-9}	0,300	3,3 10^{-9}	1,6 10^{-9}	9,7 10^{-10}	5,5 10^{-10}	4,4 10^{-10}
W-187	23,9 h	0,600	5,5 10^{-9}	0,300	4,3 10^{-9}	2,2 10^{-9}	1,3 10^{-9}	7,8 10^{-10}	6,3 10^{-10}
W-188	69,4 d	0,600	2,1 10^{-8}	0,300	1,5 10^{-8}	7,7 10^{-9}	4,6 10^{-9}	2,6 10^{-9}	2,1 10^{-9}
Rhenium									
Re-177	0,233 h	1,000	2,5 10^{-10}	0,800	1,4 10^{-10}	7,2 10^{-11}	4,1 10^{-11}	2,8 10^{-11}	2,2 10^{-11}
Re-178	0,220 h	1,000	2,9 10^{-10}	0,800	1,6 10^{-10}	7,9 10^{-11}	4,6 10^{-11}	3,1 10^{-11}	2,5 10^{-11}
Re-181	20,0 h	1,000	4,2 10^{-9}	0,800	2,8 10^{-9}	1,4 10^{-9}	8,2 10^{-10}	5,4 10^{-10}	4,2 10^{-10}
Re-182	2,67 d	1,000	1,4 10^{-8}	0,800	8,9 10^{-9}	4,7 10^{-9}	2,8 10^{-9}	1,8 10^{-9}	1,4 10^{-9}
Re-182	12,7 h	1,000	2,4 10^{-9}	0,800	1,7 10^{-9}	8,9 10^{-10}	5,2 10^{-10}	3,5 10^{-10}	2,7 10^{-10}
Re-184	38,0 d	1,000	8,9 10^{-9}	0,800	5,6 10^{-9}	3,0 10^{-9}	1,8 10^{-9}	1,3 10^{-9}	1,0 10^{-9}
Re-184m	165 d	1,000	1,7 10^{-8}	0,800	9,8 10^{-9}	4,9 10^{-9}	2,8 10^{-9}	1,9 10^{-9}	1,5 10^{-9}
Re-186	3,78 d	1,000	1,9 10^{-8}	0,800	1,1 10^{-8}	5,5 10^{-9}	3,0 10^{-9}	1,9 10^{-9}	1,5 10^{-9}
Re-186m	2,00 10^{5} a	1,000	3,0 10^{-8}	0,800	1,6 10^{-8}	7,6 10^{-9}	4,4 10^{-9}	2,8 10^{-9}	2,2 10^{-9}
Re-187	5,00 10^{10} a	1,000	6,8 10^{-11}	0,800	3,8 10^{-11}	1,8 10^{-11}	1,0 10^{-11}	6,6 10^{-12}	5,1 10^{-12}
Re-188	17,0 h	1,000	1,7 10^{-8}	0,800	1,1 10^{-8}	5,4 10^{-9}	2,9 10^{-9}	1,8 10^{-9}	1,4 10^{-9}
Re-188m	0,310 h	1,000	3,8 10^{-10}	0,800	2,3 10^{-10}	1,1 10^{-10}	6,1 10^{-11}	4,0 10^{-11}	3,0 10^{-11}
Re-189	1,01 d	1,000	9,8 10^{-9}	0,800	6,2 10^{-9}	3,0 10^{-9}	1,6 10^{-9}	1,0 10^{-9}	7,8 10^{-10}

Nuclide	Physical half-life	Age ≤ 1 a		Age	1—2 a	2—7 a	7—12 a	12—17 a	4 17 a
		f_1 for ≤ 1 a	h(g)	f_1 for g > 1 a	h(g)	h(g)	h(g)	h(g)	h(g)
Osmium									
Os-180	0,366 h	0,020	$1{,}6\ 10^{-10}$	0,010	$9{,}8\ 10^{-11}$	$5{,}1\ 10^{-11}$	$3{,}2\ 10^{-11}$	$2{,}2\ 10^{-11}$	$1{,}7\ 10^{-11}$
Os-181	1,75 h	0,020	$7{,}6\ 10^{-10}$	0,010	$5{,}0\ 10^{-10}$	$2{,}7\ 10^{-10}$	$1{,}7\ 10^{-10}$	$1{,}1\ 10^{-10}$	$8{,}9\ 10^{-11}$
Os-182	22,0 h	0,020	$4{,}6\ 10^{-9}$	0,010	$3{,}2\ 10^{-9}$	$1{,}7\ 10^{-9}$	$1{,}1\ 10^{-9}$	$7{,}0\ 10^{-10}$	$5{,}6\ 10^{-10}$
Os-185	94,0 d	0,020	$3{,}8\ 10^{-9}$	0,010	$2{,}6\ 10^{-9}$	$1{,}5\ 10^{-9}$	$9{,}8\ 10^{-10}$	$6{,}5\ 10^{-10}$	$5{,}1\ 10^{-10}$
Os-189m	6,00 h	0,020	$2{,}1\ 10^{-10}$	0,010	$1{,}3\ 10^{-10}$	$6{,}5\ 10^{-11}$	$3{,}8\ 10^{-11}$	$2{,}2\ 10^{-11}$	$1{,}8\ 10^{-11}$
Os-191	15,4 d	0,020	$6{,}3\ 10^{-9}$	0,010	$4{,}1\ 10^{-9}$	$2{,}1\ 10^{-9}$	$1{,}2\ 10^{-9}$	$7{,}0\ 10^{-10}$	$5{,}7\ 10^{-10}$
Os-191m	13,0 h	0,020	$1{,}1\ 10^{-9}$	0,010	$7{,}1\ 10^{-10}$	$3{,}5\ 10^{-10}$	$2{,}1\ 10^{-10}$	$1{,}2\ 10^{-10}$	$9{,}6\ 10^{-11}$
Os-193	1,25 d	0,020	$9{,}3\ 10^{-9}$	0,010	$6{,}0\ 10^{-9}$	$3{,}0\ 10^{-9}$	$1{,}8\ 10^{-9}$	$1{,}0\ 10^{-9}$	$8{,}1\ 10^{-10}$
Os-194	6,00 a	0,020	$2{,}9\ 10^{-8}$	0,010	$1{,}7\ 10^{-8}$	$8{,}8\ 10^{-9}$	$5{,}2\ 10^{-9}$	$3{,}0\ 10^{-9}$	$2{,}4\ 10^{-9}$
Iridium									
Ir-182	0,250 h	0,020	$5{,}3\ 10^{-10}$	0,010	$3{,}0\ 10^{-10}$	$1{,}5\ 10^{-10}$	$8{,}9\ 10^{-11}$	$6{,}0\ 10^{-11}$	$4{,}8\ 10^{-11}$
Ir-184	3,02 h	0,020	$1{,}5\ 10^{-9}$	0,010	$9{,}7\ 10^{-10}$	$5{,}2\ 10^{-10}$	$3{,}3\ 10^{-10}$	$2{,}1\ 10^{-10}$	$1{,}7\ 10^{-10}$
Ir-185	14,0 h	0,020	$2{,}4\ 10^{-9}$	0,010	$1{,}6\ 10^{-9}$	$8{,}6\ 10^{-10}$	$5{,}3\ 10^{-10}$	$3{,}3\ 10^{-10}$	$2{,}6\ 10^{-10}$
Ir-186	15,8 h	0,020	$3{,}8\ 10^{-9}$	0,010	$2{,}7\ 10^{-9}$	$1{,}5\ 10^{-9}$	$9{,}6\ 10^{-10}$	$6{,}1\ 10^{-10}$	$4{,}9\ 10^{-10}$
Ir-186	1,75 h	0,020	$5{,}8\ 10^{-10}$	0,010	$3{,}6\ 10^{-10}$	$2{,}1\ 10^{-10}$	$1{,}3\ 10^{-10}$	$7{,}7\ 10^{-11}$	$6{,}1\ 10^{-11}$
Ir-187	10,5 h	0,020	$1{,}1\ 10^{-9}$	0,010	$7{,}3\ 10^{-10}$	$3{,}9\ 10^{-10}$	$2{,}5\ 10^{-10}$	$1{,}5\ 10^{-10}$	$1{,}2\ 10^{-10}$
Ir-188	1,73 d	0,020	$4{,}6\ 10^{-9}$	0,010	$3{,}3\ 10^{-9}$	$1{,}8\ 10^{-9}$	$1{,}2\ 10^{-9}$	$7{,}9\ 10^{-10}$	$6{,}3\ 10^{-10}$
Ir-189	13,3 d	0,020	$2{,}5\ 10^{-9}$	0,010	$1{,}7\ 10^{-9}$	$8{,}6\ 10^{-10}$	$5{,}2\ 10^{-10}$	$3{,}0\ 10^{-10}$	$2{,}4\ 10^{-10}$
Ir-190	12,1 d	0,020	$1{,}0\ 10^{-8}$	0,010	$7{,}1\ 10^{-9}$	$3{,}9\ 10^{-9}$	$2{,}5\ 10^{-9}$	$1{,}6\ 10^{-9}$	$1{,}2\ 10^{-9}$
Ir-190m	3,10 h	0,020	$9{,}4\ 10^{-10}$	0,010	$6{,}4\ 10^{-10}$	$3{,}5\ 10^{-10}$	$2{,}3\ 10^{-10}$	$1{,}5\ 10^{-10}$	$1{,}2\ 10^{-10}$
Ir-190m	1,20 h	0,020	$7{,}9\ 10^{-11}$	0,010	$5{,}0\ 10^{-11}$	$2{,}6\ 10^{-11}$	$1{,}6\ 10^{-11}$	$1{,}0\ 10^{-11}$	$8{,}0\ 10^{-12}$
Ir-192	74,0 d	0,020	$1{,}3\ 10^{-8}$	0,010	$8{,}7\ 10^{-9}$	$4{,}6\ 10^{-9}$	$2{,}8\ 10^{-9}$	$1{,}7\ 10^{-9}$	$1{,}4\ 10^{-9}$
Ir-192m	$2{,}41\ 10^{2}$ a	0,020	$2{,}8\ 10^{-9}$	0,010	$1{,}4\ 10^{-9}$	$8{,}3\ 10^{-10}$	$5{,}5\ 10^{-10}$	$3{,}7\ 10^{-10}$	$3{,}1\ 10^{-10}$
Ir-193m	11,9 d	0,020	$3{,}2\ 10^{-9}$	0,010	$2{,}0\ 10^{-9}$	$1{,}0\ 10^{-9}$	$6{,}0\ 10^{-10}$	$3{,}4\ 10^{-10}$	$2{,}7\ 10^{-10}$

Nuclide	*Physical half-life*	*Age ≤ 1 a*		*Age*	*1—2 a*	*2—7 a*	*7—12 a*	*12—17 a*	*4 17 a*
		f_1 for ≤ 1 a	*h(g)*	*f_1 for g > 1 a*	*h(g)*	*h(g)*	*h(g)*	*h(g)*	*h(g)*
Ir-194	19,1 h	0,020	$1,5\ 10^{-8}$	0,010	$9,8\ 10^{-9}$	$4,9\ 10^{-9}$	$2,9\ 10^{-9}$	$1,7\ 10^{-9}$	$1,3\ 10^{-9}$
Ir-194m	171 d	0,020	$1,7\ 10^{-8}$	0,010	$1,1\ 10^{-8}$	$6,4\ 10^{-9}$	$4,1\ 10^{-9}$	$2,6\ 10^{-9}$	$2,1\ 10^{-9}$
Ir-195	2,50 h	0,020	$1,2\ 10^{-9}$	0,010	$7,3\ 10^{-10}$	$3,6\ 10^{-10}$	$2,1\ 10^{-10}$	$1,3\ 10^{-10}$	$1,0\ 10^{-10}$
Ir-195m	3,80 h	0,020	$2,3\ 10^{-9}$	0,010	$1,5\ 10^{-9}$	$7,3\ 10^{-10}$	$4,3\ 10^{-10}$	$2,6\ 10^{-10}$	$2,1\ 10^{-10}$
Platinum									
Pt-186	2,00 h	0,020	$7,8\ 10^{-10}$	0,010	$5,3\ 10^{-10}$	$2,9\ 10^{-10}$	$1,8\ 10^{-10}$	$1,2\ 10^{-10}$	$9,3\ 10^{-11}$
Pt-188	10,2 d	0,020	$6,7\ 10^{-9}$	0,010	$4,5\ 10^{-9}$	$2,4\ 10^{-9}$	$1,5\ 10^{-9}$	$9,5\ 10^{-10}$	$7,6\ 10^{-10}$
Pt-189	10,9 h	0,020	$1,1\ 10^{-9}$	0,010	$7,4\ 10^{-10}$	$3,9\ 10^{-10}$	$2,5\ 10^{-10}$	$1,5\ 10^{-10}$	$1,2\ 10^{-10}$
Pt-191	2,80 d	0,020	$3,1\ 10^{-9}$	0,010	$2,1\ 10^{-9}$	$1,1\ 10^{-9}$	$6,9\ 10^{-10}$	$4,2\ 10^{-10}$	$3,4\ 10^{-10}$
Pt-193	50,0 a	0,020	$3,7\ 10^{-10}$	0,010	$2,4\ 10^{-10}$	$1,2\ 10^{-10}$	$6,9\ 10^{-11}$	$3,9\ 10^{-11}$	$3,1\ 10^{-11}$
Pt-193m	4,33 d	0,020	$5,2\ 10^{-9}$	0,010	$3,4\ 10^{-9}$	$1,7\ 10^{-9}$	$9,9\ 10^{-10}$	$5,6\ 10^{-10}$	$4,5\ 10^{-10}$
Pt-195m	4,02 d	0,020	$7,1\ 10^{-9}$	0,010	$4,6\ 10^{-9}$	$2,3\ 10^{-9}$	$1,4\ 10^{-9}$	$7,9\ 10^{-10}$	$6,3\ 10^{-10}$
Pt-197	18,3 h	0,020	$4,7\ 10^{-9}$	0,010	$3,0\ 10^{-9}$	$1,5\ 10^{-9}$	$8,8\ 10^{-10}$	$5,1\ 10^{-10}$	$4,0\ 10^{-10}$
Pt-197m	1,57 h	0,020	$1,0\ 10^{-9}$	0,010	$6,1\ 10^{-10}$	$3,0\ 10^{-10}$	$1,8\ 10^{-10}$	$1,1\ 10^{-10}$	$8,4\ 10^{-11}$
Pt-199	0,513 h	0,020	$4,7\ 10^{-10}$	0,010	$2,7\ 10^{-10}$	$1,3\ 10^{-10}$	$7,5\ 10^{-11}$	$5,0\ 10^{-11}$	$3,9\ 10^{-11}$
Pt-200	12,5 h	0,020	$1,4\ 10^{-8}$	0,010	$8,8\ 10^{-9}$	$4,4\ 10^{-9}$	$2,6\ 10^{-9}$	$1,5\ 10^{-9}$	$1,2\ 10^{-9}$
Gold									
Au-193	17,6 h	0,200	$1,2\ 10^{-9}$	0,100	$8,8\ 10^{-10}$	$4,6\ 10^{-10}$	$2,8\ 10^{-10}$	$1,7\ 10^{-10}$	$1,3\ 10^{-10}$
Au-194	1,65 h	0,200	$2,9\ 10^{-9}$	0,100	$2,2\ 10^{-9}$	$1,2\ 10^{-9}$	$8,1\ 10^{-10}$	$5,3\ 10^{-10}$	$4,2\ 10^{-10}$
Au-195	183 d	0,200	$2,4\ 10^{-9}$	0,100	$1,7\ 10^{-9}$	$8,9\ 10^{-10}$	$5,4\ 10^{-10}$	$3,2\ 10^{-10}$	$2,5\ 10^{-10}$
Au-198	2,69 d	0,200	$1,0\ 10^{-8}$	0,100	$7,2\ 10^{-9}$	$3,7\ 10^{-9}$	$2,2\ 10^{-9}$	$1,3\ 10^{-9}$	$1,0\ 10^{-9}$
Au-198m	2,30 d	0,200	$1,2\ 10^{-8}$	0,100	$8,5\ 10^{-9}$	$4,4\ 10^{-9}$	$2,7\ 10^{-9}$	$1,6\ 10^{-9}$	$1,3\ 10^{-9}$
Au-199	3,14 d	0,200	$4,5\ 10^{-9}$	0,100	$3,1\ 10^{-9}$	$1,6\ 10^{-9}$	$9,5\ 10^{-10}$	$5,5\ 10^{-10}$	$4,4\ 10^{-10}$
Au-200	0,807 h	0,200	$8,3\ 10^{-10}$	0,100	$4,7\ 10^{-10}$	$2,3\ 10^{-10}$	$1,3\ 10^{-10}$	$8,7\ 10^{-11}$	$6,8\ 10^{-11}$
Au-200m	18,7 h	0,200	$9,2\ 10^{-9}$	0,100	$6,6\ 10^{-9}$	$3,5\ 10^{-9}$	$2,2\ 10^{-9}$	$1,3\ 10^{-9}$	$1,1\ 10^{-9}$

Nuclide	*Physical half-life*	*Age ≤ 1 a*		*Age*	*1—2 a*	*2—7 a*	*7—12 a*	*12—17 a*	*4 17 a*
		f_1 *for ≤ 1 a*	*h(g)*	f_1 *for g > 1 a*	*h(g)*	*h(g)*	*h(g)*	*h(g)*	*h(g)*
Au-201	0,440 h	0,200	$3,1\ 10^{-10}$	0,100	$1,7\ 10^{-10}$	$8,2\ 10^{-11}$	$4,6\ 10^{-11}$	$3,1\ 10^{-11}$	$2,4\ 10^{-11}$
Mercury									
Hg-193 (organic)	3,50 h	1,000	$3,3\ 10^{-10}$	1,000	$1,9\ 10^{-10}$	$9,8\ 10^{-11}$	$5,8\ 10^{-11}$	$3,9\ 10^{-11}$	$3,1\ 10^{-11}$
		0,800	$4,7\ 10^{-10}$	0,400	$4,4\ 10^{-10}$	$2,2\ 10^{-10}$	$1,4\ 10^{-10}$	$8,3\ 10^{-11}$	$6,6\ 10^{-11}$
Hg-193 (inorganic)	3,50 h	0,040	$8,5\ 10^{-10}$	0,020	$5,5\ 10^{-10}$	$2,8\ 10^{-10}$	$1,7\ 10^{-10}$	$1,0\ 10^{-10}$	$8,2\ 10^{-11}$
Hg-193m (organic)	11,1 h	1,000	$1,1\ 10^{-9}$	1,000	$6,8\ 10^{-10}$	$3,7\ 10^{-10}$	$2,3\ 10^{-10}$	$1,5\ 10^{-10}$	$1,3\ 10^{-10}$
		0,800	$1,6\ 10^{-9}$	0,400	$1,8\ 10^{-9}$	$9,5\ 10^{-10}$	$6,0\ 10^{-10}$	$3,7\ 10^{-10}$	$3,0\ 10^{-10}$
Hg-193m (inorganic)	11,1 h	0,040	$3,6\ 10^{-9}$	0,020	$2,4\ 10^{-9}$	$1,3\ 10^{-9}$	$8,1\ 10^{-10}$	$5,0\ 10^{-10}$	$4,0\ 10^{-10}$
Hg-194 (organic)	$2,60\ 10^{2}$ a	1,000	$1,3\ 10^{-7}$	1,000	$1,2\ 10^{-7}$	$8,4\ 10^{-8}$	$6,6\ 10^{-8}$	$5,5\ 10^{-8}$	$5,1\ 10^{-8}$
		0,800	$1,1\ 10^{-7}$	0,400	$4,8\ 10^{-8}$	$3,5\ 10^{-8}$	$2,7\ 10^{-8}$	$2,3\ 10^{-8}$	$2,1\ 10^{-8}$
Hg-194 (inorganic)	$2,60\ 10^{2}$ a	0,040	$7,2\ 10^{-9}$	0,020	$3,6\ 10^{-9}$	$2,6\ 10^{-9}$	$1,9\ 10^{-9}$	$1,5\ 10^{-9}$	$1,4\ 10^{-9}$
Hg-195 (organic)	9,90 h	1,000	$3,0\ 10^{-10}$	1,000	$2,0\ 10^{-10}$	$1,0\ 10^{-10}$	$6,4\ 10^{-11}$	$4,2\ 10^{-11}$	$3,4\ 10^{-11}$
		0,800	$4,6\ 10^{-10}$	0,400	$4,8\ 10^{-10}$	$2,5\ 10^{-10}$	$1,5\ 10^{-10}$	$9,3\ 10^{-11}$	$7,5\ 10^{-11}$
Hg-195 (inorganic)	9,90 h	0,040	$9,5\ 10^{-10}$	0,020	$6,3\ 10^{-10}$	$3,3\ 10^{-10}$	$2,0\ 10^{-10}$	$1,2\ 10^{-10}$	$9,7\ 10^{-11}$
Hg-195m (organic)	1,73 d	1,000	$2,1\ 10^{-9}$	1,000	$1,3\ 10^{-9}$	$6,8\ 10^{-10}$	$4,2\ 10^{-10}$	$2,7\ 10^{-10}$	$2,2\ 10^{-10}$
		0,800	$2,6\ 10^{-9}$	0,400	$2,8\ 10^{-9}$	$1,4\ 10^{-9}$	$8,7\ 10^{-10}$	$5,1\ 10^{-10}$	$4,1\ 10^{-10}$
Hg-195m (inorganic)	1,73 d	0,040	$5,8\ 10^{-9}$	0,020	$3,8\ 10^{-9}$	$2,0\ 10^{-9}$	$1,2\ 10^{-9}$	$7,0\ 10^{-10}$	$5,6\ 10^{-10}$
Hg-197 (organic)	2,67 d	1,000	$9,7\ 10^{-10}$	1,000	$6,2\ 10^{-10}$	$3,1\ 10^{-10}$	$1,9\ 10^{-10}$	$1,2\ 10^{-10}$	$9,9\ 10^{-11}$
		0,800	$1,3\ 10^{-9}$	0,400	$1,2\ 10^{-9}$	$6,1\ 10^{-10}$	$3,7\ 10^{-10}$	$2,2\ 10^{-10}$	$1,7\ 10^{-10}$
Hg-197 (inorganic)	2,67 d	0,040	$2,5\ 10^{-9}$	0,020	$1,6\ 10^{-9}$	$8,3\ 10^{-10}$	$5,0\ 10^{-10}$	$2,9\ 10^{-10}$	$2,3\ 10^{-10}$

Nuclide	Physical half-life	Age ≤ 1 a		Age	1—2 a	2—7 a	7—12 a	12—17 a	4 17 a
		f_1 for ≤ 1 a	h(g)	f_1 for g > 1 a	h(g)	h(g)	h(g)	h(g)	h(g)
Hg-197m (organic)	23,8 h	1,000	1,5 10^{-9}	1,000	9,5 10^{-10}	4,8 10^{-10}	2,9 10^{-10}	1,8 10^{-10}	1,5 10^{-10}
		0,800	2,2 10^{-9}	0,400	2,5 10^{-9}	1,2 10^{-9}	7,3 10^{-10}	4,2 10^{-10}	3,4 10^{-10}
Hg-197m (inorganic)	23,8 h	0,040	5,2 10^{-9}	0,020	3,4 10^{-9}	1,7 10^{-9}	1,0 10^{-9}	5,9 10^{-10}	4,7 10^{-10}
Hg-199m (organic)	0,710 h	1,000	3,4 10^{-10}	1,000	1,9 10^{-10}	9,3 10^{-11}	5,3 10^{-11}	3,6 10^{-11}	2,8 10^{-11}
		0,800	3,6 10^{-10}	0,400	2,1 10^{-10}	1,0 10^{-10}	5,8 10^{-11}	3,9 10^{-11}	3,1 10^{-11}
Hg-199m (inorganic)	0,710 h	0,040	3,7 10^{-10}	0,020	2,1 10^{-10}	1,0 10^{-10}	5,9 10^{-11}	3,9 10^{-11}	3,1 10^{-11}
Hg-203 (organic)	46,6 d	1,000	1,5 10^{-8}	1,000	1,1 10^{-8}	5,7 10^{-9}	3,6 10^{-9}	2,3 10^{-9}	1,9 10^{-9}
		0,800	1,3 10^{-8}	0,400	6,4 10^{-9}	3,4 10^{-9}	2,1 10^{-9}	1,3 10^{-9}	1,1 10^{-9}
Hg-203 (inorganic)	46,6 d	0,040	5,5 10^{-9}	0,020	3,6 10^{-9}	1,8 10^{-9}	1,1 10^{-9}	6,7 10^{-10}	5,4 10^{-10}
Thallium									
Tl-194	0,550 h	1,000	6,1 10^{-11}	1,000	3,9 10^{-11}	2,2 10^{-11}	1,4 10^{-11}	1,0 10^{-11}	8,1 10^{-12}
Tl-194m	0,546 h	1,000	3,8 10^{-10}	1,000	2,2 10^{-10}	1,2 10^{-10}	7,0 10^{-11}	4,9 10^{-11}	4,0 10^{-11}
Tl-195	1,16 h	1,000	2,3 10^{-10}	1,000	1,4 10^{-10}	7,5 10^{-11}	4,7 10^{-11}	3,3 10^{-11}	2,7 10^{-11}
Tl-197	2,84 h	1,000	2,1 10^{-10}	1,000	1,3 10^{-10}	6,7 10^{-11}	4,2 10^{-11}	2,8 10^{-11}	2,3 10^{-11}
Tl-198	5,30 h	1,000	4,7 10^{-10}	1,000	3,3 10^{-10}	1,9 10^{-10}	1,2 10^{-10}	8,7 10^{-11}	7,3 10^{-11}
Tl-198m	1,87 h	1,000	4,8 10^{-10}	1,000	3,0 10^{-10}	1,6 10^{-10}	9,7 10^{-11}	6,7 10^{-11}	5,4 10^{-11}
Tl-199	7,42 h	1,000	2,3 10^{-10}	1,000	1,5 10^{-10}	7,7 10^{-11}	4,8 10^{-11}	3,2 10^{-11}	2,6 10^{-11}
Tl-200	1,09 d	1,000	1,3 10^{-9}	1,000	9,1 10^{-10}	5,3 10^{-10}	3,5 10^{-10}	2,4 10^{-10}	2,0 10^{-10}
Tl-201	3,04 d	1,000	8,4 10^{-10}	1,000	5,5 10^{-10}	2,9 10^{-10}	1,8 10^{-10}	1,2 10^{-10}	9,5 10^{-11}
Tl-202	12,2 d	1,000	2,9 10^{-9}	1,000	2,1 10^{-9}	1,2 10^{-9}	7,9 10^{-10}	5,4 10^{-10}	4,5 10^{-10}
Tl-204	3,78 a	1,000	1,3 10^{-8}	1,000	8,5 10^{-9}	4,2 10^{-9}	2,5 10^{-9}	1,5 10^{-9}	1,2 10^{-9}
Lead[f]									
Pb-195m	0,263 h	0,600	2,6 10^{-10}	0,200	1,6 10^{-10}	8,4 10^{-11}	5,2 10^{-11}	3,5 10^{-11}	2,9 10^{-11}

Nuclide	*Physical half-life*	*Age ≤ 1 a*		*Age*	*1—2 a*	*2—7 a*	*7—12 a*	*12—17 a*	*4 17 a*
		f_1 *for ≤ 1 a*	*h(g)*	f_1 *for g > 1 a*	*h(g)*	*h(g)*	*h(g)*	*h(g)*	*h(g)*
Pb-198	2,40 h	0,600	$5,9\ 10^{-10}$	0,200	$4,8\ 10^{-10}$	$2,7\ 10^{-10}$	$1,7\ 10^{-10}$	$1,1\ 10^{-10}$	$1,0\ 10^{-10}$
Pb-199	1,50 h	0,600	$3,5\ 10^{-10}$	0,200	$2,6\ 10^{-10}$	$1,5\ 10^{-10}$	$9,4\ 10^{-11}$	$6,3\ 10^{-11}$	$5,4\ 10^{-11}$
Pb-200	21,5 h	0,600	$2,5\ 10^{-9}$	0,200	$2,0\ 10^{-9}$	$1,1\ 10^{-9}$	$7,0\ 10^{-10}$	$4,4\ 10^{-10}$	$4,0\ 10^{-10}$
Pb-201	9,40 h	0,600	$9,4\ 10^{-10}$	0,200	$7,8\ 10^{-10}$	$4,3\ 10^{-10}$	$2,7\ 10^{-10}$	$1,8\ 10^{-10}$	$1,6\ 10^{-10}$
Pb-202	$3,00\ 10^{5}$ a	0,600	$3,4\ 10^{-8}$	0,200	$1,6\ 10^{-8}$	$1,3\ 10^{-8}$	$1,9\ 10^{-8}$	$2,7\ 10^{-8}$	$8,8\ 10^{-9}$
Pb-202m	3,62 h	0,600	$7,6\ 10^{-10}$	0,200	$6,1\ 10^{-10}$	$3,5\ 10^{-10}$	$2,3\ 10^{-10}$	$1,5\ 10^{-10}$	$1,3\ 10^{-10}$
Pb-203	2,17 d	0,600	$1,6\ 10^{-9}$	0,200	$1,3\ 10^{-9}$	$6,8\ 10^{-10}$	$4,3\ 10^{-10}$	$2,7\ 10^{-10}$	$2,4\ 10^{-10}$
Pb-205	$1,43\ 10^{7}$ a	0,600	$2,1\ 10^{-9}$	0,200	$9,9\ 10^{-10}$	$6,2\ 10^{-10}$	$6,1\ 10^{-10}$	$6,5\ 10^{-10}$	$2,8\ 10^{-10}$
Pb-209	3,25 h	0,600	$5,7\ 10^{-10}$	0,200	$3,8\ 10^{-10}$	$1,9\ 10^{-10}$	$1,1\ 10^{-10}$	$6,6\ 10^{-11}$	$5,7\ 10^{-11}$
Pb-210	22,3 a	0,600	$8,4\ 10^{-6}$	0,200	$3,6\ 10^{-6}$	$2,2\ 10^{-6}$	$1,9\ 10^{-6}$	$1,9\ 10^{-6}$	$6,9\ 10^{-7}$
Pb-211	0,601 h	0,600	$3,1\ 10^{-9}$	0,200	$1,4\ 10^{-9}$	$7,1\ 10^{-10}$	$4,1\ 10^{-10}$	$2,7\ 10^{-10}$	$1,8\ 10^{-10}$
Pb-212	10,6 h	0,600	$1,5\ 10^{-7}$	0,200	$6,3\ 10^{-8}$	$3,3\ 10^{-8}$	$2,0\ 10^{-8}$	$1,3\ 10^{-8}$	$6,0\ 10^{-9}$
Pb-214	0,447 h	0,600	$2,7\ 10^{-9}$	0,200	$1,0\ 10^{-9}$	$5,2\ 10^{-10}$	$3,1\ 10^{-10}$	$2,0\ 10^{-10}$	$1,4\ 10^{-10}$
Bismuth									
Bi-200	0,606 h	0,100	$4,2\ 10^{-10}$	0,050	$2,7\ 10^{-10}$	$1,5\ 10^{-10}$	$9,5\ 10^{-11}$	$6,4\ 10^{-11}$	$5,1\ 10^{-11}$
Bi-201	1,80 h	0,100	$1,0\ 10^{-9}$	0,050	$6,7\ 10^{-10}$	$3,6\ 10^{-10}$	$2,2\ 10^{-10}$	$1,4\ 10^{-10}$	$1,2\ 10^{-10}$
Bi-202	1,67 h	0,100	$6,4\ 10^{-10}$	0,050	$4,4\ 10^{-10}$	$2,5\ 10^{-10}$	$1,6\ 10^{-10}$	$1,1\ 10^{-10}$	$8,9\ 10^{-11}$
Bi-203	11,8 h	0,100	$3,5\ 10^{-9}$	0,050	$2,5\ 10^{-9}$	$1,4\ 10^{-9}$	$9,3\ 10^{-10}$	$6,0\ 10^{-10}$	$4,8\ 10^{-10}$
Bi-205	15,3 d	0,100	$6,1\ 10^{-9}$	0,050	$4,5\ 10^{-9}$	$2,6\ 10^{-9}$	$1,7\ 10^{-9}$	$1,1\ 10^{-9}$	$9,0\ 10^{-10}$
Bi-206	6,24 d	0,100	$1,4\ 10^{-8}$	0,050	$1,0\ 10^{-8}$	$5,7\ 10^{-9}$	$3,7\ 10^{-9}$	$2,4\ 10^{-9}$	$1,9\ 10^{-9}$
Bi-207	38,0 a	0,100	$1,0\ 10^{-8}$	0,050	$7,1\ 10^{-9}$	$3,9\ 10^{-9}$	$2,5\ 10^{-9}$	$1,6\ 10^{-9}$	$1,3\ 10^{-9}$
Bi-210	5,01 d	0,100	$1,5\ 10^{-8}$	0,050	$9,7\ 10^{-9}$	$4,8\ 10^{-9}$	$2,9\ 10^{-9}$	$1,6\ 10^{-9}$	$1,3\ 10^{-9}$
Bi-210m	$3,00\ 10^{6}$ a	0,100	$2,1\ 10^{-7}$	0,050	$9,1\ 10^{-8}$	$4,7\ 10^{-8}$	$3,0\ 10^{-8}$	$1,9\ 10^{-8}$	$1,5\ 10^{-8}$
Bi-212	1,01 h	0,100	$3,2\ 10^{-9}$	0,050	$1,8\ 10^{-9}$	$8,7\ 10^{-10}$	$5,0\ 10^{-10}$	$3,3\ 10^{-10}$	$2,6\ 10^{-10}$
Bi-213	0,761 h	0,100	$2,5\ 10^{-9}$	0,050	$1,4\ 10^{-9}$	$6,7\ 10^{-10}$	$3,9\ 10^{-10}$	$2,5\ 10^{-10}$	$2,0\ 10^{-10}$

Nuclide	Physical half-life	Age ≤ 1 a		Age	1—2 a	2—7 a	7—12 a	12—17 a	4 17 a
		f_1 for ≤ 1 a	h(g)	f_1 for g > 1 a	h(g)	h(g)	h(g)	h(g)	h(g)
Bi-214	0,332 h	0,100	$1,4\ 10^{-9}$	0,050	$7,4\ 10^{-10}$	$3,6\ 10^{-10}$	$2,1\ 10^{-10}$	$1,4\ 10^{-10}$	$1,1\ 10^{-10}$
Polonium									
Po-203	0,612 h	1,000	$2,9\ 10^{-10}$	0,500	$2,4\ 10^{-10}$	$1,3\ 10^{-10}$	$8,5\ 10^{-11}$	$5,8\ 10^{-11}$	$4,6\ 10^{-11}$
Po-205	1,80 h	1,000	$3,5\ 10^{-10}$	0,500	$2,8\ 10^{-10}$	$1,6\ 10^{-10}$	$1,1\ 10^{-10}$	$7,2\ 10^{-11}$	$5,8\ 10^{-11}$
Po-207	5,83 h	1,000	$4,4\ 10^{-10}$	0,500	$5,7\ 10^{-10}$	$3,2\ 10^{-10}$	$2,1\ 10^{-10}$	$1,4\ 10^{-10}$	$1,1\ 10^{-10}$
Po-210	138 d	1,000	$2,6\ 10^{-5}$	0,500	$8,8\ 10^{-6}$	$4,4\ 10^{-6}$	$2,6\ 10^{-6}$	$1,6\ 10^{-6}$	$1,2\ 10^{-6}$
Astatine									
At-207	1,80 h	1,000	$2,5\ 10^{-9}$	1,000	$1,6\ 10^{-9}$	$8,0\ 10^{-10}$	$4,8\ 10^{-10}$	$2,9\ 10^{-10}$	$2,4\ 10^{-10}$
At-211	7,21 h	1,000	$1,2\ 10^{-7}$	1,000	$7,8\ 10^{-8}$	$3,8\ 10^{-8}$	$2,3\ 10^{-8}$	$1,3\ 10^{-8}$	$1,1\ 10^{-8}$
Francium									
Fr-222	0,240 h	1,000	$6,2\ 10^{-9}$	1,000	$3,9\ 10^{-9}$	$2,0\ 10^{-9}$	$1,3\ 10^{-9}$	$8,5\ 10^{-10}$	$7,2\ 10^{-10}$
Fr-223	0,363 h	1,000	$2,6\ 10^{-8}$	1,000	$1,7\ 10^{-8}$	$8,3\ 10^{-9}$	$5,0\ 10^{-9}$	$2,9\ 10^{-9}$	$2,4\ 10^{-9}$
Radium[(g)]									
Ra-223	11,4 d	0,600	$5,3\ 10^{-6}$	0,200	$1,1\ 10^{-6}$	$5,7\ 10^{-7}$	$4,5\ 10^{-7}$	$3,7\ 10^{-7}$	$1,0\ 10^{-7}$
Ra-224	3,66 d	0,600	$2,7\ 10^{-6}$	0,200	$6,6\ 10^{-7}$	$3,5\ 10^{-7}$	$2,6\ 10^{-7}$	$2,0\ 10^{-7}$	$6,5\ 10^{-8}$
Ra-225	14,8 d	0,600	$7,1\ 10^{-6}$	0,200	$1,2\ 10^{-6}$	$6,1\ 10^{-7}$	$5,0\ 10^{-7}$	$4,4\ 10^{-7}$	$9,9\ 10^{-8}$
Ra-226	$1,60\ 10^{3}$ a	0,600	$4,7\ 10^{-6}$	0,200	$9,6\ 10^{-7}$	$6,2\ 10^{-7}$	$8,0\ 10^{-7}$	$1,5\ 10^{-6}$	$2,8\ 10^{-7}$
Ra-227	0,703 h	0,600	$1,1\ 10^{-9}$	0,200	$4,3\ 10^{-10}$	$2,5\ 10^{-10}$	$1,7\ 10^{-10}$	$1,3\ 10^{-10}$	$8,1\ 10^{-11}$
Ra-228	5,75 a	0,600	$3,0\ 10^{-5}$	0,200	$5,7\ 10^{-6}$	$3,4\ 10^{-6}$	$3,9\ 10^{-6}$	$5,3\ 10^{-6}$	$6,9\ 10^{-7}$
Actinium									
Ac-224	2,90 h	0,005	$1,0\ 10^{-8}$	$5,0\ 10^{-4}$	$5,2\ 10^{-9}$	$2,6\ 10^{-9}$	$1,5\ 10^{-9}$	$8,8\ 10^{-10}$	$7,0\ 10^{-10}$
Ac-225	10,0 d	0,005	$4,6\ 10^{-7}$	$5,0\ 10^{-4}$	$1,8\ 10^{-7}$	$9,1\ 10^{-8}$	$5,4\ 10^{-8}$	$3,0\ 10^{-8}$	$2,4\ 10^{-8}$
Ac-226	1,21 d	0,005	$1,4\ 10^{-7}$	$5,0\ 10^{-4}$	$7,6\ 10^{-8}$	$3,8\ 10^{-8}$	$2,3\ 10^{-8}$	$1,3\ 10^{-8}$	$1,0\ 10^{-8}$
Ac-227	21,8 a	0,005	$3,3\ 10^{-5}$	$5,0\ 10^{-4}$	$3,1\ 10^{-6}$	$2,2\ 10^{-6}$	$1,5\ 10^{-6}$	$1,2\ 10^{-6}$	$1,1\ 10^{-6}$
Ac-228	6,13 h	0,005	$7,4\ 10^{-9}$	$5,0\ 10^{-4}$	$2,8\ 10^{-9}$	$1,4\ 10^{-9}$	$8,7\ 10^{-10}$	$5,3\ 10^{-10}$	$4,3\ 10^{-10}$

Nuclide	*Physical half-life*	*Age ≤ 1 a*		*Age*	*1—2 a*	*2—7 a*	*7—12 a*	*12—17 a*	*4 17 a*
		f_1 for ≤ 1 a	*h(g)*	*f_1 for g > 1 a*	*h(g)*	*h(g)*	*h(g)*	*h(g)*	*h(g)*
Thorium									
Th-226	0,515 h	0,005	4,4 10^{-9}	5,0 10^{-4}	2,4 10^{-9}	1,2 10^{-9}	6,7 10^{-10}	4,5 10^{-10}	3,5 10^{-10}
Th-227	18,7 d	0,005	3,0 10^{-7}	5,0 10^{-4}	7,0 10^{-8}	3,6 10^{-8}	2,3 10^{-8}	1,5 10^{-8}	8,8 10^{-9}
Th-228	1,91 a	0,005	3,7 10^{-6}	5,0 10^{-4}	3,7 10^{-7}	2,2 10^{-7}	1,5 10^{-7}	9,4 10^{-8}	7,2 10^{-8}
Th-229	7,34 10^{3} a	0,005	1,1 10^{-5}	5,0 10^{-4}	1,0 10^{-6}	7,8 10^{-7}	6,2 10^{-7}	5,3 10^{-7}	4,9 10^{-7}
Th-230	7,70 10^{4} a	0,005	4,1 10^{-6}	5,0 10^{-4}	4,1 10^{-7}	3,1 10^{-7}	2,4 10^{-7}	2,2 10^{-7}	2,1 10^{-7}
Th-231	1,06 d	0,005	3,9 10^{-9}	5,0 10^{-4}	2,5 10^{-9}	1,2 10^{-9}	7,4 10^{-10}	4,2 10^{-10}	3,4 10^{-10}
Th-232	1,40 10^{10} a	0,005	4,6 10^{-6}	5,0 10^{-4}	4,5 10^{-7}	3,5 10^{-7}	2,9 10^{-7}	2,5 10^{-7}	2,3 10^{-7}
Th-234	24,1 d	0,005	4,0 10^{-8}	5,0 10^{-4}	2,5 10^{-8}	1,3 10^{-8}	7,4 10^{-9}	4,2 10^{-9}	3,4 10^{-9}
Protactinium									
Pa-227	0,638 h	0,005	5,8 10^{-9}	5,0 10^{-4}	3,2 10^{-9}	1,5 10^{-9}	8,7 10^{-10}	5,8 10^{-10}	4,5 10^{-10}
Pa-228	22,0 h	0,005	1,2 10^{-8}	5,0 10^{-4}	4,8 10^{-9}	2,6 10^{-9}	1,6 10^{-9}	9,7 10^{-10}	7,8 10^{-10}
Pa-230	17,4 d	0,005	2,6 10^{-8}	5,0 10^{-4}	5,7 10^{-9}	3,1 10^{-9}	1,9 10^{-9}	1,1 10^{-9}	9,2 10^{-10}
Pa-231	3,27 10^{4} a	0,005	1,3 10^{-5}	5,0 10^{-4}	1,3 10^{-6}	1,1 10^{-6}	9,2 10^{-7}	8,0 10^{-7}	7,1 10^{-7}
Pa-232	1,31 d	0,005	6,3 10^{-9}	5,0 10^{-4}	4,2 10^{-9}	2,2 10^{-9}	1,4 10^{-9}	8,9 10^{-10}	7,2 10^{-10}
Pa-233	27,0 d	0,005	9,7 10^{-9}	5,0 10^{-4}	6,2 10^{-9}	3,2 10^{-9}	1,9 10^{-9}	1,1 10^{-9}	8,7 10^{-10}
Pa-234	6,70 h	0,005	5,0 10^{-9}	5,0 10^{-4}	3,2 10^{-9}	1,7 10^{-9}	1,0 10^{-9}	6,4 10^{-10}	5,1 10^{-10}
Uranium									
U-230	20,8 d	0,040	7,9 10^{-7}	0,020	3,0 10^{-7}	1,5 10^{-7}	1,0 10^{-7}	6,6 10^{-8}	5,6 10^{-8}
U-231	4,20 d	0,040	3,1 10^{-9}	0,020	2,0 10^{-9}	1,0 10^{-9}	6,1 10^{-10}	3,5 10^{-10}	2,8 10^{-10}
U-232	72,0 a	0,040	2,5 10^{-6}	0,020	8,2 10^{-7}	5,8 10^{-7}	5,7 10^{-7}	6,4 10^{-7}	3,3 10^{-7}
U-233	1,58 10^{5} a	0,040	3,8 10^{-7}	0,020	1,4 10^{-7}	9,2 10^{-8}	7,8 10^{-8}	7,8 10^{-8}	5,1 10^{-8}
U-234	2,44 10^{5} a	0,040	3,7 10^{-7}	0,020	1,3 10^{-7}	8,8 10^{-8}	7,4 10^{-8}	7,4 10^{-8}	4,9 10^{-8}
U-235	7,04 10^{8} a	0,040	3,5 10^{-7}	0,020	1,3 10^{-7}	8,5 10^{-8}	7,1 10^{-8}	7,0 10^{-8}	4,7 10^{-8}
U-236	2,34 10^{7} a	0,040	3,5 10^{-7}	0,020	1,3 10^{-7}	8,4 10^{-8}	7,0 10^{-8}	7,0 10^{-8}	4,7 10^{-8}

Nuclide	*Physical half-life*	*Age ≤ 1 a*		*Age*	*1—2 a*	*2—7 a*	*7—12 a*	*12—17 a*	*4 17 a*
		f_1 *for ≤ 1 a*	*h(g)*	f_1 *for g > 1 a*	*h(g)*	*h(g)*	*h(g)*	*h(g)*	*h(g)*
U-237	6,75 d	0,040	8,3 10^{-9}	0,020	5,4 10^{-9}	2,8 10^{-9}	1,6 10^{-9}	9,5 10^{-10}	7,6 10^{-10}
U-238	4,47 10^{9} a	0,040	3,4 10^{-7}	0,020	1,2 10^{-7}	8,0 10^{-8}	6,8 10^{-8}	6,7 10^{-8}	4,5 10^{-8}
U-239	0,392 h	0,040	3,4 10^{-10}	0,020	1,9 10^{-10}	9,3 10^{-11}	5,4 10^{-11}	3,5 10^{-11}	2,7 10^{-11}
U-240	14,1 h	0,040	1,3 10^{-8}	0,020	8,1 10^{-9}	4,1 10^{-9}	2,4 10^{-9}	1,4 10^{-9}	1,1 10^{-9}
Neptunium									
Np-232	0,245 h	0,005	8,7 10^{-11}	5,0 10^{-4}	5,1 10^{-11}	2,7 10^{-11}	1,7 10^{-11}	1,2 10^{-11}	9,7 10^{-12}
Np-233	0,603 h	0,005	2,1 10^{-11}	5,0 10^{-4}	1,3 10^{-11}	6,6 10^{-12}	4,0 10^{-12}	2,8 10^{-12}	2,2 10^{-12}
Np-234	4,40 d	0,005	6,2 10^{-9}	5,0 10^{-4}	4,4 10^{-9}	2,4 10^{-9}	1,6 10^{-9}	1,0 10^{-9}	8,1 10^{-10}
Np-235	1,08 a	0,005	7,1 10^{-10}	5,0 10^{-4}	4,1 10^{-10}	2,0 10^{-10}	1,2 10^{-10}	6,8 10^{-11}	5,3 10^{-11}
Np-236	1,15 10^{5} a	0,005	1,9 10^{-7}	5,0 10^{-4}	2,4 10^{-8}	1,8 10^{-8}	1,8 10^{-8}	1,8 10^{-8}	1,7 10^{-8}
Np-236	22,5 h	0,005	2,5 10^{-9}	5,0 10^{-4}	1,3 10^{-9}	6,6 10^{-10}	4,0 10^{-10}	2,4 10^{-10}	1,9 10^{-10}
Np-237	2,14 10^{6} a	0,005	2,0 10^{-6}	5,0 10^{-4}	2,1 10^{-7}	1,4 10^{-7}	1,1 10^{-7}	1,1 10^{-7}	1,1 10^{-7}
Np-238	2,12 d	0,005	9,5 10^{-9}	5,0 10^{-4}	6,2 10^{-9}	3,2 10^{-9}	1,9 10^{-9}	1,1 10^{-9}	9,1 10^{-10}
Np-239	2,36 d	0,005	8,9 10^{-9}	5,0 10^{-4}	5,7 10^{-9}	2,9 10^{-9}	1,7 10^{-9}	1,0 10^{-9}	8,0 10^{-10}
Np-240	1,08 h	0,005	8,7 10^{-10}	5,0 10^{-4}	5,2 10^{-10}	2,6 10^{-10}	1,6 10^{-10}	1,0 10^{-10}	8,2 10^{-11}
Plutonium									
Pu-234	8,80 h	0,005	2,1 10^{-9}	5,0 10^{-4}	1,1 10^{-9}	5,5 10^{-10}	3,3 10^{-10}	2,0 10^{-10}	1,6 10^{-10}
Pu-235	0,422 h	0,005	2,2 10^{-11}	5,0 10^{-4}	1,3 10^{-11}	6,5 10^{-12}	3,9 10^{-12}	2,7 10^{-12}	2,1 10^{-12}
Pu-236	2,85 a	0,005	2,1 10^{-6}	5,0 10^{-4}	2,2 10^{-7}	1,4 10^{-7}	1,0 10^{-7}	8,5 10^{-8}	8,7 10^{-8}
Pu-237	45,3 d	0,005	1,1 10^{-9}	5,0 10^{-4}	6,9 10^{-10}	3,6 10^{-10}	2,2 10^{-10}	1,3 10^{-10}	1,0 10^{-10}
Pu-238	87,7 a	0,005	4,0 10^{-6}	5,0 10^{-4}	4,0 10^{-7}	3,1 10^{-7}	2,4 10^{-7}	2,2 10^{-7}	2,3 10^{-7}
Pu-239	2,41 10^{4} a	0,005	4,2 10^{-6}	5,0 10^{-4}	4,2 10^{-7}	3,3 10^{-7}	2,7 10^{-7}	2,4 10^{-7}	2,5 10^{-7}
Pu-240	6,54 10^{3} a	0,005	4,2 10^{-6}	5,0 10^{-4}	4,2 10^{-7}	3,3 10^{-7}	2,7 10^{-7}	2,4 10^{-7}	2,5 10^{-7}
Pu-241	14,4 a	0,005	5,6 10^{-8}	5,0 10^{-4}	5,7 10^{-9}	5,5 10^{-9}	5,1 10^{-9}	4,8 10^{-9}	4,8 10^{-9}
Pu-242	3,76 10^{5} a	0,005	4,0 10^{-6}	5,0 10^{-4}	4,0 10^{-7}	3,2 10^{-7}	2,6 10^{-7}	2,3 10^{-7}	2,4 10^{-7}

Nuclide	Physical half-life	Age ≤ 1 a		Age	1—2 a	2—7 a	7—12 a	12—17 a	4 17 a
		f_1 for ≤ 1 a	h(g)	f_1 for g > 1 a	h(g)	h(g)	h(g)	h(g)	h(g)
Pu-243	4,95 h	0,005	$1,0\ 10^{-9}$	$5,0\ 10^{-4}$	$6,2\ 10^{-10}$	$3,1\ 10^{-10}$	$1,8\ 10^{-10}$	$1,1\ 10^{-10}$	$8,5\ 10^{-11}$
Pu-244	$8,26\ 10^{7}$ a	0,005	$4,0\ 10^{-6}$	$5,0\ 10^{-4}$	$4,1\ 10^{-7}$	$3,2\ 10^{-7}$	$2,6\ 10^{-7}$	$2,3\ 10^{-7}$	$2,4\ 10^{-7}$
Pu-245	10,5 h	0,005	$8,0\ 10^{-9}$	$5,0\ 10^{-4}$	$5,1\ 10^{-9}$	$2,6\ 10^{-9}$	$1,5\ 10^{-9}$	$8,9\ 10^{-10}$	$7,2\ 10^{-10}$
Pu-246	10,9 d	0,005	$3,6\ 10^{-8}$	$5,0\ 10^{-4}$	$2,3\ 10^{-8}$	$1,2\ 10^{-8}$	$7,1\ 10^{-9}$	$4,1\ 10^{-9}$	$3,3\ 10^{-9}$
Americium									
Am-237	1,22 h	0,005	$1,7\ 10^{-10}$	$5,0\ 10^{-4}$	$1,0\ 10^{-10}$	$5,5\ 10^{-11}$	$3,3\ 10^{-11}$	$2,2\ 10^{-11}$	$1,8\ 10^{-11}$
Am-238	1,63 h	0,005	$2,5\ 10^{-10}$	$5,0\ 10^{-4}$	$1,6\ 10^{-10}$	$9,1\ 10^{-11}$	$5,9\ 10^{-11}$	$4,0\ 10^{-11}$	$3,2\ 10^{-11}$
Am-239	11,9 h	0,005	$2,6\ 10^{-9}$	$5,0\ 10^{-4}$	$1,7\ 10^{-9}$	$8,4\ 10^{-10}$	$5,1\ 10^{-10}$	$3,0\ 10^{-10}$	$2,4\ 10^{-10}$
Am-240	2,12 d	0,005	$4,7\ 10^{-9}$	$5,0\ 10^{-4}$	$3,3\ 10^{-9}$	$1,8\ 10^{-9}$	$1,2\ 10^{-9}$	$7,3\ 10^{-10}$	$5,8\ 10^{-10}$
Am-241	$4,32\ 10^{2}$ a	0,005	$3,7\ 10^{-6}$	$5,0\ 10^{-4}$	$3,7\ 10^{-7}$	$2,7\ 10^{-7}$	$2,2\ 10^{-7}$	$2,0\ 10^{-7}$	$2,0\ 10^{-7}$
Am-242	16,0 h	0,005	$5,0\ 10^{-9}$	$5,0\ 10^{-4}$	$2,2\ 10^{-9}$	$1,1\ 10^{-9}$	$6,4\ 10^{-10}$	$3,7\ 10^{-10}$	$3,0\ 10^{-10}$
Am-242m	$1,52\ 10^{2}$ a	0,005	$3,1\ 10^{-6}$	$5,0\ 10^{-4}$	$3,0\ 10^{-7}$	$2,3\ 10^{-7}$	$2,0\ 10^{-7}$	$1,9\ 10^{-7}$	$1,9\ 10^{-7}$
Am-243	$7,38\ 10^{3}$ a	0,005	$3,6\ 10^{-6}$	$5,0\ 10^{-4}$	$3,7\ 10^{-7}$	$2,7\ 10^{-7}$	$2,2\ 10^{-7}$	$2,0\ 10^{-7}$	$2,0\ 10^{-7}$
Am-244	10,1 h	0,005	$4,9\ 10^{-9}$	$5,0\ 10^{-4}$	$3,1\ 10^{-9}$	$1,6\ 10^{-9}$	$9,6\ 10^{-10}$	$5,8\ 10^{-10}$	$4,6\ 10^{-10}$
Am-244m	0,433 h	0,005	$3,7\ 10^{-10}$	$5,0\ 10^{-4}$	$2,0\ 10^{-10}$	$9,6\ 10^{-11}$	$5,5\ 10^{-11}$	$3,7\ 10^{-11}$	$2,9\ 10^{-11}$
Am-245	2,05 h	0,005	$6,8\ 10^{-10}$	$5,0\ 10^{-4}$	$4,5\ 10^{-10}$	$2,2\ 10^{-10}$	$1,3\ 10^{-10}$	$7,9\ 10^{-11}$	$6,2\ 10^{-11}$
Am-246	0,650 h	0,005	$6,7\ 10^{-10}$	$5,0\ 10^{-4}$	$3,8\ 10^{-10}$	$1,9\ 10^{-10}$	$1,1\ 10^{-10}$	$7,3\ 10^{-11}$	$5,8\ 10^{-11}$
Am-246m	0,417 h	0,005	$3,9\ 10^{-10}$	$5,0\ 10^{-4}$	$2,2\ 10^{-10}$	$1,1\ 10^{-10}$	$6,4\ 10^{-11}$	$4,4\ 10^{-11}$	$3,4\ 10^{-11}$
Curium									
Cm-238	2,40 h	0,005	$7,8\ 10^{-10}$	$5,0\ 10^{-4}$	$4,9\ 10^{-10}$	$2,6\ 10^{-10}$	$1,6\ 10^{-10}$	$1,0\ 10^{-10}$	$8,0\ 10^{-11}$
Cm-240	27,0 d	0,005	$2,2\ 10^{-7}$	$5,0\ 10^{-4}$	$4,8\ 10^{-8}$	$2,5\ 10^{-8}$	$1,5\ 10^{-8}$	$9,2\ 10^{-9}$	$7,6\ 10^{-9}$
Cm-241	32,8 d	0,005	$1,1\ 10^{-8}$	$5,0\ 10^{-4}$	$5,7\ 10^{-9}$	$3,0\ 10^{-9}$	$1,9\ 10^{-9}$	$1,1\ 10^{-9}$	$9,1\ 10^{-10}$
Cm-242	163 d	0,005	$5,9\ 10^{-7}$	$5,0\ 10^{-4}$	$7,6\ 10^{-8}$	$3,9\ 10^{-8}$	$2,4\ 10^{-8}$	$1,5\ 10^{-8}$	$1,2\ 10^{-8}$
Cm-243	28,5 a	0,005	$3,2\ 10^{-6}$	$5,0\ 10^{-4}$	$3,3\ 10^{-7}$	$2,2\ 10^{-7}$	$1,6\ 10^{-7}$	$1,4\ 10^{-7}$	$1,5\ 10^{-7}$
Cm-244	18,1 a	0,005	$2,9\ 10^{-6}$	$5,0\ 10^{-4}$	$2,9\ 10^{-7}$	$1,9\ 10^{-7}$	$1,4\ 10^{-7}$	$1,2\ 10^{-7}$	$1,2\ 10^{-7}$

Nuclide	Physical half-life	Age ≤ 1 a		Age	1—2 a	2—7 a	7—12 a	12—17 a	4 17 a
		f_1 for ≤ 1 a	h(g)	f_1 for g > 1 a	h(g)	h(g)	h(g)	h(g)	h(g)
Cm-245	8,50 10^3 a	0,005	3,7 10^{-6}	5,0 10^{-4}	3,7 10^{-7}	2,8 10^{-7}	2,3 10^{-7}	2,1 10^{-7}	2,1 10^{-7}
Cm-246	4,73 10^3 a	0,005	3,7 10^{-6}	5,0 10^{-4}	3,7 10^{-7}	2,8 10^{-7}	2,2 10^{-7}	2,1 10^{-7}	2,1 10^{-7}
Cm-247	1,56 10^7 a	0,005	3,4 10^{-6}	5,0 10^{-4}	3,5 10^{-7}	2,6 10^{-7}	2,1 10^{-7}	1,9 10^{-7}	1,9 10^{-7}
Cm-248	3,39 10^5 a	0,005	1,4 10^{-5}	5,0 10^{-4}	1,4 10^{-6}	1,0 10^{-6}	8,4 10^{-7}	7,7 10^{-7}	7,7 10^{-7}
Cm-249	1,07 h	0,005	3,9 10^{-10}	5,0 10^{-4}	2,2 10^{-10}	1,1 10^{-10}	6,1 10^{-11}	4,0 10^{-11}	3,1 10^{-11}
Cm-250	6,90 10^3 a	0,005	7,8 10^{-5}	5,0 10^{-4}	8,2 10^{-6}	6,0 10^{-6}	4,9 10^{-6}	4,4 10^{-6}	4,4 10^{-6}
Berkelium									
Bk-245	4,94 d	0,005	6,1 10^{-9}	5,0 10^{-4}	3,9 10^{-9}	2,0 10^{-9}	1,2 10^{-9}	7,2 10^{-10}	5,7 10^{-10}
Bk-246	1,83 d	0,005	3,7 10^{-9}	5,0 10^{-4}	2,6 10^{-9}	1,4 10^{-9}	9,4 10^{-10}	6,0 10^{-10}	4,8 10^{-10}
Bk-247	1,38 10^3 a	0,005	8,9 10^{-6}	5,0 10^{-4}	8,6 10^{-7}	6,3 10^{-7}	4,6 10^{-7}	3,8 10^{-7}	3,5 10^{-7}
Bk-249	320 d	0,005	2,2 10^{-8}	5,0 10^{-4}	2,9 10^{-9}	1,9 10^{-9}	1,4 10^{-9}	1,1 10^{-9}	9,7 10^{-10}
Bk-250	3,22 h	0,005	1,5 10^{-9}	5,0 10^{-4}	8,5 10^{-10}	4,4 10^{-10}	2,7 10^{-10}	1,7 10^{-10}	1,4 10^{-10}
Californium									
Cf-244	0,323 h	0,005	9,8 10^{-10}	5,0 10^{-4}	4,8 10^{-10}	2,4 10^{-10}	1,3 10^{-10}	8,9 10^{-11}	7,0 10^{-11}
Cf-246	1,49 d	0,005	5,0 10^{-8}	5,0 10^{-4}	2,4 10^{-8}	1,2 10^{-8}	7,3 10^{-9}	4,1 10^{-9}	3,3 10^{-9}
Cf-248	334 d	0,005	1,5 10^{-6}	5,0 10^{-4}	1,6 10^{-7}	9,9 10^{-8}	6,0 10^{-8}	3,3 10^{-8}	2,8 10^{-8}
Cf-249	3,50 10^2 a	0,005	9,0 10^{-6}	5,0 10^{-4}	8,7 10^{-7}	6,4 10^{-7}	4,7 10^{-7}	3,8 10^{-7}	3,5 10^{-7}
Cf-250	13,1 a	0,005	5,7 10^{-6}	5,0 10^{-4}	5,5 10^{-7}	3,7 10^{-7}	2,3 10^{-7}	1,7 10^{-7}	1,6 10^{-7}
Cf-251	8,98 10^2 a	0,005	9,1 10^{-6}	5,0 10^{-4}	8,8 10^{-7}	6,5 10^{-7}	4,7 10^{-7}	3,9 10^{-7}	3,6 10^{-7}
Cf-252	2,64 a	0,005	5,0 10^{-6}	5,0 10^{-4}	5,1 10^{-7}	3,2 10^{-7}	1,9 10^{-7}	1,0 10^{-7}	9,0 10^{-8}
Cf-253	17,8 d	0,005	1,0 10^{-7}	5,0 10^{-4}	1,1 10^{-8}	6,0 10^{-9}	3,7 10^{-9}	1,8 10^{-9}	1,4 10^{-9}
Cf-254	60,5 d	0,005	1,1 10^{-5}	5,0 10^{-4}	2,6 10^{-6}	1,4 10^{-6}	8,4 10^{-7}	5,0 10^{-7}	4,0 10^{-7}
Einsteinium									
Es-250	2,10 h	0,005	2,3 10^{-10}	5,0 10^{-4}	9,9 10^{-11}	5,7 10^{-11}	3,7 10^{-11}	2,6 10^{-11}	2,1 10^{-11}
Es-251	1,38 d	0,005	1,9 10^{-9}	5,0 10^{-4}	1,2 10^{-9}	6,1 10^{-10}	3,7 10^{-10}	2,2 10^{-10}	1,7 10^{-10}

Nuclide	Physical half-life	Age ≤ 1 a		Age	1—2 a	2—7 a	7—12 a	12—17 a	4 17 a
		f_1 for ≤ 1 a	h(g)	f_1 for g > 1 a	h(g)	h(g)	h(g)	h(g)	h(g)
Es-253	20,5 d	0,005	1,7 10^{-7}	5,0 10^{-4}	4,5 10^{-8}	2,3 10^{-8}	1,4 10^{-8}	7,6 10^{-9}	6,1 10^{-9}
Es-254	276 d	0,005	1,4 10^{-6}	5,0 10^{-4}	1,6 10^{-7}	9,8 10^{-8}	6,0 10^{-8}	3,3 10^{-8}	2,8 10^{-8}
Es-254m	1,64 d	0,005	5,7 10^{-8}	5,0 10^{-4}	3,0 10^{-8}	1,5 10^{-8}	9,1 10^{-9}	5,2 10^{-9}	4,2 10^{-9}
Fermium									
Fm-252	22,7 h	0,005	3,8 10^{-8}	5,0 10^{-4}	2,0 10^{-8}	9,9 10^{-9}	5,9 10^{-9}	3,3 10^{-9}	2,7 10^{-9}
Fm-253	3,00 d	0,005	2,5 10^{-8}	5,0 10^{-4}	6,7 10^{-9}	3,4 10^{-9}	2,1 10^{-9}	1,1 10^{-9}	9,1 10^{-10}
Fm-254	3,24 h	0,005	5,6 10^{-9}	5,0 10^{-4}	3,2 10^{-9}	1,6 10^{-9}	9,3 10^{-10}	5,6 10^{-10}	4,4 10^{-10}
Fm-255	20,1 h	0,005	3,3 10^{-8}	5,0 10^{-4}	1,9 10^{-8}	9,5 10^{-9}	5,6 10^{-9}	3,2 10^{-9}	2,5 10^{-9}
Fm-257	101 d	0,005	9,8 10^{-7}	5,0 10^{-4}	1,1 10^{-7}	6,5 10^{-8}	4,0 10^{-8}	1,9 10^{-8}	1,5 10^{-8}
Mendelevium									
Md-257	5,20 h	0,005	3,1 10^{-9}	5,0 10^{-4}	8,8 10^{-10}	4,5 10^{-10}	2,7 10^{-10}	1,5 10^{-10}	1,2 10^{-10}
Md-258	55,0 d	0,005	6,3 10^{-7}	5,0 10^{-4}	8,9 10^{-8}	5,0 10^{-8}	3,0 10^{-8}	1,6 10^{-8}	1,3 10^{-8}

OBT denotes organically bound tritium.

(a) The f_1 value for 1 to 15 year olds is 0,4.

(b) The f_1 value for 1 to 15 year olds is 0,2.

(c) The f_1 value for 1 to 15 year olds is 0,3.

(d) The f_1 value for 1 to 15 year olds is 0,4.

(e) The f_1 value for 1 to 15 year olds is 0,3.

(f) The f_1 value for 1 to 15 year olds is 0,4.

(g) The f_1 value for 1 to 15 year olds is 0,3.

Table (B)
Committed effective dose per unit intake via inhalation (Sv Bq^{-1}) for members of the public

Nuclide	*Physical half-life*	*Type*	*Age ≤ 1 a*		*Age*	*1—2 a*	*2—7 a*	*7—12 a*	*12—17 a*	*> 17 a*
			f_1	*h(g)*	f_1	*h(g)*	*h(g)*	*h(g)*	*h(g)*	*h(g)*
Hydrogen										
Tritiated water	12,3 a	F	1,000	$2{,}6\ 10^{-11}$	1,000	$2{,}0\ 10^{-11}$	$1{,}1\ 10^{-11}$	$8{,}2\ 10^{-12}$	$5{,}9\ 10^{-12}$	$6{,}2\ 10^{-12}$
		M	0,200	$3{,}4\ 10^{-10}$	0,100	$2{,}7\ 10^{-10}$	$1{,}4\ 10^{-10}$	$8{,}2\ 10^{-11}$	$5{,}3\ 10^{-11}$	$4{,}5\ 10^{-11}$
		S	0,020	$1{,}2\ 10^{-9}$	0,010	$1{,}0\ 10^{-9}$	$6{,}3\ 10^{-10}$	$3{,}8\ 10^{-10}$	$2{,}8\ 10^{-10}$	$2{,}6\ 10^{-10}$
Beryllium										
Be-7	53,3 d	M	0,020	$2{,}5\ 10^{-10}$	0,005	$2{,}1\ 10^{-10}$	$1{,}2\ 10^{-10}$	$8{,}3\ 10^{-11}$	$6{,}2\ 10^{-11}$	$5{,}0\ 10^{-11}$
		S	0,020	$2{,}8\ 10^{-10}$	0,005	$2{,}4\ 10^{-10}$	$1{,}4\ 10^{-10}$	$9{,}6\ 10^{-11}$	$6{,}8\ 10^{-11}$	$5{,}5\ 10^{-11}$
Be-10	$1{,}60\ 10^{6}$ a	M	0,020	$4{,}1\ 10^{-8}$	0,005	$3{,}4\ 10^{-8}$	$2{,}0\ 10^{-8}$	$1{,}3\ 10^{-8}$	$1{,}1\ 10^{-8}$	$9{,}6\ 10^{-9}$
		S	0,020	$9{,}9\ 10^{-8}$	0,005	$9{,}1\ 10^{-8}$	$6{,}1\ 10^{-8}$	$4{,}2\ 10^{-8}$	$3{,}7\ 10^{-8}$	$3{,}5\ 10^{-8}$
Carbon										
C-11	0,340 h	F	1,000	$1{,}0\ 10^{-10}$	1,000	$7{,}0\ 10^{-11}$	$3{,}2\ 10^{-11}$	$2{,}1\ 10^{-11}$	$1{,}3\ 10^{-11}$	$1{,}1\ 10^{-11}$
		M	0,200	$1{,}5\ 10^{-10}$	0,100	$1{,}1\ 10^{-10}$	$4{,}9\ 10^{-11}$	$3{,}2\ 10^{-11}$	$2{,}1\ 10^{-11}$	$1{,}8\ 10^{-11}$
		S	0,020	$1{,}6\ 10^{-10}$	0,010	$1{,}1\ 10^{-10}$	$5{,}1\ 10^{-11}$	$3{,}3\ 10^{-11}$	$2{,}2\ 10^{-11}$	$1{,}8\ 10^{-11}$
C-14	$5{,}73\ 10^{3}$ a	F	1,000	$6{,}1\ 10^{-10}$	1,000	$6{,}7\ 10^{-10}$	$3{,}6\ 10^{-10}$	$2{,}9\ 10^{-10}$	$1{,}9\ 10^{-10}$	$2{,}0\ 10^{-10}$
		M	0,200	$8{,}3\ 10^{-9}$	0,100	$6{,}6\ 10^{-9}$	$4{,}0\ 10^{-9}$	$2{,}8\ 10^{-9}$	$2{,}5\ 10^{-9}$	$2{,}0\ 10^{-9}$
		S	0,020	$1{,}9\ 10^{-8}$	0,010	$1{,}7\ 10^{-8}$	$1{,}1\ 10^{-8}$	$7{,}4\ 10^{-9}$	$6{,}4\ 10^{-9}$	$5{,}8\ 10^{-9}$
Fluorine										
F-18	1,83 h	F	1,000	$2{,}6\ 10^{-10}$	1,000	$1{,}9\ 10^{-10}$	$9{,}1\ 10^{-11}$	$5{,}6\ 10^{-11}$	$3{,}4\ 10^{-11}$	$2{,}8\ 10^{-11}$
		M	1,000	$4{,}1\ 10^{-10}$	1,000	$2{,}9\ 10^{-10}$	$1{,}5\ 10^{-10}$	$9{,}7\ 10^{-11}$	$6{,}9\ 10^{-11}$	$5{,}6\ 10^{-11}$
		S	1,000	$4{,}2\ 10^{-10}$	1,000	$3{,}1\ 10^{-10}$	$1{,}5\ 10^{-10}$	$1{,}0\ 10^{-10}$	$7{,}3\ 10^{-11}$	$5{,}9\ 10^{-11}$
Sodium										
Na-22	2,60 a	F	1,000	$9{,}7\ 10^{-9}$	1,000	$7{,}3\ 10^{-9}$	$3{,}8\ 10^{-9}$	$2{,}4\ 10^{-9}$	$1{,}5\ 10^{-9}$	$1{,}3\ 10^{-9}$
Na-24	15,0 h	F	1,000	$2{,}3\ 10^{-9}$	1,000	$1{,}8\ 10^{-9}$	$9{,}3\ 10^{-10}$	$5{,}7\ 10^{-10}$	$3{,}4\ 10^{-10}$	$2{,}7\ 10^{-10}$

Nuclide	*Physical half-life*	*Type*	*Age ≤ 1 a*		*Age*	*1—2 a*	*2—7 a*	*7—12 a*	*12—17 a*	*> 17 a*
			f_1	*h(g)*	f_1	*h(g)*	*h(g)*	*h(g)*	*h(g)*	*h(g)*
Magnesium										
Mg-28	20,9 h	F	1,000	$5,3\ 10^{-9}$	0,500	$4,7\ 10^{-9}$	$2,2\ 10^{-9}$	$1,3\ 10^{-9}$	$7,3\ 10^{-10}$	$6,0\ 10^{-10}$
		M	1,000	$7,3\ 10^{-9}$	0,500	$7,2\ 10^{-9}$	$3,5\ 10^{-9}$	$2,3\ 10^{-9}$	$1,5\ 10^{-9}$	$1,2\ 10^{-9}$
Aluminium										
Al-26	$7,16\ 10^{5}$ a	F	0,020	$8,1\ 10^{-8}$	0,010	$6,2\ 10^{-8}$	$3,2\ 10^{-8}$	$2,0\ 10^{-8}$	$1,3\ 10^{-8}$	$1,1\ 10^{-8}$
		M	0,020	$8,8\ 10^{-8}$	0,010	$7,4\ 10^{-8}$	$4,4\ 10^{-8}$	$2,9\ 10^{-8}$	$2,2\ 10^{-8}$	$2,0\ 10^{-8}$
Silicon										
Si-31	2,62 h	F	0,020	$3,6\ 10^{-10}$	0,010	$2,3\ 10^{-10}$	$9,5\ 10^{-11}$	$5,9\ 10^{-11}$	$3,2\ 10^{-11}$	$2,7\ 10^{-11}$
		M	0,020	$6,9\ 10^{-10}$	0,010	$4,4\ 10^{-10}$	$2,0\ 10^{-10}$	$1,3\ 10^{-10}$	$8,9\ 10^{-11}$	$7,4\ 10^{-11}$
		S	0,020	$7,2\ 10^{-10}$	0,010	$4,7\ 10^{-10}$	$2,2\ 10^{-10}$	$1,4\ 10^{-10}$	$9,5\ 10^{-11}$	$7,9\ 10^{-11}$
Si-32	$4,50\ 10^{2}$ a	F	0,020	$3,0\ 10^{-8}$	0,010	$2,3\ 10^{-8}$	$1,1\ 10^{-8}$	$6,4\ 10^{-9}$	$3,8\ 10^{-9}$	$3,2\ 10^{-9}$
		M	0,020	$7,1\ 10^{-8}$	0,010	$6,0\ 10^{-8}$	$3,6\ 10^{-8}$	$2,4\ 10^{-8}$	$1,9\ 10^{-8}$	$1,7\ 10^{-8}$
		S	0,020	$2,8\ 10^{-7}$	0,010	$2,7\ 10^{-7}$	$1,9\ 10^{-7}$	$1,3\ 10^{-7}$	$1,1\ 10^{-7}$	$1,1\ 10^{-7}$
Phosphorus										
P-32	14,3 d	F	1,000	$1,2\ 10^{-8}$	0,800	$7,5\ 10^{-9}$	$3,2\ 10^{-9}$	$1,8\ 10^{-9}$	$9,8\ 10^{-10}$	$7,7\ 10^{-10}$
		M	1,000	$2,2\ 10^{-8}$	0,800	$1,5\ 10^{-8}$	$8,0\ 10^{-9}$	$5,3\ 10^{-9}$	$4,0\ 10^{-9}$	$3,4\ 10^{-9}$
P-33	25,4 d	F	1,000	$1,2\ 10^{-9}$	0,800	$7,8\ 10^{-10}$	$3,0\ 10^{-10}$	$2,0\ 10^{-10}$	$1,1\ 10^{-10}$	$9,2\ 10^{-11}$
		M	1,000	$6,1\ 10^{-9}$	0,800	$4,6\ 10^{-9}$	$2,8\ 10^{-9}$	$2,1\ 10^{-9}$	$1,9\ 10^{-9}$	$1,5\ 10^{-9}$
Sulphur										
S-35 (inorganic)	87,4 d	F	1,000	$5,5\ 10^{-10}$	0,800	$3,9\ 10^{-10}$	$1,8\ 10^{-10}$	$1,1\ 10^{-10}$	$6,0\ 10^{-11}$	$5,1\ 10^{-11}$
		M	0,200	$5,9\ 10^{-9}$	0,100	$4,5\ 10^{-9}$	$2,8\ 10^{-9}$	$2,0\ 10^{-9}$	$1,8\ 10^{-9}$	$1,4\ 10^{-9}$
		S	0,020	$7,7\ 10^{-9}$	0,010	$6,0\ 10^{-9}$	$3,6\ 10^{-9}$	$2,6\ 10^{-9}$	$2,3\ 10^{-9}$	$1,9\ 10^{-9}$
Chlorine										
Cl-36	$3,01\ 10^{5}$ a	F	1,000	$3,9\ 10^{-9}$	1,000	$2,6\ 10^{-9}$	$1,1\ 10^{-9}$	$7,1\ 10^{-10}$	$3,9\ 10^{-10}$	$3,3\ 10^{-10}$
		M	1,000	$3,1\ 10^{-8}$	1,000	$2,6\ 10^{-8}$	$1,5\ 10^{-8}$	$1,0\ 10^{-8}$	$8,8\ 10^{-9}$	$7,3\ 10^{-9}$

Nuclide	Physical half-life	Type	Age ≤ 1 a		Age	1—2 a	2—7 a	7—12 a	12—17 a	> 17 a
			f_1	$h(g)$	f_1	$h(g)$	$h(g)$	$h(g)$	$h(g)$	$h(g)$
Cl-38	0,620 h	F	1,000	$2{,}9\ 10^{-10}$	1,000	$1{,}9\ 10^{-10}$	$8{,}4\ 10^{-11}$	$5{,}1\ 10^{-11}$	$3{,}0\ 10^{-11}$	$2{,}5\ 10^{-11}$
		M	1,000	$4{,}7\ 10^{-10}$	1,000	$3{,}0\ 10^{-10}$	$1{,}4\ 10^{-10}$	$8{,}5\ 10^{-11}$	$5{,}4\ 10^{-11}$	$4{,}5\ 10^{-11}$
Cl-39	0,927 h	F	1,000	$2{,}7\ 10^{-10}$	1,000	$1{,}8\ 10^{-10}$	$8{,}4\ 10^{-11}$	$5{,}1\ 10^{-11}$	$3{,}1\ 10^{-11}$	$2{,}5\ 10^{-11}$
		M	1,000	$4{,}3\ 10^{-10}$	1,000	$2{,}8\ 10^{-10}$	$1{,}3\ 10^{-10}$	$8{,}5\ 10^{-11}$	$5{,}6\ 10^{-11}$	$4{,}6\ 10^{-11}$
Potassium										
K-40	$1{,}28\ 10^{9}$ a	F	1,000	$2{,}4\ 10^{-8}$	1,000	$1{,}7\ 10^{-8}$	$7{,}5\ 10^{-9}$	$4{,}5\ 10^{-9}$	$2{,}5\ 10^{-9}$	$2{,}1\ 10^{-9}$
K-42	12,4 h	F	1,000	$1{,}6\ 10^{-9}$	1,000	$1{,}0\ 10^{-9}$	$4{,}4\ 10^{-10}$	$2{,}6\ 10^{-10}$	$1{,}5\ 10^{-10}$	$1{,}2\ 10^{-10}$
K-43	22,6 h	F	1,000	$1{,}3\ 10^{-9}$	1,000	$9{,}7\ 10^{-10}$	$4{,}7\ 10^{-10}$	$2{,}9\ 10^{-10}$	$1{,}7\ 10^{-10}$	$1{,}4\ 10^{-10}$
K-44	0,369 h	F	1,000	$2{,}2\ 10^{-10}$	1,000	$1{,}4\ 10^{-10}$	$6{,}5\ 10^{-11}$	$4{,}0\ 10^{-11}$	$2{,}4\ 10^{-11}$	$2{,}0\ 10^{-11}$
K-45	0,333 h	F	1,000	$1{,}5\ 10^{-10}$	1,000	$1{,}0\ 10^{-10}$	$4{,}8\ 10^{-11}$	$3{,}0\ 10^{-11}$	$1{,}8\ 10^{-11}$	$1{,}5\ 10^{-11}$
Calcium(a)										
Ca-41	$1{,}40\ 10^{5}$ a	F	0,600	$6{,}7\ 10^{-10}$	0,300	$3{,}8\ 10^{-10}$	$2{,}6\ 10^{-10}$	$3{,}3\ 10^{-10}$	$3{,}3\ 10^{-10}$	$1{,}7\ 10^{-10}$
		M	0,200	$4{,}2\ 10^{-10}$	0,100	$2{,}6\ 10^{-10}$	$1{,}7\ 10^{-10}$	$1{,}7\ 10^{-10}$	$1{,}6\ 10^{-10}$	$9{,}5\ 10^{-11}$
		S	0,020	$6{,}7\ 10^{-10}$	0,010	$6{,}0\ 10^{-10}$	$3{,}8\ 10^{-10}$	$2{,}4\ 10^{-10}$	$1{,}9\ 10^{-10}$	$1{,}8\ 10^{-10}$
Ca-45	163 d	F	0,600	$5{,}7\ 10^{-9}$	0,300	$3{,}0\ 10^{-9}$	$1{,}4\ 10^{-9}$	$1{,}0\ 10^{-9}$	$7{,}6\ 10^{-10}$	$4{,}6\ 10^{-10}$
		M	0,200	$1{,}2\ 10^{-8}$	0,100	$8{,}8\ 10^{-9}$	$5{,}3\ 10^{-9}$	$3{,}9\ 10^{-9}$	$3{,}5\ 10^{-9}$	$2{,}7\ 10^{-9}$
		S	0,020	$1{,}5\ 10^{-8}$	0,010	$1{,}2\ 10^{-8}$	$7{,}2\ 10^{-9}$	$5{,}1\ 10^{-9}$	$4{,}6\ 10^{-9}$	$3{,}7\ 10^{-9}$
Ca-47	4,53 d	F	0,600	$4{,}9\ 10^{-9}$	0,300	$3{,}6\ 10^{-9}$	$1{,}7\ 10^{-9}$	$1{,}1\ 10^{-9}$	$6{,}1\ 10^{-10}$	$5{,}5\ 10^{-10}$
		M	0,200	$1{,}0\ 10^{-8}$	0,100	$7{,}7\ 10^{-9}$	$4{,}2\ 10^{-9}$	$2{,}9\ 10^{-9}$	$2{,}4\ 10^{-9}$	$1{,}9\ 10^{-9}$
		S	0,020	$1{,}2\ 10^{-8}$	0,010	$8{,}5\ 10^{-9}$	$4{,}6\ 10^{-9}$	$3{,}3\ 10^{-9}$	$2{,}6\ 10^{-9}$	$2{,}1\ 10^{-9}$
Scandium										
Sc-43	3,89 h	S	0,001	$9{,}3\ 10^{-10}$	$1{,}0\ 10^{-4}$	$6{,}7\ 10^{-10}$	$3{,}3\ 10^{-10}$	$2{,}2\ 10^{-10}$	$1{,}4\ 10^{-10}$	$1{,}1\ 10^{-10}$
Sc-44	3,93 h	S	0,001	$1{,}6\ 10^{-9}$	$1{,}0\ 10^{-4}$	$1{,}2\ 10^{-9}$	$5{,}6\ 10^{-10}$	$3{,}6\ 10^{-10}$	$2{,}3\ 10^{-10}$	$1{,}8\ 10^{-10}$
Sc-44m	2,44 d	S	0,001	$1{,}1\ 10^{-8}$	$1{,}0\ 10^{-4}$	$8{,}4\ 10^{-9}$	$4{,}2\ 10^{-9}$	$2{,}8\ 10^{-9}$	$1{,}7\ 10^{-9}$	$1{,}4\ 10^{-9}$
Sc-46	83,8 d	S	0,001	$2{,}8\ 10^{-8}$	$1{,}0\ 10^{-4}$	$2{,}3\ 10^{-8}$	$1{,}4\ 10^{-8}$	$9{,}8\ 10^{-9}$	$8{,}4\ 10^{-9}$	$6{,}8\ 10^{-9}$

Nuclide	Physical half-life	Type	Age ≤ 1 a		Age	1—2 a	2—7 a	7—12 a	12—17 a	> 17 a
			f_1	h(g)	f_1	h(g)	h(g)	h(g)	h(g)	h(g)
Sc-47	3,35 d	S	0,001	$4,0\ 10^{-9}$	$1,0\ 10^{-4}$	$2,8\ 10^{-9}$	$1,5\ 10^{-9}$	$1,1\ 10^{-9}$	$9,2\ 10^{-10}$	$7,3\ 10^{-10}$
Sc-48	1,82 d	S	0,001	$7,8\ 10^{-9}$	$1,0\ 10^{-4}$	$5,9\ 10^{-9}$	$3,1\ 10^{-9}$	$2,0\ 10^{-9}$	$1,4\ 10^{-9}$	$1,1\ 10^{-9}$
Sc-49	0,956 h	S	0,001	$3,9\ 10^{-10}$	$1,0\ 10^{-4}$	$2,4\ 10^{-10}$	$1,1\ 10^{-10}$	$7,1\ 10^{-11}$	$4,7\ 10^{-11}$	$4,0\ 10^{-11}$
Titanium										
Ti-44	47,3 a	F	0,020	$3,1\ 10^{-7}$	0,010	$2,6\ 10^{-7}$	$1,5\ 10^{-7}$	$9,6\ 10^{-8}$	$6,6\ 10^{-8}$	$6,1\ 10^{-8}$
		M	0,020	$1,7\ 10^{-7}$	0,010	$1,5\ 10^{-7}$	$9,2\ 10^{-8}$	$5,9\ 10^{-8}$	$4,6\ 10^{-8}$	$4,2\ 10^{-8}$
		S	0,020	$3,2\ 10^{-7}$	0,010	$3,1\ 10^{-7}$	$2,1\ 10^{-7}$	$1,5\ 10^{-7}$	$1,3\ 10^{-7}$	$1,2\ 10^{-7}$
Ti-45	3,08 h	F	0,020	$4,4\ 10^{-10}$	0,010	$3,2\ 10^{-10}$	$1,5\ 10^{-10}$	$9,1\ 10^{-11}$	$5,1\ 10^{-11}$	$4,2\ 10^{-11}$
		M	0,020	$7,4\ 10^{-10}$	0,010	$5,2\ 10^{-10}$	$2,5\ 10^{-10}$	$1,6\ 10^{-10}$	$1,1\ 10^{-10}$	$8,8\ 10^{-11}$
		S	0,020	$7,7\ 10^{-10}$	0,010	$5,5\ 10^{-10}$	$2,7\ 10^{-10}$	$1,7\ 10^{-10}$	$1,1\ 10^{-10}$	$9,3\ 10^{-11}$
Vanadium										
V-47	0,543 h	F	0,020	$1,8\ 10^{-10}$	0,010	$1,2\ 10^{-10}$	$5,6\ 10^{-11}$	$3,5\ 10^{-11}$	$2,1\ 10^{-11}$	$1,7\ 10^{-11}$
		M	0,020	$2,8\ 10^{-10}$	0,010	$1,9\ 10^{-10}$	$8,6\ 10^{-11}$	$5,5\ 10^{-11}$	$3,5\ 10^{-11}$	$2,9\ 10^{-11}$
V-48	16,2 d	F	0,020	$8,4\ 10^{-9}$	0,010	$6,4\ 10^{-9}$	$3,3\ 10^{-9}$	$2,1\ 10^{-9}$	$1,3\ 10^{-9}$	$1,1\ 10^{-9}$
		M	0,020	$1,4\ 10^{-8}$	0,010	$1,1\ 10^{-8}$	$6,3\ 10^{-9}$	$4,3\ 10^{-9}$	$2,9\ 10^{-9}$	$2,4\ 10^{-9}$
V-49	330 d	F	0,020	$2,0\ 10^{-10}$	0,010	$1,6\ 10^{-10}$	$7,7\ 10^{-11}$	$4,3\ 10^{-11}$	$2,5\ 10^{-11}$	$2,1\ 10^{-11}$
		M	0,020	$2,8\ 10^{-10}$	0,010	$2,1\ 10^{-10}$	$1,1\ 10^{-10}$	$6,3\ 10^{-11}$	$4,0\ 10^{-11}$	$3,4\ 10^{-11}$
Chromium										
Cr-48	23,0 h	F	0,200	$7,6\ 10^{-10}$	0,100	$6,0\ 10^{-10}$	$3,1\ 10^{-10}$	$2,0\ 10^{-10}$	$1,2\ 10^{-10}$	$9,9\ 10^{-11}$
		M	0,200	$1,1\ 10^{-9}$	0,100	$9,1\ 10^{-10}$	$5,1\ 10^{-10}$	$3,4\ 10^{-10}$	$2,5\ 10^{-10}$	$2,0\ 10^{-10}$
		S	0,200	$1,2\ 10^{-9}$	0,100	$9,8\ 10^{-10}$	$5,5\ 10^{-10}$	$3,7\ 10^{-10}$	$2,8\ 10^{-10}$	$2,2\ 10^{-10}$
Cr-49	0,702 h	F	0,200	$1,9\ 10^{-10}$	0,100	$1,3\ 10^{-10}$	$6,0\ 10^{-11}$	$3,7\ 10^{-11}$	$2,2\ 10^{-11}$	$1,9\ 10^{-11}$
		M	0,200	$3,0\ 10^{-10}$	0,100	$2,0\ 10^{-10}$	$9,5\ 10^{-11}$	$6,1\ 10^{-11}$	$4,0\ 10^{-11}$	$3,3\ 10^{-11}$
		S	0,200	$3,1\ 10^{-10}$	0,100	$2,1\ 10^{-10}$	$9,9\ 10^{-11}$	$6,4\ 10^{-11}$	$4,2\ 10^{-11}$	$3,5\ 10^{-11}$

Nuclide	*Physical half-life*	*Type*	*Age ≤ 1 a*		*Age*	*1—2 a*	*2—7 a*	*7—12 a*	*12—17 a*	*> 17 a*
			f_1	*h(g)*	f_1	*h(g)*	*h(g)*	*h(g)*	*h(g)*	*h(g)*
Cr-51	27,7 d	F	0,200	$1,7\ 10^{-10}$	0,100	$1,3\ 10^{-10}$	$6,3\ 10^{-11}$	$4,0\ 10^{-11}$	$2,4\ 10^{-11}$	$2,0\ 10^{-11}$
		M	0,200	$2,6\ 10^{-10}$	0,100	$1,9\ 10^{-10}$	$1,0\ 10^{-10}$	$6,4\ 10^{-11}$	$3,9\ 10^{-11}$	$3,2\ 10^{-11}$
		S	0,200	$2,6\ 10^{-10}$	0,100	$2,1\ 10^{-10}$	$1,0\ 10^{-10}$	$6,6\ 10^{-11}$	$4,5\ 10^{-11}$	$3,7\ 10^{-11}$
Manganese										
Mn-51	0,770 h	F	0,200	$2,5\ 10^{-10}$	0,100	$1,7\ 10^{-10}$	$7,5\ 10^{-11}$	$4,6\ 10^{-11}$	$2,7\ 10^{-11}$	$2,3\ 10^{-11}$
		M	0,200	$4,0\ 10^{-10}$	0,100	$2,7\ 10^{-10}$	$1,2\ 10^{-10}$	$7,8\ 10^{-11}$	$5,0\ 10^{-11}$	$4,1\ 10^{-11}$
Mn-52	5,59 d	F	0,200	$7,0\ 10^{-9}$	0,100	$5,5\ 10^{-9}$	$2,9\ 10^{-9}$	$1,8\ 10^{-9}$	$1,1\ 10^{-9}$	$9,4\ 10^{-10}$
		M	0,200	$8,6\ 10^{-9}$	0,100	$6,8\ 10^{-9}$	$3,7\ 10^{-9}$	$2,4\ 10^{-9}$	$1,7\ 10^{-9}$	$1,4\ 10^{-9}$
Mn-52m	0,352 h	F	0,200	$1,9\ 10^{-10}$	0,100	$1,3\ 10^{-10}$	$6,1\ 10^{-11}$	$3,8\ 10^{-11}$	$2,2\ 10^{-11}$	$1,9\ 10^{-11}$
		M	0,200	$2,8\ 10^{-10}$	0,100	$1,9\ 10^{-10}$	$8,7\ 10^{-11}$	$5,5\ 10^{-11}$	$3,4\ 10^{-11}$	$2,9\ 10^{-11}$
Mn-53	$3,70\ 10^{6}$ a	F	0,200	$3,2\ 10^{-10}$	0,100	$2,2\ 10^{-10}$	$1,1\ 10^{-10}$	$6,0\ 10^{-11}$	$3,4\ 10^{-11}$	$2,9\ 10^{-11}$
		M	0,200	$4,6\ 10^{-10}$	0,100	$3,4\ 10^{-10}$	$1,7\ 10^{-10}$	$1,0\ 10^{-10}$	$6,4\ 10^{-11}$	$5,4\ 10^{-11}$
Mn-54	312 d	F	0,200	$5,2\ 10^{-9}$	0,100	$4,1\ 10^{-9}$	$2,2\ 10^{-9}$	$1,5\ 10^{-9}$	$9,9\ 10^{-10}$	$8,5\ 10^{-10}$
		M	0,200	$7,5\ 10^{-9}$	0,100	$6,2\ 10^{-9}$	$3,8\ 10^{-9}$	$2,4\ 10^{-9}$	$1,9\ 10^{-9}$	$1,5\ 10^{-9}$
Mn-56	2,58 h	F	0,200	$6,9\ 10^{-10}$	0,100	$4,9\ 10^{-10}$	$2,3\ 10^{-10}$	$1,4\ 10^{-10}$	$7,8\ 10^{-11}$	$6,4\ 10^{-11}$
		M	0,200	$1,1\ 10^{-9}$	0,100	$7,8\ 10^{-10}$	$3,7\ 10^{-10}$	$2,4\ 10^{-10}$	$1,5\ 10^{-10}$	$1,2\ 10^{-10}$
Iron(b)										
Fe-52	8,28 h	F	0,600	$5,2\ 10^{-9}$	0,100	$3,6\ 10^{-9}$	$1,5\ 10^{-9}$	$8,9\ 10^{-10}$	$4,9\ 10^{-10}$	$3,9\ 10^{-10}$
		M	0,200	$5,8\ 10^{-9}$	0,100	$4,1\ 10^{-9}$	$1,9\ 10^{-9}$	$1,2\ 10^{-9}$	$7,4\ 10^{-10}$	$6,0\ 10^{-10}$
		S	0,020	$6,0\ 10^{-9}$	0,010	$4,2\ 10^{-9}$	$2,0\ 10^{-9}$	$1,3\ 10^{-9}$	$7,7\ 10^{-10}$	$6,3\ 10^{-10}$
Fe-55	2,70 a	F	0,600	$4,2\ 10^{-9}$	0,100	$3,2\ 10^{-9}$	$2,2\ 10^{-9}$	$1,4\ 10^{-9}$	$9,4\ 10^{-10}$	$7,7\ 10^{-10}$
		M	0,200	$1,9\ 10^{-9}$	0,100	$1,4\ 10^{-9}$	$9,9\ 10^{-10}$	$6,2\ 10^{-10}$	$4,4\ 10^{-10}$	$3,8\ 10^{-10}$
		S	0,020	$1,0\ 10^{-9}$	0,010	$8,5\ 10^{-10}$	$5,0\ 10^{-10}$	$2,9\ 10^{-10}$	$2,0\ 10^{-10}$	$1,8\ 10^{-10}$
Fe-59	44,5 d	F	0,600	$2,1\ 10^{-8}$	0,100	$1,3\ 10^{-8}$	$7,1\ 10^{-9}$	$4,2\ 10^{-9}$	$2,6\ 10^{-9}$	$2,2\ 10^{-9}$
		M	0,200	$1,8\ 10^{-8}$	0,100	$1,3\ 10^{-8}$	$7,9\ 10^{-9}$	$5,5\ 10^{-9}$	$4,6\ 10^{-9}$	$3,7\ 10^{-9}$
		S	0,020	$1,7\ 10^{-8}$	0,010	$1,3\ 10^{-8}$	$8,1\ 10^{-9}$	$5,8\ 10^{-9}$	$5,1\ 10^{-9}$	$4,0\ 10^{-9}$

Nuclide	Physical half-life	Type	Age ≤ 1 a		Age	1—2 a	2—7 a	7—12 a	12—17 a	> 17 a
			f_1	h(g)	f_1	h(g)	h(g)	h(g)	h(g)	h(g)
Fe-60	1,00 10^{5} a	F	0,600	4,4 10^{-7}	0,100	3,9 10^{-7}	3,5 10^{-7}	3,2 10^{-7}	2,9 10^{-7}	2,8 10^{-7}
		M	0,200	2,0 10^{-7}	0,100	1,7 10^{-7}	1,6 10^{-7}	1,4 10^{-7}	1,4 10^{-7}	1,4 10^{-7}
		S	0,020	9,3 10^{-8}	0,010	8,8 10^{-8}	6,7 10^{-8}	5,2 10^{-8}	4,9 10^{-8}	4,9 10^{-8}
Cobalt(c)										
Co-55	17,5 h	F	0,600	2,2 10^{-9}	0,100	1,8 10^{-9}	9,0 10^{-10}	5,5 10^{-10}	3,1 10^{-10}	2,7 10^{-10}
		M	0,200	4,1 10^{-9}	0,100	3,1 10^{-9}	1,5 10^{-9}	9,8 10^{-10}	6,1 10^{-10}	5,0 10^{-10}
		S	0,020	4,6 10^{-9}	0,010	3,3 10^{-9}	1,6 10^{-9}	1,1 10^{-9}	6,6 10^{-10}	5,3 10^{-10}
Co-56	78,7 d	F	0,600	1,4 10^{-8}	0,100	1,0 10^{-8}	5,5 10^{-9}	3,5 10^{-9}	2,2 10^{-9}	1,8 10^{-9}
		M	0,200	2,5 10^{-8}	0,100	2,1 10^{-8}	1,1 10^{-8}	7,4 10^{-9}	5,8 10^{-9}	4,8 10^{-9}
		S	0,020	2,9 10^{-8}	0,010	2,5 10^{-8}	1,5 10^{-8}	1,0 10^{-8}	8,0 10^{-9}	6,7 10^{-9}
Co-57	271 d	F	0,600	1,5 10^{-9}	0,100	1,1 10^{-9}	5,6 10^{-10}	3,7 10^{-10}	2,3 10^{-10}	1,9 10^{-10}
		M	0,200	2,8 10^{-9}	0,100	2,2 10^{-9}	1,3 10^{-9}	8,5 10^{-10}	6,7 10^{-10}	5,5 10^{-10}
		S	0,020	4,4 10^{-9}	0,010	3,7 10^{-9}	2,3 10^{-9}	1,5 10^{-9}	1,2 10^{-9}	1,0 10^{-9}
Co-58	70,8 d	F	0,600	4,0 10^{-9}	0,100	3,0 10^{-9}	1,6 10^{-9}	1,0 10^{-9}	6,4 10^{-10}	5,3 10^{-10}
		M	0,200	7,3 10^{-9}	0,100	6,5 10^{-9}	3,5 10^{-9}	2,4 10^{-9}	2,0 10^{-9}	1,6 10^{-9}
		S	0,020	9,0 10^{-9}	0,010	7,5 10^{-9}	4,5 10^{-9}	3,1 10^{-9}	2,6 10^{-9}	2,1 10^{-9}
Co-58m	9,15 h	F	0,600	4,8 10^{-11}	0,100	3,6 10^{-11}	1,7 10^{-11}	1,1 10^{-11}	5,9 10^{-12}	5,2 10^{-12}
		M	0,200	1,1 10^{-10}	0,100	7,6 10^{-11}	3,8 10^{-11}	2,4 10^{-11}	1,6 10^{-11}	1,3 10^{-11}
		S	0,020	1,3 10^{-10}	0,010	9,0 10^{-11}	4,5 10^{-11}	3,0 10^{-11}	2,0 10^{-11}	1,7 10^{-11}
Co-60	5,27 a	F	0,600	3,0 10^{-8}	0,100	2,3 10^{-8}	1,4 10^{-8}	8,9 10^{-9}	6,1 10^{-9}	5,2 10^{-9}
		M	0,200	4,2 10^{-8}	0,100	3,4 10^{-8}	2,1 10^{-8}	1,5 10^{-8}	1,2 10^{-8}	1,0 10^{-8}
		S	0,020	9,2 10^{-8}	0,010	8,6 10^{-8}	5,9 10^{-8}	4,0 10^{-8}	3,4 10^{-8}	3,1 10^{-8}
Co-60m	0,174 h	F	0,600	4,4 10^{-12}	0,100	2,8 10^{-12}	1,5 10^{-12}	1,0 10^{-12}	8,3 10^{-13}	6,9 10^{-13}
		M	0,200	7,1 10^{-12}	0,100	4,7 10^{-12}	2,7 10^{-12}	1,8 10^{-12}	1,5 10^{-12}	1,2 10^{-12}
		S	0,020	7,6 10^{-12}	0,010	5,1 10^{-12}	2,9 10^{-12}	2,0 10^{-12}	1,7 10^{-12}	1,4 10^{-12}

Nuclide	Physical half-life	Type	Age ≤ 1 a		Age	1—2 a	2—7 a	7—12 a	12—17 a	> 17 a
			f_1	$h(g)$	f_1	$h(g)$	$h(g)$	$h(g)$	$h(g)$	$h(g)$
Co-61	1,65 h	F	0,600	$2{,}1\ 10^{-10}$	0,100	$1{,}4\ 10^{-10}$	$6{,}0\ 10^{-11}$	$3{,}8\ 10^{-11}$	$2{,}2\ 10^{-11}$	$1{,}9\ 10^{-11}$
		M	0,200	$4{,}0\ 10^{-10}$	0,100	$2{,}7\ 10^{-10}$	$1{,}2\ 10^{-10}$	$8{,}2\ 10^{-11}$	$5{,}7\ 10^{-11}$	$4{,}7\ 10^{-11}$
		S	0,020	$4{,}3\ 10^{-10}$	0,010	$2{,}8\ 10^{-10}$	$1{,}3\ 10^{-10}$	$8{,}8\ 10^{-11}$	$6{,}1\ 10^{-11}$	$5{,}1\ 10^{-11}$
Co-62m	0,232 h	F	0,600	$1{,}4\ 10^{-10}$	0,100	$9{,}5\ 10^{-11}$	$4{,}5\ 10^{-11}$	$2{,}8\ 10^{-11}$	$1{,}7\ 10^{-11}$	$1{,}4\ 10^{-11}$
		M	0,200	$1{,}9\ 10^{-10}$	0,100	$1{,}3\ 10^{-10}$	$6{,}1\ 10^{-11}$	$3{,}8\ 10^{-11}$	$2{,}4\ 10^{-11}$	$2{,}0\ 10^{-11}$
		S	0,020	$2{,}0\ 10^{-10}$	0,010	$1{,}3\ 10^{-10}$	$6{,}3\ 10^{-11}$	$4{,}0\ 10^{-11}$	$2{,}5\ 10^{-11}$	$2{,}1\ 10^{-11}$
Nickel										
Ni-56	6,10 d	F	0,100	$3{,}3\ 10^{-9}$	0,050	$2{,}8\ 10^{-9}$	$1{,}5\ 10^{-9}$	$9{,}3\ 10^{-10}$	$5{,}8\ 10^{-10}$	$4{,}9\ 10^{-10}$
		M	0,100	$4{,}9\ 10^{-9}$	0,050	$4{,}1\ 10^{-9}$	$2{,}3\ 10^{-9}$	$1{,}5\ 10^{-9}$	$1{,}1\ 10^{-9}$	$8{,}7\ 10^{-10}$
		S	0,020	$5{,}5\ 10^{-9}$	0,010	$4{,}6\ 10^{-9}$	$2{,}7\ 10^{-9}$	$1{,}8\ 10^{-9}$	$1{,}3\ 10^{-9}$	$1{,}0\ 10^{-9}$
Ni-57	1,50 d	F	0,100	$2{,}2\ 10^{-9}$	0,050	$1{,}8\ 10^{-9}$	$8{,}9\ 10^{-10}$	$5{,}5\ 10^{-10}$	$3{,}1\ 10^{-10}$	$2{,}5\ 10^{-10}$
		M	0,100	$3{,}6\ 10^{-9}$	0,050	$2{,}8\ 10^{-9}$	$1{,}5\ 10^{-9}$	$9{,}5\ 10^{-10}$	$6{,}2\ 10^{-10}$	$5{,}0\ 10^{-10}$
		S	0,020	$3{,}9\ 10^{-9}$	0,010	$3{,}0\ 10^{-9}$	$1{,}5\ 10^{-9}$	$1{,}0\ 10^{-9}$	$6{,}6\ 10^{-10}$	$5{,}3\ 10^{-10}$
Ni-59	$7{,}50\ 10^{4}$ a	F	0,100	$9{,}6\ 10^{-10}$	0,050	$8{,}1\ 10^{-10}$	$4{,}5\ 10^{-10}$	$2{,}8\ 10^{-10}$	$1{,}9\ 10^{-10}$	$1{,}8\ 10^{-10}$
		M	0,100	$7{,}9\ 10^{-10}$	0,050	$6{,}2\ 10^{-10}$	$3{,}4\ 10^{-10}$	$2{,}1\ 10^{-10}$	$1{,}4\ 10^{-10}$	$1{,}3\ 10^{-10}$
		S	0,020	$1{,}7\ 10^{-9}$	0,010	$1{,}5\ 10^{-9}$	$9{,}5\ 10^{-10}$	$5{,}9\ 10^{-10}$	$4{,}6\ 10^{-10}$	$4{,}4\ 10^{-10}$
Ni-63	96,0 a	F	0,100	$2{,}3\ 10^{-9}$	0,050	$2{,}0\ 10^{-9}$	$1{,}1\ 10^{-9}$	$6{,}7\ 10^{-10}$	$4{,}6\ 10^{-10}$	$4{,}4\ 10^{-10}$
		M	0,100	$2{,}5\ 10^{-9}$	0,050	$1{,}9\ 10^{-9}$	$1{,}1\ 10^{-9}$	$7{,}0\ 10^{-10}$	$5{,}3\ 10^{-10}$	$4{,}8\ 10^{-10}$
		S	0,020	$4{,}8\ 10^{-9}$	0,010	$4{,}3\ 10^{-9}$	$2{,}7\ 10^{-9}$	$1{,}7\ 10^{-9}$	$1{,}3\ 10^{-9}$	$1{,}3\ 10^{-9}$
Ni-65	2,52 h	F	0,100	$4{,}4\ 10^{-10}$	0,050	$3{,}0\ 10^{-10}$	$1{,}4\ 10^{-10}$	$8{,}5\ 10^{-11}$	$4{,}9\ 10^{-11}$	$4{,}1\ 10^{-11}$
		M	0,100	$7{,}7\ 10^{-10}$	0,050	$5{,}2\ 10^{-10}$	$2{,}4\ 10^{-10}$	$1{,}6\ 10^{-10}$	$1{,}0\ 10^{-10}$	$8{,}5\ 10^{-11}$
		S	0,020	$8{,}1\ 10^{-10}$	0,010	$5{,}5\ 10^{-10}$	$2{,}6\ 10^{-10}$	$1{,}7\ 10^{-10}$	$1{,}1\ 10^{-10}$	$9{,}0\ 10^{-11}$
Ni-66	2,27 d	F	0,100	$5{,}7\ 10^{-9}$	0,050	$3{,}8\ 10^{-9}$	$1{,}6\ 10^{-9}$	$1{,}0\ 10^{-9}$	$5{,}1\ 10^{-10}$	$4{,}2\ 10^{-10}$
		M	0,100	$1{,}3\ 10^{-8}$	0,050	$9{,}4\ 10^{-9}$	$4{,}5\ 10^{-9}$	$2{,}9\ 10^{-9}$	$2{,}0\ 10^{-9}$	$1{,}6\ 10^{-9}$
		S	0,020	$1{,}5\ 10^{-8}$	0,010	$1{,}0\ 10^{-8}$	$5{,}0\ 10^{-9}$	$3{,}2\ 10^{-9}$	$2{,}2\ 10^{-9}$	$1{,}8\ 10^{-9}$

Nuclide	Physical half-life	Type	Age ≤ 1 a		Age	1—2 a	2—7 a	7—12 a	12—17 a	> 17 a
			f_1	h(g)	f_1	h(g)	h(g)	h(g)	h(g)	h(g)
Copper										
Cu-60	0,387 h	F	1,000	$2,1\ 10^{-10}$	0,500	$1,6\ 10^{-10}$	$7,5\ 10^{-11}$	$4,6\ 10^{-11}$	$2,8\ 10^{-11}$	$2,3\ 10^{-11}$
		M	1,000	$3,0\ 10^{-10}$	0,500	$2,2\ 10^{-10}$	$1,0\ 10^{-10}$	$6,5\ 10^{-11}$	$4,0\ 10^{-11}$	$3,3\ 10^{-11}$
		S	1,000	$3,1\ 10^{-10}$	0,500	$2,2\ 10^{-10}$	$1,1\ 10^{-10}$	$6,7\ 10^{-11}$	$4,2\ 10^{-11}$	$3,4\ 10^{-11}$
Cu-61	3,41 h	F	1,000	$3,1\ 10^{-10}$	0,500	$2,7\ 10^{-10}$	$1,3\ 10^{-10}$	$7,9\ 10^{-11}$	$4,5\ 10^{-11}$	$3,7\ 10^{-11}$
		M	1,000	$4,9\ 10^{-10}$	0,500	$4,4\ 10^{-10}$	$2,1\ 10^{-10}$	$1,4\ 10^{-10}$	$9,1\ 10^{-11}$	$7,4\ 10^{-11}$
		S	1,000	$5,1\ 10^{-10}$	0,500	$4,5\ 10^{-10}$	$2,2\ 10^{-10}$	$1,4\ 10^{-10}$	$9,6\ 10^{-11}$	$7,8\ 10^{-11}$
Cu-64	12,7 h	F	1,000	$2,8\ 10^{-10}$	0,500	$2,7\ 10^{-10}$	$1,2\ 10^{-10}$	$7,6\ 10^{-11}$	$4,2\ 10^{-11}$	$3,5\ 10^{-11}$
		M	1,000	$5,5\ 10^{-10}$	0,500	$5,4\ 10^{-10}$	$2,7\ 10^{-10}$	$1,9\ 10^{-10}$	$1,4\ 10^{-10}$	$1,1\ 10^{-10}$
		S	1,000	$5,8\ 10^{-10}$	0,500	$5,7\ 10^{-10}$	$2,9\ 10^{-10}$	$2,0\ 10^{-10}$	$1,3\ 10^{-10}$	$1,2\ 10^{-10}$
Cu-67	2,58 d	F	1,000	$9,5\ 10^{-10}$	0,500	$8,0\ 10^{-10}$	$3,5\ 10^{-10}$	$2,2\ 10^{-10}$	$1,2\ 10^{-10}$	$1,0\ 10^{-10}$
		M	1,000	$2,3\ 10^{-9}$	0,500	$2,0\ 10^{-9}$	$1,1\ 10^{-9}$	$8,1\ 10^{-10}$	$6,9\ 10^{-10}$	$5,5\ 10^{-10}$
		S	1,000	$2,5\ 10^{-9}$	0,500	$2,1\ 10^{-9}$	$1,2\ 10^{-9}$	$8,9\ 10^{-10}$	$7,7\ 10^{-10}$	$6,1\ 10^{-10}$
Zinc										
Zn-62	9,26 h	F	1,000	$1,7\ 10^{-9}$	0,500	$1,7\ 10^{-9}$	$7,7\ 10^{-10}$	$4,6\ 10^{-10}$	$2,5\ 10^{-10}$	$2,0\ 10^{-10}$
		M	0,200	$4,5\ 10^{-9}$	0,100	$3,5\ 10^{-9}$	$1,6\ 10^{-9}$	$1,0\ 10^{-9}$	$6,0\ 10^{-10}$	$5,0\ 10^{-10}$
		S	0,020	$5,1\ 10^{-9}$	0,010	$3,4\ 10^{-9}$	$1,8\ 10^{-9}$	$1,1\ 10^{-9}$	$6,6\ 10^{-10}$	$5,5\ 10^{-10}$
Zn-63	0,635 h	F	1,000	$2,1\ 10^{-10}$	0,500	$1,4\ 10^{-10}$	$6,5\ 10^{-11}$	$4,0\ 10^{-11}$	$2,4\ 10^{-11}$	$2,0\ 10^{-11}$
		M	0,200	$3,4\ 10^{-10}$	0,100	$2,3\ 10^{-10}$	$1,0\ 10^{-10}$	$6,6\ 10^{-11}$	$4,2\ 10^{-11}$	$3,5\ 10^{-11}$
		S	0,020	$3,6\ 10^{-10}$	0,010	$2,4\ 10^{-10}$	$1,1\ 10^{-10}$	$6,9\ 10^{-11}$	$4,4\ 10^{-11}$	$3,7\ 10^{-11}$
Zn-65	244 d	F	1,000	$1,5\ 10^{-8}$	0,500	$1,0\ 10^{-8}$	$5,7\ 10^{-9}$	$3,8\ 10^{-9}$	$2,5\ 10^{-9}$	$2,2\ 10^{-9}$
		M	0,200	$8,5\ 10^{-9}$	0,100	$6,5\ 10^{-9}$	$3,7\ 10^{-9}$	$2,4\ 10^{-9}$	$1,9\ 10^{-9}$	$1,6\ 10^{-9}$
		S	0,020	$7,6\ 10^{-9}$	0,010	$6,7\ 10^{-9}$	$4,4\ 10^{-9}$	$2,9\ 10^{-9}$	$2,4\ 10^{-9}$	$2,0\ 10^{-9}$
Zn-69	0,950 h	F	1,000	$1,1\ 10^{-10}$	0,500	$7,4\ 10^{-11}$	$3,2\ 10^{-11}$	$2,1\ 10^{-11}$	$1,2\ 10^{-11}$	$1,1\ 10^{-11}$
		M	0,200	$2,2\ 10^{-10}$	0,100	$1,4\ 10^{-10}$	$6,5\ 10^{-11}$	$4,4\ 10^{-11}$	$3,1\ 10^{-11}$	$2,6\ 10^{-11}$
		S	0,020	$2,3\ 10^{-10}$	0,010	$1,5\ 10^{-10}$	$6,9\ 10^{-11}$	$4,7\ 10^{-11}$	$3,4\ 10^{-11}$	$2,8\ 10^{-11}$

Nuclide	*Physical half-life*	*Type*	*Age ≤ 1 a*		*Age*	*1—2 a*	*2—7 a*	*7—12 a*	*12—17 a*	*> 17 a*
			f_1	*h(g)*	f_1	*h(g)*	*h(g)*	*h(g)*	*h(g)*	*h(g)*
Zn-69m	13,8 h	F	1,000	$6,6\ 10^{-10}$	0,500	$6,7\ 10^{-10}$	$3,0\ 10^{-10}$	$1,8\ 10^{-10}$	$9,9\ 10^{-11}$	$8,2\ 10^{-11}$
		M	0,200	$2,1\ 10^{-9}$	0,100	$1,5\ 10^{-9}$	$7,5\ 10^{-10}$	$5,0\ 10^{-10}$	$3,0\ 10^{-10}$	$2,4\ 10^{-10}$
		S	0,020	$2,2\ 10^{-9}$	0,010	$1,7\ 10^{-9}$	$8,2\ 10^{-10}$	$5,4\ 10^{-10}$	$3,3\ 10^{-10}$	$2,7\ 10^{-10}$
Zn-71m	3,92 h	F	1,000	$6,2\ 10^{-10}$	0,500	$5,5\ 10^{-10}$	$2,6\ 10^{-10}$	$1,6\ 10^{-10}$	$9,1\ 10^{-11}$	$7,4\ 10^{-11}$
		M	0,200	$1,3\ 10^{-9}$	0,100	$9,4\ 10^{-10}$	$4,6\ 10^{-10}$	$2,9\ 10^{-10}$	$1,9\ 10^{-10}$	$1,5\ 10^{-10}$
		S	0,020	$1,4\ 10^{-9}$	0,010	$1,0\ 10^{-9}$	$4,9\ 10^{-10}$	$3,1\ 10^{-10}$	$2,0\ 10^{-10}$	$1,6\ 10^{-10}$
Zn-72	1,94 d	F	1,000	$4,3\ 10^{-9}$	0,500	$3,5\ 10^{-9}$	$1,7\ 10^{-9}$	$1,0\ 10^{-9}$	$5,9\ 10^{-10}$	$4,9\ 10^{-10}$
		M	0,200	$8,8\ 10^{-9}$	0,100	$6,5\ 10^{-9}$	$3,4\ 10^{-9}$	$2,3\ 10^{-9}$	$1,5\ 10^{-9}$	$1,2\ 10^{-9}$
		S	0,020	$9,7\ 10^{-9}$	0,010	$7,0\ 10^{-9}$	$3,6\ 10^{-9}$	$2,4\ 10^{-9}$	$1,6\ 10^{-9}$	$1,3\ 10^{-9}$
Gallium										
Ga-65	0,253 h	F	0,010	$1,1\ 10^{-10}$	0,001	$7,3\ 10^{-11}$	$3,4\ 10^{-11}$	$2,1\ 10^{-11}$	$1,3\ 10^{-11}$	$1,1\ 10^{-11}$
		M	0,010	$1,6\ 10^{-10}$	0,001	$1,1\ 10^{-10}$	$4,8\ 10^{-11}$	$3,1\ 10^{-11}$	$2,0\ 10^{-11}$	$1,7\ 10^{-11}$
Ga-66	9,40 h	F	0,010	$2,8\ 10^{-9}$	0,001	$2,0\ 10^{-9}$	$9,2\ 10^{-10}$	$5,7\ 10^{-10}$	$3,0\ 10^{-10}$	$2,5\ 10^{-10}$
		M	0,010	$4,5\ 10^{-9}$	0,001	$3,1\ 10^{-9}$	$1,5\ 10^{-9}$	$9,2\ 10^{-10}$	$5,3\ 10^{-10}$	$4,4\ 10^{-10}$
Ga-67	3,26 d	F	0,010	$6,4\ 10^{-10}$	0,001	$4,6\ 10^{-10}$	$2,2\ 10^{-10}$	$1,4\ 10^{-10}$	$7,7\ 10^{-11}$	$6,4\ 10^{-11}$
		M	0,010	$1,4\ 10^{-9}$	0,001	$1,0\ 10^{-9}$	$5,0\ 10^{-10}$	$3,6\ 10^{-10}$	$3,0\ 10^{-10}$	$2,4\ 10^{-10}$
Ga-68	1,13 h	F	0,010	$2,9\ 10^{-10}$	0,001	$1,9\ 10^{-10}$	$8,8\ 10^{-11}$	$5,4\ 10^{-11}$	$3,1\ 10^{-11}$	$2,6\ 10^{-11}$
		M	0,010	$4,6\ 10^{-10}$	0,001	$3,1\ 10^{-10}$	$1,4\ 10^{-10}$	$9,2\ 10^{-11}$	$5,9\ 10^{-11}$	$4,9\ 10^{-11}$
Ga-70	0,353 h	F	0,010	$9,5\ 10^{-11}$	0,001	$6,0\ 10^{-11}$	$2,6\ 10^{-11}$	$1,6\ 10^{-11}$	$1,0\ 10^{-11}$	$8,8\ 10^{-12}$
		M	0,010	$1,5\ 10^{-10}$	0,001	$9,6\ 10^{-11}$	$4,3\ 10^{-11}$	$2,8\ 10^{-11}$	$1,8\ 10^{-11}$	$1,6\ 10^{-11}$
Ga-72	14,1 h	F	0,010	$2,9\ 10^{-9}$	0,001	$2,2\ 10^{-9}$	$1,0\ 10^{-9}$	$6,4\ 10^{-10}$	$3,6\ 10^{-10}$	$2,9\ 10^{-10}$
		M	0,010	$4,5\ 10^{-9}$	0,001	$3,3\ 10^{-9}$	$1,6\ 10^{-9}$	$1,0\ 10^{-9}$	$6,5\ 10^{-10}$	$5,3\ 10^{-10}$
Ga-73	4,91 h	F	0,010	$6,7\ 10^{-10}$	0,001	$4,5\ 10^{-10}$	$2,0\ 10^{-10}$	$1,2\ 10^{-10}$	$6,4\ 10^{-11}$	$5,4\ 10^{-11}$
		M	0,010	$1,2\ 10^{-9}$	0,001	$8,4\ 10^{-10}$	$4,0\ 10^{-10}$	$2,6\ 10^{-10}$	$1,7\ 10^{-10}$	$1,4\ 10^{-10}$

Nuclide	Physical half-life	Type	Age ≤ 1 a		Age	1—2 a	2—7 a	7—12 a	12—17 a	> 17 a
			f_1	$h(g)$	f_1	$h(g)$	$h(g)$	$h(g)$	$h(g)$	$h(g)$
Germanium										
Ge-66	2,27 h	F	1,000	$4,5\ 10^{-10}$	1,000	$3,5\ 10^{-10}$	$1,8\ 10^{-10}$	$1,1\ 10^{-10}$	$6,7\ 10^{-11}$	$5,4\ 10^{-11}$
		M	1,000	$6,4\ 10^{-10}$	1,000	$4,8\ 10^{-10}$	$2,5\ 10^{-10}$	$1,6\ 10^{-10}$	$1,1\ 10^{-10}$	$9,1\ 10^{-11}$
Ge-67	0,312 h	F	1,000	$1,7\ 10^{-10}$	1,000	$1,1\ 10^{-10}$	$4,9\ 10^{-11}$	$3,1\ 10^{-11}$	$1,8\ 10^{-11}$	$1,5\ 10^{-11}$
		M	1,000	$2,5\ 10^{-10}$	1,000	$1,6\ 10^{-10}$	$7,3\ 10^{-11}$	$4,6\ 10^{-11}$	$2,9\ 10^{-11}$	$2,5\ 10^{-11}$
Ge-68	288 d	F	1,000	$5,4\ 10^{-9}$	1,000	$3,8\ 10^{-9}$	$1,8\ 10^{-9}$	$1,1\ 10^{-9}$	$6,3\ 10^{-10}$	$5,2\ 10^{-10}$
		M	1,000	$6,0\ 10^{-8}$	1,000	$5,0\ 10^{-8}$	$3,0\ 10^{-8}$	$2,0\ 10^{-8}$	$1,6\ 10^{-8}$	$1,4\ 10^{-8}$
Ge-69	1,63 d	F	1,000	$1,2\ 10^{-9}$	1,000	$9,0\ 10^{-10}$	$4,6\ 10^{-10}$	$2,8\ 10^{-10}$	$1,7\ 10^{-10}$	$1,3\ 10^{-10}$
		M	1,000	$1,8\ 10^{-9}$	1,000	$1,4\ 10^{-9}$	$7,4\ 10^{-10}$	$4,9\ 10^{-10}$	$3,6\ 10^{-10}$	$2,9\ 10^{-10}$
Ge-71	11,8 d	F	1,000	$6,0\ 10^{-11}$	1,000	$4,3\ 10^{-11}$	$2,0\ 10^{-11}$	$1,1\ 10^{-11}$	$6,1\ 10^{-12}$	$4,8\ 10^{-12}$
		M	1,000	$1,2\ 10^{-10}$	1,000	$8,6\ 10^{-11}$	$4,1\ 10^{-11}$	$2,4\ 10^{-11}$	$1,3\ 10^{-11}$	$1,1\ 10^{-11}$
Ge-75	1,38 h	F	1,000	$1,6\ 10^{-10}$	1,000	$1,0\ 10^{-10}$	$4,3\ 10^{-11}$	$2,8\ 10^{-11}$	$1,7\ 10^{-11}$	$1,5\ 10^{-11}$
		M	1,000	$2,9\ 10^{-10}$	1,000	$1,9\ 10^{-10}$	$8,9\ 10^{-11}$	$6,1\ 10^{-11}$	$4,4\ 10^{-11}$	$3,6\ 10^{-11}$
Ge-77	11,3 h	F	1,000	$1,3\ 10^{-9}$	1,000	$9,5\ 10^{-10}$	$4,7\ 10^{-10}$	$2,9\ 10^{-10}$	$1,7\ 10^{-10}$	$1,4\ 10^{-10}$
		M	1,000	$2,3\ 10^{-9}$	1,000	$1,7\ 10^{-9}$	$8,8\ 10^{-10}$	$6,0\ 10^{-10}$	$4,5\ 10^{-10}$	$3,7\ 10^{-10}$
Ge-78	1,45 h	F	1,000	$4,3\ 10^{-10}$	1,000	$2,9\ 10^{-10}$	$1,4\ 10^{-10}$	$8,9\ 10^{-11}$	$5,5\ 10^{-11}$	$4,5\ 10^{-11}$
		M	1,000	$7,3\ 10^{-10}$	1,000	$5,0\ 10^{-10}$	$2,5\ 10^{-10}$	$1,6\ 10^{-10}$	$1,2\ 10^{-10}$	$9,5\ 10^{-11}$
Arsenic										
As-69	0,253 h	M	1,000	$2,1\ 10^{-10}$	0,500	$1,4\ 10^{-10}$	$6,3\ 10^{-11}$	$4,0\ 10^{-11}$	$2,5\ 10^{-11}$	$2,1\ 10^{-11}$
As-70	0,876 h	M	1,000	$5,7\ 10^{-10}$	0,500	$4,3\ 10^{-10}$	$2,1\ 10^{-10}$	$1,3\ 10^{-10}$	$8,3\ 10^{-11}$	$6,7\ 10^{-11}$
As-71	2,70 d	M	1,000	$2,2\ 10^{-9}$	0,500	$1,9\ 10^{-9}$	$1,0\ 10^{-9}$	$6,8\ 10^{-10}$	$5,0\ 10^{-10}$	$4,0\ 10^{-10}$
As-72	1,08 d	M	1,000	$5,9\ 10^{-9}$	0,500	$5,7\ 10^{-9}$	$2,7\ 10^{-9}$	$1,7\ 10^{-9}$	$1,1\ 10^{-9}$	$9,0\ 10^{-10}$
As-73	80,3 d	M	1,000	$5,4\ 10^{-9}$	0,500	$4,0\ 10^{-9}$	$2,3\ 10^{-9}$	$1,5\ 10^{-9}$	$1,2\ 10^{-9}$	$1,0\ 10^{-9}$
As-74	17,8 d	M	1,000	$1,1\ 10^{-8}$	0,500	$8,4\ 10^{-9}$	$4,7\ 10^{-9}$	$3,3\ 10^{-9}$	$2,6\ 10^{-9}$	$2,1\ 10^{-9}$
As-76	1,10 d	M	1,000	$5,1\ 10^{-9}$	0,500	$4,6\ 10^{-9}$	$2,2\ 10^{-9}$	$1,4\ 10^{-9}$	$8,8\ 10^{-10}$	$7,4\ 10^{-10}$

Nuclide	*Physical half-life*	*Type*	*Age ≤ 1 a*		*Age*	*1—2 a*	*2—7 a*	*7—12 a*	*12—17 a*	*> 17 a*
			f_1	*h(g)*	f_1	*h(g)*	*h(g)*	*h(g)*	*h(g)*	*h(g)*
As-77	1,62 d	M	1,000	2,2 10^{-9}	0,500	1,7 10^{-9}	8,9 10^{-10}	6,2 10^{-10}	5,0 10^{-10}	3,9 10^{-10}
As-78	1,51 h	M	1,000	8,0 10^{-10}	0,500	5,8 10^{-10}	2,7 10^{-10}	1,7 10^{-10}	1,1 10^{-10}	8,9 10^{-11}
Selenium										
Se-70	0,683 h	F	1,000	3,9 10^{-10}	0,800	3,0 10^{-10}	1,5 10^{-10}	9,0 10^{-11}	5,1 10^{-11}	4,2 10^{-11}
		M	0,200	6,5 10^{-10}	0,100	4,7 10^{-10}	2,3 10^{-10}	1,4 10^{-10}	8,9 10^{-11}	7,3 10^{-11}
		S	0,020	6,8 10^{-10}	0,010	4,8 10^{-10}	2,3 10^{-10}	1,5 10^{-10}	9,4 10^{-11}	7,6 10^{-11}
Se-73	7,15 h	F	1,000	7,7 10^{-10}	0,800	6,5 10^{-10}	3,3 10^{-10}	2,1 10^{-10}	1,0 10^{-10}	8,0 10^{-11}
		M	0,200	1,6 10^{-9}	0,100	1,2 10^{-9}	5,9 10^{-10}	3,8 10^{-10}	2,4 10^{-10}	1,9 10^{-10}
		S	0,020	1,8 10^{-9}	0,010	1,3 10^{-9}	6,3 10^{-10}	4,0 10^{-10}	2,6 10^{-10}	2,1 10^{-10}
Se-73m	0,650 h	F	1,000	9,3 10^{-11}	0,800	7,2 10^{-11}	3,5 10^{-11}	2,3 10^{-11}	1,1 10^{-11}	9,2 10^{-12}
		M	0,200	1,8 10^{-10}	0,100	1,3 10^{-10}	6,1 10^{-11}	3,9 10^{-11}	2,5 10^{-11}	2,0 10^{-11}
		S	0,020	1,9 10^{-10}	0,010	1,3 10^{-10}	6,5 10^{-11}	4,1 10^{-11}	2,6 10^{-11}	2,2 10^{-11}
Se-75	120 d	F	1,000	7,8 10^{-9}	0,800	6,0 10^{-9}	3,4 10^{-9}	2,5 10^{-9}	1,2 10^{-9}	1,0 10^{-9}
		M	0,200	5,4 10^{-9}	0,100	4,5 10^{-9}	2,5 10^{-9}	1,7 10^{-9}	1,3 10^{-9}	1,1 10^{-9}
		S	0,020	5,6 10^{-9}	0,010	4,7 10^{-9}	2,9 10^{-9}	2,0 10^{-9}	1,6 10^{-9}	1,3 10^{-9}
Se-79	6,50 10^{4} a	F	1,000	1,6 10^{-8}	0,800	1,3 10^{-8}	7,7 10^{-9}	5,6 10^{-9}	1,5 10^{-9}	1,1 10^{-9}
		M	0,200	1,4 10^{-8}	0,100	1,1 10^{-8}	6,9 10^{-9}	4,9 10^{-9}	3,3 10^{-9}	2,6 10^{-9}
		S	0,020	2,3 10^{-8}	0,010	2,0 10^{-8}	1,3 10^{-8}	8,7 10^{-9}	7,6 10^{-9}	6,8 10^{-9}
Se-81	0,308 h	F	1,000	8,6 10^{-11}	0,800	5,4 10^{-11}	2,3 10^{-11}	1,5 10^{-11}	9,2 10^{-12}	8,0 10^{-12}
		M	0,200	1,3 10^{-10}	0,100	8,5 10^{-11}	3,8 10^{-11}	2,5 10^{-11}	1,6 10^{-11}	1,4 10^{-11}
		S	0,020	1,4 10^{-10}	0,010	8,9 10^{-11}	3,9 10^{-11}	2,6 10^{-11}	1,7 10^{-11}	1,5 10^{-11}
Se-81m	0,954 h	F	1,000	1,8 10^{-10}	0,800	1,2 10^{-10}	5,4 10^{-11}	3,4 10^{-11}	1,9 10^{-11}	1,6 10^{-11}
		M	0,200	3,8 10^{-10}	0,100	2,5 10^{-10}	1,2 10^{-10}	8,0 10^{-11}	5,8 10^{-11}	4,7 10^{-11}
		S	0,020	4,1 10^{-10}	0,010	2,7 10^{-10}	1,3 10^{-10}	8,5 10^{-11}	6,2 10^{-11}	5,1 10^{-11}

Nuclide	Physical half-life	Type	Age ≤ 1 a		Age	1—2 a	2—7 a	7—12 a	12—17 a	> 17 a
			f_1	h(g)	f_1	h(g)	h(g)	h(g)	h(g)	h(g)
Se-83	0,375 h	F	1,000	$1,7\ 10^{-10}$	0,800	$1,2\ 10^{-10}$	$5,8\ 10^{-11}$	$3,6\ 10^{-11}$	$2,1\ 10^{-11}$	$1,8\ 10^{-11}$
		M	0,200	$2,7\ 10^{-10}$	0,100	$1,9\ 10^{-10}$	$9,2\ 10^{-11}$	$5,9\ 10^{-11}$	$3,9\ 10^{-11}$	$3,2\ 10^{-11}$
		S	0,020	$2,8\ 10^{-10}$	0,010	$2,0\ 10^{-10}$	$9,6\ 10^{-11}$	$6,2\ 10^{-11}$	$4,1\ 10^{-11}$	$3,4\ 10^{-11}$
Bromine										
Br-74	0,422 h	F	1,000	$2,5\ 10^{-10}$	1,000	$1,8\ 10^{-10}$	$8,6\ 10^{-11}$	$5,3\ 10^{-11}$	$3,2\ 10^{-11}$	$2,6\ 10^{-11}$
		M	1,000	$3,6\ 10^{-10}$	1,000	$2,5\ 10^{-10}$	$1,2\ 10^{-10}$	$7,5\ 10^{-11}$	$4,6\ 10^{-11}$	$3,8\ 10^{-11}$
Br-74m	0,691 h	F	1,000	$4,0\ 10^{-10}$	1,000	$2,8\ 10^{-10}$	$1,3\ 10^{-10}$	$8,1\ 10^{-11}$	$4,8\ 10^{-11}$	$3,9\ 10^{-11}$
		M	1,000	$5,9\ 10^{-10}$	1,000	$4,1\ 10^{-10}$	$1,9\ 10^{-10}$	$1,2\ 10^{-10}$	$7,5\ 10^{-11}$	$6,2\ 10^{-11}$
Br-75	1,63 h	F	1,000	$2,9\ 10^{-10}$	1,000	$2,1\ 10^{-10}$	$9,7\ 10^{-11}$	$5,9\ 10^{-11}$	$3,5\ 10^{-11}$	$2,9\ 10^{-11}$
		M	1,000	$4,5\ 10^{-10}$	1,000	$3,1\ 10^{-10}$	$1,5\ 10^{-10}$	$9,7\ 10^{-11}$	$6,5\ 10^{-11}$	$5,3\ 10^{-11}$
Br-76	16,2 h	F	1,000	$2,2\ 10^{-9}$	1,000	$1,7\ 10^{-9}$	$8,4\ 10^{-10}$	$5,1\ 10^{-10}$	$3,0\ 10^{-10}$	$2,4\ 10^{-10}$
		M	1,000	$3,0\ 10^{-9}$	1,000	$2,3\ 10^{-9}$	$1,2\ 10^{-9}$	$7,5\ 10^{-10}$	$5,0\ 10^{-10}$	$4,1\ 10^{-10}$
Br-77	2,33 d	F	1,000	$5,3\ 10^{-10}$	1,000	$4,4\ 10^{-10}$	$2,2\ 10^{-10}$	$1,3\ 10^{-10}$	$7,7\ 10^{-11}$	$6,2\ 10^{-11}$
		M	1,000	$6,3\ 10^{-10}$	1,000	$5,1\ 10^{-10}$	$2,7\ 10^{-10}$	$1,6\ 10^{-10}$	$1,1\ 10^{-10}$	$8,4\ 10^{-11}$
Br-80	0,290 h	F	1,000	$7,1\ 10^{-11}$	1,000	$4,4\ 10^{-11}$	$1,8\ 10^{-11}$	$1,2\ 10^{-11}$	$6,9\ 10^{-12}$	$5,9\ 10^{-12}$
		M	1,000	$1,1\ 10^{-10}$	1,000	$6,5\ 10^{-11}$	$2,8\ 10^{-11}$	$1,8\ 10^{-11}$	$1,1\ 10^{-11}$	$9,4\ 10^{-12}$
Br-80m	4,42 h	F	1,000	$4,3\ 10^{-10}$	1,000	$2,8\ 10^{-10}$	$1,2\ 10^{-10}$	$7,2\ 10^{-11}$	$4,0\ 10^{-11}$	$3,3\ 10^{-11}$
		M	1,000	$6,8\ 10^{-10}$	1,000	$4,5\ 10^{-10}$	$2,1\ 10^{-10}$	$1,4\ 10^{-10}$	$9,3\ 10^{-11}$	$7,6\ 10^{-11}$
Br-82	1,47 d	F	1,000	$2,7\ 10^{-9}$	1,000	$2,2\ 10^{-9}$	$1,2\ 10^{-9}$	$7,0\ 10^{-10}$	$4,2\ 10^{-10}$	$3,5\ 10^{-10}$
		M	1,000	$3,8\ 10^{-9}$	1,000	$3,0\ 10^{-9}$	$1,7\ 10^{-9}$	$1,1\ 10^{-9}$	$7,9\ 10^{-10}$	$6,3\ 10^{-10}$
Br-83	2,39 h	F	1,000	$1,7\ 10^{-10}$	1,000	$1,1\ 10^{-10}$	$4,7\ 10^{-11}$	$3,0\ 10^{-11}$	$1,8\ 10^{-11}$	$1,6\ 10^{-11}$
		M	1,000	$3,5\ 10^{-10}$	1,000	$2,3\ 10^{-10}$	$1,1\ 10^{-10}$	$7,7\ 10^{-11}$	$5,9\ 10^{-11}$	$4,8\ 10^{-11}$
Br-84	0,530 h	F	1,000	$2,4\ 10^{-10}$	1,000	$1,6\ 10^{-10}$	$7,1\ 10^{-11}$	$4,4\ 10^{-11}$	$2,6\ 10^{-11}$	$2,2\ 10^{-11}$
		M	1,000	$3,7\ 10^{-10}$	1,000	$2,4\ 10^{-10}$	$1,1\ 10^{-10}$	$6,9\ 10^{-11}$	$4,4\ 10^{-11}$	$3,7\ 10^{-11}$

Nuclide	*Physical half-life*	*Type*	*Age ≤ 1 a*		*Age*	*1—2 a*	*2—7 a*	*7—12 a*	*12—17 a*	*> 17 a*
			f_1	$h(g)$	f_1	$h(g)$	$h(g)$	$h(g)$	$h(g)$	$h(g)$
Rubidium										
Rb-79	0,382 h	F	1,000	$1,6\ 10^{-10}$	1,000	$1,1\ 10^{-10}$	$5,0\ 10^{-11}$	$3,2\ 10^{-11}$	$1,9\ 10^{-11}$	$1,6\ 10^{-11}$
Rb-81	4,58 h	F	1,000	$3,2\ 10^{-10}$	1,000	$2,5\ 10^{-10}$	$1,2\ 10^{-10}$	$7,1\ 10^{-11}$	$4,2\ 10^{-11}$	$3,4\ 10^{-11}$
Rb-81m	0,533 h	F	1,000	$6,2\ 10^{-11}$	1,000	$4,6\ 10^{-11}$	$2,2\ 10^{-11}$	$1,4\ 10^{-11}$	$8,5\ 10^{-12}$	$7,0\ 10^{-12}$
Rb-82m	6,20 h	F	1,000	$8,6\ 10^{-10}$	1,000	$7,3\ 10^{-10}$	$3,9\ 10^{-10}$	$2,3\ 10^{-10}$	$1,4\ 10^{-10}$	$1,1\ 10^{-10}$
Rb-83	86,2 d	F	1,000	$4,9\ 10^{-9}$	1,000	$3,8\ 10^{-9}$	$2,0\ 10^{-9}$	$1,3\ 10^{-9}$	$7,9\ 10^{-10}$	$6,9\ 10^{-10}$
Rb-84	32,8 d	F	1,000	$8,6\ 10^{-9}$	1,000	$6,4\ 10^{-9}$	$3,1\ 10^{-9}$	$2,0\ 10^{-9}$	$1,2\ 10^{-9}$	$1,0\ 10^{-9}$
Rb-86	18,7 d	F	1,000	$1,2\ 10^{-8}$	1,000	$7,7\ 10^{-9}$	$3,4\ 10^{-9}$	$2,0\ 10^{-9}$	$1,1\ 10^{-9}$	$9,3\ 10^{-10}$
Rb-87	$4,70\ 10^{10}$ a	F	1,000	$6,0\ 10^{-9}$	1,000	$4,1\ 10^{-9}$	$1,8\ 10^{-9}$	$1,1\ 10^{-9}$	$6,0\ 10^{-10}$	$5,0\ 10^{-10}$
Rb-88	0,297 h	F	1,000	$1,9\ 10^{-10}$	1,000	$1,2\ 10^{-10}$	$5,2\ 10^{-11}$	$3,2\ 10^{-11}$	$1,9\ 10^{-11}$	$1,6\ 10^{-11}$
Rb-89	0,253 h	F	1,000	$1,4\ 10^{-10}$	1,000	$9,3\ 10^{-11}$	$4,3\ 10^{-11}$	$2,7\ 10^{-11}$	$1,6\ 10^{-11}$	$1,4\ 10^{-11}$
Strontium(d)										
Sr-80	1,67 h	F	0,600	$7,8\ 10^{-10}$	0,300	$5,4\ 10^{-10}$	$2,4\ 10^{-10}$	$1,4\ 10^{-10}$	$7,9\ 10^{-11}$	$7,1\ 10^{-11}$
		M	0,200	$1,4\ 10^{-9}$	0,100	$9,0\ 10^{-10}$	$4,1\ 10^{-10}$	$2,5\ 10^{-10}$	$1,5\ 10^{-10}$	$1,3\ 10^{-10}$
		S	0,020	$1,5\ 10^{-9}$	0,010	$9,4\ 10^{-10}$	$4,3\ 10^{-10}$	$2,7\ 10^{-10}$	$1,6\ 10^{-10}$	$1,4\ 10^{-10}$
Sr-81	0,425 h	F	0,600	$2,1\ 10^{-10}$	0,300	$1,5\ 10^{-10}$	$6,7\ 10^{-11}$	$4,1\ 10^{-11}$	$2,4\ 10^{-11}$	$2,1\ 10^{-11}$
		M	0,200	$3,3\ 10^{-10}$	0,100	$2,2\ 10^{-10}$	$1,0\ 10^{-10}$	$6,6\ 10^{-11}$	$4,2\ 10^{-11}$	$3,5\ 10^{-11}$
		S	0,020	$3,4\ 10^{-10}$	0,010	$2,3\ 10^{-10}$	$1,1\ 10^{-10}$	$6,9\ 10^{-11}$	$4,4\ 10^{-11}$	$3,7\ 10^{-11}$
Sr-82	25,0 d	F	0,600	$2,8\ 10^{-8}$	0,300	$1,5\ 10^{-8}$	$6,6\ 10^{-9}$	$4,6\ 10^{-9}$	$3,2\ 10^{-9}$	$2,1\ 10^{-9}$
		M	0,200	$5,5\ 10^{-8}$	0,100	$4,0\ 10^{-8}$	$2,1\ 10^{-8}$	$1,4\ 10^{-8}$	$1,0\ 10^{-8}$	$8,9\ 10^{-9}$
		S	0,020	$6,1\ 10^{-8}$	0,010	$4,6\ 10^{-8}$	$2,5\ 10^{-8}$	$1,7\ 10^{-8}$	$1,2\ 10^{-8}$	$1,1\ 10^{-8}$
Sr-83	1,35 d	F	0,600	$1,4\ 10^{-9}$	0,300	$1,1\ 10^{-9}$	$5,5\ 10^{-10}$	$3,4\ 10^{-10}$	$2,0\ 10^{-10}$	$1,6\ 10^{-10}$
		M	0,200	$2,5\ 10^{-9}$	0,100	$1,9\ 10^{-9}$	$9,5\ 10^{-10}$	$6,0\ 10^{-10}$	$3,9\ 10^{-10}$	$3,1\ 10^{-10}$
		S	0,020	$2,8\ 10^{-9}$	0,010	$2,0\ 10^{-9}$	$1,0\ 10^{-9}$	$6,5\ 10^{-10}$	$4,2\ 10^{-10}$	$3,4\ 10^{-10}$

Nuclide	*Physical half-life*	*Type*	*Age ≤ 1 a*		*Age*	*1—2 a*	*2—7 a*	*7—12 a*	*12—17 a*	*> 17 a*
			f_1	*h(g)*	f_1	*h(g)*	*h(g)*	*h(g)*	*h(g)*	*h(g)*
Sr-85	64,8 d	F	0,600	4,4 10^{-9}	0,300	2,3 10^{-9}	1,1 10^{-9}	9,6 10^{-10}	8,3 10^{-10}	3,8 10^{-10}
		M	0,200	4,3 10^{-9}	0,100	3,1 10^{-9}	1,8 10^{-9}	1,2 10^{-9}	8,8 10^{-10}	6,4 10^{-10}
		S	0,020	4,4 10^{-9}	0,010	3,7 10^{-9}	2,2 10^{-9}	1,3 10^{-9}	1,0 10^{-9}	8,1 10^{-10}
Sr-85m	1,16 h	F	0,600	2,4 10^{-11}	0,300	1,9 10^{-11}	9,6 10^{-12}	6,0 10^{-12}	3,7 10^{-12}	2,9 10^{-12}
		M	0,200	3,1 10^{-11}	0,100	2,5 10^{-11}	1,3 10^{-11}	8,0 10^{-12}	5,1 10^{-12}	4,1 10^{-12}
		S	0,020	3,2 10^{-11}	0,010	2,6 10^{-11}	1,3 10^{-11}	8,3 10^{-12}	5,4 10^{-12}	4,3 10^{-12}
Sr-87m	2,80 h	F	0,600	9,7 10^{-11}	0,300	7,8 10^{-11}	3,8 10^{-11}	2,3 10^{-11}	1,3 10^{-11}	1,1 10^{-11}
		M	0,200	1,6 10^{-10}	0,100	1,2 10^{-10}	5,9 10^{-11}	3,8 10^{-11}	2,5 10^{-11}	2,0 10^{-11}
		S	0,020	1,7 10^{-10}	0,010	1,2 10^{-10}	6,2 10^{-11}	4,0 10^{-11}	2,6 10^{-11}	2,1 10^{-11}
Sr-89	50,5 d	F	0,600	1,5 10^{-8}	0,300	7,3 10^{-9}	3,2 10^{-9}	2,3 10^{-9}	1,7 10^{-9}	1,0 10^{-9}
		M	0,200	3,3 10^{-8}	0,100	2,4 10^{-8}	1,3 10^{-8}	9,1 10^{-9}	7,3 10^{-9}	6,1 10^{-9}
		S	0,020	3,9 10^{-8}	0,010	3,0 10^{-8}	1,7 10^{-8}	1,2 10^{-8}	9,3 10^{-9}	7,9 10^{-9}
Sr-90	29,1 a	F	0,600	1,3 10^{-7}	0,300	5,2 10^{-8}	3,1 10^{-8}	4,1 10^{-8}	5,3 10^{-8}	2,4 10^{-8}
		M	0,200	1,5 10^{-7}	0,100	1,1 10^{-7}	6,5 10^{-8}	5,1 10^{-8}	5,0 10^{-8}	3,6 10^{-8}
		S	0,020	4,2 10^{-7}	0,010	4,0 10^{-7}	2,7 10^{-7}	1,8 10^{-7}	1,6 10^{-7}	1,6 10^{-7}
Sr-91	9,50 h	F	0,600	1,4 10^{-9}	0,300	1,1 10^{-9}	5,2 10^{-10}	3,1 10^{-10}	1,7 10^{-10}	1,6 10^{-10}
		M	0,200	3,1 10^{-9}	0,100	2,2 10^{-9}	1,1 10^{-9}	6,9 10^{-10}	4,4 10^{-10}	3,7 10^{-10}
		S	0,020	3,5 10^{-9}	0,010	2,5 10^{-9}	1,2 10^{-9}	7,7 10^{-10}	4,9 10^{-10}	4,1 10^{-10}
Sr-92	2,71 h	F	0,600	9,0 10^{-10}	0,300	7,1 10^{-10}	3,3 10^{-10}	2,0 10^{-10}	1,0 10^{-10}	9,8 10^{-11}
		M	0,200	1,9 10^{-9}	0,100	1,4 10^{-9}	6,5 10^{-10}	4,1 10^{-10}	2,5 10^{-10}	2,1 10^{-10}
		S	0,020	2,2 10^{-9}	0,010	1,5 10^{-9}	7,0 10^{-10}	4,5 10^{-10}	2,7 10^{-10}	2,3 10^{-10}
Yttrium										
Y-86	14,7 h	M	0,001	3,7 10^{-9}	1,0 10^{-4}	2,9 10^{-9}	1,5 10^{-9}	9,3 10^{-10}	5,6 10^{-10}	4,5 10^{-10}
		S	0,001	3,8 10^{-9}	1,0 10^{-4}	3,0 10^{-9}	1,5 10^{-9}	9,6 10^{-10}	5,8 10^{-10}	4,7 10^{-10}
Y-86m	0,800 h	M	0,001	2,2 10^{-10}	1,0 10^{-4}	1,7 10^{-10}	8,7 10^{-11}	5,6 10^{-11}	3,4 10^{-11}	2,7 10^{-11}
		S	0,001	2,3 10^{-10}	1,0 10^{-4}	1,8 10^{-10}	9,0 10^{-11}	5,7 10^{-11}	3,5 10^{-11}	2,8 10^{-11}

Nuclide	Physical half-life	Type	Age ≤ 1 a		Age	1—2 a	2—7 a	7—12 a	12—17 a	> 17 a
			f_1	h(g)	f_1	h(g)	h(g)	h(g)	h(g)	h(g)
Y-87	3,35 d	M	0,001	2,7 10^{-9}	1,0 10^{-4}	2,1 10^{-9}	1,1 10^{-9}	7,0 10^{-10}	4,7 10^{-10}	3,7 10^{-10}
		S	0,001	2,8 10^{-9}	1,0 10^{-4}	2,2 10^{-9}	1,1 10^{-9}	7,3 10^{-10}	5,0 10^{-10}	3,9 10^{-10}
Y-88	107 d	M	0,001	1,9 10^{-8}	1,0 10^{-4}	1,6 10^{-8}	1,0 10^{-8}	6,7 10^{-9}	4,9 10^{-9}	4,1 10^{-9}
		S	0,001	2,0 10^{-8}	1,0 10^{-4}	1,7 10^{-8}	9,8 10^{-9}	6,6 10^{-9}	5,4 10^{-9}	4,4 10^{-9}
Y-90	2,67 d	M	0,001	1,3 10^{-8}	1,0 10^{-4}	8,4 10^{-9}	4,0 10^{-9}	2,6 10^{-9}	1,7 10^{-9}	1,4 10^{-9}
		S	0,001	1,3 10^{-8}	1,0 10^{-4}	8,8 10^{-9}	4,2 10^{-9}	2,7 10^{-9}	1,8 10^{-9}	1,5 10^{-9}
Y-90m	3,19 h	M	0,001	7,2 10^{-10}	1,0 10^{-4}	5,7 10^{-10}	2,8 10^{-10}	1,8 10^{-10}	1,1 10^{-10}	9,5 10^{-11}
		S	0,001	7,5 10^{-10}	1,0 10^{-4}	6,0 10^{-10}	2,9 10^{-10}	1,9 10^{-10}	1,2 10^{-10}	1,0 10^{-10}
Y-91	58,5 d	M	0,001	3,9 10^{-8}	1,0 10^{-4}	3,0 10^{-8}	1,6 10^{-8}	1,1 10^{-8}	8,4 10^{-9}	7,1 10^{-9}
		S	0,001	4,3 10^{-8}	1,0 10^{-4}	3,4 10^{-8}	1,9 10^{-8}	1,3 10^{-8}	1,0 10^{-8}	8,9 10^{-9}
Y-91m	0,828 h	M	0,001	7,0 10^{-11}	1,0 10^{-4}	5,5 10^{-11}	2,9 10^{-11}	1,8 10^{-11}	1,2 10^{-11}	1,0 10^{-11}
		S	0,001	7,4 10^{-11}	1,0 10^{-4}	5,9 10^{-11}	3,1 10^{-11}	2,0 10^{-11}	1,4 10^{-11}	1,1 10^{-11}
Y-92	3,54 h	M	0,001	1,8 10^{-9}	1,0 10^{-4}	1,2 10^{-9}	5,3 10^{-10}	3,3 10^{-10}	2,0 10^{-10}	1,7 10^{-10}
		S	0,001	1,9 10^{-9}	1,0 10^{-4}	1,2 10^{-9}	5,5 10^{-10}	3,5 10^{-10}	2,1 10^{-10}	1,8 10^{-10}
Y-93	10,1 h	M	0,001	4,4 10^{-9}	1,0 10^{-4}	2,9 10^{-9}	1,3 10^{-9}	8,1 10^{-10}	4,7 10^{-10}	4,0 10^{-10}
		S	0,001	4,6 10^{-9}	1,0 10^{-4}	3,0 10^{-9}	1,4 10^{-9}	8,5 10^{-10}	5,0 10^{-10}	4,2 10^{-10}
Y-94	0,318 h	M	0,001	2,8 10^{-10}	1,0 10^{-4}	1,8 10^{-10}	8,1 10^{-11}	5,0 10^{-11}	3,1 10^{-11}	2,7 10^{-11}
		S	0,001	2,9 10^{-10}	1,0 10^{-4}	1,9 10^{-10}	8,4 10^{-11}	5,2 10^{-11}	3,3 10^{-11}	2,8 10^{-11}
Y-95	0,178 h	M	0,001	1,5 10^{-10}	1,0 10^{-4}	9,8 10^{-11}	4,4 10^{-11}	2,8 10^{-11}	1,8 10^{-11}	1,5 10^{-11}
		S	0,001	1,6 10^{-10}	1,0 10^{-4}	1,0 10^{-10}	4,5 10^{-11}	2,9 10^{-11}	1,8 10^{-11}	1,6 10^{-11}
Zirconium										
Zr-86	16,5 h	F	0,020	2,4 10^{-9}	0,002	1,9 10^{-9}	9,5 10^{-10}	5,9 10^{-10}	3,4 10^{-10}	2,7 10^{-10}
		M	0,020	3,4 10^{-9}	0,002	2,6 10^{-9}	1,3 10^{-9}	8,4 10^{-10}	5,2 10^{-10}	4,2 10^{-10}
		S	0,020	3,5 10^{-9}	0,002	2,7 10^{-9}	1,4 10^{-9}	8,7 10^{-10}	5,4 10^{-10}	4,3 10^{-10}

Nuclide	Physical half-life	Type	Age ≤ 1 a		Age	1—2 a	2—7 a	7—12 a	12—17 a	> 17 a
			f_1	h(g)	f_1	h(g)	h(g)	h(g)	h(g)	h(g)
Zr-88	83,4 d	F	0,020	6,9 10^{-9}	0,002	8,3 10^{-9}	5,6 10^{-9}	4,7 10^{-9}	3,6 10^{-9}	3,5 10^{-9}
		M	0,020	8,5 10^{-9}	0,002	7,8 10^{-9}	5,1 10^{-9}	3,6 10^{-9}	3,0 10^{-9}	2,6 10^{-9}
		S	0,020	1,3 10^{-8}	0,002	1,2 10^{-8}	7,7 10^{-9}	5,2 10^{-9}	4,3 10^{-9}	3,6 10^{-9}
Zr-89	3,27 d	F	0,020	2,6 10^{-9}	0,002	2,0 10^{-9}	9,9 10^{-10}	6,1 10^{-10}	3,6 10^{-10}	2,9 10^{-10}
		M	0,020	3,7 10^{-9}	0,002	2,8 10^{-9}	1,5 10^{-9}	9,6 10^{-10}	6,5 10^{-10}	5,2 10^{-10}
		S	0,020	3,9 10^{-9}	0,002	2,9 10^{-9}	1,5 10^{-9}	1,0 10^{-9}	6,8 10^{-10}	5,5 10^{-10}
Zr-93	1,53 10^{6} a	F	0,020	3,5 10^{-9}	0,002	4,8 10^{-9}	5,3 10^{-9}	9,7 10^{-9}	1,8 10^{-8}	2,5 10^{-8}
		M	0,020	3,3 10^{-9}	0,002	3,1 10^{-9}	2,8 10^{-9}	4,1 10^{-9}	7,5 10^{-9}	1,0 10^{-8}
		S	0,020	7,0 10^{-9}	0,002	6,4 10^{-9}	4,5 10^{-9}	3,3 10^{-9}	3,3 10^{-9}	3,3 10^{-9}
Zr-95	64,0 d	F	0,020	1,2 10^{-8}	0,002	1,1 10^{-8}	6,4 10^{-9}	4,2 10^{-9}	2,8 10^{-9}	2,5 10^{-9}
		M	0,020	2,0 10^{-8}	0,002	1,6 10^{-8}	9,7 10^{-9}	6,8 10^{-9}	5,9 10^{-9}	4,8 10^{-9}
		S	0,020	2,4 10^{-8}	0,002	1,9 10^{-8}	1,2 10^{-8}	8,3 10^{-9}	7,3 10^{-9}	5,9 10^{-9}
Zr-97	16,9 h	F	0,020	5,0 10^{-9}	0,002	3,4 10^{-9}	1,5 10^{-9}	9,1 10^{-10}	4,8 10^{-10}	3,9 10^{-10}
		M	0,020	7,8 10^{-9}	0,002	5,3 10^{-9}	2,8 10^{-9}	1,8 10^{-9}	1,1 10^{-9}	9,2 10^{-10}
		S	0,020	8,2 10^{-9}	0,002	5,6 10^{-9}	2,9 10^{-9}	1,9 10^{-9}	1,2 10^{-9}	8,9 10^{-10}
Niobium										
Nb-88	0,238 h	F	0,020	1,8 10^{-10}	0,010	1,3 10^{-10}	6,3 10^{-11}	3,9 10^{-11}	2,4 10^{-11}	1,9 10^{-11}
		M	0,020	2,5 10^{-10}	0,010	1,8 10^{-10}	8,5 10^{-11}	5,3 10^{-11}	3,3 10^{-11}	2,7 10^{-11}
		S	0,020	2,6 10^{-10}	0,010	1,8 10^{-10}	8,7 10^{-11}	5,5 10^{-11}	3,5 10^{-11}	2,8 10^{-11}
Nb-89	2,03 h	F	0,020	7,0 10^{-10}	0,010	4,8 10^{-10}	2,2 10^{-10}	1,3 10^{-10}	7,4 10^{-11}	6,1 10^{-11}
		M	0,020	1,1 10^{-9}	0,010	7,6 10^{-10}	3,6 10^{-10}	2,2 10^{-10}	1,4 10^{-10}	1,1 10^{-10}
		S	0,020	1,2 10^{-9}	0,010	7,9 10^{-10}	3,7 10^{-10}	2,3 10^{-10}	1,5 10^{-10}	1,2 10^{-10}
Nb-89	1,10 h	F	0,020	4,0 10^{-10}	0,010	2,9 10^{-10}	1,4 10^{-10}	8,3 10^{-11}	4,8 10^{-11}	3,9 10^{-11}
		M	0,020	6,2 10^{-10}	0,010	4,3 10^{-10}	2,1 10^{-10}	1,3 10^{-10}	8,2 10^{-11}	6,8 10^{-11}
		S	0,020	6,4 10^{-10}	0,010	4,4 10^{-10}	2,1 10^{-10}	1,4 10^{-10}	8,6 10^{-11}	7,1 10^{-11}

Nuclide	Physical half-life	Type	Age ≤ 1 a		Age	1—2 a	2—7 a	7—12 a	12—17 a	> 17 a
			f_1	$h(g)$	f_1	$h(g)$	$h(g)$	$h(g)$	$h(g)$	$h(g)$
Nb-90	14,6 h	F	0,020	3,5 10^{-9}	0,010	2,7 10^{-9}	1,3 10^{-9}	8,2 10^{-10}	4,7 10^{-10}	3,8 10^{-10}
		M	0,020	5,1 10^{-9}	0,010	3,9 10^{-9}	1,9 10^{-9}	1,3 10^{-9}	7,8 10^{-10}	6,3 10^{-10}
		S	0,020	5,3 10^{-9}	0,010	4,0 10^{-9}	2,0 10^{-9}	1,3 10^{-9}	8,1 10^{-10}	6,6 10^{-10}
Nb-93m	13,6 a	F	0,020	1,8 10^{-9}	0,010	1,4 10^{-9}	7,0 10^{-10}	4,4 10^{-10}	2,7 10^{-10}	2,2 10^{-10}
		M	0,020	3,1 10^{-9}	0,010	2,4 10^{-9}	1,3 10^{-9}	8,2 10^{-10}	5,9 10^{-10}	5,1 10^{-10}
		S	0,020	7,4 10^{-9}	0,010	6,5 10^{-9}	4,0 10^{-9}	2,5 10^{-9}	1,9 10^{-9}	1,8 10^{-9}
Nb-94	2,03 10^{4} a	F	0,020	3,1 10^{-8}	0,010	2,7 10^{-8}	1,5 10^{-8}	1,0 10^{-8}	6,7 10^{-9}	5,8 10^{-9}
		M	0,020	4,3 10^{-8}	0,010	3,7 10^{-8}	2,3 10^{-8}	1,6 10^{-8}	1,3 10^{-8}	1,1 10^{-8}
		S	0,020	1,2 10^{-7}	0,010	1,2 10^{-7}	8,3 10^{-8}	5,8 10^{-8}	5,2 10^{-8}	4,9 10^{-8}
Nb-95	35,1 d	F	0,020	4,1 10^{-9}	0,010	3,1 10^{-9}	1,6 10^{-9}	1,2 10^{-9}	7,5 10^{-10}	5,7 10^{-10}
		M	0,020	6,8 10^{-9}	0,010	5,2 10^{-9}	3,1 10^{-9}	2,2 10^{-9}	1,9 10^{-9}	1,5 10^{-9}
		S	0,020	7,7 10^{-9}	0,010	5,9 10^{-9}	3,6 10^{-9}	2,5 10^{-9}	2,2 10^{-9}	1,8 10^{-9}
Nb-95m	3,61 d	F	0,020	2,3 10^{-9}	0,010	1,6 10^{-9}	7,0 10^{-10}	4,2 10^{-10}	2,4 10^{-10}	2,0 10^{-10}
		M	0,020	4,3 10^{-9}	0,010	3,1 10^{-9}	1,7 10^{-9}	1,2 10^{-9}	1,0 10^{-9}	7,9 10^{-10}
		S	0,020	4,6 10^{-9}	0,010	3,4 10^{-9}	1,9 10^{-9}	1,3 10^{-9}	1,1 10^{-9}	8,8 10^{-10}
Nb-96	23,3 h	F	0,020	3,1 10^{-9}	0,010	2,4 10^{-9}	1,2 10^{-9}	7,3 10^{-10}	4,2 10^{-10}	3,4 10^{-10}
		M	0,020	4,7 10^{-9}	0,010	3,6 10^{-9}	1,8 10^{-9}	1,2 10^{-9}	7,8 10^{-10}	6,3 10^{-10}
		S	0,020	4,9 10^{-9}	0,010	3,7 10^{-9}	1,9 10^{-9}	1,2 10^{-9}	8,3 10^{-10}	6,6 10^{-10}
Nb-97	1,20 h	F	0,020	2,2 10^{-10}	0,010	1,5 10^{-10}	6,8 10^{-11}	4,2 10^{-11}	2,5 10^{-11}	2,1 10^{-11}
		M	0,020	3,7 10^{-10}	0,010	2,5 10^{-10}	1,2 10^{-10}	7,7 10^{-11}	5,2 10^{-11}	4,3 10^{-11}
		S	0,020	3,8 10^{-10}	0,010	2,6 10^{-10}	1,2 10^{-10}	8,1 10^{-11}	5,5 10^{-11}	4,5 10^{-11}
Nb-98	0,858 h	F	0,020	3,4 10^{-10}	0,010	2,4 10^{-10}	1,1 10^{-10}	6,9 10^{-11}	4,1 10^{-11}	3,3 10^{-11}
		M	0,020	5,2 10^{-10}	0,010	3,6 10^{-10}	1,7 10^{-10}	1,1 10^{-10}	6,8 10^{-11}	5,6 10^{-11}
		S	0,020	5,3 10^{-10}	0,010	3,7 10^{-10}	1,8 10^{-10}	1,1 10^{-10}	7,1 10^{-11}	5,8 10^{-11}

Nuclide	Physical half-life	Type	Age ≤ 1 a		Age	1—2 a	2—7 a	7—12 a	12—17 a	> 17 a
			f_1	h(g)	f_1	h(g)	h(g)	h(g)	h(g)	h(g)
Molybdenum										
Mo-90	5,67 h	F	1,000	1,2 10^{-9}	0,800	1,1 10^{-9}	5,3 10^{-10}	3,2 10^{-10}	1,9 10^{-10}	1,5 10^{-10}
		M	0,200	2,6 10^{-9}	0,100	2,0 10^{-9}	9,9 10^{-10}	6,5 10^{-10}	4,2 10^{-10}	3,4 10^{-10}
		S	0,020	2,8 10^{-9}	0,010	2,1 10^{-9}	1,1 10^{-9}	6,9 10^{-10}	4,5 10^{-10}	3,6 10^{-10}
Mo-93	3,50 10^{3} a	F	1,000	3,1 10^{-9}	0,800	2,6 10^{-9}	1,7 10^{-9}	1,3 10^{-9}	1,1 10^{-9}	1,0 10^{-9}
		M	0,200	2,2 10^{-9}	0,100	1,8 10^{-9}	1,1 10^{-9}	7,9 10^{-10}	6,6 10^{-10}	5,9 10^{-10}
		S	0,020	6,0 10^{-9}	0,010	5,8 10^{-9}	4,0 10^{-9}	2,8 10^{-9}	2,4 10^{-9}	2,3 10^{-9}
Mo-93m	6,85 h	F	1,000	7,3 10^{-10}	0,800	6,4 10^{-10}	3,3 10^{-10}	2,0 10^{-10}	1,2 10^{-10}	9,6 10^{-11}
		M	0,200	1,2 10^{-9}	0,100	9,7 10^{-10}	5,0 10^{-10}	3,2 10^{-10}	2,0 10^{-10}	1,6 10^{-10}
		S	0,020	1,3 10^{-9}	0,010	1,0 10^{-9}	5,2 10^{-10}	3,4 10^{-10}	2,1 10^{-10}	1,7 10^{-10}
Mo-99	2,75 d	F	1,000	2,3 10^{-9}	0,800	1,7 10^{-9}	7,7 10^{-10}	4,7 10^{-10}	2,6 10^{-10}	2,2 10^{-10}
		M	0,200	6,0 10^{-9}	0,100	4,4 10^{-9}	2,2 10^{-9}	1,5 10^{-9}	1,1 10^{-9}	8,9 10^{-10}
		S	0,020	6,9 10^{-9}	0,010	4,8 10^{-9}	2,4 10^{-9}	1,7 10^{-9}	1,2 10^{-9}	9,9 10^{-10}
Mo-101	0,244 h	F	1,000	1,4 10^{-10}	0,800	9,7 10^{-11}	4,4 10^{-11}	2,8 10^{-11}	1,7 10^{-11}	1,4 10^{-11}
		M	0,200	2,2 10^{-10}	0,100	1,5 10^{-10}	7,0 10^{-11}	4,5 10^{-11}	3,0 10^{-11}	2,5 10^{-11}
		S	0,020	2,3 10^{-10}	0,010	1,6 10^{-10}	7,2 10^{-11}	4,7 10^{-11}	3,1 10^{-11}	2,6 10^{-11}
Technetium										
Tc-93	2,75 h	F	1,000	2,4 10^{-10}	0,800	2,1 10^{-10}	1,1 10^{-10}	6,7 10^{-11}	4,0 10^{-11}	3,2 10^{-11}
		M	0,200	2,7 10^{-10}	0,100	2,3 10^{-10}	1,2 10^{-10}	7,5 10^{-11}	4,4 10^{-11}	3,5 10^{-11}
		S	0,020	2,8 10^{-10}	0,010	2,3 10^{-10}	1,2 10^{-10}	7,6 10^{-11}	4,5 10^{-11}	3,5 10^{-11}
Tc-93m	0,725 h	F	1,000	1,2 10^{-10}	0,800	9,8 10^{-11}	4,9 10^{-11}	2,9 10^{-11}	1,8 10^{-11}	1,4 10^{-11}
		M	0,200	1,4 10^{-10}	0,100	1,1 10^{-10}	5,4 10^{-11}	3,4 10^{-11}	2,1 10^{-11}	1,7 10^{-11}
		S	0,020	1,4 10^{-10}	0,010	1,1 10^{-10}	5,4 10^{-11}	3,4 10^{-11}	2,1 10^{-11}	1,7 10^{-11}
Tc-94	4,88 h	F	1,000	8,9 10^{-10}	0,800	7,5 10^{-10}	3,9 10^{-10}	2,3 10^{-10}	1,4 10^{-10}	1,1 10^{-10}
		M	0,200	9,8 10^{-10}	0,100	8,1 10^{-10}	4,2 10^{-10}	2,6 10^{-10}	1,6 10^{-10}	1,2 10^{-10}
		S	0,020	9,9 10^{-10}	0,010	8,2 10^{-10}	4,3 10^{-10}	2,7 10^{-10}	1,6 10^{-10}	1,3 10^{-10}

Nuclide	*Physical half-life*	*Type*	*Age ≤ 1 a*		*Age*	*1—2 a*	*2—7 a*	*7—12 a*	*12—17 a*	*> 17 a*
			f_1	*h(g)*	f_1	*h(g)*	*h(g)*	*h(g)*	*h(g)*	*h(g)*
Tc-94m	0,867 h	F	1,000	4,8 10^{-10}	0,800	3,4 10^{-10}	1,6 10^{-10}	8,6 10^{-11}	5,2 10^{-11}	4,1 10^{-11}
		M	0,200	4,4 10^{-10}	0,100	3,0 10^{-10}	1,4 10^{-10}	8,8 10^{-11}	5,5 10^{-11}	4,5 10^{-11}
		S	0,020	4,3 10^{-10}	0,010	3,0 10^{-10}	1,4 10^{-10}	8,8 10^{-11}	5,6 10^{-11}	4,6 10^{-11}
Tc-95	20,0 h	F	1,000	7,5 10^{-10}	0,800	6,3 10^{-10}	3,3 10^{-10}	2,0 10^{-10}	1,2 10^{-10}	9,6 10^{-11}
		M	0,200	8,3 10^{-10}	0,100	6,9 10^{-10}	3,6 10^{-10}	2,2 10^{-10}	1,3 10^{-10}	1,0 10^{-10}
		S	0,020	8,5 10^{-10}	0,010	7,0 10^{-10}	3,6 10^{-10}	2,3 10^{-10}	1,4 10^{-10}	1,1 10^{-10}
Tc-95m	61,0 d	F	1,000	2,4 10^{-9}	0,800	1,8 10^{-9}	9,3 10^{-10}	5,7 10^{-10}	3,6 10^{-10}	2,9 10^{-10}
		M	0,200	4,9 10^{-9}	0,100	4,0 10^{-9}	2,3 10^{-9}	1,5 10^{-9}	1,1 10^{-9}	8,8 10^{-10}
		S	0,020	6,0 10^{-9}	0,010	5,0 10^{-9}	2,7 10^{-9}	1,8 10^{-9}	1,5 10^{-9}	1,2 10^{-9}
Tc-96	4,28 d	F	1,000	4,2 10^{-9}	0,800	3,4 10^{-9}	1,8 10^{-9}	1,1 10^{-9}	7,0 10^{-10}	5,7 10^{-10}
		M	0,200	4,7 10^{-9}	0,100	3,9 10^{-9}	2,1 10^{-9}	1,3 10^{-9}	8,6 10^{-10}	6,8 10^{-10}
		S	0,020	4,8 10^{-9}	0,010	3,9 10^{-9}	2,1 10^{-9}	1,4 10^{-9}	8,9 10^{-10}	7,0 10^{-10}
Tc-96m	0,858 h	F	1,000	5,3 10^{-11}	0,800	4,1 10^{-11}	2,1 10^{-11}	1,3 10^{-11}	7,7 10^{-12}	6,2 10^{-12}
		M	0,200	5,6 10^{-11}	0,100	4,4 10^{-11}	2,3 10^{-11}	1,4 10^{-11}	9,3 10^{-12}	7,4 10^{-12}
		S	0,020	5,7 10^{-11}	0,010	4,4 10^{-11}	2,3 10^{-11}	1,5 10^{-11}	9,5 10^{-12}	7,5 10^{-12}
Tc-97	2,60 10^{6} a	F	1,000	5,2 10^{-10}	0,800	3,7 10^{-10}	1,7 10^{-10}	9,4 10^{-11}	5,6 10^{-11}	4,3 10^{-11}
		M	0,200	1,2 10^{-9}	0,100	1,0 10^{-9}	5,7 10^{-10}	3,6 10^{-10}	2,8 10^{-10}	2,2 10^{-10}
		S	0,020	5,0 10^{-9}	0,010	4,8 10^{-9}	3,3 10^{-9}	2,2 10^{-9}	1,9 10^{-9}	1,8 10^{-9}
Tc-97m	87,0 d	F	1,000	3,4 10^{-9}	0,800	2,3 10^{-9}	9,8 10^{-10}	5,6 10^{-10}	3,0 10^{-10}	2,7 10^{-10}
		M	0,200	1,3 10^{-8}	0,100	1,0 10^{-8}	6,1 10^{-9}	4,4 10^{-9}	4,1 10^{-9}	3,2 10^{-9}
		S	0,020	1,6 10^{-8}	0,010	1,3 10^{-8}	7,8 10^{-9}	5,7 10^{-9}	5,2 10^{-9}	4,1 10^{-9}
Tc-98	4,20 10^{6} a	F	1,000	1,0 10^{-8}	0,800	6,8 10^{-9}	3,2 10^{-9}	1,9 10^{-9}	1,2 10^{-9}	9,7 10^{-10}
		M	0,200	3,5 10^{-8}	0,100	2,9 10^{-8}	1,7 10^{-8}	1,2 10^{-8}	1,0 10^{-8}	8,3 10^{-9}
		S	0,020	1,1 10^{-7}	0,010	1,1 10^{-7}	7,6 10^{-8}	5,4 10^{-8}	4,8 10^{-8}	4,5 10^{-8}

Nuclide	Physical half-life	Type	Age ≤ 1 a		Age	1—2 a	2—7 a	7—12 a	12—17 a	> 17 a
			f_1	$h(g)$	f_1	$h(g)$	$h(g)$	$h(g)$	$h(g)$	$h(g)$
Tc-99	2,13 10^5 a	F	1,000	4,0 10^{-9}	0,800	2,5 10^{-9}	1,0 10^{-9}	5,9 10^{-10}	3,6 10^{-10}	2,9 10^{-10}
		M	0,200	1,7 10^{-8}	0,100	1,3 10^{-8}	8,0 10^{-9}	5,7 10^{-9}	5,0 10^{-9}	4,0 10^{-9}
		S	0,020	4,1 10^{-8}	0,010	3,7 10^{-8}	2,4 10^{-8}	1,7 10^{-8}	1,5 10^{-8}	1,3 10^{-8}
Tc-99m	6,02 h	F	1,000	1,2 10^{-10}	0,800	8,7 10^{-11}	4,1 10^{-11}	2,4 10^{-11}	1,5 10^{-11}	1,2 10^{-11}
		M	0,200	1,3 10^{-10}	0,100	9,9 10^{-11}	5,1 10^{-11}	3,4 10^{-11}	2,4 10^{-11}	1,9 10^{-11}
		S	0,020	1,3 10^{-10}	0,010	1,0 10^{-10}	5,2 10^{-11}	3,5 10^{-11}	2,5 10^{-11}	2,0 10^{-11}
Tc-101	0,237 h	F	1,000	8,5 10^{-11}	0,800	5,6 10^{-11}	2,5 10^{-11}	1,6 10^{-11}	9,7 10^{-12}	8,2 10^{-12}
		M	0,200	1,1 10^{-10}	0,100	7,1 10^{-11}	3,2 10^{-11}	2,1 10^{-11}	1,4 10^{-11}	1,2 10^{-11}
		S	0,020	1,1 10^{-10}	0,010	7,3 10^{-11}	3,3 10^{-11}	2,2 10^{-11}	1,4 10^{-11}	1,2 10^{-11}
Tc-104	0,303 h	F	1,000	2,7 10^{-10}	0,800	1,8 10^{-10}	8,0 10^{-11}	4,6 10^{-11}	2,8 10^{-11}	2,3 10^{-11}
		M	0,200	2,9 10^{-10}	0,100	1,9 10^{-10}	8,6 10^{-11}	5,4 10^{-11}	3,3 10^{-11}	2,8 10^{-11}
		S	0,020	2,9 10^{-10}	0,010	1,9 10^{-10}	8,7 10^{-11}	5,4 10^{-11}	3,4 10^{-11}	2,9 10^{-11}
Ruthenium										
Ru-94	0,863 h	F	0,100	2,5 10^{-10}	0,050	1,9 10^{-10}	9,0 10^{-11}	5,4 10^{-11}	3,1 10^{-11}	2,5 10^{-11}
		M	0,100	3,8 10^{-10}	0,050	2,8 10^{-10}	1,3 10^{-10}	8,4 10^{-11}	5,2 10^{-11}	4,2 10^{-11}
		S	0,020	4,0 10^{-10}	0,010	2,9 10^{-10}	1,4 10^{-10}	8,7 10^{-11}	5,4 10^{-11}	4,4 10^{-11}
Ru-97	2,90 d	F	0,100	5,5 10^{-10}	0,050	4,4 10^{-10}	2,2 10^{-10}	1,3 10^{-10}	7,7 10^{-11}	6,2 10^{-11}
		M	0,100	7,7 10^{-10}	0,050	6,1 10^{-10}	3,1 10^{-10}	2,0 10^{-10}	1,3 10^{-10}	1,0 10^{-10}
		S	0,020	8,1 10^{-10}	0,010	6,3 10^{-10}	3,3 10^{-10}	2,1 10^{-10}	1,4 10^{-10}	1,1 10^{-10}
Ru-103	39,3 d	F	0,100	4,2 10^{-9}	0,050	3,0 10^{-9}	1,5 10^{-9}	9,3 10^{-10}	5,6 10^{-10}	4,8 10^{-10}
		M	0,100	1,1 10^{-8}	0,050	8,4 10^{-9}	5,0 10^{-9}	3,5 10^{-9}	3,0 10^{-9}	2,4 10^{-9}
		S	0,020	1,3 10^{-8}	0,010	1,0 10^{-8}	6,0 10^{-9}	4,2 10^{-9}	3,7 10^{-9}	3,0 10^{-9}
Ru-105	4,44 h	F	0,100	7,1 10^{-10}	0,050	5,1 10^{-10}	2,3 10^{-10}	1,4 10^{-10}	7,9 10^{-11}	6,5 10^{-11}
		M	0,100	1,3 10^{-9}	0,050	9,2 10^{-10}	4,5 10^{-10}	3,0 10^{-10}	2,0 10^{-10}	1,7 10^{-10}
		S	0,020	1,4 10^{-9}	0,010	9,8 10^{-10}	4,8 10^{-10}	3,2 10^{-10}	2,2 10^{-10}	1,8 10^{-10}

Nuclide	Physical half-life	Type	Age ≤ 1 a		Age	1—2 a	2—7 a	7—12 a	12—17 a	> 17 a
			f_1	h(g)	f_1	h(g)	h(g)	h(g)	h(g)	h(g)
Ru-106	1,01 a	F	0,100	7,2 10^{-8}	0,050	5,4 10^{-8}	2,6 10^{-8}	1,6 10^{-8}	9,2 10^{-9}	7,9 10^{-9}
		M	0,100	1,4 10^{-7}	0,050	1,1 10^{-7}	6,4 10^{-8}	4,1 10^{-8}	3,1 10^{-8}	2,8 10^{-8}
		S	0,020	2,6 10^{-7}	0,010	2,3 10^{-7}	1,4 10^{-7}	9,1 10^{-8}	7,1 10^{-8}	6,6 10^{-8}
Rhodium										
Rh-99	16,0 d	F	0,100	2,6 10^{-9}	0,050	2,0 10^{-9}	9,9 10^{-10}	6,2 10^{-10}	3,8 10^{-10}	3,2 10^{-10}
		M	0,100	4,5 10^{-9}	0,050	3,5 10^{-9}	2,0 10^{-9}	1,3 10^{-9}	9,6 10^{-10}	7,7 10^{-10}
		S	0,100	4,9 10^{-9}	0,050	3,8 10^{-9}	2,2 10^{-9}	1,3 10^{-9}	1,1 10^{-9}	8,7 10^{-10}
Rh-99m	4,70 h	F	0,100	2,4 10^{-10}	0,050	2,0 10^{-10}	1,0 10^{-10}	6,1 10^{-11}	3,5 10^{-11}	2,8 10^{-11}
		M	0,100	3,1 10^{-10}	0,050	2,5 10^{-10}	1,3 10^{-10}	8,0 10^{-11}	4,9 10^{-11}	3,9 10^{-11}
		S	0,100	3,2 10^{-10}	0,050	2,6 10^{-10}	1,3 10^{-10}	8,2 10^{-11}	5,1 10^{-11}	4,0 10^{-11}
Rh-100	20,8 h	F	0,100	2,1 10^{-9}	0,050	1,8 10^{-9}	9,1 10^{-10}	5,6 10^{-10}	3,3 10^{-10}	2,6 10^{-10}
		M	0,100	2,7 10^{-9}	0,050	2,2 10^{-9}	1,1 10^{-9}	7,1 10^{-10}	4,3 10^{-10}	3,4 10^{-10}
		S	0,100	2,8 10^{-9}	0,050	2,2 10^{-9}	1,2 10^{-9}	7,3 10^{-10}	4,4 10^{-10}	3,5 10^{-10}
Rh-101	3,20 a	F	0,100	7,4 10^{-9}	0,050	6,1 10^{-9}	3,5 10^{-9}	2,3 10^{-9}	1,5 10^{-9}	1,4 10^{-9}
		M	0,100	9,8 10^{-9}	0,050	8,0 10^{-9}	4,9 10^{-9}	3,4 10^{-9}	2,8 10^{-9}	2,3 10^{-9}
		S	0,100	1,9 10^{-8}	0,050	1,7 10^{-8}	1,1 10^{-8}	7,4 10^{-9}	6,2 10^{-9}	5,4 10^{-9}
Rh-101m	4,34 d	F	0,100	8,4 10^{-10}	0,050	6,6 10^{-10}	3,3 10^{-10}	2,0 10^{-10}	1,2 10^{-10}	9,7 10^{-11}
		M	0,100	1,3 10^{-9}	0,050	9,8 10^{-10}	5,2 10^{-10}	3,5 10^{-10}	2,5 10^{-10}	1,9 10^{-10}
		S	0,100	1,3 10^{-9}	0,050	1,0 10^{-9}	5,5 10^{-10}	3,7 10^{-10}	2,7 10^{-10}	2,1 10^{-10}
Rh-102	2,90 a	F	0,100	3,3 10^{-8}	0,050	2,8 10^{-8}	1,7 10^{-8}	1,1 10^{-8}	7,9 10^{-9}	7,3 10^{-9}
		M	0,100	3,0 10^{-8}	0,050	2,5 10^{-8}	1,5 10^{-8}	1,0 10^{-8}	7,9 10^{-9}	6,9 10^{-9}
		S	0,100	5,4 10^{-8}	0,050	5,0 10^{-8}	3,5 10^{-8}	2,4 10^{-8}	2,0 10^{-8}	1,7 10^{-8}
Rh-102m	207 d	F	0,100	1,2 10^{-8}	0,050	8,7 10^{-9}	4,4 10^{-9}	2,7 10^{-9}	1,7 10^{-9}	1,5 10^{-9}
		M	0,100	2,0 10^{-8}	0,050	1,6 10^{-8}	9,0 10^{-9}	6,0 10^{-9}	4,7 10^{-9}	4,0 10^{-9}
		S	0,100	3,0 10^{-8}	0,050	2,5 10^{-8}	1,5 10^{-8}	1,0 10^{-8}	8,2 10^{-9}	7,1 10^{-9}

Nuclide	*Physical half-life*	*Type*	*Age ≤ 1 a*		*Age*	*1—2 a*	*2—7 a*	*7—12 a*	*12—17 a*	*> 17 a*
			f_1	$h(g)$	f_1	$h(g)$	$h(g)$	$h(g)$	$h(g)$	$h(g)$
Rh-103m	0,935 h	F	0,100	8,6 10^{-12}	0,050	5,9 10^{-12}	2,7 10^{-12}	1,6 10^{-12}	1,0 10^{-12}	8,6 10–13
		M	0,100	1,9 10^{-11}	0,050	1,2 10^{-11}	6,3 10^{-12}	4,0 10^{-12}	3,0 10^{-12}	2,5 10^{-12}
		S	0,100	2,0 10^{-11}	0,050	1,3 10^{-11}	6,7 10^{-12}	4,3 10^{-12}	3,2 10^{-12}	2,7 10^{-12}
Rh-105	1,47 d	F	0,100	1,0 10^{-9}	0,050	6,9 10^{-10}	3,0 10^{-10}	1,8 10^{-10}	9,6 10^{-11}	8,2 10^{-11}
		M	0,100	2,2 10^{-9}	0,050	1,6 10^{-9}	7,4 10^{-10}	5,2 10^{-10}	4,1 10^{-10}	3,2 10^{-10}
		S	0,100	2,4 10^{-9}	0,050	1,7 10^{-9}	8,0 10^{-10}	5,6 10^{-10}	4,5 10^{-10}	3,5 10^{-10}
Rh-106m	2,20 h	F	0,100	5,7 10^{-10}	0,050	4,5 10^{-10}	2,2 10^{-10}	1,4 10^{-10}	8,0 10^{-11}	6,5 10^{-11}
		M	0,100	8,2 10^{-10}	0,050	6,3 10^{-10}	3,2 10^{-10}	2,0 10^{-10}	1,3 10^{-10}	1,1 10^{-10}
		S	0,100	8,5 10^{-10}	0,050	6,5 10^{-10}	3,3 10^{-10}	2,1 10^{-10}	1,4 10^{-10}	1,1 10^{-10}
Rh-107	0,362 h	F	0,100	8,9 10^{-11}	0,050	5,9 10^{-11}	2,6 10^{-11}	1,7 10^{-11}	1,0 10^{-11}	9,0 10^{-12}
		M	0,100	1,4 10^{-10}	0,050	9,3 10^{-11}	4,2 10^{-11}	2,8 10^{-11}	1,9 10^{-11}	1,6 10^{-11}
		S	0,100	1,5 10^{-10}	0,050	9,7 10^{-11}	4,4 10^{-11}	2,9 10^{-11}	1,9 10^{-11}	1,7 10^{-11}
Palladium										
Pd-100	3,63 d	F	0,050	3,9 10^{-9}	0,005	3,0 10^{-9}	1,5 10^{-9}	9,7 10^{-10}	5,8 10^{-10}	4,7 10^{-10}
		M	0,050	5,2 10^{-9}	0,005	4,0 10^{-9}	2,2 10^{-9}	1,4 10^{-9}	9,9 10^{-10}	8,0 10^{-10}
		S	0,050	5,3 10^{-9}	0,005	4,1 10^{-9}	2,2 10^{-9}	1,5 10^{-9}	1,0 10^{-9}	8,5 10^{-10}
Pd-101	8,27 h	F	0,050	3,6 10^{-10}	0,005	2,9 10^{-10}	1,4 10^{-10}	8,6 10^{-11}	4,9 10^{-11}	3,9 10^{-11}
		M	0,050	4,8 10^{-10}	0,005	3,8 10^{-10}	1,9 10^{-10}	1,2 10^{-10}	7,5 10^{-11}	5,9 10^{-11}
		S	0,050	5,0 10^{-10}	0,005	3,9 10^{-10}	2,0 10^{-10}	1,2 10^{-10}	7,8 10^{-11}	6,2 10^{-11}
Pd-103	17,0 d	F	0,050	9,7 10^{-10}	0,005	6,5 10^{-10}	3,0 10^{-10}	1,9 10^{-10}	1,1 10^{-10}	8,9 10^{-11}
		M	0,050	2,3 10^{-9}	0,005	1,6 10^{-9}	9,0 10^{-10}	5,9 10^{-10}	4,5 10^{-10}	3,8 10^{-10}
		S	0,050	2,5 10^{-9}	0,005	1,8 10^{-9}	1,0 10^{-10}	6,8 10^{-9}	5,3 10^{-10}	4,5 10^{-10}
Pd-107	6,50 10^{6} a	F	0,050	2,6 10^{-10}	0,005	1,8 10^{-10}	8,2 10^{-11}	5,2 10^{-11}	3,1 10^{-11}	2,5 10^{-11}
		M	0,050	6,5 10^{-10}	0,005	5,0 10^{-10}	2,6 10^{-10}	1,5 10^{-10}	1,0 10^{-10}	8,5 10^{-11}
		S	0,050	2,2 10^{-9}	0,005	2,0 10^{-9}	1,3 10^{-9}	7,8 10^{-10}	6,2 10^{-10}	5,9 10^{-10}

Nuclide	*Physical half-life*	*Type*	*Age ≤ 1 a*		*Age*	*1—2 a*	*2—7 a*	*7—12 a*	*12—17 a*	*> 17 a*
			f_1	*h(g)*	f_1	*h(g)*	*h(g)*	*h(g)*	*h(g)*	*h(g)*
Pd-109	13,4 h	F	0,050	1,5 10^{-9}	0,005	9,9 10^{-10}	4,2 10^{-10}	2,6 10^{-10}	1,4 10^{-10}	1,2 10^{-10}
		M	0,050	2,6 10^{-9}	0,005	1,8 10^{-9}	8,8 10^{-10}	5,9 10^{-10}	4,3 10^{-10}	3,4 10^{-10}
		S	0,050	2,7 10^{-9}	0,005	1,9 10^{-9}	9,3 10^{-10}	6,3 10^{-10}	4,6 10^{-10}	3,7 10^{-10}
Silver										
Ag-102	0,215 h	F	0,100	1,2 10^{-10}	0,050	8,6 10^{-11}	4,2 10^{-11}	2,6 10^{-11}	1,5 10^{-11}	1,3 10^{-11}
		M	0,100	1,6 10^{-10}	0,050	1,1 10^{-10}	5,5 10^{-11}	3,4 10^{-11}	2,1 10^{-11}	1,7 10^{-11}
		S	0,020	1,6 10^{-10}	0,010	1,2 10^{-10}	5,6 10^{-11}	3,5 10^{-11}	2,2 10^{-11}	1,8 10^{-11}
Ag-103	1,09 h	F	0,100	1,4 10^{-10}	0,050	1,0 10^{-10}	4,9 10^{-11}	3,0 10^{-11}	1,8 10^{-11}	1,4 10^{-11}
		M	0,100	2,2 10^{-10}	0,050	1,6 10^{-10}	7,6 10^{-11}	4,8 10^{-11}	3,2 10^{-11}	2,6 10^{-11}
		S	0,020	2,3 10^{-10}	0,010	1,6 10^{-10}	7,9 10^{-11}	5,1 10^{-11}	3,3 10^{-11}	2,7 10^{-11}
Ag-104	1,15 h	F	0,100	2,3 10^{-10}	0,050	1,9 10^{-10}	9,8 10^{-11}	5,9 10^{-11}	3,5 10^{-11}	2,8 10^{-11}
		M	0,100	2,9 10^{-10}	0,050	2,3 10^{-10}	1,2 10^{-10}	7,4 10^{-11}	4,5 10^{-11}	3,6 10^{-11}
		S	0,020	2,9 10^{-10}	0,010	2,4 10^{-10}	1,2 10^{-10}	7,6 10^{-11}	4,6 10^{-11}	3,7 10^{-11}
Ag-104m	0,558 h	F	0,100	1,6 10^{-10}	0,050	1,1 10^{-10}	5,5 10^{-11}	3,4 10^{-11}	2,0 10^{-11}	1,6 10^{-11}
		M	0,100	2,3 10^{-10}	0,050	1,6 10^{-10}	7,7 10^{-11}	4,8 10^{-11}	3,0 10^{-11}	2,5 10^{-11}
		S	0,020	2,4 10^{-10}	0,010	1,7 10^{-10}	8,0 10^{-11}	5,0 10^{-11}	3,1 10^{-11}	2,6 10^{-11}
Ag-105	41,0 d	F	0,100	3,9 10^{-9}	0,050	3,4 10^{-9}	1,7 10^{-9}	1,0 10^{-9}	6,4 10^{-10}	5,4 10^{-10}
		M	0,100	4,5 10^{-9}	0,050	3,5 10^{-9}	2,0 10^{-9}	1,3 10^{-9}	9,0 10^{-10}	7,3 10^{-10}
		S	0,020	4,5 10^{-9}	0,010	3,6 10^{-9}	2,1 10^{-9}	1,3 10^{-9}	1,0 10^{-9}	8,1 10^{-10}
Ag-106	0,399 h	F	0,100	9,4 10^{-11}	0,050	6,4 10^{-11}	2,9 10^{-11}	1,8 10^{-11}	1,1 10^{-11}	9,1 10^{-12}
		M	0,100	1,4 10^{-10}	0,050	9,5 10^{-11}	4,4 10^{-11}	2,8 10^{-11}	1,8 10^{-11}	1,5 10^{-11}
		S	0,020	1,5 10^{-10}	0,010	9,9 10^{-11}	4,5 10^{-11}	2,9 10^{-11}	1,9 10^{-11}	1,6 10^{-11}
Ag-106m	8,41 d	F	0,100	7,7 10^{-9}	0,050	6,1 10^{-9}	3,2 10^{-9}	2,1 10^{-9}	1,3 10^{-9}	1,1 10^{-9}
		M	0,100	7,2 10^{-9}	0,050	5,8 10^{-9}	3,2 10^{-9}	2,1 10^{-9}	1,4 10^{-9}	1,1 10^{-9}
		S	0,020	7,0 10^{-9}	0,010	5,7 10^{-9}	3,2 10^{-9}	2,1 10^{-9}	1,4 10^{-9}	1,1 10^{-9}

Nuclide	*Physical half-life*	*Type*	*Age ≤ 1 a*		*Age*	*1—2 a*	*2—7 a*	*7—12 a*	*12—17 a*	*> 17 a*
			f_1	*h(g)*	f_1	*h(g)*	*h(g)*	*h(g)*	*h(g)*	*h(g)*
Ag-108m	$1,27\ 10^{2}$ a	F	0,100	$3,5\ 10^{-8}$	0,050	$2,8\ 10^{-8}$	$1,6\ 10^{-8}$	$1,0\ 10^{-8}$	$6,9\ 10^{-9}$	$6,1\ 10^{-9}$
		M	0,100	$3,3\ 10^{-8}$	0,050	$2,7\ 10^{-8}$	$1,7\ 10^{-8}$	$1,1\ 10^{-8}$	$8,6\ 10^{-9}$	$7,4\ 10^{-9}$
		S	0,020	$8,9\ 10^{-8}$	0,010	$8,7\ 10^{-8}$	$6,2\ 10^{-8}$	$4,4\ 10^{-8}$	$3,9\ 10^{-8}$	$3,7\ 10^{-8}$
Ag-110m	250 d	F	0,100	$3,5\ 10^{-8}$	0,050	$2,8\ 10^{-8}$	$1,5\ 10^{-8}$	$9,7\ 10^{-9}$	$6,3\ 10^{-9}$	$5,5\ 10^{-9}$
		M	0,100	$3,5\ 10^{-8}$	0,050	$2,8\ 10^{-8}$	$1,7\ 10^{-8}$	$1,2\ 10^{-8}$	$9,2\ 10^{-9}$	$7,6\ 10^{-9}$
		S	0,020	$4,6\ 10^{-8}$	0,010	$4,1\ 10^{-8}$	$2,6\ 10^{-8}$	$1,8\ 10^{-8}$	$1,5\ 10^{-8}$	$1,2\ 10^{-8}$
Ag-111	7,45 d	F	0,100	$4,8\ 10^{-9}$	0,050	$3,2\ 10^{-9}$	$1,4\ 10^{-9}$	$8,8\ 10^{-10}$	$4,8\ 10^{-10}$	$4,0\ 10^{-10}$
		M	0,100	$9,2\ 10^{-9}$	0,050	$6,6\ 10^{-9}$	$3,5\ 10^{-9}$	$2,4\ 10^{-9}$	$1,9\ 10^{-9}$	$1,5\ 10^{-9}$
		S	0,020	$9,9\ 10^{-9}$	0,010	$7,1\ 10^{-9}$	$3,8\ 10^{-9}$	$2,7\ 10^{-9}$	$2,1\ 10^{-9}$	$1,7\ 10^{-9}$
Ag-112	3,12 h	F	0,100	$9,8\ 10^{-10}$	0,050	$6,4\ 10^{-10}$	$2,8\ 10^{-10}$	$1,7\ 10^{-10}$	$9,1\ 10^{-11}$	$7,6\ 10^{-11}$
		M	0,100	$1,7\ 10^{-9}$	0,050	$1,1\ 10^{-9}$	$5,1\ 10^{-10}$	$3,2\ 10^{-10}$	$2,0\ 10^{-10}$	$1,6\ 10^{-10}$
		S	0,020	$1,8\ 10^{-9}$	0,010	$1,2\ 10^{-9}$	$5,4\ 10^{-10}$	$3,4\ 10^{-10}$	$2,1\ 10^{-10}$	$1,7\ 10^{-10}$
Ag-115	0,333 h	F	0,100	$1,6\ 10^{-10}$	0,050	$1,0\ 10^{-10}$	$4,6\ 10^{-11}$	$2,9\ 10^{-11}$	$1,7\ 10^{-11}$	$1,5\ 10^{-11}$
		M	0,100	$2,5\ 10^{-10}$	0,050	$1,7\ 10^{-10}$	$7,6\ 10^{-11}$	$4,9\ 10^{-11}$	$3,2\ 10^{-11}$	$2,7\ 10^{-11}$
		S	0,020	$2,7\ 10^{-10}$	0,010	$1,7\ 10^{-10}$	$8,0\ 10^{-11}$	$5,2\ 10^{-11}$	$3,4\ 10^{-11}$	$2,9\ 10^{-11}$
Cadmium										
Cd-104	0,961 h	F	0,100	$2,0\ 10^{-10}$	0,050	$1,7\ 10^{-10}$	$8,7\ 10^{-11}$	$5,2\ 10^{-11}$	$3,1\ 10^{-11}$	$2,4\ 10^{-11}$
		M	0,100	$2,6\ 10^{-10}$	0,050	$2,1\ 10^{-10}$	$1,1\ 10^{-10}$	$6,9\ 10^{-11}$	$4,2\ 10^{-11}$	$3,4\ 10^{-11}$
		S	0,100	$2,7\ 10^{-10}$	0,050	$2,2\ 10^{-10}$	$1,1\ 10^{-10}$	$7,0\ 10^{-11}$	$4,4\ 10^{-11}$	$3,5\ 10^{-11}$
Cd-107	6,49 h	F	0,100	$2,3\ 10^{-10}$	0,050	$1,7\ 10^{-10}$	$7,4\ 10^{-11}$	$4,6\ 10^{-11}$	$2,5\ 10^{-11}$	$2,1\ 10^{-11}$
		M	0,100	$5,2\ 10^{-10}$	0,050	$3,7\ 10^{-10}$	$2,0\ 10^{-10}$	$1,3\ 10^{-10}$	$8,8\ 10^{-11}$	$8,3\ 10^{-11}$
		S	0,100	$5,5\ 10^{-10}$	0,050	$3,9\ 10^{-10}$	$2,1\ 10^{-10}$	$1,4\ 10^{-10}$	$9,7\ 10^{-11}$	$7,7\ 10^{-11}$
Cd-109	1,27 a	F	0,100	$4,5\ 10^{-8}$	0,050	$3,7\ 10^{-8}$	$2,1\ 10^{-8}$	$1,4\ 10^{-8}$	$9,3\ 10^{-9}$	$8,1\ 10^{-9}$
		M	0,100	$3,0\ 10^{-8}$	0,050	$2,3\ 10^{-8}$	$1,4\ 10^{-8}$	$9,5\ 10^{-9}$	$7,8\ 10^{-9}$	$6,6\ 10^{-9}$
		S	0,100	$2,7\ 10^{-8}$	0,050	$2,1\ 10^{-8}$	$1,3\ 10^{-8}$	$8,9\ 10^{-9}$	$7,6\ 10^{-9}$	$6,2\ 10^{-9}$

Nuclide	Physical half-life	Type	Age ≤ 1 a		Age	1—2 a	2—7 a	7—12 a	12—17 a	> 17 a
			f_1	$h(g)$	f_1	$h(g)$	$h(g)$	$h(g)$	$h(g)$	$h(g)$
Cd-113	9,30 10^{15} a	F	0,100	2,6 10^{-7}	0,050	2,4 10^{-7}	1,7 10^{-7}	1,4 10^{-7}	1,2 10^{-7}	1,2 10^{-7}
		M	0,100	1,2 10^{-7}	0,050	1,0 10^{-7}	7,6 10^{-8}	6,1 10^{-8}	5,7 10^{-8}	5,5 10^{-8}
		S	0,100	7,8 10^{-8}	0,050	5,8 10^{-8}	4,1 10^{-8}	3,0 10^{-8}	2,7 10^{-8}	2,6 10^{-8}
Cd-113m	13,6 a	F	0,100	3,0 10^{-7}	0,050	2,7 10^{-7}	1,8 10^{-7}	1,3 10^{-7}	1,1 10^{-7}	1,1 10^{-7}
		M	0,100	1,4 10^{-7}	0,050	1,2 10^{-7}	8,1 10^{-8}	6,0 10^{-8}	5,3 10^{-8}	5,2 10^{-8}
		S	0,100	1,1 10^{-7}	0,050	8,4 10^{-8}	5,5 10^{-8}	3,9 10^{-8}	3,3 10^{-8}	3,1 10^{-8}
Cd-115	2,23 d	F	0,100	4,0 10^{-9}	0,050	2,6 10^{-9}	1,2 10^{-9}	7,5 10^{-10}	4,3 10^{-10}	3,5 10^{-10}
		M	0,100	6,7 10^{-9}	0,050	4,8 10^{-9}	2,4 10^{-9}	1,7 10^{-9}	1,2 10^{-9}	9,8 10^{-10}
		S	0,100	7,2 10^{-9}	0,050	5,1 10^{-9}	2,6 10^{-9}	1,8 10^{-9}	1,3 10^{-9}	1,1 10^{-9}
Cd-115m	44,6 d	F	0,100	4,6 10^{-8}	0,050	3,2 10^{-8}	1,5 10^{-8}	1,0 10^{-8}	6,4 10^{-9}	5,3 10^{-9}
		M	0,100	4,0 10^{-8}	0,050	2,5 10^{-8}	1,4 10^{-8}	9,4 10^{-9}	7,3 10^{-9}	6,2 10^{-9}
		S	0,100	3,9 10^{-8}	0,050	3,0 10^{-8}	1,7 10^{-8}	1,1 10^{-8}	8,9 10^{-9}	7,7 10^{-9}
Cd-117	2,49 h	F	0,100	7,4 10^{-10}	0,050	5,2 10^{-10}	2,4 10^{-10}	1,5 10^{-10}	8,1 10^{-11}	6,7 10^{-11}
		M	0,100	1,3 10^{-9}	0,050	9,3 10^{-10}	4,5 10^{-10}	2,9 10^{-10}	2,0 10^{-10}	1,6 10^{-10}
		S	0,100	1,4 10^{-9}	0,050	9,8 10^{-10}	4,8 10^{-10}	3,1 10^{-10}	2,1 10^{-10}	1,7 10^{-10}
Cd-117m	3,36 h	F	0,100	8,9 10^{-10}	0,050	6,7 10^{-10}	3,3 10^{-10}	2,0 10^{-10}	1,1 10^{-10}	9,4 10^{-11}
		M	0,100	1,5 10^{-9}	0,050	1,1 10^{-9}	5,5 10^{-10}	3,6 10^{-10}	2,4 10^{-10}	2,0 10^{-10}
		S	0,100	1,5 10^{-9}	0,050	1,1 10^{-9}	5,7 10^{-10}	3,8 10^{-10}	2,6 10^{-10}	2,1 10^{-10}
Indium										
In-109	4,20 h	F	0,040	2,6 10^{-10}	0,020	2,1 10^{-10}	1,0 10^{-10}	6,3 10^{-11}	3,6 10^{-11}	2,9 10^{-11}
		M	0,040	3,3 10^{-10}	0,020	2,6 10^{-10}	1,3 10^{-10}	8,4 10^{-11}	5,3 10^{-11}	4,2 10^{-11}
In-110	4,90 h	F	0,040	8,2 10^{-10}	0,020	7,1 10^{-10}	3,7 10^{-10}	2,3 10^{-10}	1,3 10^{-10}	1,1 10^{-10}
		M	0,040	9,9 10^{-10}	0,020	8,3 10^{-10}	4,4 10^{-10}	2,7 10^{-10}	1,6 10^{-10}	1,3 10^{-10}
In-110	1,15 h	F	0,040	3,0 10^{-10}	0,020	2,1 10^{-10}	9,9 10^{-11}	6,0 10^{-11}	3,5 10^{-11}	2,8 10^{-11}
		M	0,040	4,5 10^{-10}	0,020	3,1 10^{-10}	1,5 10^{-10}	9,2 10^{-11}	5,8 10^{-11}	4,7 10^{-11}

Nuclide	Physical half-life	Type	Age ≤ 1 a		Age	1—2 a	2—7 a	7—12 a	12—17 a	> 17 a
			f_1	h(g)	f_1	h(g)	h(g)	h(g)	h(g)	h(g)
In-111	2,83 d	F	0,040	$1,2\ 10^{-9}$	0,020	$8,6\ 10^{-10}$	$4,2\ 10^{-10}$	$2,6\ 10^{-10}$	$1,5\ 10^{-10}$	$1,3\ 10^{-10}$
		M	0,040	$1,5\ 10^{-9}$	0,020	$1,2\ 10^{-9}$	$6,2\ 10^{-10}$	$4,1\ 10^{-10}$	$2,9\ 10^{-10}$	$2,3\ 10^{-10}$
In-112	0,240 h	F	0,040	$4,4\ 10^{-11}$	0,020	$3,0\ 10^{-11}$	$1,3\ 10^{-11}$	$8,7\ 10^{-12}$	$5,4\ 10^{-12}$	$4,7\ 10^{-12}$
		M	0,040	$6,5\ 10^{-11}$	0,020	$4,4\ 10^{-11}$	$2,0\ 10^{-11}$	$1,3\ 10^{-11}$	$8,7\ 10^{-12}$	$7,4\ 10^{-12}$
In-113m	1,66 h	F	0,040	$1,0\ 10^{-10}$	0,020	$7,0\ 10^{-11}$	$3,2\ 10^{-11}$	$2,0\ 10^{-11}$	$1,2\ 10^{-11}$	$9,7\ 10^{-12}$
		M	0,040	$1,6\ 10^{-10}$	0,020	$1,1\ 10^{-10}$	$5,5\ 10^{-11}$	$3,6\ 10^{-11}$	$2,4\ 10^{-11}$	$2,0\ 10^{-11}$
In-114m	49,5 d	F	0,040	$1,2\ 10^{-7}$	0,020	$7,7\ 10^{-8}$	$3,4\ 10^{-8}$	$1,9\ 10^{-8}$	$1,1\ 10^{-8}$	$9,3\ 10^{-9}$
		M	0,040	$4,8\ 10^{-8}$	0,020	$3,3\ 10^{-8}$	$1,6\ 10^{-8}$	$1,0\ 10^{-8}$	$7,8\ 10^{-9}$	$6,1\ 10^{-9}$
In-115	$5,10\ 10^{15}$ a	F	0,040	$8,3\ 10^{-7}$	0,020	$7,8\ 10^{-7}$	$5,5\ 10^{-7}$	$5,0\ 10^{-7}$	$4,2\ 10^{-7}$	$3,9\ 10^{-7}$
		M	0,040	$3,0\ 10^{-7}$	0,020	$2,8\ 10^{-7}$	$2,1\ 10^{-7}$	$1,9\ 10^{-7}$	$1,7\ 10^{-7}$	$1,6\ 10^{-7}$
In-115m	4,49 h	F	0,040	$2,8\ 10^{-10}$	0,020	$1,9\ 10^{-10}$	$8,4\ 10^{-11}$	$5,1\ 10^{-11}$	$2,8\ 10^{-11}$	$2,4\ 10^{-11}$
		M	0,040	$4,7\ 10^{-10}$	0,020	$3,3\ 10^{-10}$	$1,6\ 10^{-10}$	$1,0\ 10^{-10}$	$7,2\ 10^{-11}$	$5,9\ 10^{-11}$
In-116m	0,902 h	F	0,040	$2,5\ 10^{-10}$	0,020	$1,9\ 10^{-10}$	$9,2\ 10^{-11}$	$5,7\ 10^{-11}$	$3,4\ 10^{-11}$	$2,8\ 10^{-11}$
		M	0,040	$3,6\ 10^{-10}$	0,020	$2,7\ 10^{-10}$	$1,3\ 10^{-10}$	$8,5\ 10^{-11}$	$5,6\ 10^{-11}$	$4,5\ 10^{-11}$
In-117	0,730 h	F	0,040	$1,4\ 10^{-10}$	0,020	$9,7\ 10^{-11}$	$4,5\ 10^{-11}$	$2,8\ 10^{-11}$	$1,7\ 10^{-11}$	$1,5\ 10^{-11}$
		M	0,040	$2,3\ 10^{-10}$	0,020	$1,6\ 10^{-10}$	$7,5\ 10^{-11}$	$5,0\ 10^{-11}$	$3,5\ 10^{-11}$	$2,9\ 10^{-11}$
In-117m	1,94 h	F	0,040	$3,4\ 10^{-10}$	0,020	$2,3\ 10^{-10}$	$1,0\ 10^{-10}$	$6,2\ 10^{-11}$	$3,5\ 10^{-11}$	$2,9\ 10^{-11}$
		M	0,040	$6,0\ 10^{-10}$	0,020	$4,0\ 10^{-10}$	$1,9\ 10^{-10}$	$1,3\ 10^{-10}$	$8,7\ 10^{-11}$	$7,2\ 10^{-11}$
In-119m	0,300 h	F	0,040	$1,2\ 10^{-10}$	0,020	$7,3\ 10^{-11}$	$3,1\ 10^{-11}$	$2,0\ 10^{-11}$	$1,2\ 10^{-11}$	$1,0\ 10^{-11}$
		M	0,040	$1,8\ 10^{-10}$	0,020	$1,1\ 10^{-10}$	$4,9\ 10^{-11}$	$3,2\ 10^{-11}$	$2,0\ 10^{-11}$	$1,7\ 10^{-11}$
Tin										
Sn-110	4,00 h	F	0,040	$1,0\ 10^{-9}$	0,020	$7,6\ 10^{-10}$	$3,6\ 10^{-10}$	$2,2\ 10^{-10}$	$1,2\ 10^{-10}$	$9,9\ 10^{-11}$
		M	0,040	$1,5\ 10^{-9}$	0,020	$1,1\ 10^{-9}$	$5,1\ 10^{-10}$	$3,2\ 10^{-10}$	$1,9\ 10^{-10}$	$1,6\ 10^{-10}$
Sn-111	0,588 h	F	0,040	$7,7\ 10^{-11}$	0,020	$5,4\ 10^{-11}$	$2,6\ 10^{-11}$	$1,6\ 10^{-11}$	$9,4\ 10^{-12}$	$7,8\ 10^{-12}$
		M	0,040	$1,1\ 10^{-10}$	0,020	$8,0\ 10^{-11}$	$3,8\ 10^{-11}$	$2,5\ 10^{-11}$	$1,6\ 10^{-11}$	$1,3\ 10^{-11}$

Nuclide	*Physical half-life*	*Type*	*Age ≤ 1 a*		*Age*	*1—2 a*	*2—7 a*	*7—12 a*	*12—17 a*	*> 17 a*
			f_1	$h(g)$	f_1	$h(g)$	$h(g)$	$h(g)$	$h(g)$	$h(g)$
Sn-113	115 d	F	0,040	$5{,}1\ 10^{-9}$	0,020	$3{,}7\ 10^{-9}$	$1{,}8\ 10^{-9}$	$1{,}1\ 10^{-9}$	$6{,}4\ 10^{-10}$	$5{,}4\ 10^{-10}$
		M	0,040	$1{,}3\ 10^{-8}$	0,020	$1{,}0\ 10^{-8}$	$5{,}8\ 10^{-9}$	$4{,}0\ 10^{-9}$	$3{,}2\ 10^{-9}$	$2{,}7\ 10^{-9}$
Sn-117m	13,6 d	F	0,040	$3{,}3\ 10^{-9}$	0,020	$2{,}2\ 10^{-9}$	$1{,}0\ 10^{-9}$	$6{,}1\ 10^{-10}$	$3{,}4\ 10^{-10}$	$2{,}8\ 10^{-10}$
		M	0,040	$1{,}0\ 10^{-8}$	0,020	$7{,}7\ 10^{-9}$	$4{,}6\ 10^{-9}$	$3{,}4\ 10^{-9}$	$3{,}1\ 10^{-9}$	$2{,}4\ 10^{-9}$
Sn-119m	293 d	F	0,040	$3{,}0\ 10^{-9}$	0,020	$2{,}2\ 10^{-9}$	$1{,}0\ 10^{-9}$	$6{,}0\ 10^{-10}$	$3{,}4\ 10^{-10}$	$2{,}8\ 10^{-10}$
		M	0,040	$1{,}0\ 10^{-8}$	0,020	$7{,}9\ 10^{-9}$	$4{,}7\ 10^{-9}$	$3{,}1\ 10^{-9}$	$2{,}6\ 10^{-9}$	$2{,}2\ 10^{-9}$
Sn-121	1,13 d	F	0,040	$7{,}7\ 10^{-10}$	0,020	$5{,}0\ 10^{-10}$	$2{,}2\ 10^{-10}$	$1{,}3\ 10^{-10}$	$7{,}0\ 10^{-11}$	$6{,}0\ 10^{-11}$
		M	0,040	$1{,}5\ 10^{-9}$	0,020	$1{,}1\ 10^{-9}$	$5{,}1\ 10^{-10}$	$3{,}6\ 10^{-10}$	$2{,}9\ 10^{-10}$	$2{,}3\ 10^{-10}$
Sn-121m	55,0 a	F	0,040	$6{,}9\ 10^{-9}$	0,020	$5{,}4\ 10^{-9}$	$2{,}8\ 10^{-9}$	$1{,}6\ 10^{-9}$	$9{,}4\ 10^{-10}$	$8{,}0\ 10^{-10}$
		M	0,040	$1{,}9\ 10^{-8}$	0,020	$1{,}5\ 10^{-8}$	$9{,}2\ 10^{-9}$	$6{,}4\ 10^{-9}$	$5{,}5\ 10^{-9}$	$4{,}5\ 10^{-9}$
Sn-123	129 d	F	0,040	$1{,}4\ 10^{-8}$	0,020	$9{,}9\ 10^{-9}$	$4{,}5\ 10^{-9}$	$2{,}6\ 10^{-9}$	$1{,}4\ 10^{-9}$	$1{,}2\ 10^{-9}$
		M	0,040	$4{,}0\ 10^{-8}$	0,020	$3{,}1\ 10^{-8}$	$1{,}8\ 10^{-8}$	$1{,}2\ 10^{-8}$	$9{,}5\ 10^{-9}$	$8{,}1\ 10^{-9}$
Sn-123m	0,668 h	F	0,040	$1{,}4\ 10^{-10}$	0,020	$8{,}9\ 10^{-11}$	$3{,}9\ 10^{-11}$	$2{,}5\ 10^{-11}$	$1{,}5\ 10^{-11}$	$1{,}3\ 10^{-11}$
		M	0,040	$2{,}3\ 10^{-10}$	0,020	$1{,}5\ 10^{-10}$	$7{,}0\ 10^{-11}$	$4{,}6\ 10^{-11}$	$3{,}2\ 10^{-11}$	$2{,}7\ 10^{-11}$
Sn-125	9,64 d	F	0,040	$1{,}2\ 10^{-8}$	0,020	$8{,}0\ 10^{-9}$	$3{,}5\ 10^{-9}$	$2{,}0\ 10^{-9}$	$1{,}1\ 10^{-9}$	$8{,}9\ 10^{-10}$
		M	0,040	$2{,}1\ 10^{-8}$	0,020	$1{,}5\ 10^{-8}$	$7{,}6\ 10^{-9}$	$5{,}0\ 10^{-9}$	$3{,}6\ 10^{-9}$	$3{,}1\ 10^{-9}$
Sn-126	$1{,}00\ 10^{5}$ a	F	0,040	$7{,}3\ 10^{-8}$	0,020	$5{,}9\ 10^{-8}$	$3{,}2\ 10^{-8}$	$2{,}0\ 10^{-8}$	$1{,}3\ 10^{-8}$	$1{,}1\ 10^{-8}$
		M	0,040	$1{,}2\ 10^{-7}$	0,020	$1{,}0\ 10^{-7}$	$6{,}2\ 10^{-8}$	$4{,}1\ 10^{-8}$	$3{,}3\ 10^{-8}$	$2{,}8\ 10^{-8}$
Sn-127	2,10 h	F	0,040	$6{,}6\ 10^{-10}$	0,020	$4{,}7\ 10^{-10}$	$2{,}3\ 10^{-10}$	$1{,}4\ 10^{-10}$	$7{,}9\ 10^{-11}$	$6{,}5\ 10^{-11}$
		M	0,040	$1{,}0\ 10^{-9}$	0,020	$7{,}4\ 10^{-10}$	$3{,}7\ 10^{-10}$	$2{,}4\ 10^{-10}$	$1{,}6\ 10^{-10}$	$1{,}3\ 10^{-10}$
Sn-128	0,985 h	F	0,040	$5{,}1\ 10^{-10}$	0,020	$3{,}6\ 10^{-10}$	$1{,}7\ 10^{-10}$	$1{,}0\ 10^{-10}$	$6{,}1\ 10^{-11}$	$5{,}0\ 10^{-11}$
		M	0,040	$8{,}0\ 10^{-10}$	0,020	$5{,}5\ 10^{-10}$	$2{,}7\ 10^{-10}$	$1{,}7\ 10^{-10}$	$1{,}1\ 10^{-10}$	$9{,}2\ 10^{-11}$
Antimony										
Sb-115	0,530 h	F	0,200	$8{,}1\ 10^{-11}$	0,100	$5{,}9\ 10^{-11}$	$2{,}8\ 10^{-11}$	$1{,}7\ 10^{-11}$	$1{,}0\ 10^{-11}$	$8{,}5\ 10^{-12}$
		M	0,020	$1{,}2\ 10^{-10}$	0,010	$8{,}3\ 10^{-11}$	$4{,}0\ 10^{-11}$	$2{,}5\ 10^{-11}$	$1{,}6\ 10^{-11}$	$1{,}3\ 10^{-11}$
		S	0,020	$1{,}2\ 10^{-10}$	0,010	$8{,}6\ 10^{-11}$	$4{,}1\ 10^{-11}$	$2{,}6\ 10^{-11}$	$1{,}7\ 10^{-11}$	$1{,}4\ 10^{-11}$

Nuclide	Physical half-life	Type	Age ≤ 1 a		Age	1—2 a	2—7 a	7—12 a	12—17 a	> 17 a
			f_1	$h(g)$	f_1	$h(g)$	$h(g)$	$h(g)$	$h(g)$	$h(g)$
Sb-116	0,263 h	F	0,200	$8{,}4\ 10^{-11}$	0,100	$6{,}2\ 10^{-11}$	$3{,}0\ 10^{-11}$	$1{,}9\ 10^{-11}$	$1{,}1\ 10^{-11}$	$9{,}1\ 10^{-12}$
		M	0,020	$1{,}1\ 10^{-10}$	0,010	$8{,}2\ 10^{-11}$	$4{,}0\ 10^{-11}$	$2{,}5\ 10^{-11}$	$1{,}5\ 10^{-11}$	$1{,}3\ 10^{-11}$
		S	0,020	$1{,}2\ 10^{-10}$	0,010	$8{,}5\ 10^{-11}$	$4{,}1\ 10^{-11}$	$2{,}6\ 10^{-11}$	$1{,}6\ 10^{-11}$	$1{,}3\ 10^{-11}$
Sb-116m	1,00 h	F	0,200	$2{,}6\ 10^{-10}$	0,100	$2{,}1\ 10^{-10}$	$1{,}1\ 10^{-10}$	$6{,}6\ 10^{-11}$	$4{,}0\ 10^{-11}$	$3{,}2\ 10^{-11}$
		M	0,020	$3{,}6\ 10^{-10}$	0,010	$2{,}8\ 10^{-10}$	$1{,}5\ 10^{-10}$	$9{,}1\ 10^{-11}$	$5{,}9\ 10^{-11}$	$4{,}7\ 10^{-11}$
		S	0,020	$3{,}7\ 10^{-10}$	0,010	$2{,}9\ 10^{-10}$	$1{,}5\ 10^{-10}$	$9{,}4\ 10^{-11}$	$6{,}1\ 10^{-11}$	$4{,}9\ 10^{-11}$
Sb-117	2,80 h	F	0,200	$7{,}7\ 10^{-11}$	0,100	$6{,}0\ 10^{-11}$	$2{,}9\ 10^{-11}$	$1{,}8\ 10^{-11}$	$1{,}0\ 10^{-11}$	$8{,}5\ 10^{-12}$
		M	0,020	$1{,}2\ 10^{-10}$	0,010	$9{,}1\ 10^{-11}$	$4{,}6\ 10^{-11}$	$3{,}0\ 10^{-11}$	$2{,}0\ 10^{-11}$	$1{,}6\ 10^{-11}$
		S	0,020	$1{,}3\ 10^{-10}$	0,010	$9{,}5\ 10^{-11}$	$4{,}8\ 10^{-11}$	$3{,}1\ 10^{-11}$	$2{,}2\ 10^{-11}$	$1{,}7\ 10^{-11}$
Sb-118m	5,00 h	F	0,200	$7{,}3\ 10^{-10}$	0,100	$6{,}2\ 10^{-10}$	$3{,}3\ 10^{-10}$	$2{,}0\ 10^{-10}$	$1{,}2\ 10^{-10}$	$9{,}3\ 10^{-11}$
		M	0,020	$9{,}3\ 10^{-10}$	0,010	$7{,}6\ 10^{-10}$	$4{,}0\ 10^{-10}$	$2{,}5\ 10^{-10}$	$1{,}5\ 10^{-10}$	$1{,}2\ 10^{-10}$
		S	0,020	$9{,}5\ 10^{-10}$	0,010	$7{,}8\ 10^{-10}$	$4{,}1\ 10^{-10}$	$2{,}5\ 10^{-10}$	$1{,}5\ 10^{-10}$	$1{,}2\ 10^{-10}$
Sb-119	1,59 d	F	0,200	$2{,}7\ 10^{-10}$	0,100	$2{,}0\ 10^{-10}$	$9{,}4\ 10^{-11}$	$5{,}5\ 10^{-11}$	$2{,}9\ 10^{-11}$	$2{,}3\ 10^{-11}$
		M	0,020	$4{,}0\ 10^{-10}$	0,010	$2{,}8\ 10^{-10}$	$1{,}3\ 10^{-10}$	$7{,}9\ 10^{-11}$	$4{,}4\ 10^{-11}$	$3{,}5\ 10^{-11}$
		S	0,020	$4{,}1\ 10^{-10}$	0,010	$2{,}9\ 10^{-10}$	$1{,}4\ 10^{-10}$	$8{,}2\ 10^{-11}$	$4{,}5\ 10^{-11}$	$3{,}6\ 10^{-11}$
Sb-120	5,76 d	F	0,200	$4{,}1\ 10^{-9}$	0,100	$3{,}3\ 10^{-9}$	$1{,}8\ 10^{-9}$	$1{,}1\ 10^{-9}$	$6{,}7\ 10^{-10}$	$5{,}5\ 10^{-10}$
		M	0,020	$6{,}3\ 10^{-9}$	0,010	$5{,}0\ 10^{-9}$	$2{,}8\ 10^{-9}$	$1{,}8\ 10^{-9}$	$1{,}3\ 10^{-9}$	$1{,}0\ 10^{-9}$
		S	0,020	$6{,}6\ 10^{-9}$	0,010	$5{,}3\ 10^{-9}$	$2{,}9\ 10^{-9}$	$1{,}9\ 10^{-9}$	$1{,}4\ 10^{-9}$	$1{,}1\ 10^{-9}$
Sb-120	0,265 h	F	0,200	$4{,}6\ 10^{-11}$	0,100	$3{,}1\ 10^{-11}$	$1{,}4\ 10^{-11}$	$8{,}9\ 10^{-12}$	$5{,}4\ 10^{-12}$	$4{,}6\ 10^{-12}$
		M	0,020	$6{,}6\ 10^{-11}$	0,010	$4{,}4\ 10^{-11}$	$2{,}0\ 10^{-11}$	$1{,}3\ 10^{-11}$	$8{,}3\ 10^{-12}$	$7{,}0\ 10^{-12}$
		S	0,020	$6{,}8\ 10^{-11}$	0,010	$4{,}6\ 10^{-11}$	$2{,}1\ 10^{-11}$	$1{,}4\ 10^{-11}$	$8{,}7\ 10^{-12}$	$7{,}3\ 10^{-12}$
Sb-122	2,70 d	F	0,200	$4{,}2\ 10^{-9}$	0,100	$2{,}8\ 10^{-9}$	$1{,}4\ 10^{-9}$	$8{,}4\ 10^{-10}$	$4{,}4\ 10^{-10}$	$3{,}6\ 10^{-10}$
		M	0,020	$8{,}3\ 10^{-9}$	0,010	$5{,}7\ 10^{-9}$	$2{,}8\ 10^{-9}$	$1{,}8\ 10^{-9}$	$1{,}3\ 10^{-9}$	$1{,}0\ 10^{-9}$
		S	0,020	$8{,}8\ 10^{-9}$	0,010	$6{,}1\ 10^{-9}$	$3{,}0\ 10^{-9}$	$2{,}0\ 10^{-9}$	$1{,}4\ 10^{-9}$	$1{,}1\ 10^{-9}$

Nuclide	*Physical half-life*	*Type*	*Age ≤ 1 a*		*Age*	*1—2 a*	*2—7 a*	*7—12 a*	*12—17 a*	*> 17 a*
			f_1	*h(g)*	f_1	*h(g)*	*h(g)*	*h(g)*	*h(g)*	*h(g)*
Sb-124	60,2 d	F	0,200	1,2 10^{-8}	0,100	8,8 10^{-9}	4,3 10^{-9}	2,6 10^{-9}	1,6 10^{-9}	1,3 10^{-9}
		M	0,020	3,1 10^{-8}	0,010	2,4 10^{-8}	1,4 10^{-8}	9,6 10^{-9}	7,7 10^{-9}	6,4 10^{-9}
		S	0,020	3,9 10^{-8}	0,010	3,1 10^{-8}	1,8 10^{-8}	1,3 10^{-8}	1,0 10^{-8}	8,6 10^{-9}
Sb-124m	0,337 h	F	0,200	2,7 10^{-11}	0,100	1,9 10^{-11}	9,0 10^{-12}	5,6 10^{-12}	3,4 10^{-12}	2,8 10^{-12}
		M	0,020	4,3 10^{-11}	0,010	3,1 10^{-11}	1,5 10^{-11}	9,6 10^{-12}	6,5 10^{-12}	5,4 10^{-12}
		S	0,020	4,6 10^{-11}	0,010	3,3 10^{-11}	1,6 10^{-11}	1,0 10^{-11}	7,2 10^{-12}	5,9 10^{-12}
Sb-125	2,77 a	F	0,200	8,7 10^{-9}	0,100	6,8 10^{-9}	3,7 10^{-9}	2,3 10^{-9}	1,5 10^{-9}	1,4 10^{-9}
		M	0,020	2,0 10^{-8}	0,010	1,6 10^{-8}	1,0 10^{-8}	6,8 10^{-9}	5,8 10^{-9}	4,8 10^{-9}
		S	0,020	4,2 10^{-8}	0,010	3,8 10^{-8}	2,4 10^{-8}	1,6 10^{-8}	1,4 10^{-8}	1,2 10^{-8}
Sb-126	12,4 d	F	0,200	8,8 10^{-9}	0,100	6,6 10^{-9}	3,3 10^{-9}	2,1 10^{-9}	1,2 10^{-9}	1,0 10^{-9}
		M	0,020	1,7 10^{-8}	0,010	1,3 10^{-8}	7,4 10^{-9}	5,1 10^{-9}	3,5 10^{-9}	2,8 10^{-9}
		S	0,020	1,9 10^{-8}	0,010	1,5 10^{-8}	8,2 10^{-9}	5,0 10^{-9}	4,0 10^{-9}	3,2 10^{-9}
Sb-126m	0,317 h	F	0,200	1,2 10^{-10}	0,100	8,2 10^{-11}	3,8 10^{-11}	2,4 10^{-11}	1,5 10^{-11}	1,2 10^{-11}
		M	0,020	1,7 10^{-10}	0,010	1,2 10^{-10}	5,5 10^{-11}	3,5 10^{-11}	2,3 10^{-11}	1,9 10^{-11}
		S	0,020	1,8 10^{-10}	0,010	1,2 10^{-10}	5,7 10^{-11}	3,7 10^{-11}	2,4 10^{-11}	2,0 10^{-11}
Sb-127	3,85 d	F	0,200	5,1 10^{-9}	0,100	3,5 10^{-9}	1,6 10^{-9}	9,7 10^{-10}	5,2 10^{-10}	4,3 10^{-10}
		M	0,020	1,0 10^{-8}	0,010	7,3 10^{-9}	3,9 10^{-9}	2,7 10^{-9}	2,1 10^{-9}	1,7 10^{-9}
		S	0,020	1,1 10^{-8}	0,010	7,9 10^{-9}	4,2 10^{-9}	3,0 10^{-9}	2,3 10^{-9}	1,9 10^{-9}
Sb-128	9,01 h	F	0,200	2,1 10^{-9}	0,100	1,7 10^{-9}	8,3 10^{-10}	5,1 10^{-10}	2,9 10^{-10}	2,3 10^{-10}
		M	0,020	3,3 10^{-9}	0,010	2,5 10^{-9}	1,2 10^{-9}	7,9 10^{-10}	5,0 10^{-10}	4,0 10^{-10}
		S	0,020	3,4 10^{-9}	0,010	2,6 10^{-9}	1,3 10^{-9}	8,3 10^{-10}	5,2 10^{-10}	4,2 10^{-10}
Sb-128	0,173 h	F	0,200	9,8 10^{-11}	0,100	6,9 10^{-11}	3,2 10^{-11}	2,0 10^{-11}	1,2 10^{-11}	1,0 10^{-11}
		M	0,020	1,3 10^{-10}	0,010	9,2 10^{-11}	4,3 10^{-11}	2,7 10^{-11}	1,7 10^{-11}	1,4 10^{-11}
		S	0,020	1,4 10^{-10}	0,010	9,4 10^{-11}	4,4 10^{-11}	2,8 10^{-11}	1,8 10^{-11}	1,5 10^{-11}

Nuclide	Physical half-life	Type	*Age ≤ 1 a*		*Age*	*1—2 a*	*2—7 a*	*7—12 a*	*12—17 a*	*> 17 a*
			f_1	*h(g)*	f_1	*h(g)*	*h(g)*	*h(g)*	*h(g)*	*h(g)*
Sb-129	4,32 h	F	0,200	$1,1\ 10^{-9}$	0,100	$8,2\ 10^{-10}$	$3,8\ 10^{-10}$	$2,3\ 10^{-10}$	$1,3\ 10^{-10}$	$1,0\ 10^{-10}$
		M	0,020	$2,0\ 10^{-9}$	0,010	$1,4\ 10^{-9}$	$6,8\ 10^{-10}$	$4,4\ 10^{-10}$	$2,9\ 10^{-10}$	$2,3\ 10^{-10}$
		S	0,020	$2,1\ 10^{-9}$	0,010	$1,5\ 10^{-9}$	$7,2\ 10^{-10}$	$4,6\ 10^{-10}$	$3,0\ 10^{-10}$	$2,5\ 10^{-10}$
Sb-130	0,667 h	F	0,200	$3,0\ 10^{-10}$	0,100	$2,2\ 10^{-10}$	$1,1\ 10^{-10}$	$6,6\ 10^{-11}$	$4,0\ 10^{-11}$	$3,3\ 10^{-11}$
		M	0,020	$4,5\ 10^{-10}$	0,010	$3,2\ 10^{-10}$	$1,6\ 10^{-10}$	$9,8\ 10^{-11}$	$6,3\ 10^{-11}$	$5,1\ 10^{-11}$
		S	0,020	$4,6\ 10^{-10}$	0,010	$3,3\ 10^{-10}$	$1,6\ 10^{-10}$	$1,0\ 10^{-10}$	$6,5\ 10^{-11}$	$5,3\ 10^{-11}$
Sb-131	0,383 h	F	0,200	$3,5\ 10^{-10}$	0,100	$2,8\ 10^{-10}$	$1,4\ 10^{-10}$	$7,7\ 10^{-11}$	$4,6\ 10^{-11}$	$3,5\ 10^{-11}$
		M	0,020	$3,9\ 10^{-10}$	0,010	$2,6\ 10^{-10}$	$1,3\ 10^{-10}$	$8,0\ 10^{-11}$	$5,3\ 10^{-11}$	$4,4\ 10^{-11}$
		S	0,020	$3,8\ 10^{-10}$	0,010	$2,6\ 10^{-10}$	$1,2\ 10^{-10}$	$7,9\ 10^{-11}$	$5,3\ 10^{-11}$	$4,4\ 10^{-11}$
Tellurium										
Te-116	2,49 h	F	0,600	$5,3\ 10^{-10}$	0,300	$4,2\ 10^{-10}$	$2,1\ 10^{-10}$	$1,3\ 10^{-10}$	$7,2\ 10^{-11}$	$5,8\ 10^{-11}$
		M	0,200	$8,6\ 10^{-10}$	0,100	$6,4\ 10^{-10}$	$3,2\ 10^{-10}$	$2,0\ 10^{-10}$	$1,3\ 10^{-10}$	$1,0\ 10^{-10}$
		S	0,020	$9,1\ 10^{-10}$	0,010	$6,7\ 10^{-10}$	$3,3\ 10^{-10}$	$2,1\ 10^{-10}$	$1,4\ 10^{-10}$	$1,1\ 10^{-10}$
Te-121	17,0 d	F	0,600	$1,7\ 10^{-9}$	0,300	$1,4\ 10^{-9}$	$7,2\ 10^{-10}$	$4,6\ 10^{-10}$	$2,9\ 10^{-10}$	$2,4\ 10^{-10}$
		M	0,200	$2,3\ 10^{-9}$	0,100	$1,9\ 10^{-9}$	$1,0\ 10^{-9}$	$6,8\ 10^{-10}$	$4,7\ 10^{-10}$	$3,8\ 10^{-10}$
		S	0,020	$2,4\ 10^{-9}$	0,010	$2,0\ 10^{-9}$	$1,1\ 10^{-9}$	$7,2\ 10^{-10}$	$5,1\ 10^{-10}$	$4,1\ 10^{-10}$
Te-121m	154 d	F	0,600	$1,4\ 10^{-8}$	0,300	$1,0\ 10^{-8}$	$5,3\ 10^{-9}$	$3,3\ 10^{-9}$	$2,1\ 10^{-9}$	$1,8\ 10^{-9}$
		M	0,200	$1,9\ 10^{-8}$	0,100	$1,5\ 10^{-8}$	$8,8\ 10^{-9}$	$6,1\ 10^{-9}$	$5,1\ 10^{-9}$	$4,2\ 10^{-9}$
		S	0,020	$2,3\ 10^{-8}$	0,010	$1,9\ 10^{-8}$	$1,2\ 10^{-8}$	$8,1\ 10^{-9}$	$6,9\ 10^{-9}$	$5,7\ 10^{-9}$
Te-123	$1,00\ 10^{13}$ a	F	0,600	$1,1\ 10^{-8}$	0,300	$9,1\ 10^{-9}$	$6,2\ 10^{-9}$	$4,8\ 10^{-9}$	$4,0\ 10^{-9}$	$3,9\ 10^{-9}$
		M	0,200	$5,6\ 10^{-9}$	0,100	$4,4\ 10^{-9}$	$3,0\ 10^{-9}$	$2,3\ 10^{-9}$	$2,0\ 10^{-9}$	$1,9\ 10^{-9}$
		S	0,020	$5,3\ 10^{-9}$	0,010	$5,0\ 10^{-9}$	$3,5\ 10^{-9}$	$2,4\ 10^{-9}$	$2,1\ 10^{-9}$	$2,0\ 10^{-9}$
Te-123m	120 d	F	0,600	$9,8\ 10^{-9}$	0,300	$6,8\ 10^{-9}$	$3,4\ 10^{-9}$	$1,9\ 10^{-9}$	$1,1\ 10^{-9}$	$9,5\ 10^{-10}$
		M	0,200	$1,8\ 10^{-8}$	0,100	$1,3\ 10^{-8}$	$8,0\ 10^{-9}$	$5,7\ 10^{-9}$	$5,0\ 10^{-9}$	$4,0\ 10^{-9}$
		S	0,020	$2,0\ 10^{-8}$	0,010	$1,6\ 10^{-8}$	$9,8\ 10^{-9}$	$7,1\ 10^{-9}$	$6,3\ 10^{-9}$	$5,1\ 10^{-9}$

Nuclide	*Physical half-life*	*Type*	*Age ≤ 1 a*		*Age*	*1—2 a*	*2—7 a*	*7—12 a*	*12—17 a*	*> 17 a*
			f_1	$h(g)$	f_1	$h(g)$	$h(g)$	$h(g)$	$h(g)$	$h(g)$
Te-125m	58,0 d	F	0,600	$6{,}2\ 10^{-9}$	0,300	$4{,}2\ 10^{-9}$	$2{,}0\ 10^{-9}$	$1{,}1\ 10^{-9}$	$6{,}1\ 10^{-10}$	$5{,}1\ 10^{-10}$
		M	0,200	$1{,}5\ 10^{-8}$	0,100	$1{,}1\ 10^{-8}$	$6{,}6\ 10^{-9}$	$4{,}8\ 10^{-9}$	$4{,}3\ 10^{-9}$	$3{,}4\ 10^{-9}$
		S	0,020	$1{,}7\ 10^{-8}$	0,010	$1{,}3\ 10^{-8}$	$7{,}8\ 10^{-9}$	$5{,}8\ 10^{-9}$	$5{,}3\ 10^{-9}$	$4{,}2\ 10^{-9}$
Te-127	9,35 h	F	0,600	$4{,}3\ 10^{-10}$	0,300	$3{,}2\ 10^{-10}$	$1{,}4\ 10^{-10}$	$8{,}5\ 10^{-11}$	$4{,}5\ 10^{-11}$	$3{,}9\ 10^{-11}$
		M	0,200	$1{,}0\ 10^{-9}$	0,100	$7{,}3\ 10^{-10}$	$3{,}6\ 10^{-10}$	$2{,}4\ 10^{-10}$	$1{,}6\ 10^{-10}$	$1{,}3\ 10^{-10}$
		S	0,020	$1{,}2\ 10^{-9}$	0,010	$7{,}9\ 10^{-10}$	$3{,}9\ 10^{-10}$	$2{,}6\ 10^{-10}$	$1{,}7\ 10^{-10}$	$1{,}4\ 10^{-10}$
Te-127m	109 d	F	0,600	$2{,}1\ 10^{-8}$	0,300	$1{,}4\ 10^{-8}$	$6{,}5\ 10^{-9}$	$3{,}5\ 10^{-9}$	$2{,}0\ 10^{-9}$	$1{,}5\ 10^{-9}$
		M	0,200	$3{,}5\ 10^{-8}$	0,100	$2{,}6\ 10^{-8}$	$1{,}5\ 10^{-8}$	$1{,}1\ 10^{-8}$	$9{,}2\ 10^{-9}$	$7{,}4\ 10^{-9}$
		S	0,020	$4{,}1\ 10^{-8}$	0,010	$3{,}3\ 10^{-8}$	$2{,}0\ 10^{-8}$	$1{,}4\ 10^{-8}$	$1{,}2\ 10^{-8}$	$9{,}8\ 10^{-9}$
Te-129	1,16 h	F	0,600	$1{,}8\ 10^{-10}$	0,300	$1{,}2\ 10^{-10}$	$5{,}1\ 10^{-11}$	$3{,}2\ 10^{-11}$	$1{,}9\ 10^{-11}$	$1{,}6\ 10^{-11}$
		M	0,200	$3{,}3\ 10^{-10}$	0,100	$2{,}2\ 10^{-10}$	$9{,}9\ 10^{-11}$	$6{,}5\ 10^{-11}$	$4{,}4\ 10^{-11}$	$3{,}7\ 10^{-11}$
		S	0,020	$3{,}5\ 10^{-10}$	0,010	$2{,}3\ 10^{-10}$	$1{,}0\ 10^{-10}$	$6{,}9\ 10^{-11}$	$4{,}7\ 10^{-11}$	$3{,}9\ 10^{-11}$
Te-129m	33,6 d	F	0,600	$2{,}0\ 10^{-8}$	0,300	$1{,}3\ 10^{-8}$	$5{,}8\ 10^{-9}$	$3{,}1\ 10^{-9}$	$1{,}7\ 10^{-9}$	$1{,}3\ 10^{-9}$
		M	0,200	$3{,}5\ 10^{-8}$	0,100	$2{,}6\ 10^{-8}$	$1{,}4\ 10^{-8}$	$9{,}8\ 10^{-9}$	$8{,}0\ 10^{-9}$	$6{,}6\ 10^{-9}$
		S	0,020	$3{,}8\ 10^{-8}$	0,010	$2{,}9\ 10^{-8}$	$1{,}7\ 10^{-8}$	$1{,}2\ 10^{-8}$	$9{,}6\ 10^{-9}$	$7{,}9\ 10^{-9}$
Te-131	0,417 h	F	0,600	$2{,}3\ 10^{-10}$	0,300	$2{,}0\ 10^{-10}$	$9{,}9\ 10^{-11}$	$5{,}3\ 10^{-11}$	$3{,}3\ 10^{-11}$	$2{,}3\ 10^{-11}$
		M	0,200	$2{,}6\ 10^{-10}$	0,100	$1{,}7\ 10^{-10}$	$8{,}1\ 10^{-11}$	$5{,}2\ 10^{-11}$	$3{,}5\ 10^{-11}$	$2{,}8\ 10^{-11}$
		S	0,020	$2{,}4\ 10^{-10}$	0,010	$1{,}6\ 10^{-10}$	$7{,}4\ 10^{-11}$	$4{,}9\ 10^{-11}$	$3{,}3\ 10^{-11}$	$2{,}8\ 10^{-11}$
Te-131m	1,25 d	F	0,600	$8{,}7\ 10^{-9}$	0,300	$7{,}6\ 10^{-9}$	$3{,}9\ 10^{-9}$	$2{,}0\ 10^{-9}$	$1{,}2\ 10^{-9}$	$8{,}6\ 10^{-10}$
		M	0,200	$7{,}9\ 10^{-9}$	0,100	$5{,}8\ 10^{-9}$	$3{,}0\ 10^{-9}$	$1{,}9\ 10^{-9}$	$1{,}2\ 10^{-9}$	$9{,}4\ 10^{-10}$
		S	0,020	$7{,}0\ 10^{-9}$	0,010	$5{,}1\ 10^{-9}$	$2{,}6\ 10^{-9}$	$1{,}8\ 10^{-9}$	$1{,}1\ 10^{-9}$	$9{,}1\ 10^{-10}$
Te-132	3,26 d	F	0,600	$2{,}2\ 10^{-8}$	0,300	$1{,}8\ 10^{-8}$	$8{,}5\ 10^{-9}$	$4{,}2\ 10^{-9}$	$2{,}6\ 10^{-9}$	$1{,}8\ 10^{-9}$
		M	0,200	$1{,}6\ 10^{-8}$	0,100	$1{,}3\ 10^{-8}$	$6{,}4\ 10^{-9}$	$4{,}0\ 10^{-9}$	$2{,}6\ 10^{-9}$	$2{,}0\ 10^{-9}$
		S	0,020	$1{,}5\ 10^{-8}$	0,010	$1{,}1\ 10^{-8}$	$5{,}8\ 10^{-9}$	$3{,}8\ 10^{-9}$	$2{,}5\ 10^{-9}$	$2{,}0\ 10^{-9}$

Nuclide	Physical half-life	Type	Age ≤ 1 a		Age	1—2 a	2—7 a	7—12 a	12—17 a	> 17 a
			f_1	$h(g)$	f_1	$h(g)$	$h(g)$	$h(g)$	$h(g)$	$h(g)$
Te-133	0,207 h	F	0,600	$2,4\ 10^{-10}$	0,300	$2,1\ 10^{-10}$	$9,6\ 10^{-11}$	$4,6\ 10^{-11}$	$2,8\ 10^{-11}$	$1,9\ 10^{-11}$
		M	0,200	$2,0\ 10^{-10}$	0,100	$1,3\ 10^{-10}$	$6,1\ 10^{-11}$	$3,8\ 10^{-11}$	$2,4\ 10^{-11}$	$2,0\ 10^{-11}$
		S	0,020	$1,7\ 10^{-10}$	0,010	$1,2\ 10^{-10}$	$5,4\ 10^{-11}$	$3,5\ 10^{-11}$	$2,2\ 10^{-11}$	$1,9\ 10^{-11}$
Te-133m	0,923 h	F	0,600	$1,0\ 10^{-9}$	0,300	$8,9\ 10^{-10}$	$4,1\ 10^{-10}$	$2,0\ 10^{-10}$	$1,2\ 10^{-10}$	$8,1\ 10^{-11}$
		M	0,200	$8,5\ 10^{-10}$	0,100	$5,8\ 10^{-10}$	$2,8\ 10^{-10}$	$1,7\ 10^{-10}$	$1,1\ 10^{-10}$	$8,7\ 10^{-11}$
		S	0,020	$7,4\ 10^{-10}$	0,010	$5,1\ 10^{-10}$	$2,5\ 10^{-10}$	$1,6\ 10^{-10}$	$1,0\ 10^{-10}$	$8,4\ 10^{-11}$
Te-134	0,696 h	F	0,600	$4,7\ 10^{-10}$	0,300	$3,7\ 10^{-10}$	$1,8\ 10^{-10}$	$1,0\ 10^{-10}$	$6,0\ 10^{-11}$	$4,7\ 10^{-11}$
		M	0,200	$5,5\ 10^{-10}$	0,100	$3,9\ 10^{-10}$	$1,9\ 10^{-10}$	$1,2\ 10^{-10}$	$8,1\ 10^{-11}$	$6,6\ 10^{-11}$
		S	0,020	$5,6\ 10^{-10}$	0,010	$4,0\ 10^{-10}$	$1,9\ 10^{-10}$	$1,3\ 10^{-10}$	$8,4\ 10^{-11}$	$6,8\ 10^{-11}$
Iodine										
I-120	1,35 h	F	1,000	$1,3\ 10^{-9}$	1,000	$1,0\ 10^{-9}$	$4,8\ 10^{-10}$	$2,3\ 10^{-10}$	$1,4\ 10^{-10}$	$1,0\ 10^{-10}$
		M	0,200	$1,1\ 10^{-9}$	0,100	$7,3\ 10^{-10}$	$3,4\ 10^{-10}$	$2,1\ 10^{-10}$	$1,3\ 10^{-10}$	$1,0\ 10^{-10}$
		S	0,020	$1,0\ 10^{-9}$	0,010	$6,9\ 10^{-10}$	$3,2\ 10^{-10}$	$2,0\ 10^{-10}$	$1,2\ 10^{-10}$	$1,0\ 10^{-10}$
I-120m	0,883 h	F	1,000	$8,6\ 10^{-10}$	1,000	$6,9\ 10^{-10}$	$3,3\ 10^{-10}$	$1,8\ 10^{-10}$	$1,1\ 10^{-10}$	$8,2\ 10^{-11}$
		M	0,200	$8,2\ 10^{-10}$	0,100	$5,9\ 10^{-10}$	$2,9\ 10^{-10}$	$1,8\ 10^{-10}$	$1,1\ 10^{-10}$	$8,7\ 10^{-11}$
		S	0,020	$8,2\ 10^{-10}$	0,010	$5,8\ 10^{-10}$	$2,8\ 10^{-10}$	$1,8\ 10^{-10}$	$1,1\ 10^{-10}$	$8,8\ 10^{-11}$
I-121	2,12 h	F	1,000	$2,3\ 10^{-10}$	1,000	$2,1\ 10^{-10}$	$1,1\ 10^{-10}$	$6,0\ 10^{-11}$	$3,8\ 10^{-11}$	$2,7\ 10^{-11}$
		M	0,200	$2,1\ 10^{-10}$	0,100	$1,5\ 10^{-10}$	$7,8\ 10^{-11}$	$4,9\ 10^{-11}$	$3,2\ 10^{-11}$	$2,5\ 10^{-11}$
		S	0,020	$1,9\ 10^{-10}$	0,010	$1,4\ 10^{-10}$	$7,0\ 10^{-11}$	$4,5\ 10^{-11}$	$3,0\ 10^{-11}$	$2,4\ 10^{-11}$
I-123	13,2 h	F	1,000	$8,7\ 10^{-10}$	1,000	$7,9\ 10^{-10}$	$3,8\ 10^{-10}$	$1,8\ 10^{-10}$	$1,1\ 10^{-10}$	$7,4\ 10^{-11}$
		M	0,200	$5,3\ 10^{-10}$	0,100	$3,9\ 10^{-10}$	$2,0\ 10^{-10}$	$1,2\ 10^{-10}$	$8,2\ 10^{-11}$	$6,4\ 10^{-11}$
		S	0,020	$4,3\ 10^{-10}$	0,010	$3,2\ 10^{-10}$	$1,7\ 10^{-10}$	$1,1\ 10^{-10}$	$7,6\ 10^{-11}$	$6,0\ 10^{-11}$
I-124	4,18 d	F	1,000	$4,7\ 10^{-8}$	1,000	$4,5\ 10^{-8}$	$2,2\ 10^{-8}$	$1,1\ 10^{-8}$	$6,7\ 10^{-9}$	$4,4\ 10^{-9}$
		M	0,200	$1,4\ 10^{-8}$	0,100	$9,3\ 10^{-9}$	$4,6\ 10^{-9}$	$2,5\ 10^{-9}$	$1,6\ 10^{-9}$	$1,2\ 10^{-9}$
		S	0,020	$6,2\ 10^{-9}$	0,010	$4,4\ 10^{-9}$	$2,2\ 10^{-9}$	$1,4\ 10^{-9}$	$9,4\ 10^{-10}$	$7,7\ 10^{-10}$

Nuclide	*Physical half-life*	*Type*	*Age ≤ 1 a*		*Age*	*1—2 a*	*2—7 a*	*7—12 a*	*12—17 a*	*> 17 a*
			f_1	$h(g)$	f_1	$h(g)$	$h(g)$	$h(g)$	$h(g)$	$h(g)$
I-125	60,1 d	F	1,000	$2,0\ 10^{-8}$	1,000	$2,3\ 10^{-8}$	$1,5\ 10^{-8}$	$1,1\ 10^{-8}$	$7,2\ 10^{-9}$	$5,1\ 10^{-9}$
		M	0,200	$6,9\ 10^{-9}$	0,100	$5,6\ 10^{-9}$	$3,6\ 10^{-9}$	$2,6\ 10^{-9}$	$1,8\ 10^{-9}$	$1,4\ 10^{-9}$
		S	0,020	$2,4\ 10^{-9}$	0,010	$1,8\ 10^{-9}$	$1,0\ 10^{-9}$	$6,7\ 10^{-10}$	$4,8\ 10^{-10}$	$3,8\ 10^{-10}$
I-126	13,0 d	F	1,000	$8,1\ 10^{-8}$	1,000	$8,3\ 10^{-8}$	$4,5\ 10^{-8}$	$2,4\ 10^{-8}$	$1,5\ 10^{-8}$	$9,8\ 10^{-9}$
		M	0,200	$2,4\ 10^{-8}$	0,100	$1,7\ 10^{-8}$	$9,5\ 10^{-9}$	$5,5\ 10^{-9}$	$3,8\ 10^{-9}$	$2,7\ 10^{-9}$
		S	0,020	$8,3\ 10^{-9}$	0,010	$5,9\ 10^{-9}$	$3,3\ 10^{-9}$	$2,2\ 10^{-9}$	$1,8\ 10^{-9}$	$1,4\ 10^{-9}$
I-128	0,416 h	F	1,000	$1,5\ 10^{-10}$	1,000	$1,1\ 10^{-10}$	$4,7\ 10^{-11}$	$2,7\ 10^{-11}$	$1,6\ 10^{-11}$	$1,3\ 10^{-11}$
		M	0,200	$1,9\ 10^{-10}$	0,100	$1,2\ 10^{-10}$	$5,3\ 10^{-11}$	$3,4\ 10^{-11}$	$2,2\ 10^{-11}$	$1,9\ 10^{-11}$
		S	0,020	$1,9\ 10^{-10}$	0,010	$1,2\ 10^{-10}$	$5,4\ 10^{-11}$	$3,5\ 10^{-11}$	$2,3\ 10^{-11}$	$2,0\ 10^{-11}$
I-129	$1,57\ 10^{7}$ a	F	1,000	$7,2\ 10^{-8}$	1,000	$8,6\ 10^{-8}$	$6,1\ 10^{-8}$	$6,7\ 10^{-8}$	$4,6\ 10^{-8}$	$3,6\ 10^{-8}$
		M	0,200	$3,6\ 10^{-8}$	0,100	$3,3\ 10^{-8}$	$2,4\ 10^{-8}$	$2,4\ 10^{-8}$	$1,9\ 10^{-8}$	$1,5\ 10^{-8}$
		S	0,020	$2,9\ 10^{-8}$	0,010	$2,6\ 10^{-8}$	$1,8\ 10^{-8}$	$1,3\ 10^{-8}$	$1,1\ 10^{-8}$	$9,8\ 10^{-9}$
I-130	12,4 h	F	1,000	$8,2\ 10^{-9}$	1,000	$7,4\ 10^{-9}$	$3,5\ 10^{-9}$	$1,6\ 10^{-9}$	$1,0\ 10^{-9}$	$6,7\ 10^{-10}$
		M	0,200	$4,3\ 10^{-9}$	0,100	$3,1\ 10^{-9}$	$1,5\ 10^{-9}$	$9,2\ 10^{-10}$	$5,8\ 10^{-10}$	$4,5\ 10^{-10}$
		S	0,020	$3,3\ 10^{-9}$	0,010	$2,4\ 10^{-9}$	$1,2\ 10^{-9}$	$7,9\ 10^{-10}$	$5,1\ 10^{-10}$	$4,1\ 10^{-10}$
I-131	8,04 d	F	1,000	$7,2\ 10^{-8}$	1,000	$7,2\ 10^{-8}$	$3,7\ 10^{-8}$	$1,9\ 10^{-8}$	$1,1\ 10^{-8}$	$7,4\ 10^{-9}$
		M	0,200	$2,2\ 10^{-8}$	0,100	$1,5\ 10^{-8}$	$8,2\ 10^{-9}$	$4,7\ 10^{-9}$	$3,4\ 10^{-9}$	$2,4\ 10^{-9}$
		S	0,020	$8,8\ 10^{-9}$	0,010	$6,2\ 10^{-9}$	$3,5\ 10^{-9}$	$2,4\ 10^{-9}$	$2,0\ 10^{-9}$	$1,6\ 10^{-9}$
I-132	2,30 h	F	1,000	$1,1\ 10^{-9}$	1,000	$9,6\ 10^{-10}$	$4,5\ 10^{-10}$	$2,2\ 10^{-10}$	$1,3\ 10^{-10}$	$9,4\ 10^{-11}$
		M	0,200	$9,9\ 10^{-10}$	0,100	$7,3\ 10^{-10}$	$3,6\ 10^{-10}$	$2,2\ 10^{-10}$	$1,4\ 10^{-10}$	$1,1\ 10^{-10}$
		S	0,020	$9,3\ 10^{-10}$	0,010	$6,8\ 10^{-10}$	$3,4\ 10^{-10}$	$2,1\ 10^{-10}$	$1,4\ 10^{-10}$	$1,1\ 10^{-10}$
I-132m	1,39 h	F	1,000	$9,6\ 10^{-10}$	1,000	$8,4\ 10^{-10}$	$4,0\ 10^{-10}$	$1,9\ 10^{-10}$	$1,2\ 10^{-10}$	$7,9\ 10^{-11}$
		M	0,200	$7,2\ 10^{-10}$	0,100	$5,3\ 10^{-10}$	$2,6\ 10^{-10}$	$1,6\ 10^{-10}$	$1,1\ 10^{-10}$	$8,7\ 10^{-11}$
		S	0,020	$6,6\ 10^{-10}$	0,010	$4,8\ 10^{-10}$	$2,4\ 10^{-10}$	$1,6\ 10^{-10}$	$1,1\ 10^{-10}$	$8,5\ 10^{-11}$

Nuclide	Physical half-life	Type	Age ≤ 1 a		Age	1—2 a	2—7 a	7—12 a	12—17 a	> 17 a
			f_1	h(g)	f_1	h(g)	h(g)	h(g)	h(g)	h(g)
I-133	20,8 h	F	1,000	1,9 10^{-8}	1,000	1,8 10^{-8}	8,3 10^{-9}	3,8 10^{-9}	2,2 10^{-9}	1,5 10^{-9}
		M	0,200	6,6 10^{-9}	0,100	4,4 10^{-9}	2,1 10^{-9}	1,2 10^{-9}	7,4 10^{-10}	5,5 10^{-10}
		S	0,020	3,8 10^{-9}	0,010	2,9 10^{-9}	1,4 10^{-9}	9,0 10^{-10}	5,3 10^{-10}	4,3 10^{-10}
I-134	0,876 h	F	1,000	4,6 10^{-10}	1,000	3,7 10^{-10}	1,8 10^{-10}	9,7 10^{-11}	5,9 10^{-11}	4,5 10^{-11}
		M	0,200	4,8 10^{-10}	0,100	3,4 10^{-10}	1,7 10^{-10}	1,0 10^{-10}	6,7 10^{-11}	5,4 10^{-11}
		S	0,020	4,8 10^{-10}	0,010	3,4 10^{-10}	1,7 10^{-10}	1,1 10^{-10}	6,8 10^{-11}	5,5 10^{-11}
I-135	6,61 h	F	1,000	4,1 10^{-9}	1,000	3,7 10^{-9}	1,7 10^{-9}	7,9 10^{-10}	4,8 10^{-10}	3,2 10^{-10}
		M	0,200	2,2 10^{-9}	0,100	1,6 10^{-9}	7,8 10^{-10}	4,7 10^{-10}	3,0 10^{-10}	2,4 10^{-10}
		S	0,020	1,8 10^{-9}	0,010	1,3 10^{-9}	6,5 10^{-10}	4,2 10^{-10}	2,7 10^{-10}	2,2 10^{-10}
Caesium										
Cs-125	0,750 h	F	1,000	1,2 10^{-10}	1,000	8,3 10^{-11}	3,9 10^{-11}	2,4 10^{-11}	1,4 10^{-11}	1,2 10^{-11}
		M	0,200	2,0 10^{-10}	0,100	1,4 10^{-10}	6,5 10^{-11}	4,2 10^{-11}	2,7 10^{-11}	2,2 10^{-11}
		S	0,020	2,1 10^{-10}	0,010	1,4 10^{-10}	6,8 10^{-11}	4,4 10^{-11}	2,8 10^{-11}	2,3 10^{-11}
Cs-127	6,25 h	F	1,000	1,6 10^{-10}	1,000	1,3 10^{-10}	6,9 10^{-11}	4,2 10^{-11}	2,5 10^{-11}	2,0 10^{-11}
		M	0,200	2,8 10^{-10}	0,100	2,2 10^{-10}	1,1 10^{-10}	7,3 10^{-11}	4,6 10^{-11}	3,6 10^{-11}
		S	0,020	3,0 10^{-10}	0,010	2,3 10^{-10}	1,2 10^{-10}	7,6 10^{-11}	4,8 10^{-11}	3,8 10^{-11}
Cs-129	1,34 d	F	1,000	3,4 10^{-10}	1,000	2,8 10^{-10}	1,4 10^{-10}	8,7 10^{-11}	5,2 10^{-11}	4,2 10^{-11}
		M	0,200	5,7 10^{-10}	0,100	4,6 10^{-10}	2,4 10^{-10}	1,5 10^{-10}	9,1 10^{-11}	7,3 10^{-11}
		S	0,020	6,3 10^{-10}	0,010	4,9 10^{-10}	2,5 10^{-10}	1,6 10^{-10}	9,7 10^{-11}	7,7 10^{-11}
Cs-130	0,498 h	F	1,000	8,3 10^{-11}	1,000	5,6 10^{-11}	2,5 10^{-11}	1,6 10^{-11}	9,4 10^{-12}	7,8 10^{-12}
		M	0,200	1,3 10^{-10}	0,100	8,7 10^{-11}	4,0 10^{-11}	2,5 10^{-11}	1,6 10^{-11}	1,4 10^{-11}
		S	0,020	1,4 10^{-10}	0,010	9,0 10^{-11}	4,1 10^{-11}	2,6 10^{-11}	1,7 10^{-11}	1,4 10^{-11}
Cs-131	9,69 d	F	1,000	2,4 10^{-10}	1,000	1,7 10^{-10}	8,4 10^{-11}	5,3 10^{-11}	3,2 10^{-11}	2,7 10^{-11}
		M	0,200	3,5 10^{-10}	0,100	2,6 10^{-10}	1,4 10^{-10}	8,5 10^{-11}	5,5 10^{-11}	4,4 10^{-11}
		S	0,020	3,8 10^{-10}	0,010	2,8 10^{-10}	1,4 10^{-10}	9,1 10^{-11}	5,9 10^{-11}	4,7 10^{-11}

Nuclide	Physical half-life	Type	Age ≤ 1 a		Age	1—2 a	2—7 a	7—12 a	12—17 a	> 17 a
			f_1	$h(g)$	f_1	$h(g)$	$h(g)$	$h(g)$	$h(g)$	$h(g)$
Cs-132	6,48 d	F	1,000	$1{,}5\ 10^{-9}$	1,000	$1{,}2\ 10^{-9}$	$6{,}4\ 10^{-10}$	$4{,}1\ 10^{-10}$	$2{,}7\ 10^{-10}$	$2{,}3\ 10^{-10}$
		M	0,200	$1{,}9\ 10^{-9}$	0,100	$1{,}5\ 10^{-9}$	$8{,}4\ 10^{-10}$	$5{,}4\ 10^{-10}$	$3{,}7\ 10^{-10}$	$2{,}9\ 10^{-10}$
		S	0,020	$2{,}0\ 10^{-9}$	0,010	$1{,}6\ 10^{-9}$	$8{,}7\ 10^{-10}$	$5{,}6\ 10^{-10}$	$3{,}8\ 10^{-10}$	$3{,}0\ 10^{-10}$
Cs-134	2,06 a	F	1,000	$1{,}1\ 10^{-8}$	1,000	$7{,}3\ 10^{-9}$	$5{,}2\ 10^{-9}$	$5{,}3\ 10^{-9}$	$6{,}3\ 10^{-9}$	$6{,}6\ 10^{-9}$
		M	0,200	$3{,}2\ 10^{-8}$	0,100	$2{,}6\ 10^{-8}$	$1{,}6\ 10^{-8}$	$1{,}2\ 10^{-8}$	$1{,}1\ 10^{-8}$	$9{,}1\ 10^{-9}$
		S	0,020	$7{,}0\ 10^{-8}$	0,010	$6{,}3\ 10^{-8}$	$4{,}1\ 10^{-8}$	$2{,}8\ 10^{-8}$	$2{,}3\ 10^{-8}$	$2{,}0\ 10^{-8}$
Cs-134m	2,90 h	F	1,000	$1{,}3\ 10^{-10}$	1,000	$8{,}6\ 10^{-11}$	$3{,}8\ 10^{-11}$	$2{,}5\ 10^{-11}$	$1{,}6\ 10^{-11}$	$1{,}4\ 10^{-11}$
		M	0,200	$3{,}3\ 10^{-10}$	0,100	$2{,}3\ 10^{-10}$	$1{,}2\ 10^{-10}$	$8{,}3\ 10^{-11}$	$6{,}6\ 10^{-11}$	$5{,}4\ 10^{-11}$
		S	0,020	$3{,}6\ 10^{-10}$	0,010	$2{,}5\ 10^{-10}$	$1{,}3\ 10^{-10}$	$9{,}2\ 10^{-11}$	$7{,}4\ 10^{-11}$	$6{,}0\ 10^{-11}$
Cs-135	$2{,}30\ 10^{6}$ a	F	1,000	$1{,}7\ 10^{-9}$	1,000	$9{,}9\ 10^{-10}$	$6{,}2\ 10^{-10}$	$6{,}1\ 10^{-10}$	$6{,}8\ 10^{-10}$	$6{,}9\ 10^{-10}$
		M	0,200	$1{,}2\ 10^{-8}$	0,100	$9{,}3\ 10^{-9}$	$5{,}7\ 10^{-9}$	$4{,}1\ 10^{-9}$	$3{,}8\ 10^{-9}$	$3{,}1\ 10^{-9}$
		S	0,020	$2{,}7\ 10^{-8}$	0,010	$2{,}4\ 10^{-8}$	$1{,}6\ 10^{-8}$	$1{,}1\ 10^{-8}$	$9{,}5\ 10^{-9}$	$8{,}6\ 10^{-9}$
Cs-135m	0,883 h	F	1,000	$9{,}2\ 10^{-11}$	1,000	$7{,}8\ 10^{-11}$	$4{,}1\ 10^{-11}$	$2{,}4\ 10^{-11}$	$1{,}5\ 10^{-11}$	$1{,}2\ 10^{-11}$
		M	0,200	$1{,}2\ 10^{-10}$	0,100	$9{,}9\ 10^{-11}$	$5{,}2\ 10^{-11}$	$3{,}2\ 10^{-11}$	$1{,}9\ 10^{-11}$	$1{,}5\ 10^{-11}$
		S	0,020	$1{,}2\ 10^{-10}$	0,010	$1{,}0\ 10^{-10}$	$5{,}3\ 10^{-11}$	$3{,}3\ 10^{-11}$	$2{,}0\ 10^{-11}$	$1{,}6\ 10^{-11}$
Cs-136	13,1 d	F	1,000	$7{,}3\ 10^{-9}$	1,000	$5{,}2\ 10^{-9}$	$2{,}9\ 10^{-9}$	$2{,}0\ 10^{-9}$	$1{,}4\ 10^{-9}$	$1{,}2\ 10^{-9}$
		M	0,200	$1{,}3\ 10^{-8}$	0,100	$1{,}0\ 10^{-8}$	$6{,}0\ 10^{-9}$	$3{,}7\ 10^{-9}$	$3{,}1\ 10^{-9}$	$2{,}5\ 10^{-9}$
		S	0,020	$1{,}5\ 10^{-8}$	0,010	$1{,}1\ 10^{-8}$	$5{,}7\ 10^{-9}$	$4{,}1\ 10^{-9}$	$3{,}5\ 10^{-9}$	$2{,}8\ 10^{-9}$
Cs-137	30,0 a	F	1,000	$8{,}8\ 10^{-9}$	1,000	$5{,}4\ 10^{-9}$	$3{,}6\ 10^{-9}$	$3{,}7\ 10^{-9}$	$4{,}4\ 10^{-9}$	$4{,}6\ 10^{-9}$
		M	0,200	$3{,}6\ 10^{-8}$	0,100	$2{,}9\ 10^{-8}$	$1{,}8\ 10^{-8}$	$1{,}3\ 10^{-8}$	$1{,}1\ 10^{-8}$	$9{,}7\ 10^{-9}$
		S	0,020	$1{,}1\ 10^{-7}$	0,010	$1{,}0\ 10^{-7}$	$7{,}0\ 10^{-8}$	$4{,}8\ 10^{-8}$	$4{,}2\ 10^{-8}$	$3{,}9\ 10^{-8}$
Cs-138	0,536 h	F	1,000	$2{,}6\ 10^{-10}$	1,000	$1{,}8\ 10^{-10}$	$8{,}1\ 10^{-11}$	$5{,}0\ 10^{-11}$	$2{,}9\ 10^{-11}$	$2{,}4\ 10^{-11}$
		M	0,200	$4{,}0\ 10^{-10}$	0,100	$2{,}7\ 10^{-10}$	$1{,}3\ 10^{-10}$	$7{,}8\ 10^{-11}$	$4{,}9\ 10^{-11}$	$4{,}1\ 10^{-11}$
		S	0,020	$4{,}2\ 10^{-10}$	0,010	$2{,}8\ 10^{-10}$	$1{,}3\ 10^{-10}$	$8{,}2\ 10^{-11}$	$5{,}1\ 10^{-11}$	$4{,}3\ 10^{-11}$

Nuclide	Physical half-life	Type	Age ≤ 1 a		Age	1—2 a	2—7 a	7—12 a	12—17 a	> 17 a
			f_1	h(g)	f_1	h(g)	h(g)	h(g)	h(g)	h(g)
Barium[(e)]										
Ba-126	1,61 h	F	0,600	6,7 10^{-10}	0,200	5,2 10^{-10}	2,4 10^{-10}	1,4 10^{-10}	6,9 10^{-11}	7,4 10^{-11}
		M	0,200	1,0 10^{-9}	0,100	7,0 10^{-10}	3,2 10^{-10}	2,0 10^{-10}	1,2 10^{-10}	1,0 10^{-10}
		S	0,020	1,1 10^{-9}	0,010	7,2 10^{-10}	3,3 10^{-10}	2,1 10^{-10}	1,3 10^{-10}	1,1 10^{-10}
Ba-128	2,43 d	F	0,600	5,9 10^{-9}	0,200	5,4 10^{-9}	2,5 10^{-9}	1,4 10^{-9}	7,4 10^{-10}	7,6 10^{-10}
		M	0,200	1,1 10^{-8}	0,100	7,8 10^{-9}	3,7 10^{-9}	2,4 10^{-9}	1,5 10^{-9}	1,3 10^{-9}
		S	0,020	1,2 10^{-8}	0,010	8,3 10^{-9}	4,0 10^{-9}	2,6 10^{-9}	1,6 10^{-9}	1,4 10^{-9}
Ba-131	11,8 d	F	0,600	2,1 10^{-9}	0,200	1,4 10^{-9}	7,1 10^{-10}	4,7 10^{-10}	3,1 10^{-10}	2,2 10^{-10}
		M	0,200	3,7 10^{-9}	0,100	3,1 10^{-9}	1,6 10^{-9}	1,1 10^{-9}	9,7 10^{-10}	7,6 10^{-10}
		S	0,020	4,0 10^{-9}	0,010	3,0 10^{-9}	1,8 10^{-9}	1,3 10^{-9}	1,1 10^{-9}	8,7 10^{-10}
Ba-131m	0,243 h	F	0,600	2,7 10^{-11}	0,200	2,1 10^{-11}	1,0 10^{-11}	6,7 10^{-12}	4,7 10^{-12}	4,0 10^{-12}
		M	0,200	4,8 10^{-11}	0,100	3,3 10^{-11}	1,7 10^{-11}	1,2 10^{-11}	9,0 10^{-12}	7,4 10^{-12}
		S	0,020	5,0 10^{-11}	0,010	3,5 10^{-11}	1,8 10^{-11}	1,2 10^{-11}	9,5 10^{-12}	7,8 10^{-12}
Ba-133	10,7 a	F	0,600	1,1 10^{-8}	0,200	4,5 10^{-9}	2,6 10^{-9}	3,7 10^{-9}	6,0 10^{-9}	1,5 10^{-9}
		M	0,200	1,5 10^{-8}	0,100	1,0 10^{-8}	6,4 10^{-9}	5,1 10^{-9}	5,5 10^{-9}	3,1 10^{-9}
		S	0,020	3,2 10^{-8}	0,010	2,9 10^{-8}	2,0 10^{-8}	1,3 10^{-8}	1,1 10^{-8}	1,0 10^{-8}
Ba-133m	1,62 d	F	0,600	1,4 10^{-9}	0,200	1,1 10^{-9}	4,9 10^{-10}	3,1 10^{-10}	1,5 10^{-10}	1,8 10^{-10}
		M	0,200	3,0 10^{-9}	0,100	2,2 10^{-9}	1,0 10^{-9}	6,9 10^{-10}	5,2 10^{-10}	4,2 10^{-10}
		S	0,020	3,1 10^{-9}	0,010	2,4 10^{-9}	1,1 10^{-9}	7,6 10^{-10}	5,8 10^{-10}	4,6 10^{-10}
Ba-135m	1,20 d	F	0,600	1,1 10^{-9}	0,200	1,0 10^{-9}	4,6 10^{-10}	2,5 10^{-10}	1,2 10^{-10}	1,4 10^{-10}
		M	0,200	2,4 10^{-9}	0,100	1,8 10^{-9}	8,9 10^{-10}	5,4 10^{-10}	4,1 10^{-10}	3,3 10^{-10}
		S	0,020	2,7 10^{-9}	0,010	1,9 10^{-9}	8,6 10^{-10}	5,9 10^{-10}	4,5 10^{-10}	3,6 10^{-10}
Ba-139	1,38 h	F	0,600	3,3 10^{-10}	0,200	2,4 10^{-10}	1,1 10^{-10}	6,0 10^{-11}	3,1 10^{-11}	3,4 10^{-11}
		M	0,200	5,4 10^{-10}	0,100	3,5 10^{-10}	1,6 10^{-10}	1,0 10^{-10}	6,6 10^{-11}	5,6 10^{-11}
		S	0,020	5,7 10^{-10}	0,010	3,6 10^{-10}	1,6 10^{-10}	1,1 10^{-10}	7,0 10^{-11}	5,9 10^{-11}

Nuclide	Physical half-life	Type	Age ≤ 1 a		Age	1—2 a	2—7 a	7—12 a	12—17 a	> 17 a
			f_1	h(g)	f_1	h(g)	h(g)	h(g)	h(g)	h(g)
Ba-140	12,7 d	F	0,600	$1,4\ 10^{-8}$	0,200	$7,8\ 10^{-9}$	$3,6\ 10^{-9}$	$2,4\ 10^{-9}$	$1,6\ 10^{-9}$	$1,0\ 10^{-9}$
		M	0,200	$2,7\ 10^{-8}$	0,100	$2,0\ 10^{-8}$	$1,1\ 10^{-8}$	$7,6\ 10^{-9}$	$6,2\ 10^{-9}$	$5,1\ 10^{-9}$
		S	0,020	$2,9\ 10^{-8}$	0,010	$2,2\ 10^{-8}$	$1,2\ 10^{-8}$	$8,6\ 10^{-9}$	$7,1\ 10^{-9}$	$5,8\ 10^{-9}$
Ba-141	0,305 h	F	0,600	$1,9\ 10^{-10}$	0,200	$1,4\ 10^{-10}$	$6,4\ 10^{-11}$	$3,8\ 10^{-11}$	$2,1\ 10^{-11}$	$2,1\ 10^{-11}$
		M	0,200	$3,0\ 10^{-10}$	0,100	$2,0\ 10^{-10}$	$9,3\ 10^{-11}$	$5,9\ 10^{-11}$	$3,8\ 10^{-11}$	$3,2\ 10^{-11}$
		S	0,020	$3,2\ 10^{-10}$	0,010	$2,1\ 10^{-10}$	$9,7\ 10^{-11}$	$6,2\ 10^{-11}$	$4,0\ 10^{-11}$	$3,4\ 10^{-11}$
Ba-142	0,177 h	F	0,600	$1,3\ 10^{-10}$	0,200	$9,6\ 10^{-11}$	$4,5\ 10^{-11}$	$2,7\ 10^{-11}$	$1,6\ 10^{-11}$	$1,5\ 10^{-11}$
		M	0,200	$1,8\ 10^{-10}$	0,100	$1,3\ 10^{-10}$	$6,1\ 10^{-11}$	$3,9\ 10^{-11}$	$2,5\ 10^{-11}$	$2,1\ 10^{-11}$
		S	0,020	$1,9\ 10^{-10}$	0,010	$1,3\ 10^{-10}$	$6,2\ 10^{-11}$	$4,0\ 10^{-11}$	$2,6\ 10^{-11}$	$2,2\ 10^{-11}$
Lanthanum										
La-131	0,983 h	F	0,005	$1,2\ 10^{-10}$	$5,0\ 10^{-4}$	$8,7\ 10^{-11}$	$4,2\ 10^{-11}$	$2,6\ 10^{-11}$	$1,5\ 10^{-11}$	$1,3\ 10^{-11}$
		M	0,005	$1,8\ 10^{-10}$	$5,0\ 10^{-4}$	$1,3\ 10^{-10}$	$6,4\ 10^{-11}$	$4,1\ 10^{-11}$	$2,8\ 10^{-11}$	$2,3\ 10^{-11}$
La-132	4,80 h	F	0,005	$1,0\ 10^{-9}$	$5,0\ 10^{-4}$	$7,7\ 10^{-10}$	$3,7\ 10^{-10}$	$2,2\ 10^{-10}$	$1,2\ 10^{-10}$	$1,0\ 10^{-10}$
		M	0,005	$1,5\ 10^{-9}$	$5,0\ 10^{-4}$	$1,1\ 10^{-9}$	$5,4\ 10^{-10}$	$3,4\ 10^{-10}$	$2,0\ 10^{-10}$	$1,6\ 10^{-10}$
La-135	19,5 h	F	0,005	$1,0\ 10^{-10}$	$5,0\ 10^{-4}$	$7,7\ 10^{-11}$	$3,8\ 10^{-11}$	$2,3\ 10^{-11}$	$1,3\ 10^{-11}$	$1,0\ 10^{-11}$
		M	0,005	$1,3\ 10^{-10}$	$5,0\ 10^{-4}$	$1,0\ 10^{-10}$	$4,9\ 10^{-11}$	$3,0\ 10^{-11}$	$1,7\ 10^{-11}$	$1,4\ 10^{-11}$
La-137	$6,00\ 10^{4}$ a	F	0,005	$2,5\ 10^{-8}$	$5,0\ 10^{-4}$	$2,3\ 10^{-8}$	$1,5\ 10^{-8}$	$1,1\ 10^{-8}$	$8,9\ 10^{-9}$	$8,7\ 10^{-9}$
		M	0,005	$8,6\ 10^{-9}$	$5,0\ 10^{-4}$	$8,1\ 10^{-9}$	$5,6\ 10^{-9}$	$4,0\ 10^{-9}$	$3,6\ 10^{-9}$	$3,6\ 10^{-9}$
La-138	$1,35\ 10^{11}$ a	F	0,005	$3,7\ 10^{-7}$	$5,0\ 10^{-4}$	$3,5\ 10^{-7}$	$2,4\ 10^{-7}$	$1,8\ 10^{-7}$	$1,6\ 10^{-7}$	$1,5\ 10^{-7}$
		M	0,005	$1,3\ 10^{-7}$	$5,0\ 10^{-4}$	$1,2\ 10^{-7}$	$9,1\ 10^{-8}$	$6,8\ 10^{-8}$	$6,4\ 10^{-8}$	$6,4\ 10^{-8}$
La-140	1,68 d	F	0,005	$5,8\ 10^{-9}$	$5,0\ 10^{-4}$	$4,2\ 10^{-9}$	$2,0\ 10^{-9}$	$1,2\ 10^{-9}$	$6,9\ 10^{-10}$	$5,7\ 10^{-10}$
		M	0,005	$8,8\ 10^{-9}$	$5,0\ 10^{-4}$	$6,3\ 10^{-9}$	$3,1\ 10^{-9}$	$2,0\ 10^{-9}$	$1,3\ 10^{-9}$	$1,1\ 10^{-9}$
La-141	3,93 h	F	0,005	$8,6\ 10^{-10}$	$5,0\ 10^{-4}$	$5,5\ 10^{-10}$	$2,3\ 10^{-10}$	$1,4\ 10^{-10}$	$7,5\ 10^{-11}$	$6,3\ 10^{-11}$
		M	0,005	$1,4\ 10^{-9}$	$5,0\ 10^{-4}$	$9,3\ 10^{-10}$	$4,3\ 10^{-10}$	$2,8\ 10^{-10}$	$1,8\ 10^{-10}$	$1,5\ 10^{-10}$
La-142	1,54 h	F	0,005	$5,3\ 10^{-10}$	$5,0\ 10^{-4}$	$3,8\ 10^{-10}$	$1,8\ 10^{-10}$	$1,1\ 10^{-10}$	$6,3\ 10^{-11}$	$5,2\ 10^{-11}$
		M	0,005	$8,1\ 10^{-10}$	$5,0\ 10^{-4}$	$5,7\ 10^{-10}$	$2,7\ 10^{-10}$	$1,7\ 10^{-10}$	$1,1\ 10^{-10}$	$8,9\ 10^{-11}$

Nuclide	Physical half-life	Type	Age ≤ 1 a		Age	1—2 a	2—7 a	7—12 a	12—17 a	> 17 a
			f_1	$h(g)$	f_1	$h(g)$	$h(g)$	$h(g)$	$h(g)$	$h(g)$
La-143	0,237 h	F	0,005	1,4 10^{-10}	5,0 10^{-4}	8,6 10^{-11}	3,7 10^{-11}	2,3 10^{-11}	1,4 10^{-11}	1,2 10^{-11}
		M	0,005	2,1 10^{-10}	5,0 10^{-4}	1,3 10^{-10}	6,0 10^{-11}	3,9 10^{-11}	2,5 10^{-11}	2,1 10^{-11}
Cerium										
Ce-134	3,00 d	F	0,005	7,6 10^{-9}	5,0 10^{-4}	5,3 10^{-9}	2,3 10^{-9}	1,4 10^{-9}	7,7 10^{-10}	5,7 10^{-10}
		M	0,005	1,1 10^{-8}	5,0 10^{-4}	7,6 10^{-9}	3,7 10^{-9}	2,4 10^{-9}	1,5 10^{-9}	1,3 10^{-9}
		S	0,005	1,2 10^{-8}	5,0 10^{-4}	8,0 10^{-9}	3,8 10^{-9}	2,5 10^{-9}	1,6 10^{-9}	1,3 10^{-9}
Ce-135	17,6 h	F	0,005	2,3 10^{-9}	5,0 10^{-4}	1,7 10^{-9}	8,5 10^{-10}	5,3 10^{-10}	3,0 10^{-10}	2,4 10^{-10}
		M	0,005	3,6 10^{-9}	5,0 10^{-4}	2,7 10^{-9}	1,4 10^{-9}	8,9 10^{-10}	5,9 10^{-10}	4,8 10^{-10}
		S	0,005	3,7 10^{-9}	5,0 10^{-4}	2,8 10^{-9}	1,4 10^{-9}	9,4 10^{-10}	6,3 10^{-10}	5,0 10^{-10}
Ce-137	9,00 h	F	0,005	7,5 10^{-11}	5,0 10^{-4}	5,6 10^{-11}	2,7 10^{-11}	1,6 10^{-11}	8,7 10^{-12}	7,0 10^{-12}
		M	0,005	1,1 10^{-10}	5,0 10^{-4}	7,6 10^{-11}	3,6 10^{-11}	2,2 10^{-11}	1,2 10^{-11}	9,8 10^{-12}
		S	0,005	1,1 10^{-10}	5,0 10^{-4}	7,8 10^{-11}	3,7 10^{-11}	2,3 10^{-11}	1,3 10^{-11}	1,0 10^{-11}
Ce-137m	1,43 d	F	0,005	1,6 10^{-9}	5,0 10^{-4}	1,1 10^{-9}	4,6 10^{-10}	2,8 10^{-10}	1,5 10^{-10}	1,2 10^{-10}
		M	0,005	3,1 10^{-9}	5,0 10^{-4}	2,2 10^{-9}	1,1 10^{-9}	6,7 10^{-10}	5,1 10^{-10}	4,1 10^{-10}
		S	0,005	3,3 10^{-9}	5,0 10^{-4}	2,3 10^{-9}	1,0 10^{-9}	7,3 10^{-10}	5,6 10^{-10}	4,4 10^{-10}
Ce-139	138 d	F	0,005	1,1 10^{-8}	5,0 10^{-4}	8,5 10^{-9}	4,5 10^{-9}	2,8 10^{-9}	1,8 10^{-9}	1,5 10^{-9}
		M	0,005	7,5 10^{-9}	5,0 10^{-4}	6,1 10^{-9}	3,6 10^{-9}	2,5 10^{-9}	2,1 10^{-9}	1,7 10^{-9}
		S	0,005	7,8 10^{-9}	5,0 10^{-4}	6,3 10^{-9}	3,9 10^{-9}	2,7 10^{-9}	2,4 10^{-9}	1,9 10^{-9}
Ce-141	32,5 d	F	0,005	1,1 10^{-8}	5,0 10^{-4}	7,3 10^{-9}	3,5 10^{-9}	2,0 10^{-9}	1,2 10^{-9}	9,3 10^{-10}
		M	0,005	1,4 10^{-8}	5,0 10^{-4}	1,1 10^{-8}	6,3 10^{-9}	4,6 10^{-9}	4,1 10^{-9}	3,2 10^{-9}
		S	0,005	1,6 10^{-8}	5,0 10^{-4}	1,2 10^{-8}	7,1 10^{-9}	5,3 10^{-9}	4,8 10^{-9}	3,8 10^{-9}
Ce-143	1,38 d	F	0,005	3,6 10^{-9}	5,0 10^{-4}	2,3 10^{-9}	1,0 10^{-9}	6,2 10^{-10}	3,3 10^{-10}	2,7 10^{-10}
		M	0,005	5,6 10^{-9}	5,0 10^{-4}	3,9 10^{-9}	1,9 10^{-9}	1,3 10^{-9}	9,3 10^{-10}	7,5 10^{-10}
		S	0,005	5,9 10^{-9}	5,0 10^{-4}	4,1 10^{-9}	2,1 10^{-9}	1,4 10^{-9}	1,0 10^{-9}	8,3 10^{-10}

Nuclide	*Physical half-life*	*Type*	*Age ≤ 1 a*		*Age*	*1—2 a*	*2—7 a*	*7—12 a*	*12—17 a*	*> 17 a*
			f_1	*h(g)*	f_1	*h(g)*	*h(g)*	*h(g)*	*h(g)*	*h(g)*
Ce-144	284 d	F	0,005	$3,6\ 10^{-7}$	$5,0\ 10^{-4}$	$2,7\ 10^{-7}$	$1,4\ 10^{-7}$	$7,8\ 10^{-8}$	$4,8\ 10^{-8}$	$4,0\ 10^{-8}$
		M	0,005	$1,9\ 10^{-7}$	$5,0\ 10^{-4}$	$1,6\ 10^{-7}$	$8,8\ 10^{-8}$	$5,5\ 10^{-8}$	$4,1\ 10^{-8}$	$3,6\ 10^{-8}$
		S	0,005	$2,1\ 10^{-7}$	$5,0\ 10^{-4}$	$1,8\ 10^{-7}$	$1,1\ 10^{-7}$	$7,3\ 10^{-8}$	$5,8\ 10^{-8}$	$5,3\ 10^{-8}$
Praseodymium										
Pr-136	0,218 h	M	0,005	$1,3\ 10^{-10}$	$5,0\ 10^{-4}$	$8,8\ 10^{-11}$	$4,2\ 10^{-11}$	$2,6\ 10^{-11}$	$1,6\ 10^{-11}$	$1,3\ 10^{-11}$
		S	0,005	$1,3\ 10^{-10}$	$5,0\ 10^{-4}$	$9,0\ 10^{-11}$	$4,3\ 10^{-11}$	$2,7\ 10^{-11}$	$1,7\ 10^{-11}$	$1,4\ 10^{-11}$
Pr-137	1,28 h	M	0,005	$1,8\ 10^{-10}$	$5,0\ 10^{-4}$	$1,3\ 10^{-10}$	$6,1\ 10^{-11}$	$3,9\ 10^{-11}$	$2,4\ 10^{-11}$	$2,0\ 10^{-11}$
		S	0,005	$1,9\ 10^{-10}$	$5,0\ 10^{-4}$	$1,3\ 10^{-10}$	$6,4\ 10^{-11}$	$4,0\ 10^{-11}$	$2,5\ 10^{-11}$	$2,1\ 10^{-11}$
Pr-138m	2,10 h	M	0,005	$5,9\ 10^{-10}$	$5,0\ 10^{-4}$	$4,5\ 10^{-10}$	$2,3\ 10^{-10}$	$1,4\ 10^{-10}$	$9,0\ 10^{-11}$	$7,2\ 10^{-11}$
		S	0,005	$6,0\ 10^{-10}$	$5,0\ 10^{-4}$	$4,7\ 10^{-10}$	$2,4\ 10^{-10}$	$1,5\ 10^{-10}$	$9,3\ 10^{-11}$	$7,4\ 10^{-11}$
Pr-139	4,51 h	M	0,005	$1,5\ 10^{-10}$	$5,0\ 10^{-4}$	$1,1\ 10^{-10}$	$5,5\ 10^{-11}$	$3,5\ 10^{-11}$	$2,3\ 10^{-11}$	$1,8\ 10^{-11}$
		S	0,005	$1,6\ 10^{-10}$	$5,0\ 10^{-4}$	$1,2\ 10^{-10}$	$5,7\ 10^{-11}$	$3,7\ 10^{-11}$	$2,4\ 10^{-11}$	$2,0\ 10^{-11}$
Pr-142	19,1 h	M	0,005	$5,3\ 10^{-9}$	$5,0\ 10^{-4}$	$3,5\ 10^{-9}$	$1,6\ 10^{-9}$	$1,0\ 10^{-9}$	$6,2\ 10^{-10}$	$5,2\ 10^{-10}$
		S	0,005	$5,5\ 10^{-9}$	$5,0\ 10^{-4}$	$3,7\ 10^{-9}$	$1,7\ 10^{-9}$	$1,1\ 10^{-9}$	$6,6\ 10^{-10}$	$5,5\ 10^{-10}$
Pr-142m	0,243h	M	0,005	$6,7\ 10^{-11}$	$5,0\ 10^{-4}$	$4,5\ 10^{-11}$	$2,0\ 10^{-11}$	$1,3\ 10^{-11}$	$7,9\ 10^{-12}$	$6,6\ 10^{-12}$
		S	0,005	$7,0\ 10^{-11}$	$5,0\ 10^{-4}$	$4,7\ 10^{-11}$	$2,2\ 10^{-11}$	$1,4\ 10^{-11}$	$8,4\ 10^{-12}$	$7,0\ 10^{-12}$
Pr-143	13,6 d	M	0,005	$1,2\ 10^{-8}$	$5,0\ 10^{-4}$	$8,4\ 10^{-9}$	$4,6\ 10^{-9}$	$3,2\ 10^{-9}$	$2,7\ 10^{-9}$	$2,2\ 10^{-9}$
		S	0,005	$1,3\ 10^{-8}$	$5,0\ 10^{-4}$	$9,2\ 10^{-9}$	$5,1\ 10^{-9}$	$3,6\ 10^{-9}$	$3,0\ 10^{-9}$	$2,4\ 10^{-9}$
Pr-144	0,288 h	M	0,005	$1,9\ 10^{-10}$	$5,0\ 10^{-4}$	$1,2\ 10^{-10}$	$5,0\ 10^{-11}$	$3,2\ 10^{-11}$	$2,1\ 10^{-11}$	$1,8\ 10^{-11}$
		S	0,005	$1,9\ 10^{-10}$	$5,0\ 10^{-4}$	$1,2\ 10^{-10}$	$5,2\ 10^{-11}$	$3,4\ 10^{-11}$	$2,1\ 10^{-11}$	$1,8\ 10^{-11}$
Pr-145	5,98 h	M	0,005	$1,6\ 10^{-9}$	$5,0\ 10^{-4}$	$1,0\ 10^{-9}$	$4,7\ 10^{-10}$	$3,0\ 10^{-10}$	$1,9\ 10^{-10}$	$1,6\ 10^{-10}$
		S	0,005	$1,6\ 10^{-9}$	$5,0\ 10^{-4}$	$1,1\ 10^{-9}$	$4,9\ 10^{-10}$	$3,2\ 10^{-10}$	$2,0\ 10^{-10}$	$1,7\ 10^{-10}$
Pr-147	0,227 h	M	0,005	$1,5\ 10^{-10}$	$5,0\ 10^{-4}$	$1,0\ 10^{-10}$	$4,8\ 10^{-11}$	$3,1\ 10^{-11}$	$2,1\ 10^{-11}$	$1,8\ 10^{-11}$
		S	0,005	$1,6\ 10^{-10}$	$5,0\ 10^{-4}$	$1,1\ 10^{-10}$	$5,0\ 10^{-11}$	$3,3\ 10^{-11}$	$2,2\ 10^{-11}$	$1,8\ 10^{-11}$

Nuclide	Physical half-life	Type	Age ≤ 1 a		Age	1—2 a	2—7 a	7—12 a	12—17 a	> 17 a
			f_1	$h(g)$	f_1	$h(g)$	$h(g)$	$h(g)$	$h(g)$	$h(g)$
Neodymium										
Nd-136	0,844 h	M	0,005	4,6 10^{-10}	5,0 10^{-4}	3,2 10^{-10}	1,6 10^{-10}	9,8 10^{-11}	6,3 10^{-11}	5,1 10^{-11}
		S	0,005	4,8 10^{-10}	5,0 10^{-4}	3,3 10^{-10}	1,6 10^{-10}	1,0 10^{-10}	6,6 10^{-11}	5,4 10^{-11}
Nd-138	5,04 h	M	0,005	2,3 10^{-9}	5,0 10^{-4}	1,7 10^{-9}	7,7 10^{-10}	4,8 10^{-10}	2,8 10^{-10}	2,3 10^{-10}
		S	0,005	2,4 10^{-9}	5,0 10^{-4}	1,8 10^{-9}	8,0 10^{-10}	5,0 10^{-10}	3,0 10^{-10}	2,5 10^{-10}
Nd-139	0,495 h	M	0,005	9,0 10^{-11}	5,0 10^{-4}	6,2 10^{-11}	3,0 10^{-11}	1,9 10^{-11}	1,2 10^{-11}	9,9 10^{-12}
		S	0,005	9,4 10^{-11}	5,0 10^{-4}	6,4 10^{-11}	3,1 10^{-11}	2,0 10^{-11}	1,3 10^{-11}	1,0 10^{-11}
Nd-139m	5,50 h	M	0,005	1,1 10^{-9}	5,0 10^{-4}	8,8 10^{-10}	4,5 10^{-10}	2,9 10^{-10}	1,8 10^{-10}	1,5 10^{-10}
		S	0,005	1,2 10^{-9}	5,0 10^{-4}	9,1 10^{-10}	4,6 10^{-10}	3,0 10^{-10}	1,9 10^{-10}	1,5 10^{-10}
Nd-141	2,49 h	M	0,005	4,1 10^{-11}	5,0 10^{-4}	3,1 10^{-11}	1,5 10^{-11}	9,6 10^{-12}	6,0 10^{-12}	4,8 10^{-12}
		S	0,005	4,3 10^{-11}	5,0 10^{-4}	3,2 10^{-11}	1,6 10^{-11}	1,0 10^{-11}	6,2 10^{-12}	5,0 10^{-12}
Nd-147	11,0 d	M	0,005	1,1 10^{-8}	5,0 10^{-4}	8,0 10^{-9}	4,5 10^{-9}	3,2 10^{-9}	2,6 10^{-9}	2,1 10^{-9}
		S	0,005	1,2 10^{-8}	5,0 10^{-4}	8,6 10^{-9}	4,9 10^{-9}	3,5 10^{-9}	3,0 10^{-9}	2,4 10^{-9}
Nd-149	1,73 h	M	0,005	6,8 10^{-10}	5,0 10^{-4}	4,6 10^{-10}	2,2 10^{-10}	1,5 10^{-10}	1,0 10^{-10}	8,4 10^{-11}
		S	0,005	7,1 10^{-10}	5,0 10^{-4}	4,8 10^{-10}	2,3 10^{-10}	1,5 10^{-10}	1,1 10^{-10}	8,9 10^{-11}
Nd-151	0,207 h	M	0,005	1,5 10^{-10}	5,0 10^{-4}	9,9 10^{-11}	4,6 10^{-11}	3,0 10^{-11}	2,0 10^{-11}	1,7 10^{-11}
		S	0,005	1,5 10^{-10}	5,0 10^{-4}	1,0 10^{-10}	4,8 10^{-11}	3,1 10^{-11}	2,1 10^{-11}	1,7 10^{-11}
Promethium										
Pm-141	0,348 h	M	0,005	1,4 10^{-10}	5,0 10^{-4}	9,4 10^{-11}	4,3 10^{-11}	2,7 10^{-11}	1,7 10^{-11}	1,4 10^{-11}
		S	0,005	1,5 10^{-10}	5,0 10^{-4}	9,7 10^{-11}	4,4 10^{-11}	2,8 10^{-11}	1,8 10^{-11}	1,5 10^{-11}
Pm-143	265 d	M	0,005	6,2 10^{-9}	5,0 10^{-4}	5,4 10^{-9}	3,3 10^{-9}	2,2 10^{-9}	1,7 10^{-9}	1,5 10^{-9}
		S	0,005	5,5 10^{-9}	5,0 10^{-4}	4,8 10^{-9}	3,1 10^{-9}	2,1 10^{-9}	1,7 10^{-9}	1,4 10^{-9}
Pm-144	363 d	M	0,005	3,1 10^{-8}	5,0 10^{-4}	2,8 10^{-8}	1,8 10^{-8}	1,2 10^{-8}	9,3 10^{-9}	8,2 10^{-9}
		S	0,005	2,6 10^{-8}	5,0 10^{-4}	2,4 10^{-8}	1,6 10^{-8}	1,1 10^{-8}	8,9 10^{-9}	7,5 10^{-9}
Pm-145	17,7 a	M	0,005	1,1 10^{-8}	5,0 10^{-4}	9,8 10^{-9}	6,4 10^{-9}	4,3 10^{-9}	3,7 10^{-9}	3,6 10^{-9}
		S	0,005	7,1 10^{-9}	5,0 10^{-4}	6,5 10^{-9}	4,3 10^{-9}	2,9 10^{-9}	2,4 10^{-9}	2,3 10^{-9}

Nuclide	Physical half-life	Type	Age ≤ 1 a		Age	1—2 a	2—7 a	7—12 a	12—17 a	> 17 a
			f_1	h(g)	f_1	h(g)	h(g)	h(g)	h(g)	h(g)
Pm-146	5,53 a	M	0,005	$6,4\ 10^{-8}$	$5,0\ 10^{-4}$	$5,9\ 10^{-8}$	$3,9\ 10^{-8}$	$2,6\ 10^{-8}$	$2,2\ 10^{-8}$	$2,1\ 10^{-8}$
		S	0,005	$5,3\ 10^{-8}$	$5,0\ 10^{-4}$	$4,9\ 10^{-8}$	$3,3\ 10^{-8}$	$2,2\ 10^{-8}$	$1,9\ 10^{-8}$	$1,7\ 10^{-8}$
Pm-147	2,62 a	M	0,005	$2,1\ 10^{-8}$	$5,0\ 10^{-4}$	$1,8\ 10^{-8}$	$1,1\ 10^{-8}$	$7,0\ 10^{-9}$	$5,7\ 10^{-9}$	$5,0\ 10^{-9}$
		S	0,005	$1,9\ 10^{-8}$	$5,0\ 10^{-4}$	$1,6\ 10^{-8}$	$1,0\ 10^{-8}$	$6,8\ 10^{-9}$	$5,8\ 10^{-9}$	$4,9\ 10^{-9}$
Pm-148	5,37 d	M	0,005	$1,5\ 10^{-8}$	$5,0\ 10^{-4}$	$1,0\ 10^{-8}$	$5,2\ 10^{-9}$	$3,4\ 10^{-9}$	$2,4\ 10^{-9}$	$2,0\ 10^{-9}$
		S	0,005	$1,5\ 10^{-8}$	$5,0\ 10^{-4}$	$1,1\ 10^{-8}$	$5,5\ 10^{-9}$	$3,7\ 10^{-9}$	$2,6\ 10^{-9}$	$2,2\ 10^{-9}$
Pm-148m	41,3 d	M	0,005	$2,4\ 10^{-8}$	$5,0\ 10^{-4}$	$1,9\ 10^{-8}$	$1,1\ 10^{-8}$	$7,7\ 10^{-9}$	$6,3\ 10^{-9}$	$5,1\ 10^{-9}$
		S	0,005	$2,5\ 10^{-8}$	$5,0\ 10^{-4}$	$2,0\ 10^{-8}$	$1,2\ 10^{-8}$	$8,3\ 10^{-9}$	$7,1\ 10^{-9}$	$5,7\ 10^{-9}$
Pm-149	2,21 d	M	0,005	$5,0\ 10^{-9}$	$5,0\ 10^{-4}$	$3,5\ 10^{-9}$	$1,7\ 10^{-9}$	$1,1\ 10^{-9}$	$8,3\ 10^{-10}$	$6,7\ 10^{-10}$
		S	0,005	$5,3\ 10^{-9}$	$5,0\ 10^{-4}$	$3,6\ 10^{-9}$	$1,8\ 10^{-9}$	$1,2\ 10^{-9}$	$9,0\ 10^{-10}$	$7,3\ 10^{-10}$
Pm-150	2,68 h	M	0,005	$1,2\ 10^{-9}$	$5,0\ 10^{-4}$	$7,9\ 10^{-10}$	$3,8\ 10^{-10}$	$2,4\ 10^{-10}$	$1,5\ 10^{-10}$	$1,2\ 10^{-10}$
		S	0,005	$1,2\ 10^{-9}$	$5,0\ 10^{-4}$	$8,2\ 10^{-10}$	$3,9\ 10^{-10}$	$2,5\ 10^{-10}$	$1,6\ 10^{-10}$	$1,3\ 10^{-10}$
Pm-151	1,18 d	M	0,005	$3,3\ 10^{-9}$	$5,0\ 10^{-4}$	$2,5\ 10^{-9}$	$1,2\ 10^{-9}$	$8,3\ 10^{-10}$	$5,3\ 10^{-10}$	$4,3\ 10^{-10}$
		S	0,005	$3,4\ 10^{-9}$	$5,0\ 10^{-4}$	$2,6\ 10^{-9}$	$1,3\ 10^{-9}$	$7,9\ 10^{-10}$	$5,7\ 10^{-10}$	$4,6\ 10^{-10}$
Samarium										
Sm-141	0,170 h	M	0,005	$1,5\ 10^{-10}$	$5,0\ 10^{-4}$	$1,0\ 10^{-10}$	$4,7\ 10^{-11}$	$2,9\ 10^{-11}$	$1,8\ 10^{-11}$	$1,5\ 10^{-11}$
Sm-141m	0,377 h	M	0,005	$3,0\ 10^{-10}$	$5,0\ 10^{-4}$	$2,1\ 10^{-10}$	$9,7\ 10^{-11}$	$6,1\ 10^{-11}$	$3,9\ 10^{-11}$	$3,2\ 10^{-11}$
Sm-142	1,21 h	M	0,005	$7,5\ 10^{-10}$	$5,0\ 10^{-4}$	$4,8\ 10^{-10}$	$2,2\ 10^{-10}$	$1,4\ 10^{-10}$	$8,5\ 10^{-11}$	$7,1\ 10^{-11}$
Sm-145	340 d	M	0,005	$8,1\ 10^{-9}$	$5,0\ 10^{-4}$	$6,8\ 10^{-9}$	$4,0\ 10^{-9}$	$2,5\ 10^{-9}$	$1,9\ 10^{-9}$	$1,6\ 10^{-9}$
Sm-146	$1,03\ 10^{8}$ a	M	0,005	$2,7\ 10^{-5}$	$5,0\ 10^{-4}$	$2,6\ 10^{-5}$	$1,7\ 10^{-5}$	$1,2\ 10^{-5}$	$1,1\ 10^{-5}$	$1,1\ 10^{-5}$
Sm-147	$1,06\ 10^{11}$ a	M	0,005	$2,5\ 10^{-5}$	$5,0\ 10^{-4}$	$2,3\ 10^{-5}$	$1,6\ 10^{-5}$	$1,1\ 10^{-5}$	$9,6\ 10^{-6}$	$9,6\ 10^{-6}$
Sm-151	90,0 a	M	0,005	$1,1\ 10^{-8}$	$5,0\ 10^{-4}$	$1,0\ 10^{-8}$	$6,7\ 10^{-9}$	$4,5\ 10^{-9}$	$4,0\ 10^{-9}$	$4,0\ 10^{-9}$
Sm-153	1,95 d	M	0,005	$4,2\ 10^{-9}$	$5,0\ 10^{-4}$	$2,9\ 10^{-9}$	$1,5\ 10^{-9}$	$1,0\ 10^{-9}$	$7,9\ 10^{-10}$	$6,3\ 10^{-10}$
Sm-155	0,368 h	M	0,005	$1,5\ 10^{-10}$	$5,0\ 10^{-4}$	$9,9\ 10^{-11}$	$4,4\ 10^{-11}$	$2,9\ 10^{-11}$	$2,0\ 10^{-11}$	$1,7\ 10^{-11}$
Sm-156	9,40 h	M	0,005	$1,6\ 10^{-9}$	$5,0\ 10^{-4}$	$1,1\ 10^{-9}$	$5,8\ 10^{-10}$	$3,5\ 10^{-10}$	$2,7\ 10^{-10}$	$2,2\ 10^{-10}$

Nuclide	*Physical half-life*	*Type*	*Age ≤ 1 a*		*Age*	*1—2 a*	*2—7 a*	*7—12 a*	*12—17 a*	*> 17 a*
			f_1	*h(g)*	f_1	*h(g)*	*h(g)*	*h(g)*	*h(g)*	*h(g)*
Europium										
Eu-145	5,94 d	M	0,005	3,6 10^{-9}	5,0 10^{-4}	2,9 10^{-9}	1,6 10^{-9}	1,0 10^{-9}	6,8 10^{-10}	5,5 10^{-10}
Eu-146	4,61 d	M	0,005	5,5 10^{-9}	5,0 10^{-4}	4,4 10^{-9}	2,4 10^{-9}	1,5 10^{-9}	1,0 10^{-9}	8,0 10^{-10}
Eu-147	24,0 d	M	0,005	4,9 10^{-9}	5,0 10^{-4}	3,7 10^{-9}	2,2 10^{-9}	1,6 10^{-9}	1,3 10^{-9}	1,1 10^{-9}
Eu-148	54,5 d	M	0,005	1,4 10^{-8}	5,0 10^{-4}	1,2 10^{-8}	6,8 10^{-9}	4,6 10^{-9}	3,2 10^{-9}	2,6 10^{-9}
Eu-149	93,1 d	M	0,005	1,6 10^{-9}	5,0 10^{-4}	1,3 10^{-9}	7,3 10^{-10}	4,7 10^{-10}	3,5 10^{-10}	2,9 10^{-10}
Eu-150	34,2 a	M	0,005	1,1 10^{-7}	5,0 10^{-4}	1,1 10^{-7}	7,8 10^{-8}	5,7 10^{-8}	5,3 10^{-8}	5,3 10^{-8}
Eu-150	12,6 h	M	0,005	1,6 10^{-9}	5,0 10^{-4}	1,1 10^{-9}	5,2 10^{-10}	3,4 10^{-10}	2,3 10^{-10}	1,9 10^{-10}
Eu-152	13,3 a	M	0,005	1,1 10^{-7}	5,0 10^{-4}	1,0 10^{-7}	7,0 10^{-8}	4,9 10^{-8}	4,3 10^{-8}	4,2 10^{-8}
Eu-152m	9,32 h	M	0,005	1,9 10^{-9}	5,0 10^{-4}	1,3 10^{-9}	6,6 10^{-10}	4,2 10^{-10}	2,4 10^{-10}	2,2 10^{-10}
Eu-154	8,80 a	M	0,005	1,6 10^{-7}	5,0 10^{-4}	1,5 10^{-7}	9,7 10^{-8}	6,5 10^{-8}	5,6 10^{-8}	5,3 10^{-8}
Eu-155	4,96 a	M	0,005	2,6 10^{-8}	5,0 10^{-4}	2,3 10^{-8}	1,4 10^{-8}	9,2 10^{-9}	7,6 10^{-9}	6,9 10^{-9}
Eu-156	15,2 d	M	0,005	1,9 10^{-8}	5,0 10^{-4}	1,4 10^{-8}	7,7 10^{-9}	5,3 10^{-9}	4,2 10^{-9}	3,4 10^{-9}
Eu-157	15,1 h	M	0,005	2,5 10^{-9}	5,0 10^{-4}	1,9 10^{-9}	8,9 10^{-10}	5,9 10^{-10}	3,5 10^{-10}	2,8 10^{-10}
Eu-158	0,765 h	M	0,005	4,3 10^{-10}	5,0 10^{-4}	2,9 10^{-10}	1,3 10^{-10}	8,5 10^{-11}	5,6 10^{-11}	4,7 10^{-11}
Gadolinium										
Gd-145	0,382 h	F	0,005	1,3 10^{-10}	5,0 10^{-4}	9,6 10^{-11}	4,7 10^{-11}	2,9 10^{-11}	1,7 10^{-11}	1,4 10^{-11}
		M	0,005	1,8 10^{-10}	5,0 10^{-4}	1,3 10^{-10}	6,2 10^{-11}	3,9 10^{-11}	2,4 10^{-11}	2,0 10^{-11}
Gd-146	48,3 d	F	0,005	2,9 10^{-8}	5,0 10^{-4}	2,3 10^{-8}	1,2 10^{-8}	7,8 10^{-9}	5,1 10^{-9}	4,4 10^{-9}
		M	0,005	2,8 10^{-8}	5,0 10^{-4}	2,2 10^{-8}	1,3 10^{-8}	9,3 10^{-9}	7,9 10^{-9}	6,4 10^{-9}
Gd-147	1,59 d	F	0,005	2,1 10^{-9}	5,0 10^{-4}	1,7 10^{-9}	8,4 10^{-10}	5,3 10^{-10}	3,1 10^{-10}	2,6 10^{-10}
		M	0,005	2,8 10^{-9}	5,0 10^{-4}	2,2 10^{-9}	1,1 10^{-9}	7,5 10^{-10}	5,1 10^{-10}	4,0 10^{-10}
Gd-148	93,0 a	F	0,005	8,3 10^{-5}	5,0 10^{-4}	7,6 10^{-5}	4,7 10^{-5}	3,2 10^{-5}	2,6 10^{-5}	2,6 10^{-5}
		M	0,005	3,2 10^{-5}	5,0 10^{-4}	2,9 10^{-5}	1,9 10^{-5}	1,3 10^{-5}	1,2 10^{-5}	1,1 10^{-5}
Gd-149	9,40 d	F	0,005	2,6 10^{-9}	5,0 10^{-4}	2,0 10^{-9}	8,0 10^{-10}	5,1 10^{-10}	3,1 10^{-10}	2,6 10^{-10}
		M	0,005	3,6 10^{-9}	5,0 10^{-4}	3,0 10^{-9}	1,5 10^{-9}	1,1 10^{-9}	9,2 10^{-10}	7,3 10^{-10}

Nuclide	Physical half-life	Type	Age ≤ 1 a		Age	1—2 a	2—7 a	7—12 a	12—17 a	> 17 a
			f_1	$h(g)$	f_1	$h(g)$	$h(g)$	$h(g)$	$h(g)$	$h(g)$
Gd-151	120 d	F	0,005	6,3 10^{-9}	5,0 10^{-4}	4,9 10^{-9}	2,5 10^{-9}	1,5 10^{-9}	9,2 10^{-10}	7,8 10^{-10}
		M	0,005	4,5 10^{-9}	5,0 10^{-4}	3,5 10^{-9}	2,0 10^{-9}	1,3 10^{-9}	1,0 10^{-9}	8,6 10^{-10}
Gd-152	1,08 10^{14} a	F	0,005	5,9 10^{-5}	5,0 10^{-4}	5,4 10^{-5}	3,4 10^{-5}	2,4 10^{-5}	1,9 10^{-5}	1,9 10^{-5}
		M	0,005	2,1 10^{-5}	5,0 10^{-4}	1,9 10^{-5}	1,3 10^{-5}	8,9 10^{-6}	7,9 10^{-6}	8,0 10^{-6}
Gd-153	242 d	F	0,005	1,5 10^{-8}	5,0 10^{-4}	1,2 10^{-8}	6,5 10^{-9}	3,9 10^{-9}	2,4 10^{-9}	2,1 10^{-9}
		M	0,005	9,9 10^{-9}	5,0 10^{-4}	7,9 10^{-9}	4,8 10^{-9}	3,1 10^{-9}	2,5 10^{-9}	2,1 10^{-9}
Gd-159	18,6 h	F	0,005	1,2 10^{-9}	5,0 10^{-4}	8,9 10^{-10}	3,8 10^{-10}	2,3 10^{-10}	1,2 10^{-10}	1,0 10^{-10}
		M	0,005	2,2 10^{-9}	5,0 10^{-4}	1,5 10^{-9}	7,3 10^{-10}	4,9 10^{-10}	3,4 10^{-10}	2,7 10^{-10}
Terbium										
Tb-147	1,65 h	M	0,005	6,7 10^{-10}	5,0 10^{-4}	4,8 10^{-10}	2,3 10^{-10}	1,5 10^{-10}	9,3 10^{-11}	7,6 10^{-11}
Tb-149	4,15 h	M	0,005	2,1 10^{-8}	5,0 10^{-4}	1,5 10^{-8}	9,6 10^{-9}	6,6 10^{-9}	5,8 10^{-9}	4,9 10^{-9}
Tb-150	3,27 h	M	0,005	1,0 10^{-9}	5,0 10^{-4}	7,4 10^{-10}	3,5 10^{-10}	2,2 10^{-10}	1,3 10^{-10}	1,1 10^{-10}
Tb-151	17,6 h	M	0,005	1,6 10^{-9}	5,0 10^{-4}	1,2 10^{-9}	6,3 10^{-10}	4,2 10^{-10}	2,8 10^{-10}	2,3 10^{-10}
Tb-153	2,34 d	M	0,005	1,4 10^{-9}	5,0 10^{-4}	1,0 10^{-9}	5,4 10^{-10}	3,6 10^{-10}	2,3 10^{-10}	1,9 10^{-10}
Tb-154	21,4 h	M	0,005	2,7 10^{-9}	5,0 10^{-4}	2,1 10^{-9}	1,1 10^{-9}	7,1 10^{-10}	4,5 10^{-10}	3,6 10^{-10}
Tb-155	5,32 d	M	0,005	1,4 10^{-9}	5,0 10^{-4}	1,0 10^{-9}	5,6 10^{-10}	3,4 10^{-10}	2,7 10^{-10}	2,2 10^{-10}
Tb-156	5,34 d	M	0,005	7,0 10^{-9}	5,0 10^{-4}	5,4 10^{-9}	3,0 10^{-9}	2,0 10^{-9}	1,5 10^{-9}	1,2 10^{-9}
Tb-156m	1,02 d	M	0,005	1,1 10^{-9}	5,0 10^{-4}	9,4 10^{-10}	4,7 10^{-10}	3,3 10^{-10}	2,7 10^{-10}	2,1 10^{-10}
Tb-156m	5,00 h	M	0,005	6,2 10^{-10}	5,0 10^{-4}	4,5 10^{-10}	2,4 10^{-10}	1,7 10^{-10}	1,2 10^{-10}	9,6 10^{-11}
Tb-157	1,50 10^{2} a	M	0,005	3,2 10^{-9}	5,0 10^{-4}	3,0 10^{-9}	2,0 10^{-9}	1,4 10^{-9}	1,2 10^{-9}	1,2 10^{-9}
Tb-158	1,50 10^{2} a	M	0,005	1,1 10^{-7}	5,0 10^{-4}	1,0 10^{-7}	7,0 10^{-8}	5,1 10^{-8}	4,7 10^{-8}	4,6 10^{-8}
Tb-160	72,3 d	M	0,005	3,2 10^{-8}	5,0 10^{-4}	2,5 10^{-8}	1,5 10^{-8}	1,0 10^{-8}	8,6 10^{-9}	7,0 10^{-9}
Tb-161	6,91 d	M	0,005	6,6 10^{-9}	5,0 10^{-4}	4,7 10^{-9}	2,6 10^{-9}	1,9 10^{-9}	1,6 10^{-9}	1,3 10^{-9}
Dysprosium										
Dy-155	10,0 h	M	0,005	5,6 10^{-10}	5,0 10^{-4}	4,4 10^{-10}	2,3 10^{-10}	1,5 10^{-10}	9,6 10^{-11}	7,7 10^{-11}
Dy-157	8,10 h	M	0,005	2,4 10^{-10}	5,0 10^{-4}	1,9 10^{-10}	9,9 10^{-11}	6,2 10^{-11}	3,8 10^{-11}	3,0 10^{-11}

Nuclide	Physical half-life	Type	Age ≤ 1 a		Age	1—2 a	2—7 a	7—12 a	12—17 a	> 17 a
			f_1	$h(g)$	f_1	$h(g)$	$h(g)$	$h(g)$	$h(g)$	$h(g)$
Dy-159	144 d	M	0,005	$2,1\ 10^{-9}$	$5,0\ 10^{-4}$	$1,7\ 10^{-9}$	$9,6\ 10^{-10}$	$6,0\ 10^{-10}$	$4,4\ 10^{-10}$	$3,7\ 10^{-10}$
Dy-165	2,33 h	M	0,005	$5,2\ 10^{-10}$	$5,0\ 10^{-4}$	$3,4\ 10^{-10}$	$1,6\ 10^{-10}$	$1,1\ 10^{-10}$	$7,2\ 10^{-11}$	$6,0\ 10^{-11}$
Dy-166	3,40 d	M	0,005	$1,2\ 10^{-8}$	$5,0\ 10^{-4}$	$8,3\ 10^{-9}$	$4,4\ 10^{-9}$	$3,0\ 10^{-9}$	$2,3\ 10^{-9}$	$1,9\ 10^{-9}$
Holmium										
Ho-155	0,800 h	M	0,005	$1,7\ 10^{-10}$	$5,0\ 10^{-4}$	$1,2\ 10^{-10}$	$5,8\ 10^{-11}$	$3,7\ 10^{-11}$	$2,4\ 10^{-11}$	$2,0\ 10^{-11}$
Ho-157	0,210 h	M	0,005	$3,4\ 10^{-11}$	$5,0\ 10^{-4}$	$2,5\ 10^{-11}$	$1,3\ 10^{-11}$	$8,0\ 10^{-12}$	$5,1\ 10^{-12}$	$4,2\ 10^{-12}$
Ho-159	0,550 h	M	0,005	$4,6\ 10^{-11}$	$5,0\ 10^{-4}$	$3,3\ 10^{-11}$	$1,7\ 10^{-11}$	$1,1\ 10^{-11}$	$7,5\ 10^{-12}$	$6,1\ 10^{-12}$
Ho-161	2,50 h	M	0,005	$5,7\ 10^{-11}$	$5,0\ 10^{-4}$	$4,0\ 10^{-11}$	$2,0\ 10^{-11}$	$1,2\ 10^{-11}$	$7,5\ 10^{-12}$	$6,0\ 10^{-12}$
Ho-162	0,250 h	M	0,005	$2,1\ 10^{-11}$	$5,0\ 10^{-4}$	$1,5\ 10^{-11}$	$7,2\ 10^{-12}$	$4,8\ 10^{-12}$	$3,4\ 10^{-12}$	$2,8\ 10^{-12}$
Ho-162m	1,13 h	M	0,005	$1,5\ 10^{-10}$	$5,0\ 10^{-4}$	$1,1\ 10^{-10}$	$5,8\ 10^{-11}$	$3,8\ 10^{-11}$	$2,6\ 10^{-11}$	$2,1\ 10^{-11}$
Ho-164	0,483 h	M	0,005	$6,8\ 10^{-11}$	$5,0\ 10^{-4}$	$4,5\ 10^{-11}$	$2,1\ 10^{-11}$	$1,4\ 10^{-11}$	$9,9\ 10^{-12}$	$8,4\ 10^{-12}$
Ho-164m	0,625 h	M	0,005	$9,1\ 10^{-11}$	$5,0\ 10^{-4}$	$5,9\ 10^{-11}$	$3,0\ 10^{-11}$	$2,0\ 10^{-11}$	$1,3\ 10^{-11}$	$1,2\ 10^{-11}$
Ho-166	1,12 d	M	0,005	$6,0\ 10^{-9}$	$5,0\ 10^{-4}$	$4,0\ 10^{-9}$	$1,9\ 10^{-9}$	$1,2\ 10^{-9}$	$7,9\ 10^{-10}$	$6,5\ 10^{-10}$
Ho-166m	$1,20\ 10^{3}$ a	M	0,005	$2,6\ 10^{-7}$	$5,0\ 10^{-4}$	$2,5\ 10^{-7}$	$1,8\ 10^{-7}$	$1,3\ 10^{-7}$	$1,2\ 10^{-7}$	$1,2\ 10^{-7}$
Ho-167	3,10 h	M	0,005	$5,2\ 10^{-10}$	$5,0\ 10^{-4}$	$3,6\ 10^{-10}$	$1,8\ 10^{-10}$	$1,2\ 10^{-10}$	$8,7\ 10^{-11}$	$7,1\ 10^{-11}$
Erbium										
Er-161	3,24 h	M	0,005	$3,8\ 10^{-10}$	$5,0\ 10^{-4}$	$2,9\ 10^{-10}$	$1,5\ 10^{-10}$	$9,5\ 10^{-11}$	$6,0\ 10^{-11}$	$4,8\ 10^{-11}$
Er-165	10,4 h	M	0,005	$7,2\ 10^{-11}$	$5,0\ 10^{-4}$	$5,3\ 10^{-11}$	$2,6\ 10^{-11}$	$1,6\ 10^{-11}$	$9,6\ 10^{-12}$	$7,9\ 10^{-12}$
Er-169	9,30 d	M	0,005	$4,7\ 10^{-9}$	$5,0\ 10^{-4}$	$3,5\ 10^{-9}$	$2,0\ 10^{-9}$	$1,5\ 10^{-9}$	$1,3\ 10^{-9}$	$1,0\ 10^{-9}$
Er-171	7,52 h	M	0,005	$1,8\ 10^{-9}$	$5,0\ 10^{-4}$	$1,2\ 10^{-9}$	$5,9\ 10^{-10}$	$3,9\ 10^{-10}$	$2,7\ 10^{-10}$	$2,2\ 10^{-10}$
Er-172	2,05 d	M	0,005	$6,6\ 10^{-9}$	$5,0\ 10^{-4}$	$4,7\ 10^{-9}$	$2,5\ 10^{-9}$	$1,7\ 10^{-9}$	$1,4\ 10^{-9}$	$1,1\ 10^{-9}$
Thulium										
Tm-162	0,362 h	M	0,005	$1,3\ 10^{-10}$	$5,0\ 10^{-4}$	$9,6\ 10^{-11}$	$4,7\ 10^{-11}$	$3,0\ 10^{-11}$	$1,9\ 10^{-11}$	$1,6\ 10^{-11}$
Tm-166	7,70 h	M	0,005	$1,3\ 10^{-9}$	$5,0\ 10^{-4}$	$9,9\ 10^{-10}$	$5,2\ 10^{-10}$	$3,3\ 10^{-10}$	$2,2\ 10^{-10}$	$1,7\ 10^{-10}$
Tm-167	9,24 d	M	0,005	$5,6\ 10^{-9}$	$5,0\ 10^{-4}$	$4,1\ 10^{-9}$	$2,3\ 10^{-9}$	$1,7\ 10^{-9}$	$1,4\ 10^{-9}$	$1,1\ 10^{-9}$
Tm-170	129 d	M	0,005	$3,6\ 10^{-8}$	$5,0\ 10^{-4}$	$2,8\ 10^{-8}$	$1,6\ 10^{-8}$	$1,1\ 10^{-8}$	$8,5\ 10^{-9}$	$7,0\ 10^{-9}$

Nuclide	*Physical half-life*	*Type*	*Age ≤ 1 a*		*Age*	*1—2 a*	*2—7 a*	*7—12 a*	*12—17 a*	*> 17 a*
			f_1	*h(g)*	f_1	*h(g)*	*h(g)*	*h(g)*	*h(g)*	*h(g)*
Tm-171	1,92 a	M	0,005	6,8 10^{-9}	5,0 10^{-4}	5,7 10^{-9}	3,4 10^{-9}	2,0 10^{-9}	1,6 10^{-9}	1,4 10^{-9}
Tm-172	2,65 d	M	0,005	8,4 10^{-9}	5,0 10^{-4}	5,8 10^{-9}	2,9 10^{-9}	1,9 10^{-9}	1,4 10^{-9}	1,1 10^{-9}
Tm-173	8,24 h	M	0,005	1,5 10^{-9}	5,0 10^{-4}	1,0 10^{-9}	5,0 10^{-10}	3,3 10^{-10}	2,2 10^{-10}	1,8 10^{-10}
Tm-175	0,253 h	M	0,005	1,6 10^{-10}	5,0 10^{-4}	1,1 10^{-10}	5,0 10^{-11}	3,3 10^{-11}	2,2 10^{-11}	1,8 10^{-11}
Ytterbium										
Yb-162	0,315 h	M	0,005	1,1 10^{-10}	5,0 10^{-4}	7,9 10^{-11}	3,9 10^{-11}	2,5 10^{-11}	1,6 10^{-11}	1,3 10^{-11}
		S	0,005	1,2 10^{-10}	5,0 10^{-4}	8,2 10^{-11}	4,0 10^{-11}	2,6 10^{-11}	1,7 10^{-11}	1,4 10^{-11}
Yb-166	2,36 d	M	0,005	4,7 10^{-9}	5,0 10^{-4}	3,5 10^{-9}	1,9 10^{-9}	1,3 10^{-9}	9,0 10^{-10}	7,2 10^{-10}
		S	0,005	4,9 10^{-9}	5,0 10^{-4}	3,7 10^{-9}	2,0 10^{-9}	1,3 10^{-9}	9,6 10^{-10}	7,7 10^{-10}
Yb-167	0,292 h	M	0,005	4,4 10^{-11}	5,0 10^{-4}	3,1 10^{-11}	1,6 10^{-11}	1,1 10^{-11}	7,9 10^{-12}	6,5 10^{-12}
		S	0,005	4,6 10^{-11}	5,0 10^{-4}	3,2 10^{-11}	1,7 10^{-11}	1,1 10^{-11}	8,4 10^{-12}	6,9 10^{-12}
Yb-169	32,0 d	M	0,005	1,2 10^{-8}	5,0 10^{-4}	8,7 10^{-9}	5,1 10^{-9}	3,7 10^{-9}	3,2 10^{-9}	2,5 10^{-9}
		S	0,005	1,3 10^{-8}	5,0 10^{-4}	9,8 10^{-9}	5,9 10^{-9}	4,2 10^{-9}	3,7 10^{-9}	3,0 10^{-9}
Yb-175	4,19 d	M	0,005	3,5 10^{-9}	5,0 10^{-4}	2,5 10^{-9}	1,4 10^{-9}	9,8 10^{-10}	8,3 10^{-10}	6,5 10^{-10}
		S	0,005	3,7 10^{-9}	5,0 10^{-4}	2,7 10^{-9}	1,5 10^{-9}	1,1 10^{-9}	9,2 10^{-10}	7,3 10^{-10}
Yb-177	1,90 h	M	0,005	5,0 10^{-10}	5,0 10^{-4}	3,3 10^{-10}	1,6 10^{-10}	1,1 10^{-10}	7,8 10^{-11}	6,4 10^{-11}
		S	0,005	5,3 10^{-10}	5,0 10^{-4}	3,5 10^{-10}	1,7 10^{-10}	1,2 10^{-10}	8,4 10^{-11}	6,9 10^{-11}
Yb-178	1,23 h	M	0,005	5,9 10^{-10}	5,0 10^{-4}	3,9 10^{-10}	1,8 10^{-10}	1,2 10^{-10}	8,5 10^{-11}	7,0 10^{-11}
		S	0,005	6,2 10^{-10}	5,0 10^{-4}	4,1 10^{-10}	1,9 10^{-10}	1,3 10^{-10}	9,1 10^{-11}	7,5 10^{-11}
Lutetium										
Lu-169	1,42 d	M	0,005	2,3 10^{-9}	5,0 10^{-4}	1,8 10^{-9}	9,5 10^{-10}	6,3 10^{-10}	4,4 10^{-10}	3,5 10^{-10}
		S	0,005	2,4 10^{-9}	5,0 10^{-4}	1,9 10^{-9}	1,0 10^{-9}	6,7 10^{-10}	4,8 10^{-10}	3,8 10^{-10}
Lu-170	2,00 d	M	0,005	4,3 10^{-9}	5,0 10^{-4}	3,4 10^{-9}	1,8 10^{-9}	1,2 10^{-9}	7,8 10^{-10}	6,3 10^{-10}
		S	0,005	4,5 10^{-9}	5,0 10^{-4}	3,5 10^{-9}	1,8 10^{-9}	1,2 10^{-9}	8,2 10^{-10}	6,6 10^{-10}
Lu-171	8,22 d	M	0,005	5,0 10^{-9}	5,0 10^{-4}	3,7 10^{-9}	2,1 10^{-9}	1,2 10^{-9}	9,8 10^{-10}	8,0 10^{-10}
		S	0,005	4,7 10^{-9}	5,0 10^{-4}	3,9 10^{-9}	2,0 10^{-9}	1,4 10^{-9}	1,1 10^{-9}	8,8 10^{-10}

Nuclide	*Physical half-life*	*Type*	*Age ≤ 1 a*		*Age*	*1—2 a*	*2—7 a*	*7—12 a*	*12—17 a*	*> 17 a*
			f_1	*h(g)*	f_1	*h(g)*	*h(g)*	*h(g)*	*h(g)*	*h(g)*
Lu-172	6,70 d	M	0,005	8,7 10^{-9}	5,0 10^{-4}	6,7 10^{-9}	3,8 10^{-9}	2,6 10^{-9}	1,8 10^{-9}	1,4 10^{-9}
		S	0,005	9,3 10^{-9}	5,0 10^{-4}	7,1 10^{-9}	4,0 10^{-9}	2,8 10^{-9}	2,0 10^{-9}	1,6 10^{-9}
Lu-173	1,37 a	M	0,005	1,0 10^{-8}	5,0 10^{-4}	8,5 10^{-9}	5,1 10^{-9}	3,2 10^{-9}	2,5 10^{-9}	2,2 10^{-9}
		S	0,005	1,0 10^{-8}	5,0 10^{-4}	8,7 10^{-9}	5,4 10^{-9}	3,6 10^{-9}	2,9 10^{-9}	2,4 10^{-9}
Lu-174	3,31 a	M	0,005	1,7 10^{-8}	5,0 10^{-4}	1,5 10^{-8}	9,1 10^{-9}	5,8 10^{-9}	4,7 10^{-9}	4,2 10^{-9}
		S	0,005	1,6 10^{-8}	5,0 10^{-4}	1,4 10^{-8}	8,9 10^{-9}	5,9 10^{-9}	4,9 10^{-9}	4,2 10^{-9}
Lu-174m	142 d	M	0,005	1,9 10^{-8}	5,0 10^{-4}	1,4 10^{-8}	8,6 10^{-9}	5,4 10^{-9}	4,3 10^{-9}	3,7 10^{-9}
		S	0,005	2,0 10^{-8}	5,0 10^{-4}	1,5 10^{-8}	9,2 10^{-9}	6,1 10^{-9}	5,0 10^{-9}	4,2 10^{-9}
Lu-176	3,60 10^{10} a	M	0,005	1,8 10^{-7}	5,0 10^{-4}	1,7 10^{-7}	1,1 10^{-7}	7,8 10^{-8}	7,1 10^{-8}	7,0 10^{-8}
		S	0,005	1,5 10^{-7}	5,0 10^{-4}	1,4 10^{-7}	9,4 10^{-8}	6,5 10^{-8}	5,9 10^{-8}	5,6 10^{-8}
Lu-176m	3,68 h	M	0,005	8,9 10^{-10}	5,0 10^{-4}	5,9 10^{-10}	2,8 10^{-10}	1,9 10^{-10}	1,2 10^{-10}	1,1 10^{-10}
		S	0,005	9,3 10^{-10}	5,0 10^{-4}	6,2 10^{-10}	3,0 10^{-10}	2,0 10^{-10}	1,2 10^{-10}	1,2 10^{-10}
Lu-177	6,71 d	M	0,005	5,3 10^{-9}	5,0 10^{-4}	3,8 10^{-9}	2,2 10^{-9}	1,6 10^{-9}	1,4 10^{-9}	1,1 10^{-9}
		S	0,005	5,7 10^{-9}	5,0 10^{-4}	4,1 10^{-9}	2,4 10^{-9}	1,7 10^{-9}	1,5 10^{-9}	1,2 10^{-9}
Lu-177m	161 d	M	0,005	5,8 10^{-8}	5,0 10^{-4}	4,6 10^{-8}	2,8 10^{-8}	1,9 10^{-8}	1,6 10^{-8}	1,3 10^{-8}
		S	0,005	6,5 10^{-8}	5,0 10^{-4}	5,3 10^{-8}	3,2 10^{-8}	2,3 10^{-8}	2,0 10^{-8}	1,6 10^{-8}
Lu-178	0,473 h	M	0,005	2,3 10^{-10}	5,0 10^{-4}	1,5 10^{-10}	6,6 10^{-11}	4,3 10^{-11}	2,9 10^{-11}	2,4 10^{-11}
		S	0,005	2,4 10^{-10}	5,0 10^{-4}	1,5 10^{-10}	6,9 10^{-11}	4,5 10^{-11}	3,0 10^{-11}	2,6 10^{-11}
Lu-178m	0,378 h	M	0,005	2,6 10^{-10}	5,0 10^{-4}	1,8 10^{-10}	8,3 10^{-11}	5,6 10^{-11}	3,8 10^{-11}	3,2 10^{-11}
		S	0,005	2,7 10^{-10}	5,0 10^{-4}	1,9 10^{-10}	8,7 10^{-11}	5,8 10^{-11}	4,0 10^{-11}	3,3 10^{-11}
Lu-179	4,59 h	M	0,005	9,9 10^{-10}	5,0 10^{-4}	6,5 10^{-10}	3,0 10^{-10}	2,0 10^{-10}	1,2 10^{-10}	1,1 10^{-10}
		S	0,005	1,0 10^{-9}	5,0 10^{-4}	6,8 10^{-10}	3,2 10^{-10}	2,1 10^{-10}	1,3 10^{-10}	1,2 10^{-10}
Hafnium										
Hf-170	16,0 h	F	0,020	1,4 10^{-9}	0,002	1,1 10^{-9}	5,4 10^{-10}	3,4 10^{-10}	2,0 10^{-10}	1,6 10^{-10}
		M	0,020	2,2 10^{-9}	0,002	1,7 10^{-9}	8,7 10^{-10}	5,8 10^{-10}	3,9 10^{-10}	3,2 10^{-10}

Nuclide	Physical half-life	Type	Age ≤ 1 a		Age	1—2 a	2—7 a	7—12 a	12—17 a	> 17 a
			f_1	h(g)	f_1	h(g)	h(g)	h(g)	h(g)	h(g)
Hf-172	1,87 a	F	0,020	$1,5\ 10^{-7}$	0,002	$1,3\ 10^{-7}$	$7,8\ 10^{-8}$	$4,9\ 10^{-8}$	$3,5\ 10^{-8}$	$3,2\ 10^{-8}$
		M	0,020	$8,1\ 10^{-8}$	0,002	$6,9\ 10^{-8}$	$4,3\ 10^{-8}$	$2,8\ 10^{-8}$	$2,3\ 10^{-8}$	$2,0\ 10^{-8}$
Hf-173	24,0 h	F	0,020	$6,6\ 10^{-10}$	0,002	$5,0\ 10^{-10}$	$2,5\ 10^{-10}$	$1,5\ 10^{-10}$	$8,9\ 10^{-11}$	$7,4\ 10^{-11}$
		M	0,020	$1,1\ 10^{-9}$	0,002	$8,2\ 10^{-10}$	$4,3\ 10^{-10}$	$2,9\ 10^{-10}$	$2,0\ 10^{-10}$	$1,6\ 10^{-10}$
Hf-175	70,0 d	F	0,020	$5,4\ 10^{-9}$	0,002	$4,0\ 10^{-9}$	$2,1\ 10^{-9}$	$1,3\ 10^{-9}$	$8,5\ 10^{-10}$	$7,2\ 10^{-10}$
		M	0,020	$5,8\ 10^{-9}$	0,002	$4,5\ 10^{-9}$	$2,6\ 10^{-9}$	$1,8\ 10^{-9}$	$1,4\ 10^{-9}$	$1,2\ 10^{-9}$
Hf-177m	0,856 h	F	0,020	$3,9\ 10^{-10}$	0,002	$2,8\ 10^{-10}$	$1,3\ 10^{-10}$	$8,5\ 10^{-11}$	$5,2\ 10^{-11}$	$4,4\ 10^{-11}$
		M	0,020	$6,5\ 10^{-10}$	0,002	$4,7\ 10^{-10}$	$2,3\ 10^{-10}$	$1,5\ 10^{-10}$	$1,1\ 10^{-10}$	$9,0\ 10^{-11}$
Hf-178m	31,0 a	F	0,020	$6,2\ 10^{-7}$	0,002	$5,8\ 10^{-7}$	$4,0\ 10^{-7}$	$3,1\ 10^{-7}$	$2,7\ 10^{-7}$	$2,6\ 10^{-7}$
		M	0,020	$2,6\ 10^{-7}$	0,002	$2,4\ 10^{-7}$	$1,7\ 10^{-7}$	$1,3\ 10^{-7}$	$1,2\ 10^{-7}$	$1,2\ 10^{-7}$
Hf-179m	25,1 d	F	0,020	$9,7\ 10^{-9}$	0,002	$6,8\ 10^{-9}$	$3,4\ 10^{-9}$	$2,1\ 10^{-9}$	$1,2\ 10^{-9}$	$1,1\ 10^{-9}$
		M	0,020	$1,7\ 10^{-8}$	0,002	$1,3\ 10^{-8}$	$7,6\ 10^{-9}$	$5,5\ 10^{-9}$	$4,8\ 10^{-9}$	$3,8\ 10^{-9}$
Hf-180m	5,50 h	F	0,020	$5,4\ 10^{-10}$	0,002	$4,1\ 10^{-10}$	$2,0\ 10^{-10}$	$1,3\ 10^{-10}$	$7,2\ 10^{-11}$	$5,9\ 10^{-11}$
		M	0,020	$9,1\ 10^{-10}$	0,002	$6,8\ 10^{-10}$	$3,6\ 10^{-10}$	$2,4\ 10^{-10}$	$1,7\ 10^{-10}$	$1,3\ 10^{-10}$
Hf-181	42,4 d	F	0,020	$1,3\ 10^{-8}$	0,002	$9,6\ 10^{-9}$	$4,8\ 10^{-9}$	$2,8\ 10^{-9}$	$1,7\ 10^{-9}$	$1,4\ 10^{-9}$
		M	0,020	$2,2\ 10^{-8}$	0,002	$1,7\ 10^{-8}$	$9,9\ 10^{-9}$	$7,1\ 10^{-9}$	$6,3\ 10^{-9}$	$5,0\ 10^{-9}$
Hf-182	$9,00\ 10^{6}$ a	F	0,020	$6,5\ 10^{-7}$	0,002	$6,2\ 10^{-7}$	$4,4\ 10^{-7}$	$3,6\ 10^{-7}$	$3,1\ 10^{-7}$	$3,1\ 10^{-7}$
		M	0,020	$2,4\ 10^{-7}$	0,002	$2,3\ 10^{-7}$	$1,7\ 10^{-7}$	$1,3\ 10^{-7}$	$1,3\ 10^{-7}$	$1,3\ 10^{-7}$
Hf-182m	1,02 h	F	0,020	$1,9\ 10^{-10}$	0,002	$1,4\ 10^{-10}$	$6,6\ 10^{-11}$	$4,2\ 10^{-11}$	$2,6\ 10^{-11}$	$2,1\ 10^{-11}$
		M	0,020	$3,2\ 10^{-10}$	0,002	$2,3\ 10^{-10}$	$1,2\ 10^{-10}$	$7,8\ 10^{-11}$	$5,6\ 10^{-11}$	$4,6\ 10^{-11}$
Hf-183	1,07 h	F	0,020	$2,5\ 10^{-10}$	0,002	$1,7\ 10^{-10}$	$7,9\ 10^{-11}$	$4,9\ 10^{-11}$	$2,8\ 10^{-11}$	$2,4\ 10^{-11}$
		M	0,020	$4,4\ 10^{-10}$	0,002	$3,0\ 10^{-10}$	$1,5\ 10^{-10}$	$9,8\ 10^{-11}$	$7,0\ 10^{-11}$	$5,7\ 10^{-11}$
Hf-184	4,12 h	F	0,020	$1,4\ 10^{-9}$	0,002	$9,6\ 10^{-10}$	$4,3\ 10^{-10}$	$2,7\ 10^{-10}$	$1,4\ 10^{-10}$	$1,2\ 10^{-10}$
		M	0,020	$2,6\ 10^{-9}$	0,002	$1,8\ 10^{-9}$	$8,9\ 10^{-10}$	$5,9\ 10^{-10}$	$4,0\ 10^{-10}$	$3,3\ 10^{-10}$

Nuclide	Physical half-life	Type	Age ≤ 1 a		Age	1—2 a	2—7 a	7—12 a	12—17 a	> 17 a
			f_1	$h(g)$	f_1	$h(g)$	$h(g)$	$h(g)$	$h(g)$	$h(g)$
Tantalum										
Ta-172	0,613 h	M	0,010	$2,8\ 10^{-10}$	0,001	$1,9\ 10^{-10}$	$9,3\ 10^{-11}$	$6,0\ 10^{-11}$	$4,0\ 10^{-11}$	$3,3\ 10^{-11}$
		S	0,010	$2,9\ 10^{-10}$	0,001	$2,0\ 10^{-10}$	$9,8\ 10^{-11}$	$6,3\ 10^{-11}$	$4,2\ 10^{-11}$	$3,5\ 10^{-11}$
Ta-173	3,65 h	M	0,010	$8,8\ 10^{-10}$	0,001	$6,2\ 10^{-10}$	$3,0\ 10^{-10}$	$2,0\ 10^{-10}$	$1,3\ 10^{-10}$	$1,1\ 10^{-10}$
		S	0,010	$9,2\ 10^{-10}$	0,001	$6,5\ 10^{-10}$	$3,2\ 10^{-10}$	$2,1\ 10^{-10}$	$1,4\ 10^{-10}$	$1,1\ 10^{-10}$
Ta-174	1,20 h	M	0,010	$3,2\ 10^{-10}$	0,001	$2,2\ 10^{-10}$	$1,1\ 10^{-10}$	$7,1\ 10^{-11}$	$5,0\ 10^{-11}$	$4,1\ 10^{-11}$
		S	0,010	$3,4\ 10^{-10}$	0,001	$2,3\ 10^{-10}$	$1,1\ 10^{-10}$	$7,5\ 10^{-11}$	$5,3\ 10^{-11}$	$4,3\ 10^{-11}$
Ta-175	10,5 h	M	0,010	$9,1\ 10^{-10}$	0,001	$7,0\ 10^{-10}$	$3,7\ 10^{-10}$	$2,4\ 10^{-10}$	$1,5\ 10^{-10}$	$1,2\ 10^{-10}$
		S	0,010	$9,5\ 10^{-10}$	0,001	$7,3\ 10^{-10}$	$3,8\ 10^{-10}$	$2,5\ 10^{-10}$	$1,6\ 10^{-10}$	$1,3\ 10^{-10}$
Ta-176	8,08 h	M	0,010	$1,4\ 10^{-9}$	0,001	$1,1\ 10^{-9}$	$5,7\ 10^{-10}$	$3,7\ 10^{-10}$	$2,4\ 10^{-10}$	$1,9\ 10^{-10}$
		S	0,010	$1,4\ 10^{-9}$	0,001	$1,1\ 10^{-9}$	$5,9\ 10^{-10}$	$3,8\ 10^{-10}$	$2,5\ 10^{-10}$	$2,0\ 10^{-10}$
Ta-177	2,36 d	M	0,010	$6,5\ 10^{-10}$	0,001	$4,7\ 10^{-10}$	$2,5\ 10^{-10}$	$1,5\ 10^{-10}$	$1,2\ 10^{-10}$	$9,6\ 10^{-11}$
		S	0,010	$6,9\ 10^{-10}$	0,001	$5,0\ 10^{-10}$	$2,7\ 10^{-10}$	$1,7\ 10^{-10}$	$1,3\ 10^{-10}$	$1,1\ 10^{-10}$
Ta-178	2,20 h	M	0,010	$4,4\ 10^{-10}$	0,001	$3,3\ 10^{-10}$	$1,7\ 10^{-10}$	$1,1\ 10^{-10}$	$8,0\ 10^{-11}$	$6,5\ 10^{-11}$
		S	0,010	$4,6\ 10^{-10}$	0,001	$3,4\ 10^{-10}$	$1,8\ 10^{-10}$	$1,2\ 10^{-10}$	$8,5\ 10^{-11}$	$6,8\ 10^{-11}$
Ta-179	1,82 a	M	0,010	$1,2\ 10^{-9}$	0,001	$9,6\ 10^{-10}$	$5,5\ 10^{-10}$	$3,5\ 10^{-10}$	$2,6\ 10^{-10}$	$2,2\ 10^{-10}$
		S	0,010	$2,4\ 10^{-9}$	0,001	$2,1\ 10^{-9}$	$1,3\ 10^{-9}$	$8,3\ 10^{-10}$	$6,4\ 10^{-10}$	$5,6\ 10^{-10}$
Ta-180	$1,00\ 10^{13}$ a	M	0,010	$2,7\ 10^{-8}$	0,001	$2,2\ 10^{-8}$	$1,3\ 10^{-8}$	$9,2\ 10^{-9}$	$7,9\ 10^{-9}$	$6,4\ 10^{-9}$
		S	0,010	$7,0\ 10^{-8}$	0,001	$6,5\ 10^{-8}$	$4,5\ 10^{-8}$	$3,1\ 10^{-8}$	$2,8\ 10^{-8}$	$2,6\ 10^{-8}$
Ta-180m	8,10 h	M	0,010	$3,1\ 10^{-10}$	0,001	$2,2\ 10^{-10}$	$1,1\ 10^{-10}$	$7,4\ 10^{-11}$	$4,8\ 10^{-11}$	$4,4\ 10^{-11}$
		S	0,010	$3,3\ 10^{-10}$	0,001	$2,3\ 10^{-10}$	$1,2\ 10^{-10}$	$7,9\ 10^{-11}$	$5,2\ 10^{-11}$	$4,2\ 10^{-11}$
Ta-182	115 d	M	0,010	$3,2\ 10^{-8}$	0,001	$2,6\ 10^{-8}$	$1,5\ 10^{-8}$	$1,1\ 10^{-8}$	$9,5\ 10^{-9}$	$7,6\ 10^{-9}$
		S	0,010	$4,2\ 10^{-8}$	0,001	$3,4\ 10^{-8}$	$2,1\ 10^{-8}$	$1,5\ 10^{-8}$	$1,3\ 10^{-8}$	$1,0\ 10^{-8}$
Ta-182m	0,264 h	M	0,010	$1,6\ 10^{-10}$	0,001	$1,1\ 10^{-10}$	$4,9\ 10^{-11}$	$3,4\ 10^{-11}$	$2,4\ 10^{-11}$	$2,0\ 10^{-11}$
		S	0,010	$1,6\ 10^{-10}$	0,001	$1,1\ 10^{-10}$	$5,2\ 10^{-11}$	$3,6\ 10^{-11}$	$2,5\ 10^{-11}$	$2,1\ 10^{-11}$

Nuclide	Physical half-life	Type	*Age ≤ 1 a*		*Age*	*1—2 a*	*2—7 a*	*7—12 a*	*12—17 a*	*> 17 a*
			f_1	*h(g)*	f_1	*h(g)*	*h(g)*	*h(g)*	*h(g)*	*h(g)*
Ta-183	5,10 d	M	0,010	$1{,}0\ 10^{-8}$	0,001	$7{,}4\ 10^{-9}$	$4{,}1\ 10^{-9}$	$2{,}9\ 10^{-9}$	$2{,}4\ 10^{-9}$	$1{,}9\ 10^{-9}$
		S	0,010	$1{,}1\ 10^{-8}$	0,001	$8{,}0\ 10^{-9}$	$4{,}5\ 10^{-9}$	$3{,}2\ 10^{-9}$	$2{,}7\ 10^{-9}$	$2{,}1\ 10^{-9}$
Ta-184	8,70 h	M	0,010	$3{,}2\ 10^{-9}$	0,001	$2{,}3\ 10^{-9}$	$1{,}1\ 10^{-9}$	$7{,}5\ 10^{-10}$	$5{,}0\ 10^{-10}$	$4{,}1\ 10^{-10}$
		S	0,010	$3{,}4\ 10^{-9}$	0,001	$2{,}4\ 10^{-9}$	$1{,}2\ 10^{-9}$	$7{,}9\ 10^{-10}$	$5{,}4\ 10^{-10}$	$4{,}3\ 10^{-10}$
Ta-185	0,816 h	M	0,010	$3{,}8\ 10^{-10}$	0,001	$2{,}5\ 10^{-10}$	$1{,}2\ 10^{-10}$	$7{,}7\ 10^{-11}$	$5{,}4\ 10^{-11}$	$4{,}5\ 10^{-11}$
		S	0,010	$4{,}0\ 10^{-10}$	0,001	$2{,}6\ 10^{-10}$	$1{,}2\ 10^{-10}$	$8{,}2\ 10^{-11}$	$5{,}7\ 10^{-11}$	$4{,}8\ 10^{-11}$
Ta-186	0,175 h	M	0,010	$1{,}6\ 10^{-10}$	0,001	$1{,}1\ 10^{-10}$	$4{,}8\ 10^{-11}$	$3{,}1\ 10^{-11}$	$2{,}0\ 10^{-11}$	$1{,}7\ 10^{-11}$
		S	0,010	$1{,}6\ 10^{-10}$	0,001	$1{,}1\ 10^{-10}$	$5{,}0\ 10^{-11}$	$3{,}2\ 10^{-11}$	$2{,}1\ 10^{-11}$	$1{,}8\ 10^{-11}$
Tungsten										
W-176	2,30 h	F	0,600	$3{,}3\ 10^{-10}$	0,300	$2{,}7\ 10^{-10}$	$1{,}4\ 10^{-10}$	$8{,}6\ 10^{-11}$	$5{,}0\ 10^{-11}$	$4{,}1\ 10^{-11}$
W-177	2,25 h	F	0,600	$2{,}0\ 10^{-10}$	0,300	$1{,}6\ 10^{-10}$	$8{,}2\ 10^{-11}$	$5{,}1\ 10^{-11}$	$3{,}0\ 10^{-11}$	$2{,}4\ 10^{-11}$
W-178	21,7 d	F	0,600	$7{,}2\ 10^{-10}$	0,300	$5{,}4\ 10^{-10}$	$2{,}5\ 10^{-10}$	$1{,}6\ 10^{-10}$	$8{,}7\ 10^{-11}$	$7{,}2\ 10^{-11}$
W-179	0,625 h	F	0,600	$9{,}3\ 10^{-12}$	0,300	$6{,}8\ 10^{-12}$	$3{,}3\ 10^{-12}$	$2{,}0\ 10^{-12}$	$1{,}2\ 10^{-12}$	9,2 10–13
W-181	121 d	F	0,600	$2{,}5\ 10^{-10}$	0,300	$1{,}9\ 10^{-10}$	$9{,}2\ 10^{-11}$	$5{,}7\ 10^{-11}$	$3{,}2\ 10^{-11}$	$2{,}7\ 10^{-11}$
W-185	75,1 d	F	0,600	$1{,}4\ 10^{-9}$	0,300	$1{,}0\ 10^{-9}$	$4{,}4\ 10^{-10}$	$2{,}7\ 10^{-10}$	$1{,}4\ 10^{-10}$	$1{,}2\ 10^{-10}$
W-187	23,9 h	F	0,600	$2{,}0\ 10^{-9}$	0,300	$1{,}5\ 10^{-9}$	$7{,}0\ 10^{-10}$	$4{,}3\ 10^{-10}$	$2{,}3\ 10^{-10}$	$1{,}9\ 10^{-10}$
W-188	69,4 d	F	0,600	$7{,}1\ 10^{-9}$	0,300	$5{,}0\ 10^{-9}$	$2{,}2\ 10^{-9}$	$1{,}3\ 10^{-9}$	$6{,}8\ 10^{-10}$	$5{,}7\ 10^{-10}$
Rhenium										
Re-177	0,233 h	F	1,000	$9{,}4\ 10^{-11}$	0,800	$6{,}7\ 10^{-11}$	$3{,}2\ 10^{-11}$	$1{,}9\ 10^{-11}$	$1{,}2\ 10^{-11}$	$9{,}7\ 10^{-12}$
		M	1,000	$1{,}1\ 10^{-10}$	0,800	$7{,}9\ 10^{-11}$	$3{,}9\ 10^{-11}$	$2{,}5\ 10^{-11}$	$1{,}7\ 10^{-11}$	$1{,}4\ 10^{-11}$
Re-178	0,220 h	F	1,000	$9{,}9\ 10^{-11}$	0,800	$6{,}8\ 10^{-11}$	$3{,}1\ 10^{-11}$	$1{,}9\ 10^{-11}$	$1{,}2\ 10^{-11}$	$1{,}0\ 10^{-11}$
		M	1,000	$1{,}3\ 10^{-10}$	0,800	$8{,}5\ 10^{-11}$	$3{,}9\ 10^{-11}$	$2{,}6\ 10^{-11}$	$1{,}7\ 10^{-11}$	$1{,}4\ 10^{-11}$
Re-181	20,0 h	F	1,000	$2{,}0\ 10^{-9}$	0,800	$1{,}4\ 10^{-9}$	$6{,}7\ 10^{-10}$	$3{,}8\ 10^{-10}$	$2{,}3\ 10^{-10}$	$1{,}8\ 10^{-10}$
		M	1,000	$2{,}1\ 10^{-9}$	0,800	$1{,}5\ 10^{-9}$	$7{,}4\ 10^{-10}$	$4{,}6\ 10^{-10}$	$3{,}1\ 10^{-10}$	$2{,}5\ 10^{-10}$
Re-182	2,67 d	F	1,000	$6{,}5\ 10^{-9}$	0,800	$4{,}7\ 10^{-9}$	$2{,}2\ 10^{-9}$	$1{,}3\ 10^{-9}$	$8{,}0\ 10^{-10}$	$6{,}4\ 10^{-10}$
		M	1,000	$8{,}7\ 10^{-9}$	0,800	$6{,}3\ 10^{-9}$	$3{,}4\ 10^{-9}$	$2{,}2\ 10^{-9}$	$1{,}5\ 10^{-9}$	$1{,}2\ 10^{-9}$

Nuclide	Physical half-life	Type	Age ≤ 1 a		Age	1—2 a	2—7 a	7—12 a	12—17 a	> 17 a
			f_1	h(g)	f_1	h(g)	h(g)	h(g)	h(g)	h(g)
Re-182	12,7 h	F	1,000	1,3 10^{-9}	0,800	1,0 10^{-9}	4,9 10^{-10}	2,8 10^{-10}	1,7 10^{-10}	1,4 10^{-10}
		M	1,000	1,4 10^{-9}	0,800	1,1 10^{-9}	5,7 10^{-10}	3,6 10^{-10}	2,5 10^{-10}	2,0 10^{-10}
Re-184	38,0 d	F	1,000	4,1 10^{-9}	0,800	2,9 10^{-9}	1,4 10^{-9}	8,6 10^{-10}	5,4 10^{-10}	4,4 10^{-10}
		M	1,000	9,1 10^{-9}	0,800	6,8 10^{-9}	4,0 10^{-9}	2,8 10^{-9}	2,4 10^{-9}	1,9 10^{-9}
Re-184m	165 d	F	1,000	6,6 10^{-9}	0,800	4,6 10^{-9}	2,0 10^{-9}	1,2 10^{-9}	7,3 10^{-10}	5,9 10^{-10}
		M	1,000	2,9 10^{-8}	0,800	2,2 10^{-8}	1,3 10^{-8}	9,3 10^{-9}	8,1 10^{-9}	6,5 10^{-9}
Re-186	3,78 d	F	1,000	7,3 10^{-9}	0,800	4,7 10^{-9}	2,0 10^{-9}	1,1 10^{-9}	6,6 10^{-10}	5,2 10^{-10}
		M	1,000	8,7 10^{-9}	0,800	5,7 10^{-9}	2,8 10^{-9}	1,8 10^{-9}	1,4 10^{-9}	1,1 10^{-9}
Re-186m	2,00 10^{5} a	F	1,000	1,2 10^{-8}	0,800	7,0 10^{-9}	2,9 10^{-9}	1,7 10^{-9}	1,0 10^{-9}	8,3 10^{-10}
		M	1,000	5,9 10^{-8}	0,800	4,6 10^{-8}	2,7 10^{-8}	1,8 10^{-8}	1,4 10^{-8}	1,2 10^{-8}
Re-187	5,00 10^{10} a	F	1,000	2,6 10^{-11}	0,800	1,6 10^{-11}	6,8 10^{-12}	3,8 10^{-12}	2,3 10^{-12}	1,8 10^{-12}
		M	1,000	5,7 10^{-11}	0,800	4,1 10^{-11}	2,0 10^{-11}	1,2 10^{-11}	7,5 10^{-12}	6,3 10^{-12}
Re-188	17,0 h	F	1,000	6,5 10^{-9}	0,800	4,4 10^{-9}	1,9 10^{-9}	1,0 10^{-9}	6,1 10^{-10}	4,6 10^{-10}
		M	1,000	6,0 10^{-9}	0,800	4,0 10^{-9}	1,8 10^{-9}	1,0 10^{-9}	6,8 10^{-10}	5,4 10^{-10}
Re-188m	0,310 h	F	1,000	1,4 10^{-10}	0,800	9,1 10^{-11}	4,0 10^{-11}	2,1 10^{-11}	1,3 10^{-11}	1,0 10^{-11}
		M	1,000	1,3 10^{-10}	0,800	8,6 10^{-11}	4,0 10^{-11}	2,7 10^{-11}	1,6 10^{-11}	1,3 10^{-11}
Re-189	1,01 d	F	1,000	3,7 10^{-9}	0,800	2,5 10^{-9}	1,1 10^{-9}	5,8 10^{-10}	3,5 10^{-10}	2,7 10^{-10}
		M	1,000	3,9 10^{-9}	0,800	2,6 10^{-9}	1,2 10^{-9}	7,6 10^{-10}	5,5 10^{-10}	4,3 10^{-10}
Osmium										
Os-180	0,366 h	F	0,020	7,1 10^{-11}	0,010	5,3 10^{-11}	2,6 10^{-11}	1,6 10^{-11}	1,0 10^{-11}	8,2 10^{-12}
		M	0,020	1,1 10^{-10}	0,010	7,9 10^{-11}	3,9 10^{-11}	2,5 10^{-11}	1,7 10^{-11}	1,4 10^{-11}
		S	0,020	1,1 10^{-10}	0,010	8,2 10^{-11}	4,1 10^{-11}	2,6 10^{-11}	1,8 10^{-11}	1,5 10^{-11}
Os-181	1,75 h	F	0,020	3,0 10^{-10}	0,010	2,3 10^{-10}	1,1 10^{-10}	7,0 10^{-11}	4,1 10^{-11}	3,3 10^{-11}
		M	0,020	4,5 10^{-10}	0,010	3,4 10^{-10}	1,8 10^{-10}	1,1 10^{-10}	7,6 10^{-11}	6,2 10^{-11}
		S	0,020	4,7 10^{-10}	0,010	3,6 10^{-10}	1,8 10^{-10}	1,2 10^{-10}	8,1 10^{-11}	6,5 10^{-11}

Nuclide	Physical half-life	Type	Age ≤ 1 a		Age	1—2 a	2—7 a	7—12 a	12—17 a	> 17 a
			f_1	$h(g)$	f_1	$h(g)$	$h(g)$	$h(g)$	$h(g)$	$h(g)$
Os-182	22,0 h	F	0,020	1,6 10^{-9}	0,010	1,2 10^{-9}	6,0 10^{-10}	3,7 10^{-10}	2,1 10^{-10}	1,7 10^{-10}
		M	0,020	2,5 10^{-9}	0,010	1,9 10^{-9}	1,0 10^{-9}	6,6 10^{-10}	4,5 10^{-10}	3,6 10^{-10}
		S	0,020	2,6 10^{-9}	0,010	2,0 10^{-9}	1,0 10^{-9}	6,9 10^{-10}	4,8 10^{-10}	3,8 10^{-10}
Os-185	94,0 d	F	0,020	7,2 10^{-9}	0,010	5,8 10^{-9}	3,1 10^{-9}	1,9 10^{-9}	1,2 10^{-9}	1,1 10^{-9}
		M	0,020	6,6 10^{-9}	0,010	5,4 10^{-9}	2,9 10^{-9}	2,0 10^{-9}	1,5 10^{-9}	1,3 10^{-9}
		S	0,020	7,0 10^{-9}	0,010	5,8 10^{-9}	3,6 10^{-9}	2,4 10^{-9}	1,9 10^{-9}	1,6 10^{-9}
Os-189m	6,00 h	F	0,020	3,8 10^{-11}	0,010	2,8 10^{-11}	1,2 10^{-11}	7,0 10^{-12}	3,5 10^{-12}	2,5 10^{-12}
		M	0,020	6,5 10^{-11}	0,010	4,1 10^{-11}	1,8 10^{-11}	1,1 10^{-11}	6,0 10^{-12}	5,0 10^{-12}
		S	0,020	6,8 10^{-11}	0,010	4,3 10^{-11}	1,9 10^{-11}	1,2 10^{-11}	6,3 10^{-12}	5,3 10^{-12}
Os-191	15,4 d	F	0,020	2,8 10^{-9}	0,010	1,9 10^{-9}	8,5 10^{-10}	5,3 10^{-10}	3,0 10^{-10}	2,5 10^{-10}
		M	0,020	8,0 10^{-9}	0,010	5,8 10^{-9}	3,4 10^{-9}	2,4 10^{-9}	2,0 10^{-9}	1,7 10^{-9}
		S	0,020	9,0 10^{-9}	0,010	6,5 10^{-9}	3,9 10^{-9}	2,7 10^{-9}	2,3 10^{-9}	1,9 10^{-9}
Os-191m	13,0 h	F	0,020	3,0 10^{-10}	0,010	2,0 10^{-10}	8,8 10^{-11}	5,4 10^{-11}	2,9 10^{-11}	2,4 10^{-11}
		M	0,020	7,8 10^{-10}	0,010	5,4 10^{-10}	3,1 10^{-10}	2,1 10^{-10}	1,7 10^{-10}	1,4 10^{-10}
		S	0,020	8,5 10^{-10}	0,010	6,0 10^{-10}	3,4 10^{-10}	2,4 10^{-10}	2,0 10^{-10}	1,6 10^{-10}
Os-193	1,25 d	F	0,020	1,9 10^{-9}	0,010	1,2 10^{-9}	5,2 10^{-10}	3,2 10^{-10}	1,8 10^{-10}	1,6 10^{-10}
		M	0,020	3,8 10^{-9}	0,010	2,6 10^{-9}	1,3 10^{-9}	8,4 10^{-10}	5,9 10^{-10}	4,8 10^{-10}
		S	0,020	4,0 10^{-9}	0,010	2,7 10^{-9}	1,3 10^{-9}	9,0 10^{-10}	6,4 10^{-10}	5,2 10^{-10}
Os-194	6,00 a	F	0,020	8,7 10^{-8}	0,010	6,8 10^{-8}	3,4 10^{-8}	2,1 10^{-8}	1,3 10^{-8}	1,1 10^{-8}
		M	0,020	9,9 10^{-8}	0,010	8,3 10^{-8}	4,8 10^{-8}	3,1 10^{-8}	2,4 10^{-8}	2,1 10^{-8}
		S	0,020	2,6 10^{-7}	0,010	2,4 10^{-7}	1,6 10^{-7}	1,1 10^{-7}	8,8 10^{-8}	8,5 10^{-8}
Iridium										
Ir-182	0,250 h	F	0,020	1,4 10^{-10}	0,010	9,8 10^{-11}	4,5 10^{-11}	2,8 10^{-11}	1,7 10^{-11}	1,4 10^{-11}
		M	0,020	2,1 10^{-10}	0,010	1,4 10^{-10}	6,7 10^{-11}	4,3 10^{-11}	2,8 10^{-11}	2,3 10^{-11}
		S	0,020	2,2 10^{-10}	0,010	1,5 10^{-10}	6,9 10^{-11}	4,4 10^{-11}	2,9 10^{-11}	2,4 10^{-11}

Nuclide	*Physical half-life*	*Type*	*Age ≤ 1 a*		*Age*	*1—2 a*	*2—7 a*	*7—12 a*	*12—17 a*	*> 17 a*
			f_1	*h(g)*	f_1	*h(g)*	*h(g)*	*h(g)*	*h(g)*	*h(g)*
Ir-184	3,02 h	F	0,020	5,7 10^{-10}	0,010	4,4 10^{-10}	2,1 10^{-10}	1,3 10^{-10}	7,6 10^{-11}	6,2 10^{-11}
		M	0,020	8,6 10^{-10}	0,010	6,4 10^{-10}	3,2 10^{-10}	2,1 10^{-10}	1,4 10^{-10}	1,1 10^{-10}
		S	0,020	8,9 10^{-10}	0,010	6,6 10^{-10}	3,4 10^{-10}	2,2 10^{-10}	1,4 10^{-10}	1,2 10^{-10}
Ir-185	14,0 h	F	0,020	8,0 10^{-10}	0,010	6,1 10^{-10}	2,9 10^{-10}	1,8 10^{-10}	1,0 10^{-10}	8,2 10^{-11}
		M	0,020	1,3 10^{-9}	0,010	9,7 10^{-10}	4,9 10^{-10}	3,2 10^{-10}	2,2 10^{-10}	1,8 10^{-10}
		S	0,020	1,4 10^{-9}	0,010	1,0 10^{-9}	5,2 10^{-10}	3,4 10^{-10}	2,3 10^{-10}	1,9 10^{-10}
Ir-186	15,8 h	F	0,020	1,5 10^{-9}	0,010	1,2 10^{-9}	5,9 10^{-10}	3,6 10^{-10}	2,1 10^{-10}	1,7 10^{-10}
		M	0,020	2,2 10^{-9}	0,010	1,7 10^{-9}	8,8 10^{-10}	5,8 10^{-10}	3,8 10^{-10}	3,1 10^{-10}
		S	0,020	2,3 10^{-9}	0,010	1,8 10^{-9}	9,2 10^{-10}	6,0 10^{-10}	4,0 10^{-10}	3,2 10^{-10}
Ir-186	1,75 h	F	0,020	2,1 10^{-10}	0,010	1,6 10^{-10}	7,7 10^{-11}	4,8 10^{-11}	2,8 10^{-11}	2,3 10^{-11}
		M	0,020	3,3 10^{-10}	0,010	2,4 10^{-10}	1,2 10^{-10}	7,7 10^{-11}	5,1 10^{-11}	4,2 10^{-11}
		S	0,020	3,4 10^{-10}	0,010	2,5 10^{-10}	1,2 10^{-10}	8,1 10^{-11}	5,4 10^{-11}	4,4 10^{-11}
Ir-187	10,5 h	F	0,020	3,6 10^{-10}	0,010	2,8 10^{-10}	1,4 10^{-10}	8,2 10^{-11}	4,6 10^{-11}	3,7 10^{-11}
		M	0,020	5,8 10^{-10}	0,010	4,3 10^{-10}	2,2 10^{-10}	1,4 10^{-10}	9,2 10^{-11}	7,4 10^{-11}
		S	0,020	6,0 10^{-10}	0,010	4,5 10^{-10}	2,3 10^{-10}	1,5 10^{-10}	9,7 10^{-11}	7,9 10^{-11}
Ir-188	1,73 d	F	0,020	2,0 10^{-9}	0,010	1,6 10^{-9}	8,0 10^{-10}	5,0 10^{-10}	2,9 10^{-10}	2,4 10^{-10}
		M	0,020	2,7 10^{-9}	0,010	2,1 10^{-9}	1,1 10^{-9}	7,5 10^{-10}	5,0 10^{-10}	4,0 10^{-10}
		S	0,020	2,8 10^{-9}	0,010	2,2 10^{-9}	1,2 10^{-9}	7,8 10^{-10}	5,2 10^{-10}	4,2 10^{-10}
Ir-189	13,3 d	F	0,020	1,2 10^{-9}	0,010	8,2 10^{-10}	3,8 10^{-10}	2,4 10^{-10}	1,3 10^{-10}	1,1 10^{-10}
		M	0,020	2,7 10^{-9}	0,010	1,9 10^{-9}	1,1 10^{-9}	7,7 10^{-10}	6,4 10^{-10}	5,2 10^{-10}
		S	0,020	3,0 10^{-9}	0,010	2,2 10^{-9}	1,3 10^{-9}	8,7 10^{-10}	7,3 10^{-10}	6.0 10^{-10}
Ir-190	12,1 d	F	0,020	6,2 10^{-9}	0,010	4,7 10^{-9}	2,4 10^{-9}	1,5 10^{-9}	9,1 10^{-10}	7,7 10^{-10}
		M	0,020	1,1 10^{-8}	0,010	8,6 10^{-9}	4,4 10^{-9}	3,1 10^{-9}	2,7 10^{-9}	2,1 10^{-9}
		S	0,020	1,1 10^{-8}	0,010	9,4 10^{-9}	4,8 10^{-9}	3,5 10^{-9}	3,0 10^{-9}	2,4 10^{-9}

Nuclide	Physical half-life	Type	Age ≤ 1 a		Age	1—2 a	2—7 a	7—12 a	12—17 a	> 17 a
			f_1	$h(g)$	f_1	$h(g)$	$h(g)$	$h(g)$	$h(g)$	$h(g)$
Ir-190m	3,10 h	F	0,020	$4{,}2\ 10^{-10}$	0,010	$3{,}4\ 10^{-10}$	$1{,}7\ 10^{-10}$	$1{,}0\ 10^{-10}$	$6{,}0\ 10^{-11}$	$4{,}9\ 10^{-11}$
		M	0,020	$6{,}0\ 10^{-10}$	0,010	$4{,}7\ 10^{-10}$	$2{,}4\ 10^{-10}$	$1{,}5\ 10^{-10}$	$9{,}9\ 10^{-11}$	$7{,}9\ 10^{-11}$
		S	0,020	$6{,}2\ 10^{-10}$	0,010	$4{,}8\ 10^{-10}$	$2{,}5\ 10^{-10}$	$1{,}6\ 10^{-10}$	$1.0\ 10^{-10}$	$8{,}3\ 10^{-11}$
Ir-190m	1,20 h	F	0,020	$3{,}2\ 10^{-11}$	0,010	$2{,}4\ 10^{-11}$	$1{,}2\ 10^{-11}$	$7{,}2\ 10^{-12}$	$4{,}3\ 10^{-12}$	$3{,}6\ 10^{-12}$
		M	0,020	$5{,}7\ 10^{-11}$	0,010	$4{,}2\ 10^{-11}$	$2.0\ 10^{-11}$	$1{,}4\ 10^{-11}$	$1{,}2\ 10^{-11}$	$9{,}3\ 10^{-12}$
		S	0,020	$5{,}5\ 10^{-11}$	0,010	$4{,}5\ 10^{-11}$	$2{,}2\ 10^{-11}$	$1{,}6\ 10^{-11}$	$1{,}3\ 10^{-11}$	$1{,}0\ 10^{-11}$
Ir-192	74,0 d	F	0,020	$1{,}5\ 10^{-8}$	0,010	$1{,}1\ 10^{-8}$	$5{,}7\ 10^{-9}$	$3{,}3\ 10^{-9}$	$2{,}1\ 10^{-9}$	$1{,}8\ 10^{-9}$
		M	0,020	$2{,}3\ 10^{-8}$	0,010	$1{,}8\ 10^{-8}$	$1{,}1\ 10^{-8}$	$7{,}6\ 10^{-9}$	$6{,}4\ 10^{-9}$	$5{,}2\ 10^{-9}$
		S	0,020	$2{,}8\ 10^{-8}$	0,010	$2{,}2\ 10^{-8}$	$1{,}3\ 10^{-8}$	$9{,}5\ 10^{-9}$	$8{,}1\ 10^{-9}$	$6{,}6\ 10^{-9}$
Ir-192m	$2{,}41\ 10^{2}$ a	F	0,020	$2{,}7\ 10^{-8}$	0,010	$2{,}3\ 10^{-8}$	$1{,}4\ 10^{-8}$	$8{,}2\ 10^{-9}$	$5{,}4\ 10^{-9}$	$4{,}8\ 10^{-9}$
		M	0,020	$2{,}3\ 10^{-8}$	0,010	$2{,}1\ 10^{-8}$	$1{,}3\ 10^{-8}$	$8{,}4\ 10^{-9}$	$6{,}6\ 10^{-9}$	$5{,}8\ 10^{-9}$
		S	0,020	$9{,}2\ 10^{-8}$	0,010	$9{,}1\ 10^{-8}$	$6{,}5\ 10^{-8}$	$4{,}5\ 10^{-8}$	$4{,}0\ 10^{-8}$	$3{,}9\ 10^{-8}$
Ir-193m	11,9 d	F	0,020	$1{,}2\ 10^{-9}$	0,010	$8{,}4\ 10^{-10}$	$3{,}7\ 10^{-10}$	$2{,}2\ 10^{-10}$	$1{,}2\ 10^{-10}$	$1{,}0\ 10^{-10}$
		M	0,020	$4{,}8\ 10^{-9}$	0,010	$3{,}5\ 10^{-9}$	$2{,}1\ 10^{-9}$	$1{,}5\ 10^{-9}$	$1{,}4\ 10^{-9}$	$1{,}1\ 10^{-9}$
		S	0,020	$5{,}4\ 10^{-9}$	0,010	$4{,}0\ 10^{-9}$	$2{,}4\ 10^{-9}$	$1{,}8\ 10^{-9}$	$1{,}6\ 10^{-9}$	$1{,}3\ 10^{-9}$
Ir-194	19,1 h	F	0,020	$2{,}9\ 10^{-9}$	0,010	$1{,}9\ 10^{-9}$	$8{,}1\ 10^{-10}$	$4{,}9\ 10^{-10}$	$2{,}5\ 10^{-10}$	$2{,}1\ 10^{-10}$
		M	0,020	$5{,}3\ 10^{-9}$	0,010	$3{,}5\ 10^{-9}$	$1{,}6\ 10^{-9}$	$1{,}0\ 10^{-9}$	$6{,}3\ 10^{-10}$	$5{,}2\ 10^{-10}$
		S	0,020	$5{,}5\ 10^{-9}$	0,010	$3{,}7\ 10^{-9}$	$1{,}7\ 10^{-9}$	$1{,}1\ 10^{-9}$	$6{,}7\ 10^{-10}$	$5{,}6\ 10^{-10}$
Ir-194m	171 d	F	0,020	$3{,}4\ 10^{-8}$	0,010	$2{,}7\ 10^{-8}$	$1{,}4\ 10^{-8}$	$9{,}5\ 10^{-9}$	$6{,}2\ 10^{-9}$	$5{,}4\ 10^{-9}$
		M	0,020	$3{,}9\ 10^{-8}$	0,010	$3{,}2\ 10^{-8}$	$1{,}9\ 10^{-8}$	$1{,}3\ 10^{-8}$	$1{,}1\ 10^{-8}$	$9{,}0\ 10^{-9}$
		S	0,020	$5{,}0\ 10^{-8}$	0,010	$4{,}2\ 10^{-8}$	$2{,}6\ 10^{-8}$	$1{,}8\ 10^{-8}$	$1{,}5\ 10^{-8}$	$1{,}3\ 10^{-8}$
Ir-195	2,50 h	F	0,020	$2{,}9\ 10^{-10}$	0,010	$1{,}9\ 10^{-10}$	$8{,}1\ 10^{-11}$	$5{,}1\ 10^{-11}$	$2{,}9\ 10^{-11}$	$2{,}4\ 10^{-11}$
		M	0,020	$5{,}4\ 10^{-10}$	0,010	$3{,}6\ 10^{-10}$	$1{,}7\ 10^{-10}$	$1{,}1\ 10^{-10}$	$8{,}1\ 10^{-11}$	$6{,}7\ 10^{-11}$
		S	0,020	$5{,}7\ 10^{-10}$	0,010	$3{,}8\ 10^{-10}$	$1{,}8\ 10^{-10}$	$1{,}2\ 10^{-10}$	$8{,}7\ 10^{-11}$	$7{,}1\ 10^{-11}$

Nuclide	Physical half-life	Type	Age ≤ 1 a		Age	1—2 a	2—7 a	7—12 a	12—17 a	> 17 a
			f_1	h(g)	f_1	h(g)	h(g)	h(g)	h(g)	h(g)
Ir-195m	3,80 h	F	0,020	6,9 10^{-10}	0,010	4,8 10^{-10}	2,1 10^{-10}	1,3 10^{-10}	7,2 10^{-11}	6,0 10^{-11}
		M	0,020	1,2 10^{-9}	0,010	8,6 10^{-10}	4,2 10^{-10}	2,7 10^{-10}	1.9 10^{-10}	1,6 10^{-10}
		S	0,020	1,3 10^{-9}	0,010	9,0 10^{-10}	4,4 10^{-10}	2,9 10^{-10}	2,0 10^{-10}	1,7 10^{-10}
Platinum										
Pt-186	2,00 h	F	0,020	3,0 10^{-10}	0,010	2,4 10^{-10}	1,2 10^{-10}	7,2 10^{-11}	4,1 10^{-11}	3,3 10^{-11}
Pt-188	10,2 d	F	0,020	3,6 10^{-9}	0,010	2,7 10^{-9}	1,3 10^{-9}	8,4 10^{-10}	5,0 10^{-10}	4,2 10^{-10}
Pt-189	10,9 h	F	0,020	3,8 10^{-10}	0,010	2,9 10^{-10}	1,4 10^{-10}	8,4 10^{-11}	4,7 10^{-11}	3,8 10^{-11}
Pt-191	2,80 d	F	0,020	1,1 10^{-9}	0,010	7,9 10^{-10}	3,7 10^{-10}	2,3 10^{-10}	1,3 10^{-10}	1,1 10^{-10}
Pt-193	50,0 a	F	0,020	2,2 10^{-10}	0,010	1,6 10^{-10}	7,2 10^{-11}	4,3 10^{-11}	2,5 10^{-11}	2,1 10^{-11}
Pt-193m	4,33 d	F	0,020	1,6 10^{-9}	0,010	1,0 10^{-9}	4,5 10^{-10}	2,7 10^{-10}	1,4 10^{-10}	1,2 10^{-10}
Pt-195m	4,02 d	F	0,020	2,2 10^{-9}	0,010	1,5 10^{-9}	6,4 10^{-10}	3,9 10^{-10}	2,1 10^{-10}	1,8 10^{-10}
Pt-197	18,3 h	F	0,020	1,1 10^{-9}	0,010	7,3 10^{-10}	3,1 10^{-10}	1,9 10^{-10}	1,0 10^{-10}	8,5 10^{-11}
Pt-197m	1,57 h	F	0,020	2,8 10^{-10}	0,010	1,8 10^{-10}	7,9 10^{-11}	4,9 10^{-11}	2,8 10^{-11}	2,4 10^{-11}
Pt-199	0,513 h	F	0,020	1,3 10^{-10}	0,010	8,3 10^{-11}	3,6 10^{-11}	2,3 10^{-11}	1,4 10^{-11}	1,2 10^{-11}
Pt-200	12,5 h	F	0,020	2,6 10^{-9}	0,010	1,7 10^{-9}	7,2 10^{-10}	5,1 10^{-10}	2,6 10^{-10}	2,2 10^{-10}
Gold										
Au-193	17,6 h	F	0,200	3,7 10^{-10}	0,100	2,8 10^{-10}	1,3 10^{-10}	7,9 10^{-11}	4,3 10^{-11}	3,6 10^{-11}
		M	0,200	7,5 10^{-10}	0,100	5,6 10^{-10}	2,8 10^{-10}	1,9 10^{-10}	1,4 10^{-10}	1,1 10^{-10}
		S	0,200	7,9 10^{-10}	0,100	5,9 10^{-10}	3,0 10^{-10}	2,0 10^{-10}	1,5 10^{-10}	1,2 10^{-10}
Au-194	1,65 d	F	0,200	1,2 10^{-9}	0,100	9,6 10^{-10}	4,9 10^{-10}	3,0 10^{-10}	1,8 10^{-10}	1,4 10^{-10}
		M	0,200	1,7 10^{-9}	0,100	1,4 10^{-9}	7,1 10^{-10}	4,6 10^{-10}	2,9 10^{-10}	2,3 10^{-10}
		S	0,200	1,7 10^{-9}	0,100	1,4 10^{-9}	7,3 10^{-10}	4,7 10^{-10}	3,0 10^{-10}	2,4 10^{-10}
Au-195	183 d	F	0,200	7,2 10^{-10}	0,100	5,3 10^{-10}	2,5 10^{-10}	1,5 10^{-10}	8,1 10^{-11}	6,6 10^{-11}
		M	0,200	5,2 10^{-9}	0,100	4,1 10^{-9}	2,4 10^{-9}	1,6 10^{-9}	1,4 10^{-9}	1,1 10^{-9}
		S	0,200	8,1 10^{-9}	0,100	6,6 10^{-9}	3,9 10^{-9}	2,6 10^{-9}	2,1 10^{-9}	1,7 10^{-9}

Nuclide	*Physical half-life*	*Type*	*Age ≤ 1 a*		*Age*	*1—2 a*	*2—7 a*	*7—12 a*	*12—17 a*	*> 17 a*
			f_1	*h(g)*	f_1	*h(g)*	*h(g)*	*h(g)*	*h(g)*	*h(g)*
Au-198	2,69 d	F	0,200	2,4 10^{-9}	0,100	1,7 10^{-9}	7,6 10^{-10}	4,7 10^{-10}	2,5 10^{-10}	2,1 10^{-10}
		M	0,200	5,0 10^{-9}	0,100	4,1 10^{-9}	1,9 10^{-9}	1,3 10^{-9}	9,7 10^{-10}	7,8 10^{-10}
		S	0,200	5,4 10^{-9}	0,100	4,4 10^{-9}	2,0 10^{-9}	1,4 10^{-9}	1,1 10^{-9}	8,6 10^{-10}
Au-198m	2,30 d	F	0,200	3,3 10^{-9}	0,100	2,4 10^{-9}	1,1 10^{-9}	6,9 10^{-10}	3,7 10^{-10}	3,2 10^{-10}
		M	0,200	8,7 10^{-9}	0,100	6,5 10^{-9}	3,6 10^{-9}	2,6 10^{-9}	2,2 10^{-9}	1,8 10^{-9}
		S	0,200	9,5 10^{-9}	0,100	7,1 10^{-9}	4,0 10^{-9}	2,9 10^{-9}	2,5 10^{-9}	2,0 10^{-9}
Au-199	3,14 d	F	0,200	1,1 10^{-9}	0,100	7,9 10^{-10}	3,5 10^{-10}	2,2 10^{-10}	1,1 10^{-10}	9,8 10^{-11}
		M	0,200	3,4 10^{-9}	0,100	2,5 10^{-9}	1,4 10^{-9}	1,0 10^{-9}	9,0 10^{-10}	7,1 10^{-10}
		S	0,200	3,8 10^{-9}	0,100	2,8 10^{-9}	1,6 10^{-9}	1,2 10^{-9}	1,0 10^{-9}	7,9 10^{-10}
Au-200	0,807 h	F	0,200	1,9 10^{-10}	0,100	1,2 10^{-10}	5,2 10^{-11}	3,2 10^{-11}	1,9 10^{-11}	1,6 10^{-11}
		M	0,200	3,2 10^{-10}	0,100	2,1 10^{-10}	9,3 10^{-11}	6,0 10^{-11}	4,0 10^{-11}	3,3 10^{-11}
		S	0,200	3,4 10^{-10}	0,100	2,1 10^{-10}	9,8 10^{-11}	6,3 10^{-11}	4,2 10^{-11}	3,5 10^{-11}
Au-200m	18,7 h	F	0,200	2,7 10^{-9}	0,100	2,1 10^{-9}	1,0 10^{-9}	6,4 10^{-10}	3,6 10^{-10}	2,9 10^{-10}
		M	0,200	4,8 10^{-9}	0,100	3,7 10^{-9}	1,9 10^{-9}	1,2 10^{-9}	8,4 10^{-10}	6,8 10^{-10}
		S	0,200	5,1 10^{-9}	0,100	3,9 10^{-9}	2,0 10^{-9}	1,3 10^{-9}	8,9 10^{-10}	7,2 10^{-10}
Au-201	0,440 h	F	0,200	9,0 10^{-11}	0,100	5,7 10^{-11}	2,5 10^{-11}	1,6 10^{-11}	1,0 10^{-11}	8,7 10^{-12}
		M	0,200	1,5 10^{-10}	0,100	9,6 10^{-11}	4,3 10^{-11}	2,9 10^{-11}	2,0 10^{-11}	1,7 10^{-11}
		S	0,200	1,5 10^{-10}	0,100	1,0 10^{-10}	4,5 10^{-11}	3,0 10^{-11}	2,1 10^{-11}	1,7 10^{-11}
Mercury										
Hg-193 (organic)	3,50 h	F	0,800	2,2 10^{-10}	0,400	1,8 10^{-10}	8,2 10^{-11}	5,0 10^{-11}	2,9 10^{-11}	2,4 10^{-11}
Hg-193 (inorganic)	3,50 h	F	0,040	2,7 10^{-10}	0,020	2,0 10^{-10}	8,9 10^{-11}	5,5 10^{-11}	3,1 10^{-11}	2,6 10^{-11}
		M	0,040	5,3 10^{-10}	0,020	3,8 10^{-10}	1,9 10^{-10}	1,3 10^{-10}	9,2 10^{-11}	7,5 10^{-11}
Hg-193m (organic)	11,1 h	F	0,800	8,4 10^{-10}	0,400	7,6 10^{-10}	3,7 10^{-10}	2,2 10^{-10}	1,3 10^{-10}	1,0 10^{-10}
Hg-193m (inorganic)	11,1 h	F	0,040	1,1 10^{-9}	0,020	8,5 10^{-10}	4,1 10^{-10}	2,5 10^{-10}	1,4 10^{-10}	1,1 10^{-10}
		M	0,040	1,9 10^{-9}	0,020	1,4 10^{-9}	7,2 10^{-10}	4,7 10^{-10}	3,2 10^{-10}	2,6 10^{-10}

Nuclide	*Physical half-life*	*Type*	*Age ≤ 1 a*		*Age*	*1—2 a*	*2—7 a*	*7—12 a*	*12—17 a*	*> 17 a*
			f_1	*h(g)*	f_1	*h(g)*	*h(g)*	*h(g)*	*h(g)*	*h(g)*
Hg-194 (organic)	2,60 10^{2} a	F	0,800	4,9 10^{-8}	0,400	3,7 10^{-8}	2,4 10^{-8}	1,9 10^{-8}	1,5 10^{-8}	1,4 10^{-8}
Hg-194 (inorganic)	2,60 10^{2} a	F	0,040	3,2 10^{-8}	0,020	2,9 10^{-8}	2,0 10^{-8}	1,6 10^{-8}	1,4 10^{-8}	1,3 10^{-8}
		M	0,040	2,1 10^{-8}	0,020	1,9 10^{-8}	1,3 10^{-8}	1,0 10^{-8}	8,9 10^{-9}	8,3 10^{-9}
Hg-195 (organic)	9,90 h	F	0,800	2,0 10^{-10}	0,400	1,8 10^{-10}	8,5 10^{-11}	5,1 10^{-11}	2,8 10^{-11}	2,3 10^{-11}
Hg-195 (inorganic)	9,90 h	F	0,040	2,7 10^{-10}	0,020	2,0 10^{-10}	9,5 10^{-11}	5,7 10^{-11}	3,1 10^{-11}	2,5 10^{-11}
		M	0,040	5,3 10^{-10}	0,020	3,9 10^{-10}	2,0 10^{-10}	1,3 10^{-10}	9,0 10^{-11}	7,3 10^{-11}
Hg-195m (organic)	1,73 d	F	0,800	1,1 10^{-9}	0,400	9,7 10^{-10}	4,4 10^{-10}	2,7 10^{-10}	1,4 10^{-10}	1,2 10^{-10}
Hg-195m (inorganic)	1,73 d	F	0,040	1,6 10^{-9}	0,020	1,1 10^{-9}	5,1 10^{-10}	3,1 10^{-10}	1,7 10^{-10}	1,4 10^{-10}
		M	0,040	3,7 10^{-9}	0,020	2,6 10^{-9}	1,4 10^{-9}	8,5 10^{-10}	6,7 10^{-10}	5,3 10^{-10}
Hg-197 (organic)	2,67 d	F	0,800	4,7 10^{-10}	0,400	4,0 10^{-10}	1,8 10^{-10}	1,1 10^{-10}	5,8 10^{-11}	4,7 10^{-11}
Hg-197 (inorganic)	2,67 d	F	0,040	6,8 10^{-10}	0,020	4,7 10^{-10}	2,1 10^{-10}	1,3 10^{-10}	6,8 10^{-11}	5,6 10^{-11}
		M	0,040	1,7 10^{-9}	0,020	1,2 10^{-9}	6,6 10^{-10}	4,6 10^{-10}	3,8 10^{-10}	3,0 10^{-10}
Hg-197m (organic)	23,8 h	F	0,800	9,3 10^{-10}	0,400	7,8 10^{-10}	3,4 10^{-10}	2,1 10^{-10}	1,1 10^{-10}	9,6 10^{-11}
Hg-197m (inorganic)	23,8 h	F	0,040	1,4 10^{-9}	0,020	9,3 10^{-10}	4,0 10^{-10}	2,5 10^{-10}	1,3 10^{-10}	1,1 10^{-10}
		M	0,040	3,5 10^{-9}	0,020	2,5 10^{-9}	1,1 10^{-9}	8,2 10^{-10}	6,7 10^{-10}	5,3 10^{-10}
Hg-199m (organic)	0,710 h	F	0,800	1,4 10^{-10}	0,400	9,6 10^{-11}	4,2 10^{-11}	2,7 10^{-11}	1,7 10^{-11}	1,5 10^{-11}
Hg-199m (inorganic)	0,710 h	F	0,040	1,4 10^{-10}	0,020	9,6 10^{-11}	4,2 10^{-11}	2,7 10^{-11}	1,7 10^{-11}	1,5 10^{-11}
		M	0,040	2,5 10^{-10}	0,020	1,7 10^{-10}	7,9 10^{-11}	5,4 10^{-11}	3,8 10^{-11}	3,2 10^{-11}
Hg-203 (organic)	46,6 d	F	0,800	5,7 10^{-9}	0,400	3,7 10^{-9}	1,7 10^{-9}	1,1 10^{-9}	6,6 10^{-10}	5,6 10^{-10}
Hg-203 (inorganic)	46,6 d	F	0,040	4,2 10^{-9}	0,020	2,9 10^{-9}	1,4 10^{-9}	9,0 10^{-10}	5,5 10^{-10}	4,6 10^{-10}
		M	0,040	1,0 10^{-8}	0,020	7,9 10^{-9}	4,7 10^{-9}	3,4 10^{-9}	3,0 10^{-9}	2,4 10^{-9}
Thallium										
Tl-194	0,550 h	F	1,000	3,6 10^{-11}	1,000	3,0 10^{-11}	1,5 10^{-11}	9,2 10^{-12}	5,5 10^{-12}	4,4 10^{-12}

Nuclide	Physical half-life	Type	Age ≤ 1 a		Age	1—2 a	2—7 a	7—12 a	12—17 a	> 17 a
			f_1	h(g)	f_1	h(g)	h(g)	h(g)	h(g)	h(g)
Tl-194m	0,546 h	F	1,000	$1{,}7\ 10^{-10}$	1,000	$1{,}2\ 10^{-10}$	$6{,}1\ 10^{-11}$	$3{,}8\ 10^{-11}$	$2{,}3\ 10^{-11}$	$1{,}9\ 10^{-11}$
Tl-195	1,16 h	F	1,000	$1{,}3\ 10^{-10}$	1,000	$1{,}0\ 10^{-10}$	$5{,}3\ 10^{-11}$	$3{,}2\ 10^{-11}$	$1{,}9\ 10^{-11}$	$1{,}5\ 10^{-11}$
Tl-197	2,84 h	F	1,000	$1{,}3\ 10^{-10}$	1,000	$9{,}7\ 10^{-11}$	$4{,}7\ 10^{-11}$	$2{,}9\ 10^{-11}$	$1{,}7\ 10^{-11}$	$1{,}4\ 10^{-11}$
Tl-198	5,30 h	F	1,000	$4{,}7\ 10^{-10}$	1,000	$4{,}0\ 10^{-10}$	$2{,}1\ 10^{-10}$	$1{,}3\ 10^{-10}$	$7{,}5\ 10^{-11}$	$6{,}0\ 10^{-11}$
Tl-198m	1,87 h	F	1,000	$3{,}2\ 10^{-10}$	1,000	$2{,}5\ 10^{-10}$	$1{,}2\ 10^{-10}$	$7{,}5\ 10^{-11}$	$4{,}5\ 10^{-11}$	$3{,}7\ 10^{-11}$
Tl-199	7,42 h	F	1,000	$1{,}7\ 10^{-10}$	1,000	$1{,}3\ 10^{-10}$	$6{,}4\ 10^{-11}$	$3{,}9\ 10^{-11}$	$2{,}3\ 10^{-11}$	$1{,}9\ 10^{-11}$
Tl-200	1,09 d	F	1,000	$1{,}0\ 10^{-9}$	1,000	$8{,}7\ 10^{-10}$	$4{,}6\ 10^{-10}$	$2{,}8\ 10^{-10}$	$1{,}6\ 10^{-10}$	$1{,}3\ 10^{-10}$
Tl-201	3,04 d	F	1,000	$4{,}5\ 10^{-10}$	1,000	$3{,}3\ 10^{-10}$	$1{,}5\ 10^{-10}$	$9{,}4\ 10^{-11}$	$5{,}4\ 10^{-11}$	$4{,}4\ 10^{-11}$
Tl-202	12,2 d	F	1,000	$1{,}5\ 10^{-9}$	1,000	$1{,}2\ 10^{-9}$	$5{,}9\ 10^{-10}$	$3{,}8\ 10^{-10}$	$2{,}3\ 10^{-10}$	$1{,}9\ 10^{-10}$
Tl-204	3,78 a	F	1,000	$5{,}0\ 10^{-9}$	1,000	$3{,}3\ 10^{-9}$	$1{,}5\ 10^{-9}$	$8{,}8\ 10^{-10}$	$4{,}7\ 10^{-10}$	$3{,}9\ 10^{-10}$
Lead[(f)]										
Ph-195m	0,263 h	F	0,600	$1{,}3\ 10^{-10}$	0,200	$1{,}0\ 10^{-10}$	$4{,}9\ 10^{-11}$	$3{,}1\ 10^{-11}$	$1{,}9\ 10^{-11}$	$1{,}6\ 10^{-11}$
		M	0,200	$2{,}0\ 10^{-10}$	0,100	$1{,}5\ 10^{-10}$	$7{,}1\ 10^{-11}$	$4{,}6\ 10^{-11}$	$3{,}1\ 10^{-11}$	$2{,}5\ 10^{-11}$
		S	0,020	$2{,}1\ 10^{-10}$	0,010	$1{,}5\ 10^{-10}$	$7{,}4\ 10^{-11}$	$4{,}8\ 10^{-11}$	$3{,}2\ 10^{-11}$	$2{,}7\ 10^{-11}$
Pb-198	2,40 h	F	0,600	$3{,}4\ 10^{-10}$	0,200	$2{,}9\ 10^{-10}$	$1{,}5\ 10^{-10}$	$8{,}9\ 10^{-11}$	$5{,}2\ 10^{-11}$	$4{,}3\ 10^{-11}$
		M	0,200	$5{,}0\ 10^{-10}$	0,100	$4{,}0\ 10^{-10}$	$2{,}1\ 10^{-10}$	$1{,}3\ 10^{-10}$	$8{,}3\ 10^{-11}$	$6{,}6\ 10^{-11}$
		S	0,020	$5{,}4\ 10^{-10}$	0,010	$4{,}2\ 10^{-10}$	$2{,}2\ 10^{-10}$	$1{,}4\ 10^{-10}$	$8{,}7\ 10^{-11}$	$7{,}0\ 10^{-11}$
Pb-199	1,50 h	F	0,600	$1{,}9\ 10^{-10}$	0,200	$1{,}6\ 10^{-10}$	$8{,}2\ 10^{-11}$	$4{,}9\ 10^{-11}$	$2{,}9\ 10^{-11}$	$2{,}3\ 10^{-11}$
		M	0,200	$2{,}8\ 10^{-10}$	0,100	$2{,}2\ 10^{-10}$	$1{,}1\ 10^{-10}$	$7{,}1\ 10^{-11}$	$4{,}5\ 10^{-11}$	$3{,}6\ 10^{-11}$
		S	0,020	$2{,}9\ 10^{-10}$	0,010	$2{,}3\ 10^{-10}$	$1{,}2\ 10^{-10}$	$7{,}4\ 10^{-11}$	$4{,}7\ 10^{-11}$	$3{,}7\ 10^{-11}$
Pb-200	21,5 h	F	0,600	$1{,}1\ 10^{-9}$	0,200	$9{,}3\ 10^{-10}$	$4{,}6\ 10^{-10}$	$2{,}8\ 10^{-10}$	$1{,}6\ 10^{-10}$	$1{,}4\ 10^{-10}$
		M	0,200	$2{,}2\ 10^{-9}$	0,100	$1{,}7\ 10^{-9}$	$8{,}6\ 10^{-10}$	$5{,}7\ 10^{-10}$	$4{,}1\ 10^{-10}$	$3{,}3\ 10^{-10}$
		S	0,020	$2{,}4\ 10^{-9}$	0,010	$1{,}8\ 10^{-9}$	$9{,}2\ 10^{-10}$	$6{,}2\ 10^{-10}$	$4{,}4\ 10^{-10}$	$3{,}5\ 10^{-10}$
Pb-201	9,40 h	F	0,600	$4{,}8\ 10^{-10}$	0,200	$4{,}1\ 10^{-10}$	$2{,}0\ 10^{-10}$	$1{,}2\ 10^{-10}$	$7{,}1\ 10^{-11}$	$6{,}0\ 10^{-11}$
		M	0,200	$8{,}0\ 10^{-10}$	0,100	$6{,}4\ 10^{-10}$	$3{,}3\ 10^{-10}$	$2{,}1\ 10^{-10}$	$1{,}4\ 10^{-10}$	$1{,}1\ 10^{-10}$
		S	0,020	$8{,}8\ 10^{-10}$	0,010	$6{,}7\ 10^{-10}$	$3{,}5\ 10^{-10}$	$2{,}2\ 10^{-10}$	$1{,}5\ 10^{-10}$	$1{,}2\ 10^{-10}$

Nuclide	Physical half-life	Type	Age ≤ 1 a		Age	1—2 a	2—7 a	7—12 a	12—17 a	> 17 a
			f_1	$h(g)$	f_1	$h(g)$	$h(g)$	$h(g)$	$h(g)$	$h(g)$
Pb-202	$3{,}00\ 10^{5}$ a	F	0,600	$1{,}9\ 10^{-8}$	0,200	$1{,}3\ 10^{-8}$	$8{,}9\ 10^{-9}$	$1{,}3\ 10^{-8}$	$1{,}8\ 10^{-8}$	$1{,}1\ 10^{-8}$
		M	0,200	$1{,}2\ 10^{-8}$	0,100	$8{,}9\ 10^{-9}$	$6{,}2\ 10^{-9}$	$6{,}7\ 10^{-9}$	$8{,}7\ 10^{-9}$	$6{,}3\ 10^{-9}$
		S	0,020	$2{,}8\ 10^{-8}$	0,010	$2{,}8\ 10^{-8}$	$2{,}0\ 10^{-8}$	$1{,}4\ 10^{-8}$	$1{,}3\ 10^{-8}$	$1{,}2\ 10^{-8}$
Pb-202m	3,62 h	F	0,600	$4{,}7\ 10^{-10}$	0,200	$4{,}0\ 10^{-10}$	$2{,}1\ 10^{-10}$	$1{,}3\ 10^{-10}$	$7{,}5\ 10^{-11}$	$6{,}2\ 10^{-11}$
		M	0,200	$6{,}9\ 10^{-10}$	0,100	$5{,}6\ 10^{-10}$	$2{,}9\ 10^{-10}$	$1{,}9\ 10^{-10}$	$1{,}2\ 10^{-10}$	$9{,}5\ 10^{-11}$
		S	0,020	$7{,}3\ 10^{-10}$	0,010	$5{,}8\ 10^{-10}$	$3{,}0\ 10^{-10}$	$1{,}9\ 10^{-10}$	$1{,}3\ 10^{-10}$	$1{,}0\ 10^{-10}$
Pb-203	2,17 d	F	0,600	$7{,}2\ 10^{-10}$	0,200	$5{,}8\ 10^{-10}$	$2{,}8\ 10^{-10}$	$1{,}7\ 10^{-10}$	$9{,}9\ 10^{-11}$	$8{,}5\ 10^{-11}$
		M	0,200	$1{,}3\ 10^{-9}$	0,100	$1{,}0\ 10^{-9}$	$5{,}4\ 10^{-10}$	$3{,}6\ 10^{-10}$	$2{,}5\ 10^{-10}$	$2{,}0\ 10^{-10}$
		S	0,020	$1{,}5\ 10^{-9}$	0,010	$1{,}1\ 10^{-9}$	$5{,}8\ 10^{-10}$	$3{,}8\ 10^{-10}$	$2{,}8\ 10^{-10}$	$2{,}2\ 10^{-10}$
Pb-205	$1{,}43\ 10^{7}$ a	F	0,600	$1{,}1\ 10^{-9}$	0,200	$6{,}9\ 10^{-10}$	$4{,}0\ 10^{-10}$	$4{,}1\ 10^{-10}$	$4{,}3\ 10^{-10}$	$3{,}3\ 10^{-10}$
		M	0,200	$1{,}1\ 10^{-9}$	0,100	$7{,}7\ 10^{-10}$	$4{,}3\ 10^{-10}$	$3{,}2\ 10^{-10}$	$2{,}9\ 10^{-10}$	$2{,}5\ 10^{-10}$
		S	0,020	$2{,}9\ 10^{-9}$	0,010	$2{,}7\ 10^{-9}$	$1{,}7\ 10^{-9}$	$1{,}1\ 10^{-9}$	$9{,}2\ 10^{-10}$	$8{,}5\ 10^{-10}$
Pb-209	3,25 h	F	0,600	$1{,}8\ 10^{-10}$	0,200	$1{,}2\ 10^{-10}$	$5{,}3\ 10^{-11}$	$3{,}4\ 10^{-11}$	$1{,}9\ 10^{-11}$	$1{,}7\ 10^{-11}$
		M	0,200	$4{,}0\ 10^{-10}$	0,100	$2{,}7\ 10^{-10}$	$1{,}3\ 10^{-10}$	$9{,}2\ 10^{-11}$	$6{,}9\ 10^{-11}$	$5{,}6\ 10^{-11}$
		S	0,020	$4{,}4\ 10^{-10}$	0,010	$2{,}9\ 10^{-10}$	$1{,}4\ 10^{-10}$	$9{,}9\ 10^{-11}$	$7{,}5\ 10^{-11}$	$6{,}1\ 10^{-11}$
Pb-210	22,3 a	F	0,600	$4{,}7\ 10^{-6}$	0,200	$2{,}9\ 10^{-6}$	$1{,}5\ 10^{-6}$	$1{,}4\ 10^{-6}$	$1{,}3\ 10^{-6}$	$9{,}0\ 10^{-7}$
		M	0,200	$5{,}0\ 10^{-6}$	0,100	$3{,}7\ 10^{-6}$	$2{,}2\ 10^{-6}$	$1{,}5\ 10^{-6}$	$1{,}3\ 10^{-6}$	$1{,}1\ 10^{-6}$
		S	0,020	$1{,}8\ 10^{-5}$	0,010	$1{,}8\ 10^{-5}$	$1{,}1\ 10^{-5}$	$7{,}2\ 10^{-6}$	$5{,}9\ 10^{-6}$	$5{,}6\ 10^{-6}$
Pb-211	0,601 h	F	0,600	$2{,}5\ 10^{-8}$	0,200	$1{,}7\ 10^{-8}$	$8{,}7\ 10^{-9}$	$6.1\ 10^{-9}$	$4{,}6\ 10^{-9}$	$3{,}9\ 10^{-9}$
		M	0,200	$6{,}2\ 10^{-8}$	0,100	$4{,}5\ 10^{-8}$	$2{,}5\ 10^{-8}$	$1{,}9\ 10^{-8}$	$1{,}4\ 10^{-8}$	$1{,}1\ 10^{-8}$
		S	0,020	$6{,}6\ 10^{-8}$	0,010	$4{,}8\ 10^{-8}$	$2{,}7\ 10^{-8}$	$2{,}0\ 10^{-8}$	$1{,}5\ 10^{-8}$	$1{,}2\ 10^{-8}$
Pb-212	10,6 h	F	0,600	$1{,}9\ 10^{-7}$	0,200	$1{,}2\ 10^{-7}$	$5{,}4\ 10^{-8}$	$3{,}5\ 10^{-8}$	$2{,}0\ 10^{-8}$	$1{,}8\ 10^{-8}$
		M	0,200	$6{,}2\ 10^{-7}$	0,100	$4{,}6\ 10^{-7}$	$3{,}0\ 10^{-7}$	$2{,}2\ 10^{-7}$	$2{,}2\ 10^{-7}$	$1{,}7\ 10^{-7}$
		S	0,020	$6{,}7\ 10^{-7}$	0,010	$5{,}0\ 10^{-7}$	$3{,}3\ 10^{-7}$	$2{,}5\ 10^{-7}$	$2{,}4\ 10^{-7}$	$1{,}9\ 10^{-7}$

Nuclide	Physical half-life	Type	Age ≤ 1 a		Age	1—2 a	2—7 a	7—12 a	12—17 a	> 17 a
			f_1	$h(g)$	f_1	$h(g)$	$h(g)$	$h(g)$	$h(g)$	$h(g)$
Pb-214	0,447 h	F	0,600	2,2 10^{-8}	0,200	1,5 10^{-8}	6,9 10^{-9}	4,8 10^{-9}	3,3 10^{-9}	2,8 10^{-9}
		M	0,200	6,4 10^{-8}	0,100	4,6 10^{-8}	2,6 10^{-8}	1,9 10^{-8}	1,4 10^{-8}	1,4 10^{-8}
		S	0,020	6,9 10^{-8}	0,010	5,0 10^{-8}	2,8 10^{-8}	2,1 10^{-8}	1,5 10^{-8}	1,5 10^{-8}
Bismuth										
Bi-200	0,606 h	F	0,100	1,9 10^{-10}	0,050	1,5 10^{-10}	7,4 10^{-11}	4,5 10^{-11}	2,7 10^{-11}	2,2 10^{-11}
		M	0,100	2,5 10^{-10}	0,050	1,9 10^{-10}	9,9 10^{-11}	6,3 10^{-11}	4,1 10^{-11}	3,3 10^{-11}
Bi-201	1,80 h	F	0,100	4,0 10^{-10}	0,050	3,1 10^{-10}	1,5 10^{-10}	9,3 10^{-11}	5,4 10^{-11}	4,4 10^{-11}
		M	0,100	5,5 10^{-10}	0,050	4,1 10^{-10}	2,0 10^{-10}	1,3 10^{-10}	8,3 10^{-11}	6,6 10^{-11}
Bi-202	1,67 h	F	0,100	3,4 10^{-10}	0,050	2,8 10^{-10}	1,5 10^{-10}	9,0 10^{-11}	5,3 10^{-11}	4,3 10^{-11}
		M	0,100	4,2 10^{-10}	0,050	3,4 10^{-10}	1,8 10^{-10}	1,1 10^{-10}	6,9 10^{-11}	5,5 10^{-11}
Bi-203	11,8 h	F	0,100	1,5 10^{-9}	0,050	1,2 10^{-9}	6,4 10^{-10}	4,0 10^{-10}	2,3 10^{-10}	1,9 10^{-10}
		M	0,100	2,0 10^{-9}	0,050	1,6 10^{-9}	8,2 10^{-10}	5,3 10^{-10}	3,3 10^{-10}	2,6 10^{-10}
Bi-205	15,3 d	F	0,100	3,0 10^{-9}	0,050	2,4 10^{-9}	1,3 10^{-9}	8,0 10^{-10}	4,7 10^{-10}	3,8 10^{-10}
		M	0,100	5,5 10^{-9}	0,050	4,4 10^{-9}	2,5 10^{-9}	1,6 10^{-9}	1,2 10^{-9}	9,3 10^{-10}
Bi-206	6,24 d	F	0,100	6,1 10^{-9}	0,050	4,8 10^{-9}	2,5 10^{-9}	1,6 10^{-9}	9,1 10^{-10}	7,4 10^{-10}
		M	0,100	1,0 10^{-8}	0,050	8,0 10^{-9}	4,4 10^{-9}	2,9 10^{-9}	2,1 10^{-9}	1,7 10^{-9}
Bi-207	38,0 a	F	0,100	4,3 10^{-9}	0,050	3,3 10^{-9}	1,7 10^{-9}	1,0 10^{-9}	6,0 10^{-10}	4,9 10^{-10}
		M	0,100	2,3 10^{-8}	0,050	2,0 10^{-8}	1,2 10^{-8}	8,2 10^{-9}	6,5 10^{-9}	5,6 10^{-9}
Bi-210	5,01 d	F	0,100	1,1 10^{-8}	0,050	6,9 10^{-9}	3,2 10^{-9}	2,1 10^{-9}	1,3 10^{-9}	1,1 10^{-9}
		M	0,100	3,9 10^{-7}	0,050	3,0 10^{-7}	1,9 10^{-7}	1,3 10^{-7}	1,1 10^{-7}	9,3 10^{-8}
Bi-210m	3,00 10^{6} a	F	0,100	4,1 10^{-7}	0,050	2,6 10^{-7}	1,3 10^{-7}	8,3 10^{-8}	5,6 10^{-8}	4,6 10^{-8}
		M	0,100	1,5 10^{-5}	0,050	1,1 10^{-5}	7,0 10^{-6}	4,8 10^{-6}	4,1 10^{-6}	3,4 10^{-6}
Bi-212	1,01 h	F	0,100	6,5 10^{-8}	0,050	4,5 10^{-8}	2,1 10^{-8}	1,5 10^{-8}	1,0 10^{-8}	9,1 10^{-9}
		M	0,100	1,6 10^{-7}	0,050	1,1 10^{-7}	6,0 10^{-8}	4,4 10^{-8}	3,8 10^{-8}	3,1 10^{-8}
Bi-213	0,761 h	F	0,100	7,7 10^{-8}	0,050	5,3 10^{-8}	2,5 10^{-8}	1,7 10^{-8}	1,2 10^{-8}	1,0 10^{-8}
		M	0,100	1,6 10^{-7}	0,050	1,2 10^{-7}	6,0 10^{-8}	4,4 10^{-8}	3,6 10^{-8}	3,0 10^{-8}

Nuclide	*Physical half-life*	*Type*	*Age ≤ 1 a*		*Age*	*1—2 a*	*2—7 a*	*7—12 a*	*12—17 a*	*> 17 a*
			f_1	*h(g)*	f_1	*h(g)*	*h(g)*	*h(g)*	*h(g)*	*h(g)*
Bi-214	0,332 h	F	0,100	5,0 10^{-8}	0,050	3,5 10^{-8}	1,6 10^{-8}	1,1 10^{-8}	8,2 10^{-9}	7,1 10^{-9}
		M	0,100	8,7 10^{-8}	0,050	6,1 10^{-8}	3,1 10^{-8}	2,2 10^{-8}	1,7 10^{-8}	1,4 10^{-8}
Polonium										
Po-203	0,612 h	F	0,200	1,9 10^{-10}	0,100	1,5 10^{-10}	7,7 10^{-11}	4,7 10^{-11}	2,8 10^{-11}	2,3 10^{-11}
		M	0,200	2,7 10^{-10}	0,100	2,1 10^{-10}	1,1 10^{-10}	6,7 10^{-11}	4,3 10^{-11}	3,5 10^{-11}
		S	0,020	2,8 10^{-10}	0,010	2,2 10^{-10}	1,1 10^{-10}	7,0 10^{-11}	4,5 10^{-11}	3,6 10^{-11}
Po-205	1,80 h	F	0,200	2,6 10^{-10}	0,100	2,1 10^{-10}	1,1 10^{-10}	6,6 10^{-11}	4,1 10^{-11}	3,3 10^{-11}
		M	0,200	4,0 10^{-10}	0,100	3,1 10^{-10}	1,7 10^{-10}	1,1 10^{-10}	8,1 10^{-11}	6,5 10^{-11}
		S	0,020	4,2 10^{-10}	0,010	3,2 10^{-10}	1,8 10^{-10}	1,2 10^{-10}	8,5 10^{-11}	6,9 10^{-11}
Po-207	5,83 h	F	0,200	4,8 10^{-10}	0,100	4,0 10^{-10}	2,1 10^{-10}	1,3 10^{-10}	7,3 10^{-11}	5,8 10^{-11}
		M	0,200	6,2 10^{-10}	0,100	5,1 10^{-10}	2,6 10^{-10}	1,6 10^{-10}	9,9 10^{-11}	7,8 10^{-11}
		S	0,020	6,6 10^{-10}	0,010	5,3 10^{-10}	2,7 10^{-10}	1,7 10^{-10}	1,0 10^{-10}	8,2 10^{-11}
Po-210	138 d	F	0,200	7,4 10^{-6}	0,100	4,8 10^{-6}	2,2 10^{-6}	1,3 10^{-6}	7,7 10^{-7}	6,1 10^{-7}
		M	0,200	1,5 10^{-5}	0,100	1,1 10^{-5}	6,7 10^{-6}	4,6 10^{-6}	4,0 10^{-6}	3,3 10^{-6}
		S	0,020	1,8 10^{-5}	0,010	1,4 10^{-5}	8,6 10^{-6}	5,9 10^{-6}	5,1 10^{-6}	4,3 10^{-6}
Astatine										
At-207	1,80 h	F	1,000	2,4 10^{-9}	1,000	1,7 10^{-9}	8,9 10^{-10}	5,9 10^{-10}	4,0 10^{-10}	3,3 10^{-10}
		M	1,000	9,2 10^{-9}	1,000	6,7 10^{-9}	4,3 10^{-9}	3,1 10^{-9}	2,9 10^{-9}	2,3 10^{-9}
At-211	7,21 h	F	1,000	1,4 10^{-7}	1,000	9,7 10^{-8}	4,3 10^{-8}	2,8 10^{-8}	1,7 10^{-8}	1,6 10^{-8}
		M	1,000	5,2 10^{-7}	1,000	3,7 10^{-7}	1,9 10^{-7}	1,4 10^{-7}	1,3 10^{-7}	1,1 10^{-7}
Francium										
Fr-222	0,240 h	F	1,000	9,1 10^{-8}	1,000	6,3 10^{-8}	3,0 10^{-8}	2,1 10^{-8}	1,6 10^{-8}	1,4 10^{-8}
Fr-223	0,363 h	F	1,000	1,1 10^{-8}	1,000	7,3 10^{-9}	3,2 10^{-9}	1,9 10^{-9}	1,0 10^{-9}	8,9 10^{-10}

Nuclide	*Physical half-life*	*Type*	*Age ≤ 1 a*		*Age*	*1—2 a*	*2—7 a*	*7—12 a*	*12—17 a*	*> 17 a*
			f_1	*h(g)*	*f_1*	*h(g)*	*h(g)*	*h(g)*	*h(g)*	*h(g)*
Radium[(g)]										
Ra-223	11,4 d	F	0,600	3,0 10^{-6}	0,200	1,0 10^{-6}	4,9 10^{-7}	4,0 10^{-7}	3,3 10^{-7}	1,2 10^{-7}
		M	0,200	2,8 10^{-5}	0,100	2,1 10^{-5}	1,3 10^{-5}	9,9 10^{-6}	9,4 10^{-6}	7,4 10^{-6}
		S	0,020	3,2 10^{-5}	0,010	2,4 10^{-5}	1,5 10^{-5}	1,1 10^{-5}	1,1 10^{-5}	8,7 10^{-6}
Ra-224	3,66 d	F	0,600	1,5 10^{-6}	0,200	6,0 10^{-7}	2,9 10^{-7}	2,2 10^{-7}	1,7 10^{-7}	7,5 10^{-8}
		M	0,200	1,1 10^{-5}	0,100	8,2 10^{-6}	5,3 10^{-6}	3,9 10^{-6}	3,7 10^{-6}	3,0 10^{-6}
		S	0,020	1,2 10^{-5}	0,010	9,2 10^{-6}	5,9 10^{-6}	4,4 10^{-6}	4,2 10^{-6}	3,4 10^{-6}
Ra-225	14,8 d	F	0,600	4,0 10^{-6}	0,200	1,2 10^{-6}	5,6 10^{-7}	4,6 10^{-7}	3,8 10^{-7}	1,3 10^{-7}
		M	0,200	2,4 10^{-5}	0,100	1,8 10^{-5}	1,1 10^{-5}	8,4 10^{-6}	7,9 10^{-6}	6,3 10^{-6}
		S	0,020	2,8 10^{-5}	0,010	2,2 10^{-5}	1,4 10^{-5}	1,0 10^{-5}	9,8 10^{-6}	7,7 10^{-6}
Ra-226	1,60 103 a	F	0,600	2,6 10^{-6}	0,200	9,4 10^{-7}	5,5 10^{-7}	7,2 10^{-7}	1,3 10^{-6}	3,6 10^{-7}
		M	0,200	1,5 10^{-5}	0,100	1,1 10^{-5}	7,0 10^{-6}	4,9 10^{-6}	4,5 10^{-6}	3,5 10^{-6}
		S	0,020	3,4 10^{-5}	0,010	2,9 10^{-5}	1,9 10^{-5}	1,2 10^{-5}	1,0 10^{-5}	9,5 10^{-6}
Ra-227	0,703 h	F	0,600	1,5 10^{-9}	0,200	1,2 10^{-9}	7,8 10^{-10}	6,1 10^{-10}	5,3 10^{-10}	4,6 10^{-10}
		M	0,200	8,0 10^{-10}	0,100	6,7 10^{-10}	4,4 10^{-10}	3,2 10^{-10}	2,9 10^{-10}	2,8 10^{-10}
		S	0,020	1,0 10^{-9}	0,010	8,5 10^{-10}	4,4 10^{-10}	2,9 10^{-10}	2,4 10^{-10}	2,2 10^{-10}
Ra-228	5,75 a	F	0,600	1,7 10^{-5}	0,200	5,7 10^{-6}	3,1 10^{-6}	3,6 10^{-6}	4,6 10^{-6}	9,0 10^{-7}
		M	0,200	1,5 10^{-5}	0,100	1,0 10^{-5}	6,3 10^{-6}	4,6 10^{-6}	4,4 10^{-6}	2,6 10^{-6}
		S	0,020	4,9 10^{-5}	0,010	4,8 10^{-5}	3,2 10^{-5}	2,0 10^{-5}	1,6 10^{-5}	1,6 10^{-5}
Actinium										
Ac-224	2,90 h	F	0,005	1,3 10^{-7}	5,0 10^{-4}	8,9 10^{-8}	4,7 10^{-8}	3,1 10^{-8}	1,4 10^{-8}	1,1 10^{-8}
		M	0,005	4,2 10^{-7}	5,0 10^{-4}	3,2 10^{-7}	2,0 10^{-7}	1,5 10^{-7}	1,4 10^{-7}	1,1 10^{-7}
		S	0,005	4,6 10^{-7}	5,0 10^{-4}	3,5 10^{-7}	2,2 10^{-7}	1,7 10^{-7}	1,6 10^{-7}	1,3 10^{-7}
Ac-225	10,0 d	F	0,005	1,1 10^{-5}	5,0 10^{-4}	7,7 10^{-6}	4,0 10^{-6}	2,6 10^{-6}	1,1 10^{-6}	8,8 10^{-7}
		M	0,005	2,8 10^{-5}	5,0 10^{-4}	2,1 10^{-5}	1,3 10^{-5}	1,0 10^{-5}	9,3 10^{-6}	7,4 10^{-6}
		S	0,005	3,1 10^{-5}	5,0 10^{-4}	2,3 10^{-5}	1,5 10^{-5}	1,1 10^{-5}	1,1 10^{-5}	8,5 10^{-6}

Nuclide	Physical half-life	Type	Age ≤ 1 a		Age	1—2 a	2—7 a	7—12 a	12—17 a	> 17 a
			f_1	h(g)	f_1	h(g)	h(g)	h(g)	h(g)	h(g)
Ac-226	1,21 d	F	0,005	1,5 10^{-6}	5,0 10^{-4}	1,1 10^{-6}	4,0 10^{-7}	2,6 10^{-7}	1,2 10^{-7}	9,6 10^{-8}
		M	0,005	4,3 10^{-6}	5,0 10^{-4}	3,2 10^{-6}	2,1 10^{-6}	1,5 10^{-6}	1,5 10^{-6}	1,2 10^{-6}
		S	0,005	4,7 10^{-6}	5,0 10^{-4}	3,5 10^{-6}	2,3 10^{-6}	1,7 10^{-6}	1,6 10^{-6}	1,3 10^{-6}
Ac-227	21,8 a	F	0,005	1,7 10^{-3}	5,0 10^{-4}	1,6 10^{-3}	1,0 10^{-3}	7,2 10^{-4}	5,6 10^{-4}	5,5 10^{-4}
		M	0,005	5,7 10^{-4}	5,0 10^{-4}	5,5 10^{-4}	3,9 10^{-4}	2,6 10^{-4}	2,3 10^{-4}	2,2 10^{-4}
		S	0,005	2,2 10^{-4}	5,0 10^{-4}	2,0 10^{-4}	1,3 10^{-4}	8,7 10^{-5}	7,6 10^{-5}	7,2 10^{-5}
Ac-228	6,13 h	F	0,005	1,8 10^{-7}	5,0 10^{-4}	1,6 10^{-7}	9,7 10^{-8}	5,7 10^{-8}	2,9 10^{-8}	2,5 10^{-8}
		M	0,005	8,4 10^{-8}	5,0 10^{-4}	7,3 10^{-8}	4,7 10^{-8}	2,9 10^{-8}	2,0 10^{-8}	1,7 10^{-8}
		S	0,005	6,4 10^{-8}	5,0 10^{-4}	5,3 10^{-8}	3,3 10^{-8}	2,2 10^{-8}	1,9 10^{-8}	1,6 10^{-8}
Thorium										
Th-226	0,515 h	F	0,005	1,4 10^{-7}	5,0 10^{-4}	1,0 10^{-7}	4,8 10^{-8}	3,4 10^{-8}	2,5 10^{-8}	2,2 10^{-8}
		M	0,005	3,0 10^{-7}	5,0 10^{-4}	2,1 10^{-7}	1,1 10^{-7}	8,3 10^{-8}	7,0 10^{-8}	5,8 10^{-8}
		S	0,005	3,1 10^{-7}	5,0 10^{-4}	2,2 10^{-7}	1,2 10^{-7}	8,8 10^{-8}	7,5 10^{-8}	6,1 10^{-8}
Th-227	18,7 d	F	0,005	8,4 10^{-6}	5,0 10^{-4}	5,2 10^{-6}	2,6 10^{-6}	1,6 10^{-6}	1,0 10^{-6}	6,7 10^{-7}
		M	0,005	3,2 10^{-5}	5,0 10^{-4}	2,5 10^{-5}	1,6 10^{-5}	1,1 10^{-5}	1,1 10^{-5}	8,5 10^{-6}
		S	0,005	3,9 10^{-5}	5,0 10^{-4}	3,0 10^{-5}	1,9 10^{-5}	1,4 10^{-5}	1,3 10^{-5}	1,0 10^{-5}
Th-228	1,91 a	F	0,005	1,8 10^{-4}	5,0 10^{-4}	1,5 10^{-4}	8,3 10^{-5}	5,2 10^{-5}	3,6 10^{-5}	2,9 10^{-5}
		M	0,005	1,3 10^{-4}	5,0 10^{-4}	1,1 10^{-4}	6,8 10^{-5}	4,6 10^{-5}	3,9 10^{-5}	3,2 10^{-5}
		S	0,005	1,6 10^{-4}	5,0 10^{-4}	1,3 10^{-4}	8,2 10^{-5}	5,5 10^{-5}	4,7 10^{-5}	4,0 10^{-5}
Th-229	7,34 10^{3} a	F	0,005	5,4 10^{-4}	5,0 10^{-4}	5,1 10^{-4}	3,6 10^{-4}	2,9 10^{-4}	2,4 10^{-4}	2,4 10^{-4}
		M	0,005	2,3 10^{-4}	5,0 10^{-4}	2,1 10^{-4}	1,6 10^{-4}	1,2 10^{-4}	1,1 10^{-4}	1,1 10^{-4}
		S	0,005	2,1 10^{-4}	5,0 10^{-4}	1,9 10^{-4}	1,3 10^{-4}	8,7 10^{-5}	7,6 10^{-5}	7,1 10^{-5}
Th-230	7,70 10^{4} a	F	0,005	2,1 10^{-4}	5,0 10^{-4}	2,0 10^{-4}	1,4 10^{-4}	1,1 10^{-4}	9,9 10^{-5}	1,0 10^{-4}
		M	0,005	7,7 10^{-5}	5,0 10^{-4}	7,4 10^{-5}	5,5 10^{-5}	4,3 10^{-5}	4,2 10^{-5}	4,3 10^{-5}
		S	0,005	4,0 10^{-5}	5,0 10^{-4}	3,5 10^{-5}	2,4 10^{-5}	1,6 10^{-5}	1,5 10^{-5}	1,4 10^{-5}

Nuclide	Physical half-life	Type	Age ≤ 1 a		Age	1—2 a	2—7 a	7—12 a	12—17 a	> 17 a
			f_1	$h(g)$	f_1	$h(g)$	$h(g)$	$h(g)$	$h(g)$	$h(g)$
Th-231	1,06 d	F	0,005	$1,1\ 10^{-9}$	$5,0\ 10^{-4}$	$7,2\ 10^{-10}$	$2,6\ 10^{-10}$	$1,6\ 10^{-10}$	$9,2\ 10^{-11}$	$7,8\ 10^{-11}$
		M	0,005	$2,2\ 10^{-9}$	$5,0\ 10^{-4}$	$1,6\ 10^{-9}$	$8,0\ 10^{-10}$	$4,8\ 10^{-10}$	$3,8\ 10^{-10}$	$3,1\ 10^{-10}$
		S	0,005	$2,4\ 10^{-9}$	$5,0\ 10^{-4}$	$1,7\ 10^{-9}$	$7,6\ 10^{-10}$	$5,2\ 10^{-10}$	$4,1\ 10^{-10}$	$3,3\ 10^{-10}$
Th-232	$1,40\ 10^{10}$ a	F	0,005	$2,3\ 10^{-4}$	$5,0\ 10^{-4}$	$2,2\ 10^{-4}$	$1,6\ 10^{-4}$	$1,3\ 10^{-4}$	$1,2\ 10^{-4}$	$1,1\ 10^{-4}$
		M	0,005	$8,3\ 10^{-5}$	$5,0\ 10^{-4}$	$8,1\ 10^{-5}$	$6,3\ 10^{-5}$	$5,0\ 10^{-5}$	$4,7\ 10^{-5}$	$4,5\ 10^{-5}$
		S	0,005	$5,4\ 10^{-5}$	$5,0\ 10^{-4}$	$5,0\ 10^{-5}$	$3,7\ 10^{-5}$	$2,6\ 10^{-5}$	$2,5\ 10^{-5}$	$2,5\ 10^{-5}$
Th-234	24,1 d	F	0,005	$4,0\ 10^{-8}$	$5,0\ 10^{-4}$	$2,5\ 10^{-8}$	$1,1\ 10^{-8}$	$6,1\ 10^{-9}$	$3,5\ 10^{-9}$	$2,5\ 10^{-9}$
		M	0,005	$3,9\ 10^{-8}$	$5,0\ 10^{-4}$	$2,9\ 10^{-8}$	$1,5\ 10^{-8}$	$1,0\ 10^{-8}$	$7,9\ 10^{-9}$	$6,6\ 10^{-9}$
		S	0,005	$4,1\ 10^{-8}$	$5,0\ 10^{-4}$	$3,1\ 10^{-8}$	$1,7\ 10^{-8}$	$1,1\ 10^{-8}$	$9,1\ 10^{-9}$	$7,7\ 10^{-9}$
Protactinium										
Pa-227	0,638 h	M	0,005	$3,6\ 10^{-7}$	$5,0\ 10^{-4}$	$2,6\ 10^{-7}$	$1,4\ 10^{-7}$	$1,0\ 10^{-7}$	$9,0\ 10^{-8}$	$7,4\ 10^{-8}$
		S	0,005	$3,8\ 10^{-7}$	$5,0\ 10^{-4}$	$2,8\ 10^{-7}$	$1,5\ 10^{-7}$	$1,1\ 10^{-7}$	$8,1\ 10^{-8}$	$8,0\ 10^{-8}$
Pa-228	22,0 h	M	0,005	$2,6\ 10^{-7}$	$5,0\ 10^{-4}$	$2,1\ 10^{-7}$	$1,3\ 10^{-7}$	$8,8\ 10^{-8}$	$7,7\ 10^{-8}$	$6,4\ 10^{-8}$
		S	0,005	$2,9\ 10^{-7}$	$5,0\ 10^{-4}$	$2,4\ 10^{-7}$	$1,5\ 10^{-7}$	$1,0\ 10^{-7}$	$9,1\ 10^{-8}$	$7,5\ 10^{-8}$
Pa-230	17,4 d	M	0,005	$2,4\ 10^{-6}$	$5,0\ 10^{-4}$	$1,8\ 10^{-6}$	$1,1\ 10^{-6}$	$8,3\ 10^{-7}$	$7,6\ 10^{-7}$	$6,1\ 10^{-7}$
		S	0,005	$2,9\ 10^{-6}$	$5,0\ 10^{-4}$	$2,2\ 10^{-6}$	$1,4\ 10^{-6}$	$1,0\ 10^{-6}$	$9,6\ 10^{-7}$	$7,6\ 10^{-7}$
Pa-231	$3,27\ 10^{4}$ a	M	0,005	$2,2\ 10^{-4}$	$5,0\ 10^{-4}$	$2,3\ 10^{-4}$	$1,9\ 10^{-4}$	$1,5\ 10^{-4}$	$1,5\ 10^{-4}$	$1,4\ 10^{-4}$
		S	0,005	$7,4\ 10^{-5}$	$5,0\ 10^{-4}$	$6,9\ 10^{-5}$	$5,2\ 10^{-5}$	$3,9\ 10^{-5}$	$3,6\ 10^{-5}$	$3,4\ 10^{-5}$
Pa-232	1,31 d	M	0,005	$1,9\ 10^{-8}$	$5,0\ 10^{-4}$	$1,8\ 10^{-8}$	$1,4\ 10^{-8}$	$1,1\ 10^{-8}$	$1,0\ 10^{-8}$	$1,0\ 10^{-8}$
		S	0,005	$1,0\ 10^{-8}$	$5,0\ 10^{-4}$	$8,7\ 10^{-9}$	$5,9\ 10^{-9}$	$4,1\ 10^{-9}$	$3,7\ 10^{-9}$	$3,5\ 10^{-9}$
Pa-233	27,0 d	M	0,005	$1,5\ 10^{-8}$	$5,0\ 10^{-4}$	$1,1\ 10^{-8}$	$6,5\ 10^{-9}$	$4,7\ 10^{-9}$	$4,1\ 10^{-9}$	$3,3\ 10^{-9}$
		S	0,005	$1,7\ 10^{-8}$	$5,0\ 10^{-4}$	$1,3\ 10^{-8}$	$7,5\ 10^{-9}$	$5,5\ 10^{-9}$	$4,9\ 10^{-9}$	$3,9\ 10^{-9}$
Pa-234	6,70 h	M	0,005	$2,8\ 10^{-9}$	$5,0\ 10^{-4}$	$2,0\ 10^{-9}$	$1,0\ 10^{-9}$	$6,8\ 10^{-10}$	$4,7\ 10^{-10}$	$3,8\ 10^{-10}$
		S	0,005	$2,9\ 10^{-9}$	$5,0\ 10^{-4}$	$2,1\ 10^{-9}$	$1,1\ 10^{-9}$	$7,1\ 10^{-10}$	$5,0\ 10^{-10}$	$4,0\ 10^{-10}$

Nuclide	*Physical half-life*	*Type*	*Age ≤ 1 a*		*Age*	*1—2 a*	*2—7 a*	*7—12 a*	*12—17 a*	*> 17 a*
			f_1	$h(g)$	f_1	$h(g)$	$h(g)$	$h(g)$	$h(g)$	$h(g)$
Uranium										
U-230	20,8 d	F	0,040	$3,2\ 10^{-6}$	0,020	$1,5\ 10^{-6}$	$7,2\ 10^{-7}$	$5,4\ 10^{-7}$	$4,1\ 10^{-7}$	$3,8\ 10^{-7}$
		M	0,040	$4,9\ 10^{-5}$	0,020	$3,7\ 10^{-5}$	$2,4\ 10^{-5}$	$1,8\ 10^{-5}$	$1,7\ 10^{-5}$	$1,3\ 10^{-5}$
		S	0,020	$5,8\ 10^{-5}$	0,002	$4,4\ 10^{-5}$	$2,8\ 10^{-5}$	$2,1\ 10^{-5}$	$2,0\ 10^{-5}$	$1,6\ 10^{-5}$
U-231	4,20 d	F	0,040	$8,9\ 10^{-10}$	0,020	$6,2\ 10^{-10}$	$3,1\ 10^{-10}$	$1,4\ 10^{-10}$	$1,0\ 10^{-10}$	$6,2\ 10^{-11}$
		M	0,040	$2,4\ 10^{-9}$	0,020	$1,7\ 10^{-9}$	$9,4\ 10^{-10}$	$5,5\ 10^{-10}$	$4,6\ 10^{-10}$	$3,8\ 10^{-10}$
		S	0,020	$2,6\ 10^{-9}$	0,002	$1,9\ 10^{-9}$	$9,0\ 10^{-10}$	$6,1\ 10^{-10}$	$4,9\ 10^{-10}$	$4,0\ 10^{-10}$
U-232	72,0 a	F	0,040	$1,6\ 10^{-5}$	0,020	$1,0\ 10^{-5}$	$6,9\ 10^{-6}$	$6,8\ 10^{-6}$	$7,5\ 10^{-6}$	$4,0\ 10^{-6}$
		M	0,040	$3,0\ 10^{-5}$	0,020	$2,4\ 10^{-5}$	$1,6\ 10^{-5}$	$1,1\ 10^{-5}$	$1,0\ 10^{-5}$	$7,8\ 10^{-6}$
		S	0,020	$1,0\ 10^{-4}$	0,002	$9,7\ 10^{-5}$	$6,6\ 10^{-5}$	$4,3\ 10^{-5}$	$3,8\ 10^{-5}$	$3,7\ 10^{-5}$
U-233	$1,58\ 10^{5}$ a	F	0,040	$2,2\ 10^{-6}$	0,020	$1,4\ 10^{-6}$	$9,4\ 10^{-7}$	$8,4\ 10^{-7}$	$8,6\ 10^{-7}$	$5,8\ 10^{-7}$
		M	0,040	$1,5\ 10^{-5}$	0,020	$1,1\ 10^{-5}$	$7,2\ 10^{-6}$	$4,9\ 10^{-6}$	$4,3\ 10^{-6}$	$3,6\ 10^{-6}$
		S	0,020	$3,4\ 10^{-5}$	0,002	$3,0\ 10^{-5}$	$1,9\ 10^{-5}$	$1,2\ 10^{-5}$	$1,1\ 10^{-5}$	$9,6\ 10^{-6}$
U-234	$2,44\ 10^{5}$ a	F	0,040	$2,1\ 10^{-6}$	0,020	$1,4\ 10^{-6}$	$9,0\ 10^{-7}$	$8,0\ 10^{-7}$	$8,2\ 10^{-7}$	$5,6\ 10^{-7}$
		M	0,040	$1,5\ 10^{-5}$	0,020	$1,1\ 10^{-5}$	$7,0\ 10^{-6}$	$4,8\ 10^{-6}$	$4,2\ 10^{-6}$	$3,5\ 10^{-6}$
		S	0,020	$3,3\ 10^{-5}$	0,002	$2,9\ 10^{-5}$	$1,9\ 10^{-5}$	$1,2\ 10^{-5}$	$1,0\ 10^{-5}$	$9,4\ 10^{-6}$
U-235	$7,04\ 10^{8}$ a	F	0,040	$2,0\ 10^{-6}$	0,020	$1,3\ 10^{-6}$	$8,5\ 10^{-7}$	$7,5\ 10^{-7}$	$7,7\ 10^{-7}$	$5,2\ 10^{-7}$
		M	0,040	$1,3\ 10^{-5}$	0,020	$1,0\ 10^{-5}$	$6,3\ 10^{-6}$	$4,3\ 10^{-6}$	$3,7\ 10^{-6}$	$3,1\ 10^{-6}$
		S	0,020	$3,0\ 10^{-5}$	0,002	$2,6\ 10^{-5}$	$1,7\ 10^{-5}$	$1,1\ 10^{-5}$	$9,2\ 10^{-6}$	$8,5\ 10^{-6}$
U-236	$2,34\ 10^{7}$ a	F	0,040	$2,0\ 10^{-6}$	0,020	$1,3\ 10^{-6}$	$8,5\ 10^{-7}$	$7,5\ 10^{-7}$	$7,8\ 10^{-7}$	$5,3\ 10^{-7}$
		M	0,040	$1,4\ 10^{-5}$	0,020	$1,0\ 10^{-5}$	$6,5\ 10^{-6}$	$4,5\ 10^{-6}$	$3,9\ 10^{-6}$	$3,2\ 10^{-6}$
		S	0,020	$3,1\ 10^{-5}$	0,002	$2,7\ 10^{-5}$	$1,8\ 10^{-5}$	$1,1\ 10^{-5}$	$9,5\ 10^{-6}$	$8,7\ 10^{-6}$
U-237	6,75 d	F	0,040	$1,8\ 10^{-9}$	0,020	$1,5\ 10^{-9}$	$6,6\ 10^{-10}$	$4,2\ 10^{-10}$	$1,9\ 10^{-10}$	$1,8\ 10^{-10}$
		M	0,040	$7,8\ 10^{-9}$	0,020	$5,7\ 10^{-9}$	$3,3\ 10^{-9}$	$2,4\ 10^{-9}$	$2,1\ 10^{-9}$	$1,7\ 10^{-9}$
		S	0,020	$8,7\ 10^{-9}$	0,002	$6,4\ 10^{-9}$	$3,7\ 10^{-9}$	$2,7\ 10^{-9}$	$2,4\ 10^{-9}$	$1,9\ 10^{-9}$

Nuclide	Physical half-life	Type	Age ≤ 1 a		Age	1—2 a	2—7 a	7—12 a	12—17 a	> 17 a
			f_1	h(g)	f_1	h(g)	h(g)	h(g)	h(g)	h(g)
U-238	4,47 10^{9} a	F	0,040	1,9 10^{-6}	0,020	1,3 10^{-6}	8,2 10^{-7}	7,3 10^{-7}	7,4 10^{-7}	5,0 10^{-7}
		M	0,040	1,2 10^{-5}	0,020	9,4 10^{-6}	5,9 10^{-6}	4,0 10^{-6}	3,4 10^{-6}	2,9 10^{-6}
		S	0,020	2,9 10^{-5}	0,002	2,5 10^{-5}	1,6 10^{-5}	1,0 10^{-5}	8,7 10^{-6}	8,0 10^{-6}
U-239	0,392 h	F	0,040	1,0 10^{-10}	0,020	6,6 10^{-11}	2,9 10^{-11}	1,9 10^{-11}	1,2 10^{-11}	1,0 10^{-11}
		M	0,040	1,8 10^{-10}	0,020	1,2 10^{-10}	5,6 10^{-11}	3,8 10^{-11}	2,7 10^{-11}	2,2 10^{-11}
		S	0,020	1,9 10^{-10}	0,002	1,2 10^{-10}	5,9 10^{-11}	4,0 10^{-11}	2,9 10^{-11}	2,4 10^{-11}
U-240	14,1 h	F	0,040	2,4 10^{-9}	0,020	1,6 10^{-9}	7,1 10^{-10}	4,5 10^{-10}	2,3 10^{-10}	2,0 10^{-10}
		M	0,040	4,6 10^{-9}	0,020	3,1 10^{-9}	1,7 10^{-9}	1,1 10^{-9}	6,5 10^{-10}	5,3 10^{-10}
		S	0,020	4,9 10^{-9}	0,002	3,3 10^{-9}	1,6 10^{-9}	1,1 10^{-9}	7,0 10^{-10}	5,8 10^{-10}
Neptunium										
NP-232	0,245 h	F	0,005	2,0 10^{-10}	5,0 10^{-4}	1,9 10^{-10}	1,2 10^{-10}	1,1 10^{-10}	1,1 10^{-10}	1,2 10^{-10}
		M	0,005	8,9 10^{-11}	5,0 10^{-4}	8,1 10^{-11}	5,5 10^{-11}	4,5 10^{-11}	4,7 10^{-11}	5,0 10^{-11}
		S	0,005	1,2 10^{-10}	5,0 10^{-4}	9,7 10^{-11}	5,8 10^{-11}	3,9 10^{-11}	2,5 10^{-11}	2,4 10^{-11}
Np-233	0,603 h	F	0,005	1,1 10^{-11}	5,0 10^{-4}	8,7 10^{-12}	4,2 10^{-12}	2,5 10^{-12}	1,4 10^{-12}	1,1 10^{-12}
		M	0,005	1,5 10^{-11}	5,0 10^{-4}	1,1 10^{-11}	5,5 10^{-12}	3,3 10^{-12}	2,1 10^{-12}	1,6 10^{-12}
		S	0,005	1,5 10^{-11}	5,0 10^{-4}	1,2 10^{-11}	5,7 10^{-12}	3,4 10^{-12}	2,1 10^{-12}	1,7 10^{-12}
Np-234	4,40 d	F	0,005	2,9 10^{-9}	5,0 10^{-4}	2,2 10^{-9}	1,1 10^{-9}	7,2 10^{-10}	4,3 10^{-10}	3,5 10^{-10}
		M	0,005	3,8 10^{-9}	5,0 10^{-4}	3,0 10^{-9}	1,6 10^{-9}	1,0 10^{-9}	6,5 10^{-10}	5,3 10^{-10}
		S	0,005	3,9 10^{-9}	5,0 10^{-4}	3,1 10^{-9}	1,6 10^{-9}	1,0 10^{-9}	6,8 10^{-10}	5,5 10^{-10}
Np-235	1,08 a	F	0,005	4,2 10^{-9}	5,0 10^{-4}	3,5 10^{-9}	1,9 10^{-9}	1,1 10^{-9}	7,5 10^{-10}	6,3 10^{-10}
		M	0,005	2,3 10^{-9}	5,0 10^{-4}	1,9 10^{-9}	1,1 10^{-9}	6,8 10^{-10}	5,1 10^{-10}	4,2 10^{-10}
		S	0,005	2,6 10^{-9}	5,0 10^{-4}	2,2 10^{-9}	1,3 10^{-9}	8,3 10^{-10}	6,3 10^{-10}	5,2 10^{-10}
Np-236	1,15 10^{5} a	F	0,005	8,9 10^{-6}	5,0 10^{-4}	9,1 10^{-6}	7,2 10^{-6}	7,5 10^{-6}	7,9 10^{-6}	8,0 10^{-6}
		M	0,005	3,0 10^{-6}	5,0 10^{-4}	3,1 10^{-6}	2,7 10^{-6}	2,7 10^{-6}	3,1 10^{-6}	3,2 10^{-6}
		S	0,005	1,6 10^{-6}	5,0 10^{-4}	1,6 10^{-6}	1,3 10^{-6}	1,0 10^{-6}	1,0 10^{-6}	1,0 10^{-6}

Nuclide	Physical half-life	Type	Age ≤ 1 a		Age	1—2 a	2—7 a	7—12 a	12—17 a	> 17 a
			f_1	$h(g)$	f_1	$h(g)$	$h(g)$	$h(g)$	$h(g)$	$h(g)$
Np-236	22,5 h	F	0,005	2,8 10^{-8}	5,0 10^{-4}	2,6 10^{-8}	1,5 10^{-8}	1,1 10^{-8}	8,9 10^{-9}	9,0 10^{-9}
		M	0,005	1,6 10^{-8}	5,0 10^{-4}	1,4 10^{-8}	8,9 10^{-9}	6,2 10^{-9}	5,6 10^{-9}	5,3 10^{-9}
		S	0,005	1,6 10^{-8}	5,0 10^{-4}	1,3 10^{-8}	8,5 10^{-9}	5,7 10^{-9}	4,8 10^{-9}	4,2 10^{-9}
Np-237	2,14 10^{6} a	F	0,005	9,8 10^{-5}	5,0 10^{-4}	9,3 10^{-5}	6,0 10^{-5}	5,0 10^{-5}	4,7 10^{-5}	5,0 10^{-5}
		M	0,005	4,4 10^{-5}	5,0 10^{-4}	4,0 10^{-5}	2,8 10^{-5}	2,2 10^{-5}	2,2 10^{-5}	2,3 10^{-5}
		S	0,005	3,7 10^{-5}	5,0 10^{-4}	3,2 10^{-5}	2,1 10^{-5}	1,4 10^{-5}	1,3 10^{-5}	1,2 10^{-5}
Np-238	2,12 d	F	0,005	9,0 10^{-9}	5,0 10^{-4}	7,9 10^{-9}	4,8 10^{-9}	3,7 10^{-9}	3,3 10^{-9}	3,5 10^{-9}
		M	0,005	7,3 10^{-9}	5,0 10^{-4}	5,8 10^{-9}	3,4 10^{-9}	2,5 10^{-9}	2,2 10^{-9}	2,1 10^{-9}
		S	0,005	8,1 10^{-9}	5,0 10^{-4}	6,2 10^{-9}	3,2 10^{-9}	2,1 10^{-9}	1,7 10^{-9}	1,5 10^{-9}
Np-239	2,36 d	F	0,005	2,6 10^{-9}	5,0 10^{-4}	1,4 10^{-9}	6,3 10^{-10}	3,8 10^{-10}	2,1 10^{-10}	1,7 10^{-10}
		M	0,005	5,9 10^{-9}	5,0 10^{-4}	4,2 10^{-9}	2,0 10^{-9}	1,4 10^{-9}	1,2 10^{-9}	9,3 10^{-10}
		S	0,005	5,6 10^{-9}	5,0 10^{-4}	4,0 10^{-9}	2,2 10^{-9}	1,6 10^{-9}	1,3 10^{-9}	1,0 10^{-9}
Np-240	1,08 h	F	0,005	3,6 10^{-10}	5,0 10^{-4}	2,6 10^{-10}	1,2 10^{-10}	7,7 10^{-11}	4,7 10^{-11}	4,0 10^{-11}
		M	0,005	6,3 10^{-10}	5,0 10^{-4}	4,4 10^{-10}	2,2 10^{-10}	1,4 10^{-10}	1,0 10^{-10}	8,5 10^{-11}
		S	0,005	6,5 10^{-10}	5,0 10^{-4}	4,6 10^{-10}	2,3 10^{-10}	1,5 10^{-10}	1,1 10^{-10}	9,0 10^{-11}
Plutonium										
Pu-234	8,80 h	F	0,005	3,0 10^{-8}	5,0 10^{-4}	2,0 10^{-8}	9,8 10^{-9}	5,7 10^{-9}	3,6 10^{-9}	3,0 10^{-9}
		M	0,005	7,8 10^{-8}	5,0 10^{-4}	5,9 10^{-8}	3,7 10^{-8}	2,8 10^{-8}	2,6 10^{-8}	2,1 10^{-8}
		S	1,0 10^{-4}	8,7 10^{-8}	1,0 10^{-5}	6,6 10^{-8}	4,2 10^{-8}	3,1 10^{-8}	3,0 10^{-8}	2,4 10^{-8}
Pu-235	0,422 h	F	0,005	1,0 10^{-11}	5,0 10^{-4}	7,9 10^{-12}	3,9 10^{-12}	2,2 10^{-12}	1,3 10^{-12}	1,0 10^{-12}
		M	0,005	1,3 10^{-11}	5,0 10^{-4}	1,0 10^{-11}	5,0 10^{-12}	2,9 10^{-12}	1,9 10^{-12}	1,4 10^{-12}
		S	1,0 10^{-4}	1,3 10^{-11}	1,0 10^{-5}	1,0 10^{-11}	5,1 10^{-12}	3,0 10^{-12}	1,9 10^{-12}	1,5 10^{-12}
Pu-236	2,85 a	F	0,005	1,0 10^{-4}	5,0 10^{-4}	9,5 10^{-5}	6,1 10^{-5}	4,4 10^{-5}	3,7 10^{-5}	4,0 10^{-5}
		M	0,005	4,8 10^{-5}	5,0 10^{-4}	4,3 10^{-5}	2,9 10^{-5}	2,1 10^{-5}	1,9 10^{-5}	2,0 10^{-5}
		S	1,0 10^{-4}	3,6 10^{-5}	1,0 10^{-5}	3,1 10^{-5}	2,0 10^{-5}	1,4 10^{-5}	1,2 10^{-5}	1,0 10^{-5}

Nuclide	Physical half-life	Type	Age ≤ 1 a		Age	1—2 a	2—7 a	7—12 a	12—17 a	> 17 a
			f_1	$h(g)$	f_1	$h(g)$	$h(g)$	$h(g)$	$h(g)$	$h(g)$
Pu-237	45,3 d	F	0,005	$2{,}2\ 10^{-9}$	$5{,}0\ 10^{-4}$	$1{,}6\ 10^{-9}$	$7{,}9\ 10^{-10}$	$4{,}8\ 10^{-10}$	$2{,}9\ 10^{-10}$	$2{,}6\ 10^{-10}$
		M	0,005	$1{,}9\ 10^{-9}$	$5{,}0\ 10^{-4}$	$1{,}4\ 10^{-9}$	$8{,}2\ 10^{-10}$	$5{,}4\ 10^{-10}$	$4{,}3\ 10^{-10}$	$3{,}5\ 10^{-10}$
		S	$1{,}0\ 10^{-4}$	$2{,}0\ 10^{-9}$	$1{,}0\ 10^{-5}$	$1{,}5\ 10^{-9}$	$8{,}8\ 10^{-10}$	$5{,}9\ 10^{-10}$	$4{,}8\ 10^{-10}$	$3{,}9\ 10^{-10}$
Pu-238	87,7 a	F	0,005	$2{,}0\ 10^{-4}$	$5{,}0\ 10^{-4}$	$1{,}9\ 10^{-4}$	$1{,}4\ 10^{-4}$	$1{,}1\ 10^{-4}$	$1{,}0\ 10^{-4}$	$1{,}1\ 10^{-4}$
		M	0,005	$7{,}8\ 10^{-5}$	$5{,}0\ 10^{-4}$	$7{,}4\ 10^{-5}$	$5{,}6\ 10^{-5}$	$4{,}4\ 10^{-5}$	$4{,}3\ 10^{-5}$	$4{,}6\ 10^{-5}$
		S	$1{,}0\ 10^{-4}$	$4{,}5\ 10^{-5}$	$1{,}0\ 10^{-5}$	$4{,}0\ 10^{-5}$	$2{,}7\ 10^{-5}$	$1{,}9\ 10^{-5}$	$1{,}7\ 10^{-5}$	$1{,}6\ 10^{-5}$
Pu-239	$2{,}41\ 10^{4}$ a	F	0,005	$2{,}1\ 10^{-4}$	$5{,}0\ 10^{-4}$	$2{,}0\ 10^{-4}$	$1{,}5\ 10^{-4}$	$1{,}2\ 10^{-4}$	$1{,}1\ 10^{-4}$	$1{,}2\ 10^{-4}$
		M	0,005	$8{,}0\ 10^{-5}$	$5{,}0\ 10^{-4}$	$7{,}7\ 10^{-5}$	$6{,}0\ 10^{-5}$	$4{,}8\ 10^{-5}$	$4{,}7\ 10^{-5}$	$5{,}0\ 10^{-5}$
		S	$1{,}0\ 10^{-4}$	$4{,}3\ 10^{-5}$	$1{,}0\ 10^{-5}$	$3{,}9\ 10^{-5}$	$2{,}7\ 10^{-5}$	$1{,}9\ 10^{-5}$	$1{,}7\ 10^{-5}$	$1{,}6\ 10^{-5}$
Pu-240	$6{,}54\ 10^{3}$ a	F	0,005	$2{,}1\ 10^{-4}$	$5{,}0\ 10^{-4}$	$2{,}0\ 10^{-4}$	$1{,}5\ 10^{-4}$	$1{,}2\ 10^{-4}$	$1{,}1\ 10^{-4}$	$1{,}2\ 10^{-4}$
		M	0,005	$8{,}0\ 10^{-5}$	$5{,}0\ 10^{-4}$	$7{,}7\ 10^{-5}$	$6{,}0\ 10^{-5}$	$4{,}8\ 10^{-5}$	$4{,}7\ 10^{-5}$	$5{,}0\ 10^{-5}$
		S	$1{,}0\ 10^{-4}$	$4{,}3\ 10^{-5}$	$1{,}0\ 10^{-5}$	$3{,}9\ 10^{-5}$	$2{,}7\ 10^{-5}$	$1{,}9\ 10^{-5}$	$1{,}7\ 10^{-5}$	$1{,}6\ 10^{-5}$
Pu-241	14,4 a	F	0,005	$2{,}8\ 10^{-6}$	$5{,}0\ 10^{-4}$	$2{,}9\ 10^{-6}$	$2{,}6\ 10^{-6}$	$2{,}4\ 10^{-6}$	$2{,}2\ 10^{-6}$	$2{,}3\ 10^{-6}$
		M	0,005	$9{,}1\ 10^{-7}$	$5{,}0\ 10^{-4}$	$9{,}7\ 10^{-7}$	$9{,}2\ 10^{-7}$	$8{,}3\ 10^{-7}$	$8{,}6\ 10^{-7}$	$9{,}0\ 10^{-7}$
		S	$1{,}0\ 10^{-4}$	$2{,}2\ 10^{-7}$	$1{,}0\ 10^{-5}$	$2{,}3\ 10^{-7}$	$2{,}0\ 10^{-7}$	$1{,}7\ 10^{-7}$	$1{,}7\ 10^{-7}$	$1{,}7\ 10^{-7}$
Pu-242	$3{,}76\ 10^{5}$ a	F	0,005	$2{,}0\ 10^{-4}$	$5{,}0\ 10^{-4}$	$1{,}9\ 10^{-4}$	$1{,}4\ 10^{-4}$	$1{,}2\ 10^{-4}$	$1{,}1\ 10^{-4}$	$1{,}1\ 10^{-4}$
		M	0,005	$7{,}6\ 10^{-5}$	$5{,}0\ 10^{-4}$	$7{,}3\ 10^{-5}$	$5{,}7\ 10^{-5}$	$4{,}5\ 10^{-5}$	$4{,}5\ 10^{-5}$	$4{,}8\ 10^{-5}$
		S	$1{,}0\ 10^{-4}$	$4{,}0\ 10^{-5}$	$1{,}0\ 10^{-5}$	$3{,}6\ 10^{-5}$	$2{,}5\ 10^{-5}$	$1{,}7\ 10^{-5}$	$1{,}6\ 10^{-5}$	$1{,}5\ 10^{-5}$
Pu-243	4,95 h	F	0,005	$2{,}7\ 10^{-10}$	$5{,}0\ 10^{-4}$	$1{,}9\ 10^{-10}$	$8{,}8\ 10^{-11}$	$5{,}7\ 10^{-11}$	$3{,}5\ 10^{-11}$	$3{,}2\ 10^{-11}$
		M	0,005	$5{,}6\ 10^{-10}$	$5{,}0\ 10^{-4}$	$3{,}9\ 10^{-10}$	$1{,}9\ 10^{-10}$	$1{,}3\ 10^{-10}$	$8{,}7\ 10^{-11}$	$8{,}3\ 10^{-11}$
		S	$1{,}0\ 10^{-4}$	$6{,}0\ 10^{-10}$	$1{,}0\ 10^{-5}$	$4{,}1\ 10^{-10}$	$2{,}0\ 10^{-10}$	$1{,}4\ 10^{-10}$	$9{,}2\ 10^{-11}$	$8{,}6\ 10^{-11}$
Pu-244	$8{,}26\ 10^{7}$ a	F	0,005	$2{,}0\ 10^{-4}$	$5{,}0\ 10^{-4}$	$1{,}9\ 10^{-4}$	$1{,}4\ 10^{-4}$	$1{,}2\ 10^{-4}$	$1{,}1\ 10^{-4}$	$1{,}1\ 10^{-4}$
		M	0,005	$7{,}4\ 10^{-5}$	$5{,}0\ 10^{-4}$	$7{,}2\ 10^{-5}$	$5{,}6\ 10^{-5}$	$4{,}5\ 10^{-5}$	$4{,}4\ 10^{-5}$	$4{,}7\ 10^{-5}$
		S	$1{,}0\ 10^{-4}$	$3{,}9\ 10^{-5}$	$1{,}0\ 10^{-5}$	$3{,}5\ 10^{-5}$	$2{,}4\ 10^{-5}$	$1{,}7\ 10^{-5}$	$1{,}5\ 10^{-5}$	$1{,}5\ 10^{-5}$

Nuclide	*Physical half-life*	*Type*	*Age ≤ 1 a*		*Age*	*1—2 a*	*2—7 a*	*7—12 a*	*12—17 a*	*> 17 a*
			f_1	$h(g)$	f_1	$h(g)$	$h(g)$	$h(g)$	$h(g)$	$h(g)$
Pu-245	10,5 h	F	0,005	1,8 10^{-9}	5,0 10^{-4}	1,3 10^{-9}	5,6 10^{-10}	3,5 10^{-10}	1,9 10^{-10}	1,6 10^{-10}
		M	0,005	3,6 10^{-9}	5,0 10^{-4}	2,5 10^{-9}	1,2 10^{-9}	8,0 10^{-10}	5,0 10^{-10}	4,0 10^{-10}
		S	1,0 10^{-4}	3,8 10^{-9}	1,0 10^{-5}	2,6 10^{-9}	1,3 10^{-9}	8,5 10^{-10}	5,4 10^{-10}	4,3 10^{-10}
Pu-246	10,9 d	F	0,005	2,0 10^{-8}	5,0 10^{-4}	1,4 10^{-8}	7,0 10^{-9}	4,4 10^{-9}	2,8 10^{-9}	2,5 10^{-9}
		M	0,005	3,5 10^{-8}	5,0 10^{-4}	2,6 10^{-8}	1,5 10^{-8}	1,1 10^{-8}	9,1 10^{-9}	7,4 10^{-9}
		S	1,0 10^{-4}	3,8 10^{-8}	1,0 10^{-5}	2,8 10^{-8}	1,6 10^{-8}	1,2 10^{-8}	1,0 10^{-8}	8,0 10^{-9}
Americium										
Am-237	1,22 h	F	0,005	9,8 10^{-11}	5,0 10^{-4}	7,3 10^{-11}	3,5 10^{-11}	2,2 10^{-11}	1,3 10^{-11}	1,1 10^{-11}
		M	0,005	1,7 10^{-10}	5,0 10^{-4}	1,2 10^{-10}	6,2 10^{-11}	4,1 10^{-11}	3,0 10^{-11}	2,5 10^{-11}
		S	0,005	1,7 10^{-10}	5,0 10^{-4}	1,3 10^{-10}	6,5 10^{-11}	4,3 10^{-11}	3,2 10^{-11}	2,6 10^{-11}
Am-238	1,63 h	F	0,005	4,1 10^{-10}	5,0 10^{-4}	3,8 10^{-10}	2,5 10^{-10}	2,0 10^{-10}	1,8 10^{-10}	1,9 10^{-10}
		M	0,005	3,1 10^{-10}	5,0 10^{-4}	2,6 10^{-10}	1,3 10^{-10}	9,6 10^{-11}	8,8 10^{-11}	9,0 10^{-11}
		S	0,005	2,7 10^{-10}	5,0 10^{-4}	2,2 10^{-10}	1,3 10^{-10}	8,2 10^{-11}	6,1 10^{-11}	5,4 10^{-11}
Am-239	11,9 h	F	0,005	8,1 10^{-10}	5,0 10^{-4}	5,8 10^{-10}	2,6 10^{-10}	1,6 10^{-10}	9,1 10^{-11}	7,6 10^{-11}
		M	0,005	1,5 10^{-9}	5,0 10^{-4}	1,1 10^{-9}	5,6 10^{-10}	3,7 10^{-10}	2,7 10^{-10}	2,2 10^{-10}
		S	0,005	1,6 10^{-9}	5,0 10^{-4}	1,1 10^{-9}	5,9 10^{-10}	4,0 10^{-10}	2,5 10^{-10}	2,4 10^{-10}
Am-240	2,12 d	F	0,005	2,0 10^{-9}	5,0 10^{-4}	1,7 10^{-9}	8,8 10^{-10}	5,7 10^{-10}	3,6 10^{-10}	2,3 10^{-10}
		M	0,005	2,9 10^{-9}	5,0 10^{-4}	2,2 10^{-9}	1,2 10^{-9}	7,7 10^{-10}	5,3 10^{-10}	4,3 10^{-10}
		S	0,005	3,0 10^{-9}	5,0 10^{-4}	2,3 10^{-9}	1,2 10^{-9}	7,8 10^{-10}	5,3 10^{-10}	4,3 10^{-10}
Am-241	4,32 10^{2} a	F	0,005	1,8 10^{-4}	5,0 10^{-4}	1,8 10^{-4}	1,2 10^{-4}	1,0 10^{-4}	9,2 10^{-5}	9,6 10^{-5}
		M	0,005	7,3 10^{-5}	5,0 10^{-4}	6,9 10^{-5}	5,1 10^{-5}	4,0 10^{-5}	4,0 10^{-5}	4,2 10^{-5}
		S	0,005	4,6 10^{-5}	5,0 10^{-4}	4,0 10^{-5}	2,7 10^{-5}	1,9 10^{-5}	1,7 10^{-5}	1,6 10^{-5}
Am-242	16,0 h	F	0,005	9,2 10^{-8}	5,0 10^{-4}	7,1 10^{-8}	3,5 10^{-8}	2,1 10^{-8}	1,4 10^{-8}	1,1 10^{-8}
		M	0,005	7,6 10^{-8}	5,0 10^{-4}	5,9 10^{-8}	3,6 10^{-8}	2,4 10^{-8}	2,1 10^{-8}	1,7 10^{-8}
		S	0,005	8,0 10^{-8}	5,0 10^{-4}	6,2 10^{-8}	3,9 10^{-8}	2,7 10^{-8}	2,4 10^{-8}	2,0 10^{-8}

Nuclide	*Physical half-life*	*Type*	*Age ≤ 1 a*		*Age*	*1—2 a*	*2—7 a*	*7—12 a*	*12—17 a*	*> 17 a*
			f_1	*h(g)*	f_1	*h(g)*	*h(g)*	*h(g)*	*h(g)*	*h(g)*
Am-242m	1,52 10^{2} a	F	0,005	1,6 10^{-4}	5,0 10^{-4}	1,5 10^{-4}	1,1 10^{-4}	9,4 10^{-5}	8,8 10^{-5}	9,2 10^{-5}
		M	0,005	5,2 10^{-5}	5,0 10^{-4}	5,3 10^{-5}	4,1 10^{-5}	3,4 10^{-5}	3,5 10^{-5}	3,7 10^{-5}
		S	0,005	2,5 10^{-5}	5,0 10^{-4}	2,4 10^{-5}	1,7 10^{-5}	1,2 10^{-5}	1,1 10^{-5}	1,1 10^{-5}
Am-243	7,38 10^{3} a	F	0,005	1,8 10^{-4}	5,0 10^{-4}	1,7 10^{-4}	1,2 10^{-4}	1,0 10^{-4}	9,1 10^{-5}	9,6 10^{-5}
		M	0,005	7,2 10^{-5}	5,0 10^{-4}	6,8 10^{-5}	5,0 10^{-5}	4,0 10^{-5}	4,0 10^{-5}	4,1 10^{-5}
		S	0,005	4,4 10^{-5}	5,0 10^{-4}	3,9 10^{-5}	2,6 10^{-5}	1,8 10^{-5}	1,6 10^{-5}	1,5 10^{-5}
Am-244	10,1 h	F	0,005	1,0 10^{-8}	5,0 10^{-4}	9,2 10^{-9}	5,6 10^{-9}	4,1 10^{-9}	3,5 10^{-9}	3,7 10^{-9}
		M	0,005	6,0 10^{-9}	5,0 10^{-4}	5,0 10^{-9}	3,2 10^{-9}	2,2 10^{-9}	2,0 10^{-9}	2,0 10^{-9}
		S	0,005	6,1 10^{-9}	5,0 10^{-4}	4,8 10^{-9}	2,4 10^{-9}	1,6 10^{-9}	1,4 10^{-9}	1,2 10^{-9}
Am-244m	0,433 h	F	0,005	4,6 10^{-10}	5,0 10^{-4}	4,0 10^{-10}	2,4 10^{-10}	1,8 10^{-10}	1,5 10^{-10}	1,6 10^{-10}
		M	0,005	3,3 10^{-10}	5,0 10^{-4}	2,1 10^{-10}	1,3 10^{-10}	9,2 10^{-11}	8,3 10^{-11}	8,4 10^{-11}
		S	0,005	3,0 10^{-10}	5,0 10^{-4}	2,2 10^{-10}	1,2 10^{-10}	8,1 10^{-11}	5,5 10^{-11}	5,7 10^{-11}
Am-245	2,05 h	F	0,005	2,1 10^{-10}	5,0 10^{-4}	1,4 10^{-10}	6,2 10^{-11}	4,0 10^{-11}	2,4 10^{-11}	2,1 10^{-11}
		M	0,005	3,9 10^{-10}	5,0 10^{-4}	2,6 10^{-10}	1,3 10^{-10}	8,7 10^{-11}	6,4 10^{-11}	5,3 10^{-11}
		S	0,005	4,1 10^{-10}	5,0 10^{-4}	2,8 10^{-10}	1,3 10^{-10}	9,2 10^{-11}	6,8 10^{-11}	5,6 10^{-11}
Am-246	0,650 h	F	0,005	3,0 10^{-10}	5,0 10^{-4}	2,0 10^{-10}	9,3 10^{-11}	6,1 10^{-11}	3,8 10^{-11}	3,3 10^{-11}
		M	0,005	5,0 10^{-10}	5,0 10^{-4}	3,4 10^{-10}	1,6 10^{-10}	1,1 10^{-10}	7,9 10^{-11}	6,6 10^{-11}
		S	0,005	5,3 10^{-10}	5,0 10^{-4}	3,6 10^{-10}	1,7 10^{-10}	1,2 10^{-10}	8,3 10^{-11}	6,9 10^{-11}
Am-246m	0,417 h	F	0,005	1,3 10^{-10}	5,0 10^{-4}	8,9 10^{-11}	4,2 10^{-11}	2,6 10^{-11}	1,6 10^{-11}	1,4 10^{-11}
		M	0,005	1,9 10^{-10}	5,0 10^{-4}	1,3 10^{-10}	6,1 10^{-11}	4,0 10^{-11}	2,6 10^{-11}	2,2 10^{-11}
		S	0,005	2,0 10^{-10}	5,0 10^{-4}	1,4 10^{-10}	6,4 10^{-11}	4,1 10^{-11}	2,7 10^{-11}	2,3 10^{-11}
Curium										
Cm-238	2,40 h	F	0,005	7,7 10^{-9}	5,0 10^{-4}	5,4 10^{-9}	2,6 10^{-9}	1,8 10^{-9}	9,2 10^{-10}	7,8 10^{-10}
		M	0,005	2,1 10^{-8}	5,0 10^{-4}	1,5 10^{-8}	7,9 10^{-9}	5,9 10^{-9}	5,6 10^{-9}	4,5 10^{-9}
		S	0,005	2,2 10^{-8}	5,0 10^{-4}	1,6 10^{-8}	8,6 10^{-9}	6,4 10^{-9}	6,1 10^{-9}	4,9 10^{-9}

Nuclide	Physical half-life	Type	Age ≤ 1 a		Age	1—2 a	2—7 a	7—12 a	12—17 a	> 17 a
			f_1	h(g)	f_1	h(g)	h(g)	h(g)	h(g)	h(g)
Cm-240	27,0 d	F	0,005	$8,3\ 10^{-6}$	$5,0\ 10^{-4}$	$6,3\ 10^{-6}$	$3,2\ 10^{-6}$	$2,0\ 10^{-6}$	$1,5\ 10^{-6}$	$1,3\ 10^{-6}$
		M	0,005	$1,2\ 10^{-5}$	$5,0\ 10^{-4}$	$9,1\ 10^{-6}$	$5,8\ 10^{-6}$	$4,2\ 10^{-6}$	$3,8\ 10^{-6}$	$3,2\ 10^{-6}$
		S	0,005	$1,3\ 10^{-5}$	$5,0\ 10^{-4}$	$9,9\ 10^{-6}$	$6,4\ 10^{-6}$	$4,6\ 10^{-6}$	$4,3\ 10^{-6}$	$3,5\ 10^{-6}$
Cm-241	32,8 d	F	0,005	$1,1\ 10^{-7}$	$5,0\ 10^{-4}$	$8,9\ 10^{-8}$	$4,9\ 10^{-8}$	$3,5\ 10^{-8}$	$2,8\ 10^{-8}$	$2,7\ 10^{-8}$
		M	0,005	$1,3\ 10^{-7}$	$5,0\ 10^{-4}$	$1,0\ 10^{-7}$	$6,6\ 10^{-8}$	$4,8\ 10^{-8}$	$4,4\ 10^{-8}$	$3,7\ 10^{-8}$
		S	0,005	$1,4\ 10^{-7}$	$5,0\ 10^{-4}$	$1,1\ 10^{-7}$	$6,9\ 10^{-8}$	$4,9\ 10^{-8}$	$4,5\ 10^{-8}$	$3,7\ 10^{-8}$
Cm-242	163 d	F	0,005	$2,7\ 10^{-5}$	$5,0\ 10^{-4}$	$2,1\ 10^{-5}$	$1,0\ 10^{-5}$	$6,1\ 10^{-6}$	$4,0\ 10^{-6}$	$3,3\ 10^{-6}$
		M	0,005	$2,2\ 10^{-5}$	$5,0\ 10^{-4}$	$1,8\ 10^{-5}$	$1,1\ 10^{-5}$	$7,3\ 10^{-6}$	$6,4\ 10^{-6}$	$5,2\ 10^{-6}$
		S	0,005	$2,4\ 10^{-5}$	$5,0\ 10^{-4}$	$1,9\ 10^{-5}$	$1,2\ 10^{-5}$	$8,2\ 10^{-6}$	$7,3\ 10^{-6}$	$5,9\ 10^{-6}$
Cm-243	28,5 a	F	0,005	$1,6\ 10^{-4}$	$5,0\ 10^{-4}$	$1,5\ 10^{-4}$	$9,5\ 10^{-5}$	$7,3\ 10^{-5}$	$6,5\ 10^{-5}$	$6,9\ 10^{-5}$
		M	0,005	$6,7\ 10^{-5}$	$5,0\ 10^{-4}$	$6,1\ 10^{-5}$	$4,2\ 10^{-5}$	$3,1\ 10^{-5}$	$3,0\ 10^{-5}$	$3,1\ 10^{-5}$
		S	0,005	$4,6\ 10^{-5}$	$5,0\ 10^{-4}$	$4,0\ 10^{-5}$	$2,6\ 10^{-5}$	$1,8\ 10^{-5}$	$1,6\ 10^{-5}$	$1,5\ 10^{-5}$
Cm-244	18,1 a	F	0,005	$1,5\ 10^{-4}$	$5,0\ 10^{-4}$	$1,3\ 10^{-4}$	$8,3\ 10^{-5}$	$6,1\ 10^{-5}$	$5,3\ 10^{-5}$	$5,7\ 10^{-5}$
		M	0,005	$6,2\ 10^{-5}$	$5,0\ 10^{-4}$	$5,7\ 10^{-5}$	$3,7\ 10^{-5}$	$2,7\ 10^{-5}$	$2,6\ 10^{-5}$	$2,7\ 10^{-5}$
		S	0,005	$4,4\ 10^{-5}$	$5,0\ 10^{-4}$	$3,8\ 10^{-5}$	$2,5\ 10^{-5}$	$1,7\ 10^{-5}$	$1,5\ 10^{-5}$	$1,3\ 10^{-5}$
Cm-245	$8,50\ 10^{3}$ a	F	0,005	$1,9\ 10^{-4}$	$5,0\ 10^{-4}$	$1,8\ 10^{-4}$	$1,2\ 10^{-4}$	$1,0\ 10^{-4}$	$9,4\ 10^{-5}$	$9,9\ 10^{-5}$
		M	0,005	$7,3\ 10^{-5}$	$5,0\ 10^{-4}$	$6,9\ 10^{-5}$	$5,1\ 10^{-5}$	$4,1\ 10^{-5}$	$4,1\ 10^{-5}$	$4,2\ 10^{-5}$
		S	0,005	$4,5\ 10^{-5}$	$5,0\ 10^{-4}$	$4,0\ 10^{-5}$	$2,7\ 10^{-5}$	$1,9\ 10^{-5}$	$1,7\ 10^{-5}$	$1,6\ 10^{-5}$
Cm-246	$4,73\ 10^{3}$ a	F	0,005	$1,9\ 10^{-4}$	$5,0\ 10^{-4}$	$1,8\ 10^{-4}$	$1,2\ 10^{-4}$	$1,0\ 10^{-4}$	$9,4\ 10^{-5}$	$9,8\ 10^{-5}$
		M	0,005	$7,3\ 10^{-5}$	$5,0\ 10^{-4}$	$6,9\ 10^{-5}$	$5,1\ 10^{-5}$	$4,1\ 10^{-5}$	$4,1\ 10^{-5}$	$4,2\ 10^{-5}$
		S	0,005	$4,6\ 10^{-5}$	$5,0\ 10^{-4}$	$4,0\ 10^{-5}$	$2,7\ 10^{-5}$	$1,9\ 10^{-5}$	$1,7\ 10^{-5}$	$1,6\ 10^{-5}$
Cm-247	$1,56\ 10^{7}$ a	F	0,005	$1,7\ 10^{-4}$	$5,0\ 10^{-4}$	$1,6\ 10^{-4}$	$1,1\ 10^{-4}$	$9,4\ 10^{-5}$	$8,6\ 10^{-5}$	$9,0\ 10^{-5}$
		M	0,005	$6,7\ 10^{-5}$	$5,0\ 10^{-4}$	$6,3\ 10^{-5}$	$4,7\ 10^{-5}$	$3,7\ 10^{-5}$	$3,7\ 10^{-5}$	$3,9\ 10^{-5}$
		S	0,005	$4,1\ 10^{-5}$	$5,0\ 10^{-4}$	$3,6\ 10^{-5}$	$2,4\ 10^{-5}$	$1,7\ 10^{-5}$	$1,5\ 10^{-5}$	$1,4\ 10^{-5}$

Nuclide	*Physical half-life*	*Type*	*Age ≤ 1 a*		*Age*	*1—2 a*	*2—7 a*	*7—12 a*	*12—17 a*	*> 17 a*
			f_1	*h(g)*	f_1	*h(g)*	*h(g)*	*h(g)*	*h(g)*	*h(g)*
Cm-248	3,39 10^{5} a	F	0,005	6,8 10^{-4}	5,0 10^{-4}	6,5 10^{-4}	4,5 10^{-4}	3,7 10^{-4}	3,4 10^{-4}	3,6 10^{-4}
		M	0,005	2,5 10^{-4}	5,0 10^{-4}	2,4 10^{-4}	1,8 10^{-4}	1,4 10^{-4}	1,4 10^{-4}	1,5 10^{-4}
		S	0,005	1,4 10^{-4}	5,0 10^{-4}	1,2 10^{-4}	8,2 10^{-5}	5,6 10^{-5}	5,0 10^{-5}	4,8 10^{-5}
Cm-249	1,07 h	F	0,005	1,8 10^{-10}	5,0 10^{-4}	9,8 10^{-11}	5,9 10^{-11}	4,6 10^{-11}	4,0 10^{-11}	4,0 10^{-11}
		M	0,005	2,4 10^{-10}	5,0 10^{-4}	1,6 10^{-10}	8,2 10^{-11}	5,8 10^{-11}	3,7 10^{-11}	3,3 10^{-11}
		S	0,005	2,4 10^{-10}	5,0 10^{-4}	1,6 10^{-10}	7,8 10^{-11}	5,3 10^{-11}	3,9 10^{-11}	3,3 10^{-11}
Cm-250	6,90 10^{3} a	F	0,005	3,9 10^{-3}	5,0 10^{-4}	3,7 10^{-3}	2,6 10^{-3}	2,1 10^{-3}	2,0 10^{-3}	2,1 10^{-3}
		M	0,005	1,4 10^{-3}	5,0 10^{-4}	1,3 10^{-3}	9,9 10^{-4}	7,9 10^{-4}	7,9 10^{-4}	8,4 10^{-4}
		S	0,005	7,2 10^{-4}	5,0 10^{-4}	6,5 10^{-4}	4,4 10^{-4}	3,0 10^{-4}	2,7 10^{-4}	2,6 10^{-4}
Berkelium										
Bk-245	4,94 d	M	0,005	8,8 10^{-9}	5,0 10^{-4}	6,6 10^{-9}	4,0 10^{-9}	2,9 10^{-9}	2,6 10^{-9}	2,1 10^{-9}
Bk-246	1,83 d	M	0,005	2,1 10^{-9}	5,0 10^{-4}	1,7 10^{-9}	9,3 10^{-10}	6,0 10^{-10}	4,0 10^{-10}	3,3 10^{-10}
Bk-247	1,38 10^{3} a	M	0,005	1,5 10^{-4}	5,0 10^{-4}	1,5 10^{-4}	1,1 10^{-4}	7,9 10^{-5}	7,2 10^{-5}	6,9 10^{-5}
Bk-249	320 d	M	0,005	3,3 10^{-7}	5,0 10^{-4}	3,3 10^{-7}	2,4 10^{-7}	1,8 10^{-7}	1,6 10^{-7}	1,6 10^{-7}
Bk-250	3,22 h	M	0,005	3,4 10^{-9}	5,0 10^{-4}	3,1 10^{-9}	2,0 10^{-9}	1,3 10^{-9}	1,1 10^{-9}	1,0 10^{-9}
Californium										
Cf-244	0,323 h	M	0,005	7,6 10^{-8}	5,0 10^{-4}	5,4 10^{-8}	2,8 10^{-8}	2,0 10^{-8}	1,6 10^{-8}	1,4 10^{-8}
Cf-246	1,49 d	M	0,005	1,7 10^{-6}	5,0 10^{-4}	1,3 10^{-6}	8,3 10^{-7}	6,1 10^{-7}	5,7 10^{-7}	4,5 10^{-7}
Cf-248	334 d	M	0,005	3,8 10^{-5}	5,0 10^{-4}	3,2 10^{-5}	2,1 10^{-5}	1,4 10^{-5}	1,0 10^{-5}	8,8 10^{-6}
Cf-249	350 10^{2} a	M	0,005	1,6 10^{-4}	5,0 10^{-4}	1,5 10^{-4}	1,1 10^{-4}	8,0 10^{-5}	7,2 10^{-5}	7,0 10^{-5}
Cf-250	13,1 a	M	0,005	1,1 10^{-4}	5,0 10^{-4}	9,8 10^{-5}	6,6 10^{-5}	4,2 10^{-5}	3,5 10^{-5}	3,4 10^{-5}
Cf-251	8,98 10^{2} a	M	0,005	1,6 10^{-4}	5,0 10^{-4}	1,5 10^{-4}	1,1 10^{-4}	8,1 10^{-5}	7,3 10^{-5}	7,1 10^{-5}
Cf-252	2,64 a	M	0,005	9,7 10^{-5}	5,0 10^{-4}	8,7 10^{-5}	5,6 10^{-5}	3,2 10^{-5}	2,2 10^{-5}	2,0 10^{-5}
Cf-253	17,8 d	M	0,005	5,4 10^{-6}	5,0 10^{-4}	4,2 10^{-6}	2,6 10^{-6}	1,9 10^{-6}	1,7 10^{-6}	1,3 10^{-6}
Cf-254	60,5 d	M	0,005	2,5 10^{-4}	5,0 10^{-4}	1,9 10^{-4}	1,1 10^{-4}	7,0 10^{-5}	4,8 10^{-5}	4,1 10^{-5}

Nuclide	*Physical half-life*	*Type*	*Age ≤ 1 a*		*Age*	*1—2 a*	*2—7 a*	*7—12 a*	*12—17 a*	*> 17 a*
			f_1	*h(g)*	f_1	*h(g)*	*h(g)*	*h(g)*	*h(g)*	*h(g)*
Einsteinium										
Es-250	2,10 h	M	0,005	$2{,}0\ 10^{-9}$	$5{,}0\ 10^{-4}$	$1{,}8\ 10^{-9}$	$1{,}2\ 10^{-9}$	$7{,}8\ 10^{-10}$	$6{,}4\ 10^{-10}$	$6{,}3\ 10^{-10}$
Es-251	1,38 d	M	0,005	$7{,}9\ 10^{-9}$	$5{,}0\ 10^{-4}$	$6{,}0\ 10^{-9}$	$3{,}9\ 10^{-9}$	$2{,}8\ 10^{-9}$	$2{,}6\ 10^{-9}$	$2{,}1\ 10^{-9}$
Es-253	20,5 d	M	0,005	$1{,}1\ 10^{-5}$	$5{,}0\ 10^{-4}$	$8{,}0\ 10^{-6}$	$5{,}1\ 10^{-6}$	$3{,}7\ 10^{-6}$	$3{,}4\ 10^{-6}$	$2{,}7\ 10^{-6}$
Es-254	276 d	M	0,005	$3{,}7\ 10^{-5}$	$5{,}0\ 10^{-4}$	$3{,}1\ 10^{-5}$	$2{,}0\ 10^{-5}$	$1{,}3\ 10^{-5}$	$1{,}0\ 10^{-5}$	$8{,}6\ 10^{-6}$
Es-254m	1,64 d	M	0,005	$1{,}7\ 10^{-6}$	$5{,}0\ 10^{-4}$	$1{,}3\ 10^{-6}$	$8{,}4\ 10^{-7}$	$6{,}3\ 10^{-7}$	$5{,}9\ 10^{-7}$	$4{,}7\ 10^{-7}$
Fermium										
Fm-252	22,7 h	M	0,005	$1{,}2\ 10^{-6}$	$5{,}0\ 10^{-4}$	$9{,}0\ 10^{-7}$	$5{,}8\ 10^{-7}$	$4{,}3\ 10^{-7}$	$4{,}0\ 10^{-7}$	$3{,}2\ 10^{-7}$
Fm-253	3,00 d	M	0,005	$1{,}5\ 10^{-6}$	$5{,}0\ 10^{-4}$	$1{,}2\ 10^{-6}$	$7{,}3\ 10^{-7}$	$5{,}4\ 10^{-7}$	$5{,}0\ 10^{-7}$	$4{,}0\ 10^{-7}$
Fm-254	3,24 h	M	0,005	$3{,}2\ 10^{-7}$	$5{,}0\ 10^{-4}$	$2{,}3\ 10^{-7}$	$1{,}3\ 10^{-7}$	$9{,}8\ 10^{-8}$	$7{,}6\ 10^{-8}$	$6{,}1\ 10^{-8}$
Fm-255	20,1 h	M	0,005	$1{,}2\ 10^{-6}$	$5{,}0\ 10^{-4}$	$7{,}3\ 10^{-7}$	$4{,}7\ 10^{-7}$	$3{,}5\ 10^{-7}$	$3{,}4\ 10^{-7}$	$2{,}7\ 10^{-7}$
Fm-257	101 d	M	0,005	$3{,}3\ 10^{-5}$	$5{,}0\ 10^{-4}$	$2{,}6\ 10^{-5}$	$1{,}6\ 10^{-5}$	$1{,}1\ 10^{-5}$	$8{,}8\ 10^{-6}$	$7{,}1\ 10^{-6}$
Mendelevium										
Md-257	5,20 h	M	0,005	$1{,}0\ 10^{-7}$	$5{,}0\ 10^{-4}$	$8{,}2\ 10^{-8}$	$5{,}1\ 10^{-8}$	$3{,}6\ 10^{-8}$	$3{,}1\ 10^{-8}$	$2{,}5\ 10^{-8}$
Md-258	55,0 d	M	0,005	$2{,}4\ 10^{-5}$	$5{,}0\ 10^{-4}$	$1{,}9\ 10^{-5}$	$1{,}2\ 10^{-5}$	$8{,}6\ 10^{-6}$	$7{,}3\ 10^{-6}$	$5{,}9\ 10^{-6}$

Type F denotes fast clearance from the lung.
Type M denotes moderate clearance from the lung.
Type S denotes slow clearance from the lung.

(a) The f_1 value for 1 to 15 year olds for Type F is 0,4.
(b) The f_1 value for 1 to 15 year olds for Type F is 0,2.
(c) The f_1 value for 1 to 15 year olds for Type F is 0,3.
(d) *The f_1 value for 1 to 15 year olds for Type F is 0,4.*
(e) The f_1 value for 1 to 15 year olds for Type F is 0,3.
(f) The f_1 value for 1 to 15 year olds for Type F is 0,4.
(g) The f_1 value for 1 to 15 year olds for Type F is 0,3.

Table (C.1)
Effective dose coefficients (Sv Bq^{-1})

Nuclide	*Physical half-life*	*Inhalation*				*Ingestion*	
		Type	f_1	$h(g)_{1\mu m}$	$h(g)_{5\mu m}$	f_1	$h(g)$
Hydrogen							
Tritiated water	12,3 a	See Table (C.2) for inhalation doses				1,000	1,8 10^{-11}
OBT	12,3 a	See Table (C.2) for inhalation doses				1,000	4,2 10^{-11}
Beryllium							
Be-7	53,3 d	M	0,005	4,8 10^{-11}	4,3 10^{-11}	0,005	2,8 10^{-11}
		S	0,005	5,2 10^{-11}	4,6 10^{-11}		
Be-10	1,60 106 a	M	0,005	9,1 10^{-9}	6,7 10^{-9}	0,005	1,1 10^{-9}
		S	0,005	3,2 10^{-8}	1,9 10^{-8}		
Carbon							
C-11	0,340 h	See Table (C.2) for inhalation doses				1,000	2,4 10^{-11}
C-14	5,73 103 a	See Table (C.2) for inhalation doses				1,000	5,8 10^{-10}
Fluorine							
F-18	1,83 h	F	1,000	3,0 10^{-11}	5,4 10^{-11}	1,000	4,9 10^{-11}
		M	1,000	5,7 10^{-11}	8,9 10^{-11}		
		S	1,000	6,0 10^{-11}	9,3 10^{-11}		
Sodium							
Na-22	2,60 a	F	1,000	1,3 10^{-9}	2,0 10^{-9}	1,000	3,2 10^{-9}
Na-24	15,0 h	F	1,000	2,9 10^{-10}	5,3 10^{-10}	1,000	4,3 10^{-10}
Magnesium							
Mg-28	20,9 h	F	0,500	6,4 10^{-10}	1,1 10^{-9}	0,500	2,2 10^{-9}
		M	0,500	1,2 10^{-9}	1,7 10^{-9}		
Aluminium							
Al-26	7,16 105 a	F	0,010	1,1 10^{-8}	1,4 10^{-8}	0,010	3,5 10^{-9}
		M	0,010	1,8 10^{-8}	1,2 10^{-8}		
Silicon							
Si-31	2,62 h	F	0,010	2,9 10^{-11}	5,1 10^{-11}	0,010	1,6 10^{-10}
		M	0,010	7,5 10^{-11}	1,1 10^{-10}		
		S	0,010	8,0 10^{-11}	1,1 10^{-10}		
Si-32	4,50 102 a	F	0,010	3,2 10^{-9}	3,7 10^{-9}	0,010	5,6 10^{-10}
		M	0,010	1,5 10^{-8}	9,6 10^{-9}		
		S	0,010	1,1 10^{-7}	5,5 10^{-8}		
Phosphorus							
P-32	14,3 d	F	0,800	8,0 10^{-10}	1,1 10^{-9}	0,800	2,4 10^{-9}
		M	0,800	3,2 10^{-9}	2,9 10^{-9}		
P-33	25,4 d	F	0,800	9,6 10^{-11}	1,4 10^{-10}	0,800	2,4 10^{-10}
		M	0,800	1,4 10^{-9}	1,3 10^{-9}		
Sulphur							
S-35 (inorganic)	87,4 d	F	0,800	5,3 10^{-11}	8,0 10^{-10}	0,800	1,4 10^{-10}
		M	0,800	1,3 10^{-9}	1,1 10^{-9}	0,100	1,9 10^{-10}
S-35 (organic)	87,4 d	See Table (C.2) for inhalation doses				1,000	7,7 10^{-10}

Nuclide	*Physical half-life*	*Inhalation*				*Ingestion*	
		Type	f_1	$h(g)_{1\mu m}$	$h(g)_{5\mu m}$	f_1	$h(g)$
Chlorine							
Cl-36	3,01 105 a	F	1,000	3,4 10^{-10}	4,9 10^{-10}	1,000	9,3 10^{-10}
		M	1,000	6,9 10^{-9}	5,1 10^{-9}		
Cl-38	0,620 h	F	1,000	2,7 10^{-11}	4,6 10^{-11}	1,000	1,2 10^{-10}
		M	1,000	4,7 10^{-11}	7,3 10^{-11}		
Cl-39	0,927 h	F	1,000	2,7 10^{-11}	4,8 10^{-11}	1,000	8,5 10^{-11}
		M	1,000	4,8 10^{-11}	7,6 10^{-11}		
Potassium							
K-40	1,28 109 a	F	1,000	2,1 10^{-9}	3,0 10^{-9}	1,000	6,2 10^{-9}
K-42	12,4 h	F	1,000	1,3 10^{-10}	2,0 10^{-10}	1,000	4,3 10^{-10}
K-43	22,6 h	F	1,000	1,5 10^{-10}	2,6 10^{-10}	1,000	2,5 10^{-10}
K-44	0,369 h	F	1,000	2,1 10^{-11}	3,7 10^{-11}	1,000	8,4 10^{-11}
K-45	0,333 h	F	1,000	1,6 10^{-11}	2,8 10^{-11}	1,000	5,4 10^{-11}
Calcium							
Ca-41	1,40 105 a	M	0,300	1,7 10^{-10}	1,9 10^{-10}	0,300	2,9 10^{-10}
Ca-45	163 d	M	0,300	2,7 10^{-9}	2,3 10^{-9}	0,300	7,6 10^{-10}
Ca-47	4,53 d	M	0,300	1,8 10^{-9}	2,1 10^{-9}	0,300	1,6 10^{-9}
Scandium							
Sc-43	3,89 h	S	1,0$10^{-4}$	1,2 10^{-10}	1,8 10^{-10}	1,0$10^{-4}$	1,9 10^{-10}
Sc-44	3,93 h	S	1,0$10^{-4}$	1,9 10^{-10}	3,0 10^{-10}	1,0$10^{-4}$	3,5 10^{-10}
Sc-44m	2,44 d	S	1,0$10^{-4}$	1,5 10^{-9}	2,0 10^{-9}	1,0$10^{-4}$	2,4 10^{-9}
Sc-46	83,8 d	S	1,0$10^{-4}$	6,4 10^{-9}	4,8 10^{-9}	1,0$10^{-4}$	1,5 10^{-9}
Sc-47	3,35 d	S	1,0$10^{-4}$	7,0 10^{-10}	7,3 10^{-10}	1,0$10^{-4}$	5,4 10^{-10}
Sc-48	1,82 d	S	1,0$10^{-4}$	1,1 10^{-9}	1,6 10^{-9}	1,0$10^{-4}$	1,7 10^{-9}
Sc-49	0,956 h	S	1,0$10^{-4}$	4,1 10^{-11}	6,1 10^{-11}	1,0$10^{-4}$	8,2 10^{-11}
Titanium							
Ti-44	47,3 a	F	0,010	6,1 10^{-8}	7,2 10^{-8}	0,010	5,8 10^{-9}
		M	0,010	4,0 10^{-8}	2,7 10^{-8}		
		S	0,010	1,2 10^{-7}	6,2 10^{-8}		
Ti-45	3,08 h	F	0,010	4,6 10^{-11}	8,3 10^{-11}	0,010	1,5 10^{-10}
		M	0,010	9,1 10^{-11}	1,4 10^{-10}		
		S	0,010	9,6 10^{-11}	1,5 10^{-10}		
Vanadium							
V-47	0,543 h	F	0,010	1,9 10^{-11}	3,2 10^{-11}	0,010	6,3 10^{-11}
		M	0,010	3,1 10^{-11}	5,0 10^{-11}		
V-48	16,2 d	F	0,010	1,1 10^{-9}	1,7 10^{-9}	0,010	2,0 10^{-9}
		M	0,010	2,3 10^{-9}	2,7 10^{-9}		
V-49	330 d	F	0,010	2,1 10^{-11}	2,6 10^{-11}	0,010	1,8 10^{-11}
		M	0,010	3,2 10^{-11}	2,3 10^{-11}		
Chromium							
Cr-48	23,0 h	F	0,100	1,0 10^{-10}	1,7 10^{-10}	0,100	2,0 10^{-10}
		M	0,100	2,0 10^{-10}	2,3 10^{-10}	0,010	2,0 10^{-10}
		S	0,100	2,2 10^{-10}	2,5 10^{-10}		
Cr-49	0,702 h	F	0,100	2,0 10^{-11}	3,5 10^{-11}	0,100	6,1 10^{-11}
		M	0,100	3,5 10^{-11}	5,6 10^{-11}	0,010	6,1 10^{-11}
		S	0,100	3,7 10^{-11}	5,9 10^{-11}		

Nuclide	*Physical half-life*	*Inhalation*				*Ingestion*	
		Type	f_1	$h(g)_{1\mu m}$	$h(g)_{5\mu m}$	f_1	$h(g)$
Cr-51	27,7 d	F	0,100	2,1 10^{-11}	3,0 10^{-11}	0,100	3,8 10^{-11}
		M	0,100	3,1 10^{-11}	3,4 10^{-11}	0,010	3,7 10^{-11}
		S	0,100	3,6 10^{-11}	3,6 10^{-11}		
Manganese							
Mn-51	0,770 h	F	0,100	2,4 10^{-11}	4,2 10^{-11}	0,100	9,3 10^{-11}
		M	0,100	4,3 10^{-11}	6,8 10^{-11}		
Mn-52	5,59 d	F	0,100	9,9 10^{-10}	1,6 10^{-9}	0,100	1,8 10^{-9}
		M	0,100	1,4 10^{-9}	1,8 10^{-9}		
Mn-52m	0,352 h	F	0,100	2,0 10^{-11}	3,5 10^{-11}	0,100	6,9 10^{-11}
		M	0,100	3,0 10^{-11}	5,0 10^{-11}		
Mn-53	3,70 106 a	F	0,100	2,9 10^{-11}	3,6 10^{-11}	0,100	3,0 10^{-11}
		M	0,100	5,2 10^{-11}	3,6 10^{-11}		
Mn-54	312 d	F	0,100	8,7 10^{-10}	1,1 10^{-9}	0,100	7,1 10^{-10}
		M	0,100	1,5 10^{-9}	1,2 10^{-9}		
Mn-56	2,58 h	F	0,100	6,9 10^{-11}	1,2 10^{-10}	0,100	2,5 10^{-10}
		M	0,100	1,3 10^{-10}	2,0 10^{-10}		
Iron							
Fe-52	8,28 h	F	0,100	4,1 10^{-10}	6,9 10^{-10}	0,100	1,4 10^{-9}
		M	0,100	6,3 10^{-10}	9,5 10^{-10}		
Fe-55	2,70 a	F	0,100	7,7 10^{-10}	9,2 10^{-10}	0,100	3,3 10^{-10}
		M	0,100	3,7 10^{-10}	3,3 10^{-10}		
Fe-59	44,5 d	F	0,100	2,2 10^{-9}	3,0 10^{-9}	0,100	1,8 10^{-9}
		M	0,100	3,5 10^{-9}	3,2 10^{-9}		
Fe-60	1,00 105 a	F	0,100	2,8 10^{-7}	3,3 10^{-7}	0,100	1,1 10^{-7}
		M	0,100	1,3 10^{-7}	1,2 10^{-7}		
Cobalt							
Co-55	17,5 h	M	0,100	5,1 10^{-10}	7,8 10^{-10}	0,100	1,0 10^{-9}
		S	0,050	5,5 10^{-10}	8,3 10^{-10}	0,050	1,1 10^{-9}
Co-56	78,7 d	M	0,100	4,6 10^{-9}	4,0 10^{-9}	0,100	2,5 10^{-9}
		S	0,050	6,3 10^{-9}	4,9 10^{-9}	0,050	2,3 10^{-9}
Co-57	271 d	M	0,100	5,2 10^{-10}	3,9 10^{-10}	0,100	2,1 10^{-10}
		S	0,050	9,4 10^{-10}	6,0 10^{-10}	0,050	1,9 10^{-10}
Co-58	70,8 d	M	0,100	1,5 10^{-9}	1,4 10^{-9}	0,100	7,4 10^{-10}
		S	0,050	2,0 10^{-9}	1,7 10^{-9}	0,050	7,0 10^{-10}
Co-58m	9,15 h	M	0,100	1,3 10^{-11}	1,5 10^{-11}	0,100	2,4 10^{-11}
		S	0,050	1,6 10^{-11}	1,7 10^{-11}	0,050	2,4 10^{-11}
Co-60	5,27 a	M	0,100	9,6 10^{-9}	7,1 10^{-9}	0,100	3,4 10^{-9}
		S	0,050	2,9 10^{-8}	1,7 10^{-8}	0,050	2,5 10^{-9}
Co-60m	0,174 h	M	0,100	1,1 10^{-12}	1,2 10^{-12}	0,100	1,7 10^{-12}
		S	0,050	1,3 10^{-12}	1,2 10^{-12}	0,050	1,7 10^{-12}
Co-61	1,65 h	M	0,100	4,8 10^{-11}	7,1 10^{-11}	0,100	7,4 10^{-11}
		S	0,050	5,1 10^{-11}	7,5 10^{-11}	0,050	7,4 10^{-11}
Co-62m	0,232 h	M	0,100	2,1 10^{-11}	3,6 10^{-11}	0,100	4,7 10^{-11}
		S	0,050	2,2 10^{-11}	3,7 10^{-11}	0,050	4,7 10^{-11}

Nuclide	*Physical half-life*	*Inhalation*				*Ingestion*	
		Type	f_1	$h(g)_{1\mu m}$	$h(g)_{5\mu m}$	f_1	$h(g)$
Nickel							
Ni-56	6,10 d	F	0,050	$5{,}1\ 10^{-10}$	$7{,}9\ 10^{-10}$	0,050	$8{,}6\ 10^{-10}$
		M	0,050	$8{,}6\ 10^{-10}$	$9{,}6\ 10^{-10}$		
Ni-57	1,50 d	F	0,050	$2{,}8\ 10^{-10}$	$5{,}0\ 10^{-10}$	0,050	$8{,}7\ 10^{-10}$
		M	0,050	$5{,}1\ 10^{-10}$	$7{,}6\ 10^{-10}$		
Ni-59	7,50 104 a	F	0,050	$1{,}8\ 10^{-10}$	$2{,}2\ 10^{-10}$	0,050	$6{,}3\ 10^{-11}$
		M	0,050	$1{,}3\ 10^{-10}$	$9{,}4\ 10^{-11}$		
Ni-63	96,0 a	F	0,050	$4{,}4\ 10^{-10}$	$5{,}2\ 10^{-10}$	0,050	$1{,}5\ 10^{-10}$
		M	0,050	$4{,}4\ 10^{-10}$	$3{,}1\ 10^{-10}$		
Ni-65	2,52 h	F	0,050	$4{,}4\ 10^{-11}$	$7{,}5\ 10^{-11}$	0,050	$1{,}8\ 10^{-10}$
		M	0,050	$8{,}7\ 10^{-11}$	$1{,}3\ 10^{-10}$		
Ni-66	2,27 d	F	0,050	$4{,}5\ 10^{-10}$	$7{,}6\ 10^{-10}$	0,050	$3{,}0\ 10^{-9}$
		M	0,050	$1{,}6\ 10^{-9}$	$1{,}9\ 10^{-9}$		
Copper							
Cu-60	0,387 h	F	0,500	$2{,}4\ 10^{-11}$	$4{,}4\ 10^{-11}$	0,500	$7{,}0\ 10^{-11}$
		M	0,500	$3{,}5\ 10^{-11}$	$6{,}0\ 10^{-11}$		
		S	0,500	$3{,}6\ 10^{-11}$	$6{,}2\ 10^{-11}$		
Cu-61	3,41 h	F	0,500	$4{,}0\ 10^{-11}$	$7{,}3\ 10^{-11}$	0,500	$1{,}2\ 10^{-10}$
		M	0,500	$7{,}6\ 10^{-11}$	$1{,}2\ 10^{-10}$		
		S	0,500	$8{,}0\ 10^{-11}$	$1{,}2\ 10^{-10}$		
Cu-64	12,7 h	F	0,500	$3{,}8\ 10^{-11}$	$6{,}8\ 10^{-11}$	0,500	$1{,}2\ 10^{-10}$
		M	0,500	$1{,}1\ 10^{-10}$	$1{,}5\ 10^{-10}$		
		S	0,500	$1{,}2\ 10^{-10}$	$1{,}5\ 10^{-10}$		
Cu-67	2,58 d	F	0,500	$1{,}1\ 10^{-10}$	$1{,}8\ 10^{-10}$	0,500	$3{,}4\ 10^{-10}$
		M	0,500	$5{,}2\ 10^{-10}$	$5{,}3\ 10^{-10}$		
		S	0,500	$5{,}8\ 10^{-10}$	$5{,}8\ 10^{-10}$		
Zinc							
Zn-62	9,26 h	S	0,500	$4{,}7\ 10^{-10}$	$6{,}6\ 10^{-10}$	0,500	$9{,}4\ 10^{-10}$
Zn-63	0,635 h	S	0,500	$3{,}8\ 10^{-11}$	$6{,}1\ 10^{-11}$	0,500	$7{,}9\ 10^{-11}$
Zn-65	244 d	S	0,500	$2{,}9\ 10^{-9}$	$2{,}8\ 10^{-9}$	0,500	$3{,}9\ 10^{-9}$
Zn-69	0,950 h	S	0,500	$2{,}8\ 10^{-11}$	$4{,}3\ 10^{-11}$	0,500	$3{,}1\ 10^{-11}$
Zn-69m	13,8 h	S	0,500	$2{,}6\ 10^{-10}$	$3{,}3\ 10^{-10}$	0,500	$3{,}3\ 10^{-10}$
Zn-71m	3,92 h	S	0,500	$1{,}6\ 10^{-10}$	$2{,}4\ 10^{-10}$	0,500	$2{,}4\ 10^{-10}$
Zn-72	1,94 d	S	0,500	$1{,}2\ 10^{-9}$	$1{,}5\ 10^{-9}$	0,500	$1{,}4\ 10^{-9}$
Gallium							
Ga-65	0,253 h	F	0,001	$1{,}2\ 10^{-11}$	$2{,}0\ 10^{-11}$	0,001	$3{,}7\ 10^{-11}$
		M	0,001	$1{,}8\ 10^{-11}$	$2{,}9\ 10^{-11}$		
Ga-66	9,40 h	F	0,001	$2{,}7\ 10^{-10}$	$4{,}7\ 10^{-10}$	0,001	$1{,}2\ 10^{-9}$
		M	0,001	$4{,}6\ 10^{-10}$	$7{,}1\ 10^{-10}$		
Ga-67	3,26 d	F	0,001	$6{,}8\ 10^{-11}$	$1{,}1\ 10^{-10}$	0,001	$1{,}9\ 10^{-10}$
		M	0,001	$2{,}3\ 10^{-10}$	$2{,}8\ 10^{-10}$		
Ga-68	1,13 h	F	0,001	$2{,}8\ 10^{-11}$	$4{,}9\ 10^{-11}$	0,001	$1{,}0\ 10^{-10}$
		M	0,001	$5{,}1\ 10^{-11}$	$8{,}1\ 10^{-11}$		
Ga-70	0,353 h	F	0,001	$9{,}3\ 10^{-12}$	$1{,}6\ 10^{-11}$	0,001	$3{,}1\ 10^{-11}$
		M	0,001	$1{,}6\ 10^{-11}$	$2{,}6\ 10^{-11}$		

Nuclide	*Physical half-life*	*Inhalation*				*Ingestion*	
		Type	f_1	$h(g)_{1\mu m}$	$h(g)_{5\mu m}$	f_1	$h(g)$
Ga-72	14,1 h	F	0,001	$3{,}1\ 10^{-10}$	$5{,}6\ 10^{-10}$	0,001	$1{,}1\ 10^{-9}$
		M	0,001	$5{,}5\ 10^{-10}$	$8{,}4\ 10^{-10}$		
Ga-73	4,91 h	F	0,001	$5{,}8\ 10^{-11}$	$1{,}0\ 10^{-10}$	0,001	$2{,}6\ 10^{-10}$
		M	0,001	$1{,}5\ 10^{-10}$	$2{,}0\ 10^{-10}$		
Germanium							
Ge-66	2,27 h	F	1,000	$5{,}7\ 10^{-11}$	$9{,}9\ 10^{-11}$	1,000	$1{,}0\ 10^{-10}$
		M	1,000	$9{,}2\ 10^{-11}$	$1{,}3\ 10^{-10}$		
Ge-67	0,312 h	F	1,000	$1{,}6\ 10^{-11}$	$2{,}8\ 10^{-11}$	1,000	$6{,}5\ 10^{-11}$
		M	1,000	$2{,}6\ 10^{-11}$	$4{,}2\ 10^{-11}$		
Ge-68	288 d	F	1,000	$5{,}4\ 10^{-10}$	$8{,}3\ 10^{-10}$	1,000	$1{,}3\ 10^{-9}$
		M	1,000	$1{,}3\ 10^{-8}$	$7{,}9\ 10^{-9}$		
Ge-69	1,63 d	F	1,000	$1{,}4\ 10^{-10}$	$2{,}5\ 10^{-10}$	1,000	$2{,}4\ 10^{-10}$
		M	1,000	$2{,}9\ 10^{-10}$	$3{,}7\ 10^{-10}$		
Ge-71	11,8 d	F	1,000	$5{,}0\ 10^{-12}$	$7{,}8\ 10^{-12}$	1,000	$1{,}2\ 10^{-11}$
		M	1,000	$1{,}0\ 10^{-11}$	$1{,}1\ 10^{-11}$		
Ge-75	1,38 h	F	1,000	$1{,}6\ 10^{-11}$	$2{,}7\ 10^{-11}$	1,000	$4{,}6\ 10^{-11}$
		M	1,000	$3{,}7\ 10^{-11}$	$5{,}4\ 10^{-11}$		
Ge-77	11,3 h	F	1,000	$1{,}5\ 10^{-10}$	$2{,}5\ 10^{-10}$	1,000	$3{,}3\ 10^{-10}$
		M	1,000	$3{,}6\ 10^{-10}$	$4{,}5\ 10^{-10}$		
Ge-78	1,45 h	F	1,000	$4{,}8\ 10^{-11}$	$8{,}1\ 10^{-11}$	1,000	$1{,}2\ 10^{-10}$
		M	1,000	$9{,}7\ 10^{-11}$	$1{,}4\ 10^{-10}$		
Arsenic							
As-69	0,253 h	M	0,500	$2{,}2\ 10^{-11}$	$3{,}5\ 10^{-11}$	0,500	$5{,}7\ 10^{-11}$
As-70	0,876 h	M	0,500	$7{,}2\ 10^{-11}$	$1{,}2\ 10^{-10}$	0,500	$1{,}3\ 10^{-10}$
As-71	2,70 d	M	0,500	$4{,}0\ 10^{-10}$	$5{,}0\ 10^{-10}$	0,500	$4{,}6\ 10^{-10}$
As-72	1,08 d	M	0,500	$9{,}2\ 10^{-10}$	$1{,}3\ 10^{-9}$	0,500	$1{,}8\ 10^{-9}$
As-73	80,3 d	M	0,500	$9{,}3\ 10^{-10}$	$6{,}5\ 10^{-10}$	0,500	$2{,}6\ 10^{-10}$
As-74	17,8 d	M	0,500	$2{,}1\ 10^{-9}$	$1{,}8\ 10^{-9}$	0,500	$1{,}3\ 10^{-9}$
As-76	1,10 d	M	0,500	$7{,}4\ 10^{-10}$	$9{,}2\ 10^{-10}$	0,500	$1{,}6\ 10^{-9}$
As-77	1,62 d	M	0,500	$3{,}8\ 10^{-10}$	$4{,}2\ 10^{-10}$	0,500	$4{,}0\ 10^{-10}$
As-78	1,51 h	M	0,500	$9{,}2\ 10^{-11}$	$1{,}4\ 10^{-10}$	0,500	$2{,}1\ 10^{-10}$
Selenium							
Se-70	0,683 h	F	0,800	$4{,}5\ 10^{-11}$	$8{,}2\ 10^{-11}$	0,800	$1{,}2\ 10^{-10}$
		M	0,800	$7{,}3\ 10^{-11}$	$1{,}2\ 10^{-10}$	0,050	$1{,}4\ 10^{-10}$
Se-73	7,15 h	F	0,800	$8{,}6\ 10^{-11}$	$1{,}5\ 10^{-10}$	0,800	$2{,}1\ 10^{-10}$
		M	0,800	$1{,}6\ 10^{-10}$	$2{,}4\ 10^{-10}$	0,050	$3{,}9\ 10^{-10}$
Se-73m	0,650 h	F	0,800	$9{,}9\ 10^{-12}$	$1{,}7\ 10^{-11}$	0,800	$2{,}8\ 10^{-11}$
		M	0,800	$1{,}8\ 10^{-11}$	$2{,}7\ 10^{-11}$	0,050	$4{,}1\ 10^{-11}$
Se-75	120 d	F	0,800	$1{,}0\ 10^{-9}$	$1{,}4\ 10^{-9}$	0,800	$2{,}6\ 10^{-9}$
		M	0,800	$1{,}4\ 10^{-9}$	$1{,}7\ 10^{-9}$	0,050	$4{,}1\ 10^{-10}$
Se-79	6,50 104 a	F	0,800	$1{,}2\ 10^{-9}$	$1{,}6\ 10^{-9}$	0,800	$2{,}9\ 10^{-9}$
		M	0,800	$2{,}9\ 10^{-9}$	$3{,}1\ 10^{-9}$	0,050	$3{,}9\ 10^{-10}$
Se-81	0,308 h	F	0,800	$8{,}6\ 10^{-12}$	$1{,}4\ 10^{-11}$	0,800	$2{,}7\ 10^{-11}$
		M	0,800	$1{,}5\ 10^{-11}$	$2{,}4\ 10^{-11}$	0,050	$2{,}7\ 10^{-11}$

Nuclide	*Physical half-life*	*Inhalation*				*Ingestion*	
		Type	f_1	$h(g)_{1\mu m}$	$h(g)_{5\mu m}$	f_1	$h(g)$
Se-81m	0,954 h	F	0,800	1,7 10^{-11}	3,0 10^{-11}	0,800	5,3 10^{-11}
		M	0,800	4,7 10^{-11}	6,8 10^{-11}	0,050	5,9 10^{-11}
Se-83	0,375 h	F	0,800	1,9 10^{-11}	3,4 10^{-11}	0,800	4,7 10^{-11}
		M	0,800	3,3 10^{-11}	5,3 10^{-11}	0,050	5,1 10^{-11}
Bromine							
Br-74	0,422 h	F	1,000	2,8 10^{-11}	5,0 10^{-11}	1,000	8,4 10^{-11}
		M	1,000	4,1 10^{-11}	6,8 10^{-11}		
Br-74m	0,691 h	F	1,000	4,2 10^{-11}	7,5 10^{-11}	1,000	1,4 10^{-10}
		M	1,000	6,5 10^{-11}	1,1 10^{-10}		
Br-75	1,63 h	F	1,000	3,1 10^{-11}	5,6 10^{-11}	1,000	7,9 10^{-11}
		M	1,000	5,5 10^{-11}	8,5 10^{-11}		
Br-76	16,2 h	F	1,000	2,6 10^{-10}	4,5 10^{-10}	1,000	4,6 10^{-10}
		M	1,000	4,2 10^{-10}	5,8 10^{-10}		
Br-77	2,33 d	F	1,000	6,7 10^{-11}	1,2 10^{-10}	1,000	9,6 10^{-11}
		M	1,000	8,7 10^{-11}	1,3 10^{-10}		
Br-80	0,290 h	F	1,000	6,3 10^{-12}	1,1 10^{-11}	1,000	3,1 10^{-11}
		M	1,000	1,0 10^{-11}	1,7 10^{-11}		
Br-80m	4,42 h	F	1,000	3,5 10^{-11}	5,8 10^{-11}	1,000	1,1 10^{-10}
		M	1,000	7,6 10^{-11}	1,0 10^{-10}		
Br-82	1,47 d	F	1,000	3,7 10^{-10}	6,4 10^{-10}	1,000	5,4 10^{-10}
		M	1,000	6,4 10^{-10}	8,8 10^{-10}		
Br-83	2,39 h	F	1,000	1,7 10^{-11}	2,9 10^{-11}	1,000	4,3 10^{-11}
		M	1,000	4,8 10^{-11}	6,7 10^{-11}		
Br-84	0,530 h	F	1,000	2,3 10^{-11}	4,0 10^{-11}	1,000	8,8 10^{-11}
		M	1,000	3,9 10^{-11}	6,2 10^{-11}		
Rubidium							
Rb-79	0,382 h	F	1,000	1,7 10^{-11}	3,0 10^{-11}	1,000	5,0 10^{-11}
Rb-81	4,58 h	F	1,000	3,7 10^{-11}	6,8 10^{-11}	1,000	5,4 10^{-11}
Rb-81m	0,533 h	F	1,000	7,3 10^{-12}	1,3 10^{-11}	1,000	9,7 10^{-12}
Rb-82m	6,20 h	F	1,000	1,2 10^{-10}	2,2 10^{-10}	1,000	1,3 10^{-10}
Rb-83	86,2 d	F	1,000	7,1 10^{-10}	1,0 10^{-9}	1,000	1,9 10^{-9}
Rb-84	32,8 d	F	1,000	1,1 10^{-9}	1,5 10^{-9}	1,000	2,8 10^{-9}
Rb-86	18,6 d	F	1,000	9,6 10^{-10}	1,3 10^{-9}	1,000	2,8 10^{-9}
Rb-87	4,70 1010 a	F	1,000	5,1 10^{-10}	7,6 10^{-10}	1,000	1,5 10^{-9}
Rb-88	0,297 h	F	1,000	1,7 10^{-11}	2,8 10^{-11}	1,000	9,0 10^{-11}
Rb-89	0,253 h	F	1,000	1,4 10^{-11}	2,5 10^{-11}	1,000	4,7 10^{-11}
Strontium							
Sr-80	1,67 h	F	0,300	7,6 10^{-11}	1,3 10^{-10}	0,300	3,4 10^{-10}
		S	0,010	1,4 10^{-10}	2,1 10^{-10}	0,010	3,5 10^{-10}
Sr-81	0,425 h	F	0,300	2,2 10^{-11}	3,9 10^{-11}	0,300	7,7 10^{-11}
		S	0,010	3,8 10^{-11}	6,1 10^{-11}	0,010	7,8 10^{-11}
Sr-82	25,0 d	F	0,300	2,2 10^{-9}	3,3 10^{-9}	0,300	6,1 10^{-9}
		S	0,010	1,0 10^{-8}	7,7 10^{-9}	0,010	6,0 10^{-9}
Sr-83	1,35 d	F	0,300	1,7 10^{-10}	3,0 10^{-10}	0,300	4,9 10^{-10}
		S	0,010	3,4 10^{-10}	4,9 10^{-10}	0,010	5,8 10^{-10}

Nuclide	Physical half-life	Inhalation				Ingestion	
		Type	f_1	$h(g)_{1\mu m}$	$h(g)_{5\mu m}$	f_1	$h(g)$
Sr-85	64,8 d	F	0,300	3,9 10^{-10}	5,6 10^{-10}	0,300	5,6 10^{-10}
		S	0,010	7,7 10^{-10}	6,4 10^{-10}	0,010	3,3 10^{-10}
Sr-85m	1,16 h	F	0,300	3,1 10^{-12}	5,6 10^{-12}	0,300	6,1 10^{-12}
		S	0,010	4,5 10^{-12}	7,4 10^{-12}	0,010	6,1 10^{-12}
Sr-87m	2,80 h	F	0,300	1,2 10^{-11}	2,2 10^{-11}	0,300	3,0 10^{-11}
		S	0,010	2,2 10^{-11}	3,5 10^{-11}	0,010	3,3 10^{-11}
Sr-89	50,5 d	F	0,300	1,0 10^{-9}	1,4 10^{-9}	0,300	2,6 10^{-9}
		S	0,010	7,5 10^{-9}	5,6 10^{-9}	0,010	2,3 10^{-9}
Sr-90	29,1 a	F	0,300	2,4 10^{-8}	3,0 10^{-8}	0,300	2,8 10^{-8}
		S	0,010	1,5 10^{-7}	7,7 10^{-8}	0,010	2,7 10^{-9}
Sr-91	9,50 h	F	0,300	1,7 10^{-10}	2,9 10^{-10}	0,300	6,5 10^{-10}
		S	0,010	4,1 10^{-10}	5,7 10^{-10}	0,010	7,6 10^{-10}
Sr-92	2,71 h	F	0,300	1,1 10^{-10}	1,8 10^{-10}	0,300	4,3 10^{-10}
		S	0,010	2,3 10^{-10}	3,4 10^{-10}	0,010	4,9 10^{-10}
Yttrium							
Y-86	14,7 h	M	1,0 10^{-4}	4,8 10^{-10}	8,0 10^{-10}	1,0 10^{-4}	9,6 10^{-10}
		S	1,0 10^{-4}	4,9 10^{-10}	8,1 10^{-10}		
Y-86m	0,800 h	M	1,0 10^{-4}	2,9 10^{-11}	4,8 10^{-11}	1,0 10^{-4}	5,6 10^{-11}
		S	1,0 10^{-4}	3,0 10^{-11}	4,9 10^{-11}		
Y-87	3,35 d	M	1,0 10^{-4}	3,8 10^{-10}	5,2 10^{-10}	1,0 10^{-4}	5,5 10^{-10}
		S	1,0 10^{-4}	4,0 10^{-10}	5,3 10^{-10}		
Y-88	107 d	M	1,0 10^{-4}	3,9 10^{-9}	3,3 10^{-9}	1,0 10^{-4}	1,3 10^{-9}
		S	1,0 10^{-4}	4,1 10^{-9}	3,0 10^{-9}		
Y-90	2,67 d	M	1,0 10^{-4}	1,4 10^{-9}	1,6 10^{-9}	1,0 10^{-4}	2,7 10^{-9}
		S	1,0 10^{-4}	1,5 10^{-9}	1,7 10^{-9}		
Y-90m	3,19 h	M	1,0 10^{-4}	9,6 10^{-11}	1,3 10^{-10}	1,0 10^{-4}	1,7 10^{-10}
		S	1,0 10^{-4}	1,0 10^{-10}	1,3 10^{-10}		
Y-91	58,5 d	M	1,0 10^{-4}	6,7 10^{-9}	5,2 10^{-9}	1,0 10^{-4}	2,4 10^{-9}
		S	1,0 10^{-4}	8,4 10^{-9}	6,1 10^{-9}		
Y-91m	0,828 h	M	1,0 10^{-4}	1,0 10^{-11}	1,4 10^{-11}	1,0 10^{-4}	1,1 10^{-11}
		S	1,0 10^{-4}	1,1 10^{-11}	1,5 10^{-11}		
Y-92	3,54 h	M	1,0 10^{-4}	1,9 10^{-10}	2,7 10^{-10}	1,0 10^{-4}	4,9 10^{-10}
		S	1,0 10^{-4}	2,0 10^{-10}	2,8 10^{-10}		
Y-93	10,1 h	M	1,0 10^{-4}	4,1 10^{-10}	5,7 10^{-10}	1,0 10^{-4}	1,2 10^{-9}
		S	1,0 10^{-4}	4,3 10^{-10}	6,0 10^{-10}		
Y-94	0,318 h	M	1,0 10^{-4}	2,8 10^{-11}	4,4 10^{-11}	1,0 10^{-4}	8,1 10^{-11}
		S	1,0 10^{-4}	2,9 10^{-11}	4,6 10^{-11}		
Y-95	0,178 h	M	1,0 10^{-4}	1,6 10^{-11}	2,5 10^{-11}	1,0 10^{-4}	4,6 10^{-11}
		S	1,0 10^{-4}	1,7 10^{-11}	2,6 10^{-11}		
Zirconium							
Zr-86	16,5 h	F	0,002	3,0 10^{-10}	5,2 10^{-10}	0,002	8,6 10^{-10}
		M	0,002	4,3 10^{-10}	6,8 10^{-10}		
		S	0,002	4,5 10^{-10}	7,0 10^{-10}		

Nuclide	*Physical half-life*	*Inhalation*				*Ingestion*	
		Type	f_1	$h(g)_{1\mu m}$	$h(g)_{5\mu m}$	f_1	$h(g)$
Zr-88	83,4 d	F	0,002	3,5 10^{-9}	4,1 10^{-9}	0,002	3,3 10^{-10}
		M	0,002	2,5 10^{-9}	1,7 10^{-9}		
		S	0,002	3,3 10^{-9}	1,8 10^{-9}		
Zr-89	3,27 d	F	0,002	3,1 10^{-10}	5,2 10^{-10}	0,002	7,9 10^{-10}
		M	0,002	5,3 10^{-10}	7,2 10^{-10}		
		S	0,002	5,5 10^{-10}	7,5 10^{-10}		
Zr-93	1,53 106 a	F	0,002	2,5 10^{-8}	2,9 10^{-8}	0,002	2,8 10^{-10}
		M	0,002	9,6 10^{-9}	6,6 10^{-9}		
		S	0,002	3,1 10^{-9}	1,7 10^{-9}		
Zr-95	64,0 d	F	0,002	2,5 10^{-9}	3,0 10^{-9}	0,002	8,8 10^{-10}
		M	0,002	4,5 10^{-9}	3,6 10^{-9}		
		S	0,002	5,5 10^{-9}	4,2 10^{-9}		
Zr-97	16,9 h	F	0,002	4,2 10^{-10}	7,4 10^{-10}	0,002	2,1 10^{-9}
		M	0,002	9,4 10^{-10}	1,3 10^{-9}		
		S	0,002	1,0 10^{-9}	1,4 10^{-9}		
Niobium							
Nb-88	0,238 h	M	0,010	2,9 10^{-11}	4,8 10^{-11}	0,010	6,3 10^{-11}
		S	0,010	3,0 10^{-11}	5,0 10^{-11}		
Nb-89	2,03 h	M	0,010	1,2 10^{-10}	1,8 10^{-10}	0,010	3,0 10^{-10}
		S	0,010	1,3 10^{-10}	1,9 10^{-10}		
Nb-89	1,10 h	M	0,010	7,1 10^{-11}	1,1 10^{-10}	0,010	1,4 10^{-10}
		S	0,010	7,4 10^{-11}	1,2 10^{-10}		
Nb-90	14,6 h	M	0,010	6,6 10^{-10}	1,0 10^{-9}	0,010	1,2 10^{-9}
		S	0,010	6,9 10^{-10}	1,1 10^{-9}		
Nb-93m	13,6 a	M	0,010	4,6 10^{-10}	2,9 10^{-10}	0,010	1,2 10^{-10}
		S	0,010	1,6 10^{-9}	8,6 10^{-10}		
Nb-94	2,03 104 a	M	0,010	1,0 10^{-8}	7,2 10^{-9}	0,010	1,7 10^{-9}
		S	0,010	4,5 10^{-8}	2,5 10^{-8}		
Nb-95	35,1 d	M	0,010	1,4 10^{-9}	1,3 10^{-9}	0,010	5,8 10^{-10}
		S	0,010	1,6 10^{-9}	1,3 10^{-9}		
Nb-95m	3,61 d	M	0,010	7,6 10^{-10}	7,7 10^{-10}	0,010	5,6 10^{-10}
		S	0,010	8,5 10^{-10}	8,5 10^{-10}		
Nb-96	23,3 h	M	0,010	6,5 10^{-10}	9,7 10^{-10}	0,010	1,1 10^{-9}
		S	0,010	6,8 10^{-9}	1,0 10^{-10}		
Nb-97	1,20 h	M	0,010	4,4 10^{-11}	6,9 10^{-11}	0,010	6,8 10^{-11}
		S	0,010	4,7 10^{-11}	7,2 10^{-11}		
Nb-98	0,858 h	M	0,010	5,9 10^{-11}	9,6 10^{-11}	0,010	1,1 10^{-10}
		S	0,010	6,1 10^{-11}	9,9 10^{-11}		
Molybdenum							
Mo-90	5,67 h	F	0,800	1,7 10^{-10}	2,9 10^{-10}	0,800	3,1 10^{-10}
		S	0,050	3,7 10^{-10}	5,6 10^{-10}	0,050	6,2 10^{-10}
Mo-93	3,50 103 a	F	0,800	1,0 10^{-9}	1,4 10^{-9}	0,800	2,6 10^{-9}
		S	0,050	2,2 10^{-9}	1,2 10^{-9}	0,050	2,0 10^{-10}
Mo-93m	6,85 h	F	0,800	1,0 10^{-10}	1,9 10^{-10}	0,800	1,6 10^{-10}
		S	0,050	1,8 10^{-10}	3,0 10^{-10}	0,050	2,8 10^{-10}

Nuclide	Physical half-life	Inhalation				Ingestion	
		Type	f_1	$h(g)_{1\mu m}$	$h(g)_{5\mu m}$	f_1	$h(g)$
Mo-99	2,75 d	F	0,800	2,3 10^{-10}	3,6 10^{-10}	0,800	7,4 10^{-10}
		S	0,050	9,7 10^{-10}	1,1 10^{-9}	0,050	1,2 10^{-9}
Mo-101	0,244 h	F	0,800	1,5 10^{-11}	2,7 10^{-11}	0,800	4,2 10^{-11}
		S	0,050	2,7 10^{-11}	4,5 10^{-11}	0,050	4,2 10^{-11}
Technetium							
Tc-93	2,75 h	F	0,800	3,4 10^{-11}	6,2 10^{-11}	0,800	4,9 10^{-11}
		M	0,800	3,6 10^{-11}	6,5 10^{-11}		
Tc-93m	0,725 h	F	0,800	1,5 10^{-11}	2,6 10^{-11}	0,800	2,4 10^{-11}
		M	0,800	1,7 10^{-11}	3,1 10^{-11}		
Tc-94	4,88 h	F	0,800	1,2 10^{-10}	2,1 10^{-10}	0,800	1,8 10^{-10}
		M	0,800	1,3 10^{-10}	2,2 10^{-10}		
Tc-94m	0,867 h	F	0,800	4,3 10^{-11}	6,9 10^{-11}	0,800	1,1 10^{-10}
		M	0,800	4,9 10^{-11}	8,0 10^{-11}		
Tc-95	20,0 h	F	0,800	1,0 10^{-10}	1,8 10^{-10}	0,800	1,6 10^{-10}
		M	0,800	1,0 10^{-10}	1,8 10^{-10}		
Tc-95m	61,0 d	F	0,800	3,1 10^{-10}	4,8 10^{-10}	0,800	6,2 10^{-10}
		M	0,800	8,7 10^{-10}	8,6 10^{-10}		
Tc-96	4,28 d	F	0,800	6,0 10^{-10}	9,8 10^{-10}	0,800	1,1 10^{-9}
		M	0,800	7,1 10^{-10}	1,0 10^{-9}		
Tc-96m	0,858 h	F	0,800	6,5 10^{-12}	1,1 10^{-11}	0,800	1,3 10^{-11}
		M	0,800	7,7 10^{-12}	1,1 10^{-11}		
Tc-97	2,60 106 a	F	0,800	4,5 10^{-11}	7,2 10^{-11}	0,800	8,3 10^{-11}
		M	0,800	2,1 10^{-10}	1,6 10^{-10}		
Tc-97m	87,0 d	F	0,800	2,8 10^{-10}	4,0 10^{-10}	0,800	6,6 10^{-10}
		M	0,800	3,1 10^{-9}	2,7 10^{-9}		
Tc-98	4,20 106 a	F	0,800	1,0 10^{-9}	1,5 10^{-9}	0,800	2,3 10^{-9}
		M	0,800	8,1 10^{-9}	6,1 10^{-9}		
Tc-99	2,13 105 a	F	0,800	2,9 10^{-10}	4,0 10^{-10}	0,800	7,8 10^{-10}
		M	0,800	3,9 10^{-9}	3,2 10^{-9}		
Tc-99m	6,02 h	F	0,800	1,2 10^{-11}	2,0 10^{-11}	0,800	2,2 10^{-11}
		M	0,800	1,9 10^{-11}	2,9 10^{-11}		
Tc-101	0,237 h	F	0,800	8,7 10^{-12}	1,5 10^{-11}	0,800	1,9 10^{-11}
		M	0,800	1,3 10^{-11}	2,1 10^{-11}		
Tc-104	0,303 h	F	0,800	2,4 10^{-11}	3,9 10^{-11}	0,800	8,1 10^{-11}
		M	0,800	3,0 10^{-11}	4,8 10^{-11}		
Ruthenium							
Ru-94	0,863 h	F	0,050	2,7 10^{-11}	4,9 10^{-11}	0,050	9,4 10^{-11}
		M	0,050	4,4 10^{-11}	7,2 10^{-11}		
		S	0,050	4,6 10^{-11}	7,4 10^{-11}		
Ru-97	2,90 d	F	0,050	6,7 10^{-11}	1,2 10^{-10}	0,050	1,5 10^{-10}
		M	0,050	1,1 10^{-10}	1,6 10^{-10}		
		S	0,050	1,1 10^{-10}	1,6 10^{-10}		
Ru-103	39,3 d	F	0,050	4,9 10^{-10}	6,8 10^{-10}	0,050	7,3 10^{-10}
		M	0,050	2,3 10^{-9}	1,9 10^{-9}		
		S	0,050	2,8 10^{-9}	2,2 10^{-9}		

Nuclide	*Physical half-life*	*Inhalation*				*Ingestion*	
		Type	f_1	$h(g)_{1\mu m}$	$h(g)_{5\mu m}$	f_1	$h(g)$
Ru-105	4,44 h	F	0,050	$7{,}1\ 10^{-11}$	$1{,}3\ 10^{-10}$	0,050	$2{,}6\ 10^{-10}$
		M	0,050	$1{,}7\ 10^{-10}$	$2{,}4\ 10^{-10}$		
		S	0,050	$1{,}8\ 10^{-10}$	$2{,}5\ 10^{-10}$		
Ru-106	1,01 a	F	0,050	$8{,}0\ 10^{-9}$	$9{,}8\ 10^{-9}$	0,050	$7{,}0\ 10^{-9}$
		M	0,050	$2{,}6\ 10^{-8}$	$1{,}7\ 10^{-8}$		
		S	0,050	$6{,}2\ 10^{-8}$	$3{,}5\ 10^{-8}$		
Rhodium							
Rh-99	16,0 d	F	0,050	$3{,}3\ 10^{-10}$	$4{,}9\ 10^{-10}$	0,050	$5{,}1\ 10^{-10}$
		M	0,050	$7{,}3\ 10^{-10}$	$8{,}2\ 10^{-10}$		
		S	0,050	$8{,}3\ 10^{-10}$	$8{,}9\ 10^{-10}$		
Rh-99m	4,70 h	F	0,050	$3{,}0\ 10^{-11}$	$5{,}7\ 10^{-11}$	0,050	$6{,}6\ 10^{-11}$
		M	0,050	$4{,}1\ 10^{-11}$	$7{,}2\ 10^{-11}$		
		S	0,050	$4{,}3\ 10^{-11}$	$7{,}3\ 10^{-11}$		
Rh-100	20,8 h	F	0,050	$2{,}8\ 10^{-10}$	$5{,}1\ 10^{-10}$	0,050	$7{,}1\ 10^{-10}$
		M	0,050	$3{,}6\ 10^{-10}$	$6{,}2\ 10^{-10}$		
		S	0,050	$3{,}7\ 10^{-10}$	$6{,}3\ 10^{-10}$		
Rh-101	3,20 a	F	0,050	$1{,}4\ 10^{-9}$	$1{,}7\ 10^{-9}$	0,050	$5{,}5\ 10^{-10}$
		M	0,050	$2{,}2\ 10^{-9}$	$1{,}7\ 10^{-9}$		
		S	0,050	$5{,}0\ 10^{-9}$	$3{,}1\ 10^{-9}$		
Rh-101m	4,34 d	F	0,050	$1{,}0\ 10^{-10}$	$1{,}7\ 10^{-10}$	0,050	$2{,}2\ 10^{-10}$
		M	0,050	$2{,}0\ 10^{-10}$	$2{,}5\ 10^{-10}$		
		S	0,050	$2{,}1\ 10^{-10}$	$2{,}7\ 10^{-10}$		
Rh-102	2,90 a	F	0,050	$7{,}3\ 10^{-9}$	$8{,}9\ 10^{-9}$	0,050	$2{,}6\ 10^{-9}$
		M	0,050	$6{,}5\ 10^{-9}$	$5{,}0\ 10^{-9}$		
		S	0,050	$1{,}6\ 10^{-8}$	$9{,}0\ 10^{-9}$		
Rh-102m	207 d	F	0,050	$1{,}5\ 10^{-9}$	$1{,}9\ 10^{-9}$	0,050	$1{,}2\ 10^{-9}$
		M	0,050	$3{,}8\ 10^{-9}$	$2{,}7\ 10^{-9}$		
		S	0,050	$6{,}7\ 10^{-9}$	$4{,}2\ 10^{-9}$		
Rh-103m	0,935 h	F	0,050	$8{,}6\ 10^{-13}$	$1{,}2\ 10^{-12}$	0,050	$3{,}8\ 10^{-12}$
		M	0,050	$2{,}3\ 10^{-12}$	$2{,}4\ 10^{-12}$		
		S	0,050	$2{,}5\ 10^{-12}$	$2{,}5\ 10^{-12}$		
Rh-105	1,47 d	F	0,050	$8{,}7\ 10^{-11}$	$1{,}5\ 10^{-10}$	0,050	$3{,}7\ 10^{-10}$
		M	0,050	$3{,}1\ 10^{-10}$	$4{,}1\ 10^{-10}$		
		S	0,050	$3{,}4\ 10^{-10}$	$4{,}4\ 10^{-10}$		
Rh-106m	2,20 h	F	0,050	$7{,}0\ 10^{-11}$	$1{,}3\ 10^{-10}$	0,050	$1{,}6\ 10^{-10}$
		M	0,050	$1{,}1\ 10^{-10}$	$1{,}8\ 10^{-10}$		
		S	0,050	$1{,}2\ 10^{-10}$	$1{,}9\ 10^{-10}$		
Rh-107	0,362 h	F	0,050	$9{,}6\ 10^{-12}$	$1{,}6\ 10^{-11}$	0,050	$2{,}4\ 10^{-11}$
		M	0,050	$1{,}7\ 10^{-11}$	$2{,}7\ 10^{-11}$		
		S	0,050	$1{,}7\ 10^{-11}$	$2{,}8\ 10^{-11}$		
Palladium							
Pd-100	3,63 d	F	0,005	$4{,}9\ 10^{-10}$	$7{,}6\ 10^{-10}$	0,005	$9{,}4\ 10^{-10}$
		M	0,005	$7{,}9\ 10^{-10}$	$9{,}5\ 10^{-10}$		
		S	0,005	$8{,}3\ 10^{-10}$	$9{,}7\ 10^{-10}$		

Nuclide	*Physical half-life*	*Inhalation*				*Ingestion*	
		Type	f_1	$h(g)_{1\mu m}$	$h(g)_{5\mu m}$	f_1	$h(g)$
Pd-101	8,27 h	F	0,005	4,2 10^{-11}	7,5 10^{-11}	0,005	9,4 10^{-11}
		M	0,005	6,2 10^{-11}	9,8 10^{-11}		
		S	0,005	6,4 10^{-11}	1,0 10^{-10}		
Pd–103	17,0 d	F	0,005	9,0 10^{-11}	1,2 10^{-10}	0,005	1,9 10^{-10}
		M	0,005	3,5 10^{-10}	3,0 10^{-10}		
		S	0,005	4,0 10^{-10}	2,9 10^{-10}		
Pd-107	6,50 106 a	F	0,005	2,6 10^{-11}	3,3 10^{-11}	0,005	3,7 10^{-11}
		M	0,005	8,0 10^{-11}	5,2 10^{-11}		
		S	0,005	5,5 10^{-10}	2,9 10^{-10}		
Pd-109	13,4 h	F	0,005	1,2 10^{-10}	2,1 10^{-10}	0,005	5,5 10^{-10}
		M	0,005	3,4 10^{-10}	4,7 10^{-10}		
		S	0,005	3,6 10^{-10}	5,0 10^{-10}		
Silver							
Ag-102	0,215 h	F	0,050	1,4 10^{-11}	2,4 10^{-11}	0,050	4,0 10^{-11}
		M	0,050	1,8 10^{-11}	3,2 10^{-11}		
		S	0,050	1,9 10^{-11}	3,2 10^{-11}		
Ag-103	1,09 h	F	0,050	1,6 10^{-11}	2,8 10^{-11}	0,050	4,3 10^{-11}
		M	0,050	2,7 10^{-11}	4,3 10^{-11}		
		S	0,050	2,8 10^{-11}	4,5 10^{-11}		
Ag-104	1,15 h	F	0,050	3,0 10^{-11}	5,7 10^{-11}	0,050	6,0 10^{-11}
		M	0,050	3,9 10^{-11}	6,9 10^{-11}		
		S	0,050	4,0 10^{-11}	7,1 10^{-11}		
Ag-104m	0,558 h	F	0,050	1,7 10^{-11}	3,1 10^{-11}	0,050	5,4 10^{-11}
		M	0,050	2,6 10^{-11}	4,4 10^{-11}		
		S	0,050	2,7 10^{-11}	4,5 10^{-11}		
Ag-105	41,0 d	F	0,050	5,4 10^{-10}	8,0 10^{-10}	0,050	4,7 10^{-10}
		M	0,050	6,9 10^{-10}	7,0 10^{-10}		
		S	0,050	7,8 10^{-10}	7,3 10^{-10}		
Ag-106	0,399 h	F	0,050	9,8 10^{-12}	1,7 10^{-11}	0,050	3,2 10^{-11}
		M	0,050	1,6 10^{-11}	2,6 10^{-11}		
		S	0,050	1,6 10^{-11}	2,7 10^{-11}		
Ag-106m	8,41 d	F	0,050	1,1 10^{-9}	1,6 10^{-9}	0,050	1,5 10^{-9}
		M	0,050	1,1 10^{-9}	1,5 10^{-9}		
		S	0,050	1,1 10^{-9}	1,4 10^{-9}		
Ag-108m	1,27 102 a	F	0,050	6,1 10^{-9}	7,3 10^{-9}	0,050	2,3 10^{-9}
		M	0,050	7,0 10^{-9}	5,2 10^{-9}		
		S	0,050	3,5 10^{-8}	1,9 10^{-8}		
Ag-110m	250 d	F	0,050	5,5 10^{-9}	6,7 10^{-9}	0,050	2,8 10^{-9}
		M	0,050	7,2 10^{-9}	5,9 10^{-9}		
		S	0,050	1,2 10^{-8}	7,3 10^{-9}		
Ag-111	7,45 d	F	0,050	4,1 10^{-10}	5,7 10^{-10}	0,050	1,3 10^{-9}
		M	0,050	1,5 10^{-9}	1,5 10^{-9}		
		S	0,050	1,7 10^{-9}	1,6 10^{-9}		

Nuclide	*Physical half-life*	*Inhalation*				*Ingestion*	
		Type	f_1	$h(g)_{1\mu m}$	$h(g)_{5\mu m}$	f_1	$h(g)$
Ag-112	3,12 h	F	0,050	8,2 10^{-11}	1,4 10^{-10}	0,050	4,3 10^{-10}
		M	0,050	1,7 10^{-10}	2,5 10^{-10}		
		S	0,050	1,8 10^{-10}	2,6 10^{-10}		
Ag-115	0,333 h	F	0,050	1,6 10^{-11}	2,6 10^{-11}	0,050	6,0 10^{-11}
		M	0,050	2,8 10^{-11}	4,3 10^{-11}		
		S	0,050	3,0 10^{-11}	4,4 10^{-11}		
Cadmium							
Cd-104	0,961 h	F	0,050	2,7 10^{-11}	5,0 10^{-11}	0,050	5,8 10^{-11}
		M	0,050	3,6 10^{-11}	6,2 10^{-11}		
		S	0,050	3,7 10^{-11}	6,3 10^{-11}		
Cd-107	6,49 h	F	0,050	2,3 10^{-11}	4,2 10^{-11}	0,050	6,2 10^{-11}
		M	0,050	8,1 10^{-11}	1,0 10^{-10}		
		S	0,050	8,7 10^{-11}	1,1 10^{-10}		
Cd-109	1,27 a	F	0,050	8,1 10^{-9}	9,6 10^{-9}	0,050	2,0 10^{-9}
		M	0,050	6,2 10^{-9}	5,1 10^{-9}		
		S	0,050	5,8 10^{-9}	4,4 10^{-9}		
Cd-113	9,30 1015 a	F	0,050	1,2 10^{-7}	1,4 10^{-7}	0,050	2,5 10^{-8}
		M	0,050	5,3 10^{-8}	4,3 10^{-8}		
		S	0,050	2,5 10^{-8}	2,1 10^{-8}		
Cd-113m	13,6 a	F	0,050	1,1 10^{-7}	1,3 10^{-7}	0,050	2,3 10^{-8}
		M	0,050	5,0 10^{-8}	4,0 10^{-8}		
		S	0,050	3,0 10^{-8}	2,4 10^{-8}		
Cd-115	2,23 d	F	0,050	3,7 10^{-10}	5,4 10^{-10}	0,050	1,4 10^{-9}
		M	0,050	9,7 10^{-10}	1,2 10^{-9}		
		S	0,050	1,1 10^{-9}	1,3 10^{-9}		
Cd-115m	44,6 d	F	0,050	5,3 10^{-9}	6,4 10^{-9}	0,050	3,3 10^{-9}
		M	0,050	5,9 10^{-9}	5,5 10^{-9}		
		S	0,050	7,3 10^{-9}	5,5 10^{-9}		
Cd-117	2,49 h	F	0,050	7,3 10^{-11}	1,3 10^{-10}	0,050	2,8 10^{-10}
		M	0,050	1,6 10^{-10}	2,4 10^{-10}		
		S	0,050	1,7 10^{-10}	2,5 10^{-10}		
Cd-117m	3,36 h	F	0,050	1,0 10^{-10}	1,9 10^{-10}	0,050	2,8 10^{-10}
		M	0,050	2,0 10^{-10}	3,1 10^{-10}		
		S	0,050	2,1 10^{-10}	3,2 10^{-10}		
Indium							
In-109	4,20 h	F	0,020	3,2 10^{-11}	5,7 10^{-11}	0,020	6,6 10^{-11}
		M	0,020	4,4 10^{-11}	7,3 10^{-11}		
In-110	4,90 h	F	0,020	1,2 10^{-10}	2,2 10^{-10}	0,020	2,4 10^{-10}
		M	0,020	1,4 10^{-10}	2,5 10^{-10}		
In-110	1,15 h	F	0,020	3,1 10^{-11}	5,5 10^{-11}	0,020	1,0 10^{-10}
		M	0,020	5,0 10^{-11}	8,1 10^{-11}		
In-111	2,83 d	F	0,020	1,3 10^{-10}	2,2 10^{-10}	0,020	2,9 10^{-10}
		M	0,020	2,3 10^{-10}	3,1 10^{-10}		
In-112	0,240 h	F	0,020	5,0 10^{-12}	8,6 10^{-12}	0,020	1,0 10^{-11}
		M	0,020	7,8 10^{-12}	1,3 10^{-11}		

Nuclide	*Physical half-life*	*Inhalation*				*Ingestion*	
		Type	f_1	$h(g)_{1\mu m}$	$h(g)_{5\mu m}$	f_1	$h(g)$
In-113m	1,66 h	F	0,020	$1,0\ 10^{-11}$	$1,9\ 10^{-11}$	0,020	$2,8\ 10^{-11}$
		M	0,020	$2,0\ 10^{-11}$	$3,2\ 10^{-11}$		
In-114m	49,5 d	F	0,020	$9,3\ 10^{-9}$	$1,1\ 10^{-8}$	0,020	$4,1\ 10^{-9}$
		M	0,020	$5,9\ 10^{-9}$	$5,9\ 10^{-9}$		
In-115	5,10 1015 a	F	0,020	$3,9\ 10^{-7}$	$4,5\ 10^{-7}$	0,020	$3,2\ 10^{-8}$
		M	0,020	$1,5\ 10^{-7}$	$1,1\ 10^{-7}$		
In-115m	4,49 h	F	0,020	$2,5\ 10^{-11}$	$4,5\ 10^{-11}$	0,020	$8,6\ 10^{-11}$
		M	0,020	$6,0\ 10^{-11}$	$8,7\ 10^{-11}$		
In-116m	0,902 h	F	0,020	$3,0\ 10^{-11}$	$5,5\ 10^{-11}$	0,020	$6,4\ 10^{-11}$
		M	0,020	$4,8\ 10^{-11}$	$8,0\ 10^{-11}$		
In-117	0,730 h	F	0,020	$1,6\ 10^{-11}$	$2,8\ 10^{-11}$	0,020	$3,1\ 10^{-11}$
		M	0,020	$3,0\ 10^{-11}$	$4,8\ 10^{-11}$		
In-117m	1,94 h	F	0,020	$3,1\ 10^{-11}$	$5,5\ 10^{-11}$	0,020	$1,2\ 10^{-10}$
		M	0,020	$7,3\ 10^{-11}$	$1,1\ 10^{-10}$		
In-119m	0,300 h	F	0,020	$1,1\ 10^{-11}$	$1,8\ 10^{-11}$	0,020	$4,7\ 10^{-11}$
		M	0,020	$1,8\ 10^{-11}$	$2,9\ 10^{-11}$		
Tin							
Sn-110	4,00 h	F	0,020	$1,1\ 10^{-10}$	$1,9\ 10^{-10}$	0,020	$3,5\ 10^{-10}$
		M	0,020	$1,6\ 10^{-10}$	$2,6\ 10^{-10}$		
Sn-111	0,588 h	F	0,020	$8,3\ 10^{-12}$	$1,5\ 10^{-11}$	0,020	$2,3\ 10^{-11}$
		M	0,020	$1,4\ 10^{-11}$	$2,2\ 10^{-11}$		
Sn-113	115 d	F	0,020	$5,4\ 10^{-10}$	$7,9\ 10^{-10}$	0,020	$7,3\ 10^{-10}$
		M	0,020	$2,5\ 10^{-9}$	$1,9\ 10^{-9}$		
Sn-117m	13,6 d	F	0,020	$2,9\ 10^{-10}$	$3,9\ 10^{-10}$	0,020	$7,1\ 10^{-10}$
		M	0,020	$2,3\ 10^{-9}$	$2,2\ 10^{-9}$		
Sn-119m	293 d	F	0,020	$2,9\ 10^{-10}$	$3,6\ 10^{-10}$	0,020	$3,4\ 10^{-10}$
		M	0,020	$2,0\ 10^{-9}$	$1,5\ 10^{-9}$		
Sn-121	1,13 d	F	0,020	$6,4\ 10^{-11}$	$1,0\ 10^{-10}$	0,020	$2,3\ 10^{-10}$
		M	0,020	$2,2\ 10^{-10}$	$2,8\ 10^{-10}$		
Sn-121m	55,0 a	F	0,020	$8,0\ 10^{-10}$	$9,7\ 10^{-10}$	0,020	$3,8\ 10^{-10}$
		M	0,020	$4,2\ 10^{-9}$	$3,3\ 10^{-9}$		
Sn-123	129 d	F	0,020	$1,2\ 10^{-9}$	$1,6\ 10^{-9}$	0,020	$2,1\ 10^{-9}$
		M	0,020	$7,7\ 10^{-9}$	$5,6\ 10^{-9}$		
Sn-123m	0,668 h	F	0,020	$1,4\ 10^{-11}$	$2,4\ 10^{-11}$	0,020	$3,8\ 10^{-11}$
		M	0,020	$2,8\ 10^{-11}$	$4,4\ 10^{-11}$		
Sn-125	9,64 d	F	0,020	$9,2\ 10^{-10}$	$1,3\ 10^{-9}$	0,020	$3,1\ 10^{-9}$
		M	0,020	$3,0\ 10^{-9}$	$2,8\ 10^{-9}$		
Sn-126	1,00 105 a	F	0,020	$1,1\ 10^{-8}$	$1,4\ 10^{-8}$	0,020	$4,7\ 10^{-9}$
		M	0,020	$2,7\ 10^{-8}$	$1,8\ 10^{-8}$		
Sn-127	2,10 h	F	0,020	$6,9\ 10^{-11}$	$1,2\ 10^{-10}$	0,020	$2,0\ 10^{-10}$
		M	0,020	$1,3\ 10^{-10}$	$2,0\ 10^{-10}$		
Sn-128	0,985 h	F	0,020	$5,4\ 10^{-11}$	$9,5\ 10^{-11}$	0,020	$1,5\ 10^{-10}$
		M	0,020	$9,6\ 10^{-11}$	$1,5\ 10^{-10}$		

Nuclide	Physical half-life	Inhalation				Ingestion	
		Type	f_1	$h(g)_{1\mu m}$	$h(g)_{5\mu m}$	f_1	$h(g)$
Antimony							
Sb-115	0,530 h	F	0,100	$9{,}2\ 10^{-12}$	$1{,}7\ 10^{-11}$	0,100	$2{,}4\ 10^{-11}$
		M	0,010	$1{,}4\ 10^{-11}$	$2{,}3\ 10^{-11}$		
Sb-116	0,263 h	F	0,100	$9{,}9\ 10^{-12}$	$1{,}8\ 10^{-11}$	0,100	$2{,}6\ 10^{-11}$
		M	0,010	$1{,}4\ 10^{-11}$	$2{,}3\ 10^{-11}$		
Sb-116m	1,00 h	F	0,100	$3{,}5\ 10^{-11}$	$6{,}4\ 10^{-11}$	0,100	$6{,}7\ 10^{-11}$
		M	0,010	$5{,}0\ 10^{-11}$	$8{,}5\ 10^{-11}$		
Sb-117	2,80 h	F	0,100	$9{,}3\ 10^{-12}$	$1{,}7\ 10^{-11}$	0,100	$1{,}8\ 10^{-11}$
		M	0,010	$1{,}7\ 10^{-11}$	$2{,}7\ 10^{-11}$		
Sb-118m	5,00 h	F	0,100	$1{,}0\ 10^{-10}$	$1{,}9\ 10^{-10}$	0,100	$2{,}1\ 10^{-10}$
		M	0,010	$1{,}3\ 10^{-10}$	$2{,}3\ 10^{-10}$		
Sb-119	1,59 d	F	0,100	$2{,}5\ 10^{-11}$	$4{,}5\ 10^{-11}$	0,100	$8{,}1\ 10^{-11}$
		M	0,010	$3{,}7\ 10^{-11}$	$5{,}9\ 10^{-11}$		
Sb-120	5,76 d	F	0,100	$5{,}9\ 10^{-10}$	$9{,}8\ 10^{-10}$	0,100	$1{,}2\ 10^{-9}$
		M	0,010	$1{,}0\ 10^{-9}$	$1{,}3\ 10^{-9}$		
Sb-120	0,265 h	F	0,100	$4{,}9\ 10^{-12}$	$8{,}5\ 10^{-12}$	0,100	$1{,}4\ 10^{-11}$
		M	0,010	$7{,}4\ 10^{-12}$	$1{,}2\ 10^{-11}$		
Sb-122	2,70 d	F	0,100	$3{,}9\ 10^{-10}$	$6{,}3\ 10^{-10}$	0,100	$1{,}7\ 10^{-9}$
		M	0,010	$1{,}0\ 10^{-9}$	$1{,}2\ 10^{-9}$		
Sb-124	60,2 d	F	0,100	$1{,}3\ 10^{-9}$	$1{,}9\ 10^{-9}$	0,100	$2{,}5\ 10^{-9}$
		M	0,010	$6{,}1\ 10^{-9}$	$4{,}7\ 10^{-9}$		
Sb-124m	0,337 h	F	0,100	$3{,}0\ 10^{-12}$	$5{,}3\ 10^{-12}$	0,100	$8{,}0\ 10^{-12}$
		M	0,010	$5{,}5\ 10^{-12}$	$8{,}3\ 10^{-12}$		
Sb-125	2,77 a	F	0,100	$1{,}4\ 10^{-9}$	$1{,}7\ 10^{-9}$	0,100	$1{,}1\ 10^{-9}$
		M	0,010	$4{,}5\ 10^{-9}$	$3{,}3\ 10^{-9}$		
Sb-126	12,4 d	F	0,100	$1{,}1\ 10^{-9}$	$1{,}7\ 10^{-9}$	0,100	$2{,}4\ 10^{-9}$
		M	0,010	$2{,}7\ 10^{-9}$	$3{,}2\ 10^{-9}$		
Sb-126m	0,317 h	F	0,100	$1{,}3\ 10^{-11}$	$2{,}3\ 10^{-11}$	0,100	$3{,}6\ 10^{-11}$
		M	0,010	$2{,}0\ 10^{-11}$	$3{,}3\ 10^{-11}$		
Sb-127	3,85 d	F	0,100	$4{,}6\ 10^{-10}$	$7{,}4\ 10^{-10}$	0,100	$1{,}7\ 10^{-9}$
		M	0,010	$1{,}6\ 10^{-9}$	$1{,}7\ 10^{-9}$		
Sb-128	9,01 h	F	0,100	$2{,}5\ 10^{-10}$	$4{,}6\ 10^{-10}$	0,100	$7{,}6\ 10^{-10}$
		M	0,010	$4{,}2\ 10^{-10}$	$6{,}7\ 10^{-10}$		
Sb-128	0,173 h	F	0,100	$1{,}1\ 10^{-11}$	$1{,}9\ 10^{-11}$	0,100	$3{,}3\ 10^{-11}$
		M	0,010	$1{,}5\ 10^{-11}$	$2{,}6\ 10^{-11}$		
Sb-129	4,32 h	F	0,100	$1{,}1\ 10^{-10}$	$2{,}0\ 10^{-10}$	0,100	$4{,}2\ 10^{-10}$
		M	0,010	$2{,}4\ 10^{-10}$	$3{,}5\ 10^{-10}$		
Sb-130	0,667 h	F	0,100	$3{,}5\ 10^{-11}$	$6{,}3\ 10^{-11}$	0,100	$9{,}1\ 10^{-11}$
		M	0,010	$5{,}4\ 10^{-11}$	$9{,}1\ 10^{-11}$		
Sb-131	0,383 h	F	0,100	$3{,}7\ 10^{-11}$	$5{,}9\ 10^{-11}$	0,100	$1{,}0\ 10^{-10}$
		M	0,010	$5{,}2\ 10^{-11}$	$8{,}3\ 10^{-11}$		
Tellurium							
Te-116	2,49 h	F	0,300	$6{,}3\ 10^{-11}$	$1{,}2\ 10^{-10}$	0,300	$1{,}7\ 10^{-10}$
		M	0,300	$1{,}1\ 10^{-10}$	$1{,}7\ 10^{-10}$		

Nuclide	*Physical half-life*	*Inhalation*				*Ingestion*	
		Type	f_1	$h(g)_{1\mu m}$	$h(g)_{5\mu m}$	f_1	$h(g)$
Te-121	17,0 d	F	0,300	$2,5\ 10^{-10}$	$3,9\ 10^{-10}$	0,300	$4,3\ 10^{-10}$
		M	0,300	$3,9\ 10^{-10}$	$4,4\ 10^{-10}$		
Te-121m	154 d	F	0,300	$1,8\ 10^{-9}$	$2,3\ 10^{-9}$	0,300	$2,3\ 10^{-9}$
		M	0,300	$4,2\ 10^{-9}$	$3,6\ 10^{-9}$		
Te-123	1,00 1013 a	F	0,300	$4,0\ 10^{-9}$	$5,0\ 10^{-9}$	0,300	$4,4\ 10^{-9}$
		M	0,300	$2,6\ 10^{-9}$	$2,8\ 10^{-9}$		
Te-123m	120 d	F	0,300	$9,7\ 10^{-10}$	$1,2\ 10^{-9}$	0,300	$1,4\ 10^{-9}$
		M	0,300	$3,9\ 10^{-9}$	$3,4\ 10^{-9}$		
Te-125m	58,0 d	F	0,300	$5,1\ 10^{-10}$	$6,7\ 10^{-10}$	0,300	$8,7\ 10^{-10}$
		M	0,300	$3,3\ 10^{-9}$	$2,9\ 10^{-9}$		
Te-127	9,35 h	F	0,300	$4,2\ 10^{-11}$	$7,2\ 10^{-11}$	0,300	$1,7\ 10^{-10}$
		M	0,300	$1,2\ 10^{-10}$	$1,8\ 10^{-10}$		
Te-127m	109 d	F	0,300	$1,6\ 10^{-9}$	$2,0\ 10^{-9}$	0,300	$2,3\ 10^{-9}$
		M	0,300	$7,2\ 10^{-9}$	$6,2\ 10^{-9}$		
Te-129	1,16 h	F	0,300	$1,7\ 10^{-11}$	$2,9\ 10^{-11}$	0,300	$6,3\ 10^{-11}$
		M	0,300	$3,8\ 10^{-11}$	$5,7\ 10^{-11}$		
Te-129m	33,6 d	F	0,300	$1,3\ 10^{-9}$	$1,8\ 10^{-9}$	0,300	$3,0\ 10^{-9}$
		M	0,300	$6,3\ 10^{-9}$	$5,4\ 10^{-9}$		
Te-131	0,417 h	F	0,300	$2,3\ 10^{-11}$	$4,6\ 10^{-11}$	0,300	$8,7\ 10^{-11}$
		M	0,300	$3,8\ 10^{-11}$	$6,1\ 10^{-11}$		
Te-131m	1,25 d	F	0,300	$8,7\ 10^{-10}$	$1,2\ 10^{-9}$	0,300	$1,9\ 10^{-9}$
		M	0,300	$1,1\ 10^{-9}$	$1,6\ 10^{-9}$		
Te-132	3,26 d	F	0,300	$1,8\ 10^{-9}$	$2,4\ 10^{-9}$	0,300	$3,7\ 10^{-9}$
		M	0,300	$2,2\ 10^{-9}$	$3,0\ 10^{-9}$		
Te-133	0,207 h	F	0,300	$2,0\ 10^{-11}$	$3,8\ 10^{-11}$	0,300	$7,2\ 10^{-11}$
		M	0,300	$2,7\ 10^{-11}$	$4,4\ 10^{-11}$		
Te-133m	0,923 h	F	0,300	$8,4\ 10^{-11}$	$1,2\ 10^{-10}$	0,300	$2,8\ 10^{-10}$
		M	0,300	$1,2\ 10^{-10}$	$1,9\ 10^{-10}$		
Te-134	0,696 h	F	0,300	$5,0\ 10^{-11}$	$8,3\ 10^{-11}$	0,300	$1,1\ 10^{-10}$
		M	0,300	$7,1\ 10^{-11}$	$1,1\ 10^{-10}$		
Iodine							
I-120	1,35 h	F	1,000	$1,0\ 10^{-10}$	$1,9\ 10^{-10}$	1,000	$3,4\ 10^{-10}$
I-120m	0,883 h	F	1,000	$8,7\ 10^{-11}$	$1,4\ 10^{-10}$	1,000	$2,1\ 10^{-10}$
I-121	2,12 h	F	1,000	$2,8\ 10^{-11}$	$3,9\ 10^{-11}$	1,000	$8,2\ 10^{-11}$
I-123	13,2 h	F	1,000	$7,6\ 10^{-11}$	$1,1\ 10^{-10}$	1,000	$2,1\ 10^{-10}$
I-124	4,18 d	F	1,000	$4,5\ 10^{-9}$	$6,3\ 10^{-9}$	1,000	$1,3\ 10^{-8}$
I-125	60,1 d	F	1,000	$5,3\ 10^{-9}$	$7,3\ 10^{-9}$	1,000	$1,5\ 10^{-8}$
I-126	13,0 d	F	1,000	$1,0\ 10^{-8}$	$1,4\ 10^{-8}$	1,000	$2,9\ 10^{-8}$
I-128	0,416 h	F	1,000	$1,4\ 10^{-11}$	$2,2\ 10^{-11}$	1,000	$4,6\ 10^{-11}$
I-129	1,57 107 a	F	1,000	$3,7\ 10^{-8}$	$5,1\ 10^{-8}$	1,000	$1,1\ 10^{-7}$
I-130	12,4 h	F	1,000	$6,9\ 10^{-10}$	$9,6\ 10^{-10}$	1,000	$2,0\ 10^{-9}$
I-131	8,04 d	F	1,000	$7,6\ 10^{-9}$	$1,1\ 10^{-8}$	1,000	$2,2\ 10^{-8}$
I-132	2,30 h	F	1,000	$9,6\ 10^{-11}$	$2,0\ 10^{-10}$	1,000	$2,9\ 10^{-10}$
I-132m	1,39 h	F	1,000	$8,1\ 10^{-11}$	$1,1\ 10^{-10}$	1,000	$2,2\ 10^{-10}$
I-133	20,8 h	F	1,000	$1,5\ 10^{-9}$	$2,1\ 10^{-9}$	1,000	$4,3\ 10^{-9}$

Nuclide	Physical half-life	Inhalation				Ingestion	
		Type	f_1	$h(g)_{1\mu m}$	$h(g)_{5\mu m}$	f_1	$h(g)$
I-134	0,876 h	F	1,000	4,8 10^{-11}	7,9 10^{-11}	1,000	1,1 10^{-10}
I-135	6,61 h	F	1,000	3,3 10^{-10}	4,6 10^{-10}	1,000	9,3 10^{-10}
Caesium							
Cs-125	0,750 h	F	1,000	1,3 10^{-11}	2,3 10^{-11}	1,000	3,5 10^{-11}
Cs-127	6,25 h	F	1,000	2,2 10^{-11}	4,0 10^{-11}	1,000	2,4 10^{-11}
Cs-129	1,34 d	F	1,000	4,5 10^{-11}	8,1 10^{-11}	1,000	6,0 10^{-11}
Cs-130	0,498 h	F	1,000	8,4 10^{-12}	1,5 10^{-11}	1,000	2,8 10^{-11}
Cs-131	9,69 d	F	1,000	2,8 10^{-11}	4,5 10^{-11}	1,000	5,8 10^{-11}
Cs-132	6,48 d	F	1,000	2,4 10^{-10}	3,8 10^{-10}	1,000	5,0 10^{-10}
Cs-134	2,06 a	F	1,000	6,8 10^{-9}	9,6 10^{-9}	1,000	1,9 10^{-8}
Cs-134m	2,90 h	F	1,000	1,5 10^{-11}	2,6 10^{-11}	1,000	2,0 10^{-11}
Cs-135	2,30 106 a	F	1,000	7,1 10^{-10}	9,9 10^{-10}	1,000	2,0 10^{-9}
Cs-135m	0,883 h	F	1,000	1,3 10^{-11}	2,4 10^{-11}	1,000	1,9 10^{-11}
Cs-136	13,1 d	F	1,000	1,3 10^{-9}	1,9 10^{-9}	1,000	3,0 10^{-9}
Cs-137	30,0 a	F	1,000	4,8 10^{-9}	6,7 10^{-9}	1,000	1,3 10^{-8}
Cs-138	0,536 h	F	1,000	2,6 10^{-11}	4,6 10^{-11}	1,000	9,2 10^{-11}
Barium							
Ba-126	1,61 h	F	0,100	7,8 10^{-11}	1,2 10^{-10}	0,100	2,6 10^{-10}
Ba-128	2,43 h	F	0,100	8,0 10^{-10}	1,3 10^{-9}	0,100	2,7 10^{-9}
Ba-131	11,8 d	F	0,100	2,3 10^{-10}	3,5 10^{-10}	0,100	4,5 10^{-10}
Ba-131m	0,243 h	F	0,100	4,1 10^{-12}	6,4 10^{-12}	0,100	4,9 10^{-12}
Ba-133	10,7 a	F	0,100	1,5 10^{-9}	1,8 10^{-9}	0,100	1,0 10^{-9}
Ba-133m	1,62 d	F	0,100	1,9 10^{-10}	2,8 10^{-10}	0,100	5,5 10^{-10}
Ba-135m	1,20 d	F	0,100	1,5 10^{-10}	2,3 10^{-10}	0,100	4,5 10^{-10}
Ba-139	1,38 h	F	0,100	3,5 10^{-11}	5,5 10^{-11}	0,100	1,2 10^{-10}
Ba-140	12,7 d	F	0,100	1,0 10^{-9}	1,6 10^{-9}	0,100	2,5 10^{-9}
Ba-141	0,305 h	F	0,100	2,2 10^{-11}	3,5 10^{-11}	0,100	7,0 10^{-11}
Ba-142	0,177 h	F	0,100	1,6 10^{-11}	2,7 10^{-11}	0,100	3,5 10^{-11}
Lanthanum							
La-131	0,983 h	F	5,0$10^{-4}$	1,4 10^{-11}	2,4 10^{-11}	5,0$10^{-4}$	3,5 10^{-11}
		M	5,0$10^{-4}$	2,3 10^{-11}	3,6 10^{-11}		
La-132	4,80 h	F	5,0$10^{-4}$	1,1 10^{-10}	2,0 10^{-10}	5,0$10^{-4}$	3,9 10^{-10}
		M	5,0$10^{-4}$	1,7 10^{-10}	2,8 10^{-10}		
La-135	19,5 h	F	5,0$10^{-4}$	1,1 10^{-11}	2,0 10^{-11}	5,0$10^{-4}$	3,0 10^{-11}
		M	5,0$10^{-4}$	1,5 10^{-11}	2,5 10^{-11}		
La-137	6,00 104 a	F	5,0$10^{-4}$	8,6 10^{-9}	1,0 10^{-8}	5,0$10^{-4}$	8,1 10^{-11}
		M	5,0$10^{-4}$	3,4 10^{-9}	2,3 10^{-9}		
La-138	1,35 1011 a	F	5,0$10^{-4}$	1,5 10^{-7}	1,8 10^{-7}	5,0$10^{-4}$	1,1 10^{-9}
		M	5,0$10^{-4}$	6,1 10^{-8}	4,2 10^{-8}		
La-140	1,68 d	F	5,0$10^{-4}$	6,0 10^{-10}	1,0 10^{-9}	5,0$10^{-4}$	2,0 10^{-9}
		M	5,0$10^{-4}$	1,1 10^{-9}	1,5 10^{-9}		
La-141	3,93 h	F	5,0$10^{-4}$	6,7 10^{-11}	1,1 10^{-10}	5,0$10^{-4}$	3,6 10^{-10}
		M	5,0$10^{-4}$	1,5 10^{-10}	2,2 10^{-10}		
La-142	1,54 h	F	5,0$10^{-4}$	5,6 10^{-11}	1,0 10^{-10}	5,0$10^{-4}$	1,8 10^{-10}
		M	5,0$10^{-4}$	9,3 10^{-11}	1,5 10^{-10}		

Nuclide	*Physical half-life*	*Inhalation*				*Ingestion*	
		Type	f_1	$h(g)_{1\mu m}$	$h(g)_{5\mu m}$	f_1	$h(g)$
La-143	0,237 h	F	5,010^{-4}	1,2 10^{-11}	2,0 10^{-11}	5,010^{-4}	5,6 10^{-11}
		M	5,010^{-4}	2,2 10^{-11}	3,3 10^{-11}		
Cerium							
Ce-134	3,00 d	M	5,010^{-4}	1,3 10^{-9}	1,5 10^{-9}	5,010^{-4}	2,5 10^{-9}
		S	5,010^{-4}	1,3 10^{-9}	1,6 10^{-9}		
Ce-135	17,6 h	M	5,010^{-4}	4,9 10^{-10}	7,3 10^{-10}	5,010^{-4}	7,9 10^{-10}
		S	5,010^{-4}	5,1 10^{-10}	7,6 10^{-10}		
Ce-137	9,00 h	M	5,010^{-4}	1,0 10^{-11}	1,8 10^{-11}	5,010^{-4}	2,5 10^{-11}
		S	5,010^{-4}	1,1 10^{-11}	1,9 10^{-11}		
Ce-137m	1,43 d	M	5,010^{-4}	4,0 10^{-10}	5,5 10^{-10}	5,010^{-4}	5,4 10^{-10}
		S	5,010^{-4}	4,3 10^{-10}	5,9 10^{-10}		
Ce-139	138 d	M	5,010^{-4}	1,6 10^{-9}	1,3 10^{-9}	5,010^{-4}	2,6 10^{-10}
		S	5,010^{-4}	1,8 10^{-9}	1,4 10^{-9}		
Ce-141	32,5 d	M	5,010^{-4}	3,1 10^{-9}	2,7 10^{-9}	5,010^{-4}	7,1 10^{-10}
		S	5,010^{-4}	3,6 10^{-9}	3,1 10^{-9}		
Ce-143	1,38 d	M	5,010^{-4}	7,4 10^{-10}	9,5 10^{-10}	5,010^{-4}	1,1 10^{-9}
		S	5,010^{-4}	8,1 10^{-10}	1,0 10^{-9}		
Ce-144	284 d	M	5,010^{-4}	3,4 10^{-8}	2,3 10^{-8}	5,010^{-4}	5,2 10^{-9}
		S	5,010^{-4}	4,9 10^{-8}	2,9 10^{-8}		
Praseodymium							
Pr-136	0,218 h	M	5,010^{-4}	1,4 10^{-11}	2,4 10^{-11}	5,010^{-4}	3,3 10^{-11}
		S	5,010^{-4}	1,5 10^{-11}	2,5 10^{-11}		
Pr-137	1,28 h	M	5,010^{-4}	2,1 10^{-11}	3,4 10^{-11}	5,010^{-4}	4,0 10^{-11}
		S	5,010^{-4}	2,2 10^{-11}	3,5 10^{-11}		
Pr-138m	2,10 h	M	5,010^{-4}	7,6 10^{-11}	1,3 10^{-10}	5,010^{-4}	1,3 10^{-10}
		S	5,010^{-4}	7,9 10^{-11}	1,3 10^{-10}		
Pr-139	4,51 h	M	5,010^{-4}	1,9 10^{-11}	2,9 10^{-11}	5,010^{-4}	3,1 10^{-11}
		S	5,010^{-4}	2,0 10^{-11}	3,0 10^{-11}		
Pr-142	19,1 h	M	5,010^{-4}	5,3 10^{-10}	7,0 10^{-10}	5,010^{-4}	1,3 10^{-9}
		S	5,010^{-4}	5,6 10^{-10}	7,4 10^{-10}		
Pr-142m	0,243 h	M	5,010^{-4}	6,7 10^{-12}	8,9 10^{-12}	5,010^{-4}	1,7 10^{-11}
		S	5,010^{-4}	7,1 10^{-12}	9,4 10^{-12}		
Pr-143	13,6 d	M	5,010^{-4}	2,1 10^{-9}	1,9 10^{-9}	5,010^{-4}	1,2 10^{-9}
		S	5,010^{-4}	2,3 10^{-9}	2,2 10^{-9}		
Pr-144	0,288 h	M	5,010^{-4}	1,8 10^{-11}	2,9 10^{-11}	5,010^{-4}	5,0 10^{-11}
		S	5,010^{-4}	1,9 10^{-11}	3,0 10^{-11}		
Pr-145	5,98 h	M	5,010^{-4}	1,6 10^{-10}	2,5 10^{-10}	5,010^{-4}	3,9 10^{-10}
		S	5,010^{-4}	1,7 10^{-10}	2,6 10^{-10}		
Pr-147	0,227 h	M	5,010^{-4}	1,8 10^{-11}	2,9 10^{-11}	5,010^{-4}	3,3 10^{-11}
		S	5,010^{-4}	1,9 10^{-11}	3,0 10^{-11}		
Neodymium							
Nd-136	0,844 h	M	5,010^{-4}	5,3 10^{-11}	8,5 10^{-11}	5,010^{-4}	9,9 10^{-11}
		S	5,010^{-4}	5,6 10^{-11}	8,9 10^{-11}		
Nd-138	5,04 h	M	5,010^{-4}	2,4 10^{-10}	3,7 10^{-10}	5,010^{-4}	6,4 10^{-10}
		S	5,010^{-4}	2,6 10^{-10}	3,8 10^{-10}		

Nuclide	*Physical half-life*	*Inhalation*				*Ingestion*	
		Type	f_1	$h(g)_{1\mu m}$	$h(g)_{5\mu m}$	f_1	$h(g)$
Nd-139	0,495 h	M	$5,010^{-4}$	1,0 10^{-11}	1,7 10^{-11}	$5,010^{-4}$	2,0 10^{-11}
		S	$5,010^{-4}$	1,1 10^{-11}	1,7 10^{-11}		
Nd-139m	5,50 h	M	$5,010^{-4}$	1,5 10^{-10}	2,5 10^{-10}	$5,010^{-4}$	2,5 10^{-10}
		S	$5,010^{-4}$	1,6 10^{-10}	2,5 10^{-10}		
Nd-141	2,49 h	M	$5,010^{-4}$	5,1 10^{-12}	8,5 10^{-12}	$5,010^{-4}$	8,3 10^{-12}
		S	$5,010^{-4}$	5,3 10^{-12}	8,8 10^{-12}		
Nd-147	11,0 d	M	$5,010^{-4}$	2,0 10^{-9}	1,9 10^{-9}	$5,010^{-4}$	1,1 10^{-9}
		S	$5,010^{-4}$	2,3 10^{-9}	2,1 10^{-9}		
Nd-149	1,73 h	M	$5,010^{-4}$	8,5 10^{-11}	1,2 10^{-10}	$5,010^{-4}$	1,2 10^{-10}
		S	$5,010^{-4}$	9,0 10^{-11}	1,3 10^{-10}		
Nd-151	0,207 h	M	$5,010^{-4}$	1,7 10^{-11}	2,8 10^{-11}	$5,010^{-4}$	3,0 10^{-11}
		S	$5,010^{-4}$	1,8 10^{-11}	2,9 10^{-11}		
Promethium							
Pm-141	0,348 h	M	$5,010^{-4}$	1,5 10^{-11}	2,4 10^{-11}	$5,010^{-4}$	3,6 10^{-11}
		S	$5,010^{-4}$	1,6 10^{-11}	2,5 10^{-11}		
Pm-143	265 d	M	$5,010^{-4}$	1,4 10^{-9}	9,6 10^{-10}	$5,010^{-4}$	2,3 10^{-10}
		S	$5,010^{-4}$	1,3 10^{-9}	8,3 10^{-10}		
Pm-144	363 d	M	$5,010^{-4}$	7,8 10^{-9}	5,4 10^{-9}	$5,010^{-4}$	9,7 10^{-10}
		S	$5,010^{-4}$	7,0 10^{-9}	3,9 10^{-9}		
Pm-145	17,7 a	M	$5,010^{-4}$	3,4 10^{-9}	2,4 10^{-9}	$5,010^{-4}$	1,1 10^{-10}
		S	$5,010^{-4}$	2,1 10^{-9}	1,2 10^{-9}		
Pm-146	5,53 a	M	$5,010^{-4}$	1,9 10^{-8}	1,3 10^{-8}	$5,010^{-4}$	9,0 10^{-10}
		S	$5,010^{-4}$	1,6 10^{-8}	9,0 10^{-9}		
Pm-147	2,62 a	M	$5,010^{-4}$	4,7 10^{-9}	3,5 10^{-9}	$5,010^{-4}$	2,6 10^{-10}
		S	$5,010^{-4}$	4,6 10^{-9}	3,2 10^{-9}		
Pm-148	5,37 d	M	$5,010^{-4}$	2,0 10^{-9}	2,1 10^{-9}	$5,010^{-4}$	2,7 10^{-9}
		S	$5,010^{-4}$	2,1 10^{-9}	2,2 10^{-9}		
Pm-148m	41,3 d	M	$5,010^{-4}$	4,9 10^{-9}	4,1 10^{-9}	$5,010^{-4}$	1,8 10^{-9}
		S	$5,010^{-4}$	5,4 10^{-9}	4,3 10^{-9}		
Pm-149	2,21 d	M	$5,010^{-4}$	6,6 10^{-10}	7,6 10^{-10}	$5,010^{-4}$	9,9 10^{-10}
		S	$5,010^{-4}$	7,2 10^{-10}	8,2 10^{-10}		
Pm-150	2,68 h	M	$5,010^{-4}$	1,3 10^{-10}	2,0 10^{-10}	$5,010^{-4}$	2,6 10^{-10}
		S	$5,010^{-4}$	1,4 10^{-10}	2,1 10^{-10}		
Pm-151	1,18 d	M	$5,010^{-4}$	4,2 10^{-10}	6,1 10^{-10}	$5,010^{-4}$	7,3 10^{-10}
		S	$5,010^{-4}$	4,5 10^{-10}	6,4 10^{-10}		
Samarium							
Sm-141	0,170 h	M	$5,010^{-4}$	1,6 10^{-11}	2,7 10^{-11}	$5,010^{-4}$	3,9 10^{-11}
Sm-141m	0,377 h	M	$5,010^{-4}$	3,4 10^{-11}	5,6 10^{-11}	$5,010^{-4}$	6,5 10^{-11}
Sm-142	1,21 h	M	$5,010^{-4}$	7,4 10^{-11}	1,1 10^{-10}	$5,010^{-4}$	1,9 10^{-10}
Sm-145	340 d	M	$5,010^{-4}$	1,5 10^{-9}	1,1 10^{-9}	$5,010^{-4}$	2,1 10^{-10}
Sm-146	1,03 108 a	M	$5,010^{-4}$	9,9 10^{-6}	6,7 10^{-6}	$5,010^{-4}$	5,4 10^{-8}
Sm-147	1,06 1011 a	M	$5,010^{-4}$	8,9 10^{-6}	6,1 10^{-6}	$5,010^{-4}$	4,9 10^{-8}
Sm-151	90,0 a	M	$5,010^{-4}$	3,7 10^{-9}	2,6 10^{-9}	$5,010^{-4}$	9,8 10^{-11}
Sm-153	1,95 d	M	$5,010^{-4}$	6,1 10^{-10}	6,8 10^{-10}	$5,010^{-4}$	7,4 10^{-10}
Sm-155	0,368 h	M	$5,010^{-4}$	1,7 10^{-11}	2,8 10^{-11}	$5,010^{-4}$	2,9 10^{-11}

Nuclide	*Physical half-life*	*Inhalation*				*Ingestion*	
		Type	f_1	$h(g)_{1\mu m}$	$h(g)_{5\mu m}$	f_1	$h(g)$
Sm-156	9,40 h	M	$5,010^{-4}$	$2,1\ 10^{-10}$	$2,8\ 10^{-10}$	$5,010^{-4}$	$2,5\ 10^{-10}$
Europium							
Eu-145	5,94 d	M	$5,010^{-4}$	$5,6\ 10^{-10}$	$7,3\ 10^{-10}$	$5,010^{-4}$	$7,5\ 10^{-10}$
Eu-146	4,61 d	M	$5,010^{-4}$	$8,2\ 10^{-10}$	$1,2\ 10^{-9}$	$5,010^{-4}$	$1,3\ 10^{-9}$
Eu-147	24,0 d	M	$5,010^{-4}$	$1,0\ 10^{-9}$	$1,0\ 10^{-9}$	$5,010^{-4}$	$4,4\ 10^{-10}$
Eu-148	54,5 d	M	$5,010^{-4}$	$2,7\ 10^{-9}$	$2,3\ 10^{-9}$	$5,010^{-4}$	$1,3\ 10^{-9}$
Eu-149	93,1 d	M	$5,010^{-4}$	$2,7\ 10^{-10}$	$2,3\ 10^{-10}$	$5,010^{-4}$	$1,0\ 10^{-10}$
Eu-150	34,2 a	M	$5,010^{-4}$	$5,0\ 10^{-8}$	$3,4\ 10^{-8}$	$5,010^{-4}$	$1,3\ 10^{-9}$
Eu-150	12,6 h	M	$5,010^{-4}$	$1,9\ 10^{-10}$	$2,8\ 10^{-10}$	$5,010^{-4}$	$3,8\ 10^{-10}$
Eu-152	13,3 a	M	$5,010^{-4}$	$3,9\ 10^{-8}$	$2,7\ 10^{-8}$	$5,010^{-4}$	$1,4\ 10^{-9}$
Eu-152m	9,32 h	M	$5,010^{-4}$	$2,2\ 10^{-10}$	$3,2\ 10^{-10}$	$5,010^{-4}$	$5,0\ 10^{-10}$
Eu-154	8,80 a	M	$5,010^{-4}$	$5,0\ 10^{-8}$	$3,5\ 10^{-8}$	$5,010^{-4}$	$2,0\ 10^{-9}$
Eu-155	4,96 a	M	$5,010^{-4}$	$6,5\ 10^{-9}$	$4,7\ 10^{-9}$	$5,010^{-4}$	$3,2\ 10^{-10}$
Eu-156	15,2 d	M	$5,010^{-4}$	$3,3\ 10^{-9}$	$3,0\ 10^{-9}$	$5,010^{-4}$	$2,2\ 10^{-9}$
Eu-157	15,1 h	M	$5,010^{-4}$	$3,2\ 10^{-10}$	$4,4\ 10^{-10}$	$5,010^{-4}$	$6,0\ 10^{-10}$
Eu-158	0,765 h	M	$5,010^{-4}$	$4,8\ 10^{-11}$	$7,5\ 10^{-11}$	$5,010^{-4}$	$9,4\ 10^{-11}$
Gadolinium							
Gd-145	0,382 h	F	$5,010^{-4}$	$1,5\ 10^{-11}$	$2,6\ 10^{-11}$	$5,010^{-4}$	$4,4\ 10^{-11}$
		M	$5,010^{-4}$	$2,1\ 10^{-11}$	$3,5\ 10^{-11}$		
Gd-146	48,3 d	F	$5,010^{-4}$	$4,4\ 10^{-9}$	$5,2\ 10^{-9}$	$5,010^{-4}$	$9,6\ 10^{-10}$
		M	$5,010^{-4}$	$6,0\ 10^{-9}$	$4,6\ 10^{-9}$		
Gd-147	1,59 d	F	$5,010^{-4}$	$2,7\ 10^{-10}$	$4,5\ 10^{-10}$	$5,010^{-4}$	$6,1\ 10^{-10}$
		M	$5,010^{-4}$	$4,1\ 10^{-10}$	$5,9\ 10^{-10}$		
Gd-148	93,0 a	F	$5,010^{-4}$	$2,5\ 10^{-5}$	$3,0\ 10^{-5}$	$5,010^{-4}$	$5,5\ 10^{-8}$
		M	$5,010^{-4}$	$1,1\ 10^{-5}$	$7,2\ 10^{-6}$		
Gd-149	9,40 d	F	$5,010^{-4}$	$2,6\ 10^{-10}$	$4,5\ 10^{-10}$	$5,010^{-4}$	$4,5\ 10^{-10}$
		M	$5,010^{-4}$	$7,0\ 10^{-10}$	$7,9\ 10^{-10}$		
Gd-151	120 d	F	$5,010^{-4}$	$7,8\ 10^{-10}$	$9,3\ 10^{-10}$	$5,010^{-4}$	$2,0\ 10^{-10}$
		M	$5,010^{-4}$	$8,1\ 10^{-10}$	$6,5\ 10^{-10}$		
Gd-152	1,08 1014 a	F	$5,010^{-4}$	$1,9\ 10^{-5}$	$2,2\ 10^{-5}$	$5,010^{-4}$	$4,1\ 10^{-8}$
		M	$5,010^{-4}$	$7,4\ 10^{-6}$	$5,0\ 10^{-6}$		
Gd-153	242 d	F	$5,010^{-4}$	$2,1\ 10^{-9}$	$2,5\ 10^{-9}$	$5,010^{-4}$	$2,7\ 10^{-10}$
		M	$5,010^{-4}$	$1,9\ 10^{-9}$	$1,4\ 10^{-9}$		
Gd-159	18,6 h	F	$5,010^{-4}$	$1,1\ 10^{-10}$	$1,8\ 10^{-10}$	$5,010^{-4}$	$4,9\ 10^{-10}$
		M	$5,010^{-4}$	$2,7\ 10^{-10}$	$3,9\ 10^{-10}$		
Terbium							
Tb-147	1,65 h	M	$5,010^{-4}$	$7,9\ 10^{-11}$	$1,2\ 10^{-10}$	$5,010^{-4}$	$1,6\ 10^{-10}$
Tb-149	4,15 h	M	$5,010^{-4}$	$4,3\ 10^{-9}$	$3,1\ 10^{-9}$	$5,010^{-4}$	$2,5\ 10^{-10}$
Tb-150	3,27 h	M	$5,010^{-4}$	$1,1\ 10^{-10}$	$1,8\ 10^{-10}$	$5,010^{-4}$	$2,5\ 10^{-10}$
Tb-151	17,6 h	M	$5,010^{-4}$	$2,3\ 10^{-10}$	$3,3\ 10^{-10}$	$5,010^{-4}$	$3,4\ 10^{-10}$
Tb-153	2,34 d	M	$5,010^{-4}$	$2,0\ 10^{-10}$	$2,4\ 10^{-10}$	$5,010^{-4}$	$2,5\ 10^{-10}$
Tb-154	21,4 h	M	$5,010^{-4}$	$3,8\ 10^{-10}$	$6,0\ 10^{-10}$	$5,010^{-4}$	$6,5\ 10^{-10}$
Tb-155	5,32 d	M	$5,010^{-4}$	$2,1\ 10^{-10}$	$2,5\ 10^{-10}$	$5,010^{-4}$	$2,1\ 10^{-10}$
Tb-156	5,34 d	M	$5,010^{-4}$	$1,2\ 10^{-9}$	$1,4\ 10^{-9}$	$5,010^{-4}$	$1,2\ 10^{-9}$
Tb-156m	1,02 d	M	$5,010^{-4}$	$2,0\ 10^{-10}$	$2,3\ 10^{-10}$	$5,010^{-4}$	$1,7\ 10^{-10}$

Nuclide	*Physical half-life*	*Inhalation*				*Ingestion*	
		Type	f_1	$h(g)_{1\mu m}$	$h(g)_{5\mu m}$	f_1	$h(g)$
Tb-156m	5,00 h	M	5,010^{-4}	9,2 10^{-11}	1,3 10^{-10}	5,010^{-4}	8,1 10^{-11}
Tb-157	1,50 102 a	M	5,010^{-4}	1,1 10^{-9}	7,9 10^{-10}	5,010^{-4}	3,4 10^{-11}
Tb-158	1,50 102 a	M	5,010^{-4}	4,3 10^{-8}	3,0 10^{-8}	5,010^{-4}	1,1 10^{-9}
Tb-160	72,3 d	M	5,010^{-4}	6,6 10^{-9}	5,4 10^{-9}	5,010^{-4}	1,6 10^{-9}
Tb-161	6,91 d	M	5,010^{-4}	1,2 10^{-9}	1,2 10^{-9}	5,010^{-4}	7,2 10^{-10}
Dysprosium							
Dy-155	10,0 h	M	5,010^{-4}	8,0 10^{-11}	1,2 10^{-10}	5,010^{-4}	1,3 10^{-10}
Dy-157	8,10 h	M	5,010^{-4}	3,2 10^{-11}	5,5 10^{-11}	5,010^{-4}	6,1 10^{-11}
Dy-159	144 d	M	5,010^{-4}	3,5 10^{-10}	2,5 10^{-10}	5,010^{-4}	1,0 10^{-10}
Dy-165	2,33 h	M	5,010^{-4}	6,1 10^{-11}	8,7 10^{-11}	5,010^{-4}	1,1 10^{-10}
Dy-166	3,40 d	M	5,010^{-4}	1,8 10^{-9}	1,8 10^{-9}	5,010^{-4}	1,6 10^{-9}
Holmium							
Ho-155	0,800 h	M	5,010^{-4}	2,0 10^{-11}	3,2 10^{-11}	5,010^{-4}	3,7 10^{-11}
Ho-157	0,210 h	M	5,010^{-4}	4,5 10^{-12}	7,6 10^{-12}	5,010^{-4}	6,5 10^{-12}
Ho-159	0,550 h	M	5,010^{-4}	6,3 10^{-12}	1,0 10^{-11}	5,010^{-4}	7,9 10^{-12}
Ho-161	2,50 h	M	5,010^{-4}	6,3 10^{-12}	1,0 10^{-11}	5,010^{-4}	1,3 10^{-11}
Ho-162	0,250 h	M	5,010^{-4}	2,9 10^{-12}	4,5 10^{-12}	5,010^{-4}	3,3 10^{-12}
Ho-162m	1,13 h	M	5,010^{-4}	2,2 10^{-11}	3,3 10^{-11}	5,010^{-4}	2,6 10^{-11}
Ho-164	0,483 h	M	5,010^{-4}	8,6 10^{-12}	1,3 10^{-11}	5,010^{-4}	9,5 10^{-12}
Ho-164m	0,625 h	M	5,010^{-4}	1,2 10^{-11}	1,6 10^{-11}	5,010^{-4}	1,6 10^{-11}
Ho-166	1,12 d	M	5,010^{-4}	6,6 10^{-10}	8,3 10^{-10}	5,010^{-4}	1,4 10^{-9}
Ho-166m	1,20 103 a	M	5,010^{-4}	1,1 10^{-7}	7,8 10^{-8}	5,010^{-4}	2,0 10^{-9}
Ho-167	3,10 h	M	5,010^{-4}	7,1 10^{-11}	1,0 10^{-10}	5,010^{-4}	8,3 10^{-11}
Erbium							
Er-161	3,24 h	M	5,010^{-4}	5,1 10^{-11}	8,5 10^{-11}	5,010^{-4}	8,0 10^{-11}
Er-165	10,4 h	M	5,010^{-4}	8,3 10^{-12}	1,4 10^{-11}	5,010^{-4}	1,9 10^{-11}
Er-169	9,30 d	M	5,010^{-4}	9,8 10^{-10}	9,2 10^{-10}	5,010^{-4}	3,7 10^{-10}
Er-171	7,52 h	M	5,010^{-4}	2,2 10^{-10}	3,0 10^{-10}	5,010^{-4}	3,6 10^{-10}
Er-172	2,05 d	M	5,010^{-4}	1,1 10^{-9}	1,2 10^{-9}	5,010^{-4}	1,0 10^{-9}
Thulium							
Tm-162	0,362 h	M	5,010^{-4}	1,6 10^{-11}	2,7 10^{-11}	5,010^{-4}	2,9 10^{-11}
Tm-166	7,70 h	M	5,010^{-4}	1,8 10^{-10}	2,8 10^{-10}	5,010^{-4}	2,8 10^{-10}
Tm-167	9,24 d	M	5,010^{-4}	1,1 10^{-9}	1,0 10^{-9}	5,010^{-4}	5,6 10^{-10}
Tm-170	129 d	M	5,010^{-4}	6,6 10^{-9}	5,2 10^{-9}	5,010^{-4}	1,3 10^{-9}
Tm-171	1,92 a	M	5,010^{-4}	1,3 10^{-9}	9,1 10^{-10}	5,010^{-4}	1,1 10^{-10}
Tm-172	2,65 d	M	5,010^{-4}	1,1 10^{-9}	1,4 10^{-9}	5,010^{-4}	1,7 10^{-9}
Tm-173	8,24 h	M	5,010^{-4}	1,8 10^{-10}	2,6 10^{-10}	5,010^{-4}	3,1 10^{-10}
Tm-175	0,253 h	M	5,010^{-4}	1,9 10^{-11}	3,1 10^{-11}	5,010^{-4}	2,7 10^{-11}
Ytterbium							
Yb-162	0,315 h	M	5,010^{-4}	1,4 10^{-11}	2,2 10^{-11}	5,010^{-4}	2,3 10^{-11}
		S	5,010^{-4}	1,4 10^{-11}	2,3 10^{-11}		
Yb-166	2,36 d	M	5,010^{-4}	7,2 10^{-10}	9,1 10^{-10}	5,010^{-4}	9,5 10^{-10}
		S	5,010^{-4}	7,6 10^{-10}	9,5 10^{-10}		
Yb-167	0,292 h	M	5,010^{-4}	6,5 10^{-12}	9,0 10^{-12}	5,010^{-4}	6,7 10^{-12}
		S	5,010^{-4}	6,9 10^{-12}	9,5 10^{-12}		

Nuclide	*Physical half-life*	*Inhalation*				*Ingestion*	
		Type	f_1	$h(g)_{1\mu m}$	$h(g)_{5\mu m}$	f_1	$h(g)$
Yb-169	32,0 d	M	$5,010^{-4}$	$2,4\ 10^{-9}$	$2,1\ 10^{-9}$	$5,010^{-4}$	$7,1\ 10^{-10}$
		S	$5,010^{-4}$	$2,8\ 10^{-9}$	$2,4\ 10^{-9}$		
Yb-175	4,19 d	M	$5,010^{-4}$	$6,3\ 10^{-10}$	$6,4\ 10^{-10}$	$5,010^{-4}$	$4,4\ 10^{-10}$
		S	$5,010^{-4}$	$7,0\ 10^{-10}$	$7,0\ 10^{-10}$		
Yb-177	1,90 h	M	$5,010^{-4}$	$6,4\ 10^{-11}$	$8,8\ 10^{-11}$	$5,010^{-4}$	$9,7\ 10^{-11}$
		S	$5,010^{-4}$	$6,9\ 10^{-11}$	$9,4\ 10^{-11}$		
Yb-178	1,23 h	M	$5,010^{-4}$	$7,1\ 10^{-11}$	$1,0\ 10^{-10}$	$5,010^{-4}$	$1,2\ 10^{-10}$
		S	$5,010^{-4}$	$7,6\ 10^{-11}$	$1,1\ 10^{-10}$		
Lutetium							
Lu-169	1,42 d	M	$5,010^{-4}$	$3,5\ 10^{-10}$	$4,7\ 10^{-10}$	$5,010^{-4}$	$4,6\ 10^{-10}$
		S	$5,010^{-4}$	$3,8\ 10^{-10}$	$4,9\ 10^{-10}$		
Lu-170	2,00 d	M	$5,010^{-4}$	$6,4\ 10^{-10}$	$9,3\ 10^{-10}$	$5,010^{-4}$	$9,9\ 10^{-10}$
		S	$5,010^{-4}$	$6,7\ 10^{-10}$	$9,5\ 10^{-10}$		
Lu-171	8,22 d	M	$5,010^{-4}$	$7,6\ 10^{-10}$	$8,8\ 10^{-10}$	$5,010^{-4}$	$6,7\ 10^{-10}$
		S	$5,010^{-4}$	$8,3\ 10^{-10}$	$9,3\ 10^{-10}$		
Lu-172	6,70 d	M	$5,010^{-4}$	$1,4\ 10^{-9}$	$1,7\ 10^{-9}$	$5,010^{-4}$	$1,3\ 10^{-9}$
		S	$5,010^{-4}$	$1,5\ 10^{-9}$	$1,8\ 10^{-9}$		
Lu-173	1,37 a	M	$5,010^{-4}$	$2,0\ 10^{-9}$	$1,5\ 10^{-9}$	$5,010^{-4}$	$2,6\ 10^{-10}$
		S	$5,010^{-4}$	$2,3\ 10^{-9}$	$1,4\ 10^{-9}$		
Lu-174	3,31 a	M	$5,010^{-4}$	$4,0\ 10^{-9}$	$2,9\ 10^{-9}$	$5,010^{-4}$	$2,7\ 10^{-10}$
		S	$5,010^{-4}$	$3,9\ 10^{-9}$	$2,5\ 10^{-9}$		
Lu-174m	142 d	M	$5,010^{-4}$	$3,4\ 10^{-9}$	$2,4\ 10^{-9}$	$5,010^{-4}$	$5,3\ 10^{-10}$
		S	$5,010^{-4}$	$3,8\ 10^{-9}$	$2,6\ 10^{-9}$		
Lu-176	3,60 1010 a	M	$5,010^{-4}$	$6,6\ 10^{-8}$	$4,6\ 10^{-8}$	$5,010^{-4}$	$1,8\ 10^{-9}$
		S	$5,010^{-4}$	$5,2\ 10^{-8}$	$3,0\ 10^{-8}$		
Lu-176m	3,68 h	M	$5,010^{-4}$	$1,1\ 10^{-10}$	$1,5\ 10^{-10}$	$5,010^{-4}$	$1,7\ 10^{-10}$
		S	$5,010^{-4}$	$1,2\ 10^{-10}$	$1,6\ 10^{-10}$		
Lu-177	6,71 d	M	$5,010^{-4}$	$1,0\ 10^{-9}$	$1,0\ 10^{-9}$	$5,010^{-4}$	$5,3\ 10^{-10}$
		S	$5,010^{-4}$	$1,1\ 10^{-9}$	$1,1\ 10^{-9}$		
Lu-177m	161 d	M	$5,010^{-4}$	$1,2\ 10^{-8}$	$1,0\ 10^{-8}$	$5,010^{-4}$	$1,7\ 10^{-9}$
		S	$5,010^{-4}$	$1,5\ 10^{-8}$	$1,2\ 10^{-8}$		
Lu-178	0,473 h	M	$5,010^{-4}$	$2,5\ 10^{-11}$	$3,9\ 10^{-11}$	$5,010^{-4}$	$4,7\ 10^{-11}$
		S	$5,010^{-4}$	$2,6\ 10^{-11}$	$4,1\ 10^{-11}$		
Lu-178m	0,378 h	M	$5,010^{-4}$	$3,3\ 10^{-11}$	$5,4\ 10^{-11}$	$5,010^{-4}$	$3,8\ 10^{-11}$
		S	$5,010^{-4}$	$3,5\ 10^{-11}$	$5,6\ 10^{-11}$		
Lu-179	4,59 h	M	$5,010^{-4}$	$1,1\ 10^{-10}$	$1,6\ 10^{-10}$	$5,010^{-4}$	$2,1\ 10^{-10}$
		S	$5,010^{-4}$	$1,2\ 10^{-10}$	$1,6\ 10^{-10}$		
Hafnium							
Hf-170	16,0 h	F	0,002	$1,7\ 10^{-10}$	$2,9\ 10^{-10}$	0,002	$4,8\ 10^{-10}$
		M	0,002	$3,2\ 10^{-10}$	$4,3\ 10^{-10}$		
Hf-172	1,87 a	F	0,002	$3,2\ 10^{-8}$	$3,7\ 10^{-8}$	0,002	$1,0\ 10^{-9}$
		M	0,002	$1,9\ 10^{-8}$	$1,3\ 10^{-8}$		
Hf-173	24,0 h	F	0,002	$7,9\ 10^{-11}$	$1,3\ 10^{-10}$	0,002	$2,3\ 10^{-10}$
		M	0,002	$1,6\ 10^{-10}$	$2,2\ 10^{-10}$		

Nuclide	*Physical half-life*	*Inhalation*				*Ingestion*	
		Type	f_1	$h(g)_{1\mu m}$	$h(g)_{5\mu m}$	f_1	$h(g)$
Hf-175	70,0 d	F	0,002	7,2 10^{-10}	8,7 10^{-10}	0,002	4,1 10^{-10}
		M	0,002	1,1 10^{-9}	8,8 10^{-10}		
Hf-177m	0,856 h	F	0,002	4,7 10^{-11}	8,4 10^{-11}	0,002	8,1 10^{-11}
		M	0,002	9,2 10^{-11}	1,5 10^{-10}		
Hf-178m	31,0 a	F	0,002	2,6 10^{-7}	3,1 10^{-7}	0,002	4,7 10^{-9}
		M	0,002	1,1 10^{-7}	7,8 10^{-8}		
Hf-179m	25,1 d	F	0,002	1,1 10^{-9}	1,4 10^{-9}	0,002	1,2 10^{-9}
		M	0,002	3,6 10^{-9}	3,2 10^{-9}		
Hf-180m	5,50 h	F	0,002	6,4 10^{-11}	1,2 10^{-10}	0,002	1,7 10^{-10}
		M	0,002	1,4 10^{-10}	2,0 10^{-10}		
Hf-181	42,4 d	F	0,002	1,4 10^{-9}	1,8 10^{-9}	0,002	1,1 10^{-9}
		M	0,002	4,7 10^{-9}	4,1 10^{-9}		
Hf-182	9,00 106 a	F	0,002	3,0 10^{-7}	3,6 10^{-7}	0,002	3,0 10^{-9}
		M	0,002	1,2 10^{-7}	8,3 10^{-8}		
Hf-182m	1,02 h	F	0,002	2,3 10^{-11}	4,0 10^{-11}	0,002	4,2 10^{-11}
		M	0,002	4,7 10^{-11}	7,1 10^{-11}		
Hf-183	1,07 h	F	0,002	2,6 10^{-11}	4,4 10^{-11}	0,002	7,3 10^{-11}
		M	0,002	5,8 10^{-11}	8,3 10^{-11}		
Hf-184	4,12 h	F	0,002	1,3 10^{-10}	2,3 10^{-10}	0,002	5,2 10^{-10}
		M	0,002	3,3 10^{-10}	4,5 10^{-10}		
Tantalum							
Ta-172	0,613 h	M	0,001	3,4 10^{-11}	5,5 10^{-11}	0,001	5,3 10^{-11}
		S	0,001	3,6 10^{-11}	5,7 10^{-11}		
Ta-173	3,65 h	M	0,001	1,1 10^{-10}	1,6 10^{-10}	0,001	1,9 10^{-10}
		S	0,001	1,2 10^{-10}	1,6 10^{-10}		
Ta-174	1,20 h	M	0,001	4,2 10^{-11}	6,3 10^{-11}	0,001	5,7 10^{-11}
		S	0,001	4,4 10^{-11}	6,6 10^{-11}		
Ta-175	10,5 h	M	0,001	1,3 10^{-10}	2,0 10^{-10}	0,001	2,1 10^{-10}
		S	0,001	1,4 10^{-10}	2,0 10^{-10}		
Ta-176	8,08 h	M	0,001	2,0 10^{-10}	3,2 10^{-10}	0,001	3,1 10^{-10}
		S	0,001	2,1 10^{-10}	3,3 10^{-10}		
Ta-177	2,36 d	M	0,001	9,3 10^{-11}	1,2 10^{-10}	0,001	1,1 10^{-10}
		S	0,001	1,0 10^{-10}	1,3 10^{-10}		
Ta-178	2,20 h	M	0,001	6,6 10^{-11}	1,0 10^{-10}	0,001	7,8 10^{-11}
		S	0,001	6,9 10^{-11}	1,1 10^{-10}		
Ta-179	1,82 a	M	0,001	2,0 10^{-10}	1,3 10^{-10}	0,001	6,5 10^{-11}
		S	0,001	5,2 10^{-10}	2,9 10^{-10}		
Ta-180	1,00 1013 a	M	0,001	6,0 10^{-9}	4,6 10^{-9}	0,001	8,4 10^{-10}
		S	0,001	2,4 10^{-8}	1,4 10^{-8}		
Ta-180m	8,10 h	M	0,001	4,4 10^{-11}	5,8 10^{-11}	0,001	5,4 10^{-11}
		S	0,001	4,7 10^{-11}	6,2 10^{-11}		
Ta-182	115 d	M	0,001	7,2 10^{-9}	5,8 10^{-9}	0,001	1,5 10^{-9}
		S	0,001	9,7 10^{-9}	7,4 10^{-9}		
Ta-182m	0,264 h	M	0,001	2,1 10^{-11}	3,4 10^{-11}	0,001	1,2 10^{-11}
		S	0,001	2,2 10^{-11}	3,6 10^{-11}		

Nuclide	Physical half-life	Inhalation				Ingestion	
		Type	f_1	$h(g)_{1\mu m}$	$h(g)_{5\mu m}$	f_1	$h(g)$
Ta-183	5,10 d	M	0,001	$1{,}8\ 10^{-9}$	$1{,}8\ 10^{-9}$	0,001	$1{,}3\ 10^{-9}$
		S	0,001	$2{,}0\ 10^{-9}$	$2{,}0\ 10^{-9}$		
Ta-184	8,70 h	M	0,001	$4{,}1\ 10^{-10}$	$6{,}0\ 10^{-10}$	0,001	$6{,}8\ 10^{-10}$
		S	0,001	$4{,}4\ 10^{-10}$	$6{,}3\ 10^{-10}$		
Ta-185	0,816 h	M	0,001	$4{,}6\ 10^{-11}$	$6{,}8\ 10^{-11}$	0,001	$6{,}8\ 10^{-11}$
		S	0,001	$4{,}9\ 10^{-11}$	$7{,}2\ 10^{-11}$		
Ta-186	0,175 h	M	0,001	$1{,}8\ 10^{-11}$	$3{,}0\ 10^{-11}$	0,001	$3{,}3\ 10^{-11}$
		S	0,001	$1{,}9\ 10^{-11}$	$3{,}1\ 10^{-11}$		
Tungsten							
W-176	2,30 h	F	0,300	$4{,}4\ 10^{-11}$	$7{,}6\ 10^{-11}$	0,300	$1{,}0\ 10^{-10}$
						0,010	$1{,}1\ 10^{-10}$
W-177	2,25 h	F	0,300	$2{,}6\ 10^{-11}$	$4{,}6\ 10^{-11}$	0,300	$5{,}8\ 10^{-11}$
						0,010	$6{,}1\ 10^{-11}$
W-178	21,7 d	F	0,300	$7{,}6\ 10^{-11}$	$1{,}2\ 10^{-10}$	0,300	$2{,}2\ 10^{-10}$
						0,010	$2{,}5\ 10^{-10}$
W-179	0,625 h	F	0,300	$9{,}9\ 10^{-13}$	$1{,}8\ 10^{-12}$	0,300	$3{,}3\ 10^{-12}$
						0,010	$3{,}3\ 10^{-12}$
W-181	121 d	F	0,300	$2{,}8\ 10^{-11}$	$4{,}3\ 10^{-11}$	0,300	$7{,}6\ 10^{-11}$
						0,010	$8{,}2\ 10^{-11}$
W-185	75,1 d	F	0,300	$1{,}4\ 10^{-10}$	$2{,}2\ 10^{-10}$	0,300	$4{,}4\ 10^{-10}$
						0,010	$5{,}0\ 10^{-10}$
W-187	23,9 h	F	0,300	$2{,}0\ 10^{-10}$	$3{,}3\ 10^{-10}$	0,300	$6{,}3\ 10^{-10}$
						0,010	$7{,}1\ 10^{-10}$
W-188	69,4 d	F	0,300	$5{,}9\ 10^{-10}$	$8{,}4\ 10^{-10}$	0,300	$2{,}1\ 10^{-9}$
						0,010	$2{,}3\ 10^{-9}$
Rhenium							
Re-177	0,233 h	F	0,800	$1{,}0\ 10^{-11}$	$1{,}7\ 10^{-11}$	0,800	$2{,}2\ 10^{-11}$
		M	0,800	$1{,}4\ 10^{-11}$	$2{,}2\ 10^{-11}$		
Re-178	0,220 h	F	0,800	$1{,}1\ 10^{-11}$	$1{,}8\ 10^{-11}$	0,800	$2{,}5\ 10^{-11}$
		M	0,800	$1{,}5\ 10^{-11}$	$2{,}4\ 10^{-11}$		
Re-181	20,0 h	F	0,800	$1{,}9\ 10^{-10}$	$3{,}0\ 10^{-10}$	0,800	$4{,}2\ 10^{-10}$
		M	0,800	$2{,}5\ 10^{-10}$	$3{,}7\ 10^{-10}$		
Re-182	2,67 d	F	0,800	$6{,}8\ 10^{-10}$	$1{,}1\ 10^{-9}$	0,800	$1{,}4\ 10^{-9}$
		M	0,800	$1{,}3\ 10^{-9}$	$1{,}7\ 10^{-9}$		
Re-182	12,7 h	F	0,800	$1{,}5\ 10^{-10}$	$2{,}4\ 10^{-10}$	0,800	$2{,}7\ 10^{-10}$
		M	0,800	$2{,}0\ 10^{-10}$	$3{,}0\ 10^{-10}$		
Re-184	38,0 d	F	0,800	$4{,}6\ 10^{-10}$	$7{,}0\ 10^{-10}$	0,800	$1{,}0\ 10^{-9}$
		M	0,800	$1{,}8\ 10^{-9}$	$1{,}8\ 10^{-9}$		
Re-184m	165 d	F	0,800	$6{,}1\ 10^{-10}$	$8{,}8\ 10^{-10}$	0,800	$1{,}5\ 10^{-9}$
		M	0,800	$6{,}1\ 10^{-9}$	$4{,}8\ 10^{-9}$		
Re-186	3,78 d	F	0,800	$5{,}3\ 10^{-10}$	$7{,}3\ 10^{-10}$	0,800	$1{,}5\ 10^{-9}$
		M	0,800	$1{,}1\ 10^{-9}$	$1{,}2\ 10^{-9}$		
Re-186m	2,00 105 a	F	0,800	$8{,}5\ 10^{-10}$	$1{,}2\ 10^{-9}$	0,800	$2{,}2\ 10^{-9}$
		M	0,800	$1{,}1\ 10^{-8}$	$7{,}9\ 10^{-9}$		

Nuclide	Physical half-life	Inhalation				Ingestion	
		Type	f_1	$h(g)_{1\mu m}$	$h(g)_{5\mu m}$	f_1	$h(g)$
Re-187	5,00 1010 a	F	0,800	$1{,}9\ 10^{-12}$	$2{,}6\ 10^{-12}$	0,800	$5{,}1\ 10^{-12}$
		M	0,800	$6{,}0\ 10^{-12}$	$4{,}6\ 10^{-12}$		
Re-188	17,0 h	F	0,800	$4{,}7\ 10^{-10}$	$6{,}6\ 10^{-10}$	0,800	$1{,}4\ 10^{-9}$
		M	0,800	$5{,}5\ 10^{-10}$	$7{,}4\ 10^{-10}$		
Re-188m	0,3 10 h	F	0,800	$1{,}0\ 10^{-11}$	$1{,}6\ 10^{-11}$	0,800	$3{,}0\ 10^{-11}$
		M	0,800	$1{,}4\ 10^{-11}$	$2{,}0\ 10^{-11}$		
Re-189	1,01 d	F	0,800	$2{,}7\ 10^{-10}$	$4{,}3\ 10^{-10}$	0,800	$7{,}8\ 10^{-10}$
		M	0,800	$4{,}3\ 10^{-10}$	$6{,}0\ 10^{-10}$		
Osmium							
Os-180	0,366 h	F	0,010	$8{,}8\ 10^{-12}$	$1{,}6\ 10^{-11}$	0,010	$1{,}7\ 10^{-11}$
		M	0,010	$1{,}4\ 10^{-11}$	$2{,}4\ 10^{-11}$		
		S	0,010	$1{,}5\ 10^{-11}$	$2{,}5\ 10^{-11}$		
Os-181	1,75 h	F	0,010	$3{,}6\ 10^{-11}$	$6{,}4\ 10^{-11}$	0,010	$8{,}9\ 10^{-11}$
		M	0,010	$6{,}3\ 10^{-11}$	$9{,}6\ 10^{-11}$		
		S	0,010	$6{,}6\ 10^{-11}$	$1{,}0\ 10^{-10}$		
Os-182	22,0 h	F	0,010	$1{,}9\ 10^{-10}$	$3{,}2\ 10^{-10}$	0,010	$5{,}6\ 10^{-10}$
		M	0,010	$3{,}7\ 10^{-10}$	$5{,}0\ 10^{-10}$		
		S	0,010	$3{,}9\ 10^{-10}$	$5{,}2\ 10^{-10}$		
Os-185	94,0 d	F	0,010	$1{,}1\ 10^{-9}$	$1{,}4\ 10^{-9}$	0,010	$5{,}1\ 10^{-10}$
		M	0,010	$1{,}2\ 10^{-9}$	$1{,}0\ 10^{-9}$		
		S	0,010	$1{,}5\ 10^{-9}$	$1{,}1\ 10^{-9}$		
Os-189m	6,00 h	F	0,010	$2{,}7\ 10^{-12}$	$5{,}2\ 10^{-12}$	0,010	$1{,}8\ 10^{-11}$
		M	0,010	$5{,}1\ 10^{-12}$	$7{,}6\ 10^{-12}$		
		S	0,010	$5{,}4\ 10^{-12}$	$7{,}9\ 10^{-12}$		
Os-191	15,4 d	F	0,010	$2{,}5\ 10^{-10}$	$3{,}5\ 10^{-10}$	0,010	$5{,}7\ 10^{-10}$
		M	0,010	$1{,}5\ 10^{-9}$	$1{,}3\ 10^{-9}$		
		S	0,010	$1{,}8\ 10^{-9}$	$1{,}5\ 10^{-9}$		
Os-191m	13,0 h	F	0,010	$2{,}6\ 10^{-11}$	$4{,}1\ 10^{-11}$	0,010	$9{,}6\ 10^{-11}$
		M	0,010	$1{,}3\ 10^{-10}$	$1{,}3\ 10^{-10}$		
		S	0,010	$1{,}5\ 10^{-10}$	$1{,}4\ 10^{-10}$		
Os-193	1,25 d	F	0,010	$1{,}7\ 10^{-10}$	$2{,}8\ 10^{-10}$	0,010	$8{,}1\ 10^{-10}$
		M	0,010	$4{,}7\ 10^{-10}$	$6{,}4\ 10^{-10}$		
		S	0,010	$5{,}1\ 10^{-10}$	$6{,}8\ 10^{-10}$		
Os-194	6,00 a	F	0,010	$1{,}1\ 10^{-8}$	$1{,}3\ 10^{-8}$	0,010	$2{,}4\ 10^{-9}$
		M	0,010	$2{,}0\ 10^{-8}$	$1{,}3\ 10^{-8}$		
		S	0,010	$7{,}9\ 10^{-8}$	$4{,}2\ 10^{-8}$		
Iridium							
Ir-182	0,250 h	F	0,010	$1{,}5\ 10^{-11}$	$2{,}6\ 10^{-11}$	0,010	$4{,}8\ 10^{-11}$
		M	0,010	$2{,}4\ 10^{-11}$	$3{,}9\ 10^{-11}$		
		S	0,010	$2{,}5\ 10^{-11}$	$4{,}0\ 10^{-11}$		
Ir-184	3,02 h	F	0,010	$6{,}7\ 10^{-11}$	$1{,}2\ 10^{-10}$	0,010	$1{,}7\ 10^{-10}$
		M	0,010	$1{,}1\ 10^{-10}$	$1{,}8\ 10^{-10}$		
		S	0,010	$1{,}2\ 10^{-10}$	$1{,}9\ 10^{-10}$		

Nuclide	Physical half-life	Inhalation				Ingestion	
		Type	f_1	$h(g)_{1\mu m}$	$h(g)_{5\mu m}$	f_1	$h(g)$
Ir-185	14,0 h	F	0,010	8,8 10^{-11}	1,5 10^{-10}	0,010	2,6 10^{-10}
		M	0,010	1,8 10^{-10}	2,5 10^{-10}		
		S	0,010	1,9 10^{-10}	2,6 10^{-10}		
Ir-186	15,8 h	F	0,010	1,8 10^{-10}	3,3 10^{-10}	0,010	4,9 10^{-10}
		M	0,010	3,2 10^{-10}	4,8 10^{-10}		
		S	0,010	3,3 10^{-10}	5,0 10^{-10}		
Ir-186	1,75 h	F	0,010	2,5 10^{-11}	4,5 10^{-11}	0,010	6,1 10^{-11}
		M	0,010	4,3 10^{-11}	6,9 10^{-11}		
		S	0,010	4,5 10^{-11}	7,1 10^{-11}		
Ir-187	10,5 h	F	0,010	4,0 10^{-11}	7,2 10^{-11}	0,010	1,2 10^{-10}
		M	0,010	7,5 10^{-11}	1,1 10^{-10}		
		S	0,010	7,9 10^{-11}	1,2 10^{-10}		
Ir-188	1,73 d	F	0,010	2,6 10^{-10}	4,4 10^{-10}	0,010	6,3 10^{-10}
		M	0,010	4,1 10^{-10}	6,0 10^{-10}		
		S	0,010	4,3 10^{-10}	6,2 10^{-10}		
Ir-189	13,3 d	F	0,010	1,1 10^{-10}	1,7 10^{-10}	0,010	2,4 10^{-10}
		M	0,010	4,8 10^{-10}	4,1 10^{-10}		
		S	0,010	5,5 10^{-10}	4,6 10^{-10}		
Ir-190	12,1 d	F	0,010	7,9 10^{-10}	1,2 10^{-9}	0,010	1,2 10^{-9}
		M	0,010	2,0 10^{-9}	2,3 10^{-9}		
		S	0,010	2,3 10^{-9}	2,5 10^{-9}		
Ir-190m	3,10 h	F	0,010	5,3 10^{-11}	9,7 10^{-11}	0,010	1,2 10^{-10}
		M	0,010	8,3 10^{-11}	1,4 10^{-10}		
		S	0,010	8,6 10^{-11}	1,4 10^{-10}		
Ir-190m	1,20 h	F	0,010	3,7 10^{-12}	5,6 10^{-12}	0,010	8,0 10^{-12}
		M	0,010	9,0 10^{-12}	1,0 10^{-11}		
		S	0,010	1,0 10^{-11}	1,1 10^{-11}		
Ir-192	74,0 d	F	0,010	1,8 10^{-9}	2,2 10^{-9}	0,010	1,4 10^{-9}
		M	0,010	4,9 10^{-9}	4,1 10^{-9}		
		S	0,010	6,2 10^{-9}	4,9 10^{-9}		
Ir-192m	2,41 102 a	F	0,010	4,8 10^{-9}	5,6 10^{-9}	0,010	3,1 10^{-10}
		M	0,010	5,4 10^{-9}	3,4 10^{-9}		
		S	0,010	3,6 10^{-8}	1,9 10^{-8}		
Ir-193m	11,9 d	F	0,010	1,0 10^{-10}	1,6 10^{-10}	0,010	2,7 10^{-10}
		M	0,010	1,0 10^{-9}	9,1 10^{-10}		
		S	0,010	1,2 10^{-9}	1,0 10^{-9}		
Ir-194	19,1 h	F	0,010	2,2 10^{-10}	3,6 10^{-10}	0,010	1,3 10^{-9}
		M	0,010	5,3 10^{-10}	7,1 10^{-10}		
		S	0,010	5,6 10^{-10}	7,5 10^{-10}		
Ir-194m	171 d	F	0,010	5,4 10^{-9}	6,5 10^{-9}	0,010	2,1 10^{-9}
		M	0,010	8,5 10^{-9}	6,5 10^{-9}		
		S	0,010	1,2 10^{-8}	8,2 10^{-9}		
Ir-195	2,50 h	F	0,010	2,6 10^{-11}	4,5 10^{-11}	0,010	1,0 10^{-10}
		M	0,010	6,7 10^{-11}	9,6 10^{-11}		
		S	0,010	7,2 10^{-11}	1,0 10^{-10}		

Nuclide	Physical half-life	Inhalation				Ingestion	
		Type	f_1	$h(g)_{1\mu m}$	$h(g)_{5\mu m}$	f_1	$h(g)$
Ir-195m	3,80 h	F	0,010	6,5 10^{-11}	1,1 10^{-10}	0,010	2,1 10^{-10}
		M	0,010	1,6 10^{-10}	2,3 10^{-10}		
		S	0,010	1,7 10^{-10}	2,4 10^{-10}		
Platinum							
Pt-186	2,00 h	F	0,010	3,6 10^{-11}	6,6 10^{-11}	0,010	9,3 10^{-11}
Pt-188	10,2 d	F	0,010	4,3 10^{-10}	6,3 10^{-10}	0,010	7,6 10^{-10}
Pt-189	10,9 h	F	0,010	4,1 10^{-11}	7,3 10^{-11}	0,010	1,2 10^{-10}
Pt-191	2,80 d	F	0,010	1,1 10^{-10}	1,9 10^{-10}	0,010	3,4 10^{-10}
Pt-193	50,0 a	F	0,010	2,1 10^{-11}	2,7 10^{-11}	0,010	3,1 10^{-11}
Pt-193m	4,33 d	F	0,010	1,3 10^{-10}	2,1 10^{-10}	0,010	4,5 10^{-10}
Pt-195m	4,02 d	F	0,010	1,9 10^{-10}	3,1 10^{-10}	0,010	6,3 10^{-10}
Pt-197	18,3 h	F	0,010	9,1 10^{-11}	1,6 10^{-10}	0,010	4,0 10^{-10}
Pt-197m	1,57 h	F	0,010	2,5 10^{-11}	4,3 10^{-11}	0,010	8,4 10^{-11}
Pt-199	0,513 h	F	0,010	1,3 10^{-11}	2,2 10^{-11}	0,010	3,9 10^{-11}
Pt-200	12,5 h	F	0,010	2,4 10^{-10}	4,0 10^{-10}	0,010	1,2 10^{-9}
Gold							
Au-193	17,6 h	F	0,100	3,9 10^{-11}	7,1 10^{-11}	0,100	1,3 10^{-10}
		M	0,100	1,1 10^{-10}	1,5 10^{-10}		
		S	0,100	1,2 10^{-10}	1,6 10^{-10}		
Au-194	1,64 d	F	0,100	1,5 10^{-10}	2,8 10^{-10}	0,100	4,2 10^{-10}
		M	0,100	2,4 10^{-10}	3,7 10^{-10}		
		S	0,100	2,5 10^{-10}	3,8 10^{-10}		
Au-195	183 d	F	0,100	7,1 10^{-11}	1,2 10^{-10}	0,100	2,5 10^{-10}
		M	0,100	1,0 10^{-9}	8,0 10^{-10}		
		S	0,100	1,6 10^{-9}	1,2 10^{-9}		
Au-198	2,69 d	F	0,100	2,3 10^{-10}	3,9 10^{-10}	0,100	1,0 10^{-9}
		M	0,100	7,6 10^{-10}	9,8 10^{-10}		
		S	0,100	8,4 10^{-10}	1,1 10^{-9}		
Au-198m	2,30 d	F	0,100	3,4 10^{-10}	5,9 10^{-10}	0,100	1,3 10^{-9}
		M	0,100	1,7 10^{-9}	2,0 10^{-9}		
		S	0,100	1,9 10^{-9}	1,9 10^{-9}		
Au-199	3,14 d	F	0,100	1,1 10^{-10}	1,9 10^{-10}	0,100	4,4 10^{-10}
		M	0,100	6,8 10^{-10}	6,8 10^{-10}		
		S	0,100	7,5 10^{-10}	7,6 10^{-10}		
Au-200	0,807 h	F	0,100	1,7 10^{-11}	3,0 10^{-11}	0,100	6,8 10^{-11}
		M	0,100	3,5 10^{-11}	5,3 10^{-11}		
		S	0,100	3,6 10^{-11}	5,6 10^{-11}		
Au-200m	18,7 h	F	0,100	3,2 10^{-10}	5,7 10^{-10}	0,100	1,1 10^{-9}
		M	0,100	6,9 10^{-10}	9,8 10^{-10}		
		S	0,100	7,3 10^{-10}	1,0 10^{-9}		
Au-201	0,440 h	F	0,100	9,2 10^{-12}	1,6 10^{-11}	0,100	2,4 10^{-11}
		M	0,100	1,7 10^{-11}	2,8 10^{-11}		
		S	0,100	1,8 10^{-11}	2,9 10^{-11}		
Mercury							
Hg-193 (organic)	3,50 h	F	0,400	2,6 10^{-11}	4,7 10^{-11}	1,000	3,1 10^{-11}
						0,400	6,6 10^{-11}

Nuclide	Physical half-life	Inhalation				Ingestion	
		Type	f_1	$h(g)_{1\mu m}$	$h(g)_{5\mu m}$	f_1	$h(g)$
Hg-193 (inorganic)	3,50 h	F	0,020	2,8 10^{-11}	5,0 10^{-11}	0,020	8,2 10^{-11}
		M	0,020	7,5 10^{-11}	1,0 10^{-10}		
Hg-193m (organic)	11,1 h	F	0,400	1,1 10^{-10}	2,0 10^{-10}	1,000	1,3 10^{-10}
						0,400	3,0 10^{-10}
Hg-193m (inorganic)	11,1 h	F	0,020	1,2 10^{-10}	2,3 10^{-10}	0,020	4,0 10^{-10}
		M	0,020	2,6 10^{-10}	3,8 10^{-10}		
Hg-194 (organic)	2,60 102 a	F	0,400	1,5 10^{-8}	1,9 10^{-8}	1,000	5,1 10^{-8}
						0,400	2,1 10^{-8}
Hg-194 (inorganic)	2,60 102 a	F	0,020	1,3 10^{-8}	1,5 10^{-8}	0,020	1,4 10^{-9}
		M	0,020	7,8 10^{-9}	5,3 10^{-9}		
Hg-195 (organic)	9,90 h	F	0,400	2,4 10^{-11}	4,4 10^{-11}	1,000	3,4 10^{-11}
						0,400	7,5 10^{-11}
Hg-195 (inorganic)	9,90 h	F	0,020	2,7 10^{-11}	4,8 10^{-11}	0,020	9,7 10^{-11}
		M	0,020	7,2 10^{-11}	9,2 10^{-11}		
Hg-195m (organic)	1,73 d	F	0,400	1,3 10^{-10}	2,2 10^{-10}	1,000	2,2 10^{-10}
						0,400	4,1 10^{-10}
Hg-195m (inorganic)	1,73 d	F	0,020	1,5 10^{-10}	2,6 10^{-10}	0,020	5,6 10^{-10}
		M	0,020	5,1 10^{-10}	6,5 10^{-10}		
Hg-197 (organic)	2,67 d	F	0,400	5,0 10^{-11}	8,5 10^{-11}	1,000	9,9 10^{-11}
						0,400	1,7 10^{-10}
Hg-197 (inorganic)	2,67 d	F	0,020	6,0 10^{-11}	1,0 10^{-10}	0,020	2,3 10^{-10}
		M	0,020	2,9 10^{-10}	2,8 10^{-10}		
Hg-197m (organic)	23,8 h	F	0,400	1,0 10^{-10}	1,8 10^{-10}	1,000	1,5 10^{-10}
						0,400	3,4 10^{-10}
Hg-197m (inorganic)	23,8 h	F	0,020	1,2 10^{-10}	2,1 10^{-10}	0,020	4,7 10^{-10}
		M	0,020	5,1 10^{-10}	6,6 10^{-10}		
Hg-199m (organic)	0,7 10 h	F	0,400	1,6 10^{-11}	2,7 10^{-11}	1,000	2,8 10^{-11}
						0,400	3,1 10^{-11}
Hg-199m (inorganic)	0,7 10 h	F	0,020	1,6 10^{-11}	2,7 10^{-11}	0,020	3,1 10^{-11}
		M	0,020	3,3 10^{-11}	5,2 10^{-11}		
Hg-203 (organic)	46,6 d	F	0,400	5,7 10^{-10}	7,5 10^{-10}	1,000	1,9 10^{-9}
						0,400	1,1 10^{-9}
Hg-203 (inorganic)	46,6 d	F	0,020	4,7 10^{-10}	5,9 10^{-10}	0,020	5,4 10^{-10}
		M	0,020	2,3 10^{-9}	1,9 10^{-9}		
Thallium							
Tl-194	0,550 h	F	1,000	4,8 10^{-12}	8,9 10^{-12}	1,000	8,1 10^{-12}
Tl-194m	0,546 h	F	1,000	2,0 10^{-11}	3,6 10^{-11}	1,000	4,0 10^{-11}
Tl-195	1,16 h	F	1,000	1,6 10^{-11}	3,0 10^{-11}	1,000	2,7 10^{-11}
Tl-197	2,84 h	F	1,000	1,5 10^{-11}	2,7 10^{-11}	1,000	2,3 10^{-11}
Tl-198	5,30 h	F	1,000	6,6 10^{-11}	1,2 10^{-10}	1,000	7,3 10^{-11}
Tl-198m	1,87 h	F	1,000	4,0 10^{-11}	7,3 10^{-11}	1,000	5,4 10^{-11}
Tl-199	7,42 h	F	1,000	2,0 10^{-11}	3,7 10^{-11}	1,000	2,6 10^{-11}
Tl-200	1,09 d	F	1,000	1,4 10^{-10}	2,5 10^{-10}	1,000	2,0 10^{-10}
Tl-201	3,04 d	F	1,000	4,7 10^{-11}	7,6 10^{-11}	1,000	9,5 10^{-11}
Tl-202	12,2 d	F	1,000	2,0 10^{-10}	3,1 10^{-10}	1,000	4,5 10^{-10}

Nuclide	Physical half-life	Inhalation				Ingestion	
		Type	f_1	$h(g)_{1\mu m}$	$h(g)_{5\mu m}$	f_1	$h(g)$
Tl-204	3,78 a	F	1,000	4,4 10^{-10}	6,2 10^{-10}	1,000	1,3 10^{-9}
Lead							
Pb-195m	0,263 h	F	0,200	1,7 10^{-11}	3,0 10^{-11}	0,200	2,9 10^{-11}
Pb-198	2,40 h	F	0,200	4,7 10^{-11}	8,7 10^{-11}	0,200	1,0 10^{-10}
Pb-199	1,50 h	F	0,200	2,6 10^{-11}	4,8 10^{-11}	0,200	5,4 10^{-11}
Pb-200	21,5 h	F	0,200	1,5 10^{-10}	2,6 10^{-10}	0,200	4,0 10^{-10}
Pb-201	9,40 h	F	0,200	6,5 10^{-11}	1,2 10^{-10}	0,200	1,6 10^{-10}
Pb-202	3,00 105 a	F	0,200	1,1 10^{-8}	1,4 10^{-8}	0,200	8,7 10^{-9}
Pb-202m	3,62 h	F	0,200	6,7 10^{-11}	1,2 10^{-10}	0,200	1,3 10^{-10}
Pb-203	2,17 d	F	0,200	9,1 10^{-11}	1,6 10^{-10}	0,200	2,4 10^{-10}
Pb-205	1,43 107 a	F	0,200	3,4 10^{-10}	4,1 10^{-10}	0,200	2,8 10^{-10}
Pb-209	3,25 h	F	0,200	1,8 10^{-11}	3,2 10^{-11}	0,200	5,7 10^{-11}
Pb-210	22,3 a	F	0,200	8,9 10^{-7}	1,1 10^{-6}	0,200	6,8 10^{-7}
Pb-211	0,601 h	F	0,200	3,9 10^{-9}	5,6 10^{-9}	0,200	1,8 10^{-10}
Pb-212	10,6 h	F	0,200	1,9 10^{-8}	3,3 10^{-8}	0,200	5,9 10^{-9}
Pb-214	0,447 h	F	0,200	2,9 10^{-9}	4,8 10^{-9}	0,200	1,4 10^{-10}
Bismuth							
Bi-200	0,606 h	F	0,050	2,4 10^{-11}	4,2 10^{-11}	0,050	5,1 10^{-11}
		M	0,050	3,4 10^{-11}	5,6 10^{-11}		
Bi-201	1,80 h	F	0,050	4,7 10^{-11}	8,3 10^{-11}	0,050	1,2 10^{-10}
		M	0,050	7,0 10^{-11}	1,1 10^{-10}		
Bi-202	1,67 h	F	0,050	4,6 10^{-11}	8,4 10^{-11}	0,050	8,9 10^{-11}
		M	0,050	5,8 10^{-11}	1,0 10^{-10}		
Bi-203	11,8 h	F	0,050	2,0 10^{-10}	3,6 10^{-10}	0,050	4,8 10^{-10}
		M	0,050	2,8 10^{-10}	4,5 10^{-10}		
Bi-205	15,3 d	F	0,050	4,0 10^{-10}	6,8 10^{-10}	0,050	9,0 10^{-10}
		M	0,050	9,2 10^{-10}	1,0 10^{-9}		
Bi-206	6,24 d	F	0,050	7,9 10^{-10}	1,3 10^{-9}	0,050	1,9 10^{-9}
		M	0,050	1,7 10^{-9}	2,1 10^{-9}		
Bi-207	38,0 a	F	0,050	5,2 10^{-10}	8,4 10^{-10}	0,050	1,3 10^{-9}
		M	0,050	5,2 10^{-9}	3,2 10^{-9}		
Bi-210	5,01 d	F	0,050	1,1 10^{-9}	1,4 10^{-9}	0,050	1,3 10^{-9}
		M	0,050	8,4 10^{-8}	6,0 10^{-8}		
Bi-210m	3,00 106 a	F	0,050	4,5 10^{-8}	5,3 10^{-8}	0,050	1,5 10^{-8}
		M	0,050	3,1 10^{-6}	2,1 10^{-6}		
Bi-212	1,01 h	F	0,050	9,3 10^{-9}	1,5 10^{-8}	0,050	2,6 10^{-10}
		M	0,050	3,0 10^{-8}	3,9 10^{-8}		
Bi-213	0,761 h	F	0,050	1,1 10^{-8}	1,8 10^{-8}	0,050	2,0 10^{-10}
		M	0,050	2,9 10^{-8}	4,1 10^{-8}		
Bi-214	0,332 h	F	0,050	7,2 10^{-9}	1,2 10^{-8}	0,050	1,1 10^{-10}
		M	0,050	1,4 10^{-8}	2,1 10^{-8}		
Polonium							
Po-203	0,612 h	F	0,100	2,5 10^{-11}	4,5 10^{-11}	0,100	5,2 10^{-11}
		M	0,100	3,6 10^{-11}	6,1 10^{-11}		

Nuclide	Physical half-life	Inhalation				Ingestion	
		Type	f_1	$h(g)_{1\mu m}$	$h(g)_{5\mu m}$	f_1	$h(g)$
Po-205	1,80 h	F	0,100	3,5 10^{-11}	6,0 10^{-11}	0,100	5,9 10^{-11}
		M	0,100	6,4 10^{-11}	8,9 10^{-11}		
Po-207	5,83 h	F	0,100	6,3 10^{-11}	1,2 10^{-10}	0,100	1,4 10^{-10}
		M	0,100	8,4 10^{-11}	1,5 10^{-10}		
Po-210	138 d	F	0,100	6,0 10^{-7}	7,1 10^{-7}	0,100	2,4 10^{-7}
		M	0,100	3,0 10^{-6}	2,2 10^{-6}		
Astatine							
At-207	1,80 h	F	1,000	3,5 10^{-10}	4,4 10^{-10}	1,000	2,3 10^{-10}
		M	1,000	2,1 10^{-9}	1,9 10^{-9}		
At-211	7,21 h	F	1,000	1,6 10^{-8}	2,7 10^{-8}	1,000	1,1 10^{-8}
		M	1,000	9,8 10^{-8}	1,1 10^{-7}		
Francium							
Fr-222	0,240 h	F	1,000	1,4 10^{-8}	2,1 10^{-8}	1,000	7,1 10^{-10}
Fr-223	0,363 h	F	1,000	9,1 10^{-10}	1,3 10^{-9}	1,000	2,3 10^{-9}
Radium							
Ra-223	11,4 d	M	0,200	6,9 10^{-6}	5,7 10^{-6}	0,200	1,0 10^{-7}
Ra-224	3,66 d	M	0,200	2,9 10^{-6}	2,4 10^{-6}	0,200	6,5 10^{-8}
Ra-225	14,8 d	M	0,200	5,8 10^{-6}	4,8 10^{-6}	0,200	9,5 10^{-8}
Ra-226	1,60 103 a	M	0,200	3,2 10^{-6}	2,2 10^{-6}	0,200	2,8 10^{-7}
Ra-227	0,703 h	M	0,200	2,8 10^{-10}	2,1 10^{-10}	0,200	8,4 10^{-11}
Ra-228	5,75 a	M	0,200	2,6 10^{-6}	1,7 10^{-6}	0,200	6,7 10^{-7}
Actinium							
Ac-224	2,90 h	F	$5,010^{-4}$	1,1 10^{-8}	1,3 10^{-8}	$5,010^{-4}$	7,0 10^{-10}
		M	$5,010^{-4}$	1,0 10^{-7}	8,9 10^{-8}		
		S	$5,010^{-4}$	1,2 10^{-7}	9,9 10^{-8}		
Ac-225	10,0 d	F	$5,010^{-4}$	8,7 10^{-7}	1,0 10^{-6}	$5,010^{-4}$	2,4 10^{-8}
		M	$5,010^{-4}$	6,9 10^{-6}	5,7 10^{-6}		
		S	$5,010^{-4}$	7,9 10^{-6}	6,5 10^{-6}		
Ac-226	1,21 d	F	$5,010^{-4}$	9,5 10^{-8}	2,2 10^{-7}	$5,010^{-4}$	1,0 10^{-8}
		M	$5,010^{-4}$	1,1 10^{-6}	9,2 10^{-7}		
		S	$5,010^{-4}$	1,2 10^{-6}	1,0 10^{-6}		
Ac-227	21,8 a	F	$5,010^{-4}$	5,4 10^{-4}	6,3 10^{-4}	$5,010^{-4}$	1,1 10^{-6}
		M	$5,010^{-4}$	2,1 10^{-4}	1,5 10^{-4}		
		S	$5,010^{-4}$	6,6 10^{-5}	4,7 10^{-5}		
Ac-228	6,13 h	F	$5,010^{-4}$	2,5 10^{-8}	2,9 10^{-8}	$5,010^{-4}$	4,3 10^{-10}
		M	$5,010^{-4}$	1,6 10^{-8}	1,2 10^{-8}		
		S	$5,010^{-4}$	1,4 10^{-8}	1,2 10^{-8}		
Thorium							
Th-226	0,515 h	M	$5,010^{-4}$	5,5 10^{-8}	7,4 10^{-8}	$5,010^{-4}$	3,5 10^{-10}
		S	$2,010^{-4}$	5,9 10^{-8}	7,8 10^{-8}	$2,010^{-4}$	3,6 10^{-10}
Th-227	18,7 d	M	$5,010^{-4}$	7,8 10^{-6}	6,2 10^{-6}	$5,010^{-4}$	8,9 10^{-9}
		S	$2,010^{-4}$	9,6 10^{-6}	7,6 10^{-6}	$2,010^{-4}$	8,4 10^{-9}
Th-228	1,91 a	M	$5,010^{-4}$	3,1 10^{-5}	2,3 10^{-5}	$5,010^{-4}$	7,0 10^{-8}
		S	$2,010^{-4}$	3,9 10^{-5}	3,2 10^{-5}	$2,010^{-4}$	3,5 10^{-8}

Nuclide	*Physical half-life*	*Inhalation*				*Ingestion*	
		Type	f_1	$h(g)_{1\mu m}$	$h(g)_{5\mu m}$	f_1	$h(g)$
Th-229	7,34 103 a	M	5,010^{-4}	9,9 10^{-5}	6,9 10^{-5}	5,010^{-4}	4,8 10^{-7}
		S	2,010^{-4}	6,5 10^{-5}	4,8 10^{-5}	2,010^{-4}	2,0 10^{-7}
Th-230	7,70 104 a	M	5,010^{-4}	4,0 10^{-5}	2,8 10^{-5}	5,010^{-4}	2,1 10^{-7}
		S	2,010^{-4}	1,3 10^{-5}	7,2 10^{-6}	2,010^{-4}	8,7 10^{-8}
Th-231	1,06 d	M	5,010^{-4}	2,9 10^{-10}	3,7 10^{-10}	5,010^{-4}	3,4 10^{-10}
		S	2,010^{-4}	3,2 10^{-10}	4,0 10^{-10}	2,010^{-4}	3,4 10^{-10}
Th-232	1,40 1010 a	M	5,010^{-4}	4,2 10^{-5}	2,9 10^{-5}	5,010^{-4}	2,2 10^{-7}
		S	2,010^{-4}	2,3 10^{-5}	1,2 10^{-5}	2,010^{-4}	9,2 10^{-8}
Th-234	24,1 d	M	5,010^{-4}	6,3 10^{-9}	5,3 10^{-9}	5,010^{-4}	3,4 10^{-9}
		S	2,010^{-4}	7,3 10^{-9}	5,8 10^{-9}	2,010^{-4}	3,4 10^{-9}
Protactinium							
Pa-227	0,638 h	M	5,010^{-4}	7,0 10^{-8}	9,0 10^{-8}	5,010^{-4}	4,5 10^{-10}
		S	5,010^{-4}	7,6 10^{-8}	9,7 10^{-8}		
Pa-228	22,0 h	M	5,010^{-4}	5,9 10^{-8}	4,6 10^{-8}	5,010^{-4}	7,8 10^{-10}
		S	5,010^{-4}	6,9 10^{-8}	5,1 10^{-8}		
Pa-230	17,4 h	M	5,010^{-4}	5,6 10^{-7}	4,6 10^{-7}	5,010^{-4}	9,2 10^{-10}
		S	5,010^{-4}	7,1 10^{-7}	5,7 10^{-7}		
Pa-231	3,27 104 a	M	5,010^{-4}	1,3 10^{-4}	8,9 10^{-5}	5,010^{-4}	7,1 10^{-7}
		S	5,010^{-4}	3,2 10^{-5}	1,7 10^{-5}		
Pa-232	1,31 d	M	5,010^{-4}	9,5 10^{-9}	6,8 10^{-9}	5,010^{-4}	7,2 10^{-10}
		S	5,010^{-4}	3,2 10^{-9}	2,0 10^{-9}		
Pa-233	27,0 d	M	5,010^{-4}	3,1 10^{-9}	2,8 10^{-9}	5,010^{-4}	8,7 10^{-10}
		S	5,010^{-4}	3,7 10^{-9}	3,2 10^{-9}		
Pa-234	6,70 h	M	5,010^{-4}	3,8 10^{-10}	5,5 10^{-10}	5,010^{-4}	5,1 10^{-10}
		S	5,010^{-4}	4,0 10^{-10}	5,8 10^{-10}		
Uranium							
U-230	20,8 d	F	0,020	3,6 10^{-7}	4,2 10^{-7}	0,020	5,5 10^{-8}
		M	0,020	1,2 10^{-5}	1,0 10^{-5}	0,002	2,8 10^{-8}
		S	0,002	1,5 10^{-5}	1,2 10^{-5}		
U-231	4,20 d	F	0,020	8,3 10^{-11}	1,4 10^{-10}	0,020	2,8 10^{-10}
		M	0,020	3,4 10^{-10}	3,7 10^{-10}	0,002	2,8 10^{-10}
		S	0,002	3,7 10^{-10}	4,0 10^{-10}		
U-232	72,0 a	F	0,020	4,0 10^{-6}	4,7 10^{-6}	0,020	3,3 10^{-7}
		M	0,020	7,2 10^{-6}	4,8 10^{-6}	0,002	3,7 10^{-8}
		S	0,002	3,5 10^{-5}	2,6 10^{-5}		
U-233	1,58 105 a	F	0,020	5,7 10^{-7}	6,6 10^{-7}	0,020	5,0 10^{-8}
		M	0,020	3,2 10^{-6}	2,2 10^{-6}	0,002	8,5 10^{-9}
		S	0,002	8,7 10^{-6}	6,9 10^{-6}		
U-234	2,44 105 a	F	0,020	5,5 10^{-7}	6,4 10^{-7}	0,020	4,9 10^{-8}
		M	0,020	3,1 10^{-6}	2,1 10^{-6}	0,002	8,3 10^{-9}
		S	0,002	8,5 10^{-6}	6,8 10^{-6}		
U-235	7,04 108 a	F	0,020	5,1 10^{-7}	6,0 10^{-7}	0,020	4,6 10^{-8}
		M	0,020	2,8 10^{-6}	1,8 10^{-6}	0,002	8,3 10^{-9}
		S	0,002	7,7 10^{-6}	6,1 10^{-6}		

Nuclide	*Physical half-life*	*Inhalation*				*Ingestion*	
		Type	f_1	$h(g)_{1\mu m}$	$h(g)_{5\mu m}$	f_1	$h(g)$
U-236	2,34 107 a	F	0,020	$5,2\ 10^{-7}$	$6,1\ 10^{-7}$	0,020	$4,6\ 10^{-8}$
		M	0,020	$2,9\ 10^{-6}$	$1,9\ 10^{-6}$	0,002	$7,9\ 10^{-9}$
		S	0,002	$7,9\ 10^{-6}$	$6,3\ 10^{-6}$		
U-237	6,75 d	F	0,020	$1,9\ 10^{-10}$	$3,3\ 10^{-10}$	0,020	$7,6\ 10^{-10}$
		M	0,020	$1,6\ 10^{-9}$	$1,5\ 10^{-9}$	0,002	$7,7\ 10^{-10}$
		S	0,002	$1,8\ 10^{-9}$	$1,7\ 10^{-9}$		
U-238	4,47 109 a	F	0,020	$4,9\ 10^{-7}$	$5,8\ 10^{-7}$	0,020	$4,4\ 10^{-8}$
		M	0,020	$2,6\ 10^{-6}$	$1,6\ 10^{-6}$	0,002	$7,6\ 10^{-9}$
		S	0,002	$7,3\ 10^{-6}$	$5,7\ 10^{-6}$		
U-239	0,392 h	F	0,020	$1,1\ 10^{-11}$	$1,8\ 10^{-11}$	0,020	$2,7\ 10^{-11}$
		M	0,020	$2,3\ 10^{-11}$	$3,3\ 10^{-11}$	0,002	$2,8\ 10^{-11}$
		S	0,002	$2,4\ 10^{-11}$	$3,5\ 10^{-11}$		
U-240	14,1 h	F	0,020	$2,1\ 10^{-10}$	$3,7\ 10^{-10}$	0,020	$1,1\ 10^{-9}$
		M	0,020	$5,3\ 10^{-10}$	$7,9\ 10^{-10}$	0,002	$1,1\ 10^{-9}$
		S	0,002	$5,7\ 10^{-10}$	$8,4\ 10^{-10}$		
Neptunium							
Np-232	0,245 h	M	$5,010^{-4}$	$4,7\ 10^{-11}$	$3,5\ 10^{-11}$	$5,010^{-4}$	$9,7\ 10^{-12}$
Np-233	0,603 h	M	$5,010^{-4}$	$1,7\ 10^{-12}$	$3,0\ 10^{-12}$	$5,010^{-4}$	$2,2\ 10^{-12}$
Np-234	4,40 d	M	$5,010^{-4}$	$5,4\ 10^{-10}$	$7,3\ 10^{-10}$	$5,010^{-4}$	$8,1\ 10^{-10}$
Np-235	1,08 a	M	$5,010^{-4}$	$4,0\ 10^{-10}$	$2,7\ 10^{-10}$	$5,010^{-4}$	$5,3\ 10^{-11}$
Np-236	1,15 105 a	M	$5,010^{-4}$	$3,0\ 10^{-6}$	$2,0\ 10^{-6}$	$5,010^{-4}$	$1,7\ 10^{-8}$
Np-236	22,5 h	M	$5,010^{-4}$	$5,0\ 10^{-9}$	$3,6\ 10^{-9}$	$5,010^{-4}$	$1,9\ 10^{-10}$
Np-237	2,14 106 a	M	$5,010^{-4}$	$2,1\ 10^{-5}$	$1,5\ 10^{-5}$	$5,010^{-4}$	$1,1\ 10^{-7}$
Np-238	2,12 d	M	$5,010^{-4}$	$2,0\ 10^{-9}$	$1,7\ 10^{-9}$	$5,010^{-4}$	$9,1\ 10^{-10}$
Np-239	2,36 d	M	$5,010^{-4}$	$9,0\ 10^{-10}$	$1,1\ 10^{-9}$	$5,010^{-4}$	$8,0\ 10^{-10}$
Np-240	1,08 h	M	$5,010^{-4}$	$8,7\ 10^{-11}$	$1,3\ 10^{-10}$	$5,010^{-4}$	$8,2\ 10^{-11}$
Plutonium							
Pu-234	8,80 h	M	$5,010^{-4}$	$1,9\ 10^{-8}$	$1,6\ 10^{-8}$	$5,010^{-4}$	$1,6\ 10^{-10}$
		S	$1,010^{-5}$	$2,2\ 10^{-8}$	$1,8\ 10^{-8}$	$1,010^{-5}$	$1,5\ 10^{-10}$
					$1,0\ 10^{-4}$	$1,610^{-10}$	
Pu-235	0,422 h	M	$5,010^{-4}$	$1,5\ 10^{-12}$	$2,5\ 10^{-12}$	$5,010^{-4}$	$2,1\ 10^{-12}$
		S	$1,010^{-5}$	$1,6\ 10^{-12}$	$2,6\ 10^{-12}$	$1,010^{-5}$	$2,1\ 10^{-12}$
					$1,0\ 10^{-4}$	$2,110^{-12}$	
Pu-236	2,85 a	M	$5,010^{-4}$	$1,8\ 10^{-5}$	$1,3\ 10^{-5}$	$5,010^{-4}$	$8,6\ 10^{-8}$
		S	$1,010^{-5}$	$9,6\ 10^{-6}$	$7,4\ 10^{-6}$	$1,010^{-5}$	$6,3\ 10^{-9}$
						$1,010^{-4}$	$2,1\ 10^{-8}$
Pu-237	45,3 d	M	$5,010^{-4}$	$3,3\ 10^{-10}$	$2,9\ 10^{-10}$	$5,010^{-4}$	$1,0\ 10^{-10}$
		S	$1,010^{-5}$	$3,6\ 10^{-10}$	$3,0\ 10^{-10}$	$1,010^{-5}$	$1,0\ 10^{-10}$
						$1,010^{-4}$	$1,0\ 10^{-10}$
Pu-238	87,7 a	M	$5,010^{-4}$	$4,3\ 10^{-5}$	$3,0\ 10^{-5}$	$5,010^{-4}$	$2,3\ 10^{-7}$
		S	$1,010^{-5}$	$1,5\ 10^{-5}$	$1,1\ 10^{-5}$	$1,010^{-5}$	$8,8\ 10^{-9}$
						$1,010^{-4}$	$4,9\ 10^{-8}$
Pu-239	2,41 104 a	M	$5,010^{-4}$	$4,7\ 10^{-5}$	$3,2\ 10^{-5}$	$5,010^{-4}$	$2,5\ 10^{-7}$
		S	$1,010^{-5}$	$1,5\ 10^{-5}$	$8,3\ 10^{-6}$	$1,010^{-5}$	$9,0\ 10^{-9}$
					$1,0\ 10^{-4}$	$5,310^{-8}$	

Nuclide	Physical half-life	Inhalation				Ingestion	
		Type	f_1	$h(g)_{1\mu m}$	$h(g)_{5\mu m}$	f_1	$h(g)$
Pu-240	6,54 103 a	M	$5{,}010^{-4}$	$4{,}7\ 10^{-5}$	$3{,}2\ 10^{-5}$	$5{,}010^{-4}$	$2{,}5\ 10^{-7}$
		S	$1{,}010^{-5}$	$1{,}5\ 10^{-5}$	$8{,}3\ 10^{-6}$	$1{,}010^{-5}$	$9{,}0\ 10^{-9}$
						$1{,}010^{-4}$	$5{,}3\ 10^{-8}$
Pu-241	14,4 a	M	$5{,}010^{-4}$	$8{,}5\ 10^{-7}$	$5{,}8\ 10^{-7}$	$5{,}010^{-4}$	$4{,}7\ 10^{-9}$
		S	$1{,}010^{-5}$	$1{,}6\ 10^{-7}$	$8{,}4\ 10^{-8}$	$1{,}010^{-5}$	$1{,}1\ 10^{-10}$
						$1{,}010^{-4}$	$9{,}6\ 10^{-10}$
Pu-242	3,76 105 a	M	$5{,}010^{-4}$	$4{,}4\ 10^{-5}$	$3{,}1\ 10^{-5}$	$5{,}010^{-4}$	$2{,}4\ 10^{-7}$
		S	$1{,}010^{-5}$	$1{,}4\ 10^{-5}$	$7{,}7\ 10^{-6}$	$1{,}010^{-5}$	$8{,}6\ 10^{-9}$
					$1{,}0\ 10^{-4}$	$5{,}010^{-8}$	
Pu-243	4,95 h	M	$5{,}010^{-4}$	$8{,}2\ 10^{-11}$	$1{,}1\ 10^{-10}$	$5{,}010^{-4}$	$8{,}5\ 10^{-11}$
		S	$1{,}010^{-5}$	$8{,}5\ 10^{-11}$	$1{,}1\ 10^{-10}$	$1{,}010^{-5}$	$8{,}5\ 10^{-11}$
						$1{,}010^{-4}$	$8{,}5\ 10^{-11}$
Pu-244	8,26 107 a	M	$5{,}010^{-4}$	$4{,}4\ 10^{-5}$	$3{,}0\ 10^{-5}$	$5{,}010^{-4}$	$2{,}4\ 10^{-7}$
		S	$1{,}010^{-5}$	$1{,}3\ 10^{-5}$	$7{,}4\ 10^{-6}$	$1{,}010^{-5}$	$1{,}1\ 10^{-8}$
						$1{,}010^{-4}$	$5{,}2\ 10^{-8}$
Pu-245	10,5 h	M	$5{,}010^{-4}$	$4{,}5\ 10^{-10}$	$6{,}1\ 10^{-10}$	$5{,}010^{-4}$	$7{,}2\ 10^{-10}$
		S	$1{,}010^{-5}$	$4{,}8\ 10^{-10}$	$6{,}5\ 10^{-10}$	$1{,}010^{-5}$	$7{,}2\ 10^{-10}$
						$1{,}010^{-4}$	$7{,}2\ 10^{-10}$
Pu-246	10,9 d	M	$5{,}010^{-4}$	$7{,}0\ 10^{-9}$	$6{,}5\ 10^{-9}$	$5{,}010^{-4}$	$3{,}3\ 10^{-9}$
		S	$1{,}010^{-5}$	$7{,}6\ 10^{-9}$	$7{,}0\ 10^{-9}$	$1{,}010^{-5}$	$3{,}3\ 10^{-9}$
						$1{,}010^{-4}$	$3{,}3\ 10^{-9}$
Americium							
Am-237	1,22 h	M	$5{,}010^{-4}$	$2{,}5\ 10^{-11}$	$3{,}6\ 10^{-11}$	$5{,}010^{-4}$	$1{,}8\ 10^{-11}$
Am-238	1,63 h	M	$5{,}010^{-4}$	$8{,}5\ 10^{-11}$	$6{,}6\ 10^{-11}$	$5{,}010^{-4}$	$3{,}2\ 10^{-11}$
Am-239	11,9 h	M	$5{,}010^{-4}$	$2{,}2\ 10^{-10}$	$2{,}9\ 10^{-10}$	$5{,}010^{-4}$	$2{,}4\ 10^{-10}$
Am-240	2,12 d	M	$5{,}010^{-4}$	$4{,}4\ 10^{-10}$	$5{,}9\ 10^{-10}$	$5{,}010^{-4}$	$5{,}8\ 10^{-10}$
Am-241	4,32 102 a	M	$5{,}010^{-4}$	$3{,}9\ 10^{-5}$	$2{,}7\ 10^{-5}$	$5{,}010^{-4}$	$2{,}0\ 10^{-7}$
Am-242	16,0 h	M	$5{,}010^{-4}$	$1{,}6\ 10^{-8}$	$1{,}2\ 10^{-8}$	$5{,}010^{-4}$	$3{,}0\ 10^{-10}$
Am-242m	1,52 102 a	M	$5{,}010^{-4}$	$3{,}5\ 10^{-5}$	$2{,}4\ 10^{-5}$	$5{,}010^{-4}$	$1{,}9\ 10^{-7}$
Am-243	7,38 103 a	M	$5{,}010^{-4}$	$3{,}9\ 10^{-5}$	$2{,}7\ 10^{-5}$	$5{,}010^{-4}$	$2{,}0\ 10^{-7}$
Am-244	10,1 h	M	$5{,}010^{-4}$	$1{,}9\ 10^{-9}$	$1{,}5\ 10^{-9}$	$5{,}010^{-4}$	$4{,}6\ 10^{-10}$
Am-244m	0,433 h	M	$5{,}010^{-4}$	$7{,}9\ 10^{-11}$	$6{,}2\ 10^{-11}$	$5{,}010^{-4}$	$2{,}9\ 10^{-11}$
Am-245	2,05 h	M	$5{,}010^{-4}$	$5{,}3\ 10^{-11}$	$7{,}6\ 10^{-11}$	$5{,}010^{-4}$	$6{,}2\ 10^{-11}$
Am-246	0,650 h	M	$5{,}010^{-4}$	$6{,}8\ 10^{-11}$	$1{,}1\ 10^{-10}$	$5{,}010^{-4}$	$5{,}8\ 10^{-11}$
Am-246m	0,417 h	M	$5{,}010^{-4}$	$2{,}3\ 10^{-11}$	$3{,}8\ 10^{-11}$	$5{,}010^{-4}$	$3{,}4\ 10^{-11}$
Curium							
Cm-238	2,40 h	M	$5{,}010^{-4}$	$4{,}1\ 10^{-9}$	$4{,}8\ 10^{-9}$	$5{,}010^{-4}$	$8{,}0\ 10^{-11}$
Cm-240	27,0 d	M	$5{,}010^{-4}$	$2{,}9\ 10^{-6}$	$2{,}3\ 10^{-6}$	$5{,}010^{-4}$	$7{,}6\ 10^{-9}$
Cm-241	32,8 d	M	$5{,}010^{-4}$	$3{,}4\ 10^{-8}$	$2{,}6\ 10^{-8}$	$5{,}010^{-4}$	$9{,}1\ 10^{-10}$
Cm-242	163 d	M	$5{,}010^{-4}$	$4{,}8\ 10^{-6}$	$3{,}7\ 10^{-6}$	$5{,}010^{-4}$	$1{,}2\ 10^{-8}$
Cm-243	28,5 a	M	$5{,}010^{-4}$	$2{,}9\ 10^{-5}$	$2{,}0\ 10^{-5}$	$5{,}010^{-4}$	$1{,}5\ 10^{-7}$
Cm-244	18,1 a	M	$5{,}010^{-4}$	$2{,}5\ 10^{-5}$	$1{,}7\ 10^{-5}$	$5{,}010^{-4}$	$1{,}2\ 10^{-7}$
Cm-245	8,50 103 a	M	$5{,}010^{-4}$	$4{,}0\ 10^{-5}$	$2{,}7\ 10^{-5}$	$5{,}010^{-4}$	$2{,}1\ 10^{-7}$
Cm-246	4,73 103 a	M	$5{,}010^{-4}$	$4{,}0\ 10^{-5}$	$2{,}7\ 10^{-5}$	$5{,}010^{-4}$	$2{,}1\ 10^{-7}$
Cm-247	1,56 107 a	M	$5{,}010^{-4}$	$3{,}6\ 10^{-5}$	$2{,}5\ 10^{-5}$	$5{,}010^{-4}$	$1{,}9\ 10^{-7}$

Nuclide	*Physical half-life*	*Inhalation*				*Ingestion*	
		Type	f_1	$h(g)_{1\mu m}$	$h(g)_{5\mu m}$	f_1	$h(g)$
Cm-248	3,39 105 a	M	5,010^{-4}	1,4 10^{-4}	9,5 10^{-5}	5,010^{-4}	7,7 10^{-7}
Cm-249	1,07 h	M	5,010^{-4}	3,2 10^{-11}	5,1 10^{-11}	5,010^{-4}	3,1 10^{-11}
Cm-250	6,90 103 a	M	5,010^{-4}	7,9 10^{-4}	5,4 10^{-4}	5,010^{-4}	4,4 10^{-6}
Berkelium							
Bk-245	4,94 d	M	5,010^{-4}	2,0 10^{-9}	1,8 10^{-9}	5,010^{-4}	5,7 10^{-10}
Bk-246	1,83 d	M	5,010^{-4}	3,4 10^{-10}	4,6 10^{-10}	5,010^{-4}	4,8 10^{-10}
Bk-247	1,38 103 a	M	5,010^{-4}	6,5 10^{-5}	4,5 10^{-5}	5,010^{-4}	3,5 10^{-7}
Bk-249	320 d	M	5,010^{-4}	1,5 10^{-7}	1,0 10^{-7}	5,010^{-4}	9,7 10^{-10}
Bk-250	3,22 h	M	5,010^{-4}	9,6 10^{-10}	7,1 10^{-10}	5,010^{-4}	1,4 10^{-10}
Californium							
Cf-244	0,323 h	M	5,010^{-4}	1,3 10^{-8}	1,8 10^{-8}	5,010^{-4}	7,0 10^{-11}
Cf-246	1,49 d	M	5,010^{-4}	4,2 10^{-7}	3,5 10^{-7}	5,010^{-4}	3,3 10^{-9}
Cf-248	334 d	M	5,010^{-4}	8,2 10^{-6}	6,1 10^{-6}	5,010^{-4}	2,8 10^{-8}
Cf-249	3,50 102 a	M	5,010^{-4}	6,6 10^{-5}	4,5 10^{-5}	5,010^{-4}	3,5 10^{-7}
Cf-250	13,1 a	M	5,010^{-4}	3,2 10^{-5}	2,2 10^{-5}	5,010^{-4}	1,6 10^{-7}
Cf-251	8,98 102 a	M	5,010^{-4}	6,7 10^{-5}	4,6 10^{-5}	5,010^{-4}	3,6 10^{-7}
Cf-252	2,64 a	M	5,010^{-4}	1,8 10^{-5}	1,3 10^{-5}	5,010^{-4}	9,0 10^{-8}
Cf-253	17,8 d	M	5,010^{-4}	1,2 10^{-6}	1,0 10^{-6}	5,010^{-4}	1,4 10^{-9}
Cf-254	60,5 d	M	5,010^{-4}	3,7 10^{-5}	2,2 10^{-5}	5,010^{-4}	4,0 10^{-7}
Einsteinium							
Es-250	2,10 h	M	5,010^{-4}	5,9 10^{-10}	4,2 10^{-10}	5,010^{-4}	2,1 10^{-11}
Es-251	1,38 d	M	5,010^{-4}	2,0 10^{-9}	1,7 10^{-9}	5,010^{-4}	1,7 10^{-10}
Es-253	20,5 d	M	5,010^{-4}	2,5 10^{-6}	2,1 10^{-6}	5,010^{-4}	6,1 10^{-9}
Es-254	276 d	M	5,010^{-4}	8,0 10^{-6}	6,0 10^{-6}	5,010^{-4}	2,8 10^{-8}
Es-254m	1,64 d	M	5,010^{-4}	4,4 10^{-7}	3,7 10^{-7}	5,010^{-4}	4,2 10^{-9}
Fermium							
Fm-252	22,7 h	M	5,010^{-4}	3,0 10^{-7}	2,6 10^{-7}	5,010^{-4}	2,7 10^{-9}
Fm-253	3,00 d	M	5,010^{-4}	3,7 10^{-7}	3,0 10^{-7}	5,010^{-4}	9,1 10^{-10}
Fm-254	3,24 h	M	5,010^{-4}	5,6 10^{-8}	7,7 10^{-8}	5,010^{-4}	4,4 10^{-10}
Fm-255	20,1 h	M	5,010^{-4}	2,5 10^{-7}	2,6 10^{-7}	5,010^{-4}	2,5 10^{-9}
Fm-257	101 d	M	5,010^{-4}	6,6 10^{-6}	5,2 10^{-6}	5,010^{-4}	1,5 10^{-8}
Mendelevium							
Md-257	5,20 h	M	5,010^{-4}	2,3 10^{-8}	2,0 10^{-8}	5,010^{-4}	1,2 10^{-10}
Md-258	55,0 d	M	5,010^{-4}	5,5 10^{-6}	4,4 10^{-6}	5,010^{-4}	1,3 10^{-8}

OBT — Organically bound tritium.

Type F denotes fast absorption from lung.

Type M denotes moderate absorption from lung.

Type S denotes slow absorption from lung.

Table (C.2)
Effective dose coefficients for soluble or reactive gases

Nuclide/chemical form	$t_{1/2}$	*h(g) (Sv Bq^{-1})*
Tritium gas	12,3 a	$1,8\ 10^{-15}$
Tritiated water	12,3 a	$1,8\ 10^{-11}$
Organically bound tritium	12,3 a	$4,1\ 10^{-11}$
Carbon-11 vapour	0,34 h	$3,2\ 10^{-12}$
Carbon-11 dioxide	0,34 h	$2,2\ 10^{12}$
Carbon-11 monoxide	0,34 h	$1,2\ 10^{12}$
Carbon-14 vapour	$5,73\ 10^{3}$ a	$5,8\ 10^{-10}$
Carbon-14 dioxide	$5,73\ 10^{3}$ a	$6,5\ 10^{-12}$
Carbon-14 monoxide	$5,73\ 10^{3}$ a	$8,0\ 10^{-13}$
Sulphur-35 vapour	87,4 d	$1,2\ 10^{-10}$
Nickel-56 carbonyl	6,10 d	$1,2\ 10^{-9}$
Nickel-57 carbonyl	1,50 d	$5,6\ 10^{-10}$
Nickel-59 carbonyl	$7,50\ 10^{4}$ a	$8,3\ 10^{-10}$
Nickel-63 carbonyl	96,0 a	$2,0\ 10^{-9}$
Nickel-65 carbonyl	2,52 h	$3,6\ 10^{-10}$
Nickel-66 carbonyl	2,27 d	$1,6\ 10^{-9}$
Iodine-120 vapour	1,35 h	$3,0\ 10^{-10}$
Iodine-120m vapour	0,88 h	$1,8\ 10^{-10}$
Iodine-121 vapour	2,12 h	$8,6\ 10^{-11}$
Iodine-123 vapour	13,2 h	$2,1\ 10^{-10}$
Iodine-124 vapour	4,18 d	$1,2\ 10^{-8}$
Iodine-125 vapour	60,1 d	$1,4\ 10^{-8}$
Iodine-126 vapour	13,0 d	$2,6\ 10^{-8}$
Iodine-128 vapour	0,42 h	$6,5\ 10^{-11}$
Iodine-129 vapour	$1,57\ 10^{7}$ a	$9,6\ 10^{-8}$
Iodine-130 vapour	12,4 h	$1,9\ 10^{-9}$
Iodine-131 vapour	8,04 d	$2,0\ 10^{-8}$
Iodine-132 vapour	2,30 h	$3,1\ 10^{-10}$
Iodine-132m vapour	1,39 h	$2,7\ 10^{-10}$
Iodine-133 vapour	20,8 h	$4,0\ 10^{-9}$
Iodine-134 vapour	0,88 h	$1,5\ 10^{-10}$
Iodine-135 vapour	6,61 h	$9,2\ 10^{-10}$
Mercury-193 vapour	3,50 h	$1,1\ 10^{-9}$
Mercury-193m vapour	11,1 h	$3,1\ 10^{-9}$
Mercury-194 vapour	$2,60\ 10^{2}$ a	$4,0\ 10^{-8}$
Mercury-195 vapour	9,90 h	$1,4\ 10^{-9}$
Mercury-195m vapour	1,73 d	$8,2\ 10^{-9}$
Mercury-197 vapour	2,67 d	$4,4\ 10^{-9}$
Mercury-197m vapour	23,8 h	$5,8\ 10^{-9}$
Mercury-199m vapour	0,71 h	$1,8\ 10^{-10}$
Mercury-203 vapour	46,60 d	$7,0\ 10^{-9}$

Table (D)
Compounds and f_1 values used for the calculation of ingestion dose coefficients

Element	f_1	*Compounds*
Hydrogen	1,000	Ingestion of tritiated water
	1,000	Organically bound tritium
Beryllium	0,005	All compounds
Carbon	1,000	Labelled organic compounds
Fluorine	1,000	All compounds
Sodium	1,000	All compounds
Magnesium	0,500	All compounds
Aluminium	0,010	All compounds
Silicon	0,010	All compounds
Phosphorus	0,800	All compounds
Sulphur	0,800	Inorganic compounds
	0,100	Elemental sulphur
	1,000	Organic sulphur
Chlorine	1,000	All compounds
Potassium	1,000	All compounds
Calcium	0,300	All compounds
Scandium	$1,0\ 10^{-4}$	All compounds
Titanium	0,010	All compounds
Vanadium	0,010	All compounds
Chromium	0,100	Hexavalent compounds
	0,010	Trivalent compounds
Manganese	0,100	All compounds
Iron	0,100	All compounds
Cobalt	0,100	Unspecified compounds
	0,050	Oxides, hydroxides and inorganic compounds
Nickel	0,050	All compounds
Copper	0,500	All compounds
Zinc	0,500	All compounds
Gallium	0,001	All compounds
Germanium	1,000	All compounds
Arsenic	0,500	All compounds
Selenium	0,800	Unspecified compounds
	0,050	Elemental selenium and selenides
Bromine	1,000	All compounds
Rubidium	1,000	All compounds
Strontium	0,300	Unspecified compounds
	0,010	Strontium titanate ($SrTiO_3$)
Yttrium	$1,0\ 10^{-4}$	All compounds
Zirconium	0,002	All compounds
Niobium	0,010	All compounds
Molybdenum	0,800	Unspecified compounds
	0,050	Molybdenum sulphide
Technetium	0,800	All compounds
Ruthenium	0,050	All compounds

Element	f_1	*Compounds*
Rhodium	0,050	All compounds
Palladium	0,005	All compounds
Silver	0,050	All compounds
Cadmium	0,050	All inorganic compounds
Indium	0,020	All compounds
Tin	0,020	All compounds
Antimony	0,100	All compounds
Tellurium	0,300	All compounds
Iodine	1,000	All compounds
Caesium	1,000	All compounds
Barium	0,100	All compounds
Lanthanum	$5{,}0\ 10^{-4}$	All compounds
Cerium	$5{,}0\ 10^{-4}$	All compounds
Praseodymium	$5{,}0\ 10^{-4}$	All compounds
Neodymium	$5{,}0\ 10^{-4}$	All compounds
Promethium	$5{,}0\ 10^{-4}$	All compounds
Samarium	$5{,}0\ 10^{-4}$	All compounds
Europium	$5{,}0\ 10^{-4}$	All compounds
Gadolinium	$5{,}0\ 10^{-4}$	All compounds
Terbium	$5{,}0\ 10^{-4}$	All compounds
Dysprosium	$5{,}0\ 10^{-4}$	All compounds
Holmium	$5{,}0\ 10^{-4}$	All compounds
Erbium	$5{,}0\ 10^{-4}$	All compounds
Thulium	$5{,}0\ 10^{-4}$	All compounds
Ytterbium	$5{,}0\ 10^{-4}$	All compounds
Lutetium	$5{,}0\ 10^{-4}$	All compounds
Hafnium	0,002	All compounds
Tantalum	0,001	All compounds
Tungsten	0,300	Unspecified compounds
	0,010	Tungstic acid
Rhenium	0,800	All compounds
Osmium	0,010	All compounds
Iridium	0,010	All compounds
Platinum	0,010	All compounds
Gold	0,100	All compounds
Mercury	0,020	All inorganic compounds
Mercury	1,000	Methyl mercury
	0,400	Unspecified organic compounds
Thallium	1,000	All compounds
Lead	0,200	All compounds
Bismuth	0,050	All compounds
Polonium	0,100	All compounds
Astatine	1,000	All compounds
Francium	1,000	All compounds
Radium	0,200	All compounds
Actinium	$5{,}0\ 10^{-4}$	All compounds

Element	f_1	*Compounds*
Thorium	5,0 10^{-4}	Unspecified compounds
	2,0 10^{-4}	Oxides and hydroxides
Protactinium	5,0 10^{-4}	All compounds
Uranium	0,020	Unspecified compounds
	0,002	Most tetravalent compounds, e.g., UO_2, U_3O_8, UF_4
Neptunium	5,0 10^{-4}	All compounds
Plutonium	5,0 10^{-4}	Unspecified compounds
	1,0 10^{-4}	Nitrates
	1,0 10^{-4}	Insoluble oxides
Americium	5,0 10^{-4}	All compounds
Curium	5,0 10^{-4}	All compounds
Berkelium	5,0 10^{-4}	All compounds
Californium	5,0 10^{-4}	All compounds
Einsteinium	5,0 10^{-4}	All compounds
Fermium	5,0 10^{-4}	All compounds
Mendelevium	5,0 10^{-4}	All compounds

Table (E)
Compounds, lung absorption types and f_1 values used for the calculation of inhalation dose coefficients

Element	*Absorption type(s)*	f_1	*Compounds*
Beryllium	M	0,005	Unspecified compounds
	S	0,005	Oxides, halides and nitrates
Fluorine	F	1,000	Determined by combining cation
	M	1,000	Determined by combining cation
	S	1,000	Determined by combining cation
Sodium	F	1,000	All compounds
Magnesium	F	0,500	Unspecified compounds
	M	0,500	Oxides, hydroxides, carbides, halides and nitrates
Aluminium	F	0,010	Unspecified compounds
	M	0,010	Oxides, hydroxides, carbides, halides, nitrates and metallic aluminium
Silicon	F	0,010	Unspecified compounds
	M	0,010	Oxides, hydroxides, carbides and nitrates
	S	0,010	Aluminosilicate glass aerosol
Phosphorus	F	0,800	Unspecified compounds
	M	0,800	Some phosphates: determined by combining cation
Sulphur	F	0,800	Sulphides and sulphates: determined by combining cation
	M	0,800	Elemental sulphur. Sulphides and sulphates: determined by combining cation
Chlorine	F	1,000	Determined by combining cation
	M	1,000	Determined by combining cation
Potassium	F	1,000	All compounds
Calcium	M	0,300	All compounds

Element	*Absorption type(s)*	f_1	*Compounds*
Scandium	S	$1{,}0\ 10^{-4}$	All compounds
Titanium	F	0,010	Unspecified compounds
	M	0,010	Oxides, hydroxides, carbides, halides and nitrates
	S	0,010	Strontium titanate ($SrTiO_3$)
Vanadium	F	0,010	Unspecified compounds
	M	0,010	Oxides, hydroxides, carbides and halides
Chromium	F	0,100	Unspecified compounds
	M	0,100	Halides and nitrates
	S	0,100	Oxides and hydroxides
Manganese	F	0,100	Unspecified compounds
	M	0,100	Oxides, hydroxides, halides and nitrates
Iron	F	0,100	Unspecified compounds
	M	0,100	Oxides, hydroxides and halides
Cobalt	M	0,100	Unspecified compounds
	S	0,050	Oxides, hydroxides, halides and nitrates
Nickel	F	0,050	Unspecified compounds
	M	0,050	Oxides, hydroxides and carbides
Copper	F	0,500	Unspecified inorganic compounds
	M	0,500	Sulphides, halides and nitrates
	S	0,500	Oxides and hydroxides
Zinc	S	0,500	All compounds
Gallium	F	0,001	Unspecified compounds
	M	0,001	Oxides, hydroxides, carbides, halides and nitrates
Germanium	F	1,000	Unspecified compounds
	M	1,000	Oxides, sulphides and halides
Arsenic	M	0,500	All compounds
Selenium	F	0,800	Unspecified inorganic compounds
	M	0,800	Elemental selenium, oxides, hydroxides and carbides
Bromine	F	1,000	Determined by combining cation
	M	1,000	Determined by combining cation
Rubidium	F	1,000	All compounds
Strontium	F	0,300	Unspecified compounds
	S	0,010	Strontium titanate ($SrTiO_3$)
Yttrium	M	$1{,}0\ 10^{-4}$	Unspecified compounds
	S	$1{,}0\ 10^{-4}$	Oxides and hydroxides
Zirconium	F	0,002	Unspecified compounds
	M	0,002	Oxides, hydroxides, halides and nitrates
	S	0,002	Zirconium carbide
Niobium	M	0,010	Unspecified compounds
	S	0,010	Oxides and hydroxides
Molybdenum	F	0,800	Unspecified compounds
	S	0,050	Molybdenum sulphide, oxides and hydroxides
Technetium	F	0,800	Unspecified compounds
	M	0,800	Oxides, hydroxides, halides and nitrates

Element	*Absorption type(s)*	f_1	*Compounds*
Ruthenium	F	0,050	Unspecified compounds
	M	0,050	Halides
	S	0,050	Oxides and hydroxides
Rhodium	F	0,050	Unspecified compounds
	M	0,050	Halides
	S	0,050	Oxides and hydroxides
Palladium	F	0,005	Unspecified compounds
	M	0,005	Nitrates and halides
	S	0,005	Oxides and hydroxides
Silver	F	0,050	Unspecified compounds and metallic silver
	M	0,050	Nitrates and sulphides
	S	0,050	Oxides and hydroxides, carbides
Cadmium	F	0,050	Unspecified compounds
	M	0,050	Sulphides, halides and nitrates
	S	0,050	Oxides and hydroxides
Indium	F	0,020	Unspecified compounds
	M	0,020	Oxides, hydroxides, halides and nitrates
Tin	F	0,020	Unspecified compounds
	M	0,020	Stannic phosphate, sulphides, oxides, hydroxides, halides and nitrates
Antimony	F	0,100	Unspecified compounds
	M	0,010	Oxides, hydroxides, halides, sulphides, sulphates and nitrates
Tellurium	F	0,300	Unspecified compounds
	M	0,300	Oxides, hydroxides and nitrates
Iodine	F	1,000	All compounds
Caesium	F	1,000	All compounds
Barium	F	0,100	All compounds
Lanthanum	F	$5{,}0\ 10^{-4}$	Unspecified compounds
	M	$5{,}0\ 10^{-4}$	Oxides and hydroxides
Cerium	M	$5{,}0\ 10^{-4}$	Unspecified compounds
	S	$5{,}0\ 10^{-4}$	Oxides, hydroxides and fluorides
Praseodymium	M	$5{,}0\ 10^{-4}$	Unspecified compounds
	S	$5{,}0\ 10^{-4}$	Oxides, hydroxides, carbides and fluorides
Neodymium	M	$5{,}0\ 10^{-4}$	Unspecified compounds
	S	$5{,}0\ 10^{-4}$	Oxides, hydroxides, carbides and fluorides
Promethium	M	$5{,}0\ 10^{-4}$	Unspecified compounds
	S	$5{,}0\ 10^{-4}$	Oxides, hydroxides, carbides and fluorides
Samarium	M	$5{,}0\ 10^{-4}$	All compounds
Europium	M	$5{,}0\ 10^{-4}$	All compounds
Gadolinium	F	$5{,}0\ 10^{-4}$	Unspecified compounds
	M	$5{,}0\ 10^{-4}$	Oxides, hydroxides and fluorides
Terbium	M	$5{,}0\ 10^{-4}$	All compounds
Dysprosium	M	$5{,}0\ 10^{-4}$	All compounds
Holmium	M	$5{,}0\ 10^{-4}$	Unspecified compounds

Element	*Absorption type(s)*	f_1	*Compounds*
Erbium	M	5,0 10^{-4}	All compounds
Thulium	M	5,0 10^{-4}	All compounds
Ytterbium	M	5,0 10^{-4}	Unspecified compounds
	S	5,0 10^{-4}	Oxides, hydroxides and fluorides
Lutetium	M	5,0 10^{-4}	Unspecified compounds
	S	5,0 10^{-4}	Oxides, hydroxides and fluorides
Hafnium	F	0,002	Unspecified compounds
	M	0,002	Oxides, hydroxides, halides, carbides and nitrates
Tantalum	M	0,001	Unspecified compounds
	S	0,001	Elemental tantalum, oxides, hydroxides, halides, carbides, nitrates and nitrides
Tungsten	F	0,300	All compounds
Rhenium	F	0,800	Unspecified compounds
	M	0,800	Oxides, hydroxides, halides and nitrates
Osmium	F	0,010	Unspecified compounds
	M	0,010	Halides and nitrates
	S	0,010	Oxides and hydroxides
Iridium	F	0,010	Unspecified compounds
	M	0,010	Metallic iridium, halides and nitrates
	S	0,010	Oxides and hydroxides
Platinum	F	0,010	All compounds
Gold	F	0,100	Unspecified compounds
	M	0,100	Halides and nitrates
	S	0,100	Oxides and hydroxides
Mercury	F	0,020	Sulphates
	M	0,020	Oxides, hydroxides, halides, nitrates and sulphides
Mercury	F	0,400	All organic compounds
Thallium	F	1,000	All compounds
Lead	F	0,200	All compounds
Bismuth	F	0,050	Bismuth nitrate
	M	0,050	Unspecified compounds
Polonium	F	0,100	Unspecified compounds
	M	0,100	Oxides, hydroxides and nitrates
Astatine	F	1,000	Determined by combining cation
	M	1,000	Determined by combining cation
Francium	F	1,000	All compounds
Radium	M	0,200	All compounds
Actinium	F	5,0 10^{-4}	Unspecified compounds
	M	5,0 10^{-4}	Halides and nitrates
	S	5,0 10^{-4}	Oxides and hydroxides
Thorium	M	5,0 10^{-4}	Unspecified compounds
	S	2,0 10^{-4}	Oxides and hydroxides
Protactinium	M	5,0 10^{-4}	Unspecified compounds
	S	5,0 10^{-4}	Oxides and hydroxides

Element	*Absorption type(s)*	f_1	*Compounds*
Uranium	F	0,020	Most hexavalent compounds, e.g., UF_6, UO_2F_2 and $UO_2(NO_3)_2$
	M	0,020	Less soluble compounds, e.g., UO_3, UF_4, UCl_4 and most other hexavalent compounds
	S	0,002	Highly insoluble compounds, e.g., UO_2 and U_3O_8
Neptunium	M	$5{,}0\ 10^{-4}$	All compounds
Plutonium	M	$5{,}0\ 10^{-4}$	Unspecified compounds
	S	$1{,}0\ 10^{-5}$	Insoluble oxides
Americium	M	$5{,}0\ 10^{-4}$	All compounds
Curium	M	$5{,}0\ 10^{-4}$	All compounds
Berkelium	M	$5{,}0\ 10^{-4}$	All compounds
Californium	M	$5{,}0\ 10^{-4}$	All compounds
Einsteinium	M	$5{,}0\ 10^{-4}$	All compounds
Fermium	M	$5{,}0\ 10^{-4}$	All compounds
Mendelevium	M	$5{,}0\ 10^{-4}$	All compounds

DIRECTIVE 2000/53/EC DIRECTIVE 2000/53/EC OF THE EUROPEAN PARLIAMENT AND OF THE COUNCIL

of 18 September 2000

ON END-OF-LIFE VEHICLES

THE EUROPEAN PARIAMENT AND THE COUNCIL OF THE EUROPEAN UNION,

Having regard to the Treaty establishing the European Community, and in particular Article 175(1) thereof,

Having regard to the proposal from the Commission,

Having regard to the opinion of the Economic and Social Committee,

Having consulted the Committee of the Regions,

Acting in accordance with the procedure referred to in Article 251 of the Treaty in the light of the joint text approved by the Conciliation Committee on 23 May 2000,

Whereas

(1) The different national measures concerning end-of life vehicles should be harmonised in order, first, to minimise the impact of end-of life vehicles on the environment, thus contributing to the protection, preservation and improvement of the quality of the environment and energy conservation, and, second, to ensure the smooth operation of the internal market and avoid distortions of competition in the Community.

(2) A Community-wide framework is necessary in order to ensure coherence between national approaches in attaining the objectives stated above, particularly with a view to the design of vehicles for recycling and recovery, to the requirements for collection and treatment facilities, and to the attainment of the targets for reuse, recycling and recovery, taking into account the principle of subsidiarity and the polluter-pays principle.

(3) Every year end-of life vehicles in the Community generate between 8 and 9 million tonnes of waste, which must be managed correctly.

(4) In order to implement the precautionary and preventive principles and in line with the Community strategy for waste management, the generation of waste must be avoided as much as possible.

(5) It is a further fundamental principle that waste should be reused and recovered, and that preference be given to reuse and recycling.

(6) Member States should take measures to ensure that economic operators set up systems for the collection, treatment and recovery of end-of life vehicles.

(7) Member States should ensure that the last holder and/or owner can deliver the end-of life vehicle to an authorised treatment facility without any cost as a result of the vehicle having no or a negative, market value. Member States should ensure that producers meet all, or a significant part of, the costs of the implementation of these measures; the normal functioning of market forces should not be hindered.

(8) This Directive should cover vehicles and end-of life vehicles, including their components and materials, as well as spare and replacement parts, without prejudice to safety standards, air emissions and noise control.

(9) This Directive should be understood as having borrowed, where appropriate, the terminology used by several existing directives, namely Council Directive 67/548/EEC of 27 June 1967 on the approximation of laws, regulations and administrative provisions relating to the classification, packaging and labelling of dangerous substances, Council Directive 70/156/EEC of 6 February 1970 on the approximation of the laws of the Member States relating to the type-approval of motor vehicles and their trailers, and Council Directive 75/442/EEC of 15 July 1975 on waste.

(10) Vintage vehicles, meaning historic vehicles or vehicles of value to collectors or intended for museums, kept in a proper and environmentally sound manner, either ready for use or stripped into parts, are not covered by the definition of waste laid down by Directive 75/442/EEC and do not fall within the scope of this Directive.

(11) It is important that preventive measures be applied from the conception phase of the vehicle onwards and take the form, in particular, of reduction and control of hazardous substances in vehicles, in order to prevent their release into the environment, to facilitate recycling and to avoid the disposal of hazardous waste. In particular the use of lead, mercury, cadmium and hexavalent chromium should be prohibited. These heavy metals should only be used in certain applications according to a list which will be regularly reviewed. This will help to ensure that certain materials and components do not become shredder residues, and are not incinerated or disposed of in landfills.

(12) The recycling of all plastics from end-of life vehicles should be continuously improved. The Commission is currently examining the environmental impacts of PVC. The Commission will, on the basis of this work, make proposals as appropriate as to the use of PVC including considerations for vehicles.

(13) The requirements for dismantling, reuse and recycling of end-of life vehicles and their components should be integrated in the design and production of new vehicles.

(14) The development of markets for recycled materials should be encouraged.

(15) In order to ensure that end-of life vehicles are discarded without endangering the environment, appropriate collection systems should be set up.

(16) A certificate of destruction, to be used as a condition for the de-registration of end-of life vehicles, should be introduced. Member States without a de-registration system should set up a system according to which a certificate of destruction is notified to the relevant competent authority when the end-of life vehicle is transferred to a treatment facility.

(17) This Directive does not prevent Member States from granting, where appropriate, temporary deregistrations of vehicles.

(18) Collection and treatment operators should be allowed to operate only when they have received a permit or, in case a registration is used instead of a permit, specific conditions have been complied with.

(19) The recyclability and recoverability of vehicles should be promoted.

(20) It is important to lay down requirements for storage and treatment operations in order to prevent negative impacts on the environment and to avoid the emergence of distortions in trade and competition.

(21) In order to achieve results in the short term and to give operators, consumers and public authorities the necessary perspective for the longer term, quantified targets for reuse, recycling and recovery to be achieved by economic operators should be set.

(22) Producers should ensure that vehicles are designed and manufactured in such a way as to allow the quantified targets for reuse, recycling and recovery to be achieved. To this end the Commission will promote the preparation of European standards and will take the other necessary measures in order to amend the pertinent European vehicle type-approval legislation.

(23) Member States should ensure that in implementing the provisions of this Directive competition is preserved, in particular as regards the access of small and medium-sized enterprises to the collection, dismantling, treatment and recycling market.

(24) In order to facilitate the dismantling and recovery, in particular recycling of end-of life vehicles, vehicle manufacturers should provide authorised treatment facilities with all requisite dismantling information, in particular for hazardous materials.

(25) The preparation of European standards, where appropriate, should be promoted. Vehicle manufacturers and material producers should use component and material coding standards, to be established by the Commission assisted by the relevant committee. In the preparation of these standards the Commission will take account, as appropriate, of the work going on in this area in the relevant international forums.

(26) Community-wide data on end-of life vehicles are needed in order to monitor the implementation of the objectives of this Directive.
(27) Consumers have to be adequately informed in order to adjust their behaviour and attitudes; to this end information should be made available by the relevant economic operators.
(28) Member States may choose to implement certain provisions by means of agreements with the economic sector concerned, provided that certain conditions are met.
(29) The adaptation to scientific and technical progress of the requirements for treatment facilities and for the use of hazardous substances and, as well as the adoption of minimum standards for the certificate of destruction, the formats for the database and the implementation measures necessary to control compliance with the quantified targets should be effected by the Commission under a Committee procedure.
(30) The measures to be taken for the implementation of this Directive should be adopted in accordance with Council Decision 1999/468/EC of 28 June 1999 laying down the procedures for the exercise of implementing powers conferred on the Commission.
(31) Member States may apply the provisions of this Directive in advance of the date set out therein, provided such measures are compatible with the Treaty,

HAVE ADOPTED THIS DIRECTIVE:

Article 1

Objectives

This Directive lays down measures which aim, as a first priority, at the prevention of waste from vehicles and, in addition, at the reuse, recycling and other forms of recovery of end-of life vehicles and their components so as to reduce the disposal of waste, as well as at the improvement in the environmental performance of all of the economic operators involved in the life cycle of vehicles and especially the operators directly involved in the treatment of end-of life vehicles.

Article 2

Definitions

For the purposes of this Directive:

1. "vehicle" means any vehicle designated as category M1 or N1 defined in Annex IIA to Directive 70/156/EEC, and three wheel motor vehicles as defined in Directive 92/61/EEC, but excluding motor tricycles;
2. "end-of life vehicle" means a vehicle which is waste within the meaning of Article 1(a) of Directive 75/442/EEC;
3. "producer" means the vehicle manufacturer or the professional importer of a vehicle into a Member State;
4. "prevention" means measures aiming at the reduction of the quantity and the harmfulness for the environment of end-of life vehicles, their materials and substances;
5. "treatment" means any activity after the end-of life vehicle has been handed over to a facility for depollution, dismantling, shearing, shredding, recovery or preparation for disposal of the shredder wastes, and any other operation carried out for the recovery and/or disposal of the end-of life vehicle and its components;
6. "reuse" means any operation by which components of end-of life vehicles are used for the same purpose for which they were conceived;
7. "recycling" means the reprocessing in a production process of the waste materials for the original purpose or for other purposes but excluding energy recovery. Energy recovery means the use of combustible waste as a means to generate energy through direct incineration with or without other waste but with recovery of the heat;

8. "recovery" means any of the applicable operations provided for in Annex IIB to Directive 75/442/EEC;
9. "disposal" means any of the applicable operations provided for in Annex IIA to Directive 75/442/EEC;
10. "economic operators" means producers, distributors, collectors, motor vehicle insurance companies, dismantlers, shredders, recoverers, recyclers and other treatment operators of end-of life vehicles, including their components and materials;

[11. "hazardous substance" means any substance which fulfils the criteria for any of the following hazard classes or categories set out in Annex I of Regulation (EC) No 1272/2008 of the European Parliament and of the Council of 16 December 2008 on classification, labelling and packaging of substances and mixtures [];
   (a) hazard classes 2.1 to 2.4, 2.6 and 2.7, 2.8 types A and B, 2.9, 2.10, 2.12, 2.13 categories 1 and 2, 2.14 categories 1 and 2, 2.15 types A to F;
   (b) hazard classes 3.1 to 3.6, 3.7 adverse effects on sexual function and fertility or on development, 3.8 effects other than narcotic effects, 3.9 and 3.10;
   (c) hazard class 4.1;
   (d) hazard class 5.1.][1]

12. "shredder" means any device used for tearing into pieces or fragmenting end-of life vehicles, including for the purpose of obtaining directly reusable metal scrap;
13. "dismantling information" means all information required for the correct and environmentally sound treatment of end-of life vehicles. It shall be made available to authorised treatment facilities by vehicle manufacturers and component producers in the form of manuals or by means of electronic media (e.g. CD-ROM, on-line services).

Amendment

1 Substituted by Directive 2008/112/EC of the European Parliament and of the Council of 16 December 2008 amending Council Directives 76/768/EEC, 88/378/EEC, 1999/13/EC and Directives 2000/53/EC, 2002/96/EC and 2004/42/EC of the European Parliament and of the Council in order to adapt them to Regulation (EC) No 1272/2008 on classification, labelling and packaging of substances and mixtures, Article 4.

Article 3

Scope

1. This Directive shall cover vehicles and end-of life vehicles, including their components and materials. Without prejudice to Article 5(4), third subparagraph, this shall apply irrespective of how the vehicle has been serviced or repaired during use and irrespective of whether it is equipped with components supplied by the producer or with other components whose fitting as spare or replacement parts accords with the appropriate Community provisions or domestic provisions.

2. This Directive shall apply without prejudice to existing Community legislation and relevant national legislation, in particular as regards safety standards, air emissions and noise controls and the protection of soil and water.

3. Where a producer only makes or imports vehicles that are exempt from Directive 70/156/EEC by virtue of Article 8(2)(a) thereof, Member States may exempt that producer and his vehicles from Articles 7(4), 8 and 9 of this Directive.

4. Special-purpose vehicles as defined in the second indent of Article 4(1)(a) of Directive 70/156/EEC shall be excluded from the provisions of Article 7 of this Directive.

5. For three-wheel motor vehicles only Articles 5(1), 5(2) and 6 of this Directive shall apply.

Article 4

Prevention

1. In order to promote the prevention of waste Member States shall encourage, in particular:

(a) vehicle manufacturers, in liaison with material and equipment manufacturers, to limit the use of hazardous substances in vehicles and to reduce them as far as possible from the conception of the vehicle onwards, so as in particular to prevent their release into the environment, make recycling easier, and avoid the need to dispose of hazardous waste;

(b) the design and production of new vehicles which take into full account and facilitate the dismantling, reuse and recovery, in particular the recycling, of end-of life vehicles, their components and materials;

(c) vehicle manufacturers, in liaison with material and equipment manufacturers, to integrate an increasing quantity of recycled material in vehicles and other products, in order to develop the markets for recycled materials.

2.

(a) Member States shall ensure that materials and components of vehicles put on the market after 1 July 2003 do not contain lead, mercury, cadmium or hexavalent chromium other than in cases listed in Annex II under the conditions specified therein;

(b) [Annex II shall be amended on a regular basis, according to technical and scientific progress, in order to:][1]

  (i) as necessary, establish maximum concentration values up to which the existence of the substances referred to in subparagraph (a) in specific materials and components of vehicles shall be tolerated;

  (ii) exempt certain materials and components of vehicles from the provisions of subparagraph (a) if the use of these substances is unavoidable;

  (iii) delete materials and components of vehicles from Annex II if the use of these substances is avoidable;

  (iv) under points (i) and (ii) designate those materials and components of vehicles that can be stripped before further treatment; they shall be labelled or made identifiable by other appropriate means;

  [The measures referred to in points (i) to (iv), designed to amend non-essential elements of this Directive, shall be adopted in accordance with the regulatory procedure with scrutiny referred to in Article 11(3).][2]

(c) the Commission shall amend Annex II for the first time not later than 21 October 2001. In any case none of the exemptions listed therein shall be deleted from the Annex before 1 January 2003.

Amendments

1 Substituted by Directive 2008/33/EC of the European Parliament and of the Council of 11 March 2008 amending Directive 2000/53/EC on end-of-life vehicles, as regards the implementing powers conferred on the Commission, Article 1.1(a).

2 Inserted by Directive 2008/33/EC of the European Parliament and of the Council of 11 March 2008 amending Directive 2000/53/EC on end-of-life vehicles, as regards the implementing powers conferred on the Commission, Article 1.1(a).

Article 5

Collection

1. Member States shall take the necessary measures to ensure:

— that economic operators set up systems for the collection of all end-of life vehicles and, as far as technically feasible, of waste used parts removed when passenger cars are repaired,

— the adequate availability of collection facilities within their territory.

2. Member States shall also take the necessary measures to ensure that all end-of life vehicles are transferred to authorised treatment facilities.

3. Member States shall set up a system according to which the presentation of a certificate of destruction is a condition for deregistration of the end-of life vehicle. This certificate shall be issued to the holder and/or owner when the end-of life vehicle is transferred to a treatment

facility. Treatment facilities, which have obtained a permit in accordance with Article 6, shall be permitted to issue a certificate of destruction. Member States may permit producers, dealers and collectors on behalf of an authorised treatment facility to issue certificates of destruction provided that they guarantee that the end-of life vehicle is transferred to an authorised treatment facility and provided that they are registered with public authorities.

Issuing the certificate of destruction by treatment facilities or dealers or collectors on behalf of an authorised treatment facility does not entitle them to claim any financial reimbursement, except in cases where this has been explicitly arranged by Member States.

Member States which do not have a deregistration system at the date of entry into force of this Directive shall set up a system according to which a certificate of destruction is notified to the relevant competent authority when the end-of life vehicle is transferred to a treatment facility and shall otherwise comply with the terms of this paragraph. Member States making use of this subparagraph shall inform the Commission of the reasons thereof.

4. Member States shall take the necessary measures to ensure that the delivery of the vehicle to an authorised treatment facility in accordance with paragraph 3 occurs without any cost for the last holder and/or owner as a result of the vehicle's having no or a negative market value.

Member States shall take the necessary measures to ensure that producers meet all, or a significant part of, the costs of the implementation of this measure and/or take back end-of life vehicles under the same conditions as referred to in the first subparagraph.

Member States may provide that the delivery of end-of life vehicles is not fully free of charge if the end-of life vehicle does not contain the essential components of a vehicle, in particular the engine and the coachwork, or contains waste which has been added to the end-of life vehicle.

The Commission shall regularly monitor the implementation of the first subparagraph to ensure that it does not result in market distortions, and if necessary shall propose to the European Parliament and the Council an amendment thereto.

[5. Member States shall take the necessary measures to ensure that their competent authorities mutually recognise and accept the certificates of destruction issued in other Member States in accordance with paragraph 3.

To this end, minimum requirements for the certificate of destruction shall be established. That measure, designed to amend non-essential elements of this Directive by supplementing it, shall be adopted in accordance with the regulatory procedure with scrutiny referred to in Article 11(3).][1]

Amendment

1 Substituted by Directive 2008/33/EC of the European Parliament and of the Council of 11 March 2008 amending Directive 2000/53/EC on end-of-life vehicles, as regards the implementing powers conferred on the Commission, Article 1.2.

Article 6

Treatment

1. Member States shall take the necessary measures to ensure that all end-of life vehicles are stored (even temporarily) and treated in accordance with the general requirements laid down in Article 4 of Directive 75/442/EEC, and in compliance with the minimum technical requirements set out in Annex I to this Directive, without prejudice to national regulations on health and environment.

2. Member States shall take the necessary measures to ensure that any establishment or undertaking carrying out treatment operations obtains a permit from or be registered with the competent authorities, in compliance with Articles 9, 10 and 11 of Directive 75/442/EEC.

The derogation from the permit requirement referred to in Article 11(1)(b) of Directive 75/442/EEC may apply to recovery operations concerning waste of end-of life vehicles after they have been treated according to Annex 1(3) to this Directive if there is an inspection by the competent authorities before the registration. This inspection shall verify:

(a) type and quantities of waste to be treated;

(b) general technical requirements to be complied with;

(c) safety precautions to be taken,

in order to achieve the objectives referred to in Article 4 of Directive 75/442/EEC. This inspection shall take place once a year. Member States using the derogation shall send the results to the Commission.

3. Member States shall take the necessary measures to ensure that any establishment or undertaking carrying out treatment operations fulfils at least the following obligations in accordance with Annex I:

(a) end-of life vehicles shall be stripped before further treatment or other equivalent arrangements are made in order to reduce any adverse impact on the environment. Components or materials labelled or otherwise made identifiable in accordance with Article 4(2) shall be stripped before further treatment;

(b) hazardous materials and components shall be removed and segregated in a selective way so as not to contaminate subsequent shredder waste from end-of life vehicles;

(c) stripping operations and storage shall be carried out in such a way as to ensure the suitability of vehicle components for reuse and recovery, and in particular for recycling.

Treatment operations for depollution of end-of life vehicles as referred to in Annex I(3) shall be carried out as soon as possible.

4. Member States shall take the necessary measures to ensure that the permit or registration referred to in paragraph 2 includes all conditions necessary for compliance with the requirements of paragraphs 1, 2 and 3.

5. Member States shall encourage establishments or undertakings, which carry out treatment operations to introduce, certified environmental management systems.

[6. Annex I shall be amended according to technical and scientific progress. That measure, designed to amend non-essential elements of this Directive, shall be adopted in accordance with the regulatory procedure with scrutiny referred to in Article 11(3).][1]

Amendment

1 Inserted by Directive 2008/33/EC of the European Parliament and of the Council of 11 March 2008 amending Directive 2000/53/EC on end-of-life vehicles, as regards the implementing powers conferred on the Commission, Article 1.3.

Article 7

Reuse and recovery

1. Member States shall take the necessary measures to encourage the reuse of components which are suitable for reuse, the recovery of components which cannot be reused and the giving of preference to recycling when environmentally viable, without prejudice to requirements regarding the safety of vehicles and environmental requirements such as air emissions and noise control.

2. Member States shall take the necessary measures to ensure that the following targets are attained by economic operators:

(a) no later than 1 January 2006, for all end-of life vehicles, the reuse and recovery shall be increased to a minimum of 85 % by an average weight per vehicle and year. Within the same time limit the reuse and recycling shall be increased to a minimum of 80 % by an average weight per vehicle and year;

for vehicles produced before 1 January 1980, Member States may lay down lower targets, but not lower than 75 % for reuse and recovery and not lower than 70 % for reuse and recycling. Member States making use of this subparagraph shall inform the Commission and the other Member States of the reasons therefor;

(b) no later than 1 January 2015, for all end-of life vehicles, the reuse and recovery shall be increased to a minimum of 95 % by an average weight per vehicle and year. Within the same time limit, the re-use and recycling shall be increased to a minimum of 85 % by an average weight per vehicle and year.

By 31 December 2005 at the latest the European Parliament and the Council shall re-examine the targets referred to in paragraph (b) on the basis of a report of the Commission, accompanied by a proposal. In its report the Commission shall take into account the development of the material composition of vehicles and any other relevant environmental aspects related to vehicles.

[Detailed rules necessary to control compliance of Member States with the targets set out in the first subparagraph shall be established. When proposing such rules, the Commission shall take into account all relevant factors, inter alia, the availability of data and the issue of exports and imports of end-of-life vehicles. Those detailed rules, designed to amend non-essential elements of this Directive by supplementing it, shall be adopted in accordance with the regulatory procedure with scrutiny referred to in Article 11(3).][1]

3. On the basis of a proposal from the Commission, the European Parliament and the Council shall establish targets for reuse and recovery and for reuse and recycling for the years beyond 2015.

4. In order to prepare an amendment to Directive 70/156/EEC, the Commission shall promote the preparation of European standards relating to the dismantlability, recoverability and recyclability of vehicles. Once the standards are agreed, but in any case no later than by the end of 2001, the European Parliament and the Council, on the basis of a proposal from the Commission, shall amend Directive 70/156/EEC so that vehicles type-approved in accordance with that Directive and put on the market after three years after the amendment of the Directive 70/156/EEC are re-usable and/or recyclable to a minimum of 85 % by weight per vehicle and are re-usable and/or recoverable to a minimum of 95 % by weight per vehicle.

5. In proposing the amendment to Directive 70/156/EEC relating to the ability to be dismantled, recoverability and recyclability of vehicles, the Commission shall take into account as appropriate the need to ensure that the reuse of components does not give rise to safety or environmental hazards.

Amendment

1 Substituted by Directive 2008/33/EC of the European Parliament and of the Council of 11 March 2008 amending Directive 2000/53/EC on end-of-life vehicles, as regards the implementing powers conferred on the Commission, Article 1.4.

Article 8

Coding standards/dismantling information

1. Member States shall take the necessary measures to ensure that producers, in concert with material and equipment manufacturers, use component and material coding standards, in particular to facilitate the identification of those components and materials which are suitable for reuse and recovery.

[2. The standards referred to in paragraph 1 shall be established. When proposing such standards, the Commission shall take account of the work going on in this area in the relevant international forums and contribute to this work as appropriate. That measure, designed to amend non-essential elements of this Directive by supplementing it, shall be adopted in accordance with the regulatory procedure with scrutiny referred to in Article 11(3).][1]

3. Member States shall take the necessary measures to ensure that producers provide dismantling information for each type of new vehicle put on the market within six months after the vehicle is put on the market. This information shall identify, as far as it is needed by treatment facilities in order to comply with the provisions of this Directive, the different vehicle components and materials, and the location of all hazardous substances in the vehicles, in particular with a view to the achievement of the objectives laid down in Article 7.

4. Without prejudice to commercial and industrial confidentiality, Member States shall take the necessary measures to ensure that manufacturers of components used in vehicles make available to authorised treatment facilities, as far as it is requested by these facilities, appropriate information concerning dismantling, storage and testing of components which can be reused.

Amendment

1 Substituted by Directive 2008/33/EC of the European Parliament and of the Council of 11 March 2008 amending Directive 2000/53/EC on end-of-life vehicles, as regards the implementing powers conferred on the Commission, Article 1.5.

Article 9

Reporting and information

1. At three-year intervals Member States shall send a report to the Commission on the implementation of this Directive. The report shall be drawn up on the basis of a questionnaire or outline drafted by the Commission in accordance with the procedure laid down in Article 6 of Directive 91/692/EEC(8) with a view to establishing databases on end-of life vehicles and their treatment. The report shall contain relevant information on possible changes in the structure of motor vehicle dealing and of the collection, dismantling, shredding, recovery and recycling industries, leading to any distortion of competition between or within Member States. The questionnaire or outline shall be sent to the Member States six months before the start of the period covered by the report. The report shall be made to the Commission within nine months of the end of the three-year period covered by it.

The first report shall cover the period of three years from 21 April 2002.

Based on the above information, the Commission shall publish a report on the implementation of this Directive within nine months of receiving the reports from the Member States.

[The formats relating to the database system shall be adopted in accordance with the regulatory procedure referred to in Article 11(2).][1]

2. Member States shall require in each case the relevant economic operators to publish information on:

— the design of vehicles and their components with a view to their recoverability and recyclability,
— the environmentally sound treatment of end-of life vehicles, in particular the removal of all fluids and dismantling,
— the development and optimisation of ways to reuse, recycle and recover end-of life vehicles and their components,
— the progress achieved with regard to recovery and recycling to reduce the waste to be disposed of and to increase the recovery and recycling rates.

The producer must make this information accessible to the prospective buyers of vehicles. It shall be included in promotional literature used in the marketing of the new vehicle.

Amendment

1 Inserted by Directive 2008/33/EC of the European Parliament and of the Council of 11 March 2008 amending Directive 2000/53/EC on end-of-life vehicles, as regards the implementing powers conferred on the Commission, Article 1.6.

Article 10

Implementation

1. Member States shall bring into force the laws, regulations and administrative provisions necessary to comply with this Directive by 21 April 2002. They shall immediately inform the Commission thereof.

When Member States adopt these measures, these shall contain a reference to this Directive or shall be accompanied by such reference on the occasion of their official publication. The methods of making such a reference shall be laid down by Member States.

2. Member States shall communicate to the Commission the text of the main provisions of domestic law, which they adopt in the field governed by this Directive.

3. Provided that the objectives set out in this Directive are achieved, Member States may transpose the provisions set out in Articles 4(1), 5(1), 7(1), 8(1), 8(3) and 9(2) and specify the detailed rules of implementation of Article 5(4) by means of agreements between the competent authorities and the economic sectors concerned. Such agreements shall meet the following requirements

(a) agreements shall be enforceable;
(b) agreements need to specify objectives with the corresponding deadlines;
(c) agreements shall be published in the national official journal or an official document equally accessible to the public and transmitted to the Commission;
(d) the results achieved under an agreement shall be monitored regularly, reported to the competent authorities and to the Commission and made available to the public under the conditions set out in the agreement;
(e) the competent authorities shall make provisions to examine the progress reached under an agreement;
(f) in case of non-compliance with an agreement Member States must implement the relevant provisions of this Directive by legislative, regulatory or administrative measures.

[Article 11

Committee procedure][1]

[1. The Commission shall be assisted by the committee established by Article 18 of Directive 75/442/EEC.

2. Where reference is made to this paragraph, Articles 5 and 7 of Decision 1999/468/EC shall apply, having regard to the provisions of Article 8 thereof.

The period laid down in Article 5(6) of Decision 1999/468/EC shall be set at three months.

3. Where reference is made to this paragraph, Article 5a(1) to (4) and Article 7 of Decision 1999/468/EC shall apply, having regard to the provisions of Article 8 thereof.][1]

Amendment

1 Substituted by Directive 2008/33/EC of the European Parliament and of the Council of 11 March 2008 amending Directive 2000/53/EC on end-of-life vehicles, as regards the implementing powers conferred on the Commission, Article 1.7.

Article 12

Entry into force

1. This Directive shall enter into force on the day of its publication in the Official Journal of the European Communities.

2. Article 5(4) shall apply:
- as from 1 July 2002 for vehicles put on the market as from this date,
- as from 1 January 2007 for vehicles put on the market before the date referred to in the first indent.

3. Member States may apply Article 5(4) in advance of the dates set out in paragraph 2.

Article 13

Addressees

This Directive is addressed to the Member States.

ANNEX I
MINIMUM TECHNICAL REQUIREMENTS FOR TREATMENT IN ACCORDANCE WITH ARTICLE 6(1) AND (3)

1. Sites for storage (including temporary storage) of end-of-life vehicles prior to their treatament:
- impermeable surfaces for appropriate areas with the provision of spillage collection facilities, decanters and cleanser-degeasers,
- equipment for the treatment of water, including rainwater, in compliance with health and environmental regulations.

2. Sites for treatment:
- impermeable surfaces for appropriate areas with the provision of spillage collection facilities, decanters and cleanser-degreasers,
- appropriate storage for dismantled spare parts, including impermeable storage for oil-contaminated spare parts,
- appropriate containers for storage of batteries (with electrolyte neutralisation on site or elsewhere), filters and PCB/PCT-containing condensers,
- appropriate storage tanks for the segregated storage of end-of-life vehicle fluids: fuel, motor oil, gearbox oil, transmission oil, hydraulic oil, cooling liquids, antifreeze, brake fluids, battery acids, air-conditioning system fluids and any other fluid contained in the end-of-life vehicle,
- equipment for the treatment of water, including rainwater, in compliance with health and environmental regulations,
- appropriate storage for used tyres, including the prevention of fire hazards and excessive stockpiling.

3. Treatment operations for depollution of end-of-life vehicles:
- removal of batteries and liquified gas tanks,
- removal or neutralisation of potential explosive components, (e.g. air bags),
- removal and separate collection and storage of fuel, motor oil, transmission oil, gearbox oil, hydraulic oil, cooling liquids, antifreeze, brake fluids, air-conditioning system fluids and any other fluid contained in the end-of-life vehicle, unless they are necessary for the re-use of the parts concerned,
- removal, as far as feasible, of all components identified as containing mercury.

4. Treatment operations in order to promote recycling:
- removal or catalysts,
- removal of metal components containing copper, aluminium and magnesium if these metals are not segregated in the shredding process,
- removal of tyres and large plastic components (bumpers, dashboard, fluid containers, etc), if these materials are not segregated in the shredding process in such a way that they can be effectively recycled as materials,
- removal of glass.

5. Storage operations are to be carried out avoiding damage to components containing fluids or to recoverable components and spare parts.

[ANNEX II
MATERIALS AND COMPONENTS EXEMPT FROM ARTICLE 4(2)(A)][1]

[Materials and components	*Scope and expiry date of the exemption*	*To be labelled or made identifiable in accordance with Article 4(2)(b)(iv)*
Lead as an alloying element		
1(a). Steel for machining purposes and batch hot dip galvanised steel components containing up to 0,35 % lead by weight		
1(b). Continuously galvanised steel sheet containing up to 0,35 % lead by weight	Vehicles type approved before 1 January 2016 and spare parts for these vehicles	
2(a). Aluminium for machining purposes with a lead content up to 2 % by weight	As spare parts for vehicles put on the market before 1 July 2005	
2(b). Aluminium with a lead content up to 1,5 % by weight	As spare parts for vehicles put on the market before 1 July 2008	
2(c). Aluminium with a lead content up to 0,4 % by weight	[2]	
3. Copper alloy containing up to 4 % lead by weight	[2]	
4(a). Bearing shells and bushes	As spare parts for vehicles put on the market before 1 July 2008	
4(b). Bearing shells and bushes in engines, transmissions and air conditioning compressors	1 July 2011 and spare parts for vehicles put on the market before 1 July 2011	
Lead and lead compounds in components		
5. Batteries	[2]	X
6. Vibration dampers	Vehicles type approved before 1 January 2016 and spare parts for these vehicles	X
7(a). Vulcanising agents and stabilisers for elastomers in brake hoses, fuel hoses, air ventilation hoses, elastomer/metal parts in the chassis applications, and engine mountings	As spare parts for vehicles put on the market before 1 July 2005	
7(b). Vulcanising agents and stabilisers for elastomers in brake hoses, fuel hoses, air ventilation hoses, elastomer/metal parts in the chassis applications, and engine mountings containing up to 0,5 % lead by weight	As spare parts for vehicles put on the market before 1 July 2006	

[Materials and components	*Scope and expiry date of the exemption*	*To be labelled or made identifiable in accordance with Article 4(2)(b)(iv)*
14. As an anti-corrosion agent of the carbon steel cooling system in absorption refrigerators in motorcaravans up to 0,75 weight -% in the cooling solution except where the use of other cooling technologies is practicable (i.e. available on the market for the application in motor caravans) and does not lead to negative environmental, health and/or consumer safety impacts		X
Mercury		
15(a). Discharge lamps for headlight application	Vehicles type approved before 1 July 2012 and spare parts for these vehicles	X
15(b). Fluorescent tubes used in instrument panel displays	Vehicles type approved before 1 July 2012 and spare parts for these vehicles	X
Cadmium		
16. Batteries for electrical vehicles	As spare parts for vehicles put on the market before 31 December 2008	

[1] Dismantling if, in correlation with entry 10(a), an average threshold of 60 grams per vehicle is exceeded. For the application of this clause electronic devices not installed by the manufacturer on the production line shall not be taken into account.
[2] This exemption shall be reviewed in 2015.
[3] This exemption shall be reviewed in 2014.
[4] This exemption shall be reviewed before 1 January 2012.
[5] Dismantling if, in correlation with entries 8(a) to 8(j), an average threshold of 60 grams per vehicle is exceeded. For the application of this clause electronic devices not installed by the manufacturer on the production line shall not be taken into account.

Notes:

— A maximum concentration value up to 0,1 % by weight and in homogeneous material, for lead, hexavalent chromium and mercury and up to 0,01 % by weight in homogeneous material for cadmium shall be tolerated,

— The re-use of parts of vehicles which were already on the market at the date of expiry of an exemption shall be allowed without limitation since it is not covered by Article 4(2)(a),

— Spare parts put on the market after 1 July 2003 which are used for vehicles put on the market before 1 July 2003 shall be exempted from the provisions of Article 4(2)(a).][1]

Amendment

1 Substituted by Commission Directive 2011/37/EU of 30 March 2011 amending Annex II to Directive 2000/53/EC of the European Parliament and of the Council on end-of-life vehicles, Article 1, Annex.

EUROPEAN PARLIAMENT AND THE COUNCIL DIRECTIVE 2000/60/EC

of 23 October 2000

ESTABLISHING A FRAMEWORK FOR COMMUNITY ACTION IN THE FIELD OF WATER POLICY

THE EUROPEAN PARLIAMENT AND THE COUNCIL OF THE EUROPEAN UNION,

Having regard to the Treaty establishing the European Community, and in particular Article 175(1) thereof,

Having regard to the proposal from the Commission,

Having regard to the opinion of the Economic and Social Committee,

Having regard to the opinion of the Committee of the Regions,

Acting in accordance with the procedure laid down in Article 251 of the Treaty, and in the light of the joint text approved by the Conciliation Committee on 18 July 2000,

Whereas:

(1) Water is not a commercial product like any other but, rather, a heritage which must be protected, defended and treated as such.

(2) The conclusions of the Community Water Policy Ministerial Seminar in Frankfurt in 1988 highlighted the need for Community legislation covering ecological quality. The Council in its resolution of 28 June 1988 asked the Commission to submit proposals to improve ecological quality in Community surface waters.

(3) The declaration of the Ministerial Seminar on groundwater held at The Hague in 1991 recognised the need for action to avoid long-term deterioration of freshwater quality and quantity and called for a programme of actions to be implemented by the year 2000 aiming at sustainable management and protection of freshwater resources. In its resolutions of 25 February 1992, and 20 February 1995, the Council requested an action programme for groundwater and a revision of Council Directive 80/68/EEC of 17 December 1979 on the protection of groundwater against pollution caused by certain dangerous substances, as part of an overall policy on freshwater protection.

(4) Waters in the Community are under increasing pressure from the continuous growth in demand for sufficient quantities of good quality water for all purposes. On 10 November 1995, the European Environment Agency in its report "Environment in the European Union – 1995" presented an updated state of the environment report, confirming the need for action to protect Community waters in qualitative as well as in quantitative terms.

(5) On 18 December 1995, the Council adopted conclusions requiring, inter alia, the drawing up of a new framework Directive establishing the basic principles of sustainable water policy in the European Union and inviting the Commission to come forward with a proposal.

(6) On 21 February 1996 the Commission adopted a communication to the European Parliament and the Council on European Community water policy setting out the principles for a Community water policy.

(7) On 9 September 1996 the Commission presented a proposal for a Decision of the European Parliament and of the Council on an action programme for integrated protection and management of groundwater. In that proposal the Commission pointed to the need to establish procedures for the regulation of abstraction of freshwater and for the monitoring of freshwater quality and quantity.

(8) On 29 May 1995 the Commission adopted a communication to the European Parliament and the Council on the wise use and conservation of wetlands, which recognised the important functions they perform for the protection of water resources.

(9) It is necessary to develop an integrated Community policy on water.

(10) The Council on 25 June 1996, the Committee of the Regions on 19 September 1996, the Economic and Social Committee on 26 September 1996, and the European Parliament on 23 October 1996 all requested the Commission to come forward with a proposal for a Council Directive establishing a framework for a European water policy.

(11) As set out in Article 174 of the Treaty, the Community policy on the environment is to contribute to pursuit of the objectives of preserving, protecting and improving the quality of the environment, in prudent and rational utilisation of natural resources, and to be based on the precautionary principle and on the principles that preventive action should be taken, environmental damage should, as a priority, be rectified at source and that the polluter should pay.

(12) Pursuant to Article 174 of the Treaty, in preparing its policy on the environment, the Community is to take account of available scientific and technical data, environmental conditions in the various regions of the Community, and the economic and social development of the Community as a whole and the balanced development of its regions as well as the potential benefits and costs of action or lack of action.

(13) There are diverse conditions and needs in the Community which require different specific solutions. This diversity should be taken into account in the planning and execution of measures to ensure protection and sustainable use of water in the framework of the river basin. Decisions should be taken as close as possible to the locations where water is affected or used. Priority should be given to action within the responsibility of Member States through the drawing up of programmes of measures adjusted to regional and local conditions.

(14) The success of this Directive relies on close cooperation and coherent action at Community, Member State and local level as well as on information, consultation and involvement of the public, including users.

(15) The supply of water is a service of general interest as defined in the Commission communication on services of general interest in Europe.

(16) Further integration of protection and sustainable management of water into other Community policy areas such as energy, transport, agriculture, fisheries, regional policy and tourism is necessary. This Directive should provide a basis for a continued dialogue and for the development of strategies towards a further integration of policy areas. This Directive can also make an important contribution to other areas of cooperation between Member States, inter alia, the European spatial development perspective (ESDP).

(17) An effective and coherent water policy must take account of the vulnerability of aquatic ecosystems located near the coast and estuaries or in gulfs or relatively closed seas, as their equilibrium is strongly influenced by the quality of inland waters flowing into them. Protection of water status within river basins will provide economic benefits by contributing towards the protection of fish populations, including coastal fish populations.

(18) Community water policy requires a transparent, effective and coherent legislative framework. The Community should provide common principles and the overall framework for action. This Directive should provide for such a framework and coordinate and integrate, and, in a longer perspective, further develop the overall principles and structures for protection and sustainable use of water in the Community in accordance with the principles of subsidiarity.

(19) This Directive aims at maintaining and improving the aquatic environment in the Community. This purpose is primarily concerned with the quality of the waters concerned. Control of quantity is an ancillary element in securing good water quality and therefore measures on quantity, serving the objective of ensuring good quality, should also be established.

(20) The quantitative status of a body of groundwater may have an impact on the ecological quality of surface waters and terrestrial ecosystems associated with that groundwater body.

(21) The Community and Member States are party to various international agreements containing important obligations on the protection of marine waters from pollution, in particular the Convention on the Protection of the Marine Environment of the Baltic Sea Area, signed in Helsinki on 9 April 1992 and approved by Council Decision 94/157/EC, the Convention for the Protection of the Marine Environment of the North-East Atlantic, signed in Paris on 22 September 1992 and approved by Council Decision 98/249/EC, and the Convention for the Protection of the Mediterranean Sea Against Pollution, signed in Barcelona on 16 February 1976 and approved by Council Decision 77/585/EEC, and its Protocol for the Protection of the Mediterranean Sea Against Pollution from Land-Based Sources, signed in Athens on 17 May 1980 and approved by Council Decision 83/101/EEC. This Directive is to make a contribution towards enabling the Community and Member States to meet those obligations.

(22) This Directive is to contribute to the progressive reduction of emissions of hazardous substances to water.

(23) Common principles are needed in order to coordinate Member States' efforts to improve the protection of Community waters in terms of quantity and quality, to promote sustainable water use, to contribute to the control of transboundary water problems, to protect aquatic ecosystems, and terrestrial ecosystems and wetlands directly depending on them, and to safeguard and develop the potential uses of Community waters.

(24) Good water quality will contribute to securing the drinking water supply for the population.

(25) Common definitions of the status of water in terms of quality and, where relevant for the purpose of the environmental protection, quantity should be established. Environmental objectives should be set to ensure that good status of surface water and groundwater is achieved throughout the Community and that deterioration in the status of waters is prevented at Community level.

(26) Member States should aim to achieve the objective of at least good water status by defining and implementing the necessary measures within integrated programmes of measures, taking into account existing Community requirements. Where good water status already exists, it should be maintained. For groundwater, in addition to the requirements of good status, any significant and sustained upward trend in the concentration of any pollutant should be identified and reversed.

(27) The ultimate aim of this Directive is to achieve the elimination of priority hazardous substances and contribute to achieving concentrations in the marine environment near background values for naturally occurring substances.

(28) Surface waters and groundwaters are in principle renewable natural resources; in particular, the task of ensuring good status of groundwater requires early action and stable long-term planning of protective measures, owing to the natural time lag in its formation and renewal. Such time lag for improvement should be taken into account in timetables when establishing measures for the achievement of good status of groundwater and reversing any significant and sustained upward trend in the concentration of any pollutant in groundwater.

(29) In aiming to achieve the objectives set out in this Directive, and in establishing a programme of measures to that end, Member States may phase implementation of the programme of measures in order to spread the costs of implementation.

(30) In order to ensure a full and consistent implementation of this Directive any extensions of timescale should be made on the basis of appropriate, evident and transparent criteria and be justified by the Member States in the river basin management plans.

(31) In cases where a body of water is so affected by human activity or its natural condition is such that it may be unfeasible or unreasonably expensive to achieve good status, less stringent environmental objectives may be set on the basis of appropriate, evident and

transparent criteria, and all practicable steps should be taken to prevent any further deterioration of the status of waters.

(32) There may be grounds for exemptions from the requirement to prevent further deterioration or to achieve good status under specific conditions, if the failure is the result of unforeseen or exceptional circumstances, in particular floods and droughts, or, for reasons of overriding public interest, of new modifications to the physical characteristics of a surface water body or alterations to the level of bodies of groundwater, provided that all practicable steps are taken to mitigate the adverse impact on the status of the body of water.

(33) The objective of achieving good water status should be pursued for each river basin, so that measures in respect of surface water and groundwaters belonging to the same ecological, hydrological and hydrogeological system are coordinated.

(34) For the purposes of environmental protection there is a need for a greater integration of qualitative and quantitative aspects of both surface waters and groundwaters, taking into account the natural flow conditions of water within the hydrological cycle.

(35) Within a river basin where use of water may have transboundary effects, the requirements for the achievement of the environmental objectives established under this Directive, and in particular all programmes of measures, should be coordinated for the whole of the river basin district. For river basins extending beyond the boundaries of the Community, Member States should endeavour to ensure the appropriate coordination with the relevant non-member States. This Directive is to contribute to the implementation of Community obligations under international conventions on water protection and management, notably the United Nations Convention on the protection and use of transboundary water courses and international lakes, approved by Council Decision 95/308/EC and any succeeding agreements on its application.

(36) It is necessary to undertake analyses of the characteristics of a river basin and the impacts of human activity as well as an economic analysis of water use. The development in water status should be monitored by Member States on a systematic and comparable basis throughout the Community. This information is necessary in order to provide a sound basis for Member States to develop programmes of measures aimed at achieving the objectives established under this Directive.

(37) Member States should identify waters used for the abstraction of drinking water and ensure compliance with Council Directive 80/778/EEC of 15 July 1980 relating to the quality of water intended for human consumption.

(38) The use of economic instruments by Member States may be appropriate as part of a programme of measures. The principle of recovery of the costs of water services, including environmental and resource costs associated with damage or negative impact on the aquatic environment should be taken into account in accordance with, in particular, the polluter-pays principle. An economic analysis of water services based on long-term forecasts of supply and demand for water in the river basin district will be necessary for this purpose.

(39) There is a need to prevent or reduce the impact of incidents in which water is accidentally polluted. Measures with the aim of doing so should be included in the programme of measures.

(40) With regard to pollution prevention and control, Community water policy should be based on a combined approach using control of pollution at source through the setting of emission limit values and of environmental quality standards.

(41) For water quantity, overall principles should be laid down for control on abstraction and impoundment in order to ensure the environmental sustainability of the affected water systems.

(42) Common environmental quality standards and emission limit values for certain groups or families of pollutants should be laid down as minimum requirements in Community legislation. Provisions for the adoption of such standards at Community level should be ensured.

(43) Pollution through the discharge, emission or loss of priority hazardous substances must cease or be phased out. The European Parliament and the Council should, on a proposal from the Commission, agree on the substances to be considered for action as a priority and on specific measures to be taken against pollution of water by those substances, taking into account all significant sources and identifying the cost-effective and proportionate level and combination of controls.

(44) In identifying priority hazardous substances, account should be taken of the precautionary principle, relying in particular on the determination of any potentially adverse effects of the product and on a scientific assessment of the risk.

(45) Member States should adopt measures to eliminate pollution of surface water by the priority substances and progressively to reduce pollution by other substances which would otherwise prevent Member States from achieving the objectives for the bodies of surface water.

(46) To ensure the participation of the general public including users of water in the establishment and updating of river basin management plans, it is necessary to provide proper information of planned measures and to report on progress with their implementation with a view to the involvement of the general public before final decisions on the necessary measures are adopted.

(47) This Directive should provide mechanisms to address obstacles to progress in improving water status when these fall outside the scope of Community water legislation, with a view to developing appropriate Community strategies for overcoming them.

(48) The Commission should present annually an updated plan for any initiatives which it intends to propose for the water sector.

(49) Technical specifications should be laid down to ensure a coherent approach in the Community as part of this Directive. Criteria for evaluation of water status are an important step forward. Adaptation of certain technical elements to technical development and the standardisation of monitoring, sampling and analysis methods should be adopted by committee procedure. To promote a thorough understanding and consistent application of the criteria for characterisation of the river basin districts and evaluation of water status, the Commission may adopt guidelines on the application of these criteria.

(50) The measures necessary for the implementation of this Directive should be adopted in accordance with Council Decision 1999/468/EC of 28 June 1999 laying down the procedures for the exercise of implementing powers conferred on the Commission.

(51) The implementation of this Directive is to achieve a level of protection of waters at least equivalent to that provided in certain earlier acts, which should therefore be repealed once the relevant provisions of this Directive have been fully implemented.

(52) The provisions of this Directive take over the framework for control of pollution by dangerous substances established under Directive 76/464/EEC. That Directive should therefore be repealed once the relevant provisions of this Directive have been fully implemented.

(53) Full implementation and enforcement of existing environmental legislation for the protection of waters should be ensured. It is necessary to ensure the proper application of the provisions implementing this Directive throughout the Community by appropriate penalties provided for in Member States' legislation. Such penalties should be effective, proportionate and dissuasive,

HAVE ADOPTED THIS DIRECTIVE:

Article 1

Purpose

The purpose of this Directive is to establish a framework for the protection of inland surface waters, transitional waters, coastal waters and groundwater which:

(a) prevents further deterioration and protects and enhances the status of aquatic ecosystems and, with regard to their water needs, terrestrial ecosystems and wetlands directly depending on the aquatic ecosystems;
(b) promotes sustainable water use based on a long-term protection of available water resources;
(c) aims at enhanced protection and improvement of the aquatic environment, inter alia, through specific measures for the progressive reduction of discharges, emissions and losses of priority substances and the cessation or phasing-out of discharges, emissions and losses of the priority hazardous substances;
(d) ensures the progressive reduction of pollution of groundwater and prevents its further pollution, and
(e) contributes to mitigating the effects of floods and droughts

and thereby contributes to:

— the provision of the sufficient supply of good quality surface water and groundwater as needed for sustainable, balanced and equitable water use,
— a significant reduction in pollution of groundwater,
— the protection of territorial and marine waters, and
— achieving the objectives of relevant international agreements, including those which aim to prevent and eliminate pollution of the marine environment, by Community action under Article 16(3) to cease or phase out discharges, emissions and losses of priority hazardous substances, with the ultimate aim of achieving concentrations in the marine environment near background values for naturally occurring substances and close to zero for man-made synthetic substances.

Article 2

Definitions

For the purposes of this Directive the following definitions shall apply:

1. "Surface water" means inland waters, except groundwater; transitional waters and coastal waters, except in respect of chemical status for which it shall also include territorial waters.
2. "Groundwater" means all water which is below the surface of the ground in the saturation zone and in direct contact with the ground or subsoil.
3. "Inland water" means all standing or flowing water on the surface of the land, and all groundwater on the landward side of the baseline from which the breadth of territorial waters is measured.
4. "River" means a body of inland water flowing for the most part on the surface of the land but which may flow underground for part of its course.
5. "Lake" means a body of standing inland surface water.
6. "Transitional waters" are bodies of surface water in the vicinity of river mouths which are partly saline in character as a result of their proximity to coastal waters but which are substantially influenced by freshwater flows.
7. "Coastal water" means surface water on the landward side of a line, every point of which is at a distance of one nautical mile on the seaward side from the nearest point of the baseline from which the breadth of territorial waters is measured, extending where appropriate up to the outer limit of transitional waters.
8. "Artificial water body" means a body of surface water created by human activity.
9. "Heavily modified water body" means a body of surface water which as a result of physical alterations by human activity is substantially changed in character, as designated by the Member State in accordance with the provisions of Annex II.
10. "Body of surface water" means a discrete and significant element of surface water such as a lake, a reservoir, a stream, river or canal, part of a stream, river or canal, a transitional water or a stretch of coastal water.

11. "Aquifer" means a subsurface layer or layers of rock or other geological strata of sufficient porosity and permeability to allow either a significant flow of groundwater or the abstraction of significant quantities of groundwater.
12. "Body of groundwater" means a distinct volume of groundwater within an aquifer or aquifers.
13. "River basin" means the area of land from which all surface run-off flows through a sequence of streams, rivers and, possibly, lakes into the sea at a single river mouth, estuary or delta.
14. "Sub-basin" means the area of land from which all surface run-off flows through a series of streams, rivers and, possibly, lakes to a particular point in a water course (normally a lake or a river confluence).
15. "River basin district" means the area of land and sea, made up of one or more neighbouring river basins together with their associated groundwaters and coastal waters, which is identified under Article 3(1) as the main unit for management of river basins.
16. "Competent Authority" means an authority or authorities identified under Article 3(2) or 3(3).
17. "Surface water status" is the general expression of the status of a body of surface water, determined by the poorer of its ecological status and its chemical status.
18. "Good surface water status" means the status achieved by a surface water body when both its ecological status and its chemical status are at least "good".
19. "Groundwater status" is the general expression of the status of a body of groundwater, determined by the poorer of its quantitative status and its chemical status.
20. "Good groundwater status" means the status achieved by a groundwater body when both its quantitative status and its chemical status are at least "good".
21. "Ecological status" is an expression of the quality of the structure and functioning of aquatic ecosystems associated with surface waters, classified in accordance with Annex V.
22. "Good ecological status" is the status of a body of surface water, so classified in accordance with Annex V.
23. "Good ecological potential" is the status of a heavily modified or an artificial body of water, so classified in accordance with the relevant provisions of Annex V.
24. "Good surface water chemical status" means the chemical status required to meet the environmental objectives for surface waters established in Article 4(1)(a), that is the chemical status achieved by a body of surface water in which concentrations of pollutants do not exceed the environmental quality standards established in Annex IX and under Article 16(7), and under other relevant Community legislation setting environmental quality standards at Community level.
25. "Good groundwater chemical status" is the chemical status of a body of groundwater, which meets all the conditions set out in table 2.3.2 of Annex V.
26. "Quantitative status" is an expression of the degree to which a body of groundwater is affected by direct and indirect abstractions.
27. "Available groundwater resource" means the long-term annual average rate of overall recharge of the body of groundwater less the long-term annual rate of flow required to achieve the ecological quality objectives for associated surface waters specified under Article 4, to avoid any significant diminution in the ecological status of such waters and to avoid any significant damage to associated terrestrial ecosystems.
28. "Good quantitative status" is the status defined in table 2.1.2 of Annex V.
29. "Hazardous substances" means substances or groups of substances that are toxic, persistent and liable to bio-accumulate, and other substances or groups of substances which give rise to an equivalent level of concern.
30. "Priority substances" means substances identified in accordance with Article 16(2) and listed in Annex X. Among these substances there are "priority hazardous substances" which means substances identified in accordance with Article 16(3) and (6) for which measures have to be taken in accordance with Article 16(1) and (8).

31. "Pollutant" means any substance liable to cause pollution, in particular those listed in Annex VIII.
32. "Direct discharge to groundwater" means discharge of pollutants into groundwater without percolation throughout the soil or subsoil.
33. "Pollution" means the direct or indirect introduction, as a result of human activity, of substances or heat into the air, water or land which may be harmful to human health or the quality of aquatic ecosystems or terrestrial ecosystems directly depending on aquatic ecosystems, which result in damage to material property, or which impair or interfere with amenities and other legitimate uses of the environment.
34. "Environmental objectives" means the objectives set out in Article 4.
35. "Environmental quality standard" means the concentration of a particular pollutant or group of pollutants in water, sediment or biota which should not be exceeded in order to protect human health and the environment.
36. "Combined approach" means the control of discharges and emissions into surface waters according to the approach set out in Article 10.
37. "Water intended for human consumption" has the same meaning as under Directive 80/778/EEC, as amended by Directive 98/83/EC.
38. "Water services" means all services which provide, for households, public institutions or any economic activity:
    (a) abstraction, impoundment, storage, treatment and distribution of surface water or groundwater,
    (b) waste-water collection and treatment facilities which subsequently discharge into surface water.
39. "Water use" means water services together with any other activity identified under Article 5 and Annex II having a significant impact on the status of water.
    This concept applies for the purposes of Article 1 and of the economic analysis carried out according to Article 5 and Annex III, point (b).
40. "Emission limit values" means the mass, expressed in terms of certain specific parameters, concentration and/or level of an emission, which may not be exceeded during any one or more periods of time. Emission limit values may also be laid down for certain groups, families or categories of substances, in particular for those identified under Article 16.
    The emission limit values for substances shall normally apply at the point where the emissions leave the installation, dilution being disregarded when determining them. With regard to indirect releases into water, the effect of a waste-water treatment plant may be taken into account when determining the emission limit values of the installations involved, provided that an equivalent level is guaranteed for protection of the environment as a whole and provided that this does not lead to higher levels of pollution in the environment.
41. "Emission controls" are controls requiring a specific emission limitation, for instance an emission limit value, or otherwise specifying limits or conditions on the effects, nature or other characteristics of an emission or operating conditions which affect emissions. Use of the term "emission control" in this Directive in respect of the provisions of any other Directive shall not be held as reinterpreting those provisions in any respect.

Article 3

Coordination of administrative arrangements within river basin districts

1. Member States shall identify the individual river basins lying within their national territory and, for the purposes of this Directive, shall assign them to individual river basin districts. Small river basins may be combined with larger river basins or joined with neighbouring small basins to form individual river basin districts where appropriate. Where groundwaters do not fully follow a particular river basin, they shall be identified and assigned to the nearest or most appropriate river basin district. Coastal waters shall be identified and assigned to the nearest or most appropriate river basin district or districts.

2. Member States shall ensure the appropriate administrative arrangements, including the identification of the appropriate competent authority, for the application of the rules of this Directive within each river basin district lying within their territory.

3. Member States shall ensure that a river basin covering the territory of more than one Member State is assigned to an international river basin district. At the request of the Member States involved, the Commission shall act to facilitate the assigning to such international river basin districts.

Each Member State shall ensure the appropriate administrative arrangements, including the identification of the appropriate competent authority, for the application of the rules of this Directive within the portion of any international river basin district lying within its territory.

4. Member States shall ensure that the requirements of this Directive for the achievement of the environmental objectives established under Article 4, and in particular all programmes of measures are coordinated for the whole of the river basin district. For international river basin districts the Member States concerned shall together ensure this coordination and may, for this purpose, use existing structures stemming from international agreements. At the request of the Member States involved, the Commission shall act to facilitate the establishment of the programmes of measures.

5. Where a river basin district extends beyond the territory of the Community, the Member State or Member States concerned shall endeavour to establish appropriate coordination with the relevant non-Member States, with the aim of achieving the objectives of this Directive throughout the river basin district. Member States shall ensure the application of the rules of this Directive within their territory.

6. Member States may identify an existing national or international body as competent authority for the purposes of this Directive.

7. Member States shall identify the competent authority by the date mentioned in Article 24.

8. Member States shall provide the Commission with a list of their competent authorities and of the competent authorities of all the international bodies in which they participate at the latest six months after the date mentioned in Article 24. For each competent authority the information set out in Annex I shall be provided.

9. Member States shall inform the Commission of any changes to the information provided according to paragraph 8 within three months of the change coming into effect.

Article 4

Environmental objectives

1. In making operational the programmes of measures specified in the river basin management plans:

(a) for surface waters

- (i) Member States shall implement the necessary measures to prevent deterioration of the status of all bodies of surface water, subject to the application of paragraphs 6 and 7 and without prejudice to paragraph 8;
- (ii) Member States shall protect, enhance and restore all bodies of surface water, subject to the application of subparagraph (iii) for artificial and heavily modified bodies of water, with the aim of achieving good surface water status at the latest 15 years after the date of entry into force of this Directive, in accordance with the provisions laid down in Annex V, subject to the application of extensions determined in accordance with paragraph 4 and to the application of paragraphs 5, 6 and 7 without prejudice to paragraph 8;
- (iii) Member States shall protect and enhance all artificial and heavily modified bodies of water, with the aim of achieving good ecological potential and good surface water chemical status at the latest 15 years from the date of entry into

force of this Directive, in accordance with the provisions laid down in Annex V, subject to the application of extensions determined in accordance with paragraph 4 and to the application of paragraphs 5, 6 and 7 without prejudice to paragraph 8;

(iv) Member States shall implement the necessary measures in accordance with Article 16(1) and (8), with the aim of progressively reducing pollution from priority substances and ceasing or phasing out emissions, discharges and losses of priority hazardous substances

without prejudice to the relevant international agreements referred to in Article 1 for the parties concerned;

(b) for groundwater

(i) Member States shall implement the measures necessary to prevent or limit the input of pollutants into groundwater and to prevent the deterioration of the status of all bodies of groundwater, subject to the application of paragraphs 6 and 7 and without prejudice to paragraph 8 of this Article and subject to the application of Article 11(3)(j);

(ii) Member States shall protect, enhance and restore all bodies of groundwater, ensure a balance between abstraction and recharge of groundwater, with the aim of achieving good groundwater status at the latest 15 years after the date of entry into force of this Directive, in accordance with the provisions laid down in Annex V, subject to the application of extensions determined in accordance with paragraph 4 and to the application of paragraphs 5, 6 and 7 without prejudice to paragraph 8 of this Article and subject to the application of Article 11(3)(j);

(iii) Member States shall implement the measures necessary to reverse any significant and sustained upward trend in the concentration of any pollutant resulting from the impact of human activity in order progressively to reduce pollution of groundwater.

Measures to achieve trend reversal shall be implemented in accordance with paragraphs 2, 4 and 5 of Article 17, taking into account the applicable standards set out in relevant Community legislation, subject to the application of paragraphs 6 and 7 and without prejudice to paragraph 8;

(c) for protected areas

Member States shall achieve compliance with any standards and objectives at the latest 15 years after the date of entry into force of this Directive, unless otherwise specified in the Community legislation under which the individual protected areas have been established.

2. Where more than one of the objectives under paragraph 1 relates to a given body of water, the most stringent shall apply.

3. Member States may designate a body of surface water as artificial or heavily modified, when:

(a) the changes to the hydromorphological characteristics of that body which would be necessary for achieving good ecological status would have significant adverse effects on:

(i) the wider environment;

(ii) navigation, including port facilities, or recreation;

(iii) activities for the purposes of which water is stored, such as drinking-water supply, power generation or irrigation;

(iv) water regulation, flood protection, land drainage, or

(v) other equally important sustainable human development activities;

(b) the beneficial objectives served by the artificial or modified characteristics of the water body cannot, for reasons of technical feasibility or disproportionate costs, reasonably be achieved by other means, which are a significantly better environmental option.

Such designation and the reasons for it shall be specifically mentioned in the river basin management plans required under Article 13 and reviewed every six years.

4. The deadlines established under paragraph 1 may be extended for the purposes of phased achievement of the objectives for bodies of water, provided that no further deterioration occurs in the status of the affected body of water when all of the following conditions are met:

(a) Member States determine that all necessary improvements in the status of bodies of water cannot reasonably be achieved within the timescales set out in that paragraph for at least one of the following reasons:
   (i) the scale of improvements required can only be achieved in phases exceeding the timescale, for reasons of technical feasibility;
   (ii) completing the improvements within the timescale would be disproportionately expensive;
   (iii) natural conditions do not allow timely improvement in the status of the body of water.

(b) Extension of the deadline, and the reasons for it, are specifically set out and explained in the river basin management plan required under Article 13.

(c) Extensions shall be limited to a maximum of two further updates of the river basin management plan except in cases where the natural conditions are such that the objectives cannot be achieved within this period.

(d) A summary of the measures required under Article 11 which are envisaged as necessary to bring the bodies of water progressively to the required status by the extended deadline, the reasons for any significant delay in making these measures operational, and the expected timetable for their implementation are set out in the river basin management plan. A review of the implementation of these measures and a summary of any additional measures shall be included in updates of the river basin management plan.

5. Member States may aim to achieve less stringent environmental objectives than those required under paragraph 1 for specific bodies of water when they are so affected by human activity, as determined in accordance with Article 5(1), or their natural condition is such that the achievement of these objectives would be infeasible or disproportionately expensive, and all the following conditions are met:

(a) the environmental and socioeconomic needs served by such human activity cannot be achieved by other means, which are a significantly better environmental option not entailing disproportionate costs;

(b) Member States ensure,
   — for surface water, the highest ecological and chemical status possible is achieved, given impacts that could not reasonably have been avoided due to the nature of the human activity or pollution,
   — for groundwater, the least possible changes to good groundwater status, given impacts that could not reasonably have been avoided due to the nature of the human activity or pollution;

(c) no further deterioration occurs in the status of the affected body of water;

(d) the establishment of less stringent environmental objectives, and the reasons for it, are specifically mentioned in the river basin management plan required under Article 13 and those objectives are reviewed every six years.

6. Temporary deterioration in the status of bodies of water shall not be in breach of the requirements of this Directive if this is the result of circumstances of natural cause or force majeure which are exceptional or could not reasonably have been foreseen, in particular extreme floods and prolonged droughts, or the result of circumstances due to accidents which could not reasonably have been foreseen, when all of the following conditions have been met:

(a) all practicable steps are taken to prevent further deterioration in status and in order not to compromise the achievement of the objectives of this Directive in other bodies of water not affected by those circumstances;

(b) the conditions under which circumstances that are exceptional or that could not reasonably have been foreseen may be declared, including the adoption of the appropriate indicators, are stated in the river basin management plan;

(c) the measures to be taken under such exceptional circumstances are included in the programme of measures and will not compromise the recovery of the quality of the body of water once the circumstances are over;
(d) the effects of the circumstances that are exceptional or that could not reasonably have been foreseen are reviewed annually and, subject to the reasons set out in paragraph 4(a), all practicable measures are taken with the aim of restoring the body of water to its status prior to the effects of those circumstances as soon as reasonably practicable, and
(e) a summary of the effects of the circumstances and of such measures taken or to be taken in accordance with paragraphs (a) and (d) are included in the next update of the river basin management plan.

7. Member States will not be in breach of this Directive when:
— failure to achieve good groundwater status, good ecological status or, where relevant, good ecological potential or to prevent deterioration in the status of a body of surface water or groundwater is the result of new modifications to the physical characteristics of a surface water body or alterations to the level of bodies of groundwater, or
— failure to prevent deterioration from high status to good status of a body of surface water is the result of new sustainable human development activities

and all the following conditions are met:
(a) all practicable steps are taken to mitigate the adverse impact on the status of the body of water;
(b) the reasons for those modifications or alterations are specifically set out and explained in the river basin management plan required under Article 13 and the objectives are reviewed every six years;
(c) the reasons for those modifications or alterations are of overriding public interest and/or the benefits to the environment and to society of achieving the objectives set out in paragraph 1 are outweighed by the benefits of the new modifications or alterations to human health, to the maintenance of human safety or to sustainable development, and
(d) the beneficial objectives served by those modifications or alterations of the water body cannot for reasons of technical feasibility or disproportionate cost be achieved by other means, which are a significantly better environmental option.

8. When applying paragraphs 3, 4, 5, 6 and 7, a Member State shall ensure that the application does not permanently exclude or compromise the achievement of the objectives of this Directive in other bodies of water within the same river basin district and is consistent with the implementation of other Community environmental legislation.

9. Steps must be taken to ensure that the application of the new provisions, including the application of paragraphs 3, 4, 5, 6 and 7, guarantees at least the same level of protection as the existing Community legislation.

Article 5

Characteristics of the river basin district, review of the environmental impact of human activity and economic analysis of water use

1. Each Member State shall ensure that for each river basin district or for the portion of an international river basin district falling within its territory:
— an analysis of its characteristics,
— a review of the impact of human activity on the status of surface waters and on groundwater, and
— an economic analysis of water use

is undertaken according to the technical specifications set out in Annexes II and III and that it is completed at the latest four years after the date of entry into force of this Directive.

2. The analyses and reviews mentioned under paragraph 1 shall be reviewed, and if necessary updated at the latest 13 years after the date of entry into force of this Directive and every six years thereafter.

Article 6

Register of protected areas

1. Member States shall ensure the establishment of a register or registers of all areas lying within each river basin district which have been designated as requiring special protection under specific Community legislation for the protection of their surface water and groundwater or for the conservation of habitats and species directly depending on water. They shall ensure that the register is completed at the latest four years after the date of entry into force of this Directive.

2. The register or registers shall include all bodies of water identified under Article 7(1) and all protected areas covered by Annex IV.

3. For each river basin district, the register or registers of protected areas shall be kept under review and up to date.

Article 7

Waters used for the abstraction of drinking water

1. Member States shall identify, within each river basin district:
- all bodies of water used for the abstraction of water intended for human consumption providing more than 10 m3 a day as an average or serving more than 50 persons, and
- those bodies of water intended for such future use.

Member States shall monitor, in accordance with Annex V, those bodies of water which according to Annex V, provide more than 100 m3 a day as an average.

2. For each body of water identified under paragraph 1, in addition to meeting the objectives of Article 4 in accordance with the requirements of this Directive, for surface water bodies including the quality standards established at Community level under Article 16, Member States shall ensure that under the water treatment regime applied, and in accordance with Community legislation, the resulting water will meet the requirements of Directive 80/778/EEC as amended by Directive 98/83/EC.

3. Member States shall ensure the necessary protection for the bodies of water identified with the aim of avoiding deterioration in their quality in order to reduce the level of purification treatment required in the production of drinking water. Member States may establish safeguard zones for those bodies of water.

Article 8

Monitoring of surface water status, groundwater status and protected areas

1. Member States shall ensure the establishment of programmes for the monitoring of water status in order to establish a coherent and comprehensive overview of water status within each river basin district:
- for surface waters such programmes shall cover:
  - (i) the volume and level or rate of flow to the extent relevant for ecological and chemical status and ecological potential, and
  - (ii) the ecological and chemical status and ecological potential;
- for groundwaters such programmes shall cover monitoring of the chemical and quantitative status,
- for protected areas the above programmes shall be supplemented by those specifications contained in Community legislation under which the individual protected areas have been established.

2. These programmes shall be operational at the latest six years after the date of entry into force of this Directive unless otherwise specified in the legislation concerned. Such monitoring shall be in accordance with the requirements of Annex V.

[3. Technical specifications and standardised methods for analysis and monitoring of water status shall be laid down. Those measures, designed to amend non-essential elements of this Directive by supplementing it, shall be adopted in accordance with the regulatory procedure with scrutiny referred to in Article 21(3).][1]

Amendment

1 Substituted by Directive 2008/32/EC of the European Parliament and of the Council of 11 March 2008 amending Directive 2000/60/EC establishing a framework for Community action in the field of water policy, as regards the implementing powers conferred on the Commission, Article 1.1.

Article 9

Recovery of costs for water services

1. Member States shall take account of the principle of recovery of the costs of water services, including environmental and resource costs, having regard to the economic analysis conducted according to Annex III, and in accordance in particular with the polluter pays principle.

Member States shall ensure by 2010

— that water-pricing policies provide adequate incentives for users to use water resources efficiently, and thereby contribute to the environmental objectives of this Directive,
— an adequate contribution of the different water uses, disaggregated into at least industry, households and agriculture, to the recovery of the costs of water services, based on the economic analysis conducted according to Annex III and taking account of the polluter pays principle.

Member States may in so doing have regard to the social, environmental and economic effects of the recovery as well as the geographic and climatic conditions of the region or regions affected.

2. Member States shall report in the river basin management plans on the planned steps towards implementing paragraph 1 which will contribute to achieving the environmental objectives of this Directive and on the contribution made by the various water uses to the recovery of the costs of water services.

3. Nothing in this Article shall prevent the funding of particular preventive or remedial measures in order to achieve the objectives of this Directive.

4. Member States shall not be in breach of this Directive if they decide in accordance with established practices not to apply the provisions of paragraph 1, second sentence, and for that purpose the relevant provisions of paragraph 2, for a given water-use activity, where this does not compromise the purposes and the achievement of the objectives of this Directive. Member States shall report the reasons for not fully applying paragraph 1, second sentence, in the river basin management plans.

Article 10

The combined approach for point and diffuse sources

1. Member States shall ensure that all discharges referred to in paragraph 2 into surface waters are controlled according to the combined approach set out in this Article.

2. Member States shall ensure the establishment and/or implementation of:

(a) the emission controls based on best available techniques, or
(b) the relevant emission limit values, or
(c) in the case of diffuse impacts the controls including, as appropriate, best environmental practices

set out in:

— Council Directive 96/61/EC of 24 September 1996 concerning integrated pollution prevention and control,

- Council Directive 91/271/EEC of 21 May 1991 concerning urban waste-water treatment,
- Council Directive 91/676/EEC of 12 December 1991 concerning the protection of waters against pollution caused by nitrates from agricultural sources,
- the Directives adopted pursuant to Article 16 of this Directive,
- the Directives listed in Annex IX,
- any other relevant Community legislation at the latest 12 years after the date of entry into force of this Directive, unless otherwise specified in the legislation concerned.

3. Where a quality objective or quality standard, whether established pursuant to this Directive, in the Directives listed in Annex IX, or pursuant to any other Community legislation, requires stricter conditions than those which would result from the application of paragraph 2, more stringent emission controls shall be set accordingly.

Article 11

Programme of measures

1. Each Member State shall ensure the establishment for each river basin district, or for the part of an international river basin district within its territory, of a programme of measures, taking account of the results of the analyses required under Article 5, in order to achieve the objectives established under Article 4. Such programmes of measures may make reference to measures following from legislation adopted at national level and covering the whole of the territory of a Member State. Where appropriate, a Member State may adopt measures applicable to all river basin districts and/or the portions of international river basin districts falling within its territory.

2. Each programme of measures shall include the "basic" measures specified in paragraph 3 and, where necessary, "supplementary" measures.

3. "Basic measures" are the minimum requirements to be complied with and shall consist of:

(a) those measures required to implement Community legislation for the protection of water, including measures required under the legislation specified in Article 10 and in part A of Annex VI;

(b) measures deemed appropriate for the purposes of Article 9;

(c) measures to promote an efficient and sustainable water use in order to avoid compromising the achievement of the objectives specified in Article 4;

(d) measures to meet the requirements of Article 7, including measures to safeguard water quality in order to reduce the level of purification treatment required for the production of drinking water;

(e) controls over the abstraction of fresh surface water and groundwater, and impoundment of fresh surface water, including a register or registers of water abstractions and a requirement of prior authorisation for abstraction and impoundment. These controls shall be periodically reviewed and, where necessary, updated. Member States can exempt from these controls, abstractions or impoundments which have no significant impact on water status;

(f) controls, including a requirement for prior authorisation of artificial recharge or augmentation of groundwater bodies. The water used may be derived from any surface water or groundwater, provided that the use of the source does not compromise the achievement of the environmental objectives established for the source or the recharged or augmented body of groundwater. These controls shall be periodically reviewed and, where necessary, updated;

(g) for point source discharges liable to cause pollution, a requirement for prior regulation, such as a prohibition on the entry of pollutants into water, or for prior authorisation, or registration based on general binding rules, laying down emission controls for the pollutants concerned, including controls in accordance with Articles 10 and 16. These controls shall be periodically reviewed and, where necessary, updated;

(h) for diffuse sources liable to cause pollution, measures to prevent or control the input of pollutants. Controls may take the form of a requirement for prior regulation, such as a prohibition on the entry of pollutants into water, prior authorisation or registration based on general binding rules where such a requirement is not otherwise provided for under Community legislation. These controls shall be periodically reviewed and, where necessary, updated;

(i) for any other significant adverse impacts on the status of water identified under Article 5 and Annex II, in particular measures to ensure that the hydromorphological conditions of the bodies of water are consistent with the achievement of the required ecological status or good ecological potential for bodies of water designated as artificial or heavily modified. Controls for this purpose may take the form of a requirement for prior authorisation or registration based on general binding rules where such a requirement is not otherwise provided for under Community legislation. Such controls shall be periodically reviewed and, where necessary, updated;

(j) a prohibition of direct discharges of pollutants into groundwater subject to the following provisions:

Member States may authorise reinjection into the same aquifer of water used for geothermal purposes.

They may also authorise, specifying the conditions for:

— injection of water containing substances resulting from the operations for exploration and extraction of hydrocarbons or mining activities, and injection of water for technical reasons, into geological formations from which hydrocarbons or other substances have been extracted or into geological formations which for natural reasons are permanently unsuitable for other purposes. Such injections shall not contain substances other than those resulting from the above operations,

— reinjection of pumped groundwater from mines and quarries or associated with the construction or maintenance of civil engineering works,

— injection of natural gas or liquefied petroleum gas (LPG) for storage purposes into geological formations which for natural reasons are permanently unsuitable for other purposes,

[— injection of carbon dioxide streams for storage purposes into geological formations which for natural reasons are permanently unsuitable for other purposes, provided that such injection is made in accordance with Directive 2009/31/EC of the European Parliament and of the Council of 23 April 2009 on the geological storage of carbon dioxide or excluded from the scope of that Directive pursuant to its Article 2(2);][1]

— injection of natural gas or liquefied petroleum gas (LPG) for storage purposes into other geological formations where there is an overriding need for security of gas supply, and where the injection is such as to prevent any present or future danger of deterioration in the quality of any receiving groundwater,

— construction, civil engineering and building works and similar activities on, or in the ground which come into contact with groundwater. For these purposes, Member States may determine that such activities are to be treated as having been authorised provided that they are conducted in accordance with general binding rules developed by the Member State in respect of such activities,

— discharges of small quantities of substances for scientific purposes for characterisation, protection or remediation of water bodies limited to the amount strictly necessary for the purposes concerned

provided such discharges do not compromise the achievement of the environmental objectives established for that body of groundwater;

(k) in accordance with action taken pursuant to Article 16, measures to eliminate pollution of surface waters by those substances specified in the list of priority substances agreed pursuant to Article 16(2) and to progressively reduce pollution by other substances which would otherwise prevent Member States from achieving the objectives for the bodies of surface waters as set out in Article 4;

(l) any measures required to prevent significant losses of pollutants from technical installations, and to prevent and/or to reduce the impact of accidental pollution incidents for example as a result of floods, including through systems to detect or give warning of such events including, in the case of accidents which could not reasonably have been foreseen, all appropriate measures to reduce the risk to aquatic ecosystems.

4. "Supplementary" measures are those measures designed and implemented in addition to the basic measures, with the aim of achieving the objectives established pursuant to Article 4. Part B of Annex VI contains a non-exclusive list of such measures.

Member States may also adopt further supplementary measures in order to provide for additional protection or improvement of the waters covered by this Directive, including in implementation of the relevant international agreements referred to in Article 1.

5. Where monitoring or other data indicate that the objectives set under Article 4 for the body of water are unlikely to be achieved, the Member State shall ensure that:

— the causes of the possible failure are investigated,
— relevant permits and authorisations are examined and reviewed as appropriate,
— the monitoring programmes are reviewed and adjusted as appropriate, and
— additional measures as may be necessary in order to achieve those objectives are established, including, as appropriate, the establishment of stricter environmental quality standards following the procedures laid down in Annex V.

Where those causes are the result of circumstances of natural cause or force majeure which are exceptional and could not reasonably have been foreseen, in particular extreme floods and prolonged droughts, the Member State may determine that additional measures are not practicable, subject to Article 4(6).

6. In implementing measures pursuant to paragraph 3, Member States shall take all appropriate steps not to increase pollution of marine waters. Without prejudice to existing legislation, the application of measures taken pursuant to paragraph 3 may on no account lead, either directly or indirectly to increased pollution of surface waters. This requirement shall not apply where it would result in increased pollution of the environment as a whole.

7. The programmes of measures shall be established at the latest nine years after the date of entry into force of this Directive and all the measures shall be made operational at the latest 12 years after that date.

8. The programmes of measures shall be reviewed, and if necessary updated at the latest 15 years after the date of entry into force of this Directive and every six years thereafter. Any new or revised measures established under an updated programme shall be made operational within three years of their establishment.

Amendment

1 Substituted by Directive 2009/31/EC of the European Parliament and of the Council of 23 April 2009 on the geological storage of carbon dioxide and amending Council Directive 85/337/EEC, European Parliament and Council Directives 2000/60/EC, 2001/80/EC, 2004/35/EC, 2006/12/EC, 2008/1/EC and Regulation (EC) No 1013/2006, Article 32.

Article 12

Issues which can not be dealt with at Member State level

1. Where a Member State identifies an issue which has an impact on the management of its water but cannot be resolved by that Member State, it may report the issue to the Commission and any other Member State concerned and may make recommendations for the resolution of it.

2. The Commission shall respond to any report or recommendations from Member States within a period of six months.

Article 13

River basin management plans

1. Member States shall ensure that a river basin management plan is produced for each river basin district lying entirely within their territory.

2. In the case of an international river basin district falling entirely within the Community, Member States shall ensure coordination with the aim of producing a single international river basin management plan. Where such an international river basin management plan is not produced, Member States shall produce river basin management plans covering at least those parts of the international river basin district falling within their territory to achieve the objectives of this Directive.

3. In the case of an international river basin district extending beyond the boundaries of the Community, Member States shall endeavour to produce a single river basin management plan, and, where this is not possible, the plan shall at least cover the portion of the international river basin district lying within the territory of the Member State concerned.

4. The river basin management plan shall include the information detailed in Annex VII.

5. River basin management plans may be supplemented by the production of more detailed programmes and management plans for sub-basin, sector, issue, or water type, to deal with particular aspects of water management. Implementation of these measures shall not exempt Member States from any of their obligations under the rest of this Directive.

6. River basin management plans shall be published at the latest nine years after the date of entry into force of this Directive.

7. River basin management plans shall be reviewed and updated at the latest 15 years after the date of entry into force of this Directive and every six years thereafter.

Article 14

Public information and consultation

1. Member States shall encourage the active involvement of all interested parties in the implementation of this Directive, in particular in the production, review and updating of the river basin management plans. Member States shall ensure that, for each river basin district, they publish and make available for comments to the public, including users:

(a) a timetable and work programme for the production of the plan, including a statement of the consultation measures to be taken, at least three years before the beginning of the period to which the plan refers;

(b) an interim overview of the significant water management issues identified in the river basin, at least two years before the beginning of the period to which the plan refers;

(c) draft copies of the river basin management plan, at least one year before the beginning of the period to which the plan refers.

On request, access shall be given to background documents and information used for the development of the draft river basin management plan.

2. Member States shall allow at least six months to comment in writing on those documents in order to allow active involvement and consultation.

3. Paragraphs 1 and 2 shall apply equally to updated river basin management plans.

Article 15

Reporting

1. Member States shall send copies of the river basin management plans and all subsequent updates to the Commission and to any other Member State concerned within three months of their publication:

(a) for river basin districts falling entirely within the territory of a Member State, all river management plans covering that national territory and published pursuant to Article 13;
(b) for international river basin districts, at least the part of the river basin management plans covering the territory of the Member State.

2. Member States shall submit summary reports of:
— the analyses required under Article 5, and
— the monitoring programmes designed under Article 8
undertaken for the purposes of the first river basin management plan within three months of their completion.

3. Member States shall, within three years of the publication of each river basin management plan or update under Article 13, submit an interim report describing progress in the implementation of the planned programme of measures.

Article 16

Strategies against pollution of water

1. The European Parliament and the Council shall adopt specific measures against pollution of water by individual pollutants or groups of pollutants presenting a significant risk to or via the aquatic environment, including such risks to waters used for the abstraction of drinking water. For those pollutants measures shall be aimed at the progressive reduction and, for priority hazardous substances, as defined in Article 2(30), at the cessation or phasing-out of discharges, emissions and losses. Such measures shall be adopted acting on the proposals presented by the Commission in accordance with the procedures laid down in the Treaty.

2. The Commission shall submit a proposal setting out a list of priority substances selected amongst those which present a significant risk to or via the aquatic environment. Substances shall be prioritised for action on the basis of risk to or via the aquatic environment, identified by:
(a) risk assessment carried out under Council Regulation (EEC) No 793/93, Council Directive 91/414/EEC, and Directive 98/8/EC of the European Parliament and of the Council, or
(b) targeted risk-based assessment (following the methodology of Regulation (EEC) No 793/93) focusing solely on aquatic ecotoxicity and on human toxicity via the aquatic environment.
When necessary in order to meet the timetable laid down in paragraph 4, substances shall be prioritised for action on the basis of risk to, or via the aquatic environment, identified by a simplified risk-based assessment procedure based on scientific principles taking particular account of:
— evidence regarding the intrinsic hazard of the substance concerned, and in particular its aquatic ecotoxicity and human toxicity via aquatic exposure routes, and
— evidence from monitoring of widespread environmental contamination, and
— other proven factors which may indicate the possibility of widespread environmental contamination, such as production or use volume of the substance concerned, and use patterns.

3. The Commission's proposal shall also identify the priority hazardous substances. In doing so, the Commission shall take into account the selection of substances of concern undertaken in the relevant Community legislation regarding hazardous substances or relevant international agreements.

4. The Commission shall review the adopted list of priority substances at the latest four years after the date of entry into force of this Directive and at least every four years thereafter, and come forward with proposals as appropriate.

5. In preparing its proposal, the Commission shall take account of recommendations from the Scientific Committee on Toxicity, Ecotoxicity and the Environment, Member States, the

European Parliament, the European Environment Agency, Community research programmes, international organisations to which the Community is a party, European business organisations including those representing small and medium-sized enterprises, European environmental organisations, and of other relevant information which comes to its attention.

6. For the priority substances, the Commission shall submit proposals of controls for:

— the progressive reduction of discharges, emissions and losses of the substances concerned, and, in particular

— the cessation or phasing-out of discharges, emissions and losses of the substances as identified in accordance with paragraph 3, including an appropriate timetable for doing so. The timetable shall not exceed 20 years after the adoption of these proposals by the European Parliament and the Council in accordance with the provisions of this Article.

In doing so it shall identify the appropriate cost-effective and proportionate level and combination of product and process controls for both point and diffuse sources and take account of Community-wide uniform emission limit values for process controls. Where appropriate, action at Community level for process controls may be established on a sector-by-sector basis. Where product controls include a review of the relevant authorisations issued under Directive 91/414/EEC and Directive 98/8/EC, such reviews shall be carried out in accordance with the provisions of those Directives. Each proposal for controls shall specify arrangements for their review, updating and for assessment of their effectiveness.

7. The Commission shall submit proposals for quality standards applicable to the concentrations of the priority substances in surface water, sediments or biota.

8. The Commission shall submit proposals, in accordance with paragraphs 6 and 7, and at least for emission controls for point sources and environmental quality standards within two years of the inclusion of the substance concerned on the list of priority substances. For substances included in the first list of priority substances, in the absence of agreement at Community level six years after the date of entry into force of this Directive, Member States shall establish environmental quality standards for these substances for all surface waters affected by discharges of those substances, and controls on the principal sources of such discharges, based, inter alia, on consideration of all technical reduction options. For substances subsequently included in the list of priority substances, in the absence of agreement at Community level, Member States shall take such action five years after the date of inclusion in the list.

9. The Commission may prepare strategies against pollution of water by any other pollutants or groups of pollutants, including any pollution which occurs as a result of accidents.

10. In preparing its proposals under paragraphs 6 and 7, the Commission shall also review all the Directives listed in Annex IX. It shall propose, by the deadline in paragraph 8, a revision of the controls in Annex IX for all those substances which are included in the list of priority substances and shall propose the appropriate measures including the possible repeal of the controls under Annex IX for all other substances.

All the controls in Annex IX for which revisions are proposed shall be repealed by the date of entry into force of those revisions.

11. The list of priority substances of substances mentioned in paragraphs 2 and 3 proposed by the Commission shall, on its adoption by the European Parliament and the Council, become Annex X to this Directive. Its revision mentioned in paragraph 4 shall follow the same procedure.

Article 17

Strategies to prevent and control pollution of groundwater

1. The European Parliament and the Council shall adopt specific measures to prevent and control groundwater pollution. Such measures shall be aimed at achieving the objective of

good groundwater chemical status in accordance with Article 4(1)(b) and shall be adopted, acting on the proposal presented within two years after the entry into force of this Directive, by the Commission in accordance with the procedures laid down in the Treaty.

2. In proposing measures the Commission shall have regard to the analysis carried out according to Article 5 and Annex II. Such measures shall be proposed earlier if data are available and shall include:
(a) criteria for assessing good groundwater chemical status, in accordance with Annex II.2.2 and Annex V 2.3.2 and 2.4.5;
(b) criteria for the identification of significant and sustained upward trends and for the definition of starting points for trend reversals to be used in accordance with Annex V 2.4.4.

3. Measures resulting from the application of paragraph 1 shall be included in the programmes of measures required under Article 11.

4. In the absence of criteria adopted under paragraph 2 at Community level, Member States shall establish appropriate criteria at the latest five years after the date of entry into force of this Directive.

5. In the absence of criteria adopted under paragraph 4 at national level, trend reversal shall take as its starting point a maximum of 75 % of the level of the quality standards set out in existing Community legislation applicable to groundwater.

Article 18

Commission report

1. The Commission shall publish a report on the implementation of this Directive at the latest 12 years after the date of entry into force of this Directive and every six years thereafter, and shall submit it to the European Parliament and to the Council.

2. The report shall include the following:
(a) a review of progress in the implementation of the Directive;
(b) a review of the status of surface water and groundwater in the Community undertaken in coordination with the European Environment Agency;
(c) a survey of the river basin management plans submitted in accordance with Article 15, including suggestions for the improvement of future plans;
(d) a summary of the response to each of the reports or recommendations to the Commission made by Member States pursuant to Article 12;
(e) a summary of any proposals, control measures and strategies developed under Article 16;
(f) a summary of the responses to comments made by the European Parliament and the Council on previous implementation reports.

3. The Commission shall also publish a report on progress in implementation based on the summary reports that Member States submit under Article 15(2), and submit it to the European Parliament and the Member States, at the latest two years after the dates referred to in Articles 5 and 8.

4. The Commission shall, within three years of the publication of each report under paragraph 1, publish an interim report describing progress in implementation on the basis of the interim reports of the Member States as mentioned in Article 15(3). This shall be submitted to the European Parliament and to the Council.

5. The Commission shall convene when appropriate, in line with the reporting cycle, a conference of interested parties on Community water policy from each of the Member States, to comment on the Commission's implementation reports and to share experiences.

Participants should include representatives from the competent authorities, the European Parliament, NGOs, the social and economic partners, consumer bodies, academics and other experts.

Article 19

Plans for future Community measures

1. Once a year, the Commission shall for information purposes present to the Committee referred to in Article 21 an indicative plan of measures having an impact on water legislation which it intends to propose in the near future, including any emerging from the proposals, control measures and strategies developed under Article 16. The Commission shall make the first such presentation at the latest two years after the date of entry into force of this Directive.

2. The Commission will review this Directive at the latest 19 years after the date of its entry into force and will propose any necessary amendments to it.

[Article 20

Technical adaptations to the Directive][1]

[1. Annexes I, III and section 1.3.6 of Annex V may be adapted to scientific and technical progress taking account of the periods for review and updating of the river basin management plans as referred to in Article 13. Those measures, designed to amend non-essential elements of this Directive, shall be adopted in accordance with the regulatory procedure with scrutiny referred to in Article 21(3).

Where necessary, the Commission may adopt guidelines on the implementation of Annexes II and V in accordance with the regulatory procedure referred to in Article 21(2).

2. For the purpose of transmission and processing of data, including statistical and cartographic data, technical formats for the purpose of paragraph 1 may be adopted in accordance with the regulatory procedure referred to in Article 21(2).][1]

Amendment

1 Substituted by Directive 2008/32/EC of the European Parliament and of the Council of 11 March 2008 amending Directive 2000/60/EC establishing a framework for Community action in the field of water policy, as regards the implementing powers conferred on the Commission, Article 1.2.

[Article 21

Committee procedure][1]

[1. The Commission shall be assisted by a committee.

2. Where reference is made to this paragraph, Articles 5 and 7 of Decision 1999/468/EC shall apply, having regard to the provisions of Article 8 thereof.

The period laid down in Article 5(6) of Decision 1999/468/EC shall be set at three months.

3. Where reference is made to this paragraph, Article 5a(1) to (4) and Article 7 of Decision 1999/468/EC shall apply, having regard to the provisions of Article 8 thereof.][1]

Amendment

1 Substituted by Directive 2008/32/EC of the European Parliament and of the Council of 11 March 2008 amending Directive 2000/60/EC establishing a framework for Community action in the field of water policy, as regards the implementing powers conferred on the Commission, Article 1.2.

Article 22

Repeals and transitional provisions

1. The following shall be repealed with effect from seven years after the date of entry into force of this Directive:

— Directive 75/440/EEC of 16 June 1975 concerning the quality required of surface water intended for the abstraction of drinking water in the Member States,
— Council Decision 77/795/EEC of 12 December 1977 establishing a common procedure for the exchange of information on the quality of surface freshwater in the Community,
— Council Directive 79/869/EEC of 9 October 1979 concerning the methods of measurement and frequencies of sampling and analysis of surface water intended for the abstraction of drinking waters in the Member States.

2. The following shall be repealed with effect from 13 years after the date of entry into force of this Directive:
— Council Directive 78/659/EEC of 18 July 1978 on the quality of freshwaters needing protection or improvement in order to support fish life,
— Council Directive 79/923/EEC of 30 October 1979 on the quality required of shellfish waters,
— Council Directive 80/68/EEC of 17 December 1979 on the protection of groundwater against pollution caused by certain dangerous substances,
— Directive 76/464/EEC, with the exception of Article 6, which shall be repealed with effect from the entry into force of this Directive.

3. The following transitional provisions shall apply for Directive 76/464/EEC:
(a) the list of priority substances adopted under Article 16 of this Directive shall replace the list of substances prioritised in the Commission communication to the Council of 22 June 1982;
(b) for the purposes of Article 7 of Directive 76/464/EEC, Member States may apply the principles for the identification of pollution problems and the substances causing them, the establishment of quality standards, and the adoption of measures, laid down in this Directive.

4. The environmental objectives in Article 4 and environmental quality standards established in Annex IX and pursuant to Article 16(7), and by Member States under Annex V for substances not on the list of priority substances and under Article 16(8) in respect of priority substances for which Community standards have not been set, shall be regarded as environmental quality standards for the purposes of point 7 of Article 2 and Article 10 of Directive 96/61/EC.

5. Where a substance on the list of priority substances adopted under Article 16 is not included in Annex VIII to this Directive or in Annex III to Directive 96/61/EC, it shall be added thereto.

6. For bodies of surface water, environmental objectives established under the first river basin management plan required by this Directive shall, as a minimum, give effect to quality standards at least as stringent as those required to implement Directive 76/464/EEC.

Article 23

Penalties

Member States shall determine penalties applicable to breaches of the national provisions adopted pursuant to this Directive. The penalties thus provided for shall be effective, proportionate and dissuasive.

Article 24

Implementation

1. Member States shall bring into force the laws, regulations and administrative provisions necessary to comply with this Directive at the latest 22 December 2003. They shall forthwith inform the Commission thereof.

When Member States adopt these measures, they shall contain a reference to this Directive or shall be accompanied by such a reference on the occasion of their official publication. The methods of making such a reference shall be laid down by the Member States.

2. Member States shall communicate to the Commission the texts of the main provisions of national law which they adopt in the field governed by this Directive. The Commission shall inform the other Member States thereof.

Article 25

Entry into force

This Directive shall enter into force on the day of its publication in the Official Journal of the European Communities.

Article 26

Addressees

This Directive is addressed to the Member States.

ANNEX I
INFORMATION REQUIRED FOR THE LIST OF COMPETENT AUTHORITIES

As required under Article 3(8), the Member States shall provide the following information on all competent authorities within each of its river basin districts as well as the portion of any international river basin district lying within their territory.

(i) Name and address of the competent authority – the official name and address of the authority identified under Article 3(2).

(ii) Geographical coverage of the river basin district – the names of the main rivers within the river basin district together with a precise description of the boundaries of the river basin district. This information should as far as possible be available for introduction into a geographic information system (GIS) and/or the geographic information system of the Commission (GISCO).

(iii) Legal status of competent authority – a description of the legal status of the competent authority and, where relevant, a summary or copy of its statute, founding treaty or equivalent legal document.

(iv) Responsibilities – a description of the legal and administrative responsibilities of each competent authority and of its role within each river basin district.

(v) Membership – where the competent authority acts as a coordinating body for other competent authorities, a list is required of these bodies together with a summary of the institutional relationships established in order to ensure coordination.

(vi) International relationships – where a river basin district covers the territory of more than one Member State or includes the territory of non-Member States, a summary is required of the institutional relationships established in order to ensure coordination.

ANNEX II

1. SURFACE WATERS

1.1. Characterisation of surface water body types

Member States shall identify the location and boundaries of bodies of surface water and shall carry out an initial characterisation of all such bodies in accordance with the following methodology. Member States may group surface water bodies together for the purposes of this initial characterisation.

(i) The surface water bodies within the river basin district shall be identified as falling within either one of the following surface water categories – rivers, lakes, transitional waters or coastal waters – or as artificial surface water bodies or heavily modified surface water bodies.

(ii) For each surface water category, the relevant surface water bodies within the river basin district shall be differentiated according to type. These types are those defined using either "system A" or "system B" identified in section 1.2.

(iii) If system A is used, the surface water bodies within the river basin district shall first be differentiated by the relevant ecoregions in accordance with the geographical areas identified in section 1.2 and shown on the relevant map in Annex XI. The water bodies within each ecoregion shall then be differentiated by surface water body types according to the descriptors set out in the tables for system A.

(iv) If system B is used, Member States must achieve at least the same degree of differentiation as would be achieved using system A. Accordingly, the surface water bodies within the river basin district shall be differentiated into types using the values for the obligatory descriptors and such optional descriptors, or combinations of descriptors, as are required to ensure that type specific biological reference conditions can be reliably derived.

(v) For artificial and heavily modified surface water bodies the differentiation shall be undertaken in accordance with the descriptors for whichever of the surface water categories most closely resembles the heavily modified or artificial water body concerned.

(vi) Member States shall submit to the Commission a map or maps (in a GIS format) of the geographical location of the types consistent with the degree of differentiation required under system A.

1.2. Ecoregions and surface water body types

1.2.1. Rivers

System A

Fixed typology	*Descriptors*
Ecoregion	Ecoregions drawn on map A in Annex XI
Type	Altitude typology high: > 800 m mid altitude: 200 to 800 m lowland: < 200 m
	Size typology based on catchment area small: 10 to 100 km^2 medium: > 100 to 1000 km^2 large: > 1000 to 10000 km^2 very large: > 10000 km^2
	Geology calcareous siliceous organic

System B

Alternative characterisation	*Physical and chemical factors that determine the characteristics of the river or part of the river and hence the biological population structure and composition*
Obligatory factors	altitude latitude longitude geology size
Optional factors	distance from river source energy of flow (function of flow and slope) mean water width mean water depth mean water slope form and shape of main river bed river discharge (flow) category valley shape transport of solids acid neutralising capacity mean substratum composition chloride air temperature range mean air temperature precipitation

1.2.2. Lakes

System A

Fixed typology	*Descriptors*
Ecoregion	Ecoregions shown on map A in Annex XI
Type	Altitude typology high: > 800 m mid altitude: 200 to 800 m lowland: < 200 m Depth typology based on mean depth < 3 m 3 to 15 m > 15 m Size typology based on surface ares 0.5 to 1 km^2 1 to 10 km^2 10 to 100 km^2 > 100 km^2 Geology calcareous siliceous organic

System B

Alternative charactarisation	*Physical and chemical factors that determine the characteristics of the lake and hence the biological population structure and composition*
Obligatory factors	altitude latitude longitude depth geology size
Optional factors	mean water depth lake shape residence time mean air temperature air temperature range mixing characteristics (eg. monomictic, dimictic, polymictic) acid neutralising capacity background nutrient status mean substratum composition water level fluctuation

1.2.3. Transitional Waters

System A

Fixed typology	*Descriptors*
Ecoregion	The following as identified on map B in Annex XI: Baltic Sea Barents Sea Norwegian Sea North Sea North Atlantic Ocean Mediterranean Sea
Type	Based on mean annual salinity: < 0.5 ‰: freshwater 0.5 to < 5 ‰: oligohaline 5 to < 18 ‰: mesohaline 18 to < 30 ‰: polyhaline 30 to < 40 ‰: euhaline Based on mean tidal range: < 2 m: microtidal 2 to 4 m: mesotidal > 4 m: macrotidal

System B

Alternative charactarisation	*Physical and chemical factors that determine the characteristics of the transitional water and hence the biological population structure and composition*
Obligatory factors	latitude longitude tidal range salinity

Alternative charactarisation	*Physical and chemical factors that determine the characteristics of the transitional water and hence the biological population structure and composition*
Optional factors	depth current velocity wave exposure residence time mean water temperature mixing charactaristics turbidity mean substratum composition shape water temperature range

1.2.4. Coastal Waters

System A

Fixed typology	*Descriptors*
Ecoregion	The following as identified on map B in Annex XI: Baltic Sea Barents Sea Norwegian Sea North Sea North Atlantic Ocean Mediterranean Sea
Type	Based on mean annual salinity: < 0.5 ‰: freshwater 0.5 to < 5 ‰: oligohaline 5 to < 18 ‰: mesohaline 18 to < 30 ‰: polyhaline 30 to < 40 ‰: euhaline Based on mean depth: shallow waters: < 30 m intermediate: (30 to 100 m) deep: > 200 m

System B

Alternative charactarisation	*Physical and chemical factors that determine the characteristics of the coastal water and hence the biological population structure and composition*
Obligatory factors	latitude longitude tidal range salinity
Optional factors	current velocity wave exposure mean water temperature mixing charactaristics turbidity retention time (of enclosed bays) mean substratum composition water temperature range

1.3. Establishment of type-specific reference conditions for surface water body types

(i) For each surface water body type characterised in accordance with section 1.1, type-specific hydromorphological and physicochemical conditions shall be established representing the values of the hydromorphological and physicochemical quality elements specified in point 1.1 in Annex V for that surface water body type at high ecological status as defined in the relevant table in point 1.2 in Annex V. Type-specific biological reference conditions shall be established, representing the values of the biological quality elements specified in point 1.1 in Annex V for that surface water body type at high ecological status as defined in the relevant table in section 1.2 in Annex V.

(ii) In applying the procedures set out in this section to heavily modified or artificial surface water bodies references to high ecological status shall be construed as references to maximum ecological potential as defined in table 1.2.5 of Annex V. The values for maximum ecological potential for a water body shall be reviewed every six years.

(iii) Type-specific conditions for the purposes of points (i) and (ii) and type-specific biological reference conditions may be either spatially based or based on modelling, or may be derived using a combination of these methods. Where it is not possible to use these methods, Member States may use expert judgement to establish such conditions. In defining high ecological status in respect of concentrations of specific synthetic pollutants, the detection limits are those which can be achieved in accordance with the available techniques at the time when the type-specific conditions are to be established.

(iv) For spatially based type-specific biological reference conditions, Member States shall develop a reference network for each surface water body type. The network shall contain a sufficient number of sites of high status to provide a sufficient level of confidence about the values for the reference conditions, given the variability in the values of the quality elements corresponding to high ecological status for that surface water body type and the modelling techniques which are to be applied under paragraph (v).

(v) Type-specific biological reference conditions based on modelling may be derived using either predictive models or hindcasting methods. The methods shall use historical, palaeological and other available data and shall provide a sufficient level of confidence about the values for the reference conditions to ensure that the conditions so derived are consistent and valid for each surface water body type.

(vi) Where it is not possible to establish reliable type-specific reference conditions for a quality element in a surface water body type due to high degrees of natural variability in that element, not just as a result of seasonal variations, then that element may be excluded from the assessment of ecological status for that surface water type. In such circumstances Member States shall state the reasons for this exclusion in the river basin management plan.

1.4. Identification of Pressures

Member States shall collect and maintain information on the type and magnitude of the significant anthropogenic pressures to which the surface water bodies in each river basin district are liable to be subject, in particular the following.

Estimation and identification of significant point source pollution, in particular by substances listed in Annex VIII, from urban, industrial, agricultural and other installations and activities, based, inter alia, on information gathered under:

(i) Articles 15 and 17 of Directive 91/271/EEC;

(ii) Articles 9 and 15 of Directive 96/61/EC;

and for the purposes of the initial river basin management plan:

(iii) Article 11 of Directive 76/464/EEC; and

(iv) Directives 75/440/EC, 76/160/EEC, 78/659/EEC and 79/923/EEC.

Estimation and identification of significant diffuse source pollution, in particular by substances listed in Annex VIII, from urban, industrial, agricultural and other installations and activities; based, inter alia, on information gathered under:

(i) Articles 3, 5 and 6 of Directive 91/676/EEC;
(ii) Articles 7 and 17 of Directive 91/414/EEC;
(iii) Directive 98/8/EC;
and for the purposes of the first river basin management plan:
(iv) Directives 75/440/EEC, 76/160/EEC, 76/464/EEC, 78/659/EEC and 79/923/EEC.

Estimation and identification of significant water abstraction for urban, industrial, agricultural and other uses, including seasonal variations and total annual demand, and of loss of water in distribution systems.

Estimation and identification of the impact of significant water flow regulation, including water transfer and diversion, on overall flow characteristics and water balances.

Identification of significant morphological alterations to water bodies.

Estimation and identification of other significant anthropogenic impacts on the status of surface waters.

Estimation of land use patterns, including identification of the main urban, industrial and agricultural areas and, where relevant, fisheries and forests.

1.5. Assessment of Impact

Member States shall carry out an assessment of the susceptibility of the surface water status of bodies to the pressures identified above.

Member States shall use the information collected above, and any other relevant information including existing environmental monitoring data, to carry out an assessment of the likelihood that surface waters bodies within the river basin district will fail to meet the environmental quality objectives set for the bodies under Article 4. Member States may utilise modelling techniques to assist in such an assessment.

For those bodies identified as being at risk of failing the environmental quality objectives, further characterisation shall, where relevant, be carried out to optimise the design of both the monitoring programmes required under Article 8, and the programmes of measures required under Article 11.

2. GROUNDWATERS

2.1. Initial characterisation

Member States shall carry out an initial characterisation of all groundwater bodies to assess their uses and the degree to which they are at risk of failing to meet the objectives for each groundwater body under Article 4. Member States may group groundwater bodies together for the purposes of this initial characterisation. This analysis may employ existing hydrological, geological, pedological, land use, discharge, abstraction and other data but shall identify:

— the location and boundaries of the groundwater body or bodies,
— the pressures to which the groundwater body or bodies are liable to be subject including:
— diffuse sources of pollution
— point sources of pollution
— abstraction
— artificial recharge,
— the general character of the overlying strata in the catchment area from which the groundwater body receives its recharge,
— those groundwater bodies for which there are directly dependent surface water ecosystems or terrestrial ecosystems.

2.2. Further characterisation

Following this initial characterisation, Member States shall carry out further characterisation of those groundwater bodies or groups of bodies which have been identified as being at risk in order to establish a more precise assessment of the significance of such risk and identification of any measures to be required under Article 11. Accordingly, this characterisation shall include relevant information on the impact of human activity and, where relevant, information on:

— geological characteristics of the groundwater body including the extent and type of geological units,
— hydrogeological characteristics of the groundwater body including hydraulic conductivity, porosity and confinement,
— characteristics of the superficial deposits and soils in the catchment from which the groundwater body receives its recharge, including the thickness, porosity, hydraulic conductivity, and absorptive properties of the deposits and soils,
— stratification characteristics of the groundwater within the groundwater body,
— an inventory of associated surface systems, including terrestrial ecosystems and bodies of surface water, with which the groundwater body is dynamically linked,
— estimates of the directions and rates of exchange of water between the groundwater body and associated surface systems,
— sufficient data to calculate the long term annual average rate of overall recharge,
— characterisation of the chemical composition of the groundwater, including specification of the contributions from human activity. Member States may use typologies for groundwater characterisation when establishing natural background levels for these bodies of groundwater.

2.3. Review of the impact of human activity on groundwaters

For those bodies of groundwater which cross the boundary between two or more Member States or are identified following the initial characterisation undertaken in accordance with paragraph 2.1 as being at risk of failing to meet the objectives set for each body under Article 4, the following information shall, where relevant, be collected and maintained for each groundwater body:

(a) the location of points in the groundwater body used for the abstraction of water with the exception of:
    — points for the abstraction of water providing less than an average of 10 m3 per day, or,
    — points for the abstraction of water intended for human consumption providing less than an average of 10 m3 per day or serving less than 50 persons,
(b) the annual average rates of abstraction from such points,
(c) the chemical composition of water abstracted from the groundwater body,
(d) the location of points in the groundwater body into which water is directly discharged,
(e) the rates of discharge at such points,
(f) the chemical composition of discharges to the groundwater body, and
(g) land use in the catchment or catchments from which the groundwater body receives its recharge, including pollutant inputs and anthropogenic alterations to the recharge characteristics such as rainwater and run-off diversion through land sealing, artificial recharge, damming or drainage.

2.4. Review of the impact of changes in groundwater levels

Member States shall also identify those bodies of groundwater for which lower objectives are to be specified under Article 4 including as a result of consideration of the effects of the status of the body on:

(i) surface water and associated terrestrial ecosystems
(ii) water regulation, flood protection and land drainage
(iii) human development.

2.5. Review of the impact of pollution on groundwater quality

Member States shall identify those bodies of groundwater for which lower objectives are to be specified under Article 4(5) where, as a result of the impact of human activity, as determined in accordance with Article 5(1), the body of groundwater is so polluted that achieving good groundwater chemical status is infeasible or disproportionately expensive.

ANNEX III
ECONOMIC ANALYSIS

The economic analysis shall contain enough information in sufficient detail (taking account of the costs associated with collection of the relevant data) in order to:

(a) make the relevant calculations necessary for taking into account under Article 9 the principle of recovery of the costs of water services, taking account of long term forecasts of supply and demand for water in the river basin district and, where necessary:
 — estimates of the volume, prices and costs associated with water services, and
 — estimates of relevant investment including forecasts of such investments;

(b) make judgements about the most cost-effective combination of measures in respect of water uses to be included in the programme of measures under Article 11 based on estimates of the potential costs of such measures.

ANNEX IV
PROTECTED AREAS

1. The register of protected areas required under Article 6 shall include the following types of protected areas:

(i) areas designated for the abstraction of water intended for human consumption under Article 7;

(ii) areas designated for the protection of economically significant aquatic species;

(iii) bodies of water designated as recreational waters, including areas designated as bathing waters under Directive 76/160/EEC;

(iv) nutrient-sensitive areas, including areas designated as vulnerable zones under Directive 91/676/EEC and areas designated as sensitive areas under Directive 91/271/EEC; and

(v) areas designated for the protection of habitats or species where the maintenance or improvement of the status of water is an important factor in their protection, including relevant Natura 2000 sites designated under Directive 92/43/EEC and Directive 79/409/EEC.

2. The summary of the register required as part of the river basin management plan shall include maps indicating the location of each protected area and a description of the Community, national or local legislation under which they have been designated.

ANNEX V

1. SURFACE WATER STATUS

1.1. Quality elements for the classification of ecological status

1.1.1. Rivers

Biological elements

Composition and abundance of aquatic flora

Composition and abundance of benthic invertebrate fauna

Composition, abundance and age structure of fish fauna

Hydromorphological elements supporting the biological elements

Hydrological regime
    quantity and dynamics of water flow
    connection to groundwater bodies

River continuity

Morphological conditions
    river depth and width variation
    structure and substrate of the river bed
    structure of the riparian zone

Chemical and physico-chemical elements supporting the biological elements

General

Thermal conditions

Oxygenation conditions

Salinity

Acidification status

Nutrient conditions

Specific pollutants

Pollution by all priority substances identified as being discharged into the body of water

Pollution by other substances identified as being discharged in significant quantities into the body of water

1.1.2. Lakes

Biological elements

Composition, abundance and biomass of phytoplankton

Composition and abundance of other aquatic flora

Composition and abundance of benthic invertebrate fauna

Composition, abundance and age structure of fish fauna

Hydromorphological elements supporting the biological elements

Hydrological regime
    quantity and dynamics of water flow
    residence time
    connection to the groundwater body

Morphological conditions
    lake depth variation
    quantity, structure and substrate of the lake bed
    structure of the lake shore

Chemical and physico-chemical elements supporting the biological elements

General

Transparency

Thermal conditions

Oxygenation conditions

Salinity

Acidification status

Nutrient conditions

Specific pollutants

Pollution by all priority substances identified as being discharged into the body of water

Pollution by other substances identified as being discharged in significant quantities into the body of water

1.1.3. Transitional waters

Biological elements

Composition, abundance and biomass of phytoplankton

Composition and abundance of other aquatic flora

Composition and abundance of benthic invertebrate fauna

Composition and abundance of fish fauna

Hydro-morphological elements supporting the biological elements

Morphological conditions
    depth variation
    quantity, structure and substrate of the bed
    structure of the intertidal zone

Tidal regime
    freshwater flow
    wave exposure

Chemical and physico-chemical elements supporting the biological elements

General

Transparency

Thermal conditions

Oxygenation conditions

Salinity

Nutrient conditions

Specific pollutants

Pollution by all priority substances identified as being discharged into the body of water

Pollution by other substances identified as being discharged in significant quantities into the body of water

1.1.4. Coastal waters

Biological elements

Composition, abundance and biomass of phytoplankton

Composition and abundance of other aquatic flora

Composition and abundance of benthic invertebrate fauna

Hydromorphological elements supporting the biological elements

Morphological conditions
- depth variation
- structure and substrate of the coastal bed
- structure of the intertidal zone

Tidal regime
- direction of dominant currents
- wave exposure

Chemical and physico-chemical elements supporting the biological elements

General

Transparency

Thermal conditions

Oxygenation conditions

Salinity

Nutrient conditions

Specific pollutants

Pollution by all priority substances identified as being discharged into the body of water

Pollution by other substances identified as being discharged in significant quantities into the body of water

1.1.5. Artificial and heavily modified surface water bodies

The quality elements applicable to artificial and heavily modified surface water bodies shall be those applicable to whichever of the four natural surface water categories above most closely resembles the heavily modified or artificial water body concerned.

1.2. Normative definitions of ecological status classifications

Table 1.2
General definition for rivers, lakes, transitional waters and coastal waters

The following text provides a general definition of ecological quality. For the purposes of classification the values for the quality elements of ecological status for each surface water category are those given in tables 1.2.1 to 1.2.4 below.

Element	*High status*	*Good status*	*Moderate status*
General	There are no, or only very minor, anthropogenic alterations to the values of the physico-chemical and hydromorphological quality elements for the surface water body type from those normally associated with that type under undisturbed conditions. The values of the biological quality elements for the surface water body reflect those normally associated with that type under undisturbed conditions, and show no, or only very minor, evidence of distortion. These are the type-specific conditions and communities.	The values of the biological quality elements for the surface water body type show low levels of distortion resulting from human activity, but deviate only slightly from those normally associated with the surface water body type under undisturbed conditions.	The values of the biological quality elements for the surface water body type deviate moderately from those normally associated with the surface water body type under undisturbed conditions. The values show moderate signs of distortion resulting from human activity and are significantly more disturbed than under conditions of good status.

Waters achieving a status below moderate shall be classified as poor or bad.

Waters showing evidence of major alterations to the values of the biological quality elements for the surface water body type and in which the relevant biological communities deviate substantially from those normally associated with the surface water body type under undisturbed conditions, shall be classified as poor.

Waters showing evidence of severe alterations to the values of the biological quality elements for the surface water body type and in which large portions of the relevant biological communities normally associated with the surface water body type under undisturbed conditions are absent, shall be classified as bad.

1.2.1. Definitions for high, good and moderate ecological status in rivers

Biological quality elements

Element	*High status*	*Good status*	*Moderate status*
Phytoplankton	The taxonomic composition of phytoplankton corresponds totally or nearly totally to undisturbed conditions. The average phytoplankton abundance is wholly	There are slight changes in the composition and abundance of planktonic taxa compared to the type-specific communities. Such changes do not indicate any accelerated growth of algae resulting	The composition of planktonic taxa differs moderately from the type-specific communities. Abundance is moderately disturbed and may be such as to produce a significant undesirable

Element	*High status*	*Good status*	*Moderate status*
	consistent with the type-specific physico-chemical conditions and is not such as to significantly alter the type-specific transparency conditions. Planktonic blooms occur at a frequency and intensity which is consistent with the type-specific physico-chemical conditions.	in undesirable disturbances to the balance of organisms present in the water body or to the physico-chemical quality of the water or sediment. A slight increase in the frequency and intensity of the type-specific planktonic blooms may occur.	disturbance in the values of other biological and physico-chemical quality elements. A moderate increase in the frequency and intensity of planktonic blooms may occur. Persistent blooms may occur during summer months.
Macrophytes and phytobenthos	The taxonomic composition corresponds totally or nearly totally to undisturbed conditions. There are no detectable changes in the average macrophytic and the average phytobenthic abundance.	There are slight changes in the composition and abundance of macrophytic and phytobenthic taxa compared to the type-specific communities. Such changes do not indicate any accelerated growth of phytobenthos or higher forms of plant life resulting in undesirable disturbances to the balance of organisms present in the water body or to the physico-chemical quality of the water or sediment. The phytobenthic community is not adversely affected by bacterial tufts and coats present due to anthropogenic activity.	The composition of macrophytic and phytobenthic taxa differs moderately from the type-specific community and is significantly more distorted than at good status. Moderate changes in the average macrophytic and the average phytobenthic abundance are evident. The phytobenthic community may be interfered with and, in some areas, displaced by bacterial tufts and coats present as a result of anthropogenic activities.
Benthic invertebrate fauna	The taxonomic composition and abundance correspond totally or nearly totally to undisturbed conditions. The ratio of disturbance sensitive taxa to insensitive taxa shows no signs	There are slight changes in the composition and abundance of invertebrate taxa from the type-specific communities. The ratio of disturbance-sensitive taxa to insensitive taxa	The composition and abundance of invertebrate taxa differ moderately from the type-specific communities. Major taxonomic groups of the type-specific community are absent.

Element	*High status*	*Good status*	*Moderate status*
	of alteration from undisturbed levels. The level of diversity of invertebrate taxa shows no sign of alteration from undisturbed levels.	shows slight alteration from type-specific levels. The level of diversity of invertebrate taxa shows slight signs of alteration from type-specific levels.	The ratio of disturbance-sensitive taxa to insensitive taxa, and the level of diversity, are substantially lower than the type-specific level and significantly lower than for good status.
Fish fauna	Species composition and abundance correspond totally or nearly totally to undisturbed conditions. All the type-specific disturbance-sensitive species are present. The age structures of the fish communities show little sign of anthropogenic disturbance and are not indicative of a failure in the reproduction or development of any particular species.	There are slight changes in species composition and abundance from the type-specific communities attributable to anthropogenic impacts on physico-chemical and hydromorphological quality elements. The age structures of the fish communities show signs of disturbance attributable to anthropogenic impacts on physico-chemical or hydromorphological quality elements, and, in a few instances, are indicative of a failure in the reproduction or development of a particular species, to the extent that some age classes may be missing.	The composition and abundance of fish species differ moderately from the type-specific communities attributable to anthropogenic impacts on physico-chemical or hydromorphological quality elements. The age structure of the fish communities shows major signs of anthropogenic disturbance, to the extent that a moderate proportion of the type specific species are absent or of very low abundance.

Hydromorphological quality elements

Element	*High status*	*Good status*	*Moderate status*
Hydrological regime	The quantity and dynamics of flow, and the resultant connection to groundwaters, reflect totally, or nearly totally, undisturbed conditions.	Conditions consistent with the achievement of the values specified above for the biological quality elements.	Conditions consistent with the achievement of the values specified above for the biological quality elements.

Element	*High status*	*Good status*	*Moderate status*
River continuity	The continuity of the river is not disturbed by anthropogenic activities and allows undisturbed migration of aquatic organisms and sediment transport.	Conditions consistent with the achievement of the values specified above for the biological quality elements.	Conditions consistent with the achievement of the values specified above for the biological quality elements.
Morphological conditions	Channel patterns, width and depth variations, flow velocities, substrate conditions and both the structure and condition of the riparian zones correspond totally or nearly totally to undisturbed conditions.	Conditions consistent with the achievement of the values specified above for the biological quality elements.	Conditions consistent with the achievement of the values specified above for the biological quality elements.

Physico-chemical quality elements[(1)]

Element	*High status*	*Good status*	*Moderate status*
General conditions	The values of the physico-chemical elements correspond totally or nearly totally to undisturbed conditions. Nutrient concentrations remain within the range normally associated with undisturbed conditions. Levels of salinity, pH, oxygen balance, acid neutralising capacity and temperature do not show signs of anthropogenic disturbance and remain within the range normally associated with undisturbed conditions.	Temperature, oxygen balance, pH, acid neutralising capacity and salinity do not reach levels outside the range established so as to ensure the functioning of the type specific ecosystem and the achievement of the values specified above for the biological quality elements. Nutrient concentrations do not exceed the levels established so as to ensure the functioning of the ecosystem and the achievement of the values specified above for the biological quality elements.	Conditions consistent with the achievement of the values specified above for the biological quality elements.
Specific synthetic pollutants	Concentrations close to zero and at least below the limits of detection of the most advanced analytical techniques in general use.	Concentrations not in excess of the standards set in accordance with the procedure detailed in section 1.2.6 without prejudice to Directive 91/414/EC and Directive 98/8/EC. (< EQS)	Conditions consistent with the achievement of the values specified above for the biological quality elements.

Element	High status	Good status	Moderate status
Specific non-synthetic pollutants	Concentrations remain within the range normally associated with undisturbed conditions (background levels = bgl).	Concentrations not in excess of the standards set in accordance with the procedure detailed in section 1.2.6[2] without prejudice to Directive 91/414/EC and Directive 98/8/EC. (< EQS)	Conditions consistent with the achievement of the values specified above for the biological quality elements.

(1) The following abbreviations are used: bgl = background level, EQS = environmental quality standard.

(2) Application of the standards derived under this protocol shall not require reduction of pollutant concentrations below background levels: (EQS > bgl).

1.2.2. Definitions for high, good and moderate ecological status in lakes

Biological quality elements

Element	High status	Good status	Moderate status
Phytoplankton	The taxonomic composition and abundance of phytoplankton correspond totally or nearly totally to undisturbed conditions. The average phytoplankton biomass is consistent with the type-specific physicochemical conditions and is not such as to significantly alter the type-specific transparency conditions. Planktonic blooms occur at a frequency and intensity which is consistent with the type specific physico-chemical conditions.	There are slight changes in the composition and abundance of planktonic taxa compared to the type-specific communities. Such changes do not indicate any accelerated growth of algae resulting in undesirable disturbance to the balance of organisms present in the water body or to the physicochemical quality of the water or sediment. A slight increase in the frequency and intensity of the type specific planktonic blooms may occur.	The composition and abundance of planktonic taxa differ moderately from the type-specific communities. Biomass is moderately disturbed and may be such as to produce a significant undesirable disturbance in the condition of other biological quality elements and the physico-chemical quality of the water or sediment. A moderate increase in the frequency and intensity of planktonic blooms may occur. Persistent blooms may occur during summer months.

Element	*High status*	*Good status*	*Moderate status*
Macrophytes and phytobenthos	The taxonomic composition corresponds totally or nearly totally to undisturbed conditions. There are no detectable changes in the average macrophytic and the average phytobenthic abundance.	There are slight changes in the composition and abundance of macrophytic and phytobenthic taxa compared to the type-specific communities. Such changes do not indicate any accelerated growth of phytobenthos or higher forms of plant life resulting in undesirable disturbance to the balance of organisms present in the water body or to the physico-chemical quality of the water. The phytobenthic community is not adversely affected by bacterial tufts and coats present due to anthropogenic activity.	The composition of macrophytic and phytobenthic taxa differ moderately from the type-specific communities and are significantly more distorted than those observed at good quality. Moderate changes in the average macrophytic and the average phytobenthic abundance are evident. The phytobenthic community may be interfered with, and, in some areas, displaced by bacterial tufts and coats present as a result of anthropogenic activities.
Benthic invertebrate fauna	The taxonomic composition and abundance correspond totally or nearly totally to the undisturbed conditions. The ratio of disturbance sensitive taxa to insensitive taxa shows no signs of alteration from undisturbed levels. The level of diversity of invertebrate taxa shows no sign of alteration from undisturbed levels.	There are slight changes in the composition and abundance of invertebrate taxa compared to the type-specific communities. The ratio of disturbance sensitive taxa to insensitive taxa shows slight signs of alteration from type-specific levels. The level of diversity of invertebrate taxa shows slight signs of alteration from type-specific levels.	The composition and abundance of invertebrate taxa differ moderately from the type-specific conditions. Major taxonomic groups of the type-specific community are absent. The ratio of disturbance sensitive to insensitive taxa, and the level of diversity, are substantially lower than the type-specific level and significantly lower than for good status.

Element	*High status*	*Good status*	*Moderate status*
Fish fauna	Species composition and abundance correspond totally or nearly totally to undisturbed conditions. All the type-specific sensitive species are present. The age structures of the fish communities show little sign of anthropogenic disturbance and are not indicative of a failure in the reproduction or development of a particular species.	There are slight changes in species composition and abundance from the type-specific communities attributable to anthropogenic impacts on physico-chemical or hydromorphological quality elements. The age structures of the fish communities show signs of disturbance attributable to anthropogenic impacts on physico-chemical or hydromorphological quality elements, and, in a few instances, are indicative of a failure in the reproduction or development of a particular species, to the extent that some age classes may be missing.	The composition and abundance of fish species differ moderately from the type-specific communities attributable to anthropogenic impacts on physico-chemical or hydromorphological quality elements. The age structure of the fish communities shows major signs of disturbance, attributable to anthropogenic impacts on physico-chemical or hydromorphological quality elements, to the extent that a moderate proportion of the type specific species are absent or of very low abundance.

Hydromorphological quality elements

Element	*High status*	*Good status*	*Moderate status*
Hydrological regime	The quantity and dynamics of flow, level, residence time, and the resultant connection to groundwaters, reflect totally or nearly totally undisturbed conditions.	Conditions consistent with the achievement of the values specified above for the biological quality elements.	Conditions consistent with the achievement of the values specified above for the biological quality elements.
Morphological conditions	Lake depth variation, quantity and structure of the substrate, and both the structure and condition of the lake shore zone correspond totally or nearly totally to undisturbed conditions.	Conditions consistent with the achievement of the values specified above for the biological quality elements.	Conditions consistent with the achievement of the values specified above for the biological quality elements.

Physico-chemical quality elements[1]

Element	*High status*	*Good status*	*Moderate status*
General conditions	The values of physico-chemical elements correspond totally or nearly totally to undisturbed conditions. Nutrient concentrations remain within the range normally associated with undisturbed conditions. Levels of salinity, pH, oxygen balance, acid neutralising capacity, transparency and temperature do not show signs of anthropogenic disturbance and remain within the range normally associated with undisturbed conditions.	Temperature, oxygen balance, pH, acid neutralising capacity, transparency and salinity do not reach levels outside the range established so as to ensure the functioning of the ecosystem and the achievement of the values specified above for the biological quality elements. Nutrient concentrations do not exceed the levels established so as to ensure the functioning of the ecosystem and the achievement of the values specified above for the biological quality elements.	Conditions consistent with the achievement of the values specified above for the biological quality elements.
Specific synthetic pollutants	Concentrations close to zero and at least below the limits of detection of the most advanced analytical techniques in general use.	Concentrations not in excess of the standards set in accordance with the procedure detailed in section 1.2.6 without prejudice to Directive 91/414/EC and Directive 98/8/EC. (< EQS)	Conditions consistent with the achievement of the values specified above for the biological quality elements.
Specific non-synthetic pollutants	Concentrations remain within the range normally associated with undisturbed conditions (background levels = bgl).	Concentrations not in excess of the standards set in accordance with the procedure detailed in section 1.2.6[2] without prejudice to Directive 91/414/EC and Directive 98/8/EC. (< EQS)	Conditions consistent with the achievement of the values specified above for the biological quality elements.

(1) The following abbreviations are used: bgl = background level, EQS = environmental quality standard.

(2) Application of the standards derived under this protocol shall not require reduction of pollutant concentrations below background levels: (EQS > bgl).

1.2.3. Definitions for high, good and moderate ecological status in transitional waters

Biological quality elements

Element	*High status*	*Good status*	*Moderate status*
Phytoplankton	The composition and abundance of the phytoplanktonic taxa are consistent with undisturbed conditions. The average phytoplankton biomass is consistent with the type-specific physicochemical conditions and is not such as to significantly alter the type-specific transparency conditions. Planktonic blooms occur at a frequency and intensity which is consistent with the type specific physico-chemical conditions.	There are slight changes in the composition and abundance of phytoplanktonic taxa. There are slight changes in biomass compared to the type-specific conditions. Such changes do not indicate any accelerated growth of algae resulting in undesirable disturbance to the balance of organisms present in the water body or to the physico-chemical quality of the water. A slight increase in the frequency and intensity of the type specific planktonic blooms may occur.	The composition and abundance of phytoplanktonic taxa differ moderately from type-specific conditions. Biomass is moderately disturbed and may be such as to produce a significant undesirable disturbance in the condition of other biological quality elements. A moderate increase in the frequency and intensity of planktonic blooms may occur. Persistent blooms may occur during summer months.
Macroalgae	The composition of macroalgal taxa is consistent with undisturbed conditions. There are no detectable changes in macroalgal cover due to anthropogenic activities.	There are slight changes in the composition and abundance of macroalgal taxa compared to the type-specific communities. Such changes do not indicate any accelerated growth of phytobenthos or higher forms of plant life resulting in undesirable disturbance to the balance of organisms present in the water body or to the physico-chemical quality of the water.	The composition of macroalgal taxa differs moderately from type-specific conditions and is significantly more distorted than at good quality. Moderate changes in the average macroalgal abundance are evident and may be such as to result in an undesirable disturbance to the balance of organisms present in the water body.

Element	*High status*	*Good status*	*Moderate status*
Angiosperms	The taxonomic composition corresponds totally or nearly totally to undisturbed conditions. There are no detectable changes in angiosperm abundance due to anthropogenic activities.	There are slight changes in the composition of angiosperm taxa compared to the type-specific communities. Angiosperm abundance shows slight signs of disturbance.	The composition of the angiosperm taxa differs moderately from the type-specific communities and is significantly more distorted than at good quality. There are moderate distortions in the abundance of angiosperm taxa.
Benthic invertebrate fauna	The level of diversity and abundance of invertebrate taxa is within the range normally associated with undisturbed conditions. All the disturbance-sensitive taxa associated with undisturbed conditions are present.	The level of diversity and abundance of invertebrate taxa is slightly outside the range associated with the type-specific conditions. Most of the sensitive taxa of the type-specific communities are present.	The level of diversity and abundance of invertebrate taxa is moderately outside the range associated with the type-specific conditions. Taxa indicative of pollution are present. Many of the sensitive taxa of the type-specific communities are absent.
Fish fauna	Species composition and abundance is consistent with undisturbed conditions.	The abundance of the disturbance-sensitive species shows slight signs of distortion from type-specific conditions attributable to anthropogenic impacts on physico-chemical or hydromorphological quality elements.	A moderate proportion of the type-specific disturbance-sensitive species are absent as a result of anthropogenic impacts on physicochemical or hydromorphological quality elements.

Hydromorphological quality elements

Element	*High status*	*Good status*	*Moderate status*
Tidal regime	The freshwater flow regime corresponds totally or nearly totally to undisturbed conditions.	Conditions consistent with the achievement of the values specified above for the biological quality elements.	Conditions consistent with the achievement of the values specified above for the biological quality elements.

Element	*High status*	*Good status*	*Moderate status*
Morphological conditions	Depth variations, substrate conditions, and both the structure and condition of the intertidal zones correspond totally or nearly totally to undisturbed conditions.	Conditions consistent with the achievement of the values specified above for the biological quality elements.	Conditions consistent with the achievement of the values specified above for the biological quality elements.

Physico-chemical quality elements[(1)]

Element	*High status*	*Good status*	*Moderate status*
General conditions	Physico-chemical elements correspond totally or nearly totally to undisturbed conditions. Nutrient concentrations remain within the range normally associated with undisturbed conditions. Temperature, oxygen balance and transparency do not show signs of anthropogenic disturbance and remain within the range normally associated with undisturbed conditions.	Temperature, oxygenation conditions and transparency do not reach levels outside the ranges established so as to ensure the functioning of the ecosystem and the achievement of the values specified above for the biological quality elements. Nutrient concentrations do not exceed the levels established so as to ensure the functioning of the ecosystem and the achievement of the values specified above for the biological quality elements.	Conditions consistent with the achievement of the values specified above for the biological quality elements.
Specific synthetic pollutants	Concentrations close to zero and at least below the limits of detection of the most advanced analytical techniques in general use.	Concentrations not in excess of the standards set in accordance with the procedure detailed in section 1.2.6 without prejudice to Directive 91/414/EC and Directive 98/8/EC. (< EQS)	Conditions consistent with the achievement of the values specified above for the biological quality elements.
Specific non-synthetic pollutants	Concentrations remain within the range normally associated with undisturbed conditions (background levels = bgl).	Concentrations not in excess of the standards set in accordance with the procedure detailed in section 1.2.6[(2)] without prejudice to Directive 91/414/EC and Directive 98/8/EC. (< EQS)	Conditions consistent with the achievement of the values specified above for the biological quality elements.

(1) The following abbreviations are used: bgl = background level, EQS = environmental quality standard.
(2) Application of the standards derived under this protocol shall not require reduction of pollutant concentrations below background levels: (EQS > bgl).

1.2.4. Definitions for high, good and moderate ecological status in coastal waters

Biological quality elements

Element	*High status*	*Good status*	*Moderate status*
Phytoplankton	The composition and abundance of phytoplanktonic taxa are consistent with undisturbed conditions. The average phytoplankton biomass is consistent with the type-specific physicochemical conditions and is not such as to significantly alter the type-specific transparency conditions. Planktonic blooms occur at a frequency and intensity which is consistent with the type specific physico-chemical conditions.	The composition and abundance of phytoplanktonic taxa show slight signs of disturbance. There are slight changes in biomass compared to type-specific conditions. Such changes do not indicate any accelerated growth of algae resulting in undesirable disturbance to the balance of organisms present in the water body or to the quality of the water. A slight increase in the frequency and intensity of the type-specific planktonic blooms may occur.	The composition and abundance of planktonic taxa show signs of moderate disturbance. Algal biomass is substantially outside the range associated with type-specific conditions, and is such as to impact upon other biological quality elements. A moderate increase in the frequency and intensity of planktonic blooms may occur. Persistent blooms may occur during summer months.
Macroalgae and angiosperms	All disturbance-sensitive macroalgal and angiosperm taxa associated with undisturbed conditions are present. The levels of macroalgal cover and angiosperm abundance are consistent with undisturbed conditions.	Most disturbance-sensitive macroalgal and angiosperm taxa associated with undisturbed conditions are present. The level of macroalgal cover and angiosperm abundance show slight signs of disturbance.	A moderate number of the disturbance-sensitive macroalgal and angiosperm taxa associated with undisturbed conditions are absent. Macroalgal cover and angiosperm abundance is moderately disturbed and may be such as to result in an undesirable disturbance to the balance of organisms present in the water body.

Element	*High status*	*Good status*	*Moderate status*
Benthic invertebrate fauna	The level of diversity and abundance of invertebrate taxa is within the range normally associated with undisturbed conditions. All the disturbance-sensitive taxa associated with undisturbed conditions are present.	The level of diversity and abundance of invertebrate taxa is slightly outside the range associated with the type-specific conditions. Most of the sensitive taxa of the type-specific communities are present.	The level of diversity and abundance of invertebrate taxa is moderately outside the range associated with the type-specific conditions. Taxa indicative of pollution are present. Many of the sensitive taxa of the type-specific communities are absent.

Hydromorphological quality elements

Element	*High status*	*Good status*	*Moderate status*
Tidal regime	The freshwater flow regime and the direction and speed of dominant currents correspond totally or nearly totally to undisturbed conditions.	Conditions consistent with the achievement of the values specified above for the biological quality elements.	Conditions consistent with the achievement of the values specified above for the biological quality elements.
Morphological conditions	The depth variation, structure and substrate of the coastal bed, and both the structure and condition of the inter-tidal zones correspond totally or nearly totally to the undisturbed conditions.	Conditions consistent with the achievement of the values specified above for the biological quality elements.	Conditions consistent with the achievement of the values specified above for the biological quality elements.

Physico-chemical quality elements[1]

Element	*High status*	*Good status*	*Moderate status*
General conditions	The physico-chemical elements correspond totally or nearly totally to undisturbed conditions. Nutrient concentrations remain within the range normally associated with undisturbed conditions.	Temperature, oxygenation conditions and transparency do not reach levels outside the ranges established so as to ensure the functioning of the ecosystem and the achievement of the values specified above for the biological quality elements.	Conditions consistent with the achievement of the values specified above for the biological quality elements.

Element	*High status*	*Good status*	*Moderate status*
	Temperature, oxygen balance and transparency do not show signs of anthropogenic disturbance and remain within the ranges normally associated with undisturbed conditions.	Nutrient concentrations do not exceed the levels established so as to ensure the functioning of the ecosystem and the achievement of the values specified above for the biological quality elements.	
Specific synthetic pollutants	Concentrations close to zero and at least below the limits of detection of the most advanced analytical techniques in general use.	Concentrations not in excess of the standards set in accordance with the procedure detailed in section 1.2.6 without prejudice to Directive 91/414/EC and Directive 98/8/EC. (< EQS)	Conditions consistent with the achievement of the values specified above for the biological quality elements.
Specific non-synthetic pollutants	Concentrations remain within the range normally associated with undisturbed conditions (background levels = bgl).	Concentrations not in excess of the standards set in accordance with the procedure detailed in section 1.2.6(2) without prejudice to Directive 91/414/EC and Directive 98/8/EC. (< EQS)	Conditions consistent with the achievement of the values specified above for the biological quality elements.

(1) The following abbreviations are used: bgl = background level, EQS = environmental quality standard.

(2) Application of the standards derived under this protocol shall not require reduction of pollutant concentrations below background levels: (EQS > bgl).

1.2.5. Definitions for maximum, good and moderate ecological potential for heavily modified or artificial water bodies

Element	*Maximum ecological potential*	*Good ecological potential*	*Moderate ecological potential*
Biological quality elements	The values of the relevant biological quality elements reflect, as far as possible, those associated with the closest comparable surface water body type, given the physical conditions which result from the artificial or heavily modified characteristics of the water body.	There are slight changes in the values of the relevant biological quality elements as compared to the values found at maximum ecological potential.	There are moderate changes in the values of the relevant biological quality elements as compared to the values found at maximum ecological potential. These values are significantly more distorted than those found under good quality.

Element	*Maximum ecological potential*	*Good ecological potential*	*Moderate ecological potential*
Hydromorphological elements	The hydromorphological conditions are consistent with the only impacts on the surface water body being those resulting from the artificial or heavily modified characteristics of the water body once all mitigation measures have been taken to ensure the best approximation to ecological continuum, in particular with respect to migration of fauna and appropriate spawning and breeding grounds.	Conditions consistent with the achievement of the values specified above for the biological quality elements.	Conditions consistent with the achievement of the values specified above for the biological quality elements.
Physico-chemical elements			
General conditions	Physico-chemical elements correspond totally or nearly totally to the undisturbed conditions associated with the surface water body type most closely comparable to the artificial or heavily modified body concerned. Nutrient concentrations remain within the range normally associated with such undisturbed conditions. The levels of temperature, oxygen balance and pH are consistent with the those found in the most closely	The values for physico-chemical elements are within the ranges established so as to ensure the functioning of the ecosystem and the achievement of the values specified above for the biological quality elements. Temperature and pH do not reach levels outside the ranges established so as to ensure the functioning of the ecosystem and the achievement of the values specified above for the biological quality elements.	Conditions consistent with the achievement of the values specified above for the biological quality elements.

Element	*Maximum ecological potential*	*Good ecological potential*	*Moderate ecological potential*
	comparable surface water body types under undisturbed conditions.	Nutrient concentrations do not exceed the levels established so as to ensure the functioning of the ecosystem and the achievement of the values specified above for the biological quality elements.	
Specific synthetic pollutants	Concentrations close to zero and at least below the limits of detection of the most advanced analytical techniques in general use.	Concentrations not in excess of the standards set in accordance with the procedure detailed in section 1.2.6 without prejudice to Directive 91/414/EC and Directive 98/8/EC. (< EQS)	Conditions consistent with the achievement of the values specified above for the biological quality elements.
Specific non-synthetic pollutants	Concentrations remain within the range normally associated with the undisturbed conditions found in the surface water body type most closely comparable to the artificial or heavily modified body concerned (background levels = bgl).	Concentrations not in excess of the standards set in accordance with the procedure detailed in section 1.2.6[(1)] without prejudice to Directive 91/414/EC and Directive 98/8/EC. (< EQS)	Conditions consistent with the achievement of the values specified above for the biological quality elements.

(1) Application of the standards derived under this protocol shall not require reduction of pollutant concentrations below background levels.

1.2.6. Procedure for the setting of chemical quality standards by Member States

In deriving environmental quality standards for pollutants listed in points 1 to 9 of Annex VIII for the protection of aquatic biota, Member States shall act in accordance with the following provisions. Standards may be set for water, sediment or biota.

Where possible, both acute and chronic data shall be obtained for the taxa set out below which are relevant for the water body type concerned as well as any other aquatic taxa for which data are available. The "base set" of taxa are:

— algae and/or macrophytes
— daphnia or representative organisms for saline waters
— fish.

Setting the environmental quality standard

The following procedure applies to the setting of a maximum annual average concentration:

(i) Member States shall set appropriate safety factors in each case consistent with the nature and quality of the available data and the guidance given in section 3.3.1 of Part II of "Technical guidance document in support of Commission Directive 93/67/EEC on risk assessment for new notified substances and Commission Regulation (EC) No 1488/94 on risk assessment for existing substances" and the safety factors set out in the table below:

	Safety factor
At least one acute $L(E)C_{50}$ from each of three trophic levels of the base set	1000
One chronic NOEC (either fish of daphnia or a representative organism for saline waters)	100
Two chronic NOECs from species representing two trophic levels (fish and/or daphnia or a representative organism for saline waters and/or algae)	50
Chronic NOECs from at least three species (normally fish, daphnia or a representative organism for saline waters and algae) representing three trophic levels	10
Other cases, including field data or model ecosystems, which allow more precise safety factors to be calculated and applied	Case-by-case assessment

(ii) where data on persistence and bioaccumulation are available, these shall be taken into account in deriving the final value of the environmental quality standard;

(iii) the standard thus derived should be compared with any evidence from field studies. Where anomalies appear, the derivation shall be reviewed to allow a more precise safety factor to be calculated;

(iv) the standard derived shall be subject to peer review and public consultation including to allow a more precise safety factor to be calculated.

1.3. Monitoring of ecological status and chemical status for surface waters

The surface water monitoring network shall be established in accordance with the requirements of Article 8. The monitoring network shall be designed so as to provide a coherent and comprehensive overview of ecological and chemical status within each river basin and shall permit classification of water bodies into five classes consistent with the normative definitions in section 1.2. Member States shall provide a map or maps showing the surface water monitoring network in the river basin management plan.

On the basis of the characterisation and impact assessment carried out in accordance with Article 5 and Annex II, Member States shall for each period to which a river basin management plan applies, establish a surveillance monitoring programme and an operational monitoring programme. Member States may also need in some cases to establish programmes of investigative monitoring.

Member States shall monitor parameters which are indicative of the status of each relevant quality element. In selecting parameters for biological quality elements Member States shall identify the appropriate taxonomic level required to achieve adequate confidence and precision in the classification of the quality elements. Estimates of the level of confidence and precision of the results provided by the monitoring programmes shall be given in the plan.

1.3.1. Design of surveillance monitoring

Objective

Member States shall establish surveillance monitoring programmes to provide information for:

— supplementing and validating the impact assessment procedure detailed in Annex II,
— the efficient and effective design of future monitoring programmes,
— the assessment of long-term changes in natural conditions, and
— the assessment of long-term changes resulting from widespread anthropogenic activity.

The results of such monitoring shall be reviewed and used, in combination with the impact assessment procedure described in Annex II, to determine requirements for monitoring programmes in the current and subsequent river basin management plans.

Selection of monitoring points

Surveillance monitoring shall be carried out of sufficient surface water bodies to provide an assessment of the overall surface water status within each catchment or subcatchments within the river basin district. In selecting these bodies Member States shall ensure that, where appropriate, monitoring is carried out at points where:

— the rate of water flow is significant within the river basin district as a whole; including points on large rivers where the catchment area is greater than 2500 km^2,
— the volume of water present is significant within the river basin district, including large lakes and reservoirs,
— significant bodies of water cross a Member State boundary,
— sites are identified under the Information Exchange Decision 77/795/EEC, and

at such other sites as are required to estimate the pollutant load which is transferred across Member State boundaries, and which is transferred into the marine environment.

Selection of quality elements

Surveillance monitoring shall be carried out for each monitoring site for a period of one year during the period covered by a river basin management plan for:

— parameters indicative of all biological quality elements,
— parameters indicative of all hydromorphological quality elements,
— parameters indicative of all general physico-chemical quality elements,
— priority list pollutants which are discharged into the river basin or sub-basin, and
— other pollutants discharged in significant quantities in the river basin or sub-basin,

unless the previous surveillance monitoring exercise showed that the body concerned reached good status and there is no evidence from the review of impact of human activity in Annex II that the impacts on the body have changed. In these cases, surveillance monitoring shall be carried out once every three river basin management plans.

1.3.2. Design of operational monitoring

Operational monitoring shall be undertaken in order to:

— establish the status of those bodies identified as being at risk of failing to meet their environmental objectives, and
— assess any changes in the status of such bodies resulting from the programmes of measures.

The programme may be amended during the period of the river basin management plan in the light of information obtained as part of the requirements of Annex II or as part of this Annex, in particular to allow a reduction in frequency where an impact is found not to be significant or the relevant pressure is removed.

Selection of monitoring sites

Operational monitoring shall be carried out for all those bodies of water which on the basis of either the impact assessment carried out in accordance with Annex II or surveillance monitoring are identified as being at risk of failing to meet their environmental objectives under Article 4 and for those bodies of water into which priority list substances are discharged. Monitoring points shall be selected for priority list substances as specified in the legislation laying down the relevant environmental quality standard. In all other cases, including for priority list substances where no specific guidance is given in such legislation, monitoring points shall be selected as follows:

— for bodies at risk from significant point source pressures, sufficient monitoring points within each body in order to assess the magnitude and impact of the point source. Where a body is subject to a number of point source pressures monitoring points may be selected to assess the magnitude and impact of these pressures as a whole,
— for bodies at risk from significant diffuse source pressures, sufficient monitoring points within a selection of the bodies in order to assess the magnitude and impact of the diffuse source pressures. The selection of bodies shall be made such that they are representative of the relative risks of the occurrence of the diffuse source pressures, and of the relative risks of the failure to achieve good surface water status,
— for bodies at risk from significant hydromorphological pressure, sufficient monitoring points within a selection of the bodies in order to assess the magnitude and impact of the hydromorphological pressures. The selection of bodies shall be indicative of the overall impact of the hydromorphological pressure to which all the bodies are subject.

Selection of quality elements

In order to assess the magnitude of the pressure to which bodies of surface water are subject Member States shall monitor for those quality elements which are indicative of the pressures to which the body or bodies are subject. In order to assess the impact of these pressures, Member States shall monitor as relevant:

— parameters indicative of the biological quality element, or elements, most sensitive to the pressures to which the water bodies are subject,
— all priority substances discharged, and other pollutants discharged in significant quantities,
— parameters indicative of the hydromorphological quality element most sensitive to the pressure identified.

1.3.3. Design of investigative monitoring

Objective

Investigative monitoring shall be carried out:

— where the reason for any exceedances is unknown,
— where surveillance monitoring indicates that the objectives set out in Article 4 for a body of water are not likely to be achieved and operational monitoring has not already been established, in order to ascertain the causes of a water body or water bodies failing to achieve the environmental objectives, or
— to ascertain the magnitude and impacts of accidental pollution,

and shall inform the establishment of a programme of measures for the achievement of the environmental objectives and specific measures necessary to remedy the effects of accidental pollution.

1.3.4. Frequency of monitoring

For the surveillance monitoring period, the frequencies for monitoring parameters indicative of physico-chemical quality elements given below should be applied unless greater intervals would be justified on the basis of technical knowledge and expert judgement. For biological or hydromorphological quality elements monitoring shall be carried out at least once during the surveillance monitoring period.

For operational monitoring, the frequency of monitoring required for any parameter shall be determined by Member States so as to provide sufficient data for a reliable assessment of the status of the relevant quality element. As a guideline, monitoring should take place at intervals not exceeding those shown in the table below unless greater intervals would be justified on the basis of technical knowledge and expert judgement.

Frequencies shall be chosen so as to achieve an acceptable level of confidence and precision. Estimates of the confidence and precision attained by the monitoring system used shall be stated in the river basin management plan.

Monitoring frequencies shall be selected which take account of the variability in parameters resulting from both natural and anthropogenic conditions. The times at which monitoring is undertaken shall be selected so as to minimise the impact of seasonal variation on the results, and thus ensure that the results reflect changes in the water body as a result of changes due to anthropogenic pressure. Additional monitoring during different seasons of the same year shall be carried out, where necessary, to achieve this objective.

Quality element	*Rivers*	*Lakes*	*Transitional*	*Coastal*
Biological				
Phytoplankton	6 months	6 months	6 months	6 months
Other aquatic flora	3 years	3 years	3 years	3 years
Macro invertebrates	3 years	3 years	3 years	3 years
Fish	3 years	3 years	3 years	
Hydromorphological				
Continuity	6 years			
Hydrology	continuous	1 month		
Morphology	6 years	6 years	6 years	6 years
Physio-chemical				
Thermal conditions	3 months	3 months	3 months	3 months
Oxygenation	3 months	3 months	3 months	3 months
Salinity	3 months	3 months	3 months	
Nutrient status	3 months	3 months	3 months	3 months
Acidification status	3 months	3 months		
Other pollutants	3 months	3 months	3 months	3 months
Priority substances	1 month	1 month	1 month	1 month

1.3.5. Additional monitoring requirements for protected areas

The monitoring programmes required above shall be supplemented in order to fulfil the following requirements:

Drinking water abstraction points

Bodies of surface water designated in Article 7 which provide more than 100 m^3 a day as an average shall be designated as monitoring sites and shall be subject to such additional monitoring as may be necessary to meet the requirements of that Article. Such bodies shall be monitored for all priority substances discharged and all other substances discharged in significant quantities which could affect the status of the body of water and which are controlled under the provisions of the Drinking Water Directive. Monitoring shall be carried out in accordance with the frequencies set out below:

Community Served	*Frequency*
< 10 000	4 per year
10 000 to 30 000	8 per year
> 30 000	12 per year

Habitat and species protection areas

Bodies of water forming these areas shall be included within the operational monitoring programme referred to above where, on the basis of the impact assessment and the surveillance monitoring, they are identified as being at risk of failing to meet their environmental objectives under Article 4. Monitoring shall be carried out to assess the magnitude and impact of all relevant significant pressures on these bodies and, where necessary, to assess changes in the status of such bodies resulting from the programmes of measures. Monitoring shall continue until the areas satisfy the water-related requirements of the legislation under which they are designated and meet their objectives under Article 4.

1.3.6. Standards for monitoring of quality elements

Methods used for the monitoring of type parameters shall conform to the international standards listed below or such other national or international standards which will ensure the provision of data of an equivalent scientific quality and comparability.

Macroinvertebrate sampling

ISO 5667-3:1995 Water quality – Sampling – Part 3: Guidance on the preservation and handling of samples

EN 27828:1994 Water quality – Methods for biological sampling – Guidance on hand net sampling of benthic macroinvertebrates

EN 28265:1994 Water quality – Methods for biological sampling – Guidance on the design and use of quantitative samplers for benthic macroinvertebrates on stony substrata in shallow waters

EN ISO 9391:1995 Water quality – Sampling in deep waters for macroinvertebrates – Guidance on the design and use of colonisation, qualitative and quantitative samplers

EN ISO 8689-1:1999 Biological classification of rivers PART I: Guidance on the interpretation of biological quality data from surveys of benthic macroinvertebrates in running waters

EN ISO 8689-2:1999 Biological classification of rivers PART II: Guidance on the presentation of biological quality data from surveys of benthic macroinvertebrates in running waters

Macrophyte sampling

Relevant CEN / ISO standards when developed

Fish sampling

Relevant CEN / ISO standards when developed

Diatom sampling

Relevant CEN/ISO standards when developed

Standards for physico-chemical parameters

Any relevant CEN/ISO standards

Standards for hydromorphological parameters

Any relevant CEN/ISO standards

1.4. Classification and presentation of ecological status

1.4.1. Comparability of biological monitoring results

(i) Member States shall establish monitoring systems for the purpose of estimating the values of the biological quality elements specified for each surface water category or for heavily modified and artificial bodies of surface water. In applying the procedure set out below to heavily modified or artificial water bodies, references to ecological status should be construed as references to ecological potential. Such systems may utilise particular species or groups of species which are representative of the quality element as a whole.

(ii) In order to ensure comparability of such monitoring systems, the results of the systems operated by each Member State shall be expressed as ecological quality ratios for the purposes of classification of ecological status. These ratios shall represent the relationship between the values of the biological parameters observed for a given body of surface water and the values for these parameters in the reference conditions applicable to that body. The ratio shall be expressed as a numerical value between zero and one, with high ecological status represented by values close to one and bad ecological status by values close to zero.

(iii) Each Member State shall divide the ecological quality ratio scale for their monitoring system for each surface water category into five classes ranging from high to bad ecological status, as defined in Section 1.2, by assigning a numerical value to each of the boundaries between the classes. The value for the boundary between the classes of high and good status, and the value for the boundary between good and moderate status shall be established through the intercalibration exercise described below.

(iv) The Commission shall facilitate this intercalibration exercise in order to ensure that these class boundaries are established consistent with the normative definitions in Section 1.2 and are comparable between Member States.

(v) As part of this exercise the Commission shall facilitate an exchange of information between Members States leading to the identification of a range of sites in each ecoregion in the Community; these sites will form an intercalibration network. The network shall consist of sites selected from a range of surface water body types present within each ecoregion. For each surface water body type selected, the network shall consist of at least two sites corresponding to the boundary between the normative definitions of high and good status, and at least two sites corresponding to the boundary between the normative definitions of good and moderate status. The sites shall be selected by expert judgement based on joint inspections and all other available information.

(vi) Each Member State monitoring system shall be applied to those sites in the intercalibration network which are both in the ecoregion and of a surface water body type to which the system will be applied pursuant to the requirements of this Directive. The results of this application shall be used to set the numerical values for the relevant class boundaries in each Member State monitoring system.

[(vii) The Commission shall prepare a draft register of sites to form the intercalibration network. The final register of sites shall be established in accordance with the regulatory procedure referred to in Article 21(2).][1]

(viii) The Commission and Member States shall complete the intercalibration exercise within 18 months of the date on which the finalised register is published.

[(ix) The results of the intercalibration exercise and the values established for the Member State monitoring system classifications in accordance with points (i) to (viii) and designed to amend non-essential elements of this Directive by supplementing it, shall be adopted in accordance with the regulatory procedure with scrutiny referred to in Article 21(3) and published within six months of the completion of the intercalibration exercise.][1]

Amendment

1 Substituted by Directive 2008/32/EC of the European Parliament and of the Council of 11 March 2008 amending Directive 2000/60/EC establishing a framework for Community action in the field of water policy, as regards the implementing powers conferred on the Commission, Article 1.4.

1.4.2. Presentation of monitoring results and classification of ecological status and ecological potential

(i) For surface water categories, the ecological status classification for the body of water shall be represented by the lower of the values for the biological and physic-chemical monitoring results for the relevant quality elements classified in accordance with the first column of the table set out below. Member States shall provide a map for each river basin district illustrating the classification of the ecological status for each body of water, colour-coded in accordance with the second column of the table set out below to reflect the ecological status classification of the body of water.

Ecological status classification	*Colour code*
High	Blue
Good	Green
Moderate	Yellow
Poor	Orange
Bad	Red

(ii) For heavily modified and artificial water bodies, the ecological potential classification for the body of water shall be represented by the lower of the values for the biological and physic-chemical monitoring results for the relevant quality elements classified in accordance with the first column of the table set out below. Member States shall provide a map for each river basin district illustrating the classification of the ecological potential for each body of water, colour-coded, in respect of artificial water bodies in accordance with the second column of the table set out below, and in respect of heavily modified water bodies in accordance with the third column of that table.

Ecological potential classification	*Colour code*	
	Artificial Water Bodies	*Heavily Modified*
Good and above	Equal green and light grey stripes	Equal green and dark grey stripes
Moderate	Equal yellow and light grey stripes	Equal yellow and dark grey stripes
Poor	Equal orange and light grey stripes	Equal orange and light grey stripes
Bad	Equal red and light grey stripes	Equal red and light grey stripes

(iii) Member States shall also indicate, by a black dot on the map, those bodies of water where failure to achieve good status or good ecological potential is due to non-compliance with one or more environmental quality standards which have been established for that body of water in respect of specific synthetic and non-synthetic pollutants (in accordance with the compliance regime established by the Member State).

1.4.3. Presentation of monitoring results and classification of chemical status

Where a body of water achieves compliance with all the environmental quality standards established in Annex IX, Article 16 and under other relevant Community legislation setting environmental quality standards it shall be recorded as achieving good chemical status. If not, the body shall be recorded as failing to achieve good chemical status.

Member States shall provide a map for each river basin district illustrating the chemical status for each body of water, colour-coded in accordance with the second column of the table set out below to reflect the chemical status classification of the body of water.

Chemical status classification	*Colour code*
Good	Blue
Failing to achieve good	Red

2. GROUNDWATER

2.1. Groundwater quantitative status

2.1.1. Parameter for the classification of quantitative status

Groundwater level regime

2.1.2. Definition of quantitative status

Elements	*Good Status*
Groundwater level	The level of groundwater in the groundwater body is such that the available groundwater resource is not exceeded by the long-term annual average rate of abstraction. Accordingly, the level of groundwater is not subject to anthropogenic alterations such as would result in: — failure to achieve the environmental objectives specified under Article 4 for associates surface waters, — any significant diminution in the status of such waters, — any significant damage to terrestrial ecosystems which depend directly on the groundwater body, And alterations to flow direction resulting from level changes may occur temporarily, or continuously in a spatially limited area, but such reversals do not cause saltwater or other intrusion, and do not indicate a sustained and clearly identified anthropogenically induced trend in flow direction likely to result in such intrusions.

2.2. Monitoring of groundwater quantitative status

2.2.1. Groundwater level monitoring network

The groundwater monitoring network shall be established in accordance with the requirements of Articles 7 and 8. The monitoring network shall be designed so as to provide a reliable assessment of the quantitative status of all groundwater bodies or groups of bodies including assessment of the available groundwater resource. Member States shall provide a map or maps showing the groundwater monitoring network in the river basin management plan.

2.2.2. Density of monitoring sites

The network shall include sufficient representative monitoring points to estimate the groundwater level in each groundwater body or group of bodies taking into account short and long-term variations in recharge and in particular:

— for groundwater bodies identified as being at risk of failing to achieve environmental objectives under Article 4, ensure sufficient density of monitoring points to assess the impact of abstractions and discharges on the groundwater level,

— for groundwater bodies within which groundwater flows across a Member State boundary, ensure sufficient monitoring points are provided to estimate the direction and rate of groundwater flow across the Member State boundary.

2.2.3. Monitoring frequency

The frequency of observations shall be sufficient to allow assessment of the quantitative status of each groundwater body or group of bodies taking into account short and long-term variations in recharge. In particular:

— for groundwater bodies identified as being at risk of failing to achieve environmental objectives under Article 4, ensure sufficient frequency of measurement to assess the impact of abstractions and discharges on the groundwater level,
— for groundwater bodies within which groundwater flows across a Member State boundary, ensure sufficient frequency of measurement to estimate the direction and rate of groundwater flow across the Member State boundary.

2.2.4. Interpretation and presentation of groundwater quantitative status

The results obtained from the monitoring network for a groundwater body or group of bodies shall be used to assess the quantitative status of that body or those bodies. Subject to point 2.5. Member States shall provide a map of the resulting assessment of groundwater quantitative status, colour-coded in accordance with the following regime:

Good: green
Poor: red

2.3. Groundwater chemical status

2.3.1. Parameters for the determination of groundwater chemical status

Conductivity

Concentrations of pollutants

2.3.2. Definition of good groundwater chemical status

Elements	*Good Status*
General	The chemical composition of the groundwater body is such that the concentration of pollutants: — as specified below, do not exhibit the effects of saline or other intrusions — do not exceed the quality standards applicable under other relevant Community legislation in accordance with Article 17 — are not such as would result in failure to achieve the environmental objectives specified under Article 4 for associated surface waters nor any significant diminution of the ecological or chemical quality of such bodies nor in any significant damage to terrestrial ecosystems which depend directly on the groundwater body
Conductivity	Changes in conductivity are not indicative of saline or other intrusion into the groundwater body

2.4. Monitoring of groundwater chemical status

2.4.1. Groundwater monitoring network

The groundwater monitoring network shall be established in accordance with the requirements of Articles 7 and 8. The monitoring network shall be designed so as to provide a coherent and comprehensive overview of groundwater chemical status within each river basin and to detect the presence of long-term anthropogenically induced upward trends in pollutants.

On the basis of the characterisation and impact assessment carried out in accordance with Article 5 and Annex II, Member States shall for each period to which a river basin management plan applies, establish a surveillance monitoring programme. The results of this programme shall be used to establish an operational monitoring programme to be applied for the remaining period of the plan.

Estimates of the level of confidence and precision of the results provided by the monitoring programmes shall be given in the plan.

2.4.2. Surveillance monitoring

Objective

Surveillance monitoring shall be carried out in order to:
- supplement and validate the impact assessment procedure,
- provide information for use in the assessment of long term trends both as a result of changes in natural conditions and through anthropogenic activity.

Selection of monitoring sites

Sufficient monitoring sites shall be selected for each of the following:
- bodies identified as being at risk following the characterisation exercise undertaken in accordance with Annex II,
- bodies which cross a Member State boundary.

Selection of parameters

The following set of core parameters shall be monitored in all the selected groundwater bodies:
- oxygen content
- pH value
- conductivity
- nitrate
- ammonium

Bodies which are identified in accordance with Annex II as being at significant risk of failing to achieve good status shall also be monitored for those parameters which are indicative of the impact of these pressures.

Transboundary water bodies shall also be monitored for those parameters which are relevant for the protection of all of the uses supported by the groundwater flow.

2.4.3. Operational monitoring

Objective

Operational monitoring shall be undertaken in the periods between surveillance monitoring programmes in order to:
- establish the chemical status of all groundwater bodies or groups of bodies determined as being at risk,
- establish the presence of any long term anthropogenically induced upward trend in the concentration of any pollutant.

Selection of monitoring sites

Operational monitoring shall be carried out for all those groundwater bodies or groups of bodies which on the basis of both the impact assessment carried out in accordance with Annex II and surveillance monitoring are identified as being at risk of failing to meet objectives under Article 4. The selection of monitoring sites shall also reflect an assessment of how representative monitoring data from that site is of the quality of the relevant groundwater body or bodies.

Frequency of monitoring

Operational monitoring shall be carried out for the periods between surveillance monitoring programmes at a frequency sufficient to detect the impacts of relevant pressures but at a minimum of once per annum.

2.4.4. Identification of trends in pollutants

Member States shall use data from both surveillance and operational monitoring in the identification of long term anthropogenically induced upward trends in pollutant concentrations and the reversal of such trends. The base year or period from which trend identification is to be calculated shall be identified. The calculation of trends shall be undertaken for a body or, where appropriate, group of bodies of groundwater. Reversal of a trend shall be demonstrated statistically and the level of confidence associated with the identification stated.

2.4.5. Interpretation and presentation of groundwater chemical status

In assessing status, the results of individual monitoring points within a groundwater body shall be aggregated for the body as a whole. Without prejudice to the Directives concerned, for good status to be achieved for a groundwater body, for those chemical parameters for which environmental quality standards have been set in Community legislation:
— the mean value of the results of monitoring at each point in the groundwater body or group of bodies shall be calculated, and
— in accordance with Article 17 these mean values shall be used to demonstrate compliance with good groundwater chemical status.

Subject to point 2.5, Member States shall provide a map of groundwater chemical status, colour-coded as indicated below:

Good: green
Poor: red

Member States shall also indicate by a black dot on the map, those groundwater bodies which are subject to a significant and sustained upward trend in the concentrations of any pollutant resulting from the impact of human activity. Reversal of a trend shall be indicated by a blue dot on the map.

These maps shall be included in the river basin management plan.

2.5. Presentation of Groundwater Status

Member States shall provide in the river basin management plan a map showing for each groundwater body or groups of groundwater bodies both the quantitative status and the chemical status of that body or group of bodies, colour-coded in accordance with the requirements of points 2.2.4 and 2.4.5. Member States may choose not to provide separate maps under points 2.2.4 and 2.4.5 but shall in that case also provide an indication in accordance with the requirements of point 2.4.5 on the map required under this point, of those bodies which are subject to a significant and sustained upward trend in the concentration of any pollutant or any reversal in such a trend.

ANNEX VI
LISTS OF MEASURES TO BE INCLUDED WITHIN THE PROGRAMMES OF MEASURES

PART A

Measures required under the following Directives:
(i) The Bathing Water Directive (76/160/EEC);
(ii) The Birds Directive (79/409/EEC);
(iii) The Drinking Water Directive (80/778/EEC) as amended by Directive (98/83/EC);
(iv) The Major Accidents (Seveso) Directive (96/82/EC);
(v) The Environmental Impact Assessment Directive (85/337/EEC);
(vi) The Sewage Sludge Directive (86/278/EEC);
(vii) The Urban Waste-water Treatment Directive (91/271/EEC);
(viii) The Plant Protection Products Directive (91/414/EEC);

(ix) The Nitrates Directive (91/676/EEC);
(x) The Habitats Directive (92/43/EEC);
(xi) The Integrated Pollution Prevention Control Directive (96/61/EC).

PART B

The following is a non-exclusive list of supplementary measures which Member States within each river basin district may choose to adopt as part of the programme of measures required under Article 11(4):

(i) legislative instruments
(ii) administrative instruments
(iii) economic or fiscal instruments
(iv) negotiated environmental agreements
(v) emission controls
(vi) codes of good practice
(vii) recreation and restoration of wetlands areas
(viii) abstraction controls
(ix) demand management measures, inter alia, promotion of adapted agricultural production such as low water requiring crops in areas affected by drought
(x) efficiency and reuse measures, inter alia, promotion of water-efficient technologies in industry and water-saving irrigation techniques
(xi) construction projects
(xii) desalination plants
(xiii) rehabilitation projects
(xiv) artificial recharge of aquifers
(xv) educational projects
(xvi) research, development and demonstration projects
(xvii) other relevant measures

ANNEX VII
RIVER BASIN MANAGEMENT PLANS

A. River basin management plans shall cover the following elements:

1. a general description of the characteristics of the river basin district required under Article 5 and Annex II. This shall include:
   1.1. for surface waters:
   - mapping of the location and boundaries of water bodies,
   - mapping of the ecoregions and surface water body types within the river basin,
   - identification of reference conditions for the surface water body types;

   1.2. for groundwaters:
   - mapping of the location and boundaries of groundwater bodies;
2. a summary of significant pressures and impact of human activity on the status of surface water and groundwater, including:
   - estimation of point source pollution,
   - estimation of diffuse source pollution, including a summary of land use,
   - estimation of pressures on the quantitative status of water including abstractions,
   - analysis of other impacts of human activity on the status of water;
3. identification and mapping of protected areas as required by Article 6 and Annex IV;
4. a map of the monitoring networks established for the purposes of Article 8 and Annex V, and a presentation in map form of the results of the monitoring programmes carried out under those provisions for the status of:
   4.1. surface water (ecological and chemical);
   4.2. groundwater (chemical and quantitative);
   4.3. protected areas;

5. a list of the environmental objectives established under Article 4 for surface waters, groundwaters and protected areas, including in particular identification of instances where use has been made of Article 4(4), (5), (6) and (7), and the associated information required under that Article;
6. a summary of the economic analysis of water use as required by Article 5 and Annex III;
7. a summary of the programme or programmes of measures adopted under Article 11, including the ways in which the objectives established under Article 4 are thereby to be achieved;
   7.1. a summary of the measures required to implement Community legislation for the protection of water;
   7.2. a report on the practical steps and measures taken to apply the principle of recovery of the costs of water use in accordance with Article 9;
   7.3. a summary of the measures taken to meet the requirements of Article 7;
   7.4. a summary of the controls on abstraction and impoundment of water, including reference to the registers and identifications of the cases where exemptions have been made under Article 11(3)(e);
   7.5. a summary of the controls adopted for point source discharges and other activities with an impact on the status of water in accordance with the provisions of Article 11(3)(g) and 11(3)(i);
   7.6. an identification of the cases where direct discharges to groundwater have been authorised in accordance with the provisions of Article 11(3)(j);
   7.7. a summary of the measures taken in accordance with Article 16 on priority substances;
   7.8. a summary of the measures taken to prevent or reduce the impact of accidental pollution incidents;
   7.9. a summary of the measures taken under Article 11(5) for bodies of water which are unlikely to achieve the objectives set out under Article 4;
   7.10. details of the supplementary measures identified as necessary in order to meet the environmental objectives established;
   7.11. details of the measures taken to avoid increase in pollution of marine waters in accordance with Article 11(6);
8. a register of any more detailed programmes and management plans for the river basin district dealing with particular sub-basins, sectors, issues or water types, together with a summary of their contents;
9. a summary of the public information and consultation measures taken, their results and the changes to the plan made as a consequence;
10. a list of competent authorities in accordance with Annex I;
11. the contact points and procedures for obtaining the background documentation and information referred to in Article 14(1), and in particular details of the control measures adopted in accordance with Article 11(3)(g) and 11(3)(i) and of the actual monitoring data gathered in accordance with Article 8 and Annex V.

B. The first update of the river basin management plan and all subsequent updates shall also include:

1. a summary of any changes or updates since the publication of the previous version of the river basin management plan, including a summary of the reviews to be carried out under Article 4(4), (5), (6) and (7);
2. an assessment of the progress made towards the achievement of the environmental objectives, including presentation of the monitoring results for the period of the previous plan in map form, and an explanation for any environmental objectives which have not been reached;
3. a summary of, and an explanation for, any measures foreseen in the earlier version of the river basin management plan which have not been undertaken;
4. a summary of any additional interim measures adopted under Article 11(5) since the publication of the previous version of the river basin management plan.

ANNEX VIII
INDICATIVE LIST OF THE MAIN POLLUTANTS

1. Organohalogen compounds and substances which may form such compounds in the aquatic environment.

2. Organophosphorous compounds.

3. Organotin compounds.

4. Substances and preparations, or the breakdown products of such, which have been proved to possess carcinogenic or mutagenic properties or properties which may affect steroidogenic, thyroid, reproduction or other endocrine-related functions in or via the aquatic environment.

5. Persistent hydrocarbons and persistent and bioaccumulable organic toxic substances.

6. Cyanides.

7. Metals and their compounds.

8. Arsenic and its compounds.

9. Biocides and plant protection products.

10. Materials in suspension.

11. Substances which contribute to eutrophication (in particular, nitrates and phosphates).

12. Substances which have an unfavourable influence on the oxygen balance (and can be measured using parameters such as BOD, COD, etc.).

ANNEX IX
EMISSION LIMIT VALUES AND ENVIRONMENTAL QUALITY STANDARDS

The "limit values" and "quality objectives" established under the re Directives of Directive 76/464/EEC shall be considered emission limit values and environmental quality standards, respectively, for the purposes of this Directive. They are established in the following Directives:
(i) The Mercury Discharges Directive (82/176/EEC);
(ii) The Cadmium Discharges Directive (83/513/EEC);
(iii) The Mercury Directive (84/156/EEC);
(iv) The Hexachlorocyclohexane Discharges Directive (84/491/EEC); and
(v) The Dangerous Substance Discharges Directive (86/280/EEC).

[ANNEX X
LIST OF PRIORITY SUBSTANCES IN THE FIELD OF WATER POLICY][1]

[Number	*CAS number*[1]	*EU number*[2]	*Name of priority substance*[3]	*Identified as priority hazardous substance*
(1)	15972-60-8	240-110-8	Alachlor	
(2)	120-12-7	204-371-1	Anthracene	X
(3)	1912-24-9	217-617-8	Atrazine	
(4)	71-43-2	200-753-7	Benzene	
(5)	not applicable	not applicable	Brominated diphenylether[4]	X[5]
	32534-81-9	not applicable	Pentabromodiphenylether (congener numbers 28, 47, 99, 100, 153 and 154)	

[Number	*CAS number*[1]	*EU number*[2]	*Name of priority substance*[3]	*Identified as priority hazardous substance*
(6)	7440-43-9	231-152-8	Cadmium and its compounds	X
(7)	85535-84-8	287-476-5	Chloroalkanes, C_{10-13}[4]	X
(8)	470-90-6	207-432-0	Chlorfenvinphos	
(9)	2921-88-2	220-864-4	Chlorpyrifos (Chlorpyrifos-ethyl)	
(10)	107-06-2	203-458-1	1,2-dichloroethane	
(11)	75-09-2	200-838-9	Dichloromethane	
(12)	117-81-7	204-211-0	Di(2-ethylhexyl)phthalate (DEHP)	
(13)	330-54-1	206-354-4	Diuron	
(14)	115-29-7	204-079-4	Endosulfan	X
(15)	206-44-0	205-912-4	Fluoranthene[6]	
(16)	118-74-1	204-273-9	Hexachlorobenzene	X
(17)	87-68-3	201-765-5	Hexachlorobutadiene	X
(18)	608-73-1	210-158-9	Hexachlorocyclohexane	X
(19)	34123-59-6	251-835-4	Isoproturon	
(20)	7439-92-1	231-100-4	Lead and its compounds	
(21)	7439-97-6	231-106-7	Mercury and its compounds	X
(22)	91-20-3	202-049-5	Naphthalene	
(23)	7440-02-0	231-111-14	Nickel and its compounds	
(24)	25154-52-3	246-672-0	Nonylphenol	X
	104-40-5	203-199-4	(4-nonylphenol)	X
(25)	1806-26-4	217-302-5	Octylphenol	
	140-66-9	not applicable	(4-(1,1′,3,3′-tetramethyl-butyl)-phenol)	
(26)	608-93-5	210-172-5	Pentachlorobenzene	X
(27)	87-86-5	231-152-8	Pentachlorophenol	
(28)	not applicable	not applicable	Polyaromatic hydrocarbons	X
	50-32-8	200-028-5	(Benzo(a)pyrene)	X
	205-99-2	205-911-9	(Benzo(b)fluoranthene)	X
	191-24-2	205-883-8	(Benzo(g,h,i)perylene)	X
	207-08-9	205-916-6	(Benzo(k)fluoranthene)	X
	193-39-5	205-893-2	(Indeno(1,2,3-cd)pyrene)	X
(29)	122-34-9	204-535-2	Simazine	
(30)	not applicable	not applicable	Tributyltin compounds	X
	36643-28-4	not applicable	(Tributyltin-cation)	X
(31)	12002-48-1	234-413-4	Trichlorobenzenes	
(32)	67-66-3	200-663-8	Trichloromethane (chloroform)	
(33)	1582-09-8	216-428-8	Trifluralin	

[1] CAS: Chemical Abstracts Service.

[2] EU number: European Inventory of Existing Commercial Substances (Einecs) or European List of Notified Chemical Substances (Elincs).

[3] Where groups of substances have been selected, typical individual representatives are listed as indicative parameters (in brackets and without number). For these groups of substances, the indicative parameter must be defined through the analytical method.

[4] These groups of substances normally include a considerable number of individual compounds. At present, appropriate indicative parameters cannot be given.

[5] Only Pentabromobiphenylether (CAS-number 32534-81-9).

[6] Fluoranthene is on the list as an indicator of other, more dangerous polyaromatic hydrocarbons.][1]

Amendment

1 Substituted by Directive 2008/105/EC of the European Parliament and of the Council of 16 December 2008 on environmental quality standards in the field of water policy, amending and subsequently repealing Council Directives 82/176/EEC, 83/513/EEC, 84/156/EEC, 84/491/EEC, 86/280/EEC and amending Directive 2000/60/EC of the European Parliament and of the Council, Article 10, Annex II.

ANNEX XI

MAP A
SYSTEM A: ECOREGIONS FOR RIVERS AND LAKES

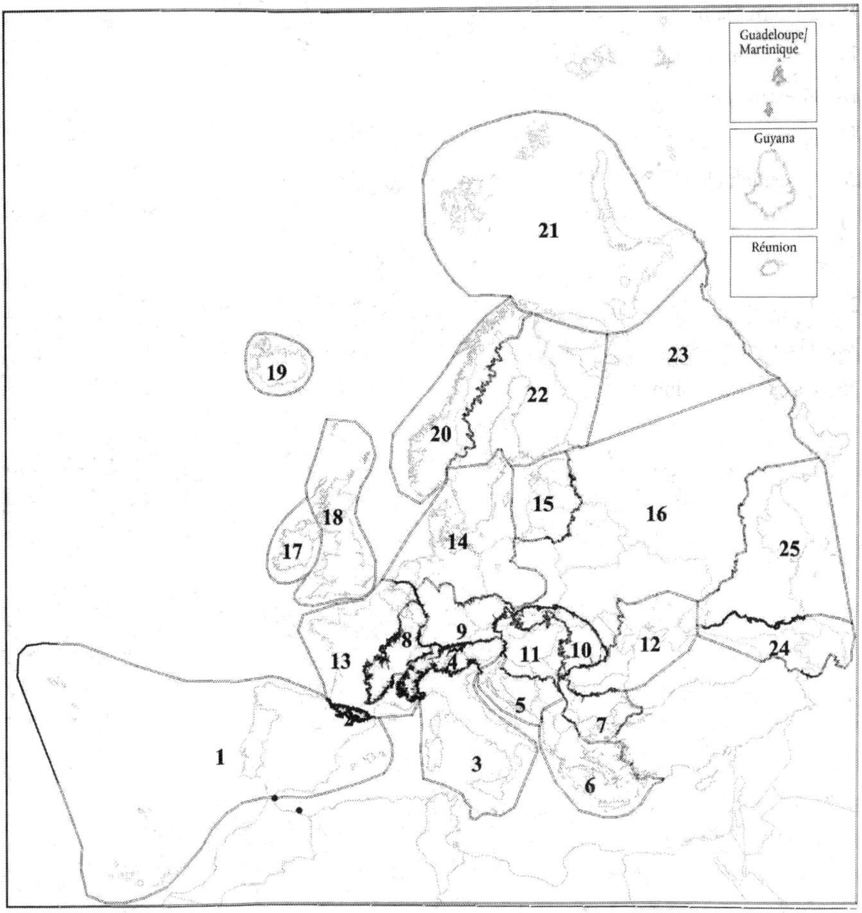

1. Iberic-Macaronesian region
2. Pyrenees

3. Italy, Corsica and Malta
4. Alps
5. Dinaric western Balkan
6. Hellenic western Balkan
7. Eastern Balkan
8. Western highlands
9. Central highlands
10. The Carpathians
11. Hungarian lowlands
12. Pontic province
13. Western plains
14. Central plains
15. Baltic province
16. Eastern plains
17. Ireland and Northern Ireland
18. Great Britain
19. Iceland
20. Borealic uplands
21. Tundra
22. Fenno-Scandian shield
23. Taiga
24. The Caucasus
25. Caspic depression

MAP B
SYSTEM A: ECOREGIONS FOR TRANSITIONAL WATERS AND COASTAL WATERS

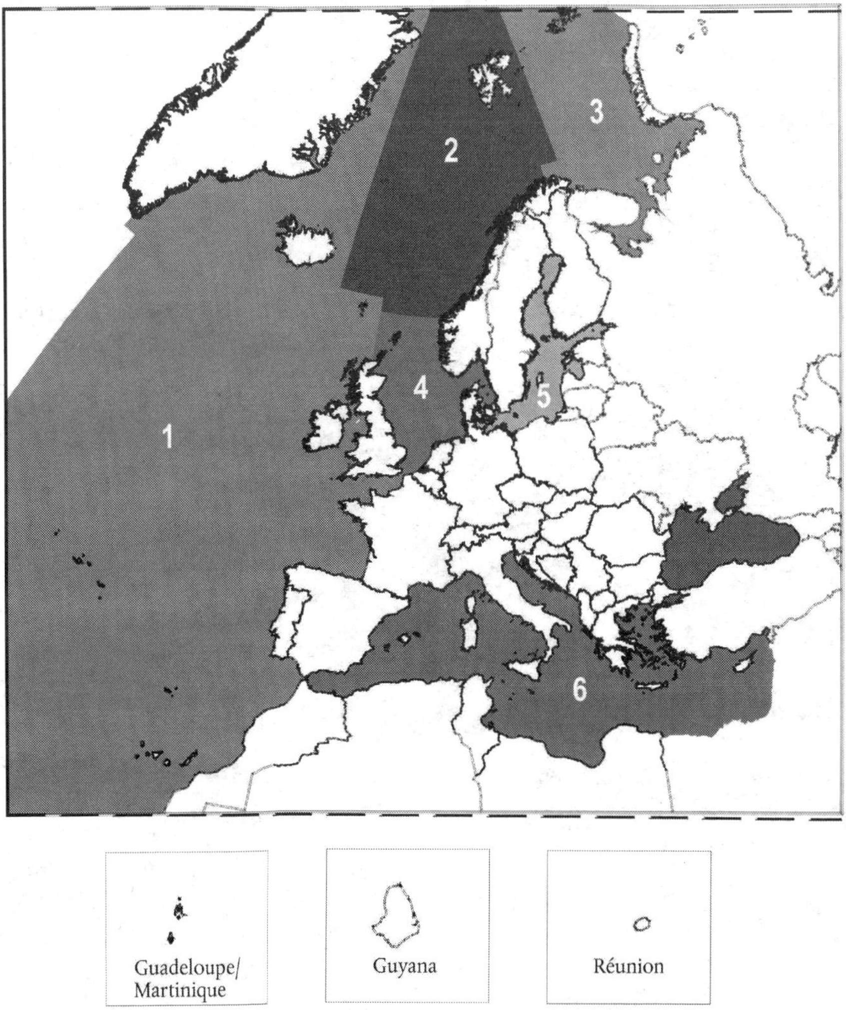

1. Atlantic Ocean
2. Norwegian Sea
3. Barents Sea
4. North Sea
5. Baltic Sea
6. Mediterranean Sea

DIRECTIVE 2000/76/EC OF THE EUROPEAN PARLIAMENT AND OF THE COUNCIL

of 4 December 2000

ON THE INCINERATION OF WASTE

THE EUROPEAN PARLIAMENT AND THE COUNCIL OF THE EUROPEAN UNION,

Having regard to the Treaty establishing the European Community, and in particular Article 175(1) thereof,

Having regard to the proposal from the Commission,

Having regard to the Opinion of the Economic and Social Committee,

Having regard to the Opinion of the Committee of the Regions,

Acting in accordance with the procedure laid down in Article 251 of the Treaty, and in the light of the joint text approved by the Conciliation Committee on 11 October 2000,

Whereas:

(1) The fifth Environment Action Programme: Towards sustainability – A European Community programme of policy and action in relation to the environment and sustainable development, supplemented by Decision No 2179/98/EC on its review, sets as an objective that critical loads and levels of certain pollutants such as nitrogen oxides (NO_x), sulphur dioxide (SO_2), heavy metals and dioxins should not be exceeded, while in terms of air quality the objective is that all people should be effectively protected against recognised health risks from air pollution. That Programme further sets as an objective a 90 % reduction of dioxin emissions of identified sources by 2005 (1985 level) and at least 70 % reduction from all pathways of cadmium (Cd), mercury (Hg) and lead (Pb) emissions in 1995.

(2) The Protocol on persistent organic pollutants signed by the Community within the framework of the United Nations Economic Commission for Europe (UN-ECE) Convention on long-range transboundary air pollution sets legally binding limit values for the emission of dioxins and furans of 0,1 ng/m; TE (Toxicity Equivalents) for installations burning more than 3 tonnes per hour of municipal solid waste, 0,5 ng/m; TE for installations burning more than 1 tonne per hour of medical waste, and 0,2 ng/m; TE for installations burning more than 1 tonne per hour of hazardous waste.

(3) The Protocol on Heavy Metals signed by the Community within the framework of the UN-ECE Convention on long-range transboundary air pollution sets legally binding limit values for the emission of particulate of 10 mg/m3 for hazardous and medical waste incineration and for the emission of mercury of 0,05 mg/m3 for hazardous waste incineration and 0,08 mg/m3 for municipal waste incineration.

(4) The International Agency for Research on Cancer and the World Health Organisation indicate that some polycyclic aromatic hydrocarbons (PAHs) are carcinogenic. Therefore, Member States may set emission limit values for PAHs among other pollutants.

(5) In accordance with the principles of subsidiarity and proportionality as set out in Article 5 of the Treaty, there is a need to take action at the level of the Community. The precautionary principle provides the basis for further measures. This Directive confines itself to minimum requirements for incineration and co-incineration plants.

(6) Further, Article 174 provides that Community policy on the environment is to contribute to protecting human health.

(7) Therefore, a high level of environmental protection and human health protection requires the setting and maintaining of stringent operational conditions, technical requirements and emission limit values for plants incinerating or co-incinerating waste within the Community. The limit values set should prevent or limit as far as practicable negative effects on the environment and the resulting risks to human health.

(8) The Communication from the Commission on the review of the Community Strategy for waste management assigns prevention of waste the first priority, followed by reuse and recovery and finally by safe disposal of waste; in its Resolution of 24 February 1997 on a Community Strategy for waste management, the Council reiterated its conviction that waste prevention should be the first priority of any rational waste policy in relation to minimising waste production and the hazardous properties of waste.

(9) In its Resolution of 24 February 1997 the Council also underlines the importance of Community criteria concerning the use of waste, the need for appropriate emission standards to apply to incineration facilities, the need for monitoring measures to be envisaged for existing incineration plants, and the need for the Commission to consider amending Community legislation in relation to the incineration of waste with energy recovery in order to avoid large-scale movements of waste for incineration or co-incineration in the Community.

(10) It is necessary to set strict rules for all plants incinerating or co-incinerating waste in order to avoid transboundary movements to plants operating at lower costs due to less stringent environmental standards.

(11) The Communication from the Commission/energy for the future: renewable sources of energy/White paper for a Community strategy and action plan takes into consideration in particular the use of biomass for energy purposes.

(12) Council Directive 96/61/EC sets out an integrated approach to pollution prevention and control in which all the aspects of an installations environmental performance are considered in an integrated manner. Installations for the incineration of municipal waste with a capacity exceeding 3 tonnes per hour and installations for the disposal or recovery of hazardous waste with a capacity exceeding 10 tonnes per day are included within the scope of the said Directive.

(13) Compliance with the emission limit values laid down by this Directive should be regarded as a necessary but not sufficient condition for compliance with the requirements of Directive 96/61/EC. Such compliance may involve more stringent emissions limit values for the pollutants envisaged by this Directive, emission limit values for other substances and other media, and other appropriate conditions.

(14) Industrial experience in the implementation of techniques for the reduction of polluting emissions from incineration plants has been acquired over a period of ten years.

(15) Council Directives 89/369/EEC and 89/429/EEC on the prevention and reduction of air pollution from municipal waste incineration plants have contributed to the reduction and control of atmospheric emissions from incineration plants. More stringent rules should now be adopted and those Directives should accordingly be repealed.

(16) The distinction between hazardous and non-hazardous waste is based principally on the properties of waste prior to incineration or co-incineration but not on differences in emissions. The same emission limit values should apply to the incineration or co-incineration of hazardous and non-hazardous waste but different techniques and conditions of incineration or co-incineration and different monitoring measures upon reception of waste should be retained.

(17) Member States should take into account Council Directive 1999/30/EC of 22 April 1999 relating to limit values for sulphur dioxide, nitrogen dioxide and oxides of nitrogen, particulate matter and lead in ambient air when implementing this Directive.

(18) The incineration of hazardous waste with a content of more than 1 % of halogenated organic substances, expressed as chlorine, has to comply with certain operational conditions in order to destroy as many organic pollutants such as dioxins as possible.

(19) The incineration of waste which contains chlorine generates flue gas residues. Such residues should be managed in a way that minimises their amount and harmfulness.

(20) There may be grounds to provide for specified exemptions to the emission limit values for some pollutants during a specified time limit and subject to specific conditions.

(21) Criteria for certain sorted combustible fraction of non-hazardous waste not suitable for recycling, should be developed in order to allow the authorisation of the reduction of the frequency of periodical measurements.

(22) A single text on the incineration of waste will improve legal clarity and enforceability. There should be a single directive for the incineration and co-incineration of hazardous and non-hazardous waste taking fully into account the substance and structure of Council Directive 94/67/EC of 16 December 1994 on the incineration of hazardous waste. Therefore Directive 94/67/EC should also be repealed.

(23) Article 4 of Council Directive 75/442/EEC of 15 July 1975 on waste requires Member States to take the necessary measures to ensure that waste is recovered or disposed of without endangering human health and without harming the environment. To this end, Articles 9 and 10 of that Directive provide that any plant or undertaking treating waste must obtain a permit from the competent authorities relating, inter alia, to the precautions to be taken.

(24) The requirements for recovering the heat generated by the incineration or co-incineration process and for minimising and recycling residues resulting from the operation of incineration or co-incineration plants will assist in meeting the objectives of Article 3 on the waste hierarchy of Directive 75/442/EEC.

(25) Incineration and co-incineration plants treating only animal waste regulated by Directive 90/667/EEC are excluded from the scope of this Directive. The Commission intends to propose a revision to the requirements of Directive 90/667 with a view to providing for high environmental standards for the incineration and co-incineration of animal waste.

(26) The permit for an incineration or co-incineration plant shall also comply with any applicable requirements laid down in Directives 91/271/EEC, 96/61/EC, 96/62/EC, 76/464/EEC, and 1999/31/EC.

(27) The co-incineration of waste in plants not primarily intended to incinerate waste should not be allowed to cause higher emissions of polluting substances in that part of the exhaust gas volume resulting from such co-incineration than those permitted for dedicated incineration plants and should therefore be subject to appropriate limitations.

(28) High-standard measurement techniques are required to monitor emissions to ensure compliance with the emission limit values for the pollutants.

(29) The introduction of emission limit values for the discharge of waste water from the cleaning of exhaust gases from incineration and co-incineration plants will limit a transfer of pollutants from the air into water.

(30) Provisions should be laid down for cases where the emission limit values are exceeded as well as for technically unavoidable stoppages, disturbances or failures of the purification devices or the measurement devices.

(31) In order to ensure transparency of the permitting process throughout the Community the public should have access to information with a view to allowing it to be involved in decisions to be taken following applications for new permits and their subsequent updates. The public should have access to reports on the functioning and monitoring of the plants burning more than three tonnes per hour in order to be informed of their potential effects on the environment and human health.

(32) The Commission should present a report both to the European Parliament and the Council based on the experience of applying this Directive, the new scientific knowledge gained, the development of the state of technology, the progress achieved in emission control techniques, and on the experience made in waste management and operation of the plants and on the development of environmental requirements, with a view to proposing, as appropriate, to adapt the related provisions of this Directive.

(33) The measures necessary for the implementation of this Directive are to be adopted in accordance with Council Decision 1999/468/EC of 28 June 1999 laying down the procedures for the exercise of implementing powers conferred on the Commission.

(34) Member States should lay down rules on penalties applicable to infringements of the provisions of this Directive and ensure that they are implemented; those penalties should be effective, proportionate and dissuasive,

HAVE ADOPTED THIS DIRECTIVE:

Article 1

Objectives

The aim of this Directive is to prevent or to limit as far as practicable negative effects on the environment, in particular pollution by emissions into air, soil, surface water and groundwater, and the resulting risks to human health, from the incineration and co-incineration of waste.

This aim shall be met by means of stringent operational conditions and technical requirements, through setting emission limit values for waste incineration and co-incineration plants within the Community and also through meeting the requirements of Directive 75/442/EEC.

Article 2

Scope

1. This Directive covers incineration and co-incineration plants.

2. The following plants shall however be excluded from the scope of this Directive:

(a) Plants treating only the following wastes:
  - (i) vegetable waste from agriculture and forestry,
  - (ii) vegetable waste from the food processing industry, if the heat generated is recovered,
  - (iii) fibrous vegetable waste from virgin pulp production and from production of paper from pulp, if it is co-incinerated at the place of production and the heat generated is recovered,
  - (iv) wood waste with the exception of wood waste which may contain halogenated organic compounds or heavy metals as a result of treatment with wood-preservatives or coating, and which includes in particular such wood waste originating from construction and demolition waste,
  - (v) cork waste,
  - (vi) radioactive waste,
  - (vii) animal carcasses as regulated by Directive 90/667/EEC without prejudice to its future amendments,
  - (viii) waste resulting from the exploration for, and the exploitation of, oil and gas resources from off-shore installations and incinerated on board the installation;

(b) Experimental plants used for research, development and testing in order to improve the incineration process and which treat less than 50 tonnes of waste per year.

Article 3

Definitions

For the purposes of this Directive:

1. "waste" means any solid or liquid waste as defined in Article 1(a) of Directive 75/442/EEC;

2. "hazardous waste" means any solid or liquid waste as defined in Article 1(4) of Council Directive 91/689/EEC of 12 December 1991 on hazardous waste.

For the following hazardous wastes, the specific requirements for hazardous waste in this Directive shall not apply:

(a) combustible liquid wastes including waste oils as defined in Article 1 of Council Directive 75/439/EEC of 16 June 1975 on the disposal of waste oils provided that they meet the following criteria:
   (i) the mass content of polychlorinated aromatic hydrocarbons, e.g. polychlorinated biphenyls (PCB) or pentachlorinated phenol (PCP) amounts to concentrations not higher than those set out in the relevant Community legislation;
   (ii) these wastes are not rendered hazardous by virtue of containing other constituents listed in Annex II to Directive 91/689/EEC in quantities or in concentrations which are inconsistent with the achievement of the objectives set out in Article 4 of Directive 75/442/EEC; and
   (iii) the net calorific value amounts to at least 30 MJ per kilogramme,

(b) any combustible liquid wastes which cannot cause, in the flue gas directly resulting from their combustion, emissions other than those from gasoil as defined in Article 1(1) of Directive 93/12/EEC or a higher concentration of emissions than those resulting from the combustion of gasoil as so defined;

3. "mixed municipal waste" means waste from households as well as commercial, industrial and institutional waste, which because of its nature and composition is similar to waste from households, but excluding fractions indicated in the Annex to Decision 94/3/EC under heading 20 01 that are collected separately at source and excluding the other wastes indicated under heading 20 02 of that Annex;

4. "incineration plant" means any stationary or mobile technical unit and equipment dedicated to the thermal treatment of wastes with or without recovery of the combustion heat generated. This includes the incineration by oxidation of waste as well as other thermal treatment processes such as pyrolysis, gasification or plasma processes in so far as the substances resulting from the treatment are subsequently incinerated.

This definition covers the site and the entire incineration plant including all incineration lines, waste reception, storage, on site pretreatment facilities, waste-fuel and air-supply systems, boiler, facilities for the treatment of exhaust gases, on-site facilities for treatment or storage of residues and waste water, stack, devices and systems for controlling incineration operations, recording and monitoring incineration conditions;

5. "co-incineration plant" means any stationary or mobile plant whose main purpose is the generation of energy or production of material products and:

— which uses wastes as a regular or additional fuel; or
— in which waste is thermally treated for the purpose of disposal.

If co-incineration takes place in such a way that the main purpose of the plant is not the generation of energy or production of material products but rather the thermal treatment of waste, the plant shall be regarded as an incineration plant within the meaning of point 4.

This definition covers the site and the entire plant including all co-incineration lines, waste reception, storage, on site pretreatment facilities, waste-, fuel- and air-supply systems, boiler, facilities for the treatment of exhaust gases, on-site facilities for treatment or storage of residues and waste water, stack devices and systems for controlling incineration operations, recording and monitoring incineration conditions;

6. "existing incineration or co-incineration plant" means an incineration or co-incineration plant:

(a) which is in operation and has a permit in accordance with existing Community legislation before 28 December 2002, or,

(b) which is authorised or registered for incineration or co-incineration and has a permit issued before 28 December 2002 in accordance with existing Community legislation, provided that the plant is put into operation not later than 28 December 2003, or

(c) which, in the view of the competent authority, is the subject of a full request for a permit, before 28 December 2002, provided that the plant is put into operation not later than 28 December 2004;

7. "nominal capacity" means the sum of the incineration capacities of the furnaces of which an incineration plant is composed, as specified by the constructor and confirmed by the operator, with due account being taken, in particular, of the calorific value of the waste, expressed as the quantity of waste incinerated per hour;

8. "emission" means the direct or indirect release of substances, vibrations, heat or noise from individual or diffuse sources in the plant into the air, water or soil;

9. "emission limit values" means the mass, expressed in terms of certain specific parameters, concentration and/or level of an emission, which may not be exceeded during one or more periods of time;

10. "dioxins and furans" means all polychlorinated dibenzo-p-dioxins and dibenzofurans listed in Annex I;

11. "operator" means any natural or legal person who operates or controls the plant or, where this is provided for in national legislation, to whom decisive economic power over the technical functioning of the plant has been delegated;

12. "permit" means a written decision (or several such decisions) delivered by the competent authority granting authorisation to operate a plant, subject to certain conditions which guarantee that the plant complies with all the requirements of this Directive. A permit may cover one or more plants or parts of a plant on the same site operated by the same operator;

13. "residue" means any liquid or solid material (including bottom ash and slag, fly ash and boiler dust, solid reaction products from gas treatment, sewage sludge from the treatment of waste waters, spent catalysts and spent activated carbon) defined as waste in Article 1(a) of Directive 75/442/EEC, which is generated by the incineration or co-incineration process, the exhaust gas or waste water treatment or other processes within the incineration or co-incineration plant.

Article 4

Application and permit

1. Without prejudice to Article 11 of Directive 75/442/EEC or to Article 3 of Directive 91/689/EEC, no incineration or co-incineration plant shall operate without a permit to carry out these activities.

2. Without prejudice to Directive 96/61/EC, the application for a permit for an incineration or co-incineration plant to the competent authority shall include a description of the measures which are envisaged to guarantee that:

(a) the plant is designed, equipped and will be operated in such a manner that the requirements of this Directive are taking into account the categories of waste to be incinerated;

(b) the heat generated during the incineration and co-incineration process is recovered as far as practicable e.g. through combined heat and power, the generating of process steam or district heating;

(c) the residues will be minimised in their amount and harmfulness and recycled where appropriate;

(d) the disposal of the residues which cannot be prevented, reduced or recycled will be carried out in conformity with national and Community legislation.

3. The permit shall be granted only if the application shows that the proposed measurement techniques for emissions into the air comply with Annex III and, as regards water, comply with Annex III paragraphs 1 and 2.

4. The permit granted by the competent authority for an incineration or co-incineration plant shall, in addition to complying with any applicable requirement laid down in Directives 91/271/EEC, 96/61/EC, 96/62/EC, 76/464/EEC and 1999/31/EC:

(a) list explicitly the categories of waste which may be treated. The list shall use at least the categories of waste set up in the European Waste Catalogue (EWC), if possible, and contain information on the quantity of waste, where appropriate;
(b) include the total waste incinerating or co-incinerating capacity of the plant;
(c) specify the sampling and measurement procedures used to satisfy the obligations imposed for periodic measurements of each air and water pollutants.

5. The permit granted by the competent authority to an incineration or co-incineration plant using hazardous waste shall in addition to paragraph 4:
(a) list the quantities of the different categories of hazardous waste which may be treated;
(b) specify the minimum and maximum mass flows of those hazardous wastes, their lowest and maximum calorific values and their maximum contents of pollutants, e.g. PCB, PCP, chlorine, fluorine, sulphur, heavy metals.

6. Without prejudice to the provisions of the Treaty, Member States may list the categories of waste to be mentioned in the permit which can be co-incinerated in defined categories of co-incineration plants.

7. Without prejudice to Directive 96/61/EC, the competent authority shall periodically reconsider and, where necessary, update permit conditions.

8. Where the operator of an incineration or co-incineration plant for non-hazardous waste is envisaging a change of operation which would involve the incineration or co-incineration of hazardous waste, this shall be regarded as a substantial change within the meaning of Article 2(10)(b) of Directive 96/61/EC and Article 12(2) of that Directive shall apply.

9. If an incineration or co-incineration plant does not comply with the conditions of the permit, in particular with the emission limit values for air and water, the competent authority shall take action to enforce compliance.

Article 5

Delivery and reception of waste

1. The operator of the incineration or co-incineration plant shall take all necessary precautions concerning the delivery and reception of waste in order to prevent or to limit as far as practicable negative effects on the environment, in particular the pollution of air, soil, surface water and groundwater as well as odours and noise, and direct risks to human health. These measures shall meet at least the requirements set out in paragraphs 3 and 4.

2. The operator shall determine the mass of each category of waste, if possible according to the EWC, prior to accepting the waste at the incineration or co-incineration plant.

3. Prior to accepting hazardous waste at the incineration or co-incineration plant, the operator shall have available information about the waste for the purpose of verifying, inter alia, compliance with the permit requirements specified in Article 4(5). This information shall cover:
(a) all the administrative information on the generating process contained in the documents mentioned in paragraph 4(a);
(b) the physical, and as far as practicable, chemical composition of the waste and all other information necessary to evaluate its suitability for the intended incineration process;
(c) the hazardous characteristics of the waste, the substances with which it cannot be mixed, and the precautions to be taken in handling the waste.

4. Prior to accepting hazardous waste at the incineration or co-incineration plant, at least the following reception procedures shall be carried out by the operator:
(a) the checking of those documents required by Directive 91/689/EEC and, where applicable, those required by Council Regulation (EEC) No 259/93 of 1 February 1993 on the supervision, and control of shipments of waste within, into and out of the European Community and by dangerous-goods transport regulations;

(b) the taking of representative samples, unless inappropriate, e.g. for infectious clinical waste, as far as possible before unloading, to verify conformity with the information provided for in paragraph 3 by carrying out controls and to enable the competent authorities to identify the nature of the wastes treated. These samples shall be kept for at least one month after the incineration.

5. The competent authorities may grant exemptions from paragraphs 2, 3 and 4 for industrial plants and undertakings incinerating or co-incinerating only their own waste at the place of generation of the waste provided that the requirements of this Directive are met.

Article 6

Operating conditions

1. Incineration plants shall be operated in order to achieve a level of incineration such that the slag and bottom ashes Total Organic Carbon (TOC) content is less than 3 % or their loss on ignition is less than 5 % of the dry weight of the material. If necessary appropriate techniques of waste pretreatment shall be used.

Incineration plants shall be designed, equipped, built and operated in such a way that the gas resulting from the process is raised, after the last injection of combustion air, in a controlled and homogeneous fashion and even under the most unfavourable conditions, to a temperature of 850 °C, as measured near the inner wall or at another representative point of the combustion chamber as authorised by the competent authority, for two seconds. If hazardous wastes with a content of more than 1 % of halogenated organic substances, expressed as chlorine, are incinerated, the temperature has to be raised to 1100 °C for at least two seconds.

Each line of the incineration plant shall be equipped with at least one auxiliary burner. This burner must be switched on automatically when the temperature of the combustion gases after the last injection of combustion air falls below 850 °C or 1100 °C as the case may be. It shall also be used during plant start-up and shut-down operations in order to ensure that the temperature of 850 °C or 1100 °C as the case may be is maintained at all times during these operations and as long as unburned waste is in the combustion chamber.

During start-up and shut-down or when the temperature of the combustion gas falls below 850 °C or 1100 °C as the case may be, the auxiliary burner shall not be fed with fuels which can cause higher emissions than those resulting from the burning of gasoil as defined in Article 1(1) of Council Directive 75/716/EEC, liquefied gas or natural gas.

2. Co-incineration plants shall be designed, equipped, built and operated in such a way that the gas resulting from the co-incineration of waste is raised in a controlled and homogeneous fashion and even under the most unfavourable conditions, to a temperature of 850 °C for two seconds. If hazardous wastes with a content of more than 1 % of halogenated organic substances, expressed as chlorine, are co-incinerated, the temperature has to be raised to 1100 °C.

3. Incineration and co-incineration plants shall have and operate an automatic system to prevent waste feed:

(a) at start-up, until the temperature of 850 °C or 1100 °C as the case may be or the temperature specified according to paragraph 4 has been reached;

(b) whenever the temperature of 850 °C or 1100 °C as the case may be or the temperature specified according to paragraph 4 is not maintained;

(c) whenever the continuous measurements required by this Directive show that any emission limit value is exceeded due to disturbances or failures of the purification devices.

4. Conditions different from those laid down in paragraph 1 and, as regards the temperature, paragraph 3 and specified in the permit for certain categories of waste or for certain thermal

processes may be authorised by the competent authority, provided the requirements of this Directive are met. Member States may lay down rules governing these authorisations. The change of the operational conditions shall not cause more residues or residues with a higher content of organic pollutants compared to those residues which could be expected under the conditions laid down in paragraph 1.

Conditions different from those laid down in paragraph 2 and, as regards the temperature, paragraph 3 and specified in the permit for certain categories of waste or for certain thermal processes may be authorised by the competent authority, provided the requirements of this Directive are met. Member States may lay down rules governing these authorisations. Such authorisation shall be conditional upon at least the provisions for emission limit values set out in Annex V for total organic carbon and CO being complied with.

In the case of co-incineration of their own waste at the place of its production in existing bark boilers within the pulp and paper industry, such authorisation shall be conditional upon at least the provisions for emission limit values set out in Annex V for total organic carbon being complied with.

All operating conditions determined under this paragraph and the results of verifications made shall be communicated by the Member State to the Commission as part of the information provided in accordance with the reporting requirements.

5. Incineration and co-incineration plants shall be designed, equipped, built and operated in such a way as to prevent emissions into the air giving rise to significant ground-level air pollution; in particular, exhaust gases shall be discharged in a controlled fashion and in conformity with relevant Community air quality standards by means of a stack the height of which is calculated in such a way as to safeguard human health and the environment.

6. Any heat generated by the incineration or the co-incineration process shall be recovered as far as practicable.

7. Infectious clinical waste should be placed straight in the furnace, without first being mixed with other categories of waste and without direct handling.

8. The management of the incineration or the co-incineration plant shall be in the hands of a natural person who is competent to manage the plant.

Article 7

Air emission limit values

1. Incineration plants shall be designed, equipped, built and operated in such a way that the emission limit values set out in Annex V are not exceeded in the exhaust gas.

2. Co-incineration plants shall be designed, equipped, built and operated in such a way that the emission limit values determined according to or set out in Annex II are not exceeded in the exhaust gas.

If in a co-incineration plant more than 40 % of the resulting heat release comes from hazardous waste, the emission limit values set out in Annex V shall apply.

3. The results of the measurements made to verify compliance with the emission limit values shall be standardised with respect to the conditions laid down in Article 11.

4. In the case of co-incineration of untreated mixed municipal waste, the limit values will be determined according to Annex V, and Annex II will not apply.

5. Without prejudice to the provisions of the Treaty, Member States may set emission limit values for polycyclic aromatic hydrocarbons or other pollutants.

Article 8

Water discharges from the cleaning of exhaust gases

1. Waste water from the cleaning of exhaust gases discharged from an incineration or co-incineration plant shall be subject to a permit granted by the competent authorities.

2. Discharges to the aquatic environment of waste water resulting from the cleaning of exhaust gases shall be limited as far as practicable, at least in accordance with the emission limit values set in Annex IV.

3. Subject to a specific provision in the permit, the waste water from the cleaning of exhaust gases may be discharged to the aquatic environment after separate treatment on condition that:
(a) the requirements of relevant Community, national and local provisions are complied with in the form of emission limit values; and
(b) the mass concentrations of the polluting substances referred to in Annex IV do not exceed the emission limit values laid down therein.

4. The emission limit values shall apply at the point where waste waters from the cleaning of exhaust gases containing the polluting substances referred to in Annex IV are discharged from the incineration or co-incineration plant.

Where the waste water from the cleaning of exhaust gases is treated on site collectively with other on-site sources of waste water, the operator shall take the measurements referred to in Article 11:
(a) on the waste water stream from the exhaust gas cleaning processes prior to its input into the collective waste water treatment plant;
(b) on the other waste water stream or streams prior to its or their input into the collective waste water treatment plant;
(c) at the point of final waste water discharge, after the treatment, from the incineration plant or co-incineration plant.

The operator shall take appropriate mass balance calculations in order to determine the emission levels in the final waste water discharge that can be attributed to the waste water arising from the cleaning of exhaust gases in order to check compliance with the emission limit values set out in Annex IV for the waste water stream from the exhaust gas cleaning process.

Under no circumstances shall dilution of waste water take place for the purpose of complying with the emission limit values set in Annex IV.

5. When waste waters from the cleaning of exhaust gases containing the polluting substances referred to in Annex IV are treated outside the incineration or co-incineration plant at a treatment plant intended only for the treatment of this sort of waste water, the emission limit values of Annex IV are to be applied at the point where the waste waters leave the treatment plant. If this off-site treatment plant is not only dedicated to treat waste water from incineration, the operator shall take the appropriate mass balance calculations, as provided for under paragraph 4(a), (b) and (c), in order to determine the emission levels in the final waste water discharge that can be attributed to the waste water arising from the cleaning of exhaust gases in order to check compliance with the emission limit values set out in Annex IV for the waste water stream from the exhaust gas cleaning process.

Under no circumstances shall dilution of waste water take place for the purpose of complying with the emission limit values set in Annex IV.

6. The permit shall:
(a) establish emission limit values for the polluting substances referred to in Annex IV, in accordance with paragraph 2 and in order to meet the requirements referred to in paragraph 3(a);
(b) set operational control parameters for waste water at least for pH, temperature and flow.

7. Incineration and co-incineration plant sites, including associated storage areas for wastes, shall be designed and in such a way as to prevent the unauthorised and accidental release of any polluting substances into soil, surface water and groundwater in accordance with the provisions provided for in relevant Community legislation. Moreover, storage capacity shall be provided for contaminated rainwater run-off from the incineration or co-incineration plant site or for contaminated water arising from spillage or fire-fighting operations.

The storage capacity shall be adequate to ensure that such waters can be tested and treated before discharge where necessary.

8. Without prejudice to the provisions of the Treaty, Member States may set emission limit values for polycyclic aromatic hydrocarbons or other pollutants.

Article 9

Residues

Residues resulting from the operation of the incineration or co-incineration plant shall be minimised in their amount and harmfulness. Residues shall be recycled, where appropriate, directly in the plant or outside in accordance with relevant Community legislation.

Transport and intermediate storage of dry residues in the form of dust, such as boiler dust and dry residues from the treatment of combustion gases, shall take place in such a way as to prevent dispersal in the environment e.g. in closed containers.

Prior to determining the routes for the disposal or recycling of the residues from incineration and co-incineration plants, appropriate tests shall be carried out to establish the physical and chemical characteristics and the polluting potential of the different incineration residues. The analysis shall concern the total soluble fraction and heavy metals soluble fraction.

Article 10

Control and monitoring

1. Measurement equipment shall be installed and techniques used in order to monitor the parameters, conditions and mass concentrations relevant to the incineration or co-incineration process.

2. The measurement requirements shall be laid down in the permit or in the conditions attached to the permit issued by the competent authority.

3. The appropriate installation and the functioning of the automated monitoring equipment for emissions into air and water shall be subject to control and to an annual surveillance test. Calibration has to be done by means of parallel measurements with the reference methods at least every three years.

4. The location of the sampling or measurement points shall be laid down by the competent authority.

5. Periodic measurements of the emissions into the air and water shall be carried out in accordance with Annex III, points 1 and 2.

Article 11

Measurement requirements

1. Member States shall, either by specification in the conditions of the permit or by general binding rules, ensure that paragraphs 2 to 12 and 17, as regards air, and paragraphs 9 and 14 to 17, as regards water, are complied with.

2. The following measurements of air pollutants shall be carried out in accordance with Annex III at the incineration and co-incineration plant:

(a) continuous measurements of the following substances: NO_x, provided that emission limit values are set, CO, total dust, TOC, HCl, HF, SO_2;

(b) continuous measurements of the following process operation parameters: temperature near the inner wall or at another representative point of the combustion chamber as authorised by the competent authority, concentration of oxygen, pressure, temperature and water vapour content of the exhaust gas;

(c) at least two measurements per year of heavy metals, dioxins and furans; one measurement at least every three months shall however be carried out for the first 12 months of operation. Member States may fix measurement periods where they have set emission limit values for polycyclic aromatic hydrocarbons or other pollutants.

3. The residence time as well as the minimum temperature and the oxygen content of the exhaust gases shall be subject to appropriate verification, at least once when the incineration or co-incineration plant is brought into service and under the most unfavourable operating conditions anticipated.

4. The continuous measurement of HF may be omitted if treatment stages for HCl are used which ensure that the emission limit value for HCl is not being exceeded. In this case the emissions of HF shall be subject to periodic measurements as laid down in paragraph 2(c).

5. The continuous measurement of the water vapour content shall not be required if the sampled exhaust gas is dried before the emissions are analysed.

6. Periodic measurements as laid down in paragraph 2(c) of HCl, HF and SO_2 instead of continuous measuring may be authorised in the permit by the competent authority in incineration or co-incineration plants, if the operator can prove that the emissions of those pollutants can under no circumstances be higher than the prescribed emission limit values.

[7. The reduction of the frequency of the periodic measurements for heavy metals from twice a year to once every two years and for dioxins and furans from twice a year to once a year may be authorised in the permit by the competent authority provided that the emissions resulting from co-incineration or incineration are below 50 % of the emission limit values determined in accordance with Annex II or Annex V respectively and that criteria for the requirements to be met are available. The Commission shall adopt measures establishing these criteria, based at least on the provisions of points (a) and (d) of the second subparagraph. Those measures, designed to amend non-essential elements of this Directive by supplementing it, shall be adopted in accordance with the regulatory procedure with scrutiny referred to in Article 17(2).][1]

Until 1 January 2005 the reduction of the frequency may be authorised even if no such criteria are available provided that:

(a) the waste to be co-incinerated or incinerated consists only of certain sorted combustible fractions of non-hazardous waste not suitable for recycling and presenting certain characteristics, and which is further specified on the basis of the assessment referred to in subparagraph (d);

(b) national quality criteria, which have been reported to the Commission, are available for these wastes;

(c) co-incineration and incineration of these wastes is in line with the relevant waste management plans referred to in Article 7 of Directive 75/442/EEC;

(d) the operator can prove to the competent authority that the emissions are under all circumstances significantly below the emission limit values set out in Annex II or Annex V for heavy metals, dioxins and furans; this assessment shall be based on information on the quality of the waste concerned and measurements of the emissions of the said pollutants;

(e) the quality criteria and the new period for the periodic measurements are specified in the permit; and

(f) all decisions on the frequency of measurements referred to in this paragraph, supplemented with information on the amount and quality of the waste concerned, shall be communicated on a yearly basis to the Commission.

8. The results of the measurements made to verify compliance with the emission limit values shall be standardised at the following conditions and for oxygen according to the formula as referred to in Annex VI:

(a) Temperature 273 K, pressure 101,3 kPa, 11 % oxygen, dry gas, in exhaust gas of incineration plants;

(b) Temperature 273 K, pressure 101,3 kPa, 3 % oxygen, dry gas, in exhaust gas of incineration of waste oil as defined in Directive 75/439/EEC;

(c) when the wastes are incinerated or co-incinerated in an oxygen-enriched atmosphere, the results of the measurements can be standardised at an oxygen content laid down by the competent authority reflecting the special circumstances of the individual case;

(d) in the case of co-incineration, the results of the measurements shall be standardised at a total oxygen content as calculated in Annex II.

When the emissions of pollutants are reduced by exhaust gas treatment in an incineration or co-incineration plant treating hazardous waste, the standardisation with respect to the oxygen contents provided for in the first subparagraph shall be done only if the oxygen content measured over the same period as for the pollutant concerned exceeds the relevant standard oxygen content.

9. All measurement results shall be recorded, processed and presented in an appropriate fashion in order to enable the competent authorities to verify compliance with the permitted operating conditions and emission limit values laid down in this Directive in accordance with procedures to be decided upon by those authorities.

10. The emission limit values for air shall be regarded as being complied with if:

(a)

— none of the daily average values exceeds any of the emission limit values set out in Annex V(a) or Annex II;

— 97 % of the daily average value over the year does not exceed the emission limit value set out in Annex V(e) first indent;

(b) either none of the half-hourly average values exceeds any of the emission limit values set out in Annex V(b), column A or, where relevant, 97 % of the half-hourly average values over the year do not exceed any of the emission limit values set out in Annex V(b), column B;

(c) none of the average values over the sample period set out for heavy metals and dioxins and furans exceeds the emission limit values set out in Annex V(c) and (d) or Annex II;

(d) the provisions of Annex V(e), second indent or Annex II, are met.

11. The half-hourly average values and the 10-minute averages shall be determined within the effective operating time (excluding the start-up and shut-off periods if no waste is being incinerated) from the measured values after having subtracted the value of the confidence interval specified in point 3 of Annex III. The daily average values shall be determined from those validated average values.

To obtain a valid daily average value no more than five half-hourly average values in any day shall be discarded due to malfunction or maintenance of the continuous measurement system. No more than ten daily average values per year shall be discarded due to malfunction or maintenance of the continuous measurement system.

12. The average values over the sample period and the average values in the case of periodical measurements of HF, HCl and SO_2 shall be determined in accordance with the requirements of Article 10(2) and (4) and Annex III.

[13. The Commission shall determine, as soon as appropriate measurement techniques are available within the Community, the date from which continuous measurements of the air emission limit values for heavy metals, dioxins and furans shall be carried out in accordance with Annex III. That measure, designed to amend non-essential elements of this Directive by supplementing it, shall be adopted in accordance with the regulatory procedure with scrutiny referred to in Article 17(2).][1]

14. The following measurements shall be carried out at the point of waste water discharge:
(a) continuous measurements of the parameters referred to in Article 8(6)(b);
(b) spot sample daily measurements of total suspended solids; Member States may alternatively provide for measurements of a flow proportional representative sample over a period of 24 hours;
(c) at least monthly measurements of a flow proportional representative sample of the discharge over a period of 24 hours of the polluting substances referred to in Article 8(3) with respect to items 2 to 10 in Annex IV;
(d) at least every six months measurements of dioxins and furans; however one measurement at least every three months shall be carried out for the first 12 months of operation. Member States may fix measurement periods where they have set emission limit values for polycyclic aromatic hydrocarbons or other pollutants.

15. The monitoring of the mass of pollutants in the treated waste water shall be done in conformity with Community legislation and laid down in the permit as well as the frequency of the measurements.

16. The emission limit values for water shall be regarded as being complied with if:
(a) for total suspended solids (polluting substance number 1), 95 % and 100 % of the measured values do not exceed the respective emission limit values as set out in Annex IV;
(b) for heavy metals (polluting substances number 2 to 10) no more than one measurement per year exceeds the emission limit values set out in Annex IV; or, if the Member State provides for more than 20 samples per year, no more than 5 % of these samples exceed the emission limit values set out in Annex IV;
(c) for dioxins and furans (polluting substance 11), the twice-yearly measurements do not exceed the emission limit value set out in Annex IV.

17. Should the measurements taken show that the emission limit values for air or water laid down in this Directive have been exceeded, the competent authorities shall be informed without delay.

Amendment

1 Substituted by Regulation (EC) No 1137/2008 of the European Parliament and of the Council of 22 October 2008 adapting a number of instruments subject to the procedure laid down in Article 251 of the Treaty to Council Decision 1999/468/EC, with regard to the regulatory procedure with scrutiny, Article 1, Annex, para 4.8.1.

Article 12

Access to information and public participation

1. Without prejudice to Council Directive 90/313/EEC and Directive 96/61/EC, applications for new permits for incineration and co-incineration plants shall be made available at one or more locations accessible to the public, such as local authority offices, for an appropriate period to enable it to comment on them before the competent authority reaches a decision. That decision, including at least a copy of the permit, and any subsequent updates, shall also be made available to the public.

2. For incineration or co-incineration plants with a nominal capacity of two tonnes or more per hour and notwithstanding Article 15(2) of Directive 96/61/EC, an annual report to be provided by the operator to the competent authority on the functioning and monitoring of the plant shall be made available to the public. This report shall, as a minimum requirement, give an account of the running of the process and the emissions into air and water compared with the emission standards in this Directive. A list of incineration or co-incineration plants

with a nominal capacity of less than two tonnes per hour shall be drawn up by the competent authority and shall be made available to the public.

Article 13

Abnormal operating conditions

1. The competent authority shall lay down in the permit the maximum permissible period of any technically unavoidable stoppages, disturbances, or failures of the purification devices or the measurement devices, during which the concentrations in the discharges into the air and the purified waste water of the regulated substances may exceed the prescribed emission limit values.

2. In the case of a breakdown, the operator shall reduce or close down operations as soon as practicable until normal operations can be restored.

3. Without prejudice to Article 6(3)(c), the incineration plant or co-incineration plant or incineration line shall under no circumstances continue to incinerate waste for a period of more than four hours uninterrupted where emission limit values are exceeded; moreover, the cumulative duration of operation in such conditions over one year shall be less than 60 hours. The 60-hour duration applies to those lines of the entire plant which are linked to one single flue gas cleaning device.

4. The total dust content of the emissions into the air of an incineration plant shall under no circumstances exceed 150 mg/m3 expressed as a half-hourly average; moreover the air emission limit values for CO and TOC shall not be exceeded. All other conditions referred to in Article 6 shall be complied with.

Article 14

Review clause

Without prejudice to Directive 96/61/EC, the Commission shall submit a report to the European Parliament and the Council before 31 December 2008 based on experience of the application of this Directive, in particular for new plants, and on the progress achieved in emission control techniques and experience in waste management. Furthermore, the report shall be based on the development of the state of technology, of experience in the operation of the plants, of environmental requirements. This report will include a specific section on the application of Annex II.1.1. and in particular on the economic and technical feasibility for existing cement kilns as referred to in the footnote to Annex II.1.1. of respecting the NO_x emission limit value for new cement kilns set out in that Annex. The report shall, as appropriate, be accompanied by proposals for revision of the related provisions of this Directive. However, the Commission shall, if appropriate, propose an amendment for Annex II.3 before the said report, if major waste streams are directed to types of co-incineration plants other than those dealt with in Annex II.1 and II.2.

Article 15

Reporting

The reports on the implementation of this Directive shall be established in accordance with the procedure laid down in Article 5 of Council Directive 91/692/EEC. The first report shall cover at least the first full three-year period after 28 December 2002 and comply with the periods referred to in Article 17 of Directive 94/67/EC and in Article 16(3) of Directive 96/61/EC. To this effect, the Commission shall elaborate the appropriate questionnaire in due time.

[Article 16

Adaptation to technical progress or new findings][1]

[The Commission shall adopt measures designed to amend non-essential elements of this Directive and adapting Articles 10, 11 and 13 and Annexes I and III to technical progress or new findings concerning the health benefits of emission reductions in accordance with the regulatory procedure with scrutiny referred to in Article 17(2).][1]

Amendment

1 Substituted by Regulation (EC) No 1137/2008 of the European Parliament and of the Council of 22 October 2008 adapting a number of instruments subject to the procedure laid down in Article 251 of the Treaty to Council Decision 1999/468/EC, with regard to the regulatory procedure with scrutiny, Article 1, Annex, para 4.8.2.

[Article 17

Committee procedure][1]

[1. The Commission shall be assisted by a committee.

2. Where reference is made to this paragraph, Article 5a(1) to (4) and Article 7 of Decision 1999/468/EC shall apply, having regard to the provisions of Article 8 thereof.][1]

Amendment

1 Substituted by Regulation (EC) No 1137/2008 of the European Parliament and of the Council of 22 October 2008 adapting a number of instruments subject to the procedure laid down in Article 251 of the Treaty to Council Decision 1999/468/EC, with regard to the regulatory procedure with scrutiny, Article 1, Annex, para 4.8.3.

Article 18

Repeal

The following shall be repealed as from 28 December 2005:
(a) Article 8(1) and the Annex to Directive 75/439/EEC;
(b) Directive 89/369/EEC;
(c) Directive 89/429/EEC;
(d) Directive 94/67/EC.

Article 19

Penalties

The Member States shall determine penalties applicable to breaches of the national provisions adopted pursuant to this Directive. The penalties thus provided for shall be effective, proportionate and dissuasive. The Member States shall notify those provisions to the Commission by 28 December 2002 at the latest and shall notify it without delay of any subsequent amendment affecting them.

Article 20

Transitional provisions

1. Without prejudice to the specific transitional provisions provided for in the Annexes to this Directive, the provisions of this Directive shall apply to existing plants as from 28 December 2005.

2. For new plants, i.e. plants not falling under the definition of "existing incineration or co-incineration plant" in Article 3(6) or paragraph 3 of this Article, this Directive, instead of the Directives mentioned in Article 18, shall apply as from 28 December 2002.

3. Stationary or mobile plants whose purpose is the generation of energy or production of material products and which are in operation and have a permit in accordance with existing Community legislation where required and which start co-incinerating waste not later than 28 December 2004 are to be regarded as existing co-incineration plants.

Article 21

Implementation

1. Member States shall bring into force the laws, regulations and administrative provisions necessary to comply with this Directive not later than 28 December 2002. They shall forthwith inform the Commission thereof.

When Member States adopt those measures, they shall contain a reference to this Directive or be accompanied by such reference on the occasion of their official publication. The methods of making such reference shall be laid down by the Member States.

2. Member States shall communicate to the Commission the text of the provisions of domestic law which they adopt in the field governed by this Directive.

Article 22

Entry into force

This Directive shall enter into force on the day of its publication in the Official Journal of the European Communities.

Article 23

Addressees

This Directive is addressed to the Member States.

ANNEX I
EQUIVALENCE FACTORS FOR DIBENZO-P-DIOXINS AND DIBENZOFURANS

For the determination of the total concentration (TE) of dioxins and furans the mass concentration of the following dibenzo-p-dioxins and dibenzofurans shall be multiplied by the following equivalence factors before summing

		Toxic equivalence factor
2, 3, 7, 8	— Tetrachlorodibenzodioxin (TCDD)	1
1, 2, 3, 7, 8	— Pentachlorodibenzodioxin (PeCDD)	0.5
1, 2, 3, 4, 7, 8	— Hexachlorodibenzodioxin (HxCDD)	0.1
1, 2, 3, 6, 7, 8	— Hexachlorodibenzodioxin (HxCDD)	0.1
1, 2, 3, 7, 8, 9	— Hexachlorodibenzodioxin (HxCDD)	0.1
1, 2, 3, 4, 6, 7, 8	— Heptachlorodibenzodioxin (HpCDD)	0.01
	— Octachlorodibenzodioxin (OCDD)	0.001
2, 3, 7, 8	— Tetrachlorodibenzofuran (TCDF)	0.1
2, 3, 4, 7, 8	— Pentachlorodibenzofuran (PeCDF)	0.5
1, 2, 3, 7, 8	— Pentachlorodibenzofuran (PeCDF)	0.05
1, 2, 3, 4, 7, 8	— Hexachlorodibenzofuran (HxCDF)	0.1

		Toxic equivalence factor
1, 2, 3, 6, 7, 8	— Hexachlorodibenzofuran (HxCDF)	0.1
1, 2, 3, 7, 8, 9	— Hexachlorodibenzofuran (HxCDF)	0.1
2, 3, 4, 6, 7, 8	— Hexachlorodibenzofuran (HxCDF)	0.1
1, 2, 3, 4, 6, 7, 8	— Heptachlorodibenzofuran (HpCDF)	0.01
1, 2, 3, 4, 7, 8, 9	— Heptachlorodibenzofuran (HpCDF)	0.01
	— Octachlorodibenzofuran (OCDF)	0.001

ANNEX II
DETERMINATION OF AIR EMISSION LIMIT VALUES FOR THE CO-INCINERATION OF WASTE

The following formula (mixing rule) is to be applied whenever a specific total emission limit value "C" has not been set out in a table in this Annex.

The limit value for each relevant pollutant and carbon monoxide in the exhaust gas resulting from the co-incineration of waste shall be calculated as follows:

$$\frac{V_{waste} \times C_{waste} + V_{proc} \times C_{proc}}{V_{waste} + V_{proc}} = C$$

V_{waste}: exhaust gas volume resulting from the incineration of waste only determined from the waste with the lowest calorific value specified in the permit and standardised at the conditions given by this Directive.

If the resulting heat release from the incineration of hazardous waste amounts to less than 10 % of the total heat released in the plant, Vwaste must be calculated from a (notional) quantity of waste that, being incinerated, would equal 10 % heat release, the total heat release being fixed.

C_{waste}: emission limit values set for incineration plants in Annex V for the relevant pollutants and carbon monoxide.

V_{proc}: exhaust gas volume resulting from the plant process including the combustion of the authorised fuels normally used in the plant (wastes excluded) determined on the basis of oxygen contents at which the emissions must be standardised as laid down in Community or national regulations. In the absence of regulations for this kind of plant, the real oxygen content in the exhaust gas without being thinned by addition of air unnecessary for the process must be used. The standardisation at the other conditions is given in this Directive.

C_{proc}: emission limit values as laid down in the tables of this annex for certain industrial sectors or in case of the absence of such a table or such values, emission limit values of the relevant pollutants and carbon monoxide in the flue gas of plants which comply with the national laws, regulations and administrative provisions for such plants while burning the normally authorised fuels (wastes excluded). In the absence of these measures the emission limit values laid down in the permit are used. In the absence of such permit values the real mass concentrations are used.

C: total emission limit values and oxygen content as laid down in the tables of this annex for certain industrial sectors and certain pollutants or in case of the absence of such a table or such values total emission limit values for CO and the relevant pollutants replacing the emission limit values as laid down in specific Annexes of this Directive. The total oxygen content to replace the oxygen content for the standardisation is calculated on the basis of the content above respecting the partial volumes.

Member States may lay down rules governing the exemptions provided for in this Annex.

II.1. Special provisions for cement kilns co-incinerating waste

Daily average values (for continuous measurements) Sample periods and other measurement requirements as in Article 7. All values in mg/m3 (Dioxins and furans ng/m3). Half-hourly average values shall only be needed in view of calculating the daily average values.

The results of the measurements made to verify compliance with the emission limit values shall be standardised at the following conditions: Temperature 273 K, pressure 101,3 kPa, 10 % oxygen, dry gas.

II.1.1. C – total emission limit values

Pollutant	*C*
Total dust	30
HCI	10
HF	1
NO_x for existing plants	800
NO_x for new plants	500[(1)]
Cd + T1	0.05
Hg	0.05
Sb + As + Pb + Cr + Co + Cu +Mn + Ni + V	0.5
Dioxins and furans	0.1

(1) For the implementation of the NO_x emission limit values, cement kilns which are in operation and have a permit in accordance with existing Community legislation and which start co-incinerating waste after the date mentioned in Article 20(3) are not to be regarded as new plants

Until 1 January 2008, exemptions for NO_x may be authorised by the competent authorities for existing wet process cement kilns or cement kilns which burn less than three tonnes of waste per hour, provided that the permit foresees a total emission limit value for NO_x of not more than 1200 mg/m^3.

Until 1 January 2008, exemptions for dust may be authorised by the competent authority for cement kilns which burn less than three tonnes of waste per hour, provided that the permit foresees a total emission limit value of not more than 50 mg/m3.

II.1.2. C – total emission limit values for SO_2 and TOC

Pollutant	*C*
SO_2	50
TOC	10

Exemptions may be authorised by the competent authority in cases where TOC and SO_2 do not result from the incineration of waste.

II.1.3. Emission limit value for CO

Emission limit values for CO can be set by the competent authority.

II.2. Special provisions for combustion plants co-incinerating waste

II.2.1. Daily average values

[Where, for large combustion plants, more stringent emission limit values are set under Directive 2001/80/EC or will be set under other Community legislation, those emission limit values shall replace, for the plants and pollutants concerned, the emission limit values laid down in the following tables (C_{proc}). In that case, the Commission shall adapt those tables to the more stringent emission limit values. Those measures, designed to amend non-essential elements of this Directive, shall be adopted in accordance with the regulatory procedure with scrutiny referred to in Article 17(2), without delay.][1]

Half-hourly average values shall only be needed in view of calculating the daily average values.

C_{proc}: C_{proc} for solid fuels expressed in mg/Nm^3 (O_2 content 6 %):

Pollutants	*< 50 MWth*	*50–100 MWth*	*100–300 MWth*	*> 300 MWth*
SO_2				
general case		850	850 to 200 (linear decrease from 100 to 300 MWth)	200
Indigenous fuels		or rate of desulphurisation ≥ 90%	or rate of desulphurisation ≥ 92%	or rate of desulphurisation ≥ 95%
NO_x		400	300	200
Dust	50	50	30	30

Until 1 January 2007 and without prejudice to relevant Community legislation, the emission limit value for NO_x does not apply to plants only co-incinerating hazardous waste.

Until 1 January 2008, exemptions for NO_x and SO_2 may be authorised by the competent authorities for existing co-incineration plants between 100 and 300 MWth using fluidised bed technology and burning solid fuels provided that the permit foresees a C_{proc} value of not more than 350 mg/Nm^3 for NO_x and not more than 850 to 400 mg/Nm^3 (linear decrease from 100 to 300 MWth) for SO_2.

C_{proc} for biomass expressed in mg/Nm^3 (O_2 content 6 %):

"Biomass" means: products consisting of any whole or part of a vegetable matter from agriculture or forestry, which can be used for the purpose of recovering its energy content as well as wastes listed in Article 2(2)(a)(i) to (v).

Pollutants	*< 50 MWth*	*50–100 MWth*	*100–300 MWth*	*> 300 MWth*
SO_2		200	200	200
NO_x		350	300	300
Dust	50	50	30	30

Until 1 January 2008, exemptions for NO_x may be authorised by the competent authorities for existing co-incineration plants between 100 and 300 MWth using fluidised bed technology and burning biomass provided that the permit foresees a C_{proc} value of not more than 350 mg/Nm^3.

C_{proc} for liquid fuels expressed in mg/Nm^3 (O_2 content 3 %):

Pollutants	*< 50 MWth*	*50–100 MWth*	*100–300 MWth*	*> 300 MWth*
SO_2		850	850 to 200 (linear decrease from 100 to 300 MWth)	200
NO_2		400	300	200
Dust	50	50	30	30

Amendment

1 Substituted by Regulation (EC) No 1137/2008 of the European Parliament and of the Council of 22 October 2008 adapting a number of instruments subject to the procedure laid down in Article 251 of the Treaty to Council Decision 1999/468/EC, with regard to the regulatory procedure with scrutiny, Article 1, Annex, para 4.8.3.

II.2.2. C – total emission limit values

C expressed in mg/Nm^3 (O_2 content 6 %). All average values over the sample period of a minimum of 30 minutes and a maximum of 8 hours:

Pollutant	*C*
Cd + T1	0.05
Hg	0.05
Sb + As + Pb + Cr + Co + Cu +Mn + Ni + V	0.5

C expressed in ng/Nm^3 (O_2 content 6 %). All average values measured over the sample period of a minimum of 6 hours and a maximum of 8 hours:

Pollutant	*C*
Dioxins and furans	0.1

II.3. Special provisions for industrial sectors not covered under II.1 or II.2 co-incinerating waste

II.3.1. C – total emission limit values:

C expressed in ng/Nm^3. All average values measured over the sample period of a minimum of 6 hours and a maximum of 8 hours:

Pollutant	*C*
Dioxins and furans	0.1

C expressed in mg/Nm^3. All average values over the sample period of a minimum of 30 minutes and a maximum of 8 hours:

Pollutant	*C*
Cd +T1	0.05
Hg	0.05

ANNEX III
MEASUREMENT TECHNIQUES

1. Measurements for the determination of concentrations of air and water polluting substances have to be carried out representatively.

2. Sampling and analysis of all pollutants including dioxins and furans as well as reference measurement methods to calibrate automated measurement systems shall be carried out as given by CEN-standards. If CEN standards are not available, ISO standards, national or international standards which will ensure the provision of data of an equivalent scientific quality shall apply.

3. At the daily emission limit value level, the values of the 95 % confidence intervals of a single measured result shall not exceed the following percentages of the emission limit values:

Carbon monoxide	10%
Sulphur dioxide	20%
Nitrogen dioxide	20%
Total dust	30%
Total organic carbon	30%
Hydrogen chloride	40%

ANNEX IV
EMISSION LIMIT VALUES FOR DISCHARGES OF WASTE WATER FROM THE CLEANING OF EXHAUST GASES

Polluting substances	*Emission limit values expressed in mass concentrations for unfiltered samples*	
1. Total suspended solids as defined by Directive 91/271/EEC	95% / 30mg/l	100% / 45mg/l
2. Mercury and its compounds, expressed as mercury (Hg)	0,03 mg/l	
3. Cadmium and its compounds, expressed as cadmium (Cd)	0,05 mg/l	
4. Thallium and its compounds, expressed as thallium (Tl)	0,05 mg/l	
5. Arsenic and its compounds, expressed as arsenic (As)	0,15 mg/l	
6. Lead and its compounds, expressed as lead (Pb)	0,2 mg/l	
7. Chromium and its compounds, expressed as chromium (Cr)	0,5 mg/l	
8. Copper and its compounds, expressed as copper (Cu)	0,5 mg/l	
9. Nickel and its compounds, expressed as nickel (Ni)	0,5 mg/l	
10. Zinc and its compounds, expressed as zinc (Zn)	1,5 mg/l	
11. Dioxins and furans, defined as the sum of the individual dioxins and furans evaluated in accordance with Annex I	0,3 ng/l	

Until 1 January 2008, exemptions for total suspended solids may be authorised by the competent authority for existing incineration plants provided the permit foresees that 80 % of the measured values do not exceed 30 mg/l and none of them exceed 45 mg/l.

ANNEX V
AIR EMISSION LIMIT VALUES

(a) Daily average values

Total dust	10 mg/m^3
Gaseous and vaporous organic substances, expressed as total organic carbon	10 mg/m^3
Hydrogen chloride (HC1)	10 mg/m^3
Hydrogen fluoride (HF)	1 mg/m^3
Sulphur dioxide (SO_2)	50 mg/m^3
Nitrogen monoxide (NO) and nitrogen dioxide (NO_2) expressed as nitrogen dioxide for existing incineration plants with a nominal capacity exceeding 6 tonnes per hour or new incineration plants	200 mg/m$^{3(*)}$
Nitrogen monoxide (NO) and nitrogen dioxide (NO_2) expressed as nitrogen dioxide for existing incineration plants with a nominal capacity exceeding 6 tonnes per hour or less	400 mg/m$^{3(*)}$

(*) until 1 January 2007 and without prejudice to relevant (Community) legislation the emission limit value for NO_x does not apply to plants only incinerating hazardous waste.

Exemptions for NO_x may be authorised by the competent authority for existing incineration plants:

— with a nominal capacity of 6 tonnes per hour, provided that the permit foresees the daily average values do not exceed 500 mg/m3 and this until 1 January 2008,

— with a nominal capacity of >6 tonnes per hour but equal or less than 16 tonnes per hour, provided the permit foresees the daily average values do not exceed 400 mg/m3 and this until 1 January 2010,

— with a nominal capacity of >16 tonnes per hour but < 25 tonnes per hour and which do not produce water discharges, provided that the permit foresees the daily average values do not exceed 400 mg/m3 and this until 1 January 2008.

Until 1 January 2008, exemptions for dust may be authorised by the competent authority for existing incinerating plants, provided that the permit foresees the daily average values do not exceed 20 mg/m3.

(b) Half-hourly average values

	(100%) A	*(97%) B*
Total dust	30 mg/m^3	10 mg/m^3
Gaseous and vaporous organic substances, expressed as total organic carbon	20 mg/m^3	10 mg/m^3
Hydrogen chloride (HC1)	60 mg/m^3	10 mg/m^3
Hydrogen fluoride (HF)	4 mg/m^3	2 mg/m^3
Sulphur dioxide (SO_2)	200 mg/m^3	50 mg/m^3
Nitrogen monoxide (NO) and nitrogen dioxide (NO_2) expressed as nitrogen dioxide for existing incineration plants with a nominal capacity exceeding 6 tonnes per hour or new incineration plants	400 mg/m^3(*)	200 mg/m^3

(*) until 1 January 2007 and without prejudice to relevant (Community) legislation the emission limit value for NO_x does not apply to plants only incinerating hazardous waste.

Until 1 January 2010, exemptions for NO_x may be authorised by the competent authority for existing incineration plants with a nominal capacity between 6 and 16 tonnes per hour, provided the half-hourly average value does not exceed 600 mg/m3 for column A or 400 mg/m3 for column B.

(c) All average values over the sample period of a minimum of 30 minutes and a maximum of 8 hours

Cadmium and its compounds, expressed as cadmium (Cd)	total 0.05 mg/m^3	total 0.1 mg/m^3(*)
Thallium and its compounds, expressed as thallium (T1)		
Mercury and its compounds, expressed as mercury (Hg)	0.05 mg/m^3	0.1 mg/m^3 (*)
Antimony and its compounds, expressed as antimony (Sb)	total 0.5 mg/m^3	total 1 mg/m^3 (*)
Arsenic and its compounds, expressed as arsenic (As)		
Lead and its compounds, expressed as lead (Pb)		
Chromium and its compounds, expressed as chromium (Cr)		
Cobalt and its compounds, expressed as cobalt (Co)		
Copper and its compounds, expressed as copper (Cu)		

Manganese and its compounds, expressed as manganese (MN)		
Nickel and its compounds, expressed as nickel (Ni)		
Vanadium and its compounds, expressed as vanadium (V)		

(*) Until 1 January 2007 average values for existing plants for which the permit to operate has been granted before 31 December 1996, and which incinerate hazardous waste only.

These average values cover also gaseous and the vapour forms of the relevant heavy metal emissions as well as their compounds.

(d) Average values shall be measured over a sample period of a minimum of 6 hours and a maximum of 8 hours. The emission limit value refers to the total concentration of dioxins and furans calculated using the concept of toxic equivalence in accordance with Annex I.

Dioxins and furans	0,1 ng/m^3

(e) The following emission limit values of carbon monoxide (CO) concentrations shall not be exceeded in the combustion gases (excluding the start-up and shut-down phase):
— 50 milligrams/m^3 of combustion gas determined as daily average value;
— 150 milligrams/m^3 of combustion gas of at least 95 % of all measurements determined as 10-minute average values or 100 mg/m^3 of combustion gas of all measurements determined as half-hourly average values taken in any 24-hour period.

Exemptions may be authorised by the competent authority for incineration plants using fluidised bed technology, provided that the permit foresees an emission limit value for carbon monoxide (CO) of not more than 100 mg/m^3 as an hourly average value.

(f) Member States may lay down rules governing the exemptions provided for in this Annex.

ANNEX VI
FORMULA TO CALCULATE THE EMISSION CONCENTRATION AT THE STANDARD PERCENTAGE OXYGEN CONCENTRATION

$$E_S = \frac{21 - O_S}{21 - O_M} \times E_M$$

E_S = calculated emission concentration at the standard percentage oxygen concentration
E_M = measured emission concentration
O_S = standard oxygen concentration
O_M = measured oxygen concentration

COUNCIL DIRECTIVE 2001/80/EC

of 23 October 2001

ON THE LIMITATION OF EMISSIONS OF CERTAIN POLLUTANTS INTO THE AIR FROM LARGE COMBUSTION PLANTS

THE EUROPEAN PARLIAMENT AND THE COUNCIL OF THE EUROPEAN UNION,

Having regard to the Treaty establishing the European Community, and in particular Article 175 thereof,

Having regard to the proposal from the Commission,

Having regard to the Opinion of the Economic and Social Committee,

Having consulted the Committee of the Regions,

Acting in accordance with the procedure laid down in Article 251 of the Treaty, in the light of the joint text approved by the Conciliation Committee on 2 August 2001,

Whereas:

(1) Council Directive 88/609/EEC of 24 November 1988 on the limitation of emissions of certain pollutants into the air from large combustion plants has contributed to the reduction and control of atmospheric emissions from large combustion plants. It should be recast in the interests of clarity.

(2) The Fifth Environmental Action Programme sets as objectives that the critical loads and levels of certain acidifying pollutants such as sulphur dioxide (SO_2) and nitrogen oxides (NO_x) should not be exceeded at any time and, as regards air quality, that all people should be effectively protected against recognised health risks from air pollution.

(3) All Member States have signed the Gothenburg Protocol of 1 December 1999 to the 1979 Convention of the United Nations Economic Commission for Europe (UNECE) on long-range transboundary air pollution to abate acidification, eutrophication and ground-level ozone, which includes, inter alia, commitments to reduce emissions of sulphur dioxide and oxides of nitrogen.

(4) The Commission has published a Communication on a Community strategy to combat acidification in which the revision of Directive 88/609/EEC was identified as being an integral component of that strategy with the long term aim of reducing emissions of sulphur dioxide and nitrogen oxides sufficiently to bring depositions and concentrations down to levels below the critical loads and levels.

(5) In accordance with the principle of subsidiarity as set out in Article 5 of the Treaty, the objective of reducing acidifying emissions from large combustion plants cannot be sufficiently achieved by the Member States acting individually and unconcerted action offers no guarantee of achieving the desired objective; in view of the need to reduce acidifying emissions across the Community, it is more effective to take action at Community level.

(6) Existing large combustion plants are significant contributors to emissions of sulphur dioxide and nitrogen oxides in the Community and it is necessary to reduce these emissions. It is therefore necessary to adapt the approach to the different characteristics of the large combustion plant sector in the Member States.

(7) Council Directive 96/61/EC of 24 September 1996 concerning integrated pollution prevention and control sets out an integrated approach to pollution prevention and control in which all the aspects of an installation's environmental performance are considered in an integrated manner; combustion installations with a rated thermal input

exceeding 50 MW are included within the scope of that Directive; pursuant to Article 15(3) of that Directive an inventory of the principal emissions and sources responsible is to be published every three years by the Commission on the basis of data supplied by the Member States. Pursuant to Article 18 of that Directive, acting on a proposal from the Commission, the Council will set emission limit values in accordance with the procedures laid down in the Treaty for which the need for Community action has been identified, on the basis, in particular, of the exchange of information provided for in Article 16 of that Directive.

(8) Compliance with the emission limit values laid down by this Directive should be regarded as a necessary but not sufficient condition for compliance with the requirements of Directive 96/61/EC regarding the use of best available techniques. Such compliance may involve more stringent emission limit values, emission limit values for other substances and other media, and other appropriate conditions.

(9) Industrial experience in the implementation of techniques for the reduction of polluting emissions from large combustion plants has been acquired over a period of 15 years.

(10) The Protocol on heavy metals to the UNECE Convention on long-range transboundary air pollution recommends the adoption of measures to reduce heavy metals emitted by certain installations. It is known that benefits from reducing dust emissions by dust abatement equipment will provide benefits on reducing particle-bound heavy metal emissions.

(11) Installations for the production of electricity represent an important part of the large combustion plant sector.

(12) Directive 96/92/EC of the European Parliament and of the Council of 19 December 1996 concerning common rules for the internal market in electricity is intended inter alia to have the effect of distributing new production capacity among new arrivals in the sector.

(13) The Community is committed to a reduction of carbon dioxide emissions. Where it is feasible the combined production of heat and electricity represents a valuable opportunity for significantly improving overall efficiency in fuel use.

(14) A significant increase in the use of natural gas for producing electricity is already underway and is likely to continue, in particular through the use of gas turbines.

(15) In view of the increase in energy production from biomass, specific emission standards for this fuel are justified.

(16) The Council Resolution of 24 February 1997 on a Community strategy for waste management emphasises the need for promoting waste recovery and states that appropriate emission standards should apply to the operation of facilities in which waste is incinerated in order to ensure a high level of protection for the environment.

(17) Industrial experience has been gained concerning techniques and equipment for the measurement of the principal pollutants emitted by large combustion plants; the European Committee for Standardisation (CEN) has undertaken work with the aim of providing a framework securing comparable measurement results within the Community and guaranteeing a high level of quality of such measurements.

(18) There is a need to improve knowledge concerning the emission of the principal pollutants from large combustion plants. In order to be genuinely representative of the level of pollution of an installation, such information should also be associated with knowledge concerning its energy consumption.

(19) This Directive is without prejudice to the time limits within which the Member States must transpose and implement Directive 88/609/EEC,

HAVE ADOPTED THIS DIRECTIVE:

Article 1

This Directive shall apply to combustion plants, the rated thermal input of which is equal to or greater than 50 MW, irrespective of the type of fuel used (solid, liquid or gaseous).

Article 2

For the purpose of this Directive:

(1) "emission" means the discharge of substances from the combustion plant into the air;

(2) "waste gases" means gaseous discharges containing solid, liquid or gaseous emissions; their volumetric flow rates shall be expressed in cubic metres per hour at standard temperature (273 K) and pressure (101,3 kPa) after correction for the water vapour content, hereinafter referred to as (Nm3/h);

(3) "emission limit value" means the permissible quantity of a substance contained in the waste gases from the combustion plant which may be discharged into the air during a given period; it shall be calculated in terms of mass per volume of the waste gases expressed in mg/Nm3, assuming an oxygen content by volume in the waste gas of 3 % in the case of liquid and gaseous fuels, 6 % in the case of solid fuels and 15 % in the case of gas turbines;

(4) "rate of desulphurisation" means the ratio of the quantity of sulphur which is not emitted into the air at the combustion plant site over a given period to the quantity of sulphur contained in the fuel which is introduced into the combustion plant facilities and which is used over the same period;

(5) "operator" means any natural or legal person who operates the combustion plant, or who has or has been delegated decisive economic power over it;

(6) "fuel" means any solid, liquid or gaseous combustible material used to fire the combustion plant with the exception of waste covered by Council Directive 89/369/EEC of 8 June 1989 on the prevention of air pollution from new municipal waste incineration plants, Council Directive 89/429/EEC of 21 June 1989 on the reduction of air pollution from existing municipal waste incineration plants, and Council Directive 94/67/EC of 16 December 1994 concerning the incineration of hazardous waste or any subsequent Community act repealing and replacing one or more of these Directives;

(7) "combustion plant" means any technical apparatus in which fuels are oxidised in order to use the heat thus generated.

This Directive shall apply only to combustion plants designed for production of energy with the exception of those which make direct use of the products of combustion in manufacturing processes. In particular, this Directive shall not apply to the following combustion plants:

(a) plants in which the products of combustion are used for the direct heating, drying, or any other treatment of objects or materials e.g. reheating furnaces, furnaces for heat treatment;

(b) post-combustion plants i.e. any technical apparatus designed to purify the waste gases by combustion which is not operated as an independent combustion plant;

(c) facilities for the regeneration of catalytic cracking catalysts;

(d) facilities for the conversion of hydrogen sulphide into sulphur;

(e) reactors used in the chemical industry;

(f) coke battery furnaces;

(g) cowpers;

(h) any technical apparatus used in the propulsion of a vehicle, ship or aircraft;

(i) gas turbines used on offshore platforms;

(j) gas turbines licensed before 27 November 2002 or which in the view of the competent authority are the subject of a full request for a licence before 27 November 2002 provided that the plant is put into operation no later than 27 November 2003 without prejudice to Article 7(1) and Annex VIII(A) and (B);

Plants powered by diesel, petrol and gas engines shall not be covered by this Directive.

Where two or more separate new plants are installed in such a way that, taking technical and economic factors into account, their waste gases could, in the judgement of the competent authorities, be discharged through a common stack, the combination formed by such plants shall be regarded as a single unit;

(8) "multi-fuel firing unit" means any combustion plant which may be fired simultaneously or alternately by two or more types of fuel;
(9) "new plant" means any combustion plant for which the original construction licence or, in the absence of such a procedure, the original operating licence was granted on or after 1 July 1987;
(10) "existing plant" means any combustion plant for which the original construction licence or, in the absence of such a procedure, the original operating licence was granted before 1 July 1987;
(11) "biomass" means products consisting of any whole or part of a vegetable matter from agriculture or forestry which can be used as a fuel for the purpose of recovering its energy content and the following waste used as a fuel:
   (a) vegetable waste from agriculture and forestry;
   (b) vegetable waste from the food processing industry, if the heat generated is recovered;
   (c) fibrous vegetable waste from virgin pulp production and from production of paper from pulp, if it is co-incinerated at the place of production and the heat generated is recovered;
   (d) cork waste;
   (e) wood waste with the exception of wood waste which may contain halogenated organic compounds or heavy metals as a result of treatment with wood preservatives or coating, and which includes in particular such wood waste originating from construction and demolition waste;
(12) "gas turbine" means any rotating machine which converts thermal energy into mechanical work, consisting mainly of a compressor, a thermal device in which fuel is oxidised in order to heat the working fluid, and a turbine.
(13) "Outermost Regions" means the French Overseas Departments with regard to France, the Azores and Madeira with regard to Portugal and the Canary Islands with regard to Spain.

Article 3

1. Not later than 1 July 1990 Member States shall draw up appropriate programmes for the progressive reduction of total annual emissions from existing plants. The programmes shall set out the timetables and the implementing procedures.

2. In accordance with the programmes mentioned in paragraph 1, Member States shall continue to comply with the emission ceilings and with the corresponding percentage reductions laid down for sulphur dioxide in Annex I, columns 1 to 6, and for oxides of nitrogen in Annex II, columns 1 to 4, by the dates specified in those Annexes, until the implementation of the provisions of Article 4 that apply to existing plants.

3. When the programmes are being carried out, Member States shall also determine the total annual emissions in accordance with Annex VIII(C).

4. If a substantial and unexpected change in energy demand or in the availability of certain fuels or certain generating installations creates serious technical difficulties for the implementation by a Member State of its programme drawn up under paragraph 1, the Commission shall, at the request of the Member State concerned and taking into account the terms of the request, take a decision to modify, for that Member State, the emission ceilings and/or the dates set out in Annexes I and II and communicate its decision to the Council and to the Member States. Any Member State may within three months refer the decision of the Commission to the Council. The Council, acting by a qualified majority, may within three months take a different decision.

Article 4

1. Without prejudice to Article 17 Member States shall take appropriate measures to ensure that all licences for the construction or, in the absence of such a procedure, for the operation of new plants which in the view of the competent authority are the subject of a full request for a

licence before 27 November 2002, provided that the plant is put into operation no later than 27 November 2003 contain conditions relating to compliance with the emission limit values laid down in part A of Annexes III to VII in respect of sulphur dioxide, nitrogen oxides and dust.

2. Member States shall take appropriate measures to ensure that all licences for the construction or, in the absence of such a procedure, for the operation of new plants, other than those covered by paragraph 1, contain conditions relating to compliance with the emission limit values laid down in part B of Annexes III to VII in respect of sulphur dioxide, nitrogen oxides and dust.

3. Without prejudice to Directive 96/61/EC and Council Directive 96/62/EC of 27 September 1996 on ambient air quality assessment and management, Member States shall, by 1 January 2008 at the latest, achieve significant emission reductions by:

(a) taking appropriate measures to ensure that all licences for the operation of existing plants contain conditions relating to compliance with the emission limit values established for new plants referred to in paragraph 1; or

(b) ensuring that existing plants are subject to the national emission reduction plan referred to in paragraph 6;

and, where appropriate, applying Articles 5, 7 and 8.

4. Without prejudice to Directives 96/61/EC and 96/62/EC, existing plants may be exempted from compliance with the emission limit values referred to in paragraph 3 and from their inclusion in the national emission reduction plan on the following conditions:

(a) the operator of an existing plant undertakes, in a written declaration submitted by 30 June 2004 at the latest to the competent authority, not to operate the plant for more than 20000 operational hours starting from 1 January 2008 and ending no later than 31 December 2015;

(b) the operator is required to submit each year to the competent authority a record of the used and unused time allowed for the plants' remaining operational life.

5. Member States may require compliance with emission limit values and time limits for implementation which are more stringent than those set out in paragraphs 1, 2, 3 and 4 and in Article 10. They may include other pollutants, and they may impose additional requirements or adaptation of plant to technical progress.

6. Member States may, without prejudice to this Directive and Directive 96/61/EC, and taking into consideration the costs and benefits as well as their obligations under Directive 2001/81/EC of the European Parliament and of the Council of 23 October 2001 on national emission ceilings for certain atmospheric pollutants and Directive 96/62/EC, define and implement a national emission reduction plan for existing plants, taking into account, inter alia, compliance with the ceilings as set out in Annexes I and II.

The national emission reduction plan shall reduce the total annual emissions of nitrogen oxides (NO_x), sulphur dioxide (SO_2) and dust from existing plants to the levels that would have been achieved by applying the emission limit values referred to in paragraph 3 to the existing plants in operation in the year 2000, (including those existing plants undergoing a rehabilitation plan in 2000, approved by the competent authority, to meet emission reductions required by national legislation) on the basis of each plant's actual annual operating time, fuel used and thermal input, averaged over the last five years of operation up to and including 2000.

The closure of a plant included in the national emission reduction plan shall not result in an increase in the total annual emissions from the remaining plants covered by the plan.

The national emission reduction plan may under no circumstances exempt a plant from the provisions laid down in relevant Community legislation, including inter alia Directive 96/61/EC.

The following conditions shall apply to national emission reduction plans:

(a) the plan shall comprise objectives and related targets, measures and timetables for reaching these objectives and targets, and a monitoring mechanism;

(b) Member States shall communicate their national emission reduction plan to the Commission no later than 27 November 2003;

(c) within six months of the communication referred to in point (b) the Commission shall evaluate whether or not the plan meets the requirements of this paragraph. When the Commission considers that this is not the case, it shall inform the Member State and within the subsequent three months the Member State shall communicate any measures it has taken in order to ensure that the requirements of this paragraph are met;

(d) the Commission shall, no later than 27 November 2002, develop guidelines to assist Member States in the preparation of their plans.

7. Not later than 31 December 2004 and in the light of progress towards protecting human health and attaining the Community's environmental objectives for acidification and for air quality pursuant to Directive 96/62/EC, the Commission shall submit a report to the European Parliament and the Council in which it shall assess:

(a) the need for further measures;

(b) the amounts of heavy metals emitted by large combustion plants;

(c) the cost-effectiveness and costs and advantages of further emission reductions in the combustion plants sector in Member States compared to other sectors;

(d) the technical and economic feasibility of such emission reductions;

(e) the effects of both the standards set for the large combustion plants sector including the provisions for indigenous solid fuels, and the competition situation in the energy market, on the environment and the internal market;

(f) any national emission reduction plans provided by Member States in accordance with paragraph 6.

The Commission shall include in its report an appropriate proposal of possible end dates or of lower limit values for the derogation contained in footnote 2 to Annex VI A.

8. The report referred to in paragraph 7 shall, as appropriate, be accompanied by related proposals, having regard to Directive 96/61/EC.

Article 5

By way of derogation from Annex III:

(1) Plants, of a rated thermal input equal to or greater than 400 MW, which do not operate more than the following numbers of hours a year (rolling average over a period of five years),

— until 31 December 2015, 2000 hours;

— from 1 January 2016, 1500 hours;

shall be subject to a limit value for sulphur dioxide emissions of 800 mg/Nm^3.

This provision shall not apply to new plants for which the licence is granted pursuant to Article 4(2).

(2) Until 31 December 1999, the Kingdom of Spain may authorise new power plants with a rated thermal input equal to or greater than 500 MW burning indigenous or imported solid fuels, commissioned before the end of 2005 and complying with the following requirements:

(a) in the case of imported solid fuels, a sulphur dioxide emission limit value of 800 mg/Nm3;

(b) in the case of indigenous solid fuels, at least a 60 % rate of desulphurisation,

provided that the total authorised capacity of such plants to which this derogation applies does not exceed:

— 2000 MWe in the case of plants burning indigenous solid fuels;

— in the case of plants burning imported solid fuels either 7500 or 50 % of all the new capacity of all plants burning solid fuels authorised up to 31 December 1999, whichever is the lower.

Article 6

In the case of new plants for which the licence is granted pursuant to Article 4(2) or plants covered by Article 10, Member States shall ensure that the technical and economic feasibility of providing for the combined generation of heat and power is examined. Where this feasibility is confirmed, bearing in mind the market and the distribution situation, installations shall be developed accordingly.

Article 7

1. Member States shall ensure that provision is made in the licences or permits referred to in Article 4 for procedures relating to malfunction or breakdown of the abatement equipment. In case of a breakdown the competent authority shall in particular require the operator to reduce or close down operations if a return to normal operation is not achieved within 24 hours, or to operate the plant using low polluting fuels. In any case the competent authority shall be notified within 48 hours. In no circumstances shall the cumulative duration of unabated operation in any twelve-month period exceed 120 hours. The competent authority may allow exceptions to the limits of 24 hours and 120 hours above in cases where, in their judgement:
(a) there is an overriding need to maintain energy supplies, or
(b) the plant with the breakdown would be replaced for a limited period by another plant which would cause an overall increase in emissions.

2. The competent authority may allow a suspension for a maximum of six months from the obligation to comply with the emission limit values provided for in Article 4 for sulphur dioxide in respect of a plant which to this end normally uses low-sulphur fuel, in cases where the operator is unable to comply with these limit values because of an interruption in the supply of low-sulphur fuel resulting from a serious shortage. The Commission shall immediately be informed of such cases.

3. The competent authority may allow a derogation from the obligation to comply with the emission limit values provided for in Article 4 in cases where a plant which normally uses only gaseous fuel, and which would otherwise need to be equipped with a waste gas purification facility, has to resort exceptionally, and for a period not exceeding 10 days except where there is an overriding need to maintain energy supplies, to the use of other fuels because of a sudden interruption in the supply of gas. The competent authority shall immediately be informed of each specific case as it arises. Member States shall inform the Commission immediately of the cases referred to in this paragraph.

Article 8

1. In the case of plants with a multi-firing unit involving the simultaneous use of two or more fuels, when granting the licence referred to in Articles 4(1) or 4(2), and in the case of such plants covered by Articles 4(3) or 10, the competent authority shall set the emission limit values as follows:
(a) firstly by taking the emission limit value relevant for each individual fuel and pollutant corresponding to the rated thermal input of the combustion plant as given in Annexes III to VII,
(b) secondly by determining fuel-weighted emission limit values, which are obtained by multiplying the above individual emission limit value by the thermal input delivered by each fuel, the product of multiplication being divided by the sum of the thermal inputs delivered by all fuels,
(c) thirdly by aggregating the fuel-weighted limit values.

2. In multi-firing units using the distillation and conversion residues from crude-oil refining for own consumption, alone or with other fuels, the provisions for the fuel with the highest emission limit value (determinative fuel) shall apply, notwithstanding paragraph 1 above, if during the operation of the combustion plant the proportion contributed by that fuel to the sum of the thermal inputs delivered by all fuels is at least 50 %.

Where the proportion of the determinative fuel is lower than 50 %, the emission limit value is determined on a pro rata basis of the heat input supplied by the individual fuels in relation to the sum of the thermal inputs delivered by all fuels as follows:

(a) firstly by taking the emission limit value relevant for each individual fuel and pollutant corresponding to the rated heat input of the combustion plant as given in Annexes III to VII,

(b) secondly by calculating the emission limit value of the determinative fuel (fuel with the highest emission limit value according to Annexes III to VII and, in the case of two fuels having the same emission limit value, the fuel with the higher thermal input); this value is obtained by multiplying the emission limit value laid down in Annexes III to VII for that fuel by a factor of two, and subtracting from this product the emission limit value of the fuel with the lowest emission limit value,

(c) thirdly by determining the fuel-weighted emission limit values, which are obtained by multiplying the calculated fuel emission limit value by the thermal input of the determinative fuel and the other individual emission limit values by the thermal input delivered by each fuel, the product of multiplication being divided by the sum of the thermal inputs delivered by all fuels,

(d) fourthly by aggregating the fuel-weighted emission limit values.

3. As an alternative to paragraph 2, the following average emission limit values for sulphur dioxide may be applied (irrespective of the fuel combination used):

(a) for plants referred to in Article 4(1) and (3): 1000 mg/Nm^3, averaged over all such plants within the refinery;

(b) for new plants referred to in Article 4(2): 600 mg/Nm^3, averaged over all such plants within the refinery, with the exception of gas turbines.

The competent authorities shall ensure that the application of this provision does not lead to an increase in emissions from existing plants.

4. In the case of plants with a multi-firing unit involving the alternative use of two or more fuels, when granting the licence referred to in Article 4(1) and (2), and in the case of such plants covered by Articles 4(3) or 10, the emission limit values set out in Annexes III to VII corresponding to each fuel used shall be applied.

Article 9

Waste gases from combustion plants shall be discharged in controlled fashion by means of a stack. The licence referred to in Article 4 and licences for combustion plants covered by Article 10 shall lay down the discharge conditions. The competent authority shall in particular ensure that the stack height is calculated in such a way as to safeguard health and the environment.

[Article 9a][1]

[1. Member States shall ensure that operators of all combustion plants with a rated electrical output of 300 megawatts or more for which the original construction licence or, in the absence of such a procedure, the original operating licence is granted after the entry into force of Directive 2009/31/EC of the European Parliament and of the Council of 23 April 2009 on the geological storage of carbon dioxide, have assessed whether the following conditions are met:

— suitable storage sites are available,

— transport facilities are technically and economically feasible,

— it is technically and economically feasible to retrofit for CO_2 capture.

2. If the conditions in paragraph 1 are met, the competent authority shall ensure that suitable space on the installation site for the equipment necessary to capture and compress CO_2 is set aside. The competent authority shall determine whether the conditions are met on the basis of the assessment referred to in paragraph 1 and other available information, particularly concerning the protection of the environment and human health.][1]

Amendment

1 Inserted by Directive 2009/31/EC of the European Parliament and of the Council of 23 April 2009 on the geological storage of carbon dioxide and amending Council Directive 85/337/EEC, European Parliament and Council Directives 2000/60/EC, 2001/80/EC, 2004/35/EC, 2006/12/EC, 2008/1/EC and Regulation (EC) No 1013/2006, Article 1, Annex, para 4.8.1.

Article 10

Where a combustion plant is extended by at least 50 MW, the emission limit values as set in part B of Annexes III to VII shall apply to the new part of the plant and shall be fixed in relation to the thermal capacity of the entire plant. This provision shall not apply in the cases referred to in Article 8(2) and (3).

Where the operator of a combustion plant is envisaging a change according to Articles 2(10)(b) and 12(2) of Directive 96/61/EC, the emission limit values as set out in part B of Annexes III to VII in respect of sulphur dioxide, nitrogen oxides and dust shall apply.

Article 11

In the case of construction of combustion plants which are likely to have significant effects on the environment in another Member State, the Member States shall ensure that all appropriate information and consultation takes place, in accordance with Article 7 of Council Directive 85/337/EEC of 27 June 1985 on the assessment of the effects of certain public and private projects on the environment.

Article 12

Member States shall take the necessary measures to ensure the monitoring, in accordance with Annex VIII(A), of emissions from the combustion plants covered by this Directive and of all other values required for the implementation of this Directive. Member States may require that such monitoring shall be carried out at the operator's expense.

Article 13

Member States shall take appropriate measures to ensure that the operator informs the competent authorities within reasonable time limits about the results of the continuous measurements, the checking of the measuring equipment, the individual measurements and all other measurements carried out in order to assess compliance with this Directive.

Article 14

1. In the event of continuous measurements, the emission limit values set out in part A of Annexes III to VII shall be regarded as having been complied with if the evaluation of the results indicates, for operating hours within a calendar year, that:

(a) none of the calendar monthly mean values exceeds the emission limit values; and

(b) in the case of:

 (i) sulphur dioxide and dust: 97 % of all the 48 hourly mean values do not exceed 110 % of the emission limit values,

 (ii) nitrogen oxides: 95 % of all the 48 hourly mean values do not exceed 110 % of the emission limit values.

The periods referred to in Article 7 as well as start-up and shut-down periods shall be disregarded.

2. In cases where only discontinuous measurements or other appropriate procedures for determination are required, the emission limit values set out in Annexes III to VII shall be regarded as having been complied with if the results of each of the series of measurements or of the other procedures defined and determined according to the rules laid down by the competent authorities do not exceed the emission limit values.

3. In the cases referred to in Article 5(2), the rates of desulphurisation shall be regarded as having been complied with if the evaluation of measurements carried out pursuant to Annex VIII, point A.3, indicates that all of the calendar monthly mean values or all of the rolling monthly mean values achieve the required desulphurisation rates.

The periods referred to in Article 7 as well as start-up and shut-down periods shall be disregarded.

4. For new plants for which the licence is granted pursuant to Article 4(2), the emission limit values shall be regarded, for operating hours within a calendar year, as complied with if:
(a) no validated daily average value exceeds the relevant figures set out in part B of Annexes III to VII, and
(b) 95 % of all the validated hourly average values over the year do not exceed 200 % of the relevant figures set out in part B of Annexes III to VII.
The "validated average values" are determined as set out in point A.6 of Annex VIII.

The periods referred to in Article 7 as well as start up and shut down periods shall be disregarded.

Article 15

1. Member States shall, not later than 31 December 1990, inform the Commission of the programmes drawn up in accordance with Article 3(1).

At the latest one year after the end of the different phases for reduction of emissions from existing plants, the Member States shall forward to the Commission a summary report on the results of the implementation of the programmes.

An intermediate report is required as well in the middle of each phase.

2. The reports referred to in paragraph 1 shall provide an overall view of:
(a) all the combustion plants covered by this Directive,
(b) emissions of sulphur dioxide, and oxides of nitrogen expressed in tonnes per annum and as concentrations of these substances in the waste gases,
(c) measures already taken or envisaged with a view to reducing emissions, and of changes in the choice of fuel used,
(d) changes in the method of operation already made or envisaged,
(e) definitive closures of combustion plants already effected or envisaged, and
(f) where appropriate, the emission limit values imposed in the programmes in respect of existing plants.
When determining the annual emissions and concentrations of pollutants in the waste gases, Member States shall take account of Articles 12, 13 and 14.

3. Member States applying Article 5 or the provisions of the Nota Bene in Annex III or the footnotes in Annex VI.A shall report thereon annually to the Commission.

Article 16

The Member States shall determine the penalties applicable to breaches of the national provisions adopted pursuant to this Directive. The penalties thus provided for shall be effective, proportionate and dissuasive.

Article 17

1. Directive 88/609/EEC shall be repealed with effect from 27 November 2002, without prejudice to paragraph 2 or to the obligations of Member States concerning the time limits for transposition and application of that Directive listed in Annex IX hereto.

2. In the case of new plants licensed before 27 November 2002 as specified in Article 4(1) of this Directive, Article 4(1), Article 5(2), Article 6, Article 15(3), Annexes III, VI, VIII and

point A.2 of Annex IX to Directive 88/609/EEC as amended by Directive 94/66/EC shall remain in effect until 1 January 2008 after which they shall be repealed.

3. References to Directive 88/609/EEC shall be construed as references to this Directive and shall be read in accordance with the correlation table in Annex X hereto.

Article 18

1. Member States shall bring into force the laws, regulations and administrative provisions necessary to comply with this Directive before 27 November 2002. They shall forthwith inform the Commission thereof.

When Member States adopt these provisions, they shall contain a reference to this Directive or shall be accompanied by such reference on the occasion of their official publication. The methods of making such reference shall be laid down by Member States.

2. For existing plant, and for new plant for which a licence is granted pursuant to Article 4(1), the provisions of point A.2 of Annex VIII shall be applied from 27 November 2004.

3. Member States shall communicate to the Commission the texts of the provisions of national law which they adopt in the field covered by this Directive.

Article 19

This Directive shall enter into force on the day of its publication in the Official Journal of the European Communities.

Article 20

This Directive is addressed to the Member States.

ANNEX I
CEILINGS AND REDUCTION TARGETS FOR EMISSION OF SO_2 FROM EXISTING PLANTS[(1)(2)]

Member State	0	1	2	3	4	5	6	7	8	9
	SO_2 emissions by large combustion plants 1980 ktonnes	Emission ceiling (ktonnes/year)			% reduction over 1980 emissions			% reduction over adjusted 1980 emissions		
		Phase 1	Phase 2	Phase 3	Phase 1	Phase 2	Phase 3	Phase 1	Phase 2	Phase 3
		1993	1998	2003	1993	1998	2003	1993	1998	2003
Belgium	530	318	212	159	–40	–60	–70	–40	–60	–70
[Bulgaria	1 734	1 410	1 300	1 190	–19	–25	–31	–19	–25	–31][1]
[Czech Republic	1 408	919	303	155	–35	–79	–89	–35	–79	–89][2]
Denmark	323	213	141	106	–34	–56	–67	–40	–60	–70
Germany	2 225	1 335	890	668	–40	–60	–70	–40	–60	–70
[Estonia	240	123	91	76	–49	–62	–68	–49	–62	–68][2]
Greece	303	320	320	320	+6	+6	+6	–45	–45	–45
Spain	2 290	2 290	1 730	1 440	0	–24	–37	–21	–40	–50
France	1 910	1 146	764	573	–40	–60	–70	–40	–60	–70
Ireland	99	124	124	124	+25	+25	+25	–29	–29	–29
Italy	2 450	1 800	1 500	900	–27	–39	–63	–40	–50	–70
[Cyprus	17	29	32	34	+71	+88	+100	+71	+88	+100
Latvia	60	40	30	25	–30	–50	–60	–30	–50	–60
Lithuania	163	52	64	75	–68	–61	–54	–68	–61	–54][2]
Luxembourg	3	1,8	1,5	1,5	–40	–50	–60	–40	–50	–50
[Hungary	720	429	448	360	–40	–38	–50	–40	–38	–50
Malta	12	13	17	14	+14	+51	+17	+14	+51	+17][2]
Netherlands	299	180	120	90	–40	–60	–70	–40	–60	–70
Portugal	115	232	270	206	+102	+135	+79	–25	–13	–34
[Poland	2 087	1 454	1 176	1 110	–30	–44	–47	–30	–44	–47][2]

Member State	*0*	*1*	*2*	*3*	*4*	*5*	*6*	*7*	*8*	*9*
	SO_2 emissions by large combustion plants 1980 ktonnes	*Emission ceiling (ktonnes/year)*			*% reduction over 1980 emissions*			*% reduction over adjusted 1980 emissions*		
		Phase 1	*Phase 2*	*Phase 3*	*Phase 1*	*Phase 2*	*Phase 3*	*Phase 1*	*Phase 2*	*Phase 3*
		1993	*1998*	*2003*	*1993*	*1998*	*2003*	*1993*	*1998*	*2003*
[Romania	561	692	503	518	23	–10	–8	23	–10	–8][1]
[Slovenia	125	122	98	49	–2	–22	–61	–2	–22	–61
Slovakia	450	177	124	86	–60	–72	–81	–60	–72	–81][2]
United Kingdom	3 883	3 106	2 330	1 553	–20	–40	–60	–20	–40	–60
Austria	90	54	36	27	–40	–60	–70	–40	–60	–70
Finland	171	102	68	51	–40	–60	–70	–40	–60	–70
Sweden	112	67	45	34	–40	–60	–70	–40	–60	–70

(1) Additional emissions may arise from capacity authorised on or after 1 July 1987.

(2) Emissions coming from combustion plants authorised before 1 July 1987 but not yet in operation before that date and which have not been taken into account in establishing the emission ceilings fixed by this Annex shall either comply with the requirements established by this Directive for new plants or be accounted for in the overall emissions from existing plants that must not exceed the ceilings fixed in this Annex.

Amendments

1 Inserted by Council Directive 2006/105/EC of 20 November 2006 adapting Directives 73/239/EEC, 74/557/EEC and 2002/83/EC in the field of environment, by reason of the accession of Bulgaria and Romania, Article 1, Annex, Pt B, para 2(a).

2 Inserted by the Act concerning the conditions of accession of the Czech Republic, the Republic of Estonia, the Republic of Cyprus, the Republic of Latvia, the Republic of Lithuania, the Republic of Hungary, the Republic of Malta, the Republic of Poland, the Republic of Slovenia and the Slovak Republic and the adjustments to the Treaties on which the European Union is founded, Article 20, Annex II, Pt 16, Ch D, para 2(a).

ANNEX II
CEILINGS AND REDUCTION TARGETS FOR EMISSIONS OF NO_X FROM EXISTING PLANTS[(1)(2)]

Member State	*0*	*1*	*2*	*3*	*4*	*5*	*6*
	NO_X emissions (as NO_2 by large combustion plants 1980 ktonnes	*NO_X emission ceilings (ktonnes/year)*		*% reduction over 1980 emissions*		*% reduction over adjusted 1980 emissions*	
		Phase 1	*Phase 2*	*Phase 1*	*Phase 2*	*Phase 1*	*Phase 2*
		1993[(3)]	*1998*	*1993*[(3)]	*1998*	*1993*[(3)]	*1998*
Belgium	110	88	66	–20	–40	–20	–40
[Bulgaria	155	125	95	–19	–39	–19	–39][1]
[Czech Republic	403	228	113	–43	–72	–43	–72][2]
Denmark	124	121	81	–3	–35	–10	–40
Germany	870	696	522	–20	–40	–20	–40
[Estonia	20	10	12	–52	–40	–52	–40]
Greece	36	70	70	+94	+94	0	0
Spain	366	368	277	+1	–24	–20	–40
France	400	320	240	–20	–40	–20	–40
Ireland	28	50	50	+79	+79	0	0
Italy	580	570	428	–2	–26	–20	–40
[Cyprus	3	5	6	+67	+100	+67	+100
Latvia	10	10	9	–4	–10	–4	–10
Lithuania	21	8	11	–62	–48	–62	–48][2]
Luxembourg	3	2,4	1,8	–20	–40	–20	–40
[Hungary	68	33	34	–51	–49	–51	–49
Malta	1,7	7	2,5	+299	+51	+299	+51][2]
Netherlands	122	98	73	–20	–40	–20	–40
Portugal	23	59	64	+157	+178	–8	0
[Poland	698	426	310	–39	–56	–39	–56][2]

Member State	0	1	2	3	4	5	6
	NO_X emissions (as NO_2 by large combustion plants 1980 ktonnes	*NO_X emission ceilings (ktonnes/year)*		*% reduction over 1980 emissions*		*% reduction over adjusted 1980 emissions*	
		Phase 1	*Phase 2*	*Phase 1*	*Phase 2*	*Phase 1*	*Phase 2*
		1993[(3)]	*1998*	*1993*[(3)]	*1998*	*1993*[(3)]	*1998*
[Romania	135	135	77	–1	–43	–1	–43][1]
[Slovenia	17	15	16	–12	–6	–12	–6
Slovakia	141	85	46	–40	–67	–40	–67][2]
United Kingdom	1 016	864	711	–15	–30	–15	–30
Austria	19	15	11	–20	–40	–20	–40
Finland	81	65	48	–20	–40	–20	–40
Sweden	31	25	19	–20	–40	–20	–40

(1) Additional emissions may arise from capacity authorised on or after 1 July 1987.

(2) Emissions coming from combustion plants authorised before 1 July 1987 but not yet in operation before that date and which have not been taken into account in establishing the emission ceilings fixed by this Annex shall either comply with the requirements established by this Directive for new plants or be accounted for in the overall emissions from existing plants that must not exceed the ceilings fixed in this Annex.

(3) Member States may for technical reasons delay for up to two years the phase 1 date for reduction in NO_x emissions by notifying the Commission within one month of the notification of this Directive.

Amendments

1 Inserted by Council Directive 2006/105/EC of 20 November 2006 adapting Directives 73/239/EEC, 74/557/EEC and 2002/83/EC in the field of environment, by reason of the accession of Bulgaria and Romania, Article 1, Annex, Pt B, para 2(b).

2 Inserted by the Act concerning the conditions of accession of the Czech Republic, the Republic of Estonia, the Republic of Cyprus, the Republic of Latvia, the Republic of Lithuania, the Republic of Hungary, the Republic of Malta, the Republic of Poland, the Republic of Slovenia and the Slovak Republic and the adjustments to the Treaties on which the European Union is founded, Article 20, Annex II, Pt 16, Ch D, para 2(b).

ANNEX III
EMISSION LIMIT VALUES FOR SO_2

Solid fuel

A. SO_2 emission limit values expressed in mg/Nm^3 (O_2 content 6 %) to be applied by new and existing plants pursuant to Article 4(1) and 4(3) respectively:

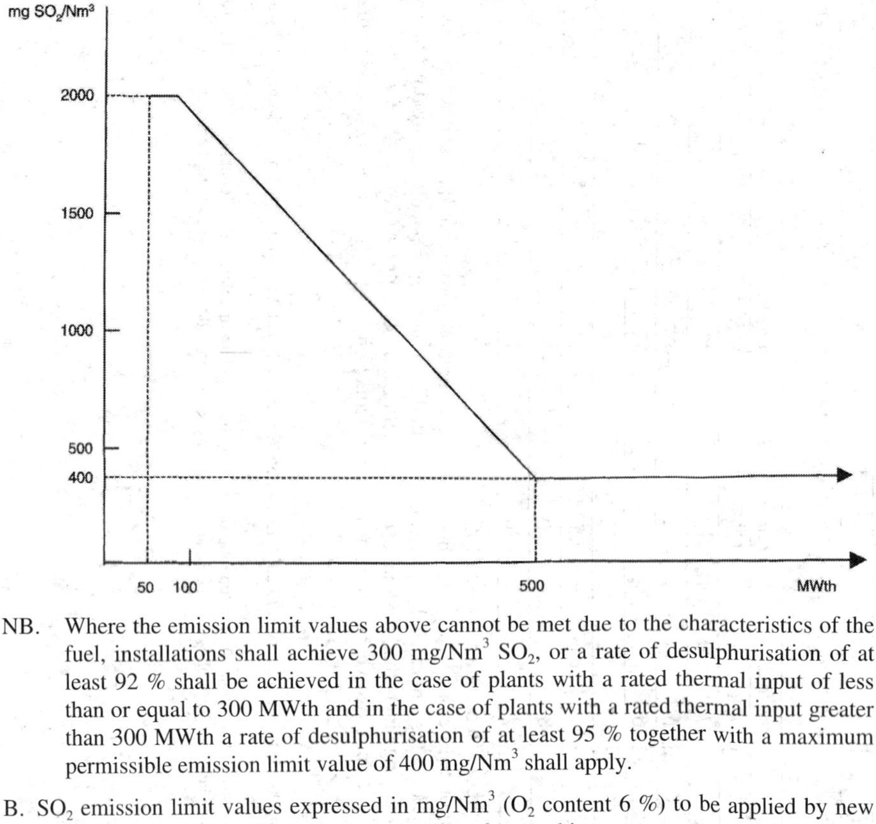

NB. Where the emission limit values above cannot be met due to the characteristics of the fuel, installations shall achieve 300 mg/Nm^3 SO_2, or a rate of desulphurisation of at least 92 % shall be achieved in the case of plants with a rated thermal input of less than or equal to 300 MWth and in the case of plants with a rated thermal input greater than 300 MWth a rate of desulphurisation of at least 95 % together with a maximum permissible emission limit value of 400 mg/Nm^3 shall apply.

B. SO_2 emission limit values expressed in mg/Nm^3 (O_2 content 6 %) to be applied by new plants pursuant to Article 4(2) with the exception of gas turbines.

Type of fuel	*50 to 100 MWth*	*100 to 300 MWth*	*> 300 MWth*
Biomass	200	200	200
General case	850	200[(1)]	200

(*) Except in the case of the "Outermost Regions" where 850 to 200 mg/Nm^3 (linear decrease) shall apply.

ANNEX IV
EMISSION LIMIT VALUES FOR SO_2

Liquid fuels

A. SO_2 emission limit values expressed in mg/Nm^3 (O_2 content 3 %) to be applied by new and existing plants pursuant to Article 4(1) and 4(3), respectively:

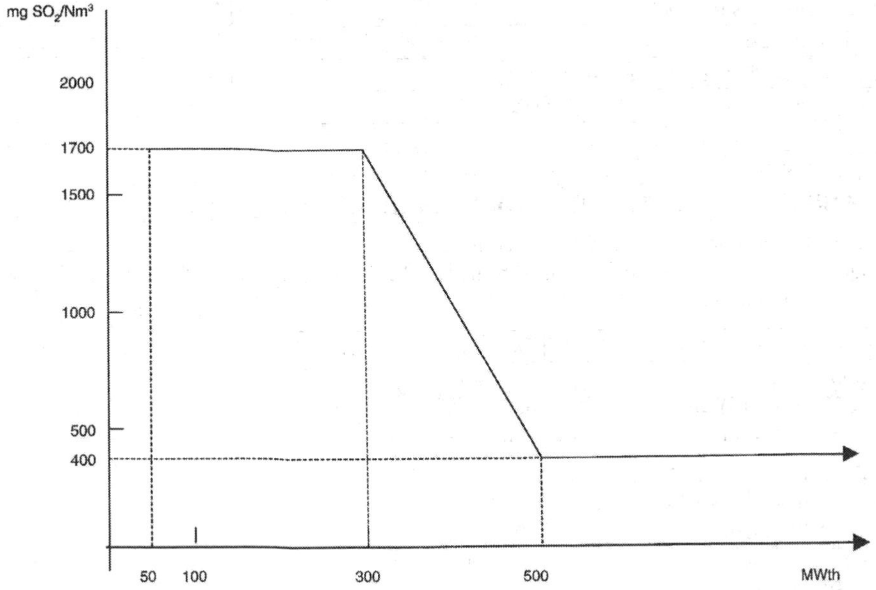

B. SO_2 emission limit values expressed in mg/Nm^3 (O_2 content 3 %) to be applied by new plants pursuant to Article 4(2) with the exception of gas turbines

50 to 100 MWth	100 to 300 MWth	> 300 Mwth
850	400 to 200 (linear decrease)(*)	200

(*) Except in the case of the "Outermost Regions" where 850 to 200 mg/Nm^3 (linear decrease shall apply.

In the case of two installations with a rated thermal input of 250 MWth on Crete and Rhodos to be licensed before 31 December 2007 the emission limit value of 1700 mg/Nm^3 shall apply.

ANNEX V
EMISSION LIMIT VALUES FOR SO_2

Gaseous fuels

A. SO_2 emission limit values expressed in mg/Nm^3 (O_2 content 3 %) to be applied by new and existing plants pursuant to Article 4(1) and 4(3), respectively:

Type of fuel	*Limit values (mg/Nm³)*
Gaseous fuels in general	35
Liquified gas	5
Lower calorific gases from gasification of refinery residues, coke oven gas, blast-furnace gas	800
Gas from gasification of coal	(*)

(*) The Council will fix the emission limit values applicable to such gas at a later stage on the basis of proposals from the Commission to be made in the light of further technical experience

B. SO_2 emission limit values expressed in mg/Nm^3 (O_2 content 3 %) to be applied by new plants pursuant to Article 4(2):

Gaseous fuels in general	35
Liquified gas	5
Low calorific gases from coke oven	400
Low calorific gases from blast furnace	200

ANNEX VI
EMISSION LIMIT VALUES FOR NO_X (MEASURED AS NO_2)

A. NO_x emission limit values expressed in mg/Nm^3 (O_2 content 6 % for solid fuels, 3 % for liquid and gaseous fuels) to be applied by new and existing plants pursuant to Article 4(1) and 4(3), respectively:

Type of fuel	*Limit values*[(1)] *(mg/Nm^3)*
Solid[(2), (3)]:	
50 to 500 MWth	600
> 500 MWth	500
From 1 January 2012	
50 to 500 MWth	600
> 500 MWth	200
Liquid:	
50 to 500 MWth	450
> 500 MWth	400
Gaseous:	
50 to 500 MWth	300
> 500 MWth	200

(1) Except in the case of the "Outermost Regions" where the following values shall apply:
Solid in general: 650;
Solid with < 10% vol comps: 1,300;
Liquid: 450; Gaseous: 350.

(2) Until 31 December 2015 plants of a rated thermal output greater than 500MW, which from 2008 onward do not operate more than 2,000 hours a year (rolling average over a period of five years) shall:
- in the case of plant licensed in accordance with Article 4 (3)(a), be subject to a limit value for nitrogen oxide emissions (measured as NO_2) of 600 mg/Nm^3;
- in the case of plant subject to a national plan under Article 4 (6), have their contributions to the national plan assessed on the basis of a limit value of 600 mg/Nm^3.

From 1 January 2016 such plants, which do not operate more than 1,500 hours a year (rolling average over a period of five years), shall be subject to a limit value for nitrogen oxide emissions (measured as NO_2) of 450 mg/Mn^3.

(3) Until 1 January 2018 in the case of plants that in the 12 month period ending on 1 January 2001 operated on, and continue to operate on, solid fuels whose volatile content is less than 10%, 1,200 mg/Nm^3 shall apply.

B. NO_x emission limit values expressed in mg/Nm^3 to be applied by new plants pursuant to Article 4(2) with the exception of gas turbines

Solid fuels (O_2 content 6 %)

Type of fuel	*50 to 100 MWth*	*100 to 300 MWth*	*> 300 MWth*
Biomass	400	300	200
General case	400	200[(*)]	200

(*) Except in the case of the "Outermost Regions" where 300 mg/Nm^3 (linear decrease) shall apply.

Liquid fuels (O_2 content 3 %)

50 to 100 MWth	*100 to 300 MWth*	*> 300 MWth*
400	200(*)	200

(*) Except in the case of the "Outermost Regions" where 300 mg/Nm^3 (linear decrease) shall apply.

In the case of two installations with a rated thermal input of 250 MWth on Crete and Rhodos to be licensed before 31 December 2007 the emission limit value of 400 mg/Nm^3 shall apply.

Gaseous fuels (O_2 content 3 %)

	50 to 300 MWth	*> 300 MWth*
Natural gas (note 1)	150	100
Other gases	200	200

Gas Turbines

NO_x emission limit values expressed in mg/Nm^3 (O_2 content 15 %) to be applied by a single gas turbine unit pursuant to Article 4(2) (the limit values apply only above 70 % load):

	> 50 MWth (thermal input at ISO conditions)
Natural gas (Note 1)	50 (Note 2)
Liquid fuels (Note 3)	120
Gaseous fuels (other than natural gas)	120

Gas turbines for emergency use that operate less than 500 hours per year are excluded from these limit values. The operator of such plants is required to submit each year to the competent authority a record of such used time.

Note 1: Natural gas is naturally occurring methane with not more than 20 % (by volume) of inerts and other constituents.

Note 2: 75 mg/Nm^3 in the following cases, where the efficiency of the gas turbine is determined at ISO base load conditions:

- gas turbines, used in combined heat and power systems having an overall efficiency greater than 75 %;
- gas turbines used in combined cycle plants having an annual average overall electrical efficiency greater than 55 %;
- gas turbines for mechanical drives.

For single cycle gas turbines not falling into any of the above categories, but having an efficiency greater than 35 % – determined at ISO base load conditions – the emission limit value shall be $50*\eta/35$ where η is the gas turbine efficiency expressed as a percentage (and at ISO base load conditions).

Note 3: This emission limit value only applies to gas turbines firing light and middle distillates.

ANNEX VII
EMISSION LIMIT VALUES FOR DUST

A. Dust emission limit values expressed in mg/Nm^3 (O_2 content 6 % for solid fuels, 3 % for liquid and gaseous fuels) to be applied by new and existing plants pursuant to Article 4(1) and 4(3), respectively:

Type of fuel	*Rated thermal input (MW)*	*Emission limit values (mg/Nm^3)*
Solid	≥ 500	50(2)
	< 500	100
Liquid(1)	all plants	50

Type of fuel	*Rated thermal input (MW)*	*Emission limit values (mg/Nm³)*
Gaseous	all plants	5 as a rule
		10 for blast furnace gas
		50 for gases produced by the steel industry that can be used elsewhere

(1) A limit value of 100 mg/Mn3 may be applied to plants with a rated thermal input of less than 500 MWth burning liquid fuel with an ash content of more than 0.06%.

(2) a limit value of 100 mg/Nm³ may be applied to plants licensed pursuant to Article 4(3) with a rated thermal input greater than or equal to 500 MWth burning solid fuel with a heat content of less than 5,800 kj/kg (net calorific value), a moisture content greater than 45% by weight, a combined moisture and ash content greater than 60% by weight and a calcium oxide content greater than 10%.

B. Dust emission limit values expressed in mg/Nm³ to be applied by new plants, pursuant to Article 4(2) with the exception of gas turbines:

Solid fuels (O_2 content 6 %)

50 to 100 MWth	*> 100 MWth*
50	30

Liquid fuels (O_2 content 3 %)

50 to 100 MWth	*> 100 MWth*
50	30

In the case of two installations with a rated thermal input of 250 MWth on Crete and Rhodos to be licensed before 31 December 2007 the emission limit value of 50 mg/Nm³ shall apply.

Gaseous fuels (O_2 content 3 %)

As a rule	5
For blast furnace gas	10
For gases produced by the steel industry which can be used elsewhere	30

ANNEX VIII
METHODS OF MEASUREMENT OF EMISSIONS

A. PROCEDURES FOR MEASURING AND EVALUATING EMISSIONS FROM COMBUSTION PLANTS.

1. Until 27 November 2004

Concentrations of SO_2, dust, NO_x shall be measured continuously in the case of new plants for which a licence is granted pursuant to Article 4(1) with a rated thermal input of more than 300 MW. However, monitoring of SO_2 and dust may be confined to discontinuous measurements or other appropriate determination procedures in cases where such measurements or procedures, which must be verified and approved by the competent authorities, may be used to obtain concentration.

In the case of new plants for which a licence is granted pursuant to Article 4(1) not covered by the first subparagraph, the competent authorities may require continuous measurements of those three pollutants to be carried out where considered necessary. Where continuous measurements are not required, discontinuous measurements or appropriate determination procedures as approved by the competent authorities shall be used regularly to evaluate the quantity of the above-mentioned substances present in the emissions.

2. From 27 November 2002 and without prejudice to Article 18(2)

Competent authorities shall require continuous measurements of concentrations of SO_2, NO_x, and dust from waste gases from each combustion plant with a rated thermal input of 100 MW or more.

By way of derogation from the first subparagraph, continuous measurements may not be required in the following cases:

— for combustion plants with a life span of less than 10000 operational hours;

— for SO_2 and dust from natural gas burning boilers or from gas turbines firing natural gas;

— for SO_2 from gas turbines or boilers firing oil with known sulphur content in cases where there is no desulphurisation equipment;

— for SO_2 from biomass firing boilers if the operator can prove that the SO_2 emissions can under no circumstances be higher than the prescribed emission limit values.

Where continuous measurements are not required, discontinuous measurements shall be required at least every six months. As an alternative, appropriate determination procedures, which must be verified and approved by the competent authorities, may be used to evaluate the quantity of the above mentioned pollutants present in the emissions. Such procedures shall use relevant CEN standards as soon as they are available. If CEN standards are not available ISO standards, national or international standards which will ensure the provision of data of an equivalent scientific quality shall apply.

3. In the case of plants which must comply with the desulphurisation rates fixed by Article 5(2) and and Annex III, the requirements concerning SO_2 emission measurements established under paragraph 2 of this point shall apply. Moreover, the sulphur content of the fuel which is introduced into the combustion plant facilities must be regularly monitored.

4. The competent authorities shall be informed of substantial changes in the type of fuel used or in the mode of operation of the plant. They shall decide whether the monitoring requirements laid down in paragraph 2 are still adequate or require adaptation.

5. The continuous measurements carried out in compliance with paragraph 2 shall include the relevant process operation parameters of oxygen content, temperature, pressure and water vapour content. The continuous measurement of the water vapour content of the exhaust gases shall not be necessary, provided that the sampled exhaust gas is dried before the emissions are analysed.

Representative measurements, i.e. sampling and analysis, of relevant pollutants and process parameters as well as reference measurement methods to calibrate automated measurement systems shall be carried out in accordance with CEN standards as soon as they are available. If CEN standards are not available ISO standards, national or international standards which will ensure the provision of data of an equivalent scientific quality shall apply.

Continuous measuring systems shall be subject to control by means of parallel measurements with the reference methods at least every year.

6. The values of the 95% confidence intervals of a single measured result shall not exceed the following percentages of the emission limit values:

Sulphur dioxide 20%
Nitrogen oxides 20%
Dust 30%

The validated hourly and daily average values shall be determined from the measured valid hourly average values after having subtracted the value of the confidence interval specified above.

Any day in which more than three hourly average values are invalid due to malfunction or maintenance of the continuous measurement system shall be invalidated. If more than ten days over a year are invalidated for such situations the competent authority shall require the operator to take adequate measures to improve the reliability of the continuous monitoring system.

B. DETERMINATION OF TOTAL ANNUAL EMISSIONS OF COMBUSTION PLANTS

Until and including 2003 the competent authorities shall obtain determination of the total annual emissions of SO_2 and NO_x from new combustion plants. When continuous monitoring is used, the operator of the combustion plant shall add up separately for each pollutant the mass of pollutant emitted each day, on the basis of the volumetric flow rates of waste gases. Where continuous monitoring is not in use, estimates of the total annual emissions shall be determined by the operator on the basis of paragraph A.1 to the satisfaction of the competent authorities.

Member States shall communicate to the Commission the total annual SO_2 and NO_x emissions of new combustion plants at the same time as the communication required under paragraph C.3 concerning the total annual emissions of existing plants.

Member States shall establish, starting in 2004 and for each subsequent year, an inventory of SO_2, NO_x and dust emissions from all combustion plants with a rated thermal input of 50 MW or more. The competent authority shall obtain for each plant operated under the control of one operator at a given location the following data:

— the total annual emissions of SO_2, NO_x and dust (as total suspended particles).
— the total annual amount of energy input, related to the net calorific value, broken down in terms of the five categories of fuel: biomass, other solid fuels, liquid fuels, natural gas, other gases.

A summary of the results of this inventory that shows the emissions from refineries separately shall be communicated to the Commission every three years within twelve months from the end of the three-year period considered. The yearly plant-by-plant data shall be made available to the Commission upon request. The Commission shall make available to the Member States a summary of the comparison and evaluation of the national inventories within twelve months of receipt of the national inventories.

Commencing on 1 January 2008 Member States shall report annually to the Commission on those existing plants declared for eligibility under Article 4(4) along with the record of the used and unused time allowed for the plants' remaining operational life.

C. DETERMINATION OF THE TOTAL ANNUAL EMISSIONS OF EXISTING PLANTS UNTIL AND INCLUDING 2003.

1. Member States shall establish, starting in 1990 and for each subsequent year until and including 2003, a complete emission inventory for existing plants covering SO_2 and NO_x:

— on a plant by plant basis for plants above 300 MWth and for refineries;
— on an overall basis for other combustion plants to which this Directive applies.

2. The methodology used for these inventories shall be consistent with that used to determine SO_2 and NO_x emissions from combustion plants in 1980.

3. The results of this inventory shall be communicated to the Commission in a conveniently aggregated form within nine months from the end of the year considered. The methodology used for establishing such emission inventories and the detailed base information shall be made available to the Commission at its request.

4. The Commission shall organise a systematic comparison of such national inventories and, if appropriate, shall submit proposals to the Council aiming at harmonising emission inventory methodologies, for the needs of an effective implementation of this Directive.

ANNEX IX
TIME-LIMITS FOR TRANSPOSITION AND IMPLEMENTATION OF THE REPEALED DIRECTIVE

(referred to in Article 17(1))

Directive	*Time-limits for transposition*	*Time-limits for application*
88/609/EEC (OJ l 336, 7.12.1988, p.1)	30 June 1990	1 July 1990
		31 December 1990
		31 December 1993
		31 December 1998
		31 December 2003
94/66/EC (OJ l 337, 24.12.1994, p.83)	24 June 1995	

ANNEX X
CORRELATION TABLE

(Referred to in Article 17(3))

This Directive	*Directive 88/609/EEC*
Article 1	Article 1
Article 2	Article 2
Article 3	Article 3
Article 4(1)	Article 4(1)
Article 4(2), (3) and (4)	
Article 4(5)	Article 4(3)
Article 4(6), (7) and (8)	
Article 5	Article 5
	Article 6
Article 6	
Article 7	Article 8
Article 8	Article 9
Article 9	Article 10
Article 10	Article 11
Article 11	Article 12
Article 12	Article 13(1)
Article 13	Article 14
Article 14	Article 15
Article 15(1), (2) and (3)	Article 16(1), (2) and (4)
Article 16	
Article 17	
Article 18(1), first subparagraph, and (3)	Article 17(1) and (2)
Article 18(1), second subparagraph, and (2) and Article 19	
Article 20	Article 18
Annexes I to VIII	Annexes I to IX
Annex IX and X	

DIRECTIVE 2001/81/EC OF THE EUROPEAN PARLIAMENT AND OF THE COUNCIL

of 23 October 2001

ON NATIONAL EMISSIONS CEILINGS FOR CERTAIN ATMOSPHERIC POLLUTANTS

THE EUROPEAN PARLIAMENT AND THE COUNCIL OF THE EUROPEAN UNION,

Having regard to the Treaty establishing the European Community, and in particular Article 175(1) thereof,

Having regard to the proposal from the Commission,

Having regard to the Opinion of the Economic and Social Committee,

Having regard to the Opinion of the Committee of the Regions,

Acting in accordance with the procedure laid down in Article 251 of the Treaty, in the light of the joint text approved by the Conciliation Committee on 2 August 2001,

Whereas:

(1) The general approach and strategy of the Fifth Environmental Action Programme was approved by the Resolution of 1 February 1993 of the Council and the Representatives of the Governments of the Member States meeting within the Council on a Community programme of policy and action in relation to the environment and sustainable development and it sets as objectives that critical loads and levels for acidification in the Community are not to be exceeded. The programme requires that all people should be effectively protected against health risks from air pollution and that permitted levels of pollution should take account of the protection of the environment. The programme also requires that guideline values from the World Health Organisation (WHO) should become mandatory at Community level.

(2) The Member States have signed the Gothenburg Protocol of 1 December 1999 to the United Nations Economic Commission for Europe (UNECE) Convention on long-range transboundary air pollution to abate acidification, eutrophication and ground-level ozone.

(3) Decision No 2179/98/EC of the European Parliament and of the Council of 24 September 1998 on the review of the European Community programme of policy and action in relation to the environment and sustainable development "Towards sustainability" specified that particular attention should be given to developing and implementing a strategy with the goal of ensuring that critical loads, in relation to exposure to acidifying, eutrophying and photochemical air pollutants, are not exceeded.

(4) Council Directive 92/72/EEC of 21 September 1992 on air pollution by ozone requires the Commission to submit to the Council a report on the evaluation of photochemical pollution in the Community, accompanied by any proposals the Commission deems appropriate on the control of air pollution by ground-level ozone and, if necessary, on reducing emissions of ozone precursors.

(5) Significant areas of the Community are exposed to depositions of acidifying and eutrophying substances at levels which have adverse effects on the environment. The WHO guideline values for the protection of human health and vegetation from photochemical pollution are substantially exceeded in all Member States.

(6) The exceedance of critical loads should therefore be gradually eliminated and guideline levels respected.

(7) At present it is not technically feasible to meet the long-term objectives of eliminating the adverse effects of acidification and reducing exposure to ground-level ozone of man and the environment to the guideline values established by the WHO. It is therefore necessary to provide for interim environmental objectives for acidification and ground-level ozone pollution, on which the necessary measures to reduce such pollution are to be based.

(8) Interim environmental objectives and the measures to meet them should take account of technical feasibility and the associated costs and benefits. Such measures should ensure that any action taken is cost-effective for the Community as a whole and should take account of the need to avoid excessive costs for any individual Member State.

(9) Transboundary pollution contributes to acidification, soil eutrophication and ground-level ozone formation, the abatement of which requires coordinated Community action.

(10) Reducing emissions of the pollutants causing acidification and exposure to ground-level ozone will also reduce soil eutrophication.

(11) A set of national ceilings for each Member State for emissions of sulphur dioxide, nitrogen oxides, volatile organic compounds and ammonia is a cost-effective way of meeting interim environmental objectives. Such emission ceilings will allow the Community and the Member States flexibility in determining how to comply with them.

(12) Member States should be responsible for implementing measures to comply with national emission ceilings. It will be necessary to evaluate progress towards compliance with the emission ceilings. National programmes for the reduction of emissions should therefore be drawn up and reported on to the Commission and should include information on the measures adopted or envisaged to comply with the emission ceilings.

(13) In accordance with the principle of subsidiarity as set out in Article 5 of the Treaty and taking account, in particular, of the precautionary principle, the objective of this Directive, namely limitation of emissions of acidifying and eutrophying pollutants and ozone precursors, cannot be sufficiently achieved by the Member States because of the transboundary nature of the pollution and can therefore be better achieved by the Community; in accordance with the principle of proportionality this Directive does not go beyond what is necessary to achieve that purpose.

(14) There should be a timely review of the progress made by Member States towards the emission ceilings, as well as a review of the extent to which implementing the ceilings is likely to meet interim environmental objectives, for the Community as a whole. Such review should consider also scientific and technical progress, developments in Community legislation and emission reductions outside the Community with special regard to progress made inter alia by the accession candidate countries. In that review, the Commission should undertake a further examination of the costs and benefits of the emission ceilings, including their cost-effectiveness, marginal costs and benefits and socio-economic impact and any impact on competitiveness. The review should also consider the limitations on the scope of this Directive.

(15) The Commission should for this purpose prepare a report to the European Parliament and the Council and, if it considers it necessary, propose appropriate amendments to this Directive taking account of the effects of any relevant Community legislation inter alia setting emission limits and product standards for relevant sources of emissions and international regulations concerning ship and aircraft emissions.

(16) Sea transport is a significant contributor to emissions of sulphur dioxide and nitrogen oxides and also to concentrations and depositions of air pollutants in the Community. Such emissions should therefore be reduced. Article 7(3) of Council Directive 1999/32/EC of 26 April 1999 relating to a reduction in the sulphur content of certain liquid fuels and amending Directive 93/12/EEC requires the Commission to consider which measures could be taken to reduce the contribution to acidification of the combustion of marine fuels other than those specified in Article 2(3) of that Directive.

(17) Member States should seek to ratify Annex VI to the International Convention for the Prevention of Pollution from Ships (MARPOL) as soon as possible.

(18) Owing to the transboundary nature of acidification and ozone pollution, the Commission should continue to examine further the need to develop harmonised Community measures, without prejudice to Article 18 of Council Directive 96/61/EC of 24 September 1996 concerning integrated pollution prevention and control, with the aim of avoiding distortion of competition, and taking into account the balance between benefits and cost of action.

(19) The provisions of this Directive should apply without prejudice to the Community legislation regulating emissions of those pollutants from specific sources and to the provisions of Council Directive 96/61/EC in relation to emission limit values and use of best available techniques.

(20) Emission inventories are necessary to monitor progress towards compliance with the emission ceilings and must be calculated in accordance with internationally agreed methodology and reported on regularly to the Commission and the European Environment Agency (EEA).

(21) Member States should lay down rules on penalties applicable to infringements of the provisions of this Directive and ensure that they are implemented. The penalties should be effective, proportionate and dissuasive.

(22) The measures necessary for the implementation of this Directive should be adopted in accordance with Council Decision 1999/468/EC of 28 June 1999 laying down the procedures for the exercise of implementing powers conferred on the Commission.

(23) The Commission and Members States should cooperate internationally with a view to achieving the objectives of this Directive,

HAVE ADOPTED THIS DIRECTIVE:

Article 1

Objective

The aim of this Directive is to limit emissions of acidifying and eutrophying pollutants and ozone precursors in order to improve the protection in the Community of the environment and human health against risks of adverse effects from acidification, soil eutrophication and ground-level ozone and to move towards the long-term objectives of not exceeding critical levels and loads and of effective protection of all people against recognised health risks from air pollution by establishing national emission ceilings, taking the years 2010 and 2020 as benchmarks, and by means of successive reviews as set out in Articles 4 and 10.

Article 2

Scope

This Directive covers emissions in the territory of the Member States and their exclusive economic zones from all sources of the pollutants referred to in Article 4 which arise as a result of human activities.

It does not cover:

(a) emissions from international maritime traffic;
(b) aircraft emissions beyond the landing and take-off cycle;
(c) for Spain, emissions in the Canary Islands;
(d) for France, emissions in the overseas departments;
(e) for Portugal, emissions in Madeira and the Azores.

Article 3

Definitions

For the purposes of this Directive:

(a) "AOT 40" means the sum of the difference between hourly concentrations of ground-level ozone greater than 80 μg/m3 (= 40 ppb) and 80 μg/m3 during daylight hours accumulated from May to July each year;
(b) "AOT 60" means the sum of the difference between hourly concentrations of ground-level ozone greater than 120 μg/m3 (=60 ppb) and 120 μg/m3 accumulated throughout the year;
(c) "critical load" means a quantitative estimate of an exposure to one or more pollutants below which significant adverse effects on specified sensitive elements of the environment do not occur, according to present knowledge;
(d) "critical level" means the concentration of pollutants in the atmosphere above which direct adverse effects on receptors, such as human beings, plants, ecosystems or materials, may occur, according to present knowledge;
(e) "emission" means the release of a substance from a point or diffuse source into the atmosphere;
(f) "grid cell" means a square 150 km × 150 km, which is the resolution used when mapping critical loads on a European scale, and also when monitoring emissions and depositions of air pollutants under the Cooperative Programme for Monitoring and Evaluation of the long-range Transmission of Air Pollutants in Europe (EMEP);
(g) "landing and take-off cycle" means a cycle represented by the following time in each operating mode: approach 4,0 minutes; taxi/ground idle 26,0 minutes, take-off 0,7 minutes; climb 2,2 minutes;
(h) "national emission ceiling" means the maximum amount of a substance expressed in kilotonnes, which may be emitted from a Member State in a calendar year;
(i) "nitrogen oxides" and "NO_x" mean nitric oxide and nitrogen dioxide, expressed as nitrogen dioxide;
(j) "ground-level ozone" means ozone in the lowermost part of the troposphere;
(k) "volatile organic compounds" and "VOC" mean all organic compounds arising from human activities, other than methane, which are capable of producing photochemical oxidants by reactions with nitrogen oxides in the presence of sunlight.

Article 4

National emission ceilings

1. By the year 2010 at the latest, Member States shall limit their annual national emissions of the pollutants sulphur dioxide (SO_2), nitrogen oxides (NO_x), volatile organic compounds (VOC) and ammonia (NH_3) to amounts not greater than the emission ceilings laid down in Annex I, taking into account any modifications made by Community measures adopted following the reports referred to in Article 9.

2. Member States shall ensure that the emission ceilings laid down in Annex I are not exceeded in any year after 2010.

Article 5

Interim environmental objectives

The national emission ceilings in Annex I shall have as their purpose to meet broadly the following interim environmental objectives, for the Community as a whole, by 2010:
(a) Acidification
The areas where critical loads are exceeded shall be reduced by at least 50 % (in each grid cell) compared with the 1990 situation.
(b) Health-related ground-level ozone exposure
The ground-level ozone load above the critical level for human health (AOT60=0) shall be reduced by two-thirds in all grid cells compared with the 1990 situation. In addition, the ground-level ozone load shall not exceed an absolute limit of 2,9 ppm.h in any grid cell.

(c) Vegetation-related ground-level ozone exposure
The ground-level ozone load above the critical level for crops and semi-natural vegetation (AOT40=3 ppm.h) shall be reduced by one-third in all grid cells compared with the 1990 situation. In addition, the ground-level ozone load shall not exceed an absolute limit of 10 ppm.h, expressed as an exceedance of the critical level of 3 ppm.h in any grid cell.

Article 6

National programmes

1. Member States shall, by 1 October 2002 at the latest, draw up programmes for the progressive reduction of national emissions of the pollutants referred to in Article 4 with the aim of complying at least with the national emission ceilings laid down in Annex I by 2010 at the latest.

2. The national programmes shall include information on adopted and envisaged policies and measures and quantified estimates of the effect of these policies and measures on emissions of the pollutants in 2010. Anticipated significant changes in the geographical distribution of national emissions shall be indicated.

3. Member States shall update and revise the national programmes as necessary by 1 October 2006.

4. Member States shall make available to the public and to appropriate organisations such as environmental organisations the programmes drawn up in accordance with paragraphs 1, 2 and 3. Information made available to the public and to organisations under this paragraph shall be clear, comprehensible and easily accessible.

Article 7

Emission inventories and projections

1. Member States shall prepare and annually update national emission inventories and emission projections for 2010 for the pollutants referred to in Article 4.

2. Member States shall establish their emission inventories and projections using the methodologies specified in Annex III.

3. The Commission, assisted by the European Environment Agency, shall, in cooperation with the Member States and on the basis of the information provided by them, establish inventories and projections of the pollutants referred to in Article 4. The inventories and projections shall be made publicly available.

[4. Any updating of the methodologies to be used in accordance with Annex III shall be adopted by the Commission. Those measures, designed to amend non-essential elements of this Directive, inter alia, by supplementing it, shall be adopted in accordance with the regulatory procedure with scrutiny referred to in Article 13(3).][1]

Amendment

1 Substituted by Regulation (EC) No 219/2009 of the European Parliament and of the Council of 11 March 2009 adapting a number of instruments subject to the procedure referred to in Article 251 of the Treaty to Council Decision 1999/468/EC with regard to the regulatory procedure with scrutiny, Article 1, Annex, para 3.5.1.

Article 8

Reports by the Member States

1. Member States shall each year, by 31 December at the latest, report their national emission inventories and their emission projections for 2010 established in accordance with Article

7 to the Commission and the European Environment Agency. They shall report their final emission inventories for the previous year but one and their provisional emission inventories for the previous year. Emission projections shall include information to enable a quantitative understanding of the key socioeconomic assumptions used in their preparation.

2. Member States shall, by 31 December 2002 at the latest, inform the Commission of the programmes drawn up in accordance with Article 6(1) and (2).

Member States shall, by 31 December 2006 at the latest, inform the Commission of the updated programmes drawn up in accordance with Article 6(3).

3. The Commission shall forward the national programmes received to the other Member States within one month of their reception.

4. The Commission shall, in accordance with the procedure set out in Article 13(2), establish provisions to ensure consistent and transparent reporting of national programmes.

Article 9

Reports by the Commission

1. In 2004 and 2008 the Commission shall report to the European Parliament and the Council on progress on the implementation of the national emission ceilings laid down in Annex I and on the extent to which the interim environmental objectives set out in Article 5 are likely to be met by 2010 and on the extent to which the long-term objectives set out in Article 1 could be met by 2020. The reports shall include an economic assessment, including cost-effectiveness, benefits, an assessment of marginal costs and benefits and the socioeconomic impact of the implementation of the national emission ceilings on particular Member States and sectors. They shall also include a review of the limitations of the scope of this Directive as defined in Article 2 and an evaluation of the extent to which further emission reductions might be necessary in order to meet the interim environmental objectives set out in Article 5. They shall take into account the reports made by Member States pursuant to Article 8(1) and (2), as well as, inter alia:

(a) any new Community legislation which may have been adopted setting emission limits and product standards for relevant sources of emissions;

(b) developments of best available techniques in the framework of the exchange of information under Article 16 of Directive 96/61/EC;

(c) emission reduction objectives for 2008 for emissions of sulphur dioxide and nitrogen oxides from existing large combustion plants, reported by Member States pursuant to Directive 2001/80/EC of the European Parliament and of the Council of 23 October 2001 on the limitation of emissions of certain pollutants into the air from large combustion plants;

(d) emission reductions and reduction commitments by third countries, with particular focus on measures to be taken in the accession candidate countries, and the possibility for further emission reductions in regions in the vicinity of the Community;

(e) any new Community legislation and any international regulations concerning ship and aircraft emissions;

(f) the development of transport and any further action to control transport emissions;

(g) developments in the field of agriculture, new livestock projections and improvements in emission reduction methods in the agricultural sector;

(h) any major changes in the energy supply market within a Member State and new forecasts reflecting the actions taken by Member States to comply with their international obligations in relation to climate change;

(i) assessment of the current and projected exceedances of critical loads and the WHO's guideline values for ground-level ozone;

(j) the possibility of identification of a proposed interim objective for reducing soil eutrophication;

(k) new technical and scientific data including an assessment of the uncertainties in:
   (i) national emission inventories;
   (ii) input reference data;
   (iii) knowledge of the transboundary transport and deposition of pollutants;
   (iv) critical loads and levels;
   (v) the model used;

   and an assessment of the resulting uncertainty in the national emission ceilings required to meet the interim environmental objectives mentioned in Article 5.

(l) whether there is a need to avoid excessive costs for any individual Member State;

(m) a comparison of model calculations with observations of acidification, eutrophication and ground-level ozone with a view to improving models;

(n) the possible use, where appropriate, of relevant economic instruments.

2. In 2012 the Commission shall report to the European Parliament and the Council on compliance with the ceilings in Annex I and on progress in relation to the interim environmental objectives in Article 5 and the long-term objectives set out in Article 1. Its report shall take account of the reports made by Member States pursuant to Article 8(1) and (2) as well as the matters listed in points (a) to (n) of paragraph 1.

Article 10

Review

1. The reports referred to in Article 9 shall take into account the factors listed in Article 9(1). In the light of these factors, of progress towards attaining the emission ceilings by the year 2010, of scientific and technical progress, and of the situation regarding progress towards attaining the interim objectives of this Directive and the long-term objectives of no exceedance of critical loads and levels and of WHO air quality guidelines for ozone, the Commission shall carry out a review of this Directive in preparation for each report.

2. In the review to be completed in 2004 an evaluation will be carried out of the indicative emission ceilings for the Community as a whole set out in Annex II. The evaluation of these indicative ceilings shall be a factor for consideration during analysis of further cost-effective actions that might be taken in order to reduce emissions of all relevant pollutants, with the aim of attaining the interim environmental objectives set out in Article 5, for the Community as a whole by 2010.

3. All reviews shall include a further investigation of the estimated costs and benefits of national emission ceilings, computed with state-of-the-art models and making use of the best available data to achieve the least possible uncertainty and taking also into account progress in the enlargement of the European Union, and of the merits of alternative methodologies, in the light of the factors listed in Article 9.

4. Without prejudice to Article 18 of Directive 96/61/EC, with the aim of avoiding distortion of competition, and taking into account the balance between benefits and costs of action, the Commission shall examine further the need to develop harmonised Community measures, for the most relevant economic sectors and products contributing to acidification, eutrophication and formation of ground-level ozone.

5. The reports referred to in Article 9 will, if appropriate, be accompanied by proposals for:

(a) modifications of the national ceilings in Annex I with the aim of meeting the interim environmental objectives of Article 5 and/or for modifications to those interim environmental objectives;

(b) possible further emission reductions with the aim of meeting, preferably by 2020, the long-term objectives of this Directive;

(c) measures to ensure compliance with the ceilings.

Article 11

Cooperation with third countries

To promote the achievement of the objective set out in Article 1, the Commission and Member States, as appropriate, shall, without prejudice to Article 300 of the Treaty, pursue bilateral and multilateral cooperation with third countries and relevant international organisations such as the United Nations Economic Commission for Europe (UNECE), the International Maritime Organization (IMO) and the International Civil Aviation Organization (ICAO), including through the exchange of information, concerning technical and scientific research and development and with the aim of improving the basis for the facilitation of emission reductions.

Article 12

Reports concerning ship and aircraft emission

1. By the end of 2002 the Commission shall report to the European Parliament and Council on the extent to which emissions from international maritime traffic contribute to acidification, eutrophication and the formation of ground-level ozone within the Community.

2. By the end of 2004 the Commission shall report to the European Parliament and Council on the extent to which emissions from aircraft beyond the landing and take-off cycle contribute to acidification, eutrophication and the formation of ground-level ozone within the Community.

3. Each report shall specify a programme of actions which could be taken at international and Community level as appropriate to reduce emissions from the sector concerned, as a basis for further consideration by the European Parliament and Council.

Article 13

Committee

1. The Commission shall be assisted by the Committee set up by Article 12 of Directive 96/62/EC, hereinafter referred to as "the Committee".

2. Where reference is made to this paragraph, Articles 4 and 7 of Decision 1999/468/EC shall apply, having regard to the provisions of Article 8 thereof.

The period referred to in Article 4(3) of Decision 1999/468/EC shall be set at three months.

[3. Where reference is made to this paragraph, Article 5a(1) to (4) and Article 7 of Decision 1999/468/EC shall apply, having regard to the provisions of Article 8 thereof.][1]

Amendment

1 Substituted by Regulation (EC) No 219/2009 of the European Parliament and of the Council of 11 March 2009 adapting a number of instruments subject to the procedure referred to in Article 251 of the Treaty to Council Decision 1999/468/EC with regard to the regulatory procedure with scrutiny, Article 1, Annex, para 3.5.2.

Article 14

Penalties

Member States shall determine the penalties applicable to breaches of the national provisions adopted pursuant to this Directive. The penalties shall be effective, proportionate and dissuasive.

Article 15

Transposition

1. Member States shall bring into force the laws, regulations and administrative provisions necessary to comply with this Directive before 27 November 2002. They shall forthwith inform the Commission thereof.

When Member States adopt those provisions, they shall contain a reference to this Directive or be accompanied by such reference on the occasion of their official publication. Member States shall determine how such reference is to be made.

2. Member States shall communicate to the Commission the text of the main provisions of national law, which they adopt in the field covered by this Directive.

Article 16

Entry into force

This Directive shall enter into force on the day of its publication in the Official Journal of the European Communities.

Article 17

Addressees

This Directive is addressed to the Member States.

[ANNEX I
NATIONAL EMISSION CEILINGS FOR SO_2, NO_X, VOC AND NH_3, TO BE ATTAINED BY 2010[(1)]][1]

[Country	*SO_2 Kilotonnes*	*NO_x Kilotonnes*	*VOC Kilotonnes*	*NH_3 Kilotonnes*
Belgium	99	176	139	74
Bulgaria[(2)]	836	247	175	108
Czech Republic	265	286	220	80
Denmark	55	127	85	69
Germany	520	1051	995	550
Estonia	100	60	49	29
Greece	523	344	261	73
Spain	746	847	662	353
France	375	810	1050	780
Ireland	42	65	55	116
Italy	475	990	1159	419
Cyprus	39	23	14	09
Latvia	101	61	136	44
Lithuania	145	110	92	84
Luxembourg	4	11	9	7
Hungary	500	198	137	90
Malta	9	8	12	3
Netherlands	50	260	185	128
Austria	39	103	159	66
Poland	1397	879	800	468
Portugal	160	250	180	90

[Country	*SO_2 Kilotonnes*	*NO_x Kilotonnes*	*VOC Kilotonnes*	*NH_3 Kilotonnes*
Romania(2)	918	437	523	210
Slovenia	27	45	40	20
Slovakia	110	130	140	39
Finland	110	170	130	31
Sweden	67	148	241	57
United Kingdom	585	1167	1200	297
EC 27	8297	9003	8848	4294

(1) These national emission ceilings are designed with the aim of broadly meeting the interim environmental objectives set out in Article 5. Meeting those objectives is expected to result in a reduction of soil eutrophication to such an extent that the Community area with depositions of nutrient nitrogen in excess of the critical loads will be reduced by about 30% compared with the situation in 1990.

(2) These national emission ceilings are temporary and are without prejudice to the review according to Article 10 of this Directive, which is to be completed in 2008.][1]

Amendment

1 Inserted by Council Directive 2006/105/EC of 20 November 2006 adapting Directives 73/239/EEC, 74/557/EEC and 2002/83/EC in the field of environment, by reason of the accession of Bulgaria and Romania, Article 1, Annex, Pt B, para 3(a).

ANNEX II
EMISSION CEILINGS FOR SO_2, NO_X AND VOC (THOUSAND TONNES)

[	*SO_2 Kilotonnes*	*NO_x Kilotonnes*	*VOC Kilotonnes*
EC 27(1)	7832	8180	7585

(1) These emission ceilings are temporary and are without prejudice to the review according to Article 10 of this Directive, which is to be completed in 2008.][1]

These emission ceilings are designed with the aim of attaining the interim environmental objectives set out in Article 5 for the Community as a whole by 2010.

Amendment

1 Inserted by Council Directive 2006/105/EC of 20 November 2006 adapting Directives 73/239/EEC, 74/557/EEC and 2002/83/EC in the field of environment, by reason of the accession of Bulgaria and Romania, Article 1, Annex, Pt B, para 3(b).

ANNEX III
METHODOLOGIES FOR EMISSION INVENTORIES AND PROJECTIONS

Member States shall establish emission inventories and projections using the methodologies agreed upon by the Convention on Long-range Transboundary Air Pollution and are requested to use the joint EMEP/CORINAIR (Air emissions inventory of the European Environment Agency) guidebook in preparing these inventories and projections.

DIRECTIVE 2002/96/EC OF THE EUROPEAN PARLIAMENT AND OF THE COUNCIL

of 27 January 2003

ON WASTE ELECTRICAL AND ELECTRONIC EQUIPMENT (WEEE)

THE EUROPEAN PARLIAMENT AND THE COUNCIL OF THE EUROPEAN UNION,

Having regard to the Treaty establishing the European Community, and in particular Article 175(1) thereof,

Having regard to the proposal from the Commission,

Having regard to the Opinion of the Economic and Social Committee,

Having regard to the Opinion of the Committee of Regions,

Acting in accordance with the procedure laid down in Article 251 of the Treaty in the light of the joint text approved by the Conciliation Committee on 8 November 2002,

Whereas:

(1) The objectives of the Community's environment policy are, in particular, to preserve, protect and improve the quality of the environment, protect human health and utilise natural resources prudently and rationally. That policy is based on the precautionary principle and principles that preventive action should be taken, that environmental damage should as a priority be rectified at source and that the polluter should pay.

(2) The Community programme of policy and action in relation to the environment and sustainable development (Fifth Environmental Action Programme) states that the achievement of sustainable development calls for significant changes in current patterns of development, production, consumption and behaviour and advocates, inter alia, the reduction of wasteful consumption of natural resources and the prevention of pollution. It mentions waste electrical and electronic equipment (WEEE) as one of the target areas to be regulated, in view of the application of the principles of prevention, recovery and safe disposal of waste.

(3) The Commission Communication of 30 July 1996 on review of the Community strategy for waste management states that, where the generation of waste cannot be avoided, it should be reused or recovered for its material or energy.

(4) The Council in its Resolution of 24 February 1997 on a Community strategy for waste management insisted on the need for promoting waste recovery with a view to reducing the quantity of waste for disposal and saving natural resources, in particular by reuse, recycling, composting and recovering energy from waste and recognised that the choice of options in any particular case must have regard to environmental and economic effects but that until scientific and technological progress is made and life-cycle analyses are further developed, reuse and material recovery should be considered preferable where and in so far as they are the best environmental options. The Council also invited the Commission to develop, as soon as possible, an appropriate follow-up to the projects of the priority waste streams programme, including WEEE.

(5) The European Parliament, in its Resolution of 14 November 1996, asked the Commission to present proposals for Directives on a number of priority waste streams, including electrical and electronic waste, and to base such proposals on the principle of producer responsibility. The European Parliament, in the same Resolution, requests the Council and the Commission to put forward proposals for cutting the volume of waste.

(6) Council Directive 75/442/EEC of 15 July 1975 on waste provides that specific rules for particular instances or supplementing those of Directive 75/442/EEC on the management of particular categories of waste may be laid down by means of individual Directives.

(7) The amount of WEEE generated in the Community is growing rapidly. The content of hazardous components in electrical and electronic equipment (EEE) is a major concern during the waste management phase and recycling of WEEE is not undertaken to a sufficient extent.

(8) The objective of improving the management of WEEE cannot be achieved effectively by Member States acting individually. In particular, different national applications of the producer responsibility principle may lead to substantial disparities in the financial burden on economic operators. Having different national policies on the management of WEEE hampers the effectiveness of recycling policies. For that reason the essential criteria should be laid down at Community level.

(9) The provisions of this Directive should apply to products and producers irrespective of the selling technique, including distance and electronic selling. In this connection the obligations of producers and distributors using distance and electronic selling channels should, as far as is practicable, take the same form and should be enforced in the same way in order to avoid other distribution channels having to bear the costs of the provisions of this Directive concerning WEEE for which the equipment was sold by distant or electronic selling.

(10) This Directive should cover all electrical and electronic equipment used by consumers and electrical and electronic equipment intended for professional use. This Directive should apply without prejudice to Community legislation on safety and health requirements protecting all actors in contact with WEEE as well as specific Community waste management legislation, in particular Council Directive 91/157/EEC of 18 March 1991 on batteries and accumulators containing certain dangerous substances.

(11) Directive 91/157/EEC needs to be revised as soon as possible, particularly in the light of this Directive.

(12) The establishment, by this Directive, of producer responsibility is one of the means of encouraging the design and production of electrical and electronic equipment which take into full account and facilitate their repair, possible upgrading, reuse, disassembly and recycling.

(13) In order to guarantee the safety and health of distributors' personnel involved in the take-back and handling of WEEE, Member States should, in accordance with national and Community legislation on safety and health requirements, determine the conditions under which take-back may be refused by distributors.

(14) Member States should encourage the design and production of electrical and electronic equipment which take into account and facilitate dismantling and recovery, in particular the re-use and recycling of WEEE, their components and materials. Producers should not prevent, through specific design features or manufacturing processes, WEEE from being reused, unless such specific design features or manufacturing processes present overriding advantages, for example with regard to the protection of the environment and/or safety requirements.

(15) Separate collection is the precondition to ensure specific treatment and recycling of WEEE and is necessary to achieve the chosen level of protection of human health and the environment in the Community. Consumers have to actively contribute to the success of such collection and should be encouraged to return WEEE. For this purpose, convenient facilities should be set up for the return of WEEE, including public collection points, where private households should be able to return their waste at least free of charge.

(16) In order to attain the chosen level of protection and harmonised environmental objectives of the Community, Member States should adopt appropriate measures to minimise the disposal of WEEE as unsorted municipal waste and to achieve a high level of separate collection of WEEE. In order to ensure that Member States strive to

set up efficient collection schemes, they should be required to achieve a high level of collection of WEEE from private households.

(17) Specific treatment for WEEE is indispensable in order to avoid the dispersion of pollutants into the recycled material or the waste stream. Such treatment is the most effective means of ensuring compliance with the chosen level of protection of the environment of the Community. Any establishment or undertakings carrying out recycling and treatment operations should comply with minimum standards to prevent negative environmental impacts associated with the treatment of WEEE. Best available treatment, recovery and recycling techniques should be used provided that they ensure human health and high environmental protection. Best available treatment, recovery and recycling techniques may be further defined in accordance with the procedures of Directive 96/61/EC.

(18) Where appropriate, priority should be given to the reuse of WEEE and its components, subassemblies and consumables. Where reuse is not preferable, all WEEE collected separately should be sent for recovery, in the course of which a high level of recycling and recovery should be achieved. In addition, producers should be encouraged to integrate recycled material in new equipment.

(19) Basic principles with regard to the financing of WEEE management have to be set at Community level and financing schemes have to contribute to high collection rates as well as to the implementation of the principle of producer responsibility.

(20) Users of electrical and electronic equipment from private households should have the possibility of returning WEEE at least free of charge. Producers should therefore finance collection from collection facilities, and the treatment, recovery and disposal of WEEE. In order to give maximum effect to the concept of producer responsibility, each producer should be responsible for financing the management of the waste from his own products. The producer should be able to choose to fulfil this obligation either individually or by joining a collective scheme. Each producer should, when placing a product on the market, provide a financial guarantee to prevent costs for the management of WEEE from orphan products from falling on society or the remaining producers. The responsibility for the financing of the management of historical waste should be shared by all existing producers in collective financing schemes to which all producers, existing on the market when the costs occur, contribute proportionately. Collective financing schemes should not have the effect of excluding niche and low-volume producers, importers and new entrants. For a transitional period, producers should be allowed to show purchasers, on a voluntary basis at the time of sale of new products, the costs of collecting, treating and disposing in an environmentally sound way of historical waste. Producers making use of this provision should ensure that the costs mentioned do not exceed the actual costs incurred.

(21) Information to users about the requirement not to dispose of WEEE as unsorted municipal waste and to collect WEEE separately, and about the collection systems and their role in the management of WEEE, is indispensable for the success of WEEE collection. Such information implies the proper marking of electrical and electronic equipment which could end up in rubbish bins or similar means of municipal waste collection.

(22) Information on component and material identification to be provided by producers is important to facilitate the management, and in particular the treatment and recovery/recycling, of WEEE.

(23) Member States should ensure that inspection and monitoring infrastructure enable the proper implementation of this Directive to be verified, having regard, inter alia, to Recommendation 2001/331/EC of the European Parliament and the Council of 4 April 2001 providing for minimum criteria for environmental inspections in the Member States.

(24) Information about the weight or, if this is not possible, the numbers of items of electrical and electronic equipment put on the market in the Community and the rates of collection, reuse (including as far as possible reuse of whole appliances), recovery/

recycling and export of WEEE collected in accordance with this Directive is necessary to monitor the achievement of the objectives of this Directive.

(25) Member States may choose to implement certain provisions of this Directive by means of agreements between the competent authorities and the economic sectors concerned provided that particular requirements are met.

(26) The adaptation to scientific and technical progress of certain provisions of the Directive, the list of products falling under the categories set out in Annex IA, the selective treatment for materials and components of WEEE, the technical requirements for storage and treatment of WEEE and the symbol for the marking of EEE should be effected by the Commission under a committee procedure.

(27) The measures necessary for the implementation of this Directive should be adopted in accordance with Council Decision 1999/468/EC of 28 June 1999 laying down the procedures for the exercise of implementing powers conferred on the Commission,

HAVE ADOPTED THIS DIRECTIVE:

Article 1

Objectives

The purpose of this Directive is, as a first priority, the prevention of waste electrical and electronic equipment (WEEE), and in addition, the reuse, recycling and other forms of recovery of such wastes so as to reduce the disposal of waste. It also seeks to improve the environmental performance of all operators involved in the life cycle of electrical and electronic equipment, e.g. producers, distributors and consumers and in particular those operators directly involved in the treatment of waste electrical and electronic equipment.

Article 2

Scope

1. This Directive shall apply to electrical and electronic equipment falling under the categories set out in Annex IA provided that the equipment concerned is not part of another type of equipment that does not fall within the scope of this Directive. Annex IB contains a list of products which fall under the categories set out in Annex IA.

2. This Directive shall apply without prejudice to Community legislation on safety and health requirements and specific Community waste management legislation.

3. Equipment which is connected with the protection of the essential interests of the security of Member States, arms, munitions and war material shall be excluded from this Directive. This does not, however, apply to products which are not intended for specifically military purposes.

Article 3

Definitions

For the purposes of this Directive, the following definitions shall apply:

(a) "electrical and electronic equipment" or "EEE" means equipment which is dependent on electric currents or electromagnetic fields in order to work properly and equipment for the generation, transfer and measurement of such currents and fields falling under the categories set out in Annex IA and designed for use with a voltage rating not exceeding 1000 Volt for alternating current and 1500 Volt for direct current;

(b) "waste electrical and electronic equipment" or "WEEE" means electrical or electronic equipment which is waste within the meaning of Article 1(a) of Directive 75/442/

EEC, including all components, subassemblies and consumables which are part of the product at the time of discarding;

(c) "prevention" means measures aimed at reducing the quantity and the harmfulness to the environment of WEEE and materials and substances contained therein;

(d) "reuse" means any operation by which WEEE or components thereof are used for the same purpose for which they were conceived, including the continued use of the equipment or components thereof which are returned to collection points, distributors, recyclers or manufacturers;

(e) "recycling" means the reprocessing in a production process of the waste materials for the original purpose or for other purposes, but excluding energy recovery which means the use of combustible waste as a means of generating energy through direct incineration with or without other waste but with recovery of the heat;

(f) "recovery" means any of the applicable operations provided for in Annex IIB to Directive 75/442/EEC;

(g) "disposal" means any of the applicable operations provided for in Annex IIA to Directive 75/442/EEC;

(h) "treatment" means any activity after the WEEE has been handed over to a facility for depollution, disassembly, shredding, recovery or [mixture][1] for disposal and any other operation carried out for the recovery and/or the disposal of the WEEE;

(i) "producer" means any person who, irrespective of the selling technique used, including by means of distance communication in accordance with Directive 97/7/EC of the European Parliament and of the Council of 20 May 1997 on the protection of consumers in respect of distance contracts:

- (i) manufactures and sells electrical and electronic equipment under his own brand,
- (ii) resells under his own brand equipment produced by other suppliers, a reseller not being regarded as the "producer" if the brand of the producer appears on the equipment, as provided for in subpoint (i), or
- (iii) imports or exports electrical and electronic equipment on a professional basis into a Member State.

Whoever exclusively provides financing under or pursuant to any finance agreement shall not be deemed a "producer" unless he also acts as a producer within the meaning of subpoints (i) to (iii);

(j) "distributor" means any person who provides electrical or electronic equipment on a commercial basis to the party who is going to use it;

(k) "WEEE from private households" means WEEE which comes from private households and from commercial, industrial, institutional and other sources which, because of its nature and quantity, is similar to that from private households;

[(l) "dangerous substance or mixture" means any mixture which has to be considered dangerous under Directive 1999/45/EC of the European Parliament and of the Council of 31 May 1999 concerning the approximation of the laws, regulations and administrative provisions of the Member States relating to the classification, packaging and labelling of dangerous [mixtures][1] or any substance which fulfils the criteria for any of the following hazard classes or categories set out in Annex I of Regulation (EC) No 1272/2008 of the European Parliament and of the Council of 16 December 2008 on classification, labelling and packaging of substances and mixtures:

- (i) hazard classes 2.1 to 2.4, 2.6 and 2.7, 2.8 types A and B, 2.9, 2.10, 2.12, 2.13 categories 1 and 2, 2.14 categories 1 and 2, 2.15 types A to F;
- (ii) hazard classes 3.1 to 3.6, 3.7 adverse effects on sexual function and fertility or on development, 3.8 effects other than narcotic effects, 3.9 and 3.10;
- (iii) hazard class 4.1;
- (iv) hazard class 5.1.][1]

(m) "finance agreement" means any loan, lease, hiring or deferred sale agreement or arrangement relating to any equipment whether or not the terms of that agreement or arrangement or any collateral agreement or arrangement provide that a transfer of ownership of that equipment will or may take place.

Amendment

1 Substituted by Directive 2008/112/EC of the European Parliament and of the Council of 16 December 2008 amending Council Directives 76/768/EEC, 88/378/EEC, 1999/13/EC and Directives 2000/53/EC, 2002/96/EC and 2004/42/EC of the European Parliament and of the Council in order to adapt them to Regulation (EC) No 1272/2008 on classification, labelling and packaging of substances and mixtures, Article 5.1, 5.2.

Article 4

Product design

Member States shall encourage the design and production of electrical and electronic equipment which take into account and facilitate dismantling and recovery, in particular the reuse and recycling of WEEE, their components and materials. In this context, Member States shall take appropriate measures so that producers do not prevent, through specific design features or manufacturing processes, WEEE from being reused, unless such specific design features or manufacturing processes present overriding advantages, for example, with regard to the protection of the environment and/or safety requirements.

Article 5

Separate collection

1. Member States shall adopt appropriate measures in order to minimise the disposal of WEEE as unsorted municipal waste and to achieve a high level of separate collection of WEEE.

2. For WEEE from private households, Member States shall ensure that by the 13 August 2005:

(a) systems are set up allowing final holders and distributors to return such waste at least free of charge. Member States shall ensure the availability and accessibility of the necessary collection facilities, taking into account in particular the population density;

(b) when supplying a new product, distributors shall be responsible for ensuring that such waste can be returned to the distributor at least free of charge on a one-to-one basis as long as the equipment is of equivalent type and has fulfilled the same functions as the supplied equipment. Member States may depart from this provision provided they ensure that returning the WEEE is not thereby made more difficult for the final holder and provided that these systems remain free of charge for the final holder. Member States making use of this provision shall inform the Commission thereof;

(c) without prejudice to the provisions of (a) and (b), producers are allowed to set up and operate individual and/or collective take-back systems for WEEE from private households provided that these are in line with the objectives of this Directive;

(d) having regard to national and Community health and safety standards, WEEE that presents a health and safety risk to personnel because of contamination may be refused for return under (a) and (b). Member States shall make specific arrangements for such WEEE.

Member States may provide for specific arrangements for the return of WEEE as under (a) and (b) if the equipment does not contain the essential components or if the equipment contains waste other than WEEE.

3. In the case of WEEE other than WEEE from private households, and without prejudice to Article 9, Member States shall ensure that producers or third parties acting on their behalf provide for the collection of such waste.

4. Member States shall ensure that all WEEE collected under paragraphs 1, 2 and 3 above is transported to treatment facilities authorised under Article 6 unless the appliances are reused as a whole. Member States shall ensure that the envisaged reuse does not lead to a circumvention of this Directive, in particular as regards Articles 6 and 7. The collection and transport of separately collected WEEE shall be carried out in a way which optimises reuse and recycling of those components or whole appliances capable of being reused or recycled.

5. Without prejudice to paragraph 1, Member States shall ensure that by 31 December 2006 at the latest a rate of separate collection of at least four kilograms on average per inhabitant per year of WEEE from private households is achieved.

The European Parliament and the Council, acting on a proposal from the Commission and taking account of technical and economic experience in the Member States, shall establish a new mandatory target by 31 December 2008. This may take the form of a percentage of the quantities of electrical and electronic equipment sold to private households in the preceding years.

Article 6

Treatment

1. Member States shall ensure that producers or third parties acting on their behalf, in accordance with Community legislation, set up systems to provide for the treatment of WEEE using best available treatment, recovery and recycling techniques. The systems may be set up by producers individually and/or collectively. To ensure compliance with Article 4 of Directive 75/442/EEC, the treatment shall, as a minimum, include the removal of all fluids and a selective treatment in accordance with Annex II to this Directive.

[Annex II may be amended in order to introduce other treatment technologies ensuring at least the same level of protection for human health and the environment. Those measures, designed to amend non-essential elements of this Directive, shall be adopted in accordance with the regulatory procedure with scrutiny referred to in Article 14(3).][1]

For the purposes of environmental protection, Member States may set up minimum quality standards for the treatment of collected WEEE. Member States which opt for such quality standards shall inform the Commission thereof, which shall publish these standards.

2. Member States shall ensure that any establishment or undertaking carrying out treatment operations obtains a permit from the competent authorities, in compliance with Articles 9 and 10 of Directive 75/442/EEC.

The derogation from the permit requirement referred to in Article 11(1)(b) of Directive 75/442/EEC may apply to recovery operations concerning WEEE if an inspection is carried out by the competent authorities before the registration in order to ensure compliance with Article 4 of Directive 75/442/EEC.

The inspection shall verify:
(a) the type and quantities of waste to be treated;
(b) the general technical requirements to be complied with;
(c) the safety precautions to be taken.
The inspection shall be carried out at least once a year and the results shall be communicated by the Member States to the Commission.

3. Member States shall ensure that any establishment or undertaking carrying out treatment operations stores and treats WEEE in compliance with the technical requirements set out in Annex III.

4. Member States shall ensure that the permit or the registration referred to in paragraph 2 includes all conditions necessary for compliance with the requirements of paragraphs 1 and 3 and for the achievement of the recovery targets set out in Article 7.

5. The treatment operation may also be undertaken outside the respective Member State or the Community provided that the shipment of WEEE is in compliance with Council Regulation (EEC) No 259/93 of 1 February 1993 on the supervision and control of shipments of waste within, into and out of the European Community.

WEEE exported out of the Community in line with Council Regulation (EEC) No 259/93, Council Regulation (EC) No 1420/1999 of 29 April 1999 establishing common rules and procedures to apply to shipments to certain non-OECD countries of certain types of waste and Commission Regulation (EC) No 1547/1999 of 12 July 1999 determining the control procedures under Council Regulation (EEC) No 259/93 to apply to shipments of certain types of waste to certain countries to which OECD Decision C(92)39 final does not apply, shall only count for the fulfilment of obligations and targets of Article 7(1) and (2) of this Directive if the exporter can prove that the recovery, reuse and/or recycling operation took place under conditions that are equivalent to the requirements of this Directive.

6. Member States shall encourage establishments or undertakings which carry out treatment operations to introduce certified environmental management systems in accordance with Regulation (EC) No 761/2001 of the European Parliament and of the Council of 19 March 2001 allowing voluntary participation by organisations in a Community eco-management and audit scheme (EMAS).

Amendment

1 Substituted by Directive 2008/34/EC of the European Parliament and of the Council of 11 March 2008 amending Directive 2002/96/EC on waste electrical and electronic equipment (WEEE), as regards the implementing powers conferred on the Commission, Article 1.1.

Article 7

Recovery

1. Member States shall ensure that producers or third parties acting on their behalf set up systems either on an individual or on a collective basis, in accordance with Community legislation, to provide for the recovery of WEEE collected separately in accordance with Article 5. Member States shall give priority to the reuse of whole appliances. Until the date referred to in paragraph 4, such appliances shall not be taken into account for the calculation of the targets set out in paragraph 2.

2. Regarding WEEE sent for treatment in accordance with Article 6, Member States shall ensure that, by 31 December 2006, producers meet the following targets:

(a) for WEEE falling under categories 1 and 10 of Annex IA,
- the rate of recovery shall be increased to a minimum of 80 % by an average weight per appliance, and
- component, material and substance reuse and recycling shall be increased to a minimum of 75 % by an average weight per appliance;

(b) for WEEE falling under categories 3 and 4 of Annex IA,
- the rate of recovery shall be increased to a minimum of 75 % by an average weight per appliance, and
- component, material and substance reuse and recycling shall be increased to a minimum of 65 % by an average weight per appliance;

(c) for WEEE falling under categories 2, 5, 6, 7 and 9 of Annex IA,
- the rate of recovery shall be increased to a minimum of 70 % by an average weight per appliance, and
- component, material and substance reuse and recycling shall be increased to a minimum of 50 % by an average weight per appliance;

(d) for gas discharge lamps, the rate of component, material and substance reuse and recycling shall reach a minimum of 80 % by weight of the lamps.

3. Member States shall ensure that, for the purpose of calculating these targets, producers or third parties acting on their behalf keep records on the mass of WEEE, their components, materials or substances when entering (input) and leaving (output) the treatment facility and/or when entering (input) the recovery or recycling facility.

[Detailed rules for monitoring the compliance of Member States with the targets set out in paragraph 2, including specifications for materials, shall be established. Those measures, designed to amend non-essential elements of this Directive by supplementing it, shall be adopted in accordance with the regulatory procedure with scrutiny referred to in Article 14(3).][1]

4. The European Parliament and the Council, acting on a proposal from the Commission, shall establish new targets for recovery and reuse/recycling, including for the reuse of whole appliances as appropriate, and for the products falling under category 8 of Annex IA, by 31 December 2008. This shall be done with account being taken of the environmental benefits of electrical and electronic equipment in use, such as improved resource efficiency resulting from developments in the areas of materials and technology. Technical progress in reuse, recovery and recycling, products and materials, and the experience gained by the Member States and the industry, shall also be taken into account.

5. Member States shall encourage the development of new recovery, recycling and treatment technologies.

Amendment

1 Substituted by Directive 2008/34/EC of the European Parliament and of the Council of 11 March 2008 amending Directive 2002/96/EC on waste electrical and electronic equipment (WEEE), as regards the implementing powers conferred on the Commission, Article 1.2.

Article 8

Financing in respect of WEEE from private households

1. Member States shall ensure that, by 13 August 2005, producers provide at least for the financing of the collection, treatment, recovery and environmentally sound disposal of WEEE from private households deposited at collection facilities, set up under Article 5(2).

2. For products put on the market later than 13 August 2005, each producer shall be responsible for financing the operations referred to in paragraph 1 relating to the waste from his own products. The producer can choose to fulfil this obligation either individually or by joining a collective scheme.

Member States shall ensure that each producer provides a guarantee when placing a product on the market showing that the management of all WEEE will be financed and that producers clearly mark their products in accordance with Article 11(2). This guarantee shall ensure that the operations referred to in paragraph 1 relating to this product will be financed. The guarantee may take the form of participation by the producer in appropriate schemes for the financing of the management of WEEE, a recycling insurance or a blocked bank account.

The costs of collection, treatment and environmentally sound disposal shall not be shown separately to purchasers at the time of sale of new products.

3. The responsibility for the financing of the costs of the management of WEEE from products put on the market before the date referred to in paragraph 1 (historical waste) shall be provided by one or more systems to which all producers, existing on the market when the respective costs occur, contribute proportionately, e.g. in proportion to their respective share of the market by type of equipment.

Member States shall ensure that for a transitional period of eight years (10 years for category 1 of Annex IA) after entry into force of this Directive, producers are allowed to show purchasers, at the time of sale of new products, the costs of collection, treatment and disposal in an environmentally sound way. The costs mentioned shall not exceed the actual costs incurred.

4. Member States shall ensure that producers supplying electrical or electronic equipment by means of distance communication also comply with the requirements set out in this Article for the equipment supplied in the Member State where the purchaser of that equipment resides.

[Article 9

Financing in respect of WEEE from users other than private households][1]

[1. Member States shall ensure that, by 13 August 2005, the financing of the costs for the collection, treatment, recovery and environmentally sound disposal of WEEE from users other than private households from products put on the market after 13 August 2005 is to be provided for by producers.

Member States shall ensure that, by 13 August 2005, for WEEE from products put on the market before 13 August 2005 (historical waste), the financing of the costs of management is as set out in the third and fourth subparagraphs.

For historical waste being replaced by new equivalent products or by new products fulfilling the same function, the financing of the costs shall be provided for by producers of those products when supplying them. Member States may, as an alternative, provide that users other than private households also be made, partly or totally, responsible for this financing.

For other historical waste, the financing of the costs shall be provided for by the users other than private households.

2. Producers and users other than private households may, without prejudice to this Directive, conclude agreements stipulating other financing methods.][1]

Amendment

1 Substituted by Directive 2003/108/EC of the European Parliament and of the Council of 8 December 2003 amending Directive 2002/96/EC on waste electrical and electronic equipment (WEEE), Article 1.

Article 10

Information for users

1. Member States shall ensure that users of electrical and electronic equipment in private households are given the necessary information about:

(a) the requirement not to dispose of WEEE as unsorted municipal waste and to collect such WEEE separately;

(b) the return and collection systems available to them;

(c) their role in contributing to reuse, recycling and other forms of recovery of WEEE;

(d) the potential effects on the environment and human health as a result of the presence of hazardous substances in electrical and electronic equipment;

(e) the meaning of the symbol shown in Annex IV.

2. Member States shall adopt appropriate measures so that consumers participate in the collection of WEEE and to encourage them to facilitate the process of reuse, treatment and recovery.

3. With a view to minimising the disposal of WEEE as unsorted municipal waste and to facilitating its separate collection, Member States shall ensure that producers appropriately mark electrical and electronic equipment put on the market after 13 August 2005 with the symbol shown in Annex IV. In exceptional cases, where this is necessary because of the size or the function of the product, the symbol shall be printed on the packaging, on the instructions for use and on the warranty of the electrical and electronic equipment.

4. Member States may require that some or all of the information referred to in paragraphs 1 to 3 shall be provided by producers and/or distributors, e.g. in the instructions for use or at the point of sale.

Article 11

Information for treatment facilities

1. In order to facilitate the reuse and the correct and environmentally sound treatment of WEEE, including maintenance, upgrade, refurbishment and recycling, Member States shall

take the necessary measures to ensure that producers provide reuse and treatment information for each type of new EEE put on the market within one year after the equipment is put on the market. This information shall identify, as far as it is needed by reuse centres, treatment and recycling facilities in order to comply with the provisions of this Directive, the different EEE components and materials, as well as the location of dangerous substances and [mixtures][1] in EEE. It shall be made available to reuse centres, treatment and recycling facilities by producers of EEE in the form of manuals or by means of electronic media (e.g. CD-ROM, online services).

2. Member States shall ensure that any producer of an electrical or electronic appliance put on the market after 13 August 2005 is clearly identifiable by a mark on the appliance. Furthermore, in order to enable the date upon which the appliance was put on the market to be determined unequivocally, a mark on the appliance shall specify that the latter was put on the market after 13 August 2005 The Commission shall promote the preparation of European standards for this purpose.

Amendment

1 Substituted by Directive 2008/112/EC of the European Parliament and of the Council of 16 December 2008 amending Council Directives 76/768/EEC, 88/378/EEC, 1999/13/EC and Directives 2000/53/EC, 2002/96/EC and 2004/42/EC of the European Parliament and of the Council in order to adapt them to Regulation (EC) No 1272/2008 on classification, labelling and packaging of substances and mixtures, Article 5.1.

Article 12

Information and reporting

1. Member States shall draw up a register of producers and collect information, including substantiated estimates, on an annual basis on the quantities and categories of electrical and electronic equipment put on their market, collected through all routes, reused, recycled and recovered within the Member States, and on collected waste exported, by weight or, if this is not possible, by numbers.

Member States shall ensure that producers supplying electrical and electronic equipment by means of distance communication provide information on the compliance with the requirements of Article 8(4) and on the quantities and categories of electrical and electronic equipment put on the market of the Member State where the purchaser of that equipment resides.

Member States shall ensure that the information required is transmitted to the Commission on a two-yearly basis within 18 months after the end of the period covered. The first set of information shall cover the years 2005 and 2006. The information shall be provided in a format which shall be established within one year after the entry into force of this Directive in accordance with the procedure referred to in Article 14(2) with a view to establishing databases on WEEE and its treatment.

Member States shall provide for adequate information exchange in order to comply with this paragraph, in particular for treatment operations as referred to in Article 6(5).

2. Without prejudice to the requirements of paragraph 1, Member States shall send a report to the Commission on the implementation of this Directive at three-year intervals. The report shall be drawn up on the basis of a questionnaire or outline drafted by the Commission in accordance with the procedure laid down in Article 6 of Council Directive 91/692/EEC of 23 December 1991 standardising and rationalising reports on the implementation of certain Directives relating to the environment(19). The questionnaire or outline shall be sent to the Member States six months before the start of the period covered by the report. The report shall be made available to the Commission within nine months of the end of the three-year period covered by it.

The first three-year report shall cover the period from 2004 to 2006.

The Commission shall publish a report on the implementation of this Directive within nine months after receiving the reports from the Member States.

[Article 13

Adaptation to scientific and technical progress][1]

[Any amendments which are necessary in order to adapt Article 7(3), Annex IB (in particular with a view to possibly adding luminaires in households, filament bulbs and photovoltaic products, i.e. solar panels), Annex II (in particular taking into account new technical developments for the treatment of WEEE), and Annexes III and IV to scientific and technical progress shall be adopted. Those measures, designed to amend non-essential elements of this Directive, shall be adopted in accordance with the regulatory procedure with scrutiny referred to in Article 14(3).

Before the annexes are amended the Commission shall, inter alia, consult producers of electrical and electronic equipment, recyclers, treatment operators and environmental organisations and employees' and consumer associations.][1]

Amendment

1 Substituted by Directive 2008/34/EC of the European Parliament and of the Council of 11 March 2008 amending Directive 2002/96/EC on waste electrical and electronic equipment (WEEE), as regards the implementing powers conferred on the Commission, Article 1.3.

Article 14

Committee

1. The Commission shall be assisted by the Committee set up by Article 18 of Directive 75/442/EEC.

2. Where reference is made to this paragraph, Articles 5 and 7 of Decision 1999/468/EC shall apply, having regard to Article 8 thereof.

The period laid down in Article 5(6) of Decision 1999/468/EC shall be set at three months.

[3. Where reference is made to this paragraph, Article 5a(1) to (4) and Article 7 of Decision 1999/468/EC shall apply, having regard to the provisions of Article 8 thereof.][1]

Amendment

1 Substituted by Directive 2008/34/EC of the European Parliament and of the Council of 11 March 2008 amending Directive 2002/96/EC on waste electrical and electronic equipment (WEEE), as regards the implementing powers conferred on the Commission, Article 1.4.

Article 15

Penalties

Member States shall determine penalties applicable to breaches of the national provisions adopted pursuant to this Directive. The penalties thus provided for shall be effective, proportionate and dissuasive.

Article 16

Inspection and monitoring

Member States shall ensure that inspection and monitoring enable the proper implementation of this Directive to be verified.

Article 17

Transposition

1. Member States shall bring into force the laws, regulations and administrative provisions necessary to comply with this Directive by 13 August 2004. They shall immediately inform the Commission thereof.

When Member States adopt these measures, they shall contain a reference to this Directive or be accompanied by such reference on the occasion of their official publication. The methods of making such a reference shall be laid down by the Member States.

2. Member States shall communicate to the Commission the text of all laws, regulations and administrative provisions adopted in the field covered by this Directive.

3. Provided that the objectives set out in this Directive are achieved, Member States may transpose the provisions set out in Articles 6(6), 10(1) and 11 by means of agreements between the competent authorities and the economic sectors concerned. Such agreements shall meet the following requirements:

(a) agreements shall be enforceable;
(b) agreements shall specify objectives with the corresponding deadlines;
(c) agreements shall be published in the national official journal or an official document equally accessible to the public and transmitted to the Commission;
(d) the results achieved shall be monitored regularly, reported to the competent authorities and the Commission and made available to the public under the conditions set out in the agreement;
(e) the competent authorities shall ensure that the progress reached under the agreement is examined;
(f) in case of non-compliance with the agreement Member States must implement the relevant provisions of this Directive by legislative, regulatory or administrative measures.

4.

(a) Greece and Ireland which, because of their overall:
 — recycling infrastructure deficit,
 — geographical circumstances such as the large number of small islands and the presence of rural and mountain areas,
 — low population density, and
 — low level of EEE consumption,

 are unable to reach either the collection target mentioned in the first subparagraph of Article 5(5) or the recovery targets mentioned in Article 7(2) and which, under the third subparagraph of Article 5(2) of Council Directive 1999/31/EC of 26 April 1999 on the landfill of waste(20), may apply for an extension of the deadline mentioned in that Article,

 may extend the periods referred to in Articles 5(5) and 7(2) of this Directive by up to 24 months.

 These Member States shall inform the Commission of their Decisions at the latest at the time of transposition of this Directive.

(b) The Commission shall inform other Member States and the European Parliament of these decisions.

5. Within five years after the entry into force of this Directive, the Commission shall submit a report to the European Parliament and the Council based on the experience of the application of this Directive, in particular as regards separate collection, treatment, recovery and financing systems. Furthermore the report shall be based on the development of the state of technology, experience gained, environmental requirements and the functioning of the internal market. The report shall, as appropriate, be accompanied by proposals for revision of the relevant provisions of this Directive.

Article 18

Entry into force

This Directive shall enter into force on the day of its publication in the Official Journal of the European Union.

Article 19

Addressees

This Directive is addressed to the Member States.

ANNEX IA
CATEGORIES OF ELECTRICAL AND ELECTRONIC EQUIPMENT COVERED BY THIS DIRECTIVE

1. Large household appliances
2. Small household appliances
3. IT and telecommunications equipment
4. Consumer equipment
5. Lighting equipment
6. Electrical and electronic tools (with the exception of large-scale stationary industrial tools)
7. Toys, leisure and sports equipment
8. Medical devices (with the exception of all implanted and infected products)
9. Monitoring and control instruments
10. Automatic dispensers

ANNEX IB
LIST OF PRODUCTS WHICH SHALL BE TAKEN INTO ACCOUNT FOR THE PURPOSE OF THIS DIRECTIVE AND WHICH FALL UNDER THE CATEGORIES OF ANNEX IA

1. LARGE HOUSEHOLD APPLIANCES

Large cooling appliances

Refrigerators

Freezers

Other large appliances used for refrigeration, conservation and storage of food

Washing machines

Clothes dryers

Dish washing machines

Cooking

Electric stoves

Electric hot plates

Microwaves

Other large appliances used for cooking and other processing of food

Electric heating appliances

Electric radiators

Other large appliances for heating rooms, beds, seating furniture

Electric fans

Air conditioner appliances

Other fanning, exhaust ventilation and conditioning equipment

2. SMALL HOUSEHOLD APPLIANCES

Vacuum cleaners

Carpet sweepers

Other appliances for cleaning

Appliances used for sewing, knitting, weaving and other processing for textiles

Irons and other appliances for ironing, mangling and other care of clothing

Toasters

Fryers

Grinders, coffee machines and equipment for opening or sealing containers or packages

Electric knives

Appliances for hair-cutting, hair drying, tooth brushing, shaving, massage and other body care appliances

Clocks, watches and equipment for the purpose of measuring, indicating or registering time

Scales

3. IT AND TELECOMMUNICATIONS EQUIPMENT

Centralised data processing:

Mainframes

Minicomputers

Printer units

Personal computing:

Personal computers (CPU, mouse, screen and keyboard included)

Laptop computers (CPU, mouse, screen and keyboard included)

Notebook computers

Notepad computers

Printers

Copying equipment

Electrical and electronic typewriters

Pocket and desk calculators

and other products and equipment for the collection, storage, processing, presentation or communication of information by electronic means

User terminals and systems

Facsimile

Telex

Telephones

Pay telephones

Cordless telephones

Cellular telephones

Answering systems

and other products or equipment of transmitting sound, images or other information by telecommunications

4. CONSUMER EQUIPMENT

Radio sets

Television sets

Videocameras

Video recorders

Hi-fi recorders

Audio amplifiers

Musical instruments

And other products or equipment for the purpose of recording or reproducing sound or images, including signals or other technologies for the distribution of sound and image than by telecommunications

5. LIGHTING EQUIPMENT

Luminaires for fluorescent lamps with the exception of luminaires in households

Straight fluorescent lamps

Compact fluorescent lamps

High intensity discharge lamps, including pressure sodium lamps and metal halide lamps

Low pressure sodium lamps

Other lighting or equipment for the purpose of spreading or controlling light with the exception of filament bulbs

6. ELECTRICAL AND ELECTRONIC TOOLS (WITH THE EXCEPTION OF LARGE-SCALE STATIONARY INDUSTRIAL TOOLS)

Drills

Saws

Sewing machines

Equipment for turning, milling, sanding, grinding, sawing, cutting, shearing, drilling, making holes, punching, folding, bending or similar processing of wood, metal and other materials

Tools for riveting, nailing or screwing or removing rivets, nails, screws or similar uses

Tools for welding, soldering or similar use

Equipment for spraying, spreading, dispersing or other treatment of liquid or gaseous substances by other means

Tools for mowing or other gardening activities

7. TOYS, LEISURE AND SPORTS EQUIPMENT

Electric trains or car racing sets

Hand-held video game consoles

Video games

Computers for biking, diving, running, rowing, etc.

Sports equipment with electric or electronic components

Coin slot machines

8. MEDICAL DEVICES (WITH THE EXCEPTION OF ALL IMPLANTED AND INFECTED PRODUCTS)

Radiotherapy equipment

Cardiology

Dialysis

Pulmonary ventilators

Nuclear medicine

Laboratory equipment for in-vitro diagnosis

Analysers

Freezers

Fertilization tests

Other appliances for detecting, preventing, monitoring, treating, alleviating illness, injury or disability

9. MONITORING AND CONTROL INSTRUMENTS

Smoke detector

Heating regulators

Thermostats

Measuring, weighing or adjusting appliances for household or as laboratory equipment

Other monitoring and control instruments used in industrial installations (e.g. in control panels)

10. AUTOMATIC DISPENSERS

Automatic dispensers for hot drinks

Automatic dispensers for hot or cold bottles or cans

Automatic dispensers for solid products

Automatic dispensers for money

All appliances which deliver automatically all kind of products

ANNEX II
SELECTIVE TREATMENT FOR MATERIALS AND COMPONENTS OF WASTE ELECTRICAL AND ELECTRONIC EQUIPMENT IN ACCORDANCE WITH ARTICLE 6(1)

1. As a minimum the following substances, [mixtures][1] and components have to be removed from any separately collected WEEE:

— polychlorinated biphenyls (PCB) containing capacitors in accordance with Council Directive 96/59/EC of 16 September 1996 on the disposal of polychlorinated biphenyls and polychlorinated terphenyls (PCB/PCT),

— mercury containing components, such as switches or backlighting lamps,

— batteries,

— printed circuit boards of mobile phones generally, and of other devices if the surface of the printed circuit board is greater than 10 square centimetres,

— toner cartridges, liquid and pasty, as well as colour toner,

— plastic containing brominated flame retardants,

— asbestos waste and components which contain asbestos,

— cathode ray tubes,

— chlorofluorocarbons (CFC), hydrochlorofluorocarbons (HCFC) or hydrofluorocarbons (HFC), hydrocarbons (HC),

— gas discharge lamps,

— liquid crystal displays (together with their casing where appropriate) of a surface greater than 100 square centimetres and all those back-lighted with gas discharge lamps,

— external electric cables,

[— components containing refractory ceramic fibres as described in part 3 of Annex VI to Regulatin (EC) No 1272/2008,][1]

— components containing radioactive substances with the exception of components that are below the exemption thresholds set in Article 3 of and Annex I to Council Directive 96/29/Euratom of 13 May 1996 laying down basic safety standards for the protection of the health of workers and the general public against the dangers arising from ionising radiation,

— electrolyte capacitors containing substances of concern (height > 25 mm, diameter > 25 mm or proportionately similar volume)

These substances, [mixtures][1] and components shall be disposed of or recovered in compliance with Article 4 of Council Directive 75/442/EEC.

2. The following components of WEEE that is separately collected have to be treated as indicated:

— cathode ray tubes: The fluorescent coating has to be removed,

— equipment containing gases that are ozone depleting or have a global warming potential (GWP) above 15, such as those contained in foams and refrigeration circuits: the gases must be properly extracted and properly treated. Ozone-depleting gases must be treated in accordance with Regulation (EC) No 2037/2000 of the European Parliament and of the Council of 29 June 2000 on substances that deplete the ozone layer.

— gas discharge lamps: The mercury shall be removed.

3. Taking into account environmental considerations and the desirability of reuse and recycling, paragraphs 1 and 2 shall be applied in such a way that environmentally-sound reuse and recycling of components or whole appliances is not hindered.

[4. Acting in accordance with the regulatory procedure with scrutiny referred to in Article 14(3), the Commission shall evaluate as a matter of priority whether the entries regarding printed circuit boards for mobile phones and liquid crystal displays are to be amended.][2]

Amendments

1 Substituted by Directive 2008/112/EC of the European Parliament and of the Council of 16 December 2008 amending Council Directives 76/768/EEC, 88/378/EEC, 1999/13/EC and Directives 2000/53/EC, 2002/96/EC and 2004/42/EC of the European Parliament and of the Council in order to adapt them to Regulation (EC) No 1272/2008 on classification, labelling and packaging of substances and mixtures, Article 5.1, 5.4.

2 Substituted by Directive 2008/34/EC of the European Parliament and of the Council of 11 March 2008 amending Directive 2002/96/EC on waste electrical and electronic equipment (WEEE), as regards the implementing powers conferred on the Commission, Article 1.5.

ANNEX III
TECHNICAL REQUIREMENTS IN ACCORDANCE WITH ARTICLE 6(3)

1. Sites for storage (including temporary storage) of WEEE prior to their treatment (without prejudice to the requirements of Council Directive 1999/31/EC):

— impermeable surfaces for appropriate areas with the provision of spillage collection facilities and, where appropriate, decanters and cleanser-degreasers,

— weatherproof covering for appropriate areas.

2. Sites for treatment of WEEE:

— balances to measure the weight of the treated waste,

— impermeable surfaces and waterproof covering for appropriate areas with the provision of spillage collection facilities and, where appropriate, decanters and cleanser-degreasers,

— appropriate storage for disassembled spare parts,

— appropriate containers for storage of batteries, PCBs/PCTs containing capacitors and other hazardous waste such as radioactive waste,

— equipment for the treatment of water in compliance with health and environmental regulations.

ANNEX IV
SYMBOL FOR THE MARKING OF ELECTRICAL AND ELECTRONIC EQUIPMENT

The symbol indicating separate collection for electrical and electronic equipment consists of the crossed-out wheeled bin, as shown below. The symbol must be printed visibly, legibly and indelibly.

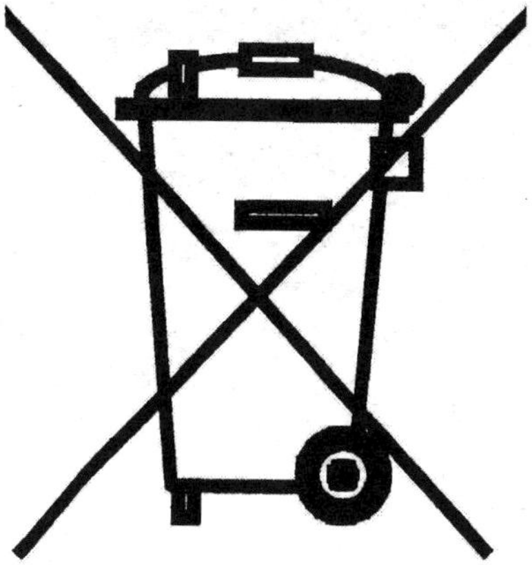

DIRECTIVE 2003/4/EC OF THE EUROPEAN PARLIAMENT AND OF THE COUNCIL

of 28 January 2003

ON PUBLIC ACCESS TO ENVIRONMENTAL INFORMATION AND REPEALING COUNCIL DIRECTIVE 90/313/EEC

THE EUROPEAN PARLIAMENT AND THE COUNCIL OF THE EUROPEAN UNION,

Having regard to the Treaty establishing the European Community, and in particular Article 175(1) thereof,

Having regard to the proposal from the Commission,

Having regard to the opinion of the European Economic and Social Committee,

Having regard to the opinion of the Committee of the Regions,

Acting in accordance with the procedure laid down in Article 251 of the Treaty in the light of the joint text approved by the Conciliation Committee on 8 November 2002,

Whereas:

(1) Increased public access to environmental information and the dissemination of such information contribute to a greater awareness of environmental matters, a free exchange of views, more effective participation by the public in environmental decision-making and, eventually, to a better environment.

(2) Council Directive 90/313/EEC of 7 June 1990 on the freedom of access to information on the environment initiated a process of change in the manner in which public authorities approach the issue of openness and transparency, establishing measures for the exercise of the right of public access to environmental information which should be developed and continued. This Directive expands the existing access granted under Directive 90/313/EEC.

(3) Article 8 of that Directive requires Member States to report to the Commission on the experience gained, in the light of which the Commission is required to make a report to the European Parliament and to the Council together with any proposal for revision of the Directive which it may consider appropriate.

(4) The report produced under Article 8 of that Directive identifies concrete problems encountered in the practical application of the Directive.

(5) On 25 June 1998 the European Community signed the UN/ECE Convention on Access to Information, Public Participation in Decision-Making and Access to Justice in Environmental Matters ("the Aarhus Convention"). Provisions of Community law must be consistent with that Convention with a view to its conclusion by the European Community.

(6) It is appropriate in the interest of increased transparency to replace Directive 90/313/EEC rather than to amend it, so as to provide interested parties with a single, clear and coherent legislative text.

(7) Disparities between the laws in force in the Member States concerning access to environmental information held by public authorities can create inequality within the Community as regards access to such information or as regards conditions of competition.

(8) It is necessary to ensure that any natural and legal person has a right of access to environmental information held by or for public authorities without his having to state an interest.

(9) It is also necessary that public authorities make available and disseminate environmental information to the general public to the widest extent possible, in particular by using information and communication technologies. The future development of these technologies should be taken into account in the reporting on, and reviewing of, this Directive.

(10) The definition of environmental information should be clarified so as to encompass information in any form on the state of the environment, on factors, measures or activities affecting or likely to affect the environment or designed to protect it, on cost-benefit and economic analyses used within the framework of such measures or activities and also information on the state of human health and safety, including the contamination of the food chain, conditions of human life, cultural sites and built structures in as much as they are, or may be, affected by any of those matters.

(11) To take account of the principle in Article 6 of the Treaty, that environmental protection requirements should be integrated into the definition and implementation of Community policies and activities, the definition of public authorities should be expanded so as to encompass government or other public administration at national, regional or local level whether or not they have specific responsibilities for the environment. The definition should likewise be expanded to include other persons or bodies performing public administrative functions in relation to the environment under national law, as well as other persons or bodies acting under their control and having public responsibilities or functions in relation to the environment.

(12) Environmental information which is physically held by other bodies on behalf of public authorities should also fall within the scope of this Directive.

(13) Environmental information should be made available to applicants as soon as possible and within a reasonable time and having regard to any timescale specified by the applicant.

(14) Public authorities should make environmental information available in the form or format requested by an applicant unless it is already publicly available in another form or format or it is reasonable to make it available in another form or format. In addition, public authorities should be required to make all reasonable efforts to maintain the environmental information held by or for them in forms or formats that are readily reproducible and accessible by electronic means.

(15) Member States should determine the practical arrangements under which such information is effectively made available. These arrangements shall guarantee that the information is effectively and easily accessible and progressively becomes available to the public through public telecommunications networks, including publicly accessible lists of public authorities and registers or lists of environmental information held by or for public authorities.

(16) The right to information means that the disclosure of information should be the general rule and that public authorities should be permitted to refuse a request for environmental information in specific and clearly defined cases. Grounds for refusal should be interpreted in a restrictive way, whereby the public interest served by disclosure should be weighed against the interest served by the refusal. The reasons for a refusal should be provided to the applicant within the time limit laid down in this Directive.

(17) Public authorities should make environmental information available in part where it is possible to separate out any information falling within the scope of the exceptions from the rest of the information requested.

(18) Public authorities should be able to make a charge for supplying environmental information but such a charge should be reasonable. This implies that, as a general rule, charges may not exceed actual costs of producing the material in question. Instances where advance payment will be required should be limited. In particular cases, where public authorities make available environmental information on a commercial basis, and where this is necessary in order to guarantee the continuation of collecting and publishing such information, a market-based charge is considered to be reasonable; an advance payment may be required. A schedule of charges should be published and

made available to applicants together with information on the circumstances in which a charge may be levied or waived.

(19) Applicants should be able to seek an administrative or judicial review of the acts or omissions of a public authority in relation to a request.

(20) Public authorities should seek to guarantee that when environmental information is compiled by them or on their behalf, the information is comprehensible, accurate and comparable. As this is an important factor in assessing the quality of the information supplied the method used in compiling the information should also be disclosed upon request.

(21) In order to increase public awareness in environmental matters and to improve environmental protection, public authorities should, as appropriate, make available and disseminate information on the environment which is relevant to their functions, in particular by means of computer telecommunication and/or electronic technology, where available.

(22) This Directive should be evaluated every four years, after its entry into force, in the light of experience and after submission of the relevant reports by the Member States, and be subject to revision on that basis. The Commission should submit an evaluation report to the European Parliament and the Council.

(23) Since the objectives of the proposed Directive cannot be sufficiently achieved by the Member States and can therefore be better achieved at Community level, the Community may adopt measures, in accordance with the principle of subsidiarity as set out in Article 5 of the Treaty. In accordance with the principle of proportionality, as set out in that Article, this Directive does not go beyond what is necessary in order to achieve those objectives.

(24) The provisions of this Directive shall not affect the right of a Member State to maintain or introduce measures providing for broader access to information than required by this Directive,

HAVE ADOPTED THIS DIRECTIVE:

Article 1

Objectives

The objectives of this Directive are:

(a) to guarantee the right of access to environmental information held by or for public authorities and to set out the basic terms and conditions of, and practical arrangements for, its exercise; and

(b) to ensure that, as a matter of course, environmental information is progressively made available and disseminated to the public in order to achieve the widest possible systematic availability and dissemination to the public of environmental information. To this end the use, in particular, of computer telecommunication and/or electronic technology, where available, shall be promoted.

Article 2

Definitions

For the purposes of this Directive:

1. "Environmental information" shall mean any information in written, visual, aural, electronic or any other material form on:

   (a) the state of the elements of the environment, such as air and atmosphere, water, soil, land, landscape and natural sites including wetlands, coastal and marine areas, biological diversity and its components, including genetically modified organisms, and the interaction among these elements;

(b) factors, such as substances, energy, noise, radiation or waste, including radioactive waste, emissions, discharges and other releases into the environment, affecting or likely to affect the elements of the environment referred to in (a);
(c) measures (including administrative measures), such as policies, legislation, plans, programmes, environmental agreements, and activities affecting or likely to affect the elements and factors referred to in (a) and (b) as well as measures or activities designed to protect those elements;
(d) reports on the implementation of environmental legislation;
(e) cost-benefit and other economic analyses and assumptions used within the framework of the measures and activities referred to in (c); and
(f) the state of human health and safety, including the contamination of the food chain, where relevant, conditions of human life, cultural sites and built structures inasmuch as they are or may be affected by the state of the elements of the environment referred to in (a) or, through those elements, by any of the matters referred to in (b) and (c).

2. "Public authority" shall mean:
(a) government or other public administration, including public advisory bodies, at national, regional or local level;
(b) any natural or legal person performing public administrative functions under national law, including specific duties, activities or services in relation to the environment; and
(c) any natural or legal person having public responsibilities or functions, or providing public services, relating to the environment under the control of a body or person falling within (a) or (b).

Member States may provide that this definition shall not include bodies or institutions when acting in a judicial or legislative capacity. If their constitutional provisions at the date of adoption of this Directive make no provision for a review procedure within the meaning of Article 6, Member States may exclude those bodies or institutions from that definition.

3. "Information held by a public authority" shall mean environmental information in its possession which has been produced or received by that authority.
4. "Information held for a public authority" shall mean environmental information which is physically held by a natural or legal person on behalf of a public authority.
5. "Applicant" shall mean any natural or legal person requesting environmental information.
6. "Public" shall mean one or more natural or legal persons, and, in accordance with national legislation or practice, their associations, organisations or groups.

Article 3

Access to environmental information upon request

1. Member States shall ensure that public authorities are required, in accordance with the provisions of this Directive, to make available environmental information held by or for them to any applicant at his request and without his having to state an interest.

2. Subject to Article 4 and having regard to any timescale specified by the applicant, environmental information shall be made available to an applicant:
(a) as soon as possible or, at the latest, within one month after the receipt by the public authority referred to in paragraph 1 of the applicant's request; or
(b) within two months after the receipt of the request by the public authority if the volume and the complexity of the information is such that the one-month period referred to in (a) cannot be complied with. In such cases, the applicant shall be informed as soon as possible, and in any case before the end of that one-month period, of any such extension and of the reasons for it.

3. If a request is formulated in too general a manner, the public authority shall as soon as possible, and at the latest within the timeframe laid down in paragraph 2(a), ask the applicant to specify the request and shall assist the applicant in doing so, e.g. by providing information on the use of the public registers referred to in paragraph 5(c). The public authorities may, where they deem it appropriate, refuse the request under Article 4(1)(c).

4. Where an applicant requests a public authority to make environmental information available in a specific form or format (including in the form of copies), the public authority shall make it so available unless:

(a) it is already publicly available in another form or format, in particular under Article 7, which is easily accessible by applicants; or

(b) it is reasonable for the public authority to make it available in another form or format, in which case reasons shall be given for making it available in that form or format.

For the purposes of this paragraph, public authorities shall make all reasonable efforts to maintain environmental information held by or for them in forms or formats that are readily reproducible and accessible by computer telecommunications or by other electronic means.

The reasons for a refusal to make information available, in full or in part, in the form or format requested shall be provided to the applicant within the time limit referred to in paragraph 2(a).

5. For the purposes of this Article, Member States shall ensure that:

(a) officials are required to support the public in seeking access to information;

(b) lists of public authorities are publicly accessible; and

(c) the practical arrangements are defined for ensuring that the right of access to environmental information can be effectively exercised, such as:

— the designation of information officers;

— the establishment and maintenance of facilities for the examination of the information required,

— registers or lists of the environmental information held by public authorities or information points, with clear indications of where such information can be found.

Member States shall ensure that public authorities inform the public adequately of the rights they enjoy as a result of this Directive and to an appropriate extent provide information, guidance and advice to this end.

Article 4

Exceptions

1. Member States may provide for a request for environmental information to be refused if:

(a) the information requested is not held by or for the public authority to which the request is addressed. In such a case, where that public authority is aware that the information is held by or for another public authority, it shall, as soon as possible, transfer the request to that other authority and inform the applicant accordingly or inform the applicant of the public authority to which it believes it is possible to apply for the information requested;

(b) the request is manifestly unreasonable;

(c) the request is formulated in too general a manner, taking into account Article 3(3);

(d) the request concerns material in the course of completion or unfinished documents or data;

(e) the request concerns internal communications, taking into account the public interest served by disclosure.

Where a request is refused on the basis that it concerns material in the course of completion, the public authority shall state the name of the authority preparing the material and the estimated time needed for completion.

2. Member States may provide for a request for environmental information to be refused if disclosure of the information would adversely affect:

(a) the confidentiality of the proceedings of public authorities, where such confidentiality is provided for by law;
(b) international relations, public security or national defence;
(c) the course of justice, the ability of any person to receive a fair trial or the ability of a public authority to conduct an enquiry of a criminal or disciplinary nature;
(d) the confidentiality of commercial or industrial information where such confidentiality is provided for by national or Community law to protect a legitimate economic interest, including the public interest in maintaining statistical confidentiality and tax secrecy;
(e) intellectual property rights;
(f) the confidentiality of personal data and/or files relating to a natural person where that person has not consented to the disclosure of the information to the public, where such confidentiality is provided for by national or Community law;
(g) the interests or protection of any person who supplied the information requested on a voluntary basis without being under, or capable of being put under, a legal obligation to do so, unless that person has consented to the release of the information concerned;
(h) the protection of the environment to which such information relates, such as the location of rare species.

The grounds for refusal mentioned in paragraphs 1 and 2 shall be interpreted in a restrictive way, taking into account for the particular case the public interest served by disclosure. In every particular case, the public interest served by disclosure shall be weighed against the interest served by the refusal. Member States may not, by virtue of paragraph 2(a), (d), (f), (g) and (h), provide for a request to be refused where the request relates to information on emissions into the environment.

Within this framework, and for the purposes of the application of subparagraph (f), Member States shall ensure that the requirements of Directive 95/46/EC of the European Parliament and of the Council of 24 October 1995 on the protection of individuals with regard to the processing of personal data and on the free movement of such data are complied with(6).

3. Where a Member State provides for exceptions, it may draw up a publicly accessible list of criteria on the basis of which the authority concerned may decide how to handle requests.

4. Environmental information held by or for public authorities which has been requested by an applicant shall be made available in part where it is possible to separate out any information falling within the scope of paragraphs 1(d) and (e) or 2 from the rest of the information requested.

5. A refusal to make available all or part of the information requested shall be notified to the applicant in writing or electronically, if the request was in writing or if the applicant so requests, within the time limits referred to in Article 3(2)(a) or, as the case may be, (b). The notification shall state the reasons for the refusal and include information on the review procedure provided for in accordance with Article 6.

Article 5

Charges

1. Access to any public registers or lists established and maintained as mentioned in Article 3(5) and examination in situ of the information requested shall be free of charge.

2. Public authorities may make a charge for supplying any environmental information but such charge shall not exceed a reasonable amount.

3. Where charges are made, public authorities shall publish and make available to applicants a schedule of such charges as well as information on the circumstances in which a charge may be levied or waived.

Article 6

Access to justice

1. Member States shall ensure that any applicant who considers that his request for information has been ignored, wrongfully refused (whether in full or in part), inadequately answered or otherwise not dealt with in accordance with the provisions of Articles 3, 4 or 5, has access to a procedure in which the acts or omissions of the public authority concerned can be reconsidered by that or another public authority or reviewed administratively by an independent and impartial body established by law. Any such procedure shall be expeditious and either free of charge or inexpensive.

2. In addition to the review procedure referred to in paragraph 1, Member States shall ensure that an applicant has access to a review procedure before a court of law or another independent and impartial body established by law, in which the acts or omissions of the public authority concerned can be reviewed and whose decisions may become final. Member States may furthermore provide that third parties incriminated by the disclosure of information may also have access to legal recourse.

3. Final decisions under paragraph 2 shall be binding on the public authority holding the information. Reasons shall be stated in writing, at least where access to information is refused under this Article.

Article 7

Dissemination of environmental information

1. Member States shall take the necessary measures to ensure that public authorities organise the environmental information which is relevant to their functions and which is held by or for them, with a view to its active and systematic dissemination to the public, in particular by means of computer telecommunication and/or electronic technology, where available.

The information made available by means of computer telecommunication and/or electronic technology need not include information collected before the entry into force of this Directive unless it is already available in electronic form.

Member States shall ensure that environmental information progressively becomes available in electronic databases which are easily accessible to the public through public telecommunication networks.

2. The information to be made available and disseminated shall be updated as appropriate and shall include at least:

(a) texts of international treaties, conventions or agreements, and of Community, national, regional or local legislation, on the environment or relating to it;

(b) policies, plans and programmes relating to the environment;

(c) progress reports on the implementation of the items referred to in (a) and (b) when prepared or held in electronic form by public authorities;

(d) the reports on the state of the environment referred to in paragraph 3;

(e) data or summaries of data derived from the monitoring of activities affecting, or likely to affect, the environment;

(f) authorisations with a significant impact on the environment and environmental agreements or a reference to the place where such information can be requested or found in the framework of Article 3;

(g) environmental impact studies and risk assessments concerning the environmental elements referred to in Article 2(1)(a) or a reference to the place where the information can be requested or found in the framework of Article 3.

3. Without prejudice to any specific reporting obligations laid down by Community legislation, Member States shall take the necessary measures to ensure that national, and,

where appropriate, regional or local reports on the state of the environment are published at regular intervals not exceeding four years; such reports shall include information on the quality of, and pressures on, the environment.

4. Without prejudice to any specific obligation laid down by Community legislation, Member States shall take the necessary measures to ensure that, in the event of an imminent threat to human health or the environment, whether caused by human activities or due to natural causes, all information held by or for public authorities which could enable the public likely to be affected to take measures to prevent or mitigate harm arising from the threat is disseminated, immediately and without delay.

5. The exceptions in Article 4(1) and (2) may apply in relation to the duties imposed by this Article.

6. Member States may satisfy the requirements of this Article by creating links to Internet sites where the information can be found.

Article 8

Quality of environmental information

1. Member States shall, so far as is within their power, ensure that any information that is compiled by them or on their behalf is up to date, accurate and comparable.

2. Upon request, public authorities shall reply to requests for information pursuant to Article 2(1)b, reporting to the applicant on the place where information, if available, can be found on the measurement procedures, including methods of analysis, sampling, and pre-treatment of samples, used in compiling the information, or referring to a standardised procedure used.

Article 9

Review procedure

1. Not later than 14 February 2009, Member States shall report on the experience gained in the application of this Directive.

They shall communicate the report to the Commission not later than 14 August 2009.

No later than 14 February 2004, the Commission shall forward to the Member States a guidance document setting out clearly the manner in which it wishes the Member States to report.

2. In the light of experience and taking into account developments in computer telecommunication and/or electronic technology, the Commission shall make a report to the European Parliament and to the Council together with any proposal for revision, which it may consider appropriate.

Article 10

Implementation

Member States shall bring into force the laws, regulations and administrative provisions necessary to comply with this Directive by 14 February 2005. They shall forthwith inform the Commission thereof.

When Member States adopt these measures, they shall contain a reference to this Directive or shall be accompanied by such reference on the occasion of their official publication. The methods of making such reference shall be laid down by Member States.

Article 11

Repeal

Directive 90/313/EEC is hereby repealed with effect from 14 February 2005.

References to the repealed Directive shall be construed as referring to this Directive and shall be read in accordance with the correlation table in the Annex.

Article 12

Entry into force

This Directive shall enter into force on the day of its publication in the Official Journal of the European Union.

Article 13

Addressees

This Directive is addressed to the Member States.

ANNEX
CORRELATION TABLE

Directive 90/313/EEC	*This Directive*
Article 1	Article 1(a) Article 1(b)
Article 2(a) Article 2(b) — — — —	Article 2(1) Article 2(2) Article 2(3) Article 2(4) Article 2(5) Article 2(6)
Article 3(1) Article 3(2) Article 3(3) Article 3(4) — — —	Article 3(1) and Article 3(5) Article 4(2) and Article 4(4) Article 4(1)(b), (c), (d) and (e) Article 3(2) and Article 4(5) Article 4(1)(a) Article 3(3) Article 3(4)
Article 4 —	Article 6(1) and Article 6(2) Article 6(3)
Article 5 — —	Article 5(1) Article 5(2) Article 5(3)
Article 6	Article 2(2)(c), Article 3(1)
Article 7 — — — —	Article 7(1), (2) and (3) Article 7(4) Article 7(5) Article 7(6) Article 8
Article 8	Article 9
Article 9	Article 10
Article 10	Article 13
—	Article 11
—	Article 12

COUNCIL DECISION 2003/33/EC

of 19 December 2002

ESTABLISHING CRITERIA AND PROCEDURES FOR THE ACCEPTANCE OF WASTE AT LANDFILLS PURSUANT TO ARTICLE 16 OF AND ANNEX II TO DIRECTIVE 1999/31/EC

THE COUNCIL FO THE EUROPEAN UNION,

Having regard to the Treaty establishing the European Community,

Having regard to Council Directive 1999/31/EC of 26 April 1999 on the landfill of waste, and in particular Article 16 thereof and Annex II thereto,

Whereas:

(1) Pursuant to Article 16 of Directive 1999/31/EC, the Commission is to adopt specific criteria and/or test methods and associated limit values for each class of landfill.

(2) A procedure should be laid down to determine the acceptability of waste at landfills.

(3) Limit values and other criteria should be set for waste acceptable at the different classes of landfills.

(4) The test methods to be used for determining the acceptability of waste at landfills should be determined.

(5) It is appropriate from a technical point of view to exempt from the criteria and procedures set out in the Annex to this Decision those wastes generated by the extractive industry that are deposited on-site.

(6) A suitably short transition period should be granted to Member States to develop the necessary system to apply this Decision and a further brief transition period may be necessary for Member States to ensure the application of the limit values.

(7) The measures provided for in this Decision are not in accordance with the opinion of the Committee established by Article 18 of Council Directive 75/442/EEC of 15 July 1975 on waste. They therefore have to be adopted by the Council in accordance with Article 18(4) of that Directive,

HAS ADOPTED THIS DECISION:

Article 1

This Decision establishes the criteria and procedures for the acceptance of waste at landfills in accordance with the principles set out in Directive 1999/31/EC and in particular Annex II thereto.

Article 2

Member States shall apply the procedure as set out in section 1 of the Annex to this Decision to determine the acceptability of waste at landfills.

Article 3

Member States shall ensure that waste is accepted at a landfill only if it fulfils the acceptance criteria of the relevant landfill class as set out in section 2 of the Annex to this Decision.

Article 4

The sampling and testing methods listed in section 3 of the Annex to this Decision shall be used for determining the acceptability of waste at landfills.

Article 5

Without prejudice to existing Community legislation, the criteria and procedures as set out in the Annex to this Decision shall not apply to waste resulting from prospecting, extraction, treatment and storage of mineral resources nor from the working of quarries, when they are deposited on-site. In the absence of specific Community legislation, Member States shall apply national criteria and procedures.

Article 6

Any amendments necessary for future updating of this Decision to scientific and technical progress shall be adopted by the Commission, assisted by the Committee established under Article 18 of Directive 75/442/EEC, for example adjustment of the parameters in the lists of limit values and/or development of acceptance criteria and limit values for additional subcategories of landfills for non-hazardous waste.

Article 7

1. This Decision shall take effect on 16 July 2004.
2. Member States shall apply the criteria set out in section 2 of the Annex to this Decision by 16 July 2005.

Article 8

This Decision is addressed to the Member States.

ANNEX
CRITERIA AND PROCEDURES FOR THE ACCEPTANCE OF WASTE AT LANDFILLS

Introduction

This Annex lays down the uniform waste classification and acceptance procedure according to Annex II to Directive 1999/31/EC on the landfill of waste (the "Landfill Directive").

In accordance with Article 176 of the Treaty, Member States are not prevented from maintaining or introducing more stringent protective measures than those established in this Annex, provided that such measures are compatible with the Treaty. Such measures shall be notified to the Commission. This could be of particular relevance with reference to the limit values for cadmium and mercury in section 2. Member States may also introduce limit values for components not included in section 2.

Section 1 of this Annex lays down the procedure to determine the acceptability of waste at landfills. This procedure consists of the basic characterisation, compliance testing and on-site verification as defined in section 3 of Annex II to the Landfill Directive.

Section 2 of this Annex lays down the acceptance criteria for each landfill class. Waste may be accepted at a landfill only if it fulfils the acceptance criteria of the relevant landfill class as laid down in section 2 of this Annex.

Section 3 of this Annex lists the methods to be used for the sampling and testing of waste.

Appendix A defines the safety assessment to be carried out for underground storage.

Appendix B is an informative Annex providing an overview of the landfill options available within the Directive and examples of possible subcategorisation of landfills' non-hazardous waste.

1. PROCEDURE FOR THE ACCEPTANCE OF WASTE AT LANDFILLS

1.1. Basic characterisation

Basic characterisation is the first step in the acceptance procedure and constitutes a full characterisation of the waste by gathering all the necessary information for a safe disposal of the waste in the long term. Basic characterisation is required for each type of waste.

1.1.1. Functions of basic characterisation

(a) Basic information on the waste (type and origin, composition, consistency, leachability and – where necessary and available – other characteristic properties)

(b) Basic information for understanding the behaviour of waste in landfills and options for treatment as laid out in Article 6(a) of the Landfill Directive

(c) Assessing waste against limit values

(d) Detection of key variables (critical parameters) for compliance testing and options for simplification of compliance testing (leading to a significant decrease of constituents to be measured, but only after demonstration of relevant information). Characterisation may deliver ratios between basic characterisation and results of simplified test procedures as well as frequency for compliance testing.

If the basic characterisation of waste shows that the waste fulfils the criteria for a landfill class as laid down in section 2 of this Annex, the waste is deemed to be acceptable at this landfill class. If this is not the case, the waste is not acceptable at this landfill class.

The producer of the waste or, in default, the person responsible for its management, is responsible for ensuring that the characterisation information is correct.

The operator shall keep records of the required information for a period to be defined by the Member State.

1.1.2. Fundamental requirements for basic characterisation of the waste

(a) Source and origin of the waste

(b) Information on the process producing the waste (description and characteristics of raw materials and products)

(c) Description of the waste treatment applied in compliance with Article 6(a) of the Landfill Directive, or a statement of reasons why such treatment is not considered necessary

(d) Data on the composition of the waste and the leaching behaviour, where relevant

(e) Appearance of the waste (smell, colour, physical form)

(f) Code according to the European waste list (Commission Decision 2001/118/EC)

(g) For hazardous waste in case of mirror entries: the relevant hazard properties according to Annex III to Council Directive 91/689/EEC of 12 December 1991 on hazardous waste

(h) Information to prove that the waste does not fall under the exclusions of Article 5(3) of the Landfill Directive

(i) The landfill class at which the waste may be accepted

(j) If necessary, additional precautions to be taken at the landfill

(k) Check if the waste can be recycled or recovered.

1.1.3. Testing

As a general rule waste must be tested to obtain the above information. In addition to the leaching behaviour, the composition of the waste must be known or determined by testing. The tests used for basic characterisation must always include those to be used for compliance testing.

The content of the characterisation, the extent of laboratory testing required and the relationship between basic characterisation and compliance checking depends on the type of waste. A differentiation can be made between:

(a) wastes that are regularly generated in the same process;
(b) wastes that are not regularly generated.

The characterisations outlined in points (a) and (b) will provide information that can be directly compared with acceptance criteria for the relevant class of landfill and, in addition, descriptive information can be supplied (e.g. the consequences of depositing with municipal waste).

(a) Wastes regularly generated in the same process

These are individual and consistent wastes regularly generated in the same process, where:

— the installation and the process generating the waste are well known and the input materials to the process and the process itself are well defined,
— the operator of the installation provides all necessary information and informs the operator of the landfill of changes to the process (especially changes to the input material).

The process will often be at a single installation. The waste can also be from different installations, if it can be identified as single stream with common characteristics within known boundaries (e.g. bottom ash from the incineration of municipal waste).

For these wastes the basic characterisation will comprise the fundamental requirements listed in section 1.1.2 and especially the following:

— compositional range for the individual wastes,
— range and variability of characteristic properties,
— if required, the leachability of the wastes determined by a batch leaching test and/or a percolation test and/or a pH dependence test,
— key variables to be tested on a regular basis.

If the waste is produced in the same process in different installations, information must be given on the scope of the evaluation. Consequently, a sufficient number of measurements must be taken to show the range and variability of the characteristic properties of the waste. The waste can then be considered characterised and shall subsequently be subject to compliance testing only, unless significant change in the generation processes occur.

For wastes from the same process in the same installation, the results of the measurements may show only minor variations of the properties of the waste in comparison with the appropriate limit values. The waste can then be considered characterised, and shall subsequently be subject to compliance testing only, unless significant changes in the generation process occur.

Waste from facilities for the bulking or mixing of waste, from waste transfer stations or mixed waste streams from waste collectors, can vary considerably in their properties. This must be taken into consideration in the basic characterisation. Such wastes may fall under case (b).

(b) Wastes that are not regularly generated

These wastes are not regularly generated in the same process in the same installation and are not part of a well-characterised waste stream. Each batch produced of such waste will need to be characterised. The basic characterisation shall include the fundamental requirements for basic characterisation. As each batch produced has to be characterised, no compliance testing is needed.

1.1.4. Cases where testing is not required

Testing for basic characterisation can be dispensed with in the following cases:

(a) the waste is on a list of wastes not requiring testing as laid down in section 2 of this Annex;
(b) all the necessary information, for the basic characterisation, is known and duly justified to the full satisfaction of the competent authority;
(c) certain waste types where testing is impractical or where appropriate testing procedures and acceptance criteria are unavailable. This must be justified and documented, including the reasons why the waste is deemed acceptable at this landfill class.

1.2. Compliance testing

When waste has been deemed acceptable for a landfill class on the basis of a basic characterisation pursuant to section 1, it shall subsequently be subject to compliance testing to determine if it complies with the results of the basic characterisation and the relevant acceptance criteria as laid down in section 2.

The function of compliance testing is periodically to check regularly arising waste streams.

The relevant parameters to be tested are determined in the basic characterisation. Parameters should be related to basic characterisation information; only a check on critical parameters (key variables), as determined in the basic characterisation, is necessary. The check has to show that the waste meets the limit values for the critical parameters.

The tests used for compliance testing shall be one or more of those used in the basic characterisation. The testing shall consist at least of a batch leaching test. For this purpose the methods listed under section 3 shall be used.

Wastes that are exempted from the testing requirements for basic characterisation in section 1.1.4(a) and section 1.1.4(c) are also exempted from compliance testing. They will, however, need checking for compliance with basic characterisation information other than testing.

Compliance testing shall be carried out at least once a year and the operator must, in any event, ensure that compliance testing is carried out in the scope and frequency determined by basic characterisation.

Records of the test results shall be kept for a period that will be determined by the Member State.

1.3. On-site verification

Each load of waste delivered to a landfill shall be visually inspected before and after unloading. The required documentation shall be checked.

For waste deposited by the waste producer at a landfill in his control, this verification may be made at the point of dispatch.

The waste may be accepted at the landfill, if it is the same as that which has been subjected to basic characterisation and compliance testing and which is described in the accompanying documents. If this is not the case, the waste must not be accepted.

Member States shall determine the testing requirements for on-site verification, including where appropriate rapid test methods.

Upon delivery, samples shall be taken periodically. The samples taken shall be kept after acceptance of the waste for a period that will be determined by the Member State (not less than one month; see Article 11(b) of the Landfill Directive.

2. WASTE ACCEPTANCE CRITERIA

This section sets out the criteria for the acceptance of waste at each landfill class, including criteria for underground storage.

In certain circumstances, up to three times higher limit values for specific parameters listed in this section (other than dissolved organic carbon (DOC) in sections 2.1.2.1, 2.2.2, 2.3.1 and 2.4.1, BTEX, PCBs and mineral oil in section 2.1.2.2, total organic carbon (TOC) and pH in section 2.3.2 and loss on ignition (LOI) and/or TOC in section 2.4.2, and restricting the possible increase of the limit value for TOC in section 2.1.2.2 to only two times the limit value) are acceptable, if

— the competent authority gives a permit for specified wastes on a case-by-case basis for the recipient landfill, taking into account the characteristics of the landfill and its surroundings, and

— emissions (including leachate) from the landfill, taking into account the limits for those specific parameters in this section, will present no additional risk to the environment according to a risk assessment.

Member States shall report to the Commission on the annual number of permits issued under this provision. The reports shall be sent to the Commission at intervals of three years as part of the reporting on the implementation of the Landfill Directive in accordance with the specifications laid down in Article 15 thereof.

Member States shall define criteria for compliance with the limit values set out in this section.

2.1. Criteria for landfills for inert waste

2.1.1. List of wastes acceptable at landfills for inert waste without testing

Wastes on the following short list are assumed to fulfil the criteria as set out in the definition of inert waste in Article 2(e) of the Landfill Directive and the criteria listed in section 2.1.2. The wastes can be admitted without testing at a landfill for inert waste.

The waste must be a single stream (only one source) of a single waste type. Different wastes contained in the list may be accepted together, provided they are from the same source.

In case of suspicion of contamination (either from visual inspection or from knowledge of the origin of the waste) testing should be applied or the waste refused. If the listed wastes are contaminated or contain other material or substances such as metals, asbestos, plastics, chemicals, etc. to an extent which increases the risk associated with the waste sufficiently to justify their disposal in other classes of landfills, they may not be accepted in a landfill for inert waste.

If there is a doubt that the waste fulfils the definition of inert waste according to Article 2(e) of the Landfill Directive and the criteria listed in section 2.1.2 or about the lack of contamination of the waste, testing must be applied. For this purpose the methods listed under section 3 shall be used.

EWC code	*Description*	*Restrictions*
1011 03	Waste glass-based fibrous materials	Only without organic binders
1501 07	Glass packaging Glas	
1701 01	Concrete	Selected C & D waste only(*)
1701 02	Bricks	Selected C & D waste only(*)
1701 03	Tiles and ceramics	Selected C & D waste only(*)
1701 07	Mixtures of concrete, bricks, tiles and ceramics	Selected C & D waste only(*)
1702 02	Glass	
1705 04	Soil and stones	Excluding topsoil, peat; excluding soil and stones from contaminated sites
1912 05	Glass	
2001 02	Glass	Separately collected glass only
2002 02	Soil and stones	Only from garden and parks waste; Excluding top soil, peat

(*) Selected construction and demolition waste (C & D waste): with low contents of other types of materials (like metals, plastic, soil, organics, wood, rubber, etc). The origin of the waste must be known.

— No C & D waste from constructions, polluted with inorganic or organic dangerous substances, e.g. because of production processes in the construction, soil pollution, storage and usage of pesticides or other dangerous substances, etc., unless it is made clear that the demolished construction was not significantly polluted.

— No C & D waste from constructions, treated, covered or painted with materials, containing dangerous substances in significant amounts.

Waste not appearing on this list must be subject to testing as laid down under section 1 to determine if it fulfils the criteria for waste acceptable at landfills for inert waste as set out in section 2.1.2.

2.1.2. Limit values for waste acceptable at landfills for inert waste

2.1.2.1. Leaching limit values

The following leaching limit values apply for waste acceptable at landfills for inert waste, calculated at liquid to solid ratios (L/S) of 2 l/kg and 10 l/kg for total release and directly expressed in mg/l for C0 (the first eluate of percolation test at L/S = 0,1 l/kg). Member States shall determine which of the test methods (see section 3) and corresponding limit values in the table should be used.

Component	*L/S = 2 l/kg*	*L/S = 10 l/kg*	*C_0 (percolation test)*
	mg/kg dry substance	*mg/kg dry substance*	*mg/l*
As	0,1	0,5	0,06
Ba	7	20	4
Cd	0,03	0,04	0,02
Cr total	0,2	0,5	0,1
Cu	0,9	2	0,6
Hg	0,003	0,01	0,002
Mo	0,3	0,5	0,2
Ni	0,2	0,4	0,12
Pb	0,2	0,5	0,15
Sb	0,02	0,06	0,1
Se	0,06	0,1	0,04
Zn	2	4	1,2
Chloride	550	800	460
Fluoride	4	10	2,5
Sulphate	560(*)	1 000(*)	1 500
Phenol index	0,5	1	0,3
DOC(**)	240	500	160
TDS(***)	2 500	4 000	—

(*) If the waste does not meet these values for sulphate, it may still be considered as complying with the acceptance criteria if the leaching does not exceed either of the following values: 1 500 mg/l as C0 at L/S = 0,1 l/kg and 6 000 mg/kg at L/S = 10 l/kg. It will be necessary to use a percolation test to determine the limit value at L/S = 0,1 l/kg under initial equilibrium conditions, whereas the value at L/S = 10 l/kg maybe determined either by a batch leaching test or by a percolation test under conditions approaching local equilibrium.

(**) If the waste does not meet these values for DOC at its own pH value, it may alternatively be tested at L/S = 10 l/kg and a pH between 7,5 and 8,0. The waste maybe considered as complying with the acceptance criteria for DOC, if the result of this determination does not exceed 500 mg/kg. (A draft method based on prEN 14429 is available).

(***) The values for total dissolved solids (TDS) can be used alternativelyto the values for sulphate and chloride.

2.1.2.2. Limit values for total content of organic parameters

In addition to the leaching limit values under section 2.1.2.1, inert wastes must meet the following additional limit values:

Parameter	*Value mg/kg*
TOC (total organic carbon)	30 000(*)
BTEX (benzene, toluene, ethylbenzene and xylenes)	6
PCBs (polychlorinated biphenyls, 7 congeners)	1
Mineral oil (C10 to C40)	500
PAHs (polycyclic aromatic hydrocarbons)	Member States to set limit value

(*) In the case of soils, a higher limit value maybe admitted bythe competent authority, provided the DOC value of 500 mg/kg is achieved at L/S = 10 l/kg, either at the soil's own pH or at a pH value between 7,5 and 8,0.

2.2. Criteria for landfills for non-hazardous waste

Member States may create subcategories of landfills for non-hazardous waste.

In this Annex limit values are laid down only for non-hazardous waste, which is landfilled in the same cell with stable, non-reactive hazardous waste.

2.2.1. Wastes acceptable at landfills for non-hazardous waste without testing

Municipal waste as defined in Article 2(b) of the Landfill Directive that is classified as non-hazardous in Chapter 20 of the European waste list, separately collected non-hazardous fractions of household wastes and the same non-hazardous materials from other origins can be admitted without testing at landfills for non-hazardous waste.

The wastes may not be admitted if they have not been subjected to prior treatment according to Article 6(a) of the Landfill Directive, or if they are contaminated to an extent which increases the risk associated with the waste sufficiently to justify their disposal in other facilities.

They may not be accepted in cells, where stable, non-reactive hazardous waste is accepted pursuant to Article 6(c)(iii) of the Landfill Directive.

2.2.2. Limit values for non-hazardous waste

The following limit values apply to granular non-hazardous waste accepted in the same cell as stable, non-reactive hazardous waste, calculated at L/S = 2 and 10 l/kg for total release and directly expressed in mg/l for C0 (in the first eluate of percolation test at L/S = 0,1 l/kg). Granular wastes include all wastes that are not monolithic. Member States shall determine which of the test methods (see section 3) and corresponding limit values in the table should be used.

Components	*L/S = 2 l/kg*	*L/S = 10 l/kg*	*C_0(percolation test)*
	mg/kg dry substance	*mg/kg dry substance*	*mg/l*
As	0,4	2	0,3
Ba	30	100	20
Cd	0,6	1	0,3
Cr total	4	10	2,5
Cu	25	50	30
Hg	0,05	0,2	0,03
Mo	5	10	3,5
Ni	5	10	3
Pb	5	10	3

Components	*L/S = 2 l/kg*	*L/S = 10 l/kg*	*C_0(percolation test)*
	mg/kg dry substance	*mg/kg dry substance*	*mg/l*
Sb	0,2	0,7	0,15
Se	0,3	0,5	0,2
Zn	25	50	15
Chloride	10 000	15 000	8 500
Fluoride	60	150	40
Sulphate	10 000	20 000	7 000
DOC(*)	380	800	250
TDS(**)	40 000	60 000	—

(*) If the waste does not meet these values for DOC at its own pH, it may alternatively be tested at L/S = 10 l/kg and a pH of 7,5-8,0. The waste maybe considered as complying with the acceptance criteria for DOC, if the result of this determination does not exceed 800 mg/kg (A draft method based on prEN 14429 is available).

(**) The values for TDS can be used alternatively to the values for sulphate and chloride.

Member States shall set criteria for monolithic waste to provide the same level of environmental protection given by the above limit values.

2.2.3. Gypsum waste

Non-hazardous gypsum-based materials should be disposed of only in landfills for non-hazardous waste in cells where no biodegradable waste is accepted. The limit values for TOC and DOC given in sections 2.3.2 and 2.3.1 shall apply to wastes landfilled together with gypsum-based materials.

2.3. Criteria for hazardous waste acceptable at landfills for non-hazardous waste pursuant to Article 6(c)(iii)

Stable, non-reactive means that the leaching behaviour of the waste will not change adversely in the long-term, under landfill design conditions or foreseeable accidents:

— in the waste alone (for example, by biodegradation),
— under the impact of long-term ambient conditions (for example, water, air, temperature, mechanical constraints),
— by the impact of other wastes (including waste products such as leachate and gas).

2.3.1. Leaching limit values

The following leaching limit values apply to granular hazardous waste acceptable at landfills for non-hazardous waste, calculated at L/S = 2 and 10 l/kg for total release and directly expressed in mg/l for C0 (the first eluate of percolation test at L/S = 0,1 l/kg). Granular wastes include all wastes that are not monolithic. Member States shall determine which of the test methods and corresponding limit values should be used.

Components	*L/S = 2 l/kg*	*L/S = 10 l/kg*	*C_0(percolation test)*
	mg/kg dry substance	*mg/kg dry substance*	*mg/l*
As	0,4	2	0,3
Ba	30	100	20
Cd	0,6	1	0,3
Cr total	4	10	2,5
Cu	25	50	30
Hg	0,05	0,2	0,03
Mo	5	10	3,5

Components	*L/S = 2 l/kg*	*L/S = 10 l/kg*	C_0 *(percolation test)*
	mg/kg dry substance	*mg/kg dry substance*	*mg/l*
Ni	5	10	3
Pb	5	10	3
Sb	0,2	0,7	0,15
Se	0,3	0,5	0,2
Zn	25	50	15
Chloride	10 000	15 000	8 500
Fluoride	60	150	40
Sulphate	10 000	20 000	7 000
DOC(*)	380	800	250
TDS(**)	40 000	60 000	—

(*) If the waste does not meet these values for DOC at its own pH, it may alternatively be tested at L/S = 10 l/kg and a pH of 7,5-8,0. The waste maybe considered as complying with the acceptance criteria for DOC, if the result of this determination does not exceed 800 mg/kg (A draft method based on prEN 14429 is available).

(**) The values for TDS can be used alternatively to the values for sulphate and chloride.

Member States shall set criteria for monolithic waste to provide the same level of environmental protection given by the above limit values.

2.3.2. *Other criteria*

In addition to the leaching limit values under section 2.3.1, granular wastes must meet the following additional criteria:

Parameter	*Value*
TOC (total organic carbon)	5 %(*)
pH Minimum	6
ANC (acid neutralisation capacity)	Must be evaluated

(*) If this value is not achieved, a higher limit value maybe admitted bythe competent authority, provided that the DOC value of 800 mg/kg is achieved at L/S = 10 l/kg, either at the material's own pH or at a pH value between 7,5 and 8,0.

Member States must set criteria to ensure that the waste will have sufficient physical stability and bearing capacity.

Member States shall set criteria to ensure that hazardous monolithic wastes are stable and non-reactive before acceptance in landfills for non-hazardous waste.

2.3.3. *Asbestos waste*

Construction materials containing asbestos and other suitable asbestos waste may be landfilled at landfills for non-hazardous waste in accordance with Article 6(c)(iii) of the Landfill Directive without testing.

For landfills receiving construction materials containing asbestos and other suitable asbestos waste the following requirements must be fulfilled:

— the waste contains no other hazardous substances than bound asbestos, including fibres bound by a binding agent or packed in plastic,
— the landfill accepts only construction material containing asbestos and other suitable asbestos waste. These wastes may also be landfilled in a separate cell of a landfill for non-hazardous waste, if the cell is sufficiently self-contained,

— in order to avoid dispersion of fibres, the zone of deposit is covered daily and before each compacting operation with appropriate material and, if the waste is not packed, it is regularly sprinkled,
— a final top cover is put on the landfill/cell in order to avoid the dispersion of fibres,
— no works are carried out on the landfill/cell that could lead to a release of fibres (e.g. drilling of holes),
— after closure a plan is kept of the location of the landfill/cell indicating that asbestos wastes have been deposited,
— appropriate measures are taken to limit the possible uses of the land after closure of the landfill in order to avoid human contact with the waste.

For landfills receiving only construction material containing asbestos, the requirements set out in Annex I, point 3.2 and 3.3 of the Landfill Directive can be reduced, if the above requirements are fulfilled.

2.4. Criteria for waste acceptable at landfills for hazardous waste

2.4.1. Leaching limit values

The following leaching limit values apply for granular waste acceptable at landfills for hazardous waste, calculated at L/S = 2 and 10 l/kg for total release and directly expressed in mg/l for C0 (in the first eluate of percolation test at L/S = 0,1 l/kg). Granular wastes include all wastes that are not monolithic. Member States shall determine which of the test methods and corresponding limit values in the table should be used.

Components	*L/S = 2 l/kg*	*L/S = 10 l/kg*	*C_0 (percolation test)*
	mg/kg dry substance	*mg/kg dry substance*	*mg/l*
As	6	25	3
Ba	100	300	60
Cd	3	5	1,7
Cr total	25	70	15
Cu	50	100	60
Hg	0,5	2	0,3
Mo	20	30	10
Ni	20	40	12
Pb	25	50	15
Sb	2	5	1
Se	4	7	3
Zn	90	200	60
Chloride	17 000	25 000	15 000
Fluoride	200	500	120
Sulphate	25 000	50 000	17 000
DOC(*)	480	1 000	320
TDS(**)	70 000	100 000	—

(*) If the waste does not meet these values for DOC at its own pH, it may alternatively be tested at L/S = 10 l/kg and a pH of 7,5-8,0. The waste maybe considered as complying with the acceptance criteria for DOC, if the result of this determination does not exceed 1 000 mg/kg. (A draft method based on prEN 14429 is available.)

(**) The values for TDS can be used alternatively to the values for sulphate and chloride.

Member States shall set criteria for monolithic waste to provide the same level of environmental protection given by the above limit values.

2.4.2. Other criteria

In addition to the leaching limit values under section 2.4.1, hazardous wastes must meet the following additional criteria:

Parameter	*Value*
LOI(*)	10 %
TOC(*)	6 %(**)
ANC (acid neutralisation capacity)	Must be evaluated

(*) Either LOI or TOC must be used.

(**) If this value is not achieved, a higher limit value maybe admitted by the competent authority, provided that the DOC value of 1 000 mg/kg is achieved at L/S = 10 l/kg, either at the material's own pH or at a pH value between 7,5 and 8,0.

2.5. Criteria for underground storage

For the acceptance of waste in underground storage sites, a site-specific safety assessment as defined in Annex A must be carried out. Waste may be accepted only if it is compatible with the site-specific safety assessment.

At underground storage sites for inert waste, only waste that fulfils the criteria set out in section 2.1 may be accepted.

At underground storage sites for non-hazardous waste, only waste that fulfils the criteria set out in section 2.2 or in section 2.3 may be accepted.

At underground storage sites for hazardous waste, waste may be accepted only if it is compatible with the site-specific safety assessment. In this case, the criteria set out in section 2.4 do not apply. However, the waste must be subject to the acceptance procedure as set out in section 1.

3. SAMPLING AND TEST METHODS

Sampling and testing for basic characterisation and compliance testing shall be carried out by independent and qualified persons and institutions. Laboratories shall have proven experience in waste testing and analysis and an efficient quality assurance system.

Member States may decide that:

1. the sampling may be carried out by producers of waste or operators under the condition that sufficient supervision of independent and qualified persons or institutions ensures that the objectives set out in this Decision are achieved;
2. the testing of the waste may be carried out by producers of waste or operators if they have set up an appropriate quality assurance system including periodic independent checking.

As long as a CEN standard is not available as formal EN, Member States will use either national standards or procedures or the draft CEN standard, when it has reached the prEN stage.

The following methods shall be used.

Sampling

For the sampling of waste – for basic characterisation, compliance testing and on-site verification testing – a sampling plan shall be developed according to part 1 of the sampling standard currently developed by CEN.

General waste properties

EN 13137	Determination of TOC in waste, sludge and sediments
prEN 14346	Calculation of dry matter by determination of dry residue or water content

Leaching tests

prEN 14405	Leaching behaviour test – Up-flow percolation test (Up-flow percolation test for inorganic constituents)
EN 12457/1-4	Leaching — Compliance test for leaching of granular waste materials and sludges: part 1: L/S = 2 l/kg, particle size <4 mm part 2: L/S = 10 l/kg, particle size <4 mm part 3: L/S = 2 and 8 l/kg, particle size <4 mm part 4: L/S = 10 l/kg, particle size < 10 mm

Digestion of raw waste

EN 13657	Digestion for subsequent determination of aqua regia soluble portion of elements (partial digestion of the solid waste prior to elementary analysis, leaving the silicate matrix intact)
EN 13656	Microwave-assisted digestion with hydrofluoric (HF), nitric (HNO3) and hydrochloric (HCl) acid mixture for subsequent determination of elements (total digestion of the solid waste prior to elementary analysis)

Analysis

ENV 12506	Analysis of eluates — Determination of pH, As, Ba, Cd, Cl, Co, Cr, CrVI, Cu, Mo, Ni, NO_2, Pb, total S, SO_4, V and Zn (analysis of inorganic constituents of solid waste and/or its eluate; major, minor and trace elements)
ENV 13370	Analysis of eluates — Determination of ammonium, AOX, conductivity, Hg, phenol index, TOC, easilyliberatable CN, F (analysis of inorganic constituents of solid waste and/or its eluate (anions))
prEN 14039	Determination of hydrocarbon content in the range of C10 to C40 by gas chromatography

This list will be amended when more CEN standards are available.

For tests and analyses, for which CEN methods are not (yet) available, the methods used must be approved by the competent authorities.

APPENDIX A
SAFETY ASSESSMENT FOR ACCEPTANCE OF WASTE IN UNDERGROUND STORAGE

1. SAFETY PHILOSOPHY FOR UNDERGROUND STORAGE: ALL TYPES

1.1. The importance of the geological barrier

Isolation of wastes from the biosphere is the ultimate objective for the final disposal of wastes in underground storage. The wastes, the geological barrier and the cavities, including any engineered structures constitute a system that together with all other technical aspects must fulfil the corresponding requirements.

The requirements of the Water Framework Directive (2000/60/EC) can be fulfilled only by demonstrating the long-term safety of the installation (see section 1.2.7). Article 11(3)(j) of Directive 2000/60/EC generally prohibits the direct discharge of pollutants into groundwater. Article 4(1)(b)(i) of Directive 2000/60/EC requires Member States to take measures to prevent the deterioration of the status of all bodies of groundwater.

1.2. Site-specific risk assessment

The assessment of risk requires the identification of:

— the hazard (in this case the deposited wastes),
— the receptors (in this case the biosphere and possibly groundwater),
— the pathways by which substances from the wastes may reach the biosphere, and
— the assessment of impact of substances that may reach the biosphere.

Acceptance criteria for underground storage are to be derived from, inter alia, the analysis of the host rock, so it must be confirmed that no site-related conditions specified in Annex I to the Landfill Directive (with an exemption of Annex I(2), (3), (4) and (5)) are of relevance.

The acceptance criteria for underground storage can be obtained only by referring to the local conditions. This requires a demonstration of the suitability of the strata for establishing a storage, i.e. an assessment of the risks to containment, taking into account the overall system of the waste, engineered structures and cavities and the host rock body.

The site specific risk assessment of the installation must be carried out for both the operational and post-operational phases. From these assessments, the required control and safety measures can be derived and the acceptance criteria can be developed.

An integrated performance assessment analysis shall be prepared, including the following components:

1. geological assessment;
2. geomechanical assessment;
3. hydrogeological assessment;
4. geochemical assessment;
5. biosphere impact assessment;
6. assessment of the operational phase;
7. long-term assessment;
8. assessment of the impact of all the surface facilities at the site.

1.2.1. Geological assessment

A thorough investigation or knowledge of the geological setting of a site is required. This includes investigations and analyses of kind of rocks, soils and the topography. The geological assessment should demonstrate the suitability of the site for underground storage. The location, frequency and structure of any faulting or fracturing in surrounding geological strata and the potential impact of seismic activity on these structures should be included. Alternative site locations should be considered.

1.2.2. Geomechanical assessment

The stability of the cavities must be demonstrated by appropriate investigations and predictions. The deposited waste must be part of this assessment. The processes should be analysed and documented in a systematic way.

The following should be demonstrated:

1. that during and after the formation of the cavities, no major deformation is to be expected either in the cavity itself or at the earth surface which could impair the operability of the underground storage or provide a pathway to the biosphere;
2. that the load-bearing capacity of the cavity is sufficient to prevent its collapse during operation;
3. that the deposited material must have the necessary stability compatible with the geo-mechanical properties of the host rock.

1.2.3. Hydrogeological assessment

A thorough investigation of the hydraulic properties is required to assess the groundwater flow pattern in the surrounding strata based on information on the hydraulic conductivity of the rock mass, fractures and the hydraulic gradients.

The site-specific assessments outlined in section 1.2 for the wastes to be accepted at an underground storage should demonstrate that the level of isolation from the biosphere is acceptable. The criteria have to be fulfilled under storage conditions.

2.4. Acceptance conditions

Wastes can be deposited only in an underground storage securely separated from mining activities.

Wastes that might react with each other must be defined and classified in groups of compatibility; the different groups of compatibility must be physically separated in the storage.

3. ADDITIONAL CONSIDERATIONS: SALT MINES

3.1. Importance of the geological barrier

In the safety philosophy for salt mines, the rock surrounding the waste has a two-fold role:

— it acts as host rock in which the wastes are encapsulated;

— together with the overlying and underlying impermeable rock strata (e.g. anhydrite), it acts as a geological barrier intended to prevent groundwater entering the landfill and, where necessary, effectively to stop liquids or gases escaping from the disposal area. Where this geological barrier is pierced by shafts and boreholes, these must be sealed during operation to secure against ingress of water, and must be hermetically closed after the underground landfill ceases to operate. If mineral extraction continues longer than the landfill operation, the disposal area must, after the landfill has ceased operating, be sealed with a hydraulically impermeable dam which is constructed according to the calculated hydraulically operative pressure corresponding to the depth, so that water which may seep into the still operating mine cannot penetrate through to the landfill area;

— in salt mines, the salt is considered to provide total containment. The wastes will only make contact with the biosphere in the case of an accident or an event in geological time such as earth movement or erosion (for example, associated with sea-level rise). The waste is unlikely to change in storage, and the consequences of such failure scenarios must be considered.

3.2. Long-term assessment

The demonstration of long-term safety of underground disposal in a salt rock should be principally undertaken by designating the salt rock as the barrier rock. Salt rock fulfils the requirement of being impermeable to gases and liquids, of being able to encase the waste because of its convergent behaviour and of confining it entirely at the end of the transformation process.

The convergent behaviour of the salt rock thus does not contradict the requirement to have stable cavities in the operation phase. The stability is important, in order to guarantee the operational safety and in order to maintain the integrity of the geological barrier over unlimited time, so that there is continued protection of the biosphere. The wastes should be isolated permanently from the biosphere. Controlled subsidence of the overburden or other defects over long time are acceptable only if it can be shown, that only rupture-free transformations will occur, the integrity of the geological barrier is maintained and no pathways are formed by which water would be able to contact the wastes or the wastes or components of the waste migrate to the biosphere.

4. ADDITIONAL CONSIDERATIONS: HARD ROCK

Deep storage in hard rock is here defined as an underground storage at several hundred metres depth, where hard rock includes various igneous rocks, e.g. granite or gneiss, it may also include sedimentary rocks, e.g. limestone and sandstone.

4.1. Safety philosophy

A deep storage in hard rock is a feasible way to avoid burdening future generations with the responsibility of the wastes since it should be constructed to be passive and with no need for maintenance. Furthermore, the construction should not obstruct recovery of the wastes or the ability to undertake future corrective measures. It should also be designed to ensure that negative environmental effects or liabilities resulting from the activities of present generations do not fall upon future generations.

In the safety philosophy of underground disposal of wastes, the main concept is isolation of the waste from the biosphere, as well as natural attenuation of any pollutants leaking from the waste. For certain types of hazardous substances and waste, a need has been identified to protect the society and the environment against sustained exposure over extended periods of time. An extended period of time implies several thousands of years. Such levels of protection can be achieved by deep storage in hard rock. A deep storage for waste in hard rock can be located either in a former mine, where the mining activities have come to an end, or in a new storage facility.

In the case of hard-rock storage, total containment is not possible. In this case, an underground storage needs to be constructed so that natural attenuation of the surrounding strata mediates the effect of pollutants to the extent that they have no irreversible negative effects on the environment. This means that the capacity of the near environment to attenuate and degrade pollutants will determine the acceptability of a release from such a facility.

The requirements of the EU Water Framework Directive (2000/60/EC) can only be fulfilled by demonstrating the long-term safety of the installation (see section 1.2.7). The performance of a deep storage system must be assessed in a holistic way, accounting for the coherent function of different components of the system. In a deep storage in hard rock, the storage will reside below the groundwater table. Article 11(3)(j) of the Directive generally prohibits the direct discharge of pollutants into groundwater. Article 4(1)(b)(i) of the Directive requires Member States to take measures to prevent the deterioration of the status of all bodies of groundwater. For a deep storage in the hard rock, this requirement is respected in that any discharges of hazardous substances from the storage will not reach the biosphere, including the upper parts of the groundwater system accessible for the biosphere, in amounts or concentrations that will cause adverse effects. Therefore the water flow paths to and in the biosphere should be evaluated. The impact of variability on the geohydraulic system should assessed.

Gas formation may occur in deep storage in hard rock due to long-term deterioration of waste, packaging and engineered structures. Therefore, this must be considered in the design of premises for a deep storage in hard rock.

APPENDIX B
OVERVIEW OF LANDFILLING OPTIONS PROVIDED BY THE LANDFILL DIRECTIVE

Introduction

Figure 1 gives an overview of the landfilling possibilities for waste provided by the Landfill Directive together with some examples of subcategories of the main classes of landfills. The starting point (upper left corner) is a waste which should be landfilled. In accordance with Article 6(a) of the Landfill Directive, some treatment is required prior to landfilling for most wastes. The general definition of "treatment" is relatively broad and to a large extent left to the competent authorities in the Member States. It is assumed that the waste does not belong to any of the categories listed in Article 5(3) of the Landfill Directive.

Inert-waste landfill

The first question to ask could be whether or not the waste is classified as hazardous. If the waste is not hazardous (according to the Hazardous Waste Directive (91/689/EC) and the current waste list), the next question could be whether or not the waste is inert. If it meets the criteria for waste to be landfilled at an inert landfill (class A, see figure 1 and table 1), the waste may be placed at an inert landfill.

Inert waste may alternatively be placed in landfills for non-hazardous waste provided it fulfils the appropriate criteria (which it generally should).

Non-hazardous waste landfill, including subcategories

If the waste is neither hazardous nor inert, then it must be non-hazardous, and it should go to a landfill for non-hazardous waste. Member States may define subcategories of landfills for non-hazardous waste in accordance with their national waste management strategies as long as the requirements of the Landfill Directive are met. Three major subcategories of non-hazardous waste landfills are shown in figure 1: landfill for inorganic waste with low organic/biodegradable content (B1), landfill for organic waste (B2), and landfill for mixed non-hazardous waste with substantial contents of both organic/biodegradable and inorganic materials. Category B1 sites can be subdivided further into sites for wastes that do not meet the criteria set out in section 2.2.2 for inorganic non-hazardous wastes that may be co-disposed with stable, non reactive hazardous wastes (B1a) and sites for wastes that do meet those criteria (B1b). Category B2 sites may, for example, be further subdivided into bioreactor landfills and landfills for less reactive, biologically treated waste. Further subclassification of non-hazardous landfills may be desired by some Member States, and monofills and landfills for solidified/monolithic waste may be defined within each subcategory (see the footnote below table 1). National acceptance criteria may be developed by the Member States to ensure proper allocation of non-hazardous waste to the various subcategories of non-hazardous waste landfills. If sub-classification of non-hazardous waste landfills is not desired, all non-hazardous waste (subject of course to the provisions of Articles 3 and 5 of the Landfill Directive) may go to a landfill for mixed non-hazardous waste (class B3).

Placement of stable, non-reactive hazardous waste in landfill for non-hazardous waste

If the waste is hazardous (according to Directive 91/689/EC and the current waste list), the treatment may have enabled the waste to meet the criteria for placement of stable, non-reactive hazardous waste in non-hazardous waste landfills within cells for inorganic waste with low organic/biodegradable content that meet the criteria in section 2.2.2 (class B1b). The waste may be granular (rendered chemically stable) or solidified/monolithic.

Hazardous waste landfill

If the hazardous waste does not meet the criteria for placement in a class B1b landfill or cell for non-hazardous waste, the next question could be whether or not it meets the criteria for acceptance at a landfill for hazardous waste (class C). If the criteria are met, then the waste may be placed at a hazardous waste landfill.

If the criteria for acceptance at a hazardous waste landfill are not met, the waste may be subjected to further treatment and tested again against the criteria, until they are met.

Underground storage

Alternatively, the waste may be tested against the criteria for underground storage. If the criteria are met, the waste may go to an underground storage facility for hazardous waste (landfill class D_{HAZ}). If the underground storage criteria are not met, the waste may be subjected to further treatment and tested again.

Although underground storage is likely to be reserved for special hazardous wastes, this subcategory may in principle be used also for inert waste (class D_{INERT}) and non-hazardous waste (class $D_{NON\text{-}HAZ}$).

Figure 1
Diagram showing the landfilling options provided by the Landfill Directive

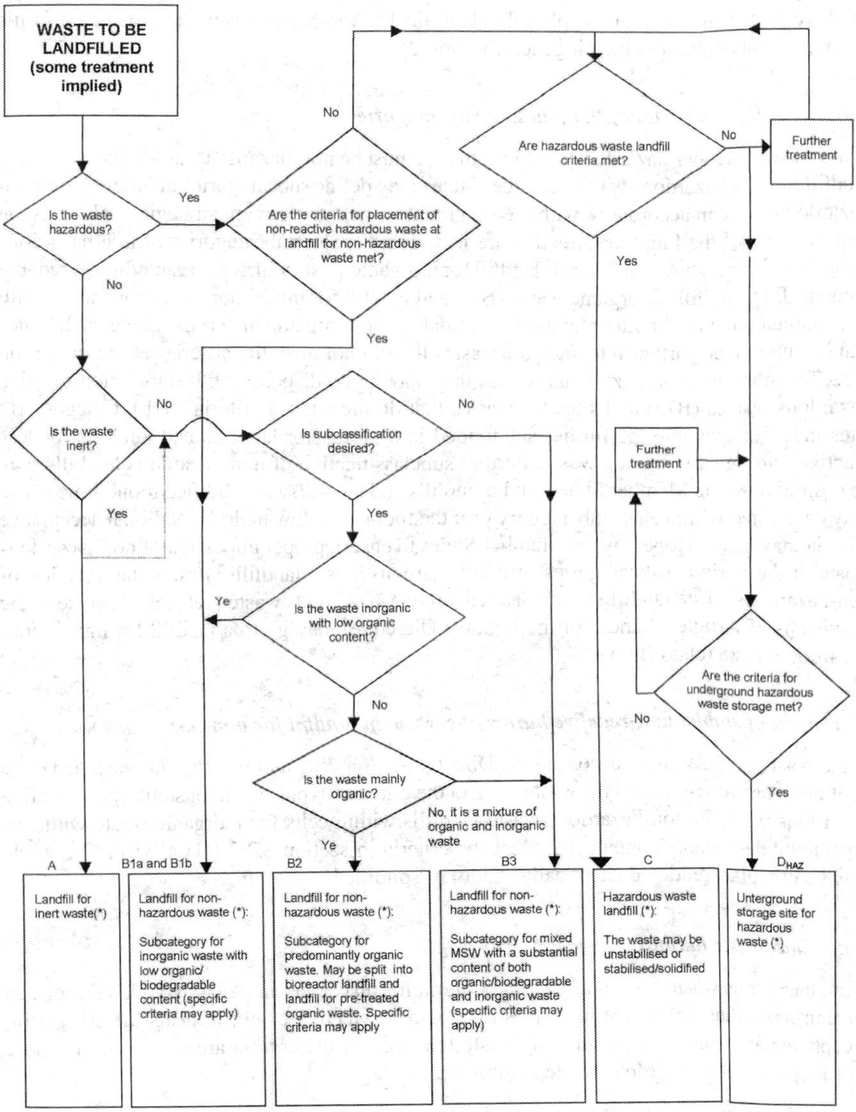

(*) In principle, underground storage is also possible for inert and non-hazardous waste.

Table 1
Overview of landfill classes and examples of subcategories

Landfill class	Major subcategories (underground storage facilities, monofills and landfills for solidified, monolithic[(*)] waste possible for all landfill classes)	ID	Acceptance criteria
Landfill for inert waste	Landfill accepting inert waste	A	Criteria for leaching and for content of organic components are set at EU level (section 2.1.2). Criteria for content of inorganic components maybe set at Member State level.
Landfill for non-hazardous waste	Landfill for inorganic non-hazardous waste with a low content of organic/ biodegradable matter, where the wastes do not meet the criteria set out in section 2.2.2. for those inorganic non-hazardous wastes that maybe landfilled together with stable, nonreactive hazardous waste	B1a	Criteria for leaching and total content are not set at EU level
	Landfill for inorganic non-hazardous waste with a low content of organic/ biodegradable matter	B1b	Criteria for leaching and content of organics (TOC) and other properties are set at EU level, common for granular non-hazardous waste and for stable, non-reactive hazardous waste (section 2.2). Additional stability criteria for the latter are to be set at Member State level. Criteria for monolithic waste must be set at Member State level
	Landfill for organic non-hazardous waste	B2	Criteria for leaching and total content are not set at EU level
	Landfill for mixed non-hazardous waste with substantial contents of both organic/biodegradable waste and inorganic waste.	B3	Criteria for leaching and total content are not set at EU level
Landfill for hazardous waste	Surface landfill for hazardous waste	C	Criteria for leaching for granular hazardous waste and total content of certain components have been laid down at EU level (section 2.4). Criteria for monolithic waste must be set at Member State level Additional criteria on content of contaminants can be set at MS level
	Underground storage site	D_{HAZ}	Special requirements at EU level are listed in Annex A

(*) Monolithic waste subcategories are only relevant for B1, C and D_{HAZ}, and possibly A.

DIRECTIVE 2003/35/EC OF THE EUROPEAN PARLIAMENT AND OF THE COUNCIL

of 26 May 2003

PROVIDING FOR PUBLIC PARTICIPATION IN RESPECT OF THE DRAWING UP OF CERTAIN PLANS AND PROGRAMMES RELATING TO THE ENVIRONMENT AND AMENDING WITH REGARD TO PUBLIC PARTICIPATION AND ACCESS TO JUSTICE COUNCIL DIRECTIVES 85/337/EEC AND 96/61/EC

THE EUROPEAN PARLIAMENT AND THE COUNCIL OF THE EUROPEAN UNION,

Having regard to the Treaty establishing the European Community, and in particular Article 175 thereof,

Having regard to the proposal from the Commission,

Having regard to the opinion of the European Economic and Social Committee,

Having regard to the opinion of the Committee of the Regions,

Acting in accordance with the procedure laid down in Article 251 of the Treaty, in the light of the joint text approved by the Conciliation Committee on 15 January 2003,

Whereas:

(1) Community legislation in the field of the environment aims to contribute to preserving, protecting and improving the quality of the environment and protecting human health.

(2) Community environmental legislation includes provisions for public authorities and other bodies to take decisions which may have a significant effect on the environment as well as on personal health and well-being.

(3) Effective public participation in the taking of decisions enables the public to express, and the decision-maker to take account of, opinions and concerns which may be relevant to those decisions, thereby increasing the accountability and transparency of the decision-making process and contributing to public awareness of environmental issues and support for the decisions taken.

(4) Participation, including participation by associations, organisations and groups, in particular non-governmental organisations promoting environmental protection, should accordingly be fostered, including inter alia by promoting environmental education of the public.

(5) On 25 June 1998 the Community signed the UN/ECE Convention on Access to Information, Public Participation in Decision-Making and Access to Justice in Environmental Matters (the Århus Convention). Community law should be properly aligned with that Convention with a view to its ratification by the Community.

(6) Among the objectives of the Århus Convention is the desire to guarantee rights of public participation in decision-making in environmental matters in order to contribute to the protection of the right to live in an environment which is adequate for personal health and well-being.

(7) Article 6 of the Århus Convention provides for public participation in decisions on the specific activities listed in Annex I thereto and on activities not so listed which may have a significant effect on the environment.

(8) Article 7 of the Århus Convention provides for public participation concerning plans and programmes relating to the environment.

(9) Article 9(2) and (4) of the Århus Convention provides for access to judicial or other procedures for challenging the substantive or procedural legality of decisions, acts or omissions subject to the public participation provisions of Article 6 of the Convention.

(10) Provision should be made in respect of certain Directives in the environmental area which require Member States to produce plans and programmes relating to the environment but which do not contain sufficient provisions on public participation, so as to ensure public participation consistent with the provisions of the Århus Convention, in particular Article 7 thereof. Other relevant Community legislation already provides for public participation in the preparation of plans and programmes and, for the future, public participation requirements in line with the Århus Convention will be incorporated into the relevant legislation from the outset.

(11) Council Directive 85/337/EEC of 27 June 1985 on the assessment of the effects of certain public and private projects on the environment, and Council Directive 96/61/EC of 24 September 1996 concerning integrated pollution prevention and control should be amended to ensure that they are fully compatible with the provisions of the Århus Convention, in particular Article 6 and Article 9(2) and (4) thereof.

(12) Since the objective of the proposed action, namely to contribute to the implementation of the obligations arising under the Århus Convention, cannot be sufficiently achieved by the Member States and can therefore, by reason of the scale and effects of the action, be better achieved at Community level, the Community may adopt measures in accordance with the principle of subsidiarity as set out in Article 5 of the Treaty. In accordance with the principle of proportionality, as set out in that Article, this Directive does not go beyond what is necessary in order to achieve that objective,

HAVE ADOPTED THIS DIRECTIVE:

Article 1

Objective

The objective of this Directive is to contribute to the implementation of the obligations arising under the Århus Convention, in particular by:

(a) providing for public participation in respect of the drawing up of certain plans and programmes relating to the environment;

(b) improving the public participation and providing for provisions on access to justice within Council Directives 85/337/EEC and 96/61/EC.

Article 2

Public participation concerning plans and programmes

1. For the purposes of this Article, "the public" shall mean one or more natural or legal persons and, in accordance with national legislation or practice, their associations, organisations or groups.

2. Member States shall ensure that the public is given early and effective opportunities to participate in the preparation and modification or review of the plans or programmes required to be drawn up under the provisions listed in Annex I.

To that end, Member States shall ensure that:

(a) the public is informed, whether by public notices or other appropriate means such as electronic media where available, about any proposals for such plans or programmes or for their modification or review and that relevant information about such proposals is made available to the public including inter alia information about the right to participate in decision-making and about the competent authority to which comments or questions may be submitted;

(b) the public is entitled to express comments and opinions when all options are open before decisions on the plans and programmes are made;

(c) in making those decisions, due account shall be taken of the results of the public participation;

(d) having examined the comments and opinions expressed by the public, the competent authority makes reasonable efforts to inform the public about the decisions taken and the reasons and considerations upon which those decisions are based, including information about the public participation process.

3. Member States shall identify the public entitled to participate for the purposes of paragraph 2, including relevant non-governmental organisations meeting any requirements imposed under national law, such as those promoting environmental protection.

The detailed arrangements for public participation under this Article shall be determined by the Member States so as to enable the public to prepare and participate effectively.

Reasonable time-frames shall be provided allowing sufficient time for each of the different stages of public participation required by this Article.

4. This Article shall not apply to plans and programmes designed for the sole purpose of serving national defence or taken in case of civil emergencies.

5. This Article shall not apply to plans and programmes set out in Annex I for which a public participation procedure is carried out under Directive 2001/42/EC of the European Parliament and of the Council of 27 June 2001 on the assessment of the effects of certain plans and programmes on the environment or under Directive 2000/60/EC of the European Parliament and of the Council of 23 October 2000 establishing a framework for Community action in the field of water policy.

[*Articles 3 and 4 are not reproduced.*]

Article 5

Reporting and review

By 25 June 2009, the Commission shall send a report on the application and effectiveness of this Directive to the European Parliament and to the Council. With a view to further integrating environmental protection requirements, in accordance with Article 6 of the Treaty, and taking into account the experience acquired in the application of this Directive in the Member States, such a report will be accompanied by proposals for amendment of this Directive, if appropriate. In particular, the Commission will consider the possibility of extending the scope of this Directive to other plans and programmes relating to the environment.

Article 6

Implementation

Member States shall bring into force the laws, regulations and administrative provisions necessary to comply with this Directive by 25 June 2005 at the latest. They shall forthwith inform the Commission thereof.

When Member States adopt these measures, they shall contain a reference to this Directive or shall be accompanied by such a reference on the occasion of their official publication. The methods of making such reference shall be laid down by Member States.

Article 7

Entry into force

This Directive shall enter into force on the day of its publication in the Official Journal of the European Union.

Article 8

Addressees

This Directive is addressed to the Member States.

ANNEX I
PROVISIONS FOR PLANS AND PROGRAMMES REFERRED TO IN ARTICLE 2

(a) Article 7(1) of Council Directive 75/442/EEC of 15 July 1975 on waste.

(b) Article 6 of Council Directive 91/157/EEC of 18 March 1991 on batteries and accumulators containing certain dangerous substances.

(c) Article 5(1) of Council Directive 91/676/EEC of 12 December 1991 concerning the protection of waters against pollution caused by nitrates from agricultural sources.

(d) Article 6(1) of Council Directive 91/689/EEC of 12 December 1991 on hazardous waste.

(e) Article 14 of Directive 94/62/EC of the European Parliament and of the Council of 20 December 1994 on packaging and packaging waste.

(f) Article 8(3) of Council Directive 96/62/EC of 27 September 1996 on ambient air quality assessment and management.

[*Annex II is not reproduced.*]

DIRECTIVE 2003/87/EC OF THE EUROPEAN PARLIAMENT AND OF THE COUNCIL

of 13 October 2003

ESTABLISHING A SCHEME FOR GREENHOUSE GAS EMISSION ALLOWANCE TRADING WITHIN THE COMMUNITY AND AMENDING COUNCIL DIRECTIVE 96/61/EC

THE EUROPEAN PARLIAMENT AND THE COUNCIL OF THE EUROPEAN UNION,

Having regard to the Treaty establishing the European Community, and in particular Article 175(1) thereof,

Having regard to the proposal from the Commission,

Having regard to the opinion of the European Economic and Social Committee,

Having regard to the opinion of the Committee of the Regions,

Acting in accordance with the procedure laid down in Article 251 of the Treaty,

Whereas:

(1) The Green Paper on greenhouse gas emissions trading within the European Union launched a debate across Europe on the suitability and possible functioning of greenhouse gas emissions trading within the European Union. The European Climate Change Programme has considered Community policies and measures through a multi-stakeholder process, including a scheme for greenhouse gas emission allowance trading within the Community (the Community scheme) based on the Green Paper. In its Conclusions of 8 March 2001, the Council recognised the particular importance of the European Climate Change Programme and of work based on the Green Paper, and underlined the urgent need for concrete action at Community level.

(2) The Sixth Community Environment Action Programme established by Decision No 1600/2002/EC of the European Parliament and of the Council identifies climate change as a priority for action and provides for the establishment of a Community-wide emissions trading scheme by 2005. That Programme recognises that the Community is committed to achieving an 8 % reduction in emissions of greenhouse gases by 2008 to 2012 compared to 1990 levels, and that, in the longer-term, global emissions of greenhouse gases will need to be reduced by approximately 70 % compared to 1990 levels.

(3) The ultimate objective of the United Nations Framework Convention on Climate Change, which was approved by Council Decision 94/69/EC of 15 December 1993 concerning the conclusion of the United Nations Framework Convention on Climate Change, is to achieve stabilisation of greenhouse gas concentrations in the atmosphere at a level which prevents dangerous anthropogenic interference with the climate system.

(4) Once it enters into force, the Kyoto Protocol, which was approved by Council Decision 2002/358/EC of 25 April 2002 concerning the approval, on behalf of the European Community, of the Kyoto Protocol to the United Nations Framework Convention on Climate Change and the joint fulfilment of commitments thereunder, will commit the Community and its Member States to reducing their aggregate anthropogenic emissions of greenhouse gases listed in Annex A to the Protocol by 8 % compared to 1990 levels in the period 2008 to 2012.

(5) The Community and its Member States have agreed to fulfil their commitments to reduce anthropogenic greenhouse gas emissions under the Kyoto Protocol jointly, in accordance with Decision 2002/358/EC. This Directive aims to contribute to fulfilling

the commitments of the European Community and its Member States more effectively, through an efficient European market in greenhouse gas emission allowances, with the least possible diminution of economic development and employment.

(6) Council Decision 93/389/EEC of 24 June 1993 for a monitoring mechanism of Community CO_2 and other greenhouse gas emissions, established a mechanism for monitoring greenhouse gas emissions and evaluating progress towards meeting commitments in respect of these emissions. This mechanism will assist Member States in determining the total quantity of allowances to allocate.

(7) Community provisions relating to allocation of allowances by the Member States are necessary to contribute to preserving the integrity of the internal market and to avoid distortions of competition.

(8) Member States should have regard when allocating allowances to the potential for industrial process activities to reduce emissions.

(9) Member States may provide that they only issue allowances valid for a five-year period beginning in 2008 to persons in respect of allowances cancelled, corresponding to emission reductions made by those persons on their national territory during a three-year period beginning in 2005.

(10) Starting with the said five-year period, transfers of allowances to another Member State will involve corresponding adjustments of assigned amount units under the Kyoto Protocol.

(11) Member States should ensure that the operators of certain specified activities hold a greenhouse gas emissions permit and that they monitor and report their emissions of greenhouse gases specified in relation to those activities.

(12) Member States should lay down rules on penalties applicable to infringements of this Directive and ensure that they are implemented. Those penalties must be effective, proportionate and dissuasive.

(13) In order to ensure transparency, the public should have access to information relating to the allocation of allowances and to the results of monitoring of emissions, subject only to restrictions provided for in Directive 2003/4/EC of the European Parliament and of the Council of 28 January 2003 on public access to environmental information.

(14) Member States should submit a report on the implementation of this Directive drawn up on the basis of Council Directive 91/692/EEC of 23 December 1991 standardising and rationalising reports on the implementation of certain Directives relating to the environment.

(15) The inclusion of additional installations in the Community scheme should be in accordance with the provisions laid down in this Directive, and the coverage of the Community scheme may thereby be extended to emissions of greenhouse gases other than carbon dioxide, inter alia from aluminium and chemicals activities.

(16) This Directive should not prevent any Member State from maintaining or establishing national trading schemes regulating emissions of greenhouse gases from activities other than those listed in Annex I or included in the Community scheme, or from installations temporarily excluded from the Community scheme.

(17) Member States may participate in international emissions trading as Parties to the Kyoto Protocol with any other Party included in Annex B thereto.

(18) Linking the Community scheme to greenhouse gas emission trading schemes in third countries will increase the cost-effectiveness of achieving the Community emission reductions target as laid down in Decision 2002/358/EC on the joint fulfilment of commitments.

(19) Project-based mechanisms including Joint Implementation (JI) and the Clean Development Mechanism (CDM) are important to achieve the goals of both reducing global greenhouse gas emissions and increasing the cost-effective functioning of the Community scheme. In accordance with the relevant provisions of the Kyoto Protocol and Marrakech Accords, the use of the mechanisms should be supplemental to domestic action and domestic action will thus constitute a significant element of the effort made.

(20) This Directive will encourage the use of more energy-efficient technologies, including combined heat and power technology, producing less emissions per unit of output, while the future directive of the European Parliament and of the Council on the promotion of cogeneration based on useful heat demand in the internal energy market will specifically promote combined heat and power technology.

(21) Council Directive 96/61/EC of 24 September 1996 concerning integrated pollution prevention and control establishes a general framework for pollution prevention and control, through which greenhouse gas emissions permits may be issued. Directive 96/61/EC should be amended to ensure that emission limit values are not set for direct emissions of greenhouse gases from an installation subject to this Directive and that Member States may choose not to impose requirements relating to energy efficiency in respect of combustion units or other units emitting carbon dioxide on the site, without prejudice to any other requirements pursuant to Directive 96/61/EC.

(22) This Directive is compatible with the United Nations Framework Convention on Climate Change and the Kyoto Protocol. It should be reviewed in the light of developments in that context and to take into account experience in its implementation and progress achieved in monitoring of emissions of greenhouse gases.

(23) Emission allowance trading should form part of a comprehensive and coherent package of policies and measures implemented at Member State and Community level. Without prejudice to the application of Articles 87 and 88 of the Treaty, where activities are covered by the Community scheme, Member States may consider the implications of regulatory, fiscal or other policies that pursue the same objectives. The review of the Directive should consider the extent to which these objectives have been attained.

(24) The instrument of taxation can be a national policy to limit emissions from installations temporarily excluded.

(25) Policies and measures should be implemented at Member State and Community level across all sectors of the European Union economy, and not only within the industry and energy sectors, in order to generate substantial emissions reductions. The Commission should, in particular, consider policies and measures at Community level in order that the transport sector makes a substantial contribution to the Community and its Member States meeting their climate change obligations under the Kyoto Protocol.

(26) Notwithstanding the multifaceted potential of market-based mechanisms, the European Union strategy for climate change mitigation should be built on a balance between the Community scheme and other types of Community, domestic and international action.

(27) This Directive respects the fundamental rights and observes the principles recognised in particular by the Charter of Fundamental Rights of the European Union.

(28) The measures necessary for the implementation of this Directive should be adopted in accordance with Council Decision 1999/468/EC of 28 June 1999 laying down the procedures for the exercise of implementing powers conferred on the Commission.

(29) As the criteria (1), (5) and (7) of Annex III cannot be amended through comitology, amendments in respect of periods after 2012 should only be made through codecision.

(30) Since the objective of the proposed action, the establishment of a Community scheme, cannot be sufficiently achieved by the Member States acting individually, and can therefore by reason of the scale and effects of the proposed action be better achieved at Community level, the Community may adopt measures, in accordance with the principle of subsidiarity as set out in Article 5 of the Treaty. In accordance with the principle of proportionality, as set out in that Article, this Directive does not go beyond what is necessary in order to achieve that objective,

HAVE ADOPTED THIS DIRECTIVE:

[Chapter I
General Provisions][1]

Article 1

Subject matter

This Directive establishes a scheme for greenhouse gas emission allowance trading within the Community (hereinafter referred to as the "Community scheme") in order to promote reductions of greenhouse gas emissions in a cost-effective and economically efficient manner.

[This Directive also provides for the reductions of greenhouse gas emissions to be increased so as to contribute to the levels of reductions that are considered scientifically necessary to avoid dangerous climate change.

This Directive also lays down provisions for assessing and implementing a stricter Community reduction commitment exceeding 20 %, to be applied upon the approval by the Community of an international agreement on climate change leading to greenhouse gas emission reductions exceeding those required in Article 9, as reflected in the 30 % commitment endorsed by the European Council of March 2007.][2]

Amendments

1 Inserted by Directive 2008/101/EC of the European Parliament and of the Council of 19 November 2008 amending Directive 2003/87/EC so as to include aviation activities in the scheme for greenhouse gas emission allowance trading within the Community, Article 1.2.

2 Inserted by Directive 2009/29/EC of the European Parliament and of the Council of 23 April 2009 amending Directive 2003/87/EC so as to improve and extend the greenhouse gas emission allowance trading scheme of the Community, Article 1.1.

Article 2

Scope

1. This Directive shall apply to emissions from the activities listed in Annex I and greenhouse gases listed in Annex II.

2. This Directive shall apply without prejudice to any requirements pursuant to Directive 96/61/EC.

[3. The application of this Directive to the airport of Gibraltar is understood to be without prejudice to the respective legal positions of the Kingdom of Spain and the United Kingdom with regard to the dispute over sovereignty over the territory in which the airport is situated.][1]

Amendment

1 Inserted by Directive 2008/101/EC of the European Parliament and of the Council of 19 November 2008 amending Directive 2003/87/EC so as to include aviation activities in the scheme for greenhouse gas emission allowance trading within the Community, Article 1.2.

Article 3

Definitions

For the purposes of this Directive the following definitions shall apply:

(a) "allowance" means an allowance to emit one tonne of carbon dioxide equivalent during a specified period, which shall be valid only for the purposes of meeting the requirements of this Directive and shall be transferable in accordance with the provisions of this Directive;

[(b) "emissions" means the release of greenhouse gases into the atmosphere from sources in an installation or the release from an aircraft performing an aviation activity listed in Annex I of the gases specified in respect of that activity;][1]

[(c) "greenhouse gases" means the gases listed in Annex II and other gaseous constituents of the atmosphere, both natural and anthropogenic, that absorb and re-emit infrared radiation;][2]

(d) "greenhouse gas emissions permit" means the permit issued in accordance with Articles 5 and 6;

(e) "installation" means a stationary technical unit where one or more activities listed in Annex I are carried out and any other directly associated activities which have a technical connection with the activities carried out on that site and which could have an effect on emissions and pollution;

(f) "operator" means any person who operates or controls an installation or, where this is provided for in national legislation, to whom decisive economic power over the technical functioning of the installation has been delegated;

(g) "person" means any natural or legal person;

[(h) "new entrant" means:

— any installation carrying out one or more of the activities indicated in Annex I, which has obtained a greenhouse gas emissions permit for the first time after 30 June 2011;
— any installation carrying out an activity which is included in the Community scheme pursuant to Article 24(1) or (2) for the first time, or
— any installation carrying out one or more of the activities indicated in Annex I or an activity which is included in the Community scheme pursuant to Article 24(1) or (2), which has had a significant extension after 30 June 2011, only in so far as this extension is concerned;][2]

(i) "the public" means one or more persons and, in accordance with national legislation or practice, associations, organisations or groups of persons;

(j) "tonne of carbon dioxide equivalent" means one metric tonne of carbon dioxide (CO_2) or an amount of any other greenhouse gas listed in Annex II with an equivalent global-warming potential.

[(k) "Annex I Party" means a Party listed in Annex I to the United Nations Framework Convention on Climate Change (UNFCCC) that has ratified the Kyoto Protocol as specified in Article 1(7) of the Kyoto Protocol;

(l) "project activity" means a project activity approved by one or more Annex I Parties in accordance with Article 6 or Article 12 of the Kyoto Protocol and the decisions adopted pursuant to the UNFCCC or the Kyoto Protocol;

(m) "emission reduction unit" or "ERU" means a unit issued pursuant to Article 6 of the Kyoto Protocol and the decisions adopted pursuant to the UNFCCC or the Kyoto Protocol;

(n) "certified emission reduction" or "CER" means a unit issued pursuant to Article 12 of the Kyoto Protocol and the decisions adopted pursuant to the UNFCCC or the Kyoto Protocol;][3]

[(o) "aircraft operator" means the person who operates an aircraft at the time it performs an aviation activity listed in Annex I or, where that person is not known or is not identified by the owner of the aircraft, the owner of the aircraft;

(p) "commercial air transport operator" means an operator that, for remuneration, provides scheduled or non-scheduled air transport services to the public for the carriage of passengers, freight or mail;

(q) "administering Member State" means the Member State responsible for administering the Community scheme in respect of an aircraft operator in accordance with Article 18a;

(r) "attributed aviation emissions" means emissions from all flights falling within the aviation activities listed in Annex I which depart from an aerodrome situated in the territory of a Member State and those which arrive in such an aerodrome from a third country;

(s) "historical aviation emissions" means the mean average of the annual emissions in the calendar years 2004, 2005 and 2006 from aircraft performing an aviation activity listed in Annex I;][4]

[(t) "combustion" means any oxidation of fuels, regardless of the way in which the heat, electrical or mechanical energy produced by this process is used, and any other directly associated activities, including waste gas scrubbing;

(u) "electricity generator" means an installation that, on or after 1 January 2005, has produced electricity for sale to third parties, and in which no activity listed in Annex I is carried out other than the "combustion of fuels".][5]

Amendments

1 Substituted by Directive 2008/101/EC of the European Parliament and of the Council of 19 November 2008 amending Directive 2003/87/EC so as to include aviation activities in the scheme for greenhouse gas emission allowance trading within the Community, Article 1.3(a).

2 Substituted by Directive 2009/29/EC of the European Parliament and of the Council of 23 April 2009 amending Directive 2003/87/EC so as to improve and extend the greenhouse gas emission allowance trading scheme of the Community, Article 1.2(a), (b).

3 Inserted by Directive 2004/101/EC of the European Parliament and of the Council of 27 October 2004 amending Directive 2003/87/EC establishing a scheme for greenhouse gas emission allowance trading within the Community, in respect of the Kyoto Protocol's project mechanisms, Article 1.1.

4 Inserted by Directive 2008/101/EC of the European Parliament and of the Council of 19 November 2008 amending Directive 2003/87/EC so as to include aviation activities in the scheme for greenhouse gas emission allowance trading within the Community, Article 1.3(b).

5 Inserted by Directive 2009/29/EC of the European Parliament and of the Council of 23 April 2009 amending Directive 2003/87/EC so as to improve and extend the greenhouse gas emission allowance trading scheme of the Community, Article 1.2(c).

[Chapter II
Aviation

Article 3a

Scope][1]

[The provisions of this Chapter shall apply to the allocation and issue of allowances in respect of aviation activities listed in Annex I.][1]

Amendment

1 Inserted by Directive 2008/101/EC of the European Parliament and of the Council of 19 November 2008 amending Directive 2003/87/EC so as to include aviation activities in the scheme for greenhouse gas emission allowance trading within the Community, Article 1.4.

[Article 3b

Aviation activities][1]

[By 2 August 2009, the Commission shall, in accordance with the regulatory procedure referred to in Article 23(2), develop guidelines on the detailed interpretation of the aviation activities listed in Annex I.][1]

Amendment

1 Inserted by Directive 2008/101/EC of the European Parliament and of the Council of 19 November 2008 amending Directive 2003/87/EC so as to include aviation activities in the scheme for greenhouse gas emission allowance trading within the Community, Article 1.4.

[Article 3c

Total quantity of allowances for aviation][1]

[1. For the period from 1 January 2012 to 31 December 2012, the total quantity of allowances to be allocated to aircraft operators shall be equivalent to 97 % of the historical aviation emissions.

2. For the period referred to in [Article 13(1)][2] beginning on 1 January 2013, and, in the absence of any amendments following the review referred to in Article 30(4), for each

subsequent period, the total quantity of allowances to be allocated to aircraft operators shall be equivalent to 95 % of the historical aviation emissions multiplied by the number of years in the period.

This percentage may be reviewed as part of the general review of this Directive.

3. The Commission shall review the total quantity of allowances to be allocated to aircraft operators in accordance with Article 30(4).

4. By 2 August 2009, the Commission shall decide on the historical aviation emissions, based on best available data, including estimates based on actual traffic information. That decision shall be considered within the Committee referred to in Article 23(1).][1]

Amendments

1 Inserted by Directive 2008/101/EC of the European Parliament and of the Council of 19 November 2008 amending Directive 2003/87/EC so as to include aviation activities in the scheme for greenhouse gas emission allowance trading within the Community, Article 1.4.

2 Substituted by Directive 2009/29/EC of the European Parliament and of the Council of 23 April 2009 amending Directive 2003/87/EC so as to improve and extend the greenhouse gas emission allowance trading scheme of the Community, Article 1.3.

[Article 3d

Method of allocation of allowances for aviation through auctioning][1]

[1. In the period referred to in Article 3c(1), 15 % of allowances shall be auctioned.

2. From 1 January 2013, 15 % of allowances shall be auctioned. This percentage may be increased as part of the general review of this Directive.

3. A Regulation shall be adopted containing detailed provisions for the auctioning by Member States of allowances not required to be issued free of charge in accordance with paragraphs 1 and 2 of this Article or Article 3f(8). The number of allowances to be auctioned in each period by each Member State shall be proportionate to its share of the total attributed aviation emissions for all Member States for the reference year reported pursuant to Article 14(3) and verified pursuant to Article 15. For the period referred to in Article 3c(1), the reference year shall be 2010 and for each subsequent period referred to in Article 3c the reference year shall be the calendar year ending 24 months before the start of the period to which the auction relates.

That Regulation, designed to amend non-essential elements of this Directive by supplementing it, shall be adopted in accordance with the regulatory procedure with scrutiny referred to in Article 23(3).

4. It shall be for Member States to determine the use to be made of revenues generated from the auctioning of allowances. Those revenues should be used to tackle climate change in the EU and third countries, inter alia, to reduce greenhouse gas emissions, to adapt to the impacts of climate change in the EU and third countries, especially developing countries, to fund research and development for mitigation and adaptation, including in particular in the fields of aeronautics and air transport, to reduce emissions through low-emission transport and to cover the cost of administering the Community scheme. The proceeds of auctioning should also be used to fund contributions to the Global Energy Efficiency and Renewable Energy Fund, and measures to avoid deforestation. Member States shall inform the Commission of actions taken pursuant to this paragraph.

5. Information provided to the Commission pursuant to this Directive does not free Member States from the notification obligation laid down in Article 88(3) of the Treaty.][1]

Amendment

1 Inserted by Directive 2008/101/EC of the European Parliament and of the Council of 19 November 2008 amending Directive 2003/87/EC so as to include aviation activities in the scheme for greenhouse gas emission allowance trading within the Community, Article 1.4.

[Article 3e

Allocation and issue of allowances to aircraft operators][1]

[1. For each period referred to in Article 3c, each aircraft operator may apply for an allocation of allowances that are to be allocated free of charge. An application may be made by submitting to the competent authority in the administering Member State verified tonne-kilometre data for the aviation activities listed in Annex I performed by that aircraft operator for the monitoring year. For the purposes of this Article, the monitoring year shall be the calendar year ending 24 months before the start of the period to which it relates in accordance with Annexes IV and V or, in relation to the period referred to in Article 3c(1), 2010. Any application shall be made at least 21 months before the start of the period to which it relates or, in relation to the period referred to in Article 3c(1), by 31 March 2011.

2. At least 18 months before the start of the period to which the application relates or, in relation to the period referred to in Article 3c (1), by 30 June 2011, Member States shall submit applications received under paragraph 1 to the Commission.

3. At least 15 months before the start of each period referred to in Article 3c(2) or, in relation to the period referred to in Article 3c(1), by 30 September 2011, the Commission shall calculate and adopt a decision setting out:

(a) the total quantity of allowances to be allocated for that period in accordance with Article 3c;

(b) the number of allowances to be auctioned in that period in accordance with Article 3d;

(c) the number of allowances in the special reserve for aircraft operators in that period in accordance with Article 3f(1);

(d) the number of allowances to be allocated free of charge in that period by subtracting the number of allowances referred to in points (b) and (c) from the total quantity of allowances decided upon under point (a); and

(e) the benchmark to be used to allocate allowances free of charge to aircraft operators whose applications were submitted to the Commission in accordance with paragraph 2.

The benchmark referred to in point (e), expressed as allowances per tonne-kilometre, shall be calculated by dividing the number of allowances referred to in point (d) by the sum of the tonne-kilometre data included in applications submitted to the Commission in accordance with paragraph 2.

4. Within three months from the date on which the Commission adopts a decision under paragraph 3, each administering Member State shall calculate and publish:

(a) the total allocation of allowances for the period to each aircraft operator whose application it submitted to the Commission in accordance with paragraph 2, calculated by multiplying the tonnekilometre data included in the application by the benchmark referred to in paragraph 3(e); and

(b) the allocation of allowances to each aircraft operator for each year, which shall be determined by dividing its total allocation of allowances for the period calculated under point (a) by the number of years in the period for which that aircraft operator is performing an aviation activity listed in Annex I.

5. By 28 February 2012 and by 28 February of each subsequent year, the competent authority of the administering Member State shall issue to each aircraft operator the number of allowances allocated to that aircraft operator for that year under this Article or Article 3f.][1]

Amendments

1 Inserted by Directive 2008/101/EC of the European Parliament and of the Council of 19 November 2008 amending Directive 2003/87/EC so as to include aviation activities in the scheme for greenhouse gas emission allowance trading within the Community, Article 1.4.

[Article 3f

Special reserve for certain aircraft operators][1]

[1. In each period referred to in Article 3c(2), 3 % of the total quantity of allowances to be allocated shall be set aside in a special reserve for aircraft operators:

(a) who start performing an aviation activity falling within Annex I after the monitoring year for which tonne-kilometre data was submitted under Article 3e(1) in respect of a period referred to in Article 3c(2); or

(b) whose tonne-kilometre data increases by an average of more than 18 % annually between the monitoring year for which tonnekilometre data was submitted under Article 3e(1) in respect of a period referred to in Article 3c(2) and the second calendar year of that period; and whose activity under point (a), or additional activity under point (b), is not in whole or in part a continuation of an aviation activity previously performed by another aircraft operator.

2. An aircraft operator who is eligible under paragraph 1 may apply for a free allocation of allowances from the special reserve by making an application to the competent authority of its administering Member State. Any application shall be made by 30 June in the third year of the period referred to in Article 3c(2) to which it relates. An allocation to an aircraft operator under paragraph 1(b) shall not exceed 1 000 000 allowances.

3. An application under paragraph 2 shall:

(a) include verified tonne-kilometre data in accordance with Annexes IV and V for the aviation activities listed in Annex I performed by the aircraft operator in the second calendar year of the period referred to in Article 3c(2) to which the application relates;

(b) provide evidence that the criteria for eligibility under paragraph 1 are fulfilled; and

(c) in the case of aircraft operators falling within paragraph 1(b), state:

  (i) the percentage increase in tonne-kilometres performed by that aircraft operator between the monitoring year for which tonnekilometre data was submitted under Article 3e(1) in respect of a period referred to in Article 3c(2) and the second calendar year of that period;

  (ii) the absolute growth in tonne-kilometres performed by that aircraft operator between the monitoring year for which tonne-kilometre data was submitted under Article 3e(1) in respect of a period referred to in Article 3c(2) and the second calendar year of that period; and

  (iii) the absolute growth in tonne-kilometres performed by that aircraft operator between the monitoring year for which tonne-kilometre data was submitted under Article 3e(1) in respect of a period referred to in Article 3c(2) and the second calendar year of that period which exceeds the percentage specified in paragraph 1(b).

4. No later than six months from the deadline for making an application under paragraph 2, Member States shall submit applications received under that paragraph to the Commission.

5. No later than 12 months from the deadline for making an application under paragraph 2, the Commission shall decide on the benchmark to be used to allocate allowances free of charge to aircraft operators whose applications were submitted to the Commission in accordance with paragraph 4. Subject to paragraph 6, the benchmark shall be calculated by dividing the number of the allowances in the special reserve by the sum of:

(a) the tonne-kilometre data for aircraft operators falling within paragraph 1(a) included in applications submitted to the Commission in accordance with paragraphs 3(a) and 4; and

(b) the absolute growth in tonne-kilometres exceeding the percentage specified in paragraph 1(b) for aircraft operators falling within paragraph 1(b) included in applications submitted to the Commission in accordance with paragraphs 3(c)(iii) and 4.

6. The benchmark referred to in paragraph 5 shall not result in an annual allocation per tonne-kilometre greater than the annual allocation per tonne-kilometre to aircraft operators under Article 3e(4).

7. Within three months from the date on which the Commission adopts a decision under paragraph 5, each administering Member State shall calculate and publish:

(a) the allocation of allowances from the special reserve to each aircraft operator whose application it submitted to the Commission in accordance with paragraph 4. This allocation shall be calculated by multiplying the benchmark referred to in paragraph 5 by:
 (i) in the case of an aircraft operator falling within paragraph 1(a), the tonne-kilometre data included in the application submitted to the Commission under paragraphs 3(a) and 4;
 (ii) in the case of an aircraft operator falling within paragraph 1(b), the absolute growth in tonne-kilometres exceeding the percentage specified in paragraph 1(b) included in the application submitted to the Commission under paragraphs 3(c)(iii) and 4; and

(b) the allocation of allowances to each aircraft operator for each year, which shall be determined by dividing its allocation of allowances under point (a) by the number of full calendar years remaining in the period referred to in Article 3c(2) to which the allocation relates.

8. Any unallocated allowances in the special reserve shall be auctioned by Member States.

9. The Commission may establish detailed rules on the operation of the special reserve under this Article, including the assessment of compliance with eligibility criteria under paragraph 1. Those measures, designed to amend non-essential elements of this Directive by supplementing it, shall be adopted in accordance with the regulatory procedure with scrutiny referred to in Article 23(3).][1]

Amendment

1 Inserted by Directive 2008/101/EC of the European Parliament and of the Council of 19 November 2008 amending Directive 2003/87/EC so as to include aviation activities in the scheme for greenhouse gas emission allowance trading within the Community, Article 1.4.

[Article 3g

Monitoring and reporting plans][1]

[The administering Member State shall ensure that each aircraft operator submits to the competent authority in that Member State a monitoring plan setting out measures to monitor and report emissions and tonne-kilometre data for the purpose of an application under Article 3e and that such plans are approved by the competent authority in accordance with [the regulation referred to in Article 14][2].][1]

Amendments

1 Inserted by Directive 2008/101/EC of the European Parliament and of the Council of 19 November 2008 amending Directive 2003/87/EC so as to include aviation activities in the scheme for greenhouse gas emission allowance trading within the Community, Article 1.4.

2 Substituted by Directive 2009/29/EC of the European Parliament and of the Council of 23 April 2009 amending Directive 2003/87/EC so as to improve and extend the greenhouse gas emission allowance trading scheme of the Community, Article 1.4.

[Chapter III
Stationary installations

Article 3h

Scope][1]

[The provisions of this Chapter shall apply to greenhouse gas emissions permits and the allocation and issue of allowances in respect of activities listed in Annex I other than aviation activities.][1]

Amendment

1 Inserted by Directive 2008/101/EC of the European Parliament and of the Council of 19 November 2008 amending Directive 2003/87/EC so as to include aviation activities in the scheme for greenhouse gas emission allowance trading within the Community, Article 1.5.

[Article 4

Greenhouse gas emissions permits][1]

[Member States shall ensure that, from 1 January 2005, no installation undertakes any activity listed in Annex I resulting in emissions specified in relation to that activity unless its operator holds a permit issued by a competent authority in accordance with Articles 5 and 6, or the installation is excluded from the Community scheme pursuant to Article 27. This shall also apply to installations opted in under Article 24.][1]

Amendment

1 Substituted by Directive 2009/29/EC of the European Parliament and of the Council of 23 April 2009 amending Directive 2003/87/EC so as to improve and extend the greenhouse gas emission allowance trading scheme of the Community, Article 1.5.

Article 5

Applications for greenhouse gas emissions permits

An application to the competent authority for a greenhouse gas emissions permit shall include a description of:

(a) the installation and its activities including the technology used;

(b) the raw and auxiliary materials, the use of which is likely to lead to emissions of gases listed in Annex I;

(c) the sources of emissions of gases listed in Annex I from the installation; and

[(d) the measures planned to monitor and report emissions in accordance with the regulation referred to in Article 14.][1]

The application shall also include a non-technical summary of the details referred to in the first subparagraph.

Amendment

1 Substituted by Directive 2009/29/EC of the European Parliament and of the Council of 23 April 2009 amending Directive 2003/87/EC so as to improve and extend the greenhouse gas emission allowance trading scheme of the Community, Article 1.6.

Article 6

Conditions for and contents of the greenhouse gas emissions permit

1. The competent authority shall issue a greenhouse gas emissions permit granting authorisation to emit greenhouse gases from all or part of an installation if it is satisfied that the operator is capable of monitoring and reporting emissions.

A greenhouse gas emissions permit may cover one or more installations on the same site operated by the same operator.

[The competent authority shall, at least every five years, review the greenhouse gas emissions permit and make any amendments as are appropriate.][1]

2. Greenhouse gas emissions permits shall contain the following:

(a) the name and address of the operator;

(b) a description of the activities and emissions from the installation;

[(c) a monitoring plan that fulfils the requirements under the regulation referred to in Article 14. Member States may allow operators to update monitoring plans without changing the permit. Operators shall submit any updated monitoring plans to the competent authority for approval;][2]

(d) reporting requirements; and

[(e) an obligation to surrender allowances, other than allowances issued under Chapter II, equal to the total emissions of the installation in each calendar year, as verified in accordance with Article 15, within four months following the end of that year.][3]

Amendments

1 Inserted by Directive 2009/29/EC of the European Parliament and of the Council of 23 April 2009 amending Directive 2003/87/EC so as to improve and extend the greenhouse gas emission allowance trading scheme of the Community, Article 1.7(a).

2 Substituted by Directive 2009/29/EC of the European Parliament and of the Council of 23 April 2009 amending Directive 2003/87/EC so as to improve and extend the greenhouse gas emission allowance trading scheme of the Community, Article 1.7(b).

3 Inserted by Directive 2008/101/EC of the European Parliament and of the Council of 19 November 2008 amending Directive 2003/87/EC so as to include aviation activities in the scheme for greenhouse gas emission allowance trading within the Community, Article 1.6.

[Article 7

Changes relating to installations][1]

[The operator shall inform the competent authority of any planned changes to the nature or functioning of the installation, or any extension or significant reduction of its capacity, which may require updating the greenhouse gas emissions permit. Where appropriate, the competent authority shall update the permit. Where there is a change in the identity of the installation's operator, the competent authority shall update the permit to include the name and address of the new operator.][1]

Amendment

1 Substituted by Directive 2009/29/EC of the European Parliament and of the Council of 23 April 2009 amending Directive 2003/87/EC so as to improve and extend the greenhouse gas emission allowance trading scheme of the Community, Article 1.8.

Article 8

Coordination with Directive 96/61/EC

Member States shall take the necessary measures to ensure that, where installations carry out activities that are included in Annex I to Directive 96/61/EC, the conditions of, and procedure for, the issue of a greenhouse gas emissions permit are coordinated with those for the permit provided for in that Directive. The requirements of Articles 5, 6 and 7 of this Directive may be integrated into the procedures provided for in Directive 96/61/EC.

[Article 9

Community-wide quantity of allowances][1]

[The Community-wide quantity of allowances issued each year starting in 2013 shall decrease in a linear manner beginning from the mid-point of the period from 2008 to 2012. The quantity shall decrease by a linear factor of 1,74 % compared to the average annual total quantity of allowances issued by Member States in accordance with the Commission Decisions on their national allocation plans for the period from 2008 to 2012.

The Commission shall, by 30 June 2010, publish the absolute Community-wide quantity of allowances for 2013, based on the total quantities of allowances issued or to be issued by the Member States in accordance with the Commission Decisions on their national allocation plans for the period from 2008 to 2012.

The Commission shall review the linear factor and submit a proposal, where appropriate, to the European Parliament and to the Council as from 2020, with a view to the adoption of a decision by 2025.][1]

Amendment

1 Substituted by Directive 2009/29/EC of the European Parliament and of the Council of 23 April 2009 amending Directive 2003/87/EC so as to improve and extend the greenhouse gas emission allowance trading scheme of the Community, Article 1.9.

[Article 9a

Adjustment of the Community-wide quantity of allowances][1]

[1. In respect of installations that were included in the Community scheme during the period from 2008 to 2012 pursuant to Article 24(1), the quantity of allowances to be issued from 1 January 2013 shall be adjusted to reflect the average annual quantity of allowances issued in respect of those installations during the period of their inclusion, adjusted by the linear factor referred to in Article 9.

2. In respect of installations carrying out activities listed in Annex I, which are only included in the Community scheme from 2013 onwards, Member States shall ensure that the operators of such installations submit to the relevant competent authority duly substantiated and independently verified emissions data in order for them to be taken into account for the adjustment of the Community-wide quantity of allowances to be issued.

Any such data shall be submitted, by 30 April 2010, to the relevant competent authority in accordance with the provisions adopted pursuant to Article 14(1).

If the data submitted are duly substantiated, the competent authority shall notify the Commission thereof by 30 June 2010 and the quantity of allowances to be issued, adjusted by the linear factor referred to in Article 9, shall be adjusted accordingly. In the case of installations emitting greenhouse gases other than CO_2, the competent authority may notify a lower amount of emissions according to the emission reduction potential of those installations.

3. The Commission shall publish the adjusted quantities referred to in paragraphs 1 and 2 by 30 September 2010.

4. In respect of installations which are excluded from the Community scheme in accordance with Article 27, the Community-wide quantity of allowances to be issued from 1 January 2013 shall be adjusted downwards to reflect the average annual verified emissions of those installations in the period from 2008 to 2010, adjusted by the linear factor referred to in Article 9.][1]

Amendment

1 Inserted by Directive 2009/29/EC of the European Parliament and of the Council of 23 April 2009 amending Directive 2003/87/EC so as to improve and extend the greenhouse gas emission allowance trading scheme of the Community, Article 1.10.

[Article 10

Auctioning of allowances][1]

[1. From 2013 onwards, Member States shall auction all allowances which are not allocated free of charge in accordance with Article 10a and 10c. By 31 December 2010, the Commission shall determine and publish the estimated amount of allowances to be auctioned.

2. The total quantity of allowances to be auctioned by each Member State shall be composed as follows:

(a) 88 % of the total quantity of allowances to be auctioned being distributed amongst Member States in shares that are identical to the share of verified emissions under the Community scheme for 2005 or the average of the period from 2005 to 2007, whichever one is the highest, of the Member State concerned;

(b) 10 % of the total quantity of allowances to be auctioned being distributed amongst certain Member States for the purpose of solidarity and growth within the Community, thereby increasing the amount of allowances that those Member States auction under point (a) by the percentages specified in Annex IIa; and

(c) 2 % of the total quantity of allowances to be auctioned being distributed amongst Member States the greenhouse gas emissions of which were, in 2005, at least 20 % below their emissions in the base year applicable to them under the Kyoto Protocol. The distribution of this percentage amongst the Member States concerned is set out in Annex IIb.

For the purposes of point (a), in respect of Member States which did not participate in the Community scheme in 2005, their share shall be calculated using their verified emissions under the Community scheme in 2007.

If necessary, the percentages referred to in points (b) and (c) shall be adapted in a proportional manner to ensure that the distribution is 10 % and 2 % respectively.

3. Member States shall determine the use of revenues generated from the auctioning of allowances. At least 50 % of the revenues generated from the auctioning of allowances referred to in paragraph 2, including all revenues from the auctioning referred to in paragraph 2, points (b) and (c), or the equivalent in financial value of these revenues, should be used for one or more of the following:

(a) to reduce greenhouse gas emissions, including by contributing to the Global Energy Efficiency and Renewable Energy Fund and to the Adaptation Fund as made operational by the Poznan Conference on Climate Change (COP 14 and COP/MOP 4), to adapt to the impacts of climate change and to fund research and development as well as demonstration projects for reducing emissions and for adaptation to climate change, including participation in initiatives within the framework of the European Strategic Energy Technology Plan and the European Technology Platforms;

(b) to develop renewable energies to meet the commitment of the Community to using 20 % renewable energies by 2020, as well as to develop other technologies contributing to the transition to a safe and sustainable low-carbon economy and to help meet the commitment of the Community to increase energy efficiency by 20 % by 2020;

(c) measures to avoid deforestation and increase afforestation and reforestation in developing countries that have ratified the international agreement on climate change, to transfer technologies and to facilitate adaptation to the adverse effects of climate change in these countries;

(d) forestry sequestration in the Community;

(e) the environmentally safe capture and geological storage of CO_2, in particular from solid fossil fuel power stations and a range of industrial sectors and subsectors, including in third countries;

(f) to encourage a shift to low-emission and public forms of transport;

(g) to finance research and development in energy efficiency and clean technologies in the sectors covered by this Directive;

(h) measures intended to increase energy efficiency and insulation or to provide financial support in order to address social aspects in lower and middle income households;

(i) to cover administrative expenses of the management of the Community scheme.

Member States shall be deemed to have fulfilled the provisions of this paragraph if they have in place and implement fiscal or financial support policies, including in particular in developing countries, or domestic regulatory policies, which leverage financial support, established for the purposes set out in the first subparagraph and which have a value equivalent to at least 50 % of the revenues generated from the auctioning of allowances referred to in paragraph 2, including all revenues from the auctioning referred to in paragraph 2, points (b) and (c).

Member States shall inform the Commission as to the use of revenues and the actions taken pursuant to this paragraph in their reports submitted under Decision No 280/2004/EC.

4. By 30 June 2010, the Commission shall adopt a regulation on timing, administration and other aspects of auctioning to ensure that it is conducted in an open, transparent, harmonised and non-discriminatory manner. To this end, the process should be predictable, in particular

as regards the timing and sequencing of auctions and the estimated volumes of allowances to be made available.

Auctions shall be designed to ensure that:
(a) operators, and in particular any SMEs covered by the Community scheme, have full, fair and equitable access;
(b) all participants have access to the same information at the same time and that participants do not undermine the operation of the auction;
(c) the organisation and participation in auctions is cost-efficient and undue administrative costs are avoided; and
(d) access to allowances is granted for small emitters.

That measure, designed to amend non-essential elements of this Directive by supplementing it, shall be adopted in accordance with the regulatory procedure with scrutiny referred to in Article 23(3).

Member States shall report on the proper implementation of the auctioning rules for each auction, in particular with respect to fair and open access, transparency, price formation and technical and operational aspects. These reports shall be submitted within one month of the auction concerned and shall be published on the Commission's website.

5. The Commission shall monitor the functioning of the European carbon market. Each year, it shall submit a report to the European Parliament and to the Council on the functioning of the carbon market including the implementation of the auctions, liquidity and the volumes traded. If necessary, Member States shall ensure that any relevant information is submitted to the Commission at least two months before the Commission adopts the report.][1]

Amendment

1 Substituted by Directive 2009/29/EC of the European Parliament and of the Council of 23 April 2009 amending Directive 2003/87/EC so as to improve and extend the greenhouse gas emission allowance trading scheme of the Community, Article 1.11.

[Article 10a

Transitional Community-wide rules for harmonised free allocation][1]

[1. By 31 December 2010, the Commission shall adopt Community-wide and fully-harmonised implementing measures for the allocation of the allowances referred to in paragraphs 4, 5, 7 and 12, including any necessary provisions for a harmonised application of paragraph 19.

Those measures, designed to amend non-essential elements of this Directive by supplementing it, shall be adopted in accordance with the regulatory procedure with scrutiny referred to in Article 23(3).

The measures referred to in the first subparagraph shall, to the extent feasible, determine Community-wide ex-ante benchmarks so as to ensure that allocation takes place in a manner that provides incentives for reductions in greenhouse gas emissions and energy efficient techniques, by taking account of the most efficient techniques, substitutes, alternative production processes, high efficiency cogeneration, efficient energy recovery of waste gases, use of biomass and capture and storage of CO_2, where such facilities are available, and shall not provide incentives to increase emissions. No free allocation shall be made in respect of any electricity production, except for cases falling within Article 10c and electricity produced from waste gases.

For each sector and subsector, in principle, the benchmark shall be calculated for products rather than for inputs, in order to maximise greenhouse gas emissions reductions and energy efficiency savings throughout each production process of the sector or the subsector concerned.

In defining the principles for setting ex-ante benchmarks in individual sectors and subsectors, the Commission shall consult the relevant stakeholders, including the sectors and subsectors concerned.

The Commission shall, upon the approval by the Community of an international agreement on climate change leading to mandatory reductions of greenhouse gas emissions comparable to those of the Community, review those measures to provide that free allocation is only to take place where this is fully justified in the light of that agreement.

2. In defining the principles for setting ex-ante benchmarks in individual sectors or subsectors, the starting point shall be the average performance of the 10 % most efficient installations in a sector or subsector in the Community in the years 2007-2008. The Commission shall consult the relevant stakeholders, including the sectors and subsectors concerned.

The regulations pursuant to Articles 14 and 15 shall provide for harmonised rules on monitoring, reporting and verification of production-related greenhouse gas emissions with a view to determining the ex-ante benchmarks.

3. Subject to paragraphs 4 and 8, and notwithstanding Article 10c, no free allocation shall be given to electricity generators, to installations for the capture of CO_2, to pipelines for transport of CO_2 or to CO_2 storage sites.

4. Free allocation shall be given to district heating as well as to high efficiency cogeneration, as defined by Directive 2004/8/EC, for economically justifiable demand, in respect of the production of heating or cooling. In each year subsequent to 2013, the total allocation to such installations in respect of the production of that heat shall be adjusted by the linear factor referred to in Article 9.

5. The maximum annual amount of allowances that is the basis for calculating allocations to installations which are not covered by paragraph 3 and are not new entrants shall not exceed the sum of:

(a) the annual Community-wide total quantity, as determined pursuant to Article 9, multiplied by the share of emissions from installations not covered by paragraph 3 in the total average verified emissions, in the period from 2005 to 2007, from installations covered by the Community scheme in the period from 2008 to 2012; and

(b) the total average annual verified emissions from installations in the period from 2005 to 2007 which are only included in the Community scheme from 2013 onwards and are not covered by paragraph 3, adjusted by the linear factor, as referred to in Article 9.

A uniform cross-sectoral correction factor shall be applied if necessary.

6. Member States may also adopt financial measures in favour of sectors or subsectors determined to be exposed to a significant risk of carbon leakage due to costs relating to greenhouse gas emissions passed on in electricity prices, in order to compensate for those costs and where such financial measures are in accordance with state aid rules applicable and to be adopted in this area.

Those measures shall be based on ex-ante benchmarks of the indirect emissions of CO_2 per unit of production. The ex-ante benchmarks shall be calculated for a given sector or subsector as the product of the electricity consumption per unit of production corresponding to the most efficient available technologies and of the CO_2 emissions of the relevant European electricity production mix.

7. Five percent of the Community-wide quantity of allowances determined in accordance with Articles 9 and 9a over the period from 2013 to 2020 shall be set aside for new entrants, as the maximum that may be allocated to new entrants in accordance with the rules adopted pursuant to paragraph 1 of this Article. Allowances in this Community-wide reserve that are neither allocated to new entrants nor used pursuant to paragraph 8, 9 or 10 of this Article over the period from 2013 to 2020 shall be auctioned by the Member States, taking into account the level to which installations in Member States have benefited from this reserve, in accordance with Article 10(2) and, for detailed arrangements and timing, Article 10(4), and the relevant implementing provisions.

Allocations shall be adjusted by the linear factor referred to in Article 9.

No free allocation shall be made in respect of any electricity production by new entrants.

By 31 December 2010, the Commission shall adopt harmonised rules for the application of the definition of "new entrant", in particular in relation to the definition of "significant extensions".

Those measures, designed to amend non-essential elements of this Directive by supplementing it, shall be adopted in accordance with the regulatory procedure with scrutiny referred to in Article 23(3).

8. Up to 300 million allowances in the new entrants' reserve shall be available until 31 December 2015 to help stimulate the construction and operation of up to 12 commercial demonstration projects that aim at the environmentally safe capture and geological storage (CCS) of CO2 as well as demonstration projects of innovative renewable energy technologies, in the territory of the Union.

The allowances shall be made available for support for demonstration projects that provide for the development, in geographically balanced locations, of a wide range of CCS and innovative renewable energy technologies that are not yet commercially viable. Their award shall be dependent upon the verified avoidance of CO_2 emissions.

Projects shall be selected on the basis of objective and transparent criteria that include requirements for knowledge-sharing. Those criteria and the measures shall be adopted in accordance with the regulatory procedure with scrutiny referred to in Article 23(3), and shall be made available to the public.

Allowances shall be set aside for the projects that meet the criteria referred to in the third subparagraph. Support for these projects shall be given via Member States and shall be complementary to substantial co-financing by the operator of the installation. They could also be co-financed by the Member State concerned, as well as by other instruments. No project shall receive support via the mechanism under this paragraph that exceeds 15 % of the total number of allowances available for this purpose. These allowances shall be taken into account under paragraph 7.

9. Lithuania, which, pursuant to Article 1 of Protocol No 4 on the Ignalina nuclear power plant in Lithuania, annexed to the 2003 Act of Accession, has committed to the closure of unit 2 of the Ignalina Nuclear Power Plant by 31 December 2009, may, if the total verified emissions of Lithuania in the period from 2013 to 2015 within the Community scheme exceed the sum of the free allowances issued to installations in Lithuania for electricity production emissions in that period and three-eighths of the allowances to be auctioned by Lithuania for the period from 2013 to 2020, claim allowances from the new entrants reserve for auctioning in accordance with the regulation referred to in Article 10(4). The maximum amount of such allowances shall be equivalent to the excess emissions in that period to the extent that this excess is due to increased emissions from electricity generation, minus any quantity by which allocations in that Member State in the period from 2008 to 2012 exceeded verified emissions within the Community scheme in Lithuania during that period. Any such allowances shall be taken into account under paragraph 7.

10. Any Member State with an electricity network which is interconnected with Lithuania and which, in 2007, imported more than 15 % of its domestic electricity consumption from Lithuania for its own consumption, and where emissions have increased due to investment in new electricity generation, may apply paragraph 9 mutatis mutandis under the conditions set out in that paragraph.

11. Subject to Article 10b, the amount of allowances allocated free of charge under paragraphs 4 to 7 of this Article in 2013 shall be 80 % of the quantity determined in accordance with the measures referred to in paragraph 1. Thereafter the free allocation shall decrease each year by equal amounts resulting in 30 % free allocation in 2020, with a view to reaching no free allocation in 2027.

12. Subject to Article 10b, in 2013 and in each subsequent year up to 2020, installations in sectors or subsectors which are exposed to a significant risk of carbon leakage shall

be allocated, pursuant to paragraph 1, allowances free of charge at 100 % of the quantity determined in accordance with the measures referred to in paragraph 1.

13. By 31 December 2009 and every five years thereafter, after discussion in the European Council, the Commission shall determine a list of the sectors or subsectors referred to in paragraph 12 on the basis of the criteria referred to in paragraphs 14 to 17.

Every year the Commission may, at its own initiative or at the request of a Member State, add a sector or subsector to the list referred to in the first subparagraph if it can be demonstrated, in an analytical report, that this sector or subsector satisfies the criteria in paragraphs 14 to 17, following a change that has a substantial impact on the sector's or subsector's activities.

For the purpose of implementing this Article, the Commission shall consult the Member States, the sectors or subsectors concerned and other relevant stakeholders.

Those measures, designed to amend non-essential elements of this Directive by supplementing it, shall be adopted in accordance with the regulatory procedure with scrutiny referred to in Article 23(3).

14. In order to determine the sectors or subsectors referred to in paragraph 12, the Commission shall assess, at Community level, the extent to which it is possible for the sector or subsector concerned, at the relevant level of disaggregation, to pass on the direct cost of the required allowances and the indirect costs from higher electricity prices resulting from the implementation of this Directive into product prices without significant loss of market share to less carbon efficient installations outside the Community. These assessments shall be based on an average carbon price according to the Commission's impact assessment accompanying the package of implementation measures for the EU's objectives on climate change and renewable energy for 2020 and, if available, trade, production and value added data from the three most recent years for each sector or subsector.

15. A sector or subsector shall be deemed to be exposed to a significant risk of carbon leakage if:

(a) the sum of direct and indirect additional costs induced by the implementation of this Directive would lead to a substantial increase of production costs, calculated as a proportion of the gross value added, of at least 5 %; and

(b) the intensity of trade with third countries, defined as the ratio between the total value of exports to third countries plus the value of imports from third countries and the total market size for the Community (annual turnover plus total imports from third countries), is above 10 %.

16. Notwithstanding paragraph 15, a sector or subsector is also deemed to be exposed to a significant risk of carbon leakage if:

(a) the sum of direct and indirect additional costs induced by the implementation of this Directive would lead to a particularly high increase of production costs, calculated as a proportion of the gross value added, of at least 30 %; or

(b) the intensity of trade with third countries, defined as the ratio between the total value of exports to third countries plus the value of imports from third countries and the total market size for the Community (annual turnover plus total imports from third countries), is above 30 %.

17. The list referred to in paragraph 13 may be supplemented after completion of a qualitative assessment, taking into account, where the relevant data are available, the following criteria:

(a) the extent to which it is possible for individual installations in the sector or subsector concerned to reduce emission levels or electricity consumption, including, as appropriate, the increase in production costs that the related investment may entail, for instance on the basis of the most efficient techniques;

(b) current and projected market characteristics, including when trade exposure or direct and indirect cost increase rates are close to one of the thresholds mentioned in paragraph 16;

(c) profit margins as a potential indicator of long-run investment or relocation decisions.

18. The list referred to in paragraph 13 shall be determined after taking into account, where the relevant data are available, the following:

(a) the extent to which third countries, representing a decisive share of global production of products in sectors or subsectors deemed to be at risk of carbon leakage, firmly commit to reducing greenhouse gas emissions in the relevant sectors or subsectors to an extent comparable to that of the Community and within the same time-frame; and

(b) the extent to which the carbon efficiency of installations located in these countries is comparable to that of the Community.

19. No free allocation shall be given to an installation that has ceased its operations, unless the operator demonstrates to the competent authority that this installation will resume production within a specified and reasonable time. Installations for which the greenhouse gas emissions permit has expired or has been withdrawn and installations for which the operation or resumption of operation is technically impossible shall be considered to have ceased operations.

20. The Commission shall, as part of the measures adopted under paragraph 1, include measures for defining installations that partially cease to operate or significantly reduce their capacity, and measures for adapting, as appropriate, the level of free allocations given to them accordingly.][1]

Amendment

1 Inserted by Directive 2009/29/EC of the European Parliament and of the Council of 23 April 2009 amending Directive 2003/87/EC so as to improve and extend the greenhouse gas emission allowance trading scheme of the Community, Article 1.12.

[Article 10b

Measures to support certain energy-intensive industries in the event of carbon leakage][1]

[1. By 30 June 2010, the Commission shall, in the light of the outcome of the international negotiations and the extent to which these lead to global greenhouse gas emission reductions, and after consulting with all relevant social partners, submit to the European Parliament and to the Council an analytical report assessing the situation with regard to energy-intensive sectors or subsectors that have been determined to be exposed to significant risks of carbon leakage. This shall be accompanied by any appropriate proposals, which may include:

(a) adjustment of the proportion of allowances received free of charge by those sectors or subsectors under Article 10a;

(b) inclusion in the Community scheme of importers of products which are produced by the sectors or subsectors determined in accordance with Article 10a;

(c) assessment of the impact of carbon leakage on Member States' energy security, in particular where the electricity connections with the rest of the Union are insufficient and where there are electricity connections with third countries, and appropriate measures in this regard.

Any binding sectoral agreements which lead to global greenhouse gas emissions reductions of the magnitude required to effectively address climate change, and which are monitorable, verifiable and subject to mandatory enforcement arrangements shall also be taken into account when considering what measures are appropriate.

2. The Commission shall assess, by 31 March 2011, whether the decisions made regarding the proportion of allowances received free of charge by sectors or subsectors in accordance with paragraph 1, including the effect of setting ex-ante benchmarks in accordance with Article 10a(2), are likely to significantly affect the quantity of allowances to be auctioned by Member States in accordance with Article 10(2)(b), compared to a scenario with full auctioning for all sectors in 2020. It shall, if appropriate, submit adequate proposals to the European Parliament and to the Council, taking into account the possible distributional effects of such proposals.][1]

Amendment

1 Inserted by Directive 2009/29/EC of the European Parliament and of the Council of 23 April 2009 amending Directive 2003/87/EC so as to improve and extend the greenhouse gas emission allowance trading scheme of the Community, Article 1.12.

[Article 10c

Option for transitional free allocation for the modernisation of electricity generation][1]

[1. By derogation from Article 10a(1) to (5), Member States may give a transitional free allocation to installations for electricity production in operation by 31 December 2008 or to installations for electricity production for which the investment process was physically initiated by the same date, provided that one of the following conditions is met:

(a) in 2007, the national electricity network was not directly or indirectly connected to the network interconnected system operated by the Union for the Coordination of Transmission of Electricity (UCTE);

(b) in 2007, the national electricity network was only directly or indirectly connected to the network operated by UCTE through a single line with a capacity of less than 400 MW; or

(c) in 2006, more than 30 % of electricity was produced from a single fossil fuel, and the GDP per capita at market price did not exceed 50 % of the average GDP per capita at market price of the Community.

The Member State concerned shall submit to the Commission a national plan that provides for investments in retrofitting and upgrading of the infrastructure and clean technologies. The national plan shall also provide for the diversification of their energy mix and sources of supply for an amount equivalent, to the extent possible, to the market value of the free allocation with respect to the intended investments, while taking into account the need to limit as far as possible directly linked price increases. The Member State concerned shall submit to the Commission, every year, a report on investments made in upgrading infrastructure and clean technologies. Investment undertaken from 25 June 2009 may be counted for this purpose.

2. Transitional free allocations shall be deducted from the quantity of allowances that the respective Member State would otherwise auction pursuant to Article 10(2). In 2013, the total transitional free allocation shall not exceed 70 % of the annual average verified emissions in 2005–2007 from such electricity generators for the amount corresponding to the gross final national consumption of the Member State concerned and shall gradually decrease, resulting in no free allocation in 2020. For those Member States which did not participate in the Community scheme in 2005, the relevant emissions shall be calculated using their verified Community scheme emissions under the Community scheme in 2007.

The Member State concerned may determine that the allowances allocated pursuant to this Article may only be used by the operator of the installation concerned for surrendering allowances pursuant to Article 12(3) with respect to emissions of the same installation during the year for which the allowances are allocated.

3. Allocations to operators shall be based on the allocation under the verified emissions in 2005–2007 or an ex-ante efficiency benchmark based on the weighted average of emission levels of most greenhouse gas efficient electricity production covered by the Community scheme for installations using different fuels. The weighting may reflect the shares of the different fuels in electricity production in the Member State concerned. The Commission shall, in accordance with the regulatory procedure referred to in Article 23(2), provide guidance to ensure that the allocation methodology avoids undue distortions of competition and minimises negative impacts on the incentives to reduce emissions.

4. Any Member State applying this Article shall require benefiting electricity generators and network operators to report every 12 months on the implementation of their investments referred to in the national plan. Member States shall report on this to the Commission and shall make such reports public.

5. Any Member State that intends to allocate allowances on the basis of this Article shall, by 30 September 2011, submit to the Commission an application containing the proposed allocation methodology and individual allocations. An application shall contain:

(a) evidence that the Member State meets at least one of the conditions set out in paragraph 1;

(b) a list of the installations covered by the application and the amount of allowances to be allocated to each installation in accordance with paragraph 3 and the Commission guidance;

(c) the national plan referred to in the second subparagraph of paragraph 1;

(d) monitoring and enforcement provisions with respect to the intended investments pursuant to the national plan;

(e) information showing that the allocations do not create undue distortions of competition.

6. The Commission shall assess the application taking into account the elements set out in paragraph 5 and may reject the application, or any aspect thereof, within six months of receiving the relevant information.

7. Two years before the end of the period during which a Member State may give transitional free allocation to installations for electricity production in operation by 31 December 2008, the Commission shall assess the progress made in the implementation of the national plan. If the Commission considers, on request of the Member State concerned, that there is a need for a possible extension of that period, it may submit to the European Parliament and to the Council appropriate proposals, including the conditions that would have to be met in the case of an extension of that period.][1]

Amendment

1 Inserted by Directive 2009/29/EC of the European Parliament and of the Council of 23 April 2009 amending Directive 2003/87/EC so as to improve and extend the greenhouse gas emission allowance trading scheme of the Community, Article 1.12.

[Article 11

National implementation measures][1]

[1. Each Member State shall publish and submit to the Commission, by 30 September 2011, the list of installations covered by this Directive in its territory and any free allocation to each installation in its territory calculated in accordance with the rules referred to in Article 10a(1) and Article 10c.

2. By 28 February of each year, the competent authorities shall issue the quantity of allowances that are to be allocated for that year, calculated in accordance with Articles 10, 10a and 10c.

3. Member States may not issue allowances free of charge under paragraph 2 to installations whose inscription in the list referred to in paragraph 1 has been rejected by the Commission.][1]

Amendment

1 Substituted by Directive 2009/29/EC of the European Parliament and of the Council of 23 April 2009 amending Directive 2003/87/EC so as to improve and extend the greenhouse gas emission allowance trading scheme of the Community, Article 1.13.

[Chapter IV
Provisions applying to aviation and stationary installations][1]

[[Article 11a

Use of CERs and ERUs from project activities in the Community scheme before the entry into force of an international agreement on climate change][2]**]**[3]

[[1. Without prejudice to the application of Article 28(3) and (4), paragraphs 2 to 7 of this Article shall apply.

2. To the extent that the levels of CER and ERU use, allowed to operators or aircraft operators by Member States for the period from 2008 to 2012, have not been used up or an entitlement to use credits is granted under paragraph 8, operators may request the competent authority to issue allowances to them valid from 2013 onwards in exchange for CERs and ERUs issued in respect of emission reductions up until 2012 from project types which were eligible for use in the Community scheme during the period from 2008 to 2012.

Until 31 March 2015, the competent authority shall make such an exchange on request.

3. To the extent that the levels of CER and ERU use, allowed to operators or aircraft operators by Member States for the period from 2008 to 2012, have not been used up or an entitlement to use credits is granted under paragraph 8, competent authorities shall allow operators to exchange CERs and ERUs from projects that were registered before 2013 issued in respect of emission reductions from 2013 onwards for allowances valid from 2013 onwards.

The first subparagraph shall apply to CERs and ERUs for all project types which were eligible for use in the Community scheme during the period from 2008 to 2012.

4. To the extent that the levels of CER and ERU use, allowed to operators or aircraft operators by Member States for the period from 2008 to 2012, have not been used up or an entitlement to use credits is granted under paragraph 8, competent authorities shall allow operators to exchange CERs issued in respect of emission reductions from 2013 onwards for allowances from new projects started from 2013 onwards in LDCs.

The first subparagraph shall apply to CERs for all project types which were eligible for use in the Community scheme during the period from 2008 to 2012, until those countries have ratified a relevant agreement with the Community or until 2020, whichever is the earlier.

5. To the extent that the levels of CER and ERU use, allowed to operators or aircraft operators by Member States for the period from 2008 to 2012, have not been used up or an entitlement to use credits is granted under paragraph 8 and in the event that the negotiations on an international agreement on climate change are not concluded by 31 December 2009, credits from projects or other emission reducing activities may be used in the Community scheme in accordance with agreements concluded with third countries, specifying levels of use. In accordance with such agreements, operators shall be able to use credits from project activities in those third countries to comply with their obligations under the Community scheme.

6. Any agreements referred to in paragraph 5 shall provide for the use of credits in the Community scheme from project types which were eligible for use in the Community scheme during the period from 2008 to 2012, including renewable energy or energy efficiency technologies which promote technological transfer and sustainable development. Any such agreement may also provide for the use of credits from projects where the baseline used is below the level of free allocation under the measures referred to in Article 10a or below the levels required by Community legislation.

7. Once an international agreement on climate change has been reached, only credits from projects from third countries which have ratified that agreement shall be accepted in the Community scheme from 1 January 2013.

8. All existing operators shall be allowed to use credits during the period from 2008 to 2020 up to either the amount allowed to them during the period from 2008 to 2012, or to an amount corresponding to a percentage, which shall not be set below 11 %, of their allocation during the period from 2008 to 2012, whichever is the highest.

Operators shall be able to use credits beyond the 11 % provided for in the first subparagraph, up to an amount which results in their combined free allocation in the period from 2008 to 2012 and overall project credits entitlement equal to a certain percentage of their verified emissions in the period from 2005 to 2007.

New entrants, including new entrants in the period from 2008 to 2012 which received neither free allocation nor an entitlement to use CERs and ERUs in the period from 2008–2012, and new sectors shall be able to use credits up to an amount corresponding to a percentage, which shall not be set below 4,5 %, of their verified emissions during the period from 2013 to 2020. Aircraft operators shall be able to use credits up to an amount corresponding to a percentage, which shall not be set below 1,5 %, of their verified emissions during the period from 2013 to 2020.

Measures shall be adopted to specify the exact percentages which shall apply under the first, second and third subparagraphs. At least one-third of the additional amount which is to be distributed to existing operators beyond the first percentage referred to in the first subparagraph shall be distributed to the operators which had the lowest level of combined average free allocation and project credit use in the period from 2008 to 2012.

Those measures shall ensure that the overall use of credits allowed does not exceed 50 % of the Community-wide reductions below the 2005 levels of the existing sectors under the Community scheme over the period from 2008 to 2020 and 50 % of the Community-wide reductions below the 2005 levels of new sectors and aviation over the period from the date of their inclusion in the Community scheme to 2020.

Those measures, designed to amend non-essential elements of this Directive by supplementing it, shall be adopted in accordance with the regulatory procedure with scrutiny referred to in Article 23(3).

9. From 1 January 2013, measures may be applied to restrict the use of specific credits from project types.

Those measures shall also set the date from which the use of credits under paragraphs 1 to 4 shall be in accordance with these measures. That date shall be, at the earliest, six months from the adoption of the measures or, at the latest, three years from their adoption.

Those measures, designed to amend non-essential elements of this Directive by supplementing it, shall be adopted in accordance with the regulatory procedure with scrutiny referred to in Article 23(3). The Commission shall consider submitting to the Committee a draft of the measures to be taken where a Member State so requests.][2]][3]

Amendments

1 Inserted by Directive 2008/101/EC of the European Parliament and of the Council of 19 November 2008 amending Directive 2003/87/EC so as to include aviation activities in the scheme for greenhouse gas emission allowance trading within the Community, Article 1.7.

2 Substituted by Directive 2009/29/EC of the European Parliament and of the Council of 23 April 2009 amending Directive 2003/87/EC so as to improve and extend the greenhouse gas emission allowance trading scheme of the Community, Article 1.13.

3 Inserted by Directive 2004/101/EC of the European Parliament and of the Council of 27 October 2004 amending Directive 2003/87/EC establishing a scheme for greenhouse gas emission allowance trading within the Community, in respect of the Kyoto Protocol's project mechanisms, Article 1.2.

[Article 11b

Project activities][1]

[1. Member States shall take all necessary measures to ensure that baselines for project activities, as defined by subsequent decisions adopted under the UNFCCC or the Kyoto Protocol, undertaken in countries having signed a Treaty of Accession with the Union fully comply with the acquis communautaire, including the temporary derogations set out in that Treaty of Accession.

[The Community and its Member States shall only authorise project activities where all project participants have headquarters either in a country that has concluded the international agreement relating to such projects or in a country or sub-federal or regional entity which is linked to the Community scheme pursuant to Article 25.][2]

2. Except as provided for in paragraphs 3 and 4, Member States hosting project activities shall ensure that no ERUs or CERs are issued for reductions or limitations of greenhouse gas emissions from [activities][3] falling within the scope of this Directive.

3. Until 31 December 2012, for JI and CDM project activities which reduce or limit directly the emissions of an installation falling within the scope of this Directive, ERUs and CERs may be issued only if an equal number of allowances is cancelled by the operator of that installation.

4. Until 31 December 2012, for JI and CDM project activities which reduce or limit indirectly the emission level of installations falling within the scope of this Directive, ERUs and CERs may be issued only if an equal number of allowances is cancelled from the national registry of the Member State of the ERUs' or CERs' origin.

5. A Member State that authorises private or public entities to participate in project activities shall remain responsible for the fulfilment of its obligations under the UNFCCC and the Kyoto Protocol and shall ensure that such participation is consistent with the relevant guidelines, modalities and procedures adopted pursuant to the UNFCCC or the Kyoto Protocol.

6. In the case of hydroelectric power production project activities with a generating capacity exceeding 20 MW, Member States shall, when approving such project activities, ensure that relevant international criteria and guidelines, including those contained in the World Commission on Dams November 2000 Report "Dams and Development — A New Framework for Decision-Making", will be respected during the development of such project activities.

[7. Provisions for the implementation of paragraphs 3 and 4, particularly in respect of the avoidance of double counting, shall be adopted by the Commission in accordance with the regulatory procedure referred to in Article 23(2). The Commission shall adopt provisions for the implementation of paragraph 5 of this Article where the host party meets all eligibility requirements for JI project activities. Those measures, designed to amend non-essential elements of this Directive, by supplementing it, shall be adopted in accordance with the regulatory procedure with scrutiny referred to in Article 23(3).][4]][1]

Amendments

1 Inserted by Directive 2004/101/EC of the European Parliament and of the Council of 27 October 2004 amending Directive 2003/87/EC establishing a scheme for greenhouse gas emission allowance trading within the Community, in respect of the Kyoto Protocol's project mechanisms, Article 1.2.

2 Inserted by Directive 2009/29/EC of the European Parliament and of the Council of 23 April 2009 amending Directive 2003/87/EC so as to improve and extend the greenhouse gas emission allowance trading scheme of the Community, Article 1.14.

3 Substituted by Directive 2008/101/EC of the European Parliament and of the Council of 19 November 2008 amending Directive 2003/87/EC so as to include aviation activities in the scheme for greenhouse gas emission allowance trading within the Community, Article 1.9.

4 Inserted by Regulation (EC) No 219/2009 of the European Parliament and of the Council of 11 March 2009 adapting a number of instruments subject to the procedure referred to in Article 251 of the Treaty to Council Decision 1999/468/EC with regard to the regulatory procedure with scrutiny, Article 1, Annex, para 3.6.1.

Article 12

Transfer, surrender and cancellation of allowances

1. Member States shall ensure that allowances can be transferred between:

(a) persons within the Community;

(b) persons within the Community and persons in third countries, where such allowances are recognised in accordance with the procedure referred to in Article 25 without restrictions other than those contained in, or adopted pursuant to, this Directive.

[1a. The Commission shall, by 31 December 2010, examine whether the market for emissions allowances is sufficiently protected from insider dealing or market manipulation and, if appropriate, shall bring forward proposals to ensure such protection. The relevant provisions of Directive 2003/6/EC of the European Parliament and of the Council of 28 January 2003 on insider dealing and market manipulation (market abuse) (may be used with any appropriate adjustments needed to apply them to trade in commodities.][1]

2. Member States shall ensure that allowances issued by a competent authority of another Member State are recognised for the purpose [of meeting an aircraft operator's obligations under paragraph 2a or][2] of meeting an operator's obligations under paragraph 3.

[2a. Administering Member States shall ensure that, by 30 April each year, each aircraft operator surrenders a number of allowances equal to the total emissions during the preceding calendar year from aviation activities listed in Annex I for which it is the aircraft operator, as verified in accordance with Article 15. Member States shall ensure that allowances surrendered in accordance with this paragraph are subsequently cancelled.][2]

[3. Member States shall ensure that, by 30 April each year, the operator of each installation surrenders a number of allowances, other than allowances issued under Chapter II, equal to the total emissions from that installation during the preceding calendar year as verified in accordance with Article 15, and that these are subsequently cancelled.][3]

[3a. An obligation to surrender allowances shall not arise in respect of emissions verified as captured and transported for permanent storage to a facility for which a permit is in force in accordance with Directive 2009/31/EC of the European Parliament and of the Council of 23 April 2009 on the geological storage of carbon dioxide.][1]

4. Member States shall take the necessary steps to ensure that allowances will be cancelled at any time at the request of the person holding them.

[5. Paragraphs 1 and 2 apply without prejudice to Article 10c.][1]

Amendments

1 Inserted by Directive 2009/29/EC of the European Parliament and of the Council of 23 April 2009 amending Directive 2003/87/EC so as to improve and extend the greenhouse gas emission allowance trading scheme of the Community, Article 1.15.

2 Inserted by Directive 2008/101/EC of the European Parliament and of the Council of 19 November 2008 amending Directive 2003/87/EC so as to include aviation activities in the scheme for greenhouse gas emission allowance trading within the Community, Article 1.10(a), (b).

3 Substituted by Directive 2008/101/EC of the European Parliament and of the Council of 19 November 2008 amending Directive 2003/87/EC so as to include aviation activities in the scheme for greenhouse gas emission allowance trading within the Community, Article 1.10(c).

[Article 13

Validity of allowances][1]

[1. Allowances issued from 1 January 2013 onwards shall be valid for emissions during periods of eight years beginning on 1 January 2013.

2. Four months after the beginning of each period referred to in paragraph 1, allowances which are no longer valid and have not been surrendered and cancelled in accordance with Article 12 shall be cancelled by the competent authority.

Member States shall issue allowances to persons for the current period to replace any allowances held by them which are cancelled in accordance with the first subparagraph.][1]

Amendment

1 Substituted by Directive 2009/29/EC of the European Parliament and of the Council of 23 April 2009 amending Directive 2003/87/EC so as to improve and extend the greenhouse gas emission allowance trading scheme of the Community, Article 1.16.

[Article 14

Guidelines for monitoring and reporting of emissions][1]

[1. By 31 December 2011, the Commission shall adopt a regulation for the monitoring and reporting of emissions and, where relevant, activity data, from the activities listed in Annex

I, for the monitoring and reporting of tonne-kilometre data for the purpose of an application under Articles 3e or 3f, which shall be based on the principles for monitoring and reporting set out in Annex IV and shall specify the global warming potential of each greenhouse gas in the requirements for monitoring and reporting emissions for that gas.

That measure, designed to amend non-essential elements of this Directive by supplementing it, shall be adopted in accordance with the regulatory procedure with scrutiny referred to in Article 23(3).

2. The regulation referred to in paragraph 1 shall take into account the most accurate and up-to-date scientific evidence available, in particular from the IPCC, and may also specify requirements for operators to report on emissions associated with the production of goods produced by energy intensive industries which may be subject to international competition. That regulation may also specify requirements for this information to be verified independently.

Those requirements may include reporting on levels of emissions from electricity generation covered by the Community scheme associated with the production of such goods.

3. Member States shall ensure that each operator of an installation or an aircraft operator monitors and reports the emissions from that installation during each calendar year, or, from 1 January 2010, the aircraft which it operates, to the competent authority after the end of that year in accordance with the regulation referred to in paragraph 1.

4. The regulation referred to in paragraph 1 may include requirements on the use of automated systems and data exchange formats to harmonise communication on the monitoring plan, the annual emission report and the verification activities between the operator, the verifier and competent authorities.][1]

Amendment

1 Substituted by Directive 2009/29/EC of the European Parliament and of the Council of 23 April 2009 amending Directive 2003/87/EC so as to improve and extend the greenhouse gas emission allowance trading scheme of the Community, Article 1.17.

[Article 15

[Verification and accreditation][1]][2]

[Member States shall ensure that the reports submitted by operators and aircraft operators pursuant to Article 14(3) are verified in accordance with the criteria set out in Annex V and any detailed provisions adopted by the Commission in accordance with this Article, and that the competent authority is informed thereof.

Member States shall ensure that an operator or aircraft operator whose report has not been verified as satisfactory in accordance with the criteria set out in Annex V and any detailed provisions adopted by the Commission in accordance with this Article by 31 March each year for emissions during the preceding year cannot make further transfers of allowances until a report from that operator or aircraft operator has been verified as satisfactory.

The Commission may adopt detailed provisions for the verification of reports submitted by aircraft operators pursuant to Article 14(3) and applications under Articles 3e and 3f, including the verification procedures to be used by verifiers, in accordance with the regulatory procedure referred to in Article 23(2).

[By 31 December 2011, the Commission shall adopt a regulation for the verification of emission reports based on the principles set out in Annex V and for the accreditation and supervision of verifiers. It shall specify conditions for the accreditation and withdrawal of accreditation, for mutual recognition and peer evaluation of accreditation bodies, as appropriate.

That measure, designed to amend non-essential elements of this Directive by supplementing it, shall be adopted in accordance with the regulatory procedure with scrutiny referred to in Article 23(3).][3]][2]

Amendments

1 Substituted by Directive 2009/29/EC of the European Parliament and of the Council of 23 April 2009 amending Directive 2003/87/EC so as to improve and extend the greenhouse gas emission allowance trading scheme of the Community, Article 1.18(a).

2 Substituted by Directive 2008/101/EC of the European Parliament and of the Council of 19 November 2008 amending Directive 2003/87/EC so as to include aviation activities in the scheme for greenhouse gas emission allowance trading within the Community, Article 1.13.

3 Inserted by Directive 2008/101/EC of the European Parliament and of the Council of 19 November 2008 amending Directive 2003/87/EC so as to include aviation activities in the scheme for greenhouse gas emission allowance trading within the Community, Article 1.18(b).

[Article 15a

Disclosure of information and professional secrecy][1]

[Member States and the Commission shall ensure that all decisions and reports relating to the quantity and allocation of allowances and to the monitoring, reporting and verification of emissions are immediately disclosed in an orderly manner ensuring non-discriminatory access.

Information covered by professional secrecy may not be disclosed to any other person or authority except by virtue of the applicable laws, regulations or administrative provisions.][1]

Amendment

1 Inserted by Directive 2009/29/EC of the European Parliament and of the Council of 23 April 2009 amending Directive 2003/87/EC so as to improve and extend the greenhouse gas emission allowance trading scheme of the Community, Article 1.19.

Article 16

Penalties

1. Member States shall lay down the rules on penalties applicable to infringements of the national provisions adopted pursuant to this Directive and shall take all measures necessary to ensure that such rules are implemented. The penalties provided for must be effective, proportionate and dissuasive. Member States shall notify these provisions to the Commission ...[1] and shall notify it without delay of any subsequent amendment affecting them.

[2. Member States shall ensure publication of the names of operators and aircraft operators who are in breach of requirements to surrender sufficient allowances under this Directive.

3. Member States shall ensure that any operator or aircraft operator who does not surrender sufficient allowances by 30 April of each year to cover its emissions during the preceding year shall be held liable for the payment of an excess emissions penalty. The excess emissions penalty shall be EUR 100 for each tonne of carbon dioxide equivalent emitted for which the operator or aircraft operator has not surrendered allowances. Payment of the excess emissions penalty shall not release the operator or aircraft operator from the obligation to surrender an amount of allowances equal to those excess emissions when surrendering allowances in relation to the following calendar year.][2]

[4. The excess emissions penalty relating to allowances issued from 1 January 2013 onwards shall increase in accordance with the European index of consumer prices.][3]

[5. In the event that an aircraft operator fails to comply with the requirements of this Directive and where other enforcement measures have failed to ensure compliance, its administering Member State may request the Commission to decide on the imposition of an operating ban on the aircraft operator concerned.

6. Any request by an administering Member State under paragraph 5 shall include:

(a) evidence that the aircraft operator has not complied with its obligations under this Directive;

(b) details of the enforcement action which has been taken by that Member State;
(c) a justification for the imposition of an operating ban at Community level; and
(d) a recommendation for the scope of an operating ban at Community level and any conditions that should be applied.

7. When requests such as those referred to in paragraph 5 are addressed to the Commission, the Commission shall inform the other Member States through their representatives on the Committee referred to in Article 23(1) in accordance with the Committee's Rules of Procedure.

8. The adoption of a decision following a request pursuant to paragraph 5 shall be preceded, when appropriate and practicable, by consultations with the authorities responsible for regulatory oversight of the aircraft operator concerned. Whenever possible, consultations shall be held jointly by the Commission and the Member States.

9. When the Commission is considering whether to adopt a decision following a request pursuant to paragraph 5, it shall disclose to the aircraft operator concerned the essential facts and considerations which form the basis for such decision. The aircraft operator concerned shall be given an opportunity to submit written comments to the Commission within 10 working days from the date of disclosure.

10. At the request of a Member State, the Commission may, in accordance with the regulatory procedure referred to in Article 23(2), adopt a decision to impose an operating ban on the aircraft operator concerned.

11. Each Member State shall enforce, within its territory, any decisions adopted under paragraph 10. It shall inform the Commission of any measures taken to implement such decisions.

12. Where appropriate, detailed rules shall be established in respect of the procedures referred to in this Article. Those measures, designed to amend non-essential elements of this Directive by supplementing it, shall be adopted in accordance with the regulatory procedure with scrutiny referred to in Article 23(3).][4]

Amendments

1 Repealed by Directive 2008/101/EC of the European Parliament and of the Council of 19 November 2008 amending Directive 2003/87/EC so as to include aviation activities in the scheme for greenhouse gas emission allowance trading within the Community, Article 1.14(a).

2 Substituted by Directive 2008/101/EC of the European Parliament and of the Council of 19 November 2008 amending Directive 2003/87/EC so as to include aviation activities in the scheme for greenhouse gas emission allowance trading within the Community, Article 1.14(b).

3 Substitued by Directive 2009/29/EC of the European Parliament and of the Council of 23 April 2009 amending Directive 2003/87/EC so as to improve and extend the greenhouse gas emission allowance trading scheme of the Community, Article 1.20.

4 Inserted by Directive 2008/101/EC of the European Parliament and of the Council of 19 November 2008 amending Directive 2003/87/EC so as to include aviation activities in the scheme for greenhouse gas emission allowance trading within the Community, Article 1.14(c).

[Article 17

Access to information][1]

[Decisions relating to the allocation of allowances, information on project activities in which a Member State participates or authorises private or public entities to participate, and the reports of emissions required under the greenhouse gas emissions permit and held by the competent authority, shall be made available to the public in accordance with Directive 2003/4/EC.][1]

Amendment

1 Substituted by Directive 2004/101/EC of the European Parliament and of the Council of 27 October 2004 amending Directive 2003/87/EC establishing a scheme for greenhouse gas emission allowance trading within the Community, in respect of the Kyoto Protocol's project mechanisms, Article 1.3.

Article 18

Competent authority

Member States shall make the appropriate administrative arrangements, including the designation of the appropriate competent authority or authorities, for the implementation of the rules of this Directive. Where more than one competent authority is designated, the work of these authorities undertaken pursuant to this Directive must be coordinated.

[Member States shall in particular ensure coordination between their designated focal point for approving project activities pursuant to Article 6 (1)(a) of the Kyoto Protocol and their designated national authority for the implementation of Article 12 of the Kyoto Protocol respectively designated in accordance with subsequent decisions adopted under the UNFCCC or the Kyoto Protocol.][1]

Amendment

1 Inserted by Directive 2004/101/EC of the European Parliament and of the Council of 27 October 2004 amending Directive 2003/87/EC establishing a scheme for greenhouse gas emission allowance trading within the Community, in respect of the Kyoto Protocol's project mechanisms, Article 1.4.

[Article 18a

Administering Member State][1]

[1. The administering Member State in respect of an aircraft operator shall be:

(a) in the case of an aircraft operator with a valid operating licence granted by a Member State in accordance with the provisions of Council Regulation (EEC) No 2407/92 of 23 July 1992 on licensing of air carriers, the Member State which granted the operating licence in respect of that aircraft operator; and

(b) in all other cases, the Member State with the greatest estimated attributed aviation emissions from flights performed by that aircraft operator in the base year.

2. Where in the first two years of any period referred to in Article 3c, none of the attributed aviation emissions from flights performed by an aircraft operator falling within paragraph 1(b) of this Article are attributed to its administering Member State, the aircraft operator shall be transferred to another administering Member State in respect of the next period. The new administering Member State shall be the Member State with the greatest estimated attributed aviation emissions from flights performed by that aircraft operator during the first two years of the previous period.

3. Based on the best available information, the Commission shall:

(a) before 1 February 2009, publish a list of aircraft operators which performed an aviation activity listed in Annex I on or after 1 January 2006 specifying the administering Member State for each aircraft operator in accordance with paragraph 1; and

(b) before 1 February of each subsequent year, update the list to include aircraft operators which have subsequently performed an aviation activity listed in Annex I.

4. The Commission may, in accordance with the regulatory procedure referred to in Article 23(2), develop guidelines relating to the administration of aircraft operators under this Directive by administering Member States.

5. For the purposes of paragraph 1, "base year" means, in relation to an aircraft operator which started operating in the Community after 1 January 2006, the first calendar year of operation, and in all other cases, the calendar year starting on 1 January 2006.][1]

Amendment

1 Inserted by Directive 2008/101/EC of the European Parliament and of the Council of 19 November 2008 amending Directive 2003/87/EC so as to include aviation activities in the scheme for greenhouse gas emission allowance trading within the Community, Article 1.15.

[Article 18b

Assistance from Eurocontrol][1]

[For the purposes of carrying out its obligations under Articles 3c(4) and 18a, the Commission may request the assistance of Eurocontrol or another relevant organisation and may conclude to that effect any appropriate agreements with those organisations.][1]

Amendments

1 Inserted by Directive 2008/101/EC of the European Parliament and of the Council of 19 November 2008 amending Directive 2003/87/EC so as to include aviation activities in the scheme for greenhouse gas emission allowance trading within the Community, Article 1.15.

Article 19

Registries

[1. Allowances issued from 1 January 2012 onwards shall be held in the Community registry for the execution of processes pertaining to the maintenance of the holding accounts opened in the Member State and the allocation, surrender and cancellation of allowances under the Commission Regulation referred to in paragraph 3.

Each Member State shall be able to fulfil the execution of authorised operations under the UNFCCC or the Kyoto Protocol.][1]

2. Any person may hold allowances. The registry shall be accessible to the public and shall contain separate accounts to record the allowances held by each person to whom and from whom allowances are issued or transferred.

[3. In order to implement this Directive, the Commission shall adopt a Regulation for a standardised and secured system of registries in the form of standardised electronic databases containing common data elements to track the issue, holding, transfer and cancellation of allowances, to provide for public access and confidentiality as appropriate and to ensure that there are no transfers which are incompatible with the obligations resulting from the Kyoto Protocol. That Regulation shall also include provisions concerning the use and identification of CERs and ERUs in the Community scheme and the monitoring of the level of such use. That measure, designed to amend non-essential elements of this Directive by supplementing it, shall be adopted in accordance with the regulatory procedure with scrutiny referred to in Article 23(3).][2]

[4. The Regulation referred to in paragraph 3 shall contain appropriate modalities for the Community registry to undertake transactions and other operations to implement arrangements referred to in Article 25(1b). That Regulation shall also include processes for the change and incident management for the Community registry with regard to issues in paragraph 1 of this Article. It shall contain appropriate modalities for the Community registry to ensure that initiatives of the Member States pertaining to efficiency improvement, administrative cost management and quality control measures are possible.][3]

Amendments

1 Substituted by Directive 2009/29/EC of the European Parliament and of the Council of 23 April 2009 amending Directive 2003/87/EC so as to improve and extend the greenhouse gas emission allowance trading scheme of the Community, Article 1.21(a).

2 Substituted by Regulation (EC) No 219/2009 of the European Parliament and of the Council of 11 March 2009 adapting a number of instruments subject to the procedure referred to in Article 251 of the Treaty to Council Decision 1999/468/EC with regard to the regulatory procedure with scrutiny, Article 1, Annex, para 3.6.3.

3 Inserted by Directive 2009/29/EC of the European Parliament and of the Council of 23 April 2009 amending Directive 2003/87/EC so as to improve and extend the greenhouse gas emission allowance trading scheme of the Community, Article 1.21(b).

Article 20

Central Administrator

1. The Commission shall designate a Central Administrator to maintain an independent transaction log recording the issue, transfer and cancellation of allowances.

2. The Central Administrator shall conduct an automated check on each transaction in registries through the independent transaction log to ensure there are no irregularities in the issue, transfer and cancellation of allowances.

3. If irregularities are identified through the automated check, the Central Administrator shall inform the Member State or Member States concerned who shall not register the transactions in question or any further transactions relating to the allowances concerned until the irregularities have been resolved.

Article 21

Reporting by Member States

1. Each year the Member States shall submit to the Commission a report on the application of this Directive. [That report shall pay particular attention to the arrangements for the allocation of allowances, the operation of registries, the application of the implementing measures on monitoring and reporting, verification and accreditation and issues relating to compliance with this Directive and on the fiscal treatment of allowances, if any.][1] The first report shall be sent to the Commission by 30 June 2005. The report shall be drawn up on the basis of a questionnaire or outline drafted by the Commission in accordance with the procedure laid down in Article 6 of Directive 91/692/EEC. The questionnaire or outline shall be sent to Member States at least six months before the deadline for the submission of the first report.

2. On the basis of the reports referred to in paragraph 1, the Commission shall publish a report on the application of this Directive within three months of receiving the reports from the Member States.

[3. The Commission shall organise an exchange of information between the competent authorities of the Member States concerning developments relating to issues of allocation, the use of ERUs and CERs in the Community scheme, the operation of registries, monitoring, reporting, verification, accreditation, information technology, and compliance with this Directive.][1]

Amendment

1 Substituted by Directive 2009/29/EC of the European Parliament and of the Council of 23 April 2009 amending Directive 2003/87/EC so as to improve and extend the greenhouse gas emission allowance trading scheme of the Community, Article 1.22.

[Article 21a

Support of capacity-building activities][1]

[In accordance with the UNFCCC, the Kyoto Protocol and any subsequent decision adopted for their implementation, the Commission and the Member States shall endeavour to support capacity-building activities in developing countries and countries with economies in transition in order to help them take full advantage of JI and the CDM in a manner that supports their sustainable development strategies and to facilitate the engagement of entities in JI and CDM project development and implementation.][1]

Amendment

1 Inserted by Directive 2004/101/EC of the European Parliament and of the Council of 27 October 2004 amending Directive 2003/87/EC establishing a scheme for greenhouse gas emission allowance trading within the Community, in respect of the Kyoto Protocol's project mechanisms, Article 1.7.

[Article 22

Amendments to the Annexes][1]

[The Annexes to this Directive, with the exception of Annexes I, IIa and IIb, may be amended in the light of the reports provided for in Article 21 and of the experience of the application of this Directive. Annexes IV and V may be amended in order to improve the monitoring, reporting and verification of emissions.

Those measures, designed to amend non-essential elements of this Directive, inter alia, by supplementing it, shall be adopted in accordance with the regulatory procedure with scrutiny referred to in Article 23(3).][1]

Amendment

1 Substituted by Directive 2009/29/EC of the European Parliament and of the Council of 23 April 2009 amending Directive 2003/87/EC so as to improve and extend the greenhouse gas emission allowance trading scheme of the Community, Article 1.23.

Article 23

Committee

1. The Commission shall be assisted by the committee instituted by Article 8 of Decision 93/389/EEC.

2. Where reference is made to this paragraph, Articles 5 and 7 of Decision 1999/468/EC shall apply, having regard to the provisions of Article 8 thereof.

The period laid down in Article 5(6) of Decision 1999/468/EC shall be set at three months.

[3. Where reference is made to this paragraph, Article 5a(1) to (4) and Article 7 of Decision 1999/468/EC shall apply, having regard to the provisions of Article 8 thereof.][1]

[4. Where reference is made to this paragraph, Article 4 and 7 of Decision 1999/468/EC shall apply, having regard to the provisions of Article 8 thereof.][2]

Amendments

1 Substituted by Regulation (EC) No 219/2009 of the European Parliament and of the Council of 11 March 2009 adapting a number of instruments subject to the procedure referred to in Article 251 of the Treaty to Council Decision 1999/468/EC with regard to the regulatory procedure with scrutiny, Article 1, Annex, para 3.6.5.

2 Inserted by Directive 2009/29/EC of the European Parliament and of the Council of 23 April 2009 amending Directive 2003/87/EC so as to improve and extend the greenhouse gas emission allowance trading scheme of the Community, Article 1.24.

[Article 24

Procedures for unilateral inclusion of additional activities and gases][1]

[1. From 2008, Member States may apply emission allowance trading in accordance with this Directive to activities and to greenhouse gases which are not listed in Annex I, taking into account all relevant criteria, in particular the effects on the internal market, potential distortions of competition, the environmental integrity of the Community scheme and the reliability of the planned monitoring and reporting system, provided that inclusion of such activities and greenhouse gases is approved by the Commission

(a) in accordance with the regulatory procedure referred to in Article 23(2), if the inclusion refers to installations which are not covered by Annex I; or

(b) in accordance with the regulatory procedure with scrutiny referred to in Article 23(3), if the inclusion refers to activities and greenhouse gases which are not listed in Annex I. Those measures are designed to amend non-essential elements of this Directive by supplementing it.

2. When the inclusion of additional activities and gases is approved, the Commission may at the same time authorise the issue of additional allowances and may authorise other Member States to include such additional activities and gases.

3. On the initiative of the Commission or at the request of a Member State, a regulation may be adopted on the monitoring of, and reporting on, emissions concerning activities, installations and greenhouse gases which are not listed as a combination in Annex I, if that monitoring and reporting can be carried out with sufficient accuracy.

That measure, designed to amend non-essential elements of this Directive by supplementing it, shall be adopted in accordance with the regulatory procedure with scrutiny referred to in Article 23(3).][1]

Amendment

1 Substituted by Directive 2009/29/EC of the European Parliament and of the Council of 23 April 2009 amending Directive 2003/87/EC so as to improve and extend the greenhouse gas emission allowance trading scheme of the Community, Article 1.25.

[Article 24a

Harmonised rules for projects that reduce emissions][1]

[1. In addition to the inclusions provided for in Article 24, implementing measures for issuing allowances or credits in respect of projects administered by Member States that reduce greenhouse gas emissions not covered by the Community scheme may be adopted.

Those measures, designed to amend non-essential elements of this Directive by supplementing it, shall be adopted in accordance with the regulatory procedure with scrutiny referred to in Article 23(3).

Any such measures shall not result in the double-counting of emission reductions nor impede the undertaking of other policy measures to reduce emissions not covered by the Community scheme. Measures shall only be adopted where inclusion is not possible in accordance with Article 24, and the next review of the Community scheme shall consider harmonising the coverage of those emissions across the Community.

2. Implementing measures that set out the details for crediting in respect of Community-level projects referred to in paragraph 1 may be adopted.

Those measures, designed to amend non-essential elements of this Directive by supplementing it, shall be adopted in accordance with the regulatory procedure with scrutiny referred to in Article 23(3).

3. A Member State can refuse to issue allowances or credits in respect of certain types of projects that reduce greenhouse gas emissions on its own territory.

Such projects will be executed on the basis of the agreement of the Member State in which the project takes place.][1]

Amendment

1 Inserted by Directive 2009/29/EC of the European Parliament and of the Council of 23 April 2009 amending Directive 2003/87/EC so as to improve and extend the greenhouse gas emission allowance trading scheme of the Community, Article 1.26.

Article 25

Links with other greenhouse gas emissions trading schemes

1. Agreements should be concluded with third countries listed in Annex B to the Kyoto Protocol which have ratified the Protocol to provide for the mutual recognition of allowances between the Community scheme and other greenhouse gas emissions trading schemes in accordance with the rules set out in Article 300 of the Treaty.

[1a. Agreements may be made to provide for the recognition of allowances between the Community scheme and compatible mandatory greenhouse gas emissions trading systems with absolute emissions caps established in any other country or in sub-federal or regional entities.

1b. Non-binding arrangements may be made with third countries or with sub-federal or regional entities to provide for administrative and technical coordination in relation to allowances in the Community scheme or other mandatory greenhouse gas emissions trading systems with absolute emissions caps.][1]

[2. Where an agreement referred to in paragraph 1 has been concluded, the Commission shall adopt any necessary provisions relating to the mutual recognition of allowances under that agreement. Those measures, designed to amend non-essential elements of this Directive, by supplementing it, shall be adopted in accordance with the regulatory procedure with scrutiny referred to in Article 23(3).][2]

Amendments

1 Inserted by Directive 2009/29/EC of the European Parliament and of the Council of 23 April 2009 amending Directive 2003/87/EC so as to improve and extend the greenhouse gas emission allowance trading scheme of the Community, Article 1.27.

2 Substituted by Regulation (EC) No 219/2009 of the European Parliament and of the Council of 11 March 2009 adapting a number of instruments subject to the procedure referred to in Article 251 of the Treaty to Council Decision 1999/468/EC with regard to the regulatory procedure with scrutiny, Article 1, Annex, para 3.6.7.

[Article 25a

Third country measures to reduce the climate change impact of aviation][1]

[1. Where a third country adopts measures for reducing the climate change impact of flights departing from that country which land in the Community, the Commission, after consulting with that third country, and with Member States within the Committee referred to in Article 23(1), shall consider options available in order to provide for optimal interaction between the Community scheme and that country's measures.

Where necessary, the Commission may adopt amendments to provide for flights arriving from the third country concerned to be excluded from the aviation activities listed in Annex I or to provide for any other amendments to the aviation activities listed in Annex I which are required by an agreement pursuant to the fourth subparagraph. Those measures, designed to amend non-essential elements of thisDirective, shall be adopted in accordance with the regulatory procedure with scrutiny referred to in Article 23(3).

The Commission may propose to the European Parliament and the Council any other amendments to this Directive.

The Commission may also, where appropriate, make recommendations to the Council in accordance with Article 300(1) of the Treaty to open negotiations with a view to concluding an agreement with the third country concerned.

2. The Community and its Member States shall continue to seek an agreement on global measures to reduce greenhouse gas emissions from aviation. In the light of any such agreement, the Commission shall consider whether amendments to this Directive as it applies to aircraft operators are necessary.][1]

Amendment

1 Inserted by Directive 2008/101/EC of the European Parliament and of the Council of 19 November 2008 amending Directive 2003/87/EC so as to include aviation activities in the scheme for greenhouse gas emission allowance trading within the Community, Article 1.18.

[*Article 26 is not reproduced.*][1]

[Article 27

Exclusion of small installations subject to equivalent measures][1]

[1. Following consultation with the operator, Member States may exclude from the Community scheme installations which have reported to the competent authority emissions of less than 25 000 tonnes of carbon dioxide equivalent and, where they carry out combustion activities, have a rated thermal input below 35 MW, excluding emissions from biomass, in each of the three years preceding the notification under point (a), and which are subject to measures that will achieve an equivalent contribution to emission reductions, if the Member State concerned complies with the following conditions:

(a) it notifies the Commission of each such installation, specifying the equivalent measures applying to that installation that will achieve an equivalent contribution to emission reductions that are in place, before the list of installations pursuant to Article 11(1) has to be submitted and at the latest when this list is submitted to the Commission;

(b) it confirms that monitoring arrangements are in place to assess whether any installation emits 25 000 tonnes or more of carbon dioxide equivalent, excluding emissions from biomass, in any one calendar year. Member States may allow simplified monitoring, reporting and verification measures for installations with average annual verified emissions between 2008 and 2010 which are below 5 000 tonnes a year, in accordance with Article 14;

(c) it confirms that if any installation emits 25 000 tonnes or more of carbon dioxide equivalent, excluding emissions from biomass, in any one calendar year or the measures applying to that installation that will achieve an equivalent contribution to emission reductions are no longer in place, the installation will be reintroduced into the Community scheme;

(d) it publishes the information referred to in points (a), (b) and (c) for public comment.

Hospitals may also be excluded if they undertake equivalent measures.

2. If, following a period of three months from the date of notification for public comment, the Commission does not object within a further period of six months, the exclusion shall be deemed approved.

Following the surrender of allowances in respect of the period during which the installation is in the Community scheme, the installation shall be excluded and the Member State shall no longer issue free allowances to the installation pursuant to Article 10a.

3. When an installation is reintroduced into the Community scheme pursuant to paragraph 1(c), any allowances issued pursuant to Article 10a shall be granted starting with the year of the reintroduction. Allowances issued to these installations shall be deducted from the quantity to be auctioned pursuant to Article 10(2) by the Member State in which the installation is situated.

Any such installation shall stay in the Community scheme for the rest of the trading period.

4. For installations which have not been included in the Community scheme during the period from 2008 to 2012, simplified requirements for monitoring, reporting and verification may be applied for determining emissions in the three years preceding the notification under paragraph 1 point (a).][1]

Amendment

1 Substituted by Directive 2009/29/EC of the European Parliament and of the Council of 23 April 2009 amending Directive 2003/87/EC so as to improve and extend the greenhouse gas emission allowance trading scheme of the Community, Article 1.28.

[Article 28

Adjustments applicable upon the approval by the Community of an international agreement on climate change][1]

[1. Within three months of the signature by the Community of an international agreement on climate change leading, by 2020, to mandatory reductions of greenhouse gas emissions exceeding 20 % compared to 1990 levels, as reflected in the 30 % reduction commitment as endorsed by the European Council of March 2007, the Commission shall submit a report assessing, in particular, the following elements:

(a) the nature of the measures agreed upon in the framework of the international negotiations as well as the commitments made by other developed countries to comparable emission reductions to those of the Community and the commitments made by economically more advanced developing countries to contributing adequately according to their responsibilities and respective capabilities;

(b) the implications of the international agreement on climate change, and consequently, options required at Community level, in order to move to the more ambitious 30 % reduction target in a balanced, transparent and equitable way, taking into account work under the Kyoto Protocol's first commitment period;

(c) the Community manufacturing industries' competitiveness in the context of carbon leakage risks;

(d) the impact of the international agreement on climate change on other Community economic sectors;

(e) the impact on the Community agriculture sector, including carbon leakage risks;

(f) the appropriate modalities for including emissions and removals related to land use, land use change and forestry in the Community;

(g) afforestation, reforestation, avoided deforestation and forest degradation in third countries in the event of the establishment of any internationally recognised system in this context;

(h) the need for additional Community policies and measures in view of the greenhouse gas reduction commitments of the Community' and of Member States.

2. On the basis of the report referred to in paragraph 1, the Commission shall, as appropriate, submit a legislative proposal to the European Parliament and to the Council amending this Directive pursuant to paragraph 1, with a view to the amending Directive entering into force upon the approval by the Community of the international agreement on climate change and in view of the emission reduction commitment to be implemented under that agreement.

The proposal shall be based upon the principles of transparency, economic efficiency and cost-effectiveness, as well as fairness and solidarity in the distribution of efforts between Member States.

3. The proposal shall allow, as appropriate, operators to use, in addition to the credits provided for in this Directive, CERs, ERUs or other approved credits from third countries which have ratified the international agreement on climate change.

4. The proposal shall also include, as appropriate, any other measures needed to help reach the mandatory reductions in accordance with paragraph 1 in a transparent, balanced and equitable way and, in particular, shall include implementing measures to provide for the use of additional types of project credits by operators in the Community scheme to those referred to in paragraphs 2 to 5 of Article 11a or the use by such operators of other mechanisms created under the international agreement on climate change, as appropriate.

5. The proposal shall include the appropriate transitional and suspensive measures pending the entry into force of the international agreement on climate change.][1]

Amendment

1 Substituted by Directive 2009/29/EC of the European Parliament and of the Council of 23 April 2009 amending Directive 2003/87/EC so as to improve and extend the greenhouse gas emission allowance trading scheme of the Community, Article 1.28.

[Article 29

Report to ensure the better functioning of the carbon market][1]

[If, on the basis of the regular reports on the carbon market referred to in Article 10(5), the Commission has evidence that the carbon market is not functioning properly, it shall submit a report to the European Parliament and to the Council. The report may be accompanied, if appropriate, by proposals aiming at increasing transparency of the carbon market and addressing measures to improve its functioning.][1]

Amendment

1 Substituted by Directive 2009/29/EC of the European Parliament and of the Council of 23 April 2009 amending Directive 2003/87/EC so as to improve and extend the greenhouse gas emission allowance trading scheme of the Community, Article 1.28.

[Article 29a

Measures in the event of excessive price fluctuations][1]

[1. If, for more than six consecutive months, the allowance price is more than three times the average price of allowances during the two preceding years on the European carbon market, the Commission shall immediately convene a meeting of the Committee established by Article 9 of Decision No 280/2004/EC.

2. If the price evolution referred to in paragraph 1 does not correspond to changing market fundamentals, one of the following measures may be adopted, taking into account the degree of price evolution:

(a) a measure which allows Member States to bring forward the auctioning of a part of the quantity to be auctioned;

(b) a measure which allows Member States to auction up to 25 % of the remaining allowances in the new entrants reserve.

Those measures shall be adopted in accordance with the management procedure referred to in Article 23(4).

3. Any measure shall take utmost account of the reports submitted by the Commission to the European Parliament and to the Council pursuant to Article 29, as well as any other relevant information provided by Member States.

4. The arrangements for the application of these provisions shall be laid down in the regulation referred to in Article 10(4).][1]

Amendment

1 Inserted by Directive 2009/29/EC of the European Parliament and of the Council of 23 April 2009 amending Directive 2003/87/EC so as to improve and extend the greenhouse gas emission allowance trading scheme of the Community, Article 1.29.

Article 30

Review and further development

1. On the basis of progress achieved in the monitoring of emissions of greenhouse gases, the Commission may make a proposal to the European Parliament and the Council by 31 December 2004 to amend Annex I to include other activities and emissions of other greenhouse gases listed in Annex II.

2. On the basis of experience of the application of this Directive and of progress achieved in the monitoring of emissions of greenhouse gases and in the light of developments in the international context, the Commission shall draw up a report on the application of this Directive, considering:

(a) how and whether Annex I should be amended to include other relevant sectors, inter alia the chemicals, aluminium and transport sectors, activities and emissions of other greenhouse gases listed in Annex II, with a view to further improving the economic efficiency of the scheme;
(b) the relationship of Community emission allowance trading with the international emissions trading that will start in 2008;
(c) further harmonisation of the method of allocation (including auctioning for the time after 2012) and of the criteria for national allocation plans referred to in Annex III;
[(d) the use of credits from project activities, including the need for harmonisation of the allowed use of ERUs and CERs in the Community scheme;][1]
(e) the relationship of emissions trading with other policies and measures implemented at Member State and Community level, including taxation, that pursue the same objectives;
(f) whether it is appropriate for there to be a single Community registry;
(g) the level of excess emissions penalties, taking into account, inter alia, inflation;
(h) the functioning of the allowance market, covering in particular any possible market disturbances;
(i) how to adapt the Community scheme to an enlarged European Union;
(j) pooling;
(k) the practicality of developing Community-wide benchmarks as a basis for allocation, taking into account the best available techniques and cost-benefit analysis.
[(l) the impact of project mechanisms on host countries, particularly on their development objectives, whether JI and CDM hydroelectric power production project activities with a generating capacity exceeding 500 MW and having negative environmental or social impacts have been approved, and the future use of CERs or ERUs resulting from any such hydroelectric power production project activities in the Community scheme;
(m) the support for capacity-building efforts in developing countries and countries with economies in transition;
(n) the modalities and procedures for Member States' approval of domestic project activities and for the issuing of allowances in respect of emission reductions or limitations resulting from such activities from 2008;
(o) technical provisions relating to the temporary nature of credits and the limit of 1 % for eligibility for land use, land-use change and forestry project activities as established in Decision 17/CP.7, and provisions relating to the outcome of the evaluation of potential risks associated with the use of genetically modified organisms and potentially invasive alien species by afforestation and reforestation project activities, to allow operators to use CERs and ERUs resulting from land use, land-use change and forestry project activities in the Community scheme from 2008, in accordance with the decisions adopted pursuant to the UNFCCC or the Kyoto Protocol.][2]

The Commission shall submit this report to the European Parliament and the Council by 30 June 2006, accompanied by proposals as appropriate.

[3. In advance of each period referred to in Article 11(2), each Member State shall publish in its national allocation plan its intended use of ERUs and CERs and the percentage of the allocation to each installation up to which operators are allowed to use ERUs and CERs in the Community scheme for that period. The total use of ERUs and CERs shall be consistent with the relevant supplementarity obligations under the Kyoto Protocol and the UNFCCC and the decisions adopted thereunder.

Member States shall, in accordance with Article 3 of Decision No 280/2004/EC of the European Parliament and of the Council of 11 February 2004 concerning a mechanism for monitoring Community greenhouse gas emissions and for implementing the Kyoto Protocol, report to the Commission every two years on the extent to which domestic action actually constitutes a significant element of the efforts undertaken at national level, as well as the extent to which use of the project mechanisms is actually supplemental to domestic action, and the ratio between them, in accordance with the relevant provisions of the Kyoto

Protocol and the decisions adopted thereunder. The Commission shall report on this in accordance with Article 5 of the said Decision. In the light of this report, the Commission shall, if appropriate, make legislative or other proposals to complement provisions adopted by Member States to ensure that use of the mechanisms is supplemental to domestic action within the Community.][1]

[4. By 1 December 2014 the Commission shall, on the basis of monitoring and experience of the application of this Directive, review the functioning of this Directive in relation to aviation activities in Annex I and may make proposals to the European Parliament and the Council pursuant to Article 251 of the Treaty as appropriate. The Commission shall give consideration in particular to:

(a) the implications and impacts of this Directive as regards the overall functioning of the Community scheme;
(b) the functioning of the aviation allowance market, covering in particular any possible market disturbances;
(c) the environmental effectiveness of the Community scheme and the extent by which the total quantity of allowances to be allocated to aircraft operators under Article 3c should be reduced in line with overall EU emissions reduction targets;
(d) the impact of the Community scheme on the aviation sector, including issues of competitiveness, taking into account in particular the effect of climate change policies implemented for aviation outside the EU;
(e) continuing with the special reserve for aircraft operators, taking into account the likely convergence of growth rates across the industry;
(f) the impact of the Community scheme on the structural dependency on aviation transport of islands, landlocked regions, peripheral regions and the outermost regions of the Community;
(g) whether a gateway system should be included to facilitate the trading of allowances between aircraft operators and operators of installations whilst ensuring that no transactions would result in a net transfer of allowances from aircraft operators to operators of installations;
(h) the implications of the exclusion thresholds as specified in Annex I in terms of certified maximum take-off mass and number of flights per year performed by an aircraft operator;
(i) the impact of the exemption from the Community scheme of certain flights performed in the framework of public service obligations imposed in accordance with Council Regulation (EEC) No 2408/92 of 23 July 1992 on access for Community air carriers to intra-Community air routes;
(j) developments, including the potential for future developments, in the efficiency of aviation and in particular the progress towards meeting the Advisory Council for Aeronautics Research in Europe (ACARE) goal to develop and demonstrate technologies able to reduce fuel consumption by 50 % by 2020 and whether further measures to increase efficiency are necessary;
(k) developments in scientific understanding on the climate change impacts of contrails and cirrus clouds caused by aviation with a view to proposing effective mitigation measures.

The Commission shall then report to the European Parliament and the Council.][3]

Amendments

1 Substituted by Directive 2004/101/EC of the European Parliament and of the Council of 27 October 2004 amending Directive 2003/87/EC establishing a scheme for greenhouse gas emission allowance trading within the Community, in respect of the Kyoto Protocol's project mechanisms, Article 1.8(a), (c).

2 Inserted by Directive 2004/101/EC of the European Parliament and of the Council of 27 October 2004 amending Directive 2003/87/EC establishing a scheme for greenhouse gas emission allowance trading within the Community, in respect of the Kyoto Protocol's project mechanisms, Article 1.8(b).

3 Inserted by Directive 2008/101/EC of the European Parliament and of the Council of 19 November 2008 amending Directive 2003/87/EC so as to include aviation activities in the scheme for greenhouse gas emission allowance trading within the Community, Article 1.20.

[Chapter V
Final provisions][1]

Article 31

Implementation

1. Member States shall bring into force the laws, regulations and administrative provisions necessary to comply with this Directive by 31 December 2003 at the latest. They shall forthwith inform the Commission thereof. The Commission shall notify the other Member States of these laws, regulations and administrative provisions.

When Member States adopt these measures, they shall contain a reference to this Directive or be accompanied by such a reference on the occasion of their official publication. The methods of making such reference shall be laid down by Member States.

2. Member States shall communicate to the Commission the text of the provisions of national law which they adopt in the field covered by this Directive. The Commission shall inform the other Member States thereof.

Amendment

1 Inserted by Directive 2008/101/EC of the European Parliament and of the Council of 19 November 2008 amending Directive 2003/87/EC so as to include aviation activities in the scheme for greenhouse gas emission allowance trading within the Community, Article 1.21.

Article 32

Entry into force

This Directive shall enter into force on the day of its publication in the Official Journal of the European Union.

Article 33

Addressees

This Directive is addressed to the Member States.

[ANNEX I
CATEGORIES OF ACTIVITIES TO WHICH THIS DIRECTIVE APPLIES][1]

[1. Installations or parts of installations used for research, development and testing of new products and processes and installations exclusively using biomass are not covered by this Directive.

2. The thresholds values given below generally refer to production capacities or outputs. Where several activities falling under the same category are carried out in the same installation, the capacities of such activities are added together.

3. When the total rated thermal input of an installation is calculated in order to decide upon its inclusion in the Community scheme, the rated thermal inputs of all technical units which are part of it, in which fuels are combusted within the installation, are added together. These units could include all types of boilers, burners, turbines, heaters, furnaces, incinerators, calciners, kilns, ovens, dryers, engines, fuel cells, chemical looping combustion units, flares, and thermal or catalytic post-combustion units. Units with a rated thermal input under 3 MW and units which use exclusively biomass shall not be taken into account for the purposes of this calculation. "Units using exclusively biomass" includes units which use fossil fuels only during startup or shut-down of the unit.

4. If a unit serves an activity for which the threshold is not expressed as total rated thermal input, the threshold of this activity shall take precedence for the decision about the inclusion in the Community scheme.

5. When the capacity threshold of any activity in this Annex is found to be exceeded in an installation, all units in which fuels are combusted, other than units for the incineration of hazardous or municipal waste, shall be included in the greenhouse gas emission permit.

6. From 1 January 2012 all flights which arrive at or depart from an aerodrome situated in the territory of a Member State to which the Treaty applies shall be included.

Activities	*Greenhouse gases*
Combustion of fuels in installations with a total rated thermal input exceeding 20 MW (except in installations for the incineration of hazardous or municipal waste)	Carbon dioxide
Refining of mineral oil	Carbon dioxide
Production of coke	Carbon dioxide
Metal ore (including sulphide ore) sintering, including palletisation	Carbon dioxide
Production of pig iron or steel (primary or secondary fusion) including continuous casting, with a capacity exceeding 2,5 tonnes per hour	Carbon dioxide
Production or processing of ferrous metals (including ferro-alloys) where combustion units with a total rated thermal input exceeding 20 MW are operated. Processing includes, inter alia, rolling mills, re-heaters, annealing furnaces, smitheries, foundries,coating and pickling	Carbon dioxide
Production of primary aluminium	Carbon dioxide and perfluorocarbons
Production of secondary aluminium wherecombustion units with a total rated thermalinput exceeding 20 MW are operated	Carbon dioxide
Production or processing of non-ferrous metals, including production of alloys, refining, foundry casting, etc., where combustion units with a total rated thermal input (including fuels used as reducing agents) exceeding 20 MW are operated	Carbon dioxide
Production of cement clinker in rotary kilns with a production capacity exceeding 500 tonnes per day or in other furnaces with a production capacity exceeding 50 tonnes per day	Carbon dioxide
Production of lime or calcination of dolomite or magnesite in rotary kilns or in other furnaces with a production capacity exceeding 50 tonnes per day	Carbon dioxide
Manufacture of glass including glass fibre with a melting capacity exceeding 20 tonnes per day	Carbon dioxide
Manufacture of ceramic products by firing, in particular roofing tiles, bricks, refractory bricks, tiles, stoneware or porcelain, with a production capacity exceeding 75 tonnes per day	Carbon dioxide
Manufacture of mineral wool insulation material using glass, rock or slag with a melting capacity exceeding 20 tonnes per day	Carbon dioxide
Drying or calcination of gypsum or production of plaster boards and other gypsum products, where combustion units with a total rated thermal input exceeding 20 MW are operated	Carbon dioxide
Production of pulp from timber or other fibrous materials	Carbon dioxide
Production of paper or cardboard with a production capacity exceeding 20 tonnes per day	Carbon dioxide

Activities	*Greenhouse gases*
Production of carbon black involving the carbonisation of organic substances such as oils, tars, cracker and distillation residues, where combustion units with a total rated thermal input exceeding 20 MW are operated	Carbon dioxide
Production of nitric acid	Carbon dioxide and nitrous oxide
Production of adipic acid	Carbon dioxide and nitrous oxide
Production of glyoxal and glyoxylic acid	Carbon dioxide and nitrous oxide
Production of ammonia	Carbon dioxide
Production of bulk organic chemicals by cracking, reforming, partial or full oxidation or by similar processes, with a production capacity exceeding 100 tonnes per day	Carbon dioxide
Production of hydrogen (H_2) and synthesis gas by reforming or partial oxidation with a production capacity exceeding 25 tonnes per day	Carbon dioxide
Production of soda ash (Na_2CO_3) and sodium bicarbonate ($NaHCO_3$)	Carbon dioxide
Capture of greenhouse gases from installations covered by this Directive for the purpose of transport and geological storage in a storage site permitted under Directive 2009/31/EC	Carbon dioxide
Transport of greenhouse gases by pipelines for geological storage in a storage site permitted under Directive 2009/31/EC	Carbon dioxide
Geological storage of greenhouse gases in a storage site permitted under Directive 2009/31/EC	Carbon dioxide
Aviation Flights which depart from or arrive in an aerodrome situated in the territory of a MemberState to which the Treaty applies. This activity shall not include: (a) flights performed exclusively for the transport, on official mission, of a reigning Monarch and his immediate family, Heads of State, Heads of Government and Government Ministers, of a country other than a Member State, where this is substantiated by an appropriate status indicator in the flight plan; (b) military flights performed by military aircraft and customs and police flights; (c) flights related to search and rescue, firefighting flights, humanitarian flights and emergency medical service flights authorised by the appropriate competent authority; (d) any flights performed exclusively under visual flight rules as defined in Annex 2 to the Chicago Convention; (e) flights terminating at the aerodrome from which the aircraft has taken off and during which no intermediate landing has been made; (f) training flights performed exclusively for the purpose of obtaining a licence, or a rating in the case of cockpit flight crew where this is substantiated by an appropriate remark in the flight plan provided that the flight does not serve for the transport of passengers and/or cargo or for the positioning or ferrying of the aircraft; (g) flights performed exclusively for the purpose of scientific research or for the purpose of checking, testing or certifying aircraft or equipment whether airborne or ground-based;	Carbon dioxide

Activities	*Greenhouse gases*
(h) flights performed by aircraft with a certified maximum take-off mass of less than 5 700 kg;	
(i) flights performed in the framework of public service obligations imposed in accordance with Regulation (EEC) No 2408/92 on routes within outermost regions, as specified in Article 299(2) of the Treaty, or on routes where the capacity offered does not exceed 30 000 seats per year; and	
(j) flights which, but for this point, would fall within this activity, performed by a commercial air transport operator operating either: — fewer than 243 flights per period for three consecutive four-month periods, or — flights with total annual emissions lower than 10 000 tonnes per year.	
Flights performed exclusively for the transport, on official mission, of a reigning Monarch and his immediate family, Heads of State, Heads of Government and Government Ministers, of a MemberState may not be excluded under this point.][1]	

Amendment

1 Substituted by Directive 2009/29/EC of the European Parliament and of the Council of 23 April 2009 amending Directive 2003/87/EC so as to improve and extend the greenhouse gas emission allowance trading scheme of the Community, Article 1.30, Annex I.

ANNEX II
GREENHOUSE GASES REFERRED TO IN ARTICLES 3 AND 30

Carbon dioxide (CO_2)

Methane (CH_4)

Nitrous Oxide (N_2O)

Hydrofluorocarbons (HFCs)

Perfluorocarbons (PFCs)

Sulphur Hexafluoride (SF_6)

[ANNEX IIA
INCREASES IN THE PERCENTAGE OF ALLOWANCES TO BE AUCTIONED BY MEMBER STATES PURSUANT TO ARTICLE 10(2)(A), FOR THE PURPOSE OF COMMUNITY SOLIDARITY AND GROWTH IN ORDER TO REDUCE EMISSIONS AND ADAPT TO THE EFFECTS OF CLIMATE CHANGE][1]

[Member state	*Share*
Belgium	10%
Bulgaria	53%
Czech Repbublic	31%
Estonia	42%
Greece	17%

[Member state	*Share*
Spain	13%
Italy	2%
Cyprus	20%
Latvia	56%
Lithuania	46%
Luxembourg	10%
Hungary	28%
Malta	23%
Poland	39%
Portugal	16%
Romania	53%
Slovenia	20%
Slovakia	41%
Sweden	10%][1]

Amendment

1 Inserted by Directive 2009/29/EC of the European Parliament and of the Council of 23 April 2009 amending Directive 2003/87/EC so as to improve and extend the greenhouse gas emission allowance trading scheme of the Community, Article 1.31, Annex II.

[ANNEX IIB
DISTRIBUTION OF ALLOWANCES TO BE AUCTIONED BY MEMBER STATES PURSUANT TO ARTICLE 10(2)(C) REFLECTING EARLY EFFORTS OF SOME MEMBER STATES TO ACHIEVE 20% REDUCTION OF GREENHOUSE GAS EMISSIONS][1]

[Member State	*Distribution of the 2% against the Kyoto base in percentages*
Bulgaria	15%
Czech Republic	4%
Estonia	6%
Hungary	5%
Latvia	4%
Lithuania	7%
Poland	27%
Romania	29%
Slovakia	3%][1]

Amendment

1 Inserted by Directive 2009/29/EC of the European Parliament and of the Council of 23 April 2009 amending Directive 2003/87/EC so as to improve and extend the greenhouse gas emission allowance trading scheme of the Community, Article 1.31, Annex II.

[*Annex III was repealed by Directive 2009/29/EC of the European Parliament and of the Council of 23 April 2009 amending Directive 2003/87/EC so as to improve and extend the greenhouse gas emission allowance trading scheme of the Community, Article 1.32.*]

ANNEX IV
PRINCIPLES FOR MONITORING AND REPORTING REFERRED TO IN ARTICLE 14(1)

[PART A
MONITORING AND REPORTING OF EMISSIONS FROM STATIONARY INSTALLATIONS][1]

Monitoring of carbon dioxide emissions

Emissions shall be monitored either by calculation or on the basis of measurement.

Calculation

Calculations of emissions shall be performed using the formula:

Activity data × Emission factor × Oxidation factor

Activity data (fuel used, production rate etc.) shall be monitored on the basis of supply data or measurement.

Accepted emission factors shall be used. Activity-specific emission factors are acceptable for all fuels. Default factors are acceptable for all fuels except non-commercial ones (waste fuels such as tyres and industrial process gases). Seam-specific defaults for coal, and EU-specific or producer country-specific defaults for natural gas shall be further elaborated. IPCC default values are acceptable for refinery products. The emission factor for biomass shall be zero.

If the emission factor does not take account of the fact that some of the carbon is not oxidised, then an additional oxidation factor shall be used. If activity-specific emission factors have been calculated and already take oxidation into account, then an oxidation factor need not be applied.

Default oxidation factors developed pursuant to Directive 96/61/EC shall be used, unless the operator can demonstrate that activity-specific factors are more accurate.

A separate calculation shall be made for each activity, installation and for each fuel.

Measurement

Measurement of emissions shall use standardised or accepted methods, and shall be corroborated by a supporting calculation of emissions.

Monitoring of emissions of other greenhouse gases

[Standardised or accepted methods shall be used, developed by the Commission in collaboration with all relevant stakeholders. Those measures, designed to amend non-essential elements of this Directive, by supplementing it, shall be adopted in accordance with the regulatory procedure with scrutiny referred to in Article 23(3).][2]

Reporting of emissions

Each operator shall include the following information in the report for an installation:

A. Data identifying the installation, including:
- Name of the installation;
- Its address, including postcode and country;
- Type and number of Annex I activities carried out in the installation;
- Address, telephone, fax and email details for a contact person; and
- Name of the owner of the installation, and of any parent company.

B. For each Annex I activity carried out on the site for which emissions are calculated:
- Activity data;
- Emission factors;

— Oxidation factors;
— Total emissions; and
— Uncertainty.

C. For each Annex I activity carried out on the site for which emissions are measured:
— Total emissions;
— Information on the reliability of measurement methods; and
— Uncertainty.

D. For emissions from combustion, the report shall also include the oxidation factor, unless oxidation has already been taken into account in the development of an activity-specific emission factor.

Member States shall take measures to coordinate reporting requirements with any existing reporting requirements in order to minimise the reporting burden on businesses.

Amendments

1 Inserted by Directive 2008/101/EC of the European Parliament and of the Council of 19 November 2008 amending Directive 2003/87/EC so as to include aviation activities in the scheme for greenhouse gas emission allowance trading within the Community, Article 1.22, Annex, para 2(a).

2 Substituted by Regulation (EC) No 219/2009 of the European Parliament and of the Council of 11 March 2009 adapting a number of instruments subject to the procedure referred to in Article 251 of the Treaty to Council Decision 1999/468/EC with regard to the regulatory procedure with scrutiny, Article 1, Annex, para 3.6.8.

[PART B
MONITORING AND REPORTING OF EMISSIONS FROM AVIATION ACTIVITIES][1]

[Monitoring of carbon dioxide emissions

Emissions shall be monitored by calculation. Emissions shall be calculated using the formula:
Fuel consumption × emission factor

Fuel consumption shall include fuel consumed by the auxiliary power unit. Actual fuel consumption for each flight shall be used wherever possible and shall be calculated using the formula:

Amount of fuel contained in aircraft tanks once fuel uplift for the flight is complete – amount of fuel contained in aircraft tanks once fuel uplift for subsequent flight is complete + fuel uplift for that subsequent flight.

If actual fuel consumption data are not available, a standardised tiered method shall be used to estimate fuel consumption data based on best available information.

Default IPCC emission factors, taken from the 2006 IPCC Inventory Guidelines or subsequent updates of these Guidelines, shall be used unless activity-specific emission factors identified by independent accredited laboratories using accepted analytical methods are more accurate. The emission factor for biomass shall be zero.

A separate calculation shall be made for each flight and for each fuel.

Reporting of emissions

Each aircraft operator shall include the following information in its report under Article 14(3):

A. Data identifying the aircraft operator, including:
— name of the aircraft operator,
— its administering Member State,
— its address, including postcode and country and, where different, its contact address in the administering Member State,
— the aircraft registration numbers and types of aircraft used in the period covered by the report to perform the aviation activities listed in Annex I for which it is the aircraft operator,

- the number and issuing authority of the air operator certificate and operating licence under which the aviation activities listed in Annex I for which it is the aircraft operator were performed,
- address, telephone, fax and e-mail details for a contact person, and
- name of the aircraft owner.

B. For each type of fuel for which emissions are calculated:

- fuel consumption,
- emission factor,
- total aggregated emissions from all flights performed during the period covered by the report which fall within the aviation activities listed in Annex I for which it is the aircraft operator,
- aggregated emissions from:
  - all flights performed during the period covered by the report which fall within the aviation activities listed in Annex I for which it is the aircraft operator and which departed from an aerodrome situated in the territory of a Member State and arrived at an aerodrome situated in the territory of the same Member State,
  - all other flights performed during the period covered by the report which fall within the aviation activities listed in Annex I for which it is the aircraft operator,
- aggregated emissions from all flights performed during the period covered by the report which fall within the aviation activities listed in Annex I for which it is the aircraft operator and which:
  - departed from each Member State, and
  - arrived in each Member State from a third country,
- uncertainty.

Monitoring of tonne-kilometre data for the purpose of Articles 3e and 3f

For the purpose of applying for an allocation of allowances in accordance with Article 3e(1) or Article 3f(2), the amount of aviation activity shall be calculated in tonne-kilometres using the following formula:

$$\text{tonne-kilometres} = \text{distance} \times \text{payload}$$

where:

"distance" means the great circle distance between the aerodrome of departure and the aerodrome of arrival plus an additional fixed factor of 95 km; and

"payload" means the total mass of freight, mail and passengers carried.

For the purposes of calculating the payload:

- the number of passengers shall be the number of persons on-board excluding crew members,
- an aircraft operator may choose to apply either the actual or standard mass for passengers and checked baggage contained in its mass and balance documentation for the relevant flights or a default value of 100 kg for each passenger and his checked baggage.

Reporting of tonne-kilometre data for the purpose of Articles 3e and 3f

Each aircraft operator shall include the following information in its application under Article 3e(1) or Article 3f(2):

A. Data identifying the aircraft operator, including:

- name of the aircraft operator,
- its administering Member State,
- its address, including postcode and country and, where different, its contact address in the administering Member State,

— the aircraft registration numbers and types of aircraft used during the year covered by the application to perform the aviation activities listed in Annex I for which it is the aircraft operator,
— the number and issuing authority of the air operator certificate and operating licence under which the aviation activities listed in Annex I for which it is the aircraft operator were performed,
— address, telephone, fax and e-mail details for a contact person, and
— name of the aircraft owner.

B. Tonne-kilometre data:
— number of flights by aerodrome pair,
— number of passenger-kilometres by aerodrome pair,
— number of tonne-kilometres by aerodrome pair,
— chosen method for calculation of mass for passengers and checked baggage,
— total number of tonne-kilometres for all flights performed during the year to which the report relates falling within the aviation activities listed in Annex I for which it is the aircraft operator.][1]

Amendment

1 Inserted by Directive 2008/101/EC of the European Parliament and of the Council of 19 November 2008 amending Directive 2003/87/EC so as to include aviation activities in the scheme for greenhouse gas emission allowance trading within the Community, Article 1.22, Annex, para 2(b).

ANNEX V
CRITERIA FOR VERIFICATION REFERRED TO IN ARTICLE 15

[PART A
VERIFICATION OF EMISSIONS FROM STATIONARY INSTALLATIONS][1]

General Principles

1. Emissions from each activity listed in Annex I shall be subject to verification.

2. The verification process shall include consideration of the report pursuant to Article 14(3) and of monitoring during the preceding year. It shall address the reliability, credibility and accuracy of monitoring systems and the reported data and information relating to emissions, in particular:
(a) the reported activity data and related measurements and calculations;
(b) the choice and the employment of emission factors;
(c) the calculations leading to the determination of the overall emissions; and
(d) if measurement is used, the appropriateness of the choice and the employment of measuring methods.

3. Reported emissions may only be validated if reliable and credible data and information allow the emissions to be determined with a high degree of certainty. A high degree of certainty requires the operator to show that:
(a) the reported data is free of inconsistencies;
(b) the collection of the data has been carried out in accordance with the applicable scientific standards; and
(c) the relevant records of the installation are complete and consistent.

4. The verifier shall be given access to all sites and information in relation to the subject of the verification.

5. The verifier shall take into account whether the installation is registered under the Community eco-management and audit scheme (EMAS).

COUNCIL DIRECTIVE 2003/122/EURATOM

of 22 December 2003

ON THE CONTROL OF HIGH-ACTIVITY SEALED RADIOACTIVE SOURCES AND ORPHAN SOURCES

THE COUNCIL OF THE EUROPEAN UNION,

Having regard to the Treaty establishing the European Atomic Energy Community, and in particular Articles 31(2) and 32 thereof,

Having regard to the proposal from the Commission, drawn up after obtaining the opinion of a group of persons appointed by the Scientific and Technical Committee from among scientific experts in the Member States, in accordance with Article 31 of the Treaty,

After consulting the European Economic and Social Committee,

Having regard to the opinion of the European Parliament,

Whereas:

(1) Article 30 of the Treaty requires basic standards to be laid down within the Community for the protection of the health of workers and the general public against the dangers arising from ionising radiation.

(2) Council Directive 96/29/Euratom of 13 May 1996 laying down basic safety standards for the protection of the health of workers and the general public against the dangers arising from ionising radiation, continues the line of directives laying down basic safety standards since 1959.

(3) Article 4(1)(e) of Directive 96/29/Euratom requires prior authorisation for, amongst other practices, the use of radioactive sources for industrial radiography or processing of products or research or the exposure of persons for medical treatment. It is appropriate to extend this requirement to all practices involving high-activity radioactive sources in order further to reduce the likelihood of accidents involving such sources.

(4) Prior to authorisation, adequate arrangements and provision for the safe management of sources should exist.

(5) The International Atomic Energy Agency (IAEA) issues regulations for the safe transport of radioactive material that include activity limits for the requirements of the regulations, which should provide an appropriate basis for defining high-activity sealed radioactive sources within the scope of this Directive.

(6) In Directive 96/29/Euratom exemption values were laid down for the reporting of a practice to the authorities. These values were defined in that Directive on the basis of a negligible level of risk. As the requirements of this Directive should not put an administrative burden on the holders of small sources that is not commensurate with the possible health detriment, the definition of high activity radioactive sources should not be extended to the exemption levels of Directive 96/29/Euratom.

(7) Shipments of sealed sources between Member States are subject to the procedure established by Council Regulation (Euratom) No 1493/93 of 8 June 1993 on shipments of radioactive substances between Member States.

(8) Although the legal requirements deriving from existing legislation at Community and at national level ensure basic protection, high-activity sources still imply considerable potential risks for human health and for the environment and therefore need to be subject to a strict control from the time they are manufactured to the time they are placed in a recognised installation for their long-term storage or disposal.

(9) Prevention of radiological accidents and injuries requires the location of each high-activity source to be known, recorded and verified from the time the source is

manufactured or imported into the Community to the time it is placed in a recognised installation for its long-term storage or disposal or it is exported from the Community. Changes in the situation of a high-activity source, e.g. its location or use, should also be recorded and notified. Physical or financial obstacles should not hinder any appropriate reuse, recycling or disposal of such sources when disused under any reasonably foreseeable circumstances.

(10) Cases of unintentional exposure should be notified to the competent authority.

(11) Movements within the Community of high-activity sources make it necessary to harmonise the control of and information on such sources through the application of minimum criteria.

(12) Experience shows that, despite the existence of an appropriate regulatory framework, control of high-activity sources may nevertheless be lost. Furthermore, the existence of orphan sources resulting from past activities requires that specific initiatives be undertaken.

(13) Accordingly, it is necessary to provide for the identification, marking and recording of each high-activity source as well as for the specific training and informing of all those involved in activities relating to the use of sources. However, the marking of existing high-activity sources by engraving or stamping by persons other than the manufacturer could be problematic and should be avoided. It is also advisable to provide appropriate training and information for those who may deal accidentally with orphan sources.

(14) It is also necessary to provide for suitable means of dealing with orphan high-activity sources for international cooperation and exchange of information in this area, for inspection and, finally, for making financial provision for cases in which the original holder either cannot be identified or, even if identified, is found to be insolvent.

(15) The Member States should lay down rules on penalties applicable to infringements of the provisions of this Directive and ensure that they are implemented; those penalties should be effective, proportionate and dissuasive,

HAS ADOPTED THIS DIRECTIVE:

Article 1

Purpose and scope

1. The purpose of this Directive is to prevent exposure of workers and the public to ionising radiation arising from inadequate control of high-activity sealed radioactive sources and orphan sources and to harmonise controls in place in the Member States by defining specific requirements ensuring that each such source is kept under control.

2. This Directive applies to high-activity sources as defined in Article 2. Member States may exclude sources from the scope of this Directive once their activity has fallen below the exemption levels specified in Directive 96/29/Euratom.

3. The minimum obligations resulting from this Directive supplement those set out in Directive 96/29/Euratom.

Article 2

Definitions

For the purpose of this Directive, the following definitions shall apply:

(a) "orphan source" means a sealed source, the activity level of which, at the time of its discovery, is above the exemption level referred to in Article 3(2)(a) of Directive 96/29/Euratom, and which is not under regulatory control, either because it has never been under regulatory control or because it has been abandoned, lost, misplaced, stolen or transferred, without proper notification of the competent authority, to a new holder or without informing the recipient;

(b) "high-activity source", hereinafter referred to as "source", means a sealed source containing a radionuclide whose activity at the time of manufacture or, if this is not known, of the first placing on the market is equal to or exceeds the relevant activity level specified in Annex I;
(c) "practice" has the meaning given to it by Directive 96/29/Euratom;
(d) "authorisation" means permission granted in a document by competent authorities, on request, to carry out a practice involving a source;
(e) "competent authority" means any authority designated by a Member State to carry out tasks in accordance with this Directive;
(f) "disused source" means a source which is no longer used or intended to be used for the practice for which authorisation was granted;
(g) "holder" means any natural or legal person who is responsible under national law for a source, including manufacturers, suppliers and users of sources but excluding "recognised installations";
(h) "manufacturer" means any natural or legal person who manufactures a source;
(i) "recognised installation" means a facility located in the territory of a Member State authorised by the competent authorities of that State in accordance with national law for the long-term storage or disposal of sources or an installation duly authorised under national law for the interim storage of sources;
(j) "exposed worker" has the meaning given to it by Directive 96/29/Euratom;
(k) "sealed source" has the meaning given to it by Directive 96/29/Euratom and includes the capsule, where applicable, enclosing the radioactive material as an integral part of the source;
(l) "supplier" means any natural or legal person who supplies or makes available a source;
(m) "transfer" of a source means a transfer of a source from one holder to another one;
(n) "source container" means the containment of a sealed source not being an integral part of the source, but meant for transport, handling, etc.

Article 3

Authorisation

1. Member States shall require the holder to obtain prior authorisation for any practice involving a source, including taking possession of a source.

2. Member States shall ensure that, before issuing authorisation:
(a) adequate arrangements, including those arising from this Directive, have been made for the safe management of sources, including when they become disused sources. These latter arrangements may provide for the transfer of these sources to the supplier or their placement in a recognised installation or an obligation for the manufacturer or the supplier to receive these sources;
(b) adequate provision, by way of a financial security or any other equivalent means appropriate to the source in question, have been made for the safe management of sources when they become disused sources, including the case where the holder becomes insolvent or goes out of business.

3. Member States shall ensure that the authorisation covers:
(a) responsibilities;
(b) minimum staff competencies, including information and training;
(c) minimum source, source container and additional equipment performance criteria;
(d) requirements for emergency procedures and communication links;
(e) work procedures to be followed;
(f) maintenance of equipment, sources and containers;
(g) adequate management of disused sources, including agreements regarding the transfer, if appropriate, of disused sources to a supplier, another authorised holder or a recognised installation.

Article 4

Transfers

Member States shall set up a system to enable them to be adequately informed of individual transfers of sources.

Article 5

Records

1. The holder shall keep records of all sources under his responsibility, their location and their transfer. The records shall include the information set out in Annex II. This information may be recorded on a standard record sheet pursuant to paragraph 5.

2. The holder shall provide the competent authority with an electronic or written copy of all or part of the records referred to in paragraph 1, as required by the Member State concerned,

— without undue delay, at the time of the establishment of such records, which should be as soon as possible after the source is acquired,
— at intervals, to be determined by Member States/competent authorities, of not more than 12 months thereafter,
— if the situation indicated on the information sheet has changed,
— without undue delay on the closure of the records for a specific source when the holder no longer holds this source; in this case the name of the holder or recognised installation to which the source is transferred shall be included,
— without undue delay on the closure of such records when the holder no longer holds any sources, and
— whenever so requested by the competent authority.

The holder's records shall be available for inspection by the competent authority.

3. The competent authorities shall keep records of authorised holders and of the sources they hold. These records shall include the radionuclide involved, the activity at the time of manufacture, or if this activity is not known, the activity at the time of the first placing on the market or at the time the holder acquired the source, and the type of source.

4. The competent authorities shall keep the records up to date, taking transfers into account, among other factors.

5. The Commission shall make available in electronic format the standard record sheet for the records set out in Annex II.

6. The Commission may, in accordance with the procedure referred to in Article 17, update the required information set out in Annex II and the standard record sheet for the records set out in Annex II.

Article 6

Requirements for holders

Each holder of sources shall:

(a) ensure that suitable tests, such as leak tests based on international standards, are undertaken regularly in order to check and maintain the integrity of each source;

(b) regularly verify, at specific intervals which may be determined by Member States, that each source and, where relevant, the equipment containing the source, is still present and in apparently good condition at its place of use or of storage;

(c) ensure that each fixed and mobile source is subject to adequate documented measures, such as written protocols and procedures, aimed at preventing unauthorised access to or loss or theft of the source or its damage by fire;

(d) promptly notify the competent authority of any loss, theft or unauthorised use of a source, arrange for a check on the integrity of each source after any event, including fire, that may have damaged the source and, if appropriate, inform the competent authority thereof and of the measures taken;
(e) return each disused source to the supplier or place it in a recognised installation or transfer it to another authorised holder unless otherwise agreed by the competent authority, without undue delay after termination of the use;
(f) ascertain that, before a transfer is made, the recipient holds appropriate authorisation;
(g) promptly notify the competent authority of any incident or accident resulting in unintentional exposure of a worker or a member of the public.

Article 7

Identification and marking

1. The manufacturer shall identify or, in the case of sources imported from outside the Community, the supplier shall ensure that each source is identified by a unique number. This number shall be engraved or stamped on the source, where practicable.

This number shall also be engraved or stamped on the source container. If this is not feasible or in the case of reusable transport containers, the source container shall at least have information on the nature of the source.

The manufacturer or the supplier shall ensure that the source container and, where practicable, the source are marked and labelled with an appropriate sign to warn people of the radiation hazard.

The manufacturer shall provide a photograph of each manufactured source design type and of the typical source container.

2. The holder shall ensure that each source is accompanied by written information indicating that the source is identified and marked in compliance with paragraph 1 and that the markings and labels referred to in paragraph 1 remain legible. The information shall include photographs of the source, source container, transport packaging, device and equipment as appropriate.

Article 8

Training and information

1. When arranging information and training in the field of radiation protection in compliance with Article 22 of Directive 96/29/Euratom, the holder shall ensure that such training includes specific requirements for the safe management of sources.

The information and training shall place particular emphasis on the necessary safety requirements and shall contain specific information on possible consequences of the loss of adequate control of sources.

The information and training shall be repeated at regular intervals and documented, with a view to preparing the relevant workers adequately for such events.

The relevant information and training shall be addressed to exposed workers.

2. Member States shall provide encouragement to ensure that the management and workers in installations where orphan sources are most likely to be found or processed (e.g. large metal scrap yards and major metal scrap recycling plants), and the management and workers in significant nodal transit points (e.g. customs posts), are
(a) informed of the possibility that they may be confronted with a source;
(b) advised and trained in the visual detection of sources and of their containers;
(c) informed of basic facts about ionising radiation and its effects;
(d) informed of and trained in the action to be taken on site in the event of the detection or suspected detection of a source.

Article 9

Orphan sources

1. Member States shall ensure that the competent authorities are prepared, or have made provision, including assignment of responsibilities, to recover orphan sources and to deal with radiological emergencies due to orphan sources and have drawn up appropriate response plans and measures.

2. Member States shall ensure that specialised technical advice and assistance is promptly made available to the persons, not normally involved in operations subject to radiation protection requirements, who suspect the presence of an orphan source. The primary aim of advice and assistance shall be the protection of workers and members of the public from radiation and the safety of the source.

3. Member States shall encourage the establishment of systems aimed at detecting orphan sources in places such as large metal scrap yards and major metal scrap recycling installations where orphan sources may generally be encountered, or at significant nodal transit points, wherever appropriate, such as customs posts.

4. Member States shall ensure that campaigns are organised, as appropriate, to recover orphan sources left behind from past activities.

The campaigns may include the financial participation of Member States in the costs of recovering, managing and disposing of the sources and may also include surveys of historical records of authorities, such as customs, and of holders, such as research institutes, material testing institutes or hospitals.

Article 10

Financial security for orphan sources

Member States shall ensure that, on the basis of arrangements to be decided by Member States, a system of financial security is established or any other equivalent means to cover intervention costs relating to the recovery of orphan sources and which may result from implementation of the requirements set out in Article 9.

Article 11

International cooperation and information exchange

Each Member State shall promptly exchange information and cooperate with other relevant Member States or third countries and with relevant international organisations as regards loss, removal, theft or discovery of sources and as regards related follow-up or investigations, without prejudice to relevant confidentiality requirements and relevant national regulations.

Article 12

Inspections

Member States shall establish or maintain a system of inspection to enforce the provisions introduced in compliance with this Directive.

Article 13

Competent authority

1. Member States shall designate the competent authority to carry out tasks in accordance with this Directive.

2. Member States shall forward to the Commission the name and the address of the competent authority and all necessary information for rapidly communicating with such authorities.

3. Where Member States have more than one competent authority, they shall designate one point of contact to act as an interface with correspondents in other Member States.

4. Member States shall forward to the Commission any changes to the data referred to in paragraphs 2 and 3.

5. The Commission shall communicate the information referred to in paragraphs 2, 3 and 4 to all competent authorities in the Community and shall publish it periodically in the Official Journal of the European Union, at intervals of no more than two years.

Article 14

Report on experience

By 31 December 2010, Member States shall report to the Commission on the experience gained in the implementation of this Directive, including consideration of any effect which Article 1(2) may have had.

On that basis, the Commission shall submit a report to the European Parliament, the Council and the European Economic and Social Committee.

Article 15

Penalties

Member States shall determine the penalties applicable to breaches of the national provisions adopted pursuant to this Directive. The penalties shall be effective, proportionate and dissuasive.

Article 16

Transposition

1. Member States shall bring into force the laws, regulations and administrative provisions necessary to comply with this Directive before 31 December 2005.

Member States may provide, as regards sources placed on the market before the date referred to in the first subparagraph, that:

(a) Articles 3 to 6 shall not apply until 31 December 2007;

(b) Article 7 shall not apply, with the exception of the following requirements which shall apply by 31 December 2007 at the latest:
   - the holder shall ensure that, if practicable, each such source and the source container are accompanied by written information to identify the source and its nature,
   - the holder shall ensure that, if practicable, each such source, if practicable, and the source container are labelled with an appropriate sign to warn people of the radiation hazard.

Where these measures are adopted by the Member States, they shall contain a reference to this Directive or shall be accompanied by such reference on the occasion of their official publication. The methods of making such reference shall be laid down by Member States.

2. Member States shall communicate to the Commission the text of the main provisions of national law which they adopt in the field covered by this Directive, together with a table showing how the provisions of this Directive correspond to the national provisions adopted.

Article 17

Committee

The Commission shall be assisted in performing the tasks laid down in Article 5(6) by an Advisory Committee composed of the representatives of the Member States and chaired by the representative of the Commission.

The representative of the Commission shall submit to the Committee a draft of the measures to be taken. The Committee shall deliver its opinion on the draft within a time limit which the Chairman may lay down according to the urgency of the matter, if necessary by taking a vote.

The opinion of the Committee shall be recorded in the minutes; in addition, each Member State shall have the right to ask to have its position recorded in the minutes.

The Commission shall take the utmost account of the opinion delivered by the Committee. It shall inform the Committee of the manner in which its opinion has been take into account.

Article 18

Entry into force

This Directive shall enter into force on the day of its publication in the Official Journal of the European Union.

Article 19

This Directive is addressed to the Member States.

ANNEX I
ACTIVITY LEVELS

For radionuclides not listed in the table below, but referred to in Annex I, Table A, of Directive 96/29/Euratom, the relevant activity level is one hundredth of the corresponding A1 value given in the IAEA Regulations for the safe transport of radioactive materials.

Element (Atomic number)	*Radionuclide*	*Activity level (Bq)*
Iron (26)	Fe-55	4×10^{11}
Cobalt (27)	Co-60	4×10^{9}
Selenium (34)	Se-75	3×10^{10}
Krypton (36)	Kr-85	1×10^{11}
Strontium (38)	Sr-90[(a)]	3×10^{9}
Palladium (46)	Pd-103[(a)]	4×10^{11}
Iodine (53)	I-125	2×10^{11}
Caesium (55)	Cs-137[(a)]	2×10^{10}
Promethium (61)	Pm-147	4×10^{11}
Gadolinium (64)	Gd-153	1×10^{11}
Thulium (69)	Tm-170	3×10^{10}
Iridium (77)	Ir-192	1×10^{10}
Thallium (69)	Tl-204	1×10^{10}
Radium (88)	Ra-226[(b)]	2×10^{11}
Plutonium (94)	Pu-238[(a)]	1×10^{11}
Americium (95)	Am-241[(b)]	1×10^{11}
Californium (98)	Cf-252	5×10^{8}

(a) The activity level includes contributions from daughter nuclides with half-lives less than 10 days.
(b) Includes neutron sources with beryllium.

ANNEX II
STANDARD RECORD SHEET FOR HIGH-ACTIVITY SEALED SOURCES (HASS) *(OPTIONAL IN ITALICS)*

1. **HASS identification number:**	2. **Identification of authorised holder** Name: Address: Country: Manufacturer ☐ Supplier ☐ User ☐	3. **Location of HASS** (Use or storage) if not the same as in 2. Name: Address: Fixed use ☐ Storage (mobile) ☐
4. **Registration** Date of start of registration: Date of transfer of registration to historic file:	5. **Authorisation** Number: Date of issue: Date of expiry:	6. **Operational control of HASS** Date: Date: Date: Date:
7. **HASS characteristic** Radionuclide: Activity at the date of manufacturing or of the first placing on the market: Date of manufacturing: Manufacturer/Supplier: (1) Name: Address: Country: Physical and chemical characteristics:	8. **Receipt of HASS** Date of receipt: Receipt from Name: Address: Country: Manufacturer ☐ Supplier ☐ Another user ☐	Date: Date: Date: Date: Date: Date: Date: Date:
Source type identification: *Capsule identification:* *ISO classsification:* *ANSI classsification:* *Special form certificate:*	9. **Transfer of HASS** Date of transfer Transfer to: Name: Address: Country: Manufacturer ☐ Supplier ☐ Another user ☐ Recognised installation	10. **Further information** *Loss* ☐ *Date of Loss:* *Theft* ☐ *Date of Theft:* *yes* ☐ *no* ☐ *Finding:* *date:* *place:* *Other information:*

(1) Where the manufacturer of the sources is established outside the Community, the name and address of the importer-supplier may be provided instead.

DIRECTIVE 2004/35/EC OF THE EUROPEAN PARLIAMENT AND OF THE COUNCIL

of 21 April 2004

ON ENVIRONMENTAL LIABILITY WITH REGARD TO THE PREVENTION AND REMEDYING OF ENVIRONMENTAL DAMAGE

THE EUROPEAN PARLIAMENT AND THE COUNCIL OF THE EUROPEAN UNION,

Having regard to the Treaty establishing the European Community, and in particular Article 175(1) thereof,

Having regard to the proposal from the Commission,

Having regard to the Opinion of the European Economic and Social Committee,

After consulting the Committee of the Regions,

Acting in accordance with the procedure laid down in Article 251 of the Treaty, in the light of the joint text approved by the Conciliation Committee on 10 March 2004,

Whereas:

(1) There are currently many contaminated sites in the Community, posing significant health risks, and the loss of biodiversity has dramatically accelerated over the last decades. Failure to act could result in increased site contamination and greater loss of biodiversity in the future. Preventing and remedying, insofar as is possible, environmental damage contributes to implementing the objectives and principles of the Community's environment policy as set out in the Treaty. Local conditions should be taken into account when deciding how to remedy damage.

(2) The prevention and remedying of environmental damage should be implemented through the furtherance of the "polluter pays" principle, as indicated in the Treaty and in line with the principle of sustainable development. The fundamental principle of this Directive should therefore be that an operator whose activity has caused the environmental damage or the imminent threat of such damage is to be held financially liable, in order to induce operators to adopt measures and develop practices to minimise the risks of environmental damage so that their exposure to financial liabilities is reduced.

(3) Since the objective of this Directive, namely to establish a common framework for the prevention and remedying of environmental damage at a reasonable cost to society, cannot be sufficiently achieved by the Member States and can therefore be better achieved at Community level by reason of the scale of this Directive and its implications in respect of other Community legislation, namely Council Directive 79/409/EEC of 2 April 1979 on the conservation of wild birds, Council Directive 92/43/EEC of 21 May 1992 on the conservation of natural habitats and of wild fauna and flora, and Directive 2000/60/EC of the European Parliament and of the Council of 23 October 2000 establishing a framework for Community action in the field of water policy, the Community may adopt measures in accordance with the principle of subsidiarity as set out in Article 5 of the Treaty. In accordance with the principle of proportionality, as set out in that Article, this Directive does not go beyond what is necessary in order to achieve that objective.

(4) Environmental damage also includes damage caused by airborne elements as far as they cause damage to water, land or protected species or natural habitats.

(5) Concepts instrumental for the correct interpretation and application of the scheme provided for by this Directive should be defined especially as regards the definition of environmental damage. When the concept in question derives from other relevant Community legislation, the same definition should be used so that common criteria can be used and uniform application promoted.

(6) Protected species and natural habitats might also be defined by reference to species and habitats protected in pursuance of national legislation on nature conservation. Account should nevertheless be taken of specific situations where Community, or equivalent national, legislation allows for certain derogations from the level of protection afforded to the environment.

(7) For the purposes of assessing damage to land as defined in this Directive the use of risk assessment procedures to determine to what extent human health is likely to be adversely affected is desirable.

(8) This Directive should apply, as far as environmental damage is concerned, to occupational activities which present a risk for human health or the environment. Those activities should be identified, in principle, by reference to the relevant Community legislation which provides for regulatory requirements in relation to certain activities or practices considered as posing a potential or actual risk for human health or the environment.

(9) This Directive should also apply, as regards damage to protected species and natural habitats, to any occupational activities other than those already directly or indirectly identified by reference to Community legislation as posing an actual or potential risk for human health or the environment. In such cases the operator should only be liable under this Directive whenever he is at fault or negligent.

(10) Express account should be taken of the Euratom Treaty and relevant international conventions and of Community legislation regulating more comprehensively and more stringently the operation of any of the activities falling under the scope of this Directive. This Directive, which does not provide for additional rules of conflict of laws when it specifies the powers of the competent authorities, is without prejudice to the rules on international jurisdiction of courts as provided, inter alia, in Council Regulation (EC) No 44/2001 of 22 December 2000 on jurisdiction and the recognition and enforcement of judgments in civil and commercial matters. This Directive should not apply to activities the main purpose of which is to serve national defence or international security.

(11) This Directive aims at preventing and remedying environmental damage, and does not affect rights of compensation for traditional damage granted under any relevant international agreement regulating civil liability.

(12) Many Member States are party to international agreements dealing with civil liability in relation to specific fields. These Member States should be able to remain so after the entry into force of this Directive, whereas other Member States should not lose their freedom to become parties to these agreements.

(13) Not all forms of environmental damage can be remedied by means of the liability mechanism. For the latter to be effective, there need to be one or more identifiable polluters, the damage should be concrete and quantifiable, and a causal link should be established between the damage and the identified polluter(s). Liability is therefore not a suitable instrument for dealing with pollution of a widespread, diffuse character, where it is impossible to link the negative environmental effects with acts or failure to act of certain individual actors.

(14) This Directive does not apply to cases of personal injury, to damage to private property or to any economic loss and does not affect any right regarding these types of damages.

(15) Since the prevention and remedying of environmental damage is a task directly contributing to the pursuit of the Community's environment policy, public authorities should ensure the proper implementation and enforcement of the scheme provided for by this Directive.

(16) Restoration of the environment should take place in an effective manner ensuring that the relevant restoration objectives are achieved. A common framework should

be defined to that end, the proper application of which should be supervised by the competent authority.

(17) Appropriate provision should be made for those situations where several instances of environmental damage have occurred in such a manner that the competent authority cannot ensure that all the necessary remedial measures are taken at the same time. In such a case, the competent authority should be entitled to decide which instance of environmental damage is to be remedied first.

(18) According to the "polluter-pays" principle, an operator causing environmental damage or creating an imminent threat of such damage should, in principle, bear the cost of the necessary preventive or remedial measures. In cases where a competent authority acts, itself or through a third party, in the place of an operator, that authority should ensure that the cost incurred by it is recovered from the operator. It is also appropriate that the operators should ultimately bear the cost of assessing environmental damage and, as the case may be, assessing an imminent threat of such damage occurring.

(19) Member States may provide for flat-rate calculation of administrative, legal, enforcement and other general costs to be recovered.

(20) An operator should not be required to bear the costs of preventive or remedial actions taken pursuant to this Directive in situations where the damage in question or imminent threat thereof is the result of certain events beyond the operator's control. Member States may allow that operators who are not at fault or negligent shall not bear the cost of remedial measures, in situations where the damage in question is the result of emissions or events explicitly authorised or where the potential for damage could not have been known when the event or emission took place.

(21) Operators should bear the costs relating to preventive measures when those measures should have been taken as a matter of course in order to comply with the legislative, regulatory and administrative provisions regulating their activities or the terms of any permit or authorisation.

(22) Member States may establish national rules covering cost allocation in cases of multiple party causation. Member States may take into account, in particular, the specific situation of users of products who might not be held responsible for environmental damage in the same conditions as those producing such products. In this case, apportionment of liability should be determined in accordance with national law.

(23) Competent authorities should be entitled to recover the cost of preventive or remedial measures from an operator within a reasonable period of time from the date on which those measures were completed.

(24) It is necessary to ensure that effective means of implementation and enforcement are available, while ensuring that the legitimate interests of the relevant operators and other interested parties are adequately safeguarded. Competent authorities should be in charge of specific tasks entailing appropriate administrative discretion, namely the duty to assess the significance of the damage and to determine which remedial measures should be taken.

(25) Persons adversely affected or likely to be adversely affected by environmental damage should be entitled to ask the competent authority to take action. Environmental protection is, however, a diffuse interest on behalf of which individuals will not always act or will not be in a position to act. Non-governmental organisations promoting environmental protection should therefore also be given the opportunity to properly contribute to the effective implementation of this Directive.

(26) The relevant natural or legal persons concerned should have access to procedures for the review of the competent authority's decisions, acts or failure to act.

(27) Member States should take measures to encourage the use by operators of any appropriate insurance or other forms of financial security and the development of financial security instruments and markets in order to provide effective cover for financial obligations under this Directive.

(28) Where environmental damage affects or is likely to affect several Member States, those Member States should cooperate with a view to ensuring proper and effective

preventive or remedial action in respect of any environmental damage. Member States may seek to recover the costs for preventive or remedial actions.

(29) This Directive should not prevent Member States from maintaining or enacting more stringent provisions in relation to the prevention and remedying of environmental damage; nor should it prevent the adoption by Member States of appropriate measures in relation to situations where double recovery of costs could occur as a result of concurrent action by a competent authority under this Directive and by a person whose property is affected by the environmental damage.

(30) Damage caused before the expiry of the deadline for implementation of this Directive should not be covered by its provisions.

(31) Member States should report to the Commission on the experience gained in the application of this Directive so as to enable the Commission to consider, taking into account the impact on sustainable development and future risks to the environment, whether any review of this Directive is appropriate,

HAVE ADOPTED THIS DIRECTIVE:

Article 1

Subject matter

The purpose of this Directive is to establish a framework of environmental liability based on the "polluter-pays" principle, to prevent and remedy environmental damage.

Article 2

Definitions

For the purpose of this Directive the following definitions shall apply:

1. "environmental damage" means:
   (a) damage to protected species and natural habitats, which is any damage that has significant adverse effects on reaching or maintaining the favourable conservation status of such habitats or species. The significance of such effects is to be assessed with reference to the baseline condition, taking account of the criteria set out in Annex I;
   Damage to protected species and natural habitats does not include previously identified adverse effects which result from an act by an operator which was expressly authorised by the relevant authorities in accordance with provisions implementing Article 6(3) and (4) or Article 16 of Directive 92/43/EEC or Article 9 of Directive 79/409/EEC or, in the case of habitats and species not covered by Community law, in accordance with equivalent provisions of national law on nature conservation.
   (b) water damage, which is any damage that significantly adversely affects the ecological, chemical and/or quantitative status and/or ecological potential, as defined in Directive 2000/60/EC, of the waters concerned, with the exception of adverse effects where Article 4(7) of that Directive applies;
   (c) land damage, which is any land contamination that creates a significant risk of human health being adversely affected as a result of the direct or indirect introduction, in, on or under land, of substances, preparations, organisms or micro-organisms;
2. "damage" means a measurable adverse change in a natural resource or measurable impairment of a natural resource service which may occur directly or indirectly;
3. "protected species and natural habitats" means:
   (a) the species mentioned in Article 4(2) of Directive 79/409/EEC or listed in Annex I thereto or listed in Annexes II and IV to Directive 92/43/EEC;

(b) the habitats of species mentioned in Article 4(2) of Directive 79/409/EEC or listed in Annex I thereto or listed in Annex II to Directive 92/43/EEC, and the natural habitats listed in Annex I to Directive 92/43/EEC and the breeding sites or resting places of the species listed in Annex IV to Directive 92/43/EEC; and

(c) where a Member State so determines, any habitat or species, not listed in those Annexes which the Member State designates for equivalent purposes as those laid down in these two Directives;

4. "conservation status" means:

(a) in respect of a natural habitat, the sum of the influences acting on a natural habitat and its typical species that may affect its long-term natural distribution, structure and functions as well as the long-term survival of its typical species within, as the case may be, the European territory of the Member States to which the Treaty applies or the territory of a Member State or the natural range of that habitat;

The conservation status of a natural habitat will be taken as "favourable" when:

— its natural range and areas it covers within that range are stable or increasing,

— the specific structure and functions which are necessary for its long-term maintenance exist and are likely to continue to exist for the foreseeable future, and

— the conservation status of its typical species is favourable, as defined in (b);

(b) in respect of a species, the sum of the influences acting on the species concerned that may affect the long-term distribution and abundance of its populations within, as the case may be, the European territory of the Member States to which the Treaty applies or the territory of a Member State or the natural range of that species;

The conservation status of a species will be taken as "favourable" when:

— population dynamics data on the species concerned indicate that it is maintaining itself on a long-term basis as a viable component of its natural habitats,

— the natural range of the species is neither being reduced nor is likely to be reduced for the foreseeable future, and

— there is, and will probably continue to be, a sufficiently large habitat to maintain its populations on a long-term basis;

5. "waters" mean all waters covered by Directive 2000/60/EC;

6. "operator" means any natural or legal, private or public person who operates or controls the occupational activity or, where this is provided for in national legislation, to whom decisive economic power over the technical functioning of such an activity has been delegated, including the holder of a permit or authorisation for such an activity or the person registering or notifying such an activity;

7. "occupational activity" means any activity carried out in the course of an economic activity, a business or an undertaking, irrespectively of its private or public, profit or non-profit character;

8. "emission" means the release in the environment, as a result of human activities, of substances, preparations, organisms or micro-organisms;

9. "imminent threat of damage" means a sufficient likelihood that environmental damage will occur in the near future;

10. "preventive measures" means any measures taken in response to an event, act or omission that has created an imminent threat of environmental damage, with a view to preventing or minimising that damage;

11. "remedial measures" means any action, or combination of actions, including mitigating or interim measures to restore, rehabilitate or replace damaged natural resources and/or impaired services, or to provide an equivalent alternative to those resources or services as foreseen in Annex II;

12. "natural resource" means protected species and natural habitats, water and land;
13. "services" and "natural resources services" mean the functions performed by a natural resource for the benefit of another natural resource or the public;
14. "baseline condition" means the condition at the time of the damage of the natural resources and services that would have existed had the environmental damage not occurred, estimated on the basis of the best information available;
15. "recovery", including "natural recovery", means, in the case of water, protected species and natural habitats the return of damaged natural resources and/or impaired services to baseline condition and in the case of land damage, the elimination of any significant risk of adversely affecting human health;
16. "costs" means costs which are justified by the need to ensure the proper and effective implementation of this Directive including the costs of assessing environmental damage, an imminent threat of such damage, alternatives for action as well as the administrative, legal, and enforcement costs, the costs of data collection and other general costs, monitoring and supervision costs.

Article 3

Scope

1. This Directive shall apply to:
(a) environmental damage caused by any of the occupational activities listed in Annex III, and to any imminent threat of such damage occurring by reason of any of those activities;
(b) damage to protected species and natural habitats caused by any occupational activities other than those listed in Annex III, and to any imminent threat of such damage occurring by reason of any of those activities, whenever the operator has been at fault or negligent.

2. This Directive shall apply without prejudice to more stringent Community legislation regulating the operation of any of the activities falling within the scope of this Directive and without prejudice to Community legislation containing rules on conflicts of jurisdiction.

3. Without prejudice to relevant national legislation, this Directive shall not give private parties a right of compensation as a consequence of environmental damage or of an imminent threat of such damage.

Article 4

Exceptions

1. This Directive shall not cover environmental damage or an imminent threat of such damage caused by:
(a) an act of armed conflict, hostilities, civil war or insurrection;
(b) a natural phenomenon of exceptional, inevitable and irresistible character.

2. This Directive shall not apply to environmental damage or to any imminent threat of such damage arising from an incident in respect of which liability or compensation falls within the scope of any of the International Conventions listed in Annex IV, including any future amendments thereof, which is in force in the Member State concerned.

3. This Directive shall be without prejudice to the right of the operator to limit his liability in accordance with national legislation implementing the Convention on Limitation of Liability for Maritime Claims (LLMC), 1976, including any future amendment to the Convention, or the Strasbourg Convention on Limitation of Liability in Inland Navigation (CLNI), 1988, including any future amendment to the Convention.

4. This Directive shall not apply to such nuclear risks or environmental damage or imminent threat of such damage as may be caused by the activities covered by the Treaty establishing the

European Atomic Energy Community or caused by an incident or activity in respect of which liability or compensation falls within the scope of any of the international instruments listed in Annex V, including any future amendments thereof.

5. This Directive shall only apply to environmental damage or to an imminent threat of such damage caused by pollution of a diffuse character, where it is possible to establish a causal link between the damage and the activities of individual operators.

6. This Directive shall not apply to activities the main purpose of which is to serve national defence or international security nor to activities the sole purpose of which is to protect from natural disasters.

Article 5

Preventive action

1. Where environmental damage has not yet occurred but there is an imminent threat of such damage occurring, the operator shall, without delay, take the necessary preventive measures.

2. Member States shall provide that, where appropriate, and in any case whenever an imminent threat of environmental damage is not dispelled despite the preventive measures taken by the operator, operators are to inform the competent authority of all relevant aspects of the situation, as soon as possible.

3. The competent authority may, at any time:
(a) require the operator to provide information on any imminent threat of environmental damage or in suspected cases of such an imminent threat;
(b) require the operator to take the necessary preventive measures;
(c) give instructions to the operator to be followed on the necessary preventive measures to be taken; or
(d) itself take the necessary preventive measures.

4. The competent authority shall require that the preventive measures are taken by the operator. If the operator fails to comply with the obligations laid down in paragraph 1 or 3(b) or (c), cannot be identified or is not required to bear the costs under this Directive, the competent authority may take these measures itself.

Article 6

Remedial action

1. Where environmental damage has occurred the operator shall, without delay, inform the competent authority of all relevant aspects of the situation and take:
(a) all practicable steps to immediately control, contain, remove or otherwise manage the relevant contaminants and/or any other damage factors in order to limit or to prevent further environmental damage and adverse effects on human health or further impairment of services and
(b) the necessary remedial measures, in accordance with Article 7.

2. The competent authority may, at any time:
(a) require the operator to provide supplementary information on any damage that has occurred;
(b) take, require the operator to take or give instructions to the operator concerning, all practicable steps to immediately control, contain, remove or otherwise manage the relevant contaminants and/or any other damage factors in order to limit or to prevent further environmental damage and adverse effect on human health, or further impairment of services;
(c) require the operator to take the necessary remedial measures;

(d) give instructions to the operator to be followed on the necessary remedial measures to be taken; or
(e) itself take the necessary remedial measures.

3. The competent authority shall require that the remedial measures are taken by the operator. If the operator fails to comply with the obligations laid down in paragraph 1 or 2(b), (c) or (d), cannot be identified or is not required to bear the costs under this Directive, the competent authority may take these measures itself, as a means of last resort.

Article 7

Determination of remedial measures

1. Operators shall identify, in accordance with Annex II, potential remedial measures and submit them to the competent authority for its approval, unless the competent authority has taken action under Article 6(2)(e) and (3).

2. The competent authority shall decide which remedial measures shall be implemented in accordance with Annex II, and with the cooperation of the relevant operator, as required.

3. Where several instances of environmental damage have occurred in such a manner that the competent authority cannot ensure that the necessary remedial measures are taken at the same time, the competent authority shall be entitled to decide which instance of environmental damage must be remedied first.

In making that decision, the competent authority shall have regard, inter alia, to the nature, extent and gravity of the various instances of environmental damage concerned, and to the possibility of natural recovery. Risks to human health shall also be taken into account.

4. The competent authority shall invite the persons referred to in Article 12(1) and in any case the persons on whose land remedial measures would be carried out to submit their observations and shall take them into account.

Article 8

Prevention and remediation costs

1. The operator shall bear the costs for the preventive and remedial actions taken pursuant to this Directive.

2. Subject to paragraphs 3 and 4, the competent authority shall recover, inter alia, via security over property or other appropriate guarantees from the operator who has caused the damage or the imminent threat of damage, the costs it has incurred in relation to the preventive or remedial actions taken under this Directive.

However, the competent authority may decide not to recover the full costs where the expenditure required to do so would be greater than the recoverable sum or where the operator cannot be identified.

3. An operator shall not be required to bear the cost of preventive or remedial actions taken pursuant to this Directive when he can prove that the environmental damage or imminent threat of such damage:
(a) was caused by a third party and occurred despite the fact that appropriate safety measures were in place; or
(b) resulted from compliance with a compulsory order or instruction emanating from a public authority other than an order or instruction consequent upon an emission or incident caused by the operator's own activities.

In such cases Member States shall take the appropriate measures to enable the operator to recover the costs incurred.

4. The Member States may allow the operator not to bear the cost of remedial actions taken pursuant to this Directive where he demonstrates that he was not at fault or negligent and that the environmental damage was caused by:

(a) an emission or event expressly authorised by, and fully in accordance with the conditions of, an authorisation conferred by or given under applicable national laws and regulations which implement those legislative measures adopted by the Community specified in Annex III, as applied at the date of the emission or event;

(b) an emission or activity or any manner of using a product in the course of an activity which the operator demonstrates was not considered likely to cause environmental damage according to the state of scientific and technical knowledge at the time when the emission was released or the activity took place.

5. Measures taken by the competent authority in pursuance of Article 5(3) and (4) and Article 6(2) and (3) shall be without prejudice to the liability of the relevant operator under this Directive and without prejudice to Articles 87 and 88 of the Treaty.

Article 9

Cost allocation in cases of multiple party causation

This Directive is without prejudice to any provisions of national regulations concerning cost allocation in cases of multiple party causation especially concerning the apportionment of liability between the producer and the user of a product.

Article 10

Limitation period for recovery of costs

The competent authority shall be entitled to initiate cost recovery proceedings against the operator, or if appropriate, a third party who has caused the damage or the imminent threat of damage in relation to any measures taken in pursuance of this Directive within five years from the date on which those measures have been completed or the liable operator, or third party, has been identified, whichever is the later.

Article 11

Competent authority

1. Member States shall designate the competent authority(ies) responsible for fulfilling the duties provided for in this Directive.

2. The duty to establish which operator has caused the damage or the imminent threat of damage, to assess the significance of the damage and to determine which remedial measures should be taken with reference to Annex II shall rest with the competent authority. To that effect, the competent authority shall be entitled to require the relevant operator to carry out his own assessment and to supply any information and data necessary.

3. Member States shall ensure that the competent authority may empower or require third parties to carry out the necessary preventive or remedial measures.

4. Any decision taken pursuant to this Directive which imposes preventive or remedial measures shall state the exact grounds on which it is based. Such decision shall be notified forthwith to the operator concerned, who shall at the same time be informed of the legal remedies available to him under the laws in force in the Member State concerned and of the time-limits to which such remedies are subject.

Article 12

Request for action

1. Natural or legal persons:
(a) affected or likely to be affected by environmental damage or
(b) having a sufficient interest in environmental decision making relating to the damage or, alternatively,
(c) alleging the impairment of a right, where administrative procedural law of a Member State requires this as a precondition,

shall be entitled to submit to the competent authority any observations relating to instances of environmental damage or an imminent threat of such damage of which they are aware and shall be entitled to request the competent authority to take action under this Directive.

What constitutes a "sufficient interest" and "impairment of a right" shall be determined by the Member States.

To this end, the interest of any non-governmental organisation promoting environmental protection and meeting any requirements under national law shall be deemed sufficient for the purpose of subparagraph (b). Such organisations shall also be deemed to have rights capable of being impaired for the purpose of subparagraph (c).

2. The request for action shall be accompanied by the relevant information and data supporting the observations submitted in relation to the environmental damage in question.

3. Where the request for action and the accompanying observations show in a plausible manner that environmental damage exists, the competent authority shall consider any such observations and requests for action. In such circumstances the competent authority shall give the relevant operator an opportunity to make his views known with respect to the request for action and the accompanying observations.

4. The competent authority shall, as soon as possible and in any case in accordance with the relevant provisions of national law, inform the persons referred to in paragraph 1, which submitted observations to the authority, of its decision to accede to or refuse the request for action and shall provide the reasons for it.

5. Member States may decide not to apply paragraphs 1 and 4 to cases of imminent threat of damage.

Article 13

Review procedures

1. The persons referred to in Article 12(1) shall have access to a court or other independent and impartial public body competent to review the procedural and substantive legality of the decisions, acts or failure to act of the competent authority under this Directive.

2. This Directive shall be without prejudice to any provisions of national law which regulate access to justice and those which require that administrative review procedures be exhausted prior to recourse to judicial proceedings.

Article 14

Financial security

1. Member States shall take measures to encourage the development of financial security instruments and markets by the appropriate economic and financial operators, including financial mechanisms in case of insolvency, with the aim of enabling operators to use financial guarantees to cover their responsibilities under this Directive.

2. The Commission, before 30 April 2010 shall present a report on the effectiveness of the Directive in terms of actual remediation of environmental damages, on the availability

at reasonable costs and on conditions of insurance and other types of financial security for the activities covered by Annex III. The report shall also consider in relation to financial security the following aspects: a gradual approach, a ceiling for the financial guarantee and the exclusion of low-risk activities. In the light of that report, and of an extended impact assessment, including a cost-benefit analysis, the Commission shall, if appropriate, submit proposals for a system of harmonised mandatory financial security.

Article 15

Cooperation between Member States

1. Where environmental damage affects or is likely to affect several Member States, those Member States shall cooperate, including through the appropriate exchange of information, with a view to ensuring that preventive action and, where necessary, remedial action is taken in respect of any such environmental damage.

2. Where environmental damage has occurred, the Member State in whose territory the damage originates shall provide sufficient information to the potentially affected Member States.

3. Where a Member State identifies damage within its borders which has not been caused within them it may report the issue to the Commission and any other Member State concerned; it may make recommendations for the adoption of preventive or remedial measures and it may seek, in accordance with this Directive, to recover the costs it has incurred in relation to the adoption of preventive or remedial measures.

Article 16

Relationship with national law

1. This Directive shall not prevent Member States from maintaining or adopting more stringent provisions in relation to the prevention and remedying of environmental damage, including the identification of additional activities to be subject to the prevention and remediation requirements of this Directive and the identification of additional responsible parties.

2. This Directive shall not prevent Member States from adopting appropriate measures, such as the prohibition of double recovery of costs, in relation to situations where double recovery could occur as a result of concurrent action by a competent authority under this Directive and by a person whose property is affected by environmental damage.

Article 17

Temporal application

This Directive shall not apply to:

- damage caused by an emission, event or incident that took place before the date referred to in Article 19(1),
- damage caused by an emission, event or incident which takes place subsequent to the date referred to in Article 19(1) when it derives from a specific activity that took place and finished before the said date,
- damage, if more than 30 years have passed since the emission, event or incident, resulting in the damage, occurred.

Article 18

Reports and review

1. Member States shall report to the Commission on the experience gained in the application of this Directive by 30 April 2013 at the latest. The reports shall include the information and data set out in Annex VI.

2. On that basis, the Commission shall submit a report to the European Parliament and to the Council before 30 April 2014, which shall include any appropriate proposals for amendment.

3. The report, referred to in paragraph 2, shall include a review of:

(a) the application of:

— Article 4(2) and (4) in relation to the exclusion of pollution covered by the international instruments listed in Annexes IV and V from the scope of this Directive, and

— Article 4(3) in relation to the right of an operator to limit his liability in accordance with the international conventions referred to in Article 4(3).

The Commission shall take into account experience gained within the relevant international for a, such as the IMO and Euratom and the relevant international agreements, as well as the extent to which these instruments have entered into force and/or have been implemented by Member States and/or have been modified, taking account of all relevant instances of environmental damage resulting from such activities and the remedial action taken and the differences between the liability levels in Member States, and considering the relationship between shipowners' liability and oil receivers' contributions, having due regard to any relevant study undertaken by the International Oil Pollution Compensation Funds.

(b) the application of this Directive to environmental damage caused by genetically modified organisms (GMOs), particularly in the light of experience gained within relevant international for a and Conventions, such as the Convention on Biological Diversity and the Cartagena Protocol on Biosafety, as well as the results of any incidents of environmental damage caused by GMOs;

(c) the application of this Directive in relation to protected species and natural habitats;

(d) the instruments that may be eligible for incorporation into Annexes III, IV and V.

Article 19

Implementation

1. Member States shall bring into force the laws, regulations and administrative provisions necessary to comply with this Directive by 30 April 2007. They shall forthwith inform the Commission thereof.

When Member States adopt those measures, they shall contain a reference to this Directive or shall be accompanied by such a reference on the occasion of their official publication. The methods of making such reference shall be laid down by Member States.

2. Member States shall communicate to the Commission the text of the main provisions of national law which they adopt in the field covered by this Directive together with a table showing how the provisions of this Directive correspond to the national provisions adopted.

Article 20

Entry into force

This Directive shall enter into force on the day of its publication in the Official Journal of the European Union.

Article 21

Addressees

This Directive is addressed to the Member States.

ANNEX I
CRITERIA REFERRED TO IN ARTICLE 2(1)(A)

The significance of any damage that has adverse effects on reaching or maintaining the favourable conservation status of habitats or species has to be assessed by reference to the conservation status at the time of the damage, the services provided by the amenities they produce and their capacity for natural regeneration. Significant adverse changes to the baseline condition should be determined by means of measurable data such as:

— the number of individuals, their density or the area covered,
— the role of the particular individuals or of the damaged area in relation to the species or to the habitat conservation, the rarity of the species or habitat (assessed at local, regional and higher level including at Community level),
— the species' capacity for propagation (according to the dynamics specific to that species or to that population), its viability or the habitat's capacity for natural regeneration (according to the dynamics specific to its characteristic species or to their populations),
— the species' or habitat's capacity, after damage has occurred, to recover within a short time, without any intervention other than increased protection measures, to a condition which leads, solely by virtue of the dynamics of the species or habitat, to a condition deemed equivalent or superior to the baseline condition.

Damage with a proven effect on human health must be classified as significant damage.

The following does not have to be classified as significant damage:

— negative variations that are smaller than natural fluctuations regarded as normal for the species or habitat in question,
— negative variations due to natural causes or resulting from intervention relating to the normal management of sites, as defined in habitat records or target documents or as carried on previously by owners or operators,
— damage to species or habitats for which it is established that they will recover, within a short time and without intervention, either to the baseline condition or to a condition which leads, solely by virtue of the dynamics of the species or habitat, to a condition deemed equivalent or superior to the baseline condition.

ANNEX II
REMEDYING OF ENVIRONMENTAL DAMAGE

This Annex sets out a common framework to be followed in order to choose the most appropriate measures to ensure the remedying of environmental damage.

1. REMEDIATION OF DAMAGE TO WATER OR PROTECTED SPECIES OR NATURAL HABITATS

Remedying of environmental damage, in relation to water or protected species or natural habitats, is achieved through the restoration of the environment to its baseline condition by way of primary, complementary and compensatory remediation, where:

(a) "Primary" remediation is any remedial measure which returns the damaged natural resources and/or impaired services to, or towards, baseline condition;
(b) "Complementary" remediation is any remedial measure taken in relation to natural resources and/or services to compensate for the fact that primary remediation does not result in fully restoring the damaged natural resources and/or services;
(c) "Compensatory" remediation is any action taken to compensate for interim losses of natural resources and/or services that occur from the date of damage occurring until primary remediation has achieved its full effect;
(d) "interim losses" means losses which result from the fact that the damaged natural resources and/or services are not able to perform their ecological functions or provide services to other natural resources or to the public until the primary or complementary

measures have taken effect. It does not consist of financial compensation to members of the public.

Where primary remediation does not result in the restoration of the environment to its baseline condition, then complementary remediation will be undertaken. In addition, compensatory remediation will be undertaken to compensate for the interim losses.

Remedying of environmental damage, in terms of damage to water or protected species or natural habitats, also implies that any significant risk of human health being adversely affected be removed.

1.1. Remediation objectives

Purpose of primary remediation

1.1.1. The purpose of primary remediation is to restore the damaged natural resources and/or services to, or towards, baseline condition.

Purpose of complementary remediation

1.1.2. Where the damaged natural resources and/or services do not return to their baseline condition, then complementary remediation will be undertaken. The purpose of complementary remediation is to provide a similar level of natural resources and/or services, including, as appropriate, at an alternative site, as would have been provided if the damaged site had been returned to its baseline condition. Where possible and appropriate the alternative site should be geographically linked to the damaged site, taking into account the interests of the affected population.

Purpose of compensatory remediation

1.1.3. Compensatory remediation shall be undertaken to compensate for the interim loss of natural resources and services pending recovery. This compensation consists of additional improvements to protected natural habitats and species or water at either the damaged site or at an alternative site. It does not consist of financial compensation to members of the public.

1.2. Identification of remedial measures

Identification of primary remedial measures

1.2.1. Options comprised of actions to directly restore the natural resources and services towards baseline condition on an accelerated time frame, or through natural recovery, shall be considered.

Identification of complementary and compensatory remedial measures

1.2.2. When determining the scale of complementary and compensatory remedial measures, the use of resource-to-resource or service-to-service equivalence approaches shall be considered first. Under these approaches, actions that provide natural resources and/or services of the same type, quality and quantity as those damaged shall be considered first. Where this is not possible, then alternative natural resources and/or services shall be provided. For example, a reduction in quality could be offset by an increase in the quantity of remedial measures.

1.2.3. If it is not possible to use the first choice resource-to-resource or service-to-service equivalence approaches, then alternative valuation techniques shall be used. The competent authority may prescribe the method, for example monetary valuation, to determine the extent of the necessary complementary and compensatory remedial measures. If valuation of the lost resources and/or services is practicable, but valuation of the replacement natural resources and/or services cannot be performed within a reasonable time-frame or at a reasonable cost, then the competent authority may choose remedial measures whose cost is equivalent to the estimated monetary value of the lost natural resources and/or services.

The complementary and compensatory remedial measures should be so designed that they provide for additional natural resources and/or services to reflect time preferences and the time profile of the remedial measures. For example, the longer the period of time before the baseline condition is reached, the greater the amount of compensatory remedial measures that will be undertaken (other things being equal).

1.3. Choice of the remedial options

1.3.1. The reasonable remedial options should be evaluated, using best available technologies, based on the following criteria:
— The effect of each option on public health and safety,
— The cost of implementing the option,
— The likelihood of success of each option,
— The extent to which each option will prevent future damage, and avoid collateral damage as a result of implementing the option,
— The extent to which each option benefits to each component of the natural resource and/or service,
— The extent to which each option takes account of relevant social, economic and cultural concerns and other relevant factors specific to the locality,
— The length of time it will take for the restoration of the environmental damage to be effective,
— The extent to which each option achieves the restoration of site of the environmental damage,
— The geographical linkage to the damaged site.

1.3.2. When evaluating the different identified remedial options, primary remedial measures that do not fully restore the damaged water or protected species or natural habitat to baseline or that restore it more slowly can be chosen. This decision can be taken only if the natural resources and/or services foregone at the primary site as a result of the decision are compensated for by increasing complementary or compensatory actions to provide a similar level of natural resources and/or services as were foregone. This will be the case, for example, when the equivalent natural resources and/or services could be provided elsewhere at a lower cost. These additional remedial measures shall be determined in accordance with the rules set out in section 1.2.2.

1.3.3. Notwithstanding the rules set out in section 1.3.2. and in accordance with Article 7(3), the competent authority is entitled to decide that no further remedial measures should be taken if:
(a) the remedial measures already taken secure that there is no longer any significant risk of adversely affecting human health, water or protected species and natural habitats, and
(b) the cost of the remedial measures that should be taken to reach baseline condition or similar level would be disproportionate to the environmental benefits to be obtained.

2. REMEDIATION OF LAND DAMAGE

The necessary measures shall be taken to ensure, as a minimum, that the relevant contaminants are removed, controlled, contained or diminished so that the contaminated land, taking account of its current use or approved future use at the time of the damage, no longer poses any significant risk of adversely affecting human health. The presence of such risks shall be assessed through risk-assessment procedures taking into account the characteristic and function of the soil, the type and concentration of the harmful substances, preparations, organisms or micro-organisms, their risk and the possibility of their dispersion. Use shall be ascertained on the basis of the land use regulations, or other relevant regulations, in force, if any, when the damage occurred.

If the use of the land is changed, all necessary measures shall be taken to prevent any adverse effects on human health.

If land use regulations, or other relevant regulations, are lacking, the nature of the relevant area where the damage occurred, taking into account its expected development, shall determine the use of the specific area.

A natural recovery option, that is to say an option in which no direct human intervention in the recovery process would be taken, shall be considered.

ANNEX III
ACTIVITIES REFERRED TO IN ARTICLE 3(1)

1. The operation of installations subject to permit in pursuance of Council Directive 96/61/EC of 24 September 1996 concerning integrated pollution prevention and control. That means all activities listed in Annex I of Directive 96/61/EC with the exception of installations or parts of installations used for research, development and testing of new products and processes.

2. Waste management operations, including the collection, transport, recovery and disposal of waste and hazardous waste, including the supervision of such operations and after-care of disposal sites, subject to permit or registration in pursuance of Council Directive 75/442/EEC of 15 July 1975 on waste and Council Directive 91/689/EEC of 12 December 1991 on hazardous waste.

Those operations include, inter alia, the operation of landfill sites under Council Directive 1999/31/EC of 26 April 1999 on the landfill of waste and the operation of incineration plants under Directive 2000/76/EC of the European Parliament and of the Council of 4 December 2000 on the incineration of waste.

For the purpose of this Directive, Member States may decide that those operations shall not include the spreading of sewage sludge from urban waste water treatment plants, treated to an approved standard, for agricultural purposes.

3. All discharges into the inland surface water, which require prior authorisation in pursuance of Council Directive 76/464/EEC of 4 May 1976 on pollution caused by certain dangerous substances, discharged into the aquatic environment of the Community.

4. All discharges of substances into groundwater which require prior authorisation in pursuance of Council Directive 80/68/EEC of 17 December 1979 on the protection of groundwater against pollution caused by certain dangerous substances.

5. The discharge or injection of pollutants into surface water or groundwater which require a permit, authorisation or registration in pursuance of Directive 2000/60/EC.

6. Water abstraction and impoundment of water subject to prior authorisation in pursuance of Directive 2000/60/EC.

7. Manufacture, use, storage, processing, filling, release into the environment and onsite transport of

(a) dangerous substances as defined in Article 2(2) of Council Directive 67/548/EEC of 27 June 1967 on the approximation of the laws, regulations and administrative provisions of the Member States relating to the classification, packaging and labelling of dangerous substances;

(b) dangerous preparations as defined in Article 2(2) of Directive 1999/45/EC of the European Parliament and of the Council of 31 May 1999 concerning the approximation of the laws, regulations and administrative provisions of the Member States relating to the classification, packaging and labelling of dangerous preparations;

(c) plant protection products as defined in Article2(1) of Council Directive 91/414/EEC of 15 July 1991 concerning the placing of plant protection products on the market;

(d) biocidal products as defined in Article 2(1)(a) of Directive 98/8/EC of the European Parliament and of the Council of 16 February 1998 concerning the placing of biocidal products on the market.

8. Transport by road, rail, inland waterways, sea or air of dangerous goods or polluting goods as defined either in Annex A to Council Directive 94/55/EC of 21 November 1994 on the approximation of the laws of the Member States with regard to the transport of dangerous goods by road or in the Annex to Council Directive 96/49/EC of 23 July 1996 on the approximation of the laws of the Member States with regard to the transport of dangerous goods by rail or as defined in Council Directive 93/75/EEC of 13 September 1993 concerning minimum requirements for vessels bound for or leaving Community ports and carrying dangerous or polluting goods.

9. The operation of installations subject to authorisation in pursuance of Council Directive 84/360/EEC of 28 June 1984 on the combating of air pollution from industrial plants in relation to the release into air of any of the polluting substances covered by the aforementioned Directive.

10. Any contained use, including transport, involving genetically modified micro-organisms as defined by Council Directive 90/219/EEC of 23 April 1990 on the contained use of genetically modified micro-organisms.

11. Any deliberate release into the environment, transport and placing on the market of genetically modified organisms as defined by Directive 2001/18/EC of the European Parliament and of the Council.

12. Transboundary shipment of waste within, into or out of the European Union, requiring an authorisation or prohibited in the meaning of Council Regulation (EEC) No 259/93 of 1 February 1993 on the supervision and control of shipments of waste within, into and out of the European Community.

[13. The management of extractive waste pursuant to Directive 2006/21/EC of the European Parliament and of the Council of 15 March 2006 on the management of waste from extractive industries.][1]

[14. The operation of storage sites pursuant to Directive 2009/31/EC of the European Parliament and of the Council of 23 April 2009 on the geological storage of carbon dioxide.][2]

Amendments

1 Inserted by Directive 2006/21/EC of the European Parliament and of the Council of 15 March 2006 on the management of waste from extractive industries and amending Directive 2004/35/EC – Statement by the European Parliament, the Council and the Commission, Article 15.

2 Inserted by Directive 2009/31/EC of the European Parliament and of the Council of 23 April 2009 on the geological storage of carbon dioxide and amending Council Directive 85/337/EEC, European Parliament and Council Directives 2000/60/EC, 2001/80/EC, 2004/35/EC, 2006/12/EC, 2008/1/EC and Regulation (EC) No 1013/2006, Article 34.

ANNEX IV
INTERNATIONAL CONVENTIONS REFERRED TO IN ARTICLE 4(2)

(a) the International Convention of 27 November 1992 on Civil Liability for Oil Pollution Damage;

(b) the International Convention of 27 November 1992 on the Establishment of an International Fund for Compensation for Oil Pollution Damage;

(c) the International Convention of 23 March 2001 on Civil Liability for Bunker Oil Pollution Damage;

(d) the International Convention of 3 May 1996 on Liability and Compensation for Damage in Connection with the Carriage of Hazardous and Noxious Substances by Sea;

(e) the Convention of 10 October 1989 on Civil Liability for Damage Caused during Carriage of Dangerous Goods by Road, Rail and Inland Navigation Vessels.

ANNEX V
INTERNATIONAL INSTRUMENTS REFERRED TO IN ARTICLE 4(4)

(a) the Paris Convention of 29 July 1960 on Third Party Liability in the Field of Nuclear Energy and the Brussels Supplementary Convention of 31 January 1963;
(b) the Vienna Convention of 21 May 1963 on Civil Liability for Nuclear Damage;
(c) the Convention of 12 September 1997 on Supplementary Compensation for Nuclear Damage;
(d) the Joint Protocol of 21 September 1988 relating to the Application of the Vienna Convention and the Paris Convention;
(e) the Brussels Convention of 17 December 1971 relating to Civil Liability in the Field of Maritime Carriage of Nuclear Material.

ANNEX VI
INFORMATION AND DATA REFERRED TO IN ARTICLE 18(1)

The reports referred to in Article 18(1) shall include a list of instances of environmental damage and instances of liability under this Directive, with the following information and data for each instance:

1. Type of environmental damage, date of occurrence and/or discovery of the damage and date on which proceedings were initiated under this Directive.
2. Activity classification code of the liable legal person(s).
3. Whether there has been resort to judicial review proceedings either by liable parties or qualified entities. (The type of claimants and the outcome of proceedings shall be specified.)
4. Outcome of the remediation process.
5. Date of closure of proceedings.

Member States may include in their reports any other information and data they deem useful to allow a proper assessment of the functioning of this Directive, for example:

1. Costs incurred with remediation and prevention measures, as defined in this Directive:
   — paid for directly by liable parties, when this information is available;
   — recovered ex post facto from liable parties;
   — unrecovered from liable parties. (Reasons for non-recovery should be specified.)
2. Results of the actions to promote and the implementation of the financial security instruments used in accordance with this Directive.
3. An assessment of the additional administrative costs incurred annually by the public administration in setting up and operating the administrative structures needed to implement and enforce this Directive.

REGULATION 850/2004/EC OF THE EUROPEAN PARLIAMENT AND OF THE COUNCIL

of 29 April 2004

ON PERSISTENT ORGANIC POLLUTANTS AND AMENDING DIRECTIVE 79/117/EEC

THE EUROPEAN PARLIAMENT AND THE COUNCIL OF THE EUROPEAN UNION,

Having regard to the Treaty establishing the European Community, and in particular Article 175(1) thereof,

Having regard to the proposal from the Commission

Having regard to the Opinion of the European Economic and Social Committee

After consulting the Committee of the Regions, acting in accordance with the procedure laid down in Article 251 of the Treaty

Whereas:

(1) This Regulation primarily concerns environmental protection and the protection of human health. The legal basis is therefore Article 175(1) of the Treaty.

(2) The Community is seriously concerned by the continuous release of persistent organic pollutants into the environment. These chemical substances are transported across international boundaries far from their sources and they persist in the environment, bioaccumulate through the food web, and pose a risk to human health and the environment. Further measures need therefore to be taken in order to protect human health and the environment against these pollutants.

(3) In view of its responsibilities for the protection of the environment, the Community signed on 24 June 1998 the Protocol to the 1979 Convention on Long-Range Transboundary Air Pollution on Persistent Organic Pollutants, hereinafter "the Protocol", and on 22 May 2001 the Stockholm Convention on Persistent Organic Pollutants, hereinafter "the Convention".

(4) While legislation at Community level relating to persistent organic pollutants has been put in place, its main deficiencies are that there is an absence of, or incomplete legislation on, prohibition of the production and use of any of the currently listed chemicals, that there is no framework to subject additional persistent organic pollutant substances to prohibitions, restrictions or elimination, nor any framework to prevent the production and use of new substances that exhibit persistent organic pollutant characteristics. No emission reduction targets, as such, have been set at Community level and the current release inventories do not cover all sources of persistent organic pollutants.

(5) In order to ensure coherent and effective implementation of the Community's obligations under the Protocol and the Convention, it is necessary to establish a common legal framework, within which to take measures designed in particular to eliminate the production, placing on the market and use of intentionally produced persistent organic pollutants. Furthermore, persistent organic pollutants' characteristics should be taken into consideration in the framework of the relevant Community assessment and authorisation schemes.

(6) Coordination and coherence should be ensured when implementing at Community level the provisions of the Rotterdam, Stockholm and Basel Conventions and when participating in the development of the Strategic Approach to International Chemicals Management (SAICM) within the United Nations framework.

(7) Moreover, considering that the provisions of this Regulation are underpinned by the precautionary principle as set forth in the Treaty, and mindful of Principle 15 of the Rio

Declaration on Environment and Development and in view of the aim of elimination, where feasible, of the release of persistent organic pollutants into the environment, it is appropriate in certain cases to provide for control measures stricter than those under the Protocol and the Convention.

(8) In the future, the proposed REACH Regulation could be an appropriate instrument by which to implement the necessary control measures on production, placing on the market and use of the listed substances and the control measures on existing and new chemicals and pesticides exhibiting persistent organic pollutants' characteristics. However, without prejudice to the future REACH Regulation and since it is important to implement these control measures on the listed substances of the Protocol and the Convention as soon as possible, this Regulation should for now implement those measures.

(9) In the Community, the placing on the market and use of most of the persistent organic pollutants listed in the Protocol or the Convention has already been phased out as a result of the prohibitions laid down in Council Directive 79/117/EEC of 21 December 1978 prohibiting the placing on the market and use of plant protection products containing certain active substances and Council Directive 76/769/EEC of 27 July 1976 on the approximation of the laws, regulations and administrative provisions of the Member States relating to restrictions on the marketing and use of certain dangerous substances and preparations. However, in order to fulfil the Community's obligations under the Protocol and the Convention and to minimise the release of persistent organic pollutants, it is necessary and appropriate also to prohibit the production of those substances and to restrict exemptions to a minimum so that exemptions only apply where a substance fulfils an essential function in a specific application.

(10) Exports of substances covered by the Convention and exports of lindane are regulated by Regulation (EC) No 304/2003 of the European Parliament and of the Council of 28 January 2003 concerning the export and import of dangerous chemicals.

(11) The production and use of hexachlorocyclohexane (HCH), including lindane, is subject to restrictions under the Protocol but not totally prohibited. That substance is still used in some Member States and therefore it is not possible to prohibit immediately all existing uses. However, in view of the harmful properties of HCH and the possible risks related to its release into the environment, its production and uses should be confined to a minimum and ultimately phased out by the end of 2007 at the latest.

(12) Obsolete or carelessly managed stockpiles of persistent organic pollutants may seriously endanger the environment and human health through, for instance, contamination of soil and ground water. It is appropriate, therefore, to adopt provisions that go beyond the provisions laid down in the Convention. Stockpiles of prohibited substances should be treated as waste, while stockpiles of substances the production or use of which is still allowed should be notified to the authorities and properly supervised. In particular, existing stockpiles which consist of or contain banned persistent organic pollutants should be managed as waste as soon as possible. If other substances are banned in the future, their stocks should also be destroyed without delay and no new stockpiles should be built up. In view of the particular problems of certain new Member States, adequate financial and technical assistance should be provided through existing Community financial instruments, such as the Cohesion and Structural Funds.

(13) In line with the Communication from the Commission on the Community Strategy for Dioxins, Furans and Polychlorinated Biphenyls (PCBs), and with the Protocol and the Convention, releases of persistent organic pollutants which are unintentional by-products of industrial processes should be identified and reduced as soon as possible with the ultimate aim of elimination, where feasible. Appropriate national action plans, covering all sources and measures, including those provided for under existing Community legislation, should be drawn up and implemented to reduce the releases continuously and cost-effectively as soon as possible. To this end, appropriate tools should be developed in the framework of the Convention.

(14) In line with that Communication, appropriate programmes and mechanisms should be established to provide adequate monitoring data on the presence of dioxins, furans and PCBs in the environment. However, it is necessary to ensure that appropriate tools are available and can be used under economically and technically viable conditions.

(15) Under the Convention, the persistent organic pollutant content in waste is to be destroyed or irreversibly transformed into substances that do not exhibit similar characteristics, unless other operations are environmentally preferable. Since current Community legislation on waste does not lay down specific rules as regards those substances, they should be laid down in this Regulation. To ensure a high level of protection, common concentration limits for the substances in waste should be established before 31 December 2005.

(16) The importance of identifying and separating waste consisting of, containing or contaminated by persistent organic pollutants at source in order to minimise the spreading of these chemicals into other waste is recognised. Council Directive 91/689/EEC of 12 December 1991 on hazardous waste established Community rules on the management of hazardous waste obliging Member States to take the necessary measures to require that establishments and undertakings which dispose of, recover, collect or transport hazardous waste do not mix different categories of hazardous waste or mix hazardous waste with non-hazardous waste.

(17) The Convention provides that each Party is to draw up a plan for the implementation of its obligations under the Convention. Member States should provide opportunities for public participation in drawing up their implementation plans. Since the Community and the Member States share competence in that regard, implementation plans should be drawn up both at national and Community level. Cooperation and an exchange of information between the Commission and the authorities of the Member States should be promoted.

(18) In accordance with the Convention and the Protocol, information on persistent organic pollutants should be provided to other Parties. The exchange of information with third countries not party to those Agreements should also be promoted.

(19) Public awareness of the hazards that persistent organic pollutants pose to the health of present and future generations as well as to the environment, particularly in developing countries, is often lacking, and wide-scale information is therefore needed to increase the level of caution and gain support for restrictions and bans. In accordance with the Convention, public awareness programmes on these substances, especially for the most vulnerable groups, as well as training of workers, scientists, educators, technical and managerial personnel should be promoted and facilitated.

(20) Upon request and within available resources, the Commission and the Member States should cooperate in providing appropriate and timely technical assistance designed especially to strengthen the capacity of developing countries and countries with economies in transition to implement the Convention. Technical assistance should include the development and implementation of suitable alternative products, methods and strategies, inter alia, to the use of DDT in disease vector control which, under the Convention, can only be used in accordance with World Health Organisation recommendations and guidelines and when locally safe, effective and affordable alternatives are not available to the country in question.

(21) There should be regular evaluation of the effectiveness of the measures taken to reduce releases of persistent organic pollutants. To that end, Member States should report regularly to the Commission, in particular as regards release inventories, notified stockpiles and the production and placing on the market of restricted substances. The Commission, in cooperation with Member States, should develop a common format for Member States' reports.

(22) The Convention and the Protocol provide that Parties thereto may propose other substances for international action and consequently additional substances may be listed under those Agreements, in which case this Regulation should be amended accordingly. Furthermore, it should be possible to modify the existing entries in Annexes to this

Regulation, inter alia for the purposes of adapting them to scientific and technical progress.

(23) When Annexes to this Regulation are amended to implement any listings of an additional, intentionally produced persistent organic pollutant in the Protocol or in the Convention, it should be included in Annex II, instead of Annex I, only in exceptional cases and when duly justified.

(24) The measures necessary for the implementation of this Regulation should be adopted in accordance with Council Decision 1999/468/EC of 28 June 1999 laying down the procedures for the exercise of implementing powers conferred on the Commission.

(25) In order to ensure transparency, impartiality and consistency at the level of enforcement activities, Member States should lay down rules on penalties applicable to infringements of the provisions of this Regulation and ensure that they are implemented. Those penalties should be effective, proportionate and dissuasive, since non-compliance can result in damage to human health and the environment. Information on infringements of the provisions of this Regulation should be made public, where appropriate.

(26) Since the objectives of this Regulation, namely to protect the environment and human health from persistent organic pollutants, cannot be sufficiently achieved by the Member States, owing to the transboundary effects of those pollutants, and can therefore be better achieved at Community level, the Community may adopt measures, in accordance with the principle of subsidiarity as set out in Article 5 of the Treaty. In accordance with the principle of proportionality, as set out in that Article, this Regulation does not go beyond what is necessary in order to achieve those objectives.

(27) In the light of the above, Directive 79/117/EEC should be amended.

HAVE ADOPTED THIS REGULATION:

Article 1

Objective and scope

1. Taking into account, in particular, the precautionary principle, the objective of this Regulation is to protect human health and the environment from persistent organic pollutants by prohibiting, phasing out as soon as possible, or restricting the production, placing on the market and use of substances subject to the Stockholm Convention on Persistent Organic Pollutants, hereinafter "the Convention", or the 1998 Protocol to the 1979 Convention on Long-Range Transboundary Air Pollution on Persistent Organic Pollutants, hereinafter "the Protocol", and by minimising, with a view to eliminating where feasible as soon as possible, releases of such substances, and by establishing provisions regarding waste consisting of, containing or contaminated by any of these substances.

2. Articles 3 and 4 shall not apply to waste consisting of, containing or contaminated by any substance listed in Annexes I or II.

Article 2

Definitions

For the purposes of this Regulation:

(a) "placing on the market" means supplying or making available to third persons against payment or free of charge. Imports into the customs territory of the Community shall also be deemed to be placed on the market;

(b) "article" means an object composed of one or more substances and/or preparations which during production is given a specific shape, surface or design determining its end use function to a greater extent than its chemical composition does;

(c) "substance" is as defined in Article 2 of Council Directive 67/548/EEC;

(d) "preparation" is as defined in Article 2 of Directive 67/548/EEC;

(e) "waste" is as defined in Article 1(a) of Council Directive 75/442/EEC;
(f) "disposal" is as defined in Article 1(e) of Directive 75/442/EEC;
(g) "recovery" is as defined in Article 1(f) of Directive 75/442/EEC.

Article 3

Control of production, placing on the market and use

1. The production, placing on the market and use of substances listed in Annex I, whether on their own, in preparations or as constituents of articles, shall be prohibited.

2. The production, placing on the market and use of substances listed in Annex II, whether on their own, in preparations or as constituents of articles, shall be restricted in accordance with the conditions set out in that Annex.

3. Member States and the Commission shall, within the assessment and authorisation schemes for existing and new chemicals and pesticides under the relevant Community legislation, take into consideration the criteria set out in paragraph 1 of Annex D to the Convention and take appropriate measures to control existing chemicals and pesticides and prevent the production, placing on the market and use of new chemicals and pesticides, which exhibit characteristics of persistent organic pollutants.

Article 4

Exemptions from control measures

1. Article 3 shall not apply in the case of:
(a) a substance used for laboratory-scale research or as a reference standard;
(b) a substance occurring as an unintentional trace contaminant in substances, preparations or articles.

2. Article 3 shall not apply in respect of substances occurring as a constituent of articles produced before or on the date of entry into force of this Regulation until six months after the date of its entry into force. Article 3 shall not apply in the case of a substance occurring as a constituent of articles already in use before or on the date of entry into force of this Regulation. However, immediately upon becoming aware of articles referred to in the first and second subparagraph, a Member State shall inform the Commission accordingly. Whenever the Commission is so informed or otherwise learns of such articles, it shall, where appropriate, notify the Secretariat of the Convention accordingly without further delay.

3. Where a substance is listed in Part A of Annex I or in Part A of Annex II, a Member State wishing to permit, until the deadline specified in the relevant Annex, the production and use of that substance as a closed-system site-limited intermediate shall notify accordingly the Secretariat of the Convention.

However, such notification may be made only if the following conditions are satisfied:
(a) an annotation has been entered in the relevant Annex expressly to the effect that such production and use of that substance may be permitted;
(b) the manufacturing process will transform the substance into one or more other substances that do not exhibit the characteristics of a persistent organic pollutant;
(c) it is not expected that either humans or the environment will be exposed to any significant quantities of the substance during its production and use, as shown through assessment of that closed system in accordance with Commission Directive 2001/59/EC

The notification shall be communicated also to the other Member States and to the Commission and shall give details of actual or estimated total production and use of the substance concerned and the nature of the closed-system site-limited process, specifying the amount of any non-transformed and unintentional trace contamination by any persistent organic pollutant starting material in the final product.

The deadlines referred to in the first subparagraph may be amended in cases where, following a repeat notification from the Member State concerned to the Secretariat of the Convention, express or tacit consent is issued under the Convention for the continued production and use of the substance for another period.

Article 5

Stockpiles

1. The holder of a stockpile, which consists of or contains any substance listed in Annex I or Annex II, for which no use is permitted, shall manage that stockpile as waste and in accordance with Article 7.

2. The holder of a stockpile greater than 50 kg, consisting of or containing any substance listed in Annex I or Annex II, and the use of which is permitted shall provide the competent authority of the Member State in which the stockpile is established with information concerning the nature and size of that stockpile. Such information shall be provided within 12 months of the entry into force of this Regulation and of amendments to Annexes I or II and annually thereafter until the deadline specified in Annex I or II for restricted use. The holder shall manage the stockpile in a safe, efficient and environmentally sound manner.

3. Member States shall monitor the use and management of notified stockpiles.

Article 6

Release reduction, minimisation and elimination

1. Within two years of the date of entry into force of this Regulation, Member States shall draw up and maintain release inventories for the substances listed in Annex III into air, water and land in accordance with their obligations under the Convention and the Protocol.

2. A Member State shall communicate its action plan on measures to identify, characterise and minimise with a view to eliminating where feasible as soon as possible the total releases developed in accordance with its obligations under the Convention, to both the Commission and the other Member States as part of its national implementation plan, pursuant to Article 8. The action plan shall include measures to promote the development and, where it deems appropriate, shall require the use of substitute or modified materials, products and processes to prevent the formation and release of the substances listed in Annex III.

3. Member States shall, when considering proposals to construct new facilities or significantly to modify existing facilities using processes that release chemicals listed in Annex III, without prejudice to Council Directive 1996/61/EC, give priority consideration to alternative processes, techniques or practices that have similar usefulness but which avoid the formation and release of substances listed in Annex III.

Article 7

Waste management

1. Producers and holders of waste shall undertake all reasonable efforts to avoid, where feasible, contamination of this waste with substances listed in Annex IV.

2. Notwithstanding Directive 96/59/EC, waste consisting of, containing or contaminated by any substance listed in Annex IV shall be disposed of or recovered, without undue delay and in accordance with Annex V, part 1 in such a way as to ensure that the persistent organic pollutant content is destroyed or irreversibly transformed so that the remaining waste and releases do not exhibit the characteristics of persistent organic pollutants. In carrying out such a disposal or recovery, any substance listed in Annex IV may be isolated from the waste, provided that this substance is subsequently disposed of in accordance with the first subparagraph.

3. Disposal or recovery operations that may lead to recovery, recycling, reclamation or re-use of the substances listed in Annex IV shall be prohibited.

4. By way of derogation from paragraph 2:

[(a) waste containing or contaminated by any substance listed in Annex IV may be otherwise disposed of or recovered in accordance with the relevant Community legislation, provided that the content of the listed substances in the waste is below the concentration limits to be specified in Annex IV. Those measures, designed to amend non-essential elements of this Regulation, shall be adopted in accordance with the regulatory procedure with scrutiny referred to in Article 17(3). Until such time as concentration limits are established in accordance with such procedure, the competent authority of a Member State may adopt or apply concentration limits or specific technical requirements in respect of the disposal or recovery of waste under this point;][1]

(b) a Member State or the competent authority designated by that Member State may, in exceptional cases, allow wastes listed in Annex V, part 2 containing or contaminated by any substance listed in Annex IV up to concentration limits to be specified in Annex V, part 2, to be otherwise dealt with in accordance with a method listed in Annex V, part 2 provided that:
   (i) the holder concerned has demonstrated to the satisfaction of the competent authority of the Member State concerned that decontamination of the waste in relation to substances listed in Annex IV was not feasible, and that destruction or irreversible transformation of the persistent organic pollutant content, performed in accordance with best environmental practice or best available techniques, does not represent the environmentally preferable option and the competent authority has subsequently authorised the alternative operation;
   (ii) this operation is in accordance with the relevant Community legislation and the conditions laid down in relevant additional measures referred to in paragraph 6; and
   (iii) the Member State concerned has informed the other Member States and the Commission of its authorisation and the justification for it.

5. [Concentration limits in Annex V, part 2 shall be established by the Commission for the purposes of paragraph 4(b) of this Article. Those measures, designed to amend non-essential elements of this Regulation, shall be adopted in accordance with the regulatory procedure with scrutiny referred to in Article 17(3).][1]

Until such time as these concentration limits are established:

(a) the competent authority may adopt or apply concentration limits or specific technical requirements in respect of waste being dealt with under paragraph 4(b);

(b) where waste is being dealt with under paragraph 4(b), the holders concerned shall provide information on the persistent organic pollutant content of the waste to the competent authority.

6. The Commission may, where appropriate, and taking into consideration technical developments and relevant international guidelines and decisions and any authorisations granted by a Member State, or the competent authority designated by that Member State in accordance with paragraph 4 and Annex V, adopt additional measures relating to the implementation of this Article. The Commission shall define a format for the submission of the information by Member States in accordance with paragraph 4(b)(iii). Such measures shall be decided in accordance with the procedure laid down in Article 17(2).

7. The Commission shall, before 31 December 2009, review the derogations in paragraph 4 in the light of international and technical developments, in particular with regard to their environmental preferability.

Amendment

1 Inserted by Regulation (EC) No 219/2009 of the European Parliament and of the Council of 11 March 2009 adapting a number of instruments subject to the procedure referred to in Article 251 of the Treaty to Council Decision 1999/468/EC with regard to the regulatory procedure with scrutiny, Article 1, Annex, para 3.7.1.

Article 8

Implementation plans

1. When preparing their national implementation plans, Member States shall, in accordance with their national procedures, give the public early and effective opportunities to participate in this process.

2. As soon as a Member State has adopted its national implementation plan in accordance with its obligations under the Convention, it shall communicate it both to the Commission and to the other Member States.

3. When preparing their implementation plans, the Commission and the Member States shall exchange information on the content, as appropriate.

4. The Commission shall, within two years of the entry into force of this Regulation, draw up a plan for the implementation of Community obligations under the Convention. As soon as the Commission has adopted the Community implementation plan, it shall communicate it to the Member States. The Commission shall review and update the Community implementation plan, as appropriate.

Article 9

Monitoring

The Commission and the Member States shall establish, in close cooperation, appropriate programmes and mechanisms, consistent with the state of the art, for the regular provision of comparable monitoring data on the presence of dioxins, furans and PCBs as identified in Annex III in the environment. When establishing such programmes and mechanisms, due account shall be taken of developments under the Protocol and the Convention.

Article 10

Information exchange

1. The Commission and the Member States shall facilitate and undertake the exchange within the Community and with third countries of information relevant to the reduction, minimisation or elimination, where feasible, of the production, use and release of persistent organic pollutants and to alternatives to those substances, specifying the risks and the economic and social costs related to such alternatives.

2. The Commission and Member States, as appropriate, shall promote and facilitate with regard to persistent organic pollutants:

(a) awareness programmes, including relating to their health and environmental effects and their alternatives and on the reduction or elimination of their production, use and release, especially for
  - (i) policy and decision makers,
  - (ii) particularly vulnerable groups;

(b) the provision of public information;

(c) training, including workers, scientists, educators and technical and managerial personnel.

3. Without prejudice to Directive 2003/4/EC of the European Parliament and of the Council of 28 January 2003 on public access to environmental information, information on health and safety of humans and the environment shall not be regarded as confidential. The Commission and the Member States that exchange other information with a third country shall protect any confidential information as mutually agreed.

Article 11

Technical assistance

In accordance with Articles 12 and 13 of the Convention, the Commission and the Member States shall cooperate in providing appropriate and timely technical and financial assistance to developing countries and countries with economies in transition to assist them, upon request and within available resources and taking into account their particular needs, to develop and strengthen their capacity to fully implement their obligations under the Convention. Such support may also be channelled through non-governmental organisations.

Article 12

Reporting

1. Member States shall every three years forward to the Commission information on the application of this Regulation, including information on infringements and penalties.

2. Member States shall provide the Commission every year with statistical data on the actual or estimated total production and placing on the market of any substance listed in Annex I or II.

3. Within three years of the date of entry into force of this Regulation and every three years thereafter, Member States shall provide the Commission with:
(a) summary information compiled from the notifications, concerning stockpiles, received pursuant to Article 5(2);
(b) summary information compiled from the release inventories drawn up pursuant to Article 6(1);
(c) summary information on the presence of dioxins, furans and PCBs as identified in Annex III in the environment, as compiled pursuant to Article 9.

4. As regards the data and information to be provided by Member States pursuant to paragraphs 1, 2 and 3, the Commission shall develop in advance a common format in accordance with the procedure referred to in Article 16(2).

5. Regarding the substances listed in the Convention, the Commission shall, at intervals to be determined by the Conference of the Parties of the Convention, compile a report on the basis of the information provided by the Member States in accordance with paragraph 2 and communicate it to the Secretariat of the Convention.

6. The Commission shall every three years compile a report on the application of this Regulation and shall integrate it with the information already available in the context of the EPER, as established by Commission Decision 2000/479/EC, and CORINAIR Emission Inventory of EMEP (Cooperative Programme for Monitoring and Evaluation of the Long-Range Transmission of Air Pollutants in Europe), and with the information provided by the Member States under paragraphs 1, 2 and 3 to form a synthesis report. This report shall include information on the use of derogations as referred to in Article 7(4). It shall forward a summary of the synthesis report to the European Parliament and to the Council and make it available to the public without delay.

Article 13

Penalties

Member States shall lay down the rules on penalties applicable to infringements of the provisions of this Regulation and shall take all measures necessary to ensure that they are implemented. The penalties provided for must be effective, proportionate and dissuasive. The Member States shall notify those provisions to the Commission one year after entry into force of this Regulation at the latest and shall notify it without delay of any subsequent amendment affecting them.

[Article 14

Amendment of Annexes][1]

[1. Whenever a substance is listed in the Convention or the Protocol, the Commission shall, where appropriate, amend Annexes I, II and III accordingly.

Those measures, designed to amend non-essential elements of this Regulation, shall be adopted in accordance with the regulatory procedure with scrutiny referred to in Article 16(3).

2. Whenever a substance is listed in the Convention or the Protocol, the Commission shall, where appropriate, amend Annex IV accordingly.

Those measures, designed to amend non-essential elements of this Regulation, shall be adopted in accordance with the regulatory procedure with scrutiny referred to in Article 17(3).

3. The Commission shall adopt modifications to the existing entries in Annexes I, II and III, including their adaptation to scientific and technical progress.

Those measures, designed to amend non-essential elements of this Regulation, shall be adopted in accordance with the regulatory procedure with scrutiny referred to in Article 16(3).

4. The Commission shall adopt modifications to the existing entries in Annex IV and modifications to Annex V, including their adaptation to scientific and technical progress.

Those measures, designed to amend non-essential elements of this Regulation, shall be adopted in accordance with the regulatory procedure with scrutiny referred to in Article 17(3).][1]

Amendment

1 Inserted by Regulation (EC) No 219/2009 of the European Parliament and of the Council of 11 March 2009 adapting a number of instruments subject to the procedure referred to in Article 251 of the Treaty to Council Decision 1999/468/EC with regard to the regulatory procedure with scrutiny, Article 1, Annex, para 3.7.2.

Article 15

Competent authorities

Each Member State shall designate the competent authority or authorities responsible for the administrative tasks required by this Regulation. It shall inform the Commission of such designation at the latest three months after the entry into force of this Regulation.

Article 16

Committee for general matters

1. The Commission shall be assisted by the Committee established by Article 29 of Directive 67/548/EEC for all matters under this Regulation except for those relating to waste.

2. Where reference is made to this paragraph, Articles 5 and 7 of Decision 1999/468/EC shall apply, having regard to the provisions of Article 8 thereof.

The period laid down in Article 5(6) of Decision 1999/468/EC shall be set at three months.

[3. Where reference is made to this paragraph, Article 5a(1) to (4) and Article 7 of Decision 1999/468/EC shall apply, having regard to the provisions of Article 8 thereof.][1]

Amendment

1 Inserted by Regulation (EC) No 219/2009 of the European Parliament and of the Council of 11 March 2009 adapting a number of instruments subject to the procedure referred to in Article 251 of the Treaty to Council Decision 1999/468/EC with regard to the regulatory procedure with scrutiny, Article 1, Annex, para 3.7.3.

Article 17

Committee for waste matters

1. The Commission shall be assisted by the Committee established by Article 18 of Directive 75/442/EEC, for matters relating to waste under this Regulation.

2. Where reference is made to this paragraph, Articles 5 and 7 of Decision 1999/468/EC shall apply, having regard to the provisions of Article 8 thereof.

The period laid down in Article 5(6) of Decision 1999/468/EC shall be set at three months.

[3. Where reference is made to this paragraph, Article 5a(1) to (4) and Article 7 of Decision 1999/468/EC shall apply, having regard to the provisions of Article 8 thereof.][1]

Amendment

1 Inserted by Regulation (EC) No 219/2009 of the European Parliament and of the Council of 11 March 2009 adapting a number of instruments subject to the procedure referred to in Article 251 of the Treaty to Council Decision 1999/468/EC with regard to the regulatory procedure with scrutiny, Article 1, Annex, para 3.7.4.

[*Article 18 is not reproduced.*]

Article 19

Entry into force

This Regulation shall enter into force on the twentieth day following that of its publication in the Official Journal of the European Union.

This Regulation shall be binding in its entirety and directly applicable in all Member States.

[ANNEX I

PART A – SUBSTANCES LISTED IN THE CONVENTION AND IN THE PROTOCOL AS WELL AS SUBSTANCES LISTED ONLY IN THE CONVENTION][1]

[Substance	*CAS No*	*EC No*	*Specific exemption on intermediate use or other specification*
Tetrabromodiphenyl ether $C_{12}H_6Br_4O$			1. For the purposes of this entry, Article 4(1)(b) shall apply to concentrations of Tetrabromodiphenyl ether equal to or below 10 mg/kg (0,001 % by weight) when it occurs in substances, preparations, articles or as constituents of the flame-retarded parts of articles. 2. By way of derogation, the production, placing on the market and use of the following shall be allowed: (a) without prejudice to subparagraph (b), articles and preparations containing concentrations below 0,1 % of tetrabromodiphenyl ether by weight when produced partially or fully from recycled materials or materials from waste prepared for re-use; (b) electrical and electronic equipment within the scope of Directive 2002/95/EC of the European Parliament and Council. 3. Use of articles already in use in the Union before 25 August 2010 containing Tetrabromodiphenyl ether as a constituent of such articles shall be allowed. Article 4(2), third and fourth subparagraphs shall apply in relation to such articles.
Pentabromodiphenyl ether $C_{12}H_5Br_5O$			1. For the purposes of this entry, Article 4(1)(b) shall apply to concentrations of pentabromodiphenyl ether equal to or below 10 mg/kg (0,001 % by weight) when it occurs in substances, preparations, articles or as constituents of the flame-retarded parts of articles. 2. By way of derogation, the production, placing on the market and use of the following shall be allowed: (a) without prejudice to subparagraph (b), articles and preparations containing concentrations below 0,1 % of pentabromodiphenyl ether by weight when produced partially or fully from recycled materials or materials from waste prepared for re-use; (b) electrical and electronic equipment within the scope of Directive 2002/95/EC.

[Substance	*CAS No*	*EC No*	*Specific exemption on intermediate use or other specification*
			3. Use of articles already in use in the Union before 25 August 2010 containing Pentabromodiphenyl ether as a constituent of such articles shall be allowed. Article 4(2), third and fourth subparagraphs shall apply in relation to such articles.
Hexabromodiphenyl ether $C_{12}H_4Br_6O$			1. For the purposes of this entry, Article 4(1)(b) shall apply to concentrations of hexabromodiphenyl ether equal to or below 10 mg/kg (0,001 % by weight) when it occurs in substances, preparations, articles or as constituents of the flame-retarded parts of articles. 2. By way of derogation, the production, placing on the market and use of the following shall be allowed: (a) without prejudice to subparagraph (b), articles and preparations containing concentrations below 0,1 % of hexabromobiphenyl ether by weight when produced partially or fully from recycled materials or materials from waste prepared for re-use; (b) electrical and electronic equipment within the scope of Directive 2002/95/EC. 3. Use of articles already in use in the Union before 25 August 2010 containing Hexabromodiphenyl ether as a constituent of such articles shall be allowed. Article 4(2), third and fourth subparagraphs shall apply in relation to such articles.
Heptabromodiphenyl ether $C_{12}H_3Br_7O$			1. For the purposes of this entry, Article 4(1)(b) shall apply to concentrations of heptabromodiphenyl ether equal to or below 10 mg/kg (0,001 % by weight) when it occurs in substances, preparations, articles or as constituents of the flame-retarded parts of articles. 2. By way of derogation, the production, placing on the market and use of the following shall be allowed: (a) without prejudice to subparagraph (b), articles and preparations containing concentrations below 0,1 % of heptabromodiphenyl ether by weight when produced partially or fully from recycled materials or materials from waste prepared for re-use; (b) electrical and electronic equipment within the scope of Directive 2002/95/EC. 3. Use of articles already in use in the Union before 25 August 2010 containing Heptabromodiphenyl ether as a constituent of such articles shall be allowed. Article 4(2), third and fourth subparagraphs shall apply in relation to such articles.

[*Substance*	*CAS No*	*EC No*	*Specific exemption on intermediate use or other specification*
Perfluorooctane sulfonic acid and its derivatives (PFOS) $C_8F_{17}SO_2X$ (X = OH, Metal salt (O-M$^+$), halide, amide, and other derivatives including polymers)			1. For the purposes of this entry, Article 4(1)(b) shall apply to concentrations of PFOS equal to or below 10 mg/kg (0,001 % by weight) when it occurs in substances or in preparations. 2. For the purposes of this entry, Article 4(1) (b) shall apply to concentrations of PFOS in semi-finished products or articles, or parts thereof, if the concentration of PFOS is lower than 0,1 % by weight calculated with reference to the mass of structurally or micro-structurally distinct parts that contain PFOS or, for textiles or other coated materials, if the amount of PFOS is lower than 1 μg/m^2 of the coated material. 3. Use of articles already in use in the Union before 25 August 2010 containing PFOS as a constituent of such articles shall be allowed. Article 4(2), third and fourth subparagraphs shall apply in relation to such articles. 4. Fire-fighting foams that were placed on the market before 27 December 2006 may be used until 27 June 2011. 5. If the quantity released into the environment is minimised, production and placing on the market is allowed for the following specific uses provided that Member States report to the Commission every four years on progress made to eliminate PFOS: (a) until 26 August 2015, wetting agents for use in controlled electroplating systems; (b) photoresists or anti reflective coatings for photolithography processes; (c) photographic coatings applied to films, papers, or printing plates; (d) mist suppressants for non-decorative hard chromium (VI) plating in closed loop systems; (e) hydraulic fluids for aviation. Where derogations in points (a) to (e) above concern the production or use in an installation within the scope of Directive 2008/1/EC of the European Parliament and of the Council, the relevant best available techniques for the prevention and minimisation of emissions of PFOS described in the information published by the Commission pursuant to Article 17(2), second subparagraph, of Directive 2008/1/EC shall apply. As soon as new information on details of uses and safer alternative substances or technologies for the uses in points (b) to (e) becomes available, the Commission shall review the derogations in the second subparagraph so that:

[Substance	CAS No	EC No	Specific exemption on intermediate use or other specification
			(i) the uses of PFOS will be phased out as soon as the use of safer alternatives is technically and economically feasible, (ii) a derogation can only be continued for essential uses for which safer alternatives do not exist and where the efforts undertaken to find safer alternatives have been reported on, (iii) releases of PFOS into the environment have been minimised by applying best available techniques. [6. Once standards are adopted by the European Committee for Standardisation (CEN) they shall be used as the analytical test methods for demonstrating the conformity of substances, preparations and articles to paragraphs 1 and 2.][2]
DDT (1,1,1-trichloro-2,2-bis(4-chlorophenyl)-ethane)	50-29-3	200-024-3	—
Chlordane	57-74-9	200-349-0	—
Hexachlorocyclohexanes, including lindane	58-89-9 319-84-6 319-85-7 608-73-1	200-401-2 206-270-8 206-271-3 210-168-9	—
Dieldrin	60-57-1	200-484-5	—
Endrin	72-20-8	200-775-7	—
Heptachlor	76-44-8	200-962-3	—
[Endosulfan	115-29-7 959-98-8 33213-65-9	204-079-4	1. Placing on the market and use of articles produced before or on 10 July 2012 containing endosulfan as a constituent of such articles shall be allowed until 10 January 2013. 2. Placing on the market and use of articles already in use before or on 10 July 2012 containing endosulfan as a constituent of such articles shall be allowed. 3. Article 4(2), third and fourth subparagraphs shall apply to articles referred to in paragraphs 1 and 2.][3]
Hexachlorobenzene	118-74-1	200-273-9	—

[Substance	*CAS No*	*EC No*	*Specific exemption on intermediate use or other specification*
Chlordecone	143-50-0	205-601-3	—
Aldrin	309-00-2	206-215-8	—
Pentachlorobenzene	608-93-5	210-172-5	—
Polychlorinated Biphenyls (PCB)	1336-36-3 and others	215-648-1 and others	Without prejudice to Directive 96/59/EC, articles already in use at the time of the entry into force of this Regulation are allowed to be used
Mirex	2385-85-5	219-196-6	—
Toxaphene	8001-35-2	232-283-3	—
Hexabromobiphenyl	36355-01-8	252-994-2	—][1]

Amendments

1 Substituted by Commission Regulation (EU) No 757/2010 of 24 August 2010 amending Regulation (EC) No 850/2004 of the European Parliament and of the Council on persistent organic pollutants as regards Annexes I and III, Article 1, Annex, para (1).

2 Substituted by Commission Regulation (EU) No 519/2012 of 19 June 2012 amending Regulation (EC) No 850/2004 of the European Parliament and of the Council on persistent organic pollutants as regards Annex I, Article 1, Annex, para (1)(a).

3 Inserted by Commission Regulation (EU) No 519/2012 of 19 June 2012 amending Regulation (EC) No 850/2004 of the European Parliament and of the Council on persistent organic pollutants as regards Annex I, Article 1, Annex, para (1)(b).

[PART B — SUBSTANCES LISTED ONLY IN THE PROTOCOL][1]

[Substance	*CAS No*	*EC No*	*Specific exemption on intermediate use or other specification*
[Hexachlorobutadiene	87-68-3	201-765-5	1. Placing on the market and use of articles produced before or on 10 July 2012 containing hexachlorobutadiene as a constituent of such articles shall be allowed until 10 January 2013. 2. Placing on the market and use of articles already in use before or on 10 July 2012 containing hexachlorobutadiene as a constituent of such articles shall be allowed. 3. Article 4(2), third and fourth subparagraphs shall apply to articles referred to in paragraphs 1 and 2.

[Substance	CAS No	EC No	Specific exemption on intermediate use or other specification
Polychlorinated naphthalenes[(*)]			1. Placing on the market and use of articles produced before or on 10 July 2012 containing polychlorinated naphthalenes as a constituent of such articles shall be allowed until 10 January 2013. 2. Placing on the market and use of articles already in use before or on 10 July 2012 containing polychlorinated naphthalenes as a constituent of such articles shall be allowed. 3. Article 4(2), third and fourth subparagraphs shall apply to articles referred to in paragraphs 1 and 2.
Alkanes C10-C13, chloro (short-chain chlorinated paraffins) (SCCPs)	85535-84-8	287-476-5	1. By way of derogation, the production, placing on the market and use of substances or preparations containing SCCPs in concentrations lower than 1 % by weight shall be allowed. 2. By way of derogation, the production, placing on the market, and use of the following applications shall be allowed provided that Member States report to the Commission no later than 2015 and every four years thereafter on the progress made to eliminate SCCPs: (a) fire retardants in rubber used in conveyor belts in the mining industry; (b) fire retardants in dam sealants.3.Placing on the market and use of articles produced before or on 10 July 2012 containing SCCPs as a constituent of such articles shall be allowed until 10 January 2013. 4. Placing on the market and use of articles already in use before or on 10 July 2012 containing SCCPs as a constituent of articles shall be allowed. 5. Article 4(2), third and fourth subparagraphs shall apply to articles referred to in paragraphs 1 and 2. As soon as new information on details of uses and safer alternative substances or technologies become available, the Commission shall review the derogations set out in point 2 so that the uses of SCCPs be phased out.

(*) Polychlorinated naphthalenes means chemical compounds based on the naphthalene ring system, where one or more hydrogen atoms have been replaced by chlorine atoms.][2]][1]

Amendments

1 Substituted by Commission Regulation (EU) No 757/2010 of 24 August 2010 amending Regulation (EC) No 850/2004 of the European Parliament and of the Council on persistent organic pollutants as regards Annexes I and III, Article 1, Annex, para (1).

2 Inserted by Commission Regulation (EU) No 519/2012 of 19 June 2012 amending Regulation (EC) No 850/2004 of the European Parliament and of the Council on persistent organic pollutants as regards Annex I, Article 1, Annex, para (1)(b).

ANNEX II
LIST OF SUBSTANCES SUBJECT TO RESTRICTIONS

PART A – SUBSTANCES LISTED IN THE CONVENTION AND IN THE PROTOCOL

Substance	*CAS No*	*EC No*	*Conditions of restriction*
—			

PART B – SUBSTANCES LISTED ONLY IN THE PROTOCOL

Substance	*CAS No*	*EC No*	*Conditions of restriction*
—			

ANNEX III
LIST OF SUBSTANCES SUBJECT TO RELEASE REDUCTION PROVISIONS

Substance CAS No

Polychlorinated dibenzo-p-dioxins and dibenzofurans (PCDD/PCDF)

Hexachlorobenzene (HCB) (CAS No: 118-74-1)

Polychlorinated biphenyls (PCB)

Polycyclic aromatic hydrocarbons (PAHs)[(1)]

[Pentachlorobenzene (CAS No 608-93-5)][1]

(1) For the purpose of emission inventories, the following four compound indicators shall be used: benzo(a)pyrene, benzo(b) fluoranthene, benzo(k)fluoranthene and indeno(1,2,3-cd)pyrene.

Amendment

1 Inserted by Commission Regulation (EU) No 757/2010 of 24 August 2010 amending Regulation (EC) No 850/2004 of the European Parliament and of the Council on persistent organic pollutants as regards Annexes I and III, Article 1, Annex, para (2).

[ANNEX IV
LIST OF SUBSTANCES SUBJECT TO WASTE MANAGEMENT PROVISIONS SET OUT IN ARTICLE 7][1]

Substance	*CAS No*	*EC No*	*Concentration limit referred to in Article 7(4)(a)*
Tetrabromodiphenyl ether $C_{12}H_6Br_4O$			
Pentabromodiphenyl ether $C_{12}H_5Br_5O$			
Hexabromodiphenyl ether $C_{12}H_4Br_6O$			
Heptabromodiphenyl ether $C_{12}H_3Br_7O$			

Substance	*CAS No*	*EC No*	*Concentration limit referred to in Article 7(4)(a)*
Perfluorooctane sulfonic acid and its derivatives (PFOS) $C_8F_{17}SO_2X$ (X = OH, Metal salt (O-M^+), halide, amide, and other derivatives including polymers)			
Polychlorinated dibenzo-p-dioxins and dibenzofurans (PCDD/PCDF)			15 μg/kg[(1)]
DDT (1,1,1-trichloro-2,2-bis (4-chlorophenyl)ethane)	50-29-3	200-024-3	50 mg/kg
Chlordane	57-74-9	200-349-0	50 mg/kg
Hexachlorocyclohexanes, including lindane	58-89-9	210-168-9	50 mg/kg
319-84-6	200-401-2		
319-85-7	206-270-8		
608-73-1	206-271-3		
Dieldrin	60-57-1	200-484-5	50 mg/kg
Endrin	72-20-8	200-775-7	50 mg/kg
Heptachlor	76-44-8	200-962-3	50 mg/kg
Hexachlorobenzene	118-74-1	200-273-9	50 mg/kg
Chlordecone	143-50-0	205-601-3	50 mg/kg
Aldrin	309-00-2	206-215-8	50 mg/kg
Pentachlorobenzene	608-93-5	210-172-5	50 mg/kg
Polychlorinated Biphenyls (PCB)	1336-36-3 and others	215-648-1	50 mg/kg[(2)]
Mirex	2385-85-5	219-196-6	50 mg/kg
Toxaphene	8001-35-2	232-283-3	50 mg/kg
Hexabromobiphenyl	36355-01-8	252-994-2	50 mg/kg

(1) The limit is calculated as PCDD and PCDF according to the following toxic equivalency factors (TEFs):

PCDD	*TEF*
2,3,7,8-TeCDD	1
1,2,3,7,8-PeCDD	1
1,2,3,4,7,8-HxCDD	0,1
1,2,3,6,7,8-HxCDD	0,1
1,2,3,7,8,9-HxCDD	0,1
1,2,3,4,6,7,8-HpCDD	0,01
OCDD	0,0003
PCDF	*TEF*
2,3,7,8-TeCDF	0,1
1,2,3,7,8-PeCDF	0,03
2,3,4,7,8-PeCDF	0,3
1,2,3,4,7,8-HxCDF	0,1
1,2,3,6,7,8-HxCDF	0,1
1,2,3,7,8,9-HxCDF	0,1

PCDD	*TEF*
2,3,4,6,7,8-HxCDF	0,1
1,2,3,4,6,7,8-HpCDF	0,01
1,2,3,4,7,8,9-HpCDF	0,01
OCDF	0,0003

(2) Where applicable, the calculation method laid down in European standards EN 12766-1 and EN 12766-2 shall be applied.

Amendment

1 Substituted by Commission Regulation (EU) No 756/2010 of 24 August 2010 amending Regulation (EC) No 850/2004 of the European Parliament and of the Council on persistent organic pollutants as regards Annexes IV and V, Article 1.1, Annex I.

ANNEX V
WASTE MANAGEMENT

PART 1
DISPOSAL AND RECOVERY UNDER ARTICLE 7(2)

The following disposal and recovery operations, as provided for in Annex IIA and IIB of Directive 75/442/EEC, are permitted for the purposes of Article 7(2) when applied in such a way as to ensure that the persistent organic pollutant content is destroyed or irreversibly transformed

D9 Physico-chemical treatment

D10 Incineration on land

R1 Use principally as a fuel or other means to generate energy, excluding waste containing PCBs,

[R4 Recycling/reclamation of metals and metal compounds, under the following conditions: The operations are restricted to residues from iron- and steel-making processes such as dusts or sludges from gas treatment or mill scale or zinc-containing filter dusts from steelworks, dusts from gas cleaning systems of copper smelters and similar wastes and lead-containing leaching residues of the non-ferrous metal production. Waste containing PCBs is excluded. The operations are restricted to processes for the recovery of iron and iron alloys (blast furnace, shaft furnace and hearth furnace) and non-ferrous metals (Waelz rotary kiln process, bath melting processes using vertical or horizontal furnaces), provided the facilities meet as minimum requirements the emission limit values for PCDDs and PCDFs laid down in Directive 2000/76/EC of the European Parliament and of the Council of 4 December 2000 on the incineration of waste, whether or not the processes are subject to that Directive, and without prejudice to the other provisions of Directive 2000/76/EC where it applies and to the provisions of Directive 96/61/EC.][1]

Pre-treatment operation prior to destruction or irreversible transformation pursuant to this Part of this Annex may be performed, provided that a substance listed in Annex IV that is isolated from the waste during the pre-treatment is subsequently disposed of in accordance with this Part of this Annex. [Where only part of a product or waste, such as waste equipment, contains or is contaminated with persistent organic pollutants, it shall be separated and then disposed of in accordance with the requirements of this Regulation.][1] In addition, repackaging and temporary storage operations may be performed prior to such pre-treatment or prior to destruction or irreversible transformation pursuant to this part of this Annex.

Amendment

1 Inserted by Commission Regulation (EC) No 304/2009 of 14 April 2009 amending Annexes IV and V to Regulation (EC) No 850/2004 of the European Parliament and of the Council as regards the treatment of waste containing persistent organic pollutants in thermal and metallurgical production processes, Article 1, Annex, para 2(a).

[PART 2
WASTES AND OPERATIONS TO WHICH ARTICLE 7(4)(B) APPLIES][1]

[The following operations are permitted for the purposes of Article 7(4)(b) in respect of the wastes specified, defined by the six-digit code as classified in Commission Decision 2000/532/EC.

[Pre-treatment operations prior to permanent storage pursuant to this part of this Annex may be performed, provided that a substance listed in Annex IV that is isolated from the waste during the pre-treatment is subsequently disposed of in accordance with Part 1 of this Annex. In addition, repackaging and temporary storage operations may be performed prior to such pre-treatment or prior to permanent storage pursuant to this part of this Annex.][2]

[Wastes as classified in Commission Decision 2000/532/EC		*Maximum concentration limits of substances listed in Annex IV*[(1)]	*Operation*
10	Wastes from thermal processess	Aldrin: 5000 mg/kg; Chlordane: 5000 mg/kg; Chlordecone: 5000 mg/kg; DDT (1,1,1-trichloro-2,2-bis (4-chlorophenyl) ethane): 5000 mg/kg; Dieldrin: 5000 mg/kg; Endrin: 5000 mg/kg; Heptabromodiphenyl ether (C12H3Br7O); Heptachlor: 5000 mg/kg; Hexabromobiphenyl: 5000 mg/kg; Hexabromodiphenyl ether (C12H4Br6O); Hexachlorobenzene: 5000 mg/kg; Hexachlorocyclohexanes, including lindane: 5000 mg/kg; Mirex: 5000 mg/kg; Pentabromodiphenyl ether ($C_{12}H_5Br_5O$); Pentachlorobenzene: 5000 mg/kg; Perfluorooctane sulfonic acid and its derivatives (PFOS) ($C_8F_{17}SO_2X$) (X = OH, Metal salt ($O-M^+$), halide, amide, and other derivatives including polymers); Polychlorinated Biphenyls (PCB)[(3)]: 50 mg/kg;	Permanent storage shall be allowed only when all the following conditions are met: 1. the storage takes place in one of the following locations: — safe, deep, underground, hard rock formations, — salt mines, — a landfill site for hazardous waste, provided that the waste is solidified or partly stabilised where technically feasible as required for classification of the waste in Subchapter 1903 of Decision 2000/532/EC; 2. the provisions of Council Directive 1999/31/EC and Council Decision 2003/33/EC were respected; 3. it has been demonstrated that the selected operation is environmentally preferable.
10 01	Wastes from power stations and other combustion plants (except 19)		
10 01 14 *[(2)]	Bottom ash, slag and boiler dust from co-incineration containing dangerous substances		
10 01 16 *	Fly ash from co-incineration containing dangerous substances		
10 02	Wastes from the iron and steel industry		
10 02 07 *	Solid wastes from gas treatment containing dangerous substances		
10 03	Wastes from aluminium thermal metallurgy		
10 03 04 *	Primary production slag		
10 03 08 *	Salt slag from secondary production		
10 03 09 *	Black dross from secondary production		
10 03 19 *	Flue-gas dust containing dangerous substances		
10 03 21 *	Other particulates and dust (including ball mill dust) containing dangerous substances		

[Wastes as classified in Commission Decision 2000/532/EC		*Maximum concentration limits of substances listed in Annex IV*[1]	*Operation*
10 03 29 *	Wastes from treatment of salt slag and black dross containing dangerous substances	Polychlorinated dibenzo-p-dioxins and dibenzofurans (PCDD/PCDF)[4]: 5 mg/kg; Tetrabromodiphenyl ether ($C_{12}H_6Br_4O$); Toxaphene: 5000 mg/kg;	
10 04	Wastes from lead thermal metallurgy		
10 04 01 *	Slag from primary and secondary production		
10 04 02 *	Dross and skimming from primary and secondary production		
10 04 04 *	Flue-gas dust		
10 04 05 *	Other particulates and dust		
10 04 06 *	Solid wastes from gas treatment		
10 05	Wastes from zinc thermal metallurgy		
10 05 03 *	Flue-gas dust		
10 05 05 *	Solid waste from gas treatment		
10 06	Wastes from copper thermal metallurgy		
10 06 03 *	Flue-gas dust		
10 06 06 *	Solid wastes from gas treatment		
10 08	Wastes from other non-ferrous thermal metallurgy		
10 08 08 *	Salt slag from primary and secondary production		
10 08 15 *	Flue-gas dust containing dangerous substances		
10 09	Wastes from casting of ferrous pieces		
10 09 09 *	Flue-gas dust containing dangerous substances		
16	Wastes not otherwise specified in the list		
16 11	Waste linings and refractories		

[Wastes as classified in Commission Decision 2000/532/EC		*Maximum concentration limits of substances listed in Annex IV*[(1)]	*Operation*
16 11 01 *	Carbon-based linings and refractories from metallurgical processes containing dangerous substances		
16 11 03 *	Other linings and refractories from metallurgical processes containing dangerous substances		
17	Constructions and demolition wastes (including excavated soil from contaminated sites)		
17 01	Concrete, bricks, tiles and ceramics		
17 01 06 *	Mixtures of, or separate fractions of concrete, bricks, tiles and ceramics containing dangerous substances		
17 05	Soil including excavated soil from contaminated sites, stones and dredging spoil		
17 05 03 *	Inorganic fraction of soil and stones containing dangerous substances		
17 09	Other construction and demolition wastes		
17 09 02 *	Construction and demolition wastes containing PCB, excluding PCB containing equipment		
17 09 03 *	Other construction and demolition wastes containing dangerous substances		

[Wastes as classified in Commission Decision 2000/532/EC		*Maximum concentration limits of substances listed in Annex IV*[(1)]	*Operation*
19	Wastes from waste management facilities, off-site waste water treatment plants and the preparation of water intended for human consumption and water from industrial use		
19 01	Wastes from incineration or pyrolysis of waste		
19 01 07 *	Solid wastes from gas treatment		
19 01 11 *	Bottom ash and slag containing dangerous substances		
19 01 13 *	Fly ash containing dangerous substances		
19 01 15 *	Boiler dust containing dangerous substances		
19 04	Vitrified waste and waste from vitrification		
19 04 02 *	Fly ash and other flue-gas treatment wastes		
19 04 03 *	Non-vitrified solid phase		

(1) These limits apply exclusively to a landfill site for hazardous waste and do not apply to permanent underground storage facilities for hazardous wastes, including salt mines.

(2) Any waste marked with an asterisk * is considered as hazardous waste pursuant to Directive 91/689/EEC and subject to the provisions of that Directive.

(3) The calculation method laid down in European standards EN 12766-1 and EN 12766-2 shall apply.

(4) The limit is calculated as PCDD and PCDF according to the following toxic equivalency factors (TEFs):

PCDD	*TEF*
2,3,7,8-TeCDD	1
1,2,3,7,8-PeCDD	1
1,2,3,4,7,8-HxCDD	0,1
1,2,3,6,7,8-HxCDD	0,1
1,2,3,7,8,9-HxCDD	0,1
1,2,3,4,6,7,8-HpCDD	0,01
OCDD	0,0003
PCDF	*TEF*
2,3,7,8-TeCDF	0,1
1,2,3,7,8-PeCDF	0,03
2,3,4,7,8-PeCDF	0,3
1,2,3,4,7,8-HxCDF	0,1
1,2,3,6,7,8-HxCDF	0,1
1,2,3,7,8,9-HxCDF	0,1
PCDD	*TEF*
2,3,4,6,7,8-HxCDF	0,1
1,2,3,4,6,7,8-HpCDF	0,01
1,2,3,4,7,8,9-HpCDF	0,01
OCDF	0,0003][3]][1]

Amendments

1 Substituted by Council Regulation (EC) No 172/2007 of 16 February 2007 amending Annex V to Regulation (EC) No 850/2004 of the European Parliament and of the Council on persistent organic pollutants, Article 1, Annex.

2 Inserted by Commission Regulation (EC) No 323/2007 of 26 March 2007 amending Annex V to Regulation (EC) No 850/2004 of the European Parliament and of the Council on persistent organic pollutants and amending Directive 79/117/EEC, Article 1, Annex.

3 Substituted by Commission Regulation (EU) No 756/2010 of 24 August 2010 amending Regulation (EC) No 850/2004 of the European Parliament and of the Council on persistent organic pollutants as regards Annexes IV and V, Article 1.2, Annex II.

DIRECTIVE 2006/7/EC OF THE EUROPEAN PARLIAMENT AND OF THE COUNCIL

of 15 February 2006

ON THE MANAGEMENT OF BATHING WATER QUALITY AND REPEALING DIRECTIVE 76/160/EEC

THE EUROPEAN PARLIAMENT AND THE COUNCIL OF THE EUROPEAN UNION,

Having regard to the Treaty establishing the European Community, and in particular Article 175(1) thereof,

Having regard to the proposal from the Commission,

Having regard to the opinion of the European Economic and Social Committee,

Having regard to the opinion of the Committee of the Regions,

Acting in accordance with the procedure laid down in Article 251 of the Treaty, in the light of the joint text approved by the Conciliation Committee on 8 December 2005,

Whereas:

(1) Building on the Commission's Communication on sustainable development, the European Council has singled out objectives as general guidance for future development in priority areas such as natural resources and public health.

(2) Water is a scarce natural resource, the quality of which should be protected, defended, managed and treated as such. Surface waters in particular are renewable resources with a limited capacity to recover from adverse impacts from human activities.

(3) Community policy on the environment should aim at a high level of protection, and contribute to pursuing the objectives of preserving, protecting and improving the quality of the environment and of protecting human health.

(4) In December 2000, the Commission adopted a Communication to the European Parliament and the Council on the development of a new bathing water policy and initiated a large-scale consultation of all interested and involved parties. The main outcome of this consultation was general support for the development of a new Directive based on the latest scientific evidence and paying particular attention to wider public participation.

(5) Decision No 1600/2002/EC of the European Parliament and of the Council of 22 July 2002 laying down the Sixth Community Environment Action Programme contains a commitment to ensuring a high level of protection of bathing water, including by revising Council Directive 76/160/EEC of 8 December 1975 concerning the quality of bathing water.

(6) Pursuant to the Treaty, in preparing policy on the environment the Community is, inter alia, to take account of available scientific and technical data. This Directive should use scientific evidence in implementing the most reliable indicator parameters for predicting microbiological health risk and to achieve a high level of protection. Further epidemiological studies should be undertaken urgently concerning the health risks associated with bathing, particularly in fresh water.

(7) In order to increase efficiency and wise use of resources, this Directive needs to be closely coordinated with other Community legislation on water, such as Council Directives 91/271/EEC of 21 May 1991 concerning urban waste-water treatment, 91/676/EEC of 12 December 1991 concerning the protection of waters against pollution caused by nitrates from agricultural sources and Directive 2000/60/EC of the

European Parliament and of the Council of 23 October 2000 establishing a framework for Community action in the field of water policy.

(8) Appropriate information on planned measures and progress on implementation should be disseminated to stakeholders. The public should receive appropriate and timely information on the results of the monitoring of bathing water quality and risk management measures in order to prevent health hazards, especially in the context of predictable short-term pollution or abnormal situations. New technology that allows the public to be informed in an efficient and comparable way on bathing waters across the Community should be applied.

(9) For the purpose of monitoring, harmonised methods and practices of analysis need to be applied. Observation and quality assessment over an extended period are necessary in order to achieve a realistic bathing water classification.

(10) Compliance should be a matter of appropriate management measures and quality assurance, not merely of measuring and calculation. A system of bathing water profiles is therefore appropriate to provide a better understanding of risks as a basis for management measures. In parallel, particular attention should be attached to adherence to quality standards and coherent transition from Directive 76/160/EEC.

(11) On 17 February 2005 the Community ratified the UNECE Convention on Access to Information, Public Participation in Decision-Making and Access to Justice in Environmental Matters (the Århus Convention). It is therefore appropriate for this Directive to include provisions on public access to information and to provide for public participation in its implementation to supplement Directive 2003/4/EC of the European Parliament and of the Council of 28 January 2003 on public access to environmental information and Directive 2003/35/EC of the European Parliament and of the Council of 26 May 2003 providing for public participation in respect of the drawing up of certain plans and programmes relating to the environment.

(12) Since the objectives of this Directive, namely the attainment by the Member States, on the basis of common standards, of a good bathing water quality and a high level of protection throughout the Community, cannot be sufficiently achieved by the Member States and can be better achieved at Community level, the Community may adopt measures, in accordance with the principle of subsidiarity as set out in Article 5 of the Treaty. In accordance with the principle of proportionality, as set out in that Article, this Directive does not go beyond what is necessary in order to achieve those objectives.

(13) The measures necessary for the implementation of this Directive should be adopted in accordance with Council Decision 1999/468/EC of 28 June 1999 laying down the procedures for the exercise of implementing powers conferred on the Commission.

(14) The continued importance of a Community bathing water policy is evident each bathing season as it protects the public from accidental and chronic pollution discharged in or near Community bathing areas. The overall quality of bathing waters has improved considerably since Directive 76/160/EEC came into force. However, that Directive reflects the state of knowledge and experience of the early 1970. Patterns of bathing water use have since changed, as has the state of scientific and technical knowledge. Therefore, that Directive should be repealed,

HAVE ADOPTED THIS DIRECTIVE:

Chapter I
General Provisions

Article 1

Purpose and scope

1. This Directive lays down provisions for:

(a) the monitoring and classification of bathing water quality;

(b) the management of bathing water quality; and
(c) the provision of information to the public on bathing water quality.

2. The purpose of this Directive is to preserve, protect and improve the quality of the environment and to protect human health by complementing Directive 2000/60/EC.

3. This Directive shall apply to any element of surface water where the competent authority expects a large number of people to bathe and has not imposed a permanent bathing prohibition, or issued permanent advice against bathing (hereinafter bathing water). It shall not apply to:
(a) swimming pools and spa pools;
(b) confined waters subject to treatment or used for therapeutic purposes;
(c) artificially created confined waters separated from surface water and groundwater.

Article 2

Definitions

For the purposes of this Directive, the following definitions shall apply:
1. the terms "surface water", "groundwater", "inland water", "transitional waters", "coastal water" and "river basin" have the same meaning as in Directive 2000/60/EC;
2. "competent authority" means the authority or authorities that a Member State has designated to ensure compliance with the requirements of this Directive or any other authority or body to which that role has been delegated;
3. "permanent" means, in relation to a bathing prohibition or advice against bathing, lasting for at least one whole bathing season;
4. "large number" means, in relation to bathers, a number that the competent authority considers to be large having regard, in particular, to past trends or to any infrastructure or facilities provided, or other measures taken, to promote bathing;
5. "pollution" means the presence of microbiological contamination or other organisms or waste affecting bathing water quality and presenting a risk to bathers' health as referred to in Articles 8 and 9 and Annex I, column A;
6. "bathing season" means the period during which large numbers of bathers can be expected.
7. "management measures" means the following measures undertaken with respect to bathing water:
   (a) establishing and maintaining a bathing water profile;
   (b) establishing a monitoring calendar;
   (c) monitoring bathing water;
   (d) assessing bathing water quality;
   (e) classifying bathing water;
   (f) identifying and assessing causes of pollution that might affect bathing waters and impair bathers' health;
   (g) giving information to the public;
   (h) taking action to prevent bathers' exposure to pollution;
   (i) taking action to reduce the risk of pollution;
8. "short-term pollution" means microbiological contamination as referred to in Annex I, column A, that has clearly identifiable causes, is not normally expected to affect bathing water quality for more than approximately 72 hours after the bathing water quality is first affected and for which the competent authority has established procedures to predict and deal with as set out in Annex II;
9. "abnormal situation" means an event or combination of events impacting on bathing water quality at the location concerned and not expected to occur on average more than once every four years;
10. "set of bathing water quality data" means data obtained in accordance with Article 3;
11. "bathing water quality assessment" means the process of evaluating bathing water quality, using the assessment method defined in Annex II;

12. "cyanobacterial proliferation" means an accumulation of cyanobacteria in the form of a bloom, mat or scum;
13. the term "public concerned" has the same meaning as in Council Directive 85/337/EEC of 27 June 1985 on the assessment of the effects of certain public and private projects on the environment.

Chapter II
Quality and management of bathing water

Article 3

Monitoring

1. Member States shall annually identify all bathing waters and define the length of the bathing season. They shall do so for the first time before the start of the first bathing season after 24 March 2008.

2. Member States shall ensure that monitoring of the parameters set out in Annex I, column A, takes place in accordance with Annex IV.

3. The monitoring point shall be the location within the bathing water where:
(a) most bathers are expected; or
(b) the greatest risk of pollution is expected, according to the bathing water profile.

4. A monitoring calendar for each bathing water shall be established before the start of each bathing season and for the first time before the start of the third full bathing season after the entry into force of this Directive. Monitoring shall take place no later than four days after the date specified in the monitoring calendar.

5. Member States may introduce monitoring of the parameters set out in Annex I, column A, during the first full bathing season following the entry into force of this Directive. In that case, monitoring shall take place with the frequency specified in Annex IV. The results of such monitoring may be used to build up the sets of bathing water quality data referred to in Article 4. As soon as Member States introduce monitoring under this Directive, monitoring of the parameters set out in the Annex to Directive 76/160/EEC may cease.

6. Samples taken during short-term pollution may be disregarded. They shall be replaced by samples taken in accordance with Annex IV.

7. During abnormal situations, the monitoring calendar referred to in paragraph 4 may be suspended. It shall be resumed as soon as possible after the end of the abnormal situation. New samples shall be taken as soon as possible after the end of the abnormal situation to replace samples that are missing due to the abnormal situation.

8. Member States shall report any suspension of the monitoring calendar to the Commission, giving the reasons for the suspension. They shall provide such reports on the occasion of the next annual report provided for in Article 13 at the latest.

9. Member States shall ensure that the analysis of bathing water quality takes place in accordance with the reference methods specified in Annex I and the rules set out in Annex V. However, Member States may permit the use of other methods or rules if they can demonstrate that the results obtained are equivalent to those obtained using the methods specified in Annex I and the rules set out in Annex V. Member States that permit the use of such equivalent methods or rules shall provide the Commission with all relevant information about the methods or rules used and their equivalence.

Article 4

Bathing water quality assessment

1. Member States shall ensure that sets of bathing water quality data are compiled through the monitoring of the parameters set out in Annex I, column A.

2. Bathing water quality assessments shall be carried out:
(a) in relation to each bathing water;
(b) after the end of each bathing season;
(c) on the basis of the set of bathing water quality data compiled in relation to that bathing season and the three preceding bathing seasons; and
(d) in accordance with the procedure set out in Annex II.
However, a Member State may decide to carry out bathing water quality assessments on the basis of the set of bathing water quality data compiled in relation to the preceding three bathing seasons only. If it so decides, it shall notify the Commission beforehand. It shall also notify the Commission if it subsequently decides to revert to carrying out assessments on the basis of four bathing seasons. Member States may not change the applicable assessment period more than once every five years.

3. Sets of bathing water data used to carry out bathing water quality assessments shall always comprise at least 16 samples or, in the special circumstances referred to in Annex IV, paragraph 2, 12 samples.

4. However, provided that either:
— the requirement of paragraph 3 is satisfied, or
— the set of bathing water data used to carry out the assessment comprises at least eight samples, in the case of bathing waters with a bathing season not exceeding eight weeks,
a bathing water quality assessment may be carried out on the basis of a set of bathing water quality data relating to fewer than four bathing seasons if:
(a) the bathing water is newly identified;
(b) any changes have occurred that are likely to affect the classification of the bathing water in accordance with Article 5, in which case the assessment shall be carried out on the basis of a set of bathing water quality data consisting solely of the results for samples collected since the changes occurred; or
(c) the bathing water had already been assessed in accordance with Directive 76/160/EEC, in which case equivalent data gathered under that Directive shall be used and, for this purpose, parameters 2 and 3 of the Annex to Directive 76/160/EEC shall be deemed to be equivalent to parameters 2 and 1 of column A of Annex I to this Directive.

5. Member States may subdivide or group together existing bathing waters in the light of bathing water quality assessments. They may group existing bathing waters together only if these waters:
(a) are contiguous;
(b) received similar assessments for the preceding four years in accordance with paragraphs 2, 3 and 4(c); and
(c) have bathing water profiles all of which identify common risk factors or the absence thereof.

Article 5

Classification and quality status of bathing waters

1. As a result of the bathing water quality assessment carried out in accordance with Article 4, Member States shall, in accordance with the criteria set out in Annex II, classify bathing water as:
(a) “poor”;
(b) “sufficient”;
(c) “good”; or
(d) “excellent”.

2. The first classification according to the requirements of this Directive shall be completed by the end of the 2015 bathing season.

3. Member States shall ensure that, by the end of the 2015 bathing season, all bathing waters are at least "sufficient". They shall take such realistic and proportionate measures as they consider appropriate with a view to increasing the number of bathing waters classified as "excellent" or "good".

4. However, notwithstanding the general requirement of paragraph 3, bathing waters may temporarily be classified as "poor" and still remain in compliance with this Directive. In such cases, Member States shall ensure that the following conditions are satisfied:

(a) in respect of each bathing water classified as "poor", the following measures shall be taken with effect from the bathing season that follows its classification:
   (i) adequate management measures, including a bathing prohibition or advice against bathing, with a view to preventing bathers' exposure to pollution;
   (ii) identification of the causes and reasons for the failure to achieve "sufficient" quality status;
   (iii) adequate measures to prevent, reduce or eliminate the causes of pollution; and
   (iv) in accordance with Article 12, alerting the public by a clear and simple warning sign and informing them of the causes of the pollution and measures taken, on the basis of the bathing water profile.

(b) If a bathing water is classified as "poor" for five consecutive years, a permanent bathing prohibition or permanent advice against bathing shall be introduced. However, a Member State may introduce a permanent bathing prohibition or permanent advice against bathing before the end of the five-year period if it considers that the achievement of "sufficient" quality would be infeasible or disproportionately expensive.

Article 6

Bathing water profiles

1. Member States shall ensure that bathing water profiles are established in accordance with Annex III. Each bathing water profile may cover a single bathing water or more than one contiguous bathing waters. Bathing water profiles shall be established for the first time by 24 March 2011.

2. Bathing water profiles shall be reviewed and updated as provided for in Annex III.

3. When establishing, reviewing and updating bathing water profiles, adequate use shall be made of data obtained from monitoring and assessments carried out pursuant to Directive 2000/60/EC that are relevant for this Directive.

Article 7

Management measures in exceptional circumstances

Member States shall ensure that timely and adequate management measures are taken when they are aware of unexpected situations that have, or could reasonably be expected to have, an adverse impact on bathing water quality and on bathers' health. Such measures shall include information to the public and, if necessary, a temporary bathing prohibition.

Article 8

Cyanobacterial risks

1. When the bathing water profile indicates a potential for cyanobacterial proliferation, appropriate monitoring shall be carried out to enable timely identification of health risks.

2. When cyanobacterial proliferation occurs and a health risk has been identified or presumed, adequate management measures shall be taken immediately to prevent exposure, including information to the public.

Article 9

Other parameters

1. When the bathing water profile indicates a tendency for proliferation of macro-algae and/ or marine phytoplankton, investigations shall be undertaken to determine their acceptability and health risks and adequate management measures shall be taken, including information to the public.

2. Bathing waters shall be inspected visually for pollution such as tarry residues, glass, plastic, rubber or any other waste. When such pollution is found, adequate management measures shall be taken, including, if necessary, information to the public.

Article 10

Cooperation on transboundary waters

Wherever a river basin gives rise to transboundary impacts on bathing water quality, the Member States involved shall cooperate as appropriate in implementing this Directive, including through the appropriate exchange of information and joint action to control those impacts.

Chapter III
Exchange of information

Article 11

Public participation

Member States shall encourage public participation in the implementation of this Directive and shall ensure the provision of opportunities for the public concerned:
— to find out how to participate, and
— to formulate suggestions, remarks or complaints.
This shall relate, in particular, to the establishment, review and updating of lists of bathing waters in accordance with Article 3(1). Competent authorities shall take due account of any information obtained.

Article 12

Information to the public

1. Member States shall ensure that the following information is actively disseminated and promptly made available during the bathing season in an easily accessible place in the near vicinity of each bathing water:
(a) the current bathing water classification and any bathing prohibition or advice against bathing referred to in this Article by means of a clear and simple sign or symbol;
(b) a general description of the bathing water, in non-technical language, based on the bathing water profile established in accordance with Annex III;
(c) in the case of bathing waters subject to short-term pollution:
  — notification that the bathing water is subject to short-term pollution,
  — an indication of the number of days on which bathing was prohibited or advised against during the preceding bathing season because of such pollution, and
  — a warning whenever such pollution is predicted or present,
(d) information on the nature and expected duration of abnormal situations during such events;
(e) whenever bathing is prohibited or advised against, a notice advising the public and giving reasons;

(f) whenever a permanent bathing prohibition or permanent advice against bathing is introduced, the fact that the area concerned is no longer a bathing water and the reasons for its declassification; and

(g) an indication of sources of more complete information in accordance with paragraph 2.

2. Member States shall use appropriate media and technologies, including the Internet, to disseminate actively and promptly the information concerning bathing waters referred to in paragraph 1 and also the following information in several languages, when appropriate:

(a) a list of bathing waters;

(b) the classification of each bathing water over the last three years and its bathing water profile, including the results of monitoring carried out in accordance with this Directive since the last classification;

(c) in the case of bathing waters classified as being "poor", information on the causes of pollution and measures taken with a view to preventing bathers' exposure to pollution and to tackle its causes as referred to in Article 5(4); and

(d) in the case of bathing waters subject to short-term pollution, general information on:
- — conditions likely to lead to short-term pollution,
- — the likelihood of such pollution and its likely duration,
- — the causes of the pollution and measures taken with a view to preventing bathers' exposure to pollution and to tackle its causes.

The list referred to in point (a) shall be available each year before the start of the bathing season. The results of the monitoring referred to in point (b) shall be made available on the Internet upon completion of the analysis.

3. The information referred to in paragraphs 1 and 2 shall be disseminated as soon as it is available and with effect from the start of the fifth bathing season after 24 March 2008.

4. Member States and the Commission shall, wherever possible, provide information to the public using geo-referenced technology and present it in a clear and coherent manner, in particular through the use of signs and symbols.

Article 13

Reports

1. Member States shall provide the Commission with the results of the monitoring and with the bathing water quality assessment for each bathing water, as well as with a description of significant management measures taken. Member States shall provide this information annually by 31 December in relation to the preceding bathing season. They shall begin providing it once the first bathing water quality assessment has been carried out in accordance with Article 4.

2. Member States shall notify the Commission annually before the start of the bathing season of all waters identified as bathing waters, including the reason for any change compared to the preceding year. They shall do so for the first time before the start of the first bathing season after 24 March 2008.

3. When monitoring of bathing water has started under this Directive, annual reporting to the Commission in accordance with paragraph 1 shall continue to take place pursuant to Directive 76/160/EEC until a first assessment can be made under this Directive. During that period, parameter 1 of the Annex to Directive 76/160/EEC shall not be taken into account in the annual report, and parameters 2 and 3 of the Annex to Directive 76/160/EEC shall be assumed to be equivalent to parameters 2 and 1 of column A of Annex I to this Directive.

4. The Commission shall publish an annual summary report on bathing water quality in the Community, including bathing water classifications, conformity with this Directive and significant management measures undertaken. The Commission shall publish this report by 30 April every year, including via the Internet. When establishing the report the Commission

shall, wherever possible, make best use of data collection, assessment and presentation systems under related Community legislation, in particular Directive 2000/60/EC.

Chapter IV
Final provisions

Article 14

Report and review

1. The Commission shall, by 2008, submit a report to the European Parliament and to the Council. The report shall have particular regard to:
(a) the results of an appropriate European epidemiological study conducted by the Commission in collaboration with Member States;
(b) other scientific, analytical and epidemiological developments relevant to the parameters for bathing water quality, including in relation to viruses; and
(c) World Health Organisation recommendations.

2. Member States shall, by the end of 2014, submit written observations to the Commission on that report including on the need for any further research or assessments which may be required to assist the Commission in its review of this Directive under paragraph 3.

3. In the light of the report, the Member States' written observations and an extended impact assessment and bearing in mind experience gained from implementing this Directive, the Commission shall, no later than 2020, review this Directive with particular regard to the parameters for bathing water quality, including whether it would be appropriate to phase out the "sufficient" classification or modify the applicable standards, and shall present if necessary appropriate legislative proposals in accordance with Article 251 of the Treaty.

[Article 15

Technical adaptations and implementing measures][1]

[1. The Commission shall, in accordance with the regulatory procedure referred to in Article 16(2), lay down the following:
(a) detailed rules for the implementation of Article 8(1), Article 12(1)(a) and Article 12(4);
(b) guidelines for a common method for the assessment of single samples.

2. The Commission shall adopt the following measures:
(a) the specification of EN/ISO standard on the equivalence of microbiological methods for the purposes of Article 3(9);
(b) any amendments necessary in order to adapt the methods of analysis for the parameters set out in Annex I in the light of scientific and technical progress;
(c) any amendments necessary in order to adapt Annex V in the light of scientific and technical progress.

Those measures, designed to amend non-essential elements of this Directive, inter alia, by supplementing it, shall be adopted in accordance with the regulatory procedure with scrutiny referred to in Article 16(3).

3. The Commission shall present a draft of the measures to be taken in accordance with paragraph 1(a) with respect to Article 12(1)(a) by 24 March 2010. Before doing so, it shall consult representatives of Member States, regional and local authorities, relevant tourist and consumer organisations and other interested parties. After the adoption of relevant rules, it shall publicise them via the Internet.][1]

Amendment

1 Substituted by Regulation (EC) No 596/2009 of the European Parliament and of the Council of 18 June 2009 adapting a number of instruments subject to the procedure referred to in Article 251 of the Treaty to Council Decision 1999/468/EC with regard to the regulatory procedure with scrutiny, Article 1, Annex, para 2.5.1.

Article 16

Committee procedure

1. The Commission shall be assisted by a committee.

2. Where reference is made to this paragraph, Articles 5 and 7 of Decision 1999/468/EC shall apply, having regard to the provisions of Article 8 thereof.

The period laid down in Article 5(6) of Decision 1999/468/EC shall be set at three months.

[3. Where reference is made to this paragraph, Article 5a(1) to (4) and Article 7 of Decision 1999/468/EC shall apply, having regard to the provisions of Article 8 thereof.][1]

Amendment

1 Substituted by Regulation (EC) No 596/2009 of the European Parliament and of the Council of 18 June 2009 adapting a number of instruments subject to the procedure referred to in Article 251 of the Treaty to Council Decision 1999/468/EC with regard to the regulatory procedure with scrutiny, Article 1, Annex, para 2.5.2.

Article 17

Repeal

1. Directive 76/160/EEC is hereby repealed with effect from 31 December 2014. Subject to paragraph 2, this repeal shall be without prejudice to Member States' obligations concerning the time limits for transposition and application set out in the repealed Directive.

2. As soon as a Member State has taken all necessary legal, administrative and practical measures to comply with this Directive, this Directive will be applicable, replacing Directive 76/160/EEC.

3. References to the repealed Directive 76/160/EEC shall be construed as being made to this Directive.

Article 18

Implementation

1. Member States shall bring into force the laws, regulations and administrative provisions necessary to comply with this Directive by 24 March 2008. They shall forthwith inform the Commission thereof.

When Member States adopt these measures, they shall contain a reference to this Directive or shall be accompanied by such a reference on the occasion of their official publication. The methods of making such reference shall be laid down by Member States.

2. Member States shall communicate to the Commission the texts of the main provisions of national law that they adopt in the field covered by this Directive.

Article 19

Entry into force

This Directive shall enter into force on the 20th day following its publication in the Official Journal of the European Union.

Article 20

Addressees

This Directive is addressed to Member States.

ANNEX I

FOR INLAND WATERS

	A	B	C	D	E
	Parameter	*Excellent quality*	*Good quality*	*Sufficient*	*Reference methods of analysis*
1	Intestinal enterococci (cfu/100 ml)	200(1)	400(1)	330(2)	ISO 7899-1 or ISO 7899-2
2	Escherichia coli (cfu/100 ml)	500(1)	1000(1)	900(2)	ISO 9308-3 or ISO 9308-1

(1) Based upon a 95 percentile evaluation. See Annex II.
(2) Based upon a 90 percentile evaluation. See Annex II.

FOR COASTAL WATERS AND TRANSITIONAL WATERS

	A	B	C	D	E
	Parameter	*Excellent quality*	*Good quality*	*Sufficient*	*Reference methods of analysis*
1	Intestinal enterococci (cfu/100 ml)	100(1)	200(1)	185(2)	ISO 7899-1 or ISO 7899-2
2	Escherichia coli (cfu/100 ml)	250(1)	500(1)	500(2)	ISO 9308-3 or ISO 9308-1

(1) Based upon a 95 percentile evaluation. See Annex II.
(2) Based upon a 90 percentile evaluation. See Annex II.

ANNEX II
BATHING WATER ASSESSMENT AND CLASSIFICATION

1. POOR QUALITY

Bathing waters are to be classified as "poor" if, in the set of bathing water quality data for the last assessment period, the percentile values for microbiological enumerations are worse than the "sufficient" values set out in Annex I, column D.

2. SUFFICIENT QUALITY

Bathing waters are to be classified as "sufficient":

1. if, in the set of bathing water quality data for the last assessment period, the percentile values for microbiological enumerations are equal to or better than the "sufficient" values set out in Annex I, column D; and
2. if the bathing water is subject to short-term pollution, on condition that:
   - (i) adequate management measures are being taken, including surveillance, early warning systems and monitoring, with a view to preventing bathers' exposure by means of a warning or, where necessary, a bathing prohibition;
   - (ii) adequate management measures are being taken to prevent, reduce or eliminate the causes of pollution; and
   - (iii) the number of samples disregarded in accordance with Article 3(6) because of short-term pollution during the last assessment period represented no more than 15 % of the total number of samples provided for in the monitoring calendars established for that period, or no more than one sample per bathing season, whichever is the greater.

3. GOOD QUALITY

Bathing waters are to be classified as "good":

1. if, in the set of bathing water quality data for the last assessment period, the percentile values for microbiological enumerations are equal to or better than the "good quality" values set out in Annex I, column C; and
2. if the bathing water is subject to short-term pollution, on condition that:
   (i) adequate management measures are being taken, including surveillance, early warning systems and monitoring, with a view to preventing bathers' exposure, by means of a warning or, where necessary, a bathing prohibition;
   (ii) adequate management measures are being taken to prevent, reduce or eliminate the causes of pollution; and
   (iii) the number of samples disregarded in accordance with Article 3(6) because of short-term pollution during the last assessment period represented no more than 15 % of the total number of samples provided for in the monitoring calendars established for that period, or no more than one sample per bathing season, whichever is the greater.

4. EXCELLENT QUALITY

Bathing waters are to be classified as "excellent":

1. if, in the set of bathing water quality data for the last assessment period, the percentile values for microbiological enumerations are equal to or better than the "excellent quality" values set out in Annex I, column B; and
2. if the bathing water is subject to short-term pollution, on condition that:
   (i) adequate management measures are being taken, including surveillance, early warning systems and monitoring, with a view to preventing bathers' exposure, by means of a warning or, where necessary, a bathing prohibition;
   (ii) adequate management measures are being taken to prevent, reduce or eliminate the causes of pollution; and
   (iii) the number of samples disregarded in accordance with Article 3(6) because of short-term pollution during the last assessment period represented no more than 15 % of the total number of samples provided for in the monitoring calendars established for that period, or no more than one sample per bathing season, whichever is the greater.

ANNEX III
THE BATHING WATER PROFILE

1. The bathing water profile referred to in Article 6 is to consist of:

(a) a description of the physical, geographical and hydrological characteristics of the bathing water, and of other surface waters in the catchment area of the bathing water concerned, that could be a source of pollution, which are relevant to the purpose of this Directive and as provided for in Directive 2000/60/EC;

(b) an identification and assessment of causes of pollution that might affect bathing waters and impair bathers' health;

(c) an assessment of the potential for proliferation of cyanobacteria;

(d) an assessment of the potential for proliferation of macro-algae and/or phytoplankton;

(e) if the assessment under point (b) shows that there is a risk of short-term pollution, the following information:

- the anticipated nature, frequency and duration of expected short-term pollution,
- details of any remaining causes of pollution, including management measures taken and the time schedule for their elimination,
- management measures taken during short-term pollution and the identity and contact details of bodies responsible for taking such action,

(f) the location of the monitoring point.

2. In the case of bathing waters classified as "good", "sufficient" or "poor", the bathing water profile is to be reviewed regularly to assess whether any of the aspects listed in paragraph 1 have changed. If necessary, it is to be updated. The frequency and scope of reviews is to be determined on the basis of the nature and severity of the pollution. However, they are to comply with at least the provisions and to take place with at least the frequency specified in the following table.

Bathing water classification	*"Good"*	*"Sufficient"*	*"Poor"*
Reviews are to take place at least every	four years	three years	two years
Aspects to be reviewed (points of paragraph 1)	(a) to (f)	(a) to (f)	(a) to (f)

In the case of bathing waters previously classified as "excellent", the bathing water profiles need be reviewed and, if necessary, updated only if the classification changes to "good", "sufficient" or "poor". The review is to cover all aspects mentioned in paragraph 1.

3. In the event of significant construction works or significant changes in the infrastructure in or in the vicinity of the bathing water, the bathing water profile is to be updated before the start of the next bathing season.

4. The information referred to in paragraph 1(a) and (b) is to be provided on a detailed map whenever practicable.

5. Other relevant information may be attached or included if the competent authority considers it appropriate.

ANNEX IV
BATHING WATER MONITORING

1. One sample is to be taken shortly before the start of each bathing season. Taking account of this extra sample and subject to paragraph 2, no fewer than four samples are to be taken and analysed per bathing season.

2. However, only three samples need be taken and analysed per bathing season in the case of a bathing water that either:
(a) has a bathing season not exceeding eight weeks; or
(b) is situated in a region subject to special geographical constraints.

3. Sampling dates are to be distributed throughout the bathing season, with the interval between sampling dates never exceeding one month.

4. In the event of short-term pollution, one additional sample is to be taken to confirm that the incident has ended. This sample is not to be part of the set of bathing water quality data. If necessary to replace a disregarded sample, an additional sample is to be taken seven days after the end of the short-term pollution.

ANNEX V
RULES ON THE HANDLING OF SAMPLES FOR MICROBIOLOGICAL ANALYSES

1. SAMPLING POINT

Where possible, samples are to be taken 30 centimetres below the water's surface and in water that is at least one metre deep.

2. STERILISATION OF SAMPLE BOTTLES

Sample bottles are:

— to undergo sterilisation in an autoclave for at least 15 minutes at 121°C, or
— to undergo dry sterilisation at between 160°C and 170°C for at least one hour, or
— to be irradiated sample containers obtained directly from manufacturer.

3. SAMPLING

The volume of the sampling bottle/container is to depend on the quantity of water needed for each parameter to be tested. The minimum content is generally 250 ml.

Sample containers are to be of transparent and non-coloured material (glass, polyethene or polypropylene).

In order to prevent accidental contamination of the sample, the sampler is to employ an aseptic technique to maintain the sterility of the sample bottles. There is no further need for sterile equipment (such as sterile surgical gloves or tongs or sample pole) if this is done properly.

The sample is to be clearly identified in indelible ink on the sample and on the sampling form.

4. STORAGE AND TRANSPORT OF SAMPLES BEFORE ANALYSIS

Water samples are to be protected at all stages of transport from exposure to light, in particular direct sunlight.

The sample is to be conserved at a temperature of around 4°C, in a cool box or refrigerator (depending on climate) until arrival at the laboratory. If the transport to the laboratory is likely to take more than four hours, then transport in a refrigerator is required.

The time between sampling and analysis is to be kept as short as possible. It is recommended that samples be analysed on the same working day. If this is not possible for practical reasons, then the samples shall be processed within no more than 24 hours. In the meantime, they shall be stored in the dark and at a temperature of 4°C ± 3°C.

DIRECTIVE 2006/11/EC OF THE EUROPEAN PARLIAMENT AND OF THE COUNCIL

of 15 February 2006

ON POLLUTION CAUSED BY CERTAIN DANGEROUS SUBSTANCES DISCHARGED INTO THE AQUATIC ENVIRONMENT OF THE COMMUNITY

THE EUROPEAN PARLIAMENT AND THE COUNCIL OF THE EUROPEAN UNION,

Having regard to the Treaty establishing the European Community, and in particular Article 175(1) thereof,

Having regard to the proposal from the Commission,

Having regard to the opinion of the European Economic and Social Committee,

After consulting the Committee of the Regions,

Acting in accordance with the procedure laid down in Article 251 of the Treaty,

Whereas:

(1) Council Directive 76/464/EEC of 4 May 1976 on pollution caused by certain dangerous substances discharged into the aquatic environment of the Community has been significantly amended on several occasions. In order to clarify matters, a codification of the provisions in question should be drawn up.

(2) There is a need for general and simultaneous action by the Member States to protect the aquatic environment of the Community from pollution, particularly that caused by certain persistent, toxic and bioaccumulable substances.

(3) Several conventions are designed to protect international watercourses and the marine environment from pollution. It is important to ensure the coordinated implementation of these conventions.

(4) Discrepancies between the provisions applicable in the various Member States with regard to the discharge of certain dangerous substances into the aquatic environment may give rise to unequal conditions of competition and thus have a direct influence on the functioning of the internal market.

(5) Decision No 1600/2002/EC of the European Parliament and of the Council of 22 July 2002 laying down the Sixth Community Environment Action Programme, provides for a number of measures to protect fresh water and sea water from certain pollutants.

(6) In order to ensure effective protection of the aquatic environment of the Community, it is necessary to establish a first list, called List I, of certain individual substances selected mainly on the basis of their toxicity, persistence and bioaccumulation, with the exception of those which are biologically harmless or which are rapidly converted into substances which are biologically harmless, and a second list, called List II, containing substances which have a deleterious effect on the aquatic environment, which can, however, be confined to a given area and which depends on the characteristics and location of the water into which such substances are discharged. Any discharge of these substances should be subject to prior authorisation which specifies emission standards.

(7) Pollution through the discharge of the various dangerous substances within List I must be eliminated. Limit values were fixed by the Directives referred to in Annex IX to Directive 2000/60/EC of the European Parliament and of the Council of 23 October 2000 establishing a framework for Community action in the field of water policy. Article 16 of Directive 2000/60/EC provides for the procedures for developing the control measures and environmental quality standards applicable to priority substances.

(8) It is necessary to reduce water pollution caused by the substances within List II. To this end Member States should establish programmes which incorporate environmental quality standards for water, drawn up in compliance with Council Directives, where they exist. The emission standards applicable to such substances should be calculated in terms of these environmental quality standards.

(9) It is appropriate for one or more Member States to be able, individually or jointly, to take measures more stringent than those provided for under this Directive.

(10) An inventory of discharges of certain particularly dangerous substances into the aquatic environment of the Community should be drawn up in order to know where they originated.

(11) It may be necessary to revise and, where required, supplement Lists I and II of Annex I on the basis of experience, if appropriate by transferring certain substances from List II to List I.

(12) This Directive should be without prejudice to the obligations of the Member States relating to the time limits for transposition into national law of the Directives set out in Part B of Annex II,

HAVE ADOPTED THIS DIRECTIVE:

Article 1

Subject to Article 7, this Directive shall apply to:

(a) inland surface water;

(b) territorial waters;

(c) internal coastal waters.

Article 2

For the purposes of this Directive:

(a) "inland surface water" means all static or flowing fresh surface water situated in the territory of one or more Member States;

(b) "internal coastal waters" means waters on the landward side of the base line from which the breadth of territorial waters is measured, extending, in the case of watercourses, up to the fresh water limit;

(c) "fresh water limit" means the place in the watercourse where, at low tide and in a period of low fresh water flow, there is an appreciable increase in salinity due to the presence of sea water;

(d) "discharge" means the introduction into the waters referred to in Article 1 of any substances in List I or List II of Annex I, with the exception of:

   (i) discharges of dredgings;

   (ii) operational discharges from ships in territorial waters;

   (iii) dumping from ships in territorial waters;

(e) "pollution" means the discharge by man, directly or indirectly, of substances or energy into the aquatic environment, the results of which are such as to cause hazards to human health, harm to living resources and to aquatic ecosystems, damage to amenities or interference with other legitimate uses of water.

Article 3

Member States shall take the appropriate steps to eliminate pollution of the waters referred to in Article 1 by the dangerous substances in the families and groups of substances in List I of Annex I, hereinafter referred to as "List I substances", and to reduce pollution of the said waters by the dangerous substances in the families and groups of substances in List II of Annex I, hereinafter referred to as "List II substances", in accordance with this Directive.

Article 4

With regard to List I substances:

(a) all discharges into the waters referred to in Article 1 which are liable to contain any such substance, shall require prior authorisation by the competent authority of the Member State concerned;

(b) the authorisation shall lay down emission standards with regard to discharges of any such substance into the waters referred to in Article 1 and, where this is necessary for the implementation of this Directive, to discharges of any such substance into sewers;

(c) authorisations may be granted for a limited period only. They may be renewed, taking into account any changes in the emission limit values laid down by the Directives referred to in Annex IX to Directive 2000/60/EC.

Article 5

1. The emission standards laid down in the authorisations granted pursuant to Article 4 shall determine:

(a) the maximum concentration of a substance permissible in a discharge. In the case of dilution, the emission limit value laid down by the Directives referred to in Annex IX to Directive 2000/60/EC shall be divided by the dilution factor;

(b) the maximum quantity of a substance permissible in a discharge during one or more specified periods of time, expressed, if necessary, as a unit of weight of the pollutant per unit of the characteristic element of the polluting activity (e.g. unit of weight per unit of raw material or per product unit).

2. For each authorisation, the competent authority of the Member State concerned may, if necessary, impose more stringent emission standards than those resulting from the application of the emission limit values laid down by the Directives referred to in Annex IX to Directive 2000/60/EC, taking into account in particular the toxicity, persistence and bioaccumulation of the substance concerned in the environment into which it is discharged.

3. If the discharger states that he is unable to comply with the required emission standards, or if this situation is evident to the competent authority in the Member State concerned, authorisation shall be refused.

4. Should the emission standards not be complied with, the competent authority in the Member State concerned shall take all appropriate steps to ensure that the conditions of authorisation are fulfilled and, if necessary, that the discharge is prohibited.

Article 6

1. In order to reduce pollution of the waters referred to in Article 1 by List II substances, Member States shall establish programmes in the implementation of which they shall apply in particular the methods referred to in paragraphs 2 and 3.

2. All discharges into the waters referred to in Article 1 which are liable to contain any List II substances, shall require prior authorisation by the competent authority in the Member State concerned, in which emission standards shall be laid down. Such standards shall be based on the environmental quality standards, which shall be fixed as provided for in paragraph 3.

3. The programmes referred to in paragraph 1 shall include environmental quality standards for water; these shall be laid down in accordance with Council Directives, where they exist.

4. The programmes may also include specific provisions governing the composition and use of substances or groups of substances and products and shall take into account the latest economically feasible technical developments.

5. The programmes shall set deadlines for their implementation.

6. Summaries of the programmes and the results of their implementation shall be communicated to the Commission.

7. The Commission, together with the Member States, shall arrange for regular comparisons of the programmes in order to ensure sufficient coordination in their implementation. If it sees fit, it shall submit relevant proposals to the European Parliament and to the Council to this end.

Article 7

Member States shall take all appropriate steps to implement measures adopted by them pursuant to this Directive in such a way as not to increase the pollution of waters to which Article 1 does not apply. They shall in addition prohibit all acts which intentionally or unintentionally circumvent the provisions of this Directive.

Article 8

The application of the measures taken pursuant to this Directive may on no account lead, either directly or indirectly, to increased pollution of the waters referred to in Article 1.

Article 9

Where appropriate, one or more Member States may individually or jointly take more stringent measures than those provided for under this Directive.

Article 10

The competent authority shall draw up an inventory of the discharges into the waters referred to in Article 1 which may contain List I substances to which emission standards are applicable.

Article 11

1. At intervals of three years, and for the first time for the period 1993 to 1995 inclusive, Member States shall send information to the Commission on the implementation of this Directive, in the form of a sectoral report which shall also cover other pertinent Community Directives. This report shall be drawn up on the basis of a questionnaire or outline drafted by the Commission in accordance with the procedure referred to in Article 6 of Council Directive 91/692/EEC of 23 December 1991 standardising and rationalising reports on the implementation of certain Directives relating to the environment. The questionnaire or outline shall be sent to the Member States six months before the start of the period covered by the report. The report shall be sent to the Commission within nine months of the end of the three-year period covered by it.

The Commission shall publish a Community report on the implementation of the Directive within nine months of receiving the reports from the Member States.

2. Information acquired as a result of the application of paragraph 1 shall be used only for the purpose for which it was requested.

3. The Commission and the competent authorities of the Member States, their officials and other servants shall not disclose information acquired by them pursuant to this Directive and of a kind covered by the obligation of professional secrecy.

4. The provisions of paragraphs 2 and 3 shall not prevent publication of general information or surveys which do not contain information relating to particular undertakings or associations of undertakings.

Article 12

The European Parliament and the Council, acting on a proposal from the Commission, which shall act on its own initiative or at the request of a Member State, shall revise and, where necessary, supplement Lists I and II of Annex I on the basis of experience, if appropriate, by transferring certain List II substances to List I.

Article 13

Directive 76/464/EEC is hereby repealed, without prejudice to the obligations of the Member States relating to the time limits for transposition into national law of the Directives set out in Part B of Annex II.

References to the repealed Directive shall be construed as references to this Directive and should be read in accordance with the correlation table in Annex III.

Article 14

This Directive shall enter into force on the 20th day following its publication in the Official Journal of the European Union.

Article 15

This Directive is addressed to the Member States.

ANNEX I

LIST I OF FAMILIES AND GROUPS OF SUBSTANCES

List I contains certain individual substances which belong to the following families and groups of substances, selected mainly on the basis of their toxicity, persistence and bioaccumulation, with the exception of those which are biologically harmless or which are rapidly converted into substances which are biologically harmless:

1. organohalogen compounds and substances which may form such compounds in the aquatic environment;
2. organophosphorus compounds;
3. organotin compounds;
4. substances which have been proved to possess carcinogenic properties in or via the aquatic environment;
5. mercury and its compounds;
6. cadmium and its compounds;
7. persistent mineral oils and hydrocarbons of petroleum origin;

and for the purposes of implementing Articles 3, 7, 8 and 12:

8. persistent synthetic substances which may float, remain in suspension or sink and which may interfere with any use of the waters.

LIST II OF FAMILIES AND GROUPS OF SUBSTANCES

List II contains:

- substances belonging to the families and groups of substances in List I for which the emission limit values laid down by the Directives referred to in Annex IX to Directive 2000/60/EC have not been determined by those Directives,
- certain individual substances and categories of substances belonging to the families and groups of substances listed below,

and which have a deleterious effect on the aquatic environment, which can, however, be confined to a given area and which depends on the characteristics and location of the water into which such substances are discharged.

Families and groups of substances referred to in the second indent

1. The following metalloids and metals and their compounds:

1. zinc
2. copper
3. nickel

4. chromium
5. lead
6. selenium
7. arsenic
8. antimony
9. molybdenum
10. titanium
11. tin
12. barium
13. beryllium
14. boron
15. uranium
16. vanadium
17. cobalt
18. thalium
19. tellurium
20. silver

2. Biocides and their derivatives not appearing in List I.

3. Substances which have a deleterious effect on the taste and/or smell of the products for human consumption derived from the aquatic environment, and compounds liable to give rise to such substances in water.

4. Toxic or persistent organic compounds of silicon, and substances which may give rise to such compounds in water, excluding those which are biologically harmless or are rapidly converted in water into harmless substances.

5. Inorganic compounds of phosphorus and elemental phosphorus.

6. Non-persistent mineral oils and hydrocarbons of petroleum origin.

7. Cyanides, fluorides.

8. Substances which have an adverse effect on the oxygen balance, particularly:ammonia, nitrites.

Statement on Article 7

With regard to the discharge of waste water into the open sea by means of pipelines, Member States undertake to lay down requirements which shall be not less stringent than those imposed by this Directive.

ANNEX II

PART A
REPEALED DIRECTIVE WITH ITS SUCCESSIVE AMENDMENT (REFERRED TO IN ARTICLE 13)

Council Directive 76/464/EEC (OJ L 129, 18.5.1976, p. 23)	
Council Directive 91/692/EEC (OJ L 377, 31.12.1991, p. 48)	Annex I, point (a) only
Directive 2000/60/EC of the European Parliament and of the Council (OJ L 327, 22.12.2000, p. 1)	Only as regards the reference in Article 22(2), fourth indent, to Article 6 of Directive 76/464/EEC

PART B
LIST OF TIME LIMITS FOR TRANSPOSITION INTO NATIONAL LAW (REFERRED TO IN ARTICLE 13)

Directive	*Time limit for transposition*
76/464/EEC	—
91/692/EEC	1 January 1993
2000/60/EC	22 December 2003

ANNEX III
CORRELATION TABLE

Directive 76/464/EEC	*This Directive*
Article 1(1), introductory wording	Article 1, introductory wording
Article 1(1), first indent	Article 1(a)
Article 1(1), second indent	Article 1(b)
Article 1(1), third indent	Article 1(c)
Article 1(1), fourth indent	—
Article 1(2), introductory wording	Article 2, introductory wording
Article 1(2)(a), (b) and (c)	Article 2(a), (b) and (c)
Article 1(2)(d), first indent	Article 2(d)(i)
Article 1(2)(d), second indent	Article 2(d)(ii)
Article 1(2)(d), third indent	Article 2(d)(iii)
Article 1(2)(e)	Article 2(e)
Article 2	Article 3
Article 3, introductory wording	Article 4, introductory wording
Article 3, point 1	Article 4(a)
Article 3, point 2	Article 4(b)
Article 3, point 3	—
Article 3, point 4	Article 4(c)
Article 4	—
Article 5	Article 5
Article 7	Article 6
Article 8	Article 7
Article 9	Article 8
Article 10	Article 9
Article 11	Article 10
Article 12	—
Article 13	Article 11
Article 14	Article 12
—	Article 13
—	Article 14
Article 15	Article 15
Annex	Annex I
—	Annex II
—	Annex III

DIRECTIVE 2006/21/EC OF THE EUROPEAN PARLIAMENT AND OF THE COUNCIL

of 15 March 2006

ON THE MANAGEMENT OF WASTE FROM EXTRACTIVE INDUSTRIES AND AMENDING DIRECTIVE 2004/35/EC

THE EUROPEAN PARLIAMENT AND THE COUNCIL OF THE EUROPEAN UNION,

Having regard to the Treaty establishing the European Community, and in particular Article 175(1) thereof,

Having regard to the proposal from the Commission,

Having regard to the opinion of the European Economic and Social Committee,

Having regard to the opinion of the Committee of the Regions,

Acting in accordance with the procedure laid down in Article 251 of the Treaty, in the light of the joint text approved by the Conciliation Committee on 8 December 2005,

Whereas:

(1) The Communication of the Commission entitled "Safe operation of mining activities: a follow-up to recent mining accidents" sets out as one of its priority actions an initiative to regulate the management of waste from the extractive industries. This action is designed to complement initiatives pursuant to Directive 2003/105/EC of the European Parliament and of the Council of 16 December 2003 amending Council Directive 96/82/EC on the control of major-accident hazards involving dangerous substances as well as the production of a best available technique document covering the management of waste rock and tailings from mining activities under the auspices of Council Directive 96/61/EC of 24 September 1996 concerning integrated pollution prevention and control.

(2) In its Resolution of 5 July 2001 concerning that Communication, the European Parliament strongly supported the need for a Directive on waste from the extractive industries.

(3) Decision No 1600/2002/EC of the European Parliament and of the Council of 22 July 2002 laying down the Sixth Community Environment Action Programme sets as the objective for wastes that are still generated that the level of their hazardousness should be reduced and that they should present as little risk as possible, that preference should be given to recovery and especially to recycling, that the quantity of waste for disposal should be minimised and should be safely disposed of, and that waste intended for disposal should be treated as closely as possible to the place of its generation to the extent that this does not lead to a decrease in the efficiency of waste treatment operations. Decision No 1600/2002/EC also prescribes as a priority action, with reference to accidents and disasters, the development of measures to help prevent major accident hazards, with special regard to those arising from mining, and the development of measures on mining waste. Decision No 1600/2002/EC also sets as a priority action the promotion of sustainable management of extractive industries with a view to reducing their environmental impact.

(4) In accordance with the objectives of Community policy on the environment, it is necessary to lay down minimum requirements in order to prevent or reduce as far as possible any adverse effects on the environment or on human health which are brought about as a result of the management of waste from the extractive industries, such as tailings (i.e. the waste solids or slurries that remain after the treatment of minerals by a number of techniques), waste rock and overburden (i.e. the material that extractive

operations move during the process of accessing an ore or mineral body, including during the pre-production development stage), and topsoil (i.e. the upper layer of the ground) provided that they constitute waste as defined in Council Directive 75/442/EEC of 15 July 1975 on waste.

(5) In accordance with paragraph 24 of the Johannesburg Plan of Implementation on Sustainable Development adopted within the framework of the United Nations at the 2002 World Summit on Sustainable Development, it is necessary to protect the natural resource base of economic and social development and reverse the current trend in natural resource degradation by managing the natural resource base in a sustainable and integrated manner.

(6) Accordingly, this Directive should cover the management of waste from land-based extractive industries, that is to say, the waste arising from the prospecting, extraction (including the pre-production development stage), treatment and storage of mineral resources and from the working of quarries. However, such management should reflect the principles and priorities identified in Directive 75/442/EEC, which, in accordance with Article 2(1)(b)(ii) thereof, continues to apply to any aspects of the management of waste from the extractive industries which are not covered by this Directive.

(7) In order to avoid duplication and disproportionate administrative requirements, the scope of this Directive should be limited to those particular operations considered to be a priority for the purposes of meeting its objectives.

(8) Accordingly, the provisions of this Directive should not apply to those waste streams which, albeit generated in the course of mineral extraction or treatment operations, are not directly linked to the extraction or treatment process, e.g. food waste, waste oil, end-of-life vehicles, spent batteries and accumulators. The management of such waste should be subject to the provisions of Directive 75/442/EEC or of Council Directive 1999/31/EC of 26 April 1999 on the landfill of waste or any other relevant Community legislation, as is the case for waste generated at a prospecting, extraction or treatment site and transported to a location that is not a waste facility according to this Directive.

(9) Nor should this Directive apply to waste resulting from the offshore prospecting, extraction and treatment of mineral resources or to the injection of water and re-injection of pumped groundwater, while inert waste, non-hazardous prospecting waste, unpolluted soil and waste resulting from the extraction, treatment and storage of peat should be covered only by a limited set of requirements due to their lower environmental risks. For non-hazardous non-inert waste, Member States may reduce or waive certain requirements. However, these exemptions should not apply to Category A waste facilities.

(10) Moreover, while covering the management of waste from the extractive industries which may be radioactive, this Directive should not cover such aspects as are specific to radioactivity, which are a matter dealt with under the Treaty establishing the European Atomic Energy Community (Euratom).

(11) In order to remain true to the principles and priorities identified in Directive 75/442/EEC and, in particular, Articles 3 and 4 thereof, Member States should ensure that operators engaged in the extractive industry take all necessary measures to prevent or reduce as far as possible any negative effects, actual or potential, on the environment or on human health which are brought about as a result of the management of waste from the extractive industries.

(12) These measures should be based, inter alia, on the concept of best available techniques as defined in Directive 96/61/EC and, when such techniques are applied, it is for the Member States to determine how the technical characteristics of the waste facility, its geographical location and local environmental conditions can, where appropriate, be taken into consideration.

(13) Member States should ensure that operators in the extractive industry draw up appropriate waste management plans for the prevention or minimisation, treatment, recovery and disposal of extractive waste. Such plans should be structured in such a way as to ensure appropriate planning of waste management options with a view to

minimising waste generation and its harmfulness, and encouraging waste recovery. Moreover, waste from the extractive industries should be characterised with respect to its composition in order to ensure that, as far as possible, such waste reacts only in predictable ways.

(14) In order to minimise the risk of accidents and to guarantee a high level of protection for the environment and human health, Member States should ensure that each operator of a Category A waste facility adopts and applies a major-accident prevention policy for waste. In terms of preventive measures, this should entail the delivery of a safety management system, emergency plans to be used in the event of accidents and the dissemination of safety information to persons likely to be affected by a major accident. In the event of an accident, operators should be required to provide the competent authorities with all the relevant information necessary to mitigate actual or potential environmental damage. These particular requirements should not apply to those waste facilities from the extractive industries falling within the scope of Directive 96/82/EC.

(15) A waste facility should not be classified in Category A solely on the basis of risks to the safety and health protection of workers in the extractive industries covered by other Community legislation, in particular Directives 92/91/EEC and 92/104/EEC.

(16) Because of the special nature of the management of waste from the extractive industries, it is necessary to introduce specific application and permit procedures in respect of waste facilities used to receive such waste. In addition, Member States should take the necessary measures to ensure that the competent authorities periodically reconsider and, where necessary, update permit conditions.

(17) Member States should be required to ensure that, in accordance with the UNECE Convention on Access to Information, Public Participation in Decision-making and Access to Justice in Environmental Matters of 25 June 1998 (Aarhus Convention), the public are informed of the application for a waste management permit and the public concerned are consulted prior to the granting of a waste management permit.

(18) It is necessary to indicate clearly the requirements with which waste facilities servicing the extractive industries should comply as regards location, management, control, closure and preventive and protective measures to be taken against any threat to the environment in the short and long-term perspectives, and more especially against the pollution of groundwater by leachate infiltration into the soil.

(19) It is necessary to define clearly Category A waste facilities used to service waste from the extractive industries, taking into account the likely effects of any pollution resulting from the operation of such a facility or from an accident in which waste escapes from such a facility.

(20) Waste placed back into the excavation voids either for their rehabilitation or for construction purposes related to the mineral extraction process, such as the building or maintenance within voids of means of access for machinery, haulage ramps, bulkheads, safety barricades or berms, needs also to be subject to certain requirements in order to protect surface water and/or groundwater, secure the stability of such waste, and ensure appropriate monitoring upon cessation of such activities. Accordingly, such waste should not be subject to the requirements of this Directive which relate exclusively to "waste facilities", except for the requirements mentioned in the specific provision on excavation voids.

(21) With a view to ensuring the proper construction and maintenance of waste facilities servicing waste from the extractive industries, Member States should take appropriate measures to ensure that the design, location and management of such facilities is carried out by technically competent persons. It is necessary to ensure that the training and knowledge acquired by operators and staff afford them the necessary skills. In addition, competent authorities should satisfy themselves that operators ensure suitable arrangements with respect to the construction and maintenance of a new waste facility or to any extension or modification of an existing waste facility, including in the after-closure phase.

(22) It is necessary to establish monitoring procedures during the operation and after-closure of waste facilities. An after-closure period for monitoring and control of Category A waste facilities should be laid down proportionate to the risk posed by the individual waste facility, in a way similar to that required by Directive 1999/31/EC.

(23) It is necessary to define when and how a waste facility servicing the extractive industries should be closed and to set out the obligations and responsibilities to be met by the operator during the after-closure period.

(24) Member States should require operators of the extractive industries to apply monitoring and management controls in order to prevent water and soil pollution and to identify any adverse effect that their waste facilities may have on the environment or on human health. In addition, for the purposes of minimising water pollution, the discharge of waste into any receiving body of water should comply with Directive 2000/60/EC of the European Parliament and of the Council of 23 October 2000 establishing a framework for Community action in the field of water policy. Furthermore, concentrations in tailings ponds of cyanide and cyanide compounds from certain extractive industries should, in view of their harmful and toxic effects, be reduced to the lowest possible levels, using best available techniques. Maximum concentration thresholds should be set accordingly and, in any case, in line with the specific requirements of this Directive to prevent such effects.

(25) The operator of a waste facility servicing the extractive industries should be required to lodge a financial guarantee or equivalent in accordance with procedures to be decided by the Member States ensuring that all the obligations flowing from the permit will be fulfilled, including those relating to the closure and after-closure of the waste facility. The financial guarantee should be sufficient to cover the cost of rehabilitation of the land affected by the waste facility, which includes the waste facility itself, as described in the waste management plan prepared pursuant to Article 5 and required by the Article 7 permit, by a suitably qualified and independent third party. It is also necessary for such a guarantee to be provided prior to the commencement of deposition operations in the waste facility and to be periodically adjusted. In addition, in accordance with the polluter pays principle and with Directive 2004/35/EC of the European Parliament and of the Council of 21 April 2004 on environmental liability with regard to the prevention and remedying of environmental damage, it is important to clarify that an operator of a waste facility servicing the extractive industries is subject to appropriate liability in respect of environmental damage caused by its operations or the imminent threat of such damage.

(26) In the case of the operation of waste facilities servicing the extractive industries that are likely to have significant adverse transboundary effects on the environment and any resultant risks to human health, in the territory of another Member State, there should be a common procedure in place to facilitate consultation among neighbouring countries. This should be done with a view to ensuring that there is an adequate exchange of information between authorities and that the public are duly informed of any such waste facilities that could have adverse effects for the environment of that other Member State.

(27) It is necessary for Member States to ensure that competent authorities organise an effective system of inspections or equivalent control measures in respect of waste facilities servicing the extractive industries. Without prejudice to the obligations of the operator under the permit, prior to the commencement of deposition operations there should be an inspection to check that the permit conditions have been complied with. In addition, Member States should ensure that operators and their successors maintain up-to-date records relating to such waste facilities and that operators transfer to their successors information concerning the state of the waste facility and its operations.

(28) Member States should send regular reports to the Commission on the implementation of this Directive, including information on accidents or near-accidents. On the basis of those reports, the Commission should report to the European Parliament and the Council.

(29) Member States should lay down rules on penalties for infringement of this Directive and ensure that they are implemented. Those penalties should be effective, proportionate and dissuasive.

(30) It is necessary for Member States to ensure that an inventory of closed, including abandoned, waste facilities located on their territory is drawn up in order to identify those which cause serious negative environmental impacts or have the potential of becoming in the medium or short term a serious threat to human health or the environment. These inventories should provide a basis for an appropriate programme of measures.

(31) The Commission should ensure an appropriate exchange of scientific and technical information on how to carry out an inventory of closed waste facilities at Member State level and on the development of methodologies to assist Member States in complying with this Directive when rehabilitating closed waste facilities. Moreover, an exchange of information should be ensured within and between Member States on the best available techniques.

(32) With a view to the consistent application of Article 6 of the Treaty, environmental protection requirements must be integrated into the implementation of Community policies and activities with a view to promoting sustainable development.

(33) This Directive could be a useful instrument to be taken into account when verifying that projects receiving Community funding in the context of development aid include the necessary measures to prevent or reduce as far as possible negative effects on the environment. Such an approach is consistent with Article 6 of the Treaty, particularly with regard to integrating environmental protection requirements into the Community's policy in the sphere of development cooperation.

(34) The objective of this Directive, that is to say, improving the management of waste from the extractive industries, cannot be sufficiently achieved by the Member States acting alone because the mismanagement of such waste may cause pollution of a transboundary nature. Under the polluter pays principle it is necessary, inter alia, to take into account any damage to the environment caused by waste from the extractive industries, and different national applications of that principle may lead to substantial disparities in the financial burden on economic operators. Moreover, the existence of different national policies on the management of waste from the extractive industries hampers the aim of ensuring a minimum level of safe and responsible management of such waste and maximising its recovery throughout the Community. Therefore, since by reason of the scale and effects of this Directive, its objective can be better achieved at Community level, the Community may adopt measures, in accordance with the principle of subsidiarity, as set out in Article 5 of the Treaty. In accordance with the principle of proportionality, as set out in that Article, this Directive does not go beyond what is necessary in order to achieve this objective.

(35) The measures necessary for the implementation of this Directive should be adopted in accordance with Council Decision 1999/468/EC of 28 June 1999 laying down the procedures for the exercise of implementing powers conferred on the Commission.

(36) The operation of waste facilities existing at the moment of transposition of this Directive should be regulated in order to take the necessary measures, within a specified period of time, for their adaptation to the requirements of this Directive.

(37) In accordance with paragraph 34 of the Interinstitutional agreement on better law-making, Member States are encouraged to draw up, for themselves and in the interest of the Community, their own tables, which will, as far as possible, illustrate the correlation between this Directive and the transposition measures and to make them public,

HAVE ADOPTED THIS DIRECTIVE:

Article 1

Subject matter

This Directive provides for measures, procedures and guidance to prevent or reduce as far as possible any adverse effects on the environment, in particular water, air, soil, fauna and flora and landscape, and any resultant risks to human health, brought about as a result of the management of waste from the extractive industries.

Article 2

Scope

1. Subject to paragraphs 2 and 3, this Directive covers the management of waste resulting from the prospecting, extraction, treatment and storage of mineral resources and the working of quarries, hereinafter "extractive waste".

2. The following shall be excluded from the scope of this Directive:

(a) waste which is generated by the prospecting, extraction and treatment of mineral resources and the working of quarries, but which does not directly result from those operations;

(b) waste resulting from the offshore prospecting, extraction and treatment of mineral resources;

(c) injection of water and re-injection of pumped groundwater as defined in the first and second indents of Article 11(3)(j) of Directive 2000/60/EC, to the extent authorised by that Article.

3. Inert waste and unpolluted soil resulting from the prospecting, extraction, treatment and storage of mineral resources and the working of quarries and waste resulting from the extraction, treatment and storage of peat shall not be subject to Articles 7, 8, 11(1) and (3), 12, 13(6), 14 and 16, unless deposited in a Category A waste facility.

The competent authority may reduce or waive the requirements for the deposit of non-hazardous waste generated from the prospecting of mineral resources, except oil and evaporites other than gypsum and anhydrite, as well as for the deposit of unpolluted soil and of waste resulting from the extraction, treatment and storage of peat as long as it is satisfied that the requirements of Article 4 are met.

Member States may reduce or waive the requirements of Articles 11(3), 12(5) and (6), 13(6), 14 and 16 for non-hazardous non-inert waste, unless deposited in a Category A waste facility.

4. Without prejudice to other Community legislation, waste which falls within the scope of this Directive shall not be subject to Directive 1999/31/EC.

Article 3

Definitions

For the purposes of this Directive:

(1) "waste" is as defined in Article 1(a) of Directive 75/442/EEC;

(2) "hazardous waste" is as defined in Article 1(4) of Council Directive 91/689/EEC of 12 December 1991 on hazardous waste;

(3) "inert waste" means waste that does not undergo any significant physical, chemical or biological transformations. Inert waste will not dissolve, burn or otherwise physically or chemically react, biodegrade or adversely affect other matter with which it comes into contact in a way likely to give rise to environmental pollution or harm human health. The total leachability and pollutant content of the waste and the ecotoxicity of

the leachate must be insignificant, and in particular not endanger the quality of surface water and/or groundwater;

(4) "unpolluted soil" means soil that is removed from the upper layer of the ground during extractive activities and that is not deemed to be polluted under the national law of the Member State where the site is located or under Community law;

(5) "mineral resource" or "mineral" means a naturally occurring deposit in the earth's crust of an organic or inorganic substance, such as energy fuels, metal ores, industrial minerals and construction minerals, but excluding water;

(6) "extractive industries" means all establishments and undertakings engaged in surface or underground extraction of mineral resources for commercial purposes, including extraction by drilling boreholes, or treatment of the extracted material;

(7) "off-shore" means that area of the sea and seabed extending from the low water mark of ordinary or medium tides outwards;

(8) "treatment" means the mechanical, physical, biological, thermal or chemical process or combination of processes carried out on mineral resources, including from the working of quarries, with a view to extracting the mineral, including size change, classification, separation and leaching, and the re-processing of previously discarded waste, but excluding smelting, thermal manufacturing processes (other than the burning of limestone) and metallurgical processes;

(9) "tailings" means the waste solids or slurries that remain after the treatment of minerals by separation processes (e.g. crushing, grinding, size-sorting, flotation and other physico-chemical techniques) to remove the valuable minerals from the less valuable rock;

(10) "heap" means an engineered facility for the deposit of solid waste on the surface;

(11) "dam" means an engineered structure designed to retain or confine water and/or waste within a pond;

(12) "pond" means a natural or engineered facility for disposing of fine-grained waste, normally tailings, along with varying amounts of free water, resulting from the treatment of mineral resources and from the clearing and recycling of process water;

(13) "weak acid dissociable cyanide" means cyanide and cyanide compounds that are dissociated with a weak acid at a defined pH;

(14) "leachate" means any liquid percolating through the deposited waste and emitted from or contained within a waste facility, including polluted drainage, which may adversely affect the environment if not appropriately treated;

(15) "waste facility" means any area designated for the accumulation or deposit of extractive waste, whether in a solid or liquid state or in solution or suspension, for the following time-periods:

- no time-period for Category A waste facilities and facilities for waste characterised as hazardous in the waste management plan;
- a period of more than six months for facilities for hazardous waste generated unexpectedly;
- a period of more than one year for facilities for non-hazardous non-inert waste;
- a period of more than three years for facilities for unpolluted soil, non-hazardous prospecting waste, waste resulting from the extraction, treatment and storage of peat and inert waste.

Such facilities are deemed to include any dam or other structure serving to contain, retain, confine or otherwise support such a facility, and also to include, but not be limited to, heaps and ponds, but excluding excavation voids into which waste is replaced, after extraction of the mineral, for rehabilitation and construction purposes;

(16) "major accident" means an occurrence on site in the course of an operation involving the management of extractive waste in any establishment covered by this Directive, leading to a serious danger to human health and/or the environment, whether immediately or over time, on-site or off-site;

(17) "dangerous substance" means a substance, mixture or preparation which is dangerous within the meaning of Directive 67/548/EEC or Directive 1999/45/EC;

(18) "best available techniques" is as defined in Article 2(11) of Directive 96/61/EC;

(19) "receiving body of water" means surface waters, groundwater, transitional waters and coastal water as defined in Article 2(1), (2), (6) and (7) of Directive 2000/60/EC, respectively;

(20) "rehabilitation" means the treatment of the land affected by a waste facility in such a way as to restore the land to a satisfactory state, with particular regard to soil quality, wild life, natural habitats, freshwater systems, landscape and appropriate beneficial uses;

(21) "prospecting" means the search for mineral deposits of economic value, including sampling, bulk sampling, drilling and trenching, but excluding any works required for the development of such deposits, and any activities directly associated with an existing extractive operation;

(22) "the public" means one or more natural or legal persons and, in accordance with national legislation or practice, their associations, organisations or groups;

(23) "the public concerned" means the public affected or likely to be affected by, or having an interest in, the environmental decision-making under Articles 6 and 7 of this Directive; for the purposes of this definition, non-governmental organisations promoting environmental protection and meeting any requirement under national law shall be deemed to have such an interest;

(24) "operator" means the natural or legal person responsible for the management of extractive waste, in accordance with the national law of the Member State in which waste management takes place, including in respect of temporary storage of extractive waste as well as the operational and the after-closure phases;

(25) "waste holder" means the producer of the extractive waste or the natural or legal person who is in possession of it;

(26) "competent person" means a natural person who has the technical knowledge and experience, as defined by the national law of the Member State in which the person operates, to perform the duties arising from this Directive;

(27) "competent authority" means the authority or authorities which a Member State designates as responsible for performing the duties arising from this Directive;

(28) "site" means all land at a distinct geographic location under the management control of an operator;

(29) "substantial change" means a change in the structure or operation of a waste facility that, in the opinion of the competent authority, may have significant negative effects on human health or the environment.

Article 4

General requirements

1. Member States shall take the necessary measures to ensure that extractive waste is managed without endangering human health and without using processes or methods which could harm the environment, and in particular without risk to water, air, soil and fauna and flora, without causing a nuisance through noise or odours and without adversely affecting the landscape or places of special interest. Member States shall also take the necessary measures to prohibit the abandonment, dumping or uncontrolled depositing of extractive waste.

2. Member States shall ensure that the operator takes all measures necessary to prevent or reduce as far as possible any adverse effects on the environment and human health brought about as a result of the management of extractive waste. This includes the management of any waste facility, also after its closure, and the prevention of major accidents involving that facility and the limiting of their consequences for the environment and human health.

3. The measures referred to in paragraph 2 shall be based, inter alia, on the best available techniques, without prescribing the use of any technique or specific technology, but taking into account the technical characteristics of the waste facility, its geographical location and the local environmental conditions.

Article 5

Waste management plan

1. Member States shall ensure that the operator draws up a waste management plan for the minimisation, treatment, recovery and disposal of extractive waste, taking account of the principle of sustainable development.

2. The objectives of the waste management plan shall be:

(a) to prevent or reduce waste production and its harmfulness, in particular by considering:

  (i) waste management in the design phase and in the choice of the method used for mineral extraction and treatment;

  (ii) the changes that the extractive waste may undergo in relation to an increase in surface area and exposure to conditions above ground;

  (iii) placing extractive waste back into the excavation void after extraction of the mineral, as far as is technically and economically feasible and environmentally sound in accordance with existing environmental standards at Community level and with the requirements of this Directive where relevant;

  (iv) putting topsoil back in place after the closure of the waste facility or, if this is not practically feasible, reusing topsoil elsewhere;

  (v) using less dangerous substances for the treatment of mineral resources;

(b) to encourage the recovery of extractive waste by means of recycling, reusing or reclaiming such waste, where this is environmentally sound in accordance with existing environmental standards at Community level and with the requirements of this Directive where relevant;

(c) to ensure short and long-term safe disposal of the extractive waste, in particular by considering, during the design phase, management during the operation and after-closure of a waste facility and by choosing a design which:

  (i) requires minimal and, if possible, ultimately no monitoring, control and management of the closed waste facility;

  (ii) prevents or at least minimises any long-term negative effects, for example attributable to migration of airborne or aquatic pollutants from the waste facility; and

  (iii) ensures the long-term geotechnical stability of any dams or heaps rising above the pre-existing ground surface.

3. The waste management plan shall contain at least the following elements:

(a) where applicable, the proposed classification for the waste facility in accordance with the criteria laid down in Annex III:

  — where a Category A waste facility is required, a document demonstrating that a major-accident prevention policy, a safety management system for implementing it and an internal emergency plan will be put into effect in accordance with Article 6(3);

  — when the operator considers that a Category A waste facility is not required, sufficient information justifying this, including an identification of possible accident hazards;

(b) waste characterisation in accordance with Annex II and a statement of the estimated total quantities of extractive waste to be produced during the operational phase;

(c) a description of the operation generating such waste and of any subsequent treatment to which it is subject;

(d) a description of how the environment and human health may be adversely affected by the deposit of such waste and the preventive measures to be taken in order to minimise environmental impact during operation and after closure, including the aspects referred to in Article 11(2) (a), (b), (d) and (e);

(e) the proposed control and monitoring procedures pursuant to Articles 10, when applicable, and 11(2)(c);

(f) the proposed plan for closure, including rehabilitation, after-closure procedures and monitoring as provided for in Article 12;
(g) measures for the prevention of water status deterioration in accordance with Directive 2000/60/EC and for the prevention or minimisation of air and soil pollution pursuant to Article 13;
(h) a survey of the condition of the land to be affected by the waste facility.

The waste management plan shall provide sufficient information to enable the competent authority to evaluate the operator's ability to meet the objectives of the waste management plan as set out in paragraph 2 and his obligations under this Directive. The plan shall explain, in particular, how the option and method chosen as mentioned in paragraph 2(a)(i) will fulfil the objectives of the waste management plan as laid down in paragraph 2(a).

4. The waste management plan shall be reviewed every five years and/or amended, as appropriate, in the event of substantial changes to the operation of the waste facility or to the waste deposited. Any amendments shall be notified to the competent authority.

5. Plans produced pursuant to other national or Community legislation and containing the information specified in paragraph 3 may be used where this obviates the unnecessary duplication of information and the repetition of work by the operator, on condition that all requirements under paragraphs 1 to 4 are met.

6. The competent authority shall approve the waste management plan on the basis of procedures to be decided by the Member States and shall monitor its implementation.

Article 6

Major-accident prevention and information

1. This Article shall apply to Category A waste facilities, save for those waste facilities falling within the scope of Directive 96/82/EC.

2. Without prejudice to other Community legislation, and in particular Directives 92/91/EEC and 92/104/EEC, Member States shall ensure that major-accident hazards are identified and that the necessary features are incorporated into the design, construction, operation and maintenance, closure and after-closure of the waste facility in order to prevent such accidents and to limit their adverse consequences for human health and/or the environment, including any transboundary impacts.

3. For the purposes of the requirements under paragraph 2, each operator shall, before the start of operations, draw up a major-accident prevention policy for the management of extractive waste and put into effect a safety management system implementing it, in accordance with the elements set out in Section 1 of Annex I, and shall also put into effect an internal emergency plan specifying the measures to be taken on site in the event of an accident.

As part of that policy, the operator shall appoint a safety manager responsible for the implementation and periodic supervision of the major-accident prevention policy.

The competent authority shall draw up an external emergency plan specifying the measures to be taken off-site in the event of an accident. As part of the application for a permit the operator shall provide the competent authority with the information necessary to enable the latter to draw up that plan.

4. The emergency plans referred to in paragraph 3 shall have the following objectives:
(a) to contain and control major accidents and other incidents so as to minimise their effects, and in particular to limit damage to human health and the environment;
(b) to implement the measures necessary to protect human health and the environment from the effects of major accidents and other incidents;
(c) to communicate the necessary information to the public and to the relevant services or authorities in the area;

(d) to provide for the rehabilitation, restoration and clean-up of the environment following a major accident.

Member States shall ensure that, in the event of a major accident, the operator immediately provides the competent authority with all the information required to help minimise its consequences for human health and to assess and minimise the extent, actual or potential, of the environmental damage.

5. Member States shall ensure that the public concerned are given early and effective opportunities to participate in the preparation or review of the external emergency plan to be drawn up in accordance with paragraph 3. To that end, the public concerned shall be informed about any such proposal and relevant information shall be made available, including, inter alia, information about the right to participate in the decision-making process and about the competent authority to which comments and questions may be submitted.

Member States shall ensure that the public concerned is entitled to express comments within reasonable time frames and that, in the decision on the external emergency plan, due account is taken of these comments.

6. Member States shall ensure that information on safety measures and on the action required in the event of an accident, containing at least the elements listed in Section 2 of Annex I, is provided, free of charge and as a matter of course, to the public concerned.

That information shall be reviewed every three years and, where necessary, updated.

Article 7

Application and permit

1. No waste facility shall be allowed to operate without a permit granted by the competent authority. The permit shall contain the elements specified in paragraph 2 of this Article and shall clearly indicate the category of the waste facility in accordance with the criteria referred to in Article 9.

Subject to compliance with all requirements under this Article, any permit produced pursuant to other national or Community legislation may be combined to form a single permit, where such a format obviates the unnecessary duplication of information and the repetition of work by the operator or competent authority. The details specified in paragraph 2 can be covered by one single permit or several permits, provided that all requirements under this Article are complied with.

2. The application for a permit shall contain at least the following details:
(a) the identity of the operator;
(b) the proposed location of the waste facility, including any possible alternative locations;
(c) the waste management plan pursuant to Article 5;
(d) adequate arrangements by way of a financial guarantee or equivalent, as required under Article 14;
(e) the information provided by the operator in accordance with Article 5 of Directive 85/337/EEC if an environmental impact assessment is required under that Directive.

3. The competent authority shall only grant a permit if it is satisfied that:
(a) the operator complies with the relevant requirements under this Directive;
(b) the management of waste does not conflict directly or otherwise interfere with the implementation of the relevant waste management plan or plans referred to in Article 7 of Directive 75/442/EEC.

4. Member States shall take the necessary measures to ensure that competent authorities periodically reconsider and, where necessary, update permit conditions:
— where there are substantial changes in the operation of the waste facility or the waste deposited;

— on the basis of monitoring results reported by the operator pursuant to Article 11(3) or inspections carried out pursuant to Article 17;
— in the light of information exchange on substantial changes in best available techniques under Article 21(3).

5. The information contained in a permit granted under this Article shall be made available to the competent national and Community statistical authorities where requested for statistical purposes. Sensitive information of a purely commercial nature, such as information concerning business relations and cost components and the volume of economic mineral reserves, shall not be made public.

Article 8

Public participation

1. The public shall be informed, by public notices or other appropriate means, such as electronic media where available, of the following matters early in the procedure for granting a permit or, at the latest, as soon as the information can reasonably be provided:
(a) the application for a permit;
(b) where applicable, the fact that a decision concerning an application for a permit is subject to consultation between the Member States in accordance with Article 16;
(c) details of the competent authorities responsible for taking the decision, those from which relevant information can be obtained, those to which comments or questions can be submitted, and details of the time schedule for transmitting comments or questions;
(d) the nature of possible decisions;
(e) where applicable, the details relating to a proposal for the updating of a permit or of permit conditions;
(f) an indication of the times and places where, or the means by which, the relevant information will be made available;
(g) details of the arrangements for public participation made pursuant to paragraph 7.

2. Member States shall ensure that, within appropriate time frames, the following are made available to the public concerned:
(a) in accordance with national legislation, the main reports and advice transmitted to the competent authority at the time when the public were informed in accordance with paragraph 1;
(b) in accordance with the provisions of Directive 2003/4/EC of the European Parliament and of the Council of 28 January 2003 on public access to environmental information, any information in addition to that referred to in paragraph 1 of this Article which is relevant for the decision in accordance with Article 7 of this Directive and which only becomes available after the time the public have been informed in accordance with paragraph 1 of this Article.

3. Member States shall take appropriate measures to ensure that the public are informed, in accordance with paragraph 1 of this Article, of an update of permit conditions in accordance with Article 7(4).

4. The public concerned shall be entitled to express comments and opinions to the competent authority before a decision is taken.

5. The results of the consultations held pursuant to this Article shall be duly taken into account in the taking of a decision.

6. When a decision has been taken the competent authority shall, in accordance with the appropriate procedures, inform the public concerned and shall make the following information available to the public concerned:
(a) the content of the decision, including a copy of the permit;
(b) the reasons and considerations on which the decision is based.

7. The detailed arrangements for public participation under this Article shall be determined by the Member States so as to enable the public concerned to prepare and participate effectively.

Article 9

Classification system for waste facilities

For the purposes of this Directive, the competent authorities shall classify a waste facility as Category A in accordance with the criteria set out in Annex III.

Article 10

Excavation voids

1. Member States shall ensure that the operator, when placing extractive waste back into the excavation voids for rehabilitation and construction purposes, whether created through surface or underground extraction, takes appropriate measures in order to:

(1) secure the stability of the extractive waste in accordance, mutatis mutandis, with Article 11(2);

(2) prevent the pollution of soil, surface water and groundwater in accordance, mutatis mutandis, with Article 13(1), (3) and (5);

(3) ensure the monitoring of the extractive waste and the excavation void in accordance, mutatis mutandis, with Article 12(4) and (5).

2. Directive 1999/31/EC shall continue to apply to the waste other than extractive waste used for filling in excavation voids as appropriate.

Article 11

Construction and management of waste facilities

1. Member States shall take appropriate measures to ensure that the management of a waste facility is in the hands of a competent person and that technical development and training of staff are provided.

2. The competent authority shall satisfy itself that, in constructing a new waste facility or modifying an existing waste facility, the operator ensures that:

(a) the waste facility is suitably located, taking into account in particular Community or national obligations relating to protected areas, and geological, hydrological, hydrogeological, seismic and geotechnical factors, and is designed so as to meet the necessary conditions for, in the short and long-term perspectives, preventing pollution of the soil, air, groundwater or surface water, taking into account especially Directives 76/464/EEC, 80/68/EEC and 2000/60/EC, and ensuring efficient collection of contaminated water and leachate as and when required under the permit, and reducing erosion caused by water or wind as far as it is technically possible and economically viable;

(b) the waste facility is suitably constructed, managed and maintained to ensure its physical stability and to prevent pollution or contamination of soil, air, surface water or groundwater in the short and long-term perspectives as well as to minimise as far as possible damage to landscape;

(c) there are suitable plans and arrangements for regular monitoring and inspection of the waste facility by competent persons and for taking action in the event of results indicating instability or water or soil contamination;

(d) suitable arrangements are made for the rehabilitation of the land and the closure of the waste facility;

(e) suitable arrangements are made for the after-closure phase of the waste facility.

Records of the monitoring and inspections referred to in point (c) shall be kept, together with permit documentation, in order to ensure the appropriate hand-over of information, particularly in the event of a change of operator.

3. The operator shall, without undue delay and in any event not later than 48 hours thereafter, notify the competent authority of any events likely to affect the stability of the waste facility and any significant adverse environmental effects revealed by the control and monitoring procedures of the waste facility. The operator shall implement the internal emergency plan, where applicable, and follow any other instruction from the competent authority as to the corrective measures to be taken.

The operator shall bear the costs of the measures to be undertaken.

At a frequency to be determined by the competent authority, and in any event at least once a year, the operator shall report, on the basis of aggregated data, all monitoring results to the competent authorities for the purposes of demonstrating compliance with permit conditions and increasing knowledge of waste and waste facility behaviour. On the basis of this report the competent authority may decide that validation by an independent expert is necessary.

Article 12

Closure and after-closure procedures for waste facilities

1. Member States shall take measures to ensure compliance with paragraphs 2 to 5.

2. A waste facility shall only start the closure procedure if one of the following conditions is satisfied:
(a) the relevant conditions stated in the permit are met;
(b) authorisation is granted by the competent authority, at the request of the operator;
(c) the competent authority issues a reasoned decision to that effect.

3. A waste facility may be considered as finally closed only after the competent authority has, without undue delay, carried out a final on-site inspection, assessed all the reports submitted by the operator, certified that the land affected by a waste facility has been rehabilitated and communicated to the operator its approval of the closure.

That approval shall not in any way reduce the operator's obligations under the conditions of the permit or otherwise in law.

4. The operator shall be responsible for the maintenance, monitoring, control and corrective measures in the after-closure phase for as long as may be required by the competent authority, taking into account the nature and duration of the hazard, save where the competent authority decides to take over such tasks from the operator, after a waste facility has been finally closed and without prejudice to any national or Community legislation governing the liability of the waste holder.

5. When considered necessary by the competent authority, in order to fulfil relevant environmental requirements set out in Community legislation, in particular those in Directives 76/464/EEC, 80/68/EEC and 2000/60/EC, following closure of a waste facility, the operator shall, inter alia, control the physical and chemical stability of the facility and minimise any negative environmental effect, in particular with respect to surface and groundwater, by ensuring that:
(a) all the structures pertaining to the facility are monitored and conserved, with control and measuring apparatus always ready for use;
(b) where applicable, overflow channels and spillways are kept clean and free.

6. Following closure of a waste facility, the operator shall, without delay, notify the competent authority of any events or developments likely to affect the stability of the waste facility, and any significant adverse environmental effects revealed by the relevant control and monitoring procedures. The operator shall implement the internal emergency plan, where applicable, and

follow any other instruction from the competent authority as to the corrective measures to be taken.

The operator shall bear the costs of the measures to be undertaken.

In cases and at a frequency to be determined by the competent authority, the operator shall report, on the basis of aggregated data, all monitoring results to the competent authorities for the purposes of demonstrating compliance with permit conditions and increasing knowledge of waste and waste facility behaviour.

Article 13

Prevention of water status deterioration, air and soil pollution

1. The competent authority shall satisfy itself that the operator has taken the necessary measures in order to meet Community environmental standards, in particular to prevent, in accordance with Directive 2000/60/EC, the deterioration of current water status, inter alia, by:

(a) evaluating the leachate generation potential, including contaminant content of the leachate, of the deposited waste during both the operational and after-closure phase of the waste facility, and determining the water balance of the waste facility;

(b) preventing or minimising leachate generation and surface water or groundwater and soil from being contaminated by the waste;

(c) collecting and treating contaminated water and leachate from the waste facility to the appropriate standard required for their discharge.

2. The competent authority shall ensure that the operator has taken adequate measures to prevent or reduce dust and gas emissions.

3. Where, on the basis of an assessment of environmental risks, taking into account, in particular, Directives 76/464/EEC, 80/68/EEC or 2000/60/EC, as applicable, the competent authority has decided that collection and treatment of leachate is not necessary or it has been established that the waste facility poses no potential hazard to soil, groundwater or surface water, the requirements set out in points (b) and (c) of paragraph 1 may be reduced or waived accordingly.

4. Member States shall make the disposal of extractive waste, whether in solid, slurry or liquid form, into any receiving body of water other than one constructed for the purpose of disposing of extractive waste conditional upon compliance by the operator with the relevant requirements of Directives 76/464/EEC, 80/68/EEC and 2000/60/EC.

5. When placing extractive waste back into excavation voids, whether created through surface or underground extraction, which will be allowed to flood after closure, the operator shall take the necessary measures to prevent or minimise water status deterioration and soil pollution in accordance, mutatis mutandis, with paragraphs (1) and (3).The operator shall provide the competent authority with the information necessary to ensure compliance with Community obligations, in particular those in Directive 2000/60/EC.

6. In the case of a pond involving the presence of cyanide, the operator shall ensure that the concentration of weak acid dissociable cyanide in the pond is reduced to the lowest possible level using best available techniques and, in any case, at waste facilities which have previously been granted a permit or have already been in operation on 1 May 2008 that the concentration of weak acid dissociable cyanide at the point of discharge of the tailings from the processing plant into the pond does not exceed 50 ppm as from 1 May 2008, 25 ppm as from 1 May 2013, 10 ppm as from 1 May 2018 and 10 ppm at waste facilities which are granted a permit after 1 May 2008.

If the competent authority so requests, the operator shall demonstrate, through a risk assessment that takes site-specific conditions into account, that those concentration limits need not be further lowered.

Article 14

Financial guarantee

1. The competent authority shall, prior to the commencement of any operations involving the accumulation or deposit of extractive waste in a waste facility, require a financial guarantee (e.g. in the form of a financial deposit, including industry-sponsored mutual guarantee funds) or equivalent, in accordance with procedures to be decided by the Member States, so that:

(a) all obligations under the permit issued pursuant to this Directive, including after-closure provisions, are discharged;

(b) there are funds readily available at any given time for the rehabilitation of the land affected by the waste facility, as described in the waste management plan prepared pursuant to Article 5 and required by the Article 7 permit.

2. The calculation of the guarantee referred to in paragraph 1 shall be made on the basis of:

(a) the likely environmental impact of the waste facility, taking into account in particular the category of the waste facility, the characteristics of the waste and the future use of the rehabilitated land;

(b) the assumption that independent and suitably qualified third parties will assess and perform any rehabilitation work needed.

3. The size of the guarantee shall be periodically adjusted in accordance with any rehabilitation work needed to be carried out on the land affected by the waste facility, as described in the waste management plan prepared pursuant to Article 5 and required by the Article 7 permit.

4. Where the competent authority approves closure in accordance with Article 12(3), it shall provide the operator with a written statement releasing him from the guarantee obligation referred to in paragraph 1 of this Article with the exception of after-closure obligations as referred to in Article 12(4).

[*Article 15 is not reproduced.*]

Article 16

Transboundary effects

1. Where a Member State in which a waste facility is situated is aware that the operation of a Category A waste facility is likely to have significant adverse effects on the environment of, and any resultant risks to human health in, another Member State, or where a Member State likely to be thus affected so requests, the Member State in whose territory the application for a permit pursuant to Article 7 was submitted shall forward the information provided pursuant to that Article to the other Member State at the same time as it makes it available to its own nationals.

Such information shall serve as a basis for any consultation necessary within the context of bilateral relations between the two Member States on a reciprocal and equivalent basis.

2. Within the framework of their bilateral relations, Member States shall ensure that in the cases referred to in paragraph 1 the applications are also made available for an appropriate period of time to the public concerned of the Member State likely to be affected so that they will have the right to comment on them before the competent authority reaches its decision.

3. Member States shall ensure that, in the event of an accident involving a waste facility as referred to in paragraph 1 of this Article, information provided by the operator to the competent authority pursuant to Article 6(4) is immediately forwarded to the other Member State in order to help minimise the consequences of the accident for human health and to assess and minimise the extent of the actual or potential environmental damage.

Article 17

Inspections by the competent authority

1. Prior to the commencement of deposit operations and at regular intervals thereafter, including the after-closure phase, to be decided by the Member State concerned, the competent authority shall inspect any waste facility covered by Article 7 in order to ensure that it complies with the relevant conditions of the permit. An affirmative finding shall in no way reduce the responsibility of the operator under the conditions of the permit.

2. Member States shall require the operator to keep up-to-date records of all waste management operations and make them available for inspection by the competent authority and to ensure that, in the event of a change of operator during the management of a waste facility, there is an appropriate transfer of relevant up-to-date information and records relating to the waste facility.

Article 18

Obligation to report

1. At intervals of three years Member States shall transmit to the Commission a report on the implementation of this Directive. The report shall be drawn up on the basis of a questionnaire or outline to be adopted by the Commission in accordance with the procedure referred to in Article 23(2). The report shall be transmitted to the Commission within nine months of the end of the three-year period covered by it.

The Commission shall publish a report on the implementation of this Directive within nine months of receiving the reports from the Member States.

2. Every year Member States shall transmit to the Commission information on events notified by the operators in accordance with Articles 11(3) and 12(6). The Commission shall make this information available to the Member States upon request. Without prejudice to Community law on public access to environmental information, Member States shall in their turn make the information available to members of the public concerned on request.

Article 19

Penalties

The Member States shall lay down rules on penalties for infringement of the provisions of national law adopted pursuant to this Directive and shall take all measures necessary to ensure that they are implemented. The penalties provided for shall be effective, proportionate and dissuasive.

Article 20

Inventory of closed waste facilities

Member States shall ensure that an inventory of closed waste facilities, including abandoned waste facilities, located on their territory which cause serious negative environmental impacts or have the potential of becoming in the medium or short term a serious threat to human health or the environment is drawn up and periodically updated. Such an inventory, to be made available to the public, shall be carried out by 1 May 2012, taking into account the methodologies as referred to in Article 21, if available.

Article 21

Exchange of information

1. The Commission, assisted by the Committee referred to in Article 23, shall ensure that there is an appropriate exchange of technical and scientific information between Member States, with a view to developing methodologies relating to:

(a) the implementation of Article 20;

(b) the rehabilitation of those closed waste facilities identified under Article 20 in order to satisfy the requirements of Article 4. Such methodologies shall allow for the establishment of the most appropriate risk assessment procedures and remedial actions having regard to the variation of geological, hydrogeological and climatological characteristics across Europe.

2. Member States shall ensure that the competent authority follows or is informed of developments in best available techniques.

3. The Commission shall organise an exchange of information between Member States and the organisations concerned on best available techniques, associated monitoring and developments in them. The Commission shall publish the results of the exchange of information.

[Article 22][1]

[1. The Commission shall, in accordance with the regulatory procedure referred to in Article 23(2), adopt the following:

(a) provisions necessary for the harmonisation and regular transmission of the information referred to in Article 7(5) and Article 12(6);

(b) technical guidelines for the establishment of the financial guarantee in accordance with the requirements of Article 14(2);

(c) technical guidelines for inspections in accordance with Article 17.

2. The Commission shall lay down provisions necessary for the following, prioritising points (b), (c) and (d):

(a) the implementation of Article 13(6), including technical requirements relating to the definition of weak acid dissociable cyanide and its measurement method;

(b) the completion of the technical requirements for waste characterisation contained in Annex II;

(c) the interpretation of the definition contained in point 3 of Article 3;

(d) the definition of the criteria for the classification of waste facilities in accordance with Annex III;

(e) the determination of any harmonised standards for sampling and analysis methods needed for the technical implementation of this Directive.

Those measures, designed to amend non-essential elements of this Directive, inter alia, by supplementing it, shall be adopted in accordance with the regulatory procedure with scrutiny referred to in Article 23(3).

3. The Commission shall make the necessary amendments to the Annexes for the purpose of adapting them to scientific and technical progress. Those amendments shall be made with a view to achieving a high level of environmental protection.

Those measures, designed to amend non-essential elements of this Directive, shall be adopted in accordance with the regulatory procedure with scrutiny referred to in Article 23(3).][1]

Amendment

1 Substituted by Regulation (EC) No 596/2009 of the European Parliament and of the Council of 18 June 2009 adapting a number of instruments subject to the procedure referred to in Article 251 of the Treaty to Council Decision 1999/468/EC with regard to the regulatory procedure with scrutiny, Article 1, Annex, para 2.6.1.

Article 23

Committee

1. The Commission shall be assisted by the Committee established by Article 18 of Directive 75/442/EEC, hereinafter "the Committee".

2. Where reference is made to this paragraph, Articles 5 and 7 of Decision 1999/468/EC shall apply, having regard to the provisions of Article 8 thereof.

The period laid down in Article 5(6) of Decision 1999/468/EC shall be set at three months.

[3. Where reference is made to this paragraph, Article 5a(1) to (4) and Article 7 of Decision 1999/468/EC shall apply, having regard to the provisions of Article 8 thereof.][1]

Amendment

1 Substituted by Regulation (EC) No 596/2009 of the European Parliament and of the Council of 18 June 2009 adapting a number of instruments subject to the procedure referred to in Article 251 of the Treaty to Council Decision 1999/468/EC with regard to the regulatory procedure with scrutiny, Article 1, Annex, para 2.6.2.

Article 24

Transitional provision

1. Member States shall ensure that any waste facility which has been granted a permit or which is already in operation on 1 May 2008 complies with the provisions of this Directive by 1 May 2012, except for those set out in Article 14(1) for which compliance must be ensured by 1 May 2014 and for those set out in Article 13(6) for which compliance must be ensured in accordance with the timetable laid down therein.

2. Paragraph 1 shall not apply to waste facilities closed by 1 May 2008.

3. Member States shall ensure that, from 1 May 2006 and notwithstanding any closure of a waste facility after that date and before 1 May 2008, extractive waste is managed in a way that does not prejudice the fulfilment of Article 4(1) of this Directive, and other applicable environmental requirements set out in Community legislation, including Directive 2000/60/EC.

4. Articles 5, 6(3) to (5), 7, 8, 12(1) and (2) and 14(1) to (3) shall not apply to those waste facilities that:

— stopped accepting waste before 1 May 2006,
— are completing the closure procedures in accordance with the applicable Community or national legislation or programmes approved by the competent authority, and
— will be effectively closed by 31 December 2010.

Member States shall notify such cases to the Commission by 1 August 2008 and ensure that these facilities are managed in a way that does not prejudice the achievement of the objectives of this Directive, in particular the objectives of Article 4(1), and those of any other Community legislation, including Directive 2000/60/EC.

Article 25

Transposition

1. Member States shall bring into force the laws, regulations and administrative provisions necessary to comply with this Directive before 1 May 2008. They shall forthwith inform the Commission thereof.

When Member States adopt these measures, they shall contain a reference to this Directive or shall be accompanied by such reference on the occasion of their official publication. The methods of making such reference shall be laid down by Member States.

2. Member States shall communicate to the Commission the text of the provisions of national law which they adopt in the field covered by this Directive.

Article 26

Entry into force

This Directive shall enter into force on the 20th day following its publication in the Official Journal of the European Union.

Article 27

Addressees

This Directive is addressed to the Member States.

ANNEX I
MAJOR-ACCIDENT PREVENTION POLICY AND INFORMATION TO BE COMMUNICATED TO THE PUBLIC CONCERNED

1. MAJOR-ACCIDENT PREVENTION POLICY

The operator's major-accident prevention policy and safety management system should be proportionate to the major-accident hazards presented by the waste facility. For the purpose of implementing them, account shall be taken of the following elements:

(1) the major-accident prevention policy should include the operator's overall aims and principles of action with respect to the control of major-accident hazards;

(2) the safety management system should include the part of the general management system which includes the organisational structure, responsibilities, practices, procedures, processes and resources for determining and implementing the major-accident prevention policy;

(3) the following issues shall be addressed by the safety management system:

- (a) organisation and personnel — the roles and responsibilities of personnel involved in the management of major hazards at all levels in the organisation; identification of training needs of such personnel and the provision of the training so identified; and involvement of employees and, where appropriate, subcontractors;
- (b) identification and evaluation of major hazards — adoption and implementation of procedures for systematically identifying major hazards arising from normal and abnormal operations and assessment of their likelihood and severity;
- (c) operational control — adoption and implementation of procedures and instructions for safe operation, including maintenance of plant, processes, equipment and temporary stoppages;
- (d) management of change — adoption and implementation of procedures for planning modifications to, or the design of, new waste facilities;
- (e) planning for emergencies — adoption and implementation of procedures to identify foreseeable emergencies by systematic analysis and to prepare, test and review emergency plans to respond to such emergencies;
- (f) monitoring performance — adoption and implementation of procedures for the ongoing assessment of compliance with the objectives set by the operator's major-accident prevention policy and safety management system, and the mechanisms for investigation and taking corrective action in case of non-compliance. The procedures should cover the operator's system for reporting major accidents or near misses, particularly those involving failure of protective measures, and their investigation and follow-up on the basis of lessons learnt;

(g) audit and review — adoption and implementation of procedures for periodic systematic assessment of the major-accident prevention policy and the effectiveness and suitability of the safety management system; the documented review of performance of the policy and safety management system and its updating by senior management.

2. INFORMATION TO BE COMMUNICATED TO THE PUBLIC CONCERNED

(1) Name of operator and address of the waste facility.
(2) Identification, by position held, of the person providing the information.
(3) Confirmation that the waste facility is subject to the regulations and/or administrative provisions implementing this Directive and, when applicable, that the information relevant to the elements referred to in Article 6(2) has been submitted to the competent authority.
(4) An explanation in clear and simple terms of the activity or activities undertaken at the site.
(5) The common names or the generic names or the general danger classification of the substances and preparations involved at the waste facility as well as waste which could give rise to a major accident, with an indication of their principal dangerous characteristics.
(6) General information relating to the nature of the major-accident hazards, including their potential effects on the surrounding population and environment.
(7) Adequate information on how the surrounding population concerned are to be warned and kept informed in the event of a major accident.
(8) Adequate information on the actions the population concerned should take, and on the behaviour they should adopt, in the event of a major accident.
(9) Confirmation that the operator is required to make adequate arrangements on site, in particular liaison with the emergency services, to deal with major accidents and to minimise their effects.
(10) A reference to the external emergency plan drawn up to cope with any off-site effects from an accident. This should include advice to co-operate with any instructions or requests from the emergency services at the time of an accident.
(11) Details of where further relevant information can be obtained, subject to the requirements of confidentiality laid down in national legislation.

ANNEX II
WASTE CHARACTERISATION

The waste to be deposited in a facility shall be characterised in such a way as to guarantee the long-term physical and chemical stability of the structure of the facility and to prevent major accidents. The waste characterisation shall include, where appropriate and in accordance with the category of the waste facility, the following aspects:

(1) description of expected physical and chemical characteristics of the waste to be deposited in the short and the long term, with particular reference to its stability under surface atmospheric/meteorological conditions, taking account of the type of mineral or minerals to be extracted and the nature of any overburden and/or gangue minerals that will be displaced in the course of the extractive operations;
(2) classification of the waste according to the relevant entry in Decision 2000/532/EC, with particular regard to its hazardous characteristics;
(3) description of the chemical substances to be used during treatment of the mineral resource and their stability;
(4) description of the method of deposition;
(5) waste transport system to be employed.

ANNEX III
CRITERIA FOR DETERMINING THE CLASSIFICATION OF WASTE FACILITIES

A waste facility shall be classified under category A if:

— a failure or incorrect operation, e.g. the collapse of a heap or the bursting of a dam, could give rise to a major accident, on the basis of a risk assessment taking into account factors such as the present or future size, the location and the environmental impact of the waste facility; or

— it contains waste classified as hazardous under Directive 91/689/EEC above a certain threshold; or

— it contains substances or preparations classified as dangerous under Directives 67/548/EEC or 1999/45/EC above a certain threshold.

COUNCIL DIRECTIVE 2006/117/EURATOM

of 20 November 2006

ON THE SUPERVISION AND CONTROL OF SHIPMENTS OF RADIOACTIVE WASTE AND SPENT FUEL

THE COUNCIL OF THE EUROPEAN UNION,

Having regard to the Treaty establishing the European Atomic Energy Community, and in particular Articles 31(2) and 32 thereof,

Having regard to the proposal from the Commission drawn up after obtaining the opinion of a group of persons appointed by the Scientific and Technical Committee from among scientific experts in the Member States, in accordance with Article 31 of the Treaty, and after having consulted the European Economic and Social Committee,

Having regard to the opinion of the European Parliament,

Whereas:

(1) Operations involved in shipments of radioactive waste or spent fuel are subject to a number of requirements under Community and international legal instruments regarding in particular the safe transport of radioactive material and the conditions under which radioactive waste or spent fuel is disposed of or stored in the country of destination.

(2) Further to these requirements, the health protection of workers and the general public requires that shipments of radioactive waste or spent fuel between Member States and into and out of the Community be subject to a compulsory and common system of prior authorisation.

(3) As stated in Council Resolution of 22 May 2002 on the establishment of national systems for surveillance and control of the presence of radioactive materials in the recycling of metallic materials in the Member States, it is important to minimise the radiological risk deriving from the presence of radioactive materials among metallic materials destined for recycling.

(4) Council Directive 92/3/Euratom of 3 February 1992 on the supervision and control of shipments of radioactive waste between Member States and into and out of the Community established a Community system of strict control and prior authorisation for shipments of radioactive waste that has proved satisfactory. It needs, nevertheless, to be amended in the light of experience in order to clarify and add concepts and definitions, to address situations that had been omitted in the past, to simplify the existing procedure for the shipment of radioactive waste between Member States and to guarantee consistency with other Community and international provisions, and in particular with the Joint Convention on the Safety of Spent Fuel Management and on the Safety of Radioactive Waste Management (hereinafter referred to as Joint Convention), to which the Community acceded on 2 January 2006.

(5) In the framework of the Fifth Phase of the SLIM (Simpler Legislation for the Internal Market) initiative, a working group of representatives of Member States and of users was set up in order to address a number of concerns expressed by users of Directive 92/3/Euratom, while bringing it into line with current international rules and instruments.

(6) The procedure laid down in Directive 92/3/Euratom has been applied in practice only to shipments of spent fuel for which no further use is intended, considered thus as "radioactive waste" for the purposes of that Directive. From a radiological point of view, excluding the application of such supervision and control procedure to spent fuel where it is intended for reprocessing is not justified. It is therefore appropriate that this Directive cover all shipments of spent fuel, whether it is intended for disposal or for reprocessing.

(7) Each Member State should remain fully responsible for the choice of its own policy on the management of the nuclear waste and spent fuel within its jurisdiction, some choosing reprocessing of spent fuel, others aiming at final disposal of spent fuel with no other use foreseen. This Directive should therefore be without prejudice to the right of Member States to export their spent fuel for reprocessing and nothing in this Directive should imply that a Member State of destination has to accept shipments of radioactive waste and spent fuel for final treatment or disposal except in the case of reshipment. Any refusal of such shipments should be justified on the basis of the criteria set out in this Directive.

(8) Simplification of the existing procedure should not hamper the existing rights of the Member States to object to, or impose conditions in relation to, a shipment of radioactive waste which require their consent. Objections should not be arbitrary and should be founded on relevant national, Community or international law. This Directive should be without prejudice to rights and obligations under international law, and in particular to the exercise, by ships and aircraft, of maritime, river and air navigation rights and freedoms, as provided for under international law.

(9) The possibility for a Member State of destination or of transit to refuse the automatic procedure for granting consent to shipments imposes an unjustified administrative burden and generates uncertainty. The mandatory acknowledgement of receipt of the application by the authorities of the countries of destination and transit, together with the extension of the period for granting consent, should allow tacit approval to be assumed with a high degree of certainty.

(10) The "authorisations" for shipments in the sense of this Directive should not replace any specific national requirements for the shipments such as transport licences.

(11) To protect human health and the environment against the dangers arising from radioactive waste, account should be taken of risks occurring outside the Community. In the case of radioactive waste and spent fuel leaving the Community, the third country of destination should not only be informed of the shipment, but should also give its consent to it.

(12) The competent authorities of the Member State of destination should cooperate and liaise with the other competent authorities involved in order to avoid undue delays and to ensure a smooth operation of the consent procedure laid down by this Directive.

(13) The requirement that the person responsible for the shipment take corrective safety measures where necessary in case of shipment failure should not prevent the application of mechanisms established by the Member States at national level.

(14) The requirement that the holder be liable for costs arising in case of shipment failure should not prevent that mechanisms established by the Member States at national level or any contractual arrangement between the holder and any other person involved in the shipment, apply.

(15) While radioactive waste should, as far as is compatible with the safe management of such material, be disposed of in the State in which it was generated it is recognized that Member States should promote agreements between themselves in order to facilitate the safe and efficient management of radioactive waste or spent fuel from Member States that produced it in small quantities and where the establishment of appropriate facilities would not be justified from a radiological point of view.

(16) When an arrangement between a consignee in a third country and a holder in a third country has been concluded pursuant to Article 27 of the Joint Convention, the same arrangement could be used for the purpose of this Directive.

(17) For the purposes of this Directive and in the light of past experience it is appropriate to adapt the existing standard document. For the sake of clarity the obligation to establish the new standard document by the date of transposition of this Directive should be laid down. However, should this deadline not be met, transitional provisions should provide for the use of the existing standard document. Moreover, clear rules on the use of languages should allow for legal certainty and prevent unjustified delays.

(18) Periodical reporting from Member States to the Commission and from the Commission to the European Parliament, to the Council and to the European Economic and Social Committee should provide a useful overview of authorisations given Community-wide and should identify possible difficulties encountered in practice by the Member States and solutions applied.

(19) Council Directive 96/29/Euratom of 13 May 1996 laying down basic safety standards for the protection of the health of workers and the general public against the dangers arising from ionising radiation, applies, inter alia, to the transport, import to and export from the Community of radioactive substances and provides for a reporting and authorisation system of practices involving ionising radiation. Those provisions are therefore relevant to the field covered by this Directive.

(20) In the light of the foregoing, it is necessary, for reasons of clarity, to repeal and replace Directive 92/3/Euratom. This Directive should not prejudice the obligations of the Member States concerning the deadlines for transposition into national law and application of the repealed Directive.

(21) In accordance with paragraph 34 of the interinstitutional agreement on better law making Member States are encouraged to draw up, for themselves and in the interest of the Community, their own tables which will, as far as possible, illustrate the correlation between this Directive and the transposition measures and to make them public,

HAS ADOPTED THIS DIRECTIVE:

Chapter 1
Preliminary provisions

Article 1

Subject matter and scope

1. This Directive lays down a Community system of supervision and control of transboundary shipments of radioactive waste and spent fuel, so as to guarantee an adequate protection of the population.

2. This Directive shall apply to transboundary shipments of radioactive waste or spent fuel whenever:

(a) the country of origin or the country of destination or any country of transit is a Member State of the Community; and

(b) the quantities and concentration of the consignment exceed the levels laid down in Article 3(2) points (a) and (b) of Directive 96/29/Euratom.

3. This Directive shall not apply to shipments of disused sources to a supplier or manufacturer of radioactive sources or to a recognised installation.

4. This Directive shall not apply to shipments of radioactive materials recovered, through reprocessing, for further use.

5. This Directive shall not apply to transboundary shipments of waste that contains only naturally occurring radioactive material which does not arise from practices.

6. This Directive is without prejudice to rights and obligations under international law.

Article 2

Reshipments related to processing and reprocessing operations

This Directive shall not affect the right of a Member State or an undertaking in the Member State to which:

(a) radioactive waste is to be shipped for processing; or

(b) other material is to be shipped with the purpose to recover the radioactive waste,

to return the radioactive waste after treatment to its country of origin. Nor shall it affect the right of a Member State or an undertaking in that Member State to which spent fuel is to be shipped for reprocessing to return to its country of origin radioactive waste recovered from the reprocessing operation.

Article 3

Transboundary shipments of spent fuel for reprocessing

Without prejudice to the competence of each Member State to define its own spent fuel cycle policy, this Directive shall not affect the right of a Member State to export spent fuel for reprocessing, taking into account the principles of the nuclear common market, in particular the free movement of goods. Those shipments and exports shall be supervised and controlled in accordance with the procedures laid down in this Directive.

Article 4

Reshipment related to non-authorised shipments and undeclared radioactive waste

This Directive shall not affect the right of a Member State to safely return to its country of origin:

(a) shipments of radioactive waste and spent fuel which fall under the scope of this Directive but which were not duly authorised in accordance with this directive; and

(b) radioactively contaminated waste or material containing a radioactive source where this material has not been declared as radioactive waste by the country of origin.

Article 5

Definitions

For the purposes of this Directive the following definitions shall apply:

1. "radioactive waste" means radioactive material in gaseous, liquid or solid form for which no further use is foreseen by the countries of origin and destination, or by a natural or legal person whose decision is accepted by these countries, and which is controlled as radioactive waste by a regulatory body under the legislative and regulatory framework of the countries of origin and destination;
2. "spent fuel" means nuclear fuel that has been irradiated in and permanently removed from a reactor core; spent fuel may either be considered as usable resource that can be reprocessed or be destined for final disposal with no further use foreseen and treated as radioactive waste;
3. "reprocessing" means a process or operation, the purpose of which is to extract radioactive isotopes from spent fuel for further use;
4. "shipment" means the whole of operations involved in moving radioactive waste or spent fuel from the country or the Member State of origin to the country or the Member State of destination;
5. "intra-community shipment" means a shipment carried out where the country of origin and the country of destination are Member States;
6. "extra-community shipment" means a shipment carried out where the country of origin and/or the country of destination are third countries;
7. "disposal" means the emplacement of radioactive waste or spent fuel in an authorised facility without the intention of retrieval;
8. "storage" means the holding of radioactive waste or spent fuel in a facility that provides for its containment, with the intention of retrieval;
9. "holder" means any natural or legal person who, before carrying out a shipment of radioactive waste or spent fuel is responsible under the applicable national law for such materials and plans to carry out a shipment to a consignee;

10. "consignee" means any natural or legal person to whom radioactive waste or spent fuel is shipped;
11. "country or Member State of origin" and "country or Member State of destination" respectively means any country or Member State from which a shipment is planned to be initiated or is initiated, and any country or Member State to which a shipment is planned or takes place;
12. "country or Member State of transit" means any country or Member State other than the country or the Member State of origin or the country or the Member State of destination, through the territory of which a shipment is planned or takes place;
13. "competent authorities" means any authority which, under the law or regulations of the countries of origin, transit or destination, are empowered to implement the system of supervision and control of shipments of radioactive waste or spent fuel;
14. "sealed source" has the meaning given to it by Directive 96/29/Euratom and includes the capsule, where applicable, enclosing the radioactive material as an integral part of the source;
15. "disused source" means a sealed source which is no longer used or intended to be used for the practice for which authorisation was granted;
16. "recognised installation" means a facility located in the territory of a country authorised by the competent authorities of that country in accordance with national law for the long-term storage or disposal of sealed sources or an installation duly authorised under national law for the interim storage of sealed sources;
17. "duly completed application" means the standard document that complies with all the requirements, as established in accordance with Article 17.

Chapter 2
Intra-community shipments

Article 6

Application for shipment authorisation

1. A holder who plans to carry out an intra-Community shipment of radioactive waste or spent fuel or to arrange for such a shipment to be carried out shall submit a duly completed application for authorisation to the competent authorities of the Member State of origin.

2. The application may be sent in respect of more than one shipment, provided that:

(a) the radioactive waste or the spent fuel to which it relates essentially has the same physical, chemical and radioactive characteristics; and

(b) the shipments are to be made from the same holder to the same consignee and involve the same competent authorities, and

(c) where shipments involve transit through third countries, such transit is via the same frontier post of entry to and/or exit from the Community and via the same frontier post(s) of the third country or countries concerned, unless otherwise agreed between the competent authorities concerned.

Article 7

Transmission of the application to the competent authorities

1. The competent authorities of the Member State of origin shall send the duly completed application referred to in Article 6 for consent to the competent authorities of the Member State of destination and of the Member States of transit, if any.

2. The competent authorities of the Member States involved shall take the necessary measures to ensure that all information regarding shipments covered by this Directive is handled with due care and protected against any misuse.

Article 8

Acknowledgement of receipt and request for information

1. Within 20 days following the receipt of the application, the competent authorities of the Member State of destination and transit shall verify that the application is duly completed, within the meaning of Article 5(17).

2. In case the application is duly completed, the competent authorities of the Member State of destination shall send an acknowledgement of receipt to the competent authorities of the Member State of origin and copy it to the other competent authorities concerned, not later than 10 days after expiry of the 20 days period set out in paragraph 1.

3. If any of the competent authorities of the Member States concerned consider that the application is not duly completed, they shall request the missing information from the competent authorities of the Member State of origin and inform the other competent authorities of such request. This request shall be made not later than the expiry of the period set out in paragraph 1.

The competent authorities of the Member State of origin shall transmit the requested information to the competent authorities concerned.

Not later than 10 days after the date of receipt of the missing information and not earlier than after expiry of the 20 days period set out in paragraph 1, the competent authorities of the Member State of destination shall send an acknowledgement of receipt to the competent authorities of the Member State of origin and copy it to the other competent authorities concerned.

4. The time periods set out in paragraphs 1, 2 and 3 for issuing the acknowledgement of receipt may be shortened if the competent authorities of destination and transit are satisfied that the application is duly completed.

Article 9

Consent and refusal

1. Not later than two months from the date of acknowledgement of receipt the competent authorities of all Member States concerned shall notify the competent authorities of the Member State of origin of their consent, or of the conditions which they consider necessary for giving their consent, or of their refusal to grant consent.

However, the competent authorities of the Member State of destination or of any Member State of transit may request a further period of not more than one month in addition to the period referred to in the first subparagraph to make their position known.

2. If upon expiry of the periods set out in paragraph 1, no reply has been received from the competent authorities of the Member State of destination and/or the intended Member State of transit, those countries shall be deemed to have given their consent for the shipment requested.

3. Reasons shall be given by Member States for any refusal to grant consent, or for conditions attached to their consent, which shall be based:

(a) for Member States of transit, on the relevant national, Community or international legislation applicable to the transport of radioactive material;

(b) for the Member State of destination, on relevant legislation applicable to the management of radioactive waste or spent fuel or on relevant national, Community or international legislation applicable to the transport of radioactive material.

Any conditions imposed by the competent authorities of the Member States, whether they are the country of transit or of destination, may not be more stringent than those laid down for similar shipments within those Member States.

4. The Member State or States which gave consent to transit for a given shipment may not refuse to give consent to reshipment in the following cases:

(a) when the initial consent concerned material being shipped for treatment or reprocessing purposes, if the reshipment concerns radioactive waste or other products equivalent to the original material after treatment or reprocessing, and all relevant legislation is respected;

(b) under the circumstances described in Article 12, if the reshipment is undertaken on the same conditions and with the same specifications.

5. Unjustified delays and/or lack of cooperation by the competent authorities of another Member State shall be reported to the Commission.

Article 10

Authorisation of shipments

1. If all the consents necessary for shipment have been given, the competent authorities of the Member State of origin shall be entitled to authorise the holder to carry out the shipment and shall inform the competent authorities of the Member State of destination and of any Member State or third country of transit accordingly.

2. The authorisation referred to in paragraph 1 shall not in any way affect the responsibility of the holder, the transporters, the owner, the consignee or any other natural or legal person involved in the shipment.

3. A single authorisation may cover more than one shipment, where the conditions set out in Article 6(2) are met.

4. Any authorisation shall be valid for a period of not more than three years.

When establishing this period of validity, Member States shall take into account any conditions set out in the consent given by the Member States of destination or of transit.

Article 11

Acknowledgement of receipt of the shipment

1. Within 15 days of receipt, the consignee shall send the competent authorities of the Member State of destination an acknowledgement of receipt of each shipment.

2. The competent authorities of the Member State of destination shall send copies of the acknowledgement of receipt to the Member State of origin and any Member State or third country of transit.

3. The competent authorities of the Member State of origin shall send a copy of the acknowledgement of receipt to the original holder.

Article 12

Shipment failure

1. The Member State of destination, origin or transit may decide that the shipment may not be completed if the conditions for shipment are no longer complied with in accordance with this Directive, or are not in accordance with the authorisations or consents given pursuant to this Directive.

Such Member State shall forthwith inform the competent authorities of the other Member States involved in the shipment of this decision.

2. Where a shipment cannot be completed or if the conditions for shipment are not complied with in accordance with this Directive, the competent authorities of the Member State of origin

shall ensure that the radioactive waste or the spent fuel in question is taken back by the holder, unless an alternative safe arrangement can be made. These competent authorities shall ensure that the person responsible for the shipment takes corrective safety measures where necessary.

3. The holder shall be liable for costs arising in cases where the shipment cannot or may not be completed.

Chapter 3
Extra-community shipments

Article 13

Imports into the Community

1. Where radioactive waste or spent fuel falling within the scope of this Directive is to enter the Community from a third country and the country of destination is a Member State, the consignee shall submit an application for authorisation to the competent authorities of that Member State. The application may be sent in respect of more than one shipment, under the conditions set out in Article 6(2).

The application shall include evidence that the consignee has made an arrangement with the holder established in the third country, and which has been accepted by the competent authorities of that third country, obliging that holder to take back the radioactive waste or the spent fuel where a shipment cannot be completed in accordance with this Directive, as provided for in paragraph 5 of this Article.

2. The competent authorities of the Member State of destination shall send the application referred to in paragraph 1 for consent to the competent authorities of the Member States of transit, if any.

Articles 8 and 9 shall apply.

3. If all the consents necessary for the shipment have been granted, the competent authorities of the Member State of destination shall be entitled to authorise the consignee to carry out the shipment and shall inform the competent authorities of any Member State or third country of origin or of transit accordingly.

Article 10(2), (3) and (4) shall apply.

4. Within 15 days of receipt of the shipment, the consignee shall send the competent authorities of the Member State of destination an acknowledgement of receipt of each shipment. The competent authorities of the Member State of destination shall send copies of the acknowledgement to the country of origin and to any Member State or third country of transit.

5. The Member State of destination or any Member State of transit may decide that the shipment may not be completed if the conditions for shipment are no longer complied with in accordance with this Directive, or are not in accordance with the authorisations or consents issued pursuant to this Directive. Such Member State shall forthwith inform the competent authorities of the country of origin of this decision.

6. The consignee shall be liable for costs arising in cases where the shipment cannot or may not be completed.

Article 14

Transit through the Community

1. Where radioactive waste or spent fuel is to enter the Community from a third country and the country of destination is not a Member State, the natural or legal person who has the responsibility for managing the shipment within the Member State through whose customs

post radioactive waste or spent fuel is first to enter the Community (first Member State of transit) shall submit an application for authorisation to the competent authorities of that Member State. The application may be sent in respect of more than one shipment, under the conditions set out in Article 6(2).

The application shall include evidence that the consignee established in the third country has made an arrangement with the holder established in the third country, and accepted by the competent authorities of that third country, obliging that holder to take back radioactive waste or the spent fuel where a shipment cannot be completed in accordance with this Directive, as provided for in paragraph 5 of this Article.

2. The competent authorities of the first Member State of transit shall send the application referred to in paragraph 1 for consent to the competent authorities of other Member States of transit, if any.

Articles 8 and 9 shall apply.

3. If all the consents necessary for shipment have been granted, the competent authorities of the first Member State of transit shall be entitled to authorise the person responsible referred to in paragraph 1 to carry out the shipment and shall inform the competent authorities of any other Member State or third country of transit or of origin accordingly.

Article 10(2), (3) and (4) shall apply.

4. The person responsible referred to in paragraph 1 shall notify the competent authorities of the first Member State of transit that the radioactive waste or spent fuel has reached its destination in the third country within 15 days of the date of arrival and shall indicate the last customs post in the Community through which the shipment passed.

The notification shall be substantiated by a declaration or certification by the consignee stating that the radioactive waste or spent fuel has reached its proper destination and indicating the customs post of entry in the third country.

5. A Member State of transit may decide that the shipment may not be completed if the conditions for shipment are no longer complied with in accordance with this Directive, or are not in accordance with the authorisations or consents issued pursuant to this Directive. Such Member State shall forthwith inform the competent authorities of the country of origin of this decision. The person responsible referred to in paragraph 1 shall be liable for costs arising in cases where the shipment cannot or may not be completed.

Article 15

Exports out of the Community

1. Where radioactive waste or spent fuel is to be exported from the Community to a third country, the holder shall submit an application for authorisation to the competent authorities of the Member State of origin. The application may be sent in respect of more than one shipment, under the conditions set out in Article 6(2).

2. The competent authorities of the Member State of origin shall:

(a) notify the competent authorities of the country of destination of the planned shipment and ask their consent; and

(b) send the application referred to in paragraph 1 for consent to the competent authorities of the Member States of transit, if any.

Article 8 shall apply.

3. If all the consents necessary for shipment have been given, the competent authorities of the Member State of origin shall be entitled to authorise the holder to carry out the shipment and shall inform the competent authorities of the third country of destination and of any Member State or third country of transit accordingly.

Article 10(2), (3) and (4) shall apply.

4. The holder shall notify the competent authorities of the Member State of origin that the radioactive waste or spent fuel has reached its destination in the third country within 15 days of the date of arrival and shall indicate the last customs post in the Community through which the shipment passed.

The notification shall be substantiated by a declaration or certification by the consignee stating that the radioactive waste or spent fuel has reached its proper destination and indicating the customs post of entry in the third country.

5. The Member State of origin or any Member State of transit may decide that the shipment may not be completed if the conditions for shipment are no longer complied with in accordance with this Directive, or are not in accordance with the authorisations or consents issued pursuant to this Directive. Such Member State of transit shall forthwith inform the competent authorities of the Member State of origin of this decision.

Article 12(2) and (3), shall apply.

Article 16

Prohibited exports

1. The competent authorities of Member States shall not authorise shipments:

(a) to a destination south of latitude 60° south; or

(b) to a State which is party to the Partnership Agreement between the members of the African, Caribbean and Pacific Group of States of the one part, and the European Community and its Member States, of the other part, (Cotonou ACP-EC Agreement) which is not a Member State, without prejudice to Article 2, or

(c) to a third country which does not, in the opinion of the competent authorities of the Member State of origin, in accordance with the criteria referred to in paragraph 2 of this Article, have the administrative and technical capacity and regulatory structure to manage the radioactive waste or spent fuel safely, as stated in the Joint Convention. In coming to an opinion on this issue, Member States shall take duly into account any relevant information from other Member States. In this respect, Member States shall inform the Commission and the Advisory committee, as set up under Article 21 on a yearly basis.

2. The Commission shall, in accordance with the procedure laid down in Article 21, establish criteria, taking due account of, inter alia, relevant safety standards of the International Atomic Energy Agency (IAEA), facilitating Member States to evaluate whether requirements for exports are met.

Chapter 4
General provisions

Article 17

Use of a standard document

1. A standard document shall be used for all shipments within the scope of this Directive.

2. The Commission shall, in accordance with the procedure laid down in Article 21, establish the standard document which shall include as an Annex a list of the minimum requirements of a duly completed application.

The standard document and its Annexes shall be published in the Official Journal of the European Union and be made available in electronic form not later than 25 December 2008. If necessary, it shall be updated following the same procedure.

3. The application for authorisation shall be completed and any further documentation and information referred to in Articles 10, 13, 14 and 15 shall be supplied in a language that is acceptable to the competent authorities of the Member State to whom the application for authorisation is submitted in accordance with this Directive.

An authenticated translation shall be supplied by the holder at the request of the competent authorities of the country of destination or transit in a language acceptable to them.

4. Any additional requirements for authorising a shipment shall be attached to the standard document.

5. Without prejudice to any other accompanying documents required under other relevant legal provisions, the completed standard document certifying that the authorisation procedure has been duly complied with shall accompany each shipment falling under the scope of this Directive, including cases where the authorisation relates to more than one shipment in a single document.

6. These documents shall be available to the competent authorities of the country of origin and destination and any country of transit.

Article 18

Competent authorities

1. Member States shall forward to the Commission not later than 25 December 2008 the name(s) and the address(es) of the competent authority or authorities and all necessary information for rapidly communicating with such authorities.

2. Member States shall regularly forward to the Commission any changes to such data.

Article 19

Transmission

1. The Commission shall, in accordance with the procedure laid down in Article 21, establish recommendations for a secure and effective system of transmission of the documents and information relating to the provisions of this Directive.

2. The Commission shall establish and maintain an electronic communication platform to publish;
(a) the name(s) and address(es) of the competent authority or authorities of each Member State;
(b) the languages acceptable to the competent authorities of each Member State; and
(c) all general conditions and additional requirements, if any, necessary for the competent authorities of each Member State to authorise a shipment.

Article 20

Regular reports

1. By 25 December 2011 and every three years afterwards, Member States shall forward to the Commission reports on the implementation of this Directive.

2. On the basis of these reports, the Commission shall, in accordance with the procedure laid down in Article 21, establish a summary report for the European Parliament, the Council and the European Economic and Social Committee, paying particular attention to the implementation of Article 4.

Article 21

Advisory committee

1. In performing the tasks laid down in Articles 16(2), 17(2), 19(1) and Article 20(2) the Commission shall be assisted by a Committee of an advisory nature composed of representatives of the Member States and chaired by a representative of the Commission (hereinafter referred to as the Committee).

2. The representative of the Commission shall submit to the Committee a draft of the measures to be taken. The Committee shall deliver its opinion on the draft within a time limit which the Chairman may lay down according to the urgency of the matter, if necessary by taking a vote.

3. The opinion shall be recorded in the minutes. Each Member State shall have the right to ask to have its position recorded in the minutes.

4. The Commission shall take account of the opinion delivered by the Committee. It shall inform the Committee of the manner in which its opinion has been taken into account.

Article 22

Transposition

1. Member States shall bring into force the laws, regulations and administrative provisions necessary to comply with this Directive before 25 December 2008. They shall forthwith inform the Commission thereof.

When they are adopted by the Member States, these measures shall contain a reference to this Directive or shall be accompanied by such reference on the occasion of their official publication. The methods of making such reference shall be laid down by Member States.

2. Member States shall communicate to the Commission the text of the main provisions of national law which they adopt in the field covered by this Directive.

[*Article 23 is not reproduced.*]

Article 24

Transitional provisions

1. Where the application for authorisation has been duly approved by or submitted to the competent authorities of the country of origin before 25 December 2008, Directive 92/3/Euratom shall apply to all shipment operations covered by the same authorisation.

2. When deciding on applications for authorisation submitted before 25 December 2008, for more than one shipment of radioactive waste or spent fuel to a third country of destination, the Member State of origin shall take account of all relevant circumstances, and in particular:

(a) the planned time schedule for carrying out all shipments covered by the same application;

(b) the justification for including all shipments in the same application;

(c) the appropriateness of authorising a number of shipments lower than that covered by the application.

3. Until the standard document provided for in Article 17 of this Directive becomes available, the standard document established by Commission Decision 93/552/Euratom shall be used mutatis mutandis for the purposes of this Directive.

Article 25

Entry into force

This Directive shall enter into force on the 20th day following its publication in the Official Journal of the European Union.

Article 26

This Directive is addressed to the Member States.

ANNEX
CORRELATION TABLE

Directive 92/3/Euratom	*This Directive*
Article 1	Article 1
Article 2	Article 5
Article 3	First recital
Article 4, first subparagraph, first sentence	Article 6(1)
Article 4, first subparagraph, second sentence	Article 7(1)
Article 4, second subparagraph	Article 17(1)
Article 4, third subparagraph	none
Article 5(1)	Article 6(2)
Article 5(2)	Article 10(4)
Article 6(1), first subparagraph	Article 9(1)
Article 6(1), second subparagraph	Article 17(1)
Article 6(2)	Article 9(3)
Article 6(3)	Article 9(1), second subparagraph
Article 6(4)	Article 9(2)
Article 7, first subparagraph	Article 10(1)
Article 7, second subparagraph	Article 17(1)
Article 7, third subparagraph	Article 10(2)
Article 8	Article 17(5)
Article 9(1), first part of the sentence	Article 11(1)
Article 9(1), end part of the sentence	Article 17(1)
Article 9(2), first sentence	Article 11(2)
Article 9(2), second sentence	Article 11(3)
Article 10(1)	Article 13
Article 10(1), end of the first sentence	Article 17(1)
Article 10(2)	Article 14
Article 10(3)	Article 13
Article 11	Article 16(1)
Article 12(1)	Article 15(1)
Article 12(2)	Article 15(3)
Article 12(3)	Article 10(2)
Article 12(4)	Article 17(1)
Article 12(5)	Article 15(4), first subparagraph
Article 12(6)	Article 15(4), second subparagraph
Article 13	Article 1(3)
Article 14	Article 2
Article 15(1)	Article 12(2)
Article 15(2)	Article 13(1), second subparagraph
Article 16	Article 9(4)
Article 17	Article 18
Article 18	Article 20

Directive 92/3/Euratom	*This Directive*
Article 19	Article 21
Article 20, (first, second and third indents)	Article 17(1)
Article 20, fourth indent	Article 16(2)
Article 20, fifth indent	Article 20(2)
Article 21	Article 22
Article 22	Article 26
	Article 3(new)
	Article 4(new)
	Article 8(new)
	Article 19(new)
	Article 23(new)
	Article 24(new)
	Article 25(new)

DIRECTIVE 2006/118/EC OF THE EUROPEAN PARLIAMENT AND OF THE COUNCIL

of 12 December 2006

ON THE PROTECTION OF GROUNDWATER AGAINST POLLUTION AND DETERIORATION

THE EUROPEAN PARLIAMENT AND THE COUNCIL OF THE EUROPEAN UNION,

Having regard to the Treaty establishing the European Community, and in particular Article 175(1) thereof,

Having regard to the proposal from the Commission,

Having regard to the Opinion of the European Economic and Social Committee,

Having regard to the Opinion of the Committee of the Regions,

Acting in accordance with the procedure laid down in Article 251 of the Treaty, in the light of the joint text approved by the Conciliation Committee on 28 November 2006,

Whereas:

(1) Groundwater is a valuable natural resource and as such should be protected from deterioration and chemical pollution. This is particularly important for groundwater-dependent ecosystems and for the use of groundwater in water supply for human consumption.

(2) Groundwater is the most sensitive and the largest body of freshwater in the European Union and, in particular, also a main source of public drinking water supplies in many regions.

(3) Groundwater in bodies of water used for the abstraction of drinking water or intended for such future use must be protected in such a way that deterioration in the quality of such bodies of water is avoided in order to reduce the level of purification treatment required in the production of drinking water, in accordance with Article 7(2) and (3) of Directive 2000/60/EC of the European Parliament and of the Council of 23 October 2000 establishing a framework for Community action in the field of water policy.

(4) Decision No 1600/2002/EC of the European Parliament and of the Council of 22 July 2002 laying down the Sixth Community Environment Action Programme includes the objective to achieve water quality levels that do not give rise to significant impacts on, and risks to, human health and the environment.

(5) In order to protect the environment as a whole, and human health in particular, detrimental concentrations of harmful pollutants in groundwater must be avoided, prevented or reduced

(6) Directive 2000/60/EC sets out general provisions for the protection and conservation of groundwater. As provided for in Article 17 of that Directive, measures to prevent and control groundwater pollution should be adopted, including criteria for assessing good groundwater chemical status and criteria for the identification of significant and sustained upward trends and for the definition of starting points for trend reversals.

(7) Having regard to the need to achieve consistent levels of protection for groundwater, quality standards and threshold values should be established, and methodologies based on a common approach developed, in order to provide criteria for the assessment of the chemical status of bodies of groundwater.

(8) Quality standards for nitrates, plant protection products and biocides should be set as Community criteria for the assessment of the chemical status of bodies of groundwater, and consistency should be ensured with Council Directive 91/676/EEC of 12 December

1991 concerning the protection of waters against pollution caused by nitrates from agricultural sources, Council Directive 91/414/EEC of 15 July 1991 concerning the placing of plant protection products on the market, and Directive 98/8/EC of the European Parliament and of the Council of 16 February 1998 concerning the placing of biocidal products on the market, respectively.

(9) The protection of groundwater may in some areas require a change in farming or forestry practices, which could entail a loss of income. The Common Agricultural Policy provides for funding mechanisms to implement measures to comply with Community standards, namely through Council Regulation (EC) No 1698/2005 of 20 September 2005 on support for rural development by the European Agricultural Fund for Rural Development (EAFRD). With regard to groundwater protection measures, it will be the Member States' responsibility to choose their priorities and projects.

(10) Groundwater chemical status provisions do not apply to high naturally-occurring levels of substances or ions or their indicators, contained either in a body of groundwater or in associated bodies of surface water, due to specific hydro-geological conditions, which are not covered by the definition of pollution. Equally, they do not apply to temporary, spatially-limited changes in flow direction and chemical composition, which are not regarded as intrusions.

(11) Criteria should be established for the identification of any significant and sustained upward trends in pollutant concentrations and for the definition of the starting point for trend reversal, taking into account the likelihood of adverse effects on associated aquatic ecosystems or dependent terrestrial ecosystems.

(12) Member States should, where possible, use statistical procedures, provided they comply with international standards and contribute to the comparability of results of monitoring between Member States over long periods.

(13) In accordance with the third indent of Article 22(2) of Directive 2000/60/EC, Council Directive 80/68/EEC of 17 December 1979 on the protection of groundwater against pollution by certain dangerous substances is to be repealed with effect from 22 December 2013. It is necessary to ensure the continuity of the protection provided by Directive 80/68/EEC with regard to measures aimed at preventing or limiting both direct and indirect inputs of pollutants into groundwater.

(14) It is necessary to distinguish between hazardous substances, inputs of which should be prevented, and other pollutants, inputs of which should be limited. Annex VIII to Directive 2000/60/EC, listing the main pollutants relevant for the water environment, should be used to identify hazardous and non-hazardous substances which present an existing or potential risk of pollution.

(15) Measures to prevent or limit inputs of pollutants into bodies of groundwater used for or intended for future use for the abstraction of water intended for human consumption, as referred to in Article 7(1) of Directive 2000/60/EC, should, in accordance with Article 7(2) of that Directive, include such measures as are necessary to ensure that under the water treatment regime applied, and in accordance with Community legislation, the resulting water will meet the requirements of Council Directive 98/83/EC of 3 November 1998 on the quality of water intended for human consumption. Those measures may also include, in accordance with Article 7(3) of Directive 2000/60/EC, the establishment by Member States of safeguard zones of such size as the competent national body deems necessary to protect drinking water supplies. Such safeguard zones may cover the whole territory of a Member State.

(16) In order to ensure consistent protection of groundwater, Member States sharing bodies of groundwater should coordinate their activities in respect of monitoring, the setting of threshold values, and the identification of relevant hazardous substances.

(17) Reliable and comparable methods for groundwater monitoring are an important tool for assessment of groundwater quality and also for choosing the most appropriate measures. Articles 8(3) and 20 of Directive 2000/60/EC provide for the adoption of standardised methods for analysis and monitoring of water status and, where necessary, of guidelines on implementation including monitoring.

(18) In certain circumstances, Member States should be authorised to grant exemptions from measures to prevent or limit the input of pollutants into groundwater. Any exemptions should be based on transparent criteria and be detailed in the river basin management plans.
(19) The impact on the level of environmental protection and on the functioning of the internal market of different groundwater threshold values to be defined by the Member States should be analysed.
(20) Research should be conducted in order to provide better criteria for ensuring groundwater ecosystem quality and protection. Where necessary, the findings obtained should be taken into account when implementing or revising this Directive. Such research, as well as dissemination of knowledge, experience and research findings, needs to be encouraged and funded.
(21) It is necessary to provide for transitional measures to apply during the period between the date of implementation of this Directive and the date from which Directive 80/68/EEC is repealed.
(22) Directive 2000/60/EC sets out the requirement of controls including a requirement for prior authorisation of artificial recharge or augmentation of bodies of groundwater, provided that the use of the source does not compromise the achievement of the environmental objectives established for the source or the recharged or augmented body of groundwater.
(23) Directive 2000/60/EC includes in Article 11(2) and Part B of Annex VI on the programme of measures a non-exclusive list of supplementary measures which Member States may choose to adopt as part of the programme of measures, inter alia:
— legislative instruments,
— administrative instruments, and
— negotiated agreements for the protection of the environment.
(24) The measures necessary for the implementation of this Directive should be adopted in accordance with Council Decision 1999/468/EC of 28 June 1999 laying down the procedures for the exercise of implementing powers conferred on the Commission.
(25) In particular, it is necessary to follow the regulatory procedure with scrutiny as regards measures of general scope designed to amend non-essential elements of this Directive, inter alia by deleting some of those elements or by supplementing this Directive by adding new non-essential elements to it,

HAVE ADOPTED THIS DIRECTIVE:

Article 1

Purpose

1. This Directive establishes specific measures as provided for in Article 17(1) and (2) of Directive 2000/60/EC in order to prevent and control groundwater pollution. These measures include in particular:
(a) criteria for the assessment of good groundwater chemical status; and
(b) criteria for the identification and reversal of significant and sustained upward trends and for the definition of starting points for trend reversals.

2. This Directive also complements the provisions preventing or limiting inputs of pollutants into groundwater already contained in Directive 2000/60/EC, and aims to prevent the deterioration of the status of all bodies of groundwater.

Article 2

Definitions

For the purposes of this Directive, the following definitions shall apply in addition to those laid down in Article 2 of Directive 2000/60/EC:

1) "groundwater quality standard" means an environmental quality standard expressed as the concentration of a particular pollutant, group of pollutants or indicator of pollution in groundwater, which should not be exceeded in order to protect human health and the environment;
2) "threshold value" means a groundwater quality standard set by Member States in accordance with Article 3;
3) "significant and sustained upward trend" means any statistically and environmentally significant increase of concentration of a pollutant, group of pollutants, or indicator of pollution in groundwater for which trend reversal is identified as being necessary in accordance with Article 5;
4) "input of pollutants into groundwater" means the direct or indirect introduction of pollutants into groundwater as a result of human activity;
5) "background level" means the concentration of a substance or the value of an indicator in a body of groundwater corresponding to no, or only very minor, anthropogenic alterations to undisturbed conditions;
6) "baseline level" means the average value measured at least during the reference years 2007 and 2008 on the basis of monitoring programmes implemented under Article 8 of Directive 2000/60/EC or, in the case of substances identified after these reference years, during the first period for which a representative period of monitoring data is available.

Article 3

Criteria for assessing groundwater chemical status

1. For the purposes of the assessment of the chemical status of a body or a group of bodies of groundwater pursuant to Section 2.3 of Annex V to Directive 2000/60/EC, Member States shall use the following criteria:
(a) groundwater quality standards as referred to in Annex I;
(b) threshold values to be established by Member States in accordance with the procedure set out in Part A of Annex II for the pollutants, groups of pollutants and indicators of pollution which, within the territory of a Member State, have been identified as contributing to the characterisation of bodies or groups of bodies of groundwater as being at risk, taking into account at least the list contained in Part B of Annex II.

The threshold values applicable to good chemical status shall be based on the protection of the body of groundwater in accordance with Part A, points 1, 2 and 3 of Annex II, having particular regard to its impact on, and interrelationship with, associated surface waters and directly dependent terrestrial ecosystems and wetlands and shall inter alia take into account human toxicology and ecotoxicology knowledge.

2. Threshold values can be established at the national level, at the level of the river basin district or the part of the international river basin district falling within the territory of a Member State, or at the level of a body or a group of bodies of groundwater.

3. Member States shall ensure that, for bodies of groundwater shared by two or more Member States and for bodies of groundwater within which groundwater flows across a Member State's boundary, the establishment of threshold values is subject to coordination between the Member States concerned, in accordance with Article 3(4) of Directive 2000/60/EC.

4. Where a body or a group of bodies of groundwater extends beyond the territory of the Community, the Member State(s) concerned shall endeavour to establish threshold values in coordination with the non-Member State(s) concerned, in accordance with Article 3(5) of Directive 2000/60/EC.

5. Member States shall establish threshold values pursuant to paragraph 1(b) for the first time by 22 December 2008.

All threshold values established shall be published in the river basin management plans to be submitted in accordance with Article 13 of Directive 2000/60/EC, and including a summary of the information set out in Part C of Annex II to this Directive.

6. Member States shall amend the list of threshold values whenever new information on pollutants, groups of pollutants, or indicators of pollution indicates that a threshold value should be set for an additional substance, that an existing threshold value should be amended, or that a threshold value previously removed from the list should be re-inserted, in order to protect human health and the environment.

Threshold values can be removed from the list when the body of groundwater concerned is no longer at risk from the corresponding pollutants, groups of pollutants, or indicators of pollution.

Any such changes to the list of threshold values shall be reported in the context of the periodic review of the river basin management plans.

7. The Commission shall publish a report by 22 December 2009 on the basis of the information provided by Member States in accordance with paragraph 5.

Article 4

Procedure for assessing groundwater chemical status

1. Member States shall use the procedure described in paragraph 2 to assess the chemical status of a body of groundwater. Where appropriate, Member States may group bodies of groundwater in accordance with Annex V to Directive 2000/60/EC when carrying out this procedure.

2. A body or a group of bodies of groundwater shall be considered to be of good chemical status when:

(a) the relevant monitoring demonstrates that the conditions set out in Table 2.3.2 of Annex V to Directive 2000/60/EC are being met; or

(b) the values for the groundwater quality standards listed in Annex I and the relevant threshold values established in accordance with Article 3 and Annex II are not exceeded at any monitoring point in that body or group of bodies of groundwater; or

(c) the value for a groundwater quality standard or threshold value is exceeded at one or more monitoring points but an appropriate investigation in accordance with Annex III confirms that:

 (i) on the basis of the assessment referred to in paragraph 3 of Annex III, the concentrations of pollutants exceeding the groundwater quality standards or threshold values are not considered to present a significant environmental risk, taking into account, where appropriate, the extent of the body of groundwater which is affected;

 (ii) the other conditions for good groundwater chemical status set out in Table 2.3.2 in Annex V to Directive 2000/60/EC are being met, in accordance with paragraph 4 of Annex III to this Directive;

 (iii) for bodies of groundwater identified in accordance with Article 7(1) of Directive 2000/60/EC, the requirements of Article 7(3) of that Directive are being met, in accordance with paragraph 4 of Annex III to this Directive;

 (iv) the ability of the body of groundwater or of any of the bodies in the group of bodies of groundwater to support human uses has not been significantly impaired by pollution.

3. Choice of the groundwater monitoring sites has to satisfy the requirements of Section 2.4 of Annex V to Directive 2000/60/EC on being designed so as to provide a coherent and comprehensive overview of groundwater chemical status and to provide representative monitoring data.

4. Member States shall publish a summary of the assessment of groundwater chemical status in the river basin management plans in accordance with Article 13 of Directive 2000/60/EC.

This summary, established at the level of the river basin district or the part of the international river basin district falling within the territory of a Member State, shall also include an explanation as to the manner in which exceedances of groundwater quality standards or threshold values at individual monitoring points have been taken into account in the final assessment.

5. If a body of groundwater is classified as being of good chemical status in accordance with paragraph 2(c), Member States, in accordance with Article 11 of Directive 2000/60/EC, shall take such measures as may be necessary to protect aquatic ecosystems, terrestrial ecosystems and human uses of groundwater dependent on the part of the body of groundwater represented by the monitoring point or points at which the value for a groundwater quality standard or the threshold value has been exceeded.

Article 5

Identification of significant and sustained upward trends and the definition of starting points for trend reversals

1. Member States shall identify any significant and sustained upward trend in concentrations of pollutants, groups of pollutants or indicators of pollution found in bodies or groups of bodies of groundwater identified as being at risk and define the starting point for reversing that trend, in accordance with Annex IV.

2. Member States shall, in accordance with Part B of Annex IV, reverse trends which present a significant risk of harm to the quality of aquatic ecosystems or terrestrial ecosystems, to human health, or to actual or potential legitimate uses of the water environment, through the programme of measures referred to in Article 11 of Directive 2000/60/EC, in order progressively to reduce pollution and prevent deterioration of groundwater.

3. Member States shall define the starting point for trend reversal as a percentage of the level of the groundwater quality standards set out in Annex I and of the threshold values established pursuant to Article 3, on the basis of the identified trend and the environmental risk associated therewith, in accordance with Part B, point 1 of Annex IV.

4. In the river basin management plans to be submitted in accordance with Article 13 of Directive 2000/60/EC, Member States shall summarise:

(a) the way in which the trend assessment from individual monitoring points within a body or a group of bodies of groundwater has contributed to identifying, in accordance with Section 2.5 of Annex V to that Directive, that those bodies are subject to a significant and sustained upward trend in concentration of any pollutant or a reversal of that trend; and

(b) the reasons for the starting points defined pursuant to paragraph 3.

5. Where necessary to assess the impact of existing plumes of pollution in bodies of groundwater that may threaten the achievement of the objectives in Article 4 of Directive 2000/60/EC, and in particular, those plumes resulting from point sources and contaminated land, Member States shall carry out additional trend assessments for identified pollutants in order to verify that plumes from contaminated sites do not expand, do not deteriorate the chemical status of the body or group of bodies of groundwater, and do not present a risk for human health and the environment. The results of these assessments shall be summarised in the river basin management plans to be submitted in accordance with Article 13 of Directive 2000/60/EC.

Article 6

Measures to prevent or limit inputs of pollutants into groundwater

1. In order to achieve the objective of preventing or limiting inputs of pollutants into groundwater, established in accordance with Article 4(1)(b)(i) of Directive 2000/60/EC, Member States shall ensure that the programme of measures established in accordance with Article 11 of that Directive includes:

(a) all measures necessary to prevent inputs into groundwater of any hazardous substances, without prejudice to paragraphs 2 and 3. In identifying such substances, Member States shall in particular take account of hazardous substances belonging to the families or groups of pollutants referred to in points 1 to 6 of Annex VIII to Directive 2000/60/EC, as well as of substances belonging to the families or groups of pollutants referred to in points 7 to 9 of that Annex, where these are considered to be hazardous;

(b) for pollutants listed in Annex VIII to Directive 2000/60/EC which are not considered hazardous, and any other non-hazardous pollutants not listed in that Annex considered by Member States to present an existing or potential risk of pollution, all measures necessary to limit inputs into groundwater so as to ensure that such inputs do not cause deterioration or significant and sustained upward trends in the concentrations of pollutants in groundwater. Such measures shall take account, at least, of established best practice, including the Best Environmental Practice and Best Available Techniques specified in the relevant Community legislation.

For the purpose of establishing measures referred to in points (a) or (b), Member States may, as a first step, identify the circumstances under which the pollutants listed in Annex VIII to Directive 2000/60/EC, in particular essential metals and their compounds referred to in point 7 of that Annex, are to be considered hazardous or non-hazardous.

2. Inputs of pollutants from diffuse sources of pollution having an impact on the groundwater chemical status shall be taken into account whenever technically possible.

3. Without prejudice to any more stringent requirements in other Community legislation, Member States may exempt from the measures required by paragraph 1 inputs of pollutants that are:

(a) the result of direct discharges authorised in accordance with Article 11(3)(j) of Directive 2000/60/EC;

(b) considered by the competent authorities to be of a quantity and concentration so small as to obviate any present or future danger of deterioration in the quality of the receiving groundwater;

(c) the consequences of accidents or exceptional circumstances of natural cause that could not reasonably have been foreseen, avoided or mitigated;

(d) the result of artificial recharge or augmentation of bodies of groundwater authorised in accordance with Article 11(3)(f) of Directive 2000/60/EC;

(e) in the view of the competent authorities incapable, for technical reasons, of being prevented or limited without using:

    (i) measures that would increase risks to human health or to the quality of the environment as a whole; or

    (ii) disproportionately costly measures to remove quantities of pollutants from, or otherwise control their percolation in, contaminated ground or subsoil; or

(f) the result of interventions in surface waters for the purposes, amongst others, of mitigating the effects of floods and droughts, and for the management of waters and waterways, including at international level. Such activities, including cutting, dredging, relocation and deposition of sediments in surface water, shall be conducted in accordance with general binding rules, and, where applicable, with permits and authorisations issued on the basis of such rules, developed by the Member States for that purpose, provided that such inputs do not compromise the achievement of the environmental objectives established for the water bodies concerned in accordance with Article 4(1)(b) of Directive 2000/60/EC.

The exemptions provided for in points (a) to (f) may be used only where the Member States' competent authorities have established that efficient monitoring of the bodies of groundwater concerned, in accordance with point 2.4.2 of Annex V to Directive 2000/60/EC, or other appropriate monitoring, is being carried out.

4. The competent authorities of the Member States shall keep an inventory of the exemptions referred to in paragraph 3 for the purpose of notification, upon request, to the Commission.

Article 7

Transitional arrangements

In the period between 16 January 2009 and 22 December 2013, any new authorisation procedure pursuant to Articles 4 and 5 of Directive 80/68/EEC shall take into account the requirements set out in Articles 3, 4 and 5 of this Directive.

Article 8

Technical adaptations

1. Parts A and C of Annex II and Annexes III and IV may be amended, in the light of scientific and technical progress, in accordance with the regulatory procedure with scrutiny referred to in Article 9(2), taking into consideration the period for reviewing and updating river basin management plans, as referred to in Article 13(7) of Directive 2000/60/EC.

2. Part B of Annex II may be amended, in accordance with the regulatory procedure with scrutiny referred to in Article 9(2), in order to add new pollutants or indicators.

Article 9

Committee procedure

1. The Commission shall be assisted by a committee.

2. Where reference is made to this paragraph, Article 5a (1) to (4) and Article 7 of Decision 1999/468/EC shall apply, having regard to the provisions of Article 8 thereof.

Article 10

Review

Without prejudice to Article 8, the Commission shall review Annexes I and II to this Directive by 16 January 2013, and thereafter every six years. Based on the review, it shall, if appropriate, come forward with legislative proposals, in accordance with the procedure laid down in Article 251 of the Treaty, to amend Annexes I and/or II. In its review and in preparing any proposal, the Commission shall take account of all relevant information, which might include the results of the monitoring programmes implemented under Article 8 of Directive 2000/60/EC, of Community research programmes, and/or of recommendations from the Scientific Committee on Health and Environmental Risks, Member States, the European Parliament, the European Environment Agency, European business organisations and European environmental organisations.

Article 11

Evaluation

The report by the Commission provided for under Article 18(1) of Directive 2000/60/EC shall for groundwater include an evaluation of the functioning of this Directive in relation to other relevant environmental legislation, including consistency therewith.

Article 12

Implementation

Member States shall bring into force the laws, regulations and administrative provisions necessary to comply with this Directive before 16 January 2009. They shall forthwith inform the Commission thereof.

When Member States adopt these measures, they shall contain a reference to this Directive or shall be accompanied by such reference on the occasion of their official publication. The methods of making such reference shall be laid down by Member States.

Article 13

Entry into force

This Directive shall enter into force on the twentieth day following that of its publication in the Official Journal of the European Union.

Article 14

Addressees

This Directive is addressed to the Member States.

ANNEX I
GROUNDWATER QUALITY STANDARDS

1. For the purposes of assessing groundwater chemical status in accordance with Article 4, the following groundwater quality standards will be the quality standards referred to in Table 2.3.2 in Annex V to Directive 2000/60/EC and established in accordance with Article 17 of that Directive.

Pollutant	*Quality standards*
Nitrates	50 mg/l
Active substances in pesticides, including their relevant metabolites, degradation and reaction products(1)	0,1 μg/l 0,5 μg/l (total)(2)

(1) 'Pesticides' means plant protection products and biocidal products as defined in Article 2 of Directive 91/414/EEC and in Article 2 of Directive 98/8/EC, respectively.

(2) 'Total' means the sum of all individual pesticides detected and quantified in the monitoring procedure, including their relevant metabolites, degradation and reaction products.

2. The results of the application of the quality standards for pesticides in the manner specified for the purposes of this Directive will be without prejudice to the results of the risk assessment procedures required by Directive 91/414/EEC or Directive 98/8/EC.

3. Where, for a given body of groundwater, it is considered that the groundwater quality standards could result in failure to achieve the environmental objectives specified in Article 4 of Directive 2000/60/EC for associated bodies of surface water, or in any significant diminution of the ecological or chemical quality of such bodies, or in any significant damage to terrestrial ecosystems which depend directly on the body of groundwater, more stringent threshold values will be established in accordance with Article 3 and Annex II to this Directive. Programmes and measures required in relation to such a threshold value will also apply to activities falling within the scope of Directive 91/676/EEC.

ANNEX II
THRESHOLD VALUES FOR GROUNDWATER POLLUTANTS AND INDICATORS OF POLLUTION

PART A
GUIDELINES FOR THE ESTABLISHMENT OF THRESHOLD VALUES BY MEMBER STATES IN ACCORDANCE WITH ARTICLE 3

Member States will establish threshold values for all pollutants and indicators of pollution which, pursuant to the characterisation performed in accordance with Article 5 of Directive 2000/60/EC, characterise bodies or groups of bodies of groundwater as being at risk of failing to achieve good groundwater chemical status.

Threshold values will be established in such a way that, should the monitoring results at a representative monitoring point exceed the thresholds, this will indicate a risk that one or more of the conditions for good groundwater chemical status referred to in Article 4(2)(c)(ii), (iii) and (iv) are not being met.

When establishing threshold values, Member States will consider the following guidelines:

1) the determination of threshold values should be based on:
   (a) the extent of interactions between groundwater and associated aquatic and dependent terrestrial ecosystems;
   (b) the interference with actual or potential legitimate uses or functions of groundwater;
   (c) all pollutants which characterise bodies of groundwater as being at risk, taking into account the minimum list set out in part B;
   (d) hydro-geological characteristics including information on background levels and water balance;
2) the determination of threshold values should also take account of the origins of the pollutants, their possible natural occurrence, their toxicology and dispersion tendency, their persistence and their bioaccumulation potential;
3) wherever elevated background levels of substances or ions or their indicators occur due to natural hydro-geological reasons, these background levels in the relevant body of groundwater shall be taken into account when establishing threshold values;
4) the determination of threshold values should be supported by a control mechanism for the data collected, based on an evaluation of data quality, analytical considerations, and background levels for substances which may occur both naturally and as a result of human activities.

PART B
MINIMUM LIST OF POLLUTANTS AND THEIR INDICATORS FOR WHICH MEMBER STATES HAVE TO CONSIDER ESTABLISHING THRESHOLD VALUES IN ACCORDANCE WITH ARTICLE 3

1. Substances or ions or indicators which may occur both naturally and/or as a result of human activities

   Arsenic
   Cadmium
   Lead
   Mercury
   Ammonium
   Chloride
   Sulphate

2. Man-made synthetic substances

   Trichloroethylene
   Tetrachloroethylene

3. Parameters indicative of saline or other intrusions
   Conductivity

PART C
INFORMATION TO BE PROVIDED BY MEMBER STATES WITH REGARD TO THE POLLUTANTS AND THEIR INDICATORS FOR WHICH THRESHOLD VALUES HAVE BEEN ESTABLISHED

Member States will summarise, in the river basin management plans to be submitted in accordance with Article 13 of Directive 2000/60/EC, the way the procedure set out in Part A of this Annex has been followed.

In particular, Member States will provide, where feasible:
(a) information on the number of bodies or groups of bodies of groundwater characterised as being at risk and on the pollutants and indicators of pollution which contribute to this classification, including the observed concentrations/values;
(b) information on each of the bodies of groundwater characterised as being at risk, in particular the size of the bodies, the relationship between the bodies of groundwater and the associated surface waters and directly dependent terrestrial ecosystems, and, in the case of naturally-occurring substances, the natural background levels in the bodies of groundwater;
(c) the threshold values, whether they apply at the national level, at the level of the river basin district or the part of the international river basin district falling within the territory of the Member State, or at the level of a body or a group of bodies of groundwater;
(d) the relationship between the threshold values and:
  (i) in the case of naturally-occurring substances, the observed background levels,
  (ii) the environmental quality objectives and other standards for water protection that exist at national, Community or international level, and
  (iii) any relevant information concerning the toxicology, eco-toxicology, persistence, bioaccumulation potential, and dispersion tendency of the pollutants.

ANNEX III
ASSESSMENT OF GROUNDWATER CHEMICAL STATUS

1. The assessment procedure for determining the chemical status of a body or a group of bodies of groundwater will be carried out in relation to all bodies or groups of bodies of groundwater characterised as being at risk and in relation to each of the pollutants which contribute to the body or group of bodies of groundwater being so characterised.

2. In undertaking any investigations referred to in Article 4(2)(c), Member States will take into account:
(a) the information collected as part of the characterisation to be carried out in accordance with Article 5 of Directive 2000/60/EC and with Sections 2.1, 2.2 and 2.3 of Annex II thereto;
(b) the results of the groundwater monitoring network obtained in accordance with Section 2.4 of Annex V to Directive 2000/60/EC; and
(c) any other relevant information including a comparison of the annual arithmetic mean concentration of the relevant pollutants at a monitoring point with the groundwater quality standards set out in Annex I and the threshold values set by Member States in accordance with Article 3 and Annex II.

3. For the purposes of investigating whether the conditions for good groundwater chemical status referred to in Article 4(2)(c)(i) and (iv) are met, Member States will, where relevant and necessary, and on the basis of appropriate aggregations of the monitoring results, supported where necessary by concentration estimations based on a conceptual model of the body or group of bodies of groundwater, estimate the extent of the body of groundwater having

an annual arithmetic mean concentration of a pollutant higher than a groundwater quality standard or a threshold value.

4. For the purposes of investigating whether the conditions for good groundwater chemical status referred to in Article 4(2)(c)(ii) and (iii) are met, Member States will, where relevant and necessary, and on the basis of relevant monitoring results and of a suitable conceptual model of the body of groundwater, assess:
(a) the impact of the pollutants in the body of groundwater;
(b) the amounts and the concentrations of the pollutants being, or likely to be, transferred from the body of groundwater to the associated surface waters or directly dependent terrestrial ecosystems;
(c) the likely impact of the amounts and concentrations of the pollutants transferred to the associated surface waters and directly dependent terrestrial ecosystems;
(d) the extent of any saline or other intrusions into the body of groundwater; and
(e) the risk from pollutants in the body of groundwater to the quality of water abstracted, or intended to be abstracted, from the body of groundwater for human consumption.

5. Member States will present the groundwater chemical status of a body or a group of bodies of groundwater on maps in accordance with Sections 2.4.5 and 2.5 of Annex V to Directive 2000/60/EC. In addition, Member States will indicate on these maps all monitoring points where groundwater quality standards and/or threshold values are exceeded, where relevant and feasible.

ANNEX IV
IDENTIFICATION AND REVERSAL OF SIGNIFICANT AND SUSTAINED UPWARD TRENDS

PART A
IDENTIFICATION OF SIGNIFICANT AND SUSTAINED UPWARD TRENDS

Member States will identify significant and sustained upward trends in all bodies or groups of bodies of groundwater that are characterised as being at risk in accordance with Annex II to Directive 2000/60/EC, taking into account the following requirements:
1) in accordance with Section 2.4 of Annex V to Directive 2000/60/EC, the monitoring programme will be so designed as to detect significant and sustained upward trends in concentrations of the pollutants identified pursuant to Article 3 of this Directive;
2) the procedure for the identification of significant and sustained upward trends will be based on the following elements:
   (a) monitoring frequencies and monitoring locations will be selected such as are sufficient to:
      (i) provide the information necessary to ensure that such upward trends can be distinguished from natural variation with an adequate level of confidence and precision;
      (ii) enable such upward trends to be identified in sufficient time to allow measures to be implemented in order to prevent, or at least mitigate as far as practicable, environmentally significant detrimental changes in groundwater quality. This identification will be carried out for the first time by 2009, if possible, and will take into account existing data, in the context of the report on trend identification within the first river basin management plan referred to in Article 13 of Directive 2000/60/EC, and at least every six years thereafter;
      (iii) take into account the physical and chemical temporal characteristics of the body of groundwater, including groundwater flow conditions and recharge rates and percolation time through soil or subsoil;

(b) the methods of monitoring and analysis used will conform to international quality control principles, including, if relevant, CEN or national standardised methods, to ensure equivalent scientific quality and comparability of the data provided;

(c) the assessment will be based on a statistical method, such as regression analysis, for trend analysis in time series of individual monitoring points;

(d) in order to avoid bias in trend identification, all measurements below the quantification limit will be set to half of the value of the highest quantification limit occurring in time series, except for total pesticides;

3) the identification of significant and sustained upward trends in the concentrations of substances which occur both naturally and as a result of human activities will consider the baseline levels and, where such data are available, the data collected before the start of the monitoring programme in order to report on trend identification within the first river basin management plan referred to in Article 13 of Directive 2000/60/EC.

PART B
STARTING POINTS FOR TREND REVERSALS

Member States will reverse identified significant and sustained upward trends, in accordance with Article 5, taking into account the following requirements:

1) the starting point for implementing measures to reverse significant and sustained upward trends will be when the concentration of the pollutant reaches 75 % of the parametric values of the groundwater quality standards set out in Annex I and of the threshold values established pursuant to Article 3, unless:

(a) an earlier starting point is required to enable trend reversal measures to prevent most cost-effectively, or at least mitigate as far as possible, any environmentally significant detrimental changes in groundwater quality;

(b) a different starting point is justified where the detection limit does not allow for establishing the presence of a trend at 75 % of the parametric values; or

(c) the rate of increase and the reversibility of the trend are such that a later starting point for trend reversal measures would still enable such measures to prevent most cost-effectively, or at least mitigate as far as possible, any environmentally significant detrimental changes in groundwater quality. Such later starting point may not lead to any delay in achieving the deadline for the environmental objectives.

For activities falling within the scope of Directive 91/676/EEC, the starting point for implementing measures to reverse significant and sustained upward trends will be established in accordance with that Directive and with Directive 2000/60/EC and, in particular, adhering to environmental objectives for water protection as set out in Article 4 of Directive 2000/60/EC;

2) once a starting point has been established for a body of groundwater characterised as being at risk in accordance with Section 2.4.4 of Annex V to Directive 2000/60/EC and pursuant to point 1 above, it will not be changed during the six-year cycle of the river basin management plan required in accordance with Article 13 of Directive 2000/60/EC;

3) trend reversals will be demonstrated, taking into account relevant monitoring provisions contained in Part A, point 2.

REGULATION 1013/2006/EC OF THE EUROPEAN PARLIAMENT AND OF THE COUNCIL

of 14 June 2006

ON SHIPMENTS OF WASTE

THE EUROPEAN PARLIAMENT AND THE COUNCIL OF THE EUROPEAN UNION,

Having regard to the Treaty establishing the European Community, and in particular Article 175(1) thereof,

Having regard to the proposal from the Commission,

Having regard to the opinion of the European Economic and Social Committee,

After consulting the Committee of the Regions,

Acting in accordance with the procedure laid down in Article 251 of the Treaty,

Whereas:

(1) The main and predominant objective and component of this Regulation is the protection of the environment, its effects on international trade being only incidental.

(2) Council Regulation (EEC) No 259/93 of 1 February 1993 on the supervision and control of shipments of waste within, into and out of the European Community has already been significantly amended on several occasions and requires further amendment. It is necessary, in particular, to incorporate in that Regulation the content of Commission Decision 94/774/EC of 24 November 1994 concerning the standard consignment note referred to in Council Regulation (EEC) No 259/93 and of Commission Decision 1999/412/EC of 3 June 1999 concerning a questionnaire for the reporting obligation of Member States pursuant to Article 41(2) of Council Regulation (EEC) No 259/93. Regulation (EEC) No 259/93 should therefore be replaced in the interests of clarity.

(3) Council Decision 93/98/EEC concerned the conclusion, on behalf of the Community, of the Basel Convention of 22 March 1989 on the control of transboundary movements of hazardous wastes and their disposal, to which the Community has been a Party since 1994. By adopting Regulation (EEC) No 259/93, the Council has established rules to curtail and to control such movements designed, inter alia, to make the existing Community system for the supervision and control of waste movements comply with the requirements of the Basel Convention.

(4) Council Decision 97/640/EC concerned the approval, on behalf of the Community, of the amendment to the Basel Convention, as laid down in Decision III/1 of the Conference of the Parties. By that amendment, all exports of hazardous waste destined for disposal from countries listed in Annex VII to the Convention to countries not listed therein were prohibited, as were, with effect from 1 January 1998, all such exports of the hazardous waste referred to in Article 1(1)(a) of the Convention and destined for recovery. Regulation (EEC) No 259/93 was amended accordingly by Council Regulation (EC) No 120/97.

(5) In view of the fact that the Community has approved Decision C(2001)107/Final of the OECD Council concerning the revision of Decision C(92)39/Final on the control of transboundary movements of wastes destined for recovery operations (OECD Decision), in order to harmonise waste lists with the Basel Convention and revise certain other requirements, it is necessary to incorporate the content of that Decision in Community legislation.

(6) The Community has signed the Stockholm Convention of 22 May 2001 on persistent organic pollutants.

(7) It is important to organise and regulate the supervision and control of shipments of waste in a way which takes account of the need to preserve, protect and improve the quality of the environment and human health and which promotes a more uniform application of the Regulation throughout the Community.

(8) It is also important to bear in mind the requirement laid down in Article 4(2)(d) of the Basel Convention that shipments of hazardous waste are to be reduced to a minimum, consistent with environmentally sound and efficient management of such waste.

(9) Furthermore, it is important to bear in mind the right of each Party to the Basel Convention, pursuant to Article 4(1) thereof, to prohibit the import of hazardous waste or of waste listed in Annex II to that Convention.

(10) Shipments of waste generated by armed forces or relief organisations should be excluded from the scope of this Regulation when imported into the Community in certain situations (including transit within the Community when the waste enters the Community). The requirements of international law and international agreements should be respected in relation to such shipments. In such cases, any competent authority of transit and the competent authority of destination in the Community should be informed in advance concerning the shipment and its destination.

(11) It is necessary to avoid duplication with Regulation (EC) No 1774/2002 of the European Parliament and of the Council of 3 October 2002 laying down health rules concerning animal by-products not intended for human consumption, which already contains provisions covering the overall consignment, channelling and movement (collection, transport, handling, processing, use, recovery or disposal, record keeping, accompanying documents and traceability) of animal by-products within, into and out of the Community.

(12) The Commission should report by the date of entry into force of this Regulation on the relationship between the existing sectoral legislation on animal and public health and the provisions of this Regulation, and should submit by that date any proposals needed to bring such legislation into line with this Regulation in order to achieve an equivalent level of control.

(13) Although the supervision and control of shipments of waste within a Member State is a matter for that Member State, national systems concerning shipments of waste should take account of the need for coherence with the Community system in order to ensure a high level of protection of the environment and human health.

(14) In the case of shipments of waste destined for disposal operations and waste not listed in Annex III, IIIA or IIIB destined for recovery operations, it is appropriate to ensure optimum supervision and control by requiring prior written consent to such shipments. Such a procedure should in turn entail prior notification, which enables the competent authorities to be duly informed so that they can take all necessary measures for the protection of human health and the environment. It should also enable those authorities to raise reasoned objections to such a shipment.

(15) In the case of shipments of waste listed in Annex III, IIIA or IIIB destined for recovery operations, it is appropriate to ensure a minimum level of supervision and control by requiring such shipments to be accompanied by certain information.

(16) In view of the need for uniform application of this Regulation and for the proper functioning of the internal market, it is necessary in the interests of efficiency to require that notifications be processed through the competent authority of dispatch.

(17) It is also important to clarify the system of financial guarantees or equivalent insurance.

(18) Considering the responsibility of waste producers for the environmentally sound management of waste, the notification and movement documents for waste shipments should, where practicable, be filled in by the waste producers.

(19) It is necessary to provide procedural safeguards for the notifier, both in the interests of legal certainty and to ensure uniform application of this Regulation and the proper functioning of the internal market.

(20) In the case of shipments of waste for disposal, Member States should take into account the principles of proximity, priority for recovery and self-sufficiency at Community and

national levels, in accordance with Directive 2006/12/EC of the European Parliament and of the Council of 5 April 2006 on waste, by taking measures in accordance with the Treaty to prohibit generally or partially or to object systematically to such shipments. Account should also be taken of the requirement laid down in Directive 2006/12/EC, whereby Member States are to establish an integrated and adequate network of waste disposal installations, in order to enable the Community as a whole to become self-sufficient in waste disposal and the Member States to move towards that aim individually, taking into account geographical circumstances or the need for specialised installations for certain types of waste. Member States should also be able to ensure that the waste management facilities covered by Council Directive 96/61/EC of 24 September 1996 concerning integrated pollution prevention and control apply best available techniques as defined in that Directive in compliance with the permit of the facility, and that the waste is treated in accordance with legally binding environmental protection standards in relation to disposal operations established in Community legislation.

(21) In the case of shipments of waste destined for recovery, Member States should be able to ensure that the waste management facilities covered by Directive 96/61/EC apply best available techniques as defined in that Directive in compliance with the permit of the facility. Member States should also be able to ensure that waste is treated in accordance with legally binding environmental protection standards in relation to recovery operations established in Community legislation and that, taking account of Article 7(4) of Directive 2006/12/EC, waste is treated in accordance with waste management plans established pursuant to that Directive with the purpose of ensuring the implementation of legally binding recovery or recycling obligations established in Community legislation.

(22) The development of mandatory requirements for waste facilities and the treatment of specific waste materials at Community level, in addition to the existing provisions of Community law, can contribute to the creation of a high level of environmental protection across the Community, assist in the creation of a level playing field for recycling and help to ensure that the development of an economically viable internal market for recycling is not hindered. Therefore there is a need to develop a Community level playing field for recycling through the application of common standards in certain areas, as appropriate and including in relation to secondary materials, in order to increase the quality of recycling. The Commission should submit, as appropriate, proposals for such standards for certain wastes and certain recycling facilities as soon as practicable based on further examination in the context of the waste strategy and taking into account existing Community legislation and legislation in the Member States. In the interim, it should be possible, under certain conditions, to object to planned shipments where the related recovery would not be in accordance with national legislation in the country of dispatch relating to the recovery of waste. In the interim, the Commission should also keep under review the situation regarding possible undesired shipments of waste to the new Member States and, if necessary, submit appropriate proposals to deal with such situations.

(23) Member States should be required to ensure that, in accordance with the United Nations Economic Commission for Europe (UNECE) Convention on Access to Information, Public Participation in Decision-making and Access to Justice in Environmental Matters of 25 June 1998 (Aarhus Convention), the relevant competent authorities make publicly available by appropriate means information on notifications of shipments, where such information is not confidential under national or Community legislation.

(24) An obligation should be laid down to the effect that waste from a shipment that cannot be completed as intended is to be taken back to the country of dispatch or recovered or disposed of in an alternative way.

(25) It should also be made compulsory for the person whose action is the cause of an illegal shipment to take back the waste involved or make alternative arrangements for its recovery or disposal. Failing that, the competent authorities of dispatch or destination, as appropriate, should intervene themselves.

(26) It is necessary, in order to protect the environment of the countries concerned, to clarify the scope of the prohibition laid down in accordance with the Basel Convention of exports from the Community of any waste destined for disposal in a third country other than an EFTA (European Free Trade Association) country.

(27) Countries that are Parties to the Agreement on the European Economic Area may adopt the control procedures provided for shipments within the Community.

(28) It is also necessary, in order to protect the environment of the countries concerned, to clarify the scope of the prohibition of exports of hazardous waste destined for recovery in a country to which the OECD Decision does not apply, also laid down in accordance with the Basel Convention. In particular, it is necessary to clarify the list of waste to which that prohibition applies and to ensure that it also includes the waste listed in Annex II to the Basel Convention, namely waste collected from households and residues from the incineration of household waste.

(29) Specific arrangements should be maintained for exports of non-hazardous waste destined for recovery in countries to which the OECD Decision does not apply and provision should be made for them to be further streamlined at a later date.

(30) Imports into the Community of waste for disposal should be permitted where the exporting country is a Party to the Basel Convention. Imports into the Community of waste for recovery should be permitted where the exporting country is one to which the OECD Decision applies or is a Party to the Basel Convention. In other cases, however, imports should be allowed only if the exporting country is bound by a bilateral or multilateral agreement or arrangement compatible with Community legislation and in accordance with Article 11 of the Basel Convention, except when this is not possible during situations of crisis, peacemaking, peacekeeping or war.

(31) This Regulation should be applied in accordance with international maritime law.

(32) This Regulation should reflect the rules regarding exports and imports of waste to and from the overseas countries and territories laid down in Council Decision 2001/822/EC of 27 November 2001 on the association of the overseas countries and territories with the European Community (Overseas Association Decision).

(33) The necessary steps should be taken to ensure that, in accordance with Directive 2006/12/EC and other Community legislation on waste, waste shipped within the Community and waste imported into the Community is managed, throughout the period of shipment and including recovery or disposal in the country of destination, without endangering human health and without using processes or methods which could harm the environment. As regards exports from the Community that are not prohibited, efforts should be made to ensure that the waste is managed in an environmentally sound manner throughout the period of shipment and including recovery or disposal in the third country of destination. The facility which receives the waste should be operated in accordance with human health and environmental protection standards that are broadly equivalent to those established in Community legislation. A list of non-binding guidelines should be established in which guidance may be sought on environmentally sound management.

(34) Member States should provide the Commission with information concerning the implementation of this Regulation, both through the reports submitted to the Secretariat of the Basel Convention and on the basis of a separate questionnaire.

(35) It is necessary to ensure the safe and environmentally sound management of ship dismantling in order to protect human health and the environment. Furthermore, it should be noted that a ship may become waste as defined in Article 2 of the Basel Convention and that at the same time it may be defined as a ship under other international rules. It is important to recall that work is ongoing, involving inter-agency cooperation between International Labour Organisation (ILO), International Maritime Organisation (IMO) and the Secretariat of the Basel Convention, to establish mandatory requirements at the global level ensuring an efficient and effective solution to the problem of ship dismantling.

(36) Efficient international cooperation regarding control of shipments of waste is instrumental in ensuring that shipments of hazardous waste are controlled. Information exchange, shared responsibility and cooperative efforts between the Community and its Member States and third countries should be promoted with a view to ensuring sound management of waste.

(37) Certain Annexes to this Regulation should be adopted by the Commission in accordance with the procedure referred to in Article 18(3) of Directive 2006/12/EC. This procedure should also apply to the amendment of the Annexes to take account of scientific and technical progress, of modifications in the relevant Community legislation or of events connected to the OECD Decision or to the Basel Convention and other related international conventions and agreements.

(38) In preparing the instructions for completing the notification and movement documents to be set out in Annex IC, the Commission, taking into account the OECD Decision and the Basel Convention, should specify, inter alia, that the notification and movement documents should, as far as possible, be on two pages and what the precise timing is for completion of the notification and movement documents in Annex IA and IB, taking into account Annex II. In addition, where terminology and requirements differ between the OECD Decision or the Basel Convention and this Regulation, the specific requirements should be clarified.

(39) In considering the mixtures of wastes to be added in Annex IIIA, the following information should be considered, inter alia: the properties of the waste, such as its possible hazardous characteristics, its potential for contamination and its physical state; the management aspects, such as the technological capacity to recover the waste, and the environmental benefits arising from the recovery operation, including whether the environmentally sound management of the waste may be impaired. The Commission should progress towards the completion of this Annex as far as possible before the date of entry into force of this Regulation and complete this task at the latest six months after that date.

(40) Additional measures related to the implementation of this Regulation should also be adopted by the Commission in accordance with the procedure referred to in Article 18(3) of Directive 2006/12/EC. These measures should include a method for calculating the financial guarantee or equivalent insurance to be completed by the Commission, if possible, before the date of application of this Regulation.

(41) The measures necessary for the implementation of this Regulation should be adopted in accordance with Council Decision 1999/468/EC of 28 June 1999 laying down the procedures for the exercise of implementing powers conferred on the Commission.

(42) Since the objective of this Regulation, namely to ensure protection of the environment when waste is subject to shipment, cannot be sufficiently achieved by the Member States and can therefore, by reason of the scale and effects thereof, be better achieved at Community level, the Community may adopt measures in accordance with the principle of subsidiarity as set out in Article 5 of the Treaty. In accordance with the principle of proportionality, as set out in that Article, this Regulation does not go beyond what is necessary in order to achieve that objective,

HAVE ADOPTED THIS REGULATION:

Title I
Scope and definitions

Article 1

Scope

1. This Regulation establishes procedures and control regimes for the shipment of waste, depending on the origin, destination and route of the shipment, the type of waste shipped and the type of treatment to be applied to the waste at its destination.

2. This Regulation shall apply to shipments of waste:
(a) between Member States, within the Community or with transit through third countries;
(b) imported into the Community from third countries;
(c) exported from the Community to third countries;
(d) in transit through the Community, on the way from and to third countries.

3. The following shall be excluded from the scope of this Regulation:
(a) the offloading to shore of waste, including waste water and residues, generated by the normal operation of ships and offshore platforms, provided that such waste is subject to the requirements of the International Convention for the Prevention of Pollution from Ships, 1973, as modified by the Protocol of 1978 relating thereto (Marpol 73/78), or other binding international instruments;
(b) waste generated on board vehicles, trains, aeroplanes and ships, until such waste is offloaded in order to be recovered or disposed of;
(c) shipments of radioactive waste as defined in Article 2 of Council Directive 92/3/Euratom of 3 February 1992 on the supervision and control of shipments of radioactive waste between Member States and into and out of the Community;
(d) shipments which are subject to the approval requirements of Regulation (EC) No 1774/2002;
(e) shipments of the waste referred to in point 1(b)(ii), (iv) and (v) of Article 2 of Directive 2006/12/EC, where such shipments are already covered by other Community legislation containing similar provisions;
(f) shipments of waste from the Antarctic into the Community which are in accordance with the requirements of the Protocol on Environmental Protection to the Antarctic Treaty (1991);
(g) imports into the Community of waste generated by armed forces or relief organisations in situations of crisis, peacemaking or peacekeeping operations where such waste is shipped, by the armed forces or relief organisations concerned or on their behalf, directly or indirectly to the country of destination. In such cases, any competent authority of transit and the competent authority of destination in the Community shall be informed in advance concerning the shipment and its destination;
[(h) shipments of CO2 for the purposes of geological storage in accordance with Directive 2009/31/EC of the European Parliament and of the Council of 23 April 2009 on the geological storage of carbon dioxide.][1]

4. Shipments of waste from the Antarctic to countries outside the Community, which transit through the Community, shall be subject to Articles 36 and 49.

5. Shipments of waste exclusively within a Member State shall be subject only to Article 33.

Amendment

1 Inserted by Directive 2009/31/EC of the European Parliament and of the Council of 23 April 2009 on the geological storage of carbon dioxide and amending Council Directive 85/337/EEC, European Parliament and Council Directives 2000/60/EC, 2001/80/EC, 2004/35/EC, 2006/12/EC, 2008/1/EC and Regulation (EC) No 1013/2006, Article 36.

Article 2

Definitions

For the purposes of this Regulation:
1. "waste" is as defined in Article 1(1)(a) of Directive 2006/12/EC;
2. "hazardous waste" is as defined in Article 1(4) of Council Directive 91/689/EEC of 12 December 1991 on hazardous waste;
3. "mixture of wastes" means waste that results from an intentional or unintentional mixing of two or more different wastes and for which mixture no single entry exists in Annexes III, IIIB, IV and IVA. Waste shipped in a single shipment of wastes, consisting of two or more wastes, where each waste is separated, is not a mixture of wastes;

4. "disposal" is as defined in Article 1(1)(e) of Directive 2006/12/EC;
5. "interim disposal" means disposal operations D 13 to D 15 as defined in Annex II A to Directive 2006/12/EC;
6. "recovery" is as defined in Article 1(1)(f) of Directive 2006/12/EC;
7. "interim recovery" means recovery operations R 12 and R 13 as defined in Annex II B to Directive 2006/12/EC;
8. "environmentally sound management" means taking all practicable steps to ensure that waste is managed in a manner that will protect human health and the environment against adverse effects which may result from such waste;
9. "producer" is anyone whose activities produce waste (original producer) and/or anyone who carries out pre-processing, mixing or other operations resulting in a change in the nature or composition of this waste (new producer) (as defined in Article 1(1)(b) of Directive 2006/12/EC);
10. "holder" is the producer of the waste or the natural or legal person who is in possession of it (and as defined in Article 1(1)(c) of Directive 2006/12/EC);
11. "collector" is anyone carrying out waste collection as defined in Article 1(1)(g) of Directive 2006/12/EC;
12. "dealer" is anyone who acts in the role of principal to purchase and subsequently sell waste, including such dealers who do not take physical possession of the waste, and as referred to in Article 12 of Directive 2006/12/EC;
13. "broker" is anyone arranging the recovery or disposal of waste on behalf of others, including such brokers who do not take physical possession of the waste, as referred to in Article 12 of Directive 2006/12/EC;
14. "consignee" means the person or undertaking under the jurisdiction of the country of destination to whom or to which the waste is shipped for recovery or disposal;
15. "notifier" means:
    (a) in the case of a shipment originating from a Member State, any natural or legal person under the jurisdiction of that Member State who intends to carry out a shipment of waste or intends to have a shipment of waste carried out and to whom the duty to notify is assigned. The notifier is one of the persons or bodies listed below, selected in accordance with the ranking established in this listing:
        (i) the original producer, or
        (ii) the licensed new producer who carries out operations prior to shipment, or
        (iii) a licensed collector who, from various small quantities of the same type of waste collected from a variety of sources, has assembled the shipment which is to start from a single notified location, or
        (iv) a registered dealer who has been authorised in writing by the original producer, new producer or licensed collector specified in (i), (ii) and (iii) to act on his/her behalf as notifier,
        (v) a registered broker who has been authorised in writing by the original producer, new producer or licensed collector specified in (i), (ii) and (iii) to act on his/her behalf as notifier,
        (vi) where all of the persons specified in (i), (ii), (iii), (iv) and (v) if applicable, are unknown or insolvent, the holder.

        Should a notifier specified in (iv) or (v) fail to fulfil any of the take-back obligations set out in Articles 22 to 25, the original producer, new producer or licensed collector specified in (i), (ii) or (iii) respectively who authorised that dealer or broker to act on his/her behalf shall be deemed to be the notifier for the purposes of the said take-back obligations. In circumstances of illegal shipment notified by a dealer or broker specified in (iv) or (v), the person specified in (i), (ii) or (iii) who authorised that dealer or broker to act on his/her behalf shall be deemed to be the notifier for the purposes of this Regulation;
    (b) in the case of import into, or transit through, the Community of waste that does not originate in a Member State, any of the following natural or legal persons under the jurisdiction of the country of dispatch who intends to carry out a

shipment of waste or intends to have, or who has had, a shipment of waste carried out, being either:

(i) the person designated by the law of the country of dispatch; or, in the absence of any such designation,

(ii) the holder at the time the export took place;

16. "Basel Convention" means the Basel Convention of 22 March 1989 on the control of transboundary movements of hazardous wastes and their disposal;

17. "OECD Decision" means Decision C(2001)107/Final of the OECD Council concerning the revision of Decision C(92)39/Final on control of transboundary movements of wastes destined for recovery operations;

18. "competent authority" means:

(a) in the case of Member States, the body designated by the Member State concerned in accordance with Article 53; or

(b) in the case of a non-Member State that is a Party to the Basel Convention, the body designated by that country as the competent authority for the purposes of that Convention in accordance with Article 5 thereof; or

(c) in the case of any country not referred to in either (a) or (b), the body that has been designated as the competent authority by the country or region concerned or, in the absence of such designation, the regulatory authority for the country or region, as appropriate, which has jurisdiction over shipments of waste for recovery or disposal or transit, as the case may be;

19. "competent authority of dispatch" means the competent authority for the area from which the shipment is planned to be initiated or is initiated;

20. "competent authority of destination" means the competent authority for the area to which the shipment is planned or takes place, or in which waste is loaded prior to recovery or disposal in an area not under the national jurisdiction of any country;

21. "competent authority of transit" means the competent authority for any country, other than that of the competent authority of dispatch or destination, through which the shipment is planned or takes place;

22. "country of dispatch" means any country from which a shipment of waste is planned to be initiated or is initiated;

23. "country of destination" means any country to which a shipment of waste is planned or takes place for recovery or disposal therein, or for the purpose of loading prior to recovery or disposal in an area not under the national jurisdiction of any country;

24. "country of transit" means any country, other than the country of dispatch or destination, through which a shipment of waste is planned or takes place;

25. "area under the national jurisdiction of a country" means any land or marine area within which a state exercises administrative and regulatory responsibility in accordance with international law as regards the protection of human health or the environment;

26. "overseas countries and territories" means the overseas countries and territories as listed in Annex IA to Decision 2001/822/EC;

27. "customs office of export from the Community" is the customs office as defined in Article 161(5) of Council Regulation (EEC) No 2913/92 of 12 October 1992 establishing the Community Customs Code;

28. "customs office of exit from the Community" is the customs office as defined in Article 793(2) of Commission Regulation (EEC) No 2454/93 of 2 July 1993 laying down provisions for the implementation of Council Regulation (EEC) No 2913/92 establishing the Community Customs Code;

29. "customs office of entry into the Community" is the customs office where waste brought into the customs territory of the Community shall be conveyed to in accordance with Article 38(1) of Regulation (EEC) No 2913/92;

30. "import" means any entry of waste into the Community but excluding transit through the Community;

31. "export" means the action of waste leaving the Community but excluding transit through the Community;

32. "transit" means a shipment of waste or a planned shipment of waste through one or more countries other than the country of dispatch or destination;
33. "transport" means the carriage of waste by road, rail, air, sea or inland waterways;
34. "shipment" means the transport of waste destined for recovery or disposal which is planned or takes place:
    (a) between a country and another country; or
    (b) between a country and overseas countries and territories or other areas, under that country's protection; or
    (c) between a country and any land area which is not part of any country under international law; or
    (d) between a country and the Antarctic; or
    (e) from one country through any of the areas referred to above; or
    (f) within a country through any of the areas referred to above and which originates in and ends in the same country; or
    (g) from a geographic area not under the jurisdiction of any country, to a country;
35. "illegal shipment" means any shipment of waste effected:
    (a) without notification to all competent authorities concerned pursuant to this Regulation; or
    (b) without the consent of the competent authorities concerned pursuant to this Regulation; or
    (c) with consent obtained from the competent authorities concerned through falsification, misrepresentation or fraud; or
    (d) in a way which is not specified materially in the notification or movement documents; or
    (e) in a way which results in recovery or disposal in contravention of Community or international rules; or
    (f) contrary to Articles 34, 36, 39, 40, 41 and 43; or
    (g) which, in relation to shipments of waste as referred to in Article 3(2) and (4), has resulted from:
        (i) the waste being discovered not to be listed in Annexes III, IIIA or IIIB, or
        (ii) non-compliance with Article 3(4),
        (iii) the shipment being effected in a way which is not specified materially in the document set out in Annex VII.

Title II
Shipments within the Community with or without transit through third countries

Article 3

Overall procedural framework

1. Shipments of the following wastes shall be subject to the procedure of prior written notification and consent as laid down in the provisions of this Title:

(a) if destined for disposal operations:
    all wastes;

(b) if destined for recovery operations:
    (i) wastes listed in Annex IV, which include, inter alia, wastes listed in Annexes II and VIII to the Basel Convention,
    (ii) wastes listed in Annex IVA,
    (iii) wastes not classified under one single entry in either Annex III, IIIB, IV or IVA,
    (iv) mixtures of wastes not classified under one single entry in either Annex III, IIIB, IV or IVA unless listed in Annex IIIA.

2. Shipments of the following wastes destined for recovery shall be subject to the general information requirements laid down in Article 18, if the amount of waste shipped exceeds 20 kg:

(a) waste listed in Annex III or IIIB;

(b) mixtures, not classified under one single entry in Annex III, of two or more wastes listed in Annex III, provided that the composition of these mixtures does not impair their environmentally sound recovery and provided that such mixtures are listed in Annex IIIA, in accordance with Article 58.

3. For wastes listed in Annex III, in exceptional cases, the relevant provisions shall apply as if they had been listed in Annex IV, if they display any of the hazardous characteristics listed in Annex III to Directive 91/689/EEC. These cases shall be treated in accordance with Article 58.

4. Shipments of waste explicitly destined for laboratory analysis to assess either its physical or chemical characteristics or to determine its suitability for recovery or disposal operations shall not be subject to the procedure of prior written notification and consent as described in paragraph 1. Instead, the procedural requirements of Article 18 shall apply. The amount of such waste exempted when explicitly destined for laboratory analysis shall be determined by the minimum quantity reasonably needed to adequately perform the analysis in each particular case, and shall not exceed 25 kg.

5. Shipments of mixed municipal waste (waste entry 20 03 01) collected from private households, including where such collection also covers such waste from other producers, to recovery or disposal facilities shall, in accordance with this Regulation, be subject to the same provisions as shipments of waste destined for disposal.

Chapter 1
Prior written notification and consent

Article 4

Notification

Where the notifier intends to ship waste as referred to in Article 3(1)(a) or (b), he/she shall submit a prior written notification to and through the competent authority of dispatch and, if submitting a general notification, comply with Article 13.

When a notification is submitted, the following requirements shall be fulfilled:

1. notification and movement documents:
   Notification shall be effected by means of the following documents:
   (a) the notification document set out in Annex IA; and
   (b) the movement document set out in Annex IB.
   In submitting a notification, the notifier shall fill in the notification document and, where relevant, the movement document.

   When the notifier is not the original producer in accordance with point 15(a)(i) of Article 2, the notifier shall ensure that this producer or one of the persons indicated in point 15(a)(ii) or (iii) of Article 2, where practicable, also signs the notification document set out in Annex IA.

   The notification document and the movement document shall be issued to the notifier by the competent authority of dispatch;
2. information and documentation in the notification and movement documents:
   The notifier shall supply on, or annex to, the notification document information and documentation as listed in Annex II, Part 1. The notifier shall supply on, or annex to, the movement document information and documentation referred to in Annex II, Part 2, to the extent possible at the time of notification.

   A notification shall be considered properly carried out when the competent authority of dispatch is satisfied that the notification document and movement document have been completed in accordance with the first subparagraph;
3. additional information and documentation:
   If requested by any of the competent authorities concerned, the notifier shall supply

additional information and documentation. A list of additional information and documentation that may be requested is set out in Annex II, Part 3.

A notification shall be considered properly completed when the competent authority of destination is satisfied that the notification document and the movement document have been completed and that the information and documentation as listed in Annex II, Parts 1 and 2, as well as any additional information and documentation requested in accordance with this paragraph and as listed in Annex II, Part 3, have been supplied by the notifier;

4. conclusion of a contract between the notifier and the consignee:
The notifier shall conclude a contract as described in Article 5 with the consignee for the recovery or disposal of the notified waste.

Evidence of this contract or a declaration certifying its existence in accordance with Annex IA shall be supplied to the competent authorities involved at the time of notification. A copy of the contract or such evidence to the satisfaction of the competent authority concerned shall be provided by the notifier or consignee upon request by the competent authority;

5. establishment of a financial guarantee or equivalent insurance:
A financial guarantee or equivalent insurance shall be established as described in Article 6. A declaration to this effect shall be made by the notifier through completion of the appropriate part of the notification document set out in Annex IA.

The financial guarantee or equivalent insurance (or if the competent authority so allows, evidence of that guarantee or insurance or a declaration certifying its existence) shall be supplied as part of the notification document at the time of notification or, if the competent authority so allows, pursuant to national legislation, at such time before the shipment starts;

6. Coverage of the notification:
A notification shall cover the shipment of waste from its initial place of dispatch and including its interim and non-interim recovery or disposal.

If subsequent interim or non-interim operations take place in a country other than the first country of destination, the non-interim operation and its destination shall be indicated in the notification and Article 15(f) shall apply.

Only one waste identification code shall be covered for each notification, except for:

(a) wastes not classified under one single entry in either Annex III, IIIB, IV or IVA. In this case, only one type of waste shall be specified;

(b) mixtures of wastes not classified under one single entry in either Annex III, IIIB, IV or IVA unless listed in Annex IIIA. In this case, the code for each fraction of the waste shall be specified in order of importance.

Article 5

Contract

1. All shipments of waste for which notification is required shall be subject to the requirement of the conclusion of a contract between the notifier and the consignee for the recovery or disposal of the notified waste.

2. The contract shall be concluded and effective at the time of notification and for the duration of the shipment until a certificate is issued in accordance with Article 15(e), Article 16(e) or, where appropriate, Article 15(d).

3. The contract shall include obligations:

(a) on the notifier to take the waste back if the shipment or the recovery or disposal has not been completed as intended or if it has been effected as an illegal shipment, in accordance with Article 22 and Article 24(2);

(b) on the consignee to recover or dispose of the waste if it has been effected as an illegal shipment, in accordance with Article 24(3); and

(c) on the facility to provide, in accordance with Article 16(e), a certificate that the waste has been recovered or disposed of, in accordance with the notification and the conditions specified therein and the requirements of this Regulation.

4. If the waste shipped is destined for interim recovery or disposal operations, the contract shall include the following additional obligations:

(a) the obligation on the facility of destination to provide, in accordance with Article 15(d) and, where appropriate, Article 15(e), the certificates that the waste has been recovered or disposed of in accordance with the notification and the conditions specified therein and the requirements of this Regulation; and

(b) the obligation on the consignee to submit, where applicable, a notification to the initial competent authority of the initial country of dispatch in accordance with Article 15(f) (ii).

5. If the waste is shipped between two establishments under the control of the same legal entity, the contract may be replaced by a declaration by the entity in question undertaking to recover or dispose of the notified waste.

Article 6

Financial guarantee

1. All shipments of waste for which notification is required shall be subject to the requirement of a financial guarantee or equivalent insurance covering:

(a) costs of transport;

(b) costs of recovery or disposal, including any necessary interim operation; and

(c) costs of storage for 90 days.

2. The financial guarantee or equivalent insurance is intended to cover costs arising in the context of:

(a) cases where a shipment or the recovery or disposal cannot be completed as intended, as referred to in Article 22; and

(b) cases where a shipment or the recovery or disposal is illegal as referred to in Article 24.

3. The financial guarantee or equivalent insurance shall be established by the notifier or by another natural or legal person on its behalf and shall be effective at the time of the notification or, if the competent authority which approves the financial guarantee or equivalent insurance so allows, at the latest when the shipment starts, and shall apply to the notified shipment at the latest when the shipment starts.

4. The competent authority of dispatch shall approve the financial guarantee or equivalent insurance, including the form, wording and amount of the cover.

However, in cases of import into the Community, the competent authority of destination in the Community shall review the amount of cover and, if necessary, approve an additional financial guarantee or equivalent insurance.

5. The financial guarantee or equivalent insurance shall be valid for and cover a notified shipment and completion of recovery or disposal of the notified waste.

The financial guarantee or equivalent insurance shall be released when the competent authority concerned has received the certificate referred to in Article 16(e) or, where appropriate, in Article 15(e) as regards interim recovery or disposal operations.

6. By way of derogation from paragraph 5, if the waste shipped is destined for interim recovery or disposal operations and a further recovery or disposal operation takes place in

the country of destination, the financial guarantee or equivalent insurance may be released when the waste leaves the interim facility and the competent authority concerned has received the certificate referred to in Article 15(d). In this case, any further shipment to a recovery or disposal facility shall be covered by a new financial guarantee or equivalent insurance unless the competent authority of destination is satisfied that such a financial guarantee or equivalent insurance is not required. In these circumstances, the competent authority of destination shall be responsible for obligations arising in the case of an illegal shipment or for take-back where the shipment or the further recovery or disposal operation cannot be completed as intended.

7. The competent authority within the Community which has approved the financial guarantee or equivalent insurance shall have access thereto and shall make use of the funding, including for the purpose of payments to other authorities concerned, in order to meet the obligations arising in accordance with Articles 23 and 25.

8. In the case of a general notification pursuant to Article 13, a financial guarantee or equivalent insurance covering parts of the general notification may be established, instead of one covering the entire general notification. In such cases, the financial guarantee or equivalent insurance shall apply to the shipment at the latest when the notified shipment it covers starts.

The financial guarantee or equivalent insurance shall be released when the competent authority concerned has received the certificate referred to in Article 16(e) or, where appropriate, in Article 15(e) as regards interim recovery or disposal operations for the relevant waste. Paragraph 6 shall apply mutatis mutandis.

9. Member States shall inform the Commission of provisions of national law adopted pursuant to this Article.

Article 7

Transmission of the notification by the competent authority of dispatch

1. Once the notification has been properly carried out, as described in the second subparagraph, point 2 of Article 4, the competent authority of dispatch shall retain a copy of the notification and transmit the notification to the competent authority of destination with copies to any competent authority(ies) of transit, and shall inform the notifier of the transmission. This shall be done within three working days of receipt of the notification.

2. If the notification is not properly carried out, the competent authority of dispatch shall request information and documentation from the notifier in accordance with the second subparagraph, point 2 of Article 4.

This shall be done within three working days of receipt of the notification.

In such cases the competent authority of dispatch shall have three working days following the receipt of the information and/or documentation requested in which to comply with paragraph 1.

3. Once the notification has been properly carried out, as described in the second subparagraph, point 2 of Article 4, the competent authority of dispatch may decide, within three working days, not to proceed with the notification, if it has objections to the shipment in accordance with Articles 11 and 12.

It shall immediately inform the notifier of its decision and of these objections.

4. If, within 30 days of receipt of the notification, the competent authority of dispatch has not transmitted the notification as required under paragraph 1, it shall provide the notifier with a reasoned explanation upon his/her request. This shall not apply when the request for information, referred to in paragraph 2, has not been complied with.

Article 8

Requests for information and documentation by the competent authorities concerned and acknowledgement by the competent authority of destination

1. Following the transmission of the notification by the competent authority of dispatch, if any of the competent authorities concerned considers that additional information and documentation is required as referred to in the second subparagraph, point 3 of Article 4, it shall request such information and documentation from the notifier and inform the other competent authorities of such request. This shall be done within three working days of receipt of the notification. In such cases the competent authorities concerned shall have three working days following the receipt of the information and documentation requested in which to inform the competent authority of destination.

2. When the competent authority of destination considers that the notification has been properly completed, as described in the second subparagraph, point 3 of Article 4, it shall send an acknowledgement to the notifier and copies to the other competent authorities concerned. This shall be done within three working days of receipt of the properly completed notification.

3. If, within 30 days of receipt of the notification, the competent authority of destination has not acknowledged the notification as required under paragraph 2, it shall provide the notifier, upon his/her request, with a reasoned explanation.

Article 9

Consents by the competent authorities of destination, dispatch and transit and time periods for transport, recovery or disposal

1. The competent authorities of destination, dispatch and transit shall have 30 days following the date of transmission of the acknowledgement by the competent authority of destination in accordance with Article 8 in which to take one of the following duly reasoned decisions in writing as regards the notified shipment:
(a) consent without conditions;
(b) consent with conditions in accordance with Article 10; or
(c) objections in accordance with Articles 11 and 12.

Tacit consent by the competent authority of transit may be assumed if no objection is lodged within the said 30-day time limit.

2. The competent authorities of destination, dispatch and, where appropriate, transit shall transmit their decision and the reasons therefor to the notifier in writing within the 30-day time limit referred to in paragraph 1, with copies to the other competent authorities concerned.

3. The competent authorities of destination, dispatch and, where appropriate, transit shall signify their written consent by appropriately stamping, signing and dating the notification document or their copies thereof.

4. A written consent to a planned shipment shall expire one calendar year after it is issued or on such later date as is indicated in the notification document. However, this shall not apply if a shorter period is indicated by the competent authorities concerned.

5. Tacit consent to a planned shipment shall expire one calendar year after the expiry of the 30-day time limit referred to in paragraph 1.

6. The planned shipment may take place only after fulfilment of the requirements of Article 16(a) and (b) and during the period of validity of the tacit or written consents of all competent authorities.

7. The recovery or disposal of waste in relation to a planned shipment shall be completed no later than one calendar year from the receipt of the waste by the facility, unless a shorter period is indicated by the competent authorities concerned.

8. The competent authorities concerned shall withdraw their consent when they have knowledge that:

(a) the composition of the waste is not as notified; or

(b) the conditions imposed on the shipment are not respected; or

(c) the waste is not recovered or disposed of in compliance with the permit of the facility that performs the said operation; or

(d) the waste is to be, or has been, shipped, recovered or disposed of in a way that is not in accordance with the information supplied on, or annexed to, the notification and movement documents.

9. Any withdrawal of consent shall be transmitted by means of official notice to the notifier with copies to the other competent authorities concerned and to the consignee.

Article 10

Conditions for a shipment

1. The competent authorities of dispatch, destination and transit may, within 30 days following the date of transmission of the acknowledgement of the competent authority of destination in accordance with Article 8, lay down conditions in connection with their consent to a notified shipment. Such conditions may be based on one or more of the reasons specified in either Article 11 or Article 12.

2. The competent authorities of dispatch, destination and transit may also, within the 30-day time limit referred to in paragraph 1, lay down conditions in respect of the transport of waste within their jurisdiction. Such transport conditions shall not be more stringent than those laid down in respect of similar shipments occurring wholly within their jurisdiction and shall take due account of existing agreements, in particular relevant international agreements.

3. The competent authorities of dispatch, destination and transit may also, within the 30-day time limit referred to in paragraph 1, lay down a condition that their consent is to be considered withdrawn if the financial guarantee or equivalent insurance is not applicable at the latest when the notified shipment starts, as required by Article 6(3).

4. Conditions shall be transmitted to the notifier in writing by the competent authority that lays them down, with copies to the competent authorities concerned.

Conditions shall be supplied on, or annexed to, the notification document by the relevant competent authority.

5. The competent authority of destination may also, within the 30-day time limit referred to in paragraph 1, lay down a condition that the facility which receives the waste shall keep a regular record of inputs, outputs and/or balances for wastes and the related recovery or disposal operations as contained in the notification, and for the period of validity of the notification. Such records shall be signed by a person legally responsible for the facility and be sent to the competent authority of destination within one month of completion of the notified recovery or disposal operation.

Article 11

Objections to shipments of waste destined for disposal

1. Where a notification is submitted regarding a planned shipment of waste destined for disposal, the competent authorities of destination and dispatch may, within 30 days following the date of transmission of the acknowledgement of the competent authority of destination in accordance with Article 8, raise reasoned objections based on one or more of the following grounds and in accordance with the Treaty:

(a) that the planned shipment or disposal would not be in accordance with measures taken to implement the principles of proximity, priority for recovery and self-sufficiency at

Community and national levels in accordance with Directive 2006/12/EC, to prohibit generally or partially or to object systematically to shipments of waste; or

(b) that the planned shipment or disposal would not be in accordance with national legislation relating to environmental protection, public order, public safety or health protection concerning actions taking place in the objecting country; or

(c) that the notifier or the consignee has previously been convicted of illegal shipment or some other illegal act in relation to environmental protection. In this case, the competent authorities of dispatch and destination may refuse all shipments involving the person in question in accordance with national legislation; or

(d) that the notifier or the facility has repeatedly failed to comply with Articles 15 and 16 in connection with past shipments; or

(e) that the Member State wishes to exercise its right pursuant to Article 4(1) of the Basel Convention to prohibit the import of hazardous waste or of waste listed in Annex II to that Convention; or

(f) that the planned shipment or disposal conflicts with obligations resulting from international conventions concluded by the Member State(s) concerned or the Community; or

(g) that the planned shipment or disposal is not in accordance with Directive 2006/12/EC, in particular Articles 5 and 7 thereof, while taking into account geographical circumstances or the need for specialised installations for certain types of waste:

  (i) in order to implement the principle of self-sufficiency at Community and national levels, or

  (ii) in cases where the specialised installation has to dispose of waste from a nearer source and the competent authority has given priority to this waste, or

  (iii) in order to ensure that shipments are in accordance with waste management plans, or

(h) that the waste will be treated in a facility which is covered by Directive 96/61/EC, but which does not apply best available techniques as defined in Article 9(4) of that Directive in compliance with the permit of the facility; or

(i) that the waste is mixed municipal waste collected from private households (waste entry 20 03 01); or

(j) that the waste concerned will not be treated in accordance with legally binding environmental protection standards in relation to disposal operations established in Community legislation (also in cases where temporary derogations are granted).

2. The competent authority(ies) of transit may, within the 30-day time limit referred to in paragraph 1, raise reasoned objections based only on paragraph 1(b), (c), (d) and (f).

3. In the case of hazardous waste produced in a Member State of dispatch in such a small quantity overall per year that the provision of new specialised disposal installations within that Member State would be uneconomic, paragraph 1(a) shall not apply.

The competent authority of destination shall cooperate with the competent authority of dispatch which considers that this paragraph and not paragraph 1(a) should apply, with a view to resolving the issue bilaterally.

[If there is no satisfactory solution, either Member State may refer the matter to the Commission. The issue shall then be determined in accordance with the regulatory procedure referred to in Article 59a(2).][1]

4. If, within the 30-day time limit referred to in paragraph 1, the competent authorities consider that the problems which gave rise to their objections have been resolved, they shall immediately inform the notifier in writing, with copies to the consignee and to the other competent authorities concerned.

5. If the problems giving rise to the objections have not been resolved within the 30-day time limit referred to in paragraph 1, the notification shall cease to be valid. In cases where the notifier still intends to carry out the shipment, a new notification shall be submitted, unless all the competent authorities concerned and the notifier agree otherwise.

6. Measures taken by Member States in accordance with paragraph 1(a), to prohibit generally or partially or to object systematically to shipments of waste destined for disposal, or in accordance with paragraph 1(e), shall immediately be notified to the Commission which shall inform the other Member States.

Amendment

1 Substituted by Regulation (EC) No 219/2009 of the European Parliament and of the Council of 11 March 2009 adapting a number of instruments subject to the procedure referred to in Article 251 of the Treaty to Council Decision 1999/468/EC with regard to the regulatory procedure with scrutiny, Article 1, Annex, para 3.9.1.

Article 12

Objections to shipments of waste destined for recovery

1. Where a notification is submitted regarding a planned shipment of waste destined for recovery, the competent authorities of destination and dispatch may, within 30 days following the date of transmission of the acknowledgement of the competent authority of destination in accordance with Article 8, raise reasoned objections based on one or more of the following grounds and in accordance with the Treaty:

(a) that the planned shipment or recovery would not be in accordance with Directive 2006/12/EC, in particular Articles 3, 4, 7 and 10 thereof; or

(b) that the planned shipment or recovery would not be in accordance with national legislation relating to environmental protection, public order, public safety or health protection concerning actions taking place in the objecting country; or

(c) that the planned shipment or recovery would not be in accordance with national legislation in the country of dispatch relating to the recovery of waste, including where the planned shipment would concern waste destined for recovery in a facility which has lower treatment standards for the particular waste than those of the country of dispatch, respecting the need to ensure the proper functioning of the internal market;

This shall not apply if:

(i) there is corresponding Community legislation, in particular related to waste, and if requirements that are at least as stringent as those laid down in the Community legislation have been introduced in national legislation transposing such Community legislation,

(ii) the recovery operation in the country of destination takes place under conditions that are broadly equivalent to those prescribed in the national legislation of the country of dispatch,

(iii) the national legislation in the country of dispatch, other than that covered by (i), has not been notified in accordance with Directive 98/34/EC of the European Parliament and of the Council of 22 June 1998 laying down a procedure for the provision of information in the field of technical standards and regulations and of rules on Information Society services, where required by that Directive, or

(d) that the notifier or the consignee has previously been convicted of illegal shipment or some other illegal act in relation to environmental protection. In this case, the competent authorities of dispatch and destination may refuse all shipments involving the person in question in accordance with national legislation; or

(e) that the notifier or the facility has repeatedly failed to comply with Articles 15 and 16 in connection with past shipments; or

(f) that the planned shipment or recovery conflicts with obligations resulting from international conventions concluded by the Member State(s) concerned or the Community; or

(g) that the ratio of the recoverable and non-recoverable waste, the estimated value of the materials to be finally recovered or the cost of the recovery and the cost of the disposal of the non-recoverable fraction do not justify the recovery, having regard to economic and/or environmental considerations; or

(h) that the waste shipped is destined for disposal and not for recovery; or

(i) that the waste will be treated in a facility which is covered by Directive 96/61/EC, but which does not apply best available techniques as defined in Article 9(4) of that Directive in compliance with the permit of the facility; or

(j) that the waste concerned will not be treated in accordance with legally binding environmental protection standards in relation to recovery operations, or legally binding recovery or recycling obligations established in Community legislation (also in cases where temporary derogations are granted); or

(k) that the waste concerned will not be treated in accordance with waste management plans drawn up pursuant to Article 7 of Directive 2006/12/EC with the purpose of ensuring the implementation of legally binding recovery or recycling obligations established in Community legislation.

2. The competent authority(ies) of transit may, within the 30-day time limit referred to in paragraph 1, raise reasoned objections to the planned shipment based only on paragraph 1(b), (d), (e) and (f).

3. If, within the 30-day time limit referred to in paragraph 1, the competent authorities consider that the problems which gave rise to their objections have been resolved, they shall immediately inform the notifier in writing, with copies to the consignee and to the other competent authorities concerned.

4. If the problems giving rise to the objections are not resolved within the 30-day time limit referred to in paragraph 1, the notification shall cease to be valid. In cases where the notifier still intends to carry out the shipment, a new notification shall be submitted, unless all the competent authorities concerned and the notifier agree otherwise.

5. Objections raised by competent authorities in accordance with paragraph 1(c) shall be reported by Member States to the Commission in accordance with Article 51.

6. The Member State of dispatch shall inform the Commission and the other Member States of the national legislation on which objections raised by competent authorities in accordance with paragraph 1(c) may be based, and shall state to which waste and waste recovery operations those objections apply, before such legislation is invoked in order to raise reasoned objections.

Article 13

General notification

1. The notifier may submit a general notification to cover several shipments if, in the case of each shipment:

(a) the waste has essentially similar physical and chemical characteristics; and

(b) the waste is shipped to the same consignee and the same facility; and

(c) the route of the shipment as indicated in the notification document is the same.

2. If, owing to unforeseen circumstances, the same route cannot be followed, the notifier shall inform the competent authorities concerned as soon as possible and, if possible, before the shipment starts if the need for modification is already known.

Where the route modification is known before the shipment starts and involves competent authorities other than those concerned by the general notification, the general notification may not be used and a new notification shall be submitted.

3. The competent authorities concerned may make their agreement to the use of a general notification subject to the subsequent provision of additional information and documentation, in accordance with the second subparagraph, points 2 and 3 of Article 4.

Article 14

Pre-consented recovery facilities

1. The competent authorities of destination which have jurisdiction over specific recovery facilities may decide to issue pre-consents to such facilities.

Such decisions shall be limited to a specific period and may be revoked at any time.

2. In the case of a general notification submitted in accordance with Article 13, the period of validity of the consent referred to in Article 9(4) and (5) may be extended to up to three years by the competent authority of destination in agreement with the other competent authorities concerned.

3. Competent authorities which decide to issue a pre-consent to a facility in accordance with paragraphs 1 and 2 shall inform the Commission and, where appropriate, the OECD Secretariat of:

(a) the name, registration number and address of the recovery facility;
(b) the description of technologies employed, including R-code(s);
(c) the wastes as listed in Annexes IV and IVA or the wastes to which the decision applies;
(d) the total pre-consented quantity;
(e) the period of validity;
(f) any change in the pre-consent;
(g) any change in the information notified; and
(h) any revocation of the pre-consent.

For this purpose the form set out in Annex VI shall be used.

4. By way of derogation from Articles 9, 10 and 12, the consent given in accordance with Article 9, conditions imposed in accordance with Article 10 or objections raised in accordance with Article 12 by the competent authorities concerned shall be subject to a time limit of seven working days following the date of transmission of the acknowledgement of the competent authority of destination in accordance with Article 8.

5. Notwithstanding paragraph 4, the competent authority of dispatch may decide that more time is needed in order to receive further information or documentation from the notifier.

In such cases, the competent authority shall, within seven working days, inform the notifier in writing with copies to the other competent authorities concerned.

The total time needed shall not exceed 30 days following the date of transmission of the acknowledgement of the competent authority of destination in accordance with Article 8.

Article 15

Additional provisions regarding interim recovery and disposal operations

Shipments of waste destined for interim recovery or disposal operations shall be subject to the following additional provisions:

(a) Where a shipment of waste is destined for an interim recovery or disposal operation, all the facilities where subsequent interim as well as non-interim recovery and disposal operations are envisaged shall also be indicated in the notification document in addition to the initial interim recovery or disposal operation.

(b) The competent authorities of dispatch and destination may give their consent to a shipment of waste destined for an interim recovery or disposal operation only if there are no grounds for objection, in accordance with Articles 11 or 12, to the shipment(s) of waste to the facilities performing any subsequent interim or non-interim recovery or disposal operations.

(c) Within three days of the receipt of the waste by the facility which carries out this interim recovery or disposal operation, that facility shall provide confirmation in writing that the waste has been received.

This confirmation shall be supplied on, or annexed to, the movement document. The said facility shall send signed copies of the movement document containing this confirmation to the notifier and to the competent authorities concerned.

(d) As soon as possible, but no later than 30 days after completion of the interim recovery or disposal operation, and no later than one calendar year, or a shorter period in accordance with Article 9(7), following the receipt of the waste, the facility carrying out this operation shall, under its responsibility, certify that the interim recovery or disposal has been completed.

This certificate shall be contained in, or annexed to, the movement document.

The said facility shall send signed copies of the movement document containing this certificate to the notifier and to the competent authorities concerned.

(e) When a recovery or disposal facility which carries out an interim recovery or disposal operation delivers the waste for any subsequent interim or non-interim recovery or disposal operation to a facility located in the country of destination, it shall obtain as soon as possible but no later than one calendar year following delivery of the waste, or a shorter period in accordance with Article 9(7), a certificate from that facility that the subsequent non-interim recovery or disposal operation has been completed.

The said facility that carries out an interim recovery or disposal operation shall promptly transmit the relevant certificate(s) to the notifier and the competent authorities concerned, identifying the shipment(s) to which the certificate(s) pertain.

(f) When a delivery as described in subparagraph (e) is made to a facility respectively located:

(i) in the initial country of dispatch or in another Member State, a new notification shall be required in accordance with the provisions of this Title, or

(ii) in a third country, a new notification shall be required in accordance with the provisions of this Regulation, with the addition that the provisions concerning the competent authorities concerned shall also apply to the initial competent authority of the initial country of dispatch.

Article 16

Requirements following consent to a shipment

After consent has been given to a notified shipment by the competent authorities involved, all undertakings involved shall complete the movement document, or, in the case of a general notification, the movement documents at the points indicated, sign it or them and retain a copy or copies. The following requirements shall be fulfilled:

(a) Completion of the movement document by the notifier: once the notifier has received consent from the competent authorities of dispatch, destination and transit or, in relation to the competent authority of transit, can assume tacit consent, he/she shall insert the actual date of shipment and otherwise complete the movement document to the extent possible.

(b) Prior information regarding actual start of shipment: the notifier shall send signed copies of the then completed movement document, as described in point (a), to the competent authorities concerned and to the consignee at least three working days before the shipment starts.

(c) Documents to accompany each transport: the notifier shall retain a copy of the movement document. The movement document and copies of the notification document containing the written consents and the conditions of the competent authorities concerned shall accompany each transport. The movement document shall be retained by the facility which receives the waste.

(d) Written confirmation of receipt of the waste by the facility: within three days of receipt of the waste, the facility shall provide confirmation in writing that the waste has been received.

This confirmation shall be contained in, or annexed to, the movement document.

The facility shall send signed copies of the movement document containing this confirmation to the notifier and to the competent authorities concerned.

(e) Certificate for non-interim recovery or disposal by the facility: as soon as possible, but no later than 30 days after completion of the non-interim recovery or disposal operation, and no later than one calendar year, or a shorter period in accordance with Article 9(7), following receipt of the waste, the facility carrying out the operation shall, under its responsibility, certify that the non-interim recovery or disposal has been completed.

This certificate shall be contained in, or annexed to, the movement document.

The facility shall send signed copies of the movement document containing this certificate to the notifier and to the competent authorities concerned.

Article 17

Changes in the shipment after consent

1. If any essential change is made to the details and/or conditions of the consented shipment, including changes in the intended quantity, route, routing, date of shipment or carrier, the notifier shall inform the competent authorities concerned and the consignee immediately and, where possible, before the shipment starts.

2. In such cases a new notification shall be submitted, unless all the competent authorities concerned consider that the proposed changes do not require a new notification.

3. Where such changes involve competent authorities other than those concerned in the original notification, a new notification shall be submitted.

Chapter 2
General information requirements

Article 18

Waste to be accompanied by certain information

1. Waste as referred to in Article 3(2) and (4) that is intended to be shipped shall be subject to the following procedural requirements:

(a) In order to assist the tracking of shipments of such waste, the person under the jurisdiction of the country of dispatch who arranges the shipment shall ensure that the waste is accompanied by the document contained in Annex VII.

(b) The document contained in Annex VII shall be signed by the person who arranges the shipment before the shipment takes place and shall be signed by the recovery facility or the laboratory and the consignee when the waste in question is received.

2. The contract referred to in Annex VII between the person who arranges the shipment and the consignee for recovery of the waste shall be effective when the shipment starts and shall include an obligation, where the shipment of waste or its recovery cannot be completed as intended or where it has been effected as an illegal shipment, on the person who arranges the shipment or, where that person is not in a position to complete the shipment of waste or its recovery (for example, is insolvent), on the consignee, to:

(a) take the waste back or ensure its recovery in an alternative way; and

(b) provide, if necessary, for its storage in the meantime.

The person who arranges the shipment or the consignee shall provide a copy of the contract upon request by the competent authority concerned.

3. For inspection, enforcement, planning and statistical purposes, Member States may in accordance with national legislation require information as referred to in paragraph 1 on shipments covered by this Article.

4. The information referred to in paragraph 1 shall be treated as confidential where this is required by Community and national legislation.

Chapter 3
General requirements

Article 19

Prohibition on mixing waste during shipment

From the start of the shipment to the receipt in a recovery or disposal facility, waste, as specified on the notification document or as referred to in Article 18, shall not be mixed with other waste.

Article 20

Keeping of documents and information

1. All documents sent to or by the competent authorities in relation to a notified shipment shall be kept in the Community for at least three years from the date when the shipment starts, by the competent authorities, the notifier, the consignee and the facility which receives the waste.

2. Information given pursuant to Article 18(1) shall be kept in the Community for at least three years from the date when the shipment starts, by the person who arranges for the shipment, the consignee and the facility which receives the waste.

Article 21

Public access to notifications

The competent authorities of dispatch or destination may make publicly available by appropriate means, such as the Internet, information on notifications of shipments they have consented to, where such information is not confidential under national or Community legislation.

Chapter 4
Take-back obligations

Article 22

Take-back when a shipment cannot be completed as intended

1. Where any of the competent authorities concerned becomes aware that a shipment of waste, including its recovery or disposal, cannot be completed as intended in accordance with the terms of the notification and movement documents and/or contract referred to in the second subparagraph, point 4 of Article 4 and in Article 5, it shall immediately inform the competent authority of dispatch. Where a recovery or disposal facility rejects a shipment received, it shall immediately inform the competent authority of destination.

2. The competent authority of dispatch shall ensure that, except in cases referred to in paragraph 3, the waste in question is taken back to its area of jurisdiction or elsewhere within the country of dispatch by the notifier as identified in accordance with the ranking established in point 15 of Article 2, or, if impracticable, by that competent authority itself or by a natural or legal person on its behalf.

This shall take place within 90 days, or such other period as may be agreed between the competent authorities concerned, after the competent authority of dispatch becomes aware or has been advised in writing by the competent authorities of destination or transit that the consented shipment of waste or its recovery or disposal cannot be completed and has been informed of the reason(s) therefor. Such advice may result from information submitted to the competent authorities of destination or transit, inter alia, by other competent authorities.

3. The take-back obligation in paragraph 2 shall not apply if the competent authorities of dispatch, transit and destination involved in disposing of or recovering the waste are satisfied that the waste can be recovered or disposed of in an alternative way in the country of destination or elsewhere by the notifier or, if impracticable, by the competent authority of dispatch or by a natural or legal person on its behalf.

The take-back obligation in paragraph 2 shall not apply if the waste shipped has, in the course of the operation at the facility concerned, been irreversibly mixed with other waste before a competent authority concerned has become aware of the fact that the notified shipment cannot be completed as referred to in paragraph 1. Such mixture shall be recovered or disposed of in an alternative way in accordance with the first subparagraph.

4. In cases of take-back as referred to in paragraph 2, a new notification shall be submitted, unless the competent authorities concerned agree that a duly reasoned request by the initial competent authority of dispatch is sufficient.

A new notification, where appropriate, shall be submitted by the initial notifier or, if impracticable, by any other natural or legal persons identified in accordance with point 15 of Article 2, or, if impracticable, by the initial competent authority of dispatch or by a natural or legal person on its behalf.

No competent authority shall oppose or object to the return of waste from a shipment that cannot be completed or to the related recovery and disposal operation.

5. In cases of alternative arrangements outside the initial country of destination as referred to in paragraph 3, a new notification, where appropriate, shall be submitted by the initial notifier or, if impracticable, by any other natural or legal persons identified in accordance with point 15 of Article 2, or, if impracticable, by the initial competent authority of dispatch or by a natural or legal person on its behalf.

When such a new notification is submitted by the notifier, this notification shall also be submitted to the competent authority of the initial country of dispatch.

6. In cases of alternative arrangements in the initial country of destination as referred to in paragraph 3, a new notification shall not be required and a duly reasoned request shall suffice. Such a duly reasoned request, seeking agreement to the alternative arrangement, shall be transmitted to the competent authority of destination and dispatch by the initial notifier or, if impracticable, to the competent authority of destination by the initial competent authority of dispatch.

7. If no new notification is to be submitted in accordance with paragraphs 4 or 6, a new movement document shall be completed in accordance with Article 15 or Article 16 by the initial notifier or, if impracticable, by any other natural or legal persons identified in accordance with point 15 of Article 2, or, if impracticable, by the initial competent authority of dispatch or by a natural or legal person on its behalf.

If a new notification is submitted by the initial competent authority of dispatch in accordance with paragraphs 4 or 5, a new financial guarantee or equivalent insurance shall not be required.

8. The obligation of the notifier and the subsidiary obligation of the country of dispatch to take the waste back or arrange for alternative recovery or disposal shall end when the facility issues the certificate of non-interim recovery or disposal as referred to in Article 16(e) or, where appropriate, in Article 15(e). In the cases of interim recovery or disposal referred to in Article 6(6), the subsidiary obligation of the country of dispatch shall end when the facility issues the certificate referred to in Article 15(d).

If a facility issues a certificate of recovery or disposal in such a way as to result in an illegal shipment, with the consequence that the financial guarantee is released, Article 24(3) and Article 25(2) shall apply.

9. Where waste from a shipment which cannot be completed, including its recovery or disposal, is discovered within a Member State, the competent authority with jurisdiction over the area where the waste was discovered shall be responsible for ensuring that arrangements are made for the safe storage of the waste pending its return or non-interim recovery or disposal in an alternative way.

Article 23

Costs for take-back when a shipment cannot be completed

1. Costs arising from the return of waste from a shipment that cannot be completed, including costs of its transport, recovery or disposal pursuant to Article 22(2) or (3) and, from the date on which the competent authority of dispatch becomes aware that a shipment of waste or its recovery or disposal cannot be completed, storage costs pursuant to Article 22(9) shall be charged:

(a) to the notifier as identified in accordance with the ranking established in point 15 of Article 2; or, if impracticable;
(b) to other natural or legal persons as appropriate; or, if impracticable;
(c) to the competent authority of dispatch; or, if impracticable;
(d) as otherwise agreed between the competent authorities concerned.

2. This Article shall be without prejudice to Community and national provisions concerning liability.

Article 24

Take-back when a shipment is illegal

1. Where a competent authority discovers a shipment that it considers to be an illegal shipment, it shall immediately inform the other competent authorities concerned.

2. If an illegal shipment is the responsibility of the notifier, the competent authority of dispatch shall ensure that the waste in question is:

(a) taken back by the notifier de facto; or, if no notification has been submitted;
(b) taken back by the notifier de jure; or, if impracticable;
(c) taken back by the competent authority of dispatch itself or by a natural or legal person on its behalf; or, if impracticable;
(d) alternatively recovered or disposed of in the country of destination or dispatch by the competent authority of dispatch itself or by a natural or legal person on its behalf; or, if impracticable;
(e) alternatively recovered or disposed of in another country by the competent authority of dispatch itself or by a natural or legal person on its behalf if all the competent authorities concerned agree.

This take-back, recovery or disposal shall take place within 30 days, or such other period as may be agreed between the competent authorities concerned after the competent authority of dispatch becomes aware of or has been advised in writing by the competent authorities of destination or transit of the illegal shipment and informed of the reason(s) therefor. Such advice may result from information submitted to the competent authorities of destination or transit, inter alia, by other competent authorities.

In cases of take-back as referred to in (a), (b) and (c), a new notification shall be submitted, unless the competent authorities concerned agree that a duly reasoned request by the initial competent authority of dispatch is sufficient.

The new notification shall be submitted by the person or authority listed in (a), (b) or (c) and in accordance with that order.

No competent authority shall oppose or object to the return of waste of an illegal shipment. In the case of alternative arrangements as referred to in (d) and (e) by the competent authority of dispatch, a new notification shall be submitted by the initial competent authority of dispatch or by a natural or legal person on its behalf unless the competent authorities concerned agree that a duly reasoned request by that authority is sufficient.

3. If an illegal shipment is the responsibility of the consignee the competent authority of destination shall ensure that the waste in question is recovered or disposed of in an environmentally sound manner:
(a) by the consignee; or, if impracticable,
(b) by the competent authority itself or by a natural or legal person on its behalf.
This recovery or disposal shall take place within 30 days, or such other period as may be agreed between the competent authorities concerned after the competent authority of destination becomes aware of or has been advised in writing by the competent authorities of dispatch or transit of the illegal shipment and informed of the reason(s) therefor. Such advice may result from information submitted to the competent authorities of dispatch and transit, inter alia, by other competent authorities.

To this end, the competent authorities concerned shall cooperate, as necessary, in the recovery or disposal of the waste.

4. If no new notification is to be submitted, a new movement document shall be completed in accordance with Article 15 or 16 by the person responsible for take-back or, if impracticable, by the initial competent authority of dispatch.

If a new notification is submitted by the initial competent authority of dispatch, a new financial guarantee or equivalent insurance shall not be required.

5. In particular in cases where responsibility for the illegal shipment cannot be imputed to either the notifier or the consignee, the competent authorities concerned shall cooperate to ensure that the waste in question is recovered or disposed of.

6. In the cases of interim recovery or disposal referred to in Article 6(6) where an illegal shipment is discovered after completion of the interim recovery or disposal operation, the subsidiary obligation of the country of dispatch to take the waste back or arrange for alternative recovery or disposal shall end when the facility has issued the certificate referred to in Article 15(d).

If a facility issues a certificate of recovery or disposal in such a way as to result in an illegal shipment, with the consequence that the financial guarantee is released, paragraph 3 and Article 25(2) shall apply.

7. Where the waste of an illegal shipment is discovered within a Member State, the competent authority with jurisdiction over the area where the waste was discovered shall be responsible for ensuring that arrangements are made for the safe storage of the waste pending its return or non-interim recovery or disposal in an alternative way.

8. Articles 34 and 36 shall not apply in cases where illegal shipments are returned to the country of dispatch and that country of dispatch is a country covered by the prohibitions set out in those Articles.

9. In the case of an illegal shipment as defined in point 35(g) of Article 2, the person who arranges the shipment shall be subject to the same obligations established in this Article as the notifier.

10. This Article shall be without prejudice to Community and national provisions concerning liability.

Article 25

Costs for take-back when a shipment is illegal

1. Costs arising from the take-back of waste of an illegal shipment, including costs of its transport, recovery or disposal pursuant to Article 24(2) and, from the date on which the competent authority of dispatch becomes aware that a shipment is illegal, storage costs pursuant to Article 24(7), shall be charged to:

(a) the notifier de facto, as identified in accordance with the ranking established in point 15 of Article 2; or, if no notification has been submitted;
(b) the notifier de jure or other natural or legal persons as appropriate; or, if impracticable;
(c) the competent authority of dispatch.

2. Costs arising from recovery or disposal pursuant to Article 24(3), including possible transport and storage costs pursuant to Article 24(7), shall be charged to:

(a) the consignee; or, if impracticable;
(b) the competent authority of destination.

3. Costs arising from recovery or disposal pursuant to Article 24(5), including possible transport and storage costs pursuant to Article 24(7), shall be charged to:

(a) the notifier, as identified in accordance with the ranking established in point 15 of Article 2, and/or the consignee, depending upon the decision by the competent authorities involved; or, if impracticable,
(b) other natural or legal persons as appropriate; or, if impracticable,
(c) the competent authorities of dispatch and destination.

4. In the case of an illegal shipment as defined in point 35(g) of Article 2, the person who arranges the shipment shall be subject to the same obligations established in this Article as the notifier.

5. This Article shall be without prejudice to Community and national provisions concerning liability.

Chapter 5
General administrative provisions

Article 26

Format of the communications

1. The information and documents listed below may be submitted by post:

(a) notification of a planned shipment pursuant to Articles 4 and 13;
(b) request for information and documentation pursuant to Articles 4, 7 and 8;
(c) submission of information and documentation pursuant to Articles 4, 7 and 8;
(d) written consent to a notified shipment pursuant to Article 9;
(e) conditions for a shipment pursuant to Article 10;
(f) objections to a shipment pursuant to Articles 11 and 12;
(g) information on decisions to issue pre-consents to specific recovery facilities pursuant to Article 14(3);
(h) written confirmation of receipt of the waste pursuant to Articles 15 and 16;
(i) certificate for recovery or disposal of the waste pursuant to Articles 15 and 16;
(j) prior information regarding actual start of the shipment pursuant to Article 16;
(k) information on changes in the shipment after consent pursuant to Article 17; and
(l) written consents and movement documents to be sent pursuant to Titles IV, V and VI.

2. Subject to the agreement of the competent authorities concerned and the notifier, the documents referred to in paragraph 1 may alternatively be submitted using any of the following methods of communication:

(a) by fax; or
(b) by fax followed by post; or
(c) by e-mail with digital signature. In this case, any stamp or signature required shall be replaced by the digital signature; or
(d) by e-mail without digital signature followed by post.

3. The documents to accompany each transport in accordance with Article 16(c) and Article 18 may be in an electronic form with digital signatures if they can be made readable at any time during the transport and if this is acceptable to the competent authorities concerned.

4. Subject to the agreement of the competent authorities concerned and of the notifier, the information and documents listed in paragraph 1 may be submitted and exchanged by means of electronic data interchange with electronic signature or electronic authentication in accordance with Directive 1999/93/EC of the European Parliament and of the Council of 13 December 1999 on a Community framework for electronic signatures, or a comparable electronic authentication system which provides the same level of security. In such cases, organisational arrangements concerning the flow of electronic data interchange may be made.

Article 27

Language

1. Any notification, information, documentation or other communication submitted pursuant to the provisions of this Title shall be supplied in a language acceptable to the competent authorities concerned.

2. The notifier shall provide the competent authorities concerned with authorised translation(s) into a language which is acceptable to them, should they so request.

Article 28

Disagreement on classification issues

1. If the competent authorities of dispatch and of destination cannot agree on the classification as regards the distinction between waste and non-waste, the subject matter shall be treated as if it were waste. This shall be without prejudice to the right of the country of destination to deal with the shipped material in accordance with its national legislation, following arrival of the shipped material and where such legislation is in accordance with Community or international law.

2. If the competent authorities of dispatch and of destination cannot agree on the classification of the notified waste as being listed in Annex III, IIIA, IIIB or IV, the waste shall be regarded as listed in Annex IV.

3. If the competent authorities of dispatch and destination cannot agree on the classification of the waste treatment operation notified as being recovery or disposal, the provisions regarding disposal shall apply.

4. Paragraphs 1 to 3 shall apply only for the purposes of this Regulation, and shall be without prejudice to rights of interested parties to resolve any dispute related to these questions before a court of law or tribunal.

Article 29

Administrative costs

Appropriate and proportionate administrative costs of implementing the notification and supervision procedures and usual costs of appropriate analyses and inspections may be charged to the notifier.

Article 30

Border-area agreements

1. In exceptional cases, and if the specific geographical or demographical situation warrants such a step, Member States may conclude bilateral agreements making the notification procedure for shipments of specific flows of waste less stringent in respect of cross-border shipments to the nearest suitable facility located in the border area between the two Member States concerned.

2. Such bilateral agreements may also be concluded where waste is shipped from and treated in the country of dispatch but transits another Member State.

3. Member States may also conclude such agreements with countries that are Parties to the Agreement on the European Economic Area.

4. Such agreements shall be notified to the Commission before they take effect.

Chapter 6
Shipments within the Community with transit via third countries

Article 31

Shipments of waste destined for disposal

Where a shipment of waste takes place within the Community with transit via one or more third countries, and the waste is destined for disposal, the competent authority of dispatch shall, in addition to the provisions of this Title, ask the competent authority in the third countries whether it wishes to send its written consent to the planned shipment:

(a) in the case of Parties to the Basel Convention, within 60 days, unless it has waived this right in accordance with the terms of that Convention; or

(b) in the case of countries not Parties to the Basel Convention, within a period agreed between the competent authorities.

Article 32

Shipments of waste destined for recovery

1. When a shipment of waste takes place within the Community with transit via one or more third countries to which the OECD Decision does not apply, and the waste is destined for recovery, Article 31 shall apply.

2. When a shipment of waste takes place within the Community, including shipments between localities in the same Member State, with transit via one or more third countries to which the OECD Decision applies, and the waste is destined for recovery, the consent referred to in Article 9 may be provided tacitly, and if no objection has been lodged or no conditions have been specified, the shipment may start 30 days after the date of transmission of the acknowledgement by the competent authority of destination in accordance with Article 8.

Title III
Shipments exclusively within Member States

Article 33

Application of this Regulation to shipments exclusively within Member States

1. Member States shall establish an appropriate system for the supervision and control of shipments of waste exclusively within their jurisdiction. This system shall take account of the need for coherence with the Community system established by Titles II and VII.

2. Member States shall inform the Commission of their system for supervision and control of shipments of waste. The Commission shall inform the other Member States thereof.

3. Member States may apply the system provided for in Titles II and VII within their jurisdiction.

Title IV
Exports from the Community to third countries

Chapter 1
Exports of waste for disposal

Article 34

Export prohibited except to EFTA countries

1. All exports of waste from the Community destined for disposal shall be prohibited.

2. The prohibition in paragraph 1 shall not apply to exports of waste destined for disposal in EFTA countries which are also Parties to the Basel Convention.

3. However, exports of waste for disposal to an EFTA country Party to the Basel Convention shall also be prohibited:
(a) where the EFTA country prohibits imports of such waste; or
(b) if the competent authority of dispatch has reason to believe that the waste will not be managed in an environmentally sound manner, as referred to in Article 49, in the country of destination concerned.

4. This provision shall be without prejudice to the take-back obligations as laid down in Articles 22 and 24.

Article 35

Procedures when exporting to EFTA countries

1. Where waste is exported from the Community and destined for disposal in EFTA countries Parties to the Basel Convention, the provisions of Title II shall apply mutatis mutandis, with the adaptations and additions listed in paragraphs 2 and 3.

2. The following adaptations shall apply:
(a) the competent authority of transit outside the Community shall have 60 days following the date of transmission of its acknowledgement of receipt of the notification in which to request additional information on the notified shipment, to provide, if the country concerned has decided not to require prior written consent and has informed the other Parties thereof in accordance with Article 6(4) of the Basel Convention, tacit consent or to give a written consent with or without conditions; and
(b) the competent authority of dispatch in the Community shall take the decision to consent to the shipment as referred to in Article 9 only after having received written consent from the competent authority of destination and, where appropriate, the tacit or written consent of the competent authority of transit outside the Community, and not earlier than 61 days following the date of transmission of the acknowledgement by the competent authority of transit. The competent authority of dispatch may take the decision before the conclusion of the 61-day time limit if it has the written consent of the other competent authorities concerned.

3. The following additional provisions shall apply:
(a) the competent authority of transit in the Community shall acknowledge the receipt of the notification to the notifier;

(b) the competent authorities of dispatch and, where appropriate, transit in the Community shall send a stamped copy of their decisions to consent to the shipment to the customs office of export and to the customs office of exit from the Community;
(c) a copy of the movement document shall be delivered by the carrier to the customs office of export and the customs office of exit from the Community;
(d) as soon as the waste has left the Community, the customs office of exit from the Community shall send a stamped copy of the movement document to the competent authority of dispatch in the Community stating that the waste has left the Community;
(e) if, 42 days after the waste has left the Community, the competent authority of dispatch in the Community has received no information from the facility about receipt of the waste, it shall without delay inform the competent authority of destination; and
(f) the contract referred to in the second subparagraph, point 4 of Article 4 and in Article 5 shall stipulate that:
  (i) if a facility issues an incorrect certificate of disposal with the consequence that the financial guarantee is released, the consignee shall bear the costs arising from the duty to return the waste to the area of jurisdiction of the competent authority of dispatch and from its recovery or disposal in an alternative and environmentally sound manner,
  (ii) within three days of receipt of the waste for disposal, the facility shall send signed copies of the completed movement document, except for the certificate of disposal referred to in subpoint iii, to the notifier and the competent authorities concerned, and
  (iii) as soon as possible but no later than 30 days after completion of disposal, and no later than one calendar year following the receipt of the waste the facility shall, under its responsibility, certify that the disposal has been completed and shall send signed copies of the movement document containing this certification to the notifier and to the competent authorities concerned.

4. The shipment may take place only if:
(a) the notifier has received written consent from the competent authorities of dispatch, destination and, where appropriate, transit outside the Community and if the conditions laid down are met;
(b) a contract between the notifier and consignee has been concluded and is effective, as required in the second subparagraph, point 4 of Article 4 and in Article 5;
(c) a financial guarantee or equivalent insurance has been established and is effective, as required in the second subparagraph, point 5 of Article 4 and in Article 6; and
(d) environmentally sound management, as referred to in Article 49, is ensured.

5. Where waste is exported, it shall be destined for disposal operations within a facility which, under applicable national law, is operating or is authorised to operate in the country of destination.

6. If a customs office of export or a customs office of exit from the Community discovers an illegal shipment, it shall without delay inform the competent authority in the country of the customs office which shall:
(a) without delay inform the competent authority of dispatch in the Community; and
(b) ensure detention of the waste until the competent authority of dispatch has decided otherwise and has communicated that decision in writing to the competent authority in the country of the customs office in which the waste is detained.

Chapter 2
Exports of waste for recovery

Section 1
Exports to non-OECD Decision countries

Article 36

Exports prohibition

1. Exports from the Community of the following wastes destined for recovery in countries to which the OECD Decision does not apply are prohibited:
(a) wastes listed as hazardous in Annex V;
(b) wastes listed in Annex V, Part 3;
(c) hazardous wastes not classified under one single entry in Annex V;
(d) mixtures of hazardous wastes and mixtures of hazardous wastes with non-hazardous wastes not classified under one single entry in Annex V;
(e) wastes that the country of destination has notified to be hazardous under Article 3 of the Basel Convention;
(f) wastes the import of which has been prohibited by the country of destination; or
(g) wastes which the competent authority of dispatch has reason to believe will not be managed in an environmentally sound manner, as referred to in Article 49, in the country of destination concerned.

2. This provision shall be without prejudice to the take-back obligations as set out in Articles 22 and 24.

3. Member States may, in exceptional cases, adopt provisions to determine, on the basis of documentary evidence provided in an appropriate way by the notifier, that a specific hazardous waste listed in Annex V is excluded from the export prohibition if it does not display any of the properties listed in Annex III to Directive 91/689/EEC, taking into account, as regards the properties H3 to H8, H10 and H11 defined in that Annex, the limit values laid down in Commission Decision 2000/532/EC of 3 May 2000 replacing Decision 94/3/EC establishing a list of wastes pursuant to Article 1(a) of Council Directive 75/442/EEC on waste and Council Decision 94/904/EC establishing a list of hazardous waste pursuant to Article 1(4) of Council Directive 91/689/EEC on hazardous waste.

4. The fact that waste is not listed as hazardous in Annex V, or that it is listed in Annex V, Part 1, List B, shall not preclude, in exceptional cases, characterisation of such waste as hazardous and therefore subject to the export prohibition if it displays any of the properties listed in Annex III to Directive 91/689/EEC, taking into account, as regards the properties H3 to H8, H10 and H11 defined in that Annex, the limit values laid down in Commission Decision 2000/532/EC, as provided for in Article 1(4), second indent, of Directive 91/689/EEC and in the introductory paragraph of Annex III to this Regulation.

5. In the cases referred to in paragraphs 3 and 4, the Member State concerned shall inform the envisaged country of destination prior to taking a decision. Member States shall notify such cases to the Commission before the end of each calendar year. The Commission shall forward the information to all Member States and to the Secretariat of the Basel Convention. On the basis of the information provided, the Commission may make comments and, where appropriate, adapt Annex V in accordance with Article 58.

Article 37

Procedures when exporting waste listed in Annex III or IIIA

1. In the case of waste which is listed in Annex III or IIIA and the export of which is not prohibited under Article 36, the Commission shall, within 20 days of the entry into force of

this Regulation, send a written request to each country to which the OECD Decision does not apply, seeking:

(i) confirmation in writing that the waste may be exported from the Community for recovery in that country, and
(ii) an indication as to which control procedure, if any, would be followed in the country of destination.

Each country to which the OECD Decision does not apply shall be given the following options:

(a) a prohibition; or
(b) a procedure of prior written notification and consent as described in Article 35; or
(c) no control in the country of destination.

2. Before the date of application of this Regulation, the Commission shall adopt a Regulation taking into account all replies received pursuant to paragraph 1 and shall inform the Committee established pursuant to Article 18 of Directive 2006/12/EC.

If a country has not issued a confirmation as referred to in paragraph 1 or if a country for any reason has not been contacted, paragraph 1(b) shall apply.

The Commission shall periodically update the Regulation adopted.

3. If a country indicates in its reply that certain shipments of waste are not subject to any control, Article 18 shall apply mutatis mutandis to such shipments.

4. Where waste is exported, it shall be destined for recovery operations within a facility which, under applicable national law, is operating or is authorised to operate in the country of destination.

5. In the case of a shipment of waste not classified under one single entry in Annex III or a shipment of mixtures of wastes not classified under one single entry in Annex III or IIIA or a shipment of waste classified in Annex IIIB, and provided that the export is not prohibited pursuant to Article 36, paragraph 1(b) of this Article shall apply.

Section 2
Exports to OECD-Decision countries

Article 38

Exports of waste listed in Annexes III, IIIA, IIIB, IV and IVA

1. Where waste listed in Annexes III, IIIA, IIIB, IV and IVA, waste not classified or mixtures of wastes not classified under one single entry in either Annex III, IV or IVA are exported from the Community and destined for recovery in countries to which the OECD Decision applies, with or without transit through countries to which the OECD Decision applies, the provisions of Title II shall apply mutatis mutandis, with the adaptations and additions listed in paragraphs 2, 3 and 5.

2. The following adaptations shall apply:

(a) mixtures of wastes listed in Annex IIIA destined for an interim operation shall be subject to the procedure of prior written notification and consent if any subsequent interim or non-interim recovery or disposal operation is to take place in a country to which the OECD Decision does not apply;
(b) waste listed in Annex IIIB shall be subject to the procedure of prior written notification and consent;
(c) the consent as required in accordance with Article 9 may be provided in the form of tacit consent from the competent authority of destination outside the Community.

3. As regards exports of waste listed in Annexes IV and IVA, the following additional provisions shall apply:

(a) the competent authorities of dispatch and, where appropriate, transit in the Community shall send a stamped copy of their decisions to consent to the shipment to the customs office of export and to the customs office of exit from the Community;
(b) a copy of the movement document shall be delivered by the carrier to the customs office of export and customs office of exit from the Community;
(c) as soon as the waste has left the Community, the customs office of exit from the Community shall send a stamped copy of the movement document to the competent authority of dispatch in the Community stating that the waste has left the Community;
(d) if, 42 days after the waste has left the Community, the competent authority of dispatch in the Community has received no information from the facility about receipt of the waste, it shall without delay inform the competent authority of destination; and
(e) the contract referred to in the second subparagraph, point 4 of Article 4 and in Article 5 shall stipulate that:
    (i) if a facility issues an incorrect certificate of recovery with the consequence that the financial guarantee is released, the consignee shall bear the costs arising from the duty to return the waste to the area of jurisdiction of the competent authority of dispatch and from its recovery or disposal in an alternative and environmentally sound manner,
    (ii) within three days of receipt of the waste for recovery, the facility shall send signed copies of the completed movement document, except for the certificate of recovery referred to in subpoint iii, to the notifier and the competent authorities concerned, and
    (iii) as soon as possible but no later than 30 days after completion of recovery, and no later than one calendar year following the receipt of the waste the facility shall, under its responsibility, certify that the recovery has been completed and shall send signed copies of the movement document containing this certification to the notifier and to the competent authorities concerned.

4. The shipment may take place only if:
(a) the notifier has received written consent from the competent authorities of dispatch, destination and, where appropriate, transit or, if tacit consent from the competent authorities of destination and transit outside the Community is provided or can be assumed and if the conditions laid down are met;
(b) Article 35(4)(b), (c) and (d) is complied with.

5. If an export as described in paragraph 1 of waste listed in Annexes IV and IVA is in transit through a country to which the OECD Decision does not apply, the following adaptations shall apply:
(a) the competent authority of transit to which the OECD Decision does not apply shall have 60 days following the date of transmission of its acknowledgement of receipt of the notification in which to request additional information on the notified shipment, to provide, if the country concerned has decided not to require prior written consent and has informed the other Parties thereof in accordance with Article 6(4) of the Basel Convention, tacit consent or to give a written consent with or without conditions; and
(b) the competent authority of dispatch in the Community shall take the decision to consent to the shipment as referred to in Article 9 only after having received tacit or written consent from that competent authority of transit to which the OECD Decision does not apply, and not earlier than 61 days following the date of transmission of the acknowledgement of the competent authority of transit. The competent authority of dispatch may take the decision before the conclusion of the 61-day time limit if it has the written consent of the other competent authorities concerned.

6. Where waste is exported, it shall be destined for recovery operations within a facility which, under applicable national law, is operating or is authorised to operate in the country of destination.

7. If a customs office of export or a customs office of exit from the Community discovers an illegal shipment, it shall without delay inform the competent authority in the country of the customs office which shall:
(a) without delay inform the competent authority of dispatch in the Community; and
(b) ensure detention of the waste until the competent authority of dispatch has decided otherwise and has communicated that decision in writing to the competent authority in the country of the customs office in which the waste is detained.

Chapter 3
General provisions

Article 39

Exports to the Antarctic

Exports of waste from the Community to the Antarctic shall be prohibited.

Article 40

Exports to overseas countries or territories

1. Exports from the Community of waste destined for disposal in overseas countries or territories shall be prohibited.

2. As regards exports of waste destined for recovery in overseas countries or territories, the prohibition set out in Article 36 shall apply mutatis mutandis.

3. As regards exports of waste destined for recovery in overseas countries or territories not covered by the prohibition set out in paragraph 2, the provisions of Title II shall apply mutatis mutandis.

Title V
Imports into the Community from third countries

Chapte 1
Imports of waste for disposal

Article 41

Imports prohibited except from a country Party to the Basel Convention or with an agreement in place or from other areas during situations of crisis or war

1. Imports into the Community of waste destined for disposal shall be prohibited except those from:
(a) countries which are Parties to the Basel Convention; or
(b) other countries with which the Community, or the Community and its Member States, have concluded bilateral or multilateral agreements or arrangements compatible with Community legislation and in accordance with Article 11 of the Basel Convention; or
(c) other countries with which individual Member States have concluded bilateral agreements or arrangements in accordance with paragraph 2; or
(d) other areas in cases where, on exceptional grounds during situations of crisis, peacemaking, peacekeeping or war, no bilateral agreements or arrangements pursuant to points (b) or (c) can be concluded or where a competent authority in the country of dispatch has either not been designated or is unable to act.

2. In exceptional cases, individual Member States may conclude bilateral agreements and arrangements for the disposal of specific waste in those Member States, where such waste

will not be managed in an environmentally sound manner, as referred to in Article 49, in the country of dispatch.

These agreements and arrangements shall be compatible with Community legislation and in accordance with Article 11 of the Basel Convention.

These agreements and arrangements shall guarantee that the disposal operations will be carried out in an authorised facility and will comply with the requirements for environmentally sound management.

These agreements and arrangements shall also guarantee that the waste is produced in the country of dispatch and that disposal will be carried out exclusively in the Member State which has concluded the agreement or arrangement.

These agreements or arrangements shall be notified to the Commission prior to their conclusion. However, in emergency situations they may be notified up to one month after conclusion.

3. Bilateral or multilateral agreements or arrangements entered into in accordance with paragraph 1(b) and (c) shall be based upon the procedural requirements of Article 42.

4. The countries referred to in paragraph 1(a), (b) and (c) shall be required to present a prior duly reasoned request to the competent authority of the Member State of destination on the basis that they do not have and cannot reasonably acquire the technical capacity and the necessary facilities in order to dispose of the waste in an environmentally sound manner.

Article 42

Procedural requirements for imports from a country Party to the Basel Convention or from other areas during situations of crisis or war

1. Where waste is imported into the Community and destined for disposal from countries Parties to the Basel Convention, the provisions of Title II shall apply mutatis mutandis, with the adaptations and additions listed in paragraphs 2 and 3.

2. The following adaptations shall apply:
(a) the competent authority of transit outside the Community shall have 60 days following the date of transmission of its acknowledgement of receipt of the notification in which to request additional information on the notified shipment, to provide, if the country concerned has decided not to require prior written consent and has informed the other Parties thereof in accordance with Article 6(4) of the Basel Convention, tacit consent or to give a written consent with or without conditions; and
(b) in the cases referred to in Article 41(1)(d) involving situations of crisis, peacemaking, peacekeeping or war, the consent of the competent authorities of dispatch shall not be required.

3. The following additional provisions shall apply:
(a) the competent authority of transit in the Community shall acknowledge the receipt of the notification to the notifier, with copies to the competent authorities concerned;
(b) the competent authorities of destination and, where appropriate, transit in the Community shall send a stamped copy of their decisions to consent to the shipment to the customs office of entry into the Community;
(c) a copy of the movement document shall be delivered by the carrier to the customs office of entry into the Community; and
(d) having carried out the necessary customs formalities, the customs office of entry into the Community shall send a stamped copy of the movement document to the competent authorities of destination and transit in the Community, stating that the waste has entered the Community.

4. The shipment may take place only if:

(a) the notifier has received written consent from the competent authorities of dispatch, destination and, where appropriate, transit and if the conditions laid down are met;
(b) a contract between the notifier and consignee has been concluded and is effective, as required in the second subparagraph, point 4 of Article 4 and in Article 5;
(c) a financial guarantee or equivalent insurance has been established and is effective, as required in the second subparagraph, point 5 of Article 4 and in Article 6; and
(d) environmentally sound management, as referred to in Article 49, is ensured.

5. If a customs office of entry into the Community discovers an illegal shipment, it shall without delay inform the competent authority in the country of the customs office which shall:
(a) without delay inform the competent authority of destination in the Community which shall inform the competent authority of dispatch outside the Community; and
(b) ensure detention of the waste until the competent authority of dispatch outside the Community has decided otherwise and has communicated that decision in writing to the competent authority in the country of the customs office in which the waste is detained.

Chapter 2
Imports of waste for recovery

Article 43

Imports prohibited except from an OECD Decision country or a country Party to the Basel Convention or with an agreement in place or from other areas during situations of crisis or war

1. All imports into the Community of waste destined for recovery shall be prohibited except those from:
(a) countries to which the OECD Decision applies; or
(b) other countries which are Parties to the Basel Convention; or
(c) other countries with which the Community, or the Community and its Member States, have concluded bilateral or multilateral agreements or arrangements compatible with Community legislation and in accordance with Article 11 of the Basel Convention; or
(d) other countries with which individual Member States have concluded bilateral agreements or arrangements in accordance with paragraph 2; or
(e) other areas in cases where, on exceptional grounds during situations of crisis, peacemaking, peacekeeping or war, no bilateral agreements or arrangements pursuant to points (b) or (c) can be concluded or where a competent authority in the country of dispatch has either not been designated or is unable to act.

2. In exceptional cases, individual Member States may conclude bilateral agreements and arrangements for the recovery of specific waste in those Member States, where such waste will not be managed in an environmentally sound manner, as referred to in Article 49, in the country of dispatch.

In such cases Article 41(2) shall apply.

3. Bilateral or multilateral agreements or arrangements entered into in accordance with paragraph 1(c) and (d) shall be based upon the procedural requirements of Article 42 in so far as may be relevant.

Article 44

Procedural requirements for imports from an OECD Decision country or from other areas during situations of crisis or war

1. Where waste destined for recovery is imported into the Community from countries and through countries to which the OECD Decision applies, the provisions of Title II shall apply mutatis mutandis, with the adaptations and additions listed in paragraphs 2 and 3.

2. The following adaptations shall apply:

(a) the consent as required in accordance with Article 9 may be provided in the form of tacit consent from the competent authority of dispatch outside the Community;

(b) prior written notification in accordance with Article 4 may be submitted by the notifier; and

(c) in the cases referred to in Article 43(1)(e) involving situations of crisis, peacemaking, peacekeeping or war, the consent of the competent authorities of dispatch shall not be required.

3. In addition, Article 42(3)(b), (c) and (d) shall be complied with.

4. The shipment may take place only if:

(a) the notifier has received written consent from the competent authorities of dispatch, destination and, where appropriate, transit or if tacit consent from the competent authority of dispatch outside the Community is provided or can be assumed and if the conditions laid down are met;

(b) a contract between the notifier and consignee has been concluded and is effective, as required in the second subparagraph, point 4 of Article 4 and in Article 5;

(c) a financial guarantee or equivalent insurance has been established and is effective, as required in the second subparagraph, point 5 of Article 4 and in Article 6; and

(d) environmentally sound management, as referred to in Article 49, is ensured.

5. If a customs office of entry into the Community discovers an illegal shipment, it shall without delay inform the competent authority in the country of the customs office which shall:

(a) without delay inform the competent authority of destination in the Community which shall inform the competent authority of dispatch outside the Community; and

(b) ensure detention of the waste until the competent authority of dispatch outside the Community has decided otherwise and has communicated that decision in writing to the competent authority in the country of the customs office in which the waste is detained.

Article 45

Procedural requirements for imports from a non-OECD Decision country Party to the Basel Convention or from other areas during situations of crisis or war

Where waste destined for recovery is imported into the Community:

(a) from a country to which the OECD Decision does not apply; or

(b) through any country to which the OECD Decision does not apply and which is also Party to the Basel Convention,

Article 42 shall apply mutatis mutandis.

Chapter 3
General provisions

Article 46

Imports from overseas countries or territories

1. Where waste is imported into the Community from overseas countries or territories, Title II shall apply mutatis mutandis.

2. One or more overseas countries and territories and the Member State to which they are linked may apply national procedures to shipments from the overseas country or territory to that Member State.

3. Member States which apply paragraph 2 shall notify the Commission of the national procedures applied.

Title VI
Transit through the Community from and to third countries

Chapter 1
Transit of waste for disposal

Article 47

Transit through the Community of waste destined for disposal

Where waste destined for disposal is shipped through Member States from and to third countries, Article 42 shall apply mutatis mutandis, with the adaptations and additions listed below:

(a) the first and last competent authority of transit in the Community shall, where appropriate, send a stamped copy of the decisions to consent to the shipment or, if they have provided tacit consent, a copy of the acknowledgement in accordance with Article 42(3)(a) to the customs offices of entry into and exit from the Community respectively; and

(b) as soon as the waste has left the Community, the customs office of exit from the Community shall send a stamped copy of the movement document to the competent authority(ies) of transit in the Community, stating that the waste has left the Community.

Chapter 2
Transit of waste for recovery

Article 48

Transit through the Community of waste destined for recovery

1. Where waste destined for recovery is shipped through Member States from and to a country to which the OECD Decision does not apply, Article 47 shall apply mutatis mutandis.

2. Where waste destined for recovery is shipped through Member States from and to a country to which the OECD Decision applies, Article 44 shall apply mutatis mutandis, with the adaptations and additions listed below:

(a) the first and last competent authority of transit in the Community shall, where appropriate, send a stamped copy of the decisions to consent to the shipment or, if they have provided tacit consent, a copy of the acknowledgement in accordance with Article 42(3)(a) to the customs offices of entry into and exit from the Community respectively; and

(b) as soon as the waste has left the Community, the customs office of exit from the Community shall send a stamped copy of the movement document to the competent authority(ies) of transit in the Community, stating that the waste has left the Community.

3. Where waste destined for recovery is shipped through Member States from a country to which the OECD Decision does not apply to a country to which the OECD Decision applies or vice versa, paragraph 1 shall apply as regards the country to which the OECD Decision does not apply and paragraph 2 shall apply as regards the country to which the OECD Decision applies.

Title VII
Other provisions

Chapter 1
Additional obligations

Article 49

Protection of the environment

1. The producer, the notifier and other undertakings involved in a shipment of waste and/or its recovery or disposal shall take the necessary steps to ensure that any waste they ship is managed without endangering human health and in an environmentally sound manner throughout the period of shipment and during its recovery and disposal. In particular, when the shipment takes place in the Community, the requirements of Article 4 of Directive 2006/12/EC and other Community legislation on waste shall be respected.

2. In the case of exports from the Community, the competent authority of dispatch in the Community shall:
(a) require and endeavour to secure that any waste exported is managed in an environmentally sound manner throughout the period of shipment, including recovery as referred to in Articles 36 and 38 or disposal as referred to in Article 34, in the third country of destination;
(b) prohibit an export of waste to third countries if it has reason to believe that the waste will not be managed in accordance with the requirements of point (a).

Environmentally sound management may, inter alia, be assumed as regards the waste recovery or disposal operation concerned, if the notifier or the competent authority in the country of destination can demonstrate that the facility which receives the waste will be operated in accordance with human health and environmental protection standards that are broadly equivalent to standards established in Community legislation.

This assumption shall, however, be without prejudice to the overall assessment of environmentally sound management throughout the period of shipment and including recovery or disposal in the third country of destination.

For the purposes of seeking guidance on environmentally sound management, the guidelines listed in Annex VIII may be considered.

3. In the case of imports into the Community, the competent authority of destination in the Community shall:
(a) require and take the necessary steps to ensure that any waste shipped into its area of jurisdiction is managed without endangering human health and without using processes or methods which could harm the environment, and in accordance with Article 4 of Directive 2006/12/EC and other Community legislation on waste throughout the period of shipment, including recovery or disposal in the country of destination;
(b) prohibit an import of waste from third countries if it has reason to believe that the waste will not be managed in accordance with the requirements of point (a).

Article 50

Enforcement in Member States

1. Member States shall lay down the rules on penalties applicable for infringement of the provisions of this Regulation and shall take all measures necessary to ensure that they are implemented. The penalties provided for must be effective, proportionate and dissuasive. Member States shall notify the Commission of their national legislation relating to prevention and detection of illegal shipments and penalties for such shipments.

2. Member States shall, by way of measures for the enforcement of this Regulation, provide, inter alia, for inspections of establishments and undertakings in accordance with Article 13 of Directive 2006/12/EC, and for spot checks on shipments of waste or on the related recovery or disposal.

3. Checks on shipments may take place in particular:
(a) at the point of origin, carried out with the producer, holder or notifier;
(b) at the destination, carried out with the consignee or the facility;
(c) at the frontiers of the Community; and/or
(d) during the shipment within the Community.

4. Checks on shipments shall include the inspection of documents, the confirmation of identity and, where appropriate, physical checking of the waste.

5. Member States shall cooperate, bilaterally or multilaterally, with one another in order to facilitate the prevention and detection of illegal shipments.

6. Member States shall identify those members of their permanent staff responsible for the cooperation referred to in paragraph 5 and identify the focal point(s) for the physical checks referred to in paragraph 4. The information shall be sent to the Commission which shall distribute a compiled list to the correspondents referred to in Article 54.

7. At the request of another Member State, a Member State may take enforcement action against persons suspected of being engaged in the illegal shipment of waste who are present in that Member State.

Article 51

Reports by Member States

1. Before the end of each calendar year, each Member State shall send the Commission a copy of the report for the previous calendar year which, in accordance with Article 13(3) of the Basel Convention, it has drawn up and submitted to the Secretariat of that Convention.

2. Before the end of each calendar year, Member States shall also draw up a report for the previous year based on the additional reporting questionnaire in Annex IX, and shall send it to the Commission.

3. The reports drawn up by Member States in accordance with paragraphs 1 and 2 shall be submitted to the Commission in an electronic version.

4. The Commission shall establish every three years a report, based on these reports, on the implementation of this Regulation by the Community and its Member States.

Article 52

International cooperation

Member States, where appropriate and necessary in liaison with the Commission, shall cooperate with other Parties to the Basel Convention and inter-State organisations, inter alia, via the exchange and/or sharing of information, the promotion of environmentally sound technologies and the development of appropriate codes of good practice.

Article 53

Designation of competent authorities

Member States shall designate the competent authority or authorities responsible for the implementation of this Regulation. Each Member State shall designate only one single competent authority of transit.

Article 54

Designation of correspondents

Member States and the Commission shall each designate one or more correspondents responsible for informing or advising persons or undertakings making enquiries. The Commission correspondent shall forward to the correspondents of the Member States any questions put to him/her which concern the latter, and vice versa.

Article 55

Designation of customs offices of entry into and exit from the Community

Member States may designate specific customs offices of entry into and exit from the Community for shipments of waste entering and leaving the Community. If Member States decide to designate such customs offices, no shipment of waste shall be allowed to use any other frontier crossing points within a Member State for the purposes of entering or leaving the Community.

Article 56

Notification of, and information regarding, designations

1. Member States shall notify the Commission of designations of:
(a) competent authorities, pursuant to Article 53;
(b) correspondents, pursuant to Article 54; and,
(c) where appropriate, customs offices of entry into and exit from the Community, pursuant to Article 55.

2. In relation to those designations, Member States shall notify the Commission of the following information:
(a) name(s);
(b) postal address(es);
(c) e-mail address(es);
(d) telephone number(s);
(e) fax number(s); and
(f) languages acceptable to the competent authorities.

3. Member States shall immediately notify the Commission of any changes in this information.

4. This information as well as any changes in the information shall be submitted to the Commission in an electronic as well as a paper version if so required.

5. The Commission shall publish on its web-site lists of the designated competent authorities, correspondents and customs offices of entry into and exit from the Community, and shall update these lists as appropriate.

Chapter 2
Other provisions

Article 57

Meeting of the correspondents

The Commission shall, if requested by Member States or if otherwise appropriate, periodically hold a meeting of the correspondents to examine the questions raised by the implementation of this Regulation. Relevant stakeholders shall be invited to such meetings, or parts of meetings, where all Member States and the Commission are in agreement that this is appropriate.

[Article 58

Amendment of Annexes][1]

[1. The Commission may amend the Annexes to take account of scientific and technical progress. Those measures, designed to amend non-essential elements of this Regulation, shall be adopted in accordance with the regulatory procedure with scrutiny referred to in Article 59a(3). In addition:

(a) Annexes I, II, III, IIIA, IV and V shall be amended to take account of changes agreed under the Basel Convention and the OECD Decision;

(b) unclassified wastes may be added to Annex IIIB, IV or V on a provisional basis pending a decision on their inclusion in the relevant Annexes to the Basel Convention or to the OECD Decision;

(c) following the submission of a request by a Member State, mixtures of two or more wastes listed in Annex III may be considered for inclusion in Annex IIIA in the cases referred to in Article 3(2) on a provisional basis pending a decision on their inclusion in the relevant Annexes to the Basel Convention or to the OECD Decision. Annex IIIA may contain the proviso that one or more of the entries therein shall not apply for exports to countries to which the OECD Decision does not apply;

(d) the exceptional cases referred to in Article 3(3) shall be determined and, where necessary, such waste shall be added to Annexes IVA and V and deleted from Annex III;

(e) Annex V shall be amended to reflect agreed changes to the list of hazardous waste adopted in accordance with Article 1(4) of Directive 91/689/EEC;

(f) Annex VIII shall be amended to reflect relevant international conventions and agreements.

2. When amending Annex IX, the Committee established by Council Directive 91/692/EEC of 23 December 1991 standardising and rationalising reports on the implementation of certain Directives relating to the environment shall be fully associated with the deliberations.][1]

Amendment

1 Substituted by Regulation (EC) No 219/2009 of the European Parliament and of the Council of 11 March 2009 adapting a number of instruments subject to the procedure referred to in Article 251 of the Treaty to Council Decision 1999/468/EC with regard to the regulatory procedure with scrutiny, Article 1, Annex, para 3.9.2.

[Article 59

Additional measures][1]

[1. The Commission may adopt, in accordance with the regulatory procedure referred to in Article 59a(2), the following additional measures related to the implementation of this Regulation:

(a) guidelines for the application of Article 12(1)(g);

(b) guidelines on the application of Article 15 in relation to the identification and tracking of waste undergoing substantial changes in the interim recovery or disposal operation;

(c) guidelines for the cooperation of competent authorities with regard to illegal shipments as referred to in Article 24;

(d) technical and organisational requirements for the practical implementation of electronic data interchange for the submission of documents and information in accordance with Article 26(4);

(e) further guidance concerning the use of languages referred to in Article 27;

(f) further clarification of the procedural requirements of Title II as regards their application to exports, imports and transit of waste from, to, and through the Community;

(g) further recommendations concerning undefined legal terms.

2. The Commission may adopt implementing measures concerning the following:

(a) a method for calculating the financial guarantee or equivalent insurance as set out in Article 6;

(b) further conditions and requirements in relation to pre-consented recovery facilities as referred to in Article 14.

Those measures, designed to amend non-essential elements of this Regulation by supplementing it, shall be adopted in accordance with the regulatory procedure with scrutiny referred to in Article 59a(3).][1]

Amendment

1 Substituted by Regulation (EC) No 219/2009 of the European Parliament and of the Council of 11 March 2009 adapting a number of instruments subject to the procedure referred to in Article 251 of the Treaty to Council Decision 1999/468/EC with regard to the regulatory procedure with scrutiny, Article 1, Annex, para 3.9.3.

[Article 59a

Committee procedure][1]

[1. The Commission shall be assisted by the committee set up by Article 18(1) of Directive 2006/12/EC.

2. Where reference is made to this paragraph, Articles 5 and 7 of Decision 1999/468/EC shall apply, having regard to the provisions of Article 8 thereof.

The period laid down in Article 5(6) of Decision 1999/468/EC shall be set at three months.

3. Where reference is made to this paragraph, Article 5a(1) to (4) and Article 7 of Decision 1999/468/EC shall apply, having regard to the provisions of Article 8 thereof.][1]

Amendment

1 Inserted by Regulation (EC) No 219/2009 of the European Parliament and of the Council of 11 March 2009 adapting a number of instruments subject to the procedure referred to in Article 251 of the Treaty to Council Decision 1999/468/EC with regard to the regulatory procedure with scrutiny, Article 1, Annex, para 3.9.4.

Article 60

Review

1. By 15 July 2006, the Commission shall complete its review of the relationship between existing sectoral legislation on animal and public health, including shipments of waste covered by Regulation (EC) No 1774/2002, and the provisions of this Regulation. If necessary, this review shall be accompanied by appropriate proposals with a view to achieving an equivalent level of procedures and control regime for the shipment of such waste.

2. Within five years from 12 July 2007, the Commission shall review the implementation of Article 12(1)(c), including its effect on environment protection and the functioning of the internal market. If necessary, this review shall be accompanied by appropriate proposals to amend this provision.

[*Article 61 is not reproduced.*]

Article 62

Transition rules

1. Any shipment that has been notified and for which the competent authority of destination has given acknowledgement before 12 July 2007 shall be subject to the provisions of Regulation (EEC) No 259/93.

2. Any shipment for which the competent authorities concerned have given their consent pursuant to Regulation (EEC) No 259/93 shall be completed not later than one year from 12 July 2007.

3. Reporting pursuant to Article 41(2) of Regulation (EEC) No 259/93 and Article 51 of this Regulation for the year 2007 shall be based on the questionnaire contained in Decision 1999/412/EC.

Article 63

Transitional arrangements for certain Member States

1. Until 31 December 2010, all shipments to Latvia of waste for recovery listed in Annexes III and IV and shipments of waste for recovery not listed in those Annexes shall be subject to the procedure of prior written notification and consent in accordance with Title II.

By way of derogation from Article 12, the competent authorities shall object to shipments of waste for recovery listed in Annexes III and IV and shipments of waste for recovery not listed in those Annexes destined for a facility benefiting from a temporary derogation from certain provisions of Directive 96/61/EC during the period in which the temporary derogation is applied to the facility of destination.

2. Until 31 December 2012, all shipments to Poland of waste for recovery listed in Annex III shall be subject to the procedure of prior written notification and consent in accordance with Title II.

By way of derogation from Article 12, until 31 December 2007, the competent authorities may raise objections to shipments to Poland for recovery of the following waste listed in Annexes III and IV in conformity with the grounds for objection laid down in Article 11:

B2020 and GE020 (glass waste)
B2070
B2080
B2100
B2120
B3010 and GH013 (solid plastic waste)
B3020 (paper waste)
B3140 (waste pneumatic tyres)
Y46
Y47
A1010 and A1030 (only the indents referring to arsenic and mercury)
A1060
A1140
A2010
A2020
A2030
A2040
A3030
A3040
A3070
A3120
A3130
A3160
A3170
A3180 (applies only in respect of polychlorinated naphthalenes (PCN))
A4010
A4050
A4060
A4070
A4090
AB030
AB070

AB120
AB130
AB150
AC060
AC070
AC080
AC150
AC160
AC260
AD150

[With the exception of glass waste, paper waste and waste pneumatic tyres, this period may be extended until no later than 31 December 2012 in accordance with the regulatory procedure referred to in Article 59a(2).][1]

By way of derogation from Article 12, until 31 December 2012, the competent authorities may raise objections in conformity with the grounds for objection laid down in Article 11 to shipments to Poland of:

(a) the following waste for recovery listed in Annex IV:
A2050
A3030
A3180, except polychlorinated naphthalenes (PCN)
A3190
A4110
A4120
RB020
and of

(b) waste for recovery not listed in the Annexes.

By way of derogation from Article 12, competent authorities shall object to shipments of waste for recovery listed in Annexes III and IV and shipments of waste for recovery not listed in those Annexes destined for a facility benefiting from a temporary derogation from certain provisions of Directive 96/61/EC during the period in which the temporary derogation is applied to the facility of destination.

3. Until 31 December 2011, all shipments to Slovakia of waste for recovery listed in Annexes III and IV and shipments of waste for recovery not listed in those Annexes shall be subject to the procedure of prior written notification and consent in accordance with Title II.

By way of derogation from Article 12, the competent authorities shall object to shipments of waste for recovery listed in Annexes III and IV and shipments of waste for recovery not listed in those Annexes destined for a facility benefiting from a temporary derogation from certain provisions of Directives 94/67/EC and 96/61/EC, Directive 2000/76/EC of the European Parliament and of the Council of 4 December 2000 on the incineration of waste, and Directive 2001/80/EC of the European Parliament and of the Council of 23 October 2001 on the limitation of emissions of certain pollutants into the air from large combustion plants during the period in which the temporary derogation is applied to the facility of destination.

4. Until 31 December 2014, all shipments to Bulgaria of waste for recovery listed in Annex III shall be subject to the procedure of prior written notification and consent in accordance with Title II.

By way of derogation from Article 12, until 31 December 2009, the Bulgarian competent authorities may raise objections to shipments to Bulgaria for recovery of the following waste listed in Annexes III and IV in conformity with the grounds for objection laid down in Article 11:

B2070
B2080
B2100

B2120
Y46
Y47
A1010 and A1030 (only the indents referring to arsenic and mercury)
A1060
A1140
A2010
A2020
A2030
A2040
A3030
A3040
A3070
A3120
A3130
A3160
A3170
A3180 (applies only in respect of polychlorinated naphthalenes (PCN))
A4010
A4050
A4060
A4070
A4090
AB030
AB070
AB120
AB130
AB150
AC060
AC070
AC080
AC150
AC160
AC260
AD150

[This period may be extended until no later than 31 December 2012 in accordance with the regulatory procedure referred to in Article 59a(2).][1]

By way of derogation from Article 12, until 31 December 2009, the Bulgarian competent authorities may raise objections in conformity with the grounds for objection laid down in Article 11 to shipments to Bulgaria of:

(a) the following waste for recovery listed in Annex IV:
A2050
A3030
A3180, except polychlorinated naphthalenes (PCN)
A3190
A4110
A4120
RB020
and of

(b) waste for recovery not listed in those Annexes.

By way of derogation from Article 12, the Bulgarian competent authorities shall object to shipments of waste for recovery listed in Annexes III and IV and shipments of waste for recovery not listed in those Annexes destined for a facility benefiting from a temporary derogation from certain provisions of Directive 96/61/EC or Directive 2001/80/EC during the period in which the temporary derogation is applied to the facility of destination.

5. Until 31 December 2015, all shipments to Romania of waste for recovery listed in Annex III shall be subject to the procedure of prior written notification and consent in accordance with Title II.

By way of derogation from Article 12, until 31 December 2011, the Romanian competent authorities may raise objections to shipments to Romania for recovery of the following waste listed in Annexes III and IV in conformity with the grounds for objection laid down in Article 11:

B2070
B2100, except waste alumina
B2120
B4030
Y46
Y47
A1010 and A1030 (only the indents referring to arsenic, mercury and thallium)
A1060
A1140
A2010
A2020
A2030
A3030
A3040
A3050
A3060
A3070
A3120
A3130
A3140
A3150
A3160
A3170
A3180 (applies only in respect of polychlorinated naphthalenes (PCN))
A4010
A4030
A4040
A4050
A4080
A4090
A4100
A4160
AA060
AB030
AB120
AC060
AC070
AC080
AC150
AC160
AC260
AC270
AD120
AD150

[This period may be extended until no later than 31 December 2015 in accordance with the regulatory procedure referred to in Article 59a(2).][1]

By way of derogation from Article 12, until 31 December 2011, the Romanian competent authorities may raise objections in conformity with the grounds for objection laid down in Article 11 to shipments to Romania of:

(a) the following waste for recovery listed in Annex IV:
A2050
A3030
A3180, except polychlorinated naphthalenes (PCN)
A3190
A4110
A4120
RB020
and of

(b) waste for recovery not listed in those Annexes.

[This period may be extended until no later than 31 December 2015 in accordance with the regulatory procedure referred to in Article 59a(2).][1]

By way of derogation from Article 12, the Romanian competent authorities shall object to shipments of waste for recovery listed in Annexes III and IV and shipments of waste for recovery not listed in those Annexes destined for a facility benefiting from a temporary derogation from certain provisions of Directive 96/61/EC, Directive 2000/76/EC or Directive 2001/80/EC during the period in which the temporary derogation is applied to the facility of destination.

6. When reference is made in this Article to Title II in relation to waste listed in Annex III, Article 3(2), Article 4, second subparagraph, point 5, and Articles 6, 11, 22, 23, 24, 25 and 31 shall not apply.

Amendment

1 Substituted by Regulation (EC) No 219/2009 of the European Parliament and of the Council of 11 March 2009 adapting a number of instruments subject to the procedure referred to in Article 251 of the Treaty to Council Decision 1999/468/EC with regard to the regulatory procedure with scrutiny, Article 1, Annex, para 3.9.5.

Article 64

Entry into force and application

1. This Regulation shall enter into force on the third day following that of its publication in the Official Journal of the European Union.

It shall apply from 12 July 2007.

2. Should the date of accession of Bulgaria or Romania be later than the date of application specified in paragraph 1, Article 63(4) and (5) shall, by way of derogation from paragraph 1 of this Article, apply from the date of accession.

3. Subject to the agreement of the Member States concerned, Article 26(4) may be applied before 12 July 2007.

This Regulation shall be binding in its entirety and directly applicable in all Member States.

[ANNEX IA
NOTIFICATION DOCUMENT FOR TRANSBOUNDARY MOVEMENTS OR SHIPMENTS OF WASTE EU][1]

[

1. Exporter — notifier Registration No:
Name:
Address:
Contact person:
Tel.: Fax:
E-mail:

3. Notification No:
Notification concerning
A. (i) Individual shipment: ☐ (ii) Multiple shipments: ☐
B. (i) Disposal (1): ☐ (ii) Recovery: ☐
C. Pre-consented recovery facility (2) (3) Yes ☐ No ☐

4. Total intended number of shipments:

2. Importer — consignee Registration No:
Name:
Address:
Contact person:
Tel.: Fax:
E-mail:

5. Total intended quantity (4):
Tonnes (Mg):
m^3:

6. Intended period of time for shipment(s) (4):
First departure: Last departure:

7. Packaging type(s) (5):
Special handling requirements (6): Yes ☐ No ☐

8. Intended carrier(s) Registration No:
Name (7):
Address:
Contact person:
Tel.: Fax:
E-mail:
Means of transport (5):

11. Disposal/recovery operation(s) (2)
D-code/R-code (5):
Technology employed (6):
Reason for export (1) (6):

12. Designation and composition of the waste (6):

9. Waste generator(s) — producer(s) (1) (7) (8) Registration No:
Name:
Address:
Contact person:
Tel.: Fax:
E-mail:
Site and process of generation (6)

13. Physical characteristics (5):

10. Disposal facility (2): ☐ **or recovery facility** (2): ☐
Registration No:
Name:
Address:
Contact person:
Tel.: Fax:
E-mail:
Actual site of disposal/recovery:

14. Waste identification *(fill in relevant codes)*
(i) Basel Annex VIII (or IX if applicable):
(ii) OECD code (if different from (i)):
(iii) EC list of wastes:
(iv) National code in country of export:
(v) National code in country of import:
(vi) Other (specify):
(vii) Y-code:
(viii) H-code (5):
(ix) UN class (5):
(x) UN number:
(xi) UN shipping name:
(xii) Customs code(s) (HS):

15. (a) Countries/States concerned, (b) code No of competent authorities where applicable, (c) specific points of exit or entry (border crossing or port)

State of export — dispatch	State(s) of transit (entry and exit)			State of import — destination
(a)				
(b)				
(c)				

16. Customs offices of entry and/or exit and/or export (European Community):
Entry: Exit: Export:

17. Exporter's — notifier's/generator's — producer's (1) **declaration:**
I certify that the information is complete and correct to my best knowledge. I also certify that legally enforceable written contractual obligations have been entered into and that any applicable insurance or other financial guarantee is or shall be in force covering the transboundary movement.
Exporter's — notifier's name: Date: Signature:
Generator's — producer's name: Date: Signature:

18. Number of annexes attached

FOR USE BY COMPETENT AUTHORITIES

19. Acknowledgement from the relevant competent authority of countries of import — destination/transit (1)**/export — dispatch** (9):
Country:
Notification received on:
Acknowledgement sent on:
Name of competent authority:
Stamp and/or signature:

20. Written consent (1) (8) **to the movement provided by the competent authority of** (country):
Consent given on:
Consent valid from: until:
Specific conditions: No: ☐ If Yes, see block 21 (6): ☐
Name of competent authority:
Stamp and/or signature:

21. Specific conditions on consenting to the movement or reasons for objecting

(1) Required by the Basel Convention.
(2) In the case of an R12/R13 or D13-D15 operation, also attach corresponding information on any subsequent R12/R13 or D13-D15 facilities and on the subsequent R1-R11 or D1-D12 facilit(y)ies when required.
(3) To be completed for movements within the OECD area and only if B(ii) applies.
(4) Attach detailed list if multiple shipments.
(5) See list of abbreviations and codes on the next page.
(6) Attach details if necessary.
(7) Attach list if more than one.
(8) If required by national legislation.
(9) If applicable under the OECD Decision.

List of abbreviations and codes used in the notification document

DISPOSAL OPERATIONS (block 11)

D1 Deposit into or onto land (e.g. landfill, etc.)
D2 Land treatment (e.g., biodegradation of liquid or sludgy discards in soils, etc.)
D3 Deep injection (e.g. injection of pumpable discards into wells, salt domes or naturally occurring repositories, etc.)
D4 Surface impoundment (e.g. placement of liquid or sludge discards into pits, ponds or lagoons, etc.)
D5 Specially engineered landfill (e.g. placement into lined discrete cells which are capped and isolated from one another and the environment, etc.)
D6 Release into a water body except seas/oceans
D7 Release into seas/oceans including sea-bed insertion
D8 Biological treatment not specified elsewhere in this list which results in final compounds or mixtures which are discarded by means of any of the operations in this list
D9 Physico-chemical treatment not specified elsewhere in this list which results in final compounds or mixtures which are discarded by means of any of the operations in this list (e.g. evaporation, drying, calcination, etc.)
D10 Incineration on land
D11 Incineration at sea
D12 Permanent storage (e.g. emplacement of containers in a mine, etc.)
D13 Blending or mixing prior to submission to any of the operations in this list
D14 Repackaging prior to submission to any of the operations in this list
D15 Storage pending any of the operations in this list

RECOVERY OPERATIONS (block 11)

R1 Use as a fuel (other than in direct incineration) or other means to generate energy (Basel/OECD) — Use principally as a fuel or other means to generate energy (EU)
R2 Solvent reclamation/regeneration
R3 Recycling/reclamation of organic substances which are not used as solvents
R4 Recycling/reclamation of metals and metal compounds
R5 Recycling/reclamation of other inorganic materials
R6 Regeneration of acids or bases
R7 Recovery of components used for pollution abatement
R8 Recovery of components from catalysts
R9 Used oil re-refining or other reuses of previously used oil
R10 Land treatment resulting in benefit to agriculture or ecological improvement
R11 Uses of residual materials obtained from any of the operations numbered R1-R10
R12 Exchange of wastes for submission to any of the operations numbered R1-R11
R13 Accumulation of material intended for any operation in this list.

PACKAGING TYPES (block 7)

1. Drum
2. Wooden barrel
3. Jerrican
4. Box
5. Bag
6. Composite packaging
7. Pressure receptacle
8. Bulk
9. Other (specify)

MEANS OF TRANSPORT (block 8)

R = Road
T = Train/rail
S = Sea
A = Air
W = Inland waterways

PHYSICAL CHARACTERISTICS (block 13)

1. Powdery/powder
2. Solid
3. Viscous/paste
4. Sludgy
5. Liquid
6. Gaseous
7. Other (specify)

H-CODE AND UN CLASS (block 14)

UN Class	H-code	Characteristics
1	H1	Explosive
3	H3	Flammable liquids
4.1	H4.1	Flammable solids
4.2	H4.2	Substances or wastes liable to spontaneous combustion
4.3	H4.3	Substances or wastes which, in contact with water, emit flammable gases
5.1	H5.1	Oxidising
5.2	H5.2	Organic peroxides
6.1	H6.1	Poisonous (acute)
6.2	H6.2	Infectious substances
8	H8	Corrosives
9	H10	Liberation of toxic gases in contact with air or water
9	H11	Toxic (delayed or chronic)
9	H12	Ecotoxic
9	H13	Capable, by any means, after disposal of yielding another material, e.g., leachate, which possesses any of the characteristics listed above

Further information, in particular related to waste identification (block 14), i.e. on Basel Annexes VIII and IX codes, OECD codes and Y-codes, can be found in a Guidance/Instruction Manual available from the OECD and the Secretariat of the Basel Convention.'

][1]

Amendment

1 Substituted by Commission Regulation (EC) No 1379/2007 of 26 November 2007 amending Annexes IA, IB, VII and VIII of Regulation (EC) No 1013/2006 of the European Parliament and of the Council on shipments of waste, for the purposes of taking account of technical progress and changes agreed under the Basel Convention, Article 1, Annex I.

ANNEX IB
MOVEMENT DOCUMENT FOR TRANSBOUNDARY MOVEMENTS OR SHIPMENTS OF EU WASTE

[

1. Corresponding to notification No:

2. Serial/total number of shipments /

3. Exporter — notifier Registration No:
Name:
Address:
Contact person:
Tel.: Fax:
E-mail:

4. Importer — consignee Registration No:
Name:
Address:
Contact person:
Tel.: Fax:
E-mail:

5. Actual quantity: Tonnes (Mg): m³:

6. Actual date of shipment:

7. Packaging Type(s) (1): Number of packages:
Special handling requirements: (2) Yes: ☐ No: ☐

8.(a) 1st carrier (3):
Registration No:
Name:
Address:
Tel.:
Fax:
E-mail:

8.(b) 2nd carrier (3):
Registration No:
Name:
Address:
Tel.:
Fax:
E-mail:

8.(c) Last carrier (3):
Registration No:
Name:
Address:
Tel.:
Fax:
E-mail:

- - - - - - - *To be completed by carrier's representative* - - - - - - -

More than three carriers (2) ☐

Means of transport (1):
Date of transfer:
Signature:

Means of transport (1):
Date of transfer:
Signature:

Means of transport (1):
Date of transfer:
Signature:

9. Waste generator(s) — producer(s) (4) (5) (6):
Registration No:
Name:
Address:
Contact person:
Tel.: Fax:
E-mail:
Site of generation (2):

10. Disposal facility ☐ **or recovery facility** ☐
Registration No:
Name:
Address:
Contact person:
Tel.: Fax:
E-mail:
Actual site of disposal/recovery (2)

11. Disposal/recovery operation(s)
D-code/R-code (1):

12. Designation and composition of the waste (2):

13. Physical characteristics (1):

14. Waste identification *(fill in relevant codes)*
(i) Basel Annex VIII (or IX if applicable):
(ii) OECD code (if different from (i)):
(iii) EC list of wastes:
(iv) National code in country of export
(v) National code in country of import:
(vi) Other (specify):
(vii) Y-code:
(viii) H-code (1):
(ix) UN class (1):
(x) UN number:
(xi) UN shipping name:
(xii) Customs code(s) (HS):

15. Exporter's — notifier's/generator's — producer's (4) **declaration:**
I certify that the above information is complete and correct to my best knowledge. I also certify that legally enforceable written contractual obligations have been entered into, that any applicable insurance or other financial guarantee is in force covering the transboundary movement and that all necessary consents have been received from the competent authorities of the countries concerned.
Name: Date: Signature:

16. For use by any person involved in the transboundary movement in case additional information is required

17. Shipment received by importer — consignee (if not facility):
Name: Date: Signature:

TO BE COMPLETED BY DISPOSAL/RECOVERY FACILITY

18. Shipment received at disposal facility ☐ **or recovery facility** ☐
Date of reception: Accepted: ☐ Rejected (*): ☐
Quantity received: Tonnes (Mg): m³:
(*) immediately contact competent authorities
Approximate date of disposal/recovery:
Disposal/recovery operation (1):
Name:
Date:
Signature:

19. I certify that the disposal/recovery of the waste described above has been completed
Name:
Date:
Signature and stamp:

(1) See list of abbreviations and codes on the next page.
(2) Attach details if necessary.
(3) If more than three carriers, attach information as required in blocks 8 (a, b, c).
(4) Required by the Basel Convention.
(5) Attach list if more than one.
(6) If required by national legislation.

FOR USE BY CUSTOMS OFFICES (if required by national legislation)			
20. Country of export — dispatch or customs office of exit The waste described in this movement document left the country on: Signature: Stamp:		**21. Country of import — destination or customs office of entry** The waste described in this movement document entered the country on: Signature: Stamp:	
22. Stamps of customs offices of transit countries			
Name of country: Entry:	Exit:	Name of country: Entry:	Exit:
Name of country: Entry:	Exit:	Name of country: Entry:	Exit:

List of abbreviations and codes used in the movement document

DISPOSAL OPERATIONS (block 11)

D1 Deposit into or onto land (e.g. landfill, etc.)
D2 Land treatment (e.g. biodegradation of liquid or sludgy discards in soils, etc.)
D3 Deep injection (e.g., injection of pumpable discards into wells, salt domes or naturally occurring repositories, etc.)
D4 Surface impoundment (e.g., placement of liquid or sludge discards into pits, ponds or lagoons, etc.)
D5 Specially engineered landfill (e.g. placement into lined discrete cells which are capped and isolated from one another and the environment, etc.)
D6 Release into a water body except seas/oceans
D7 Release into seas/oceans including sea-bed insertion
D8 Biological treatment not specified elsewhere in this list which results in final compounds or mixtures which are discarded by means of any of the operations in this list
D9 Physico-chemical treatment not specified elsewhere in this list which results in final compounds or mixtures which are discarded by means of any of the operations in this list (e.g., evaporation, drying, calcination, etc.)
D10 Incineration on land
D11 Incineration at sea
D12 Permanent storage (e.g. emplacement of containers in a mine, etc.)
D13 Blending or mixing prior to submission to any of the operations in this list
D14 Repackaging prior to submission to any of the operations in this list
D15 Storage pending any of the operations in this list

RECOVERY OPERATIONS (block 11)

R1 Use as a fuel (other than in direct incineration) or other means to generate energy (Basel/OECD) — Use principally as a fuel or other means to generate energy (EU)
R2 Solvent reclamation/regeneration
R3 Recycling/reclamation of organic substances which are not used as solvents
R4 Recycling/reclamation of metals and metal compounds
R5 Recycling/reclamation of other inorganic materials
R6 Regeneration of acids or bases
R7 Recovery of components used for pollution abatement
R8 Recovery of components from catalysts
R9 Used oil re-refining or other reuses of previously used oil
R10 Land treatment resulting in benefit to agriculture or ecological improvement
R11 Uses of residual materials obtained from any of the operations numbered R1 to R10
R12 Exchange of wastes for submission to any of the operations numbered R1 to R11
R13 Accumulation of material intended for any operation in this list

PACKAGING TYPES (block 7)

1. Drum
2. Wooden barrel
3. Jerrican
4. Box
5. Bag
6. Composite packaging
7. Pressure receptacle
8. Bulk
9. Other (specify)

MEANS OF TRANSPORT (block 8)

R = Road
T = Train/rail
S = Sea
A = Air
W = Inland waterways

PHYSICAL CHARACTERISTICS (block 13)

1. Powdery/powder
2. Solid
3. Viscous/paste
4. Sludgy
5. Liquid
6. Gaseous
7. Other (specify)

H-CODE AND UN CLASS (block 14)

UN Class	H-code	Characteristics
1	H1	Explosive
3	H3	Flammable liquids
4.1	H4.1	Flammable solids
4.2	H4.2	Substances or wastes liable to spontaneous combustion
4.3	H4.3	Substances or wastes which, in contact with water, emit flammable gases
5.1	H5.1	Oxidising
5.2	H5.2	Organic peroxides
6.1	H6.1	Poisonous (acute)
6.2	H6.2	Infectious substances
8	H8	Corrosives
9	H10	Liberation of toxic gases in contact with air or water
9	H11	Toxic (delayed or chronic)
9	H12	Ecotoxic
9	H13	Capable, by any means, after disposal of yielding another material, e.g., leachate, which possesses any of the characteristics listed above

Further information, in particular related to waste identification (block 14), i.e. on Basel Annexes VIII and IX codes, OECD codes and Y-codes, can be found in a Guidance/instruction Manual available from the OECD and the Secretariat of the Basel Convention.'

][1]

Amendment

1 Substituted by Commission Regulation (EC) No 1379/2007 of 26 November 2007 amending Annexes IA, IB, VII and VIII of Regulation (EC) No 1013/2006 of the European Parliament and of the Council on shipments of waste, for the purposes of taking account of technical progress and changes agreed under the Basel Convention, Article 1, Annex II.

[ANNEX IC
SPECIFIC INSTRUCTIONS FOR COMPLETING THE NOTIFICATION AND MOVEMENT DOCUMENTS

I. INTRODUCTION][1]

1. The present instructions provide the necessary explanations for completing the notification and movement documents. Both documents are compatible with the Basel Convention, the OECD Decision (which only covers shipments of wastes destined for recovery operations within the OECD area) and this Regulation, since they take into account the specific requirements set out in these three instruments. Because the documents have been made broad enough to cover all three instruments, however, not all blocks in the document will be applicable to all of the instruments and it therefore may not be necessary to complete all of the blocks in a given case. Any specific requirements relating to only one control system have been indicated with the use of footnotes. It is also possible that national implementing legislation may use terminology that differs from that adopted in the Basel Convention and the OECD Decision. For example, the term "shipment" is used in this Regulation instead of "movement" and the titles of the notification and movement documents therefore reflect this variation by employing the term "movement/shipment".

2. The documents include both the term "disposal" and "recovery", because the terms are defined differently in the three instruments. The European Community Regulation and the OECD Decision use the term "disposal" to refer to disposal operations listed in Annex IV.A of the Basel Convention and Appendix 5.A of the OECD Decision and "recovery" for recovery operations listed in Annex IV.B of the Basel Convention and Appendix 5.B of the OECD Decision. In the Basel Convention itself, however, the term "disposal" is used to refer to both disposal and recovery operations.

3. The competent authorities of dispatch are responsible for providing and issuing the notification and movement documents (in both paper and electronic versions). When doing so, they will use a numbering system, which allows a particular consignment of waste to be traced. The numbering system should be prefixed with the country code of the country of dispatch that can be found in the ISO standard 3166 abbreviation list. Within the EU, the two-digits country code must be followed by a space. This may be followed by an optional code of up to four digits specified by the competent authority of dispatch followed by a space. The numbering system must end with a six-digit number. For illustration, if the country code is XY and the six-digit number 123456, the notification number would be XY 123456 if no optional code were specified. Where an optional code, for example 12, is specified, the notification number would be XY 12 123456. However, in case a notification or movement document is transmitted electronically and no optional code is specified, "0000" should be inserted instead of the optional code (e.g. XY 0000 123456); in case an optional code of less than four digits is specified, for example 12, the notification number would be XY 0012 123456.

4. Countries may wish to issue the documents in a paper size format that conforms to their national standards (normally ISO A4, as recommended by the United Nations). In order to facilitate their use internationally, however, and to take into account the difference between ISO A4 and the paper size used in North America, the frame size of the forms should not be greater than 183 × 262 mm with margins aligned at the top and the left side of the paper. The notification document (block 1-block 21 including footnotes) should be on one page and the list of abbreviations and codes used in the notification document should be on a second page. With regard to the movement document, block 1-block 19 including footnotes should be on one page and block 20-22 and the list of abbreviations and codes used in the movement document should be on a second page.][1]

Amendment

1 Substituted by Commission Regulation (EC) No 669/2008 of 15 July 2008 on completing Annex IC of Regulation (EC) No 1013/2006 of the European Parliament and of the Council on shipments of waste, Article 1, Annex.

[II. PURPOSE OF THE NOTIFICATION AND MOVEMENT DOCUMENTS][1]

[5. The notification document is intended to provide the competent authorities concerned with the information they need to assess the acceptability of proposed waste shipments. It also provides space for them to acknowledge receipt of the notification and, where required, to consent in writing to a proposed shipment.

6. The movement document is intended to travel with a consignment of waste at all times from the moment it leaves the waste producer to its arrival at a disposal or recovery facility in another country. Each person who takes charge of a shipment (carriers and possibly consignee) is to sign the movement document either upon delivery or receipt of the wastes in question. There are also spaces in the movement document for recording passage of the consignment through the customs offices of all countries concerned (required by this Regulation). Finally, the document is to be used by the relevant disposal or recovery facility to certify that the waste has been received and that the recovery or disposal operation has been completed.][1]

Amendment

1 Substituted by Commission Regulation (EC) No 669/2008 of 15 July 2008 on completing Annex IC of Regulation (EC) No 1013/2006 of the European Parliament and of the Council on shipments of waste, Article 1, Annex.

[III. GENERAL REQUIREMENTS]

[7. A planned shipment subject to the procedure of prior written notification and consent may take place only after the notification and movement documents have been completed pursuant to this Regulation, taking into account Articles 16(a) and 16(b), and during the period of validity of the written or tacit consents of all competent authorities concerned.

8. Those filling out printed copies of the documents should use typescript or block capitals in permanent ink throughout. Signatures should always be written in permanent ink and the name of the authorised representative should accompany the signature in capital letters. In the event of a minor mistake, for example the use of the wrong code for a waste, a correction can be made with the approval of the competent authorities. The new text must be marked and signed or stamped, and the date of the modification must be noted. For major changes or corrections, a new form must be completed.

9. The forms have also been designed to be easily completed electronically. Where this is done, appropriate security measures should be taken against any misuse of the forms. Any changes made to a completed form with the approval of the competent authorities should be visible. When using electronic forms transmitted by e-mail, a digital signature is necessary.

10. To simplify translation, the documents require a code, rather than text, for the completion of several blocks. Where text is required, however, it must be in a language acceptable to the competent authorities in the country of destination and, where required, to the other concerned authorities.

11. A six-digit format should be used to indicate the date. For example, 29 January 2006 should be shown as 29.01.06 (Day.Month.Year).

12. Where it is necessary to add annexes to the documents providing additional information, each annex should include the reference number of the relevant document and cite the block to which it relates.][1]

Amendment

1 Substituted by Commission Regulation (EC) No 669/2008 of 15 July 2008 on completing Annex IC of Regulation (EC) No 1013/2006 of the European Parliament and of the Council on shipments of waste, Article 1, Annex.

[IV. SPECIFIC INSTRUCTIONS FOR COMPLETING THE NOTIFICATION DOCUMENT][1]

[13. The notifier is to complete blocks 1–18 (except the notification number in block 3) at the time of notification. In some third countries which are not OECD member countries, the competent authority of dispatch may complete these blocks. When the notifier is not the same person as the original producer, this producer or one of the persons indicated in point 15(a) (ii) or (iii) of Article 2 is, where practicable, also to sign in block 17 as specified in the second subparagraph, point 1 of Article 4, and Annex II, Part 1, point 26.

14. Blocks 1 (See Annex II, Part 1, points 2 and 4) and 2 (Annex II, Part 1, point 6): Provide the required information (give registration number only where applicable, address including the name of the country and telephone and fax numbers including the country code; contact person should be responsible for the shipment including if incidents during shipment occur). In some third countries, information relating to the competent authority of dispatch may be given instead. The notifier may be a dealer or broker in accordance with point 15 of Article 2 of this Regulation. In this case, provide a copy of the contract or evidence of the contract (or a declaration certifying its existence) between the producer, new producer or collector and the broker or dealer in an annex (see Annex II, Part 1, point 23). The phone and fax numbers and the e-mail address should facilitate contact of all relevant persons at any time regarding an incident during shipment.

15. Normally, the consignee would be the disposal or recovery facility given in block 10. In some cases, however, the consignee may be another person, for example a dealer, a broker, or a corporate body, such as the headquarters or mailing address of the receiving disposal or recovery facility in block 10. In order to act as a consignee, a dealer, broker or corporate body must be under the jurisdiction of the country of destination and possess or have some other form of legal control over the waste at the moment the shipment arrives in the country of destination. In such cases, information relating to the dealer, broker or corporate body should be completed in block 2.

16. Block 3 (See Annex II, Part 1, points 1, 5, 11 and 19): When issuing a notification document, a competent authority will, according to its own system, provide an identification number which will be printed in this block (see paragraph 3 above). Under A, "individual shipment" refers to a single notification and "multiple shipments" to a general notification. Under B, give the type of operation the waste being shipped is destined for. Under C, pre-consent refers to Article 14 of this Regulation.

17. Blocks 4 (See Annex II, Part 1, point 1), 5 (See Annex II, Part 1, point 17) and 6 (See Annex II, Part 1, point 12): Give the number of shipments in block 4 and the intended date of a single shipment or, for multiple shipments, the dates of the first and last shipments, in block 6. In block 5, give the estimated minimum and maximum weight in tonnes (1 tonne equals 1 megagram (Mg) or 1000 kg) of the waste. In some third countries, giving the volume in cubic metres (1 cubic metre equals 1000 litres) or other metric units, such as kilograms or litres, may also be acceptable. When other metric units are used, the unit of measure may be indicated and the unit in the document may be crossed out. The total quantity shipped must not exceed the maximum quantity declared in block 5. The intended period of time for shipments in block 6 may not exceed one year, with the exception of multiple shipments to pre-consented recovery facilities according to Article 14 of this Regulation (see paragraph 16), for which the intended period of time may not exceed three years. All shipments must take place within the validity period of the written or tacit consents of all competent authorities concerned issued by the competent authorities according to Article 9(6) of this Regulation. In the case of multiple shipments, some third countries may, based on the Basel Convention, require the expected dates or the expected frequency and the estimated quantity of each shipment to be quoted in blocks 5 and 6 or attached in an annex. Where a competent authority issues a written consent to the shipment and the validity period of that consent in block 20 differs from the period indicated in block 6, the decision of the competent authority overrides the information in block 6.

18. Block 7 (See Annex II, Part 1, point 18): Types of packaging should be indicated using the codes provided in the list of abbreviations and codes attached to the notification document. If special handling precautions are required, such as those required by producers' handling instructions for employees, health and safety information, including information on dealing with spillage, and instructions in writing for the transport of dangerous goods, tick the appropriate box and attach the information in an annex.

19. Block 8 (See Annex II, Part 1, points 7 and 13): Provide the required information (give registration number only where applicable, address including the name of the country and telephone and fax numbers including the country code; contact person should be responsible for the shipment). If more than one carrier is involved, append to the notification document a complete list giving the required information for each carrier. Where the transport is organised by a forwarding agent, the agent's details and the respective information on actual carriers should be provided in an annex. Provide evidence of registration of the carrier(s) regarding waste transports (e.g. a declaration certifying its existence) in an annex (see Annex II, Part 1, point 15). Means of transport should be indicated using the abbreviations provided in the list of abbreviations and codes attached to the notification document.

20. Block 9 (See Annex II, Part 1, points 3 and 16): Provide the required information on the producer of the waste. The registration number of the producer should be given where applicable. If the notifier is the producer of the waste then write "Same as block 1". If the waste has been produced by more than one producer, write "See attached list" and append a list providing the requested information for each producer. Where the producer is not known, give the name of the person in possession or control of such waste (holder). Also provide information on the process by which the waste was produced and the site of production.

21. Block 10 (See Annex II, Part 1, point 5): Provide the required information (give destination of the shipment by ticking either disposal or recovery facility, registration number only where applicable and actual site of disposal or recovery if it is different from the address of the facility). If the disposer or recoverer is also the consignee, state here "Same as block 2". If the disposal or recovery operation is a D13–D15 or R12 or R13 operation (according to Annexes IIA or IIB of Directive 2006/12/EC on waste), the facility performing the operation should be mentioned in block 10, as well as the location where the operation will be performed. In such a case, corresponding information on the subsequent facility or facilities, where any subsequent R12/R13 or D13–D15 operation and the D1–D12 or R1–R11 operation or operations takes or take place or may take place should be provided in an annex. If the recovery or disposal facility is listed in Annex I, Category 5 of Directive 96/61/EC of 24 September 1996 on integrated pollution and prevention control, evidence (e.g. a declaration certifying its existence) of a valid permit issued in accordance with Articles 4 and 5 of that Directive must be provided in an annex in case a facility is located in the European Community.

22. Block 11 (See Annex II, Part 1, points 5, 19 and 20): Indicate the type of recovery or disposal operation by using R-codes or D-codes of Annexes IIA or IIB of Directive 2006/12/EC on waste (see also the list of abbreviations and codes attached to the notification document). If the disposal or recovery operation is a D13–D15 or R12 or R13 operation, corresponding information on the subsequent operations (any R12/R13 or D13–D15 as well as D1–D12 or R1–R11) should be provided in an annex. Also indicate the technology to be employed. If the waste is destined for recovery, provide the planned method of disposal for the non-recoverable fraction after recovery, the amount of recovered material in relation to non-recoverable waste, the estimated value of the recovered material and the cost of recovery and the cost of disposal of the non-recoverable fraction in an annex. In addition, in cases of imports into the Community of wastes destined for disposal, indicate a prior duly motivated request from the country of dispatch according Article 41(4) of this Regulation under "reason for export" and attach this request in an annex. Some third countries outside the OECD may, based on the Basel Convention, also require that the reason for export is specified.

23. Block 12 (See Annex II, Part 1, point 16): Give the name or names by which the material is commonly known or the commercial name and the names of its major constituents (in

terms of quantity and/or hazard) and their relative concentrations (expressed as a percentage), if known. In the case of a mixture of wastes, provide the same information for the different fractions and indicate which fractions are destined for recovery. A chemical analysis of the composition of the waste may be requested in accordance with Annex II Part 3 point 7 of this Regulation. Attach further information in an annex if necessary.

24. Block 13 (See Annex II, Part 1, point 16). Indicate physical characteristics of the waste at normal temperatures and pressures.

25. Block 14 (See Annex II, Part 1, point 16): State the code that identifies the waste according to Annexes III, IIIA, IIIB, IV or IVA of this Regulation. Give the code according to the system adopted under the Basel Convention (under subheading (i) in block 14) and, where applicable, the systems adopted in the OECD Decision (under subheading (ii)) and other accepted classification systems (under subheadings (iii) to (xii)). According to the second subparagraph, point 6 of Article 4 of this Regulation, give only one waste code (from Annexes III, IIIA, IIIB, IV or IVA of this Regulation) with the following two exceptions: In the case of wastes not classified under one single entry in either Annex III, IIIB, IV or IVA, give only one type of waste. In the case of mixtures of wastes not classified under one single entry in either Annex III, IIIB, IV or IVA, unless listed in Annex IIIA, provide the code of each fraction of the waste in order of importance (in an annex if necessary).

(a) Subheading (i): Basel Convention Annex VIII codes should be used for wastes that are subject to the procedure of prior written notification and consent (see Part I of Annex IV of this Regulation); Basel Annex IX codes should be used for wastes that are not usually subject to the procedure of prior written notification and consent but which, for a specific reason such as contamination by hazardous substances (cf. paragraph 1 of Annex III of this Regulation) or different classification according to Article 63 of this Regulation or national regulations, are subject to the procedure of prior written notification and consent (see Part I of Annex III of this Regulation). Basel Annexes VIII and IX can be found in Annex V of this Regulation, in the text of the Basel Convention as well as in the Instruction Manual available from the Secretariat of the Basel Convention. If a waste is not listed in Annexes VIII or IX of the Basel Convention, insert "not listed".

(b) Subheading (ii): OECD member countries should use OECD codes for wastes listed in Part II of Annexes III and IV of this Regulation, i.e. wastes that have no equivalent listing in the Annexes of the Basel Convention or that have a different level of control under this Regulation from the one required by the Basel Convention. If a waste is not listed in Part II of Annexes III and IV of this Regulation, insert "not listed".

(c) Subheading (iii): European Union Member States should use the codes included in the European Community list of wastes (see Commission Decision 2000/532/EC as amended). Such codes may also be included in Annex IIIB of this Regulation.

(d) Subheadings (iv) and (v): Where applicable, national identification codes other than the EC list of wastes used in the country of dispatch and, if known, in the country of destination should be used. Such codes may be included in Annexes IIIA, IIIB or IVA of this Regulation.

(e) Subheading (vi): If useful or required by the relevant competent authorities, add here any other code or additional information that would facilitate the identification of the waste.

(f) Subheading (vii): State the appropriate Y-code or Y-codes according to the "Categories of wastes to be controlled" (see Annex I of the Basel Convention and Appendix 1 of the OECD Decision), or according to the "Categories of wastes requiring special consideration" given in Annex II of the Basel Convention (see Annex IV Part I of this Regulation or Appendix 2 of the Basel Instruction Manual), if it or they exist(s). Y-codes are not required by this Regulation and the OECD Decision except where the waste shipment falls under one of the two "Categories requiring special consideration" under the Basel Convention (Y46 and Y47 or Annex II wastes), in which case the Basel Y-code should be indicated. Nevertheless, indicate the Y-code or Y-codes for wastes defined as hazardous according Article 1(1)(a) of the Basel Convention in order to fulfil the reporting requirements under the Basel Convention.

(g) Subheading (viii): If applicable, state here the appropriate H-code or H-codes, i.e. the codes indicating the hazardous characteristics exhibited by the waste (see the list of abbreviations and codes attached to the notification document). If there is no hazardous characteristics covered by the Basel Convention, but the waste is hazardous according to Annex III of Directive 91/689/EEC on hazardous waste, state the H-code or H-codes according to this Annex III and insert "EC" after the H code (e.g. H14 EC).

(h) Subheading (ix): If applicable, state here the United Nations class or classes which indicate the hazardous characteristics of the waste according to the United Nations classification (see the list of abbreviations and codes attached to the notification document) and are required to comply with international rules for the transport of dangerous goods (see the United Nations Recommendations on the Transport of Dangerous Goods. Model Regulations (Orange Book), latest edition).

(i) Subheadings (x and xi): If applicable, state here the appropriate United Nations number or numbers and United Nations shipping name or names. These are used to identify the waste according to the United Nations classification system and are required to comply with international rules for transport of dangerous goods (see the United Nations Recommendations on the Transport of Dangerous Goods. Model Regulations (Orange Book), latest edition).

(j) Subheading (xii): If applicable, state here customs code or codes, which allow identification of the waste by customs offices (see the list of codes and commodities in the "Harmonised commodity description and coding system" produced by the World Customs Organisation).

26. Block 15 (See Annex II, Part 1, points 8-10, 14): On line (a) of block 15, provide the name of the countries of dispatch, transit and destination or the codes for each country by using the ISO standard 3166 abbreviations. On line (b), provide, where applicable, the code number of the respective competent authority for each country and on line (c) insert the name of the border crossing or port and, where applicable, the customs office code number as the point of entry to or exit from a particular country. For transit countries give the information in line (c) for points of entry and exit. If more than three transit countries are involved in a particular shipment, attach the appropriate information in an annex. Provide the intended route between points of exit and entry, including possible alternatives, also in cases of unforeseen circumstances, in an annex.

27. Block 16 (See Annex II, Part 1, point 14): Provide the required information in case shipments enter, pass through or leave the European Union.

28. Block 17 (See Annex II, Part 1, points 21-22 and 24-26): Each copy of the notification document is to be signed and dated by the notifier (or by dealer or broker if acting as a notifier) before being forwarded to the competent authorities of the countries concerned. In some third countries, the competent authority of dispatch may sign and date. When the notifier is not the same person as the original producer, this producer, the new producer or the collector is, where practicable, also to sign and date; it is noted that this may not be practicable in cases where there are several producers (definitions regarding practicability may be contained in national legislation). Further, where the producer is not known, the person in possession or control of the waste (holder) should sign. This declaration should also certify the existence of insurance against liability for damage to third parties. Some third countries may require proof of insurance or other financial guarantees and a contract to accompany the notification document.

29. Block 18: Indicate the number of annexes containing any additional information supplied with the notification document. Each annex must include a reference to the notification number to which it relates, which is indicated in the corner of block 3.

30. Block 19: Under the Basel Convention, the competent authority or authorities of the country or countries of destination (where applicable) and transit issue such an acknowledgement.

Under the OECD Decision, the competent authority of the country of destination issues the acknowledgement. Some third countries may, according to their national legislation, require that the competent authority of dispatch also issues an acknowledgement.

31. Blocks 20 and 21: Block 20 is for use by competent authorities of any country concerned when providing a written consent. The Basel Convention (except if a country has decided not to require written consent with regard to transit and has informed the other Parties thereof in accordance with Article 6(4) of the Basel Convention) and certain countries always require a written consent (according Article 9(1) of this Regulation, a competent authority of transit may provide a tacit consent) whereas the OECD Decision does not require a written consent. Indicate the name of the country (or its code by using the ISO standard 3166 abbreviations). If the shipment is subject to specific conditions, the competent authority in question should tick the appropriate box and specify the conditions in block 21 or in an annex to the notification document. If a competent authority wishes to object to the shipment it should do so by writing "OBJECTION" in block 20. Block 21, or a separate letter, may then be used to explain the reasons for the objection.][1]

Amendment

1 Substituted by Commission Regulation (EC) No 669/2008 of 15 July 2008 on completing Annex IC of Regulation (EC) No 1013/2006 of the European Parliament and of the Council on shipments of waste, Article 1, Annex.

[V. SPECIFIC INSTRUCTIONS FOR COMPLETING THE MOVEMENT DOCUMENT][1]

[32. At the time of notification, the notifier is to complete blocks 3, 4 and 9–14. After receipt of the consents from the competent authorities of dispatch, destination and transit or, in relation to the competent authority of transit, tacit consent can be assumed, and before the actual start of the shipment, the notifier is to complete blocks 2, 5–8 (except the means of transport, the date of transfer and the signature), 15 and, if appropriate, 16. In some third countries which are not OECD member countries, the competent authority of dispatch may complete these blocks instead of the notifier. At the time of taking possession of the consignment, the carrier or its representative is to complete the means of transport, the date of transfer and the signature, which appear in blocks 8(a) to 8(c) and, if appropriate, 16. The consignee is to complete block 17 in the event that it is not the disposer or recoverer and when it takes charge of a shipment of waste after it arrives in the country of destination and, if appropriate, 16.

33. Block 1: The competent authority of dispatch is to enter the notification number (this is to be copied from block 3 in the notification document).

34. Block 2 (See Annex II, Part 2, point 1): For a general notification for multiple shipments, enter the serial number of the shipment and the total intended number of shipments indicated in block 4 in the notification document (for example, enter "4/11" for the fourth shipment out of eleven intended shipments under the general notification in question). In the case of a single notification, enter "1/1".

35. Blocks 3 and 4: Reproduce the same information on the notifier and consignee as given in blocks 1 and 2 in the notification document.

36. Block 5 (See Annex II, Part 2, point 6): Give the actual weight in tonnes (1 tonne equals 1 megagram (Mg) or 1000 kg of the waste. In some third countries, giving the volume in cubic metres (1 cubic metre equals 1000 litres) or other metric units, such as kilograms or litres, may be acceptable. When other metric units are used, the unit of measure may be indicated and the unit in the form may be crossed out. Attach, wherever possible, copies of weighbridge tickets.

37. Block 6 (See Annex II, Part 2, point 2): Enter the date when the shipment actually starts (see also instructions on block 6 of the notification document).

38. Block 7 (See Annex II, Part 2, points 7 and 8): Types of packaging should be indicated using the codes provided in the list of abbreviations and codes attached to the movement

document. If special handling precautions are required, such as those prescribed by producers' handling instructions for employees, health and safety information, including information on dealing with spillage, and transport emergency cards, tick the appropriate box and attach the information in an annex. Also enter the number of packages making up the consignment.

39. Blocks 8 (a), (b) and (c) (See Annex II, Part 2, points 3 and 4): Provide the required information (give registration number only where applicable, address including the name of the country and telephone and fax numbers including the country code). When more than three carriers are involved, appropriate information on each carrier should be attached to the movement document. The means of transport, the date of transfer and a signature should be provided by the carrier or carrier's representative taking possession of the consignment. A copy of the signed movement document is to be retained by the notifier. Upon each successive transfer of the consignment, the new carrier or carrier's representative taking possession of the consignment will have to comply with the same request and also sign the document. A copy of the signed document is to be retained by the previous carrier.

40. Block 9: Reproduce the information given in block 9 of the notification document.

41. Blocks 10 and 11: Reproduce the information given in blocks 10 and 11 in the notification document. If the disposer or recoverer is also the consignee, write in block 10: "Same as block 4". If the disposal or recovery operation is a D13–D15 or R12 or R13 operation (according to Annexes IIA or IIB of Directive 2006/12/EC on waste), the information on the facility performing the operation provided in block 10 is sufficient. No further information on any subsequent facilities performing R12/R13 or D13–D15 operations and the subsequent facility(ies) performing the D1–D12 or R1–R11 operation(s) needs to be included in the movement document.

42. Blocks 12, 13 and 14: Reproduce the information given in blocks 12, 13 and 14 in the notification document.

43. Block 15 (See Annex II, Part 2, point 9): At the time of shipment, the notifier (or the dealer or broker if acting as a notifier) shall sign and date the movement document. In some third countries, the competent authority of dispatch, or the generator of the waste according to the Basel Convention, may sign and date the movement document. According to Article 16(c) of this Regulation, enclose copies of the notification document containing the written consent, including any conditions, of the competent authorities concerned with the movement document. Some third countries may require originals to be enclosed.

44. Block 16 (See Annex II, Part 2, point 5): This block can be used by any person involved in a shipment (notifier or the competent authority of dispatch, as appropriate, consignee, any competent authority, carrier) in specific cases where more detailed information is required by national legislation concerning a particular item (for example, information on the port where a transfer to another transport mode occurs, the number of containers and their identification number, or additional proof or stamps indicating that the shipment has been consented by the competent authorities). Give the routing (point of exit from and entry into each country concerned, including customs offices of entry into and/or exit from and/or export from the Community) and route (route between points of exit and entry), including possible alternatives, also in case of unforeseen circumstances either in block 16 or attach it in an annex.

45. Block 17: This block is to be completed by the consignee in the event that it is not the disposer or recoverer (cf. paragraph 15 above) and in case the consignee takes charge of the waste after the shipment arrives in the country of destination.

46. Block 18: This block is to be completed by the authorised representative of the disposal or recovery facility upon receipt of the waste consignment. Tick the box of the appropriate type of facility. With regard to the quantity received, please refer to the specific instructions on block 5 (paragraph 36). A signed copy of the movement document is given to the last carrier. If the shipment is rejected for any reason, the representative of the disposal or recovery facility must immediately contact his or her competent authority. According to Article 16(d) or, if

appropriate, 15(c) of this Regulation and the OECD Decision, signed copies of the movement document must be sent within three days to the notifier and the competent authorities in the countries concerned (with the exception of those OECD transit countries which have informed the OECD Secretariat that they do not wish to receive such copies of the movement document). The original movement document shall be retained by the disposal or recovery facility.

47. Receipt of the waste consignment must be certified by any facility performing any disposal or recovery operation, including any D13–D15 or R12 or R13 operation. A facility performing any D13D15 or R12/R13 operation or a D1–D12 or R1–11 operation subsequent to a D13–D15 or R12 or R13 operation in the same country, is not, however, required to certify receipt of the consignment from the D13–D15 or R12 or R13 facility. Thus, block 18 does not need to be used for the final receipt of the consignment in such a case. Indicate also the type of disposal or recovery operation by using R-codes or D codes of Annexes IIA or IIB of Directive 2006/12/EC on waste and the approximate date by which the disposal or recovery of waste will be completed.

48. Block 19: This block is to be completed by the disposer or recoverer to certify the completion of the disposal or recovery of the waste. According to Article 16(e) or, if appropriate, 15(d) of this Regulation and the OECD Decision, signed copies of the movement document with block 19 completed should be sent to the notifier and competent authorities of dispatch, transit (not required by the OECD Decision) and destination as soon as possible, but no later than 30 days after the completion of the recovery or disposal and no later than one calendar year following the receipt of the waste. Some third countries which are not OECD member countries may require in accordance with the Basel Convention that signed copies of the document with block 19 completed must be sent to the notifier and the competent authority of dispatch. For disposal or recovery operations D13–D15 or R12 or R13, the information on the facility performing such an operation provided in block 10 is sufficient, and no further information on any subsequent facilities performing R12/R13 or D13–D15 operations and the subsequent facility(ies) performing the D1–D12 or R1–R11 operation(s) need be included in the movement document.

49. The disposal or recovery of waste must be certified by any facility performing any disposal or recovery operation, including a D13–D15 or R12 or R13 operation. Therefore, a facility performing any D13–D15 or R12/R13 operation or a D1–D12 or R1–R11 operation, subsequent to a D13–D15 or R12 or R13 operation in the same country, should not use block 19 to certify the recovery or disposal of the waste, since this block will already have been completed by the D13–D15 or R12 or R13 facility. The means of certifying disposal or recovery in this particular case must be ascertained by each country.

50. Blocks 20, 21 and 22: The blocks must be used for control by customs offices at the borders of the Community.][1]

Amendment

1 Substituted by Commission Regulation (EC) No 669/2008 of 15 July 2008 on completing Annex IC of Regulation (EC) No 1013/2006 of the European Parliament and of the Council on shipments of waste, Article 1, Annex.

ANNEX II
INFORMATION AND DOCUMENTATION RELATED TO NOTIFICATION

PART 1: INFORMATION TO BE SUPPLIED ON, OR ANNEXED TO, THE NOTIFICATION DOCUMENT:

1. Serial number or other accepted identifier of the notification document and intended total number of shipments.

2. Notifier's name, address, telephone number, fax number, e-mail address, registration number and contact person.

3. If the notifier is not the producer: producer's (producers') name, address, telephone number, fax number, e-mail address and contact person.

4. Dealer's (dealers') or broker's (brokers') name, address, telephone number, fax number, e-mail address and contact person, where the notifier has authorised him in accordance with point 15 of Article 2.

5. Recovery or disposal facility's name, address, telephone number, fax number, e-mail address, registration number, contact person, technologies employed and possible status as pre-consented in accordance with Article 14.

If the waste is destined for an interim recovery or disposal operation, similar information regarding all facilities where subsequent interim and non-interim recovery or disposal operations are envisaged shall be indicated.

If the recovery or disposal facility is listed in Annex I, Category 5 of Directive 96/61/EC, evidence (e.g. a declaration certifying its existence) of a valid permit issued in accordance with Articles 4 and 5 of that Directive shall be provided.

6. Consignee's name, address, telephone number, fax number, e-mail address, registration number and contact person.

7. Intended carrier's (carriers') and/or their agent's (agents') name, address, telephone number, fax number, e-mail address, registration number and contact person.

8. Country of dispatch and relevant competent authority.

9. Countries of transit and relevant competent authorities.

10. Country of destination and relevant competent authority.

11. Single notification or general notification. If general notification, period of validity requested.

12. Date(s) envisaged for start of the shipment(s).

13. Means of transport envisaged.

14. Intended routing (point of exit from and entry into each country concerned, including customs offices of entry into and/or exit from and/or export from the Community) and intended route (route between points of exit and entry), including possible alternatives, also in case of unforeseen circumstances.

15. Evidence of registration of the carrier(s) regarding waste transports (e.g. a declaration certifying its existence).

16. Designation of the waste on the appropriate list, the source(s), description, composition and any hazardous characteristics. In the case of waste from various sources, also a detailed inventory of the waste.

17. Estimated maximum and minimum quantities.

18. Type of packaging envisaged.

19. Specification of the recovery or disposal operation(s) as referred to in Annexes II A and II B to Directive 2006/12/EC.

20. If the waste is destined for recovery:
(a) the planned method of disposal for the non-recoverable fraction after recovery;
(b) the amount of recovered material in relation to non-recoverable waste;
(c) the estimated value of the recovered material;
(d) the cost of recovery and the cost of disposal of the non-recoverable fraction.

21. Evidence of insurance against liability for damage to third parties (e.g. a declaration certifying its existence).

22. Evidence of a contract (or a declaration certifying its existence) between the notifier and consignee for the recovery or disposal of the waste that has been concluded and is effective at the time of the notification, as required in the second subparagraph, point 4 of Article 4 and in Article 5.

23. A copy of the contract or evidence of the contract (or a declaration certifying its existence) between the producer, new producer or collector and the broker or dealer, in the event that the broker or dealer acts as notifier.

24. Evidence of a financial guarantee or equivalent insurance (or a declaration certifying its existence if the competent authority so allows) that has been established and is effective at the time of the notification or, if the competent authority which approves the financial guarantee or equivalent insurance so allows, at the latest when the shipment starts, as required in the second subparagraph, point 5 of Article 4 and in Article 6.

25. Certification by the notifier that the information is complete and correct to the best of his/her knowledge.

26. When the notifier is not the producer in accordance with point 15(a)(i) of Article 2, the notifier shall ensure that the producer or one of the persons indicated in point 15(a)(ii) or (iii) of Article 2, where practicable, also signs the notification document provided for in Annex IA.

PART 2: INFORMATION TO BE SUPPLIED ON, OR ANNEXED TO, THE MOVEMENT DOCUMENT:

Supply all information listed in Part 1, updated in accordance with the points set out below, and the other additional information specified:

1. Serial and total number of shipments.

2. Date shipment started.

3. Means of transport.

4. Carrier's (carriers') name, address, telephone number, fax number and e-mail address.

5. Routing (point of exit from and entry into each country concerned, including customs offices of entry into and/or exit from and/or export from the Community) and route (route between points of exit and entry), including possible alternatives, also in case of unforeseen circumstances.

6. Quantities.

7. Type of packaging.

8. Any special precautions to be taken by the carrier(s).

9. Declaration by the notifier that all necessary consents have been received from the competent authorities of the countries concerned. This declaration must be signed by the notifier.

10. Appropriate signatures for each custody transfer.

PART 3: ADDITIONAL INFORMATION AND DOCUMENTATION THAT MAY BE REQUESTED BY THE COMPETENT AUTHORITIES:

1. The type and duration of the authorisation pursuant to which the recovery or disposal facility operates.

2. Copy of the permit issued in accordance with Articles 4 and 5 of Directive 96/61/EC.

3. Information concerning the measures to be taken to ensure transport safety.

4. The transport distance(s) between the notifier and the facility, including possible alternative routes, also in case of unforeseen circumstances and, in the event of intermodal transport, the place where the transfer will take place.

5. Information about costs of transport between the notifier and the facility.

6. Copy of the registration of the carrier(s) regarding the waste transport.

7. Chemical analysis of the composition of the waste.

8. Description of the production process of the waste.

9. Description of the treatment process of the facility which receives the waste.

10. The financial guarantee or equivalent insurance or a copy thereof.

11. Information concerning the calculation of the financial guarantee or equivalent insurance as required in the second subparagraph, point 5 of Article 4 and in Article 6.

12. Copy of the contracts referred to in Part 1, points 22 and 23.

13. Copy of the policy of insurance against liability for damage to third parties.

14. Any other information which is pertinent to the assessment of the notification in accordance with this Regulation and national legislation.

ANNEX III
LIST OF WASTES SUBJECT TO THE GENERAL INFORMATION REQUIREMENTS LAID DOWN IN ARTICLE 18 ("GREEN LISTED WASTE")

Regardless of whether or not wastes are included on this list, they may not be subject to the general information requirements laid down in Article 18 if they are contaminated by other materials to an extent which

(a) increases the risks associated with the wastes sufficiently to render them appropriate for submission to the procedure of prior written notification and consent, when taking into account the hazardous characteristics listed in Annex III to Directive 91/689/EEC; or

(b) prevents the recovery of the wastes in an environmentally sound manner.

PART I

The following wastes will be subject to the general information requirements laid down in Article 18:

Wastes listed in Annex IX to the Basel Convention.

[For the purposes of this Regulation:

(a) any reference to list A in Annex IX to the Basel Convention shall be understood as a reference to Annex IV to this Regulation;

(b) in Basel entry B1020, the term "bulk finished form" includes all metallic non-dispersible (3) forms of the scrap listed therein;

(c) Basel entry B1030 shall read: "Residues containing refractory metals";

(d) the part of Basel entry B1100 that refers to "Slags from copper processing" etc., does not apply and (OECD) entry GB040 in Part II applies instead;

(e) Basel entry B1110 does not apply and (OECD) entries GC010 and GC020 in Part II apply instead;

(f) Basel entry B2050 does not apply and (OECD) entry GG040 in Part II applies instead;

(g) the reference in Basel entry B3010 to fluorinated polymer wastes shall be deemed to include polymers and co-polymers of fluorinated ethylene (PTFE).][1]

Amendment

1 Substituted by Commission Regulation (EU) No 413/2010 of 12 May 2010 amending Annexes III, IV and V to Regulation (EC) No 1013/2006 of the European Parliament and of the Council on shipments of waste so as to take account of changes adopted by OECD Council Decision C (2008) 156, Article 1, Annex, para 1.

PART II

The following wastes will also be subject to the general information requirements laid down in Article 18:

Metal bearing wastes arising from melting, smelting and refining of metals		
GB040	7112 262030 262090	Slags from precious metals and copper processing for further refining
Other wastes containing metals		
GC010		Electrical assemblies consisting only of metals or alloys
GC020		Electronic scrap (e.g. printed circuit boards, electronic components, wire, etc.) and reclaimed electronic components suitable for base and precious metal recovery
GC030	ex 890800	Vessels and other floating structures for breaking up, properly emptied of any cargo and other materials arising from the operation of the vessel which may have been classified as a dangerous substance or waste
GC050		Spent fluid catalytic cracking (FCC) catalysts (e.g. aluminium oxide, zeolites)
Glass waste in non-dispersible form		
GE020	ex 7001 ex 701939	Glass fibre waste
Ceramic wastes in non-dispersible form		
GF010		Ceramic wastes which have been fired after shaping, including ceramic vessels (before and/or after use) I
Other wastes containing principally inorganic constituents, which may contain metals and organic materials		
GG030	ex 2621	Bottom ash and slag tap from coal fired power plants I
GG040	ex 2621	Coal fired power plants fly ash
Solid plastic wastes		
GH013	391530 ex 390410—40	Polymers of vinyl chloride
Wastes arising from tanning and fellmongery operations and leather use		
GN010	ex 050200	Waste of pigs', hogs' or boars' bristles and hair or of badger hair and other brush making hair
GN020	ex 050300	Horsehair waste, whether or not put up as a layer with or without supporting material
GN030	ex 050590	Waste of skins and other parts of birds, with their feathers or down, of feathers and parts of feathers (whether or not with trimmed edges) and down, not further worked than cleaned, disinfected or treated for preservation

[ANNEX IIIA
MIXTURES OF TWO OR MORE WASTES LISTED IN ANNEX III AND NOT CLASSIFIED UNDER ONE SINGLE ENTRY AS REFERRED TO IN ARTICLE 3(2)][1]

[1. Regardless of whether or not mixtures are included on this list, they may not be subject to the general information requirements laid down in Article 18 if they are contaminated by other materials to an extent which:

(a) increases the risks associated with the wastes sufficiently to render them appropriate for submission to the procedure of prior written notification and consent, when taking into account the hazardous characteristics listed in Annex III to Directive 91/689/EEC; or
(b) prevents the recovery of the wastes in an environmentally sound manner.

[2. The following mixtures of wastes are included in this Annex:
(a) mixtures of wastes classified under Basel entries B1010 and B1050;
(b) mixtures of wastes classified under Basel entries B1010 and B1070;
(c) mixtures of wastes classified under Basel entries B3040 and B3080;
(d) mixtures of wastes classified under (OECD) entry GB040 and under Basel entry B1100 restricted to hard zinc spelter, zinc-containing drosses, aluminium skimmings (or skims) excluding salt slag and wastes of refractory linings, including crucibles, originating from copper smelting;
(e) mixtures of wastes classified under (OECD) entry GB040, under Basel entry B1070 and under Basel entry B1100 restricted to wastes of refractory linings, including crucibles, originating from copper smelting.
The entries referred to in points (d) and (e) shall not apply for exports to countries to which the OECD Decision does not apply.][2]

[3. The following mixtures of wastes classified under separate indents or sub-indents of one single entry are included in this Annex:
(a) mixtures of wastes classified under Basel entry B1010;
(b) mixtures of wastes classified under Basel entry B2010;
(c) mixtures of wastes classified under Basel entry B2030;
(d) mixtures of wastes classified under Basel entry B3010 and listed under Scrap plastic of non-halogenated polymers and copolymers;
(e) mixtures of wastes classified under Basel entry B3010 and listed under Cured waste resins or condensation products;
(f) mixtures of wastes classified under Basel entry B3010 and listed under Perfluoro alkoxyl alkane;
(g) mixtures of wastes classified under Basel entry B3020 restricted to unbleached paper or paperboard or of corrugated paper or paperboard, other paper or paperboard, made mainly of bleached chemical pulp, not coloured in the mass, paper or paperboard made mainly of mechanical pulp (for example, newspapers, journals and similar printed matter);
(h) mixtures of wastes classified under Basel entry B3030;
(i) mixtures of wastes classified under Basel entry B3040;
(j) mixtures of wastes classified under Basel entry B3050.][3]][1]

Amendments

1 Substituted by Commission Regulation (EC) No 308/2009 of 15 April 2009 amending, for the purposes of adaptation to scientific and technical progress, Annexes IIIA and VI to Regulation (EC) No 1013/2006 of the European Parliament and of the Council on shipments of waste, Article 1, Annex, para 1.

2 Substituted by Commission Regulation (EU) No 664/2011 of 11 July 2011 amending Regulation (EC) No 1013/2006 of the European Parliament and of the Council on shipments of waste to include certain mixtures of wastes in Annex IIIA thereto, Article 1, Annex, para (1).

3 Inserted by Commission Regulation (EU) No 664/2011 of 11 July 2011 amending Regulation (EC) No 1013/2006 of the European Parliament and of the Council on shipments of waste to include certain mixtures of wastes in Annex IIIA thereto, Article 1, Annex, para (2).

[ANNEX IIIB ADDITIONAL GREEN LISTED WASTE AWAITING INCLUSION IN THE RELEVANT ANNEXES TO THE BASEL CONVENTION OR THE OECD DECISION AS REFERRED TO IN ARTICLE 58(1)(B)][1]

[1. Regardless of whether or not wastes are included on this list, they may not be subject to the general information requirements laid down in Article 18 if they are contaminated by other materials to an extent which:

(a) increases the risks associated with the wastes sufficiently to render them appropriate for submission to the procedure of prior written notification and consent, when taking into account the hazardous characteristics listed in Annex III to Directive 2008/98/EC of the European Parliament and of the Council; or
(b) prevents the recovery of the wastes in an environmentally sound manner.

2. The following wastes are included in this Annex:
BEU01 Pressure sensitive adhesive label laminate waste containing raw materials used in label material production not covered by Basel entry B3020
BEU02 Non-separable plastic fraction from the pre-treatment of used liquid packages
BEU03 Non-separable plastic-aluminium fraction from the pre-treatment of used liquid packages
BEU04 Composite packaging consisting of mainly paper and some plastic, not containing residues and not covered by Basel entry B3020
BEU05 Clean biodegradable waste from agriculture, horticulture, forestry, gardens, parks and cemeteries

3. The shipments of waste listed in this Annex are without prejudice to the provisions of Council Directive 2000/29/EC, including measures adopted pursuant to Article 16(3) thereof.][1]

Amendment
1 Substituted by Commission Regulation (EU) No 135/2012 of 16 February 2012 amending Regulation (EC) No 1013/2006 of the European Parliament and of the Council on shipments of waste to include certain unclassified wastes in Annex IIIB thereto, Article 1, Annex.

ANNEX IV
LIST OF WASTES SUBJECT TO THE PROCEDURE OF PRIOR WRITTEN NOTIFICATION AND CONSENT ("AMBER" LISTED WASTE)

PART I

The following wastes will be subject to the procedure of prior written notification and consent:

Wastes listed in Annexes II and VIII to the Basel Convention.

For the purposes of this Regulation:
(a) Any reference to list B in Annex VIII to the Basel Convention shall be understood as a reference to Annex III to this Regulation.
(b) In Basel entry A1010, the term "excluding such wastes specifically listed on List B (Annex IX)" is a reference both to Basel entry B1020 and the note on B1020 in Annex III to this Regulation, Part I(b).
(c) Basel entries A1180 and A2060 do not apply and OECD entries GC010, GC020 and GG040 in Annex III, Part II apply instead when appropriate.
(d) Basel entry A4050 includes spent potlinings from aluminium smelting because they contain Y33 inorganic cyanides. If the cyanides have been destroyed, spent potlinings are assigned to Part II entry AB120 because they contain Y32, inorganic fluorine compounds excluding calcium fluoride.

PART II

The following wastes will also be subject to the procedure of prior written notification and consent:

Metal bearing wastes		
[AA010	261900	Dross, scalings and other wastes from the iron and steel industry][1]
AA060	262050	Vanadium ashes and residues

Metal bearing wastes		
AA190	810420 ex 810430	Magnesium waste and scrap that is flammable, pyrophoric or emits, upon contact with water, flammable gases in dangerous quantities
Wastes containing principally inorganic constituents, which may contain metals and organic materials		
AB030		Wastes from non-cyanide based systems which arise from surface treatment of metals
AB070		Sands used in foundry operations
AB120	ex 281290 ex 3824	Inorganic halide compounds, not elsewhere specified or included
AB130		Used blasting grit
AB150	ex 382490	Unrefined calcium sulphite and calcium sulphate from flue gas desulphurisation (FGD) ǀ
Wastes containing principally organic constituents, which may contain metals and inorganic materials		
AC060	ex 381900	Hydraulic fluids
AC070	ex 381900	Brake fluids
AC080	ex 382000	Antifreeze fluids
AC150		Chlorofluorocarbons
AC160		Halons
AC170	ex 440310	Treated cork and wood wastes
AC250		Surface active agents (surfactants)
AC260	ex 3101	Liquid pig manure; faeces
AC270		Sewage sludge
Wastes which may contain either inorganic or organic constituents		
AD090	ex 382490	Wastes from production, formulation and use of reprographic and photographic chemicals and materials not elsewhere specified or included
AD100		Wastes from non-cyanide based systems which arise from surface treatment of plastics
AD120	ex 391400 ex 3915	Ion exchange resins
AD150		Naturally occurring organic material used as a filter medium (such as bio-filters)
Wastes containing principally inorganic constituents, which may contain metals and organic materials		
RB020	ex 6815	Ceramic based fibres of physico-chemical characteristics similar to those of asbestos

Amendment

1 Substituted by Commission Regulation (EU) No 413/2010 of 12 May 2010 amending Annexes III, IV and V to Regulation (EC) No 1013/2006 of the European Parliament and of the Council on shipments of waste so as to take account of changes adopted by OECD Council Decision C (2008) 156, Article 1, Annex, para 2.

ANNEX IVA
WASTE LISTED IN ANNEX III BUT SUBJECT TO THE PROCEDURE OF PRIOR WRITTEN NOTIFICATION AND CONSENT (ARTICLE 3(3))

ANNEX V
WASTE SUBJECT TO THE EXPORT PROHIBITION IN ARTICLE 36

INTRODUCTORY NOTES

1. This Annex applies without prejudice to Directives 91/689/EEC and 2006/12/EC.

2. This Annex consists of three parts, Parts 2 and 3 of which apply only when Part 1 is not applicable. Consequently, to determine whether a specific waste is listed in this Annex, an initial check must be made to ascertain whether the waste is listed in Part 1 of this Annex, and, if it does not, whether it is listed in Part 2, and, if it does not, whether it is listed in Part 3.

Part 1 is divided into two sub-sections: List A lists wastes which are classified as hazardous by Article 1(1)(a) of the Basel Convention, and therefore covered by the export prohibition, and List B lists wastes which are not covered by Article 1(1)(a) of the Basel Convention, and therefore not covered by the export prohibition.

Thus, if a waste is listed in Part 1, a check must be made to ascertain whether it is listed in List A or in List B. Only if a waste is not listed in either List A or List B of Part 1, must a check be made to ascertain whether it is listed either among the hazardous waste listed in Part 2 (i.e. types of waste marked with an asterisk) or in Part 3, and if this is the case, it is covered by the export prohibition.

3. Wastes listed in List B of Part 1 or which are among the non-hazardous waste listed in Part 2 (i.e. wastes not marked with an asterisk) are covered by the export prohibition if they are contaminated by other materials to an extent which

(a) increases the risks associated with the waste sufficiently to render it appropriate for submission to the procedure of prior written notification and consent, when taking into account the hazardous characteristics listed in Annex III to Directive 91/689/EEC; or

(b) prevents the recovery of the waste in an environmentally sound manner.

PART 1

List A (Annex VIII to the Basel Convention)

A1 Metal and metal bearing wastes

A1010 Metal wastes and waste consisting of alloys of any of the following:

— Antimony
— Arsenic
— Beryllium
— Cadmium
— Lead
— Mercury
— Selenium
— Tellurium
— Thallium

but excluding such wastes specifically listed on list B.

A1020 Waste having as constituents or contaminants, excluding metal waste in massive form, any of the following:

— Antimony; antimony compounds
— Beryllium; beryllium compounds
— Cadmium; cadmium compounds

— Lead; lead compounds
— Selenium; selenium compounds
— Tellurium; tellurium compounds

A1030 Wastes having as constituents or contaminants any of the following:
— Arsenic; arsenic compounds
— Mercury; mercury compounds
— Thallium; thallium compounds

A1040 Wastes having as constituents any of the following:
— Metal carbonyls
— Hexavalent chromium compounds

A1050 Galvanic sludges

A1060 Waste liquors from the pickling of metals

A1070 Leaching residues from zinc processing, dust and sludges such as jarosite, hematite, etc.

A1080 Waste zinc residues not included on list B, containing lead and cadmium in concentrations sufficient to exhibit Annex III characteristics

A1090 Ashes from the incineration of insulated copper wire

A1100 Dusts and residues from gas cleaning systems of copper smelters

A1110 Spent electrolytic solutions from copper electrorefining and electrowinning operations

A1120 Waste sludges, excluding anode slimes, from electrolyte purification systems in copper electrorefining and electrowinning operations

A1130 Spent etching solutions containing dissolved copper

A1140 Waste cupric chloride and copper cyanide catalysts

A1150 Precious metal ash from incineration of printed circuit boards not included on list B

A1160 Waste lead-acid batteries, whole or crushed

A1170 Unsorted waste batteries excluding mixtures of only list B batteries. Waste batteries not specified on list B containing Annex I constituents to an extent to render them hazardous

A1180 Waste electrical and electronic assemblies or scrap containing components such as accumulators and other batteries included on list A, mercury-switches, glass from cathode-ray tubes and other activated glass and PCB-capacitors, or contaminated with Annex I constituents (e.g. cadmium, mercury, lead, polychlorinated biphenyl) to an extent that they possess any of the characteristics contained in Annex III (note the related entry on list B, B1110)

A1190 Waste metal cables coated or insulated with plastics containing or contaminated with coal tar, PCB, lead, cadmium, other organohalogen compounds or other Annex I constituents, to the extent that they exhibit Annex III characteristics

A2 Wastes containing principally inorganic constituents, which may contain metals and organic materials

A2010 Glass waste from cathode-ray tubes and other activated glasses

A2020 Waste inorganic fluorine compounds in the form of liquids or sludges but excluding such wastes specified on list B

A2030 Waste catalysts but excluding such wastes specified on list B

A2040 Waste gypsum arising from chemical industry processes, when containing Annex I constituents to the extent that it exhibits an Annex III hazardous characteristic (note the related entry on list B, B2080)

A2050 Waste asbestos (dusts and fibres)

A2060 Coal-fired power plant fly-ash containing Annex I substances in concentrations sufficient to exhibit Annex III characteristics (note the related entry on list B, B2050)

A3 Wastes containing principally organic constituents, which may contain metals and inorganic materials

A3010 Waste from the production or processing of petroleum coke and bitumen

A3020 Waste mineral oils unfit for their originally intended use

A3030 Wastes that contain, consist of or are contaminated with leaded anti-knock compound sludges

A3040 Waste thermal (heat transfer) fluids

A3050 Wastes from production, formulation and use of resins, latex, plasticisers, glues/adhesives excluding such wastes specified on list B (note the related entry on list B, B4020)

A3060 Waste nitrocellulose

A3070 Waste phenols, phenol compounds including chlorophenol in the form of liquids or sludges

A3080 Waste ethers not including those specified on list B

A3090 Waste leather dust, ash, sludges and flours when containing hexavalent chromium compounds or biocides (note the related entry on list B, B3100)

A3100 Waste paring and other waste of leather or of composition leather not suitable for the manufacture of leather articles containing hexavalent chromium compounds or biocides (note the related entry on list B, B3090)

A3110 Fellmongery wastes containing hexavalent chromium compounds or biocides or infectious substances (note the related entry on list B, B3110)

A3120 Fluff — light fraction from shredding

A3130 Waste organic phosphorous compounds

A3140 Waste non-halogenated organic solvents but excluding such wastes specified on list B

A3150 Waste halogenated organic solvents

A3160 Waste halogenated or unhalogenated non-aqueous distillation residues arising from organic solvent recovery operations

A3170 Wastes arising from the production of aliphatic halogenated hydrocarbons (such as chloromethane, dichloro-ethane, vinyl chloride, vinylidene chloride, allyl chloride and epichlorhydrin)

A3180 Wastes, substances and articles containing, consisting of or contaminated with polychlorinated biphenyl (PCB), polychlorinated terphenyl (PCT), polychlorinated naphthalene (PCN) or polybrominated biphenyl (PBB), or any other polybrominated analogues of these compounds, at a concentration level of 50 mg/kg or more

A3190 Waste tarry residues (excluding asphalt cements) arising from refining, distillation and any pyrolitic treatment of organic materials

A3200 Bituminous material (asphalt waste) from road construction and maintenance, containing tar (note the related entry on list B B2130)

A4 Wastes which may contain either inorganic or organic constituents

A4010 Wastes from the production, preparation and use of pharmaceutical products but excluding such wastes specified on list B

A4020 Clinical and related wastes; that is wastes arising from medical, nursing, dental, veterinary, or similar practices, and wastes generated in hospitals or other facilities during the investigation or treatment of patients, or research projects

A4030 Wastes from the production, formulation and use of biocides and phytopharmaceuticals, including waste pesticides and herbicides which are off-specification, out-dated, or unfit for their originally intended use

A4040 Wastes from the manufacture, formulation and use of wood-preserving chemicals

A4050 Wastes that contain, consist of or are contaminated with any of the following:

— Inorganic cyanides, excepting precious-metal-bearing residues in solid form containing traces of inorganic cyanides
— Organic cyanides

A4060 Waste oils/water, hydrocarbons/water mixtures, emulsions

A4070 Wastes from the production, formulation and use of inks, dyes, pigments, paints, lacquers, varnish excluding any such waste specified on list B (note the related entry on list B, B4010)

A4080 Wastes of an explosive nature (but excluding such wastes specified on list B)

A4090 Waste acidic or basic solutions, other than those specified in the corresponding entry on list B (note the related entry on list B, B2120)

A4100 Wastes from industrial pollution control devices for cleaning of industrial off-gases but excluding such wastes specified on list B

A4110 Wastes that contain, consist of or are contaminated with any of the following:

— any congenor of polychlorinated dibenzo-furan
— any congenor of polychlorinated dibenzo-dioxin

A4120 Wastes that contain, consist of or are contaminated with peroxides

A4130 Waste packages and containers containing Annex I substances in concentrations sufficient to exhibit Annex III hazard characteristics

A4140 Waste consisting of or containing off-specification or out-dated chemicals corresponding to Annex I categories and exhibiting Annex III hazard characteristics

A4150 Waste chemical substances arising from research and development or teaching activities which are not identified and/or are new and whose effects on human health and/or the environment are not known

A4160 Spent activated carbon not included on list B (note the related entry on list B, B2060)

List B (Annex IX to the Basel Convention)

B1 Metal and metal bearing wastes

B1010 Metal and metal-alloy wastes in metallic, non-dispersible form:

— Precious metals (gold, silver, the platinum group, but not mercury)
— Iron and steel scrap
— Copper scrap
— Nickel scrap
— Aluminium scrap
— Zinc scrap
— Tin scrap
— Tungsten scrap
— Molybdenum scrap
— Tantalum scrap
— Magnesium scrap

- Cobalt scrap
- Bismuth scrap
- Titanium scrap
- Zirconium scrap
- Manganese scrap
- Germanium scrap
- Vanadium scrap
- Scrap of Hafnium, Indium, Niobium, Rhenium and Gallium
- Thorium scrap
- Rare earths scrap
- Chromium scrap

B1020 Clean, uncontaminated metal scrap, including alloys, in bulk finished form (sheet, plate, beams, rods, etc.):

- Antimony scrap
- Beryllium scrap
- Cadmium scrap
- Lead scrap (but excluding lead-acid batteries)
- Selenium scrap
- Tellurium scrap

B1030 Refractory metals containing residues

B1031 Molybdenum, tungsten, titanium, tantalum, niobium and rhenium metal and metal alloy wastes in metallic dispersible form (metal powder), excluding such wastes as specified in list A under entry A1050, Galvanic sludges.

B1040 Scrap assemblies from electrical power generation not contaminated with lubricating oil, PCB or PCT to an extent to render them hazardous

B1050 Mixed non-ferrous metal, heavy fraction scrap, not containing Annex I materials in concentrations sufficient to exhibit Annex III characteristics

B1060 Waste Selenium and Tellurium in metallic elemental form including powder

B1070 Waste of copper and copper alloys in dispersible form, unless they contain Annex I constituents to an extent that they exhibit Annex III characteristics

B1080 Zinc ash and residues including zinc alloys residues in dispersible form unless containing Annex I constituents in concentration such as to exhibit Annex III characteristics or exhibiting hazard characteristic H4.3

B1090 Waste batteries conforming to a specification, excluding those made with lead, cadmium or mercury

B1100 Metal-bearing wastes arising from melting, smelting and refining of metals:

- Hard zinc spelter
- Zinc-containing drosses:
  - Galvanising slab zinc top dross (>90 % Zn)
  - Galvanising slab zinc bottom dross (>92 % Zn)
  - Zinc die casting dross (>85 % Zn)
  - Hot dip galvanisers slab zinc dross (batch) (>92 % Zn)
  - Zinc skimmings
- Aluminium skimmings (or skims) excluding salt slag
- Slags from copper processing for further processing or refining not containing arsenic, lead or cadmium to an extent that they exhibit Annex III hazard characteristics
- Wastes of refractory linings, including crucibles, originating from copper smelting
- Slags from precious metals processing for further refining
- Tantalum bearing tin slags with less than 0,5 % tin

B1110 Electrical and electronic assemblies:

— Electronic assemblies consisting only of metals or alloys
— Waste electrical and electronic assemblies or scrap (including printed circuit boards) not containing components such as accumulators and other batteries included on list A, mercury-switches, glass from cathode-ray tubes and other activated glass and PCB-capacitors, or not contaminated with Annex I constituents (e.g. cadmium, mercury, lead, polychlorinated biphenyl) or from which these have been removed, to an extent that they do not possess any of the characteristics contained in Annex III (note the related entry on list A, A1180)
— Electrical and electronic assemblies (including printed circuit boards, electronic components and wires) destined for direct re-use and not for recycling or final disposal

B1115 Waste metal cables coated or insulated with plastics, not included in list A1190, excluding those destined for Annex IVA operations or any other disposal operations involving, at any stage, uncontrolled thermal processes, such as open-burning

B1120 Spent catalysts excluding liquids used as catalysts, containing any of:
— Transition Metals, excluding waste catalysts (spent catalysts, liquid used catalysts or other catalysts) on list A
Scandium, Vanadium, Manganese, Cobalt, Copper, Yttrium, Niobium, Hafnium, Tungsten, Titanium, Chromium, Iron, Nickel, Zinc, Zirconium, Molybdenum, Tantalum, Rhenium
— Lanthanides (rare earth metals):
Lanthanum, Praseodymium, Samarium, Gadolinium, Dysprosium, Erbium, Ytterbium, Cerium, Neodym, Europium, Terbium, Holmium, Thulium, Lutetium

B1130 Cleaned spent precious-metal-bearing catalysts

B1140 Precious-metal-bearing residues in solid form which contain traces of inorganic cyanides

B1150 Precious metals and alloy wastes (gold, silver, the platinum group, but not mercury) in a dispersible, non-liquid form with appropriate packaging and labelling

B1160 Precious-metal ash from the incineration of printed circuit boards (note the related entry on list A, A1150)

B1170 Precious-metal ash from the incineration of photographic film

B1180 Waste photographic film containing silver halides and metallic silver

B1190 Waste photographic paper containing silver halides and metallic silver

B1200 Granulated slag arising from the manufacture of iron and steel

B1210 Slag arising from the manufacture of iron and steel including slags as a source of TiO2 and Vanadium

B1220 Slag from zinc production, chemically stabilised, having a high iron content (above 20 %) and processed according to industrial specifications (e.g. DIN 4301) mainly for construction

B1230 Mill scaling arising from the manufacture of iron and steel

B1240 Copper oxide mill-scale

B1250 Waste end-of-life motor vehicles, containing neither liquids nor other hazardous components

B2 Wastes containing principally inorganic constituents, which may contain metals and organic materials

B2010 Wastes from mining operations in non-dispersible form:
— Natural graphite waste
— Slate waste, whether or not roughly trimmed or merely cut, by sawing or otherwise

— Mica waste
— Leucite, nepheline and nepheline syenite waste
— Feldspar waste
— Fluorspar waste
— Silica wastes in solid form excluding those used in foundry operations

B2020 Glass waste in non-dispersible form:
— Cullet and other waste and scrap of glass except for glass from cathode-ray tubes and other activated glasses

B2030 Ceramic wastes in non-dispersible form:
— Cermet wastes and scrap (metal ceramic composites)
— Ceramic based fibres not elsewhere specified or included

B2040 Other wastes containing principally inorganic constituents:
— Partially refined calcium sulphate produced from flue-gas desulphurisation (FGD)
— Waste gypsum wallboard or plasterboard arising from the demolition of buildings
— Slag from copper production, chemically stabilised, having a high iron content (above 20 %) and processed according to industrial specifications (e.g. DIN 4301 and DIN 8201) mainly for construction and abrasive applications
— Sulphur in solid form
— Limestone from the production of calcium cyanamide (having a pH less than 9)
— Sodium, potassium, calcium chlorides
— Carborundum (silicon carbide)
— Broken concrete
— Lithium-Tantalum and Lithium-Niobium containing glass scraps

B2050 Coal-fired power plant fly-ash, not included on list A (note the related entry on list A, A2060)

B2060 Spent activated carbon not containing any Annex I constituents to an extent they exhibit Annex III characteristics, for example, carbon resulting from the treatment of potable water and processes of the food industry and vitamin production (note the related entry on list A A4160)

B2070 Calcium fluoride sludge

B2080 Waste gypsum arising from chemical industry processes not included on list A (note the related entry on list A, A2040)

B2090 Waste anode butts from steel or aluminium production made of petroleum coke or bitumen and cleaned to normal industry specifications (excluding anode butts from chlor alkali electrolyses and from metallurgical industry)

B2100 Waste hydrates of aluminium and waste alumina and residues from alumina production excluding such materials used for gas cleaning, flocculation or filtration processes

B2110 Bauxite residue (red mud) (pH moderated to less than 11,5)

B2120 Waste acidic or basic solutions with a pH greater than 2 and less than 11,5, which are not corrosive or otherwise hazardous (note the related entry on list A, A4090)

B2130 Bituminous material (asphalt waste) from road construction and maintenance, not containing tar (note the related entry on list A A3200)

B3 Wastes containin principally organic constituents, which may contain metals and inorganic materials

B3010 Solid plastic waste:

The following plastic or mixed plastic materials, provided they are not mixed with other wastes and are prepared to a specification:

— Scrap plastic of non-halogenated polymers and copolymers, including but not limited to the following:
  — ethylene
  — styrene
  — polypropylene
  — polyethylene terephthalate
  — acrylonitrile
  — butadiene
  — polyacetals
  — polyamides
  — polybutylene terephthalate
  — polycarbonates
  — polyethers
  — polyphenylene sulphides
  — acrylic polymers
  — alkanes C10-C13 (plasticiser)
  — polyurethane (not containing CFCs)
  — polysiloxanes
  — polymethyl methacrylate
  — polyvinyl alcohol
  — polyvinyl butyral
  — polyvinyl acetate
— Cured waste resins or condensation products including the following:
  — urea formaldehyde resins
  — phenol formaldehyde resins
  — melamine formaldehyde resins
  — expoxy resins
  — alkyd resins
  — polyamides
— The following fluorinated polymer wastes:
  — Perfluoroethylene/propylene (FEP)
  — Perfluoro alkoxyl alkane
  — Tetrafluoroethylene/per fluoro vinyl ether (PFA)
  — Tetrafluoroethylene/per fluoro methylvinyl ether (MFA)
  — Polyvinylfluoride (PVF)
  — Polyvinylidenefluoride (PVDF)

B3020 Paper, paperboard and paper product wastes

The following materials, provided they are not mixed with hazardous wastes:

Waste and scrap of paper or paperboard of:
— unbleached paper or paperboard or of corrugated paper or paperboard
— other paper or paperboard, made mainly of bleached chemical pulp, not coloured in the mass
— paper or paperboard made mainly of mechanical pulp (for example, newspapers, journals and similar printed matter)
— other, including but not limited to
  1. laminated paperboard;
  2. unsorted scrap

B3030 Textile wastes

The following materials, provided they are not mixed with other wastes and are prepared to a specification:
— Silk waste (including cocoons unsuitable for reeling, yarn waste and garnetted stock)
  — not carded or combed
  — other

- Waste of wool or of fine or coarse animal hair, including yarn waste but excluding garnetted stock
  - noils of wool or of fine animal hair
  - other waste of wool or of fine animal hair
  - waste of coarse animal hair
- Cotton waste (including yarn waste and garnetted stock)
  - yarn waste (including thread waste)
  - garnetted stock
  - other
- Flax tow and waste
- Tow and waste (including yarn waste and garnetted stock) of true hemp (Cannabis sativa L.)
- Tow and waste (including yarn waste and garnetted stock) of jute and other textile bast fibres (excluding flax, true hemp and ramie)
- Tow and waste (including yarn waste and garnetted stock) of sisal and other textile fibres of the genus Agave
- Tow, noils and waste (including yarn waste and garnetted stock) of coconut
- Tow, noils and waste (including yarn waste and garnetted stock) of abaca (Manila hemp or Musa textilis Nee)
- Tow, noils and waste (including yarn waste and garnetted stock) of ramie and other vegetable textile fibres, not elsewhere specified or included
- Waste (including noils, yarn waste and garnetted stock) of man-made fibres
  - of synthetic fibres
  - of artificial fibres
- Worn clothing and other worn textile articles
- Used rags, scrap twine, cordage, rope and cables and worn out articles of twine, cordage, rope or cables of textile
  - sorted
  - other

B3035 Waste textile floor coverings, carpets

B3040 Rubber wastes

The following materials, provided they are not mixed with other wastes:
- Waste and scrap of hard rubber (e.g. ebonite)
- Other rubber wastes (excluding such wastes specified elsewhere)

B3050 Untreated cork and wood waste:
- Wood waste and scrap, whether or not agglomerated in logs, briquettes, pellets or similar forms
- Cork waste: crushed, granulated or ground cork

B3060 Wastes arising from agro-food industries provided it is not infectious:
- Wine lees
- Dried and sterilised vegetable waste, residues and byproducts, whether or not in the form of pellets, or a kind used in animal feeding, not elsewhere specified or included
- Degras: residues resulting from the treatment of fatty substances or animal or vegetable waxes
- Waste of bones and horn-cores, unworked, defatted, simply prepared (but not cut to shape), treated with acid or degelatinised
- Fish waste
- Cocoa shells, husks, skins and other cocoa waste
- Other wastes from the agro-food industry excluding by-products which meet national and international requirements and standards for human or animal consumption

B3065 Waste edible fats and oils of animal or vegetable origin (e.g. frying oils), provided they do not exhibit an Annex III characteristic

B3070 The following wastes:
— Waste of human hair
— Waste straw
— Deactivated fungus mycelium from penicillin production to be used as animal feed

B3080 Waste parings and scrap of rubber

B3090 Paring and other wastes of leather or of composition leather not suitable for the manufacture of leather articles, excluding leather sludges, not containing hexavalent chromium compounds and biocides (note the related entry on list A, A3100)

B3100 Leather dust, ash, sludges or flours not containing hexavalent chromium compounds or biocides (note the related entry on list A, A3090)

B3110 Fellmongery wastes not containing hexavalent chromium compounds or biocides or infectious substances (note the related entry on list A, A3110)

B3120 Wastes consisting of food dyes

B3130 Waste polymer ethers and waste non-hazardous monomer ethers incapable of forming peroxides

B3140 Waste pneumatic tyres, excluding those destined for Annex IVA operations

B4 Wastes which may contain either inorganic or organic constituents

B4010 Wastes consisting mainly of water-based/latex paints, inks and hardened varnishes not containing organic solvents, heavy metals or biocides to an extent to render them hazardous (note the related entry on list A, A4070)

B4020 Wastes from production, formulation and use of resins, latex, plasticisers, glues/adhesives, not listed on list A, free of solvents and other contaminants to an extent that they do not exhibit Annex III characteristics, e.g. water based, or glues based on casein starch, dextrin, cellulose ethers, polyvinyl alcohols (note the related entry on list A, A3050)

B4030 Used single use cameras, with batteries not included on list A

PART 2

Wastes listed in the Annex to Decision 2000/532/EC

01 Wastes resulting from exploration, mining, quarrying, and physical and chemical treatment of minerals

01 01 wastes from mineral excavation
01 01 01 wastes from mineral metalliferous excavation
01 01 02 wastes from mineral non-metalliferous excavation

01 03 wastes from physical and chemical processing of metalliferous minerals
01 03 04* acid-generating tailings from processing of sulphide ore
01 03 05* other tailings containing dangerous substances
01 03 06 tailings other than those mentioned in 01 03 04 and 01 03 05
01 03 07* other wastes containing dangerous substances from physical and chemical processing of metalliferous minerals
01 03 08 dusty and powdery wastes other than those mentioned in 01 03 07
01 03 09 red mud from alumina production other than the wastes mentioned in 01 03 07
01 03 99 wastes not otherwise specified

01 04 wastes from physical and chemical processing of non-metalliferous minerals
01 04 07* wastes containing dangerous substances from physical and chemical processing of non-metalliferous minerals

01 04 08 waste gravel and crushed rocks other than those mentioned in 01 04 07
01 04 09 waste sand and clays
01 04 10 dusty and powdery wastes other than those mentioned in 01 04 07
01 04 11 wastes from potash and rock-salt processing other than those mentioned in 01 04 07
01 04 12 tailings and other wastes from washing and cleaning of minerals other than those mentioned in 01 04 07 and 01 04 11
01 04 13 wastes from stone cutting and sawing other than those mentioned in 01 04 07
01 04 99 wastes not otherwise specified

01 05 drilling muds and other drilling wastes
01 05 04 fresh-water drilling muds and wastes
01 05 05* oil-containing drilling muds and wastes
01 05 06* drilling muds and other drilling wastes containing dangerous substances
01 05 07 barite-containing drilling muds and wastes other than those mentioned in 01 05 05 and 01 05 06
01 05 08 chloride-containing drilling muds and wastes other than those mentioned in 01 05 05 and 01 05 06
01 05 99 wastes not otherwise specified

Wastes marked with an asterisk are considered to be hazardous waste pursuant to Directive 91/689/EEC. When identifying a waste in the list below, the introduction to the Annex of Decision 2000/532/EC is relevant.

02 Wastes from agriculture, horticulture, aquaculture, forestry, hunting and fishing, food preparation and processing

02 01 wastes from agriculture, horticulture, aquaculture, forestry, hunting and fishing
02 01 01 sludges from washing and cleaning
02 01 02 animal-tissue waste
02 01 03 plant-tissue waste
02 01 04 waste plastics (except packaging)
02 01 06 animal faeces, urine and manure (including spoiled straw), effluent, collected separately and treated off-site
02 01 07 wastes from forestry
02 01 08* agrochemical waste containing dangerous substances
02 01 09 agrochemical waste other than those mentioned in 02 01 08
02 01 10 waste metal
02 01 99 wastes not otherwise specified

02 02 wastes from the preparation and processing of meat, fish and other foods of animal origin
02 02 01 sludges from washing and cleaning
02 02 02 animal-tissue waste
02 02 03 materials unsuitable for consumption or processing
02 02 04 sludges from on-site effluent treatment
02 02 99 wastes not otherwise specified

02 03 wastes from fruit, vegetables, cereals, edible oils, cocoa, coffee, tea and tobacco preparation and processing; conserve production; yeast and yeast extract production, molasses preparation and fermentation
02 03 01 sludges from washing, cleaning, peeling, centrifuging and separation
02 03 02 wastes from preserving agents
02 03 03 wastes from solvent extraction
02 03 04 materials unsuitable for consumption or processing
02 03 05 sludges from on-site effluent treatment
02 03 99 wastes not otherwise specified

02 04 wastes from sugar processing
02 04 01 soil from cleaning and washing beet
02 04 02 off-specification calcium carbonate
02 04 03 sludges from on-site effluent treatment
02 04 99 wastes not otherwise specified

02 05 wastes from the dairy products industry
02 05 01 materials unsuitable for consumption or processing
02 05 02 sludges from on-site effluent treatment
02 05 99 wastes not otherwise specified

02 06 wastes from the baking and confectionery industry
02 06 01 materials unsuitable for consumption or processing
02 06 02 wastes from preserving agents
02 06 03 sludges from on-site effluent treatment
02 06 99 wastes not otherwise specified

02 07 wastes from the production of alcoholic and non-alcoholic beverages (except coffee, tea and cocoa)
02 07 01 wastes from washing, cleaning and mechanical reduction of raw materials
02 07 02 wastes from spirits distillation
02 07 03 wastes from chemical treatment
02 07 04 materials unsuitable for consumption or processing
02 07 05 sludges from on-site effluent treatment
02 07 99 wastes not otherwise specified

03 Wastes from wood processing and the production of panels and furniture, pulp, paper and cardboard

03 01 wastes from wood processing and the production of panels and furniture
03 01 01 waste bark and cork
03 01 04* sawdust, shavings, cuttings, wood, particle board and veneer containing dangerous substances
03 01 05 sawdust, shavings, cuttings, wood, particle board and veneer other than those mentioned in 03 01 04
03 01 99 wastes not otherwise specified

03 02 wastes from wood preservation
03 02 01* non-halogenated organic wood preservatives
03 02 02* organochlorinated wood preservatives
03 02 03* organometallic wood preservatives
03 02 04* inorganic wood preservatives
03 02 05* other wood preservatives containing dangerous substances
03 02 99 wood preservatives not otherwise specified

03 03 wastes from pulp, paper and cardboard production and processing
03 03 01 waste bark and wood
03 03 02 green liquor sludge (from recovery of cooking liquor)
03 03 05 de-inking sludges from paper recycling
03 03 07 mechanically separated rejects from pulping of waste paper and cardboard
03 03 08 wastes from sorting of paper and cardboard destined for recycling
03 03 09 lime mud waste
03 03 10 fibre rejects, fibre-, filler- and coating sludges from mechanical separation
03 03 11 sludges from on-site effluent treatment other than those mentioned in 03 03 10
03 03 99 wastes not otherwise specified

04 Wastes from the leather, fur and textile industries

04 01 wastes from the leather and fur industry

04 01 01	fleshings and lime split wastes
04 01 02	liming waste
04 01 03*	degreasing wastes containing solvents without a liquid phase
04 01 04	tanning liquor containing chromium
04 01 05	tanning liquor free of chromium
04 01 06	sludges, in particular from on-site effluent treatment containing chromium
04 01 07	sludges, in particular from on-site effluent treatment free of chromium
04 01 08	waste tanned leather (blue sheetings, shavings, cuttings, buffing dust) containing chromium
04 01 09	wastes from dressing and finishing
04 01 99	wastes not otherwise specified

04 02 wastes from the textile industry

04 02 09	wastes from composite materials (impregnated textile, elastomer, plastomer)
04 02 10	organic matter from natural products (e.g. grease, wax)
04 02 14*	wastes from finishing containing organic solvents
04 02 15	wastes from finishing other than those mentioned in 04 02 14
04 02 16*	dyestuffs and pigments containing dangerous substances
04 02 17	dyestuffs and pigments other than those mentioned in 04 02 16
04 02 19*	sludges from on-site effluent treatment containing dangerous substances
04 02 20	sludges from on-site effluent treatment other than those mentioned in 4 02 19 I
04 02 21	wastes from unprocessed textile fibres
04 02 22	wastes from processed textile fibres
04 02 99	wastes not otherwise specified

05 Wastes from petroleum refining, natural gas purification and pyrolytic treatment of coal

05 01 wastes from petroleum refining

05 01 02*	desalter sludges
05 01 03*	tank bottom sludges
05 01 04*	acid alkyl sludges
05 01 05*	oil spills
05 01 06*	oily sludges from maintenance operations of the plant or equipment
05 01 07*	acid tars
05 01 08*	other tars
05 01 09*	sludges from on-site effluent treatment containing dangerous substances
05 01 10	sludges from on-site effluent treatment other than those mentioned in 05 01 09
05 01 11*	wastes from cleaning of fuels with bases
05 01 12*	oil containing acids
05 01 13	boiler feedwater sludges
05 01 14	wastes from cooling columns
05 01 15*	spent filter clays
05 01 16	sulphur-containing wastes from petroleum desulphurisation
05 01 17	bitumen
05 01 99	wastes not otherwise specified

05 06 wastes from the pyrolytic treatment of coal

05 06 01*	acid tars
05 06 03*	other tars
05 06 04	waste from cooling columns
05 06 99	wastes not otherwise specified

05 07 wastes from natural gas purification and transportation

05 07 01*	wastes containing mercury
05 07 02	wastes containing sulphur
05 07 99	wastes not otherwise specified

06 Wastes from inorganic chemical processes

06 01 wastes from the manufacture, formulation, supply and use (MFSU) of acids
06 01 01* sulphuric acid and sulphurous acid
06 01 02* hydrochloric acid
06 01 03* hydrofluoric acid
06 01 04* phosphoric and phosphorous acid
06 01 05* nitric acid and nitrous acid
06 01 06* other acids
06 01 99 wastes not otherwise specified

06 02 wastes from the MFSU of bases
06 02 01* calcium hydroxide
06 02 03* ammonium hydroxide
06 02 04* sodium and potassium hydroxide
06 02 05* other bases
06 02 99 wastes not otherwise specified

06 03 wastes from the MFSU of salts and their solutions and metallic oxides
06 03 11* solid salts and solutions containing cyanides
06 03 13* solid salts and solutions containing heavy metals
06 03 14 solid salts and solutions other than those mentioned in 06 03 11 and 06 03 13
06 03 15* metallic oxides containing heavy metals
06 03 16 metallic oxides other than those mentioned in 06 03 15
06 03 99 wastes not otherwise specified

06 04 metal-containing wastes other than those mentioned in 06 03
06 04 03* wastes containing arsenic
06 04 04* wastes containing mercury
06 04 05* wastes containing other heavy metals
06 04 99 wastes not otherwise specified

06 05 sludges from on-site effluent treatment
06 05 02* sludges from on-site effluent treatment containing dangerous substances
06 05 03 sludges from on-site effluent treatment other than those mentioned in 06 05 02

06 06 wastes from the MFSU of sulphur chemicals, sulphur chemical processes and desulphurisation processes
06 06 02* wastes containing dangerous sulphides
06 06 03 wastes containing sulphides other than those mentioned in 06 06 02
06 06 99 wastes not otherwise specified

06 07 wastes from the MFSU of halogens and halogen chemical processes
06 07 01* wastes containing asbestos from electrolysis
06 07 02* activated carbon from chlorine production
06 07 03* barium sulphate sludge containing mercury
06 07 04* solutions and acids, e.g. contact acid
06 07 99 wastes not otherwise specified

06 08 wastes from the MFSU of silicon and silicon derivatives
06 08 02* wastes containing dangerous chlorosilanes
06 08 99 wastes not otherwise specified

06 09 wastes from the MSFU of phosphorous chemicals and phosphorous chemical processes
06 09 02 phosphorous slag
06 09 03* calcium-based reaction wastes containing or contaminated with dangerous substances
06 09 04 calcium-based reaction wastes other than those mentioned in 06 09 03
06 09 99 wastes not otherwise specified

06 10 wastes from the MFSU of nitrogen chemicals, nitrogen chemical processes and fertiliser manufacture

06 10 02*	wastes containing dangerous substances
06 10 99	wastes not otherwise specified

06 11 wastes from the manufacture of inorganic pigments and opacificiers

06 11 01	calcium-based reaction wastes from titanium dioxide production
06 11 99	wastes not otherwise specified

06 13 wastes from inorganic chemical processes not otherwise specified

06 13 01*	inorganic plant protection products, wood-preserving agents and other biocides.
06 13 02*	spent activated carbon (except 06 07 02)
06 13 03	carbon black
06 13 04*	wastes from asbestos processing
06 13 05*	soot
06 13 99	wastes not otherwise specified

07 Wastes from organic chemical processes

07 01 wastes from the manufacture, formulation, supply and use (MFSU) of basic organic chemicals

07 01 01*	aqueous washing liquids and mother liquors
07 01 03*	organic halogenated solvents, washing liquids and mother liquors
07 01 04*	other organic solvents, washing liquids and mother liquors
07 01 07*	halogenated still bottoms and reaction residues
07 01 08*	other still bottoms and reaction residues
07 01 09*	halogenated filter cakes and spent absorbents
07 01 10*	other filter cakes and spent absorbents
07 01 11*	sludges from on-site effluent treatment containing dangerous substances
07 01 12	sludges from on-site effluent treatment other than those mentioned in 07 01 11
07 01 99	wastes not otherwise specified

07 02 wastes from the MFSU of plastics, synthetic rubber and man-made fibres

07 02 01*	aqueous washing liquids and mother liquors
07 02 03*	organic halogenated solvents, washing liquids and mother liquors
07 02 04*	other organic solvents, washing liquids and mother liquors
07 02 07*	halogenated still bottoms and reaction residues
07 02 08*	other still bottoms and reaction residues
07 02 09*	halogenated filter cakes and spent absorbents
07 02 10*	other filter cakes and spent absorbents
07 02 11*	sludges from on-site effluent treatment containing dangerous substances
07 02 12	sludges from on-site effluent treatment other than those mentioned in 07 02 11
07 02 13	waste plastic
07 02 14*	wastes from additives containing dangerous substances
07 02 15	wastes from additives other than those mentioned in 07 02 14
07 02 16*	wastes containing dangerous silicones
07 02 17	waste containing silicones other than those mentioned in 07 02 16
07 02 99	wastes not otherwise specified

07 03 wastes from the MFSU of organic dyes and pigments (except 06 11)

07 03 01*	aqueous washing liquids and mother liquors
07 03 03*	organic halogenated solvents, washing liquids and mother liquors
07 03 04*	other organic solvents, washing liquids and mother liquors
07 03 07*	halogenated still bottoms and reaction residues
07 03 08*	other still bottoms and reaction residues
07 03 09*	halogenated filter cakes and spent absorbents
07 03 10*	other filter cakes and spent absorbents

07 03 11* sludges from on-site effluent treatment containing dangerous substances
07 03 12 sludges from on-site effluent treatment other than those mentioned in 07 03 11
07 03 99 wastes not otherwise specified

07 04 wastes from the MFSU of organic plant protection products (except 02 01 08 and 02 01 09), wood preserving agents (except 03 02) and other biocides
07 04 01* aqueous washing liquids and mother liquors
07 04 03* organic halogenated solvents, washing liquids and mother liquors
07 04 04* other organic solvents, washing liquids and mother liquors
07 04 07* halogenated still bottoms and reaction residues
07 04 08* other still bottoms and reaction residues
07 04 09* halogenated filter cakes and spent absorbents
07 04 10* other filter cakes and spent absorbents
07 04 11* sludges from on-site effluent treatment containing dangerous substances
07 04 12 sludges from on-site effluent treatment other than those mentioned in 07 04 11
07 04 13* solid wastes containing dangerous substances
07 04 99 wastes not otherwise specified

07 05 wastes from the MFSU of pharmaceuticals
07 05 01* aqueous washing liquids and mother liquors
07 05 03* organic halogenated solvents, washing liquids and mother liquors
07 05 04* other organic solvents, washing liquids and mother liquors
07 05 07* halogenated still bottoms and reaction residues
07 05 08* other still bottoms and reaction residues
07 05 09* halogenated filter cakes and spent absorbents
07 05 10* other filter cakes and spent absorbents
07 05 11* sludges from on-site effluent treatment containing dangerous substances
07 05 12 sludges from on-site effluent treatment other than those mentioned in 07 05 11
07 05 13* solid wastes containing dangerous substances
07 05 14 solid wastes other than those mentioned in 07 05 13
07 05 99 wastes not otherwise specified

07 06 wastes from the MFSU of fats, grease, soaps, detergents, disinfectants and cosmetics
07 06 01* aqueous washing liquids and mother liquors
07 06 03* organic halogenated solvents, washing liquids and mother liquors
07 06 04* other organic solvents, washing liquids and mother liquors
07 06 07* halogenated still bottoms and reaction residues
07 06 08* other still bottoms and reaction residues
07 06 09* halogenated filter cakes and spent absorbents
07 06 10* other filter cakes and spent absorbents
07 06 11* sludges from on-site effluent treatment containing dangerous substances
07 06 12 sludges from on-site effluent treatment other than those mentioned in 07 06 11
07 06 99 wastes not otherwise specified

07 07 wastes from the MFSU of fine chemicals and chemical products not otherwise specified
07 07 01* aqueous washing liquids and mother liquors
07 07 03* organic halogenated solvents, washing liquids and mother liquors
07 07 04* other organic solvents, washing liquids and mother liquors
07 07 07* halogenated still bottoms and reaction residues
07 07 08* other still bottoms and reaction residues
07 07 09* halogenated filter cakes and spent absorbents
07 07 10* other filter cakes and spent absorbents
07 07 11* sludges from on-site effluent treatment containing dangerous substances
07 07 12 sludges from on-site effluent treatment other than those mentioned in 07 07 11
07 07 99 wastes not otherwise specified

08 Wastes from the manufacture, formulation, supply and use (MFSU) of coatings (paints, varnishes and vitreous enamels), adhesives, sealants and printing inks

08 01 wastes from MFSU and removal of paint and varnish

08 01 11*	waste paint and varnish containing organic solvents or other dangerous substances
08 01 12	waste paint and varnish other than those mentioned in 08 01 11
08 01 13*	sludges from paint or varnish containing organic solvents or other dangerous substances
08 01 14	sludges from paint or varnish other than those mentioned in 08 01 13
08 01 15*	aqueous sludges containing paint or varnish containing organic solvents or other dangerous substances
08 01 16	aqueous sludges containing paint or varnish other than those mentioned in 08 01 15
08 01 17*	wastes from paint or varnish removal containing organic solvents or other dangerous substances
08 01 18	wastes from paint or varnish removal other than those mentioned in 08 01 17
08 01 19*	aqueous suspensions containing paint or varnish containing organic solvents or other dangerous substances
08 01 20	aqueous suspensions containing paint or varnish other than those mentioned in 08 01 19
08 01 21*	waste paint or varnish remover
08 01 99	wastes not otherwise specified

08 02 wastes from MFSU of other coatings (including ceramic materials)

08 02 01	waste coating powders
08 02 02	aqueous sludges containing ceramic materials
08 02 03	aqueous suspensions containing ceramic materials
08 02 99	wastes not otherwise specified

08 03 wastes from MFSU of printing inks

08 03 07	aqueous sludges containing ink
08 03 08	aqueous liquid waste containing ink
08 03 12*	waste ink containing dangerous substances
08 03 13	waste ink other than those mentioned in 08 03 12
08 03 14*	ink sludges containing dangerous substances
08 03 15	ink sludges other than those mentioned in 08 03 14
08 03 16*	waste etching solutions
08 03 17*	waste printing toner containing dangerous substances
08 03 18	waste printing toner other than those mentioned in 08 03 17
08 03 19*	disperse oil
08 03 99	wastes not otherwise specified

08 04 wastes from MFSU of adhesives and sealants (including waterproofing products)

08 04 09*	waste adhesives and sealants containing organic solvents or other dangerous substances
08 04 10	waste adhesives and sealants other than those mentioned in 08 04 09
08 04 11*	adhesive and sealant sludges containing organic solvents or other dangerous substances
08 04 12	adhesive and sealant sludges other than those mentioned in 08 04 11
08 04 13*	aqueous sludges containing adhesives or sealants containing organic solvents or other dangerous substances
08 04 14	aqueous sludges containing adhesives or sealants other than those mentioned in 08 04 13
08 04 15*	aqueous liquid waste containing adhesives or sealants containing organic solvents or other dangerous substances
08 04 16	aqueous liquid waste containing adhesives or sealants other than those mentioned in 08 04 15

08 04 17* rosin oil
08 04 99 wastes not otherwise specified

08 05 wastes not otherwise specified in 08
08 05 01* waste isocyanates

09 Wastes from the photographic industry

09 01 wastes from the photographic industry
09 01 01* water-based developer and activator solutions
09 01 02* water-based offset plate developer solutions
09 01 03* solvent-based developer solutions
09 01 04* fixer solutions
09 01 05* bleach solutions and bleach fixer solutions
09 01 06* wastes containing silver from on-site treatment of photographic wastes
09 01 07 photographic film and paper containing silver or silver compounds
09 01 08 photographic film and paper free of silver or silver compounds
09 01 10 single-use cameras without batteries
09 01 11* single-use cameras containing batteries included in 16 06 01, 16 06 02 or 16 06 03
09 01 12 single-use cameras containing batteries other than those mentioned in 09 01 11
09 01 13* aqueous liquid waste from on-site reclamation of silver other than those mentioned in 09 01 06
09 01 99 wastes not otherwise specified

10 Wastes from thermal processes

10 01 wastes from power stations and other combustion plants (except 19)
10 01 01 bottom ash, slag and boiler dust (excluding boiler dust mentioned in 10 01 04)
10 01 02 coal fly ash
10 01 03 fly ash from peat and untreated wood
10 01 04* oil fly ash and boiler dust
10 01 05 calcium-based reaction wastes from flue-gas desulphurisation in solid form
10 01 07 calcium-based reaction wastes from flue-gas desulphurisation in sludge form
10 01 09* sulphuric acid
10 01 13* fly ash from emulsified hydrocarbons used as fuel
10 01 14* bottom ash, slag and boiler dust from coincineration containing dangerous substances
10 01 15 bottom ash, slag and boiler dust from coincineration other than those mentioned in 10 01 14
10 01 16* fly ash from coincineration containing dangerous substances
10 01 17 fly ash from coincineration other than those mentioned in 10 01 16
10 01 18* wastes from gas cleaning containing dangerous substances
10 01 19 wastes from gas cleaning other than those mentioned in 10 01 05, 10 01 07 and 10 01 18
10 01 20* sludges from on-site effluent treatment containing dangerous substances
10 01 21 sludges from on-site effluent treatment other than those mentioned in 10 01 20
10 01 22* aqueous sludges from boiler cleansing containing dangerous substances
10 01 23 aqueous sludges from boiler cleansing other than those mentioned in 10 01 22
10 01 24 sands from fluidised beds
10 01 25 wastes from fuel storage and preparation of coal-fired power plants
10 01 26 wastes from cooling-water treatment
10 01 99 wastes not otherwise specified

10 02 wastes from the iron and steel industry
10 02 02 unprocessed slag
10 02 07* solid wastes from gas treatment containing dangerous substances

10 02 08	solid wastes from gas treatment other than those mentioned in 10 02 07
10 02 10	mill scales
10 02 11*	wastes from cooling-water treatment containing oil
10 02 12	wastes from cooling-water treatment other than those mentioned in 10 02 11
10 02 13*	sludges and filter cakes from gas treatment containing dangerous substances
10 02 14	sludges and filter cakes from gas treatment other than those mentioned in 10 02 13
10 02 15	other sludges and filter cakes
10 02 99	wastes not otherwise specified

10 03 wastes from aluminium thermal metallurgy

10 03 02	anode scraps
10 03 04*	primary production slags
10 03 05	waste alumina
10 03 08*	salt slags from secondary production
10 03 09*	black drosses from secondary production
10 03 15*	skimmings that are flammable or emit, upon contact with water, flammable gases in dangerous quantities
10 03 16	skimmings other than those mentioned in 10 03 15
10 03 17*	tar-containing wastes from anode manufacture
10 03 18	carbon-containing wastes from anode manufacture other than those mentioned in 10 03 17
10 03 19*	flue-gas dust containing dangerous substances
10 03 20	flue-gas dust other than those mentioned in 10 03 19
10 03 21*	other particulates and dust (including ball-mill dust) containing dangerous substances
10 03 22	other particulates and dust (including ball-mill dust) other than those mentioned in 10 03 21
10 03 23*	solid wastes from gas treatment containing dangerous substances
10 03 24	solid wastes from gas treatment other than those mentioned in 10 03 23
10 03 25*	sludges and filter cakes from gas treatment containing dangerous substances
10 03 26	sludges and filter cakes from gas treatment other than those mentioned in 10 03 25
10 03 27*	wastes from cooling-water treatment containing oil
10 03 28	wastes from cooling-water treatment other than those mentioned in 10 03 27
10 03 29*	wastes from treatment of salt slags and black drosses containing dangerous substances
10 03 30	wastes from treatment of salt slags and black drosses other than those mentioned in 10 03 29
10 03 99	wastes not otherwise specified

10 04 wastes from lead thermal metallurgy

10 04 01*	slags from primary and secondary production
10 04 02*	dross and skimmings from primary and secondary production
10 04 03*	calcium arsenate
10 04 04*	flue-gas dust
10 04 05*	other particulates and dust
10 04 06*	solid wastes from gas treatment
10 04 07*	sludges and filter cakes from gas treatment
10 04 09*	wastes from cooling-water treatment containing oil
10 04 10	wastes from cooling-water treatment other than those mentioned in 10 04 09
10 04 99	wastes not otherwise specified

10 05 wastes from zinc thermal metallurgy

10 05 01	slags from primary and secondary production
10 05 03*	flue-gas dust
10 05 04	other particulates and dust

10 05 05*	solid waste from gas treatment
10 05 06*	sludges and filter cakes from gas treatment
10 05 08*	wastes from cooling-water treatment containing oil
10 05 09	wastes from cooling-water treatment other than those mentioned in 10 05 08
10 05 10*	dross and skimmings that are flammable or emit, upon contact with water, flammable gases in dangerous quantities
10 05 11	dross and skimmings other than those mentioned in 10 05 10
10 05 99	wastes not otherwise specified

10 06 wastes from copper thermal metallurgy

10 06 01	dross and skimmings from primary and secondary production
10 06 02	slags from primary and secondary production
10 06 03*	flue-gas dust
10 06 04	other particulates and dust
10 06 06*	solid wastes from gas treatment
10 06 07*	sludges and filter cakes from gas treatment
10 06 09*	wastes from cooling-water treatment containing oil
10 06 10	wastes from cooling-water treatment other than those mentioned in 10 06 09
10 06 99	wastes not otherwise specified

10 07 wastes from silver, gold and platinum thermal metallurgy

10 07 01	slags from primary and secondary production
10 07 02	dross and skimmings from primary and secondary production
10 07 03	solid wastes from gas treatment
10 07 04	other particulates and dust
10 07 05	sludges and filter cakes from gas treatment
10 07 07*	wastes from cooling-water treatment containing oil
10 07 08	wastes from cooling-water treatment other than those mentioned in 10 07 07
10 07 99	wastes not otherwise specified

10 08 wastes from other non-ferrous thermal metallurgy

10 08 04*	particulates and dust
10 08 08*	salt slag from primary and secondary production
10 08 09	other slags
10 08 10*	dross and skimmings that are flammable or emit, upon contact with water, flammable gases in dangerous quantities
10 08 11	dross and skimmings other than those mentioned in 10 08 10
10 08 12*	tar-containing wastes from anode manufacture
10 08 13	carbon-containing wastes from anode manufacture other than those mentioned in 10 08 12
10 08 14	anode scrap
10 08 15*	flue-gas dust containing dangerous substances
10 08 16	flue-gas dust other than those mentioned in 10 08 15
10 08 17*	sludges and filter cakes from flue-gas treatment containing dangerous substances
10 08 18	sludges and filter cakes from flue-gas treatment other than those mentioned in 10 08 17
10 08 19*	wastes from cooling-water treatment containing oil
10 08 20	wastes from cooling-water treatment other than those mentioned in 10 08 19
10 08 99	wastes not otherwise specified

10 09 wastes from casting of ferrous pieces

10 09 03	furnace slag
10 09 05*	casting cores and moulds which have not undergone pouring containing dangerous substances
10 09 06	casting cores and moulds which have not undergone pouring other than those mentioned in 10 09 05

10 09 07* casting cores and moulds which have undergone pouring containing dangerous substances
10 09 08 casting cores and moulds which have undergone pouring other than those mentioned in 10 09 07
10 09 09* flue-gas dust containing dangerous substances
10 09 10 flue-gas dust other than those mentioned in 10 09 09
10 09 11* other particulates containing dangerous substances
10 09 12 other particulates other than those mentioned in 10 09 11
10 09 13* waste binders containing dangerous substances
10 09 14 waste binders other than those mentioned in 10 09 13
10 09 15* waste crack-indicating agent containing dangerous substances
10 09 16 waste crack-indicating agent other than those mentioned in 10 09 15
10 09 99 wastes not otherwise specified

10 10 wastes from casting of non-ferrous pieces
10 10 03 furnace slag
10 10 05* casting cores and moulds which have not undergone pouring containing dangerous substances
10 10 06 casting cores and moulds which have not undergone pouring other than those mentioned in 10 10 05
10 10 07* casting cores and moulds which have undergone pouring containing dangerous substances
10 10 08 casting cores and moulds which have undergone pouring other than those mentioned in 10 10 07
10 10 09* flue-gas dust containing dangerous substances
10 10 10 flue-gas dust other than those mentioned in 10 10 09
10 10 11* other particulates containing dangerous substances
10 10 12 other particulates other than those mentioned in 10 10 11
10 10 13* waste binders containing dangerous substances
10 10 14 waste binders other than those mentioned in 10 10 13
10 10 15* waste crack-indicating agent containing dangerous substances
10 10 16 waste crack-indicating agent other than those mentioned in 10 10 15
10 10 99 wastes not otherwise specified

10 11 wastes from manufacture of glass and glass products
10 11 03 waste glass-based fibrous materials
10 11 05 particulates and dust
10 11 09* waste preparation mixture before thermal processing containing dangerous substances
10 11 10 waste preparation mixture before thermal processing other than those mentioned in 10 11 09
10 11 11* waste glass in small particles and glass powder containing heavy metals (e.g. from cathode ray tubes)
10 11 12 waste glass other than those mentioned in 10 11 11
10 11 13* glass-polishing and -grinding sludge containing dangerous substances
10 11 14 glass-polishing and -grinding sludge other than those mentioned in 10 11 13
10 11 15* solid wastes from flue-gas treatment containing dangerous substances
10 11 16 solid wastes from flue-gas treatment other than those mentioned in 10 11 15
10 11 17* sludges and filter cakes from flue-gas treatment containing dangerous substances
10 11 18 sludges and filter cakes from flue-gas treatment other than those mentioned in 10 11 17
10 11 19* solid wastes from on-site effluent treatment containing dangerous substances
10 11 20 solid wastes from on-site effluent treatment other than those mentioned in 10 11 19
10 11 99 wastes not otherwise specified

10 12 wastes from manufacture of ceramic goods, bricks, tiles and construction products

10 12 01 waste preparation mixture before thermal processing
10 12 03 particulates and dust
10 12 05 sludges and filter cakes from gas treatment
10 12 06 discarded molds
10 12 08 waste ceramics, bricks, tiles and construction products (after thermal processing)
10 12 09* solid wastes from gas treatment containing dangerous substances
10 12 10 solid wastes from gas treatment other than those mentioned in 10 12 09
10 12 11* wastes from glazing containing heavy metals
10 12 12 wastes from glazing other than those mentioned in 10 12 11
10 12 13 sludge from on-site effluent treatment
10 12 99 wastes not otherwise specified

10 13 wastes from manufacture of cement, lime and plaster and articles and products made from them
10 13 01 waste preparation mixture before thermal processing
10 13 04 wastes from calcination and hydration of lime
10 13 06 particulates and dust (except 10 13 12 and 10 13 13)
10 13 07 sludges and filter cakes from gas treatment
10 13 09* wastes from asbestos-cement manufacture containing asbestos
10 13 10 wastes from asbestos-cement manufacture other than those mentioned in 10 13 09
10 13 11 wastes from cement-based composite materials other than those mentioned in 10 13 09 and 10 13 10
10 13 12* solid wastes from gas treatment containing dangerous substances
10 13 13 solid wastes from gas treatment other than those mentioned in 10 13 12
10 13 14 waste concrete and concrete sludge
10 13 99 wastes not otherwise specified

10 14 waste from crematoria
10 14 01* waste from gas cleaning containing mercury

11 Wastes from chemical surface treatment and coating of metals and other materials; non-ferrous hydro-metallurgy

11 01 wastes from chemical surface treatment and coating of metals and other materials (e.g. galvanic processes, zinc coating processes, pickling processes, etching, phosphatising, alkaline degreasing, anodising)
11 01 05* pickling acids
11 01 06* acids not otherwise specified
11 01 07* pickling bases
11 01 08* phosphatising sludges
11 01 09* sludges and filter cakes containing dangerous substances
11 01 10 sludges and filter cakes other than those mentioned in 11 01 09
11 01 11* aqueous rinsing liquids containing dangerous substances
11 01 12 aqueous rinsing liquids other than those mentioned in 11 01 11
11 01 13* degreasing wastes containing dangerous substances
11 01 14 degreasing wastes other than those mentioned in 11 01 13
11 01 15* eluate and sludges from membrane systems or ion exchange systems containing dangerous substances
11 01 16* saturated or spent ion exchange resins
11 01 98* other wastes containing dangerous substances
11 01 99 wastes not otherwise specified

11 02 wastes from non-ferrous hydrometallurgical processes
11 02 02* sludges from zinc hydrometallurgy (including Jarosite, goethite)
11 02 03 wastes from the production of anodes for aqueous electrolytical processes

11 02 05* wastes from copper hydrometallurgical processes containing dangerous substances
11 02 06 wastes from copper hydrometallurgical processes other than those mentioned in 11 02 05
11 02 07* other wastes containing dangerous substances
11 02 99 wastes not otherwise specified

11 03 sludges and solids from tempering processes
11 03 01* wastes containing cyanide
11 03 02* other wastes

11 05 wastes from hot galvanising processes
11 05 01 hard zinc
11 05 02 zinc ash
11 05 03* solid wastes from gas treatment
11 05 04* spent flux
11 05 99 wastes not otherwise specified

12 Wastes from shaping and physical and mechanical surface treatment of metals and plastics

12 01 wastes from shaping and physical and mechanical surface treatment of metals and plastics
12 01 01 ferrous metal filings and turnings
12 01 02 ferrous metal dust and particles
12 01 03 non-ferrous metal filings and turnings
12 01 04 non-ferrous metal dust and particles
12 01 05 plastics shavings and turnings
12 01 06* mineral-based machining oils containing halogens (except emulsions and solutions)
12 01 07* mineral-based machining oils free of halogens (except emulsions and solutions)
12 01 08* machining emulsions and solutions containing halogens
12 01 09* machining emulsions and solutions free of halogens
12 01 10* synthetic machining oils
12 01 12* spent waxes and fats
12 01 13 welding wastes
12 01 14* machining sludges containing dangerous substances
12 01 15 machining sludges other than those mentioned in 12 01 14
12 01 16* waste blasting material containing dangerous substances
12 01 17 waste blasting material other than those mentioned in 12 01 16
12 01 18* metal sludge (grinding, honing and lapping sludge) containing oil
12 01 19* readily biodegradable machining oil
12 01 20* spent grinding bodies and grinding materials containing dangerous substances
12 01 21 spent grinding bodies and grinding materials other than those mentioned in 12 01 20
12 01 99 wastes not otherwise specified

12 03 wastes from water and steam degreasing processes (except 11)
12 03 01* aqueous washing liquids
12 03 02* steam degreasing wastes

13 Oil wastes and wastes of liquid fuels (except edible oils, and those in chapters 05, 12 and 19)

13 01 waste hydraulic oils
13 01 01* hydraulic oils, containing PCBs
13 01 04* chlorinated emulsions
13 01 05* non-chlorinated emulsions

13 01 09* mineral-based chlorinated hydraulic oils
13 01 10* mineral based non-chlorinated hydraulic oils
13 01 11* synthetic hydraulic oils
13 01 12* readily biodegradable hydraulic oils
13 01 13* other hydraulic oils

13 02 waste engine, gear and lubricating oils
13 02 04* mineral-based chlorinated engine, gear and lubricating oils
13 02 05* mineral-based non-chlorinated engine, gear and lubricating oils
13 02 06* synthetic engine, gear and lubricating oils
13 02 07* readily biodegradable engine, gear and lubricating oils
13 02 08* other engine, gear and lubricating oils

13 03 waste insulating and heat transmission oils
13 03 01* insulating or heat transmission oils containing PCBs
13 03 06* mineral-based chlorinated insulating and heat transmission oils other than those mentioned in 13 03 01
13 03 07* mineral-based non-chlorinated insulating and heat transmission oils
13 03 08* synthetic insulating and heat transmission oils
13 03 09* readily biodegradable insulating and heat transmission oils
13 03 10* other insulating and heat transmission oils

13 04 bilge oils
13 04 01* bilge oils from inland navigation
13 04 02* bilge oils from jetty sewers
13 04 03* bilge oils from other navigation

13 05 oil/water separator contents
13 05 01* solids from grit chambers and oil/water separators
13 05 02* sludges from oil/water separators
13 05 03* interceptor sludges
13 05 06* oil from oil/water separators
13 05 07* oily water from oil/water separators
13 05 08* mixtures of wastes from grit chambers and oil/water separators

13 07 wastes of liquid fuels
13 07 01* fuel oil and diesel
13 07 02* petrol
13 07 03* other fuels (including mixtures)

13 08 oil wastes not otherwise specified
13 08 01* desalter sludges or emulsions
13 08 02* other emulsions
13 08 99* wastes not otherwise specified

14 Waste organic solvents, refrigerants and propellants (except 07 and 08)

14 06 waste organic solvents, refrigerants and foam/aerosol propellants
14 06 01* chlorofluorocarbons, HCFC, HFC
14 06 02* other halogenated solvents and solvent mixtures
14 06 03* other solvents and solvent mixtures
14 06 04* sludges or solid wastes containing halogenated solvents
14 06 05* sludges or solid wastes containing other solvents

15 Waste packaging, absorbents, wiping cloths, filter materials and protective clothing not otherwise specified

15 01 packaging (including separately collected municipal packaging waste)
15 01 01 paper and cardboard packaging

15 01 02 plastic packaging
15 01 03 wooden packaging
15 01 04 metallic packaging
15 01 05 composite packaging
15 01 06 mixed packaging
15 01 07 glass packaging
15 01 09 textile packaging
15 01 10* packaging containing residues of or contaminated by dangerous substances
15 01 11* metallic packaging containing a dangerous solid porous matrix (e.g. asbestos), including empty pressure containers

15 02 absorbents, filter materials, wiping cloths and protective clothing
15 02 02* absorbents, filter materials (including oil filters not otherwise specified), wiping cloths, protective clothing contaminated by dangerous substances
15 02 03 absorbents, filter materials, wiping cloths and protective clothing other than those mentioned in 15 02 02

16 Wastes not otherwise specified in the list

16 01 end-of-life vehicles from different means of transport (including off-road machinery) and wastes from dismantling of end-of-life vehicles and vehicle maintenance (except 13, 14, 16 06 and 16 08)
16 01 03 end-of-life tyres
16 01 04* end-of-life vehicles
16 01 06 end-of-life vehicles, containing neither liquids nor other hazardous components
16 01 07* oil filters
16 01 08* components containing mercury
16 01 09* components containing PCBs
16 01 10* explosive components (e.g. air bags)
16 01 11* brake pads containing asbestos
16 01 12 brake pads other than those mentioned in 16 01 11
16 01 13* brake fluids
16 01 14* antifreeze fluids containing dangerous substances
16 01 15 antifreeze fluids other than those mentioned in 16 01 14
16 01 16 tanks for liquefied gas
16 01 17 ferrous metal
16 01 18 non-ferrous metal
16 01 19 plastic
16 01 20 glass
16 01 21* hazardous components other than those mentioned in 16 01 07 to 16 01 11 and 16 01 13 and 16 01 14
16 01 22 components not otherwise specified
16 01 99 wastes not otherwise specified

16 02 wastes from electrical and electronic equipment
16 02 09* transformers and capacitors containing PCBs
16 02 10* discarded equipment containing or contaminated by PCBs other than those mentioned in 16 02 09
16 02 11* discarded equipment containing chlorofluorocarbons, HCFC, HFC
16 02 12* discarded equipment containing free asbestos
16 02 13* discarded equipment containing hazardous components other than those mentioned in 16 02 09 to 16 02 12
16 02 14 discarded equipment other than those mentioned in 16 02 09 to 16 02 13
16 02 15* hazardous components removed from discarded equipment
16 02 16 components removed from discarded equipment other than those mentioned in 16 02 15

16 03 off-specification batches and unused products
16 03 03* inorganic wastes containing dangerous substances
16 03 04 inorganic wastes other than those mentioned in 16 03 03
16 03 05* organic wastes containing dangerous substances
16 03 06 organic wastes other than those mentioned in 16 03 05

16 04 waste explosives
16 04 01* waste ammunition
16 04 02* fireworks wastes
16 04 03* other waste explosives

16 05 gases in pressure containers and discarded chemicals
16 05 04* gases in pressure containers (including halons) containing dangerous substances
16 05 05 gases in pressure containers other than those mentioned in 16 05 04
16 05 06* laboratory chemicals consisting of or containing dangerous substances including mixtures of laboratory chemicals
16 05 07* discarded inorganic chemicals consisting of or containing dangerous substances
16 05 08* discarded organic chemicals consisting of or containing dangerous substances
16 05 09 discarded chemicals other than those mentioned in 16 05 06, 16 05 07 or 16 05 08

16 06 batteries and accumulators
16 06 01* lead batteries
16 06 02* Ni-Cd batteries
16 06 03* mercury-containing batteries
16 06 04 alkaline batteries (except 16 06 03)
16 06 05 other batteries and accumulators
16 06 06* separately collected electrolyte from batteries and accumulators

16 07 wastes from transport tank, storage tank and barrel cleaning (except 05 and 13)
16 07 08* wastes containing oil
16 07 09* wastes containing other dangerous substances
16 07 99 wastes not otherwise specified

16 08 spent catalysts
16 08 01 spent catalysts containing gold, silver, rhenium, rhodium, palladium, iridium or platinum (except 16 08 07)
16 08 02* spent catalysts containing dangerous transition metals or dangerous transition metal compounds
16 08 03 spent catalysts containing transition metals or transition metal compounds not otherwise specified
16 08 04 spent fluid catalytic cracking catalysts (except 16 08 07)
16 08 05* spent catalysts containing phosphoric acid
16 08 06* spent liquids used as catalysts
16 08 07* spent catalysts contaminated with dangerous substances

16 09 oxidising substances
16 09 01* permanganates, e.g. potassium permanganate
16 09 02* chromates, e.g. potassium chromate, potassium or sodium dichromate
16 09 03* peroxides, e.g. hydrogen peroxide
16 09 04* oxidising substances, not otherwise specified

16 10 aqueous liquid wastes destined for off-site treatment
16 10 01* aqueous liquid wastes containing dangerous substances
16 10 02 aqueous liquid wastes other than those mentioned in 16 10 01
16 10 03* aqueous concentrates containing dangerous substances
16 10 04 aqueous concentrates other than those mentioned in 16 10 03

16 11 waste linings and refractories

16 11 01* carbon-based linings and refractories from metallurgical processes containing dangerous substances
16 11 02 carbon-based linings and refractories from metallurgical processes others than those mentioned in 16 11 01
16 11 03* other linings and refractories from metallurgical processes containing dangerous substances
16 11 04 other linings and refractories from metallurgical processes other than those mentioned in 16 11 03
16 11 05* linings and refractories from non-metallurgical processes containing dangerous substances
16 11 06 linings and refractories from non-metallurgical processes others than those mentioned in 16 11 05

17 Construction and demolition wastes (including excavated soil from contaminated sites)

17 01 concrete, bricks, tiles and ceramics
17 01 01 concrete
17 01 02 bricks
17 01 03 tiles and ceramics
17 01 06* mixtures of, or separate fractions of concrete, bricks, tiles and ceramics containing dangerous substances
17 01 07 mixtures of concrete, bricks, tiles and ceramics other than those mentioned in 17 01 06

17 02 wood, glass and plastic
17 02 01 wood
17 02 02 glass
17 02 03 plastic
17 02 04* glass, plastic and wood containing or contaminated with dangerous substances

17 03 bituminous mixtures, coal tar and tarred products
17 03 01* bituminous mixtures containing coal tar
17 03 02 bituminous mixtures other than those mentioned in 17 03 01
17 03 03* coal tar and tarred products

17 04 metals (including their alloys)
17 04 01 copper, bronze, brass
17 04 02 aluminium
17 04 03 lead
17 04 04 zinc
17 04 05 iron and steel
17 04 06 tin
17 04 07 mixed metals
17 04 09* metal waste contaminated with dangerous substances
17 04 10* cables containing oil, coal tar and other dangerous substances
17 04 11 cables other than those mentioned in 17 04 10

17 05 soil (including excavated soil from contaminated sites), stones and dredging spoil
17 05 03* soil and stones containing dangerous substances
17 05 04 soil and stones other than those mentioned in 17 05 03
17 05 05* dredging spoil containing dangerous substances
17 05 06 dredging spoil other than those mentioned in 17 05 05
17 05 07* track ballast containing dangerous substances
17 05 08 track ballast other than those mentioned in 17 05 07

17 06 insulation materials and asbestos-containing construction materials
17 06 01* insulation materials containing asbestos
17 06 03* other insulation materials consisting of or containing dangerous substances

17 06 04 insulation materials other than those mentioned in 17 06 01 and 17 06 03
17 06 05* construction materials containing asbestos

17 08 gypsum-based construction material
17 08 01* gypsum-based construction materials contaminated with dangerous substances
17 08 02 gypsum-based construction materials other than those mentioned in 17 08 01

17 09 other construction and demolition wastes
17 09 01* construction and demolition wastes containing mercury
17 09 02* construction and demolition wastes containing PCB (e.g. PCB-containing sealants, PCB-containing resin-based floorings, PCB-containing sealed glazing units, PCB-containing capacitors)
17 09 03* other construction and demolition wastes (including mixed wastes) containing dangerous substances
17 09 04 mixed construction and demolition wastes other than those mentioned in 17 09 01, 17 09 02 and 17 09 03

18 Wastes from human or animal healthcare and/or related research (except kitchen and restaurant wastes not arising from immediate health care)

18 01 wastes from natal care, diagnosis, treatment or prevention of disease in humans
18 01 01 sharps (except 18 01 03)
18 01 02 body parts and organs including blood bags and blood preserves (except 18 01 03)
18 01 03* wastes whose collection and disposal is subject to special requirements in order to prevent infection
18 01 04 wastes whose collection and disposal is not subject to special requirements in order to prevent infection (e.g. dressings, plaster casts, linen, disposable clothing, diapers)
18 01 06* chemicals consisting of or containing dangerous substances
18 01 07 chemicals other than those mentioned in 18 01 06
18 01 08* cytotoxic and cytostatic medicines
18 01 09 medicines other than those mentioned in 18 01 08
18 01 10* amalgam waste from dental care

18 02 wastes from research, diagnosis, treatment or prevention of disease involving animals
18 02 01 sharps (except 18 02 02)
18 02 02* wastes whose collection and disposal is subject to special requirements in order to prevent infection
18 02 03 wastes whose collection and disposal is not subject to special requirements in order to prevent infection
18 02 05* chemicals consisting of or containing dangerous substances
18 02 06 chemicals other than those mentioned in 18 02 05
18 02 07* cytotoxic and cytostatic medicines
18 02 08 medicines other than those mentioned in 18 02 07

19 Wastes from waste management facilities, off-site waste water treatment plants and the preparation of water intended for human consumption and water for industrial use

19 01 wastes from incineration or pyrolysis of waste
19 01 02 ferrous materials removed from bottom ash
19 01 05* filter cake from gas treatment
19 01 06* aqueous liquid wastes from gas treatment and other aqueous liquid wastes
19 01 07* solid wastes from gas treatment
19 01 10* spent activated carbon from flue-gas treatment
19 01 11* bottom ash and slag containing dangerous substances
19 01 12 bottom ash and slag other than those mentioned in 19 01 11
19 01 13* fly ash containing dangerous substances

19 01 14 fly ash other than those mentioned in 19 01 13
19 01 15* boiler dust containing dangerous substances
19 01 16 boiler dust other than those mentioned in 19 01 15
19 01 17* pyrolysis wastes containing dangerous substances
19 01 18 pyrolysis wastes other than those mentioned in 19 01 17
19 01 19 sands from fluidised beds
19 01 99 wastes not otherwise specified

19 02 wastes from physico/chemical treatments of waste (including dechromatation, decyanidation, neutralisation)
19 02 03 premixed wastes composed only of non hazardous wastes
19 02 04* premixed wastes composed of at least one hazardous waste
19 02 05* sludges from physico/chemical treatment containing dangerous substances
19 02 06 sludges from physico/chemical treatment other than those mentioned in 19 02 05
19 02 07* oil and concentrates from separation
19 02 08* liquid combustible wastes containing dangerous substances
19 02 09* solid combustible wastes containing dangerous substances
19 02 10 combustible wastes other than those mentioned in 19 02 08 and 19 02 09
19 02 11* other wastes containing dangerous substances
19 02 99 wastes not otherwise specified

19 03 stabilised/solidified wastes
19 03 04* wastes marked as hazardous, partly stabilised
19 03 05 stabilised wastes other than those mentioned in 19 03 04
19 03 06* wastes marked as hazardous, solidified
19 03 07 solidified wastes other than those mentioned in 19 03 06

19 04 vitrified waste and wastes from vitrification
19 04 01 vitrified waste
19 04 02* fly ash and other flue-gas treatment wastes
19 04 03* non-vitrified solid phase
19 04 04 aqueous liquid wastes from vitrified waste tempering

19 05 wastes from aerobic treatment of solid wastes
19 05 01 non-composted fraction of municipal and similar wastes
19 05 02 non-composted fraction of animal and vegetable waste
19 05 03 off-specification compost
19 05 99 wastes not otherwise specified

19 06 wastes from anaerobic treatment of waste
19 06 03 liquor from anaerobic treatment of municipal waste
19 06 04 digestate from anaerobic treatment of municipal waste
19 06 05 liquor from anaerobic treatment of animal and vegetable waste
19 06 06 digestate from anaerobic treatment of animal and vegetable waste
19 06 99 wastes not otherwise specified

19 07 landfill leachate
19 07 02* landfill leachate containing dangerous substances
19 07 03 landfill leachate other than those mentioned in 19 07 02

19 08 wastes from waste water treatment plants not otherwise specified
19 08 01 screenings
19 08 02 waste from desanding
19 08 05 sludges from treatment of urban waste water
19 08 06* saturated or spent ion exchange resins
19 08 07* solutions and sludges from regeneration of ion exchangers
19 08 08* membrane system waste containing heavy metals
19 08 09 grease and oil mixture from oil/water separation containing only edible oil and fats

19 08 10* grease and oil mixture from oil/water separation other than those mentioned in 19 08 09
19 08 11* sludges containing dangerous substances from biological treatment of industrial waste water
19 08 12 sludges from biological treatment of industrial waste water other than those mentioned in 19 08 11
19 08 13* sludges containing dangerous substances from other treatment of industrial waste water
19 08 14 sludges from other treatment of industrial waste water other than those mentioned in 19 08 13
19 08 99 wastes not otherwise specified

19 09 wastes from the preparation of water intended for human consumption or water for industrial use
19 09 01 solid waste from primary filtration and screenings
19 09 02 sludges from water clarification
19 09 03 sludges from decarbonation
19 09 04 spent activated carbon
19 09 05 saturated or spent ion exchange resins
19 09 06 solutions and sludges from regeneration of ion exchangers
19 09 99 wastes not otherwise specified

19 10 wastes from shredding of metal-containing wastes
19 10 01 iron and steel waste
19 10 02 non-ferrous waste
19 10 03* fluff — light fraction and dust containing dangerous substances
19 10 04 fluff — light fraction and dust other than those mentioned in 19 10 03
19 10 05* other fractions containing dangerous substances
19 10 06 other fractions other than those mentioned in 19 10 05

19 11 wastes from oil regeneration
19 11 01* spent filter clays
19 11 02* acid tars
19 11 03* aqueous liquid wastes
19 11 04* wastes from cleaning of fuel with bases
19 11 05* sludges from on-site effluent treatment containing dangerous substances
19 11 06 sludges from on-site effluent treatment other than those mentioned in 19 11 05
19 11 07* wastes from flue-gas cleaning
19 11 99 wastes not otherwise specified

19 12 wastes from the mechanical treatment of waste (e.g. sorting, crushing, compacting, pelletising) not otherwise specified
19 12 01 paper and cardboard
19 12 02 ferrous metal
19 12 03 non-ferrous metal
19 12 04 plastic and rubber
19 12 05 glass
19 12 06* wood containing dangerous substances
19 12 07 wood other than that mentioned in 19 12 06
19 12 08 textiles
19 12 09 minerals (e.g. sand, stones)
19 12 10 combustible waste (refuse derived fuel)
19 12 11* other wastes (including mixtures of materials) from mechanical treatment of waste containing dangerous substances
19 12 12 other wastes (including mixtures of materials) from mechanical treatment of wastes other than those mentioned in 19 12 11

19 13 wastes from soil and groundwater remediation

19 13 01* solid wastes from soil remediation containing dangerous substances
19 13 02 solid wastes from soil remediation other than those mentioned in 19 13 01
19 13 03* sludges from soil remediation containing dangerous substances
19 13 04 sludges from soil remediation other than those mentioned in 19 13 03
19 13 05* sludges from groundwater remediation containing dangerous substances
19 13 06 sludges from groundwater remediation other than those mentioned in 19 13 05
19 13 07* aqueous liquid wastes and aqueous concentrates from groundwater remediation containing dangerous substances
19 13 08 aqueous liquid wastes and aqueous concentrates from groundwater remediation other than those mentioned in 19 13 07

20 Municipal wastes (household waste and similar commercial, industrial and institutional wastes) including separately collected fractions

20 01 separately collected fractions (except 15 01)
20 01 01 paper and cardboard
20 01 02 glass
20 01 08 biodegradable kitchen and canteen waste
20 01 10 clothes
20 01 11 textiles
20 01 13* solvents
20 01 14* acids
20 01 15* alkalines
20 01 17* photochemicals
20 01 19* pesticides
20 01 21* fluorescent tubes and other mercury-containing waste
20 01 23* discarded equipment containing chlorofluorocarbons
20 01 25 edible oil and fat
20 01 26* oil and fat other than those mentioned in 20 01 25
20 01 27* paint, inks, adhesives and resins containing dangerous substances
20 01 28 paint, inks, adhesives and resins other than those mentioned in 20 01 27
20 01 29* detergents containing dangerous substances
20 01 30 detergents other than those mentioned in 20 01 29
20 01 31* cytotoxic and cytostatic medicines
20 01 32 medicines other than those mentioned in 20 01 31
20 01 33* batteries and accumulators included in 16 06 01, 16 06 02 or 16 06 03 and unsorted batteries and accumulators containing these batteries
20 01 34 batteries and accumulators other than those mentioned in 20 01 33
20 01 35* discarded electrical and electronic equipment other than those mentioned in 20 01 21 and 20 01 23 containing hazardous components
20 01 36 discarded electrical and electronic equipment other than those mentioned in 20 01 21, 20 01 23 and 20 01 35
20 01 37* wood containing dangerous substances
20 01 38 wood other than that mentioned in 20 01 37
20 01 39 plastics
20 01 40 metals
20 01 41 wastes from chimney sweeping
20 01 99 other fractions not otherwise specified

20 02 garden and park wastes (including cemetery waste)
20 02 01 biodegradable waste
20 02 02 soil and stones
20 02 03 other non-biodegradable wastes

20 03 other municipal wastes
20 03 01 mixed municipal waste
20 03 02 waste from markets

20 03 03 street-cleaning residues
20 03 04 septic tank sludge
20 03 06 waste from sewage cleaning
20 03 07 bulky waste
20 03 99 municipal wastes not otherwise specified

PART 3

List A (Annex II to the Basel Convention)

Y46 Waste collected from households

Y47 Residues arising from the incineration of household wastes

List B (Waste from Appendix 4, Part II of the OECD Decision

Metal bearing wastes		
[AA 010	261900	Dross, scalings and other wastes from the iron and steel industry][1]
AA 060	262050	Vanadium ashes and residues
AA 190	810420 ex 810430	Magnesium waste and scrap that is flammable, pyrophoric or emits, upon contact with water, flammable gases in dangerous quantities
Wastes containing principally inorganic constituents, which may contain metals and organic materials		
AB 030		Wastes from non-cyanide based systems which arise from surface treatment of metals
AB 070		Sands used in foundry operations
AB 120	ex 281290 ex 3824	Inorganic halide compounds, not elsewhere specified or included I
AB150	ex 382490	Unrefined calcium sulphite and calcium sulphate from flue gas desulphurisation (FGD)
Wastes containing principally organic constituents, which may contain metals and inorganic materials		
AC060	ex 381900	Hydraulic fluids
AC070	ex 382000	Antifreeze fluids
AC080	ex 381900	Brake fluids
AC150		Chlorofluorocarbons
AC160		Halons
AC170	ex 440310	Treated cork and wood wastes
Wastes which may contain either inorganic or organic constituents		
AD090	ex 382490	Wastes from production, formulation and use of reprographic and photographic chemicals and materials not elsewhere specified or included
AD100		Wastes from non-cyanide based systems which arise from surface treatment of plastics
AD120	ex 391400 ex 3915	Ion exchange resins
AD150		Naturally occurring organic material used as a filter medium (such as bio-filters)
Wastes containing principally inorganic constituents, which may contain metals and organic materials		
RB020	ex 6815	Ceramic based fibres of physico-chemical characteristics similar to those of asbestos

Amendment

1 Substituted by Commission Regulation (EU) No 413/2010 of 12 May 2010 amending Annexes III, IV and V to Regulation (EC) No 1013/2006 of the European Parliament and of the Council on shipments of waste so as to take account of changes adopted by OECD Council Decision C (2008) 156, Article 1, Annex, para 3.

[ANNEX VI FORM FOR PRE-CONSENTED FACILITIES (ARTICLE 14)][1]

[

Competent authority	Recovery facility				Waste identification	Period of validity		Total pre-consented quantity
	Name and number of the recovery facility	Address	Recovery operation (+ R-code)	Technologies employed	(code)	from	to	(tonnes (Mg))

][1]

Amendments

1 Substituted by Commission Regulation (EC) No 308/2009 of 15 April 2009 amending, for the purposes of adaptation to scientific and technical progress, Annexes IIIA and VI to Regulation (EC) No 1013/2006 of the European Parliament and of the Council on shipments of waste, Article 1, Annex, para 2.

[ANNEX VII INFORMATION ACCOMPANYING SHIPMENTS OF WASTE AS REFERRED TO IN ARTICLE 3(2) AND (4)][1]

[

Consignment information (1)

1. Person who arranges the shipment Name: Address: Contact person: Tel.: Fax: E-mail:	**2. Importer/consignee** Name: Address: Contact person: Tel.: Fax: E-mail:
3. Actual quantity: Tonnes (Mg): m^3:	**4. Actual date of shipment:**

5.(a) First carrier (2): Name: Address: Contact person: Tel.: Fax: E-mail: Means of transport: Date of transfer: Signature:	**5.(b) Second carrier:** Name: Address: Contact person: Tel.: Fax: E-mail: Means of transport: Date of transfer: Signature:	**5.(c) Third carrier:** Name: Address: Contact person: Tel.: Fax: E-mail: Means of transport: Date of transfer: Signature:

6. Waste generator (3) **Original producer(s), new producer(s) or collector:** Name: Address: Contact person: Tel.: Fax: E-mail:	**8. Recovery operation (or if appropriate disposal operation in the case of waste referred to in Article 3(4)):** R-code/D-code: **9. Usual description of the waste:**
7. Recovery facility ☐ **Laboratory** ☐ Name: Address: Contact person: Tel.: Fax: E-mail:	**10. Waste identification** *(fill in relevant codes)*: (i) Basel Annex IX: (ii) OECD *(if different from (i))*: (iii) EC list of wastes: (iv) National code:

11. Countries/States concerned:

Export/dispatch	Transit			Import/destination

12. Declaration of the person who arranges the shipment: I certify that the above information is complete and correct to my best knowledge. I also certify that effective written contractual obligations have been entered into with the consignee *(not required in the case of waste referred to in Article 3(4))*:

Name: Date: Signature:

13. Signature upon receipt of the waste by the consignee:

Name: Date: Signature:

TO BE COMPLETED BY THE RECOVERY FACILITY OR BY THE LABORATORY:

14. Shipment received at recovery facility ☐ **or laboratory** ☐ Quantity received: Tonnes (Mg): m^3:

Name: Date: Signature:

(1) Information accompanying shipments of green listed waste and destined for recovery or waste destined for laboratory analysis pursuant to Regulation (EC) No 1013/2006. For completing this document, see also the corresponding specific instructions as contained in Annex IC of Regulation (EC) No 1013/2006.
(2) If more than three carriers, attach information as required in blocks 5 (a), (b), (c).
(3) When the person who arranges the shipment is not the producer or collector, information about the producer or collector shall be provided.'

][1]

Amendment

1 Substituted by Commission Regulation (EC) No 1379/2007 of 26 November 2007 amending Annexes IA, IB, VII and VIII of Regulation (EC) No 1013/2006 of the European Parliament and of the Council on shipments of waste, for the purposes of taking account of technical progress and changes agreed under the Basel Convention, Article 1, Annex III.

[ANNEX VIII
GUIDELINES ON ENVIRONMENTALLY SOUND MANAGEMENT (ARTICLE 49)][1]

[I. Guidelines adopted under the Basel Convention:

1. Technical Guidelines on the Environmentally Sound Management of Biomedical and Health Care Wastes (Y1; Y3);
2. Technical Guidelines on the Environmentally Sound Management of Waste Lead Acid Batteries;
3. Technical Guidelines on the Environmentally Sound Management of the Full and Partial Dismantling of Ships;
4. Technical Guidelines on the Environmentally Sound Recycling/Reclamation of Metals and Metal Compounds (R4);
5. Updated General Technical Guidelines for the Environmentally Sound Management of Wastes Consisting of, Containing or Contaminated with Persistent Organic Pollutants (POPs);
6. Updated Technical Guidelines for the Environmentally Sound Management of Wastes Consisting of, Containing or Contaminated with Polychlorinated Biphenyls (PCBs), Polychlorinated Terphenyls (PCTs) or Polybrominated Biphenyls (PBBs);
7. Technical Guidelines for the Environmentally Sound Management of Wastes Consisting of, Containing or Contaminated with the Pesticides Aldrin, Chlordane, Dieldrin, Endrin, Heptachlor, Hexachlorobenzene (HCB), Mirex or Toxaphene or with HCB as an Industrial Chemical;
8. Technical Guidelines for the Environmentally Sound Management of Wastes Consisting of, Containing or Contaminated with 1,1,1-trichloro-2,2-bis (4 chlorophenyl)ethane (DDT);
9. Technical Guidelines for the Environmentally Sound Management of Wastes Containing or Contaminated with Unintentionally Produced Polychlorinated Dibenzo-p-dioxins (PCDDs), Polychlorinated Dibenzofurans (PCDFs), Hexachlorobenzene (HCB) or Polychlorinated Biphenyls (PCBs).

II. Guidelines adopted by the OECD:

Technical guidance for the environmentally sound management of specific waste streams:

Used and scrap personal computers.

III. Guidelines adopted by the International Maritime Organisation (IMO):

Guidelines on ship recycling.

IV. Guidelines adopted by the International Labour Organisation (ILO):

Safety and health in shipbreaking: guidelines for Asian countries and Turkey.]1

Amendment

1 Substituted by Commission Regulation (EC) No 1379/2007 of 26 November 2007 amending Annexes IA, IB, VII and VIII of Regulation (EC) No 1013/2006 of the European Parliament and of the Council on shipments of waste, for the purposes of taking account of technical progress and changes agreed under the Basel Convention, Article 1, Annex IV.

ANNEX IX
ADDITONAL QUESTIONNAIRE FOR REPORTS BY MEMBER STATES PURSUANT TO ARTICLE 51(2)

Article 11(1)(a)	**Information on the measures taken to prohibit generally or partially shipments of waste between Member States** **In order to implement the principles of proximity, priority for recovery and self-sufficiency at Community and national levels in accordance with Directive 2006/12/EC** Has this provision been applied? Yes ☐ No ☐ *(please tick ✓ as appropriate)* If yes, please provide details of the measures taken: …………………………………… …………………………………… …………………………………… …………………………………… Additional remarks: …………………………………… …………………………………… …………………………………… …………………………………… **Information on the measures taken to object systematically to shipments of waste between Member States** **In order to implement the principles of proximity, priority for recovery and self-sufficiency at Community and national levels in accordance with Directive 2006/12/EC** Has this provision been applied? Yes ☐ No ☐ *(please tick ✓ as appropriate)* If yes, please provide details of the measures taken: …………………………………… …………………………………… …………………………………… …………………………………… Additional remarks: …………………………………… …………………………………… …………………………………… ……………………………………
Article 11(1)(e)	**Information on the prohibition of the import of waste** Has this provision been applied? Yes ☐ No ☐ *(please tick ✓ as appropriate)* If yes, please provide details of the measures taken: …………………………………… …………………………………… …………………………………… ……………………………………

Article 11(3)	**Information on exceptions to the implementation of the principle of proximity, priority for recovery and self-sufficiency** **In the case of hazardous waste produced in a Member State of dispatch in such a small quantity overall per year that the provision of new specialised disposal installations within that State would be uneconomic** Have you asked any Member State to apply this exception? Yes ☐ No ☐ *(please tick ✓ as appropriate)* If yes, please complete Table 1 and give details below of any bilateral solution found pursuant to Article 11(3): .... Have you received any request from Member States to apply this exception? Yes ☐ No ☐ *(please tick ✓ as appropriate)* If yes, please complete Table 1 and give details below of any bilateral solution found pursuant to Article 11(3): ....
Article 11(1)(g)	**Information on objections to planned shipments or disposal on the basis of their not being in accordance with Directive 2006/12/EC** Has this provision been applied? Yes ☐ No ☐ *(please tick ✓ as appropriate)* If yes, please complete Table 2.
Article 12(5)	**Information on objections to planned shipments or recovery on the basis of their not being in accordance with Article 12(1)(c)** Has this provision been applied? Yes ☐ No ☐ *(please tick ✓ as appropriate)* If yes, please complete Table 3.
Article 14	**Information on decisions by competent authorities having jurisdiction over specific recovery facilities to issue pre-consents to such facilities** Has there been any case? Yes ☐ No ☐ *(please tick ✓ as appropriate)* If yes, please complete Table 4.

Article 33	**Information on the Member States' system for the supervision and control of shipments of waste exclusively within their jurisdiction** Is there a system for the supervision and control of shipments of waste within the jurisdiction? Yes ☐ No ☐ *(please tick ✓ as appropriate)* If there is such a system, do you apply the system provided for in Titles II and VII of the Regulation? Yes ☐ No ☐ *(please tick ✓ as appropriate)* If you apply a different system from that provided for in Titles II and VII of the Regulation, please give details of the system applied: ... ...
Article 24 and Article 50(1)	**Information on illegal shipments of waste** Has there been any case? Yes ☐ No ☐ *(please tick ✓ as appropriate)* If yes, please complete Table 5. Please provide information on how illegal shipments of waste are prevented, detected and penalised under national legislation: ... ...
Article 50(2)	**Information on spot checks on shipments of waste or on the related recovery or disposal** Number of checks on shipments of waste or on the related recovery or disposal: Number of supposed illegal shipments ascertained during these checks: Additional remarks: ... ...
Article 6	**Information on a financial guarantee or equivalent insurance covering costs for transport, recovery or disposal and storage of waste, including cases referred to in Articles 22 and 24** Please provide details on the provisions of national law adopted pursuant to this Article: ... ...
Article 55	**Information on any customs offices designated by Member States for shipments of waste entering and leaving the Community** Has there been any designation? Yes ☐ No ☐ *(please tick ✓ as appropriate)* If yes, please complete Table 6.

Note for completion of the tables:

D codes and R codes are those referred to in Annexes IIA and IIB to Directive 2006/12/EC.

Waste identification codes are those referred to in Annexes III, IIIA, IIIB, IV and IVA to this Regulation.

Table 1

Information on exceptions to the implementation of the principles of proximity, priority for recovery and self-sufficiency (Article 11(3))

Waste identification (code)	Quantity (kg/litres)	Country of destination (De)/ country of dispatch (Di)	Disposal operation D code	Referral of the matter to the Commission (Yes/No)

Table 2

Objections to planned shipments or disposal (Article 11(1)(g))

Waste identification (code)	Quantity (kg/litres)	Country of transit (T)/ country of dispatch (Di)	Reasons for the objection (please tick ✓ as appropriate)			Inrichting	
			Article 11(1)(g)(i)	Article 11(1)(g)(ii)	Article 11(1)(g)(iii)	Name (in case of Article 11(1)(g)(ii))	Disposal operation D code

Table 3

Objections to planned shipments or recovery (Article 12(1)(c))

Waste identification (code)	Quantity (kg/litres)	Country of destination	Reasons for the objection *and details of relevant national legislation*	Facility *(in the country of destination)*	
				Name	Recovery operation R code

Table 4

Information on decisions by competent authorities to issue pre-consents (Article 14)

Competent authority	Recovery facility				Waste identification (code)	Period of validity		Revocation (date)
	Name and No	Address	Recovery operation R code	Technologies employed		From	To	

Table 5

Information on illegal shipments of waste (*) (Article 24 and Article 50(1))

Waste identification (code)	Quantity (kg/litres)	Country of destination (De) and country of dispatch (Di)	Identification of the reason for illegality (possible reference to violated Articles)	Responsible for illegality (*please tick ✓ as appropriate*)			Measures taken including possible penalties
				Notifier	Consignee	Other	

(*) Information on cases which have been closed during the reporting period.

Table 6

Information on any specific customs offices designated by Member States for shipments of waste entering and leaving the Community (Article 55)

Customs office		
Office	Location	Import/export countries controlled

DIRECTIVE 2008/1/EC OF THE EUROPEAN PARLIAMENT AND OF THE COUNCIL

of 15 January 2008

CONCERNING INTEGRATED POLLUTION PREVENTION AND CONTROL

THE EUROPEAN PARLIAMENT AND THE COUNCIL OF THE EUROPEAN UNION,

Having regard to the Treaty establishing the European Community, and in particular Article 175(1) thereof,

Having regard to the proposal from the Commission,

Having regard to the opinion of the European Economic and Social Committee,

After consulting the Committee of the Regions,

Acting in accordance with the procedure laid down in Article 251 of the Treaty,

Whereas:

(1) Council Directive 96/61/EC of 24 September 1996 concerning integrated pollution prevention and control has been substantially amended several times. In the interests of clarity and rationality the said Directive should be codified.

(2) The objectives and principles of the Community's environment policy, as set out in Article 174 of the Treaty, consist in particular of preventing, reducing and as far as possible eliminating pollution by giving priority to intervention at source and ensuring prudent management of natural resources, in compliance with the "polluter pays" principle and the principle of pollution prevention.

(3) The Fifth Environmental Action Programme, the broad outline of which was approved by the Council and the Representatives of the Governments of the Member States, meeting within the Council, in the Resolution of 1 February 1993 on a Community programme of policy and action in relation to the environment and sustainable development, accorded priority to integrated pollution control as an important part of the move towards a more sustainable balance between human activity and socioeconomic development, on the one hand, and the resources and regenerative capacity of nature, on the other.

(4) The implementation of an integrated approach to reduce pollution requires action at Community level in order to modify and supplement existing Community legislation concerning the prevention and control of pollution from industrial plants.

(5) Council Directive 84/360/EEC of 28 June 1984 on the combating of air pollution from industrial plants introduced a general framework requiring authorisation prior to any operation or substantial modification of industrial installations which may cause air pollution.

(6) Directive 2006/11/EC of the European Parliament and of the Council of 15 February 2006 on pollution caused by certain dangerous substances discharged into the aquatic environment of the Community provides for an authorisation requirement for the discharge of those substances.

(7) Although Community legislation exists on the combating of air pollution and the prevention or minimisation of the discharge of dangerous substances into water, there is no comparable Community legislation aimed at preventing or minimising emissions into soil.

(8) Different approaches to controlling emissions into the air, water or soil separately may encourage the shifting of pollution between the various environmental media rather than protecting the environment as a whole.

(9) The objective of an integrated approach to pollution control is to prevent emissions into air, water or soil wherever this is practicable, taking into account waste management, and, where it is not, to minimise them in order to achieve a high level of protection for the environment as a whole.

(10) This Directive should establish a general framework for integrated pollution prevention and control. It should lay down the measures necessary to implement integrated pollution prevention and control in order to achieve a high level of protection for the environment as a whole. Application of the principle of sustainable development should be promoted by an integrated approach to pollution control.

(11) The provisions of this Directive should apply without prejudice to the provisions of Council Directive 85/337/EEC of 27 June 1985 on the assessment of the effects of certain public and private projects on the environment. When information or conclusions obtained further to the application of that Directive have to be taken into consideration for the granting of authorisation, this Directive should not affect the implementation of Directive 85/337/EEC.

(12) Member States should take the necessary steps in order to ensure that the operator of the industrial activities referred to in this Directive is complying with the general principles of certain basic obligations. For that purpose it would suffice for the competent authorities to take those general principles into account when laying down the authorisation conditions.

(13) Some of the provisions adopted pursuant to this Directive must be applied to existing installations after 30 October 2007 and others had to be applied as from 30 October 1999.

(14) In order to tackle pollution problems more effectively and efficiently, environmental aspects should be taken into consideration by the operator. Those aspects should be communicated to the competent authority or authorities so that they can satisfy themselves, before granting a permit, that all appropriate preventive or pollution-control measures have been laid down. Very different application procedures may give rise to different levels of environmental protection and public awareness. Therefore, applications for permits under this Directive should include minimum data.

(15) Full coordination of the authorisation procedure and conditions between competent authorities should make it possible to achieve the highest practicable level of protection for the environment as a whole.

(16) The competent authority or authorities should grant or amend a permit only when integrated environmental protection measures for air, water and land have been laid down.

(17) The permit should include all necessary measures to fulfil the authorisation conditions in order thus to achieve a high level of protection for the environment as a whole. Without prejudice to the authorisation procedure, those measures may also be the subject of general binding requirements.

(18) Emission limit values, parameters or equivalent technical measures should be based on the best available techniques, without prescribing the use of one specific technique or technology and taking into consideration the technical characteristics of the installation concerned, its geographical location and local environmental conditions. In all cases the authorisation conditions should lay down provisions on minimising long-distance or transfrontier pollution and ensure a high level of protection for the environment as a whole.

(19) It is for the Member States to determine how the technical characteristics of the installation concerned, its geographical location and local environmental conditions can, where appropriate, be taken into consideration.

(20) When an environmental quality standard requires more stringent conditions than those that can be achieved by using the best available techniques, supplementary conditions

should in particular be required by the permit, without prejudice to other measures that may be taken to comply with the environmental quality standards.

(21) Because best available techniques will change with time, particularly in the light of technical advances, the competent authorities should monitor or be informed of such progress.

(22) Changes to an installation may give rise to pollution. The competent authority or authorities should therefore be notified of any change which might affect the environment. Substantial changes to plant must be subject to the granting of prior authorisation in accordance with this Directive.

(23) The authorisation conditions should be periodically reviewed and if necessary updated. Under certain conditions, they should in any event be re-examined.

(24) Effective public participation in the taking of decisions should enable the public to express, and the decision-maker to take account of, opinions and concerns which may be relevant to those decisions, thereby increasing the accountability and transparency of the decision-making process and contributing to public awareness of environmental issues and support for the decisions taken. In particular, the public should have access to information on the operation of installations and their potential effect on the environment, and, before any decision is taken, to information relating to applications for permits for new installations or substantial changes and to the permits themselves, their updating and the relevant monitoring data.

(25) Participation, including participation by associations, organisations and groups, in particular non-governmental organisations promoting environmental protection, should accordingly be fostered, including by promoting environmental education of the public.

(26) On 25 June 1998 the Community signed the UNECE Convention on Access to Information, Public Participation in Decision-Making and Access to Justice in Environmental Matters (the Århus Convention). Among the objectives of the Århus Convention is the desire to guarantee rights of public participation in decision-making in environmental matters in order to contribute to the protection of the right to live in an environment which is adequate for personal health and well-being.

(27) The development and exchange of information at Community level about best available techniques should help to redress the technological imbalances in the Community, should promote the worldwide dissemination of limit values and techniques used in the Community and should help the Member States in the efficient implementation of this Directive.

(28) Reports on the implementation and effectiveness of this Directive should be drawn up regularly.

(29) This Directive is concerned with installations whose potential for pollution, and therefore transfrontier pollution, is significant. Transboundary consultation should be organised where applications relate to the licensing of new installations or substantial changes to installations which are likely to have significant negative environmental effects. The applications relating to such proposals or substantial changes should be available to the public of the Member State likely to be affected.

(30) The need for action may be identified at Community level to lay down emission limit values for certain categories of installation and pollutant covered by this Directive. The European Parliament and the Council should set such emission limit values in accordance with the provisions of the Treaty.

(31) The provisions of this Directive should apply without prejudice to Community provisions on health and safety at the workplace.

(32) This Directive should be without prejudice to the obligations of the Member States relating to the time-limits for transposition into national law of the Directives as set out in Annex VI, Part B,

HAVE ADOPTED THIS DIRECTIVE:

Article 1

Purpose and scope

The purpose of this Directive is to achieve integrated prevention and control of pollution arising from the activities listed in Annex I. It lays down measures designed to prevent or, where that is not practicable, to reduce emissions in the air, water and land from the abovementioned activities, including measures concerning waste, in order to achieve a high level of protection of the environment taken as a whole, without prejudice to Directive 85/337/EEC and other relevant Community provisions.

Article 2

Definitions

For the purposes of this Directive the following definitions shall apply:

1. "substance" means any chemical element and its compounds, with the exception of radioactive substances within the meaning of Council Directive 96/29/Euratom of 13 May 1996 laying down basic safety standards for the protection of the health of workers and the general public against the dangers arising from ionizing radiation and genetically modified organisms within the meaning of Council Directive 90/219/EEC of 23 April 1990 on the contained use of genetically modified micro-organisms and Directive 2001/18/EC of the European Parliament and of the Council of 12 March 2001 on the deliberate release into the environment of genetically modified organisms;
2. "pollution" means the direct or indirect introduction, as a result of human activity, of substances, vibrations, heat or noise into the air, water or land which may be harmful to human health or the quality of the environment, result in damage to material property, or impair or interfere with amenities and other legitimate uses of the environment;
3. "installation" means a stationary technical unit where one or more activities listed in Annex I are carried out, and any other directly associated activities which have a technical connection with the activities carried out on that site and which could have an effect on emissions and pollution;
4. "existing installation" means an installation which on 30 October 1999, in accordance with legislation existing before that date, was in operation or was authorised or, in the view of the competent authority, was the subject of a full request for authorisation, provided that that installation was put into operation no later than 30 October 2000;
5. "emission" means the direct or indirect release of substances, vibrations, heat or noise from individual or diffuse sources in the installation into the air, water or land;
6. "emission limit values" means the mass, expressed in terms of certain specific parameters, concentration and/or level of an emission, which may not be exceeded during one or more periods of time; emission limit values may also be laid down for certain groups, families or categories of substances, in particular for those listed in Annex III. The emission limit values for substances normally apply at the point where the emissions leave the installation, any dilution being disregarded when determining them; with regard to indirect releases into water, the effect of a water treatment plant may be taken into account when determining the emission limit values of the installation involved, provided that an equivalent level is guaranteed for the protection of the environment as a whole and provided this does not lead to higher levels of pollution in the environment, without prejudice to Directive 2006/11/EC or the Directives implementing it;
7. "environmental quality standard" means the set of requirements which must be fulfilled at a given time by a given environment or particular part thereof, as set out in Community legislation;
8. "competent authority" means the authority or authorities or bodies responsible under the legal provisions of the Member States for carrying out the obligations arising from this Directive;

Article 7

Integrated approach to issuing permits

Member States shall take the measures necessary to ensure that the conditions of, and procedure for the grant of, the permit are fully coordinated where more than one competent authority is involved, in order to guarantee an effective integrated approach by all authorities competent for this procedure.

Article 8

Decisions

Without prejudice to other requirements laid down in national or Community legislation, the competent authority shall grant a permit containing conditions guaranteeing that the installation complies with the requirements of this Directive or, if it does not, shall refuse to grant the permit.

All permits granted and modified permits must include details of the arrangements made for air, water and land protection as referred to in this Directive.

Article 9

Conditions of the permit

1. Member States shall ensure that the permit includes all measures necessary for compliance with the requirements of Articles 3 and 10 for the granting of permits in order to achieve a high level of protection for the environment as a whole by means of protection of the air, water and land.

2. In the case of a new installation or a substantial change where Article 4 of Directive 85/337/EEC applies, any relevant information obtained or conclusion arrived at pursuant to Articles 5, 6 and 7 of that Directive shall be taken into consideration for the purposes of granting the permit.

3. The permit shall include emission limit values for polluting substances, in particular those listed in Annex III, likely to be emitted from the installation concerned in significant quantities, having regard to their nature and their potential to transfer pollution from one medium to another (water, air and land). If necessary, the permit shall include appropriate requirements ensuring protection of the soil and ground water and measures concerning the management of waste generated by the installation. Where appropriate, limit values may be supplemented or replaced by equivalent parameters or technical measures.

For installations under point 6.6 in Annex I, emission limit values laid down in accordance with this paragraph shall take into account practical considerations appropriate to these categories of installation.

Where emissions of a greenhouse gas from an installation are specified in Annex I to Directive 2003/87/EC of the European Parliament and of the Council of 13 October 2003 establishing a scheme for greenhouse gas emission allowance trading within the Community in relation to an activity carried out in that installation, the permit shall not include an emission limit value for direct emissions of that gas unless it is necessary to ensure that no significant local pollution is caused.

For activities listed in Annex I to Directive 2003/87/EC, Member States may choose not to impose requirements relating to energy efficiency in respect of combustion units or other units emitting carbon dioxide on the site.

Where necessary, the competent authorities shall amend the permit as appropriate.

The third, fourth and fifth subparagraphs shall not apply to installations temporarily excluded from the scheme for greenhouse gas emission allowance trading within the Community in accordance with Article 27 of Directive 2003/87/EC.

4. Without prejudice to Article 10, the emission limit values and the equivalent parameters and technical measures referred to in paragraph 3 shall be based on the best available techniques, without prescribing the use of any technique or specific technology, but taking into account the technical characteristics of the installation concerned, its geographical location and the local environmental conditions. In all circumstances, the conditions of the permit shall contain provisions on the minimisation of long-distance or transboundary pollution and ensure a high level of protection for the environment as a whole.

5. The permit shall contain suitable release monitoring requirements, specifying measurement methodology and frequency, evaluation procedure and an obligation to supply the competent authority with data required for checking compliance with the permit.

For installations under point 6.6 in Annex I, the measures referred to in this paragraph may take account of costs and benefits.

6. The permit shall contain measures relating to conditions other than normal operating conditions. Thus, where there is a risk that the environment may be affected, appropriate provision shall be made for start-up, leaks, malfunctions, momentary stoppages and definitive cessation of operations.

The permit may also contain temporary derogations from the requirements of paragraph 4 if a rehabilitation plan approved by the competent authority ensures that these requirements will be met within six months and if the project leads to a reduction of pollution.

7. The permit may contain such other specific conditions for the purposes of this Directive as the Member State or competent authority may think fit.

8. Without prejudice to the obligation to implement a permit procedure pursuant to this Directive, Member States may prescribe certain requirements for certain categories of installations in general binding rules instead of including them in individual permit conditions, provided that an integrated approach and an equivalent high level of environmental protection as a whole are ensured.

Article 10

Best available techniques and environmental quality standards

Where an environmental quality standard requires stricter conditions than those achievable by the use of the best available techniques, additional measures shall in particular be required in the permit, without prejudice to other measures which might be taken to comply with environmental quality standards.

Article 11

Developments in best available techniques

Member States shall ensure that the competent authority follows or is informed of developments in best available techniques.

Article 12

Changes by operators to installations

1. Member States shall take the necessary measures to ensure that the operator informs the competent authorities of any planned change in the operation. Where appropriate, the competent authorities shall update the permit or the conditions.

2. Member States shall take the necessary measures to ensure that no substantial change planned by the operator is made without a permit issued in accordance with this Directive. The application for a permit and the decision by the competent authority must cover those parts of the installation and those aspects listed in Article 6 that may be affected by the change. The relevant provisions of Article 3, Articles 6 to 10 and Article 15(1), (2) and (3) shall apply mutatis mutandis.

Article 13

Reconsideration and updating of permit conditions by the competent authority

1. Member States shall take the necessary measures to ensure that competent authorities periodically reconsider and, where necessary, update permit conditions.

2. The reconsideration shall be undertaken in any event where:

(a) the pollution caused by the installation is of such significance that the existing emission limit values of the permit need to be revised or new such values need to be included in the permit;

(b) substantial changes in the best available techniques make it possible to reduce emissions significantly without imposing excessive costs;

(c) the operational safety of the process or activity requires other techniques to be used;

(d) new provisions of Community or national legislation so dictate.

Article 14

Compliance with permit conditions

Member States shall take the necessary measures to ensure that:

(a) the conditions of the permit are complied with by the operator when operating the installation;

(b) the operator regularly informs the competent authority of the results of the monitoring of releases and without delay of any incident or accident significantly affecting the environment;

(c) operators of installations afford the representatives of the competent authority all necessary assistance to enable them to carry out any inspections within the installation, to take samples and to gather any information necessary for the performance of their duties for the purposes of this Directive.

Article 15

Access to information and public participation in the permit procedure

1. Member States shall ensure that the public concerned is given early and effective opportunities to participate in the procedure for:

(a) issuing a permit for new installations;

(b) issuing a permit for any substantial change;

(c) updating of a permit or permit conditions for an installation in accordance with Article 13(2)(a).

The procedure set out in Annex V shall apply for the purposes of such participation.

2. The results of monitoring of releases as required under the permit conditions referred to in Article 9 and held by the competent authority shall be made available to the public.

3. Paragraphs 1 and 2 shall apply subject to the restrictions laid down in Article 4(1), (2) and (4) of Directive 2003/4/EC of the European Parliament and of the Council of 28 January 2003 on public access to environmental information.

4. When a decision has been taken, the competent authority shall inform the public in accordance with the appropriate procedures and shall make available to the public the following information:

(a) the content of the decision, including a copy of the permit and of any conditions and any subsequent updates; and

(b) having examined the concerns and opinions expressed by the public concerned, the reasons and considerations on which the decision is based, including information on the public participation process.

Article 16

Access to justice

1. Member States shall ensure that, in accordance with the relevant national legal system, members of the public concerned have access to a review procedure before a court of law or another independent and impartial body established by law to challenge the substantive or procedural legality of decisions, acts or omissions subject to the public participation provisions of this Directive when:

(a) they have a sufficient interest; or

(b) they maintain the impairment of a right, where administrative procedural law of a Member State requires this as a precondition.

2. Member States shall determine at what stage the decisions, acts or omissions may be challenged.

3. What constitutes a sufficient interest and impairment of a right shall be determined by the Member States, consistently with the objective of giving the public concerned wide access to justice. To this end, the interest of any non-governmental organisation promoting environmental protection and meeting any requirements under national law shall be deemed sufficient for the purpose of paragraph 1(a).

Such organisations shall also be deemed to have rights capable of being impaired for the purpose of paragraph 1(b).

4. The provisions of this Article shall not exclude the possibility of a preliminary review procedure before an administrative authority and shall not affect the requirement of exhaustion of administrative review procedures prior to recourse to judicial review procedures, where such a requirement exists under national law.

Any such procedure shall be fair, equitable, timely and not prohibitively expensive.

5. In order to further the effectiveness of the provisions of this Article, Member States shall ensure that practical information is made available to the public on access to administrative and judicial review procedures.

Article 17

Exchange of information

1. With a view to exchanging information, Member States shall take the necessary measures to send the Commission every three years, and for the first time before 30 April 2001, the available representative data on the limit values laid down by specific category of activities in accordance with Annex I and, if appropriate, the best available techniques from which those values are derived in accordance with, in particular, Article 9. On subsequent occasions the data shall be supplemented in accordance with the procedures laid down in paragraph 3 of this Article.

2. The Commission shall organise an exchange of information between Member States and the industries concerned on best available techniques, associated monitoring, and developments in them.

Every three years the Commission shall publish the results of the exchanges of information.

3. At intervals of three years, and for the first time for the period 30 October 1999 to 30 October 2002 inclusive, Member States shall send information to the Commission on the implementation of this Directive in the form of a report. The report shall be drawn up on the basis of a questionnaire or outline drafted by the Commission in accordance with the procedure laid down in Article 6(2) of Council Directive 91/692/EEC of 23 December 1991 standardising and rationalising reports on the implementation of certain Directives relating to the environment. The questionnaire or outline shall be sent to the Member States six months before the start of the period covered by the report. The report shall be submitted to the Commission within nine months of the end of the three-year period covered by it.

The Commission shall publish a Community report on the implementation of the Directive within nine months of receiving the reports from the Member States.

The Commission shall submit the Community report to the European Parliament and to the Council, accompanied by proposals if necessary.

4. Member States shall establish or designate the authority or authorities which are to be responsible for the exchange of information under paragraphs 1, 2 and 3 and shall inform the Commission accordingly.

Article 18

Transboundary effects

1. Where a Member State is aware that the operation of an installation is likely to have significant negative effects on the environment of another Member State, or where a Member State likely to be significantly affected so requests, the Member State in whose territory the application for a permit pursuant to Article 4 or Article 12(2) was submitted shall forward to the other Member State any information required to be given or made available pursuant to Annex V at the same time as it makes it available to its own nationals. Such information shall serve as a basis for any consultations necessary in the framework of the bilateral relations between the two Member States on a reciprocal and equivalent basis.

2. Within the framework of their bilateral relations, Member States shall see to it that in the cases referred to in paragraph 1 the applications are also made available for an appropriate period of time to the public of the Member State likely to be affected so that it will have the right to comment on them before the competent authority reaches its decision.

3. The results of any consultations pursuant to paragraphs 1 and 2 must be taken into consideration when the competent authority reaches a decision on the application.

4. The competent authority shall inform any Member State which has been consulted pursuant to paragraph 1 of the decision reached on the application and shall forward to it the information referred to in Article 15(4). That Member State shall take the measures necessary to ensure that that information is made available in an appropriate manner to the public concerned in its own territory.

Article 19

Community emission limit values

1. Where the need for Community action has been identified, on the basis, in particular, of the exchange of information provided for in Article 17, the European Parliament and the Council, acting on a proposal from the Commission, shall set emission limit values, in accordance with the procedures laid down in the Treaty, for:

(a) the categories of installations listed in Annex I except for the landfills covered by points 5,1 and 5,4 of that Annex,

and

(b) the polluting substances referred to in Annex III.

2. In the absence of Community emission limit values defined pursuant to this Directive, the relevant emission limit values contained in the Directives listed in Annex II and in other Community legislation shall be applied as minimum emission limit values pursuant to this Directive for the installations listed in Annex I.

3. Without prejudice to the requirements of this Directive, the technical requirements applicable for the landfills covered by points 5,1 and 5,4 of Annex I, have been fixed in Council Directive 1999/31/EC of 26 April 1999 on the landfill of waste.

Article 20

Transitional provisions

1. The provisions of Directive 84/360/EEC, the provisions of Articles 4, 5 and 6(2) of Directive 2006/11/EC and the relevant provisions concerning authorisation systems in the Directives listed in Annex II shall apply, without prejudice to the exceptions provided for in Directive 2001/80/EC, to existing installations in respect of activities listed in Annex I until the measures required pursuant to Article 5 of this Directive have been taken by the competent authorities.

2. The relevant provisions concerning authorisation systems in the Directives listed in Annex II shall not, in respect of the activities listed in Annex I, apply to installations which are not existing installations within the meaning of point 4 of Article 2.

3. Directive 84/360/EEC shall be repealed on 30 October 2007.

Acting on a proposal from the Commission, the Council or the European Parliament and the Council shall, where necessary, amend the relevant provisions of the Directives listed in Annex II in order to adapt them to the requirements of this Directive before 30 October 2007.

Article 21

Communication

Member States shall communicate to the Commission the texts of the main provisions of national law which they adopt in the field covered by this Directive.

[*Article 22 is not reproduced.*]

Article 23

Entry into force

This Directive shall enter into force on the 20th day following its publication in the Official Journal of the European Union.

Article 24

Addressees

This Directive is addressed to the Member States.

ANNEX I
CATEGORIES OF INDUSTRIAL ACTIVITIES REFERRED TO IN ARTICLE 1

1. Installations or parts of installations used for research, development and testing of new products and processes are not covered by this Directive.

2. The threshold values given below generally refer to production capacities or outputs. Where one operator carries out several activities falling under the same subheading in the same installation or on the same site, the capacities of such activities are added together.

1. ENERGY INDUSTRIES

1.1. Combustion installations with a rated thermal input exceeding 50 MW.

1.2. Mineral oil and gas refineries.

1.3. Coke ovens.

1.4. Coal gasification and liquefaction plants.

2. PRODUCTION AND PROCESSING OF METALS

2.1. Metal ore (including sulphide ore) roasting or sintering installations.

2.2. Installations for the production of pig iron or steel (primary or secondary fusion) including continuous casting, with a capacity exceeding 2,5 tonnes per hour.

2.3. Installations for the processing of ferrous metals:
(a) hot-rolling mills with a capacity exceeding 20 tonnes of crude steel per hour;
(b) smitheries with hammers the energy of which exceeds 50 kilojoules per hammer, where the calorific power used exceeds 20 MW;
(c) application of protective fused metal coats with an input exceeding 2 tonnes of crude steel per hour.

2.4. Ferrous metal foundries with a production capacity exceeding 20 tonnes per day.

2.5. Installations:
(a) for the production of non-ferrous crude metals from ore, concentrates or secondary raw materials by metallurgical, chemical or electrolytic processes;
(b) for the smelting, including the alloyage, of non-ferrous metals, including recovered products, (refining, foundry casting, etc.) with a melting capacity exceeding 4 tonnes per day for lead and cadmium or 20 tonnes per day for all other metals.

2.6. Installations for surface treatment of metals and plastic materials using an electrolytic or chemical process where the volume of the treatment vats exceeds 30 m^3.

3. MINERAL INDUSTRY

3.1. Installations for the production of cement clinker in rotary kilns with a production capacity exceeding 500 tonnes per day or lime in rotary kilns with a production capacity exceeding 50 tonnes per day or in other furnaces with a production capacity exceeding 50 tonnes per day.

3.2. Installations for the production of asbestos and the manufacture of asbestos-based products.

3.3. Installations for the manufacture of glass including glass fibre with a melting capacity exceeding 20 tonnes per day.

3.4. Installations for melting mineral substances including the production of mineral fibres with a melting capacity exceeding 20 tonnes per day.

3.5. Installations for the manufacture of ceramic products by firing, in particular roofing tiles, bricks, refractory bricks, tiles, stoneware or porcelain, with a production capacity exceeding 75 tonnes per day, and/or with a kiln capacity exceeding 4 m^3 and with a setting density per kiln exceeding 300 kg/m^3.

4. CHEMICAL INDUSTRY

Production within the meaning of the categories of activities contained in this section means the production on an industrial scale by chemical processing of substances or groups of substances listed in points 4.1 to 4.6.

4.1. Chemical installations for the production of basic organic chemicals, such as:
(a) simple hydrocarbons (linear or cyclic, saturated or unsaturated, aliphatic or aromatic);
(b) oxygen-containing hydrocarbons such as alcohols, aldehydes, ketones, carboxylic acids, esters, acetates, ethers, peroxides, epoxy resins;
(c) sulphurous hydrocarbons;
(d) nitrogenous hydrocarbons such as amines, amides, nitrous compounds, nitro compounds or nitrate compounds, nitriles, cyanates, isocyanates;
(e) phosphorus-containing hydrocarbons;
(f) halogenic hydrocarbons;
(g) organometallic compounds;
(h) basic plastic materials (polymers, synthetic fibres and cellulose-based fibres);
(i) synthetic rubbers;
(j) dyes and pigments;
(k) surface-active agents and surfactants.

4.2. Chemical installations for the production of basic inorganic chemicals, such as:
(a) gases, such as ammonia, chlorine or hydrogen chloride, fluorine or hydrogen fluoride, carbon oxides, sulphur compounds, nitrogen oxides, hydrogen, sulphur dioxide, carbonyl chloride;
(b) acids, such as chromic acid, hydrofluoric acid, phosphoric acid, nitric acid, hydrochloric acid, sulphuric acid, oleum, sulphurous acids;
(c) bases, such as ammonium hydroxide, potassium hydroxide, sodium hydroxide;
(d) salts, such as ammonium chloride, potassium chlorate, potassium carbonate, sodium carbonate, perborate, silver nitrate;
(e) non-metals, metal oxides or other inorganic compounds such as calcium carbide, silicon, silicon carbide.

4.3. Chemical installations for the production of phosphorous-, nitrogen- or potassium-based fertilisers (simple or compound fertilisers).

4.4. Chemical installations for the production of basic plant health products and of biocides.

4.5. Installations using a chemical or biological process for the production of basic pharmaceutical products.

4.6. Chemical installations for the production of explosives.

5. WASTE MANAGEMENT

Without prejudice to Article 11 of Directive 2006/12/EC or Article 3 of Council Directive 91/689/EEC of 12 December 1991 on hazardous waste:

5.1. Installations for the disposal or recovery of hazardous waste as defined in the list referred to in Article 1(4) of Directive 91/689/EEC, as defined in Annexes II A and II B (operations R1, R5, R6, R8 and R9) to Directive 2006/12/EC and in Council Directive 75/439/EEC of 16 June 1975 on the disposal of waste oils, with a capacity exceeding 10 tonnes per day.

5.2. Installations for the incineration of municipal waste (household waste and similar commercial, industrial and institutional wastes) with a capacity exceeding 3 tonnes per hour.

5.3. Installations for the disposal of non-hazardous waste as defined in Annex II A to Directive 2006/12/EC under headings D8 and D9, with a capacity exceeding 50 tonnes per day.

5.4. Landfills receiving more than 10 tonnes per day or with a total capacity exceeding 25000 tonnes, excluding landfills of inert waste.

6. OTHER ACTIVITIES

6.1. Industrial plants for the production of:
(a) pulp from timber or other fibrous materials;
(b) paper and cardboard with a production capacity exceeding 20 tonnes per day.

6.2. Plants for the pre-treatment (operations such as washing, bleaching, mercerisation) or dyeing of fibres or textiles where the treatment capacity exceeds 10 tonnes per day.

6.3. Plants for the tanning of hides and skins where the treatment capacity exceeds 12 tonnes of finished products per day.

6.4.
(a) Slaughterhouses with a carcase production capacity greater than 50 tonnes per day.
(b) Treatment and processing intended for the production of food products from:
— animal raw materials (other than milk) with a finished product production capacity greater than 75 tonnes per day,
— vegetable raw materials with a finished product production capacity greater than 300 tonnes per day (average value on a quarterly basis).
(c) Treatment and processing of milk, the quantity of milk received being greater than 200 tonnes per day (average value on an annual basis).

6.5. Installations for the disposal or recycling of animal carcases and animal waste with a treatment capacity exceeding 10 tonnes per day.

6.6. Installations for the intensive rearing of poultry or pigs with more than:
(a) 40000 places for poultry;
(b) 2000 places for production pigs (over 30 kg); or
(c) 750 places for sows.

6.7. Installations for the surface treatment of substances, objects or products using organic solvents, in particular for dressing, printing, coating, degreasing, waterproofing, sizing, painting, cleaning or impregnating, with a consumption capacity of more than 150 kg per hour or more than 200 tonnes per year.

6.8. Installations for the production of carbon (hard-burnt coal) or electrographite by means of incineration or graphitisation.

[6.9. Capture of CO_2 streams from installations covered by this Directive for the purposes of geological storage pursuant to Directive 2009/31/EC of the European Parliament and of the Council of 23 April 2009 on the geological storage of carbon dioxide.][1]

Amendment
1 Inserted by Directive 2009/31/EC of the European Parliament and of the Council of 23 April 2009 on the geological storage of carbon dioxide and amending Council Directive 85/337/EEC, European Parliament and Council Directives 2000/60/EC, 2001/80/EC, 2004/35/EC, 2006/12/EC, 2008/1/EC and Regulation (EC) No 1013/2006, Article 37.

ANNEX II
LIST OF THE DIRECTIVES REFERRED TO IN ARTICLES 19(2), (3) AND 20

1. Council Directive 87/217/EEC of 19 March 1987 on the prevention and reduction of environmental pollution by asbestos.

2. Council Directive 82/176/EEC of 22 March 1982 on limit values and quality objectives for mercury discharges by the chlor-alkali electrolysis industry.

3. Council Directive 83/513/EEC of 26 September 1983 on limit values and quality objectives for cadmium discharges.

4. Council Directive 84/156/EEC of 8 March 1984 on limit values and quality objectives for mercury discharges by sectors other than the chlor-alkali electrolysis industry.

5. Council Directive 84/491/EEC of 9 October 1984 on limit values and quality objectives for discharges of hexachlorocyclohexane.

6. Council Directive 86/280/EEC of 12 June 1986 on limit values and quality objectives for discharges of certain dangerous substances included in List I of the Annex to Directive 76/464/EEC.

7. Directive 2000/76/EC of the European Parliament and of the Council of 4 December 2000 on the incineration of waste.

8. Council Directive 92/112/EEC of 15 December 1992 on procedures for harmonising the programmes for the reduction and eventual elimination of pollution caused by waste from the titanium dioxide industry.

9. Directive 2001/80/EC of the European Parliament and of the Council of 23 October 2001 on the limitation of emissions of certain pollutants into the air from large combustion plants.

10. Directive 2006/11/EC of the European Parliament and of the Council of 15 February 2006 on pollution caused by certain dangerous substances discharged into the aquatic environment of the Community.

11. Directive 2006/12/EC of the European Parliament and of the Council of 5 April 2006 on waste.

12. Council Directive 75/439/EEC of 16 June 1975 on the disposal of waste oils.

13. Council Directive 91/689/EEC of 12 December 1991 on hazardous waste.

14. Council Directive 1999/31/EC of 26 April 1999 on the landfill of waste.

ANNEX III
INDICATIVE LIST OF THE MAIN POLLUTING SUBSTANCES TO BE TAKEN INTO ACCOUNT IF THEY ARE RELEVANT FOR FIXING EMISSION LIMIT VALUES

Air

1. Sulphur dioxide and other sulphur compounds.

2. Oxides of nitrogen and other nitrogen compounds.

3. Carbon monoxide.

4. Volatile organic compounds.

5. Metals and their compounds.

6. Dust.

7. Asbestos (suspended particulates, fibres).

8. Chlorine and its compounds.

9. Fluorine and its compounds.

10. Arsenic and its compounds.

11. Cyanides.

12. Substances and preparations which have been proved to possess carcinogenic or mutagenic properties or properties which may affect reproduction via the air.

13. Polychlorinated dibenzodioxins and polychlorinated dibenzofurans.

Water

1. Organohalogen compounds and substances which may form such compounds in the aquatic environment.

2. Organophosphorus compounds.

3. Organotin compounds.

4. Substances and preparations which have been proved to possess carcinogenic or mutagenic properties or properties which may affect reproduction in or via the aquatic environment.

5. Persistent hydrocarbons and persistent and bioaccumulable organic toxic substances.

6. Cyanides.

7. Metals and their compounds.

8. Arsenic and its compounds.

9. Biocides and plant health products.

10. Materials in suspension.

11. Substances which contribute to eutrophication (in particular, nitrates and phosphates).

12. Substances which have an unfavourable influence on the oxygen balance (and can be measured using parameters such as BOD, COD, etc.).

ANNEX IV

Considerations to be taken into account generally or in specific cases when determining best available techniques, as defined in Article 2(12), bearing in mind the likely costs and benefits of a measure and the principles of precaution and prevention:

1. the use of low-waste technology;
2. the use of less hazardous substances;
3. the furthering of recovery and recycling of substances generated and used in the process and of waste, where appropriate;
4. comparable processes, facilities or methods of operation which have been tried with success on an industrial scale;
5. technological advances and changes in scientific knowledge and understanding;
6. the nature, effects and volume of the emissions concerned;
7. the commissioning dates for new or existing installations;
8. the length of time needed to introduce the best available technique;
9. the consumption and nature of raw materials (including water) used in the process and energy efficiency;
10. the need to prevent or reduce to a minimum the overall impact of the emissions on the environment and the risks to it;
11. the need to prevent accidents and to minimise the consequences for the environment;
12. the information published by the Commission pursuant to Article 17(2), second subparagraph, or by international organisations.

ANNEX V
PUBLIC PARTICIPATION IN DECISION-MAKING

1. The public shall be informed (by public notices or other appropriate means such as electronic media where available) of the following matters early in the procedure for the taking of a decision or, at the latest, as soon as the information can reasonably be provided:

(a) the application for a permit or, as the case may be, the proposal for the updating of a permit or of permit conditions in accordance with Article 15(1), including the description of the elements listed in Article 6(1);

(b) where applicable, the fact that a decision is subject to a national or transboundary environmental impact assessment or to consultations between Member States in accordance with Article 18;

(c) details of the competent authorities responsible for taking the decision, those from which relevant information can be obtained, those to which comments or questions can be submitted, and details of the time schedule for transmitting comments or questions;

(d) the nature of possible decisions or, where there is one, the draft decision;

(e) where applicable, the details relating to a proposal for the updating of a permit or of permit conditions;

(f) an indication of the times and places where, or means by which, the relevant information will be made available;

(g) details of the arrangements for public participation and consultation made pursuant to point 5.

2. Member States shall ensure that, within appropriate time-frames, the following is made available to the public concerned:

(a) in accordance with national legislation, the main reports and advice issued to the competent authority or authorities at the time when the public concerned were informed in accordance with point 1;

(b) in accordance with the provisions of Directive 2003/4/EC, information other than that referred to in point 1 which is relevant for the decision in accordance with Article 8 and which only becomes available after the time the public concerned was informed in accordance with point 1.

3. The public concerned shall be entitled to express comments and opinions to the competent authority before a decision is taken.

4. The results of the consultations held pursuant to this Annex must be taken into due account in the taking of a decision.

5. The detailed arrangements for informing the public (for example by bill posting within a certain radius or publication in local newspapers) and consulting the public concerned (for example by written submissions or by way of a public inquiry) shall be determined by the Member States. Reasonable time-frames for the different phases shall be provided, allowing sufficient time for informing the public and for the public concerned to prepare and participate effectively in environmental decision-making subject to the provisions of this Annex.

ANNEX VI

PART A
REPEALED DIRECTIVE WITH ITS SUCCESSIVE AMENDMENTS (REFERRED TO IN ARTICLE 22)

Council Directive 96/61/EC (OJ L 257, 10.10.1996, p. 26).	
Directive 2003/35/EC of the European Parliament and of the Council (OJ L 156, 25.6.2003, p. 17)	only Article 4 and Annex II
Directive 2003/87/EC of the European Parliament and of the Council (OJ L 275, 25.10.2003, p. 32).	only Article 26
Regulation (EC) No 1882/2003 of the European Parliament and of the Council (OJ L 284, 31.10.2003, p. 1)	only point (61) of Annex III
Regulation (EC) No 166/2006 of the European Parliament and of the Council (OJ L 33, 4.2.2006, p. 1).	only Article 21(2)

PART B
LIST OF TIME-LIMITS FOR TRANSPOSITION INTO NATIONAL LAW (REFERRED TO IN ARTICLE 22)

Directive	*Time-limit for transposition*
96/61/EC	30 October 1999
2003/35/EC	25 June 2005
2003/87/EC	31 December 2003

ANNEX VII
CORRELATION TABLE

Directive 96/61/EC	*This Directive*
Article 1	Article 1
Article 2, introductory words	Article 2, introductory words
Article 2(1-9)	Article 2(1-9)
Article 2(10)(a)	Article 2(10)
Article 2(10)(b)	Article 2(11)
Article 2(11), first subparagraph, introductory wording	Article 2(12), first subparagraph, introductory wording
Article 2(11), first subparagraph, first indent	Article 2(12), first subparagraph, (a)
Article 2(11), first subparagraph, second indent	Article 2(12), first subparagraph, (b)
Article 2(11), first subparagraph, third indent	Article 2(12), first subparagraph, (c)
Article 2(11), second subparagraph	Article 2(12), second subparagraph
Article 2(12)	Article 2(13)
Article 2(13)	Article 2(14)
Article 2(14)	Article 2(15)
Article 3, first subparagraph	Article 3(1)
Article 3, second subparagraph	Article 3(2)
Article 4	Article 4
Article 5	Article 5
Article 6(1), first subparagraph, introductory wording	Article 6(1), first subparagraph, introductory wording
Article 6(1), first subparagraph, first to tenth indent	Article 6(1), first subparagraph, (a) to (j)
Article 6(1), second subparagraph	Article 6(1), second subparagraph
Article 6(2)	Article 6(2)
Article 7 to 12	Article 7 to 12
Article 13(1)	Article 13(1)
Article 13(2), introductory wording	Article 13(2), introductory wording
Article 13(2), first to fourth indent	Article 13(2)(a) to (d)
Article 14, introductory wording	Article 14, introductory wording
Article 14, first to third indent	Article 14(a) to (c)
Article 15(1), first subparagraph, introductory wording	Article 15(1), first subparagraph, introductory wording
Article 15(1), first subparagraph, first to third indent	Article 15(1), first subparagraph, (a) to (c)
Article 15(1), second subparagraph	Article 15(1), second subparagraph

Directive 96/61/EC	*This Directive*
Article 15(2)	Article 15(2)
Article 15(4)	Article 15(3)
Article 15(5)	Article 15(4)
Article 15a, first subparagraph, introductory and final words	Article 16(1)
Article 15a, first subparagraph, (a) and (b)	Article 16(1)(a) and (b)
Article 15a, second subparagraph	Article 16(2)
Article 15a, third subparagraph, first and second sentence	Article 16(3), first subparagraph
Article 15a, third subparagraph, third sentence	Article 16(3), second subparagraph
Article 15a, fourth subparagraph	Article 16(4), first subparagraph
Article 15a, fifth subparagraph	Article 16(4), second subparagraph
Article 15a, sixth subparagraph	Article 16(5)
Article 16	Article 17
Article 17	Article 18
Article 18(1), introductory and final words	Article 19(1)
Article 18(1), first and second indent	Article 19(1)(a) and (b)
Article 18(2), first subparagraph	Article 19(2)
Article 18(2), second subparagraph	Article 19(3)
Article 19	—
Article 20(1)	Article 20(1)
Article 20(2)	Article 20(2)
Article 20(3), first subparagraph	Article 20(3), first subparagraph
Article 20(3), second subparagraph	—
Article 20(3), third subparagraph	Article 20(3), second subparagraph
Article 21(1)	—
Article 21(2)	Article 21
—	Article 22
Article 22	Article 23
Article 23	Article 24
Annex I	Annex I
Annex II	Annex II
Annex III	Annex III
Annex IV	Annex IV
Annex V	Annex V
—	Annex VI
—	Annex VII

COUNCIL DIRECTIVE 2008/98/EC

of 19 November 2008

ON WASTE AND REPEALING CERTAIN DIRECTIVES

THE EUROPEAN PARLIAMENT AND THE COUNCIL OF THE EUROPEAN UNION,

Having regard to the Treaty establishing the European Community, and in particular Article 175(1) thereof,

Having regard to the proposal from the Commission,

Having regard to the opinion of the European Economic and Social Committee,

Having regard to the opinion of the Committee of the Regions,

Acting in accordance with the procedure laid down in Article 251 of the Treaty,

Whereas:

(1) Directive 2006/12/EC of the European Parliament and of the Council of 5 April 2006 on waste establishes the legislative framework for the handling of waste in the Community. It defines key concepts such as waste, recovery and disposal and puts in place the essential requirements for the management of waste, notably an obligation for an establishment or undertaking carrying out waste management operations to have a permit or to be registered and an obligation for the Member States to draw up waste management plans. It also establishes major principles such as an obligation to handle waste in a way that does not have a negative impact on the environment or human health, an encouragement to apply the waste hierarchy and, in accordance with the polluter-pays principle, a requirement that the costs of disposing of waste must be borne by the holder of waste, by previous holders or by the producers of the product from which the waste came.

(2) Decision No 1600/2002/EC of the European Parliament and of the Council of 22 July 2002 laying down the Sixth Community Environment Action Programme calls for the development or revision of the legislation on waste, including a clarification of the distinction between waste and non-waste, and for the development of measures regarding waste prevention and management, including the setting of targets.

(3) The Commission communication of 27 May 2003 towards a Thematic Strategy on the prevention and recycling of waste noted the need to assess the existing definitions of recovery and disposal, the need for a generally applicable definition of recycling and a debate on the definition of waste.

(4) In its resolution of 20 April 2004 on the abovementioned communication, the European Parliament called on the Commission to consider extending Council Directive 96/61/EC of 24 September 1996 concerning integrated pollution prevention and control to the waste sector as a whole. It also asked the Commission to differentiate clearly between recovery and disposal and to clarify the distinction between waste and non-waste.

(5) In its conclusions of 1 July 2004, the Council called on the Commission to bring forward a proposal for the revision of certain aspects of Directive 75/442/EEC, repealed and replaced by Directive 2006/12/EC, in order to clarify the distinction between waste and non-waste and that between recovery and disposal.

(6) The first objective of any waste policy should be to minimise the negative effects of the generation and management of waste on human health and the environment. Waste policy should also aim at reducing the use of resources, and favour the practical application of the waste hierarchy.

(7) In its Resolution of 24 February 1997 on a Community strategy for waste management, the Council confirmed that waste prevention should be the first priority of waste management, and that re-use and material recycling should be preferred to energy recovery from waste, where and insofar as they are the best ecological options.

(8) It is therefore necessary to revise Directive 2006/12/EC in order to clarify key concepts such as the definitions of waste, recovery and disposal, to strengthen the measures that must be taken in regard to waste prevention, to introduce an approach that takes into account the whole life-cycle of products and materials and not only the waste phase, and to focus on reducing the environmental impacts of waste generation and waste management, thereby strengthening the economic value of waste. Furthermore, the recovery of waste and the use of recovered materials should be encouraged in order to conserve natural resources. In the interests of clarity and readability, Directive 2006/12/EC should be repealed and replaced by a new directive.

(9) Since most significant waste management operations are now covered by Community legislation in the field of environment, it is important that this Directive be adapted to that approach. An emphasis on the environmental objectives laid down in Article 174 of the Treaty would bring the environmental impacts of waste generation and waste management more sharply into focus throughout the life-cycle of resources. Consequently, the legal basis for this Directive should be Article 175.

(10) Effective and consistent rules on waste treatment should be applied, subject to certain exceptions, to movable property which the holder discards or intends or is required to discard.

(11) The waste status of uncontaminated excavated soils and other naturally occurring material which are used on sites other than the one from which they were excavated should be considered in accordance with the definition of waste and the provisions on by-products or on the end of waste status under this Directive.

(12) Regulation (EC) No 1774/2002 of the European Parliament and of the Council of 3 October 2002 laying down health rules concerning animal by-products not intended for human consumption provides, inter alia, for proportionate controls as regards the collection, transport, processing, use and disposal of all animal by-products including waste of animal origin, preventing it from presenting a risk to animal and public health. It is therefore necessary to clarify the link with that Regulation, avoiding duplication of rules by excluding from the scope of this Directive animal by-products where they are intended for uses that are not considered waste operations.

(13) In the light of the experience gained in applying Regulation (EC) No 1774/2002, it is appropriate to clarify the scope of waste legislation and of its provisions on hazardous waste as regards animal by-products regulated by Regulation (EC) No 1774/2002. Where animal by-products pose potential health risks, the appropriate legal instrument to address these risks is Regulation (EC) No 1774/2002 and unnecessary overlaps with waste legislation should be avoided.

(14) The classification of waste as hazardous waste should be based, inter alia, on the Community legislation on chemicals, in particular concerning the classification of preparations as hazardous, including concentration limit values used for that purpose. Hazardous waste should be regulated under strict specifications in order to prevent or limit, as far as possible, the potential negative effects on the environment and on human health due to inappropriate management. Furthermore, it is necessary to maintain the system by which waste and hazardous waste have been classified in accordance with the list of the types of waste as last established by Commission Decision 2000/532/EC, in order to encourage a harmonised classification of waste and ensure the harmonised determination of hazardous waste within the Community.

(15) It is necessary to distinguish between the preliminary storage of waste pending its collection, the collection of waste and the storage of waste pending treatment. Establishments or undertakings that produce waste in the course of their activities should not be regarded as engaged in waste management and subject to authorisation for the storage of their waste pending its collection.

(16) Preliminary storage of waste within the definition of collection is understood as a storage activity pending its collection in facilities where waste is unloaded in order to permit its preparation for further transport for recovery or disposal elsewhere. The distinction between preliminary storage of waste pending collection and the storage of waste pending treatment should be made, in view of the objective of this Directive, according to the type of waste, the size and time period of storage and the objective of the collection. This distinction should be made by the Member States. The storage of waste prior to recovery for a period of three years or longer and the storage of waste prior to disposal for a period of one year or longer is subject to Council Directive 1999/31/EC of 26 April 1999 on the landfill of waste.

(17) Waste collection schemes which are not conducted on a professional basis should not be subject to registration as they present a lower risk and contribute to the separate collection of waste. Examples of such schemes are waste medicines collected by pharmacies, take-back schemes in shops for consumer goods and community schemes in schools.

(18) Definitions of prevention, re-use, preparing for re-use, treatment and recycling should be included in this Directive, in order to clarify the scope of these concepts.

(19) The definitions of recovery and disposal need to be modified in order to ensure a clear distinction between the two concepts, based on a genuine difference in environmental impact through the substitution of natural resources in the economy and recognising the potential benefits to the environment and human health of using waste as a resource. In addition, guidelines may be developed in order to clarify cases where this distinction is difficult to apply in practice or where the classification of the activity as recovery does not match the real environmental impact of the operation.

(20) This Directive should also clarify when the incineration of municipal solid waste is energy-efficient and may be considered a recovery operation.

(21) Disposal operations consisting of release to seas and oceans including sea bed insertion are also regulated by international conventions, in particular the Convention on the Prevention of Marine Pollution by Dumping of Wastes and Other Matter, done at London on 13 November 1972, and the 1996 Protocol thereto as amended in 2006.

(22) There should be no confusion between the various aspects of the waste definition, and appropriate procedures should be applied, where necessary, to by-products that are not waste, on the one hand, or to waste that ceases to be waste, on the other hand. In order to specify certain aspects of the definition of waste, this Directive should clarify:

— when substances or objects resulting from a production process not primarily aimed at producing such substances or objects are by-products and not waste. The decision that a substance is not waste can be taken only on the basis of a coordinated approach, to be regularly updated, and where this is consistent with the protection of the environment and human health. If the use of a by-product is allowed under an environmental licence or general environmental rules, this can be used by Member States as a tool to decide that no overall adverse environmental or human health impacts are expected to occur; an object or substance should be regarded as being a by-product only when certain conditions are met. Since by-products fall into the category of products, exports of by-products should meet the requirements of the relevant Community legislation; and

— when certain waste ceases to be waste, laying down end-of-waste criteria that provide a high level of environmental protection and an environmental and economic benefit; possible categories of waste for which "end-of-waste" specifications and criteria should be developed are, among others, construction and demolition waste, some ashes and slags, scrap metals, aggregates, tyres, textiles, compost, waste paper and glass. For the purposes of reaching end-of-waste status, a recovery operation may be as simple as the checking of waste to verify that it fulfils the end-of-waste criteria.

(23) In order to verify or calculate if the recycling and recovery targets set in European Parliament and Council Directive 94/62/EC of 20 December 1994 on packaging and

packaging waste, Directive 2000/53/EC of the European Parliament and of the Council of 18 September 2000 on end-of life vehicles, Directive 2002/96/EC of the European Parliament and of the Council of 27 January 2003 on waste electrical and electronic equipment (WEEE) and Directive 2006/66/EC of the European Parliament and of the Council of 6 September 2006 on batteries and accumulators and waste batteries and accumulators as well as other relevant Community legislation are met, the amounts of waste which have ceased to be waste should be accounted for as recycled and recovered waste when the recycling or recovery requirements of that legislation are satisfied.

(24) On the basis of the definition of waste, in order to promote certainty and consistency, the Commission may adopt guidelines to specify in certain cases when substances or objects become waste. Such guidelines may be developed inter alia for electrical and electronic equipment and vehicles.

(25) It is appropriate that costs be allocated in such a way as to reflect the real costs to the environment of the generation and management of waste.

(26) The polluter-pays principle is a guiding principle at European and international levels. The waste producer and the waste holder should manage the waste in a way that guarantees a high level of protection of the environment and human health.

(27) The introduction of extended producer responsibility in this Directive is one of the means to support the design and production of goods which take into full account and facilitate the efficient use of resources during their whole life-cycle including their repair, re-use, disassembly and recycling without compromising the free circulation of goods on the internal market.

(28) This Directive should help move the EU closer to a "recycling society", seeking to avoid waste generation and to use waste as a resource. In particular, the Sixth Community Environment Action Programme calls for measures aimed at ensuring the source separation, collection and recycling of priority waste streams. In line with that objective and as a means to facilitating or improving its recovery potential, waste should be separately collected if technically, environmentally and economically practicable, before undergoing recovery operations that deliver the best overall environmental outcome. Member States should encourage the separation of hazardous compounds from waste streams if necessary to achieve environmentally sound management.

(29) Member States should support the use of recyclates, such as recovered paper, in line with the waste hierarchy and with the aim of a recycling society, and should not support the landfilling or incineration of such recyclates whenever possible.

(30) In order to implement the precautionary principle and the principle of preventive action enshrined in Article 174(2) of the Treaty, it is necessary to set general environmental objectives for the management of waste within the Community. By virtue of those principles, it is for the Community and the Member States to establish a framework to prevent, reduce and, in so far as is possible, eliminate from the outset the sources of pollution or nuisance by adopting measures whereby recognised risks are eliminated.

(31) The waste hierarchy generally lays down a priority order of what constitutes the best overall environmental option in waste legislation and policy, while departing from such hierarchy may be necessary for specific waste streams when justified for reasons of, inter alia, technical feasibility, economic viability and environmental protection.

(32) It is necessary, in order to enable the Community as a whole to become self-sufficient in waste disposal and in the recovery of mixed municipal waste collected from private households and to enable the Member States to move towards that aim individually, to make provision for a network of cooperation as regards disposal installations and installations for the recovery of mixed municipal waste collected from private households, taking into account geographical circumstances and the need for specialised installations for certain types of waste.

(33) For the purposes of applying Regulation (EC) No 1013/2006 of the European Parliament and of the Council of 14 June 2006 on shipments of waste, mixed municipal waste as referred to in Article 3(5) of that Regulation remains mixed municipal waste even when

it has been subject to a waste treatment operation that has not substantially altered its properties.

(34) It is important that hazardous waste be labelled in accordance with international and Community standards. However, where such waste is collected separately from households, this should not result in householders being obliged to complete the requisite documentation.

(35) It is important, in accordance with the waste hierarchy, and for the purpose of reduction of greenhouse gas emissions originating from waste disposal on landfills, to facilitate the separate collection and proper treatment of bio-waste in order to produce environmentally safe compost and other bio-waste based materials. The Commission, after an assessment on the management of bio-waste, will submit proposals for legislative measures, if appropriate.

(36) Technical minimum standards concerning waste treatment activities not covered by Directive 96/61/EC may be adopted where there is evidence that a benefit would be gained in terms of protecting human health and the environment and where a coordinated approach to the implementation of this Directive would ensure the protection of human health and the environment.

(37) It is necessary to specify further the scope and content of the waste management planning obligation, and to integrate into the process of developing or revising waste management plans the need to take into account the environmental impacts of the generation and management of waste. Account should also be taken, where appropriate, of the waste planning requirements laid down in Article 14 of Directive 94/62/EC and of the strategy for the reduction of biodegradable waste going to landfills, referred to in Article 5 of Directive 1999/31/EC.

(38) Member States may apply environmental authorisations or general environmental rules to certain waste producers without compromising the proper functioning of the internal market.

(39) According to Regulation (EC) No 1013/2006, Member States may take the measures necessary to prevent shipments of waste which are not in accordance with their waste management plans. By way of derogation from that Regulation, Member States should be allowed to limit incoming shipments to incinerators classified as recovery, where it has been established that national waste would have to be disposed of or that waste would have to be treated in a way that is not consistent with their waste management plans. It is recognised that certain Member States may not be able to provide a network comprising the full range of final recovery facilities within their territory.

(40) In order to improve the way in which waste prevention actions are taken forward in the Member States and to facilitate the circulation of best practice in this area, it is necessary to strengthen the provisions relating to waste prevention and to introduce a requirement for the Member States to develop waste prevention programmes concentrating on the key environmental impacts and taking into account the whole life-cycle of products and materials. Such measures should pursue the objective of breaking the link between economic growth and the environmental impacts associated with the generation of waste. Stakeholders, as well as the general public, should have the opportunity to participate in the drawing up of the programmes, and should have access to them once drawn up, in line with Directive 2003/35/EC of the European Parliament and of the Council of 26 May 2003 providing for public participation in respect of the drawing up of certain plans and programmes relating to the environment. Waste prevention and decoupling objectives should be developed covering, as appropriate, the reduction of the adverse impacts of waste and of the amounts of waste generated.

(41) In order to move towards a European recycling society with a high level of resource efficiency, targets for preparing for re-use and recycling of waste should be set. Member States maintain different approaches to the collection of household wastes and wastes of a similar nature and composition. It is therefore appropriate that such targets take account of the different collection systems in different Member States. Waste streams

from other origins similar to household waste include waste referred to in entry 20 of the list established by Commission Decision 2000/532/EC.

(42) Economic instruments can play a crucial role in the achievement of waste prevention and management objectives. Waste often has value as a resource, and the further application of economic instruments may maximise environmental benefits. The use of such instruments at the appropriate level should therefore be encouraged while stressing that individual Member States can decide on their use.

(43) Certain provisions on the handling of waste, laid down in Council Directive 91/689/EEC of 12 December 1991 on hazardous waste, should be amended in order to remove obsolete provisions and to improve the clarity of the text. In the interests of simplifying Community legislation, they should be integrated into this Directive. In order to clarify the operation of the mixing ban laid down in Directive 91/689/EEC, and to protect the environment and human health, the exemptions to the mixing ban should additionally comply with best available techniques as defined in Directive 96/61/EC. Directive 91/689/EEC should therefore be repealed.

(44) In the interests of the simplification of Community legislation and the reflection of environmental benefits, the relevant provisions of Council Directive 75/439/EEC of 16 June 1975 on the disposal of waste oils should be integrated into this Directive. Directive 75/439/EEC should therefore be repealed. The management of waste oils should be conducted in accordance with the priority order of the waste hierarchy, and preference should be given to options that deliver the best overall environmental outcome. The separate collection of waste oils remains crucial to their proper management and the prevention of damage to the environment from their improper disposal.

(45) Member States should provide for effective, proportionate and dissuasive penalties to be imposed on natural and legal persons responsible for waste management, such as waste producers, holders, brokers, dealers, transporters and collectors, establishments or undertakings which carry out waste treatment operations and waste management schemes, in cases where they infringe the provisions of this Directive. Member States may also take action to recover the costs of non-compliance and remedial measures, without prejudice to Directive 2004/35/EC of the European Parliament and of the Council of 21 April 2004 on environmental liability with regard to the prevention and remedying of environmental damage.

(46) The measures necessary for the implementation of this Directive should be adopted in accordance with Council Decision 1999/468/EC of 28 June 1999 laying down the procedures for the exercise of implementing powers conferred on the Commission.

(47) In particular, the Commission should be empowered to establish criteria regarding a number of issues such as the conditions under which an object is to be considered a by-product, the end-of-waste status and the determination of waste which is considered as hazardous, as well as to establish detailed rules on the application and calculation methods for verifying compliance with the recycling targets set out in this Directive. Furthermore, the Commission should be empowered to adapt the annexes to technical and scientific progress and to specify the application of the formula for incineration facilities referred to in Annex II, R1. Since those measures are of general scope and are designed to amend non-essential elements of this Directive, by supplementing it with new non-essential elements, they must be adopted in accordance with the regulatory procedure with scrutiny provided for in Article 5a of Decision 1999/468/EC.

(48) In accordance with paragraph 34 of the interinstitutional agreement on better law-making, Member States are encouraged to draw up, for themselves and in the interest of the Community, their own tables, illustrating, as far as possible, the correlation between this Directive and the transposition measures and to make them public.

(49) Since the objective of this Directive, namely the protection of the environment and human health, cannot be sufficiently achieved by the Member States and can therefore, by reasons of the scale or effects of the Directive, be better achieved at Community level, the Community may adopt measures, in accordance with the principle of subsidiarity as

set out in Article 5 of the Treaty. In accordance with the principle of proportionality, as set out in that Article, this Directive does not go beyond what is necessary in order to achieve that objective,

HAVE ADOPTED THIS DIRECTIVE:

Chapter I
Subject matter, scope and definitions

Article 1

Subject matter and scope

This Directive lays down measures to protect the environment and human health by preventing or reducing the adverse impacts of the generation and management of waste and by reducing overall impacts of resource use and improving the efficiency of such use.

Article 2

Exclusions from the scope

1. The following shall be excluded from the scope of this Directive:
(a) gaseous effluents emitted into the atmosphere;
(b) land (in situ) including unexcavated contaminated soil and buildings permanently connected with land;
(c) uncontaminated soil and other naturally occurring material excavated in the course of construction activities where it is certain that the material will be used for the purposes of construction in its natural state on the site from which it was excavated;
(d) radioactive waste;
(e) decommissioned explosives;
(f) faecal matter, if not covered by paragraph 2(b), straw and other natural non-hazardous agricultural or forestry material used in farming, forestry or for the production of energy from such biomass through processes or methods which do not harm the environment or endanger human health.

2. The following shall be excluded from the scope of this Directive to the extent that they are covered by other Community legislation:
(a) waste waters;
(b) animal by-products including processed products covered by Regulation (EC) No 1774/2002, except those which are destined for incineration, landfilling or use in a biogas or composting plant;
(c) carcasses of animals that have died other than by being slaughtered, including animals killed to eradicate epizootic diseases, and that are disposed of in accordance with Regulation (EC) No 1774/2002;
(d) waste resulting from prospecting, extraction, treatment and storage of mineral resources and the working of quarries covered by Directive 2006/21/EC of the European Parliament and of the Council of 15 March 2006 on the management of waste from extractive industries.

3. Without prejudice to obligations under other relevant Community legislation, sediments relocated inside surface waters for the purpose of managing waters and waterways or of preventing floods or mitigating the effects of floods and droughts or land reclamation shall be excluded from the scope of this Directive if it is proved that the sediments are non-hazardous.

4. Specific rules for particular instances, or supplementing those of this Directive, on the management of particular categories of waste, may be laid down by means of individual Directives.

Article 3

Definitions

For the purposes of this Directive, the following definitions shall apply:

1. "waste" means any substance or object which the holder discards or intends or is required to discard;
2. "hazardous waste" means waste which displays one or more of the hazardous properties listed in Annex III;
3. "waste oils" means any mineral or synthetic lubrication or industrial oils which have become unfit for the use for which they were originally intended, such as used combustion engine oils and gearbox oils, lubricating oils, oils for turbines and hydraulic oils;
4. "bio-waste" means biodegradable garden and park waste, food and kitchen waste from households, restaurants, caterers and retail premises and comparable waste from food processing plants;
5. "waste producer" means anyone whose activities produce waste (original waste producer) or anyone who carries out pre-processing, mixing or other operations resulting in a change in the nature or composition of this waste;
6. "waste holder" means the waste producer or the natural or legal person who is in possession of the waste;
7. "dealer" means any undertaking which acts in the role of principal to purchase and subsequently sell waste, including such dealers who do not take physical possession of the waste;
8. "broker" means any undertaking arranging the recovery or disposal of waste on behalf of others, including such brokers who do not take physical possession of the waste;
9. "waste management" means the collection, transport, recovery and disposal of waste, including the supervision of such operations and the after-care of disposal sites, and including actions taken as a dealer or broker;
10. "collection" means the gathering of waste, including the preliminary sorting and preliminary storage of waste for the purposes of transport to a waste treatment facility;
11. "separate collection" means the collection where a waste stream is kept separately by type and nature so as to facilitate a specific treatment;
12. "prevention" means measures taken before a substance, material or product has become waste, that reduce:
    (a) the quantity of waste, including through the re-use of products or the extension of the life span of products;
    (b) the adverse impacts of the generated waste on the environment and human health; or
    (c) the content of harmful substances in materials and products;
13. "re-use" means any operation by which products or components that are not waste are used again for the same purpose for which they were conceived;
14. "treatment" means recovery or disposal operations, including preparation prior to recovery or disposal;
15. "recovery" means any operation the principal result of which is waste serving a useful purpose by replacing other materials which would otherwise have been used to fulfil a particular function, or waste being prepared to fulfil that function, in the plant or in the wider economy. Annex II sets out a non-exhaustive list of recovery operations;
16. "preparing for re-use" means checking, cleaning or repairing recovery operations, by which products or components of products that have become waste are prepared so that they can be re-used without any other pre-processing;
17. "recycling" means any recovery operation by which waste materials are reprocessed into products, materials or substances whether for the original or other purposes. It includes the reprocessing of organic material but does not include energy recovery and the reprocessing into materials that are to be used as fuels or for backfilling operations;

18. "regeneration of waste oils" means any recycling operation whereby base oils can be produced by refining waste oils, in particular by removing the contaminants, the oxidation products and the additives contained in such oils;
19. "disposal" means any operation which is not recovery even where the operation has as a secondary consequence the reclamation of substances or energy. Annex I sets out a non-exhaustive list of disposal operations;
20. "best available techniques" means best available techniques as defined in Article 2(11) of Directive 96/61/EC.

Article 4

Waste hierarchy

1. The following waste hierarchy shall apply as a priority order in waste prevention and management legislation and policy:
(a) prevention;
(b) preparing for re-use;
(c) recycling;
(d) other recovery, e.g. energy recovery; and
(e) disposal.

2. When applying the waste hierarchy referred to in paragraph 1, Member States shall take measures to encourage the options that deliver the best overall environmental outcome. This may require specific waste streams departing from the hierarchy where this is justified by life-cycle thinking on the overall impacts of the generation and management of such waste.

Member States shall ensure that the development of waste legislation and policy is a fully transparent process, observing existing national rules about the consultation and involvement of citizens and stakeholders.

Member States shall take into account the general environmental protection principles of precaution and sustainability, technical feasibility and economic viability, protection of resources as well as the overall environmental, human health, economic and social impacts, in accordance with Articles 1 and 13.

Article 5

By-products

1. A substance or object, resulting from a production process, the primary aim of which is not the production of that item, may be regarded as not being waste referred to in point (1) of Article 3 but as being a by-product only if the following conditions are met:
(a) further use of the substance or object is certain;
(b) the substance or object can be used directly without any further processing other than normal industrial practice;
(c) the substance or object is produced as an integral part of a production process; and
(d) further use is lawful, i.e. the substance or object fulfils all relevant product, environmental and health protection requirements for the specific use and will not lead to overall adverse environmental or human health impacts.

2. On the basis of the conditions laid down in paragraph 1, measures may be adopted to determine the criteria to be met for specific substances or objects to be regarded as a by-product and not as waste referred to in point (1) of Article 3. Those measures, designed to amend non-essential elements of this Directive by supplementing it, shall be adopted in accordance with the regulatory procedure with scrutiny referred to in Article 39(2).

Article 6

End-of-waste status

1. Certain specified waste shall cease to be waste within the meaning of point (1) of Article 3 when it has undergone a recovery, including recycling, operation and complies with specific criteria to be developed in accordance with the following conditions:

(a) the substance or object is commonly used for specific purposes;

(b) a market or demand exists for such a substance or object;

(c) the substance or object fulfils the technical requirements for the specific purposes and meets the existing legislation and standards applicable to products; and

(d) the use of the substance or object will not lead to overall adverse environmental or human health impacts.

The criteria shall include limit values for pollutants where necessary and shall take into account any possible adverse environmental effects of the substance or object.

2. The measures designed to amend non-essential elements of this Directive by supplementing it relating to the adoption of the criteria set out in paragraph 1 and specifying the type of waste to which such criteria shall apply shall be adopted in accordance with the regulatory procedure with scrutiny referred to in Article 39(2). End-of-waste specific criteria should be considered, among others, at least for aggregates, paper, glass, metal, tyres and textiles.

3. Waste which ceases to be waste in accordance with paragraphs 1 and 2, shall also cease to be waste for the purpose of the recovery and recycling targets set out in Directives 94/62/EC, 2000/53/EC, 2002/96/EC and 2006/66/EC and other relevant Community legislation when the recycling or recovery requirements of that legislation are satisfied.

4. Where criteria have not been set at Community level under the procedure set out in paragraphs 1 and 2, Member States may decide case by case whether certain waste has ceased to be waste taking into account the applicable case law. They shall notify the Commission of such decisions in accordance with Directive 98/34/EC of the European Parliament and of the Council of 22 June 1998 laying down a procedure for the provision of information in the field of technical standards and regulations and of rules on Information Society services where so required by that Directive.

Article 7

List of waste

1. The measures designed to amend non-essential elements of this Directive relating to the updating of the list of waste established by Decision 2000/532/EC shall be adopted in accordance with the regulatory procedure with scrutiny referred to in Article 39(2). The list of waste shall include hazardous waste and shall take into account the origin and composition of the waste and, where necessary, the limit values of concentration of hazardous substances. The list of waste shall be binding as regards determination of the waste which is to be considered as hazardous waste. The inclusion of a substance or object in the list shall not mean that it is waste in all circumstances. A substance or object shall be considered to be waste only where the definition in point (1) of Article 3 is met.

2. A Member State may consider waste as hazardous waste where, even though it does not appear as such on the list of waste, it displays one or more of the properties listed in Annex III. The Member State shall notify the Commission of any such cases without delay. It shall record them in the report provided for in Article 37(1) and shall provide the Commission with all relevant information. In the light of notifications received, the list shall be reviewed in order to decide on its adaptation.

3. Where a Member State has evidence to show that specific waste that appears on the list as hazardous waste does not display any of the properties listed in Annex III, it may consider that

waste as non-hazardous waste. The Member State shall notify the Commission of any such cases without delay and shall provide the Commission with the necessary evidence. In the light of notifications received, the list shall be reviewed in order to decide on its adaptation.

4. The reclassification of hazardous waste as non-hazardous waste may not be achieved by diluting or mixing the waste with the aim of lowering the initial concentrations of hazardous substances to a level below the thresholds for defining waste as hazardous.

5. The measures designed to amend non-essential elements of this Directive relating to the revision of the list in order to decide on its adaptation pursuant to paragraphs 2 and 3 shall be adopted in accordance with the regulatory procedure with scrutiny referred to in Article 39(2).

6. Member States may consider waste as non-hazardous waste in accordance with the list of waste referred to in paragraph 1.

7. The Commission shall ensure that the list of waste and any review of this list adhere, as appropriate, to principles of clarity, comprehensibility and accessibility for users, particularly small and medium-sized enterprises (SMEs).

Chapter II
General requirements

Article 8

Extended producer responsibility

1. In order to strengthen the re-use and the prevention, recycling and other recovery of waste, Member States may take legislative or non-legislative measures to ensure that any natural or legal person who professionally develops, manufactures, processes, treats, sells or imports products (producer of the product) has extended producer responsibility.

Such measures may include an acceptance of returned products and of the waste that remains after those products have been used, as well as the subsequent management of the waste and financial responsibility for such activities. These measures may include the obligation to provide publicly available information as to the extent to which the product is re-usable and recyclable.

2. Member States may take appropriate measures to encourage the design of products in order to reduce their environmental impacts and the generation of waste in the course of the production and subsequent use of products, and in order to ensure that the recovery and disposal of products that have become waste take place in accordance with Articles 4 and 13.

Such measures may encourage, inter alia, the development, production and marketing of products that are suitable for multiple use, that are technically durable and that are, after having become waste, suitable for proper and safe recovery and environmentally compatible disposal.

3. When applying extended producer responsibility, Member States shall take into account the technical feasibility and economic viability and the overall environmental, human health and social impacts, respecting the need to ensure the proper functioning of the internal market.

4. The extended producer responsibility shall be applied without prejudice to the responsibility for waste management as provided for in Article 15(1) and without prejudice to existing waste stream specific and product specific legislation.

Article 9

Prevention of waste

Following the consultation of stakeholders, the Commission shall submit to the European Parliament and the Council the following reports accompanied, if appropriate, by proposals for measures required in support of the prevention activities and the implementation of the waste prevention programmes referred to in Article 29 covering:

(a) by the end of 2011, an interim report on the evolution of waste generation and the scope of waste prevention, including the formulation of a product eco-design policy addressing both the generation of waste and the presence of hazardous substances in waste, with a view to promoting technologies focusing on durable, re-usable and recyclable products;

(b) by the end of 2011, the formulation of an action plan for further support measures at European level seeking, in particular, to change current consumption patterns;

(c) by the end of 2014, the setting of waste prevention and decoupling objectives for 2020, based on best available practices including, if necessary, a revision of the indicators referred to in Article 29(4).

Article 10

Recovery

1. Member States shall take the necessary measures to ensure that waste undergoes recovery operations, in accordance with Articles 4 and 13.

2. Where necessary to comply with paragraph 1 and to facilitate or improve recovery, waste shall be collected separately if technically, environmentally and economically practicable and shall not be mixed with other waste or other material with different properties.

Article 11

Re-use and recycling

1. Member States shall take measures, as appropriate, to promote the re-use of products and preparing for re-use activities, notably by encouraging the establishment and support of re-use and repair networks, the use of economic instruments, procurement criteria, quantitative objectives or other measures.

Member States shall take measures to promote high quality recycling and, to this end, shall set up separate collections of waste where technically, environmentally and economically practicable and appropriate to meet the necessary quality standards for the relevant recycling sectors.

Subject to Article 10(2), by 2015 separate collection shall be set up for at least the following: paper, metal, plastic and glass.

2. In order to comply with the objectives of this Directive, and move towards a European recycling society with a high level of resource efficiency, Member States shall take the necessary measures designed to achieve the following targets:

(a) by 2020, the preparing for re-use and the recycling of waste materials such as at least paper, metal, plastic and glass from households and possibly from other origins as far as these waste streams are similar to waste from households, shall be increased to a minimum of overall 50 % by weight;

(b) by 2020, the preparing for re-use, recycling and other material recovery, including backfilling operations using waste to substitute other materials, of non-hazardous construction and demolition waste excluding naturally occurring material defined in category 17 05 04 in the list of waste shall be increased to a minimum of 70 % by weight.

3. The Commission shall establish detailed rules on the application and calculation methods for verifying compliance with the targets set out in paragraph 2 of this Article, considering Regulation (EC) No 2150/2002 of the European Parliament and of the Council of 25 November 2002 on waste statistics. These can include transition periods for Member States which, in 2008, recycled less than 5 % of either categories of waste referred to in paragraph 2. Those

measures, designed to amend non-essential elements of this Directive by supplementing it, shall be adopted in accordance with the regulatory procedure with scrutiny referred to in Article 39(2) of this Directive.

4. By 31 December 2014 at the latest, the Commission shall examine the measures and the targets referred to in paragraph 2 with a view to, if necessary, reinforcing the targets and considering the setting of targets for other waste streams. The report of the Commission, accompanied by a proposal if appropriate, shall be sent to the European Parliament and the Council. In its report, the Commission shall take into account the relevant environmental, economic and social impacts of setting the targets.

5. Every three years, in accordance with Article 37, Member States shall report to the Commission on their record with regard to meeting the targets. If targets are not met, this report shall include the reasons for failure and the actions the Member State intends to take to meet those targets.

Article 12

Disposal

Member States shall ensure that, where recovery in accordance with Article 10(1) is not undertaken, waste undergoes safe disposal operations which meet the provisions of Article 13 on the protection of human health and the environment.

Article 13

Protection of human health and the environment

Member States shall take the necessary measures to ensure that waste management is carried out without endangering human health, without harming the environment and, in particular:

(a) without risk to water, air, soil, plants or animals;
(b) without causing a nuisance through noise or odours; and
(c) without adversely affecting the countryside or places of special interest.

Article 14

Costs

1. In accordance with the polluter-pays principle, the costs of waste management shall be borne by the original waste producer or by the current or previous waste holders.

2. Member States may decide that the costs of waste management are to be borne partly or wholly by the producer of the product from which the waste came and that the distributors of such product may share these costs.

Chapter III
Waste management

Article 15

Responsibility for waste management

1. Member States shall take the necessary measures to ensure that any original waste producer or other holder carries out the treatment of waste himself or has the treatment handled by a dealer or an establishment or undertaking which carries out waste treatment operations or arranged by a private or public waste collector in accordance with Articles 4 and 13.

2. When the waste is transferred from the original producer or holder to one of the natural or legal persons referred to in paragraph 1 for preliminary treatment, the responsibility for

carrying out a complete recovery or disposal operation shall not be discharged as a general rule.

Without prejudice to Regulation (EC) No 1013/2006, Member States may specify the conditions of responsibility and decide in which cases the original producer is to retain responsibility for the whole treatment chain or in which cases theresponsibility of the producer and the holder can be shared or delegated among the actors of the treatment chain.

3. Member States may decide, in accordance with Article 8, that the responsibility for arranging waste management is to be borne partly or wholly by the producer of the product from which the waste came and that distributors of such product may share this responsibility.

4. Member States shall take the necessary measures to ensure that, within their territory, the establishments or undertakings which collect or transport waste on a professional basis deliver the waste collected and transported to appropriate treatment installations respecting the provisions of Article 13.

Article 16

Principles of self-sufficiency and proximity

1. Member States shall take appropriate measures, in cooperation with other Member States where this is necessary or advisable, to establish an integrated and adequate network of waste disposal installations and of installations for the recovery of mixed municipal waste collected from private households, including where such collection also covers such waste from other producers, taking into account best available techniques.

By way of derogation from Regulation (EC) No 1013/2006, Member States may, in order to protect their network, limit incoming shipments of waste destined to incinerators that are classified as recovery, where it has been established that such shipments would result in national waste having to be disposed of or waste having to be treated in a way that is not consistent with their waste management plans. Member States shall notify the Commission of any such decision. Member States may also limit outgoing shipments of waste on environmental grounds as set out in Regulation (EC) No 1013/2006.

2. The network shall be designed to enable the Community as a whole to become self-sufficient in waste disposal as well as in the recovery of waste referred to in paragraph 1, and to enable Member States to move towards that aim individually, taking into account geographical circumstances or the need for specialised installations for certain types of waste.

3. The network shall enable waste to be disposed of or waste referred to in paragraph 1 to be recovered in one of the nearest appropriate installations, by means of the most appropriate methods and technologies, in order to ensure a high level of protection for the environment and public health.

4. The principles of proximity and self-sufficiency shall not mean that each Member State has to possess the full range of final recovery facilities within that Member State.

Article 17

Control of hazardous waste

Member States shall take the necessary action to ensure that the production, collection and transportation of hazardous waste, as well as its storage and treatment, are carried out in conditions providing protection for the environment and human health in order to meet the provisions of Article 13, including action to ensure traceability from production to final destination and control of hazardous waste in order to meet the requirements of Articles 35 and 36.

Article 18

Ban on the mixing of hazardous waste

1. Member States shall take the necessary measures to ensure that hazardous waste is not mixed, either with other categories of hazardous waste or with other waste, substances or materials. Mixing shall include the dilution of hazardous substances.

2. By way of derogation from paragraph 1, Member States may allow mixing provided that:
(a) the mixing operation is carried out by an establishment or undertaking which has obtained a permit in accordance with Article 23;
(b) the provisions of Article 13 are complied with and the adverse impact of the waste management on human health and the environment is not increased; and
(c) the mixing operation conforms to best available techniques.

3. Subject to technical and economic feasibility criteria, where hazardous waste has been mixed in a manner contrary to paragraph 1, separation shall be carried out where possible and necessary in order to comply with Article 13.

Article 19

Labelling of hazardous waste

1. Member States shall take the necessary measures to ensure that, in the course of collection, transport and temporary storage, hazardous waste is packaged and labelled in accordance with the international and Community standards in force.

2. Whenever hazardous waste is transferred within a Member State, it shall be accompanied by an identification document, which may be in electronic format, containing the appropriate data specified in Annex IB to Regulation (EC) No 1013/2006.

Article 20

Hazardous waste produced by households

Articles 17, 18, 19 and 35 shall not apply to mixed waste produced by households.

Articles 19 and 35 shall not apply to separate fractions of hazardous waste produced by households until they are accepted for collection, disposal or recovery by an establishment or an undertaking which has obtained a permit or has been registered in accordance with Articles 23 or 26.

Article 21

Waste oils

1. Without prejudice to the obligations related to the management of hazardous waste laid down in Articles 18 and 19, Member States shall take the necessary measures to ensure that:
(a) waste oils are collected separately, where this is technically feasible;
(b) waste oils are treated in accordance with Articles 4 and 13;
(c) where this is technically feasible and economically viable, waste oils of different characteristics are not mixed and waste oils are not mixed with other kinds of waste or substances, if such mixing impedes their treatment.

2. For the purposes of separate collection of waste oils and their proper treatment, Member States may, according to their national conditions, apply additional measures such as technical requirements, producer responsibility, economic instruments or voluntary agreements.

3. If waste oils, according to national legislation, are subject to requirements of regeneration, Member States may prescribe that such waste oils shall be regenerated if technically feasible

and, where Articles 11 or 12 of Regulation (EC) No 1013/2006 apply, restrict the transboundary shipment of waste oils from their territory to incineration or co-incineration facilities in order to give priority to the regeneration of waste oils.

Article 22

Bio-waste

Member States shall take measures, as appropriate, and in accordance with Articles 4 and 13, to encourage:
(a) the separate collection of bio-waste with a view to the composting and digestion of bio-waste;
(b) the treatment of bio-waste in a way that fulfils a high level of environmental protection;
(c) the use of environmentally safe materials produced from bio-waste.
The Commission shall carry out an assessment on the management of bio-waste with a view to submitting a proposal if appropriate. The assessment shall examine the opportunity of setting minimum requirements for bio-waste management and quality criteria for compost and digestate from bio-waste, in order to guarantee a high level of protection for human health and the environment.

Chapter IV
Permits and registrations

Article 23

Issue of permits

1. Member States shall require any establishment or undertaking intending to carry out waste treatment to obtain a permit from the competent authority.

Such permits shall specify at least the following:
(a) the types and quantities of waste that may be treated;
(b) for each type of operation permitted, the technical and any other requirements relevant to the site concerned;
(c) the safety and precautionary measures to be taken;
(d) the method to be used for each type of operation;
(e) such monitoring and control operations as may be necessary;
(f) such closure and after-care provisions as may be necessary.

2. Permits may be granted for a specified period and may be renewable.

3. Where the competent authority considers that the intended method of treatment is unacceptable from the point of view of environmental protection, in particular when the method is not in accordance with Article 13, it shall refuse to issue the permit.

4. It shall be a condition of any permit covering incineration or co-incineration with energy recovery that the recovery of energy take place with a high level of energy efficiency.

5. Provided that the requirements of this Article are complied with, any permit produced pursuant to other national or Community legislation may be combined with the permit required under paragraph 1 to form a single permit, where such a format obviates the unnecessary duplication of information and the repetition of work by the operator or the competent authority.

Article 24

Exemptions from permit requirements

Member States may exempt from the requirement laid down in Article 23(1) establishments or undertakings for the following operations:

(a) disposal of their own non-hazardous waste at the place of production; or
(b) recovery of waste.

Article 25

Conditions for exemptions

1. Where a Member State wishes to allow exemptions, as provided for in Article 24, it shall lay down, in respect of each type of activity, general rules specifying the types and quantities of waste that may be covered by an exemption, and the method of treatment to be used.

Those rules shall be designed to ensure that waste is treated in accordance with Article 13. In the case of disposal operations referred to in point (a) of Article 24 those rules should consider best available techniques.

2. In addition to the general rules provided for in paragraph 1, Member States shall lay down specific conditions for exemptions relating to hazardous waste, including types of activity, as well as any other necessary requirement for carrying out different forms of recovery and, where relevant, the limit values for the content of hazardous substances in the waste as well as the emission limit values.

3. Member States shall inform the Commission of the general rules laid down pursuant to paragraphs 1 and 2.

Article 26

Registration

Where the following are not subject to permit requirements, Member States shall ensure that the competent authority keeps a register of:
(a) establishments or undertakings which collect or transport waste on a professional basis;
(b) dealers or brokers; and
(c) establishments or undertakings which are subject to exemptions from the permit requirements pursuant to Article 24.

Where possible, existing records held by the competent authority shall be used to obtain the relevant information for this registration process in order to reduce the administrative burden.

Article 27

Minimum standards

1. Technical minimum standards for treatment activities which require a permit pursuant to Article 23 may be adopted where there is evidence that a benefit in terms of the protection of human health and the environment would be gained from such minimum standards. Those measures, designed to amend non-essential elements of this Directive by supplementing it, shall be adopted in accordance with the regulatory procedure with scrutiny referred to in Article 39(2).

2. Such minimum standards shall cover only those waste treatment activities that are not covered by Directive 96/61/EC or are not appropriate for coverage by that Directive.

3. Such minimum standards shall:
(a) be directed to the main environmental impacts of the waste treatment activity;
(b) ensure that the waste is treated in accordance with Article 13;
(c) take into account best available techniques; and
(d) as appropriate, include elements regarding the quality of treatment and the process requirements.

4. Minimum standards for activities that require registration pursuant to points (a) and (b) of Article 26 shall be adopted where there is evidence that a benefit in terms of the protection of human health and the environment or in avoiding disruption to the internal market would be gained from such minimum standards, including elements regarding the technical qualification of collectors, transporters, dealers or brokers.

Those measures, designed to amend non-essential elements of this Directive by supplementing it, shall be adopted in accordance with the regulatory procedure with scrutiny referred to in Article 39(2).

Chapter V
Plans and programmes

Article 28

Waste management plans

1. Member States shall ensure that their competent authorities establish, in accordance with Articles 1, 4, 13 and 16, one or more waste management plans.

Those plans shall, alone or in combination, cover the entire geographical territory of the Member State concerned.

2. The waste management plans shall set out an analysis of the current waste management situation in the geographical entity concerned, as well as the measures to be taken to improve environmentally sound preparing for re-use, recycling, recovery and disposal of waste and an evaluation of how the plan will support the implementation of the objectives and provisions of this Directive.

3. The waste management plans shall contain, as appropriate and taking into account the geographical level and coverage of the planning area, at least the following:

(a) the type, quantity and source of waste generated within the territory, the waste likely to be shipped from or to the national territory, and an evaluation of the development of waste streams in the future;

(b) existing waste collection schemes and major disposal and recovery installations, including any special arrangements for waste oils, hazardous waste or waste streams addressed by specific Community legislation;

(c) an assessment of the need for new collection schemes, the closure of existing waste installations, additional waste installation infrastructure in accordance with Article 16, and, if necessary, the investments related thereto;

(d) sufficient information on the location criteria for site identification and on the capacity of future disposal or major recovery installations, if necessary;

(e) general waste management policies, including planned waste management technologies and methods, or policies for waste posing specific management problems.

4. The waste management plan may contain, taking into account the geographical level and coverage of the planning area, the following:

(a) organisational aspects related to waste management including a description of the allocation of responsibilities between public and private actors carrying out the waste management;

(b) an evaluation of the usefulness and suitability of the use of economic and other instruments in tackling various waste problems, taking into account the need to maintain the smooth functioning of the internal market;

(c) the use of awareness campaigns and information provision directed at the general public or at a specific set of consumers;

(d) historical contaminated waste disposal sites and measures for their rehabilitation.

5. Waste management plans shall conform to the waste planning requirements laid down in Article 14 of Directive 94/62/EC and the strategy for the implementation of the reduction of biodegradable waste going to landfills, referred to in Article 5 of Directive 1999/31/EC.

Article 29

Waste prevention programmes

1. Member States shall establish, in accordance with Articles 1 and 4, waste prevention programmes not later than 12 December 2013.

Such programmes shall be integrated either into the waste management plans provided for in Article 28 or into other environmental policy programmes, as appropriate, or shall function as separate programmes. If any such programme is integrated into the waste management plan or into other programmes, the waste prevention measures shall be clearly identified.

2. The programmes provided for in paragraph 1 shall set out the waste prevention objectives. Member States shall describe the existing prevention measures and evaluate the usefulness of the examples of measures indicated in Annex IV or other appropriate measures.

The aim of such objectives and measures shall be to break the link between economic growth and the environmental impacts associated with the generation of waste.

3. Member States shall determine appropriate specific qualitative or quantitative benchmarks for waste prevention measures adopted in order to monitor and assess the progress of the measures and may determine specific qualitative or quantitative targets and indicators, other than those referred to in paragraph 4, for the same purpose.

4. Indicators for waste prevention measures may be adopted in accordance with the regulatory procedure referred to in Article 39(3).

5. The Commission shall create a system for sharing information on best practice regarding waste prevention and shall develop guidelines in order to assist the Member States in the preparation of the Programmes.

Article 30

Evaluation and review of plans and programmes

1. Member States shall ensure that the waste management plans and waste prevention programmes are evaluated at least every sixth year and revised as appropriate and, where relevant, in accordance with Articles 9 and 11.

2. The European Environment Agency is invited to include in its annual report a review of progress in the completion and implementation of waste prevention programmes.

Article 31

Public participation

Member States shall ensure that relevant stakeholders and authorities and the general public have the opportunity to participate in the elaboration of the waste management plans and waste prevention programmes, and have access to them once elaborated, in accordance with Directive 2003/35/EC or, if relevant, Directive 2001/42/EC of the European Parliament and of the Council of 27 June 2001 on the assessment of the effects of certain plans and programmes on the environment. They shall place the plans and programmes on a publicly available website.

Article 32

Cooperation

Member States shall cooperate as appropriate with the other Member States concerned and the Commission to draw up the waste management plans and the waste prevention programmes in accordance with Articles 28 and 29.

Article 33

Information to be submitted to the Commission

1. Member States shall inform the Commission of the waste management plans and waste prevention programmes referred to in Articles 28 and 29, once adopted, and of any substantial revisions to the plans and programmes.

2. The format for notifying the information on the adoption and substantial revisions of those plans and programmes shall be adopted in accordance with the regulatory procedure referred to in Article 39(3).

Chapter VI
Inspections and records

Article 34

Inspections

1. Establishments or undertakings which carry out waste treatment operations, establishments or undertakings which collect or transport waste on a professional basis, brokers and dealers, and establishments or undertakings which produce hazardous waste shall be subject to appropriate periodic inspections by the competent authorities.

2. Inspections concerning collection and transport operations shall cover the origin, nature, quantity and destination of the waste collected and transported.

3. Member States may take account of registrations obtained under the Community Eco-Management and Audit Scheme (EMAS), in particular regarding the frequency and intensity of inspections.

Article 35

Record keeping

1. The establishments or undertakings referred to in Article 23(1), the producers of hazardous waste and the establishments and undertakings which collect or transport hazardous waste on a professional basis, or act as dealers and brokers of hazardous waste, shall keep a chronological record of the quantity, nature and origin of the waste, and, where relevant, the destination, frequency of collection, mode of transport and treatment method foreseen in respect of the waste, and shall make that information available, on request, to the competent authorities.

2. For hazardous waste, the records shall be preserved for at least three years except in the case of establishments and undertakings transporting hazardous waste which must keep such records for at least 12 months.

Documentary evidence that the management operations have been carried out shall be supplied at the request of the competent authorities or of a previous holder.

3. Member States may require the producers of non-hazardous waste to comply with paragraphs 1 and 2.

Article 36

Enforcement and penalties

1. Member States shall take the necessary measures to prohibit the abandonment, dumping or uncontrolled management of waste.

2. Members States shall lay down provisions on the penalties applicable to infringements of the provisions of this Directive and shall take all measures necessary to ensure that they are implemented. The penalties shall be effective, proportionate and dissuasive.

Chapter VII
Final provisions

Article 37

Reporting and reviewing

1. Every three years, Member States shall inform the Commission of the implementation of this Directive by submitting a sectoral report in an electronic form. This report shall also contain information on the management of waste oil and on the progress achieved in the implementation of the waste prevention programmes and, as appropriate, information on measures as foreseen by Article 8 on extended producer responsibility.

The report shall be drawn up on the basis of a questionnaire or outline established by the Commission in accordance with the procedure referred to in Article 6 of Council Directive 91/692/EEC of 23 December 1991 standardising and rationalising reports on the implementation of certain Directives relating to the environment. The report shall be submitted to the Commission within nine months of the end of the three year period covered by it.

2. The Commission shall send the questionnaire or outline to the Member States six months before the start of the period covered by the sectoral report.

3. The Commission shall publish a report on the implementation of this Directive within nine months of receiving the sectoral reports from the Member States in accordance with paragraph 1.

4. In the first report that intervenes by 12 December 2014, the Commission shall review the implementation of this Directive, including the energy efficiency provisions, and will present a proposal for revision if appropriate. The report shall also assess the existing Member State waste prevention programmes, objectives and indicators and shall review the opportunity of Community level programmes, including producer responsibility schemes for specific waste streams, targets, indicators and measures related to recycling, as well as material and energy recovery operations that may contribute to fulfilling the objectives set out in Articles 1 and 4 more effectively.

Article 38

Interpretation and adaptation to technical progress

1. The Commission may develop guidelines for the interpretation of the definitions of recovery and disposal.

If necessary, the application of the formula for incineration facilities referred to in Annex II, R1, shall be specified. Local climatic conditions may be taken into account, such as the severity of the cold and the need for heating insofar as they influence the amounts of energy that can technically be used or produced in the form of electricity, heating, cooling or processing steam. Local conditions of the outermost regions as recognised in the fourth subparagraph of Article 299(2) of the Treaty and of the territories mentioned in Article 25 of the 1985 Act of Accession may also be taken into account. This measure, designed to amend non-essential elements of this Directive, shall be adopted in accordance with the regulatory procedure with scrutiny referred to in Article 39(2).

2. The Annexes may be amended in the light of scientific and technical progress. Those measures, designed to amend non-essential elements of this Directive, shall be adopted in accordance with the regulatory procedure with scrutiny referred to in Article 39(2).

Article 39

Committee procedure

1. The Commission shall be assisted by a committee.

2. Where reference is made to this paragraph, Article 5a(1) to (4) and Article 7 of Decision 1999/468/EC shall apply, having regard to the provisions of Article 8 thereof.

3. Where reference is made to this paragraph, Articles 5 and 7 of Decision 1999/468/EC shall apply, having regard to the provisions of Article 8 thereof.

The period laid down in Article 5(6) of Decision 1999/468/EC shall be set at three months.

Article 40

Transposition

1. Member States shall bring into force the laws, regulations and administrative provisions necessary to comply with this Directive by 12 December 2010.

When Member States adopt these measures, they shall contain a reference to this Directive or shall be accompanied by such reference on the occasion of their official publication. The methods of making such reference shall be laid down by Member States.

2. Member States shall communicate to the Commission the text of the main provisions of national law which they adopt in the field covered by this Directive.

[*Article 41 is not reproduced.*]

Article 42

Entry into force

This Directive shall enter into force on the twentieth day following that of its publication in the Official Journal of the European Union.

Article 43

Addressees

This Directive is addressed to the Member States.

ANNEX I
DISPOSAL OPERATIONS

D 1 Deposit into or on to land (e.g. landfill, etc.)

D 2 Land treatment (e.g. biodegradation of liquid or sludgy discards in soils, etc.)

D 3 Deep injection (e.g. injection of pumpable discards into wells, salt domes or naturally occurring repositories, etc.)

D 4 Surface impoundment (e.g. placement of liquid or sludgy discards into pits, ponds or lagoons, etc.)

D 5 Specially engineered landfill (e.g. placement into lined discrete cells which are capped and isolated from one another and the environment, etc.)

D 6 Release into a water body except seas/oceans

D 7 Release to seas/oceans including sea-bed insertion

D 8 Biological treatment not specified elsewhere in this Annex which results in final compounds or mixtures which are discarded by means of any of the operations numbered D 1 to D 12

D 9 Physico-chemical treatment not specified elsewhere in this Annex which results in final compounds or mixtures which are discarded by means of any of the operations numbered D 1 to D 12 (e.g. evaporation, drying, calcination, etc.)

D 10 Incineration on land

D 11 Incineration at sea(*)

D 12 Permanent storage (e.g. emplacement of containers in a mine, etc.)

D 13 Blending or mixing prior to submission to any of the operations numbered D 1 to D 12(**)

D 14 Repackaging prior to submission to any of the operations numbered D 1 to D 13

D 15 Storage pending any of the operations numbered D 1 to D 14 (excluding temporary storage, pending collection, on the site where the waste is produced)(***)

(*) This operation is prohibited by EU legislation and international conventions.
(**) If there is no other D code appropriate, this can include preliminary operations prior to disposal including pre-processing such as, inter alia, sorting, crushing, compacting, pelletising, drying, shredding, conditioning or separating prior to submission to any of the operations numbered D1 to D12.
(***) Temporary storage means preliminary storage according to point (10) of Article 3.

ANNEX II
RECOVERY OPERATIONS

R 1 Use principally as a fuel or other means to generate energy(*)

R 2 Solvent reclamation/regeneration

R 3 Recycling/reclamation of organic substances which are not used as solvents (including composting and other biological transformation processes)(**)

R 4 Recycling/reclamation of metals and metal compounds

R 5 Recycling/reclamation of other inorganic materials(***)

R 6 Regeneration of acids or bases

R 7 Recovery of components used for pollution abatement

R 8 Recovery of components from catalysts

R 9 Oil re-refining or other reuses of oil

R 10 Land treatment resulting in benefit to agriculture or ecological improvement

R 11 Use of waste obtained from any of the operations numbered R 1 to R 10

R 12 Exchange of waste for submission to any of the operations numbered R 1 to R 11(****)

R 13 Storage of waste pending any of the operations numbered R 1 to R 12 (excluding temporary storage, pending collection, on the site where the waste is produced)(*****)

(*) This includes incineration facilities dedicated to the processing of municipal solid waste only where their energy efficiency is equal to or above:
- 0,60 for installations in operation and permitted in accordance with applicable Community legislation before 1 January 2009,
- 0,65 for installations permitted after 31 December 2008,

using the following formula:

Energy efficiency = (Ep – (Ef + Ei))/(0,97 × (Ew + Ef))

In which:

Ep means annual energy produced as heat or electricity. It is calculated with energy in the form of electricity being multiplied by 2,6 and heat produced for commercial use multiplied by 1,1 (GJ/year)

Ef means annual energy input to the system from fuels contributing to the production of steam (GJ/year)

Ew means annual energy contained in the treated waste calculated using the net calorific value of the waste (GJ/year)

Ei means annual energy imported excluding Ew and Ef (GJ/year)

0,97 is a factor accounting for energy losses due to bottom ash and radiation.

This formula shall be applied in accordance with the reference document on Best Available Techniques for waste incineration.

(**) This includes gasification and pyrolisis using the components as chemicals.

(***) This includes soil cleaning resulting in recovery of the soil and recycling of inorganic construction materials.

(****) If there is no other R code appropriate, this can include preliminary operations prior to recovery including pre-processing such as, inter alia, dismantling, sorting, crushing, compacting, pelletising, drying, shredding, conditioning, repackaging, separating, blending or mixing prior to submission to any of the operations numbered R1 to R11.

(*****) Temporary storage means preliminary storage according to point (10) of Article 3.

ANNEX III
PROPERTIES OF WASTE WHICH RENDER IT HAZARDOUS

H 1 "Explosive": substances and preparations which may explode under the effect of flame or which are more sensitive to shocks or friction than dinitrobenzene.

H 2 "Oxidizing": substances and preparations which exhibit highly exothermic reactions when in contact with other substances, particularly flammable substances.

H 3-A "Highly flammable"

— liquid substances and preparations having a flash point below 21 °C (including extremely flammable liquids), or
— substances and preparations which may become hot and finally catch fire in contact with air at ambient temperature without any application of energy, or
— solid substances and preparations which may readily catch fire after brief contact with a source of ignition and which continue to burn or to be consumed after removal of the source of ignition, or
— gaseous substances and preparations which are flammable in air at normal pressure, or
— substances and preparations which, in contact with water or damp air, evolve highly flammable gases in dangerous quantities.

H 3-B "Flammable": liquid substances and preparations having a flash point equal to or greater than 21 °C and less than or equal to 55 °C.

H 4 "Irritant": non-corrosive substances and preparations which, through immediate, prolonged or repeated contact with the skin or mucous membrane, can cause inflammation.

H 5 "Harmful": substances and preparations which, if they are inhaled or ingested or if they penetrate the skin, may involve limited health risks.

H 6 "Toxic": substances and preparations (including very toxic substances and preparations) which, if they are inhaled or ingested or if they penetrate the skin, may involve serious, acute or chronic health risks and even death.

H 7 "Carcinogenic": substances and preparations which, if they are inhaled or ingested or if they penetrate the skin, may induce cancer or increase its incidence.

H 8 "Corrosive": substances and preparations which may destroy living tissue on contact.

H 9 "Infectious": substances and preparations containing viable micro-organisms or their toxins which are known or reliably believed to cause disease in man or other living organisms.

H 10 "Toxic for reproduction": substances and preparations which, if they are inhaled or ingested or if they penetrate the skin, may induce non-hereditary congenital malformations or increase their incidence.

H 11 "Mutagenic": substances and preparations which, if they are inhaled or ingested or if they penetrate the skin, may induce hereditary genetic defects or increase their incidence.

H 12 Waste which releases toxic or very toxic gases in contact with water, air or an acid.

H 13(*) "Sensitizing": substances and preparations which, if they are inhaled or if they penetrate the skin, are capable of eliciting a reaction of hypersensitization such that on further exposure to the substance or preparation, characteristic adverse effects are produced.

H 14 "Ecotoxic": waste which presents or may present immediate or delayed risks for one or more sectors of the environment.

H 15 Waste capable by any means, after disposal, of yielding another substance, e.g. a leachate, which possesses any of the characteristics listed above.

Notes

1. Attribution of the hazardous properties "toxic" (and "very toxic"), "harmful", "corrosive", "irritant", "carcinogenic", "toxic to reproduction", "mutagenic" and "eco-toxic" is made on the basis of the criteria laid down by Annex VI, to Council Directive 67/548/EEC of 27 June 1967 on the approximation of laws, regulations and administrative provisions relating to the classification, packaging and labelling of dangerous substances.

2. Where relevant the limit values listed in Annex II and III to Directive 1999/45/EC of the European Parliament and of the Council of 31 May 1999 concerning the approximation of the laws, regulations and administrative provisions of the Member States relating to the classification, packaging and labelling of dangerous preparations shall apply.

Test methods

The methods to be used are described in Annex V to Directive 67/548/EEC and in other relevant CEN-notes.

(*) As far as testing methods are available.

ANNEX IV
EXAMPLES OF WASTE PREVENTION MEASURES REFERRED TO IN ARTICLE 29

Measures that can affect the framework conditions related to the generation of waste

1. The use of planning measures, or other economic instruments promoting the efficient use of resources.

2. The promotion of research and development into the area of achieving cleaner and less wasteful products and technologies and the dissemination and use of the results of such research and development.

3. The development of effective and meaningful indicators of the environmental pressures associated with the generation of waste aimed at contributing to the prevention of waste generation at all levels, from product comparisons at Community level through action by local authorities to national measures.

Measures that can affect the design and production and distribution phase

4. The promotion of eco-design (the systematic integration of environmental aspects into product design with the aim to improve the environmental performance of the product throughout its whole life cycle).

5. The provision of information on waste prevention techniques with a view to facilitating the implementation of best available techniques by industry.

6. Organise training of competent authorities as regards the insertion of waste prevention requirements in permits under this Directive and Directive 96/61/EC.

7. The inclusion of measures to prevent waste production at installations not falling under Directive 96/61/EC. Where appropriate, such measures could include waste prevention assessments or plans.

8. The use of awareness campaigns or the provision of financial, decision making or other support to businesses. Such measures are likely to be particularly effective where they are aimed at, and adapted to, small and medium sized enterprises and work through established business networks.

9. The use of voluntary agreements, consumer/producer panels or sectoral negotiations in order that the relevant businesses or industrial sectors set their own waste prevention plans or objectives or correct wasteful products or packaging.

10. The promotion of creditable environmental management systems, including EMAS and ISO 14001.

Measures that can affect the consumption and use phase

11. Economic instruments such as incentives for clean purchases or the institution of an obligatory payment by consumers for a given article or element of packaging that would otherwise be provided free of charge.

12. The use of awareness campaigns and information provision directed at the general public or a specific set of consumers.

13. The promotion of creditable eco-labels.

14. Agreements with industry, such as the use of product panels such as those being carried out within the framework of Integrated Product Policies or with retailers on the availability of waste prevention information and products with a lower environmental impact.

15. In the context of public and corporate procurement, the integration of environmental and waste prevention criteria into calls for tenders and contracts, in line with the Handbook on environmental public procurement published by the Commission on 29 October 2004.

16. The promotion of the reuse and/or repair of appropriate discarded products or of their components, notably through the use of educational, economic, logistic or other measures such as support to or establishment of accredited repair and reuse-centres and networks especially in densely populated regions.

ANNEX V
CORRELATION TABLE

Directive 2006/12/EC	*This Directive*
Article 1(1)(a)	Article 3(1)
Article 1(1)(b)	Article 3(5)
Article 1(1)(c)	Article 3(6)
Article 1(1)(d)	Article 3(9)

Directive 2006/12/EC	*This Directive*
Article 1(1)(e)	Article 3(19)
Article 1(1)(f)	Article 3(15)
Article 1(1)(g)	Article 3(10)
Article 1(2)	Article 7
Article 2(1)	Article 2(1)
Article 2(1)(a)	Article 2(1)(a)
Article 2(1)(b)	Article 2(2)
Article 2(1)(b)(i)	Article 2(1)(d)
Article 2(1)(b)(ii)	Article 2(2)(d)
Article 2(1)(b)(iii)	Article 2(1)(f) and (2)(c)
Article 2(1)(b)(iv)	Article 2(2)(a)
Article 2(1)(b)(v)	Article 2(1)(e)
Article 2(2)	Article 2(4)
Article 3(1)	Article 4
Article 4(1)	Article 13
Article 4(2)	Article 36(1)
Article 5	Article 16
Article 6	—
Article 7	Article 28
Article 8	Article 15
Article 9	Article 23
Article 10	Article 23
Article 11	Articles 24 and 25
Article 12	Article 26
Article 13	Article 34
Article 14	Article 35
Article 15	Article 14
Article 16	Article 37
Article 17	Article 38
Article 18(1)	Article 39(1)
—	Article 39(2)
Article 18(2)	—
Article 18(3)	Article 39(3)
Article 19	Article 40
Article 20	—
Article 21	Article 42
Article 22	Article 43
Annex I	—
Annex IIA	Annex I
Annex IIB	Annex II

Directive 75/439/EEC	*This Directive*
Article 1(1)	Article 3(18)
Article 2	Articles 13 and 21
Article 3(1) and (2)	—
Article 3(3)	Article 13

Directive 75/439/EEC	*This Directive*
Article 4	Article 13
Article 5(1)	—
Article 5(2)	—
Article 5(3)	—
Article 5(4)	Articles 26 and 34
Article 6	Article 23
Article 7(a)	Article 13
Article 7(b)	—
Article 8(1)	—
Article 8(2)(a)	. —
Article 8(2)(b)	—
Article 8(3)	—
Article 9	—
Article 10(1)	Article 18
Article 10(2)	Article 13
Article 10(3) and (4)	—
Article 10(5)	Articles 19, 21, 25, 34 and 35
Article 11	—
Article 12	Article 35
Article 13(1)	Article 34
Article 13(2)	—
Article 14	—
Article 15	—
Article 16	—
Article 17	—
Article 18	Article 37
Article 19	—
Article 20	—
Article 21	—
Article 22	—
Annex I	—

Directive 91/689/EEC	*This Directive*
Article 1(1)	—
Article 1(2)	—
Article 1(3)	—
Article 1(4)	Articles 3(2) and 7
Article 1(5)	Article 20
Article 2(1)	Article 23
Article 2(2)-(4)	Article 18
Article 3	Articles 24, 25 and 26
Article 4(1)	Article 34(1)
Article 4(2)(3)	Article 35
Article 5(1)	Article 19(1)
Article 5(2)	Article 34(2)
Article 5(3)	Article 19(2)

Directive 91/689/EEC	*This Directive*
Article 6	Article 28
Article 7	—
Article 8	—
Article 9	—
Article 10	—
Article 11	—
Article 12	—
Annexes I and II	—
Annex III	Annex III

DIRECTIVE 2008/105/EC OF THE EUROPEAN PARLIAMENT AND OF THE COUNCIL

of 16 December 2008

ON ENVIRONMENTAL QUALITY STANDARDS IN THE FIELD OF WATER POLICY, AMENDING AND SUBSEQUENTLY REPEALING COUNCIL DIRECTIVES 82/176/EEC, 83/513/EEC, 84/156/EEC, 84/491/EEC, 86/280/EEC AND AMENDING DIRECTIVE 2000/60/EC OF THE EUROPEAN PARLIAMENT AND OF THE COUNCIL

THE EUROPEAN PARLIAMENT AND THE COUNCIL OF THE EUROPEAN UNION,

Having regard to the Treaty establishing the European Community, and in particular Article 175(1) thereof,

Having regard to the proposal from the Commission,

Having regard to the opinion of the European Economic and Social Committee,

After consulting the Committee of the Regions,

Acting in accordance with the procedure laid down in Article 251 of the Treaty,

Whereas:

(1) Chemical pollution of surface water presents a threat to the aquatic environment with effects such as acute and chronic toxicity to aquatic organisms, accumulation in the ecosystem and losses of habitats and biodiversity, as well as a threat to human health. As a matter of priority, causes of pollution should be identified and emissions should be dealt with at source, in the most economically and environmentally effective manner.

(2) As set out in second sentence of Article 174(2) of the Treaty, Community policy on the environment is to be based on the precautionary principle and on the principles that preventive action should be taken, that environmental damage should, as a priority, be rectified at source and that the polluter should pay.

(3) Pursuant to Article 174(3) of the Treaty, in preparing its policy on the environment, the Community is to take account of the available scientific and technical data, environmental conditions in the various regions of the Community, the economic and social development of the Community as a whole and the balanced development of its regions as well as the potential benefits and costs of action or lack of action.

(4) Decision No 1600/2002/EC of the European Parliament and of the Council of 22 July 2002 laying down the Sixth Community Environment Action Programme states that environment and health and quality of life are among the key environmental priorities of that Programme, highlighting in particular the need to establish more specific legislation in the field of water policy.

(5) Directive 2000/60/EC of the European Parliament and of the Council of 23 October 2000 establishing a framework for Community action in the field of water policy lays down a strategy against pollution of water and requires further specific measures for pollution control and environmental quality standards (EQS). This Directive lays down EQS in accordance with the provisions and objectives of Directive 2000/60/EC.

(6) In accordance with Article 4 of Directive 2000/60/EC, and in particular paragraph 1(a), Member States should implement the necessary measures in accordance with Article 16(1) and (8) of that Directive, with the aim of progressively reducing pollution from priority substances and ceasing or phasing out emissions, discharges and losses of priority hazardous substances.

(7) Numerous Community acts have been adopted since the year 2000 which constitute emission control measures in accordance with Article 16 of Directive 2000/60/EC for individual priority substances. Moreover, many environmental protection measures fall under the scope of other existing Community legislation. Therefore priority should be given to implementing and revising existing instruments rather than establishing new controls.

(8) As regards emission controls of priority substances from point and diffuse sources, as referred to in Article 16 of Directive 2000/60/EC, it seems more cost-effective and proportionate for Member States to include, where necessary, in addition to the implementation of other existing Community legislation, appropriate control measures, pursuant to Article 10 of Directive 2000/60/EC, in the programme of measures to be developed for each river basin district in accordance with Article 11 of that Directive.

(9) Member States should improve the knowledge and data available on sources of priority substances and ways in which pollution occurs in order to identify targeted and effective control options. Member States should, inter alia, monitor sediment and biota, as appropriate, at an adequate frequency to provide sufficient data for a reliable long-term trend analysis of those priority substances that tend to accumulate in sediment and/or biota. The results of the monitoring, including monitoring of sediment and biota, should, as far as required by Article 3 of Decision No 2455/2001/EC of the European Parliament and of the Council of 20 November 2001 establishing the list of priority substances in the field of water policy, be made available in order to inform future Commission proposals under Article 16(4) and (8) of Directive 2000/60/EC.

(10) Decision No 2455/2001/EC sets out the first list of 33 substances or groups of substances that have been prioritised for action at Community level. Among those priority substances, certain substances have been identified as priority hazardous substances for which Member States should implement necessary measures with the aim of ceasing or phasing out emissions, discharges and losses. For substances occurring naturally or through natural processes, the cessation or phasing-out of emissions, discharges and losses from all potential sources is impossible. Some substances have been under review and should be classified. The Commission should continue to review the list of priority substances, prioritising substances for action on the basis of agreed criteria that demonstrate the risk to, or via, the aquatic environment, in accordance with the timetable provided for in Article 16 of Directive 2000/60/EC, and bring forward proposals as appropriate.

(11) In the interests of the Community and for a more effective regulation of surface water protection, it is appropriate to set up EQS for pollutants classified as priority substances at Community level and to leave it to Member States to lay down, where necessary, rules for remaining pollutants at national level, subject to the application of relevant Community rules. None the less, eight pollutants which fall under the scope of Council Directive 86/280/EEC of 12 June 1986 on limit values and quality objectives for discharges of certain dangerous substances included in List I of the Annex to Directive 76/464/EEC, and which form part of the group of substances for which Member States should implement measures with the aim of achieving good chemical status by 2015, subject to Articles 2 and 4 of Directive 2000/60/EC, were not included in the list of priority substances. However, the common standards established for those pollutants proved to be useful and it is therefore appropriate to maintain their regulation at Community level.

(12) Consequently, the provisions concerning current environmental quality objectives laid down in Council Directive 82/176/EEC of 22 March 1982 on limit values and quality objectives for mercury discharges by the chlor-alkali electrolysis industry, Council Directive 83/513/EEC of 26 September 1983 on limit values and quality objectives for cadmium discharges, Council Directive 84/156/EEC of 8 March 1984 on limit values and quality objectives for mercury discharges by sectors other than the chlor-alkali electrolysis industry, Council Directive 84/491/EEC of 9 October 1984 on limit values and quality objectives for discharges of hexachlorocyclohexane and Directive 86/280/EEC will become superfluous and should be deleted.

(13) The aquatic environment can be affected by chemical pollution both in the short- and long- term, and therefore both acute and chronic effects data should be used as the basis for establishing the EQS. In order to ensure that the aquatic environment and human health are adequately protected, EQS expressed as an annual average value should be established at a level providing protection against long-term exposure, and maximum allowable concentrations should be established to protect against short-term exposure.

(14) In accordance with the rules set out in section 1.3.4 of Annex V to Directive 2000/60/EC, when monitoring compliance with the EQS, including those expressed as maximum allowable concentrations, Member States may introduce statistical methods, such as a percentile calculation, to deal with outliers, that is extreme deviations from the mean, and false readings in order to ensure an acceptable level of confidence and precision. To ensure the comparability of monitoring between Member States, it is appropriate to provide for the establishment of detailed rules for such statistical methods through a committee procedure.

(15) For the majority of substances the establishment of EQS values at Community level should, at this stage, be limited to surface water only. However, as regards hexachlorobenzene, hexachlorobutadiene and mercury, it is not possible to ensure protection against indirect effects and secondary poisoning at Community level by EQS for surface water alone. It is therefore appropriate to establish EQS for biota at Community level for those three substances. In order to allow Member States flexibility depending on their monitoring strategy, Member States should be able either to monitor and apply those EQS for biota, or to establish stricter EQS for surface water providing the same level of protection.

(16) Furthermore, Member States should be able to establish EQS for sediment and/or biota at national level and apply those EQS instead of the EQS for water set out in this Directive. Such EQS should be established through a transparent procedure involving notifications to the Commission and other Member States so as to ensure a level of protection equivalent to the EQS for water set up at Community level. The Commission should summarise these notifications in its reports on the implementation of Directive 2000/60/EC. Moreover, sediment and biota remain important matrices for the monitoring of certain substances with significant accumulation potential. In order to assess long-term impacts of anthropogenic activity and trends, Member States should take measures, subject to Article 4 of Directive 2000/60/EC, with the aim of ensuring that existing levels of contamination in biota and sediments will not significantly increase.

(17) In accordance with Article 13 of, and Annex VII(A)(5) to, Directive 2000/60/EC, any exemptions to the application of the EQS for priority substances applied to water bodies in accordance with Article 4(4), (5) and (6) of that Directive, taking into account Article 4(8) and (9) thereof, should be reported in the river basin management plans. Provided that the requirements of Article 4 of Directive 2000/60/EC including conditions for exemptions are met, activities, including dredging and shipping, leading to discharges, emissions and losses of priority substances can take place.

(18) Member States have to comply with Council Directive 98/83/EC of 3 November 1998 on the quality of water intended for human consumption and manage the surface water bodies used for abstraction of drinking water in accordance with Article 7 of Directive 2000/60/EC. This Directive should therefore be implemented without prejudice to those requirements which may require more stringent standards.

(19) In the vicinity of discharges from point sources, concentrations of pollutants are usually higher than the ambient concentrations in water. Therefore, Member States should be able to make use of mixing zones, so long as they do not affect the compliance of the rest of the body of surface water with the relevant EQS. The extent of mixing zones should be restricted to the proximity of the point of discharge and should be proportionate. In accordance with Article 3(4) of Directive 2000/60/EC, Member States should ensure, as appropriate, that the requirements for the achievement of the environmental objectives set out in Article 4 of that Directive are coordinated for the whole of the river basin district, including the designation of mixing zones in transboundary water bodies.

(20) It is necessary to check compliance with the objectives for cessation or phase-out, and reduction, as specified in Article 4(1)(a) of Directive 2000/60/EC, and to make the assessment of compliance with these obligations transparent, in particular as regards the consideration of significant emissions, discharges and losses as a result of human activities. Further, a timetable for cessation or phase-out, and reduction, can only be related to an inventory. It should also be possible to assess the application of Article 4(4) to (7) of Directive 2000/60/EC. An appropriate tool is likewise needed for the quantification of losses of substances occurring naturally, or resulting from natural processes, in which case complete cessation or phase-out from all potential sources is impossible. In order to meet those needs, each Member State should establish an inventory of emissions, discharges and losses for each river basin district or part of a river basin district in its territory.

(21) In order to avoid duplication of work by establishing those inventories and to ensure the coherence of those inventories with other existing tools in the area of surface water protection, Member States should use information collected under Directive 2000/60/EC and under Regulation (EC) No 166/2006 of the European Parliament and Council of 18 January 2006 concerning the establishment of a European Pollutant Release and Transfer Register.

(22) In order to ensure consistent protection of surface water, Member States sharing bodies of surface water should coordinate their monitoring activities and, as appropriate, the compilation of inventories.

(23) In order better to reflect their needs, Member States should be able to choose an appropriate one-year reference period for measuring the basic entries of the inventory. However, account should be taken of the fact that the losses from the application of pesticides may vary considerably from one year to another because of different application rates, for instance as a result of different climatic conditions. Therefore, Member States should be able to opt for a three-year reference period for certain substances covered by Council Directive 91/414/EEC of 15 July 1991 concerning the placing of plant protection products on the market.

(24) In order to optimise the use of the inventory, it is appropriate to fix a deadline for the Commission to verify that emissions, discharges and losses are making progress towards compliance with the objectives set out in Article 4(1)(a) of Directive 2000/60/EC, subject to Article 4(4) and (5) of that Directive.

(25) Technical guidelines should be developed to contribute to the harmonisation of methodologies used by Member States to establish the inventories of emissions, discharges and losses, including losses from pollution accumulated in sediments.

(26) Several Member States are affected by pollution the source of which lies outside their national jurisdiction. It is therefore appropriate to make clear that a Member State would not be in breach of its obligations under this Directive as a result of the exceeding of an EQS due to such transboundary pollution, provided that certain conditions were met and that it had taken advantage, as appropriate, of the relevant provisions of Directive 2000/60/EC.

(27) On the basis of reports from Member States, in accordance with Article 15 of Directive 2000/60/EC, the Commission should review the need to amend existing acts and the need for additional specific Community-wide measures, such as emission controls, and, if appropriate, make relevant proposals. The Commission should report the conclusions of this review to the European Parliament and to the Council in the context of the report under Article 18(1) of Directive 2000/60/EC. In making any proposals for emission control measures, having regard to Article 10 of Directive 2000/60/EC, the Commission should take into account existing emission control requirements, such as those under Directive 2008/1/EC of the European Parliament and of the Council of 15 January 2008 concerning integrated pollution prevention and control, and the latest developments on pollution abatement technology.

(28) The criteria for identifying substances that are persistent, bioaccumulative and toxic, as well as substances of other equivalent concern, notably very persistent and very

bioaccumulative, as referred to in Directive 2000/60/EC, are established in the Technical Guidance Document for Risk Assessment in support of Commission Directive 93/67/EEC of 20 July 1993 laying down the principles for assessment of risks to man and the environment of substances notified in accordance with Council Directive 67/548/EEC, Directive 98/8/EC of the European Parliament and of the Council of 16 February 1998 concerning the placing of biocidal products on the market and Regulation (EC) No 1907/2006 of the European Parliament and of the Council of 18 December 2006 concerning the Registration, Evaluation, Authorisation and Restriction of Chemicals (REACH) and establishing a European Chemicals Agency. In order to ensure consistency of Community legislation, only those criteria should be applied to the substances under review according to Decision No 2455/2001/EC, and Annex X to Directive 2000/60/EC should be replaced accordingly.

(29) The obligations laid down in the Directives listed in Annex IX to Directive 2000/60/EC are already incorporated in Directive 2008/1/EC and in Directive 2000/60/EC and, at least, the same level of protection is guaranteed if the EQS are maintained or reviewed. In order to ensure a consistent approach to chemical pollution of surface waters and to simplify and clarify the existing Community legislation in that area, it is appropriate to repeal, pursuant to Directive 2000/60/EC, with effect from 22 December 2012, Directives 82/176/EEC, 83/513/EEC, 84/156/EEC, 84/491/EEC and 86/280/EEC.

(30) The recommendations referred to in Directive 2000/60/EC, in particular those of the Scientific Committee on Toxicity, Ecotoxicity and the Environment, have been considered.

(31) In accordance with paragraph 34 of the Interinstitutional Agreement on better law-making, Member States are encouraged to draw up, for themselves and in the interests of the Community, their own tables illustrating, as far as possible, the correlation between this Directive and the transposition measures, and to make them public.

(32) Since the objective of this Directive, namely that of achieving of good surface water chemical status by laying down EQS for priority substances and certain other pollutants, cannot be sufficiently achieved by the Member States and can therefore, by reason of maintaining the same level of protection of surface water throughout the Community, be better achieved at Community level, the Community may adopt measures, in accordance with the principle of subsidiarity as set out in Article 5 of the Treaty. In accordance with the principle of proportionality, as set out in that Article, this Directive does not go beyond what is necessary in order to achieve that objective.

(33) The measures necessary for the implementation of this Directive should be adopted in accordance with Council Decision 1999/468/EC of 28 June 1999 laying down the procedures for the exercise of implementing powers conferred on the Commission.

(34) In particular, the Commission should be empowered to amend point 3 of part B of Annex I to this Directive. Since that measure is of general scope and is designed to amend non-essential elements of this Directive, or to supplement it by the addition of new non-essential elements, it must be adopted in accordance with the regulatory procedure with scrutiny provided for in Article 5a of Decision 1999/468/EC,

HAVE ADOPTED THIS DIRECTIVE:

Article 1

Subject matter

This Directive lays down environmental quality standards (EQS) for priority substances and certain other pollutants as provided for in Article 16 of Directive 2000/60/EC, with the aim of achieving good surface water chemical status and in accordance with the provisions and objectives of Article 4 of that Directive.

Article 2

Definitions

For the purposes of this Directive, the definitions laid down in Article 2 of Directive 2000/60/EC shall apply.

Article 3

Environmental quality standards

1. In accordance with Article 1 of this Directive and Article 4 of Directive 2000/60/EC, Member States shall apply the EQS laid down in Part A of Annex I to this Directive for bodies of surface water.

Member States shall apply the EQS for bodies of surface water in accordance with the requirements laid down in Part B of Annex I.

2. Member States may opt to apply EQS for sediment and/or biota instead of those laid down in Part A of Annex I in certain categories of surface water. Member States that apply this option shall:

(a) apply, for mercury and its compounds, an EQS of 20 μg/kg, and/or for hexachlorobenzene, an EQS of 10 μg/kg, and/or for hexachlorobutadiene, an EQS of 55 μg/kg, these EQS being for prey tissue (wet weight), choosing the most appropriate indicator from among fish, molluscs, crustaceans and other biota;

(b) establish and apply EQS other than those mentioned in point (a) for sediment and/or biota for specified substances. These EQS shall offer at least the same level of protection as the EQS for water set out in Part A of Annex I;

(c) determine, for the substances mentioned in points (a) and (b), the frequency of monitoring in biota and/or sediment. However, monitoring shall take place at least once every year, unless technical knowledge and expert judgment justify another interval; and

(d) notify the Commission and other Member States, through the Committee referred to in Article 21 of Directive 2000/60/EC, of the substances for which EQS have been established in accordance with point (b), the reasons and basis for using this approach, the alternative EQS established, including the data and the methodology by which alternative EQS were derived, the categories of surface water to which they would apply, and the frequency of monitoring planned, together with the justification for that frequency.

The Commission shall include a summary of notifications pursuant to point (d) above and to note 9 to Part A of Annex I in the reports published in accordance with Article 18 of Directive 2000/60/EC.

3. Member States shall arrange for the long-term trend analysis of concentrations of those priority substances listed in Part A of Annex I that tend to accumulate in sediment and/or biota, giving particular consideration to substances numbers 2, 5, 6, 7, 12, 15, 16, 17, 18, 20, 21, 26, 28 and 30, on the basis of monitoring of water status carried out in accordance with Article 8 of Directive 2000/60/EC. They shall take measures aimed at ensuring, subject to Article 4 of Directive 2000/60/EC,that such concentrations do not significantly increase in sediment and/or relevant biota.

Member States shall determine the frequency of monitoring in sediment and/or biota so as to provide sufficient data for a reliable long-term trend analysis. As a guideline, monitoring should take place every three years, unless technical knowledge and expert judgment justify another interval.

4. The Commission shall examine technical and scientific progress, including the conclusion of risk assessments as referred to in Article 16(2)(a) and (b) of Directive 2000/60/EC and information from the registration of substances made publicly available according to Article

119 of Regulation (EC) No 1907/2006, and, if necessary, propose that the EQS laid down in Part A of Annex I to this Directive be revised in accordance with the procedure laid down in Article 251 of the Treaty in line with the timetable provided for in Article 16(4) of Directive 2000/60/EC.

5. Point 3 of Part B of Annex I to this Directive may be amended in accordance with the regulatory procedure with scrutiny referred to in Article 9(3) of this Directive.

Article 4

Mixing zones

1. Member States may designate mixing zones adjacent to points of discharge. Concentrations of one or more substances listed in Part A of Annex I may exceed the relevant EQS within such mixing zones if they do not affect the compliance of the rest of the body of surface water with those standards.

2. Member States that designate mixing zones shall include in river basin management plans produced in accordance with Article 13 of Directive 2000/60/EC a description of:
(a) the approaches and methodologies applied to define such zones; and
(b) measures taken with a view to reducing the extent of the mixing zones in the future, such as those pursuant to Article 11(3)(k) of Directive 2000/60/EC or by reviewing permits referred to in Directive 2008/1/EC or prior regulations referred to in Article 11(3)(g) of Directive 2000/60/EC.

3. Member States that designate mixing zones shall ensure that the extent of any such zone is:
(a) restricted to the proximity of the point of discharge;
(b) proportionate, having regard to the concentrations of pollutants at the point of discharge and to the conditions on emissions of pollutants contained in the prior regulations, such as authorisations and/or permits, referred to in Article 11(3)(g) of Directive 2000/60/EC and any other relevant Community law, in accordance with the application of best available techniques and Article 10 of Directive 2000/60/EC, in particular after those prior regulations are reviewed.

4. Technical guidelines for the identification of mixing zones shall be adopted in accordance with the regulatory procedure referred to in Article 9(2) of this Directive.

Article 5

Inventory of emissions, discharges and losses

1. On the basis of the information collected in accordance with Articles 5 and 8 of Directive 2000/60/EC, under Regulation (EC) No 166/2006 and other available data, Member States shall establish an inventory, including maps, if available, of emissions, discharges and losses of all priority substances and pollutants listed in Part A of Annex I to this Directive for each river basin district or part of a river basin district lying within their territory including their concentrations in sediment and biota, as appropriate.

2. The reference period for the estimation of pollutant values to be entered in the inventories referred to in paragraph 1 shall be one year between 2008 and 2010.

However, for priority substances or pollutants covered by Directive 91/414/EEC, the entries may be calculated as the average of the years 2008, 2009 and 2010.

3. Member States shall communicate the inventories established pursuant to paragraph 1 of this Article, including the respective reference periods, to the Commission in accordance with the reporting requirements under Article 15(1) of Directive 2000/60/EC.

4. Member States shall update their inventories as part of the reviews of the analyses specified in Article 5(2) of Directive 2000/60/EC.

The reference period for the establishment of values in the updated inventories shall be the year before that analysis is to be completed. For priority substances or pollutants covered by Directive 91/414/EEC, the entries may be calculated as the average of the three years before the completion of that analysis.

Member States shall publish the updated inventories in their updated river basin management plans as laid down in Article 13(7) of Directive 2000/60/EC.

5. The Commission shall, by 2018, verify that emissions, discharges and losses as reflected in the inventory are making progress towards compliance with the reduction or cessation objectives laid down in Article 4(1)(a)(iv) of Directive 2000/60/EC, subject to Article 4(4) and (5) of that Directive.

6. Technical guidelines for the establishment of inventories shall be adopted in accordance with the regulatory procedure referred to in Article 9(2) of this Directive.

Article 6

Transboundary pollution

1. A Member State shall not be in breach of its obligations under this Directive as a result of the exceedance of an EQS if it can demonstrate that:
(a) the exceedance was due to a source of pollution outside its national jurisdiction;
(b) it was unable as a result of such transboundary pollution to take effective measures to comply with the relevant EQS; and
(c) it had applied the coordination mechanisms set out in Article 3 of Directive 2000/60/EC and, as appropriate, taken advantage of the provisions of Article 4(4), (5) and (6) of that Directive for those water bodies affected by transboundary pollution.

2. Member States shall use the mechanism laid down in Article 12 of Directive 2000/60/EC to provide the Commission with necessary information in the circumstances set out in paragraph 1 of this Article and with a summary of the measures taken in relation to transboundary pollution in the relevant river basin management plan in accordance with the reporting requirements under Article 15(1) of Directive 2000/60/EC.

Article 7

Reporting and review

1. On the basis of reports from Member States, including reports in accordance with Article 12 of Directive 2000/60/EC and in particular those on transboundary pollution, the Commission shall review the need to amend existing acts and the need for additional specific Community-wide measures, such as emission controls.

2. The Commission shall report to the European Parliament and to the Council in the context of the report prepared in accordance with Article 18(1) of Directive 2000/60/EC, on:
(a) the conclusions of the review referred to in paragraph 1 of this Article;
(b) measures taken to reduce the extent of mixing zones designated in accordance with Article 4(1) of this Directive;
(c) the outcome of the verification referred to in Article 5(5) of this Directive;
(d) the situation regarding pollution originating outside the territory of the Community.
The Commission shall, if appropriate, accompany the report with relevant proposals.

Article 8

Review of Annex X to Directive 2000/60/EC

Within the framework of the review of Annex X to Directive 2000/60/EC, as provided for in Article 16(4) of that Directive, the Commission shall consider inter alia the substances set out in Annex III to this Directive for possible identification as priority substances or priority hazardous substances. The Commission shall report the outcome of its review to the European Parliament and to the Council by 13 January 2011. It shall accompany the report, if appropriate, with relevant proposals, in particular proposals to identify new priority substances or priority hazardous substances or to identify certain priority substances as priority hazardous substances and to set corresponding EQS for surface water, sediment or biota, as appropriate.

Article 9

Committee procedure

1. The Commission shall be assisted by the Committee referred to in Article 21(1) of Directive 2000/60/EC.

2. Where reference is made to this paragraph, Articles 5 and 7 of Decision 1999/468/EC shall apply, having regard to the provisions of Article 8 thereof.

The period laid down in Article 5(6) of Decision 1999/468/EC shall be set at three months.

3. Where reference is made to this paragraph, Article 5a(1) to (4) and Article 7 of Decision 1999/468/EC shall apply, having regard to the provisions of Article 8 thereof.

[*Articles 10, 11 and 12 are not reproduced.*]

Article 13

Transposition

1. Member States shall bring into force the laws, regulations and administrative provisions necessary to comply with this Directive by 13 July 2010.

When Member States adopt those measures, they shall contain a reference to this Directive or be accompanied by such a reference on the occasion of their official publication. Member States shall determine how such reference is to be made.

2. Member States shall communicate to the Commission the text of the main provisions of national law which they adopt in the field covered by this Directive.

Article 14

Entry into force

This Directive shall enter into force on the 20th day following its publication in the Official Journal of the European Union.

Article 15

Addressees

This Directive is addressed to the Member States.

ANNEX I
ENVIRONMENTAL QUALITY STANDARDS FOR PRIORITY SUBSTANCES AND CERTAIN OTHER POLLUTANTS

PART A: ENVIRONMENTAL QUALITY STANDARDS (EQS)

AA: annual average;

MAC: maximum allowable concentration.

Unit: [μg/l]

(1)	*(2)*	*(3)*	*(4)*	*(5)*	*(6)*	*(7)*
No	*Name of substance*	*CAS number*[(1)]	*AA-EQS*[(2)] *Inland surface waters*[(3)]	*AA-EQS*[(2)] *Other surface waters*	*MAC-EQS*[(4)] *Inland surface waters*[(3)]	*MAC-EQS*[(4)] *Other surface waters*
(1)	Alachlor	15972-60-8	0,3	0,3	0,7	0,7
(2)	Anthracene	120-12-7	0,1	0,1	0,4	0,4
(3)	Atrazine	1912-24-9	0,6	0,6	2,0	2,0
(4)	Benzene	71-43-2	10	8	50	50
(5)	Brominated diphenylether[(5)]	32534-81-9	0,0005	0,0002	not applicable	not applicable
(6)	Cadmium and its compounds (depending on water hardness classes)[(6)]	7440-43-9	≤ 0,08 (Class 1)	0,2	≤ 0,45 (Class 1)	≤ 0,45 (Class 1)
			0,08 (Class 2)		0,45 (Class 2)	0,45 (Class 2)
			0,09 (Class 3)		0,6 (Class 3)	0,6 (Class 3)
			0,15 (Class 4)		0,9 (Class 4)	0,9 (Class 4)
			0,25 (Class 5)		1,5 (Class 5)	1,5 (Class 5)
(6a)	Carbon-tetrachloride[(7)]	56-23-5	12	12	not applicable	not applicable
(7)	C10-13 Chloroalkanes	85535-84-8	0,4	0,4	1,4	1,4
(8)	Chlorfenvinphos	470-90-6	0,1	0,1	0,3	0,3
(9)	Chlorpyrifos (Chlorpyrifos-ethyl)	2921-88-2	0,03	0,03	0,1	0,1
(9a)	Cyclodiene pesticides:		Σ= 0,01	Σ = 0,005	not applicable	not applicable
	Aldrin[(7)]	309-00-2				
	Dieldrin[(7)]	60-57-1				
	Endrin[(7)]	72-20-8				
	Isodrin[(7)]	465-73-6				
(9b)	DDT total[(7)(8)]	not applicable	0,025	0,025	not applicable	not applicable
	para-para-DDT[(7)]	50-29-3	0,01	0,01	not applicable	not applicable
(10)	1,2-Dichloroethane	107-06-2	10	10	not applicable	not applicable

(1)	*(2)*	*(3)*	*(4)*	*(5)*	*(6)*	*(7)*
No	*Name of substance*	*CAS number*[1]	*AA-EQS*[2] *Inland surface waters*[3]	*AA-EQS*[2] *Other surface waters*	*MAC-EQS*[4] *Inland surface waters*[3]	*MAC-EQS*[4] *Other surface waters*
(11)	Dichloromethane	75-09-2	20	20	not applicable	not applicable
(12)	Di(2-ethylhexyl)-phthalate (DEHP)	117-81-7	1,3	1,3	not applicable	not applicable
(13)	Diuron	330-54-1	0,2	0,2	1,8	1,8
(14)	Endosulfan	115-29-7	0,005	0,0005	0,01	0,004
(15)	Fluoranthene	206-44-0	0,1	0,1	1	1
(16)	Hexachloro-benzene	118-74-1	0,01[9]	0,01[9]	0,05	0,05
(17)	Hexachloro-butadiene	87-68-3	0,1[9]	0,1[9]	0,6	0,6
(18)	Hexachloro-cyclohexane	608-73-1	0,02	0,002	0,04	0,02
(19)	Isoproturon	34123-59-6	0,3	0,3	1,0	1,0
(20)	Lead and its compounds	7439-92-1	7,2	7,2	not applicable	not applicable
(21)	Mercury and its compounds	7439-97-6	0,05[9]	0,05[9]	0,07	0,07
(22)	Naphthalene	91-20-3	2,4	1,2	not applicable	not applicable
(23)	Nickel and its compounds	7440-02-0	20	20	not applicable	not applicable
(24)	Nonylphenol (4-Nonylphenol)	104-40-5	0,3	0,3	2,0	2,0
(25)	Octylphenol ((4-(1,1′,3,3′-tetramethylbutyl)-phenol))	140-66-9	0,1	0,01	not applicable	not applicable
(26)	Pentachloro-benzene	608-93-5	0,007	0,0007	not applicable	not applicable
(27)	Pentachloro-phenol	87-86-5	0,4	0,4	1	1
(28)	Polyaromatic hydrocarbons (PAH)[10]	not applicable	not applicable	not applicable	not applicable	not applicable
	Benzo(a)pyrene	50-32-8	0,05	0,05	0,1	0,1
	Benzo(b)fluor-anthene	205-99-2	$\Sigma = 0,03$	$\Sigma = 0,03$	not applicable	not applicable
	Benzo(k)fluor-anthene	207-08-9				
	Benzo(g,h,i)-perylene	191-24-2	$\Sigma = 0,002$	$\Sigma = 0,002$	not applicable	not applicable
	Indeno(1,2,3-cd)-pyrene	193-39-5				

(1)	(2)	(3)	(4)	(5)	(6)	(7)
No	*Name of substance*	*CAS number*[1]	*AA-EQS*[2] *Inland surface waters*[3]	*AA-EQS*[2] *Other surface waters*	*MAC-EQS*[4] *Inland surface waters*[3]	*MAC-EQS*[4] *Other surface waters*
(29)	Simazine	122-34-9	1	1	4	4
(29a)	Tetrachloro-ethylene[7]	127-18-4	10	10	not applicable	not applicable
(29b)	Trichloro-ethylene[7]	79-01-6	10	10	not applicable	not applicable
(30)	Tributyltin compounds (Tributhyltin-cation)	36643-28-4	0,0002	0,0002	0,0015	0,0015
(31)	Trichloro-benzenes	12002-48-1	0,4	0,4	not applicable	not applicable
(32)	Trichloro-methane	67-66-3	2,5	2,5	not applicable	not applicable
(33)	Trifluralin	1582-09-8	0,03	0,03	not applicable	not applicable

(1) CAS: Chemical Abstracts Service.
(2) This parameter is the EQS expressed as an annual average value (AA-EQS). Unless otherwise specified, it applies to the total concentration of all isomers.
(3) Inland surface waters encompass rivers and lakes and related artificial or heavily modified water bodies.
(4) This parameter is the EQS expressed as a maximum allowable concentration (MAC-EQS). Where the MAC-EQS are marked as "not applicable", the AA-EQS values are considered protective against short-term pollution peaks in continuous discharges since they are significantly lower than the values derived on the basis of acute toxicity.
(5) For the group of priority substances covered by brominated diphenylethers (No 5) listed in Decision No 2455/2001/EC, an EQS is established only for congener numbers 28, 47, 99, 100, 153 and 154.
(6) For cadmium and its compounds (No 6) the EQS values vary depending on the hardness of the water as specified in five class categories (Class 1: < 40 mg CaCO3/l, Class 2: 40 to < 50 mg CaCO3/l, Class 3: 50 to < 100 mg CaCO3/l, Class 4: 100 to < 200 mg CaCO3/l and Class 5: ≥ 200 mg CaCO3/l).
(7) This substance is not a priority substance but one of the other pollutants for which the EQS are identical to those laid down in the legislation that applied prior to 13 January 2009.
(8) DDT total comprises the sum of the isomers 1,1,1-trichloro-2,2 bis (p-chlorophenyl) ethane (CAS number 50-29-3; EU number 200-024-3); 1,1,1-trichloro-2 (o-chlorophenyl)-2-(p-chlorophenyl) ethane (CAS number 789-02-6; EU number 212-332-5); 1,1-dichloro-2,2 bis (p-chlorophenyl) ethylene (CAS number 72-55-9; EU number 200-784-6); and 1,1-dichloro-2,2 bis (p-chlorophenyl) ethane (CAS number 72-54-8; EU number 200-783-0).
(9) If Member States do not apply EQS for biota they shall introduce stricter EQS for water in order to achieve the same level of protection as the EQS for biota set out in Article 3(2) of this Directive. They shall notify the Commission and other Member States, through the Committee referred to in Article 21 of Directive 2000/60/EC, of the reasons and basis for using this approach, the alternative EQS for water established, including the data and the methodology by which the alternative EQS were derived, and the categories of surface water to which they would apply.
(10) For the group of priority substances of polyaromatic hydrocarbons (PAH) (No 28), each individual EQS is applicable, i.e. the EQS for Benzo(a)pyrene, the EQS for the sum of Benzo(b)fluoranthene and Benzo(k)fluoranthene and the EQS for the sum of Benzo(g,h,i)perylene and Indeno(1,2,3-cd)pyrene must be met.

PART B: APPLICATION OF THE EQS SET OUT IN PART A

1. Columns 4 and 5 of the table: For any given surface water body, applying the AA-EQS means that, for each representative monitoring point within the water body, the arithmetic mean of the concentrations measured at different times during the year does not exceed the standard.

The calculation of the arithmetic mean, the analytical method used and, where there is no appropriate analytical method meeting the minimum performance criteria, the method of applying an EQS must be in accordance with implementing acts adopting technical specifications for chemical monitoring and quality of analytical results, in accordance with Directive 2000/60/EC.

2. Columns 6 and 7 of the table: For any given surface water body, applying the MAC-EQS means that the measured concentration at any representative monitoring point within the water body does not exceed the standard.

However, in accordance with section 1.3.4 of Annex V to Directive 2000/60/EC, Member States may introduce statistical methods, such as a percentile calculation, to ensure an acceptable level of confidence and precision for determining compliance with the MAC-EQS.

If they do so, such statistical methods shall comply with detailed rules laid down in accordance with the regulatory procedure referred to in Article 9(2) of this Directive.

3. With the exception of cadmium, lead, mercury and nickel (hereinafter "metals") the EQS set up in this Annex are expressed as total concentrations in the whole water sample. In the case of metals the EQS refers to the dissolved concentration, i.e. the dissolved phase of a water sample obtained by filtration through a 0,45 μm filter or any equivalent pre-treatment.

Member States may, when assessing the monitoring results against the EQS, take into account:
(a) natural background concentrations for metals and their compounds, if they prevent compliance with the EQS value; and
(b) hardness, pH or other water quality parameters that affect the bioavailability of metals.

[*Annex II is not reproduced.*]

ANNEX III
SUBSTANCES SUBJECT TO REVIEW FOR POSSIBLE IDENTIFICATION AS PRIORITY SUBSTANCES OR PRIORITY HAZARDOUS SUBSTANCES

CAS Number	*EU Number*	*Name of substance*
1066-51-9	—	AMPA
25057-89-0	246-585-8	Bentazon
80-05-7		Bisphenol-A
115-32-2	204-082-0	Dicofol
60-00-4	200-449-4	EDTA
57-12-5		Free cyanide
1071-83-6	213-997-4	Glyphosate
7085-19-0	230-386-8	Mecoprop (MCPP)
81-15-2	201-329-4	Musk xylene
1763-23-1		Perfluorooctane sulphonic acid (PFOS)
124495-18-7	—	Quinoxyfen (5,7-dichloro-4-(p-fluorophenoxy)quinoline)
		Dioxins
		PCB

DIRECTIVE 2009/31/EC OF THE EUROPEAN PARLIAMENT AND OF THE COUNCIL

of 23 April 2009

ON THE GEOLOGICAL STORAGE OF CARBON DIOXIDE AND AMENDING COUNCIL DIRECTIVE 85/337/EEC, EUROPEAN PARLIAMENT AND COUNCIL DIRECTIVES 2000/60/EC, 2001/80/EC, 2004/35/EC, 2006/12/EC, 2008/1/EC AND REGULATION (EC) NO 1013/2006

THE EUROPEAN PARLIAMENT AND THE COUNCIL OF THE EUROPEAN UNION,

Having regard to the Treaty establishing the European Community, and in particular Article 175(1) thereof,

Having regard to the proposal from the Commission,

Having regard to the opinion of the European Economic and Social Committee,

After consulting the Committee of the Regions,

Acting in accordance with the procedure laid down in Article 251 of the Treaty,

Whereas:

(1) The ultimate objective of the United Nations Framework Convention on Climate Change, which was approved by Council Decision 94/69/EC of 15 December 1993, is to stabilise greenhouse gas concentrations in the atmosphere at a level that would prevent dangerous anthropogenic interference with the climate system.

(2) The Sixth Community Environment Action Programme established by Decision No 1600/2002/EC of the European Parliament and of the Council of 22 July 2002 identifies climate change as a priority for action. That programme recognises that the Community is committed to achieving an 8 % reduction in emissions of greenhouse gases by 2008 to 2012 compared to 1990 levels, and that, in the longer term, global emissions of greenhouse gases will need to be reduced by approximately 70 % compared to 1990 levels.

(3) The Commission Communication of 10 January 2007 entitled "Limiting global climate change to two degrees Celsius – The way ahead for 2020 and beyond" clarifies that in the context of the envisaged global reduction of greenhouse gas emissions of 50 % by 2050, a reduction in greenhouse gas emissions of 30 % in the developed world by 2020 is required, rising to 60 %-80 % by 2050, that this reduction is technically feasible and the benefits far outweigh the costs, but that, to achieve it, all mitigation options must be harnessed.

(4) Carbon dioxide capture and geological storage (CCS) is a bridging technology that will contribute to mitigating climate change. It consists of the capture of carbon dioxide (CO_2) from industrial installations, its transport to a storage site and its injection into a suitable underground geological formation for the purposes of permanent storage. This technology should not serve as an incentive to increase the share of fossil fuel power plants. Its development should not lead to a reduction of efforts to support energy saving policies, renewable energies and other safe and sustainable low carbon technologies, both in research and financial terms.

(5) Preliminary estimates, carried out with a view to assessing the impact of the Directive and referred to in the impact assessment of the Commission, indicate that seven million tonnes of CO_2 could be stored by 2020, and up to 160 million tonnes by 2030, assuming a 20 % reduction in greenhouse gas emissions by 2020 and provided that CCS obtains

private, national and Community support and proves to be an environmentally safe technology. The CO_2 emissions avoided in 2030 could account for some 15 % of the reductions required in the Union.

(6) The Second European Climate Change Programme, which was established by the Commission Communication of 9 February 2005 entitled "Winning the Battle Against Global Climate Change" to prepare and examine future climate policy in the Community, set up a Working Group on Carbon Capture and Geological Storage. The Working Group's mandate was to explore CCS as a means of reducing climate change. The Working Group published a detailed report on the topic of regulation, which was adopted in June 2006. It stressed the need for the development of both policy and regulatory frameworks for CCS and urged the Commission to undertake further research into the subject.

(7) The Commission Communication of 10 January 2007 entitled "Sustainable power generation from fossil fuels: aiming for near-zero emissions from coal after 2020" reiterated the need for a regulatory framework based on an integrated risk assessment for CO_2 leakage, including site selection requirements designed to minimise the risk of leakage, monitoring and reporting regimes to verify storage and adequate remediation of any damage that may occur. The Communication set out an action plan for the Commission in this area during 2007, which required the development of a sound management framework for CCS, including the work on the regulatory framework, incentive framework, and support programmes, as well as external elements, for example technology cooperation with key countries on CCS.

(8) The European Council of March 2007 also urged the Member States and the Commission to work towards strengthening research and development and developing the necessary technical, economic and regulatory framework in order to remove existing legal barriers and to bring environmentally safe CCS to deployment with new fossil power plants, if possible by 2020.

(9) The European Council of March 2008 recalled that the objective of proposing a regulatory framework on CCS was to ensure that this novel technology would be deployed in an environmentally safe way.

(10) The European Council of June 2008 called on the Commission to bring forward as soon as possible a mechanism to incentivise Member State and private sector investments to ensure the construction and operation by 2015 of up to 12 CCS demonstration plants.

(11) Each of the different components of CCS, namely capture, transport and storage of CO_2, has been the object of pilot projects on a smaller scale than that required for their industrial application. These components still need to be integrated into a complete CCS process, technological costs need to be reduced and more and better scientific knowledge has to be gathered. It is therefore important that Community efforts on CCS demonstration within an integrated policy framework start as soon as possible, including, in particular, a legal framework for the environmentally safe application of CO_2 storage, incentives, notably for further research and development, efforts by means of demonstration projects, and public awareness measures.

(12) At the international level, legal barriers to the geological storage of CO_2 in geological formations under the seabed have been removed through the adoption of related risk management frameworks under the 1996 London Protocol to the 1972 Convention on the Prevention of Marine Pollution by Dumping of Wastes and Other Matter (1996 London Protocol) and under the Convention for the Protection of the Marine Environment of the North-East Atlantic (OSPAR Convention).

(13) In 2006, the Contracting Parties to the 1996 London Protocol adopted amendments to the Protocol. These amendments allow and regulate the storage of CO_2 streams from CO_2 capture processes in geological formations under the seabed.

(14) The Contracting Parties to the OSPAR Convention in 2007 adopted amendments to the Annexes to the Convention to allow the storage of CO_2 in geological formations under the seabed, a Decision to ensure environmentally safe storage of CO_2 streams in geological formations, and OSPAR Guidelines for Risk Assessment and Management

of that activity. They also adopted a Decision to prohibit placement of CO_2 into the water-column of the sea and on the seabed, because of the potential negative effects.

(15) At Community level, a number of legislative instruments are already in place to manage some of the environmental risks of CCS, in particular regarding capture and transport of CO_2, and they should be used where possible.

(16) Directive 2008/1/EC of the European Parliament and of the Council of 15 January 2008 concerning integrated pollution prevention and control is suitable for regulating, in respect of certain industrial activities, the risks of CO_2 capture to the environment and human health and, as a result, should be applied to the capture of CO_2 streams for the purposes of geological storage from installations covered by that Directive.

(17) Council Directive 85/337/EEC of 27 June 1985 on the assessment of the effects of certain public and private projects on the environment should be applied to the capture and transport of CO_2 streams for the purposes of geological storage. It should also apply to storage sites pursuant to this Directive.

(18) This Directive should apply to the geological storage of CO_2 within the territory of the Member States, in their exclusive economic zones and on their continental shelves. The Directive should not apply to projects with a total intended storage below 100 kilotonnes, undertaken for research, development or testing of new products and processes. This threshold would also seem appropriate for the purposes of other relevant Community legislation. The storage of CO_2 in storage complexes extending beyond the territorial scope of this Directive and the storage of CO_2 in the water column should not be permitted.

(19) Member States should retain the right to determine the areas within their territory from which storage sites may be selected. This includes the right of Member States not to allow any storage in parts or on the whole of their territory, or to give priority to any other use of the underground, such as exploration, production and storage of hydrocarbons or geothermal use of aquifers. In this context, Member States should in particular give due consideration to other energy-related options for the use of a potential storage site, including options which are strategic for the security of the Member State's energy supply or for the development of renewable sources of energy. The selection of the appropriate storage site is crucial to ensure that the stored CO_2 will be completely and permanently contained. Member States should, in selecting storage sites, take account of their geological characteristics, for example seismicity, in the most objective and effective way possible. A site should therefore only be selected as a storage site, if there is no significant risk of leakage, and if in any case no significant environmental or health impacts are likely to occur. This should be determined through a characterisation and assessment of a potential storage complex pursuant to specific requirements.

(20) Enhanced Hydrocarbon Recovery (EHR) refers to the recovery of hydrocarbons in addition to those extracted by water injection or other means. EHR is not in itself included in the scope of this Directive. However, where EHR is combined with geological storage of CO_2, the provisions of this Directive for the environmentally safe storage of CO_2 should apply. In that case, the provisions of this Directive concerning leakage are not intended to apply to quantities of CO_2 released from surface installations which do not exceed what is necessary in the normal process of extraction of hydrocarbons, and which do not compromise the security of the geological storage or adversely affect the surrounding environment. Such releases are covered by the inclusion of storage sites in Directive 2003/87/EC of the European Parliament and of the Council of 13 October 2003 establishing a scheme for greenhouse gas emission allowance trading within the Community, which requires surrender of emissions trading allowances for any leaked emissions.

(21) Member States should make available to the public environmental information relating to geological storage of CO_2 in accordance with applicable Community legislation.

(22) Member States which intend to allow geological storage of CO_2 in their territory should undertake an assessment of the storage capacity available within their territory. The Commission should organise an exchange of information and best practices between

those Member States, in the context of the exchange of information provided for in this Directive.

(23) Member States should determine in which cases exploration is required to generate the information necessary for the site selection. Exploration, that is activities intruding into the subsurface, should be made subject to a permit requirement. Member States do not need to set admission criteria for procedures for granting exploration permits, but where they do, they should at least ensure that the procedures for the granting of exploration permits are open to all entities possessing the necessary capacities. Member States should also ensure that the permits are granted on the basis of objective, published and non-discriminatory criteria. In order to protect and encourage exploration investments, exploration permits should be granted for a limited volume area and for a limited time during which the holder of the permit should have the sole right to explore the potential CO_2 storage complex. Member States should ensure that no conflicting uses of the complex are permitted during this time. If no activities are carried out within a reasonable time, Member States should ensure that the exploration permit is withdrawn and can be granted to other entities.

(24) Storage sites should not be operated without a storage permit. The storage permit should be the core instrument to ensure that the substantial requirements of this Directive are met and that geological storage therefore takes place in an environmentally safe way. In the granting of the storage permit, priority should be given to the holder of the exploration permit over competitors, as the former will generally have made substantial investments.

(25) In the early phase of the implementation of this Directive, to ensure consistency in implementation of the requirements of this Directive across the Community, all storage permit applications should be made available to the Commission after receipt. The draft storage permits should be transmitted to the Commission to enable it to issue an opinion on the draft permits within four months of their receipt. The national authorities should take this opinion into consideration when taking a decision on the permit and should justify any departure from the Commission's opinion. The review at Community level should also help to enhance public confidence in CCS.

(26) The competent authority should review and where necessary update or withdraw the storage permit if, inter alia, it has been notified of leakages or significant irregularities, if the reports submitted by the operators or the inspections carried out show non-compliance with permit conditions or if it is made aware of any other failure by the operator to comply with the permit conditions. After the withdrawal of a permit, the competent authority should either issue a new permit or close the storage site. In the meantime, the competent authority should take over the responsibility for the storage site, including specific legal obligations. Costs incurred should be recovered from the former operator.

(27) It is necessary to impose on the composition of the CO_2 stream constraints that are consistent with the primary purpose of geological storage, which is to isolate CO_2 emissions from the atmosphere, and that are based on the risks that contamination may pose to the safety and security of the transport and storage network and to the environment and human health. To this end, the composition of the CO_2 stream should be verified prior to injection and storage. The composition of the CO_2 stream is the result of the processes at the capture installations. Following inclusion of capture installations in Directive 85/337/EEC, an environmental impact assessment has to be carried out in the capture permit process. Inclusion of capture installations in Directive 2008/1/EC further ensures that best available techniques to improve the composition of the CO_2 stream have to be established and applied. In addition, in accordance with this Directive, the operator of the storage site should only accept and inject CO_2 streams if an analysis of the composition, including corrosive substances, of the streams, and a risk assessment have been carried out, and if the risk assessment has shown that the contamination levels of the CO_2 stream are in line with the composition criteria referred to in this Directive.

(28) Monitoring is essential to assess whether injected CO_2 is behaving as expected, whether any migration or leakage occurs, and whether any identified leakage is damaging the environment or human health. To that end, Member States should ensure that during the operational phase, the operator monitors the storage complex and the injection facilities on the basis of a monitoring plan designed pursuant to specific monitoring requirements. The plan should be submitted to and approved by the competent authority. In the case of geological storage under the seabed, monitoring should further be adapted to the specific conditions for the management of CCS in the marine environment.

(29) The operator should report, inter alia, the results of the monitoring to the competent authority at least once a year. In addition, Member States should establish a system of inspections to ensure that the storage site is operated in compliance with the requirements of this Directive.

(30) Provisions are required concerning liability for damage to the local environment and the climate, resulting from any failure of permanent containment of CO_2. Liability for environmental damage (damage to protected species and natural habitats, water and land) is regulated by Directive 2004/35/EC of the European Parliament and of the Council of 21 April 2004 on environmental liability with regard to the prevention and remedying of environmental damage, which should be applied to the operation of storage sites pursuant to this Directive. Liability for climate damage as a result of leakages is covered by the inclusion of storage sites in Directive 2003/87/EC, which requires surrender of emissions trading allowances for any leaked emissions. In addition, this Directive should establish the obligation on the operator of the storage site to take corrective measures in case of leakages or significant irregularities on the basis of a corrective measures plan submitted to and approved by the competent national authority. Where the operator fails to take the necessary corrective measures, these measures should be taken by the competent authority, which should recover the costs from the operator.

(31) A storage site should be closed if the relevant conditions stated in the permit have been complied with, upon request from the operator after authorisation of the competent authority, or if the competent authority so decides after the withdrawal of a storage permit.

(32) After a storage site has been closed, the operator should remain responsible for maintenance, monitoring and control, reporting, and corrective measures pursuant to the requirements of this Directive on the basis of a post-closure plan submitted to and approved by the competent authority as well as for all ensuing obligations under other relevant Community legislation until the responsibility for the storage site is transferred to the competent authority.

(33) The responsibility for the storage site, including specific legal obligations, should be transferred to the competent authority, if and when all available evidence indicates that the stored CO_2 will be completely and permanently contained. To this end, the operator should submit a report to the competent authority for approval of the transfer. In the early phase of the implementation of this Directive, to ensure consistency in implementation of the requirements of this Directive across the Community, all reports should be made available to the Commission after receipt. The draft approval decisions should be transmitted to the Commission to enable it to issue an opinion on the draft approval decisions within four months of their receipt. The national authorities should take this opinion into consideration when taking a decision on the approval and should justify any departure from the Commission's opinion. The review of draft approval decisions should, in the same way as the review of draft storage permits at Community level, also help to enhance public confidence in CCS.

(34) Liabilities other than those covered by this Directive, Directive 2003/87/EC and Directive 2004/35/EC, in particular concerning the injection phase, the closure of the storage site and the period after transfer of legal obligations to the competent authority, should be dealt with at national level.

(35) After the transfer of responsibility, monitoring should be reduced to a level which still allows for identification of leakages or significant irregularities, but should again be

intensified if leakages or significant irregularities are identified. There should be no recovery of costs incurred by the competent authority from the former operator after the transfer of responsibility except in the case of fault on the part of the operator prior to the transfer of responsibility for the storage site.

(36) Financial provision should be made in order to ensure that closure and post-closure obligations, obligations arising from inclusion under Directive 2003/87/EC, and obligations under this Directive to take corrective measures in case of leakages or significant irregularities, can be met. Member States should ensure that financial provision, by way of financial security or any other equivalent, is made by the potential operator so that it is valid and effective before commencement of injection.

(37) National authorities may, after transfer of responsibility, have to bear costs, such as monitoring costs, associated with CO_2 storage. A financial contribution should therefore be made available by the operator to the competent authority, before the transfer of responsibility takes place and on the basis of arrangements to be decided by Member States. This financial contribution should at least cover the anticipated cost of monitoring for a period of 30 years. The level of the financial contribution should be determined on the basis of guidelines to be adopted by the Commission to help ensure consistency in implementation of the requirements of this Directive across the Community.

(38) Access to CO_2 transport networks and storage sites, irrespective of the geographical location of potential users within the Union, could become a condition for entry into or competitive operation within the internal electricity and heat market, depending on the relative prices of carbon and CCS. It is therefore appropriate to make arrangements for potential users to obtain such access. This should be done in a manner to be determined by each Member State, applying the objectives of fair, open and non-discriminatory access and taking into account, inter alia, the transport and storage capacity which is available or can reasonably be made available as well as the proportion of its CO_2 reduction obligations pursuant to international legal instruments and to Community legislation intended to be met through CCS. Pipelines for CO_2 transport should, where possible, be designed so as to facilitate access of CO_2 streams meeting reasonable minimum composition thresholds. Member States should also establish dispute settlement mechanisms to enable expeditious settlement of disputes regarding access to transport networks and storage sites.

(39) Provisions are required to ensure that, in cases of transboundary CO_2 transport, transboundary storage sites or transboundary storage complexes, the competent authorities of the Member States concerned meet jointly the requirements of this Directive and of all other Community legislation.

(40) The competent authority should establish and maintain a register of the storage permits granted and of all closed storage sites and surrounding storage complexes, including maps of their spatial extent to be taken into consideration by the competent national authorities in relevant planning and permitting procedures. The register should also be reported to the Commission.

(41) Member States should submit reports on the implementation of this Directive on the basis of questionnaires drawn up by the Commission pursuant to Council Directive 91/692/EEC of 23 December 1991 standardising and rationalising reports on the implementation of certain Directives relating to the environment.

(42) Member States should lay down rules on penalties applicable to infringements of the national provisions adopted pursuant to this Directive. Those penalties should be effective, proportionate and dissuasive.

(43) The measures necessary for the implementation of this Directive should be adopted in accordance with Council Decision 1999/468/EC of 28 June 1999 laying down the procedures for the exercise of implementing powers conferred on the Commission.

(44) In particular the Commission should be empowered to amend the Annexes. Since those measures are of general scope and are designed to amend non-essential elements of this Directive, they must be adopted in accordance with the regulatory procedure with scrutiny provided for in Article 5a of Decision 1999/468/EC.

(45) Directive 85/337/EEC should be amended to cover capture and transport of CO_2 streams for the purposes of geological storage as well as storage sites pursuant to this Directive. Directive 2004/35/EC should be amended to cover the operation of storage sites pursuant to this Directive. Directive 2008/1/EC should be amended to cover capture of CO_2 streams for the purposes of geological storage from installations covered by that Directive.

(46) The adoption of this Directive should ensure a high level of protection of the environment and human health from the risks posed by the geological storage of CO_2. For this reason, Directive 2006/12/EC of the European Parliament and of the Council of 5 April 2006 on waste and Regulation (EC) No 1013/2006 of the European Parliament and of the Council of 14 June 2006 on shipments of waste should be amended so as to exclude CO_2 captured and transported for the purposes of geological storage from the scope of application of those instruments. Directive 2000/60/EC of the European Parliament and of the Council of 23 October 2000 establishing a framework for Community action in the field of water policy should also be amended to allow for injection of CO_2 into saline aquifers for the purposes of geological storage. Any such injection is subject to the provisions of Community legislation on the protection of groundwater, and must be in accordance with Article 4(1)(b) of Directive 2000/60/EC and with Directive 2006/118/EC of the European Parliament and of the Council of 12 December 2006 on the protection of groundwater against pollution and deterioration.

(47) The transition to low-carbon power generation requires that, in the case of fossil fuel power generation, new investments be made in such a way as to facilitate substantial reductions in emissions. To this end, Directive 2001/80/EC of the European Parliament and of the Council of 23 October 2001 on the limitation of emissions of certain pollutants into the air from large combustion plants should be amended to require that all combustion plants of a specified capacity, for which the original construction licence or the original operating licence is granted after the entry into force of this Directive, have suitable space on the installation site for the equipment necessary to capture and compress CO_2 if suitable storage sites are available, and if CO_2 transport and retrofitting for CO_2 capture are technically and economically feasible. The economic feasibility of the transport and retrofitting should be assessed taking into account the anticipated costs of avoided CO_2 for the particular local conditions in the case of retrofitting and the anticipated costs of CO_2 allowances in the Community. The projections should be based on the latest evidence; a review of technical options and an analysis of uncertainties in the assessment processes should also be undertaken. The competent authority should determine whether these conditions are met on the basis of an assessment made by the operator and other available information, particularly concerning the protection of the environment and human health.

(48) The Commission should, by 30 June 2015, conduct a review of this Directive in the light of the experience gained in the early phase of its implementation and make proposals for its revision as appropriate.

(49) Since the objective of this Directive, namely the establishment of a legal framework for the environmentally safe storage of CO_2, cannot be sufficiently achieved by the Member States acting individually, and can therefore, by reason of its scale and effects, be better achieved at Community level, the Community may adopt measures in accordance with the principle of subsidiarity as set out in Article 5 of the Treaty. In accordance with the principle of proportionality, as set out in that Article, this Directive does not go beyond what is necessary in order to achieve that objective.

(50) In accordance with point 34 of the Interinstitutional agreement on better law-making, Member States are encouraged to draw up, for themselves and in the interest of the Community, their own tables, which will, as far as possible, illustrate the correlation between this Directive and the transposition measures and to make them public.

(51) The application of this Directive is without prejudice to Articles 87 and 88 of the Treaty,

HAVE ADOPTED THIS DIRECTIVE:

Chapter 1
Subject matter, scope and definitions

Article 1

Subject matter and purpose

1. This Directive establishes a legal framework for the environmentally safe geological storage of carbon dioxide (CO_2) to contribute to the fight against climate change.

2. The purpose of environmentally safe geological storage of CO_2 is permanent containment of CO_2 in such a way as to prevent and, where this is not possible, eliminate as far as possible negative effects and any risk to the environment and human health.

Article 2

Scope and prohibition

1. This Directive shall apply to the geological storage of CO_2 in the territory of the Member States, their exclusive economic zones and on their continental shelves within the meaning of the United Nations Convention on the Law of the Sea (Unclos).

2. This Directive shall not apply to geological storage of CO_2, with a total intended storage below 100 kilotonnes, undertaken for research, development or testing of new products and processes.

3. The storage of CO_2 in a storage site with a storage complex extending beyond the area referred to in paragraph 1 shall not be permitted.

4. The storage of CO_2 in the water column shall not be permitted.

Article 3

Definitions

For the purposes of this Directive the following definitions shall apply:

1. "geological storage of CO_2" means injection accompanied by storage of CO_2 streams in underground geological formations;
2. "water column" means the vertically continuous mass of water from the surface to the bottom sediments of a water body;
3. "storage site" means a defined volume area within a geological formation used for the geological storage of CO_2 and associated surface and injection facilities;
4. "geological formation" means a lithostratigraphical subdivision within which distinct rock layers can be found and mapped;
5. "leakage" means any release of CO_2 from the storage complex;
6. "storage complex" means the storage site and surrounding geological domain which can have an effect on overall storage integrity and security; that is, secondary containment formations;
7. "hydraulic unit" means a hydraulically connected pore space where pressure communication can be measured by technical means and which is bordered by flow barriers, such as faults, salt domes, lithological boundaries, or by the wedging out or outcropping of the formation;
8. "exploration" means the assessment of potential storage complexes for the purposes of geologically storing CO_2 by means of activities intruding into the subsurface such as drilling to obtain geological information about strata in the potential storage complex and, as appropriate, carrying out injection tests in order to characterise the storage site;
9. "exploration permit" means a written and reasoned decision authorising exploration, and specifying the conditions under which it may take place, issued by the competent authority pursuant to the requirements of this Directive;

10. "operator" means any natural or legal, private or public person who operates or controls the storage site or to whom decisive economic power over the technical functioning of the storage site has been delegated according to national legislation;
11. "storage permit" means a written and reasoned decision or decisions authorising the geological storage of CO_2 in a storage site by the operator, and specifying the conditions under which it may take place, issued by the competent authority pursuant to the requirements of this Directive;
12. "substantial change" means any change not provided for in the storage permit, which may have significant effects on the environment or human health;
13. "CO_2 stream" means a flow of substances that results from CO_2 capture processes;
14. "waste" means the substances defined as waste in Article 1(1)(a) of Directive 2006/12/EC;
15. "CO_2 plume" means the dispersing volume of CO_2 in the geological formation;
16. "migration" means the movement of CO_2 within the storage complex;
17. "significant irregularity" means any irregularity in the injection or storage operations or in the condition of the storage complex itself, which implies the risk of a leakage or risk to the environment or human health;
18. "significant risk" means a combination of a probability of occurrence of damage and a magnitude of damage that cannot be disregarded without calling into question the purpose of this Directive for the storage site concerned;
19. "corrective measures" means any measures taken to correct significant irregularities or to close leakages in order to prevent or stop the release of CO_2 from the storage complex;
20. "closure" of a storage site means the definitive cessation of CO_2 injection into that storage site;
21. "post-closure" means the period after the closure of a storage site, including the period after the transfer of responsibility to the competent authority;
22. "transport network" means the network of pipelines, including associated booster stations, for the transport of CO_2 to the storage site.

Chapter 2
Selection of storage sites and exploration permits

Article 4

Selection of storage sites

1. Member States shall retain the right to determine the areas from which storage sites may be selected pursuant to the requirements of this Directive. This includes the right of Member States not to allow for any storage in parts or in the whole of their territory.

2. Member States which intend to allow geological storage of CO_2 in their territory shall undertake an assessment of the storage capacity available in parts or in the whole of their territory, including by allowing exploration pursuant to Article 5. The Commission may organise an exchange of information and best practices between those Member States, in the context of the exchange of information provided for in Article 27.

3. The suitability of a geological formation for use as a storage site shall be determined through a characterisation and assessment of the potential storage complex and surrounding area pursuant to the criteria specified in Annex I.

4. A geological formation shall only be selected as a storage site, if under the proposed conditions of use there is no significant risk of leakage, and if no significant environmental or health risks exist.

Article 5

Exploration permits

1. Where Member States determine that exploration is required to generate the information necessary for selection of storage sites pursuant to Article 4, they shall ensure that no such exploration takes place without an exploration permit.

Where appropriate, monitoring of injection tests may be included in the exploration permit.

2. Member States shall ensure that the procedures for the granting of exploration permits are open to all entities possessing the necessary capacities and that the permits are granted or refused on the basis of objective, published and non-discriminatory criteria.

3. The duration of a permit shall not exceed the period necessary to carry out the exploration for which it is granted. However, the Member States may extend the validity of the permit where the stipulated duration is insufficient to complete the exploration concerned and where the exploration has been performed in accordance with the permit. Exploration permits shall be granted in respect of a limited volume area.

4. The holder of an exploration permit shall have the sole right to explore the potential CO_2 storage complex. Member States shall ensure that no conflicting uses of the complex are permitted during the period of validity of the permit.

Chapter 3
Storage permits

Article 6

Storage permits

1. Member States shall ensure that no storage site is operated without a storage permit, that there shall be only one operator for each storage site, and that no conflicting uses are permitted on the site.

2. Member States shall ensure that the procedures for the granting of storage permits are open to all entities possessing the necessary capacities and that the permits are granted on the basis of objective, published and transparent criteria.

3. Without prejudice to the requirements of this Directive, priority for the granting of a storage permit for a particular site shall be given to the holder of the exploration permit for that site, provided that the exploration of that site is completed, that any condition set in the exploration permit has been complied with, and that the application for a storage permit is made during the period of validity of the exploration permit. Member States shall ensure that no conflicting uses of the complex are allowed during the permit procedure.

Article 7

Applications for storage permits

Applications to the competent authority for storage permits shall include at least the following information:

1. the name and address of the potential operator;
2. proof of the technical competence of the potential operator;
3. the characterisation of the storage site and storage complex and an assessment of the expected security of the storage pursuant to Article 4(3) and (4);
4. the total quantity of CO_2 to be injected and stored, as well as the prospective sources and transport methods, the composition of CO_2 streams, the injection rates and pressures, and the location of injection facilities;
5. a description of measures to prevent significant irregularities;
6. a proposed monitoring plan pursuant to Article 13(2);

7. a proposed corrective measures plan pursuant to Article 16(2);
8. a proposed provisional post-closure plan pursuant to Article 17(3);
9. the information provided pursuant to Article 5 of Directive 85/337/EEC;
10. proof that the financial security or other equivalent provision as required under Article 19 will be valid and effective before commencement of the injection.

Article 8

Conditions for storage permits

The competent authority shall issue a storage permit only if the following conditions are met:

1. the competent authority, on the basis of the application submitted pursuant to Article 7 and of any other relevant information, is satisfied that:
   (a) all relevant requirements of this Directive and of other relevant Community legislation are met;
   (b) the operator is financially sound and technically competent and reliable to operate and control the site and that professional and technical development and training of the operator and all staff are provided;
   (c) in the case of more than one storage site in the same hydraulic unit, the potential pressure interactions are such that both sites can simultaneously meet the requirements of this Directive;
2. the competent authority has considered any opinion of the Commission on the draft permit issued pursuant to Article 10.

Article 9

Contents of storage permits

The permit shall contain at least the following:

1. the name and address of the operator;
2. the precise location and delimitation of the storage site and storage complex, and information concerning the hydraulic unit;
3. the requirements for storage operation, the total quantity of CO_2 authorised to be geologically stored, the reservoir pressure limits, and the maximum injection rates and pressures;
4. the requirements for the composition of the CO_2 stream and the CO_2 stream acceptance procedure pursuant to Article 12, and, if necessary, further requirements for injection and storage in particular to prevent significant irregularities;
5. the approved monitoring plan, the obligation to implement the plan and requirements for updating it pursuant to Article 13 as well as the reporting requirements pursuant to Article 14;
6. the requirement to notify the competent authority in the event of leakages or significant irregularities, the approved corrective measures plan and the obligation to implement the corrective measures plan in the event of leakages or significant irregularities pursuant to Article 16;
7. the conditions for closure and the approved provisional post-closure plan referred to in Article 17;
8. any provisions on changes, review, updating and withdrawal of the storage permit pursuant to Article 11;
9. the requirement to establish and maintain the financial security or any other equivalent pursuant to Article 19.

Article 10

Commission review of draft storage permits

1. Member States shall make the permit applications available to the Commission within one month after receipt. They shall also make available other related material that shall be taken

into account by the competent authority when it seeks to make a decision on the award of a storage permit. They shall inform the Commission of all draft storage permits and any other material taken into consideration for the adoption of the draft decision. Within four months after receipt of the draft storage permit, the Commission may issue a non-binding opinion on it. If the Commission decides not to issue an opinion, it shall inform the Member State within one month of submission of the draft permit and state its reasons.

2. The competent authority shall notify the final decision to the Commission, and where it departs from the Commission opinion it shall state its reasons.

Article 11

Changes, review, update and withdrawal of storage permits

1. The operator shall inform the competent authority of any changes planned in the operation of the storage site, including changes concerning the operator. Where appropriate, the competent authority shall update the storage permit or the permit conditions.

2. Member States shall ensure that no substantial change is implemented without a new or updated storage permit issued in accordance with this Directive. Annex II, point 13, first indent of Directive 85/337/EEC shall apply in such cases.

3. The competent authority shall review and where necessary update or, as a last resort, withdraw the storage permit:

(a) if it has been notified or made aware of any leakages or significant irregularities pursuant to Article 16(1);

(b) if the reports submitted pursuant to Article 14 or the environmental inspections carried out pursuant to Article 15 show non-compliance with permit conditions or risks of leakages or significant irregularities;

(c) if it is aware of any other failure by the operator to meet the permit conditions;

(d) if it appears necessary on the basis of the latest scientific findings and technological progress; or

(e) without prejudice to points (a) to (d), five years after issuing the permit and every 10 years thereafter.

4. After a permit has been withdrawn pursuant to paragraph 3, the competent authority shall either issue a new storage permit or close the storage site pursuant to Article 17(1)(c). Until a new storage permit has been issued, the competent authority shall temporarily take over all legal obligations relating to acceptance criteria where the competent authority decides to continue CO_2 injections, monitoring and corrective measures pursuant to the requirements laid down in this Directive, the surrender of allowances in cases of leakage pursuant to Directive 2003/87/EC and preventive and remedial action pursuant to Articles 5(1) and 6(1) of Directive 2004/35/EC. The competent authority shall recover any costs incurred from the former operator, including by drawing on the financial security referred to in Article 19. In case of closure of the storage site pursuant to Article 17(1)(c), Article 17(4) shall apply.

Chapter 4
Operation, closure and post-closure obligations

Article 12

CO_2 stream acceptance criteria and procedure

1. A CO_2 stream shall consist overwhelmingly of carbon dioxide. To this end, no waste or other matter may be added for the purpose of disposing of that waste or other matter. However, a CO_2 stream may contain incidental associated substances from the source, capture or injection process and trace substances added to assist in monitoring and verifying CO_2 migration. Concentrations of all incidental and added substances shall be below levels that would:

(a) adversely affect the integrity of the storage site or the relevant transport infrastructure;
(b) pose a significant risk to the environment or human health; or
(c) breach the requirements of applicable Community legislation.

2. The Commission shall, if appropriate, adopt guidelines to help identify the conditions applicable on a case by case basis for respecting the criteria laid down in paragraph 1.

3. Member States shall ensure that the operator:
(a) accepts and injects CO_2 streams only if an analysis of the composition, including corrosive substances, of the streams and a risk assessment have been carried out, and if the risk assessment has shown that the contamination levels are in line with the conditions referred to in paragraph 1;
(b) keeps a register of the quantities and properties of the CO_2 streams delivered and injected, including the composition of those streams.

Article 13

Monitoring

1. Member States shall ensure that the operator carries out monitoring of the injection facilities, the storage complex (including where possible the CO_2 plume), and where appropriate the surrounding environment for the purpose of:
(a) comparison between the actual and modelled behaviour of CO_2 and formation water, in the storage site;
(b) detecting significant irregularities;
(c) detecting migration of CO_2;
(d) detecting leakage of CO_2;
(e) detecting significant adverse effects for the surrounding environment, including in particular on drinking water, for human populations, or for users of the surrounding biosphere;
(f) assessing the effectiveness of any corrective measures taken pursuant to Article 16;
(g) updating the assessment of the safety and integrity of the storage complex in the short and long term, including the assessment of whether the stored CO_2 will be completely and permanently contained.

2. The monitoring shall be based on a monitoring plan designed by the operator pursuant to the requirements laid down in Annex II, including details on the monitoring in accordance with the guidelines established pursuant to Article 14 and Article 23(2) of Directive 2003/87/EC, submitted to and approved by the competent authority pursuant to Article 7(6) and Article 9(5) of this Directive. The plan shall be updated pursuant to the requirements laid down in Annex II and in any case every five years to take account of changes to the assessed risk of leakage, changes to the assessed risks to the environment and human health, new scientific knowledge, and improvements in best available technology. Updated plans shall be re-submitted for approval to the competent authority.

Article 14

Reporting by the operator

At a frequency to be determined by the competent authority, and in any event at least once a year, the operator shall submit to the competent authority:
1. all results of the monitoring pursuant to Article 13 in the reporting period, including information on the monitoring technology employed;
2. the quantities and properties of the CO_2 streams delivered and injected, including composition of those streams, in the reporting period, registered pursuant to Article 12(3)(b);
3. proof of the putting in place and maintenance of the financial security pursuant to Article 19 and Article 9(9);

4. any other information the competent authority considers relevant for the purposes of assessing compliance with storage permit conditions and increasing the knowledge of CO_2 behaviour in the storage site.

Article 15

Inspections

1. Member States shall ensure that the competent authorities organise a system of routine and non-routine inspections of all storage complexes within the scope of this Directive for the purposes of checking and promoting compliance with the requirements of the Directive and of monitoring the effects on the environment and on human health.

2. Inspections should include activities such as visits of the surface installations, including the injection facilities, assessing the injection and monitoring operations carried out by the operator, and checking all relevant records kept by the operator.

3. Routine inspections shall be carried out at least once a year until three years after closure and every five years until transfer of responsibility to the competent authority has occurred. They shall examine the relevant injection and monitoring facilities as well as the full range of relevant effects from the storage complex on the environment and on human health.

4. Non-routine inspections shall be carried out:
(a) if the competent authority has been notified or made aware of leakages or significant irregularities pursuant to Article 16(1);
(b) if the reports pursuant to Article 14 have shown insufficient compliance with the permit conditions;
(c) to investigate serious complaints related to the environment or human health;
(d) in other situations where the competent authority considers this appropriate.

5. Following each inspection, the competent authority shall prepare a report on the results of the inspection. The report shall evaluate compliance with the requirements of this Directive and indicate whether or not further action is necessary. The report shall be communicated to the operator concerned and shall be publicly available in accordance with relevant Community legislation within two months of the inspection.

Article 16

Measures in case of leakages or significant irregularities

1. Member States shall ensure that in the event of leakages or significant irregularities, the operator immediately notifies the competent authority, and takes the necessary corrective measures, including measures related to the protection of human health. In cases of leakages and significant irregularities which imply the risk of leakage, the operator shall also notify the competent authority pursuant to Directive 2003/87/EC.

2. The corrective measures referred to in paragraph 1 shall be taken as a minimum on the basis of a corrective measures plan submitted to and approved by the competent authority pursuant to Article 7(7) and Article 9(6).

3. The competent authority may at any time require the operator to take the necessary corrective measures, as well as measures related to the protection of human health. These may be additional to or different from those laid out in the corrective measures plan. The competent authority may also at any time take corrective measures itself.

4. If the operator fails to take the necessary corrective measures, the competent authority shall take the necessary corrective measures itself.

5. The competent authority shall recover the costs incurred in relation to the measures referred to in paragraphs 3 and 4 from the operator, including by drawing on the financial security pursuant to Article 19.

Article 17

Closure and post-closure obligations

1. A storage site shall be closed:
(a) if the relevant conditions stated in the permit have been met;
(b) at the substantiated request of the operator, after authorisation of the competent authority; or
(c) if the competent authority so decides after the withdrawal of a storage permit pursuant to Article 11(3).

2. After a storage site has been closed pursuant to points (a) or (b) of paragraph 1, the operator remains responsible for monitoring, reporting and corrective measures, pursuant to the requirements laid down in this Directive, and for all obligations relating to the surrender of allowances in case of leakages pursuant to Directive 2003/87/EC and preventive and remedial actions pursuant to Articles 5 to 8 of Directive 2004/35/EC until the responsibility for the storage site is transferred to the competent authority pursuant to Article 18(1) to (5) of this Directive. The operator shall also be responsible for sealing the storage site and removing the injection facilities.

3. The obligations referred to in paragraph 2 shall be fulfilled on the basis of a post-closure plan designed by the operator based on best practice and in accordance with the requirements laid down in Annex II. A provisional post-closure plan shall be submitted to and approved by the competent authority pursuant to Article 7(8) and Article 9(7). Prior to the closure of a storage site pursuant to points (a) or (b) of paragraph 1 of this Article, the provisional post-closure plan shall be:
(a) updated as necessary, taking account of risk analysis, best practice and technological improvements;
(b) submitted to the competent authority for its approval; and
(c) approved by the competent authority as the definitive post-closure plan.

4. After a storage site has been closed pursuant to paragraph 1(c), the competent authority shall be responsible for monitoring and corrective measures pursuant to the requirements laid down in this Directive and for all obligations relating to the surrender of allowances in case of leakages pursuant to Directive 2003/87/EC and preventive and remedial action pursuant to Articles 5(1) and 6(1) of Directive 2004/35/EC. The post-closure requirements pursuant to this Directive shall be fulfilled by the competent authority on the basis of the provisional post-closure plan referred to in paragraph 3 of this Article, which shall be updated as necessary.

5. The competent authority shall recover from the operator the costs incurred in relation to the measures referred to in paragraph 4, including by drawing on the financial security pursuant to Article 19.

Article 18

Transfer of responsibility

1. Where a storage site has been closed pursuant to points (a) or (b) of Article 17(1), all legal obligations relating to monitoring and corrective measures pursuant to the requirements laid down in this Directive, the surrender of allowances in the event of leakages pursuant to Directive 2003/87/EC and preventive and remedial action pursuant to Articles 5(1) and 6(1) of Directive 2004/35/EC, shall be transferred to the competent authority on its own initiative or upon request from the operator, if the following conditions are met:
(a) all available evidence indicates that the stored CO_2 will be completely and permanently contained;
(b) a minimum period, to be determined by the competent authority has elapsed. This minimum period shall be no shorter than 20 years, unless the competent authority is convinced that the criterion referred to in point (a) is complied with before the end of that period;

(c) the financial obligations referred to in Article 20 have been fulfilled;
(d) the site has been sealed and the injection facilities have been removed.

2. The operator shall prepare a report documenting that the condition referred to in paragraph 1(a) has been met and shall submit it to the competent authority for the latter to approve the transfer of responsibility. This report shall demonstrate, at least:
(a) the conformity of the actual behaviour of the injected CO_2 with the modelled behaviour;
(b) the absence of any detectable leakage;
(c) that the storage site is evolving towards a situation of long-term stability.
The Commission may adopt guidelines on the assessment of the matters referred to in points (a), (b) and (c) of the first subparagraph, highlighting therein any implications for the technical criteria relevant to the determination of the minimum periods referred to in paragraph 1(b).

3. Where the competent authority is satisfied that the conditions referred to in points (a) and (b) of paragraph 1 are met, it shall prepare a draft decision of approval of the transfer of responsibility. The draft decision shall specify the method for determining that the conditions referred to in paragraph 1(d) have been met as well as any updated requirements for the sealing of the storage site and for the removal of injection facilities.

If the competent authority considers that the conditions referred to in points (a) and (b) of paragraph 1 are not met, it shall inform the operator of its reasons.

4. Member States shall make the reports referred to in paragraph 2 available to the Commission within one month after receipt. They shall also make available other related material that shall be taken into account by the competent authority when it prepares a draft decision of approval on the transfer of responsibility. They shall inform the Commission of all draft decisions of approval prepared by the competent authority pursuant to paragraph 3, including any other material taken into consideration for arriving at its conclusion. Within four months after receipt of the draft decision of approval, the Commission may issue a non-binding opinion on it. If the Commission decides not to issue an opinion, it shall inform the Member State within one month of submission of the draft decision of approval and state its reasons.

5. Where the competent authority is satisfied that the conditions referred to in points (a) to (d) of paragraph 1 are complied with, it shall adopt the final decision and notify that decision to the operator. The competent authority shall also notify the final decision to the Commission, and where it departs from the Commission opinion it shall state its reasons.

6. After the transfer of responsibility, routine inspections provided for in Article 15(3) shall cease and monitoring may be reduced to a level which allows for detection of leakages or significant irregularities. If any leakages or significant irregularities are detected, monitoring shall be intensified as required to assess the scale of the problem and the effectiveness of corrective measures.

7. In cases where there has been fault on the part of the operator, including cases of deficient data, concealment of relevant information, negligence, wilful deceit or a failure to exercise due diligence, the competent authority shall recover from the former operator the costs incurred after the transfer of responsibility has taken place. Without prejudice to Article 20, there shall be no further recovery of costs after the transfer of responsibility.

8. Where a storage site has been closed pursuant to Article 17(1)(c), transfer of responsibility shall be deemed to take place if and when all available evidence indicates that the stored CO_2 will be completely and permanently contained, and after the site has been sealed and the injection facilities have been removed.

Article 19

Financial security

1. Member States shall ensure that proof that adequate provisions can be established, by way of financial security or any other equivalent, on the basis of arrangements to be decided

by the Member States, is presented by the potential operator as part of the application for a storage permit. This is in order to ensure that all obligations arising under the permit issued pursuant to this Directive, including closure and post-closure requirements, as well as any obligations arising from inclusion of the storage site under Directive 2003/87/EC, can be met. This financial security shall be valid and effective before commencement of injection.

2. The financial security shall be periodically adjusted to take account of changes to the assessed risk of leakage and the estimated costs of all obligations arising under the permit issued pursuant to this Directive as well as any obligations arising from inclusion of the storage site under Directive 2003/87/EC.

3. The financial security or any other equivalent referred to in paragraph 1 shall remain valid and effective:

(a) after a storage site has been closed pursuant to points (a) or (b) of Article 17(1), until the responsibility for the storage site is transferred to the competent authority pursuant to Article 18(1) to (5);

(b) after the withdrawal of a storage permit pursuant to Article 11(3):
  (i) until a new storage permit has been issued;
  (ii) where the site is closed pursuant to Article 17(1)(c), until the transfer of responsibility pursuant to Article 18(8), provided the financial obligations referred to in Article 20 have been fulfilled.

Article 20

Financial mechanism

1. Member States shall ensure that the operator, on the basis of arrangements to be decided by the Member States, makes a financial contribution available to the competent authority before the transfer of responsibility pursuant to Article 18 has taken place. The contribution from the operator shall take into account those criteria referred to in Annex I and elements relating to the history of storing CO_2 relevant to determining the post-transfer obligations, and cover at least the anticipated cost of monitoring for a period of 30 years. This financial contribution may be used to cover the costs borne by the competent authority after the transfer of responsibility to ensure that the CO_2 is completely and permanently contained in geological storage sites after the transfer of responsibility.

2. The Commission may adopt guidelines for the estimation of the costs referred to in paragraph 1 to be developed in consultation with Member States with a view to ensuring transparency and predictability for operators.

Chapter 5
Third-party access

Article 21

Access to transport network and storage sites

1. Member States shall take the necessary measures to ensure that potential users are able to obtain access to transport networks and to storage sites for the purposes of geological storage of the produced and captured CO_2, in accordance with paragraphs 2, 3 and 4.

2. The access referred to in paragraph 1 shall be provided in a transparent and non-discriminatory manner determined by the Member State. The Member State shall apply the objectives of fair and open access, taking into account:

(a) the storage capacity which is or can reasonably be made available within the areas determined under Article 4, and the transport capacity which is or can reasonably be made available;

(b) the proportion of its CO_2 reduction obligations pursuant to international legal instruments and to Community legislation that it intends to meet through capture and geological storage of CO_2;

(c) the need to refuse access where there is an incompatibility of technical specifications which cannot be reasonably overcome;

(d) the need to respect the duly substantiated reasonable needs of the owner or operator of the storage site or of the transport network and the interests of all other users of the storage or the network or relevant processing or handling facilities who may be affected.

3. Transport network operators and operators of storage sites may refuse access on the grounds of lack of capacity. Duly substantiated reasons shall be given for any refusal.

4. Member States shall take the measures necessary to ensure that the operator refusing access on the grounds of lack of capacity or a lack of connection makes any necessary enhancements as far as it is economic to do so or when a potential customer is willing to pay for them, provided this would not negatively impact on the environmental security of transport and geological storage of CO_2.

Article 22

Dispute settlement

1. Member States shall ensure that they have in place dispute settlement arrangements, including an authority independent of the parties with access to all relevant information, to enable disputes relating to access to transport networks and to storage sites to be settled expeditiously, taking into account the criteria referred to in Article 21(2) and the number of parties which may be involved in negotiating such access.

2. In the event of cross-border disputes, the dispute settlement arrangements of the Member State having jurisdiction over the transport network or the storage site to which access has been refused shall be applied. Where, in cross-border disputes, more than one Member State covers the transport network or storage site concerned, the Member States concerned shall consult with a view to ensuring that this Directive is applied consistently.

Chapter 6
General provisions

Article 23

Competent authority

Member States shall establish or designate the competent authority or authorities responsible for fulfilling the duties established under this Directive. Where more than one competent authority is designated, Member States shall establish arrangements for the coordination of the work of those authorities undertaken pursuant to this Directive.

Article 24

Transboundary cooperation

In cases of transboundary transport of CO_2, transboundary storage sites or transboundary storage complexes, the competent authorities of the Member States concerned shall jointly meet the requirements of this Directive and of other relevant Community legislation.

Article 25

Registers

1. The competent authority shall establish and maintain:

(a) a register of the storage permits granted; and
(b) a permanent register of all closed storage sites and surrounding storage complexes, including maps and sections of their spatial extent and available information relevant for assessing that the stored CO_2 will be completely and permanently contained.

2. The registers referred to in paragraph 1 shall be taken into consideration by the competent national authorities in relevant planning procedures and when permitting any activity that could affect or be affected by the geological storage of CO_2 in the registered storage sites.

Article 26

Information to the public

Member States shall make available to the public environmental information relating to the geological storage of CO_2 in accordance with the applicable Community legislation.

Article 27

Reporting by Member States

1. Every three years the Member States shall submit to the Commission a report on the implementation of this Directive, including the register referred to in Article 25(1)(b). The first report shall be sent to the Commission by 30 June 2011. The report shall be drawn up on the basis of a questionnaire or outline drafted by the Commission in accordance with the procedure referred to in Article 6 of Directive 91/692/EEC. The questionnaire or outline shall be sent to Member States at least six months before the deadline for the submission of the report.

2. The Commission shall organise an exchange of information between the competent authorities of the Member States concerning the implementation of this Directive.

Article 28

Penalties

The Member States shall lay down the rules on penalties applicable to infringements of the national provisions adopted pursuant to this Directive and shall take all measures necessary to ensure that they are implemented. The penalties provided for must be effective, proportionate and dissuasive. The Member States shall notify those provisions to the Commission by 25 June 2011 and shall notify it without delay of any subsequent amendment affecting them.

Article 29

Amendments of Annexes

Measures may be adopted to amend the Annexes. Those measures, designed to amend non-essential elements of this Directive, shall be adopted in accordance with the regulatory procedure with scrutiny referred to in Article 30(2).

Article 30

Committee procedure

1. The Commission shall be assisted by the Climate Change Committee.

2. Where reference is made to this paragraph, Article 5a(1) to (4) and Article 7 of Decision 1999/468/EC shall apply, having regard to the provisions of Article 8 thereof.

Chapter 7
Amendments

[*Articles 31 to 37 are not reproduced.*]

Chapter 8
Final provisions

Article 38

Review

1. The Commission shall transmit to the European Parliament and to the Council a report on the implementation of this Directive within nine months of receiving the reports referred to in Article 27.

2. In the report transmitted by 31 March 2015, the Commission shall assess in particular, on the basis of experience with the implementation of this Directive, in light of the experience with CCS and taking into account technical progress and the most recent scientific knowledge:

— whether permanent containment of CO_2 in such a way as to prevent and reduce as far as possible negative effects on the environment and any resulting risk to human health and the environmental and human safety of CCS has been sufficiently demonstrated,
— whether the procedures regarding the Commission's reviews of the draft storage permits, referred to in Article 10, and the draft decisions on transfer of responsibility, referred to in Article 18, are still required,
— experience with the provisions on CO_2 stream acceptance criteria and procedure referred to in Article 12,
— experience with the provisions on third-party access referred to in Articles 21 and 22 and with the provisions on transboundary cooperation pursuant to Article 24,
— the provisions applicable to combustion plants with a rated electrical output of 300 megawatts or more referred to in Article 9a of Directive 2001/80/EC,
— prospects for geological storage of CO_2 in third countries,
— further development and updating of the criteria referred to in Annex I and Annex II,
— experience with incentives for applying CCS on installations combusting biomass,
— the need for further regulation on environmental risks related to CO_2 transport,

and shall present a proposal for revision of the Directive if appropriate.

3. Where permanent containment of CO_2 in such way as to prevent and, where this is not possible, eliminate as far as possible negative effects and any risk to the environment and human health, and the environmental and human safety of CCS have been sufficiently demonstrated, as well as its economic feasibility, the review shall examine whether it is needed and practicable to establish a mandatory requirement for emission performance standards for new electricity-generating large combustion installations pursuant to Article 9a of Directive 2001/80/EC.

Article 39

Transposition and transitional measures

1. Member States shall bring into force the laws, regulations and administrative provisions necessary to comply with this Directive by 25 June 2011. They shall forthwith communicate to the Commission the text of those measures.

When Member States adopt these measures, they shall contain a reference to this Directive or shall be accompanied by such reference on the occasion of their official publication. The methods of making such reference shall be laid down by Member States.

2. Member States shall communicate to the Commission the text of the main provisions of national law which they adopt in the field covered by this Directive.

3. Member States shall ensure that the following storage sites falling within the scope of this Directive are operated in accordance with the requirements of this Directive by 25 June 2012:

(a) storage sites used in accordance with existing legislation on 25 June 2009;

(b) storage sites authorised in accordance with such legislation before or on 25 June 2009, provided that the sites are used not later than one year after that date.

Articles 4 and 5, Article 7(3), Article 8(2) and Article 10 shall not apply in these cases.

Article 40

Entry into force

This Directive shall enter into force on the 20th day following its publication in the Official Journal of the European Union.

Article 41

Addressees

This Directive is addressed to the Member States.

ANNEX I
CRITERIA FOR THE CHARACTERISATION AND ASSESSMENT OF THE POTENTIAL STORAGE COMPLEX AND SURROUNDING AREA REFERRED TO IN ARTICLE 4(3)

The characterisation and assessment of the potential storage complex and surrounding area referred to in Article 4(3) shall be carried out in three steps according to best practices at the time of the assessment and to the following criteria. Derogations from one or more of these criteria may be permitted by the competent authority provided the operator has demonstrated that the capacity of the characterisation and assessment to enable the determinations pursuant to Article 4 is not affected.

Step 1: Data collection

Sufficient data shall be accumulated to construct a volumetric and three-dimensional static (3-D)-earth model for the storage site and storage complex, including the caprock, and the surrounding area, including the hydraulically connected areas. This data shall cover at least the following intrinsic characteristics of the storage complex:

(a) geology and geophysics;

(b) hydrogeology (in particular existence of ground water intended for consumption);

(c) reservoir engineering (including volumetric calculations of pore volume for CO_2 injection and ultimate storage capacity);

(d) geochemistry (dissolution rates, mineralisation rates);

(e) geomechanics (permeability, fracture pressure);

(f) seismicity;

(g) presence and condition of natural and man-made pathways, including wells and boreholes which could provide leakage pathways.

The following characteristics of the complex vicinity shall be documented:

(h) domains surrounding the storage complex that may be affected by the storage of CO_2 in the storage site;

(i) population distribution in the region overlying the storage site;

(j) proximity to valuable natural resources (including in particular Natura 2000 areas pursuant to Council Directive 79/409/EEC of 2 April 1979 on the conservation of wild birds and Council Directive 92/43/EEC of 21 May 1992 on the conservation of natural habitats and of wild fauna and flora, potable groundwater and hydrocarbons);

(k) activities around the storage complex and possible interactions with these activities (for example, exploration, production and storage of hydrocarbons, geothermal use of aquifers and use of underground water reserves);
(l) proximity to the potential CO_2 source(s) (including estimates of the total potential mass of CO_2 economically available for storage) and adequate transport networks.

Step 2: Building the three-dimensional static geological earth model

Using the data collected in Step 1, a three-dimensional static geological earth model, or a set of such models, of the candidate storage complex, including the caprock and the hydraulically connected areas and fluids shall be built using computer reservoir simulators. The static geological earth model(s) shall characterise the complex in terms of:
(a) geological structure of the physical trap;
(b) geomechanical, geochemical and flow properties of the reservoir overburden (caprock, seals, porous and permeable horizons) and surrounding formations;
(c) fracture system characterisation and presence of any human-made pathways;
(d) areal and vertical extent of the storage complex;
(e) pore space volume (including porosity distribution);
(f) baseline fluid distribution;
(g) any other relevant characteristics.
The uncertainty associated with each of the parameters used to build the model shall be assessed by developing a range of scenarios for each parameter and calculating the appropriate confidence limits. Any uncertainty associated with the model itself shall also be assessed.

Step 3: Characterisation of the storage dynamic behaviour, sensitivity characterisation, risk assessment

The characterisations and assessment shall be based on dynamic modelling, comprising a variety of time-step simulations of CO_2 injection into the storage site using the three-dimensional static geological earth model(s) in the computerised storage complex simulator constructed under Step 2.

Step 3.1: Characterisation of the storage dynamic behaviour

At least the following factors shall be considered:
(a) possible injection rates and CO_2 stream properties;
(b) the efficacy of coupled process modelling (that is, the way various single effects in the simulator(s) interact);
(c) reactive processes (that is, the way reactions of the injected CO_2 with in situ minerals feedback in the model);
(d) the reservoir simulator used (multiple simulations may be required in order to validate certain findings);
(e) short and long-term simulations (to establish CO_2 fate and behaviour over decades and millennia, including the rate of dissolution of CO_2 in water).
The dynamic modelling shall provide insight into:
(f) pressure and temperature of the storage formation as a function of injection rate and accumulative injection amount over time;
(g) areal and vertical extent of CO_2 vs time;
(h) the nature of CO_2 flow in the reservoir, including phase behaviour;
(i) CO_2 trapping mechanisms and rates (including spill points and lateral and vertical seals);
(j) secondary containment systems in the overall storage complex;
(k) storage capacity and pressure gradients in the storage site;
(l) the risk of fracturing the storage formation(s) and caprock;
(m) the risk of CO_2 entry into the caprock;

(n) the risk of leakage from the storage site (for example, through abandoned or inadequately sealed wells);
(o) the rate of migration (in open-ended reservoirs);
(p) fracture sealing rates;
(q) changes in formation(s) fluid chemistry and subsequent reactions (for example, pH change, mineral formation) and inclusion of reactive modelling to assess affects;
(r) displacement of formation fluids;
(s) increased seismicity and elevation at surface level.

Step 3.2: Sensitivity characterisation

Multiple simulations shall be undertaken to identify the sensitivity of the assessment to assumptions made about particular parameters. The simulations shall be based on altering parameters in the static geological earth model(s), and changing rate functions and assumptions in the dynamic modelling exercise. Any significant sensitivity shall be taken into account in the risk assessment.

Step 3.3: Risk assessment

The risk assessment shall comprise, inter alia, the following:

3.3.1. Hazard characterisation

Hazard characterisation shall be undertaken by characterising the potential for leakage from the storage complex, as established through dynamic modelling and security characterisation described above. This shall include consideration of, inter alia:

(a) potential leakage pathways;
(b) potential magnitude of leakage events for identified leakage pathways (flux rates);
(c) critical parameters affecting potential leakage (for example maximum reservoir pressure, maximum injection rate, temperature, sensitivity to various assumptions in the static geological Earth model(s));
(d) secondary effects of storage of CO_2, including displaced formation fluids and new substances created by the storing of CO_2;
(e) any other factors which could pose a hazard to human health or the environment (for example physical structures associated with the project).

The hazard characterisation shall cover the full range of potential operating conditions to test the security of the storage complex.

3.3.2. Exposure assessment — based on the characteristics of the environment and the distribution and activities of the human population above the storage complex, and the potential behaviour and fate of leaking CO_2 from potential pathways identified under Step 3.3.1.

3.3.3. Effects assessment — based on the sensitivity of particular species, communities or habitats linked to potential leakage events identified under Step 3.3.1. Where relevant it shall include effects of exposure to elevated CO_2 concentrations in the biosphere (including soils, marine sediments and benthic waters (asphyxiation; hypercapnia) and reduced pH in those environments as a consequence of leaking CO_2). It shall also include an assessment of the effects of other substances that may be present in leaking CO_2 streams (either impurities present in the injection stream or new substances formed through storage of CO_2). These effects shall be considered at a range of temporal and spatial scales, and linked to a range of different magnitudes of leakage events.

3.3.4. Risk characterisation — this shall comprise an assessment of the safety and integrity of the site in the short and long term, including an assessment of the risk of leakage under the proposed conditions of use, and of the worst-case environment and health impacts. The risk characterisation shall be conducted based on the hazard, exposure and effects assessment. It shall include an assessment of the sources of uncertainty identified during the steps of characterisation and assessment of storage site and when feasible, a description of the possibilities to reduce uncertainty.

ANNEX II
CRITERIA FOR ESTABLISHING AND UPDATING THE MONITORING PLAN REFERRED TO IN ARTICLE 13(2) AND FOR POST-CLOSURE MONITORING

1. ESTABLISHING AND UPDATING THE MONITORING PLAN

The monitoring plan referred to in Article 13(2) shall be established according to the risk assessment analysis carried out in Step 3 of Annex I, and updated with the purpose of meeting the monitoring requirements laid out in Article 13(1) according to the following criteria:

1.1. Establishing the plan

The monitoring plan shall provide details of the monitoring to be deployed at the main stages of the project, including baseline, operational and post-closure monitoring. The following shall be specified for each phase:

(a) parameters monitored;
(b) monitoring technology employed and justification for technology choice;
(c) monitoring locations and spatial sampling rationale;
(d) frequency of application and temporal sampling rationale.

The parameters to be monitored are identified so as to fulfil the purposes of monitoring. However, the plan shall in any case include continuous or intermittent monitoring of the following items:

(e) fugitive emissions of CO_2 at the injection facility;
(f) CO_2 volumetric flow at injection wellheads;
(g) CO_2 pressure and temperature at injection wellheads (to determine mass flow);
(h) chemical analysis of the injected material;
(i) reservoir temperature and pressure (to determine CO_2 phase behaviour and state).

The choice of monitoring technology shall be based on best practice available at the time of design. The following options shall be considered and used as appropriate:

(j) technologies that can detect the presence, location and migration paths of CO_2 in the subsurface and at surface;
(k) technologies that provide information about pressure-volume behaviour and areal/vertical distribution of CO_2-plume to refine numerical 3-D simulation to the 3-D-geological models of the storage formation established pursuant to Article 4 and Annex I;
(l) technologies that can provide a wide areal spread in order to capture information on any previously undetected potential leakage pathways across the areal dimensions of the complete storage complex and beyond, in the event of significant irregularities or migration of CO_2 out of the storage complex.

1.2. Updating the plan

The data collected from the monitoring shall be collated and interpreted. The observed results shall be compared with the behaviour predicted in dynamic simulation of the 3-D-pressure-volume and saturation behaviour undertaken in the context of the security characterisation pursuant to Article 4 and Annex I Step 3.

Where there is a significant deviation between the observed and the predicted behaviour, the 3-D model shall be recalibrated to reflect the observed behaviour. The recalibration shall be based on the data observations from the monitoring plan, and where necessary to provide confidence in the recalibration assumptions, additional data shall be obtained.

Steps 2 and 3 of Annex I shall be repeated using the recalibrated 3-D model(s) so as to generate new hazard scenarios and flux rates and to revise and update the risk assessment.

Where new CO_2 sources, pathways and flux rates or observed significant deviations from previous assessments are identified as a result of history matching and model recalibration, the monitoring plan shall be updated accordingly.

2. POST-CLOSURE MONITORING

Post-closure monitoring shall be based on the information collected and modelled during the implementation of the monitoring plan referred to in Article 13(2) and above in point 1.2 of this Annex. It shall serve in particular to provide information required for the determination of Article 18(1).

DIRECTIVE 2009/147/EC OF THE EUROPEAN PARLIAMENT AND OF THE COUNCIL

of 30 November 2009

ON THE CONSERVATION OF WILD BIRDS

THE EUROPEAN PARLIAMENT AND THE COUNCIL OF THE EUROPEAN UNION,

Having regard to the Treaty establishing the European Community, and in particular Article 175(1) thereof,

Having regard to the proposal from the Commission,

Having regard to the opinion of the European Economic and Social Committee,

Acting in accordance with the procedure laid down in Article 251 of the Treaty,

Whereas:

(1) Council Directive 79/409/EEC of 2 April 1979 on the conservation of wild birds has been substantially amended several times. In the interests of clarity and rationality the said Directive should be codified.

(2) Decision No 1600/2002/EC of the European Parliament and of the Council of 22 July 2002 laying down the Sixth Community Environment Action Programme calls for specific action for biodiversity, including to protect birds and their habitats.

(3) A large number of species of wild birds naturally occurring in the European territory of the Member States are declining in number, very rapidly in some cases. This decline represents a serious threat to the conservation of the natural environment, particularly because of the biological balances threatened thereby.

(4) The species of wild birds naturally occurring in the European territory of the Member States are mainly migratory species. Such species constitute a common heritage and effective bird protection is typically a trans-frontier environment problem entailing common responsibilities.

(5) The conservation of the species of wild birds naturally occurring in the European territory of the Member States is necessary in order to attain the Community's objectives regarding the improvement of living conditions and sustainable development.

(6) The measures to be taken must apply to the various factors which may affect the numbers of birds, namely the repercussions of man's activities and in particular the destruction and pollution of their habitats, capture and killing by man and the trade resulting from such practices; the stringency of such measures should be adapted to the particular situation of the various species within the framework of a conservation policy.

(7) Conservation is aimed at the long-term protection and management of natural resources as an integral part of the heritage of the peoples of Europe. It makes it possible to control natural resources and governs their use on the basis of the measures necessary for the maintenance and adjustment of the natural balances between species as far as is reasonably possible.

(8) The preservation, maintenance or restoration of a sufficient diversity and area of habitats is essential to the conservation of all species of birds. Certain species of birds should be the subject of special conservation measures concerning their habitats in order to ensure their survival and reproduction in their area of distribution. Such measures must also take account of migratory species and be coordinated with a view to setting up a coherent whole.

(9) In order to prevent commercial interests from exerting a possible harmful pressure on exploitation levels, it is necessary to impose a general ban on marketing and to restrict

all derogation to those species whose biological status so permits, account being taken of the specific conditions obtaining in the different regions.

(10) Because of their high population level, geographical distribution and reproductive rate in the Community as a whole, certain species may be hunted, which constitutes acceptable exploitation where certain limits are established and respected, as such hunting must be compatible with maintenance of the population of these species at a satisfactory level.

(11) The various means, devices or methods of large-scale or non-selective capture or killing and hunting with certain forms of transport must be banned because of the excessive pressure which they exert or may exert on the numbers of the species concerned.

(12) Because of the importance which may be attached to certain specific situations, provision should be made for the possibility of derogations on certain conditions and subject to monitoring by the Commission.

(13) The conservation of birds and, in particular, migratory birds still presents problems which call for scientific research. Such research will also make it possible to assess the effectiveness of the measures taken.

(14) Care should be taken in consultation with the Commission to see that the introduction of any species of wild bird not naturally occurring in the European territory of the Member States does not cause harm to local flora and fauna.

(15) The Commission will every three years prepare and transmit to the Member States a composite report based on information submitted by the Member States on the application of national provisions introduced pursuant to this Directive.

(16) The measures necessary for the implementation of this Directive should be adopted in accordance with Council Decision 1999/468/EC of 28 June 1999 laying down the procedures for the exercise of implementing powers conferred on the Commission.

(17) In particular, the Commission should be empowered to amend certain Annexes in the light of scientific and technical progress. Since those measures are of general scope and are designed to amend non-essential elements of this Directive, they must be adopted in accordance with the regulatory procedure with scrutiny provided for in Article 5a of Decision 1999/468/EC.

(18) This Directive should be without prejudice to the obligations of the Member States relating to the time limits for transposition into national law of the directives set out in Annex VI, Part B,

HAVE ADOPTED THIS DIRECTIVE:

Article 1

1. This Directive relates to the conservation of all species of naturally occurring birds in the wild state in the European territory of the Member States to which the Treaty applies. It covers the protection, management and control of these species and lays down rules for their exploitation.

2. It shall apply to birds, their eggs, nests and habitats.

Article 2

Member States shall take the requisite measures to maintain the population of the species referred to in Article 1 at a level which corresponds in particular to ecological, scientific and cultural requirements, while taking account of economic and recreational requirements, or to adapt the population of these species to that level.

Article 3

1. In the light of the requirements referred to in Article 2, Member States shall take the requisite measures to preserve, maintain or re-establish a sufficient diversity and area of habitats for all the species of birds referred to in Article 1.

2. The preservation, maintenance and re-establishment of biotopes and habitats shall include primarily the following measures:
(a) creation of protected areas;
(b) upkeep and management in accordance with the ecological needs of habitats inside and outside the protected zones;
(c) re-establishment of destroyed biotopes;
(d) creation of biotopes.

Article 4

1. The species mentioned in Annex I shall be the subject of special conservation measures concerning their habitat in order to ensure their survival and reproduction in their area of distribution.

In this connection, account shall be taken of:
(a) species in danger of extinction;
(b) species vulnerable to specific changes in their habitat;
(c) species considered rare because of small populations or restricted local distribution;
(d) other species requiring particular attention for reasons of the specific nature of their habitat.
Trends and variations in population levels shall be taken into account as a background for evaluations.

Member States shall classify in particular the most suitable territories in number and size as special protection areas for the conservation of these species in the geographical sea and land area where this Directive applies.

2. Member States shall take similar measures for regularly occurring migratory species not listed in Annex I, bearing in mind their need for protection in the geographical sea and land area where this Directive applies, as regards their breeding, moulting and wintering areas and staging posts along their migration routes. To this end, Member States shall pay particular attention to the protection of wetlands and particularly to wetlands of international importance.

3. Member States shall send the Commission all relevant information so that it may take appropriate initiatives with a view to the coordination necessary to ensure that the areas provided for in paragraphs 1 and 2 form a coherent whole which meets the protection requirements of these species in the geographical sea and land area where this Directive applies.

4. In respect of the protection areas referred to in paragraphs 1 and 2, Member States shall take appropriate steps to avoid pollution or deterioration of habitats or any disturbances affecting the birds, in so far as these would be significant having regard to the objectives of this Article. Outside these protection areas, Member States shall also strive to avoid pollution or deterioration of habitats.

Article 5

Without prejudice to Articles 7 and 9, Member States shall take the requisite measures to establish a general system of protection for all species of birds referred to in Article 1, prohibiting in particular:
(a) deliberate killing or capture by any method;
(b) deliberate destruction of, or damage to, their nests and eggs or removal of their nests;
(c) taking their eggs in the wild and keeping these eggs even if empty;
(d) deliberate disturbance of these birds particularly during the period of breeding and rearing, in so far as disturbance would be significant having regard to the objectives of this Directive;
(e) keeping birds of species the hunting and capture of which is prohibited.

Article 6

1. Without prejudice to paragraphs 2 and 3, Member States shall prohibit, for all the bird species referred to in Article 1, the sale, transport for sale, keeping for sale and the offering for sale of live or dead birds and of any readily recognisable parts or derivatives of such birds.

2. The activities referred to in paragraph 1 shall not be prohibited in respect of the species referred to in Annex III, Part A, provided that the birds have been legally killed or captured or otherwise legally acquired.

3. Member States may, for the species listed in Annex III, Part B, allow within their territory the activities referred to in paragraph 1, making provision for certain restrictions, provided that the birds have been legally killed or captured or otherwise legally acquired.

Member States wishing to grant such authorisation shall first of all consult the Commission with a view to examining jointly with the latter whether the marketing of specimens of such species would result or could reasonably be expected to result in the population levels, geographical distribution or reproductive rate of the species being endangered throughout the Community. Should this examination prove that the intended authorisation will, in the view of the Commission, result in any one of the aforementioned species being thus endangered or in the possibility of their being thus endangered, the Commission shall forward a reasoned recommendation to the Member State concerned stating its opposition to the marketing of the species in question. Should the Commission consider that no such risk exists, it shall inform the Member State concerned accordingly.

The Commission's recommendation shall be published in the Official Journal of the European Union.

Member States granting authorisation pursuant to this paragraph shall verify at regular intervals that the conditions governing the granting of such authorisation continue to be fulfilled.

Article 7

1. Owing to their population level, geographical distribution and reproductive rate throughout the Community, the species listed in Annex II may be hunted under national legislation. Member States shall ensure that the hunting of these species does not jeopardise conservation efforts in their distribution area.

2. The species referred to in Annex II, Part A may be hunted in the geographical sea and land area where this Directive applies.

3. The species referred to in Annex II, Part B may be hunted only in the Member States in respect of which they are indicated.

4. Member States shall ensure that the practice of hunting, including falconry if practised, as carried on in accordance with the national measures in force, complies with the principles of wise use and ecologically balanced control of the species of birds concerned and that this practice is compatible as regards the population of these species, in particular migratory species, with the measures resulting from Article 2.

They shall see in particular that the species to which hunting laws apply are not hunted during the rearing season or during the various stages of reproduction.

In the case of migratory species, they shall see in particular that the species to which hunting regulations apply are not hunted during their period of reproduction or during their return to their rearing grounds.

Member States shall send the Commission all relevant information on the practical application of their hunting regulations.

Article 8

1. In respect of the hunting, capture or killing of birds under this Directive, Member States shall prohibit the use of all means, arrangements or methods used for the large-scale or non-selective capture or killing of birds or capable of causing the local disappearance of a species, in particular the use of those listed in Annex IV, point (a).

2. Moreover, Member States shall prohibit any hunting from the modes of transport and under the conditions mentioned in Annex IV, point (b).

Article 9

1. Member States may derogate from the provisions of Articles 5 to 8, where there is no other satisfactory solution, for the following reasons:

(a)
- — in the interests of public health and safety,
- — in the interests of air safety,
- — to prevent serious damage to crops, livestock, forests, fisheries and water,
- — for the protection of flora and fauna;

(b) for the purposes of research and teaching, of re-population, of re-introduction and for the breeding necessary for these purposes;

(c) to permit, under strictly supervised conditions and on a selective basis, the capture, keeping or other judicious use of certain birds in small numbers.

2. The derogations referred to in paragraph 1 must specify:

(a) the species which are subject to the derogations;

(b) the means, arrangements or methods authorised for capture or killing;

(c) the conditions of risk and the circumstances of time and place under which such derogations may be granted;

(d) the authority empowered to declare that the required conditions obtain and to decide what means, arrangements or methods may be used, within what limits and by whom;

(e) the controls which will be carried out.

3. Each year the Member States shall send a report to the Commission on the implementation of paragraphs 1 and 2.

4. On the basis of the information available to it, and in particular the information communicated to it pursuant to paragraph 3, the Commission shall at all times ensure that the consequences of the derogations referred to in paragraph 1 are not incompatible with this Directive. It shall take appropriate steps to this end.

Article 10

1. Member States shall encourage research and any work required as a basis for the protection, management and use of the population of all species of bird referred to in Article 1. Particular attention shall be paid to research and work on the subjects listed in Annex V.

2. Member States shall send the Commission any information required to enable it to take appropriate measures for the coordination of the research and work referred to in paragraph 1.

Article 11

Member States shall see that any introduction of species of bird which do not occur naturally in the wild state in the European territory of the Member States does not prejudice the local flora and fauna. In this connection they shall consult the Commission.

Article 12

1. Member States shall forward to the Commission every three years, starting from 7 April 1981, a report on the implementation of national provisions taken under this Directive.

2. The Commission shall prepare every three years a composite report based on the information referred to in paragraph 1. That part of the draft report covering the information supplied by a Member State shall be forwarded to the authorities of the Member State in question for verification. The final version of the report shall be forwarded to the Member States.

Article 13

Application of the measures taken pursuant to this Directive may not lead to deterioration in the present situation as regards the conservation of the species of birds referred to in Article 1.

Article 14

Member States may introduce stricter protective measures than those provided for under this Directive.

Article 15

Such amendments as are necessary for adapting Annexes I and V to technical and scientific progress shall be adopted. Those measures, designed to amend non-essential elements of this Directive, shall be adopted in accordance with the regulatory procedure with scrutiny referred to in Article 16(2).

Article 16

1. The Commission shall be assisted by the Committee for Adaptation to Technical and Scientific Progress.

2. Where reference is made to this paragraph, Article 5a(1) to (4) and Article 7 of Decision 1999/468/EC shall apply, having regard to the provisions of Article 8 thereof.

Article 17

Member States shall communicate to the Commission the texts of the main provisions of national law which they adopt in the field governed by this Directive.

Article 18

Directive 79/409/EEC, as amended by the acts listed in Annex VI, Part A, is repealed, without prejudice to the obligations of the Member States relating to the time limits for transposition into national law of the Directives set out in Annex VI, Part B.

References to the repealed Directive shall be construed as references to this Directive and shall be read in accordance with the correlation table in Annex VII.

Article 19

This Directive shall enter into force on the 20th day following its publication in the Official Journal of the European Union.

Article 20

This Directive is addressed to the Member States.

ANNEX I

GAVIIFORMES
Gaviidae
    Gavia stellata
    Gavia arctica
    Gavia immer

PODICIPEDIFORMES
Podicipedidae
    Podiceps auritus

PROCELLARIIFORMES
Procellariidae
Pterodroma madeira
Pterodroma feae
Bulweria bulwerii
Calonectris diomedea
Puffinus puffinus mauretanicus (Puffinus mauretanicus)
Puffinus yelkouan
Puffinus assimilis
Hydrobatidae
Pelagodroma marina
Hydrobates pelagicus
Oceanodroma leucorhoa
Oceanodroma castro

PELECANIFORMES
Pelecanidae
Pelecanus onocrotalus
Pelecanus crispus
Phalacrocoracidae
Phalacrocorax aristotelis desmarestii
Phalacrocorax pygmeus

CICONIIFORMES
Ardeidae
Botaurus stellaris
Ixobrychus minutus
Nycticorax nycticorax
Ardeola ralloides
Egretta garzetta
Egretta alba (Ardea alba)
Ardea purpurea
Ciconiidae
Ciconia nigra
Ciconia ciconia
Threskiornithidae
Plegadis falcinellus
Platalea leucorodia

PHOENICOPTERIFORMES
Phoenicopteridae
Phoenicopterus ruber

ANSERIFORMES
Anatidae
Cygnus bewickii (Cygnus columbianus bewickii)
Cygnus cygnus
Anser albifrons flavirostris
Anser erythropus
Branta leucopsis
Branta ruficollis
Tadorna ferruginea
Marmaronetta angustirostris
Aythya nyroca
Polysticta stelleri
Mergus albellus (Mergellus albellus)
Oxyura leucocephala

FALCONIFORMES
Pandionidae
- Pandion haliaetus

Accipitridae
- Pernis apivorus
- Elanus caeruleus
- Milvus migrans
- Milvus milvus
- Haliaeetus albicilla
- Gypaetus barbatus
- Neophron percnopterus
- Gyps fulvus
- Aegypius monachus
- Circaetus gallicus
- Circus aeruginosus
- Circus cyaneus
- Circus macrourus
- Circus pygargus
- Accipiter gentilis arrigonii
- Accipiter nisus granti
- Accipiter brevipes
- Buteo rufinus
- Aquila pomarina
- Aquila clanga
- Aquila heliaca
- Aquila adalberti
- Aquila chrysaetos
- Hieraaetus pennatus
- Hieraaetus fasciatus
- Falco vespertinus
- Falco columbarius
- Falco eleonorae
- Falco biarmicus

Falconidae
- Falco naumanni
- Falco cherrug
- Falco rusticolus
- Falco peregrinus

GALLIFORMES
Tetraonidae
- Bonasa bonasia
- Lagopus mutus pyrenaicus
- Lagopus mutus helveticus
- Tetrao tetrix tetrix
- Tetrao urogallus

Phasianidae
- Alectoris graeca
- Alectoris barbara
- Perdix perdix italica
- Perdix perdix hispaniensis

GRUIFORMES
Turnicidae
- Turnix sylvatica

Gruidae
- Grus grus

Rallidae
- Porzana porzana
- Porzana parva
- Porzana pusilla
- Crex crex
- Porphyrio porphyrio
- Fulica cristata

Otididae
- Tetrax tetrax
- Chlamydotis undulata
- Otis tarda

CHARADRIIFORMES

Recurvirostridae
- Himantopus himantopus
- Recurvirostra avosetta

Burhinidae
- Burhinus oedicnemus

Glareolidae
- Cursorius cursor
- Glareola pratincola

Charadriidae
- Charadrius alexandrinus
- Charadrius morinellus (Eudromias morinellus)
- Pluvialis apricaria
- Hoplopterus spinosus

Scolopacidae
- Calidris alpina schinzii
- Philomachus pugnax
- Gallinago media
- Limosa lapponica
- Numenius tenuirostris
- Tringa glareola
- Xenus cinereus (Tringa cinerea)
- Phalaropus lobatus

Laridae
- Larus melanocephalus
- Larus genei
- Larus audouinii
- Larus minutus

Sternidae
- Gelochelidon nilotica (Sterna nilotica)
- Sterna caspia
- Sterna sandvicensis
- Sterna dougallii
- Sterna hirundo
- Sterna paradisaea
- Sterna albifrons
- Chlidonias hybridus
- Chlidonias niger

Alcidae
- Uria aalge ibericus

PTEROCLIFORMES

Pteroclididae
- Pterocles orientalis
- Pterocles alchata

COLUMBIFORMES
Columbidae
Columba palumbus azorica
Columba trocaz
Columba bollii
Columba junoniae

STRIGIFORMES
Strigidae
Bubo bubo
Nyctea scandiaca
Surnia ulula
Glaucidium passerinum
Strix nebulosa
Strix uralensis
Asio flammeus
Aegolius funereus

CAPRIMULGIFORMES
Caprimulgidae
Caprimulgus europaeus

APODIFORMES
Apodidae
Apus caffer

CORACIIFORMES
Alcedinidae
Alcedo atthis
Coraciidae
Coracias garrulus

PICIFORMES
Picidae
Picus canus
Dryocopus martius
Dendrocopos major canariensis
Dendrocopos major thanneri
Dendrocopos syriacus
Dendrocopos medius
Dendrocopos leucotos
Picoides tridactylus

PASSERIFORMES
Alaudidae
Chersophilus duponti
Melanocorypha calandra
Calandrella brachydactyla
Galerida theklae
Lullula arborea
Motacillidae
Anthus campestris
Troglodytidae
Troglodytes troglodytes fridariensis
Muscicapidae (Turdinae)
Luscinia svecica
Saxicola dacotiae
Oenanthe leucura

Oenanthe cypriaca
Oenanthe pleschanka
Muscicapidae (Sylviinae)
Acrocephalus melanopogon
Acrocephalus paludicola
Hippolais olivetorum
Sylvia sarda
Sylvia undata
Sylvia melanothorax
Sylvia rueppelli
Sylvia nisoria
Muscicapidae (Muscicapinae)
Ficedula parva
Ficedula semitorquata
Ficedula albicollis
Paridae
Parus ater cypriotes
Sittidae
Sitta krueperi
Sitta whiteheadi
Certhiidae
Certhia brachydactyla dorotheae
Laniidae
Lanius collurio
Lanius minor
Lanius nubicus
Corvidae
Pyrrhocorax pyrrhocorax
Fringillidae (Fringillinae)
Fringilla coelebs ombriosa
Fringilla teydea
Fringillidae (Carduelinae)
Loxia scotica
Bucanetes githagineus
Pyrrhula murina (Pyrrhula pyrrhula murina)
Emberizidae (Emberizinae)
Emberiza cineracea
Emberiza hortulana
Emberiza caesia

ANNEX II

PART A

ANSERIFORMES
Anatidae
Anser fabalis
Anser anser
Branta canadensis
Anas penelope
Anas strepera
Anas crecca
Anas platyrhynchos
Anas acuta
Anas querquedula

Anas clypeata
Aythya ferina
Aythya fuligula

GALLIFORMES
Tetraonidae
Lagopus lagopus scoticus et hibernicus
Lagopus mutus
Phasianidae
Alectoris graeca
Alectoris rufa
Perdix perdix
Phasianus colchicus

GRUIFORMES
Rallidae
Fulica atra

CHARADRIIFORMES
Scolopacidae
Lymnocryptes minimus
Gallinago gallinago
Scolopax rusticola

COLUMBIFORMES
Columbidae
Columba livia
Columba palumbus

PART B

ANSERIFORMES
Anatidae
Cygnus olor
Anser brachyrhynchus
Anser albifrons
Branta bernicla
Netta rufina
Aythya marila
Somateria mollissima
Clangula hyemalis
Melanitta nigra
Melanita fusca
Bucephala clangula
Mergus serrator
Mergus merganser

GALLIFORMES
Meleagridae
Meleagris gallopavo
Tetraonidae
Bonasa bonasia
Lagopus lagopus lagopus
Tetrao tetrix
Tetrao urogallus
Phasianidae
Francolinus francolinus
Alectoris barbara

Alectoris chukar
Coturnix coturnix

GRUIFORMES
Rallidae
Rallus aquaticus
Gallinula chloropus

CHARADRIIFORMES
Haematopodidae
Haematopus ostralegus
Charadriidae
Pluvialis apricaria
Pluvialis squatarola
Vanellus vanellus
Scolopacidae
Calidris canutus
Philomachus pugnax
Limosa limosa
Limosa lapponica
Numenius phaeopus
Numenius arquata
Tringa erythropus
Tringa totanus
Tringa nebularia
Laridae
Larus ridibundus
Larus canus
Larus fuscus
Larus argentatus
Larus cachinnans
Larus marinus

COLUMBIFORMES
Columbidae
Columba oenas
Streptopelia decaocto
Streptopelia turtur

PASSERIFORMES
Alaudidae
Alauda arvensis
Muscicapidae
Turdus merula
Turdus pilaris
Turdus philomelos
Turdus iliacus
Turdus viscivorus
Sturnidae
Sturnus vulgaris
Corvidae
Garrulus glandarius
Pica pica
Corvus monedula
Corvus frugilegus
Corvus corone

	BE	BG	CZ	DK	DE	EE	EL	ES	FR	IE	IT	CY	LV	LT	LU	HU	MT	NL	AT	PL	PT	RO	SI	SK	FI	SE	UK
Calidris canutus				+					+																		
Philomachus pugnax									+		+						+										
Limosa limosa				+					+																		
Limosa lapponica				+					+																		+
Numenius phaeopus				+					+																		+
Numenius arquata				+					+	+																	+
Tringa erythropus				+					+																		
Tringa totanus				+					+		+																+
Tringa nebularia				+					+																		
Larus ridibundus	+			+	+	+		+								+			+					+		+	
Larus canus				+	+	+																			+	+	
Larus fuscus				+	+																						
Larus argentatus	+			+	+	+							+												+	+	
Larus cachinnans								+								+											
Larus marinus				+	+	+																			+	+	
Columba oenas							+	+	+			+									+	+					
Streptopelia decaocto		+	+	+	+				+			+				+			+			+		+			
Streptopelia turtur		+					+	+	+		+	+					+		+		+	+					
Alauda arvensis							+		+		+	+					+					+					
Turdus merula							+		+		+	+					+				+					+	
Turdus pilaris						+	+	+	+		+	+					+		+		+	+			+	+	
Turdus philomelos							+	+	+		+	+					+				+	+					
Turdus iliacus							+	+	+		+	+					+				+	+					
Turdus viscivorus							+	+	+			+					+				+	+					
Sturnus vulgaris		+					+	+	+			+				+	+				+	+					
Garrulus glandarius	+			+	+				+		+				+	+		+			+	+	+	+		+	+
Pica pica	+	+	+	+	+		+	+	+		+	+	+		+	+		+			+	+	+	+	+	+	+
Corvus monedula		+					+	+				+						+				+			+	+	+

	BE	BG	CZ	DK	DE	EE	EL	ES	FR	IE	IT	CY	LV	LT	LU	HU	MT	NL	AT	PL	PT	RO	SI	SK	FI	SE	UK
Calidris canutus				+					+																		
Philomachus pugnax									+		+						+										
Limosa limosa				+					+																		
Limosa lapponica				+					+																		+
Numenius phaeopus				+					+																		+
Numenius arquata				+					+	+																	+
Tringa erythropus				+					+																		
Tringa totanus				+					+		+																+
Tringa nebularia				+					+																		
Larus ridibundus	+			+	+	+		+								+			+					+		+	
Larus canus				+	+	+																			+	+	
Larus fuscus				+	+																						
Larus argentatus	+			+	+	+							+												+	+	
Larus cachinnans								+								+											
Larus marinus				+	+	+																			+	+	
Columba oenas							+	+	+			+									+	+					
Streptopelia decaocto		+	+	+	+				+			+				+			+			+		+			
Streptopelia turtur		+					+	+	+		+	+					+		+		+	+					
Alauda arvensis							+		+		+	+					+					+					
Turdus merula							+		+		+	+					+				+					+	
Turdus pilaris						+	+	+	+		+	+					+		+		+	+			+	+	
Turdus philomelos							+	+	+		+	+					+				+	+					
Turdus iliacus							+	+	+		+	+					+				+	+					
Turdus viscivorus							+	+	+			+					+				+	+					
Sturnus vulgaris		+					+	+	+			+				+	+				+	+					
Garrulus glandarius	+			+	+				+		+				+	+		+			+	+	+	+		+	+
Pica pica	+	+	+	+	+		+	+	+		+	+	+		+	+		+			+	+	+	+	+	+	+
Corvus monedula		+					+	+				+						+				+			+	+	+

	BE	BG	CZ	DK	DE	EE	EL	ES	FR	IE	IT	CY	LV	LT	LU	HU	MT	NL	AT	PL	PT	RO	SI	SK	FI	SE	UK
Corvus frugilegus		+				+			+					+		+						+		+		+	+
Corvus corone	+	+	+	+	+	+	+	+	+		+	+	+	+	+	+		+			+	+	+	+	+	+	+

AT = Österreich, BE = Belgique/België, BG = България, CY = Κύπρος, CZ = Česká republika, DE = Deutschland, DK = Danmark, EE = Eesti, ES = España, FI = Suomi/Finland, FR = France, EL = Ελλάδα, HU = Magyarország, IE = Ireland, IT = Italia, LT = Lietuva, LU = Luxembourg, LV = Latvija, MT = Malta, NL = Nederland, PL = Polska, PT = Portugal, RO = România, SE = Sverige, SI = Slovenija, SK = Slovensko, UK = United Kingdom.

+ = Member States which under Article 7(3) may authorise hunting of the species listed.

ANNEX III

PART A

ANSERIFORMES
Anatidae
    Anas platyrhynchos

GALLIFORMES
Tetraonidae
    Lagopus lagopus lagopus, scoticus et hibernicus
Phasianidae
    Alectoris rufa
    Alectoris barbara
    Perdix perdix
    Phasianus colchicus

COLUMBIFORMES
Columbidae
    Columba palumbus

PART B

ANSERIFORMES
Anatidae
    Anser albifrons albifrons
    Anser anser
    Anas penelope
    Anas crecca
    Anas acuta
    Anas clypeata
    Aythya ferina
    Aythya fuligula
    Aythya marila
    Somateria mollissima
    Melanitta nigra

GALLIFORMES
Tetraonidae
    Lagopus mutus
    Tetrao tetrix britannicus
    Tetrao urogallus

GRUIFORMES
Rallidae
    Fulica atra

CHARADRIIFORMES
Charadriidae
    Pluvialis apricaria
Scolopacidae
    Lymnocryptes minimus
    Gallinago gallinago
    Scolopax rusticola

ANNEX IV

(a)

— Snares (with the exception of Finland and Sweden for the capture of Lagopus lagopus lagopus and Lagopus mutus north of latitude 58° N), limes, hooks, live birds which are blind or mutilated used as decoys, tape recorders, electrocuting devices,
— artificial light sources, mirrors, devices for illuminating targets, sighting devices for night shooting comprising an electronic image magnifier or image converter,
— explosives,
— nets, traps, poisoned or anaesthetic bait,
— semi-automatic or automatic weapons with a magazine capable of holding more than two rounds of ammunition;

(b)

— aircraft, motor vehicles,
— boats driven at a speed exceeding five kilometres per hour. On the open sea, Member States may, for safety reasons, authorise the use of motor-boats with a maximum speed of 18 kilometres per hour. Member States shall inform the Commission of any authorisations granted.

ANNEX V

(a) National lists of species in danger of extinction or particularly endangered species, taking into account their geographical distribution.
(b) Listing and ecological description of areas particularly important to migratory species on their migratory routes and as wintering and nesting grounds.
(c) Listing of data on the population levels of migratory species as shown by ringing.
(d) Assessing the influence of methods of taking wild birds on population levels.
(e) Developing or refining ecological methods for preventing the type of damage caused by birds.
(f) Determining the role of certain species as indicators of pollution.
(g) Studying the adverse effect of chemical pollution on population levels of bird species.

ANNEX VI

PART A
REPEALED DIRECTIVE WITH LIST OF ITS SUCCESSIVE AMENDMENTS (REFERRED TO IN ARTICLE 18)

Council Directive 79/409/EEC (OJ L 103, 25.4.1979, p. 1)

1979 Act of Accession, Annex I, point XIII.1.F (OJ L 291, 19.11.1979, p. 111)

Council Directive 81/854/EEC (OJ L 319, 7.11.1981, p. 3)

Commission Directive 85/411/EEC (OJ L 233, 30.8.1985, p. 33)

1985 Act of Accession, Annex I, points X.1.(h) and X.6 (OJ L 302, 15.11.1985, p. 218)

Council Directive 86/122/EEC (OJ L 100, 16.4.1986, p. 22)

Commission Directive 91/244/EEC (OJ L 115, 8.5.1991, p. 41)

Council Directive 94/24/EC (OJ L 164, 30.6.1994, p. 9)

1994 Act of Accession, Annex I, point VIII.E.1 (OJ C 241, 29.8.1994, p. 175)

Commission Directive 97/49/EC (OJ L 223, 13.8.1997, p. 9)

Council Regulation (EC) No 807/2003 (OJ L 122, 16.5.2003, p. 36)	only Annex III, point 29
2003 Act of Accession, Annex II, point 16.C.1 (OJ L 236, 23.9.2003, p. 667)	
Council Directive 2006/105/EC (OJ L 363, 20.12.2006, p. 368)	only as regards the reference, in Article 1, to Directive 79/409/EEC and point A.1 of the Annex
Directive 2008/102/EC of the European Parliament and of the Council (OJ L 323, 3.12.2008, p. 31)	

Part B
List of time limits for transposition into national law
(referred to in Article 18)

Directives	*Time limit for transposition*
79/409/EEC	7 April 1981
81/854/EEC	—
85/411/EEC	31 July 1986
86/122/EEC	—
91/244/EEC	31 July 1992
94/24/EC	29 September 1995
97/49/EC	30 September 1998
2006/105/EC	1 January 2007
2008/102/EC	—

ANNEX VII
CORRELATION TABLE

Directive 79/409/EEC	*This Directive*
Article 1(1) and (2)	Article 1(1) and (2)
Article 1(3)	—
Articles 2 to 5	Articles 2 to 5
Article 6(1), (2) and (3)	Article 6(1), (2) and (3)
Article 6(4)	—
Article 7(1), (2) and (3)	Article 7(1), (2) and (3)
Article 7(4), first sentence	Article 7(4), first subparagraph
Article 7(4), second sentence	Article 7(4), second subparagraph
Article 7(4), third sentence	Article 7(4), third subparagraph
Article 7(4), fourth sentence	Article 7(4), fourth subparagraph
Article 8	Article 8
Article 9(1)	Article 9(1)
Article 9(2), introductory wording	Article 9(2), introductory wording
Article 9(2), first indent	Article 9(2), point (a)
Article 9(2), second indent	Article 9(2), point (b)
Article 9(2), third indent	Article 9(2), point (c)
Article 9(2), fourth indent	Article 9(2), point (d)
Article 9(2), fifth indent	Article 9(2), point (e)

Directive 79/409/EEC	*This Directive*
Article 9(3)	Article 9(3)
Article 9(4)	Article 9(4)
Article 10(1)	Article 10(1), first sentence
Article 10(2), first sentence	Article 10(1), second sentence
Article 10(2), second sentence	Article 10(2)
Articles 11 to 15	Articles 11 to 15
Article 16(1)	—
Article 17	Article 16
Article 18(1)	—
Article 18(2)	Article 17
—	Article 18
—	Article 19
Article 19	Article 20
Annex I	Annex I
Annex II/1	Annex II, Part A
Annex II/2	Annex II, Part B
Annex III/1	Annex III, Part A
Annex III/2	Annex III, Part B
Annex IV	Annex IV
Annex V	Annex V
—	Annex VI
—	Annex VII

REGULATION 1005/2009/EC OF THE EUROPEAN PARLIAMENT AND OF THE COUNCIL

of 16 September 2009

ON SUBSTANCES THAT DEPLETE THE OZONE LAYER

THE EUROPEAN PARLIAMENT AND THE COUNCIL OF THE EUROPEAN UNION,

Having regard to the Treaty establishing the European Community, and in particular Article 175(1) thereof,

Having regard to the proposal from the Commission,

Having regard to the opinion of the European Economic and Social Committee,

After consulting the Committee of the Regions,

Acting in accordance with the procedure laid down in Article 251 of the Treaty,

Whereas:

(1) Regulation (EC) No 2037/2000 of the European Parliament and of the Council of 29 June 2000 on substances that deplete the ozone layer has been substantially amended several times. Since further amendments are to be made, it should be recast in the interests of clarity.

(2) It is established that continued emissions of ozone-depleting substances (ODS) cause significant damage to the ozone layer. There is clear evidence of a decrease in the atmospheric burden of ODS and some early signs of stratospheric ozone recovery have been observed. However, the recovery of the ozone layer to the concentrations level existing before 1980 is not projected to take place before the middle of the 21st century. Increased UV-B radiation resulting from ozone depletion therefore persists as a significant threat to health and environment. At the same time, most of these substances have high global warming potential and are contributory factors towards increasing the temperature of the planet. Further efficient measures need therefore to be taken in order to protect human health and the environment against adverse effects resulting from such emissions and to avoid risking further delay in the recovery of the ozone layer.

(3) In view of its responsibilities for the environment and trade, the Community, pursuant to Council Decision 88/540/EEC, has become a Party to the Vienna Convention for the Protection of the Ozone Layer and the Montreal Protocol on Substances that Deplete the Ozone Layer (hereinafter "the Protocol").

(4) Many ODS are greenhouse gases but are not controlled under the United Nations Framework Convention for Climate Change and its Kyoto Protocol on the assumption that the Protocol will phase out ODS. Despite progress made by the Protocol, the task of phasing out ODS still needs to be completed in the European Union and globally, whilst bearing in mind that at present many alternatives to ODS have a high global warming potential. It is therefore necessary to minimise and eliminate the production and use of ODS wherever technically feasible alternatives with low global warming potential are available.

(5) Additional measures for the protection of the ozone layer were adopted by the Parties to the Protocol, most recently at their meeting in Montreal in September 2007 and in Doha in November 2008. It is necessary for action to be taken at Community level to comply with the Community's obligations under the Protocol and in particular to implement the accelerated phase out of hydrochlorofluorocarbons with due consideration to the risks of phasing in alternatives with high global warming potential.

(6) Following the concerns stated in the 2006 Report of the Scientific Assessment Panel related to the accelerating growth of production and consumption of

hydrochlorofluorocarbons in developing countries, the Parties to the Protocol in 2007 adopted Decision XIX/6 at their 19th Meeting providing for an accelerated phase-out schedule for hydrochlorofluorocarbons. Following that Decision the production phase-out date should be brought forward from 2025 to 2020.

(7) Under Regulation (EC) No 2037/2000, as from 2010, virgin hydrochlorofluorocarbons can no longer be used for the maintenance or servicing of refrigeration and air conditioning equipment. In order to minimise the risk of illegal use of virgin hydrochlorofluorocarbons as recycled or reclaimed material, only reclaimed or recycled material should be used in maintenance or servicing operations. The re-selling of recycled hydrochlorofluorocarbons should be prohibited, and recycled hydrochlorofluorocarbons should only be used when recovered from such equipment and only by the undertaking which carried out or mandated the recovery. For consistency this exemption should also apply to heat pump equipment.

(8) In view of the wide availability of technologies and alternative substances for replacing ODS, it is appropriate in certain cases to provide for control measures which are stricter than those provided for in Regulation (EC) No 2037/2000 and stricter than those in the Protocol.

(9) Under Regulation (EC) No 2037/2000 the production and placing on the market of chlorofluorocarbons, other fully halogenated chlorofluorocarbons, halons, carbon tetrachloride, 1,1,1-trichloroethane, hydrobromofluorocarbons, bromochloromethane and methyl bromide have been phased out and the placing on the market of those substances and of products and equipment containing those substances is thus prohibited. It is now also appropriate to progressively generalise the ban on the use of those substances for the maintenance or servicing of such equipment.

(10) Even after the phase out of controlled substances the Commission should, under certain conditions, grant exemptions for essential laboratory and analytical uses. In particular, Decision X/14 of the Parties to the Protocol establishes criteria for granting of exemptions for those uses. The Commission should be empowered to establish conditions for essential laboratory and analytical uses. To avoid an increase in the quantities used for these purposes, producers and importers should not be allowed to significantly increase the quantities placed on the market. Specific conditions decided by the Parties for the placing on the market of substances for those uses should be integrated into this Regulation to ensure compliance with them.

(11) The availability of alternatives to methyl bromide has been reflected in more substantial reductions in its production and consumption compared to the Protocol, as well as in Commission Decision 2008/753/EC of 18 September 2008 concerning the non-inclusion of methyl bromide in Annex I to Council Directive 91/414/EEC and the withdrawal of authorisations for plant protection products containing that substance and in Directive 98/8/EC of the European Parliament and of the Council of 16 February 1998 concerning the placing of biocidal products on the market. The exemption for critical uses of methyl bromide should cease completely whilst temporarily allowing the possibility to grant a derogation in emergency situations in the case of unexpected pests or disease outbreaks where such emergency use is to be permitted under Council Directive 91/414/EEC of 15 July 1991 concerning the placing of plant protection products on the market and Directive 98/8/EC. In such cases measures to minimise emissions, such as the use of virtually impermeable films for soil fumigation, should be specified.

(12) In view of Commission Regulation (EC) No 2032/2003 of 4 November 2003 on the second phase of the 10-year work programme referred to in Article 16(2) of Directive 98/8/EC of the European Parliament and of the Council concerning the placing of biocidal products on the market, which banned the use of methyl bromide as a biocide by 1 September 2006, and Decision 2008/753/EC, which banned the use of methyl bromide as a plant protection product by 18 March 2010, the use of methyl bromide for quarantine and pre-shipment applications should also be banned by 18 March 2010.

(13) The Protocol, in Article 2F, requires the Parties to endeavour to ensure that the use of hydrochlorofluorocarbons is limited to those applications where more environmentally

suitable alternative substances or technologies are not available. In view of the availability of alternative and substitute technologies, the placing on the market and use of hydrochlorofluorocarbons as well as of products and equipment containing or relying on hydrochlorofluorocarbons can be further limited. Decision VI/13 of the Parties to the Protocol provides that the evaluation of alternatives to hydrochlorofluorocarbons should take into account such factors as ozone-depleting potential, energy efficiency, potential flammability, toxicity, global warming potential and the potential impacts on the effective use and phase out of chlorofluorocarbons and halons. The Parties concluded in that decision that hydrochlorofluorocarbon controls under the Protocol should be considerably tightened to protect the ozone layer and to reflect the availability of alternatives.

(14) Control measures regarding products and equipment containing controlled substances should be extended to products and equipment relying on those substances in order to prevent circumventions of the restrictions under this Regulation. By covering additionally products and equipment for which the design, the use or the proper functioning requires the presence of a controlled substance, a potential opportunity to place on the market, import or export products or equipment which do not contain controlled substances at that moment, but which would have to be refilled at a later date, is eliminated. Furthermore, exemptions for products and equipment manufactured before the entry into force of the control measures should be removed as they are no longer relevant and might constitute a risk of illegal placing on the market or trade.

(15) Controlled substances as well as products and equipment containing or relying on controlled substances from States not party to the Protocol should not be imported. Furthermore, the export of products and equipment containing or relying on hydrochlorofluorocarbons after the entry into force of a ban on use of those products and equipment or of controlled substances for their maintenance or servicing in the Community should be prohibited in order to avoid the building-up of banks of those substances in countries where sufficient destruction facilities are not available.

(16) The licensing system for controlled substances includes the authorisation of exports of controlled substances, in order to improve the monitoring of and control of trade in ODS and to allow for exchange of information between Parties. That licensing system should be extended to products and equipment containing or relying on controlled substances.

(17) To improve the monitoring and control of trade the licensing should cover not only the entry of goods into the customs territory for release for free circulation in the Community but also the entry under other customs procedures or for customs-approved treatments and uses. Transit through the customs territory of the Community, temporary storage, customs warehousing and the free zone procedure should still be possible without licensing in order to avoid unnecessary burdens on operators and customs authorities. Shipments to or from a territory of a Member State that is not part of the customs territory of the Community or not covered by this Regulation, but which is covered by the Member State's ratification of the Protocol should not create unnecessary burdens to Member States in relation to licensing and reporting provided that the obligations of this Regulation and the Protocol are complied with.

(18) Before issuing import and export licences the Commission should be enabled to verify with the competent authorities of the third country concerned whether the intended transaction would comply with the requirements applicable in that country, in order to avoid illegal and unwanted trade.

(19) Council Directive 67/548/EEC of 27 June 1967 on the approximation of laws, regulations and administrative provisions relating to the classification, packaging and labelling of dangerous substances, Directive 1999/45/EC of the European Parliament and of the Council of 31 May 1999 concerning the approximation of the laws, regulations and administrative provisions of the Member States relating to the classification, packaging and labelling of dangerous preparations and Regulation (EC) No 1272/2008 of the European Parliament and of the Council of 16 December 2008

on classification, labelling and packaging of substances and mixtures provide for the labelling of substances classified as ODS and the labelling of mixtures containing such substances. As ODS produced for feedstock, process agent, laboratory and analytical uses can be released for free circulation in the Community, they should be distinguished from those substances produced for other uses, in order to avoid any diversions of controlled substances intended for feedstock, as a process agent or for laboratory and analytical uses to other uses which are controlled under this Regulation. Furthermore, in order to inform end users and to facilitate the enforcement of this Regulation also products and equipment containing or relying on such substances should be so labelled during maintenance or servicing.

(20) To reduce the release of controlled substances into the atmosphere, provision should be made for the recovery of used controlled substances and the prevention of leakages of controlled substances.

(21) The Protocol requires reporting on trade in ODS. Annual reporting should therefore be required from producers, importers and exporters of controlled substances. In order to enable the Commission to streamline the reporting procedures to comply with the Protocol and avoid duplications in the process, destruction facilities should also report directly to the Commission. To ensure compliance with reporting obligations under the Protocol and to improve their practical application the Commission should be empowered to modify the reporting requirements for Member States and undertakings. In view of the envisaged development of Internet-based reporting tools the Commission should, as appropriate, draft measures to adapt the reporting requirements as soon as the relevant reporting tools are in place.

(22) The protection of individuals with regard to the processing of personal data by the Member States is governed by Directive 95/46/EC of the European Parliament and of the Council of 24 October 1995 on the protection of individuals with regard to the processing of personal data and on the free movement of such data and the protection of individuals with regard to the processing of personal data by the Commission is governed by Regulation (EC) No 45/2001 of the European Parliament and of the Council of 18 December 2000 on the protection of individuals with regard to the processing of personal data by the Community institutions and bodies and on the free movement of such data in particular as regards the requirements of confidentiality and security of processing, the transfer of personal data from the Commission to the Member States, the lawfulness of processing, and the rights of data subjects to information, access to and rectification of their personal data.

(23) Member States should carry out inspections, taking a risk-based approach in order to ensure compliance with all provisions of this Regulation and thus targeting those activities representing the highest risk of illegal trade or emission of controlled substances. Recommendation 2001/331/EC of the European Parliament and of the Council of 4 April 2001 providing for minimum criteria for environmental inspections in the Member States should provide guidance for the carrying out of inspections by Member States.

(24) In view of the continuing innovation in the sectors covered by this Regulation, the Commission should regularly review this Regulation and, if appropriate, make proposals, in particular on the exemptions and derogations provided for when technically and economically feasible alternatives to the use of controlled substances become available, to further strengthen the protection of the ozone layer and simultaneously reduce greenhouse gases emissions. In order to ensure compliance with the Protocol, the Commission should be empowered to align Annexes to this Regulation with decisions of the Parties, in particular with those concerning approved destruction methods, conditions for the placing on the market of controlled substances for essential laboratory and analytical uses, and processes in which controlled substances may be used as process agents.

(25) The measures necessary for the implementation of this Regulation should be adopted in accordance with Council Decision 1999/468/EC of 28 June 1999 laying down the procedures for the exercise of implementing powers conferred on the Commission.

(26) In particular, the Commission should be empowered to determine the form and content of labels for controlled substances produced, placed on the market or used as feedstock, as process agent or for laboratory and analytical uses; to amend Annex III on processes for which controlled substances may be used as process agents; to amend the maximum amount of controlled substances that may be used as process agents or emitted from process agents uses; to amend Annex V on conditions for placing on the market and further distribution of controlled substances for laboratory and analytical uses; to determine a mechanism for the allocation of quotas for controlled substances for laboratory and analytical uses; to amend Annex VI; to adopt modifications and time frames for the phasing out of the critical uses of halons; to amend the list of items required to be stated in an application for a licence; to adopt additional monitoring measures on trade in controlled substances or new substances and of products and equipment containing or relying on controlled substances; to adopt rules applicable to the release for free circulation in the Community of products and equipment imported from any State not party to the Protocol which were produced using controlled substances; to amend Annex VII on destruction technologies; to establish a list with products and equipment for which the recovery for destruction or destruction without prior recovery of controlled substances should be considered technically and economically feasible and therefore mandatory; to adopt minimum qualification requirements for personnel; to establish a list of technologies and practices to be used by undertakings to prevent and minimise any leakage and emission of controlled substances; to include new substances in Annex II and to amend reporting requirements for Member States and undertakings. Since those measures are of general scope and are designed to amend non-essential elements of this Regulation, inter alia, by supplementing it with new non-essential elements, they must be adopted in accordance with the regulatory procedure with scrutiny provided for in Article 5a of Decision 1999/468/EC.

(27) Directive 2006/12/EC of the European Parliament and of the Council of 5 April 2006 on waste and Council Directive 91/689/EEC of 12 December 1991 on hazardous waste provide for measures on the environmentally sound disposal and recovery of waste and controls on hazardous waste. In this regard, special attention should be paid to ODS in construction and demolition waste and in equipment falling within the scope of Directive 2002/96/EC of the European Parliament and of the Council of 27 January 2003 on waste electrical and electronic equipment (WEEE). In accordance with the Protocol only technologies approved by the Parties may be applied to the destruction of controlled substances. The relevant decisions of the Parties should therefore be incorporated in this Regulation to ensure that only those technologies are applied, provided that their application is compatible with Community and national legislation on waste.

(28) A flexible mechanism should be established to introduce reporting obligations for substances identified as ozone depleting, to allow for assessing the magnitude of their environmental impact and to ensure that those new substances which have been identified as having a significant ozone-depleting potential are subject to control measures. In this context, special attention should be paid to the role of very short-lived substances, having regard, in particular, to the 2006 United Nations Environment Programme/World Meteorological Organisation (UNEP/WMO) ozone assessment, which concluded that the ozone-depleting potential of those substances is greater than previously assessed.

(29) Member States should lay down rules on penalties applicable to infringements of the provisions of this Regulation and ensure that they are implemented. Those penalties should be effective, proportionate and dissuasive.

(30) Since the objectives of this Regulation, namely to ensure compliance with the Community's obligations as party to the Protocol and to address a transboundary environmental problem with global impact whilst regulating intra-Community and external trade in ODS and products and equipment containing or relying on those substances, cannot be sufficiently achieved by the Member States acting individually

and can therefore be better achieved at Community level, the Community may adopt measures, in accordance with the principle of subsidiarity, as set out in Article 5 of the Treaty. In accordance with the principle of proportionality, as set out in that Article, this Regulation does not go beyond what is necessary in order to achieve those objectives,

HAVE ADOPTED THIS REGULATION:

CHAPTER I
GENERAL PROVISIONS

Article 1

Subject matter

This Regulation lays down rules on the production, import, export, placing on the market, use, recovery, recycling, reclamation and destruction of substances that deplete the ozone layer, on the reporting of information related to those substances and on the import, export, placing on the market and use of products and equipment containing or relying on those substances.

Article 2

Scope

This Regulation shall apply to controlled substances, to new substances and to products and equipment containing or relying on controlled substances.

Article 3

Definitions

For the purposes of this Regulation:

1. "Protocol" means the 1987 Montreal Protocol on Substances that Deplete the Ozone Layer, as last amended and adjusted;
2. "Party" means any party to the Protocol;
3. "State not party to the Protocol" means, with respect to a particular controlled substance, any State or regional economic integration organisation that has not agreed to be bound by the provisions of the Protocol applicable to that substance;
4. "controlled substances" means substances listed in Annex I, including their isomers, whether alone or in a mixture, and whether they are virgin, recovered, recycled or reclaimed;
5. "chlorofluorocarbons" means the controlled substances listed in Group I of Annex I, including their isomers;
6. "halons" means the controlled substances listed in Group III of Annex I, including their isomers;
7. "carbon tetrachloride" means the controlled substance specified in Group IV of Annex I;
8. "methyl bromide" means the controlled substance specified in Group VI of Annex I;
9. "hydrochlorofluorocarbons" means the controlled substances listed in Group VIII of Annex I, including their isomers;
10. "new substances" means substances listed in Annex II, whether alone or in a mixture, and whether they are virgin, recovered, recycled or reclaimed;
11. "feedstock" means any controlled substance or new substance that undergoes chemical transformation in a process in which it is entirely converted from its original composition and whose emissions are insignificant;
12. "process agents" means controlled substances used as chemical process agents in the applications listed in Annex III;

13. "producer" means any natural or legal person producing controlled substances or new substances within the Community;
14. "production" means the amount of controlled substances or new substances produced, including the amount produced, intentionally or inadvertently, as a by-product unless that by-product is destroyed as part of the manufacturing process or following a documented procedure ensuring compliance with this Regulation and the Community and national legislation on waste. No amount recovered, recycled or reclaimed shall be considered as "production", nor shall any insignificant amount unavoidably incorporated in products in trace quantities or emitted during manufacturing;
15. "ozone-depleting potential" or "ODP" means the figure specified in Annexes I and II representing the potential effect of each controlled substance or new substance on the ozone layer;
16. "calculated level" means a quantity determined by multiplying the quantity of each controlled substance by its ozone-depleting potential and by adding together, for each group of controlled substances in Annex I separately, the resulting figures;
17. "industrial rationalisation" means the transfer either between Parties or within a Member State of all or a portion of the calculated level of production of one producer to another, for the purpose of optimising economic efficiency or responding to anticipated shortfalls in supply as a result of plant closures;
18. "import" means the entry of substances, products and equipment covered by this Regulation into the customs territory of the Community as far as the territory is covered by a Member State's ratification of the Protocol and this Regulation applies;
19. "export" means the exit from the customs territory of the Community, in so far as the territory is covered by a Member State's ratification of the Protocol and by this Regulation, of substances, products and equipment covered by this Regulation which have the status of Community goods or the re-export of substances, products and equipment covered by this Regulation if they have the status of non-Community goods;
20. "placing on the market" means the supplying or making available to third persons within the Community for payment or free of charge, and includes the release for free circulation in the Community as referred to in Regulation (EC) No 450/2008. In respect of products and equipment being part of immovable property or part of means of transport this refers only to the supplying or making available within the Community for the first time;
21. "use" means the utilisation of controlled substances or new substances in the production, maintenance or servicing, including refilling, of products and equipment or in other processes;
22. "heat pump" means a device or installation that extracts heat at low temperatures from air, water or earth and supplies heat;
23. "recovery" means the collection and the storage of controlled substances from products and equipment or containers during maintenance or servicing or before disposal;
24. "recycling" means the reuse of a recovered controlled substance following a basic cleaning process;
25. "reclamation" means the reprocessing of a recovered controlled substance in order to meet the equivalent performance of a virgin substance, taking into account its intended use;
26. "undertaking" means any natural or legal person which:
    - (a) produces, recovers, recycles, reclaims, uses or destroys controlled substances or new substances;
    - (b) imports such substances;
    - (c) exports such substances;
    - (d) places such substances on the market; or
    - (e) operates refrigeration, air conditioning or heat pump equipment, or fire protection systems, which contain controlled substances;
27. "quarantine applications" means treatments to prevent the introduction, establishment or spread of quarantine pests (including diseases), or to ensure their official control, where:

— official control is that performed by, or authorised by, a national plant, animal or environmental protection or health authority,
— quarantine pests are pests of potential importance to the areas endangered thereby and not yet present there, or present but not widely distributed, and being officially controlled;

28. "pre-shipment applications" means those non-quarantine applications applied no more than 21 days prior to export to meet the official requirements of the importing country or official requirements of the exporting country existing before 7 December 1995. Official requirements are those which are performed by, or authorised by, a national plant, animal, environmental, health or stored product authority;
29. "products and equipment relying on controlled substances" means products and equipment which do not function without controlled substances, not including those products and equipment used for the production, processing, recovery, recycling, reclamation or destruction of controlled substances;
30. "virgin substances" means substances which have not previously been used;
31. "products and equipment" means all products and equipment except containers used for the transportation or storage of controlled substances.

CHAPTER II
PROHIBITIONS

Article 4

Production of controlled substances

The production of controlled substances shall be prohibited.

Article 5

Placing on the market and use of controlled substances

1. The placing on the market and the use of controlled substances shall be prohibited.

2. Controlled substances shall not be placed on the market in non-refillable containers, except for laboratory and analytical uses as referred to in Article 10 and Article 11(2).

3. This Article shall not apply to controlled substances in products and equipment.

Article 6

Placing on the market of products and equipment containing or relying on controlled substances

1. The placing on the market of products and equipment containing or relying on controlled substances shall be prohibited, with the exception of products and equipment for which the use of the respective controlled substance is authorised in accordance with Article 10, Article 11(2) or Article 13 or has been authorised on the basis of Article 3(1) of Regulation (EC) No 2037/2000.

2. Except for uses referred to in Article 13(1), fire protection systems and fire extinguishers containing halons shall be prohibited and shall be decommissioned.

CHAPTER III
EXEMPTIONS AND DEROGATIONS

Article 7

Production, placing on the market and use of controlled substances as feedstock

1. By way of derogation from Articles 4 and 5, controlled substances may be produced, placed on the market and used as feedstock.

2. Controlled substances produced or placed on the market as feedstock may only be used for that purpose. As of 1 July 2010, containers of such substances shall be labelled with a clear indication that the substance may only be used as feedstock. Where such substances are required to be labelled in accordance with Directive 67/548/EEC, Directive 1999/45/EC or Regulation (EC) No 1272/2008, such indication shall be included in the label referred to in those Directives or in the supplemental information part of the label as referred to in Article 25(3) of that Regulation.

The Commission may determine the form and content of the label to be used. Those measures, designed to amend non-essential elements of this Regulation, inter alia, by supplementing it, shall be adopted in accordance with the regulatory procedure with scrutiny referred to in Article 25(3).

Article 8

Production, placing on the market and use of controlled substances as process agents

1. By way of derogation from Articles 4 and 5, controlled substances may be produced, placed on the market and used as process agents.

2. Controlled substances may only be used as process agents in installations existing on 1 September 1997, and where emissions are insignificant.

3. Controlled substances produced or placed on the market as process agents may only be used for that purpose. As of 1 July 2010, containers of such substances shall be labelled with a clear indication that those substances may only be used as process agents. Where such substances are required to be labelled in accordance with Directive 67/548/EEC, Directive 1999/45/EC or Regulation (EC) No 1272/2008, such indication shall be included in the label referred to in those Directives or in the supplemental information part of the label as referred to in Article 25(3) of that Regulation.

The Commission may determine the form and content of the label to be used. Those measures, designed to amend non-essential elements of this Regulation, inter alia, by supplementing it, shall be adopted in accordance with the regulatory procedure with scrutiny referred to in Article 25(3).

4. The Commission shall, if appropriate, in accordance with the management procedure referred to in Article 25(2), establish a list of undertakings in which the use of controlled substances as process agents shall be permitted, laying down maximum quantities that may be used for make-up or for consumption as process agents and emission levels for each of the undertakings concerned.

The maximum amount of controlled substances that may be used as process agents within the Community shall not exceed 1083 metric tonnes per year.

The maximum amount of controlled substances that may be emitted from process agent uses within the Community shall not exceed 17 metric tonnes per year.

5. In the light of new information or technical developments or decisions taken by the Parties, the Commission shall, if appropriate:

(a) amend Annex III;

(b) amend the maximum amount of controlled substances that may be used as process agents or emitted from process agent uses as referred to in the second and third subparagraphs of paragraph 4.

Those measures, designed to amend non-essential elements of this Regulation, shall be adopted in accordance with the regulatory procedure with scrutiny referred to in Article 25(3).

Article 9

Placing on the market of controlled substances for destruction or reclamation and of products and equipment containing or relying on controlled substances for destruction

By way of derogation from Articles 5 and 6, controlled substances and products and equipment containing or relying on controlled substances may be placed on the market for destruction within the Community in accordance with the requirements for destruction referred to in Article 22(1). Controlled substances may also be placed on the market for reclamation within the Community.

Article 10

Essential laboratory and analytical uses of controlled substances other than hydrochlorofluorocarbons

1. By way of derogation from Articles 4 and 5, controlled substances other than hydrochlorofluorocarbons may be produced, placed on the market and used for essential laboratory and analytical uses, subject to registration and licensing in accordance with this Article.

2. The Commission shall, if appropriate, in accordance with the management procedure referred to in Article 25(2), determine any essential laboratory and analytical uses for which the production and import of controlled substances other than hydrochlorofluorocarbons may be permitted in the Community, the respective quantities, the period for which the exemption shall be valid and those users which may take advantage of those essential laboratory and analytical uses.

3. Controlled substances produced or placed on the market for essential laboratory and analytical uses may only be used for that purpose. As of 1 July 2010, containers containing such substances shall be labelled with a clear indication that the substance may only be used for laboratory and analytical uses. Where such substances are required to be labelled in accordance with Directive 67/548/EEC, Directive 1999/45/EC or Regulation (EC) No 1272/2008, such indication shall be included in the label referred to in those Directives or in the supplemental information part of the label as referred to in Article 25(3) of that Regulation.

The Commission may determine the form and content of the label to be used. Those measures, designed to amend non-essential elements of this Regulation, shall be adopted in accordance with the regulatory procedure with scrutiny referred to in Article 25(3).

Controlled substances referred to in the first subparagraph shall only be placed on the market and further distributed under the conditions set out in Annex V. The Commission may amend that Annex. Those measures, designed to amend non-essential elements of this Regulation, shall be adopted in accordance with the regulatory procedure with scrutiny referred to in Article 25(3).

4. Any undertaking using controlled substances other than hydrochlorofluorocarbons for essential laboratory and analytical uses shall register with the Commission, indicating the substances being used, the purpose, the estimated annual consumption and the suppliers of those substances, and shall update that information when changes occur.

5. By the date specified in a notice issued by the Commission, producers and importers supplying the undertaking referred to in paragraph 4 or using controlled substances for their own account shall declare to the Commission the foreseen demand for the period specified in the notice, specifying the nature and quantities of controlled substances needed.

6. The Commission shall issue licences to producers and importers of controlled substances, other than hydrochlorofluorocarbons, produced or imported for essential laboratory and analytical uses and shall notify them of the use for which they have authorisation and the substances and quantities thereof that they are authorised to place on the market or to use for

their own account. The quantity annually authorised under licences for individual producers and importers shall not exceed 130 % of the annual average of the calculated level of controlled substances licensed for the producer or importer for essential laboratory and analytical uses in the years 2007 to 2009.

The total quantity annually authorised under licences, including licences for hydrochlorofluorocarbons under Article 11(2), shall not exceed 110 ODP tonnes. Remaining quantities may be allocated to producers and importers which did not place on the market or use controlled substances, for their own account for essential laboratory and analytical uses in the years 2007 to 2009.

The Commission shall determine a mechanism for the allocation of quotas to producers and importers. Those measures, designed to amend non-essential elements of this Regulation, inter alia, by supplementing it, shall be adopted in accordance with the regulatory procedure with scrutiny referred to in Article 25(3).

7. A producer may be authorised by the competent authority of the Member State in which that producer's relevant production is situated to produce the controlled substances referred to in paragraph 1 for the purpose of meeting the requests licensed in accordance with paragraph 6.

The competent authority of the Member State concerned shall notify the Commission in advance of its intention to issue any such authorisation.

8. To the extent permitted by the Protocol, the competent authority of the Member State in which a producer's relevant production is situated may authorise that producer to produce or to exceed the calculated levels of production laid down in paragraph 6 in order to satisfy any essential laboratory and analytical uses of Parties at their request.

The competent authority of the Member State concerned shall notify the Commission in advance of its intention to issue any such authorisation.

Article 11

Production, placing on the market and use of hydrochlorofluorocarbons and placing on the market of products and equipment containing or relying on hydrochlorofluorocarbons

1. By way of derogation from Article 4, hydrochlorofluorocarbons may be produced provided that each producer ensures the following:

(a) the calculated level of its production of hydrochlorofluorocarbons in the period from 1 January 2010 to 31 December 2010 and in each 12-month period thereafter until 31 December 2013 does not exceed 35 % of the calculated level of its production of hydrochlorofluorocarbons in 1997;

(b) the calculated level of its production of hydrochlorofluorocarbons in the period from 1 January 2014 to 31 December 2014 and in each 12-month period thereafter until 31 December 2016 does not exceed 14 % of the calculated level of its production of hydrochlorofluorocarbons in 1997;

(c) the calculated level of its production of hydrochlorofluorocarbons in the period from 1 January 2017 to 31 December 2017 and in each 12-month period thereafter until 31 December 2019 does not exceed 7 % of the calculated level of its production of hydrochlorofluorocarbons in 1997;

(d) it produces no hydrochlorofluorocarbons after 31 December 2019.

2. By way of derogation from Article 4 and Article 5(1), hydrochlorofluorocarbons may be produced, placed on the market and used for laboratory and analytical uses.

Article 10(3) to (7) shall apply mutatis mutandis.

3. By way of derogation from Article 5, until 31 December 2014, reclaimed hydrochlorofluorocarbons may be placed on the market and used for the maintenance or servicing of existing refrigeration, air-conditioning and heat pump equipment, provided that the container is labelled with an indication that the substance has been reclaimed and with information on the batch number and name and address of the reclamation facility.

4. Until 31 December 2014, recycled hydrochlorofluorocarbons may be used for the maintenance or servicing of existing refrigeration, air-conditioning and heat pump equipment provided that they have been recovered from such equipment and may only be used by the undertaking which carried out the recovery as part of maintenance or servicing or for which the recovery as part of maintenance or servicing was carried out.

5. By way of derogation from Article 5, until 31 December 2019, hydrochlorofluorocarbons may be placed on the market for repackaging and subsequent export. Any undertaking carrying out the repackaging and subsequent export of hydrochlorofluorocarbons shall register with the Commission, indicating the controlled substances concerned, their estimated annual demand and the suppliers of those substances, and shall update this information when changes occur.

6. When reclaimed or recycled hydrochlorofluorocarbons are used for maintenance or servicing, the refrigeration, air-conditioning and heat pump equipment concerned shall be labelled with an indication of the type of substance, its quantity contained in the equipment and the label elements set out in Annex I to Regulation (EC) No 1272/2008 for substances or mixtures classified as Hazardous to the Ozone Layer.

7. Undertakings operating the equipment referred to in paragraph 4 containing a fluid charge of 3 kg or more shall keep a record of the quantity and type of substance recovered and added, and of the company or technician which performed the maintenance or servicing.

Undertakings using reclaimed or recycled hydrochlorofluorocarbons for maintenance or servicing shall keep a record of the undertakings that have supplied reclaimed hydrochlorofluorocarbons and of the source of recycled hydrochlorofluorocarbons.

8. By way of derogation from Articles 5 and 6, the Commission may, following a request by a competent authority of a Member State and in accordance with the management procedure referred to in Article 25(2), authorise a time-limited exemption to allow the use and placing on the market of hydrochlorofluorocarbons and of products and equipment containing or relying on hydrochlorofluorocarbons where it is demonstrated that, for a particular use, technically and economically feasible alternative substances or technologies are not available or cannot be used.

This exemption may not be authorised for a period which extends beyond 31 December 2019.

Article 12

Quarantine and pre-shipment applications and emergency uses of methyl bromide

1. By way of derogation from Article 5(1), until 18 March 2010, methyl bromide may be placed on the market and used for quarantine and for pre-shipment applications for treatment of goods for export provided that the placing on the market and use of methyl bromide are allowed respectively under national legislation in accordance with Directive 91/414/EEC and Directive 98/8/EC.

Methyl bromide may only be used on sites approved by the competent authorities of the Member State concerned and, if economically and technically feasible, subject to the condition that at least 80 % of methyl bromide released from the consignment is recovered.

2. The calculated level of methyl bromide which undertakings place on the market or use for their own account in the period from 1 January 2010 to 18 March 2010 shall not exceed 45 ODP tonnes.

Each undertaking shall ensure that the calculated level of methyl bromide which it places on the market or uses for its own account for quarantine and pre-shipment applications shall not exceed 21 % of the average of the calculated level of methyl bromide which it placed on the market or used for its own account for quarantine and pre-shipment in the years 2005 to 2008.

3. In an emergency, where unexpected outbreaks of particular pests or diseases so require, the Commission may, at the request of the competent authority of a Member State, authorise the temporary production, placing on the market and use of methyl bromide, provided that the placing on the market and use of methyl bromide are allowed respectively under Directive 91/414/EEC and Directive 98/8/EC.

Such authorisation shall apply for a period not exceeding 120 days and to a quantity not exceeding 20 metric tonnes and shall specify measures to be taken to reduce emissions during use.

Article 13

Critical uses of halons and decommissioning of equipment containing halons

1. By way of derogation from Article 5(1), halons may be placed on the market and used for critical uses set out in Annex VI. Halons may only be placed on the market by undertakings authorised by the competent authority of the Member State concerned to store halons for critical uses.

2. The Commission shall review Annex VI and, if appropriate, adopt modifications and time-frames for the phasing out of the critical uses by defining cut-off dates for new applications and end dates for existing applications, taking into account the availability of technically and economically feasible alternatives or technologies that are acceptable from the standpoint of environment and health.

Those measures, designed to amend non-essential elements of this Regulation, inter alia, by supplementing it, shall be adopted in accordance with the regulatory procedure with scrutiny referred to in Article 25(3).

3. Fire protection systems and fire extinguishers containing halons applied in uses referred to in paragraph 1 shall be decommissioned by the end dates to be specified in Annex VI.

4. The Commission may, at the request of the competent authority of a Member State and in accordance with the management procedure referred to in Article 25(2), grant derogations from end dates for existing applications or cut-off dates for new applications, provided those dates have been specified in Annex VI in accordance with paragraph 2, for specific cases where it is demonstrated that no technically and economically feasible alternative is available.

Article 14

Transfer of rights and industrial rationalisation

1. Any producer or importer entitled to place controlled substances on the market or use them for its own account may transfer that right in respect of all or any quantities of the respective group of substances fixed in accordance with this Article to any other producer or importer of that group of substances within the Community. Any such transfer shall be notified in advance to the Commission. The transfer of the right to place on the market or use shall not imply the further right to produce or to import.

2. To the extent permitted by the Protocol, the competent authority of the Member State in which a producer's relevant production is situated may authorise that producer to exceed the calculated levels of production laid down in Article 10 and Article 11(2) for the purpose of industrial rationalisation within the Member State concerned, provided that the calculated levels of production of that Member State do not exceed the sum of the calculated levels of production of its domestic producers as laid down in Article 10 and Article 11(2) for the

periods in question. The competent authority of the Member State concerned shall notify the Commission in advance of its intention to issue any such authorisation.

3. To the extent permitted by the Protocol, the Commission may, in agreement with the competent authority of the Member State in which a producer's relevant production is situated, authorise that producer to exceed the calculated levels of production laid down in Article 10 and Article 11(2) for the purpose of industrial rationalisation between Member States, provided that the combined calculated levels of production of the Member States concerned do not exceed the sum of the calculated levels of production of their domestic producers as laid down in Article 10 and Article 11(2) for the periods in question. The agreement of the competent authority of the Member State in which it is intended to reduce production shall also be required.

4. To the extent permitted by the Protocol, the Commission may, in agreement with both the competent authority of the Member State in which a producer's relevant production is situated and the government of the third country Party concerned, authorise a producer to combine the calculated levels of production laid down in Article 10 and Article 11(2) with the calculated levels of production allowed to a producer in a third country Party under the Protocol and that producer's national legislation for the purpose of industrial rationalisation with a third country Party, provided that the combined calculated levels of production by the two producers do not exceed the sum of the calculated levels of production allowed to the Community producer under Article 10 and Article 11(2) and the calculated levels of production allowed to the third country Party producer under the Protocol and any relevant national legislation.

CHAPTER IV
TRADES

Article 15

Imports of controlled substances or of products and equipment containing or relying on controlled substances

1. Imports of controlled substances or of products and equipment other than personal effects containing or relying on those substances, shall be prohibited.

2. The prohibition set out in paragraph 1 shall not apply to imports of:

(a) controlled substances to be used for laboratory and analytical uses referred to in Article 10 and Article 11(2);

(b) controlled substances to be used as feedstock;

(c) controlled substances to be used as process agents;

(d) controlled substances for destruction by technologies referred to in Article 22(2);

(e) until 31 December 2019, hydrochlorofluorocarbons to be repackaged and subsequently re-exported no later than 31 December of the following calendar year to a Party where the consumption or import of that hydrochlorofluorocarbon is not prohibited;

(f) methyl bromide for emergency uses referred to in Article 12(3) or, until 31 December 2014, for repackaging and subsequent re-export for quarantine and pre-shipment applications provided that the re-export takes place during the year of import;

(g) recovered, recycled or reclaimed halons, under the condition that they are only imported for critical uses referred to in Article 13(1), by undertakings authorised by the competent authority of the Member State concerned to store halons for critical uses;

(h) products and equipment containing or relying on controlled substances for destruction, where applicable by technologies referred to in Article 22(2);

(i) products and equipment containing or relying on controlled substances to satisfy laboratory and analytical uses referred to in Article 10 and Article 11(2);

(j) products and equipment containing or relying on halon to satisfy critical uses referred to in Article 13(1);

(k) products and equipment containing hydrochlorofluorocarbons for which the placing on the market has been authorised in accordance with Article 11(5).

3. Imports referred to in paragraph 2, with the exception of imports for transit through the customs territory of the Community or imports under the temporary storage, customs warehousing or free zone procedure as referred to in Regulation (EC) No 450/2008, provided that they remain in the customs territory of the Community no longer than 45 days and that they are not subsequently presented for release for free circulation in the Community, destroyed or processed, shall be subject to the presentation of an import licence. Those licences shall be issued by the Commission after verification of compliance with Articles 16 and 20.

Article 16

Release for free circulation in the Community of imported controlled substances

1. The release for free circulation in the Community of imported controlled substances shall be subject to quantitative limits. The Commission shall determine those limits and allocate quotas to undertakings for the period from 1 January to 31 December 2010 and for each 12-month period thereafter in accordance with the management procedure referred to in Article 25(2).

The quotas referred to in the first subparagraph shall be allocated only for the following substances:

(a) controlled substances if they are used for laboratory and analytical, or critical uses, referred to in Article 10, Article 11(2) and Article 13;
(b) controlled substances if they are used as feedstock;
(c) controlled substances if they are used as process agents.

2. By the date specified in a notice issued by the Commission, importers of substances referred to in points (a), (b) and (c) of paragraph 1 shall declare to the Commission the anticipated demand, specifying the nature and quantities of controlled substances needed. On the basis of those declarations the Commission shall establish quantitative limits to the imports of substances referred to in points (a), (b) and (c) of paragraph 1.

Article 17

Export of controlled substances or of products and equipment containing or relying on controlled substances

1. Exports of controlled substances or of products and equipment other than personal effects containing or relying on those substances, shall be prohibited.

2. The prohibition set out in paragraph 1 shall not apply to exports of:

(a) controlled substances to be used for essential laboratory and analytical uses referred to in Article 10;
(b) controlled substances to be used as feedstock;
(c) controlled substances to be used as process agents;
(d) products and equipment containing or relying on controlled substances produced in accordance with Article 10(7) or imported under point (h) or (i) of Article 15(2);
(e) recovered, recycled or reclaimed halons stored for critical uses referred to in Article 13(1) by undertakings authorised by the competent authority of a Member State and products and equipment containing or relying on halon to satisfy critical uses;
(f) virgin or reclaimed hydrochlorofluorocarbons for uses other than destruction;
(g) until 31 December 2014, methyl bromide re-exported for quarantine and pre-shipment applications;
(h) metered dose inhalers manufactured with chlorofluorocarbon the use of which has been authorised on the basis of Article 3(1) of Regulation (EC) No 2037/2000.

3. By way of derogation from paragraph 1, the Commission may, following a request by a competent authority of a Member State and in accordance with the management procedure referred to in Article 25(2), authorise the export of products and equipment containing hydrochlorofluorocarbons where it is demonstrated that in view of the economic value

and the expected remaining lifetime of the specific good, the prohibition of export would impose a disproportionate burden on the exporter. Such export requires prior notification by Commission to the importing country.

4. Exports referred to in paragraphs 2 and 3 shall be subject to licensing, with the exception of re-exports subsequent to transit through the customs territory of the Community, temporary storage, customs-warehousing or free zone procedure, as referred to in Regulation (EC) No 450/2008, provided that the re-export takes place not later than 45 days after the import. That export licence shall be issued by the Commission to undertakings after verification of compliance with Article 20.

Article 18

Licensing of imports and exports

1. The Commission shall set up and operate an electronic licensing system and shall decide on applications for licences within 30 days of receipt.

2. Applications for licences referred to in Articles 15 and 17 shall be submitted using the system referred to in paragraph 1. Before submitting an application for a licence undertakings shall register in that system.

3. An application for a licence shall state the following:
(a) the names and the addresses of the importer and the exporter;
(b) the country of import and export;
(c) in the case of imports or exports of controlled substances, a description of each controlled substance, including:
  (i) the commercial description;
  (ii) the description and the Combined Nomenclature code as laid down in Annex IV;
  (iii) whether the substance is virgin, recovered, recycled or reclaimed;
  (iv) the quantity of the substance in metric kilograms;
  (v) in the case of halons, a declaration that they are to be imported or exported to satisfy a critical use referred to in Article 13(1), specifying which use;
(d) in the case of imports or exports of products and equipment containing or relying on controlled substances:
  (i) the type and nature of the products and equipment;
  (ii) for countable items the number of units, the description and the quantity per unit in metric kilograms of each controlled substance;
  (iii) for uncountable items the total quantity of the product, the description and the total net quantity, in metric kilograms, of each controlled substance;
  (iv) the country/countries of final destination of the products and equipment;
  (v) whether the controlled substance contained is virgin, recycled, recovered or reclaimed;
  (vi) in the case of imports or exports of products and equipment containing or relying on halon, a declaration that they are to be imported or exported to satisfy a critical use referred to in Article 13(1), specifying which use;
  (vii) in the case of products and equipment containing or relying on hydrochlorofluorocarbons, the reference to the Commission authorisation referred to in Article 17(3);
  (viii) the Combined Nomenclature code of the product or equipment to be imported or exported;
(e) the purpose of the proposed import, including the intended customs treatment and use, specifying where relevant the intended customs procedure;
(f) the place and expected date of the proposed import or export;
(g) the customs office where the goods will be declared;
(h) in the case of imports of controlled substances or products and equipment for destruction, the name and address of the facility where they will be destroyed;

(i) any further information deemed necessary by the competent authority of a Member State.

4. Each importer or exporter shall notify the Commission of any changes which might occur during the period of validity of the licence in relation to the data notified under paragraph 3.

5. The Commission may require a certificate attesting the nature or composition of substances to be imported or exported and may request a copy of the licence issued by the country from which the import or to which the export takes place.

6. The Commission may share the submitted data so far as necessary in specific cases with competent authorities of the Parties concerned and may reject the licence application if any relevant obligations set out in this Regulation are not complied with, or on the following grounds:

(a) in the case of an import licence, where it is established based on information from the competent authorities of the country concerned that the exporter is not an undertaking authorised to trade in the respective substance in that country;

(b) in the case of an export licence, where the competent authorities of the importing country have informed the Commission that the import of the controlled substance would constitute a case of illegal trade, or would adversely impact on the implementation of control measures of the importing country in place to comply with its obligations under the Protocol or would lead to an excess of the quantitative limits under the Protocol for that country.

7. The Commission shall make available a copy of each licence to the competent authority of the Member State concerned.

8. The Commission shall, as soon as possible, inform the applicant and the Member State concerned of any licence application rejected pursuant to paragraph 6, specifying the reason for the rejection.

9. The Commission may amend the list of items mentioned in paragraph 3 and Annex IV. Those measures, designed to amend non-essential elements of this Regulation, shall be adopted in accordance with the regulatory procedure with scrutiny referred to in Article 25(3).

Article 19

Measures for monitoring of illegal trade

The Commission may adopt additional measures for the monitoring of controlled substances or new substances and of products and equipment containing or relying on controlled substances placed under temporary storage, customs warehousing or free zone procedure or in transit through the customs territory of the Community and subsequently re-exported, on the basis of an evaluation of the potential risks of illegal trade linked to such movements, taking into account the environmental benefits and socioeconomic impacts of such measures.

Those measures, designed to amend non-essential elements of this Regulation, inter alia, by supplementing it, shall be adopted in accordance with the regulatory procedure with scrutiny referred to in Article 25(3).

Article 20

Trade with a State not party to the Protocol and a territory not covered by the Protocol

1. Import and export of controlled substances and of products and equipment containing or relying on controlled substances from and to any State not party to the Protocol shall be prohibited.

2. The Commission may adopt rules applicable to the release for free circulation in the Community of products and equipment imported from any State not party to the Protocol

which were produced using controlled substances but do not contain substances which can be positively identified as controlled substances. The identification of such products and equipment shall comply with periodical technical advice given to the Parties. Those measures, designed to amend non-essential elements of this Regulation, inter alia, by supplementing it, shall be adopted in accordance with the regulatory procedure with scrutiny referred to in Article 25(3).

3. By way of derogation from paragraph 1, trade with any State not party to the Protocol in controlled substances and products and equipment containing or relying on such substances or which are produced by means of one or more such substances may be authorised by the Commission, to the extent that the State not party to the Protocol is determined by a meeting of the Parties pursuant to Article 4(8) of the Protocol to be in full compliance with the Protocol and has submitted data to that effect as specified in Article 7 of the Protocol. The Commission shall act in accordance with the management procedure referred to in Article 25(2) of this Regulation.

4. Subject to any decision taken under the second subparagraph, paragraph 1 shall apply to any territory not covered by the Protocol as they apply to any State not party to the Protocol.

Where the authorities of a territory not covered by the Protocol are in full compliance with the Protocol and have submitted data to that effect as specified in Article 7 of the Protocol, the Commission may decide that some or all of the provisions of paragraph 1 of this Article shall not apply in respect of that territory.

The Commission shall act in accordance with the management procedure referred to in Article 25(2).

Article 21

List of products and equipment containing or relying on controlled substances

No later than 1 January 2010, the Commission shall make available a list of products and equipment which might contain or rely on controlled substances and of Combined Nomenclature codes for guidance of the Member States' customs authorities.

CHAPTER V
EMISSION CONTROL

Article 22

Recovery and destruction of used controlled substances

1. Controlled substances contained in refrigeration, air-conditioning and heat pump equipment, equipment containing solvents or fire protection systems and fire extinguishers shall, during the maintenance or servicing of equipment or before the dismantling or disposal of equipment, be recovered for destruction, recycling or reclamation.

2. Controlled substances and products containing such substances shall only be destroyed by approved technologies listed in Annex VII or, in the case of controlled substances not referred to in that Annex, by the most environmentally acceptable destruction technology not entailing excessive costs, provided that the use of those technologies complies with Community and national legislation on waste and that additional requirements under such legislation are met.

3. The Commission may amend Annex VII in order to take new technological developments into account.

Those measures, designed to amend non-essential elements of this Regulation, shall be adopted in accordance with the regulatory procedure with scrutiny referred to in Article 25(3).

4. Controlled substances contained in products and equipment other than those mentioned in paragraph 1 shall, if technically and economically feasible, be recovered for destruction, recycling or reclamation, or shall be destroyed without prior recovery, applying the technologies referred to in paragraph 2.

The Commission shall establish an Annex to this Regulation with a list of products and equipment for which the recovery of controlled substances or destruction of products and equipment without prior recovery of controlled substances shall be considered technically and economically feasible, specifying, if appropriate, the technologies to be applied. Any draft measure to establish such an Annex shall be accompanied and supported by a full economic assessment of costs and benefits, taking into account the individual circumstances of Member States.

Those measures, designed to amend non-essential elements of this Regulation, inter alia, by supplementing it, shall be adopted in accordance with the regulatory procedure with scrutiny referred to in Article 25(3).

5. Member States shall take steps to promote the recovery, recycling, reclamation and destruction of controlled substances and shall define the minimum qualification requirements for the personnel involved.

The Commission shall evaluate the measures taken by the Member States and may in the light of this evaluation and of technical and other relevant information, as appropriate, adopt measures regarding those minimum qualification requirements.

Those measures, designed to amend non-essential elements of this Regulation, inter alia, by supplementing it, shall be adopted in accordance with the regulatory procedure with scrutiny referred to in Article 25(3).

Article 23

Leakages and emissions of controlled substances

1. Undertakings shall take all precautionary measures practicable to prevent and minimise any leakages and emissions of controlled substances.

2. Undertakings operating refrigeration, air conditioning or heat pump equipment, or fire protection systems, including their circuits, which contain controlled substances shall ensure that the stationary equipment or systems:

(a) with a fluid charge of 3 kg or more of controlled substances are checked for leakage at least once every 12 months; this shall not apply to equipment with hermetically sealed systems, which are labelled as such and contain less than 6 kg of controlled substances;

(b) with a fluid charge of 30 kg or more of controlled substances are checked for leakage at least once every 6 months;

(c) with a fluid charge of 300 kg or more of controlled substances are checked for leakage at least once every 3 months;

and that any detected leakage is repaired as soon as possible and in any event within 14 days.

The equipment or system shall be checked for leakage within 1 month after a leak has been repaired to ensure that the repair has been effective.

3. Undertakings referred to in paragraph 2 shall maintain records on the quantity and type of controlled substances added and the quantity recovered during maintenance, servicing and final disposal of the equipment or system referred to in that paragraph. They shall also maintain records of other relevant information including the identification of the company or technician which performed the maintenance or servicing, as well as the dates and results of the leakage checks carried out. These records shall be made available on request to the competent authority of a Member State and to the Commission.

4. Member States shall define the minimum qualification requirements for the personnel carrying out activities referred to in paragraph 2. In the light of an evaluation of these measures taken by the Member States and of technical and other relevant information, the Commission may adopt measures regarding the harmonisation of those minimum qualification requirements.

Those measures, designed to amend non-essential elements of this Regulation, inter alia, by supplementing it, shall be adopted in accordance with the regulatory procedure with scrutiny referred to in Article 25(3).

5. Undertakings shall take all precautionary measures practicable to prevent and minimise any leakages and emissions of controlled substances used as feedstock and as process agents.

6. Undertakings shall take all precautionary measures practicable to prevent and minimise any leakage and emissions of controlled substances inadvertently produced in the course of the manufacture of other chemicals.

7. The Commission may establish a list of technologies or practices to be used by undertakings to prevent and minimise any leakage and emissions of controlled substances.

Those measures, designed to amend non-essential elements of this Regulation, inter alia, by supplementing it, shall be adopted in accordance with the regulatory procedure with scrutiny referred to in Article 25(3).

CHAPTER VI
NEW SUBSTANCES

Article 24

New substances

1. The production, import, placing on the market, use and export of new substances in Part A of Annex II are prohibited. This prohibition does not apply to new substances if they are used as feedstock or for laboratory and analytical uses, to imports for transit through the customs territory of the Community or imports under the temporary storage, customs warehousing or free zone procedure as referred to in Regulation (EC) No 450/2008, unless such imports have been assigned another customs-approved treatment or use as referred to in that Regulation, or to exports subsequent to imports already exempted.

2. The Commission shall, if appropriate, include in Part A of Annex II substances that are included in Part B of that Annex that are found to be exported, imported, produced or put on the market in significant quantities and that are found by the Scientific Assessment Panel under the Protocol to have a significant ozone-depleting potential, and shall, if appropriate, determine possible exemptions from paragraph 1.

Those measures, designed to amend non-essential elements of this Regulation, shall be adopted in accordance with the regulatory procedure with scrutiny referred to in Article 25(3).

3. In the light of relevant scientific information, the Commission shall, if appropriate, include in Part B of Annex II any substances that are not controlled substances but that are found by the Scientific Assessment Panel under the Protocol or another recognised authority of equivalent stature to have a significant ozone-depleting potential. Those measures, designed to amend non-essential elements of this Regulation, shall be adopted in accordance with the regulatory procedure with scrutiny referred to in Article 25(3).

CHAPTER VII
COMMITTEE, REPORTING, INSPECTION AND PENALTIES

Article 25

Committee

1. The Commission shall be assisted by a Committee.

2. Where reference is made to this paragraph, Articles 4 and 7 of Decision 1999/468/EC shall apply, having regard to the provisions of Article 8 thereof.

The period laid down in Article 4(3) of Decision 1999/468/EC shall be set at 1 month.

3. Where reference is made to this paragraph, Article 5a(1) to (4) and Article 7 of Decision 1999/468/EC shall apply, having regard to the provisions of Article 8 thereof.

Article 26

Reporting by the Member States

1. Each year by 30 June Member States shall report the following information in an electronic format to the Commission, for the previous calendar year:
(a) the quantities of methyl bromide authorised, pursuant to Article 12(2) and (3), for different treatments for quarantine and pre-shipment purposes used in their territory, specifying the purposes for which methyl bromide was used, and the progress in evaluating and using alternatives;
(b) the quantities of halons installed, used and stored for critical uses, pursuant to Article 13(1), the measures taken to reduce their emissions and an estimate of such emissions, and progress in evaluating and using adequate alternatives;
(c) cases of illegal trade, in particular those detected during the inspections carried out pursuant to Article 28.

2. The Commission shall, in accordance with the management procedure referred to in Article 25(2), determine the format for the submission of the information referred to in paragraph 1.

3. The Commission may amend paragraph 1.

Those measures, designed to amend non-essential elements of this Regulation, shall be adopted in accordance with the regulatory procedure with scrutiny referred to in Article 25(3).

Article 27

Reporting by undertakings

1. Each year by 31 March, each undertaking shall communicate to the Commission, sending a copy to the competent authority of the Member State concerned, the data listed in paragraphs 2 to 6 for each controlled substance and each new substance listed in Annex II for the previous calendar year.

2. Each producer shall communicate the following data:
(a) its total production of each substance referred to in paragraph 1;
(b) any production placed on the market or used for the producer's own account within the Community, separately identifying production for feedstock, process agent and other uses;
(c) any production to meet the essential laboratory and analytical uses in the Community, licensed in accordance with Article 10(6);
(d) any production authorised under Article 10(8) to satisfy essential laboratory and analytical uses of Parties;
(e) any increase in production authorised under Article 14(2), (3) and (4) in connection with industrial rationalisation;
(f) any quantity recycled, reclaimed or destroyed and the technology used for the destruction, including amounts produced and destroyed as by-product as referred to in Article 3(14);
(g) any stocks;
(h) any purchases from and sales to other producers in the Community.

3. Each importer shall communicate for each substance referred to in paragraph 1 the following data:

(a) any quantities released for free circulation in the Community, separately identifying imports for feedstock and process agent uses, for essential laboratory and analytical uses licensed in accordance with Article 10(6), for use in quarantine and pre-shipment applications and for destruction. Importers which imported controlled substances for destruction shall also communicate the actual final destination or destinations of each of the substances, providing separately for each destination the quantity of each of the substances and the name and address of destruction facility where the substance was delivered;
(b) any quantities imported under other customs procedures, separately identifying the customs procedure and the designated uses;
(c) any quantities of used substances referred to in paragraph 1 imported for recycling or reclamation;
(d) any stocks;
(e) any purchases from and sales to other undertakings in the Community;
(f) the exporting country.

4. Each exporter shall communicate for each substances referred to in paragraph 1 the following data:
(a) any quantities of such substances exported, separately identifying quantities exported to each country of destination and quantities exported for feedstock and process agent uses, essential laboratory and analytical uses, critical uses and for quarantine and pre-shipment applications;
(b) any stocks;
(c) any purchases from and sales to other undertakings in the Community;
(d) the country of destination.

5. Each undertaking destroying controlled substances referred to in paragraph 1 and not covered by paragraph 2 shall communicate the following data:
(a) any quantities of such substances destroyed, including quantities contained in products or equipment;
(b) any stocks of such substances waiting to be destroyed, including quantities contained in products or equipment;
(c) technology used for the destruction.

6. Each undertaking using controlled substances as feedstock or process agents shall communicate the following data:
(a) any quantities of such substances used as feedstock or process agents;
(b) any stocks of such substances;
(c) the processes and emissions involved.

7. Each year before 31 March, each producer or importer which holds a licence under Article 10(6) shall, for each substance for which an authorisation has been received, report to the Commission, sending a copy to the competent authority of the Member State concerned, the nature of the use, the quantities used during the previous year, the quantities held in stock, any quantities recycled, reclaimed or destroyed, and the quantity of products and equipment containing or relying on those substances placed on the Community market and/or exported.

8. The Commission shall take appropriate steps to protect the confidentiality of the information submitted to it.

9. The format of the reports referred to in paragraphs 1 to 7 shall be established in accordance with the management procedure referred to in Article 25(2).

10. The Commission may amend the reporting requirements laid down in paragraphs 1 to 7.

Those measures, designed to amend non-essential elements of this Regulation, shall be adopted in accordance with the regulatory procedure with scrutiny referred to in Article 25(3).

Article 28

Inspection

1. Member States shall conduct inspections on the compliance of undertakings with this Regulation, following a risk-based approach, including inspections on imports and exports of controlled substances as well as of products and equipment containing or relying on those substances. The competent authorities of the Member States shall carry out the investigations which the Commission considers necessary under this Regulation.

2. Subject to the agreement of the Commission and of the competent authority of the Member State within the territory of which the investigations are to be made, the officials of the Commission shall assist the officials of that authority in the performance of their duties.

3. In carrying out the tasks assigned to it by this Regulation, the Commission may obtain all necessary information from the governments and competent authorities of the Member States and from undertakings. When requesting information from an undertaking the Commission shall at the same time forward a copy of the request to the competent authority of the Member State within the territory of which the undertaking's seat is situated.

4. The Commission shall take appropriate action to promote an adequate exchange of information and cooperation between national authorities and between national authorities and the Commission.

The Commission shall take appropriate steps to protect the confidentiality of information obtained under this Article.

5. At the request of another Member State, a Member State may conduct inspections of undertakings or investigations of undertakings suspected of being engaged in the illegal movement of controlled substances and which are operating on the territory of that Member State.

Article 29

Penalties

Member States shall lay down the rules on penalties applicable to infringements of the provisions of this Regulation and shall take all measures necessary to ensure that they are implemented. The penalties provided for must be effective, proportionate and dissuasive. Member States shall notify those provisions to the Commission by 30 June 2011 at the latest and shall also notify it without delay of any subsequent amendment affecting them.

CHAPTER VIII
FINAL PROVISIONS

[*Article 30 is not reproduced.*]

Article 31

Entry into force

This Regulation shall enter into force on the 20th day following its publication in the Official Journal of the European Union.

It shall apply from 1 January 2010.

This Regulation shall be binding in its entirety and directly applicable in all Member States.

ANNEX I
CONTROLLED SUBSTANCES

Group	*Substance*			*Ozone depleting potential*[(1)]
Group I	$CFCl_3$	CFC-11	Trichlorofluoromethane	1,0
	CF_2Cl_2	CFC-12	Dichlorodifluoromethane	1,0
	$C_2F_3Cl_3$	CFC-113	Trichlorotrifluoroethane	0,8
	$C_2F_4Cl_2$	CFC-114	Dichlorotetrafluoroethane	1,0
	C_2F_5Cl	CFC-115	Chloropentafluoroethane	0,6
Group II	CF_3Cl	CFC-13	Chlorotrifluoromethane	1,0
	C_2FCl_5	CFC-111	Pentachlorofluoroethane	1,0
	$C_2F_2Cl_4$	CFC-112	Tetrachlorodifluoroethane	1,0
	C_3FCl_7	CFC-211	Heptachlorofluoropropane	1,0
	$C_3F_2Cl_6$	CFC-212	Hexachlorodifluoropropane	1,0
	$C_3F_3Cl_5$	CFC-213	Pentachlorotrifluoropropane	1,0
	$C_3F_4Cl_4$	CFC-214	Tetrachlorotetrafluoropropane	1,0
	$C_3F_5Cl_3$	CFC-215	Trichloropentafluoropropane	1,0
	$C_3F_6Cl_2$	CFC-216	Dichlorohexafluoropropane	1,0
	C_3F_7Cl	CFC-217	Chloroheptafluoropropane	1,0
Group III	CF_2BrCl	halon-1211	Bromochlorodifluoromethane	3,0
	CF_3Br	halon-1301	Bromotrifluoromethane	10,0
	C_2F4Br_2	halon-2402	Dibromotetrafluoroethane	6,0
Group IV	CCl_4	CTC	Tetrachloromethane (carbon tetrachloride)	1,1
Group V	$C_2H_3Cl_3$[(2)]	1,1,1-TCA	1,1,1-Trichloroethane (methylchloroform)	0,1
Group VI	CH_3Br	methyl bromide	Bromomethane	0,6
Group VII	$CHFBr_2$	HBFC-21 B2	Dibromofluoromethane	1,00
	CHF_2Br	HBFC-22 B1	Bromodifluoromethane	0,74
	CH_2FBr	HBFC-31 B1	Bromofluoromethane	0,73
	C_2HFBr_4	HBFC-121 B4	Tetrabromofluoroethane	0,8
	$C_2HF_2Br_3$	HBFC-122 B3	Tribromodifluoroethane	1,8
	$C_2HF_3Br_2$	HBFC-123 B2	Dibromotrifluoroethane	1,6
	C_2HF_4Br	HBFC-124 B1	Bromotetrafluoroethane	1,2
	$C_2H_2FBr_3$	HBFC-131 B3	Tribromofluoroethane	1,1
	$C_2H_2F_2Br_2$	HBFC-132 B2	Dibromodifluoroethane	1,5
	$C2H_2F_3Br$	HBFC-133 B1	Bromotrifluoroethane	1,6
	$C_2H_3FBr_2$	HBFC-141 B2	Dibromofluoroethane	1,7
	$C_2H_3F_2Br$	HBFC-142 B1	Bromodifluoroethane	1,1
	C_2H_4FBr	HBFC-151 B1	Bromofluoroethane	0,1
	C_3HFBr_6	HBFC-221 B6	Hexabromofluoropropane	1,5
	$C_3HF_2Br_5$	HBFC-222 B5	Pentabromodifluoropropane	1,9
	$C_3HF_3Br_4$	HBFC-223 B4	Tetrabromotrifluoropropane	1,8
	$C_3HF_4Br_3$	HBFC-224 B3	Tribromotetrafluoropropane	2,2
	$C_3HF_5Br_2$	HBFC-225 B2	Dibromopentafluoropropane	2,0
	C_3HF_6Br	HBFC-226 B1	Bromohexafluoropropane	3,3

Group	*Substance*			*Ozone depleting potential*[1]
Group VII *contd*	$C_3H_2FBr_5$	HBFC-231 B5	Pentabromofluoropropane	1,9
	$C_3H_2F_2Br_4$	HBFC-232 B4	Tetrabromodifluoropropane	2,1
	$C_3H_2F_3Br_3$	HBFC-233 B3	Tribromotrifluoropropane	5,6
	$C_3H_2F_4Br_2$	HBFC-234 B2	Dibromotetrafluoropropane	7,5
	$C_3H_2F_5Br$	HBFC-235 B1	Bromopentafluoropropane	1,4
	$C_3H_3FBr_4$	HBFC-241 B4	Tetrabromofluoropropane	1,9
	$C_3H_3F_2Br_3$	HBFC-242 B3	Tribromodifluoropropane	3,1
	$C_3H_3F_3Br_2$	HBFC-243 B2	Dibromotrifluoropropane	2,5
	$C_3H_3F_4Br$	HBFC-244 B1	Bromotetrafluoropropane	4,4
	$C_3H_4FBr_3$	HBFC-251 B1	Tribromofluoropropane	0,3
	$C_3H_4F_2Br_2$	HBFC-252 B2	Dibromodifluoropropane	1,0
	$C_3H_4F_3Br$	HBFC-253 B1	Bromotrifluoropropane	0,8
	$C_3H_5FBr_2$	HBFC-261 B2	Dibromofluoropropane	0,4
	$C_3H_5F_2Br$	HBFC-262 B1	Bromodifluoropropane	0,8
	C_3H_6FBr	HBFC-271 B1	Bromofluoropropane	0,7
Group VIII	$CHFCl_2$	HCFC-21[3]	Dichlorofluoromethane	0,040
	CHF_2Cl	HCFC-22[3]	Chlorodifluoromethane	0,055
	CH_2FCl	HCFC-31	Chlorofluoromethane	0,020
	C_2HFCl_4	HCFC-121	Tetrachlorofluoroethane	0,040
	$C_2HF_2Cl_3$	HCFC-122	Trichlorodifluoroethane	0,080
	$C_2HF_3Cl_2$	HCFC-123[3]	Dichlorotrifluoroethane	0,020
	C_2HF_4Cl	HCFC-124[3]	Chlorotetrafluoroethane	0,022
	$C_2H_2FCl_3$	HCFC-131	Trichlorofluoroethane	0,050
	$C_2H_2F_2Cl_2$	HCFC-132	Dichlorodifluoroethane	0,050
	$C_2H_2F_3Cl$	HCFC-133	Chlorotrifluoroethane	0,060
	$C_2H_3FCl_2$	HCFC-141	Dichlorofluoroethane	0,070
	CH_3CFCl_2	HCFC-141b[3]	1,1-Dichloro-1-fluoroethane	0,110
	$C_2H_3F_2Cl$	HCFC-142	Chlorodifluoroethane	0,070
	CH_3CF_2Cl	HCFC-142b[3]	1-Chloro-1,1-difluoroethane	0,065
	C_2H_4FCl	HCFC-151	Chlorofluoroethane	0,005
	C_3HFCl_6	HCFC-221	Hexachlorofluoropropane	0,070
	$C_3HF_2Cl_5$	HCFC-222	Pentachlorodifluoropropane	0,090
	$C_3HF_3Cl_4$	HCFC-223	Tetrachlorotrifluoropropane	0,080
	$C_3HF_4Cl_3$	HCFC-224	Trichlorotetrafluoropropane	0,090
	$C_3HF_5Cl_2$	HCFC-225	Dichloropentafluoropropane	0,070
	$CF_3CF_2CHCl_2$	HCFC-225ca[3]	3,3-Dichloro-1,1,1,2,2-pentafluoropropane	0,025
	CF_2ClCF_2CHClF	HCFC-225cb[3]	1,3-Dichloro-1,1,2,2,3-pentafluoropropane	0,033
	C_3HF_6Cl	HCFC-226	Chlorohexafluoropropane	0,100
	$C_3H_2FCl_5$	HCFC-231	Pentachlorofluoropropane	0,090
	$C_3H_2F_2Cl_4$	HCFC-232	Tetrachlorodifluoropropane	0,100
	$C_3H_2F_3Cl_3$	HCFC-233	Trichlorotrifluoropropane	0,230
	$C_3H_2F_4Cl_2$	HCFC-234	Dichlorotetrafluoropropane	0,280
	$C_3H_2F_5Cl$	HCFC-235	Chloropentafluoropropane	0,520

Group	*Substance*			*Ozone depleting potential*[(1)]
Group VIII *contd*	$C_3H_3FCl_4$	HCFC-241	Tetrachlorofluoropropane	0,090
	$C_3H_3F_2Cl_3$	HCFC-242	Trichlorodifluoropropane	0,130
	$C_3H_3F_3Cl_2$	HCFC-243	Dichlorotrifluoropropane	0,120
	$C_3H_3F_4Cl$	HCFC-244	Chlorotetrafluoropropane	0,140
	$C_3H_4FCl_3$	HCFC-251	Trichlorofluoropropane	0,010
	$C_3H_4F_2C12$	HCFC-252	Dichlorodifluoropropane	0,040
	$C_3H_4F_3Cl$	HCFC-253	Chlorotrifluoropropane	0,030
	$C_3H_5FCl_2$	HCFC-261	Dichlorofluoropropane	0,020
	$C_3H_5F_2Cl$	HCFC-262	Chlorodifluoropropane	0,020
	C_3H_6FCl	HCFC-271	Chlorofluoropropane	0,030
Group IX	CH_2BrCl	BCM	Bromochloromethane	0,12

(1) The figures relating to ozone-depleting potential are estimates based on existing knowledge and will be reviewed and revised periodically in the light of decisions taken by the Parties.
(2) This formula does not refer to 1,1,2-trichloroethane.
(3) Identifies the most commercially viable substance as prescribed in the Protocol.

ANNEX II
NEW SUBSTANCES

PART A: SUBSTANCES RESTRICTED UNDER ARTICLE 24(1)

Substance		*Ozone-depleting potential*
$CBr_2 F_2$	Dibromodifluoromethane (halon-1202)	1,25

PART B: SUBSTANCES TO BE REPORTED ON UNDER ARTICLE 27

Substance		*Ozone-depleting potential*[(1)]
C_3H_7Br	1-Bromopropane (n-propyl bromide)	0,02 — 0,10
C_2H_5Br	Bromoethane (ethyl bromide)	0,1 — 0,2
CF_3I	Trifluoroiodomethane (trifluoromethyl iodide)	0,01 — 0,02
CH_3Cl	Chloromethane (methyl chloride)	0,02

(1) The figures relating to ozone-depleting potential are estimates based on existing knowledge and will be reviewed and revised periodically in the light of decisions taken by the Parties.

ANNEX III

Processes in which controlled substances are used as process agents as referred to in Article 3(12):

(a) use of carbon tetrachloride for the elimination of nitrogen trichloride in the production of chlorine and caustic soda;

(b) use of carbon tetrachloride in the recovery of chlorine in tail gas from production of chlorine;

(c) use of carbon tetrachloride in the manufacture of chlorinated rubber;

(d) use of carbon tetrachloride in the manufacture of poly-phenylene-terephthalamide;
(e) use of CFC-12 in the photochemical synthesis of perfluoropolyetherpolyperoxide precursors of Z-perfluoropolyethers and difunctional derivatives;
(f) use of CFC-113 in the preparation of perfluoropolyether diols with high functionality;
(g) use of carbon tetrachloride in production of Cyclodime;
(h) use of hydrochlorofluorocarbons in the processes set out in points (a) to (g) when used to replace the chlorofluorocarbon or carbon tetrachloride.

ANNEX IV
GROUPS, COMBINED NOMENCLATURE CODES(1) AND DESCRIPTIONS FOR THE SUBSTANCES REFERRED TO IN ANNEX I

Group	*CN code*	*Description*
Group I	29034100	Trichlorofluoromethane
	29034200	Dichlorodifluoromethane
	29034300	Trichlorotrifluoroethanes
	29034410	Dichlorotetrafluoroethanes
	29034490	Chloropentafluoroethane
Group II	29034510	Chlorotrifluoromethane
	29034515	Pentachlorofluoroethane
	29034520	Tetrachlorodifluoroethanes
	29034525	Heptachlorofluoropropanes
	29034530	Hexachlorodifluoropropanes
	29034535	Pentachlorotrifluoropropanes
	29034540	Tetrachlorotetrafluoropropanes
	29034545	Trichloropentafluoropropanes
	29034550	Dichlorohexafluoropropanes
	29034555	Chloroheptafluoropropanes
Group III	29034610	Bromochlorodifluoromethane
	29034620	Bromotrifluoromethane
	29034690	Dibromotetrafluoroethanes
Group IV	29031400	Carbon tetrachloride
Group V	29031910	1,1,1-Trichloroethane (methyl chloroform)
Group VI	29033911	Bromomethane (methyl bromide)
Group VII	29034930	Hydrobromofluoromethanes, -ethanes or -propanes
Group VIII	29034911	Chlorodifluoromethane (HCFC-22)
	29034915	1,1-Dichloro-1-fluoroethane (HCFC-141b)
	29034919	Other Hydrochlorofluoromethanes, -ethanes or -propanes (HCFCs)
Group IX	ex 29034980	Bromochloromethane
Mixtures	38247100	Mixtures containing chlorofluorocarbons (CFCs), whether or not containing hydrochlorofluorocarbons (HCFCs), perfluorocarbons (PFCs) or hydrofluorocarbons (HFCs)
	38247200	Mixtures containing bromochlorodifluoromethane, bromotrifluoromethane or dibromotetrafluoroethanes
	38247300	Mixtures containing hydrobromofluorocarbons (HBFCs)
	38247400	Mixtures containing hydrochlorofluorocarbons (HCFCs), whether or not containing perfluorocarbons (PFCs) or hydrofluorocarbons (HFCs), but not containing chlorofluorocarbons (CFCs)

Group	*CN code*	*Description*
Mixtures *contd.*	38247500	Mixtures containing carbon tetrachloride
	38247600	Mixtures containing 1,1,1-trichloroethane (methyl chloroform)
	38247700	Mixtures containing bromomethane (methyl bromide) or bromochloromethane

(1) An "ex" before the code implies that substances other than those referred to in the column "Description" may also fall under that sub heading.

ANNEX V
CONDITIONS FOR THE PLACING ON THE MARKET AND FURTHER DISTRIBUTION OF CONTROLLED SUBSTANCES FOR ESSENTIAL LABORATORY AND ANALYTICAL USES REFERRED TO IN ARTICLE 10(3)

1. Controlled substances for essential laboratory and analytical uses shall contain only controlled substances manufactured to the following purities:

Substance	%
CTC (reagent grade)	99,5
1,1,1-trichloroethane	99,0
CFC 11	99,5
CFC 13	99,5
CFC 12	99,5
CFC 113	99,5
CFC 114	99,5
Other controlled substances with a boiling point > 20 °C	99,5
Other controlled substances with a boiling point < 20 °C	99,0

These pure controlled substances may be subsequently mixed by manufacturers, agents, or distributors with other chemicals controlled or not controlled by the Protocol as is customary for laboratory and analytical uses.

2. These high purity substances and mixtures containing controlled substances shall be supplied only in re-closable containers or high pressure cylinders smaller than three litres or in 10 millilitre or smaller glass ampoules, marked clearly as substances that deplete the ozone layer, restricted to laboratory and analytical uses and specifying that used or surplus substances should be collected and recycled, if practical. The material should be destroyed if recycling is not practical.

[ANNEX VI
CRITICAL USES OF HALONS][1]

[For the purposes of this Annex, the following definitions shall apply:

1. "Cut-off date" means the date after which halons must not be used for fire extinguishers or fire protection systems in new equipment and new facilities for the application concerned.
2. "New equipment" means equipment for which, by the cut-off date, neither of the following events has occurred:
   (a) signature of the relevant procurement or development contract;
   (b) submission of a request for type approval or type certification to the appropriate regulatory authority.

3. "New facilities" means facilities for which, by the cut-off date, neither of the following events has occurred:
   (a) signature of the relevant development contract;
   (b) submission of a request for planning consent to the appropriate regulatory authority.
4. "End date" means the date after which halons shall not be used for the application concerned and by which date the fire extinguishers or fire protection systems containing halons shall be decommissioned.
5. "Inerting" means preventing the initiation of combustion of a flammable or explosive atmosphere by means of the addition of an inhibiting or diluting agent.
6. "Cargo ship" means a ship that is not a passenger ship, is over 500 tonnes gross weight, and embarks on an international voyage, in accordance with the definition of those terms in the Safety of Life at Sea (SOLAS) Convention. The SOLAS Convention defines a "passenger ship" as "a ship that carries more than 12 passengers" and an "international voyage" as "a voyage from a country to which the present Convention applies to a port outside such country, or conversely".
7. A "normally occupied" space means a protected space in which it is necessary for persons to be present most or all of the time in order for the equipment or facility to function effectively. For military applications, the occupancy status of the protected space would be that applicable during a combat situation.
8. A "normally unoccupied" space means a protected space that is occupied for limited periods only, in particular for undertaking maintenance, and where the continual presence of persons is not necessary for the effective functioning of the equipment or facility.

Critical uses of halons

Application				*Cut-off date (31 December of the stated year)*	*End date (31 December of the stated year)*
Category of equipment or facility	*Purpose*	*Type of extinguisher*	*Type of halon*		
1. On military ground vehicles	1.1. For the protection of engine compartments	Fixed system	1301 1211 2402	2010	2035
	1.2. For the protection of crew compartments	Fixed system	1301 2402	2011	2040
	1.3. For the protection of crew compartments	Portable extinguisher	1301 1211	2011	2020
2. On military surface ships	2.1. For the protection of normally occupied machinery spaces	Fixed system	1301 2402	2010	2040
	2.2. For the protection of normally unoccupied engine spaces	Fixed system	1301 1211 2402	2010	2035
	2.3. For the protection of normally unoccupied electrical compartments	Fixed system	1301 1211	2010	2030
	2.4. For the protection of command centres	Fixed system	1301	2010	2030
	2.5. For the protection of fuel pump rooms	Fixed system	1301	2010	2030

Application				*Cut-off date (31 December of the stated year)*	*End date (31 December of the stated year)*
Category of equipment or facility	*Purpose*	*Type of extinguisher*	*Type of halon*		
2. On military surface ships *contd*	2.6. For the protection of flammable liquid storage compartments	Fixed system	1301 1211 2402	2010	2030
	2.7. For the protection of aircraft in hangars and maintenance areas	Portable extinguisher	1301 1211	2010	2016
3. On military submarines	3.1. For the protection of machinery spaces	Fixed system	1301	2010	2040
	3.2. For the protection of command centres	Fixed system	1301	2010	2040
	3.3. For the protection of diesel generator spaces	Fixed system	1301	2010	2040
	3.4. For the protection of electrical compartments	Fixed system	1301	2010	2040
4. On aircraft	4.1. For the protection of normally unoccupied cargo compartments	Fixed system	1301 1211 2402	2018	2040
	4.2. For the protection of cabins and crew compartments	Portable extinguisher	1211 2402	2014	2025
	4.3. For the protection of engine nacelles and auxiliary power units	Fixed system	1301 1211 2402	2014	2040
	4.4. For the inerting of fuel tanks	Fixed system	1301 2402	2011	2040
	4.5. For the protection of lavatory waste receptacles	Fixed system	1301 1211 2402	2011	2020
	4.6. For the protection of dry bays	Fixed system	1301 1211 2402	2011	2040
5. In oil, gas and petrochemicals facilities	5.1. For the protection of spaces where flammable liquid or gas could be released	Fixed system	1301 2402	2010	2020
6. On commercial cargo ships	6.1. For the inerting of normally occupied spaces where flammable liquid or gas could be released	Fixed system	1301 2402	1994	2016

Application				*Cut-off date (31 December of the stated year)*	*End date (31 December of the stated year)*
Category of equipment or facility	*Purpose*	*Type of extinguisher*	*Type of halon*		
7. In land-based command and communications facilities essential to national security	7.1. For the protection of normally occupied spaces	Fixed system	1301 2402	2010	2025
	7.2. For the protection of normally occupied spaces	Portable extinguisher	1211	2010	2013
	7.3. For the protection of normally unoccupied spaces	Fixed system	1301 2402	2010	2020
8. At airfields and airports	8.1. For crash rescue vehicles	Portable extinguisher	1211	2010	2016
	8.2. For the protection of aircraft in hangars and maintenance areas	Portable extinguisher	1211	2010	2016
9. In nuclear power and nuclear research facilities	9.1. For the protection of spaces where necessary to minimise risk of dispersion of radioactive matter	Fixed system	1301	2010	2020
10. In the Channel Tunnel	10.1. For the protection of technical facilities	Fixed system	1301	2010	2016
	10.2. For the protection of power cars and shuttle wagons of Channel Tunnel trains	Fixed system	1301	2010	2020
11. Other	11.1. For initial extinguishing by fire brigades where essential to personal safety	Portable extinguisher	1211	2010	2013
	11.2. For the protection of persons by military and police personnel	Portable extinguisher	1211	2010	2013][1]

Amendment

1 Substituted by Commission Regulation (EU) No 744/2010 of 18 August 2010 amending Regulation (EC) No 1005/2009 of the European Parliament and of the Council on substances that deplete the ozone layer, with regard to the critical uses of halons, Article 1, Annex.

ANNEX VII
DESTRUCTION TECHNOLOGIES REFERRED TO IN ARTICLE 22(1)

	Applicability		
Technology	*Controlled substances*(1)(2)		*Dilute sources*(3)
	Controlled substances listed in Annex I, groups I, II, IV, V, VIII	*Halons listed in Annex I group III*	*Foam*
Destruction and removal efficiency (DRE)(4)	99,99 %	99,99 %	95 %
Cement kilns	Approved(5)	Not Approved	Not applicable
Liquid injection incineration	Approved	Approved	Not applicable
Gaseous/fume oxidation	Approved	Approved	Not applicable
Municipal solid waste incineration	Not applicable	Not applicable	Approved
Reactor cracking	Approved	Not Approved	Not applicable
Rotary kiln incineration	Approved	Approved	Approved
Argon plasma arc	Approved	Approved	Not applicable
Inductively coupled radio frequency plasma	Approved	Approved	Not applicable
Microwave plasma	Approved	Not Approved	Not applicable
Nitrogen plasma arc	Approved	Not Approved	Not applicable
Gas phase catalytic dehalogenation	Approved	Not Approved	Not applicable
Superheated steam reactor	Approved	Not Approved	Not applicable

(1) Controlled substances not listed below shall be destroyed by the most environmentally acceptable destruction technology not entailing excessive costs.

(2) Concentrated sources refer to virgin, recovered and reclaimed ozone-depleting substances.

(3) Dilute sources refer to ozone-depleting substances contained in a matrix of a solid, for example foam.

(4) The DRE criterion presents technology capability on which approval of the technology is based. It does not always reflect the day-to-day performance achieved, which in itself will be controlled by national minimum standards.

(5) Approved by the Parties.

ANNEX VIII
CORRELATION TABLE

Regulation (EC) No 2037/2000	*This Regulation*
Article 1	Article 1 and 2
Article 2	Article 3
Article 3(1) first subparagraph	Article 4(1)
Article 3(1) second subparagraph	Article 10(2) and (4)
Article 3(2) point (i)	Article 4
Article 3(2) point (ii) first subparagraph	—
Article 3(2) point (ii) second subparagraph	Article 12(3)
Article 3(3)	Article 11(1)
Article 3(4)	Article 10(6) first sentence
Article 3(5)	Article 10(7)

Regulation (EC) No 2037/2000	*This Regulation*
Article 3(6)	—
Article 3(7)	Article 10(8)
Article 3(8)	Article 14(2)
Article 3(9)	Article 14(3)
Article 3(10)	Article 14(4)
Article 4(1)	Article 5(1)
Article 4(2) point (i)	Article 5(1)
Article 4(2) point (ii)	—
Article 4(2) point (iii) first subparagraph	Article 12(1) and (2)
Article 4(2) point (iii) second subparagraph	Article 26(1) point (a)
Article 4(2) point (iii) third subparagraph	Article 12(2)
Article 4(2) point (iv)	—
Article 4(3) point (i)	Article 5(1)
Article 4(3) point (ii)	—
Article 4(3) point (iii)	—
Article 4(3) point (iv)	—
Article 4(4) point (i)(a)	Article 9
Article 4(4) point (i)(b) first indent	Article 7(1) and Article 8(1)
Article 4(4) point (i)(b) second indent	Article 10(1) and Article 12(3)
Article 4(4) point (ii)	—
Article 4(4) point (iii)	—
Article 4(4) point (iv) first sentence	Article 13(1)
Article 4(4) point (iv) second sentence	Article 27(1)
Article 4(4) point (v)	Article 6(2)
Article 4(5)	Article 14(1)
Article 4(6)	Article 6
Article 4(6)	—
Article 5(1)	Article 5(1)
Article 5(2) point (a)	Article 11(2)
Article 5(2) point (b)	Article 7(1)
Article 5(2) point (c)	Article 8(1)
Article 5(3)	—
Article 5(4) first sentence	Article 11(8)
Article 5(4) second sentence	—
Article 5(5)	—
Article 5(6)	—
Article 5(7)	Article 11(8)
Article 6(1) first sentence	Article 15(3)
Article 6(1) second sentence	—
Article 6(2)	—
Article 6(3)	Article 18(3)
Article 6(4)	Article 18(5)
Article 6(5)	Article 18(9)
Article 7	Article 16(1)
Article 8	Article 20(1)
Article 9(1)	Article 20(1)

Regulation (EC) No 2037/2000	*This Regulation*
Article 9(2)	Article 21
Article 10	Article 20(2)
Article 11(1)	Article 17(1) and (2)
Article 11(2)	Article 20(1)
Article 11(3)	Article 20(1)
Article 11(4)	—
Article 12(1)	Article 17(4)
Article 12(2)	Article 18(4)
Article 12(3)	Article 18(5)
Article 12(4)	Article 18(3) and (4)
Article 13	Article 20(3)
Article 14	Article 20(4)
Article 15	—
Article 16(1)	Article 22(1)
Article 16(2)	—
Article 16(3)	Article 22(3)
Article 16(4)	—
Article 16(5)	Article 22(5)
Article 16(6)	—
Article 16(7)	—
Article 17	Article 23
Article 18	Article 25
Article 19	Article 25
Article 20(1)	Article 28(3)
Article 20(2)	Article 28(3)
Article 20(3)	Article 28(1)
Article 20(4)	Article 28(2)
Article 20(5)	Article 28(4)
Article 21	Article 29
Article 22	Article 24
Article 23	Article 30
Article 24	Article 31
Annex I	Annex I
Annex III	—
Annex IV	Annex IV
Annex V	—
Annex VI	Annex III
Annex VII	Annex VI

REGULATION 1069/2009/EU OF THE EUROPEAN PARLIAMENT AND OF THE COUNCIL

of 21 October 2009

LAYING DOWN HEALTH RULES AS REGARDS ANIMAL BY-PRODUCTS AND DERIVED PRODUCTS NOT INTENDED FOR HUMAN CONSUMPTION AND REPEALING REGULATION (EC) NO 1774/2002 (ANIMAL BY-PRODUCTS REGULATION)

THE EUROPEAN PARLIAMENT AND THE COUNCIL OF THE EUROPEAN UNION,

Having regard to the Treaty establishing the European Community, and in particular Article 152(4)(b) thereof,

Having regard to the proposal from the Commission,

Having regard to the opinion of the European Economic and Social Committee,

Having consulted the Committee of the Regions,

Acting in accordance with the procedure laid down in Article 251 of the Treaty,

Whereas:

(1) Animal by-products not intended for human consumption are a potential source of risks to public and animal health. Past crises related to outbreaks of foot-and-mouth disease, the spread of transmissible spongiform encephalopathies such as bovine spongiform encephalopathy (BSE) and the occurrence of dioxins in feedingstuffs have shown the consequences of the improper use of certain animal by-products for public and animal health, the safety of the food and feed chain and consumer confidence. In addition, such crises may also have a wider adverse impact on society as a whole, by their impact on the socioeconomic situation of the farmers and of the industrial sectors concerned and on consumer confidence in the safety of products of animal origin. Disease outbreaks could also have negative consequences for the environment, not only due to the disposal problems posed, but also as regards biodiversity.

(2) Animal by-products arise mainly during the slaughter of animals for human consumption, during the production of products of animal origin such as dairy products, and in the course of the disposal of dead animals and during disease control measures. Regardless of their source, they pose a potential risk to public and animal health and the environment. This risk needs to be adequately controlled, either by directing such products towards safe means of disposal or by using them for different purposes, provided that strict conditions are applied which minimise the health risks involved.

(3) The disposal of all animal by-products is not a realistic option, as it would lead to unsustainable costs and risks for the environment. Conversely, there is a clear interest for all citizens that, provided the health risks are minimised, a wide range of animal by-products are safely used for various applications in a sustainable manner. A wide range of animal by-products are indeed commonly used in important productive sectors, such as the pharmaceutical, feed and leather industries.

(4) New technologies have widened the possible use of animal by-products or derived products to a large number of productive sectors, in particular for the generation of energy. However, the use of those new technologies might pose health risks that must also be minimised.

(5) Community health rules for collection, transport, handling, treatment, transformation, processing, storage, placing on the market, distribution, use or disposal of animal by-products should be laid down in a coherent and comprehensive framework.

(6) Those general rules should be proportionate to the risk to public and animal health which animal by-products pose when they are dealt with by operators at different stages of the chain from collection to their use or disposal. The rules should also take into account the risks for the environment posed during those operations. The Community framework should include health rules on the placing on the market, including intra-Community trade and import, of animal by-products, where appropriate.

(7) In Regulation (EC) No 1774/2002, the European Parliament and the Council laid down Community health rules concerning animal by-products not intended for human consumption. Based on scientific advice and as an action under the Commission White Paper of 12 January 2000 on Food Safety, that Regulation introduced a set of rules aimed at protecting the safety of the food and feed chain, which is complementary to Community legislation on food and feed. Those rules have significantly improved the level of protection in the Community against the risks posed by animal by-products.

(8) Regulation (EC) No 1774/2002 introduced the classification of animal by-products into three categories according to the degree of risk involved. It requires operators to keep animal by-products of different categories separate from each other if they wish to make use of animal by-products which do not pose a significant risk to public or animal health, in particular if such products are derived from material fit for human consumption. That Regulation also introduced the principle that high-risk material should not be fed to farmed animals, and that material derived from animals is not to be fed to animals of the species from which it is derived. Pursuant to that Regulation, only material from animals which have undergone veterinary inspection is to enter the feed chain. In addition, it lays down rules for processing standards which ensure the reduction of risks.

(9) Under Article 35(2) of Regulation (EC) No 1774/2002, the Commission is to submit a report to the European Parliament and to the Council on the measures taken by the Member States to ensure compliance with that Regulation. The report is to be accompanied, if appropriate, by legislative proposals. The report was submitted on 21 October 2005 and emphasised that the principles of Regulation (EC) No 1774/2002 should be maintained. In addition, it highlighted the areas where amendments to that Regulation were considered necessary, in particular clarifications as regards the applicability of the rules to finished products, the relationship with other Community legislation and the classification of certain material. The findings of a series of fact-finding missions carried out in the Member States by the Food and Veterinary Office of the Commission (FVO) in 2004 and 2005 support those conclusions. According to the FVO, improvements are necessary as regards the traceability of the flow of animal by-products and the effectiveness and harmonisation of official controls.

(10) The Scientific Steering Committee, which was superseded by the European Food Safety Authority (EFSA) in 2002, has adopted a number of opinions concerning animal by-products. Those opinions demonstrate the need to maintain the main principles of Regulation (EC) No 1774/2002; in particular that animal by-products derived from animals shown not to be fit for human consumption as a result of a health inspection should not enter the feed chain. However, those animal by-products may be recovered and used for the production of technical or industrial products under specified health conditions.

(11) The conclusions of the Presidency of the Council on the Commission report of 21 October 2005 which were adopted in December 2005, and the subsequent consultations carried out by the Commission, have highlighted that the rules laid down in Regulation (EC) No 1774/2002 should be improved. The chief objectives of the rules on animal by-products, namely the control of risks to public and animal health and the protection of the safety of the food and feed chain, should be clearly laid down. The provisions of this Regulation should permit the achievement of those objectives.

(12) The rules on animal by-products laid down in this Regulation should apply to products that may not be used for human consumption under Community legislation, in particular

where they do not comply with food hygiene legislation or where they may not be placed on the market as food since they are unsafe either because they are injurious to health or unfit for human consumption (animal by-products "by law"). Those rules should, however, also apply to products of animal origin which do comply with certain rules regarding their possible use for human consumption, or which are raw materials for the production of products for human consumption, even if they are eventually destined for other purposes (animal by-products "by choice").

(13) In addition, in order to prevent risks arising from wild animals, bodies or parts of bodies of such animals suspected of being infected with a transmissible disease should be subject to the rules laid down in this Regulation. This inclusion should not imply an obligation to collect and dispose of bodies of wild animals that have died or that are hunted in their natural habitat. If good hunting practices are observed, intestines and other body parts of wild game may be disposed of safely on site. Such practices for the mitigation of risks are well-established in Member States and are in some cases based on cultural traditions or on national legislation which regulates the activities of hunters. Community legislation, in particular Regulation (EC) No 853/2004 of the European Parliament and of the Council of 29 April 2004 laying down specific hygiene rules for food of animal origin, lays down rules for handling of meat and animal by-products from wild game. Those rules also place the responsibility for the prevention of risks on trained persons such as hunters. In view of the potential risks for the food chain, animal by-products from killed wild game should only be subject to this Regulation in so far as food hygiene legislation applies to the placing on the market of such game and involves operations carried out by game-handling establishments. In addition, animal by-products for the preparation of game trophies should be covered by this Regulation in order to prevent animal health risks arising from such by-products.

(14) The rules laid down in this Regulation should apply to animal by-products derived from aquatic animals, other than material from vessels operating under Community food hygiene legislation. However, risk-proportionate measures should be adopted as regards the handling and disposal of material which arises on board fishing vessels from the evisceration of fish and which shows signs of disease. Such measures for the implementation of this Regulation should be adopted on the basis of a risk assessment carried out by the appropriate scientific institution in view of the available evidence regarding the effectiveness of certain measures to combat the spread of diseases communicable to humans, in particular of certain parasites.

(15) Due to the limited risks arising from materials used as raw pet food on farm or supplied to end users by food businesses, certain activities related to such raw pet food should not be covered by the rules laid down in this Regulation.

(16) It is appropriate to clarify in this Regulation which animals are to be classified as pet animals, so that by-products derived from such animals are not used in feed for farmed animals. In particular, animals kept for purposes other than farming, such as for companionship, should be classified as pet animals.

(17) For the sake of consistency of Community legislation, certain definitions set out in Regulation (EC) No 999/2001 of the European Parliament and of the Council of 22 May 2001 laying down rules for the prevention, control and eradication of certain transmissible spongiform encephalopathies and in Directive 2008/98/EC of the European Parliament and of the Council of 19 November 2008 on waste should be used in this Regulation. The reference to Council Directive 86/609/EEC of 24 November 1986 on the approximation of laws, regulations and administrative provisions of the Member States regarding the protection of animals used for experimental and other scientific purposes should be clarified.

(18) For the sake of consistency of Community legislation, the definition of "aquatic animal" as laid down in Council Directive 2006/88/EC of 24 October 2006 on animal health requirements for aquaculture animals and products thereof, and on the prevention and control of certain diseases in aquatic animals should be used in this Regulation. At the same time, aquatic invertebrates which are not covered by that definition and which

pose no risk of disease transmission should be subject to the same requirements as aquatic animals.

(19) Council Directive 1999/31/EC of 26 April 1999 on the landfill of waste specifies the conditions for the issuing of a permit for a landfill. This Regulation should provide for the disposal of animal by-products on landfills for which such a permit has been issued.

(20) The primary responsibility for carrying out operations in accordance with this Regulation should rest with operators. At the same time, the public interest in preventing risks to public and animal health requires that a collection and disposal system is in place to ensure the safe use or the safe disposal of animal by-products which may not be used, or which are not used for economic reasons. The scope of the collection and disposal system should take into account the actual amount of animal by-products which accrue in the particular Member State. It should also reflect, on a precautionary basis, the need for extended disposal capacities in the event of major outbreaks of transmissible diseases or of temporary technical failures in an existing disposal facility. Member States should be permitted to cooperate with each other and third countries provided that the objectives of this Regulation are met.

(21) It is important to determine the starting point in the life cycle of animal by-products from which the requirements of this Regulation should apply. Once a product has become an animal by-product, it should not re-enter the food chain. Special circumstances apply for the handling of certain raw materials, such as hides, handled in establishments or plants integrated at the same time into the food chain and the animal by-products chain. In those cases, the necessary measures should be taken by means of segregation to mitigate potential risks for the food chain which can arise from cross-contamination. For other establishments, risk-based conditions should be determined to prevent cross-contamination, in particular through separation between the animal by-products chain and the food chain.

(22) For reasons of legal certainty and proper control of potential risks, an end point in the manufacturing chain should be determined for products which no longer have direct relevance for the safety of the feed chain. For certain products regulated under other Community legislation, such an end point should be determined at the stage of manufacturing. Products which have reached this end point should be exempt from controls under this Regulation. In particular, products beyond the end point should be allowed to be placed on the market without restriction under this Regulation and to be handled and transported by operators which have not been approved or registered in accordance with this Regulation.

(23) However, it should be possible to modify such an end point, particularly in the case of newly emerging risks. Regulation (EC) No 1774/2002 exempts certain products, notably guano, certain hides to which particular forms of treatment such as tanning have been applied, and certain game trophies from its requirements. Similar exemptions should be provided for in the implementing measures to be adopted under this Regulation for products such as oleochemical products and the end products resulting from the production of biodiesel, under appropriate conditions.

(24) In order to ensure a high level of protection of public and animal health, Member States should continue to take the necessary measures to prevent the dispatch of animal by-products from restricted areas or establishments, in particular in the event of an outbreak of a disease listed in Council Directive 92/119/EEC of 17 December 1992 introducing general Community measures for the control of certain animal diseases and specific measures relating to swine vesicular disease.

(25) Operations with animal by-products which give rise to a considerable degree of risk to public and animal health should only be carried out in establishments or plants which have been approved in advance for such operations by the competent authority. That condition should apply in particular to processing establishments or plants and other establishments or plants which handle or store animal by-products with a direct relevance for the safety of the feed chain. It should be permitted for animal by-products of more than one category to be handled in the same establishment or plant provided

cross-contamination is prevented. It should further be permitted to amend those conditions if the amount of material for disposal and processing rises due to a major outbreak of disease, provided it is ensured that the temporary use under such amended conditions does not lead to the propagation of disease risks.

(26) However, such approvals should not be necessary for establishments or plants which process or handle certain safe materials, such as products processed to such an extent that they no longer pose a risk to public and animal health. Such establishments or plants should be registered so as to permit official control over the flow of material and ensure their traceability. That registration requirement should apply also to operators who transport animal by-products or derived products, unless they are no longer subject to any control since an end point in the chain has been determined.

(27) Establishments or plants should be approved following the submission of information to the competent authority and following a visit carried out on site which demonstrates that the requirements of this Regulation for the infrastructure and equipment of the establishment or plant will be met, so that any risks to public and animal health arising from the process used will be adequately contained. It should be possible to grant the approvals conditionally in order to allow operators to rectify deficiencies before the establishment or plant obtains full approval.

(28) Establishments or plants whose operations have already been approved in accordance with Community legislation on food hygiene should not be required to be approved or registered under this Regulation, as approvals or registrations under that Community legislation already take into account the objectives of this Regulation. However, establishments or plants which have been approved or registered under hygiene legislation should be obliged to comply with the requirements of this Regulation and subject to official controls carried out for the purposes of verifying compliance with the requirements of this Regulation.

(29) Animal by-products and derived products should be classified into three categories which reflect the degree of risk that they pose to public and animal health, on the basis of risk assessments. While animal by-products and derived products posing a high risk should only be used for purposes outside the feed chain, their use posing a lower risk should be permitted under safe conditions.

(30) Progress in science and technology may lead to the development of processes which eliminate or minimise the risks to public and animal health. Amendments to the lists of animal by-products set out in this Regulation should be possible, in order to take account of such progress. Prior to any such amendments, and in accordance with the general principles of Community legislation aimed at ensuring a high level of protection of public and animal health, a risk assessment should be carried out by the appropriate scientific institution, such as EFSA, the European Medicines Agency or the Scientific Committee for Consumer Products, depending on the type of animal by-products for which risks are to be assessed. However, it should be clear that once animal by-products of different categories are mixed, the mixture should be handled in accordance with the standards laid down for the proportion of the mixture belonging to the highest risk category.

(31) Due to the high risk to public health, animal by-products giving rise to a risk of transmissible spongiform encephalopathy (TSE) should, in particular, not be used for feed. This restriction should also apply to wild animals through which a communicable disease may be transmitted. The restriction on the feeding of animal by-products giving rise to a TSE risk should be without prejudice to the feeding rules laid down in Regulation (EC) No 999/2001.

(32) Animal by-products from animals used for experiments as defined in Directive 86/609/EEC should also be excluded from use in feed, due to the potential risks arising from those animal by-products. However, Member States may allow the use of animal by-products from animals which have been used for experiments to test new feed additives, in accordance with Regulation (EC) No 1831/2003 of the European Parliament and of the Council of 22 September 2003 on additives for use in animal nutrition.

(33) The use of certain substances and products is unlawful under Council Regulation (EEC) No 2377/90 of 26 June 1990 laying down a Community procedure for the establishment of maximum residue limits of veterinary medicinal products in food stuffs of animal origin and Council Directive 96/22/EC of 29 April 1996 concerning the prohibition on the use in stockfarming of certain substances having a hormonal or thyrostatic action and of ß agonists. In addition, Council Directive 96/23/EC of 29 April 1996 on measures to monitor certain substances and residues thereof in live animals and animal products lays down further rules on the monitoring of certain substances and residues thereof in live animals and animal products. Directive 96/23/EC also lays down rules which apply where the presence of residues of authorised substances or contaminants exceeding certain permitted levels has been established. In order to ensure the coherence of Community legislation, products of animal origin in which substances are detected in breach of Regulation (EEC) No 2377/90 and Directives 96/22/EC and 96/23/EC should be classified as Category 1 or Category 2 material, as appropriate, in view of the risk they pose to the food and feed chain.

(34) Manure and digestive tract content should not need to be disposed of, provided that proper treatment ensures that diseases are not transmitted during their application to land. Animal by-products from animals that die on farm and animals killed for the eradication of diseases should not be used in the feed chain. This restriction should also apply to imported animal by-products which are allowed into the Community, where they do not comply with Community legislation upon inspection at the Community border post, and to products which do not comply with the applicable requirements during checks carried out within the Community. Non-compliance with Directive 2000/13/EC of the European Parliament and of the Council of 20 March 2000 on the approximation of the laws of the Member States relating to the labelling, presentation and advertising of foodstuffs and with Regulation (EC) No 767/2009 of the European Parliament and of the Council of 13 July 2009 on the placing on the market and use of feed should not result in the exclusion from the feed chain of products presented for border inspection.

(35) Since the date of entry into force of Regulation (EC) No 1774/2002, the classification of certain animal by-products by default as Category 2 material limits their possible uses severely, while not necessarily being proportionate to the risks involved. Accordingly those animal by-products should be reclassified as Category 3 material, so as to allow their use for certain feeding purposes. For any other animal by-products which are not listed under one of the three categories, the categorisation by default as Category 2 material should be maintained for precautionary reasons, in particular to reinforce the general exclusion of such material from the feed chain for farmed animals, other than fur animals.

(36) Other legislation which has entered into force following the adoption of Regulation (EC) No 178/2002 of the European Parliament and of the Council of 28 January 2002 laying down the general principles and requirements of food law, establishing the European Food Safety Authority and laying down procedures in matters of food safety, namely Regulation (EC) No 852/2004 of the European Parliament and of the Council of 29 April 2004 on the hygiene of foodstuffs, Regulation (EC) No 853/2004 and Regulation (EC) No 183/2005 of the European Parliament and of the Council of 12 January 2005 laying down requirements for feed hygiene, and to which Regulation (EC) No 1774/2002 is complementary, places the primary duty of complying with Community legislation, aimed at protecting public and animal health, on the food and feed business operators. In line with that legislation, operators carrying out activities under this Regulation should also be primarily responsible for ensuring compliance with this Regulation. That obligation should be further clarified and specified as regards the means by which traceability is ensured, such as separate collection and channelling of animal by-products. Established systems ensuring traceability for products exclusively circulating at national level by other means should continue to operate, if they provide equivalent information. Every effort should be made to promote the use of electronic

and other means of documentation which do not involve paper records, as long as they ensure full traceability.

(37) A system of own checks is necessary to ensure that, within an establishment or plant, the requirements of this Regulation are fulfilled. During official controls the competent authorities should take into account the performance of own checks. In certain establishments or plants own checks should be carried out through a system based on the hazard analysis and critical control points (HACCP) principles. The HACCP principles should be based on the experience of their implementation under Community legislation on food and feed hygiene. In this respect, national guides to good practice could serve as a useful tool to facilitate the practical implementation of the HACCP principles, and of other aspects of this Regulation.

(38) Animal by-products should only be used if the risks to public and animal health are minimised in the course of their processing and the placing on the market of derived products manufactured on the basis of animal by-products. If this option is not available, the animal by-products should be disposed of under safe conditions. The options available for the use of animal by-products of the different categories should be clarified in coherence with other Community legislation. In general, the options for a higher risk category should be available for the lower risk categories as well, unless special considerations apply in view of the risk attached to certain animal by-products.

(39) Disposal of animal by-products and derived products should take place in accordance with environmental legislation regarding landfilling and waste incineration. In order to ensure consistency, incineration should take place in accordance with Directive 2000/76/EC of the European Parliament and of the Council of 4 December 2000 on the incineration of waste. Co-incineration of waste – either as a recovery or disposal operation – is subject to similar conditions regarding approval and operation to those regarding waste incineration, in particular as to air emission limit values, waste water and residue discharge, control and monitoring and measurement requirements. Consequently, direct co-incineration, without prior processing, of all three categories of materials should be permitted. In addition, specific provisions should be enacted for the approval of low and high-capacity incineration plants.

(40) The use of animal by-products or derived products as a fuel in the combustion process should be authorised and should not be considered as a waste disposal operation. However, such use should take place under conditions which ensure the protection of public and animal health, as well as the appropriate environmental standards.

(41) This Regulation should provide for the possibility to lay down parameters for processing methods regarding time, temperature and pressure for animal by-products, in particular for the methods currently referred to as methods 2 to 7 under Regulation (EC) No 1774/2002.

(42) Shells from shellfish from which the soft tissue or flesh have been removed, should be excluded from the scope of the Regulation. Due to the various practices in the Community regarding the removal of such soft tissue or flesh from shells, it should be possible to use shells from which the entire soft tissue or flesh has not been removed, provided such use does not lead to a risk arising to public and animal health. National guides to good practice could assist in the dissemination of knowledge regarding proper conditions under which such use would be possible.

(43) In view of the limited risk to public or animal health arising from such products, the competent authority should be able to authorise the preparation and application to land of biodynamic preparations, on the basis of Category 2 and Category 3 materials, as referred to in Council Regulation (EC) No 834/2007 of 28 June 2007 on organic production and labelling of organic products.

(44) Novel technologies which are being developed offer advantageous ways of generating energy on the basis of animal by-products or of providing for the safe disposal of such products. Safe disposal may take place through a combination of methods for the safe containment of animal by-products on site with established disposal methods, and through a combination of authorised processing parameters with new standards which

have been favourably assessed. In order to take account of the related progress in science and technology, such technologies should be authorised as alternative methods for the disposal or use of animal by-products throughout the Community. If a technological process has been developed by an individual, an application checked by the competent authority should be examined by EFSA before such authorisation is granted, in order to ensure that an assessment of the risk reduction potential of the process is carried out and that the rights of individuals, including the confidentiality of business information, is preserved. In order to provide advice to applicants a standard format for application should be adopted. Since that document is intended only to be indicative it should be adopted in accordance with the advisory procedure in collaboration with EFSA.

(45) It is appropriate to clarify the requirements applicable to the placing on the market of animal by-products and derived products intended for feeding purposes and of organic fertilisers and soil improvers, so as to ensure the protection of the food and feed chain. Only Category 3 material should be used for feeding farmed animals other than fur animals. Fertilisers produced on the basis of animal by-products may affect the safety of the feed and food chain. Where they have been manufactured from meat-and-bone meal derived from Category 2 material or from processed animal protein, a component, such as an inorganic or an indigestible substance, should be added in order to prevent their direct use for feeding purposes. Such mixing should not be required if the composition or packaging of products, in particular of products destined for use by the final consumer, prevents the misuse of the product for feeding purposes. When determining the components, different circumstances regarding climate and soil and the objective for the use of particular fertilisers should be taken into account.

(46) Regulation (EC) No 1523/2007 of the European Parliament and of the Council of 11 December 2007 banning the placing on the market and the import to, or export from, the Community of cat and dog fur, and products containing such fur lays down a general prohibition on the placing on the market and the import and export of cat and dog fur and products containing such fur. However, that prohibition should not affect the obligation under this Regulation to dispose of animal by-products from cats and dogs, including fur.

(47) The promotion of science and research, and artistic activities may require the use of animal by-products or derived products of all categories, sometimes in quantities below the scale of commercial exchanges. In order to facilitate the import and use of such animal by-products or derived products, the competent authority should be able to fix the conditions for such operations on a case-specific basis. Harmonised conditions should be laid down where action at a Community level is necessary.

(48) Regulation (EC) No 1774/2002 contains detailed provisions which allow, by way of derogation, the feeding of Category 2 and Category 3 materials to zoo animals. Similar provisions should be laid down in this Regulation and the feeding of certain Category 1 material should be allowed and complemented by the possibility to lay down detailed rules to control any possible risks arising to public or animal health.

(49) Regulation (EC) No 1774/2002 allows for the feeding of Category 1 material to endangered or protected species of necrophagous birds and other species living in their natural habitat, for the promotion of biodiversity. In order to provide an adequate tool for the preservation of those species, that feeding practice should continue to be permitted under this Regulation, in accordance with conditions laid down to prevent the spread of diseases. At the same time, health conditions should be laid down in the implementing measures permitting the use of such Category 1 material for feeding purposes in extensive grazing systems and for feeding to other carnivore species, such as bears and wolves. It is important that such health conditions take into account the natural consumption patterns of the species concerned as well as Community objectives for the promotion of biodiversity as referred to in the Communication from the Commission of 22 May 2006 entitled "Halting the loss of biodiversity by 2010 – and beyond".

(50) Burial and burning of animal by-products, in particular of dead animals may be justified in specific situations, in particular in remote areas, or in disease control situations

to and impose certain conditions to ensure the protection of public or animal health. In particular, Directive 76/768/EEC excludes Category 1 and Category 2 materials as part of the composition of a cosmetic product and obliges manufacturers to apply good manufacturing practices. Commission Directive 2003/32/EC introduces detailed specifications with respect to medical devices manufactured utilising tissues of animal origin.

(63) However, where those conditions have not yet been laid down in the specific Directives or where they do not cover certain risks to public and animal health, this Regulation should apply, and recourse to safeguard measures in accordance with Regulation (EC) No 178/2002 should be possible.

(64) Certain derived products do not enter the feed chain or are not applied to land which is grazed by farmed animals or from which herbage for feed is cut. Such derived products include products for technical uses, such as treated hides for leather production, processed wool for the textile industry, bone products for glue and processed material destined for petfood. Operators should be permitted to place such products on the market provided that they are either derived from raw material requiring no treatment or the treatment or the end use of the treated material ensures adequate risk control.

(65) Certain failures to comply with the rules laid down in Regulation (EC) No 1774/2002 have been revealed in a number of Member States. Accordingly, in addition to the strict enforcement of those rules, criminal and other sanctions against operators which do not comply with those rules are needed. Therefore, it is necessary that Member States lay down rules on penalties applicable to infringements of this Regulation.

(66) Since the objective of this Regulation, namely to lay down public and animal health rules for animal by-products and derived products in order to prevent and minimise risks to public and animal health arising from those products and, in particular, to protect the safety of the food and feed chain, cannot be sufficiently achieved by the Member States and can therefore be better achieved at Community level, the Community may adopt measures, in accordance with the principle of subsidiarity as set out in Article 5 of the Treaty. In accordance with the principle of proportionality, as set out in that Article, this Regulation does not go beyond what is necessary in order to achieve that objective.

(67) In order to enhance legal certainty and in the light of the Commission's general objective to simplify Community legislation, a coherent framework of rules should be laid down in this Regulation, taking into account the rules laid down in Regulation (EC) No 1774/2002, as well as the experience gained and progress made since the date of entry into force of that Regulation. Regulation (EC) No 1774/2002 should therefore be repealed and replaced by this Regulation.

(68) The measures necessary for the implementation of this Regulation should be adopted in accordance with Council Decision 1999/468/EC of 28 June 1999 laying down the procedures for the exercise of implementing powers conferred on the Commission.

(69) In order to improve coherence and clarity of Community legislation, the technical rules concerning specific operations involving animal by-products, which are currently laid down in the Annexes to Regulation (EC) No 1774/2002, as well as in implementing measures adopted by the Commission on the basis of that Regulation, should be laid down in separate implementing acts. Consultation and information of consumers and socio-professional circles concerned with issues related to this Regulation should be carried out in accordance with Commission Decision 2004/613/EC of 6 August 2004 concerning the creation of an advisory group on the food chain and animal and plant health.

(70) In particular, the Commission should be empowered to adopt rules modifying the end point in the manufacturing chain of certain derived products and establishing such an end point for certain other derived products, rules in regard to serious transmissible diseases in the presence of which the dispatch of animal by-products and derived products should not be allowed and/or the conditions allowing such a dispatch, measures changing the categorisation of animal by-products and derived products, measures regarding restrictions on the use and disposal of animal by-products and derived

products, measures laying down conditions for the application of certain derogations regarding the use, collection and disposal of animal by-products and derived products and measures authorising or rejecting a particular alternative method for the use and disposal of animal by-products and derived products.

(71) In addition, the Commission should be empowered to adopt more specific rules concerning collection and transport of animal by-products and derived products, the infrastructure, equipment and hygiene requirements for establishments or plants handling animal by-products and derived products, the conditions and technical requirements for the handling of animal by-products and derived products, including the evidence to be presented for the purpose of validation of such treatment, conditions for the placing on the market of animal by-products and derived products, requirements related to safe sourcing, safe treatment and safe end uses, conditions for the import, transit and export of animal by-products and derived products, detailed arrangements for implementing official controls including rules concerning the reference methods for microbiological analyses as well as conditions for the control of the dispatch of certain animal by-products and derived products between Member States. Since those measures are of general scope and are designed to amend non-essential elements of this Regulation, inter alia, by supplementing it with new non-essential elements, they must be adopted in accordance with the regulatory procedure with scrutiny provided for in Article 5a of Decision 1999/468/EC.

(72) On grounds of efficiency, the normal time-limits for the regulatory procedure with scrutiny should be curtailed for the adoption of measures specifying the conditions for the dispatch of animal by-products from restricted holdings, plants or zones. On grounds of urgency, it is necessary to apply the urgency procedure provided for in Article 5a(6) of Decision 1999/468/EC for the adoption of measures modifying the end point in the manufacturing chain for certain products,

HAVE ADOPTED THIS REGULATION:

Title I
General provisions

Chapter I
Common provisions

Section 1
Subject matter, scope and definitions

Article 1

Subject matter

This Regulation lays down public health and animal health rules for animal by-products and derived products, in order to prevent and minimise risks to public and animal health arising from those products, and in particular to protect the safety of the food and feed chain.

Article 2

Scope

1. This Regulation shall apply to:

(a) animal by-products and derived products which are excluded from human consumption under Community legislation; and

(b) the following products which pursuant to a decision by an operator, which shall be irreversible, are destined for purposes other than human consumption:

(i) products of animal origin which may be destined for human consumption under Community legislation;
(ii) raw materials for the production of products of animal origin.

2. This Regulation shall not apply to the following animal by-products:
(a) entire bodies or parts of wild animals, other than wild game, which are not suspected of being infected or affected with a disease communicable to humans or animals, except for aquatic animals landed for commercial purposes;
(b) entire bodies or parts of wild game which are not collected after killing, in accordance with good hunting practice, without prejudice to Regulation (EC) No 853/2004;
(c) animal by-products from wild game and from wild game meat referred to in Article 1(3)(e) of Regulation (EC) No 853/2004;
(d) oocytes, embryos and semen destined for breeding purposes;
(e) raw milk, colostrum and products derived therefrom which are obtained, kept, disposed of or used on the farm of origin;
(f) shells from shellfish with the soft tissue and flesh removed;
(g) catering waste, except if it:
   (i) originates from means of transport operating internationally;
   (ii) is destined for feeding purposes;
   (iii) is destined for processing by pressure sterilisation or for processing by methods referred to in point (b) of the first subparagraph of Article 15(1) or for transformation into biogas or for composting;
(h) without prejudice to Community environmental legislation, material from vessels complying with Regulations (EC) No 852/2004 and (EC) No 853/2004, which has arisen in the course of their fishing operations and is disposed of at sea, except material derived from on-board evisceration of fish showing signs of disease, including parasites, that are communicable to humans;
(i) raw pet food originating from retail shops, where the cutting and storage are performed solely for the purpose of supplying the consumer directly on the spot;
(j) raw pet food derived from animals which are slaughtered on the farm of origin for private domestic consumption; and
(k) excrement and urine other than manure and non-mineralised guano.

3. This Regulation shall be without prejudice to Community veterinary legislation having as its objective the control and eradication of animal diseases.

Article 3

Definitions

For the purposes of this Regulation, the following definitions shall apply:
1. "animal by-products" means entire bodies or parts of animals, products of animal origin or other products obtained from animals, which are not intended for human consumption, including oocytes, embryos and semen;
2. "derived products" means products obtained from one or more treatments, transformations or steps of processing of animal by-products;
3. "products of animal origin" means products of animal origin as defined in point 8.1 of Annex I to Regulation (EC) No 853/2004;
4. "carcase" means carcase as defined in point 1.9 of Annex I to Regulation (EC) No 853/2004;
5. "animal" means any invertebrate or vertebrate animal;
6. "farmed animal" means:
   (a) any animal that is kept, fattened or bred by humans and used for the production of food, wool, fur, feathers, hides and skins or any other product obtained from animals or for other farming purposes;
   (b) equidae;

7. "wild animal" means any animal not kept by humans;
8. "pet animal" means any animal belonging to species normally nourished and kept but not consumed, by humans for purposes other than farming;
9. "aquatic animals" means aquatic animals as defined in Article 3(1)(e) of Directive 2006/88/EC;
10. "competent authority" means the central authority of a Member State competent to ensure compliance with the requirements of this Regulation or any authority to which that competence has been delegated; it also includes, where appropriate, the corresponding authority of a third country;
11. "operator" means the natural or legal persons having an animal by-product or derived product under their actual control, including carriers, traders and users;
12. "user" means the natural or legal persons using animal by-products and derived products for special feeding purposes, for research or for other specific purposes;
13. "establishment" or "plant" means any place where any operation involving the handling of animal by-products or derived products is carried out, other than a fishing vessel;
14. "placing on the market" means any operation the purpose of which is to sell animal by-products or derived products to a third party in the Community or any other form of supply against payment or free of charge to such a third party or storage with a view to supply to such a third party;
15. "transit" means movement through the Community from the territory of a third country to the territory of another third country, other than by sea or by air;
16. "export" means movement from the Community to a third country;
17. "transmissible spongiform encephalopathies (TSEs)" means all transmissible spongiform encephalopathies as defined in Article 3(1)(a) of Regulation (EC) No 999/2001;
18. "specified risk material" means specified risk material as defined in Article 3(1)(g) of Regulation (EC) No 999/2001;
19. "pressure sterilisation" means the processing of animal by-products, after reduction in particle size to not more than 50 mm, to a core temperature of more than 133 °C for at least 20 minutes without interruption at an absolute pressure of at least 3 bar;
20. "manure" means any excrement and/or urine of farmed animals other than farmed fish, with or without litter;
21. "authorised landfill" means a landfill for which a permit has been issued in accordance with Directive 1999/31/EC;
22. "organic fertiliser" and "soil improver" means materials of animal origin used to maintain or improve plant nutrition and the physical and chemical properties and biological activities of soils, either separately or together; they may include manure, non-mineralised guano, digestive tract content, compost and digestion residues;
23. "remote area" means an area where the animal population is so small, and where disposal establishments or plants are so far away that the arrangements necessary for the collection and transport of animal by-products would be unacceptably onerous compared to local disposal;
24. "food" or "foodstuff" means food or foodstuff as defined in Article 2 of Regulation (EC) No 178/2002;
25. "feed" or "feedingstuff" means feed or feedingstuff as defined in Article 3(4) of Regulation (EC) No 178/2002;
26. "centrifuge or separator sludge" means material collected as a by-product after purification of raw milk and separation of skimmed milk and cream from raw milk;
27. "waste" means waste as defined in point 1 of Article 3 of Directive 2008/98/EC.

Section 2
Obligations

Article 4

Starting point in the manufacturing chain and obligations

1. As soon as operators generate animal by-products or derived products falling within the scope of this Regulation, they shall identify them and ensure that they are dealt with in accordance with this Regulation (starting point).

2. Operators shall ensure at all stages of collection, transport, handling, treatment, transformation, processing, storage, placing on the market, distribution, use and disposal within the businesses under their control that animal by-products and derived products satisfy the requirements of this Regulation which are relevant to their activities.

3. Member States shall monitor and verify that the relevant requirements of this Regulation are fulfilled by operators along the entire chain of animal by-products and derived products as referred to in paragraph 2. For that purpose, they shall maintain a system of official controls in accordance with relevant Community legislation.

4. Member States shall ensure that an adequate system is in place on their territory ensuring that animal by-products are:
(a) collected, identified and transported without undue delay; and
(b) treated, used or disposed of in accordance with this Regulation.

5. Member States may fulfil their obligations under paragraph 4 in cooperation with other Member States or third countries.

Article 5

End point in the manufacturing chain

1. Derived products referred to in Article 33 which have reached the stage of manufacturing regulated by the Community legislation referred to in that Article shall be regarded as having reached the end point in the manufacturing chain, beyond which they are no longer subject to the requirements of this Regulation.

Those derived products may subsequently be placed on the market without restrictions under this Regulation and shall no longer be subject to official controls in accordance with this Regulation.

The end point in the manufacturing chain may be modified:
(a) for products referred to in Article 33(a) to (d), in case of risks to animal health;
(b) for products referred to in Article 33(e) and (f), in case of risks to public or animal health.
Those measures, designed to amend non-essential elements of this Regulation, shall be adopted in accordance with the regulatory procedure with scrutiny referred to in Article 52(6).

2. For derived products referred to in Articles 35 and 36 which no longer pose any significant risk to public or animal health, an end point in the manufacturing chain may be determined, beyond which they are no longer subject to the requirements of this Regulation.

Those derived products may subsequently be placed on the market without restrictions under this Regulation and shall no longer be subject to official controls in accordance with this Regulation.

Those measures, designed to amend non-essential elements of this Regulation by supplementing it, shall be adopted in accordance with the regulatory procedure with scrutiny referred to in Article 52(5).

3. In the event of risks to public or animal health, Articles 53 and 54 of Regulation (EC) No 178/2002 concerning emergency measures shall apply mutatis mutandis to the derived products referred to in Articles 33 and 36 of this Regulation.

Section 3
Animal health restrictions

Article 6

General animal health restrictions

1. Animal by-products and derived products from susceptible species shall not be dispatched from holdings, establishments, plants or zones which are subject to restrictions:
(a) pursuant to Community veterinary legislation; or
(b) due to the presence of a serious transmissible disease:
  (i) listed in Annex I to Directive 92/119/EEC; or
  (ii) laid down in accordance with the second subparagraph.

The measures referred to in point (b)(ii) of the first subparagraph, designed to amend non-essential elements of this Regulation by supplementing it, shall be adopted in accordance with the regulatory procedure with scrutiny referred to in Article 52(4).

2. Paragraph 1 shall not apply where animal by-products and derived products are dispatched under conditions designed to prevent the spread of diseases transmissible to humans or animals.

Those measures, designed to amend non-essential elements of this Regulation by supplementing it, shall be adopted in accordance with the regulatory procedure with scrutiny referred to in Article 52(5).

Section 4
Categorisation

Article 7

Categorisation of animal by-products and derived products

1. Animal by-products shall be categorised into specific categories which reflect the level of risk to public and animal health arising from those animal by-products, in accordance with the lists laid down in Articles 8, 9 and 10.

2. Derived products shall be subject to the rules for the specific category of animal by-products from which they have been derived, unless otherwise specified in this Regulation, or provided for in measures for the implementation of this Regulation which may specify the conditions under which derived products are not subject to those rules adopted by the Commission.

3. Articles 8, 9 and 10 may be amended in order to take into account scientific progress as regards the assessment of the level of risk, provided such progress can be identified on the basis of a risk assessment carried out by the appropriate scientific institution. However, no animal by-products listed in those Articles may be removed from those lists, only changes of categorisation or additions may be made.

4. The measures referred to in paragraphs 2 and 3, designed to amend non-essential elements of this Regulation, inter alia, by supplementing it, shall be adopted in accordance with the regulatory procedure with scrutiny referred to in Article 52(4).

Article 8

Category 1 material

Category 1 material shall comprise the following animal by-products:

(a) entire bodies and all body parts, including hides and skins, of the following animals:
 (i) animals suspected of being infected by a TSE in accordance with Regulation (EC) No 999/2001 or in which the presence of a TSE has been officially confirmed;
 (ii) animals killed in the context of TSE eradication measures;
 (iii) animals other than farmed and wild animals, including in particular pet animals, zoo animals and circus animals;
 [(iv) animals used in a procedure or procedures defined in Article 3 of Directive 2010/63/EU of the European Parliament and of the Council of 22 September 2010 on the protection of animals used for scientific purposes, in cases where the competent authority decides that such animals or any of their body parts have the potential to pose serious health risks to humans or to other animals, as a result of that procedure or those procedures without prejudice to Article 3(2) of Regulation (EC) No 1831/2003;][1]
 (v) wild animals, when suspected of being infected with diseases communicable to humans or animals;
(b) the following material:
 (i) specified risk material;
 (ii) entire bodies or parts of dead animals containing specified risk material at the time of disposal;
(c) animal by-products derived from animals which have been submitted to illegal treatment as defined in Article 1(2)(d) of Directive 96/22/EC or Article 2(b) of Directive 96/23/EC;
(d) animal by-products containing residues of other substances and environmental contaminants listed in Group B(3) of Annex I to Directive 96/23/EC, if such residues exceed the permitted level laid down by Community legislation or, in the absence thereof, by national legislation;
(e) animal by-products collected during the treatment of waste water required by implementing rules adopted under point (c) of the first paragraph of Article 27:
 (i) from establishments or plants processing Category 1 material; or
 (ii) from other establishments or plants where specified risk material is being removed;
(f) catering waste from means of transport operating internationally;
(g) mixtures of Category 1 material with either Category 2 material or Category 3 material or both.

Amendment

1 Inserted by Directive 2010/63/EU of the European Parliament and of the Council of 22 September 2010 on the protection of animals used for scientific purposes, Article 63.

Article 9

Category 2 material

Category 2 material shall comprise the following animal by-products:
(a) manure, non-mineralised guano and digestive tract content;
(b) animal by-products collected during the treatment of waste water required by implementing rules adopted under point (c) of the first paragraph of Article 27:
 (i) from establishments or plants processing Category 2 material; or
 (ii) from slaughterhouses other than those covered by Article 8(e);
(c) animal by-products containing residues of authorised substances or contaminants exceeding the permitted levels as referred to in Article 15(3) of Directive 96/23/EC;
(d) products of animal origin which have been declared unfit for human consumption due to the presence of foreign bodies in those products;
(e) products of animal origin, other than Category 1 material, that are:
 (i) imported or introduced from a third country and fail to comply with Community veterinary legislation for their import or introduction into the Community except where Community legislation allows their import or introduction subject to specific restrictions or their return to the third country; or

(ii) dispatched to another Member State and fail to comply with requirements laid down or authorised by Community legislation except where they are returned with the authorisation of the competent authority of the Member State of origin;

(f) animals and parts of animals, other than those referred to in Article 8 or Article 10,

(i) that died other than by being slaughtered or killed for human consumption, including animals killed for disease control purposes;

(ii) foetuses;

(iii) oocytes, embryos and semen which are not destined for breeding purposes; and

(iv) dead-in-shell poultry;

(g) mixtures of Category 2 material with Category 3 material;

(h) animal by-products other than Category 1 material or Category 3 material.

Article 10

Category 3 material

Category 3 material shall comprise the following animal by-products:

(a) carcases and parts of animals slaughtered or, in the case of game, bodies or parts of animals killed, and which are fit for human consumption in accordance with Community legislation, but are not intended for human consumption for commercial reasons;

(b) carcases and the following parts originating either from animals that have been slaughtered in a slaughterhouse and were considered fit for slaughter for human consumption following an ante-mortem inspection or bodies and the following parts of animals from game killed for human consumption in accordance with Community legislation:

(i) carcases or bodies and parts of animals which are rejected as unfit for human consumption in accordance with Community legislation, but which did not show any signs of disease communicable to humans or animals;

(ii) heads of poultry;

(iii) hides and skins, including trimmings and splitting thereof, horns and feet, including the phalanges and the carpus and metacarpus bones, tarsus and metatarsus bones, of:

— animals, other than ruminants requiring TSE testing, and

— ruminants which have been tested with a negative result in accordance with Article 6(1) of Regulation (EC) No 999/2001;

(iv) pig bristles;

(v) feathers;

(c) animal by-products from poultry and lagomorphs slaughtered on the farm as referred to in Article 1(3)(d) of Regulation (EC) No 853/2004, which did not show any signs of disease communicable to humans or animals;

(d) blood of animals which did not show any signs of disease communicable through blood to humans or animals obtained from the following animals that have been slaughtered in a slaughterhouse after having been considered fit for slaughter for human consumption following an ante-mortem inspection in accordance with Community legislation:

(i) animals other than ruminants requiring TSE testing; and

(ii) ruminants which have been tested with a negative result in accordance with Article 6(1) of Regulation (EC) No 999/2001;

(e) animal by-products arising from the production of products intended for human consumption, including degreased bones, greaves and centrifuge or separator sludge from milk processing;

(f) products of animal origin, or foodstuffs containing products of animal origin, which are no longer intended for human consumption for commercial reasons or due to problems of manufacturing or packaging defects or other defects from which no risk to public or animal health arise;

(g) petfood and feedingstuffs of animal origin, or feedingstuffs containing animal by-products or derived products, which are no longer intended for feeding for commercial reasons or due to problems of manufacturing or packaging defects or other defects from which no risk to public or animal health arises;

(h) blood, placenta, wool, feathers, hair, horns, hoof cuts and raw milk originating from live animals that did not show any signs of disease communicable through that product to humans or animals;

(i) aquatic animals, and parts of such animals, except sea mammals, which did not show any signs of disease communicable to humans or animals;

(j) animal by-products from aquatic animals originating from establishments or plants manufacturing products for human consumption;

(k) the following material originating from animals which did not show any signs of disease communicable through that material to humans or animals:
  (i) shells from shellfish with soft tissue or flesh;
  (ii) the following originating from terrestrial animals:
    — hatchery by-products,
    — eggs,
    — egg by-products, including egg shells,
  (iii) day-old chicks killed for commercial reasons;

(l) aquatic and terrestrial invertebrates other than species pathogenic to humans or animals;

(m) animals and parts thereof of the zoological orders of Rodentia and Lagomorpha, except Category 1 material as referred to in Article 8(a)(iii), (iv) and (v) and Category 2 material as referred to in Article 9(a) to (g);

(n) hides and skins, hooves, feathers, wool, horns, hair and fur originating from dead animals that did not show any signs of disease communicable through that product to humans or animals, other than those referred to in point (b) of this Article;

(o) adipose tissue from animals which did not show any signs of disease communicable through that material to humans or animals, which were slaughtered in a slaughterhouse and which were considered fit for slaughter for human consumption following an ante-mortem inspection in accordance with Community legislation;

(p) catering waste other than as referred to in Article 8(f).

Chapter II
Disposal and use of animal by-products and derived products

Section 1
Restrictions on use

Article 11

Restrictions on use

1. The following uses of animal by-products and derived products shall be prohibited:

(a) the feeding of terrestrial animals of a given species other than fur animals with processed animal protein derived from the bodies or parts of bodies of animals of the same species;

(b) the feeding of farmed animals other than fur animals with catering waste or feed material containing or derived from catering waste;

(c) the feeding of farmed animals with herbage, either directly by grazing or by feeding with cut herbage, from land to which organic fertilisers or soil improvers, other than manure, have been applied unless the cutting or grazing takes place after the expiry of a waiting period which ensures adequate control of risks to public and animal health and is at least 21 days; and

(d) the feeding of farmed fish with processed animal protein derived from the bodies or parts of bodies of farmed fish of the same species.

2. Measures relating to the following may be laid down:

(a) the checks and controls to be carried out to ensure the application of the prohibitions referred to in paragraph 1, including detection methods and tests to be used to verify the presence of materials originating from certain species and thresholds for insignificant amounts of processed animal proteins referred to in points (a) and (d) of paragraph 1 which are caused by adventitious and technically unavoidable contamination;

(b) the conditions for the feeding of fur animals with processed animal protein derived from bodies or parts of bodies of animals of the same species; and

(c) the conditions for the feeding of farmed animals with herbage from land to which organic fertilisers or soil improvers have been applied, in particular a modification of the waiting period as referred to in paragraph 1(c).

Those measures, designed to amend non-essential elements of this Regulation by supplementing it, shall be adopted in accordance with the regulatory procedure with scrutiny referred to in Article 52(4).

Section 2
Disposal and use

Article 12

Disposal and use of Category 1 material

Category 1 material shall be:

(a) disposed of as waste by incineration:
  - (i) directly without prior processing; or
  - (ii) following processing, by pressure sterilisation if the competent authority so requires, and permanent marking of the resulting material;

(b) recovered or disposed of by co-incineration, if the Category 1 material is waste:
  - (i) directly without prior processing; or
  - (ii) following processing, by pressure sterilisation if the competent authority so requires, and permanent marking of the resulting material;

(c) in the case of Category 1 material other than material referred to in Article 8(a)(i) and (ii), disposed of by processing by pressure sterilisation, permanent marking of the resulting material and burial in an authorised landfill;

(d) in the case of Category 1 material referred to in Article 8(f), disposed of by burial in an authorised landfill;

(e) used as a fuel for combustion with or without prior processing; or

(f) used for the manufacture of derived products referred to in Articles 33, 34 and 36 and placed on the market in accordance with those Articles.

Article 13

Disposal and use of Category 2 material

Category 2 material shall be:

(a) disposed of as waste by incineration:
  - (i) directly without prior processing; or
  - (ii) following processing, by pressure sterilisation if the competent authority so requires, and permanent marking of the resulting material;

(b) recovered or disposed of by co-incineration, if the Category 2 material is waste:
  - (i) directly without prior processing; or
  - (ii) following processing, by pressure sterilisation if the competent authority so requires, and permanent marking of the resulting material;

(c) disposed of in an authorised landfill, following processing by pressure sterilisation and permanent marking of the resulting material;

(d) used for the manufacturing of organic fertilisers or soil improvers to be placed on the market in accordance with Article 32 following processing by pressure sterilisation, when applicable, and permanent marking of the resulting material;

(e) composted or transformed into biogas:

(i) following processing by pressure sterilisation and permanent marking of the resulting material; or

(ii) in the case of manure, digestive tract and its content, milk, milk-based products, colostrum, eggs and egg products which the competent authority does not consider to present a risk for the spread of any serious transmissible disease, following or without prior processing;

(f) applied to land without processing, in the case of manure, digestive tract content separated from the digestive tract, milk, milk-based products and colostrum which the competent authority does not consider to present a risk for the spread of any serious transmissible disease;

(g) in the case of material originating from aquatic animals, ensiled, composted or transformed into biogas;

(h) used as a fuel for combustion with or without prior processing; or

(i) used for the manufacture of derived products referred to in Articles 33, 34 and 36 and placed on the market in accordance with those Articles.

Article 14

Disposal and use of Category 3 material

Category 3 material shall be:

(a) disposed of as waste by incineration, with or without prior processing;

(b) recovered or disposed of by co-incineration, with or without prior processing, if the Category 3 material is waste;

(c) disposed of in an authorised landfill, following processing;

(d) processed, except in the case of Category 3 material which has changed through decomposition or spoilage so as to present an unacceptable risk to public or animal health, through that product, and used:

(i) for the manufacturing of feed for farmed animals other than fur animals, to be placed on the market in accordance with Article 31, except in the case of material referred to in Article 10(n), (o) and (p);

(ii) for the manufacturing of feed for fur animals, to be placed on the market in accordance with Article 36;

(iii) for the manufacturing of pet food, to be placed on the market in accordance with Article 35; or

(iv) for the manufacturing of organic fertilisers or soil improvers, to be placed on the market in accordance with Article 32;

(e) used for the production of raw petfood, to be placed on the market in accordance with Article 35;

(f) composted or transformed into biogas;

(g) in the case of material originating from aquatic animals, ensiled, composted or transformed into biogas;

(h) in the case of shells from shellfish, other than those referred to in Article 2(2)(f), and egg shells, used under conditions determined by the competent authority which prevent risks arising to public and animal health;

(i) used as a fuel for combustion with or without prior processing;

(j) used for the manufacture of derived products referred to in Articles 33, 34 and 36 and placed on the market in accordance with those Articles;

(k) in the case of catering waste referred to in Article 10(p) processed by pressure sterilisation or by processing methods referred to in point (b) of the first subparagraph of Article 15(1) or composted or transformed into biogas; or

(l) applied to land without processing, in the case of raw milk, colostrum and products derived therefrom, which the competent authority does not consider to present a risk of any disease communicable through those products to humans or animals.

Article 15

Implementing measures

1. Measures for the implementation of this Section may be laid down relating to the following:
(a) special conditions for the on-board handling and the disposal of material derived from on-board evisceration of fish showing signs of disease, including parasites, that are communicable to humans;
(b) processing methods for animal by-products other than pressure sterilisation, in particular as regards the parameters to be applied for those processing methods, in particular the time, temperature, pressure and size of particles;
(c) parameters for the transformation of animal by-products, including catering waste, into biogas or compost;
(d) conditions for the incineration and co-incineration of animal by-products and derived products;
(e) conditions for the combustion of animal by-products and derived products;
(f) conditions for the generation and handling of animal by-products referred to in Article 10(c);
(g) ensilage of material originating from aquatic animals;
(h) permanent marking of animal by-products;
(i) the application to land of certain animal by-products, organic fertilisers and soil improvers;
(j) the use of certain animal by-products for feeding to farmed animals; and
(k) the level of risk to public or animal health with respect to certain material which is considered as unacceptable as referred to in Article 14(d).

Those measures designed to amend non-essential elements of this Regulation, by supplementing it, shall be adopted in accordance with the regulatory procedure with scrutiny referred to in Article 52(4).

2. Pending the adoption of rules referred to:
(a) in points (c), (f) and (g) of the first subparagraph of paragraph 1, Member States may adopt or maintain national rules for:
  (i) the generation and handling of animal by-products referred to in Article 10(c);
  (ii) the transformation of animal by-products referred to in Article 10(p); and
  (iii) for the ensilage of material originating from aquatic animals;
(b) in point (a) of the first subparagraph of paragraph 1, animal by-products referred to therein may be disposed of at sea, without prejudice to Community environmental legislation.

Section 3
Derogations

Article 16

Derogations

By way of derogation from Articles 12, 13 and 14, animal by-products may be:
(a) in the case of animal by-products referred to in point (a) of the first subparagraph of Article 15(1), handled and disposed of in accordance with special conditions laid down pursuant to that point;
(b) used for research and other specific purposes in accordance with Article 17;
(c) in the case of animal by-products referred to in Article 18, used for special feeding purposes in accordance with that Article;

(d) in the case of animal by-products referred to in Article 19, disposed of in accordance with that Article;
(e) disposed of or used in accordance with alternative methods which have been authorised in accordance with Article 20, based on parameters which may include pressure sterilisation or other requirements of this Regulation or the implementing measures thereof;
(f) in the case of Category 2 and Category 3 materials and if authorised by the competent authority, used for the preparation and application to land of bio-dynamic preparations as referred to in Article 12(1)(c) of Regulation (EC) No 834/2007;
(g) in the case of Category 3 material and, if authorised by the competent authority, used for feeding to pet animals;
(h) in the case of animal by-products, except for Category 1 material, which arise in the course of surgical intervention on live animals or during birth of animals on farm and, if authorised by the competent authority, disposed of on that farm.

Article 17

Research and other specific purposes

1. The competent authority may, by way of derogation from Articles 12, 13 and 14, authorise the use of animal by-products and derived products for exhibitions, artistic activities, and for diagnostic, educational or research purposes under conditions which ensure the control of risks to public and animal health.

Such conditions shall include:
(a) the prohibition of any subsequent use of the animal by-products or derived products for other purposes; and
(b) the obligation to dispose of the animal by-products or derived products safely, or to re-dispatch them to their place of origin, if appropriate.

2. In the case of risks to public and animal health which require the adoption of measures for the whole territory of the Community, in particular in the case of newly emerging risks, harmonised conditions for the import and use of the animal by-products and derived products referred to in paragraph 1 may be laid down. Such conditions may include requirements regarding storage, packaging, identification, transport and disposal.

Those measures, designed to amend non-essential elements of this Regulation by supplementing it, shall be adopted in accordance with the regulatory procedure with scrutiny referred to in Article 52(4).

Article 18

Special feeding purposes

1. The competent authority may, by way of derogation from Articles 13 and 14, authorise, under conditions which ensure the control of risks to public and animal health, the collection and use of Category 2 material, provided that it comes from animals which were not killed or did not die as a result of the presence or suspected presence of a disease communicable to humans or animals, and of Category 3 material for feeding to:
(a) zoo animals;
(b) circus animals;
(c) reptiles and birds of prey other than zoo or circus animals;
(d) fur animals;
(e) wild animals;
(f) dogs from recognised kennels or packs of hounds;
(g) dogs and cats in shelters;
(h) maggots and worms for fishing bait.

2. The competent authority may authorise, by way of derogation from Article 12, and in accordance with the conditions laid down pursuant to paragraph 3 of this Article:

(a) the feeding of the Category 1 material referred to in Article 8(b)(ii) and of material derived from zoo animals for feeding to zoo animals; and

(b) the feeding of the Category 1 material referred to in Article 8(b)(ii) to endangered or protected species of necrophagous birds and other species living in their natural habitat, for the promotion of biodiversity.

3. Measures for the implementation of this Article may be laid down relating to the following:

(a) conditions under which the collection and use as referred to in paragraph 1 may be authorised with respect to the movement, storage and use of Category 2 material and of Category 3 material for feeding, including in the case of newly emerging risks; and

(b) conditions under which, in certain cases by way of derogation from the obligation laid down in Article 21(1), the feeding of Category 1 material as referred to in paragraph 2 of this Article may be authorised, including:

  (i) the endangered or protected species of necrophagous birds and other species in certain Member States to which such material may be fed;

  (ii) measures to prevent risks to public and animal health.

Those measures, designed to amend non-essential elements of this Regulation by supplementing it, shall be adopted in accordance with the regulatory procedure with scrutiny referred to in Article 52(4).

Article 19

Collection, transport and disposal

1. The competent authority may, by way of derogation from Articles 12, 13, 14 and 21, authorise the disposal:

(a) by burial of dead pet animals and equidae;

(b) by burning or burial on site or by other means under official supervision which prevent the transmission of risks to public and animal health of Category 1 material referred to in Article 8(a)(v) and (b)(ii), Category 2 and Category 3 materials in remote areas;

(c) by burning or burial on site or by other means under official supervision which prevent the transmission of risks to public and animal health of Category 1 material referred to in Article 8(b)(ii), Category 2 and Category 3 materials in areas where access is practically impossible or where access would only be possible under circumstances, related to geographical or climatic reasons or due to a natural disaster, which would pose a risk to the health and safety of the personnel carrying out the collection or where access would necessitate the use of disproportionate means of collection;

(d) by means other than burning or burial on site, under official supervision, in the case of Category 2 and Category 3 materials which do not pose a risk to public and animal health, when the amounts of materials do not exceed a particular volume per week, this volume being determined in relation to the nature of the activities carried out and the species of origin of the animal by-products concerned;

(e) by burning or burial on site, under conditions which prevent the transmission of risks to public and animal health, of animal by-products other than Category 1 material referred to in Article 8(a)(i) in the event of an outbreak of a notifiable disease, if transport to the nearest plant approved for processing or disposal of the animal by-products would increase the danger of propagation of health risks or, in case of a widespread outbreak of an epizootic disease, would mean that the disposal capacities of such plants were exceeded; and

(f) by burning or burial on site, under conditions which prevent the transmission of risks to public and animal health, of bees and apiculture by-products.

2. The animal population of a particular species in the remote areas referred to in paragraph 1(b) shall not exceed a maximum percentage of the animal population of this species in the Member State concerned.

3. Member States shall make available to the Commission information on:
(a) the areas that they categorise as remote areas for the purpose of applying paragraph 1(b) and the reasons for that categorisation, and updated information concerning any change to such categorisation; and
(b) the use they make of the authorisations provided for in points (c) and (d) of paragraph 1 with respect to Category 1 and Category 2 materials.

4. Measures for the implementation of this Article shall be laid down relating to the following:
(a) conditions aimed at ensuring control of risks to public and animal health in the event of burning and burial on site;
(b) the maximum percentage of the animal population as referred to in paragraph 2;
(c) the volume of animal by-products, in relation to the nature of activities and the species of origin, as referred to in paragraph 1(d); and
(d) the list of diseases referred to in paragraph 1(e).
Those measures, designed to amend non-essential elements of this Regulation by supplementing it, shall be adopted in accordance with the regulatory procedure with scrutiny referred to in Article 52(4).

Section 4
Alternative methods

Article 20

Authorisation of alternative methods

1. The procedure for authorisation of an alternative method of use or disposal of animal by-products or derived products may be initiated either by the Commission or, following an application, by a Member State or by an interested party, which may represent several interested parties.

2. Interested parties shall send their applications to the competent authority of the Member State where they intend to use the alternative method.

The competent authority shall evaluate, within a period of two months following receipt of a complete application, whether the application complies with the standard format for applications referred to in paragraph 10.

3. The competent authority shall communicate the applications of the Member States and interested parties, together with a report on its evaluation to the European Food Safety Authority (EFSA) and inform the Commission thereof.

4. When the Commission initiates the procedure for authorisation, it shall send a report on its evaluation to EFSA.

5. EFSA shall assess, within six months following receipt of a complete application, whether the method submitted ensures that risks to public or animal health are:
(a) controlled in a manner which prevents their proliferation before disposal in accordance with this Regulation or the implementing measures thereof; or
(b) reduced to a degree which is at least equivalent, for the relevant category of animal by-products, to the processing methods laid down pursuant to point (b) of the first subparagraph of Article 15(1).
EFSA shall issue an opinion on the application submitted.

6. In duly justified cases where EFSA requests additional information from applicants, the period provided for in paragraph 5 may be extended.

After consulting the Commission or the applicant, EFSA shall decide on a period within which that information shall be provided to it and inform the Commission and the applicant as appropriate of the additional period needed.

7. Where applicants wish to submit additional information on their own initiative, they shall send it directly to EFSA.

In that case the period provided for in paragraph 5 shall not be extended by an additional period.

8. EFSA shall forward its opinion to the Commission, the applicant and the competent authority of the Member State concerned.

9. Within three months following receipt of the opinion of EFSA and taking account of that opinion, the Commission shall inform the applicant of the proposed measure to be adopted in accordance with paragraph 11.

10. A standard format for applications for alternative methods shall be adopted in accordance with the advisory procedure referred to in Article 52(2).

11. Following receipt of the opinion of EFSA, the following shall be adopted:

(a) either a measure authorising an alternative method of use or disposal of animal by-products or derived products; or

(b) a measure rejecting the authorisation of such an alternative method.

Those measures, designed to amend non-essential elements of this Regulation by supplementing it, shall be adopted in accordance with the regulatory procedure with scrutiny referred to in Article 52(4).

Title II
Obligations of operators

Chapter I
General obligations

Section 1
Collection, transport and traceability

Article 21

Collection and identification as regards category and transport

1. Operators shall collect, identify and transport animal by-products without undue delay under conditions which prevent risks arising to public and animal health.

2. Operators shall ensure that animal by-products and derived products are accompanied during transport by a commercial document or, when required by this Regulation or by a measure adopted in accordance with paragraph 6, by a health certificate.

By way of derogation from the first subparagraph, the competent authority may authorise the transport of manure between two points located on the same farm or between farms and users of manure within the same Member State without a commercial document or health certificate.

3. Commercial documents and health certificates accompanying animal by-products or derived products during transport shall at least include information on the origin, the destination and the quantity of such products, and a description of the animal by-products or derived products and their marking, when such marking is required by this Regulation.

However, for animal by-products and derived products transported within the territory of a Member State, the competent authority of the Member State concerned may authorise transmission of the information referred to in the first subparagraph by way of an alternative system.

4. Operators shall collect, transport and dispose of Category 3 catering waste, in accordance with national measures foreseen in Article 13 of Directive 2008/98/EC.

5. The following shall be adopted in accordance with the regulatory procedure referred to in Article 52(3):

(a) models for commercial documents which are required to accompany animal by-products during transport; and

(b) models for health certificates and the conditions governing the way they must accompany animal by-products and derived products during transport.

6. Measures for the implementation of this Article may be laid down relating to the following:

(a) cases where a health certificate is required, having regard to the level of risk to public and animal health arising from certain derived products;

(b) cases where, by way of derogation from the first subparagraph of paragraph 2 and having regard to the low level of risk to public and animal health arising from certain animal by-products or derived products, transport of derived products may take place without the documents or certificates referred to in that paragraph;

(c) requirements for the identification, including labelling, and for the separation of different categories of animal by-products during transport; and

(d) conditions to prevent risks to public and animal health arising during the collection and transport of animal by-products, including conditions for the safe transport of those products with respect to containers, vehicles and packaging material.

Those measures, designed to amend non-essential elements of this Regulation by supplementing it, shall be adopted in accordance with the regulatory procedure with scrutiny referred to in Article 52(4).

Article 22

Traceability

1. Operators consigning, transporting or receiving animal by-products or derived products shall keep a record of consignments and related commercial documents or health certificates.

However, the first subparagraph shall not apply when an authorisation to transport animal by-products or derived products without commercial documents or health certificates has been granted in accordance with the second subparagraph of Article 21(2) or in accordance with implementing measures adopted under Article 21(6)(b).

2. The operators referred to in paragraph 1 shall have in place systems and procedures to identify:

(a) the other operators to which their animal by-products or derived products have been supplied; and

(b) the operators from whom they have been supplied.

This information shall be made available to the competent authorities on request.

3. Measures for the implementation of this Article may be adopted in accordance with the regulatory procedure referred to in Article 52(3), in particular on:

(a) the information to be made available to the competent authorities;

(b) the period of time during which this information must be kept.

Section 2
Registration and approval

Article 23

Registration of operators, establishments or plants

1. With a view to registration, operators shall:

(a) before commencing operations, notify the competent authority of any establishments or plants under their control which are active at any stage of the generation, transport, handling, processing, storage, placing on the market, distribution, use or disposal of animal by-products and derived products;

(b) provide the competent authority with information on:
  (i) the category of animal by-products or derived products under their control;
  (ii) the nature of the operations performed using animal by-products or derived products as starting material.

2. Operators shall provide the competent authority with up-to-date information on any establishments or plants under their control as referred to in point (a) of paragraph 1, including any significant change in activities such as any closure of an existing establishment or plant.

3. Detailed rules regarding registration as referred to in paragraph 1 may be adopted in accordance with the regulatory procedure referred to in Article 52(3).

4. By way of derogation from paragraph 1, no notification with a view to registration shall be required for activities with respect to which establishments generating animal by-products have already been approved or registered in accordance with Regulation (EC) No 852/2004 or Regulation (EC) No 853/2004; and for activities with respect to which establishments or plants have already been approved in accordance with Article 24 of this Regulation.

The same derogation shall apply for the activities involving the generation of animal by-products on site only, which are carried out on farms or other premises where animals are kept, bred or taken care of.

Article 24

Approval of establishments or plants

1. Operators shall ensure that establishments or plants under their control are approved by the competent authority, where such establishments or plants carry out one or more of the following activities:

(a) processing of animal by-products by pressure sterilisation, by processing methods referred to in point (b) of the first subparagraph of Article 15(1) or by alternative methods authorised in accordance with Article 20;

(b) disposal, as waste, by incineration of animal by-products and derived products, excluding establishments or plants which have a permit to operate in accordance with Directive 2000/76/EC;

(c) disposal or recovery of animal by-products and derived products, if they are waste, by co-incineration, excluding establishments or plants which have a permit to operate in accordance with Directive 2000/76/EC;

(d) use of animal by-products and derived products as fuel for combustion;

(e) manufacturing of pet food;

(f) manufacturing of organic fertilisers and soil improvers;

(g) transformation of animal by-products and/or derived products into biogas or compost;

(h) handling of animal by-products after their collection, by way of operations such as sorting, cutting, chilling, freezing, salting, removal of hides and skins or of specified risk material;

(i) storage of animal by-products;

(j) storage of derived products intended to be:
  (i) disposed of by landfill or incineration or intended to be recovered or disposed of by co-incineration;
  (ii) used as fuel for combustion;
  (iii) used as feed, excluding establishments or plants approved or registered in accordance with Regulation (EC) No 183/2005;
  (iv) used as organic fertilisers and soil improvers, excluding storage at a place of direct application.

2. The approval referred to in paragraph 1 shall specify if the establishment or plant is approved for operations with animal by-products and/or derived products of:
(a) a particular category referred to in Articles 8, 9 or 10; or
(b) more than one category referred to in Articles 8, 9 or 10, indicating if such operations are carried out:
  (i) permanently under conditions of strict separation which prevent any risk to public and animal health; or
  (ii) temporarily under conditions which prevent contamination, in response to a shortage of capacity for such products arising due to:
    — a widespread outbreak of an epizootic disease, or
    — other extraordinary and unforeseen circumstances.

Article 25

General hygiene requirements

1. Operators shall ensure that establishments or plants under their control carrying out the activities referred to in Article 24(1)(a) and (h):
(a) are constructed in a way permitting their effective cleaning and disinfection and where appropriate the construction of floors facilitates the draining of liquids;
(b) have access to adequate facilities for personal hygiene such as lavatories, changing rooms and washbasins for staff;
(c) have appropriate arrangements for protection against pests, such as insects, rodents and birds;
(d) keep installations and equipment in good condition and ensure that measuring equipment is calibrated regularly; and
(e) have appropriate arrangements for the cleaning and the disinfection of containers and vehicles in place to avoid risks of contamination.

2. Any person working in the establishment or plant referred to in paragraph 1 shall wear suitable, clean and, where necessary, protective clothing.

Where appropriate in a particular establishment or plant:
(a) persons working in the unclean sector shall not enter the clean sector without first changing their work clothes and shoes or without having disinfected them;
(b) equipment and machinery shall not be moved from the unclean to the clean sector without first being cleaned and disinfected; and
(c) the operator shall establish a procedure relating to the movements of persons in order to monitor their movements and describe the correct use of footbaths and wheel baths.

3. In establishments or plants carrying out the activities referred to in Article 24(1)(a):
(a) animal by-products shall be handled in such a way as to avoid risks of contamination;
(b) animal by-products shall be processed as soon as possible. After processing, derived products shall be handled and stored in such a way as to avoid risks of contamination;
(c) where appropriate, during any processing applied to animal by-products and derived products every part of the animal by-product and derived products shall be treated to a given temperature for a given period of time and risks of re-contamination shall be prevented;
(d) the operators shall check regularly the applicable parameters, particularly temperature, pressure, time, size of particles, where appropriate by automatic devices;
(e) cleaning procedures shall be established and documented for all parts of the establishments or plants.

Article 26

Handling of animal by-products within food businesses

1. The treatment, processing or storage of animal by-products in establishments or plants approved or registered in accordance with Article 4 of Regulation (EC) No 853/2004 or

in accordance with Article 6 of Regulation (EC) No 852/2004 shall be carried out under conditions which prevent cross-contamination and if appropriate in a dedicated part of the establishment or plant.

2. Raw materials for the production of gelatine and collagen not intended for human consumption may be stored, treated or processed in the establishments specifically authorised in accordance with Regulation (EC) No 853/2004, Annex III, Section XIV, Chapter I, point 5, and Section XV, Chapter I, point 5, provided the transmission of disease risk is prevented by segregation of such raw materials from the raw materials for the production of products of animal origin.

3. Paragraphs 1 and 2 shall apply without prejudice to more specific requirements laid down in Community veterinary legislation.

Article 27

Implementing measures

Measures for the implementation of this Section and Section 1 of this Chapter shall be laid down relating to the following:

(a) infrastructure and equipment requirements applicable within establishments or plants;

(b) hygiene requirements applicable to all types of handling of animal by-products and derived products, including measures modifying hygiene requirements for establishments or plants referred to in Article 25(1);

(c) conditions and technical requirements for the handling, treatment, transformation, processing and storage of animal by-products or derived products and conditions for treatment of waste water;

(d) evidence to be presented by the operator for the purpose of validation of the treatment, transformation and processing of animal by-products or derived products, on their ability to prevent public and animal health risks;

(e) conditions for the handling of animal by-products or derived products of more than one category referred to in Articles 8, 9 or 10 in the same establishment or plant:
  (i) where such operations are carried out separately;
  (ii) where such operations are carried out temporarily in certain circumstances;

(f) conditions for the prevention of cross-contamination when animal by-products are stored, treated or processed in a dedicated part of an establishment or plant referred to in Article 26;

(g) standard transformation parameters for biogas and composting plants;

(h) requirements applicable to the incineration or co-incineration in plants of high and low capacity as referred to in Article 24(1)(b) and (c); and

(i) requirements applicable to the combustion of animal by-products and derived products as referred to in Article 24(1)(d).

Those measures, designed to amend non-essential elements of this Regulation by supplementing it shall be adopted in accordance with the regulatory procedure with scrutiny referred to in Article 52(4).

Section 3
Own checks and hazard analysis and critical control points

Article 28

Own checks

Operators shall put in place, implement and maintain own checks in their establishments or plants in order to monitor compliance with this Regulation. They shall ensure that no animal by-products or derived products suspected or discovered not to comply with this Regulation leave the establishment or plant, unless destined for disposal.

Article 29

Hazard analysis and critical control points

1. Operators carrying out one of the following activities shall put in place, implement and maintain a permanent written procedure or procedures based on the hazard analysis and critical control points (HACCP) principles for the:
(a) processing of animal by-products;
(b) transformation of animal by-products into biogas and compost;
(c) handling and storage of more than one category of animal by-products or derived products in the same establishment or plant;
(d) manufacturing of pet food.

2. Operators as specified in paragraph 1 shall in particular:
(a) identify any hazards that must be prevented, eliminated or reduced to acceptable levels;
(b) identify the critical control points at the step or steps at which control is essential to prevent or eliminate a hazard or reduce it to acceptable levels;
(c) establish critical limits at critical control points which separate acceptability from unacceptability, for the prevention, elimination or reduction of identified hazards;
(d) establish and implement effective monitoring procedures at critical control points;
(e) establish corrective action when monitoring indicates that a critical control point is not under control;
(f) establish procedures to verify that the measures outlined in points (a) to (e) are complete and working effectively. Verification procedures shall be carried out regularly;
(g) establish documents and records commensurate with the nature and size of the businesses to demonstrate the effective application of the measures set out in points (a) to (f).

3. When any modification is made to a product, process or any stage of production, processing, storage or distribution, operators shall review their procedures and make the necessary changes.

4. Measures to facilitate the implementation of this Article may be adopted in accordance with the regulatory procedure referred to in Article 52(3).

Article 30

National guides to good practice

1. Where necessary, competent authorities shall encourage the development, dissemination and voluntary use of national guides to good practice in particular for the application of HACCP principles as referred to in Article 29. Operators may use such guides on a voluntary basis.

2. The competent authority shall assess national guides to ensure that:
(a) they have been developed in consultation with representatives of parties whose interests may be substantially affected, and have been disseminated by sectors of operators; and
(b) their contents are practicable for the sectors to which they refer.

Chapter II
Placing on the market

Section 1
Animal by-products and derived products for feeding to farmed animals excluding fur animals

Article 31

Placing on the market

1. Animal by-products and derived products destined for feeding to farmed animals, excluding fur animals, may only be placed on the market provided:

(a) they are or they are derived from Category 3 material other than material referred to in Article 10(n), (o) and (p);
(b) they have been collected or processed, as applicable, in accordance with the conditions for pressure sterilisation or other conditions to prevent risks arising to public and animal health in accordance with measures adopted pursuant to Article 15 and any measures which have been laid down in accordance with paragraph 2 of this Article; and
(c) they come from approved or registered establishments or plants, as applicable for the animal by-product or derived product concerned.

2. Measures for the implementation of this Article may be laid down relating to the public and animal health conditions for the collection, processing and treatment of animal by-products and derived products referred to in paragraph 1.

Those measures, designed to amend non-essential elements of this Regulation by supplementing it, shall be adopted in accordance with the regulatory procedure with scrutiny referred to in Article 52(4).

Section 2
Organic fertilisers and soil improvers

Article 32

Placing on the market and use

1. Organic fertilisers and soil improvers may be placed on the market and used provided:
(a) they are derived from Category 2 or Category 3 material;
(b) they have been produced in accordance with the conditions for pressure sterilisation or with other conditions to prevent risks arising to public and animal health, in accordance with the requirements laid down pursuant to Article 15 and any measures which have been laid down in accordance with paragraph 3 of this Article;
(c) they come from approved or registered establishments or plants, as applicable; and
(d) in the case of meat-and-bone meal derived from Category 2 material and processed animal proteins intended to be used as or in organic fertilisers and soil improvers, they have been mixed with a component to exclude the subsequent use of the mixture for feeding purposes and marked when required by measures adopted under paragraph 3.

In addition, digestion residues from transformation into biogas or compost may be placed on the market and used as organic fertilisers or soil improvers.

Member States may adopt or maintain national rules imposing additional conditions for or restricting the use of organic fertilisers and soil improvers, provided that such rules are justified on grounds of the protection of public and animal health.

2. By way of derogation from point (d) of paragraph 1, mixing shall not be required for materials whose use for feeding purposes is excluded due to their composition or packaging.

3. Measures for the implementation of this Article may be laid down relating to the following:
(a) public and animal health conditions for the production and use of organic fertilisers and soil improvers;
(b) components or substances for the marking of organic fertilisers or soil improvers;
(c) components to be mixed with organic fertilisers or soil improvers;
(d) supplementary conditions, such as the methods to be used for marking and the minimum proportions to be observed when preparing the mixture, in order to exclude the use of such fertilisers or soil improvers for feeding purposes; and
(e) cases where the composition or packaging allows the materials to be exempted from the mixing requirement.

Those measures, designed to amend non-essential elements of this Regulation by supplementing it, shall be adopted in accordance with the regulatory procedure with scrutiny referred to in Article 52(4).

Section 3
Derived products regulated by certain other Community legislation

Article 33

Placing on the market

Operators may place on the market the following derived products:
(a) cosmetic products as defined in Article 1(1) of Directive 76/768/EEC;
(b) active implantable medical devices as defined in Article 1(2)(c) of Directive 90/385/EEC;
(c) medical devices as defined in Article 1(2)(a) of Directive 93/42/EEC;
(d) in vitro diagnostic medical devices as defined in Article 1(2)(b) of Directive 98/79/EC;
(e) veterinary medicinal products as defined in Article 1(2) of Directive 2001/82/EC;
(f) medicinal products as defined in Article 1(2) of Directive 2001/83/EC.

Article 34

Manufacture

1. The import, collection and movement of animal by-products and derived products destined for establishments or plants for the manufacture of the derived products referred to in Article 33 and the manufacture of those derived products shall be carried out in accordance with the Community legislation referred to in that Article.

Unused material from such establishments or plants shall be disposed of in accordance with that legislation.

2. However, this Regulation shall apply where the Community legislation referred to in Article 33 does not provide for conditions controlling potential risks to public and animal health in accordance with the objectives of this Regulation.

Section 4
Other derived products

Article 35

Placing on the market of pet food

Operators may place pet food on the market provided:
(a) the products are derived:
    (i) from Category 3 material, other than material referred to in Article 10(n), (o) and (p);
    (ii) in the case of imported pet food or of pet food produced from imported materials, from Category 1 material referred to in Article 8(c), subject to conditions laid down pursuant to point (a) of the first paragraph of Article 40; or
    (iii) in the case of raw petfood, from material referred to in Article 10(a) and (b)(i) and (ii); and
(b) they ensure the control of risks to public and animal health by safe treatment in accordance with Article 38, where safe sourcing in accordance with Article 37 does not ensure sufficient control.

Article 36

Placing on the market of other derived products

Operators may place on the market derived products, other than the products referred to in Articles 31, 32, 33 and 35, provided:

(a) those products are:
  (i) not intended for use for the feeding to farmed animals or for application to land from which such animals are to be fed; or
  (ii) intended for feeding to fur animals; and
(b) they ensure the control of risks to public and animal health by:
  (i) safe sourcing in accordance with Article 37;
  (ii) safe treatment in accordance with Article 38, where safe sourcing does not ensure sufficient control; or
  (iii) verifying that the products are only used for safe end uses in accordance with Article 39 where safe treatment does not ensure sufficient control.

Article 37

Safe sourcing

1. Safe sourcing shall include the use of material:
(a) from which no unacceptable risks to public and animal health arise;
(b) which has been collected and transported from the point of collection to the manufacturing establishment or plant under conditions which exclude risks to public and animal health; or
(c) which has been imported into the Community and transported from the point of first entry to the manufacturing establishment or plant under conditions which exclude risks to public and animal health.

2. For the purpose of safe sourcing, operators shall provide documentation of the requirements of paragraph 1, including, where necessary, proof of the safety of bio-security measures taken in order to exclude risks arising to public and animal health from starting material.

Such documentation shall be kept available to the competent authority upon request.

In the case referred to in point (c) of paragraph 1, the consignments shall be accompanied by a health certificate corresponding to a model adopted in accordance with the regulatory procedure referred to in Article 52(3).

Article 38

Safe treatment

Safe treatment shall include application of a manufacturing process to the material used which reduces to an acceptable level risks to public and animal health arising from the material used or from other substances resulting from the manufacturing process.

It shall be ensured that the derived product poses no unacceptable risks to public and animal health, in particular by means of testing of the end product.

Article 39

Safe end uses

Safe end uses shall include the use of derived products:
(a) under conditions which pose no unacceptable risks to public and animal health; or
(b) which may pose a risk to public and animal health, for specific purposes provided that such use is justified by objectives set out in Community legislation, in particular for the protection of public and animal health.

Article 40

Implementing measures

Measures for the implementation of this Section may be laid down relating to the following:

(a) conditions for the placing on the market of imported pet food or of pet food produced from imported materials, from Category 1 material referred to in Article 8(c);
(b) conditions for the safe sourcing and movement of material to be used under conditions which exclude risks to public and animal health;
(c) documentation as referred to in the first subparagraph of Article 37(2);
(d) parameters for the manufacturing process as referred to in the first paragraph of Article 38, in particular as regards the application of physical or chemical treatments to the material used;
(e) testing requirements applicable to the end product; and
(f) conditions for the safe use of derived products which pose a risk to public or animal health.

Those measures, designed to amend non-essential elements of this Regulation by supplementing it, shall be adopted in accordance with the regulatory procedure with scrutiny referred to in Article 52(4).

Chapter III
Import, transit and export

Article 41

Import and transit

1. Animal by-products and derived products shall be imported into, or sent in transit through, the Community in accordance with:
(a) the relevant requirements of this Regulation and the implementing measures thereof for the particular animal by-product or derived product which are at least as stringent as those applicable to the production and marketing of such animal by-products or derived products within the Community;
(b) conditions recognised to be at least equivalent to the requirements applicable to the production and marketing of such animal by-products or derived products under Community legislation; or
(c) in the case of animal by-products and derived products referred to in Articles 33, 35 and 36, the requirements set out in those Articles.

The measures referred to in point (b) of the first subparagraph, designed to amend non-essential elements of this Regulation by supplementing it, shall be adopted in accordance with the regulatory procedure with scrutiny referred to in Article 52(4).

2. By way of derogation from paragraph 1, the import and transit of:
(a) specified risk material shall take place only in accordance with Regulation (EC) No 999/2001;
(b) animal by-products or derived products mixed or contaminated with any waste listed as hazardous in Decision 2000/532/EC shall take place only subject to the requirements of Regulation (EC) No 1013/2006;
(c) Category 1 material, Category 2 material and products derived therefrom which are not intended for the manufacture of derived products referred to in Articles 33, 35 and 36, shall only take place provided that rules for their import have been adopted in accordance with Article 42(2)(a);
(d) animal by-products and derived products destined for the purposes referred to in Article 17(1) shall take place in accordance with national measures which ensure the control of risks to public and animal health, pending the adoption of harmonised conditions referred to in Article 17(2).

3. In the case of import and transit of Category 3 material and products derived therefrom, the relevant requirements as referred to in point (a) of the first subparagraph of paragraph 1 shall be laid down.

Those requirements may specify that consignments:

(a) must come from a third country or part of a third country listed in accordance with paragraph 4;

(b) must come from establishments or plants approved or registered by the competent authority of the third country of origin and listed by that authority for that purpose; and

(c) must be accompanied at the point of entry into the Community where the veterinary checks take place by documentation such as a commercial document or a health certificate and where appropriate by a declaration, which corresponds to a model laid down pursuant to point (d) of the first subparagraph of Article 42(2).

Those measures, designed to amend non-essential elements of this Regulation by supplementing it, shall be adopted in accordance with the regulatory procedure with scrutiny referred to in Article 52(4).

Pending the adoption of the requirements referred to in points (a) and (c) of the second subparagraph, the Member States shall specify those requirements in national measures.

4. Lists of third countries or parts of third countries from which animal by-products or derived products may be imported or transit through the Community shall be drawn up in accordance with the regulatory procedure referred to in Article 52(3), taking into account in particular:

(a) the legislation of the third country;

(b) the organisation of the competent authority and its inspection services in the third country, the powers of those services, the supervision to which they are subject, and their authority to monitor effectively the application of their legislation;

(c) the actual health conditions applied to the production, manufacture, handling, storage and dispatch of products of animal origin intended for the Community;

(d) the assurances the third country can give regarding compliance with the relevant health conditions;

(e) experience of marketing the product from the third country and the results of import checks carried out;

(f) the result of any Community inspections in the third country;

(g) the health status of the livestock, other domestic animals and wildlife in the third country, having particular regard to exotic animal diseases and any aspects of the general health situation in the country which might pose a risk to public or animal health in the Community;

(h) the regularity and speed with which the third country supplies information about the existence of infectious animal diseases in its territory, in particular the diseases listed in the Terrestrial Animal Health Code and the Aquatic Animal Health Code of the World Organisation for Animal Health;

(i) the regulations on the prevention and control of infectious animal diseases in force in the third country and their implementation, including rules on imports from other third countries.

The lists of establishments or plants referred to in point (b) of the second subparagraph of paragraph 3 shall be kept up to date and communicated to the Commission and the Member States and made available to the public.

Article 42

Implementing measures

1. Measures for the implementation of Article 41 which may exclude animal by-products or derived products manufactured in certain establishments or plants from import or transit in order to protect public or animal health shall be adopted in accordance with the regulatory procedure referred to in Article 52(3).

2. Other measures for the implementation of Article 41 shall be laid down relating to the following:

(a) conditions for the import and transit of Category 1 and Category 2 materials and for products derived therefrom;
(b) restrictions regarding public or animal health applicable to imported Category 3 material or products derived therefrom which may be laid down by reference to Community lists of third countries or parts of third countries drawn up in accordance with Article 41(4) or for other public or animal health purposes;
(c) conditions for the manufacture of animal by-products or derived products in establishments or plants in third countries; such conditions may include the arrangements for controls of such establishments or plants by the competent authority concerned and may exempt certain types of establishments or plants handling animal by-products or derived products from approval or registration as referred to in point (b) of the second subparagraph of Article 41(3); and
(d) models for health certificates, commercial documents and declarations which are to accompany consignments, specifying the conditions under which it can be stated that the animal by-products or derived products concerned have been collected or manufactured in accordance with the requirements of this Regulation.

Those measures, designed to amend non-essential elements of this Regulation by supplementing it, shall be adopted in accordance with the regulatory procedure with scrutiny referred to in Article 52(4).

Article 43

Export

1. The export of animal by-products and derived products destined for incineration or landfill shall be prohibited.

2. The export of animal by-products and derived products to third countries which are not members of the OECD for use in a biogas or composting plant shall be prohibited.

3. Category 1 material, Category 2 material and products derived therefrom shall only be exported for purposes other than those referred to in paragraphs 1 and 2 provided that rules for their export have been laid down.

Those measures, designed to amend non-essential elements of this Regulation by supplementing it, shall be adopted in accordance with the regulatory procedure with scrutiny referred to in Article 52(4).

4. Article 12 of Regulation (EC) No 178/2002 concerning food and feed exported from the Community shall apply mutatis mutandis to the export of Category 3 material or products derived therefrom in compliance with this Regulation.

5. By way of derogation from paragraphs 3 and 4, the export of:
(a) specified risk material shall take place only in accordance with Regulation (EC) No 999/2001;
(b) animal by-products or derived products mixed or contaminated with any waste listed as hazardous in Decision 2000/532/EC shall take place only subject to the requirements of Regulation (EC) No 1013/2006.

Title III
Official controls and final provisions

Chapter I
Official controls

Article 44

Procedure for approval

1. The competent authority shall approve establishments or plants only where an on site visit, prior to start-up of any activity, has demonstrated that they meet the relevant requirements laid down in accordance with Article 27.

2. The competent authority may grant conditional approval if it appears, from the on site visit, that the establishment or plant meets all the infrastructure and equipment requirements with a view to ensuring the application of the operational procedures in compliance with this Regulation. It shall grant full approval only if it appears, from another on site visit carried out within three months of granting conditional approval, that the establishment or plant meets the other requirements referred to in paragraph 1. If clear progress has been made, but the establishment or plant still does not meet all of these requirements, the competent authority may extend conditional approval. However, conditional approval shall not exceed a total of six months.

3. Operators shall ensure that an establishment or plant ceases to operate if the competent authority withdraws its approval or in the case of conditional approval fails to extend it or to grant full approval.

Article 45

Official controls

1. Without prejudice to Article 5, the competent authority shall at regular intervals carry out official controls and supervision of the handling of animal by-products and derived products falling within the scope of this Regulation.

2. Articles 41 and 42 of Regulation (EC) No 882/2004 shall apply mutatis mutandis to official controls carried out to verify compliance with this Regulation.

3. The competent authority may take into account adherence to guides to good practice, when carrying out its official controls.

4. Detailed arrangements for implementing this Article, including rules concerning the reference methods for microbiological analyses, may be laid down.

Those measures, designed to amend non-essential elements of this Regulation by supplementing it, shall be adopted in accordance with the regulatory procedure with scrutiny referred to in Article 52(4).

Article 46

Suspensions, withdrawals and prohibitions on operations

1. If the official controls and supervision carried out by the competent authority reveal that one or more of the requirements of this Regulation are not met, it shall take appropriate action.

The competent authority shall in particular, as appropriate to the nature and to the gravity of the deficiencies and to the potential risks for public and animal health:

(a) suspend approvals of establishments or plants approved pursuant to this Regulation, if:

- (i) the conditions for approving or operating the establishment or plant are no longer fulfilled;
- (ii) the operator can be expected to remedy the deficiencies within a reasonable period of time; and
- (iii) the potential risks to public and animal health do not require action in accordance with point (b);

(b) withdraw approvals of establishments or plants approved pursuant to this Regulation, if:

- (i) the conditions for approving or operating the establishment or plant are no longer fulfilled; and
- (ii) the operator cannot be expected to remedy the deficiencies within a reasonable period of time:
  - — for reasons relating to the infrastructure of the establishment or plant,
  - — for reasons relating to the personal capacity of the operator or the staff under his supervision, or
  - — because of serious risks to public and animal health requiring major adjustments to the operation of the establishment or plant before the operator may apply for re-approval;

(c) impose specific conditions on establishments or plants in order to rectify existing deficiencies.

2. The competent authority shall, as appropriate to the nature and to the gravity of the deficiencies and to the potential risks for public and animal health, temporarily or permanently prohibit operators referred to in Articles 23(1) and (3) and Article 24(1) from carrying out operations under this Regulation, as appropriate, following receipt of information indicating:

(a) that the requirements of Community legislation are not met; and

(b) potential risks to public or animal health arising from such operations.

Article 47

Lists

1. Each Member State shall draw up a list of establishments, plants and operators which have been approved or registered in accordance with this Regulation within its territory.

It shall assign an official number to each approved or registered establishment, plant or operator, which identifies the establishment, plant or operator with respect to the nature of its activities.

Member States shall indicate, if applicable, an official number which has been assigned to the establishment, plant or operator under other Community legislation.

Member States shall make the lists of approved or registered establishments, plants and operators available to the Commission and other Member States.

Member States shall keep up-to-date the lists of approved or registered establishments, plants and operators and make them available to other Member States and to the public.

2. Measures for the implementation of this Article may be laid down in accordance with the regulatory procedure referred to in Article 52(3), in particular on:

(a) the format for the lists referred to in paragraph 1; and

(b) the procedure for making the lists referred to in paragraph 1 available.

Article 48

Controls for dispatch to other Member States

1. Where an operator intends to dispatch Category 1 material, Category 2 material and meat-and-bone meal or animal fat derived from Category 1 and Category 2 materials to another

Member State, it shall inform the competent authority of the Member State of origin and the competent authority of the Member State of destination.

The competent authority of the Member State of destination shall decide upon application by the operator, within a specified time period:

(a) to refuse receipt of the consignment;

(b) to accept the consignment unconditionally; or

(c) to make receipt of the consignment subject to the following conditions:

  (i) if the derived products have not undergone pressure sterilisation, it must undergo such treatment; or

  (ii) the animal by-products or derived products must comply with any conditions for the dispatch of the consignment which are justified for the protection of public and animal health in order to ensure that animal by-products and derived products are handled in accordance with this Regulation.

2. Formats for applications by operators referred to in paragraph 1 may be adopted in accordance with the regulatory procedure referred to in Article 52(3).

3. The competent authority of the Member State of origin shall inform the competent authority of the Member State of destination, by means of the Traces system in accordance with Decision 2004/292/EC, of the dispatch of each consignment sent to the Member State of destination, of

(a) animal by-products or derived products referred to in paragraph 1;

(b) processed animal protein derived from Category 3 material.

When informed of the dispatch, the competent authority of the Member State of destination shall inform the competent authority of the Member State of origin of the arrival of each consignment by means of the Traces system.

4. Category 1 and Category 2 materials, meat-and-bone meal and animal fat referred to in paragraph 1 shall be transported directly to the establishment or plant of destination, which must have been registered or approved in accordance with Articles 23, 24 and 44 or, in the case of manure, to the farm of destination.

5. When animal by-products or derived products are sent to other Member States via the territory of a third country, they shall be sent in consignments which have been sealed in the Member State of origin and shall be accompanied by a health certificate.

The sealed consignments shall re-enter the Community only via a border inspection post, in accordance with Article 6 of Directive 89/662/EEC.

6. By way of derogation from paragraphs 1 to 5, animal by-products or derived products referred to therein which have been mixed or contaminated with any waste listed as hazardous in Decision 2000/532/EC shall be sent to other Member States only subject to the requirements of Regulation (EC) No 1013/2006.

7. Measures for the implementation of this Article may be adopted relating to the following:

(a) a specified time period for the decision of the competent authority as referred to in paragraph 1;

(b) supplementary conditions for the dispatch of animal by-products or derived products referred to in paragraph 4;

(c) models for the health certificates which have to accompany consignments sent in accordance with paragraph 5; and

(d) conditions under which animal by-products or derived products intended to be used for exhibitions, artistic activities, for diagnostic, educational or research purposes may be sent to other Member States, by way of derogation from paragraph 1 to 5 of this Article.

Those measures, designed to amend non-essential elements of this Regulation by supplementing it, shall be adopted in accordance with the regulatory procedure with scrutiny referred to in Article 52(4).

8. Measures for the implementation of this Article may specify the conditions subject to which, by way of derogation from paragraphs 1 to 4, the competent authorities may allow:

(a) the dispatch of manure transported between two points located on the same farm or between farms located in the border regions of Member States sharing a common border;

(b) the dispatch of other animal by-products transported between establishments or plants located in the border regions of Member States sharing a common border; and

(c) the transport of a dead pet animal for incineration to an establishment or plant located in the border region of another Member State sharing a common border.

Those measures, designed to amend non-essential elements of this Regulation by supplementing it, shall be adopted in accordance with the regulatory procedure with scrutiny referred to in Article 52(4).

Article 49

Community controls in Member States

1. Experts from the Commission may make on-the-spot checks, in cooperation with the competent authorities of Member States, in so far as is necessary for the uniform application of this Regulation.

The Member State on whose territory the checks are made shall provide the experts with all the assistance necessary for carrying out their duties.

The Commission shall inform the competent authority of the results of the checks made.

2. Measures for the implementation of this Article may be adopted in accordance with the regulatory procedure referred to in Article 52(3), in particular on the procedure for the cooperation with national authorities.

Article 50

Application of Regulation (EC) No 882/2004 for the purposes of certain controls

1. Article 46 of Regulation (EC) No 882/2004 shall apply mutatis mutandis to Community controls in third countries carried out to verify compliance with this Regulation.

2. Article 50(1)(a) of Regulation (EC) No 882/2004 shall apply mutatis mutandis to the phased introduction of the requirements of Article 41(3) of this Regulation.

3. Article 52 of Regulation (EC) No 882/2004 shall apply mutatis mutandis to third-country controls in Member States related to operations under this Regulation.

Chapter II
Final provisions

Article 51

National provisions

Member States shall communicate to the Commission the text of the provisions of national law they adopt in areas under their competence which directly concern the proper implementation of this Regulation.

Article 52

Committee procedure

1. The Commission shall be assisted by the Standing Committee on the Food Chain and Animal Health established by Article 58(1) of Regulation (EC) No 178/2002.

2. Where reference is made to this paragraph, Articles 3 and 7 of Decision 1999/468/EC shall apply, having regard to the provisions of Article 8 thereof.

3. Where reference is made to this paragraph, Articles 5 and 7 of Decision 1999/468/EC shall apply, having regard to the provisions of Article 8 thereof.

The period laid down in Article 5(6) of Decision 1999/468/EC shall be set at three months.

4. Where reference is made to this paragraph, Article 5a(1) to (4) and Article 7 of Decision 1999/468/EC shall apply, having regard to the provisions of Article 8 thereof.

5. Where reference is made to this paragraph, Article 5a(1) to (4) and (5)(b) and Article 7 of Decision 1999/468/EC shall apply, having regard to the provisions of Article 8 thereof.

The time limits laid down in Article 5a(3)(c), (4)(b) and (4)(e) of Decision 1999/468/EC shall be two months, one month and two months respectively.

6. Where reference is made to this paragraph, Article 5a(1), (2), (4) and (6) and Article 7 of Decision 1999/468/EC shall apply, having regard to the provisions of Article 8 thereof.

Article 53

Penalties

The Member States shall lay down the rules on penalties applicable to infringements of this Regulation and shall take all measures necessary to ensure that they are implemented. The penalties provided for must be effective, proportionate and dissuasive. The Member States shall notify those provisions to the Commission by 4 June 2011 and shall notify it without delay of any subsequent amendment affecting them.

[*Article 54 is not reproduced.*]

Article 55

Transitional measure

Establishments, plants and users approved or registered in accordance with Regulation (EC) No 1774/2002 before 4 March 2011 shall be deemed to be approved or registered, as required, in accordance with this Regulation.

Article 56

Entry into force

This Regulation shall enter into force on the 20th day following its publication in the Official Journal of the European Union.

It shall apply from 4 March 2011.

This Regulation shall be binding in its entirety and directly applicable in all Member States.

ANNEX
CORRELATION TABLE

Regulation (EC) No 1774/2002	*This Regulation*
Article 1	Articles 1 and 2
Article 2	Article 3
Article 3(1)	Article 4(1) and(2)
Article 3(2)	Article 41(3), fourth subparagraph
Article 3(3)	Article 4(3), (4) and (5)
Article 4(1)	Article 8
Article 4(2)	Articles 12, 15 and 16
Article 4(3)	Article 24(h), (i) and (j)
Article 4(4)	Article 41(2)(c), Article 43(3) and (5)(a)
Article 5(1)	Article 9
Article 5(2)	Articles 13, 15 and 16
Article 5(3)	Article 24(h), (i) and (j)
Article 5(4)	Article 41(2)(c) and Article 43(3)
Article 6(1)	Article 10
Article 6(2)	Articles 14, 15 and 16
Article 6(3)	Article 24(h), (i) and (j)
Article 7	Article 21
Article 8	Article 48
Article 9	Article 22
Articles 10 to 15, 17 and 18	Articles 23, 24, 27 and 44
Article 16	Article 6
Article 19	Article 31
Article 20(1)	Articles 35 and 36
Article 20(2)	Article 32
Article 20(3)	Article 36
Article 21	—
Article 22	Article 11
Article 23	Articles 17 and 18
Article 24	Article 19
Article 25	Articles 28 and 29
Article 26	Articles 45, 46 and 47
Article 27	Article 49
Article 28	Article 35(a)(ii) and Article 41(1)
Article 29	Articles 41 and 42
Article 30	Article 41(1)(b)
Article 31	Article 50(1)
Article 32	—
Article 33	Article 52
Article 34	—
Article 35	Article 15(2) and Article 51
Article 36	—
Article 37	Article 54
Article 38	Article 56

DIRECTIVE 2010/31/EU OF THE EUROPEAN PARLIAMENT AND OF THE COUNCIL

of 19 May 2010

ON THE ENERGY PERFORMANCE OF BUILDINGS

THE EUROPEAN PARLIAMENT AND THE COUNCIL OF THE EUROPEAN UNION,

Having regard to the Treaty on the Functioning of the European Union, and in particular Article 194(2) thereof,

Having regard to the proposal from the European Commission,

Having regard to the opinion of the European Economic and Social Committee,

Having regard to the opinion of the Committee of the Regions,

Acting in accordance with the ordinary legislative procedure,

Whereas:

(1) Directive 2002/91/EC of the European Parliament and of the Council of 16 December 2002 on the energy performance of buildings has been amended. Since further substantive amendments are to be made, it should be recast in the interests of clarity.

(2) An efficient, prudent, rational and sustainable utilisation of energy applies, inter alia, to oil products, natural gas and solid fuels, which are essential sources of energy, but also the leading sources of carbon dioxide emissions.

(3) Buildings account for 40 % of total energy consumption in the Union. The sector is expanding, which is bound to increase its energy consumption. Therefore, reduction of energy consumption and the use of energy from renewable sources in the buildings sector constitute important measures needed to reduce the Union's energy dependency and greenhouse gas emissions. Together with an increased use of energy from renewable sources, measures taken to reduce energy consumption in the Union would allow the Union to comply with the Kyoto Protocol to the United Nations Framework Convention on Climate Change (UNFCCC), and to honour both its long term commitment to maintain the global temperature rise below 2 °C, and its commitment to reduce, by 2020, overall greenhouse gas emissions by at least 20 % below 1990 levels, and by 30 % in the event of an international agreement being reached. Reduced energy consumption and an increased use of energy from renewable sources also have an important part to play in promoting security of energy supply, technological developments and in creating opportunities for employment and regional development, in particular in rural areas.

(4) Management of energy demand is an important tool enabling the Union to influence the global energy market and hence the security of energy supply in the medium and long term.

(5) The European Council of March 2007 emphasised the need to increase energy efficiency in the Union so as to achieve the objective of reducing by 20 % the Union's energy consumption by 2020 and called for a thorough and rapid implementation of the priorities established in the Commission Communication entitled "Action plan for energy efficiency: realising the potential". That action plan identified the significant potential for cost-effective energy savings in the buildings sector. The European Parliament, in its resolution of 31 January 2008, called for the strengthening of the provisions of Directive 2002/91/EC, and has called at various times, on the latest occasion in its resolution of 3 February 2009 on the Second Strategic Energy Review, for the 20 % energy efficiency target in 2020 to be made binding. Moreover, Decision

No 406/2009/EC of the European Parliament and of the Council of 23 April 2009 on the effort of Member States to reduce their greenhouse gas emissions to meet the Community's greenhouse gas emission reduction commitments up to 2020, sets national binding targets for CO_2 reduction for which energy efficiency in the building sector will be crucial, and Directive 2009/28/EC of the European Parliament and of the Council of 23 April 2009 on the promotion of the use of energy from renewable sources provides for the promotion of energy efficiency in the context of a binding target for energy from renewable sources accounting for 20 % of total Union energy consumption by 2020.

(6) The European Council of March 2007 reaffirmed the Union's commitment to the Union-wide development of energy from renewable sources by endorsing a mandatory target of a 20 % share of energy from renewable sources by 2020. Directive 2009/28/EC establishes a common framework for the promotion of energy from renewable sources.

(7) It is necessary to lay down more concrete actions with a view to achieving the great unrealised potential for energy savings in buildings and reducing the large differences between Member States' results in this sector.

(8) Measures to improve further the energy performance of buildings should take into account climatic and local conditions as well as indoor climate environment and cost-effectiveness. These measures should not affect other requirements concerning buildings such as accessibility, safety and the intended use of the building.

(9) The energy performance of buildings should be calculated on the basis of a methodology, which may be differentiated at national and regional level. That includes, in addition to thermal characteristics, other factors that play an increasingly important role such as heating and air-conditioning installations, application of energy from renewable sources, passive heating and cooling elements, shading, indoor air-quality, adequate natural light and design of the building. The methodology for calculating energy performance should be based not only on the season in which heating is required, but should cover the annual energy performance of a building. That methodology should take into account existing European standards.

(10) It is the sole responsibility of Member States to set minimum requirements for the energy performance of buildings and building elements. Those requirements should be set with a view to achieving the cost-optimal balance between the investments involved and the energy costs saved throughout the lifecycle of the building, without prejudice to the right of Member States to set minimum requirements which are more energy efficient than cost-optimal energy efficiency levels. Provision should be made for the possibility for Member States to review regularly their minimum energy performance requirements for buildings in the light of technical progress.

(11) The objective of cost-effective or cost-optimal energy efficiency levels may, in certain circumstances, for example in the light of climatic differences, justify the setting by Member States of cost-effective or cost-optimal requirements for building elements that would in practice limit the installation of building products that comply with standards set by Union legislation, provided that such requirements do not constitute an unjustifiable market barrier.

(12) When setting energy performance requirements for technical building systems, Member States should use, where available and appropriate, harmonised instruments, in particular testing and calculation methods and energy efficiency classes developed under measures implementing Directive 2009/125/EC of the European Parliament and of the Council of 21 October 2009 establishing a framework for the setting of ecodesign requirements for energy-related products and Directive 2010/30/EU of the European Parliament and of the Council of 19 May 2010 on the indication by labelling and standard product information of the consumption of energy and other resources by energy-related products, with a view to ensuring coherence with related initiatives and minimise, to the extent possible, potential fragmentation of the market.

(13) This Directive is without prejudice to Articles 107 and 108 of the Treaty on the Functioning of the European Union (TFEU). The term "incentive" used in this Directive should not therefore be interpreted as constituting State aid.

(14) The Commission should lay down a comparative methodology framework for calculating cost-optimal levels of minimum energy performance requirements. Member States should use this framework to compare the results with the minimum energy performance requirements which they have adopted. Should significant discrepancies, i.e. exceeding 15 %, exist between the calculated cost-optimal levels of minimum energy performance requirements and the minimum energy performance requirements in force, Member States should justify the difference or plan appropriate steps to reduce the discrepancy. The estimated economic lifecycle of a building or building element should be determined by Member States, taking into account current practices and experience in defining typical economic lifecycles. The results of this comparison and the data used to reach these results should be regularly reported to the Commission. These reports should enable the Commission to assess and report on the progress of Member States in reaching cost-optimal levels of minimum energy performance requirements.

(15) Buildings have an impact on long-term energy consumption. Given the long renovation cycle for existing buildings, new, and existing buildings that are subject to major renovation, should therefore meet minimum energy performance requirements adapted to the local climate. As the application of alternative energy supply systems is not generally explored to its full potential, alternative energy supply systems should be considered for new buildings, regardless of their size, pursuant to the principle of first ensuring that energy needs for heating and cooling are reduced to cost-optimal levels.

(16) Major renovations of existing buildings, regardless of their size, provide an opportunity to take cost-effective measures to enhance energy performance. For reasons of cost-effectiveness, it should be possible to limit the minimum energy performance requirements to the renovated parts that are most relevant for the energy performance of the building. Member States should be able to choose to define a "major renovation" either in terms of a percentage of the surface of the building envelope or in terms of the value of the building. If a Member State decides to define a major renovation in terms of the value of the building, values such as the actuarial value, or the current value based on the cost of reconstruction, excluding the value of the land upon which the building is situated, could be used.

(17) Measures are needed to increase the number of buildings which not only fulfil current minimum energy performance requirements, but are also more energy efficient, thereby reducing both energy consumption and carbon dioxide emissions. For this purpose Member States should draw up national plans for increasing the number of nearly zero-energy buildings and regularly report such plans to the Commission.

(18) Union financial instruments and other measures are being put into place or adapted with the aim of stimulating energy efficiency-related measures. Such financial instruments at Union level include, inter alia, Regulation (EC) No 1080/2006 of the European Parliament and of the Council of 5 July 2006 on the European Regional Development Fund, amended to allow increased investments in energy efficiency in housing; the public-private partnership on a "European energy-efficient buildings" initiative to promote green technologies and the development of energy-efficient systems and materials in new and renovated buildings; the EC-European Investment Bank (EIB) initiative "EU sustainable energy financing initiative" which aims to enable, inter alia, investments for energy efficiency and the EIB-led "Marguerite Fund": the 2020 European Fund for Energy, Climate Change and Infrastructure; Council Directive 2009/47/EC of 5 May 2009 amending Directive 2006/112/EC as regards reduced rates of value added tax, structural and cohesion funds instrument Jeremie (Joint European Resources for micro to medium enterprises); the Energy Efficiency Finance Facility; the Competitiveness and Innovation Framework Programme including the Intelligent Energy Europe II Programme focused specifically on removing market barriers

related to energy efficiency and energy from renewable sources through for example the technical assistance facility ELENA (European Local Energy Assistance); the Covenant of Mayors; the Entrepreneurship and Innovation programme; the ICT Policy Support Programme 2010, and the Seventh Research Framework Programme. The European Bank for Reconstruction and Development also provides funding with the aim of stimulating energy-efficiency-related measures.

(19) Union financial instruments should be used to give practical effect to the objectives of this Directive, without however substituting national measures. In particular, they should be used for providing appropriate and innovative means of financing to catalyse investment in energy efficiency measures. They could play an important role in the development of national, regional and local energy efficiency funds, instruments, or mechanisms, which deliver such financing possibilities to private property owners, to small and medium-sized enterprises and to energy efficiency service companies.

(20) In order to provide the Commission with adequate information, Member States should draw up lists of existing and proposed measures, including those of a financial nature, other than those required by this Directive, which promote the objectives of this Directive. The existing and proposed measures listed by Member States may include, in particular, measures that aim to reduce existing legal and market barriers and encourage investments and/or other activities to increase the energy efficiency of new and existing buildings, thus potentially contributing to reducing energy poverty. Such measures could include, but should not be limited to, free or subsidised technical assistance and advice, direct subsidies, subsidised loan schemes or low interest loans, grant schemes and loan guarantee schemes. The public authorities and other institutions which provide those measures of a financial nature could link the application of such measures to the indicated energy performance and the recommendations from energy performance certificates.

(21) In order to limit the reporting burden on Member States it should be possible to integrate the reports required by this Directive into the Energy Efficiency Action Plans referred to in Article 14(2) of Directive 2006/32/EC of the European Parliament and of the Council of 5 April 2006 on energy end-use efficiency and energy services. The public sector in each Member State should lead the way in the field of energy performance of buildings, and therefore the national plans should set more ambitious targets for the buildings occupied by public authorities.

(22) The prospective buyer and tenant of a building or building unit should, in the energy performance certificate, be given correct information about the energy performance of the building and practical advice on improving such performance. Information campaigns may serve to further encourage owners and tenants to improve the energy performance of their building or building unit. Owners and tenants of commercial buildings should also be encouraged to exchange information regarding actual energy consumption, in order to ensure that all the data are available to make informed decisions about necessary improvements. The energy performance certificate should also provide information about the actual impact of heating and cooling on the energy needs of the building, on its primary energy consumption and on its carbon dioxide emissions.

(23) Public authorities should lead by example and should endeavour to implement the recommendations included in the energy performance certificate. Member States should include within their national plans measures to support public authorities to become early adopters of energy efficiency improvements and to implement the recommendations included in the energy performance certificate as soon as feasible.

(24) Buildings occupied by public authorities and buildings frequently visited by the public should set an example by showing that environmental and energy considerations are being taken into account and therefore those buildings should be subject to energy certification on a regular basis. The dissemination to the public of information on energy performance should be enhanced by clearly displaying these energy performance certificates, in particular in buildings of a certain size which are occupied by public authorities or which are frequently visited by the public, such as shops and shopping centres, supermarkets, restaurants, theatres, banks and hotels.

(25) Recent years have seen a rise in the number of air-conditioning systems in European countries. This creates considerable problems at peak load times, increasing the cost of electricity and disrupting the energy balance. Priority should be given to strategies which enhance the thermal performance of buildings during the summer period. To that end, there should be focus on measures which avoid overheating, such as shading and sufficient thermal capacity in the building construction, and further development and application of passive cooling techniques, primarily those that improve indoor climatic conditions and the micro-climate around buildings.

(26) Regular maintenance and inspection of heating and air-conditioning systems by qualified personnel contributes to maintaining their correct adjustment in accordance with the product specification and in that way ensures optimal performance from an environmental, safety and energy point of view. An independent assessment of the entire heating and air-conditioning system should occur at regular intervals during its lifecycle in particular before its replacement or upgrading. In order to minimise the administrative burden on building owners and tenants, Member States should endeavour to combine inspections and certifications as far as possible.

(27) A common approach to the energy performance certification of buildings and to the inspection of heating and air-conditioning systems, carried out by qualified and/or accredited experts, whose independence is to be guaranteed on the basis of objective criteria, will contribute to a level playing field as regards efforts made in Member States to energy saving in the buildings sector and will introduce transparency for prospective owners or users with regard to energy performance in the Union property market. In order to ensure the quality of energy performance certificates and of the inspection of heating and air-conditioning systems throughout the Union, an independent control mechanism should be established in each Member State.

(28) Since local and regional authorities are critical for the successful implementation of this Directive, they should be consulted and involved, as and when appropriate in accordance with applicable national legislation, on planning issues, the development of programmes to provide information, training and awareness-raising, and on the implementation of this Directive at national or regional level. Such consultations may also serve to promote the provision of adequate guidance to local planners and building inspectors to carry out the necessary tasks. Furthermore, Member States should enable and encourage architects and planners to properly consider the optimal combination of improvements in energy efficiency, use of energy from renewable sources and use of district heating and cooling when planning, designing, building and renovating industrial or residential areas.

(29) Installers and builders are critical for the successful implementation of this Directive. Therefore, an adequate number of installers and builders should, through training and other measures, have the appropriate level of competence for the installation and integration of the energy efficient and renewable energy technology required.

(30) Member States should take account of Directive 2005/36/EC of the European Parliament and of the Council of 7 September 2005 on the recognition of professional qualifications with regard to the mutual recognition of professional experts which are addressed by this Directive, and the Commission should continue its activities under the Intelligent Energy Europe Programme on guidelines and recommendations for standards for the training of such professional experts.

(31) In order to enhance the transparency of energy performance in the Union's non-residential property market, uniform conditions for a voluntary common certification scheme for the energy performance of non-residential buildings should be established. In accordance with Article 291 TFEU, rules and general principles concerning mechanisms for control by Member States of the Commission's exercise of implementing powers shall be laid down in advance by a regulation adopted in accordance with the ordinary legislative procedure. Pending the adoption of that new regulation, Council Decision 1999/468/EC of 28 June 1999 laying down the procedures for the exercise of implementing powers

conferred on the Commission continues to apply, with the exception of the regulatory procedure with scrutiny, which is not applicable.

(32) The Commission should be empowered to adopt delegated acts in accordance with Article 290 TFEU in respect of the adaptation to technical progress of certain parts of the general framework set out in Annex I, and in respect of the establishment of a methodology framework for calculating cost-optimal levels of minimum energy performance requirements. It is of particular importance that the Commission carry out appropriate consultations during its preparatory work, including at expert level.

(33) Since the objective of this Directive, namely of enhancing the energy performance of buildings, cannot be sufficiently achieved by the Member States, due to the complexity of the buildings sector and the inability of the national housing markets to adequately address the challenges of energy efficiency, and can by the reason of the scale and the effects of the action be better achieved at Union level, the Union may adopt measures, in accordance with the principle of subsidiarity as set out in Article 5 of the Treaty on European Union. In accordance with the principles of proportionality, as set out in that Article, this Directive does not go beyond what is necessary in order to achieve that objective.

(34) The obligation to transpose this Directive into national law should be confined to those provisions which represent a substantive change as compared with Directive 2002/91/EC. The obligation to transpose the provisions which are unchanged arises under that Directive.

(35) This Directive should be without prejudice to the obligations of the Member States relating to the time limits for transposition into national law and application of the Directive 2002/91/EC.

(36) In accordance with point 34 of the Interinstitutional Agreement on better law-making, Member States are encouraged to draw up, for themselves and in the interest of the Union, their own tables, illustrating, as far as possible, the correlation between this Directive and the transposition measures, and to make them public,

HAVE ADOPTED THIS DIRECTIVE:

Article 1

Subject matter

1. This Directive promotes the improvement of the energy performance of buildings within the Union, taking into account outdoor climatic and local conditions, as well as indoor climate requirements and cost-effectiveness.

2. This Directive lays down requirements as regards:

(a) the common general framework for a methodology for calculating the integrated energy performance of buildings and building units;

(b) the application of minimum requirements to the energy performance of new buildings and new building units;

(c) the application of minimum requirements to the energy performance of:

  (i) existing buildings, building units and building elements that are subject to major renovation;

  (ii) building elements that form part of the building envelope and that have a significant impact on the energy performance of the building envelope when they are retrofitted or replaced; and

  (iii) technical building systems whenever they are installed, replaced or upgraded;

(d) national plans for increasing the number of nearly zero-energy buildings;

(e) energy certification of buildings or building units;

(f) regular inspection of heating and air-conditioning systems in buildings; and

(g) independent control systems for energy performance certificates and inspection reports.

3. The requirements laid down in this Directive are minimum requirements and shall not prevent any Member State from maintaining or introducing more stringent measures. Such measures shall be compatible with the Treaty on the Functioning of the European Union. They shall be notified to the Commission.

Article 2

Definitions

For the purpose of this Directive, the following definitions shall apply:

1. "building" means a roofed construction having walls, for which energy is used to condition the indoor climate;
2. "nearly zero-energy building" means a building that has a very high energy performance, as determined in accordance with Annex I. The nearly zero or very low amount of energy required should be covered to a very significant extent by energy from renewable sources, including energy from renewable sources produced on-site or nearby;
3. "technical building system" means technical equipment for the heating, cooling, ventilation, hot water, lighting or for a combination thereof, of a building or building unit;
4. "energy performance of a building" means the calculated or measured amount of energy needed to meet the energy demand associated with a typical use of the building, which includes, inter alia, energy used for heating, cooling, ventilation, hot water and lighting;
5. "primary energy" means energy from renewable and non-renewable sources which has not undergone any conversion or transformation process;
6. "energy from renewable sources" means energy from renewable non-fossil sources, namely wind, solar, aerothermal, geothermal, hydrothermal and ocean energy, hydropower, biomass, landfill gas, sewage treatment plant gas and biogases;
7. "building envelope" means the integrated elements of a building which separate its interior from the outdoor environment;
8. "building unit" means a section, floor or apartment within a building which is designed or altered to be used separately;
9. "building element" means a technical building system or an element of the building envelope;
10. "major renovation" means the renovation of a building where:
    (a) the total cost of the renovation relating to the building envelope or the technical building systems is higher than 25 % of the value of the building, excluding the value of the land upon which the building is situated; or
    (b) more than 25 % of the surface of the building envelope undergoes renovation;
    Member States may choose to apply option (a) or (b).
11. "European standard" means a standard adopted by the European Committee for Standardisation, the European Committee for Electrotechnical Standardisation or the European Telecommunications Standards Institute and made available for public use;
12. "energy performance certificate" means a certificate recognised by a Member State or by a legal person designated by it, which indicates the energy performance of a building or building unit, calculated according to a methodology adopted in accordance with Article 3;
13. "cogeneration" means simultaneous generation in one process of thermal energy and electrical and/or mechanical energy;
14. "cost-optimal level" means the energy performance level which leads to the lowest cost during the estimated economic lifecycle, where:
    (a) the lowest cost is determined taking into account energy-related investment costs, maintenance and operating costs (including energy costs and savings, the category of building concerned, earnings from energy produced), where applicable, and disposal costs, where applicable; and
    (b) the estimated economic lifecycle is determined by each Member State. It refers to the remaining estimated economic lifecycle of a building where

energy performance requirements are set for the building as a whole, or to the estimated economic lifecycle of a building element where energy performance requirements are set for building elements.

The cost-optimal level shall lie within the range of performance levels where the cost benefit analysis calculated over the estimated economic lifecycle is positive;

15. "air-conditioning system" means a combination of the components required to provide a form of indoor air treatment, by which temperature is controlled or can be lowered;
16. "boiler" means the combined boiler body-burner unit, designed to transmit to fluids the heat released from burning;
17. "effective rated output" means the maximum calorific output, expressed in kW, specified and guaranteed by the manufacturer as being deliverable during continuous operation while complying with the useful efficiency indicated by the manufacturer;
18. "heat pump" means a machine, a device or installation that transfers heat from natural surroundings such as air, water or ground to buildings or industrial applications by reversing the natural flow of heat such that it flows from a lower to a higher temperature. For reversible heat pumps, it may also move heat from the building to the natural surroundings;
19. "district heating" or "district cooling" means the distribution of thermal energy in the form of steam, hot water or chilled liquids, from a central source of production through a network to multiple buildings or sites, for the use of space or process heating or cooling.

Article 3

Adoption of a methodology for calculating the energy performance of buildings

Member States shall apply a methodology for calculating the energy performance of buildings in accordance with the common general framework set out in Annex I.

This methodology shall be adopted at national or regional level.

Article 4

Setting of minimum energy performance requirements

1. Member States shall take the necessary measures to ensure that minimum energy performance requirements for buildings or building units are set with a view to achieving cost-optimal levels. The energy performance shall be calculated in accordance with the methodology referred to in Article 3. Cost-optimal levels shall be calculated in accordance with the comparative methodology framework referred to in Article 5 once the framework is in place.

Member States shall take the necessary measures to ensure that minimum energy performance requirements are set for building elements that form part of the building envelope and that have a significant impact on the energy performance of the building envelope when they are replaced or retrofitted, with a view to achieving cost-optimal levels.

When setting requirements, Member States may differentiate between new and existing buildings and between different categories of buildings.

These requirements shall take account of general indoor climate conditions, in order to avoid possible negative effects such as inadequate ventilation, as well as local conditions and the designated function and the age of the building.

A Member State shall not be required to set minimum energy performance requirements which are not cost-effective over the estimated economic lifecycle.

Minimum energy performance requirements shall be reviewed at regular intervals which shall not be longer than five years and, if necessary, shall be updated in order to reflect technical progress in the building sector.

2. Member States may decide not to set or apply the requirements referred to in paragraph 1 to the following categories of buildings:

(a) buildings officially protected as part of a designated environment or because of their special architectural or historical merit, in so far as compliance with certain minimum energy performance requirements would unacceptably alter their character or appearance;

(b) buildings used as places of worship and for religious activities;

(c) temporary buildings with a time of use of two years or less, industrial sites, workshops and non-residential agricultural buildings with low energy demand and non-residential agricultural buildings which are in use by a sector covered by a national sectoral agreement on energy performance;

(d) residential buildings which are used or intended to be used for either less than four months of the year or, alternatively, for a limited annual time of use and with an expected energy consumption of less than 25 % of what would be the result of all-year use;

(e) stand-alone buildings with a total useful floor area of less than 50 m^2.

Article 5

Calculation of cost-optimal levels of minimum energy performance requirements

1. The Commission shall establish by means of delegated acts in accordance with Articles 23, 24 and 25 by 30 June 2011 a comparative methodology framework for calculating cost-optimal levels of minimum energy performance requirements for buildings and building elements.

The comparative methodology framework shall be established in accordance with Annex III and shall differentiate between new and existing buildings and between different categories of buildings.

2. Member States shall calculate cost-optimal levels of minimum energy performance requirements using the comparative methodology framework established in accordance with paragraph 1 and relevant parameters, such as climatic conditions and the practical accessibility of energy infrastructure, and compare the results of this calculation with the minimum energy performance requirements in force.

Member States shall report to the Commission all input data and assumptions used for those calculations and the results of those calculations. The report may be included in the Energy Efficiency Action Plans referred to in Article 14(2) of Directive 2006/32/EC. Member States shall submit those reports to the Commission at regular intervals, which shall not be longer than five years. The first report shall be submitted by 30 June 2012.

3. If the result of the comparison performed in accordance with paragraph 2 shows that the minimum energy performance requirements in force are significantly less energy efficient than cost-optimal levels of minimum energy performance requirements, the Member State concerned shall justify this difference in writing to the Commission in the report referred to in paragraph 2, accompanied, to the extent that the gap cannot be justified, by a plan outlining appropriate steps to significantly reduce the gap by the next review of the energy performance requirements as referred to in Article 4(1).

4. The Commission shall publish a report on the progress of the Member States in reaching cost-optimal levels of minimum energy performance requirements.

Article 6

New buildings

1. Member States shall take the necessary measures to ensure that new buildings meet the minimum energy performance requirements set in accordance with Article 4.

For new buildings, Member States shall ensure that, before construction starts, the technical, environmental and economic feasibility of high-efficiency alternative systems such as those listed below, if available, is considered and taken into account:

(a) decentralised energy supply systems based on energy from renewable sources;
(b) cogeneration;
(c) district or block heating or cooling, particularly where it is based entirely or partially on energy from renewable sources;
(d) heat pumps.

2. Member States shall ensure that the analysis of alternative systems referred to in paragraph 1 is documented and available for verification purposes.

3. That analysis of alternative systems may be carried out for individual buildings or for groups of similar buildings or for common typologies of buildings in the same area. As far as collective heating and cooling systems are concerned, the analysis may be carried out for all buildings connected to the system in the same area.

Article 7

Existing buildings

Member States shall take the necessary measures to ensure that when buildings undergo major renovation, the energy performance of the building or the renovated part thereof is upgraded in order to meet minimum energy performance requirements set in accordance with Article 4 in so far as this is technically, functionally and economically feasible.

Those requirements shall be applied to the renovated building or building unit as a whole. Additionally or alternatively, requirements may be applied to the renovated building elements.

Member States shall in addition take the necessary measures to ensure that when a building element that forms part of the building envelope and has a significant impact on the energy performance of the building envelope, is retrofitted or replaced, the energy performance of the building element meets minimum energy performance requirements in so far as this is technically, functionally and economically feasible.

Member States shall determine these minimum energy performance requirements in accordance with Article 4.

Member States shall encourage, in relation to buildings undergoing major renovation, the consideration and taking into account of high-efficiency alternative systems, as referred to in Article 6(1), in so far as this is technically, functionally and economically feasible.

Article 8

Technical building systems

1. Member States shall, for the purpose of optimising the energy use of technical building systems, set system requirements in respect of the overall energy performance, the proper installation, and the appropriate dimensioning, adjustment and control of the technical building systems which are installed in existing buildings. Member States may also apply these system requirements to new buildings.

System requirements shall be set for new, replacement and upgrading of technical building systems and shall be applied in so far as they are technically, economically and functionally feasible.

The system requirements shall cover at least the following:

(a) heating systems;
(b) hot water systems;
(c) air-conditioning systems;

(d) large ventilation systems;

or a combination of such systems.

2. Member States shall encourage the introduction of intelligent metering systems whenever a building is constructed or undergoes major renovation, whilst ensuring that this encouragement is in line with point 2 of Annex I to Directive 2009/72/EC of the European Parliament and of the Council of 13 July 2009 concerning common rules for the internal market in electricity. Member States may furthermore encourage, where appropriate, the installation of active control systems such as automation, control and monitoring systems that aim to save energy.

Article 9

Nearly zero-energy buildings

1. Member States shall ensure that:

(a) by 31 December 2020, all new buildings are nearly zero-energy buildings; and

(b) after 31 December 2018, new buildings occupied and owned by public authorities are nearly zero-energy buildings.

Member States shall draw up national plans for increasing the number of nearly zero-energy buildings. These national plans may include targets differentiated according to the category of building.

2. Member States shall furthermore, following the leading example of the public sector, develop policies and take measures such as the setting of targets in order to stimulate the transformation of buildings that are refurbished into nearly zero-energy buildings, and inform the Commission thereof in their national plans referred to in paragraph 1.

3. The national plans shall include, inter alia, the following elements:

(a) the Member State's detailed application in practice of the definition of nearly zero-energy buildings, reflecting their national, regional or local conditions, and including a numerical indicator of primary energy use expressed in kWh/m^2 per year. Primary energy factors used for the determination of the primary energy use may be based on national or regional yearly average values and may take into account relevant European standards;

(b) intermediate targets for improving the energy performance of new buildings, by 2015, with a view to preparing the implementation of paragraph 1;

(c) information on the policies and financial or other measures adopted in the context of paragraphs 1 and 2 for the promotion of nearly zero-energy buildings, including details of national requirements and measures concerning the use of energy from renewable sources in new buildings and existing buildings undergoing major renovation in the context of Article 13(4) of Directive 2009/28/EC and Articles 6 and 7 of this Directive.

4. The Commission shall evaluate the national plans referred to in paragraph 1, notably the adequacy of the measures envisaged by the Member State in relation to the objectives of this Directive. The Commission, taking due account of the principle of subsidiarity, may request further specific information regarding the requirements set out in paragraphs 1, 2 and 3. In that case, the Member State concerned shall submit the requested information or propose amendments within nine months following the request from the Commission. Following its evaluation, the Commission may issue a recommendation.

5. The Commission shall by 31 December 2012 and every three years thereafter publish a report on the progress of Member States in increasing the number of nearly zero-energy buildings. On the basis of that report the Commission shall develop an action plan and, if necessary, propose measures to increase the number of those buildings and encourage best practices as regards the cost-effective transformation of existing buildings into nearly zero-energy buildings.

6. Member States may decide not to apply the requirements set out in points (a) and (b) of paragraph 1 in specific and justifiable cases where the cost-benefit analysis over the economic

lifecycle of the building in question is negative. Member States shall inform the Commission of the principles of the relevant legislative regimes.

Article 10

Financial incentives and market barriers

1. In view of the importance of providing appropriate financing and other instruments to catalyse the energy performance of buildings and the transition to nearly zero-energy buildings, Member States shall take appropriate steps to consider the most relevant such instruments in the light of national circumstances.

2. Member States shall draw up, by 30 June 2011, a list of existing and, if appropriate, proposed measures and instruments including those of a financial nature, other than those required by this Directive, which promote the objectives of this Directive.

Member States shall update this list every three years. Member States shall communicate these lists to the Commission, which they may do by including them in the Energy Efficiency Action Plans referred to in Article 14(2) of Directive 2006/32/EC.

3. The Commission shall examine the effectiveness of the listed existing and proposed measures referred to in paragraph 2 as well as of relevant Union instruments, in supporting the implementation of this Directive. On the basis of that examination, and taking due account of the principle of subsidiarity, the Commission may provide advice or recommendations as regards specific national schemes and coordination with Union and international financial institutions. The Commission may include its examination and possible advice or recommendations in its report on the National Energy Efficiency Plans referred to in Article 14(5) of Directive 2006/32/EC.

4. The Commission shall, where appropriate, assist upon request Member States in setting up national or regional financial support programmes with the aim of increasing energy efficiency in buildings, especially of existing buildings, by supporting the exchange of best practice between the responsible national or regional authorities or bodies.

5. In order to improve financing in support of the implementation of this Directive and taking due account of the principle of subsidiarity, the Commission shall, preferably by 2011, present an analysis on, in particular:

(a) the effectiveness, the appropriateness of the level, and the actual amount used, of structural funds and framework programmes that were used for increasing energy efficiency in buildings, especially in housing;

(b) the effectiveness of the use of funds from the EIB and other public finance institutions;

(c) the coordination of Union and national funding and other forms of support that can act as a leverage for stimulating investments in energy efficiency and the adequacy of such funds for achieving Union objectives.

On the basis of that analysis, and in accordance with the multiannual financial framework, the Commission may subsequently submit, if it considers this appropriate, proposals with respect to Union instruments to the European Parliament and the Council.

6. Member States shall take account of the cost-optimal levels of energy performance when providing incentives for the construction or major renovation of buildings.

7. The provisions of this Directive shall not prevent Member States from providing incentives for new buildings, renovations or building elements which go beyond the cost-optimal levels.

Article 11

Energy performance certificates

1. Member States shall lay down the necessary measures to establish a system of certification of the energy performance of buildings. The energy performance certificate shall include the

energy performance of a building and reference values such as minimum energy performance requirements in order to make it possible for owners or tenants of the building or building unit to compare and assess its energy performance.

The energy performance certificate may include additional information such as the annual energy consumption for non-residential buildings and the percentage of energy from renewable sources in the total energy consumption.

2. The energy performance certificate shall include recommendations for the cost-optimal or cost-effective improvement of the energy performance of a building or building unit, unless there is no reasonable potential for such improvement compared to the energy performance requirements in force.

The recommendations included in the energy performance certificate shall cover:

(a) measures carried out in connection with a major renovation of the building envelope or technical building system(s); and

(b) measures for individual building elements independent of a major renovation of the building envelope or technical building system(s).

3. The recommendations included in the energy performance certificate shall be technically feasible for the specific building and may provide an estimate for the range of payback periods or cost-benefits over its economic lifecycle.

4. The energy performance certificate shall provide an indication as to where the owner or tenant can receive more detailed information, including as regards the cost-effectiveness of the recommendations made in the energy performance certificate. The evaluation of cost effectiveness shall be based on a set of standard conditions, such as the assessment of energy savings and underlying energy prices and a preliminary cost forecast. In addition, it shall contain information on the steps to be taken to implement the recommendations. Other information on related topics, such as energy audits or incentives of a financial or other nature and financing possibilities may also be provided to the owner or tenant.

5. Subject to national rules, Member States shall encourage public authorities to take into account the leading role which they should play in the field of energy performance of buildings, inter alia, by implementing the recommendations included in the energy performance certificate issued for buildings owned by them within its validity period.

6. Certification for building units may be based:

(a) on a common certification of the whole building; or

(b) on the assessment of another representative building unit with the same energy-relevant characteristics in the same building.

7. Certification for single-family houses may be based on the assessment of another representative building of similar design and size with a similar actual energy performance quality if such correspondence can be guaranteed by the expert issuing the energy performance certificate.

8. The validity of the energy performance certificate shall not exceed 10 years.

9. The Commission shall, by 2011, in consultation with the relevant sectors, adopt a voluntary common European Union certification scheme for the energy performance of non-residential buildings. That measure shall be adopted in accordance with the advisory procedure referred to in Article 26(2). Member States are encouraged to recognise or use the scheme, or use part thereof by adapting it to national circumstances.

Article 12

Issue of energy performance certificates

1. Member States shall ensure that an energy performance certificate is issued for:

(a) buildings or building units which are constructed, sold or rented out to a new tenant; and

(b) buildings where a total useful floor area over 500 m^2 is occupied by a public authority and frequently visited by the public. On 9 July 2015, this threshold of 500 m^2 shall be lowered to 250 m^2.

The requirement to issue an energy performance certificate does not apply where a certificate, issued in accordance with either Directive 2002/91/EC or this Directive, for the building or building unit concerned is available and valid.

2. Member States shall require that, when buildings or building units are constructed, sold or rented out, the energy performance certificate or a copy thereof is shown to the prospective new tenant or buyer and handed over to the buyer or new tenant.

3. Where a building is sold or rented out in advance of construction, Member States may require the seller to provide an assessment of its future energy performance, as a derogation from paragraphs 1 and 2; in this case, the energy performance certificate shall be issued at the latest once the building has been constructed.

4. Member States shall require that when:

— buildings having an energy performance certificate,
— building units in a building having an energy performance certificate, and
— building units having an energy performance certificate,

are offered for sale or for rent, the energy performance indicator of the energy performance certificate of the building or the building unit, as applicable, is stated in the advertisements in commercial media.

5. The provisions of this Article shall be implemented in accordance with applicable national rules on joint ownership or common property.

6. Member States may exclude the categories of buildings referred to in Article 4(2) from the application of paragraphs 1, 2, 4 and 5 of this Article.

7. The possible effects of energy performance certificates in terms of legal proceedings, if any, shall be decided in accordance with national rules.

Article 13

Display of energy performance certificates

1. Member States shall take measures to ensure that where a total useful floor area over 500 m^2 of a building for which an energy performance certificate has been issued in accordance with Article 12(1) is occupied by public authorities and frequently visited by the public, the energy performance certificate is displayed in a prominent place clearly visible to the public.

On 9 July 2015, this threshold of 500 m^2 shall be lowered to 250 m^2.

2. Member States shall require that where a total useful floor area over 500 m^2 of a building for which an energy performance certificate has been issued in accordance with Article 12(1) is frequently visited by the public, the energy performance certificate is displayed in a prominent place clearly visible to the public.

3. The provisions of this Article do not include an obligation to display the recommendations included in the energy performance certificate.

Article 14

Inspection of heating systems

1. Member States shall lay down the necessary measures to establish a regular inspection of the accessible parts of systems used for heating buildings, such as the heat generator, control system and circulation pump(s), with boilers of an effective rated output for space heating purposes of more than 20 kW. That inspection shall include an assessment of the boiler efficiency and the boiler sizing compared with the heating requirements of the building. The

assessment of the boiler sizing does not have to be repeated as long as no changes were made to the heating system or as regards the heating requirements of the building in the meantime.

Member States may reduce the frequency of such inspections or lighten them as appropriate, where an electronic monitoring and control system is in place.

2. Member States may set different inspection frequencies depending on the type and effective rated output of the heating system whilst taking into account the costs of the inspection of the heating system and the estimated energy cost savings that may result from the inspection.

3. Heating systems with boilers of an effective rated output of more than 100 kW shall be inspected at least every two years.

For gas boilers, this period may be extended to four years.

4. As an alternative to paragraphs 1, 2 and 3 Member States may opt to take measures to ensure the provision of advice to users concerning the replacement of boilers, other modifications to the heating system and alternative solutions to assess the efficiency and appropriate size of the boiler. The overall impact of this approach shall be equivalent to that arising from the provisions set out in paragraphs 1, 2 and 3.

Where Member States choose to apply the measures referred to in the first subparagraph, they shall submit to the Commission a report on the equivalence of those measures to measures referred to in paragraphs 1, 2 and 3 of this Article by 30 June 2011 at the latest. Member States shall submit these reports to the Commission every three years. The reports may be included in the Energy Efficiency Action Plans referred to in Article 14(2) of Directive 2006/32/EC.

5. After receiving the national report from a Member State about the application of the option as described in paragraph 4, the Commission may request further specific information regarding the requirements and equivalence of the measures set out in that paragraph. In that case, the Member State concerned shall present the requested information or propose amendments within nine months.

Article 15

Inspection of air-conditioning systems

1. Member States shall lay down the necessary measures to establish a regular inspection of the accessible parts of air-conditioning systems of an effective rated output of more than 12 kW. The inspection shall include an assessment of the air-conditioning efficiency and the sizing compared to the cooling requirements of the building. The assessment of the sizing does not have to be repeated as long as no changes were made to this air-conditioning system or as regards the cooling requirements of the building in the meantime.

Member States may reduce the frequency of such inspections or lighten them, as appropriate, where an electronic monitoring and control system is in place.

2. The Member States may set different inspection frequencies depending on the type and effective rated output of the air-conditioning system, whilst taking into account the costs of the inspection of the air-conditioning system and the estimated energy cost savings that may result from the inspection.

3. In laying down the measures referred to in paragraphs 1 and 2 of this Article, Member States shall, as far as is economically and technically feasible, ensure that inspections are carried out in accordance with the inspection of heating systems and other technical systems referred to in Article 14 of this Directive and the inspection of leakages referred to in Regulation (EC) No 842/2006 of the European Parliament and of the Council of 17 May 2006 on certain fluorinated greenhouse gases.

4. As an alternative to paragraphs 1, 2 and 3 Member States may opt to take measures to ensure the provision of advice to users on the replacement of air-conditioning systems or on

other modifications to the air-conditioning system which may include inspections to assess the efficiency and appropriate size of the air-conditioning system. The overall impact of this approach shall be equivalent to that arising from the provisions set out in paragraphs 1, 2 and 3.

Where Member States apply the measures referred to in the first subparagraph, they shall, by 30 June 2011 at the latest, submit to the Commission a report on the equivalence of those measures to the measures referred to in paragraphs 1, 2 and 3 of this Article. Member States shall submit these reports to the Commission every three years. The reports may be included in the Energy Efficiency Action Plans referred to in Article 14(2) of Directive 2006/32/EC.

5. After receiving the national report from a Member State about the application of the option as described in paragraph 4, the Commission may request further specific information regarding the requirements and equivalence of the measures set in that paragraph. In this case, the Member State concerned shall present the requested information or propose amendments within nine months.

Article 16

Reports on the inspection of heating and air-conditioning systems

1. An inspection report shall be issued after each inspection of a heating or air-conditioning system. The inspection report shall contain the result of the inspection performed in accordance with Article 14 or 15 and include recommendations for the cost-effective improvement of the energy performance of the inspected system.

The recommendations may be based on a comparison of the energy performance of the system inspected with that of the best available feasible system and a system of similar type for which all relevant components achieve the level of energy performance required by the applicable legislation.

2. The inspection report shall be handed over to the owner or tenant of the building.

Article 17

Independent experts

Member States shall ensure that the energy performance certification of buildings and the inspection of heating systems and air-conditioning systems are carried out in an independent manner by qualified and/or accredited experts, whether operating in a self-employed capacity or employed by public bodies or private enterprises.

Experts shall be accredited taking into account their competence.

Member States shall make available to the public information on training and accreditations. Member States shall ensure that either regularly updated lists of qualified and/or accredited experts or regularly updated lists of accredited companies which offer the services of such experts are made available to the public.

Article 18

Independent control system

1. Member States shall ensure that independent control systems for energy performance certificates and reports on the inspection of heating and air-conditioning systems are established in accordance with Annex II. Member States may establish separate systems for the control of energy performance certificates and for the control of reports on the inspection of heating and air-conditioning systems.

2. The Member States may delegate the responsibilities for implementing the independent control systems.

Where the Member States decide to do so, they shall ensure that the independent control systems are implemented in compliance with Annex II.

3. Member States shall require the energy performance certificates and the inspection reports referred to in paragraph 1 to be made available to the competent authorities or bodies on request.

Article 19

Review

The Commission, assisted by the Committee established by Article 26, shall evaluate this Directive by 1 January 2017 at the latest, in the light of the experience gained and progress made during its application, and, if necessary, make proposals.

Article 20

Information

1. Member States shall take the necessary measures to inform the owners or tenants of buildings or building units of the different methods and practices that serve to enhance energy performance.

2. Member States shall in particular provide information to the owners or tenants of buildings on energy performance certificates and inspection reports, their purpose and objectives, on cost-effective ways to improve the energy performance of the building and, where appropriate, on financial instruments available to improve the energy performance of the building.

At the request of the Member States, the Commission shall assist Member States in staging information campaigns for the purposes of paragraph 1 and the first subparagraph of this paragraph, which may be dealt with in Union programmes.

3. Member States shall ensure that guidance and training are made available for those responsible for implementing this Directive. Such guidance and training shall address the importance of improving energy performance, and shall enable consideration of the optimal combination of improvements in energy efficiency, use of energy from renewable sources and use of district heating and cooling when planning, designing, building and renovating industrial or residential areas.

4. The Commission is invited to continuously improve its information services, in particular the website that has been set up as a European portal for energy efficiency in buildings directed towards citizens, professionals and authorities, in order to assist Member States in their information and awareness-raising efforts. Information displayed on this website might include links to relevant European Union and national, regional and local legislation, links to Europa websites that display the National Energy Efficiency Action Plans, links to available financial instruments, as well as best practice examples at national, regional and local level. In the context of the European Regional Development Fund, the Commission shall continue and further intensify its information services with the aim of facilitating the use of available funds by providing assistance and information to interested stakeholders, including national, regional and local authorities, on funding possibilities, taking into account the latest changes in the regulatory framework.

Article 21

Consultation

In order to facilitate the effective implementation of the Directive, Member States shall consult the stakeholders involved, including local and regional authorities, in accordance with the national legislation applicable and as relevant. Such consultation is of particular importance for the application of Articles 9 and 20.

Article 22

Adaptation of Annex I to technical progress

The Commission shall adapt points 3 and 4 of Annex I to technical progress by means of delegated acts in accordance with Articles 23, 24 and 25.

Article 23

Exercise of delegation

1. The powers to adopt the delegated acts referred to in Article 22 shall be conferred on the Commission for a period of five years beginning on 8 July 2010. The Commission shall make a report in respect of the delegated powers not later than six months before the end of the five-year period. The delegation of powers shall be automatically extended for periods of an identical duration, unless the European Parliament or the Council revokes it in accordance with Article 24.

2. Without prejudice to the deadline referred to in Article 5(1), the powers to adopt the delegated acts referred to in Article 5 shall be conferred on the Commission until 30 June 2012.

3. As soon as it adopts a delegated act, the Commission shall notify it simultaneously to the European Parliament and to the Council.

4. The powers to adopt delegated acts are conferred on the Commission subject to the conditions laid down in Articles 24 and 25.

Article 24

Revocation of the delegation

1. The delegation of powers referred to in Articles 5 and 22 may be revoked by the European Parliament or by the Council.

2. The institution which has commenced an internal procedure for deciding whether to revoke the delegation of powers shall endeavour to inform the other institution and the Commission within a reasonable time before the final decision is taken, indicating the delegated powers which could be subject to revocation and possible reasons for a revocation.

3. The decision of revocation shall put an end to the delegation of the powers specified in that decision. It shall take effect immediately or at a later date specified therein. It shall not affect the validity of the delegated acts already in force. It shall be published in the Official Journal of the European Union.

Article 25

Objections to delegated acts

1. The European Parliament or the Council may object to a delegated act within a period of two months from the date of notification.

At the initiative of the European Parliament or the Council that period shall be extended by two months.

2. If, on expiry of that period, neither the European Parliament nor the Council has objected to the delegated act it shall be published in the Official Journal of the European Union and shall enter into force on the date stated therein.

The delegated act may be published in the Official Journal of the European Union and enter into force before the expiry of that period, if the European Parliament and the Council have both informed the Commission of their intention not to raise objections.

3. If the European Parliament or the Council objects to a delegated act, it shall not enter into force. The institution which objects shall state the reasons for objecting to the delegated act.

Article 26

Committee procedure

1. The Commission shall be assisted by a Committee.

2. Where reference is made to this paragraph, Articles 3 and 7 of Decision 1999/468/EC shall apply, having regard to the provisions of Article 8 thereof.

Article 27

Penalties

Member States shall lay down the rules on penalties applicable to infringements of the national provisions adopted pursuant to this Directive and shall take all measures necessary to ensure that they are implemented. The penalties provided for must be effective, proportionate and dissuasive. Member States shall communicate those provisions to the Commission by 9 January 2013 at the latest and shall notify it without delay of any subsequent amendment affecting them.

Article 28

Transposition

1. Member States shall adopt and publish, by 9 July 2012 at the latest, the laws, regulations and administrative provisions necessary to comply with Articles 2 to 18, and with Articles 20 and 27.

They shall apply those provisions as far as Articles 2, 3, 9, 11, 12, 13, 17, 18, 20 and 27 are concerned, from 9 January 2013 at the latest.

They shall apply those provisions as far as Articles 4, 5, 6, 7, 8, 14, 15 and 16 are concerned, to buildings occupied by the public authorities from 9 January 2013 at the latest and to other buildings from 9 July 2013 at the latest.

They may defer the application of Article 12(1) and (2) to single building units that are rented out, until 31 December 2015. This shall however not result in fewer certificates being issued than would have been the case under the application of the Directive 2002/91/EC in the Member State concerned.

When Member States adopt measures, they shall contain a reference to this Directive or be accompanied by such a reference on the occasion of their official publication. They shall also include a statement that references in existing laws, regulations and administrative provisions to Directive 2002/91/EC shall be construed as references to this Directive. Member States shall determine how such reference is to be made and how that statement is to be formulated.

2. Member States shall communicate to the Commission the text of the main provisions of national law which they adopt in the field covered by this Directive.

Article 29

Repeal

Directive 2002/91/EC, as amended by the Regulation indicated in Annex IV, Part A, is hereby repealed with effect from 1 February 2012, without prejudice to the obligations of the Member

States relating to the time limit for transposition into national law and application of the Directive set out in Annex IV, Part B.

References to Directive 2002/91/EC shall be construed as references to this Directive and shall be read in accordance with the correlation table in Annex V.

Article 30

Entry into force

This Directive shall enter into force on the 20th day following its publication in the Official Journal of the European Union.

Article 31

Addressees

This Directive is addressed to the Member States.

ANNEX I
COMMON GENERAL FRAMEWORK FOR THE CALCULATION OF ENERGY PERFORMANCE OF BUILDINGS (REFERRED TO IN ARTICLE 3)

1. The energy performance of a building shall be determined on the basis of the calculated or actual annual energy that is consumed in order to meet the different needs associated with its typical use and shall reflect the heating energy needs and cooling energy needs (energy needed to avoid overheating) to maintain the envisaged temperature conditions of the building, and domestic hot water needs.

2. The energy performance of a building shall be expressed in a transparent manner and shall include an energy performance indicator and a numeric indicator of primary energy use, based on primary energy factors per energy carrier, which may be based on national or regional annual weighted averages or a specific value for on-site production.

The methodology for calculating the energy performance of buildings should take into account European standards and shall be consistent with relevant Union legislation, including Directive 2009/28/EC.

3. The methodology shall be laid down taking into consideration at least the following aspects:

(a) the following actual thermal characteristics of the building including its internal partitions:
   (i) thermal capacity;
   (ii) insulation;
   (iii) passive heating;
   (iv) cooling elements; and
   (v) thermal bridges;

(b) heating installation and hot water supply, including their insulation characteristics;

(c) air-conditioning installations;

(d) natural and mechanical ventilation which may include air-tightness;

(e) built-in lighting installation (mainly in the non-residential sector);

(f) the design, positioning and orientation of the building, including outdoor climate;

(g) passive solar systems and solar protection;

(h) indoor climatic conditions, including the designed indoor climate;

(i) internal loads.

4. The positive influence of the following aspects shall, where relevant in the calculation, be taken into account:

(a) local solar exposure conditions, active solar systems and other heating and electricity systems based on energy from renewable sources;
(b) electricity produced by cogeneration;
(c) district or block heating and cooling systems;
(d) natural lighting.

5. For the purpose of the calculation buildings should be adequately classified into the following categories:
(a) single-family houses of different types;
(b) apartment blocks;
(c) offices;
(d) educational buildings;
(e) hospitals;
(f) hotels and restaurants;
(g) sports facilities;
(h) wholesale and retail trade services buildings;
(i) other types of energy-consuming buildings.

ANNEX II
INDEPENDENT CONTROL SYSTEMS FOR ENERGY PERFORMANCE CERTIFICATES AND INSPECTION REPORTS

1. The competent authorities or bodies to which the competent authorities have delegated the responsibility for implementing the independent control system shall make a random selection of at least a statistically significant percentage of all the energy performance certificates issued annually and subject those certificates to verification.

The verification shall be based on the options indicated below or on equivalent measures:
(a) validity check of the input data of the building used to issue the energy performance certificate and the results stated in the certificate;
(b) check of the input data and verification of the results of the energy performance certificate, including the recommendations made;
(c) full check of the input data of the building used to issue the energy performance certificate, full verification of the results stated in the certificate, including the recommendations made, and on-site visit of the building, if possible, to check correspondence between specifications given in the energy performance certificate and the building certified.

2. The competent authorities or bodies to which the competent authorities have delegated the responsibility for implementing the independent control system shall make a random selection of at least a statistically significant percentage of all the inspection reports issued annually and subject those reports to verification.

ANNEX III
COMPARATIVE METHODOLOGY FRAMEWORK TO IDENTIFY COST-OPTIMAL LEVELS OF ENERGY PERFORMANCE REQUIREMENTS FOR BUILDINGS AND BUILDING ELEMENTS

The comparative methodology framework shall enable Member States to determine the energy performance of buildings and building elements and the economic aspects of measures relating to the energy performance, and to link them with a view to identifying the cost-optimal level.

The comparative methodology framework shall be accompanied by guidelines outlining how to apply this framework in the calculation of cost-optimal performance levels.

The comparative methodology framework shall allow for taking into account use patterns, outdoor climate conditions, investment costs, building category, maintenance and operating costs (including energy costs and savings), earnings from energy produced, where applicable, and disposal costs, where applicable. It should be based on relevant European standards relating to this Directive.

The Commission shall also provide:

— guidelines to accompany the comparative methodology framework; these guidelines will serve to enable the Member States to undertake the steps listed below,
— information on estimated long-term energy price developments.

For the application of the comparative methodology framework by Member States, general conditions, expressed by parameters, shall be laid down at Member State level.

The comparative methodology framework shall require Member States to:

— define reference buildings that are characterised by and representative of their functionality and geographic location, including indoor and outdoor climate conditions. The reference buildings shall cover residential and non-residential buildings, both new and existing ones,
— define energy efficiency measures to be assessed for the reference buildings. These may be measures for individual buildings as a whole, for individual building elements, or for a combination of building elements,
— assess the final and primary energy need of the reference buildings and the reference buildings with the defined energy efficiency measures applied,
— calculate the costs (i.e. the net present value) of the energy efficiency measures (as referred to in the second indent) during the expected economic lifecycle applied to the reference buildings (as referred to in the first indent) by applying the comparative methodology framework principles.

By calculating the costs of the energy efficiency measures during the expected economic lifecycle, the cost-effectiveness of different levels of minimum energy performance requirements is assessed by the Member States. This will allow the determination of cost-optimal levels of energy performance requirements.

ANNEX IV

PART A
REPEALED DIRECTIVE WITH ITS SUCCESSIVE AMENDMENT
(REFERRED TO IN ARTICLE 29)

Directive 2002/91/EC of the European Parliament and of the Council (OJ L 1, 4.1.2003, p. 65)	
Regulation (EC) No 1137/2008 of the European Parliament and of the Council (OJ L 311, 21.11.2008, p. 1)	only point 9.9 of the Annex

PART B
TIME LIMITS FOR TRANSPOSITION INTO NATIONAL LAW AND APPLICATION
(REFERRED TO IN ARTICLE 29)

Directive	*Time limit for transposition*	*Date of application*
2002/91/EC	4 January 2006	4 January 2009 as regards Articles 7, 8 and 9 only

ANNEX V
CORRELATION TABLE

Directive 2002/91/EC	*This Directive*
Article 1	Article 1
Article 2, point (1)	Article 2, point (1)
—	Article 2, points (2) and (3)
Article 2, point (2)	Article 2, point (4) and Annex I
—	Article 2, points (5), (6), (7), (8), (9), (10) and (11)
Article 2, point (3)	Article 2, point (12)
Article 2, point (4)	Article 2, point (13)
—	Article 2, point (14)
Article 2, point (5)	Article 2, point (15)
Article 2, point (6)	Article 2, point (16)
Article 2, point (7)	Article 2, point (17)
Article 2, point (8)	Article 2, point (18)
—	Article 2, point (19)
Article 3	Article 3 and Annex I
Article 4(1)	Article 4(1)
Article 4(2)	—
Article 4(3)	Article 4(2)
—	Article 5
Article 5	Article 6(1)
—	Article 6(2) and (3)
Article 6	Article 7
—	Articles 8, 9 and 10
Article 7(1) first subparagraph	Article 11(8) and Article 12(2)
Article 7(1) second subparagraph	Article 11(6)
Article 7(1) third subparagraph	Article 12(6)
Article 7(2)	Article 11(1) and (2)
—	Article 11(3), (4), (5), (7) and (9)
—	Article 12(1), (3), (4), (5) and (7)
Article 7(3)	Article 13(1) and (3)
—	Article 13(2)
Article 8, point (a)	Article 14(1) and (3)
—	Article 14(2)
Article 8, point (b)	Article 14(4)
—	Article 14(5)
Article 9	Article 15(1)
—	Article 15(2), (3), (4) and (5)
—	Article 16
Article 10	Article 17
—	Article 18
Article 11, introductory wording	Article 19
Article 11, points (a) and (b)	—
Article 12	Article 20(1) and Article 20(2) second subparagraph

Directive 2002/91/EC	*This Directive*
—	Article 20(2) first subparagraph and Article 20(3) and (4)
—	Article 21
Article 13	Article 22
—	Articles 23, 24 and 25
Article 14(1)	Article 26(1)
Article 14(2) and (3)	—
—	Article 26(2)
—	Article 27
Article 15(1)	Article 28
Article 15(2)	—
—	Article 29
Article 16	Article 30
Article 17	Article 31
Annex	Annex I
—	Annexes II to V

DIRECTIVE 2010/75/EU OF THE EUROPEAN PARLIAMENT AND OF THE COUNCIL

of 24 November 2010

ON INDUSTRIAL EMISSIONS (INTEGRATED POLLUTION PREVENTION AND CONTROL)

THE EUROPEAN PARLIAMENT AND THE COUNCIL OF THE EUROPEAN UNION,

Having regard to the Treaty on the Functioning of the European Union, and in particular Article 192(1) thereof,

Having regard to the proposal from the European Commission,

Having regard to the opinion of the European Economic and Social Committee,

Having regard to the opinion of the Committee of the Regions,

Acting in accordance with the ordinary legislative procedure,

Whereas:

(1) A number of substantial changes are to be made to Council Directive 78/176/EEC of 20 February 1978 on waste from the titanium dioxide industry, Council Directive 82/883/EEC of 3 December 1982 on procedures for the surveillance and monitoring of environments concerned by waste from the titanium dioxide industry, Council Directive 92/112/EEC of 15 December 1992 on procedures for harmonising the programmes for the reduction and eventual elimination of pollution caused by waste from the titanium dioxide industry, Council Directive 1999/13/EC of 11 March 1999 on the limitation of emissions of volatile organic compounds due to the use of organic solvents in certain activities and installations, Directive 2000/76/EC of the European Parliament and of the Council of 4 December 2000 on the incineration of waste, Directive 2001/80/EC of the European Parliament and of the Council of 23 October 2001 on the limitation of emissions of certain pollutants into the air from large combustion plants and Directive 2008/1/EC of the European Parliament and of the Council of 15 January 2008 concerning integrated pollution prevention and control. In the interests of clarity, those Directives should be recast.

(2) In order to prevent, reduce and as far as possible eliminate pollution arising from industrial activities in compliance with the "polluter pays" principle and the principle of pollution prevention, it is necessary to establish a general framework for the control of the main industrial activities, giving priority to intervention at source, ensuring prudent management of natural resources and taking into account, when necessary, the economic situation and specific local characteristics of the place in which the industrial activity is taking place.

(3) Different approaches to controlling emissions into air, water or soil separately may encourage the shifting of pollution from one environmental medium to another rather than protecting the environment as a whole. It is, therefore, appropriate to provide for an integrated approach to prevention and control of emissions into air, water and soil, to waste management, to energy efficiency and to accident prevention. Such an approach will also contribute to the achievement of a level playing field in the Union by aligning environmental performance requirements for industrial installations.

(4) It is appropriate to revise the legislation relating to industrial installations in order to simplify and clarify the existing provisions, reduce unnecessary administrative burden and implement the conclusions of the Commission Communications of 21 September 2005 on the Thematic Strategy on Air Pollution (hereinafter the Thematic Strategy on

Air Pollution), of 22 September 2006 on the Thematic Strategy for Soil Protection and of 21 December 2005 on the Thematic Strategy on the Prevention and Recycling of Waste adopted as a follow-up to Decision No 1600/2002/EC of the European Parliament and of the Council of 22 July 2002 laying down the Sixth Community Environment Action Programme. Those Communications set objectives to protect human health and the environment which cannot be met without further reductions in emissions arising from industrial activities.

(5) In order to ensure the prevention and control of pollution, each installation should operate only if it holds a permit or, in the case of certain installations and activities using organic solvents, only if it holds a permit or is registered.

(6) It is for Member States to determine the approach for assigning responsibilities to operators of installations provided that compliance with this Directive is ensured. Member States may choose to grant a permit to one responsible operator for each installation or to specify the responsibility amongst several operators of different parts of an installation. Where its current legal system provides for only one responsible operator for each installation, a Member State may decide to retain this system.

(7) In order to facilitate the granting of permits, Member States should be able to set requirements for certain categories of installations in general binding rules.

(8) It is important to prevent accidents and incidents and limit their consequences. Liability regarding the environmental consequences of accidents and incidents is a matter for relevant national law and, where applicable, other relevant Union law.

(9) In order to avoid duplication of regulation, the permit for an installation covered by Directive 2003/87/EC of the European Parliament and of the Council of 13 October 2003 establishing a scheme for greenhouse gas emission allowance trading within the Community should not include an emission limit value for direct emissions of the greenhouse gases specified in Annex I to that Directive except where it is necessary to ensure that no significant local pollution is caused or where an installation is excluded from that scheme.

(10) In accordance with Article 193 of the Treaty on the Functioning of the European Union (TFEU), this Directive does not prevent Member States from maintaining or introducing more stringent protective measures, for example greenhouse gas emission requirements, provided that such measures are compatible with the Treaties and the Commission has been notified.

(11) Operators should submit permit applications containing the information necessary for the competent authority to set permit conditions. Operators should be able to use information resulting from the application of Council Directive 85/337/EEC of 27 June 1985 on the assessment of the effects of certain public and private projects on the environment and of Council Directive 96/82/EC of 9 December 1996 on the control of major-accident hazards involving dangerous substances when submitting permit applications.

(12) The permit should include all the measures necessary to achieve a high level of protection of the environment as a whole and to ensure that the installation is operated in accordance with the general principles governing the basic obligations of the operator. The permit should also include emission limit values for polluting substances, or equivalent parameters or technical measures, appropriate requirements to protect the soil and groundwater and monitoring requirements. Permit conditions should be set on the basis of best available techniques.

(13) In order to determine best available techniques and to limit imbalances in the Union as regards the level of emissions from industrial activities, reference documents for best available techniques (hereinafter BAT reference documents') should be drawn up, reviewed and, where necessary, updated through an exchange of information with stakeholders and the key elements of BAT reference documents (hereinafter BAT conclusions') adopted through committee procedure. In this respect, the Commission should, through committee procedure, establish guidance on the collection of data, on the elaboration of BAT reference documents and on their quality assurance.

BAT conclusions should be the reference for setting permit conditions. They can be supplemented by other sources. The Commission should aim to update BAT reference documents not later than 8 years after the publication of the previous version.

(14) In order to ensure an effective and active exchange of information resulting in high-quality BAT reference documents, the Commission should establish a forum that functions in a transparent manner. Practical arrangements for the exchange of information and the accessibility of BAT reference documents should be laid down, in particular to ensure that Member States and stakeholders provide data of sufficient quality and quantity based on established guidance to enable the determination of best available techniques and emerging techniques.

(15) It is important to provide sufficient flexibility to competent authorities to set emission limit values that ensure that, under normal operating conditions, emissions do not exceed the emission levels associated with the best available techniques. To this end, the competent authority may set emission limits that differ from the emission levels associated with the best available techniques in terms of the values, periods of time and reference conditions applied, so long as it can be demonstrated, through the results of emission monitoring, that emissions have not exceeded the emission levels associated with the best available techniques. Compliance with the emission limit values that are set in permits results in emissions below those emission limit values.

(16) In order to take into account certain specific circumstances where the application of emission levels associated with the best available techniques would lead to disproportionately high costs compared to the environmental benefits, competent authorities should be able to set emission limit values deviating from those levels. Such deviations should be based on an assessment taking into account well-defined criteria. The emission limit values set out in this Directive should not be exceeded. In any event, no significant pollution should be caused and a high level of protection of the environment taken as a whole should be achieved.

(17) In order to enable operators to test emerging techniques which could provide for a higher general level of environmental protection, or at least the same level of environmental protection and higher cost savings than existing best available techniques, the competent authority should be able to grant temporary derogations from emission levels associated with the best available techniques.

(18) Changes to an installation may give rise to higher levels of pollution. Operators should notify the competent authority of any planned change which might affect the environment. Substantial changes to installations which may have significant negative effects on human health or the environment should not be made without a permit granted in accordance with this Directive.

(19) The spreading of manure contributes significantly to emissions of pollutants into air and water. With a view to meeting the objectives set out in the Thematic Strategy on Air Pollution and Union law on water protection, it is necessary for the Commission to review the need to establish the most suitable controls of these emissions through the application of best available techniques.

(20) The intensive rearing of poultry and cattle contributes significantly to emissions of pollutants into air and water. With a view to meeting the objectives set out in the Thematic Strategy on Air Pollution and in Union law on water protection, it is necessary for the Commission to review the need to establish differentiated capacity thresholds for different poultry species in order to define the scope of this Directive and to review the need to establish the most suitable controls on emissions from cattle rearing installations.

(21) In order to take account of developments in best available techniques or other changes to an installation, permit conditions should be reconsidered regularly and, where necessary, updated, in particular where new or updated BAT conclusions are adopted.

(22) In specific cases where permit reconsideration and updating identifies that a longer period than 4 years after the publication of a decision on BAT conclusions might be needed to introduce new best available techniques, competent authorities may set a

longer time period in permit conditions where this is justified on the basis of the criteria laid down in this Directive.

(23) It is necessary to ensure that the operation of an installation does not lead to a deterioration of the quality of soil and groundwater. Permit conditions should, therefore, include appropriate measures to prevent emissions to soil and groundwater and regular surveillance of those measures to avoid leaks, spills, incidents or accidents occurring during the use of equipment and during storage. In order to detect possible soil and groundwater pollution at an early stage and, therefore, to take appropriate corrective measures before the pollution spreads, the monitoring of soil and groundwater for relevant hazardous substances is also necessary. When determining the frequency of monitoring, the type of prevention measures and the extent and occurrence of their surveillance may be considered.

(24) In order to ensure that the operation of an installation does not deteriorate the quality of soil and groundwater, it is necessary to establish, through a baseline report, the state of soil and groundwater contamination. The baseline report should be a practical tool that permits, as far as possible, a quantified comparison between the state of the site described in that report and the state of the site upon definitive cessation of activities, in order to ascertain whether a significant increase in pollution of soil or groundwater has taken place. The baseline report should, therefore, contain information making use of existing data on soil and groundwater measurements and historical data related to past uses of the site.

(25) In accordance with the polluter pays principle, when assessing the level of significance of the pollution of soil and groundwater caused by the operator which would trigger the obligation to return the site to the state described in the baseline report, Member States should take into account the permit conditions that have applied over the lifetime of the activity concerned, the pollution prevention measures adopted for the installation, and the relative increase in pollution compared to the contamination load identified in the baseline report. Liability regarding pollution not caused by the operator is a matter for relevant national law and, where applicable, other relevant Union law.

(26) In order to ensure the effective implementation and enforcement of this Directive, operators should regularly report to the competent authority on compliance with permit conditions. Member States should ensure that the operator and the competent authority each take necessary measures in the event of non-compliance with this Directive and provide for a system of environmental inspections. Member States should ensure that sufficient staff are available with the skills and qualifications needed to carry out those inspections effectively.

(27) In accordance with the Århus Convention on access to information, public participation in decision-making and access to justice in environmental matters, effective public participation in decision-making is necessary to enable the public to express, and the decision-maker to take account of, opinions and concerns which may be relevant to those decisions, thereby increasing the accountability and transparency of the decision-making process and contributing to public awareness of environmental issues and support for the decisions taken. Members of the public concerned should have access to justice in order to contribute to the protection of the right to live in an environment which is adequate for personal health and well-being.

(28) The combustion of fuel in installations with a total rated thermal input below 50 MW contributes significantly to emissions of pollutants into the air. With a view to meeting the objectives set out in the Thematic Strategy on Air Pollution, it is necessary for the Commission to review the need to establish the most suitable controls on emissions from such installations. That review should take into account the specificities of combustion plants used in healthcare facilities, in particular with regard to their exceptional use in the case of emergencies.

(29) Large combustion plants contribute greatly to emissions of polluting substances into the air resulting in a significant impact on human health and the environment. In order to reduce that impact and to work towards meeting the requirements of Directive

2001/81/EC of the European Parliament and of the Council of 23 October 2001 on national emission ceilings for certain atmospheric pollutants and the objectives set out in the Thematic Strategy on Air Pollution, it is necessary to set more stringent emission limit values at Union level for certain categories of combustion plants and pollutants.

(30) The Commission should review the need to establish Union-wide emission limit values and to amend the emission limit values set out in Annex V for certain large combustion plants, taking into account the review and update of the relevant BAT reference documents. In this context, the Commission should consider the specificity of the energy systems of refineries.

(31) Due to the characteristics of certain indigenous solid fuels, it is appropriate to apply minimum desulphurisation rates rather than emission limit values for sulphur dioxide for combustion plants firing such fuels. Moreover, as the specific characteristics of oil shale may not allow the application of the same sulphur abatement techniques or the achievement of the same desulphurisation efficiency as for other fuels, a slightly lower minimum desulphurisation rate for plants using this fuel is appropriate.

(32) In the case of a sudden interruption in the supply of low-sulphur fuel or gas resulting from a serious shortage, the competent authority should be able to grant temporary derogations to allow emissions of the combustion plants concerned to exceed the emission limit values set out in this Directive.

(33) The operator concerned should not operate a combustion plant for more than 24 hours after malfunctioning or breakdown of abatement equipment and unabated operation should not exceed 120 hours in a 12-month period in order to limit the negative effects of pollution on the environment. However, where there is an overriding need for energy supplies or it is necessary to avoid an overall increase of emissions resulting from the operation of another combustion plant, competent authorities should be able to grant a derogation from those time limits.

(34) In order to ensure a high level of environmental and human health protection and to avoid transboundary movements of waste to plants operating at lower environmental standards, it is necessary to set and maintain stringent operating conditions, technical requirements and emission limit values for plants incinerating or co-incinerating waste within the Union.

(35) The use of organic solvents in certain activities and installations gives rise to emissions of organic compounds into the air which contribute to the local and transboundary formation of photochemical oxidants which causes damage to natural resources and has harmful effects on human health. It is, therefore, necessary to take preventive action against the use of organic solvents and to establish a requirement to comply with emission limit values for organic compounds and appropriate operating conditions. Operators should be allowed to comply with the requirements of a reduction scheme instead of complying with the emission limit values set out in this Directive where other measures, such as the use of low-solvent or solvent-free products or techniques, provide alternative means of achieving equivalent emission reduction.

(36) Installations producing titanium dioxide can give rise to significant pollution into air and water. In order to reduce these impacts, it is necessary to set at Union level more stringent emission limit values for certain polluting substances.

(37) With regard to the inclusion in the scope of national laws, regulations and administrative provisions brought into force in order to comply with this Directive of installations for the manufacturing of ceramic products by firings, on the basis of the characteristics of the national industrial sector, and in order to grant clear interpretation of the scope, Member States should decide whether to apply both the criteria, production capacity and kiln capacity, or just one of the two criteria.

(38) In order to simplify reporting and reduce unnecessary administrative burden, the Commission should identify methods to streamline the way in which data are made available pursuant to this Directive with the other requirements of Union law, and in particular Regulation (EC) No 166/2006 of the European Parliament and of the Council

of 18 January 2006 concerning the establishment of a European Pollutant Release and Transfer Register.

(39) In order to ensure uniform conditions for implementation, implementing powers should be conferred on the Commission to adopt guidance on the collection of data, on the drawing up of BAT reference documents and on their quality assurance, including the suitability of their content and format, to adopt decisions on BAT conclusions, to establish detailed rules on the determination of start-up and shut-down periods and for transitional national plans for large combustion plants, and to establish the type, format and frequency of information that Member States are to make available to the Commission. In accordance with Article 291 TFEU, rules and general principles concerning mechanisms for the control by Member States of the Commission's exercise of implementing powers are to be laid down in advance by a regulation adopted in accordance with the ordinary legislative procedure. Pending the adoption of that new regulation, Council Decision 1999/468/EC of 28 June 1999 laying down the procedures for the exercise of implementing powers conferred on the Commission continues to apply, with the exception of the regulatory procedure with scrutiny, which is not applicable.

(40) The Commission should be empowered to adopt delegated acts in accordance with Article 290 TFEU in respect of the setting of the date from which continuous measurements of emissions into the air of heavy metals and dioxins and furans are to be carried out, and the adaptation of certain parts of Annexes V, VI and VII to scientific and technical progress. In the case of waste incineration plants and waste co-incineration plants, this may include, inter alia, the establishment of criteria to allow derogations from continuous monitoring of total dust emissions. It is of particular importance that the Commission carry out appropriate consultations during its preparatory work, including at expert level.

(41) In order to address significant environmental pollution, for example from heavy metals and dioxins and furans, the Commission should, based on an assessment of the implementation of the best available techniques by certain activities or of the impact of those activities on the environment as a whole, present proposals for Union-wide minimum requirements for emission limit values and for rules on monitoring and compliance.

(42) Member States should lay down rules on penalties applicable to infringements of the national provisions adopted pursuant to this Directive and ensure that they are implemented. Those penalties should be effective, proportionate and dissuasive.

(43) In order to provide existing installations with sufficient time to adapt technically to the new requirements of this Directive, some of the new requirements should apply to those installations after a fixed period from the date of application of this Directive. Combustion plants need sufficient time to install the necessary abatement measures to meet the emission limit values set out in Annex V.

(44) Since the objectives of this Directive, namely to ensure a high level of environmental protection and the improvement of environmental quality, cannot be sufficiently achieved by Member States and can, therefore, by reason of the transboundary nature of pollution from industrial activities, be better achieved at Union level, the Union may adopt measures in accordance with the principle of subsidiarity as set out in Article 5 of the Treaty on European Union. In accordance with the principle of proportionality, as set out in that Article, this Directive does not go beyond what is necessary in order to achieve those objectives.

(45) This Directive respects the fundamental rights and observes the principles recognised in particular by the Charter of Fundamental Rights of the European Union. In particular, this Directive seeks to promote the application of Article 37 of that Charter.

(46) The obligation to transpose this Directive into national law should be confined to those provisions which represent a substantive change as compared with the earlier Directives. The obligation to transpose the provisions which are unchanged arises under the earlier Directives.

plant or, where this is provided for in national law, to whom decisive economic power over the technical functioning of the installation or plant has been delegated;

(16) "the public" means one or more natural or legal persons and, in accordance with national law or practice, their associations, organisations or groups;

(17) "the public concerned" means the public affected or likely to be affected by, or having an interest in, the taking of a decision on the granting or the updating of a permit or of permit conditions; for the purposes of this definition, non-governmental organisations promoting environmental protection and meeting any requirements under national law shall be deemed to have an interest;

(18) "hazardous substances" means substances or mixtures as defined in Article 3 of Regulation (EC) No 1272/2008 of the European Parliament and of the Council of 16 December 2008 on classification, labelling and packaging of substances and mixtures;

(19) "baseline report" means information on the state of soil and groundwater contamination by relevant hazardous substances;

(20) "groundwater" means groundwater as defined in point 2 of Article 2 of Directive 2000/60/EC of the European Parliament and of the Council of 23 October 2000 establishing a framework for Community action in the field of water policy;

(21) "soil" means the top layer of the Earth's crust situated between the bedrock and the surface. The soil is composed of mineral particles, organic matter, water, air and living organisms;

(22) "environmental inspection" means all actions, including site visits, monitoring of emissions and checks of internal reports and follow-up documents, verification of self-monitoring, checking of the techniques used and adequacy of the environment management of the installation, undertaken by or on behalf of the competent authority to check and promote compliance of installations with their permit conditions and, where necessary, to monitor their environmental impact;

(23) "poultry" means poultry as defined in point 1 of Article 2 of Council Directive 90/539/EEC of 15 October 1990 on animal health conditions governing intra-Community trade in, and imports from third countries of, poultry and hatching eggs;

(24) "fuel" means any solid, liquid or gaseous combustible material;

(25) "combustion plant" means any technical apparatus in which fuels are oxidised in order to use the heat thus generated;

(26) "stack" means a structure containing one or more flues providing a passage for waste gases in order to discharge them into the air;

(27) "operating hours" means the time, expressed in hours, during which a combustion plant, in whole or in part, is operating and discharging emissions into the air, excluding start-up and shut-down periods;

(28) "rate of desulphurisation" means the ratio over a given period of time of the quantity of sulphur which is not emitted into air by a combustion plant to the quantity of sulphur contained in the solid fuel which is introduced into the combustion plant facilities and which is used in the plant over the same period of time;

(29) "indigenous solid fuel" means a naturally occurring solid fuel fired in a combustion plant specifically designed for that fuel and extracted locally;

(30) "determinative fuel" means the fuel which, amongst all fuels used in a multi-fuel firing combustion plant using the distillation and conversion residues from the refining of crude-oil for own consumption, alone or with other fuels, has the highest emission limit value as set out in Part 1 of Annex V, or, in the case of several fuels having the same emission limit value, the fuel having the highest thermal input amongst those fuels;

(31) "biomass" means any of the following:

(a) products consisting of any vegetable matter from agriculture or forestry which can be used as a fuel for the purpose of recovering its energy content;

(b) the following waste:

(i) vegetable waste from agriculture and forestry;

(ii) vegetable waste from the food processing industry, if the heat generated is recovered;

(iii) fibrous vegetable waste from virgin pulp production and from production of paper from pulp, if it is co-incinerated at the place of production and the heat generated is recovered;

(iv) cork waste;

(v) wood waste with the exception of wood waste which may contain halogenated organic compounds or heavy metals as a result of treatment with wood preservatives or coating and which includes, in particular, such wood waste originating from construction and demolition waste;

(32) "multi-fuel firing combustion plant" means any combustion plant which may be fired simultaneously or alternately by two or more types of fuel;

(33) "gas turbine" means any rotating machine which converts thermal energy into mechanical work, consisting mainly of a compressor, a thermal device in which fuel is oxidised in order to heat the working fluid, and a turbine;

(34) "gas engine" means an internal combustion engine which operates according to the Otto cycle and uses spark ignition or, in case of dual fuel engines, compression ignition to burn fuel;

(35) "diesel engine" means an internal combustion engine which operates according to the diesel cycle and uses compression ignition to burn fuel;

(36) "small isolated system" means a small isolated system as defined in point 26 of Article 2 of Directive 2003/54/EC of the European Parliament and of the Council of 26 June 2003 concerning common rules for the internal market in electricity;

(37) "waste" means waste as defined in point 1 of Article 3 of Directive 2008/98/EC of the European Parliament and of the Council of 19 November 2008 on waste;

(38) "hazardous waste" means hazardous waste as defined in point 2 of Article 3 of Directive 2008/98/EC;

(39) "mixed municipal waste" means waste from households as well as commercial, industrial and institutional waste which, because of its nature and composition, is similar to waste from households, but excluding fractions indicated under heading 20 01 of the Annex to Decision 2000/532/EC that are collected separately at source and excluding the other waste indicated under heading 20 02 of that Annex;

(40) "waste incineration plant" means any stationary or mobile technical unit and equipment dedicated to the thermal treatment of waste, with or without recovery of the combustion heat generated, through the incineration by oxidation of waste as well as other thermal treatment processes, such as pyrolysis, gasification or plasma process, if the substances resulting from the treatment are subsequently incinerated;

(41) "waste co-incineration plant" means any stationary or mobile technical unit whose main purpose is the generation of energy or production of material products and which uses waste as a regular or additional fuel or in which waste is thermally treated for the purpose of disposal through the incineration by oxidation of waste as well as other thermal treatment processes, such as pyrolysis, gasification or plasma process, if the substances resulting from the treatment are subsequently incinerated;

(42) "nominal capacity" means the sum of the incineration capacities of the furnaces of which a waste incineration plant or a waste co-incineration plant is composed, as specified by the constructor and confirmed by the operator, with due account being taken of the calorific value of the waste, expressed as the quantity of waste incinerated per hour;

(43) "dioxins and furans" means all polychlorinated dibenzo-p-dioxins and dibenzofurans listed in Part 2 of Annex VI;

(44) "organic compound" means any compound containing at least the element carbon and one or more of hydrogen, halogens, oxygen, sulphur, phosphorus, silicon or nitrogen, with the exception of carbon oxides and inorganic carbonates and bicarbonates;

(45) "volatile organic compound" means any organic compound as well as the fraction of creosote, having at 293,15 K a vapour pressure of 0,01 kPa or more, or having a corresponding volatility under the particular conditions of use;

(46) "organic solvent" means any volatile organic compound which is used for any of the following:

(a) alone or in combination with other agents, and without undergoing a chemical change, to dissolve raw materials, products or waste materials;
(b) as a cleaning agent to dissolve contaminants;
(c) as a dissolver;
(d) as a dispersion medium;
(e) as a viscosity adjuster;
(f) as a surface tension adjuster;
(g) as a plasticiser;
(h) as a preservative;

(47) "coating" means coating as defined in point 8 of Article 2 of Directive 2004/42/EC of the European Parliament and of the Council of 21 April 2004 on the limitation of emissions of volatile organic compounds due to the use of organic solvents in certain paints and varnishes and vehicle refinishing products.

Article 4

Obligation to hold a permit

1. Member States shall take the necessary measures to ensure that no installation or combustion plant, waste incineration plant or waste co-incineration plant is operated without a permit.

By way of derogation from the first subparagraph, Member States may set a procedure for the registration of installations covered only by Chapter V.

The procedure for registration shall be specified in a binding act and include at least a notification to the competent authority by the operator of the intention to operate an installation.

2. Member States may opt to provide that a permit cover two or more installations or parts of installations operated by the same operator on the same site.

Where a permit covers two or more installations, it shall contain conditions to ensure that each installation complies with the requirements of this Directive.

3. Member States may opt to provide that a permit cover several parts of an installation operated by different operators. In such cases, the permit shall specify the responsibilities of each operator.

Article 5

Granting of a permit

1. Without prejudice to other requirements laid down in national or Union law, the competent authority shall grant a permit if the installation complies with the requirements of this Directive.

2. Member States shall take the measures necessary to ensure that the conditions of, and the procedures for the granting of, the permit are fully coordinated where more than one competent authority or more than one operator is involved or more than one permit is granted, in order to guarantee an effective integrated approach by all authorities competent for this procedure.

3. In the case of a new installation or a substantial change where Article 4 of Directive 85/337/EEC applies, any relevant information obtained or conclusion arrived at pursuant to Articles 5, 6, 7 and 9 of that Directive shall be examined and used for the purposes of granting the permit.

Article 6

General binding rules

Without prejudice to the obligation to hold a permit, Member States may include requirements for certain categories of installations, combustion plants, waste incineration plants or waste co-incineration plants in general binding rules.

Where general binding rules are adopted, the permit may simply include a reference to such rules.

Article 7

Incidents and accidents

Without prejudice to Directive 2004/35/EC of the European Parliament and of the Council of 21 April 2004 on environmental liability with regard to the prevention and remedying of environmental damage, in the event of any incident or accident significantly affecting the environment, Member States shall take the necessary measures to ensure that:

(a) the operator informs the competent authority immediately;

(b) the operator immediately takes the measures to limit the environmental consequences and to prevent further possible incidents or accidents;

(c) the competent authority requires the operator to take any appropriate complementary measures that the competent authority considers necessary to limit the environmental consequences and to prevent further possible incidents or accidents.

Article 8

Non-compliance

1. Member States shall take the necessary measures to ensure that the permit conditions are complied with.

2. In the event of a breach of the permit conditions, Member States shall ensure that:

(a) the operator immediately informs the competent authority;

(b) the operator immediately takes the measures necessary to ensure that compliance is restored within the shortest possible time;

(c) the competent authority requires the operator to take any appropriate complementary measures that the competent authority considers necessary to restore compliance.

Where the breach of the permit conditions poses an immediate danger to human health or threatens to cause an immediate significant adverse effect upon the environment, and until compliance is restored in accordance with points (b) and (c) of the first subparagraph, the operation of the installation, combustion plant, waste incineration plant, waste co-incineration plant or relevant part thereof shall be suspended.

Article 9

Emission of greenhouse gases

1. Where emissions of a greenhouse gas from an installation are specified in Annex I to Directive 2003/87/EC in relation to an activity carried out in that installation, the permit shall not include an emission limit value for direct emissions of that gas, unless necessary to ensure that no significant local pollution is caused.

2. For activities listed in Annex I to Directive 2003/87/EC, Member States may choose not to impose requirements relating to energy efficiency in respect of combustion units or other units emitting carbon dioxide on the site.

3. Where necessary, the competent authorities shall amend the permit as appropriate.

4. Paragraphs 1 to 3 shall not apply to installations which are temporarily excluded from the scheme for greenhouse gas emission allowance trading within the Union in accordance with Article 27 of Directive 2003/87/EC.

Chapter II
Provisions for activities listed in Annex I

Article 10

Scope

This Chapter shall apply to the activities set out in Annex I and, where applicable, reaching the capacity thresholds set out in that Annex.

Article 11

General principles governing the basic obligations of the operator

Member States shall take the necessary measures to provide that installations are operated in accordance with the following principles:
(a) all the appropriate preventive measures are taken against pollution;
(b) the best available techniques are applied;
(c) no significant pollution is caused;
(d) the generation of waste is prevented in accordance with Directive 2008/98/EC;
(e) where waste is generated, it is, in order of priority and in accordance with Directive 2008/98/EC, prepared for re-use, recycled, recovered or, where that is technically and economically impossible, it is disposed of while avoiding or reducing any impact on the environment;
(f) energy is used efficiently;
(g) the necessary measures are taken to prevent accidents and limit their consequences;
(h) the necessary measures are taken upon definitive cessation of activities to avoid any risk of pollution and return the site of operation to the satisfactory state defined in accordance with Article 22.

Article 12

Applications for permits

1. Member States shall take the necessary measures to ensure that an application for a permit includes a description of the following:
(a) the installation and its activities;
(b) the raw and auxiliary materials, other substances and the energy used in or generated by the installation;
(c) the sources of emissions from the installation;
(d) the conditions of the site of the installation;
(e) where applicable, a baseline report in accordance with Article 22(2);
(f) the nature and quantities of foreseeable emissions from the installation into each medium as well as identification of significant effects of the emissions on the environment;
(g) the proposed technology and other techniques for preventing or, where this is not possible, reducing emissions from the installation;
(h) measures for the prevention, preparation for re-use, recycling and recovery of waste generated by the installation;
(i) further measures planned to comply with the general principles of the basic obligations of the operator as provided for in Article 11;
(j) measures planned to monitor emissions into the environment;
(k) the main alternatives to the proposed technology, techniques and measures studied by the applicant in outline.

An application for a permit shall also include a non-technical summary of the details referred to in the first subparagraph.

2. Where information supplied in accordance with the requirements provided for in Directive 85/337/EEC or a safety report prepared in accordance with Directive 96/82/EC or other

information produced in response to other legislation fulfils any of the requirements of paragraph 1, that information may be included in, or attached to, the application.

Article 13

BAT reference documents and exchange of information

1. In order to draw up, review and, where necessary, update BAT reference documents, the Commission shall organise an exchange of information between Member States, the industries concerned, non-governmental organisations promoting environmental protection and the Commission.

2. The exchange of information shall, in particular, address the following:
(a) the performance of installations and techniques in terms of emissions, expressed as short- and long-term averages, where appropriate, and the associated reference conditions, consumption and nature of raw materials, water consumption, use of energy and generation of waste;
(b) the techniques used, associated monitoring, cross-media effects, economic and technical viability and developments therein;
(c) best available techniques and emerging techniques identified after considering the issues mentioned in points (a) and (b).

3. The Commission shall establish and regularly convene a forum composed of representatives of Member States, the industries concerned and non-governmental organisations promoting environmental protection.

The Commission shall obtain the opinion of the forum on the practical arrangements for the exchange of information and, in particular, on the following:
(a) the rules of procedure of the forum;
(b) the work programme for the exchange of information;
(c) guidance on the collection of data;
(d) guidance on the drawing up of BAT reference documents and on their quality assurance including the suitability of their content and format.
The guidance referred to in points (c) and (d) of the second subparagraph shall take account of the opinion of the forum and shall be adopted in accordance with the regulatory procedure referred to in Article 75(2).

4. The Commission shall obtain and make publicly available the opinion of the forum on the proposed content of the BAT reference documents and shall take into account this opinion for the procedures laid down in paragraph 5.

5. Decisions on the BAT conclusions shall be adopted in accordance with the regulatory procedure referred to in Article 75(2).

6. After the adoption of a decision in accordance with paragraph 5, the Commission shall without delay make the BAT reference document publicly available and ensure that BAT conclusions are made available in all the official languages of the Union.

7. Pending the adoption of a relevant decision in accordance with paragraph 5, the conclusions on best available techniques from BAT reference documents adopted by the Commission prior to the date referred to in Article 83 shall apply as BAT conclusions for the purposes of this Chapter except for Article 15(3) and (4).

Article 14

Permit conditions

1. Member States shall ensure that the permit includes all measures necessary for compliance with the requirements of Articles 11 and 18.

Those measures shall include at least the following:

(a) emission limit values for polluting substances listed in Annex II, and for other polluting substances, which are likely to be emitted from the installation concerned in significant quantities, having regard to their nature and their potential to transfer pollution from one medium to another;

(b) appropriate requirements ensuring protection of the soil and groundwater and measures concerning the monitoring and management of waste generated by the installation;

(c) suitable emission monitoring requirements specifying:
  (i) measurement methodology, frequency and evaluation procedure; and
  (ii) where Article 15(3)(b) is applied, that results of emission monitoring are available for the same periods of time and reference conditions as for the emission levels associated with the best available techniques;

(d) an obligation to supply the competent authority regularly, and at least annually, with:
  (i) information on the basis of results of emission monitoring referred to in point (c) and other required data that enables the competent authority to verify compliance with the permit conditions; and
  (ii) where Article 15(3)(b) is applied, a summary of the results of emission monitoring which allows a comparison with the emission levels associated with the best available techniques;

(e) appropriate requirements for the regular maintenance and surveillance of measures taken to prevent emissions to soil and groundwater pursuant to point (b) and appropriate requirements concerning the periodic monitoring of soil and groundwater in relation to relevant hazardous substances likely to be found on site and having regard to the possibility of soil and groundwater contamination at the site of the installation;

(f) measures relating to conditions other than normal operating conditions such as start-up and shut-down operations, leaks, malfunctions, momentary stoppages and definitive cessation of operations;

(g) provisions on the minimisation of long-distance or transboundary pollution;

(h) conditions for assessing compliance with the emission limit values or a reference to the applicable requirements specified elsewhere.

2. For the purpose of paragraph 1(a), emission limit values may be supplemented or replaced by equivalent parameters or technical measures ensuring an equivalent level of environmental protection.

3. BAT conclusions shall be the reference for setting the permit conditions.

4. Without prejudice to Article 18, the competent authority may set stricter permit conditions than those achievable by the use of the best available techniques as described in the BAT conclusions. Member States may establish rules under which the competent authority may set such stricter conditions.

5. Where the competent authority sets permit conditions on the basis of a best available technique not described in any of the relevant BAT conclusions, it shall ensure that:

(a) that technique is determined by giving special consideration to the criteria listed in Annex III; and

(b) the requirements of Article 15 are complied with.

Where the BAT conclusions referred to in the first subparagraph do not contain emission levels associated with the best available techniques, the competent authority shall ensure that the technique referred to in the first subparagraph ensures a level of environmental protection equivalent to the best available techniques described in the BAT conclusions.

6. Where an activity or a type of production process carried out within an installation is not covered by any of the BAT conclusions or where those conclusions do not address all the potential environmental effects of the activity or process, the competent authority shall, after prior consultations with the operator, set the permit conditions on the basis of the best available techniques that it has determined for the activities or processes concerned, by giving special consideration to the criteria listed in Annex III.

7. For installations referred to in point 6.6 of Annex I, paragraphs 1 to 6 of this Article shall apply without prejudice to the legislation relating to animal welfare.

Article 15

Emission limit values, equivalent parameters and technical measures

1. The emission limit values for polluting substances shall apply at the point where the emissions leave the installation, and any dilution prior to that point shall be disregarded when determining those values.

With regard to indirect releases of polluting substances into water, the effect of a water treatment plant may be taken into account when determining the emission limit values of the installation concerned, provided that an equivalent level of protection of the environment as a whole is guaranteed and provided this does not lead to higher levels of pollution in the environment.

2. Without prejudice to Article 18, the emission limit values and the equivalent parameters and technical measures referred to in Article 14(1) and (2) shall be based on the best available techniques, without prescribing the use of any technique or specific technology.

3. The competent authority shall set emission limit values that ensure that, under normal operating conditions, emissions do not exceed the emission levels associated with the best available techniques as laid down in the decisions on BAT conclusions referred to in Article 13(5) through either of the following:

(a) setting emission limit values that do not exceed the emission levels associated with the best available techniques. Those emission limit values shall be expressed for the same or shorter periods of time and under the same reference conditions as those emission levels associated with the best available techniques; or

(b) setting different emission limit values than those referred to under point (a) in terms of values, periods of time and reference conditions.

Where point (b) is applied, the competent authority shall, at least annually, assess the results of emission monitoring in order to ensure that emissions under normal operating conditions have not exceeded the emission levels associated with the best available techniques.

4. By way of derogation from paragraph 3, and without prejudice to Article 18, the competent authority may, in specific cases, set less strict emission limit values. Such a derogation may apply only where an assessment shows that the achievement of emission levels associated with the best available techniques as described in BAT conclusions would lead to disproportionately higher costs compared to the environmental benefits due to:

(a) the geographical location or the local environmental conditions of the installation concerned; or

(b) the technical characteristics of the installation concerned.

The competent authority shall document in an annex to the permit conditions the reasons for the application of the first subparagraph including the result of the assessment and the justification for the conditions imposed.

The emission limit values set in accordance with the first subparagraph shall, however, not exceed the emission limit values set out in the Annexes to this Directive, where applicable.

The competent authority shall in any case ensure that no significant pollution is caused and that a high level of protection of the environment as a whole is achieved.

On the basis of information provided by Member States in accordance with Article 72(1), in particular concerning the application of this paragraph, the Commission may, where necessary, assess and further clarify, through guidance, the criteria to be taken into account for the application of this paragraph.

The competent authority shall re-assess the application of the first subparagraph as part of each reconsideration of the permit conditions pursuant to Article 21.

5. The competent authority may grant temporary derogations from the requirements of paragraphs 2 and 3 of this Article and from Article 11(a) and (b) for the testing and use of emerging techniques for a total period of time not exceeding 9 months, provided that after the period specified, either the technique is stopped or the activity achieves at least the emission levels associated with the best available techniques.

Article 16

Monitoring requirements

1. The monitoring requirements referred to in Article 14(1)(c) shall, where applicable, be based on the conclusions on monitoring as described in the BAT conclusions.

2. The frequency of the periodic monitoring referred to in Article 14(1)(e) shall be determined by the competent authority in a permit for each individual installation or in general binding rules.

Without prejudice to the first subparagraph, periodic monitoring shall be carried out at least once every 5 years for groundwater and 10 years for soil, unless such monitoring is based on a systematic appraisal of the risk of contamination.

Article 17

General binding rules for activities listed in Annex I

1. When adopting general binding rules, Member States shall ensure an integrated approach and a high level of environmental protection equivalent to that achievable with individual permit conditions.

2. General binding rules shall be based on the best available techniques, without prescribing the use of any technique or specific technology in order to ensure compliance with Articles 14 and 15.

3. Member States shall ensure that general binding rules are updated to take into account developments in best available techniques and in order to ensure compliance with Article 21.

4. General binding rules adopted in accordance with paragraphs 1 to 3 shall contain a reference to this Directive or be accompanied by such a reference on the occasion of their official publication.

Article 18

Environmental quality standards

Where an environmental quality standard requires stricter conditions than those achievable by the use of the best available techniques, additional measures shall be included in the permit, without prejudice to other measures which may be taken to comply with environmental quality standards.

Article 19

Developments in best available techniques

Member States shall ensure that the competent authority follows or is informed of developments in best available techniques and of the publication of any new or updated BAT conclusions and shall make that information available to the public concerned.

Article 20

Changes by operators to installations

1. Member States shall take the necessary measures to ensure that the operator informs the competent authority of any planned change in the nature or functioning, or an extension of the installation which may have consequences for the environment. Where appropriate, the competent authority shall update the permit.

2. Member States shall take the necessary measures to ensure that no substantial change planned by the operator is made without a permit granted in accordance with this Directive.

The application for a permit and the decision by the competent authority shall cover those parts of the installation and those details listed in Article 12 which may be affected by the substantial change.

3. Any change in the nature or functioning or an extension of an installation shall be deemed to be substantial if the change or extension in itself reaches the capacity thresholds set out in Annex I.

Article 21

Reconsideration and updating of permit conditions by the competent authority

1. Member States shall take the necessary measures to ensure that the competent authority periodically reconsiders in accordance with paragraphs 2 to 5 all permit conditions and, where necessary to ensure compliance with this Directive, updates those conditions.

2. At the request of the competent authority, the operator shall submit all the information necessary for the purpose of reconsidering the permit conditions, including, in particular, results of emission monitoring and other data, that enables a comparison of the operation of the installation with the best available techniques described in the applicable BAT conclusions and with the emission levels associated with the best available techniques.

When reconsidering permit conditions, the competent authority shall use any information resulting from monitoring or inspections.

3. Within 4 years of publication of decisions on BAT conclusions in accordance with Article 13(5) relating to the main activity of an installation, the competent authority shall ensure that:

(a) all the permit conditions for the installation concerned are reconsidered and, if necessary, updated to ensure compliance with this Directive, in particular, with Article 15(3) and (4), where applicable;

(b) the installation complies with those permit conditions.

The reconsideration shall take into account all the new or updated BAT conclusions applicable to the installation and adopted in accordance with Article 13(5) since the permit was granted or last reconsidered.

4. Where an installation is not covered by any of the BAT conclusions, the permit conditions shall be reconsidered and, if necessary, updated where developments in the best available techniques allow for the significant reduction of emissions.

5. The permit conditions shall be reconsidered and, where necessary, updated at least in the following cases:

(a) the pollution caused by the installation is of such significance that the existing emission limit values of the permit need to be revised or new such values need to be included in the permit;

(b) the operational safety requires other techniques to be used;

(c) where it is necessary to comply with a new or revised environmental quality standard in accordance with Article 18.

Article 22

Site closure

1. Without prejudice to Directive 2000/60/EC, Directive 2004/35/EC, Directive 2006/118/EC of the European Parliament and of the Council of 12 December 2006 on the protection of groundwater against pollution and deterioration and to relevant Union law on soil protection, the competent authority shall set permit conditions to ensure compliance with paragraphs 3 and 4 of this Article upon definitive cessation of activities.

2. Where the activity involves the use, production or release of relevant hazardous substances and having regard to the possibility of soil and groundwater contamination at the site of the installation, the operator shall prepare and submit to the competent authority a baseline report before starting operation of an installation or before a permit for an installation is updated for the first time after 7 January 2013.

The baseline report shall contain the information necessary to determine the state of soil and groundwater contamination so as to make a quantified comparison with the state upon definitive cessation of activities provided for under paragraph 3.

The baseline report shall contain at least the following information:

(a) information on the present use and, where available, on past uses of the site;

(b) where available, existing information on soil and groundwater measurements that reflect the state at the time the report is drawn up or, alternatively, new soil and groundwater measurements having regard to the possibility of soil and groundwater contamination by those hazardous substances to be used, produced or released by the installation concerned.

Where information produced pursuant to other national or Union law fulfils the requirements of this paragraph that information may be included in, or attached to, the submitted baseline report.

The Commission shall establish guidance on the content of the baseline report.

3. Upon definitive cessation of the activities, the operator shall assess the state of soil and groundwater contamination by relevant hazardous substances used, produced or released by the installation. Where the installation has caused significant pollution of soil or groundwater by relevant hazardous substances compared to the state established in the baseline report referred to in paragraph 2, the operator shall take the necessary measures to address that pollution so as to return the site to that state. For that purpose, the technical feasibility of such measures may be taken into account.

Without prejudice to the first subparagraph, upon definitive cessation of the activities, and where the contamination of soil and groundwater at the site poses a significant risk to human health or the environment as a result of the permitted activities carried out by the operator before the permit for the installation is updated for the first time after 7 January 2013 and taking into account the conditions of the site of the installation established in accordance with Article 12(1)(d), the operator shall take the necessary actions aimed at the removal, control, containment or reduction of relevant hazardous substances, so that the site, taking into account its current or approved future use, ceases to pose such a risk.

4. Where the operator is not required to prepare a baseline report referred to in paragraph 2, the operator shall, upon definitive cessation of the activities, take the necessary actions aimed at the removal, control, containment or reduction of relevant hazardous substances, so that the site, taking into account its current or approved future use, ceases to pose any significant risk to human health or the environment due to the contamination of soil and groundwater as a result of the permitted activities and taking into account the conditions of the site of the installation established in accordance with Article 12(1)(d).

Article 23

Environmental inspections

1. Member States shall set up a system of environmental inspections of installations addressing the examination of the full range of relevant environmental effects from the installations concerned.

Member States shall ensure that operators afford the competent authorities all necessary assistance to enable those authorities to carry out any site visits, to take samples and to gather any information necessary for the performance of their duties for the purposes of this Directive.

2. Member States shall ensure that all installations are covered by an environmental inspection plan at national, regional or local level and shall ensure that this plan is regularly reviewed and, where appropriate, updated.

3. Each environmental inspection plan shall include the following:
(a) a general assessment of relevant significant environmental issues;
(b) the geographical area covered by the inspection plan;
(c) a register of the installations covered by the plan;
(d) procedures for drawing up programmes for routine environmental inspections pursuant to paragraph 4;
(e) procedures for non-routine environmental inspections pursuant to paragraph 5;
(f) where necessary, provisions on the cooperation between different inspection authorities.

4. Based on the inspection plans, the competent authority shall regularly draw up programmes for routine environmental inspections, including the frequency of site visits for different types of installations.

The period between two site visits shall be based on a systematic appraisal of the environmental risks of the installations concerned and shall not exceed 1 year for installations posing the highest risks and 3 years for installations posing the lowest risks.

If an inspection has identified an important case of non-compliance with the permit conditions, an additional site visit shall be carried out within 6 months of that inspection.

The systematic appraisal of the environmental risks shall be based on at least the following criteria:
(a) the potential and actual impacts of the installations concerned on human health and the environment taking into account the levels and types of emissions, the sensitivity of the local environment and the risk of accidents;
(b) the record of compliance with permit conditions;
(c) the participation of the operator in the Union eco-management and audit scheme (EMAS), pursuant to Regulation (EC) No 1221/2009.

The Commission may adopt guidance on the criteria for the appraisal of environmental risks.

5. Non-routine environmental inspections shall be carried out to investigate serious environmental complaints, serious environmental accidents, incidents and occurrences of non-compliance as soon as possible and, where appropriate, before the granting, reconsideration or update of a permit.

6. Following each site visit, the competent authority shall prepare a report describing the relevant findings regarding compliance of the installation with the permit conditions and conclusions on whether any further action is necessary.

The report shall be notified to the operator concerned within 2 months of the site visit taking place. The report shall be made publicly available by the competent authority in accordance with Directive 2003/4/EC of the European Parliament and of the Council of 28 January 2003 on public access to environmental information within 4 months of the site visit taking place.

Without prejudice to Article 8(2), the competent authority shall ensure that the operator takes all the necessary actions identified in the report within a reasonable period.

Article 24

Access to information and public participation in the permit procedure

1. Member States shall ensure that the public concerned are given early and effective opportunities to participate in the following procedures:

(a) the granting of a permit for new installations;

(b) the granting of a permit for any substantial change;

(c) the granting or updating of a permit for an installation where the application of Article 15(4) is proposed;

(d) the updating of a permit or permit conditions for an installation in accordance with Article 21(5)(a).

The procedure set out in Annex IV shall apply to such participation.

2. When a decision on granting, reconsideration or updating of a permit has been taken, the competent authority shall make available to the public, including via the Internet in relation to points (a), (b) and (f), the following information:

(a) the content of the decision, including a copy of the permit and any subsequent updates;

(b) the reasons on which the decision is based;

(c) the results of the consultations held before the decision was taken and an explanation of how they were taken into account in that decision;

(d) the title of the BAT reference documents relevant to the installation or activity concerned;

(e) how the permit conditions referred to in Article 14, including the emission limit values, have been determined in relation to the best available techniques and emission levels associated with the best available techniques;

(f) where a derogation is granted in accordance with Article 15(4), the specific reasons for that derogation based on the criteria laid down in that paragraph and the conditions imposed.

3. The competent authority shall also make available to the public, including via the Internet at least in relation to point (a):

(a) relevant information on the measures taken by the operator upon definitive cessation of activities in accordance with Article 22;

(b) the results of emission monitoring as required under the permit conditions and held by the competent authority.

4. Paragraphs 1, 2 and 3 of this Article shall apply subject to the restrictions laid down in Article 4(1) and (2) of Directive 2003/4/EC.

Article 25

Access to justice

1. Member States shall ensure that, in accordance with the relevant national legal system, members of the public concerned have access to a review procedure before a court of law or another independent and impartial body established by law to challenge the substantive or procedural legality of decisions, acts or omissions subject to Article 24 when one of the following conditions is met:

(a) they have a sufficient interest;

(b) they maintain the impairment of a right, where administrative procedural law of a Member State requires this as a precondition.

2. Member States shall determine at what stage the decisions, acts or omissions may be challenged.

3. What constitutes a sufficient interest and impairment of a right shall be determined by Member States, consistently with the objective of giving the public concerned wide access to justice.

To this end, the interest of any non-governmental organisation promoting environmental protection and meeting any requirements under national law shall be deemed sufficient for the purpose of paragraph 1(a).

Such organisations shall also be deemed to have rights capable of being impaired for the purpose of paragraph 1(b).

4. Paragraphs 1, 2 and 3 shall not exclude the possibility of a preliminary review procedure before an administrative authority and shall not affect the requirement of exhaustion of administrative review procedures prior to recourse to judicial review procedures, where such a requirement exists under national law.

Any such procedure shall be fair, equitable, timely and not prohibitively expensive.

5. Member States shall ensure that practical information is made available to the public on access to administrative and judicial review procedures.

Article 26

Transboundary effects

1. Where a Member State is aware that the operation of an installation is likely to have significant negative effects on the environment of another Member State, or where a Member State which is likely to be significantly affected so requests, the Member State in whose territory the application for a permit pursuant to Article 4 or Article 20(2) was submitted shall forward to the other Member State any information required to be given or made available pursuant to Annex IV at the same time as it makes it available to the public.

Such information shall serve as a basis for any consultations necessary in the framework of the bilateral relations between the two Member States on a reciprocal and equivalent basis.

2. Within the framework of their bilateral relations, Member States shall ensure that in the cases referred to in paragraph 1, the applications are also made available for an appropriate period of time to the public of the Member State likely to be affected so that it will have the right to comment on them before the competent authority reaches its decision.

3. The results of any consultations pursuant to paragraphs 1 and 2 shall be taken into consideration when the competent authority reaches a decision on the application.

4. The competent authority shall inform any Member State which has been consulted pursuant to paragraph 1 of the decision reached on the application and shall forward to it the information referred to in Article 24(2). That Member State shall take the measures necessary to ensure that that information is made available in an appropriate manner to the public concerned in its own territory.

Article 27

Emerging techniques

1. Member States shall, where appropriate, encourage the development and application of emerging techniques, in particular for those emerging techniques identified in BAT reference documents.

2. The Commission shall establish guidance to assist Member States in encouraging the development and application of emerging techniques as referred to in paragraph 1.

Chapter III
Special provisions for combustion plants

Article 28

Scope

This Chapter shall apply to combustion plants, the total rated thermal input of which is equal to or greater than 50 MW, irrespective of the type of fuel used.

This Chapter shall not apply to the following combustion plants:
(a) plants in which the products of combustion are used for the direct heating, drying, or any other treatment of objects or materials;
(b) post-combustion plants designed to purify the waste gases by combustion which are not operated as independent combustion plants;
(c) facilities for the regeneration of catalytic cracking catalysts;
(d) facilities for the conversion of hydrogen sulphide into sulphur;
(e) reactors used in the chemical industry;
(f) coke battery furnaces;
(g) cowpers;
(h) any technical apparatus used in the propulsion of a vehicle, ship or aircraft;
(i) gas turbines and gas engines used on offshore platforms;
(j) plants which use any solid or liquid waste as a fuel other than waste referred to in point (b) of point 31 of Article 3.

Article 29

Aggregation rules

1. Where the waste gases of two or more separate combustion plants are discharged through a common stack, the combination formed by such plants shall be considered as a single combustion plant and their capacities added for the purpose of calculating the total rated thermal input.

2. Where two or more separate combustion plants which have been granted a permit for the first time on or after 1 July 1987, or the operators of which have submitted a complete application for a permit on or after that date, are installed in such a way that, taking technical and economic factors into account, their waste gases could in the judgement of the competent authority, be discharged through a common stack, the combination formed by such plants shall be considered as a single combustion plant and their capacities added for the purpose of calculating the total rated thermal input.

3. For the purpose of calculating the total rated thermal input of a combination of combustion plants referred to in paragraphs 1 and 2, individual combustion plants with a rated thermal input below 15 MW shall not be considered.

Article 30

Emission limit values

1. Waste gases from combustion plants shall be discharged in a controlled way by means of a stack, containing one or more flues, the height of which is calculated in such a way as to safeguard human health and the environment.

2. All permits for installations containing combustion plants which have been granted a permit before 7 January 2013, or the operators of which have submitted a complete application for a permit before that date, provided that such plants are put into operation no later than 7 January 2014, shall include conditions ensuring that emissions into air from these plants do not exceed the emission limit values set out in Part 1 of Annex V.

All permits for installations containing combustion plants which had been granted an exemption as referred to in Article 4(4) of Directive 2001/80/EC and which are in operation after 1 January 2016, shall include conditions ensuring that emissions into the air from these plants do not exceed the emission limit values set out in Part 2 of Annex V.

3. All permits for installations containing combustion plants not covered by paragraph 2 shall include conditions ensuring that emissions into the air from these plants do not exceed the emission limit values set out in Part 2 of Annex V.

4. The emission limit values set out in Parts 1 and 2 of Annex V as well as the minimum rates of desulphurisation set out in Part 5 of that Annex shall apply to the emissions of each common stack in relation to the total rated thermal input of the entire combustion plant. Where Annex V provides that emission limit values may be applied for a part of a combustion plant with a limited number of operating hours, those limit values shall apply to the emissions of that part of the plant, but shall be set in relation to the total rated thermal input of the entire combustion plant.

5. The competent authority may grant a derogation for a maximum of 6 months from the obligation to comply with the emission limit values provided for in paragraphs 2 and 3 for sulphur dioxide in respect of a combustion plant which to this end normally uses low-sulphur fuel, in cases where the operator is unable to comply with those limit values because of an interruption in the supply of low-sulphur fuel resulting from a serious shortage.

Member States shall immediately inform the Commission of any derogation granted under the first subparagraph.

6. The competent authority may grant a derogation from the obligation to comply with the emission limit values provided for in paragraphs 2 and 3 in cases where a combustion plant using only gaseous fuel has to resort exceptionally to the use of other fuels because of a sudden interruption in the supply of gas and for this reason would need to be equipped with a waste gas purification facility. The period for which such a derogation is granted shall not exceed 10 days except where there is an overriding need to maintain energy supplies.

The operator shall immediately inform the competent authority of each specific case referred to in the first subparagraph.

Member States shall inform the Commission immediately of any derogation granted under the first subparagraph.

7. Where a combustion plant is extended, the emission limit values set out in Part 2 of Annex V shall apply to the extended part of the plant affected by the change and shall be set in relation to the total rated thermal input of the entire combustion plant. In the case of a change to a combustion plant, which may have consequences for the environment and which affects a part of the plant with a rated thermal input of 50 MW or more, the emission limit values as set out in Part 2 of Annex V shall apply to the part of the plant which has changed in relation to the total rated thermal input of the entire combustion plant.

8. The emission limit values set out in Parts 1 and 2 of Annex V shall not apply to the following combustion plants:
(a) diesel engines;
(b) recovery boilers within installations for the production of pulp.

9. For the following combustion plants, on the basis of the best available techniques, the Commission shall review the need to establish Union-wide emission limit values and to amend the emission limit values set out in Annex V:
(a) the combustion plants referred to in paragraph 8;
(b) combustion plants within refineries firing the distillation and conversion residues from the refining of crude-oil for own consumption, alone or with other fuels, taking into account the specificity of the energy systems of refineries;
(c) combustion plants firing gases other than natural gas;

(d) combustion plants in chemical installations using liquid production residues as non-commercial fuel for own consumption.

The Commission shall, by 31 December 2013, report the results of this review to the European Parliament and to the Council accompanied, if appropriate, by a legislative proposal.

Article 31

Desulphurisation rate

1. For combustion plants firing indigenous solid fuel, which cannot comply with the emission limit values for sulphur dioxide referred to in Article 30(2) and (3) due to the characteristics of this fuel, Member States may apply instead the minimum rates of desulphurisation set out in Part 5 of Annex V, in accordance with the compliance rules set out in Part 6 of that Annex and with prior validation by the competent authority of the technical report referred to in Article 72(4)(a).

2. For combustion plants firing indigenous solid fuel, which co-incinerate waste, and which cannot comply with the Cproc values for sulphur dioxide set out in points 3.1 or 3.2 of Part 4 of Annex VI due to the characteristics of the indigenous solid fuel, Member States may apply instead the minimum rates of desulphurisation set out in Part 5 of Annex V, in accordance with the compliance rules set out in Part 6 of that Annex. If Member States choose to apply this paragraph, Cwaste as referred to in point 1 of Part 4 of Annex VI shall be equal to 0 mg/Nm^3.

3. The Commission shall, by 31 December 2019, review the possibility of applying minimum rates of desulphurisation set out in Part 5 of Annex V, taking into account, in particular, the best available techniques and benefits obtained from reduced sulphur dioxide emissions.

Article 32

Transitional National Plan

1. During the period from 1 January 2016 to 30 June 2020, Member States may draw up and implement a transitional national plan covering combustion plants which were granted the first permit before 27 November 2002 or the operators of which had submitted a complete application for a permit before that date, provided that the plant was put into operation no later than 27 November 2003. For each of the combustion plants covered by the plan, the plan shall cover emissions of one or more of the following pollutants: nitrogen oxides, sulphur dioxide and dust. For gas turbines, only nitrogen oxides emissions shall be covered by the plan.

The transitional national plan shall not include any of the following combustion plants:

(a) those to which Article 33(1) applies;

(b) those within refineries firing low calorific gases from the gasification of refinery residues or the distillation and conversion residues from the refining of crude oil for own consumption, alone or with other fuels;

(c) those to which Article 35 applies;

(d) those which are granted an exemption as referred to in Article 4(4) of Directive 2001/80/EC.

2. Combustion plants covered by the plan may be exempted from compliance with the emission limit values referred to in Article 30(2) for the pollutants which are subject to the plan or, where applicable, with the rates of desulphurisation referred to in Article 31.

The emission limit values for sulphur dioxide, nitrogen oxides and dust set out in the permit for the combustion plant applicable on 31 December 2015, pursuant in particular to the requirements of Directives 2001/80/EC and 2008/1/EC, shall at least be maintained.

Combustion plants with a total rated thermal input of more than 500 MW firing solid fuels, which were granted the first permit after 1 July 1987, shall comply with the emission limit values for nitrogen oxides set out in Part 1 of Annex V.

3. For each of the pollutants it covers, the transitional national plan shall set a ceiling defining the maximum total annual emissions for all of the plants covered by the plan on the basis of each plant's total rated thermal input on 31 December 2010, its actual annual operating hours and its fuel use, averaged over the last 10 years of operation up to and including 2010.

The ceiling for the year 2016 shall be calculated on the basis of the relevant emission limit values set out in Annexes III to VII to Directive 2001/80/EC or, where applicable, on the basis of the rates of desulphurisation set out in Annex III to Directive 2001/80/EC. In the case of gas turbines, the emission limit values for nitrogen oxides set out for such plants in Part B of Annex VI to Directive 2001/80/EC shall be used. The ceilings for the years 2019 and 2020 shall be calculated on the basis of the relevant emission limit values set out in Part 1 of Annex V to this Directive or, where applicable, the relevant rates of desulphurisation set out in Part 5 of Annex V to this Directive. The ceilings for the years 2017 and 2018 shall be set providing a linear decrease of the ceilings between 2016 and 2019.

Where a plant included in the transitional national plan is closed or no longer falls within the scope of Chapter III, this shall not result in an increase in total annual emissions from the remaining plants covered by the plan.

4. The transitional national plan shall also contain provisions on monitoring and reporting that comply with the implementing rules established in accordance with Article 41(b), as well as the measures foreseen for each of the plants in order to ensure timely compliance with the emission limit values that will apply from 1 July 2020.

5. Not later than 1 January 2013, Member States shall communicate their transitional national plans to the Commission.

The Commission shall evaluate the plans and, where the Commission has raised no objections within 12 months of receipt of a plan, the Member State concerned shall consider its plan to be accepted.

When the Commission considers a plan not to be in accordance with the implementing rules established in accordance with Article 41(b), it shall inform the Member State concerned that its plan cannot be accepted. In relation to the evaluation of a new version of a plan which a Member State communicates to the Commission, the time period referred to in the second subparagraph shall be 6 months.

6. Member States shall inform the Commission of any subsequent changes to the plan.

Article 33

Limited life time derogation

1. During the period from 1 January 2016 to 31 December 2023, combustion plants may be exempted from compliance with the emission limit values referred to in Article 30(2) and with the rates of desulphurisation referred to in Article 31, where applicable, and from their inclusion in the transitional national plan referred to in Article 32 provided that the following conditions are fulfilled:

(a) the operator of the combustion plant undertakes, in a written declaration submitted by 1 January 2014 at the latest to the competent authority, not to operate the plant for more than 17500 operating hours, starting from 1 January 2016 and ending no later than 31 December 2023;

(b) the operator is required to submit each year to the competent authority a record of the number of operating hours since 1 January 2016;

(c) the emission limit values for sulphur dioxides, nitrogen oxides and dust set out in the permit for the combustion plant applicable on 31 December 2015, pursuant in particular to the requirements of Directives 2001/80/EC and 2008/1/EC, shall at least be maintained during the remaining operational life of the combustion plant. Combustion plants with a total rated thermal input of more than 500 MW firing solid fuels, which were granted the first permit after 1 July 1987, shall comply with the emission limit values for nitrogen oxides set out in Part 1 of Annex V; and

(d) the combustion plant has not been granted an exemption as referred to in Article 4(4) of Directive 2001/80/EC.

2. At the latest on 1 January 2016, each Member State shall communicate to the Commission a list of any combustion plants to which paragraph 1 applies, including their total rated thermal input, the fuel types used and the applicable emission limit values for sulphur dioxide, nitrogen oxides and dust. For plants subject to paragraph 1, Member States shall communicate annually to the Commission a record of the number of operating hours since 1 January 2016.

3. In case of a combustion plant being, on 6 January 2011, part of a small isolated system and accounting at that date for at least 35 % of the electricity supply within that system, which is unable, due to its technical characteristics, to comply with the emission limit values referred to in Article 30(2), the number of operating hours referred to in paragraph 1(a) of this Article shall be 18000, starting from 1 January 2020 and ending no later than 31 December 2023, and the date referred to in paragraph 1(b) and paragraph 2 of this Article shall be 1 January 2020.

4. In case of a combustion plant with a total rated thermal input of more than 1500 MW which started operating before 31 December 1986 and fires indigenous solid fuel with a net calorific value of less than 5800 kJ/kg, a moisture content greater than 45 % by weight, a combined moisture and ash content greater than 60 % by weight and a calcium oxide content in ash greater than 10 %, the number of operating hours referred to in paragraph 1(a) shall be 32000.

Article 34

Small isolated systems

1. Until 31 December 2019, combustion plants being, on 6 January 2011, part of a small isolated system may be exempted from compliance with the emission limit values referred to in Article 30(2) and the rates of desulphurisation referred to in Article 31, where applicable. Until 31 December 2019, the emission limit values set out in the permits of these combustion plants, pursuant in particular to the requirements of Directives 2001/80/EC and 2008/1/EC, shall at least be maintained.

2. Combustion plants with a total rated thermal input of more than 500 MW firing solid fuels, which were granted the first permit after 1 July 1987, shall comply with the emission limit values for nitrogen oxides set out in Part 1 of Annex V.

3. Where there are, on the territory of a Member State combustion plants covered by this Chapter that are part of a small isolated system, that Member State shall report to the Commission before 7 January 2013 a list of those combustion plants, the total annual energy consumption of the small isolated system and the amount of energy obtained through interconnection with other systems.

Article 35

District heating plants

1. Until 31 December 2022, a combustion plant may be exempted from compliance with the emission limit values referred to in Article 30(2) and the rates of desulphurisation referred to in Article 31 provided that the following conditions are fulfilled:

(a) the total rated thermal input of the combustion plant does not exceed 200 MW;

(b) the plant was granted a first permit before 27 November 2002 or the operator of that plant had submitted a complete application for a permit before that date, provided that it was put into operation no later than 27 November 2003;

(c) at least 50 % of the useful heat production of the plant, as a rolling average over a period of 5 years, is delivered in the form of steam or hot water to a public network for district heating; and

(d) the emission limit values for sulphur dioxide, nitrogen oxides and dust set out in its permit applicable on 31 December 2015, pursuant in particular to the requirements of Directives 2001/80/EC and 2008/1/EC, are at least maintained until 31 December 2022.

2. At the latest on 1 January 2016, each Member State shall communicate to the Commission a list of any combustion plants to which paragraph 1 applies, including their total rated thermal input, the fuel types used and the applicable emission limit values for sulphur dioxide, nitrogen oxides and dust. In addition, Member States shall, for any combustion plants to which paragraph 1 applies and during the period mentioned in that paragraph, inform the Commission annually of the proportion of useful heat production of each plant which was delivered in the form of steam or hot water to a public network for district heating, expressed as a rolling average over the preceding 5 years.

Article 36

Geological storage of carbon dioxide

1. Member States shall ensure that operators of all combustion plants with a rated electrical output of 300 megawatts or more for which the original construction licence or, in the absence of such a procedure, the original operating licence is granted after the entry into force of Directive 2009/31/EC of the European Parliament and of the Council of 23 April 2009 on the geological storage of carbon dioxide, have assessed whether the following conditions are met:
(a) suitable storage sites are available,
(b) transport facilities are technically and economically feasible,
(c) it is technically and economically feasible to retrofit for carbon dioxide capture.

2. If the conditions laid down in paragraph 1 are met, the competent authority shall ensure that suitable space on the installation site for the equipment necessary to capture and compress carbon dioxide is set aside. The competent authority shall determine whether the conditions are met on the basis of the assessment referred to in paragraph 1 and other available information, particularly concerning the protection of the environment and human health.

Article 37

Malfunction or breakdown of the abatement equipment

1. Member States shall ensure that provision is made in the permits for procedures relating to malfunction or breakdown of the abatement equipment.

2. In the case of a breakdown, the competent authority shall require the operator to reduce or close down operations if a return to normal operation is not achieved within 24 hours, or to operate the plant using low polluting fuels.

The operator shall notify the competent authority within 48 hours after the malfunction or breakdown of the abatement equipment.

The cumulative duration of unabated operation shall not exceed 120 hours in any 12-month period.

The competent authority may grant a derogation from the time limits set out in the first and third subparagraphs in one of the following cases:
(a) there is an overriding need to maintain energy supplies;
(b) the combustion plant with the breakdown would be replaced for a limited period by another plant which would cause an overall increase in emissions.

Article 38

Monitoring of emissions into air

1. Member States shall ensure that the monitoring of air polluting substances is carried out in accordance with Part 3 of Annex V.

2. The installation and functioning of the automated monitoring equipment shall be subject to control and to annual surveillance tests as set out in Part 3 of Annex V.

3. The competent authority shall determine the location of the sampling or measurement points to be used for the monitoring of emissions.

4. All monitoring results shall be recorded, processed and presented in such a way as to enable the competent authority to verify compliance with the operating conditions and emission limit values which are included in the permit.

Article 39

Compliance with emission limit values

The emission limit values for air shall be regarded as being complied with if the conditions set out in Part 4 of Annex V are fulfilled.

Article 40

Multi-fuel firing combustion plants

1. In the case of a multi-fuel firing combustion plant involving the simultaneous use of two or more fuels, the competent authority shall set the emission limit values in accordance with the following steps:

(a) taking the emission limit value relevant for each individual fuel and pollutant corresponding to the total rated thermal input of the entire combustion plant as set out in Parts 1 and 2 of Annex V;

(b) determining fuel-weighted emission limit values, which are obtained by multiplying the individual emission limit value referred to in point (a) by the thermal input delivered by each fuel, and dividing the product of multiplication by the sum of the thermal inputs delivered by all fuels,

(c) aggregating the fuel-weighted emission limit values.

2. In the case of multi-fuel firing combustion plants covered by Article 30(2), which use the distillation and conversion residues from the refining of crude-oil for own consumption, alone or with other fuels, the following emission limit values may be applied instead of the emission limit values set according to paragraph 1:

(a) where, during the operation of the combustion plant, the proportion contributed by the determinative fuel to the sum of the thermal inputs delivered by all fuels is 50 % or more, the emission limit value set in Part 1 of Annex V for the determinative fuel;

(b) where the proportion contributed by the determinative fuel to the sum of the thermal inputs delivered by all fuels is less than 50 %, the emission limit value determined in accordance with the following steps:

  (i) taking the emission limit values set out in Part 1 of Annex V for each of the fuels used, corresponding to the total rated thermal input of the combustion plant;

  (ii) calculating the emission limit value of the determinative fuel by multiplying the emission limit value, determined for that fuel according to point (i), by a factor of two, and subtracting from this product the emission limit value of the fuel used with the lowest emission limit value as set out in Part 1 of Annex V, corresponding to the total rated thermal input of the combustion plant;

  (iii) determining the fuel-weighted emission limit value for each fuel used by multiplying the emission limit value determined under points (i) and (ii) by the thermal input of the fuel concerned and by dividing the product of this multiplication by the sum of the thermal inputs delivered by all fuels;

  (iv) aggregating the fuel-weighted emission limit values determined under point (iii).

3. In the case of multi-fuel firing combustion plants covered by Article 30(2), which use the distillation and conversion residues from the refining of crude-oil for own consumption, alone

or with other fuels, the average emission limit values for sulphur dioxide set out in Part 7 of Annex V may be applied instead of the emission limit values set according to paragraphs 1 or 2 of this Article.

Article 41

Implementing rules

Implementing rules shall be established concerning:

(a) the determination of the start-up and shut-down periods referred to in point 27 of Article 3 and in point 1 of Part 4 of Annex V; and

(b) the transitional national plans referred to in Article 32 and, in particular, the setting of emission ceilings and related monitoring and reporting.

Those implementing rules shall be adopted in accordance with the regulatory procedure referred to in Article 75(2). The Commission shall make appropriate proposals not later than 7 July 2011.

Chapter IV

Special provisions for waste incineration plants and waste co-incineration plants

Article 42

Scope

1. This Chapter shall apply to waste incineration plants and waste co-incineration plants which incinerate or co-incinerate solid or liquid waste.

This Chapter shall not apply to gasification or pyrolysis plants, if the gases resulting from this thermal treatment of waste are purified to such an extent that they are no longer a waste prior to their incineration and they can cause emissions no higher than those resulting from the burning of natural gas.

For the purposes of this Chapter, waste incineration plants and waste co-incineration plants shall include all incineration lines or co-incineration lines, waste reception, storage, on site pretreatment facilities, waste-, fuel- and air-supply systems, boilers, facilities for the treatment of waste gases, on-site facilities for treatment or storage of residues and waste water, stacks, devices and systems for controlling incineration or co-incineration operations, recording and monitoring incineration or co-incineration conditions.

If processes other than oxidation, such as pyrolysis, gasification or plasma process, are applied for the thermal treatment of waste, the waste incineration plant or waste co-incineration plant shall include both the thermal treatment process and the subsequent incineration process.

If waste co-incineration takes place in such a way that the main purpose of the plant is not the generation of energy or production of material products but rather the thermal treatment of waste, the plant shall be regarded as a waste incineration plant.

2. This Chapter shall not apply to the following plants:

(a) plants treating only the following wastes:

  (i) waste listed in point (b) of point 31 of Article 3;

  (ii) radioactive waste;

  (iii) animal carcasses as regulated by Regulation (EC) No 1774/2002 of the European Parliament and of the Council of 3 October 2002 laying down health rules concerning animal by-products not intended for human consumption;

  (iv) waste resulting from the exploration for, and the exploitation of, oil and gas resources from off-shore installations and incinerated on board the installations;

(b) experimental plants used for research, development and testing in order to improve the incineration process and which treat less than 50 tonnes of waste per year.

Article 43

Definition of residue

For the purposes of this Chapter, "residue" shall mean any liquid or solid waste which is generated by a waste incineration plant or waste co-incineration plant.

Article 44

Applications for permits

An application for a permit for a waste incineration plant or waste co-incineration plant shall include a description of the measures which are envisaged to guarantee that the following requirements are met:

(a) the plant is designed, equipped and will be maintained and operated in such a manner that the requirements of this Chapter are met taking into account the categories of waste to be incinerated or co-incinerated;

(b) the heat generated during the incineration and co-incineration process is recovered as far as practicable through the generation of heat, steam or power;

(c) the residues will be minimised in their amount and harmfulness and recycled where appropriate;

(d) the disposal of the residues which cannot be prevented, reduced or recycled will be carried out in conformity with national and Union law.

Article 45

Permit conditions

1. The permit shall include the following:

(a) a list of all types of waste which may be treated using at least the types of waste set out in the European Waste List established by Decision 2000/532/EC, if possible, and containing information on the quantity of each type of waste, where appropriate;

(b) the total waste incinerating or co-incinerating capacity of the plant;

(c) the limit values for emissions into air and water;

(d) the requirements for the pH, temperature and flow of waste water discharges;

(e) the sampling and measurement procedures and frequencies to be used to comply with the conditions set for emission monitoring;

(f) the maximum permissible period of any technically unavoidable stoppages, disturbances, or failures of the purification devices or the measurement devices, during which the emissions into the air and the discharges of waste water may exceed the prescribed emission limit values.

2. In addition to the requirements set out in paragraph 1, the permit granted to a waste incineration plant or waste co-incineration plant using hazardous waste shall include the following:

(a) a list of the quantities of the different categories of hazardous waste which may be treated;

(b) the minimum and maximum mass flows of those hazardous wastes, their lowest and maximum calorific values and their maximum contents of polychlorinated biphenyls, pentachlorophenol, chlorine, fluorine, sulphur, heavy metals and other polluting substances.

3. Member States may list the categories of waste to be included in the permit which can be co-incinerated in certain categories of waste co-incineration plants.

4. The competent authority shall periodically reconsider and, where necessary, update permit conditions.

Article 46

Control of emissions

1. Waste gases from waste incineration plants and waste co-incineration plants shall be discharged in a controlled way by means of a stack the height of which is calculated in such a way as to safeguard human health and the environment.

2. Emissions into air from waste incineration plants and waste co-incineration plants shall not exceed the emission limit values set out in parts 3 and 4 of Annex VI or determined in accordance with Part 4 of that Annex.

If in a waste co-incineration plant more than 40 % of the resulting heat release comes from hazardous waste, or the plant co-incinerates untreated mixed municipal waste, the emission limit values set out in Part 3 of Annex VI shall apply.

3. Discharges to the aquatic environment of waste water resulting from the cleaning of waste gases shall be limited as far as practicable and the concentrations of polluting substances shall not exceed the emission limit values set out in Part 5 of Annex VI.

4. The emission limit values shall apply at the point where waste waters from the cleaning of waste gases are discharged from the waste incineration plant or waste co-incineration plant.

When waste waters from the cleaning of waste gases are treated outside the waste incineration plant or waste co-incineration plant at a treatment plant intended only for the treatment of this sort of waste water, the emission limit values set out in Part 5 of Annex VI shall be applied at the point where the waste waters leave the treatment plant. Where the waste water from the cleaning of waste gases is treated collectively with other sources of waste water, either on site or off site, the operator shall make the appropriate mass balance calculations, using the results of the measurements set out in point 3 of Part 6 of Annex VI in order to determine the emission levels in the final waste water discharge that can be attributed to the waste water arising from the cleaning of waste gases.

Under no circumstances shall dilution of waste water take place for the purpose of complying with the emission limit values set out in Part 5 of Annex VI.

5. Waste incineration plant sites and waste co-incineration plant sites, including associated storage areas for waste, shall be designed and operated in such a way as to prevent the unauthorised and accidental release of any polluting substances into soil, surface water and groundwater.

Storage capacity shall be provided for contaminated rainwater run-off from the waste incineration plant site or waste co-incineration plant site or for contaminated water arising from spillage or fire-fighting operations. The storage capacity shall be adequate to ensure that such waters can be tested and treated before discharge where necessary.

6. Without prejudice to Article 50(4)(c), the waste incineration plant or waste co-incineration plant or individual furnaces being part of a waste incineration plant or waste co-incineration plant shall under no circumstances continue to incinerate waste for a period of more than 4 hours uninterrupted where emission limit values are exceeded.

The cumulative duration of operation in such conditions over 1 year shall not exceed 60 hours.

The time limit set out in the second subparagraph shall apply to those furnaces which are linked to one single waste gas cleaning device.

Article 47

Breakdown

In the case of a breakdown, the operator shall reduce or close down operations as soon as practicable until normal operations can be restored.

Article 48

Monitoring of emissions

1. Member States shall ensure that the monitoring of emissions is carried out in accordance with Parts 6 and 7 of Annex VI.

2. The installation and functioning of the automated measuring systems shall be subject to control and to annual surveillance tests as set out in point 1 of Part 6 of Annex VI.

3. The competent authority shall determine the location of the sampling or measurement points to be used for monitoring of emissions.

4. All monitoring results shall be recorded, processed and presented in such a way as to enable the competent authority to verify compliance with the operating conditions and emission limit values which are included in the permit.

5. As soon as appropriate measurement techniques are available within the Union, the Commission shall, by means of delegated acts in accordance with Article 76 and subject to the conditions laid down in Articles 77 and 78, set the date from which continuous measurements of emissions into the air of heavy metals and dioxins and furans are to be carried out.

Article 49

Compliance with emission limit values

The emission limit values for air and water shall be regarded as being complied with if the conditions described in Part 8 of Annex VI are fulfilled.

Article 50

Operating conditions

1. Waste incineration plants shall be operated in such a way as to achieve a level of incineration such that the total organic carbon content of slag and bottom ashes is less than 3 % or their loss on ignition is less than 5 % of the dry weight of the material. If necessary, waste pre-treatment techniques shall be used.

2. Waste incineration plants shall be designed, equipped, built and operated in such a way that the gas resulting from the incineration of waste is raised, after the last injection of combustion air, in a controlled and homogeneous fashion and even under the most unfavourable conditions, to a temperature of at least 850 °C for at least two seconds.

Waste co-incineration plants shall be designed, equipped, built and operated in such a way that the gas resulting from the co-incineration of waste is raised in a controlled and homogeneous fashion and even under the most unfavourable conditions, to a temperature of at least 850 °C for at least two seconds.

If hazardous waste with a content of more than 1 % of halogenated organic substances, expressed as chlorine, is incinerated or co-incinerated, the temperature required to comply with the first and second subparagraphs shall be at least 1100 °C.

In waste incineration plants, the temperatures set out in the first and third subparagraphs shall be measured near the inner wall of the combustion chamber. The competent authority may authorise the measurements at another representative point of the combustion chamber.

3. Each combustion chamber of a waste incineration plant shall be equipped with at least one auxiliary burner. This burner shall be switched on automatically when the temperature of the combustion gases after the last injection of combustion air falls below the temperatures set out in paragraph 2. It shall also be used during plant start-up and shut-down operations in order to

ensure that those temperatures are maintained at all times during these operations and as long as unburned waste is in the combustion chamber.

The auxiliary burner shall not be fed with fuels which can cause higher emissions than those resulting from the burning of gas oil as defined in Article 2(2) of Council Directive 1999/32/EC of 26 April 1999 relating to a reduction in the sulphur content of certain liquid fuels, liquefied gas or natural gas.

4. Waste incineration plants and waste co-incineration plants shall operate an automatic system to prevent waste feed in the following situations:

(a) at start-up, until the temperature set out in paragraph 2 of this Article or the temperature specified in accordance with Article 51(1) has been reached;

(b) whenever the temperature set out in paragraph 2 of this Article or the temperature specified in accordance with Article 51(1) is not maintained;

(c) whenever the continuous measurements show that any emission limit value is exceeded due to disturbances or failures of the waste gas cleaning devices.

5. Any heat generated by waste incineration plants or waste co-incineration plants shall be recovered as far as practicable.

6. Infectious clinical waste shall be placed straight in the furnace, without first being mixed with other categories of waste and without direct handling.

7. Member States shall ensure that the waste incineration plant or waste co-incineration plant is operated and controlled by a natural person who is competent to manage the plant.

Article 51

Authorisation to change operating conditions

1. Conditions different from those laid down in Article 50(1), (2) and (3) and, as regards the temperature, paragraph 4 of that Article and specified in the permit for certain categories of waste or for certain thermal processes, may be authorised by the competent authority provided the other requirements of this Chapter are met. Member States may lay down rules governing these authorisations.

2. For waste incineration plants, the change of the operating conditions shall not cause more residues or residues with a higher content of organic polluting substances compared to those residues which could be expected under the conditions laid down in Article 50(1), (2) and (3).

3. Emissions of total organic carbon and carbon monoxide from waste co-incineration plants, authorised to change operating conditions according to paragraph 1 shall also comply with the emission limit values set out in Part 3 of Annex VI.

Emissions of total organic carbon from bark boilers within the pulp and paper industry co-incinerating waste at the place of its production which were in operation and had a permit before 28 December 2002 and which are authorised to change operating conditions according to paragraph 1 shall also comply with the emission limit values set out in Part 3 of Annex VI.

4. Member States shall communicate to the Commission all operating conditions authorised under paragraphs 1, 2 and 3 and the results of verifications made as part of the information provided in accordance with the reporting requirements under Article 72.

Article 52

Delivery and reception of waste

1. The operator of the waste incineration plant or waste co-incineration plant shall take all necessary precautions concerning the delivery and reception of waste in order to prevent or to

limit as far as practicable the pollution of air, soil, surface water and groundwater as well as other negative effects on the environment, odours and noise, and direct risks to human health.

2. The operator shall determine the mass of each type of waste, if possible according to the European Waste List established by Decision 2000/532/EC, prior to accepting the waste at the waste incineration plant or waste co-incineration plant.

3. Prior to accepting hazardous waste at the waste incineration plant or waste co-incineration plant, the operator shall collect available information about the waste for the purpose of verifying compliance with the permit requirements specified in Article 45(2).

That information shall cover the following:
(a) all the administrative information on the generating process contained in the documents mentioned in paragraph 4(a);
(b) the physical, and as far as practicable, chemical composition of the waste and all other information necessary to evaluate its suitability for the intended incineration process;
(c) the hazardous characteristics of the waste, the substances with which it cannot be mixed, and the precautions to be taken in handling the waste.

4. Prior to accepting hazardous waste at the waste incineration plant or waste co-incineration plant, at least the following procedures shall be carried out by the operator:
(a) the checking of the documents required by Directive 2008/98/EC and, where applicable, those required by Regulation (EC) No 1013/2006 of the European Parliament and of the Council of 14 June 2006 on shipments of waste and by legislation on transport of dangerous goods;
(b) the taking of representative samples, unless inappropriate as far as possible before unloading, to verify conformity with the information provided for in paragraph 3 by carrying out controls and to enable the competent authorities to identify the nature of the wastes treated.

The samples referred to in point (b) shall be kept for at least 1 month after the incineration or co-incineration of the waste concerned.

5. The competent authority may grant exemptions from paragraphs 2, 3 and 4 to waste incineration plants or waste co-incineration plants which are a part of an installation covered by Chapter II and only incinerate or co-incinerate waste generated within that installation.

Article 53

Residues

1. Residues shall be minimised in their amount and harmfulness. Residues shall be recycled, where appropriate, directly in the plant or outside.

2. Transport and intermediate storage of dry residues in the form of dust shall take place in such a way as to prevent dispersal of those residues in the environment.

3. Prior to determining the routes for the disposal or recycling of the residues, appropriate tests shall be carried out to establish the physical and chemical characteristics and the polluting potential of the residues. Those tests shall concern the total soluble fraction and heavy metals soluble fraction.

Article 54

Substantial change

A change of operation of a waste incineration plant or a waste co-incineration plant treating only non-hazardous waste in an installation covered by Chapter II which involves the incineration or co-incineration of hazardous waste shall be regarded as a substantial change.

Article 55

Reporting and public information on waste incineration plants and waste co-incineration plants

1. Applications for new permits for waste incineration plants and waste co-incineration plants shall be made available to the public at one or more locations for an appropriate period to enable the public to comment on the applications before the competent authority reaches a decision. That decision, including at least a copy of the permit, and any subsequent updates, shall also be made available to the public.

2. For waste incineration plants or waste co-incineration plants with a nominal capacity of 2 tonnes or more per hour, the report referred to in Article 72 shall include information on the functioning and monitoring of the plant and give account of the running of the incineration or co-incineration process and the level of emissions into air and water in comparison with the emission limit values. That information shall be made available to the public.

3. A list of waste incineration plants or waste co-incineration plants with a nominal capacity of less than 2 tonnes per hour shall be drawn up by the competent authority and shall be made available to the public.

Chapter V
Special provisions for installations and activities using organic solvents

Article 56

Scope

This chapter shall apply to activities listed in Part 1 of Annex VII and, where applicable, reaching the consumption thresholds set out in Part 2 of that Annex.

Article 57

Definitions

For the purposes of this Chapter, the following definitions shall apply:

(1) "existing installation" means an installation in operation on 29 March 1999 or which was granted a permit or registered before 1 April 2001 or the operator of which submitted a complete application for a permit before 1 April 2001, provided that that installation was put in operation no later than 1 April 2002;

(2) "waste gases" means the final gaseous discharge containing volatile organic compounds or other pollutants from a stack or abatement equipment into air;

(3) "fugitive emissions" means any emissions not in waste gases of volatile organic compounds into air, soil and water as well as solvents contained in any products, unless otherwise stated in Part 2 of Annex VII;

(4) "total emissions" means the sum of fugitive emissions and emissions in waste gases;

(5) "mixture" means mixture as defined in Article 3(2) of Regulation (EC) No 1907/2006 of the European Parliament and of the Council of 18 December 2006 concerning the Registration, Evaluation, Authorisation and Restriction of Chemicals (REACH) and establishing a European Chemicals Agency,

(6) "adhesive" means any mixture, including all the organic solvents or mixtures containing organic solvents necessary for its proper application, which is used to adhere separate parts of a product;

(7) "ink" means a mixture, including all the organic solvents or mixtures containing organic solvents necessary for its proper application, which is used in a printing activity to impress text or images on to a surface;

(8) "varnish" means a transparent coating;

(9) "consumption" means the total input of organic solvents into an installation per calendar year, or any other 12-month period, less any volatile organic compounds that are recovered for re-use;

(10) "input" means the quantity of organic solvents and their quantity in mixtures used when carrying out an activity, including the solvents recycled inside and outside the installation, and which are counted every time they are used to carry out the activity;

(11) "re-use" means the use of organic solvents recovered from an installation for any technical or commercial purpose and including use as a fuel but excluding the final disposal of such recovered organic solvent as waste;

(12) "contained conditions" means conditions under which an installation is operated so that the volatile organic compounds released from the activity are collected and discharged in a controlled way either via a stack or abatement equipment and are, therefore, not entirely fugitive;

(13) "start-up and shut-down operations" means operations excluding regularly oscillating activity phases whilst bringing an activity, an equipment item or a tank into or out of service or into or out of an idling state.

Article 58

Substitution of hazardous substances

Substances or mixtures which, because of their content of volatile organic compounds classified as carcinogens, mutagens, or toxic to reproduction under Regulation (EC) No 1272/2008, are assigned or need to carry the hazard statements H340, H350, H350i, H360D or H360F, shall be replaced, as far as possible by less harmful substances or mixtures within the shortest possible time.

Article 59

Control of emissions

1. Member States shall take the necessary measures to ensure that each installation complies with either of the following:

(a) the emission of volatile organic compounds from installations shall not exceed the emission limit values in waste gases and the fugitive emission limit values, or the total emission limit values, and other requirements laid down in Parts 2 and 3 of Annex VII are complied with;

(b) the requirements of the reduction scheme set out in Part 5 of Annex VII provided that an equivalent emission reduction is achieved compared to that achieved through the application of the emission limit values referred to in point (a).

Member States shall report to the Commission in accordance with Article 72(1) on the progress in achieving the equivalent emission reduction referred to in point (b).

2. By way of derogation from paragraph 1(a), where the operator demonstrates to the competent authority that for an individual installation the emission limit value for fugitive emissions is not technically and economically feasible, the competent authority may allow emissions to exceed that emission limit value provided that significant risks to human health or the environment are not to be expected and that the operator demonstrates to the competent authority that the best available techniques are being used.

3. By way of derogation from paragraph 1, for coating activities covered by item 8 of the table in Part 2 of Annex VII which cannot be carried out under contained conditions, the competent authority may allow the emissions of the installation not to comply with the requirements set out in that paragraph if the operator demonstrates to the competent authority that such compliance is not technically and economically feasible and that the best available techniques are being used.

4. Member States shall report to the Commission on the derogations referred to in paragraphs 2 and 3 of this Article in accordance with Article 72(2).

5. The emissions of either volatile organic compounds which are assigned or need to carry the hazard statements H340, H350, H350i, H360D or H360F or halogenated volatile organic compounds which are assigned or need to carry the hazard statements H341 or H351, shall be controlled under contained conditions as far as technically and economically feasible to safeguard public health and the environment and shall not exceed the relevant emission limit values set out in Part 4 of Annex VII.

6. Installations where two or more activities are carried out, each of which exceeds the thresholds in Part 2 of Annex VII shall:

(a) as regards the substances specified in paragraph 5, meet the requirements of that paragraph for each activity individually;
(b) as regards all other substances, either:
   (i) meet the requirements of paragraph 1 for each activity individually; or
   (ii) have total emissions of volatile organic compounds not exceeding those which would have resulted had point (i) been applied.

7. All appropriate precautions shall be taken to minimise emissions of volatile organic compounds during start-up and shut-down operations.

Article 60

Monitoring of emissions

Member States shall, either by specification in the permit conditions or by general binding rules, ensure that measurements of emissions are carried out in accordance with Part 6 of Annex VII.

Article 61

Compliance with emission limit values

The emission limit values in waste gases shall be regarded as being complied with if the conditions set out in Part 8 of Annex VII are fulfilled.

Article 62

Reporting on compliance

The operator shall supply the competent authority, on request, with data enabling the competent authority to verify compliance with either of the following:

(a) emission limit values in waste gases, fugitive emission limit values and total emission limit values;
(b) the requirements of the reduction scheme under Part 5 of Annex VII;
(c) the derogations granted in accordance with Article 59(2) and (3).

This may include a solvent management plan prepared in accordance with Part 7 of Annex VII.

Article 63

Substantial change to existing installations

1. A change of the maximum mass input of organic solvents by an existing installation averaged over 1 day, where the installation is operated at its design output under conditions other than start-up and shut-down operations and maintenance of equipment, shall be considered as substantial if it leads to an increase of emissions of volatile organic compounds of more than:

(a) 25 % for an installation carrying out either activities which fall within the lower threshold band of items 1, 3, 4, 5, 8, 10, 13, 16 or 17 of the table in Part 2 of Annex VII or, activities which fall under one of the other items of Part 2 of Annex VII, and with a solvent consumption of less than 10 tonnes per year;
(b) 10 % for all other installations.

2. Where an existing installation undergoes a substantial change, or falls within the scope of this Directive for the first time following a substantial change, that part of the installation which undergoes the substantial change shall be treated either as a new installation or as an existing installation, provided that the total emissions of the whole installation do not exceed those that would have resulted had the substantially changed part been treated as a new installation.

3. In case of a substantial change, the competent authority shall check compliance of the installation with the requirements of this Directive.

Article 64

Exchange of information on substitution of organic solvents

The Commission shall organise an exchange of information with the Member States, the industry concerned and non-governmental organisations promoting environmental protection on the use of organic solvents and their potential substitutes and techniques which have the least potential effects on air, water, soil, ecosystems and human health.

The exchange of information shall be organised on all of the following:
(a) fitness for use;
(b) potential effects on human health and occupational exposure in particular;
(c) potential effects on the environment;
(d) the economic consequences, in particular the costs and benefits of the options available.

Article 65

Access to information

1. The decision of the competent authority, including at least a copy of the permit, and any subsequent updates, shall be made available to the public.

The general binding rules applicable for installations and the list of installations subject to permitting and registration shall be made available to the public.

2. The results of the monitoring of emissions as required under Article 60 and held by the competent authority shall be made available to the public.

3. Paragraphs 1 and 2 of this Article shall apply, subject to the restrictions laid down in Article 4(1) and (2) of Directive 2003/4/EC.

Chapter VI
Special provisions for installations producing titanium dioxide

Article 66

Scope

This Chapter shall apply to installations producing titanium dioxide.

Article 67

Prohibition of the disposal of waste

Member States shall prohibit the disposal of the following waste into any water body, sea or ocean:

(a) solid waste;
(b) the mother liquors arising from the filtration phase following hydrolysis of the titanyl sulphate solution from installations applying the sulphate process; including the acid waste associated with such liquors, containing overall more than 0,5 % free sulphuric acid and various heavy metals and including such mother liquors which have been diluted until they contain 0,5 % or less free sulphuric acid;
(c) waste from installations applying the chloride process containing more than 0,5 % free hydrochloric acid and various heavy metals, including such waste which has been diluted until it contains 0,5 % or less free hydrochloric acid;
(d) filtration salts, sludges and liquid waste arising from the treatment (concentration or neutralisation) of the waste mentioned under points (b) and (c) and containing various heavy metals, but not including neutralised and filtered or decanted waste containing only traces of heavy metals and which, before any dilution, has a pH value above 5,5.

Article 68

Control of emissions into water

Emissions from installations into water shall not exceed the emission limit values set out in Part 1 of Annex VIII.

Article 69

Prevention and control of emissions into air

1. The emission of acid droplets from installations shall be prevented.

2. Emissions into air from installations shall not exceed the emission limit values set out in Part 2 of Annex VIII.

Article 70

Monitoring of emissions

1. Member States shall ensure the monitoring of emissions into water in order to enable the competent authority to verify compliance with the permit conditions and Article 68.

2. Member States shall ensure the monitoring of emissions into air in order to enable the competent authority to verify compliance with the permit conditions and Article 69. Such monitoring shall include at least monitoring of emissions as set out in Part 3 of Annex VIII.

3. Monitoring shall be carried out in accordance with CEN standards or, if CEN standards are not available, ISO, national or other international standards which ensure the provision of data of an equivalent scientific quality.

Chapter VII
Committee, transitional and final provisions

Article 71

Competent authorities

Member States shall designate the competent authorities responsible for carrying out the obligations arising from this Directive.

Article 72

Reporting by Member States

1. Member States shall ensure that information is made available to the Commission on the implementation of this Directive, on representative data on emissions and other forms

of pollution, on emission limit values, on the application of best available techniques in accordance with Articles 14 and 15, in particular on the granting of exemptions in accordance with Article 15(4), and on progress made concerning the development and application of emerging techniques in accordance with Article 27. Member States shall make the information available in an electronic format.

2. The type, format and frequency of information to be made available pursuant to paragraph 1 shall be established in accordance with the regulatory procedure referred to in Article 75(2). This shall include the determination of the specific activities and pollutants for which data referred to in paragraph 1 shall be made available.

3. For all combustion plants covered by Chapter III of this Directive, Member States shall, from 1 January 2016, establish an annual inventory of the sulphur dioxide, nitrogen oxides and dust emissions and energy input.

Taking into account the aggregation rules set out in Article 29, the competent authority shall obtain the following data for each combustion plant:

(a) the total rated thermal input (MW) of the combustion plant;
(b) the type of combustion plant: boiler, gas turbine, gas engine, diesel engine, other (specifying the type);
(c) the date of the start of operation of the combustion plant;
(d) the total annual emissions (tonnes per year) of sulphur dioxide, nitrogen oxides and dust (as total suspended particles);
(e) the number of operating hours of the combustion plant;
(f) the total annual amount of energy input, related to the net calorific value (TJ per year), broken down in terms of the following categories of fuel: coal, lignite, biomass, peat, other solid fuels (specifying the type), liquid fuels, natural gas, other gases (specifying the type).

The annual plant-by-plant data contained in these inventories shall be made available to the Commission upon request.

A summary of the inventories shall be made available to the Commission every 3 years within 12 months from the end of the three-year period considered. This summary shall show separately the data for combustion plants within refineries.

The Commission shall make available to the Member States and to the public a summary of the comparison and evaluation of those inventories in accordance with Directive 2003/4/EC within 24 months from the end of the three-year period considered.

4. Member States shall, from 1 January 2016, report the following data annually to the Commission:

(a) for combustion plants to which Article 31 applies, the sulphur content of the indigenous solid fuel used and the rate of desulphurisation achieved, averaged over each month. For the first year where Article 31 is applied, the technical justification of the non-feasibility of complying with the emission limit values referred to in Article 30(2) and (3) shall also be reported; and
(b) for combustion plants which do not operate more than 1500 operating hours per year as a rolling average over a period of 5 years, the number of operating hours per year.

Article 73

Review

1. By 7 January 2016, and every 3 years thereafter, the Commission shall submit to the European Parliament and to the Council a report reviewing the implementation of this Directive on the basis of the information referred to in Article 72.

That report shall include an assessment of the need for Union action through the establishment or updating of Union-wide minimum requirements for emission limit values and for rules on monitoring and compliance for activities within the scope of the BAT conclusions adopted during the previous three-year period, on the basis of the following criteria:

(a) the impact of the activities concerned on the environment as a whole; and

(b) the state of implementation of best available techniques for the activities concerned.

That assessment shall consider the opinion of the forum referred to in Article 13(4).

Chapter III and Annex V of this Directive shall be considered to represent the Union-wide minimum requirements in the case of large combustion plants.

The report shall be accompanied by a legislative proposal where appropriate. Where the assessment referred to in the second subparagraph identifies such a need, the legislative proposal shall include provisions establishing or updating Union-wide minimum requirements for emission limit values and for rules on monitoring and compliance assessment for the activities concerned.

2. The Commission shall, by 31 December 2012, review the need to control emissions from:

(a) the combustion of fuels in installations with a total rated thermal input below 50 MW;

(b) the intensive rearing of cattle; and

(c) the spreading of manure.

The Commission shall report the results of that review to the European Parliament and to the Council accompanied by a legislative proposal where appropriate.

3. The Commission shall report to the European Parliament and the Council, by 31 December 2011, on the establishment in Annex I of:

(a) differentiated capacity thresholds for the rearing of different poultry species, including the specific case of quail;

(b) capacity thresholds for the simultaneous rearing of different types of animals within the same installation.

The Commission shall report the results of that review to the European Parliament and to the Council accompanied by a legislative proposal where appropriate.

Article 74

Amendments of Annexes

In order to allow the provisions of this Directive to be adapted to scientific and technical progress on the basis of best available techniques, the Commission shall adopt delegated acts in accordance with Article 76 and subject to the conditions laid down in Articles 77 and 78 as regards the adaptation of Parts 3 and 4 of Annex V, Parts 2, 6, 7 and 8 of Annex VI and Parts 5, 6, 7 and 8 of Annex VII to such scientific and technical progress.

Article 75

Committee procedure

1. The Commission shall be assisted by a committee.

2. Where reference is made to this paragraph, Articles 5 and 7 of Decision 1999/468/EC shall apply, having regard to the provisions of Article 8 thereof.

The period laid down in Article 5(6) of Decision 1999/468/EC shall be set at 3 months.

Article 76

Exercise of the delegation

1. The power to adopt the delegated acts referred to in Article 48(5) and Article 74 shall be conferred on the Commission for a period of 5 years from 6 January 2011. The Commission shall draw up a report in respect of the delegated power at the latest 6 months before the end

of the five-year period. The delegation of power shall be automatically extended for periods of an identical duration, unless the European Parliament or the Council revokes it in accordance with Article 77.

2. As soon as it adopts a delegated act, the Commission shall notify it simultaneously to the European Parliament and to the Council.

3. The power to adopt delegated acts is conferred on the Commission subject to the conditions laid down in Articles 77 and 78.

Article 77

Revocation of the delegation

1. The delegation of power referred to in Article 48(5) and Article 74 may be revoked at any time by the European Parliament or by the Council.

2. The institution which has commenced an internal procedure for deciding whether to revoke a delegation of power shall endeavour to inform the other institution and the Commission within a reasonable time before the final decision is taken, indicating the delegated power which could be subject to revocation and possible reasons for a revocation.

3. The decision of revocation shall put an end to the delegation of the power specified in that decision. It shall take effect immediately or on a later date specified therein. It shall not affect the validity of the delegated acts already in force. It shall be published in the Official Journal of the European Union.

Article 78

Objections to delegated acts

1. The European Parliament or the Council may object to a delegated act within a period of 2 months from the date of notification.

At the initiative of the European Parliament or the Council that period shall be extended by 2 months.

2. If, on expiry of the period referred to in paragraph 1, neither the European Parliament nor the Council has objected to the delegated act, it shall be published in the Official Journal of the European Union and shall enter into force on the date stated therein.

The delegated act may be published in the Official Journal of the European Union and enter into force before the expiry of that period if the European Parliament and the Council have both informed the Commission of their intention not to raise objections.

3. If either the European Parliament or the Council objects to the delegated act within the period referred to in paragraph 1, it shall not enter into force. The institution which objects shall state the reasons for objecting to the delegated act.

Article 79

Penalties

Member States shall determine penalties applicable to infringements of the national provisions adopted pursuant to this Directive. The penalties thus provided for shall be effective, proportionate and dissuasive. Member States shall notify those provisions to the Commission by 7 January 2013 and shall notify it without delay of any subsequent amendment affecting them.

Article 80

Transposition

1. Member States shall bring into force the laws, regulations and administrative provisions necessary to comply with Article 2, points (8), (11) to (15), (18) to (23), (26) to (30), (34) to (38) and (41) of Article 3, Article 4(2) and (3), Article 7, Articles 8 and 10, Article 11(e) and (h), Article 12(1)(e) and (h), Article 13(7), point (ii) of Article 14(1)(c), points (d), (e), (f) and (h) of Article 14(1), Article 14(2) to (7), Article 15(2) to (5), Articles 16, 17 and 19, Article 21(2) to (5), Articles 22, 23, 24, 27, 28 and 29, Article 30(1), (2), (3), (4), (7) and (8), Articles 31, 32, 33, 34, 35, 36, 38 and 39, Article 40(2) and (3), Articles 42 and 43, Article 45(1), Article 58, Article 59(5), Article 63, Article 65(3), Articles 69, 70, 71, 72 and 79, and with the first subparagraph and points 1.1, 1.4, 2.5(b), 3.1, 4, 5, 6.1(c), 6.4(b), 6.10 and 6.11 of Annex I, Annex II, point 12 of Annex III, Annex V, point (b) of Part 1, points 2.2, 2.4, 3.1 and 3.2 of Part 4, points 2.5 and 2.6 of Part 6 and point 1.1(d) of Part 8 of Annex VI, point 2 of Part 4, point 1 of Part 5, point 3 of Part 7 of Annex VII, points 1 and 2(c) of Part 1, points 2 and 3 of Part 2 and Part 3 of Annex VIII by 7 January 2013.

They shall apply those measures from that same date.

When Member States adopt those measures, they shall contain a reference to this Directive or be accompanied by such a reference on the occasion of their official publication. The methods of making such reference shall be laid down by Member States.

2. Member States shall communicate to the Commission the text of the main provisions of national law which they adopt in the field covered by this Directive.

Article 81

Repeal

1. Directives 78/176/EEC, 82/883/EEC, 92/112/EEC, 1999/13/EC, 2000/76/EC and 2008/1/EC, as amended by the acts listed in Annex IX, Part A are repealed with effect from 7 January 2014, without prejudice to the obligations of the Member States relating to the time limits for transposition into national law and application of the Directives set out in Annex IX, Part B.

2. Directive 2001/80/EC as amended by the acts listed in Annex IX, Part A is repealed with effect from 1 January 2016, without prejudice to the obligations of the Member States relating to the time limits for transposition into national law and application of the Directives set out in Annex IX, Part B.

3. References to the repealed Directives shall be construed as references to this Directive and shall be read in accordance with the correlation table set out in Annex X.

Article 82

Transitional provisions

1. In relation to installations carrying out activities referred to in Annex I, point 1.1 for activities with a total rated thermal input exceeding 50 MW, points 1.2 and 1.3, point 1.4(a), points 2.1 to 2.6, points 3.1 to 3.5, points 4.1 to 4.6 for activities concerning production by chemical processing, points 5.1 and 5.2 for activities covered by Directive 2008/1/EC, point 5.3 (a)(i) and (ii), point 5.4, point 6.1(a) and (b), points 6.2 and 6.3, point 6.4(a), point 6.4(b) for activities covered by Directive 2008/1/EC, point 6.4(c) and points 6.5 to 6.9 which are in operation and hold a permit before 7 January 2013 or the operators of which have submitted a complete application for a permit before that date, provided that those installations are put into operation no later than 7 January 2014, Member States shall apply the laws, regulations and administrative provisions adopted in accordance with Article 80(1) from 7 January 2014 with the exception of Chapter III and Annex V.

2. In relation to installations carrying out activities referred to in Annex I, point 1.1 for activities with a total rated thermal input of 50 MW, point 1.4(b), points 4.1 to 4.6 for activities concerning production by biological processing, points 5.1 and 5.2 for activities not covered by Directive 2008/1/EC, point 5.3(a)(iii) to (v), point 5.3(b), points 5.5 and 5.6, point 6.1(c), point 6.4(b) for activities not covered by Directive 2008/1/EC and points 6.10 and 6.11 which are in operation before 7 January 2013, Member States shall apply the laws, regulations and administrative provisions adopted in accordance with this Directive from 7 July 2015 with the exception of Chapters III and IV and Annexes V and VI.

3. In relation to combustion plants referred to in Article 30(2), Member States shall, from 1 January 2016, apply the laws, regulations and administrative provisions adopted in accordance with Article 80(1) to comply with Chapter III and Annex V.

4. In relation to combustion plants referred to in Article 30(3), Member States shall no longer apply Directive 2001/80/EC from 7 January 2013.

5. In relation to combustion plants which co-incinerate waste, point 3.1 of Part 4 of Annex VI shall apply until:
(a) 31 December 2015, for combustion plants referred to in Article 30(2);
(b) 6 January 2013, for combustion plants referred to in Article 30(3).

6. Point 3.2 of Part 4 of Annex VI shall apply in relation to combustion plants which co-incinerate waste, as from:
(a) 1 January 2016, for combustion plants referred to in Article 30(2)
(b) 7 January 2013, for combustion plants referred to in Article 30(3).

7. Article 58 shall apply from 1 June 2015. Until that date, substances or mixtures which, because of their content of volatile organic compounds classified as carcinogens, mutagens, or toxic to reproduction under Regulation (EC) No 1272/2008, are assigned or need to carry the hazard statements H340, H350, H350i, H360D or H360F or the risk phrases R45, R46, R49, R60 or R61, shall be replaced, as far as possible, by less harmful substances or mixtures within the shortest possible time.

8. Article 59(5) shall apply from 1 June 2015. Until that date, the emissions of either volatile organic compounds which are assigned or need to carry the hazard statements H340, H350, H350i, H360D or H360F or the risk phrases R45, R46, R49, R60 or R61 or halogenated volatile organic compounds which are assigned or need to carry the hazard statements H341 or H351 or the risk phrases R40 or R68, shall be controlled under contained conditions, as far as technically and economically feasible, to safeguard public health and the environment and shall not exceed the relevant emission limit values set out in Part 4 of Annex VII.

9. Point 2 of Part 4 of Annex VII shall apply from 1 June 2015. Until that date, for emissions of halogenated volatile organic compounds which are assigned or need to carry the hazard statements H341 or H351 or the risk phrases R40 or R68, where the mass flow of the sum of the compounds causing the hazard statements H341 or H351 or the labelling R40 or R68 is greater than, or equal to, 100 g/h, an emission limit value of 20 mg/Nm^3 shall be complied with. The emission limit value refers to the mass sum of the individual compounds.

Article 83

Entry into force

This Directive shall enter into force on the 20th day following its publication in the Official Journal of the European Union.

Article 84

Addressees

This Directive is addressed to the Member States.

ANNEX I
CATEGORIES OF ACTIVITIES REFERRED TO IN ARTICLE 10

The threshold values given below generally refer to production capacities or outputs. Where several activities falling under the same activity description containing a threshold are operated in the same installation, the capacities of such activities are added together. For waste management activities, this calculation shall apply at the level of activities 5.1, 5.3(a) and 5.3(b).

The Commission shall establish guidance on:
(a) the relationship between waste management activities described in this Annex and those described in Annexes I and II to Directive 2008/98/EC; and
(b) the interpretation of the term "industrial scale" regarding the description of chemical industry activities described in this Annex.

1. Energy industries

1.1. Combustion of fuels in installations with a total rated thermal input of 50 MW or more

1.2. Refining of mineral oil and gas

1.3. Production of coke

1.4. Gasification or liquefaction of:
(a) coal;
(b) other fuels in installations with a total rated thermal input of 20 MW or more.

2. Production and processing of metals

2.1. Metal ore (including sulphide ore) roasting or sintering

2.2. Production of pig iron or steel (primary or secondary fusion) including continuous casting, with a capacity exceeding 2,5 tonnes per hour

2.3. Processing of ferrous metals:
(a) operation of hot-rolling mills with a capacity exceeding 20 tonnes of crude steel per hour;
(b) operation of smitheries with hammers the energy of which exceeds 50 kilojoule per hammer, where the calorific power used exceeds 20 MW;
(c) application of protective fused metal coats with an input exceeding 2 tonnes of crude steel per hour.

2.4. Operation of ferrous metal foundries with a production capacity exceeding 20 tonnes per day

2.5. Processing of non-ferrous metals:
(a) production of non-ferrous crude metals from ore, concentrates or secondary raw materials by metallurgical, chemical or electrolytic processes;
(b) melting, including the alloyage, of non-ferrous metals, including recovered products and operation of non-ferrous metal foundries, with a melting capacity exceeding 4 tonnes per day for lead and cadmium or 20 tonnes per day for all other metals.

2.6. Surface treatment of metals or plastic materials using an electrolytic or chemical process where the volume of the treatment vats exceeds 30 m^3

3. Mineral industry

3.1. Production of cement, lime and magnesium oxide:
(a) production of cement clinker in rotary kilns with a production capacity exceeding 500 tonnes per day or in other kilns with a production capacity exceeding 50 tonnes per day;
(b) production of lime in kilns with a production capacity exceeding 50 tonnes per day;

(c) production of magnesium oxide in kilns with a production capacity exceeding 50 tonnes per day.

3.2. Production of asbestos or the manufacture of asbestos-based products

3.3. Manufacture of glass including glass fibre with a melting capacity exceeding 20 tonnes per day

3.4. Melting mineral substances including the production of mineral fibres with a melting capacity exceeding 20 tonnes per day

3.5. Manufacture of ceramic products by firing, in particular roofing tiles, bricks, refractory bricks, tiles, stoneware or porcelain with a production capacity exceeding 75 tonnes per day and/or with a kiln capacity exceeding 4 m^3 and with a setting density per kiln exceeding 300 kg/m^3

4. Chemical industry

For the purpose of this section, production within the meaning of the categories of activities contained in this section means the production on an industrial scale by chemical or biological processing of substances or groups of substances listed in points 4.1 to 4.6

4.1. Production of organic chemicals, such as:
(a) simple hydrocarbons (linear or cyclic, saturated or unsaturated, aliphatic or aromatic);
(b) oxygen-containing hydrocarbons such as alcohols, aldehydes, ketones, carboxylic acids, esters and mixtures of esters, acetates, ethers, peroxides and epoxy resins;
(c) sulphurous hydrocarbons;
(d) nitrogenous hydrocarbons such as amines, amides, nitrous compounds, nitro compounds or nitrate compounds, nitriles, cyanates, isocyanates;
(e) phosphorus-containing hydrocarbons;
(f) halogenic hydrocarbons;
(g) organometallic compounds;
(h) plastic materials (polymers, synthetic fibres and cellulose-based fibres);
(i) synthetic rubbers;
(j) dyes and pigments;
(k) surface-active agents and surfactants.

4.2. Production of inorganic chemicals, such as:
(a) gases, such as ammonia, chlorine or hydrogen chloride, fluorine or hydrogen fluoride, carbon oxides, sulphur compounds, nitrogen oxides, hydrogen, sulphur dioxide, carbonyl chloride;
(b) acids, such as chromic acid, hydrofluoric acid, phosphoric acid, nitric acid, hydrochloric acid, sulphuric acid, oleum, sulphurous acids;
(c) bases, such as ammonium hydroxide, potassium hydroxide, sodium hydroxide;
(d) salts, such as ammonium chloride, potassium chlorate, potassium carbonate, sodium carbonate, perborate, silver nitrate;
(e) non-metals, metal oxides or other inorganic compounds such as calcium carbide, silicon, silicon carbide.

4.3. Production of phosphorous-, nitrogen- or potassium-based fertilisers (simple or compound fertilisers)

4.4. Production of plant protection products or of biocides

4.5. Production of pharmaceutical products including intermediates

4.6. Production of explosives

5. Waste management

5.1. Disposal or recovery of hazardous waste with a capacity exceeding 10 tonnes per day involving one or more of the following activities:

(a) biological treatment;
(b) physico-chemical treatment;
(c) blending or mixing prior to submission to any of the other activities listed in points 5.1 and 5.2;
(d) repackaging prior to submission to any of the other activities listed in points 5.1 and 5.2;
(e) solvent reclamation/regeneration;
(f) recycling/reclamation of inorganic materials other than metals or metal compounds;
(g) regeneration of acids or bases;
(h) recovery of components used for pollution abatement;
(i) recovery of components from catalysts;
(j) oil re-refining or other reuses of oil;
(k) surface impoundment.

5.2. Disposal or recovery of waste in waste incineration plants or in waste co-incineration plants:
(a) for non-hazardous waste with a capacity exceeding 3 tonnes per hour;
(b) for hazardous waste with a capacity exceeding 10 tonnes per day.

5.3.
(a) Disposal of non-hazardous waste with a capacity exceeding 50 tonnes per day involving one or more of the following activities, and excluding activities covered by Council Directive 91/271/EEC of 21 May 1991 concerning urban waste-water treatment:
   (i) biological treatment;
   (ii) physico-chemical treatment;
   (iii) pre-treatment of waste for incineration or co-incineration;
   (iv) treatment of slags and ashes;
   (v) treatment in shredders of metal waste, including waste electrical and electronic equipment and end-of-life vehicles and their components.
(b) Recovery, or a mix of recovery and disposal, of non-hazardous waste with a capacity exceeding 75 tonnes per day involving one or more of the following activities, and excluding activities covered by Directive 91/271/EEC:
   (i) biological treatment;
   (ii) pre-treatment of waste for incineration or co-incineration;
   (iii) treatment of slags and ashes;
   (iv) treatment in shredders of metal waste, including waste electrical and electronic equipment and end-of-life vehicles and their components.

When the only waste treatment activity carried out is anaerobic digestion, the capacity threshold for this activity shall be 100 tonnes per day.

5.4. Landfills, as defined in Article 2(g) of Council Directive 1999/31/EC of 26 April 1999 on the landfill of waste, receiving more than 10 tonnes of waste per day or with a total capacity exceeding 25000 tonnes, excluding landfills of inert waste

5.5. Temporary storage of hazardous waste not covered under point 5.4 pending any of the activities listed in points 5.1, 5.2, 5.4 and 5.6 with a total capacity exceeding 50 tonnes, excluding temporary storage, pending collection, on the site where the waste is generated

5.6. Underground storage of hazardous waste with a total capacity exceeding 50 tonnes

6. Other activities

6.1. Production in industrial installations of:
(a) pulp from timber or other fibrous materials;
(b) paper or card board with a production capacity exceeding 20 tonnes per day;
(c) one or more of the following wood-based panels: oriented strand board, particleboard or fibreboard with a production capacity exceeding 600 m^3 per day.

6.2. Pre-treatment (operations such as washing, bleaching, mercerisation) or dyeing of textile fibres or textiles where the treatment capacity exceeds 10 tonnes per day

6.3. Tanning of hides and skins where the treatment capacity exceeds 12 tonnes of finished products per day

6.4.
(a) Operating slaughterhouses with a carcass production capacity greater than 50 tonnes per day
(b) Treatment and processing, other than exclusively packaging, of the following raw materials, whether previously processed or unprocessed, intended for the production of food or feed from:
  (i) only animal raw materials (other than exclusively milk) with a finished product production capacity greater than 75 tonnes per day;
  (ii) only vegetable raw materials with a finished product production capacity greater than 300 tonnes per day or 600 tonnes per day where the installation operates for a period of no more than 90 consecutive days in any year;
  (iii) animal and vegetable raw materials, both in combined and separate products, with a finished product production capacity in tonnes per day greater than:
    — 75 if A is equal to 10 or more; or,
    — [300- (22,5 × A)] in any other case,
  where "A" is the portion of animal material (in percent of weight) of the finished product production capacity.
  Packaging shall not be included in the final weight of the product.
  This subsection shall not apply where the raw material is milk only.

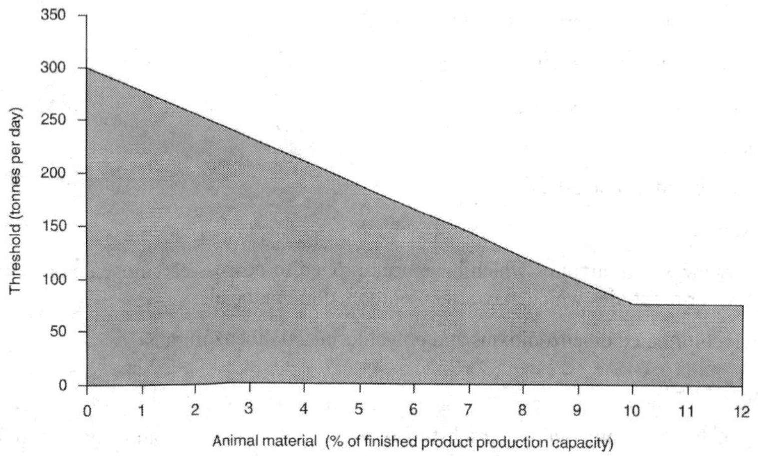

(c) Treatment and processing of milk only, the quantity of milk received being greater than 200 tonnes per day (average value on an annual basis).

6.5. Disposal or recycling of animal carcases or animal waste with a treatment capacity exceeding 10 tonnes per day

6.6. Intensive rearing of poultry or pigs:
(a) with more than 40000 places for poultry;
(b) with more than 2000 places for production pigs (over 30 kg), or
(c) with more than 750 places for sows.

6.7. Surface treatment of substances, objects or products using organic solvents, in particular for dressing, printing, coating, degreasing, waterproofing, sizing, painting, cleaning or impregnating, with an organic solvent consumption capacity of more than 150 kg per hour or more than 200 tonnes per year

6.8. Production of carbon (hard-burnt coal) or electrographite by means of incineration or graphitisation

6.9. Capture of CO_2 streams from installations covered by this Directive for the purposes of geological storage pursuant to Directive 2009/31/EC

6.10. Preservation of wood and wood products with chemicals with a production capacity exceeding 75 m^3 per day other than exclusively treating against sapstain

6.11. Independently operated treatment of waste water not covered by Directive 91/271/EEC and discharged by an installation covered by Chapter II

ANNEX II
LIST OF POLLUTING SUBSTANCES

Air

1. Sulphur dioxide and other sulphur compounds
2. Oxides of nitrogen and other nitrogen compounds
3. Carbon monoxide
4. Volatile organic compounds
5. Metals and their compounds
6. Dust including fine particulate matter
7. Asbestos (suspended particulates, fibres)
8. Chlorine and its compounds
9. Fluorine and its compounds
10. Arsenic and its compounds
11. Cyanides
12. Substances and mixtures which have been proved to possess carcinogenic or mutagenic properties or properties which may affect reproduction via the air
13. Polychlorinated dibenzodioxins and polychlorinated dibenzofurans

Water

1. Organohalogen compounds and substances which may form such compounds in the aquatic environment
2. Organophosphorus compounds
3. Organotin compounds
4. Substances and mixtures which have been proved to possess carcinogenic or mutagenic properties or properties which may affect reproduction in or via the aquatic environment
5. Persistent hydrocarbons and persistent and bioaccumulable organic toxic substances
6. Cyanides
7. Metals and their compounds
8. Arsenic and its compounds
9. Biocides and plant protection products
10. Materials in suspension
11. Substances which contribute to eutrophication (in particular, nitrates and phosphates)

12. Substances which have an unfavourable influence on the oxygen balance (and can be measured using parameters such as BOD, COD, etc.)

13. Substances listed in Annex X to Directive 2000/60/EC

ANNEX III
CRITERIA FOR DETERMINING BEST AVAILABLE TECHNIQUES

1. the use of low-waste technology;

2. the use of less hazardous substances;

3. the furthering of recovery and recycling of substances generated and used in the process and of waste, where appropriate;

4. comparable processes, facilities or methods of operation which have been tried with success on an industrial scale;

5. technological advances and changes in scientific knowledge and understanding;

6. the nature, effects and volume of the emissions concerned;

7. the commissioning dates for new or existing installations;

8. the length of time needed to introduce the best available technique;

9. the consumption and nature of raw materials (including water) used in the process and energy efficiency;

10. the need to prevent or reduce to a minimum the overall impact of the emissions on the environment and the risks to it;

11. the need to prevent accidents and to minimise the consequences for the environment;

12. information published by public international organisations.

ANNEX IV
PUBLIC PARTICIPATION IN DECISION-MAKING

1. The public shall be informed (by public notices or other appropriate means such as electronic media where available) of the following matters early in the procedure for the taking of a decision or, at the latest, as soon as the information can reasonably be provided:

(a) the application for a permit or, as the case may be, the proposal for the updating of a permit or of permit conditions in accordance with Article 21, including the description of the elements listed in Article 12(1);

(b) where applicable, the fact that a decision is subject to a national or transboundary environmental impact assessment or to consultations between Member States in accordance with Article 26;

(c) details of the competent authorities responsible for taking the decision, those from which relevant information can be obtained, those to which comments or questions can be submitted, and details of the time schedule for transmitting comments or questions;

(d) the nature of possible decisions or, where there is one, the draft decision;

(e) where applicable, the details relating to a proposal for the updating of a permit or of permit conditions;

(f) an indication of the times and places where, or means by which, the relevant information will be made available;

(g) details of the arrangements for public participation and consultation made pursuant to point 5.

2. Member States shall ensure that, within appropriate time-frames, the following is made available to the public concerned:

(a) in accordance with national law, the main reports and advice issued to the competent authority or authorities at the time when the public concerned were informed in accordance with point 1;

(b) in accordance with Directive 2003/4/EC, information other than that referred to in point 1 which is relevant for the decision in accordance with Article 5 of this Directive and which only becomes available after the time the public concerned was informed in accordance with point 1.

3. The public concerned shall be entitled to express comments and opinions to the competent authority before a decision is taken.

4. The results of the consultations held pursuant to this Annex must be taken into due account in the taking of a decision.

5. The detailed arrangements for informing the public (for example by bill posting within a certain radius or publication in local newspapers) and consulting the public concerned (for example by written submissions or by way of a public inquiry) shall be determined by the Member States. Reasonable time-frames for the different phases shall be provided, allowing sufficient time to inform the public and for the public concerned to prepare and participate effectively in environmental decision-making subject to this Annex.

ANNEX V
TECHNICAL PROVISIONS RELATING TO COMBUSTION PLANTS

PART 1
EMISSION LIMIT VALUES FOR COMBUSTION PLANTS REFERRED TO IN ARTICLE 30(2)

1. All emission limit values shall be calculated at a temperature of 273,15 K, a pressure of 101,3 kPa and after correction for the water vapour content of the waste gases and at a standardised O_2 content of 6 % for solid fuels, 3 % for combustion plants, other than gas turbines and gas engines using liquid and gaseous fuels and 15 % for gas turbines and gas engines.

2. Emission limit values (mg/Nm^3) for SO_2 for combustion plants using solid or liquid fuels with the exception of gas turbines and gas engines

Total rated thermal input (MW)	*Coal and lignite and other solid fuels*	*Biomass*	*Peat*	*Liquid fuels*
50-100	400	200	300	350
100-300	250	200	300	250
> 300	200	200	200	200

Combustion plants, using solid fuels which were granted a permit before 27 November 2002 or the operators of which had submitted a complete application for a permit before that date, provided that the plant was put into operation no later than 27 November 2003, and which do not operate more than 1500 operating hours per year as a rolling average over a period of 5 years, shall be subject to an emission limit value for SO_2 of 800 mg/Nm^3.

Combustion plants using liquid fuels, which were granted a permit before 27 November 2002 or the operators of which had submitted a complete application for a permit before that date, provided that the plant was put into operation no later than 27 November 2003, and which do not operate more than 1500 operating hours per year as a rolling average over a period of 5 years, shall be subject to an emission limit value for SO_2 of 850 mg/Nm^3 in case of plants with a total rated thermal input not exceeding 300 MW and of 400 mg/Nm^3 in case of plants with a total rated thermal input greater than 300 MW.

A part of a combustion plant discharging its waste gases through one or more separate flues within a common stack, and which does not operate more than 1500 operating hours per year as a rolling average over a period of 5 years, may be subject to the emission limit values set out in the preceding two paragraphs in relation to the total rated thermal input of the entire combustion plant. In such cases the emissions through each of those flues shall be monitored separately.

3. Emission limit values (mg/Nm^3) for SO_2 for combustion plants using gaseous fuels with the exception of gas turbines and gas engines

In general	35
Liquefied gas	5
Low calorific gases from coke oven	400
Low calorific gases from blast furnace	200

Combustion plants, firing low calorific gases from gasification of refinery residues, which were granted a permit before 27 November 2002 or the operators of which had submitted a complete application for a permit before that date, provided that the plant was put into operation no later than 27 November 2003, shall be subject to an emission limit value for SO_2 of 800 mg/Nm^3.

4. Emission limit values (mg/Nm^3) for NO_x for combustion plants using solid or liquid fuels with the exception of gas turbines and gas engines

Total rated thermal input (MW)	*Coal and lignite and other solid fuels*	*Biomass and peat*	*Liquid fuels*
50-100	300 450 in case of pulverised lignite combustion	300	450
100-300	200	250	200[(1)]
> 300	200	200	150[(1)]

(1) The emission limit value is 450 mg/Nm^3 for the firing of distillation and conversion residues from the refining of crude-oil for own consumption in combustion plants with a total rated thermal input not exceeding 500 MW which were granted a permit before 27 November 2002 or the operators of which had submitted a complete application for a permit before that date, provided that the plant was put into operation no later than 27 November 2003.

Combustion plants in chemical installations using liquid production residues as non-commercial fuel for own consumption with a total rated thermal input not exceeding 500 MW which were granted a permit before 27 November 2002 or the operators of which had submitted a complete application for a permit before that date, provided that the plant was put into operation no later than 27 November 2003, shall be subject to an emission limit value for NO_x of 450 mg/Nm^3.

Combustion plants using solid or liquid fuels with a total rated thermal input not exceeding 500 MW which were granted a permit before 27 November 2002 or the operators of which had submitted a complete application for a permit before that date, provided that the plant was put into operation no later than 27 November 2003, and which do not operate more than 1500 operating hours per year as a rolling average over a period of 5 years, shall be subject to an emission limit value for NO_x of 450 mg/Nm^3.

Combustion plants using solid fuels with a total rated thermal input greater than 500 MW, which were granted a permit before 1 July 1987 and which do not operate more than 1500 operating hours per year as a rolling average over a period of 5 years, shall be subject to an emission limit value for NO_x of 450 mg/Nm^3.

Combustion plants using liquid fuels, with a total rated thermal input greater than 500 MW which were granted a permit before 27 November 2002 or the operators of which had submitted a complete application for a permit before that date, provided that the plant was put into operation no later than 27 November 2003, and which do not operate more than 1500 operating hours per year as a rolling average over a period of 5 years, shall be subject to an emission limit value for NO_x of 400 mg/Nm^3.

A part of a combustion plant discharging its waste gases through one or more separate flues within a common stack, and which does not operate more than 1500 operating hours per year as a rolling average over a period of 5 years, may be subject to the emission limit values set out in the preceding three paragraphs in relation to the total rated thermal input of the entire combustion plant. In such cases the emissions through each of those flues shall be monitored separately.

5. Gas turbines (including combined cycle gas turbines (CCGT)) using light and middle distillates as liquid fuels shall be subject to an emission limit value for NO_x of 90 mg/Nm^3 and for CO of 100 mg/Nm^3.

Gas turbines for emergency use that operate less than 500 operating hours per year are not covered by the emission limit values set out in this point. The operator of such plants shall record the used operating hours.

6. Emission limit values (mg/Nm^3) for NO_x and CO for gas fired combustion plants

	NO_x	CO
Combustion plants firing natural gas with the exception of gas turbines and gas engines	100	100
Combustion plants firing blast furnace gas, coke oven gas or low calorific gases from gasification of refinery residues, with the exception of gas turbines and gas engines	200(4)	—
Combustion plants firing other gases, with the exception of gas turbines and gas engines	200(4)	—
Gas turbines (including CCGT), using natural gas(1) as fuel	50(2)(3)	100
Gas turbines (including CCGT), using other gases as fuel	120	—
Gas engines	100	100

(1) Natural gas is naturally occurring methane with not more than 20% (by volume) of inerts and other constituents.

(2) 75 mg/Nm^3 in the following cases where the efficiency of the gas turbine is determined at ISO base load conditions.
   (i) gas turbines used in combined heat and power systems having an overall efficiency greater than 75%
   (ii) gas turbines used in combined cycle plants having an annual average overall electrical efficiency greater than 55 %.
   (iii) gas turbines for mechanical drives.

(3) For single cycle gas turbines not falling into any of the categories mentioned under note (2), but having an efficiency greater than 35 % – determined at ISO base load conditions – the emission limit value for NO_x shall be $50 \times \eta / 35$ where η is the gas turbine efficiency at ISO base load conditions expressed as a percentage.

(4) 300 mg/Nm^3 for such combustion plants with a total rated thermal input not exceeding 500 MW which were granted a permit before 27 November 2002 or the operators of which had submitted a complete application for a permit before that date, provided that the plant was put into operation no later than 27 November 2003.

For gas turbines (including CCGT), the NO_x and CO emission limit values set out in the table contained in this point apply only above 70 % load.

For gas turbines (including CCGT) which were granted a permit before 27 November 2002 or the operators of which had submitted a complete application for a permit before that date, provided that the plant was put into operation no later than 27 November 2003, and which do not operate more than 1500 operating hours per year as a rolling average over a period of 5 years, the emission limit value for NO_x is 150 mg/Nm^3 when firing natural gas and 200 mg/Nm^3 when firing other gases or liquid fuels.

A part of a combustion plant discharging its waste gases through one or more separate flues within a common stack, and which does not operate more than 1500 operating hours per year as a rolling average over a period of 5 years, may be subject to the emission limit values set out in the preceding paragraph in relation to the total rated thermal input of the entire combustion plant. In such cases the emissions through each of those flues shall be monitored separately.

Gas turbines and gas engines for emergency use that operate less than 500 operating hours per year are not covered by the emission limit values set out in this point. The operator of such plants shall record the used operating hours.

7. Emission limit values (mg/Nm^3) for dust for combustion plants using solid or liquid fuels with the exception of gas turbines and gas engines

Total rated thermal input (MW)	*Coal and lignite and other solid fuels*	*Biomass and peat*	*Liquid fuels*(1)
50-100	30	30	30
100-300	25	20	25
> 300	20	20	20

(1) The emission limit value is 50 mg/Nm^3 for the firing of distillation and conversion residues from the refining of crude oil for own consumption in combustion plants which were granted a permit before 27 November 2002 or the operators of which had submitted a complete application for a permit before that date, provided that the plant was put into operation no later than 27 November 2003.

8. Emission limit values (mg/Nm^3) for dust for combustion plants using gaseous fuels with the exception of gas turbines and gas engines

In general	5
Blast furnace gas	10
Gases produced by the steel industry which can be used elsewhere	30

PART 2
EMISSION LIMIT VALUES FOR COMBUSTION PLANTS REFERRED TO IN ARTICLE 30(3)

1. All emission limit values shall be calculated at a temperature of 273,15 K, a pressure of 101,3 kPa and after correction for the water vapour content of the waste gases and at a standardised O_2 content of 6 % for solid fuels, 3 % for combustion plants other than gas turbines and gas engines using liquid and gaseous fuels and 15 % for gas turbines and gas engines.

In case of combined cycle gas turbines with supplementary firing, the standardised O_2 content may be defined by the competent authority, taking into account the specific characteristics of the installation concerned.

2. Emission limit values (mg/Nm^3) for SO_2 for combustion plants using solid or liquid fuels with the exception of gas turbines and gas engines

Total rated thermal input (MW)	*Coal and lignite and other solid fuels*	*Biomass*	*Peat*	*Liquid fuels*
50-100	400	200	300	350
100-300	200	200	300 250 in case of fluidised bed combustion	200
> 300	150 200 in case of circulating or pressurised fluidised bed combustion	150	150 200 in case of fluidised bed combustion	150

3. Emission limit values (mg/Nm^3) for SO_2 for combustion plants using gaseous fuels with the exception of gas turbines and gas engines

In general	35
Liquefied gas	5
Low calorific gases from coke oven	400
Low calorific gases from blast furnace	200

4. Emission limit values (mg/Nm^3) for NO_x for combustion plants using solid or liquid fuels with the exception of gas turbines and gas engines

Total rated thermal input (MW)	*Coal and lignite and other solid fuels*	*Biomass and peat*	*Liquid fuels*[(1)]
50-100	300 400 in case of pulverised lignite combustion	250	300
100-300	200	200	150
> 300	150 200 in case of pulverised lignite combustion	150	100

5. Gas turbines (including CCGT) using light and middle distillates as liquid fuels shall be subject to an emission limit value for NO_x of 50 mg/Nm^3 and for CO of 100 mg/Nm^3

Gas turbines for emergency use that operate less than 500 operating hours per year are not covered by the emission limit values set out in this point. The operator of such plants shall record the used operating hours.

6. Emission limit values (mg/Nm^3) for NO_x and CO for gas fired combustion plants

	NO_x	*CO*
Combustion plants other than gas turbines and gas engines	100	100
Gas turbines (including CCGT)	50[(1)]	100
Gas engines	75	100

(1) For single cycle gas turbines having an efficiency greater than 35 % – determined at ISO base load conditions – the emission limit value for NO_x shall be $50 \times \eta/35$ where η is the gas turbine efficiency at ISO base load conditions expressed as a percentage.

For gas turbines (including CCGT), the NO_x and CO emission limit values set out in this point apply only above 70 % load.

Gas turbines and gas engines for emergency use that operate less than 500 operating hours per year are not covered by the emission limit values set out in this point. The operator of such plants shall record the used operating hours.

7. Emission limit values (mg/Nm^3) for dust for combustion plants using solid or liquid fuels with the exception of gas turbines and gas engines

Total rated thermal input (MW)	
50-300	20
> 300	10 20 for biomass and peat

8. Emission limit values (mg/Nm^3) for dust for combustion plants using gaseous fuels with the exception of gas turbines and gas engines

In general	5
Blast furnace gas	10
Gases produced by the steel industry which can be used elsewhere	30

PART 3
EMISSION MONITORING

1. The concentrations of SO_2, NO_x and dust in waste gases from each combustion plant with a total rated thermal input of 100 MW or more shall be measured continuously.

The concentration of CO in waste gases from each combustion plant firing gaseous fuels with a total rated thermal input of 100 MW or more shall be measured continuously.

2. The competent authority may decide not to require the continuous measurements referred to in point 1 in the following cases:
(a) for combustion plants with a life span of less than 10000 operational hours;
(b) for SO_2 and dust from combustion plants firing natural gas;
(c) for SO_2 from combustion plants firing oil with known sulphur content in cases where there is no waste gas desulphurisation equipment;
(d) for SO_2 from combustion plants firing biomass if the operator can prove that the SO_2 emissions can under no circumstances be higher than the prescribed emission limit values.

3. Where continuous measurements are not required, measurements of SO_2, NO_x, dust and, for gas fired plants, also of CO shall be required at least once every 6 months.

4. For combustion plants firing coal or lignite, the emissions of total mercury shall be measured at least once per year.

5. As an alternative to the measurements of SO_2 and NO_x referred to in point 3, other procedures, verified and approved by the competent authority, may be used to determine the SO_2 and NO_x emissions. Such procedures shall use relevant CEN standards or, if CEN standards are not available, ISO, national or other international standards which ensure the provision of data of an equivalent scientific quality.

6. The competent authority shall be informed of significant changes in the type of fuel used or in the mode of operation of the plant. The competent authority shall decide whether the monitoring requirements laid down in points 1 to 4 are still adequate or require adaptation.

7. The continuous measurements carried out in accordance with point 1 shall include the measurement of the oxygen content, temperature, pressure and water vapour content of the waste gases. The continuous measurement of the water vapour content of the waste gases shall not be necessary, provided that the sampled waste gas is dried before the emissions are analysed.

8. Sampling and analysis of relevant polluting substances and measurements of process parameters as well as the quality assurance of automated measuring systems and the reference measurement methods to calibrate those systems shall be carried out in accordance with CEN standards. If CEN standards are not available, ISO, national or other international standards which ensure the provision of data of an equivalent scientific quality shall apply.

The automated measuring systems shall be subject to control by means of parallel measurements with the reference methods at least once per year.

The operator shall inform the competent authority about the results of the checking of the automated measuring systems.

9. At the emission limit value level, the values of the 95 % confidence intervals of a single measured result shall not exceed the following percentages of the emission limit values:

Carbon monoxide	10%
Sulphur dioxide	20%
Nitrogen oxides	20%
Dust	30%

10. The validated hourly and daily average values shall be determined from the measured valid hourly average values after having subtracted the value of the confidence interval specified in point 9.

Any day in which more than three hourly average values are invalid due to malfunction or maintenance of the automated measuring system shall be invalidated. If more than 10 days over a year are invalidated for such situations the competent authority shall require the operator to take adequate measures to improve the reliability of the automated measuring system.

11. In the case of plants which must comply with the rates of desulphurisation referred to in Article 31, the sulphur content of the fuel which is fired in the combustion plant shall also be regularly monitored. The competent authorities shall be informed of substantial changes in the type of fuel used.

PART 4
ASSESSMENT OF COMPLIANCE WITH EMISSION LIMIT VALUES

1. In the case of continuous measurements, the emission limit values set out in Parts 1 and 2 shall be regarded as having been complied with if the evaluation of the measurement results indicates, for operating hours within a calendar year, that all of the following conditions have been met:

(a) no validated monthly average value exceeds the relevant emission limit values set out in Parts 1 and 2;

(b) no validated daily average value exceeds 110 % of the relevant emission limit values set out in Parts 1 and 2;

(c) in cases of combustion plants composed only of boilers using coal with a total rated thermal input below 50 MW, no validated daily average value exceeds 150 % of the relevant emission limit values set out in Parts 1 and 2,

(d) 95 % of all the validated hourly average values over the year do not exceed 200 % of the relevant emission limit values set out in Parts 1 and 2.

The validated average values are determined as set out in point 10 of Part 3.

For the purpose of the calculation of the average emission values, the values measured during the periods referred to in Article 30(5) and (6) and Article 37 as well as during the start-up and shut-down periods shall be disregarded.

2. Where continuous measurements are not required, the emission limit values set out in Parts 1 and 2 shall be regarded as having been complied with if the results of each of the series of measurements or of the other procedures defined and determined according to the rules laid down by the competent authorities do not exceed the emission limit values.

PART 5
MINIMUM RATE OF DESULPHURISATION

1. Minimum rate of desulphurisation for combustion plants referred to in Article 30(2)

Total rated thermal input (MW)	*Minimum rate of desulphurisation*	
	Plants which were granted a permit before 27 November 2002 or the operators of which had submitted a complete application for a permit before that date, provided that the plant was put into operation no later than 27 November 2003	*Other plants*
50-100	80 %	92 %
100-300	90 %	92 %
> 300	96 % (1)	96 %

(1) For combustion plants firing oil shale, the minimum rate of desulphurisation is 9.5%.

2. Minimum rate of desulphurisation for combustion plants referred to in Article 30(3)

Total rated thermal input (MW)	*Minimum rate of desulphurisation*
50-100	93 %
100-300	93 %
> 300	97 %

PART 6
COMPLIANCE WITH RATE OF DESULPHURISATION

The minimum rates of desulphurisation set out in Part 5 of this Annex shall apply as a monthly average limit value.

PART 7
AVERAGE EMISSION LIMIT VALUES FOR MULTI-FUEL FIRING COMBUSTION PLANTS WITHIN A REFINERY

Average emission limit values (mg/Nm^3) for SO_2 for multi-fuel firing combustion plants within a refinery, with the exception of gas turbines and gas engines, which use the distillation and conversion residues from the refining of crude-oil for own consumption, alone or with other fuels:

(a) for combustion plants which were granted a permit before 27 November 2002 or the operators of which had submitted a complete application for a permit before that date, provided that the plant was put into operation no later than 27 November 2003: 1000 mg/Nm^3;

(b) for other combustion plants: 600 mg/Nm^3.

These emission limit values shall be calculated at a temperature of 273,15 K, a pressure of 101,3 kPa and after correction for the water vapour content of the waste gases and at a standardised O_2 content of 6 % for solid fuels and 3 % for liquid and gaseous fuels.

ANNEX VI
TECHNICAL PROVISIONS RELATING TO WASTE INCINERATION PLANTS AND WASTE CO-INCINERATION PLANTS

PART 1
DEFINITIONS

For the purpose of this Annex the following definitions shall apply:

(a) "existing waste incineration plant" means one of the following waste incineration plants:

  (i) which was in operation and had a permit in accordance with applicable Union law before 28 December 2002,

(ii) which was authorised or registered for waste incineration and had a permit granted before 28 December 2002 in accordance with applicable Union law, provided that the plant was put into operation no later than 28 December 2003,

(iii) which, in the view of the competent authority, was the subject of a full request for authorisation before 28 December 2002, provided that the plant was put into operation not later than 28 December 2004;

(b) "new waste incineration plant" means any waste incineration plant not covered by point (a).

PART 2
EQUIVALENCE FACTORS FOR DIBENZO-P-DIOXINS AND DIBENZOFURANS

For the determination of the total concentration of dioxins and furans, the mass concentrations of the following dibenzo-p-dioxins and dibenzofurans shall be multiplied by the following equivalence factors before summing:

	Toxic equivalence factor
2,3,7,8 — Tetrachlorodibenzodioxin (TCDD)	1
1,2,3,7,8 — Pentachlorodibenzodioxin (PeCDD)	0,5
1,2,3,4,7,8 — Hexachlorodibenzodioxin (HxCDD)	0,1
1,2,3,6,7,8 — Hexachlorodibenzodioxin (HxCDD)	0,1
1,2,3,7,8,9 — Hexachlorodibenzodioxin (HxCDD)	0,1
1,2,3,4,6,7,8 — Heptachlorodibenzodioxin (HpCDD)	0,01
Octachlorodibenzodioxin (OCDD)	0,001
2,3,7,8 — Tetrachlorodibenzofuran (TCDF)	0,1
2,3,4,7,8 — Pentachlorodibenzofuran (PeCDF)	0,5
1,2,3,7,8 — Pentachlorodibenzofuran (PeCDF)	0,05
1,2,3,4,7,8 — Hexachlorodibenzofuran (HxCDF)	0,1
1,2,3,6,7,8 — Hexachlorodibenzofuran (HxCDF)	0,1
1,2,3,7,8,9 — Hexachlorodibenzofuran (HxCDF)	0,1
2,3,4,6,7,8 — Hexachlorodibenzofuran (HxCDF)	0,1
1,2,3,4,6,7,8 — Heptachlorodibenzofuran (HpCDF)	0,01
1,2,3,4,7,8,9 — Heptachlorodibenzofuran (HpCDF)	0,01
Octachlorodibenzofuran (OCDF)	0,001

PART 3
AIR EMISSION LIMIT VALUES FOR WASTE INCINERATION PLANTS

1. All emission limit values shall be calculated at a temperature of 273,15 K, a pressure of 101,3 kPa and after correcting for the water vapour content of the waste gases.

They are standardised at 11 % oxygen in waste gas except in case of incineration of mineral waste oil as defined in point 3 of Article 3 of Directive 2008/98/EC, when they are standardised at 3 % oxygen, and in the cases referred to in Point 2.7 of Part 6.

1.1. Daily average emission limit values for the following polluting substances (mg/Nm^3)

Total dust	10
Gaseous and vaporous organic substances, expressed as total organic carbon (TOC)	10
Hydrogen chloride (HCl)	10
Hydrogen fluoride (HF)	1
Sulphur dioxide (SO_2)	50

Nitrogen monoxide (NO) and nitrogen dioxide (NO_2), expressed as NO_2 for existing waste incineration plants with a nominal capacity exceeding 6 tonnes per hour or new waste incineration plants	200
Nitrogen monoxide (NO) and nitrogen dioxide (NO_2), expressed as NO_2 for existing waste incineration plants with a nominal capacity of 6 tonnes per hour or less	400

1.2. Half-hourly average emission limit values for the following polluting substances (mg/ Nm^3)

	(100 %) A	(97 %) B
Total dust	30	10
Gaseous and vaporous organic substances, expressed as total organic carbon (TOC)	20	10
Hydrogen chloride (HCl)	60	10
Hydrogen fluoride (HF)	4	2
Sulphur dioxide (SO_2)	200	50
Nitrogen monoxide (NO) and nitrogen dioxide (NO_2), expressed as NO_2 for existing waste incineration plants with a nominal capacity exceeding 6 tonnes per hour or new waste incineration plants	400	200

1.3. Average emission limit values (mg/Nm^3) for the following heavy metals over a sampling period of a minimum of 30 minutes and a maximum of 8 hours

Cadmium and its compounds, expressed as cadmium (Cd)	Total: 0,05
Thallium and its compounds, expressed as thallium (Tl)	
Mercury and its compounds, expressed as mercury (Hg)	0,05
Antimony and its compounds, expressed as antimony (Sb)	Total: 0,5
Arsenic and its compounds, expressed as arsenic (As)	
Lead and its compounds, expressed as lead (Pb)	
Chromium and its compounds, expressed as chromium (Cr)	
Cobalt and its compounds, expressed as cobalt (Co)	
Copper and its compounds, expressed as copper (Cu)	
Manganese and its compounds, expressed as manganese (Mn)	
Nickel and its compounds, expressed as nickel (Ni)	
Vanadium and its compounds, expressed as vanadium (V)	

These average values cover also the gaseous and the vapour forms of the relevant heavy metal emissions as well as their compounds.

1.4. Average emission limit value (ng/Nm^3) for dioxins and furans over a sampling period of a minimum of 6 hours and a maximum of 8 hours. The emission limit value refers to the total concentration of dioxins and furans calculated in accordance with Part 2.

Dioxins and furans	0,1

1.5. Emission limit values (mg/Nm^3) for carbon monoxide (CO) in the waste gases:

(a) 50 as daily average value;

(b) 100 as half-hourly average value;

(c) 150 as 10-minute average value.

The competent authority may authorise exemptions from the emission limit values set out in this point for waste incineration plants using fluidised bed technology, provided that the permit sets an emission limit value for carbon monoxide (CO) of not more than 100 mg/Nm^3 as an hourly average value.

2. Emission limit values applicable in the circumstances described in Article 46(6) and Article 47.

The total dust concentration in the emissions into the air of a waste incineration plant shall under no circumstances exceed 150 mg/Nm^3 expressed as a half-hourly average. The air emission limit values for TOC and CO set out in points 1.2 and 1.5(b) shall not be exceeded.

3. Member States may lay down rules governing the exemptions provided for in this Part.

PART 4
DETERMINATION OF AIR EMISSION LIMIT VALUES FOR THE CO-INCINERATION OF WASTE

1. The following formula (mixing rule) shall be applied whenever a specific total emission limit value "C" has not been set out in a table in this Part.

The emission limit value for each relevant polluting substance and CO in the waste gas resulting from the co-incineration of waste shall be calculated as follows:

$$\frac{V_{waste} \times C_{waste} + V_{proc} \times C_{proc}}{V_{waste} + V_{proc}} = C$$

V_{waste}: waste gas volume resulting from the incineration of waste only determined from the waste with the lowest calorific value specified in the permit and standardised at the conditions given by this Directive.
If the resulting heat release from the incineration of hazardous waste amounts to less than 10 % of the total heat released in the plant, Vwaste must be calculated from a (notional) quantity of waste that, being incinerated, would equal 10 % heat release, the total heat release being fixed.

C_{waste}: emission limit values for waste incineration plants set out in Part 3

V_{proc}: waste gas volume resulting from the plant process including the combustion of the authorised fuels normally used in the plant (wastes excluded) determined on the basis of oxygen contents at which the emissions must be standardised as set out in Union or national law. In the absence of legislation for this kind of plant, the real oxygen content in the waste gas without being thinned by addition of air unnecessary for the process must be used.

C_{proc}: emission limit values as set out in this Part for certain industrial activities or in case of the absence of such values, emission limit values of plants which comply with the national laws, regulations and administrative provisions for such plants while burning the normally authorised fuels (wastes excluded). In the absence of these measures the emission limit values set out in the permit are used. In the absence of such permit values the real mass concentrations are used.

C: total emission limit values at an oxygen content as set out in this Part for certain industrial activities and certain polluting substances or, in case of the absence of such values, total emission limit values replacing the emission limit values as set out in specific Annexes of this Directive. The total oxygen content to replace the oxygen content for the standardisation is calculated on the basis of the content above respecting the partial volumes.
All emission limit values shall be calculated at a temperature of 273,15 K, a pressure of 101,3 kPa and after correcting for the water vapour content of the waste gases.

Member States may lay down rules governing the exemptions provided for in this Part.

2. Special provisions for cement kilns co-incinerating waste

2.1. The emission limit values set out in points 2.2 and 2.3 apply as daily average values for total dust, HCl, HF, NO_x, SO_2 and TOC (for continuous measurements), as average values over the sampling period of a minimum of 30 minutes and a maximum of 8 hours for heavy metals and as average values over the sampling period of a minimum of 6 hours and a maximum of 8 hours for dioxins and furans.

All values are standardised at 10 % oxygen.
Half-hourly average values shall only be needed in view of calculating the daily average values.

2.2. C – total emission limit values (mg/Nm^3 except for dioxins and furans) for the following –polluting substances

Polluting substance	*C*
Total dust	30
HCl	10
HF	1
NO_x	500[(1)]
Cd + Tl	0,05
Hg	0,05
Sb + As + Pb + Cr + Co + Cu + Mn + Ni + V	0,5
Dioxins and furans (ng/Nm^3)	0,1

(1) Until 1 January 2016, the competent authority may authorise exemptions from the limit value for NO_x or Lepol kilns and long rotary kilns provided that the permit sets a total emission limit value for $NO_x$of not more than 800 mg/Nm^3.

2.3. C – total emission limit values (mg/Nm^3) for SO_2 and TOC

Pollutant	*C*
SO_2	50
TOC	10

The competent authority may grant derogations for emission limit values set out in this point in cases where TOC and SO_2 do not result from the co-incineration of waste.

2.4. C- total emission limit values for CO
The competent authority may set emission limit values for CO.

3. Special provisions for combustion plants co-incinerating waste

3.1. Cproc expressed as daily average values (mg/Nm^3) valid until the date set out in Article 82(5)
For determining the total rated thermal input of the combustion plants, the aggregation rules as defined in Article 29 shall apply. Half-hourly average values shall only be needed in view of calculating the daily average values.
C_{proc} for solid fuels with the exception of biomass (O_2 content 6 %):

Polluting substances	*< 50 MWth*	*50-100 MWth*	*100 to 300 MWth*	*> 300 MWth*
SO_2	—	850	200	200
NO_x	—	400	200	200
Dust	50	50	30	30

C_{proc} for biomass (O_2 content 6 %):

Polluting substances	*< 50 MWth*	*50-100 MWth*	*100 to 300 MWth*	*> 300 MWth*
SO_2	—	200	200	200
NO_x	—	350	300	200
Dust	50	50	30	30

C_{proc} for liquid fuels (O_2 content 3 %):

Polluting substances	*< 50 MWth*	*50-100 MWth*	*100 to 300 MWth*	*> 300 MWth*
SO_2	—	850	400 to 200 (linear decrease from 100 to 300 MWth)	200
NO_x	—	400	200	200
Dust	50	50	30	30

3.2. C_{proc} expressed as daily average values (mg/Nm^3) valid from the date set out in Article 82(6)

For determining the total rated thermal input of the combustion plants, the aggregation rules as defined in Article 29 shall apply. Half-hourly average values shall only be needed in view of calculating the daily average values.

3.2.1. C_{proc} for combustion plants referred to in Article 30(2), with the exception of gas turbines and gas engines

C_{proc} for solid fuels with the exception of biomass (O_2 content 6 %):

Polluting substances	*< 50 MWth*	*50-100 MWth*	*100 to 300 MWth*	*> 300 MWth*
SO_2	—	400 for peat: 300	200 200	200 200
NO_x	—	300 for pulverised lignite: 400	200	100
Dust	50	30	25 for peat: 20	20

C_{proc} for biomass (O_2 content 6 %):

Polluting substances	*< 50 MWth*	*50-100 MWth*	*100 to 300 MWth*	*> 300 MWth*
SO_2	—	200	200	200
NO_x	—	300	250	200
Dust	50	30	20	20

C_{proc} for liquid fuels (O_2 content 3 %):

Polluting substances	*< 50 MWth*	*50-100 MWth*	*100 to 300 MWth*	*> 300 MWth*
SO_2	—	350	250	200
NO_x	—	300	250	150
Dust	50	30	30	20

3.2.2. C_{proc} for combustion plants referred to in Article 30(3), with the exception of gas turbines and gas engines

C_{proc} for solid fuels with the exception of biomass (O_2 content 6 %):

Polluting substances	*< 50 MWth*	*50-100 MWth*	*100 to 300 MWth*	*> 300 MWth*
SO_2	—	400 for peat: 300	200 for peat: 300, except in the case of fluidised bed combustion: 250	150 for circulating or pressurised fluidised bed combustion or, in case of peat firing, for all fluidised bed combustion: 200
NO_x	—	300 for peat: 250	200	150 for pulverised lignite combustion: 200
Dust	50	20	20	10 for peat: 20

C_{proc} for biomass (O_2 content 6 %):

Polluting substances	*< 50 MWth*	*50-100 MWth*	*100 to 300 MWth*	*> 300 MWth*
SO_2	—	200	200	150
NO_x	—	250	200	150
Dust	50	20	20	20

C_{proc} for liquid fuels (O_2 content 3 %):

Polluting substances	*< 50 MWth*	*50-100 MWth*	*100 to 300 MWth*	*> 300 MWth*
SO_2	—	350	200	150
NO_x	—	300	150	100
Dust	50	20	20	10

3.3. C — total emission limit values for heavy metals (mg/Nm^3) expressed as average values over the sampling period of a minimum of 30 minutes and a maximum of 8 hours (O_2 content 6 % for solid fuels and 3 % for liquid fuels)

Polluting substances	*C*
Cd + Tl	0,05
Hg	0,05
Sb + As + Pb + Cr + Co + Cu + Mn + Ni + V	0,5

3.4. C — total emission limit value (ng/Nm^3) for dioxins and furans expressed as average value measured over the sampling period of a minimum of 6 hours and a maximum of 8 hours (O_2 content 6 % for solid fuels and 3 % for liquid fuels)

Polluting substances	*C*
Dioxins and furans	0,1

4. Special provisions for waste co-incineration plants in industrial sectors not covered under Points 2 and 3 of this Part

4.1. C — total emission limit value (ng/Nm^3) for dioxins and furans expressed as average value measured over the sampling period of a minimum of 6 hours and a maximum of 8 hours:

Polluting substances	*C*
Dioxins and furans	0,1

4.2. C – total emission limit values (mg/Nm^3) for heavy metals expressed as average values over the sampling period of a minimum of 30 minutes and a maximum of 8 hours:

Polluting substances	*C*
Cd + Tl	0,05
Hg	0,05

PART 5
EMISSION LIMIT VALUES FOR DISCHARGES OF WASTE WATER FROM THE CLEANING OF WASTE GASES

Polluting substances	*Emission limit values for unfiltered samples (mg/l except for dioxins and furans)*	
1. Total suspended solids as defined in Annex I of Directive 91/271/EEC	(95 %) 30	(100 %) 45
2. Mercury and its compounds, expressed as mercury (Hg)	0,03	
3. Cadmium and its compounds, expressed as cadmium (Cd)	0,05	
4. Thallium and its compounds, expressed as thallium (Tl)	0,05	
5. Arsenic and its compounds, expressed as arsenic (As)	0,15	
6. Lead and its compounds, expressed as lead (Pb)	0,2	
7. Chromium and its compounds, expressed as chromium (Cr)	0,5	
8. Copper and its compounds, expressed as copper (Cu)	0,5	
9. Nickel and its compounds, expressed as nickel (Ni)	0,5	
10. Zinc and its compounds, expressed as zinc (Zn)	1,5	
11. Dioxins and furans	0,3 ng/l	

PART 6
MONITORING OF EMISSIONS

1. Measurement techniques

1.1. Measurements for the determination of concentrations of air and water polluting substances shall be carried out representatively.

1.2. Sampling and analysis of all polluting substances including dioxins and furans as well as the quality assurance of automated measuring systems and the reference measurement methods to calibrate them shall be carried out according to CEN-standards. If CEN standards are not available, ISO, national or other international standards which ensure the provision of data of an equivalent scientific quality shall apply. Automated measuring systems shall be subject to control by means of parallel measurements with the reference methods at least once per year.

1.3. At the daily emission limit value level, the values of the 95 % confidence intervals of a single measured result shall not exceed the following percentages of the emission limit values:

Carbon monoxide:	10 %
Sulphur dioxide:	20 %
Nitrogen dioxide:	20 %
Total dust:	30 %
Total organic carbon:	30 %

Periodic measurements of the emissions into air and water shall be carried out in accordance with points 1.1 and 1.2.

2. Measurements relating to air polluting substances

2.1. The following measurements relating to air polluting substances shall be carried out:

(a) continuous measurements of the following substances: NO_x, provided that emission limit values are set, CO, total dust, TOC, HCl, HF, SO_2;

(b) continuous measurements of the following process operation parameters: temperature near the inner wall or at another representative point of the combustion chamber as authorised by the competent authority, concentration of oxygen, pressure, temperature and water vapour content of the waste gas;

(c) at least two measurements per year of heavy metals and dioxins and furans; one measurement at least every 3 months shall, however, be carried out for the first 12 months of operation.

2.2. The residence time as well as the minimum temperature and the oxygen content of the waste gases shall be subject to appropriate verification, at least once when the waste incineration plant or waste co-incineration plant is brought into service and under the most unfavourable operating conditions anticipated.

2.3. The continuous measurement of HF may be omitted if treatment stages for HCl are used which ensure that the emission limit value for HCl is not being exceeded. In that case the emissions of HF shall be subject to periodic measurements as laid down in point 2.1(c).

2.4. The continuous measurement of the water vapour content shall not be required if the sampled waste gas is dried before the emissions are analysed.

2.5. The competent authority may decide not to require continuous measurements for HCl, HF and SO_2 in waste incineration plants or waste co-incineration plants and require periodic measurements as set out in point 2.1(c) or no measurements if the operator can prove that the emissions of those pollutants can under no circumstances be higher than the prescribed emission limit values.

The competent authority may decide not to require continuous measurements for NO_x and require periodic measurements as set out in point 2.1(c) in existing waste incineration plants with a nominal capacity of less than 6 tonnes per hour or in existing waste co-incineration plants with a nominal capacity of less than 6 tonnes per hour if the operator can prove on the basis of information on the quality of the waste concerned, the technologies used and the results of the monitoring of emissions, that the emissions of NO_x can under no circumstances be higher than the prescribed emission limit value.

2.6. The competent authority may decide to require one measurement every 2 years for heavy metals and one measurement per year for dioxins and furans in the following cases:

(a) the emissions resulting from co-incineration or incineration of waste are under all circumstances below 50 % of the emission limit values;

(b) the waste to be co-incinerated or incinerated consists only of certain sorted combustible fractions of non-hazardous waste not suitable for recycling and presenting certain characteristics, and which is further specified on the basis of the assessment referred to in point (c);

(c) the operator can prove on the basis of information on the quality of the waste concerned and the monitoring of the emissions that the emissions are under all circumstances significantly below the emission limit values for heavy metals and dioxins and furans.

2.7. The results of the measurements shall be standardised using the standard oxygen concentrations mentioned in Part 3 or calculated according to Part 4 and by applying the formula given in Part 7.

When waste is incinerated or co-incinerated in an oxygen-enriched atmosphere, the results of the measurements can be standardised at an oxygen content laid down by the competent authority reflecting the special circumstances of the individual case.

When the emissions of polluting substances are reduced by waste gas treatment in a waste incineration plant or waste co-incineration plant treating hazardous waste, the standardisation with respect to the oxygen contents provided for in the first subparagraph shall be done only if the oxygen content measured over the same period as for the polluting substance concerned exceeds the relevant standard oxygen content.

3. Measurements relating to water polluting substances

3.1. The following measurements shall be carried out at the point of waste water discharge:
- (a) continuous measurements of pH, temperature and flow;
- (b) spot sample daily measurements of total suspended solids or measurements of a flow proportional representative sample over a period of 24 hours;
- (c) at least monthly measurements of a flow proportional representative sample of the discharge over a period of 24 hours of Hg, Cd, TI, As, Pb, Cr, Cu, Ni and Zn;
- (d) at least every 6 months measurements of dioxins and furans; however, one measurement at least every 3 months shall be carried out for the first 12 months of operation.

3.2. Where the waste water from the cleaning of waste gases is treated on site collectively with other on-site sources of waste water, the operator shall take the measurements:
- (a) on the waste water stream from the waste gas cleaning processes prior to its input into the collective waste water treatment plant;
- (b) on the other waste water stream or streams prior to its or their input into the collective waste water treatment plant;
- (c) at the point of final waste water discharge, after the treatment, from the waste incineration plant or waste co-incineration plant.

PART 7
FORMULA TO CALCULATE THE EMISSION CONCENTRATION AT THE STANDARD PERCENTAGE OXYGEN CONCENTRATION

$$E_S = \frac{21 - O_S}{21 - O_M} \times E_M$$

E_S = calculated emission concentration at the standard percentage oxygen concentration
E_M = measured emission concentration
O_S = standard oxygen concentration
O_M = measured oxygen concentration

PART 8
ASSESSMENT OF COMPLIANCE WITH EMISSION LIMIT VALUES

1. Air emission limit values

1.1. The emission limit values for air shall be regarded as being complied with if:
- (a) none of the daily average values exceeds any of the emission limit values set out in point 1.1 of Part 3 or in Part 4 or calculated in accordance with Part 4;
- (b) either none of the half-hourly average values exceeds any of the emission limit values set out in column A of the table under point 1.2 of Part 3 or, where relevant, 97 % of the half-hourly average values over the year do not exceed any of the emission limit values set out in column B of the table under point 1.2 of Part 3;
- (c) none of the average values over the sampling period set out for heavy metals and dioxins and furans exceeds the emission limit values set out in points 1.3 and 1.4 of Part 3 or in Part 4 or calculated in accordance with Part 4;
- (d) for carbon monoxide (CO):
  - (i) in case of waste incineration plants:
    - — at least 97 % of the daily average values over the year do not exceed the emission limit value set out in point 1.5(a) of Part 3; and,
    - — at least 95 % of all 10-minute average values taken in any 24-hour period or all of the half-hourly average values taken in the same

period do not exceed the emission limit values set out in points 1.5(b) and (c) of Part 3; in case of waste incineration plants in which the gas resulting from the incineration process is raised to a temperature of at least 1100 °C for at least two seconds, Member States may apply an evaluation period of 7 days for the 10-minute average values;

(ii) in case of waste co-incineration plants: the provisions of Part 4 are met.

1.2. The half-hourly average values and the 10-minute averages shall be determined within the effective operating time (excluding the start-up and shut-down periods if no waste is being incinerated) from the measured values after having subtracted the value of the confidence interval specified in point 1.3 of Part 6. The daily average values shall be determined from those validated average values.

To obtain a valid daily average value no more than five half-hourly average values in any day shall be discarded due to malfunction or maintenance of the continuous measurement system. No more than ten daily average values per year shall be discarded due to malfunction or maintenance of the continuous measurement system.

1.3. The average values over the sampling period and the average values in the case of periodical measurements of HF, HCl and SO_2 shall be determined in accordance with the requirements of Articles 45(1)(e), 48(3) and point 1 of Part 6.

2. Water emission limit values

The emission limit values for water shall be regarded as being complied with if:

(a) for total suspended solids 95 % and 100 % of the measured values do not exceed the respective emission limit values as set out in Part 5;

(b) for heavy metals (Hg, Cd, TI, As, Pb, Cr, Cu, Ni and Zn) no more than one measurement per year exceeds the emission limit values set out in Part 5; or, if the Member State provides for more than 20 samples per year, no more than 5 % of these samples exceed the emission limit values set out in Part 5;

(c) for dioxins and furans, the measurement results do not exceed the emission limit value set out in Part 5.

ANNEX VII
TECHNICAL PROVISIONS RELATING TO INSTALLATIONS AND ACTIVITIES USING ORGANIC SOLVENTS

PART 1
ACTIVITIES

1. In each of the following points, the activity includes the cleaning of the equipment but not the cleaning of products unless specified otherwise.

2. Adhesive coating

Any activity in which an adhesive is applied to a surface, with the exception of adhesive coating and laminating associated with printing activities.

3. Coating activity

Any activity in which a single or multiple application of a continuous film of a coating is applied to:

(a) either of the following vehicles:

(i) new cars, defined as vehicles of category M1 in Directive 2007/46/EC of the European Parliament and of the Council of 5 September 2007 establishing a framework for the approval of motor vehicles and their trailers, and of systems, components and separate technical units intended for such vehicles and of category N1 in so far as they are coated at the same installation as M1 vehicles;

(ii) truck cabins, defined as the housing for the driver, and all integrated housing for the technical equipment, of vehicles of categories N2 and N3 in Directive 2007/46/EC;
(iii) vans and trucks, defined as vehicles of categories N1, N2 and N3 in Directive 2007/46/EC, but not including truck cabins;
(iv) buses, defined as vehicles of categories M2 and M3 in Directive 2007/46/EC;
(v) trailers, defined in categories O1, O2, O3 and O4 in Directive 2007/46/EC;

(b) metallic and plastic surfaces including surfaces of airplanes, ships, trains, etc.;
(c) wooden surfaces;
(d) textile, fabric, film and paper surfaces;
(e) leather.

Coating activities do not include the coating of substrate with metals by electrophoretic and chemical spraying techniques. If the coating activity includes a step in which the same article is printed by whatever technique used, that printing step is considered part of the coating activity. However, printing activities operated as a separate activity are not included, but may be covered by Chapter V of this Directive if the printing activity falls within the scope thereof.

4. Coil coating

Any activity where coiled steel, stainless steel, coated steel, copper alloys or aluminium strip is coated with either a film forming or laminate coating in a continuous process.

5. Dry cleaning

Any industrial or commercial activity using volatile organic compounds in an installation to clean garments, furnishing and similar consumer goods with the exception of the manual removal of stains and spots in the textile and clothing industry.

6. Footwear manufacture
Any activity of producing complete footwear or parts thereof.

7. Manufacturing of coating mixtures, varnishes, inks and adhesives

The manufacture of the above final products, and of intermediates where carried out at the same site, by mixing of pigments, resins and adhesive materials with organic solvent or other carrier, including dispersion and predispersion activities, viscosity and tint adjustments and operations for filling the final product into its container.

8. Manufacturing of pharmaceutical products

The chemical synthesis, fermentation, extraction, formulation and finishing of pharmaceutical products and, where carried out at the same site, the manufacture of intermediate products.

9. Printing

Any reproduction activity of text and/or images in which, with the use of an image carrier, ink is transferred onto whatever type of surface. It includes associated varnishing, coating and laminating techniques. However, only the following sub-processes are subject to Chapter V:

(a) flexography – a printing activity using an image carrier of rubber or elastic photopolymers on which the printing areas are above the non-printing areas, using liquid inks which dry through evaporation;
(b) heatset web offset – a web-fed printing activity using an image carrier in which the printing and non-printing area are in the same plane, where web-fed means that the material to be printed is fed to the machine from a reel as distinct from separate sheets. The non-printing area is treated to attract water and thus reject ink. The printing area is treated to receive and transmit ink to the surface to be printed. Evaporation takes place in an oven where hot air is used to heat the printed material;
(c) laminating associated to a printing activity – the adhering together of two or more flexible materials to produce laminates;
(d) publication rotogravure – a rotogravure printing activity used for printing paper for magazines, brochures, catalogues or similar products, using toluene-based inks;

(e) rotogravure – a printing activity using a cylindrical image carrier in which the printing area is below the non-printing area, using liquid inks which dry through evaporation. The recesses are filled with ink and the surplus is cleaned off the non-printing area before the surface to be printed contacts the cylinder and lifts the ink from the recesses;

(f) rotary screen printing – a web-fed printing activity in which the ink is passed onto the surface to be printed by forcing it through a porous image carrier, in which the printing area is open and the non-printing area is sealed off, using liquid inks which dry only through evaporation. Web-fed means that the material to be printed is fed into the machine from a reel as distinct from separate sheets;

(g) varnishing – an activity by which a varnish or an adhesive coating for the purpose of later sealing the packaging material is applied to a flexible material.

10. Rubber conversion

Any activity of mixing, milling, blending, calendering, extrusion and vulcanisation of natural or synthetic rubber and any ancillary operations for converting natural or synthetic rubber into a finished product.

11. Surface cleaning

Any activity except dry cleaning using organic solvents to remove contamination from the surface of material including degreasing. A cleaning activity consisting of more than one step before or after any other activity shall be considered as one surface cleaning activity. This activity does not refer to the cleaning of the equipment but to the cleaning of the surface of products.

12. Vegetable oil and animal fat extraction and vegetable oil refining activities

Any activity to extract vegetable oil from seeds and other vegetable matter, the processing of dry residues to produce animal feed, the purification of fats and vegetable oils derived from seeds, vegetable matter and/or animal matter.

13. Vehicle refinishing

Any industrial or commercial coating activity and associated degreasing activities performing either of the following:

(a) the original coating of road vehicles as defined in Directive 2007/46/EC or part of them with refinishing-type materials, where this is carried out away from the original manufacturing line;

(b) the coating of trailers (including semi-trailers) (category O in Directive 2007/46/EC).

14. Winding wire coating

Any coating activity of metallic conductors used for winding the coils in transformers and motors, etc.

15. Wood impregnation

Any activity giving a loading of preservative in timber.

16. Wood and plastic lamination

Any activity to adhere together wood and/or plastic to produce laminated products.

PART 2
THRESHOLDS AND EMISSION LIMIT VALUES

PART 2

Thresholds and emission limit values

The emission limit values in waste gases shall be calculated at a temperature of 273,15 K, and a pressure of 101,3 kPa.

	Activity (solvent consumption threshold in tonnes/year)	Threshold (solvent consumption threshold in tonnes/year)	Emission limit values in waste gases (mg C/Nm³)	Fugitive emission limit values (percentage of solvent input)		Total emission limit values		Special provisions
				New installations	Existing installations	New installations	Existing installations	
1	Heatset web offset printing (> 15)	15—25 > 25	100 20		30 (1) 30 (1)			(1) Solvent residue in finished product is not to be considered as part of fugitive emissions.
2	Publication rotogravure (> 25)		75	10	15			
3	Other rotogravure, flexography, rotary screen printing, laminating or varnishing units (> 15) rotary screen printing on textile/cardboard (> 30)	15—25 > 25 > 30 (1)	100 100 100		25 20 20			(1) Threshold for rotary screen printing on textile and on cardboard.
4	Surface cleaning using compounds specified in Article 59(5). (> 1)	1—5 > 5	20 (1) 20 (1)		15 10			(1) Limit value refers to mass of compounds in mg/Nm³, and not to total carbon.
5	Other surface cleaning (> 2)	2—10 > 10	75 (1) 75 (1)		20 (1) 15 (1)			(1) Installations which demonstrate to the competent authority that the average organic solvent content of all cleaning material used does not exceed 30 % by weight are exempt from application of these values.

	Activity (solvent consumption threshold in tonnes/year)	Threshold (solvent consumption threshold in tonnes/year)	Emission limit values in waste gases (mg C/Nm³)	Fugitive emission limit values (percentage of solvent input)		Total emission limit values		Special provisions
				New installations	Existing installations	New installations	Existing installations	
6	Vehicle coating (< 15) and vehicle refinishing	> 0,5	50 (1)		25			(1) Compliance in accordance with point 2 of Part 8 shall be demonstrated based on 15 minute average measurements.
7	Coil coating (> 25)		50 (1)	5	10			(1) For installations which use techniques which allow reuse of recovered solvents, the emission limit value shall be 150.
8	Other coating, including metal, plastic, textile (5), fabric, film and paper coating (> 5)	5—15 > 15	100 (1) (4) 50/75 (2) (3) (4)		25 (4) 20 (4)			(1) Emission limit value applies to coating application and drying processes operated under contained conditions. (2) The first emission limit value applies to drying processes, the second to coating application processes. (3) For textile coating installations which use techniques which allow reuse of recovered solvents, the emission limit value applied to coating application and drying processes taken together shall be 150. (4) Coating activities which cannot be carried out under contained conditions (such as shipbuilding, aircraft painting) may be exempted from these values, in accordance with Article 59(3). (5) Rotary screen printing on textile is covered by activity No 3.

	Activity (solvent consumption threshold in tonnes/year)	Threshold (solvent consumption threshold in tonnes/year)	Emission limit values in waste gases (mg C/Nm^3)	Fugitive emission limit values (percentage of solvent input)		Total emission limit values		Special provisions
				New installations	Existing installations	New installations	Existing installations	
9	Winding wire coating (> 5)					10 g/kg (1) 5 g/kg (2)		(1) Applies for installations where average diameter of wire ≤ 0,1 mm. (2) Applies for all other installations.
10	Coating of wooden surfaces (> 15)	15—25 > 25	100 (1) 50/75 (2)		25 20			(1) Emission limit value applies to coating application and drying processes operated under contained conditions. (2) The first value applies to drying processes, the second to coating application processes.
11	Dry cleaning					20 g/kg (1) (2)		(1) Expressed in mass of solvent emitted per kilogram of product cleaned and dried. (2) The emission limit value in point 2 of Part 4 does not apply for this activity.
12	Wood impregnation (> 25)		100 (1)		45	11 kg/m^3		(1) Emission limit value does not apply for impregnation with creosote.
13	Coating of leather (> 10)	10—25 > 25 > 10 (1)				85 g/m^2 75 g/m^2 150 g/m^2		Emission limit values are expressed in grams of solvent emitted per m^2 of product produced. (1) For leather coating activities in furnishing and particular leather goods used as small consumer goods like bags, belts, wallets, etc.

	Activity (solvent consumption threshold in tonnes/ year)	Threshold (solvent consumption threshold in tonnes/ year)	Emission limit values in waste gases (mg C/Nm^3)	Fugitive emission limit values (percentage of solvent input)		Total emission limit values		Special provisions
				New installations	Existing installations	New installations	Existing installations	
14	Footwear manufacture (> 5)					25 g per pair		Total emission limit value is expressed in grams of solvent emitted per pair of complete footwear produced.
15	Wood and plastic lamination (> 5)					30 g/m^2		
16	Adhesive coating (> 5)	5—15 > 15	50 (1) 50 (1)		25 20			(1) If techniques are used which allow reuse of recovered solvent, the emission limit value in waste gases shall be 150.
17	Manufacture of coating mixture, varnishes, inks and adhesives (> 100)	100—1 000 > 1 000	150 150		5 3	5 % of solvent input 3 % of solvent input		The fugitive emission limit value does not include solvent sold as part of a coatings mixture in a sealed container.
18	Rubber conversion (> 15)		20 (1)		25 (2)	25 % of solvent input		(1) If techniques are used which allow reuse of recovered solvent, the emission limit value in waste gases shall be 150. (2) The fugitive emission limit value does not include solvent sold as part of products or mixtures in a sealed container.

	Activity (solvent consumption threshold in tonnes/year)	Threshold (solvent consumption threshold in tonnes/year)	Emission limit values in waste gases (mg C/Nm³)	Fugitive emission limit values (percentage of solvent input)		Total emission limit values		Special provisions
				New installations	Existing installations	New installations	Existing installations	
19	Vegetable oil and animal fat extraction and vegetable oil refining activities (> 10)					Animal fat: 1,5 kg/tonne Castor: 3 kg/tonne Rape seed: 1 kg/tonne Sunflower seed: 1 kg/tonne Soya beans (normal crush): 0,8 kg/tonne Soya beans (white flakes): 1,2 kg/tonne Other seeds and other vegetable matter: 3 kg/tonne (1) 1,5 kg/tonne (2) 4 kg/tonne (3)		(1) Total emission limit values for installations processing individual batches of seeds and other vegetable matter should be set by the competent authority on a case-by-case basis, applying the best available techniques. (2) Applies to all fractionation processes excluding de-gumming (the removal of gums from the oil). (3) Applies to de-gumming.
20	Manufacturing of pharmaceutical products (> 50)		20 (1)	5 (2)	15 (2)	5 % of solvent input	15 % of solvent input	(1) If techniques are used which allow reuse of recovered solvent, the emission limit value in waste gases shall be 150. (2) The fugitive emission limit value does not include solvent sold as part of products or mixtures in a sealed container.

PART 3
EMISSION LIMIT VALUES FOR INSTALLATIONS OF THE VEHICLE COATING INDUSTRY

1. The total emission limit values are expressed in terms of grams of organic solvent emitted in relation to the surface area of product in square metres and in kilograms of organic solvent emitted in relation to the car body.

2. The surface area of any product dealt with in the table under point 3 is defined as the surface area calculated from the total electrophoretic coating area, and the surface area of any parts that might be added in successive phases of the coating process which are coated with the same coatings as those used for the product in question, or the total surface area of the product coated in the installation.

The surface of the electrophoretic coating area is calculated using the following formula:

$$\frac{2 \times \text{total weight of product shellaverage thickness of metal sheet} \times \text{density of metal sheet}}{\text{average thickness of metal sheet} \times \text{density of metal sheet}}$$

This method shall also be applied for other coated parts made out of sheets.

Computer aided design or other equivalent methods shall be used to calculate the surface area of the other parts added, or the total surface area coated in the installation.

3. The total emission limit values in the table below refer to all process stages carried out at the same installation from electrophoretic coating, or any other kind of coating process, through to the final wax and polish of topcoating inclusive, as well as solvent used in cleaning of process equipment, including spray booths and other fixed equipment, both during and outside of production time.

Activity (solvent consumption threshold in tonnes/ year)	*Production threshold (refers to annual production of coated item)*	*Total emission limit value*	
		New installations	*Existing installations*
Coating of new cars (> 15)	> 5000	45 g/m^2 or 1,3 kg/ body + 33 g/m^2	60 g/m^2 or 1,9 kg/ body + 41 g/m^2
	≤ 5000 monocoque or > 3500 chassis-built	90 g/m^2 or 1,5 kg/ body + 70 g/m^2	90 g/m^2 or 1,5 kg/ body + 70 g/m^2
		Total emission limit value (g/m^2)	
Coating of new truck cabins (> 15)	≤ 5000	65	85
	> 5000	55	75
Coating of new vans and trucks (> 15)	≤ 2500	90	120
	> 2500	70	90
Coating of new buses (> 15)	≤ 2000	210	290
	> 2000	150	225

4. Vehicle coating installations below the solvent consumption thresholds mentioned in the table under point 3 shall meet the requirements for the vehicle refinishing sector set out in Part 2.

PART 4
EMISSION LIMIT VALUES RELATING TO VOLATILE ORGANIC COMPOUNDS WITH SPECIFIC RISK PHRASES

1. For emissions of the volatile organic compounds referred to in Article 58 where the mass flow of the sum of the compounds causing the labelling referred to in that Article is greater than, or equal to, 10 g/h, an emission limit value of 2 mg/Nm^3 shall be complied with. The emission limit value refers to the mass sum of the individual compounds.

2. For emissions of halogenated volatile organic compounds which are assigned or need to carry the hazard statements H341 or H351, where the mass flow of the sum of the compounds causing the hazard statements H341 or H351 is greater than, or equal to, 100 g/h, an emission limit value of 20 mg/Nm^3 shall be complied with. The emission limit value refers to the mass sum of the individual compounds.

PART 5
REDUCTION SCHEME

1. The operator may use any reduction scheme, specially designed for his installation.

2. In the case of applying coatings, varnishes, adhesives or inks, the following scheme can be used. Where the following method is inappropriate, the competent authority may allow an operator to apply any alternative scheme achieving equivalent emission reductions to those achieved if the emission limit values of Parts 2 and 3 were to be applied. The design of the scheme shall take into account the following facts:

(a) where substitutes containing little or no solvent are still under development, a time extension shall be given to the operator to implement his emission reduction plans;

(b) the reference point for emission reductions should correspond as closely as possible to the emissions which would have resulted had no reduction action been taken.

3. The following scheme shall operate for installations for which a constant solid content of product can be assumed:

(a) The annual reference emission is calculated as follows:

 (i) The total mass of solids in the quantity of coating and/or ink, varnish or adhesive consumed in a year is determined. Solids are all materials in coatings, inks, varnishes and adhesives that become solid once the water or the volatile organic compounds are evaporated.

 (ii) The annual reference emissions are calculated by multiplying the mass determined in (i) by the appropriate factor listed in the table below. Competent authorities may adjust these factors for individual installations to reflect documented increased efficiency in the use of solids.

Activity	*Multiplication factor for use in item (a)(ii)*
Rotogravure printing; flexography printing; laminating as part of a printing activity; varnishing as part of a printing activity; wood coating; coating of textiles, fabric film or paper; adhesive coating	4
Coil coating, vehicle refinishing	3
Food contact coating, aerospace coatings	2,33
Other coatings and rotary screen printing	1,5

(b) The target emission is equal to the annual reference emission multiplied by a percentage equal to:

 (i) (the fugitive emission limit value + 15), for installations falling within item 6 and the lower threshold band of items 8 and 10 of Part 2,

 (ii) (the fugitive emission limit value + 5) for all other installations.

(c) Compliance is achieved if the actual solvent emission determined from the solvent management plan is less than or equal to the target emission.

PART 6
EMISSION MONITORING

1. Channels to which abatement equipment is connected, and which at the final point of discharge emit more than an average of 10 kg/h of total organic carbon, shall be monitored continuously for compliance.

2. In the other cases, Member States shall ensure that either continuous or periodic measurements are carried out. For periodic measurements at least three measurement values shall be obtained during each measurement exercise.

3. Measurements are not required in the case where end-of-pipe abatement equipment is not needed to comply with this Directive.

PART 7
SOLVENT MANAGEMENT PLAN

1. Principles
The solvent management plan shall be used to:
(a) verify compliance as specified in Article 62;
(b) identify future reduction options;
(c) enable provision of information on solvent consumption, solvent emissions and compliance with the requirements of Chapter V to the public.

2. Definitions
The following definitions provide a framework for the mass balance exercise.
Inputs of organic solvents (I):
I1 The quantity of organic solvents or their quantity in mixtures purchased which are used as input into the process in the time frame over which the mass balance is being calculated.
I2 The quantity of organic solvents or their quantity in mixtures recovered and reused as solvent input into the process. The recycled solvent is counted every time it is used to carry out the activity.
Outputs of organic solvents (O):
O1 Emissions in waste gases
O2 O2 Organic solvents lost in water, taking into account waste water treatment when calculating O5
O3 The quantity of organic solvents which remains as contamination or residue in products output from the process
O4 Uncaptured emissions of organic solvents into air. This includes the general ventilation of rooms, where air is released to the outside environment via windows, doors, vents and similar openings
O5 Organic solvents and/or organic compounds lost due to chemical or physical reactions (including those which are destroyed, by incineration or other waste gas or waste water treatments, or captured, as long as they are not counted under O6, O7 or O8)
O6 Organic solvents contained in collected waste
O7 Organic solvents, or organic solvents contained in mixtures, which are sold or are intended to be sold as a commercially valuable product
O8 Organic solvents contained in mixtures recovered for reuse but not as input into the process, as long as not counted under O7
O9 Organic solvents released in other ways

3. Use of the solvent management plan for verification of compliance.
The use made of the solvent management plan shall be determined by the particular requirement which is to be verified, as follows:
(a) verification of compliance with the reduction scheme as set out in Part 5, with a total emission limit value expressed in solvent emissions per unit product, or otherwise stated in Parts 2 and 3.
   (i) for all activities using the reduction scheme as set out in Part 5, the solvent management plan shall be drawn up annually to determine the consumption (C). The consumption shall be calculated according to the following equation:
   $C = I1 - O8$
   A parallel exercise shall also be undertaken to determine solids used in coating in order to derive the annual reference emission and the target emission each year.

(ii) for assessing compliance with a total emission limit value expressed in solvent emissions per unit product or otherwise stated in Parts 2 and 3, the solvent management plan shall be drawn up annually to determine the emissions (E). The emissions shall be calculated according to the following equation:

$E = F + O1$

Where F is the fugitive emission as defined in point (b)(i). The emission figure shall then be divided by the relevant product parameter.

(iii) for assessing compliance with the requirements of point (b)(ii) of Article 59(6), the solvent management plan shall be drawn up annually to determine total emissions from all activities concerned, and that figure shall then be compared with the total emissions that would have resulted had the requirements of Parts 2, 3 and 5 been met for each activity separately.

(b) Determination of fugitive emissions for comparison with the fugitive emission limit values in Part 2:

(i) The fugitive emission shall be calculated according to one of the following equations;

$F = I1 - O1 - O5 - O6 - O7 - O8$

or

$F = O2 + O3 + O4 + O9$

F shall be determined either by direct measurement of the quantities or by an equivalent method or calculation, for instance by using the capture efficiency of the process.

The fugitive emission limit value is expressed as a proportion of the input, which shall be calculated according to the following equation:

$I = I1 + I2$

(ii) Determination of fugitive emissions shall be done by a short but comprehensive set of measurements and needs not be done again until the equipment is modified.

PART 8
ASSESSMENT OF COMPLIANCE WITH EMISSION LIMIT VALUES IN WASTE GASES

1. In the case of continuous measurements the emission limit values shall be considered to be complied with if:

(a) none of the arithmetic averages of all valid readings taken during any 24-hour period of operation of an installation or activity except start-up and shut-down operations and maintenance of equipment exceeds the emission limit values,

(b) none of the hourly averages exceeds the emission limit values by more than a factor of 1,5.

2. In the case of periodic measurements the emission limit values shall be considered to be complied with if, in one monitoring exercise:

(a) the average of all the measurement values does not exceed the emission limit values,

(b) none of the hourly averages exceeds the emission limit value by more than a factor of 1,5.

3. Compliance with Part 4 shall be verified on the basis of the sum of the mass concentrations of the individual volatile organic compounds concerned. For all other cases, compliance shall be verified on the basis of the total mass of organic carbon emitted unless otherwise specified in Part 2.

4. Gas volumes may be added to the waste gas for cooling or dilution purposes where technically justified but shall not be considered when determining the mass concentration of the pollutant in the waste gas.

ANNEX VIII
TECHNICAL PROVISIONS RELATING TO INSTALLATIONS PRODUCING TITANIUM DIOXIDE

PART 1
EMISSION LIMIT VALUES FOR EMISSIONS INTO WATER

1. In case of installations using the sulphate process (as an annual average): 550 kg of sulphate per tonne of titanium dioxide produced.

2. In case of installations using the chloride process (as an annual average):
(a) 130 kg chloride per tonne of titanium dioxide produced using neutral rutile,
(b) 228 kg chloride per tonne of titanium dioxide produced using synthetic rutile,
(c) 330 kg chloride per tonne of titanium dioxide produced using slag. Installations discharging into salt water (estuarine, coastal, open sea) may be subject to an emission limit value of 450 kg chloride per tonne of titanium dioxide produced using slag.

3. For installations using the chloride process and using more than one type of ore, the emission limit values in point 2 shall apply in proportion to the quantity of the ores used.

PART 2
EMISSION LIMIT VALUES INTO AIR

1. The emission limit values which are expressed as concentrations in mass per cubic meter (Nm^3) shall be calculated at a temperature of 273,15 K, and a pressure of 101,3 kPa.

2. For dust: 50 mg/Nm^3 as an hourly average from major sources and 150 mg/Nm^3 as an hourly average from any other source.

3. For gaseous sulphur dioxide and trioxide discharged from digestion and calcination, including acid droplets calculated as SO_2 equivalent:
(a) 6 kg per tonne of titanium dioxide produced as an annual average;
(b) 500 mg/Nm^3 as an hourly average for plants for the concentration of waste acid.

4. For chlorine in the case of installations using the chloride process:
(a) 5 mg/Nm^3 as a daily average;
(b) 40 mg/Nm^3 at any time.

PART 3
EMISSION MONITORING

The monitoring of emissions into air shall include at least the continuous monitoring of:
(a) gaseous sulphur dioxide and trioxide discharged from digestion and calcination from plants for the concentration of waste acid in installations using the sulphate process;
(b) chlorine from major sources within installations using the chloride process;
(c) dust from major sources.

ANNEX IX

PART A
REPEALED DIRECTIVES WITH THEIR SUCCESSIVE AMENDMENTS (REFERRED TO IN ARTICLE 81)

Council Directive 78/176/EEC (OJ L 54, 25.2.1978, p. 19).	
Council Directive 83/29/EEC (OJ L 32, 3.2.1983, p. 28).	
Council Directive 91/692/EEC (OJ L 377, 31.12.1991, p. 48).	only Annex I, point (b)
Council Directive 82/883/EEC (OJ L 378, 31.12.1982, p. 1).	

Act of Accession of 1985	only Annex I, point X.1(o)
Act of Accession of 1994	only Annex I, point VIII.A.6
Council Regulation (EC) No 807/2003 (OJ L 122, 16.5.2003, p. 36).	only Annex III, point 34
Regulation (EC) No 219/2009 of the European Parliament and of the Council (OJ L 87, 31.3.2009, p. 109).	only Annex, point 3.1
Council Directive 92/112/EEC (OJ L 409, 31.12.1992, p. 11).	
Council Directive 1999/13/EC (OJ L 85, 29.3.1999, p. 1).	
Regulation (EC) No 1882/2003 of the European Parliament and of the Council (OJ L 284, 31.10.2003, p. 1).	only Annex I, point 17
Directive 2004/42/EC of the European Parliament and of the Council (OJ L 143, 30.4.2004, p. 87).	only Article 13(1)
Directive 2008/112/EC of the European Parliament and of the Council (OJ L 345, 23.12.2008, p. 68).	only Article 3
Directive 2000/76/EC of the European Parliament and of the Council (OJ L 332, 28.12.2000, p. 91).	
Regulation (EC) No 1137/2008 of the European Parliament and of the Council (OJ L 311, 21.11.2008, p. 1).	only Annex, point 4.8
Directive 2001/80/EC of the European Parliament and of the Council (OJ L 309, 27.11.2001, p. 1).	
Council Directive 2006/105/EC (OJ L 363, 20.12.2006, p. 368).	only Annex, part B, point 2
Directive 2009/31/EC of the European Parliament and of the Council (OJ L 140, 5.6.2009, p. 114).	only Article 33
Directive 2008/1/EC of the European Parliament and of the Council (OJ L 24, 29.1.2008, p. 8).	
Directive 2009/31/EC of the European Parliament and of the Council (OJ L 140, 5.6.2009, p. 114).	only Article 37

PART B
LIST OF TIME-LIMITS FOR TRANSPOSITION INTO NATIONAL LAW AND APPLICATION
(REFERRED TO IN ARTICLE 81)

Directive	Time-limit for transposition	Time-limit for application
78/176/EEC	25 February 1979	
82/883/EEC	31 December 1984	
92/112/EEC	15 June 1993	
1999/13/EC	1 April 2001	
2000/76/EC	28 December 2000	28 December 2002
		28 December 2005
2001/80/EC	27 November 2002	27 November 2004
2003/35/EC	25 June 2005	
2003/87/EC	31 December 2003	
2008/1/EC	30 October 1999[(1)]	30 October 1999 30 October 2007

(1) Directive 2008/1/EC is a codified version of Council Directive 96/61/EC of 24 September 1996 concerning integrated pollution prevention and control (OJ L 257, 10.10.1996, p. 26) and the time-limits for transposition and application remain in force.

ANNEX X
CORRELATION TABLE

Directive 78/176/EEC	Directive 82/883/EEC	Directive 92/112/EEC	Directive 2008/1/EC	Directive 1999/13/EC	Directive 2000/76/EC	Directive 2001/80/EC	This Directive
Article 1(1)	Article 1	Article 1					Article 66
—	—	—	—	—	—	—	Article 2
Article 1(2), point (a)			Article 2(2)				Article 3(2)
Article 1(2), point (b)					Article 3(1)		Article 3(37)
Article 1(2), points (c), (d) and (e)							—
—	—	—	—	—	—	—	Article 66
Article 2							Article 67
Article 3							Article 11, points (d) and (e)
Article 4			Article 4	Article 3, introductory wording and (1)	Article 4(1)		Article 4(1), first subparagraph
Article 5							Article 11, points (d) and (e)
Article 6							Article 11, points (d) and (e)
Article 7(1)		Article 10					Article 70(1) and 70(2), first sentence
Article 7(2) and (3)							—
—	—	—	—	—	—	—	Article 70(2), second sentence and 70(3)

Directive 78/176/EEC	Directive 82/883/EEC	Directive 92/112/EEC	Directive 2008/1/EC	Directive 1999/13/EC	Directive 2000/76/EC	Directive 2001/80/EC	This Directive
Article 8(1)							—
Article 8(2)							Article 26(1), second subparagraph
Article 9							—
Article 10							—
Article 11							Article 12
Article 12							—
Article 13(1)			Article 17(1), first subparagraph and 17(3), first subparagraph, first sentence	Article 11(1), first sentence and 11(2)			Article 72(1), first sentence
—	—	—	—	—	—	—	Article 72(1), second sentence
Article 13(2), (3) and (4)							—
Article 14							—
Article 15	Article 14	Article 12	Article 21	Article 15	Article 21	Article 18(1) and (3)	Article 80
Article 16	Article 15	Article 13	Article 23	Article 17	Article 23	Article 20	Article 84
Annex I							—
Annex II section A introductory wording and point 1							—
Annex II section A point 2							—
Annex II section B							—

Directive 78/176/EEC	Directive 82/883/EEC	Directive 92/112/EEC	Directive 2008/1/EC	Directive 1999/13/EC	Directive 2000/76/EC	Directive 2001/80/EC	This Directive
	Article 2						—
	Article 3						—
	Article 4(1) and 4(2), first subparagraph						—
	Article 4(2), second subparagraph						—
	Article 4(3) and (4)						—
	Article 5						—
	Article 6						—
	Article 7						—
	Article 8						—
	Article 9						—
	Article 10						—
	Article 11(1)			Article 13(1)	Article 17(1)		Article 75(1)
—	—	—	—	—	—	—	Article 75(2)
	Article 11(2)				Article 17(2)		—
	Article 11(3)						—
	Article 12						—

Directive 78/176/EEC	Directive 82/883/EEC	Directive 92/112/EEC	Directive 2008/1/EC	Directive 1999/13/EC	Directive 2000/76/EC	Directive 2001/80/EC	This Directive
	Article 13						—
	Annex I						—
	Annex II						—
	Annex III						—
	Annex IV						—
	Annex V						—
		Article 2(1), introductory wording					—
		Article 2(1)(a), introductory wording					—
		Article 2(1)(a), first indent					Article 67, point (a)
		Article 2(1)(a), second indent					Article 67, point (b)
		Article 2(1)(a), third indent and 2(1)(b), third indent					Article 67, point (d)
		Article 2(1)(a), fourth, fifth, sixth and seventh indent					—

Directive 78/176/EEC	Directive 82/883/EEC	Directive 92/112/EEC	Directive 2008/1/EC	Directive 1999/13/EC	Directive 2000/76/EC	Directive 2001/80/EC	This Directive
		Article 2(1)(b), introductory wording and first, fourth, fifth, sixth and seventh indent					—
		Article 2(1)(b), second indent					Article 67, point (c)
		Article 2(1)(c)					—
		Article 2(2)					—
		Article 3					Article 67
		Article 4					Article 67
		Article 5					—
		Article 6, first paragraph, introductory wording					Article 68
		Article 6, first paragraph, point (a)					Annex VIII, Part 1, point 1
		Article 6, first paragraph, point (b)					Annex VIII, Part 1, point 2
		Article 6, second paragraph					Annex VIII, Part 1, point 3
		Article 7					—
		Article 8					—

Directive 78/176/EEC	Directive 82/883/EEC	Directive 92/112/EEC	Directive 2008/1/EC	Directive 1999/13/EC	Directive 2000/76/EC	Directive 2001/80/EC	This Directive
		Article 9(1) introductory wording					Article 69(2)
		Article 9(1)(a), introductory wording					—
		Article 9(1)(a)(i)					Annex VIII, Part 2, point 2
		Article 9(1)(a)(ii)					Annex VIII, Part 2, point 3, introductory wording, and point 3(a)
		Article 9(1)(a)(iii)					Article 69(1)
		Article 9(1)(a)(iv)					Annex VIII, Part 2, point 3(b)
		Article 9(1)(a)(v)					—
		Article 9(1)(b)					Annex VIII, Part 2, point 4
		Article 9(2) and (3)					—
		Article 11					Article 11, points (d) and (e)
		Annex					—
			Article 1				Article 1

Directive 78/176/EEC	Directive 82/883/EEC	Directive 92/112/EEC	Directive 2008/1/EC	Directive 1999/13/EC	Directive 2000/76/EC	Directive 2001/80/EC	This Directive
			Article 2, introductory wording				Article 3, introductory wording
			Article 2(1)	Article 2(14)			Article 3(1)
			Article 2(3)	Article 2(1)			Article 3(3)
			Article 2(4)				—
			Article 2(5)	Article 2(9)	Article 3(8)	Article 2(1)	Article 3(4)
			Article 2(6), first sentence	Article 2(13)	Article 3(9)	Article 2(3), first part	Article 3(5)
			Article 2(6), second sentence				Article 15(1)
			Article 2(7)				Article 3(6)
			Article 2(8)	Article 2(5)			Article 71
			Article 2(9), first sentence	Article 2(7)	Article 3(12)		Article 3(7)
			Article 2(9), second sentence				Article 4(2), first subparagraph
—	—	—	—	—	—	—	Article 4(2), second subparagraph
—	—	—	—	—	—	—	Article 4(3)

Directive 78/176/EEC	Directive 82/883/EEC	Directive 92/112/EEC	Directive 2008/1/EC	Directive 1999/13/EC	Directive 2000/76/EC	Directive 2001/80/EC	This Directive
			Article 2(10)				—
—	—	—	—	—	—	—	Article 3(8)
			Article 2(11), first sentence				Article 3(9)
			Article 2(11), second sentence				Article 20(3)
			Article 2(12), first subparagraph and Annex IV, introductory wording				Article 3(10)
			Article 2(12), second subparagraph				Articles 14(5), point (a) and 14(6)
			Article 2(13)	Article 2(6)	Article 3(11)	Article 2(5)	Article 3(15)
			Article 2(14)				Article 3(16)
			Article 2(15)				Article 3(17)
—	—	—	—	—	—	—	Article 3(11) to (14), (18) to (23), (26) to (30) and (34) to (36)
			Article 3(1), introductory wording				Article 11, introductory wording
			Article 3(1), point (a)				Article 11, points (a) and (b)

Directive 78/176/EEC	Directive 82/883/EEC	Directive 92/112/EEC	Directive 2008/1/EC	Directive 1999/13/EC	Directive 2000/76/EC	Directive 2001/80/EC	This Directive
			Article 3(1), point (b)				Article 11, point (c)
			Article 3(1), point (c)				Article 11, points (d) and (e)
			Article 3(1), point (d)				Article 11, point (f)
			Article 3(1), point (e)				Article 11, point (g)
			Article 3(1), point (f)				Article 11, point (h)
			Article 3(2)				—
			Article 5(1)				—
			Article 5(2)				Article 80(1), second subparagraph
			Article 6(1), introductory wording				Article 12(1), first subparagraph, introductory wording
			Article 6(1), first subparagraph, points (a) to (d)				Article 12(1), first subparagraph, points (a) to (d)
—	—	—	—	—	—	—	Article 12(1), first subparagraph, point (e)
			Article 6(1), first subparagraph, point (e)				Article 12(1), first subparagraph, point (f)
			Article 6(1), first subparagraph, point (f)				Article 12(1), first subparagraph, point (g)

Directive 78/176/EEC	Directive 82/883/EEC	Directive 92/112/EEC	Directive 2008/1/EC	Directive 1999/13/EC	Directive 2000/76/EC	Directive 2001/80/EC	This Directive
			Article 6(1), first subparagraph, point (g)				Article 12(1), first subparagraph, point (h)
			Article 6(1), first subparagraph, point (h)				Article 12(1), first subparagraph, point (i)
			Article 6(1), first subparagraph, point (i)				Article 12(1), first subparagraph, point (j)
			Article 6(1), first subparagraph, point (j)				Article 12(1), first subparagraph, point (k)
			Article 6(1), second subpara-graph				Article 12(1), second subparagraph
			Article 6(2)				Article 12(2)
			Article 7				Article 5(2)
			Article 8, first paragraph		Article 4(3)		Article 5(1)
			Article 8, second paragraph				—
			Article 9(1), first part of sentence				Article 14(1), first subparagraph
			Article 9(1), second part of sentence				—
			Article 9(2)				Article 5(3)

Directive 78/176/EEC	Directive 82/883/EEC	Directive 92/112/EEC	Directive 2008/1/EC	Directive 1999/13/EC	Directive 2000/76/EC	Directive 2001/80/EC	This Directive
			Article 9(3), first subparagraph, first and second sentence				Article 14(1), second subparagraph, introductory wording and points (a) and (b)
			Article 9(3), first subparagraph, third sentence				Article 14(2)
—	—	—	—	—	—	—	Article 14(3), (4), and (7)
—	—	—	—	—	—	—	Article 14(5), introductory wording and point (b) of first subparagraph and Article 14(5), second subparagraph
			Article 9(3), second subpara-graph				—
			Article 9(3), third subparagraph				Article 9(1)
			Article 9(3), fourth subparagraph				Article 9(2)
			Article 9(3), fifth subparagraph				Article 9(3)
			Article 9(3), sixth subparagraph				Article 9(4)
—	—	—	—	—	—	—	Article 10

Directive 78/176/EEC	Directive 82/883/EEC	Directive 92/112/EEC	Directive 2008/1/EC	Directive 1999/13/EC	Directive 2000/76/EC	Directive 2001/80/EC	This Directive
			Article 9(4), first part of first sentence				Article 15(2)
			Article 9(4), second part of first sentence				Article 15(4), first subparagraph
—	—	—	—	—	—	—	Article 15(4), second to fifth subparagraphs and Article 15(5)
			Article 9(4), second sentence				Article 14(1), second subparagraph, point (g)
—	—	—	—	—	—	—	Article 14(1), second subparagraph, point (h)
—	—	—	—	—	—	—	Article 15(3)
—	—	—	—	—	—	—	Article 16
			Article 9(5), first subparagraph				Article 14(1), second subparagraph, point (c)(i)
—	—	—	—	—	—	—	Article 14(1), second subparagraph, point (c)(ii)
—	—	—	—	—	—	—	Article 14(1), second subparagraph, point (d)
			Article 9(5), second subpara-graph				—

Directive 78/176/EEC	Directive 82/883/EEC	Directive 92/112/EEC	Directive 2008/1/EC	Directive 1999/13/EC	Directive 2000/76/EC	Directive 2001/80/EC	This Directive
—	—	—	—	—	—	—	Article 14(1), second subparagraph, point (e)
			Article 9(6), first subparagraph				Article 14(1), second subparagraph, point (f)
			Article 9(6), second subparagraph				—
			Article 9(7)				—
			Article 9(8)				Article 6 and Article 17(1)
—	—	—	—	—	—	—	Article 17(2), (3) and (4)
			Article 10				Article 18
			Article 11				Article 19
			Article 12(1)				Article 20(1)
			Article 12(2), first sentence				Article 20(2), first subparagraph
			Article 12(2), second sentence				Article 20(2), second subparagraph
			Article 12(2), third sentence				—
			Article 13(1)				Article 21(1)

Directive 78/176/EEC	Directive 82/883/EEC	Directive 92/112/EEC	Directive 2008/1/EC	Directive 1999/13/EC	Directive 2000/76/EC	Directive 2001/80/EC	This Directive
—	—	—	—	—	—	—	Article 21(2), (3) and (4)
			Article 13(2), introductory wording				Article 21(5), introductory wording
			Article 13(2)(a)				Article 21(5), point (a)
			Article 13(2)(b)				—
			Article 13(2)(c)				Article 21(5), point (b)
			Article 13(2)(d)				—
—	—	—	—	—	—	—	Article 21(5), point (c)
—	—	—	—	—	—	—	Article 22
—	—	—	—	—	—	—	Article 23(1), first subparagraph
			Article 14, introductory wording and point (a)				Article 8(1)
			Article 14, point (b)				Article 7, point (a) and Article 14(1), point (d)(i)
—	—	—	—	—	—	—	Article 7, introductory wording and points (b) and (c)
—	—	—	—	—	—	—	Article 14(1), point (d)(ii)
			Article 14, point (c)				Article 23(1), second subparagraph

Directive 78/176/EEC	Directive 82/883/EEC	Directive 92/112/EEC	Directive 2008/1/EC	Directive 1999/13/EC	Directive 2000/76/EC	Directive 2001/80/EC	This Directive
—	—	—	—	—	—	—	Article 23(2) to (6)
			Article 15(1), first subparagraph, introductory wording and points (a) and (b)	Article 12(1), first subparagraph			Article 24(1), first subparagraph, introductory wording and points (a) and (b)
			Article 15(1), first subparagraph, point (c)				Article 24(1), first subparagraph, point (c)
			Article 15(1), second subparagraph				Article 24(1), second subparagraph
			Article 15(2)				Article 24(3)(b)
			Article 15(3)				Article 24(4)
			Article 15(4)				Article 24(2), introductory wording and points (a) and (b)
—	—	—	—	—	—	—	Article 24(2), points (c) to (f) and Article 24(3), introductory wording and point (a)
			Article 16				Article 25
			Article 17(1), second subparagraph				—
			Article 17(2), first subparagraph				Article 13(1)

Directive 78/176/EEC	Directive 82/883/EEC	Directive 92/112/EEC	Directive 2008/1/EC	Directive 1999/13/EC	Directive 2000/76/EC	Directive 2001/80/EC	This Directive
—	—	—	—	—	—	—	Article 13(2) to (7)
			Article 17(2), second subparagraph				—
			Article 17(3), first subparagraph, second and third sentence	Article 11(1), second sentence			Article 72(2)
			Article 17(3), first subparagraph, fourth sentence				—
—	—	—	—	—	—	—	Article 72(3) and (4)
			Article 17(3), second subparagraph				—
			Article 17(3), third subparagraph	Article 11(3)			Article 73(1)
—	—	—	—	—	—	—	Article 73(2)
			Article 17(4)				—
—	—	—	—	—	—	—	Article 74
—	—	—	—	—	—	—	Article 27
			Article 18			Article 11	Article 26
			Article 19				—
			Article 20				—

Directive 78/176/EEC	Directive 82/883/EEC	Directive 92/112/EEC	Directive 2008/1/EC	Directive 1999/13/EC	Directive 2000/76/EC	Directive 2001/80/EC	This Directive
			Article 21				Article 80(2)
			Article 22		Article 18	Article 17	Article 81
—	—	—	—	—	—	—	Article 82
			Article 23	Article 16	Article 22	Article 19	Article 83
—	—	—	—	—	—	—	Article 2(1)
			Annex I, paragraph 1 of introductory wording				Article 2(2)
			Annex I, paragraph 2 of introductory wording				Annex I, first subparagraph of introductory wording, first sentence
—	—	—	—	—	—	—	Annex I, first subparagraph of introductory wording, second sentence
—	—	—	—	—	—	—	Annex I, second subparagraph of intro-ductory wording
			Annex I, points 1.1 to 1.3				Annex I, points 1.1 to 1.3
			Annex I, point 1.4				Annex I, point 1.4(a)
—	—	—	—	—	—	—	Annex I, point 1.4(b)
			Annex I, point 2				Annex I, point 2
			Annex I, point 3.1				Annex I, point 3.1(a) and (b)

Directive 78/176/EEC	Directive 82/883/EEC	Directive 92/112/EEC	Directive 2008/1/EC	Directive 1999/13/EC	Directive 2000/76/EC	Directive 2001/80/EC	This Directive
—	—	—	—	—	—	—	Annex I, point 3.1(c)
			Annex I, points 3.2 to 3.5				Annex I, points 3.2 to 3.5
			Annex I, point 4				Annex I, point 4
			Annex I, point 5, introductory wording				—
			Annex I, point 5.1				Annex I, points 5.1(b), (f), (g), (i), (j) and 5.2(b)
—	—	—	—	—	—	—	Annex I, points 5.1(a), (c), (d), (e), (h), (k)
			Annex I, point 5.2				Annex I, point 5.2(a)
			Annex I, point 5.3				Annex I, point 5.3(a)(i) and (ii)
—	—	—	—	—	—	—	Annex I, point 5.3(a)(iii) to (v) and 5.3(b)
			Annex I, point 5.4				Annex I, point 5.4
—	—	—	—	—	—	—	Annex I, points 5.5 and 5.6
			Annex I, points 6.1(a) and (b)				Annex I, points 6.1(a) and (b)

Directive 78/176/EEC	Directive 82/883/EEC	Directive 92/112/EEC	Directive 2008/1/EC	Directive 1999/13/EC	Directive 2000/76/EC	Directive 2001/80/EC	This Directive
—	—	—	—	—	—	—	Annex I, point 6.1(c)
			Annex I, points 6.2 – 6.4(b)				Annex I, points 6.2 – 6.4(b)(ii)
—	—	—	—	—	—	—	Annex I, point 6.4 (b)(iii)
			Annex I, points 6.4(c) – 6.9				Annex I, points 6.4(c) – 6.9
—	—	—	—	—	—	—	Annex I, points 6.10 and 6.11
			Annex II				—
			Annex III				Annex II, 'Air', and 'Water', points 1 to 12
—	—	—	—	—	—	—	Annex II, 'Water', point 13
			Annex IV				Annex III
			Annex V				Annex IV
				Article 1			Article 56
				Article 2(2)			Article 57(1)

Directive 78/176/EEC	Directive 82/883/EEC	Directive 92/112/EEC	Directive 2008/1/EC	Directive 1999/13/EC	Directive 2000/76/EC	Directive 2001/80/EC	This Directive
				Article 2(3)			—
				Article 2(4)			Article 63(1)
				Article 2(8)			Article 4(1), third subparagraph
				Article 2(10)			Article 57(3)
				Article 2(11)			Article 57(2)
				Article 2(12)			Article 57(4)
				Article 2(15)			Article 57(5)
				Article 2(16)			Article 3(44)
				Article 2(17)			Article 3(45)
				Article 2(18)			Article 3(46)
				Article 2(19)			—
				Article 2(20)			Article 3(47)

Directive 78/176/EEC	Directive 82/883/EEC	Directive 92/112/EEC	Directive 2008/1/EC	Directive 1999/13/EC	Directive 2000/76/EC	Directive 2001/80/EC	This Directive
				Article 2(21)			Article 57(6)
				Article 2(22)			Article 57(7)
				Article 2(23)			Article 57(8)
				Article 2(24)			Article 57(9)
				Article 2(25)			Article 57(10)
				Article 2(26)			Article 57(11)
				Article 2(27)			—
				Article 2(28)			Article 63(1)
				Article 2(29)			—
				Article 2(30)			Article 57(12)
				Article 2(31)			Annex VII, Part 2, first sentence Annex VIII, Part 2, point 1
				Article 2(32)			—
				Article 2(33)			Article 57(13)

Directive 78/176/EEC	Directive 82/883/EEC	Directive 92/112/EEC	Directive 2008/1/EC	Directive 1999/13/EC	Directive 2000/76/EC	Directive 2001/80/EC	This Directive
				Article 3(2)			Article 4(1), second subparagraph
				Article 4(1), (2) and(3)			Article 4(1), first and second subparagraph
				Article 4(4)			Article 63(2)
				Article 5(1)			Article 59(1), first subparagraph, introductory wording
				Article 5(2)			Article 59(1) first subparagraph, points (a) and (b)
				Article 5(3), first subparagraph, point (a)			Article 59(2)
				Article 5(3), first subparagraph, point (b)			Article 59(3)
				Article 5(3), second subparagraph			Article 59(4)
—	—	—	—	—	—	—	Article 59(5)
				Article 5(4)			—
				Article 5(5)			Article 59(6)
				Article 5(6)			Article 58

Directive 78/176/EEC	Directive 82/883/EEC	Directive 92/112/EEC	Directive 2008/1/EC	Directive 1999/13/EC	Directive 2000/76/EC	Directive 2001/80/EC	This Directive
				Article 5(7)			Annex VII, Part 4, point 1
				Article 5(8) first subparagraph			Annex VII, Part 4, point 2
				Article 5(8) second subparagraph			—
				Article 5(9)			—
				Article 5(10)			Article 59(7)
				Article 5(11), (12) and (13)			—
				Article 6			—
				Article 7(1), introductory wording and first, second, third and fourth indent			Article 64
				Article 7(1), closing wording			—
				Article 7(2)			—
				Article 8(1)			Article 14(1), point (d), Article 60
—	—	—	—	—	—	—	Article 61
				Article 8(2)			Annex VII, Part 6, point 1

Directive 78/176/EEC	Directive 82/883/EEC	Directive 92/112/EEC	Directive 2008/1/EC	Directive 1999/13/EC	Directive 2000/76/EC	Directive 2001/80/EC	This Directive
				Article 8(3)			Annex VII, Part 6, point 2
				Article 8(4)			Annex VII Part 6, point 3
				Article 8(5)			—
				Article 9(1), first subparagraph, introductory wording			Article 62, first subparagraph, introductory wording
				Article 9(1), first subparagraph, first, second and third indent			Article 62, first subparagraph, points (a), (b) and (c)
				Article 9(1), second subparagraph			Article 62, second subparagraph
				Article 9(1), third subparagraph			Annex VII, Part 8, point 4
				Article 9(2)			Article 63(3)
				Article 9(3)			Annex VII, Part 8, point 1
				Article 9(4)			Annex VII, Part 8, point 2
				Article 9(5)			Annex VII, Part 8, point 3
				Article 10	Article 4(9)		Article 8(2)

Directive 78/176/EEC	Directive 82/883/EEC	Directive 92/112/EEC	Directive 2008/1/EC	Directive 1999/13/EC	Directive 2000/76/EC	Directive 2001/80/EC	This Directive
				Article 11(1), third to sixth sentences			—
				Article 12(1), second subparagraph			Article 65(1), first subparagraph
				Article 12(1), third subparagraph			Article 65(1), second subparagraph
				Article 12(2)			Article 65(2)
				Article 12(3)			Article 65(3)
				Article 13(2) and (3)			—
				Article 14	Article 19	Article 16	Article 79
				Annex I, first and second sentence of introductory wording			Article 56
				Annex I, third sentence of introductory wording and list of activities			Annex VII, Part 1
				Annex IIA			Annex VII, Parts 2 and 3
				Annex IIA, Part II, last sentence of paragraph 6			—
				Annex IIB, point 1, first and second sentences			Article 59(1), first subparagraph, point (b)

Directive 78/176/EEC	Directive 82/883/EEC	Directive 92/112/EEC	Directive 2008/1/EC	Directive 1999/13/EC	Directive 2000/76/EC	Directive 2001/80/EC	This Directive
				Annex IIB, point 1, third sentence			Article 59(1), second subparagraph
				Annex IIB, point 2			Annex VII, Part 5
				Annex IIB, point 2, second subparagraph (i) and table			—
				Annex III, point 1			—
				Annex III, point 2			Annex VII, Part 7, point 1
				Annex III, point 3			Annex VII, Part 7, point 2
				Annex III, point 4			Annex VII, Part 7, point 3
					Article 1, first paragraph		Article 42
					Article 1, second paragraph		—
					Article 2(1)		Article 42(1), first subparagraph
—	—	—	—	—	—	—	Article 42(1), second to fifth subparagraphs
					Article 2(2), introductory wording		Article 42(2), introductory wording
					Article 2(2)(a), introductory wording		Article 42(2)(a), introductory wording

Directive 78/176/EEC	Directive 82/883/EEC	Directive 92/112/EEC	Directive 2008/1/EC	Directive 1999/13/EC	Directive 2000/76/EC	Directive 2001/80/EC	This Directive
					Article 2(2)(a), points (i) to (v)		Article 42(2)(a), point (i)
					Article 2(2)(a), point (vi)		Article 42(2)(a), point (ii)
					Article 2(2)(a), point (vii)		Article 42(2)(a), point (iii)
					Article 2(2)(a), point (viii)		Article 42(2)(a), point (iv)
					Article 2(2)(b)		Article 42(2)(b)
					Article 3(2), first subparagraph		Article 3(38)
					Article 3(2), second subparagraph		—
					Article 3(3)		Article 3(39)
					Article 3(4), first subparagraph		Article 3(40)
					Article 3(4), second subparagraph		Article 42(1), third subparagraph
—	—	—	—	—	—	—	Article 42(1), fourth subparagraph
					Article 3(5), first subparagraph		Article 3(41)

Directive 78/176/EEC	Directive 82/883/EEC	Directive 92/112/EEC	Directive 2008/1/EC	Directive 1999/13/EC	Directive 2000/76/EC	Directive 2001/80/EC	This Directive
					Article 3(5), second subparagraph		Article 42(1), fifth subparagraph
					Article 3(5), third subparagraph		Article 42(1), third subparagraph
					Article 3(6)		Annex VI, Part 1, point (a)
					Article 3(7)		Article 3(42)
—	—	—	—	—	—	—	Annex VI, Part 1, point (b)
					Article 3(10)		Article 3(43)
					Article 3(13)		Article 43
					Article 4(2)		Article 44
					Article 4(4), introductory wording and points (a) and (b)		Article 45(1), introductory wording and points (a) and (b)
					Article 4(4), point (c)		Article 45(1), point (e)
					Article 4(5)		Article 45(2)
					Article 4(6)		Article 45(3)
					Article 4(7)		Article 45(4)

Directive 78/176/EEC	Directive 82/883/EEC	Directive 92/112/EEC	Directive 2008/1/EC	Directive 1999/13/EC	Directive 2000/76/EC	Directive 2001/80/EC	This Directive
					Article 4(8)		Article 54
					Article 5		Article 52
					Article 6(1), first subparagraph		Article 50(1)
					Article 6(1), second subparagraph and 6(2)		Article 50(2)
					Article 6(1), third subparagraph		Article 50(3), first subparagraph
					Article 6(1), first part of fourth subpara-graph		—
					Article 6(1), second part of fourth subparagraph		Article 50(3), second subparagraph
					Article 6(3)		Article 50(4)
					Article 6(4), first and second sentences of first subparagraph and Article 6(4), first and second sentences of second subparagraph		Article 51(1)

Directive 78/176/EEC	Directive 82/883/EEC	Directive 92/112/EEC	Directive 2008/1/EC	Directive 1999/13/EC	Directive 2000/76/EC	Directive 2001/80/EC	This Directive
					Article 6(4), third sentence of first subparagraph		Article 51(2)
—	—	—	—	—	Article 6(4), third sentence of second subparagraph	—	Article 51(3), first subparagraph
					Article 6(4), third subparagraph		Article 51(3), second subparagraph
					Article 6(4), fourth subparagraph		Article 51(4)
					Article 6(5), first part of sentence		—
					Article 6(5), second part of the sentence		Article 46(1)
					Article 6(6)		Article 50(5)
					Article 6(7)		Article 50(6)
					Article 6(8)		Article 50(7)
					Article 7(1) and Article 7(2), first subparagraph		Article 46(2), first subparagraph
					Article 7(2), second subparagraph		Article 46(2), second subparagraph

Directive 78/176/EEC	Directive 82/883/EEC	Directive 92/112/EEC	Directive 2008/1/EC	Directive 1999/13/EC	Directive 2000/76/EC	Directive 2001/80/EC	This Directive
					Article 7(3) and Article 11(8), first subparagraph, introductory wording		Annex VI, Part 6, first part of point 2.7
					Article 7(4)		Article 46(2), second subparagraph
					Article 7(5)		—
					Article 8(1)		Article 45(1), point (c)
					Article 8(2)		Article 46(3)
					Article 8(3)		—
					Article 8(4), first subparagraph		Article 46(4), first subparagraph
					Article 8(4), second subparagraph		Annex VI, Part 6, point 3.2
					Article 8(4), third subparagraph		—
					Article 8(4), fourth subparagraph		—
					Article 8(5)		Article 46(4), second and third subparagraph

Directive 78/176/EEC	Directive 82/883/EEC	Directive 92/112/EEC	Directive 2008/1/EC	Directive 1999/13/EC	Directive 2000/76/EC	Directive 2001/80/EC	This Directive
					Article 8(6)		Article 45(1), points (c) and (d)
					Article 8(7)		Article 46(5)
					Article 8(8)		—
					Article 9, first subparagraph		Article 53(1)
					Article 9, second subparagraph		Article 53(2)
					Article 9, third subparagraph		Article 53(3)
					Article 10(1) and (2)		—
					Article 10(3), first sentence		Article 48(2)
					Article 10(3), second sentence		—
					Article 10(4)		Article 48(3)
					Article 10(5)		Annex VI, Part 6, second part of point 1.3
					Article 11(1)		Article 48(1)
					Article 11(2)		Annex VI, Part 6, point 2.1

Directive 78/176/EEC	Directive 82/883/EEC	Directive 92/112/EEC	Directive 2008/1/EC	Directive 1999/13/EC	Directive 2000/76/EC	Directive 2001/80/EC	This Directive
					Article 11(3)		Annex VI, Part 6, point 2.2
					Article 11(4)		Annex VI, Part 6, point 2.3
					Article 11(5)		Annex VI, Part 6, point 2.4
					Article 11(6)		Annex VI, Part 6, point 2.5, first subparagraph
—	—	—	—	—	—	—	Annex VI, Part 6, point 2.5, second subparagraph
					Article 11(7), first part of first sentence of first subparagraph		Annex VI, Part 6, point 2.6, introductory wording
					Article 11(7), second part of first sentence of first subparagraph		Annex VI, Part 6, point 2.6(a)
					Article 11(7), second sentence of first subparagraph		—
					Article 11(7), second subparagraph		—
					Article 11(7), point (a)		Annex VI, Part 6, point 2.6(b)
					Article 11(7), points (b) and (c)		—

Directive 78/176/EEC	Directive 82/883/EEC	Directive 92/112/EEC	Directive 2008/1/EC	Directive 1999/13/EC	Directive 2000/76/EC	Directive 2001/80/EC	This Directive
					Article 11(7), point (d)		Annex VI, Part 6, point 2.6(c)
					Article 11(7), points (e) and (f)		—
					Article 11(8), first subparagraph, points (a) and (b)		Annex VI, Part 3, point 1
					Article 11(8), first subparagraph, point (c) and second subparagraph		Annex VI, Part 6, second subparagraph of point 2.7
					Article 11(8), first subparagraph, point (d)		Annex VI, Part 4, point 2.1, second subparagraph
					Article 11(9)		Article 48(4)
					Article 11(10)		Annex VI, Part 8, point 1.1
					Article 11(11)		Annex VI, Part 8, point 1.2
					Article 11(12)		Annex VI, Part 8, point 1.3
					Article 11(13)		Article 48(5)
—	—	—	—	—	—	—	Article 49
					Article 11(14)		Annex VI, Part 6, point 3.1
					Article 11(15)		Article 45(1), point (e)

Directive 78/176/EEC	Directive 82/883/EEC	Directive 92/112/EEC	Directive 2008/1/EC	Directive 1999/13/EC	Directive 2000/76/EC	Directive 2001/80/EC	This Directive
					Article 11(16)		Annex VI, Part 8, point 2
					Article 11(17)		Article 8(2), point (a)
					Article 12(1)		Article 55(1)
					Article 12(2), first and second sentence		Article 55(2)
					Article 12(2), third sentence		Article 55(3)
					Article 13(1)		Article 45(1), point (f)
					Article 13(2)		Article 47
					Article 13(3)		Article 46(6)
					Article 13(4)		Annex VI, Part 3, point 2
					Article 14		—
					Article 15		—
					Article 16		—
					Article 20		—
					Annex I		Annex VI, Part 2
					Annex II, first part (without numbering)		Annex VI, Part 4, point 1

Directive 78/176/EEC	Directive 82/883/EEC	Directive 92/112/EEC	Directive 2008/1/EC	Directive 1999/13/EC	Directive 2000/76/EC	Directive 2001/80/EC	This Directive
					Annex II, point 1, introductory wording		Annex VI, Part 4, point 2.1
					Annex II, points 1.1 and 1.2		Annex VI, Part 4, points 2.2 and 2.3
—	—	—	—	—	—	—	Annex VI, Part 4, point 2.4
					Annex II, point 1.3		—
					Annex II, point 2.1		Annex VI, Part 4, point 3.1
—	—	—	—	—	—	—	Annex VI, Part 4, point 3.2
					Annex II, point 2.2		Annex VI, Part 4, point 3.3 and 3.4
					Annex II, point 3		Annex VI, Part 4, point 4
					Annex III		Annex VI, Part 6, point 1
					Annex IV, table		Annex VI, Part 5
					Annex IV, final sentence		—
					Annex V, point (a), table		Annex VI, Part 3, point 1.1
					Annex V, point (a), final sentences		—
					Annex V, point (b), table		Annex VI, Part 3, point 1.2
					Annex V, point (b), final sentence		—
					Annex V, point (c)		Annex VI, Part 3, point 1.3

Directive 78/176/EEC	Directive 82/883/EEC	Directive 92/112/EEC	Directive 2008/1/EC	Directive 1999/13/EC	Directive 2000/76/EC	Directive 2001/80/EC	This Directive
					Annex V, point (d)		Annex VI, Part 3, point 1.4
					Annex V, point (e)		Annex VI, Part 3, point 1.5
					Annex V, point (f)		Annex VI, Part 3, point 3
					Annex VI		Annex VI, Part 7
						Article 1	Article 28, first subparagraph
						Article 2(2)	Annex V, Part 1, point 1 and Part 2, point 1, first subparagraph
—	—	—	—	—	—	—	Annex V, Part 1, point 1 and Part 2, point 1, second subparagraph
						Article 2(3) second part	Annex V, Part 1, point 1 and Part 2, point 1, first subparagraph
—	—	—	—	—	—	—	Annex V, Part 1, point 1 and Part 2, point 1, second subparagraph
						Article 2(4)	—
						Article 2(6), first part	Article 3(24)
						Article 2(6), second part	Article 28, second subparagraph, point (j)

Directive 78/176/EEC	Directive 82/883/EEC	Directive 92/112/EEC	Directive 2008/1/EC	Directive 1999/13/EC	Directive 2000/76/EC	Directive 2001/80/EC	This Directive
						Article 2(7), first subparagraph	Article 3(25)
						Article 2(7), second subparagraph, first sentence	—
						Article 2(7), second subparagraph, second sentence and points (a) to (i)	Article 28, second subparagraph and points (a) to (i)
						Article 2(7), second subparagraph, point (j)	—
						Article 2(7), third subparagraph	—
—	—	—	—	—	—	—	Article 29(1)
						Article 2(7), fourth subparagraph	Article 29(2)
—	—	—	—	—	—	—	Article 29(3)
						Article 2(8)	Article 3(32)
						Article 2(9)	—
						Article 2(10)	—

Directive 78/176/EEC	Directive 82/883/EEC	Directive 92/112/EEC	Directive 2008/1/EC	Directive 1999/13/EC	Directive 2000/76/EC	Directive 2001/80/EC	This Directive
						Article 2(11)	Article 3(31)
						Article 2(12)	Article 3(33)
						Article 2(13)	—
						Article 3	—
						Article 4(1)	—
						Article 4(2)	—
						Article 4(3)to 4(8)	
						Article 5(1)	Annex V, Part 1, point 2, second subparagraph
							Annex V, Part 1, point 2, first, third and fourth subparagraphs
						Article 5(2)	—
						Article 6	—
						Article 7(1)	Article 37
						Article 7(2)	Article 30(5)
						Article 7(3)	Article 30(6)

Directive 78/176/EEC	Directive 82/883/EEC	Directive 92/112/EEC	Directive 2008/1/EC	Directive 1999/13/EC	Directive 2000/76/EC	Directive 2001/80/EC	This Directive
						Article 8(1)	Article 40(1)
						Article 8(2), first part of first subparagraph	Article 40(2), first part of first subparagraph
						Article 8(2), second part of first subparagraph	—
—	—	—	—	—	—	—	Article 40(2), second part of first subparagraph
—	—	—	—	—	—	—	Article 40(2), second subparagraph
—	—	—	—	—	—	—	Article 40(3)
—	—	—	—	—	—	—	Article 41
						Article 8(2), second subpara-graph	—
						Article 8(3) and (4)	—
						Article 9	Article 30(1)
—	—	—	—	—	—	—	Article 30(2), (3) and (4)
						Article 9a	Article 36
						Article 10, first paragraph, first sentence	Article 30(7), first sentence

Directive 78/176/EEC	Directive 82/883/EEC	Directive 92/112/EEC	Directive 2008/1/EC	Directive 1999/13/EC	Directive 2000/76/EC	Directive 2001/80/EC	This Directive
—	—	—	—	—	—	—	Article 30(7), second sentence
—	—	—	—	—	—	—	Article 30(8) and (9)
—	—	—	—	—	—	—	Article 31 to 35
						Article 10, first paragraph, second sentence	—
						Article 10, second paragraph	—
						Article 12, first sentence	Article 38(1)
						Article 12, second sentence	—
—	—	—	—	—	—	—	Article 38(2), (3) and (4)
—	—	—	—	—	—	—	Article 39
						Article 13	Annex V, Part 3, third part of point 8
						Article 14	Annex V, Part 4
—	—	—	—	—	—	—	Annex V, Part 5, 6 and 7
						Article 15	—
						Article 18(2)	—
						Annex I	—
						Annex II	—
						Annex III and IV	Annex V, point 2 of Part 1 and Part 2

Directive 78/176/EEC	Directive 82/883/EEC	Directive 92/112/EEC	Directive 2008/1/EC	Directive 1999/13/EC	Directive 2000/76/EC	Directive 2001/80/EC	This Directive
						Annex V A	Annex V, Part 1, point 3
						Annex V B	Annex V, Part 2, point 3
						Annex VI A	Annex V, Part 1, points 4 and 6
—	—	—	—	—	—	—	Annex V, Part 1, point 5
						Annex VI B	Annex V, Part 2, points 4 and 6
—	—	—	—	—	—	—	Annex V, Part 2, point 5
						Annex VII A	Annex V, Part 1, points 7 and 8
						Annex VII B	Annex V, Part 2, points 7 and 8
						Annex VIII A point 1	—
						Annex VIII A point 2	Annex V, Part 3, first part of point 1 and points 2, 3 and 5
—	—	—	—	—	—	—	Annex V, Part 3, second part of point 1
—	—	—	—	—	—	—	Annex V, Part 3, point 4
						Annex VIII A point 3	—
						Annex VIII A point 4	Annex V, Part 3, point 6

Directive 78/176/EEC	Directive 82/883/EEC	Directive 92/112/EEC	Directive 2008/1/EC	Directive 1999/13/EC	Directive 2000/76/EC	Directive 2001/80/EC	This Directive
						Annex VIII A point 5	Annex V, Part 3, points 7 and 8
						Annex VIII A point 6	Annex V, Part 3, points 9 and 10
—	—	—	—	—	—	—	Annex V, Part 3, point 11
—	—	—	—	—	—	—	Annex V, Part 4
						Annex VIII B	—
						Annex VIII C	—
			Annex VI			Annex IX	Annex IX
			Annex VII			Annex X	Annex X

[COMMISSION REGULATION (EU) NO 920/2010

of 7 October 2010][1]

[ESTABLISHING A UNION REGISTRY FOR THE PERIODS ENDING 31 DECEMBER 2012 OF THE UNION EMISSIONS TRADING SCHEME PURSUANT TO DIRECTIVE 2003/87/EC OF THE EUROPEAN PARLIAMENT AND OF THE COUNCIL AND DECISION NO 280/2004/EC OF THE EUROPEAN PARLIAMENT AND OF THE COUNCIL][1]

THE EUROPEAN COMMISSION,

Having regard to the Treaty on the Functioning of the European Union,

Having regard to Directive 2003/87/EC of the European Parliament and of the Council of 13 October 2003 establishing a system for greenhouse gas emission allowance trading within the Community and amending Council Directive 96/61/EC, and in particular Article 19 thereof,

Having regard to Decision No 280/2004/EC of the European Parliament and of the Council of 11 February 2004 concerning a mechanism for monitoring Community greenhouse gas emissions and for implementing the Kyoto Protocol, and in particular the first subparagraph, second sentence, Article 6(1) thereof,

Having consulted the European Data Protection Supervisor,

Whereas:

(1) Article 6 of Decision No 280/2004/EC requires the Union and its Member States to apply the functional and technical specifications for data exchange standards for registry systems under the Kyoto Protocol, adopted by Decision 12/CMP.1 of the Conference of the Parties to the UNFCCC serving as the Meeting of the Parties to the Kyoto Protocol (hereinafter Decision 12/CMP.1), for the establishment and operation of registries and the CITL.

(2) Article 19(1) of Directive 2003/87/EC establishing greenhouse gas emission allowance trading within the Community (hereinafter ETS) requires that all allowances are held in the Union registry on accounts managed by the Member States. In order to ensure that Kyoto units and allowances can be held on the same Union registry accounts, the Union registry must also conform to the functional and technical specifications for data exchange standards for registry systems under the Kyoto Protocol, adopted by Decision 12/CMP.1,

(3) Article 20 of Directive 2003/87/EC requires that an independent transaction log (hereinafter European Union Transaction Log or EUTL) recording the issue, transfer and cancellation of allowances is established. Article 6(2) of Decision No 280/2004/EC requires that information on the issue, holding, transfer, acquisition, cancellation and withdrawal of assigned amount units, removal units, emission reduction units and certified emission reductions and the carryover of assigned amount units, emission reduction units and certified emission reductions is made available to the transaction log.

(4) Article 19(3) of Directive 2003/87/EC requires that a regulation for a standardised and secured system of registries in the form of standardised electronic databases containing common data elements to track the issue, holding, transfer and cancellation of allowances, to provide for public access and confidentiality as appropriate and to ensure that there are no transfers which are incompatible with the obligations resulting from the Kyoto Protocol is drawn up.

(5) Each registry established in accordance with Article 6 of Decision No 280/2004/EC should contain at least one Party holding account, one retirement account, and the cancellation and replacement accounts required pursuant to Decision 13/CMP.1 of the Conference of the Parties to the UNFCCC serving as the Meeting of the Parties to the Kyoto Protocol (hereinafter Decision 13/CMP.1), and the Union registry holding all allowances pursuant to Article 19 of Directive 2003/87/EC should contain management accounts and user accounts required to implement the requirements of that Directive. Each account should be created in accordance with standardised procedures to ensure the integrity of the registries system and public access to information held in this system.

(6) Each registry established in accordance with Article 6 of Decision No 280/2004/EC should issue assigned amount units (hereinafter AAUs) pursuant to Decision 13/CMP.1, whereas allowances should be issued in the Union registry. Registries established in accordance with Article 6 of Decision No 280/2004/EC should ensure that they keep a deposit of AAUs that is equal to the amount of allowances issued by them in the Union registry in order to ensure that any transactions with allowances may be followed up with corresponding transfers of AAUs via a clearing mechanism at the end of each period.

(7) As Member States have no influence on the amount of allowances that account holders will choose to bank in their registries, any potential future international limitations on the banking of AAUs that serve as deposit for issued allowances would cause serious difficulties for those registries where a disproportionate number of such allowances are held. In order to ensure that the risks Member States face in this regard are shared equally among all Member States, the clearing mechanism should be set up in a way that upon its completion, an amount of AAUs is held in the Union registry's clearing account that is equal to allowances to be banked from the 2008-12 period.

(8) Transactions with allowances within the Union registry should be carried out through a communication link involving the EUTL, whereas transactions with Kyoto units should be carried out through a communication link involving both the EUTL and the UNFCCC international transaction log (hereinafter ITL). Provisions should be adopted to ensure that Member States that are not able to issue AAUs under the Kyoto Protocol because they have no binding emission reduction commitment are able to continue their equal participation in the Union emissions trading system. Such participation would not be possible in the 2008-12 period as, unlike all other Member States, these Member States would not be able to issue allowances that are linked to AAUs recognised under the Kyoto Protocol. Such equal participation should be allowed through specific mechanisms within the Union registry.

(9) The EUTL should perform automated checks on all processes in the registries system concerning allowances, verified emissions, accounts and Kyoto units, and the ITL should perform automated checks on processes concerning Kyoto units to ensure that there are no irregularities. Processes that fail these checks should be terminated in order to ensure that transactions in the Union registries system comply with the requirements of Directive 2003/87/EC and the requirements elaborated pursuant to the UNFCCC and the Kyoto Protocol.

(10) Adequate and harmonised requirements on authentication and access rights should be applied to protect the security of information held in the integrated registries system and records concerning all processes, operators and persons in the registries system should be kept.

(11) The Central Administrator should ensure that interruptions to the operation of the registries system are kept to a minimum by taking all reasonable steps to ensure the availability of the Union registry and the EUTL and by providing for robust systems and procedures for the safeguarding of all information.

(12) The registry system should be able to accommodate the introduction of aviation into the scheme for greenhouse gas emission allowance trading within the Union from 1 January 2012 onwards. The majority of tasks emerging from the revision of the ETS, laid down

in Directive 2009/29/EC of the European Parliament and of the Council of 23 April 2009 amending Directive 2003/87/EC so as to improve and extend the greenhouse gas emission allowance trading scheme of the Community, need to be fulfilled only from 1 January 2013 onwards. Those requirements are separate from the functionalities that need to be in place in 2012 due to the introduction of aviation activities into the ETS.

(13) Because aircraft operators are entitled to surrender a different set of allowances than operators of installations, aircraft operators should be provided a different type of account, the aircraft operator holding account. Allowances issued under the EU ETS Directive's Chapter II covering aviation are different from allowances issued heretofore, since they cover emissions that are for the most part not in the scope of the Kyoto Protocol. As such, they should be marked as different from other allowances.

(14) Directive 2008/101/EC of the European Parliament and of the Council of 19 November 2008 amending Directive 2003/87/EC so as to include aviation activities in the scheme for greenhouse gas emission allowance trading within the Community required that Kyoto units or allowances backed by Kyoto units surrendered by aircraft operators shall only be retired up to the quantity equal to domestic aviation emissions. However, as Member States cannot influence the choice of aircraft operators as to whether they surrender Chapter II allowances or units that may be retired, a centralised surrendering and redistribution system should be set up that guarantees that units surrendered by aircraft operators that may be retired are collected and used first of all to cover the domestic aviation emissions of all the Member States in an equal way. Member States should decide at a later stage how to use any units thus collected that may be retired.

(15) For the purposes of implementing the ETS review and to accommodate the introduction of aviation in 2012, it is sufficient to merge on a technical level the current ETS registry functions of Member States and leave the technical implementation of Kyoto Protocol registry functions with separate Kyoto Protocol (hereinafter KP) registries operated by Member States.

(16) To implement the changes introduced by Directive 2009/29/EC and to accommodate the introduction of aviation activities into the ETS in 2012, it is sufficient to merge on a technical level the current ETS registry functions of Member States and leave the technical implementation of registry functions with separate registries operated by Member States for so long as this is necessary. However, such a solution would not be cost-effective, as it would require the maintenance in each Member State of extensive parallel information technology capacities that would be little used. Thus, it is the aim of the Commission and the Member States to work together towards the establishment of a "Consolidated System of European Registries" that would unite the KP registry-related information technology functions of all Member States.

(17) The modalities determined in this Regulation for the accounting of allowances and Kyoto units and the possibility of setting up of the Consolidated System of European Registries is without prejudice to any future decision by the European Union concerning whether to commit to a joint Union emission reduction target or to separate Member State emission reduction targets under any future international climate change treaty.

(18) According to Article 19(4) of Directive 2003/87/EC, there needs to be provision for processes for the change and incident management for the Union registry and appropriate modalities for the Union registry to ensure that initiatives of the Member States pertaining to efficiency improvement, administrative cost management and quality control measures are possible. The holding of all allowances in the Union registry should be without prejudice to the maintenance of national registries for emissions not covered by the ETS and the Union registry should provide the same quality of services as national registries.

(19) As since 2009, the occurrence of VAT-fraud, money laundering and other criminal activities has increased significantly throughout the registries system, there is a need to provide more detailed and robust rules on checking identity information provided by account holders and people requesting to open accounts. In addition, Member State authorities need to be enabled to refuse the opening of an account to those that can be

reasonably suspected of wanting to use the registries system for fraudulent purposes. Finally, detailed rules shall be provided to enable the swift and effective provision of data to law enforcement agencies, which should then be able to use data thus obtained for investigation purposes.

(20) Commission Regulation (EC) No 994/2008 of 8 October 2008 for a standardised and secured system of registries pursuant to Directive 2003/87/EC of the European Parliament and of the Council and Decision No 280/2004/EC of the European Parliament and of the Council repealed and replaced Commission Regulation (EC) No 2216/2004 of 21 December 2004 for a standardised and secured system of registries pursuant to Directive 2003/87/EC of the European Parliament and of the Council and Decision No 280/2004/EC of the European Parliament and of the Council 2012 onwards. As this Regulation substantially changes the provisions applicable from 1 January 2012 on several regulated areas, the interest of clarity requires that Regulation (EC) No 994/2008 is repealed and replaced in its entirety, while retaining the repeal and replace of Regulation (EC) No 2216/2004 provided for in Regulation (EC) No 994/2008.

(21) Since Regulation (EC) No 2216/2004 will remain in force until the end of 2011, certain partial amendments of that Regulation are necessary with immediate effect. Those amendments relate to the fight against fraud and other criminal activities and the surrendering process. Obsolete provisions should also be deleted for the sake of clarity. Since the amendments related to anti-fraud activities and to the surrendering process should be applied as soon as possible, this Regulation should enter into force immediately following its publication.

(22) Regulation (EC) No 2216/2004 should therefore be amended accordingly with immediate effect. That Regulation should be repealed as of 1 January 2012.

(23) In accordance with Directive 2003/4/EC of the European Parliament and of the Council of 28 January 2003 on public access to environmental information and repealing Council Directive 90/313/EEC and Decision 13/CMP.1, specific reports should be made public on a regular basis to ensure that the public has access to information held within the integrated system of registries, subject to certain confidentiality requirements.

(24) Union legislation concerning the protection of individuals with regard to the processing of personal data and on the free movement of such data, in particular Directive 95/46/EC of the European Parliament and of the Council of 24 October 1995 on the protection of individuals with regard to the processing of personal data and on the free movement of such data, Directive 2002/58/EC of the European Parliament and of the Council of 12 July 2002 concerning the processing of personal data and the protection of privacy in the electronic communications sector (Directive on privacy and electronic communications) and Regulation (EC) No 45/2001 of the European Parliament and of the Council of 18 December 2000 on the protection of individuals with regard to the processing of personal data by the Community institutions and bodies and on the free movement of such data, should be respected where these are applicable to information held and processed pursuant to this Regulation.

(25) The measures provided for in this Regulation are in accordance with the opinion of the Climate Change Committee,

Amendment

1 Substituted by Commission Regulation (EU) No 1193/2011 of 18 November 2011 establishing a Union Registry for the trading period commencing on 1 January 2013 , and subsequent trading periods, of the Union emissions trading scheme pursuant to Directive 2003/87/EC of the European Parliament and of the Council and Decision No 280/2004/EC of the European Parliament and of the Council and amending Commission Regulations (EC) No 2216/2004 and (EU) No 920/2010, Article 89(1).

HAS ADOPTED THIS REGULATION:

Chapter I
Subject matter and definitions

Article 1

Subject matter

[This Regulation lays down general as well as operational and maintenance requirements for the periods ending 31 December 2012 concerning the standardised and secured registries system consisting of registries, and the independent transaction log provided for in Article 20(1) of Directive 2003/87/EC and Article 6 of Decision No 280/2004/EC.][1] It also provides for a communication system between the registries system and the International Transaction Log established, operated and maintained by the Secretariat of the United Nations Framework Convention on Climate Change (UNFCCC).

Amendment

1 Substituted by Commission Regulation (EU) No 1193/2011 of 18 November 2011 establishing a Union Registry for the trading period commencing on 1 January 2013, and subsequent trading periods, of the Union emissions trading scheme pursuant to Directive 2003/87/EC of the European Parliament and of the Council and Decision No 280/2004/EC of the European Parliament and of the Council and amending Commission Regulations (EC) No 2216/2004 and (EU) No 920/2010, Article 89(2).

[Article 1a

Scope][1]

[This Regulation concerns allowances created in the Union emissions trading scheme for the periods ending 31 December 2012 and Kyoto units.][1]

Amendment

1 Inserted by Commission Regulation (EU) No 1193/2011 of 18 November 2011 establishing a Union Registry for the trading period commencing on 1 January 2013, and subsequent trading periods, of the Union emissions trading scheme pursuant to Directive 2003/87/EC of the European Parliament and of the Council and Decision No 280/2004/EC of the European Parliament and of the Council and amending Commission Regulations (EC) No 2216/2004 and (EU) No 920/2010, Article 89(3).

Article 2

Definitions

For the purposes of this Regulation, the definitions laid down in Article 3 of Directive 2003/87/EC shall apply. The following definitions shall also apply:

1. "account holder" means a person who holds an account in the registries system;
2. "Central Administrator" means the person designated by the Commission pursuant to Article 20 of Directive 2003/87/EC;
3. "competent authority" means the authority or authorities designated by a Member State pursuant to Article 18 of Directive 2003/87/EC;
4. "KP Party" means a Party to the Kyoto Protocol;
5. "trading platform" is any type of multilateral exchange that brings together or facilitates the bringing together of multiple third-party buying and selling interests as defined in Article 4 of Directive 2004/39/EC of the European Parliament and of the Council, where the interests bought and sold are in allowances or Kyoto units;
6. "verifier" means a verifier as defined in Annex I(5)(m) to Commission Decision 2007/589/EC;
7. "Assigned Amount Units" or "AAUs" are units issued pursuant to Article 7(3) of Decision No 280/2004/EC;
8. "Chapter II allowances" are allowances issued under Chapter II of Directive 2003/87/EC;

9. “Chapter III allowances” are all allowances not issued under Chapter II of Directive 2003/87/EC;
10. “long-term CERs” or “lCERs” are units issued for an afforestation or reforestation project activity under the CDM which, subject to Decision 5/CMP.1 of the Conference of the Parties serving as the meeting of the Parties to the Kyoto Protocol, expires at the end of the emission reduction crediting period of the afforestation or reforestation project activity under the CDM for which it was issued;
11. “Removal Units” or “RMUs” are units issued pursuant to Article 3 of the Kyoto Protocol;
12. “temporary CERs” or “tCERs” are units issued for an afforestation or reforestation project activity under the CDM which, subject to Decision 5/CMP.1, expires at the end of the Kyoto Protocol commitment period following the one during which it was issued;
13. “process” means an automated technical means to carry out an action relating to an account or a unit in a registry;
14. “transaction” means a process that includes the transfer of an allowance or Kyoto unit from one account to another account;
15. “surrender” means the accounting of an allowance or a Kyoto unit by an operator or aircraft operator against the verified emissions of her installation or aircraft;
16. “cancellation” means the definitive disposal of a Kyoto unit by its holder without accounting it against verified emissions;
17. “deletion” means the definitive disposal of an allowance by its holder without accounting it against verified emissions;
18. “retirement” means the accounting of a Kyoto unit by a Party to the Kyoto Protocol against the reported emissions of that Party;
19. “money laundering” means the same as defined in Articles 1(2) of Directive 2005/60/EC of the European Parliament and the Council;
20. “serious crime” means the same as defined in Article 3(5) of Directive 2005/60/EC;
21. “terrorist financing” means the same as defined in Article 1(4) of Directive 2005/60/EC;
22. “registry administrator” shall refer to the registry administrator of the Union registry or any other Kyoto Protocol registry;
23. “national administrator” shall refer to the entity responsible for managing on behalf of a Member State a set of user accounts under the jurisdiction of a Member State in the Union registry, designated in accordance with Article 6;
24. “administrator of an account” shall refer to the administrator determined for a particular type of account in the third column of Table I-I in Annex I.

[25. “directors” includes the persons effectively directing the day-to-day operations of a legal person;

26. “central European time” means central European summer time during the summer-time period as defined in Articles 1, 2 and 3 of Directive 2000/84/EC of the European Parliament and of the Council.][1]

Amendment

1 Inserted by Commission Regulation (EU) No 1193/2011 of 18 November 2011 establishing a Union Registry for the trading period commencing on 1 January 2013, and subsequent trading periods, of the Union emissions trading scheme pursuant to Directive 2003/87/EC of the European Parliament and of the Council and Decision No 280/2004/EC of the European Parliament and of the Council and amending Commission Regulations (EC) No 2216/2004 and (EU) No 920/2010, Article 89(4).

Chapter II
The registries system

Article 3

Registries

1. For the purposes of meeting their obligations as KP Parties and under Article 6 of Decision No 280/2004/EC to ensure the accurate accounting of Kyoto units, each Member State and

the Union shall operate a registry (hereinafter "KP registry") in the form of a standardised electronic database that complies with the UNFCCC's requirements concerning registries, and in particular the functional and technical specifications for data exchange standards for registry systems under the Kyoto Protocol elaborated pursuant to Decision 12/CMP.1 of the Conference of the Parties serving as the meeting of the Parties to the Kyoto Protocol.

[2. A Union Registry for the periods ending 31 December 2012 of the Union emissions trading scheme is hereby established. For the purposes of meeting their obligations under Article 19 of Directive 2003/87/EC to ensure the accurate accounting of allowances, from 1 January 2012 onwards Member States shall use the Union Registry, which shall also function as a KP registry for the European Community as a separate KP Party. The Union Registry shall provide to national administrators and account holders all the processes described in Chapters IV to VI.][1]

3. By way of derogation from paragraph 1, Member States that are not able to issue AAUs due to reasons other than being determined by the UNFCCC to be ineligible to transfer ERUs, AAUs and CERs in accordance with the provisions of Decision 11/CMP.1 of the Conference of the Parties serving as the meeting of the Parties to the Kyoto Protocol (hereinafter "Member States with no KP registry") are not required to set up a KP registry.

4. The Union registry and every other KP registry shall conform to the functional and technical specifications for data exchange standards for registry systems under the Kyoto Protocol elaborated pursuant to Decision 12/CMP.1 and comply with the hardware, network and software and security requirements set out in the Data Exchange and Technical Specifications provided for in Article 71.

Amendment

1 Substituted by Commission Regulation (EU) No 1193/2011 of 18 November 2011 establishing a Union Registry for the trading period commencing on 1 January 2013, and subsequent trading periods, of the Union emissions trading scheme pursuant to Directive 2003/87/EC of the European Parliament and of the Council and Decision No 280/2004/EC of the European Parliament and of the Council and amending Commission Regulations (EC) No 2216/2004 and (EU) No 920/2010, Article 89(5).

Article 4

European Union Transaction Log

[1. A European Union Transaction Log (EUTL), to take the form of a standardised electronic database, is hereby established, pursuant to Article 20 of Directive 2003/87/EC, for transactions within the scope of this Regulation. The EUTL shall also serve to record all information relating to the holdings and transfers of Kyoto units in accordance with Article 6(2) of Decision No 280/2004/EC.][1]

2. The Central Administrator shall operate and maintain the EUTL in accordance with the provisions of this Regulation.

3. The EUTL shall be capable of checking and recording all processes referred to under Article 3(2), and shall conform to the functional and technical specifications for data exchange standards for registry systems under the Kyoto Protocol elaborated pursuant to Decision 12/CMP.1 and comply with the hardware, network and software requirements set out in the Data Exchange and Technical Specifications provided for in Article 71.

4. The EUTL shall be capable of recording all processes described in Chapters IV to VI.

Amendment

1 Substituted by Commission Regulation (EU) No 1193/2011 of 18 November 2011 establishing a Union Registry for the trading period commencing on 1 January 2013, and subsequent trading periods, of the Union emissions trading scheme pursuant to Directive 2003/87/EC of the European Parliament and of the Council and Decision No 280/2004/EC of the European Parliament and of the Council and amending Commission Regulations (EC) No 2216/2004 and (EU) No 920/2010, Article 89(6).

Article 5

Communication links between registries, the ITL and the EUTL

1. The Union registry and every other KP registry shall maintain a communication link with the UNFCCC's International Transaction Log (hereinafter "ITL") for the purposes of communicating transactions that transfer Kyoto units to or from other KP registries.

2. The EUTL shall also maintain a communication link with the ITL for the purposes of recording and checking transfers referred to under paragraph 1. For this purpose, the ITL communicates all proposed transfers involving a KP registry to the EUTL before the transfer is recorded.

3. The Union registry shall also maintain a direct communication link with the EUTL for the purposes of checking and recording transactions that transfer allowances and the account management processes described in Chapter IV. All transactions involving allowances shall take place within the Union registry, and shall be recorded and checked by the EUTL, but not by the ITL.

4. The Climate Change Committee may decide to consolidate the external communication links, the information technology infrastructure, user account access procedures, and the mechanisms for managing KP accounts of the Union registry with those of all other KP registries into a Consolidated System of European Registries, maintained by the Central Administrator. Upon the adoption of this decision, the Commission shall propose amendments to this Regulation to define the modalities of implementing a Consolidated System of European Registries.

5. The Central Administrator may establish a restricted communication link between the EUTL and the registry of an Accession Country for the purposes of enabling such registries to communicate with the ITL through the EUTL and to record verified emissions data of operators in the EUTL. Those registries must successfully complete all testing and initialisation procedures required of registries before the establishment of this communication link.

Article 6

National administrators and KP registry administrators

1. Each Member State shall designate a national administrator. The Member State shall access and manage its own accounts and the accounts in the Union registry under its jurisdiction through its national administrator. Each Member State's national administrator shall also act as the administrator of its KP registry. The KP registry administrator shall operate and maintain the KP registry of its Member State in accordance with the provisions of this Regulation.

2. The Central Administrator shall operate and maintain the Union registry. The Central Administrator shall also act as the KP registry administrator of the EU KP registry part of the Union registry.

3. The Member States and the Commission shall ensure that there is no conflict of interest among national administrators, the Central Administrator and holders of user accounts.

4. Each Member State shall notify the Commission of the identity and contact details of its national administrator.

5. The Commission shall coordinate the implementation of this Regulation with the registry administrators of each Member State and the Central Administrator. In particular, the Commission shall consult the administrators' working group of the Climate Change Committee on issues and procedures related to the operation of registries and the implementation of this Regulation. The administrators' working group shall agree on common operational procedures for the implementation of this Regulation, including change and incident management procedures for the Union registry. Rules of procedure for the registry administrators' working group shall be adopted by the Climate Change Committee.

6. The Central Administrator, the competent authorities and national administrators shall only perform processes where these are necessary to carry out their respective functions.

Chapter III
Units

Article 7

Units

1. The Union registry shall be able to hold Chapter II allowances and Chapter III allowances.

2. Each KP registry and the Union registry shall be capable of holding AAUs, ERUs, CERs, RMUs, lCERs and tCERs (collectively referred to as "Kyoto units").

Chapter IV
Accounts

Section 1
Provisions applicable to all accounts

Article 8

Accounts

1. The Union registry shall contain the accounts listed under the headings "II. Management accounts in the Union registry" and "III. User accounts in the Union registry" in Annex I.

2. The Union registry and every other KP registry shall contain the accounts listed under the heading "I. KP Party accounts in KP registries" in Annex I.

3. The type of units that may be held by each account type are set out in Annex I, and the type of transactions that may be initiated or received by each account type are set out in Annex II.

Article 9

Account status

1. Accounts shall be in one of the following status: open, inactive, blocked or closed.

2. No processes may be initiated from blocked accounts, except for the surrendering of units, the entering of verified emissions, and the updating of account details.

3. No processes may be initiated from closed accounts. A closed account may not be re-opened, and may not receive any unit transfers.

Article 10

The administering of accounts

1. Every account shall have an administrator who is responsible for administering the account on behalf of a Member State or on behalf of the Union.

2. The administrator of an account is determined for each account type in the third column of Table I-1 in Annex I.

3. The administrator of an account shall have the responsibility to open, suspend access to or close an account, to approve authorised representatives, to permit such changes to account details that require the approval of the administrator, and to initiate transactions if this is requested by the account holder in accordance with Article 19(4).

4. User accounts shall be governed by the laws and fall under the jurisdiction of the Member State of their administrator and the units held in them shall be considered to be situated in that Member State's territory.

Article 11

Notifications from the administrators

The Central Administrator shall notify the holder and the administrator of a Union registry account of the initiation and completion or termination of any process related to the account through an automated mechanism described in the Data Exchange and Technical Specifications provided for in Article 71.

Section 2
Opening and updating of accounts

Article 12

Opening of KP Party accounts and management accounts

1. The Commission shall instruct the Central administrator to open the Union's KP Party accounts and all management accounts in the Union registry except the national allowance holding accounts.

2. The competent body of the Member State shall instruct the national administrator to open its national allowance holding account in the Union registry.

3. The instructions referred to in paragraphs 1 and 2 shall contain the information set out in Annex III.

4. Within 20 working days of the instruction, the registry administrator or the Central administrator shall open the KP Party account or management account.

Article 13

Opening of person holding accounts in the Union registry

1. A request for the opening of a person holding account in the Union registry shall be submitted to the national administrator of a Member State. The person requesting the account opening shall provide the information required by the national administrator, which shall include at least the information set out in Annex IV.

2. The Member State of the national administrator may require that EU persons requesting the account opening have their permanent residence or registration in the Member State of the national administrator administering the account.

3. Within 20 working days of the receipt of a complete set of information required in accordance with paragraph 1 and 2 and after approving the required number of authorised representatives in accordance with Article 20 the national administrator shall open a person holding account in the Union registry or inform the person requesting the account opening that it refuses to open the account.

4. …[1]

Amendment

1 Repealed by Commission Regulation (EU) No 1193/2011 of 18 November 2011 establishing a Union Registry for the trading period commencing on 1 January 2013, and subsequent trading periods, of the Union emissions trading scheme pursuant to Directive 2003/87/EC of the European Parliament and of the Council and Decision No 280/2004/EC of the European Parliament and of the Council and amending Commission Regulations (EC) No 2216/2004 and (EU) No 920/2010, Article 89(7).

[Article 13a

Opening of trading accounts in the Union Registry][1]

[From 30 June 2012, the opening of trading accounts in the Union Registry may be requested. Subject to Articles 43 and 44, the rules set out in this Regulation for person holding accounts shall apply mutatis mutandis.][1]

Amendment

1 Inserted by Commission Regulation (EU) No 1193/2011 of 18 November 2011 establishing a Union Registry for the trading period commencing on 1 January 2013, and subsequent trading periods, of the Union emissions trading scheme pursuant to Directive 2003/87/EC of the European Parliament and of the Council and Decision No 280/2004/EC of the European Parliament and of the Council and amending Commission Regulations (EC) No 2216/2004 and (EU) No 920/2010, Article 89(8).

Article 14

Opening of trading platform holding accounts in the Union registry

[1. Trading platforms may submit a request for a trading platform holding account in the Union Registry. This request shall be submitted to the national administrator. The person requesting the account shall provide information as required by the national administrator. This information shall include, at a minimum, the information set out in Annex III and evidence that the trading platform ensures a level of security equivalent or higher than the security ensured by the Union Registry in accordance with this Regulation.

2. National administrators shall ensure that external platforms conform to the technical and security requirements described in the data exchange and technical specifications provided for in Article 71.][1]

3. Within 20 working days of the receipt of the complete information required in accordance with paragraphs 1 and 2 and after approving the required number of authorised representatives in accordance with Article 20 the national administrator shall open a trading platform holding account in the Union registry or inform the person requesting the account opening that it refuses to open the account.

[4. The approval of an additional authorised representative pursuant to Article 19(2) shall not be required for transactions initiated by exempted trading platforms. A trading platform may be exempted by the national administrator upon written request if the external trading platform provides evidence that it has security arrangements in place that offer at least a level of protection afforded by the requirement in Article 19(2). The minimum technical and security requirements shall be set out in the data exchange and technical specifications provided for in Article 71. The national administrator concerned shall notify the Commission of such requests without delay. Exemptions pursuant to this paragraph shall be made public by the Commission.][1]

Amendment

1 Substituted by Commission Regulation (EU) No 1193/2011 of 18 November 2011 establishing a Union Registry for the trading period commencing on 1 January 2013, and subsequent trading periods, of the Union emissions trading scheme pursuant to Directive 2003/87/EC of the European Parliament and of the Council and Decision No 280/2004/EC of the European Parliament and of the Council and amending Commission Regulations (EC) No 2216/2004 and (EU) No 920/2010, Article 89(9), (10).

Article 15

Opening of operator holding accounts in the Union registry

1. Within 20 working days of the entry into force of a greenhouse gas emissions permit for the operation of a new installation, the competent authority issuing the permit shall provide its Member State's national administrator with the information set out in Annex VII, and the

operator shall request the national administrator to open an operator holding account in the Union registry.

2. If the competent authority so decides, the information referred to in paragraph 1 above may also be provided by the operator to the national administrator within the deadline set out in paragraph 1.

3. Within 20 working days of the receipt of all the information referred to in paragraph 1 and after approving the required number of authorised representatives in accordance with Article 20 the national administrator shall open a separate operator holding account for each installation in the Union registry.

Article 16

Opening of aircraft operator holding accounts in the Union registry

1. Within 20 working days from the approval of the monitoring plan of an aircraft operator, or by 1 January 2012, whichever is the later, the competent authority shall provide its national administrator with the information set out in Annex VIII and the aircraft operator shall request the national administrator to open an aircraft operator holding account in the Union registry. Each aircraft operator shall have one aircraft operator holding account.

2. If the competent authority so decides, the information referred to in paragraph 1 above may also be provided by the operator to the national administrator within the deadline set out in paragraph 1.

3. Within 40 working days of the receipt of the information referred to in paragraph 1. and after approving the required number of authorised representatives in accordance with Article 20 the national administrator shall open a separate aircraft operator holding account for each aircraft operator in the Union registry.

[4. The status of aircraft operator holding accounts shall be changed from blocked to open following the entry of verified emissions pursuant to Article 29 and a compliance status figure greater than or equal to 0 calculated pursuant to Article 31 paragraph 1. The status of the account shall also be changed to open at an earlier date following receipt by the national administrator of a request by the account holder to activate its account for trading, provided that such a request contains, at a minimum, any required elements specified in the data exchange and technical specifications provided for in Article 71.][1]

Amendment

1 Inserted by Commission Regulation (EU) No 1193/2011 of 18 November 2011 establishing a Union Registry for the trading period commencing on 1 January 2013, and subsequent trading periods, of the Union emissions trading scheme pursuant to Directive 2003/87/EC of the European Parliament and of the Council and Decision No 280/2004/EC of the European Parliament and of the Council and amending Commission Regulations (EC) No 2216/2004 and (EU) No 920/2010, Article 89(11).

Article 17

Opening of verifier accounts in the Union registry

1. A request for the opening of a verifier account in the Union registry shall be submitted to the national administrator. The person requesting the account opening shall provide the information required by the national administrator, which shall include the information set out in Annex IV and Annex V.

2. Within 20 working days of the receipt of all the information referred to in paragraph 1 and after approving the required number of authorised representatives in accordance with Article 20, the national administrator shall open the verifier account in the Union registry.

[Article 18

Refusal to open an account][1]

[1. The national administrator shall verify whether the information and documents provided for account opening are complete, up to date, accurate and true.

2. A national administrator may refuse to open an account:
(a) if the information and documents provided are incomplete, out of date or otherwise inaccurate or false;
(b) if the prospective account holder, or, if it is a legal person, any of the directors, is under investigation or has been convicted in the preceding five years for fraud involving allowances or Kyoto units, money laundering, terrorist financing or other serious crimes for which the account may be an instrument;
(c) if the national administrator has reasonable grounds to believe that the accounts may be used for fraud involving allowances or Kyoto units, money laundering, terrorist financing or other serious crimes;
(d) for reasons set out in national law.

3. If the national administrator refuses to open an account, the person requesting the account opening may object to the relevant authority under national law, who shall either instruct the national administrator to open the account or uphold the refusal in a reasoned decision, subject to requirements of national law that pursue a legitimate objective compatible with this Regulation and are proportionate.][1]

Amendment

1 Substituted by Commission Regulation (EU) No 1193/2011 of 18 November 2011 establishing a Union Registry for the trading period commencing on 1 January 2013, and subsequent trading periods, of the Union emissions trading scheme pursuant to Directive 2003/87/EC of the European Parliament and of the Council and Decision No 280/2004/EC of the European Parliament and of the Council and amending Commission Regulations (EC) No 2216/2004 and (EU) No 920/2010, Article 89(12).

Article 19

Authorised representatives

[1. Each account, with the exception of the verifier account, shall have at least two authorised representatives. A verifier account shall have at least one authorised representative. The authorised representatives shall initiate transactions and other processes on behalf of the account holder.

2. Accounts may have one or more additional authorised representatives. The approval of an additional authorised representative is required in addition to the approval of an authorised representative, in order to initiate a transaction, except for:
(a) transfers to an account on the trusted account list in the Union Registry of the account holder;
(b) transactions initiated by trading platforms exempted pursuant to Article 14(4); and
(c) surrender of allowances, ERUs and CERs pursuant to Chapter VI, Section 3.][1]

[2a. In addition to the authorised representatives specified in paragraph 1, accounts may have authorised representatives with view only access to the account.][2]

3. The administrator of the account may allow holders of user accounts to enable their accounts to be accessed through a trading platform. Account holders enabling their account to be accessed through a trading platform shall nominate as authorised representative a person who is already the authorised representative of a trading platform holding account.

4. If the authorised representative has no access to the internet, he may also request the administrator of the account to initiate transactions on his behalf, provided that the administrator allows such requests and access was not suspended in accordance with Article 27.

5. The Data Exchange and Technical Specifications may set a maximum number of authorised representatives and additional authorised representatives for each account type. A national administrator may set a lower maximum for its account, but the minimum number of authorised representatives must be three.

6. Authorised representatives and additional authorised representatives must be natural persons over 18 years. All authorised representatives and additional authorised representatives of a single account must be different persons but the same person can be an authorised representative or an additional authorised representative on more than one account. The Member State of the national administrator may require that at least one of the authorised representatives of user accounts must be a permanent resident in the Member State of the national administrator administering the account.

Amendments

1 Substituted by Commission Regulation (EU) No 1193/2011 of 18 November 2011 establishing a Union Registry for the trading period commencing on 1 January 2013, and subsequent trading periods, of the Union emissions trading scheme pursuant to Directive 2003/87/EC of the European Parliament and of the Council and Decision No 280/2004/EC of the European Parliament and of the Council and amending Commission Regulations (EC) No 2216/2004 and (EU) No 920/2010, Article 89(13).

2 Inserted by Commission Regulation (EU) No 1193/2011 of 18 November 2011 establishing a Union Registry for the trading period commencing on 1 January 2013, and subsequent trading periods, of the Union emissions trading scheme pursuant to Directive 2003/87/EC of the European Parliament and of the Council and Decision No 280/2004/EC of the European Parliament and of the Council and amending Commission Regulations (EC) No 2216/2004 and (EU) No 920/2010, Article 89(14).

Article 20

Nominating and approval of authorised representatives and additional authorised representatives

1. When requesting the opening of an account, the person requesting the account opening shall nominate at least two authorised representatives, and that person may nominate additional authorised representatives if this is permitted by the administrator of the account.

2. When nominating an authorised representative or additional authorised representative, the person requesting the account opening shall provide the information required by the administrator. That information shall include at least the documents and identification information on the nominee set out in Annex IX.

3. Within 20 working days of the receipt of a complete set of information required in accordance with paragraph 2 the national administrator shall approve an authorised representative or additional authorised representative, or inform the person requesting the account opening that it refuses to approve. Where evaluation of the nominee information requires more time, the administrator may once extend the evaluation process by up to 20 additional working days, and notify the extension to the person requesting the account opening.

[3a. The national administrator shall verify whether the information and documents provided for nominating an authorised representative or additional authorised representative are complete, up to date, accurate and true.

3b. A national administrator may refuse to approve an authorised representative or additional authorised representative:

(a) if the information and documents provided are incomplete, out of date or otherwise inaccurate or false;

(b) if the prospective representative is under investigation or has been convicted in the preceding five years for fraud involving allowances or Kyoto units, money laundering, terrorist financing or other serious crimes for which the account may be an instrument;

(c) for reasons set out in national law.][1]

4. If the national administrator refused to approve an authorised representative or additional authorised representative, the person requesting the account opening may object to this refusal

with the competent authority or the relevant authority under national law, who shall either instruct the national administrator to give its approval or uphold the refusal in a reasoned decision. Reasons for refusing the approval may be that the person nominated as authorised representative or additional authorised representative is under investigation for being involved in fraud involving allowances or Kyoto units, money laundering, terrorist financing or other serious crimes to which the account may be an instrument, or any other reason set out in national law.

5. The authorised representative of the ETS central clearing account shall act as the authorised representative of the Central Administrator. The authorised representative of each national allowance holding account shall act as the authorised representative of the national administrator for the Member State holding the national allowance holding account.

Amendment

1 Inserted by Commission Regulation (EU) No 1193/2011 of 18 November 2011 establishing a Union Registry for the trading period commencing on 1 January 2013, and subsequent trading periods, of the Union emissions trading scheme pursuant to Directive 2003/87/EC of the European Parliament and of the Council and Decision No 280/2004/EC of the European Parliament and of the Council and amending Commission Regulations (EC) No 2216/2004 and (EU) No 920/2010, Article 89(15).

Article 21

Updating of account information and information on authorised representatives

1. All account holders shall notify the administrator of the account within 10 working days of any changes to the information submitted for the opening of an account, and for the nomination of an authorised representative or additional authorised representative. Aircraft operators shall notify the administrator of their account within 10 working days if they have undergone a merger of two or more aircraft operators or if they have split into two or more aircraft operators. If the account holder was required to provide evidence for a particular piece of information upon opening the account or the nomination of an authorised representative or additional authorised representative, the notification of changes shall likewise be accompanied with the required evidence. Within 15 working days of the receipt of such a notification and the accompanying evidence, the administrator of the account shall update the information on the account holder or refuse updating and inform the account holder thereof. Objections to such refusals may be raised with the competent authority or the relevant authority under national law in accordance with Articles 13(4), 14(4) or 20(4).

2. The holder of a person holding account, a trading platform holding account, a verifier account or an aircraft operator holding account may not sell or divest of the ownership of its account to another person. The account holder of an operator holding account may only sell or divest of its operator holding account together with the installation linked to the operator holding account.

3. An authorised representative or additional authorised representative may not transfer its status as such to another person.

4. Any account holder may notify the recalling of authorised representatives, provided that there remain at least two authorised representatives. Within 10 working days of the receipt of such a notification, the responsible administrator shall remove the authorised representative.

5. Any account holder may nominate new authorised representatives or additional authorised representatives in accordance with the procedure set out in Article 20.

6. If the administering Member State of an aircraft operator changes in accordance with the procedure set out in Article 18a of Directive 2003/87/EC or due to the enlargement of the European Union the Central Administrator shall update the national administrator of the corresponding aircraft operator holding account. Where the administrator of an aircraft operator holding account changes, the new administrator may require the aircraft operator to submit the account opening information required by the new administrator in accordance

with Article 16 and the information required by the new administrator about authorised representatives in accordance with Article 20.

7. Except for the exception provided for in paragraph 6 above, the Member State responsible for managing an account shall not change.

[Article 21a

Trusted account list][1]

[1. From 30 June 2012, operator holding accounts, aircraft operator holding accounts, person holding accounts and trading accounts may have a trusted account list in the Union Registry.

2. Accounts held by the same account holder shall be automatically included on the trusted account list.

3. Changes to the trusted account list shall be initiated and completed through the procedure set out in Article 32a for transactions specified in Chapter VI. The change shall be confirmed by an additional authorised representative, or, if no additional authorised representative has been nominated, by another authorised representative. The delay specified in Article 32a(4) shall not apply for the deletion of accounts from the trusted account list; for all other changes to the trusted account list the delay shall be seven days.][1]

Amendment

1 Inserted by Commission Regulation (EU) No 1193/2011 of 18 November 2011 establishing a Union Registry for the trading period commencing on 1 January 2013, and subsequent trading periods, of the Union emissions trading scheme pursuant to Directive 2003/87/EC of the European Parliament and of the Council and Decision No 280/2004/EC of the European Parliament and of the Council and amending Commission Regulations (EC) No 2216/2004 and (EU) No 920/2010, Article 89(16).

Section 3
Closure of accounts

Article 22

Closure of KP Party accounts, management accounts, person holding accounts and trading platform holding accounts

Within 10 working days of the receipt of a request from the account holder to close a KP Party account in the Union registry, a management account, a person holding account or a trading platform holding account administered by it, the administrator shall close the account.

Article 23

Closure of operator holding accounts

1. The competent authority shall notify the national administrator within 10 working days of a greenhouse gas emissions permit being revoked or surrendered for an installation that is, as a result, not covered by any such permit. The competent authority shall also notify the national administrator within 10 working days when it learns that an installation has closed without notifying the competent authority. Within 10 working days of being notified by the competent authority, the national administrator shall record in the Union registry the date on which the greenhouse gas emissions permit expires. Where an installation closes without the permit expiring, the date of closure notified by the competent authority shall be recorded as the permit expiry date.

2. The national administrator may close operator holding accounts by 30 June of the year after the year in which the permit expired if the relevant installation has surrendered an amount of allowances and Kyoto units at least equal to its verified emissions.

Article 24

Closure of aircraft operator holding accounts

Aircraft operator holding accounts shall only be closed by the national administrator if it was instructed by the competent authority to do so because the competent authority has discovered that the aircraft operator merged into another aircraft operator or the aircraft operator has permanently ceased all its operations covered by Annex I to Directive 2003/87/EC, either through a notification by the account holder or through other evidence.

Article 25

Closure of verifier accounts

1. Within 10 working days of the receipt of a request from a verifier to close its account, the national administrator shall close the verifier account.

2. The competent authority may also instruct the national administrator to close a verifier account where one of the following conditions is fulfilled:
(a) the verifier's accreditation has expired or was withdrawn;
(b) the verifier ceased its operations.

Article 26

Positive balance on accounts under closure

1. If there is a positive balance of allowances or Kyoto units on an account which an administrator is to close in accordance with Articles 22 to 25 and 28, the administrator shall first request the account holder to specify another account administered by the same administrator to which such allowances or Kyoto units shall then be transferred. If the account holder has not responded to the administrator's request within 40 working days, the administrator may transfer the allowances to its national allowance holding account in the Union registry and the Kyoto units to a KP Party holding account in its KP registry.

2. If there is a positive balance of allowances or Kyoto units on an account to which access was suspended in accordance with Article 27(3), the competent authority may require in its instruction in accordance with Article 28(1) that the allowances are moved immediately to the relevant national allowance holding account and the Kyoto units are moved immediately to the relevant KP Party holding account.

Section 4
Suspension of access to accounts

Article 27

Suspension of access to accounts

1. An administrator may suspend the access of an authorised representative or an additional authorised representative to any accounts in its registry or to processes to which that authorised representative would otherwise have access if the administrator knows or has reasonable grounds to believe that the authorised representative has:
(a) attempted to access accounts or processes which he is not authorised to access;
(b) repeatedly attempted to access an account or a process using a non-matching username and password; or
(c) attempted, or is attempting, to undermine the security of the registry or the registries system.

2. An administrator may suspend the access of all authorised representatives or additional authorised representatives to a specific account where one of the following conditions is fulfilled:

(a) the account holder died without a legal successor or ceased to exist as a legal person;
(b) the account holder did not pay its fees;
(c) the account holder violated the terms and conditions applicable to the account;
(d) the account holder did not agree to the changes in the terms and conditions set by the national administrator and the Central Administrator;
(e) the account holder did not provide evidence concerning the changes to account information, or evidence concerning new account information requirements;
(f) the account holder failed to maintain the required minimum number of authorised representatives for the account;
(g) the account holder failed to maintain compliance with the Member State requirement to have an authorised representative with a permanent residence in the Member State of the administrator of the account;
(h) the account holder failed to maintain compliance with the Member State requirement that the account holder have a permanent residence or registration in the Member State of the administrator of the account.

[2a. An administrator may suspend the access of all authorised representatives or additional authorised representatives to a specific account and the possibility to initiate processes from that account:

(a) for a maximum period of two weeks if the administrator has reasonable grounds to believe that the account was used or will be used for fraud, money laundering, terrorist financing or other serious crimes; or
(b) on the basis of and in accordance with national law provisions that pursue a legitimate objective.][1]

3. The national administrator may suspend access to a person holding account or a trading platform holding account if it considers that their opening should have been refused in accordance with Article 13(3) or Article 14(3).

4. The administrator of the account shall lift the suspension immediately once the situation giving rise to the suspension is resolved.

5. The account holder may object to the suspension of its access in accordance with paragraphs 1 and 3 with the competent authority or the relevant authority under national law within 30 calendar days, who shall either instruct the national administrator to reinstate access or uphold the suspension in a reasoned decision.

6. The competent authority, or in the case of accounts in the Union registry, the Central administrator may also instruct the administrator to implement a suspension.

7. When access to a trading platform holding account is suspended, the administrator shall also suspend access enabled for the trading platform to user accounts in accordance with Article 19(3). When access of authorised representatives and additional authorised representatives of a trading platform holding account is suspended, the administrator shall also suspend their access enabled for the trading platform to user accounts in accordance with Article 19(3).

8. Where the holder of an operator holding account or aircraft operator holding account is prevented from surrendering in the 10 working days preceding the surrender deadline laid down in Article 12(2a) and 12(3) of Directive 2003/87/EC due to suspensions in accordance with paragraphs 1 and 2, the national administrator shall, if so requested by the account holder and following submission of the authorised representative's identity by means of supporting evidence, surrender the number of allowances and ERUs and CERs specified by the account holder.

Amendment

1 Inserted by Commission Regulation (EU) No 1193/2011 of 18 November 2011 establishing a Union Registry for the trading period commencing on 1 January 2013, and subsequent trading periods, of the Union

emissions trading scheme pursuant to Directive 2003/87/EC of the European Parliament and of the Council and Decision No 280/2004/EC of the European Parliament and of the Council and amending Commission Regulations (EC) No 2216/2004 and (EU) No 920/2010, Article 89(17).

Article 28

Closure of accounts and removal of authorised representative on the administrator's initiative

1. If the situation giving rise to the suspension of access to accounts pursuant to Article 27 is not resolved within a reasonable period despite repeated notifications, the competent authority may instruct the national administrator to close those person holding accounts or trading platform holding accounts where access is suspended.

2. If a person holding account has a zero balance and no transactions have been recorded during a year, the national administrator may notify the account holder that the person holding account will be closed within 40 working days unless the national administrator receives within that period a request from the account holder that the person holding account be maintained. If the national administrator does not receive any such request from the account holder, the national administrator may close the account.

3. The national administrator shall close any operator holding account when the competent authority has instructed the national administrator to close the account because there is no reasonable prospect of further allowances being surrendered by the installation's operator.

4. The national administrator may remove an authorised representative or an additional authorised representative if it considers that the approval of the authorised representative or an additional authorised representative should have been refused in accordance with Article 20(3), and in particular if it discovers that the documents and identification information provided in upon nomination were fraudulent or erroneous.

5. The account holder may object to the closure of its account in accordance with paragraph 1 or the removal of its authorised representative or additional authorised representative in accordance with paragraph 4 with the competent authority within 30 calendar days, who shall either instruct the national administrator to reinstate the account or the authorised representative or additional authorised representative or uphold the closure or removal in a reasoned decision.

Chapter V
Verified emissions and compliance

Article 29

Verified emissions data for an installation or aircraft operator

1. Before submitting annual emissions data to the Union registry, each operator and aircraft operator shall select a verifier from the verifiers registered at the national administrator administering its account. If an operator or aircraft operator is also a verifier, it may not select itself as verifier.

2. The national administrator shall enter emissions data for a year between 1 January and 31 March of the following year. Emissions data for an installation may also be entered for a year during the course of that year if the installation's greenhouse gas permit has already expired. The competent authority may decide that instead of the national administrator, the account holder or the verifier (including those competent authorities acting as verifiers) shall be responsible for entering the emissions data within the deadline set out above.

3. Annual emissions data shall be submitted using the format set out in Annex X.

[4. Upon the satisfactory verification in accordance with Article 15, first paragraph of Directive 2003/87/EC of an operator's report on the emissions from an installation during a previous year, or of an aircraft operator's report on the emissions from all aviation activities it performed during a previous year, the verifier or the competent authority shall approve the annual verified emissions.

5. The emissions approved in accordance with paragraph 4 shall be marked as verified in the Union Registry by the national administrator or the competent authority. The competent authority may decide that instead of the national administrator, the verifier shall be responsible for marking emissions as verified in the Union Registry.][1]

6. The competent authority may instruct the national administrator to correct the annual verified emissions for an installation or an aircraft operator to ensure compliance with the detailed requirements established by the Member State pursuant to Annex V to Directive 2003/87/EC, by entering the corrected verified or estimated emissions for that installation or an aircraft operator for that year into the records of the Union registry.

7. Where, on 1 May of each year, no verified emissions figure has been recorded in the Union registry for an installation or an aircraft operator for a previous year or the verified emissions figure was proven to be incorrect, any substitute emissions figure estimate entered in the Union registry shall be calculated as closely as possible in accordance with the detailed requirements established by the Member State pursuant to Annex V to Directive 2003/87/EC.

Amendment

1 Substituted by Commission Regulation (EU) No 1193/2011 of 18 November 2011 establishing a Union Registry for the trading period commencing on 1 January 2013, and subsequent trading periods, of the Union emissions trading scheme pursuant to Directive 2003/87/EC of the European Parliament and of the Council and Decision No 280/2004/EC of the European Parliament and of the Council and amending Commission Regulations (EC) No 2216/2004 and (EU) No 920/2010, Article 89(18).

Article 30

Blocking of accounts due to a failure to submit verified emissions

1. If, on 1 April of each year the annual verified emissions of an installation or aircraft operator for the preceding year have not been recorded in the Union registry, the Union registry shall set the corresponding operator holding account or aircraft operator holding account to blocked status.

2. When all overdue verified emissions of the installation or aircraft operator for the year have been recorded in the Union registry, the Union registry shall set the account to open status.

Article 31

Calculation of compliance status figures

1. On 1 May of each year, the Union registry shall determine the compliance status figure for the preceding year for every installation and aircraft operator with an open or blocked operator holding account or aircraft operator holding account by calculating the sum of all allowances, CERs and ERUs surrendered for the current period minus the sum of all verified emissions in the current period up to and including the current year, plus a correction factor.

2. The correction factor referred to in paragraph 1 shall be zero if the compliance status figure of the last year of the previous period was greater than zero, but shall remain as the compliance status figure of the last year of the previous period if this figure is less than or equal to zero.

3. The Union registry shall record the compliance status figure for every installation and aircraft operator for each year.

Article 32

Inactive aircraft operator holding accounts

1. If, by the deadline set out in Article 12(2a) of Directive 2003/87/EC for surrendering allowances, a verified emissions value of 0 is entered in the Union registry for an aircraft operator for the previous year in accordance with Article 29, the Union registry shall set the corresponding aircraft operator holding account to inactive status.

2. The Union registry shall set the account to open status when the verified emissions value for year before the current year is not 0.

Chapter VI
Transactions

Section 1
Allocation and issue of allowances

[Article 32a

Execution of transfers][1]

[1. For all transactions specified in Chapter VI that are not initiated by a trading platform, an out-of-band confirmation shall be required by the Union Registry before the transaction can be initiated. A transaction shall only be initiated where an additional authorised representative whose approval is required pursuant to Article 19(2), has confirmed the transaction out of band.

2. For all transfers of allowances and Kyoto units specified in Articles 43 and 44, the transfer shall be initiated immediately if it is confirmed between 10:00 and 16:00 central European time between Monday and Friday inclusive, with the exception of public holidays in the Member States deciding to suspend the running of the delay pursuant to paragraph 3. A transfer confirmed at any other time shall be initiated on the next day, Monday to Friday, at 10:00 central European time.

3. For all transfers of allowances and Kyoto units specified in Articles 43 and 44, except for transfers from a trading account to an account on the trusted account list of that account, a delay of 26 hours shall apply between the initiation and the transfer being communicated for finalisation pursuant to Article 70. The running of this delay shall be suspended between 00:00 and 24:00 central European time on Saturdays and Sundays. Member States may decide to also suspend the running of this delay between 00:00 and 24:00 central European time on national public holidays for a given year, subject to publication of that decision by 1 December of the previous year.

4. If an account representative suspects that a transfer was initiated fraudulently, at the latest two hours before the end of the delay provided in paragraph 3 they may request the national administrator to cancel the transfer on their behalf before the transfer is communicated for finalisation. The account holder shall report the suspected fraud to the competent national law enforcement authority immediately following the request. That report shall be forwarded to the national administrator within seven days.

5. Upon initiation pursuant to paragraphs 1 and 2, a notification shall be sent to all account representatives indicating the proposed initiation of the transfer.][1]

Amendment

1 Inserted by Commission Regulation (EU) No 1193/2011 of 18 November 2011 establishing a Union Registry for the trading period commencing on 1 January 2013, and subsequent trading periods, of the Union emissions trading scheme pursuant to Directive 2003/87/EC of the European Parliament and of the Council and Decision No 280/2004/EC of the European Parliament and of the Council and amending Commission Regulations (EC) No 2216/2004 and (EU) No 920/2010, Article 89(19).

[Article 32b

Nature of allowances and finality of transactions][1]

[1. An allowance or Kyoto unit shall be a fungible, dematerialised instrument that is tradable on the market.

2. The dematerialised nature of allowances and Kyoto units shall imply that the record of the Union Registry shall constitute prima facie and sufficient evidence of title over an allowance or Kyoto unit, and of any other matter which is by this Regulation directed or authorised to be recorded in the registry.

3. The fungibility of allowances and Kyoto units shall imply that any recovery or restitution obligations that may arise under national law in respect of an allowance or Kyoto unit shall only apply to the allowance or Kyoto unit in kind. In particular:

(a) subject to Article 51 and the reconciliation process foreseen in Article 69 of this Regulation, a transaction shall become final and irrevocable upon its finalisation pursuant to Article 70. Without prejudice to any provision of or remedy under national law that may result in a requirement or order to execute a new transaction in the registry, no law, regulation, rule or practice on the setting aside of contracts or transactions shall lead to the unwinding in the registry of a transaction that has become final and irrevocable under this Regulation;

(b) nothing within this Article shall prevent an account holder or a third party from exercising any right or claim resulting from the underlying transaction that they may have in law, including to recovery, restitution, or damages, in respect of a transaction that has become final in the registry, for instance in case of fraud or technical error, as long as this does not lead to the reversal, revocation or unwinding of the transaction in the registry.

4. A purchaser and holder of an allowance or Kyoto unit acting in good faith shall acquire title to an allowance or Kyoto unit free of any defects in the title of the transferor.][1]

Amendment

1 Inserted by Commission Regulation (EU) No 1193/2011 of 18 November 2011 establishing a Union Registry for the trading period commencing on 1 January 2013, and subsequent trading periods, of the Union emissions trading scheme pursuant to Directive 2003/87/EC of the European Parliament and of the Council and Decision No 280/2004/EC of the European Parliament and of the Council and amending Commission Regulations (EC) No 2216/2004 and (EU) No 920/2010, Article 89(19).

Article 33

National allocation plan tables

1. The EUTL shall contain one national allocation plan table for each Member State for the 2008–2012 period. National allocation plan tables shall include the following information:

(a) total number of allowances to issue to installations: in a single cell the total number of allowances that will be issued to installations for the period covered by the national allocation plan;

(b) total number of allowances not allocated to incumbent installations (reserve): in a single cell the total number of allowances (issued or purchased) that are set aside for new entrant installations and auctioning for the period covered by the national allocation plan;

(c) years: in individual cells for each of the years covered in the national allocation plan in ascending order;

(d) Installation identification code of every installation that has a valid permit at the moment: in individual cells in ascending order. The installations listed shall include installations unilaterally included under Article 24 of Directive 2003/87/EC and shall not include any installations temporarily excluded under Article 27 of Directive 2003/87/EC;

(e) Allocated allowances: the allowances to be allocated for a specified year for a specified installation shall be entered into the cell connecting that year to that installation's identification code.

2. The national allocation plan tables shall follow the format set out in Annex XI.

Article 34

Union aviation allocation table

1. The EUTL shall contain a single Union aviation allocation table for the year 2012. This table shall tabulate the following information:

(a) the total number of Chapter II allowances to be allocated in the Union in 2012;

(b) the number of Chapter II allowances already allocated for free to each account holder listed in the table;

(c) the number of Chapter II allowances not yet allocated by the Member States, shown separately for each Member State;

[(d) the identity of the receivers of the allocation (in the case of allowances allocated through auction, the receiver shall be the account set up for that purpose by Commission Regulation (EU) No 1193/2011).][1]

2. The Union aviation allocation table shall follow the format set out in Annex XII.

Amendment

1 Substituted by Commission Regulation (EU) No 1193/2011 of 18 November 2011 establishing a Union Registry for the trading period commencing on 1 January 2013, and subsequent trading periods, of the Union emissions trading scheme pursuant to Directive 2003/87/EC of the European Parliament and of the Council and Decision No 280/2004/EC of the European Parliament and of the Council and amending Commission Regulations (EC) No 2216/2004 and (EU) No 920/2010, Article 89(20).

Article 35

Entry into the EUTL of national allocation plan tables

1. At least 12 months before the start of the 2008-2012 period, each Member State shall notify to the Commission its national allocation plan table, corresponding to the decision taken under Article 11(2)of Directive 2003/87/EC.

2. If the national allocation plan table is based upon the national allocation plan notified to the Commission which was not rejected under Article 9(3) of Directive 2003/87/EC or on which the Commission has accepted proposed amendments, the Commission shall instruct the Central Administrator to enter the national allocation plan table into the EUTL.

Article 36

Entry of allocation decisions in the Union aviation allocation table

If the Chapter II allowance allocation decisions taken by Member States under Article 3e(4), of Directive 2003/87/EC with respect to the year 2012 are in conformity with Directive 2003/87/EC, the Commission shall instruct the Central Administrator to enter the allocation decisions into the Union aviation allocation table in the EUTL.

Article 37

Corrections of national allocation plan tables

1. For the 2008–2012 period, the national administrator shall carry out corrections to the national allocation plan table in the EUTL without notifying the Commission in advance, where:

(a) a new entrant was granted an allocation;
(b) the Member State has replenished the reserve through the purchase of allowances;
(c) an installation's permit has expired and any allocation not yet delivered to its account are moved to the reserve;
(d) an installation was split into two or more installations;
(e) two or more installations were merged into one installation.

Those corrections shall not change the total issued quantity of allowances set out in the national allocation plan table.

2. A Member State shall notify in advance any correction other than those referred to in paragraph 1 to its national allocation plan together with each corresponding correction in its national allocation plan table to the Commission. If the correction to the national allocation plan table is based upon the national allocation plan notified to the Commission which was not rejected under Article 9(3) of Directive 2003/87/EC or on which the Commission has accepted amendments and that correction results from improvements in data, the Commission shall instruct the Central Administrator to enter the corresponding correction into the national allocation plan table held in the EUTL.

3. Subsequent to any correction made pursuant to paragraph 2 which occurs after allowances have been issued or allocated, and which reduces the total quantity of allowances for the 2008–2012 period, the national administrator shall transfer the number and type of allowances specified by the Union registry to the Union allowance deletion account for the relevant period.

Article 38

Corrections of the Union aviation allocation table

1. The national administrator may carry out the corresponding corrections to the Union aviation allocation table in the EUTL without notifying the Commission in advance, where:
(a) a new aircraft operator started operating;
(b) an auctioneer was awarded Chapter II allowances for auctioning;
(c) an aircraft operator was split into two or more aircraft operators;
(d) two or more aircraft operators have merged into a single aircraft operator.

2. Such corrections shall not change the total quantity of Chapter II allowances set out in the Union aviation allocation table.

3. A Member State shall notify any correction other than those referred to in paragraph 1. and required to correct an over-allocation caused by an error by the Commission or a Member State to its Chapter II allowance allocation decision taken under Article 3e, paragraph (4) of Directive 2003/87/EC to the Commission. If the correction is in conformity with Directive 2003/87/EC, the Commission shall instruct the Central Administrator to correct the Union aviation allocation table on the basis of this decision and enter it into the EUTL.

4. After any correction made pursuant to paragraph 2. which occurs after Chapter II allowances have been allocated in accordance with Article 41 and which reduces the total quantity of Chapter II allowances for the 2008–2012 period, the national administrator shall, transfer the number of Chapter II allowances specified by the Central administrator to the Union allowance deletion account for the relevant period.

5. If a merger between aircraft operators involves aircraft operators that are administered by different Member States, the correction under paragraph (1)(d) shall be initiated by the national administrator administering the aircraft operator whose allocation is to be merged into the allocation of another aircraft operator. Before carrying out the correction, consent shall be obtained from the national administrator administering the aircraft operator whose allocation will incorporate the allocation of the merged aircraft operator.

Article 39

Issuance of Chapter III allowances

1. After the national allocation plan table has been entered into the EUTL, the national administrator shall, by 28 February of the first year of the 2008–12 period:

(a) transfer an amount of AAUs issued for the 2008–2012 period that is equal to the quantity of Chapter III allowances to be issued from a KP Party holding account to the ETS AAU deposit account;

(b) issue the total quantity of Chapter III allowances set out in the national allocation plan table into its national allowance holding account in the Union registry.

2. Prior to the action referred to in paragraph 1, KP registry administrators shall notify the account ID of the designated ETS AAU deposit account in their KP registry to the Central Administrator.

3. The Union registry shall assign each allowance a unique unit identification code upon their issuance in accordance with paragraph 1.

4. Member States with no KP registry shall not carry out the action under point (a) of paragraph 1.

Article 40

Allocation of Chapter III allowances

1. Without prejudice to Articles 37 and 47, by 28 February of each year, the national administrator shall transfer from the national allowance holding account to the relevant open operator holding account the proportion of the total quantity of Chapter III allowances issued which has been allocated to the corresponding installation for that year in accordance with the relevant section of the national allocation plan table.

2. Where foreseen for an installation in the national allocation plan of the Member State, the national administrator may transfer that proportion at a later date of each year.

3. If an installation is allocated additional Chapter III allowances in the national allocation plan table as a result of corrections in accordance with Article 37, the national administrator shall transfer from the national allowance holding account to the relevant open operator holding account the additionally allocated Chapter III allowances for the current year at the time when instructed to do so by the competent authority.

Article 41

Allocation of Chapter II allowances

1. After the Union aviation allocation table has been entered into the EUTL, the national administrator shall by 28 February 2012, create a quantity of Chapter II allowances on each open aircraft operator holding account that is equal to the allocation set out in the Union aviation allocation table for the holder of that account for that year.

2. The Union registry shall assign each allowance a unique unit identification code upon their creation in accordance with paragraph 1.

3. If an account holder is allocated additional Chapter II allowances in the Union aviation allocation table as a result of corrections in accordance with Article 38, the national administrator shall, when instructed by the competent authority, create an additional quantity of allocated Chapter II allowances on each open aircraft operator holding account that is equal to the additional allocation set out in the Union aviation allocation table for the holder of that account for the current year.

4. Where an inactive aircraft operator holding account does not receive allowances under paragraph 1, those allowances shall not be created in the account should it be subsequently set to open status.

Article 42

Allocation of Chapter III allowances following their sale by Member State

During the 2008–2012 period, if instructed to do so by the competent authority, following a sale of 2008–2012 Chapter III allowances by a Member State, the national administrator shall transfer a quantity of Chapter III allowances from the national allowance holding account to the holding account designated by the competent authority.

Section 2
Transfers of allowances and Kyoto units

[Article 43

Transfers of allowances by account holders][1]

[1. Subject to paragraph 2, upon request of an account holder, the Union Registry shall carry out any transfer of allowances held in its Union Registry account to any other account in the Union Registry, unless such transfer is prevented by the status of the initiating account or the type of allowances that may be held in the acquiring account in accordance with Article 8(3).

2. From 30 June 2012, the operator holding accounts, aircraft operator holding accounts, person holding accounts and trading platforms may only transfer allowances to an account on the trusted account list set up pursuant to Article 21a.][1]

Amendment

1 Substituted by Commission Regulation (EU) No 1193/2011 of 18 November 2011 establishing a Union Registry for the trading period commencing on 1 January 2013, and subsequent trading periods, of the Union emissions trading scheme pursuant to Directive 2003/87/EC of the European Parliament and of the Council and Decision No 280/2004/EC of the European Parliament and of the Council and amending Commission Regulations (EC) No 2216/2004 and (EU) No 920/2010, Article 89(21).

[Article 44

Transfers of Kyoto units by account holders][1]

[1. Subject to paragraph 2, upon request of an account holder, the Union Registry shall carry out any transfer of Kyoto units held in a Union registry account to any other account in the Union Registry or in a KP registry, unless such transfer is prevented by the status of the initiating account or the Kyoto units that may be held in the acquiring account in accordance with Article 8(3).

2. From 30 June 2012, the operator holding accounts, aircraft operator holding accounts, person holding accounts and trading platforms may only transfer Kyoto units to an account on the trusted account list set up pursuant to Article 21a.][1]

Amendment

1 Substituted by Commission Regulation (EU) No 1193/2011 of 18 November 2011 establishing a Union Registry for the trading period commencing on 1 January 2013, and subsequent trading periods, of the Union emissions trading scheme pursuant to Directive 2003/87/EC of the European Parliament and of the Council and Decision No 280/2004/EC of the European Parliament and of the Council and amending Commission Regulations (EC) No 2216/2004 and (EU) No 920/2010, Article 89(21).

Article 45

Minimum holding of Chapter III allowances in Union registry holding accounts administered by the same Member State

1. If a proposed transfer of allowances by an account holder in accordance with Article 43 would result in the total amount of 2008–12 period Chapter III allowances held in all the Union registry accounts administered by the national administrator of a particular Member State dropping below the quantity of Kyoto units required to be held in the KP registry of that Member State under Decision 11/CMP.1 as the commitment period reserve, minus the amount of Kyoto units currently held in the KP registry of that Member State outside of the ETS AAU deposit account and the cancellation account, the EUTL shall reject the proposed transfer.

2. If a proposed transfer of allowances by an account holder in accordance with Article 43 would result in the total amount of 2008–2012 period Chapter III allowances held in all the Union registry accounts administered by the national administrators of the oldest fifteen Member States dropping below the quantity of Kyoto units required to be held in the KP registries of these Member States under Decision 11/CMP.1 as the commitment period reserve of the European Union, minus the amount of Kyoto units currently held in the KP registries of those Member States outside of the ETS AAU deposit accounts and the cancellation accounts, the EUTL shall reject the proposed transfer.

Section 3
Surrender of allowances, ERUs and CERs

Article 46

Surrender of allowances

1. An operator or aircraft operator shall surrender allowances for the 2008–2012 period by proposing to the Union registry to:

(a) move a specified number of 2008–12 period allowances from the relevant operator holding account or aircraft operator holding account into the Union allowance deletion account;

(b) record the number and type of transferred allowances as surrendered for the emissions of the operator's installation or the emissions of the aircraft operator in the current period.

2. Chapter II allowances may only be surrendered by aircraft operators.

3. An allowance that was already surrendered may not be surrendered again.

Article 47

Surrender of allowances on instruction of the competent authority

If instructed to do so by the competent authority, the national administrator shall surrender part or all of the proportion of the total quantity of allowances issued which has been allocated to an installation or an aircraft operator for a specific year, by recording the number of surrendered allowances for that installation or aircraft operator for the current period.

Article 48

The surrender of CERs and ERUs

1. The surrender of ERUs and CERs by an operator in accordance with Article 11a of Directive 2003/87/EC shall take place through an operator proposing to the Union registry to:

(a) move a specified number of 2008–2012 period CERs or ERUs from the relevant operator holding account into:
 (i) a KP Party holding account of the administering Member State, in the case of accounts administered by Member States with a KP registry;
 (ii) the cancellation account of the Union registry, in the case of accounts administered by Member States with no KP registry;
(b) record the number of transferred CERs and ERUs as surrendered for the emissions of the operator's installation in the current period.

2. The surrender of ERUs and CERs by an aircraft operator in accordance with Article 11a of Directive 2003/87/EC shall take place through the aircraft operator proposing to the Union registry to:
(a) move a specified number of 2008–2012 period CERs or ERUs from the relevant aircraft operator holding account into the aviation surrender set-aside account in the Union registry;
(b) record the number of transferred CERs and ERUs as surrendered for the emissions of the aircraft operator in the current period.

3. The Union registry shall only allow surrenders of CERs and ERUs up to:
(a) the maximum quantity set by the national administrator of an operator holding account, in the case of operators;
(b) for 2012, 15 % of the number of allowances required to be surrendered pursuant to Article 12(2a) of Directive 2003/87/EC in the case of aircraft operators.

4. The Union registry shall reject any request to surrender CERs and ERUs that would surpass the maximum amount of CERs and ERUs that may be surrendered by the operators of a Member State in accordance with the national allocation plan of the Member State.

5. The Union registry shall reject any request to surrender CERs or ERUs that are prohibited from being used in the ETS in accordance with Article 11a of Directive 2003/87/EC.

6. A CER or ERU that was already surrendered may not be surrendered again nor transferred to an operator or person holding account in the EU ETS.

7. The Union registry shall provide automated processes to ensure that account holders cannot surrender units into incorrect accounts under Articles 46 and 48.

Section 4
Deletion of allowances and cancellation of Kyoto units

Article 49

Deletion of allowances

1. The Union registry shall carry out any request from an account holder pursuant to Article 12(4) of Directive 2003/87/EC to delete allowances held in the accounts of the account holder by:
(a) transferring a specified number of allowances from the relevant account into the Union allowance deletion account; and
(b) recording the number of transferred allowances as deleted for the current year.

2. Deleted allowances shall not be recorded as surrendered for any emissions.

3. The Union registry shall reject the request for the deletion of allowances if it is initiated by an account administered by a Member State that has no KP registry and it would result in a minimum deposited quantity calculated for that Member State in accordance with Article 52 that is lower than the gateway quantity calculated for that Member State in accordance with Article 53.

[Article 50

Cancellation of Kyoto units][1]

[The Union Registry shall carry out any request from an account holder pursuant to Article 12(4) of Directive 2003/87/EC to cancel Kyoto units held in the accounts of the account holder by transferring a specified type and number of Kyoto units from the relevant account into the cancellation account of the account administrator's KP registry or the cancellation account of the Union Registry.][1]

Amendment

1 Substituted by Commission Regulation (EU) No 1193/2011 of 18 November 2011 establishing a Union Registry for the trading period commencing on 1 January 2013, and subsequent trading periods, of the Union emissions trading scheme pursuant to Directive 2003/87/EC of the European Parliament and of the Council and Decision No 280/2004/EC of the European Parliament and of the Council and amending Commission Regulations (EC) No 2216/2004 and (EU) No 920/2010, Article 89(22).

Section 5
Transaction reversal

Article 51

Reversal of finalised processes initiated in error

1. If an account holder or a registry administrator acting on behalf of the account holder unintentionally or erroneously initiated one of the transactions listed in paragraph 2, the account holder may propose to the administrator of its account to carry out a reversal of the completed transaction in a written request. The request shall be duly signed by the authorised representative or representatives of the account holder that are authorised to initiate the type of transaction to be reversed and shall be posted within 5 working days of the finalisation of the process. The request shall contain a statement indicating that the transaction was initiated erroneously or unintentionally.

2. Account holders may propose the reversal of the following transactions:
(a) allocation of Chapter III allowances;
(b) allocation of Chapter II allowances;
(c) surrender of allowances;
(d) surrender of CERs and ERUs;
(e) deletion of allowances;
(f) cancellation of Kyoto units.

3. If the administrator of the account establishes that the request fulfils the conditions under paragraph 1 and the administrator agrees with the request, it may propose the reversal of the transaction in the Union registry.

4. The Union registry shall accept the proposal for reversal, block the units that are to be transferred by the reversal and forward the proposal to the Central Administrator provided that all of the following conditions are met:
[(a) the transaction to be reversed was not completed more than 30 working days prior to the account administrator's proposal in accordance with paragraph 3, except for allocation of Chapter III allowances and allocation of Chapter II allowances;][1]
(b) no operator would become non-compliant for a previous year as a result of the reversal;
(c) the destination account of the transaction to be reversed still holds the amount of units of the type that were involved in the transaction to be reversed;
(d) the transaction to be reversed was not yet followed up by a deduction in accordance with Article 52 from the minimum deposited quantity after an accounting transfer made on the basis of the transaction to be reversed;
(e) the allocation of Chapter III allowances to be reversed was carried out after the expiry date of the installation's permit.

5. The Central Administrator shall approve the proposal within 10 working days. Where the transaction to be reversed involves transfers of Kyoto units from one KP registry to another KP registry, this approval shall only be given if the ITL administrator agreed to reverse the transaction in the ITL.

6. The Union registry may complete the reversal with different units of the same unit type that are on the destination account of the transaction that is being reversed.

Amendment

1 Substituted by Commission Regulation (EU) No 1193/2011 of 18 November 2011 establishing a Union Registry for the trading period commencing on 1 January 2013, and subsequent trading periods, of the Union emissions trading scheme pursuant to Directive 2003/87/EC of the European Parliament and of the Council and Decision No 280/2004/EC of the European Parliament and of the Council and amending Commission Regulations (EC) No 2216/2004 and (EU) No 920/2010, Article 89(23).

Section 6
Accounting mechanisms

Article 52

Minimum deposited quantity on the ETS AAU deposit account

1. The EUTL shall record a minimum deposited quantity for each Member State. In the case of Member States with KP registries, the EUTL will prevent transfers of Kyoto units from their ETS AAU deposit account that would result in Kyoto unit holdings on the ETS AAU deposit account that are below the minimum deposited quantity. In the case of Member States with no KP registry, the minimum deposited quantity is a value used in the clearing process.

2. The EUTL shall add a quantity to the minimum deposited quantity after an issue of Chapter III allowances has taken place in accordance with Article 39, where the addition shall be equal to the amount of Chapter III allowances issued.

3. The EUTL shall deduct a quantity from the minimum deposited quantity immediately after:

(a) a transfer of Chapter III allowances to the Union allowance deletion account has taken place as a result of downwards correction of Chapter III allowances after their allocation in accordance with Article 37(3), where the deduction shall be equal to the amount of Chapter III allowances transferred;

(b) a set-aside of Kyoto units against surrenders of Chapter III allowances by aircraft operators in accordance with Article 54 has taken place, where the deduction shall be equal to the amount set-aside;

(c) a cancellation of Kyoto units against deletions of Chapter III allowances in accordance with Article 55(1) has taken place, where the deduction shall be equal to the quantity cancelled;

(d) a deletion of allowances set out in Article 55(2) took place, where the deduction shall be equal to the quantity deleted.

4. The Central Administrator shall carry out a deduction of a quantity from the minimum deposited quantity recorded in the EUTL after the clearing transactions in accordance with Article 56 have taken place. The deduction shall equal the total amount of Chapter III allowances surrendered by user accounts administered by the national administrator of the Member State for the 2008–12 period; plus the clearing value calculated in accordance with Article 56(3).

Article 53

Gateway quantity and gateway deposit account

1. The EUTL shall record a gateway quantity for each Member State with no KP registry.

2. The EUTL shall add a quantity to the gateway quantity after Chapter III allowances are transferred from a user account administered by a Member State with no KP registry to a user account administered by another Member State, where the addition shall be equal to the amount of Chapter III allowances transferred.

3. The EUTL shall deduct a quantity from the gateway quantity after Chapter III allowances are transferred from a user account administered by a Member State to a user account administered by a Member State with no KP registry, where the deduction shall be equal to the amount of Chapter III allowances transferred.

4. The EUTL will not allow any transfer of Chapter III allowances out of accounts administered by a Member State with no KP registry that would result in a gateway quantity that is higher than the amount of Kyoto units held in the gateway deposit account for that Member State.

5. Until 1 July 2013 or the completion of the clearing set out in Article 56, whichever is later, the EUTL will not allow any transfer of Kyoto units out of the gateway deposit account for a particular Member State with no KP registry that would result in holdings on the gateway deposit account for the Member State that are lower than the gateway quantity.

6. After 1 July 2013 or the completion of the clearing set out in Article 56, whichever is later, the Central Administrator shall reset the gateway quantity to zero and empty the gateway deposit account through transfers carried out in the following order of precedence:

(a) transfers in accordance with in Article 54(2);

(b) transfers to the ETS AAU deposit account of the Member State served by the gateway up to the quantity needed to ensure the banking of all Chapter III allowances in accordance with Article 57;

(c) transfers to the KP Party holding account of the European Union up to the amount of any previous transfers from that account to the gateway deposit account;

(d) transfers to the KP Party holding account of the Member State served by the gateway deposit account.

Article 54

Setting aside of AAUs against surrenders of Chapter III allowances by aircraft operators

1. By 5 May 2013 and each year thereafter, KP registry administrators of Member States with KP registries shall transfer to the aviation surrender set-aside account in the Union registry an amount of AAUs that is equal to the amount of Chapter III allowances surrendered for the current period by aircraft operators pursuant to Article 46 between 1 May of the preceding year and 30 April of the current year.

2. By 1 July 2013 or when the clearing process in Article 56 is completed, whichever is later, the Central Administrator shall transfer from the gateway deposit account of a Member State with no KP registry to the aviation surrender set-aside account in the Union registry an amount of Kyoto units that is equal to the lower of the following:

(a) the total amount of Chapter III allowances surrendered from aircraft operator holding accounts administered by that Member State with no KP registry;

(b) the total amount of units held on the gateway account.

Article 55

Cancellation of Kyoto units against deletions of Chapter III allowances

1. By 5 May 2013 and each year thereafter each KP registry administrator shall transfer an amount of AAUs, ERUs or CERs, but not lCERs or tCERs to the cancellation account in the Union registry. The transferred amount shall be equal to the amount of Chapter III allowances deleted in accordance with Article 49 from user accounts administered by its Member State between 1 May of the preceding year and 30 April of the current year.

2. By way of derogation from paragraph 1 a registry administrator is not obliged to transfer to the cancellation account in the Union registry amounts of AAUs, ERUs, or CERs equal to deletions which meet one of the following conditions:
(a) the deletion was carried out in an account administered by a Member State that has no KP registry;
(b) the deletion took place after 30 April of the year following the last year of the period.

Article 56

Clearing of allowance transfers

1. After the end of the 2008–2012 period, in order to ensure that transfers of Chapter III allowances between accounts administered by national administrators of different Member States are followed up with an equal amount of Kyoto units transferred between KP registries, paragraphs 2 to 4 shall apply.

2. On the first working day following 1 June 2013, or the day after all changes to minimum deposit quantities related to downwards corrections to allowances set out in Article 52(3)(a) are completed, whichever is later, the Central Administrator shall calculate a clearing value for each Member State and notify the national administrators thereof.

3. In the case of Member States with a KP registry, the clearing value shall be equal to:
(a) the minimum deposit quantity on 1 June; minus
(b) the total amount of Chapter III allowances surrendered by operators administered by the national administrator of the Member State for the 2008–12 period.

4. In the case of Member States with no KP registry, the clearing value shall be equal to the gateway quantity calculated in accordance with Article 53 on 1 June 2013.

5. Within 5 working days of the notification set out in paragraph 2, each KP registry administrator whose Member State has a positive clearing value shall transfer an amount of AAUs equal to the clearing value to the ETS central clearing account in the Union registry. In the case of Member States with no KP registry, this transfer shall be carried out by the Central Administrator from the gateway deposit account for the Member State with no KP registry.

6. Within 5 working days of the completion of the transfers set out in paragraph 5, the Central Administrator shall transfer an amount of AAUs from the ETS central clearing account in the Union registry to a KP Party holding account in the KP registry of each Member State with a negative clearing value that is equal to the positive equivalent of the clearing value. In the case of Member States with no KP registry, this amount shall be transferred to the gateway deposit account.

Article 57

Banking between periods

Within 10 working days of the completion of the clearing transactions set out in Article 56, the Union registry shall delete Chapter III allowances and Chapter II allowances valid for the 2008–2012 period held in user accounts in the Union registry and issue an equal amount of Chapter III allowances valid for the 2013–2020 period to the same accounts.

Article 58

Retirement of AAUs, ERUs or CERs against the domestic aviation emissions of aircraft operators

1. By 30 September of the year following the year of entry into force of this Regulation, the Central Administrator shall transfer an amount of Kyoto units from the aviation surrender

set-aside account in the Union registry to the Party holding account of each Member State that is equal to those verified emissions by aircraft operators that are included in the national inventory under the UNFCCC of that Member State for that year. The amounts thus transferred shall constitute of AAUs to the extent possible. If the AAUs in the aviation surrender set-aside account are not sufficient for completing all transfers, the Central Administrator shall preferentially transfer AAUs to those Member States whose domestic aviation emissions are lower than the amount of AAUs they transferred into the aviation surrender set-aside account in accordance with Article 54(1).

2. If the holdings of the aviation surrender set-aside account are not enough to carry out the transfer set out in paragraph 1, all amounts to be transferred shall be reduced with a factor that shall equal the total units held on the aviation surrender set-aside account divided by the total amount of units required to be transferred.

Chapter VII
Technical requirements of the registries system

Section I
Availability

Article 59

Availability and reliability of the Union registry and the EUTL

1. The EUTL shall respond to any message from any registry within 24 hours of its receipt.

2. The Central Administrator shall take all reasonable steps to ensure that:

(a) the Union registry is available for access by account holders 24 hours a day, 7 days a week;

(b) the communication links referred to in Article 5(1) and (2) between the Union registry and the EUTL are maintained 24 hours a day, 7 days a week;

(c) backup hardware and software necessary in the event of a breakdown in operations of the primary hardware and software is provided for;

(d) the Union registry and the EUTL respond promptly to requests made by account holders.

3. The Central Administrator shall ensure that the Union registry and EUTL incorporate robust systems and procedures for the safeguarding of all data and the prompt recovery of all data and operations in the event of a disaster.

4. The Central Administrator shall keep interruptions to the operation of the Union registry and EUTL to a minimum.

Article 60

Helpdesks

1. National administrators shall provide assistance and support to holders of accounts in the Union registry that are administered by them through national helpdesks.

2. The Central Administrator shall provide support to national administrators through a Central Helpdesk for the purposes of helping them to provide assistance in accordance with paragraph 1.

Section 2
Security, and authentication

Article 61

Authentication of registries and the EUTL

1. The identity of the Union registry shall be authenticated towards the EUTL with digital certificates and usernames and passwords as indicated in the Data Exchange and Technical Specifications provided for in Article 71.

2. The Member States and the Union shall use the digital certificates issued by the Secretariat to the UNFCCC, or an entity designated by it, to authenticate their registries to the ITL for the purposes of establishing the communication link referred to in Article 5.

Article 62

Accessing accounts in the Union registry

1. Account holders shall be able to access their accounts in the Union registry through the secure area of the Union registry. The Central administrator shall ensure that the secure area of the Union registry website is accessible through the Internet. The website of the Union registry shall be available in all languages of the European Union.

2. The Central administrator shall ensure that accounts in the Union registry where access through trading platforms in accordance with Article 19(3) is enabled and one authorised representative is also the authorised representative of a trading platform holding account are accessible to the trading platform operated by the holder of that trading platform holding account.

3. Communications between authorised representatives or trading platforms and the secure area of Union registry shall be encrypted in accordance with the security requirements set out in the Data Exchange and Technical Specifications provided for in Article 71.

4. The Central administrator shall take all necessary steps to ensure that unauthorised access to the secure area of the Union registry website does not occur.

5. If the security of the credentials of an authorised representative or additional authorised representative has been compromised, the authorised representative or additional authorised representative shall immediately inform the administrator of the account thereof and request a replacement.

Article 63

Authentication and authorisation of authorised representatives in the Union registry

1. The Union registry shall issue each authorised representative and additional authorised representative with a username and password to authenticate them for the purposes of accessing the registry.

2. An authorised representative or additional authorised representative shall only have access to the accounts within the Union registry which he is authorised to access and shall only be able to request the initiation of processes which he is authorised to request pursuant to Article 19. That access or request shall take place through a secure area of the website of the Union registry.

3. In addition to the username and password referred to in paragraph 1, national administrators shall provide secondary authentication to all accounts administered by them. The types of secondary authentication mechanisms that can be used to access the Union registry shall be set out in the Data Exchange and Technical Specifications provided for in Article 71.

Article 67

Detection of discrepancies

1. In case of processes completed through the direct communication link between the Union registry and the EUTL referred to in Article 5(2), the EUTL shall terminate any processes where it identifies discrepancies upon conducting the automated checks referred to in Article 66(2), and shall inform thereof the Union registry and the administrator of the accounts involved in the terminated transaction by returning an automated check response code. The Union registry shall immediately inform the relevant account holders that the process has been terminated.

2. In case of transactions completed through the ITL referred to in Article 5(1), the ITL shall terminate any processes where discrepancies are identified either by the ITL or the EUTL upon conducting the automated checks referred to in Article 66(2). Following a termination by the ITL, the EUTL shall also terminate the transaction. The ITL informs the administrators of the registries involved of the termination of the transaction by returning an automated check response code. If one of the registries involved is the Union registry, the Union registry shall also inform the administrator of the Union registry accounts involved in the terminated transaction by returning an automated check response code. The Union registry shall immediately inform the relevant account holders that the process has been terminated.

Article 68

Detection of discrepancies by the registries

1. The Union registry and every other KP registry shall contain check input codes and check response codes to ensure the correct interpretation of information exchanged during each process. The check codes shall correspond to those contained in the Data Exchange and Technical Specifications provided for in Article 71.

2. Prior to and during the execution of all processes the Union registry shall conduct appropriate automated checks to ensure that discrepancies are detected and incorrect processes are terminated in advance of automated checks being conducted by the EUTL.

Article 69

Reconciliation — Detection of inconsistencies by the EUTL

1. The EUTL shall periodically initiate data reconciliation to ensure that the EUTL's records of accounts, holdings of Kyoto units and allowances match the records of these holdings in the Union registry. For that purpose the EUTL shall record all processes.

2. The ITL periodically initiates data reconciliation to ensure that the ITL's records of the holdings of Kyoto units match the records of these holdings in the Union registry and every other KP registry.

3. If during the data reconciliation process referred to in paragraph 1, an irregularity, hereinafter referred to as "inconsistency", is identified by EUTL, whereby the information regarding accounts, holdings of Kyoto units and allowances provided by the Union registry as part of the periodic reconciliation process differs from the information contained in the EUTL, the EUTL shall ensure that no further processes may be completed with any of the accounts, allowances or Kyoto units which are the subject of the inconsistency. The EUTL shall immediately inform the Central Administrator and the administrators of the relevant accounts of any inconsistency.

Article 70

Finalisation of processes

1. All transactions communicated to the ITL in accordance with Article 5(1) shall be final when the ITL notifies to the EUTL that it has completed the process.

2. All transactions and other processes communicated to the EUTL in accordance with Article 5(3) shall be final when the EUTL notifies to the Union registry that it has completed the processes.

3. The data reconciliation process referred to in Article 69(1) shall be final when all inconsistencies between the information contained in the Union registry and the information contained in the EUTL for a specific time and date have been resolved, and the data reconciliation process has been successfully re-initiated and completed.

Section 4
Specifications and change management

[Article 71

Data exchange and technical specifications][1]

[1. The Commission shall make available to administrators data exchange and technical specifications necessary for exchanging data between registries and transaction logs, including the identification codes, automated checks and response codes, as well as the testing procedures and security requirements necessary for the launching of data exchange.

2. The data exchange and technical specifications shall be drawn up in consultation with the Administrators' Working Group of the Climate Change Committee and shall be consistent with the functional and technical specifications for data exchange standards for registry systems under the Kyoto Protocol elaborated pursuant to Decision 12/CMP.1.][1]

Amendment

1 Substituted by Commission Regulation (EU) No 1193/2011 of 18 November 2011 establishing a Union Registry for the trading period commencing on 1 January 2013, and subsequent trading periods, of the Union emissions trading scheme pursuant to Directive 2003/87/EC of the European Parliament and of the Council and Decision No 280/2004/EC of the European Parliament and of the Council and amending Commission Regulations (EC) No 2216/2004 and (EU) No 920/2010, Article 89(27).

Article 72

Change management

If a new version or release of a KP registry, including the Union registry is required, that registry shall complete the testing procedures set out in the Data Exchange and Technical Specifications provided for in Article 71 before a communication link is established and activated between the new version or release of that registry and the EUTL or ITL.

Chapter VIII
Records, reports, confidentiality and fees

Article 73

Records

1. The Union registry and every other KP registry shall store records concerning all processes and account holders for 15 years or until any questions of implementation relating to them have been resolved, whichever is later.

2. National administrators shall be able to access, query and export all records held in the Union registry in relation to accounts that are administered by them.

3. Records shall be stored in accordance with the data logging requirements described in the Data Exchange and Technical Specifications provided for in Article 71.

Article 74

Reporting

1. The Central Administrator shall make available the information listed in Annex XIII at the frequencies and to the recipients set out in Annex XIII in a transparent and organised manner via the EUTL website. The Central Administrator shall not release additional information held in the EUTL or in the Union registry unless this is permitted under Article 75.

2. National administrators may also make available the part of the information listed in Annex XIII that they have access to in accordance with Article 73 at the frequencies and to the recipients set out in Annex XIII in a transparent and organised manner on a site publicly accessible via the Internet. National administrators shall not release additional information held in the Union registry unless this is permitted under Article 75.

3. The EUTL website shall allow recipients of the reports listed in Annex XIII to query those reports using search facilities.

4. KP registry administrators shall comply with the requirement to publish the information relating to the issuance of ERUs specified in paragraph 46 of the Annex to Decision 13/CMP.1 of the Conference of the Parties serving as the meeting of the Parties to the Kyoto Protocol within a week after the issuance has taken place.

5. The Union registry and each KP registry shall comply with the requirement to publish the information specified in points (a), (d), (f) and l of paragraph 47 of the Annex to Decision 13/CMP.1 of the Conference of the Parties serving as the meeting of the Parties to the Kyoto Protocol on 1 January of the fifth year after the recording of the information.

6. The Union registry and each KP registry shall comply with the requirement to publish the information specified in points (b), (c), (e), and from (g) to (k) of paragraph 47 of the Annex to Decision 13/CMP.1 of the Conference of the Parties serving as the meeting of the Parties to the Kyoto Protocol on 1 January of the first year after the recording of the information.

Article 75

Confidentiality

[1. Information, including the holdings of all accounts, all transactions made, the unique unit identification code of the allowances and the unique numeric value of the unit serial number of the Kyoto units held or affected by the transaction, held in the EUTL, the Union Registry and every other KP registry shall be considered confidential except as otherwise required by Union law, or by provisions of national law that pursue a legitimate objective compatible with this Regulation and are proportionate.

2. The following entities may obtain data stored in the Union Registry and the EUTL:

(a) the law enforcement and tax authorities of a Member State;

(b) the European Anti-fraud Office of the European Commission;

(c) the European Court of Auditors;

(d) Eurojust;

(e) the competent authorities referred to in Article 11 of Directive 2003/6/EC and in Article 37(1) of Directive 2005/60/EC;

(f) competent national supervisory authorities;

(g) the national administrators of Member States and the competent authorities referred to in Article 18 of Directive 2003/87/EC.

3. Data may be provided to the entities listed under paragraph 2 upon their request to the central administrator or to a national administrator if such requests are necessary for the performance of their tasks.][1]

4. An entity receiving data in accordance with paragraph 3 shall ensure that the data received is only used for the purposes stated in the request in accordance with paragraph 3 and is not made available deliberately or accidentally to persons not involved in the intended purpose of the data use. This provision shall not preclude these entities to make the data available to other entities listed in paragraph 2, if this is necessary for the purposes stated in the request made in accordance with paragraph 3.

5. Upon their request, the Central administrator may provide access to anonymised transaction data to the entities listed in paragraph 2. for the purpose of looking for suspicious transaction patterns. Entities with such access may notify suspicious transaction patterns to other entities listed in paragraph 2.

[5a. Europol shall obtain permanent read-only access to data stored in the Union Registry and the EUTL for the purpose of the performance of its tasks in accordance with Council Decision 2009/371/JHA. Europol shall keep the Commission informed of the use it makes of the data.][2]

[6. National administrators shall make available through secure means to all other national administrators and the central administrator the names and identities of persons for whom they refused to open an account for in accordance with Article 13(3) or 14(3), or whom they refused to nominate as an authorised representative or additional authorised representative in accordance with Article 20(3) and the names and identities of the account holder, authorised representative or additional authorised representative of accounts to which access has been suspended in accordance with Articles 64 and 64a or of accounts that have been closed in accordance with Article 28.][1]

7. National administrators may decide to notify to national law enforcement authorities all transactions that involve a number of units above the amount determined by the national administrator and to notify any account that is involved in a number of transactions within a 24-hour period that is above the amount determined by the national administrator.

8. Account holders may request from the national administrator in writing that the public website of the Union registry should not display some or all of the data items in, rows 2 to 12 of Table VII-II of Annex VII.

9. Account holders may request from the national administrator in writing that the public website of the Union registry display some or all of the data items in rows 3 to 15 of Table IX-I of Annex IX.

10. Neither the EUTL nor KP registries shall require account holders to submit price information concerning allowances or Kyoto units.

Amendments

1 Substituted by Commission Regulation (EU) No 1193/2011 of 18 November 2011 establishing a Union Registry for the trading period commencing on 1 January 2013, and subsequent trading periods, of the Union emissions trading scheme pursuant to Directive 2003/87/EC of the European Parliament and of the Council and Decision No 280/2004/EC of the European Parliament and of the Council and amending Commission Regulations (EC) No 2216/2004 and (EU) No 920/2010, Article 89(28)(a), (c).

2 Inserted by Commission Regulation (EU) No 1193/2011 of 18 November 2011 establishing a Union Registry for the trading period commencing on 1 January 2013, and subsequent trading periods, of the Union emissions trading scheme pursuant to Directive 2003/87/EC of the European Parliament and of the Council and Decision No 280/2004/EC of the European Parliament and of the Council and amending Commission Regulations (EC) No 2216/2004 and (EU) No 920/2010, Article 89(28)(b).

Article 76

Fees

1. The Central Administrator shall not charge any fees to holders of accounts in the Union registry.

2. National administrators may charge reasonable fees to holders of accounts administered by them.

3. No fees shall be charged for the transactions described in Chapter VI.

4. National administrators shall notify the charged fees to the Central Administrator and shall notify it of any changes in the fees within 10 working days. The Central Administrator shall display any fees notified to it on its public website.

Chapter IX
Transitional and final provisions

Article 77

Migration and Decoupling

1. When implementing this Regulation, the following migration process shall apply:
(a) KP registry administrators shall convert any allowances held in any account that are recognised as AAUs by the ITL into AAUs by removing the allowance element from the unique unit identification code of each such AAU and transfer them into the ETS AAU deposit account in their KP registry;
(b) the Central Administrator shall:
  (i) create an amount of allowances not recognised as AAUs by the ITL in the Union registry that is equal to the amount transferred in accordance with paragraph (1)(a);
  (ii) make available in the Union registry a set of accounts equivalent to the set from which allowances were transferred in accordance with paragraph (1)(a);
  (iii) transfer an amount of allowances created in accordance with (i) to accounts referred to in (ii). The amount of allowances transferred to each such account shall be equal to the amount transferred from the equivalent account in accordance with paragraph (1)(a).

2. The KP registry administrators and the Central Administrator shall ensure that relevant historical data related to the account is transferred from the Member States' registries to the Union registry.

[2a. Before migration, person holding accounts shall be checked by national administrators to ensure that the information submitted for account opening are complete, up to date, accurate and true.][1]

3. The migration process shall be implemented in accordance with procedures defined in the Data Exchange and Technical Specifications referred to in Article 71. In the course of the migration process, operation of the registry system may be suspended by the Central Administrator for a period of up to 14 calendar days.

Amendment

1 Inserted by Commission Regulation (EU) No 1193/2011 of 18 November 2011 establishing a Union Registry for the trading period commencing on 1 January 2013, and subsequent trading periods, of the Union emissions trading scheme pursuant to Directive 2003/87/EC of the European Parliament and of the Council and Decision No 280/2004/EC of the European Parliament and of the Council and amending Commission Regulations (EC) No 2216/2004 and (EU) No 920/2010, Article 89(29).

[*Articles 78 and 79 are not reproduced.*]

Article 80

Entry into force

This Regulation shall enter into force on the day following its publication in the Official Journal of the European Union.

Articles 2 to 76 and the Annexes shall apply from 1 January 2012.

This Regulation shall be binding in its entirety and directly applicable in all Member States.

ANNEX I
TABLE I-I: ACCOUNT TYPES AND UNIT TYPES THAT MAY BE HELD IN EACH ACCOUNT TYPE

▼B

ANNEX I

Table I-I: Account types and unit types that may be held in each account type

Account type name	Account holder	Account Administrator	No of accounts of this type	Allowances (Non-Kyoto units)		Kyoto units			
				Chapter III allowances	Chapter II allowances	AAU	CER	ERU	lCER/ tCER/ RMU
I. *KP Party accounts in KP registries (including the Union registry)*									
Party holding account	KP Party	KP registry Administrator (in the Union registry: the Central Administrator)	at least 1	No	No	Yes	Yes	Yes	Yes
Cancellation account			1	No	No	Yes	Yes	Yes	Yes
Retirement account			1	No	No	Yes	Yes	Yes	Yes
ETS AAU deposit account			1	No	No	Yes	No	No	No
II. *Management accounts in the Union registry*									
National allowance holding account	Member State	Nat'l Admin of the MS holding the account	1 for each MS	Yes	Yes	No	No	No	No
ETS central clearing account	EU	Central Administrator	1	No	No	Yes	No	No	No
Gateway deposit account			1 for each MS with no KP Reg.	No	No	Yes	No	No	No
Union allowance deletion account			1	Yes	Yes	No	No	No	No
Aviation Surrender Set-Aside Account			1	No	No	Yes	Yes	Yes	No

▼B

Account type name	Account holder	Account Administrator	No of accounts of this type	Allowances (Non-Kyoto units)		Kyoto units			
				Chapter III allowances	Chapter II allowances	AAU	CER	ERU	lCER/ tCER/ RMU
III. *User accounts in the Union registry*									
Operator holding account	Operator	Nat'l Admin of the MS where installation is located	one for each installation/ aircraft operator/ person/ trading platform in MS	Yes	No	by MS (*)	Yes	Yes	by MS (*)
Aircraft Operator holding account	Aircraft operator	Nat'l Admin of the MS administering the aircraft operator		Yes	Yes	by MS (*)	Yes	Yes	by MS (*)
Person holding account	Person	Nat'l Admin that has opened the account		Yes	Yes	by MS (*)	Yes	Yes	by MS (*)
Trading Platform holding Account	Trading platform			Yes	Yes	by MS (*)	Yes	Yes	by MS (*)
Verifier Account	Verifier		One for each verifier	No	No	No	No	No	No

(*) The MS National Administrator can decide whether the account (or the account type) may hold this type of unit.

ANNEX II
TRANSACTION TYPES THAT MAY BE INITIATED AND RECEIVED BY EACH ACCOUNT TYPE (WITH THE TYPE OF UNITS THAT MY BE INVOLVED)

▼B

ANNEX II

Transaction types that may be initiated and received by each account type (with the type of units that my be involved)

Account type name	Transaction name and action type (I = Initiate, R = receive)											
	Transfer of units						Surrender of units		Deletion of allowances		Cancellation of Kyoto units	
	from a UR account		to a UR account (from a non-UR account)		between two non-UR accounts (in EEA)							
	I	R	I	R	I	R	I	R	I	R	I	R
I. KP Party accounts in the Union registry and all other KP registries												
KP Party holding account	n.a.	Yes	Yes	n.a.	Yes	Yes	No	Yes	No	No	Yes	No
Cancellation account	n.a.	Yes	No	n.a.	No	Yes	No	No	No	No	No	Yes
Retirement account	n.a.	Yes	No	n.a.	No	Yes	No	No	No	No	No	No
ETS AAU deposit account	n.a.	n.a.	Yes	n.a.	Yes	Yes	No	No	No	No	No	No
II. Management accounts in the Union registry												
ETS central clearing account	Yes	Yes	n.a.	Yes	n.a.	n.a.	No	No	No	No	No	No
Gateway deposit account (for MS with no KP registry)	Yes	Yes	n.a.	Yes	n.a.	n.a.	No	No	No	No	No	No
National allowance holding account (only for MS with KP registries)	Yes	Yes	n.a.	Yes	n.a.	n.a.	No	No	Yes	No	No	No
Union allowance deletion account	No	No	n.a.	No	n.a.	n.a.	No	Yes	No	Yes	No	No
Aviation Surrender Set-Aside Account	Yes	Yes	n.a.	Yes	n.a.	n.a.	No	Yes	No	No	Yes	No
III. User accounts in the Union registry												
Operator holding account	Yes	Yes	n.a.	Yes	n.a.	n.a.	Yes	No	Yes	No	Yes	No
Aircraft Operator holding account	Yes	Yes	n.a.	Yes	n.a.	n.a.	Yes	No	Yes	No	Yes	No
Person holding account	Yes	Yes	n.a.	Yes	n.a.	n.a.	No	No	Yes	No	Yes	No
Trading Platform holding account	Yes	Yes	n.a.	Yes	n.a.	n.a.	No	No	Yes	No	Yes	No
Verifier Account	No	No	n.a.	No	n.a.	n.a.	No	No	No	No	No	No

ANNEX III
INFORMATION TO BE SUBMITTED WITH REQUESTS FOR OPENING KP PARTY ACCOUNTS AND MANAGEMENT ACCOUNTS

2010R0920 — EN — 30.11.2011 — 001.001 — 67

▼B

ANNEX III

Information to be submitted with requests for opening KP Party accounts and management accounts

1. The information set out in Table III-I.

Table III-I: Account Details for all accounts

	A	B	C	D	E	F
Item No	Account detail item	Mandatory or Optional?	Type	Can be updated?	Is approval from NA needed for update?	Displayed on UR public website?
1	Account ID (given by UR)	M	Preset	No	n.a.	No
2	Account type	M	Choice	No	n.a.	Yes
3	Commitment period	M	Choice	No	n.a.	Yes
4	Account Holder ID (issued by UR)	M	Free	Yes	Yes	Yes
5	Account holder Name	M	Free	Yes	Yes	Yes
6	Account Identifier (given by account holder)	M	Free	Yes	No	No
7	AH Address — country	M	Choice	Yes	Yes	Yes
8	AH Address — region or state	O	Free	Yes	Yes	Yes
9	AH Address — city	M	Free	Yes	Yes	Yes
10	AH Address — postcode	M	Free	Yes	Yes	Yes
11	AH Address — street	M	Free	Yes	Yes	Yes
12	AH Address — street No	M	Free	Yes	Yes	Yes
13	AH Company registration No or ID No	M	Free	Yes	Yes	Yes
14	AH Telephone 1	M	Free	Yes	No	Yes
15	AH Telephone 2	M	Free	Yes	No	Yes
16	AH email address	M	Free	Yes	No	Yes
17	Date of Birth (for natural persons)	O	Free	No	n.a.	No
18	Place of Birth (for natural persons)	O	Free	No	n.a.	No
19	VAT registration number with country code	O	Free	Yes	Yes	No
20	Account opening date	M	Preset	No	n.a.	Yes
21	Account closing date	O	Preset	Yes	Yes	Yes

2. The account identifier shall be unique within the registry system.

[ANNEX IV
INFORMATION CONCERNING PERSON HOLDING ACCOUNTS AND TRADING PLATFORM HOLDING ACCOUNTS TO BE PROVIDED TO THE NATIONAL ADMINISTRATOR][1]

[1. The information set out in Table III-I. (The account ID and the alphanumeric identifier are to be unique within the registry system.)

2. With the exception of aircraft operators, proof that the person requesting the account opening has an open bank account in a Member State of the European Economic Area.

3. Evidence to support the identity of the natural person requesting the account opening, which may be a copy of one of the following:
(a) an identity card issued by a State that is a member of the European Economic Area or the Organisation for Economic Cooperation and Development;
(b) a passport.

4. Evidence to support the address of the permanent residence of the natural person account holder, which may be a copy of one of the following:
(a) the identity document submitted under point 3, if it contains the address of the permanent residence;
(b) any other government-issued identity document that contains the address of permanent residence;
(c) if the country of permanent residence does not issue identity documents that contain the address of permanent residence, a statement from the local authorities confirming the nominee's permanent residence;
(d) any other document that is customarily accepted in the Member State of the administrator of the account as evidence of the permanent residence of the nominee.

5. The following documents in case of a legal person requesting the account opening:
(a) a copy of the instruments establishing the legal entity and a copy of a document proving the registration of the legal entity;
(b) bank account details;
(c) a confirmation of VAT registration;
(d) information on the legal entity's beneficial owner as defined in Directive 2005/60/EC;
(e) list of directors;
(f) a copy of the annual report or of the latest audited financial statements, or if no audited financial statements available, a copy of the financial statements stamped by the tax office or the financial director.

6. Evidence to support the registered address of the legal person account holder, if this is not clear from the document submitted in accordance with point 5.

7. The criminal record of the natural person requesting the account opening or if it is a legal person, of its directors.

8. Any copy of a document submitted as evidence under this Annex must be certified as a true copy by a notary public or other similar person specified by the national administrator. Regarding documents issued outside the Member State requesting a copy, the copy must be legalised. The date of the certification or legalisation must not be more than three months prior to the date of application.

9. The administrator of the account may require that the documents submitted are accompanied with a certified translation into a language specified by the administrator.

10. Instead of obtaining paper documents, the administrator of the account may use electronic mechanisms to check the evidence to be submitted in accordance with this Annex.][1]

Amendment

1 Substituted by Commission Regulation (EU) No 1193/2011 of 18 November 2011 establishing a Union Registry for the trading period commencing on 1 January 2013, and subsequent trading periods, of the Union

emissions trading scheme pursuant to Directive 2003/87/EC of the European Parliament and of the Council and Decision No 280/2004/EC of the European Parliament and of the Council and amending Commission Regulations (EC) No 2216/2004 and (EU) No 920/2010, Article 89(30).

ANNEX V

ADDITIONAL INFORMATION CONCERNING TRADING PLATFORM HOLDING ACCOUNTS TO BE PROVIDED TO THE NATIONAL ADMINISTRATOR

1. A signed statement from the competent financial authorities of the Member State of the administrator opening the account confirming that the person requesting the account opening is authorised by that Member State as one of the following:

(a) a regulated market as defined under Article 4, paragraph 1, (14) of Directive 2004/39/EC on markets in financial instruments, as amended;

(b) a multilateral trading facility as defined under Article 4, paragraph 1, (15) of Directive 2004/39/EC on markets in financial instruments, as amended;

(c) any other exchange that is a multilateral system operated and/or managed by a market operator, which brings together or facilitates the bringing together of multiple third-party buying and selling interests in allowances or Kyoto units, including any clearing or settlement system responsible for the payment for and delivery of allowances and the management of collateral servicing the relevant regulated market or multilateral trading facility, or any other exchange.

ADDITIONAL INFORMATION CONCERNING VERIFIER ACCOUNTS TO BE PROVIDED TO THE NATIONAL ADMINISTRATOR

2. A document proving that the person requesting the account opening is accredited as a verifier in the Member State of the administrator from whom it requests the opening of an account.

ANNEX VI
CORE TERMS AND CONDITIONS

Structure and effect of core terms and conditions

1. The relationship between account holders and registry administrators.

The account holder and authorised representative's obligations

2. The account holder and authorised representative's obligations with respect to security, usernames and passwords, and access to the registry website.

3. The account holder and authorised representative's obligation to post data on the registry website and ensure that data posted is accurate.

4. The account holder and authorised representative's obligation to comply with the terms of use of the registry website.

The registry administrator's obligations

5. The registry administrator's obligation to carry out account holder's instructions.

6. The registry administrator's obligation to log the account holder's details.

7. The registry administrator's obligation to open, update or close the account in accordance with the provisions of the Regulation.

Process procedures

8. The process finalisation and confirmation provisions.

Payment

9. The terms and conditions regarding any registry fees for establishing and maintaining accounts.

Operation of the registry website

10. Provisions regarding the right of the registry administrator to make changes to the registry website.

11. Conditions of use of the registry website.

Warranties and indemnities

12. Accuracy of information.

13. Authority to initiate processes.

Modification of these core terms to reflect changes to this Regulation or changes to domestic legislation

Security and response to security breaches

14. An indication that all suspicious messages related to transactions may be passed on to national law enforcement agencies by national administrators.

Dispute resolution

15. Provisions relating to disputes between account holders.

Liability

16. The limit of liability for the registry administrator.

17. The limit of liability for the account holder.

Third party rights

Agency, notices and governing law

ANNEX VII
INFORMATION CONCERNING EACH OPERATOR HOLDING ACCOUNT TO BE PROVIDED TO THE NATIONAL ADMINISTRATOR

1. The information set out in Table III-I.

2. Under the data provided in accordance with table III-I, the operator of the installation shall be given as the account holder. The name provided for the account holder should be identical to name of the natural or legal person that is the holder of the relevant greenhouse gas permit.

3. The information set out in Tables VII-I and VII-II

Table VII-I: Account Details for operator holding accounts

	A	B	C	D	E	F
Item No	*Account detail item*	*Mandatory or Optional?*	*Type*	*Can be updated?*	*Is approval from NA needed for update?*	*Displayed on UR public website?*
1	Installation ID	M	Preset	No	—	Yes
2	Permit ID	M	Free	Yes	Yes	Yes
3	Permit entry into force date	M	Free	No	—	Yes
4	Permit expiry date	O	Free	Yes	Yes	Yes
5	Installation Name	M	Free	Yes	Yes	Yes
6	Installation Activity Type	M	Choice	Yes	Yes	Yes
7	Installation Address — country	M	Preset	Yes	Yes	Yes
8	Installation Address — region or state	O	Free	Yes	Yes	Yes
9	Installation Address — city	M	Free	Yes	Yes	Yes
10	Installation Address — postcode	M	Free	Yes	Yes	Yes
11	Installation Address — street	M	Free	Yes	Yes	Yes
12	Installation Address — street No	M	Free	Yes	Yes	Yes
13	Installation Telephone 1	M	Free	Yes	No	Yes
14	Installation Telephone 2	M	Free	Yes	No	Yes
15	Installation email address	M	Free	Yes	No	Yes
16	Parent Company	O	Free	Yes	No	Yes
17	Subsidiary Company	O	Free	Yes	No	Yes
18	EPRTR Identification Number	M	Free	Yes	No	Yes
19	Latitude	O	Free	Yes	No	Yes
20	Longitude	O	Free	Yes	No	Yes

Table VII-II: Account verifier and contact person details

	A	*B*	*C*	*D*	*E*	*F*
Item No	*Account detail item*	*Mandatory or Optional?*	*Type*	*Can be updated?*	*Is approval from NA needed for update?*	*Displayed on UR public website?*
1	Verifier	O	Choice	Yes	No	Yes
	Company name	O	Free	Yes	No	Yes(1)
	Company department	O	Free	Yes	No	Yes(1)
2	Contact Person within MS First Name	O	Free	Yes	No	Yes(1)
3	Contact Person within MS Last Name	O	Free	Yes	No	Yes(1)
4	Contact Person Address — country	O	Preset	Yes	No	Yes(1)
5	Contact Person Address — region or state	O	Free	Yes	No	Yes(1)
6	Contact Person Address — city	O	Free	Yes	No	Yes(1)
7	Contact Person Address — postcode	O	Free	Yes	No	Yes(1)
8	Contact Person Address — street	O	Free	Yes	No	Yes(1)
9	Contact Person Address — street No	O	Free	Yes	No	Yes(1)
10	Contact Person Telephone 1	O	Free	Yes	No	Yes(1)
11	Contact Person Telephone 2	O	Free	Yes	No	Yes(1)
12	Contact Person email address	O	Free	Yes	No	Yes(1)

(1) These items are not displayed if the account holder requests keeping them confidential in accordance with Article 75.

4. The name of the installation shall be identical to the name indicated in the relevant greenhouse gas permit.

ANNEX VIII
INFORMATION CONCERNING EACH AIRCRAFT OPERATOR HOLDING ACCOUNT TO BE PROVIDED TO THE REGISTRY ADMINISTRATOR

1. The information set out in Table III-I and VII-II.

2. Under the data provided in accordance with table III-I, the aircraft operator shall be given as the account holder. The name recorded for the account holder shall be identical to the name in the Monitoring Plan. In case of the name in the Monitoring Plan being obsolete, the name in the trading registry or the name used by Eurocontrol shall be used.

3. The information set out in Table VIII-I.

Table VIII-I: Account Details for Aircraft operator holding accounts

	A	*B*	*C*	*D*	*E*	*F*
Item No	*Account detail item*	*Mandatory or Optional?*	*Type*	*Can be updated?*	*Is approval from NA needed for update?*	*Displayed on UR public website?*
1	Aircraft operator ID (assigned by Union registry)	M	Free	No	—	Yes
2	Unique code under Commission Regulation (EC) No 748/2009	M	Free	Yes	Yes	Yes
3	call sign (ICAO designator)	O	Free	Yes	Yes	Yes
4	Monitoring plan ID	M	Free	Yes	Yes	Yes
5	Monitoring plan — first year of applicability	M	Free	No	—	Yes
6	Monitoring plan — year of expiry	O	Free	Yes	Yes	Yes

4. The call sign is ICAO designator in box 7 of the flight plan or, if not available, the registration marking of the aircraft.

[ANNEX IX INFORMATION CONCERNING AUTHORISED REPRESENTATIVES AND ADDITIONAL AUTHORISED REPRESENTATIVES TO BE PROVIDED TO THE ADMINISTRATOR OF THE ACCOUNT][1]

[1. The information set out in Table IX-I.

Table IX-I: Authorised representative details

	A	*B*	*C*	*D*	*E*	*F*
Item No	*Account detail item*	*Mandatory or Optional?*	*Type*	*Can be updated?*	*Is approval from NA needed for update?*	*Displayed on UR public website?*
1	Person ID	M	Free	No	n.a.	No
2	Type of AR	M	Choice	Yes	No	Yes
3	First name	M	Free	Yes	Yes	No(1)
4	Last name	M	Free	Yes	Yes	No(1)
5	Title	O	Free	Yes	No	No(1)
6	Job title	O	Free	Yes	No	No(1)
	Company name	O	Free	Yes	No	No(1)
	Company department	O	Free	Yes	No	No(1)
7	Country	M	Preset	No	n.a.	No(1)
8	Region or State	O	Free	Yes	Yes	No(1)
9	City	M	Free	Yes	Yes	No(1)
10	Postcode	M	Free	Yes	Yes	No(1)
11	Address — line 1	M	Free	Yes	Yes	No(1)
12	Address — line 2	O	Free	Yes	Yes	No(1)

	A	*B*	*C*	*D*	*E*	*F*
Item No	*Account detail item*	*Mandatory or Optional?*	*Type*	*Can be updated?*	*Is approval from NA needed for update?*	*Displayed on UR public website?*
13	Telephone 1	M	Free	Yes	No	No[(1)]
14	Mobile phone	M	Free	Yes	Yes	No[(1)]
15	E-mail address	M	Free	Yes	Yes	No
16	Date of birth	M	Free	No	n.a.	No
17	Place of birth — city	M	Free	No	n.a.	No
18	Place of birth — country	M				
18	Preferred language	O	Choice	Yes	No	No
19	Confidentiality level	O	Choice	Yes	No	No
20	AARs rights	M	Multiple choice	Yes	No	No

2. A signed statement from the account holder indicating that it wishes to nominate a particular person as authorised representative or additional authorised representative, confirming that the authorised representative has the right to initiate, or that additional authorised representative has the right to approve, transactions on behalf of the account holder and indicating any limitations to that right.

3. Evidence to support the identity of the nominee, which may be a copy of one of the following:

(a) an identity card issued by a State that is a member of the European Economic Area or the Organisation for Economic Cooperation and Development;

(b) a passport.

4. Evidence to support the address of the permanent residence of the nominee, which may be a copy of one of the following:

(a) the identity document submitted under point 3, if it contains the address of the permanent residence;

(b) any other government-issued identity document that contains the address of permanent residence;

(c) if the country of permanent residence does not issue identity documents that contain the address of permanent residence, a statement from the local authorities confirming the nominee's permanent residence;

(d) any other document that is customarily accepted in the Member State of the administrator of the account as evidence of the permanent residence of the nominee.

5. Criminal record of the nominee.

6. Any copy of a document submitted as evidence under this Annex must be certified as a true copy by a notary public or other similar person specified by the national administrator. Regarding documents issued outside the Member State requesting a copy, the copy must be legalised. The date of the certification or legalisation must not be more than three months prior to the date of application.

7. The administrator of the account may require that the documents submitted are accompanied with a certified translation into a language specified by the national administrator.

8. Instead of obtaining paper documents, the administrator of the account may use electronic mechanisms to check the evidence to be submitted in accordance with this Annex.][1]

Amendment

1 Substituted by Commission Regulation (EU) No 1193/2011 of 18 November 2011 establishing a Union Registry for the trading period commencing on 1 January 2013, and subsequent trading periods, of the Union

emissions trading scheme pursuant to Directive 2003/87/EC of the European Parliament and of the Council and Decision No 280/2004/EC of the European Parliament and of the Council and amending Commission Regulations (EC) No 2216/2004 and (EU) No 920/2010, Article 89(31).

ANNEX X
FORMATS FOR SUBMITTING ANNUAL EMISSIONS DATA

1. Emissions data for operators shall contain the information set out in Table X-I.

Table X-I: Emissions data for operators

	A	*B*	*C*
1	Installation ID:		
2	Reporting year		
	Greenhouse Gas Emissions		
		in tons	*in tons of CO_2eq*
3	CO_2 emissions		
4	N2O emissions		
5	PFC emissions		
6	Total emissions	—	Σ (C2 + C3 + C4)

2. Emissions data for aircraft operators shall contain the data set out in under paragraphs 8 and 9 of Section 8 in Annex XIV to Decision 2007/589/EC.

3. The electronic format for submitting emissions data shall be described in the Data Exchange and Technical Specifications provided for in Article 71.

ANNEX XI
NATIONAL ALLOCATION PLAN TABLE FOR THE 2008–2012 PERIOD

Row No	*Name*			*No of Chapter III allowances*	*Input ("r" stands for "row")*
	Country code of Member State				*Manual input*
1	Total number of allowances to issue to installations				Σ (r5 to r9, r12 to r16)
2	Total number of allowances in reserve				Manual input
3		Account ID of installation A			Manual input
4		Quantity to be allocated to Installation A:			
5			in year 2008		Manual input
6			in year 2009		Manual input
7			in year 2010		Manual input
8			in year 2011		Manual input
9			in year 2012		Manual input
10		Account ID of installation B			Manual input
11		Quantity to be allocated to Installation B:			
12			in year 2008		Manual input
13			in year 2009		Manual input
14			in year 2010		Manual input
15			in year 2011		Manual input
16			in year 2012		Manual input

ANNEX XII
UNION AVIATION ALLOCATION TABLE FOR THE 2008-2012 PERIOD

Row No	*Name*			*No of Chapter II allowances*	*Input ("r" stands for "row")*
1	Union-wide quantity of Chapter II allowances in 2012:				Manual input
2		Quantity still to be allocated in 2012:			(r1 × 0,15) = Σ (r3, r4, r5)
3			by MS 1:		Manual input
4			by MS 2:		Manual input
5			by MS n:		Manual input
6		Quantity already allocated for 2012			(r1 – r2) = Σ (r7, r8, r9)
7			to Aircraft Operator 1:		Manual input
8			to Aircraft Operator 2:		Manual input
9			to Account Holder n:		Manual input

ANNEX XIII
REPORTING REQUIREMENTS OF THE CENTRAL ADMINISTRATOR

Information available to the public

1. The EUTL shall display on the public website of the EUTL the following information for each account:

(a) all information indicated as to be "displayed on UR public website" in Tables III-I, VII-I, VII-II, VIII-I, IX-I. This information shall be updated every 24 hours;

(b) allowances allocated to individual account holders pursuant to Article 40 and Article 41. This information shall be updated every 24 hours;

(c) the status of the account in accordance with Article 9(1). This information shall be updated every 24 hours;

(d) the number of allowances and ERUs and CERs surrendered in accordance with Article 46, and the unit ID of the surrendered ERUs and CERs. The number of allowances and ERUs and CERs surrendered in the period from 1 January to 15 May shall only be displayed after 15 May. In the period from 15 May to 31 December, this information shall be updated every 24 hours;

(e) verified emissions figure, along with its corrections for the installation related to the operator holding account for year X shall be displayed from 1 April onwards of year (X+1);

(f) a symbol and a statement indicating whether the installation or aircraft operator related to the operator holding account surrendered a number of Kyoto units or allowances by 30 April that is at least equal to all its emissions in all past years. The symbols and the statements to be displayed are set out in Table XIII-I. The symbol shall be updated on 1 May and, except for the addition of a * in cases described under row 5 of Table XIII-I, it shall not change until the next 1 May.

Table XIII-I: Compliance statements

Row No	*Compliance status figure according to Article 31*	*Verified emissions are recorded for last complete year?*	*Symbol*	*Statement*
			to be displayed on EUTL public website	
1	0 or any positive number	Yes	A	"The number of allowances and ERUs/CERs surrendered by 30 April is greater than or equal to verified emissions"
2	any negative number	Yes	B	"The number of allowances and ERUs/CERs surrendered by 30 April is lower than verified emissions"
3	any number	No	C	"Verified emissions for preceding year were not entered until 30 April"
4	any number	No (because the allowance surrender process and/or verified emissions update process being suspended for the Member State's registry)	X	"Entering verified emissions and/or surrendering was impossible until 30 April due to the allowance surrender process and/or verified emissions update process being suspended for the Member State's registry"
5	any number	Yes or No (but subsequently updated by the competent authority)	* [added to the initial symbol]	"Verified emissions were estimated or corrected by the competent authority."

2. The EUTL shall display on the public website of the EUTL the following general information, and shall update it every 24 hours:

(a) the national allocation plan table of each Member State, including indications of any corrections made to the table in accordance with Article 37;

(b) the Union aviation allocation table, including indications of any corrections made to the table in accordance with Article 38;

(c) any set-aside table drawn up in accordance with Commission Decision 2006/780/EC;

(d) the total number of allowances, ERUs and CERs held in the Union registry in all user accounts on the previous day;

(e) a list of the unit IDs of all allowances, CERs and ERUs that were surrendered, marking those units that were moved out of the account they were surrendered into and are now held in person holding accounts or operator holding accounts. In the case of CERs and ERUs, project name, originating country and project ID shall also be displayed;

(f) a listing of the type of Kyoto units other than CERs and ERUs that can be held in user accounts administered by a particular national administrator in accordance with point 1 of Annex I;

(g) the total number of CERs and ERUs which operators in each Member State are allowed to surrender for each period pursuant to Article 11a(1) of Directive 2003/87/EC;

(h) the fees charged by national administrators in accordance with Article 76.

3. The EUTL shall display on its public website the following general information, on 30 April of each year:

(a) the percentage share of allowances surrendered in each Member State in the preceding calendar year that were surrendered from the account to which they were allocated to;

(b) the sum of verified emissions by Member State entered for the preceding calendar year as a percentage of the sum of verified emissions of the year before that year;
(c) the percentage share belonging to accounts administered by a particular Member State in the number and volume of all allowance and Kyoto unit transfer transactions in the preceding calendar year;
(d) the percentage share belonging to accounts administered by a particular Member State in the number and volume of all allowance and Kyoto unit transfer transactions in the preceding calendar year between accounts administered by different Member States.

4. The EUTL shall display on the public website of the EUTL the following information about each completed transaction recorded by the EUTL, on 1 January of the fifth year after the year of the recording of the information:
(a) account holder name and Account holder ID of the transferring account;
(b) account holder name and Account holder ID of the acquiring account;
[(c) the amount of allowances or Kyoto units involved in the transaction, without the unique unit identification code of the allowances and the unique numeric value of the unit serial number of the Kyoto units;][1]
(d) transaction identification code;
(e) date and time at which the transaction was completed (in Central European Time);
(f) The type of the transaction.

Amendment

1 Substituted by Commission Regulation (EU) No 1193/2011 of 18 November 2011 establishing a Union Registry for the trading period commencing on 1 January 2013, and subsequent trading periods, of the Union emissions trading scheme pursuant to Directive 2003/87/EC of the European Parliament and of the Council and Decision No 280/2004/EC of the European Parliament and of the Council and amending Commission Regulations (EC) No 2216/2004 and (EU) No 920/2010, Article 89(32)(a).

Information available to account holders

5. The Union registry shall display on the part of the Union registry's website only accessible to the account holder the following information, and shall update it in real time:
[(a) current holdings of allowances and Kyoto units, without unique unit identification code of the allowances and the unique numeric value of the unit serial number of the Kyoto units;][1]
(b) list of proposed transactions initiated by that account holder, detailing for each proposed transaction:
    (i) the elements in paragraph 4;
    (ii) the date and time at which the transaction was proposed (in Central European Time);
    (iii) the current status of that proposed transaction;
    (iv) any response codes returned consequent to the checks made by the registry and the EUTL;
(c) a list of allowances or Kyoto units acquired by that account as a result of completed transactions, detailing for each transaction the elements in point 4;
(d) list of allowances or Kyoto units transferred out of that account as a result of completed transactions, detailing for each transaction the elements in point 4.

Amendment

1 Substituted by Commission Regulation (EU) No 1193/2011 of 18 November 2011 establishing a Union Registry for the trading period commencing on 1 January 2013, and subsequent trading periods, of the Union emissions trading scheme pursuant to Directive 2003/87/EC of the European Parliament and of the Council and Decision No 280/2004/EC of the European Parliament and of the Council and amending Commission Regulations (EC) No 2216/2004 and (EU) No 920/2010, Article 89(32)(b).

Information available to national administrators

6. The Union registry shall display on the part of the Union registry's website only accessible to national administrators:

(a) the current balance and the transaction history of the ETS central clearing account, the Gateway deposit account, the Union allowance deletion account and the Aviation Surrender Set-Aside Account;

(b) account holders and authorised representatives whose access to any account in the Union registry was suspended by any national administrator in accordance with Article 27.

DIRECTIVE 2011/65/EU OF THE EUROPEAN PARLIAMENT AND OF THE COUNCIL

of 8 June 2011

ON THE RESTRICTION OF THE USE OF CERTAIN HAZARDOUS SUBSTANCES IN ELECTRICAL AND ELECTRONIC EQUIPMENT

THE EUROPEAN PARLIAMENT AND THE COUNCIL OF THE EUROPEAN UNION,

Having regard to the Treaty on the Functioning of the European Union, and in particular Article 114 thereof,

Having regard to the proposal from the European Commission,

Having regard to the opinion of the European Economic and Social Committee,

Having regard to the opinion of the Committee of Regions,

Acting in accordance with the ordinary legislative procedure,

Whereas:

(1) A number of substantial changes are to be made to Directive 2002/95/EC of the European Parliament and of the Council of 27 January 2003 on the restriction of the use of certain hazardous substances in electrical and electronic equipment. In the interest of clarity, that Directive should be recast.

(2) The disparities between the laws or administrative measures adopted by the Member States regarding the restriction of the use of hazardous substances in electrical and electronic equipment (EEE) could create barriers to trade and distort competition in the Union and may thereby have a direct impact on the establishment and functioning of the internal market. It therefore appears necessary to lay down rules in this field and to contribute to the protection of human health and the environmentally sound recovery and disposal of waste EEE.

(3) Directive 2002/95/EC provides that the Commission shall review the provisions of that Directive, in particular, in order to include in its scope equipment which falls within certain categories and to study the need to adapt the list of restricted substances on the basis of scientific progress, taking into account the precautionary principle, as endorsed by Council Resolution of 4 December 2000.

(4) Directive 2008/98/EC of the European Parliament and of the Council of 19 November 2008 on waste gives first priority to prevention in waste legislation. Prevention is defined, inter alia, as measures that reduce the content of harmful substances in materials and products.

(5) Council Resolution of 25 January 1988 on a Community action programme to combat environmental pollution by cadmium invited the Commission to pursue without delay the development of specific measures for such a programme. Human health also has to be protected and an overall strategy that in particular restricts the use of cadmium and stimulates research into substitutes should therefore be implemented. The Resolution stresses that the use of cadmium should be limited to cases where suitable alternatives do not exist.

(6) Regulation (EC) No 850/2004 of the European Parliament and of the Council of 29 April 2004 on persistent organic pollutants recalls that the objective of protecting the environment and human health from persistent organic pollutants cannot be sufficiently achieved by the Member States, owing to the transboundary effects of those pollutants, and can therefore be better achieved at Union level. Pursuant to that Regulation, releases of persistent organic pollutants, such as dioxins and furans, which are unintentional by-

products of industrial processes, should be identified and reduced as soon as possible with the ultimate aim of elimination, where feasible.

(7) The available evidence indicates that measures on the collection, treatment, recycling and disposal of waste EEE as set out in Directive 2002/96/EC of the European Parliament and of the Council of 27 January 2003 on waste electrical and electronic equipment (WEEE) are necessary to reduce the waste management problems associated with the heavy metals and flame retardants concerned. In spite of those measures, however, significant parts of waste EEE will continue to be found in the current disposal routes inside or outside the Union. Even if waste EEE were collected separately and submitted to recycling processes, its content of mercury, cadmium, lead, chromium VI, polybrominated biphenyls (PBB) and polybrominated diphenyl ethers (PBDE) would be likely to pose risks to health or the environment, especially when treated in less than optimal conditions.

(8) Taking into account technical and economic feasibility, including for small and medium sized enterprises (SMEs), the most effective way of ensuring a significant reduction of risks to health and the environment relating to those substances, in order to achieve the chosen level of protection in the Union, is the substitution of those substances in EEE by safe or safer materials. Restricting the use of those hazardous substances is likely to enhance the possibilities and economic profitability of recycling of waste EEE and decrease the negative impact on the health of workers in recycling plants.

(9) The substances covered by this Directive are scientifically well researched and evaluated and have been subject to different measures both at Union and at national level.

(10) The measures provided for in this Directive should take into account existing international guidelines and recommendations and should be based on an assessment of available scientific and technical information. The measures are necessary to achieve the chosen level of protection of human health and the environment, with due respect for the precautionary principle, and having regard to the risks which the absence of measures would be likely to create in the Union. The measures should be kept under review and, if necessary, adjusted to take account of available technical and scientific information. The annexes to this Directive should be reviewed periodically to take into account, inter alia, Annexes XIV and XVII to Regulation (EC) No 1907/2006 of the European Parliament and of the Council of 18 December 2006 concerning the Registration, Evaluation, Authorisation and Restriction of Chemicals (REACH) and establishing a European Chemicals Agency. In particular, the risks to human health and the environment arising from the use of Hexabromocyclododecane (HBCDD), Bis (2-ethylhexyl) phthalate (DEHP), Butyl benzyl phthalate (BBP) and Dibutyl phthalate (DBP) should be considered as a priority. With a view to further restrictions of substances, the Commission should re-investigate the substances that were subject to previous assessments, in accordance with the new criteria set out in this Directive as part of the first review.

(11) This Directive supplements the general Union waste management legislation, such as Directive 2008/98/EC and Regulation (EC) No 1907/2006.

(12) A number of definitions should be included in this Directive in order to specify its scope. In addition, the definition of "electrical and electronic equipment" should be complemented by a definition of "dependent", to cover the multipurpose character of certain products, where the intended functions of EEE are to be determined on the basis of objective characteristics, such as the design of the product and its marketing.

(13) Directive 2009/125/EC of the European Parliament and of the Council of 21 October 2009 establishing a framework for the setting of ecodesign requirements for energy-related products enables specific ecodesign requirements to be set for energy-related products which may also be covered by this Directive. Directive 2009/125/EC and the implementing measures adopted pursuant to it are without prejudice to Union waste management legislation.

(14) This Directive should apply without prejudice to Union legislation on safety and health requirements and specific Union waste management legislation, in particular Directive

2006/66/EC of the European Parliament and of the Council of 6 September 2006 on batteries and accumulators and waste batteries and accumulators and Regulation (EC) No 850/2004.

(15) The technical development of EEE without heavy metals, PBDE and PBB should be taken into account.

(16) As soon as scientific evidence is available, and taking into account the precautionary principle, the restriction of other hazardous substances, including any substances of very small size or with a very small internal or surface structure (nanomaterials) which may be hazardous due to properties relating to their size or structure, and their substitution by more environmentally friendly alternatives which ensure at least the same level of protection of consumers should be examined. To this end, the review and amendment of the list of restricted substances in Annex II should be coherent, maximise synergies with, and reflect the complementary nature of the work carried out under other Union legislation, and in particular under Regulation (EC) No 1907/2006 while ensuring the mutually independent operation of this Directive and that Regulation. Consultation with the relevant stakeholders should be carried out and specific account should be taken of the potential impact on SMEs.

(17) The development of renewable forms of energy is one of the Union's key objectives, and the contribution made by renewable energy sources to environmental and climate objectives is crucial. Directive 2009/28/EC of the European Parliament and of the Council of 23 April 2009 on the promotion of the use of energy from renewable sources recalls that there should be coherence between those objectives and other Union environmental legislation. Consequently, this Directive should not prevent the development of renewable energy technologies that have no negative impact on health and the environment and that are sustainable and economically viable.

(18) Exemptions from the substitution requirement should be permitted if substitution is not possible from the scientific and technical point of view, taking specific account of the situation of SMEs or if the negative environmental, health and consumer safety impacts caused by substitution are likely to outweigh the environmental, health and consumer safety benefits of the substitution or the reliability of substitutes is not ensured. The decision on exemptions and on the duration of possible exemptions should take into account the availability of substitutes and the socioeconomic impact of substitution. Life-cycle thinking on the overall impacts of exemptions should apply, where relevant. Substitution of the hazardous substances in EEE should also be carried out in such a way as to be compatible with the health and safety of users of EEE. The placing on the market of medical devices requires a conformity assessment procedure, according to Council Directive 93/42/EEC of 14 June 1993 concerning medical devices and Directive 98/79/EC of the European Parliament and of the Council of 27 October 1998 on in vitro diagnostic medical devices, which could require the involvement of a notified body designated by competent authorities of Member States. If such a notified body certifies that the safety of the potential substitute for the intended use in medical devices or in vitro diagnostic medical devices is not demonstrated, the use of that potential substitute will be deemed to have clear negative socioeconomic, health and consumer safety impacts. It should be possible, from the date of entry into force of this Directive, to apply for exemptions for equipment, even before the actual inclusion of that equipment in the scope of this Directive.

(19) Exemptions from the restriction for certain specific materials or components should be limited in their scope and duration, in order to achieve a gradual phase-out of hazardous substances in EEE, given that the use of those substances in such applications should become avoidable.

(20) As product reuse, refurbishment and extension of lifetime are beneficial, spare parts need to be available.

(21) Procedures for assessing the conformity of EEE subject to this Directive should be consistent with relevant Union legislation, in particular Decision No 768/2008/EC of the European Parliament and of the Council of 9 July 2008 on a common framework for

the marketing of products. Harmonising conformity assessment procedures should give manufacturers legal certainty as to what they have to provide as proof of compliance to the authorities throughout the Union.

(22) The conformity marking applicable for products at Union level, CE marking, should also apply to EEE that is subject to this Directive.

(23) The market surveillance mechanisms laid down by Regulation (EC) No 765/2008 of the European Parliament and of the Council of 9 July 2008 setting out the requirements for accreditation and market surveillance relating to the marketing of products provide the safeguard mechanisms to check compliance with this Directive.

(24) In order to ensure uniform conditions for the implementation of this Directive, particularly with regard to the guidelines and format of applications for exemptions, implementing powers should be conferred on the Commission. Those powers should be exercised in accordance with Regulation (EU) No 182/2011 of the European Parliament and of the Council of 16 February 2011 laying down the rules and general principles concerning mechanisms for control by Member States of the Commission's exercise of implementing powers.

(25) For the purposes of achieving the objectives of this Directive the Commission should be empowered to adopt delegated acts in accordance with Article 290 of the Treaty on the Functioning of the European Union in respect of amendments to Annex II, detailed rules for complying with maximum concentration values, and the adaptation of Annexes III and IV to technical and scientific progress. It is of particular importance that the Commission carry out appropriate consultations during its preparatory work, including at expert level.

(26) The obligation to transpose this Directive into national law should be confined to those provisions which represent a substantive change as compared with the earlier Directive. The obligation to transpose the provisions which are unchanged arises under the earlier Directive.

(27) This Directive should be without prejudice to the obligations of the Member States relating to the time-limits for transposition into national law and application of the Directive set out in Annex VII, Part B.

(28) When reviewing this Directive, a thorough analysis of its coherence with Regulation (EC) No 1907/2006 should be carried out by the Commission.

(29) In accordance with paragraph 34 of the Interinstitutional Agreement on better law-making, Member States are encouraged to draw up, for themselves and in the interests of the Union, their own tables, which will, as far as possible, illustrate the correlation between this Directive and their transposition measures, and to make those tables public.

(30) Since the objective of this Directive, namely to establish restrictions on the use of hazardous substances in EEE, cannot be sufficiently achieved by the Member States and can therefore, by reason of the scale of the problem and its implications in respect of other Union legislation on recovery and disposal of waste and areas of common interest, such as human health protection, be better achieved at Union level, the Union may adopt measures, in accordance with the principle of subsidiarity as set out in Article 5 of the Treaty on European Union. In accordance with the principle of proportionality, as set out in that Article, this Directive does not go beyond what is necessary in order to achieve that objective,

HAVE ADOPTED THIS DIRECTIVE:

Article 1

Subject matter

This Directive lays down rules on the restriction of the use of hazardous substances in electrical and electronic equipment (EEE) with a view to contributing to the protection of human health and the environment, including the environmentally sound recovery and disposal of waste EEE.

Article 2

Scope

1. This Directive shall, subject to paragraph 2, apply to EEE falling within the categories set out in Annex I.

2. Without prejudice to Article 4(3) and 4(4), Member States shall provide that EEE that was outside the scope of Directive 2002/95/EC, but which would not comply with this Directive, may nevertheless continue to be made available on the market until 22 July 2019.

3. This Directive shall apply without prejudice to the requirements of Union legislation on safety and health, and on chemicals, in particular Regulation (EC) No 1907/2006, as well as the requirements of specific Union waste management legislation.

4. This Directive does not apply to:

(a) equipment which is necessary for the protection of the essential interests of the security of Member States, including arms, munitions and war material intended for specifically military purposes;

(b) equipment designed to be sent into space;

(c) equipment which is specifically designed, and is to be installed, as part of another type of equipment that is excluded or does not fall within the scope of this Directive, which can fulfil its function only if it is part of that equipment, and which can be replaced only by the same specifically designed equipment;

(d) large-scale stationary industrial tools;

(e) large-scale fixed installations;

(f) means of transport for persons or goods, excluding electric two-wheel vehicles which are not type-approved;

(g) non-road mobile machinery made available exclusively for professional use;

(h) active implantable medical devices;

(i) photovoltaic panels intended to be used in a system that is designed, assembled and installed by professionals for permanent use at a defined location to produce energy from solar light for public, commercial, industrial and residential applications;

(j) equipment specifically designed solely for the purposes of research and development only made available on a business-to-business basis.

Article 3

Definitions

For the purposes of this Directive, the following definitions shall apply:

(1) "electrical and electronic equipment" or "EEE" means equipment which is dependent on electric currents or electromagnetic fields in order to work properly and equipment for the generation, transfer and measurement of such currents and fields and designed for use with a voltage rating not exceeding 1000 volts for alternating current and 1500 volts for direct current;

(2) for the purposes of point 1, "dependent " means, with regard to EEE, needing electric currents or electromagnetic fields to fulfil at least one intended function;

(3) "large-scale stationary industrial tools" means a large-scale assembly of machines, equipment, and/or components, functioning together for a specific application, permanently installed and de-installed by professionals at a given place, and used and maintained by professionals in an industrial manufacturing facility or research and development facility;

(4) "large-scale fixed installation" means a large-scale combination of several types of apparatus and, where applicable, other devices, which are assembled and installed by

professionals, intended to be used permanently in a pre-defined and dedicated location, and de-installed by professionals;

(5) "cables" means all cables with a rated voltage of less than 250 volts that serve as a connection or an extension to connect EEE to the electrical outlet or to connect two or more EEE to each other;

(6) "manufacturer" means any natural or legal person who manufactures an EEE or who has an EEE designed or manufactured and markets it under his name or trademark;

(7) "authorised representative" means any natural or legal person established within the Union who has received a written mandate from a manufacturer to act on his behalf in relation to specified tasks;

(8) "distributor" means any natural or legal person in the supply chain, other than the manufacturer or the importer, who makes an EEE available on the market;

(9) "importer" means any natural or legal person established within the Union, who places an EEE from a third country on the Union market;

(10) "economic operators" means the manufacturer, the authorised representative, the importer and the distributor;

(11) "making available on the market" means any supply of an EEE for distribution, consumption or use on the Union market in the course of a commercial activity, whether in return for payment or free of charge;

(12) "placing on the market" means making available an EEE on the Union market for the first time;

(13) "harmonised standard" means a standard adopted by one of the European standardisation bodies listed in Annex I to Directive 98/34/EC of the European Parliament and of the Council of 22 June 1998 laying down a procedure for the provision of information in the field of technical standards and regulations and of rules on Information Society services on the basis of a request made by the Commission in accordance with Article 6 of Directive 98/34/EC;

(14) "technical specification" means a document that prescribes technical requirements to be fulfilled by a product, process or service;

(15) "CE marking" means a marking by which the manufacturer indicates that the product is in conformity with the applicable requirements set out in Union harmonisation legislation providing for its affixing;

(16) "conformity assessment" means the process demonstrating whether the requirements of this Directive relating to an EEE, are met;

(17) "market surveillance" means the activities carried out and measures taken by public authorities to ensure that EEE complies with the requirements set out in this Directive and does not endanger health, safety or other issues of public interest protection;

(18) "recall" means any measure aimed at achieving the return of a product that has already been made available to the end user;

(19) "withdrawal" means any measure aimed at preventing a product in the supply chain from being made available on the market;

(20) "homogeneous material" means one material of uniform composition throughout or a material, consisting of a combination of materials, that cannot be disjointed or separated into different materials by mechanical actions such as unscrewing, cutting, crushing, grinding and abrasive processes;

(21) "medical device" means a medical device within the meaning of point (a) of Article 1(2) of Directive 93/42/EEC and which is also EEE;

(22) "in vitro diagnostic medical device" means an in vitro diagnostic medical device within the meaning of point (b) of Article 1(2) of Directive 98/79/EC;

(23) "active implantable medical device" means any active implantable medical device within the meaning of point (c) of Article 1(2) of Council Directive 90/385/EEC of 20 June 1990 on the approximation of the laws of the Member States relating to active implantable medical devices;

(24) "industrial monitoring and control instruments" means monitoring and control instruments designed for exclusively industrial or professional use;

(25) "availability of a substitute" means the ability of a substitute to be manufactured and delivered within a reasonable period of time as compared with the time required for manufacturing and delivering the substances listed in Annex II;

(26) "reliability of a substitute" means the probability that an EEE using a substitute will perform a required function without failure under stated conditions for a stated period of time;

(27) "spare part" means a separate part of an EEE that can replace a part of an EEE. The EEE cannot function as intended without that part of the EEE. The functionality of EEE is restored or is upgraded when the part is replaced by a spare part;

(28) "non-road mobile machinery made available exclusively for professional use" means machinery, with an on-board power source, the operation of which requires either mobility or continuous or semi-continuous movement between a succession of fixed working locations while working, and is made available exclusively for professional use.

Article 4

Prevention

1. Member States shall ensure that EEE placed on the market, including cables and spare parts for its repair, its reuse, updating of its functionalities or upgrading of its capacity, does not contain the substances listed in Annex II.

2. For the purposes of this Directive, no more than the maximum concentration value by weight in homogeneous materials as specified in Annex II shall be tolerated. The Commission shall adopt, by means of delegated acts in accordance with Article 20 and subject to the conditions laid down in Articles 21 and 22, detailed rules for complying with these maximum concentration values taking into account, inter alia, surface coatings.

3. Paragraph 1 shall apply to medical devices and monitoring and control instruments which are placed on the market from 22 July 2014, to in vitro diagnostic medical devices which are placed on the market from 22 July 2016 and to industrial monitoring and control instruments which are placed on the market from 22 July 2017.

4. Paragraph 1 shall not apply to cables or spare parts for the repair, the reuse, the updating of functionalities or upgrading of capacity of the following:

(a) EEE placed on the market before 1 July 2006;

(b) medical devices placed on the market before 22 July 2014;

(c) in vitro diagnostic medical devices placed on the market before 22 July 2016;

(d) monitoring and control instruments placed on the market before 22 July 2014;

(e) industrial monitoring and control instruments placed on the market before 22 July 2017;

(f) EEE which benefited from an exemption and which was placed on the market before that exemption expired as far as that specific exemption is concerned.

5. Paragraph 1 shall not apply to reused spare parts, recovered from EEE placed on the market before 1 July 2006 and used in equipment placed on the market before 1 July 2016, provided that reuse takes place in auditable closed-loop business-to-business return systems, and that the reuse of parts is notified to the consumer.

6. Paragraph 1 shall not apply to the applications listed in Annexes III and IV.

Article 5

Adaptation of the Annexes to scientific and technical progress

1. For the purposes of adapting Annexes III and IV to scientific and technical progress, and in order to achieve the objectives set out in Article 1, the Commission shall adopt by means of

individual delegated acts in accordance with Article 20 and subject to the conditions laid down in Articles 21 and 22, the following measures:

(a) inclusion of materials and components of EEE for specific applications in the lists in Annexes III and IV, provided that such inclusion does not weaken the environmental and health protection afforded by Regulation (EC) No 1907/2006 and where any of the following conditions is fulfilled:

— their elimination or substitution via design changes or materials and components which do not require any of the materials or substances listed in Annex II is scientifically or technically impracticable,

— the reliability of substitutes is not ensured,

— the total negative environmental, health and consumer safety impacts caused by substitution are likely to outweigh the total environmental, health and consumer safety benefits thereof.

Decisions on the inclusion of materials and components of EEE in the lists in Annexes III and IV and on the duration of any exemptions shall take into account the availability of substitutes and the socioeconomic impact of substitution. Decisions on the duration of any exemptions shall take into account any potential adverse impacts on innovation. Life-cycle thinking on the overall impacts of the exemption shall apply, where relevant;

(b) deletion of materials and components of EEE from the lists in Annexes III and IV where the conditions set out in point (a) are no longer fulfilled.

2. Measures adopted in accordance with point (a) of paragraph 1 shall, for categories 1 to 7, 10 and 11 of Annex I, have a validity period of up to 5 years and, for categories 8 and 9 of Annex I, a validity period of up to 7 years. The validity periods are to be decided on a case-by-case basis and may be renewed.

For the exemptions listed in Annex III as at 21 July 2011, the maximum validity period, which may be renewed, shall, for categories 1 to 7 and 10 of Annex I, be 5 years from 21 July 2011 and, for categories 8 and 9 of Annex I, 7 years from the relevant dates laid down in Article 4(3), unless a shorter period is specified.

For the exemptions listed in Annex IV as at 21 July 2011, the maximum validity period, which may be renewed, shall be 7 years from the relevant dates laid down in Article 4(3), unless a shorter period is specified.

3. An application for granting, renewing or revoking an exemption shall be made to the Commission in accordance with Annex V.

4. The Commission shall:

(a) acknowledge receipt of an application in writing within 15 days of its receipt. The acknowledgement shall state the date of receipt of the application;

(b) inform the Member States of the application without delay and make the application and any supplementary information supplied by the applicant available to them;

(c) make a summary of the application available to the public;

(d) evaluate the application and its justification.

5. An application for renewal of an exemption shall be made no later than 18 months before the exemption expires.

The Commission shall decide on an application for renewal of an exemption no later than 6 months before the expiry date of the existing exemption unless specific circumstances justify other deadlines. The existing exemption shall remain valid until a decision on the renewal application is taken by the Commission.

6. In the event that the application for renewal of an exemption is rejected or that an exemption is revoked, the exemption shall expire at the earliest 12 months, and at the latest 18 months, after the date of the decision.

7. Before Annexes are amended, the Commission shall, inter alia, consult economic operators, recyclers, treatment operators, environmental organisations and employee and consumer associations and make the comments received publicly available.

8. The Commission shall adopt a harmonised format for applications referred to in paragraph 3 of this Article as well as comprehensive guidelines for such applications, taking into account the situation of SMEs. Those implementing acts shall be adopted in accordance with the examination procedure referred to in Article 19(2).

Article 6

Review and amendment of list of restricted substances in Annex II

1. With a view to achieving the objectives set out in Article 1 and taking account of the precautionary principle, a review, based on a thorough assessment, and amendment of the list of restricted substances in Annex II shall be considered by the Commission before 22 July 2014, and periodically thereafter on its own initiative or following the submission of a proposal by a Member State containing the information referred to in paragraph 2.

The review and amendment of the list of restricted substances in Annex II shall be coherent with other legislation related to chemicals, in particular Regulation (EC) No 1907/2006, and shall take into account, inter alia, Annexes XIV and XVII to that Regulation. The review shall use publicly available knowledge obtained from the application of such legislation.

In order to review and amend Annex II, the Commission shall take special account of whether a substance, including substances of very small size or with a very small internal or surface structure, or a group of similar substances:

(a) could have a negative impact during EEE waste management operations, including on the possibilities for preparing for the reuse of waste EEE or for recycling of materials from waste EEE;

(b) could give rise, given its uses, to uncontrolled or diffuse release into the environment of the substance, or could give rise to hazardous residues, or transformation or degradation products through the preparation for reuse, recycling or other treatment of materials from waste EEE under current operational conditions;

(c) could lead to unacceptable exposure of workers involved in the waste EEE collection or treatment processes;

(d) could be replaced by substitutes or alternative technologies which have less negative impacts.

During that review, the Commission shall consult interested parties, including economic operators, recyclers, treatment operators, environmental organisations and employee and consumer associations.

2. The proposals to review and amend the list of restricted substances, or a group of similar substances, in Annex II shall contain at least the following information:

(a) precise and clear wording of the proposed restriction;

(b) references and scientific evidence for the restriction;

(c) information on the use of the substance or the group of similar substances in EEE;

(d) information on detrimental effects and exposure in particular during waste EEE management operations;

(e) information on possible substitutes and other alternatives, their availability and reliability;

(f) justification for considering a Union-wide restriction as the most appropriate measure;

(g) socioeconomic assessment.

3. The measures referred to in this Article shall be adopted by the Commission by means of delegated acts in accordance with Article 20 and subject to the conditions laid down in Articles 21 and 22.

Article 7

Obligations of manufacturers

Member States shall ensure that:

(a) when placing EEE on the market, manufacturers ensure that it has been designed and manufactured in accordance with the requirements set out in Article 4;

(b) manufacturers draw up the required technical documentation and carry out the internal production control procedure in line with module A of Annex II to Decision No 768/2008/EC or have it carried out;

(c) where compliance of EEE with the applicable requirements has been demonstrated by the procedure referred to in point (b), manufacturers draw up an EU declaration of conformity and affix the CE marking on the finished product. Where other applicable Union legislation requires the application of a conformity assessment procedure which is at least as stringent, compliance with the requirements of Article 4(1) of this Directive may be demonstrated within the context of that procedure. A single technical documentation may be drawn up;

(d) manufacturers keep the technical documentation and the EU declaration of conformity for 10 years after the EEE has been placed on the market;

(e) manufacturers ensure that procedures are in place for series production to remain in conformity. Changes in product design or characteristics and changes in the harmonised standards or in technical specifications by reference to which conformity of EEE is declared shall be adequately taken into account;

(f) manufacturers keep a register of non-conforming EEE and product recalls, and keep distributors informed thereof;

(g) manufacturers ensure that their EEE bears a type, batch or serial number or other element allowing its identification, or, where the size or nature of the EEE does not allow it, that the required information is provided on the packaging or in a document accompanying the EEE;

(h) manufacturers indicate their name, registered trade name or registered trade mark and the address at which they can be contacted on the EEE or, where that is not possible, on its packaging or in a document accompanying the EEE. The address must indicate a single point at which the manufacturer can be contacted. Where other applicable Union legislation contains provisions for the affixing of the manufacturer's name and address which are at least as stringent, those provisions shall apply;

(i) manufacturers who consider or have reason to believe that EEE which they have placed on the market is not in conformity with this Directive immediately take the necessary corrective measures to bring that EEE into conformity, to withdraw it or recall it, if appropriate, and immediately inform the competent national authorities of the Member States in which they made the EEE available to that effect, giving details, in particular, of the non-compliance and of any corrective measures taken;

(j) manufacturers, further to a reasoned request from a competent national authority, provide it with all the information and documentation necessary to demonstrate the conformity of the EEE with this Directive, in a language which can be easily understood by that authority, and that they cooperate with that authority, at its request, on any action taken to ensure compliance with this Directive of EEE which they have placed on the market.

Article 8

Obligations of authorised representatives

Member States shall ensure that:

(a) manufacturers have the possibility to appoint an authorised representative by written mandate. The obligations laid down in point (a) of Article 7 and the drawing up of technical documentation shall not form part of the authorised representative's mandate;

(b) an authorised representative performs the tasks specified in the mandate received from the manufacturer. The mandate shall allow the authorised representative to do at least the following:
- — keep the EU declaration of conformity and the technical documentation at the disposal of national surveillance authorities for 10 years following the placing on the market of the EEE,
- — further to a reasoned request from a competent national authority, provide that authority with all the information and documentation necessary to demonstrate the conformity of an EEE with this Directive,
- — cooperate with the competent national authorities, at their request, on any action taken to ensure compliance with this Directive of EEE covered by their mandate.

Article 9

Obligations of importers

Member States shall ensure that:

(a) importers place only EEE that complies with this Directive on the Union market;

(b) importers, before placing an EEE on the market, ensure that the appropriate conformity assessment procedure has been carried out by the manufacturer, and that they further ensure that the manufacturer has drawn up the technical documentation, that the EEE bears the CE marking and is accompanied by the required documents, and that the manufacturer has complied with the requirements set out in points (f) and (g) of Article 7;

(c) where an importer considers or has reason to believe that an EEE is not in conformity with Article 4, that importer does not place the EEE on the market until it has been brought into conformity, and that that importer informs the manufacturer and the market surveillance authorities to that effect;

(d) importers indicate their name, registered trade name or registered trade mark and the address at which they can be contacted on the EEE or, where that is not possible, on its packaging or in a document accompanying the EEE. Where other applicable Union legislation contains provisions for the affixing of the importer's name and address which are at least as stringent, those provisions shall apply;

(e) importers, in order to ensure compliance with this Directive, keep a register of non-compliant EEE and EEE recalls, and keep distributors informed thereof;

(f) importers who consider or have reason to believe that an EEE which they have placed on the market is not in conformity with this Directive immediately take the corrective measures necessary to bring that EEE into conformity, to withdraw it or recall it, as appropriate, and immediately inform the competent national authorities of the Member States in which they made the EEE available to that effect, giving details, in particular, of the non-compliance and of any corrective measures taken;

(g) importers keep, for 10 years following the placing on the market of the EEE, a copy of the EU declaration of conformity at the disposal of the market surveillance authorities and ensure that the technical documentation can be made available to those authorities, upon request;

(h) importers, further to a reasoned request from a competent national authority, provide it with all the information and documentation necessary to demonstrate the conformity of an EEE with this Directive in a language which can be easily understood by that authority, and that they cooperate with that authority, at its request, on any action taken to ensure compliance with this Directive of EEE which they have placed on the market.

Article 10

Obligations of distributors

Member States shall ensure that:

(a) when making an EEE available on the market, distributors act with due care in relation to the requirements applicable in particular by verifying that the EEE bears the CE marking, that it is accompanied by the required documents in a language which can be easily understood by consumers and other end-users in the Member State in which the EEE is to be made available on the market, and that the manufacturer and the importer have complied with the requirements set out in points (g) and (h) of Article 7 and in point (d) of Article 9;

(b) where a distributor considers or has reason to believe that an EEE is not in conformity with Article 4, that distributor does not make the EEE available on the market until it has been brought into conformity, and that that distributor informs the manufacturer or the importer as well as the market surveillance authorities to that effect;

(c) distributors who consider or have reason to believe that an EEE which they have made available on the market is not in conformity with this Directive make sure that the corrective measures necessary to bring that EEE into conformity, to withdraw it or recall it, as appropriate, are taken and that they immediately inform the competent national authorities of the Member States in which they made the EEE available to that effect, giving details, in particular, of the non-compliance and of any corrective measures taken;

(d) distributors, further to a reasoned request from a competent national authority, provide it with all the information and documentation necessary to demonstrate the conformity of EEE with this Directive, and that they cooperate with that authority, at its request, on any action taken to ensure the compliance with this Directive of the EEE which they have made available on the market.

Article 11

Cases in which obligations of manufacturers apply to importers and distributors

Member States shall ensure that an importer or distributor is considered a manufacturer for the purposes of this Directive and that he is subject to the obligations of the manufacturer under Article 7, where he places EEE on the market under his name or trademark or modifies EEE already placed on the market in such a way that compliance with the applicable requirements may be affected.

Article 12

Identification of economic operators

Member States shall ensure that economic operators, on request, identify the following to the market surveillance authorities, for 10 years following the placing on the market of the EEE:

(a) any economic operator who has supplied them with an EEE;

(b) any economic operator to whom they have supplied an EEE.

Article 13

EU declaration of conformity

1. The EU declaration of conformity shall state that it has been demonstrated that the requirements specified in Article 4 have been met.

2. The EU declaration of conformity shall have the model structure and shall contain the elements specified in Annex VI and shall be updated. It shall be translated into the language or languages required by the Member State on the market of which the product is placed or made available.

Where other applicable Union legislation requires the application of a conformity assessment procedure which is at least as stringent, compliance with the requirements of Article 4(1) of this Directive may be demonstrated within the context of that procedure. A single technical documentation may be drawn up.

3. By drawing up the EU declaration of conformity, the manufacturer shall assume responsibility for the compliance of the EEE with this Directive.

Article 14

General principles of the CE marking

The CE marking shall be subject to the general principles set out in Article 30 of Regulation (EC) No 765/2008.

Article 15

Rules and conditions for affixing the CE marking

1. The CE marking shall be affixed visibly, legibly and indelibly to the finished EEE or to its data plate. Where that is not possible or not warranted on account of the nature of the EEE, it shall be affixed to the packaging and to the accompanying documents.

2. The CE marking shall be affixed before the EEE is placed on the market.

3. Member States shall build upon existing mechanisms to ensure the correct application of the regime governing the CE marking and take appropriate action in the event of improper use of the CE marking. Member States shall also provide for penalties for infringements, which may include criminal sanctions for serious infringements. Those penalties shall be proportionate to the seriousness of the offence and constitute an effective deterrent against improper use.

Article 16

Presumption of conformity

1. In the absence of evidence to the contrary, Member States shall presume EEE bearing the CE marking to comply with this Directive.

2. Materials, components and EEE on which tests and measurements demonstrating compliance with the requirements of Article 4 have been performed, or which have been assessed, in accordance with harmonised standards, the references of which have been published in the Official Journal of the European Union, shall be presumed to comply with the requirements of this Directive.

Article 17

Formal objection to a harmonised standard

1. Where a Member State or the Commission considers that a harmonised standard does not entirely satisfy the requirements which it covers and which are set out in Article 4, the Commission or the Member State concerned shall bring the matter before the Committee set up pursuant to Article 5 of Directive 98/34/EC, giving its arguments. The Committee shall, after consulting the relevant European standardisation bodies, deliver its opinion without delay.

2. In the light of the Committee's opinion, the Commission shall decide to publish, not to publish, to publish with restriction, to maintain, to maintain with restriction or to withdraw the references to the harmonised standard concerned in or from the Official Journal of the European Union.

3. The Commission shall inform the European standardisation body concerned and, if necessary, request the revision of the harmonised standards concerned.

Article 18

Market surveillance and controls of EEE entering the Union market

Member States shall carry out market surveillance in accordance with Articles 15 to 29 of Regulation (EC) No 765/2008.

Article 19

Committee procedure

1. The Commission shall be assisted by the committee set up pursuant to Article 39 of Directive 2008/98/EC. That committee shall be a committee within the meaning of Regulation (EU) No 182/2011.

2. Where reference is made to this paragraph, Article 5 of Regulation (EU) No 182/2011 shall apply.

Article 20

Exercise of the delegation

1. The powers to adopt the delegated acts referred to in Article 4(2), Article 5(1) and Article 6 shall be conferred on the Commission for a period of 5 years from 21 July 2011. The Commission shall draw up a report in respect of delegated powers at the latest 6 months before the end of the 5 year period. The delegation of power shall be automatically extended for periods of an identical duration, unless the European Parliament or the Council revokes it in accordance with Article 21.

2. As soon as it adopts a delegated act, the Commission shall notify it simultaneously to the European Parliament and to the Council.

3. The powers to adopt delegated acts are conferred on the Commission subject to the conditions laid down in Articles 21 and 22.

Article 21

Revocation of the delegation

1. The delegation of power referred to in Article 4(2), Article 5(1) and Article 6 may be revoked at any time by the European Parliament or by the Council.

2. The institution which has commenced an internal procedure for deciding whether to revoke the delegation of powers shall endeavour to inform the other institution and the Commission within a reasonable time before the final decision is taken, indicating the delegated powers which could be subject to revocation and possible reasons for a revocation.

3. The decision of revocation shall put an end to the delegation of the powers specified in that decision. It shall take effect immediately or at a later date specified therein. It shall not affect the validity of the delegated acts already in force. It shall be published in the Official Journal of the European Union.

Article 22

Objections to delegated acts

1. The European Parliament or the Council may object to a delegated act within a period of 2 months from the date of notification.

At the initiative of the European Parliament or the Council that period shall be extended by 2 months.

2. If, on expiry of the period referred to in paragraph 1, neither the European Parliament nor the Council has objected to the delegated act it shall be published in the Official Journal of the European Union and shall enter into force on the date stated therein.

The delegated act may be published in the Official Journal of the European Union and enter into force before the expiry of that period if the European Parliament and the Council have both informed the Commission of their intention not to raise objections.

3. If the European Parliament or the Council objects to the delegated act within the period referred to in paragraph 1, it shall not enter into force. The institution which objects shall state the reasons for objecting to the delegated act.

Article 23

Penalties

The Member States shall lay down the rules on penalties applicable to infringements of the national provisions adopted pursuant to this Directive and shall take all measures necessary to ensure that they are implemented. The penalties provided for must be effective, proportionate and dissuasive. The Member States shall notify those provisions to the Commission by 2 January 2013 and shall notify it without delay of any subsequent amendment affecting them.

Article 24

Review

1. No later than 22 July 2014 the Commission shall examine the need to amend the scope of this Directive in respect of the EEE referred to in Article 2, and shall present a report thereon to the European Parliament and the Council accompanied by a legislative proposal, if appropriate, with respect to any additional exclusions related to that EEE.

2. No later than 22 July 2021 the Commission shall carry out a general review of this Directive, and shall present a report to the European Parliament and the Council accompanied, if appropriate, by a legislative proposal.

Article 25

Transposition

1. Member States shall adopt and publish, by 2 January 2013, the laws, regulations and administrative provisions necessary to comply with this Directive. They shall forthwith communicate to the Commission the text of those provisions.

When Member States adopt those provisions, they shall contain a reference to this Directive or be accompanied by such a reference on the occasion of their official publication. Member States shall determine how such reference is to be made.

2. Member States shall communicate to the Commission the text of the main provisions of national law which they adopt in the field covered by this Directive.

Article 26

Repeal

Directive 2002/95/EC as amended by the acts listed in Annex VII, Part A is repealed with effect from 3 January 2013 without prejudice to the obligations of the Member States relating to the time limits for transposition into national law and application of the Directive set out in Annex VII, Part B.

References to the repealed acts shall be construed as references to this Directive and shall be read in accordance with the correlation table in Annex VIII.

Article 27

Entry into force

This Directive shall enter into force on the 20th day following its publication in the Official Journal of the European Union.

Article 28

Addressees

This Directive is addressed to the Member States.

ANNEX I
CATEGORIES OF EEE COVERED BY THIS DIRECTIVE

1. Large household appliances.
2. Small household appliances.
3. IT and telecommunications equipment.
4. Consumer equipment.
5. Lighting equipment.
6. Electrical and electronic tools.
7. Toys, leisure and sports equipment.
8. Medical devices.
9. Monitoring and control instruments including industrial monitoring and control instruments.
10. Automatic dispensers.
11. Other EEE not covered by any of the categories above.

ANNEX II
RESTRICTED SUBSTANCES REFERRED TO IN ARTICLE 4(1) AND MAXIMUM CONCENTRATION VALUES TOLERATED BY WEIGHT IN HOMOGENEOUS MATERIALS

Lead (0,1 %)

Mercury (0,1 %)

Cadmium (0,01 %)

Hexavalent chromium (0,1 %)

Polybrominated biphenyls (PBB) (0,1 %)

Polybrominated diphenyl ethers (PBDE) (0,1 %)

ANNEX III
APPLICATIONS EXEMPTED FROM THE RESTRICTION IN ARTICLE 4(1)

Exemption		*Scope and dates of applicability*
1	Mercury in single capped (compact) fluorescent lamps not exceeding (per burner):	
1(a)	For general lighting purposes < 30 W: 5 mg	Expires on 31 December 2011; 3,5 mg may be used per burner after 31 December 2011 until 31 December 2012; 2,5 mg shall be used per burner after 31 December 2012
1(b)	For general lighting purposes ≥ 30 W and < 50 W: 5 mg	Expires on 31 December 2011; 3,5 mg may be used per burner after 31 December 2011
1(c)	For general lighting purposes ≥ 50 W and < 150 W: 5 mg	
1(d)	For general lighting purposes ≥ 150 W: 15 mg	
1(e)	For general lighting purposes with circular or square structural shape and tube diameter ≤ 17 mm	No limitation of use until 31 December 2011; 7 mg may be used per burner after 31 December 2011
1(f)	For special purposes: 5 mg	
2(a)	Mercury in double-capped linear fluorescent lamps for general lighting purposes not exceeding (per lamp):	
2(a)(1)	Tri-band phosphor with normal lifetime and a tube diameter < 9 mm (e.g. T2): 5 mg	Expires on 31 December 2011; 4 mg may be used per lamp after 31 December 2011
2(a)(2)	Tri-band phosphor with normal lifetime and a tube diameter ≥ 9 mm and ≤ 17 mm (e.g. T5): 5 mg	Expires on 31 December 2011; 3 mg may be used per lamp after 31 December 2011
2(a)(3)	Tri-band phosphor with normal lifetime and a tube diameter > 17 mm and ≤ 28 mm (e.g. T8): 5 mg	Expires on 31 December 2011; 3,5 mg may be used per lamp after 31 December 2011
2(a)(4)	Tri-band phosphor with normal lifetime and a tube diameter > 28 mm (e.g. T12): 5 mg	Expires on 31 December 2012; 3,5 mg may be used per lamp after 31 December 2012
2(a)(5)	Tri-band phosphor with long lifetime (≥ 25000 h): 8 mg	Expires on 31 December 2011; 5 mg may be used per lamp after 31 December 2011
2(b)	Mercury in other fluorescent lamps not exceeding (per lamp):	
2(b)(1)	Linear halophosphate lamps with tube > 28 mm (e.g. T10 and T12): 10 mg	Expires on 13 April 2012
2(b)(2)	Non-linear halophosphate lamps (all diameters): 15 mg	Expires on 13 April 2016
2(b)(3)	Non-linear tri-band phosphor lamps with tube diameter > 17 mm (e.g. T9)	No limitation of use until 31 December 2011; 15 mg may be used per lamp after 31 December 2011

Exemption		*Scope and dates of applicability*
2(b)(4)	Lamps for other general lighting and special purposes (e.g. induction lamps)	No limitation of use until 31 December 2011; 15 mg may be used per lamp after 31 December 2011
3	Mercury in cold cathode fluorescent lamps and external electrode fluorescent lamps (CCFL and EEFL) for special purposes not exceeding (per lamp):	
3(a)	Short length (≤ 500 mm)	No limitation of use until 31 December 2011; 3,5 mg may be used per lamp after 31 December 2011
3(b)	Medium length (> 500 mm and ≤ 1500 mm)	No limitation of use until 31 December 2011; 5 mg may be used per lamp after 31 December 2011
3(c)	Long length (> 1500 mm)	No limitation of use until 31 December 2011; 13 mg may be used per lamp after 31 December 2011
4(a)	Mercury in other low pressure discharge lamps (per lamp)	No limitation of use until 31 December 2011; 15 mg may be used per lamp after 31 December 2011
4(b)	Mercury in High Pressure Sodium (vapour) lamps for general lighting purposes not exceeding (per burner) in lamps with improved colour rendering index Ra > 60:	
4(b)-I	P ≤ 155 W	No limitation of use until 31 December 2011; 30 mg may be used per burner after 31 December 2011
4(b)-II	155 W < P ≤ 405 W	No limitation of use until 31 December 2011; 40 mg may be used per burner after 31 December 2011
4(b)-III	P > 405 W	No limitation of use until 31 December 2011; 40 mg may be used per burner after 31 December 2011
4(c)	Mercury in other High Pressure Sodium (vapour) lamps for general lighting purposes not exceeding (per burner):	
4(c)-I	P ≤ 155 W	No limitation of use until 31 December 2011; 25 mg may be used per burner after 31 December 2011
4(c)-II	155 W < P ≤ 405 W	No limitation of use until 31 December 2011; 30 mg may be used per burner after 31 December 2011
4(c)-III	P > 405 W	No limitation of use until 31 December 2011; 40 mg may be used per burner after 31 December 2011
4(d)	Mercury in High Pressure Mercury (vapour) lamps (HPMV)	Expires on 13 April 2015
4(e)	Mercury in metal halide lamps (MH)	

Exemption		*Scope and dates of applicability*
4(f)	Mercury in other discharge lamps for special purposes not specifically mentioned in this Annex	
5(a)	Lead in glass of cathode ray tubes	
5(b)	Lead in glass of fluorescent tubes not exceeding 0,2 % by weight	
6(a)	Lead as an alloying element in steel for machining purposes and in galvanised steel containing up to 0,35 % lead by weight	
6(b)	Lead as an alloying element in aluminium containing up to 0,4 % lead by weight	
6(c)	Copper alloy containing up to 4 % lead by weight	
7(a)	Lead in high melting temperature type solders (i.e. lead-based alloys containing 85 % by weight or more lead)	
7(b)	Lead in solders for servers, storage and storage array systems, network infrastructure equipment for switching, signalling, transmission, and network management for telecommunications	
7(c)-I	Electrical and electronic components containing lead in a glass or ceramic other than dielectric ceramic in capacitors, e.g. piezoelectronic devices, or in a glass or ceramic matrix compound	
7(c)-II	Lead in dielectric ceramic in capacitors for a rated voltage of 125 V AC or 250 V DC or higher	
7(c)-III	Lead in dielectric ceramic in capacitors for a rated voltage of less than 125 V AC or 250 V DC	Expires on 1 January 2013 and after that date may be used in spare parts for EEE placed on the market before 1 January 2013
8(a)	Cadmium and its compounds in one shot pellet type thermal cut-offs	Expires on 1 January 2012 and after that date may be used in spare parts for EEE placed on the market before 1 January 2012
8(b)	Cadmium and its compounds in electrical contacts	
9	Hexavalent chromium as an anticorrosion agent of the carbon steel cooling system in absorption refrigerators up to 0,75 % by weight in the cooling solution	
9(b)	Lead in bearing shells and bushes for refrigerant-containing compressors for heating, ventilation, air conditioning and refrigeration (HVACR) applications	
11(a)	Lead used in C-press compliant pin connector systems	May be used in spare parts for EEE placed on the market before 24 September 2010

Exemption		*Scope and dates of applicability*
11(b)	Lead used in other than C-press compliant pin connector systems	Expires on 1 January 2013 and after that date may be used in spare parts for EEE placed on the market before 1 January 2013
12	Lead as a coating material for the thermal conduction module C-ring	May be used in spare parts for EEE placed on the market before 24 September 2010
13(a)	Lead in white glasses used for optical applications	
13(b)	Cadmium and lead in filter glasses and glasses used for reflectance standards	
14	Lead in solders consisting of more than two elements for the connection between the pins and the package of microprocessors with a lead content of more than 80 % and less than 85 % by weight	Expired on 1 January 2011 and after that date may be used in spare parts for EEE placed on the market before 1 January 2011
15	Lead in solders to complete a viable electrical connection between semiconductor die and carrier within integrated circuit flip chip packages	
16	Lead in linear incandescent lamps with silicate coated tubes	Expires on 1 September 2013
17	Lead halide as radiant agent in high intensity discharge (HID) lamps used for professional reprography applications	
18(a)	Lead as activator in the fluorescent powder (1 % lead by weight or less) of discharge lamps when used as speciality lamps for diazoprinting reprography, lithography, insect traps, photochemical and curing processes containing phosphors such as SMS ($(Sr,Ba)_2MgSi_2O_7:Pb$)	Expired on 1 January 2011
18(b)	Lead as activator in the fluorescent powder (1 % lead by weight or less) of discharge lamps when used as sun tanning lamps containing phosphors such as BSP ($BaSi_2O5:Pb$)	
19	Lead with PbBiSn-Hg and PbInSn-Hg in specific compositions as main amalgam and with PbSn-Hg as auxiliary amalgam in very compact energy saving lamps (ESL)	Expires on 1 June 2011
20	Lead oxide in glass used for bonding front and rear substrates of flat fluorescent lamps used for Liquid Crystal Displays (LCDs)	Expires on 1 June 2011
21	Lead and cadmium in printing inks for the application of enamels on glasses, such as borosilicate and soda lime glasses	
23	Lead in finishes of fine pitch components other than connectors with a pitch of 0,65 mm and less	May be used in spare parts for EEE placed on the market before 24 September 2010

Exemption		*Scope and dates of applicability*
24	Lead in solders for the soldering to machined through hole discoidal and planar array ceramic multilayer capacitors	
25	Lead oxide in surface conduction electron emitter displays (SED) used in structural elements, notably in the seal frit and frit ring	
26	Lead oxide in the glass envelope of black light blue lamps	Expires on 1 June 2011
27	Lead alloys as solder for transducers used in high-powered (designated to operate for several hours at acoustic power levels of 125 dB SPL and above) loudspeakers	Expired on 24 September 2010
29	Lead bound in crystal glass as defined in Annex I (Categories 1, 2, 3 and 4) of Council Directive 69/493/EEC	
30	Cadmium alloys as electrical/mechanical solder joints to electrical conductors located directly on the voice coil in transducers used in high-powered loudspeakers with sound pressure levels of 100 dB (A) and more	
31	Lead in soldering materials in mercury free flat fluorescent lamps (which, e.g. are used for liquid crystal displays, design or industrial lighting)	
32	Lead oxide in seal frit used for making window assemblies for Argon and Krypton laser tubes	
33	Lead in solders for the soldering of thin copper wires of 100 μm diameter and less in power transformers	
34	Lead in cermet-based trimmer potentiometer elements	
36	Mercury used as a cathode sputtering inhibitor in DC plasma displays with a content up to 30 mg per display	Expired on 1 July 2010
37	Lead in the plating layer of high voltage diodes on the basis of a zinc borate glass body	
38	Cadmium and cadmium oxide in thick film pastes used on aluminium bonded beryllium oxide	
39	Cadmium in colour converting II-VI LEDs (< 10 μg Cd per mm^2 of light-emitting area) for use in solid state illumination or display systems	Expires on 1 July 2014

ANNEX IV
APPLICATIONS EXEMPTED FROM THE RESTRICTION IN ARTICLE 4(1) SPECIFIC TO MEDICAL DEVICES AND MONITORING AND CONTROL INSTRUMENTS

Equipment utilising or detecting ionising radiation

1. Lead, cadmium and mercury in detectors for ionising radiation.

2. Lead bearings in X-ray tubes.

3. Lead in electromagnetic radiation amplification devices: micro-channel plate and capillary plate.

4. Lead in glass frit of X-ray tubes and image intensifiers and lead in glass frit binder for assembly of gas lasers and for vacuum tubes that convert electromagnetic radiation into electrons.

5. Lead in shielding for ionising radiation.

6. Lead in X-ray test objects.

7. Lead stearate X-ray diffraction crystals.

8. Radioactive cadmium isotope source for portable X-ray fluorescence spectrometers.

Sensors, detectors and electrodes

1a. Lead and cadmium in ion selective electrodes including glass of pH electrodes.

1b. Lead anodes in electrochemical oxygen sensors.

1c. Lead, cadmium and mercury in infra-red light detectors.

1d. Mercury in reference electrodes: low chloride mercury chloride, mercury sulphate and mercury oxide.

Others

9. Cadmium in helium-cadmium lasers.

10. Lead and cadmium in atomic absorption spectroscopy lamps.

11. Lead in alloys as a superconductor and thermal conductor in MRI.

12. Lead and cadmium in metallic bonds to superconducting materials in MRI and SQUID detectors.

13. Lead in counterweights.

14. Lead in single crystal piezoelectric materials for ultrasonic transducers.

15. Lead in solders for bonding to ultrasonic transducers.

16. Mercury in very high accuracy capacitance and loss measurement bridges and in high frequency RF switches and relays in monitoring and control instruments not exceeding 20 mg of mercury per switch or relay.

17. Lead in solders in portable emergency defibrillators.

18. Lead in solders of high performance infrared imaging modules to detect in the range 8-14 µm.

19. Lead in Liquid crystal on silicon (LCoS) displays.

20. Cadmium in X-ray measurement filters.

ANNEX V
APPLICATIONS FOR GRANTING, RENEWING AND REVOKING EXEMPTIONS AS REFERRED TO IN ARTICLE 5

Applications for exemptions, renewal of exemptions or, mutatis mutandis, for revoking an exemption may be submitted by a manufacturer, the authorised representative of a manufacturer, or any economic operator in the supply chain and shall include at least the following:

(a) the name, address and contact details of the applicant;

(b) information on the material or component and the specific uses of the substance in the material and component for which an exemption, or its revocation, is requested and its particular characteristics;

(c) verifiable and referenced justification for an exemption, or its revocation, in line with the conditions established in Article 5;

(d) an analysis of possible alternative substances, materials or designs on a life-cycle basis, including, when available, information about independent research, peer-review studies and development activities by the applicant and an analysis of the availability of such alternatives;

(e) information on the possible preparation for reuse or recycling of materials from waste EEE, and on the provisions relating to the appropriate treatment of waste according to Annex II to Directive 2002/96/EC;

(f) other relevant information;

(g) the proposed actions to develop, request the development and/or to apply possible alternatives including a timetable for such actions by the applicant;

(h) where appropriate, an indication of the information which should be regarded as proprietary accompanied by verifiable justification;

(i) when applying for an exemption, proposal for a precise and clear wording for the exemption;

(j) a summary of the application.

ANNEX VI
EU DECLARATION OF CONFORMITY

1. No … (unique identification of the EEE):

2. Name and address of the manufacturer or his authorised representative:

3. This declaration of conformity is issued under the sole responsibility of the manufacturer (or installer):

4. Object of the declaration (identification of EEE allowing traceability. It may include a photograph, where appropriate):

5. The object of the declaration described above is in conformity with Directive 2011/65/EU of the European Parliament and of the Council of 8 June 2011 on the restriction of the use of certain hazardous substances in electrical and electronic equipment:

6. Where applicable, references to the relevant harmonised standards used or references to the technical specifications in relation to which conformity is declared:

7. Additional information:

Signed for and on behalf of:
(place and date of issue):
(name, function) (signature):

ANNEX VII

PART A
REPEALED DIRECTIVE WITH ITS SUCCESSIVE AMENDMENTS (REFERRED TO IN ARTICLE 26)

Directive 2002/95/EC of the European Parliament and of the Council	(OJ L 37, 13.2.2003, p. 19).
Commission Decision 2005/618/EC	(OJ L 214, 19.8.2005, p. 65).
Commission Decision 2005/717/EC	(OJ L 271, 15.10.2005, p. 48).
Commission Decision 2005/747/EC	(OJ L 280, 25.10.2005, p. 18).
Commission Decision 2006/310/EC	(OJ L 115, 28.4.2006, p. 38).
Commission Decision 2006/690/EC	(OJ L 283, 14.10.2006, p. 47).
Commission Decision 2006/691/EC	(OJ L 283, 14.10.2006, p. 48).
Commission Decision 2006/692/EC	(OJ L 283, 14.10.2006, p. 50).
Directive 2008/35/EC of the European Parliament and of the Council	(OJ L 81, 20.3.2008, p. 67).
Commission Decision 2008/385/EC	(OJ L 136, 24.5.2008, p. 9).
Commission Decision 2009/428/EC	(OJ L 139, 5.6.2009, p. 32).
Commission Decision 2009/443/EC	(OJ L 148, 11.6.2009, p. 27).
Commission Decision 2010/122/EU	(OJ L 49, 26.2.2010, p. 32).
Commission Decision 2010/571/EU	(OJ L 251, 25.9.2010, p. 28).

PART B
LIST OF TIME-LIMITS FOR TRANSPOSITION INTO NATIONAL LAW (REFERRED TO IN ARTICLE 26)

Directive	*Deadline for transposition*
2002/95/EC	12 August 2004
2008/35/EC	—

ANNEX VIII
CORRELATION TABLE

Directive 2002/95/EC	*This Directive*
Article 1	Article 1
Article 2(1)	Article 2(1), 2(2), Annex I
Article 2(2)	Article 2(3)
Article 2(3)	Article 2(4), introductory wording
—	Article 2(4)
Article 3(a)	Article 3(1),(2)
Article 3(b)	—
—	Article 3(6)-(28)
Article 4(1)	Article 4(1), Annex II
—	Article 4(3)-(4)
Article 4(2)	Article 4(6)
Article 4(3)	—
Article 5(1), introductory wording	Article 5(1), introductory wording
Article 5(1)(a)	Article 4(2)
Article 5(1)(b)	Article 5(1)(a), first and third indents

Directive 2002/95/EC	*This Directive*
—	Article 5(1)(a), second indent Article 5(1)(a), final paragraph
Article 5(1)(c)	Article 5(1)(b)
—	Article 5(2) Article 5(3)-(6)
Article 5(2)	Article 5(7)
—	Article 5(8)
Article 6	Article 6
—	Article 7-18
Article 7	Articles 19-22
Article 8	Article 23
Article 9	Article 25
—	Article 26
Article 10	Article 27
Article 11	Article 28
—	Annexes I-II
Annex, points 1-39	Annex III, points 1-39
—	Annexes IV, V, VI-VIII

COUNCIL DIRECTIVE 2011/70/EURATOM

of 19 July 2011

ESTABLISHING A COMMUNITY FRAMEWORK FOR THE RESPONSIBLE AND SAFE MANAGEMENT OF SPENT FUEL AND RADIOACTIVE WASTE

THE COUNCIL OF THE EUROPEAN UNION,

Having regard to the Treaty establishing the European Atomic Energy Community, and in particular Articles 31 and 32 thereof,

Having regard to the proposal from the European Commission, drawn up after obtaining the opinion of a group of persons appointed by the Scientific and Technical Committee from among scientific experts in the Member States,

Having regard to the opinion of the European Economic and Social Committee,

Having regard to the opinion of the European Parliament,

Whereas:

(1) Article 2(b) of the Treaty establishing the European Atomic Energy Community ("Euratom Treaty") provides for the establishment of uniform safety standards to protect the health of workers and of the general public.

(2) Article 30 of the Euratom Treaty provides for the establishment of basic standards for the protection of the health of workers and the general public against the dangers arising from ionising radiations.

(3) Article 37 of the Euratom Treaty requires Member States to provide the Commission with general data relating to any plan for the disposal of radioactive waste.

(4) Council Directive 96/29/Euratom establishes basic safety standards for the protection of the health of workers and the general public against the dangers arising from ionising radiation. That Directive has been supplemented by more specific legislation.

(5) As recognised by the Court of Justice of the European Union in its case-law, the provisions of Chapter 3 of the Euratom Treaty, on health and safety, form a coherent whole conferring upon the Commission powers of some considerable scope in order to protect the population and the environment against the risks of nuclear contamination.

(6) Council Decision 87/600/Euratom of 14 December 1987 on Community arrangements for the early exchange of information in the event of a radiological emergency established a framework for notification and provision of information to be used by the Member States in order to protect the general public in case of a radiological emergency. Council Directive 89/618/Euratom of 27 November 1989 on informing the general public about health protection measures to be applied and steps to be taken in the event of a radiological emergency imposed obligations on the Member States to inform the general public in the event of a radiological emergency.

(7) Council Directive 2003/122/Euratom provides for the control of high-activity sealed radioactive sources and orphan sources, including disused sources. In accordance with the Joint Convention on the Safety of Spent Fuel Management and on the Safety of Radioactive Waste Management ("the Joint Convention") and the International Atomic Energy Agency (IAEA) Code of Conduct on the Safety and Security of Radioactive Sources, and current industrial practices, disused sealed sources can be reused, recycled or disposed of. In many cases, this needs a return of the source or return of the equipment, including the source, to a supplier or a manufacturer, for requalification or processing.

(8) Directive 2006/21/EC of the European Parliament and of the Council of 15 March 2006 on the management of waste from extractive industries covers the management of waste from extractive industries which may be radioactive, but excluding such aspects as are specific to radioactivity, which are matters dealt with under the Euratom Treaty.

(9) Council Directive 2006/117/Euratom lays down a European Atomic Energy Community ("Community") system of supervision and control of transboundary shipments of radioactive waste and spent fuel. That Directive was supplemented by Commission Recommendation 2008/956/Euratom of 4 December 2008 on criteria for the export of radioactive waste and spent fuel to third countries.

(10) Council Directive 2009/71/Euratom of 25 June 2009 establishing a Community framework for the nuclear safety of nuclear installations imposes obligations on the Member States to establish and maintain a national framework for nuclear safety. While that Directive concerns principally the nuclear safety of nuclear installations, it states that it is also important to ensure the safe management of spent fuel and radioactive waste, including at storage and disposal facilities. Therefore, those facilities, addressed both in Directive 2009/71/Euratom and in this Directive, should not be subject to disproportionate or unnecessary obligations, especially as regards reporting.

(11) Directive 2003/35/EC of the European Parliament and of the Council of 26 May 2003 providing for public participation in respect of the drawing up of certain plans and programmes relating to the environment applies to certain plans and programmes within the scope of Directive 2001/42/EC of the European Parliament and of the Council of 27 June 2001 on the assessment of the effects of certain plans and programmes on the environment.

(12) Commission Recommendation 2006/851/Euratom of 24 October 2006 on the management of the financial resources for the decommissioning of nuclear installations, spent fuel and radioactive waste focuses on the adequacy of funding, its financial security and its transparency in order to ensure that the funds are only used for the intended purposes.

(13) Under the specific terms of accession of Lithuania, Slovakia and Bulgaria to the European Union, where certain nuclear power plants were subject to early shutdown, the Community has taken part in the raising of financial resources and provides financial support subject to certain conditions to various decommissioning projects, including management of radioactive waste and spent fuel.

(14) The Joint Convention, concluded under the auspices of the IAEA, represents an incentive instrument which aims at achieving and maintaining a high level of safety worldwide in spent fuel and radioactive waste management through the enhancement of national measures and international cooperation.

(15) Some Member States have already participated and intend to participate further in the US-Russian driven programme, called the Global Threat Reduction Initiative, by shipping the spent fuel of research reactors to the United States of America and to the Russian Federation.

(16) In 2006, the IAEA updated the structure of standards and published the Fundamental Safety Principles, which were jointly sponsored by the Community, the Organisation for Economic Cooperation and Development/Nuclear Energy Agency and other international organisations. Applying the Fundamental Safety Principles will facilitate the application of international safety standards and will make for greater consistency between the arrangements of different states.

(17) Following the Council's invitation to set up a High Level Group at EU level, as recorded in its Conclusions of 8 May 2007 on Nuclear Safety and Safe Management of Spent Nuclear Fuel and Radioactive Waste, the European Nuclear Safety Regulators Group (ENSREG) was set up by Commission Decision 2007/530/Euratom of 17 July 2007 on establishing the European High Level Group on Nuclear Safety and Waste Management to contribute to the achievement of the Community objectives in the field of spent fuel and radioactive waste management. The conclusions and recommendations of ENSREG were reflected in the Council Resolution of 16 December 2008 on Spent Fuel

and Radioactive Waste Management and the Council Conclusions of 10 November 2009 on the report by the European Nuclear Safety Regulators Group.

(18) The European Parliament adopted on 10 May 2007 a Resolution "Assessing Euratom – 50 Years of European nuclear energy policy" where it called for harmonised standards for radioactive waste management and invited the Commission to review the relevant drafts of its legislative proposal and submit a new proposal for a directive on radioactive waste management.

(19) While each Member State remains free to define its energy mix, all Member States generate radioactive waste from power generation or in the course of industrial, agricultural, medical and research activities, or through decommissioning of nuclear facilities or in situations of remediation and interventions.

(20) The operation of nuclear reactors generates spent fuel. Each Member State remains free to define its fuel cycle policy. The spent fuel can be regarded either as a valuable resource that may be reprocessed or as radioactive waste that is destined for direct disposal. Whatever option is chosen, the disposal of high-level waste, separated at reprocessing, or of spent fuel regarded as waste should be considered.

(21) Radioactive waste, including spent fuel considered as waste, requires containment and isolation from humans and the living environment over the long term. Its specific nature, namely that it contains radionuclides, requires arrangements to protect human health and the environment against dangers arising from ionising radiation, including disposal in appropriate facilities as the end location point. The storage of radioactive waste, including long-term storage, is an interim solution, but not an alternative to disposal.

(22) A national radioactive waste classification scheme should support those arrangements, taking fully into account the specific types and properties of radioactive waste.

(23) The typical disposal concept for low and intermediate-level waste is near-surface disposal. It is broadly accepted at the technical level that, at this time, deep geological disposal represents the safest and most sustainable option as the end point of the management of high-level waste and spent fuel considered as waste. Member States, while retaining responsibility for their respective policies in respect of the management of their spent fuel and low, intermediate or high-level radioactive waste, should include planning and implementation of disposal options in their national policies. Since the implementation and development of a disposal facility will take place over many decades, many programmes recognise the necessity of remaining flexible and adaptable, e.g. in order to incorporate new knowledge about site conditions or the possible evolution of the disposal system. The activities conducted under the Implementing Geological Disposal of Radioactive Waste Technology Platform (IGD-TP) could facilitate access to expertise and technology in this respect. To that end, reversibility and retrievability as operating and design criteria may be used to guide the technical development of a disposal system. However, those criteria should not be a substitute for a well designed disposal facility that has a defensible basis for closure. A compromise is needed as the management of radioactive waste and spent fuel is based on state-of-the-art science and technology.

(24) It should be an ethical obligation of each Member State to avoid any undue burden on future generations in respect of spent fuel and radioactive waste including any radioactive waste expected from decommissioning of existing nuclear installations. Through the implementation of this Directive Member States will have demonstrated that they have taken reasonable steps to ensure that that objective is met.

(25) The ultimate responsibility of Member States for the safety of spent fuel and radioactive waste management is a fundamental principle reaffirmed by the Joint Convention. That principle of national responsibility, as well as the principle of prime responsibility of the licence holder for the safety of spent fuel and radioactive waste management under the supervision of its competent regulatory authority, should be enhanced and the role and independence of the competent regulatory authority should be reinforced by this Directive.

(26) It is understood that the utilisation of radioactive sources by a competent regulatory authority for the purpose of carrying out its regulatory tasks does not affect its independence.

(27) Member States should ensure that adequate funding is available for the management of spent fuel and radioactive waste.

(28) Member States should establish national programmes to ensure the transposition of political decisions into clear provisions for the timely implementation of all steps of spent fuel and radioactive waste management from generation to disposal. It should be possible for such national programmes to be in the form of a single reference document or a set of documents.

(29) It is understood that national arrangements for the safety of spent fuel and radioactive waste management will be applied through some form of legal, regulatory or organisational instrument, the choice of which rests within the competence of the Member States.

(30) The different steps in spent fuel and radioactive waste management are closely interrelated. Decisions taken in one individual step may affect a subsequent step. Therefore such interdependencies should be taken into account when developing national programmes.

(31) Transparency is important in the management of spent fuel and radioactive waste. Transparency should be provided by ensuring effective public information and opportunities for all stakeholders concerned, including local authorities and the public, to participate in the decision-making processes in accordance with national and international obligations.

(32) Cooperation between Member States and at an international level could facilitate and accelerate decision-making through access to expertise and technology.

(33) Some Member States consider that the sharing of facilities for spent fuel and radioactive waste management, including disposal facilities, is a potentially beneficial, safe and cost-effective option when based on an agreement between the Member States concerned.

(34) The documentation of the decision-making process as it relates to safety should be commensurate with the levels of risk (graded approach) and should provide a basis for decisions related to the management of spent fuel and radioactive waste. This should enable the identification of areas of uncertainty on which attention needs to be focused in an assessment of safety. Safety decisions should be based on the findings of an assessment of safety and information on the robustness and reliability of that assessment and the assumptions made therein. The decision-making process should therefore be based on a collection of arguments and evidence that seek to demonstrate that the required standard of safety is achieved for a facility or activity related to the management of spent fuel and radioactive waste. In the particular case of a disposal facility, the documentation should improve understanding of those aspects influencing the safety of the disposal system, including natural (geological) and engineered barriers, and the expected development of the disposal system over time.

(35) A Member State which has no spent fuel, no immediate prospect of having spent fuel and no present or planned activities related to spent fuel, would be under a disproportionate and unnecessary obligation if it had to transpose and implement the provisions of this Directive with regard to spent fuel. Therefore, such Member States should be exempted, for as long as they have not taken a decision to develop any activity related to nuclear fuel, from the obligation to transpose and implement the provisions related to spent fuel of this Directive.

(36) A Treaty between the government of the Republic of Slovenia and the government of the Republic of Croatia on the regulation of the status and other legal relations regarding investment, exploitation and decommissioning of the Krško nuclear power plant governs the co-ownership of a nuclear power plant. That Treaty provides for shared responsibility for the management and disposal of radioactive waste and spent fuel. Therefore an exemption to certain provisions of this Directive should be laid down in order not to hinder the full implementation of that bilateral Treaty.

(37) While recognising that radiological and non-radiological hazards associated with spent fuel and radioactive waste should be taken into account in the national framework, this Directive does not cover non-radiological hazards, which fall under the Treaty on the Functioning of the European Union.

(38) Maintenance and further development of competences and skills in the management of spent fuel and radioactive waste, as an essential element to ensure high levels of safety, should be based on learning through operational experience.

(39) Scientific research and technological development supported by technical cooperation between actors may open horizons to improve the safe management of spent fuel and radioactive waste, as well as contribute to reducing the risk of the radiotoxicity of high-level waste.

(40) Peer review could serve as an excellent means of building confidence and trust in the management of radioactive waste and spent fuel in the European Union, with the aim of developing and exchanging experience and ensuring high standards,

HAS ADOPTED THIS DIRECTIVE:

Chapter 1
Scope, definitions and general principles

Article 1

Subject-matter

1. This Directive establishes a Community framework for ensuring responsible and safe management of spent fuel and radioactive waste to avoid imposing undue burdens on future generations.

2. It ensures that Member States provide for appropriate national arrangements for a high level of safety in spent fuel and radioactive waste management to protect workers and the general public against the dangers arising from ionising radiation.

3. It ensures the provision of necessary public information and participation in relation to spent fuel and radioactive waste management while having due regard to security and proprietary information issues.

4. Without prejudice to Directive 96/29/Euratom, this Directive supplements the basic standards referred to in Article 30 of the Euratom Treaty as regards the safety of spent fuel and radioactive waste.

Article 2

Scope

1. This Directive shall apply to all stages of:

(a) spent fuel management when the spent fuel results from civilian activities;

(b) radioactive waste management, from generation to disposal, when the radioactive waste results from civilian activities.

2. This Directive shall not apply to:

(a) waste from extractive industries which may be radioactive and which falls within the scope of Directive 2006/21/EC;

(b) authorised releases.

3. Article 4(4) of this Directive shall not apply to:

(a) repatriation of disused sealed sources to a supplier or manufacturer;

(b) shipment of spent fuel of research reactors to a country where research reactor fuels are supplied or manufactured, taking into account applicable international agreements;

(c) the waste and spent fuel of the existing Krško nuclear power plant, when it concerns shipments between Slovenia and Croatia.

4. This Directive shall not affect the right of a Member State or an undertaking in that Member State to return radioactive waste after processing to its country of origin where:

(a) the radioactive waste is to be shipped to that Member State or undertaking for processing; or

(b) other material is to be shipped to that Member State or undertaking with the purpose of recovering the radioactive waste.

This Directive shall not affect the right of a Member State or an undertaking in that Member State to which spent fuel is to be shipped for treatment or reprocessing to return to its country of origin radioactive waste recovered from the treatment or reprocessing operation, or an agreed equivalent.

Article 3

Definitions

For the purpose of this Directive the following definitions shall apply:

(1) "closure" means the completion of all operations at some time after the emplacement of spent fuel or radioactive waste in a disposal facility, including the final engineering or other work required to bring the facility to a condition that will be safe in the long term;

(2) "competent regulatory authority" means an authority or a system of authorities designated in a Member State in the field of regulation of the safety of spent fuel or radioactive waste management as referred to in Article 6;

(3) "disposal" means the emplacement of spent fuel or radioactive waste in a facility without the intention of retrieval;

(4) "disposal facility" means any facility or installation the primary purpose of which is radioactive waste disposal;

(5) "licence" means any legal document granted under the jurisdiction of a Member State to carry out any activity related to the management of spent fuel or radioactive waste, or to confer responsibility for siting, design, construction, commissioning, operation, decommissioning or closure of a spent fuel management facility or of a radioactive waste management facility;

(6) "licence holder" means a legal or natural person having overall responsibility for any activity or facility related to the management of spent fuel or radioactive waste as specified in a licence;

(7) "radioactive waste" means radioactive material in gaseous, liquid or solid form for which no further use is foreseen or considered by the Member State or by a legal or natural person whose decision is accepted by the Member State, and which is regulated as radioactive waste by a competent regulatory authority under the legislative and regulatory framework of the Member State;

(8) "radioactive waste management" means all activities that relate to handling, pretreatment, treatment, conditioning, storage, or disposal of radioactive waste, excluding off-site transportation;

(9) "radioactive waste management facility" means any facility or installation the primary purpose of which is radioactive waste management;

(10) "reprocessing" means a process or operation, the purpose of which is to extract fissile and fertile materials from spent fuel for further use;

(11) "spent fuel" means nuclear fuel that has been irradiated in and permanently removed from a reactor core; spent fuel may either be considered as a usable resource that can be reprocessed or be destined for disposal if regarded as radioactive waste;

(12) "spent fuel management" means all activities that relate to the handling, storage, reprocessing, or disposal of spent fuel, excluding off-site transportation;

(13) "spent fuel management facility" means any facility or installation the primary purpose of which is spent fuel management;

(14) "storage" means the holding of spent fuel or of radioactive waste in a facility with the intention of retrieval.

Article 4

General principles

1. Member States shall establish and maintain national policies on spent fuel and radioactive waste management. Without prejudice to Article 2(3), each Member State shall have ultimate responsibility for management of the spent fuel and radioactive waste generated in it.

2. Where radioactive waste or spent fuel is shipped for processing or reprocessing to a Member State or a third country, the ultimate responsibility for the safe and responsible disposal of those materials, including any waste as a by-product, shall remain with the Member State or third country from which the radioactive material was shipped.

3. National policies shall be based on all of the following principles:
(a) the generation of radioactive waste shall be kept to the minimum which is reasonably practicable, both in terms of activity and volume, by means of appropriate design measures and of operating and decommissioning practices, including the recycling and reuse of materials;
(b) the interdependencies between all steps in spent fuel and radioactive waste generation and management shall be taken into account;
(c) spent fuel and radioactive waste shall be safely managed, including in the long term with passive safety features;
(d) implementation of measures shall follow a graded approach;
(e) the costs for the management of spent fuel and radioactive waste shall be borne by those who generated those materials;
(f) an evidence-based and documented decision-making process shall be applied with regard to all stages of the management of spent fuel and radioactive waste.

4. Radioactive waste shall be disposed of in the Member State in which it was generated, unless at the time of shipment an agreement, taking into account the criteria established by the Commission in accordance with Article 16(2) of Directive 2006/117/Euratom, has entered into force between the Member State concerned and another Member State or a third country to use a disposal facility in one of them.

Prior to a shipment to a third country, the exporting Member State shall inform the Commission of the content of any such agreement and take reasonable measures to be assured that:
(a) the country of destination has concluded an agreement with the Community covering spent fuel and radioactive waste management or is a party to the Joint Convention on the Safety of Spent Fuel Management and on the Safety of Radioactive Waste Management ("the Joint Convention");
(b) the country of destination has radioactive waste management and disposal programmes with objectives representing a high level of safety equivalent to those established by this Directive; and
(c) the disposal facility in the country of destination is authorised for the radioactive waste to be shipped, is operating prior to the shipment, and is managed in accordance with the requirements set down in the radioactive waste management and disposal programme of that country of destination.

Chapter 2
Obligations

Article 5

National framework

1. Member States shall establish and maintain a national legislative, regulatory and organisational framework ("national framework") for spent fuel and radioactive waste management that allocates responsibility and provides for coordination between relevant competent bodies. The national framework shall provide for all of the following:

(a) a national programme for the implementation of spent fuel and radioactive waste management policy;

(b) national arrangements for the safety of spent fuel and radioactive waste management. The determination of how those arrangements are to be adopted and through which instrument they are to be applied rests within the competence of the Member States;

(c) a system of licensing of spent fuel and radioactive waste management activities, facilities or both, including the prohibition of spent fuel or radioactive waste management activities, of the operation of a spent fuel or radioactive waste management facility without a licence or both and, if appropriate, prescribing conditions for further management of the activity, facility or both;

(d) a system of appropriate control, a management system, regulatory inspections, documentation and reporting obligations for radioactive waste and spent fuel management activities, facilities or both, including appropriate measures for the post-closure periods of disposal facilities;

(e) enforcement actions, including the suspension of activities and the modification, expiration or revocation of a licence together with requirements, if appropriate, for alternative solutions that lead to improved safety;

(f) the allocation of responsibility to the bodies involved in the different steps of spent fuel and radioactive waste management; in particular, the national framework shall give primary responsibility for the spent fuel and radioactive waste to their generators or, under specific circumstances, to a licence holder to whom this responsibility has been entrusted by competent bodies;

(g) national requirements for public information and participation;

(h) the financing scheme(s) for spent fuel and radioactive waste management in accordance with Article 9.

2. Member States shall ensure that the national framework is improved where appropriate, taking into account operating experience, insights gained from the decision-making process referred to in Article 4(3)(f), and the development of relevant technology and research.

Article 6

Competent regulatory authority

1. Each Member State shall establish and maintain a competent regulatory authority in the field of safety of spent fuel and radioactive waste management.

2. Member States shall ensure that the competent regulatory authority is functionally separate from any other body or organisation concerned with the promotion or utilisation of nuclear energy or radioactive material, including electricity production and radioisotope applications, or with the management of spent fuel and radioactive waste, in order to ensure effective independence from undue influence on its regulatory function.

3. Member States shall ensure that the competent regulatory authority is given the legal powers and human and financial resources necessary to fulfil its obligations in connection with the national framework as described in Article 5(1)(b), (c), (d) and (e).

Article 7

Licence holders

1. Member States shall ensure that the prime responsibility for the safety of spent fuel and radioactive waste management facilities and/or activities rest with the licence holder. That responsibility can not be delegated.

2. Member States shall ensure that the national framework in place require licence holders, under the regulatory control of the competent regulatory authority, to regularly assess, verify and continuously improve, as far as is reasonably achievable, the safety of the radioactive waste

and spent fuel management facility or activity in a systematic and verifiable manner. This shall be achieved through an appropriate safety assessment, other arguments and evidence.

3. As part of the licensing of a facility or activity the safety demonstration shall cover the development and operation of an activity and the development, operation and decommissioning of a facility or closure of a disposal facility as well as the post-closure phase of a disposal facility. The extent of the safety demonstration shall be commensurate with the complexity of the operation and the magnitude of the hazards associated with the radioactive waste and spent fuel, and the facility or activity. The licensing process shall contribute to safety in the facility or activity during normal operating conditions, anticipated operational occurrences and design basis accidents. It shall provide the required assurance of safety in the facility or activity. Measures shall be in place to prevent accidents and mitigate the consequences of accidents, including verification of physical barriers and the licence holder's administrative protection procedures that would have to fail before workers and the general public would be significantly affected by ionising radiation. That approach shall identify and reduce uncertainties.

4. Member States shall ensure that the national framework require licence holders to establish and implement integrated management systems, including quality assurance, which give due priority for overall management of spent fuel and radioactive waste to safety and are regularly verified by the competent regulatory authority.

5. Member States shall ensure that the national framework require licence holders to provide for and maintain adequate financial and human resources to fulfil their obligations with respect to the safety of spent fuel and radioactive waste management as laid down in paragraphs 1 to 4.

Article 8

Expertise and skills

Member States shall ensure that the national framework require all parties to make arrangements for education and training for their staff, as well as research and development activities to cover the needs of the national programme for spent fuel and radioactive waste management in order to obtain, maintain and to further develop necessary expertise and skills.

Article 9

Financial resources

Member States shall ensure that the national framework require that adequate financial resources be available when needed for the implementation of national programmes referred to in Article 11, especially for the management of spent fuel and radioactive waste, taking due account of the responsibility of spent fuel and radioactive waste generators.

Article 10

Transparency

1. Member States shall ensure that necessary information on the management of spent fuel and radioactive waste be made available to workers and the general public. This obligation includes ensuring that the competent regulatory authority inform the public in the fields of its competence. Information shall be made available to the public in accordance with national legislation and international obligations, provided that this does not jeopardise other interests such as, inter alia, security, recognised in national legislation or international obligations.

2. Member States shall ensure that the public be given the necessary opportunities to participate effectively in the decision-making process regarding spent fuel and radioactive waste management in accordance with national legislation and international obligations.

Article 11

National programmes

1. Each Member State shall ensure the implementation of its national programme for the management of spent fuel and radioactive waste ("national programme"), covering all types of spent fuel and radioactive waste under its jurisdiction and all stages of spent fuel and radioactive waste management from generation to disposal.

2. Each Member State shall regularly review and update its national programme, taking into account technical and scientific progress as appropriate as well as recommendations, lessons learned and good practices from peer reviews.

Article 12

Contents of national programmes

1. The national programmes shall set out how the Member States intend to implement their national policies referred to in Article 4 for the responsible and safe management of spent fuel and radioactive waste to secure the aims of this Directive, and shall include all of the following:

(a) the overall objectives of the Member State's national policy in respect of spent fuel and radioactive waste management;
(b) the significant milestones and clear timeframes for the achievement of those milestones in light of the over-arching objectives of the national programme;
(c) an inventory of all spent fuel and radioactive waste and estimates for future quantities, including those from decommissioning, clearly indicating the location and amount of the radioactive waste and spent fuel in accordance with appropriate classification of the radioactive waste;
(d) the concepts or plans and technical solutions for spent fuel and radioactive waste management from generation to disposal;
(e) the concepts or plans for the post-closure period of a disposal facility's lifetime, including the period during which appropriate controls are retained and the means to be employed to preserve knowledge of that facility in the longer term;
(f) the research, development and demonstration activities that are needed in order to implement solutions for the management of spent fuel and radioactive waste;
(g) the responsibility for the implementation of the national programme and the key performance indicators to monitor progress towards implementation;
(h) an assessment of the national programme costs and the underlying basis and hypotheses for that assessment, which must include a profile over time;
(i) the financing scheme(s) in force;
(j) a transparency policy or process as referred to in Article 10;
(k) if any, the agreement(s) concluded with a Member State or a third country on management of spent fuel or radioactive waste, including on the use of disposal facilities.

2. The national programme together with the national policy may be contained in a single document or in a number of documents.

Article 13

Notification

1. Member States shall notify to the Commission their national programmes and any subsequent significant changes.

2. Within 6 months of the date of notification, the Commission may request clarification and/or express its opinion on whether the content of the national programme is in accordance with Article 12.

3. Within 6 months of receiving the Commission's reaction Member States shall provide the requested clarification and/or inform the Commission of any revision of the national programmes.

4. The Commission, when deciding on the provision of Community financial or technical assistance for spent fuel and radioactive waste management facilities or activities, shall take into account the Member States' clarifications and progress regarding the national programmes.

Article 14

Reporting

1. Member States shall submit a report to the Commission on the implementation of this Directive for the first time by 23 August 2015, and every 3 years thereafter, taking advantage of the review and reporting under the Joint Convention.

2. On the basis of the Member States' reports, the Commission shall submit to the European Parliament and the Council the following:
(a) a report on progress made with the implementation of this Directive; and
(b) an inventory of radioactive waste and spent fuel present in the Community's territory and the future prospects.

3. Member States shall periodically, and at least every 10 years, arrange for self-assessments of their national framework, competent regulatory authority, national programme and its implementation, and invite international peer review of their national framework, competent regulatory authority and/or national programme with the aim of ensuring that high safety standards are achieved in the safe management of spent fuel and radioactive waste. The outcomes of any peer review shall be reported to the Commission and the other Member States, and may be made available to the public where there is no conflict with security and proprietary information.

Chapter 3
Final provisions

Article 15

Transposition

1. Member States shall bring into force the laws, regulations and administrative provisions necessary to comply with this Directive before 23 August 2013. They shall forthwith inform the Commission thereof.

When Member States adopt these measures, they shall contain a reference to this Directive or shall be accompanied by such reference on the occasion of their official publication. The methods of making such reference shall be laid down by Member States.

2. The obligations for transposition and implementation of provisions related to spent fuel of this Directive shall not apply to Cyprus, Denmark, Estonia, Ireland, Latvia, Luxembourg and Malta for as long as they decide not to develop any activity related to nuclear fuel.

3. Member States shall communicate to the Commission the text of the main provisions of national law which they adopt in the field covered by this Directive and of any subsequent amendments to those provisions.

4. Member States shall for the first time notify to the Commission the content of their national programme covering all the items provided for in Article 12 as soon as possible, but not later than 23 August 2015.

Article 16

Entry into force

This Directive shall enter into force on the 20th day following its publication in the Official Journal of the European Union.

Article 17

Addressees

This Directive is addressed to the Member States.

DIRECTIVE 2012/19/EU OF THE EUROPEAN PARLIAMENT AND OF THE COUNCIL

of 4 July 2012

ON WASTE ELECTRICAL AND ELECTRONIC EQUIPMENT (WEEE)

THE EUROPEAN PARLIAMENT AND THE COUNCIL OF THE EUROPEAN UNION,

Having regard to the Treaty on the Functioning of the European Union, and in particular Article 192(1) thereof,

Having regard to the proposal from the European Commission,

Having regard to the opinion of the European Economic and Social Committee,

Having regard to the opinion of the Committee of the Regions,

Acting in accordance with the ordinary legislative procedure,

Whereas:

(1) A number of substantial changes are to be made to Directive 2002/96/EC of the European Parliament and of the Council of 27 January 2003 on waste electrical and electronic equipment (WEEE). In the interests of clarity, that Directive should be recast.

(2) The objectives of the Union's environment policy are, in particular, to preserve, protect and improve the quality of the environment, to protect human health and to utilise natural resources prudently and rationally. That policy is based on the precautionary principle and the principles that preventive action should be taken, that environmental damage should, as a priority, be rectified at source and that the polluter should pay.

(3) The Community programme of policy and action in relation to the environment and sustainable development (Fifth Environmental Action Programme) stated that the achievement of sustainable development calls for significant changes in current patterns of development, production, consumption and behaviour and advocates, inter alia, the reduction of wasteful consumption of natural resources and the prevention of pollution. It mentioned waste electrical and electronic equipment (WEEE) as one of the target areas to be regulated, in view of the application of the principles of prevention, recovery and safe disposal of waste.

(4) This Directive supplements the general waste management legislation of the Union, such as Directive 2008/98/EC of the European Parliament and of the Council of 19 November 2008 on waste. It refers to the definitions in that Directive, including the definitions of waste and general waste management operations. The definition of collection in Directive 2008/98/EC includes the preliminary sorting and preliminary storage of waste for the purposes of transport to a waste treatment facility. Directive 2009/125/EC of the European Parliament and of the Council establishes a framework for setting ecodesign requirements for energy-related products and enables the adoption of specific ecodesign requirements for energy-related products which may also be covered by this Directive. Directive 2009/125/EC and the implementing measures adopted pursuant thereto are without prejudice to the waste management legislation of the Union. Directive 2002/95/EC of the European Parliament and of the Council of 27 January 2003 on the restriction of the use of certain hazardous substances in electrical and electronic equipment requires the substitution of banned substances in respect of all electrical and electronic equipment (EEE) within its scope.

(5) As the market continues to expand and innovation cycles become even shorter, the replacement of equipment accelerates, making EEE a fast-growing source of waste.

While Directive 2002/95/EC has contributed effectively to reducing hazardous substances contained in new EEE, hazardous substances such as mercury, cadmium, lead, hexavalent chromium and polychlorinated biphenyls (PCBs) and ozone-depleting substances will still be present in WEEE for many years. The content of hazardous components in EEE is a major concern during the waste management phase, and recycling of WEEE is not undertaken to a sufficient extent. A lack of recycling results in the loss of valuable resources.

(6) The purpose of this Directive is to contribute to sustainable production and consumption by, as a first priority, the prevention of WEEE and, in addition, by the re-use, recycling and other forms of recovery of such wastes so as to reduce the disposal of waste and to contribute to the efficient use of resources and the retrieval of valuable secondary raw materials. It also seeks to improve the environmental performance of all operators involved in the life cycle of EEE, e.g. producers, distributors and consumers and, in particular, those operators directly involved in the collection and treatment of WEEE. In particular, different national applications of the "producer responsibility" principle may lead to substantial disparities in the financial burden on economic operators. Having different national policies on the management of WEEE hampers the effectiveness of recycling policies. For that reason, the essential criteria should be laid down at the level of the Union and minimum standards for the treatment of WEEE should be developed.

(7) The provisions of this Directive should apply to products and producers irrespective of selling technique, including distance and electronic selling. In this connection, the obligations of producers and distributors using distance and electronic selling channels should, as far as is practicable, take the same form, and should be enforced in the same way, as for other distribution channels, in order to avoid those other distribution channels having to bear the costs resulting from this Directive arising from WEEE for which the equipment was sold by distance or electronic selling.

(8) In order to fulfil the obligations pursuant to this Directive in a given Member State, a producer should be established in that Member State. By exception, to reduce existing barriers to the proper functioning of the internal market and administrative burdens, Member States should allow producers that are not established on their territory, but that are established in another Member State, to appoint an authorised representative to be responsible for fulfilling the obligations of that producer under this Directive. In addition, administrative burdens should be reduced by simplifying registration and reporting procedures and by ensuring that duplicate charges are not levied for registrations within individual Member States.

(9) This Directive should cover all EEE used by consumers and EEE intended for professional use. This Directive should apply without prejudice to Union legislation on safety and health requirements protecting all actors in contact with WEEE, as well as specific Union waste management legislation, in particular Directive 2006/66/EC of the European Parliament and of the Council of 6 September 2006 on batteries and accumulators and waste batteries and accumulators, and Union product design legislation, in particular Directive 2009/125/EC. The preparing for re-use, recovery and recycling of waste cooling equipment and the substances, mixtures or components thereof should be in accordance with the relevant legislation of the Union, in particular Regulation (EC) No 1005/2009 of the European Parliament and of the Council of 16 September 2009 on substances that deplete the ozone layer and Regulation (EC) No 842/2006 of the European Parliament and of the Council of 17 May 2006 on certain fluorinated greenhouse gases. The objectives of this Directive can be achieved without including large-scale fixed installations such as oil platforms, airport luggage transport systems or elevators within its scope. However, any equipment which is not specifically designed and installed as part of those installations, and which can fulfil its function even if it is not part of those installations, should be included in the scope of this Directive. This refers for instance to equipment such as lighting equipment or photovoltaic panels.

(10) A number of definitions should be included in this Directive in order to specify its scope. However, in the framework of a revision of the scope, the definition of EEE

should be further clarified in order to bring Member States' relevant national measures and current, applied and established practices closer together.

(11) Ecodesign requirements facilitating the re-use, dismantling and recovery of WEEE should be laid down in the framework of measures implementing Directive 2009/125/EC. In order to optimise re-use and recovery through product design, the whole life cycle of the product should be taken into account.

(12) The establishment, by this Directive, of producer responsibility is one of the means of encouraging design and production of EEE which take into full account and facilitate its repair, possible upgrading, re-use, disassembly and recycling.

(13) In order to guarantee the safety and health of distributors' personnel involved in the take-back and handling of WEEE, Member States should, in accordance with national and Union legislation on safety and health requirements, determine the conditions under which take-back may be refused by distributors.

(14) Separate collection is a precondition for ensuring specific treatment and recycling of WEEE and is necessary to achieve the chosen level of protection of human health and the environment in the Union. Consumers have to actively contribute to the success of such collection and should be encouraged to return WEEE. For this purpose, convenient facilities should be set up for the return of WEEE, including public collection points, where private households should be able to return their waste at least free of charge. Distributors have an important role in contributing to the success of WEEE collection. Therefore, collection points set up at retail shops for very small WEEE should not be subject to the registration or permit requirements of Directive 2008/98/EC.

(15) In order to attain the chosen level of protection and the harmonised environmental objectives of the Union, Member States should adopt appropriate measures to minimise the disposal of WEEE as unsorted municipal waste and to achieve a high level of separate collection of WEEE. In order to ensure that Member States strive to set up efficient collection schemes, they should be required to achieve a high level of collection of WEEE, particularly for cooling and freezing equipment containing ozone-depleting substances and fluorinated greenhouse gases, given their high environmental impact and in view of the obligations contained in Regulation (EC) No 842/2006 and Regulation (EC) No 1005/2009. Data included in the impact assessment carried out by the Commission in 2008 show that 65 % of the EEE placed on the market was already separately collected then, but more than half of this was potentially the object of improper treatment and illegal exports, and, even when properly treated, this was not reported. This leads to losses of valuable secondary raw materials, environmental degradation, and provision of inconsistent data. To avoid this, it is necessary to set an ambitious collection target and to ensure that WEEE collected is treated in an environmentally sound way and is correctly reported. It is appropriate to lay down minimum requirements for shipments of used EEE suspected to be WEEE, in the application of which Member States may have regard to any relevant Correspondents' Guidelines elaborated in the context of the implementation of Regulation (EC) No 1013/2006 of the European Parliament and of the Council of 14 June 2006 on shipments of waste. Such minimum requirements should in any case have the purpose of avoiding unwanted shipments of non-functional EEE to developing countries.

(16) The setting of ambitious collection targets should be based on the amount of WEEE generated where due account is taken of the differing life cycles of products in the Member States, of non-saturated markets and of EEE with a long life cycle. Therefore, a methodology for calculating collection rates based on WEEE generated should be developed in the near future. According to current estimates, a collection rate of 85 % of WEEE generated is broadly equivalent to a collection rate of 65 % of the average weight of EEE placed on the market in the three preceding years.

(17) Specific treatment for WEEE is indispensable in order to avoid the dispersion of pollutants in recycled material or the waste stream. Such treatment is the most effective means of ensuring compliance with the chosen level of protection of the environment of the Union. Any establishment or undertaking carrying out collection, recycling

and treatment operations should comply with minimum standards to prevent negative environmental impacts associated with the treatment of WEEE. The best available treatment, recovery and recycling techniques should be used, provided that they ensure human health and a high level of environmental protection. Best available treatment, recovery and recycling techniques may be further defined in accordance with the procedures of Directive 2008/1/EC of the European Parliament and of the Council of 15 January 2008 concerning integrated pollution prevention and control.

(18) The Scientific Committee on Emerging and Newly Identified Health Risks, in its opinion on "Risk Assessment of Products of Nanotechnology" of 19 January 2009, stated that exposure to nanomaterials that are firmly embedded in large structures, for example in electronic circuits, may occur in the waste phase and during recycling. To control possible risks to human health and the environment from the treatment of WEEE that contains nanomaterials, it is appropriate for the Commission to assess whether specific treatment may be necessary.

(19) The collection, storage, transport, treatment and recycling of WEEE as well as its preparation for re-use shall be conducted with an approach geared to protecting the environment and human health and preserving raw materials and shall aim at recycling valuable resources contained in EEE with a view to ensuring a better supply of commodities within the Union.

(20) Where appropriate, priority should be given to preparing for re-use of WEEE and its components, sub-assemblies and consumables. Where this is not preferable, all WEEE collected separately should be sent for recovery, in the course of which a high level of recycling and recovery should be achieved. In addition, producers should be encouraged to integrate recycled material in new equipment.

(21) The recovery, preparation for re-use and recycling of WEEE should be counted towards the achievement of the targets laid down in this Directive only if that recovery, preparation for re-use or recycling does not conflict with other Union or national legislation applicable to the equipment. Ensuring proper preparation for re-use, recycling and recovery of WEEE is important for sound resource management and will optimise supply of resources.

(22) Basic principles with regard to the financing of WEEE management have to be set at the level of the Union, and financing schemes have to contribute to high collection rates, as well as to the implementation of the principle of producer responsibility.

(23) Users of EEE from private households should have the possibility of returning WEEE at least free of charge. Producers should finance at least the collection from collection facilities, and the treatment, recovery and disposal of WEEE. Member States should encourage producers to take full responsibility for the WEEE collection, in particular by financing the collection of WEEE throughout the entire waste chain, including from private households, in order to avoid separately collected WEEE becoming the object of suboptimal treatment and illegal exports, to create a level playing field by harmonising producer financing across the Union and to shift payment for the collection of this waste from general tax payers to the consumers of EEE, in line with the "polluter pays" principle. In order to give maximum effect to the concept of producer responsibility, each producer should be responsible for financing the management of the waste from his own products. The producer should be able to choose to fulfil this obligation either individually or by joining a collective scheme. Each producer should, when placing a product on the market, provide a financial guarantee to prevent costs for the management of WEEE from orphan products from falling on society or the remaining producers. The responsibility for the financing of the management of historical waste should be shared by all existing producers through collective financing schemes to which all producers that exist on the market when the costs occur contribute proportionately. Collective financing schemes should not have the effect of excluding niche and low-volume producers, importers and new entrants. Collective schemes could provide for differentiated fees based on how easily products and the valuable secondary raw materials that they contain could be recycled. In the case of products which have a long

life cycle and which are now covered by this Directive, such as photovoltaic panels, the best possible use should be made of existing collection and recovery systems, provided that they meet the requirements laid down in this Directive.

(24) Producers could be allowed to show purchasers, on a voluntary basis at the time of sale of new products, the costs of collecting, treating and disposing of WEEE in an environmentally sound way. This is in line with the Commission Communication on Sustainable Consumption and Production and Sustainable Industrial Policy Action Plan, in particular with regard to smarter consumption and green public procurement.

(25) Information to users about the requirement not to dispose of WEEE as unsorted municipal waste and to collect WEEE separately and about the collection systems and their role in the management of WEEE is indispensable for the success of WEEE collection. Such information necessitates the proper marking of EEE which could end up in rubbish bins or similar means of municipal waste collection.

(26) Information on component and material identification to be provided by producers is important to facilitate the management, and in particular the treatment and recovery or recycling, of WEEE.

(27) Member States should ensure that inspection and monitoring infrastructure enables the proper implementation of this Directive to be verified, having regard, inter alia, to Recommendation 2001/331/EC of the European Parliament and of the Council of 4 April 2001 providing for minimum criteria for environmental inspections in the Member States.

(28) Member States should provide for effective, proportionate and dissuasive penalties to be imposed on natural and legal persons responsible for waste management, where they infringe the provisions of this Directive. Member States should also be able to take action to recover the costs of non-compliance and remedial measures, without prejudice to Directive 2004/35/EC of the European Parliament and of the Council of 21 April 2004 on environmental liability with regard to the prevention and remedying of environmental damage.

(29) Information about the weight of EEE placed on the market in the Union and the rates of collection, preparation for re-use, including as far as possible preparation for re-use of whole appliances, recovery or recycling and export of WEEE collected in accordance with this Directive is necessary to monitor the achievement of the objectives of this Directive. For the purposes of calculating collection rates, a common methodology for the calculation of weight of EEE should be developed to ascertain, inter alia, whether this term includes the actual weight of the entire equipment in the form in which it is marketed, including all components, sub-assemblies, accessories and consumables but excluding packaging, batteries, instructions for use and manuals.

(30) It is appropriate to allow Member States to choose to implement certain provisions of this Directive by means of agreements between the competent authorities and the economic sectors concerned, provided that particular requirements are met.

(31) In order to address difficulties faced by Member States in achieving the collection rates, to take into account technical and scientific progress and to supplement the provisions on fulfilment of recovery targets, the power to adopt acts in accordance with Article 290 of the Treaty on the Functioning of the European Union (TFEU) should be delegated to the Commission in respect of transitional adjustments for certain Member States, adaptation to technical and scientific progress and the adoption of detailed rules on WEEE exported out of the Union counting towards the fulfilment of recovery targets. It is of particular importance that the Commission carry out appropriate consultations during its preparatory work, including at expert level. The Commission, when preparing and drawing up delegated acts, should ensure a simultaneous, timely and appropriate transmission of relevant documents to the European Parliament and to the Council.

(32) In order to ensure uniform conditions for the implementation of this Directive, implementing powers should be conferred on the Commission. Those powers should be exercised in accordance with Regulation (EU) No 182/2011 of the European Parliament and of the Council of 16 February 2011 laying down the rules and general principles

concerning mechanisms for control by Member States of the Commission's exercise of implementing powers.

(33) The obligation to transpose this Directive into national law should be confined to those provisions which represent a substantive change as compared with the earlier Directives. The obligation to transpose the provisions which are unchanged arises under the earlier Directives.

(34) In accordance with the Joint Political Declaration of 28 September 2011 of Member States and the Commission on explanatory documents, Member States have undertaken to accompany, in justified cases, the notification of their transposition measures with one or more documents explaining the relationship between the components of a directive and the corresponding parts of national transposition instruments. With regard to this Directive, the legislator considers the transmission of such documents to be justified.

(35) This Directive should be without prejudice to the obligations of the Member States relating to the time limits for transposition into national law and application of the Directives set out in Annex XI, Part B.

(36) Since the objective of this Directive cannot be sufficiently achieved by the Member States and can therefore, by reason of the scale of the problem, be better achieved at the level of the Union, the Union may adopt measures, in accordance with the principle of subsidiarity as set out in Article 5 of the Treaty on European Union. In accordance with the principle of proportionality, as set out in that Article, this Directive does not go beyond what is necessary in order to achieve that objective,

HAVE ADOPTED THIS DIRECTIVE:

Article 1

Subject matter

This Directive lays down measures to protect the environment and human health by preventing or reducing the adverse impacts of the generation and management of waste from electrical and electronic equipment (WEEE) and by reducing overall impacts of resource use and improving the efficiency of such use in accordance with Articles 1 and 4 of Directive 2008/98/EC, thereby contributing to sustainable development.

Article 2

Scope

1. This Directive shall apply to electrical and electronic equipment (EEE) as follows:

(a) from 13 August 2012 to 14 August 2018 (transitional period), subject to paragraph 3, to EEE falling within the categories set out in Annex I. Annex II contains an indicative list of EEE which falls within the categories set out in Annex I;

(b) from 15 August 2018, subject to paragraphs 3 and 4, to all EEE. All EEE shall be classified within the categories set out in Annex III. Annex IV contains a non-exhaustive list of EEE which falls within the categories set out in Annex III (open scope).

2. This Directive shall apply without prejudice to the requirements of Union legislation on safety and health, on chemicals, in particular Regulation (EC) No 1907/2006 of the European Parliament and of the Council of 18 December 2006 concerning the Registration, Evaluation, Authorisation and Restriction of Chemicals (REACH), establishing a European Chemicals Agency, as well as of specific Union waste management or product design legislation.

3. This Directive shall not apply to any of the following EEE:

(a) equipment which is necessary for the protection of the essential interests of the security of Member States, including arms, munitions and war material intended for specifically military purposes;

(b) equipment which is specifically designed and installed as part of another type of equipment that is excluded from or does not fall within the scope of this Directive, which can fulfil its function only if it is part of that equipment;
(c) filament bulbs.

4. In addition to the equipment specified in paragraph 3, from 15 August 2018, this Directive shall not apply to the following EEE:
(a) equipment designed to be sent into space;
(b) large-scale stationary industrial tools;
(c) large-scale fixed installations, except any equipment which is not specifically designed and installed as part of those installations;
(d) means of transport for persons or goods, excluding electric two-wheel vehicles which are not type-approved;
(e) non-road mobile machinery made available exclusively for professional use;
(f) equipment specifically designed solely for the purposes of research and development that is only made available on a business-to-business basis;
(g) medical devices and in vitro diagnostic medical devices, where such devices are expected to be infective prior to end of life, and active implantable medical devices.

5. No later than 14 August 2015, the Commission shall review the scope of this Directive set out in point (b) of paragraph 1, including the parameters to distinguish between large and small equipment in Annex III, and shall present a report thereon to the European Parliament and to the Council. The report shall be accompanied by a legislative proposal, if appropriate.

Article 3

Definitions

1. For the purposes of this Directive, the following definitions shall apply:
(a) "electrical and electronic equipment" or "EEE" means equipment which is dependent on electric currents or electromagnetic fields in order to work properly and equipment for the generation, transfer and measurement of such currents and fields and designed for use with a voltage rating not exceeding 1000 volts for alternating current and 1500 volts for direct current;
(b) "large-scale stationary industrial tools" means a large size assembly of machines, equipment, and/or components, functioning together for a specific application, permanently installed and de-installed by professionals at a given place, and used and maintained by professionals in an industrial manufacturing facility or research and development facility;
(c) "large-scale fixed installation" means a large-size combination of several types of apparatus and, where applicable, other devices, which:
   (i) are assembled, installed and de-installed by professionals;
   (ii) are intended to be used permanently as part of a building or a structure at a pre-defined and dedicated location; and
   (iii) can only be replaced by the same specifically designed equipment;
(d) "non-road mobile machinery" means machinery, with on-board power source, the operation of which requires either mobility or continuous or semi-continuous movement between a succession of fixed working locations while working;
(e) "waste electrical and electronic equipment" or "WEEE" means electrical or electronic equipment which is waste within the meaning of Article 3(1) of Directive 2008/98/EC, including all components, sub-assemblies and consumables which are part of the product at the time of discarding;
(f) "producer" means any natural or legal person who, irrespective of the selling technique used, including distance communication within the meaning of Directive 97/7/EC of the European Parliament and of the Council of 20 May 1997 on the protection of consumers in respect of distance contracts:

(i) is established in a Member State and manufactures EEE under his own name or trademark, or has EEE designed or manufactured and markets it under his name or trademark within the territory of that Member State;

(ii) is established in a Member State and resells within the territory of that Member State, under his own name or trademark, equipment produced by other suppliers, a reseller not being regarded as the "producer" if the brand of the producer appears on the equipment, as provided for in point (i);

(iii) is established in a Member State and places on the market of that Member State, on a professional basis, EEE from a third country or from another Member State; or

(iv) sells EEE by means of distance communication directly to private households or to users other than private households in a Member State, and is established in another Member State or in a third country.

Whoever exclusively provides financing under or pursuant to any finance agreement shall not be deemed to be a "producer" unless he also acts as a producer within the meaning of points (i) to (iv);

(g) "distributor" means any natural or legal person in the supply chain, who makes an EEE available on the market. This definition does not prevent a distributor from being, at the same time, a producer within the meaning of point (f);

(h) "WEEE from private households" means WEEE which comes from private households and WEEE which comes from commercial, industrial, institutional and other sources which, because of its nature and quantity, is similar to that from private households. Waste from EEE likely to be used by both private households and users other than private households shall in any event be considered to be WEEE from private households;

(i) "finance agreement" means any loan, lease, hiring or deferred sale agreement or arrangement relating to any equipment whether or not the terms of that agreement or arrangement or any collateral agreement or arrangement provide that a transfer of ownership of that equipment will or may take place;

(j) "making available on the market" means any supply of a product for distribution, consumption or use on the market of a Member State in the course of a commercial activity, whether in return for payment or free of charge;

(k) "placing on the market" means the first making available of a product on the market within the territory of a Member State on a professional basis;

(l) "removal" means manual, mechanical, chemical or metallurgic handling with the result that hazardous substances, mixtures and components are contained in an identifiable stream or are an identifiable part of a stream within the treatment process. A substance, mixture or component is identifiable if it can be monitored to verify environmentally safe treatment;

(m) "medical device" means a medical device or accessory within the meaning of, respectively, point (a) or (b) of Article 1(2) of Council Directive 93/42/EEC of 14 June 1993 concerning medical devices which is EEE;

(n) "in vitro diagnostic medical device" means an in vitro diagnostic device or accessory within the meaning of, respectively, point (b) or (c) of Article 1(2) of Directive 98/79/EC of the European Parliament and of the Council of 27 October 1998 on in vitro diagnostic medical devices which is EEE;

(o) "active implantable medical device" means an active implantable medical device within the meaning of point (c) of Article 1(2) of Council Directive 90/385/EEC of 20 June 1990 on the approximation of the laws of the Member States relating to active implantable medical devices which is EEE.

2. In addition, the definitions of "hazardous waste", "collection", "separate collection", "prevention", "re-use", "treatment", "recovery", "preparing for re-use", "recycling" and "disposal" laid down in Article 3 of Directive 2008/98/EC shall apply.

Article 4

Product design

Member States shall, without prejudice to the requirements of Union legislation on the proper functioning of the internal market and on product design, including Directive 2009/125/EC, encourage cooperation between producers and recyclers and measures to promote the design and production of EEE, notably in view of facilitating re-use, dismantling and recovery of WEEE, its components and materials. In this context, Member States shall take appropriate measures so that the ecodesign requirements facilitating re-use and treatment of WEEE established in the framework of Directive 2009/125/EC are applied and producers do not prevent, through specific design features or manufacturing processes, WEEE from being re-used, unless such specific design features or manufacturing processes present overriding advantages, for example, with regard to the protection of the environment and/or safety requirements.

Article 5

Separate collection

1. Member States shall adopt appropriate measures to minimise the disposal of WEEE in the form of unsorted municipal waste, to ensure the correct treatment of all collected WEEE and to achieve a high level of separate collection of WEEE, notably, and as a matter of priority, for temperature exchange equipment containing ozone-depleting substances and fluorinated greenhouse gases, fluorescent lamps containing mercury, photovoltaic panels and small equipment as referred to in categories 5 and 6 of Annex III.

2. For WEEE from private households, Member States shall ensure that:

(a) systems are set up allowing final holders and distributors to return such waste at least free of charge. Member States shall ensure the availability and accessibility of the necessary collection facilities, taking into account, in particular, the population density;

(b) when supplying a new product, distributors are responsible for ensuring that such waste can be returned to the distributor at least free of charge on a one-to-one basis as long as the equipment is of equivalent type and has fulfilled the same functions as the supplied equipment. Member States may derogate from this provision provided that they ensure that returning the WEEE is not thereby made more difficult for the final holder and that it remains free of charge for the final holder. Member States making use of this derogation shall inform the Commission thereof;

(c) distributors provide for the collection, at retail shops with sales areas relating to EEE of at least 400 m^2, or in their immediate proximity, of very small WEEE (no external dimension more than 25 cm) free of charge to end-users and with no obligation to buy EEE of an equivalent type, unless an assessment shows that alternative existing collection schemes are likely to be at least as effective. Such assessments shall be available to the public. WEEE collected shall be properly treated in accordance with Article 8;

(d) without prejudice to points (a), (b) and (c), producers are allowed to set up and to operate individual and/or collective take-back systems for WEEE from private households provided that these are in line with the objectives of this Directive;

(e) having regard to national and Union health and safety standards, WEEE that presents a health and safety risk to personnel because of contamination may be refused for return under points (a), (b) and (c). Member States shall make specific arrangements for such WEEE.

Member States may provide for specific arrangements for the return of WEEE pursuant to points (a), (b) and (c) for cases in which the equipment does not contain its essential components or if the equipment contains waste other than WEEE.

3. Member States may designate the operators that are allowed to collect WEEE from private households as referred to in paragraph 2.

4. Member States may require that the WEEE deposited at collection facilities referred to in paragraphs 2 and 3 is handed over to producers or third parties acting on their behalf or is handed over, for purposes of preparing for re-use, to designated establishments or undertakings.

5. In the case of WEEE other than WEEE from private households, and without prejudice to Article 13, Member States shall ensure that producers or third parties acting on their behalf provide for the collection of such waste.

Article 6

Disposal and transport of collected WEEE

1. Member States shall prohibit the disposal of separately collected WEEE which has not yet undergone the treatment specified in Article 8.

2. Member States shall ensure that the collection and transport of separately collected WEEE is carried out in a way which allows optimal conditions for preparing for re-use, recycling and the confinement of hazardous substances.

In order to maximise preparing for re-use, Member States shall promote that, prior to any further transfer, collection schemes or facilities provide, where appropriate, for the separation at the collection points of WEEE that is to be prepared for re-use from other separately collected WEEE, in particular by granting access for personnel from re-use centres.

Article 7

Collection rate

1. Without prejudice to Article 5(1), each Member State shall ensure the implementation of the "producer responsibility" principle and, on that basis, that a minimum collection rate is achieved annually. From 2016, the minimum collection rate shall be 45 % calculated on the basis of the total weight of WEEE collected in accordance with Articles 5 and 6 in a given year in the Member State concerned, expressed as a percentage of the average weight of EEE placed on the market in the three preceding years in that Member State. Member States shall ensure that the volume of WEEE collected evolves gradually during the period from 2016 to 2019, unless the collection rate laid down in the second subparagraph has already been achieved.

From 2019, the minimum collection rate to be achieved annually shall be 65 % of the average weight of EEE placed on the market in the three preceding years in the Member State concerned, or alternatively 85 % of WEEE generated on the territory of that Member State.

Until 31 December 2015, a rate of separate collection of at least 4 kilograms on average per inhabitant per year of WEEE from private households or the same amount of weight of WEEE as was collected in that Member State on average in the three preceding years, whichever is greater, shall continue to apply.

Member States may set more ambitious rates for separate collection of WEEE and shall in such a case report this to the Commission.

2. In order to establish whether the minimum collection rate has been achieved, Member States shall ensure that information concerning the WEEE that is separately collected in accordance with Article 5 is transmitted to the Member States free of charge, including at least information on WEEE that has been:

(a) received by collection and treatment facilities;

(b) received by distributors;

(c) separately collected by producers or third parties acting on their behalf.

3. By way of derogation from paragraph 1, Bulgaria, the Czech Republic, Latvia, Lithuania, Hungary, Malta, Poland, Romania, Slovenia and Slovakia may, because of their lack of the necessary infrastructure and their low level of EEE consumption, decide to:

(a) achieve, from 14 August 2016, a collection rate that is lower than 45 % but higher than 40 % of the average weight of EEE placed on the market in the three preceding years; and

(b) postpone the achievement of the collection rate referred to in the second subparagraph of paragraph 1 until a date of their own choice which shall not be later than 14 August 2021.

4. The Commission shall be empowered to adopt delegated acts in accordance with Article 20 laying down the necessary transitional adjustments in order to address difficulties faced by Member States in adhering to the requirements laid down in paragraph 1.

5. In order to ensure uniform conditions for the implementation of this Article, the Commission shall, by 14 August 2015, adopt implementing acts establishing a common methodology for the calculation of the weight of EEE placed on the national market and a common methodology for the calculation of the quantity of WEEE generated by weight in each Member State. Those implementing acts shall be adopted in accordance with the examination procedure referred to in Article 21(2).

6. The Commission shall, by 14 August 2015, present a report to the European Parliament and to the Council on the re-examination of the deadlines relating to the collection rates referred to in paragraph 1 and on possibly setting individual collection rates for one or more categories set out in Annex III, particularly for temperature exchange equipment, photovoltaic panels, small equipment, small IT and telecommunication equipment and lamps containing mercury. The report shall, if appropriate, be accompanied by a legislative proposal.

7. If the Commission considers, on the basis of an impact study, that the collection rate based on WEEE generated requires revision, it shall submit a legislative proposal to the European Parliament and the Council.

Article 8

Proper treatment

1. Member States shall ensure that all separately collected WEEE undergoes proper treatment.

2. Proper treatment, other than preparing for re-use, and recovery or recycling operations shall, as a minimum, include the removal of all fluids and a selective treatment in accordance with Annex VII.

3. Member States shall ensure that producers or third parties acting on their behalf set up systems to provide for the recovery of WEEE using best available techniques. The systems may be set up by producers individually or collectively. Member States shall ensure that any establishment or undertaking carrying out collection or treatment operations stores and treats WEEE in compliance with the technical requirements set out in Annex VIII.

4. The Commission shall be empowered to adopt delegated acts in accordance with Article 20 concerning the amendment of Annex VII in order to introduce other treatment technologies that ensure at least the same level of protection for human health and the environment.

The Commission shall evaluate, as a matter of priority, whether the entries regarding printed circuit boards for mobile phones and liquid crystal displays need to be amended. The Commission is invited to evaluate whether amendments to Annex VII are necessary to address nanomaterials contained in EEE.

5. For the purposes of environmental protection, Member States may set up minimum quality standards for the treatment of the WEEE that has been collected.

Member States which opt for such quality standards shall inform the Commission thereof, which shall publish these standards.

The Commission shall, not later than 14 February 2013, request the European standardisation organisations to develop European standards for the treatment, including recovery, recycling and preparing for re-use, of WEEE. Those standards shall reflect the state of the art.

In order to ensure uniform conditions for the implementation of this Article, the Commission may adopt implementing acts laying down minimum quality standards based in particular on the standards developed by the European standardisation organisations. Those implementing acts shall be adopted in accordance with the examination procedure referred to in Article 21(2).

A reference to the standards adopted by the Commission shall be published.

6. Member States shall encourage establishments or undertakings which carry out treatment operations to introduce certified environmental management systems in accordance with Regulation (EC) No 1221/2009 of the European Parliament and of the Council of 25 November 2009 on the voluntary participation by organisations in a Community eco-management and audit scheme (EMAS).

Article 9

Permits

1. Member States shall ensure that any establishment or undertaking carrying out treatment operations obtains a permit from the competent authorities in compliance with Article 23 of Directive 2008/98/EC.

2. Exemptions from permit requirements, conditions for exemptions and registration shall be in compliance, respectively, with Articles 24, 25 and 26 of Directive 2008/98/EC.

3. Member States shall ensure that the permit or the registration referred to in paragraphs 1 and 2 includes all the conditions that are necessary for compliance with the requirements of Article 8(2), (3) and (5) and for the achievement of the recovery targets set out in Article 11.

Article 10

Shipments of WEEE

1. The treatment operation may also be undertaken outside the respective Member State or the Union provided that the shipment of WEEE is in compliance with Regulation (EC) No 1013/2006 and Commission Regulation (EC) No 1418/2007 of 29 November 2007 concerning the export for recovery of certain waste listed in Annex III or IIIA to Regulation (EC) No 1013/2006 of the European Parliament and of the Council to certain countries to which the OECD Decision on the control of transboundary movements of wastes does not apply.

2. WEEE exported out of the Union shall only count towards the fulfilment of obligations and targets set out in Article 11 of this Directive if, in compliance with Regulations (EC) No 1013/2006 and (EC) No 1418/2007, the exporter can prove that the treatment took place in conditions that are equivalent to the requirements of this Directive.

3. The Commission shall, not later than 14 February 2014, adopt delegated acts, in accordance with Article 20, laying down detailed rules supplementing those in paragraph 2 of this Article, in particular the criteria for the assessment of equivalent conditions.

Article 11

Recovery targets

1. Regarding all WEEE separately collected in accordance with Article 5 and sent for treatment in accordance with Articles 8, 9 and 10, Member States shall ensure that producers meet the minimum targets set out in Annex V.

2. The achievement of the targets shall be calculated, for each category, by dividing the weight of the WEEE that enters the recovery or recycling/preparing for re-use facility, after proper treatment in accordance with Article 8(2) with regard to recovery or recycling, by the weight of all separately collected WEEE for each category, expressed as a percentage.

Preliminary activities including sorting and storage prior to recovery shall not count towards the achievement of these targets.

3. In order to ensure uniform conditions for the implementation of this Article, the Commission may adopt implementing acts establishing additional rules on the calculation methods for the application of the minimum targets. Those implementing acts shall be adopted in accordance with the examination procedure referred to in Article 21(2).

4. Member States shall ensure that, for the purpose of calculating these targets, producers or third parties acting on their behalf keep records on the weight of WEEE, its components, materials or substances when leaving (output) the collection facility, entering (input) and leaving (output) the treatment facilities and when entering (input) the recovery or recycling/preparing for re-use facility.

Member States shall also ensure that, for the purposes of paragraph 6, records on the weight of products and materials when leaving (output) the recovery or recycling/preparing for re-use facility are kept.

5. Member States shall encourage the development of new recovery, recycling and treatment technologies.

6. On the basis of a report of the Commission accompanied, if appropriate, by a legislative proposal, the European Parliament and the Council shall, by 14 August 2016, re-examine the recovery targets referred to in Annex V, Part 3, examine the possibility of setting separate targets for WEEE to be prepared for re-use and re-examine the calculation method referred to in paragraph 2 with a view to analysing the feasibility of setting targets on the basis of products and materials resulting (output) from the recovery, recycling and preparation for re-use processes.

Article 12

Financing in respect of WEEE from private households

1. Member States shall ensure that producers provide at least for the financing of the collection, treatment, recovery and environmentally sound disposal of WEEE from private households that has been deposited at collection facilities set up under Article 5(2).

2. Member States may, where appropriate, encourage producers to finance also the costs occurring for collection of WEEE from private households to collection facilities.

3. For products placed on the market later than 13 August 2005, each producer shall be responsible for financing the operations referred to in paragraph 1 relating to the waste from his own products. The producer may choose to fulfil this obligation either individually or by joining a collective scheme.

Member States shall ensure that each producer provides a guarantee when placing a product on the market showing that the management of all WEEE will be financed and shall ensure that producers clearly mark their products in accordance with Article 15(2). This guarantee shall ensure that the operations referred to in paragraph 1 relating to this product will be financed. The guarantee may take the form of participation by the producer in appropriate schemes for the financing of the management of WEEE, a recycling insurance or a blocked bank account.

4. The responsibility for the financing of the costs of the management of WEEE from products placed on the market on or before 13 August 2005 ("historical waste") shall be borne by one or more systems to which all producers existing on the market when the respective costs occur

contribute proportionately, e.g. in proportion to their respective share of the market by type of equipment.

5. Member States shall take the necessary measures to ensure that appropriate mechanisms or refund procedures are developed for the reimbursement of contributions to the producers where EEE is transferred for placing on the market outside the territory of the Member State concerned. Such mechanisms or procedures may be developed by producers or third parties acting on their behalf.

6. The Commission is invited to report, by 14 August 2015, on the possibility of developing criteria to incorporate the real end-of-life costs into the financing of WEEE by producers, and to submit a legislative proposal to the European Parliament and the Council if appropriate.

Article 13

Financing in respect of WEEE from users other than private households

1. Member States shall ensure that the financing of the costs for the collection, treatment, recovery and environmentally sound disposal of WEEE from users other than private households resulting from products placed on the market after 13 August 2005 is to be provided for by producers.

For historical waste being replaced by new equivalent products or by new products fulfilling the same function, the financing of the costs shall be provided for by producers of those products when supplying them. Member States may, as an alternative, provide that users other than private households also be made, partly or totally, responsible for this financing.

For other historical waste, the financing of the costs shall be provided for by the users other than private households.

2. Producers and users other than private households may, without prejudice to this Directive, conclude agreements stipulating other financing methods.

Article 14

Information for users

1. Member States may require producers to show purchasers, at the time of sale of new products, the costs of collection, treatment and disposal in an environmentally sound way. The costs mentioned shall not exceed the best estimate of the actual costs incurred.

2. Member States shall ensure that users of EEE in private households are given the necessary information about:

(a) the requirement not to dispose of WEEE as unsorted municipal waste and to collect such WEEE separately;
(b) the return and collection systems available to them, encouraging the coordination of information on the available collection points irrespective of the producers or other operators which have set them up;
(c) their role in contributing to re-use, recycling and other forms of recovery of WEEE;
(d) the potential effects on the environment and human health as a result of the presence of hazardous substances in EEE;
(e) the meaning of the symbol shown in Annex IX.

3. Member States shall adopt appropriate measures so that consumers participate in the collection of WEEE and to encourage them to facilitate the process of re-use, treatment and recovery.

4. With a view to minimising the disposal of WEEE as unsorted municipal waste and to facilitating its separate collection, Member States shall ensure that producers appropriately mark — preferably in accordance with the European standard EN 50419 — EEE placed on

the market with the symbol shown in Annex IX. In exceptional cases, where this is necessary because of the size or the function of the product, the symbol shall be printed on the packaging, on the instructions for use and on the warranty of the EEE.

5. Member States may require that some or all of the information referred to in paragraphs 2, 3 and 4 shall be provided by producers and/or distributors, e.g. in the instructions for use, at the point of sale and through public awareness campaigns.

Article 15

Information for treatment facilities

1. In order to facilitate the preparation for re-use and the correct and environmentally sound treatment of WEEE, including maintenance, upgrade, refurbishment and recycling, Member States shall take the necessary measures to ensure that producers provide information free of charge about preparation for re-use and treatment in respect of each type of new EEE placed for the first time on the Union market within one year after the equipment is placed on the market. This information shall identify, as far as it is needed by centres which prepare for re-use and treatment and recycling facilities in order to comply with the provisions of this Directive, the different EEE components and materials, as well as the location of dangerous substances and mixtures in EEE. It shall be made available to centres which prepare for re-use and treatment and recycling facilities by producers of EEE in the form of manuals or by means of electronic media (e.g. CD-ROM, online services).

2. In order to enable the date upon which the EEE was placed on the market to be determined unequivocally, Member States shall ensure that a mark on the EEE specifies that the latter was placed on the market after 13 August 2005. Preferably, the European Standard EN 50419 shall be applied for this purpose.

Article 16

Registration, information and reporting

1. Member States shall, in accordance with paragraph 2, draw up a register of producers, including producers supplying EEE by means of distance communication. That register shall serve to monitor compliance with the requirements of this Directive.

Producers supplying EEE by means of distance communication as defined in Article 3(1)(f)(iv) shall be registered in the Member State that they sell to. Where such producers are not registered in the Member State that they are selling to, they shall be registered through their authorised representatives as referred to in Article 17(2).

2. Member States shall ensure that:

(a) each producer, or each authorised representative where appointed under Article 17, is registered as required and has the possibility of entering online in their national register all relevant information reflecting that producer's activities in that Member State;

(b) upon registering, each producer, or each authorised representative where appointed under Article 17, provides the information set out in Annex X, Part A, undertaking to update it as appropriate;

(c) each producer, or each authorised representative where appointed under Article 17, provides the information set out in Annex X, Part B;

(d) national registers provide links to other national registers on their website to facilitate, in all Member States, registration of producers or, where appointed under Article 17, authorised representatives.

3. In order to ensure uniform conditions for the implementation of this Article, the Commission shall adopt implementing acts establishing the format for registration and reporting and the frequency of reporting to the register. Those implementing acts shall be adopted in accordance with the examination procedure referred to in Article 21(2).

4. Member States shall collect information, including substantiated estimates, on an annual basis, on the quantities and categories of EEE placed on their markets, collected through all routes, prepared for re-use, recycled and recovered within the Member State, and on separately collected WEEE exported, by weight.

5. Member States shall, at three-year intervals, send a report to the Commission on the implementation of this Directive and on the information set out in paragraph 4. The implementation report shall be drawn up on the basis of a questionnaire laid down in Commission Decisions 2004/249/EC and 2005/369/EC. The report shall be made available to the Commission within nine months of the end of the three-year period covered by it.

The first report shall cover the period from 14 February 2014 to 31 December 2015.

The Commission shall publish a report on the implementation of this Directive within nine months after receiving the reports from the Member States.

Article 17

Authorised representative

1. Each Member State shall ensure that a producer as defined in Article 3(1)(f)(i) to (iii) established in another Member State is allowed, by way of exception to Article 3(1)(f) (i) to (iii), to appoint a legal or natural person established on its territory as the authorised representative that is responsible for fulfilling the obligations of that producer, pursuant to this Directive, on its territory.

2. Each Member State shall ensure that a producer as defined in Article 3(1)(f)(iv) and established on its territory, which sells EEE to another Member State in which it is not established, appoints an authorised representative in that Member State as the person responsible for fulfilling the obligations of that producer, pursuant to this Directive, on the territory of that Member State.

3. Appointment of an authorised representative shall be by written mandate.

Article 18

Administrative cooperation and exchange of information

Member States shall ensure that authorities responsible for implementing this Directive cooperate with each other, in particular to establish an adequate flow of information to ensure that producers comply with the provisions of this Directive and, where appropriate, provide each other and the Commission with information in order to facilitate the proper implementation of this Directive. The administrative cooperation and exchange of information, in particular between national registers, shall include electronic means of communication.

Cooperation shall include, inter alia, granting access to the relevant documents and information including the results of any inspections, subject to the provisions of the data protection law in force in the Member State of the authority which is requested to cooperate.

Article 19

Adaptation to scientific and technical progress

The Commission shall be empowered to adopt delegated acts in accordance with Article 20 concerning the amendments necessary in order to adapt Article 16(5) and Annexes IV, VII, VIII and IX to scientific and technical progress. When amending Annex VII, the exemptions granted under Directive 2011/65/EU of the European Parliament and of the Council of 8 June 2011 on the restriction of the use of certain hazardous substances in electrical and electronic equipment shall be taken into consideration.

Before the Annexes are amended, the Commission shall, inter alia, consult producers of EEE, recyclers, treatment operators and environmental organisations and employees' and consumer associations.

Article 20

Exercise of the delegation

1. The power to adopt delegated acts is conferred on the Commission subject to the conditions laid down in this Article.

2. The power to adopt delegated acts referred to in Article 7(4), Article 8(4), Article 10(3) and Article 19 shall be conferred on the Commission for a period of five years from 13 August 2012. The Commission shall draw up a report in respect of the delegation of power not later than nine months before the end of the five-year period. The delegation of power shall be tacitly extended for periods of an identical duration, unless the European Parliament or the Council opposes such extension not later than three months before the end of each period.

3. The delegation of power referred to in Article 7(4), Article 8(4), Article 10(3) and Article 19 may be revoked at any time by the European Parliament or by the Council. A decision to revoke shall put an end to the delegation of the power specified in that decision. It shall take effect the day following the publication of the decision in the Official Journal of the European Union or at a later date specified therein. It shall not affect the validity of any delegated acts already in force.

4. As soon as it adopts a delegated act, the Commission shall notify it simultaneously to the European Parliament and to the Council.

5. A delegated act adopted pursuant to Article 7(4), Article 8(4), Article 10(3) and Article 19 shall enter into force only if no objection has been expressed either by the European Parliament or the Council within a period of two months of notification of that act to the European Parliament and to the Council or if, before the expiry of that period, the European Parliament and the Council have both informed the Commission that they will not object. That period shall be extended by two months at the initiative of the European Parliament or of the Council.

Article 21

Committee procedure

1. The Commission shall be assisted by the Committee established by Article 39 of Directive 2008/98/EC. That committee shall be a committee within the meaning of Regulation (EU) No 182/2011.

2. Where reference is made to this paragraph, Article 5 of Regulation (EU) No 182/2011 shall apply.

Where the committee delivers no opinion, the Commission shall not adopt the draft implementing act and the third subparagraph of Article 5(4) of Regulation (EU) No 182/2011 shall apply.

Article 22

Penalties

The Member States shall lay down the rules on penalties applicable to infringements of the national provisions adopted pursuant to this Directive and shall take all measures necessary to ensure that they are implemented. The penalties provided for must be effective, proportionate and dissuasive. The Member States shall notify those provisions to the Commission by 14 February 2014 at the latest and shall notify it without delay of any subsequent amendment affecting them.

Article 23

Inspection and monitoring

1. Member States shall carry out appropriate inspections and monitoring to verify the proper implementation of this Directive.

Those inspections shall at least cover:
(a) information reported in the framework of the register of producers;
(b) shipments, in particular exports of WEEE outside the Union in compliance with Regulation (EC) No 1013/2006 and Regulation (EC) No 1418/2007; and
(c) the operations at treatment facilities in accordance with Directive 2008/98/EC and Annex VII of this Directive.

2. Member States shall ensure that shipments of used EEE suspected to be WEEE are carried out in accordance with the minimum requirements in Annex VI and shall monitor such shipments accordingly.

3. The costs of appropriate analyses and inspections, including storage costs, of used EEE suspected to be WEEE may be charged to the producers, to third parties acting on their behalf or to other persons arranging the shipment of used EEE suspected to be WEEE.

4. In order to ensure uniform conditions for the implementation of this Article and of Annex VI, the Commission may adopt implementing acts establishing additional rules on inspections and monitoring and in particular uniform conditions for the implementation of Annex VI, point 2. Those implementing acts shall be adopted in accordance with the examination procedure referred to in Article 21(2).

Article 24

Transposition

1. Member States shall bring into force the laws, regulations and administrative provisions necessary to comply with this Directive by 14 February 2014. They shall immediately communicate to the Commission the text of those provisions.

When Member States adopt those provisions, they shall contain a reference to this Directive or shall be accompanied by such reference on the occasion of their official publication. They shall also include a statement that references in existing laws, regulations and administrative provisions to the directives repealed by this Directive shall be construed as references to this Directive. Member States shall determine how such reference is to be made and how that statement is to be formulated.

2. Member States shall communicate to the Commission the text of the main provisions of national law which they adopt in the field covered by this Directive.

3. Provided that the objectives set out in this Directive are achieved, Member States may transpose the provisions set out in Article 8(6), Article 14(2) and Article 15 by means of agreements between the competent authorities and the economic sectors concerned. Such agreements shall meet the following requirements:
(a) agreements shall be enforceable;
(b) agreements shall specify objectives with the corresponding deadlines;
(c) agreements shall be published in the national official journal or an official document equally accessible to the public and transmitted to the Commission;

(d) the results achieved shall be monitored regularly, reported to the competent authorities and the Commission and made available to the public under the conditions set out in the agreement;

(e) the competent authorities shall ensure that the progress achieved under the agreement is examined;

(f) in the case of non-compliance with the agreement, Member States must implement the relevant provisions of this Directive by legislative, regulatory or administrative measures.

Article 25

Repeal

Directive 2002/96/EC as amended by the Directives listed in Annex XI, Part A is repealed with effect from 15 February 2014, without prejudice to the obligations of the Member States relating to the time limits for transposition into national law and application of the Directives set out in Annex XI, Part B.

References to the repealed Directives shall be construed as references to this Directive and shall be read in accordance with the correlation table in Annex XII.

Article 26

Entry into force

This Directive shall enter into force on the twentieth day following that of its publication in the Official Journal of the European Union.

Article 27

Addressees

This Directive is addressed to the Member States.

ANNEX I
CATEGORIES OF EEE COVERED BY THIS DIRECTIVE DURING THE TRANSITIONAL PERIOD AS PROVIDED FOR IN ARTICLE 2(1)(A)

1. Large household appliances
2. Small household appliances
3. IT and telecommunications equipment
4. Consumer equipment and photovoltaic panels
5. Lighting equipment
6. Electrical and electronic tools (with the exception of large-scale stationary industrial tools)
7. Toys, leisure and sports equipment
8. Medical devices (with the exception of all implanted and infected products)
9. Monitoring and control instruments
10. Automatic dispensers

ANNEX II
INDICATIVE LIST OF EEE WHICH FALLS WITHIN THE CATEGORIES OF ANNEX I

1. LARGE HOUSEHOLD APPLIANCES

Large cooling appliances

Refrigerators

Freezers

Other large appliances used for refrigeration, conservation and storage of food

Washing machines

Clothes dryers

Dish washing machines

Cookers

Electric stoves

Electric hot plates

Microwaves

Other large appliances used for cooking and other processing of food

Electric heating appliances

Electric radiators

Other large appliances for heating rooms, beds, seating furniture

Electric fans

Air conditioner appliances

Other fanning, exhaust ventilation and conditioning equipment

2. SMALL HOUSEHOLD APPLIANCES

Vacuum cleaners

Carpet sweepers

Other appliances for cleaning

Appliances used for sewing, knitting, weaving and other processing for textiles

Irons and other appliances for ironing, mangling and other care of clothing

Toasters

Fryers

Grinders, coffee machines and equipment for opening or sealing containers or packages

Electric knives

Appliances for hair cutting, hair drying, tooth brushing, shaving, massage and other body care appliances

Clocks, watches and equipment for the purpose of measuring, indicating or registering time

Scales

3. IT AND TELECOMMUNICATIONS EQUIPMENT

Centralised data processing:

Mainframes

Minicomputers

Printer units

Personal computing:

Personal computers (CPU, mouse, screen and keyboard included)

Laptop computers (CPU, mouse, screen and keyboard included)

Notebook computers

Notepad computers

Printers

Copying equipment

Electrical and electronic typewriters

Pocket and desk calculators

and other products and equipment for the collection, storage, processing, presentation or communication of information by electronic means

User terminals and systems

Facsimile machine (fax)

Telex

Telephones

Pay telephones

Cordless telephones

Cellular telephones

Answering systems

and other products or equipment of transmitting sound, images or other information by telecommunications

4. CONSUMER EQUIPMENT AND PHOTOVOLTAIC PANELS

Radio sets

Television sets

Video cameras

Video recorders

Hi-fi recorders

Audio amplifiers

Musical instruments

and other products or equipment for the purpose of recording or reproducing sound or images, including signals or other technologies for the distribution of sound and image than by telecommunications

Photovoltaic panels

5. LIGHTING EQUIPMENT

Luminaires for fluorescent lamps with the exception of luminaires in households

Straight fluorescent lamps

Compact fluorescent lamps

High intensity discharge lamps, including pressure sodium lamps and metal halide lamps

Low pressure sodium lamps

Other lighting or equipment for the purpose of spreading or controlling light with the exception of filament bulbs

6. ELECTRICAL AND ELECTRONIC TOOLS (WITH THE EXCEPTION OF LARGE-SCALE STATIONARY INDUSTRIAL TOOLS)

Drills

Saws

Sewing machines

Equipment for turning, milling, sanding, grinding, sawing, cutting, shearing, drilling, making holes, punching, folding, bending or similar processing of wood, metal and other materials

Tools for riveting, nailing or screwing or removing rivets, nails, screws or similar uses

Tools for welding, soldering or similar use

Equipment for spraying, spreading, dispersing or other treatment of liquid or gaseous substances by other means

Tools for mowing or other gardening activities

7. TOYS, LEISURE AND SPORTS EQUIPMENT

Electric trains or car racing sets

Hand-held video game consoles

Video games

Computers for biking, diving, running, rowing, etc.

Sports equipment with electric or electronic components

Coin slot machines

8. MEDICAL DEVICES (WITH THE EXCEPTION OF ALL IMPLANTED AND INFECTED PRODUCTS)

Radiotherapy equipment

Cardiology equipment

Dialysis equipment

Pulmonary ventilators

Nuclear medicine equipment

Laboratory equipment for in vitro diagnosis

Analysers

Freezers

Fertilization tests

Other appliances for detecting, preventing, monitoring, treating, alleviating illness, injury or disability

9. MONITORING AND CONTROL INSTRUMENTS

Smoke detector

Heating regulators

Thermostats

Measuring, weighing or adjusting appliances for household or as laboratory equipment

Other monitoring and control instruments used in industrial installations (e.g. in control panels)

10. AUTOMATIC DISPENSERS

Automatic dispensers for hot drinks

Automatic dispensers for hot or cold bottles or cans

Automatic dispensers for solid products

Automatic dispensers for money

All appliances which deliver automatically all kinds of products

ANNEX III
CATEGORIES OF EEE COVERED BY THIS DIRECTIVE

1. Temperature exchange equipment

2. Screens, monitors, and equipment containing screens having a surface greater than 100 cm^2

3. Lamps

4. Large equipment (any external dimension more than 50 cm) including, but not limited to: Household appliances; IT and telecommunication equipment; consumer equipment; luminaires; equipment reproducing sound or images, musical equipment; electrical and electronic tools; toys, leisure and sports equipment; medical devices; monitoring and control instruments; automatic dispensers; equipment for the generation of electric currents. This category does not include equipment included in categories 1 to 3.

5. Small equipment (no external dimension more than 50 cm) including, but not limited to: Household appliances; consumer equipment; luminaires; equipment reproducing sound or images, musical equipment; electrical and electronic tools; toys, leisure and sports equipment; medical devices; monitoring and control instruments; automatic dispensers; equipment for the generation of electric currents. This category does not include equipment included in categories 1 to 3 and 6.

6. Small IT and telecommunication equipment (no external dimension more than 50 cm)

ANNEX IV
NON-EXHAUSTIVE LIST OF EEE WHICH FALLS WITHIN THE CATEGORIES LISTED IN ANNEX III

1. Temperature exchange equipment

Refrigerators, Freezers, Equipment which automatically delivers cold products, Air conditioning equipment, Dehumidifying equipment, Heat pumps, Radiators containing oil and other temperature exchange equipment using fluids other than water for the temperature exchange.

2. Screens, monitors, and equipment containing screens having a surface greater than 100 cm^2
Screens, Televisions, LCD photo frames, Monitors, Laptops, Notebooks.

3. Lamps
Straight fluorescent lamps, Compact fluorescent lamps, Fluorescent lamps, High intensity discharge lamps – including pressure sodium lamps and metal halide lamps, Low pressure sodium lamps, LED.

4. Large equipment
Washing machines, Clothes dryers, Dish washing machines, Cookers, Electric stoves, Electric hot plates, Luminaires, Equipment reproducing sound or images, Musical equipment (excluding pipe organs installed in churches), Appliances for knitting and weaving, Large computer-mainframes, Large printing machines, Copying equipment, Large coin slot machines, Large medical devices, Large monitoring and control instruments, Large appliances which automatically deliver products and money, Photovoltaic panels.

5. Small equipment
Vacuum cleaners, Carpet sweepers, Appliances for sewing, Luminaires, Microwaves, Ventilation equipment, Irons, Toasters, Electric knives, Electric kettles, Clocks and Watches, Electric shavers, Scales, Appliances for hair and body care, Calculators, Radio sets, Video cameras, Video recorders, Hi-fi equipment, Musical instruments, Equipment reproducing sound or images, Electrical and electronic toys, Sports equipment, Computers for biking, diving, running, rowing, etc., Smoke detectors, Heating regulators, Thermostats, Small Electrical and electronic tools, Small medical devices, Small Monitoring and control instruments, Small Appliances which automatically deliver products, Small equipment with integrated photovoltaic panels.

6. Small IT and telecommunication equipment (no external dimension more than 50 cm)
Mobile phones, GPS, Pocket calculators, Routers, Personal computers, Printers, Telephones.

ANNEX V
MINIMUM RECOVERY TARGETS REFERRED TO IN ARTICLE 11

Part 1: Minimum targets applicable by category from 13 August 2012 until 14 August 2015 with reference to the categories listed in Annex I:

(a) for WEEE falling within category 1 or 10 of Annex I,
— 80 % shall be recovered, and
— 75 % shall be recycled;

(b) for WEEE falling within category 3 or 4 of Annex I,
— 75 % shall be recovered, and
— 65 % shall be recycled;

(c) for WEEE falling within category 2, 5, 6, 7, 8 or 9 of Annex I,
— 70 % shall be recovered, and
— 50 % shall be recycled;

(d) for gas discharge lamps, 80 % shall be recycled.

Part 2: Minimum targets applicable by category from 15 August 2015 until 14 August 2018 with reference to the categories listed in Annex I:

(a) for WEEE falling within category 1 or 10 of Annex I,
— 85 % shall be recovered, and
— 80 % shall be prepared for re-use and recycled;

(b) for WEEE falling within category 3 or 4 of Annex I,
— 80 % shall be recovered, and
— 70 % shall be prepared for re-use and recycled;

(c) for WEEE falling within category 2, 5, 6, 7, 8 or 9 of Annex I,
— 75 % shall be recovered, and
— 55 % shall be prepared for re-use and recycled;
(d) for gas discharge lamps, 80 % shall be recycled.

Part 3: Minimum targets applicable by category from 15 August 2018 with reference to the categories listed in Annex III:
(a) for WEEE falling within category 1 or 4 of Annex III,
— 85 % shall be recovered, and
— 80 % shall be prepared for re-use and recycled;
(b) for WEEE falling within category 2 of Annex III,
— 80 % shall be recovered, and
— 70 % shall be prepared for re-use and recycled;
(c) for WEEE falling within category 5 or 6 of Annex III,
— 75 % shall be recovered, and
— 55 % shall be prepared for re-use and recycled;
(d) for WEEE falling within category 3 of Annex III, 80 % shall be recycled.

ANNEX VI
MINIMUM REQUIREMENTS FOR SHIPMENTS

1. In order to distinguish between EEE and WEEE, where the holder of the object claims that he intends to ship or is shipping used EEE and not WEEE, Member States shall require the holder to have available the following to substantiate this claim:
(a) a copy of the invoice and contract relating to the sale and/or transfer of ownership of the EEE which states that the equipment is destined for direct re-use and that it is fully functional;
(b) evidence of evaluation or testing in the form of a copy of the records (certificate of testing, proof of functionality) on every item within the consignment and a protocol containing all record information according to point 3;
(c) a declaration made by the holder who arranges the transport of the EEE that none of the material or equipment within the consignment is waste as defined by Article 3(1) of Directive 2008/98/EC; and
(d) appropriate protection against damage during transportation, loading and unloading in particular through sufficient packaging and appropriate stacking of the load.

2. By way of derogation, point 1(a) and (b) and point 3 do not apply where it is documented by conclusive proof that the shipment is taking place in the framework of a business-to-business transfer agreement and that:
(a) the EEE is sent back to the producer or a third party acting on his behalf as defective for repair under warranty with the intention of re-use; or
(b) the used EEE for professional use is sent to the producer or a third party acting on his behalf or a third-party facility in countries to which Decision C(2001)107/Final of the OECD Council concerning the revision of Decision C(92)39/Final on control of transboundary movements of wastes destined for recovery operations applies, for refurbishment or repair under a valid contract with the intention of re-use; or
(c) the defective used EEE for professional use, such as medical devices or their parts, is sent to the producer or a third party acting on his behalf for root cause analysis under a valid contract, in cases where such an analysis can only be conducted by the producer or third parties acting on his behalf.

3. In order to demonstrate that the items being shipped constitute used EEE rather than WEEE, Member States shall require the following steps for testing and record keeping for used EEE to be carried out:

Step 1: Testing

(a) Functionality shall be tested and the presence of hazardous substances shall be evaluated. The tests to be conducted depend on the kind of EEE. For most of the used EEE a functionality test of the key functions is sufficient.

(b) Results of evaluation and testing shall be recorded.

Step 2: Record

(a) The record shall be fixed securely but not permanently on either the EEE itself (if not packed) or on the packaging so it can be read without unpacking the equipment.

(b) The record shall contain the following information:

- name of item (name of the equipment if listed in Annex II or Annex IV, as appropriate, and category set out in Annex I or Annex III, as appropriate),
- identification number of the item (type No) where applicable,
- year of production (if available),
- name and address of the company responsible for evidence of functionality,
- result of tests as described in step 1 (including date of the functionality test),
- kind of tests performed.

4. In addition to the documentation requested in points 1, 2 and 3, every load (e.g. shipping container, lorry) of used EEE shall be accompanied by:

(a) a relevant transport document, e.g. CMR or waybill;

(b) a declaration by the liable person on its responsibility.

5. In the absence of proof that an object is used EEE and not WEEE through the appropriate documentation required in points 1, 2, 3 and 4 and of appropriate protection against damage during transportation, loading and unloading in particular through sufficient packaging and appropriate stacking of the load, which are the obligations of the holder who arranges the transport, Member State authorities shall consider that an item is WEEE and presume that the load comprises an illegal shipment. In these circumstances the load will be dealt with in accordance with Articles 24 and 25 of Regulation (EC) No 1013/2006.

ANNEX VII
SELECTIVE TREATMENT FOR MATERIALS AND COMPONENTS OF WASTE ELECTRICAL AND ELECTRONIC EQUIPMENT REFERRED TO IN ARTICLE 8(2)

1. As a minimum the following substances, mixtures and components have to be removed from any separately collected WEEE:

- polychlorinated biphenyls (PCB) containing capacitors in accordance with Council Directive 96/59/EC of 16 September 1996 on the disposal of polychlorinated biphenyls and polychlorinated terphenyls (PCB/PCT),
- mercury containing components, such as switches or backlighting lamps,
- batteries,
- printed circuit boards of mobile phones generally, and of other devices if the surface of the printed circuit board is greater than 10 square centimetres,
- toner cartridges, liquid and paste, as well as colour toner,
- plastic containing brominated flame retardants,
- asbestos waste and components which contain asbestos,
- cathode ray tubes,
- chlorofluorocarbons (CFC), hydrochlorofluorocarbons (HCFC) or hydrofluorocarbons (HFC), hydrocarbons (HC),
- gas discharge lamps,
- liquid crystal displays (together with their casing where appropriate) of a surface greater than 100 square centimetres and all those back-lighted with gas discharge lamps,

— external electric cables,
— components containing refractory ceramic fibres as described in Commission Directive 97/69/EC of 5 December 1997 adapting to technical progress for the 23rd time Council Directive 67/548/EEC on the approximation of the laws, regulations and administrative provisions relating to the classification, packaging and labelling of dangerous substances,
— components containing radioactive substances with the exception of components that are below the exemption thresholds set in Article 3 of and Annex I to Council Directive 96/29/Euratom of 13 May 1996 laying down basic safety standards for the protection of the health of workers and the general public against the dangers arising from ionizing radiation,
— electrolyte capacitors containing substances of concern (height > 25 mm, diameter > 25 mm or proportionately similar volume).

These substances, mixtures and components shall be disposed of or recovered in compliance with Directive 2008/98/EC.

2. The following components of WEEE that is separately collected have to be treated as indicated:
— cathode ray tubes: the fluorescent coating has to be removed,
— equipment containing gases that are ozone depleting or have a global warming potential (GWP) above 15, such as those contained in foams and refrigeration circuits: the gases must be properly extracted and properly treated. Ozone-depleting gases must be treated in accordance with Regulation (EC) No 1005/2009,
— gas discharge lamps: the mercury shall be removed.

3. Taking into account environmental considerations and the desirability of preparation for re-use and recycling, points 1 and 2 shall be applied in such a way that environmentally-sound preparation for re-use and recycling of components or whole appliances is not hindered.

ANNEX VIII
TECHNICAL REQUIREMENTS REFERRED TO IN ARTICLE 8(3)

1. Sites for storage (including temporary storage) of WEEE prior to its treatment (without prejudice to the requirements of Council Directive 1999/31/EC of 26 April 1999 on the landfill of waste):
— impermeable surfaces for appropriate areas with the provision of spillage collection facilities and, where appropriate, decanters and cleanser-degreasers,
— weatherproof covering for appropriate areas.

2. Sites for treatment of WEEE:
— scales to measure the weight of the treated waste,
— impermeable surfaces and waterproof covering for appropriate areas with the provision of spillage collection facilities and, where appropriate, decanters and cleanser-degreasers,
— appropriate storage for disassembled spare parts,
— appropriate containers for storage of batteries, PCBs/PCTs containing capacitors and other hazardous waste such as radioactive waste,
— equipment for the treatment of water in compliance with health and environmental regulations.

ANNEX IX
SYMBOL FOR THE MARKING OF EEE

The symbol indicating separate collection for EEE consists of the crossed-out wheeled bin, as shown below. The symbol must be printed visibly, legibly and indelibly.

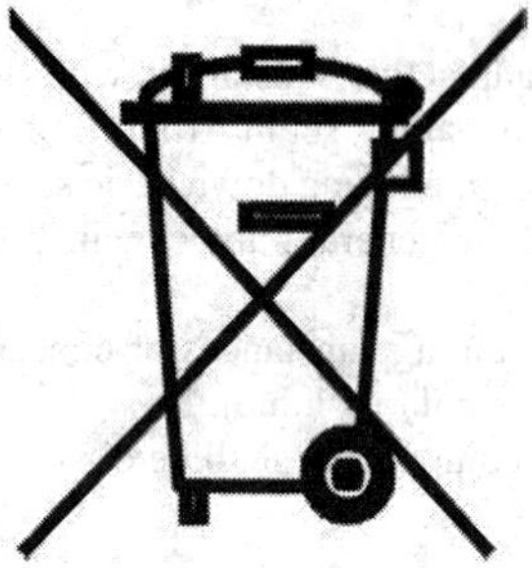

ANNEX X
INFORMATION FOR REGISTRATION AND REPORTING REFERRED TO IN ARTICLE 16

A. Information to be submitted upon registration:

1. Name and address of the producer or of the authorised representative where appointed under Article 17 (postal code and location, street name and number, country, telephone and fax number, e-mail, as well as a contact person). In the case of an authorised representative as defined in Article 17, also the contact details of the producer that is represented.
2. National identification code of the producer, including European tax number or national tax number of the producer.
3. Category of EEE set out in Annex I or III, as appropriate.
4. Type of EEE (household or other than household equipment).
5. Brand name of EEE.
6. Information on how the producer meets its responsibilities: individual or collective scheme, including information on financial guarantee.
7. Selling technique used (e.g. distance selling).
8. Declaration stating that the information provided is true.

B. Information to be submitted for reporting:

1. National identification code of the producer.
2. Reporting period.
3. Category of EEE set out in Annex I or III, as appropriate.
4. Quantity of EEE placed on the national market, by weight.
5. Quantity, by weight, of waste of EEE separately collected, recycled (including prepared for re-use), recovered and disposed of within the Member State or shipped within or outside the Union.

Note: information set out in points 4 and 5 must be given by category.

ANNEX XI

PART A
REPEALED DIRECTIVE WITH ITS SUCCESSIVE AMENDMENTS (REFERRED TO IN ARTICLE 25)

Directive 2002/96/EC on waste electrical and electronic equipment (WEEE)	(OJ L 37, 13.2.2003, p. 24)
Directive 2003/108/EC of the European Parliament and of the Council	(OJ L 345, 31.12.2003, p. 106)
Directive 2008/34/EC of the European Parliament and of the Council	(OJ L 81, 20.3.2008, p. 65)

PART B
LIST OF TIME LIMITS FOR TRANSPOSITION INTO NATIONAL LAW (REFERRED TO IN ARTICLE 25)

Directive	*Deadline for transposition*
2002/96/EC	13 August 2004
2003/108/EC	13 August 2004
2008/34/EC	—

ANNEX XII
CORRELATION TABLE

Directive 2002/96/EC	*This Directive*
Article 1	—
—	Article 1
Article 2(1)	Article 2(1)
Article 2(2)	Article 2(2)
Article 2(3)	Article 2(3)(a)
Article 2(1) (partly)	Article 2(3)(b)
Annex IB, point 5, last item	Article 2(3)(c)
Annex IB, point 8	Article 2(4)(g)
—	Article 2(4)(a) to (f) and 2(5)
Article 3(a)	Article 3(1)(a)
—	Article 3(1)(b) to (d)
Article 3(b)	Article 3(1)(e)
Article 3(c) to (h)	Article 3(2)
Article 3(i)	Article 3(1)(f)
Article 3(j)	Article 3(1)(g)
Article 3(k)	Article 3(1)(h)
Article 3(l)	—
Article 3(m)	Article 3(1)(i)
—	Article 3(1)(j) to (o)
Article 4	Article 4
Article 5(1) to (2)	Article 5(1) to (2)
—	Article 5(3) to (4)
Article 5(3)	Article 5(5)
—	Article 6(1)

Directive 2002/96/EC	*This Directive*
Article 5(4)	Article 6(2)
Article 5(5)	Article 7(1) and (2)
—	Article 8(1)
Article 6(1), first and second subparagraphs, and (3)	Article 8(2), (3) and (4)
Annex II(4)	Article 8(4), second subparagraph, first sentence
Article 6(1), third subparagraph	Article 8(5)
Article 6(6)	Article 8(6)
Article 6(2)	Article 9(1) and (2)
Article 6(4)	Article 9(3)
Article 6(5)	Article 10(1) and (2)
—	Article 10(3)
Article 7(1)	—
Article 7(2)	Article 11(1) and Annex V
—	Article 11(2)
—	Article 11(3)
Article 7(3), first subparagraph	Article 11(4)
Article 7(3), second subparagraph	—
Article 7(4)	—
Article 7(5)	Article 11(5)
—	Article 11(6)
Article 8(1)	Article 12(1)
—	Article 12(2)
Article 8(2), first and second subparagraphs	Article 12(3)
Article 8(2), third subparagraph	Article 14(1) (partly)
Article 8(3), first subparagraph	Article 12(4)
—	Article 12(5)
Article 8(3), second subparagraph	Article 14(1) (partly)
Article 8(4)	—
Article 9(1), first subparagraph	Article 13(1), first subparagraph
Article 9(1), second subparagraph	—
Article 9(1), third subparagraph	Article 13(1), second subparagraph
Article 9(1), fourth subparagraph	Article 13(1), third subparagraph
Article 9(2)	Article 13(2)
Article 10(1)	Article 14(2)
Article 10(2)	Article 14(3)
Article 10(3)	Article 14(4)
Article 10(4)	Article 14(5)
Article 11	Article 15
Article 12(1) (partly)	Article 16(1) to (3)
Article 12(1), first subparagraph (partly)	Article 16(4)
Article 12(1), second subparagraph	Article 16(1) and (2) and Article 17(2) and (3)
Article 12(1), third subparagraph	Article 16(3) and (5)
—	Article 17(1)

Directive 2002/96/EC	*This Directive*
Article 12(1), fourth subparagraph	Article 18
Article 12(2)	Article 16(5)
Article 13	Article 19
—	Article 20
Article 14	Article 21
Article 15	Article 22
Article 16	Article 23(1)
—	Article 23(2) to (4)
Article 17(1) to (3)	Article 24(1) to (3)
Article 17(4)	Article 7(3)
Article 17(5)	Article 7(4) to (7), Article 11(6) and Article 12(6)
—	Article 25
Article 18	Article 26
Article 19	Article 27
Annex IA	Annex I
Annex IB	Annex II
—	Annexes III, IV and VI
Annexes II to IV	Annexes VII to IX
—	Annexes X and XI
—	Annex XII

Part 5
International Materials

CONVENTION ON WETLANDS OF INTERNATIONAL IMPORTANCE ESPECIALLY AS WATERFOWL HABITAT

(Ramsar, 1971)

2 February 1971

UNITED NATIONS EDUCATIONAL, SCIENTIFIC AND CULTURAL ORGANIZATION (UNESCO)

THE CONTRACTING PARTIES,

RECOGNIZING the interdependence of Man and his environment;

CONSIDERING the fundamental ecological functions of wetlands as regulators of water regimes and as habitats supporting a characteristic flora and fauna, especially waterfowl;

BEING CONVINCED that wetlands constitute a resource of great economic, cultural, scientific, and recreational value, the loss of which would be irreparable;

DESIRING to stem the progressive encroachment on and loss of wetlands now and in the future;

RECOGNIZING that waterfowl in their seasonal migrations may transcend frontiers and so should be regarded as an international resource;

BEING CONFIDENT that the conservation of wetlands and their flora and fauna can be ensured by combining far-sighted national policies with co-ordinated international action;

HAVE AGREED AS FOLLOWS:

Article 1

1. For the purpose of this Convention wetlands are areas of marsh, fen, peat land or water, whether natural or artificial, permanent or temporary, with water that is static or flowing, fresh, brackish or salt, including areas of marine water the depth of which at low tide does not exceed six metres.

2. For the purpose of this Convention waterfowl are birds ecologically dependent on wetlands.

Article 2

1. Each Contracting Party shall designate suitable wetlands within its territory for inclusion in a List of Wetlands of International Importance, hereinafter referred to as "the List" which is maintained by the bureau established under Article 8. The boundaries of each wetland shall be precisely described and also delimited on a map and they may incorporate riparian and coastal zones adjacent to the wetlands, and islands or bodies of marine water deeper than six metres at low tide lying within the wetlands, especially where these have importance as waterfowl habitat.

2. Wetlands should be selected for the List on account of their international significance in terms of ecology, botany, zoology, limnology or hydrology. In the first instance wetlands of international importance to waterfowl at any season should be included.

3. The inclusion of a wetland in the List does not prejudice the exclusive sovereign rights of the Contracting Party in whose territory the wetland is situated.

4. Each Contracting Party shall designate at least one wetland to be included in the List when signing this Convention or when depositing its instrument of ratification or accession, as provided in Article 9.

5. Any Contracting Party shall have the right to add to the List further wetlands situated within its territory, to extend the boundaries of those wetlands already included by it in the List, or, because of its urgent national interests, to delete or restrict the boundaries of wetlands already included by it in the List and shall, at the earliest possible time, inform the organization or government responsible for the continuing bureau duties specified in Article 8 of any such changes.

6. Each Contracting Party shall consider its international responsibilities for the conservation, management and wise use of migratory stocks of waterfowl, both when designating entries for the List and when exercising its right to change entries in the List relating to wetlands within its territory.

Article 3

1. The Contracting Parties shall formulate and implement their planning so as to promote the conservation of the wetlands included in the List, and as far as possible the wise use of wetlands in their territory.

2. Each Contracting Party shall arrange to be informed at the earliest possible time if the ecological character of any wetland in its territory and included in the List has changed, is changing or is likely to change as the result of technological developments, pollution or other human interference. Information on such changes shall be passed without delay to the organization or government responsible for the continuing bureau duties specified in Article 8.

Article 4

1. Each Contracting Party shall promote the conservation of wetlands and waterfowl by establishing nature reserves on wetlands, whether they are included in the List or not, and provide adequately for their wardening.

2. Where a Contracting Party in its urgent national interest, deletes or restricts the boundaries of a wetland included in the List, it should as far as possible compensate for any loss of wetland resources, and in particular it should create additional nature reserves for waterfowl and for the protection, either in the same area or elsewhere, of an adequate portion of the original habitat.

3. The Contracting Parties shall encourage research and the exchange of data and publications regarding wetlands and their flora and fauna.

4. The Contracting Parties shall endeavour through management to increase waterfowl populations on appropriate wetlands.

5. The Contracting Parties shall promote the training of personnel competent in the fields of wetland research, management and wardening.

Article 5

1. The Contracting Parties shall consult with each other about implementing obligations arising from the Convention especially in the case of a wetland extending over the territories of more than one Contracting Party or where a water system is shared by Contracting Parties. They shall at the same time endeavour to coordinate and support present and future policies and regulations concerning the conservation of wetlands and their flora and fauna.

Article 6

1. There shall be established a Conference of the Contracting Parties to review and promote the implementation of this Convention. The Bureau referred to in Article 8, paragraph 1, shall

convene ordinary meetings of the Conference of the Contracting Parties at intervals of not more than three years, unless the Conference decides otherwise, and extraordinary meetings at the written requests of at least one third of the Contracting Parties. Each ordinary meeting of the Conference of the Contracting Parties shall determine the time and venue of the next ordinary meeting.

2. The Conference of the Contracting Parties shall be competent:
a) to discuss the implementation of this Convention;
b) to discuss additions to and changes in the List;
c) to consider information regarding changes in the ecological character of wetlands included in the List provided in accordance with paragraph 2 of Article 3;
d) to make general or specific recommendations to the Contracting Parties regarding the conservation, management and wise use of wetlands and their flora and fauna;
e) to request relevant international bodies to prepare reports and statistics on matters which are essentially international in character affecting wetlands;
f) to adopt other recommendations, or resolutions, to promote the functioning of this Convention.

3. The Contracting Parties shall ensure that those responsible at all levels for wetlands management shall be informed of, and take into consideration, recommendations of such Conferences concerning the conservation, management and wise use of wetlands and their flora and fauna.

4. The Conference of the Contracting Parties shall adopt rules of procedure for each of its meetings.

5. The Conference of the Contracting Parties shall establish and keep under review the financial regulations of this Convention. At each of its ordinary meetings, it shall adopt the budget for the next financial period by a two-third majority of Contracting Parties present and voting.

6. Each Contracting Party shall contribute to the budget according to a scale of contributions adopted by unanimity of the Contracting Parties present and voting at a meeting of the ordinary Conference of the Contracting Parties.

Article 7

1. The representatives of the Contracting Parties at such Conferences should include persons who are experts on wetlands or waterfowl by reason of knowledge and experience gained in scientific, administrative or other appropriate capacities.

2. Each of the Contracting Parties represented at a Conference shall have one vote, recommendations, resolutions and decisions being adopted by a simple majority of the Contracting Parties present and voting, unless otherwise provided for in this Convention.

Article 8

1. The International Union for Conservation of Nature and Natural Resources shall perform the continuing bureau duties under this Convention until such time as another organization or government is appointed by a majority of two-thirds of all Contracting Parties.

2. The continuing bureau duties shall be, inter alia:
a) to assist in the convening and organizing of Conferences specified in Article 6;
b) to maintain the List of Wetlands of International Importance and to be informed by the Contracting Parties of any additions, extensions, deletions or restrictions concerning wetlands included in the List provided in accordance with paragraph 5 of Article 2;
c) to be informed by the Contracting Parties of any changes in the ecological character of wetlands included in the List provided in accordance with paragraph 2 of Article 3;

d) to forward notification of any alterations to the List, or changes in character of wetlands included therein, to all Contracting Parties and to arrange for these matters to be discussed at the next Conference;

e) to make known to the Contracting Party concerned, the recommendations of the Conferences in respect of such alterations to the List or of changes in the character of wetlands included therein.

Article 9

1. This Convention shall remain open for signature indefinitely.

2. Any member of the United Nations or of one of the Specialized Agencies or of the International Atomic Energy Agency or Party to the Statute of the International Court of Justice may become a Party to this Convention by:
signature without reservation as to ratification;
signature subject to ratification followed by ratification;
accession.

3. Ratification or accession shall be effected by the deposit of an instrument of ratification or accession with the Director-General of the United Nations Educational, Scientific and Cultural Organization (hereinafter referred to as "the Depositary").

Article 10

1. This Convention shall enter into force four months after seven States have become Parties to this Convention in accordance with paragraph 2 of Article 9.

2. Thereafter this Convention shall enter into force for each Contracting Party four months after the day of its signature without reservation as to ratification, or its deposit of an instrument of ratification or accession.

Article 10 bis

1. This Convention may be amended at a meeting of the Contracting Parties convened for that purpose in accordance with this article.

2. Proposals for amendment may be made by any Contracting Party.

3. The text of any proposed amendment and the reasons for it shall be communicated to the organization or government performing the continuing bureau duties under the Convention (hereinafter referred to as "the Bureau") and shall promptly be communicated by the Bureau to all Contracting Parties. Any comments on the text by the Contracting Parties shall be communicated to the Bureau within three months of the date on which the amendments were communicated to the Contracting Parties by the Bureau. The Bureau shall, immediately after the last day for submission of comments, communicate to the Contracting Parties all comments submitted by that day.

4. A meeting of Contracting Parties to consider an amendment communicated in accordance with paragraph 3 shall be convened by the Bureau upon the written request of one third of the Contracting Parties. The Bureau shall consult the Parties concerning the time and venue of the meeting.

5. Amendments shall be adopted by a two-thirds majority of the Contracting Parties present and voting.

6. An amendment adopted shall enter into force for the Contracting Parties which have accepted it on the first day of the fourth month following the date on which two thirds of the Contracting Parties have deposited an instrument of acceptance with the Depositary. For each Contracting Party which deposits an instrument of acceptance after the date on which two thirds of the Contracting Parties have deposited an instrument of acceptance, the amendment

shall enter into force on the first day of the fourth month following the date of the deposit of its instrument of acceptance.

Article 11

1. This Convention shall continue in force for an indefinite period.

2. Any Contracting Party may denounce this Convention after a period of five years from the date on which it entered into force for that party by giving written notice thereof to the Depositary. Denunciation shall take effect four months after the day on which notice thereof is received by the Depositary.

Article 12

1. The Depositary shall inform all States that have signed and acceded to this Convention as soon as possible of: signatures to the Convention;
a) deposits of instruments of ratification of this Convention;
b) deposits of instruments of accession to this Convention;
c) the date of entry into force of this Convention;
d) notifications of denunciation of this Convention.

2. When this Convention has entered into force, the Depositary shall have it registered with the Secretariat of the United Nations in accordance with Article 102 of the Charter.

IN WITNESS WHEREOF, the undersigned, being duly authorized to that effect, have signed this Convention.

UNITED NATIONS FRAMEWORK CONVENTION ON CLIMATE CHANGE

1992

THE PARTIES TO THIS CONVENTION,

Acknowledging that change in the Earth's climate and its adverse effects are a common concern of humankind,

Concerned that human activities have been substantially increasing the atmospheric concentrations of greenhouse gases, that these increases enhance the natural greenhouse effect, and that this will result on average in an additional warming of the Earth's surface and atmosphere and may adversely affect natural ecosystems and humankind,

Noting that the largest share of historical and current global emissions of greenhouse gases has originated in developed countries, that per capita emissions in developing countries are still relatively low and that the share of global emissions originating in developing countries will grow to meet their social and development needs,

Aware of the role and importance in terrestrial and marine ecosystems of sinks and reservoirs of greenhouse gases,

Noting that there are many uncertainties in predictions of climate change, particularly with regard to the timing, magnitude and regional patterns thereof,

Acknowledging that the global nature of climate change calls for the widest possible cooperation by all countries and their participation in an effective and appropriate international response, in accordance with their common but differentiated responsibilities and respective capabilities and their social and economic conditions,

Recalling the pertinent provisions of the Declaration of the United Nations Conference on the Human Environment, adopted at Stockholm on 16 June 1972,

Recalling also that States have, in accordance with the Charter of the United Nations and the principles of international law, the sovereign right to exploit their own resources pursuant to their own environmental and developmental policies, and the responsibility to ensure that activities within their jurisdiction or control do not cause damage to the environment of other States or of areas beyond the limits of national jurisdiction,

Reaffirming the principle of sovereignty of States in international cooperation to address climate change,

Recognizing that States should enact effective environmental legislation, that environmental standards, management objectives and priorities should reflect the environmental and developmental context to which they apply, and that standards applied by some countries may be inappropriate and of unwarranted economic and social cost to other countries, in particular developing countries,

Recalling the provisions of General Assembly resolution 44/228 of 22 December 1989 on the United Nations Conference on Environment and Development, and resolutions 43/53 of 6 December 1988, 44/207 of 22 December 1989, 45/212 of 21 December 1990 and 46/169 of 19 December 1991 on protection of global climate for present and future generations of mankind,

Recalling also the provisions of General Assembly resolution 44/206 of 22 December 1989 on the possible adverse effects of sea-level rise on islands and coastal areas, particularly low-lying coastal areas and the pertinent provisions of General Assembly resolution 44/172 of 19 December 1989 on the implementation of the Plan of Action to Combat Desertification,

Recalling further the Vienna Convention for the Protection of the Ozone Layer, 1985, and the Montreal Protocol on Substances that Deplete the Ozone Layer, 1987, as adjusted and amended on 29 June 1990,

Noting the Ministerial Declaration of the Second World Climate Conference adopted on 7 November 1990,

Conscious of the valuable analytical work being conducted by many States on climate change and of the important contributions of the World Meteorological Organization, the United Nations Environment Programme and other organs, organizations and bodies of the United Nations system, as well as other international and intergovernmental bodies, to the exchange of results of scientific research and the coordination of research,

Recognizing that steps required to understand and address climate change will be environmentally, socially and economically most effective if they are based on relevant scientific, technical and economic considerations and continually re-evaluated in the light of new findings in these areas,

Recognizing that various actions to address climate change can be justified economically in their own right and can also help in solving other environmental problems,

Recognizing also the need for developed countries to take immediate action in a flexible manner on the basis of clear priorities, as a first step towards comprehensive response strategies at the global, national and, where agreed, regional levels that take into account all greenhouse gases, with due consideration of their relative contributions to the enhancement of the greenhouse effect,

Recognizing further that low-lying and other small island countries, countries with low-lying coastal, arid and semi-arid areas or areas liable to floods, drought and desertification, and developing countries with fragile mountainous ecosystems are particularly vulnerable to the adverse effects of climate change,

Recognizing the special difficulties of those countries, especially developing countries, whose economies are particularly dependent on fossil fuel production, use and exportation, as a consequence of action taken on limiting greenhouse gas emissions,

Affirming that responses to climate change should be coordinated with social and economic development in an integrated manner with a view to avoiding adverse impacts on the latter, taking into full account the legitimate priority needs of developing countries for the achievement of sustained economic growth and the eradication of poverty,

Recognizing that all countries, especially developing countries, need access to resources required to achieve sustainable social and economic development and that, in order for developing countries to progress towards that goal, their energy consumption will need to grow taking into account the possibilities for achieving greater energy efficiency and for controlling greenhouse gas emissions in general, including through the application of new technologies on terms which make such an application economically and socially beneficial,

Determined to protect the climate system for present and future generations,

HAVE AGREED AS FOLLOWS:

Article 1

Definitions

For the purposes of this Convention:

1. "Adverse effects of climate change" means changes in the physical environment or biota resulting from climate change which have significant deleterious effects on the composition, resilience or productivity of natural and managed ecosystems or on the operation of socio-economic systems or on human health and welfare.

2. "Climate change" means a change of climate which is attributed directly or indirectly to human activity that alters the composition of the global atmosphere and which is in addition to natural climate variability observed over comparable time periods.
3. "Climate system" means the totality of the atmosphere, hydrosphere, biosphere and geosphere and their interactions.
4. "Emissions" means the release of greenhouse gases and/or their precursors into the atmosphere over a specified area and period of time.
5. "Greenhouse gases" means those gaseous constituents of the atmosphere, both natural and anthropogenic, that absorb and re-emit infrared radiation.
6. "Regional economic integration organization" means an organization constituted by sovereign States of a given region which has competence in respect of matters governed by this Convention or its protocols and has been duly authorized, in accordance with its internal procedures, to sign, ratify, accept, approve or accede to the instruments concerned.
7. "Reservoir" means a component or components of the climate system where a greenhouse gas or a precursor of a greenhouse gas is stored.
8. "Sink" means any process, activity or mechanism which removes a greenhouse gas, an aerosol or a precursor of a greenhouse gas from the atmosphere.
9. "Source" means any process or activity which releases a greenhouse gas, an aerosol or a precursor of a greenhouse gas into the atmosphere.

Article 2

Objective

The ultimate objective of this Convention and any related legal instruments that the Conference of the Parties may adopt is to achieve, in accordance with the relevant provisions of the Convention, stabilization of greenhouse gas concentrations in the atmosphere at a level that would prevent dangerous anthropogenic interference with the climate system. Such a level should be achieved within a time frame sufficient to allow ecosystems to adapt naturally to climate change, to ensure that food production is not threatened and to enable economic development to proceed in a sustainable manner.

Article 3

Principles

In their actions to achieve the objective of the Convention and to implement its provisions, the Parties shall be guided, inter alia, by the following:

1. The Parties should protect the climate system for the benefit of present and future generations of humankind, on the basis of equity and in accordance with their common but differentiated responsibilities and respective capabilities. Accordingly, the developed country Parties should take the lead in combating climate change and the adverse effects thereof.
2. The specific needs and special circumstances of developing country Parties, especially those that are particularly vulnerable to the adverse effects of climate change, and of those Parties, especially developing country Parties, that would have to bear a disproportionate or abnormal burden under the Convention, should be given full consideration.
3. The Parties should take precautionary measures to anticipate, prevent or minimize the causes of climate change and mitigate its adverse effects. Where there are threats of serious or irreversible damage, lack of full scientific certainty should not be used as a reason for postponing such measures, taking into account that policies and measures to deal with climate change should be cost-effective so as to ensure global benefits at the lowest possible cost. To achieve this, such policies and measures should take into account different socio-economic contexts, be comprehensive, cover all relevant

sources, sinks and reservoirs of greenhouse gases and adaptation, and comprise all economic sectors. Efforts to address climate change may be carried out cooperatively by interested Parties.

4. The Parties have a right to, and should, promote sustainable development. Policies and measures to protect the climate system against human-induced change should be appropriate for the specific conditions of each Party and should be integrated with national development programmes, taking into account that economic development is essential for adopting measures to address climate change.

5. The Parties should cooperate to promote a supportive and open international economic system that would lead to sustainable economic growth and development in all Parties, particularly developing country Parties, thus enabling them better to address the problems of climate change. Measures taken to combat climate change, including unilateral ones, should not constitute a means of arbitrary or unjustifiable discrimination or a disguised restriction on international trade.

Article 4

Commitments

1. All Parties, taking into account their common but differentiated responsibilities and their specific national and regional development priorities, objectives and circumstances, shall:

(a) Develop, periodically update, publish and make available to the Conference of the Parties, in accordance with Article 12, national inventories of anthropogenic emissions by sources and removals by sinks of all greenhouse gases not controlled by the Montreal Protocol, using comparable methodologies to be agreed upon by the Conference of the Parties;

(b) Formulate, implement, publish and regularly update national and, where appropriate, regional programmes containing measures to mitigate climate change by addressing anthropogenic emissions by sources and removals by sinks of all greenhouse gases not controlled by the Montreal Protocol, and measures to facilitate adequate adaptation to climate change;

(c) Promote and cooperate in the development, application and diffusion, including transfer, of technologies, practices and processes that control, reduce or prevent anthropogenic emissions of greenhouse gases not controlled by the Montreal Protocol in all relevant sectors, including the energy, transport, industry, agriculture, forestry and waste management sectors;

(d) Promote sustainable management, and promote and cooperate in the conservation and enhancement, as appropriate, of sinks and reservoirs of all greenhouse gases not controlled by the Montreal Protocol, including biomass, forests and oceans as well as other terrestrial, coastal and marine ecosystems;

(e) Cooperate in preparing for adaptation to the impacts of climate change; develop and elaborate appropriate and integrated plans for coastal zone management, water resources and agriculture, and for the protection and rehabilitation of areas, particularly in Africa, affected by drought and desertification, as well as floods;

(f) Take climate change considerations into account, to the extent feasible, in their relevant social, economic and environmental policies and actions, and employ appropriate methods, for example impact assessments, formulated and determined nationally, with a view to minimizing adverse effects on the economy, on public health and on the quality of the environment, of projects or measures undertaken by them to mitigate or adapt to climate change;

(g) Promote and cooperate in scientific, technological, technical, socio-economic and other research, systematic observation and development of data archives related to the climate system and intended to further the understanding and to reduce or eliminate the remaining uncertainties regarding the causes, effects, magnitude and timing of climate change and the economic and social consequences of various response strategies;

(h) Promote and cooperate in the full, open and prompt exchange of relevant scientific, technological, technical, socio-economic and legal information related to the climate system and climate change, and to the economic and social consequences of various response strategies;
(i) Promote and cooperate in education, training and public awareness related to climate change and encourage the widest participation in this process, including that of non-governmental organizations; and
(j) Communicate to the Conference of the Parties information related to implementation, in accordance with Article 12.

2. The developed country Parties and other Parties included in Annex I commit themselves specifically as provided for in the following:
(a) Each of these Parties shall adopt national policies and take corresponding measures on the mitigation of climate change, by limiting its anthropogenic emissions of greenhouse gases and protecting and enhancing its greenhouse gas sinks and reservoirs. These policies and measures will demonstrate that developed countries are taking the lead in modifying longer-term trends in anthropogenic emissions consistent with the objective of the Convention, recognizing that the return by the end of the present decade to earlier levels of anthropogenic emissions of carbon dioxide and other greenhouse gases not controlled by the Montreal Protocol would contribute to such modification, and taking into account the differences in these Parties' starting points and approaches, economic structures and resource bases, the need to maintain strong and sustainable economic growth, available technologies and other individual circumstances, as well as the need for equitable and appropriate contributions by each of these Parties to the global effort regarding that objective. These Parties may implement such policies and measures jointly with other Parties and may assist other Parties in contributing to the achievement of the objective of the Convention and, in particular, that of this subparagraph; 1 This includes policies and measures adopted by regional economic integration organizations.
(b) In order to promote progress to this end, each of these Parties shall communicate, within six months of the entry into force of the Convention for it and periodically thereafter, and in accordance with Article 12, detailed information on its policies and measures referred to in subparagraph (a) above, as well as on its resulting projected anthropogenic emissions by sources and removals by sinks of greenhouse gases not controlled by the Montreal Protocol for the period referred to in subparagraph (a), with the aim of returning individually or jointly to their 1990 levels these anthropogenic emissions of carbon dioxide and other greenhouse gases not controlled by the Montreal Protocol. This information will be reviewed by the Conference of the Parties, at its first session and periodically thereafter, in accordance with Article 7;
(c) Calculations of emissions by sources and removals by sinks of greenhouse gases for the purposes of subparagraph (b) above should take into account the best available scientific knowledge, including of the effective capacity of sinks and the respective contributions of such gases to climate change. The Conference of the Parties shall consider and agree on methodologies for these calculations at its first session and review them regularly thereafter;
(d) The Conference of the Parties shall, at its first session, review the adequacy of subparagraphs (a) and (b) above. Such review shall be carried out in the light of the best available scientific information and assessment on climate change and its impacts, as well as relevant technical, social and economic information. Based on this review, the Conference of the Parties shall take appropriate action, which may include the adoption of amendments to the commitments in subparagraphs (a) and (b) above. The Conference of the Parties, at its first session, shall also take decisions regarding criteria for joint implementation as indicated in subparagraph (a) above. A second review of subparagraphs (a) and (b) shall take place not later than 31 December 1998, and thereafter at regular intervals determined by the Conference of the Parties, until the objective of the Convention is met;
(e) Each of these Parties shall:

(i) coordinate as appropriate with other such Parties, relevant economic and administrative instruments developed to achieve the objective of the Convention; and

(ii) identify and periodically review its own policies and practices which encourage activities that lead to greater levels of anthropogenic emissions of greenhouse gases not controlled by the Montreal Protocol than would otherwise occur;

(f) The Conference of the Parties shall review, not later than 31 December 1998, available information with a view to taking decisions regarding such amendments to the lists in Annexes I and II as may be appropriate, with the approval of the Party concerned;

(g) Any Party not included in Annex I may, in its instrument of ratification, acceptance, approval or accession, or at any time thereafter, notify the Depositary that it intends to be bound by subparagraphs (a) and (b) above. The Depositary shall inform the other signatories and Parties of any such notification.

3. The developed country Parties and other developed Parties included in Annex II shall provide new and additional financial resources to meet the agreed full costs incurred by developing country Parties in complying with their obligations under Article 12, paragraph 1. They shall also provide such financial resources, including for the transfer of technology, needed by the developing country Parties to meet the agreed full incremental costs of implementing measures that are covered by paragraph 1 of this Article and that are agreed between a developing country Party and the international entity or entities referred to in Article 11, in accordance with that Article. The implementation of these commitments shall take into account the need for adequacy and predictability in the flow of funds and the importance of appropriate burden sharing among the developed country Parties.

4. The developed country Parties and other developed Parties included in Annex II shall also assist the developing country Parties that are particularly vulnerable to the adverse effects of climate change in meeting costs of adaptation to those adverse effects.

5. The developed country Parties and other developed Parties included in Annex II shall take all practicable steps to promote, facilitate and finance, as appropriate, the transfer of, or access to, environmentally sound technologies and know-how to other Parties, particularly developing country Parties, to enable them to implement the provisions of the Convention. In this process, the developed country Parties shall support the development and enhancement of endogenous capacities and technologies of developing country Parties. Other Parties and organizations in a position to do so may also assist in facilitating the transfer of such technologies.

6. In the implementation of their commitments under paragraph 2 above, a certain degree of flexibility shall be allowed by the Conference of the Parties to the Parties included in Annex I undergoing the process of transition to a market economy, in order to enhance the ability of these Parties to address climate change, including with regard to the historical level of anthropogenic emissions of greenhouse gases not controlled by the Montreal Protocol chosen as a reference.

7. The extent to which developing country Parties will effectively implement their commitments under the Convention will depend on the effective implementation by developed country Parties of their commitments under the Convention related to financial resources and transfer of technology and will take fully into account that economic and social development and poverty eradication are the first and overriding priorities of the developing country Parties.

8. In the implementation of the commitments in this Article, the Parties shall give full consideration to what actions are necessary under the Convention, including actions related to funding, insurance and the transfer of technology, to meet the specific needs and concerns of developing country Parties arising from the adverse effects of climate change and/or the impact of the implementation of response measures, especially on:

(a) Small island countries;

(b) Countries with low-lying coastal areas;

(c) Countries with arid and semi-arid areas, forested areas and areas liable to forest decay;

(d) Countries with areas prone to natural disasters;
(e) Countries with areas liable to drought and desertification;
(f) Countries with areas of high urban atmospheric pollution;
(g) Countries with areas with fragile ecosystems, including mountainous ecosystems;
(h) Countries whose economies are highly dependent on income generated from the production, processing and export, and/or on consumption of fossil fuels and associated energy-intensive products; and
(i) Landlocked and transit countries.

Further, the Conference of the Parties may take actions, as appropriate, with respect to this paragraph.

9. The Parties shall take full account of the specific needs and special situations of the least developed countries in their actions with regard to funding and transfer of technology.

10. The Parties shall, in accordance with Article 10, take into consideration in the implementation of the commitments of the Convention the situation of Parties, particularly developing country Parties, with economies that are vulnerable to the adverse effects of the implementation of measures to respond to climate change. This applies notably to Parties with economies that are highly dependent on income generated from the production, processing and export, and/or consumption of fossil fuels and associated energy-intensive products and/or the use of fossil fuels for which such Parties have serious difficulties in switching to alternatives.

Article 5

Research and systematic observation

In carrying out their commitments under Article 4, paragraph 1 (g), the Parties shall:
(a) Support and further develop, as appropriate, international and intergovernmental programmes and networks or organizations aimed at defining, conducting, assessing and financing research, data collection and systematic observation, taking into account the need to minimize duplication of effort;
(b) Support international and intergovernmental efforts to strengthen systematic observation and national scientific and technical research capacities and capabilities, particularly in developing countries, and to promote access to, and the exchange of, data and analyses thereof obtained from areas beyond national jurisdiction; and
(c) Take into account the particular concerns and needs of developing countries and cooperate in improving their endogenous capacities and capabilities to participate in the efforts referred to in subparagraphs (a) and (b) above.

Article 6

Education, training and public awareness

In carrying out their commitments under Article 4, paragraph 1 (i), the Parties shall:
(a) Promote and facilitate at the national and, as appropriate, subregional and regional levels, and in accordance with national laws and regulations, and within their respective capacities:
 (i) the development and implementation of educational and public awareness programmes on climate change and its effects;
 (ii) public access to information on climate change and its effects;
 (iii) public participation in addressing climate change and its effects and developing adequate responses; and
 (iv) training of scientific, technical and managerial personnel;
(b) Cooperate in and promote, at the international level, and, where appropriate, using existing bodies:
 (i) the development and exchange of educational and public awareness material on climate change and its effects; and

(ii) the development and implementation of education and training programmes, including the strengthening of national institutions and the exchange or secondment of personnel to train experts in this field, in particular for developing countries.

Article 7

Conference of the Parties

1. A Conference of the Parties is hereby established.

2. The Conference of the Parties, as the supreme body of this Convention, shall keep under regular review the implementation of the Convention and any related legal instruments that the Conference of the Parties may adopt, and shall make, within its mandate, the decisions necessary to promote the effective implementation of the Convention. To this end, it shall:

(a) Periodically examine the obligations of the Parties and the institutional arrangements under the Convention, in the light of the objective of the Convention, the experience gained in its implementation and the evolution of scientific and technological knowledge;

(b) Promote and facilitate the exchange of information on measures adopted by the Parties to address climate change and its effects, taking into account the differing circumstances, responsibilities and capabilities of the Parties and their respective commitments under the Convention;

(c) Facilitate, at the request of two or more Parties, the coordination of measures adopted by them to address climate change and its effects, taking into account the differing circumstances, responsibilities and capabilities of the Parties and their respective commitments under the Convention;

(d) Promote and guide, in accordance with the objective and provisions of the Convention, the development and periodic refinement of comparable methodologies, to be agreed on by the Conference of the Parties, inter alia, for preparing inventories of greenhouse gas emissions by sources and removals by sinks, and for evaluating the effectiveness of measures to limit the emissions and enhance the removals of these gases;

(e) Assess, on the basis of all information made available to it in accordance with the provisions of the Convention, the implementation of the Convention by the Parties, the overall effects of the measures taken pursuant to the Convention, in particular environmental, economic and social effects as well as their cumulative impacts and the extent to which progress towards the objective of the Convention is being achieved;

(f) Consider and adopt regular reports on the implementation of the Convention and ensure their publication;

(g) Make recommendations on any matters necessary for the implementation of the Convention;

(h) Seek to mobilize financial resources in accordance with Article 4, paragraphs 3, 4 and 5, and Article 11;

(i) Establish such subsidiary bodies as are deemed necessary for the implementation of the Convention;

(j) Review reports submitted by its subsidiary bodies and provide guidance to them;

(k) Agree upon and adopt, by consensus, rules of procedure and financial rules for itself and for any subsidiary bodies;

(l) Seek and utilize, where appropriate, the services and cooperation of, and information provided by, competent international organizations and intergovernmental and non-governmental bodies; and

(m) Exercise such other functions as are required for the achievement of the objective of the Convention as well as all other functions assigned to it under the Convention.

3. The Conference of the Parties shall, at its first session, adopt its own rules of procedure as well as those of the subsidiary bodies established by the Convention, which shall include decision-making procedures for matters not already covered by decision-making procedures

stipulated in the Convention. Such procedures may include specified majorities required for the adoption of particular decisions.

4. The first session of the Conference of the Parties shall be convened by the interim secretariat referred to in Article 21 and shall take place not later than one year after the date of entry into force of the Convention. Thereafter, ordinary sessions of the Conference of the Parties shall be held every year unless otherwise decided by the Conference of the Parties.

5. Extraordinary sessions of the Conference of the Parties shall be held at such other times as may be deemed necessary by the Conference, or at the written request of any Party, provided that, within six months of the request being communicated to the Parties by the secretariat, it is supported by at least one third of the Parties.

6. The United Nations, its specialized agencies and the International Atomic Energy Agency, as well as any State member thereof or observers thereto not Party to the Convention, may be represented at sessions of the Conference of the Parties as observers. Anybody or agency, whether national or international, governmental or non-governmental, which is qualified in matters covered by the Convention, and which has informed the secretariat of its wish to be represented at a session of the Conference of the Parties as an observer, may be so admitted unless at least one third of the Parties present object. The admission and participation of observers shall be subject to the rules of procedure adopted by the Conference of the Parties.

Article 8

Secretariat

1. A secretariat is hereby established.

2. The functions of the secretariat shall be:

(a) To make arrangements for sessions of the Conference of the Parties and its subsidiary bodies established under the Convention and to provide them with services as required;

(b) To compile and transmit reports submitted to it;

(c) To facilitate assistance to the Parties, particularly developing country Parties, on request, in the compilation and communication of information required in accordance with the provisions of the Convention;

(d) To prepare reports on its activities and present them to the Conference of the Parties;

(e) To ensure the necessary coordination with the secretariats of other relevant international bodies;

(f) To enter, under the overall guidance of the Conference of the Parties, into such administrative and contractual arrangements as may be required for the effective discharge of its functions; and

(g) To perform the other secretariat functions specified in the Convention and in any of its protocols and such other functions as may be determined by the Conference of the Parties.

3. The Conference of the Parties, at its first session, shall designate a permanent secretariat and make arrangements for its functioning.

Article 9

Subsidiary body for scientific and technological advice

1. A subsidiary body for scientific and technological advice is hereby established to provide the Conference of the Parties and, as appropriate, its other subsidiary bodies with timely information and advice on scientific and technological matters relating to the Convention. This body shall be open to participation by all Parties and shall be multidisciplinary. It shall comprise government representatives competent in the relevant field of expertise. It shall report regularly to the Conference of the Parties on all aspects of its work.

2. Under the guidance of the Conference of the Parties, and drawing upon existing competent international bodies, this body shall:

(a) Provide assessments of the state of scientific knowledge relating to climate change and its effects;

(b) Prepare scientific assessments on the effects of measures taken in the implementation of the Convention;

(c) Identify innovative, efficient and state-of-the-art technologies and know-how and advise on the ways and means of promoting development and/or transferring such technologies;

(d) Provide advice on scientific programmes, international cooperation in research and development related to climate change, as well as on ways and means of supporting endogenous capacity-building in developing countries; and

(e) Respond to scientific, technological and methodological questions that the Conference of the Parties and its subsidiary bodies may put to the body.

3. The functions and terms of reference of this body may be further elaborated by the Conference of the Parties.

Article 10

Subsidiary body for implementation

1. A subsidiary body for implementation is hereby established to assist the Conference of the Parties in the assessment and review of the effective implementation of the Convention. This body shall be open to participation by all Parties and comprise government representatives who are experts on matters related to climate change. It shall report regularly to the Conference of the Parties on all aspects of its work.

2. Under the guidance of the Conference of the Parties, this body shall:

(a) Consider the information communicated in accordance with Article 12, paragraph 1, to assess the overall aggregated effect of the steps taken by the Parties in the light of the latest scientific assessments concerning climate change;

(b) Consider the information communicated in accordance with Article 12, paragraph 2, in order to assist the Conference of the Parties in carrying out the reviews required by Article 4, paragraph 2 (d); and

(c) Assist the Conference of the Parties, as appropriate, in the preparation and implementation of its decisions.

Article 11

Financial mechanism

1. A mechanism for the provision of financial resources on a grant or concessional basis, including for the transfer of technology, is hereby defined. It shall function under the guidance of and be accountable to the Conference of the Parties, which shall decide on its policies, programme priorities and eligibility criteria related to this Convention. Its operation shall be entrusted to one or more existing international entities.

2. The financial mechanism shall have an equitable and balanced representation of all Parties within a transparent system of governance.

3. The Conference of the Parties and the entity or entities entrusted with the operation of the financial mechanism shall agree upon arrangements to give effect to the above paragraphs, which shall include the following:

(a) Modalities to ensure that the funded projects to address climate change are in conformity with the policies, programme priorities and eligibility criteria established by the Conference of the Parties;

(b) Modalities by which a particular funding decision may be reconsidered in light of these policies, programme priorities and eligibility criteria;
(c) Provision by the entity or entities of regular reports to the Conference of the Parties on its funding operations, which is consistent with the requirement for accountability set out in paragraph 1 above; and
(d) Determination in a predictable and identifiable manner of the amount of funding necessary and available for the implementation of this Convention and the conditions under which that amount shall be periodically reviewed.

4. The Conference of the Parties shall make arrangements to implement the above-mentioned provisions at its first session, reviewing and taking into account the interim arrangements referred to in Article 21, paragraph 3, and shall decide whether these interim arrangements shall be maintained. Within four years thereafter, the Conference of the Parties shall review the financial mechanism and take appropriate measures.

5. The developed country Parties may also provide and developing country Parties avail themselves of, financial resources related to the implementation of the Convention through bilateral, regional and other multilateral channels.

Article 12

Communication of information related to implementation

1. In accordance with Article 4, paragraph 1, each Party shall communicate to the Conference of the Parties, through the secretariat, the following elements of information:
(a) A national inventory of anthropogenic emissions by sources and removals by sinks of all greenhouse gases not controlled by the Montreal Protocol, to the extent its capacities permit, using comparable methodologies to be promoted and agreed upon by the Conference of the Parties;
(b) A general description of steps taken or envisaged by the Party to implement the Convention; and (c) Any other information that the Party considers relevant to the achievement of the objective of the Convention and suitable for inclusion in its communication, including, if feasible, material relevant for calculations of global emission trends.

2. Each developed country Party and each other Party included in Annex I shall incorporate in its communication the following elements of information:
(a) A detailed description of the policies and measures that it has adopted to implement its commitment under Article 4, paragraphs 2 (a) and 2 (b); and
(b) A specific estimate of the effects that the policies and measures referred to in subparagraph (a) immediately above will have on anthropogenic emissions by its sources and removals by its sinks of greenhouse gases during the period referred to in Article 4, paragraph 2 (a).

3. In addition, each developed country Party and each other developed Party included in Annex II shall incorporate details of measures taken in accordance with Article 4, paragraphs 3, 4 and 5.

4. Developing country Parties may, on a voluntary basis, propose projects for financing, including specific technologies, materials, equipment, techniques or practices that would be needed to implement such projects, along with, if possible, an estimate of all incremental costs, of the reductions of emissions and increments of removals of greenhouse gases, as well as an estimate of the consequent benefits.

5. Each developed country Party and each other Party included in Annex I shall make its initial communication within six months of the entry into force of the Convention for that Party. Each Party not so listed shall make its initial communication within three years of the entry into force of the Convention for that Party, or of the availability of financial resources in accordance with Article 4, paragraph 3. Parties that are least developed countries may make

their initial communication at their discretion. The frequency of subsequent communications by all Parties shall be determined by the Conference of the Parties, taking into account the differentiated timetable set by this paragraph.

6. Information communicated by Parties under this Article shall be transmitted by the secretariat as soon as possible to the Conference of the Parties and to any subsidiary bodies concerned. If necessary, the procedures for the communication of information may be further considered by the Conference of the Parties.

7. From its first session, the Conference of the Parties shall arrange for the provision to developing country Parties of technical and financial support, on request, in compiling and communicating information under this Article, as well as in identifying the technical and financial needs associated with proposed projects and response measures under Article 4. Such support may be provided by other Parties, by competent international organizations and by the secretariat, as appropriate.

8. Any group of Parties may, subject to guidelines adopted by the Conference of the Parties, and to prior notification to the Conference of the Parties, make a joint communication in fulfilment of their obligations under this Article, provided that such a communication includes information on the fulfilment by each of these Parties of its individual obligations under the Convention.

9. Information received by the secretariat that is designated by a Party as confidential, in accordance with criteria to be established by the Conference of the Parties, shall be aggregated by the secretariat to protect its confidentiality before being made available to any of the bodies involved in the communication and review of information.

10. Subject to paragraph 9 above, and without prejudice to the ability of any Party to make public its communication at any time, the secretariat shall make communications by Parties under this Article publicly available at the time they are submitted to the Conference of the Parties.

Article 13

Resolution of questions regarding implementation

The Conference of the Parties shall, at its first session, consider the establishment of a multilateral consultative process, available to Parties on their request, for the resolution of questions regarding the implementation of the Convention.

Article 14

Settlement of disputes

1. In the event of a dispute between any two or more Parties concerning the interpretation or application of the Convention, the Parties concerned shall seek a settlement of the dispute through negotiation or any other peaceful means of their own choice.

2. When ratifying, accepting, approving or acceding to the Convention, or at any time thereafter, a Party which is not a regional economic integration organization may declare in a written instrument submitted to the Depositary that, in respect of any dispute concerning the interpretation or application of the Convention, it recognizes as compulsory ipso facto and without special agreement, in relation to any Party accepting the same obligation:

(a) Submission of the dispute to the International Court of Justice; and/or

(b) Arbitration in accordance with procedures to be adopted by the Conference of the Parties as soon as practicable, in an annex on arbitration.

A Party which is a regional economic integration organization may make a declaration with like effect in relation to arbitration in accordance with the procedures referred to in subparagraph (b) above.

3. A declaration made under paragraph 2 above shall remain in force until it expires in accordance with its terms or until three months after written notice of its revocation has been deposited with the Depositary.

4. A new declaration, a notice of revocation or the expiry of a declaration shall not in any way affect proceedings pending before the International Court of Justice or the arbitral tribunal, unless the parties to the dispute otherwise agree.

5. Subject to the operation of paragraph 2 above, if after twelve months following notification by one Party to another that a dispute exists between them, the Parties concerned have not been able to settle their dispute through the means mentioned in paragraph 1 above, the dispute shall be submitted, at the request of any of the parties to the dispute, to conciliation.

6. A conciliation commission shall be created upon the request of one of the parties to the dispute. The commission shall be composed of an equal number of members appointed by each party concerned and a chairman chosen jointly by the members appointed by each party. The commission shall render a recommendatory award, which the parties shall consider in good faith.

7. Additional procedures relating to conciliation shall be adopted by the Conference of the Parties, as soon as practicable, in an annex on conciliation.

8. The provisions of this Article shall apply to any related legal instrument which the Conference of the Parties may adopt, unless the instrument provides otherwise.

Article 15

Amendments to the Convention

1. Any Party may propose amendments to the Convention.

2. Amendments to the Convention shall be adopted at an ordinary session of the Conference of the Parties. The text of any proposed amendment to the Convention shall be communicated to the Parties by the secretariat at least six months before the meeting at which it is proposed for adoption. The secretariat shall also communicate proposed amendments to the signatories to the Convention and, for information, to the Depositary.

3. The Parties shall make every effort to reach agreement on any proposed amendment to the Convention by consensus. If all efforts at consensus have been exhausted, and no agreement reached, the amendment shall as a last resort be adopted by a three-fourths majority vote of the Parties present and voting at the meeting. The adopted amendment shall be communicated by the secretariat to the Depositary, who shall circulate it to all Parties for their acceptance.

4. Instruments of acceptance in respect of an amendment shall be deposited with the Depositary. An amendment adopted in accordance with paragraph 3 above shall enter into force for those Parties having accepted it on the ninetieth day after the date of receipt by the Depositary of an instrument of acceptance by at least three fourths of the Parties to the Convention.

5. The amendment shall enter into force for any other Party on the ninetieth day after the date on which that Party deposits with the Depositary its instrument of acceptance of the said amendment.

6. For the purposes of this Article, "Parties present and voting" means Parties present and casting an affirmative or negative vote.

Article 16

Adoption and amendment of Annexes to the Convention

1. Annexes to the Convention shall form an integral part thereof and, unless otherwise expressly provided, a reference to the Convention constitutes at the same time a reference to

any annexes thereto. Without prejudice to the provisions of Article 14, paragraphs 2 (b) and 7, such annexes shall be restricted to lists, forms and any other material of a descriptive nature that is of a scientific, technical, procedural or administrative character.

2. Annexes to the Convention shall be proposed and adopted in accordance with the procedure set forth in Article 15, paragraphs 2, 3 and 4.

3. An annex that has been adopted in accordance with paragraph 2 above shall enter into force for all Parties to the Convention six months after the date of the communication by the Depositary to such Parties of the adoption of the annex, except for those Parties that have notified the Depositary, in writing, within that period of their non-acceptance of the annex. The annex shall enter into force for Parties which withdraw their notification of non-acceptance on the ninetieth day after the date on which withdrawal of such notification has been received by the Depositary.

4. The proposal, adoption and entry into force of amendments to annexes to the Convention shall be subject to the same procedure as that for the proposal, adoption and entry into force of annexes to the Convention in accordance with paragraphs 2 and 3 above.

5. If the adoption of an annex or an amendment to an annex involves an amendment to the Convention, that annex or amendment to an annex shall not enter into force until such time as the amendment to the Convention enters into force.

Article 17

Protocols

1. The Conference of the Parties may, at any ordinary session, adopt protocols to the Convention.

2. The text of any proposed protocol shall be communicated to the Parties by the secretariat at least six months before such a session.

3. The requirements for the entry into force of any protocol shall be established by that instrument.

4. Only Parties to the Convention may be Parties to a protocol.

5. Decisions under any protocol shall be taken only by the Parties to the protocol concerned.

Article 18

Right to vote

1. Each Party to the Convention shall have one vote, except as provided for in paragraph 2 below.

2. Regional economic integration organizations, in matters within their competence, shall exercise their right to vote with a number of votes equal to the number of their member States that are Parties to the Convention. Such an organization shall not exercise its right to vote if any of its member States exercises its right, and vice versa.

Article 19

Depositary

The Secretary-General of the United Nations shall be the Depositary of the Convention and of protocols adopted in accordance with Article 17.

Article 20

Signature

This Convention shall be open for signature by States Members of the United Nations or of any of its specialized agencies or that are Parties to the Statute of the International Court of Justice and by regional economic integration organizations at Rio de Janeiro, during the United Nations Conference on Environment and Development, and thereafter at United Nations Headquarters in New York from 20 June 1992 to 19 June 1993.

Article 21

Interim arrangements

1. The secretariat functions referred to in Article 8 will be carried out on an interim basis by the secretariat established by the General Assembly of the United Nations in its resolution 45/212 of 21 December 1990, until the completion of the first session of the Conference of the Parties.

2. The head of the interim secretariat referred to in paragraph 1 above will cooperate closely with the Intergovernmental Panel on Climate Change to ensure that the Panel can respond to the need for objective scientific and technical advice. Other relevant scientific bodies could also be consulted.

3. The Global Environment Facility of the United Nations Development Programme, the United Nations Environment Programme and the International Bank for Reconstruction and Development shall be the international entity entrusted with the operation of the financial mechanism referred to in Article 11 on an interim basis. In this connection, the Global Environment Facility should be appropriately restructured and its membership made universal to enable it to fulfil the requirements of Article 11.

Article 22

Ratification, acceptance, approval or accession

1. The Convention shall be subject to ratification, acceptance, approval or accession by States and by regional economic integration organizations. It shall be open for accession from the day after the date on which the Convention is closed for signature. Instruments of ratification, acceptance, approval or accession shall be deposited with the Depositary.

2. Any regional economic integration organization which becomes a Party to the Convention without any of its member States being a Party shall be bound by all the obligations under the Convention. In the case of such organizations, one or more of whose member States is a Party to the Convention, the organization and its member States shall decide on their respective responsibilities for the performance of their obligations under the Convention. In such cases, the organization and the member States shall not be entitled to exercise rights under the Convention concurrently.

3. In their instruments of ratification, acceptance, approval or accession, regional economic integration organizations shall declare the extent of their competence with respect to the matters governed by the Convention. These organizations shall also inform the Depositary, who shall in turn inform the Parties, of any substantial modification in the extent of their competence.

Article 23

Entry into force

1. The Convention shall enter into force on the ninetieth day after the date of deposit of the fiftieth instrument of ratification, acceptance, approval or accession.

2. For each State or regional economic integration organization that ratifies, accepts or approves the Convention or accedes thereto after the deposit of the fiftieth instrument of ratification, acceptance, approval or accession, the Convention shall enter into force on the ninetieth day after the date of deposit by such State or regional economic integration organization of its instrument of ratification, acceptance, approval or accession.

3. For the purposes of paragraphs 1 and 2 above, any instrument deposited by a regional economic integration organization shall not be counted as additional to those deposited by States members of the organization.

Article 24

Reservations

No reservations may be made to the Convention.

Article 25

Withdrawal

1. At any time after three years from the date on which the Convention has entered into force for a Party, that Party may withdraw from the Convention by giving written notification to the Depositary.

2. Any such withdrawal shall take effect upon expiry of one year from the date of receipt by the Depositary of the notification of withdrawal, or on such later date as may be specified in the notification of withdrawal.

3. Any Party that withdraws from the Convention shall be considered as also having withdrawn from any protocol to which it is a Party.

Article 26

Authentic texts

The original of this Convention, of which the Arabic, Chinese, English, French, Russian and Spanish texts are equally authentic, shall be deposited with the Secretary-General of the United Nations.

IN WITNESS WHEREOF the undersigned, being duly authorized to that effect, have signed this Convention.

DONE at New York this ninth day of May one thousand nine hundred and ninety-two.

ANNEX I

Australia

Austria

Belarus[1]

Belgium

Bulgaria[1]

Canada

Croatia[1 2]

Czech Republic[1 2]

Denmark

European Economic Community

Estonia[1]

Finland

France

Germany

Greece

Hungary[1]

Iceland

Ireland

Italy

Japan

Latvia[1]

Liechtenstein[2]

Lithuania[1]

Luxembourg

Monaco[2]

Netherlands

New Zealand

Norway

Poland[1]

Portugal

Romania[1]

Russian Federation[1]

Slovakia[1 2]

Slovenia[1 2]

Spain

Sweden

Switzerland

Turkey

Ukraine[1]

United Kingdom of Great Britain and Northern Ireland

United States of America

1. Countries that are undergoing the process of transition to a market economy.
2. Countries added to Annex I by an amendment that entered into force on 13 August 1998, pursuant to decision 4/CP.3 adopted at COP.3.

ANNEX II

Australia

Austria

Belgium

Canada

Denmark

European Economic Community

Finland

France

Germany

Greece

Iceland

Ireland

Italy

Japan

Luxembourg

Netherlands

New Zealand

Norway

Portugal

Spain

Sweden

Switzerland[1]

United Kingdom of Great Britain and Northern Ireland

United States of America

1. Turkey was deleted from Annex II by an amendment that entered into force 28 June 2002, pursuant to decision 26/CP.7 adopted at COP.7.

KYOTO PROTOCOL TO THE UNITED NATIONS FRAMEWORK CONVENTION ON CLIMATE CHANGE

1997

THE PARTIES TO THIS PROTOCOL,

Being Parties to the United Nations Framework Convention on Climate Change, hereinafter referred to as "the Convention",

In pursuit of the ultimate objective of the Convention as stated in its Article 2,

Recalling the provisions of the Convention,

Being guided by Article 3 of the Convention,

Pursuant to the Berlin Mandate adopted by decision 1/CP.1 of the

Conference of the Parties to the Convention at its first session,

HAVE AGREED AS FOLLOWS:

Article 1

For the purposes of this Protocol, the definitions contained in Article 1 of the Convention shall apply. In addition:

1. "Conference of the Parties" means the Conference of the Parties to the Convention.
2. "Convention" means the United Nations Framework Convention on Climate Change, adopted in New York on 9 May 1992.
3. "Intergovernmental Panel on Climate Change" means the Intergovernmental Panel on Climate Change established in 1988 jointly by the World Meteorological Organization and the United Nations Environment Programme.
4. "Montreal Protocol" means the Montreal Protocol on Substances that Deplete the Ozone Layer, adopted in Montreal on 16 September 1987 and as subsequently adjusted and amended.
5. "Parties present and voting" means Parties present and casting an affirmative or negative vote.
6. "Party" means, unless the context otherwise indicates, a Party to this Protocol.
7. "Party included in Annex I" means a Party included in Annex I to the Convention, as may be amended, or a Party which has made a notification under Article 4, paragraph 2(g), of the Convention.

Article 2

1. Each Party included in Annex I, in achieving its quantified emission limitation and reduction commitments under Article 3, in order to promote sustainable development, shall:

(a) Implement and/or further elaborate policies and measures in accordance with its national circumstances, such as:

- (i) Enhancement of energy efficiency in relevant sectors of the national economy;
- (ii) Protection and enhancement of sinks and reservoirs of greenhouse gases not controlled by the Montreal Protocol, taking into account its commitments under relevant international environmental agreements; promotion of sustainable forest management practices, afforestation and reforestation;
- (iii) Promotion of sustainable forms of agriculture in light of climate change considerations;
- (iv) Research on, and promotion, development and increased use of, new and renewable forms of energy, of carbon dioxide sequestration technologies and of advanced and innovative environmentally sound technologies;

(v) Progressive reduction or phasing out of market imperfections, fiscal incentives, tax and duty exemptions and subsidies in all greenhouse gas emitting sectors that run counter to the objective of the Convention and application of market instruments;

(vi) Encouragement of appropriate reforms in relevant sectors aimed at promoting policies and measures which limit or reduce emissions of greenhouse gases not controlled by the Montreal Protocol;

(vii) Measures to limit and/or reduce emissions of greenhouse gases not controlled by the Montreal Protocol in the transport sector;

(viii) Limitation and/or reduction of methane emissions through recovery and use in waste management, as well as in the production, transport and distribution of energy;

(b) Cooperate with other such Parties to enhance the individual and combined effectiveness of their policies and measures adopted under this Article, pursuant to Article 4, paragraph 2(e)(i), of the Convention. To this end, these Parties shall take steps to share their experience and exchange information on such policies and measures, including developing ways of improving their comparability, transparency and effectiveness. The Conference of the Parties serving as the meeting of the Parties to this Protocol shall, at its first session or as soon as practicable thereafter, consider ways to facilitate such cooperation, taking into account all relevant information.

2. The Parties included in Annex I shall pursue limitation or reduction of emissions of greenhouse gases not controlled by the Montreal Protocol from aviation and marine bunker fuels, working through the International Civil Aviation Organization and the International Maritime Organization, respectively.

3. The Parties included in Annex I shall strive to implement policies and measures under this Article in such a way as to minimize adverse effects, including the adverse effects of climate change, effects on international trade, and social, environmental and economic impacts on other Parties, especially developing country Parties and in particular those identified in Article 4, paragraphs 8 and 9, of the Convention, taking into account Article 3 of the Convention. The Conference of the Parties serving as the meeting of the Parties to this Protocol may take further action, as appropriate, to promote the implementation of the provisions of this paragraph.

4. The Conference of the Parties serving as the meeting of the Parties to this Protocol, if it decides that it would be beneficial to coordinate any of the policies and measures in paragraph 1(a) above, taking into account different national circumstances and potential effects, shall consider ways and means to elaborate the coordination of such policies and measures.

Article 3

1. The Parties included in Annex I shall, individually or jointly, ensure that their aggregate anthropogenic carbon dioxide equivalent emissions of the greenhouse gases listed in Annex A do not exceed their assigned amounts, calculated pursuant to their quantified emission limitation and reduction commitments inscribed in Annex B and in accordance with the provisions of this Article, with a view to reducing their overall emissions of such gases by at least 5 per cent below 1990 levels in the commitment period 2008 to 2012.

[1 bis. The Parties included in Annex I shall, individually or jointly, ensure that their aggregate anthropogenic carbon dioxide equivalent emissions of the greenhouse gases listed in Annex A do not exceed their assigned amounts, calculated pursuant to their quantified emission limitation and reduction commitments inscribed in the third column of the table contained in Annex B and in accordance with the provisions of this Article, with a view to reducing their overall emissions of such gases by at least 18 per cent below 1990 levels in the commitment period 2013 to 2020.

1 ter. A Party included in Annex B may propose an adjustment to decrease the percentage inscribed in the third column of Annex B of its quantified emission limitation and reduction

commitment inscribed in the third column of the table contained in Annex B. A proposal for such an adjustment shall be communicated to the Parties by the secretariat at least three months before the meeting of the Conference of the Parties serving as the meeting of the Parties to this Protocol at which it is proposed for adoption.

1 quater. An adjustment proposed by a Party included in Annex I to increase the ambition of its quantified emission limitation and reduction commitment in accordance with Article 3, paragraph 1 ter, above shall be considered adopted by the Conference of the Parties serving as the meeting of the Parties to this Protocol unless more than three-fourths of the Parties present and voting object to its adoption. The adopted adjustment shall be communicated by the secretariat to the Depositary, who shall circulate it to all Parties, and shall enter into force on 1 January of the year following the communication by the Depositary. Such adjustments shall be binding upon Parties.][1]

2. Each Party included in Annex I shall, by 2005, have made demonstrable progress in achieving its commitments under this Protocol.

3. The net changes in greenhouse gas emissions by sources and removals by sinks resulting from direct human-induced land-use change and forestry activities, limited to afforestation, reforestation and deforestation since 1990, measured as verifiable changes in carbon stocks in each commitment period, shall be used to meet the commitments under this Article of each Party included in Annex I. The greenhouse gas emissions by sources and removals by sinks associated with those activities shall be reported in a transparent and verifiable manner and reviewed in accordance with Articles 7 and 8.

4. Prior to the first session of the Conference of the Parties serving as the meeting of the Parties to this Protocol, each Party included in Annex I shall provide, for consideration by the Subsidiary Body for Scientific and Technological Advice, data to establish its level of carbon stocks in 1990 and to enable an estimate to be made of its changes in carbon stocks in subsequent years. The Conference of the Parties serving as the meeting of the Parties to this Protocol shall, at its first session or as soon as practicable thereafter, decide upon modalities, rules and guidelines as to how, and which, additional human-induced activities related to changes in greenhouse gas emissions by sources and removals by sinks in the agricultural soils and the land-use change and forestry categories shall be added to, or subtracted from, the assigned amounts for Parties included in Annex I, taking into account uncertainties, transparency in reporting, verifiability, the methodological work of the Intergovernmental Panel on Climate Change, the advice provided by the Subsidiary Body for Scientific and Technological Advice in accordance with Article 5 and the decisions of the Conference of the Parties. Such a decision shall apply in the second and subsequent commitment periods. A Party may choose to apply such a decision on these additional human-induced activities for its first commitment period, provided that these activities have taken place since 1990.

5. The Parties included in Annex I undergoing the process of transition to a market economy whose base year or period was established pursuant to decision 9/CP.2 of the Conference of the Parties at its second session shall use that base year or period for the implementation of their commitments under this Article. Any other Party included in Annex I undergoing the process of transition to a market economy which has not yet submitted its first national communication under Article 12 of the Convention may also notify the Conference of the Parties serving as the meeting of the Parties to this Protocol that it intends to use an historical base year or period other than 1990 for the implementation of its commitments under this Article. The Conference of the Parties serving as the meeting of the Parties to this Protocol shall decide on the acceptance of such notification.

6. Taking into account Article 4, paragraph 6, of the Convention, in the implementation of their commitments under this Protocol other than those under this Article, a certain degree of flexibility shall be allowed by the Conference of the Parties serving as the meeting of the Parties to this Protocol to the Parties included in Annex I undergoing the process of transition to a market economy.

7. In the first quantified emission limitation and reduction commitment period, from 2008 to 2012, the assigned amount for each Party included in Annex I shall be equal to the percentage inscribed for it in Annex B of its aggregate anthropogenic carbon dioxide equivalent emissions of the greenhouse gases listed in Annex A in 1990, or the base year or period determined in accordance with paragraph 5 above, multiplied by five. Those Parties included in Annex I for whom land-use change and forestry constituted a net source of greenhouse gas emissions in 1990 shall include in their 1990 emissions base year or period the aggregate anthropogenic carbon dioxide equivalent emissions by sources minus removals by sinks in 1990 from land-use change for the purposes of calculating their assigned amount.

[7 bis. In the second quantified emission limitation and reduction commitment period, from 2013 to 2020, the assigned amount for each Party included in Annex I shall be equal to the percentage inscribed for it in the third column of the table contained in Annex B of its aggregate anthropogenic carbon dioxide equivalent emissions of the greenhouse gases listed in Annex A in 1990, or the base year or period determined in accordance with paragraph 5 above, multiplied by eight. Those Parties included in Annex I for whom land-use change and forestry constituted a net source of greenhouse gas emissions in 1990 shall include in their 1990 emissions base year or period the aggregate anthropogenic carbon dioxide equivalent emissions by sources minus removals by sinks in 1990 from land-use change for the purposes of calculating their assigned amount.

7 ter. Any positive difference between the assigned amount of the second commitment period for a Party included in the Annex I and average annual emissions for the first three years of the preceding commitment period multiplied by eight shall be transferred to the cancellation account of that Party.][1]

8. Any Party included in Annex I may use 1995 as its base year for hydrofluorocarbons, perfluorocarbons and sulphur hexafluoride, for the purposes of the [calculation referred to in paragraphs 7 and 7 bis above][2].

[8 bis. Any Party included in Annex I may use 1995 or 2000 as its base year for nitrogen trifluoride for the purposes of the calculation referred to in paragraph 7 bis above.][1]

9. Commitments for subsequent periods for Parties included in Annex I shall be established in amendments to Annex B to this Protocol, which shall be adopted in accordance with the provisions of Article 21, paragraph 7. The Conference of the Parties serving as the meeting of the Parties to this Protocol shall initiate the consideration of such commitments at least seven years before the end of the first commitment period referred to in paragraph 1 above.

10. Any emission reduction units, or any part of an assigned amount, which a Party acquires from another Party in accordance with the provisions of Article 6 or of Article 17 shall be added to the assigned amount for the acquiring Party.

11. Any emission reduction units, or any part of an assigned amount, which a Party transfers to another Party in accordance with the provisions of Article 6 or of Article 17 shall be subtracted from the assigned amount for the transferring Party.

[12 bis. Any units generated from market-based mechanisms to be established under the Convention or its instruments may be used by Parties included in Annex I to assist them in achieving compliance with their quantified emission limitation and reduction commitments under Article 3. Any such units which a Party acquires from another Party to the Convention shall be added to the assigned amount for the acquiring Party and subtracted from the quantity of units held by the transferring Party.

12 ter. The Conference of the Parties serving as the meeting of the Parties to this Protocol shall ensure that, where units from approved activities under market-based mechanisms referred to in paragraph 12 bis above are used by Parties included in Annex I to assist them in achieving compliance with their quantified emission limitation and reduction commitments under Article 3, a share of these units is used to cover administrative expenses, as well as

3. A Party included in Annex I may authorize legal entities to participate, under its responsibility, in actions leading to the generation, transfer or acquisition under this Article of emission reduction units.

4. If a question of implementation by a Party included in Annex I of the requirements referred to in this Article is identified in accordance with the relevant provisions of Article 8, transfers and acquisitions of emission reduction units may continue to be made after the question has been identified, provided that any such units may not be used by a Party to meet its commitments under Article 3 until any issue of compliance is resolved.

Article 7

1. Each Party included in Annex I shall incorporate in its annual inventory of anthropogenic emissions by sources and removals by sinks of greenhouse gases not controlled by the Montreal Protocol, submitted in accordance with the relevant decisions of the Conference of the Parties, the necessary supplementary information for the purposes of ensuring compliance with Article 3, to be determined in accordance with paragraph 4 below.

2. Each Party included in Annex I shall incorporate in its national communication, submitted under Article 12 of the Convention, the supplementary information necessary to demonstrate compliance with its commitments under this Protocol, to be determined in accordance with paragraph 4 below.

3. Each Party included in Annex I shall submit the information required under paragraph 1 above annually, beginning with the first inventory due under the Convention for the first year of the commitment period after this Protocol has entered into force for that Party. Each such Party shall submit the information required under paragraph 2 above as part of the first national communication due under the Convention after this Protocol has entered into force for it and after the adoption of guidelines as provided for in paragraph 4 below. The frequency of subsequent submission of information required under this Article shall be determined by the Conference of the Parties serving as the meeting of the Parties to this Protocol, taking into account any timetable for the submission of national communications decided upon by the Conference of the Parties.

4. The Conference of the Parties serving as the meeting of the Parties to this Protocol shall adopt at its first session, and review periodically thereafter, guidelines for the preparation of the information required under this Article, taking into account guidelines for the preparation of national communications by Parties included in Annex I adopted by the Conference of the Parties. The Conference of the Parties serving as the meeting of the Parties to this Protocol shall also, prior to the first commitment period, decide upon modalities for the accounting of assigned amounts.

Article 8

1. The information submitted under Article 7 by each Party included in Annex I shall be reviewed by expert review teams pursuant to the relevant decisions of the Conference of the Parties and in accordance with guidelines adopted for this purpose by the Conference of the Parties serving as the meeting of the Parties to this Protocol under paragraph 4 below. The information submitted under Article 7, paragraph 1, by each Party included in Annex I shall be reviewed as part of the annual compilation and accounting of emissions inventories and assigned amounts. Additionally, the information submitted under Article 7, paragraph 2, by each Party included in Annex I shall be reviewed as part of the review of communications.

2. Expert review teams shall be coordinated by the secretariat and shall be composed of experts selected from those nominated by Parties to the Convention and, as appropriate, by intergovernmental organizations, in accordance with guidance provided for this purpose by the Conference of the Parties.

3. The review process shall provide a thorough and comprehensive technical assessment of all aspects of the implementation by a Party of this Protocol. The expert review teams shall prepare a report to the Conference of the Parties serving as the meeting of the Parties to this Protocol, assessing the implementation of the commitments of the Party and identifying any potential problems in, and factors influencing, the fulfilment of commitments. Such reports shall be circulated by the secretariat to all Parties to the Convention. The secretariat shall list those questions of implementation indicated in such reports for further consideration by the Conference of the Parties serving as the meeting of the Parties to this Protocol.

4. The Conference of the Parties serving as the meeting of the Parties to this Protocol shall adopt at its first session, and review periodically thereafter, guidelines for the review of implementation of this Protocol by expert review teams taking into account the relevant decisions of the Conference of the Parties.

5. The Conference of the Parties serving as the meeting of the Parties to this Protocol shall, with the assistance of the Subsidiary Body for Implementation and, as appropriate, the Subsidiary Body for Scientific and Technological Advice, consider:

(a) The information submitted by Parties under Article 7 and the reports of the expert reviews thereon conducted under this Article; and

(b) Those questions of implementation listed by the secretariat under paragraph 3 above, as well as any questions raised by Parties.

6. Pursuant to its consideration of the information referred to in paragraph 5 above, the Conference of the Parties serving as the meeting of the Parties to this Protocol shall take decisions on any matter required for the implementation of this Protocol.

Article 9

1. The Conference of the Parties serving as the meeting of the Parties to this Protocol shall periodically review this Protocol in the light of the best available scientific information and assessments on climate change and its impacts, as well as relevant technical, social and economic information. Such reviews shall be coordinated with pertinent reviews under the Convention, in particular those required by Article 4, paragraph 2(d), and Article 7, paragraph 2(a), of the Convention. Based on these reviews, the Conference of the Parties serving as the meeting of the Parties to this Protocol shall take appropriate action.

2. The first review shall take place at the second session of the Conference of the Parties serving as the meeting of the Parties to this Protocol. Further reviews shall take place at regular intervals and in a timely manner.

Article 10

All Parties, taking into account their common but differentiated responsibilities and their specific national and regional development priorities, objectives and circumstances, without introducing any new commitments for Parties not included in Annex I, but reaffirming existing commitments under Article 4, paragraph 1, of the Convention, and continuing to advance the implementation of these commitments in order to achieve sustainable development, taking into account Article 4, paragraphs 3, 5 and 7, of the Convention, shall:

(a) Formulate, where relevant and to the extent possible, cost-effective national and, where appropriate, regional programmes to improve the quality of local emission factors, activity data and/or models which reflect the socio-economic conditions of each Party for the preparation and periodic updating of national inventories of anthropogenic emissions by sources and removals by sinks of all greenhouse gases not controlled by the Montreal Protocol, using comparable methodologies to be agreed upon by the Conference of the Parties, and consistent with the guidelines for the preparation of national communications adopted by the Conference of the Parties;

(b) Formulate, implement, publish and regularly update national and, where appropriate, regional programmes containing measures to mitigate climate change and measures to facilitate adequate adaptation to climate change:

(i) Such programmes would, inter alia, concern the energy, transport and industry sectors as well as agriculture, forestry and waste management. Furthermore, adaptation technologies and methods for improving spatial planning would improve adaptation to climate change; and

(ii) Parties included in Annex I shall submit information on action under this Protocol, including national programmes, in accordance with Article 7; and other Parties shall seek to include in their national communications, as appropriate, information on programmes which contain measures that the Party believes contribute to addressing climate change and its adverse impacts, including the abatement of increases in greenhouse gas emissions, and enhancement of and removals by sinks, capacity building and adaptation measures;

(c) Cooperate in the promotion of effective modalities for the development, application and diffusion of, and take all practicable steps to promote, facilitate and finance, as appropriate, the transfer of, or access to, environmentally sound technologies, know-how, practices and processes pertinent to climate change, in particular to developing countries, including the formulation of policies and programmes for the effective transfer of environmentally sound technologies that are publicly owned or in the public domain and the creation of an enabling environment for the private sector, to promote and enhance the transfer of, and access to, environmentally sound technologies;

(d) Cooperate in scientific and technical research and promote the maintenance and the development of systematic observation systems and development of data archives to reduce uncertainties related to the climate system, the adverse impacts of climate change and the economic and social consequences of various response strategies, and promote the development and strengthening of endogenous capacities and capabilities to participate in international and intergovernmental efforts, programmes and networks on research and systematic observation, taking into account Article 5 of the Convention;

(e) Cooperate in and promote at the international level, and, where appropriate, using existing bodies, the development and implementation of education and training programmes, including the strengthening of national capacity building, in particular human and institutional capacities and the exchange or secondment of personnel to train experts in this field, in particular for developing countries, and facilitate at the national level public awareness of, and public access to information on, climate change. Suitable modalities should be developed to implement these activities through the relevant bodies of the Convention, taking into account Article 6 of the Convention;

(f) Include in their national communications information on programmes and activities undertaken pursuant to this Article in accordance with relevant decisions of the Conference of the Parties; and

(g) Give full consideration, in implementing the commitments under this Article, to Article 4, paragraph 8, of the Convention.

Article 11

1. In the implementation of Article 10, Parties shall take into account the provisions of Article 4, paragraphs 4, 5, 7, 8 and 9, of the Convention.

2. In the context of the implementation of Article 4, paragraph 1, of the Convention, in accordance with the provisions of Article 4, paragraph 3, and Article 11 of the Convention, and through the entity or entities entrusted with the operation of the financial mechanism of the Convention, the developed country Parties and other developed Parties included in Annex II to the Convention shall:

(a) Provide new and additional financial resources to meet the agreed full costs incurred by developing country Parties in advancing the implementation of existing commitments under Article 4, paragraph 1(a), of the Convention that are covered in Article 10, subparagraph (a); and

(b) Also provide such financial resources, including for the transfer of technology, needed by the developing country Parties to meet the agreed full incremental costs of advancing the implementation of existing commitments under Article 4, paragraph 1, of the Convention that are covered by Article 10 and that are agreed between a developing country Party and the international entity or entities referred to in Article 11 of the Convention, in accordance with that Article.

The implementation of these existing commitments shall take into account the need for adequacy and predictability in the flow of funds and the importance of appropriate burden sharing among developed country Parties. The guidance to the entity or entities entrusted with the operation of the financial mechanism of the Convention in relevant decisions of the Conference of the Parties, including those agreed before the adoption of this Protocol, shall apply mutatis mutandis to the provisions of this paragraph.

3. The developed country Parties and other developed Parties in Annex II to the Convention may also provide, and developing country Parties avail themselves of, financial resources for the implementation of Article 10, through bilateral, regional and other multilateral channels.

Article 12

1. A clean development mechanism is hereby defined.

2. The purpose of the clean development mechanism shall be to assist Parties not included in Annex I in achieving sustainable development and in contributing to the ultimate objective of the Convention, and to assist Parties included in Annex I in achieving compliance with their quantified emission limitation and reduction commitments under Article 3.

3. Under the clean development mechanism:
(a) Parties not included in Annex I will benefit from project activities resulting in certified emission reductions; and
(b) Parties included in Annex I may use the certified emission reductions accruing from such project activities to contribute to compliance with part of their quantified emission limitation and reduction commitments under Article 3, as determined by the Conference of the Parties serving as the meeting of the Parties to this Protocol.

4. The clean development mechanism shall be subject to the authority and guidance of the Conference of the Parties serving as the meeting of the Parties to this Protocol and be supervised by an executive board of the clean development mechanism.

5. Emission reductions resulting from each project activity shall be certified by operational entities to be designated by the Conference of the Parties serving as the meeting of the Parties to this Protocol, on the basis of:
(a) Voluntary participation approved by each Party involved;
(b) Real, measurable, and long-term benefits related to the mitigation of climate change; and
(c) Reductions in emissions that are additional to any that would occur in the absence of the certified project activity.

6. The clean development mechanism shall assist in arranging funding of certified project activities as necessary.

7. The Conference of the Parties serving as the meeting of the Parties to this Protocol shall, at its first session, elaborate modalities and procedures with the objective of ensuring transparency, efficiency and accountability through independent auditing and verification of project activities.

8. The Conference of the Parties serving as the meeting of the Parties to this Protocol shall ensure that a share of the proceeds from certified project activities is used to cover administrative expenses as well as to assist developing country Parties that are particularly vulnerable to the adverse effects of climate change to meet the costs of adaptation.

9. Participation under the clean development mechanism, including in activities mentioned in paragraph 3(a) above and in the acquisition of certified emission reductions, may involve

private and/or public entities, and is to be subject to whatever guidance may be provided by the executive board of the clean development mechanism.

10. Certified emission reductions obtained during the period from the year 2000 up to the beginning of the first commitment period can be used to assist in achieving compliance in the first commitment period.

Article 13

1. The Conference of the Parties, the supreme body of the Convention, shall serve as the meeting of the Parties to this Protocol.

2. Parties to the Convention that are not Parties to this Protocol may participate as observers in the proceedings of any session of the Conference of the Parties serving as the meeting of the Parties to this Protocol. When the Conference of the Parties serves as the meeting of the Parties to this Protocol, decisions under this Protocol shall be taken only by those that are Parties to this Protocol.

3. When the Conference of the Parties serves as the meeting of the Parties to this Protocol, any member of the Bureau of the Conference of the Parties representing a Party to the Convention but, at that time, not a Party to this Protocol, shall be replaced by an additional member to be elected by and from amongst the Parties to this Protocol.

4. The Conference of the Parties serving as the meeting of the Parties to this Protocol shall keep under regular review the implementation of this Protocol and shall make, within its mandate, the decisions necessary to promote its effective implementation. It shall perform the functions assigned to it by this Protocol and shall:

(a) Assess, on the basis of all information made available to it in accordance with the provisions of this Protocol, the implementation of this Protocol by the Parties, the overall effects of the measures taken pursuant to this Protocol, in particular environmental, economic and social effects as well as their cumulative impacts and the extent to which progress towards the objective of the Convention is being achieved;

(b) Periodically examine the obligations of the Parties under this Protocol, giving due consideration to any reviews required by Article 4, paragraph 2(d), and Article 7, paragraph 2, of the Convention, in the light of the objective of the Convention, the experience gained in its implementation and the evolution of scientific and technological knowledge, and in this respect consider and adopt regular reports on the implementation of this Protocol;

(c) Promote and facilitate the exchange of information on measures adopted by the Parties to address climate change and its effects, taking into account the differing circumstances, responsibilities and capabilities of the Parties and their respective commitments under this Protocol;

(d) Facilitate, at the request of two or more Parties, the coordination of measures adopted by them to address climate change and its effects, taking into account the differing circumstances, responsibilities and capabilities of the Parties and their respective commitments under this Protocol;

(e) Promote and guide, in accordance with the objective of the Convention and the provisions of this Protocol, and taking fully into account the relevant decisions by the Conference of the Parties, the development and periodic refinement of comparable methodologies for the effective implementation of this Protocol, to be agreed on by the Conference of the Parties serving as the meeting of the Parties to this Protocol;

(f) Make recommendations on any matters necessary for the implementation of this Protocol;

(g) Seek to mobilize additional financial resources in accordance with Article 11, paragraph 2;

(h) Establish such subsidiary bodies as are deemed necessary for the implementation of this Protocol;

(i) Seek and utilize, where appropriate, the services and cooperation of, and information provided by, competent international organizations and intergovernmental and non-governmental bodies; and

(j) Exercise such other functions as may be required for the implementation of this Protocol, and consider any assignment resulting from a decision by the Conference of the Parties.

5. The rules of procedure of the Conference of the Parties and financial procedures applied under the Convention shall be applied mutatis mutandis under this Protocol, except as may be otherwise decided by consensus by the Conference of the Parties serving as the meeting of the Parties to this Protocol.

6. The first session of the Conference of the Parties serving as the meeting of the Parties to this Protocol shall be convened by the secretariat in conjunction with the first session of the Conference of the Parties that is scheduled after the date of the entry into force of this Protocol. Subsequent ordinary sessions of the Conference of the Parties serving as the meeting of the Parties to this Protocol shall be held every year and in conjunction with ordinary sessions of the Conference of the Parties, unless otherwise decided by the Conference of the Parties serving as the meeting of the Parties to this Protocol.

7. Extraordinary sessions of the Conference of the Parties serving as the meeting of the Parties to this Protocol shall be held at such other times as may be deemed necessary by the Conference of the Parties serving as the meeting of the Parties to this Protocol, or at the written request of any Party, provided that, within six months of the request being communicated to the Parties by the secretariat, it is supported by at least one third of the Parties.

8. The United Nations, its specialized agencies and the International Atomic Energy Agency, as well as any State member thereof or observers thereto not party to the Convention, may be represented at sessions of the Conference of the Parties serving as the meeting of the Parties to this Protocol as observers. Anybody or agency, whether national or international, governmental or non-governmental, which is qualified in matters covered by this Protocol and which has informed the secretariat of its wish to be represented at a session of the Conference of the Parties serving as the meeting of the Parties to this Protocol as an observer, may be so admitted unless at least one third of the Parties present object. The admission and participation of observers shall be subject to the rules of procedure, as referred to in paragraph 5 above.

Article 14

1. The secretariat established by Article 8 of the Convention shall serve as the secretariat of this Protocol.

2. Article 8, paragraph 2, of the Convention on the functions of the secretariat, and Article 8, paragraph 3, of the Convention on arrangements made for the functioning of the secretariat, shall apply mutatis mutandis to this Protocol. The secretariat shall, in addition, exercise the functions assigned to it under this Protocol.

Article 15

1. The Subsidiary Body for Scientific and Technological Advice and the Subsidiary Body for Implementation established by Articles 9 and 10 of the Convention shall serve as, respectively, the Subsidiary Body for Scientific and Technological Advice and the Subsidiary Body for Implementation of this Protocol. The provisions relating to the functioning of these two bodies under the Convention shall apply mutatis mutandis to this Protocol. Sessions of the meetings of the Subsidiary Body for Scientific and Technological Advice and the Subsidiary Body for Implementation of this Protocol shall be held in conjunction with the meetings of, respectively, the Subsidiary Body for Scientific and Technological Advice and the Subsidiary Body for Implementation of the Convention.

2. Parties to the Convention that are not Parties to this Protocol may participate as observers in the proceedings of any session of the subsidiary bodies. When the subsidiary bodies serve as the subsidiary bodies of this Protocol, decisions under this Protocol shall be taken only by those that are Parties to this Protocol.

3. When the subsidiary bodies established by Articles 9 and 10 of the Convention exercise their functions with regard to matters concerning this Protocol, any member of the Bureaux of those subsidiary bodies representing a Party to the Convention but, at that time, not a party to this Protocol, shall be replaced by an additional member to be elected by and from amongst the Parties to this Protocol.

Article 16

The Conference of the Parties serving as the meeting of the Parties to this Protocol shall, as soon as practicable, consider the application to this Protocol of, and modify as appropriate, the multilateral consultative process referred to in Article 13 of the Convention, in the light of any relevant decisions that may be taken by the Conference of the Parties. Any multilateral consultative process that may be applied to this Protocol shall operate without prejudice to the procedures and mechanisms established in accordance with Article 18.

Article 17

The Conference of the Parties shall define the relevant principles, modalities, rules and guidelines, in particular for verification, reporting and accountability for emissions trading. The Parties included in Annex B may participate in emissions trading for the purposes of fulfilling their commitments under Article 3. Any such trading shall be supplemental to domestic actions for the purpose of meeting quantified emission limitation and reduction commitments under that Article.

Article 18

The Conference of the Parties serving as the meeting of the Parties to this Protocol shall, at its first session, approve appropriate and effective procedures and mechanisms to determine and to address cases of non-compliance with the provisions of this Protocol, including through the development of an indicative list of consequences, taking into account the cause, type, degree and frequency of non-compliance. Any procedures and mechanisms under this Article entailing binding consequences shall be adopted by means of an amendment to this Protocol.

Article 19

The provisions of Article 14 of the Convention on settlement of disputes shall apply mutatis mutandis to this Protocol.

Article 20

1. Any Party may propose amendments to this Protocol.

2. Amendments to this Protocol shall be adopted at an ordinary session of the Conference of the Parties serving as the meeting of the Parties to this Protocol. The text of any proposed amendment to this Protocol shall be communicated to the Parties by the secretariat at least six months before the meeting at which it is proposed for adoption. The secretariat shall also communicate the text of any proposed amendments to the Parties and signatories to the Convention and, for information, to the Depositary.

3. The Parties shall make every effort to reach agreement on any proposed amendment to this Protocol by consensus. If all efforts at consensus have been exhausted, and no agreement reached, the amendment shall as a last resort be adopted by a three-fourths majority vote of the Parties present and voting at the meeting. The adopted amendment shall be communicated by the secretariat to the Depositary, who shall circulate it to all Parties for their acceptance.

4. Instruments of acceptance in respect of an amendment shall be deposited with the Depositary. An amendment adopted in accordance with paragraph 3 above shall enter into force for those Parties having accepted it on the ninetieth day after the date of receipt by the Depositary of an instrument of acceptance by at least three fourths of the Parties to this Protocol.

5. The amendment shall enter into force for any other Party on the ninetieth day after the date on which that Party deposits with the Depositary its instrument of acceptance of the said amendment.

Article 21

1. Annexes to this Protocol shall form an integral part thereof and, unless otherwise expressly provided, a reference to this Protocol constitutes at the same time a reference to any annexes thereto. Any annexes adopted after the entry into force of this Protocol shall be restricted to lists, forms and any other material of a descriptive nature that is of a scientific, technical, procedural or administrative character.

2. Any Party may make proposals for an annex to this Protocol and may propose amendments to annexes to this Protocol.

3. Annexes to this Protocol and amendments to annexes to this Protocol shall be adopted at an ordinary session of the Conference of the Parties serving as the meeting of the Parties to this Protocol. The text of any proposed annex or amendment to an annex shall be communicated to the Parties by the secretariat at least six months before the meeting at which it is proposed for adoption. The secretariat shall also communicate the text of any proposed annex or amendment to an annex to the Parties and signatories to the Convention and, for information, to the Depositary.

4. The Parties shall make every effort to reach agreement on any proposed annex or amendment to an annex by consensus. If all efforts at consensus have been exhausted, and no agreement reached, the annex or amendment to an annex shall as a last resort be adopted by a three-fourths majority vote of the Parties present and voting at the meeting. The adopted annex or amendment to an annex shall be communicated by the secretariat to the Depositary, who shall circulate it to all Parties for their acceptance.

5. An annex, or amendment to an annex other than Annex A or B, that has been adopted in accordance with paragraphs 3 and 4 above shall enter into force for all Parties to this Protocol six months after the date of the communication by the Depositary to such Parties of the adoption of the annex or adoption of the amendment to the annex, except for those Parties that have notified the Depositary, in writing, within that period of their non-acceptance of the annex or amendment to the annex. The annex or amendment to an annex shall enter into force for Parties which withdraw their notification of non-acceptance on the ninetieth day after the date on which withdrawal of such notification has been received by the Depositary.

6. If the adoption of an annex or an amendment to an annex involves an amendment to this Protocol, that annex or amendment to an annex shall not enter into force until such time as the amendment to this Protocol enters into force.

7. Amendments to Annexes A and B to this Protocol shall be adopted and enter into force in accordance with the procedure set out in Article 20, provided that any amendment to Annex B shall be adopted only with the written consent of the Party concerned.

Article 22

1. Each Party shall have one vote, except as provided for in paragraph 2 below.

2. Regional economic integration organizations, in matters within their competence, shall exercise their right to vote with a number of votes equal to the number of their member States that are Parties to this Protocol. Such an organization shall not exercise its right to vote if any of its member States exercises its right, and vice versa.

Article 23

The Secretary-General of the United Nations shall be the Depositary of this Protocol.

Article 24

1. This Protocol shall be open for signature and subject to ratification, acceptance or approval by States and regional economic integration organizations which are Parties to the Convention. It shall be open for signature at United Nations Headquarters in New York from 16 March 1998 to 15 March 1999. This Protocol shall be open for accession from the day after the date on which it is closed for signature. Instruments of ratification, acceptance, approval or accession shall be deposited with the Depositary.

2. Any regional economic integration organization which becomes a Party to this Protocol without any of its member States being a Party shall be bound by all the obligations under this Protocol. In the case of such organizations, one or more of whose member States is a Party to this Protocol, the organization and its member States shall decide on their respective responsibilities for the performance of their obligations under this Protocol. In such cases, the organization and the member States shall not be entitled to exercise rights under this Protocol concurrently.

3. In their instruments of ratification, acceptance, approval or accession, regional economic integration organizations shall declare the extent of their competence with respect to the matters governed by this Protocol. These organizations shall also inform the Depositary, who shall in turn inform the Parties, of any substantial modification in the extent of their competence.

Article 25

1. This Protocol shall enter into force on the ninetieth day after the date on which not less than 55 Parties to the Convention, incorporating Parties included in Annex I which accounted in total for at least 55 per cent of the total carbon dioxide emissions for 1990 of the Parties included in Annex I, have deposited their instruments of ratification, acceptance, approval or accession.

2. For the purposes of this Article, "the total carbon dioxide emissions for 1990 of the Parties included in Annex I" means the amount communicated on or before the date of adoption of this Protocol by the Parties included in Annex I in their first national communications submitted in accordance with Article 12 of the Convention.

3. For each State or regional economic integration organization that ratifies, accepts or approves this Protocol or accedes thereto after the conditions set out in paragraph 1 above for entry into force have been fulfilled, this Protocol shall enter into force on the ninetieth day following the date of deposit of its instrument of ratification, acceptance, approval or accession.

4. For the purposes of this Article, any instrument deposited by a regional economic integration organization shall not be counted as additional to those deposited by States members of the organization.

Article 26

No reservations may be made to this Protocol.

Article 27

1. At any time after three years from the date on which this Protocol has entered into force for a Party, that Party may withdraw from this Protocol by giving written notification to the Depositary.

2. Any such withdrawal shall take effect upon expiry of one year from the date of receipt by the Depositary of the notification of withdrawal, or on such later date as may be specified in the notification of withdrawal.

3. Any Party that withdraws from the Convention shall be considered as also having withdrawn from this Protocol.

Article 28

The original of this Protocol, of which the Arabic, Chinese, English, French, Russian and Spanish texts are equally authentic, shall be deposited with the Secretary-General of the United Nations.

DONE at Kyoto this eleventh day of December one thousand nine hundred and ninety-seven.

IN WITNESS WHEREOF the undersigned, being duly authorized to that effect, have affixed their signatures to this Protocol on the dates indicated.

ANNEX A

[Greenhouse gases

Carbon dioxide (CO_2)

Methane (CH_4)

Nitrous oxide (N_2O)

Hydrofluorocarbons (HFCs)

Perfluorocarbons (PFCs)

Sulphur hexafluoride (SF_6)

Nitrogen trifluoride (NF_3)][1]

Sectors/source categories

- Energy
  - Fuel combustion
    - Energy industries
    - Manufacturing industries and construction
    - Transport
    - Other sectors
    - Other
  - Fugitive emissions from fuels
    - Solid fuels
    - Oil and natural gas
    - Other

- Industrial processes
  - Mineral products
  - Chemical industry
  - Metal production
  - Other production
  - Production of halocarbons and sulphur hexafluoride
  - Consumption of halocarbons and sulphur hexafluoride
  - Other

- Solvent and other product use
  - Agriculture
  - Enteric fermentation

Manure management
Rice cultivation
Agricultural soils
Prescribed burning of savannas
Field burning of agricultural residues
Other

Waste
Solid waste disposal on land
Wastewater handling
Waste incineration
Other

Amendment

1 Substituted by an amendment adopted at the eighth session of the Conference of the Parties to the Kyoto Protocol serving as the meeting of the Parties to the Kyoto Protocol held in Doha, Qatar, in December 2012.

[1	2	3	4	5	6
Party	*Quantified emission limitation or reduction commitment (2008–2012) (percentage of base year or period)*	*Quantified emission limitation or reduction commitment (2013–2020) (percentage of base year or period)*	*Reference year*[1]	*Quantified emission limitation or reduction commitment (2013–2020) (expressed as percentage of reference year)*	*Pledges for the reduction of greenhouse gas emissions by 2020 (percentage of reference year)*[2]
Australia	108	99.5	2000	98	–5 to –15% or –25%[3]
Austria	92	80[4]	NA	NA	
Belarus[5]*		88	1990	NA	–8%
Belgium	92	80[4]	NA	NA	
Bulgaria*	92	80[4]	NA	NA	
Croatia*	95	80[6]	NA	NA	–20%/–30%[7]
Czech Republic*	92	80[4]	NA	NA	
Denmark	92	80[4]	NA	NA	
Estonia*	92	80[4]	NA	NA	
European Union	92	80[4]	NA	NA	–20%/–30%[7]
Finland	92	80[4]	NA	NA	
France	92	80[4]	NA	NA	
Germany	92	80[4]	NA	NA	
Greece	92	80[4]	NA	NA	
Hungary*	94	80[4]	NA	NA	
Iceland	110	80[8]	NA	NA	
Ireland	92	80[4]	NA	NA	
Italy	92	80[4]	NA	NA	
Kazakhstan*		95	1990	95	–7%
Latvia*	92	80[4]	NA	NA	

[1 Party	2 *Quantified emission limitation or reduction commitment (2008–2012) (percentage of base year or period)*	3 *Quantified emission limitation or reduction commitment (2013–2020) (percentage of base year or period)*	4 *Reference year*[1]	5 *Quantified emission limitation or reduction commitment (2013–2020) (expressed as percentage of reference year)*	6 *Pledges for the reduction of greenhouse gas emissions by 2020 (percentage of reference year)*[2]
Liechtenstein	92	80[4]	NA	NA	–20%/–30%[9]
Lithuania*	92	80[4]	NA	NA	
Luxembourg	92	80[4]	NA	NA	
Malta		80[4]	NA	NA	
Monaco	92	78	1990	78	–30%
Netherlands	92	80[4]	NA	NA	
Norway	101	84	1990	84	–30% to –40%[10]
Poland*	94	80[4]	NA	NA	
Portugal	92	80[4]	NA	NA	
Romania*	92	80[4]	NA	NA	
Slovakia*	92	80[4]	NA	NA	
Slovenia*	92	80[4]	NA	NA	
Spain	92	80[4]	NA	NA	
Sweden	92	80[4]	NA	NA	
Switzerland	92	84.2	1990	NA	–20% to –30%[11]
Ukraine*	100	76[12]	1990	NA	–20%
United Kingdom of Great Britain and Northern Ireland	92	80[4]	NA	NA	

Party	Quantified emission limitation or reduction commitment (2008–2012) (percentage of base year or period)
Canada[13]	94
Japan[14]	94
New Zealand[15]	100
Russian Federation[16]*	100

Abbreviation: NA = not applicable.

* Countries that are undergoing the process of transition to a market economy.

All footnotes below, except for footnotes 1, 2 and 5, have been provided through communications from the respective Parties.

1 A reference year may be used by a Party on an optional basis for its own purposes to express its quantified emission limitation or reduction commitment (QELRC) as a percentage of emissions of that year, that is not internationally binding under the Kyoto Protocol, in addition to the listing of its QELRC(s) in relation to the base year in the second and third columns of this table, which are internationally legally binding.

2 Further information on these pledges can be found in documents FCCC/SB/2011/INF.1/Rev.1 and FCCC/KP/AWG/2012/MISC.1, Add.1 and Add.2.

3 Australia's QELRC under the second commitment period of the Kyoto Protocol is consistent with the achievement of Australia's unconditional 2020 target of 5 per cent below 2000 levels. Australia retains the option later to move up within its 2020 target of 5 to 15, or 25 per cent below 2000 levels, subject to certain conditions being met. This reference retains the status of these pledges as made under the Cancun Agreements and does not amount to a new legally binding commitment under this Protocol or its associated rules and modalities.

4 The QELRCs for the European Union and its member States for a second commitment period under the Kyoto Protocol are based on the understanding that these will be fulfilled jointly with the European Union and its member States, in accordance with Article 4 of the Kyoto Protocol. The QELRCs are without prejudice to the subsequent notification by the European Union and its member States of an agreement to fulfil their commitments jointly in accordance with the provisions of the Kyoto Protocol.

5 Added to Annex B by an amendment adopted pursuant to decision 10/CMP.2. This amendment has not yet entered into force.

6 Croatia's QELRC for a second commitment period under the Kyoto Protocol is based on the understanding that it will fulfil this QELRC jointly with the European Union and its member States, in accordance with Article 4 of the Kyoto Protocol. As a consequence, Croatia's accession to the European Union shall not affect its participation in such joint fulfilment agreement pursuant to Article 4 or its QELRC.

7 As part of a global and comprehensive agreement for the period beyond 2012, the European Union reiterates its conditional offer to move to a 30 per cent reduction by 2020 compared to 1990 levels, provided that other developed countries commit themselves to comparable emission reductions and developing countries contribute adequately according to their responsibilities and respective capabilities.

8 The QELRC for Iceland for a second commitment period under the Kyoto Protocol is based on the understanding that it will be fulfilled jointly with the European Union and its member States, in accordance with Article 4 of the Kyoto Protocol.

9 The QELRC presented in column three refers to a reduction target of 20 per cent by 2020 compared to 1990 levels. Liechtenstein would consider a higher reduction target of up to 30 per cent by 2020 compared to 1990 levels under the condition that other developed countries commit themselves to comparable emission reductions and that economically more advanced developing countries contribute adequately according to their responsibilities and respective capabilities.

10 Norway's QELRC of 84 is consistent with its target of 30 per cent reduction of emissions by 2020, compared to 1990. If it can contribute to a global and comprehensive agreement where major emitting Parties agree on emission reductions in line with the 2° C target, Norway will move to a level of 40 per cent reduction for 2020 based on 1990 levels. This reference retains the status of the pledge made under the Cancun Agreements and does not amount to a new legally binding commitment under this Protocol.

11 The QELRC presented in the third column of this table refers to a reduction target of 20 per cent by 2020 compared to 1990 levels. Switzerland would consider a higher reduction target up to 30 per cent by 2020 compared to 1990 levels subject to comparable emission reduction commitments from other developed countries and

adequate contribution from developing countries according to their responsibilities and capabilities in line with the 2° C target. This reference retains the status of the pledge made under the Cancun Agreements and does not amount to a new legally binding commitment under this Protocol or its associated rules and modalities.

12 Should be full carry-over and there is no acceptance of any cancellation or any limitation on use of this legitimately acquired sovereign property.

13 On 15 December 2011, the Depositary received written notification of Canada's withdrawal from the Kyoto Protocol. This action will become effective for Canada on 15 December 2012.

14 In a communication dated 10 December 2010, Japan indicated that it does not have any intention to be under obligation of the second commitment period of the Kyoto Protocol after 2012.

15 New Zealand remains a Party to the Kyoto Protocol. It will be taking a quantified economy-wide emission reduction target under the United Nations Framework Convention on Climate Change in the period 2013 to 2020.

16 In a communication dated 8 December 2010 that was received by the secretariat on 9 December 2010, the Russian Federation indicated that it does not intend to assume a quantitative emission limitation or reduction commitment for the second commitment period.][1]

Amendment

1 Substituted by an amendment adopted at the eighth session of the Conference of the Parties to the Kyoto Protocol serving as the meeting of the Parties to the Kyoto Protocol held in Doha, Qatar, in December 2012.

CONVENTION ON ACCESS TO INFORMATION, PUBLIC PARTICIPATION IN DECISION MAKING AND ACCESS TO JUSTICE IN ENVIRONMENTAL MATTERS

on 25 June 1998

THE PARTIES TO THIS CONVENTION,

Recalling principle 1 of the Stockholm Declaration on the Human Environment,

Recalling also principle 10 of the Rio Declaration on Environment and Development,

Recalling further General Assembly resolutions 37/7 of 28 October 1982 on the World Charter for Nature and 45/94 of 14 December 1990 on the need to ensure a healthy environment for the well-being of individuals,

Recalling the European Charter on Environment and Health adopted at the First European Conference on Environment and Health of the World Health Organization in Frankfurt-am-Main, Germany, on 8 December 1989,

Affirming the need to protect, preserve and improve the state of the environment and to ensure sustainable and environmentally sound development,

Recognizing that adequate protection of the environment is essential to human well-being and the enjoyment of basic human rights, including the right to life itself,

Recognizing also that every person has the right to live in an environment adequate to his or her health and well-being, and the duty, both individually and in association with others, to protect and improve the environment for the benefit of present and future generations,

Considering that, to be able to assert this right and observe this duty, citizens must have access to information, be entitled to participate in decision-making and have access to justice in environmental matters, and acknowledging in this regard that citizens may need assistance in order to exercise their rights,

Recognizing that, in the field of the environment, improved access to information and public participation in decision-making enhance the quality and the implementation of decisions, contribute to public awareness of environmental issues, give the public the opportunity to express its concerns and enable public authorities to take due account of such concerns,

Aiming thereby to further the accountability of and transparency in decision-making and to strengthen public support for decisions on the environment,

Recognizing the desirability of transparency in all branches of government and inviting legislative bodies to implement the principles of this Convention in their proceedings,

Recognizing also that the public needs to be aware of the procedures for participation in environmental decision-making, have free access to them and know how to use them,

Recognizing further the importance of the respective roles that individual citizens, non-governmental organizations and the private sector can play in environmental protection,

Desiring to promote environmental education to further the understanding of the environment and sustainable development and to encourage widespread public awareness of, and participation in, decisions affecting the environment and sustainable development,

Noting, in this context, the importance of making use of the media and of electronic or other, future forms of communication,

Recognizing the importance of fully integrating environmental considerations in governmental decision-making and the consequent need for public authorities to be in possession of accurate, comprehensive and up-to-date environmental information,

Acknowledging that public authorities hold environmental information in the public interest,

Concerned that effective judicial mechanisms should be accessible to the public, including organizations, so that its legitimate interests are protected and the law is enforced,

Noting the importance of adequate product information being provided to consumers to enable them to make informed environmental choices,

Recognizing the concern of the public about the deliberate release of genetically modified organisms into the environment and the need for increased transparency and greater public participation in decision-making in this field,

Convinced that the implementation of this Convention will contribute to strengthening democracy in the region of the United Nations Economic Commission for Europe (ECE),

Conscious of the role played in this respect by ECE and recalling, inter alia, the ECE Guidelines on Access to Environmental Information and Public Participation in Environmental Decision-making endorsed in the Ministerial Declaration adopted at the Third Ministerial Conference "Environment for Europe" in Sofia, Bulgaria, on 25 October 1995,

Bearing in mind the relevant provisions in the Convention on Environmental Impact Assessment in a Transboundary Context, done at Espoo, Finland, on 25 February 1991, and the Convention on the Transboundary Effects of Industrial Accidents and the Convention on the Protection and Use of Transboundary Watercourses and International Lakes, both done at Helsinki on 17 March 1992, and other regional conventions,

Conscious that the adoption of this Convention will have contributed to the further strengthening of the "Environment for Europe" process and to the results of the Fourth Ministerial Conference in Aarhus, Denmark, in June 1998,

HAVE AGREED AS FOLLOWS:

Article 1

Objective

In order to contribute to the protection of the right of every person of present and future generations to live in an environment adequate to his or her health and well-being, each Party shall guarantee the rights of access to information, public participation in decision-making, and access to justice in environmental matters in accordance with the provisions of this Convention.

Article 2

Definitions

For the purposes of this Convention,

1. "Party" means, unless the text otherwise indicates, a Contracting Party to this Convention;
2. "Public authority" means:
   (a) Government at national, regional and other level;
   (b) Natural or legal persons performing public administrative functions under national law, including specific duties, activities or services in relation to the environment;
   (c) Any other natural or legal persons having public responsibilities or functions, or providing public services, in relation to the environment, under the control of a body or person falling within subparagraphs (a) or (b) above;

(d) The institutions of any regional economic integration organization referred to in article 17 which is a Party to this Convention.

This definition does not include bodies or institutions acting in a judicial or legislative capacity;

3. "Environmental information" means any information in written, visual, aural, electronic or any other material form on:

(a) The state of elements of the environment, such as air and atmosphere, water, soil, land, landscape and natural sites, biological diversity and its components, including genetically modified organisms, and the interaction among these elements;

(b) Factors, such as substances, energy, noise and radiation, and activities or measures, including administrative measures, environmental agreements, policies, legislation, plans and programmes, affecting or likely to affect the elements of the environment within the scope of subparagraph (a) above, and cost-benefit and other economic analyses and assumptions used in environmental decision-making;

(c) The state of human health and safety, conditions of human life, cultural sites and built structures, inasmuch as they are or may be affected by the state of the elements of the environment or, through these elements, by the factors, activities or measures referred to in subparagraph (b) above;

4. "The public" means one or more natural or legal persons, and, in accordance with national legislation or practice, their associations, organizations or groups;

5. "The public concerned" means the public affected or likely to be affected by, or having an interest in, the environmental decision-making; for the purposes of this definition, non-governmental organizations promoting environmental protection and meeting any requirements under national law shall be deemed to have an interest.

Article 3

General provisions

1. Each Party shall take the necessary legislative, regulatory and other measures, including measures to achieve compatibility between the provisions implementing the information, public participation and access-to-justice provisions in this Convention, as well as proper enforcement measures, to establish and maintain a clear, transparent and consistent framework to implement the provisions of this Convention.

2. Each Party shall endeavour to ensure that officials and authorities assist and provide guidance to the public in seeking access to information, in facilitating participation in decision-making and in seeking access to justice in environmental matters.

3. Each Party shall promote environmental education and environmental awareness among the public, especially on how to obtain access to information, to participate in decision-making and to obtain access to justice in environmental matters.

4. Each Party shall provide for appropriate recognition of and support to associations, organizations or groups promoting environmental protection and ensure that its national legal system is consistent with this obligation.

5. The provisions of this Convention shall not affect the right of a Party to maintain or introduce measures providing for broader access to information, more extensive public participation in decision-making and wider access to justice in environmental matters than required by this Convention.

6. This Convention shall not require any derogation from existing rights of access to information, public participation in decision-making and access to justice in environmental matters.

7. Each Party shall promote the application of the principles of this Convention in international environmental decision-making processes and within the framework of international organizations in matters relating to the environment.

8. Each Party shall ensure that persons exercising their rights in conformity with the provisions of this Convention shall not be penalized, persecuted or harassed in any way for their involvement. This provision shall not affect the powers of national courts to award reasonable costs in judicial proceedings.

9. Within the scope of the relevant provisions of this Convention, the public shall have access to information, have the possibility to participate in decision-making and have access to justice in environmental matters without discrimination as to citizenship, nationality or domicile and, in the case of a legal person, without discrimination as to where it has its registered seat or an effective centre of its activities.

Article 4

Access to environmental information

1. Each Party shall ensure that, subject to the following paragraphs of this article, public authorities, in response to a request for environmental information, make such information available to the public, within the framework of national legislation, including, where requested and subject to subparagraph (b) below, copies of the actual documentation containing or comprising such information:

(a) Without an interest having to be stated;

(b) In the form requested unless:

 (i) It is reasonable for the public authority to make it available in another form, in which case reasons shall be given for making it available in that form; or

 (ii) The information is already publicly available in another form.

2. The environmental information referred to in paragraph 1 above shall be made available as soon as possible and at the latest within one month after the request has been submitted, unless the volume and the complexity of the information justify an extension of this period up to two months after the request. The applicant shall be informed of any extension and of the reasons justifying it.

3. A request for environmental information may be refused if:

(a) The public authority to which the request is addressed does not hold the environmental information requested;

(b) The request is manifestly unreasonable or formulated in too general a manner; or

(c) The request concerns material in the course of completion or concerns internal communications of public authorities where such an exemption is provided for in national law or customary practice, taking into account the public interest served by disclosure.

4. A request for environmental information may be refused if the disclosure would adversely affect:

(a) The confidentiality of the proceedings of public authorities, where such confidentiality is provided for under national law;

(b) International relations, national defence or public security;

(c) The course of justice, the ability of a person to receive a fair trial or the ability of a public authority to conduct an enquiry of a criminal or disciplinary nature;

(d) The confidentiality of commercial and industrial information, where such confidentiality is protected by law in order to protect a legitimate economic interest. Within this framework, information on emissions which is relevant for the protection of the environment shall be disclosed;

(e) Intellectual property rights;

(f) The confidentiality of personal data and/or files relating to a natural person where that person has not consented to the disclosure of the information to the public, where such confidentiality is provided for in national law;

(g) The interests of a third party which has supplied the information requested without that party being under or capable of being put under a legal obligation to do so, and where that party does not consent to the release of the material; or

(h) The environment to which the information relates, such as the breeding sites of rare species.

The aforementioned grounds for refusal shall be interpreted in a restrictive way, taking into account the public interest served by disclosure and taking into account whether the information requested relates to emissions into the environment.

5. Where a public authority does not hold the environmental information requested, this public authority shall, as promptly as possible, inform the applicant of the public authority to which it believes it is possible to apply for the information requested or transfer the request to that authority and inform the applicant accordingly.

6. Each Party shall ensure that, if information exempted from disclosure under paragraphs 3 (c) and 4 above can be separated out without prejudice to the confidentiality of the information exempted, public authorities make available the remainder of the environmental information that has been requested.

7. A refusal of a request shall be in writing if the request was in writing or the applicant so requests. A refusal shall state the reasons for the refusal and give information on access to the review procedure provided for in accordance with article 9. The refusal shall be made as soon as possible and at the latest within one month, unless the complexity of the information justifies an extension of this period up to two months after the request. The applicant shall be informed of any extension and of the reasons justifying it.

8. Each Party may allow its public authorities to make a charge for supplying information, but such charge shall not exceed a reasonable amount. Public authorities intending to make such a charge for supplying information shall make available to applicants a schedule of charges which may be levied, indicating the circumstances in which they may be levied or waived and when the supply of information is conditional on the advance payment of such a charge.

Article 5

Collection and dissemination of environmental information

1. Each Party shall ensure that:

(a) Public authorities possess and update environmental information which is relevant to their functions;

(b) Mandatory systems are established so that there is an adequate flow of information to public authorities about proposed and existing activities which may significantly affect the environment;

(c) In the event of any imminent threat to human health or the environment, whether caused by human activities or due to natural causes, all information which could enable the public to take measures to prevent or mitigate harm arising from the threat and is held by a public authority is disseminated immediately and without delay to members of the public who may be affected.

2. Each Party shall ensure that, within the framework of national legislation, the way in which public authorities make environmental information available to the public is transparent and that environmental information is effectively accessible, inter alia, by:

(a) Providing sufficient information to the public about the type and scope of environmental information held by the relevant public authorities, the basic terms and conditions under which such information is made available and accessible, and the process by which it can be obtained;

(b) Establishing and maintaining practical arrangements, such as:
   (i) Publicly accessible lists, registers or files;
   (ii) Requiring officials to support the public in seeking access to information under this Convention; and
   (iii) The identification of points of contact; and

(c) Providing access to the environmental information contained in lists, registers or files as referred to in subparagraph (b) (i) above free of charge.

3. Each Party shall ensure that environmental information progressively becomes available in electronic databases which are easily accessible to the public through public telecommunications networks. Information accessible in this form should include:

(a) Reports on the state of the environment, as referred to in paragraph 4 below;

(b) Texts of legislation on or relating to the environment;

(c) As appropriate, policies, plans and programmes on or relating to the environment, and environmental agreements; and

(d) Other information, to the extent that the availability of such information in this form would facilitate the application of national law implementing this Convention, provided that such information is already available in electronic form.

4. Each Party shall, at regular intervals not exceeding three or four years, publish and disseminate a national report on the state of the environment, including information on the quality of the environment and information on pressures on the environment.

5. Each Party shall take measures within the framework of its legislation for the purpose of disseminating, inter alia:

(a) Legislation and policy documents such as documents on strategies, policies, programmes and action plans relating to the environment, and progress reports on their implementation, prepared at various levels of government;

(b) International treaties, conventions and agreements on environmental issues; and

(c) Other significant international documents on environmental issues, as appropriate.

6. Each Party shall encourage operators whose activities have a significant impact on the environment to inform the public regularly of the environmental impact of their activities and products, where appropriate within the framework of voluntary eco-labelling or eco-auditing schemes or by other means.

7. Each Party shall:

(a) Publish the facts and analyses of facts which it considers relevant and important in framing major environmental policy proposals;

(b) Publish, or otherwise make accessible, available explanatory material on its dealings with the public in matters falling within the scope of this Convention; and

(c) Provide in an appropriate form information on the performance of public functions or the provision of public services relating to the environment by government at all levels.

8. Each Party shall develop mechanisms with a view to ensuring that sufficient product information is made available to the public in a manner which enables consumers to make informed environmental choices.

9. Each Party shall take steps to establish progressively, taking into account international processes where appropriate, a coherent, nationwide system of pollution inventories or registers on a structured, computerized and publicly accessible database compiled through standardized reporting. Such a system may include inputs, releases and transfers of a specified range of substances and products, including water, energy and resource use, from a specified range of activities to environmental media and to on-site and offsite treatment and disposal sites.

10. Nothing in this article may prejudice the right of Parties to refuse to disclose certain environmental information in accordance with article 4, paragraphs 3 and 4.

Article 6

Public participation in decisions on specific activities

1. Each Party:
(a) Shall apply the provisions of this article with respect to decisions on whether to permit proposed activities listed in annex I;
(b) Shall, in accordance with its national law, also apply the provisions of this article to decisions on proposed activities not listed in annex I which may have a significant effect on the environment. To this end, Parties shall determine whether such a proposed activity is subject to these provisions; and
(c) May decide, on a case-by-case basis if so provided under national law, not to apply the provisions of this article to proposed activities serving national defence purposes, if that Party deems that such application would have an adverse effect on these purposes.

2. The public concerned shall be informed, either by public notice or individually as appropriate, early in an environmental decision-making procedure, and in an adequate, timely and effective manner, inter alia, of:
(a) The proposed activity and the application on which a decision will be taken;
(b) The nature of possible decisions or the draft decision;
(c) The public authority responsible for making the decision;
(d) The envisaged procedure, including, as and when this information can be provided:
    (i) The commencement of the procedure;
    (ii) The opportunities for the public to participate;
    (iii) The time and venue of any envisaged public hearing;
    (iv) An indication of the public authority from which relevant information can be obtained and where the relevant information has been deposited for examination by the public;
    (v) An indication of the relevant public authority or any other official body to which comments or questions can be submitted and of the time schedule for transmittal of comments or questions; and
    (vi) An indication of what environmental information relevant to the proposed activity is available; and
(e) The fact that the activity is subject to a national or transboundary environmental impact assessment procedure.

3. The public participation procedures shall include reasonable time-frames for the different phases, allowing sufficient time for informing the public in accordance with paragraph 2 above and for the public to prepare and participate effectively during the environmental decision-making.

4. Each Party shall provide for early public participation, when all options are open and effective public participation can take place.

5. Each Party should, where appropriate, encourage prospective applicants to identify the public concerned, to enter into discussions, and to provide information regarding the objectives of their application before applying for a permit.

6. Each Party shall require the competent public authorities to give the public concerned access for examination, upon request where so required under national law, free of charge and as soon as it becomes available, to all information relevant to the decision-making referred to in this article that is available at the time of the public participation procedure, without prejudice to the right of Parties to refuse to disclose certain information in accordance with article 4, paragraphs 3 and 4. The relevant information shall include at least, and without prejudice to the provisions of article 4:
(a) A description of the site and the physical and technical characteristics of the proposed activity, including an estimate of the expected residues and emissions;
(b) A description of the significant effects of the proposed activity on the environment;
(c) A description of the measures envisaged to prevent and/or reduce the effects, including emissions;

(d) A non-technical summary of the above;
(e) An outline of the main alternatives studied by the applicant; and
(f) In accordance with national legislation, the main reports and advice issued to the public authority at the time when the public concerned shall be informed in accordance with paragraph 2 above.

7. Procedures for public participation shall allow the public to submit, in writing or, as appropriate, at a public hearing or inquiry with the applicant, any comments, information, analyses or opinions that it considers relevant to the proposed activity.

8. Each Party shall ensure that in the decision due account is taken of the outcome of the public participation.

9. Each Party shall ensure that, when the decision has been taken by the public authority, the public is promptly informed of the decision in accordance with the appropriate procedures. Each Party shall make accessible to the public the text of the decision along with the reasons and considerations on which the decision is based.

10. Each Party shall ensure that, when a public authority reconsiders or updates the operating conditions for an activity referred to in paragraph 1, the provisions of paragraphs 2 to 9 of this article are applied mutatis mutandis, and where appropriate.

11. Each Party shall, within the framework of its national law, apply, to the extent feasible and appropriate, provisions of this article to decisions on whether to permit the deliberate release of genetically modified organisms into the environment.

Article 7

Public participation concerning plans, programmes and policies relating to the environment

Each Party shall make appropriate practical and/or other provisions for the public to participate during the preparation of plans and programmes relating to the environment, within a transparent and fair framework, having provided the necessary information to the public. Within this framework, article 6, paragraphs 3, 4 and 8, shall be applied. The public which may participate shall be identified by the relevant public authority, taking into account the objectives of this Convention. To the extent appropriate, each Party shall endeavour to provide opportunities for public participation in the preparation of policies relating to the environment.

Article 8

Public participation during the preparation of executive regulations and/or generally applicable legally binding normative instruments

Each Party shall strive to promote effective public participation at an appropriate stage, and while options are still open, during the preparation by public authorities of executive regulations and other generally applicable legally binding rules that may have a significant effect on the environment. To this end, the following steps should be taken:
(a) Time-frames sufficient for effective participation should be fixed;
(b) Draft rules should be published or otherwise made publicly available; and
(c) The public should be given the opportunity to comment, directly or through representative consultative bodies. The result of the public participation shall be taken into account as far as possible.

Article 9

Access to justice

1. Each Party shall, within the framework of its national legislation, ensure that any person who considers that his or her request for information under article 4 has been ignored,

wrongfully refused, whether in part or in full, inadequately answered, or otherwise not dealt with in accordance with the provisions of that article, has access to a review procedure before a court of law or another independent and impartial body established by law.

In the circumstances where a Party provides for such a review by a court of law, it shall ensure that such a person also has access to an expeditious procedure established by law that is free of charge or inexpensive for reconsideration by a public authority or review by an independent and impartial body other than a court of law.

Final decisions under this paragraph 1 shall be binding on the public authority holding the information. Reasons shall be stated in writing, at least where access to information is refused under this paragraph.

2. Each Party shall, within the framework of its national legislation, ensure that members of the public concerned

(a) Having a sufficient interest or, alternatively,

(b) Maintaining impairment of a right, where the administrative procedural law of a Party requires this as a precondition, have access to a review procedure before a court of law and/or another independent and impartial body established by law, to challenge the substantive and procedural legality of any decision, act or omission subject to the provisions of article 6 and, where so provided for under national law and without prejudice to paragraph 3 below, of other relevant provisions of this Convention.

What constitutes a sufficient interest and impairment of a right shall be determined in accordance with the requirements of national law and consistently with the objective of giving the public concerned wide access to justice within the scope of this Convention. To this end, the interest of any non-governmental organization meeting the requirements referred to in article 2, paragraph 5, shall be deemed sufficient for the purpose of subparagraph (a) above. Such organizations shall also be deemed to have rights capable of being impaired for the purpose of subparagraph (b) above.

The provisions of this paragraph 2 shall not exclude the possibility of a preliminary review procedure before an administrative authority and shall not affect the requirement of exhaustion of administrative review procedures prior to recourse to judicial review procedures, where such a requirement exists under national law.

3. In addition and without prejudice to the review procedures referred to in paragraphs 1 and 2 above, each Party shall ensure that, where they meet the criteria, if any, laid down in its national law, members of the public have access to administrative or judicial procedures to challenge acts and omissions by private persons and public authorities which contravene provisions of its national law relating to the environment.

4. In addition and without prejudice to paragraph 1 above, the procedures referred to in paragraphs 1, 2 and 3 above shall provide adequate and effective remedies, including injunctive relief as appropriate, and be fair, equitable, timely and not prohibitively expensive. Decisions under this article shall be given or recorded in writing. Decisions of courts, and whenever possible of other bodies, shall be publicly accessible.

5. In order to further the effectiveness of the provisions of this article, each Party shall ensure that information is provided to the public on access to administrative and judicial review procedures and shall consider the establishment of appropriate assistance mechanisms to remove or reduce financial and other barriers to access to justice.

Article 10

Meeting of the Parties

1. The first meeting of the Parties shall be convened no later than one year after the date of the entry into force of this Convention. Thereafter, an ordinary meeting of the Parties shall be held at least once every two years, unless otherwise decided by the Parties, or at the written

request of any Party, provided that, within six months of the request being communicated to all Parties by the Executive Secretary of the Economic Commission for Europe, the said request is supported by at least one third of the Parties.

2. At their meetings, the Parties shall keep under continuous review the implementation of this Convention on the basis of regular reporting by the Parties, and, with this purpose in mind, shall:

(a) Review the policies for and legal and methodological approaches to access to information, public participation in decision-making and access to justice in environmental matters, with a view to further improving them;
(b) Exchange information regarding experience gained in concluding and implementing bilateral and multilateral agreements or other arrangements having relevance to the purposes of this Convention and to which one or more of the Parties are a party;
(c) Seek, where appropriate, the services of relevant ECE bodies and other competent international bodies and specific committees in all aspects pertinent to the achievement of the purposes of this Convention;
(d) Establish any subsidiary bodies as they deem necessary;
(e) Prepare, where appropriate, protocols to this Convention;
(f) Consider and adopt proposals for amendments to this Convention in accordance with the provisions of article 14;
(g) Consider and undertake any additional action that may be required for the achievement of the purposes of this Convention;
(h) At their first meeting, consider and by consensus adopt rules of procedure for their meetings and the meetings of subsidiary bodies;
(i) At their first meeting, review their experience in implementing the provisions of article 5, paragraph 9, and consider what steps are necessary to develop further the system referred to in that paragraph, taking into account international processes and developments, including the elaboration of an appropriate instrument concerning pollution release and transfer registers or inventories which could be annexed to this Convention.

3. The Meeting of the Parties may, as necessary, consider establishing financial arrangements on a consensus basis.

4. The United Nations, its specialized agencies and the International Atomic Energy Agency, as well as any State or regional economic integration organization entitled under article 17 to sign this Convention but which is not a Party to this Convention, and any intergovernmental organization qualified in the fields to which this Convention relates, shall be entitled to participate as observers in the meetings of the Parties.

5. Any non-governmental organization, qualified in the fields to which this Convention relates, which has informed the Executive Secretary of the Economic Commission for Europe of its wish to be represented at a meeting of the Parties shall be entitled to participate as an observer unless at least one third of the Parties present in the meeting raise objections.

6. For the purposes of paragraphs 4 and 5 above, the rules of procedure referred to in paragraph 2 (h) above shall provide for practical arrangements for the admittance procedure and other relevant terms.

Article 11

Right to vote

1. Except as provided for in paragraph 2 below, each Party to this Convention shall have one vote.

2. Regional economic integration organizations, in matters within their competence, shall exercise their right to vote with a number of votes equal to the number of their member States

which are Parties to this Convention. Such organizations shall not exercise their right to vote if their member States exercise theirs, and vice versa.

Article 12

Secretariat

The Executive Secretary of the Economic Commission for Europe shall carry out the following secretariat functions:
(a) The convening and preparing of meetings of the Parties;
(b) The transmission to the Parties of reports and other information received in accordance with the provisions of this Convention; and
(c) Such other functions as may be determined by the Parties.

Article 13

Annexes

The annexes to this Convention shall constitute an integral part thereof.

Article 14

Amendments to the Convention

1. Any Party may propose amendments to this Convention.

2. The text of any proposed amendment to this Convention shall be submitted in writing to the Executive Secretary of the Economic Commission for Europe, who shall communicate it to all Parties at least ninety days before the meeting of the Parties at which it is proposed for adoption.

3. The Parties shall make every effort to reach agreement on any proposed amendment to this Convention by consensus. If all efforts at consensus have been exhausted, and no agreement reached, the amendment shall as a last resort be adopted by a three-fourths majority vote of the Parties present and voting at the meeting.

4. Amendments to this Convention adopted in accordance with paragraph 3 above shall be communicated by the Depositary to all Parties for ratification, approval or acceptance. Amendments to this Convention other than those to an annex shall enter into force for Parties having ratified, approved or accepted them on the ninetieth day after the receipt by the Depositary of notification of their ratification, approval or acceptance by at least three fourths of these Parties. Thereafter they shall enter into force for any other Party on the ninetieth day after that Party deposits its instrument of ratification, approval or acceptance of the amendments.

5. Any Party that is unable to approve an amendment to an annex to this Convention shall so notify the Depositary in writing within twelve months from the date of the communication of the adoption. The Depositary shall without delay notify all Parties of any such notification received. A Party may at any time substitute an acceptance for its previous notification and, upon deposit of an instrument of acceptance with the Depositary, the amendments to such an annex shall become effective for that Party.

6. On the expiry of twelve months from the date of its communication by the Depositary as provided for in paragraph 4 above an amendment to an annex shall become effective for those Parties which have not submitted a notification to the Depositary in accordance with the provisions of paragraph 5 above, provided that not more than one third of the Parties have submitted such a notification.

7. For the purposes of this article, "Parties present and voting" means Parties present and casting an affirmative or negative vote.

Article 15

Review of compliance

The Meeting of the Parties shall establish, on a consensus basis, optional arrangements of a non-confrontational, non-judicial and consultative nature for reviewing compliance with the provisions of this Convention. These arrangements shall allow for appropriate public involvement and may include the option of considering communications from members of the public on matters related to this Convention.

Article 16

Settlement of disputes

1. If a dispute arises between two or more Parties about the interpretation or application of this Convention, they shall seek a solution by negotiation or by any other means of dispute settlement acceptable to the parties to the dispute.

2. When signing, ratifying, accepting, approving or acceding to this Convention, or at any time thereafter, a Party may declare in writing to the Depositary that, for a dispute not resolved in accordance with paragraph 1 above, it accepts one or both of the following means of dispute settlement as compulsory in relation to any Party accepting the same obligation:
(a) Submission of the dispute to the International Court of Justice;
(b) Arbitration in accordance with the procedure set out in annex II.

3. If the parties to the dispute have accepted both means of dispute settlement referred to in paragraph 2 above, the dispute may be submitted only to the International Court of Justice, unless the parties agree otherwise.

Article 17

Signature

This Convention shall be open for signature at Aarhus (Denmark) on 25 June 1998, and thereafter at United Nations Headquarters in New York until 21 December 1998, by States members of the Economic Commission for Europe as well as States having consultative status with the Economic Commission for Europe pursuant to paragraphs 8 and 11 of Economic and Social Council resolution 36 (IV) of 28 March 1947, and by regional economic integration organizations constituted by sovereign States members of the Economic Commission for Europe to which their member States have transferred competence over matters governed by this Convention, including the competence to enter into treaties in respect of these matters.

Article 18

Depositary

The Secretary-General of the United Nations shall act as the Depositary of this Convention.

Article 19

Ratification, acceptance, approval and accession

1. This Convention shall be subject to ratification, acceptance or approval by signatory States and regional economic integration organizations.

2. This Convention shall be open for accession as from 22 December 1998 by the States and regional economic integration organizations referred to in article 17.

3. Any other State, not referred to in paragraph 2 above, that is a Member of the United Nations may accede to the Convention upon approval by the Meeting of the Parties.

4. Any organization referred to in article 17 which becomes a Party to this Convention without any of its member States being a Party shall be bound by all the obligations under this Convention. If one or more of such an organization's member States is a Party to this Convention, the organization and its member States shall decide on their respective responsibilities for the performance of their obligations under this Convention. In such cases, the organization and the member States shall not be entitled to exercise rights under this Convention concurrently.

5. In their instruments of ratification, acceptance, approval or accession, the regional economic integration organizations referred to in article 17 shall declare the extent of their competence with respect to the matters governed by this Convention. These organizations shall also inform the Depositary of any substantial modification to the extent of their competence.

Article 20

Entry into force

1. This Convention shall enter into force on the ninetieth day after the date of deposit of the sixteenth instrument of ratification, acceptance, approval or accession.

2. For the purposes of paragraph 1 above, any instrument deposited by a regional economic integration organization shall not be counted as additional to those deposited by States members of such an organization.

3. For each State or organization referred to in article 17 which ratifies, accepts or approves this Convention or accedes thereto after the deposit of the sixteenth instrument of ratification, acceptance, approval or accession, the Convention shall enter into force on the ninetieth day after the date of deposit by such State or organization of its instrument of ratification, acceptance, approval or accession.

Article 21

Withdrawal

At any time after three years from the date on which this Convention has come into force with respect to a Party, that Party may withdraw from the Convention by giving written notification to the Depositary. Any such withdrawal shall take effect on the ninetieth day after the date of its receipt by the Depositary.

Article 22

Authentic texts

The original of this Convention, of which the English, French and Russian texts are equally authentic, shall be deposited with the Secretary-General of the United Nations.

IN WITNESS WHEREOF the undersigned, being duly authorized thereto, have signed this Convention.

DONE at Aarhus (Denmark), this twenty-fifth day of June, one thousand nine hundred and ninety-eight.

ANNEX I
LIST OF ACTIVITIES REFERRED TO IN ARTICLE 6, PARAGRAPH 1 (A)

1. Energy sector:
— Mineral oil and gas refineries;
— Installations for gasification and liquefaction;

- Thermal power stations and other combustion installations with a heat input of 50 megawatts (MW)or more;
- Coke ovens;
- Nuclear power stations and other nuclear reactors including the dismantling or decommissioning of such power stations or reactors[1] (except research installations for the production and conversion of fissionable and fertile materials whose maximum power does not exceed 1 kW continuous thermal load);
- Installations for the reprocessing of irradiated nuclear fuel;
- Installations designed:
  - For the production or enrichment of nuclear fuel;
  - For the processing of irradiated nuclear fuel or high-level radioactive waste;
  - For the final disposal of irradiated nuclear fuel;
  - Solely for the final disposal of radioactive waste;
  - Solely for the storage (planned for more than 10 years) of irradiated nuclear fuels or radioactive waste in a different site than the production site.

2. Production and processing of metals:
- Metal ore (including sulphide ore) roasting or sintering installations;
- Installations for the production of pig-iron or steel (primary or secondary fusion) including continuous casting, with a capacity exceeding 2.5 tons per hour;
- Installations for the processing of ferrous metals:
  (i) Hot-rolling mills with a capacity exceeding 20 tons of crude steel per hour;
  (ii) Smitheries with hammers the energy of which exceeds 50 kilojoules per hammer, where the calorific power used exceeds 20 MW;
  (iii) Application of protective fused metal coats with an input exceeding 2 tons of crude steel per hour;
- Ferrous metal foundries with a production capacity exceeding 20 tons per day;
- Installations:
  (i) For the production of non-ferrous crude metals from ore, concentrates or secondary raw materials by metallurgical, chemical or electrolytic processes;
  (ii) For the smelting, including the alloying, of non-ferrous metals, including recovered products (refining, foundry casting, etc.), with a melting capacity exceeding 4 tons per day for lead and cadmium or 20 tons per day for all other metals;
- Installations for surface treatment of metals and plastic materials using an electrolytic or chemical process where the volume of the treatment vats exceeds 30 m^3.

3. Mineral industry:
- Installations for the production of cement clinker in rotary kilns with a production capacity exceeding 500 tons per day or lime in rotary kilns with a production capacity exceeding 50 tons per day or in other furnaces with a production capacity exceeding 50 tons per day;
- Installations for the production of asbestos and the manufacture of asbestos-based products;
- Installations for the manufacture of glass including glass fibre with a melting capacity exceeding 20 tons per day;
- Installations for melting mineral substances including the production of mineral fibres with a melting capacity exceeding 20 tons per day;
- Installations for the manufacture of ceramic products by firing, in particular roofing tiles, bricks, refractory bricks, tiles, stoneware or porcelain, with a production capacity exceeding 75 tons per day, and/or with a kiln capacity exceeding 4 m^3 and with a setting density per kiln exceeding 300 kg/m^3.

4. Chemical industry: Production within the meaning of the categories of activities contained in this paragraph means the production on an industrial scale by chemical processing of substances or groups of substances listed in subparagraphs (a) to (g):

(a) Chemical installations for the production of basic organic chemicals, such as:
  (i) Simple hydrocarbons (linear or cyclic, saturated or unsaturated, aliphatic or aromatic);
  (ii) Oxygen-containing hydrocarbons such as alcohols, aldehydes, ketones, carboxylic acids, esters, acetates, ethers, peroxides, epoxy resins;
  (iii) Sulphurous hydrocarbons;
  (iv) Nitrogenous hydrocarbons such as amines, amides, nitrous compounds, nitro compounds or nitrate compounds, nitriles, cyanates, isocyanates;
  (v) Phosphorus-containing hydrocarbons;
  (vi) Halogenic hydrocarbons;
  (vii) Organometallic compounds;
  (viii) Basic plastic materials (polymers, synthetic fibres and cellulose-based fibres);
  (ix) Synthetic rubbers;
  (x) Dyes and pigments;
  (xi) Surface-active agents and surfactants;

(b) Chemical installations for the production of basic inorganic chemicals, such as:
  (i) Gases, such as ammonia, chlorine or hydrogen chloride, fluorine or hydrogen fluoride, carbon oxides, sulphur compounds, nitrogen oxides, hydrogen, sulphur dioxide, carbonyl chloride;
  (ii) Acids, such as chromic acid, hydrofluoric acid, phosphoric acid, nitric acid, hydrochloric acid, sulphuric acid, oleum, sulphurous acids;
  (iii) Bases, such as ammonium hydroxide, potassium hydroxide, sodium hydroxide;
  (iv) Salts, such as ammonium chloride, potassium chlorate, potassium carbonate, sodium carbonate, perborate, silver nitrate;
  (v) Non-metals, metal oxides or other inorganic compounds such as calcium carbide, silicon, silicon carbide;

(c) Chemical installations for the production of phosphorous-, nitrogen- or potassium-based fertilizers (simple or compound fertilizers);

(d) Chemical installations for the production of basic plant health products and of biocides;

(e) Installations using a chemical or biological process for the production of basic pharmaceutical products;

(f) Chemical installations for the production of explosives;

(g) Chemical installations in which chemical or biological processing is used for the production of protein feed additives, ferments and other protein substances.

5. Waste management:

— Installations for the incineration, recovery, chemical treatment or landfill of hazardous waste;

— Installations for the incineration of municipal waste with a capacity exceeding 3 tons per hour;

— Installations for the disposal of non-hazardous waste with a capacity exceeding 50 tons per day;

— Landfills receiving more than 10 tons per day or with a total capacity exceeding 25 000 tons, excluding landfills of inert waste.

6. Waste-water treatment plants with a capacity exceeding 150 000 population equivalent.

7. Industrial plants for the:

(a) Production of pulp from timber or similar fibrous materials;

(b) Production of paper and board with a production capacity exceeding 20 tons per day.

8.

(a) Construction of lines for long-distance railway traffic and of airports[2] with a basic runway length of 2 100 m or more;

(b) Construction of motorways and express roads[3];

(c) Construction of a new road of four or more lanes, or realignment and/or widening of an existing road of two lanes or less so as to provide four or more lanes, where such new road, or realigned and/or widened section of road, would be 10 km or more in a continuous length.

9.
(a) Inland waterways and ports for inland-waterway traffic which permit the passage of vessels of over 1 350 tons;
(b) Trading ports, piers for loading and unloading connected to land and outside ports (excluding ferry piers) which can take vessels of over 1 350 tons.

10. Groundwater abstraction or artificial groundwater recharge schemes where the annual volume of water abstracted or recharged is equivalent to or exceeds 10 million cubic metres.

11.
(a) Works for the transfer of water resources between river basins where this transfer aims at preventing possible shortages of water and where the amount of water transferred exceeds 100 million cubic metres/year;
(b) In all other cases, works for the transfer of water resources between river basins where the multiannual average flow of the basin of abstraction exceeds 2 000 million cubic metres/year and where the amount of water transferred exceeds 5% of this flow. In both cases transfers of piped drinking water are excluded.

12. Extraction of petroleum and natural gas for commercial purposes where the amount extracted exceeds 500 tons/day in the case of petroleum and 500 000 cubic metres/day in the case of gas.

13. Dams and other installations designed for the holding back or permanent storage of water, where a new or additional amount of water held back or stored exceeds 10 million cubic metres.

14. Pipelines for the transport of gas, oil or chemicals with a diameter of more than 800 mm and a length of more than 40 km.

15. Installations for the intensive rearing of poultry or pigs with more than:
(a) 40 000 places for poultry;
(b) 2 000 places for production pigs (over 30 kg); or
(c) 750 places for sows.

16. Quarries and opencast mining where the surface of the site exceeds 25 hectares, or peat extraction, where the surface of the site exceeds 150 hectares.

17. Construction of overhead electrical power lines with a voltage of 220 kV or more and a length of more than 15 km.

18. Installations for the storage of petroleum, petrochemical, or chemical products with a capacity of 200 000 tons or more.

19. Other activities:
— Plants for the pretreatment (operations such as washing, bleaching, mercerization) or dyeing of fibres or textiles where the treatment capacity exceeds 10 tons per day;
— Plants for the tanning of hides and skins where the treatment capacity exceeds 12 tons of finished products per day;
—
  (a) Slaughterhouses with a carcass production capacity greater than 50 tons per day;
  (b) Treatment and processing intended for the production of food products from:
    (i) Animal raw materials (other than milk) with a finished product production capacity greater than 75 tons per day;
    (ii) Vegetable raw materials with a finished product production capacity greater than 300 tons per day (average value on a quarterly basis);
  (c) Treatment and processing of milk, the quantity of milk received being greater than 200 tons per day (average value on an annual basis);

— Installations for the disposal or recycling of animal carcasses and animal waste with a treatment capacity exceeding 10 tons per day;
— Installations for the surface treatment of substances, objects or products using organic solvents, in particular for dressing, printing, coating, degreasing, waterproofing, sizing, painting, cleaning or impregnating, with a consumption capacity of more than 150 kg per hour or more than 200 tons per year;
— Installations for the production of carbon (hard-burnt coal) or electrographite by means of incineration or graphitization.

20. Any activity not covered by paragraphs 1-19 above where public participation is provided for under an environmental impact assessment procedure in accordance with national legislation.

21. The provision of article 6, paragraph 1 (a) of this Convention, does not apply to any of the above projects undertaken exclusively or mainly for research, development and testing of new methods or products for less than two years unless they would be likely to cause a significant adverse effect on environment or health.

22. Any change to or extension of activities, where such a change or extension in itself meets the criteria/thresholds set out in this annex, shall be subject to article 6, paragraph 1 (a) of this Convention. Any other change or extension of activities shall be subject to article 6, paragraph 1 (b) of this Convention.

Notes

1. Nuclear power stations and other nuclear reactors cease to be such an installation when all nuclear fuel and other radioactively contaminated elements have been removed permanently from the installation site.
2. For the purposes of this Convention, "airport" means an airport which complies with the definition in the 1944 Chicago Convention setting up the International Civil Aviation Organization (Annex 14).
3. For the purposes of this Convention, "express road" means a road which complies with the definition in the European Agreement on Main International Traffic Arteries of 15 November 1975.

ANNEX II
ARBITRATION

1. In the event of a dispute being submitted for arbitration pursuant to article 16, paragraph 2, of this Convention, a party or parties shall notify the secretariat of the subject matter of arbitration and indicate, in particular, the articles of this Convention whose interpretation or application is at issue. The secretariat shall forward the information received to all Parties to this Convention.

2. The arbitral tribunal shall consist of three members. Both the claimant party or parties and the other party or parties to the dispute shall appoint an arbitrator, and the two arbitrators so appointed shall designate by common agreement the third arbitrator, who shall be the president of the arbitral tribunal. The latter shall not be a national of one of the parties to the dispute, nor have his or her usual place of residence in the territory of one of these parties, nor be employed by any of them, nor have dealt with the case in any other capacity.

3. If the president of the arbitral tribunal has not been designated within two months of the appointment of the second arbitrator, the Executive Secretary of the Economic Commission for Europe shall, at the request of either party to the dispute, designate the president within a further two-month period.

4. If one of the parties to the dispute does not appoint an arbitrator within two months of the receipt of the request, the other party may so inform the Executive Secretary of the Economic Commission for Europe, who shall designate the president of the arbitral tribunal within a

further two-month period. Upon designation, the president of the arbitral tribunal shall request the party which has not appointed an arbitrator to do so within two months. If it fails to do so within that period, the president shall so inform the Executive Secretary of the Economic Commission for Europe, who shall make this appointment within a further two-month period.

5. The arbitral tribunal shall render its decision in accordance with international law and the provisions of this Convention.

6. Any arbitral tribunal constituted under the provisions set out in this annex shall draw up its own rules of procedure.

7. The decisions of the arbitral tribunal, both on procedure and on substance, shall be taken by majority vote of its members.

8. The tribunal may take all appropriate measures to establish the facts.

9. The parties to the dispute shall facilitate the work of the arbitral tribunal and, in particular, using all means at their disposal, shall:
(a) Provide it with all relevant documents, facilities and information;
(b) Enable it, where necessary, to call witnesses or experts and receive their evidence.

10. The parties and the arbitrators shall protect the confidentiality of any information that they receive in confidence during the proceedings of the arbitral tribunal.

11. The arbitral tribunal may, at the request of one of the parties, recommend interim measures of protection.

12. If one of the parties to the dispute does not appear before the arbitral tribunal or fails to defend its case, the other party may request the tribunal to continue the proceedings and to render its final decision. Absence of a party or failure of a party to defend its case shall not constitute a bar to the proceedings.

13. The arbitral tribunal may hear and determine counter-claims arising directly out of the subject matter of the dispute.

14. Unless the arbitral tribunal determines otherwise because of the particular circumstances of the case, the expenses of the tribunal, including the remuneration of its members, shall be borne by the parties to the dispute in equal shares. The tribunal shall keep a record of all its expenses, and shall furnish a final statement thereof to the parties.

15. Any Party to this Convention which has an interest of a legal nature in the subject matter of the dispute, and which may be affected by a decision in the case, may intervene in the proceedings with the consent of the tribunal.

16. The arbitral tribunal shall render its award within five months of the date on which it is established, unless it finds it necessary to extend the time limit for a period which should not exceed five months.

17. The award of the arbitral tribunal shall be accompanied by a statement of reasons. It shall be final and binding upon all parties to the dispute. The award will be transmitted by the arbitral tribunal to the parties to the dispute and to the secretariat. The secretariat will forward the information received to all Parties to this Convention.

18. Any dispute which may arise between the parties concerning the interpretation or execution of the award may be submitted by either party to the arbitral tribunal which made the award or, if the latter cannot be seized thereof, to another tribunal constituted for this purpose in the same manner as the first.

STOCKHOLM CONVENTION ON PERSISTENT ORGANIC POLLUTANTS (POPS)

22 May 2001

INTRODUCTION

The Stockholm Convention on Persistent Organic Pollutants was adopted at a Conference of Plenipotentiaries on 22 May 2001 in Stockholm, Sweden. The Convention entered into force on 17 May 2004, ninety (90) days after submission of the fiftieth instrument of ratification, acceptance, approval or accession in respect of the Convention.

Article 18 of the Convention requires the Conference of the Parties to adopt arbitration and conciliation procedures to govern the settlement of disputes between Parties to the Convention. At its fi rst meeting, held from 2 to 6 May 2005 in Punta del Este, Uruguay, the Conference of the Parties adopted decision SC-1/2, by which it established such procedures. The procedures are set out in a new annex to the Convention, Annex G, Part I of which sets forth the arbitration procedure and Part II of which sets forth the conciliation procedure. Annex G entered into force on 31 October 2007, i.e. one (1) year after the date of the communication of its adoption by the depositary for the Convention.

At its fourth meeting, held from 4 to 8 May 2009 in Geneva, Switzerland, the Conference of the Parties, by its decisions SC-4/10 to SC-4/18, amended Annexes A, B and C to the Convention to include additional chemicals:

alpha hexachlorocyclohexane; beta hexachlorocyclohexane; chlordecone; hexabromobiphenyl; hexabromodiphenyl ether and heptabromodiphenyl ether; lindane; pentachlorobenzene; perfl uorooctane sulfonic acid, its salts and perfl uorooctane sulfonyl fluoride; and tetrabromodiphenyl ether and pentabromodiphenyl ether. On 26 August 2010, i.e. one (1) year after the date of the communication of their adoption by the depositary for the Convention, the amendments to the Annexes entered into force for all Parties, except for those that had submitted i) a notification of non-acceptance in accordance with the provisions of paragraph 3 (b) of Article 22, or ii) a declaration in accordance with paragraph 4 of Article 22 and paragraph 4 of Article 25 of the Convention, in which case such amendments shall enter into force on the ninetieth day after the date of deposit with the depositary of its instrument of ratification, acceptance, approval or accession with respect to such amendments.

Any errors identified in the text of the Convention in typing or printing, spelling, punctuation or numbering or due to lack of conformity with the original records of the Conference of Plenipotentiaries or lack of concordance between the various language versions of the text of the Stockholm Convention, all of which are deemed to be equally authentic by Article 30 of the Convention, have been corrected in accordance with paragraphs 48 to 62 of the "Summary of Practice of the Secretary-General as Depositary".

Annexes A and B to the Convention set forth a number of specific exemptions for which Parties may register in accordance with Articles 3 and 4 of the Convention. Paragraph 9 of Article 4 provides that if at any time there are no Parties registered for a given specific exemption, no new registrations may be made in respect of that exemption. As at 17 May 2009 there were no Parties registered for the specific exemptions listed in Annex A pertaining to aldrin, chlordane, dieldrin, heptachlor, hexachlorobenzene and mirex, nor for the specific exemptions listed in Annex B pertaining to DDT. In accordance with paragraph 9 of Article 4 of the Convention, therefore, no new registrations may be made with respect to those exemptions. Specific exemptions for which no new registrations may be made are indicated in grey in the version of the Stockholm Convention set out in this booklet.

This revised Stockholm Convention text therefore reflects the amendments as adopted by the fourth meeting of the Conference of the Parties in 2009 in its decisions SC-4/10 to SC-4/18.

The version of the Stockholm Convention contained in this booklet does not substitute the Certified True Copy (CTC) as deposited with the Secretary-General in New York. Should you require a CTC, you may retrieve an electronic version from the United Nations Treaty Collection website or kindly contact the Treaty Section for further assistance.

The Secretariat of the Stockholm Convention, August 2010

THE PARTIES TO THIS CONVENTION,

Recognizing that persistent organic pollutants possess toxic properties, resist degradation, bioaccumulate and are transported, through air, water and migratory species, across international boundaries and deposited far from their place of release, where they accumulate in terrestrial and aquatic ecosystems,

Aware of the health concerns, especially in developing countries, resulting from local exposure to persistent organic pollutants, in particular impacts upon women and, through them, upon future generations,

Acknowledging that the Arctic ecosystems and indigenous communities are particularly at risk because of the biomagnification of persistent organic pollutants and that contamination of their traditional foods is a public health issue,

Conscious of the need for global action on persistent organic pollutants,

Mindful of decision 19/13 C of 7 February 1997 of the Governing Council of the United Nations Environment Programme to initiate international action to protect human health and the environment through measures which will reduce and/or eliminate emissions and discharges of persistent organic pollutants,

Recalling the pertinent provisions of the relevant international environmental conventions, especially the Rotterdam Convention on the Prior Informed Consent Procedure for Certain Hazardous Chemicals and Pesticides in International Trade, and the Basel Convention on the Control of Transboundary Movements of Hazardous Wastes and their Disposal including the regional agreements developed within the framework of its Article 11,

Recalling also the pertinent provisions of the Rio Declaration on Environment and Development and Agenda 21,

Acknowledging that precaution underlies the concerns of all the Parties and is embedded within this Convention,

Recognizing that this Convention and other international agreements in the field of trade and the environment are mutually supportive,

Reaffirming that States have, in accordance with the Charter of the United Nations and the principles of international law, the sovereign right to exploit their own resources pursuant to their own environmental and developmental policies, and the responsibility to ensure that activities within their jurisdiction or control do not cause damage to the environment of other States or of areas beyond the limits of national jurisdiction,

Taking into account the circumstances and particular requirements of developing countries, in particular the least developed among them, and countries with economies in transition, especially the need to strengthen their national capabilities for the management of chemicals, including through the transfer of technology, the provision of fi nancial and technical assistance and the promotion of cooperation among the Parties,

Taking full account of the Programme of Action for the Sustainable Development of Small Island Developing States, adopted in Barbados on 6 May 1994,

Noting the respective capabilities of developed and developing countries, as well as the common but differentiated responsibilities of States as set forth in Principle 7 of the Rio Declaration on Environment and Development,

Recognizing the important contribution that the private sector and nongovernmental organizations can make to achieving the reduction and/or elimination of emissions and discharges of persistent organic pollutants,

Underlining the importance of manufacturers of persistent organic pollutants taking responsibility for reducing adverse effects caused by their products and for providing information to users, Governments and the public on the hazardous properties of those chemicals,

Conscious of the need to take measures to prevent adverse effects caused by persistent organic pollutants at all stages of their life cycle,

Reaffirming Principle 16 of the Rio Declaration on Environment and Development which states that national authorities should endeavour to promote the internalization of environmental costs and the use of economic instruments, taking into account the approach that the polluter should, in principle, bear the cost of pollution, with due regard to the public interest and without distorting international trade and investment,

Encouraging Parties not having regulatory and assessment schemes for pesticides and industrial chemicals to develop such schemes,

Recognizing the importance of developing and using environmentally sound alternative processes and chemicals,

Determined to protect human health and the environment from the harmful impacts of persistent organic pollutants,

HAVE AGREED AS FOLLOWS:

Article 1

Objective

Mindful of the precautionary approach as set forth in Principle 15 of the Rio Declaration on Environment and Development, the objective of this Convention is to protect human health and the environment from persistent organic pollutants.

Article 2

Definitions

For the purposes of this Convention:

(a) "Party" means a State or regional economic integration organization that has consented to be bound by this Convention and for which the Convention is in force;

(b) "Regional economic integration organization" means an organization constituted by sovereign States of a given region to which its member States have transferred competence in respect of matters governed by this Convention and which has been duly authorized, in accordance with its internal procedures, to sign, ratify, accept, approve or accede to this Convention;

(c) "Parties present and voting" means Parties present and casting an affirmative or negative vote.

Article 3

Measures to reduce or eliminate releases from intentional production and use

1. Each Party shall:

(a) Prohibit and/or take the legal and administrative measures necessary to eliminate:

(i) Its production and use of the chemicals listed in Annex A subject to the provisions of that Annex; and

(ii) Its import and export of the chemicals listed in Annex A in accordance with the provisions of paragraph 2; and

(b) Restrict its production and use of the chemicals listed in Annex B in accordance with the provisions of that Annex.

2. Each Party shall take measures to ensure:

(a) That a chemical listed in Annex A or Annex B is imported only:

(i) For the purpose of environmentally sound disposal as set forth in paragraph 1 (d) of Article 6; or

(ii) For a use or purpose which is permitted for that Party under Annex A or Annex B;

(b) That a chemical listed in Annex A for which any production or use specific exemption is in effect or a chemical listed in Annex B for which any production or use specific exemption or acceptable purpose is in effect, taking into account any relevant provisions in existing international prior informed consent instruments, is exported only:

(i) For the purpose of environmentally sound disposal as set forth in paragraph 1 (d) of Article 6;

(ii) To a Party which is permitted to use that chemical under Annex A or Annex B; or

(iii) To a State not Party to this Convention which has provided an annual certification to the exporting Party. Such certification shall specify the intended use of the chemical and include a statement that, with respect to that chemical, the importing State is committed to:

a. Protect human health and the environment by taking the necessary measures to minimize or prevent releases;

b. Comply with the provisions of paragraph 1 of Article 6; and

c. Comply, where appropriate, with the provisions of paragraph 2 of Part II of Annex B.

The certification shall also include any appropriate supporting documentation, such as legislation, regulatory instruments, or administrative or policy guidelines. The exporting Party shall transmit the certification to the Secretariat within sixty days of receipt.

(c) That a chemical listed in Annex A, for which production and use specific exemptions are no longer in effect for any Party, is not exported from it except for the purpose of environmentally sound disposal as set forth in paragraph 1 (d) of Article 6;

(d) For the purposes of this paragraph, the term "State not Party to this Convention" shall include, with respect to a particular chemical, a State or regional economic integration organization that has not agreed to be bound by the Convention with respect to that chemical.

3. Each Party that has one or more regulatory and assessment schemes for new pesticides or new industrial chemicals shall take measures to regulate with the aim of preventing the production and use of new pesticides or new industrial chemicals which, taking into consideration the criteria in paragraph 1 of Annex D, exhibit the characteristics of persistent organic pollutants.

4. Each Party that has one or more regulatory and assessment schemes for pesticides or industrial chemicals shall, where appropriate, take into consideration within these schemes the criteria in paragraph 1 of Annex D when conducting assessments of pesticides or industrial chemicals currently in use.

5. Except as otherwise provided in this Convention, paragraphs 1 and 2 shall not apply to quantities of a chemical to be used for laboratory-scale research or as a reference standard.

6. Any Party that has a specific exemption in accordance with Annex A or a specific exemption or an acceptable purpose in accordance with Annex B shall take appropriate measures to ensure that any production or use under such exemption or purpose is carried out in a manner that

prevents or minimizes human exposure and release into the environment. For exempted uses or acceptable purposes that involve intentional release into the environment under conditions of normal use, such release shall be to the minimum extent necessary, taking into account any applicable standards and guidelines.

Article 4

Register of specific exemptions

1. A Register is hereby established for the purpose of identifying the Parties that have specific exemptions listed in Annex A or Annex B. It shall not identify Parties that make use of the provisions in Annex A or Annex B that may be exercised by all Parties. The Register shall be maintained by the Secretariat and shall be available to the public.

2. The Register shall include:
(a) A list of the types of specific exemptions reproduced from Annex A and Annex B;
(b) A list of the Parties that have a specific exemption listed under Annex A or Annex B; and
(c) A list of the expiry dates for each registered specific exemption.

3. Any State may, on becoming a Party, by means of a notification in writing to the Secretariat, register for one or more types of specific exemptions listed in Annex A or Annex B.

4. Unless an earlier date is indicated in the Register by a Party, or an extension is granted pursuant to paragraph 7, all registrations of specific exemptions shall expire five years after the date of entry into force of this Convention with respect to a particular chemical.

5. At its first meeting, the Conference of the Parties shall decide upon its review process for the entries in the Register.

6. Prior to a review of an entry in the Register, the Party concerned shall submit a report to the Secretariat justifying its continuing need for registration of that exemption. The report shall be circulated by the Secretariat to all Parties. The review of a registration shall be carried out on the basis of all available information. Thereupon, the Conference of the Parties may make such recommendations to the Party concerned as it deems appropriate.

7. The Conference of the Parties may, upon request from the Party concerned, decide to extend the expiry date of a specific exemption for a period of up to five years. In making its decision, the Conference of the Parties shall take due account of the special circumstances of the developing country Parties and Parties with economies in transition.

8. A Party may, at any time, withdraw an entry from the Register for a specific exemption upon written notification to the Secretariat. The withdrawal shall take effect on the date specified in the notification.

9. When there are no longer any Parties registered for a particular type of specific exemption, no new registrations may be made with respect to it.

Article 5

Measures to reduce or eliminate releases from unintentional production

Each Party shall at a minimum take the following measures to reduce the total releases derived from anthropogenic sources of each of the chemicals listed in Annex C, with the goal of their continuing minimization and, where feasible, ultimate elimination:
(a) Develop an action plan or, where appropriate, a regional or subregional action plan within two years of the date of entry into force of this Convention for it, and subsequently implement it as part of its implementation plan specified in Article 7, designed to identify, characterize and address the release of the chemicals listed in

Annex C and to facilitate implementation of subparagraphs (b) to (e). The action plan shall include the following elements:

(i) An evaluation of current and projected releases, including the development and maintenance of source inventories and release estimates, taking into consideration the source categories identified in Annex C;

(ii) An evaluation of the efficacy of the laws and policies of the Party relating to the management of such releases;

(iii) Strategies to meet the obligations of this paragraph, taking into account the evaluations in (i) and (ii);

(iv) Steps to promote education and training with regard to, and awareness of, those strategies;

(v) A review every five years of those strategies and of their success in meeting the obligations of this paragraph; such reviews shall be included in reports submitted pursuant to Article 15;

(vi) A schedule for implementation of the action plan, including for the strategies and measures identified therein;

(b) Promote the application of available, feasible and practical measures that can expeditiously achieve a realistic and meaningful level of release reduction or source elimination;

(c) Promote the development and, where it deems appropriate, require the use of substitute or modified materials, products and processes to prevent the formation and release of the chemicals listed in Annex C, taking into consideration the general guidance on prevention and release reduction measures in Annex C and guidelines to be adopted by decision of the Conference of the Parties;

(d) Promote and, in accordance with the implementation schedule of its action plan, require the use of best available techniques for new sources within source categories which a Party has identified as warranting such action in its action plan, with a particular initial focus on source categories identified in Part II of Annex C. In any case, the requirement to use best available techniques for new sources in the categories listed in Part II of that Annex shall be phased in as soon as practicable but no later than four years after the entry into force of the Convention for that Party. For the identified categories, Parties shall promote the use of best environmental practices. When applying best available techniques and best environmental practices, Parties should take into consideration the general guidance on prevention and release reduction measures in that Annex and guidelines on best available techniques and best environmental practices to be adopted by decision of the Conference of the Parties;

(e) Promote, in accordance with its action plan, the use of best available techniques and best environmental practices:

(i) For existing sources, within the source categories listed in Part II of Annex C and within source categories such as those in Part III of that Annex; and

(ii) For new sources, within source categories such as those listed in Part III of Annex C which a Party has not addressed under subparagraph (d). When applying best available techniques and best environmental practices, Parties should take into consideration the general guidance on prevention and release reduction measures in Annex C and guidelines on best available techniques and best environmental practices to be adopted by decision of the Conference of the Parties;

(f) For the purposes of this paragraph and Annex C:

(i) "Best available techniques" means the most effective and advanced stage in the development of activities and their methods of operation which indicate the practical suitability of particular techniques for providing in principle the basis for release limitations designed to prevent and, where that is not practicable, generally to reduce releases of chemicals listed in Part I of Annex C and their impact on the environment as a whole. In this regard:

(ii) "Techniques" includes both the technology used and the way in which the installation is designed, built, maintained, operated and decommissioned;

(iii) "Available" techniques means those techniques that are accessible to the operator and that are developed on a scale that allows implementation in the relevant industrial sector, under economically and technically viable conditions, taking into consideration the costs and advantages; and
(iv) "Best" means most effective in achieving a high general level of protection of the environment as a whole;
(v) "Best environmental practices" means the application of the most appropriate combination of environmental control measures and strategies;
(vi) "New source" means any source of which the construction or substantial modification is commenced at least one year after the date of:
a. Entry into force of this Convention for the Party concerned; or
b. Entry into force for the Party concerned of an amendment to Annex C where the source becomes subject to the provisions of this Convention only by virtue of that amendment.

(g) Release limit values or performance standards may be used by a Party to fulfil its commitments for best available techniques under this paragraph.

Article 6

Measures to reduce or eliminate releases from stockpiles and wastes

1. In order to ensure that stockpiles consisting of or containing chemicals listed either in Annex A or Annex B and wastes, including products and articles upon becoming wastes, consisting of, containing or contaminated with a chemical listed in Annex A, B or C, are managed in a manner protective of human health and the environment, each Party shall:

(a) Develop appropriate strategies for identifying:
(i) Stockpiles consisting of or containing chemicals listed either in Annex A or Annex B; and
(ii) Products and articles in use and wastes consisting of, containing or contaminated with a chemical listed in Annex A, B or C;

(b) Identify, to the extent practicable, stockpiles consisting of or containing chemicals listed either in Annex A or Annex B on the basis of the strategies referred to in subparagraph (a);

(c) Manage stockpiles, as appropriate, in a safe, efficient and environmentally sound manner. Stockpiles of chemicals listed either in Annex A or Annex B, after they are no longer allowed to be used according to any specific exemption specified in Annex A or any specific exemption or acceptable purpose specified in Annex B, except stockpiles which are allowed to be exported according to paragraph 2 of Article 3, shall be deemed to be waste and shall be managed in accordance with subparagraph (d);

(d) Take appropriate measures so that such wastes, including products and articles upon becoming wastes, are:
(i) Handled, collected, transported and stored in an environmentally sound manner;
(ii) Disposed of in such a way that the persistent organic pollutant content is destroyed or irreversibly transformed so that they do not exhibit the characteristics of persistent organic pollutants or otherwise disposed of in an environmentally sound manner when destruction or irreversible transformation does not represent the environmentally preferable option or the persistent organic pollutant content is low, taking into account international rules, standards, and guidelines, including those that may be developed pursuant to paragraph 2, and relevant global and regional regimes governing the management of hazardous wastes;
(iii) Not permitted to be subjected to disposal operations that may lead to recovery, recycling, reclamation, direct reuse or alternative uses of persistent organic pollutants; and
(iv) Not transported across international boundaries without taking into account relevant international rules, standards and guidelines;

(e) Endeavour to develop appropriate strategies for identifying sites contaminated by chemicals listed in Annex A, B or C; if remediation of those sites is undertaken it shall be performed in an environmentally sound manner.

2. The Conference of the Parties shall cooperate closely with the appropriate bodies of the Basel Convention on the Control of Transboundary Movements of Hazardous Wastes and their Disposal to, inter alia:

(a) Establish levels of destruction and irreversible transformation necessary to ensure that the characteristics of persistent organic pollutants as specified in paragraph 1 of Annex D are not exhibited;

(b) Determine what they consider to be the methods that constitute environmentally sound disposal referred to above; and

(c) Work to establish, as appropriate, the concentration levels of the chemicals listed in Annexes A, B and C in order to define the low persistent organic pollutant content referred to in paragraph 1 (d) (ii).

Article 7

Implementation plans

1. Each Party shall:

(a) Develop and endeavour to implement a plan for the implementation of its obligations under this Convention;

(b) Transmit its implementation plan to the Conference of the Parties within two years of the date on which this Convention enters into force for it; and

(c) Review and update, as appropriate, its implementation plan on a periodic basis and in a manner to be specified by a decision of the Conference of the Parties.

2. The Parties shall, where appropriate, cooperate directly or through global, regional and sub-regional organizations, and consult their national stakeholders, including women's groups and groups involved in the health of children, in order to facilitate the development, implementation and updating of their implementation plans.

3. The Parties shall endeavour to utilize and, where necessary, establish the means to integrate national implementation plans for persistent organic pollutants in their sustainable development strategies where appropriate.

Article 8

Listing of chemicals in Annexes A, B and C

1. A Party may submit a proposal to the Secretariat for listing a chemical in Annexes A, B and/or C. The proposal shall contain the information specified in Annex D. In developing a proposal, a Party may be assisted by other Parties and/or by the Secretariat.

2. The Secretariat shall verify whether the proposal contains the information specified in Annex D. If the Secretariat is satisfied that the proposal contains the information so specified, it shall forward the proposal to the Persistent Organic Pollutants Review Committee.

3. The Committee shall examine the proposal and apply the screening criteria specified in Annex D in a flexible and transparent way, taking all information provided into account in an integrative and balanced manner.

4. If the Committee decides that:

(a) It is satisfied that the screening criteria have been fulfilled, it shall, through the Secretariat, make the proposal and the evaluation of the Committee available to all Parties and observers and invite them to submit the information specified in Annex E; or

(b) It is not satisfied that the screening criteria have been fulfilled, it shall, through the Secretariat, inform all Parties and observers and make the proposal and the evaluation of the Committee available to all Parties and the proposal shall be set aside.

5. Any Party may resubmit a proposal to the Committee that has been set aside by the Committee pursuant to paragraph 4. The resubmission may include any concerns of the Party as well as a justification for additional consideration by the Committee. If, following this procedure, the Committee again sets the proposal aside, the Party may challenge the decision of the Committee and the Conference of the Parties shall consider the matter at its next session. The Conference of the Parties may decide, based on the screening criteria in Annex D and taking into account the evaluation of the Committee and any additional information provided by any Party or observer, that the proposal should proceed.

6. Where the Committee has decided that the screening criteria have been fulfilled, or the Conference of the Parties has decided that the proposal should proceed, the Committee shall further review the proposal, taking into account any relevant additional information received, and shall prepare a draft risk profile in accordance with Annex E. It shall, through the Secretariat, make that draft available to all Parties and observers, collect technical comments from them and, taking those comments into account, complete the risk profile.

7. If, on the basis of the risk profile conducted in accordance with Annex E, the Committee decides:

(a) That the chemical is likely as a result of its long-range environmental transport to lead to significant adverse human health and/or environmental effects such that global action is warranted, the proposal shall proceed. Lack of full scientific certainty shall not prevent the proposal from proceeding. The Committee shall, through the Secretariat, invite information from all Parties and observers relating to the considerations specified in Annex F. It shall then prepare a risk management evaluation that includes an analysis of possible control measures for the chemical in accordance with that Annex; or

(b) That the proposal should not proceed, it shall, through the Secretariat, make the risk profile available to all Parties and observers and set the proposal aside.

8. For any proposal set aside pursuant to paragraph 7 (b), a Party may request the Conference of the Parties to consider instructing the Committee to invite additional information from the proposing Party and other Parties during a period not to exceed one year. After that period and on the basis of any information received, the Committee shall reconsider the proposal pursuant to paragraph 6 with a priority to be decided by the Conference of the Parties. If, following this procedure, the Committee again sets the proposal aside, the Party may challenge the decision of the Committee and the Conference of the Parties shall consider the matter at its next session. The Conference of the Parties may decide, based on the risk profile prepared in accordance with Annex E and taking into account the evaluation of the Committee and any additional information provided by any Party or observer, that the proposal should proceed. If the Conference of the Parties decides that the proposal shall proceed, the Committee shall then prepare the risk management evaluation.

9. The Committee shall, based on the risk profile referred to in paragraph 6 and the risk management evaluation referred to in paragraph 7 (a) or paragraph 8, recommend whether the chemical should be considered by the Conference of the Parties for listing in Annexes A, B and/or C. The Conference of the Parties, taking due account of the recommendations of the Committee, including any scientific uncertainty, shall decide, in a precautionary manner, whether to list the chemical, and specify its related control measures, in Annexes A, B and/or C.

Article 9

Information exchange

1. Each Party shall facilitate or undertake the exchange of information relevant to:

(a) The reduction or elimination of the production, use and release of persistent organic pollutants; and
(b) Alternatives to persistent organic pollutants, including information relating to their risks as well as to their economic and social costs.

2. The Parties shall exchange the information referred to in paragraph 1 directly or through the Secretariat.

3. Each Party shall designate a national focal point for the exchange of such information.

4. The Secretariat shall serve as a clearing-house mechanism for information on persistent organic pollutants, including information provided by Parties, intergovernmental organizations and non-governmental organizations.

5. For the purposes of this Convention, information on health and safety of humans and the environment shall not be regarded as confidential. Parties that exchange other information pursuant to this Convention shall protect any confidential information as mutually agreed.

Article 10

Public information, awareness and education

1. Each Party shall, within its capabilities, promote and facilitate:
(a) Awareness among its policy and decision makers with regard to persistent organic pollutants;
(b) Provision to the public of all available information on persistent organic pollutants, taking into account paragraph 5 of Article 9;
(c) Development and implementation, especially for women, children and the least educated, of educational and public awareness programmes on persistent organic pollutants, as well as on their health and environmental effects and on their alternatives;
(d) Public participation in addressing persistent organic pollutants and their health and environmental effects and in developing adequate responses, including opportunities for providing input at the national level regarding implementation of this Convention;
(e) Training of workers, scientists, educators and technical and managerial personnel;
(f) Development and exchange of educational and public awareness materials at the national and international levels; and
(g) Development and implementation of education and training programmes at the national and international levels.

2. Each Party shall, within its capabilities, ensure that the public has access to the public information referred to in paragraph 1 and that the information is kept up-to-date.

3. Each Party shall, within its capabilities, encourage industry and professional users to promote and facilitate the provision of the information referred to in paragraph 1 at the national level and, as appropriate, subregional, regional and global levels.

4. In providing information on persistent organic pollutants and their alternatives, Parties may use safety data sheets, reports, mass media and other means of communication, and may establish information centres at national and regional levels.

5. Each Party shall give sympathetic consideration to developing mechanisms, such as pollutant release and transfer registers, for the collection and dissemination of information on estimates of the annual quantities of the chemicals listed in Annex A, B or C that are released or disposed of.

Article 11

Research, development and monitoring

1. The Parties shall, within their capabilities, at the national and international levels, encourage and/or undertake appropriate research, development, monitoring and cooperation pertaining

to persistent organic pollutants and, where relevant, to their alternatives and to candidate persistent organic pollutants, including on their:

(a) Sources and releases into the environment;
(b) Presence, levels and trends in humans and the environment;
(c) Environmental transport, fate and transformation;
(d) Effects on human health and the environment;
(e) Socio-economic and cultural impacts;
(f) Release reduction and/or elimination; and
(g) Harmonized methodologies for making inventories of generating sources and analytical techniques for the measurement of releases.

2. In undertaking action under paragraph 1, the Parties shall, within their capabilities:

(a) Support and further develop, as appropriate, international programmes, networks and organizations aimed at defining, conducting, assessing and financing research, data collection and monitoring, taking into account the need to minimize duplication of effort;
(b) Support national and international efforts to strengthen national scientific and technical research capabilities, particularly in developing countries and countries with economies in transition, and to promote access to, and the exchange of, data and analyses;
(c) Take into account the concerns and needs, particularly in the field of financial and technical resources, of developing countries and countries with economies in transition and cooperate in improving their capability to participate in the efforts referred to in subparagraphs (a) and (b);
(d) Undertake research work geared towards alleviating the effects of persistent organic pollutants on reproductive health;
(e) Make the results of their research, development and monitoring activities referred to in this paragraph accessible to the public on a timely and regular basis; and
(f) Encourage and/or undertake cooperation with regard to storage and maintenance of information generated from research, development and monitoring.

Article 12

Technical assistance

1. The Parties recognize that rendering of timely and appropriate technical assistance in response to requests from developing country Parties and Parties with economies in transition is essential to the successful implementation of this Convention.

2. The Parties shall cooperate to provide timely and appropriate technical assistance to developing country Parties and Parties with economies in transition, to assist them, taking into account their particular needs, to develop and strengthen their capacity to implement their obligations under this Convention.

3. In this regard, technical assistance to be provided by developed country Parties, and other Parties in accordance with their capabilities, shall include, as appropriate and as mutually agreed, technical assistance for capacity building relating to implementation of the obligations under this Convention. Further guidance in this regard shall be provided by the Conference of the Parties.

4. The Parties shall establish, as appropriate, arrangements for the purpose of providing technical assistance and promoting the transfer of technology to developing country Parties and Parties with economies in transition relating to the implementation of this Convention. These arrangements shall include regional and subregional centres for capacity-building and transfer of technology to assist developing country Parties and Parties with economies in transition to fulfil their obligations under this Convention. Further guidance in this regard shall be provided by the Conference of the Parties.

5. The Parties shall, in the context of this Article, take full account of the specific needs and special situation of least developed countries and small island developing states in their actions with regard to technical assistance.

Article 13

Financial resources and mechanisms

1. Each Party undertakes to provide, within its capabilities, financial support and incentives in respect of those national activities that are intended to achieve the objective of this Convention in accordance with its national plans, priorities and programmes.

2. The developed country Parties shall provide new and additional financial resources to enable developing country Parties and Parties with economies in transition to meet the agreed full incremental costs of implementing measures which fulfil their obligations under this Convention as agreed between a recipient Party and an entity participating in the mechanism described in paragraph 6. Other Parties may also on a voluntary basis and in accordance with their capabilities provide such financial resources. Contributions from other sources should also be encouraged. The implementation of these commitments shall take into account the need for adequacy, predictability, the timely flow of funds and the importance of burden sharing among the contributing Parties.

3. Developed country Parties, and other Parties in accordance with their capabilities and in accordance with their national plans, priorities and programmes, may also provide and developing country Parties and Parties with economies in transition avail themselves of financial resources to assist in their implementation of this Convention through other bilateral, regional and multilateral sources or channels.

4. The extent to which the developing country Parties will effectively implement their commitments under this Convention will depend on the effective implementation by developed country Parties of their commitments under this Convention relating to financial resources, technical assistance and technology transfer. The fact that sustainable economic and social development and eradication of poverty are the first and overriding priorities of the developing country Parties will be taken fully into account, giving due consideration to the need for the protection of human health and the environment.

5. The Parties shall take full account of the specific needs and special situation of the least developed countries and the small island developing states in their actions with regard to funding.

6. A mechanism for the provision of adequate and sustainable financial resources to developing country Parties and Parties with economies in transition on a grant or concessional basis to assist in their implementation of the Convention is hereby defined. The mechanism shall function under the authority, as appropriate, and guidance of, and be accountable to the Conference of the Parties for the purposes of this Convention. Its operation shall be entrusted to one or more entities, including existing international entities, as may be decided upon by the Conference of the Parties. The mechanism may also include other entities providing multilateral, regional and bilateral financial and technical assistance. Contributions to the mechanism shall be additional to other financial transfers to developing country Parties and Parties with economies in transition as reflected in, and in accordance with, paragraph 2.

7. Pursuant to the objectives of this Convention and paragraph 6, the Conference of the Parties shall at its first meeting adopt appropriate guidance to be provided to the mechanism and shall agree with the entity or entities participating in the financial mechanism upon arrangements to give effect thereto. The guidance shall address, inter alia:

(a) The determination of the policy, strategy and programme priorities, as well as clear and detailed criteria and guidelines regarding eligibility for access to and utilization of financial resources including monitoring and evaluation on a regular basis of such utilization;

(b) The provision by the entity or entities of regular reports to the Conference of the Parties on adequacy and sustainability of funding for activities relevant to the implementation of this Convention;

(c) The promotion of multiple-source funding approaches, mechanisms and arrangements;

(d) The modalities for the determination in a predictable and identifiable manner of the amount of funding necessary and available for the implementation of this Convention, keeping in mind that the phasing out of persistent organic pollutants might require sustained funding, and the conditions under which that amount shall be periodically reviewed; and

(e) The modalities for the provision to interested Parties of assistance with needs assessment, information on available sources of funds and on funding patterns in order to facilitate coordination among them.

8. The Conference of the Parties shall review, not later than its second meeting and thereafter on a regular basis, the effectiveness of the mechanism established under this Article, its ability to address the changing needs of the developing country Parties and Parties with economies in transition, the criteria and guidance referred to in paragraph 7, the level of funding as well as the effectiveness of the performance of the institutional entities entrusted to operate the financial mechanism. It shall, based on such review, take appropriate action, if necessary, to improve the effectiveness of the mechanism, including by means of recommendations and guidance on measures to ensure adequate and sustainable funding to meet the needs of the Parties.

Article 14

Interim financial arrangements

The institutional structure of the Global Environment Facility, operated in accordance with the Instrument for the Establishment of the Restructured Global Environment Facility, shall, on an interim basis, be the principal entity entrusted with the operations of the financial mechanism referred to in Article 13, for the period between the date of entry into force of this Convention and the fi rst meeting of the Conference of the Parties, or until such time as the Conference of the Parties decides which institutional structure will be designated in accordance with Article 13. The institutional structure of the Global Environment Facility should fulfil this function through operational measures related specifically to persistent organic pollutants taking into account that new arrangements for this area may be needed.

Article 15

Reporting

1. Each Party shall report to the Conference of the Parties on the measures it has taken to implement the provisions of this Convention and on the effectiveness of such measures in meeting the objectives of the Convention.

2. Each Party shall provide to the Secretariat:

(a) Statistical data on its total quantities of production, import and export of each of the chemicals listed in Annex A and Annex B or a reasonable estimate of such data; and

(b) To the extent practicable, a list of the States from which it has imported each such substance and the States to which it has exported each such substance.

3. Such reporting shall be at periodic intervals and in a format to be decided by the Conference of the Parties at its first meeting.

Article 16

Effectiveness evaluation

1. Commencing four years after the date of entry into force of this Convention, and periodically thereafter at intervals to be decided by the Conference of the Parties, the Conference shall evaluate the effectiveness of this Convention.

2. In order to facilitate such evaluation, the Conference of the Parties shall, at its fi rst meeting, initiate the establishment of arrangements to provide itself with comparable monitoring data on the presence of the chemicals listed in Annexes A, B and C as well as their regional and global environmental transport. These arrangements:

(a) Should be implemented by the Parties on a regional basis when appropriate, in accordance with their technical and financial capabilities, using existing monitoring programmes and mechanisms to the extent possible and promoting harmonization of approaches;
(b) May be supplemented where necessary, taking into account the differences between regions and their capabilities to implement monitoring activities; and
(c) Shall include reports to the Conference of the Parties on the results of the monitoring activities on a regional and global basis at intervals to be specified by the Conference of the Parties.

3. The evaluation described in paragraph 1 shall be conducted on the basis of available scientific, environmental, technical and economic information, including:

(a) Reports and other monitoring information provided pursuant to paragraph 2;
(b) National reports submitted pursuant to Article 15; and
(c) Non-compliance information provided pursuant to the procedures established under Article 17.

Article 17

Non-compliance

The Conference of the Parties shall, as soon as practicable, develop and approve procedures and institutional mechanisms for determining non-compliance with the provisions of this Convention and for the treatment of Parties found to be in non-compliance.

Article 18

Settlement of disputes

1. Parties shall settle any dispute between them concerning the interpretation or application of this Convention through negotiation or other peaceful means of their own choice.

2. When ratifying, accepting, approving or acceding to the Convention, or at any time thereafter, a Party that is not a regional economic integration organization may declare in a written instrument submitted to the depositary that, with respect to any dispute concerning the interpretation or application of the Convention, it recognizes one or both of the following means of dispute settlement as compulsory in relation to any Party accepting the same obligation:

(a) Arbitration in accordance with procedures to be adopted by the Conference of the Parties in an annex as soon as practicable;
(b) Submission of the dispute to the International Court of Justice.

3. A Party that is a regional economic integration organization may make a declaration with like effect in relation to arbitration in accordance with the procedure referred to in paragraph 2 (a).

4. A declaration made pursuant to paragraph 2 or paragraph 3 shall remain in force until it expires in accordance with its terms or until three months after written notice of its revocation has been deposited with the depositary.

5. The expiry of a declaration, a notice of revocation or a new declaration shall not in any way affect proceedings pending before an arbitral tribunal or the International Court of Justice unless the parties to the dispute otherwise agree.

6. If the parties to a dispute have not accepted the same or any procedure pursuant to paragraph 2, and if they have not been able to settle their dispute within twelve months following notification by one party to another that a dispute exists between them, the dispute shall be submitted to a conciliation commission at the request of any party to the dispute. The conciliation commission shall render a report with recommendations. Additional procedures relating to the conciliation commission shall be included in an annex to be adopted by the Conference of the Parties no later than at its second meeting.

Article 19

Conference of the Parties

1. A Conference of the Parties is hereby established.

2. The first meeting of the Conference of the Parties shall be convened by the Executive Director of the United Nations Environment Programme no later than one year after the entry into force of this Convention. Thereafter, ordinary meetings of the Conference of the Parties shall be held at regular intervals to be decided by the Conference.

3. Extraordinary meetings of the Conference of the Parties shall be held at such other times as may be deemed necessary by the Conference, or at the written request of any Party provided that it is supported by at least one third of the Parties.

4. The Conference of the Parties shall by consensus agree upon and adopt at its first meeting rules of procedure and financial rules for itself and any subsidiary bodies, as well as financial provisions governing the functioning of the Secretariat.

5. The Conference of the Parties shall keep under continuous review and evaluation the implementation of this Convention. It shall perform the functions assigned to it by the Convention and, to this end, shall:

(a) Establish, further to the requirements of paragraph 6, such subsidiary bodies as it considers necessary for the implementation of the Convention;

(b) Cooperate, where appropriate, with competent international organizations and intergovernmental and non-governmental bodies; and

(c) Regularly review all information made available to the Parties pursuant to Article 15, including consideration of the effectiveness of paragraph 2 (b) (iii) of Article 3;

(d) Consider and undertake any additional action that may be required for the achievement of the objectives of the Convention.

6. The Conference of the Parties shall, at its first meeting, establish a subsidiary body to be called the Persistent Organic Pollutants Review Committee for the purposes of performing the functions assigned to that Committee by this Convention. In this regard:

(a) The members of the Persistent Organic Pollutants Review Committee shall be appointed by the Conference of the Parties. Membership of the Committee shall consist of government-designated experts in chemical assessment or management. The members of the Committee shall be appointed on the basis of equitable geographical distribution;

(b) The Conference of the Parties shall decide on the terms of reference, organization and operation of the Committee; and

(c) The Committee shall make every effort to adopt its recommendations by consensus. If all efforts at consensus have been exhausted, and no consensus reached, such recommendation shall as a last resort be adopted by a two-thirds majority vote of the members present and voting.

7. The Conference of the Parties shall, at its third meeting, evaluate the continued need for the procedure contained in paragraph 2 (b) of Article 3, including consideration of its effectiveness.

8. The United Nations, its specialized agencies and the International Atomic Energy Agency, as well as any State not Party to this Convention, may be represented at meetings of the

Conference of the Parties as observers. Anybody or agency, whether national or international, governmental or nongovernmental, qualified in matters covered by the Convention, and which has informed the Secretariat of its wish to be represented at a meeting of the Conference of the Parties as an observer may be admitted unless at least one third of the Parties present object. The admission and participation of observers shall be subject to the rules of procedure adopted by the Conference of the Parties.

Article 20

Secretariat

1. A Secretariat is hereby established.

2. The functions of the Secretariat shall be:
(a) To make arrangements for meetings of the Conference of the Parties and its subsidiary bodies and to provide them with services as required;
(b) To facilitate assistance to the Parties, particularly developing country Parties and Parties with economies in transition, on request, in the implementation of this Convention;
(c) To ensure the necessary coordination with the secretariats of other relevant international bodies;
(d) To prepare and make available to the Parties periodic reports based on information received pursuant to Article 15 and other available information;
(e) To enter, under the overall guidance of the Conference of the Parties, into such administrative and contractual arrangements as may be required for the effective discharge of its functions; and
(f) To perform the other secretariat functions specified in this Convention and such other functions as may be determined by the Conference of the Parties.

3. The secretariat functions for this Convention shall be performed by the Executive Director of the United Nations Environment Programme, unless the Conference of the Parties decides, by a three-fourths majority of the Parties present and voting, to entrust the secretariat functions to one or more other international organizations.

Article 21

Amendments to the Convention

1. Amendments to this Convention may be proposed by any Party.

2. Amendments to this Convention shall be adopted at a meeting of the Conference of the Parties. The text of any proposed amendment shall be communicated to the Parties by the Secretariat at least six months before the meeting at which it is proposed for adoption. The Secretariat shall also communicate proposed amendments to the signatories to this Convention and, for information, to the depositary.

3. The Parties shall make every effort to reach agreement on any proposed amendment to this Convention by consensus. If all efforts at consensus have been exhausted, and no agreement reached, the amendment shall as a last resort be adopted by a three-fourths majority vote of the Parties present and voting.

4. The amendment shall be communicated by the depositary to all Parties for ratification, acceptance or approval.

5. Ratification, acceptance or approval of an amendment shall be notified to the depositary in writing. An amendment adopted in accordance with paragraph 3 shall enter into force for the Parties having accepted it on the ninetieth day after the date of deposit of instruments of ratification, acceptance or approval by at least three-fourths of the Parties. Thereafter, the amendment shall enter into force for any other Party on the ninetieth day after the date on which that Party deposits its instrument of ratification, acceptance or approval of the amendment.

Article 22

Adoption and amendment of annexes

1. Annexes to this Convention shall form an integral part thereof and, unless expressly provided otherwise, a reference to this Convention constitutes at the same time a reference to any annexes thereto.

2. Any additional annexes shall be restricted to procedural, scientific, technical or administrative matters.

3. The following procedure shall apply to the proposal, adoption and entry into force of additional annexes to this Convention:

(a) Additional annexes shall be proposed and adopted according to the procedure laid down in paragraphs 1, 2 and 3 of Article 21;

(b) Any Party that is unable to accept an additional annex shall so notify the depositary, in writing, within one year from the date of communication by the depositary of the adoption of the additional annex. The depositary shall without delay notify all Parties of any such notification received. A Party may at any time withdraw a previous notification of non-acceptance in respect of any additional annex, and the annex shall thereupon enter into force for that Party subject to subparagraph (c); and

(c) On the expiry of one year from the date of the communication by the depositary of the adoption of an additional annex, the annex shall enter into force for all Parties that have not submitted a notification in accordance with the provisions of subparagraph (b).

4. The proposal, adoption and entry into force of amendments to Annex A, B or C shall be subject to the same procedures as for the proposal, adoption and entry into force of additional annexes to this Convention, except that an amendment to Annex A, B or C shall not enter into force with respect to any Party that has made a declaration with respect to amendment to those Annexes in accordance with paragraph 4 of Article 25, in which case any such amendment shall enter into force for such a Party on the ninetieth day after the date of deposit with the depositary of its instrument of ratification, acceptance, approval or accession with respect to such amendment.

5. The following procedure shall apply to the proposal, adoption and entry into force of an amendment to Annex D, E or F:

(a) Amendments shall be proposed according to the procedure in paragraphs 1 and 2 of Article 21;

(b) The Parties shall take decisions on an amendment to Annex D, E or F by consensus; and

(c) A decision to amend Annex D, E or F shall forthwith be communicated to the Parties by the depositary. The amendment shall enter into force for all Parties on a date to be specified in the decision.

6. If an additional annex or an amendment to an annex is related to an amendment to this Convention, the additional annex or amendment shall not enter into force until such time as the amendment to the Convention enters into force.

Article 23

Right to vote

1. Each Party to this Convention shall have one vote, except as provided for in paragraph 2.

2. A regional economic integration organization, on matters within its competence, shall exercise its right to vote with a number of votes equal to the number of its member States that are Parties to this Convention. Such an organization shall not exercise its right to vote if any of its member States exercises its right to vote, and vice versa.

Article 24

Signature

This Convention shall be open for signature at Stockholm by all States and regional economic integration organizations on 23 May 2001, and at the United Nations Headquarters in New York from 24 May 2001 to 22 May 2002.

Article 25

Ratification, acceptance, approval or accession

1. This Convention shall be subject to ratification, acceptance or approval by States and by regional economic integration organizations. It shall be open for accession by States and by regional economic integration organizations from the day after the date on which the Convention is closed for signature. Instruments of ratification, acceptance, approval or accession shall be deposited with the depositary.

2. Any regional economic integration organization that becomes a Party to this Convention without any of its member States being a Party shall be bound by all the obligations under the Convention. In the case of such organizations, one or more of whose member States is a Party to this Convention, the organization and its member States shall decide on their respective responsibilities for the performance of their obligations under the Convention. In such cases, the organization and the member States shall not be entitled to exercise rights under the Convention concurrently.

3. In its instrument of ratification, acceptance, approval or accession, a regional economic integration organization shall declare the extent of its competence in respect of the matters governed by this Convention. Any such organization shall also inform the depositary, who shall in turn inform the Parties, of any relevant modification in the extent of its competence.

4. In its instrument of ratification, acceptance, approval or accession, any Party may declare that, with respect to it, any amendment to Annex A, B or C shall enter into force only upon the deposit of its instrument of ratification, acceptance, approval or accession with respect thereto.

Article 26

Entry into force

1. This Convention shall enter into force on the ninetieth day after the date of deposit of the fiftieth instrument of ratification, acceptance, approval or accession.

2. For each State or regional economic integration organization that ratifies, accepts or approves this Convention or accedes thereto after the deposit of the fiftieth instrument of ratification, acceptance, approval or accession, the Convention shall enter into force on the ninetieth day after the date of deposit by such State or regional economic integration organization of its instrument of ratification, acceptance, approval or accession.

3. For the purpose of paragraphs 1 and 2, any instrument deposited by a regional economic integration organization shall not be counted as additional to those deposited by member States of that organization.

Article 27

Reservations

No reservations may be made to this Convention.

Article 28

Withdrawal

1. At any time after three years from the date on which this Convention has entered into force for a Party, that Party may withdraw from the Convention by giving written notification to the depositary.

2. Any such withdrawal shall take effect upon the expiry of one year from the date of receipt by the depositary of the notification of withdrawal, or on such later date as may be specified in the notification of withdrawal.

Article 29

Depositary

The Secretary-General of the United Nations shall be the depositary of this Convention.

Article 30

Authentic texts

The original of this Convention, of which the Arabic, Chinese, English, French, Russian and Spanish texts are equally authentic, shall be deposited with the Secretary-General of the United Nations.

IN WITNESS WHEREOF the undersigned, being duly authorized to that effect, have signed this Convention.

ANNEX A
ELIMINATION

PART I

Chemical	*Activity*	*Specific exemption*[(1)]
Aldrin* CAS No: 309-00-2	Production	None
	Use	Local ectoparasiticide Insecticide
[Alpha hexachlorocyclohexane* CAS No: 319-84-6	Production	None
	Use	None][1]
[Beta hexachlorocyclohexane* CAS No: 319-85-7	Production	None
	Use	None][1]
Chlordane* CAS No: 57-74-9	Production	As allowed for the Parties listed in the Register
	Use	Local ectoparasiticide Insecticide Termiticide Termiticide in buildings and dams Termiticide in roads Additive in plywood adhesives
[Chlordecone* CAS No: 143-50-0	Production	None
	Use	None][1]
Dieldrin* CAS No: 60-57-1	Production	None
	Use	In agricultural operations

Chemical	*Activity*	*Specific exemption*(1)
Endrin* CAS No: 72-20-8	Production	None
	Use	None
Heptachlor* CAS No: 76-44-8	Production	None
	Use	Termiticide Termiticide in structures of houses Termiticide (subterranean) Wood treatment In use in underground cable boxes
[Hexabromobiphenyl* CAS No: 36355-01-8	Production	None
	Use	None][1]
[Hexabromodiphenyl ether* and heptabromodiphenyl ether*	Production	None
	Use	Articles in accordance with the provisions of Part IV of this Annex][1]
Hexachlorobenzene CAS No: 118-74-1	Production	As allowed for the Parties listed in the Register
	Use	Intermediate Solvent in pesticide Closed system site limited intermediate(2)
[Lindane* CAS No: 58-89-9	Production	None
	Use	Human health pharmaceutical for control of head lice and scabies as second line treatment][1]
Mirex* CAS No: 2385-85-5	Production	As allowed for the Parties listed in the Register
	Use	Termiticide
[Pentachlorobenzene* CAS No: 608-93-5	Production	None
	Use	None][1]
Polychlorinated biphenyls (PCB)*	Production	None
	Use	Articles in use in accordance with the provisions of Part II of this Annex
[Technical endosulfan* (CAS No: 115-29-7) and its related isomers* (CAS No: 959-98-8 and CAS No: 33213-65-9)	Production	As allowed for the parties listed in the Register
	Use	Crop-pest complexes as listed in accordance with the provisions of part VI of this Annex][2]
[Tetrabromodiphenyl ether* and pentabromodiphenyl ether*	Production	None
	Use	Articles in accordance with the provisions of Part IV of this Annex][1]
Toxaphene* CAS No: 8001-35-2	Production	None
	Use	None

(1) Please note that, as at 17 May 2009, there were no Parties registered for the specific exemptions listed in Annex A pertaining to aldrin, chlordane, dieldrin, heptachlor, hexachlorobenzene, and mirex. Therefore, in accordance with paragraph 9 of Article 4

of the Convention, no new registrations may be made with respect to such exemptions, which appear in grey text in the table.

(2) Please note that, although the specific exemption for the use of hexachlorobenzene as closedsystem site-limited intermediate is no longer available, this use is still possible in accordance with note (iii) of Part I of this Annex.

Notes:

(i) Except as otherwise specified in this Convention, quantities of a chemical occurring as unintentional trace contaminants in products and articles shall not be considered to be listed in this Annex;

(ii) This note shall not be considered as a production and use specific exemption for purposes of paragraph 2 of Article 3. Quantities of a chemical occurring as constituents of articles manufactured or already in use before or on the date of entry into force of the relevant obligation with respect to that chemical, shall not be considered as listed in this Annex, provided that a Party has notified the Secretariat that a particular type of article remains in use within that Party. The Secretariat shall make such notifications publicly available;

(iii) This note, which does not apply to a chemical that has an asterisk following its name in the Chemical column in Part I of this Annex, shall not be considered as a production and use specific exemption for purposes of paragraph 2 of Article 3. Given that no significant quantities of the chemical are expected to reach humans and the environment during the production and use of a closed-system site limited intermediate, a Party, upon notification to the Secretariat, may allow the production and use of quantities of a chemical listed in this Annex as a closed-system site-limited intermediate that is chemically transformed in the manufacture of other chemicals that, taking into consideration the criteria in paragraph 1 of Annex D, do not exhibit the characteristics of persistent organic pollutants. This notification shall include information on total production and use of such chemical or a reasonable estimate of such information and information regarding the nature of the closed-system site limited process including the amount of any non-transformed and unintentional trace contamination of the persistent organic pollutant starting material in the final product. This procedure applies except as otherwise specified in this Annex. The Secretariat shall make such notifications available to the Conference of the Parties and to the public. Such production or use shall not be considered a production or use specific exemption. Such production and use shall cease after a ten-year period, unless the Party concerned submits a new notification to the Secretariat, in which case the period will be extended for an additional ten years unless the Conference of the Parties, after a review of the production and use decides otherwise. The notification procedure can be repeated;

(iv) All the specific exemptions in this Annex may be exercised by Parties that have registered exemptions in respect of them in accordance with Article 4 with the exception of the use of polychlorinated biphenyls in articles in use in accordance with the provisions of Part II, [and the use of hexabromodiphenyl ether and heptabromodiphenyl ether in accordance with the provisions of Part IV of this Annex, and the use of tetrabromodiphenyl ether and pentabromodiphenyl ether in accordance with the provisions of Part V of this Annex][1], which may be exercised by all Parties.

[(v) Technical endosulfan (CAS No: 115-29-7), its related isomers (CAS No: 959-98-8 and CAS No: 33213-65-9) and endosulfan sulfate (CAS No: 1031-07-8) were assessed and identified as persistent organic pollutants.][2]

Amendments

1 Inserted by decisions SC-4/10, 4/11, 4/12, 4,/13, 4/14, 4/15, 4/16 and 4/18, as adopted by the Conference of the Parties at its fourth meeting held in Geneva from 4 to 8 May 2009.

2 Inserted by decision SC-5/3, as adopted by the Conference of the Parties at its fifth meeting held in Geneva from 25 to 29 April 2011.

PART II
POLYCHLORINATED BIPHENYLS

Each Party shall:

(a) With regard to the elimination of the use of polychlorinated biphenyls in equipment (e.g. transformers, capacitors or other receptacles containing liquid stocks) by 2025, subject to review by the Conference of the Parties, take action in accordance with the following priorities:
   (i) Make determined efforts to identify, label and remove from use equipment containing greater than 10 per cent polychlorinated biphenyls and volumes greater than 5 litres;
   (ii) Make determined efforts to identify, label and remove from use equipment containing greater than 0.05 per cent polychlorinated biphenyls and volumes greater than 5 litres;
   (iii) Endeavour to identify and remove from use equipment containing greater than 0.005 per cent polychlorinated biphenyls and volumes greater than 0.05 litres;

(b) Consistent with the priorities in subparagraph (a), promote the following measures to reduce exposures and risk to control the use of polychlorinated biphenyls:
   (i) Use only in intact and non-leaking equipment and only in areas where the risk from environmental release can be minimised and quickly remedied;
   (ii) Not use in equipment in areas associated with the production or processing of food or feed;
   (iii) When used in populated areas, including schools and hospitals, all reasonable measures to protect from electrical failure which could result in a fire, and regular inspection of equipment for leaks;

(c) Notwithstanding paragraph 2 of Article 3, ensure that equipment containing polychlorinated biphenyls, as described in subparagraph (a), shall not be exported or imported except for the purpose of environmentally sound waste management;

(d) Except for maintenance and servicing operations, not allow recovery for the purpose of reuse in other equipment of liquids with polychlorinated biphenyls content above 0.005 per cent;

(e) Make determined efforts designed to lead to environmentally sound waste management of liquids containing polychlorinated biphenyls and equipment contaminated with polychlorinated biphenyls having a polychlorinated biphenyls content above 0.005 per cent, in accordance with paragraph 1 of Article 6, as soon as possible but no later than 2028, subject to review by the Conference of the Parties;

(f) In lieu of note (ii) in Part I of this Annex, endeavour to identify other articles containing more than 0.005 per cent polychlorinated biphenyls (e.g. cable-sheaths, cured caulk and painted objects) and manage them in accordance with paragraph 1 of Article 6;

(g) Provide a report every five years on progress in eliminating polychlorinated biphenyls and submit it to the Conference of the Parties pursuant to Article 15;

(h) The reports described in subparagraph (g) shall, as appropriate, be considered by the Conference of the Parties in its reviews relating to polychlorinated biphenyls. The Conference of the Parties shall review progress towards elimination of polychlorinated biphenyls at five year intervals or other period, as appropriate, taking into account such reports.

[PART III
DEFINITIONS][1]

[For the purpose of this Annex:

(a) "Hexabromodiphenyl ether and heptabromodiphenyl ether" means 2,2',4,4',5,5'-hexabromodiphenyl ether (BDE-153, CAS No: 68631-49-2), 2,2',4,4',5,6'-hexabromodiphenyl ether (BDE-154, CAS No: 207122-15-4), 2,2',3,3',4,5',6-heptabromodiphenyl ether (BDE-175, CAS No: 446255- 22-7), 2,2',3,4,4',5',6-heptabromodiphenyl ether (BDE-183, CAS No: 207122-16-5) and other hexa- and heptabromodiphenyl ethers present in commercial octabromodiphenyl ether.

(b) "Tetrabromodiphenyl ether and pentabromodiphenyl ether" means 2,2',4,4'-tetrabromodiphenyl ether (BDE-47, CAS No: 5436-43-1) and 2,2',4,4',5-pentabromodiphenyl ether (BDE-99, CAS No: 60348-60-9) and other tetra- and pentabromodiphenyl ethers present in commercial pentabromodiphenyl ether.][1]

Amendment

1 Inserted by decisions SC-4/14 and 4/18, as adopted by the Conference of the Parties at its fourth meeting held in Geneva from 4 to 8 May 2009.

[PART IV HEXABROMODIPHENYL ETHER AND HEPTABROMODIPHENYL ETHER][1]

[1. A Party may allow recycling of articles that contain or may contain hexabromodiphenyl ether and heptabromodiphenyl ether, and the use and final disposal of articles manufactured from recycled materials that contain or may contain hexabromodiphenyl ether and heptabromodiphenyl ether, provided that:

(a) The recycling and final disposal is carried out in an environmentally sound manner and does not lead to recovery of hexabromodiphenyl ether and heptabromodiphenyl ether for the purpose of their reuse;

(b) The Party takes steps to prevent exports of such articles that contain levels/ concentrations of hexabromodiphenyl ether and heptabromodiphenyl ether exceeding those permitted for the sale, use, import or manufacture of those articles within the territory of the Party; and

(c) The Party has notified the Secretariat of its intention to make use of this exemption.

2. At its sixth ordinary meeting and at every second ordinary meeting thereafter the Conference of the Parties shall evaluate the progress that Parties have made towards achieving their ultimate objective of elimination of hexabromodiphenyl ether and heptabromodiphenyl ether contained in articles and review the continued need for this specific exemption. This specific exemption shall in any case expire at the latest in 2030.][1]

Amendment

1 Inserted by decision SC-4/14, as adopted by the Conference of the Parties at its fourth meeting held in Geneva from 4 to 8 May 2009.

[PART V TETRABROMODIPHENYL ETHER AND PENTABROMODIPHENYL ETHER][1]

[1. A Party may allow recycling of articles that contain or may contain tetrabromodiphenyl ether and pentabromodiphenyl ether, and the use and final disposal of articles manufactured from recycled materials that contain or may contain tetrabromodiphenyl ether and pentabromodiphenyl ether, provided that:

(a) The recycling and final disposal is carried out in an environmentally sound manner and does not lead to recovery of tetrabromodiphenyl ether and pentabromodiphenyl ether for the purpose of their reuse;

(b) The Party does not allow this exemption to lead to the export of articles containing levels/concentrations of tetrabromodiphenyl ether and pentabromodiphenyl ether that exceed those permitted to be sold within the territory of the Party; and

(c) The Party has notified the Secretariat of its intention to make use of this exemption.

2. At its sixth ordinary meeting and at every second ordinary meeting thereafter the Conference of the Parties shall evaluate the progress that Parties have made towards achieving their ultimate objective of elimination of tetrabromodiphenyl ether and pentabromodiphenyl ether contained in articles and review the continued need for this specific exemption. This specific exemption shall in any case expire at the latest in 2030.][1]

Amendment

1 Inserted by decision SC-4/18, as adopted by the Conference of the Parties at its fourth meeting held in Geneva from 4 to 8 May 2009.

[PART VI
TECHNICAL ENDOSULFAN AND ITS RELATED ISOMERS (ENDOSULFAN)][1]

[The production and use of endosulfan shall be eliminated except for parties that have notified the Secretariat of their intention to produce and/or use it in accordance with Article 4 of the Convention. Specific exemptions may be available for the use of endosulfan for the following crop-pest complexes:

Crop	*Pest*
Apple	Aphids
Arhar, gram	Aphids, caterpillars, pea semilooper, pod borer
Bean, cowpea	Aphids, leaf miner, whiteflies
Chilli, onion, potato	Aphids, jassids
Coffee	Berry Borer, stem borer
Cotton	Aphids, cotton bollworm, jassids, leaf rollers, pink bollworm, thrips, whiteflies
Eggplant, okra	Aphids, diamondback moth, jassids, shoot and fruit borer
Groundnut	Aphids
Jute	Bihar hairy caterpillar, yellow mite
Maize	Aphids, pink borer, stem borers
Mango	Fruit flies, hoppers
Mustard	Aphids, gall midges
Rice	Gall midges, rice hispa, stem borers, white jassid
Tea	Aphids, caterpillars, flushworm, mealybugs, scale insects, smaller green leafhopper, tea geometrid, tea mosquito bug, thrips
Tobacco	Aphids, oriental tobacco budworm
Tomato	Aphids, diamondback moth, jassids, leaf miner, shoot and fruit borer, whiteflies
Wheat	Aphids, pink borer, termites][1]

Amendment

1 Inserted by decision SC-5/3, as adopted by the Conference of the Parties at its fifth meeting held in Geneva from 25 to 29 April 2011.

ANNEX B
RESTRICTION

PART I

Chemical	*Activity*	*Acceptable purpose or specific exemption*[1]
DDT (1,1,1-trichloro-2,2-bis (4-chlorophenyl)ethane) CAS No: 50-29-3	Production	Acceptable purpose: Disease vector control use in accordance with Part II of this Annex Specific exemption: Intermediate in production of dicofol Intermediate
	Use	Acceptable purpose: Disease vector control in accordance with Part II of this Annex Specific exemption: Production of dicofol Intermediate
[Perfluorooctane sulfonic acid (CAS No: 1763-23-1), its salts* and perfluorooctane sulfonyl fl uoride (CAS No: 307-35-7) *For example: potassium perfluorooctane sulfonate (CAS No: 2795-39-3); lithium perfluorooctane sulfonate (CAS No: 29457- 72-5); ammonium perfluorooctane sulfonate (CAS No: 29081-56-9); diethanolammonium perfluorooctane sulfonate (CAS No: 70225-14-8); tetraethylammonium perfluorooctane sulfonate (CAS No: 56773-42-3); didecyldimethylammonium perfluorooctane sulfonate (CAS No: 251099-16-8)	Production	Acceptable purpose: In accordance with Part III of this Annex, production of other chemicals to be used solely for the uses below. Production for uses listed below. Specifi c exemption: As allowed for Parties listed in the Register.
	Use	Acceptable purpose: In accordance with Part III of this Annex for the following acceptable purposes, or as an intermediate in the production of chemicals with the following acceptable purposes: • Photo-imaging • Photo-resist and anti-reflective coatings for semi-conductors • Etching agent for compound semiconductors and ceramic filters • Aviation hydraulic fluids • Metal plating (hard metal plating) only in closed-loop systems • Certain medical devices (such as ethylene tetrafluoroethylene copolymer (ETFE) layers and radio-opaque ETFE production, in-vitro diagnostic medical devices, and CCD colour filters) Chemical Activity Acceptable purpose or specific exemption • Fire-fighting foam • Insect baits for control of leaf-cutting ants from Atta spp. and Acromyrmex spp.

Chemical	*Activity*	*Acceptable purpose or specific exemption*[1]
		Specific exemption: For the following specific uses, or as an intermediate in the production of chemicals with the following specific uses: • Photo masks in the semiconductor and liquid crystal display (LCD) industries • Metal plating (hard metal plating) • Metal plating (decorative plating) • Electric and electronic parts for some colour printers and colour copy machines • Insecticides for control of red imported fire ants and termites • Chemically driven oil production • Carpets • Leather and apparel • Textiles and upholstery • Paper and packaging • Coatings and coating additives • Rubber and plastics][1]

1. Please note that, as at 17 May 2009, there were no Parties registered for the specific exemptions listed in Annex B pertaining to DDT. Therefore, in accordance with paragraph 9 of Article 4 of the Convention, no new registrations may be made with respect to such exemptions, which appear in grey text in the table.

Notes:

(i) Except as otherwise specified in this Convention, quantities of a chemical occurring as unintentional trace contaminants in products and articles shall not be considered to be listed in this Annex;

(ii) This note shall not be considered as a production and use acceptable purpose or specific exemption for purposes of paragraph 2 of Article 3. Quantities of a chemical occurring as constituents of articles manufactured or already in use before or on the date of entry into force of the relevant obligation with respect to that chemical, shall not be considered as listed in this Annex, provided that a Party has notified the Secretariat that a particular type of article remains in use within that Party. The Secretariat shall make such notifications publicly available;

(iii) This note shall not be considered as a production and use specific exemption for purposes of paragraph 2 of Article 3. Given that no significant quantities of the chemical are expected to reach humans and the environment during the production and use of a closed-system site-limited intermediate, a Party, upon notification to the Secretariat, may allow the production and use of quantities of a chemical listed in this Annex as a closed-system site-limited intermediate that is chemically transformed in the manufacture of other chemicals that, taking into consideration the criteria in paragraph 1 of Annex D, do not exhibit the characteristics of persistent organic pollutants. This notification shall include information on total production and use of such chemical or a reasonable estimate of such information and information regarding the nature of the closed-system site limited process including the amount of any non-transformed and unintentional trace contamination of the persistent organic pollutant starting material in the fi nal product. This procedure applies except as otherwise specified in this Annex. The Secretariat shall make such notifications available to the Conference of the Parties and to the public. Such production or use shall not be considered a production or use specific exemption. Such production and use shall cease after a ten-year period, unless the Party concerned submits a new notification to the Secretariat, in which case the period will be extended for an additional ten years unless the Conference of the Parties, after a review of the production and use decides otherwise. The notification procedure can be repeated;

(iv) All the specific exemptions in this Annex may be exercised by Parties that have registered in respect of them in accordance with Article 4.

Amendment

1 Inserted by decision SC-4/17, as adopted by the Conference of the Parties at its fourth meeting held in Geneva from 4 to 8 May 2009.

PART II DDT (1,1,1-TRICHLORO-2,2-BIS(4-CHLOROPHENYL)ETHANE)

1. The production and use of DDT shall be eliminated except for Parties that have notified the Secretariat of their intention to produce and/or use it. A DDT Register is hereby established and shall be available to the public. The Secretariat shall maintain the DDT Register.

2. Each Party that produces and/or uses DDT shall restrict such production and/or use for disease vector control in accordance with the World Health Organization recommendations and guidelines on the use of DDT and when locally safe, effective and affordable alternatives are not available to the Party in question.

3. In the event that a Party not listed in the DDT Register determines that it requires DDT for disease vector control, it shall notify the Secretariat as soon as possible in order to have its name added forthwith to the DDT Register. It shall at the same time notify the World Health Organization.

4. Every three years, each Party that uses DDT shall provide to the Secretariat and the World Health Organization information on the amount used, the conditions of such use and its relevance to that Party's disease management strategy, in a format to be decided by the Conference of the Parties in consultation with the World Health Organization.

5. With the goal of reducing and ultimately eliminating the use of DDT, the Conference of the Parties shall encourage:

(a) Each Party using DDT to develop and implement an action plan as part of the implementation plan specified in Article 7. That action plan shall include:

(i) Development of regulatory and other mechanisms to ensure that DDT use is restricted to disease vector control;

(ii) Implementation of suitable alternative products, methods and strategies, including resistance management strategies to ensure the continuing effectiveness of these alternatives;

(iii) Measures to strengthen health care and to reduce the incidence of the disease.

(b) The Parties, within their capabilities, to promote research and development of safe alternative chemical and non-chemical products, methods and strategies for Parties using DDT, relevant to the conditions of those countries and with the goal of decreasing the human and economic burden of disease. Factors to be promoted when considering alternatives or combinations of alternatives shall include the human health risks and environmental implications of such alternatives. Viable alternatives to DDT shall pose less risk to human health and the environment, be suitable for disease control based on conditions in the Parties in question and be supported with monitoring data.

6. Commencing at its first meeting, and at least every three years thereafter, the Conference of the Parties shall, in consultation with the World Health Organization, evaluate the continued need for DDT for disease vector control on the basis of available scientific, technical, environmental and economic information, including:

(a) The production and use of DDT and the conditions set out in paragraph 2;

(b) The availability, suitability and implementation of the alternatives to DDT; and

(c) Progress in strengthening the capacity of countries to transfer safely to reliance on such alternatives.

7. A Party may, at any time, withdraw its name from the DDT Registry upon written notification to the Secretariat. The withdrawal shall take effect on the date specified in the notification.

[PART III PERFLUOROOCTANE SULFONIC ACID, ITS SALTS, AND PERFLUOROOCTANE SULFONYL FLUORIDE][1]

[1. The production and use of perfluorooctane sulfonic acid (PFOS), its salts and perfluorooctane sulfonyl fl uoride (PFOSF) shall be eliminated by all Parties except as provided in Part I of this Annex for Parties that have notified the Secretariat of their intention to produce and/or use them for acceptable purposes. A Register of Acceptable Purposes is hereby established and shall be available to the public. The Secretariat shall maintain the Register of Acceptable Purposes. In the event that a Party not listed in the Register determines that it requires the use of PFOS, its salts or PFOSF for the acceptable purposes listed in Part I of this Annex it shall notify the Secretariat as soon as possible in order to have its name added forthwith to the Register.

2. Parties that produce and/or use these chemicals shall take into account, as appropriate, guidance such as that given in the relevant parts of the general guidance on best available techniques and best environmental practices given in Part V of Annex C of the Convention.

3. Every four years, each Party that uses and/or produces these chemicals shall report on progress made to eliminate PFOS, its salts and PFOSF and submit information on such progress to the Conference of the Parties pursuant to and in the process of reporting under Article 15 of the Convention.

4. With the goal of reducing and ultimately eliminating the production and/or use of these chemicals, the Conference of the Parties shall encourage:

(a) Each Party using these chemicals to take action to phase out uses when suitable alternatives substances or methods are available;

(b) Each Party using and/or producing these chemicals to develop and implement an action plan as part of the implementation plan specified in Article 7 of the Convention;

(c) The Parties, within their capabilities, to promote research on and development of safe alternative chemical and non-chemical products and processes, methods and strategies for Parties using these chemicals, relevant to the conditions of those Parties. Factors to be promoted when considering alternatives or combinations of alternatives shall include the human health risks and environmental implications of such alternatives.

5. The Conference of the Parties shall evaluate the continued need for these chemicals for the various acceptable purposes and specific exemptions on the basis of available scientific, technical, environmental and economic information, including:

(a) Information provided in the reports described in paragraph 3;

(b) Information on the production and use of these chemicals;

(c) Information on the availability, suitability and implementation of alternatives to these chemicals;

(d) Information on progress in building the capacity of countries to transfer safely to reliance on such alternatives.

6. The evaluation referred to in the preceding paragraph shall take place no later than in 2015 and every four years thereafter, in conjunction with a regular meeting of the Conference of the Parties.

7. Due to the complexity of the use and the many sectors of society involved in the use of these chemicals, there might be other uses of these chemicals of which countries are not presently aware. Parties which become aware of other uses are encouraged to inform the Secretariat as soon as possible.

8. A Party may, at any time, withdraw its name from the Register of acceptable purposes upon written notification to the Secretariat. The withdrawal shall take effect on the date specified in the notification.

9. The provisions of note (iii) of Part I of Annex B shall not apply to these chemicals.][1]

Amendment

1 Inserted by decision SC-4/17, as adopted by the Conference of the Parties at its fourth meeting held in Geneva from 4 to 8 May 2009.

ANNEX C
UNINTENTIONAL PRODUCTION

PART I PERSISTENT ORGANIC POLLUTANTS SUBJECT TO THE REQUIREMENTS OF ARTICLE 5

This Annex applies to the following persistent organic pollutants when formed and released unintentionally from anthropogenic sources:

Chemical

Hexachlorobenzene (HCB) (CAS No: 118-74-1)

Polychlorinated biphenyls (PCB)

Polychlorinated dibenzo-p-dioxins and dibenzofurans (PCDD/PCDF)

[Pentachlorobenzene (PeCB) (CAS No: 608-93-5)][1]

Amendment

1 Inserted by decision SC-4/16, as adopted by the Conference of the Parties at its fourth meeting held in Geneva from 4 to 8 May 2009.

PART II SOURCE CATEGORIES

Hexachlorobenzene, polychlorinated biphenyls, polychlorinated dibenzo-p-dioxins and dibenzofurans [and pentachlorobenzene][1] are unintentionally formed and released from thermal processes involving organic matter and chlorine as a result of incomplete combustion or chemical reactions. The following industrial source categories have the potential for comparatively high formation and release of these chemicals to the environment:

(a) Waste incinerators, including co-incinerators of municipal, hazardous or medical waste or of sewage sludge;
(b) Cement kilns firing hazardous waste;
(c) Production of pulp using elemental chlorine or chemicals generating elemental chlorine for bleaching;
(d) The following thermal processes in the metallurgical industry:
    (i) Secondary copper production;
    (ii) Sinter plants in the iron and steel industry;
    (iii) Secondary aluminium production;
    (iv) Secondary zinc production.

Amendment

1 Inserted by decision SC-4/16, as adopted by the Conference of the Parties at its fourth meeting held in Geneva from 4 to 8 May 2009.

PART III SOURCE CATEGORIES

Hexachlorobenzene, polychlorinated biphenyls, polychlorinated dibenzo-p-dioxins and dibenzofurans [and pentachlorobenzene][1] may also be unintentionally formed and released from the following source categories, including:

(a) Open burning of waste, including burning of landfill sites;
(b) Thermal processes in the metallurgical industry not mentioned in Part II;
(c) Residential combustion sources;
(d) Fossil fuel-fi red utility and industrial boilers;
(e) Firing installations for wood and other biomass fuels;
(f) Specific chemical production processes releasing unintentionally formed persistent organic pollutants, especially production of chlorophenols and chloranil;
(g) Crematoria;
(h) Motor vehicles, particularly those burning leaded gasoline;
(i) Destruction of animal carcasses;
(j) Textile and leather dyeing (with chloranil) and finishing (with alkaline extraction);
(k) Shredder plants for the treatment of end of life vehicles;
(l) Smouldering of copper cables;
(m) Waste oil refineries.

Amendment

1 Inserted by decision SC-4/16, as adopted by the Conference of the Parties at its fourth meeting held in Geneva from 4 to 8 May 2009.

PART IV DEFINITIONS

1. For the purposes of this Annex:
(a) "Polychlorinated biphenyls" means aromatic compounds formed in such a manner that the hydrogen atoms on the biphenyl molecule (two benzene rings bonded together by a single carbon-carbon bond) may be replaced by up to ten chlorine atoms; and
(b) "Polychlorinated dibenzo-p-dioxins" and "polychlorinated dibenzofurans" are tricyclic, aromatic compounds formed by two benzene rings connected by two oxygen atoms in polychlorinated dibenzo-p-dioxins and by one oxygen atom and one carbon-carbon bond in polychlorinated dibenzofurans and the hydrogen atoms of which may be replaced by up to eight chlorine atoms.

2. In this Annex, the toxicity of polychlorinated dibenzo-p-dioxins and dibenzofurans is expressed using the concept of toxic equivalency which measures the relative dioxin-like toxic activity of different congeners of polychlorinated dibenzo-p-dioxins and dibenzofurans and coplanar polychlorinated biphenyls in comparison to 2,3,7,8-tetrachlorodibenzop- dioxin. The toxic equivalent factor values to be used for the purposes of this Convention shall be consistent with accepted international standards, commencing with the World Health Organization 1998 mammalian toxic equivalent factor values for polychlorinated dibenzo-p-dioxins and dibenzofurans and coplanar polychlorinated biphenyls. Concentrations are expressed in toxic equivalents.

PART V GENERAL GUIDANCE ON BEST AVAILABLE TECHNIQUES AND BEST ENVIRONMENTAL PRACTICES

This Part provides general guidance to Parties on preventing or reducing releases of the chemicals listed in Part I.

A. General prevention measures relating to both best available techniques and best environmental practices

Priority should be given to the consideration of approaches to prevent the formation and release of the chemicals listed in Part I. Useful measures could include:
(a) The use of low-waste technology;
(b) The use of less hazardous substances;
(c) The promotion of the recovery and recycling of waste and of substances generated and used in a process;

(d) Replacement of feed materials which are persistent organic pollutants or where there is a direct link between the materials and releases of persistent organic pollutants from the source;
(e) Good housekeeping and preventive maintenance programmes;
(f) Improvements in waste management with the aim of the cessation of open and other uncontrolled burning of wastes, including the burning of landfill sites. When considering proposals to construct new waste disposal facilities, consideration should be given to alternatives such as activities to minimize the generation of municipal and medical waste, including resource recovery, reuse, recycling, waste separation and promoting products that generate less waste. Under this approach, public health concerns should be carefully considered;
(g) Minimization of these chemicals as contaminants in products;
(h) Avoiding elemental chlorine or chemicals generating elemental chlorine for bleaching.

B. Best available techniques

The concept of best available techniques is not aimed at the prescription of any specific technique or technology, but at taking into account the technical characteristics of the installation concerned, its geographical location and the local environmental conditions. Appropriate control techniques to reduce releases of the chemicals listed in Part I are in general the same. In determining best available techniques, special consideration should be given, generally or in specific cases, to the following factors, bearing in mind the likely costs and benefits of a measure and consideration of precaution and prevention:

(a) General considerations:
  (i) The nature, effects and mass of the releases concerned: techniques may vary depending on source size;
  (ii) The commissioning dates for new or existing installations;
  (iii) The time needed to introduce the best available technique;
  (iv) The consumption and nature of raw materials used in the process and its energy efficiency;
  (v) The need to prevent or reduce to a minimum the overall impact of the releases to the environment and the risks to it;
  (vi) The need to prevent accidents and to minimize their consequences for the environment;
  (vii) The need to ensure occupational health and safety at workplaces;
  (viii) Comparable processes, facilities or methods of operation which have been tried with success on an industrial scale;
  (ix) Technological advances and changes in scientific knowledge and understanding.
(b) General release reduction measures: When considering proposals to construct new facilities or significantly modify existing facilities using processes that release chemicals listed in this Annex, priority consideration should be given to alternative processes, techniques or practices that have similar usefulness but which avoid the formation and release of such chemicals. In cases where such facilities will be constructed or significantly modified, in addition to the prevention measures outlined in section A of Part V the following reduction measures could also be considered in determining best available techniques:
  (i) Use of improved methods for fl ue-gas cleaning such as thermal or catalytic oxidation, dust precipitation, or adsorption;
  (ii) Treatment of residuals, wastewater, wastes and sewage sludge by, for example, thermal treatment or rendering them inert or chemical processes that detoxify them;
  (iii) Process changes that lead to the reduction or elimination of releases, such as moving to closed systems;
  (iv) Modification of process designs to improve combustion and prevent formation of the chemicals listed in this Annex, through the control of parameters such as incineration temperature or residence time.

C. Best environmental practices

The Conference of the Parties may develop guidance with regard to best environmental practices.

ANNEX D
INFORMATION REQUIREMENTS AND SCREENING CRITERIA

1. A Party submitting a proposal to list a chemical in Annexes A, B and/or C shall identify the chemical in the manner described in subparagraph (a) and provide the information on the chemical, and its transformation products where relevant, relating to the screening criteria set out in subparagraphs (b) to (e):

(a) Chemical identity:
  - (i) Names, including trade name or names, commercial name or names and synonyms, Chemical Abstracts Service (CAS) Registry number, International Union of Pure and Applied Chemistry (IUPAC) name; and
  - (ii) Structure, including specification of isomers, where applicable, and the structure of the chemical class;

(b) Persistence:
  - (i) Evidence that the half-life of the chemical in water is greater than two months, or that its half-life in soil is greater than six months, or that its half-life in sediment is greater than six months; or
  - (ii) Evidence that the chemical is otherwise sufficiently persistent to justify its consideration within the scope of this Convention;

(c) Bio-accumulation:
  - (i) Evidence that the bio-concentration factor or bio-accumulation factor in aquatic species for the chemical is greater than 5,000 or, in the absence of such data, that the log Kow is greater than 5;
  - (ii) Evidence that a chemical presents other reasons for concern, such as high bio-accumulation in other species, high toxicity or ecotoxicity; or
  - (iii) Monitoring data in biota indicating that the bio-accumulation potential of the chemical is sufficient to justify its consideration within the scope of this Convention;

(d) Potential for long-range environmental transport:
  - (i) Measured levels of the chemical in locations distant from the sources of its release that are of potential concern;
  - (ii) Monitoring data showing that long-range environmental transport of the chemical, with the potential for transfer to a receiving environment, may have occurred via air, water or migratory species; or
  - (iii) Environmental fate properties and/or model results that demonstrate that the chemical has a potential for long-range environmental transport through air, water or migratory species, with the potential for transfer to a receiving environment in locations distant from the sources of its release. For a chemical that migrates significantly through the air, its half-life in air should be greater than two days; and

(e) Adverse effects:
  - (i) Evidence of adverse effects to human health or to the environment that justifies consideration of the chemical within the scope of this Convention; or
  - (ii) Toxicity or ecotoxicity data that indicate the potential for damage to human health or to the environment.

2. The proposing Party shall provide a statement of the reasons for concern including, where possible, a comparison of toxicity or ecotoxicity data with detected or predicted levels of a chemical resulting or anticipated from its long-range environmental transport, and a short statement indicating the need for global control.

3. The proposing Party shall, to the extent possible and taking into account its capabilities, provide additional information to support the review of the proposal referred to in paragraph 6 of Article 8. In developing such a proposal, a Party may draw on technical expertise from any source.

ANNEX E
INFORMATION REQUIREMENTS FOR THE RISK PROFILE

The purpose of the review is to evaluate whether the chemical is likely, as a result of its long-range environmental transport, to lead to significant adverse human health and/or environmental effects, such that global action is warranted. For this purpose, a risk profile shall be developed that further elaborates on, and evaluates, the information referred to in Annex D and includes, as far as possible, the following types of information:

(a) Sources, including as appropriate:
  (i) Production data, including quantity and location;
  (ii) Uses; and
  (iii) Releases, such as discharges, losses and emissions;
(b) Hazard assessment for the endpoint or endpoints of concern, including a consideration of toxicological interactions involving multiple chemicals;
(c) Environmental fate, including data and information on the chemical and physical properties of a chemical as well as its persistence and how they are linked to its environmental transport, transfer within and between environmental compartments, degradation and transformation to other chemicals. A determination of the bio-concentration factor or bioaccumulation factor, based on measured values, shall be available, except when monitoring data are judged to meet this need;
(d) Monitoring data;
(e) Exposure in local areas and, in particular, as a result of long-range environmental transport, and including information regarding bioavailability;
(f) National and international risk evaluations, assessments or profiles and labelling information and hazard classifications, as available; and
(g) Status of the chemical under international conventions.

ANNEX F
INFORMATION ON SOCIO-ECONOMIC CONSIDERATIONS

An evaluation should be undertaken regarding possible control measures for chemicals under consideration for inclusion in this Convention, encompassing the full range of options, including management and elimination. For this purpose, relevant information should be provided relating to socio-economic considerations associated with possible control measures to enable a decision to be taken by the Conference of the Parties. Such information should refl ect due regard for the differing capabilities and conditions among the Parties and should include consideration of the following indicative list of items:

(a) Efficacy and efficiency of possible control measures in meeting risk reduction goals:
  (i) Technical feasibility; and
  (ii) Costs, including environmental and health costs;
(b) Alternatives (products and processes):
  (i) Technical feasibility;
  (ii) Costs, including environmental and health costs;
  (iii) Efficacy;
  (iv) Risk;
  (v) Availability; and
  (vi) Accessibility;
(c) Positive and/or negative impacts on society of implementing possible control measures:
  (i) Health, including public, environmental and occupational health;

- (ii) Agriculture, including aquaculture and forestry;
- (iii) Biota (biodiversity);
- (iv) Economic aspects;
- (v) Movement towards sustainable development; and
- (vi) Social costs;

(d) Waste and disposal implications (in particular, obsolete stocks of pesticides and clean-up of contaminated sites):

- (i) Technical feasibility; and
- (ii) Cost;

(e) Access to information and public education;

(f) Status of control and monitoring capacity; and

(g) Any national or regional control actions taken, including information on alternatives, and other relevant risk management information.

ANNEX G
ARBITRATION AND CONCILIATION PROCEDURES FOR SETTLEMENT OF DISPUTES
(DECISION SC-1/2 OF THE CONFERENCE OF THE PARTIES)

PART I ARBITRATION PROCEDURE

The arbitration procedure for purposes of paragraph 2 (a) of Article 18 of the Convention shall be as follows:

Article 1

1. A Party may initiate recourse to arbitration in accordance with Article 18 of the Convention by written notification addressed to the other party to the dispute. The notification shall be accompanied by a statement of the claim, together with any supporting documents, and state the subject-matter of arbitration and include, in particular, the articles of the Convention the interpretation or application of which are at issue.

2. The claimant party shall notify the Secretariat that the parties are referring a dispute to arbitration pursuant to Article 18. The notification shall be accompanied by the written notification of the claimant party, the statement of claim and the supporting documents referred to in paragraph 1 above. The Secretariat shall forward the information thus received to all Parties.

Article 2

1. If a dispute is referred to arbitration in accordance with Article 1 above, an arbitral tribunal shall be established. It shall consist of three members.

2. Each of the parties to the dispute shall appoint an arbitrator and the two arbitrators so appointed shall designate by common agreement the third arbitrator, who shall be the President of the tribunal. The President of the tribunal shall not be a national of one of the parties to the dispute, nor have his or her usual place of residence in the territory of one of those parties, nor be employed by any of them, nor have dealt with the case in any other capacity.

3. In disputes between more than two parties, parties in the same interest shall appoint one arbitrator jointly by agreement.

4. Any vacancy shall be filled in the manner prescribed for the initial appointment.

5. If the parties do not agree on the subject-matter of the dispute before the President of the arbitral tribunal is designated, the arbitral tribunal shall determine the subject-matter.

Article 3

1. If one of the parties to the dispute does not appoint an arbitrator within two months of the date on which the respondent party receives the notification of the arbitration, the other party may inform the Secretary-General of the United Nations, who shall make the designation within a further two-month period.

2. If the President of the arbitral tribunal has not been designated within two months of the date of the appointment of the second arbitrator, the Secretary- General of the United Nations shall, at the request of a party, designate the President within a further two-month period.

Article 4

The arbitral tribunal shall render its decisions in accordance with the provisions of the Convention and international law.

Article 5

Unless the parties to the dispute otherwise agree, the arbitral tribunal shall determine its own rules of procedure.

Article 6

The arbitral tribunal may, at the request of one of the parties, indicate essential interim measures of protection.

Article 7

The parties to the dispute shall facilitate the work of the arbitral tribunal and, in particular, using all means at their disposal, shall:

(a) Provide it with all relevant documents, information and facilities; and

(b) Enable it, when necessary, to call witnesses or experts and receive their evidence.

Article 8

The parties and the arbitrators are under an obligation to protect the confidentiality of any information they receive in confidence during the proceedings of the arbitral tribunal.

Article 9

Unless the arbitral tribunal determines otherwise because of the particular circumstances of the case, the costs of the tribunal shall be borne by the parties to the dispute in equal shares. The tribunal shall keep a record of all its costs, and shall furnish a final statement thereof to the parties.

Article 10

A party that has an interest of a legal nature in the subject matter of the dispute which may be affected by the decision in the case may intervene in the proceedings with the consent of the tribunal.

Article 11

The tribunal may hear and determine counterclaims arising directly out of the subject matter of the dispute.

Article 12

Decisions both on procedure and substance of the arbitral tribunal shall be taken by a majority vote of its members.

Article 13

1. If one of the parties to the dispute does not appear before the arbitral tribunal or fails to defend its case, the other party may request the tribunal to continue the proceedings and to make its award. Absence of a party or a failure of a party to defend its case shall not constitute a bar to the proceedings.

2. Before rendering its final decision, the arbitral tribunal must satisfy itself that the claim is well founded in fact and law.

Article 14

The tribunal shall render its final decision within five months of the date on which it is fully constituted unless it finds it necessary to extend the time limit for a period which should not exceed five more months.

Article 15

The final decision of the arbitral tribunal shall be confined to the subject matter of the dispute and shall state the reasons on which it is based. It shall contain the names of the members who have participated and the date of the final decision. Any member of the tribunal may attach a separate or dissenting opinion to the final decision.

Article 16

The award shall be binding on the parties to the dispute. The interpretation of the Convention given by the award shall also be binding upon a Party intervening under Article 10 above insofar as it relates to matters in respect of which that Party intervened. The award shall be without appeal unless the parties to the dispute have agreed in advance to an appellate procedure.

Article 17

Any controversy which may arise between those bound by the fi nal decision in accordance with Article 16 above, as regards the interpretation or manner of implementation of that decision, may be submitted by any of them for decision to the arbitral tribunal which rendered it.

PART II CONCILIATION PROCEDURE

The conciliation procedure for purposes of paragraph 6 of Article 18 of the Convention shall be as follows:

Article 1

1. A request by a party to a dispute to establish a conciliation commission in consequence of paragraph 6 of Article 18 shall be addressed in writing to the Secretariat. The Secretariat shall forthwith inform all Parties to the Convention accordingly.

2. The conciliation commission shall, unless the parties otherwise agree, be composed of three members, one appointed by each party concerned and a President chosen jointly by those members.

Article 2

In disputes between more than two parties, parties in the same interest shall appoint their members of the commission jointly by agreement.

Article 3

If any appointments by the parties are not made within two months of the date of receipt by the Secretariat of the written request referred to in Article 1, the Secretary-General of the United Nations shall, upon request by a party, make those appointments within a further two-month period.

Article 4

If the President of the conciliation commission has not been chosen within two months of the second member of the commission being appointed, the Secretary-General of the United Nations shall, upon request by a party, designate the President within a further two-month period.

Article 5

1. The conciliation commission shall, unless the parties to the dispute otherwise agree, determine its own rules of procedure.

2. The parties and members of the commission are under an obligation to protect the confidentiality of any information they receive in confidence during the proceedings of the commission.

Article 6

The conciliation commission shall take its decisions by a majority vote of its members.

Article 7

The conciliation commission shall render a report with recommendations for resolution of the dispute within twelve months of being established, which the parties shall consider in good faith.

Article 8

Any disagreement as to whether the conciliation commission has competence to consider a matter referred to it shall be decided by the commission.

Article 9

The costs of the commission shall be borne by the parties to the dispute in shares agreed by them. The commission shall keep the record of all its costs and shall furnish a final statement thereof to the parties.

UNECE PROTOCOL ON POLLUTANT RELEASE AND TRANSFER REGISTERS

21 May 2003

THE PARTIES TO THIS PROTOCOL,

Recalling article 5, paragraph 9, and article 10, paragraph 2, of the 1998 Convention on Access to Information, Public Participation in Decision-making and Access to Justice in Environmental Matters (the Aarhus Convention),

Recognizing that pollutant release and transfer registers provide an important mechanism to increase corporate accountability, reduce pollution and promote sustainable development, as stated in the Lucca Declaration adopted at the first meeting of the Parties to the Aarhus Convention,

Having regard to principle 10 of the 1992 Rio Declaration on Environment and Development,

Having regard also to the principles and commitments agreed to at the 1992 United Nations

Conference on Environment and Development, in particular the provisions in chapter 19 of Agenda 21,

Taking note of the Programme for the Further Implementation of Agenda 21, adopted by the General Assembly of the United Nations at its nineteenth special session, 1997, in which it called for, inter alia, enhanced national capacities and capabilities for information collection, processing and dissemination, to facilitate public access to information on global environmental issues through appropriate means,

Having regard to the Plan of Implementation of the 2002 World Summit on Sustainable Development, which encourages the development of coherent, integrated information on chemicals, such as through national pollutant release and transfer registers,

Taking into account the work of the Intergovernmental Forum on Chemical Safety, in particular the 2000 Bahia Declaration on Chemical Safety, the Priorities for Action Beyond 2000 and the Pollutant Release and Transfer Register/Emission Inventory Action Plan,

Taking into account also the activities undertaken within the framework of the Inter-Organization Programme for the Sound Management of Chemicals,

Taking into account furthermore the work of the Organisation for Economic Co-operation and Development, in particular its Council Recommendation on Implementing Pollutant Release and Transfer Registers, in which the Council calls upon member countries to establish and make publicly available national pollutant release and transfer registers,

Wishing to provide a mechanism contributing to the ability of every person of present and future generations to live in an environment adequate to his or her health and well -being, by ensuring the development of publicly accessible environmental information systems,

Wishing also to ensure that the development of such systems takes into account principles contributing to sustainable development such as the precautionary approach set forth in principle 15 of the 1992 Rio Declaration on Environment and Development,

Recognizing the link between adequate environmental information systems and the exercise of the rights contained in the Aarhus Convention,

Noting the need for cooperation with other international initiatives concerning pollutants and waste, including the 2001 Stockholm Convention on Persistent Organic Pollutants and the 1989 Basel Convention on the Control of Transboundary Movements of Hazardous Wastes and their Disposal,

Recognizing that the objectives of an integrated approach to minimizing pollution and the amount of waste resulting from the operation of industrial installations and other sources are to achieve a high level of protection for the environment as a whole, to move towards sustainable and environmentally sound development and to protect the health of present and future generations,

Convinced of the value of pollutant release and transfer registers as a cost -effective tool for encouraging improvements in environmental performance, for providing public access to information on pollutants released into and transferred in and through communities, and for use by Governments in tracking trends, demonstrating progress in pollution reduction, monitoring compliance with certain international agreements, setting priorities and evaluating progress achieved through environmental policies and programmes,

Believing that pollutant release and transfer registers can bring tangible benefits to industry through the improved management of pollutants,

Noting the opportunities for using data from pollutant release and transfer registers, combined with health, environmental, demographic, economic or other types of relevant information, for the purpose of gaining a better understanding of potential problems, identifying 'hot spots', taking preventive and mitigating measures, and setting environmental management priorities,

Recognizing the importance of protecting the privacy of identified or identifiable natural persons in the processing of information reported to pollutant release and transfer registers in accordance with applicable international standards relating to data protection,

Recognizing also the importance of developing internationally compatible national pollutant release and transfer register systems to increase the comparability of data,

Noting that many member States of the United Nations Economic Commission for Europe, the European Community and the Parties to the North American Free Trade Agreement are acting to collect data on pollutant releases and transfers from various sources and to make these data publicly accessible, and recognizing especially in this area the long and valuable experience in certain countries,

Taking into account the different approaches in existing emission registers and the need to avoid duplication, and recognizing therefore that a certain degree of flexibility is needed,

Urging the progressive development of national pollutant release and transfer registers,

Urging also the establishment of links between national pollutant release and transfer registers and information systems on other releases of public concern,

HAVE AGREED AS FOLLOWS:

Article 1

Objective

The objective of this Protocol is to enhance public access to information through the establishment of coherent, integrated, nationwide pollutant release and transfer registers (PRTRs) in accordance with the provisions of this Protocol, which could facilitate public participation in environmental decision-making as well as contribute to the prevention and reduction of pollution of the environment.

Article 2

Definitions

For the purposes of this Protocol,

1. "Party" means, unless the text indicates otherwise, a State or a regional economic integration organization referred to in article 24 which has consented to be bound by this Protocol and for which the Protocol is in force;
2. "Convention" means the Convention on Access to Information, Public Participation in Decision making and Access to Justice in Environmental Matters, done at Aarhus, Denmark, on 25 June 1998;
3. "The public" means one or more natural or legal persons, and, in accordance with national legislation or practice, their associations, organizations or groups;
4. "Facility" means one or more installations on the same site, or on adjoining sites, that are owned or operated by the same natural or legal person;
5. "Competent authority" means the national authority or authorities, or any other competent body or bodies, designated by a Party to manage a national pollutant release and transfer register system;
6. "Pollutant" means a substance or a group of substances that may be harmful to the environment or to human health on account of its properties and of its introduction into the environment;
7. "Release" means any introduction of pollutants into the environment as a resul t of any human activity, whether deliberate or accidental, routine or non-routine, including spilling, emitting, discharging, injecting, disposing or dumping, or through sewer systems without final waste-water treatment;
8. "Off-site transfer" means the movement beyond the boundaries of the facility of either pollutants or waste destined for disposal or recovery and of pollutants in waste water destined for waste-water treatment;
9. "Diffuse sources" means the many smaller or scattered sources from which pollutants may be released to land, air or water, whose combined impact on those media may be significant and for which it is impractical to collect reports from each individual source;
10. The terms "national" and "nationwide" shall, with respect to the obligations under the Protocol on Parties that are regional economic integration organizations, be construed as applying to the region in question unless otherwise indicated;
11. "Waste" means substances or objects which are:
    (a) Disposed of or recovered;
    (b) Intended to be disposed of or recovered; or
    (c) Required by the provisions of national law to be disposed of or recovered;
12. "Hazardous waste" means waste that is defined as hazardous by the provisions of national law;
13. "Other waste" means waste that is not hazardous waste;
14. "Waste water" means used water containing substances or objects that is subject to regulation by national law.

Article 3

General provisions

1. Each Party shall take the necessary legislative, regulatory and other measures, and appropriate enforcement measures, to implement the provisions of this Protocol.

2. The provisions of this Protocol shall not affect the right of a Party to maintain or introduce a more extensive or more publicly accessible pollutant release and transfer register than required by this Protocol.

3. Each Party shall take the necessary measures to require that employees of a facility and members of the public who report a violation by a facility of national laws implementing this Protocol to public authorities are not penalized, persecuted or harassed by that facility or public authorities for their actions in reporting the violation.

4. In the implementation of this Protocol, each Party shall be guided by the precautionary approach as set forth in principle 15 of the 1992 Rio Declaration on Environment and Development.

5. To reduce duplicative reporting, pollutant release and transfer register systems may be integrated to the degree practicable with existing information sources such as repo rting mechanisms under licences or operating permits.

6. Parties shall strive to achieve convergence among national pollutant release and transfer registers.

Article 4

Core elements of a pollutant release and transfer register system

In accordance with this Protocol, each Party shall establish and maintain a publicly accessible national pollutant release and transfer register that:

(a) Is facility-specific with respect to reporting on point sources;
(b) Accommodates reporting on diffuse sources;
(c) Is pollutant-specific or waste-specific, as appropriate;
(d) Is multimedia, distinguishing among releases to air, land and water;
(e) Includes information on transfers;
(f) Is based on mandatory reporting on a periodic basis;
(g) Includes standardized and timely data, a limited number of standardized reporting thresholds and limited provisions, if any, for confidentiality;
(h) Is coherent and designed to be user-friendly and publicly accessible, including in electronic form;
(i) Allows for public participation in its development and modification; and
(j) Is a structured, computerized database or several linked databases maintained by the competent authority.

Article 5

Design and structure

1. Each Party shall ensure that the data held on the register referred to in article 4 are presented in both aggregated and non-aggregated forms, so that releases and transfers can be searched and identified according to:

(a) Facility and its geographical location;
(b) Activity;
(c) Owner or operator, and, as appropriate, company;
(d) Pollutant or waste, as appropriate;
(e) Each of the environmental media into which the pollutant is released; and
(f) As specified in article 7, paragraph 5, the destination of the transfer and, where appropriate, the disposal or recovery operation for waste.

2. Each Party shall also ensure that the data can be searched and identified according to those diffuse sources which have been included in the register.

3. Each Party shall design its register taking into account the possibility of its future expansion and ensuring that the reporting data from at least the ten previous reporting years are publicly accessible.

4. The register shall be designed for maximum ease of public access through electronic means, such as the Internet. The design shall allow that, under normal operating conditions, the information on the register is continuously and immediately available through electronic means.

5. Each Party should provide links in its register to its relevant existing, publicly accessible databases on subject matters related to environmental protection.

6. Each Party shall provide links in its register to the pollutant release and transfer registers of other Parties to the Protocol and, where feasible, to those of other countries.

Article 6

Scope of the register

1. Each Party shall ensure that its register includes the information on:
(a) Releases of pollutants required to be reported under article 7, paragraph 2;
(b) Off-site transfers required to be reported under article 7, paragraph 2; and
(c) Releases of pollutants from diffuse sources required under article 7, paragraph 4.

2. Having assessed the experience gained from the development of national pollutant release and transfer registers and the implementation of this Protocol, and taking into account relevant international processes, the Meeting of the Parties shall review the reporting requirements under this Protocol and shall consider the following issues in its further development:
(a) Revision of the activities specified in annex I;
(b) Revision of the pollutants specified in annex II;
(c) Revision of the thresholds in annexes I and II; and
(d) Inclusion of other relevant aspects such as information on on-site transfers, storage, the specification of reporting requirements for diffuse sources or the development of criteria for including pollutants under this Protocol.

Article 7

Reporting requirements

1. Each Party shall either:
(a) Require the owner or the operator of each individual facility within its jurisdiction that undertakes one or more of the activities specified in annex I above the applicable capacity threshold specified in annex I, column 1, and:
   (i) Releases any pollutant specified in annex II in quantities exceeding the applicable thresholds specified in annex II, column 1;
   (ii) Transfers off-site any pollutant specified in annex II in quantities exceeding the applicable threshold specified in annex II, column 2, where the Party has opted for pollutant -specific reporting of transfers pursuant to paragraph 5 (d);
   (iii) Transfers off-site hazardous waste exceeding 2 tons per year or other waste exceeding 2,000 tons per year, where the Party has opted for waste -specific reporting of transfers pursuant to paragraph 5 (d); or
   (iv) Transfers off-site any pollutant specified in annex II in waste water destined for waste-water treatment in quantities exceeding the applicable threshold specified in annex II, column 1b; to undertake the obligation imposed on that owner or operator pursuant to paragraph 2; or
(b) Require the owner or the operator of each individual facility within its jurisdiction that undertakes one or more of the activities specified in annex I at or above the employee threshold specified in annex I, column 2, and manufactures, processes or uses any pollutant specified in annex II in quantities exceeding the applicable threshold specified in annex II, column 3, to undertake the obligation imposed on that owner or operator pursuant to paragraph 2.

2. Each Party shall require the owner or operator of a facility referred to in paragraph 1 to submit the information specified in paragraphs 5 and 6, and in accordance with the requirements therein, with respect to those pollutants and wastes for which thresholds were exceeded.

3. In order to achieve the objective of this Protocol, a Party may decide with respect to a particular pollutant to apply either a release threshold or a manufacture, process or use threshold, provided that this increases the relevant information on releases or transfers available in its register.

4. Each Party shall ensure that its competent authority collects, or shall designate one or more public authorities or competent bodies to collect, the information on releases of pollutants from diffuse sources specified in paragraphs 7 and 8, for inclusion in its register.

5. Each Party shall require the owners or operators of the facilities required to report under paragraph 2 to complete and submit to its competent authority, the following information on a facility-specific basis:

(a) The name, street address, geographical location and the activity or activities of the reporting facility, and the name of the owner or operator, and, as appropriate, company;

(b) The name and numerical identifier of each pollutant required to be reported pursuant to paragraph 2;

(c) The amount of each pollutant required to be reported pursuant to paragraph 2 released from the facility to the environment in the reporting year, both in aggregate and according to whether the release is to air, to water or to land, including by underground injection;

(d) Either:

(i) The amount of each pollutant required to be reported pursuant to paragraph 2 that is transferred off-site in the reporting year, distinguishing between the amounts transferred for disposal and for recovery, and the name and address of the facility receiving the transfer; or

(ii) The amount of waste required to be reported pursuant to paragraph 2 transferred off-site in the reporting year, distinguishing between hazardous waste and other waste, for any operations of recovery or disposal, indicating respectively with 'R' or 'D' whether the waste is destined for recovery or disposal pursuant to annex III and, for transboundary movements of hazardous waste, the name and address of the recoverer or disposer of the waste and the actual recovery or disposal site receiving the transfer;

(e) The amount of each pollutant in waste water required to be reported pursuant to paragraph 2 transferred off-site in the reporting year; and

(f) The type of methodology used to derive the information referred to in subparagraphs (c) to (e), according to article 9, paragraph 2, indicating whether the information is based on measurement, calculation or estimation.

6. The information referred to in paragraph 5 (c) to (e) shall include information on releases and transfers resulting from routine activities and from extraordinary events.

7. Each Party shall present on its register, in an adequate spatial disaggregation, the information on releases of pollutants from diffuse sources for which that Party determines that data are being collected by the relevant authorities and can be practicably included. Where the Party determines that no such data exist, it shall take measures to initiate reporting on releases of relevant pollutants from one or more diffuse sources in accordance with its national priorities.

8. The information referred to in paragraph 7 shall include information on the type of methodology used to derive the information.

Article 8

Reporting cycle

1. Each Party shall ensure that the information required to be incorporated in its register is publicly available, compiled and presented on the register by calendar year. The reporting year is the calendar year to which that information relates. For each Party, the first reporting year is the calendar year after the Protocol enters into force for that Party. The reporting required under article 7 shall be annual. However, the second reporting year may be the second calendar year following the first reporting year.

2. Each Party that is not a regional economic integration organization shall ensure that the information is incorporated into its register within fifteen months from the end of each reporting year. However, the information for the first reporting year shall be incorporated into its register within two years from the end of that reporting year.

3. Each Party that is a regional economic integration organization shall ensure that the information for a particular reporting year is incorporated into its register six months after the Parties that are not regional economic integration organizations are required to do so.

Article 9

Data collection and record-keeping

1. Each Party shall require the owners or operators of the facilities subject to the reporting requirements of article 7 to collect the data needed to determine, in accordance with paragraph 2 below and with appropriate frequency, the facility's releases and off-site transfers subject to reporting under article 7 and to keep available for the competent authorities the records of the data from which the reported information was derived for a period of five years, starting from the end of the reporting year concerned. These records shall also describe the methodology used for data gathering.

2. Each Party shall require the owners or operators of the facilities subject to reporting under article 7 to use the best available information, which may include monitoring data, emission factors, mass balance equations, indirect monitoring or other calculations, engineering judgments and other methods. Where appropriate, this should be done in accordance with internationally approved methodologies.

Article 10

Quality assessment

1. Each Party shall require the owners or operators of the facilities subject to the reporting requirements of article 7, paragraph 1, to assure the quality of the information that they report.

2. Each Party shall ensure that the data contained in its register are subject to quality assessment by the competent authority, in particular as to their completeness, consistency and credibility, taking into account any guidelines that may be developed by the Meeting of the Parties.

Article 11

Public access to information

1. Each Party shall ensure public access to information contained in its pollutant release and transfer register, without an interest having to be stated, and according to the provisions of this Protocol, primarily by ensuring that its register provides for direct electronic access through public telecommunications networks.

2. Where the information contained in its register is not easily publicly accessible by direct electronic means, each Party shall ensure that its competent authority upon request provides that information by any other effective means, as soon as possible and at the latest within one month after the request has been submitted.

3. Subject to paragraph 4, each Party shall ensure that access to information contained in its register is free of charge.

4. Each Party may allow its competent authority to make a charge for reproducing and mailing the specific information referred to in paragraph 2, but such charge shall not exceed a reasonable amount.

5. Where the information contained in its register is not easily publicly accessible by direct electronic means, each Party shall facilitate electronic access to its register in publicly accessible locations, for example in public libraries, offices of local authorities or other appropriate places.

Article 12

Confidentiality

1. Each Party may authorize the competent authority to keep information held on the register confidential where public disclosure of that information would adversely affect:

(a) International relations, national defence or public security;

(b) The course of justice, the ability of a person to receive a fair trial or the ability of a public authority to conduct an enquiry of a criminal or disciplinary nature;

(c) The confidentiality of commercial and industrial information, where such confidentiality is protected by law in order to protect a legitimate economic interest;

(d) Intellectual property rights; or

(e) The confidentiality of personal data and/or files relating to a natural person if that person has not consented to the disclosure of the information to the public, where such confidentiality is provided for in national law. The aforementioned grounds for confidentiality shall be interpreted in a restrictive way, taking into account the public interest served by disclosure and whether the information relates to releases into the environment.

2. Within the framework of paragraph 1 (c), any information on releases which is relevant for the protection of the environment shall be considered for disclosure according to national law.

3. Whenever information is kept confidential according to paragraph 1, the register shall indicate what type of information has been withheld, through, for example, providing generic chemical information if possible, and for what reason it has been withheld.

Article 13

Public participation in the development of national pollutant release and transfer registers

1. Each Party shall ensure appropriate opportunities for public participation in the development of its national pollutant release and transfer register, within the framework of its national law.

2. For the purpose of paragraph 1, each Party shall provide the opportunity for free public access to the information on the proposed measures concerning the development of its national pollutant release and transfer register and for the submission of any comments, information, analyses or opinions that are relevant to the decision-making process, and the relevant authority shall take due account of such public input.

3. Each Party shall ensure that, when a decision to establish or significantly change its register has been taken, information on the decision and the considerations on which it is based are made publicly available in a timely manner.

Article 14

Access to justice

1. Each Party shall, within the framework of its national legislation, ensure that any person who considers that his or her request for information under article 11, paragraph 2, has been ignored, wrongfully refused, whether in part or in full, inadequately answered, or otherwise no t dealt with in accordance with the provisions of that paragraph has access to a review procedure before a court of law or another independent and impartial body established by law.

2. The requirements in paragraph 1 are without prejudice to the respective rights and obligations of Parties under existing treaties applicable between them dealing with the subject matter of this article.

Article 15

Capacity-building

1. Each Party shall promote public awareness of its pollutant release and transfer register, and shall ensure that assistance and guidance are provided in accessing its register and in understanding and using the information contained in it.

2. Each Party should provide adequate capacity-building for and guidance to the responsible authorities and bodies to assist them in carrying out their duties under this Protocol.

Article 16

International cooperation

1. The Parties shall, as appropriate, cooperate and assist each other:
(a) In international actions in support of the objectives of this Protocol;
(b) On the basis of mutual agreement between the Parties concerned, in implementing national systems in pursuance of this Protocol;
(c) In sharing information under this Protocol on releases and transfers within border areas; and
(d) In sharing information under this Protocol concerning transfers among Parties.

2. The Parties shall encourage cooperation among each other and with relevant international organizations, as appropriate, to promote:
(a) Public awareness at the international level;
(b) The transfer of technology; and
(c) The provision of technical assistance to Parties that are developing countries and Parties with economies in transition in matters relating to this Protocol.

Article 17

Meeting of the Parties

1. A Meeting of the Parties is hereby established. Its first session shall be convened no later than two years after the entry into force of this Protocol. Thereafter, ordinary sessions of the Meeting of the Parties shall be held sequentially with or parallel to ordinary meetings of the Parties to the Convention, unless otherwise decided by the Parties to this Protocol. The Meeting of the Parties shall hold an extraordinary session if it so decides in the course of an ordinary session or at the written request of any Party provided that, within six months of it being communicated by the Executive Secretary of the Economic Commission for Europe to all Parties, the said request is supported by at least one third of these Parties.

2. The Meeting of the Parties shall keep under continuous review the implementation and development of this Protocol on the basis of regular reporting by the Parties and, with this purpose in mind, shall:
(a) Review the development of pollutant release and transfer registers, and promote their progressive strengthening and convergence;
(b) Establish guidelines facilitating reporting by the Parties to it, bearing in mind the need to avoid duplication of effort in this regard;
(c) Establish a programme of work;
(d) Consider and, where appropriate, adopt measures to strengthen international cooperation in accordance with article 16;
(e) Establish such subsidiary bodies as it deems necessary;
(f) Consider and adopt proposals for such amendments to this Protocol and its annexes as are deemed necessary for the purposes of this Protocol, in accordance with the provisions of article 20;

(g) At its first session, consider and by consensus adopt rules of procedure for its sessions and those of its subsidiary bodies, taking into account any rul es of procedure adopted by the Meeting of the Parties to the Convention;
(h) Consider establishing financial arrangements by consensus and technical assistance mechanisms to facilitate the implementation of this Protocol;
(i) Seek, where appropriate, the services of other relevant international bodies in the achievement of the objectives of this Protocol; and
(j) Consider and take any additional action that may be required to further the objectives of this Protocol, such as the adoption of guidelines and recommendations which promote its implementation.

3. The Meeting of the Parties shall facilitate the exchange of information on the experience gained in reporting transfers using the pollutant-specific and waste-specific approaches, and shall review that experience in order to investigate the possibility of convergence between the two approaches, taking into account the public interest in information in accordance with article 1 and the overall effectiveness of national pollutant release and transfer registers.

4. The United Nations, its specialized agencies and the International Atomic Energy Agency, as well as any State or regional economic integration organization entitled under article 24 to sign this Protocol but which is not a Party to it, and any intergovernmental organization qualified in the fields to which the Protocol relates, shall be entitled to participate as observers in the sessions of the Meeting of the Parties. Their admission and participation shall be subject to the rules of procedure adopted by the Meeting of the Parties.

5. Any non-governmental organization qualified in the fields to which this Protocol relates which has informed the Executive Secretary of the Economic Commission for Europe of its wish to be represented at a session of the Meeting of the Parties shall be entitled to participate as an observer unless one third of the Parties present at the session raise objections. Their admission and participation shall be subject to the rules of procedure adopted by the Meeting of the Parties.

Article 18

Right to vote

1. Except as provided for in paragraph 2, each Party to this Protocol shall have one vote.

2. Regional economic integration organizations, in matters within their competence, shall exercise their right to vote with a number of votes equal to the number of their member States which are Parties. Such organizations shall not exercise their right to vote if their member States exercise theirs, and vice versa.

Article 19

Annexes

Annexes to this Protocol shall form an integral part thereof and, unless expressly provided otherwise, a reference to this Protocol constitutes at the same time a reference to any annexes thereto.

Article 20

Amendments

1. Any Party may propose amendments to this Protocol.

2. Proposals for amendments to this Protocol shall be considered at a session of the Meeting of the Parties.

3. Any proposed amendment to this Protocol shall be submitted in writing to the secretariat, which shall communicate it at least six months before the session at which it is proposed for adoption to all Parties, to other States and regional economic integration organizations that have consented to be bound by the Protocol and for which it has not yet entered into force and to Signatories.

4. The Parties shall make every effort to reach agreement on any proposed amendment to this Protocol by consensus. If all efforts at consensus have been exhausted, and no agreement reached, the amendment shall as a last resort be adopted by a three-fourths majority vote of the Parties present and voting at the session.

5. For the purposes of this article, "Parties present and voting" means Parties present and casting an affirmative or negative vote.

6. Any amendment to this Protocol adopted in accordance with paragraph 4 shall be communicated by the secretariat to the Depositary, who shall circulate it to all Parties, to other States and regional economic integration organizations that have consented to be bound by the Protocol and for which it has not yet entered into force and to Signatories.

7. An amendment, other than one to an annex, shall enter into force for those Parties having ratified, accepted or approved it on the ninetieth day after the date of receipt by the Depositary of the instruments of ratification, acceptance or approval by at least three fourths of those which were Parties at the time of its adoption. Thereafter it shall enter into force for any other Party on the ninetieth day after that Party deposits its instrument of ratification, acceptance or approval of the amendment.

8. In the case of an amendment to an annex, a Party that does not accept such an amendment shall so notify the Depositary in writing within twelve months from the date of its circulation by the Depositary. The Depositary shall without delay inform all Parties of any such notification received. A Party may at any time withdraw a notification of non-acceptance, whereupon the amendment to an annex shall enter into force for that Party.

9. On the expiry of twelve months from the date of its circulation by the Depositary as provided for in paragraph 6, an amendment to an annex shall enter into force for those Parties which have not submitted a notification to the Depositary in accordance with paragraph 8, provided that, at that time, not more than one third of those which were Parties at the time of the adoption of the amendment have submitted such a notification.

10. If an amendment to an annex is directly related to an amendment to this Protocol, it shall not enter into force until such time as the amendment to this Protocol enters into force.

Article 21

Secretariat

The Executive Secretary of the Economic Commission for Europe shall carry out the following secretariat functions for this Protocol:

(a) The preparation and servicing of the sessions of the Meeting of the Parties;
(b) The transmission to the Parties of reports and other information received in accordance with the provisions of this Protocol;
(c) The reporting to the Meeting of the Parties on the activities of the secretariat; and
(d) Such other functions as may be determined by the Meeting of the Parties on the basis of available resources.

Article 22

Review of compliance

At its first session, the Meeting of the Parties shall by consensus establish cooperative procedures and institutional arrangements of a non-judicial, non-adversarial and consultative nature to assess and promote compliance with the provisions of this Protocol and to address cases of non-compliance. In establishing these procedures and arrangements, the Meeting of the Parties shall consider, inter alia, whether to allow for information to be received from members of the public on matters related to this Protocol.

Article 23

Settlement of disputes

1. If a dispute arises between two or more Parties about the interpretation or application of this Protocol, they shall seek a solution by negotiation or by any other peaceful means of dispute settlement acceptable to the parties to the dispute.

2. When signing, ratifying, accepting, approving or acceding to this Protocol, or at any time thereafter, a State may declare in writing to the Depositary that, for a dispute not resolved in accordance with paragraph 1, it accepts one or both of the following means of dispute settlement as compulsory in relation to any Party accepting the same obligation:
(a) Submission of the dispute to the International Court of Justice;
(b) Arbitration in accordance with the procedure set out in annex IV.
A regional economic integration organization may make a declaration with like effect in relation to arbitration in accordance with the procedures referred to in subparagraph (b).

3. If the parties to the dispute have accepted both means of dispute settlement referred to in paragraph 2, the dispute may be submitted only to the International Court of Justice, unless the parties to the dispute agree otherwise.

Article 24

Signature

This Protocol shall be open for signature at Kiev (Ukraine) from 21 to 23 May 2003 on the occasion of the fifth Ministerial Conference "Environment for Europe," and thereafter at United Nations Headquarters in New York until 31 December 2003, by all States which are members of the United Nations and by regional economic integration organizations constituted by sovereign States members of the United Nations to which their member States have transferred competence over matters governed by this Protocol, including the competence to enter into treaties in respect of these matters.

Article 25

Depositary

The Secretary-General of the United Nations shall act as the Depositary of this Protocol.

Article 26

Ratification, acceptance, approval and accession

1. This Protocol shall be subject to ratification, acceptance or approval by signatory States and regional economic integration organizations referred to in article 24.

2. This Protocol shall be open for accession as from 1 January 2004 by the States and regional economic integration organizations referred to in article 24.

3. Any regional economic integration organization referred to in article 24 which becomes a Party without any of its member States being a Party shall be bound by all the obligations under this Protocol. If one or more member States of such an organization is a Party, the organization and its member States shall decide on their respective responsibilities for the performance of their obligations under this Protocol. In such cases, the organization and the member States shall not be entitled to exercise rights under this Protocol concurrently.

4. In their instruments of ratification, acceptance, approval or accession, the regional economic integration organizations referred to in article 24 shall declare the extent of their competence with respect to the matters governed by this Protocol. These organizations shall also inform the Depositary of any substantial modifications to the extent of their competence.

Article 27

Entry into force

1. This Protocol shall enter into force on the ninetieth day after the date of deposit of the sixteenth instrument of ratification, acceptance, approval or accession.

2. For the purposes of paragraph 1, any instrument deposited by a regional economic integration organization shall not be counted as additional to those deposited by the States members of such an organization.

3. For each State or regional economic integration organization which ratifies, accepts or approves this Protocol or accedes thereto after the deposit of the sixteenth instrument of ratification, acceptance, approval or accession, the Protocol shall enter into force on the ninetieth day after the date of deposit by such State or organization of its instrument of ratification, acceptance, approval or accession.

Article 28

Reservations

No reservations may be made to this Protocol.

Article 29

Withdrawal

At any time after three years from the date on which this Protocol has come into force with respect to a Party, that Party may withdraw from the Protocol by giving written notification to the Depositary. Any such withdrawal shall take effect on the ninetieth day after the date of its receipt by the Depositary.

Article 30

Authentic texts

The original of this Protocol, of which the English, French and Russian texts are equally authentic, shall be deposited with the Secretary-General of the United Nations.

IN WITNESS WHEREOF the undersigned, being duly authorized thereto, have signed this Protocol.

ANNEX I ACTIVITIES

No	*Activity*	*Capacity threshold (column 1)*	*Employee threshold (column 2)*
1.	Energy sector		
(a)	Mineral oil and gas refineries	*	10 employees
(b)	Installations for gasification and liquefaction *	*	
(c)	Thermal power stations and other combustion installations	With a heat input of 50 megawatts (MW)	
(d)	Coke ovens	*	
(e)	Coal rolling mills	With a capacity of 1 ton per hour	
(f)	Installations for the manufacture of coal products and solid smokeless fuel	*	
2.	Production and processing of metals		
(a)	Metal ore (including sulphide ore) roasting or sintering installations	*	10 employees
(b)	Installations for the production of pig iron or steel (primary or secondary melting) including continuous casting	With a capacity of 2.5 tons per hour	
(c)	Installations for the processing of ferrous metals:		
	(i) Hot-rolling mills	With a capacity of 20 tons of crude steel per hour	
	(ii) Smitheries with hammers	With an energy of 50 kilojoules per hammer, where the calorific power used exceeds 20 MW	
	(iii) Application of protective fused metal coats	With an input of 2 tons of crude steel per hour	
(d)	Ferrous metal foundries	With a production capacity of 20 tons per day	
(e)	Installations:		
	(i) For the production of non-ferrous crude metals from ore, concentrates or secondary raw materials by metallurgical, chemical or electrolytic processes	*	
	(ii) For the smelting, including the alloying, of non-ferrous metals, including recovered products (refining, foundry casting, etc.)	With a melting capacity of 4 tons per day for lead and cadmium or 20 tons per day for all other metals	
(f)	Installations for surface treatment of metals and plastic materials using an electrolytic or chemical process	Where the volume of the treatment vats equals 30 m^3	

No	*Activity*	*Capacity threshold (column 1)*	*Employee threshold (column 2)*
3.	Mineral industry		
(a)	Underground mining and related operations	*	10 employees
(b)	Opencast mining	Where the surface of the area being mined equals 25 hectares	
(c)	Installations for the production of:		
	(i) Cement clinker in rotary kilns	With a production capacity of 500 tons per day	
	(ii) Lime in rotary kilns	With a production capacity exceeding 50 tons per day	
	(iii) Cement clinker or lime in other furnaces	With a production capacity of 50 tons per day	
(d)	Installations for the production of asbestos and the manufacture of asbestos -based products	*	
(e)	Installations for the manufacture of glass, including glass fibre	With a melting capacity of 20 tons per day	
(f)	Installations for melting mineral substances, including the production of mineral fibres	With a melting capacity of 20 tons per day	
(g)	Installations for the manufacture of ceramic products by firing, in particular roofing tiles, bricks, refractory bricks, tiles, stoneware or porcelain	With a production capacity of 75 tons per day, or with a kiln capacity of 4 m^3 and with a setting density per kiln of 300 kg/m^3	
4.	Chemical industry		
(a)	Chemical installations for the production on an industrial scale of basic organic chemicals, such as: (i) Simple hydrocarbons (linear or cyclic, saturated or unsaturated, aliphatic or aromatic) (ii) Oxygen-containing hydrocarbons such as alcohols, aldehydes, ketones, carboxylic acids, esters, acetates, ethers, peroxides, epoxy resins (iii) Sulphurous hydrocarbons	*	10 employees

No	*Activity*	*Capacity threshold (column 1)*	*Employee threshold (column 2)*
	(iv) Nitrogenous hydrocarbons such as amines, amides, nitrous compounds, nitro compounds or nitrate compounds, nitrile s, cyanates, isocyanates (v) Phosphorus -containing hydrocarbons (vi) Halogenic hydrocarbons (vii) Organometallic compounds (viii) Basic plastic materials (polymers, synthetic fibres and cellulose-based fibres) (ix) Synthetic rubbers (x) Dyes and pigments (xi) Surface-active agents and surfactants		
(b)	Chemical installations for the production on an industrial scale of basic inorganic chemicals, such as: (i) Gases, such as ammonia, chlorine or hydrogen chloride, fluorine or hydrogen fluoride, carbon oxides, sulphur compounds, nitrogen oxides, hydrogen, sulphur dioxide, carbonyl chloride (ii) Acids, such as chromic acid, hydrofluoric acid, phosphoric acid, nitric acid, hydrochloric acid, sulphuric acid, oleum, sulphurous acids (iii) Bases, such as ammonium hydroxide, potassium hydroxide, sodium hydroxide (iv) Salts, such as ammonium chloride, potassium chlorate, potassium carbonate, sodium carbonate, perborate, silver nitrate (v) *Non-metals, metal oxides or other inorganic compounds* such as calcium carbide, silicon, silicon carbide	*	
(c)	Chemical installations for the production on an industrial scale of phosphorous -, nitrogen- or potassium based fertilizers (simple or compound fertilizers)	*	

No	*Activity*	*Capacity threshold (column 1)*	*Employee threshold (column 2)*
(d)	Chemical installations for the production on an industrial scale of basic plant health products and of biocides	*	
(e)	Installations using a chemical or biological process for the production on an industrial scale of basic pharmaceutical products	*	
(f)	Installations for the production on an industrial scale of explosives and pyrotechnic products	*	
5.	Waste and waste-water management		
(a)	Installations for the incineration, pyrolysis, recovery, chemical treatment or landfilling of hazardous waste	Receiving 10 tons per day	10 employees
(b)	Installations for the incineration of municipal waste	With a capacity of 3 tons per hour	
(c)	Installations for the disposal of non -hazardous waste	With a capacity of 50 tons per day	
(d)	Landfills (excluding landfills of inert waste)	Receiving 10 tons per day or with a total capacity of 25,000 tons	
(e)	Installations for the disposal or recycling of animal carcasses and animal waste	With a treatment capacity of 10 tons per day	
(f)	Municipal waste -water treatment plants	With a capacity of 100,000 population equivalents	
(g)	Independently operated industrial waste-water treatment plants which serve one or more activities of this annex	With a capacity of 10,000 m^3 per day	
6.	Paper and wood production and processing		
(a)	Industrial plants for the production of pulp from timber or similar fibrous materials	*	10 employees
(b)	Industrial plants for the production of paper and board and other primary wood products (such as chipboard, fibreboard and plywood)	With a production capacity of 20 tons per day	
(c)	Industrial plants for the p reservation of wood and wood products with chemicals	With a production capacity of 50 m^3 per day	

No	*Activity*	*Capacity threshold (column 1)*	*Employee threshold (column 2)*
7.	Intensive livestock production and aquaculture		
(a)	Installations for the intensive rearing of poultry or pigs	(i) With 40,000 places for poultry (ii) With 2,000 places for production pigs (over 30 kg) (iii) With 750 places for sows	10 employees
(b)	Intensive aquaculture	1,000 tons of fish and shellfish per year	
8.	Animal and vegetable products from the food and beverage sector		
(a)	Slaughterhouses	With a carcass production capacity of 50 tons per day	10 employees
(b)	Treatment and processing intended for the production of food and beverage products from:		
	(i) Animal raw materials (other than milk)	With a finished product production capacity of 75 tons per day	
	(ii) Vegetable raw materials	With a finished product production capacity of 300 tons per day (average value on a quarterly basis)	
(c)	Treatment and processing of milk	With a capacity to re ceive 200 tons of milk per day (average value on an annual basis)	
9.	Other activities		
(a)	Plants for the pretreatment (operations such as washing, bleaching, mercerization) or dyeing of fibres or textiles	With a treatment capacity of 10 tons per day	10 employees
(b)	Plants for the tanning of hides and skins	With a treatment capacity of 12 tons of finished product per day	
(c)	Installations for the surface treatment of substances, objects or products using organic solvents, in particular for dressing, printing, coating, degreasing, waterproofing, sizing, painting, cleaning or impregnating	With a consumption capacity of 150 kg per hour or 200 tons per year	
(d)	Installations for the production of carbon (hard-burnt coal) or electrographite by means of incineration or graphitization	*	
(e)	Installations for the building of, and painting or removal of paint from ships	With a capacity for ships 100 m long	

Explanatory notes:

Column 1 contains the capacity thresholds referred to article 7, paragraph 1 (a).

An asterisk (*) indicates that no capacity threshold is applicable (all facilities are subject to reporting).

Column 2 contains the employee threshold referred to in article 7, paragraph 1 (b).

"10 employees" means the equivalent of 10 full-time employees.

ANNEX II
POLLUTANTS

No.	CAS number	Pollutant	Threshold for releases (column 1)			Threshold for off-site transfers of pollutants (column 2)	Manufacture, process or use threshold (column 3)
			to air (column 1a) kg/year	to water (column 1b) kg/year	to land (column 1c) kg/year	kg/year	kg/year
1	74-82-8	Methane (CH_4)	100 000	-	-	-	*
2	630-08-0	Carbon monoxide (CO)	500 000	-	-	-	*
3	124-38-9	Carbon dioxide (CO_2)	100 million	-	-	-	*
4		Hydro-fluorocarbons (HFCs)	100	-	-	-	*
5	10024-97-2	Nitrous oxide (N_2O)	10 000	-	-	-	*
6	7664-41-7	Ammonia (NH_3)	10 000	-	-	-	10 000
7		Non-methane volatile organic compounds (NMVOC)	100 000	-	-	-	*
8		Nitrogen oxides (NO_x/NO_2)	100 000	-	-	-	*
9		Perfluorocarbons (PFCs)	100	-	-	-	*
10	2551-62-4	Sulphur hexafluoride (SF_6)	50	-	-	-	*
11		Sulphur oxides (SO_x/SO_2)	150 000	-	-	-	*
12		Total nitrogen	-	50 000	50 000	10 000	10 000
13		Total phosphorus	-	5 000	5 000	10 000	10 000
14		Hydrochlorofluorocarbons (HCFCs)	1	-	-	100	10 000
15		Chlorofluorocarbons (CFCs)	1	-	-	100	10 000
16		Halons	1	-	-	100	10 000
17	7440-38-2	Arsenic and compounds (as As)	20	5	5	50	50
18	7440-43-9	Cadmium and compounds (as Cd)	10	5	5	5	5
19	7440-47-3	Chromium and compounds (as Cr)	100	50	50	200	10 000
20	7440-50-8	Copper and compounds (as Cu)	100	50	50	500	10 000
21	7439-97-6	Mercury and compounds (as Hg)	10	1	1	5	5
22	7440-02-0	Nickel and compounds (as Ni)	50	20	20	500	10 000
23	7439-92-1	Lead and compounds (as Pb)	200	20	20	50	50
24	7440-66-6	Zinc and compounds (as Zn)	200	100	100	1 000	10 000
25	15972-60-8	Alachlor	-	1	1	5	10 000
26	309-00-2	Aldrin	1	1	1	1	1
27	1912-24-9	Atrazine	-	1	1	5	10 000
28	57-74-9	Chlordane	1	1	1	1	1
29	143-50-0	Chlordecone	1	1	1	1	1
30	470-90-6	Chlorfenvinphos	-	1	1	5	10 000
31	85535-84-8	Chloro-alkanes, C_{10}-C_{13}	-	1	1	10	10 000
32	2921-88-2	Chlorpyrifos	-	1	1	5	10 000
33	50-29-3	DDT	1	1	1	1	1
34	107-06-2	1,2-dichloroethane (EDC)	1 000	10	10	100	10 000
35	75-09-2	Dichloromethane (DCM)	1 000	10	10	100	10 000
36	60-57-1	Dieldrin	1	1	1	1	1
37	330-54-1	Diuron	-	1	1	5	10 000
38	115-29-7	Endosulphan	-	1	1	5	10 000
39	72-20-8	Endrin	1	1	1	1	1
40		Halogenated organic compounds (as AOX)	-	1 000	1 000	1 000	10 000
41	76-44-8	Heptachlor	1	1	1	1	1
42	118-74-1	Hexachlorobenzene (HCB)	10	1	1	1	5
43	87-68-3	Hexachlorobutadiene (HCBD)	-	1	1	5	10 000
44	608-73-1	1,2,3,4,5,6-hexachlorocyclohexane (HCH)	10	1	1	1	10
45	58-89-9	Lindane	1	1	1	1	1
46	2385-85-5	Mirex	1	1	1	1	1

No.	CAS number	Pollutant	Threshold for releases (column 1) to air (column 1a) kg/year	to water (column 1b) kg/year	to land (column 1c) kg/year	Threshold for off-site transfers of pollutants (column 2) kg/year	Manufacture, process or use threshold (column 3) kg/year
47		PCDD +PCDF (dioxins +furans) (as Teq)	0.001	0.001	0.001	0.001	0.001
48	608-93-5	Pentachlorobenzene	1	1	1	5	50
49	87-86-5	Pentachlorophenol (PCP)	10	1	1	5	10 000
50	1336-36-3	Polychlorinated biphenyls (PCBs)	0.1	0.1	0.1	1	50
51	122-34-9	Simazine	-	1	1	5	10 000
52	127-18-4	Tetrachloroethylene (PER)	2 000	-	-	1 000	10 000
53	56-23-5	Tetrachloromethane (TCM)	100	-	-	1 000	10 000
54	12002-48-1	Trichlorobenzenes (TCBs)	10	-	-	1 000	10 000
55	71-55-6	1,1,1-trichloroethane	100	-	-	1 000	10 000
56	79-34-5	1,1,2,2-tetrachloroethane	50	-	-	1 000	10 000
57	79-01-6	Trichloroethylene	2 000	-	-	1 000	10 000
58	67-66-3	Trichloromethane	500	-	-	1 000	10 000
59	8001-35-2	Toxaphene	1	1	1	1	1
60	75-01-4	Vinyl chloride	1 000	10	10	100	10 000
61	120-12-7	Anthracene	50	1	1	50	50
62	71-43-2	Benzene	1 000	200 (as BTEX)[a/]	200 (as BTEX)[a/]	2 000 (as BTEX)[a/]	10 000
63		Brominated diphenylethers (PBDE)	-	1	1	5	10 000
64		Nonylphenol ethoxylates (NP/NPEs) and related substances	-	1	1	5	10 000
65	100-41-4	Ethyl benzene	-	200 (as BTEX)[a/]	200 (as BTEX)[a/]	2 000 (as BTEX)[a/]	10 000
66	75-21-8	Ethylene oxide	1 000	10	10	100	10 000
67	34123-59-6	Isoproturon	-	1	1	5	10 000
68	91-20-3	Naphthalene	100	10	10	100	10 000
69		Organotin compounds (as total Sn)	-	50	50	50	10 000
70	117-81-7	Di-(2-ethyl hexyl) phthalate (DEHP)	10	1	1	100	10 000
71	108-95-2	Phenols (as total C)	-	20	20	200	10 000
72		Polycyclic aromatic hydrocarbons (PAHs)[b/]	50	5	5	50	50
73	108-88-3	Toluene	-	200 (as BTEX)[a/]	200 (as BTEX)[a/]	2 000 (as BTEX)[a/]	10 000
74		Tributyltin and compounds	-	1	1	5	10 000
75		Triphenyltin and compounds	-	1	1	5	10 000
76		Total organic carbon (TOC) (as total C or COD/3)	-	50 000	-	-	**
77	1582-09-8	Trifluralin	-	1	1	5	10 000
78	1330-20-7	Xylenes	-	200 (as BTEX)[a/]	200 (as BTEX)[a/]	2 000 (as BTEX)[a/]	10 000
79		Chlorides (as total Cl)	-	2 million	2 million	2 million	10 000[c/]
80		Chlorine and inorganic compounds (as HCl)	10 000	-	-	-	10 000
81	1332-21-4	Asbestos	1	1	1	10	10 000
82		Cyanides (as total CN)	-	50	50	500	10 000
83		Fluorides (as total F)	-	2 000	2 000	10 000	10 000[c/]
84		Fluorine and inorganic compounds (as HF)	5 000	-	-	-	10 000
85	74-90-8	Hydrogen cyanide (HCN)	200	-	-	-	10 000
86		Particulate matter (PM_{10})	50 000	-	-	-	*

Explanatory notes:

The CAS number of the pollutant means the precise identifier in Chemical Abstracts Service.

Column 1 contains the thresholds referred to in article 7, paragraph 1 (a)(i) and (iv). If the threshold in a given sub-column (air, water or land) is exceeded, reporting of releases or, for pollutants in waste water destined for waste-water treatment, transfers to the environmental medium referred to in that sub-column is required with respect to the facility in question, for those Parties which have opted for a system of reporting pursuant to article 7, paragraph 1 (a).

Column 2 contains the thresholds referred to in article 7, paragraph 1 (a)(ii). If the threshold in this column is exceeded for a given pollutant, reporting of the off-site transfer of that pollutant is required with respect to the facility in question, for those Parties which have opted for a system of reporting pursuant to article 7, paragraph 1 (a)(ii).

Column 3 contains the thresholds referred to in article 7, paragraph (1)(b). If the threshold in this column is exceeded for a given pollutant, reporting of the releases and off-site transfers of that pollutant is required with respect to the facility in question, for those Parties which have opted for a system of reporting pursuant to article 7, paragraph 1 (b).

A hyphen (-) indicates that the parameter in question does not trigger a reporting requirement.

An asterisk (*) indicates that, for this pollutant, the release threshold in column (1)(a) is to be used rather than a manufacture, process or use threshold.

A double asterisk (**) indicates that, for this pollutant, the release threshold in column (1)(b) is to be used rather than a manufacture, process or use threshold.

Footnotes:

a/ Single pollutants are to be reported if the threshold for BTEX (the sum parameter of benzene, toluene, ethyl benzene, xylene) is exceeded.

b/ Polycyclic aromatic hydrocarbons (PAHs) are to be measured as benzo(a)pyrene (50-32-8), benzo(b)fluoranthene (205-99-2), benzo(k)fluoranthene (207-08-9), indeno(1,2,3-cd)pyrene (193-39-5) (derived from the Protocol on Persistent Organic Pollutants to the Convention on Long-range Transboundary Air Pollution).

c/ As inorganic compounds.– 24 –

ANNEX III

PART A
DISPOSAL OPERATIONS ('D')

— Deposit into or onto land (e.g. landfill)
— Land treatment (e.g. biodegradation of liquid or sludgy discards in soils)
— Deep injection (e.g. injection of pumpable discards into wells, salt domes or naturally occurring repositories)
— Surface impoundment (e.g. placement of liquid or sludge discards into pits, ponds or lagoons)
— Specially engineered landfill (e.g. placement into lined discrete cells which are capped and isolated from one another and the environment)
— Release into a water body except seas/oceans
— Release into seas/oceans including sea-bed insertion
— Biological treatment not specified elsewhere in this annex which results in final compounds or mixtures which are discarded by means of any of the operations specified in this part
— Physico-chemical treatment not specified elsewhere in this annex which results in final compounds or mixtures which are discarded by means of any of the operations specified in this part (e.g. evaporation, drying, calcination, neutralization, precipitation)
— Incineration on land
— Incineration at sea
— Permanent storage (e.g. emplacement of containers in a mine)
— Blending or mixing prior to submission to any of the operations specified in this part

— Repackaging prior to submission to any of the operations specified in this part
— Storage pending any of the operations specified in this part

PART B
RECOVERY OPERATIONS ('R')

— Use as a fuel (other than in direct incineration) or other means to generate energy
— Solvent reclamation/regeneration
— Recycling/reclamation of organic substances which are not used as solvents
— Recycling/reclamation of metals and metal compounds
— Recycling/reclamation of other inorganic materials
— Regeneration of acids or bases
— Recovery of components used for pollution abatement
— Recovery of components from catalysts
— Used oil re-refining or other reuses of previously used oil
— Land treatment resulting in benefit to agriculture or ecological improvement
— Uses of residual materials obtained from any of the recovery operations specified above in this part
— Exchange of wastes for submission to any of the recovery operations specified above in this part
— Accumulation of material intended for any operation specified in this part

ANNEX IV
ARBITRATION

1. In the event of a dispute being submitted for arbitration pursuant to article 23, paragraph 2, of this Protocol, a party or parties shall notify the other party or parties to the dispute by diplomatic means as well as the secretariat of the subject matter of arbitration and indicate, in particular, the articles of this Protocol whose interpretation or application is at issue. The secretariat shall forward the information received to all Parties to this Protocol.

2. The arbitral tribunal shall consist of three members. Both the claimant party or parties and the other party or parties to the dispute shal l appoint an arbitrator, and the two arbitrators so appointed shall designate by common agreement the third arbitrator, who shall be the president of the arbitral tribunal. The latter shall not be a national of one of the parties to the dispute, nor have his or her usual place of residence in the territory of one of these parties, nor be employed by any of them, nor have dealt with the case in any other capacity.

3. If the president of the arbitral tribunal has not been designated within two months of the appointment of the second arbitrator, the Executive Secretary of the Economic Commission for Europe shall, at the request of either party to the dispute, designate the president within a further two -month period.

4. If one of the parties to the dispute does not appoint an arbitrator within two months of the notification referred to in paragraph 1, the other party may so inform the Executive Secretary of the Economic Commission for Europe, who shall designate the president of the arbitral tribunal within a further two-month period. Upon designation, the president of the arbitral tribunal shall request the party which has not appointed an arbitrator to do so within two months. If it fails to do so within that period, the president shall so inform the Executive Secretary of the Economic Commission for Europe, who shall make this appointment within a further two -month period.

5. The arbitral tribunal shall render its decision in accordance with international law and the provisions of this Protocol.

6. Any arbitral tribunal constituted under the provisions set out in this annex shall draw up its own rules of procedure.

7. The decisions of the arbitral tribunal, both on procedure and on substance, shall be taken by majority vote of its members.

8. The tribunal may take all appropriate measures to establish the facts.

9. The parties to the dispute shall facilitate the work of the arbitral tribunal and, in particular, using all means at their disposal, shall:
(a) Provide it with all relevant documents, facilities and information;
(b) Enable it, where necessary, to call witnesses or experts and receive their evidence.

10. The parties and the arbitrators shall protect the confidentiality of any information that they receive in confidence during the proceedings of the arbitral tribunal.

11. The arbitral tribunal may, at the request of one of the parties, recommend interim measures of protection.

12. If one of the parties to the dispute does not appear before the arbitral tribunal or fails to defend its case, the other party may request the tribunal to continue the proceedings and to render its final decision. Absence of a party or failure of a party to defend its case shall not constitute a bar to the proceedings. Before rendering its final decision, the arbitr al tribunal must satisfy itself that the claim is well founded in fact and law.

13. The arbitral tribunal may hear and determine counterclaims arising directly out of the subject matter of the dispute.

14. Unless the arbitral tribunal determines otherwise because of the particular circumstances of the case, the expenses of the tribunal, including the remuneration of its members, shall be borne by the parties to the dispute in equal shares. The tribunal shall keep a record of all its expenses, and shall furnish a final statement thereof to the parties.

15. Any Party to this Protocol which has an interest of a legal nature in the subject matter of the dispute, and which may be affected by a decision in the case, may intervene in the proceedings with the consent of the tribunal.

16. The arbitral tribunal shall render its award within five months of the date on which it is established, unless it finds it necessary to extend the time limit for a period which should not exceed five months.

17. The award of the arbitral tribunal shall be accompanied by a statement of reasons. It shall be final and binding upon all parties to the dispute. The award will be transmitted by the arbitral tribunal to the parties to the dispute and to the secretariat. The secretariat will forward the information received to all Parties to this Protocol.

18. Any dispute which may arise between the parties concerning the interpretation or execution of the award may be submitted by either party to the arbitral tribunal which made the award or, if the latter cannot be seized thereof, to another tribunal constituted for this purpose in the same manner as the first.